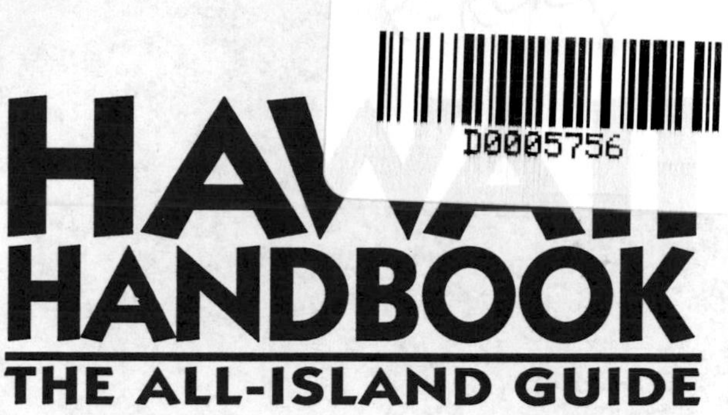
HAWAII
HANDBOOK
THE ALL-ISLAND GUIDE
D0005756

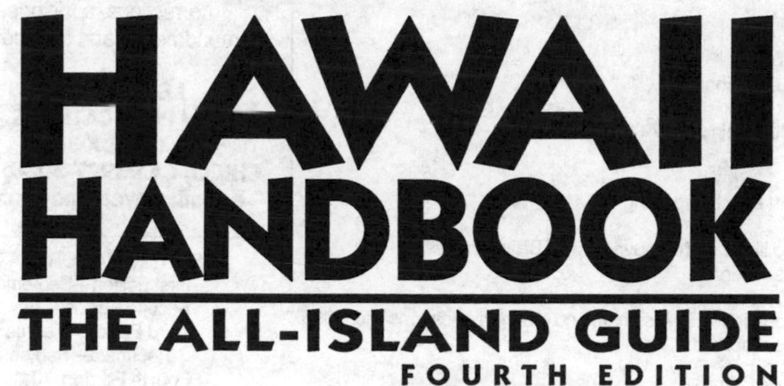

J.D. BISIGNANI

HAWAII HANDBOOK
FOURTH EDITION

Published by
Moon Publications, Inc.
P.O. Box 3040
Chico, California 95927-3040, USA

Printed by
Colorcraft Ltd., Hong Kong

ISBN 1-56691-000-5
ISSN 1078-5299

Please send all comments, corrections, additions, amendments, and critiques to:

J.D. BISIGNANI
MOON PUBLICATIONS, INC.
P.O. BOX 3040
CHICO, CA 95927-3040, USA
e-mail: travel@moon.com

PRINTING HISTORY
First Edition—September 1987
Second Edition—July 1989
Third Edition—February 1991
Reprinted—September 1994
Fourth Edition—July 1995

Editor: Pauli Galin
Copy Editors: Elizabeth Marie Kim, Valerie Sellers
Production & Design: Nancy Kennedy, David Hurst
Cartographers: Bob Race, Brian Bardwell
Index: Valerie Sellers

Front Cover Art: Roy Tabora, *Trail of Gold* courtesy of Kahn Galleries,
4569 Kukui St., Kapa'a, Kauai HI 96746

All photos by J.D. Bisignani unless otherwise noted.

Distributed in U.S.A. by Publishers Group West
Printed in Hong Kong

To Sandy B.,

who from first glance

filled my life with aloha

Love, Dad

CONTENTS

MAUI

BIG ISLAND

KAUAI

MAPS

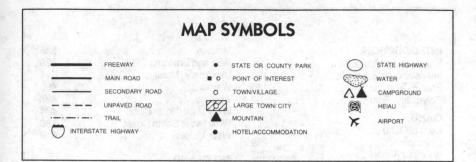

MAP SYMBOLS

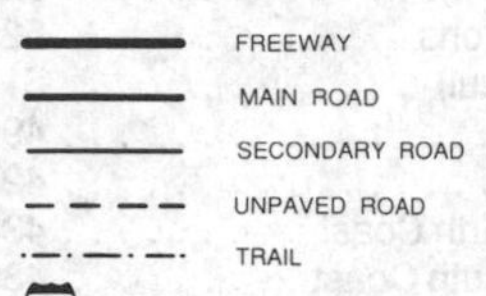

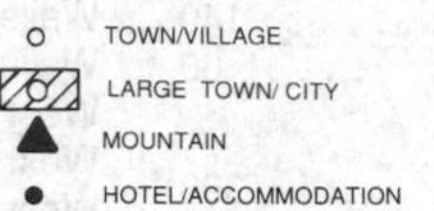

STATE HIGHWAY
WATER
CAMPGROUND
HEIAU
AIRPORT

CHARTS AND SPECIAL TOPICS

ACKNOWLEDGMENTS

Writing the acknowledgments for a book is supercharged with energy. It's a time when you look forward, hopefully, to a bright future for your work, and a time when you reflect on all that has gone into producing it. Mostly it's a time to say thank you. Thank you for the grace necessary to carry out the task, and thank you to all the wonderful people whose efforts have helped so much along the way. To the following people, I offer my most sincere thank you.

Firstly, to the Moon staff, professionals every one. As time has passed, and one book has followed another, they've become amazingly adept at their work, to the point where their mastery is a marvel to watch.

I would also like to thank the following people for their special help and consideration: Dr. Greg Leo, an adventurer and environmentalist who has done remarkable field research and provided me with invaluable information about the unique flora and fauna of Hawaii; Roger Rose of the Bishop Museum; Lee Wild, Hawaiian Mission Houses Museum; Marilyn Nicholson, State Foundation on Culture and the Arts; the Hawaii Visitors Bureau; Donna Jung, Donna Jung and Associates, who has shown confidence in me since day one; Haunani Vieira, Dollar Rent A Car; Keoni Wagner, Hawaiian Airlines; Jim and John Costello; Dr. Terry and Nancy Carolan; Elizabeth Demotte, Ritz-Carlton Mauna Lani; Barbara Schonley, Destination Molokai; Elisa Josephsohn, Public Relations; Faith Ogawa, for helping me keep the faith; Carol Zahorsky, Four Seasons Resort; Joyce Matsumoto, Halekulani Hotel; Jeanne Datz, Hilton Hotels; Nancy Daniels, Kahala Hilton; Dianne Doer, Kona Hilton; Rudy Bosma, Lanai City Service; Donn Takahashi and Carol Dawson, Maui Prince Hotel; Dennis Costa, Maui Hill; Kim Marshall, Grand Wailea Resort; Sheila Donnelly, Diana Reutter, Julie Char, Sweetie Aiwohi Nelson, Deborah Sharkey of Sheila Donnelly and Associates; Sandi Kato-Klutke, Aston Kauai Beach Villa; Barbara Sheehan, Sheraton Moana Surfrider; Sally Proctor, Aston Hotels; Norm Manzione, Suntrips; Renee Cochran and Will Titus, Colony Resorts; Linda Darling-Mann, Coco Palms Resort. To all of you, my deepest *aloha.*

IS THIS BOOK OUT OF DATE?

In today's world, things change so rapidly that it's impossible for one person to keep up with everything happening in any one place. This is particularly true in Hawaii, where situations are always in flux. Travel books are like automobiles: they require fine tuning and frequent overhauls to keep in shape. Help us keep this book in shape! We require input from our readers so that we can continue to provide the best, most current information available. Please write to let us know about any inaccuracies, new information, or misleading suggestions. Although we try to make our maps as accurate as possible, errors do occur. If you have any suggestions for improvement or places that should be included, please let us know about them.

We especially appreciate letters from female travelers, visiting expatriates, local residents, and hikers and outdoor enthusiasts. We also like hearing from experts in the field as well as from local hotel owners and individuals wishing to accommodate visitors from abroad.

As you travel through the islands, keep notes in the margins of this book. Notes written on the spot are always more accurate than those put down on paper later. If you take a photograph during your trip that you think should be included in future editions, please send it to us. Send only good slide duplicates or glossy black-and-white prints. Drawings and other artwork are also appreciated. If we use your photo or drawing, you'll be mentioned in the credits and receive a free copy of the book. Keep in mind, however, that the publisher cannot return any materials unless you include a self-addressed, stamped envelope. Moon Publications will own the rights on all material submitted. Address your letter to:

J.D. Bisignani
Moon Publications, Inc.
P.O. Box 3040
Chico, CA 95927-3040
USA

ABBREVIATIONS

AFB—Air Force Base
B&B—Bed And Breakfast
BYO—bring your own
4WD—Four-Wheel Drive
HVB—Hawaii Visitors Bureau
Hwy.—Highway
Mph—miles per hour
NWR—National Wildlife Refuge
OHA—Office of Hawaiian Affairs
PADI—Professional Association of Dive Instructors
P.O.—Post Office
Rt.—Route
S.A.S.E.—Self-addressed Stamped Envelope
SRA—State Recreation Area
YH—Youth Hostel

INTRODUCTION

"No alien land in all the world
has any deep, strong charm for me,
but that one;
no other land could
so longingly and beseechingly
haunt my sleeping and waking,
through half a lifetime,
as that one has done.
Other things leave me,
but it abides."

—Mark Twain, c. 1889

INTRODUCTION

The modern geological theory concerning the formation of the Hawaiian Islands is no less fanciful than the Polynesian legends sung about their origins. Science maintains that 30 million years ago, while the great continents were being geologically tortured into their rudimentary shapes, the Hawaiian Islands were a mere ooze of bubbling magma 20,000 feet below the surface of the primordial sea. For millions of years this molten rock flowed up through fissures in the sea floor. Slowly, layer upon layer of lava was deposited until an island rose above the surface of the sea. The great weight then sealed the fissures, whose own colossal forces progressively crept in a southwesterly direction, then burst out again and again to build the chain. The entire Pacific plate, afloat on the giant sea of molten magma, slowly glided to the northwest, carrying the newly formed islands with it.

In the beginning the spewing crack formed the Kure and Midway islands in the extreme northwestern sector of the Hawaiian chain. Today, more than 130 islands, islets, and shoals make up the Hawaiian Islands, stretching 1,600 miles across an expanse of the North Pacific. Some geologists maintain the "hot spot" now primarily under the Big Island remains relatively stationary, and the 1,600-mile spread of the Hawaiian archipelago is due to a northwestern drifting effect of three to five inches per year. With the center of activity under the Big Island, the Mauna Loa and Kilauea volcanoes regularly add more land to the only state in the U.S. that is literally still growing. About 30 miles southeast of the Big Island is Loihi Sea Mount, waiting 3,000 feet below the waves. Frequent eruptions bring it closer and closer to the surface until one day it will emerge and become the newest Hawaiian island.

THE LAND

The Hawaiian Islands sit right in the middle of the North Pacific just a touch south of the Tropic of Cancer. They take up about as much room as a flower petal floating in a swimming pool. The sea makes life possible on the islands, and the Hawaiian sea is a mostly benign benefactor providing all the basics. It is also responsible for an endless assortment of pleasure, romance,

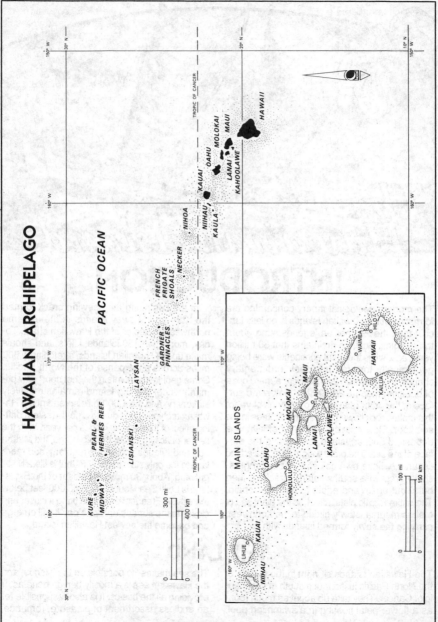

HAWAIIAN ARCHIPELAGO

and excitement, and a cultural link between Hawaii and its Polynesian counterparts. The slopes of the Hawaiian Islands rise dramatically from the sea floor, not gradually, but abruptly, like temple pillars rising straight up from Neptune's kingdom.

Physical Features

Hawaii is the southernmost state in the Union and the most westerly except for a few far-flung islands in the Alaskan Aleutians. The Tropic of Cancer runs through the state, and it shares the same latitude as Mexico City, Havana, Calcutta, and Hong Kong. It's the fourth smallest state, larger than Connecticut, Rhode Island, and Delaware. Together, its 132 shoals, reefs, islets, and islands constitute 6,450 square miles of land. The eight *major* islands of Hawaii account for over 99% of the total land area, and are home to 100% of the population (except for a staffed military installation here and there). They stretch over 400 miles of Pacific, and from northwest to southeast include: Niihau (privately owned), Kauai, Oahu, Molokai, Maui, Lanai, Kahoolawe (uninhabited), and Hawaii, the Big Island. The little-known Northwest Islands, less than one percent of the state's total land mass, are dotted across the North Pacific for over 1,100 miles running from Kure in the far north to Nihoa, about 100 miles off Kauai's north shore. The state has just over 1,000 miles of tidal shoreline, and ranges in elevation from Mauna Loa's 13,796-foot summit to Maro Reef which is often awash by the sea.

Volcanoes

The Hawaiians worshipped Pele, the fire goddess whose name translates equally well as "volcano," "fire pit," or "eruption of lava." Pele spit fire and spewed lava that cooled and formed islands, which in turn attracted billions of polyps whose skeletal remains cemented into coral reefs. The Hawaiian Islands are perfect examples of **shield volcanoes.** These are formed by a succession of gentle submarine eruptions that build an elongated dome much like a turtle shell. As the dome nears the surface of the sea, the eruptions combine with air and become extremely explosive due to the rapid temperature change and increased oxygen. Once above the surface they mellow again and steadily build upon themselves. As the island-mountain mushrooms, its weight seals off the spewing fissure below. Instead of forcing itself upward, the lava now finds less resistance by moving laterally. Eventually, the giant tube which carried lava to the top of the volcano sinks in upon itself and becomes a caldera. More eruptions occur periodically, but the lava is less dense and could be thought of as icing on a titanic cake. Then the relentless forces of wind and water take over to sculpt the raw lava into deep crevices and cuts that eventually become valleys. The smooth, once-single mountain is transformed into a miniature mountain range, while marinelife builds reefs around the islands, and the rising and falling of the surrounding seas during episodic ice ages combine with eroded soil to add or destroy coastal plains.

Lava

The Hawaiian Islands are huge mounds of cooled **basaltic lava** skirted by coral reefs, the skeletons of billions of polyps. The main components of Hawaiian lava are silica, iron oxide, magnesium, and lime. Lava flows in two distinct types for which the Hawaiian names have become universal geological terms: *'a'a* and *pahoehoe.* They are easily distinguished by appearance, but in chemical composition they are the same. Their differing appearance is due to the amount of gases contained in the flow when the lava hardens. ***'A'a*** lava is extremely rough and spiny, and will quickly tear up your shoes if you do much hiking over it. If you have the misfortune to fall down, you'll soon find out why it's called *'a'a.* ***Pahoehoe*** is a billowy, ropy lava that looks like burned pancake batter. Not nearly as dense as *'a'a,* it can form fantastic shapes and designs.

Lava actually forms molten rivers as it barrels down the steep slopes of the volcanoes. Sometimes a lava river crusts over while the molten material on the inside continues to drain, until a lava tube is formed. Such a tube characteristically has a domed roof and a flat floor and would make a very passable subway tunnel. Some tubes measure more than 20 feet in diameter. One of the best examples is the Thurston Lava Tube at Volcanoes National Park on Hawaii. Other lava oddities are **peridots** (green, gemlike stones) and clear **feldspar.**

Gray lichens that cover older volcanic flows are known as **Hawaiian snow,** and volcanic glass that has been spun into hairlike strands is known as **Pele's hair,** while congealed lava droplets are known as **Pele's tears.**

Lakes And Rivers

Hawaii has very few natural lakes because of the porousness of the lava: water tends to seep into the ground rather than form ponds or lakes. However, *underground* deposits where water has been trapped between porous lava on top and dense subterranean layers below account for many freshwater springs throughout the islands; these are tapped as a primary source for irrigating sugarcane and pineapple. Hawaii's only large natural lakes happen to be on the private island of Niihau, and are therefore seldom seen by the outside world. **Lake Waiau,** at the 13,000-foot level on the Big Island's Mauna Kea, ranks among the highest lakes in the United States. Honolulu's **Salt Lake,** once Oahu's only natural inland body of water, was bulldozed for land reclamation. No extensive rivers are found in Hawaii except the **Waimea River** on Kauai; none are navigable except for a few miles of the Waimea. The countless "streams" and "rivulets" on the main islands turn from trickles to torrents depending upon rainfall. This is of greatest concern to hikers, who can find themselves threatened by a flash flood in a valley that was the height of hospitality only a few minutes before.

Tidal Waves

Tsunami, the Japanese word for "tidal wave," ranks up there in causing the worst horror in human beings. But if you were to count all the people in Hawaii swept away by tidal waves in the last 50 years, the toll wouldn't come close to those killed on bicycles in only a few Mainland cities in just five years. A Hawaiian tsunami is actually a seismic sea wave generated by an earthquake that could easily have its origins thousands of miles away in South America or Alaska. Some waves have been clocked at speeds up to 500 miles per hour. The U.S. Geological Survey has uncovered data that indicates a 1,000-foot-high wall of water crashed into the Hawaiian Islands about 100,000 years ago. They believe a giant undersea landslide about 25 miles south of Lanai was the cause. The

HAWAII STATE ARCHIVES

engraving of Hawaii's unique pali *by Barthelme Lauvergue, c. 1836*

wave was about 15 miles wide and when it hit Lanai it stripped land more than 1,200 feet above sea level. It struck the other islands less severely, stripping land up to 800 feet above sea level. The worst tsunami in modern times have both struck Hilo on the Big Island: the one in May 1960 claimed 61 lives. Maui also experienced a catastrophic wave that inundated the Hana coast on April l, l946, taking lives and destroying much property. Other waves have inexplicably claimed no lives. The Big Island's Waipio Valley, for example, was a place of royalty that, according to ancient Hawaiian beliefs, was protected by the gods. A giant tsunami inundated Waipio in the 1940s, catching hundreds of people in its watery grasp. Unbelievably, not one person was hurt. After the wave departed, many people rushed to the valley floor to gather thousands of fish that were washed ashore. Without warning, a second towering wave struck and grabbed the people again. Although giant trees and boulders were washed out to sea, not one person was harmed even the second time around. The safest place, besides high ground well away from beach areas, is out on the open ocean where an enormous wave is perceived only as a large swell. A tidal wave is only dangerous when it is opposed by land.

Earthquakes

Earthquakes are also a concern in Hawaii and offer a double threat because they cause tsunami. If you ever feel a tremor and are close to a beach, evacuate as soon as possible. The Big Island, because of its active volcanoes, experiences hundreds of technical earthquakes every year, although 99% can only be felt on very delicate equipment. The last major quake occurred on the Big Island in late November 1975, reaching 7.2 on the Richter scale, and causing many millions of dollars' worth of damage on the island's southern portion. Tragically, yet fortunately, only two young men lost their lives when a part of the beach on which they were camping with a large party collapsed and they were drowned.

Hawaii has an elaborate warning system against natural disasters. You will notice loudspeakers high atop poles along many beaches and coastal areas; these warn of tsunami, hurricanes, and earthquakes. They are tested at 11 a.m. on the first working day of each month. All island telephone books contain a Civil Defense warning and procedures section with which you should acquaint yourself. Note the maps showing areas that have been traditionally inundated by tsunami and what procedures to follow in case an emergency occurs.

LAND STATISTICS

All figures given are approximations

WHERE	SQ. MILES	COASTLINE	ELEVATION (FT.)
ISLAND	6,450	1,052	
Hawaii	4,038	313	
Mauna Kea			13,796
Mauna Loa			13,677
Kilauea			4,093
Oahu	608	209	
Mt. Kaala			4,020
Tantalus			2,013
Diamond Head			760
Maui	729	149	
Haleakala			10,023
Puu Kukui			5,788
Kauai	553	110	
Kawaikini			5,243
Waialeale			5,148
Molokai	261	106	
Kamakou			4,970
Lanai	140	52	
Lanaihale			3,370
Niihau	73	50	
Paniau			1,281
Kahoolawe	45	36	
Lua Makika			1,477
Northwestern Islands (total)	32	25	
Nihoa			910
Lehua			702

CLIMATE

Of the wide variety of reasons for visiting Hawaii, most people have at least one in common: the weather! Nowhere on the face of the earth do human beings feel more physically comfortable than in Hawaii, and a happy body almost always means a happy mind and spirit too. Cooling trade winds, low humidity, high pressure, clear sunny days, negative ionization from the sea, and an almost total lack of industrial pollution combine to make Hawaii *the* most healthful spot in America.

"So Good" Weather

The ancient Hawaiians had words to describe climatic specifics such as rain, wind, fog, and even snow, but they didn't have a general word for *weather.* The reason is that the weather is just about the same throughout the year

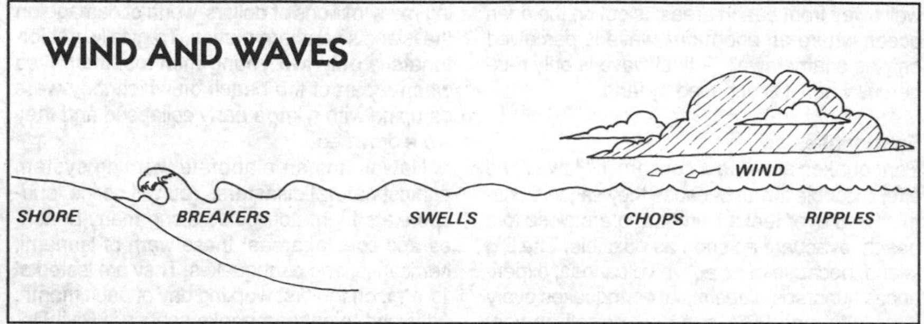

and depends more on where you are on any given island than on what season it is. The Hawaiians did distinguish between *kau* (summer, May-October) and *hoo'ilo* (winter, November-April), but this distinction included social, religious, and even navigational factors, far beyond a mere distinction of weather variations. The average daytime temperature throughout Hawaii is about 80° F, with the average winter day registering 78°, and the average summer day raising the thermometer only seven degrees to 85°. Nighttime temperatures drop less than 10°. Altitude, however, does drop temperatures about three degrees for every 1,000 feet; if you intend to visit the mountain peaks of Haleakala, Mauna Loa, or Mauna Kea (all over 10,000 feet), expect the temperature to be at least 30° cooler than at sea level. The lowest temperatures ever recorded in Hawaii were atop Haleakala in January 1961 when the mercury dropped well below freezing to a mere 11°; the hottest day occurred in 1931 in the Puna District of the Big Island with a scorching (for Hawaii) 100°.

The Trade Winds

One reason Hawaiian temperatures are both constant and moderate is the trade winds. These breezes are so prevailing that the northeast sides of the islands are always referred to as **windward,** regardless of where the wind happens to be blowing on any given day. You can count on the *trades* to be blowing an average of 300 days per year: hardly missing a day during summer, and half the time in winter. They blow throughout the day, but are strong during the heat of the afternoon and weaken at night. Just when you need a cooling breeze, there they are, and when the temperature drops at night, it's as if someone turned down a giant fan. The trade winds are also a factor in keeping down the humidity. They will suddenly disappear, however, usually in winter, and might not resume for a few weeks. The Tropic of Cancer runs through the center of Hawaii, yet its famed oppressively hot and muggy weather is joyfully absent. Honolulu, on the same latitude as sweaty Hong Kong and Havana, has only a 50-60% daily humidity factor.

Kona Winds

Kona means "leeward" in Hawaiian, and when the trades stop blowing these southerly winds often take over. To anyone from Hawaii, "*kona* wind" is euphemistic for bad weather: bringing in hot sticky air. Luckily they are most common from October to April when they appear roughly half the time. The temperatures drop slightly during the winter so these hot winds are tolerable, and even useful for moderating the thermometer. In the summer they are awful, but luckily again they hardly ever blow during this season. A ***kona* storm** is another matter. These subtropical low-pressure storms develop west of the Hawaiian Islands, and as they move easterly draw winds up from the south. Usual only in winter, they can cause considerable damage to crops and real estate. There is no real pattern to *kona* storms—some years they come every few weeks while other years they don't appear at all.

Rain

Hardly a day goes by when it isn't raining somewhere on *all* the main islands. If this amazes you, just consider each island to be a mini-continent: it would be the same as expecting no rain anywhere in North America on any given day. All islands have a windward (northeast, wet) and leeward (southwest, dry) side. It rains much more on the windward side, and much more often during winter than summer. (However, *kona* storms, because they come from the south, hit the islands' leeward sides most often.) Another important rain factor is the mountains, which act like water magnets. Moist winds gather around them and eventually build rain clouds. The ancient Hawaiians used these clouds and the reflected green light on their underbellies to spot land from great distances. Precipitation mostly occurs at or below the 3,000-foot level; thus, the upper slopes of taller mountains such as Haleakala are quite dry. The average annual rainfall on the seas surrounding Hawaii is only 25 inches, while a few miles inland around the windward slopes of mountains it can be 250 inches! A dramatic example of this phenomenon is seen by comparing Lahaina and Mt. Puu Kukui, only seven miles distant from each other on West Maui. Hot, arid Lahaina has an annual rainfall of only 17 inches; Puu Kukui can receive close to 40 *feet* of rainfall a year, rivaling Mt. Waialeale on Kauai as the "wettest spot on earth." Another point to remember is where there's rain there's also an incredible explosion of colorful flowers like an overgrown natural hothouse. You'll find this effect mostly on the windward sides of the islands. Conversely, the best beach weather is on the leeward sides: Kaanapali, Waikiki, Kailua-Kona, Poipu. They all sit in the "rain shadows" of interior mountains, and if it happens to be raining at one leeward beach, just move down the road to the next. One more thing about Hawaiian rains—they aren't very nasty. Much of the time just a light drizzle, they hardly ever last all day. Because they are mostly locálized, you can often spot them by looking for rainbows. Rain should never spoil your outings in Hawaii. Just "hang loose, brah," and go to the sunshine.

Bad Weather

With all this talk of ideal weather it might seem like there isn`t any bad. Read on. When a storm does hit an island it can be bleak and miserable. The worst storms are in the winter and often have the warped sense of humor to drop their heaviest rainfalls on areas that are normally quite dry. It's not infrequent for a storm to dump more than three inches of rain an hour; this can go as high as 10, making Hawaiian rainfalls some of the heaviest on earth.

Hawaii has also been hit with some walloping **hurricanes** in the last few decades; there haven't been many but they've been destructive. The vast majority of hurricanes originate far to the southeast off the coasts of Mexico and Latin America. Most of them pass harmlessly south of Hawaii but some, swept along by *kona* winds, strike the islands. The most recent and destructive was Hurricane Iniki, which battered the islands in 1992. It had its greatest effect on Kauai and on the leeward coast of Oahu. Iniki carried a destructive price tag of $1.5 billion. (For more information see "Climate" under "The Land" in the Kauai introduction.)

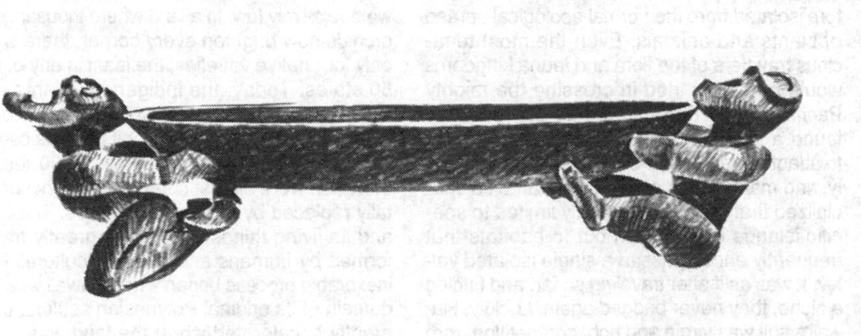

BOB RACE

DIANA LASICH HARPER

FLORA AND FAUNA

Anyone who loves a mystery will be intrigued by the speculation about how plants and animals first came to Hawaii. Most people's idea of an island paradise includes swaying palms, dense mysterious jungles ablaze with wildflowers, and luscious fruits just waiting to be plucked. In fact, for millions of years the Hawaiian chain consisted of raw and barren islands where no plants grew and no birds sang. Why? Because they are geological orphans that spontaneously popped up in the middle of the Pacific Ocean. The islands, more than 2,000 miles from any continental landfall, were therefore isolated from the normal ecological spread of plants and animals. Even the most tenacious travelers of the flora and fauna kingdoms would be sorely tried in crossing the mighty Pacific. Those that made it by pure chance found a totally foreign ecosystem. They had to adapt or perish. The survivors evolved quickly, and many plants and birds became so specialized that they were not only limited to specific islands in the chain but to habitats that frequently encompassed a single isolated valley. It was as if after traveling so far, and finding a niche, they never budged again. Luckily, Hawaii's soil was virgin and rich, competition from other plants or animals was nonexistent, and the climate was sufficiently varied and nearly perfect for most growing things.

The evolution of plants and animals on the isolated islands was astonishingly rapid. A tremendous change in environment, coupled with a limited gene pool, accelerated natural selection. For example, many plants lost their protective thorns and spines because there were no grazing animals or birds to destroy them. Before settlement, Hawaii had no fruits, vegetables, coconut palms, edible land animals, conifers, mangroves, or banyans. Tropical flowers, wild and vibrant as we know them today, were relatively few. In a land where thousands of orchids now brighten every corner, there were only four native varieties, the least in any of the 50 states. Today, the indigenous plants and animals have the highest rate of extinction anywhere on earth. By the beginning of this century, native plants growing below 1,500 feet in elevation were almost completely extinct or totally replaced by introduced species. The land and its living things have been greatly transformed by humans and their agriculture. This inexorable process began when Hawaii was the domain of its original Polynesian settlers, then greatly accelerated when the land was inundated by Western peoples.

The Greening Of Hawaii

The first *deliberate* migrants to Hawaii were Polynesians from the Marquesas Islands. Many of their voyages were undertaken when life on their native islands became intolerable. They were prompted mostly by defeat in war, or by growing island populations that overtaxed the available food supply. Whatever the reasons, the migrations were deliberate and permanent. The first colonizers were known as "the land seekers" in the old Marquesan language—probably advance scouting parties who proved true the ancient chants, which sung of a land to the north. Once they discovered Hawaii, their return voyage to the southern homeland was relatively easy. They had the favorable trade winds at their backs, plus the certainty of sailing into familiar waters. Later both men and women would set out for the new land in canoes laden with seeds and plant cuttings necessary for survival, as well as animals for both consumption and sacrifice.

Not all the domesticated plants and animals came at once, but the colonizers brought enough to get started. The basic food plants included taro, banana, coconut, sugarcane, breadfruit, and yams. The Polynesians also brought the paper mulberry from which *tapa* was made, and the ti plant necessary for cooking and making offerings at *heiau*. Various gourds were grown to be used as bowls, containers, and even helmets for Hawaiian-style defensive armor. Arrowroot and turmeric were used in cooking and by the healing *kahuna* as medicines. *Awa* was brought by the high priests to be used in rituals; it was chewed, and the resulting juice was spat into a bowl where it fermented and became a mind-altering intoxicant. Bamboo, the natural wonder material, was planted and used for countless purposes. The only domesticated animals taken to the new land were pigs, dogs, and chickens. Rats also made the journey as stowaways.

In the new land the Polynesians soon found native plants that they incorporated and put to good use. Some included: *olona,* which made the best-known fiber cord anywhere in the world and later was eagerly accepted by sailing ships as new rigging and as a trade item; koa, an excellent hardwood used for the manufacture of highly prized calabashes and the hulls of magnificent seagoing canoes; *kukui* (candlenut), eaten as a tasty nut, strung to make lei, or burned as a source of light like a natural candle. For a thousand years a distinct Hawaiian culture formed in relative isolation. When the first whites came they found a people who had become intimately entwined with their environment. The relationship between Hawaiians and the *aina* (land) was spiritual, physical, and emotional: they were one.

Note: Also see "Flora and Fauna" in the introductions to the various travel chapters for plants and animals specifically confined to, or more common on, those particular islands. Also see the Index "Flora, Fauna" along with specific listings in the Index.

PLANTS, FLOWERS, AND TREES

Much like the Polynesian settlers who followed, the drifters, castaways, and shanghaied of the plant and animal kingdom were the first to reach Hawaii. Botanists say spores and seeds were carried aloft into the upper atmosphere by powerful winds, then made lucky landings on the islands. Some hardy seeds came with the tides and managed to sprout and grow once they hit land. Others were carried on the feathers and feet of migratory birds, while some made the trip in birds' digestive tracts and were ignominiously deposited with their droppings. This chance seeding of Hawaii obviously took a very long time: scientists estimate one plant arrival and establishment every 20,000-30,000 years. By latest count over 1,700 distinct species of endemic (only Hawaiian) and indigenous (other islands of Polynesia) plants have been cataloged throughout the island chain. It is reasonably certain all of these plants were introduced by only 250 original immigrants; the 168 different Hawaiian ferns, for example, are the result of approximately 13 colonists. Most of the seeds and spores are believed to have come from Asia and Indonesia, and evidence of this spread can be seen in related plant species common to many Polynesian islands. Other endemic species such as the koa tree, which the Hawaiians put to great use in canoe building, have close relatives only in Australia. No other group of islands between Hawaii and Australia have such trees; the reason remains a mystery. Many plants and grasses came from North and South

America and can be identified with common ancestors still there. Some species have become so totally Hawaiian that relatives are found nowhere else on earth. This last category has either evolved so dramatically they can no longer be recognized, or their common ancestors have long been extinct from the original environment. An outstanding example in this category is the silversword *(ahinahina),* found in numbers only atop Haleakala on Maui, with a few specimens extant on the volcanoes of the Big Island.

Hawaii's Flora

Hawaii's indigenous plants, flowers, and trees are fascinating and beautiful, but unfortunately, like everything else native, are quickly disappearing. The majority of flora considered exotic by visitors was introduced either by the original Polynesians or by later white settlers. The Polynesians who colonized Hawaii brought foodstuffs, including coconuts, bananas, taro, breadfruit, sweet potatoes, yams, and sugarcane. They also carried along gourds to use as containers, the *awa* plant to make a basic intoxicant, and the ti plant to use for offerings or to string into hula skirts. Non-Hawaiian settlers over the years have brought mangos, papayas, passion fruit, pineapples, and many other tropical fruits and vegetables associated with the islands. Also, most of the flowers, including protea, plumeria, anthuriums, orchids, heliconia, ginger, and most hibiscus, have come from every continent on earth. Tropical America, Asia, Java, India, and China have contributed their most beautiful and delicate blooms. Hawaii is blessed with national and state parks, gardens, undisturbed rainforests, private reserves, and commercial nurseries that offer an exhaustive botanical survey of the island. The following is a sampling of the common native and introduced flora that add dazzling color and exotic tastes to the landscape.

Native Trees

Koa and ohia are two native trees still seen on the main islands. Both have been greatly reduced by the foraging of introduced cattle and goats, and through logging and forest fires.

The koa, a form of acacia, is Hawaii's finest native tree. It can grow to over 70 feet high and has a strong, straight trunk that can measure more than 10 feet in circumference. Koa is a quickly growing legume that fixes nitrogen in the soil. It is believed the tree originated in Africa, then migrated to Australia, where dry conditions caused the elimination of leaves. When koa came to the Pacific Islands, instead of reverting to the true leaf, it just broadened its leaf stem into sickle-shaped, leaflike foliage that produces an inconspicuous, pale-yellow flower. When the tree is young or damaged it will revert to the original feathery, fernlike leaf that evolved in Africa millions of years ago. Koa does best in well-drained soil in deep forest areas, but scruffy specimens will grow in poorer soil. The Hawaiians used koa as the main log for their dugout canoes, and elaborate ceremonies were performed when a log was cut and dragged to a canoe shed. Koa wood was also preferred for paddles, spears, even surfboards. Today it is still, unfortunately, considered an excellent furniture wood; and although fine specimens can be found in the reserve of Hawaii Volcanoes National Park on the Big Island, loggers elsewhere are harvesting the last of the big trees.

The ohia is a survivor and therefore the most abundant of all the native Hawaiian trees. Coming in a variety of shapes and sizes, it grows

KAREN McKINLEY

koa

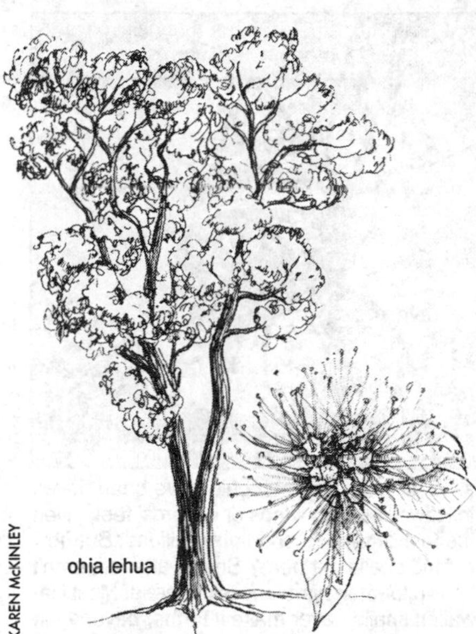
KAREN McKINLEY

ohia lehua

as miniature trees in wet bogs or as 100-foot giants on cool, dark slopes at higher elevations. This tree is often the first life in new lava flows. The ohia produces a tuftlike flower—usually red, but occasionally orange, yellow, or white, the latter being very rare and elusive—that resembles a natural pompon. The flower was considered sacred to Pele; it was said she would cause a rainstorm if you picked ohia blossoms without the proper prayers. The flowers were fashioned into lei that resembled feather boas. The strong, hard wood was used to make canoes, poi bowls, and especially temple images. Ohia logs were also used as railroad ties and shipped to the Mainland from Pahoa. It's believed that the "golden spike" linking rail lines between the U.S. East and West coasts was driven into a Puna ohia log when the two railroads came together in Ogden, Utah.

Note: For more on the *kukui* nut tree see "Hawaiian Folk Medicine and Cures" under "Health and Safety" later in this chapter.

Lobelia

More species of lobelia grow in Hawaii than anywhere else in the world. A common garden flower elsewhere, in Hawaii it grows to tree height. You'll see some unique species covered with hair or with spikes. The lobelia flower is tiny and resembles a miniature orchid with curved and pointed ends, like the beak of the native *'i'iwi.* This bird feeds on the flower's nectar; it's obvious that both evolved in Hawaii together and exhibit the strange phenomenon of nature mimicking nature.

Tropical Rainforests

When it comes to pure and diverse natural beauty, the U.S. is one of the finest pieces of real estate on earth. As if purple mountains' majesty and fruited plains weren't enough, it even received a tiny, living emerald of tropical rainforest. A tropical rainforest is where the earth itself takes a breath and exhales pure sweet oxygen through its vibrant, living green canopy. Though these forests—located in the territories of Puerto Rico and the Virgin Islands, and in the state of Hawaii—comprise only one-half of one percent of the world's total, they must be preserved. The U.S. Congress passed two bills in 1986 designed to protect the unique biological diversity of its tropical areas, but their destruction has continued unabated. The lowland rainforests of Hawaii, populated mostly by native ohia trees, are being razed. Landowners slash, burn, and bulldoze them to create more land for cattle and agriculture, and, most distressingly, for wood chips to generate electricity! Introduced wild boar gouge the forest floor, exposing sensitive roots and leaving tiny fetid ponds where mosquito larvae thrive. Feral goats roam the forests like hoofed locusts and strip all vegetation within reach. Maui's Nature Conservancy Preserve in Waikamoi has managed to fence in a speck of this forest, keeping it safe from these animals for the time being. Almost half of the birds classified in the U.S. as endangered live in Hawaii, and almost all of these make their homes in the rainforests. For example, Maui's rainforests have yielded the *poouli,* a new species of bird discovered only in 1974. Another forest survey in 1981 rediscovered the Bishop's *'o'o,* a bird thought to be extinct at the turn of the century. We can only lament the passing of the rainforests that have already fallen to ignorance, but if this ill-fated destruction continues on a global level, we will be lamenting our own passing. We must nurture the rainforests that remain, and with simple enlightenment, let them be.

HAWAII'S ANIMALS

No one knows for sure, but it's highly probable the first animal arrivals in Hawaii were insects. Again the theory is most were blown here by ancient hurricanes or drifted here imbedded in floating logs and other pieces of wood. Like the plants that preceded them, their success and rapid evolution were phenomenal. A pregnant female had to make the impossible journey, then happen upon a suitable medium in which to deposit her eggs. Here, at least, they would be free from predators and parasites with a good chance of developing to maturity. Again the gene pool was highly restricted and the environment so foreign that an amazing variety of evolutionary changes occurred. Biologists believe only 150 original insect species are responsible for the more than 10,000 species that occur in Hawaii today. Of these 10,000, nearly 98% are found nowhere else on earth. Many are restricted to only one island, and most are dependent on a single species of plant or fruit. For this reason, when Hawaiian plants become extinct, many insects disappear as well.

It's very probable there were no pests before humans arrived. The first Polynesians introduced flies, lice, and fleas. Westerners brought the indestructible cockroach, mosquito larvae in their ships' stores of water, termites, ants, and all the plant pests that could hitch a ride in the cuttings and fruits intended for planting. Today visitors will note the stringent agricultural controls at airports. Some complain about the inconvenience, but they should know that in the past 50 years over 700 new insect species have become established in Hawaii. Many are innocent enough, while others cause great problems for Hawaii's agriculture.

Land Snails

People have the tendency to ignore snails until they step on one, and then they find them repulsive. But Hawaiian snails are some of the most remarkable and beautiful in the world. It's one thing to accept the possibility that a few in-

LOUISE FOOTE

sects or plant spores could have been driven to Hawaii by high winds or on birds' feet, given the fact of their uncountable billions. But how did the snails get here? Snails, after all, aren't known for their nimbleness or speed. Most Hawaiian snails never make it farther beyond the tree in which they're born. Yet over 1,000 snail varieties are found in Hawaii, and most are inexplicably found nowhere else. The Polynesians didn't bring them, seawater kills them, and it would have to be a mighty big bird that didn't notice one clinging to its foot. Biologists have puzzled over Hawaiian snails for years. One, J.T. Gulick, wrote in 1858, "These Achatinellinae [tree snails] never came from Noah's ark." Tree snails are found on Oahu, Maui, Molokai, and Lanai, but not on Kauai. Kauai has its own land dwellers, and the Big Island has land snails that have moved into the trees. Like all the other endemic species, Hawaiian land snails now face extinction. Of the estimated 1,000 species existing when the Europeans came, 600 are now gone forever, and many others are threatened. Agriculture, the demise of native flora, and the introduction of new species add up to a bleak future for the snails.

Drosophila, The Hawaiian Fly

Most people hardly pay attention to flies, unless one lands on their plate lunch. But geneticists from throughout the world, and especially from the University of Hawaii, make special pilgrimages to the volcano area of the Big Island

and to Maui just to study the native Hawaiian drosophila. This critter is related to the fruit fly and housefly, but there are hundreds of singularly unique native species. The Hawaiian ecosystem is very simple and straightforward, so geneticists can trace the evolutionary changes from species to subspecies through mating behavior. The scientists compare the drosophila species between the two islands and chart the differences. Major discoveries in evolutionary genetics have been made through these studies.

Coral

Whether you're an avid scuba diver or novice snorkeler, you'll become aware of Maui's underwater coral gardens and grottoes whenever you peer at the fantastic seascapes below the waves. Although there is plenty of it, the coral in Hawaii doesn't do as well as in other more equatorial areas because the water is too wild and it's not quite as warm. Coral looks like a plant fashioned from colorful stone, but it's really the skeleton of tiny animals, zoophytes, that eat algae in order to live. Coral grows best on the west side of Maui where the water is quite still, the days more sunny, and the algae can thrive. Many of Hawaii's reefs have been dying in the last 20 years, and no one seems to know why. Pesticides, used in agriculture, have been pointed to as a possible cause.

Indigenous Land Animals

Before humans arrived, Hawaii had a paucity of higher forms of land animals. There were no amphibians and no reptiles, and except for a profusion of birdlife, insects, and snails, only two other animals were present: the **monk seal** and the **hoary bat,** both highly specialized mammals.

The monk seal has close relatives in the Caribbean and Mediterranean, although the Caribbean relatives are now believed to be extinct, making the monk seal one of the two tropical seals left on earth. It's believed that the monk seal's ancestors entered the Pacific about 200,000 years ago when the Isthmus of Panama was submerged. When the land rose, no more seals arrived, and the monk seal became indigenous to Hawaii. The main habitat for the Hawaiian monk seal is the outer islands, from the French Frigate Atolls north to Kure Island, but infrequently a seal is spotted on the shores of one of the main islands. Though the seals' existence was known to the native Hawaiians, who called them *ilio-holo-i-kauaua* ("dog running in the toughness"), they didn't seem to play much of a role in their folklore or ecosystem. Whalers and traders certainly knew of their existence, hunting them for food and sometimes for skins. This kind of pressure almost wiped out the small seal population in the 18th century. Scientists were largely unaware of the monk seal until early this century. Finally, the seals were recognized as an endangered species and put under the protection of the Hawaiian Islands National Wildlife Refuge, where they remain in a touch-and-go battle against extinction. Today it's estimated that only 1,000 individuals are left.

The hoary bat (*pe'apo'a*) is a remarkable migratory animal that reached Hawaii from North and South America under its own power. The Hawaiian hoary bat no longer migrates, but its continental relatives still range far and wide. The Hawaiian bat has become somewhat smaller and reddish in color over the years, distinguishing it from its larger, darker brown cousins. The main population is on the Big Island, with a smaller breeding ground on Kauai. The bats normally live at altitudes below 4,000 feet, but some have been observed on Mauna Loa and Mauna Kea above 6,000 feet. Sometimes bats are spotted on the other main islands, but it remains uncertain whether they inhabit the islands or simply fly there from their established colonies. The hoary bat is a solitary creature that spends the daylight hours hanging from the branches of trees. It doesn't live in caves like others of its species. Look for them over Hilo Bay on the Big Island at sunset.

BIRDLIFE

One of the great tragedies of natural history is the continuing demise of Hawaiian birdlife. Perhaps only 15 original species of birds remain of the more than 70 native families that thrived before the coming of humans. Experts believe that the ancient Hawaiians annihilated about 40 species, including seven species of geese, a rare one-legged owl, ibis, lovebirds, sea eagles, and hunting creepers. Since the arrival of Captain Cook in 1778, 23 species have become extinct, with 31 more in danger. Hawaii's endangered birds account for more than 50% of the birds listed in the U.S. Sport Fisheries and Wildlife's *Red Book* that cites rare and endangered animals. In the last 200 years, more than four times as many birds have become extinct in Hawaii as in all of North America. These figures unfortunately suggest that a full 40% of Hawaii's endemic birds no longer exist. Almost all of Oahu's native birds are gone and few indigenous Hawaiian birds can be found on any island below the 3,000-foot level.

Native birds have been reduced in number because of multiple factors. The original Polynesians helped wipe out many species. They altered large areas for farming, and burned off patches of pristine forests. Also, bird feathers were highly prized for the making of lei, for featherwork in capes and helmets, and for the large *kahili* fans that indicated rank among the *ali'i*. Introduced exotic birds and the new diseases they carried are another major reason for reduction of native bird numbers, along with predation by the mongoose and rat—especially upon ground-nesting birds. Bird malaria and bird pox were also devastating to the native species. Mosquitoes, unknown in Hawaii until a ship named the *Wellington* introduced them at Lahaina in 1826 through larvae carried in its water barrels, infected most native birds, causing a rapid reduction in birdlife. Feral pigs rooting deep in the rainforests knock over ferns and small trees, creating muddy pools in which mosquito larvae thrive. However, the most damaging factor by far is the assault upon native forests by agriculture and land developers. The vast majority of Hawaiian birds evolved into specialists. They lived in only one small area and ate a very limited number of plants or insects, which once removed or altered soon caused the death of the birds.

Preservation

Theodore Roosevelt established the Northwest Islands as a National Wildlife Reserve in the early 20th century, and efforts have continued since then to preserve Hawaii's unique avifauna. Many fine organizations are fighting the battle to preserve Hawaii's natural heritage, including: Hawaii Audubon Society, University of Hawaii, U.S. Fish and Wildlife Service, World Wildlife Fund, and Hawaii Department of Natural Resources. While visiting Hawaii make sure to obey all rules regarding the natural environment. Never disturb nesting birds or their habitat while hiking. Be careful with fire and never cut living trees. If you spot an injured or dead bird do not pick it up, but report it to the local office of the U.S. Fish and Wildlife Service. Only through a conscientious effort of all concerned does Hawaii's wildlife stand a chance of surviving.

Hawaiian Honeycreepers

A most amazing family of all the birds on the face of earth is one known as Drepanididae, or Hawaiian honeycreepers. There are more than 40 distinct types of honeycreepers, although many more are suspected to have become extinct even before the arrival of Captain Cook, when a record was started. All are believed to have evolved from *a single* ancestral species. The honeycreepers have differing body types. Some look like finches, while others resemble warblers, thrushes, blackbirds, parrots, and even woodpeckers. Their bills range from long, pointed honeysuckers to tough, hooked nutcrackers. They are the most divergently evolved birds in the world. If Darwin, who studied the birds of the Galapagos Islands, had come to Hawaii, he would have found bird evolution that would make the Galapagos seem like child's play.

More Endangered Endemic Birds

Maui is the last home of the **crested honeycreeper** *(akohe'kohe)*. It once lived on Molokai but no longer. Its habitat is the windward slope of Haleakala, from the 4,500- to the 6,500-foot level. A rather large bird, averaging seven inches, it's predominantly black. Its throat and breast are tipped with gray feathers; bright orange decks its neck and underbelly. A distinctive fluff of feathers forms a crown. It primarily eats ohia flowers, and it's believed the crown feathers gather pollen and help propagate the ohia. The **Maui parrotbill** is another endangered bird found only on the slopes of Haleakala above 5,000 feet. It has an olive green back and yellow body. Its most distinctive feature is the parrotlike bill it uses to crack branches and pry out larvae. Two endangered waterbirds are the **Hawaiian stilt** *(ae'o)* and the **Hawaiian coot** *(alae*

pueo

ke'oke'o). The stilt is a 16-inch, very thin wading bird. It is primarily black with a white belly. Its long, sticklike legs are pink. It lives on Maui at Kanaha and Kealia ponds. The adults will pretend to be hurt, putting on an excellent "broken-wing" performance in order to lure predators away from their nests. The Hawaiian coot is a web-footed waterbird that resembles a duck. Found on all the main islands but mostly on Maui and Kauai, it has dull gray feathers, a white bill, and white tail feathers. It builds a large floating nest and vigorously defends its young. The **dark-rumped petrel** is slightly different than others in its family that are primarily marine birds. This petrel is found around the visitors center at Haleakala Crater about an hour after dusk from May to October.

Survivors

The *amakihi* and the *'i'iwi* are endemic birds not endangered at the moment. The *amakihi* is one of the most common native birds. Yellowish-green, it frequents the high branches of ohia, koa, and sandalwood looking for insects, nectar, or fruit. It's less specialized than most other Hawaiian birds, the main reason for its continued existence. The *'i'iwi* is a bright red bird with a salmon-colored hooked bill. It's found only on Maui, Hawaii, and Kauai in forests above 2,000 feet. It, too, feeds on a variety of insects and flowers. The *'i'iwi* is known for its harsh voice that sounds like a squeaking hinge, but is also capable of a melodious song.

The *poouli* is a dark brown, five-inch bird with a black mask and dark brown feet. Its tail is short, and it sports a conical bill. It was saved from extinction through efforts of the Sierra Club and Audubon Society, who successfully had it listed as the newest addition to the Federal List of Endangered Species. The bird has one remaining stronghold deep in the forests of Maui.

Pueo

This Hawaiian owl is found on all of the main islands, but mostly on Maui, especially in Haleakala Crater. The *pueo* is one of the oldest examples of an *aumakua* (family-protecting spirit) in Hawaiian mythology. It was an especially benign and helpful guardian. Old Hawaiian stories abound in which a *pueo* came to the aid of a warrior in distress or a whole defeated army. Arriving at a tree in which a *pueo* had alighted, the soldiers are safe from their pursuers and are under the protection of "the wings of an owl." The many introduced barn owls in Hawaii are easily distinguished from a *pueo* by their heart-shaped faces. The *pueo* is about 15 inches tall with a mixture of brown and white feathers. The eyes are large, round, and yellow, and the legs are heavily feathered, unlike those of a barn owl. *Pueo* chicks are a distinct yellow.

The *Nene*

The *nene,* or Hawaiian goose, deserves special mention because it is Hawaii's state bird and is making a comeback from the edge of extinction. The *nene* is found only on the slopes of Mauna Loa, Hualalai, and Mauna Kea on the Big Island, and in Haleakala Crater on Maui. It was extinct on Maui until a few birds were returned there in 1957, but some experts maintain the *nene* lived naturally only on the Big Island. *Nene* are raised at the Wildfowl Trust in Slimbridge, England, which placed the first birds at Haleakala, and at the Hawaiian Fish and Game Station at Pohakuloa, along the Saddle Road on Hawaii. By the 1940s, fewer than 50 birds lived in the wild. Now approximately 125 birds live on Haleakala and 500 on the Big Island. Although the birds can be raised successfully in captivity, their life in the wild is still in question.

The *nene* is believed to be a descendant of the Canada goose, which it resembles. Geese are migratory birds that form strong kinship ties, mating for life. It's speculated a migrating goose became disabled, and along with its loyal mate, remained in Hawaii. The *nene* is smaller than its Canadian cousin, has lost a great deal of webbing in its feet, and is perfectly at home away from water, foraging and nesting on rugged and bleak lava flows. The *nene* is a perfect symbol of Hawaii: let it be, and it will live.

WHALES

Perhaps it's their tremendous size and graceful power, coupled with a dancer's delicacy of movement, that render whales so esthetically and emotionally captivating. In fact, many people claim they feel a spirit-bond to these obviously intelligent mammals that at one time shared dry land with us and then reevolved into creatures of the great seas. Experts often remark whales exhibit behavior akin to the highest social virtues. For example, whales rely much more on learned behavior than on instinct, the sign of a highly evolved intelligence. Gentle mothers and protective "escort" males join to teach the young to survive. They display loyalty and bravery in times of distress, and innate gentleness and curiosity. Their "songs," especially those of the humpbacks, fascinate scientists and are considered a unique form of communication in the animal kingdom. Hawaii, especially the shallow and warm waters around Maui, is home to migrating humpback whales every year from November to May. Here, they winter, mate, give birth, and nurture their young until returning to food-rich northern waters in the spring. It's hoped that humankind can peacefully share the oceans with these magnificent giants forever. Then, perhaps, we will have taken the first steps toward saving ourselves.

Evolution And Socialization

Many millions of years ago, for an unknown reason, animals similar to cows were genetically triggered to leave the land and readapt to the sea. Known as cetaceans, this order contains about 80 species of whales, porpoises, and dolphins. Being mammals, cetaceans are warm-blooded and maintain a body temperature of 96°, only 2.5 degrees less than humans. After a gestation period of about one year, whales give birth to fully formed young, which usually enter the world tail first. The mother whale spins quickly to snap the umbilical cord, then places herself under the newborn and lifts it to the surface to take its first breath. A whale must be taught to swim or it will drown like any other air-breathing mammal. The baby whale, nourished by its mother's rich milk, becomes a member of an extended family, or **pod,** through which it's cared for, socialized, and protected by many "nannies."

Physiology

The best way to spot a whale is to look for its "spout," a misty spray forced from a blowhole—really the whale's nostrils that have moved from its snout to just behind its head. The spray from the spout is not water, but highly compressed air heated by the whale's body and expelled with such force that it condenses into a fine mist. A whale's tail is called a fluke; unlike the vertical tail of fish, a whale's tail is horizontal. The fluke, a marvelous appendage for propelling the whale through the water, is a vestige of the pelvis. It's so powerful that a 40-ton humpback can lift itself completely out of the water with only three strokes of its fluke. A whale's flippers are used to guide it through the water. The bones in the flippers closely resemble those of the human arm and hand; small, delicate bones at the ends of the flippers look like fingers and joints. On a humpback the flippers can be one-third as long as the body and supple enough to bend over its back, like a human reaching over the shoulder to scratch an itch.

A whale's eyes are functional but very small and not the primary sensors. Instead, the whale has developed keen hearing; the ears are small holes about as big around as the lead of a pencil. They have protective wax plugs that build up over the years. Like the growth rings in a tree, the ear plugs can be counted to determine the age of a whale; its life span is about the same as that of a human being. Because of strong ocean currents, and because of the myriad dangers inherent in being at sea, whales enjoy a very light sleep, more like a rest similar to humans just awakening, a state that is not fully conscious but aware.

Types Of Whales

Although all whales, dolphins, and porpoises are cetaceans, they are arbitrarily divided according to length. Whales are longer than 30 feet; dolphins range 6-30 feet; and porpoises are less than six feet long. There are basically two types of whales: toothed, which includes the sperm, killer, and pilot whales, as well as porpoises and dolphins; and baleen, including the blue, minke, right, fin, and humpback.

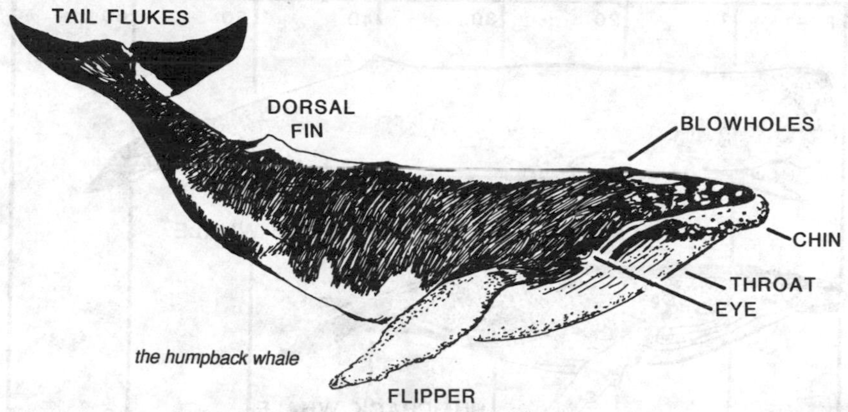

the humpback whale

Toothed whales feed by capturing and tearing their prey with their teeth. The killer whale or orca is the best known of the toothed whales. With its distinctive black-and-white markings and propensity for aquabatics, it's a favorite at marine parks around the world. The orca hunts other cetaceans, oftentimes attacking in packs to overcome larger whales. A killer whale in the wild lives about four times as long as a well-cared-for one in captivity.

A baleen whale eats by gliding through the water with its mouth open, sucking in marine plankton and tiny shrimplike creatures called krill. The whale then expels the water and captures the food in row after row of a prickly, fingernail-like substance called baleen.

Hawaiian Whales And Dolphins

The role of whales and dolphins in Hawaiian culture seems quite limited. Unlike fish, which were intimately known and individually named, only two generic names described whales: *kohola* ("whale"), and *palaoa* ("sperm whale"). Dolphins were lumped together under one name, *nai'a;* Hawaiians were known to harvest dolphins on occasion by herding them onto a beach. Whale jewelry was worn by the *ali'i.* The most coveted ornament came from a sperm whale's tooth, called a *lei niho palaoa,* which was carved into one large curved pendant. Sperm whales have upward of 50 teeth, ranging in size 4-12 inches and weighing up to two pounds. One whale could provide numerous pendants. The most famous whale in Hawaiian waters is the humpback, but others often sighted include the sperm, killer, false killer, pilot, Cuvier's, Blainsville, and pygmy killer. There are technically no porpoises, but dolphins include the common, bottlenose, spinner, white-sided, broad- and slender-beaked, and rough-toothed. The mahimahi, a favorite eating fish found on many menus, is commonly referred to as a dolphin but is unrelated and is a true fish, not a cetacean.

The Humpbacks Of Maui

The humpback gets its name from its style of exposing its dorsal fin when it dives, which gives it a humped appearance. Its dorsal fin also puts it into the **roqual** family. There are about 7,000-8,000 humpback whales alive today, down from an estimated 100,000 at the turn of the century. The remaining whales are divided into three separate global populations: North Atlantic, North Pacific, and South Pacific groups. About 600 North Pacific humpbacks migrate from coastal Alaska beginning in November. Migration peaks in February, when humpbacks congregate mostly in the waters off Maui, with a smaller group heading for the waters off Kona on Hawaii. Within the last few years, all of the waters surrounding Maui County (including the Lahaina Roads but not the water around Kahoolawe) have been designated as the **Hawaiian Islands Humpback Whale National Marine Sanctuary.** This will hopefully ensure a perpetual safe haven for the whales.

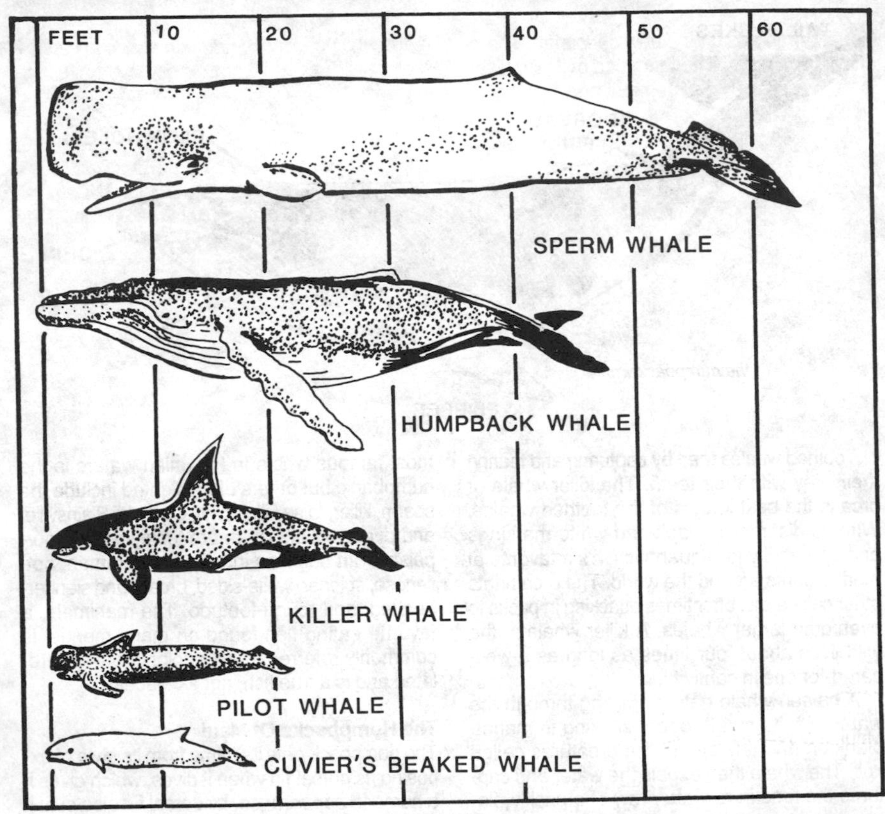

An adult humpback is 45 feet long and weighs in at a svelte 40 tons (80,000 pounds). It comes to Hawaii mainly to give birth to a single 2,000-pound, relatively blubberless calf. It nurses its calf for about one year and becomes impregnated again the next. While in Hawaiian waters the humpbacks generally don't eat. They wait until returning to Alaska, where they gorge themselves on krill. It's estimated they can live off their blubber without peril for six months. They have enormous mouths stretching one-third the length of their bodies, which is filled with over 600 rows of baleen, a prickly, fingernail-like substance. Humpbacks have been known to blow air underwater to create giant bubble-nets that help corral krill. They rush in with mouths agape and dine on their catch.

Like other baleen whales, humpbacks feed in relatively shallow waters and sound (dive) for periods lasting a maximum of about 25 minutes. In comparison, the sperm whale, a toothed bottom-feeder, can stay down for over an hour. On the surface a humpback will breathe about once every two minutes. They also sleep on the surface or just below it.

A distinctive feature of the humpback is the 15-foot flipper it can bend over its back. The flippers and tail flukes have white markings that differ between individuals, much like human fingerprints. These markings are used to identify individual migrating humpbacks. Scientists photograph the distinctive tails and send prints to Seattle, Washington, a center of whale research. There a computer analysis identifies the individual or records it as a new specimen. Thereafter, any sightings become part of its life history. The humpback is the most aquabatic of all whales and it is a thrilling sight to see one of these agile giants leap from the water, creating a monumental splash.

The Humpback's Song

Unlike other whales, humpbacks have the special ability to sing. They create their melodies by grunting, shrieking, and moaning. No one knows exactly what the songs represent, but it's clear they're a form of communication. The singers appear to be "escort males" who tag along with, and seem to guard, a mother and her calf. Some scientists believe these are lone males and perhaps the song is territorial, or a mating call. The songs are exact renditions that last 20 minutes or longer and are repeated for hours. Amazingly, all the whales know and sing the same song, and the song changes from year to year. The notes are so forceful they can be heard above and below the water for miles. Some of the deep bass notes carry underwater for 100 miles.

Good recordings of the humpbacks' songs can be heard aboard the *Carthaginian II,* a restored 19th-century square-rigged ship just to the right of the loading dock in Lahaina Harbor on Maui. It serves as a floating museum dedicated to whales and whaling. As you descend into the ship's hold and bright sunlight fades to cool shadow, you become a visitor in the watery world of the humpback whale. The mysterious songs of the humpback provide the background music and set the mood. Sit on comfortable captain's chairs and watch the excellent audio-visual display. The photos of whales are by Flip Nicklin, courtesy of the National Geographic Society. The *Carthaginian II* is a project of the Lahaina Restoration Foundation, P.O. Box 338, Lahaina, Maui HI 96761, tel. 661-3262. The foundation is a nonprofit organization dedicated to educational and historical restoration in Lahaina (see "Lahaina" in the West Maui chapter).

Whaling History

Humans have known about whales for many thousands of years. A Minoan palace on the island of Crete depicts whales on a 5,000-year-old mural. The first whalers were probably Norwegians who used stone harpoon heads to capture their prey over 4,000 years ago. Inuit have long engaged in whaling as a means of survival, and for centuries many peoples living along coastal waters have harpooned migrating whales that ventured close to shore. The Basques had a thriving medieval whaling industry in the 12th century centered in the Bay of Biscay, until they wiped out all the Biscayan right whales. The height of the classic whaling industry that inspired Melville's *Moby Dick* occurred from 1820 until 1860. The international whaling capital perfectly situated in the center of the winter whaling grounds was Lahaina, Maui. At that time 900 sailing ships roamed the globe in search of whales. Of these, 700 were American, and they started the trend away from coastal to pelagic whaling by bringing their try-pots (blubber pots) aboard ship.

Although the killing was great during these years, every part of the whale was needed and used: blubber, meat, bone, teeth. Whale oil, the main product, was a superior lighting fuel and lubricant unmatched until petroleum came into general use in the mid-19th century. Today, every single whale by-product can be manufactured synthetically and there's absolutely no primary need to justify slaughtering whales.

During the great whaling days, the whales actually had a fighting chance. After all, they were hunted by men in wooden sailing ships that depended upon favorable winds. Once a whale was sighted by a sailor perched high in the rigging using a low-powered telescope, a small boat heaved off; after desperate rowing and dangerous maneuvering, the master harpooner threw his shaft by hand. Once the whale was dead, it took every able-bodied man to haul it in.

Today, however, modern methods have wiped out every trace of daring and turned the hunt into technologically assisted slaughter. Low-flying aircraft radio the whales' locations to huge factory-ships that track them with radar and sonar. Once the pod is spotted, super-swift launches tear into them, firing cannon-propelled harpoons with lethal exploding tips. The killer launches keep firing until every whale in the pod is dead, and the huge factory-ship follows behind, merely scooping up the lifeless carcasses and hauling them aboard with diesel winches.

Many pirate whalers still roam the seas. The worst example of modern hunting perpetrated by these racketeers occurred in the Bahamas in 1971. A ship ironically carrying the name of *the* classic conservation group, *Sierra,* succeeded in wiping out every single humpback whale that wintered in Bahamian waters. Since 1971 not one whale has been sighted in the Bahamas, and whalewatchers lament they will never return.

The Last Whalers

Thanks to world opinion and the efforts of benign but aggressive organizations such as Greenpeace and Earth Trust, the **International Whaling Commission** (IWC), a voluntary group of 17 nations, now sets standards and passes quotas on the number and species of whales that can be killed. Over the last 18 years the blue, right, gray, bowhead, and humpback have become totally protected. However, many great whales such as the sperm, minke, sei, and fin are still hunted. Also, the IWC has no power of enforcement except public opinion and possible voluntary economic sanction. In some countries, the whaling industry is the *only* means of livelihood to coastal people whose economy is depressed and difficult already. A proposed quota of 10,000 minke whales will be hunted in Antarctica this year, mainly by Norway, Greenland, and Iceland. They will sell their catches to Japan, where whale meat brings up to $200 per pound.

The Japanese technically stay within their quotas, but they hire and outfit these and other nationals to hunt whales for them. Their main argument is that whaling is a traditional industry upon which they rely for food and jobs. This is patently false. Hardly more than 100 years old, pelagic whaling is a new industry to the Japanese. Much of the Japanese whale meat becomes pet food anyway, which is mainly exported.

Amazingly, a recent poll taken in Japan by the Whale and Dolphin Society of London found that 69% of the people opposed whaling. Finally, through the efforts of *ICEARCH* (International Cetacean Education And Research Conference), the first pillars of a bridge were laid between Japanese and Western scientists who are dedicated to finding a way for humans and whales to live in harmony. In April 1993 these scientists came together on Maui for the first time to discuss the issue.

Whalewatching

If you're in Hawaii from late November to early May, you have an excellent chance of spotting a humpback. You can often see a whale from a vantage point on land, but this is nowhere near as thrilling as seeing them close up from a boat. Either way, binoculars are a must. Telephoto and zoom lenses are also useful, and you might even get a nifty photo in the bargain. But don't waste your film unless you have a fairly high-powered zoom: fixed-lens cameras give pictures with a lot of ocean and a tiny black speck. If you're lucky enough to see a whale breach (jump clear of the water), keep watching—they often repeat this a number of times. If a whale dives and lifts its fluke high in the air, expect it to be down for at least 15 minutes and not come up in the same spot. Other times a whale will dive shallowly, then bob up and down quite often. If you time your arrival near sunset, even if you don't see a whale you'll enjoy a mind-boggling light show. (For whalewatching tours see "Sightseeing Tours" in the individual travel chapters.)

BOB RACE

HISTORY

THE ROAD FROM TAHITI

Until the 1820s, when New England missionaries began a phonetic rendering of the Hawaiian language, the past was kept vividly alive by the sonorous voices of special *kahuna* who chanted the sacred *mele*. The chants were beautiful, flowing word pictures that captured the essence of every aspect of life. These *mele* praised the land *(mele aina),* royalty *(mele ali'i),* and life's tender aspects *(mele aloha).* Chants were dedicated to friendship, hardship, and favorite children. Entire villages sometimes joined together to compose a *mele*—every word was chosen carefully, and the wise old *kupuna* would decide if the words were lucky or unlucky. Some *mele* were bawdy or funny on the surface but contained secret meanings, often bitingly sarcastic, that ridiculed an inept or cruel leader. The most important chants took listeners back into the dim past before people lived in Hawaii. From these genealogies *(ko'ihonua),* the *ali'i* derived the right to rule, since these chants went back to the gods Wakea and Papa from whom the *ali'i* were directly descended.

The Kumulipo

The great genealogies, finally compiled in the late 1800s by order of King Kalakaua, were collectively known as *The Kumulipo, A Hawaiian Creation Chant,* basically a Polynesian account of Genesis. Other chants related to the beginning of this world, but *The Kumulipo* sums it all up and is generally considered the best. The chant relates that after the beginning of time, there is a period of darkness. The darkness, however, mysteriously brims with spontaneous life; during this period plants and animals are born, as well as Kumulipo, the man, and Po'ele, the woman. In the eighth chant darkness gives way to light and the gods descend to earth. Wakea is "the sky father" and Papa is "the earth mother," whose union gives birth to the islands of Hawaii. First born is Hawaii, followed by Maui, then Kahoolawe. Apparently, Papa becomes bushed after three consecutive births and decides to vacation in Tahiti. While Papa is away recovering from postpartum depression and working on her tan, Wakea gets lonely and takes Kaula as his second wife; she bears him the island-child of Lanai. Not fully cheered up, but getting the hang of it, Wakea takes a third wife, Hina, who promptly bears the island of Molokai.

Meanwhile, Papa gets wind of these shenanigans, returns from Polynesia, and retaliates by taking up with Lua, a young and virile god. She soon gives birth to the island of Oahu. Papa and Wakea finally decide that they really are meant for each other and reconcile to conceive Kauai, Niihau, Kaula, and Nihoa. These two progenitors are the source from which the *ali'i* ultimately traced their lineage, and from which they derived their god-ordained power to rule.

Basically, there are two major genealogical families: the **Nana'ulu,** who became the royal *ali'i* of Oahu and Kauai; and the **Ulu,** who provided the royalty of Maui and Hawaii. The best sources of information on Hawaiian myth and legend are Martha Beckwith's *Hawaiian Mythology* and the monumental three-volume opus *An Account of the Polynesian Race* compiled by Abraham Fornander from 1878-85. Fornander, after settling in Hawaii, married an *ali'i* from Molokai and had an illustrious career as a journalist, Maui circuit judge, and finally Supreme Court justice. For years Fornander sent scribes to every corner of the kingdom to listen to the elder *kupuna.* They returned with firsthand accounts, which he dutifully recorded.

Polynesians

Since prehistory, Polynesians have been seafaring people whose origins cannot be completely traced. They seem to have come from Southeast Asia mostly through the gateway of Indonesia, and their racial strain pulls features from all three dominant races: Caucasian, Negro, and Asian. They learned to navigate on tame narrow waterways along Indonesia and New Guinea, then fanned out eastward into the great Pacific. They sailed northeast to the low islands of Micronesia and southwest to Fiji, the New Hebrides (now called Vanuatu), and New Caledonia. Fiji is regarded as the "cradle of Polynesian culture"; carbon dating places humans there as early as 3,500 B.C. Many races blended on Fiji, until finally the Negroid became dominant and the Polynesians moved on. Wandering, they discovered and settled Samoa and Tonga, then ranged far east to populate Tahiti, Easter Island, and the Marquesas. Ultimately, they became the masters of the "Polynesian Triangle," which measures more than 5,000 miles on each leg, stretching across both the North and South Pacific studded with islands. The great Maori kingdom of New Zealand is the southern apex of the triangle, with Easter Island marking the point farthest east; Hawaii, farthest north, was the last to be settled.

Migrations And Explorations

Ancient legends common throughout the South Pacific speak of a great Polynesian culture that existed on the island of Raiatea about 150 miles north of Tahiti. Here a powerful priesthood held sway in an enormous *heiau* in the Opoa district called Toputapuatea. Kings from throughout Polynesia came here to worship. Human sacrifice was common, as it was believed that the essence of the spirit could be utilized and controlled in this life; therefore the mana of Toputapuatea was great. Defeated warriors and commoners were used as living rollers to drag canoes up onto the beach, while corpses were dismembered and hung in trees. The power of the priests of Opoa lasted for many generations, evoking trembling fear in even the bravest warrior just by the mention of their name. Finally, their power waned and Polynesians lost their centralized culture, but the constant coming and going from Raiatea for centuries sharpened the Polynesians' already excellent sailing skills and convinced them that the world was vast and that unlimited opportunities existed to better their lot.

LOUISE FOOTE

The Polynesians, attuned to every nuance in their environment, noticed a migratory land bird called the golden plover arrived from the north every year. They reasoned that since the plover was not a seabird, there must be land to the north.

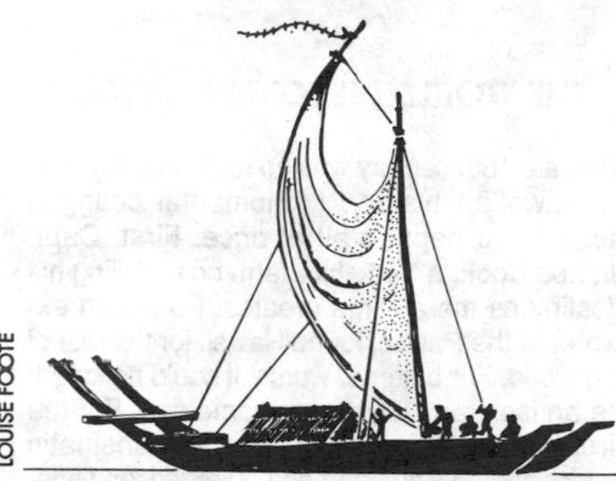

LOUISE FOOTE

The canoe hull was a log shaped by masterly stone adze work. The sides were planks drilled and sewn together with fiber cord.

Now explorers, many left to look for the "heavenly homeland to the north." Samoans called it *Savai'i;* Tongans *Hawai;* Rarotongans *Avalki;* and Society Islanders *Havai'i.* Others abandoned the small islands throughout Polynesia where population pressures exceeded the limits of natural resources, prompting famine. Furthermore, Polynesians were very warlike among themselves; power struggles between members of a ruling family were common, as were marauders from other islands. So, driven by hunger or warfare, countless refugee Polynesians headed north. Joining them were a few who undoubtedly went for the purely human reason of wanderlust.

The Great Navigators

No one knows exactly when the first Polynesians arrived in Hawaii, but the great deliberate migrations from the southern islands seem to have taken place A.D. 500-800; anthropologists keep pushing the date backward as new evidence becomes available. Even before that, however, it's reasonable to assume that the first people to set foot on Hawaii were probably fishermen, or perhaps defeated warriors whose canoes were blown hopelessly northward into unfamiliar waters. They arrived by a combination of extraordinary good luck and an uncanny ability to sail and navigate without instruments, using the sun by day and the moon and rising stars by night. They could feel the water and determine direction by swells, tides, and currents. The movements of fish and cloud formations were also utilized to give direction. Since their arrival was probably an accident, they were unprepared to settle on the fertile but barren lands, having no stock animals, plant cuttings, or women. Forced to return southward, many undoubtedly lost their lives at sea, but a few wild-eyed stragglers must have made it home to tell tales of a paradise to the north where land was plentiful and the sea bounteous. This is affirmed by ancient navigational chants from Tahiti, Moorea, and Bora Bora, which passing from father to son revealed how to follow the stars to the "heavenly homeland in the north." Possibly a few migrations followed, but it's known that for centuries there was no real reason for a mass exodus, so the chants alone remained and eventually became shadowy legend.

From Where They Came

It's generally agreed that the first planned migrations were from the violent cannibal islands that Spanish explorers called the Marquesas, 11 islands in extreme eastern Polynesia. The islands themselves are harsh and inhospitable, breeding a toughness into these people that enabled them to withstand the hardships of long, unsure ocean voyages and years of resettlement. Marquesans were a fiercely independent people whose chiefs could rise from the ranks because of bravery or intelligence. They must have also been a savage-looking lot. Both men and women tattooed themselves in complex blue patterns from head to foot. The warriors carried massive, intricately designed ironwood war clubs and wore carved whale teeth in slits in their earlobes that eventually stretched to their shoulders. They shaved the sides of their heads with sharks' teeth, tied their hair in two topknots that looked like horns, and rubbed their heavily muscled and tattooed bodies with scented coconut oils. Their cults worshipped mummified ancestors; the bodies of warriors of defeated neighboring tribes were consumed. They were masters at building great double-hulled canoes launched from huge canoe sheds. Two hulls were fastened together to form a catamaran, and a hut in the center provided shelter in bad weather. The average voyaging canoe was 60-80 feet long and could comfortably hold an extended family of about 30 people. These small family bands carried all the staples they would need in the new lands.

The New Lands

For five centuries the Marquesans settled and lived peacefully on the new land, as if Hawaii's *aloha* spirit overcame most of their fierceness. The tribes coexisted in relative harmony, especially since there was no competition for land. Cannibalism died out. There was much coming and going between Hawaii and Polynesia as new people came to settle for hundreds of years. Then, it appears that in the 12th century a deliberate exodus of warlike Tahitians arrived and subjugated the settled islanders. They came to conquer. This incursion had a terrific significance on the Hawaiian religious and social system. Oral tradition relates that a Tahitian priest, Paao, found the mana or power of the Hawaiian chiefs to be low, signifying that their gods were weak. Paao built a *heiau* at Wahaula on the Big Island, then introduced the warlike god Ku and the rigid *kapu* system through which the new rulers became dominant. Voyages between Tahiti and Hawaii continued for about 100 years and Tahitian customs, legends, and language became the Hawaiian way of life. Then suddenly, for no recorded or apparent reason, the voyages discontinued and Hawaii returned to total isolation.

The islands remained forgotten for almost 500 years until the indomitable English seaman, Capt. James Cook, sighted Oahu on January 18, 1778 and stepped ashore at Waimea on Kauai two days later. At that time Hawaii's isolation was so complete that even the Polynesians had forgotten about it. On an earlier voyage, Tupaia, a high priest from Raiatea, had accompanied Captain Cook as he sailed throughout Polynesia. Tupaia demonstrated his vast knowledge of existing archipelagos throughout the South Pacific by naming over 130 islands and drawing a map that included the Tonga group, the Cook Islands, the Marquesas, even tiny Pitcairn, a rock in far eastern Polynesia where the mutinous crew of the *Bounty* found solace. In mentioning the Marquesas, Tupaia said, *"He ma'a te ka'ata,"* which means "Food is man" or simply "Cannibals!" But remarkably absent from Tupaia's vast knowledge was the existence of Easter Island, New Zealand, and Hawaii.

The next waves of people to Hawaii would be white, and the Hawaiian world would be changed quickly and forever.

THE WORLD DISCOVERS HAWAII

The late 18th century was an extraordinary time in Hawaiian history. Monumental changes seemed to happen all at once. First, Capt. James Cook, a Yorkshire farm boy fulfilling his destiny as the all-time greatest European explorer of the Pacific, found Hawaii for the rest of the world. For better or worse, it could no longer be an isolated Polynesian homeland. For the first time in Hawaiian history, a charismatic leader named Kamehameha emerged, and after a long civil war he united the islands into one centralized kingdom. The death of Captain Cook in Hawaii marked the beginning of a long series of tragic misunderstandings between whites and natives. When Kamehameha died, the old religious system of *kapu* came to an end, leaving the Hawaiians in a spiritual vortex. Many takers arrived to fill the void: missionaries after souls, whalers after their prey and a good time, traders and planters after profits and a home. The islands were opened and devoured like ripe fruit. Powerful nations, including Russia, Great Britain, France, and the United States, yearned to bring this strategic Pacific jewel under their influence. The 19th century brought the demise of the Hawaiian people as a dominant

HAWAII STATE ARCHIVES

Captain James Cook

political force in their own land and with it the end of Hawaii as a sovereign monarchy. An almost bloodless yet bitter military coup followed by a brief Hawaiian Republic ended in annexation by the United States. As the U.S. became completely entrenched politically and militarily, a new social and economic order was founded on the plantation system. Amazingly rapid population growth occurred with the importation of plantation workers from Asia and Europe, which yielded a unique cosmopolitan blend of races like none elsewhere on earth. By the dawning of the 20th century, the face of old Hawaii had been altered forever; the "sacred homeland in the north" was hurled into the modern age. The attack on Pearl Harbor saw a tremendous loss of life and brought Hawaii closer to the U.S. by a baptism of blood. Finally, on August 21, 1959, after 59 years as a "territory," Hawaii officially became America's 50th state.

Captain Cook Sights Hawaii

In 1776 Capt. James Cook set sail for the Pacific from Plymouth, England, on his third and final expedition into this still vastly unexplored region of the world. On a fruitless quest for the fabled Northwest Passage across the North American continent, he sailed down the coast of Africa, rounded the Cape of Good Hope, crossed the Indian Ocean, and traveled past New Zealand, Tasmania, and the Friendly Islands (where an unsuccessful plot was hatched by the *friendly* natives to murder him). On January 18, 1778, Captain Cook's 100-foot flagship HMS *Resolution* and its 90-foot companion HMS *Discovery* sighted Oahu. Two days later, they sighted Kauai and went ashore at the village of Waimea on January 20, 1778. Though anxious to get on with his mission, Cook decided to make a quick sortie to investigate this new land and reprovision his ships. He did, however, take time to remark in his diary about the close resemblance of these newfound people to others he had encountered as far south as New Zealand, and marveled at their widespread habitation across the Pacific.

The first trade was some brass medals for a mackerel. Cook also stated that he had never before met natives so astonished by a ship, and that they had an amazing fascination for iron. There is even some conjecture that a Spanish ship under one Captain Gaetano had landed in Hawaii as early as the 16th century, trading a few scraps of iron that the Hawaiians valued even more than the Europeans valued gold. It was also noted that the Hawaiian women gave themselves freely to the sailors with the apparent good wishes of the island men. This was actually a ploy by the *kahuna* to test if the white newcomers were gods or men—gods didn't need women. These sailors proved immediately mortal. Cook, who was also a physician, tried valiantly to keep the 66 men (out of 112) who had measurable cases of V.D. away from the women. The task proved impossible as women literally swarmed the ships; when Cook returned less than a year later, it was logged that signs of V.D. were already apparent on some natives' faces.

Cook was impressed with the Hawaiians' swimming ability and with their well-bred manners. They had happy dispositions and sticky fingers, stealing any object made of metal, especially nails. The first item stolen was a butcher's cleaver. An unidentified native grabbed it, plunged overboard, swam to shore, and waved his booty in triumph. The Hawaiians didn't seem to care for beads and were not at all impressed with a mirror. Cook provisioned his ships by trading chisels for hogs, while common sailors gleefully traded nails for sex. Landing parties were sent inland to fill casks with fresh water. On one such excursion a Mr. Williamson, who was eventually drummed out of the Royal Navy for cowardice, unnecessarily shot and killed a native. After a brief stop on Niihau, the ships sailed away, but both groups were indelibly impressed with the memory of each other.

Cook Returns

Almost a year later, when winter weather forced Cook to return from the coast of Alaska, his discovery began to take on far-reaching significance. Cook had named Hawaii the Sandwich Islands, in honor of one of his patrons, John Montague, the Earl of Sandwich. On this return voyage, he spotted Maui on November 26, 1778. After eight weeks of seeking a suitable harbor, the ships bypassed it, but not before the coastline was duly drawn by Lt. William Bligh, one of Cook's finest and most trusted officers. (Bligh would find his own drama almost 10 years later as commander of the infamous HMS *Bounty*.) The *Discovery* and *Resolution* finally found safe anchorage at Kealakekua Bay on the Kona coast of the Big Island. It is very lucky for history that on board was Mr. Anderson, ship's chronicler, who left a handwritten record of the strange and tragic events that followed. Even more important were the drawings of John Webber, ship's artist, who rendered invaluable impressions in superb drawings and etchings. Other noteworthy men aboard were George Vancouver, who would lead the first British return to Hawaii after Cook's death and introduce many fruits, vegetables, cattle, sheep, and goats; and James Burney, who would become a long-standing leading authority on the Pacific.

The Great God Lono Returns

By all accounts Cook was a humane and just captain, greatly admired by his men. Unlike many other supremacists of that time, he was known to have a respectful attitude toward any people he discovered, treating them as equals and recognizing the significance of their cultures. Not known as a violent man, he would use his superior weapons against natives only in an absolute case of self-defense. His hardened crew had been at sea facing untold hardship for almost three years; returning to Hawaii was truly like reentering paradise.

A strange series of coincidences sailed with Cook into Kealakekua Bay on January 16, 1779. It was *makahiki* time, a period of rejoicing and festivity dedicated to the fertility god of the earth, Lono. Normal *kapu* days were suspended and willing partners freely enjoyed each other sexually. There was also dancing, feasting, and the islands' version of the Olympic Games. It was long held in Hawaiian legend that the great god Lono would return to earth. Lono's image was a small wooden figure perched on a tall, mastlike crossbeam; hanging from the crossbeam were long, white sheets of tapa. Who else could Cook be but Lono, and what else could his ships with their masts and white sails be but his sacred floating *heiau?* This explained the Hawaiians' previous fascination with his ships, but to add to the remarkable coincidence, Kealakekua Harbor happened to be considered Lono's private sacred harbor. Natives from throughout the land prostrated themselves and paid homage to the returning god. Cook was taken ashore and brought to Lono's sacred temple, where he was afforded the highest respect. The ships badly needed fresh supplies so the Hawaiians readily gave all they had, stretching their own provisions to the limit. To the sailors' delight, this included full measures of the *aloha* spirit.

The Fatal Misunderstandings

After an uproarious welcome and generous hospitality for over a month, it became obvious that the newcomers were beginning to overstay their welcome. During the interim a seaman named William Watman died, convincing the Hawaiians that the *haole* were indeed mortals, not gods. Watman was buried at Hikiau Heiau, where a plaque commemorates the event to this day. Incidents of petty theft began to increase dramatically. The lesser chiefs indicated it was time to leave by "rubbing the Englishmen's bellies." Inadvertently many *kapu* were broken by the English, and once-friendly relations became strained. Finally, the ships sailed away on February 4, 1779.

After plying terrible seas for only a week, *Resolution's* foremast was damaged. Cook sailed back into Kealakekua Bay, dragging the mast ashore on February 13. The natives, now totally hostile, hurled rocks at the sailors. Orders were given to load muskets with ball; firearms had previously only been loaded with shot and a light charge. Confrontations increased when some Hawaiians stole a small boat and Cook's men set after them, capturing the fleeing canoe that held an *ali'i* named Palea. The English treated him roughly; to the Hawaiians' horror, they even smacked him on the head with a paddle. The Hawaiians then furiously attacked the marines, who abandoned the small boat.

Cook Goes Down

Next the Hawaiians stole a small cutter from the *Discovery* that had been moored to a buoy and partially sunk to protect it from the sun. For the first time Captain Cook became furious. He ordered Captain Clerk of the *Discovery* to sail to the southeast end of the bay and stop any canoe trying to leave Kealakekua. Cook then made a fatal error in judgment. He decided to take nine armed marines ashore in an attempt to convince

HAWAII STATE ARCHIVES

The Death of Captain Cook *by John Webber, ship's artist on Cook's third Pacific exploration, c. 1779*

the venerable King Kalaniopuu to accompany him back aboard ship, where he would hold him for ransom in exchange for the cutter. The old king agreed, but his wife prevailed upon him not to trust the *haole*. Kalaniopuu sat down on the beach to think while the tension steadily grew.

Meanwhile, a group of marines fired upon a canoe trying to leave the bay. A lesser chief, Nookemai, was killed. The crowd around Cook and his men reached an estimated 20,000. Warriors outraged by the killing of the chief armed themselves with clubs and protective straw-mat armor. One bold warrior advanced on Cook and struck him with his *pahoa*. In retaliation, Cook drew a tiny pistol lightly loaded with shot and fired at the warrior. His bullets spent themselves on the straw armor and fell harmlessly to the ground. The Hawaiians went wild. Lieutenant Molesworth Phillips, in charge of the nine marines, began a withering fire; Cook himself slew two natives.

Overpowered by sheer numbers, the marines headed for boats standing offshore, while Lieutenant Phillips lay wounded. It is believed that Captain Cook, the greatest Western seaman ever to enter the Pacific, stood helplessly in knee-deep water instead of making for the boats because he could not swim! Hopelessly surrounded, he was knocked on the head. Countless warriors then passed a knife around and hacked and mutilated his lifeless body. A sad Lieutenant King lamented in his diary, "Thus fell our great and excellent commander."

The Final Chapter

Captain Clerk, now in charge, settled his men and prevailed upon the Hawaiians to return Cook's body. On the morning of February 16 a grisly piece of charred meat was brought aboard: the Hawaiians, according to their custom, had afforded Cook the highest honor by baking his body in an underground oven to remove the flesh from the bones. On February 17 a group of Hawaiians in a canoe taunted the marines by brandishing Cook's hat. The English, strained to the limit and thinking that Cook was being desecrated, finally broke. Foaming with blood-lust, they leveled their cannons and muskets on shore and shot anything that moved. It is believed that Kamehameha the Great was wounded in this flurry, along with four *ali'i;* 25 *maka'ainana* (commoners) were killed. Finally, on February 21, 1779, the bones of Capt. James Cook's hands, skull, arms, and legs were returned and tearfully buried at sea. A common seaman, one Mr. Zimmerman, summed up the feelings of all who sailed under Cook when he wrote, ". . . he was our leading star." The English sailed next morning after dropping off their Hawaiian girlfriends who were still aboard.

Captain Clerk, in bad health, carried on with the fruitless search for the Northwest Passage. He died and was buried at the Siberian village of Petropavlovisk. England was at war with upstart colonists in America, so the return of the expedition warranted little fanfare. The *Resolution* was converted into an army transport to fight the pesky Americans; the once-proud *Discovery* was reduced to a convict ship ferrying inmates to Botany Bay, Australia. Mrs. Cook, the great captain's steadfast and chaste wife, lived to the age of 93, surviving all her children. She was given a stipend of 200 pounds per year and finished her days surrounded by Cook's mementos, observing the anniversary of his death to the very end by fasting and reading from the Bible.

THE UNIFICATION OF OLD HAWAII

Hawaii was already in a state of political turmoil and civil war when Cook arrived. In the 1780s the islands were roughly divided into three kingdoms: venerable Kalaniopuu ruled Hawaii and the Hana district of Maui; wily and ruthless warrior-king Kahekili ruled Maui, Kahoolawe, Lanai, and later Oahu; and Kaeo, Kahekili's brother, ruled Kauai. War ravaged the land until a remarkable chief, Kamehameha, rose and subjugated all the islands under one rule. Kamehameha initiated a dynasty that would last for about 100 years, until the independent monarchy of Hawaii forever ceased to be. To add a zing to this brewing political stew, Westerners and their technology were beginning to come in ever-increasing numbers. In 1786, Captain La Pérouse and his French exploration party landed in what's now La Perouse Bay near Lahaina, foreshadowing European attention to the islands. In 1786 two American captains, Portlock and Dixon, made landfall in Hawaii. Also, it was known that a fortune could be made on the fur trade between the Pacific Northwest and Canton, China; stopping in Hawaii could make it feasible. After this was reported, the fate of Hawaii was sealed.

Hawaii under Kamehameha was ready to enter its "golden age." The social order was medieval, with the *ali'i* as knights owing their military allegiance to the king, and the serflike *maka'ainana* paying tribute and working the lands. The priesthood of *kahuna* filled the posts of advisors, sorcerers, navigators, doctors, and historians. This was Polynesian Hawaii at its apex. But like the uniquely Hawaiian silversword, the old culture blossomed, and as soon as it did, began to wither. Ever since, all that was purely Hawaiian has been supplanted by the relentless foreign influences that began bearing down upon it.

Young Kamehameha

The greatest native son of Hawaii, Kamehameha, was born under mysterious circumstances in the Kohala District, probably in 1753. He was royal born to Keoua Kupuapaikalaninui, the chief of Kohala, and Kekuiapoiwa, a chieftess from Kona. Accounts vary, but one claims that before his birth, a *kahuna* prophesied that this child would grow to be a "killer of chiefs." Because of this, the local chiefs conspired to murder the infant. When Kekuiapoiwa's time came, she secretly went to the royal birthing stones near Mookini Heiau and delivered Kamehameha. She entrusted her baby to a manservant and instructed him to hide the child. He headed for the rugged and remote coast around Kapaau. Here Kamehameha was raised in the mountains, mostly by men. Always alone, he earned the nickname "the lonely one."

Kamehameha was a man noticed by everyone; there was no doubt he was a force to be reckoned with. He had met Captain Cook when the *Discovery* unsuccessfully tried to land at Hana on Maui. While aboard, he made a lasting impression, distinguishing himself from the multitude of natives swarming the ships by his royal bearing. Lieutenant James King, in a diary entry, remarked that Kamehameha was a fierce-looking man, almost ugly, but that he was obviously intelligent, observant, and very good-natured. Kamehameha received his early military training from his uncle Kalaniopuu, the great king of Hawaii and Hana who fought fierce battles against Alapai, the usurper who stole his hereditary lands. After regaining Hawaii, Kalaniopuu returned to his Hana district and turned his attention to conquering all of Maui. During this period young Kamehameha distinguished himself as a ferocious warrior and earned the nickname of "the hard-shelled crab," even though old Kahekili, Maui's king, almost annihilated Kalaniopuu's army at the sand hills of Wailuku.

When the old king neared death, he passed on the kingdom to his son Kiwalao. He also, however, empowered Kamehameha as the keeper of the family war god Kukailimoku: Ku of the Bloody Red Mouth, Ku the Destroyer.

HAWAII STATE ARCHIVES

Kamehameha I as drawn by Louis Choris, ship's artist for the Von Kotzebue expedition, c. 1816. Supposedly it was the only time Kamehameha sat to have his portrait rendered.

Oddly enough, Kamehameha had been born not 500 yards from Ku's great *heiau* at Kohala, and had heard the chanting and observed the ceremonies dedicated to this fierce god from his first breath. Soon after Kalaniopuu died, Kamehameha found himself in a bitter war that he did not seek against his two cousins, Kiwalao and his brother Keoua, with the island of Hawaii at stake. The skirmish lasted nine years until Kamehameha's armies met the two brothers at Mokuohai in an indecisive battle in which Kiwalao was killed. The result was a shaky truce with Keoua, a much-embittered enemy. During this fighting, Kahekili of Maui conquered Oahu, where he built a house of the skulls and bones of his adversaries as a reminder of his omnipotence. He also extended his will to Kauai by marrying his half-brother to a high-ranking chieftess of that island. A new factor would resolve this stalemate of power—the coming of the *haole*.

The Olowalu Massacre

In 1790 the American merchant ship *Ella Nora,* commanded by Yankee Capt. Simon Metcalfe, was looking for a harbor after its long voyage from the Pacific Northwest. Following a day behind was the *Fair American,* a tiny ship sailed by Metcalfe's son Thomas and a crew of five. Simon Metcalfe, perhaps by necessity, was a stern and humorless man who would broach no interference. While his ship was anchored at Olowalu, a beach area about five miles east of Lahaina, some natives slipped close in their canoes and stole a small boat, killing a seaman in the process. Metcalfe decided to trick the Hawaiians by first negotiating a truce and then unleashing full fury upon them. Signaling he was willing to trade, he invited canoes of innocent natives to visit his ship. In the meantime, he ordered that all cannons and muskets be readied with scatter shot. When the canoes were within hailing distance, he ordered his crew to fire at will. Over 100 people were slain; the Hawaiians remembered this killing as "the day of spilled brains." Metcalfe then sailed away to Kealakekua Bay and in an unrelated incident succeeded in insulting Kameiamoku, a ruling chief, who vowed to annihilate the next *haole* ship he saw.

Fate sent him the *Fair American* and young Thomas Metcalfe. The little ship was entirely overrun by superior forces. In the ensuing battle, the mate, Isaac Davis, so distinguished himself by open acts of bravery that his life alone was spared. Kameiamoku later turned over both Davis and the ship to Kamehameha. Meanwhile, while harbored at Kealakekua, the senior Metcalfe sent John Young to reconnoiter. Kamehameha, having learned of the capture of the *Fair American,* detained Young so he could not report, and Metcalfe, losing patience, marooned his own man and sailed off to Canton. (Metcalfe never learned of the fate of his son Thomas, and was later killed with another son while trading with the Native Americans along the Pacific coast of the Mainland.) Kamehameha quickly realized the significance of his two captives and the *Fair American* with its brace of small cannons. He appropriated the ship and made Davis and Young trusted advisors, eventually raising them to the rank of chief. They would all play a significant role in the unification of Hawaii.

Kamehameha The Great

Later in 1790, supported by the savvy of Davis and Young and the cannons from the *Fair American* (which he mounted on carts), Kamehameha invaded Maui, using Hana as his power base. The island's defenders under Kalaniekupule, son of Kahekili who was lingering on Oahu, were totally demoralized, then driven back into the death trap of Iao Valley. There, Kamehameha's forces annihilated them. No mercy was expected and none given, although mostly commoners were slain with no significant *ali'i* falling to the victors. So many were killed in this sheer-walled, inescapable valley that the battle was called *"ka pani wai,"* which means "the damming of the waters"—literally with dead bodies.

While Kamehameha was fighting on Maui, his old nemesis Keoua was busy running amok back on Hawaii, again pillaging Kamehameha's lands. The great warrior returned home flushed with victory, but in two battles could not subdue Keoua. Finally, Kamehameha had a prophetic dream in which he was told that Ku would lead him to victory over all the lands of Hawaii if he would build a *heiau* to the war god at Kawaihae. Even before the temple was finished, old Kahekili attempted to invade Waipio, Kamehameha's stronghold. But Kamehameha summoned Davis and Young, and with the *Fair American* and an enormous fleet of war canoes defeated Kahekili at Waimanu. Kahekili had no choice but to accept the indomitable Kamehameha as the king of Maui, although he himself remained the administrative head until his death in 1794.

Now only Keoua remained in the way and he would be defeated not by war, but by the great mana of Ku. While Keoua's armies were crossing the desert on the southern slopes of Kilauea, the fire goddess Pele trumpeted her disapproval and sent a huge cloud of poisonous gas and mud-ash into the air. It descended upon and instantly killed the middle legions of Keoua's armies and their families. The footprints of this ill-fated army remain to this day outlined in the mud-ash as clearly as if they were deliberately encased in wet cement. Keoua's intuition told him that the victorious mana of the gods had swung to Kamehameha and that his own fate was sealed. Kamehameha sent word that he wanted Keoua to meet with him at Ku's newly dedicated temple in Kawaihae. Both knew that Keoua must die. Riding proudly in his canoe, the old nemesis came gloriously outfitted in the red-and-gold feathered cape and helmet signifying his exalted rank. When he stepped ashore he was felled by Kamehameha's warriors. His body was ceremoniously laid upon the altar along with 11 others who were slaughtered and dedicated to Ku, of the Maggot-dripping Mouth.

Increasing Contact

By the time Kamehameha had won the Big Island, Hawaii was becoming a regular stopover for numerous ships seeking the lucrative sandalwood trade with China. In February 1791, Capt. George Vancouver, still seeking the Northwest Passage, returned to Kealakekua where he was greeted by a throng of 30,000. The captain at once recognized Kamehameha, who was wearing a Chinese dressing gown that he had received in tribute from another chief who in turn had received it directly from the hands of Cook himself. The diary of a crew member, Thomas Manby, relates that Kamehameha, missing his front teeth, was more fierce-looking than ever as he approached the ship in an elegant double-hulled canoe sporting 46 rowers. The king invited all to a great feast prepared for them on the beach. Kamehameha's appetite matched his tremendous size. It was noted that he ate two sizable fish, a king-sized bowl of poi, a small pig, and an entire baked dog. Kamehameha personally entertained the English by putting on a mock battle in which he deftly avoided spears by rolling, tumbling, and catching them in midair, all the while hurling his own spear a great distance. The English reciprocated by firing cannon bursts into the air, creating an impromptu fireworks display. Kamehameha requested from Vancouver a full table setting with which he was provided, but his request for firearms was prudently denied. Captain Vancouver became a trusted advisor of Kamehameha and told him about the white people's form of worship. He even interceded for Kamehameha with his headstrong queen, Kaahumanu, and coaxed her from her hiding place under a rock when she sought refuge at Pu'uhonua O Honaunau. The captain gave gifts of beef cattle, fowl, and breeding stock of sheep and goats. The ship's naturalist, Archibald Menzies, was the first *haole* to climb Mauna Kea; he also introduced a large assortment of fruits and vegetables. The Hawaiians were cheerful and outgoing, and showed remorse when they

HAWAII STATE ARCHIVES

Captain George Vancouver

indicated that the remainder of Cook's bones had been buried at a temple close to Kealakekua. John Young, by this time firmly entrenched into Hawaiian society, made no request to sail away with Vancouver. During the next two decades of Kamehameha's rule, the French, Russians, English, and Americans discovered the great whaling waters off Hawaii. Their increasing visits shook and finally tumbled the ancient religion and social order of *kapu*.

Finishing Touches

After Keoua was laid to rest, it was only a matter of time until Kamehameha consolidated his power over all of Hawaii. In 1794 the old warrior Kahekili of Maui died and gave Oahu to his son, Kalanikupule, while Kauai and Niihau went to his brother Kaeo. In wars between the two, Kalanikupule was victorious, though he did not possess the grit of his father nor the great mana of Kamehameha. He had previously murdered a Captain Brown, who had anchored in Honolulu, and seized his ship, the *Jackal.* With the aid of this ship, Kalanikupule now determined to attack Kamehameha. However, while en route, the sailors regained control of their ship and cruised to the Big Island to inform and join with Kamehameha. An army of 16,000 was raised and sailed for Maui, where they met only token resistance, destroyed Lahaina, pillaged the countryside, and subjugated Molokai in one bloody battle.

The war canoes sailed next for Oahu and the final showdown. The great army landed at Waikiki, and though defenders fought bravely, giving up Oahu by the inch, they were steadily driven into the surrounding mountains. The beleaguered army made its last stand at Nuuanu Pali, a great precipice in the mountains behind present-day Honolulu. Kamehameha's warriors mercilessly drove the enemy into the great abyss. Kalanikupule, who hid in the mountains, was captured after a few months and sacrificed to Ku, the Snatcher of Lands, thereby ending the struggle for power.

Kamehameha put down a revolt on Hawaii in 1796. The king of Kauai, Kaumuali, accepting the inevitable, recognized Kamehameha as supreme ruler without suffering the ravages of a needless war. Kamehameha, for the first time in Hawaiian history, was the undisputed ruler of all the islands of "the heavenly homeland in the north."

Kamehameha's Rule

Kamehameha was as gentle in victory as he was ferocious in battle. Under his rule, which lasted until his death on May 8, 1819, Hawaii enjoyed a peace unlike any the warring islands had ever known. The king moved his royal court to Lahaina, where in 1803 he built the "Brick Palace," Hawaii's first permanent building. The benevolent tyrant also enacted the "Law of the Splintered Paddle." This law, which protected the weak from the exploitation of the strong, had its origins in an incident of many years before. A brave defender of a small overwhelmed village had broken a paddle over Kamehameha's head and taught the chief—literally in one stroke—about the nobility of the commoner.

However, just as Old Hawaii reached its "golden age," its demise was at hand. The relentless waves of *haole* both innocently and determinedly battered the old ways into the ground. With the foreign ships came prosperity and fanciful new goods after which the *ali'i* lusted. The *maka'ainana* were worked mercilessly to provide sandalwood for the China trade. This was the first "boom" economy to hit the islands, but it set the standard of exploitation that would follow. Kamehameha built an observation tower in Lahaina to watch for ships, many of which were his own returning laden with riches from the world at large. In the last years of his life Kamehameha returned to his beloved Kona coast, where he enjoyed the excellent fishing renowned to this day. He had taken Hawaii from the darkness of warfare into the light of peace. He died true to the religious and moral *kapu* of his youth, the only ones he had ever known, and with him died a unique way of life. Two loyal retainers buried his bones after the baked flesh had been ceremoniously stripped away. A secret burial cave was chosen so that no one could desecrate the remains of the great chief, thereby absorbing his mana. The tomb's whereabouts remains unknown, and disturbing the dead remains one of the strictest *kapu* to this day. The Lonely One's kingdom would pass to his son, Liholiho, but true power would be in the hands of his beloved and feisty wife Kaahumanu. As Kamehameha's spirit drifted from this earth, two forces sailing around Cape Horn would forever change Hawaii: the missionaries and the whalers.

MISSIONARIES AND WHALERS

The year 1819 was of the utmost significance in Hawaiian history. It marked the death of Kamehameha, the overthrow of the ancient *kapu* system, the arrival of the first "whaler" in Lahaina, and the departure from New England of Calvinist missionaries determined to convert the heathen islands. Great changes began to rattle the old order to its foundations. With the *kapu* system and the ancient gods abandoned (except for the fire goddess Pele of Kilauea), a great void permeated the souls of the Hawaiians. In the coming decades Hawaii, also coveted by Russia, France, and England, was finally consumed by America. The islands had the first American school, printing press, and newspaper (the *Polynesian*) west of the Mississippi. Lahaina, in its heyday, became the world's greatest whaling port, accommodating over 500 ships during its peak years.

The Royal Family

Maui's Hana District provided Hawaii with one of its greatest queens, Kaahumanu, born in 1768 in a cave within walking distance of Hana Harbor. At the age of 17 she became the third of Kamehameha's 21 wives and eventually the love of his life. At first she proved to be totally independent and unmanageable and was known to openly defy her king by taking numerous lovers. Kamehameha placed a *kapu* on her body and even had her attended by horribly deformed hunchbacks in an effort to curb her carnal appetites, but she continued to flaunt his authority. Young Kaahumanu had no love for her great, lumbering, unattractive husband, but in time (even Captain Vancouver was pressed into service as a marriage counselor) she learned to love him dearly. She in turn became his favorite wife, although she remained childless throughout her life. Kamehameha's first wife was the supremely royal Keopuolani, who so outranked even him that the king himself had to approach her naked and crawling on his belly. Keopuolani produced the royal children Liholiho and Kauikeaouli, who became King Kamehameha II and III, respectively. Just before Kamehameha I died in 1819 he appointed Liholiho his successor, but he also had the wisdom to make Kaahumanu the *kuhina nui* or queen regent. Initially, Liholiho was weak and became a drunkard. Later he became a good ruler, but he was always supported by his royal mother Keopuolani and by the ever-formidable Kaahumanu.

Kapu Is *Pau*

Kaahumanu was greatly loved and respected by the people. On public occasions, she donned Kamehameha's royal cloak and spear: so attired and infused with the king's mana, she demonstrated that she was the real leader of Hawaii. For six months after Kamehameha's death, Kaahumanu counseled Liholiho on what he must do. The wise *kuhina nui* knew that the old ways were *pau* ("finished") and that Hawaii could not hope to function in a rapidly changing world under the *kapu* system. In November 1819, Kaahumanu and Keopuolani prevailed upon Liholiho to break two of the oldest and most sacred *kapu* by eating with women and by allowing women to eat previously forbidden foods such as bananas and certain fish. Heav-

HAWAII STATE ARCHIVES

the great Queen Kaahumanu, by ship's artist Louis Choris from the Otto Von Kotzebue expedition, c. 1816

ily fortified with strong drink and attended by other high-ranking chiefs and a handful of foreigners, Kaahumanu and Liholiho ate together in public. This feast became known as *Ai Noa* ("free eating"). As the first morsels passed Kaahumanu's lips, the ancient gods of Hawaii tumbled. Throughout the land, revered *heiau* were burned and abandoned and the idols knocked to the ground. Now the people had nothing but their weakened inner selves to rely on. Nothing and no one could answer their prayers; their spiritual lives were empty and in shambles.

Missionaries

Into this spiritual vortex sailed the brig *Thaddeus* on April 4, 1820. It had set sail from Boston on October 23, 1819, lured to the Big Island by Henry Opukahaia, a local boy born at Napoopoo in 1792. Coming ashore at Kailua-Kona, the reverends Bingham and Thurston were granted a one-year trial missionary period by King Liholiho. They established themselves on the Big Island and Oahu and from there began the transformation of Hawaii. The missionaries were people of God, but also practical-minded Yankees. They brought education, enterprise, and most importantly, unlike the transient seafarers, a commitment to stay and build. By 1824 the new faith had such a foothold that Chieftess Keopuolani climbed to the firepit atop Kilauea and defied Pele. This was even more striking than the previous breaking of the food *kapu* because the strength of Pele could actually be seen. Keopuolani ate forbidden *ohelo* berries and cried out, "Jehovah is my God." Over the next decades the governing of Hawaii slipped away from the Big Island and moved to the new port cities of Lahaina and later, Honolulu. In 1847, the Parker Ranch began with a two-acre grant given to John Parker. He coupled this with 360 acres given to his *ali'i* wife Kipikane by the land division known as the Great *Mahele.*

Rapid Conversions

The year 1824 also marked the death of Keopuolani, who was given a Christian burial. She had set the standard by accepting Christianity, and a number of the *ali'i* had followed the queen's lead. Liholiho had sailed off to England, where he and his wife contracted measles and died. Their bodies were returned by the British in 1825, on the HMS *Blonde* captained by Lord Byron, cousin of *the* Lord Byron. During these years, Kaahumanu allied herself with Reverend Richards, pastor of the first mission in the islands, and together they wrote Hawaii's first code of laws based upon the Ten Commandments. Foremost was the condemnation of murder, theft, brawling, and the desecration of the Sabbath by work or play. The early missionaries had the best of intentions, but like all zealots they were blinded by the singleminded-

Kamehameha III

ness that was also their greatest ally. They weren't surgically selective in their destruction of native beliefs. *Anything* native was felt to be inferior, and they set about wiping out all traces of the old ways. In their rampage they reduced the Hawaiian culture to ashes, plucking self-will and determination from the hearts of a once-proud people. More so than the whalers, they terminated the Hawaiian way of life.

The Early Seamen

A good portion of the common seamen of the early 19th century came from the dregs of the Western world. Many a whoremongering drunkard had awoken from a stupor and found himself on the pitching deck of a ship, discovering to his dismay that he had been "pressed into naval service." For the most part these sailors were filthy, uneducated, lawless rabble. Their present situation was dim, their future hopeless, and they would live to be 30 if they were lucky and didn't die from scurvy or a thousand other miserable fates. They snatched brief pleasure in every port and jumped ship at every opportunity, especially in an easy berth like Lahaina. They displayed the worst elements of Western culture—which the Hawaiians naively mimicked. In exchange for *aloha* they gave drunkenness, sloth, and insidious death by disease. By the 1850s the population of native Hawaiians tumbled from the estimated 300,000 reported by Captain Cook in 1778 to barely 60,000. Common conditions such as colds, flu, venereal disease, and sometimes smallpox and cholera decimated the Hawaiians, who had no natural immunities to these foreign ailments. By the time the missionaries arrived, *hapa haole* children were common in Lahaina streets.

The earliest merchant ships to the islands were owned or skippered by lawless opportunists who had come seeking sandalwood after first filling their holds with furs from the Pacific Northwest. Aided by *ali'i* hungry for manufactured goods and Western finery, they raped Hawaiian forests of this fragrant wood so coveted in China. Next, droves of sailors came in search of whales. The whalers, decent men at home, left their morals back in the Atlantic and lived by the slogan "no conscience east of the Cape." The delights of Hawaii were just too tempting for most.

Two Worlds Tragically Collide

The 1820s were a time of confusion and soul-searching for the Hawaiians. When Kamehameha II died the kingdom passed to Kauikeaouli (Kamehameha III), who made his lifelong residence in Lahaina. The young king was only nine years old when the title passed to him, but his power was secure because Kaahumanu was still a vibrant *kuhina nui*. The young prince, more so than any other, was raised in the cultural confusion of the times. His childhood was spent during the very cusp of the change from old ways to new, and he was often pulled in two directions by vastly differing beliefs. Since he was royal born, he was bound by age-old Hawaiian tradition to mate and produce an heir with the highest-ranking *ali'i* in the kingdom. This mate happened to be his younger sister, the Princess Nahienaena. To the old Hawaiian advisors, this arrangement was perfectly acceptable and encouraged. To the increasingly influential missionaries, incest was an unimaginable abomination in the eyes of God.

The problem was compounded by the fact that Kamehameha III and Nahienaena were drawn to each other and were deeply in love. The young king could not stand the mental pressure imposed by conflicting worlds. He became a teenage alcoholic too royal to be restrained by anyone in the kingdom, and his bouts of drunkenness and womanizing were both legendary and scandalous.

Meanwhile, Nahienaena was even more pressured because she was a favorite of the missionaries, baptized into the church at age 12. She too vacillated between the old and the new. At times a pious Christian, at others she drank all night and took numerous lovers. As the prince and princess grew into their late teens, they became even more attached to each other and hardly made an attempt to keep their relationship from the missionaries. Whenever possible, they lived together in a grass house built for the princess by her father.

In 1832, the great Kaahumanu died, leaving the king on his own. In 1833, at the age of 18, Kamehameha III announced that the "regency" was over and that all the lands in Hawaii were his personally, and that he alone was the ultimate law. Almost immediately, however, he decreed that his half-sister Kinau would be "premier," signifying that he would leave the actual running of the kingdom in her hands. Kamehameha III fell into total drunken confusion, until one night he attempted suicide. After this episode he seemed to straighten up a bit and mostly kept a low profile. In 1836, Princess Nahienaena was convinced by the missionaries to take a husband. She married Leleiohoku, a chief from the Big Island, but continued to sleep with her brother. It is uncertain who fathered the child, but Nahienaena gave birth to a baby boy in September 1836. The young prince survived for only a few hours, and Nahienaena never recovered from her convalescence. She died in December 1836 and was laid to rest in the mausoleum next to her mother, Keopuolani, on the royal island in Mokuhina Pond (still in existence in modern-day Lahaina). After the death of his sister, Kamehameha III became a sober and righteous ruler. Often seen paying his respects at the royal mausoleum, he ruled longer than any other king until his death in 1854.

The Missionaries Prevail

In 1823, the first mission was established in Lahaina under the pastorage of Reverend Richards and his wife. Within a few years, many of the notable *ali'i* had been, at least in appearance, converted to Christianity. By 1828 the cornerstones for Wainee Church, the first stone church on the Island, were laid just behind the palace of Kamehameha III. The struggle between missionaries and whalers centered around public drunkenness and the servicing of sailors by native women. The normally God-fearing whalers had signed on for perilous duty that lasted up to three years, and when they anchored in Lahaina they demanded their pleasure. The missionaries were instrumental in placing a curfew on sailors and prohibiting native women from boarding ships, which had become customary. These measures certainly did not stop the liaisons between sailor and *wahine,* but they did impose a modicum of social sanction and tolled the end of the wide-open days. The sailors were outraged; in 1825 the crew from the *Daniel* attacked the home of the meddler, Reverend Richards. A year later a similar incident occurred. In 1827, confined and lonely sailors from the whaler *John Palmer* fired their cannons at Reverend Richards' newly built home.

Slowly the tensions eased, and by 1836 many sailors were regulars at the Seamen's Chapel adjacent to the Baldwin home. Unfortunately, even the missionaries couldn't stop the pesky mosquito from entering the islands through the port of Lahaina. The mosquitoes arrived from Mexico in 1826 aboard the merchant ship *Wellington.* They were inadvertently carried as larvae in the water barrels and democratically pestered everyone in the islands from that day forward, regardless of race, religion, or creed.

Lahaina Becomes A Cultural Center

By 1831, Lahaina was firmly established as a seat of Western influence in Hawaii. That year marked the founding of Lahainaluna School, the first *real* American school west of the Rockies. Virtually a copy of a New England normal school, it attracted the best students, both native and white, from throughout the kingdom. By 1834, Lahainaluna had an operating printing press publishing the islands' first newspaper, the *Torch of Hawaii,* starting a lucrative printing industry centered in Lahaina that dominated not only the islands but also California for many years.

An early native student was David Malo. He was brilliant and well educated, but more importantly, he remembered the "old ways." One of the first Hawaiians to realize his native land was being swallowed up by the newcomers, Malo compiled the first history of pre-contact Hawaii. The resulting book, *Hawaiian Antiquities,* became a reference masterpiece which has yet to be eclipsed. David Malo insisted that the printing be done in Hawaiian, not English. Malo is buried in the mountains above Lahainaluna where, by his own request, he is "high above the tide of foreign invasion." By the 1840s, Lahaina was firmly established as the "whaling capital of the world"; the peak year 1846 saw 395 whaling ships anchored here. A census in 1846 reported that Lahaina was home to 3,445 natives, 112 permanent *haole,* 600 sailors, and over 500 dogs. The populace was housed in 882 grass houses, 155 adobe houses, and 59 relatively permanent stone and wooden framed structures. Lahaina would probably have remained the islands' capital, had Kamehameha III not moved the royal capital to the burgeoning port of Honolulu on the island of Oahu.

Foreign Influence

By the 1840s Honolulu was becoming the center of commerce in the islands; when Kamehameha III moved the royal court there from Lahaina, the ascendant fate of the new capital was guaranteed. In 1843, Lord Paulet, commander of the warship *Carysfort,* forced Kamehameha III to sign a treaty ceding Hawaii to the British. London, however, repudiated this act, and Hawaii's independence was restored within a few months when Queen Victoria sent Admiral Thomas as her personal agent of good intentions. The king memorialized the turn of events by a speech in which he uttered the phrase, *Ua mau ke ea o ka aina i ka pono* ("The life of the land is preserved in righteousness"), now Hawaii's motto. The French used similar bullying tactics to force an unfavorable treaty on the Hawaiians in 1839; as part of these heavy-handed negotiations they exacted a payment of $20,000 and the right of Catholics to enjoy religious freedom in the islands. In 1842 the U.S. recognized and guaranteed Hawaii's independence without a formal treaty, and by 1860 over 80% of the islands' trade was with America.

The Great *Mahele*

In 1840 Kamehameha III ended his autocratic rule and instituted a constitutional monarchy. This brought about the Hawaiian Bill of Rights, but the most far-reaching change was the transition to private ownership of land. Formerly, all land belonged to the ruling chief, who gave wedge-shaped parcels called *ahupua'a* to lesser chiefs to be worked for him. The commoners did the real labor, their produce heavily taxed by the *ali'i.* The fortunes of war, the death of a chief, or the mere whim of a superior could force a commoner off the land. The Hawaiians, however, could not think in terms of "owning" land. No one could *possess* land; one could only *use* land, and its *ownership* was a strange and foreign concept. (As a result, naive Hawaiians gave up their lands for a song to unscrupulous traders, which remains an integral, unrectified problem to this day.)

In 1847 Kamehameha III and his advisors separated the lands of Hawaii into three groupings: crown land (belonging to the king), government land (belonging to the chiefs), and the people's land (the largest parcels). In 1848, 245 *ali'i* entered their land claims in the *Mahele Book,* assuring them ownership. In 1850 the commoners were given title in fee simple to the lands they cultivated and lived on as tenants, not including house lots in towns. Commoners without land could buy small *kuleana* (farms) from the government at 50 cents per acre. In 1850, foreigners were also allowed to purchase land in fee simple, and the ownership of Hawaii from that day forward slipped steadily from the hands of its indigenous people.

KING SUGAR

The sugar industry began at Hana, Maui in 1849. A whaler named George Wilfong hauled four blubber pots ashore and set them up on a rocky hill in the middle of 60 acres he had planted in sugar. A team of oxen turned "crushing rollers" and the cane juice flowed down an open

indentured Japanese plantation workers and mounted overseer

trough into the pots, under which an attending native kept a fire roaring. Wilfong's methods of refining were crude but the resulting high-quality sugar turned a neat profit in Lahaina. The main problem was labor. The Hawaiians, who made excellent whalers, were basically indentured workers. They became extremely disillusioned with their contracts, which could last up to 10 years. Most of their wages were eaten up by manufactured commodities sold at the company store, and it didn't take long for them to realize that they were little more than slaves. At every opportunity they either left the area or just refused to work.

Imported Labor

The **Masters and Servants Act of 1850,** which allowed importation of laborers under the contract system, ostensibly guaranteed an endless supply of cheap labor for the plantations. Chinese laborers were imported, but were too enterprising to remain in the fields for a meager $3 per month. They left as soon as opportunity permitted, and went into business as small merchants and retailers. In the meantime, Wilfong had sold out, releasing most of the Hawaiians previously under contract, and his plantation fell into disuse. In 1860 two Danish brothers, August and Oscar Unna, bought land at Hana to raise sugar. They solved the labor problem by importing Japanese laborers who were extremely hard-working and easily managed. The workday lasted 10 hours, six days a week, for a salary of $20 per month with housing and medical care thrown in. Plantation life was very structured, with stringent rules governing even bedtimes and lights out. A worker was fined for being late or for smoking on the job. The Japanese couldn't function under these circumstances, and improvements in benefits and housing were slowly gained.

Sugar Grows

The demand for "Sandwich Island Sugar" grew as California was populated during the gold rush, and increased dramatically when the American Civil War demanded a constant supply. The only sugar plantations on the Mainland were small plots confined to the Confederate states, whose products would hardly be bought by the Union and whose fields, later in the war, were destroyed. By the 1870s it was clear to the planters, still mainly New Englanders, that the U.S. was their market; they tried often to gain closer ties and favorable tariffs. The Americans also planted rumors that the British were interested in annexing Hawaii; this put pressure on the U.S. Congress to pass the long-desired **Reciprocity Act,** which would exempt sugar from import duty. It finally passed in 1875, in exchange for U.S. long-range rights to the strategic naval port of Pearl Harbor, among other concessions. These agreements gave increased political power to a small group of American planters whose outlooks were similar to those of the post-Civil War South, where a few powerful whites were the virtual masters of a multitude of dark-skinned laborers. Sugar was now big business and the Hana District alone exported almost 3,000 tons per year. All of Hawaii would have to reckon with the "sugar barons."

Changing Society

The sugar plantation system changed life in Hawaii physically, spiritually, politically, and economically. Now boatloads of workers came not only from Japan, but from Portugal, Germany, and even Russia. The white-skinned workers were most often the field foremen (*luna*). With the immigrants came new religions, new animals and plants, unique cuisines, and a plantation language known as pidgin, or better yet, *da'kine*. Many Asians, and to a lesser extent the other groups including the white plantation owners, intermarried with Hawaiians. A new class of people properly termed "cosmopolitan" but more familiarly and aptly known as "locals" was emerging. These were the people of multiple racial backgrounds who couldn't exactly say *what* they were but it was clear to all just *who* they were. The plantation owners became the new "chiefs" of Hawaii who could carve up the land and dispense favors. The Hawaiian monarchy was soon eliminated.

A KINGDOM PASSES

The fate of Lahaina's Wainee Church through the years has been a symbol of the political and economic climate of the times. Its construction heralded the beginning of missionary dominance in 1828. It was destroyed by a tornado or "ghost wind" in 1858, just when whaling began to falter and the previously dominant missionaries began losing their control to the merchants and planters. In 1894, Wainee Church was burned to the ground by royalists supporting the besieged Queen Liliuokalani. Rebuilding was begun in 1897—while Hawaii was a republic ruled by the sugar planters—with a grant from H.P. Baldwin. It wasn't until 1947 that Wainee was finally completed and remodeled.

HAWAII STATE ARCHIVES

Robert Louis Stevenson with King Kalakaua, the last king of Hawaii

The Beginning Of The End

Like the Hawaiian people themselves, the Kamehameha dynasty in the mid-1800s was dying from within. King Kamehameha IV (Alexander Liholiho) ruled 1854-63; his only child died in 1862. He was succeeded by his older brother Kamehameha V (Lot Kamehameha), who ruled until 1872. With his passing the Kamehameha line ended. William Lunalilo, elected king in 1873 by popular vote, was of royal, but not Kamehameha, lineage. He died after only a year in office, and being a bachelor left no heirs. He was succeeded by David Kalakaua, known far and wide as "The Merrie Monarch," who made a world tour and was well received wherever he went. He built Iolani Palace in Honolulu and was personally in favor of closer ties with the U.S., helping push through the Reciprocity Act. Kalakaua died in 1891 and was replaced by his sister Lydia Liliuokalani, last of the Hawaiian monarchs.

The Revolution

When Liliuokalani took office in 1891, the native population was at a low of 40,000 and she felt that the U.S. had too much influence over her homeland. She was known to personally favor the English over the Americans. She attempted to replace the liberal constitution of 1887 (adopted by her pro-American brother) with an autocratic mandate in which she would have had much more political and economic control of the islands. When the McKinley Tariff of 1890 brought a decline in sugar profits, she made no attempt to improve the situation. Thus, the planters saw her as a political obstacle to their economic growth; most of Hawaii's American planters and merchants were in favor of a rebellion. She would have to go! A central spokesperson and firebrand was Lorrin Thurston, a Honolulu publisher who, with a central core of about 30 men, challenged the Hawaiian monarchy. Although Liliuokalani rallied some support and had a small military potential in her personal guard, the coup was ridiculously easy—it took only one casualty. Captain John Good shot a Hawaiian policeman in the arm and that did it. Naturally, the conspirators could not have succeeded without some solid assurances from a secret contingent in the U.S. Congress as well as outgoing president Benjamin Harrison, who favored Hawaii's annexation. Marines from the *Boston* went ashore to "protect American lives," and on January 17, 1893, the Hawaiian monarchy came to an end.

The provisional government was headed by Sanford B. Dole, who became president of the Hawaiian Republic. Liliuokalani surrendered not to the conspirators but to U.S. Ambassador John Stevens. She believed that the U.S. government, which had assured her of Hawaiian independence, would be outraged by the overthrow and would come to her aid. Incoming president Grover Cleveland *was* outraged and Hawaii wasn't immediately annexed as expected. When queried about what she would do with the conspirators if she were reinstated, Liliuokalani said that they would be hung as traitors. The racist press of the times, which portrayed the Hawaiians as half-civilized, bloodthirsty heathens, publicized this widely. Since the conspirators were the leading citizens of the land, the queen's words proved untimely. In January 1895 a small, ill-fated counterrevolution headed by Liliuokalani failed, and she was placed under house arrest in Iolani Palace. Officials of the republic insisted that she use her married name (Mrs. John Dominis) to sign the documents forcing her to abdicate her throne. She was also forced to swear allegiance to the new republic. Liliuokalani went on to write *Hawaii's Story* and the lyric ballad "Aloha O'e." She never forgave the conspirators and remained "queen" to the Hawaiians until her death in 1917.

Annexation

The overwhelming majority of Hawaiians opposed annexation and desired to restore the monarchy. But they were prevented from voting by the new republic because they couldn't meet the imposed property and income qualifications—a transparent ruse by the planters to control the majority. Most *haole* were racist and believed that the "common people" could not be entrusted with the vote because they were childish and incapable of ruling themselves. The fact that the Hawaiians had existed quite well for 1,000 years before white people even reached Hawaii was never considered. The Philippine theater of the Spanish-American War also prompted annexation. One of the strongest proponents was Alfred Mahon, a brilliant naval strategist who, with support from Theodore Roosevelt, argued that the U.S. military must have Hawaii in order to be a viable force in the Pacif-

HAWAII STATE ARCHIVES

Queen Liliuokalani

HAWAII STATE ARCHIVES

Sanford B. Dole reads the proclamation inaugurating the Hawaiian Republic on July 4, 1894.

ic. In addition, Japan, victorious in its recent war with China, protested the American intention to annex, and in so doing prompted even moderates to support annexation for fear that the Japanese themselves coveted the prize. On July 7, 1898, President McKinley signed the annexation agreement, and this "tropical fruit" was finally put into America's basket.

MODERN TIMES

Hawaii entered the 20th century totally transformed. The old Hawaiian language, religion, culture, and leadership were gone; Western dress, values, education, and recreation were the norm. Native Hawaiians were now unseen citizens who lived in dwindling numbers in remote areas. The plantations, new centers of social order, had a strong Asian flavor; more than 75% of their workforce was Asian. There was a small white middle class, an all-powerful white elite, and a single political party ruled by that elite. Education, however, was always highly prized, and by the turn of the century all racial groups were encouraged to attend school. By 1900, almost 90% of Hawaiians were literate (far above the national norm) and schooling was mandatory for children ages 6-15. Intermarriage was accepted, and there was a mixing of the races like nowhere else on earth. The military became increasingly important to Hawaii. It brought in money and jobs, dominating the island economy. The Japanese attack on Pearl Harbor, which began U.S. involvement in WW II, bound Hawaii to America forever. Once the islands had been baptized by blood, the average Mainlander felt that Hawaii was American soil. A movement among Hawaiians to become part of the United States began to grow. They wanted a real voice in Washington, not merely a voteless delegate as provided under their territory status. Hawaii became the 50th state in 1959 and the jumbo-jet revolution of the 1960s made it easily accessible to growing numbers of tourists from all over the world.

Military History

A few military strategists realized the importance of Hawaii early in the 19th century, but most didn't recognize the advantages until the Spanish-American War. It was clearly an unsinkable ship in the middle of the Pacific from which the U.S. could launch military operations. Troops were stationed at Camp McKinley, at the foot of Diamond Head, the main military compound until it became obsolete in 1907. Pearl Harbor was first surveyed in 1872 by General Schofield. Later, a military base named in his honor, Schofield Barracks, was a main military post in central Oahu. It housed the U.S. 5th Cavalry in 1909 and was heavily bombed by the Japanese at the outset of WW II. Pearl Harbor, dredged in 1908, was officially opened on December 11, 1911. The first warship to enter was the cruiser *California*. Ever since, the military has been a

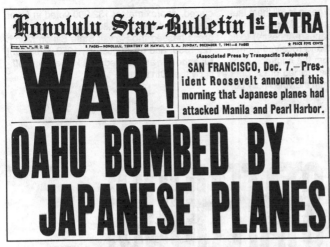

Honolulu Star-Bulletin 1st EXTRA

8 PAGES—HONOLULU, TERRITORY OF HAWAII, U. S. A., SUNDAY, DECEMBER 7, 1941—8 PAGES ★ PRICE FIVE CENTS

WAR!

(Associated Press by Transpacific Telephone)

SAN FRANCISCO, Dec. 7.—President Roosevelt announced this morning that Japanese planes had attacked Manila and Pearl Harbor.

OAHU BOMBED BY JAPANESE PLANES

The Honolulu Star Bulletin *banner headline announces the official beginning of U.S. involvement in WWII on Sunday December 7, 1941.*

mainstay of Island economy. Unfortunately, there has been long-standing bad blood between locals and military personnel. Each group has tended to look down upon the other.

Pearl Harbor Attack

On the morning of December 7, 1941, the Japanese carrier *Akagi,* flying the battle flag of the famed Admiral Togo of the Russo-Japanese War, received and broadcast over its PA system island music from Honolulu station KGMB. Deep in the bowels of the ship a radio man listened for a much different message, coming thousands of miles from the Japanese mainland. When the ironically poetic message "east wind rain" was received, the attack was launched. At the end of the day, 2,325 U.S. servicemen and 57 civilians were dead; 188 planes were destroyed; 18 major warships were sunk or heavily damaged; and the U.S. was at war. Japanese casualties were extremely light. The ignited conflict would rage for four years until Japan, through Nagasaki and Hiroshima, was vaporized into submission. At the end of hostilities, Hawaii would never again be considered separate from America.

Statehood

A number of economic and political reasons explain why the ruling elite of Hawaii desired statehood, but put simply, the vast majority of people who lived here, especially after WW II, considered themselves Americans. The first serious mention of making "The Sandwich Islands" a state was in the 1850s under President Franklin Pierce, but it wasn't taken seriously until the monarchy was overthrown in the 1890s. For the next 50 years statehood proposals were made repeatedly to Congress, but there was stiff opposition, especially from the southern states. With Hawaii a territory, an import quota system beneficial to Mainland producers could be enacted on produce, especially sugar. Also, there was prejudice against creating a state in a place where the majority of the populace was not white. This situation was illuminated by the infamous Massie Rape Case of 1931 (see "Caucasians" under "The People" later in this chapter for details), which went down as one of the greatest miscarriages of justice in American history.

During WW II, Hawaii was placed under martial law, but no serious attempt to intern the Japanese population was made, as in California. There were simply too many Japanese, who went on to gain the respect of the American people by their outstanding fighting record during the war. Hawaii's own 100th Battalion became the famous 442nd Regimental Combat Team, which gained notoriety by saving the Lost Texas Battalion during the Battle of the Bulge and went on to be *the* most decorated battalion in all of WW II. When these GIs returned home, *no one* was going to tell them that they were not loyal Americans. Many of these AJAs (Americans of Japanese Ancestry) took advantage of the GI Bill and received higher education. They were from the common people, not the elite, and they rallied grassroots support for statehood. When the vote finally occurred, approximately 132,900 voted in favor of statehood with only 7,800 votes against. Congress passed the Hawaii State Bill on March 12, 1959, and on August 21, 1959, President Eisenhower announced that Hawaii was officially the 50th state.

STATEHOOD!

House Roll Call Results, Page 16; Senate, Page 14

Bill Is Sent To President

10¢

Statehood Booms Isle Stock Prices

Ike Delighted Hawaii Got Statehood

Honolulu Star-Bulletin

Stock Final

Special Radio, Phone Lines Flash News

Sirens, Bells Herald Statehood Arrival

BOB RACE

GOVERNMENT

Being the newest state in America, Hawaii has had the chance to scrutinize the others, pick their best attributes, and learn from their past mistakes. The government of the State of Hawaii is in essence no different from any other except that it is streamlined and, in theory, more efficient. There are only two levels: state and county. There are no town or city governments to deal with, and added bureaucracy is theoretically eliminated. Unfortunately, some of the state-run agencies, like the centralized Board of Education, have become "red-tape" monsters. Hawaii, in anticipation of becoming a state, drafted a constitution in 1950 and was ready to go when statehood was ratified. Politics and government are taken seriously in the "Aloha State," which consistently turns in the best national voting record per capita. For example, in the election to ratify statehood, hardly a ballot went uncast, with 95% of the voters opting for statehood. In the first state elections that followed, 173,000 of 180,000 registered voters voted. The bill carried every island of Hawaii except for Niihau, where, coincidentally, the majority of people (total population 250, or so) are of relatively pure Hawaiian blood.

State Government

Hawaii's state legislature has 76 members, with 51 elected seats in the House of Representatives, and 25 in the State Senate. Members serve two- and four-year terms respectively. All officials come from 76 separate electorates based on population, which sometimes makes for strange political bedfellows. For example, Maui's split 5th Senatorial District and 9th Representative District share one member from each with both Lanai and Molokai. These districts combine some of the island's richest condo and resort communities on Maui's Kaanapali coast with Lanai, where many people are Filipino field workers, and with economically depressed Molokai, where 80% of the native Hawaiians live on welfare.

Oahu, which has the largest number of voters, elects 19 of 25 senators and 39.7 of 51 representatives, giving this island a majority in both houses. Maui, in comparison, elects 2.2 state senators and four representatives.

The state is divided into four administrative counties: the **County of Kauai,** covering Kauai and Niihau; the **City and County of Honolulu,** which encompasses Oahu and includes all of the Northwestern Hawaiian Islands; the **County of Hawaii,** covering the Big Island; and the **County of Maui,** administering the islands of Maui, Lanai, Molokai, and uninhabited Kahoolawe, with the county seat at Wailuku on Maui.

Branches Of Government

The **State Legislature** is the collective body of the House of Representatives and the Senate. They meet during a once-yearly legislative session that begins on the third Wednesday of January and lasts for 90 working days. (These sessions are oftentimes extended and special sessions are frequently called.) The Legislature primarily focuses on taxes, new laws, and appropriations. The **Executive Branch** is headed by the governor and lieutenant governor, both elected on a statewide basis for four years with a two-term maximum. The governor has the right to appoint the heads of 20 state departments outlined in the constitution. The department appointees must be approved by the Senate, and they usually hold office as long as the appointing administration. The present governor is John Waihee III, first ethnically Hawaiian governor in the United States. Mr. Waihee has held this office since 1986. The **Judiciary** is headed by a state Supreme Court of five justices, an appeals court, and four circuit courts. All are appointed by the governor and serve for 10 years with Senate approval. There are 27 district courts which have local jurisdiction; the judges are appointed for six-year terms by the chief justice of the Supreme Court.

Special Departments

The Department of Education is headed by a board of 13 nonpartisan representatives elected for four-year terms, 10 from Oahu and three from the other islands. The board has the right to appoint the Superintendent of Schools. Many praise the centralized board as a democratic body offering equal educational opportunity to all districts of Hawaii regardless of sociofinancial status. Detractors say that the centralized board provides "equal educational mediocrity" to all. The University of Hawaii is governed by a Board of Regents appointed by the governor. They choose the president of the university.

Political History

The politics of Hawaii before WW II was a self-serving yet mostly benevolent oligarchy. The one real political party was Republican, controlled by the Hawaiian Sugar Planters Association. The planters felt that, having made Hawaii a paradise, they should rule because they had "right on their side." The Baldwin family of Maui *was* the government, with such supporters as the Rice family, which controlled Kauai, and William (Doc) Hill of Hawaii. These were the preeminent families of the islands; all were represented on the boards of the Big Five corporations that ruled Hawaii economically by controlling sugar, transportation, and utilities. An early native politician was Prince Jonah Kuhio Kalanianaole, a brother to Liliuokalani, who joined with the Republicans to gain perks for himself and for his own people. Nepotism and political hoopla were the order of those days. The Republicans, in coalition with the native Hawaiians, maintained a majority over the large racial groups such as the Japanese and Filipinos who, left to their own devices, would have been Democrats. The Republicans also used unfair literacy laws, land ownership qualifications, and proof of birth in Hawaii to control the large numbers of immigrant workers who could threaten their ruling position. It was even alleged that during elections a pencil was hung on a string over the Republican ballot: if Hawaiians wanted to vote Democratic, they would have to pull the string to the other side of the voting booth. The telltale angle would be a giveaway. They would be unemployed the next day.

The Democrats Rise To Power

The Democrats were plagued with poor leadership and internal factionalism in the early years. Their first real rise to power began in 1935 when the International Longshoremen's and Warehousemen's Union (ILWU) formed a branch in Hilo on the Big Island. In 1937, an incident known as the "Hilo Massacre" occurred when policemen fired on and wounded 25 striking stevedores, which was the catalyst needed to bind labor together. Thereafter, the ILWU, under the leadership of Jack Hall, became a major factor in the Democratic party. Their relationship was strained in later years when the ILWU was linked to Communism, but during the early days, whomever the ILWU supported in the Democratic Party won.

The Democrats began to take over after WW II when returning Japanese servicemen become active in politics. The Japanese by this time were the largest ethnic group in Hawaii. A central character during the late 1940s and '50s was Jack Burns. Although a *haole,* this simple man was known to be for "the people" regardless of their ethnic background. During the war, as a police captain he made clear his view that he considered the Japanese exemplary Americans. The Japanese community never forgot this, and were instrumental in Burns's election as governor, both in 1962 and 1966. The majority of people in the Asian ethnic groups in Hawaii tended to remain Democrat even after they climbed the socioeconomic ladder. The first special election after statehood saw the governorship go to the previously appointed Republican Governor William Quinn, and the lieutenant governorship to another Republican, James Kealoha, of Hawaiian-Chinese ancestry. The first congressperson elected was Japanese-American, Democrat Daniel Inouye. Since then, every governor has been a Democrat and one out of every two political offices is held by a person of Japanese extraction. Former governor George Ariyoshi is the first Japanese governor in the United States.

OFFICE OF HAWAIIAN AFFAIRS

In 1979, constitutional mandate created the Office of Hawaiian Affairs (OHA). This remarkable piece of legislature recognized, for the first time since the fall of the monarchy in 1893, the special plight of native Hawaiians. For 75 years, no one in government was eager to face the "native question," but since 1979, OHA has opened a Pandora's box of litigation and accusation. For example, in 1983, a presidential commission investigated U.S. involvement in the overthrow of Hawaii's last queen, Liliuokalani, to decide if the federal government owed reparations to her Hawaiian people. After listening to testimony from thousands attesting to personal family loss of land and freedom, complete with old deeds documenting their claims, the commission concluded the U.S. was guiltless and native Hawaiians had nothing coming from Uncle Sam. Jaws dropped, and even those opposed to native Hawaiian rights couldn't believed this *white*wash. Then-governor George Ariyoshi said in a newspaper interview, "A recent congressional study did not accurately portray what went on here at the turn of the century. . . . To say that the monarchy was not overthrown . . . is something that I cannot accept. It is not historically true."

Trouble In Paradise

Since then, OHA, as the vanguard of native political activism, has focused on gaining moneys guaranteed in the state constitution as recently as 1959 for "ceded lands." It has also been instrumental in regaining disputed Hawaiian lands and has helped in the fight to save the sacred island of Kahoolawe, currently uninhabited and until recently used as a bombing target since WW II. To simply state a complex issue, native Hawaiians have been eligible for benefits from revenues accrued from ceded lands and haven't been receiving them. These lands (1.8 million acres) were crown and government lands belonging to the Hawaiian monarchy and, therefore, to its subjects. When the kingdom was overthrown, the lands passed on to the short-lived Republic, followed by the U.S. Protectorate, and then finally to the state in 1959. No one disputed these lands belonged to *the people,* who were entitled to money collected from rents and leases. For the last 26 years, however, these tens of millions of dollars have gone into a "general fund" used by various state agencies such as the Department of Transportation and the Department of Land and Natural Resources; the state is extremely reluctant to turn these funds over to what they derisively call an "unconstitutional special interest group." A Constitutional Convention in 1988 supposedly addressed this issue, but many problems still exist.

Native Hawaiian Rights

The question has always been, "Just what is a native Hawaiian?" The answer has always been ambiguous. The government has used the "blood quantum" as a measuring stick. This is simply the percentage of Hawaiian blood in a person's ancestry—customarily 50% qualifies a person as *Hawaiian.* The issue is compounded by the fact that no other group of people has been so racially intermarried for so many years. Even though many people have direct ancestry to pre-Republic Hawaiians, they don't have enough "Hawaiian-ness" to qualify. An overwhelming number of these people fall into the category of "locals": they "feel" Hawaiian, but blood-wise they're not. They suffer all of the negativity of second-class citizens and reap none of the benefits accorded Hawaiians. Those who do qualify according to blood quantum don't have the numbers or the political clout necessary to get results. In fact, many people involved with OHA would not qualify themselves, at least not according to the blood quantum! Strong factionalism within the native Hawaiian movement itself threatens its credibility. Many people who do qualify by the blood quantum view the others as impinging on their rightful claims. The most vocal activists point out only a coalition of people who have Hawaiian blood, combined with those who "identify" with the movement, will get results. Political firebrands maintain "anti-Hawaiian rights" lobbyists such as the tourist industry, airlines, and large corporations are now stronger than the Hawaiians. They advise the only way the Hawaiian rights movement can win is to become active "political warriors" and vote for legislators who will support their cause. The rhetoric of OHA is reminiscent of that of the equal rights movement of the 1960s.

Obviously compromise is necessary. Perhaps certain social entitlements (such as tuition grants) could be equal for all, whereas money and land entitlements could be granted by percentages equal to the claiming person's "blood quantum." OHA members appeal directly to the Hawaiian people and can build political constituencies at a grassroots level. Since they are elected by the people and not appointed by the government (the case with the Hawaiian Home Lands Department and the trustees of the Bishop Estate, two other *supposedly* Hawaiian institutions), the status quo political parties of Hawaii are wary of them. Their candidates may be opposed and defeated in the future. What makes the issue even more ludicrous is that some of the state's most powerful corporate families opposed to Hawaiian rights have direct lineage to not only pre-Republic Hawaiian ancestors, but to Hawaiian royalty. They themselves would receive "entitlements" from the ceded land according to blood quantum, but socioeconomically they are the natural enemies of OHA. The problem is difficult and it is improbable that all concerned will get satisfaction. OHA maintains offices at 711 Kapiolani Blvd., Honolulu, HI 96813, tel. (808) 586-3777. They publish a newspaper entitled *Ka Wai Ola O OHA* (The Living Waters of OHA), which is available upon request.

Note: The island of Kahoolawe, used as a bombing range and controlled by the U.S. Navy since WW II, was recently returned to the State of Hawaii by the federal government. **Ohana,** a grassroots political group, is very much involved with the future administration of the island. For complete details see the Kahoolawe chapter.

BOB RACE

ECONOMY

Hawaii's mid-Pacific location makes it perfect for two primary sources of income: tourism and the military. Tourists come in anticipation of endless golden days on soothing beaches, while the military is provided with the strategic position of an unsinkable battleship. Each nets Hawaii about $5 billion annually, which should keep flowing smoothly into the foreseeable future, increasing proportionally with the times. These revenues mostly remain aloof from the normal ups and downs of the mainland U.S. economy. Together they make up 60% of the islands' income, and both attract either gung-ho enthusiasts or rabidly negative detractors. The remaining 40% comes in descending proportions from manufacturing, construction, and agriculture, mainly sugar and pineapples, both of which are suffering financial doldrums. As long as the sun shines and the balance of global power requires a military presence, the economic stability of Hawaii is guaranteed.

TOURISM

"The earthly paradise! Don't you want to go to it? Why, of course!" This was the opening line of *The Hawaiian Guide Book* by Henry Whitney that appeared in 1875. In print for 25 years, it sold for 60 cents during a time when a roundtrip sea voyage between San Francisco and Honolulu cost $125. The technique is a bit dated, but the human desires remain the same: some of us seek paradise, all seek escape, some are drawn to play out a drama in a beautiful setting. Tourists have been coming to Hawaii ever since steamship service began in the 1860s. Until WW II, luxury liners carried the financial elite on exclusive voyages to the islands. By the 1920s 10,000 visitors a year were spending almost $5 million dollars—cementing the bond between Hawaii and tourism.

A $25,000 prize offered by James Dole of pineapple fame sparked a transpacific air race in 1927. The success of these aerial daredevils proved that commercial air travel to Hawaii was feasible. Two years later, **Hawaiian Air** was offering regularly scheduled flights between the major islands. By 1950 airplanes had captured over 50% of the transportation market, and ocean voyages were relegated to "specialty travel," catering to the elite. By 1960 the large airbuses made their debut; 300,000 tourists arrived on eight designated airlines. The Boeing 747 began operating in 1969. These enormous planes could carry hundreds of passengers at reasonable rates, so travel to Hawaii became possible for the average-income person. In 1970, two million arrived, and by 1980 close to four million passengers arrived on 22 international air carriers. The first hotel in Honolulu was the **Hawaiian,** built in 1872. It was pre-dated by **Volcano House,** which overlooks Kilauea Crater on the Big Island, and was built in 1866. The coral-pink **Royal Hawaiian,** built in 1927, is Waikiki's graciously aging grande dame, a symbol of days gone by. As late as the 1950s it had Waikiki Beach almost to itself. Only 10,000 hotel units were available in 1960; today there are over 60,000, and thousands of condos as well.

Tourists: Who, When, And Where

Tourism-based income outstripped pineapples and sugar by the mid-'60s and the boom was on. Longtime residents could even feel a physical change in air temperature: many trees were removed from Honolulu to build parking lots, and reflected sunlight made Honolulu much hotter and at times unbearable. Even the trade winds, known to moderate temperatures, were not up to that task. So many people from the outlying farming communities were attracted to work in the hotels, there was a poi famine in 1967. But for the most part, islanders knew their economic future was tied to the "nonpolluting" industry of tourism. Most visitors (75%) are Americans, and the largest numbers come from the West Coast. Sun-seeking refugees from frigid Alaska, however, make up the greatest proportional number, according to population figures. The remaining arrivals are, in descending order of numbers, from Japan, Canada, Australia, and England. Europe, as a whole, sends proportionately fewer visitors than North America or Asia, while the least amount come from South America.

The Japanese market is constantly growing, with over a million Japanese visitors per year now arriving. This is particularly beneficial to the tourist market because the average Western tourist spends about $150 per day, while his or her Japanese counterpart spends just over $300 per day. However, a Japanese tourist stays only about five days, shorter than the typical visit. Up until very recently the Japanese traveled only in groups and primarily stayed on Oahu. Now the trend is to travel independently, or to come with a group and then peel off, with a hefty percentage heading for the Neighbor Islands.

The typical visitor is fairly affluent, about 35 years old, with 20% more women than men arriving. The average age is a touch higher than in most vacation areas because it reflects an inflated proportion of retirees heading for Hawaii, especially Honolulu, to fulfill a lifelong "dream" vacation. A typical stay lasts about 12 days, down from a month in the 1950s; a full 50% are repeat visitors. On any given day there are about 80,000 travelers on Oahu, 25,000 on Maui, and about 8,000 each on Kauai and Hawaii. Molokai and Lanai get so few the figures are hardly counted.

In 1964 only 10% of the islands' hotel rooms were on the Neighbor Islands, but by 1966 the figure jumped to 25%, with more than 70% of tourists opting to visit the Neighbor Islands. Today five out of 10 hotel rooms are on the Neighbor Islands, with the figure steadily rising. The overwhelming number of tourists are on package tours, and the largest number of people congregate on Oahu in Waikiki, which has a 74% average hotel occupancy and attracts two times as many visitors as do the Neighbor Islands together. Obviously, Waikiki is still most people's idea of paradise. Those seeking a more intimate experience can have it with a 20-minute flight from Oahu to a Neighbor Island. Joaquin Miller, the 19th-century poet of the Sierras, said, "I tell you my boy, the man who has not seen the Sandwich Islands, in this one great ocean's warm heart, has not seen the world." The times have certainly changed, but the sentiments of most visitors to Hawaii remain consistently the same.

Tourism-Related Problems

Tourism is both boon and blight to Hawaii. It is the root cause of two problems: one environmental, the other socioeconomic. The environmental impact is obvious and best described in the lament of songstress Joni Mitchell: "They paved paradise and put up a parking lot." Simply, tourism can draw too many people to an area and overburden it. In the process, it stresses the very land and destroys the natural beauty that attracted people in the first place. Tourists come to Hawaii for what has been called its "ambient resource": a balanced collage of indulgent climate, invigorating waters, intoxicating scenery, and exotic people all wrapped up neatly in one area which can both soothe and excite at the same time. It is in the best interest of Hawaii to preserve this "resource."

Most point to Oahu's Waikiki as a prime example of development gone mad. It is supersaturated, and amazingly enough, hotel owners themselves are trying to keep development in check. Two prime examples of the best and the worst development can be found on Maui's south shore at Kihei and Wailea, less than five miles apart. Kihei looks like a high-rise, low-income, federally funded housing project. You can bet those who made a killing building here don't live here. Just down the road, Wailea is a model of what development could and should be. The architecture is tasteful, low-rise, unobtrusive, and done with people and the preservation of the scenery in mind. It's obviously more exclusive, but access points to the beaches are open to everyone and the view is still there for all to enjoy. It points the way for development standards of the future.

Changing Lifestyle

Like the land, humans are stressed by tourism. Local people, who once took the "Hawaiian lifestyle" for granted, became displaced and estranged in their own land. Some areas, predominantly along gorgeous beaches that were average- to low-income communities, are now overdeveloped with prices going through the roof. The locals are not only forced to move out, but often must come back as service personnel in the tourist industry and cater to the very people who displaced them. At one time the psychological blow was softened because, after all, the newcomers were merely benign tourists who would stay a short time, spend a wad of money, and leave. Today, condos are being built and a different sort of visitor is arriving. Many condo owners are in the above-average income bracket: well-educated businesspeople and professionals. The average condo owner is a Mainlander who purchases one as a second or retirement home. These people are not islanders and have a tough time relating to the locals, who naturally feel resentment. Moreover, since they don't *leave* like normal tourists, they use all community facilities, find those special nooks and crannies for shopping or sunbathing once exclusively the domain of locals, and have a say as voters in community governments. The islanders have become more and more disenfranchised. Many believe the new order instigated by tourism is similar to what has always existed in Hawaii: a few from the privileged class being catered to by many from the working class. In a way it's an extension of the plantation system, but instead of carrying pineapples, most islanders find themselves carrying luggage, cocktails, or broiled fish. One argument, however, remains undeniable: whether it's people or pineapples, one has to make a living. The days of a little grass shack on a sunny beach aren't gone, but you need a steady job or a wallet full of credit cards to afford one.

THE MILITARY

Hawaii is the most militarized state in the U.S.: all five services are represented. Oahu is the headquarters of CINCPAC (Commander in Chief Pacific), which controls 70% of earth's surface from California to the east coast of Africa and to both poles. The U.S. military presence dates back to 1887, when Pearl Harbor was given to the Navy as part of the "Sugar Reciprocity Treaty." The sugar planters were given favorable "duty-free" treatment on their sugar, while the U.S. Navy was allowed exclusive rights to one of the best harbors in the Pacific. In 1894, when the monarchy was being overthrown by the sugar planters, the USS *Boston* sent a contingency of marines ashore to "keep order," which really amounted to a show of force, backing the revolution. The Spanish-American War saw U.S. troops billeted at Camp McKinley at the foot of Diamond Head, and Schofield Barracks opened to receive the 5th Cavalry in 1909. Pearl Harbor's flames ignited WW II and there has been no looking back since then.

About 60,000 military personnel are stationed in Hawaii, with a slightly higher number of dependents. The U.S. Navy and Marines combined have the most personnel with about 36,000, followed by 17,000 Army, 6,000 Air

Force, and 1,000 or so Coast Guard personnel. Besides this, 20,000 civilian support personnel account for 65% of all federal jobs in Hawaii. The combined military services are one of the largest landholders, with over 242,000 acres, accounting for six percent of Hawaiian land. The two major holdings are the 100,000-acre Pohahuloa Training Area on Hawaii and 100,000 acres on Oahu, which is a full 26% of the entire island. The Army controls 71% of the military lands, followed by the Navy at 25%; the remainder goes to the Air Force and a few small installations to the Coast Guard.

The Military Has No *Aloha*

Not everyone is thrilled about the strong military presence in Hawaii. Two factions, native Hawaiians and anti-nuclear groups, are downright angry. Radical contingencies of "native Hawaiian-rights groups" consider Hawaii an independent country, besieged and "occupied" by the U.S. government. They date their loss of independence to Liliuokalani's overthrow in 1894. The vast majority of ethnic Hawaiians, though they consider themselves Americans, are concerned with loss of their rightful homelands, with no financial reparation, and a continuing destruction and disregard for their traditional religious and historical sites. A long list of grievances is cited by native Hawaiian action groups, but the best and clearest example is the controversy over the sacred island, Kahoolawe, which until recently was used as a bombing target by the Navy. (For more information see the Kahoolawe chapter.)

The second controversy raised by the military presence focuses on Hawaii as a nuclear target. The ultimate goal of the anti-nuclear protestors is to see the Pacific, and the entire world, free from nuclear arms. They see Hawaii as a big arsenal used by international power merchants on the Mainland as both pawn and watchdog. There is no doubt Hawaii is a nuclear target, and the anti-nuke groups say if war breaks out the Hawaiian Islands will be reduced to cinders. The military naturally counters that a strong Hawaii is a deterrent to nuclear war and that Hawaii is not only a powerful offensive weapon, but one of the best-defended regions of the world. Unfortunately, when you are on an island there is no place to go: like a boxer in a ring, you can run, but you can't hide. Anyone interested in the nuclear controversy can contact the U.S. Nuclear Free Pacific Network, 942 Market St., Rm. 711, San Francisco, CA 94102.

SUGAR

Sugarcane *(ko)* was brought to Hawaii by its original settlers and was known throughout Polynesia. Its cultivation was well established and duly noted by Captain Cook when he first sighted the islands. The native Hawaiians used vari-

Missiles stand ready to defend the U.S. Battleship Hawaii.

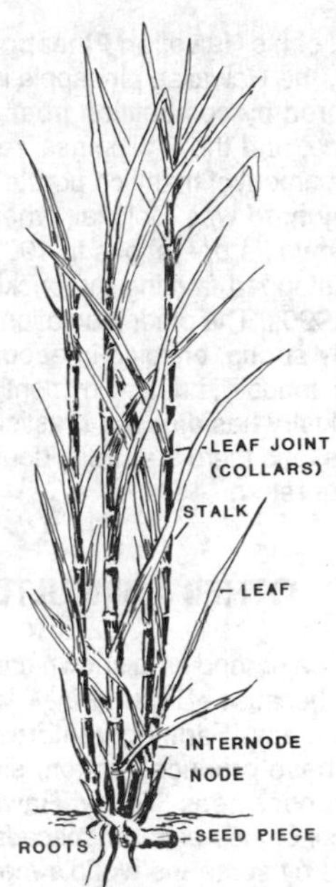

young sugarcane

ous strains of sugarcane for food, rituals, and medicine. It was never refined, but the stalk was chewed and juice was pressed from it. It was used as food during famine, as an ingredient in many otherwise unpalatable medicines, and especially as a love potion. Commercial growing started with a failure on Oahu in 1825, followed by a successful venture a decade later on Kauai. This original plantation, now part of the McBryde Sugar Co., is still productive. The industry received a technological boost in 1850 when a centrifuge, engineered by David Weston of the Honolulu Iron Works, was installed at a plantation on East Maui. It was used to spin the molasses out of the cooked syrup, leaving a crude crystal.

Hawaii's biggest market has always been the mainland U.S. Demand rose dramatically during the California gold rush of 1849-50, and again a decade later during the American Civil War. At first Hawaiian sugar had a poor reputation that almost killed its export market, but with technological advances it became the best-quality sugar available in the last century.

Irrigation And Profit Politics

In 1876 the **Reciprocity Treaty** freed Hawaiian sugar from import duty. Now a real fortune could be made. One entrepreneur, **Claus Spreckels,** a sugar-beet magnate from California, became the reigning Sugar King in Hawaii. His state-of-the-art refineries on Maui employed every modern convenience, including electric lighting; he was also instrumental in building marvelous irrigation ditches necessary to grow sugar on once-barren land. The biggest hurdle to commercial sugarcane growing has always been water. One pound of sugar requires one ton of water, or about 250 gallons. A real breakthrough came when the growers reasoned that fresh water in the form of rain must seep through the lava and be stored underground. Fresh water will furthermore float atop heavier salt water and therefore be recoverable by a series of vertical wells and tunnels. By 1898, planters were tapping this underground supply of water, and sugar could be produced in earnest as an export crop.

The Plantation System

Sugarcane also produced the plantation system, which was in many ways socially comparable to that of the pre-Civil War South. It was the main cause of the cosmopolitan mixture of races found in Hawaii today. Workers were in great demand, and the sugar growers scoured the globe looking for likely sources. Importing plantation workers started by liberalizing **The Masters and Servants Act;** this basically allowed the importation of conscripted workers. Even during its heyday, people with consciences felt that this system was no different from slavery. The first conscripts were Chinese, followed by Japanese, and then a myriad of people including other Polynesians, Germans, Norwegians, Spanish, Portuguese, Puerto Ricans, Filipinos, and even a few freed slaves from the southern U.S. (For further coverage see "The People" later in this chapter.)

Today, with production down on Oahu, Maui, Kauai, and Hawaii, yearly sugar sales have fallen from those a few years ago when they were a hefty $500 million, although the state's sugarcane-producing farms, and their attendant refineries, still employ a hefty amount of the islands' workforce. Newcomers, startled by what appear to be brush fires, are actually witnessing the burning of sugarcane prior to harvesting. Some sugar lands, such as those along Kaanapali on Maui, coexist side by side with a developed tourist area. Hawaii's sugarcane industry is still healthy and solvent, producing over nine million tons of cane annually. If profits remain sweet, cane as a cash crop will flourish for many years to come.

PINEAPPLES

Next to cane, the majority of Hawaii's cultivated lands yield pineapples. The main farms are on Oahu and on the northwest tip of Maui, with Lanai, once the world's largest pineapple plantation, now out of business. Pineapples were brought to the islands by **Don Francisco Marin,** an early Spanish agronomist, in the 1820s. Fresh pineapples were exported as early as 1850 to San Francisco, and a few cases of canned fruit appeared in 1876 at Hawaii's pavilion at the U.S. Centennial Exposition in Philadelphia. Old varieties of pineapples were pithier and pricklier than the modern variety. Today's large, luscious, golden fruits are the "smooth cayenne" variety from Jamaica, introduced by Captain Kidwell in 1886.

Dole

But Hawaiian pineapple, as we know it, is synonymous with one man, **James Dole,** who actually *made* the industry at the turn of this century. Jim Dole started growing pineapples on a 60-acre homestead in Wahiawa, Oahu. He felt that America was ready to add this fruit to its diet and that "canning" would be the conveyance. By 1903, he was shipping canned fruit from his Iwilei plant and by 1920 pineapples were a familiar item in most American homes. Hawaii was at that time the largest producer in the world. In 1922, Jim Dole bought the entire island of Lanai, whose permanent residents numbered only about 100, and started the world's largest pineapple plantation. (For more information see the Lanai chapter.) By all accounts, Jim Dole was an exemplary human being, but he could never learn to "play ball" with the economic powers that ruled Hawaii, namely "The Big Five." They ruined him by 1932 and took control of his **Hawaiian Pineapple Company.** Today, the Hawaiian pineapple industry is beleaguered by competition from Asia, Central America, and the Philippines, resulting in the abandonment of many corporate farms. Hit especially hard was Molokai, where Del Monte shut down its operations in 1982, and Lanai, which stopped farming the prickly fruits in the early 1990s. The other plantations are still reasonably strong, bringing in about $200 million dollars annually, but employment in the pineapple industry has dropped drastically in the last decade, and there are strong doubts these jobs will ever return.

OTHER AGRICULTURE

Every major food crop known can be grown in Hawaii because of its amazingly varied climates and rich soil. Farming ventures through the years have produced cotton, sisal, rice, and even rubber trees. Today, Hawaii is a major producer of the Australian macadamia nut, considered by some the world's most useful and delicious nut. The islands' fresh exotic fruits are unsurpassed; juices and nectars made from papaya, passion fruit, and guava are becoming well known worldwide. Dazzling flowers such as protea, carnations, orchids, and anthuriums are also commercially grown. Hawaii has a very healthy livestock industry, headed by the Big Island's quarter-million-acre Parker Ranch, the largest singly owned cattle ranch in the United States. Poultry, dairy, and pork are also produced on many farms. The only coffee grown in the U.S. is found on the slopes of Mauna Loa in the Kona District of the Big Island. "Kona coffee" is of gourmet quality and well regarded for its aroma and rich flavor. Recently, chocolate manufacture was introduced to the Big Island, and production of this fine sweet is in full operation. *Pakalolo* (marijuana) is the most lucrative cash crop, but no official economic records exist. It's grown by enterprising gardeners on all the islands (see "Health and Safety" in the Out and About chapter for more about *pakalolo*).

Hawaiian waters are alive with fish, but its commercial fleet is woefully small and obsolete. Fishing revenues amount to only $35 million per year, which is ludicrous in a land where fish is the obvious natural bounty. Native Hawaiians were masters of aquaculture, routinely building fishponds and living from their harvest. Where once there were hundreds of fishponds, only a handful are in use today. The main aquaculture is growing freshwater prawns; the state is considered the world leader, although there are less than 25 prawn farms operating at a yearly value of only $2.5 million. With all of these foodstuffs, unbelievable as it may sound, Hawaii must import much of its food. Hawaii can feed *itself,* but it cannot support the six million hungry tourists who come to sample its superb and diverse cuisine every year.

ECONOMIC POWER

The Big Five Corporations

Until statehood, Hawaii was ruled economically by a consortium of corporations known as the "Big Five": **C. Brewer and Co.,** sugar, ranching, and chemicals, founded in 1826; **Theo. H. Davies & Co.,** sugar, investments, insurance, and transportation, founded in 1845; **Amfac Inc.** (originally H. Hackfield Inc.—a German firm that changed its name and ownership during the anti-German sentiment of WW I to American Factors), sugar, insurance, and land development, founded in 1849; **Castle and Cooke Inc.,** (Dole) pineapple, food packing, and land development, founded in 1851; and **Alexander and Baldwin Inc.,** shipping, sugar, and pineapple, founded in 1895. This economic oligarchy ruled Hawaii with a steel grip in a velvet glove.

With members on every important corporate board, they controlled all major commerce, including banking, shipping, insurance, hotel development, agriculture, utilities, and wholesale and retail merchandising. Anyone trying to buck the system was ground to dust, finding it suddenly impossible to do business in the islands. The Big Five were made up of the islands' oldest and most well-established *haole* families; all included bloodlines from Hawaii's own nobility. They looked among themselves for suitable husbands and wives, so that breaking in from the outside even through marriage was hardly possible. The only time they were successfully challenged prior to statehood was when Sears, Roebuck and Co. opened a store on Oahu.

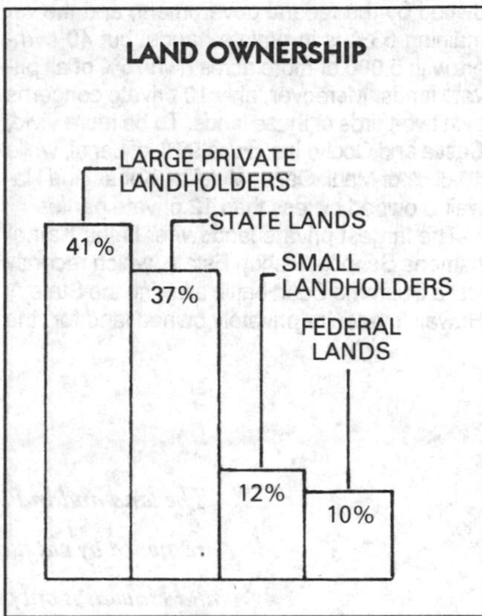

Closing ranks, the Big Five decreed that their steamships would not carry Sears's freight. When Sears threatened to buy its own steamship line, the Big Five relented.

Actually, statehood, and more to the point, tourism, broke their oligarchy. After 1960 too much money was at stake for Mainland-based corporations to ignore. Eventually the grip of the Big Five was loosened, but they are still enormously powerful and richer than ever. These days, however, they don't control everything; now their power is land. With only five other major landholders, they control 65% of the privately held land in Hawaii.

Land Ownership

Hawaii, landwise, is a small pie. Its slices are not at all well divided. There are 6,425 square miles of land, 98% of which make up the six main inhabited islands. This figure does not include Niihau, which is privately owned by the Robinson family and inhabited by the last remaining pure-blooded Hawaiiansl; nor does it include Kahoolawe, the uninhabited, former Navy bombing target just off Maui's south shore, which was only returned to state control in 1994. Of the 4,045,511 acres that make up the inhabited islands, 37% is owned by the state, 10% is owned by the federal government, and the remaining 53% is in private hands, but 40 owners with 5,000 or more acres own 75% of all private lands. Moreover, only 10 private concerns own two-thirds of these lands. To be more vivid, Castle and Cooke Inc. owns 99% of Lanai, while 40-60% of Maui, Oahu, Molokai, Kauai, and Hawaii is owned by less than 12 private parties.

The largest private landowner is the Kamehameha Schools/Bishop Estate, which recently lost a Supreme Court battle allowing the State of Hawaii to acquire privately owned land for "the public good." More than in any other state, Hawaiian landowners tend to lease land rather than sell it, and many private homes are on rented ground. This was the case with many homes rented from the Bishop Estate. The state acquired the land and resold it to long-term lease holders. These lands had previously earned a slow but steady profit for native Hawaiians. As land prices continue to rise, only the very rich land developers are able to purchase long-term leases, and the "people" of Hawaii continue to become even more land poor.

"The land and industries of Hawaii

are owned by old families and large corporations,

and Hawaii is only so large."

—Jack London, c. 1916

THE PEOPLE

The people of Hawaii are no longer *in* the human race; they've already *won* it. Nowhere else on earth can you find such a kaleidoscopic mixture of people. Every major race is accounted for, with over 50 ethnic groups adding not only their genes, but their customs, traditions, and outlooks. The modern Hawaiian is the future's "everyman": a blending of all races. Interracial marriage has been long accepted in Hawaii, and people are so mixed it's already difficult to place them in a specific racial category. Besides the original Hawaiians, themselves a mixed race of Polynesians, people in the islands have multiple ancestor combinations. Hawaii is the most racially integrated state in the U.S., and although the newest, it epitomizes the time-honored American ideal of the melting-pot society.

THE ISSUE OF RACE

This polyracial society should be a model of understanding and tolerance, and in most ways it is, but there are still racial tensions. People tend to identify with one group, and though not openly hostile, they do look disparagingly on others. Some racial barbs maintain the Chinese are grasping, the Japanese too cold and calculating, the *haole* materialistic, Hawaiians lackadaisical, and Filipinos emotional. In Hawaii this labeling tendency is a bit modified because *people*, as individuals, are not usually discriminated against, but their *group* may be. Another factor is individuals identify with a group not along strict blood lines, but more by a "feeling of identity." If a white/Japanese man married a Hawaiian/Chinese woman, they would be accepted by all groups concerned. Their children, moreover, would be what they chose to be and, more to the point, what they "felt" like.

There are no ghettos as such, but there are traditional areas where people of similar racial strains live, and where outsiders are made to feel unwelcome. For example, the Waianae district of Oahu is considered a strong "Hawaiian" area where other people may meet with hostility; the Kahala area of Oahu mostly attracts upwardly mobile whites; on the island of Lanai,

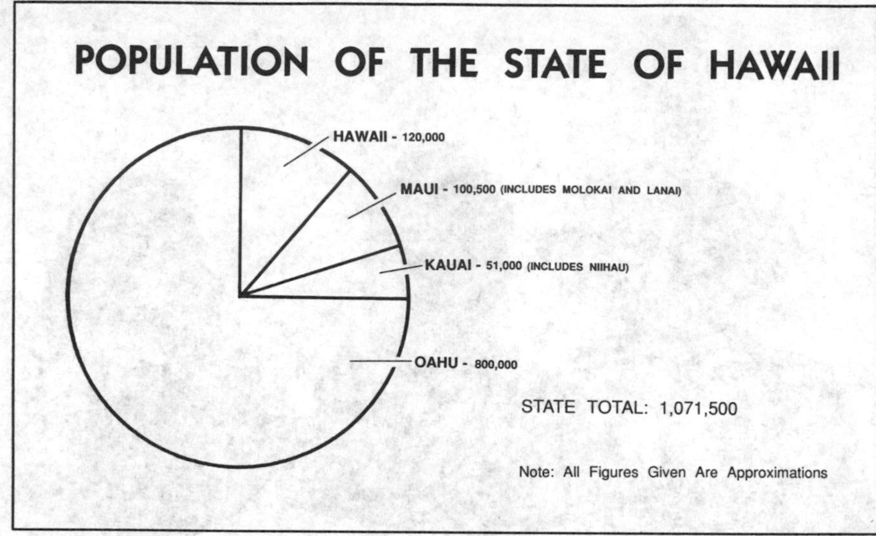

Japanese managers don't live among Filipino workers. Some clubs make it difficult for non-whites to become members; certain Japanese, Chinese, and Filipino organizations attract only members from these ethnic groups; and Hawaiian *ohana* would question any person seeking to join unless he or she had some Hawaiian blood. Generally, however, the vast majority of people get along with each other and mix with no discernible problems.

The real catalyst responsible for most racial acceptance is the Hawaiian public school system. Education has always been highly regarded in Hawaii; the classroom has long been integrated. Thanks to a standing tradition of progressive education, democracy and individualism have always been basic maxims taught in the classroom. The racial situation in Hawaii is far from perfect, but it does point the way to the future in which all people can live side by side with respect and dignity.

Who, What, And Where

Hawaii has an approximate population of 1,100,000, which includes 120,000 permanently stationed military personnel and their dependents. (All numbers used in this section are approximations.) It has the highest ratio of population to immigration in the U.S., and is the only state where whites are not the majority. White people are, however, the fastest growing group, due primarily to immigration from the U.S. West Coast. About 60% of Hawaiian residents were born in Hawaii; 25% were born on the mainland U.S.; and 15% are foreign-born. The average age is 29, and men slightly outnumber women. This is due to the large concentration of predominantly male military personnel, and to the substantial number of older bachelor plantation workers who came during the first part of this century and never found wives. The population has grown steadily in recent times, but has fluctuated wildly in the past. In 1876, it reached its lowest ebb with only 55,000 permanent residents. This was the era of large sugar plantations; their constant demand for labor was the primary cause of importing various peoples from around the world, and led to Hawaii's racially integrated society. WW II saw the population swell from 400,000 to 900,000. These 500,000 military personnel left at war's end, but many returned to settle after getting a taste of island living. Of the one million plus people in the islands today, 835,000 live on Oahu, with 377,000 in the Honolulu metropolitan area. The rest are distributed as follows: 120,000 on Hawaii, with 36,000 in Hilo;

91,000 on Maui, the largest concentration around Wailuku/Kahului with 25,000; 50,000 on Kauai, including 230 pure-blooded Hawaiians on Niihau; 7,000 on Molokai; and just over 2,000 on Lanai. The overall population density is 164 people per square mile, equal to that of California, with Honolulu claiming more than 1,400 people per square mile, and Maui the second most densely populated island with only 105 people per square mile. City dwellers outnumber those living in the country by four to one. The average household size ranges from just over one person in Honolulu, to 3.1 persons per household throughout the remainder of the state.

THE HAWAIIANS

The drama of the native Hawaiians is a tragedy: it ends in their demise as a viable people. When Captain Cook discovered Hawaii in 1778, an estimated 300,000 natives were living in harmony with their surroundings; within 100 years a scant 50,000 demoralized and dejected Hawaiians existed almost as wards of the state. Today, although 115,000 people claim varying degrees of Hawaiian blood, experts say less than 1,000 can lay claim to being pure Hawaiian, and that's stretching it. A resurgence of Hawaiian ethnic pride is sweeping the islands as many people trace their roots and attempt to absorb the finer aspects of their ancestral lifestyle. It's easy to see why they could be bitter over what they've lost, since they're now strangers in their own land, much like Native Americans. The overwhelming majority of Hawaiians are of mixed heritage, and the wisest take the best from all worlds. From the Hawaiian side comes simplicity, love of the land, and acceptance of people. It is the Hawaiian legacy of *aloha* that remains immortal and adds the special elusive quality that "is" Hawaii.

Polynesian Roots

The Polynesians' original root stock is muddled and remains an anthropological mystery. It's believed they were nomadic wanderers who migrated from both the Indian subcontinent and Southeast Asia through Indonesia, where they learned to sail and navigate on protected waterways. As they migrated, they honed their sailing skills until they could take on the Pacific, and absorbed other cultures and races until they coalesced into Polynesians. Abraham Fornander, still considered a major authority on the subject, wrote in his *Account of the Polynesian Race* (1885) that the Polynesians started as a white race, heavily influenced by contact with the Cushite, Chaldeo-Arabian civilization. He estimated their arrival in Hawaii at A.D. 600 based on Hawaiian genealogical chants. Modern science seems to bear this date out, but remains skeptical on his other surmises.

Thousands of years before Europeans even imagined the existence of a Pacific Ocean, Polynesians had populated the far-flung islands of the "Polynesian Triangle" stretching from New Zealand in the south, thousands of miles east to Easter Island, and finally to Hawaii, the northern apex. Similar language, gods, foods, and crafts add credibility to this theory. Other more fanciful versions are all long on conjecture and short on evidence. For example, Atlantis, the most "found" lost continent in history, pops up again, with the Hawaiians the supposed remnants of this advanced civilization. The slim proof is the Hawaiian *kahuna,* so well versed in the curative arts they had to be Atlantians. In fact, they not only made it to Hawaii, but also to the Philippines, where their secret powers have been passed on to the faith healers of today. That the Hawaiians are the "lost tribe of Israel" is another theory, but this too is wild conjecture.

The "Land Seekers"

The intrepid Polynesians who actually settled Hawaii are believed to have come from the Marquesas Islands, 1,000 miles south of Hawaii and a few hundred miles east. The Marquesans were cannibals known for their tenacity and strength, two attributes that would serve them well. They left their own islands because of war and famine; these migrations went on for centuries. Ships' logs mention Marquesan seagoing canoes setting sail in search of new land as late as the mid-19th century. The first navigator-explorers, advance scouting parties, were referred to as "land seekers." They were led northward by a few terse words sung in a chant that gave a general direction and promised some guiding stars (probably recounting the wild adventures of canoes blown far off course that somehow managed to return to the southern islands of Polynesia). The land seekers were familiar with the stars, currents, habits of land birds, and countless other subliminal clues that are overlooked by "civilized" people.

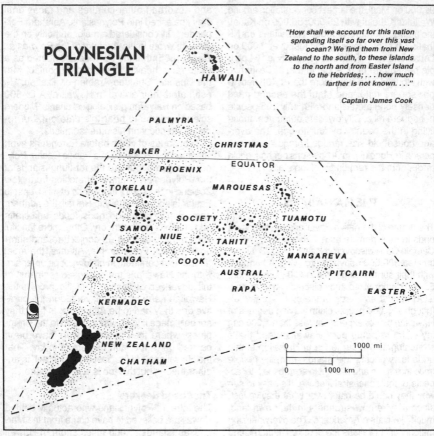

After finding Hawaii, they were aided in their voyage home by favorable trade winds and familiar waters. They set sail again in canoes laden with hopeful families and all the foodstuffs necessary to colonize a new land, anticipating a one-way ride with no return. Over the centuries, the fierce Marquesans mellowed into Hawaiians, and formed a new benevolent culture based on the fertility god Lono. Then, in the 12th century, a ferocious army of Tahitians invaded Hawaii and supplanted not only the ruling chiefs but also the gentler gods with their war god Ku, who demanded human sacrifice. Abruptly, contact with Polynesia stopped. Some say the voyages, always fraught with danger, were no longer necessary. Hawaii was forgotten by the Polynesians, and the Hawaiians became the most rarified race in the world. It was to these people that Captain Cook in 1778 brought the outside world. Finding Polynesians stretched so far and wide across the Pacific, he declared them "the most extensive nation upon earth."

The "Little People" Of Hawaii

The Mu, Wa, Eepa, and Wao are all "little people" of Hawaii, but the most famous are the

Menehune. As a group they resemble the trolls and leprechauns of Europe, but so many stories concern them that they appear to have actually existed in Hawaii at one time. Even in the late 18th century, an official census noted King Kaumualii of Kauai had 65 Menehune, who were said to live in Wainiha Valley. It's held the Menehune drove out the Mu and the Wa. They also differed slightly in appearance. The Menehune are about two to three feet tall with hairy, well-muscled bodies. Their red faces have thick noses, protruding foreheads, and long eyebrows, and their hair is stringy. They love to frolic, especially by rolling down hills into the sea, and their favorite foods are shrimp and poi. They seldom speak, but their chatter sounds like the low growling of a dog. Nocturnal creatures, Menehune are frightened of owls and dogs.

The Mu are mute, while the Wa are noted for their loud blustering shouts. The Mu were thought to be black-skinned and to live deep in the forest on a diet of bananas. All had their specialties, but the Menehune were stone masons par excellence. Many feats involving stonework are attributed to the Menehune. The most famous is the "Menehune Ditch" on Kauai. They finished their monumental tasks in one night, disappearing by daybreak. Even in the 1950s, masons building with stone near Diamond Head insisted their work was disturbed at night, and a *kahuna* had to be called in to appease the Menehune. After that, all went well.

In a more scientific vein, the Tahitian word for Menehune means "commoner." Many feel they were non-Polynesian aboriginals who somehow made it to the islands, and co-mingled with Hawaiians until their chiefs became alarmed their little race would vanish. (Mohikia and Analike are the respective names of a Menehune prince and princess who married Hawaiians and whose names have been preserved in legend.) The Menehune assembled en masse and supposedly floated away on an island descended from the heavens called "Kuaihelani." Some say they headed for the far-flung outer islands of Necker and Nihoa, where, oddly enough, stone gods found there are unlike any on the other Hawaiian islands. But there the trail grows cold. Today, island mothers warn their misbehaving toddlers the Menehune will come and take them away, but in most stories they are actually pixielike and benign.

The Demise Of Hawaiians

When Captain Cook stepped ashore on Waimea, Kauai, on the morning of January 20, 1778, he discovered a population of 300,000 natives living in perfect harmony with their surroundings. Their agrarian society had flourished in the last thousand years. However, the ecological system of Hawaii has always been exceptionally fragile, its people included. White arrivals found a great people who were large, strong, and virile, but when it came to fighting even minor diseases they proved as delicate as hothouse flowers. To exacerbate the situation, the Hawaiians were totally uninhibited in sex between willing partners. Unfortunately, white sailors were laden with syphilis, gonorrhea, and all manner of other germs and common European diseases. Captain Cook tried desperately to keep sexually diseased members of his crew away from Hawaiian women, but it was impossible. The *hospitality* of Hawaiian women was legendary, and promises of "paradise" were actually used as a lure to get sailors for perilous cruises into the Pacific that could last for years. When Cook returned from the north in less than one year, there were already natives with telltale signs of venereal disease.

Fatal Flaws

Hawaiian women brought venereal disease home, and it spread like wildfire. By the time the missionaries came in 1820 and halted the widespread fornication, the native population was only 140,000, half of what it had been only 40 years after initial contact. In 1804 alone, perhaps 100,000 died from *okuu* (either typhoid or cholera). In the next 50 years measles, mumps, influenza, and tuberculosis ravaged the people. In 1853 a smallpox epidemic ate further into the doomed and weakened Hawaiian race, and leprosy ranged far and wide in the land. In addition, during the whaling years, at least 25% of all able-bodied Hawaiian men sailed away, never to return. By 1880 King Kalaukaua had only 48,000 Hawaiian subjects, a cataclysmic decrease of 82% of the original population. Wherever the king went, he would beseech his people, *"Hooulu lahui"* ("Increase the race"), but it was already too late. Nature itself had turned

Native Hawaiians lived a more and more humble existence as time passed them by.

its back on these once-proud people. Many of their marriages were barren and in 1874 when only 1,400 children were born, a full 75% died in infancy. The final coup de grace was intermarriage. With so many interracial marriages, the Hawaiians literally bred themselves out of existence.

Painful Adjustments

In the last century, the old paternalism inherent in the Hawaiian caste system was carried on by the ruling *haole* families. The remaining Hawaiians looked to the ruling class of whites as they had to their own *ali'i,* and for many years this attitude discouraged self help. Many Hawaiians fervently accepted the Christianity that had supplanted their own religion because it was a haven against a rapidly changing world in which they felt more and more alienated. Though Hawaiians were not favored as good plantation workers and were branded as lazy, they were actually hard and dedicated workers. Like all people attuned to their environment, they chose to work in the cool of the mornings and late afternoons, and could make no sense of laboring in the intense heat of the day. As fishermen they were unparalleled, and also made excellent cowboys on the ranches, preferring the open ranges to the constricting plantation fields.

Hawaiians readily engaged in politics and were impressed with all the hoopla and fanfare. They attended rallies, performed hula and songs, and in most instances sided with the whites against the Asians. They were known to accept money for their votes and almost considered it the obligation of the leader, whom they regarded as a sort of chief, to grease their palms. Educated Hawaiians tended to become lawyers, judges, policeman, and teachers, and there is still a disproportionate number of Hawaiians, population-wise, in these fields. Hawaiians were somewhat racist toward the Japanese and Chinese. However, they would readily intermarry because, true to *aloha,* they accepted individual "people" even though they might be prejudiced against their group. In 1910, although the native population was greatly reduced, there are still twice as many full-blooded Hawaiians as mixed bloods. By 1940 mixed-blood Hawaiians were the fastest-growing group, and full bloods the fastest declining.

Hawaiians Today

Many Hawaiians moved to the cities and became more and more disenfranchised. Their folk society stressed openness and a giving nature, but downplayed the individual and the ownership of private property. These cultural traits made them easy targets for users and schemers. After repeated unfair treatment, they became either apathetic or angry. About 138,000 people living in Hawaii have *some* Hawaiian blood. Most surveys reveal that although they number only 13% of the population, they account for almost 50% of the financially destitute families, arrests, and illegitimate births. Niihau, a privately owned island, is home to about 250 pureblood Hawaiians, the largest concentration per capita in the islands. The Robinson family, which owns the island, restricts visitors to invited guests only. The second largest concentration of people with Hawaiian blood is on Molokai, where 3,200 Hawaiians, living mostly on Hawaiian Homes lands, make up 49% of the population. The majority of part- or full-blooded Hawaiians, 92,000 or so, live on Oahu, where they are particularly strong in the hotel and entertainment fields. People of Hawaiian extraction are a delight to meet, and visitors so lucky as to be befriended by one long regard this friendship as the highlight of their travels. The Hawaiians have always given their *aloha* freely and it is we who must accept it as a precious gift.

THE CHINESE

Next to Yankees from New England, the Chinese are the oldest migrant group in Hawaii. Since the beginning, their influence has far outshone their meager numbers. They have long been the backbone of the small, privately owned retail trade. They brought to Hawaii, along with their individuality, Confucianism, Taoism, and Buddhism. Though many became Christians, the flavor of their Asian traditions still lingers. The Chinese population of about 68,000 makes up only six percent of the state's total, and the vast majority (63,000) reside on Oahu. Their key to success has been indefatigable hard work, the shrewdness to seize a good opportunity, and above all, an almost fanatical desire to educate their children. As an ethnic group they have the least amount of crime, the highest per capita income, and a disproportionate number of professionals, and remain some of Hawaii's most prominent citizens.

The First Chinese

No one knows his name, but a Chinese person is credited with being the first one in Hawaii to refine sugar. This Asian wanderer tried his hand at crude refining on Lanai in 1802. He failed, but other Chinese were operating sugar mills by 1830. Within 20 years, the plantations desperately needed workers, and the first Chinese laborers were 195 coolies from Amoy who arrived in 1852 under the newly passed Masters and Servants Act. These conscripted laborers were contracted for three to five years, and given $3 per month plus room and board. This was for 12 hours a day, six days per week—absolutely miserable wages even in 1852. The Chinese almost always left the plantations the minute their contracts expired. They then went into business for themselves and promptly monopolized the restaurant and small shop trade.

Bad Feelings

When they left the plantations, they were universally resented, due to prejudice, Chinese xenophobia, and their success in business. The first Chinese peddler in Honolulu was mentioned as early as 1823. The Chinese Consul in Hawaii was very conservative and sided with the plantation owners, giving his own people no support. When leprosy became epidemic in the islands, it was blamed on the Chinese. The Hawaiians called it *pake* disease, their derisive name for Chinese men (which oddly enough was an endearment in China meaning "uncle"). Although leprosy cannot be blamed solely on the Chinese, a boatload of Chinese immigrants did bring smallpox in 1880. At the turn of the century, a smallpox epidemic broke out again in Honolulu's Chinatown (half the residents were really Japanese), and it was promptly burnt to the ground by the authorities. Amidst all this negativity, some intrepid souls prospered. The greatest phenomenon was Chun Afong who, with little more than determination, became a millionaire by 1857, raised 16 children, and almost singlehandedly created the Chinese bourgeoisie in Hawaii. The Chinese were also responsible for making rice Hawaii's second most important crop from 1867 until 1872. It was another Chinese person, Ah In, who brought the first water buffalo used to cultivate rice during this period.

The Chinese Exclusion Act

Although reforms on the plantations were forthcoming, the Chinese preferred the retail trade. In 1880 half of all plantation workers were Chinese, by 1900 10%, and by 1959, only 300 Chinese worked on plantations. When the "powers that were" decided Hawaii needed compliant laborers, not competitive businesspeople, the monarchy passed the Chinese Exclusion Act in 1886, forbidding any more Chinese contract laborers from entering Hawaii. Still, 15,000 more Chinese were contracted in the next few years. In 1900 there were about 25,000 Chinese in Ha-

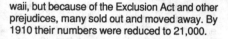

Many believed the devastating Chinatown fire of 1900 was deliberately allowed to burn in order to displace the Chinese population.

HAWAII STATE ARCHIVES

waii, but because of the Exclusion Act and other prejudices, many sold out and moved away. By 1910 their numbers were reduced to 21,000.

The Chinese Niche

Although most residents considered all Chinese the same, they were actually quite different. The majority comprised two distinct ethnic groups from Kwangtung Province in southern China—the Punti, who made up 75% of the immigrants—and the Hakka, who made up the remainder. The Hakka had invaded Punti lands over a thousand years previously and lived in the hills overlooking the Punti villages, never mixing. But in Hawaii, they mixed out of necessity. Few Chinese women came at first, so a Chinese man gladly accepted any Chinese woman as a wife, regardless of her ethnic background. The Chinese were also one of the first groups to willingly intermarry with the Hawaiians, and the men gained a reputation of being exceptionally caring husbands. By the 1930s, there was still resentment, but the Japanese were receiving most of the negative scrutiny by then, and the Chinese were firmly entrenched in the merchant class. Their thrift, hard work, and family solidarity had paid off. The Chinese accepted the social order and kept a low profile. During Hawaii's turbulent labor movements of the 1930s and '40s, the Chinese community produced *not one* labor leader, radical intellectual, or left-wing politician. When Hawaii became a state, one of the two first senators was Hiram Fong, a racially mixed Chinese. Since statehood, the Chinese community has carried on business as usual, as they continue to rise even further, both economically and socially.

THE JAPANESE

Conjecture holds a few Japanese castaways, who floated to Hawaii long before Captain Cook, introduced iron, because the islanders seemed to be familiar with it before white explorers arrived. Most scholars refute this claim and say Portuguese or Spanish ships lost in the Pacific introduced iron. Nevertheless, shipwrecked Japanese did make it to the islands. The most famous episode involved Jirokichi who, lost at sea for 10 months, was rescued by Captain Cathcart of Nantucket in 1839. Cathcart brought him to Hawaii, where Jirokichi boarded with prominent families. This adventure-filled episode is recounted in the Japanese classic *Ban Tan* (Stories of the Outside World) written by the scribe Yuten-sei. The first *official* arrivals were a group of ambassadors sent by the *shogun* to negotiate with the U.S. in Washington. They stopped en route at Honolulu in March 1860, only seven years after Commodore Perry and his famous "Black Ships" had roused Japan from its self-imposed 200-year slumber. A small group of Japanese plantation workers arrived in 1868, though mass migration was politically blocked for almost 20 years, and Japanese laborers didn't start coming in large numbers until 1886. King Kalakaua, among others, proposed

Japanese be brought as contract laborers in 1881; the thinking went that millions of Japanese subsistence farmers held promise as an inexhaustible supply of hardworking, uncomplaining, inexpensive, resolute workers. In 1886, when famine struck Japan, the Japanese government allowed farmers mainly from southern Honshu, Kyushu, and Okinawa to emigrate. Among these were members of Japan's little-talked-about untouchable caste, called *eta* or *burakumin* in Japan and *chorinbo* in Hawaii. They gratefully seized this opportunity to better their lot, an impossibility in their homeland.

The Japanese Arrive

The first Japanese migrants were almost all men. Under Robert Irwin, the American agent for recruiting the Japanese, almost 27,000 Japanese came, for which he received a fee of $5 per head. The contract workers received $9 plus room and board, and an additional $6 for a working wife. This pay was for a 26-workday month at 10 hours per day in the fields or 12 hours in a factory. Between 1897-1908, migration was a steady 70% men, 30% women. Afterwards, the "Gentlemen's Agreement," a euphemism for racism against the "yellow peril," halted most immigration. By 1900 over 60,000 Japanese had arrived, constituting the largest ethnic group. Until 1907 most Japanese longed to return home and faithfully sent back part of their pay to help support their families. Eventually, a full 50% did return to Japan, but the others began to consider Hawaii their home and resolved to settle . . . if they could get wives! Between 1908 and 1924, "picture brides" arrived whose marriages had been arranged *(omiai)* by family members back home. These women clung to the old ways and reinforced the Japanese ethnic identity. Excellent plantation workers, they set about making their rude camps into model villages. They felt an obligation that extended from individual to family, village, and their new country. As peasants, they were imbued with a feeling of a natural social order which they readily accepted . . . if treated fairly.

Changing Attitudes

Unfortunately some plantation *luna* were brutal, and Japanese laborers were mistreated, exploited, and made to live in indecent conditions on the plantations. In unusual protest, they formed their first trade union under Yasutaro Soga in 1908 and gained better treatment and higher wages. In 1919 an unsuccessful statewide plantation strike headed by the Federation of Japanese Labor lasted seven bitter months, earning the lasting mistrust of the establishment. By the 1930s, the Japanese, frustrated at being passed over for advancement because they were nonwhite, began to move from the plantations, opening retail stores and small businesses. By WW II they owned 50% of retail stores and accounted for 56% of household domestics. Many became small farmers, especially in Kona, where they began to grow coffee. They also accounted for Hawaii's fledgling fishing fleet and would brave the deep waters in their small, seaworthy sampans. Like the Chinese, they were committed to bettering themselves and placed education above all else. Unlike the Chinese, they did not marry outside their ethnic group and remained, relatively, racially intact.

Americans Of Japanese Ancestry (AJAs)

Parents of most Japanese children born in Hawaii before WW II were *issei* (first generation), who considered themselves apart from other Americans and clung to the notion of "we Japanese." They held traditional beliefs of unwavering family loyalty, and to propagate their values and customs they supported Japanese-language schools, which 80% of their children attended before the war. This group, who were never "disloyal," were, however, "prideful" in being Japanese. Some diehards even refused to believe Japan lost WW II and were shamed by their former homeland's unconditional surrender.

Their children, the *nissei* or second generation, were a different breed. In one generation they had become Americans through that basic melting pot called a schoolroom. They put into practice the high Japanese virtues of obligation, duty, and loyalty to the homeland—which was now, unquestionably, America. After Pearl Harbor was bombed, many people were terrified that the Hawaiian Japanese would be disloyal to America and would serve as spies and even as advance combatants for imperial Japan. The FBI kept close tabs on the Japanese community, and the menace of the "enemy within" prompted the decision to place Hawaii under martial law for the duration of the war. Because of their sheer numbers it was impossible to place the Hawaiian Japanese into concentration camps as was done in California, but prejudice and suspicion toward them, especially from Mainland military personnel, was fierce.

AJAs As GIs

Although Japanese had formed a battalion during WW I, they were insulted by being considered unacceptable as American soldiers in WW II. Those already in the armed services were relieved of any duty involving weapons. Those who knew better supported the AJAs. One was Jack Burns, a Honolulu policeman, who stated unequivocally that the AJAs were trustworthy. They never forgot his support, and thanks to a huge Japanese vote he was elected governor in 1963. Also, it has since been noted that not a single instance of Japanese sabotage, spying, or disloyalty was ever reported in Hawaii. Some American Japanese volunteered to serve in labor battalions, and because of their flawless work and loyalty, it was decided to put out a call for a few hundred volunteers to form a combat unit. Over 10,000 rushed to sign up!

AJAs formed two distinguished units in WW II—the **100th Infantry Battalion** and, later, the **442nd Regimental Combat Team.** They landed in Italy at Salerno and even fought from Guadalcanal to Okinawa. They distinguished themselves as the most decorated unit in American military history. They made excellent newspaper copy; their exploits hit front pages around the nation. They were immortalized as the rescuers of a Texas company pinned down during the Battle of the Bulge. These Texans became known as "The Lost Battalion" and have periodic reunions with the AJA GIs who risked and lost so much to bring them to safety.

The Japanese-American GIs returned as "our boys."

The AJAs Return

The AJAs returned home to a grateful country. In Hawaii, at first, they were accused of being cocky. Actually, they were refusing to revert to the pre-war status of second-class citizens and began to assert their rights as citizens who had defended their country. Many took advantage of the GI Bill and received college educations. The "Big Five" Corporations for the first time accepted former AJA officers as executives, and the old order began to wobble. Many Japanese became involved in Hawaiian politics, and the first elected member to Congress was Daniel Inouye, who had lost an arm fighting in the war. Hawaii's former governor, George Ariyoshi, was the country's first Japanese-American to reach such high office.

Today, one out of every two political offices in Hawaii is held by a Japanese. In one of those weird quirks of fate, it is now the Hawaiian Japanese who are accused by other ethnic groups of engaging in unfair political practices, nepotism, and reverse discrimination. It's often heard that "if you're not Japanese, forget about getting a government job." Many of these accusations against AJAs are undoubtedly motivated by jealousy, but their record of social fairness is not without blemish, and true to their custom of family loyalty, they do stick together. Heavily into the "professions," they're committed to climbing the social ladder. The AJAs of Hawaii, now indistinguishable from "the establishment," enjoy a higher standard of living than most and are motivated to get the best education possible for their children. AJA men are still the least likely to marry outside of their ethnic group.

CAUCASIANS

White people have a distinction from other ethnic groups in Hawaii—they are all lumped together as one. You can be anything from a Norwegian dock worker to a Greek shipping tycoon, but if your skin is white, you're a *haole*. What's more, you could have arrived at Waikiki from Missoula, Montana, in the last 24 hours, or your *kama'aina* family can go back five generations, but again, if you're white, you're a *haole*. The word *haole* has a floating connotation that depends upon the spirit in which it's used. It can mean anything from a derisive "honky" or "cracker" to nothing more than "white person." The exact Hawaiian meaning is clouded, but some say it meant "a man of no background," because white people couldn't chant a genealogical *kanaenae* telling the Hawaiians who they were. *Haole* then became euphemized into "foreign white man" and today simply "white person."

White History

Next to Hawaiians, white people have the oldest stake in Hawaii. Settlers in earnest since the missionaries of the 1820s, they were established long before any other migrant group. From last century until statehood, old *haole* families owned and controlled everything, and although they were benevolent, philanthropic, and paternalistic, they were also racist. They felt (not without certain justification) they had "made" Hawaii, and they had the right to rule. Established *kama'aina* families, many of whom made up the boards of the "Big Five" or owned huge plantations, formed an inner social circle closed to the outside except through marriage. Their paternalism, which they accepted with grave responsibility, at first extended only to the Hawaiians, who saw them as replacing their own *ali'i*. Asians were primarily considered "instruments of production." These supremacist attitudes tended to drag on until recent times. Today, they're responsible for the sometimes sour relations between white and nonwhite people in the islands. Since the *haole* had the power over other ethnic groups for so long, they have offended each group at one time or another. Today's white people are resented to a certain degree for these past acts, although they were in no way involved.

White Plantation Workers

In the 1880s, the white landowners looked around and felt surrounded and outnumbered by Asians. Many figured these people would one day be a political force to be reckoned with, so they tried to import white people for plantation work. Some of the imported workers included: 600 Scandinavians in 1881; 1,400 Germans during 1881-85; 400 Poles during 1897-98; and 2,400 Russians during 1909-12. None worked out. Europeans were accustomed to much higher wages and better living conditions than provided on the plantations. Although they were workers, not considered the equals of the ruling elite, they were expected to act like a special class and were treated preferentially, receiving higher wages for the same jobs performed by Asians. Even so, they proved troublesome to the landowners, unwilling to work under the prevailing conditions; they were especially resentful of Hawaiian *luna*. Most moved quickly to the Mainland, and the Poles and Russians even staged strikes after only months on the job. A contingency of Scots, who first came as mule skinners and gained a reputation for hard work and frugality, became successful plantation managers and supervisors. There were so many on the Hamakua Coast of the Big Island that it was dubbed the "Scotch Coast." The Germans and Scandinavians were well received and climbed the social ladder rapidly, becoming professionals and skilled workers. The Depression years, not as economically disastrous in Hawaii, brought more whites seeking opportunity.

These new folks, many from the U.S. south and west, tended to be even more racist toward brown-skinned people and Asians than the *kama'aina haoles.* They made matters worse and competed intensely for jobs.

The Massie Rape Case

The racial tension generated during this period came to a head in 1931 with the infamous Massie Rape Case. Thomas Massie, a naval officer, and his young wife Thalia attended a party at the Officers Club. After drinking and dancing all evening, they got into a row and Thalia rushed out in a huff. A few hours later, Thalia was at home, confused and hysterical, claiming to have been raped by some local men. On the most circumstantial evidence, Joseph Kahahawai and four friends of mixed ethnic background were accused. In a highly controversial trial rife with racial tensions, the verdict ended in a hung jury. While a new trial was being set, Kahahawai and his friends were out on bail. Seeking revenge, Thomas Massie and Grace Fortescue, Thalia's mother, kidnapped Joseph Kahahawai with a plan of extracting a confession from him. They were aided by two enlisted men assigned to guard Thalia. While questioning Joseph, they killed him and attempted to dump his body in the sea but were apprehended. Another controversial trial—this time for Mrs. Fortescue, Massie, and the accomplices—followed. Clarence Darrow, the famous lawyer, sailed to Hawaii to defend them. For killing Kahahawai, these people served *one hour* of imprisonment in the judge's private chambers. The other four, acquitted with Joseph Kahahawai, maintain innocence of the rape to this day. Later, the Massies divorced, and Thalia went on to become a depressed alcoholic who, sadly, took her own life.

The Portuguese

The last time anyone looked, Portugal was still attached to the European continent, but for some anomalous reason the Portuguese weren't considered *haole.* This was because they weren't part of the ruling elite, but merely workers, showing that at one time the word *haole* implied social standing and not just skin color. About 12,000 arrived during 1878-87 and another 6,000 came during 1906-13. They were accompanied during the latter period by 8,000 Spanish, who were considered one and the same. Most of the Portuguese were illiterate peasants from Madeira and the Azores, while the Spanish hailed from Andalusia. The majority of Spanish and some Portuguese tended to leave for California as soon as they made passage money. Those who remained were well received because they were white, but not *haole,* making a perfect "buffer" ethnic group. Unlike other Europeans, they would take any job, worked hard, and accepted authority. Committed to staying in Hawaii, they rose to be skilled workers and the *luna* class on the plantations. However, the Portuguese did not invest as much in education and became very racist toward the upwardly mobile Asians, seeing them as a threat to job security. By 1920 27,000 Portuguese made up 11% of the population. After that they tended to blend with the other ethnic groups and weren't counted separately. Portuguese men married within their ethnic group, but a good portion of Portuguese women married other white men and became closer to the *haole* group, while another large portion chose Hawaiian mates.

Although they didn't originate pidgin English (see "Language" later in this chapter), the unique melodious quality of their native tongue did give pidgin a certain lilt it has today. Also, the ukulele ("jumping flea") was closely patterned after a Portuguese stringed folk instrument.

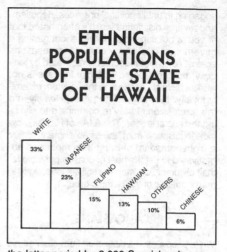

ETHNIC POPULATIONS OF THE STATE OF HAWAII

WHITE	JAPANESE	FILIPINO	HAWAIIAN	OTHERS	CHINESE
33%	23%	15%	13%	10%	6%

The White Population

Today all white people together make up the largest racial, if not ethnic, group in the islands at 33% (about 330,000) of the population. Percentage-wise, they are spread evenly throughout Kauai, Oahu, Maui, and the Big Island, with much smaller percentages on Molokai and Lanai. Numerically, the vast majority (260,000) live on Oahu, in the more fashionable central valley and southeastern sections. Heavy white concentrations are also found on the Kihei and Kaanapali coasts of Maui and the north Kona coast of Hawaii. The white population is also the fastest growing in the islands; most people resettling in Hawaii are white Americans predominantly from the West Coast.

FILIPINOS AND OTHERS

The Filipinos who came to Hawaii brought high hopes of making a fortune and returning home as rich heroes: for most this dream never came true. Filipinos were American nationals since the Spanish-American War of 1898, and as such weren't subject to the immigration laws that curtailed the importation of Asian workers at the turn of the century. Fifteen families arrived in 1906, but a large number came in 1924 as strikebreakers. The majority who came were illiterate Ilocano peasants from the northern Philippines with about 10% Visayans from the central cities. The Visayans were not as hardworking or thrifty, but were much more sophisticated. From the first, Filipinos were looked down upon by the other immigrant groups, and considered particularly uncouth by the Japanese. They put the least value on education of any group and, even by 1930, only half could speak rudimentary English, while the majority remained illiterate. They were billeted in the worst housing, performed the most menial jobs, and were the last hired and first fired. One big deterrent which kept Filipinos from becoming a part of mainstream society was the lack of Filipino women to marry, and they clung to the idea of returning home. In 1930 there were 30,000 men and only 360 women. This hopeless situation caused a great deal of prostitution and homosexual behavior, and many of these terribly lonely bachelors would feast and drink on weekends and engage in their gruesome but exciting pastime of cockfighting on Sunday. When some did manage to find wives, their mates were inevitably part Hawaiian.

Today, there are still plenty of old Filipino bachelors who never managed to get home, and the Sunday cockfight remains a way of life. Filipinos constitute 15% of Hawaii's population, with almost 71% living on Oahu. The largest concentration, however, is on Lanai, where 1,100 Filipino pineapple workers make up 60% of that island's population. Many of these men are new arrivals with the same dream held by their countrymen for over 70 years. Many visitors to Hawaii mistake Filipinos for Hawaiians because of their dark skin. This case of mistaken identity irritates Hawaiians and Filipinos alike, although some streetwise Filipinos claim to be Hawaiians because being Hawaiian is *in,* and it goes over well with tourists, especially young women. For the most part, these people are hardworking, dependable laborers who do tough jobs for little recognition. They still remain low on the social totem pole and have not yet organized to stand up for their rights.

Other Groups

About 10% of Hawaii's population is a conglomerate of other ethnic groups. Of these, the largest is Korean, numbering about 14,000 people today.

About 8,000 Koreans came to Hawaii from 1903 until 1905, when their government halted emigration. During the same period about 6,000 Puerto Ricans arrived, but they have become so assimilated that only 4,000 people in Hawaii today consider themselves Puerto Rican. There were also two attempts made last century to import other Polynesians to strengthen the dying Hawaiian race, but they were failures. In 1869 only 126 central Polynesian natives could be lured to Hawaii, and during 1878-85, 2,500 Gilbert Islanders arrived. Both groups became immediately disenchanted with Hawaii. They pined away for their own islands and departed for home as soon as possible.

Today, however, 12,000 Samoans have settled in Hawaii, and with more on the way they are the fastest-growing minority in the state. For inexplicable reasons, Samoans and native

Hawaiians get along extremely poorly and have the worst racial tensions and animosity of any groups. The Samoans ostensibly should represent the archetypal Polynesians the Hawaiians are seeking, but it doesn't work that way. Samoans are criticized by Hawaiians for their hot tempers, lingering feuds, and petty jealousies. They're clannish and are often the butt of "dumb" jokes. This racism seems especially ridiculous, but that's the way it is.

Just to add a bit more exotic spice to the stew, there are about 27,000 African-Americans and other blacks, a few thousand Native Americans including 100 or so Inuits and Aleuts, and a smattering of Vietnamese refugees living on the islands.

HAWAII STATE ARCHIVES

by ship's artist Wm. Ellis, c. 1791

RELIGION

The Lord saw fit to keep His island paradise secret from humankind for a few million years, but once we finally arrived we were awfully thankful. Hawaii cometimes appears a floating tabernacle—everywhere you look there's a church, temple, shrine, or *heiau*. The islands are either very holy, or a powerful lot of sinning's going on to require so many houses of prayer. Actually, it's just America's "right to worship" concept fully employed . . . in microcosm. Everyone who came to Hawaii brought their own forms of devotion. The Polynesian Hawaiians praised the primordial creators, Wakea and Papa, from whom their pantheon of animist-inspired gods sprang. Obviously, to a modern world these old gods would never do. There were simply too many, and belief in them was looked down upon as mere superstition, the folly of semi-civilized pagans. So, the famous missionaries of the 1820s brought Congregational Christianity and the "true path to heaven." Unfortunately, the Catholics, Mormons, Reformed Mormons, Adventists, Episcopalians, Unitarians, Christian Scientists, Lutherans, Baptists, Jehovah's Witnesses, Salvation Army, and every other major and minor denomination of Christianity that followed in their wake brought their own brando of enlightenment. The Chinese and Japanese established all the major sects of Buddhism, Confucianism, Taoism, and Shintoism. Today, Allah is praised, the Torah is chanted in Jewish synagogues, and nirvana is available at a variety of Hindu temples. If the spirit moves you, a Hare Krishna devotee will be glad to point you in the right direction and give you a "free" flower for only a dollar or two. If the world is still too much with you, you might find peace at a Church of Scientology, or meditate at a Kundalini yoga institute, or perhaps find relief at a local assembly of Baha'i. Regardless, rejoice, because in Hawaii you'll find not only paradise, but maybe even salvation.

THE WATERS OF KANE

The Polynesian Hawaiians worshipped nature. They saw its forces manifested in a multiplicity of forms to which they ascribed godlike powers.

Daily life was based on this animistic philosophy. Hand-picked and specially trained storytellers chanted the exploits of the gods. These ancient tales, kept alive in a special oral tradition called *moolelo,* were recited only by day. Entranced listeners encircled the chanter and, out of respect for the gods and in fear of their wrath, were forbidden to move once the tale was begun. This was serious business in which a person's life could be at stake; it was not like the telling of *ka'ao* which were simple fictions, tall tales of ancient heroes, related for amusement and to pass the long nights. Any object, animate or inanimate, could be a god. All could be infused with mana, especially a dead body or a respected ancestor. *Ohana* had personal family gods called *aumakua* on whom they called in times of danger or strife. Children of gods, called *kupua,* were thought to live among men, distinguished either for their beauty and strength or for their ugliness and terror. Hawaiians believed processions of dead *ali'i* called "Marchers of the Night" wandered through the land of the living, and unless you were properly protected it could mean death if they looked upon you. Simple ghosts known as *akua lapu* merely frightened people. Waterfalls, trees, springs, and a thousand forms of nature were the manifestations of *akua li'i,* "little spirits" that could be invoked at any time for help or protection.

Behind all of these beliefs was an innate sense of natural balance and order, and the idea that everything had its opposite. The time of darkness when only the gods lived was *po.* When the great gods descended to earth and created light, this was *ao,* and humanity was born. All of these *moolelo* are part of *The Kumulipo,* the great chant that records the Hawaiian version of creation. From the time the gods descended and touched earth at Ku Moku on Lanai, the genealogies were kept. Unlike in the Bible, these included the noble families of female as well as male *ali'i.*

Heiau And Idols

The basic *heiau* (temple) was a masterfully built and fitted rectangular stone wall varying in size from as large as a basketball court to the size of a football field. Once the restraining outer walls were built, the interior was backfilled with smaller stones, and the top dressing was expertly laid and then rolled, perhaps with a log, to form a pavementlike surface. All that remains of Hawaii's many *heiau* are the stone platforms. The buildings—made from perishable wood, leaves and grass—have long since disappeared. At some dreaded *heiau* humans were sacrificed. Tradition says this barbaric custom began at Wahaula Heiau on the Big Island in the 12th century, introduced by a ferocious Tahitian priest named Paao. Other *heiau,* such as Pu'uhonua O Honaunau, also on the Big Island, were temples of refuge where the weak, widowed, orphaned, and vanquished could find sanctuary. Within *heiau,* ceremonies were conducted by the priestly *kahuna.* Offerings of chickens, dogs, fish, fruit, and tapa were laid on the *lele,* a huge stone altar, in hopes the gods would act favorably toward the people. Some buildings held the bones of dead *ali'i,* infused with their mana. Other structures were god houses in which idols resided, while still others were oracle towers from which prophecies were made. The gods were honored by *ali'i* and *maka'ainana* alike, but the *kahuna* prayed for the *ali'i,* while the commoners represented themselves. There was a patron god for every aspect of life, especially farming and fishing, but gods could be invoked for everything from weaving to help for thieves! Men and women had their own gods, with rituals governing birth, cutting the umbilical cord, sickness, and death. Ceremonies, often lasting for many days, were conducted by *kahuna,* many of whom had highly specialized functions. Two of the most interesting were: *kahuna kilikilo,* who could see a person die in a dream and save his or her life through offerings of white dogs, chickens, tapa, and *awa;* and *kahuna kaula,* semi-hermits who could fortell the future.

All worshipped the gods in the form of idols, which were fashioned from wood, feathers, and stone. Some figures were over six feet tall, and crowned with elaborate head pieces. Figures were often pointed at the end so they could be stuck into the ground. Until eyes, made from pearl shell, were fitted or carved, the idol was dormant. With eyes, it was alive. The hair used was often human, and the arms and legs were usually flexed. The mouth was either gaping or formed a figure "8" on its side, and was usually lined with glistening dog teeth. Also made were small figures of woven basketry, expertly cov-

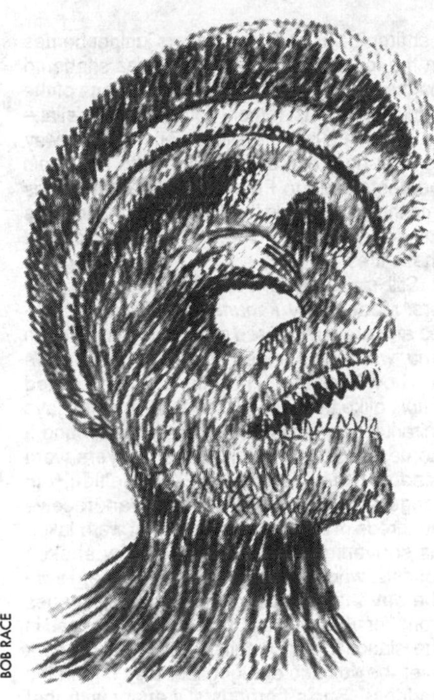

Ku

ered with red and yellow feathers taken from specific birds by men whose only work was to roam the forests in search of them. It made no difference who or what you were in old Hawaii, the gods were ever-present, and they played a direct and active role in your life.

GREAT GODS

Ku

The progenitors of the gods were Wakea, the "sky father," and Papa, the "earth mother," but the actual gods worshipped in Hawaii were Ku, Kane and Kanaloa, and Lono. Ku was a universal god who represented the male aspect of nature, and Hina, the moon goddess, was his female counterpart. Ku was prayed to at sunrise and Hina at sunset. Ku's maleness was represented with pointed stones, while flat ones symbolized Hina's womanhood. Ku ruled the forest, land, mountains, farming, and fishing—his benevolent side. But Ku was better known as the god of war. It was Ku who demanded human sacrifice, especially in times of calamity or in preparation for battle. At times, Ku was represented by an ohia log, and a human sacrifice was made in the forest where it was cut and also at the post hole that held it upright at the *heiau.* When Ku was invoked, the strict and serious ceremonies could go on for over a week. The entire *aha* (assembly) kept complete silence and sat ramrod straight with the left leg and hand crossed over the right leg and hand in an attitude called *neepu.* At a precise command everyone simultaneously pointed their right hands heavenward. Anyone caught dozing or daydreaming, or who for some reason missed the command, instantly became the main course for Ku's lunch.

Kamehameha the Great carried a portable Ku into battle with him at all times, known as Kukailimoku ("the Snatcher of Lands"). It was held that during battle this effigy, whose gaping mouth gleamed with canine incisors, would cry out in a loud voice and stir Kamehameha's warriors on to victory. After a battle, the slain enemies were taken to the *heiau* and placed upon Ku's altar with their arms encircling two pigs. Now Ku became Kuwahailo ("of the Dripping Maggot Mouth"). With Ku's killing nature appeased, the people would pray for good crops, good fishing, and fertile wives. The scales were balanced and life went on.

Kane And Kanaloa

Kane is the Hawaiian word for "man" or "husband," and he was the leading god of worship when the missionaries arrived. God of life, ancestor of all Hawaiians, Kane is the center of the Hawaiian creation myth, whose events are amazingly similar to those of Genesis. Kane comes forward from *po* (darkness) into *ao* (light), and with the help of Ku and Lono, fashions a man from clay gathered from the four cardinal points of the compass. Once the body is formed, the gods breathe (some say spit) into the mouth and nostrils and give it life. The man is placed upon a paradise island, *Kalani i hauola,* and a wife is fashioned for him out of his right side. Like Adam and Eve, these two break the law by eating from the forbidden tree and are driven from paradise by the sacred white albatross of Kane.

Kane is a forgiving god who demands no human sacrifice, because all life is sacred to him. He is a god of a higher order, not usually rendered as an idol. Instead he was symbolized as a single upright male stone splashed with oil and wrapped in white tapa. Kanaloa, the antithesis of Kane, was represented as a great squid, and often likened to the Christian devil. He warred with Kane and was driven out of heaven along with his minions. Kanaloa became the ruler of the dead, and was responsible for "black" sorcery and for poisonous things. However, these two gods were often linked together. For example, prayers would be offered to Kane when a canoe was built, and to Kanaloa to provide favorable winds. Farmers and diviners often prayed simultaneously to Kane and Kanaloa. Both gods were intimately connected to water and the narcotic beverage *awa.*

Pele

The Hawaiian gods were toppled literally and figuratively in 1819, and began to fade from the minds of people. Two that remained prominent were Madame Pele, the fire goddess, who resides at Kilauea Volcano on Hawaii, and the demigod Maui, who is like Paul Bunyan and Ulysses rolled into one. Many versions account for how Pele wound up living in Kilauea firepit, but they all follow a general outline. It seems the beautiful young goddess, from a large family of gods, was struck by wanderlust. Tucking her young sister, in the convenient form of an egg, under her armpit, she set out to see the world. Fortune had its ups and downs in store for young Pele. For one, she was ravished by a real swine, Kamapua'a the pig god. Moreover, she fought desperately with her sister, Namaka o Kahai, over the love of a handsome young chief; Pele's sister stalked her and smashed her bones on the Hana coast of Maui at a spot called *Kaiwi o Pele* (the Bones of Pele).

Pulling herself back together, Pele set out to make a love nest for her lover and herself. She chose the firepit at Kilauea Volcano and has long been held responsible for its lava flows along with anything else that deals with heat or fire. Pele can change her form from a withered old woman to a ravishing beauty; her moods can change from gentle to fiery hot. She is traditionally appeased with *ohelo* berries cast into her firepit, but lately she prefers juniper berries in the form of gin. Pele's myth was shattered by the Hawaiian queen Keopuolani, one of the earliest and most fervent converts to Christianity. In the 1820s this brave queen made her way to Kilauea firepit and defiantly ate the *ohelo* berries sacred to Pele. She then cast stones into the pit and cried in a loud voice, "Jehovah is my god . . . it is my God, not Pele, that kindled these fires."

Still, stories abound of Pele's continuing powers. Modern-day *kahuna* are always consulted and prayers offered over construction of an *imu,* which falls under Pele's fire domain. It's said by traditional Hawaiians and educated *haole* alike that when Kilauea erupts, the lava miraculously stops before or circles around a homestead over which proper prayers were made to the fire goddess. In addition, the rangers at Volcanoes National Park receive hundreds of stones every year that were taken as souvenirs and then returned by shaken tourists, who claim bad luck stalked them from the day they removed Pele's sacred stones from her volcano. And, no one who has lived in the islands for any length of time will carry pork over the volcano at night, lest they offend the goddess. She's perhaps still angry with that swine, Kama pua'a.

The Strifes Of Maui

Of all the heroes and mythological figures of Polynesia, Maui is the best known. His "strifes" are like the great Greek epics, and they make excellent tales of daring that elders loved to relate to youngsters around the evening campfire. Maui was abandoned by his mother Hina of Fire, when he was an infant. She wrapped him in her hair and cast him upon the sea, where she expected him to die, but he lived and returned home to become her favorite. She knew then he was a born hero and had strength far beyond that of mortals. His first exploit was to "lift the sky." In those days the sky hung so low humans had to crawl around on all fours. A seductive young woman approached Maui and asked him to use his great strength to lift the sky. In fine heroic fashion this big boy agreed if the beautiful woman would, euphemistically, "give him a drink from her gourd." He then obliged her by lifting the sky.

The territory of humans was small at the time, and Maui then decided more land was needed, so he conspired to "fish up islands." He decended into the land of the dead and petitioned an ancestress to fashion him a hook out of her jawbone. She obliged, and created the mythical hook *Manai Ikalanl.* Maul then secured a sacred bird, the *alae,* that he intended to use for bait. He bid his brothers to paddle him far out to sea, and when he arrived at the deepest spot, he lowered *Manai ikalani* baited with the sacred bird. His sister, Hina of the Sea, placed it into the mouth of "Old One Tooth" who held land fast to the bottom of the waters. Maui then exhorted his brothers to row, but warned them not to look back. They strained at the oars, and slowly a great land mass rose. One brother, overcome by curiosity, looked back, and when he did so, the land shattered into all of the islands of Polynesia.

Maui desired to serve humankind further. People were without fire and the secret was held by the sacred *alae,* who had learned it from Maui's beneficent ancestress. She had given Maui her burning fingernails, but he oafishly kept dropping them into streams until all had fizzled out, and he had totally irritated this generous relative. She pursued Maui trying to burn him to a cinder. Maui desperately chanted for rain to put out her scorching fires. When she saw her fires being quenched, she hid her fire in the barks of special trees and informed common mud hens where they could be found, but first made them promise never to tell humans. Maui learned of this, captured a mud hen, and threatened to wring its neck unless it gave up the secret. The bird tried trickery and told Maui first to rub together the stems of sugarcane, then of banana and even of *taro.* None worked, and Maui's determined rubbing is why these plants have hollow roots today. Finally, with Maui's hands tightening around the mud hen's neck, the bird confessed fire could be found in the *hau* tree and also the sandalwood, which Maui named *ili aha* ("fire bark"). Maui then rubbed all the feathers of the mud hen's head for being so deceitful, and that's why their crown is featherless today.

Maui's greatest deed, however, was snaring the sun and exacting his promise to go slower across the heavens. The people had complained of not enough daylight hours to fish or farm. Maui's mother could not dry her tapa cloth because the sun rose and set so quickly. When she asked her son to help, Maui went to his blind grandmother for assistance. She lived on the slopes of Haleakala and was responsible for cooking the sun's bananas that he ate in passing every day. Maui kept stealing his granny's bananas until she agreed to help. She told him to personally weave 16 strong ropes and to make nooses out of his sister's hair. Some say these weavings came from her head, but other versions insist that it was no doubt Hina's pubic hair that had the power to hold "Sunny Boy." Maui positioned himself, and as each of the 16 rays of the sun came across Haleakela, he snared them until the sun was defenseless and had to bargain for his life. Maui agreed to free him if he promised to go more slowly. The sun agreed, and Haleakala ("The House of the Sun") became his home.

Lono And The Makahiki Festival

Lono was a benevolent god of clouds, harvest, and rain. In a fit of temper he killed his wife, whom he thought unfaithful. When he discovered his grave error, he roamed the countryside challenging everyone he met to a boxing match. Boxing later became an event of the Makahiki, the Harvest Festival, held in his honor. Lono decided to leave his island home, but promised one day to return on a floating island. Every year at the beginning of *ho'oilo* (winter), starting in October, the Makahiki was held. It was a jubilant time of harvest when taxes were collected and most *kapu* were lifted. It ended sometime in February, and then the new year began. During this time great sporting events included surfing, boxing, sledding, and a form of bowling. At night, people feasted at luau to the rhythm of drums and hula. Fertility was honored, and willing partners from throughout the land coupled and husbands and wives shared their mates in the tradition of *punalua.*

Lono's idol was an *akua loa,* a slender 15-foot pole with his small image perched atop. Another pole fastened at the top formed a cross. Hanging from the cross pole were long banners of white tapa cloth and it was festooned with the feathers and skins of seabirds. To this image the *kahuna* offered red and white fish, black coconut, and immature *awa.* This image, called

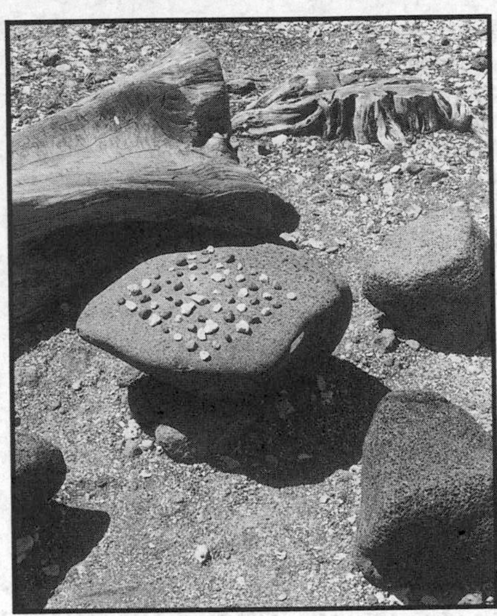

konane board, Hawaiian checkers often played during the Makahiki Festival

"Long God," proceeded in a procession clockwise around the island. It was met at every *ahupua'a* (land division) by the chief of that region, and new tapa was offered by the chieftess along with roasted taro. The *maka'ainana* came and offered their produce from sea and land and so the taxes were collected. At the end of the festival a naked man representing the god Kohoali'i ate the eyeball of a fish and one of a human victim and proclaimed the New Year.

It was just during the Makahiki that Captain Cook sailed into Kealakekua Bay. *Kahuna* saw his great "floating islands" and proclaimed the return of Lono. Uncannily, the masts of the sailing ships draped in canvas looked remarkably like Lono's idol. Cook himself was particularly tall and white-skinned, and many natives at first sight fell to their knees and worshipped him as "Lono returned."

THE CASTE *(KAPU)* SYSTEM

All was not heavenly in paradise due to horrible wars, but the people mainly lived quiet, ordered lives based on a strict caste society and the *kapu* system. Famine was contained to a regional level. The population was kept in check by herbal birth-control potions, crude abortions, and infanticide, especially of baby girls. The strict caste system was determined by birth, which there was no chance of changing. The highest rank was the ***ali'i,*** the chiefs and royalty. The impeccable genealogies of the *ali'i* were traced back to the gods themselves, and recorded in chants *(mo'o ali'i)* memorized and sung by professionals called *ku'auhau.* Ranking passed from both father and mother, and custom dictated the first mating of an *ali'i* be with a person of equal rank. After a child was produced, the *ali'i* was free to mate with lesser *ali'i* or even with a commoner. The custom of ***punalua,*** the sharing of mates, was practiced throughout Hawaiian society. Moreover, incest was not only condoned but sanctioned among *ali'i.* To conceive an offspring of the highest rank, *ni'au pi'o* ("coconut leaf looped back on itself"), the parents were required to be full brothers and sisters. These offspring were so sacred they were considered *akua* ("living god"), and people of all rank had to literally crawl on their stomachs in their presence. *Ali'i* who ran society's affairs were of lesser rank, and they were the real functionaries. The two most important were the land supervisors *(konohiki)* and caste priests *(kahuna).* The *konohiki* were in charge of the *ahupua'a,* pie-shaped land divisions running from mountain to sea. The common people came in contact with these *ali'i* as they also collected taxes and ruled as judges among the people.

Kahuna were highly skilled people whose advice was sought before any major undertaking such as building a house, hollowing a canoe log, or even offering a prayer. The *mo'o kahuna* were the priests of Ku and Lono, in charge of praying and following rituals. These powerful *ali'i* kept strict secrets and laws concerning their various functions. The *kahuna* dedicated to Ku were severe: it was they who sought human sacrifice. The *kahuna* of Lono were more comforting to the people, but were of lesser rank than the Ku *kahuna.* Other *kahuna* were not *ali'i* but commoners. The two most important were the healers *(kahuna lapa'au),* and the black magicians *(kahuna ana'ana),* who could pray a person to death. The *kahuna lapa'au* had a pharmacopoeia of herbs and spices that could

JACQUES ARAGO, HAWAII STATE ARCHIVES

Punishment of a kapu-*breaker was harsh and swift.*

cure over 250 diseases. They employed baths and massage, and used various colored stones to outline the human body and accurately pinpoint not only the organs but the internal origins of illness. The *kahuna ana'ana* were given a wide berth by the people, who did everything possible to stay on their good side! The *kahuna ana'ana* could be hired to cast a love spell over a person or cause untimely death; they seldom had to send a reminder of payment.

The common people were called the ***maka'ainana,*** "people of the land." They were the farmers, craftspeople, and fishermen. Their land was owned by the *ali'i,* but they were not bound to it. If the local *ali'i* was cruel or unfair, the *maka'ainana* had the right to leave. Very unjust *ali'i* were even put to death by their own people, with no retribution if their accusations proved true. The *maka'ainana* mostly loved their local *ali'i,* and vice versa. *Maka'ainana* who lived close to the *ali'i* and could be counted on as warriors in times of trouble were called *kanaka no lua kaua,* "a man for the heat of battle." They were treated with greater favor than those who lived in the backcountry, *kanaka no hii kua,* whose lesser standing opened them up to discrimination and cruelty. All *maka'ainana* formed extended families *(ohana)* and usually lived on the same section of land *(ahupua'a).* Inland farmers would barter their produce with fishermen; thus all shared equally in the bounty of the land and sea.

A special group ***(kauwa)*** was a landless untouchable caste confined to living on reservations. Their origins were obviously Polynesian, but they appeared to be descendents of castaways who had survived and become perhaps the aboriginals of Hawaii before the main migrations. It was *kapu* for anyone to go onto *kauwa* lands; doing so meant instant death. A *kauwa* driven by necessity to leave his lands was required to cover his head with tapa cloth, his eyes focused on the ground in a humble manner. If a human sacrifice was needed, the *kahuna* simply summoned a *kauwa,* who had no recourse but to mutely comply. Through the years after discovery by Cook, the *kauwa* became obscured as a class and mingled with the remainder of the population. But even to this day, calling someone *kauwa,* which now supposedly only means servant, is still considered a fight-provoking insult.

Kapu And Daily Life

A strict division of labor existed between men and women. Only men were permitted to have anything to do with taro, a foodstuff so sacred it had a greater *kapu* than humans themselves. Men pounded poi and served it to women. Men were also the fishermen and builders of houses, canoes, irrigation ditches, and walls. Women tended gardens and were responsible for making tapa and tending to shoreline fishing. The entire family lived in the common house *(hale noa).* But certain things were *kapu* between the sexes. The primary *kapu* were entrance by a woman into the *mua* (men's house) and eating with men. Certain foods such as pork and bananas were forbidden to women. It was *kapu* for a man to have intercourse before going fishing, engaging in battle, or attending a religious ceremony. Young boys lived with the women until they underwent circumcision *(pule ipu),* after which they were required to keep the *kapu* of men.

Ali'i could also declare a *kapu,* and often did so. Certain lands or fishing areas were temporarily made *kapu* so they could revitalize. Even today, it is *kapu* for anyone to remove all the *opihi* (a type of limpet) from a rock. The great King Kamehameha I placed a *kapu* on the body of his notoriously unfaithful child bride, Kaahumanu. It didn't work! The greatest *kapu (kapu moe)* was afforded to the highest ranking *ali'i:* anyone coming into their presence had to prostrate themselves. Lesser ranking *ali'i* were afforded the *kapu noho:* lessers had to sit or kneel in their presence. Commoners could not let their shadows fall upon an *ali'i* or enter their houses except through a special door. Breaking a *kapu* meant immediate death.

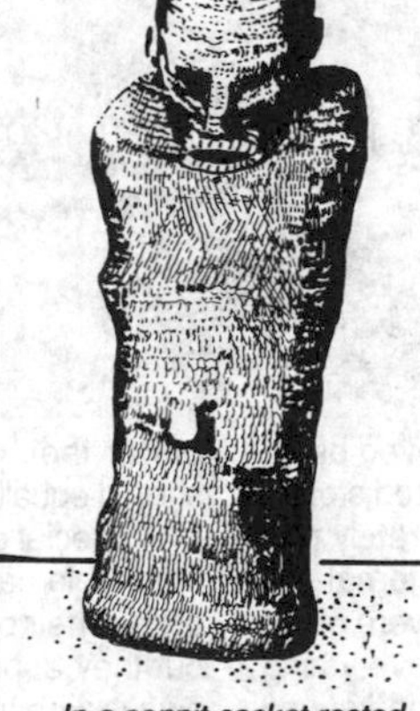

In a sennit casket rested the bones of the dead.

LOUISE FOOTE

Fun And Games

The native Hawaiians loved sports. A type of "Olympiad" was held each year during the Makahiki Festival. Events included boxing, swimming, diving, surfing, and running. A form of bowling used polished, wheel-shaped stones that tested for distance and accuracy. Hawaiians also enjoyed a more cerebral, chesslike game called *konane.* Intricately carved *konane* boards survive to this day. Hawaiians built special downhill courses for a runnered bobsled called a *holua.* They could coast over wet grasses or leaves for 200 yards. Strangely enough, the Hawaiians developed a bow and arrow but never employed it in warfare. It was merely a toy for shooting at targets or rats.

The greatest sport of all was surfing. **Surfing** originated with the Hawaiians, and many old records recount this singularly exhilarating activity. The boards, made of various woods, were greatly cared for, measuring up to 15 feet long and six inches thick. James King, a lieutenant with Cook, was "altogether astonished" by surfing, and Reverend Ellis wrote in 1826, ". . . to see fifty or a hundred persons riding on an immense billow . . . for a distance of several hundred yards together is one of the most novel and interesting sports a foreigner can witness in the islands."

Ghosts

The Hawaiians had countless superstitions and ghost legends, but two of the more interesting involve astral travel of the soul, and the "death marchers." The soul, *uhane,* was considered by Hawaiians to be totally free and independent of its body, *kino.* The soul could separate, leaving the body asleep or very drowsy. This disincorporated soul *(hihi'o)* could visit people and was considered quite different from a *lapu,* an ordinary spirit of a dead person. A *kahuna* could immediately recognize if a person's *uhane* had left his or her body, and a special wreath was placed upon his or her head for protection and to facilitate reentry. A person confronted by an apparition could test to see if it was indeed dead or still alive by placing leaves of an *ape* plant upon the ground. If the leaves tore when they were walked upon, the spirit was human, but if they remained intact it was a ghost. Also, you could sneak up and startle the vision and if it disappeared it was a ghost; or if no reflection of the face appeared when it drank water from an offered calabash, it was a ghost. Unfortunately, there were no instructions to follow once you had determined you indeed had a ghost on your hands. Maybe it was better not to know! Some people would sprinkle salt and water around their houses, but this only kept away evil spirits, not ghosts.

There are also many stories of *kahuna* restoring souls to a dead bodies. First the *kahuna* had to catch one and keep it in a gourd. He then placed beautiful tapa and fragrant flowers and herbs about the body to make it more enticing. Slowly, the *kahuna* would coax the soul out of the gourd, which reentered the body through the big toe.

Death Marchers

One inexplicable phenomenon that many people attest to is *ka huakai o ka po,* "Marchers of the Night." This march of the dead is fatal if you gaze upon it, unless one of the marchers happens to be a friendly ancestor who will protect you. The peak time for "the march" is 7:30 p.m.-2 a.m. The marchers can be dead *ali'i* and warriors, the gods themselves, or the lesser *aumakua.* When the *aumakua* march there is usually chanting and music. *Ali'i* marches are more somber. The entire procession, lit by torches, often stops at the house of a relative and might even carry him or her away. When the gods themselves march, there is often thunder, lightning, and heavy seas. The sky is lit with torches, and they walk six abreast, three gods and three goddesses. If you get in the way of a march, remove your clothing and prostrate yourself. If the marching gods or *aumakua* happen to be ones to which you pray, you might be spared. If it's a march of the *ali'i,* you might make it if you lie face upward and feign death. If you *do* see a death march, the last thing you'll worry about is lying naked on the ground and looking ridiculous.

MISSIONARIES ONE AND ALL

In Hawaii when you say "missionaries," it usually refers to the small, determined band of Congregationalists who arrived aboard the Brig *Thaddeus* in 1820 and the "companies" or "packets" that reinforced them over the next 40 years. They were sent from Boston by the American Board of Commissioners for Foreign Missions (ABCFM), who learned of the "godless plight" of the Hawaiian people from returning sailors and from the few Hawaiians who had come to America to study. A young man named Opukahaia was instrumental in bringing the missionaries to Hawaii. An orphan befriended by a captain and taken to New England, he studied theology and was obsessed with the desire to return home to save his people from sure damnation. His widely read accounts of life in Hawaii were the direct cause of the formation of the Pioneer Company to the Sandwich Islands Missions. Unfortunately, Opukahaia died in New England from typhus in 1819, the year before the missionaries sailed.

The missionaries' first task was to Christianize and civilize. They met with extreme hostility—not from the natives, but from sailors and traders content with the open debauchery and wanton whoremongering that was the status quo in 1820s Hawaii. Many incidents of direct confrontation between these two factions even included the cannonading of missionary homes by American sea captains who were denied the customary services of island women thanks to the meddlesome "do-gooders." Actually, the situation was much closer to the sentiments of James Jarves, who wrote, "The missionary was a far more useful and agreeable man than his catechism would indicate; and the trader was not so bad a man as the missionary would make him out to be." The missionary's aim was conversion, but the fortuitous by-product was education that raised the consciousness of every Hawaiian regardless of religious affiliation.

The American Board of Missions officially ended its support in 1863, and in 40 short years considered Hawaii a civilized nation well on the road to modernity. Some of Hawaii's finest museums and grandest architecture are part of the missionary legacy. Some of the most notable are: Mokuaikaua Church in Kona, Hawaii, the first Christian church founded in 1820; the Lyman House Museum of Hilo; Kawaiahao Church in Honolulu, founded 1821, and next door the superb Mission House Museum; Wainee Church, the first stone church in Hawaii, founded in Lahaina in 1828, and the Baldwin Home just down Front Street; and Lahainaluna High School and Printing House, the first American school and publishing house west of the Rockies. The churches, but especially the homes and museums, not only offer a glimpse of religious life, but are some of the finest "windows" into 19th-century America. Their collections of artifacts, utensils, and general memorabilia put the life and times of 18th-century Yankees in a setting that could hardly be more different than New England.

Bonanza For Missionaries

Although the missionaries were the first, they by no means had the field to themselves. Hot on the same religious trail came the Catholics—French Sacred Hearts led by Father Bachelot, who arrived in Honolulu in July 1827 aboard the *La Comete*. Immediately, Queen Kaahumanu, who had been converted by the Congregationalists, ordered them to leave. They refused. For the next 10 years the Catholic priests and their converts met with open hostility and persecution which, in true missionary fashion, only strengthened their resolve. The humiliation of a young convert, Juliana Keawahine, who was tied to a tree and scourged, became a religious rallying point. After this incident the persecutions stopped. Honolulu's Our Lady of Peace Cathedral was completed in 1843 and Ahuimanu Catholic School, Oahu's counterpart to Lahainaluna, opened for instruction in 1846. Today, Roman Catholicism, with 290,000 adherents, is the single largest religious group in Hawaii.

The Saints Come Marching In

A strange episode in Hawaii's history involved the Mormons. In 1850, the Latter-Day Saints arrived direct from missionary work in California gold fields. By 1852, George Cannon had already translated the *Book of Mormon* into Hawaiian. The five original Mormon missionaries spent every moment traveling and converting the Hawaiians. They had a grand plan of constructing a "City of Joseph" on Lanai, where they managed to gain a large tract of land. In 1858 the Mormon Wars broke out in Utah and the missionaries were called home. One of their band, Walter Murray Gibson, who stayed to manage the fledgling Mormon Church, became one of the most controversial and singularly strange fixtures in Hawaiian politics. When the Mormons returned in 1864, they found Gibson had indeed carried on the "City of Joseph," but had manipulated all of the deeds and land grants into his personal possession. Furthermore, he had set himself up as an omnipotent grand patriarch and openly denounced the polygamous beliefs of the Mormons of the day. Immediately excommunicated, Gibson was abandoned to his fate and the Mormons moved to Oahu where they founded a sugar plantation and temple in Laie.

The Mormon Church now has approximately 32,000 members, the largest Protestant denomination in Hawaii. Their settlement on Oahu at Laie is now home to an impressive Mormon Temple and an island branch of Brigham Young University. Close by, the Mormons also operate the Polynesian Cultural Center, which is one of the top five tourist attractions in all of Hawaii.

As for Gibson, he was elected to the legislature in 1876 and became a private counselor to King Kalaukaua. In 1882, he worked himself into the office of "Premier," which he ran like a petty dictator. One of his more visionary suggestions was to import Japanese labor. Two of his most ridiculous were to drive non-Hawaiians from the islands (excluding himself) and to gather Oceania into one Pacific nation with Hawaii at the forefront. By 1887 he and Kalaukaua had so infuriated the sugar planters that Gibson was railroaded out of the islands and Kalaukaua was forced to sign a constitution that greatly limited his power. Gibson died in 1888 and his daughter Talulah and her husband sold the lands on Lanai for a song, after they tried but failed to grow sugarcane.

Non-Christian

By the turn of this century, Shintoism (brought by the Japanese) and Buddhism (brought by both the Japanese and Chinese) were firmly established in Hawaii. The first official Buddhist Temple was Hongpa Hongwanji, established on Oahu in 1889. All Buddhist sects combined have about 170,000 parishioners; there are perhaps 50,000 Shintoists. The Hindu religion has 2,000 adherents, with about the same number of Jewish people living throughout Hawaii, though only one synagogue, Temple Emanuel, is on Oahu. About 10,000 people are in new religious movements and lesser-known faiths such as Baha'i and Unitarianism. The largest number of people in Hawaii (300,000) remain unaffiliated.

LANGUAGE

Hawaii is part of America and people speak English here, but that's not the whole story. If you turn on the TV to catch the evening news, you'll hear "Walter Cronkite" English, unless of course you happen to tune in to a Japanese-language broadcast designed for tourists from that country. You can easily pick up a Chinese-language newspaper or groove to the music on a Filipino radio station, but let's not confuse the issue. All your needs and requests at airports, car-rental agencies, restaurants, hotels, or wherever you happen to travel will be completely understood, as well as answered, in English. However, when you happen to overhear islanders speaking, what they're saying will sound somewhat familiar but you won't be able to pick up all the words, and the beat and melody of the language will be noticeably different.

Hawaii, like New England, the Deep South, and the Midwest, has its own unmistakable linguistic regionalism. The ethnic peoples who make up Hawaii have enriched the English spoken here with words, expressions, and subtle shades of meaning that are commonly used and understood throughout the islands. The greatest influence on English has come from the Hawaiian language itself, and words such as aloha, hula, and muumuu are familiarly used and understood by most Americans.

Other migrant peoples, especially the Chinese, Japanese, and Portuguese, influenced the local dialect to such an extent that the simplified plantation lingo they spoke has become known as pidgin. A fun and enriching part of the "island experience" is picking up a few words of Hawaiian and pidgin. English is the official language of the state, business, education, and perhaps even the mind; but pidgin is the language of the people, the emotions, and life; while Hawaiian remains the language of the heart and the soul.

Note: Many Hawaiian words are commonly used in English, appear in English dictionaries, and therefore would ordinarily be subject to the rules of English grammar. The Hawaiian language, however, does not pluralize nouns by adding an "s"; the singular and plural are differentiated in context. For purposes of this book, and to highlight rather than denigrate the Hawaiian culture, the Hawaiian style of pluralization will be followed for common Hawaiian words. The following are some examples of plural Hawaiian nouns treated this way in this book: *haole* (not haoles), hula, *kahuna,* lei, *nene.*

PIDGIN

The dictionary definition of pidgin is: a simplified language with a rudimentary grammar used as a means of communication between people speaking different languages. Hawaiian pidgin is a little more complicated than that. It had its roots during the plantation days of last century when white owners and *luna* (foremen) had to communicate with recently arrived Chinese, Japanese, and Portuguese laborers. It was designed as a simple language of the here and now, and was primarily concerned with the necessary functions of working, eating, and sleeping. It has an economical noun-verb-object structure (not necessarily in that order).

Hawaiian words make up most of pidgin's non-English vocabulary. It includes a good smattering of Chinese, Japanese, and Samoan; the distinctive rising inflection is provided by the melodious Mediterranean lilt of the Portuguese. Pidgin is not a stagnant language. It's kept alive by hip new words introduced by people who are "so radical," or especially by slang words introduced by teenagers. It's a colorful English, like "jive" or "ghettoese" spoken by African-North Americans, and is as regionally unique as the speech of Cajuns from Louisiana's bayous. *Maka'ainana* of all socioethnic backgrounds understand pidgin. Most islanders are proud of it, while some consider it low-class jargon. The Hawaiian House of Representatives has given pidgin an official sanction, and most people feel that it adds a real local style and should be preserved.

Pidgin Lives

Pidgin is first learned at school where all students, regardless of background, are exposed to it. The pidgin spoken by young people today is "fo' real" different from that of their parents. It's no longer only plantation talk but has moved to the streets and picked up sophistication. At one time there was an academic movement to exterminate it, but that idea died away with the same thinking that insisted on making left-handed people write with their right hand. It is strange, however, that pidgin has become the unofficial language of Hawaii's grassroots movement, when it actually began as a white owners' language that was used to supplant Hawaiian and other languages brought to the islands.

Although hip young *haole* use pidgin all the time, it has gained the connotation of being the language of the nonwhite locals, and is part of the "us against them" way of thinking. All local people, *haole* or not, consider pidgin their own island language, and don't really like it when it's used by *malihini* (newcomers). If you're in the islands long enough, you don't have to bother learning pidgin; it'll learn you. There's a book sold all over the islands called *Pidgin to da Max,* written by (you guessed it) a *haole* from Nebraska named Doug Simonson. You might not be able to understand what's being said by locals speaking pidgin (that's usually the idea), but you should be able to *feel* what's meant.

CAPSULE PIDGIN

The following commonly used words and expressions should give you an idea of pidgin. It really can't be written properly, merely approximated, but for now, *"Brah, study da' kine an' bimbye you be hele on, brah! OK? Lesgo."*

an' den—and then? big deal; so what's next; how boring

bimbye—after a while; bye and bye. "Bimbye, you learn pidgin."

blalah—brother, but actually only refers to a large, heavy-set, good-natured Hawaiian man

brah—all the bros in Hawaii are brahs; brother; pal. Used to call someone's attention. One of the most common words used even among people who are not acquainted. After a fill-up at a gas station, a person would say "T'anks, brah."

cockaroach—steal; rip off. If you really want to find out what *cockaroach* means, leave your camera on your beach blanket when you take a little dip.

da' kine—a catchall word of many meanings that epitomizes the essence of pidgin. *Da' kine* is easily used as a euphemism for pidgin and is substituted whenever the speaker is at a loss for a word or wants to generalize. It can mean: you know? watchamacallit; of that type.

geev um—give it to them; give them hell; go for it. Can be used as an encouragement. If a surfer is riding a great wave, the people on the beach might yell, "Geev um, brah!"

hana ho—again. Especially after a concert the audience shouts, "Hana ho!" (One more!).

hele on—right on! hip; with it; groovy

howzit?—as in "howzit brah?" what's happening? how is it going? The most common greeting, used in place of the more formal "How do you do?"

hu hu—angry! "You put the make on the wrong da' kine wahine brah, and you in da' kine trouble, if you get one big Hawaiian blalah plenty hu hu."

kapu—a Hawaiian word meaning forbidden. If *kapu* is written on a gate or posted on a tree it means "No trespassing." *Kapu*-breakers are still very unpopular in the islands.

lesgo—let's go! do it!

li'dis an' li'dat—like this or that; a catch-all grouping especially if you want to avoid details; like, ya' know?

lolo buggah—stupid or crazy guy (person). Words to a tropical island song go, "I want to find the lolo who stole my pakalolo."

mo' bettah—real good! great idea. An island sentiment used to be, "Mo' bettah you *come* Hawaii." Now it has subtly changed to, "Mo' bettah you *visit* Hawaii."

ono—number one! delicious; great; groovy. "Hawaii is ono, brah!"

pakalolo—literally "crazy smoke"; marijuana; grass; reefer. "Hey, brah! Maui-wowie da' kine ono pakalolo."

pakiki head—stubborn; bull-headed

pau—a Hawaiian word meaning finished; done; over and done with. *Pau hana* means end of work or quitting time. Once used by plantation workers, now used by everyone.

stink face—basically frowning at someone; using facial expression to show displeasure; hard looks. What you'll get if you give local people a hard time.
swell head—burned up; angry
talk story—spinning yarns; shooting the breeze; throwing the bull; a rap session. If you're lucky enough to be around to hear *kupuna* (elders) "talk story," you can hear some fantastic tales in the tradition of old Hawaii.
tita—sister, but only used to describe a fun-loving, down-to-earth country girl
waddascoops—what's the scoop? what's up? what's happening?

HAWAIIAN

The Hawaiian language sways like a palm tree in a gentle wind. Its words are as melodious as a love song. Linguists say that you can learn a lot about people through their language; when you hear Hawaiian you think of gentleness and love, and it's hard to imagine the ferocious side so evident in Hawaii's past. With its many Polynesian root words easily traced to Indonesian and Malay, Hawaiian is obviously from this same stock. The Hawaiian spoken today is very different from old Hawaiian. Its greatest metamorphosis occurred when the missionaries began to write it down in the 1820s. There is a movement to reestablish the Hawaiian language, and courses in it are offered at the University of Hawaii. Many scholars have put forth translations of Hawaiian, but there are endless, volatile disagreements in the academic sector about the real meanings of Hawaiian words. Hawaiian is no longer spoken as a language except on Niihau, and the closest tourists will come to it are in place-names, street names, and words that have become part of common usage, such as *aloha* and *mahalo*. A few old Hawaiians still speak it at home and there are sermons in Hawaiian at some local churches. Kawaiahao Church in downtown Honolulu is the most famous of these. (See the Glossary for a list of commonly used Hawaiian words.)

Wiki Wiki Hawaiian

Thanks to the missionaries, the Hawaiian language is rendered phonetically using only 12 letters. They are the five vowels, a-e-i-o-u, sounded as they are in Italian; and seven consonants, h-k-l-m-n-p-w, sounded as they are in English. Sometimes "w" is pronounced as "v," but this only occurs in the middle of a word and always follows a vowel. A consonant is always followed by a vowel, forming two-letter syllables, but vowels are often found in pairs or even triplets. A slight oddity about Hawaiian is the glottal stop. This is an abrupt break in sound in the middle of a word, such as "oh-oh" in English and is denoted in this book by an apostrophe (').

THE ALPHABET.

VOWELS.	Names.	SOUND. Ex. in Eng.	Ex. in Hawaii.
A a	â	as in *father*,	la—sun.
E e	a	— *tele*,	hemo—cast off.
I i	e	— *marine*,	marie—quiet.
O o	o	— *over*,	ono—sweet.
U u	oo	—*rule*,	nui—large.

CONSONANTS.	Names.	CONSONANTS.	Names.
B b	be	N n	nu
D d	de	P p	pi
H h	he	R r	ro
K k	ke	T t	ti
L l	la	V v	vi
M m	mu	W w	we

The following are used in spelling foreign words:

F f	fe	S s	se
G g	ge	Y y	yi

1

cover page of the first Hawaiian primer, showing the phonetic rendering of the ancient Hawaiian language before five of the consonants were dropped

A good example is *ali'i*; or even better, the Oahu town of Ha'iku, which means "abrupt break."

Pronunciation Key

For those unfamiliar with the sounds of Italian or other Romance languages, the vowels are sounded as follows:

A—in stressed syllables, long **"a"** as in **"ah"** (that feels good!). For example, Haleakala (Hah lay ah kah lah). Unstressed syllables get a short **"a"** as in "**a**gain" or "**a**bove." For example, Kamehameha (**Kamehameha**).

E—short **"e"** as in "p**e**n" or "d**e**nt" (Hal**e**). Long **"e"** sounded as "ay" as in "sw**ay**" or "d**ay**." For example, the Hawaiian goose (**nene**) is a "nay nay," not a "knee knee."

I—long **"i"** as in "s**ee**" or "w**e**" (Hawa**ii** or pal**i**).

O—round **"o"** as in "n**o**" or "**o**h" (k**o**a or **o**n**o**).

U—round **"u"** as in "d**o**" or "st**ew**" (kap**u** or P**u**na).

Diphthongs

There are eight vowel pairs known as "diphthongs" (ae-ai-ao-au-ei-eu-oi-ou). These are the sounds made by gliding from one vowel to another within a syllable. The stress is placed on the first vowel. In English, examples would be s**oi**l and **eu**phoria. Common examples in Hawaiian are lei (lay) and *heiau.*

Stress

The best way to learn which syllables are stressed in Hawaiian is by listening closely. It becomes obvious after a while. Some vowel sounds are held longer than others; these can occur at the beginning of a word, such as the first "a" in *aina,* or in the middle of a word, like the first "a" in *lanai.* Again, it's a matter of tuning your ear and paying attention. No one is going to give you a hard time if you mispronounce a word. It's good, however, to pay close attention to the pronunciation of street and place-names, because many Hawaiian words sound alike and a misplaced vowel here or there could be the difference between getting where you want to go and getting lost.

CAPSULE HAWAIIAN

The list on the following pages will give you a "taste" of Hawaiian and provide a basic vocabulary of words you are likely to hear. Becoming familiar with them is not a strict necessity, but they will definitely enhance your experience and make it more congenial when talking with local people. You'll soon notice that many islanders spice their speech with certain words, especially when they're speaking "pidgin," and you too can use them just as soon as you feel comfortable. You might even discover some Hawaiian words so perfectly expressive they'll become a regular part of your vocabulary. Many Hawaiian words have actually made it into the English dictionary. Place-names, historical names, and descriptive terms used throughout the text may not appear in the lists below, but will be cited in the glossary at the back of the book. Also see "Capsule Pidgin," "Food," and "Getting Around" for applicable Hawaiian words and phrases in these categories. The definitions given are not exhaustive, but are generally considered the most common.

BASIC VOCABULARY

'a'a—rough clinker lava. *'A'a* has become the correct geological term to describe this type of lava found anywhere in the world.

ae—yes

akamai—smart; clever; wise

ali'i—Hawaiian nobility

aloha—the most common greeting in the islands. Can mean hello or goodbye, welcome or farewell. It can also convey romantic love, affection, or best wishes.

aole—no

hale—house or building; often combined with other words to name a specific place such as Haleakala ("House of the Sun"), or Hale Pai at Lahainaluna, meaning "Printing House"

hana—work; combined with *pau* means end of work or quitting time

haole—a word that at one time meant foreigner, but now means a white person or Caucasian. Many etymological definitions have been put forth, but none satisfy everyone. Some feel it signified a person without a background, because the first white arrivals could not chant their genealogies as was common to Hawaiians.

hapai—pregnant. Used by all ethnic groups when a *keiki* is on the way.

hapa—half, as in a mixed-blooded person being refered to as *hapa haolo*

heiau—traditional Hawaiian temple. A platform made of skillfully fitted rocks, upon which structures were built and offerings made to the gods.

holomuu—ankle-length dress much more fitted than a muumuu, often worn on formal occasions

hoolaulea—any happy event, but especially a family outing or picnic

hoomalimali—sweet talk; flattery

hu hu—angry; irritated; mad

huli huli—barbecue, as in *huli huli* chicken

hula—native Hawaiian dance capturing the rhythm of the islands in swaying hips and stories told by lyrically moving hands

hui—group; meeting; society. Often used to refer to Chinese businesspeople or family members who pool their money to get businesses started.

imu—underground oven filled with hot rocks and used for baking. The main cooking feature at a luau, used to steam-bake the pork and other succulent dishes. Traditionally the tending of the *imu* was for men only.

ipo—sweetheart; lover; girl- or boyfriend

kahuna—priest; sorcerer; doctor; skillful person. *Kahuna* had tremendous power in old Hawaii, which they used for both good and evil. The *kahuna ana'ana* was a feared individual because he practiced "black magic" and could pray a person to death, while a *kahuna lapa'au* was a medical practitioner bringing aid and comfort to the people.

kalua—roasted underground in an *imu.* A favorite island food is *kalua* pork.

kama'aina—child of the land; old-timer; longtime island resident of any ethnic background; resident of Hawaii or native son. Oftentimes, hotels and airlines offer discounts called *"kama'aina* rates" to anyone who can prove island residency.

kane—means man, but is actually used to signify a husband or boyfriend. Written on a door, it means "Men's Room."

kapu—forbidden; taboo; keep out; do not touch

kaukau—slang word meaning food or chow; grub. Some of the best eating in Hawaii is from *"kaukau* wagons," which are trucks from which plate lunches and other morsels are sold.

keiki—child or children; used by all ethnic groups. "Have you hugged your *keiki* today?"

kokua—help. As in, "Your *kokua* is needed to keep Hawaii free from litter."

kona wind—muggy subtropical wind that blows from the south and hits the leeward side of the islands. It usually brings sticky hot weather and one of the few times when air-conditioning is appreciated.

kupuna—grandparent or old-timer; usually means someone who has gained wisdom. The statewide school system now invites *kapuna* to talk to the children about the old ways and methods.

lanai—veranda or porch. You'll pay more for a hotel room if it has a lanai with an ocean view.

lei—traditional garland of flowers or vines. One of Hawaii's most beautiful customs. Given at any auspicious occasion, but especially when arriving or leaving Hawaii.

limu—edible seaweed gathered from the shoreline. It makes an excellent salad, and is used to garnish many island dishes—a favorite at luau.

lomi lomi—traditional Hawaiian massage; also, a vinegared salad made of raw salmon, chopped onions, and spices

lua—the toilet; the head; the bathroom

luau—Hawaiian feast featuring poi, *imu*-baked pork, and other traditional foods. A good luau provides some of the best gastronomical delights in the world.

mahalo—thanks; thank you. *Mahalo nui* means big thanks or thank you very much.

mahu—homosexual; often used derisively like "fag" or "queer"

makai—toward the sea; used by most islanders when giving directions

malihini—what you are if you have just arrived: a newcomer; a tenderfoot; a recent arrival

manuahi—free; gratis; extra

manini—stingy; tight. A Hawaiianized word taken from the name of Don Francisco Marin, who was instrumental in bringing many fruits and plants to Hawaii. He was known for never sharing any of the bounty from his substantial gardens on Vineyard Street in Honolulu; therefore his name came to mean stingy.

mauka—toward the mountains; used by most islanders when giving directions

mauna—mountain. Often combined with other words to be more descriptive, as in Mauna Kea ("White Mountain").

(continues)

moana—the ocean; the sea. Many businesses and hotels as well as place-names have *moana* as part of their name.

muumuu—garment introduced by the missionaries to cover the nakedness of the Hawaiians. A "Mother Hubbard," a long dress with a high neckline that has become fashionable attire for almost any occasion in Hawaii.

ohana—family; the fundamental social division; extended family. Now used to denote a social organization with "grass roots," as in the "Save Kahoolawe Ohana."

okolehau—literally "iron bottom"; a traditional booze made from ti root; *okole* means your "rear end" and *hau* means iron, which was descriptive of the huge blubber pots in which *okolehau* was made. Also, if you drink too much it'll surely knock you on your *okole*.

ono—delicious; delightful; the best. *Ono ono* means "extra or absolutely" delicious.

opu—belly; stomach

pahoehoe—smooth ropey lava that looks like burnt pancake batter. *Pahoehoe* is now the correct geological term used to describe this type of lava found anywhere in the world.

pakalolo—"crazy smoke"; marijuana; grass; smoke; dope

pali—cliff; precipice. Hawaii's geology makes them quite common. The most famous are the *pali* of Oahu, where a major battle was fought.

paniolo—Hawaiian cowboy. Derived from the Spanish *espaniola*. The first cowboys brought in during the early 19th century were Mexicans from California.

pau—finished; done; completed. Often combined into *pau hana*, which means end of work or quitting time.

pilau—stink; smells bad; stench

pilikia—trouble of any kind, big or small; bad times

pono—righteous or excellent

poi—glutinous paste made from the pounded corm of taro which, slightly fermented, has a light sour taste. Purplish in color, it is a staple at luau, where it is called one-, two-, or three-finger poi, depending upon its thickness.

puka—hole of any size. *Puka* is used by all island residents and can be employed when talking about a tiny *puka* in a rubber boat or a *puka* (tunnel) through a mountain.

punee—bed; narrow couch. Used by all ethnic groups. To recline on a *punee* on a breezy lanai is a true island treat.

pu pu—appetizer; snack; hors d'oeuvres; can be anything from cheese and crackers to sushi. Oftentimes, bars or nightclubs offer them free.

pupule—crazy; nuts; out of your mind

tapa—traditional paper cloth made from beaten bark. Intricate designs were stamped in using beaters, and color was added with natural dyes. The tradition was lost in Hawaii, but it is now making a comeback and provides some of the most beautiful folk art in the islands.

tutu—grandmother; granny; older woman. Used by all as a term of respect and endearment.

ukulele—*uku* means "flea" and *lele* means "jumping," thus ukulele means "jumping flea," which was the way the Hawaiians perceived the quick finger movements on the banjo-type Portuguese folk instrument called a *cavaquinho*. The ukulele quickly became synonymous with the islands.

wahine—young woman; female; girl; wife. Used by all ethnic groups. When written on a door means "Women's Room."

wai—fresh water; drinking water

wela—hot. *Wela kahao* is a "hot time" or "making whoopee."

wiki—quickly; fast; in a hurry. Often seen as *wiki wiki* (very fast), as in "Wiki Wiki Messenger Service."

USEFUL PHRASES

Aloha ahiahi—Good evening

Aloha au ia oe—I love you!

Aloha kakahiaka—Good morning

aloha nui loa—much love; fondest regards

Hauoli la hanau—Happy Birthday

Hauoli makahiki hou—Happy New Year

komo mai—please come in; enter; welcome

Mele Kalikimaka—Merry Christmas

okole maluna—bottoms up; salute; cheers; kampai

BOB RACE

OUT AND ABOUT

SPORTS AND RECREATION

Hawaii is a playground for young and old with sports, games, and activities galore. Everyone can find something they enjoy, and most activities are free, relatively cheap, or once-in-a-lifetime thrills that are worth the money. The sea is the ideal playground. You can swim, snorkel, scuba, surf, fish, sail, canoe, kayak, sailboard, bodysurf, parasail, cruise, or stroll along the shore picking up shells or exploring tidepools. Every island offers tennis and golf, along with plenty of horseback riding, hiking, hunting, and freshwater fishing. Spectator sports like baseball, basketball, polo, and especially football are popular, and the Kona coast of the Big Island is a mecca for world-class triathletes. Whatever your desire or physical abilities may be, there'll be some activity that strikes your fancy in Hawaii.

One of the best tonics for relaxation is to play hard at something you thoroughly enjoy, so you're deliciously tired and fulfilled at day's end. For you this might be hooking onto an 800-pound marlin that'll test you to the limit, or perhaps just giving yourself to the sea and floating on gentle waves. Hawaii is guaranteed to thrill the young, invigorate the once young, put a twinkle in your eye, and add a bounce to your step.

Note

The following sports and recreation overview is designed to give you an idea of what's available. They'll all be covered in depth in the travel chapters. There you'll also find specific entries for localized sports like horseback riding, Jet Skiing, water-skiing, snow skiing, parasailing, kayaking, and much more. Whatever else you may do in Hawaii, you owe it to yourself to do one thing: enjoy it!

SCUBA AND SNORKELING

If you think that Hawaii is beautiful above the sea, wait until you explore below. The warm tropical waters and coral growth make it a fascinating haven for reef fish and aquatic plantlife. Snorkel and dive sites, varying in difficulty and challenge, are accessible from all islands. Sites can be totally hospitable ones where families, snorkeling for the first time, can have an exciting but safe frolic; or they can be accessible only to the experienced diver. Every island has dive shops where you can rent or buy equipment, and where dive boats and instruction on all levels can be arranged. You'll soon discover Hawaiian waters are remarkably clear with excellent visibility. Below, fish in every fathomable color parade by. Lavender clusters of coral, red-and-gold coral trees, and over 1,500 different types of shells carpet the ocean floor. In some spots (like Oahu's Hanauma Bay) the fish are so accustomed to humans they'll eat bread from your hand. In other spots, lurking moray eels add the zest of danger. Sharks and barracuda pose less danger than scraping your knee on the coral or being driven against the rocks by a heavy swell. There are enormous but harmless sea bass and a profusion of sea turtles. All this awaits you below Hawaii's waters.

Scuba

If you're a scuba diver you'll have to show your "C Card" before local shops will rent you gear, fill your tanks, or take you on a charter dive. Plenty of outstanding scuba instructors will give you lessons toward certification, and they're especially reasonable because of the stiff competition. Prices vary, but you can take a four- to five-day semiprivate (PADI) certification course including all equipment for about $375. Divers unaccustomed to Hawaiian waters should not dive alone regardless of their experience. Most opt for dive tours to special dive grounds guaranteed to please. These vary also, but an *accompanied* single-tank dive where no boat is involved goes for about $65. For a single-tank boat dive, expect to spend $65-85. There are charter dives, night dives, and photography dives. Most companies pick you up at your hotel, take you to the site, and return you home. Basic equipment rental costs $25-35 for the day, and most times the water is so mild you'll only need the top of a wetsuit.

Snorkeling

Scuba diving takes expensive special equipment, skills, and athletic ability. Snorkeling in comparison is much simpler and enjoyable to anyone who can swim. In about 15 minutes you can be taught the fundamentals of snorkeling, so you're comfortable and confident in the water—you really don't need formal instructions. Other snorkelers or dive shop attendants can tell you enough to get you started. Because you can breathe without lifting your head, you get great propulsion from the fins and hardly ever need to use your arms. You can go for much greater distances and spend longer in the water than if you were swimming. Experienced snorkelers make an art of this sport and you too can see and do amazing things with a mask, snorkel, and flippers. Don't, however, get a false sense of invincibility and exceed your limitations.

Gear And Excursions

You can buy or rent equipment in dive shops and in department stores. Sometimes condos and hotels offer free snorkeling equipment for their guests, but if you have to rent it, don't do it at a hotel or condo; go to a dive shop where it's much cheaper. Expect to spend $7 a day for mask, fins, and snorkel. Scuba divers can rent gear for about $30 from most shops. A special option is underwater cameras. Rental of camera, film included, is about $10. Many boats will take you out snorkeling or diving. Prices range from about $40 (half day, four hours) to $70 (full day, eight hours). See sections on sightseeing tours and sports in the individual travel chapters for many boats that do it all, from deep-sea fishing to moonlight cruises. Also, activities centers can arrange these excursions for no extra charge.

SURFING, WINDSURFING, AND BOOGIE BOARDING

Surfing

Surfing is a sport indigenous to Hawaii. When the first white people arrived, they were astonished to see natives paddling out to meet the ships on long carved boards, then gracefully riding them in to shore on crests of waves. The Hawaiians called surfing *he'enalu* (to "slide on a wave"). The newcomers were fascinated by this sport, recording it in engravings and woodcuts, which were marvelled at around the world. Meanwhile, the Polynesians left records of surfing in petroglyphs and in *mele* of past exploits. Early in the century, the most famous waterman of all time, Duke Kahanamoku, won an Olympic medal for swimming. He then became a one-man traveling show, introducing surfing to California and Australia. Surfing later became a lifestyle, spread far and wide by the songs of the Beach Boys in the '60s. Now surfing is a world-famous sport complete with championships, movies, magazines, and advanced board technology.

It takes years of practice to become good, but with determination, good swimming ability, and a sense of balance you can learn the fundamentals in a short time. One of the safest places, offering ideal conditions to learn, is Waikiki. The sea is just right for the beginner, and legions of beachboys offer lessons. At surf shops on all islands you can rent a board for very reasonable prices. The boards of the ancient *ali'i* were up to 20 feet long and weighed over 150 pounds, but today's board is made from ultralight foam plastic covered in fiberglass. They're about six feet long and weigh 12 pounds or so. Innovations occur every day in surfing, but one is the changeable "skeg" or rudder allowing you to surf in variable conditions. The sport of surfing is still male-dominated, but women champions have been around for years. The most famous surfing beach in the world is Sunset Beach and the Banzai Pipeline on North Shore Oahu. Every year the nationally televised Pro-Tour Surfing Championship is held here, usually in late November and December. It's only a matter of time before surfing becomes an Olympic sport. One of the most brilliant books ever written on surfing is *Surfing, The Ultimate Pleasure,* by Leonard Lueras and designed by Fred Bechlen. Published by Workman Publishing of New York, it can be found at almost every surf shop.

Sailboarding

Many people call this relatively new sport "windsurfing," though that is actually the name of one of the most famous manufacturers of sailboards. For this combination of surfing and sailing, the equipment is a rather large and stable surfboard mounted with a highly maneuverable sail. The sport may sound difficult, but most people find it slightly easier than surfing because you're mobilized by the wind and not at the mercy of the waves. You don't have to "read" the waves as well as a surfer, and as with riding a bicycle, as long as you keep moving, you can hold your balance. Boards and lessons are available on all the major islands. Sailboards are slightly more expensive than surfboards to rent, but you should be in business for about $35.

Boogie Boards

If surfing or sailboarding are a bit too much for you, try a boogie board—a foam board about three feet long that you lie on from the waist up. With the help of flippers for maneuverability, you can get tremendous rides on boogie boards. You can learn to ride in minutes and it's much faster, easier, and more thrilling than bodysurfing. Boogie boards are for sale all over the islands and are relatively cheap. You can rent one from a dive or surf shop for a couple bucks, or buy your own for $35-70.

GONE FISHING

Hawaii has some of the most exciting and productive "blue waters" in all the world. You'll find a statewide "sport fishing fleet" made up of skippers and crews who are experienced professional anglers. You can also fish from jetties, piers, rocks, and shores. If rod and reel don't strike your fancy, try the old-fashioned throw net, or take along a spear when you go snorkeling or scuba diving. There's nighttime torch fishing that requires special skills and equipment, and freshwater fishing in public areas. Streams and irrigation ditches yield introduced trout, bass, and catfish. While you're at it, you might want to try crabbing for Kona and Samoan crabs, or working low-tide areas after sundown hunting "squid" (really octopus), a tantalizing island delicacy.

Deep-Sea Fishing

Most game-fishing boats work the blue waters on the calmer leeward sides of the islands. Some skippers, carrying anglers who are accustomed to the sea, will also work the much rougher windward coasts and island channels where the fish bite just as well. Trolling is the preferred method of deep-sea fishing; this is done usually in waters of 1,000-2,000 fathoms (a fathom is six feet). The skipper will either "area fish," which means running in a crisscross pattern over a known productive area; or "ledge fish," which involves trolling over submerged ledges where game fish

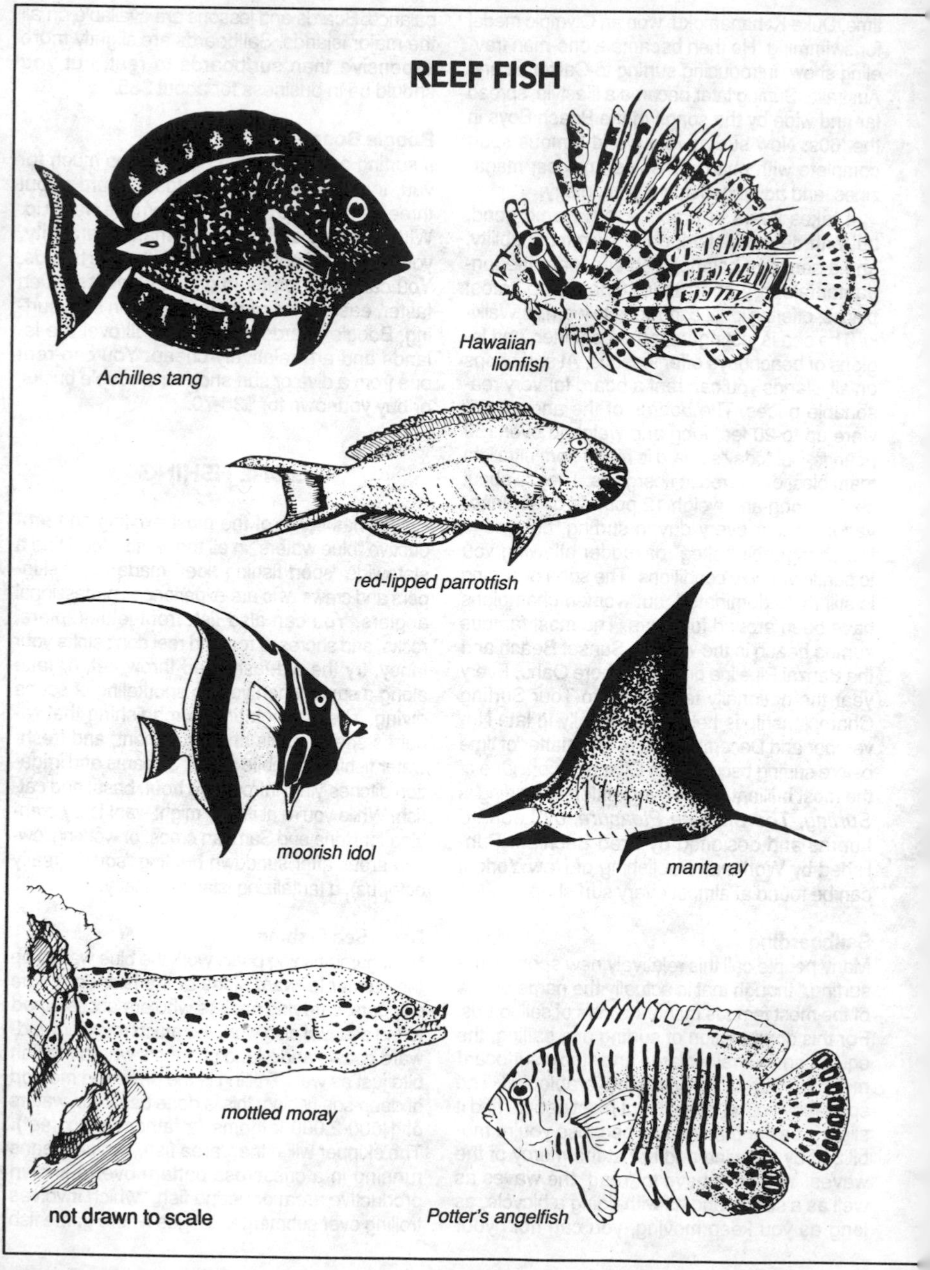

REEF FISH

Achilles tang
Hawaiian lionfish
red-lipped parrotfish
moorish idol
manta ray
mottled moray
Potter's angelfish
not drawn to scale

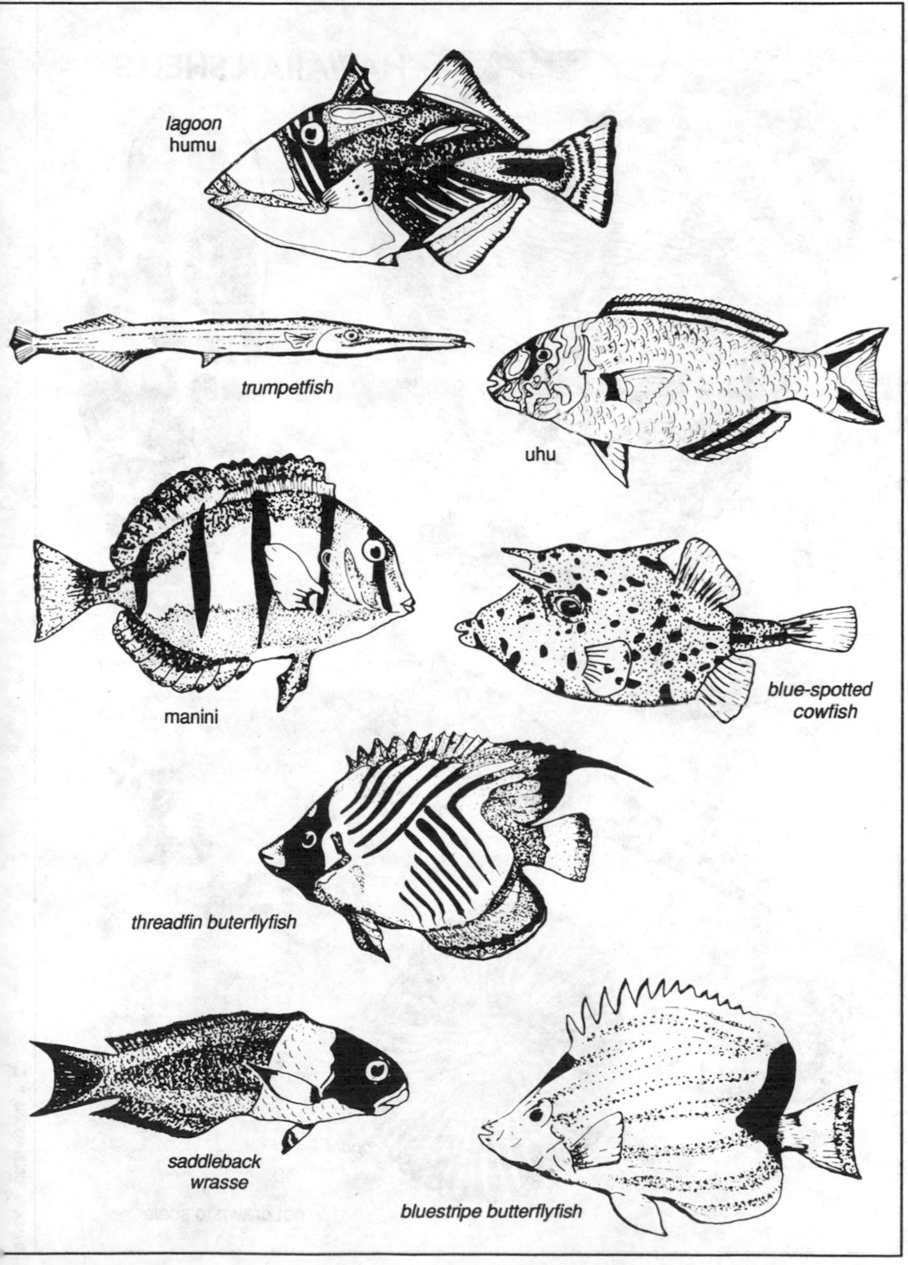
lagoon
humu
trumpetfish
uhu
manini
blue-spotted
cowfish
threadfin buterflyfish
saddleback
wrasse
bluestripe butterflyfish

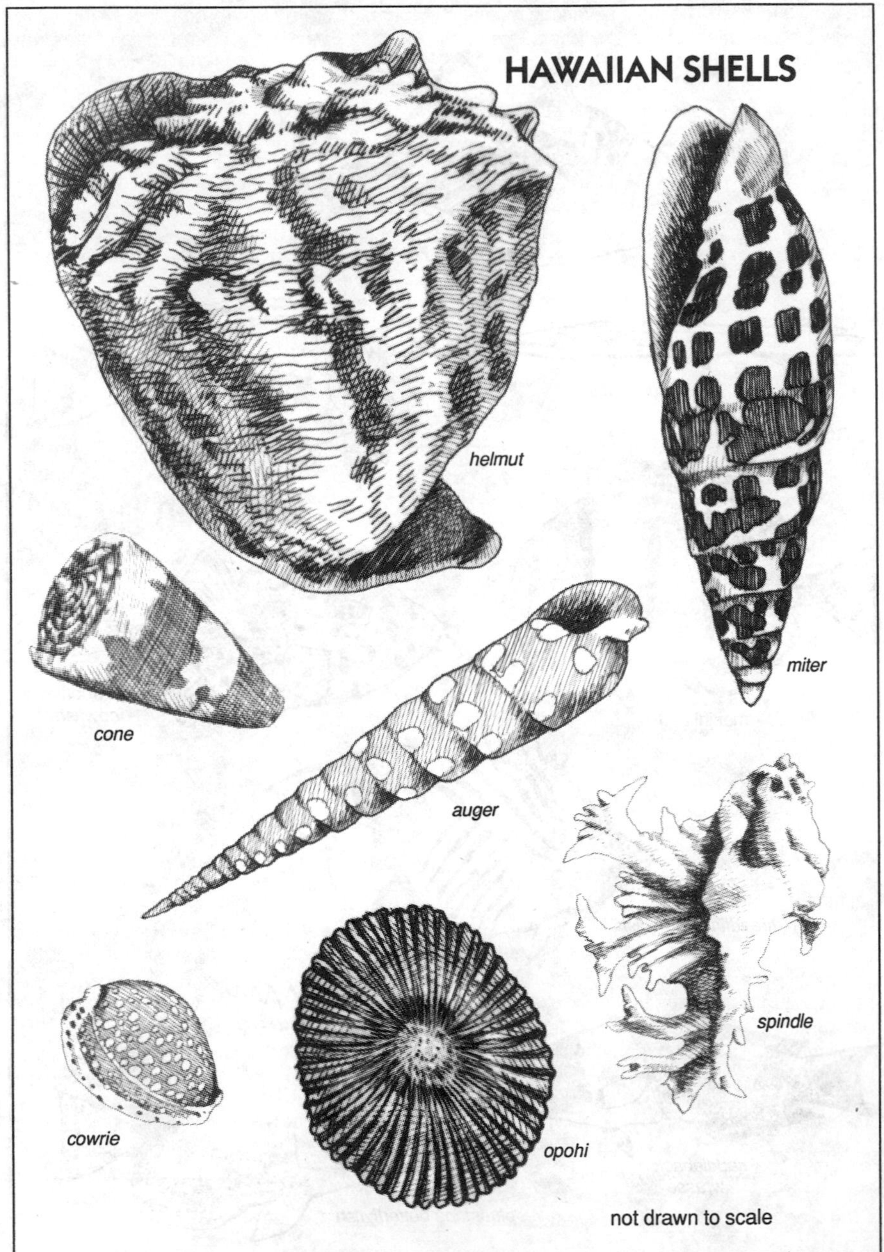
HAWAIIAN SHELLS
helmut
miter
cone
auger
spindle
cowrie
opohi
not drawn to scale
© MOON PUBLICATIONS, INC.

are known to feed. The most advanced marine technology, available on many boats, sends sonar bleeps searching for fish. On deck, the crew and anglers scan the horizon in the age-old Hawaiian tradition—searching for seabirds clustered in an area, feeding on bait fish pursued to the surface by the huge and aggressive game fish. "Still fishing," or "bottom fishing" with hand lines, can yield some tremendous fish.

The Game Fish

The most thrilling game fish in Hawaiian waters is marlin, generically known as "billfish" or *a'u* to the locals. The king of them is the blue marlin, with record catches well over 1,000 pounds. There are also striped marlin and sailfish, which often go over 200 pounds. The best times for marlin are during spring, summer, and fall. The fishing tapers off in January and picks up again by late February. "Blues" can be caught year-round, but, oddly enough, when they stop biting it seems as though the striped marlin pick up. Second to the marlin is tuna. *Ahi* (yellowfin tuna) is caught in Hawaiian waters at depths of 100-1,000 fathoms. It can weigh 300 pounds, but 25-100 pounds is common. There's also *aku* (skipjack tuna), and the delicious *ono,* which averages 20-40 pounds.

Mahimahi is another strong-fighting, deep-water game fish abundant in Hawaii. A delicious fish, it can weigh up to 70 pounds. Shore fishing and bait-casting yield *papio,* a jack tuna. *Akule,* a scad, (locally called *halalu*), is a smallish schooling fish that comes close to shore and is great to catch on light tackle. *Ulua* is a shore fish that can be found in tidepools. It's excellent eating, and averages two to three pounds. *O'io* is a bonefish that comes close to shore to spawn. It's caught by bait-casting and bottom fishing with cut bait. Though bony, it's a favorite for fish cakes and *poki. Awa* is a schooling fish that loves brackish water. It can get up to three feet long, and is a good fighter. A favorite for throw netters, it's even raised commercially in fishponds. Besides these there are plenty of goatfish, mullet, mackerel, and snapper; various sharks; and even salmon.

"Blue Water" Areas

One of the most famous fishing spots in Hawaii is the **Penguin Banks** off the west coast of Molokai and the south coast of Oahu. The "Chicken Farm" at the southern tip of the Penguin Banks has great trolling waters for marlin and mahimahi. The calm waters off the Waianae Coast of Oahu yield marlin and *ahi.* The Kona coast of Hawaii with its crystal waters is the most famous marlin grounds in Hawaii. Every year the **Hawaiian International Billfish Tournament** draws anglers from around the world to Kona. The marlin are found in 1,000 fathoms of water, but close in on the Kona coast you can hook *ono* and hand line for *onaga* and *kahala.* Maui fishermen usually head for the waters formed by the triangle of Maui, Lanai, and Kahoolawe where they troll for marlin, *mahi,* and *ono,* or bottom fish for snapper. The waters around Kahoolawe are also good. Kauai has excellent fishing waters year-round, with *ono, ahi,* and marlin along the ledges. Large schools of *ahi* come to Kauai in the spring, and the fishing is fabulous with possible 200-pound catches.

Charter Boats

The charter boats of Hawaii come in all shapes and sizes, but all are staffed by professional, competent crews and captains with intimate knowledge of Hawaiian waters. Prices vary but expect to spend $85-150 on a share basis. The average number of fishermen per boat is six, and most boats rent all day for $750. You can also arrange half days, and bigger boats with more anglers can cost as little as $50 per person. Tackle weighing 30-130 pounds is carried on the boats and is part of the service. Oftentimes soft drinks are supplied, but usually you carry your own lunch. It is customary for the crew to be given any fish that are caught, but naturally this doesn't apply to trophy fish; the crew is also glad to cut off steaks and fillets for your personal use. Honolulu's Kewalo Basin, only a few minutes from Waikiki, has the largest fleet of charter boats. Pokai Bay also has a fleet, and many charter boats sail out of Kaneohe Bay. On the Big Island, Kailua-Kona has the largest concentration of charter boats, with some boats out of Kawaihae. Maui boats come out of Lahaina or Maalaea Bay. Molokai has a small fleet berthed in Kaunakakai Harbor, and on Kauai most boats sail out of Nawiliwili Bay.

Freshwater Fishing

Due to Hawaii's unique geology, only a handful of natural lakes and rivers are good for fishing. The state maintains five "Public Fishing Areas" spread over Kauai, Oahu, and Hawaii. None are found on Maui, Lanai, or Molokai. Public fishing areas include: on Oahu, **Wahiawa Public Area,** a 300-acre irrigation reservoir primarily for sugarcane located near Wahiawa in central Oahu, and **Nuuanu Resevoir no. 4,** located in the Koolau Mountains above Honolulu; on Kauai, **Koke'e Public Fishing Area,** located north of Kekaha, with 13 miles of stream, two miles of irrigation ditches, and a 15-acre reservoir offering only rainbow trout; on Hawaii, **Waiakea Public Area,** a 26-acre pond within the city of Hilo, and **Kohala Reservoir** on the north coast.

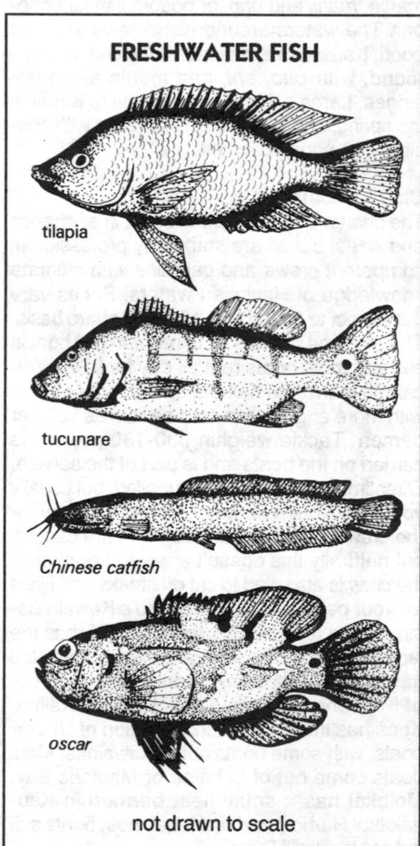

Freshwater Fish And Rules

Hawaii has only one native freshwater game fish, the *'o'opu.* This gobie is an oddball with fused ventral fins. It grows to 12 inches and is found on all islands, especially Kauai. Introduced species include largemouth and smallmouth bass, bluegills, catfish, *tucunare,* oscar, carp, and *tilapia.* The only trout to survive is the rainbow, found only in the streams of Kauai. The *tucunare* is a tough-fighting, good-tasting game fish introduced from South America, similar to the oscar, from the same region. Both have been compared to bass, but are of a different family. The *tilapia* is from Africa and has become common in Hawaii's irrigation ditches. It's a "mouth breeder" and the young will take refuge in their parents' protective jaws even a few weeks after hatching. The snakehead is an eel-like fish that inhabits reservoirs and is a great fighter. The channel catfish can grow to over 20 pounds and bites best after sundown. There's also the carp, and with its broad tail and tremendous strength, it's the poor person's game fish. All of these species are best caught with light spinning tackle, or with a bamboo pole and a trusty old worm.

Fishing licenses are good for one year, from July 1 to June 30. Licenses for nonresidents are obtained from the Division of Conservation and Resources Enforcement on Oahu, tel. (808) 548-8766, or from most sporting goods stores. For free booklets and information write Division of Aquatic Resources, 1151 Punchbowl St., Honolulu, HI 96813. All game fish may be taken year-round, except trout. Trout, found only on Kauai, may be taken for 16 days commencing on the first Saturday of August. Thereafter, for the remainder of August and September, trout can be taken only on Saturday, Sunday, and state holidays.

HUNTING

Most people don't think of Hawaii as a place to hunt, but actually it's quite good. Seven species of introduced game animals are regularly hunted, and 16 species of game birds. Not all

LOUISE FOOTE

feral pig

species of game animals are open on all islands, but every island offers hunting. Please refer to "Sports" in the travel chapters for full details on hunting on particular islands.

General Hunting Rules

Hunting licenses are mandatory to hunt on public, private, or military land anywhere in Hawaii. They're good for one year beginning July 1. They cost $7.50 residents, $15 nonresidents, free to senior citizens. Licenses are available from the various offices of the Division of Forestry and Wildlife (see "Sources of Information," below) and from sporting goods stores. This government organization also sets and enforces the rules, so contact them with any questions. Generally, hunting hours are from a half hour before sunrise to a half hour after sunset. At times, there are "checking stations," where the hunter must check in before and after hunting.

Rifles must have greater than a 1,200-foot-pound muzzle velocity. Shotguns larger than .20 gauge are allowed, and muzzleloaders must have a .45 caliber bore or larger. Bows must have a minimum draw of 45 pounds for straight bows and 30 pounds for compounds. Arrows must be broadheads. Dogs are permitted only for some birds and game, and smaller caliber rifles and shotguns are permitted with their use, along with spears and knives. Hunters must wear orange safety cloth on front and back no smaller than a 12-inch square. Certain big game species are hunted only by lottery selection; contact the Division of Forestry and Wildlife two months in advance. Guide service is not mandatory, but is advised if you're unfamiliar with hunting in Hawaii. You can hunt on private land only with permission, and you must possess a valid hunting license. Guns and ammunition brought into Hawaii must be registered with the chief of police of the corresponding county within 48 hours of arrival.

Sources Of Information

Hunting rules and regulations are always subject to change. Also, environmental considerations often change bag limits and seasons. Make sure to check with the Division of Forestry and Wildlife for the most current information. Request "Rules Regulating Game Bird Hunting, Field Trails and Commercial Shooting Preserves," "Rules Regulating Game Mammal Hunting," and "Hunting in Hawaii." Direct inquiries to: Department of Land and Natural Resources, Division of Forestry and Wildlife Office, 1151 Punchbowl St., Honolulu, HI 96813, tel. (808) 548-2861; on Maui, 54 S. High St., P.O. Box 1015, Wailuku, HI 96793, tel. (808) 244-4352; on Hawaii, Box 4849, Hilo, HI 96720, tel. (808) 961-7221; on Lanai, 338 8th St., Lanai City, HI 96763, tel. (808) 565-6688; on Kauai, 3060 Eiwa St., Box 1671, Lihue, HI 96766, tel. (808) 245-4444; on Molokai, Puu Kapeelua Ave., Hoolehua, HI 96729, tel. (808) 553-5415.

Game Animals

All game animals have been introduced to Hawaii. Some are adapting admirably and becoming well entrenched, while the existence of others is still precarious. **Axis deer** originated in India and were brought to Lanai and Molokai, where they're doing well. The small herd on Maui is holding its own. Their unique flavor makes them one of the best wild meats, and they're hunted on Molokai and Lanai in March and April, by public lottery. **Feral pigs** are escaped domestic pigs that have gone wild and are found on all islands except Lanai. The stock is a mixture of original Polynesian pigs and those that came later. Because the pigs are hunted with dogs and usually killed with a spear or long knife, pig hunting is not recommended for the timid or tender-hearted. These beasts' four-inch tusks and fighting spirit make them tough and dangerous. **Feral goats** come in a variety of colors. Found on all islands except Lanai, they have been known to cause erosion and are considered a pest in some areas, especially on Haleakala. Openly hunted on all islands, their meat when done properly is considered delicious. **Black-**

tailed deer come from the Rocky Mountains. Forty were released on Kauai in 1961; the herd is now stabilized at around 400 and they're hunted in October by public lottery. **Mouflon sheep** are native to Corsica and Sardinia. They do well on Lanai and on the windswept slopes of Mauna Loa and Mauna Kea, where they're hunted at various times by public lottery. **Feral sheep** haunt the slopes of Mauna Kea and Mauna Loa at 7,000-12,000 feet. They travel in flocks and destroy vegetation. It takes determination and a good set of lungs to bag one, especially with a bow and arrow. **Pronghorn antelope** on Lanai, **feral cattle** on the Big Island, and **rock wallabies** from Australia, who now make their home on Oahu, are not hunted.

Game Birds

A number of game birds are found on most of the islands. Bag limits and hunting seasons vary, so check with the Division of Forestry and Wildlife for details. The **ring-necked pheasant** is one of the best game birds, and is found on all the islands. The **kalij pheasant** from Nepal is found only on the Big Island, where the **green pheasant** is also prevalent, with some found on Oahu and Maui. **Francolins,** gray and black, from India and the Sudan, are similar to partridges. They are hunted on all islands with dogs and are great roasted. There are also **chukar** from Tibet, found on the slopes of all islands; a number of **quail,** including the **Japanese** and **California** varieties; **doves;** and the **wild Rio Grande turkey** found on all islands except Kauai and Oahu (although a few of the "featherless variety" have been known to walk the streets of Waikiki).

GOLF AND TENNIS

People addicted to chasing that little white ball around the links are going to be delighted with Hawaii. You can golf every day of the year on over 60 golf courses scattered around the state. Many are open to the public, and are built along some of the most spectacular scenery in the world, where pounding surf or flower-dappled mountains form the backdrop. Many courses have pros and pro shops, and a profusion of hotels offer "golfing specials." You'll find everything from Lanai's nine-hole Cavendish Golf Course, where you put your money in an envelope on the honor system, to some of the most highly praised, exclusive, and exciting golf courses in the world. Master builders such as Robert Trent Jones, Jack Nicklaus, and Robert Trent Jones Jr. have laid out links in the islands where major tournaments, such as the Kemper Open, are yearly events. Fees range from as little as $10 for some little nine-holers up to $150 and more at exclusive resorts.

Tennis courts are found on every island of Hawaii and enjoyed by locals and visitors on a year-round basis. County courts are open to the public, as are some hotel and private courts where fees range from complimentary to about $6 for nonhotel guests. Most courts are of Laykold or Plexipave asphalt. Many of the hotel courts and some of the public courts are lighted.

Gambel's quail, left; gray francolin, right

BOB RACE

CAMPING AND HIKING

A major aspect of the "Hawaii experience" is found in the simple beauty of nature and the outdoors. Visitors come to Hawaii to luxuriate at resorts and dine in fine restaurants, but everyone heads for the sand and surf, and most are captivated by the lush mountainous interior. What better way to savor this natural beauty than by hiking slowly through it or pitching a tent in the middle of it? Hawaii offers a full range of hiking and camping, and what's more, most of it is easily accessible and free. Camping facilities are located near many choice beaches and amid the most scenic areas in the islands. They range in amenities from full housekeeping cabins to primitive hike-in sites. Some restrictions to hiking apply because much of the land is privately owned, so you may require advance permission. But plenty of public access trails along the coast and deep into the interior would fill the itineraries of even the most intrepid trekkers. If you enjoy the great outdoors on the Mainland, you'll be thrilled by these "mini-continents," where in one day you can go from the frosty summits of alpine wonderlands down into baking cactus-covered deserts and emerge through jungle foliage onto a sun-soaked subtropical shore.

Camping Note

Individual state, county, and national parks, along with directions on how to get there, are described under "Camping and Hiking" in their respective travel chapters.

NATIONAL PARKS

Hawaii's two National Parks sit atop volcanoes: **Haleakela National Park** on Maui, and **Hawaii Volcanoes National Park** centered around Kilauea Crater on the Big Island. Camping is free at both, and permits are not required except for the cabins and campgrounds inside Haleakala crater. Get free information by writing to the individual park headquarters listed in the respective travel chapters or from the **National Park Service,** 300 Ala Moana Blvd., Honolulu, HI 96850, tel. (808) 546-7584.

STATE PARKS

Hawaii's 67 state parks (plus or minus) are managed by the Department of Land and Natural

Resources, through their Division of State Parks branch offices on each island. These parks include everything from historical sites like Iolani Palace in downtown Honolulu to wildland accessible only by trail. Some are for looking at, some are restricted to day use, and at 16 or so (which change periodically without notice) there is overnight camping. At seven of these 16 state parks, A-frames, self-contained cabins, or group accommodations are available on a fee basis with reservations necessary. At the others, camping is free, but permits are required. RVs are technically not allowed.

Permits And Rules

Camping permits are good for a maximum stay of five nights at any one park. A permit to the same person for the same park is again available only after 30 days have elapsed. Campgrounds are open every day on the Neighbor Islands, but closed Wednesday and Thursday on Oahu. Arrive after 2 p.m. and check out by 11 a.m., except again on Oahu where Wednesday checkout is 8 a.m. You must be 18 for park permits; anyone under that age must be accompanied by an adult. Alcoholic beverages are prohibited, along with nude sunbathing and swimming. Plants and wildlife are protected, but reasonable amounts of fruits and seeds may be gathered for personal consumption. Fires are allowed on cookstoves or in designated pits only. Dogs and other pets must be under control at all times, and are not permitted to run around unleashed. Hunting and freshwater fishing are allowed in season with a license, and ocean fishing is permitted except when disallowed by posting. Permits are required for certain trails, pavilions, and remote camps, so check.

Cabins And Shelters

Housekeeping cabins, A-frames, and group lodges are available at seven state parks throughout the state. See specific travel chapters for charts detailing locations. As with camping, permits are required and have the same five-day maximum-stay limitations. Reservations are necessary because of popularity, and a 50% deposit at time of confirmation is required. There is a three-day cancellation requirement for refunds, with payment made in cash, money order, or certified check. If you pay by personal check, it must be received 30 days before arrival so cashing procedures are possible. The balance is due on arrival; check in is 2 p.m., checkout 11 a.m.

State Park Permit-Issuing Offices

Permits can be reserved two months in advance by writing a letter including your name, address, phone number, number in your party, type of permit requested, and duration of stay. They can be picked up on arrival with proof of identification. Office hours are Mon.-Fri. 8 a.m.-4:15 p.m. Usually, camping permits are no problem (Oahu excepted, see "Camping and Hiking" in the Oahu chapter Introduction) to secure on the day you arrive, but reserving ensures you a space and alleviates anxiety. The permits are available from the following offices: **Oahu,** Division of State Parks, 1151 Punchbowl St., Honolulu, HI 96813, tel. (808) 548-7455; **Hawaii,** Div. of State Parks, 75 Aupuni St., Hilo, HI 96720, tel. (808) 961-7200; **Maui and Molokai,** Division of State Parks, 54 High St., Wailuku, HI 96793, tel. (808) 244-4354; **Kauai,** Division of State Parks, State Bldg., 3060 Eiwa and Hardy Streets, Box 1671, Lihue, HI 96766, tel. (808) 245-4444. For lodging at **Kokee State Park,** Kauai, write Kokee Lodge, Box 819, Waimea, HI 96796, tel. (808) 335-6061.

COUNTY PARKS

The state of Hawaii is broken up into counties, and the counties control their own parks. Over 100 of these are scattered primarily along the coastlines, and are generally referred to as **beach parks.** Most are for day use only, where visitors fish, swim, snorkel, surf, picnic, and sunbathe, but over 36 beach parks have overnight camping. The rules governing their use vary slightly from county to county, but most have about the same requirements as state parks. The main difference is that, along with a use permit, most county parks charge a fee for overnight use. Again, the differences between individual parks are too numerous to mention, but the majority have a central pavilion for cooking, restrooms, and cold-water showers (solar heated at a few). Some have individual fire pits, picnic tables, and electricity (usually only at the central pavilion). RVs are allowed to park in appropriate spaces.

Fees And Permits

The fees are quite reasonable at $1-3 per night, per person, children about 50 cents each. One safety point to consider is that beach parks are open to the general public and most are used with regularity. Quite a few people pass through, and your chances of encountering a hassle or rip-off are slightly higher (see "Theft and Hassles" under "Health and Safety" later in this chapter for safety tips). To get a permit and pay your fees for use of a county park, either write in advance, or visit one of the following issuing offices. Most will accept reservations months in advance, with offices generally open during normal working hours. Write or visit the Department of Parks and Recreation, County Parks: **Oahu,** 650 S. King St., Honolulu, HI 96813, tel. (808) 523-4525; **Maui,** War Memorial Gym, Wailuku, HI 96793, tel. (808) 244-5514; **Hawaii,** 25 Aupuni St., Hilo, HI 96720, tel. (808) 961-8311; **Kauai,** 4191 Hardy St., Lihue, HI 96766, tel. (808) 245-4982, or during off hours Lihue Police Station, 3060 Umi St., Lihue, HI 96766, tel. (808) 245-6721; **Molokai,** County Bldg., Kaunakakai, HI 96748, tel. (808) 553-5141.

EQUIPMENT, INFORMATION, AND SAFETY

Hiking Groups And Information

The following organizations can provide information on wildlife, conservation, and organized hiking trips. The **Department of Land and Natural Resources,** Division of Forestry and Wildlife, 1151 Punchbowl St., Honolulu, HI 96813, tel. (808) 548-2861, is helpful in providing trail maps, accessibility information, hunting and fishing regulations, and general forest rules. Their "Recreation Map" (one for each island) is excellent and free. **Hawaiian Trail and Mountain Club,** Box 2238, Honolulu 96804, meets behind Iolani Palace on Saturday at 10 a.m., and Sunday at 8 a.m. Their hikes are announced in the *Honolulu Star Bulletin*'s "Pulse of Paradise" column. **Hawaii Audubon Society** can be reached at Box 22832, Honolulu, HI 96822. **Sierra Club,** 1212 University Ave., Honolulu, HI 96826, tel. (808) 538-6616, can provide you with a packet describing Hawaii's trails, charted by island, along with their physical characteristics and information on obtaining maps and permits. The packet costs $3, postage paid.

For well-written and detailed hiking guides complete with maps, check out *Oahu Trails, Maui Trails, Hawaii Trails,* and *Kauai Trails* by Kathy Morey, published by Wilderness Press, 2440 Bancroft Way, Berkeley, CA 94704.

Equipment

Like everything else you take to Hawaii, your camping and hiking equipment should be lightweight and durable. Camping equipment size and weight should not cause a problem with baggage requirements on airlines: if it does, it's a tip-off that you're hauling too much. One odd piece of luggage you might bring along is a small **styrofoam cooler** packed with equipment. Exchange the equipment for food items when you get to Hawaii. If you intend to car camp successfully and keep food prices down, you'll definitely need the cooler. You can also buy one on arrival for only a few dollars. You'll need a lightweight **tent,** preferably with a rainfly and a sewn-in floor. This will save you from getting wet and miserable, and will keep out mosquitoes, cockroaches, ants, and the few stinging insects on Oahu.

Sleeping bags are a good idea, although you can get along at sea level with only a blanket. Down-filled bags are necessary for Haleakala, Mauna Kea, Mauna Loa, or any high-elevation camping—you'll freeze without one. **Campstoves** are needed because there's very little wood in some volcanic areas, it's often wet in the deep forest, and open fires are often prohibited. If you'll be car-camping, take along a multiburner stove; for trekking, a backpacker's stove will be necessary. The grills found at some campgrounds are popular with many families who go often to the beach parks for open-air dinners. You can buy a very inexpensive charcoal grill at many variety stores throughout Hawaii.

It's a great idea to take along a **lantern.** This will add safety to car-camping. Definitely take a **flashlight,** replacement batteries, and a few small **candles.** A complete **first-aid kit** can be the difference between life and death, and is worth the extra bulk. Hikers, especially those leaving the coastal areas, should take **rain gear,** plastic ground cloth, utility knife, compass, safety whistle, mess kit, water purification tablets, canteen, nylon twine, and waterproof matches. You can find plenty of stores that sell, and a few stores that rent, camping equipment; see "Camping Equipment" in the *Yellow Pages* and "Shopping" in the following travel chapters.

Safety

There are two things in Hawaii you must keep your eye on to remain safe: humans and nature. The general rule is: the farther you get away from towns, the safer you'll be from human-induced hassles. If possible, don't hike or camp alone, especially if you're a woman. Don't leave your valuables in your tent, and always carry your money, papers, and camera with you. (See "Theft and Hassles" under "Health and Safety" later in this chapter.) Don't tempt the locals by being overly friendly or unfriendly, and make yourself scarce if they're drinking. While hiking, remember many trails are well maintained, but trailhead markers are often missing. The trails themselves can be muddy, which can make them treacherously slippery and oftentimes knee-deep. Always bring food because you cannot, in most cases, forage from the land. Water in most streams is biologically polluted and will give you bad stomach problems if you drink it without purifying it first, either through boiling or with tablets. For your part, please don't use the streams as a toilet.

Precautions

Always tell a ranger or official of your hiking intentions. Supply an itinerary and your expected route, then stick to it. Twilight is short in the islands, and night sets in rapidly. In June sunrise and sunset are around 6 a.m. and 7 p.m., in December they occur at 7 a.m. and 6 p.m. If lost, walk on ridges and avoid the gulches, which have more obstacles and make it harder for rescuers to spot you. If you become lost at night, stay put, light a fire if possible, and keep as dry as you can.

Hawaii is made of volcanic rock which is brittle and crumbly. Never attempt to climb steep *pali* (cliffs). Every year people are stranded and fatalities occur on the *pali*. Be careful of elevation sickness, especially on Haleakala, Mauna Loa, and Mauna Kea. The best cure is to head down as soon as possible.

Heat can cause you to lose water and salt. If you become woozy or weak, rest, take salt, and drink water as you need it. Remember, it takes much more water to restore a dehydrated person than to keep hydrated; take small frequent sips. Be mindful of flash floods. Small creeks can turn into raging torrents with upland rains. Never camp in a dry creekbed. Fog is only encountered at the 1,500- to 5,000-foot level, but be careful of disorientation. Generally, stay within your limits, be careful, and enjoy yourself.

Topographical And Nautical Charts

For in-depth topographical maps, write **U.S. Geological Survey,** Federal Center, Denver, CO 80225. In Hawaii, a wide range of topographical maps can be purchased at **Trans-Pacific Instrument Co.,** 1406 Colburn St., Honolulu, HI 96817, tel. (808) 841-7538. For nautical charts, write **National Ocean Service,** 6501 Lafayette Ave., Riverdale, MD 20737-1199, tel. (301) 436-6990.

SUE STRANGIO EVERETT

FESTIVALS, HOLIDAYS, AND EVENTS

In addition to all the American national holidays, Hawaii celebrates its own festivals, pageants, and ethnic fairs, and puts on a multitude of specialized exhibits. They occur throughout the year, some particular to only one island or locality, while others such as Aloha Week and Lei Day are celebrated on all the islands. Some of the smaller local happenings are semi-spontaneous, so there's no *exact* date when they're held. These are some of the most rewarding, because they provide the best times to have fun with the local people. At festival time, everyone is welcome. Check local newspapers and the free island magazines for exact dates of events.

JANUARY

Early January

Start the New Year off right by climbing to the top of Koko Crater on Oahu for a ***Hauoli Makahiki Hou,*** a great way to focus on the horizons of the coming year and a great hangover remedy. Check with HVB for details. Or, continue the party with the **Sunshine Music Festival** rock concert at Diamond Head Crater.

Thump in the New Year with a traditional Japanese **Mochi Pounding Festival** at Volcano Art Center, Volcanoes National Park, Hawaii.

January Sports

January's first Saturday brings the **Hula Bowl Game** to Aloha Stadium, Honolulu. This annual game is a college all-star football classic. Call Aloha Stadium, tel. (808) 488-7731 for details.

The **Molokai Challenge,** a new biathlon, is held along Molokai's amazing north coast. Watch a three-mile run and a kayak race against time and the power of the sea.

The **Kauai Loves You Triathlon** is at lovely Hanalei Bay, Kauai. Amateurs and professionals are welcome. Covered by CBS, it can occur in December.

Athletes gear up with the Big Island **Triathlon Invitational** held in late December or early January. This three-day event ranges all over the island and includes an overnight stay at Volcanoes National Park.

Over a thousand runners participate in **The Volcano Wilderness Marathon and Rim Runs.** The truly energetic run 26 miles through the Big Island's desolate Kau Desert and 10 miles around the crater rim.

The grueling **Maui Triathlon,** Kaanapali, Maui, is a very competitive sporting event with world-class athletes running for top prizes.

NFL Pro Bowl at Aloha Stadium, Honolulu, is the annual all-star football game offering the best from both conferences. Call Aloha Stadium, tel. (808) 488-7731, for details.

Late January
Robert Burns Night at the Ilikai Hotel, Honolulu, is when local and visiting Scots from Canada and the Mainland celebrate the birthday of Scotland's poet Robert Burns.

The **Cherry Blossom Festival** in Honolulu can begin in late January and last through March. The fun includes a Japanese cultural and trade show, tea ceremony, flower arranging, queen pageant, and coronation ball. Check newspapers and free tourist magazines for dates and times of various Japanese cultural events.

The Narcissus Festival in Honolulu's Chinatown starts with the parade and festivities of Chinese New Year, which can be anytime from mid-January to early February. The city sparkles with lion dances in the street, fireworks, a beauty pageant, and a coronation ball.

FEBRUARY

Early February
The **Punahou School Carnival,** in Honolulu, with its arts, crafts, and a huge rummage sale, is held at one of Hawaii's oldest and most prestigious high schools. Great ethnic foods, and you'd be surprised at what Hawaii's oldest and most established families donate to the rummage sale.

The **Hawaiian Open International Golf Tournament** tees off in Honolulu at the exclusive Waialae Country Club. A king's ransom in prize money lures the best PGA golfers to this tournament, which is beginning its second decade.

February offers everything from the links to skiing at the **Mauna Kea Ski Meet** atop the Big Island's 13,000-foot volcano—weather and snow conditions dictate the exact time, which can vary from early January to March. Skiers from around the world compete in downhill and cross-country events.

Mid To Late February
The **Carole Kai Bed Race** is a fund-raising race of crazies pushing decorated beds down Front Street in Lahaina, Maui, and at the Kukui Grove Center in Lihue, Kauai. It's also held in Honolulu in early March.

The **Haleiwa Sea Spree** on Oahu's North Shore is a four-day, action-packed event with surfing championships, outrigger canoe races, and ancient Hawaiian sports. An around-the-island bicycle race tops it off.

Enjoy the authentic Western flavor of the **Great Waikoloa Horse Races and Rodeo** at Waikoloa Stables, Waikoloa, Hawaii. Major rodeo events draw skilled *paniolo* from around the islands.

The **Annual Keauhou-Kona Triathlon** at Keauhou Bay, Big Island, equals half the Ironman World Triathlon Championship requirements. Open to athletes unable to enter the Ironman and anyone in good health, it allows relay team racing for the grueling events.

The **Captain Cook Festival** is held at Waimea, Kauai, the spot where the intrepid Pacific explorer first made contact. Food, entertainment, and a partial marathon add to the fun.

Buffalo's Annual Big Board Surfing Classic at Makaha Beach, Oahu, features the best of the classic board riders along with an authentic cultural event complete with entertainment, crafts, and food. The two-day competitions are held the last weekend in February and again on the first weekend in March.

MARCH

Early March brings the **Annual Maui Marathon** along island roads from Wailuku to Lahaina, Maui. For information contact the Valley Isle Road Runners at tel. (808) 242-6042.

The **Kukini Run** follows an ancient trail through Kahakuloa Valley on Maui's northwest coast.

The **Carole Kai Bed Race** heads down Kalakaua Avenue in Waikiki. A free concert is given at the Waikiki Shell the night before. Appearances by Hawaii's name entertainers are part of this fun-filled charity fund-raiser.

Mid-March rumbles in with the **Kona Stampede** at Honaunau Arena, Honaunau, Kona,

Hawaii. *Paniolo* provide plenty of action during the full range of rodeo events.

The more *genteel* **Polo Season** starts in March and lasts until September. International teams come to Dillingham Field, Mokuleia, Oahu, for the competition.

Bagpipes herald late March at the **Hawaiian Highland Gathering,** Richardson's Field, Pearl Harbor, Oahu. Clans gather for Scottish games, competitions, ethnic foods, highland dancing, and pipe bands. Enjoy Scotsmen in kilts and lei too.

Music And Dance
The **Hawaiian Song Festival and Song Composing Contest** at Kapiolani Park Bandstand in Waikiki determines the year's best Hawaiian song and attracts top-name entertainers.

Honolulu's **Emerald Ball** is an elegant affair sponsored by the Society of the Friendly Sons of St. Patrick and features dinner and dancing to a big-name band. At this time the St. Patrick's Day Parade winds along Kalakaua Ave. in Waikiki.

Competition among secondary-school students of Hawaiian ancestry marks the **Kamehameha Schools Annual Song Contest** held at the Blaisdell Center Arena, Honolulu. For information call Kamehameha Schools at tel. (808) 842-8211.

March For Women
Mid-month features feminine beauty, grace, and athletic ability at the **Miss Maui Pageant** at Baldwin High School, Wailuku, Maui; **Miss Kauai Pageant** at Kauai War Memorial Convention Hall, Lihue, Kauai; and **Miss Aloha Hawaii Pageant** at Hilo Civic Auditorium, Hilo, Hawaii.

The prestigious **LPGA Women's Kemper Open** chooses one of the islands' best golf courses for this annual event that features the Helene Curtis Pro-Am, and draws the world's best women golfers.

March For The Prince
The end of March is dedicated to Prince Kuhio, a member of the royal family and Hawaii's first delegate to the U.S. Congress. **Prince Kuhio Day** is a state holiday honoring Hawaii's Prince Kuhio held on March 26, his birthday. Celebrations are held at the Prince Kuhio Federal Building, Oahu.

The **Prince Kuhio Festival** at Lihue, Kauai, features festivities from the era of Prince Kuhio along with canoe races and a royal ball.

The **Prince Kuhio Rodeo** is held at Po'oku Stables, in Princeville, Kauai.

APRIL

Easter Sunday's **Sunrise Service** at the National Memorial Cemetery of The Pacific, Punchbowl Crater, Honolulu, is a moving ceremony that shouldn't be missed if you're in the islands at that time.

The **Annual Hawaiian Festival of Music** at Waikiki Shell, Honolulu, is a grand and lively music competition of groups from all over the islands and the mainland. This music-lovers' smorgasbord offers everything from symphony to swing and all beats in between.

Wesak or Buddha Day is on the closest Sunday to April 8, and celebrates the birthday of Gautama Buddha. Ornate offerings of tropical flowers are placed at temple altars throughout Hawaii. Enjoy the sunrise ceremonies at Kapiolani Park, Honolulu, with Japanese in their best *kimonos* along with flower festivals, pageants, and dance programs in many island temples.

Mid To Late April
The **Aloha Basketball Classic** at the Blaisdell Center Arena, Honolulu, brings top college seniors who are invited to Hawaii to participate in charity games made up of four teams. Contact Blaisdell Center, tel. (808) 527-5400.

The **Paniolo Ski Meet** is exciting skiing atop the Big Island's Mauna Kea, conditions permitting.

The **Merrie Monarch Festival** in Hilo sways with the best hula dancers that the islands' *hula halau* have to offer. Gentle but stiff competition features both ancient and modern dances. The festival runs for a week on a variable schedule from year to year. It's immensely popular with islanders, and hotels, cars, and flights are booked solid.

The **Kona Sports Festival** in Kailua-Kona, Hawaii, is a solid week of sports entertainment and frivolity held toward the end of the month.

MAY

Early May

May 1 is May Day to the communist world, but in Hawaii red is only one of the colors when everyone dons a lei for **Lei Day.** Festivities abound throughout Hawaii, but there are special goings-on at Kapiolani Park, Waikiki.

The **Captain Cook Festival** at Kailua-Kona offers Hawaiian games, music, and fishing.

Costumed pageants, canoe races, and a beard-judging contest commemorate times past at the **Lahaina Whaling Spree,** Lahaina, Maui.

The **Pacific Handcrafters Guild Fair** at Ala Moana Park, Honolulu, is a perfect opportunity to see the "state of the arts" in Hawaii when the islands' best artists gather in one spot to sell their creations.

Look skyward on May 5, **Japanese Boys' Day,** and you'll see paper carp (koi) flying from rooftops. Carp symbolize the virtues of strength and courage. The number of koi kites corresponds to the number of sons in the family, with the largest on top for the eldest, and so on down the line.

Mid To Late May

Armed Forces Week brings military open houses, concerts, and displays in and around the islands. Hawaii is the most militarized state in the U.S. and this fact becomes obvious. Call Military Relations, tel. (808) 438-9761, for details.

Filipino Fiesta is a month-long celebration of the islands' Filipino population. Food, various festivities, and a beauty contest are part of the fiesta.

Costumed riders from the annals of Hawaiian history ride again at **Hawaii on Horseback.** Horsemanship and a Western flair mark these days held in and around Waimea and the Parker Ranch on the Big Island.

Annual Western Week at Honokaa on the Big Island is a fun-filled week with a Western theme. It includes a cookout, parade, rodeo, and dance.

Memorial Day in Hawaii is special with military services held at Honolulu's National Memorial Cemetery of the Pacific on the last Monday in May.

Agricultural exhibits, down-home cooking, entertainment, and fresh produce are presented for four weekends starting in late May at the **50th State Fair,** at Aloha Stadium, Honolulu, tel. (808) 536-5492.

JUNE

Early June

The **Kauai County Fair** at the Kauai War Memorial Convention Hall, Lihue, is a typical county fair offering the best in agriculture that the island has to offer.

Hawaii's best artists and craftspeople come to the **Mission Houses Museum Fancy Fair** in Honolulu. Browse while enjoying homemade food and entertainment. Call (808) 531-0481 for details.

King Kamehameha Day

June 11 is a state holiday honoring Kamehameha the Great, with festivities on all islands. Check local papers for times and particulars. The following are the main events: Oahu holds a lei-draping ceremony at the King Kamehameha statue at the Civic Center in downtown Honolulu, along with parades complete with floats and pageantry featuring a *ho'olaule'a* (street party) in Waikiki; Kailua-Kona on the Big Island is hospitable with a *ho'olaule'a,* parades, art demonstrations, entertainment, and contests; on Kauai enjoy parades, *ho'olaule'a,* arts, and crafts centered around the Kauai County Building; Maui's Lahaina and Kahului are decked out for parades and pageants. Also, the Kamehameha Day Invitational Archery Tournament is held at the Kahului Armory and Valley Isle Archers Field Range.

The **Kamehameha Ski Meet** is in early June when bikini-clad contestants add a little extra spice on those moguls.

Mid To Late June

The Brigham Young University at Laie, Oahu, swings with the **Annual King Kamehameha Traditional Hula and Chant Competition.**

The **Annual Upcountry Fun Fair** at the Eddie Tam Center, Makawao, Maui, is an old-fashioned farm fair right in the heart of Maui's *paniolo* country. Crafts, food, and competitions are part of the fair.

The **Annual Hawaiian Festival Of Music** at the Waikiki Shell, Honolulu, is a repeat of the

April festivities but no less of a music-lovers' delight, as competing local and Mainland bands play everything from symphony to swing.

Hilo, Hawaii, flashes its brilliant colors with the **Annual Hilo Orchid Society Show** at the Hilo Civic Auditorium, and the **Annual Big Island Bonsai Show,** Wailoa Center, Hilo (both sometimes scheduled for early July).

Dancing is part of the **Annual Japan Festival** in Honolulu at Kapiolani Park and the Blaisdell Center. Also, ***Bon Odori,*** the Japanese festival of departed souls, featuring dances and candle-lighting ceremonies, is held at numerous Buddhist temples throughout the islands. A special *bon odori* festival is offered at Haleiwa Jodo Mission, Haleiwa, Oahu. These festivities change yearly and can be held anytime from late June to early August.

JULY

The week of the **Fourth of July** offers the all-American sport of rodeo along with parades on every island. Don't miss the following if possible: **July Fourth Parker Ranch Rodeo And Horse Races,** Paniolo Park, Waimea, Hawaii. The epitome of rodeo by Hawaii's top cowboys. The setting is the Parker Ranch, the largest privately owned ranch in all of America, including Texas, *pardner!*

The **Annual Naalehu Rodeo,** Naalehu, Hawaii, offers rodeo events, motorcycle and dune buggy races, luau, food booths, and Hawaiian entertainment.

Makawao Statewide Rodeo at the Oskie Rice Arena, Makawao, Maui, is an old-time upcountry rodeo that can't be beat for fun and entertainment anywhere in the country.

The **Hawaiian Islands Tall Ships Parade** floats off Oahu on the Fourth of July. Tall-masted ships from throughout the islands parade from Koko Head to Sand Island and back to Diamond Head. A rare treat and taste of days gone by.

July Sports

Sporting events throughout July feature races and competitions both on land and at sea. The **Big Island Marathon** in Hilo is a full and half marathon starting and ending at the Hilo Hawaiian Hotel.

The **Tin Man Triathlon,** Honolulu, gathers over 1,000 triathletes to swim 800 meters, bike 25 miles, and finish with a 10,000-meter (6.2-mile) run around Diamond Head and back to Kapiolani Park in Waikiki.

Run To The Sun from Kahului, Maui, is a grueling 37.5-mile ultra-marathon from sea level to Maui's 10,000-foot Haleakala. Held in June or August.

The **Annual Pan Am Windsurfing Pacific Cup** is held at various beaches around Oahu, determined by wind conditions.

Boats from ports around the world sail to Oahu for the **Pan Am Clipper Cup Series.** They navigate a series of triangles off Waikiki, along with one nonstop race from Ala Wai Harbor to Molokai, and an around-the-state nonstop race.

The **Trans Pacific Race** from Los Angeles to Honolulu sails during odd-numbered years. Yachties arrive throughout the month and converge on Ala Wai Yacht basin, where "party" is the password. They head off for Hanalei Bay, Kauai, to begin the year's yachting season.

Four-person teams of one pro and three amateurs compete in the 54-hole **Mauna Kea Beach Hotel's Annual Pro-Am Golf Tournament** held at the hotel links along the Big Island's Kohala Coast.

Mid To Late July

The **International Festival Of The Pacific** in mid-July features a "Pageant of Nations" in Hilo. Folk dances, complete with authentic costumes from throughout Asia and the Pacific, add a rare excitement to the festivities. Contact the Japanese Chamber of Commerce, tel. (808) 961-6123, for details.

The **Prince Lot Hula Festival** in Honolulu is a great chance for visitors to see "authentic" hula from some of the finest *hula halau* in the islands. Held at Moanalua Gardens, tel. (808) 839-5334.

Hundreds of ukulele players from throughout the islands come to Waikiki's Kapiolani Park Bandstand for the **Annual Ukulele Festival.**

Take the opportunity to see the "state of the arts" all in one locality. Browse, buy, and eat ethnic foods at various stalls of the **Pacific Handcrafters Fair** at Thomas Square, Honolulu.

The beauty and grace of one of Hawaii's ethnic groups is apparent at the **Miss Hawaii Filipina Pageant,** Naniloa Hotel, Hilo.

The **Annual Honomu Village Fair,** Honomu, Hawaii, starts with a 46-mile Volcano-to-Honomu team relay race followed by mountainball and volleyball. There's plenty of local foods, and arts and crafts.

AUGUST

Early August
Honolulu Zoo Day in Waikiki is a day of family fun when "kids" of all ages get an up-close look at the animals, along with a full day of entertainment.

The **Annual Hanalei Stampede** is held at the Po'oku Stables, Princeville, Kauai.

Recent hula graduates from Honolulu's Summer Fun classes perform at the **Hula Festival,** Kapiolani Park, Waikiki. Dancers of all ages, shapes, and sizes perform some amazing bodily gyrations.

Chamber music by nationally acclaimed artists fills the Kapalua Bay Hotel on Maui for the **Kapalua Music Festival,** one of Hawaii's few formal occasions.

The first August weekend is **Establishment Day,** with traditional hula and lei workshops presented at the Big Island's Pu'ukohola Heiau, where traditional artifacts are also on display.

Mid-August
The **Kona Hawaiian Billfish Tournament** in the waters off Kona, Hawaii, brings American teams seeking entry to the **Annual Hawaiian International Billfish Tournament,** held about one week later.

Hula, artifacts, workshops in lei-making, Hawaiian language, and other ancient skills are the focus of **Establishment Day** at Pu'ukohola Heiau on the Big Island. The day is extremely educational and packed with family fun. Puukohala Heiau, tel. (808) 882-7218.

The macadamia nut harvest is celebrated with sporting events, horse racing, and a "Harvest Ball" at the **Macadamia Nut Harvest festival,** Honokaa, Hawaii.

August 17 is **Admissions Day,** a state holiday recognizing the day Hawaii became a state.

Late August
The **Hawaiian Open State Tennis Championships** is held at various courts around Honolulu and offers substantial prizes.

At the **Kauai County Fair,** gardeners, stockmen, and craftspeople of the "Garden Island" display their wares at the War Memorial Center in Lihue. Pageantry, great local foods, and terrific bargains are to be had.

Terminally cute children ages 5-12 dance for the **Queen Liliuokalani Keiki Hula Competition** at the Kamehameha Schools, Honolulu.

SEPTEMBER

In early September don't miss the **Parker Ranch Round-Up Rodeo,** Paniolo Park, Waimea, Hawaii; or the **Maui County Rodeo,** Makawao, Maui.

Athletes compete in the **Waikiki Rough Water Swim,** a two-mile, open-ocean swim from Sans Souci Beach to Duke Kahanamoku Beach. Open to all ages and ability levels. Also, the **Garden Island Marathon And Half Marathon** starts at the Sheraton Hotel, Kapa'a, Kauai.

Mid-September
The **Annual Seiko Super Tennis Tournament** at Wailea, Maui, is a championship tennis competition with leading professional team players.

The **Million Dollar Golden Marlin Fishing Tournament** catches plenty of fishermen at Kailua-Kona, Hawaii.

The **Hawaii County Fair** at Hilo, Hawaii, is an old-time fair held on the grounds of Hilo Civic Auditorium.

Aloha Week
Late September brings festivities on all of the islands, as everyone celebrates Hawaii's own "intangible quality," *aloha.* There are parades, luau, historical pageants, balls, and various entertainment. The spirit of *aloha* is infectious and all are welcomed to join in. Check local papers and tourist literature for happenings near you.

The **Molokai To Oahu Canoe Race** for women (men in October) takes off at the end of September in Hawaiian-stlye canoes from a remote beach on Molokai to Fort DeRussy in

Honolulu. In crossing, the teams must navigate the always-rough Kaiwi Channel.

OCTOBER

Early October
A fall show of the best works of guild members (perfect for early-bird Christmas shopping) is featured at the **Pacific Handcrafters Guild,** Ala Moana Center Gallery, Honolulu.

The **Maui County Fair** at the fairgrounds in Kahului is the oldest in Hawaii.

The **Makahiki Festival** at Waimea Falls Park, an 800-acre tropical preserve on Oahu, features Hawaiian games, crafts, and dances reminiscent of the great *makahiki* celebrations of ancient Hawaii.

The **Molokai To Oahu Canoe Race** for men (women in September) navigates Hawaiian-style canoes across the rough Kaiwi Channel from a remote beach on Molokai to Fort DeRussy, Honolulu.

Where else would you expect to find German *oompah* bands, succulent *Wiener schnitzel und bier* than at Honolulu's **Oktoberfest?** At the Budweiser Warehouse, 99-877 Iwaena St., Halawa Park, noon-10:00 p.m.

Mid To Late October
Watch the boys from throughout Oceania smash, clash, and collide in the rough-and-tumble **Pan Am International Rugby Club Tournament** held at Queen Kapiolani Park, Honolulu, during odd-numbered years.

The **Annual Orchid Plant And Flower Show** displays Hawaii's copious and glorious flowers at the Blaisdell Center Exhibition Hall, Honolulu, tel. (808) 527-5400.

The later part of the month is a superb time to visit the world's best museum of Polynesian and Hawaiian culture during the **Bishop Museum Festival.** Arts, crafts, plants, and tours of the museum and planetarium provide a full day of fun and entertainment for the family. Bishop Museum, Honolulu, tel. (808) 847-3511.

When they really "wanna have fun," superathletes come to the **Ironman World Triathlon Championship** at Kailua-Kona, Hawaii. A 2.4-mile open-ocean swim, followed by a 112-mile bike ride and topped off by a full marathon, is their idea of a good day. For information call the Ironman office, tel. (808) 528-2050.

The **Kapalua International Championship Of Golf,** at Kapalua, Maui, is one of the best pro tournaments, drawing the world's best golfers for one of the world's largest purses. Runs through early November.

NOVEMBER

Early November
Taste the best and only coffee commercially grown in the U.S. at the **Annual Kona Coffee Festival,** Kailua-Kona, Hawaii. Parades, arts and crafts, ethnic food, and entertainment are part of the festivities.

Na Mele O'Maui Festival, Kaanapali and Lahaina, Maui, is a time when old Hawaii comes alive through art, dances, and music.

At the **Ho'olaulea in Waianae,** Waianae, Oahu, the military lets down its hair and puts on a display accompanied by top entertainers, food, and music in this very ethnic area. An all-day event; for information call Army Community Relations at (808) 438-9761.

Mid-November
Here's your chance to see polo at the **Michelob Polo Cup And Bar-B-Que,** Olinda Polo Field, Makawao, Maui.

The **Annual King Kalakaua Keiki Hula Festival** is for children from around the state who come to Kailua-Kona, Hawaii, to perform. Plenty of fun, but the competition is serious.

November 11, **Veterans Day,** is a national holiday celebrated by a large parade from Fort DeRussy to Queen Kapiolani Park, Waikiki. (However, all islands have a parade.) For information, call the American Legion, tel. (808) 949-1140.

Christmas In November
Hui Noeau Christmas Craft Fair is an annual event offering gifts, decorations, and food for hungry shoppers. Held at Kaluanui Museum, Makawao, Maui.

Christmas In The Country atop Hawaii's volcano is a delight during which merrymakers frolic in the crisp air around a blazing fire, drinking hot toddies. Plenty of arts and crafts, food, and Santa for the *keiki* (children) at Volcano Art Center, Hawaii Volcanoes National Park, Hawaii, tel. (808) 976-7676.

The **YWCA Festival Of Trees** presents Christmas crafts, ornaments, and decorated trees on display and for sale at the YMCA, Hilo, Hawaii, tel. (808) 935-7141.

Quality items are offered by Hawaii's top craftspeople in an open air bazaar at the **Annual Christmas Fair** of the Mission Houses Museum, Honolulu, tel. (808) 531-0481.

Late November

The best surfers in the world come to the best surfing beaches on Oahu for the **Hawaiian Pro-Surfing Championships.** Wave action determines sites except for the **Men's Masters,** which is always held at Banzai Pipeline, North Shore, Oahu. Big money and national TV coverage bring out the best in everyone.

The Honolulu Academy of Arts, Honolulu, tel. (808) 538-3693, showcases some of Hawaii's finest contemporary artists at its **Artists Of Hawaii Annual Exhibition.**

DECEMBER

Early December

The **Kauai Junior Miss Presentation,** Kauai War Memorial Convention Hall, Lihue, is where young hopefuls get their first taste of the "big time."

The **Hawaii International Film Festival** at the East West Center, Honolulu, screens some of the best art films from the "East," "West," and Oceania.

Christmas Celebrations

Christmas Fantasyland Of Trees at Honokaa, Hawaii, is an early showing of gaily decorated trees. The right Christmas spirit auctions them off for charity.

The **Festival Of Trees** is when the business community pitches in and offers for sale gaily decorated trees, donating the proceeds to charity. It's held at the Coco Palms Hotel Queen's Audience Hall, Lihue, Kauai.

The **Kauai Museum Holiday Festival** is an annual Christmas event known for attracting the island's best in handcrafted items and home-baked goodies. Call for information at the Kauai Museum, Lihue, Kauai, tel. (808) 245-6931.

The **Kamehameha Schools Christmas Concert** is open to everyone and lifts the Christmas spirit at the Blaisdell Center Concert Hall, Honolulu, tel. (808) 842-8211.

The open-air **Pacific Handcrafters Guild Christmas Fair,** Thomas Square, Honolulu, presents the best by the best, just in time for Christmas. Pacific Handcrafters, tel. (808) 732-4913.

Mid To Late December

The **Annual Honolulu Marathon** is an "institution" in marathon races, attracting the best runners from around the world, and includes TV coverage.

The people of Hilo celebrate a New England Christmas in memory of the missionaries with **A Christmas Tradition.** Held at the Lyman House Memorial Museum, Hilo, tel. (808) 935-5021.

A Christmas Tradition features the distinctive touches of a New England-style Christmas at the Lyman House Memorial Museum, Hilo, tel. 935-5021.

Bodhi Day is ushered in with ceremonies at Buddhist temples to commemorate Buddha's day of enlightenment on all the islands.

The **Christmas Concert** by the Kauai High School Band and Chorus performs a medley of classic, contemporary, and Hawaiian Christmas carols and tunes. At the Kauai War Memorial Convention Hall, Lihue, tel. (808) 245-6422.

On **New Year's Eve** hold onto your hat, because they do it up big in Hawaii. Merriment and alcohol flow all over the islands. Firecrackers are illegal, but they go off everywhere. Beware of hangovers and "amateur" drunken drivers.

December Sports

At the **Mauna Kea Beach Hotel's Annual Invitational Golf Tournament** men and women play at this fabulous golf course on the Kohala Coast, Hawaii.

The **Kapalua-Betsey Nagelson Tennis Invitational** is a select field of women pros and amateurs held at Kapalua, Maui, Tennis Garden.

The **Annual Rainbow Classic** is an invitational tournament of collegiate basketball teams held at Blaisdell Center Arena, Honolulu, tel. (808) 948-7523.

The **Aloha Bowl Game** is collegiate football with top teams from the Mainland coming to Aloha Stadium, Honolulu, tel. (808) 488-7731.

PERFORMING ARTS EVENTS

The following organizations offer top-notch performances at various times throughout the year: **Honolulu Symphony,** tel. (808) 537-6191; **Hawaii Opera Theatre,** tel. (808) 521-6537; **Honolulu Community Theatre,** tel. (808) 734-0274; and **Hawaii Performing Arts Company Theatre,** tel. (808) 988-6131.

Ticketing

The Connection, a computerized ticketing service, open 24 hours, tel. (808) 945-2867 or (800) 333-3388, handles all kinds of event ticketing for concerts, sporting events, theater performances, visiting Broadway plays, and most family attractions. You can call before you arrive in Hawaii and the tickets will be waiting for you at the venue's "Will Call Window." The Connection also has outlets at all JR Music and House of Music stores on Oahu and Maui. Payment is by cash or major credit card.

yellow ginger

BOB RACE

ARTS AND CRAFTS

Referring to Hawaii as "paradise" is about as hackneyed as you can get, but when you combine it into "artists' paradise" it's the absolute truth. Something about the place evokes art (or at least personal expression) from most people. The islands are like a magnet: they not only draw artists to them, but they draw art *from* the artists. The list of literary figures who visited Hawaii and had something inspirational to say reads like a freshman survey in literature: William Henry Dana, Herman Melville, Mark Twain, Robert Louis Stevenson, Jack London, Somerset Maugham, Joaquin Miller, and of course, James Michener.

The inspiration comes from the astounding natural surroundings. The land is so beautiful yet so raw; the ocean's power and rhythm are primal and ever-present; the riotous colors of flowers and fruit leap from the deep-green jungle background. Crystal water beads and pale mists turn the mountains into mystic temples, while rainbows ride the crests of waves. The stunning variety of faces begging to be rendered suggests that all the world sent delegations to the islands. And in most cases it did! Inspiration is everywhere, as is art, good or bad.

Sometimes the artwork is overpowering in itself and in its sheer volume. Though geared to the tourist's market of cheap souvenirs, there is hardly a shop in Hawaii that doesn't sell some item that falls into the general category of "art." You can find everything from carved monkey-face coconut shells to true masterpieces. The Polynesian Hawaiians were master craftspeople, and their legacy still lives in a wide variety of woodcarvings, basketry, and weavings. The hula is art in swaying motion, and the true form is rigorously studied and taken very seriously. There is hardly a resort area that doesn't offer the "bump and grind" tourist's hula, and even these revues are accompanied by proficient local musicians. Nightclubs offer "slack key" balladeers; island music performed on ukuleles and on Hawaii's own steel guitars spills from many lounges.

Vibrant fabrics that catch the spirit of the islands are rendered into muumuu and aloha shirts at countless local factories. They're almost a mandatory purchase! Pottery, heavily influenced by the Japanese, is a well-developed craft at numerous kilns. Local artisans fashion delicate jewelry from coral and olivine, while some ply the whaler's legacy of etching on ivory, called scrimshaw. There are fine traditions of quilting, flower art in lei, and street artists working in everything from airbrush to glass. The following is an overview; for local offerings please see "Shopping" in the travel chapters.

ARTS OF OLD HAWAII

Since everything in old Hawaii had to be fashioned by hand, almost every object was either a work of art or at least a highly refined craft. With the "civilizing" of the natives, most of the "old ways" disappeared, including the old arts and crafts. Most authentic Hawaiian art exists only in museums, but with the resurgence of Hawaiian roots, many old arts are being revitalized, and a few artists are becoming proficient.

Magnificent Canoes

The most respected artisans in old Hawaii were the canoe makers. With little more than a stone adze and a pump drill, they built canoes that could carry 200 people and last for generations—sleek, well proportioned, and infinitely seaworthy. The main hull was usually a gigantic koa log, and the gunwale planks were minutely drilled and sewn to the sides with sennit rope. Apprenticeships lasted for years, and a young man knew that he had graduated when one day he was nonchalantly asked to sit down and eat with the master builders. Small family-sized canoes with outriggers were used for fishing and perhaps carried a spear rack; large oceangoing double-hulled canoes were used for migration and warfare. On these, the giant logs had been adzed to about two inches thick. A mainsail woven from pandanus was mounted on a central platform, and the boat was steered by two long paddles. The hull was dyed with plant juices and charcoal, and the entire village helped launch the canoe in a ceremony called "drinking the sea."

Carving And Weaving

Wood was a primary material, and craftspeople turned out well-proportioned and distinctive calabashes made mostly from koa. Their luster and intricate grain were brought out with hand rubbing. Temple idols were a major product of woodcarving. A variety of stone artifacts was turned out, including poi pounders, mirrors, fish sinkers, and small idols.

Hawaiians became the *best* basket makers and mat weavers in all of Polynesia. *Ulana* (mats) were made from *lau hala* (pandanus) leaves. Once split, the spine was removed and the leaves stored in large rolls. When needed they were soaked, pounded, and then fashioned into various floor coverings and sleeping mats. Intricate geometrical pattterns were woven in, and the edges were rolled and well fashioned. Coconut palms were not used to make mats in old Hawaii, but a wide variety of basketry was made from the aerial root *'ie'ie.* The shapes varied according to use. Some baskets were tall and narrow, some were cones, others were flat like trays, while many were woven around gourds and calabashes.

A strong tradition of weaving and carving has survived in Hawaii, and the time-tested material of *lau hala* is still the best, although much is now made from coconut fronds. You can purchase anything from beach mats to a woven hat, and all share the desirable qualities of strength, lightness, and air flow.

Featherwork

This highly refined art was found only on the islands of Tahiti, New Zealand, and Hawaii, while the fashioning of feather helmets and idols was unique to Hawaii alone. Favorite colors were red and yellow, which came only in a very limited number on a few

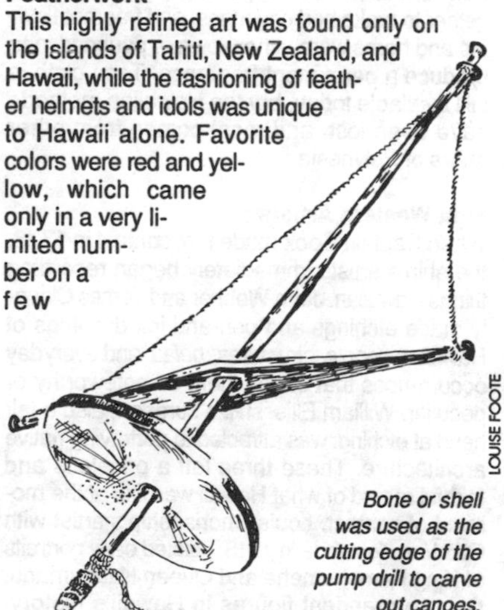

Bone or shell was used as the cutting edge of the pump drill to carve out canoes.

birds such as the *'o'o, 'i'iwi, mamo,* and *apapane.* Professional bird hunters in old Hawaii paid their taxes to *ali'i* in prized feathers. The feathers were fastened to a woven net of *olona* cord and made into helmets, idols, and beautiful flowing capes and cloaks. These resplendent garments were made and worn only by men, especially during battle when a fine cloak became a great trophy of war. Featherwork was also employed in the making of *kahili* and lei which were highly prized by the noble *ali'i* women.

The ali'i *wore magnificent feathered capes that signified their rank.*

Tapa Cloth

Tapa, cloth made from tree bark, was common throughout Polynesia and was a woman's art. A few trees such as the *wauke* and *mamaki* produced the best cloth, but a variety of other bark types could be utilized. First the raw bark was pounded into a feltlike pulp and beaten together to form strips. The beaters had distinctive patterns that also helped make the cloth supple. The strips were then decorated by stamping, using a form of block printing, and dyed with natural colors from plants and sea animals in shades of gray, purple, pink, and red. They were even painted with natural brushes made from pandanus fruit, with an overall gray color made from charcoal. The tapa cloth was sewn together to make bed coverings, and fragrant flowers and herbs were either sewn or pounded in to produce a permanent fragrance. Tapa cloth is still available today, but the Hawaiian methods have been lost, and most comes from other areas of Polynesia.

First Western Artists

When Captain Cook made first contact in 1778, the ship's artists immediately began recording things Hawaiian. John Webber and James Cleveley made etchings and pen-and-ink drawings of Hawaiian people, structures, *heiau,* and everyday occurrences that struck them as noteworthy or peculiar. William Ellis, ship's surgeon, also a fair hand at etching, was attracted to portraying native architecture. These three left a priceless and faithful record of what Hawaii was like at the moment of contact. Louis Choris, ship's artist with Otto Von Kotzebue in 1816, painted early portraits of King Kamehameha and Queen Kaahumanu, the two grandest figures in Hawaii's history. Jacques Arago, aboard the *Uranie* with the French Captain de Freycinet in 1819, recorded some gruesome customs of punishment of *kapu* breakers, and made many drawings of island people. Robert Dampier, who sailed on the *Blonde,* the ship that returned King Liholiho's body from England, recorded one of the earliest landscapes of Honolulu, a site which has continued to be depicted more on film by tourists than almost any other city on earth. These early artists set a trend that continues unabated to this day; artists endeavor to "capture" Hawaii, and they do so with every artistic medium available.

Modern Masters

Countless artists working at all levels of accomplishment try to match their skills to the vigor and beauty of the islands. Some have set the standards, and their names have become synonymous with Hawaiian art. Heading this list of luminaries are Huc Luquiens, Madge Tennent, Tadashi Sato, Jean Charlot, and John Kelly.

Madge Tennent (1889-1972) was an Englishwoman who came to Hawaii via Samoa after spending years in South Africa and New Zealand. She worked in oils that she applied liberally and in bold strokes. Enamored with the people of Hawaii, her portraits are of a race striking in appearance and noble in character. Her works, along with those of other island artists, are displayed at the Tennent Art Foundation, on the slopes of Punchbowl on Oahu.

Huc Luquiens, former chair of the art department at the University of Hawaii, was a master at etching, and was especially accomplished in drypoint. His works, mainly island landscapes, are displayed in the Hawaiiana Collection of the Honolulu Academy of Arts.

Maui-born Tadashi Sato, a superbly accomplished muralist, has produced such famous mosaics as the 30-foot "Aquarius" at the state capitol in Honolulu, and the 60-foot "Portals of Immortality" at the Maui Memorial Gymnasium in Lahaina.

Frenchman Jean Charlot perfected his mural art in Mexico before coming to Hawaii in 1949. He is renowned for his frescoes and became a well-known art critic and the grand old man of Hawaiian art. He died in 1979 at the ripe old age of 90. John M. Kelly was in love with Hawaiian women; his etchings of them are both inspired and technically flawless. Kelly was infinitely patient, rendering his subjects in the minutest detail.

These artists are the "Big Five of Hawaiian Art"; their accomplishments a gauge of what Hawaii can inspire in an artist. By observing their works you can get an instant art course and a comparative view of the state of the arts in Hawaii.

Contemporary Artists

The crop of new artists making their mark always seems bounteous and their works, heavily influenced by the "feeling of Hawaii," continue to be superb. Every island has art galleries, co-ops, or unofficial art centers. One of the finest groups of island artists can be found at the **Sunday Art Mart,** which recently changed its official name to **Artists of Oahu, Sunday Exhibit.** It's located along the "fence" of the Honolulu Zoo fronting Kapiolani Park. These artists, along with others around the islands, will be discussed in their respective travel chapters, so check. The following list of artists, with a short description of their work, is by no means exhaustive. It merely shows the wide range of artwork available.

Richard Fields, a former Californian, now lives on Maui. The fascinating beauty of the *aina* is the inspiration for his suprarealistic paintings of birds, mountains, clouds, flowers, and waterfalls. Richard creates his rich renditions using a mixed media of airbrush, acrylic, india ink, and stencils. His works are as striking and as inspiring as the ever-changing beauty of the islands.

Roy Tabora specializes in dramatic seascapes of windwhipped palm trees and crashing surf illuminated by glorious sunsets. His work is a dramatic crescendo of sea, surf, and spirit, entwined to capture the awesome power that is Hawaii.

George Sumner paints surrealistic yet superreal renderings of dolphins hovering in the stratosphere. One painting depicts two magnificent gulls winging their way past a mythical Hawaiian waterfall along a silhouetted *pali.*

James Hoyle, a longtime Kauai resident, captures the spirit of Hawaii through color and movement. His media are oil, pastel, and polymer that he applies on canvas in a distinctive style of macro-pointillism. Each daub, like a melted jelly bean, is a fantastic deep purple, orange, magenta, yellow, or green. The result is a blazing sunset swirling with color backlighting a tortured lava mountain that broods over a tiny pool of water speckled with green taro. The sense that permeates all of Hoyle's work is that in humankind cannot conquer nature, but must learn to live in harmony with the *aina* which is very much alive.

A minute down the road from Hoyle's studio is the **Lele Aka Studio and Gallery,** wild with fantastic demons rising from the sea, and goddesses with silvery moonbeams emanating from their foreheads. In stark contrast, portraits depict the lovely bright faces of Kauai's children.

Robert Nelson is a Maui artist who superbly transmits the integrated mystical life of land and sea. His watercolors are often diffused with the strange filtered light found beneath the waves. A conservationist, he has often depicted the gentle frolicking life of the whales that visit Hawaiian waters.

Bill Christian is a master of scrimshaw, which he renders on slate. He also produces fine oil paintings of the sea and old salts. A world-class artist, he has had his works displayed at art galleries on Maui as well as at the Smithsonian and at the New Bedford Massachusetts Whaling Museum.

Pegge Hopper is often compared with Madge Tennent. She works in bold colors and strokes. Her subject matter is islanders, especially the delicacy and inner strength of women. Her works are displayed at various galleries, particularly on Maui and Oahu, and are often available in limited-edition serigraphs.

John Costello, an Oahu artist, specializes in pointillism to capture the waves, women, and flora of Hawaii in a sensitive and mystical way. He co-owns and operates Kaala Art and Rainbow Island T's with his brother Jim in Haleiwa on North Shore Oahu. John's work as well as that of local artists is showcased in their small shop.

Alapai Hanapi is a traditionalist sculptor re-creates the motifs of his Hawaiian ancestors. He works in wood and stone with tools that he fashions himself. His driving force is cultural awareness and through his art he tells of the old ways. He lives with his wife and three daughters near an old fishpond on eastern Molokai. His work is known for its simplicity and is available at art shows periodically held throughout the islands.

Al Furtado is a freelance artist working in Honolulu. He specializes in capturing the movement of Hawaiian dance. His depictions are often larger than life, with a strong sense of vitality and motion.

Daniel Wang was born in Shanghai, where he learned the art of Chinese watercolors. Although born deaf and mute, he speaks loudly, clearly, and beautifully through his art. Daniel has a special technique in which the palm of his hand becomes his artistic tool. He can transmit intense inner emotions directly from his body to the canvas.

The following is a potpourri of distinguished artists displayed at various galleries around the islands. Any work bearing their name is authentic island art considered superior by fellow artists. William Waterfall, photographer; Satoru Abe, sculptor; Ruthadell Anderson, weaver; Betty Tseng Yu-ho Ecke, *dsui* painter; Claude Horan, sculptor, ceramics; Erica Karawina, stained glass; Ron Kowalke, painter; Ben Norris, painter; Louis Pohl, printmaker; Mamoru Sato, sculptor; Tadashi Sato, painter; Reuben Tam, painter; Jean Williams, weaver; John Wisnosky, painter; and John Young, painter.

Hawaiian Maiden *by John Costello*

ARTS TO BUY

Wild Hawaiian shirts or bright muumuu, especially when worn on the Mainland, have the magical effect of making wearers "feel" like they're in Hawaii, while at the same time eliciting spontaneous smiles from passersby. Maybe it's the colors, or perhaps it's the "vibe" that signifies "party time" or "hang loose," but nothing says Hawaii like alohawear does. There are more than a dozen fabric houses in Hawaii turning out distinctive patterns, and many dozens of factories creating their own personalized designs. Oftentimes these factories have attached retail outlets, but in any case you can find hundreds of shops selling alohawear. Aloha shirts were the brilliant idea of a Chinese merchant in Honolulu, who used to hand-tailor them and sell them to the tourists who arrived by ship in the glory days before WW II. They were an instant success. Muumuu or "Mother Hubbards" were the idea of missionaries, who were appalled by Hawaiian women running about au naturel and insisted on covering their new Christian converts from head to foot. Now the roles are reversed, and it's Mainlanders who come to Hawaii and immediately strip down to as little clothing as possible.

Alohawear

At one time exclusively made of cotton, or from manmade yet naturally based rayon, tropical clothing is best when made of these traditional materials. Beware, however: polyester has slowly crept into the market. No material could possibly be worse than polyester for the island climate, so when buying your alohawear make sure to check the label for material content. Muumuu now come in a variety of styles and can be worn for the entire spectrum of social occasions in Hawaii. Aloha shirts are still basically cut the same as always, but the patterns have undergone changes, and apart from the original flowers and ferns, modern shirts might depict an island scene, giving the impression of a silkscreen painting. A basic good-quality muumuu or aloha shirt starts at about $25 and is guaranteed to be worth its price in good times and happy smiles. The connoisseur might want to purchase *The Hawaiian Shirt, Its Art and History,* by R. Thomas Steele. It's illustrated with more than 150 shirts that are now considered works of art by collectors the world over.

Scrimshaw

This art of etching and carving on bone and ivory has become an island tradition handed down from the times of the old whaling ships. Although scrimshaw can be found throughout Hawaii, the center remains in the old whaling capital of Lahaina. Along Front Street are numerous shops specializing in scrimshaw. Today, pieces are carved on fossilized walrus ivory gathered by Inuit and shipped to Hawaii. The ivory comes in a variety of shades from pure white to mocha, depending upon the mineral content of the earth in which it was buried. Elephant ivory or whale bone is no longer used because of ecological considerations, but there is a "gray market" in Pacific walrus tusks. Inuit can legally hunt the walrus. They then make a few minimal scratches on the tusks which technically qualifies them as "Native American art" and free of most governmental restrictions. The tusks are then sent to Hawaii as art objects, but the superficial scratches are immediately removed and the ivory is reworked by artisans. Scrimshaw is made into everything from belt buckles to delicate earrings and even into coffee-table centerpieces. The prices can go from a few dollars up into the thousands.

Woodcarvings

One Hawaiian art that has not died out is woodcarving. This art was extremely well developed among the old Hawaiians and they almost exclusively used koa because of its density, strength, and natural luster. It was turned into canoes, woodware, and furniture for the *ali'i.* Koa is becoming increasingly scarce, but many items are still available, though costly. Milo and monkeypod are also excellent woods for carving and have largely replaced koa. You can buy tikis, bowls, and furniture at numerous shops. Countless inexpensive carved items are sold at variety stores, such as hula dancers or salad servers, but most are imported from Asia or the Philippines and can be bought at any variety store.

Weaving

The minute you arrive in Hawaii you should shell out $2 for a woven beach mat. This is a necessity, not a frivolous purchase, but the mat definitely won't have been made in Hawaii. What is made in Hawaii is traditional *lau hala* weaving from the leaves *(lau)* of the pandanus *(hala)* tree. These leaves vary greatly in length, with the largest over six feet, and they have a thorny spine that must be removed before they can be worked. The color ranges from light tan to dark brown. The leaves are cut into strips from one-eighth to one inch wide and are then employed in weaving. Any variety of items can be made or at least covered in *lau hala*. It makes great purses, mats, baskets, and table mats.

A *lau hala* hat is absolutely superb but should not be confused with a palm-frond hat. A *lau hala* hat is amazingly supple and even when squashed will pop back into shape. A good one is expensive ($25) and with proper care will last for years. All *lau hala* should be given a light application of mineral oil on a monthly basis, especially if it's exposed to the sun. Iron flat items under a damp cloth and keep purses and baskets stuffed with paper when not in use. Palm fronds also are widely used in weaving. They, too, are a great natural raw material, but not as good as *lau hala*. Almost any item woven from palm, such as a beach bag, makes a good authentic yet inexpensive gift or souvenir, and is available in countless shops.

Gift Items

Jewelry is always an appreciated gift, especially if it's distinctive, and Hawaii has some of the most original. The sea provides the basic raw materials of pink, gold, and black coral, and it's so beautiful that it holds the same fascination as gemstones. Harvesting the coral is very dangerous work. The Lahaina beds off Maui have one of the best black coral lodes in the islands, but unlike reef coral these trees grow at depths bordering the outer limits of a scuba diver's capabilities. Only the best can dive 180 feet after the black coral, and about one diver per year dies in pursuit of it. Conservationists have placed great pressure on the harvesters of these deep corals, and the State of Hawaii has created strict limits and guidelines that must be followed by the firms and divers involved.

Pink coral has long been treasured by humans. The Greeks considered it a talisman for good health, and there's even evidence that it has been coveted since the Stone Age. Coral jewelry is on sale at many shops throughout Hawaii, its value determined by the color of the coral and the workmanship.

Puka shells (with small, naturally occurring holes) and *opihi* shells are also made into jewelry. Many times these items are very inexpensive, yet they are authentic and great purchases for the price. Hanging macrame planters festooned with seashells are usually quite affordable and sold at roadside stands along with shells.

BOB RACE

scrimshaw

Hawaii produces unique food items appreciated by many. Various-sized jars of macadamia nuts and butters are great gifts, as are tins of rich, gourmet-quality Kona coffee, the only coffee produced in the United States. Guava, pineapple, passion fruit, and mango are often gift-boxed into assortments of jams, jellies, and spicy chutneys. And for that special person in your life, you can bring home perfumes and colognes in exotic island fragrances of gardenia, plumeria, and ginger. All of the above items are reasonably priced, lightweight, and easy to carry.

LANGUAGE OF THE LEI

The goddess Hiiaka is Pele's youngest sister, and although many gods are depicted wearing flower garlands, the lei is most associated with her. Perhaps this is because Hiiaka is the goddess of mercy and protection, qualities which the lei is deemed to symbolize. Hiiaka traveled throughout the islands destroying evil spirits wherever she found them. In the traditional translation of "The Song of the Islands" by Rev. Samuel Kapu, the last verses read, "We all call to you, answer us o Hiiaka, the woman who travels the seas. This is the conclusion of our song, o wreaths of Hawaii, respond to our call." A special day, May 1, is Lei Day in Hawaii. It started in 1928 as a project of Don Blanding, an island poet.

Hardly a more beautiful tradition exists anywhere in the world than placing a flower garland around the neck of someone special. The traditional time to give a lei is when someone is arriving or departing the islands, so every airport has lei sellers, mostly older women who have a little booth at the entrance to the airport. But lei are worn on every occasion, from marriages to

ART INFORMATION

This section includes the names and addresses of guilds, centers, and organizations that dispense information on Hawaiian arts and crafts.

Arts Council of Hawaii, P.O. Box 50225, Honolulu, HI 96850, tel. 524-7120; Karl Ichida, executive director. A citizens' advocacy group for the arts providing technical assistance and information to individuals and groups. Publishes the *Cultural Climate,* a newsletter covering what's happening in the arts of Hawaii. Includes a calendar of events, feature articles, and editorials. Membership fee, $15, includes newsletter; nonmembers, 50 cents per issue.

Bishop Museum, 1525 Bernice St., Honolulu, HI 96819, tel. 847-3511. The world's *best* museum covering Polynesia and Hawaii. Exhibits, galleries, archives, demonstrations of Hawaiian crafts, and a planetarium. On the premises, Shop Pacifica has a complete selection of books and publications on all aspects of Hawaiian art and culture. Shouldn't be missed.

Contemporary Arts Center, 605 Kapiolani Blvd., Honolulu, HI 96813, tel. 525-8047. Promotes public awareness of contemporary art by providing gallery space, publicity, and exposure for local artists. Also houses a permanent collection and monthly exhibitions.

East Hawaii Cultural Council, P.O. Box 1312, Hilo, HI 96721. Publishes the *The Center Newspaper,* a monthly newsletter of what's happening artistically and culturally primarily on the Big Island. Includes a good monthly calendar of events with listings from exhibit openings to movies.

East-West Center Culture Learning Institute, Burns Hall 4076, 1777 East-West Rd., Honolulu, HI 96848, tel. 944-7691. At University of Hawaii campus. Dedicated to the sharing, exhibiting, and appreciation of arts, culture, and crafts from throughout Asia and the Western world. Bimonthly *Centerviews* includes an events calendar and topical editorials on the Pacific. Free.

East-West Journal, 1633 Kapiolani Blvd., Honolulu, HI 96814. Yearly guide to exhibition galleries featuring the work of locally renowned artists.

Hawaii Craftsmen, P.O. Box 22145, Honolulu, HI 96823, tel. 523-1974. Increases awareness of Hawaiian crafts through programs, exhibitions, workshops, lectures, and demonstrations.

Honolulu Academy of Arts, 900 S. Beretania St., Honolulu, HI 96814, tel. 532-8700. Collects, preserves, and exhibits works of art. Offers public art education programs related to their collections. Also offers tours, classes, lectures, films, and a variety of publications.

Honolulu Symphony Society, 1000 Bishop St., Honolulu, HI 96813, tel. 537-6171. Provides professional-level music, primarily symphonic concerts.

Pacific Handcrafters Guild, P.O. Box 15491, Honolulu, HI 96818, tel. 538-7227. Focuses on developing and preserving handicrafts in Hawaii and the Pacific. Sponsors three major crafts fairs annually.

State Foundation on Culture and the Arts, 335 Merchant St., Room 202, Honolulu, HI 96813, tel. 586-0300. Begun by state legislature in 1965 to preserve Hawaii's diverse cultural and artistic heritage. Publishes *Hawaii Cultural Resource Directory,* which lists most of the art organizations, galleries, councils, co-ops, and guilds throughout Hawaii. Very complete.

University of Hawaii at Manoa Art Gallery, 2535 The Mall, Honolulu, HI 96822, tel. 948-6888. Showcases contemporary artwork. Theme changes periodically.

funerals, and are equally apt to appear around the lovely neck of a hula dancer or as a floral hatband on the grizzled head of an old *paniolo,* or even draped around his horse's neck. In old Hawaii lei were given to the local *ali'i* as a sign of affection. When two warring chiefs sat together and wove a lei, it meant the end of hostilities and symbolized the circle of peace.

Lei Making

Any flower or blossom can be strung into a lei, but the most common are carnations or the lovely smelling plumeria. Lei, like babies, are all beautiful, but special lei are highly prized by those who know what to look for. Of the different stringing styles, the most common is *kui*—stringing the flower through the middle or side. Most "airport-quality" lei are of this type. The *humuhumu* style, reserved for making flat lei, is made by sewing flowers and ferns to a ti, banana, or sometimes *hala* leaf. A *humuhumu* lei makes an excellent hatband. *Wili* is the winding together of greenery, ferns, and flowers into short, bouquet-type lengths. The most traditional form is *hili,* which requires no stringing at all but involves braiding fragrant ferns and leaves such as *maile.* If flowers are interwoven, the *hili* becomes the *haku* style, the most difficult and most beautiful type of lei.

The Lei Of The Land

Every major island is symbolized by its own lei made from a distinctive flower, shell, or fern. Each island has its own official color as well, though it doesn't necessarily correspond to the color of the island's lei.

The island of Hawaii's lei is made from the red (or rare creamy white or orange) *lehua* blossom. The *lehua* tree grows from sea level to 9,000 feet and produces an abundance of tufted flowers. The official color of Hawaii Island, like the lava from its active volcanoes, is red.

Kauai, oldest of the main islands, is represented by the *mokihana* lei and the regal color purple. The *mokihana* tree produces a small, cubelike fruit that smells like anise. Green when strung into Kauai's lei, the fruit turn a dark brown and keep their scent for months.

Maui is the pink island; its lei is the corresponding small pink rose called the *lokelani.* Not native but imported, in recent years they've fallen prey to a rose beetle. When they're scarce, a substitute *roselani* is used for Maui's lei.

Molokai is the silvery green island, and its lei is fashioned from the green leaves and small white flowers of the *kukui* tree. After it's shaped and polished, the *kukui* nut makes some of the most permanent and beautiful lei for sale in Hawaii. *Kukui* nut lei are quite common and make excellent gifts. Although not the official lei of any island, they could easily be the official lei representing all the islands.

Lanai has one of the most traditional forms of lei in Hawaii. Both its color and its lei are represented by the orange *kaunaoa.* This plant commonly grows along beaches and roadsides. Its orange, leafless stems are twisted into strands to form a lei.

Oahu, the color of the sun, is garlanded by the yellow *ilima.* This flower is reminiscent of the *'o'o* bird whose yellow feathers made the finest capes in Hawaii. The *ilima* often bears double yellow flowers and will infrequently produce a light red flower too rare to be used in lei.

Kahoolawe, the sacred island now used as a naval target range, is given the color gray (hope-

lei for sale, Honolulu c. 1920

HAWAII STATE ARCHIVES

fully not as in "battleship") and is represented by the silvery leaves and small, white, sweet-scented flowers of the *hinahina.* This heliotrope grows on sandy beaches just above the high-water mark, and is a very common plant throughout the Pacific.

Niihau, the Forbidden Island, is home to some of the last remaining pure-blooded Hawaiians and takes the color white. The island's lei is the rare *pupu* shell. This white shell sometimes has brown spots and is less than one-half inch long. The shell was once the home of a mollusk that died on the offshore reef. These *pupu* lei, considered fine jewelry, fetch a handsome price. Very cheap facsimiles made of *pikake* shells are sold everywhere; most have been imported from the Cook and Society islands of the South Pacific.

BOB RACE

Hawaiian lei

The last island is the semi-submerged volcano of Molokini, just off Maui's south shore. Molokini is represented by the very traditional lei made from *limu kala,* a brown, coarse seaweed with feathery spiny leaves that makes a boa-type lei.

Besides these island lei, two others must be mentioned. A lei made from *maile* is perhaps the most traditional of all. *Maile* is a green, leafy vine. Its stiff, bonelike inner stem is removed, leaving the leaves and pliable bark intact, which are then twisted into lei. They might be ordinary to look at, but they have a delicious smell that is Hawaii. *Maile* is often used in conjunction with flowers to make top-notch lei. *Lauae* is a common fern with large, coarse, shiny leaves. It is used to fluff out many lei and when bruised, the leaves have a mild scent of *maile.* Lei have one quality that is unsurpassed: they feel just as good to give as they do to receive.

HULA

The hula was and is more than an ethnic dance; it is the soul of Hawaii expressed in motion. It began as a form of worship during religious ceremonies and was only danced by highly trained men. It gradually evolved into a form of entertainment, but in no regard was it sexual. The hula was the opera, theater, and lecture hall of the islands all rolled into one. It was history portrayed in the performing arts. In the beginning an androgynous deity named Laka descended to earth and taught men how to dance the hula. In time the male aspect of Laka departed for the heavens, but the female aspect remained. The female Laka set up her own special hula *heiau* at Haena Point on the Na Pali coast of Kauai, where it still exists. As time went on women were allowed to learn the hula. Scholars surmise that men became too busy wresting a living from the land to maintain the art form. Most likely, it was the dance's swaying movements and primal rhythm that attracted the women. And once they began showing off what nature had bestowed upon them, what chief in his right mind was going to tell them to stop?!

Men did retain a type of hula for themselves called *lua.* This was a form of martial art employed in hand-to-hand combat. It included paralyzing holds, bone-crunching punches, and thrusting with spears and clubs. It evolved into a ritualized warfare dance called *hula kui.* During the 19th century, the hula almost vanished because the missionaries considered it vile and heathen. King Kalakaua is generally regarded as saving it during the 1800s, when he formed his own troupe and encouraged the dancers to learn the old hula. Many of the original dances were forgotten, but some were retained and are performed to this day. Although professional dancers were highly trained, everyone took part in the hula. *Ali'i,* commoners, young, and old all danced. Early drawings by ships' artists like Arago, Choris, and Webber recorded hula scenes. Old folks even did it sitting down if their legs were too weak to perform some of the gyrations.

Hula Training

Only the most beautiful, graceful, and elegant girls were chosen to enter the hula *halau* (school). At one time, the *halau* was a temple in its own right and the girls who entered at the ages of four or five would emerge as accomplished dancers in their early teens to begin lifelong careers of the highest honor. In the *halau,* the *haumana* (pupils) were under the strict and total guidance of the *kumu* (teacher), and many *kapu* were placed upon them. The hula was a subordination of gross strength into a sublime coupling of grace and elegance. Once a woman became a proficient and accomplished dancer, her hula showed a personal, semi-spontaneous interpretation based upon past experiences. Today, *hula halau* are active on every island, teaching hula, and keeping the old ways and culture alive. Performers still spend years perfecting their techniques. They show off their accomplishments during the fierce competition of the Merrie Monarch Festival in Hilo every April. The winning *halau* is praised and recognized throughout the islands.

The Special World Of Hula

Hawaiian hula was never performed in grass skirts; tapa or ti-leaf skirts were worn. Grass skirts came to Hawaii from the Gilbert Islands, and if you see grass and cellophane skirts in a "hula revue," it's not traditional. Almost every major resort offering entertainment or a luau also offers a revue. Most times, young island beauties accompanied by local musicians put on a floor show for the tourists. It'll be fun, but it won't be traditional. A hula dancer has to learn how to control every part of her/his body, including facial expressions, which help set the mood. The correct chanting of the *mele* is an integral part of the performance. These story chants, accompanied by musical instruments, make the hula very much like opera; it is especially similar in the way the tale unfolds. The hands are extremely important and provide instant background scenery. For example, if the hands are thrust outward in an aggressive manner, this can mean a battle; if they sway gently overhead, they refer to the gods or to creation; they can easily become rain, clouds, sun, sea, or moon. Watch the hands to get the gist of the story, though in the words of one wiseguy, "You watch the parts you like, and I'll watch the parts I like!" The motion of swaying hips can denote a long walk, a canoe ride, or sexual intercourse. Foot motion can portray a battle, a walk, or any kind of conveyance. The overall effect is multidirectional synchronized movement.

Hula Music

Accompaniment is provided by chants called *mele* or *oli* and by a wide variety of instruments. The *ipu* is a primary hula instrument made of two gourds fastened together. It's thumped on a mat and slapped with the hand. In the background is the steady rhythm of the *pahu,* a large bass drum made from a hollowed coconut or breadfruit tree log, and covered with a sharkskin membrane. Hawaii's largest drum, it was sometimes placed on a pedestal and used in ceremonies at the *heiau.* The *uli uli* is a gourd or coconut filled with shells or pebbles and used like rattles, while *ili ili* are stones clicked together like castanets. The *punui* is a small drum made from a coconut shell half and beaten in counterpoint to the *ipu.* Oftentimes it was played by the hula dancer, who had it fastened to her body as a knee drum. The *puili* is a length of bamboo split at one end to look like a whisk, and struck against the body to make a rattling noise, while the *kaekaekee* and *kalau* are bamboo cut to various lengths and struck to make a rudimentary xylophonic sound. Two unique instruments are the *kupee niho ilio,* a dog's tooth rattle worn as an ankle bracelet by men only, now replaced by sea shells; and an *ohe hano ihu,* a nose flute of bamboo that accompanied chants. None of these instruments are actually necessary to perform a hula. All that's needed are a dancer and a chant.

THAT GOOD OLD ISLAND MUSIC

The missionaries usually take a beating when it's recounted how much Hawaiian culture they destroyed while "civilizing" the natives. However, they seem to have done one thing right. They introduced the Hawaiians to the diatonic musical scale and immediately opened a door to latent and superbly harmonious talent. Before the missionaries, the Hawaiians knew little about melody. Though sonorous, their *mele* were repetitive chants in which the emphasis was placed on historical accuracy and not on "making music." The Hawaiians, in short, didn't *sing* in the European manner. But within a few years of the missionaries' arrival, they were belting out good old Christian hymns, and one of their favorite pastimes became group and individual singing.

Early in the 1800s, Spanish *vaqueros* from California were imported to teach the Hawaiians how to be cowboys. With them came guitars and moody ballads. The Hawaiian *paniolos* (cowboys) quickly learned how to punch cows and croon away the long lonely nights on the range. Immigrants who came along a little later in the 19th century, especially from Portugal, helped create a Hawaiian-style music. Their biggest influence was a small, four-stringed instrument called a *braga* or *cavaquinho.* One owned by Augusto Dias was the prototype of a homegrown Hawaiian instrument that became known as the ukulele. "Jumping flea," the translation of ukulele, is an appropriate name devised by the Hawaiians when they saw how nimble the fingers were as they "jumped" over the strings.

The Merry Monarch, King Kalakaua, and Queen Liliuokalani were both patrons of the arts who furthered the Hawaiian musical identity at the turn of the century. Kalakaua revived the hula and was also a gifted lyricist and balladeer. He wrote the words to "Hawaii Pono," which became the national anthem of Hawaii and later the state anthem. Liliuokalani wrote the hauntingly beautiful "Aloha Oe," which is often pointed to as the "spirit of Hawaii" in music. Detractors say that its melody is extremely close to the old Christian hymn, "Rock Beside the Sea," but the lyrics are so beautiful and perfectly fitted that this doesn't matter.

Just prior to Kalakaua's reign a Prussian bandmaster, Capt. Henri Berger, was invited to head the fledgling Royal Hawaiian Band, which he turned into a very respectable orchestra lauded by many visitors to the islands. Berger was open-minded and learned to love Hawaiian music. He collaborated with Kalakaua and other island musicians to incorporate their music into a Western format. He headed the band for 43 years until 1915, and was instrumental in making music a serious pursuit of talented Hawaiians.

Popular Hawaiian Music

Hawaiian music has a unique twang, a special feeling that says the same thing to everyone who hears it: "Relax, sit back in the moonlight, watch the swaying palms as the surf sings a lullaby." This special sound is epitomized by the bouncy ukulele, the falsettos of Hawaiian crooners, and the smooth ring of the "steel" or "Hawaiian" guitar. The steel guitar is a variation originated by Joseph Kekuku in the 1890s. Stories abound of how Joseph Kekuku devised this instrument; the most popular versions say that Joe dropped his comb or pocketknife on his guitar strings and liked what he heard. Driven by the faint rhythm of an inner sound, he went to the machine shop at the Kamehameha Schools and turned out a steel bar for sliding over the strings. To complete the sound he changed the cat-gut strings to steel and raised them so they wouldn't hit the frets. Voila!—Hawaiian music as the world knows it today.

The first melodious strains of **slack-key guitar** can be traced back to the time of Kamehameha III, when Spanish cowboys (the forerunners of Hawaiian *paniolos*) from California were brought to the kingdom to run the wild cattle that had grown steadily in number ever since killing them was made *kapu* by Kamehameha I. The white people's gift had become a menace, increasing to the point where they were attacking grass houses for fodder. The Spanish cowboys roped, branded, and corralled them, and living up to the cowboy image, would pass lonesome nights on the range singing and playing their guitars. The Hawaiians, who became excellent cowboys, and with their ears recently tuned by the missionaries, picked up the melodies accompanied by the strange new instrument, and quickly Hawaiianized them. The Spanish had their way of tuning the guitar, and played difficult and aggressive music that did not sit well with Hawaiians, who were much more gentle and casual in their manners.

Hawaiians soon became adept at making their own music. At first, one person played the melody, but it lacked fullness. There was no body to the sound. So, as one *paniolo* fooled with the melody, another soon learned to play bass, which added depth. But, a player was often alone, and by experimenting learned that he could get the right hand going with the melody, and at the same time could play the bass note with the thumb to improve the sound. Singers also learned that they could "open tune" the guitar to match their rich voices.

Due to *kahunaism,* Hawaiians believed knowledge was sacred, and what is sacred should be treated with utmost respect, which meant keeping it secret, except from sincere apprentices. Guitar playing became a personal artform whose secrets were closely guarded, handed down only to family members, and only to those who showed ability and determination. When old-time slack-key guitar players were done strumming, they loosened all the strings so no one could figure out how they had them tuned. If they were playing, and some folks came by who were interested and weren't part of the family, the Hawaiians stopped what they were doing, put their guitars down, and put their feet across the strings to wait for the folks to go away. As time went on, more and more Hawaiians began to play slack key, and a common repertoire emerged.

An accomplished musician could easily figure out the simple songs, once they had figured out how the family had tuned the guitar. One of the most popular tunings was the "open G." Old Hawaiian folks called it the "taro patch tune." Different songs came out, and if you were in their family and were interested in the guitar, they took the time to sit down and teach you. The way they taught was straightforward and a test of your sincerity at the same time. The old master would start to play. He just wanted you to listen, get a feel for the music, not any more than that. You brought your guitar and *listened.* When you felt it, you played it, and the knowledge was transferred. Today, only a handful of slack-key guitar players know how to play the classic tunes classically. The best-known and perhaps greatest slack-key player was Gabby Pahinui, with The Sons of Hawaii. He passed away recently, but left many recordings behind. A slack-key master still singing and playing is Raymond Kane. Raymond now teaches a handful of students his wonderful and haunting music. Not one of his students are from his own family, and most are *haole* musicians trying to preserve the classical method of playing.

Hawaiian music received its biggest boost from a remarkable radio program known as "Hawaii Calls." This program sent out its music from the Banyan Court of the Moana Hotel from 1935 until 1975. At its peak in the mid-1950s, it was syndicated on over 700 radio stations throughout the world. Ironically, Japanese pilots heading for Pearl Harbor tuned in island music as a signal beam. Some internationally famous classic tunes came out of the '40s and '50s. Jack Pitman composed "Beyond the Reef" in 1948; over 300 artists have recorded it and it has sold well over 12 million records. Other million-sellers include: "Sweet Leilani," "Lovely Hula Hands," "The Crosseyed Mayor of Kaunakakai," and "The Hawaiian Wedding Song."

By the 1960s, Hawaiian music began to die. Just too corny and light for those turbulent years, it belonged to the older generation and the good times that followed WW II. One man was instrumental in keeping Hawaiian music alive during this period. Don Ho, with his "Tiny Bubbles," became the token Hawaiian musician of the '60s and early '70s. He's persevered long enough to become a legend in his own time, and his Polynesian Extravaganza at the Hilton Hawaiian Village packed visitors in until the early 1990s (see "Entertainment" in the Waikiki chapter). Al Harrington, "The South Pacific Man," until his recent retirement had another Honolulu "big revue" that drew large crowds. Of this type of entertainment, perhaps the most Hawaiian is Danny Kaleikini, still performing at the Kahala Hilton, who entertains his audience with dances, Hawaiian anecdotes, and tunes on the traditional Hawaiian nose flute.

The Beat Goes On

Beginning in the mid-'70s islanders began to assert their cultural identity. One of the unifying factors was the coming of age of "Hawaiian" music. It graduated from the "little grass shack" novelty tune and began to include sophisticated jazz, rock, and contemporary rhythms. Accomplished musicians whose roots were in traditional island music began to highlight their tunes with this distinctive sound. The best embellish their arrangements with ukuleles, steel guitars, and traditional percussion and melodic instruments. Some excellent modern recording artists have become island institutions. The local people say that you know if the Hawaiian harmonies are good if they give you "chicken skin."

Each year special music awards, **Na Hoku Hanohano,** or Hoku for short, are given to distinguished island musicians. The following are recent Hoku winners considered by their contemporaries to be among the best in Hawaii. If they're playing while you're there, don't miss them. **Loyal Garner,** who was awarded Female Vocalist of the Year for "I Shall Sing," is a truly wonderful artist. **Del Beazley,** who walked away

RADIO STATIONS

STATION	DIAL NUMBER	REMARKS
OAHU		
KCCN	AM 1420	Hawaiian music 24 hours. Indiscriminate selections will either delight or exasperate.
KDEO	AM 940, FM 102	Country
KPOI	FM 98	Rock
MAUI		
KAIM	AM 870, FM 95.5	Contemporary
KAOI	FM 95	Stereo
KPOA	FM 93.5	Hawaiian music 19 hours a day. Tropical jazz five hours a day.
HAWAII		
KBIG	FM 98	
KHLO	AM 850	Country
KIPA	AM 620	Contemporary and requests
KKON	AM 790	Contemporary
KPUA	AM 670	Contemporary
KOAS	FM 92.1	Contemporary
KAUAI		
KFMN	FM 97	Contemporary, oldies
KONG	AM 570, FM 93.5	Contemporary and requests
KUAI	AM 720	Contemporary, surf report

Note: Not all stations may be received on all islands.

with top honors for Male Vocalist of the Year, Contemporary Hawaiian Album, and Song of the Year, all from his fantastic album "Night and Day," is a wonderful performer. **Makaha Sons Of Niihau** captured a number of Hoku for Best Traditional Hawaiian Album, Best Group, and Album of the Year for their fantastic work "Ho'oluana." Led by Israel Kamakawiwoole, they are the best and shouldn't be missed. Best Contemporary Album went to **Hawaiian Style Band** for "Vanishing Treasures," while Single of the Year was awarded to **Bryan Kessler & Me No Hoa Aloha** for "Heiau," a haunting melody. Instrumental Album of the Year was awarded to **Susan Gillespie and Susi Hussong** for "Wedding Music," and Most Promising Artist was taken by **Kealohi** for "Kealohi."

Past winners of Hoku who have become renowned performers include: **Brothers Cazimero,** who are blessed with beautiful harmonic voices; **Krush,** who are highly regarded for their contemporary sounds; **The Peter Moon Band,** fantastic performers with a strong traditional sound; **Karen Keawehawai'i,** who has a sparkling voice and can be very funny when the mood strikes her; and **Henry Kapono,** formerly of Cecilio and Kapono, who keeps a low profile but is an incredible performer and excellent songwriter. His shows are noncommercial and very special. **Cecilio** is now teamed up with **Maggie Herron;** they are hot together and have a strong following in Honolulu. **The Beamer Brothers** are excellent performers, and can be seen at various nightspots.

Some top-notch performers with a strong following are: Ledward Kaapana; Mango; Oliver Kelly; Ka'eo; Na Leo Pilimehana, whose "Local Boys" recently won a Hoku for Best Single; Freitas Brothers; Brickwood Galuteria, who won a double Hoku for Best Male Vocalist and Most Promising Artist; and Third Road Delite.

Classical And Chamber Music

A wide assortment of classical and chamber music is offered in Hawaii. The following organizations sponsor concerts throughout the year: Chamber Music Hawaii, 905 Spencer St., No. 404, Honolulu, HI 96822, tel. (808) 531-6617; Classical Guitar Society of Hawaii, 1229 D. Waimanu, Honolulu, HI 96814, tel. (808) 537-6451; The Ensemble Players Guild, Box 50225, Honolulu, HI 96850, tel. (808) 735-1173; Hawaii Concert Society, Box 663, Hilo, HI 96721, tel. (808) 935- 5831; Honolulu Symphony Society, 1000 Bishop St., Suite 901, Honolulu, HI 96813, tel. (808) 537-6171; Kauai Concert Association, 5867 Haaheo Pl., Kapa'a, HI 96746, tel. (808) 822-7593; Maui Philharmonic Society, 2274 S. Kihei Rd., Kihei, HI 96753, tel. (808) 879-2962.

ACCOMMODATIONS

Hawaii's accommodations won't disappoint anyone. It has an exceptionally wide range of places to stay with varieties both in style and in price. You can camp on a totally secluded beach three days down a hiking trail, have a dream vacation at one of the undisputed top resorts in the world, or get a package deal including a week's lodging in one of many island hotels for less than you would spend for a hotel at home. If you want to experience the islands as if you lived here, bed and breakfasts are becoming popular and easy to arrange. Condominiums are plentiful, and great for extended stays for families who want to set up home away from home, or for a group of friends who want to save money by sharing costs. There is a smattering of youth hostels, YM/WCAs, and home exchanges. If you're a student, a summer session at the University of Hawaii can mix education and fun.

Hawaii makes the greater part of its living from visitors, and all concerned desire to keep Hawaiian standards up and vacationers coming back. This means accommodations in Hawaii are operated by professionals who know the business of pleasing people. This adds up to benefits for you. Rooms in even the more moderate hotels are clean; the standard of services ranges from adequate to luxurious pampering. With the tips and advice given below, you should be able to find a place to stay that will match your taste and your pocketbook. For specifics, please refer to "Accommodations" in each of the travel chapters.

HOTELS

Even with the wide variety of other accommodations available, most vistors, at least first-timers, tend to stay in hotels. At one time, hotels were the only places to stay, and characters like Mark Twain were berthed at Kilauea's rude Volcano House, while millionaires and nobility sailed for Waikiki where they stayed in luxury at the Moana Hotel or Royal Hawaiian, which both still stand as vintage reminders of days past. Maui's Pioneer Inn dates from the turn of the century, and if you were Hawaii-bound, these and a handful that haven't survived were about all that was offered. Today, there are about 65,000 hotel rooms statewide, and every year more hotels are built and older ones renovated. They come in all shapes and sizes, from 10-room family-run affairs to high-rise giants. A trend turned some into condominiums, while the Neighbor Islands have learned an aesthetic lesson from Waikiki and built low-rise resorts that don't obstruct the view and that blend more readily with the surroundings. Whatever accommodation you want, you'll find it in Hawaii.

Types Of Hotel Rooms

Most readily available and least expensive is a bedroom with bath, the latter sometimes shared in the more inexpensive hotels. Some hotels also offer a studio, a large sitting room that converts to a bedroom; a suite, a bedroom with sitting room; or an apartmen that has a full kitchen plus at least one bedroom. Kitchenettes are often available; each contains a refrigerator, sink, and stove usually in a small corner nook or fitted together as one space-saving unit. A kitchenette costs a bit more, but saves you a bundle by allowing you to prepare some of your own meals. To get that vacation feeling while keeping costs down, eat breakfast in, pack a lunch for the day, and go out to dinner. If you rent a kitchenette, make sure all the appliances work as soon as you arrive. If they don't, notify the front desk immediately, and if the hotel will not rectify the situation ask to be moved or for a reduced rate. Hawaii has cockroaches (see "Health and Safety" later in this chapter), so put all food away.

Hotel Rates: Add 10% Room Tax

Every year Hawaiian hotels welcome in the New Year by hiking their rates by about 10%. A room that was $100 this year will be $110 next year, and so on. Hawaii, because of its gigantic tourist flow and tough competition, offers hotel rooms at rates universally lower than those of most developed resort areas around the world. Package deals, especially to Waikiki, almost throw in a week's lodging for the price of an air ticket. The basic **daily rate** is geared toward double occupancy; singles are hit in the pocketbook. Single rates are cheaper than doubles, but never as low as half the double rate; the most you get off is 40%. **Weekly and monthly** rates will save you approximately 10% off the daily rate. Make sure to ask because this information won't be volunteered. Many hotels will charge for a double and then add an additional charge ($10-25) for extra persons. Some hotels, not always the budget ones, let you cram in as many as can sleep on the floor for no additional charge, so again, ask. Others have a policy of **minimum stay,** usually three days, but their rates can be cheaper.

Hawaii's **peak season** runs from just before Christmas until after Easter, and then again in early summer. Rooms are at a premium then, and peak-season rates are an extra 10% above the normal daily rate. Oftentimes hotels will also suspend weekly and monthly rates during peak season. The **off-peak** season is in late summer and fall, when rooms are easy to come by and most hotels offer off-peak rates. Here, subtract about 10% from the normal rate.

In Hawaiian hotels you always pay more for a good view. Terms vary slightly, but usually "oceanfront" means your room faces the ocean and most of your view is unimpeded. "Ocean view" is slightly more vague. It could be a decent view, or it could require standing on the dresser and craning your neck to catch a tiny slice of the sea sandwiched between two skyscrapers. Rooms are also designated and priced upward as **standard, superior, and deluxe.** As you go up, this could mean larger rooms with more amenities or can merely signify a better view.

Plenty of hotels offer the **family plan,** which allows children under a certain age to stay in their parents' room free, if they use the existing bedding. If another bed or crib is required, there is an additional charge. Only a limited number of hotels offer the **American plan,** in which breakfast and dinner are included with the night's lodging. Many hotels provide a refrigerator and a heating unit to make coffee and tea.

Paying, Deposits, And Reservations

The vast majority of Hawaiian hotels accept foreign and domestic traveler's checks, personal checks preapproved by the management, foreign cash, and most major credit cards. Reservations are always the best policy, and they're easily made through travel agents or by directly contacting the hotel. In all cases, bring documentation of your confirmed reservations with you in case of a mix-up.

Deposits are not always required to make reservations, but they do secure them. Some hotels require the first night's payment in advance. Reservations without a deposit can be legally released if the room is not claimed by 6 p.m. Remember, too, that letters "requesting reservations" are not the same as "confirmed reservations." In letters, include your dates of stay, type of room you want, and price. Once the hotel answers your letter, "confirm" your reservations with a phone call or follow-up letter and make sure that the hotel sends you a copy of the confirmation. All hotels and resorts have **cancellation requirements** for refunding deposits. The time limit on these can be as little as 24 hours before arrival, to a full 30 days. Some hotels require full **advance payment** for your stay, especially during peak season, or during times of crowded special events such as the Merrie Monarch Festival in Hilo. Be aware of the time required for a cancellation notice *before* making your reservation deposit, especially when dealing with advance payment. If you have confirmed reservations, especially with a deposit, and there is no room for you, or one that doesn't meet prearranged requirements, you should be given the option of accepting alternate accommodations. You are owed the difference in room rates if there is any. If there is no room whatsoever, the hotel is required to find you one at another comparable hotel and refund your deposit in full.

Amenities

All hotels have some of them, and some hotels have all of them. Air-conditioning is available in most, but under normal circumstances you won't need it. Balmy trade winds flow through louvered windows and doors in many hotels. Casablanca room fans are better. TVs are often included in the rate, but not always. In-room phones are frequently provided, but a service charge is usually tacked on, even for local calls. Swimming pools are very common, even though the hotel may sit right on the beach.

There is always a restaurant of some sort, a coffee shop or two, a bar, a cocktail lounge, and sometimes a sundries shop. Some hotels also offer tennis courts or golf courses either as part of the premises or affiliated with the hotel; usually an activities desk can book you into a variety of daily outings. Plenty of hotels offer laundromats on the premises, and hotel towels can be used at the beach. Bellhops get about $1 per bag, and maid service is free, though maids are customarily tipped $1-2 per day, or a bit more if kitchenettes are involved. Parking is free. Hotels can often arrange special services like babysitters, all kinds of lessons, and entertainment. A few even lend bicycles and some snorkeling equipment. They'll receive and send mail for you, cash your traveler's checks, and take messages.

CONDOMINIUMS

Hawaii was one of the first states struck by the condominium phenomenon; it began in the 1950s and has increased ever since. Now condos are almost as common as hotels, and renting one is just about as easy. Condos, unlike hotel rooms, are privately owned apartments normally part of a complex or high-rise. The condo is usually an absentee owner's second or vacation home. An on-premises condo manager rents out vacant units and is responsible for maintenance and security.

Things To Know

Staying in a condo has advantages and disadvantages over staying in a hotel. The method of paying for and reserving a condo is just about the same as for a hotel. However, requirements for deposits, final payments, and cancellation charges are much stiffer than in hotels. Make absolutely sure you understand these requirements when you make your reservations. The main qualitative difference between a condo and a hotel is amenities. At a condo, you're more on your own. You're temporarily renting an apartment, so there won't be any bellhops, and rarely a bar, restaurant, or lounge on the premises, though many times you'll find a sundries store. The main lobby, instead of having that grand entrance feel of many hotels, is more like an apartment house entrance, although there might be a front desk. A condo can be an efficiency (one big room), but most are one- or multiple-bedroom affairs with complete kitchens. Reasonable housekeeping items should be provided: linens, furniture, and a fully equipped kitchen. Most have TVs and phones, but remember the furnishings are provided by the owner. You can find brand-new furnishings that are top of the line, right down to garage sale bargains. Inquire about the furnishings when you make your reservations. Maid service might be included on a limited basis (for example once weekly), or you might have to pay for it if you require a maid.

Condos usually require a minimum stay, although some will rent on a daily basis, like hotels. Minimum stays when applicable are often three days, but seven is also commonplace, and during peak season, two weeks isn't unheard of. Swimming pools are common, and depending on the "theme" of the condo, you can find saunas, weight rooms, jacuzzis, or tennis courts. Rates are about 10-15% higher than at comparable hotels, with hardly any difference between doubles and singles. A nominal extra is charged for more than two people; condos can normally accommodate four to six guests. You can find clean, decent condos for as little as $200 per week, all the way up to exclusive apartments for well over $1000 per week. Their real advantage is for families, friends who want to share, and especially long-term stays for which you will always get a special rate. The kitchen facilities save a great deal on dining costs, and it's common to find units with their own mini-washers and dryers. Parking space is ample for guests, and like hotels, plenty of stay/drive deals are offered.

Hotel/Condominium Information

The best source of hotel/condo information is the **Hawaii Visitors Bureau.** While planning your trip, either visit one nearby or write to them in Hawaii. (Addresses are listed in the "Hawaii Visitors Bureau" section under "Information and Services" later in this chapter.) Request a copy of their free and current ***Member Accommodation Guide.*** This handy booklet lists all the hotel/condo members of the HVB. Listings include addresses, phone numbers, facilities, rates, and general tips. Understand that these are not all of the hotels/condos in Hawaii, just members of HVB.

BED AND BREAKFAST

Bed-and-breakfast (B&B) inns are hardly a new idea. The Bible talks of the hospitable hosts who opened the gates of their homes and invited the wayfarer in to spend the night. B&Bs have a long tradition in Europe and were commonplace in Revolutionary America. Now, lodging in a private home called a bed and breakfast is becoming increasingly fashionable throughout America, and Hawaii is no exception. Not only can you visit the Big Island, you can "live" there for a time with a host family and share an intimate experience of daily life.

Points To Consider

The primary feature of B&B homes is that every one is privately owned, and therefore uniquely different from every other. The range of B&Bs is as wide as the living standards in America. You'll find everything from a semi-mansion in the most fashionable residential area to a little grass shack offered by a down-home fisherman and his family. This means that it's particularly important for the guest to choose a host family with whom his or her lifestyle is compatible.

Unlike at a hotel or a condo, you'll be living *with* a host (usually a family), although your room will be private, with private baths and separate entrances being quite common. You don't just "check in" at a B&B. In Hawaii you go through agencies (listed below) which act as go-betweens, matching host and guest. Write to them and they'll send you a booklet with a complete description of the B&B, its general location, the fees charged, and a good idea of the lifestyle of your host family. With the reservations application they'll include a questionnaire that will basically determine your profile: Are you single? Do you have children? Smoker? etc., as well as arrival and departure dates and all pertinent particulars.

Since B&Bs are run by individual families, the times they will accept guests can vary according to what's happening in their lives. This makes it imperative to write well in advance: three months is good; earlier is too long and too many things can change. Four weeks is about the minimum time required to make all necessary arrangements. Expect a minimum stay (three days is common) and a maximum stay. B&Bs are not long-term housing, although it's hoped that guest and host will develop a friendship and that future stays can be as long as both desire.

B&B Agencies

One of the most experienced agencies, **Bed And Breakfast Honolulu Statewide,** at 3242 Kaohinanai Dr., Honolulu, HI 96817, tel. (808) 595-7533 or (800) 288-4666, owned and operated by Marylee and Gene Bridges, began in 1982. Since then, they've become masters at finding visitors the perfect accommodations to match their desires, needs, and pocketbooks. Their repertoire of guest homes offers more than 400 rooms, with half on Oahu and the other half scattered around the state. Accommodations from Marylee and Gene are more personally tailored than a hotel room. When you phone, they'll match your needs to their computerized in-house guidelines. B&B Honolulu Statewide also features bargain package deals for inter-island fly-car rentals. If you have special needs and are coming during peak season, reserve up to four months in advance; normal bookings are perfect with two months lead time. But, don't count them out if you just show up at the airport. Rooms can't be guaranteed, but they'll do their best to find you a place to stay.

Another top-notch B&B agency is **Bed and Breakfast Hawaii,** operated by Evelyn Warner and Al Davis. They've been running this service since 1978, and their reputation is excellent. B&B Hawaii has a yearly membership fee of $10. For this they mail you their "Directory of Homes," a periodic "hot sheet" of new listings, and pertinent guest applications; add $1 handling. Write Bed and Breakfast Hawaii, Box 449, Kapa'a, HI 96746. Phone info and reservations at (808) 822-7771 or (800) 733-1632.

Bed and Breakfast Maui Style is the oldest B&B agency operating on Maui. The friendly host, Jeanne Rominger, can arrange a stay on Maui as well as on any of the other islands, including Molokai. Accommodations range from a room in a private home to one-bedroom apartments. Write Bed and Breakfast Maui Style, P.O. Box 886, Kihei, HI 96753, tel. (808) 879-7865.

Following are other well-known agencies. **Go Native Hawaii** will send you a directory and information if you write to them at 65 Halaulani Pl., Box 11418, Hilo, HI 96721, tel. (808) 935-4178 or (800) 662-8483. **Pacific Hawaii Bed And Breakfast** at 602 Kailua Rd., Suite 107C, Kailua, HI 96734, tel. (808) 486-8838 or (800) 999-6026, lists homes throughout the state, but especially around Kailua/Kaneohe on Oahu's upscale windward coast. Four agencies specializing in beachfront villas, luxury condominiums, and exclusive estates are **Villas of Hawaii,** 4218 Waialae Ave., Suite 203, Honolulu, HI 96816, tel. (808) 735-9000; **All Islands B&B,** at 823 Kainui, Kailua, HI 96734, tel. (808) 263-2342 or (800) 542-0344, owned and operated by Ann Carlin and Peggy Frazier (a new and energetic agency with over 300 host homes that prides itself on personalized attention); **Premier Connections of Hawaii,** at 1993 S. Kihei Rd., Suite 209, Kihei, HI 96753; and **Vacation Locations Hawaii,** Box 1689, Kihei, HI 96753, tel. (808) 874-0077. Information on B&Bs can also be obtained from the **American Board of Bed and Breakfast Association,** Box 23294, Washington, D.C. 20026.

OTHER ACCOMMODATIONS

Youth Hostels And YM/WCAs

YM/WCAs are quite limited in Hawaii. They vary as far as private room and bath are concerned, so each should be contacted individually. Prices vary too, but expect to pay $15 single. Men or women are accepted at respective Ys unless otherwise stated. Oahu has five Ys, and Maui and Kauai each have one. You can get information by writing **YMCA Central Branch,** 401 Atkinson Dr., Honolulu, HI 96814, tel. (808) 941-3344; Maui YMCA, J. Walter Cameron Center, 95 Mahalani St., Wailuku, HI 96793, tel. (808) 244-3153; YMCA of Kauai, Box 1786, Lihue, HI 96766, tel. (808) 742-1182 or 742-1200. Refer to "Accommodations" in the travel chapters for particulars on the Ys.

There is only one official **American YH** in Hawaii, located in Honolulu and always busy. Other unaffiliated YHs exist in Waikiki as well. You can make reservations (see "Accommodations" in the Honolulu and Waikiki chapters for addresses). **Elderhostel,** 100 Boylston St., Suite 200, Boston, MA 02116, offers noncredit courses at Hawaii Loa College, Oahu. The **University of Hawaii** has two six-week summer sessions beginning in late May and again in early July offering along with the coursework reasonable rates in residence halls (mandatory meals) and in apartments on campus. For complete information see "Accommodations" in the Honolulu chapter.

Home Exchanges

One other method of staying in Hawaii, open to homeowners, is to offer the use of your home for use of a home in Hawaii. You do this by listing your home with an agency that facilitates the exchange and publishes a descriptive directory. To list your home and to find out what is available, write: Vacation Exchange Club, 12006 111th Ave., Youngtown, AZ 85363; or Interservice Home Exchange, Box 87, Glen Echo, MD 20812.

DIANA LASICH HARPER

FOOD AND DRINK

Hawaii is a gastronome's Shangri-La, a sumptuous smorgasbord in every sense of the word. The varied ethnic groups that have come to Hawaii in the last 200 years have brought their own special enthusiasms and cultures, and lucky for all, they didn't forget their cookpots, hearty appetites, and taste buds.

The Polynesians who first arrived found a fertile but barren land. Immediately they set about growing taro, coconuts, and bananas, and raising chickens, pigs, fish, and dogs, though the latter were reserved for nobility. Harvests were bountiful and the islanders thanked the gods with the traditional feast called the luau. The underground oven, the *imu,* baked most of the dishes, and participants were encouraged to feast while relaxing on straw mats and enjoying the hula and various entertainments. The luau is as popular as ever, and a treat that's guaranteed to delight anyone with a sense of eating adventure.

The missionaries and sailors came next and their ships' holds carried barrels of ingredients for puddings, pies, dumplings, gravies, and roasts—the sustaining "American foods" of New England farms. The mid-1800s saw the arrival of boatloads of Chinese and Japanese peasants, who wasted no time making rice instead of bread the staple of the islands. The Chinese added their exotic spices, creating complex Sichuan dishes as well as workers' basics like chop suey. The Japanese introduced shoyu, sashimi, boxed *(bento)* lunches, delicate tempura, and rich, filling noodle soups. The Portuguese brought their luscious Mediterranean dishes with tomatoes and peppers surrounding plump spicy sausages, nutritious bean soups, and mouthwatering sweet treats like *malasadas* and *pao dolce* (sweet bread). Koreans carried crocks of zesty *kimchi,* and quickly fired up barbecue pits for *pulgogi,* a traditional marinated beef cooked over an open fire. Filipinos served up their tart *adobo* stews of fish, meat, or chicken in a rich sauce of vinegar and garlic.

Recently, Thai and Vietnamese restaurants have been offering their irresistible dishes side

Hawaiian family eating poi, by A. Plum, c. 1846

HAWAII STATE ARCHIVES

by side with restaurants offering fiery burritos from Mexico and elegant cream sauces from France. The ocean breezes of Hawaii not only cool the skin, but waft some of the most delectable aromas on earth, to make the taste buds thrill and the spirit soar.

Special Note

Nothing is sweeter to the appetite than reclining on a beach and deciding just what dish will make your taste buds laugh that night. Kick back, close your eyes, and let the smells and tastes of past meals drift into your consciousness. The following should help you decide exactly what you're in the mood for, and give you an idea of Hawaii's dishes and their ingredients. Particular restaurants, eateries, stores, and shops will be covered in the travel chapters under "Food" and "Shopping."

HAWAIIAN FOODS

Hawaiian foods, oldest of the island dishes, are wholesome, well prepared, and delicious. All you have to do upon arrival is notice the size of some of the "local boys" (and women) to know that food is to them a happy and serious business. An oft-heard island joke is that "local men don't eat until they're full, they eat until they're tired." Many Hawaiian dishes have become standard fare at restaurants, eaten at one time or another by anyone who spends time in the islands. Hawaiian food in general is called *kaukau,* cooked food is *kapahaki,* and something broiled is called *kaola.* All of these prefixes on a menu will let you know that Hawaiian food is served. Usually inexpensive, it will definitely fill you up and keep you going.

Traditional Favorites

In old Hawaii, although the sea meant life, many more people were farmers than fishermen. They cultivated neat garden plots of taro, sugarcane, breadfruit, and various sweet potatoes *(uala).* They raised pigs and barkless dogs *(ilio),* and prized *moa* (chicken) for their feathers and meat, but found eating the eggs repulsive. Their only farming implement was the *'o'o,* a sharpened hardwood digging stick. The Hawaiians were the best farmers of Polynesia, and the first thing they planted was taro, a tuberous root created by the gods at the same time as humans. This main staple of the old Hawaiians was pounded into poi, a glutinous purple paste. Poi comes in liquid consistencies referred to as "one-, two, or three-finger poi." The fewer fingers you need to eat it, the thicker it is. Poi is one of the most nutritious carbohydrates known, but people unaccustomed to it find it bland and tasteless, although some of the best, fermented for a day or so, has an acidic bite. Poi is made to be eaten *with* something, but locals who love it pop it in their mouths and smack their lips.

Those unaccustomed to it will suffer constipation if they eat too much.

A favorite popular desert is *haupia,* a custard made from coconut. *Limu* is a generic term for edible seaweed, which many people still gather from the shoreline and eat as a salad, or mix with ground *kukui* nuts and salt as a relish. A favorite Hawaiian snack is *opihi,* small shellfish (limpets) that cling to rocks. People who gather them always leave some for the future. They are cut from the shell and eaten raw by all peoples of Hawaii. As testament to their popularity they sell for $150 per gallon in Honolulu. A general term that has come to mean "hors d'oeuvres" in Hawaii is *pu pu.* Originally the name of a small shellfish, it is now used by everyone for any "munchy" considered a finger food. A traditional liquor made from ti root is *okolehao.* It literally means "iron bottom," reminiscent of the iron blubber pots in which it was fermented.

Luau

Thick cookbooks are filled with common Hawaiian dishes, but you can get a good sampling at a well-done luau. The central feature is the *imu,* an underground oven. Basically, a shallow hole is dug and lined with stones upon which a roaring fire is kindled. Once the fire dies down and the stones are super-heated, the ashes are swept away and the *imu* is ready for cooking. At one time only men could cook in this fashion; it was *kapu* for women. These restrictions have long been lifted, but men still seem to do most of the pit cooking, while women primarily serve. The main dish at a luau is *kalua* pork. *Kalua* refers to any dish baked underground. A whole pig *(pua'a)* is wrapped in ti and banana leaves and placed in the pit's hot center. The pig's stomach cavity is filled with more hot stones; surrounding it are bundles of food wrapped in ti leaves. These savory bundles, *lau lau,* contain the side dishes: fish, chicken, poi, sweet potatoes, breadfruit, and bananas. The entire contents are then covered with multiple layers of banana, ti, or sometimes ginger leaves, and a final coating of earth. A long tube of bamboo may stick from the *imu* so that water (for steam) can be added. In about four hours the coverings are removed and the luau begins. You are encouraged to recline on *lau hala* mats placed around the central dining area, although tables and chairs are provided. There are forks and plates, but traditionally it is proper to use your fingers and a sturdy banana leaf as a plate. Professional luau cooks pride themselves on their methods of cooking and their food, and for a fixed price you can gorge yourself like an ancient *ali'i.* All luau supply entertainment, and exotic drinks flow like the tides. Your biggest problem after one of these extravaganzas will be finding the strength to rise from your *lau hala* mat.

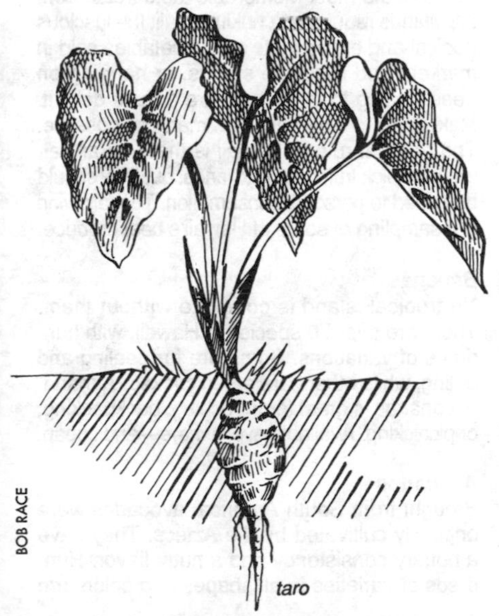
BOB RACE

taro

Luau range in price $40-55 per person. The price often includes admission to the theme parks at which many are now presented. The least expensive, most authentic, and best luau are often put on by local churches or community groups. They are not held on a regular basis, so make sure to peruse the free tourist literature where they advertise.

INTERNATIONAL DISHES

Chinese and Japanese cuisines have a strong influence on island cooking, and their well-known spices and ingredients are creatively used in many recipes. Other cuisines, such as Filipino,

Korean, and Portuguese, are not as well known, but are now becoming standard island fare.

Chinese

Tens of thousands of fortune cookies yield their little springs of wisdom every day to hungry diners throughout Hawaii. The Chinese, who came to Hawaii as plantation workers, soon discovered a brighter economic future by striking out on their own. Almost from the beginning, these immigrants opened restaurants. The tradition is still strong, and if the smallest town in Hawaii has a restaurant at all, it's probably Chinese. These restaurants are some of the least expensive, especially at lunchtime when prices are lower. In them, you'll find the familiar chop suey, chow mein, Peking duck, and fried rice. Takeout is common and makes a good, inexpensive picnic lunch.

Japanese

For the uninitiated, Japanese food is simple, aesthetically pleasing, and delicious. *Sushi* bars are plentiful, especially in Honolulu, using the freshest fish from local waters. Some common dishes include: teriyaki chicken, fish, or steak, which is grilled in a marinated shoyu (soy) sauce base; tempura, or mouth-sized bites of fish and vegetables dipped in a flour and egg batter and deep fried; sukiyaki, or vegetables, meat, mushrooms, tofu, and vermicelli you cook at your table in a prepared stock kept boiling with a little burner, then dip the morsels into a mixture of egg and shoyu; *shabu shabu,* similar to sukiyaki though without noodles and with the emphasis on beef; *donburi,* ("various ingredients on rice in a bowl"), such as *ten donburi,* battered shrimp on rice; and various tofu dishes and miso soup, which provide some of the highest sources of nonmeat protein. Japanese restaurants span the entire economic range, from elegant and expensive to hole-in-the-wall eateries where the surroundings are basic but the food is fit for a samurai. Above all, cleanliness is guaranteed.

Filipino

Most people have never sampled Filipino food. This cuisine is spicy with plenty of exotic sauces. The following is a sampling found in most Filipino restaurants: *singang,* sour soup made from fish, shrimp, or vegetables, that has an acidic base from fruits like tamarind; *adobo,* a generic term for anything (chicken and pork are standards) stewed in vinegar and garlic; *lumpia,* a Filipino spring roll; *pancit,* many variations of noodles made into ravioli-like bundles stuffed with pork or other meats; *lechon,* a whole suckling pig stuffed and roasted; *siopao,* a steam-heated dough ball filled with chicken or other tasty ingredients; and *halo halo,* a confection of shaved ice smothered in preserved fruits and canned milk.

Korean

Those who have never dined on Korean dishes are in for a sumptuous treat: *kalbitang,* a beef rib soup in a thin but tasty broth; *pulgogi,* marinated beef and vegetables grilled over an open flame; *pulkalbi,* beef ribs grilled over an open flame; *pibimbap,* a large bowl of rice smothered with beef, chicken, and vegetables that you mix together before eating; *kimchi,* fermented cabbage and hot spices made into a zesty "slaw"; *kimchi chigyae,* a stew of *kimchi,* pork, vegetables, and spices in a thick soup base.

TROPICAL FRUITS AND VEGETABLES

Some of the most memorable taste treats from the islands require no cooking at all: the luscious tropical and exotic fruits and vegetables sold in markets and roadside stands, or hanging on trees waiting to be picked, are a taste delight. Make sure to experience as many as possible. The general rule in Hawaii is that you are allowed to pick fruit on public lands, but they should be limited to personal consumption. The following is a sampling of some of Hawaii's best produce.

Bananas

No tropical island is complete without them. There are over 70 species in Hawaii, with hundreds of variations. Some are for peeling and eating, while others are eaten cooked. A "hand" of bananas is great for munching, backpacking, or picnicking. Available everywhere—and cheap.

Avocados

Brought from South America, avocados were originally cultivated by the Aztecs. They have a buttery consistency and a nutty flavor. Hundreds of varieties in all shapes and colors are

DIANA LASICH HARPER

breadfruit

available fresh year-round. They have the highest fat content of any fruit next to the olive.

Coconuts
What tropical paradise would be complete without coconuts? Indeed, these were some of the first plants brought by the Polynesians. When children were born, coconut trees were planted for them so they'd have fruit throughout their lifetimes. Truly tropical fruits, they know no season. Drinking nuts are large and green, and when shaken you can hear the milk inside. You get about a quart of fluid from each. It takes skill to open one, but a machete can handle anything. Cut the stem end flat so that it will stand, then bore a hole into the pointed end and put in a straw or hollow bamboo. Coconut water is slightly acidic and helps balance alkaline foods. Spoon meat is a custardlike gel on the inside of drinking nuts. Sprouted coconut meat is also an excellent food. Split open a sprouted nut, and inside is the yellow fruit, like moist sponge cake. "Millionaire's salad" is made from the heart of a coconut palm. At one time an entire tree was cut down to get to the heart, which is just inside the trunk below the fronds and is like an artichoke heart except that it's about the size of a watermelon. In a downed tree, the heart stays good for about two weeks.

Breadfruit
This island staple provides a great deal of carbohydrate, but many people find the baked, boiled, or fried fruit bland. It grows all over the islands and is really thousands of little fruits growing together to form a ball.

Mangos
These are some of the most delicious fruits known to humans. They grow wild all over the islands; the ones on the leeward sides of the islands ripen April-June, while the ones on the windward sides can last until October. They're found in the wild on trees up to 60 feet tall, and the problem is to stop eating them once you start!

Papaya
This truly tropical fruit has no real season but is mostly available in the summer. They grow on branchless trees and are ready to pick as soon as any yellow appears on them. Of the many varieties, the "solo papaya," meant to be eaten by one person, is the best. Split them in half, scrape out the seeds and have at them with a spoon.

Passion Fruit
Known by their island name of *lilikoi,* passion fruit make excellent juice and pies. They're small yellow fruit (similar to lemons but smooth-skinned) mostly available in summer and fall, and many wild ones grow on vines, waiting to be picked. Slice off the stem end, scoop the seedy pulp out with your tongue, and you'll know why they're called "passion fruit."

Guava
These small round yellow fruits are abundant in the wild, where they are ripe from early summer to late fall. Considered a pest—so pick all you want. A good source of vitamin C, they're great for juice, jellies, and desserts.

Macadamia Nuts
The king of nuts was brought from Australia in 1892. Now it's the state's fourth largest agricultural product. Available roasted, candied, or buttered.

Litchi
Litchi are called nuts but are really small fruit with thin red shells. They have sweet, juicy white flesh when fresh, and appear nutlike when dried.

Other Fruit
Besides the above, you'll find pineapples, oranges, limes, kumquats, thimbleberries, and blackberries, as well as carambolas, wild cherry tomatoes, and tamarinds.

FISH AND SEAFOOD

Anyone who loves fresh fish and seafood has come to the right place. Island restaurants specialize in seafood, and it's available everywhere. Pound for pound, seafood is one of the best dining bargains in Hawaii. You'll find it served in every kind of restaurant, and often the fresh catch of the day is proudly displayed on ice in a glass case. The following is a sampling of the best.

Mahimahi
This excellent eating fish is one of the most common and least expensive in Hawaii. It's referred to as a "dolphin," but is definitely a fish and not a mammal at all. Mahimahi can weigh 10-65 pounds; the flesh is light and moist, and the fish is broadest at the head. When caught it's a dark olive color, but after a while the skin turns iridescent—blue, green, and yellow. It can be served as a main course, or as a patty in a fish sandwich.

A'u
This true island delicacy is a broadbill swordfish or marlin. It's expensive even in Hawaii because the damn thing's so hard to catch. The meat is moist, white, and truly superb. If it's offered on the menu, order it. It'll cost a bit more, but you won't be disappointed.

Ono
Ono means "delicious" in Hawaiian so that should tip you off to the taste of this "wahoo," or king mackerel. *Ono* is regarded as one of the finest eating fishes in the ocean, and its white, flaky meat lives up to its name.

Manini
These five-inch fish are some of the most abundant in Hawaii and live in about 10 feet of water. They school and won't bite a hook but are easily taken with spear or net. Not often on a menu, but they're favorites with local people who know best.

Ulua
This member of the "Jack Crevalle" family ranges 15-100 pounds. Its flesh is white and has a steaklike texture. Delicious and often found on menus on all the islands.

Uku
This firm-fleshed fish is a gray snapper that's a favorite with local people. The meat is light and firm, and grills well.

Ahi
A yellowfin tuna with a distinctive pinkish meat, *ahi,* one of the island's best fish, is a great favorite cooked, or uncooked in sushi bars.

Seafood Potpourri
Moi is the Hawaiian word for "king." This fish has large eyes and a sharklike head. Considered one of the finest eating fishes in Hawaii, it's best during the autumn months.

'A'ama are the ubiquitous little black crabs that you'll spot on rocks and around pier areas. For fun, local fishermen try to catch them with poles, but the more efficient way is to throw a fish head into a plastic bucket and wait for the crabs to crawl in and trap themselves. The *'a'ama* are about as big as two fingers and make delicious eating.

Limu is edible seaweed that has been gathered as a garnish since pre-contact times, and is frequently found on traditional island menus. There's no other seaweed except *limu* in Hawaii. Because of this, the heavy, fishy-ocean smell that people associate with the sea but which is actually that of seaweed is absent in Hawaii.

Other island seafood found on menus include: *aloalo,* like tiny lobsters; crawfish, plentiful in taro fields and irrigation ditches; *ahipalaka,* albacore tuna; various octopus (squid or calamari); and shark of various types.

MUNCHIES AND ISLAND TREATS

Certain finger foods, fast foods, and island treats are unique to Hawaii. Some are meals in themselves, others are snacks. Here are some of the best and most popular.

Pu Pu
Pronounced as in "Winnie the Pooh Pooh," these are finger foods and hors d'oeuvres. They're everything from crackers to cracked crab. Often, they're free at lounges and bars

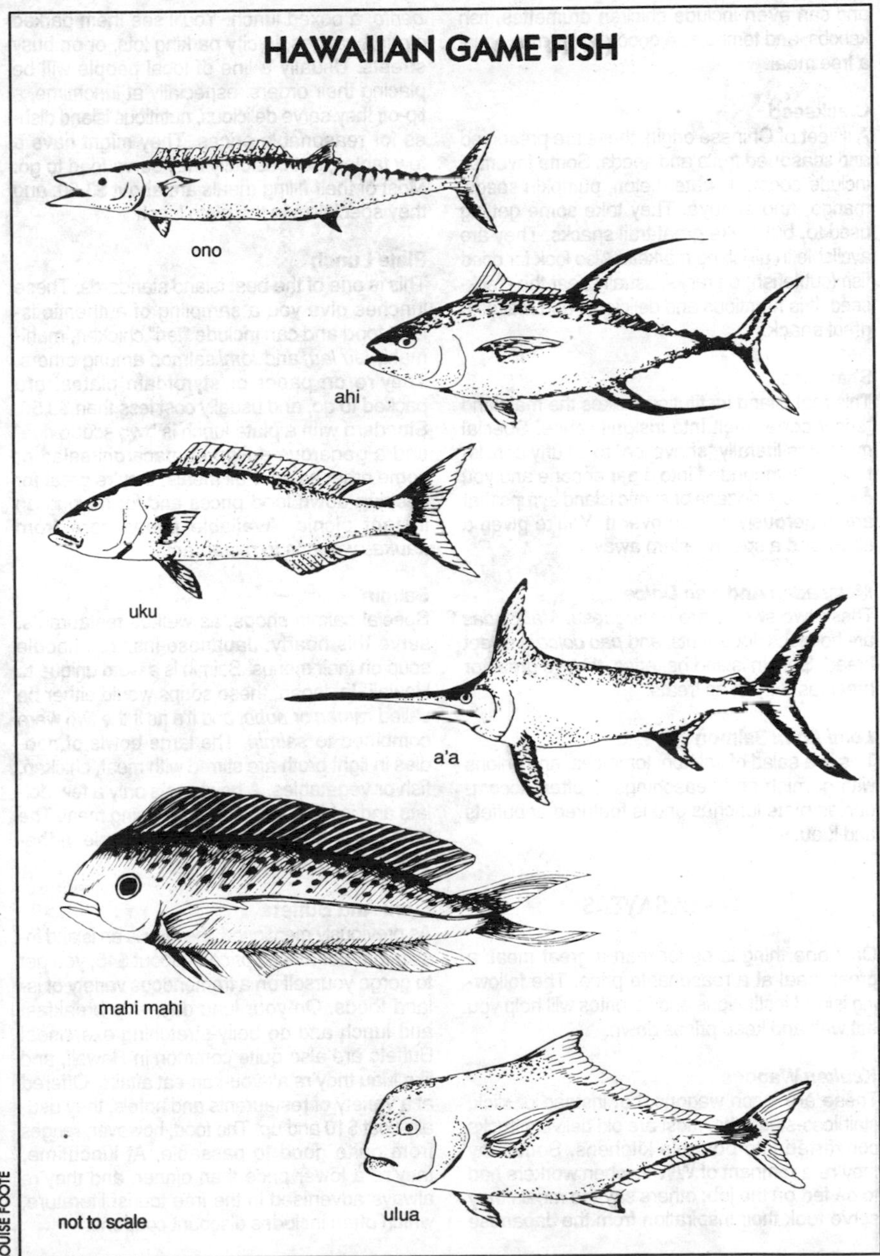
HAWAIIAN GAME FISH
ono
ahi
uku
a'a
mahi mahi
ulua
not to scale
LOUISE FOOTE

and can even include chicken drumettes, fish kabobs, and tempura. A good display may equal a free meal.

Crackseed

A sweet of Chinese origin, these are preserved and seasoned fruits and seeds. Some favorites include coconut, watermelon, pumpkin seeds, mango, and papaya. They take some getting used to, but make great trail snacks. They are available in all island markets. Also look for dried fish (cuttlefish) on racks, usually near the crackseed. It is nutritious and delicious, and makes a great snack.

Shave Ice

This real island institution makes the mainland "snow cone" melt into insignificance. Special machines literally "shave ice" to a fluffy consistency. It's mounded into a paper cone and you choose from dozens of exotic island syrups that are generously poured over it. You're given a straw and a spoon—slurp away.

Malasadas* And *Pao Dolce

These two sweets are Portuguese. *Malasadas* are holeless doughnuts, and *pao dolce* is sweet bread. Sold in island bakeries, they're great for breakfast or just as treats.

***Lomi Lomi* Salmon**

This is a salad of salmon, tomatoes, and onions with garnish and seasonings. It often accompanies plate lunches and is featured at buffets and luau.

MONEY-SAVERS

Only one thing is better than a great meal: a great meal at a reasonable price. The following island institutions and favorites will help you eat well and keep prices down.

***Kaukau* Wagons**

These are lunch wagons, but instead of slick, stainless-steel jobs, most are old delivery trucks converted into portable kitchens. Some say they're a remnant of WW II, when workers had to be fed on the job; others say the meals they serve took their inspiration from the Japanese *bento,* a boxed lunch. You'll see them parked along beaches, in city parking lots, or on busy streets. Usually a line of local people will be placing their orders, especially at lunchtime, a tip-off they serve delicious, nutritious island dishes for reasonable prices. They might have a few tables, but basically they serve food to go. Most of their filling meals are about $3.50, and they specialize in the plate lunch.

Plate Lunch

This is one of the best island standards. These lunches give you a sampling of authentic island food and can include "teri" chicken, mahimahi, *lau lau,* and *lomi* salmon among others. They're on paper or styrofoam plates, are packed to go, and usually cost less than $3.50. Standard with a plate lunch is "two scoop rice" and a generous dollop of macaroni salad or some other salad. Full meals, they're great for keeping down food prices and for making an instant picnic. Available everywhere from *kaukau* wagons to restaurants.

Saimin

Special saimin shops, as well as restaurants, serve this hearty, Japanese-inspired noodle soup on their menus. Saimin is a word unique to Hawaii. In Japan, these soups would either be called *ramen* or *soba,* and it's as if the two were combined to *saimin.* The large bowls of noodles in light broth are stirred with meat, chicken, fish or vegetables. A bowl costs only a few dollars and is big enough for an evening meal. The best place to eat saimin is a little hole-in-the-wall run by a family.

Luau And Buffets

As previously mentioned, the luau is an island institution. For a fixed price of about $45, you get to gorge yourself on a tremendous variety of island foods. On your luau day, skip breakfast and lunch and do belly-stretching exercises! Buffets are also quite common in Hawaii, and like luau they're all-you-can-eat affairs. Offered at a variety of restaurants and hotels, they usually cost $10 and up. The food, however, ranges from quite good to passable. At lunchtime, they're a lower price than dinner, and they're always advertised in the free tourist literature, which often includes discount coupons.

Tips

Even some of the island's best restaurants in the fanciest hotels offer "early-bird specials"—regular menu dinners offered to diners who come in before the usual dinner hour, which is approximately 6 p.m. You pay as little as half the normal price and can dine in luxury on some of the best foods. They are often advertised in free tourist literature, which sometimes includes coupons for reduced-price meals: two for one, or limited dinners at much lower prices. Hawaii also has the full contingency of American fast-food chains including, Jack in the Box, McDonald's, Shakey's Pizza, and Kentucky Fried Chicken.

ISLAND DRINKS

To complement the fine dining in the islands, bartenders have been busy creating their own tasty concoctions. The full range of beers, wines, and standard drinks is served in Hawaii, but for a real treat you should try mixed drinks inspired by the islands.

Beer

A locally brewed beer, **Primo,** manufactured under the auspices of the Joseph Schlitz Brewing Co. of Milwaukee, is a serviceable American brew in the German style, but lacks the full, hearty flavor of the European imports. In the early '70s it enjoyed an estimated 65% of the local market share, the highest in the nation, but after a bad batch was inadvertently released, sales plummeted and the local share fell to five percent, where it has since remained.

In the early 1990s two local breweries folded: the Pacific Brewing Company that produced **Maui Lager** and the Honolulu Brewing Company that produced **Koolau Lager,** among others. Both breweries were critically acclaimed, but both geared their beers to the full-bodied European taste. Local beer drinkers enjoy a much lighter brew, so sales of the new beers never really took off. Undaunted, Paula Thompson, a young and energetic ad executive turned *bier meister,* has brewed small batches of beer in her Kula home for years. A visiting uncle, involved in an Oregon brewery, suggested after tasting and enjoying one of her beers, that Maui was perfect for a microbrewery of its own. Paula agreed, but to keep start-up costs down, she brews her **Whale Ale** and **Aloha Lager** at the Blitz Weinhard Brewery in Portland, Oregon. Once the beer has been established, she hopes to move operations to Maui.

Another island entrepreneur, Marcus Bender, with more capital, will open the Hawaii Brewery Development Co. on a 22-acre site on the Big Island of Hawaii, where the Planning Commission has already approved the project. Eager to bypass the pitfalls that swallowed past local breweries, Bender, going for volume, is positioning his **Big Island Beer** to compete directly with Budweiser, Coors, and Miller, avoiding the upscale market dominated by the imports.

Coffee

Kona coffee is the only coffee grown in America. It comes from the Kona District of the Big Island and it is a rich, aromatic, truly fine coffee. If it's offered on the menu, have a cup.

Drinking Laws

There are no state-run liquor stores; all kinds of spirits, wines, and beers are available in markets and shops, generally open during normal business hours, seven days a week. The drinking age is 21, and no towns are "dry." Legal hours for serving drinks depend on the type of establishment. Hours generally are: hotels, 6 a.m.-4 a.m.; discos, and nightclubs where there is dancing, 10 a.m.-4 a.m.; bars and lounges where there is no dancing, 6 a.m.-2 a.m. Most restaurants serve alcohol, and in many that don't, you can bring your own.

Exotic Drinks

To make your experience complete, you must order a colorful island drink. Most look very innocent because they come in pineapples, coconut shells, or tall frosted glasses. They're often garnished with little umbrellas or sparklers, and most have enough fruit in them to give you your vitamins for the day. Rum is used as the basis of many of them; it's been an island favorite since it was introduced by the whalers of last century. Here are some of the most famous: mai tai, a mixture of light and dark rum, orange curaçao, orange and almond flavoring, and lemon juice; chi chi, a simple concoction of vodka, pineapple juice, and coconut syrup, a real sleeper because it tastes like a milk shake; Blue Hawaii, vodka and blue curaçao; planter's punch, light rum, grenadine, bitters, and lemon juice—a great thirst quencher; and Singapore Sling, a sparkling mixture of gin, cherry brandy, and lemon juice.

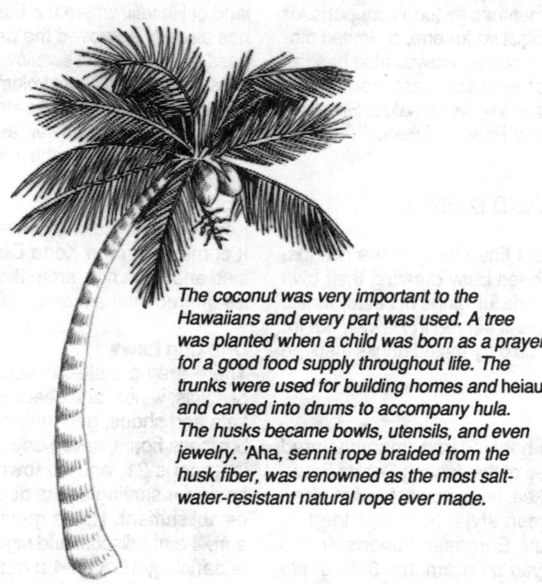

The coconut was very important to the Hawaiians and every part was used. A tree was planted when a child was born as a prayer for a good food supply throughout life. The trunks were used for building homes and heiau *and carved into drums to accompany hula. The husks became bowls, utensils, and even jewelry.* 'Aha, *sennit rope braided from the husk fiber, was renowned as the most salt-water-resistant natural rope ever made.*

GETTING THERE

With the number of visitors each year approaching six million, and double that number of travelers passing through, Hawaii is one of the easiest places in the world to get to . . . by plane. About 10 large U.S. airlines (and other small ones) fly to and from the islands; about the same number of foreign carriers, mostly from Asia and Oceania, touch down on a daily basis. In 1978 airlines were "deregulated." In 1984, the reign of the Civil Aeronautics Board (CAB), which controlled exactly which airlines flew where and how much they could charge, ended. Routes, prices, and schedules were thrown open to free competition. Airlines that had previously monopolized preferred destinations found competitors prying loose their strangleholds. Thus, Hawaii is now one of the most hotly contested air markets in the world. The competition between carriers is fierce, and this makes for "sweet deals" and a wide choice of fares for the money-wise traveler. It also makes for pricing chaos. It's impossible to give airline prices that will hold true for more than a month, if that long.But it's comforting to know flights to Hawaii are cheaper today than they have been in years, and mile for mile are one of the best travel bargains in the industry. What's really important is to be familiar with the alternatives at your disposal, so you can make an informed travel selection. Now more than ever you should work with a sharp travel agent who's on your side.

Note: Handicapped travelers, please see "Services for the Disabled" under "Health and Safety" later in this chapter.

Brief Airline History

On May 20-21, 1927, the people of the world were mesmerized by the heroic act of Charles Lindbergh, The Lone Eagle, as he safely piloted his sturdy craft, *The Spirit of St. Louis,* across the Atlantic. With the Atlantic barrier broken, it took only four days for Jim Dole, of pineapple fame, to announce an air race from the West Coast to Hawaii. He offered the same first prize of $25,000 that Lindbergh had claimed, and to sweeten the pot he offered $10,500 for second place. The **Dole Air Derby** applied only to civilian flights, though the military was already at work attempting the Pacific crossing.

In August 1925, a Navy flying boat took off from near San Francisco, piloted by Comdr. John Rodgers. The seaplane flew without difficulty across the wide Pacific's expanse, but ran out of gas just north of the Hawaiian Islands and had to put down in a stormy sea. Communication devices went dead and the mission was given up as lost. Heroically, Rodgers and his crew made crude sails from the wing's fabric and sailed the plane to within 12 miles of Kauai, where they were spotted by an incredulous submarine crew. On June 28, 1927, Army lieutenants Maitland and Hegenberger successfully flew a Fokker trimotor land plane, *The Bird of Paradise,* from Oakland to Oahu in just under 26 hours.

On July 14, 1927, independent of the air derby, two indomitable pilots, Smith and Bronte, flew their *City of Oakland* from its namesake to a forced landing on the shoreline of Molokai. On August 16, 1927, eight planes lined up in Oakland to start the derby. The first to take off was the *Woolaroc,* piloted by Art Goebel and Bill Davis. It went on to win the race and claim the prize in just over 26 hours. Second place went to the appropriately named *Aloha,* crewed by Martin Jensen and Paul Schluter, coming in two hours behind the *Woolaroc.* Unfortunately, two planes were lost in the crossing and two more in the rescue attempt, which accounted

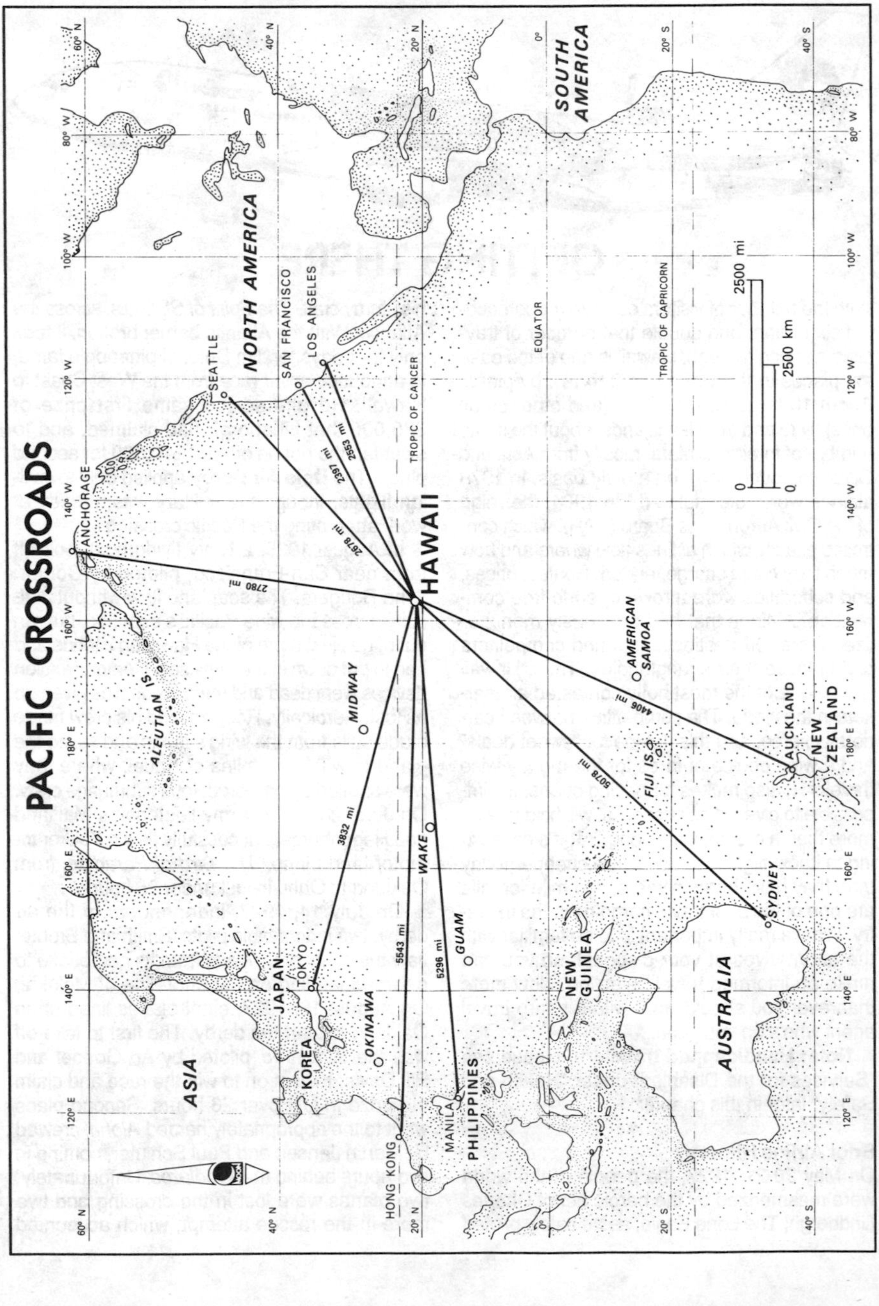

PACIFIC CROSSROADS

ASIA
JAPAN
KOREA
TOKYO
OKINAWA
HONG KONG
MANILA
PHILIPPINES
GUAM
WAKE
MIDWAY
ALEUTIAN IS.
ANCHORAGE
SEATTLE
SAN FRANCISCO
LOS ANGELES
NORTH AMERICA
SOUTH AMERICA
HAWAII
AMERICAN SAMOA
FIJI IS.
AUCKLAND
NEW ZEALAND
SYDNEY
AUSTRALIA
NEW GUINEA
TROPIC OF CANCER
EQUATOR
TROPIC OF CAPRICORN
2780 mi
2678 mi
2397 mi
2553 mi
3832 mi
5543 mi
5296 mi
5078 mi
4406 mi
0 2500 mi
0 2500 km
60° N
40° N
20° N
0°
20° S
40° S
120° E
140° E
160° E
180° E
160° W
140° W
120° W
100° W
80° W

for a total of 12 dead. However, the race proved that flying to Hawaii was indeed feasible.

WINGS TO HAWAII

There are two categories of airlines you can take to Hawaii: **domestic,** meaning American-owned, and **foreign**-owned. An American law, penned at the turn of the century to protect American shipping, says only an American carrier can transport you to and from two American cities. In the airline industry, this law is still very much in effect. It means, for example, that if you want to fly roundtrip San Francisco-Honolulu, you *must* fly on a domestic carrier, such as United or Pan Am. If, however, you are flying San Francisco to Tokyo, you are at liberty to fly a "foreign" airline such as Japan Air Lines, and you may even have a stopover in Hawaii, but you must continue on to Tokyo or some other foreign city and cannot fly JAL back to San Francisco. Canadians have no problem flying Canadian Pacific roundtrip from Toronto to Honolulu because this route does not connect two American cities, and so it is with all foreign travel to and from Hawaii. Travel agents know this, but if you're planning your own trip be aware of this fact and know that if you're flying roundtrip it must be on a domestic carrier.

Kinds Of Flights

The three kinds of flights are the "milk run," direct, and nonstop. Milk runs are the least convenient. On these, you board a carrier, say in your home town, fly it to a gateway city, change planes and carriers, fly on to the West Coast, change again, and then fly to Hawaii. They're a hassle—your bags have a much better chance of getting lost, you waste time in airports, and to top it off, they're not any cheaper. Avoid them if you can.

On direct flights you fly from point A to point B without changing planes; it doesn't mean that you don't land in between. Direct flights do land usually once to board and deplane passengers, but you sit cozily on the plane along with your luggage and off you go again. Nonstop is just that, but can cost a bit more. You board and when the doors open again you're in Hawaii. All flights from the West Coast gateway cities are nonstop, "God willing," because there is only the Pacific in between!

Travel Agents

At one time people went to a travel agent the same way they went to a barber or beautician . . . loyally sticking with one. Most agents are reputable professionals who know what they're doing. They should be members of the American Society of Travel Agents (ASTA) and licensed by the Air Traffic Conference (ATC). Most have the inside track on the best deals, and they'll save you countless hours calling 800 numbers and listening to elevator music while on hold. Unless you require them to make very special arrangements, their services are free—the airlines and hotels they book you into pay their commission.

If you've done business with a travel agent in the past, and were satisfied with the services and prices, by all means stick with him or her. If no such positive rapport exists, then shop around. Ask friends or relatives for recommendations; if you can't get any endorsements go to the *Yellow Pages*. Call two or three travel agents to compare prices. Make sure to give them equal information and be as precise as possible. Tell them where and when you want to go, how long you want to stay, what class you want to travel, and any special requirements. Write down their information. It's amazing how confusing travel plans can be when you have to keep track of flight numbers, times, prices, and all the preparation info. When you compare, don't look only for the cheapest price. Check for convenience in flights, hotel amenities, and any other fringe benefits that might be included. Then make your choice of agents; if they are willing to give you individualized service, stick with them from this point on.

Agents become accustomed to offering the same deals to many clients because they're familiar with making the arrangements and they worked well in the past. Sometimes these are indeed the best, but if they don't suit you, don't be railroaded into accepting them. Any good agent will work with you. After all, it's your trip and your money.

Package Tours

For the independent traveler, practical package deals that include only flight, car, and lodging are okay. Agents put these together all the time and they just might be the best, but if they don't suit you, make arrangements separately. A package *tour* is totally different. On these you get your hand held by an escort, eat where they want you to eat, go where they want you to go, and watch Hawaii slide by your bus window. For some people this might be the way, but most should avoid the package tour. You'll see Hawaii best on your own, and if you want a tour you can arrange one there, often cheaper. Once arrangements have been made with your travel agent, make sure to take all receipts and letters of confirmation (hotel, car) with you to Hawaii. They probably won't be needed, but if they are, nothing will work better in getting results.

Mainland And International Fares

There are many categories of airline fares, but only three apply to the average traveler: first class, coach, and excursion (APEX). Traveling **first class** seats you in the front of the plane, gives you free drinks and movie headsets, a wider choice of meals, more leg room, and access to VIP lounges, if they exist. There are no restrictions, no penalties for advance-booking cancellations or rebooking of return flights, and no minimum-stay requirements.

Coach, the way most people fly, is totally adequate. You sit in the plane's main compartment behind first class. Your seats are comfortable, but you don't have as much leg room or as wide a choice of meals. Movie headsets and drinks cost you a few dollars, but that's about it. Coach offers many of the same benefits of first class and costs about 30% less. You can buy tickets up until takeoff; you have no restrictions on minimum or maximum stays; you receive liberal stopover privileges; and you can cash in your return ticket or change your return date with no penalties.

Excursion or advance payment excursion (APEX) fares are the cheapest. You are accommodated on the plane exactly the same as if you were flying coach. There are, however, some restrictions. You must book and pay for your ticket in advance (7-14 days). At the same time, you must book your return flight, and under most circumstances you can't change either without paying a penalty. Also, your stopovers are severely limited and you will have a minimum/maximum stay period. Only a limited number of seats on any one plane are set aside for APEX fares, so book as early as you can. Also, if you must change travel plans, you can go to the airport and get on as a standby passenger using a discounted ticket, even if the airline doesn't have an official standby policy. There's always the risk you won't get on, but you do have a chance, as well as priority over an actual standby customer.

Standby is exactly what its name implies: you go to the airport and wait around to see if any flights going to Hawaii have an empty seat. You can save some money, but cannot have a firm itinerary or limited time. Since Hawaii is such a popular destination, standbys can wait days before catching a plane. A company called **Stand Bys Ltd.** offers an up-to-the-minute newsletter and an 800 number which gives you information on charter flights that haven't sold out. The service costs $45 per year, but you can save 15-60% on most tickets. For information write to Stand Bys Ltd., 26711 Northwestern Hwy., Southfield, MI 48034, tel. (313) 352-4876.

Active and retired **military personnel** and their dependents are offered special fares on airlines and in military hostels. An excellent resource book listing these special fares and more is *Space-A* ($11.75 for book and first-class postage), available from Military Travel News, Box 9, Oakton, VA 22124. Plenty of money-saving tips.

Charters

Charter flights were at one time only for groups or organizations that had memberships in travel clubs. Now they're open to the general public. A charter flight is an entire plane or a "block" of seats purchased at a quantity discount by a charter company and then sold to customers. Because they are bought at wholesale prices, charter fares can be the cheapest available. As in package deals, only take a charter flight if it is a "fly only," or perhaps includes a car. You don't need one that includes a guide and a bus. Most importantly, make sure the charter company is reputable. They should belong to the same organizations (ASTA and ATC) as most travel agents. If not, check them out at the local chamber of commerce.

More restrictions apply to charters than to any other flights. You must pay in advance. If you cancel after a designated time, you can be penalized severely or lose your money entirely. You cannot change departure or return dates and times. However, up to 10 days before departure the charter company is legally able to cancel, raise the price by 10%, or change time and dates. They must return your money if cancellation occurs, or if changed arrangements are unacceptable to you. Mostly they are on the up-and-up and flights go smoothly, but there are horror stories. Be careful. Be wise. Investigate!

Tips

Flights from the West Coast take about five hours; you gain two hours over Pacific Standard Time when you land in Hawaii. From the East Coast it takes about 11 hours and you gain five hours over Eastern Standard Time. Try to fly Mon.-Thurs., when flights are cheaper and easier to book. Pay for your ticket as soon as your plans are firm. If prices go up no charge is added, but merely booking doesn't guarantee the lowest price. Make sure the airlines, hotels, and car agencies get your phone number too, not only your travel agent's, in case any problems with availability arise (travel agents are often closed on weekends). It's not necessary, but it's a good idea to call and reconfirm flights 24-72 hours in advance.

First-row (bulkhead) seats are good for people who need more leg room, but bad for watching the movie. Airlines will give you special meals (vegetarian, kosher, low cal, low salt) often at no extra charge, but you must notify them in advance. If you're "bumped" from an overbooked flight, you're entitled to a comparable flight to your destination within one hour. If more than an hour elapses, you get denied-boarding compensation which goes up proportionately with the amount of time you're held up. Sometimes this is cash or a voucher for another flight to be used in the future. You don't have to accept what an airline offers on the spot, if you feel they aren't being fair.

Taking your pet cat or dog (seeing-eye dog too) can pose great problems. See "Pets and Quarantine" under "What to Take" later in this chapter.

When To Go

The prime tourist season starts two weeks before Christmas and lasts until Easter. It picks up again with summer vacation in early June and ends once more in late August. If possible, avoid these times of year. Everything is usually booked solid and prices are inflated. Hotel, airline, and car reservations, which are a must, are often hard to coordinate. You can save 10-50% and a lot of hassle if you go in the artificially created off-season, September to early December, and mid-April (after Easter) until early June. You'll not only find the prices better, but the beaches, hikes, campgrounds and restaurants will be less crowded. The people will be happier to see you, too.

Traveling With Children

Fares for children ages 2-12 are 50% of the adult fare; children under two not occupying a seat travel free. If you're traveling with an infant or active toddler, book your flight well in advance and request the bulkhead seat or first row in any section and a bassinet if available. Many carriers have fold-down cribs with restraints for baby's safety and comfort. Toddlers appreciate the extra space provided by the front-row seats. Be sure to reconfirm, and arrive early to ensure this special seating. On long flights you'll be glad you took these extra pains.

Although most airlines have coloring books, puppets, etc., to keep your child busy, it's always a good idea to bring your own. These can make the difference between a pleasant flight and a harried ordeal. Also, remember to bring baby bottles, formula, diapers, and other necessities, as many airlines may not be equipped with exactly what you need. Make all inquiries ahead of time so you're not caught unprepared.

Baggage

You are allowed two free pieces of checked-on luggage and a carry-on bag. The two checked pieces can weigh up to 70 pounds each; a charge is levied for extra weight. The larger bag can have an overall added dimension (height plus width plus length) of 62 inches; the smaller, 55 inches. Your carry-on must fit under your seat or in the overhead storage compartment. Purses and camera bags are not counted as carry-ons and may be taken aboard. Surfboards

The Honolulu Advertiser EXTRA
Hawaii's Territorial Newspaper

HONOLULU, TERRITORY OF HAWAII, U.S.A., WEDNESDAY MORNING, APRIL 17, 1935. PRICE FIVE CENTS

CLIPPER LANDS AT 8:00

Thousands See Flight's Start At Golden Gate

Heavily-Laden Ship In Graceful Takeoff from Bay Waters; Routine Job to Crew

An Early Morning Caller

Reaches Honolulu At 7:04; Cruises Over Island Until Crowds Arrive At Air Base

Giant Plane Sets New Record for Westbound Hop; Could Easily Have Made Better Time But Delayed Landing for Spectators

At exactly 8 a. m. the 19-ton Pan American Clipper Ship came to a graceful landing at the fleet air base in Pearl Harbor, completing her flight from Alameda Airport to Honolulu in 19 hours and 48 minutes, and bettering the previous record for a westbound crossing of 24 hours and 45 minutes, made by the mass flight of the U. S. navy patrol squadron in January, 1934, by the wide margin of four hours and three minutes.

But the giant plane, commanded by Captain Edwin Musick, reached Honolulu at 7:04 o'clock and could have landed less than ten minutes later. To accommodate the crowds and the welcoming committee Captain Musick circled over the city and kept her aloft until 8 o'clock.

Aided by the trade winds over approximately the last 500 miles the clipper ship came along at speeds ranging from 115 to 160 miles an hour and could have made faster time had speed been her object. Almost perfect visibility and weather prevailed throughout the flight.

Advertiser Signs Wood

Here's Log Of Clipper Since Hop From Coast

Receptions Ready Today

Naval And Civilian Officials To Greet Men

Pan American Airlines, now out of business, opened Hawaii to mass air travel with this historic 19 hour and 48 minute flight on Wednesday, April 17, 1935.

and bicycles are about $15 extra. Although they make great mementos, remove all previous baggage tags from your luggage; they can confuse handlers. Attach a sturdy luggage tag with your name and address on the handle, or stick a label on the bag itself. Put your name and address inside the bag, and the address where you'll be staying in Hawaii if possible. Carry your cosmetics, identification, money, prescriptions, tickets, reservations, change of underwear, camera equipment, and perhaps a change of shirt or blouse in your carry-on.

Visas

Entering Hawaii is like entering anywhere else in the U.S. Foreign nationals must have a current passport and proper visa, an ongoing or return air ticket, and sufficient funds for the proposed stay in Hawaii. Canadians do not need a visa or passport, but must have proper identification such as passport, driver's license, or birth certificate.

Leaving Hawaii

Remember that before you leave Hawaii for the Mainland, all of your bags are subject to an **agricultural inspection,** a usually painless procedure taking only a minute or two. To facilitate your departure, leave all bags unlocked until after inspection. There are no restrictions on beach sand, coconuts, dried flower arrangements, fresh flower lei, pineapples, certified pest-free plants, seashells, seed lei, and wood roses. However, avocado, litchi, and papaya must be treated before departure. Some other restricted items are berries, fresh gardenias, roses, jade plants, live insects, snails, cotton, plants in soil, soil itself, and sugarcane.

DOMESTIC CARRIERS

The following are the major domestic carriers to and from Hawaii. The planes used are primarily DC-10s and 747s, with a smaller 727 flown now and again. A list of the "gateway cities" from which they fly direct and nonstop flights is given, but "connecting cities" are not. All flights, by all carriers, land at Honolulu International Airport except the limited direct flights to Maui and Hawaii. Only the established companies are listed. Entrepreneurial small airlines such as the now-defunct Hawaii Express pop up now and again and specialize in dirt-cheap fares. There is a hectic frenzy to buy their tickets, and business is great for a while, but then the established companies lower their fares and the gamblers fold.

Hawaiian Air

One of Hawaii's own domestic airlines has entered the Mainland market. They operate a daily flight from Los Angeles and San Francisco to Honolulu, with periodic flights from Anchorage, Las Vegas, Portland, and Seattle. The "common fare" ticket price includes an ongoing flight to any of the Neighbor Islands, and if you're leaving Hawaii, a free flight from a Neighbor Island to the link-up in Honolulu. Senior-citizen discounts for people age 60 or older are offered on transpacific and interisland flights. Hawaiian Air's transpacific schedule features flights between Honolulu and points in the South Pacific nearly every day: flights depart for Pago Pago and American Samoa, half continuing on to Apia and Western Samoa, and the rest flying to Tonga, with additional flights to New Zealand, Guam, Tahiti, and Rarotonga. Hawaiian Air offers special discount deals with Dollar rental cars and select major-island hotels. Contact Hawaiian Air at (800) 367-5320 Mainland, or (800) 882-8811 in Hawaii.

United Airlines
Since their first island flight in 1947, United has become top dog in flights to Hawaii. Their Mainland routes connect over 100 cities to Honolulu. The main gateways for direct flights are San Francisco, Los Angeles, San Diego, Seattle, Portland, Chicago, New York, Denver, and Toronto. They also offer direct flights to Maui from San Francisco, Los Angeles, and Chicago, and from Los Angeles to the Big Island. United offers a number of packages, including flight and hotel on Oahu, and flight, hotel, and car on the Neighbor Islands. They inter-line with Aloha Airlines and deal with Hertz rental cars. They're the "big guys" and they intend to stay that way—their packages are hard to beat. Call (800) 241-6522.

American Airlines
American offers direct flights to Honolulu from Los Angeles, San Francisco, Dallas, and Chicago. They also fly from Los Angeles and San Francisco to Maui, with a connection in Honolulu. Call (800) 433-7300.

Continental
Flights from all Mainland cities to Honolulu connect via Los Angeles and San Francisco. Also available are direct flights from Australia and New Zealand to Honolulu. Call (800) 525-0280 or (800) 231-0856 for international information.

Northwest
Northwest flies from Los Angeles, San Francisco, and Portland via Seattle. There are onward flights to Tokyo, Osaka, Okinawa, Manila, Hong Kong, Taipei, and Seoul. Call (800) 225-2525.

Delta Air Lines
In 1985, Delta entered the Hawaiian market; when it bought out Western Airlines its share became even bigger. They have nonstop flights to Honolulu from Dallas/Fort Worth, Los Angeles, San Francisco, and San Diego; and now flights to Kahului, Maui, via Los Angeles or Honolulu. Call (800) 221-1212.

FOREIGN CARRIERS

The following carriers operate throughout Oceania but have no U.S. flying rights. This means in order for you to vacation in Hawaii using one of these carriers, your flight must originate or terminate in a foreign city. Though you can have a stopover in Honolulu with a connecting flight to a Neighbor Island, if you've purchased a flight on Japan Air Lines from San Francisco to Tokyo, you can stop in Hawaii, but you must then carry on to Tokyo. Failure to do so will result in a stiff fine, and the balance of your ticket will not be refunded.

Canadian Airlines International
Nonstop flights from Canada to Honolulu originate in Vancouver, Toronto, and Calgary; nonstop Pacific flights go to Fiji, Auckland, and Sydney, with connecting flights to other Pacific cities. Call (800) 426-7007.

Air New Zealand
Flights link New Zealand, Australia, and Fiji with Los Angeles via Honolulu. Also offered are a remarkable APEX fare from Los Angeles to New Zealand, with stops in Honolulu and Fiji; and a Super Pass fare that lets you stop in eight cities between Los Angeles and Australia. Occasionally, other special fares are offered. Call (800) 262-1234 for current information.

Japan Air Lines
The Japanese are the second-largest group, next to Americans, to visit Hawaii. JAL flights to Honolulu originate in Tokyo, Nagoya, and Osaka. There are no JAL flights between the Mainland and Hawaii. Call (800) 525-3663.

Philippine Airlines
Philippine Airlines flies between Los Angeles or San Francisco and Manila via Honolulu. Con-

nections in Manila are available to most Asian cities. Call (800) 435-9725.

Qantas
Daily flights depart from San Francisco and Los Angeles for Sydney via Honolulu. Stopovers are possible in Fiji and Tahiti. Call (800) 622-0850.

China Airlines
Routes from Los Angeles to Taipei with stopovers in Honolulu and Tokyo are possible, but flights are not available year-round. There are connections from Taipei to most Asian capitals. Call (800) 227-5118.

Korean Air
Korean Air offers some of the least expensive flights to Asia. Flights leave only from Los Angeles, stop in Honolulu, then continue either directly to Seoul or stop over in Tokyo, with connections to many Asian cities. Call (800) 421-8200.

Air Tungaru
Limited flights are available from Kiribati to Honolulu via Christmas Island and Tarawa. In Hawaii, call (808) 735-3994.

Air Nauru
The South Pacific's richest island offers flights throughout Polynesia, including most major islands, with connections to Japan, Taipei, Hong Kong, Manila, Singapore, and Australia. In Hawaii, call (808) 531-9766.

TRAVEL BY SHIP

American Hawaii Cruises
This American cruise ship company operates two 800-passenger ships, the SS *Independence* and the SS *Constitution.* These ships offer similar seven-day itineraries that circumnavigate and call at the four main islands. Their fares range from an inside "thrifty cabin" at $1095 to a luxury owner's suite for $3950. Children under 16 are often given special rates and cruise free June-Sept. when they share a cabin with their parents. You board the ship in Honolulu after a plane flight to the islands arranged by American Hawaii Cruises. Each ship is a luxury seagoing hotel and gourmet restaurant; swimming pools, health clubs, movies, and nightclubs are part of the amenities. For details contact American Hawaii Cruises, 550 Kearny St., San Francisco, CA 94108, tel. (800) 765-7000; from Canada call collect (415) 392-9400.

Alternatives
Other companies offering varied cruises include **P&O Lines,** which operates the *Sea Princess* through the South Pacific, making port at Honolulu on its way from the West Coast once a year.

Royal Cruise Line out of Los Angeles, or Auckland alternatively, sails the *Royal Odyssey,* which docks in Honolulu on its South Pacific and Orient cruise at a cost of $2200-4000.

The **Holland America Line** sails the *Rotterdam* on its 108-day Grand Circle cruise, departing Fort Lauderdale, passing around South America, and calling at Honolulu as it heads for Asia. Prices are $20,000-70,000. Call (800) 426-0327.

Society Expeditions offers a 42-day cruise throughout the South Pacific departing from Honolulu. Fares range $3000-9000. Call (800) 426-7794.

Information
Most travel agents can provide information on the above cruise lines. If you're especially interested in traveling by freighter, contact **Freighter Travel Club of America,** Box 12693, Salem, OR 97309; or **Ford's Freighter Travel Guide,** Box 505, 22151 Clarendon St., Woodland Hills, CA 91367.

TOUR COMPANIES

Many tour companies advertise packages to Hawaii in large city newspapers every week. They offer very reasonable airfares, car rentals, and accommodations. Without trying, you can get roundtrip airfare from the West Coast and a week in Hawaii for $400-500 using one of these companies. The following companies offer great deals and have excellent reputations. This list is by no means exhaustive.

SunTrips
This California-based tour and charter company sells vacations all over the world. They're pri-

marily a wholesale company, but will work with the general public. SunTrips often works with American Trans-Air, tel. (800) 225-9920, when flying to Hawaii. American Trans-Air answers their phones Mon.-Fri. during normal business hours only. When you receive your SunTrips tickets, you are given discount vouchers for places to stay that are convenient to the airport of departure. Many of these hotels have complimentary airport pickup service, and will allow you to park your car, free of charge, for up to 14 days, which saves a considerable amount on airport parking fees. SunTrips does not offer assigned seating until you get to the airport. They recommend you get there two hours in advance, and they ain't kidding! This is the price you pay for getting such inexpensive air travel. SunTrips usually has a deal with a car-rental company. Remember everyone on your incoming flight is offered the same deal, and all make a beeline for the rental car's shuttle van after landing and securing their baggage. If you have a traveling companion, work together to beat the rush by leaving your companion to fetch the baggage while you head directly for the van as soon as you arrive. Pick your car up, then return for your partner and the bags. Even if you're alone, you could zip over to the car-rental center and then return for your bags without having them sit very long on the carousel. Contact SunTrips, 100 Park Center, Box 18505, San Jose, CA 95158, tel. (800) 662-9292, (800) 786-8747 in California, (808) 941-2697 in Honolulu.

Council Travel Services

These full-service, budget-travel specialists are a subsidiary of the nonprofit Council on International Educational Exchange, and the official U.S. representative to the International Student Travel Conference. They'll custom-design trips and programs for everyone from senior citizens to college students. Bona fide students have extra advantages, however, including eligibility for the International Student Identification Card (CISC), which often gets you discount fares and waived entrance fees. Groups and business travelers are also welcome. For full information, write to Council Travel Services at one of these offices: 919 Irving St. #102, San Francisco, CA 94122, tel. (415) 566-6222; or 205 E. 42nd St., New York, NY 10017, tel. (212) 661-1450. Other offices are in Austin, Berkeley, Boston, Davis, Long Beach, Los Angeles, Miami, Portland, San Diego, and Seattle.

S.T.A. Travel

You don't have to be a student to avail yourself of their services. Their main office in Los Angeles is at 7202 Melrose Ave., Los Angeles, CA 90046, tel. (213) 934-8722. S.T.A. also maintains offices in Boston, Cambridge, New York, Philadelphia, San Francisco, and Washington, D.C., and has affiliates in Toronto and Vancouver, as well as throughout Australia and Europe.

Nature Expeditions International

These quality tours have nature as the theme. Trips are 15-day, four-island, natural-history expeditions, with an emphasis on plants, birds, and geology. Their guides are experts in their fields and give personable and attentive service. Contact Nature Expeditions International at 474 Willamette, Box 11496, Eugene, OR 97440, tel. (503) 484-6529 or (800) 869-0639.

Ocean Voyages

This unique company offers seven- and 10-day itineraries aboard a variety of yachts in the Hawaiian Islands. The yachts, equipped to carry 2-10 passengers, ensure individualized training in sailing. The vessels sail throughout the islands, exploring hidden bays and coves, and berth at different ports as they go. This opportunity is for anyone who wishes to see the islands in a timeless fashion, thrilling to sights experienced by the first Polynesian settlers and Western explorers. For rates and information contact Ocean Voyages, 1709 Bridgeway, Sausalito, CA 94965, tel. (415) 332-4681.

Island Holiday Tours

This established, Hawaii-based company offers flights with American and United, and rental cars through Budget. Arrangements can also be made for tours, luau, helicopter rides, etc., on all islands. Contact Island Holiday Tours, 2255 Kuhio Ave., Honolulu, HI 96815, tel. (800) 448-6877.

Pleasant Hawaiian Holidays

A California-based company specializing in Hawaii, Pleasant Hawaiian Holidays makes arrangements for flights, accommodations, and transportation only. At 2404 Townsgate Rd., Westlake Village, CA 91361, tel. (800) 242-9244.

EcoTours To Hawaii

Sierra Club Trips offers Hawaii trips for nature lovers interested in an outdoor experience. Various trips include hikes over Maui's Haleakala, kayaking along the Na Pali Coast of Kauai, and a family camping spree in Kauai's Koke'e region. All trips are led by experienced guides and are open to Sierra Club members only ($33 per year to join). For information contact the Sierra Club Outing Department, 730 Polk St., San Francisco, CA 94109, tel. (415) 776-2211.

Earthwatch allows you to become part of an expeditionary team dedicated to conservation and the study of the natural environment. An expedition might include studying dolphins in Kewalo Basin Marine Mammal Laboratory, or observing the ubiquitous mongoose from a hut high atop Mauna Kea. Basically, you become an assistant field researcher—your lodgings might be a dorm room at the University of Hawaii, and your meals might come from a remote camp kitchen. Fees vary and are tax deductible. If you are interested in this learning experience, contact Earthwatch, 680 Mt. Auburn St., Box 403-P, Watertown, MA 02272, tel. (617) 926-8200.

Backroads, 1516 5th St., Suite PR, Berkeley, CA 94710, tel. (510) 527-1555 or (800) 462-2848, arranges easy-on-the-environment bicycle and hiking trips to the Big Island. Basic tours include: six-day hiking/camping tour $698; six-day hiking/inn tour $1295; eight-day bicycle/inn tour $1495; and five-day bicycle/camping tour $649. Prices include hotel/inn accommodations or tent when applicable, most meals, and professional guide service. Airfare is not included, and bicycles and sleeping bags can be rented (BYO okay) for reasonable rates.

Far Horizons, Box 1529, 16 Fern Ln., San Anselmo, CA 94960, tel. (800) 552-4575, specializes in cultural discovery trips. A 12-day trip visits the islands of Hawaii, Lanai, and Oahu. Led by archaeologist Dr. Georgia Lee, an expert on Polynesian rock art, the expedition features stops at Hawaii's most famous *heiau,* petroglyph fields, museums, and historical homes. The cost is $3695 per person and includes transpacific and internal flights, accommodations, ground transportation, most meals, and entry fees.

Crane Tours, 15101 Magnolia Blvd., Sherman Oaks, CA 91403, tel. (800) 653-2545, owned and operated by Bill Crane, has been taking people kayaking and backpacking to the Big Island, Maui, and Kauai since 1976. Basic prices for these eco-adventures start at $650, with the most expensive tour around $800 (airfare not included).

DIANA LASICH HARPER

The plumeria has become the maki *(death) flower often planted at cemeteries because of its perpetual blooms.*

GETTING AROUND

BY AIR

Interisland air travel is highly developed, economical, and completely convenient. You can go almost anywhere at anytime on everything from wide-bodied jets to single-engine air taxis. Hawaiians take flying for granted, using planes the way most people use buses. A shopping excursion to Honolulu from a Neighbor Island is commonplace, as is a trip from the city for a picnic at a quiet beach. The longest flight, just over an hour, is from Kauai to Hawaii, including a stopover at one of the islands in between. The moody sea can be uncooperative to mass transit, but the skies above Hawaii are generally clear and perfect for flying. Their infrequent gloomier moments can delay flights, but the major airlines of Hawaii have been flying nonstop ever since Hawaiian Air's maiden flight in 1929. The fares are competitive, the schedules convenient, and the service friendly.

Brief History

Little more than a motorized kite, the *Hawaiian Skylark* was the first plane to fly in Hawaii. On New Year's Day, 1911, it circled a Honolulu polo field, where 3,000 spectators, including Queen Liliuokalani, witnessed history. Hawaiians have been soaring above their lovely islands ever since. The first paying customer, Mrs. Newmann, took off on a $15 joy ride in 1913 with a Chinese aviator named Tom Gunn. In February 1920, Charles Fern piloted the first interisland customer roundtrip from Honolulu to Maui for $150. He worked for Charles Stoffer, who started the first commercial airline the year before with one Curtiss bi-plane, affectionately known as "Charlie's Crate." For about 10 years sporadic attempts at interisland service amounted to little more than extended joy rides to deliver the day's newspaper from Honolulu. The James Dole Air Race in 1927 proved transpacific flight was possible, but interisland passenger service didn't really begin until Stanley C. Kennedy, a WW I flier and heir to Inter-Island Steam Navigation Co., began Inter-Island Airways in January 1929. For a dozen years he ran Sikorsky Amphibians, considered the epitome of safety. By 1941 he converted to the venerable workhorse, the DC-3, and changed the company name to **Hawaiian Air.**

By 1948, Hawaiian Air was unopposed in the interisland travel market, because regularly scheduled boats had already become obsolete. However, in 1946 a fledgling airline named Trans-Pacific opened for business. A non-scheduled airline with only one war surplus DC-3, they carried a hunting party of businessmen to Molokai on their maiden flight. By June 1952, they were a regularly scheduled airline in stiff competition with Hawaiian Air and had changed their name to **Aloha Airlines.** Both airlines had their financial glory days and woes over the next decade; by the end of the '60s both were flying interisland jets.

A healthy crop of small unscheduled airlines known as "air taxis" always darted about the wings of the large airlines, flying to minor airfields and performing flying services uneconomical for the bigger airlines. Most of these tiny, often one-plane air taxis were swatted from the air like gnats whenever the economy went sour or tourism went sluggish. They had names like Peacock and Rainbow, and after a brief flash of wings, they were gone.

INTERISLAND CARRIERS

The only effective way for most visitors to travel between the Hawaiian Islands is by air. Luckily, Hawaii has excellent air transportation that boasts one of the industry's safest flight records. The following airlines have competitive prices, with interisland flights about $75 each way. You can also save money (about $15) if you *take the first or last daily scheduled flight.* This offer usually applies only to flights to and from Honolulu, but do check because the policy often changes. Another alternative is to purchase a booklet containing six **flight vouchers.** You save about $7 per ticket, and they are *transferable.* Just book a flight as usual and present the filled-in voucher to board the plane. Vouchers are perfect for families or groups of friends, and can be purchased at any ticket office or at Honolulu International Airport.

Hawaiian Air, tel. (800) 367-5320 Mainland, (800) 882-8811 Hawaii, is not only the oldest airline in Hawaii, it is also the biggest. It flies

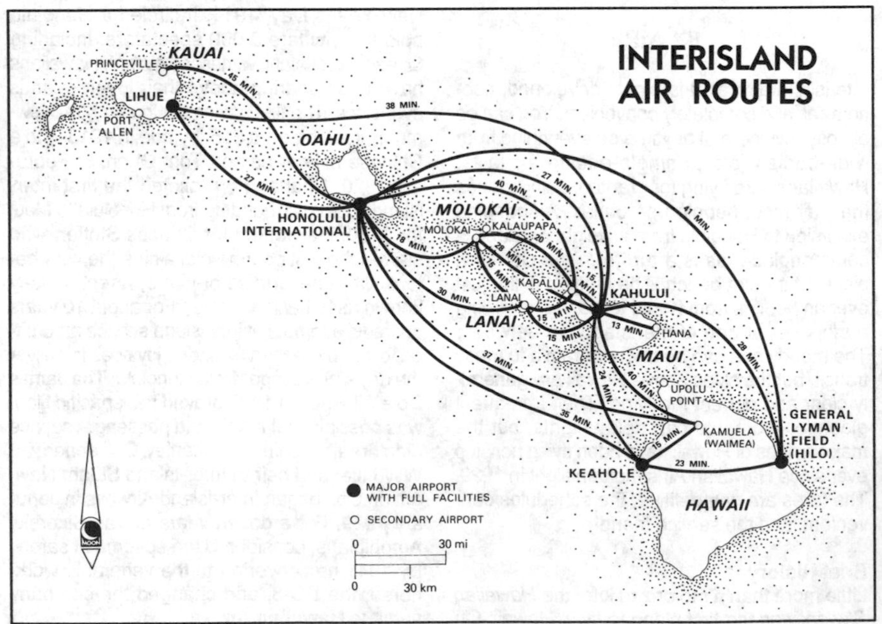

more aircraft, to more airports, more times per day than any other airline in Hawaii. It services all islands, including Molokai and Lanai, and boasts a top-notch fleet of DC-9 jets for its longer flights, and modern Dash-7 turbo-props (50 passengers) for its shorter runs.

Aloha Airlines, tel. (808) 935-5771, (800) 367-5250, is also an old and venerable Hawaiian company with plenty of flights connecting Oahu to Kauai, Maui, and both Kona and Hilo on Hawaii.

Aloha Island Air, tel. (800) 323-3345 Mainland, (800) 652-6541 Hawaii, offers scheduled flights to and from Honolulu, Princeville on Kauai, Molokai, and Lanai; and from Kahului, Kapalua, and Hana airports on Maui. They fly comfortable 18-passenger Twin Otter De Havilland aircraft.

Commuter/Charter Airlines

Hawaii has a good but dwindling selection of "commuter/charter airlines" offering some regularly scheduled flights, air tours, and special flights to small airports the big carriers don't service. They're so handy and personalized they might be considered "air taxis." All use smaller aircraft that seat about 12 people, and fly low enough so their normal interisland flights are like air tours. Stories abound of passengers being invited to ride copilot, or of a pilot going out of his way to show off a glimmering coastline or a beautiful waterfall. Many times you get the sense it's "your" flight and the airline is doing everything possible to make it memorable. Specific schedules are listed in the "Getting There-Getting Around" sections of the travel chapters. The commuter airlines are limited in plane size and routes serviced. Among themselves, prices are very competitive, but, except on their specialty runs, they tend to be more expensive than the three major interisland carriers. They're also not as generous on baggage allowance. You'll be charged more for the extra bulk, or some of it may not be allowed to accompany you on the plane.

Companies include: **Big Island Air,** tel. (808) 329-4868, or (800) 303-8868., operating out of Kailua-Kona, with a regularly scheduled flight between Kona and Hilo on the Big Island only, along with charter service and flightsee tours around the Big Island; **Air Molokai,** tel. (808) 553-3636 or (808) 877-0026, with scheduled flights between Molokai and Maui, and charter flights to Lanai; **Paragon Air,** tel. (808) 244-

3356, (800) 428-1231, with charter flights to all of Hawaii's airports.

Air Tours And Helicopters

Scores of air-tour companies specialize in personalized flights around the islands. These are not economical as travel between islands. A growing number of helicopters also fly in the islands. They too offer air tours and adventures: Waimea Canyon, Haleakala, and Kilauea when it's spouting lava are some of their more popular sightseeing tours. Many land in remote areas, so you can enjoy your own private waterfall and views. Look for listings in "Sightseeing Tours" in the various travel chapter introductions.

CAR RENTALS

Does Hawaii really have more rental cars than pineapples? Oahu's *Yellow Pages* have eight pages of listings for car rental agencies. There are over 40 firms on Maui, a few dozen on the Big Island, 20 or so on Kauai. Molokai has a handful, and even Lanai has one or two. You can rent anything from a 60-passenger Scenic-cruiser, to a 60cc moped. Even so, if you visit the islands during peak tourist frenzy without reserving your wheels in advance, you'll be marooned at the airport.

The tremendous field of cars and agencies from which to choose is cheaper than anywhere else in America. Special deals come and go like tropical rain showers; swashbuckling price slashings and come-ons are all over the rental car market. A little knowledge combined with some shrewd shopping around can save you a bundle. And renting a car is the best way to see the islands if you're going to be here for a limited time. Outside of Oahu, it simply isn't worthwhile to hassle with the poor public transportation system or rely on your thumb.

Requirements

A variety of requirements are imposed on the renter by car agencies, but the most important clauses are common. Some of the worst practices being challenged are no rentals to people under 25 and over 70, military personnel, or Hawaiian residents! Before renting, check that you fulfill the requirements. Generally, you must be 21, although some agencies rent to 18-year-olds, while others still require you to be 25. You must possess a valid driver's license, with licenses from most countries accepted, but if you are not American, get an International Driver's License to be safe. You should have a major credit card in your name. This is the easiest way to rent a car. Some companies will take a deposit, but it will be very stiff. It could easily be $50 per day on top of your rental fees and sometimes much more. In addition, they may require a credit check on the spot, complete with phone calls to your employer and bank. If you damage the car, charges will be deducted from your deposit, and the car company itself determines the extent of the damages. Some companies *will not* rent you a car without a major credit card in your name, no matter how much of a deposit you are willing to leave.

When To Rent

On this one, you'll have to make up your own mind, because it's a "bet" that you can either win or lose big. But it's always good to know the odds before you plop down your money. You can reserve your car in advance when you book your air ticket, or play the field when you get there. If you book in advance, you'll obviously have a car waiting for you, but the deal you made is the deal you'll get—it may or may not be the best around. On the other hand, if you wait, you can often take advantage of excellent on-the-spot deals. However, you're betting cars are available. You might be totally disappointed and unable to rent a car at all, or you might make a honey of a deal.

If you're arriving during the peak seasons of Christmas, Easter, or late summer vacation, *absolutely book your car in advance.* They are all accounted for during this period, and even if you can find a junker from a fly-by-night, they'll price-gouge you mercilessly. If you're going off-peak, you stand a good chance of getting the car you want at the price you want. It's generally best to book ahead; the majority of car companies have toll-free 800 numbers (listed below). It's suggested you at least call them for an opinion of your chances of getting a car upon your intended arrival if you choose not to reserve.

Rates

If you pick up a car rental brochure at a travel agency, notice the prices for Hawaii rentals are about the lowest in the U.S. The two rate options for renting are **mileage** and **flat rate.** A third type, **mileage/minimum,** is generally a bad idea unless you plan to do some heavy-duty driving. Mileage rate costs less per day, but you are charged for every mile driven. Mileage rates are best if you drive less than 30 miles per day—but even on an island that isn't much! The flat rate is best, providing a fixed daily rate and unlimited mileage. With either rate, you buy the gas; don't buy the cheapest because the poor performance from low octane eats up your savings.

Discounts of 10-15% for weekend, weekly, and monthly rates are available. It's sometimes cheaper to rent a car for the week even if you're only going to use it for five days. Both weekly and monthly rates can be split between Neighbor Islands.

Warning: If you keep your car beyond your contract, you'll be charged the highest daily rate unless you notify the rental agency beforehand. Don't keep your car longer than the contract without notifying the company. They are *quick* to send out their repossession specialists. You might find your car gone, a warrant for your arrest, and an extra charge. A simple courtesy call notifying the company of your intentions saves a lot of headaches and hassle.

What Wheels To Rent

The super-cheap rates on the eye-catcher brochures refer to subcompact standard shifts. The price goes up with the size of the car and with an automatic transmission. As with options on a new car, the more luxury, the more you pay. If you can drive a standard shift, get one: they're cheaper to rent and operate. Because many Hawaiian roads are twisty affairs, you'll appreciate the downshifting ability and extra control of a standard shift. AM/FM radios are good to have for entertainment and for weather and surf conditions. If you have the choice, take a car with cloth seats instead of sticky vinyl.

The average price of a subcompact standard shift, without a/c, is $30 per day, $120 per week (add about $8 per day—$50 per week—for an automatic), but rates vary widely. Luxury cars are about $10 per day more, with a comparable weekly rate. Most of the car companies, local and national, offer special rates and deals. These deals fluctuate too rapidly to give any hard-and-fast information. They are common, however, so make sure to inquire. Also, peak periods have "black outs" when normally good deals no longer apply.

Insurance

Before signing your car rental agreement, you'll be offered "insurance" for around $10 per day. Since insurance is already built into the contract (don't expect the rental agency to point this out), what you're really buying is a waiver on the deductible ($500-1000), in case you crack up the car. If you have insurance at home, you will almost always have coverage on a rental car, including your normal deductible, but not all policies are the same, so check with your agent. Also, if you haven't bought their waiver, and you have a mishap, the rental agencies will put a claim against your major credit card on the spot for the amount of deductible, even if you can prove your insurance will cover it. They'll tell you to collect from your insurance company because they don't want to be left holding the bag on an across-the-waters claim. If you have a good policy with a small deductible, it's hardly worth paying the extra money for the waiver, but if your own policy is inadequate, buy the insurance. Also, most **major credit cards** offer complimentary car rental insurance as an incentive to use their cards to rent the car. Simply call your credit card company to see if this service is included.

Driving Tips

Protect your children as you would at home with car seats. Their rental prices vary considerably: Alamo offers them free of charge; National charges $3 per day; Hertz needs 48 hours' notice; Dollar gives them free, but they're not always available at all locations. Almost every agency can make arrangements if you give them enough notice. Check before you go and if all else fails, bring one from home.

There are few differences between driving in Hawaii and on the Mainland. Just remember many people on the roads are tourists and can be confused about where they're going. Since many drivers are from somewhere else, there's hardly a "regular style" of driving in the islands. A farmer from Iowa accustomed to poking along on back roads can be sandwiched between a frenetic New Yorker who's trying to drive over his roof and a super-polite but horribly confused Japanese tourist who normally drives on the left.

In Hawaii, drivers don't honk their horns except to say hello, or in an emergency. It's considered rude, and honking to hurry someone might earn you a knuckle sandwich. Hawaiian drivers reflect the climate: they're relaxed and polite. Oftentimes, they'll brake to let you turn left when they're coming at you. They may assume you'll do the same, so be ready, after a perfunctory turn signal from another driver, for him or her to turn across your lane. The more rural the area, the more apt this is to happen.

It may seem like common sense, but remember to slow down when you enter the little towns strung along the circle-island route. It's easy to bomb along on the highway and flash through these towns, missing some of Hawaii's best scenery. Also, rural children expect *you* to be watchful, and will assume that you are going to stop for them when they dart onto the crosswalks.

Oahu's **H-1, H-2, and H-3 freeways** throw many Mainlanders a Polynesian "screwball." Accustomed to driving on superhighways, Mainlanders assume these are the same. They're not. Oahu's superhighways are much more convoluted than most Mainland counterparts. Subliminally they look like normal freeways, except they've been tied into Hawaiian knots. There are split-offs, crossroads, and exits in the middle of exits. Stay alert and don't be lulled into complacency.

BYO Car

If you want to bring your own car, write for information to: Director of Finance, Division of Licenses, 1455 S. Beretania St., Honolulu, HI 96814. However, unless you'll be in Hawaii for a minimum of six months and will spend all your time on one island, don't even think about it. It's an expensive proposition and takes time and plenty of arrangements. From California, the cost is at least $600 to Honolulu, and an additional $100 to any other island. To save on rental costs, it would be better to buy and sell a car in the islands, or to lease for an extended period.

Four-Wheel-Drives

For normal touring, it is unnecessary to rent 4WDs in Hawaii except on Lanai where they're a must, or if you really want to get off the beaten track on the other islands. They are expensive ($65-85 per day) and uneconomical, and you simply don't need them. If you still want one, most car rental agencies have them. Because their numbers are limited, reservations are absolutely necessary.

CAR RENTAL AGENCIES

When you arrive at any of Hawaii's airports, you'll walk the gauntlet of car rental booths and courtesy phones shoulder to shoulder along the main hallways. Of the two categories of car rental agencies in Hawaii, each has its advantage. The first category is the big international firms like Dollar, National, Hertz, Avis, and Budget. These big guys are familiar and easy to work with, sometimes offer special fly/drive deals with airlines, and live up to their promises. If you want your rental experience to be hassle-free, they're the ones. Also, don't be prejudiced against them just because they're so well known; sometimes they offer the best deals.

Hawaii has spawned a good crop of local entrepreneurial rental agencies. Their deals and cars can range, like rummage-sale treasures, from great finds to pure junk. These companies have the advantage of being able to cut deals on the spot. If nothing is moving from their lot on the day you arrive, you might get a real bargain. Unfortunately, mixed in this category is a hodgepodge of fly-by-nights. Some of these are small, but adequate, while others are a rip-off. Their cars are bad, their service is worse, and they have more hidden costs than a Monopoly board.

National Agencies

All of the following national companies are represented in Hawaii. The **local phone numbers** given are for Honolulu only, while the 800 numbers can be reached from the Mainland and Canada. Call for details.

One of the best national firms with an excellent reputation for service and prices is **Dollar Rent A Car,** tel. (808) 944-1544, (800) 367-7006, (800) 342-7398 in Hawaii. Their deals and service can't be beat.

Others include: **National Car Rental,** tel. (808) 831-3800, (800) 227-7368; **Hertz,** tel. (808) 831-3500, (800) 654-3131; **Avis,** tel. (808) 834-5536, (800) 331-1212, (800) 831-8000 in Hawaii; **Budget,** tel. (808) 922-3600, (800) 527-0700; **Alamo,** tel. (808) 845-7511, (800) 327-9633; and **Sears,** accepting Sears credit cards, tel. (808) 599-2205, (800) 451-3600.

Car Pick-Up

The majority of agencies listed above have booths at all of the airport terminal buildings throughout Hawaii. If they don't, they have clearly marked courtesy phones in the lobbies. Just pick one up and they'll give directions on where to wait, then come fetch you in their shuttle.

BY BOAT

Ironically, in the country's only island state complete with a long sailing history, modern shipping, and port towns, ferry service between the islands, except for sails between Maui and Lanai, and between Maui and Molokai, is nonexistent. Periodically, there is a cry to reinstate some sort of coastal and interisland boat or ferry service. Some say visitors and islanders alike would enjoy the experience and be able to travel more economically. Others argue the Hawaiian waters are as dangerous and unpredictable as ever, and no evidence of need or enough passen-

MAUI PRINCESS SAILING SCHEDULE

For information and reservations:
on Molokai call 553-5736
on Maui call 661-5857
Mainland toll-free (800) 533-5800

Depart:	Kaunakakai, Molokai	5:45 a.m.
Arrive:	Lahaina, Maui slip 3	7:15 a.m.
Depart:	Lahaina, Maui slip 3	7:30 a.m.
Arrive:	Kaunakakai, Molokai	8:45 a.m.
Depart:	Kaunakakai, Molokai	3:45 p.m.
Arrive:	Lahaina, Maui slip 3	4:45 p.m.
Depart:	Lahaina, Maui slip 3	5:00 p.m.
Arrive:	Kaunakakai, Molokai	6:45 p.m.

gers exists. A few skippers run pleasure craft between Maui-Molokai-Lanai and are willing to take on passengers, but this is a hit-and-miss situation based on space. These special situations will be discussed in the appropriate travel chapters under "Getting Around." For now, interisland travelers have to be content with seeing the islands from the air.

PUBLIC TRANSPORTATION

Public transportation is very limited in Hawaii except for Oahu's exemplary **TheBus.** TheBus, tel. (808) 848-5555, can take you just about anywhere you want to go on Oahu for only 85 cents (students, children, and seniors are cheaper; see "Getting Around" in the Oahu Introduction for details). Carrying over 230,000 passengers per day, it's a model of what a bus system should be.

The MTS Line, popularly called the **Hele On Bus Company,** tel. (808) 935-8241 or (808) 961-6722, is a woefully slow, very local bus system that tries to service the Big Island. It's cheap and okay for short hops, but too infrequent and slow for long distances. Travelers say they consistently make better time hitchhiking between Hilo and Kona than waiting for Hele On to waddle by.

Bus service, except for a few limited runs in specific areas is not available on the other islands (check all island "Getting Around" sections for details). There are a few remaining novelty pedicabs in Waikiki, many hotel shuttles to and from airports, and convenience buses from some major resorts to nearby beaches and shopping centers, but that's about all the "public transportation" in Hawaii.

Ongoing Public Transportation

For those continuing on to the Mainland and wishing to procure a **Greyhound** "Ameripass" (sorry, not valid in Hawaii), this can be done in Hawaii. Write or visit Greyhound International, 550 Paiea St., Suite 104, Honolulu, HI 96819, tel. (808) 893-1909. Send a $75 money order (for up-to-the-minute prices call any Greyhound terminal) for seven days of unlimited travel in the U.S., with the name of the person using the pass. For $12 per day more, you get an extension if the pass is renewed before the initial seven-day period runs out.

HITCHHIKING

Hitchhiking varies from island to island, both in legality and method of thumbing a ride. On Oahu, hitchhiking is legal, and you use the tried-and-true style of facing traffic and waving your thumb—but you can only hitchhike from bus stops. Not many people hitchhike and the pickings are reasonably easy, but TheBus is only 85 cents for anywhere you want to go, and the paltry sum you save by hitchhiking is lost in "seeing time." It's legal to hitch on Kauai and the police don't bother you on Hawaii. Remember Hawaii is indeed a "big" island; be prepared to take some time getting from one end to the other. Though on Lanai and Molokai hitching is illegal, hardly any policemen are to be seen. If they stop, it will probably be just to warn you, but note the traffic is light on both islands. On Maui, thumbing a ride is illegal and the police will write you a ticket. You must learn a new and obviously transparent charade to hitch successfully. Basically: thumb at your side, stand by the road, face traffic, and smile. Everyone knows you're hitching, but that's the game.

In general, you will get a ride, eventually, but in comparison to the amount of traffic going by, it isn't easy. Two things against you: many of the drivers are tourists and don't want to bother with hitchhikers, and many locals don't want to bother with nonlocal hitchhikers. When you do get a ride, most of the time it will be from a *haole* who is either a tourist on his or her own or a new island resident. If you are hitchhiking along a well-known beach area, perhaps in your bathing suit and obviously not going far, you can get a ride more easily. Women should exercise caution as they do everywhere else in the U.S. and avoid hitchhiking alone.

SIGHTSEEING TOURS

Tours offered on all the major islands will literally let you cover an individual island from top to bottom; you can walk it, drive it, sail around it, fly over it, or see it from below the water. Please see the travel chapters' "Sightseeing Tours" sections for information on particular islands. For snorkel/scuba, deep-sea fishing, and horseback-riding tours, see the "Sports and Recreation" sections in the individual travel chapters.

Ecotourism In Hawaii

The following is a partial list of organizations, both public and private, offering environmentally sound tours and outings throughout the Hawaiian Islands.

American Friends Service Committee, 2426 Oahu Ave., Honolulu, HI 96822, tel. (808) 988-6266 (Hawaii "Land Seminars").

EcoTours of Hawaii/Hawaiian Walkways, Box 2193, Kamuela, HI 96743, tel. (808) 885-7759 (sea kayaking and mountain biking).

Eye of the Whale/Earthwalk Tours, Box 652, Davisville, RI 02854, tel. (401) 539-2401 (sailing and hiking).

Hawaii Audubon Society, 212 Merchant St., Suite 320, Honolulu, HI 96813, tel. (808) 528-1432 (hikes and talks).

Hawaii Volcanoes National Park/Interpretation, Box 52, Hawaii Volcanoes National Park, HI 96718, tel. (808) 967-7311 (hikes and talks).

The Nature Conservancy, 1116 Smith St., Suite 201, Honolulu, HI 96817, tel. (808) 537-4508 (hikes).

Sierra Club, Moku Loa Group, Box 1137, Hilo, HI 96721, tel. (808) 961-6978 (hikes and service trips).

Note: Also see "Camping and Hiking" in this chapter and "Flora and Fauna" in the General Introduction for more information.

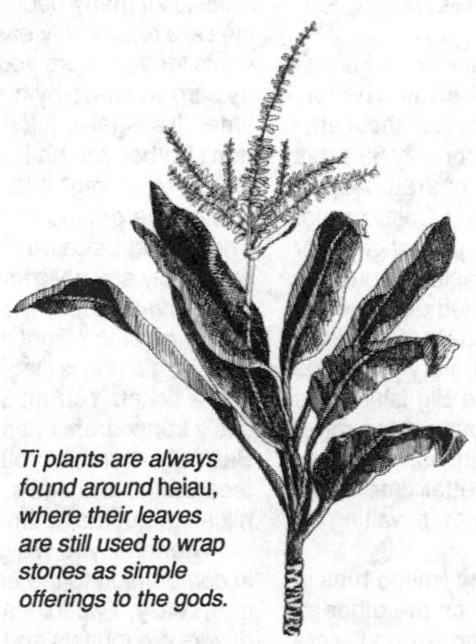

Ti plants are always found around heiau*, where their leaves are still used to wrap stones as simple offerings to the gods.*

DIANA LASICH HARPER

BOB RACE

HEALTH AND SAFETY

In a recent survey published by *Science Digest,* Hawaii was cited as the healthiest state in the U.S. in which to live. Indeed, Hawaiian citizens live longer than anywhere else in America: men to 74 years and women to 78. Lifestyle, heredity, and diet help with these figures, but Hawaii is also an oasis in the middle of the ocean, and germs just have a tougher time getting here. There are no cases of malaria, cholera, or yellow fever. Because of a strict quarantine law, rabies is also nonexistent. On the other hand, tooth decay, perhaps because of a wide use of sugar and the enzymes present in certain tropical fruits, is 30% above the national average. With the perfect weather, a multitude of fresh-air activities, soothing negative ionization from the sea, and a generally relaxed and carefree lifestyle, everyone feels better there. Hawaii is just what the doctor ordered: a beautiful, natural health spa. That's one of its main draws. The food and water are perfectly safe, and the air quality is the best in the country.

Handling The Sun

Don't become a victim of your own exuberance. People can't wait to strip down and lie on the sand like beached whales, but the tropical sun will burn you to a cinder if you're silly. The burning rays come through easier in Hawaii because of the sun's angle, and you don't feel them as much because there's always a cool breeze. The worst part of the day is 11 a.m.-3 p.m. You'll just have to force yourself to go slowly. Don't worry; you'll be able to flaunt your best souvenir, your golden Hawaiian tan, to your green-with-envy friends when you get home. It's better than showing them a boiled lobster body with peeling skin! If your skin is snowflake white, 15 minutes per side on the first day is plenty. Increase by 15-minute intervals every day, which will allow you a full hour per side by the fourth day. Have faith; this is enough to give you a deep golden, uniform tan.

Haole Rot

A peculiar condition caused by the sun is referred to locally as *haole* rot. It's called this because it supposedly affects only white people, but you'll notice some dark-skinned people with the same condition. Basically, the skin becomes mottled with white spots that refuse to tan. You get a blotchy effect, mostly on the shoulders and back. Dermatologists have a fancy name for it, and they'll give you a fancy prescription with a not-so-fancy price tag to cure it. It's common knowledge throughout the islands that Selsun Blue shampoo has some ingredient that stops the white mottling effect. Wash your hair with it and then make sure to rub the lather over the affected areas, and it should clear up.

Bugs

Everyone, in varying degrees, has an aversion to vermin and creepy crawlers. Hawaii isn't infested with a wide variety, but it does have its share. Mosquitoes were unknown in the islands until their larvae stowed away in the water barrels of the *Wellington* in 1826 and were introduced at Lahaina. They bred in the tropical climate and rapidly spread to all the islands. They are a particular nuisance in the rainforests. Be prepared, and bring a natural repellent like citronella oil, available in most health stores on the islands, or a commercial product available in all groceries or drugstores. Campers will be happy to have mosquito coils to burn at night as well.

Cockroaches are very democratic insects. They hassle all strata of society equally. They breed well in Hawaii, and most hotels are at war with them, trying desperately to keep them from being spotted by guests. One comforting thought is that in Hawaii they aren't a sign of filth or dirty housekeeping. They love the climate like everyone else, and it's a real problem keeping them under control.

Poisonous Plants

A number of plants in Hawaii, mostly imported, contain toxins. In almost every case you have to eat a quantity of them before they'll do you any real harm. The following is a partial list of the most common poisonous plants you'll encounter and the parts to avoid: poinsettia—leaves, stems, and sap; oleander—all parts; azalea—all parts; crown flower—juice; lantana—berries; castor bean—all parts; bird of paradise—seeds; coral plant—seeds.

Pollution In Paradise

Calling Hawaii the healthiest state in America doesn't mean that it has totally escaped pollution. It is the only state, however, in which all of the natural beauty is protected by state law, with a statewide zoning and a general development plan. For example, the absence of billboard advertising is due to the pioneering work of a women's club, "The Outdoor Circle," which was responsible for an anti-billboard law passed in 1927. It's strictly enforced, but unfortunately high-rise and ill-advised development have obscured some of the lovely views that these far-sighted women were trying to preserve. Numerous environmental controversies, including nuclear proliferation and the ill effects of rampant development, rage on the islands.

The most obvious infringements occur on Oahu, with 80% of the islands' population, which places the greatest stress on the environment. An EPA study found that almost 20% of Oahu's wells have unacceptably high concentrations of DBCP and TCP. Because of Hawaii's unique water lenses (fresh water trapped by layers of lava), this fact is particularly onerous. The "Great Oahu Milk Crisis" of 1982 saw dairies shut down when their milk was found to have abnormally high concentrations of heptachlor, a chemical used in the pineapple industry. This was traced to when the tops of pineapple plants were sold as fodder, which tainted the milk.

Widespread concern existed over a 1,500-unit development on the Waianae coast known as West Beach. According to environmentalists, the recently completed development will not only put a major strain on diminishing water resources, but impinge on one of the last fruitful fishing areas near long-established homes of native Hawaiians. Oahu's H-3 Freeway was cut across an ecologically sensitive mountain range, and an alternative biomass energy plant is denuding the islands of its remaining indigenous ohia trees. On the Big Island, plans are always lurking for resort development on South Point and even in the magnificent Waipio Valley. Also on the Big Island, a thermal energy plant has been bitterly challenged because its builders insist on locating it in the middle of sensitive rainforest when other, more ecologically acceptable sites are readily available. And just to be pesky, the Mediterranean fruit fly made its appearance and Malathion had to be sprayed. Compared to those in many states, these conditions are small potatoes, but they lucidly point out the holistic global concept that no place on earth is immune to the

by ship's artist Francis Olmsted, c. 1840

ravages of pollution. (See individual travel chapters for more information.)

Environmental Resource Groups

Anyone interested in Hawaii's environmental issues can contact the following for more information: **Hawaii Green Movement,** Box 61508, Honolulu, HI 96839; **Sierra Club Legal Defense Fund,** 212 Merchant St., Suite 202, Honolulu, HI 96813, tel. (808) 599-2436; **Pele Defense Fund,** Box 404, Volcano, HI 96875, tel. (808) 935-1663; and **Rainforest Action Network,** 301 Broadway, Suite A, San Francisco, CA 94133, tel. (415) 398-4404.

Environment Hawaii, 733 Bishop St., Honolulu, HI 96813, tel. (808) 934-0115, individual subscription rate $35 per year, is a savvy monthly newsletter that focuses on environmental and political issues facing Hawaii today. The well-researched and concisely written newsletter attempts to be fair to all parties concerned, explaining both sides to most controversies. Short on preaching and long on common sense, *Environment Hawaii* is an excellent resource for anyone interested in sociopolitical and environmental issues.

For environmental tours see "Sightseeing Tours" under "Getting Around" earlier in this chapter.

WATER SAFETY

Hawaii has one very sad claim to fame: more people drown here than anywhere else in the world. Moreover, there are dozens of yearly swimming victims with broken necks and backs or with injuries from scuba and snorkeling accidents. These statistics shouldn't keep you out of the sea, because it is indeed beautiful—benevolent in most cases—and a major reason to go to Hawaii. But if you're foolish, the sea will bounce you like a basketball and suck you away for good. The best remedy is to avoid situations you can't handle. Don't let anyone dare you into a situation that makes you uncomfortable. "Macho men" who know nothing about the power of the sea will be tumbled into Cabbage Patch Kids dolls in short order. Ask lifeguards or beach attendants about conditions, and follow their advice. If local people refuse to go in, there's a good reason. Even experts get in trouble in Hawaiian waters. Some beaches, such as Waikiki, are as gentle as lambs and you would have to tie an anchor around your neck to drown there. Others, especially on the north coasts during the winter months, are frothing giants.

While beachcombing, or especially when walking out on rocks, never turn your back to the sea. Be aware of undertows (the waves drawing back into the sea). They can knock you off your feet. Before entering the water, study it for rocks, breakers, reefs, and riptides. Riptides are powerful currents, like rivers in the sea, that can drag you out. Mostly they peter out not too far from shore, and you can often see their choppy waters on the surface. If you get caught in a "rip," don't fight to swim directly against it; you'll lose and only exhaust yourself. Swim diagonally across it, while going along with it, and try to stay parallel to the shore. Don't waste all your lung power yelling, and rest by floating.

When bodysurfing, never ride straight in; come to shore at a 45° angle. Remember, waves come in sets. Little ones can be followed by giants, so watch the action awhile instead of plunging right in. Standard procedure is to duck under a breaking wave. You can survive even thunderous oceans using this technique. Don't try to swim through a heavy froth and never turn your back and let it smash you. Don't swim alone if possible, and obey all warning signs. Hawaiians want to entertain you and they don't put up signs just to waste money. The last rule is, "If in doubt, stay out."

Yikes!

Sharks live in all the oceans of the world. Most mind their own business and stay away from

This "denizen of the deep" is much more afraid of you than you are of it.

shore. Hawaiian sharks are well fed—on fish—and don't usually bother with unsavory humans. If you encounter a shark, don't panic. Never thrash around because this will trigger their attack instinct. If they come close, scream loudly.

Portuguese man-of-wars put out long, floating tentacles that sting if they touch you. Don't wash the sting off with fresh water, as this will only aggravate it. Hot salt water will take away the sting, as will alcohol (the drinking or rubbing kind), after-shave lotion, and meat tenderizer (MSG), which can be found in any supermarket and many Chinese restaurants.

Coral can give you a nasty cut, and it's known to cause infections because it's a living organism. Wash the cut immediately and apply an antiseptic. Keep the cut clean and covered, and watch for infection.

Poisonous sea urchins, such as the lacquer-black *wana,* can be beautiful creatures. They are found in shallow tidepools and will hurt you if you step on them. Their spines will break off, enter your foot, and burn like blazes. There are cures. Vinegar and wine poured on the wound will stop the burning. If not available, the Hawaiian solution is urine. It might seem ignominious to have someone pee on your foot, but it'll put the fire out. The spines will disintegrate in a few days, and there are generally no long-term effects.

Hawaiian reefs also have their share of moray eels. These creatures are ferocious in appearance, but will never initiate an attack. You'll have to poke around in their holes while snorkeling or scuba diving to get them to attack. Sometimes this is inadvertent on the diver's part, so be careful where you stick your hand while underwater.

HAWAIIAN FOLK MEDICINE AND CURES

Hawaiian folk medicine is well developed, and its cures for common ailments have been used effectively for centuries. Hawaiian *kahuna* were highly regarded for their medicinal skills, and Hawaiians were by far some of the healthiest people in the world until the coming of the Europeans. Many folk remedies and cures are used to this day and, what's more, they work. Many of the common plants and fruits you'll encounter provide some of the best remedies. When roots and seeds and special exotic plants are used, the preparation of the medicine is as painstaking as in a modern pharmacy. These prescriptions are exact and take an expert to prepare. They should never be prepared or administered by an amateur.

Common Curative Plants

Arrowroot, for diarrhea, is a powerful narcotic used in rituals and medicines. The pepper plant (*Piper methisticum*) is chewed and the juice is spat into a container for fermenting. Used as a medicine for urinary tract infections, rheumatism, and asthma, it also induces sleep and cures headaches. A poultice for wounds is made from the skins of ripe bananas. Peelings have a powerful antibiotic quality and contain vitamins A, B, and C, phosphorous, calcium, and iron. The nectar from the plant was fed to babies as a vitamin juice. Breadfruit sap is used for healing cuts and as a moisturizing lotion. Coconut is used to make moisturizing oil, and the juice was chewed, spat into the hand, and used as a shampoo. Guava is a source of vitamins A, B, and C. Hibiscus has been used as a laxative. *Kukui* nut oil makes a gargle for sore throats and a laxative, plus the flowers are used to cure diarrhea. *Noni,* an unappetizing hand-grenade-shaped fruit that you wouldn't want to eat unless you had to, reduces tumors, diabetes, and high blood pressure, and the juice is good for diarrhea. Sugarcane sweetens many concoctions, and the juice of toasted cane was a tonic for sick babies. Sweet potato is used as a tonic during pregnancy and juiced as a gargle for phlegm. Tamarind is a natural laxative and contains the most acid and sugar of any fruit on earth. Taro has been used for lung infections and thrush, and as a suppository. Yams are good for coughs, vomiting, constipation, and appendicitis.

Commonly Treated Ailments

For arthritis make a poultice of *koali* and Hawaiian salt; cover the area and keep warm. A bad-breath gargle is made from the *hapu'u* fern. The latex from inside the leaves of aloe is great for soothing burns and sunburn, as well as for innumerable skin problems. If you get chapped lips or windburned skin, use oil from the *hinu honu.* A headache is lessened with *awa* or *ape.* Calm nervousness with *awa* and *lomi lomi,* Hawaiian-style massage. To get rid of a raspy sore throat, chew the bark of the root of the *uhaloa.* A toothache is eased by the sticky narcotic juice from the *pua kala* seed, a prickly poppy.

Lomi Lomi

This traditional Hawaiian massage is of exceptional therapeutic value. It has been practiced since very early times and is especially useful in cases of fatigue, general body aches, preventive medicine, and sports injuries. When Otto Von Kotzebue arrived in 1824, he noted, ". . . Queen Nomahana, after feasting heartily, turned on her back, whereupon a tall fellow sprang upon her body and kneaded it unmercifully with his knees and fists as if it had been the dough of bread. Digestion was so assisted that the queen resumed her feasting." *Lomi lomi* practitioners must be accredited by the state.

MEDICAL AND EMERGENCY SERVICES

Emergency: Dial 911

The following hospitals provide emergency room, long-term, and acute care. **Oahu:** Kaiser Foundation Hospital, 1697 Ala Moana Blvd., Honolulu, tel. (808) 949-5811. They have an emergency room and are closest to Waikiki. They demand payment before treatment. Queen's Medical Center, 1301 Punchbowl, Honolulu, tel. (808) 538-9011; St. Francis Hospital, 2230 Liliha, Honolulu, tel. 547-6551. **Maui:** Kula Hospital, 204 Kula Hwy., tel. (808) 878-1221; Maui Memorial, Kaahumanu Ave., Wailuku, tel. (808) 244-9056. **Molokai:** Molokai General, Kaunakakai, tel. (808) 553-5331. **Lanai:** Lanai Community Hospital, Lanai City, tel. (808) 565-6411. **Hawaii:** Hilo Hospital, 1190 Waianuenue Ave., Hilo, tel. (808) 961-4211; Kona Hospital, Kailua-Kona, tel. (808) 322-9311. **Kauai:** Wilcox Memorial Hospital, 3420 Kuhio Hwy., Lihue, tel. (808) 245-1100.

Alternative Medicine

Most ethnic groups who migrated to Hawaii brought along their own cures. The Chinese and Japanese are especially known for their unique and effective medicines, such as herbal medicine, acupuncture, and shiatsu. Hawaii also has a huge selection of chiropractors and its own form of massage called *lomi lomi.* The *Yellow Pages* on all islands list holistic practitioners, herbalists, and naturopaths.

The time-honored Chinese therapy of acupuncture is available throughout the islands. On Oahu contact the Hawaiian Association of Certified Acupuncturists, Box 11202, Honolulu 96828, tel. (808) 941-7771, for referrals to state-licensed acupuncturists throughout the islands.

All types of massage are available throughout the islands. If you look in the *Yellow Pages,* you'll find everything from shiatsu and *lomi lomi* to "escort services" that masquerade their real profession as massage. It's easy to tell the ads of legitimate massage practitioners offering therapeutic holistic massage. Check listings under "holistic practitioners" as well as "massage."

Note
For detailed information on medical services, alternative medicine, and massage see the individual travel chapters' "Information and Services" sections.

SERVICES FOR THE DISABLED

A physically disabled person can have a wonderful time in Hawaii; all that's needed is a little pre-planning. The following general advice should help you plan.

Commission On Persons With Disabilities

This commission was designed with the express purpose of aiding handicapped people. It is a source of invaluable information and distributes self-help booklets free of charge. Any handicapped person heading to Hawaii should write first or visit their offices on arrival. For the *Aloha Guide To Accessibility* ($3) write or visit the head office at: Commission on Persons With Disabilities, 500 Ala Moana Blvd., Honolulu, HI 96813, tel. (808) 586-8121; on Maui, 54 High St., Wailuku, Maui, HI 96793, tel. (808) 243-5441; on Kauai, 3060 Eiwa St. #207, Lihue, Kauai, HI 96766, tel. (808) 241-3308; on Hawaii, P.O. Box 1641, Hilo, HI 96820, tel. (808) 933-7747.

General Information

The key for a smooth trip is to make as many arrangements ahead of time as possible. Tell the transportation companies and hotels you'll be dealing with the nature of your handicap in advance so they can make arrangements to accommodate you. Bring your medical records and notify medical establishments of your arrival if you'll need their services. Travel with a friend or make arrangements for an aide on arrival (see "Maui Services," below). Bring your own wheelchair if possible and let airlines know if it is battery-powered; boarding interisland carriers requires steps. No problem: they'll board you early on special lifts, but they must know that you're coming. Many hotels and restaurants accommodate disabled persons, but always call ahead just to make sure.

KAREN McKINLEY

KUKUI (CANDLENUT)

Reaching heights of 80 feet, the *kukui* (candlenut) was a veritable department store to the Hawaiians, who made use of almost every part of this utilitarian giant. Its nuts, bark, or flowers were ground into potions and salves to be taken as a general tonic, applied to ulcers and cuts as an effective antibiotic, or administered internally as a cure for constipation or asthma attacks. The bark was mixed with water and the resulting juice was used as a dye in tattooing, tapa-cloth making, and canoe painting, and as a preservative for fishnets. The oily nuts were burned as a light source in stone holders, and ground and eaten as a condiment called *inamona.* Polished nuts took on a beautiful sheen and were strung as lei. Lastly, the wood itself was hollowed into canoes and used as fishnet floats.

Oahu Services

At Honolulu International, handicapped parking spaces are on the fourth floor of the parking garage near the elevator closest to the interisland terminal. Know that the airport shuttle, the **Wiki Wiki Bus,** has steps. **Medical services** are available 24 hours through the Honolulu County Medical Society, tel. (808) 536-6988; **airport medical services** at tel. (808) 836-3341; and **visitor information** at tel. (808) 836-6417. For getting around, the City of Honolulu has a free curb-to-curb service for disabled persons, called **Handi-Van.** You must make arrangements for a pass 24 hours in advance. For a free handicapped bus pass for disabled but ambulatory people, write Handi-Van Pass, or Handicapped Bus Pass, 650 S. King St., Honolulu 96813, tel. (808) 524-4626. A private special taxi company is **Handi-Cabs of the Pacific** in Honolulu at tel. (808) 524-3866. **Avis** will rent cars with hand controls, tel. (808) 836-5511.

For **medical equipment** the following Honolulu establishments rent all kinds of apparatus: **AAA Medical,** tel. (808) 538-7021; **Abbey Rents,** tel. (808) 537-2922; **Medical Supplies,** tel. (808) 845-9522; **Honolulu Orthopedic,** tel. (808) 536-6661. For **medical support and help** the following provide nurses, companions, and health aides (all require advance notice): **Hawaii Center for Independent Living,** tel. (808) 537-1941; **Travel-Well International,** tel. (808) 689-5420; **Voluntary Action Center,** tel. (808) 536-7234.

Maui Services

Parking spaces for the handicapped are directly in front of Kahului Airport's main terminal. The restaurant here has steps, so food will be brought to you in the cocktail lounge. There are no special emergency medical services, but visitor information is available at (808) 877-6431. There is no centralized medical service, but **Maui Memorial Hospital** in Wailuku will make references, tel. 244-9056. Getting around can be tough because there is virtually no public transportaion on Maui, and no tours or companies to accommodate nonambulatory persons. However, both **Hertz** and **Avis** rent cars with hand controls. Health care is provided by **Maui Center for Independent Living,** tel. (808) 242-4966. Medical equipment is available at **Hawaiian Rentals,** tel. (808) 877-7684, and **Maui Rents,** tel. (808) 877-5827. Special recreation activities referrals are made by **Easter Seal Society,** tel. (808) 877-4443, or by the **Commission on Persons with Disabilities,** tel. (808) 243-5441.

Over The Rainbow, 186 Mehani Circle, Kihei, HI 96753, tel. (808) 879-5521, is a private company, owned and operated by Dave McKown, who has traveled the world with his brother, a paraplegic. Dave knows firsthand the obstacles faced by disabled people. Over The Rainbow provides: a full-service travel agency, with bookings into hotels, condos, and private homes set up for the handicapped; an activities desk featuring everything from water sports to helicopter rides; u-drive cars and vans with hand controls and wheelchair lifts; airport arrangements; and scenic tours.

On December 30, 1993, a measure was passed to make four Maui beaches wheelchair accessible: Kihei's Kamaole Beaches I, II, and III, and Kahului's Kanaha Beach park. Construction, mandated to be finished within a year, will include large, clearly marked parking spaces, and an elevated boardwalk leading to the beach. Contact Maui's Department of Parks and Recreation, tel. (808) 243-7626, for complete and up-to-the-minute details.

Kauai Services

At Lihue Airport, handicapped parking is available in an adjacent lot and across the street in the metered area.

For **emergency services,** call (808) 245-3773; visitor info, call (808) 246-1440. For medical services, **Kauai Medical Group** at Wilcox Hospital will refer, tel. (808) 245-1500. For emergency room, long-term, and acute care contact **Wilcox Memorial Hospital,** 3420 Kuhio Hwy., Lihue, tel. (808) 245-1100.

To get around, arrangements can be made if the following are contacted well in advance: the county's **Office of Elderly Affairs,** tel. (808) 245-7230; and **Akita Enterprises,** tel. (808) 245-5344. **Avis** will install hand controls on cars, but they need a month's notice. There are very few sidewalks and fewer cut curbs on Kauai and none in Lihue. Special **parking permits** (legal anywhere, anytime) are available from the police station in Lihue. Medical equipment rentals are available from: **American Cancer Society,** tel. (808) 245-2942; **Pay 'n Save,** tel. (808) 245-6776; **Easter Seals,** tel. (808) 245-6983. For medical support and help contact **Kauai Center for Independent Living,** tel. (808) 245-4034.

Hawaii Island Services

At Hilo Airport there are no facilities for deplaning nonambulatory people from propeller planes, only from jets and on the jetways. Interisland flights should be arranged only on jets. Ramps and a special elevator provide access in the bi-level terminal. Parking is convenient in designated areas. At Kona Airport, boarding and deplaning is possible for the handicapped. Ramps make the terminal accessible. To get around, **Handi-Vans** are available in Hilo, tel. (808) 961-6722. **Kamealoha Unlimited** has specially equipped vans, tel. (808) 966-7244. **Parking permits** are available from the Department of Finance, tel. (808) 961-8231. Medical help, nurses, and companions can be arranged through **Big Island Center for Independent Living,** tel. (808) 935-3777. Doctors are referred by **Hilo Hospital,** tel. (808) 961-4211, and by **Kona Hospital,** tel. (808) 322-9311. Medical equipment is available from **Kamealoha Unlimited,** tel. (808) 966-7244; **Medi-Home,** tel. (808) 969-1123; **Pacific Rentall,** tel. (808) 935-2974.

PROSTITUTION

Though the small towns and villages are as safe as you can find anywhere in America, Hawaii isn't all good clean fun. Wherever there's constant tourist flow, a huge military presence, and high cost of living, there will be those people mama warned you about. Most of the heavy night action occurs in Waikiki, Oahu, around Kuhio and Kalakaua avenues, and on Chinatown's Hotel Street. Something about the *vibe* exudes sexuality. The land is raw and wild, and the settings are intoxicating. All those glistening bodies under the tropical sun and the carefree lifestyle are super-conducive to you know what! It's long been known as a great place for boy meets girl, or whomever, but there is also "play for pay."

Prostitution—The Way It Was

Ever since the first ship arrived in 1778, Hawaii has known prostitution. At that time, a sailor paid for a night with a woman with one iron nail. Funny, today they'll take a plastic card. Prostitution, rampant until the missionaries arrived in 1819, was a major cause of the tragic population decline of the Hawaiian race. The tradition carried on into this century. Iwilei was a notorious red-light district in Honolulu at the turn of the century. The authorities, many of whom were clientele, not only turned a blind eye to this scene, but semilegalized it. A policeman was stationed inside the "stockade" and police rules were listed on the five entrances. The women were required to have a weekly VD checkup from the Board of Health, and without a current disease-free certificate they couldn't work. Iwilei was even considered by some to be an attraction: when Somerset Maugham passed through the islands in 1916 on his way to Russia as a spy for England, he was taken here as if on a sightseeing tour. The long-established military presence in Hawaii has also helped keep prostitution a flourishing business. During WW II, troops were entertained by prostitutes in the streets, at houses of prostitution, and at dance halls. The consensus of the military commanders was that prostitution was a necessary evil, needed to keep up the morale of the troops.

The Scene Today

You can go two ways on the "sleaze" scene in Hawaii: ignore it or remain aloof and never see any; or look for and find it with no trouble. The following is neither a condemnation nor an endorsement of how you should act and what you should do. It's merely the facts and the choice is up to you.

The two areas notorious for prostitution today are Kuhio and Kalakaua avenues in Waikiki, Oahu, which are geared toward the tourist; and Hotel Street in downtown Honolulu, for servicemen and a much rougher trade. All sorts of women solicit on Kuhio and Kalakaua avenues —whites, blacks, and Asians—but the majority are young white women from the Mainland. They cruise along in the old-fashioned style, meeting eyes and giving the nod. As long as they keep walking, the police won't roust them. They talk business on the street and then take their john to a nearby backstreet hotel, where he'll be required to pay for the room. Prices vary with the services sought.

The prostitutes in Waikiki number about 300. Most hang out across the street from the police station on Kalakaua or in front of the Hyatt. There was a great influx when Los Angeles cracked down on prostitution for the 1984 Olympics, and Honolulu inherited many of that city's displaced streetwalkers. Most hookers prefer Japanese clientele, followed by the general tourist, and lastly, the always-broke serviceman. In the terse words of one streetwalker queried about the preference for Japanese, "They're small, clean, fast, and they pay a lot." If anyone in Waikiki can speak Japanese, a hooker can. Most are not "equal opportunity employees." Western guys, whether white or black, don't stand much of a chance. The prostitutes are after the Japanese in a sort of crazy payback. The Japanese fish American waters, and the "pros" of Waikiki hook big Japanese fish.

A Honolulu policeman on his Kuhio Avenue beat said, "I can't do anything if they keep walking. It's a free country. Besides, I'm not here to teach anyone morals. . . . Last week a john "fell" out of an eight-story window and a prostitute was found with her throat slit. . . . I'm just on the front lines fighting herpes and AIDS. Just fighting herpes and AIDS, man." The average guy won't have any hassles with a Waikiki prostitue. Mostly it's a straightforward business transaction, but unlike during the days of Iwilei, there is no official control or VD testing.

Then there is Chinatown's Hotel Street (see "Chinatown Nights" in the Honolulu chapter), as rough as guts. The girls are shabby, the bars and strip joints are shabbier, and the vibe is heavy.

Male prostitutes frequent most of the beaches of Honolulu and Waikiki. Most transactions take place during the day. Although many men make legitimate livings as "beachboys" instructing in surfing and the like, some are also prostitutes. It's up to the customer to decide how far the "lessons" proceed.

Massage Parlors, Etc.

Besides streetwalkers, Honolulu and some of the Neighbor Islands have their share of massage parlors, escort services, and exotic dance joints. Most are in Honolulu, and some will even fly their practitioners to the Neighbor Islands if necessary. For massage parlors and escort services you can let your fingers do the walking—through 14 pages in the Honolulu *Yellow Pages* alone. Oddly enough, the "massage" listing is preceded by one for "marketing" and followed by one for "meat." Many legitimate massage practitioners in Hawaii can offer the best therapeutic massages in a variety of disciplines, including shiatsu, *lomi lomi,* and Swedish. Unfortunately, they share the same listings with the other kind of massage parlors. If the *Yellow Pages* listing reads something like "Fifi's Playthings—We'll rub it day or night, wherever it is," this should tip you off. Such parlors usually offer escort services too, for both men and women.

Honolulu also has a number of exotic dance clubs, many along Kapiolani Boulevard (see "Entertainment" in the Honolulu chapter). Basically, they're strip joints with a twist. The dancers are attractive women brought over from the Mainland. They can easily make $150 per night dancing, and the majority are not prostitutes. An act lasts for three songs, and gets raunchier as it goes. If you invite a dancer to have a drink, it'll cost you $10, but it will be a real drink. This gets you nothing but conversation. The price of a patron's drink isn't as inflated as the scene would suggest, and some think it a bargain with a naked woman bumping and grinding just five feet away. Working the sexually agitated male crowd are women who can best be described as "lap sitters." They're almost always older Korean women who've been through the mill. They'll charge you $20 for a fake drink called *niko hana* ("nothing"), and then try to entice you over to a dark corner table, where they'll chisel out $20 more for all you can manage, or are brave enough to do, in a dark corner of a nightclub. Their chief allies are dim lights and booze.

ILLEGAL DRUGS

The use and availability of illegal, controlled, and recreational drugs are about the same in Hawaii as throughout the rest of America. Cocaine constitutes the fastest-growing recreational drug, and it's available on the streets of the main cities, especially Honolulu. Although most dealers are small-time, the drug is brought in by organized crime. The underworld here is mostly populated by men of Asian descent, and the Japanese *yakuza* is said recently to have heightened involvement in Hawaiian organized crime.

A newer drug menace hitting the Honolulu streets is known as "ice." Ice is smokable methamphetamine that will wire a user for up to 24 hours. The high lasts longer, and is cheaper, than cocaine or its derivative, "crack." Users become quickly dependent, despondent, and violent because ice robs them of their sleep, along with their dignity. Its use is particularly prevalent among late-night workers. Many of the violent deaths in Honolulu have been linked to the growing use of ice.

However, the main drug available and commonly used in Hawaii is marijuana, which is locally called *pakalolo*. There are also three varieties of psychoactive mushrooms that contain the hallucinogen psilocybin. They grow wild but are considered illegal controlled substances.

Pakalolo Growing

About 25 years ago, mostly *haole* hippies from the Mainland began growing pot in the more remote sections of the islands, such as Puna on Hawaii and around Hana on Maui. They discovered what legitimate planters had known for 200 years: plant a broomstick in Hawaii, treat it right, and it'll grow. *Pakalolo,* after all, is only a weed, and it grows in Hawaii like wildfire. The locals quickly got into the act when they realized they, too, could grow a "money tree." As a matter of fact, they began resenting the *haole* usurpers, and a quiet and sometimes dangerous feud has been going on ever since. Much is made of the viciousness of the backcountry "growers" of Hawaii. There are tales of booby traps and armed patrols guarding their plants in the hills, but mostly it's a cat-and-mouse game between the authorities and the growers. If you, as a tourist, are tramping about in the forest and happen upon someone's "patch," don't touch anything. Just back off and you'll be okay. Pot has the largest monetary turnover of any crop in the islands, and as such, is now considered a major source of agricultural revenue. There are all kinds of local names and varieties of pot in Hawaii, the most potent being "Kona Gold," "Puna Butter," and "Maui Wowie." These names are all becoming passé.

THEFT AND HASSLES

From the minute you sit behind the wheel of your rental car you'll be warned not to leave valuables unattended and to lock your car up tighter than a drum. Signs warning about theft at most major tourist attractions help fuel your paranoia. Many hotel rooms offer coin-operated safes, so you can lock your valuables away and relax while getting sunburned. Stories abound about purse snatchings and surly locals just itching to give you a hard time. Well, they're all true to a degree, but Hawaii's reputation is much worse than the reality. In Hawaii you'll have to observe two golden laws: if you look for trouble, you'll find it; and a fool and his camera are soon parted.

Theft

The majority of theft in Hawaii is of the "sneak thief" variety. If you leave your hotel door unlocked, a camera sitting on the seat of your rental car, or valuables on your beach towel, you'll be inviting a very obliging thief to pad away with your stuff. You have to learn to take precautions, but they won't be anything like those employed in rougher areas like South America or Southeast Asia—just normal American precautions.

If you must walk alone at night, stay on the main streets in well-lit areas. Always lock your hotel door and windows and place all valuable jewelry in the hotel safe. When you leave your hotel for the beach, there is absolutely no reason to carry all your traveler's checks, credit cards, or a big wad of money. Just take what you'll need for drinks and lunch. If you're uptight about leaving any money in your beach bag, stick it in your bathing suit or bikini. American money is just as negotiable if it is damp. Don't leave your camera or portable stereo on the beach unattended. Ask a person nearby to watch it for you while you go for a dip. Most people won't mind at all, and you can repay the favor.

While sightseeing in your shiny new rental car, which immediately brands you as a tourist, again, don't take more than what you'll need for the day. Why people leave a camera sitting on the seat of their car is a mystery! Many people lock valuables away in the trunk, but remember most good car thieves can "jimmy" it as quickly as you can open it with your key. If you must, for some reason, leave your camera or valuables in your car, lock them in the trunk or consider putting them under the hood. Thieves usually don't look there, and on most modern cars you can only pop the hood with a lever on the inside of the car. It's not fail-safe, but it's worth a try.

Campers face special problems because their entire scene is open to thievery. Most campgrounds don't have any real security, but who, after all, wants to fence an old tent or a used sleeping bag? Many tents have zippers that can be secured with a small padlock. If you want to go trekking and are afraid to leave your gear in the campgrounds, take a large green garbage bag with you. Transport your gear down the trail and then walk off through some thick brush. Put your gear in the garbage bag and bury it under leaves and other light camouflage. That's about as safe as you can be. You can also use a variation on this technique instead of leaving your valuables in your rental car.

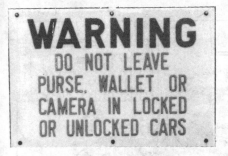

Hassles

Another self-perpetuating myth about Hawaii is that "the natives are restless." An undeniable animosity exists between locals, especially those with some Hawaiian blood, and *haole.* Fortunately, this prejudice is directed mostly at the group and not at the individual. The locals are resentful of those *haole* who came, took their land, and relegated them to second-class citizenship. They realize this is not the average tourist and they can tell what you are at a glance. Tourists usually are treated with understanding and are given a type of immunity. Besides, Hawaiians are still among the most friendly, giving, and understanding people on earth.

Haole who live in Hawaii might tell you stories of their children having trouble at school. They could even mention an unhappy situation at some schools called "beat-up-a-*haole*" day, and you might hear that if you're a *haole* it's not a matter of *if* you'll be beaten up, but *when.* Truthfully, most of this depends upon your attitude and your sensitivity. The locals feel infringed upon, so don't fuel these feelings. If you're at a beach park and there is a group of local people in one area, don't crowd them. If you go into a local bar and you're the only one of your ethnic group in sight, you shouldn't have to be told to leave. Much of the hassle involves drinking. Booze brings out the worst prejudice on all sides. If you're invited to a beach party, and the local guys start getting drunk, make this your exit call. Don't wait until it's too late.

Most trouble seems to be directed toward white men. White women are mostly immune from being beaten up, but they have to beware of the violence of sexual abuse and rape. Although plenty of local women marry white men, it's not a good idea for a white man to try to pick up a local woman. If you're known in the area and have been properly introduced, that's another story. Also, women out for the night in bars or discos can be approached if they're not in the company of local men. If you are with your bikini-clad girlfriend, and a bunch of local guys are, say, drinking beer at a beach park, don't go over and try to be friendly and ask, "What's up?" You, and especially your girlfriend, just might find out. Maintain your own dignity and self-respect by treating others with dignity and respect. Most times you'll reap what you sow.

"Some were rapacious exploiters, seeking to deceive, loot and leave. Hawaii has known them by the thousands through the years."

—Edward Joesting

SUE STRANGIO EVERETT

WHAT TO TAKE

It's a snap to pack for a visit to Hawaii. Everything is on your side. The weather is moderate and uniform on the whole, and the style of dress is delightfully casual. The rule of thumb is to pack lightly: few items, and light clothing both in color and weight. What you'll need will depend largely on your itinerary and your desires. Are you drawn to the nightlife, the outdoors, or both? If you forget something at home, it won't be a disaster. You can buy everything you'll need in Hawaii. As a matter of fact, Hawaiian clothing, such as muumuu and aloha shirts, is one of the best purchases you can make, both in comfort and style. It's quite feasible to bring only one or two changes of clothing with the express purpose of outfitting yourself while here. Prices on bathing suits, bikinis, and summer wear in general are quite reasonable.

Matters Of Taste

A grand conspiracy in Hawaii adhered to by everyone—tourist, traveler, and resident—is to "hang loose" and dress casually. Best of all, alohawear is just about all you'll need for comfort and virtually every occasion. The classic muumuu is large and billowy, and aloha shirts are made to be worn outside the pants. The best of both are made of cool cotton. Rayon is a natural fiber that isn't too bad, but polyester is hot, sticky, and inauthentic. Not all muumuu are of the "tent persuasion." Some are very fashionable and form-fitted with peek-a-boo slits up the side, down the front, or around the back. A *holomuu* is a muumuu fitted at the waist with a flowing skirt to the ankles. It is not only elegant, but perfect for "stepping out."

In The Cold And Rain

Two occasions for which you'll have to consider dressing warmly are visits to mountaintops and boat rides when wind and ocean sprays are a factor. You can conquer both with a jogging suit (sweat suit) and a featherweight, water-resistant windbreaker. If you intend to visit Mauna Kea or Mauna Loa, it'll be downright chilly. Your jogging suit with a hooded windbreaker/raincoat will do the trick for all occasions. If you're going to camp or trek, you should add another layer, a woolen sweater being one of the best. Wool is the only natural fiber that retains most of its warmth-giving properties even if it gets wet. Several varieties of "fleece" synthetics currently on the market also have this ability. If your hands get cold, put a pair of socks over them. Tropical rain showers can happen at any time so you might consider a fold-up umbrella, but the sun quickly breaks through and the warming winds blow.

Shoes

Dressing your feet is hardly a problem. You'll most often wear zoris (rubber thongs) for going to and from the beach, leather sandals for strolling and dining, and jogging shoes for trekking and sightseeing. A few discos require dress shoes, but it's hardly worth bringing them just for that. If you plan on heavy-duty trekking, you'll definitely want your hiking boots. Lava, especially *'a'a*, is murderous on shoes. Most backcountry trails are rugged and muddy, and you'll need those good old lug soles for traction. If you plan moderate hikes, consider bringing rubberized ankle supports to complement your jogging shoes. Most drugstores sell them, and the best are a rubberized sock with toe and heel cut out.

Specialty Items

Following is a list of specialty items you might consider bringing along. They're not necessities but most will definitely come in handy. A pair of binoculars really enhances sightseeing—great for viewing birds and sweeping panoramas, and almost a necessity if you're going whalewatching. A folding, Teflon-bottomed travel iron makes up for cotton's one major shortcoming, wrinkles; you can't always count on hotels to have irons. Nylon twine and miniature clothespins are handy for drying garments, especially bathing suits. Commercial and hotel laundromats abound, but many times you'll get by with hand-washing a few items in the sink. A transistor radio/tape recorder provides news, weather, and entertainment, and can be used to record impressions, island music, and a running commentary for your slide show. An inflatable raft for riding waves, along with flippers, mask, and snorkel, can easily be bought in Hawaii but don't weigh much or take up much space in your luggage. If you'll be camping, trekking, or boating with only seawater available for bathing, take along "Sea Saver Soap," available from good sporting goods stores. This special soap will lather in seawater and rinse away the sticky salt residue with it.

For The Camper

If you don't want to take it with you, camping gear can be purchased or rented while in Hawaii. Besides the above, you should consider taking the following: framed backpack or the convertible packs that turn into suitcases, daypack, matches in a waterproof container, all-purpose knife, mess kit, eating utensils, flashlight (remove batteries), candle, nylon cord, and sewing kit (dental floss works as thread). Take a first-aid kit containing Band-Aids, all-purpose antiseptic cream, alcohol swabs, tourniquet string, cotton balls, elastic bandage, razor blade, Telfa pads, and a small mirror for viewing private nooks and crannies. A light sleeping bag is good, although your fleecy jogging suit with a ground pad and light blanket or even your rain poncho will be sufficient. Definitely bring a down bag for Haleakala or mountainous areas. In a film container pack a few nails, safety pins, fishhooks, line, and bendable wire. Nothing else does what these do and they're all handy for a million and one uses.

Basic Necessities

As previously mentioned, you really have to consider only two "modes" of dressing in Hawaii: beachwear and casual clothing. The following list is designed for the mid-range traveler carrying one suitcase or a backpack. Remember there are laundromats, and you'll be spending a considerable amount of time in your bathing suit. Consider one or two pairs of light cotton slacks for going out and about, and one pair of jeans for trekking, or better yet, corduroys which can serve both purposes; two or three casual sundresses—muumuu are great; three or four pairs of shorts for beachwear and for sightseeing; four to five short-sleeved shirts or blouses and one long-sleeved; three or four colored and printed T-shirts that can be worn anytime from trekking to strolling; a beach coverup—the short terry-cloth type is the best; a brimmed hat for rain and sun—the crushable floppy type is great for purse or daypack; two or three pairs of socks are sufficient, nylons you won't need; two bathing suits (nylon ones dry quickest); plastic bags to hold wet bathing suits and laundry; five to six pairs of underwear; towels (optional, because hotels provide them, even for the beach); a first-aid kit, pocket-size is sufficient; suntan lotion and insect repellent; a daypack or large beach bag. And don't forget your windbreaker, perhaps a shawl for the evening, and an all-purpose jogging suit.

Pets And Quarantine
Hawaii has a very rigid pet quarantine policy designed to keep rabies and other Mainland diseases from reaching the state. All domestic pets are subject to **90 days' quarantine,** regardless of the fact they may have current veterinary shot certificates. Unless you are contemplating a move to Hawaii, it is not feasible to take pets. For complete information, contact the Department of Agriculture, Animal Quarantine Division, 99-770 Moanalua Rd., Honolulu, HI 96701, tel. (808) 488-8461.

INFORMATION AND SERVICES

This section is dedicated to the practical side of travel, the nuts and bolts you'll need to make your stay in Hawaii easier, more efficient, and more convenient. In it you'll find the names, addresses, and phone numbers of useful and helpful organizations and offices. Information, such as business hours, currency, and emergency phone numbers, is listed, as well as a smattering of little-known facts and tidbits related to Hawaii. This information should help you get what you want, or at least point you in the right direction. Good luck!

HAWAII VISITORS BUREAU

In 1903 the Hawaiian Promotion Committee thought tourism could be the economic wave of the future. They began the "Hawaii Tourist Bureau," which became the Hawaii Visitors Bureau. The **HVB** is now a top-notch organization providing help and information to Hawaii's visitors. Anyone contemplating a trip to Hawaii should visit or write the HVB for any specific information they may require. Their advice, and excellent brochures on virtually every facet of living, visiting, or simply enjoying Hawaii, are free. The materials they offer are too voluminous to list, but for basics, request individual island brochures (including maps), and ask for their "Member Accommodation Guide" and "Member Restaurant Guide." Allow two to three weeks for a reply.

Hawaii Visitors Bureau Offices
In Hawaii, **statewide HVB** offices include: HVB Administrative Office, Waikiki Business Plaza, 2270 Kalakaua Ave., Suite 801, Honolulu, HI 96815, tel. (808) 923-1811; Big Island HVB, 250 Keawe St., Hilo, HI 96720, tel. (808) 961-5797; Kauai HVB, 3016 Umi St., Suite 207, Lihue, HI 96766, tel. (808) 245-3971; HVB Kona Branch, 75-5719 W. Ali'i Dr., Kailua-Kona, HI 96740, tel. (808) 329-7787; Maui HVB, 250 Alamaha St., Suite N-16, Kahului, HI 96732, tel. (808) 244-3530.

North America HVB offices are:

HVB Canada, 205-1624 56th St., Delta, B.C., Canada V4L 2B1, tel. (604) 943-8555

HVB Chicago, 180 N. Michigan Ave., Suite 2210, Chicago, IL 60601, tel. (312) 236-0632

HVB Los Angeles, Central Plaza, 3440 Wilshire Blvd., Room 610, Los Angeles, CA 90010, tel. (213) 385-5301

HVB New York, Empire State Bldg., Suite 808, New York, NY 10018, tel. (212) 947-0717

HVB San Francisco, Suite 450, 50 California St., San Francisco, CA 94111, tel. (415) 392-8173

HVB Washington D.C., 1511 K St. NW, Suite 415, Washington, D.C. 20005, tel. (202) 393-6752

European HVB offices are:

HVB Belgium, Rue Couperin, #87 Bis, Boncelles 4100, tel. 32-41-38-1517

HVB Germany, c/o Hans Regh Assoc., Postfach 930 247, Ginnheimer Landstrasse 1, D-6000, Frankfurt, tel. 49-69-70-4013

HVB United Kingdom, 14 The Green, Richmond, TW9 1PX, England, tel. 44-81-332-6969

Asia/Pacific HVB offices are:

HVB Australia, c/o Walshes World, 92 Pitt St., Sydney, N.S.W. 2000, tel. 61-2-235-0194

The "HVB Warrior" is posted alongside the roadway, marking sites of cultural and historical importance.

HVB Hong Kong, Suite 3702-A, EIE Tower, Bond Centre, Queensway, Central, Hong Kong, tel. 852-526-0387

HVB Japan, Hibiya Kokusai Bldg., 11th Fl., 2-2-3 Uchisaiwaicho, Chiyoda-ku, Tokyo 100, tel. 011-81-3-3580-2481

HVB Korea, c/o Travel Press, 2nd Fl., Westin Chosun Hotel, C.P.O. Box 6445, Seoul 100-070, tel. 82-2-757-6781

HVB Malaysia, c/o Pacific World Travel, 2.5 & 2.6 Angkasa Raya Bldg., Jalan Ampag, Kuala Lumpur 50450, tel. 60-3-244-8449

HVB New Zealand, c/o Walshes World, 87 Queen St., 2nd Fl., Dingwall Bldg., Auckland, tel. 64-9-379-3708

HVB Singapore, c/o Pacific Leisure, 3 Seah St. #01-04, Singapore 0718, tel. 65-338-1612

HVB Taiwan, c/o Federal Transportation Co., 8th Fl., Nanking E. Road, Section 3, Taipei, tel. 886-2-507-8133

HVB Thailand, c/o ADAT Sales, 8th Fl., Maneeya Center Bldg., 518/5 Ploenchit Rd., Bangkok 10330, tel. 66-2-255-6838

FOREIGN CONSULATES

All of the foreign consulates and diplomatic offices are located in Honolulu. Most major European, Asian, and Oceanic nations, along with many South American countries, have delegates in Honolulu. They are listed under "Consulates" in the Oahu *Yellow Pages*.

TELEPHONES

Area Code: 808

The telephone system on the main islands is modern and comparable to any system on the Mainland. You can "direct dial" from Hawaii to the Mainland and 70 foreign countries. Undersea cables and satellite communications ensure top-quality phone service. Public telephones are found at hotels, street booths, restaurants, most public buildings, and some beach parks. It is common to have a phone in most hotel rooms and condominiums, though a service charge is usually collected, even on local calls. The **area code** for all islands is **808.**

Rates

Like everywhere else in the U.S., long-distance rates go down at 5 p.m. and again at 11 p.m. until 8 a.m. the next morning. From Friday at 5 p.m. until Monday morning at 8 a.m. rates are cheapest. Local calls from public telephones (anywhere on the same island is a local call) cost 25 cents. Calling between islands is a toll call, and the price depends on when and from where you call and how long you speak. Emergency calls are always free. For directory assistance: local, 1-411; interisland, 1-555-1212; Mainland, 1-area code-555-1212; toll free, 1-800-555-1212.

Helpful Numbers

Police, fire, ambulance: On all islands dial 911. **Coast Guard Rescue:** Oahu, 536-4336; Maui, 244-5256; Kauai, 245-4521; Hawaii, 935-6370.

Civil defense: In case of natural disaster such as hurricanes or *tsunami* when on Oahu call 523-4121; Maui, 244-7721; Kauai, 245-4001; Hawaii, 935-0031.

Crisis and self-help centers: Oahu, 521-4555; Maui, 244-7407; Kauai, 245-7838; Hawaii, 329-9111.

The area code for all Hawaii is 808

Consumer protection: If you encounter problems finding accommodations, bad service, or downright rip-offs, try the following all on Oahu: Chamber of Commerce, 531-411; Hawaii Hotel Association, 923-0407; Office of Consumer Protection, 548-2540.

OTHER PRACTICALITIES

Time Zones

There is no daylight saving time in Hawaii. When daylight saving time is not in effect on the Mainland, Hawaii is two hours behind the West Coast, four hours behind the Midwest, and five hours behind the East Coast. Hawaii, being just east of the International Date Line, is almost a full day behind most Asian and Oceanic cities. Hours behind these countries and cities are: Japan, 19 hours; Singapore, 18 hours; Sydney, 20 hours; New Zealand, 22 hours; Fiji, 22 hours.

Electricity

The same electrical current applies in Hawaii as on the U.S. Mainland and is uniform throughout the islands. The system functions on 110 volts, 60 cycles of alternating current (AC). Appliances from Japan will work, but there is some danger of burn out, while those requiring the normal European current of 220 will not work.

MONEY AND FINANCES

Currency

U.S. currency is among the drabbest in the world. It's all the same size and color; those unfamiliar with it should spend some time getting acquainted so they don't make costly mistakes. U.S. coinage in use is one cent, five cents, 10 cents, 25 cents, 50 cents, and $1 (uncommon); paper currency is $1, $2, (uncommon), $5, $10, $20, $50, $100. Bills larger than $100 are not in common usage.

Banks

Full-service banks tend to open slightly earlier than Mainland banks, Mon.-Fri. 8:30 a.m.-3 p.m., except for late hours on Friday when most banks remain open until 6 p.m. Of most value to travelers, banks sell and cash traveler's checks, give cash advances on credit cards, and exchange and sell foreign currency.

Traveler's Checks

Traveler's checks are accepted throughout Hawaii at hotels, restaurants, car rental agencies, and most stores and shops. However, to be readily acceptable they should be in American currency. Some larger hotels dealing frequently with Japanese and Canadians will accept their currency. Banks accept foreign currency traveler's checks, but it'll mean an extra trip and inconvenience. It's best to get most of your traveler's checks in $20-50 denominations; anything larger will be hard to cash in smaller shops and boutiques, though not in hotels.

Credit Cards

More and more business is transacted in Hawaii using credit cards. Almost every form of accommodation, shop, restaurant, and amusement accepts them. For renting a car they're a must. With credit card insurance readily available, they're as safe as traveler's checks and sometimes even more convenient. Write down the numbers of your cards in case they're stolen. Don't rely on them completely because some establishments won't accept them, or perhaps won't accept the kind you carry. The most readily accepted credit cards are MasterCard and Visa, followed by American Express, Diners Club, and Carte Blanche. Most banks, for a fee, will give you cash advances on your credit cards.

POST OFFICE

Post offices are located in all major towns and cities. Most larger hotels also offer limited postal services. Normal business hours are Mon.-Fri. 8 or 8:30 a.m.-4:30 or 5 p.m., Saturday 8 a.m.-noon.

Receiving Mail

The simplest way to receive mail is to have it sent to your lodgings if you'll be there long enough to receive it. Have it addresssed to you in care of your hotel or condo, and include the room number if you know it. It'll be in your box at the front desk. If you plan frequent moves, or a multiple-island itinerary with short stays on each island, have mail sent "General Delivery" to a post office in a town you plan to visit. The post office will hold your mail in general delivery for 30 days. It takes about five days for a first-class letter to arrive in Hawaii from the Mainland. It's a good idea to notify the postmaster of the post office where you will be receiving mail of the dates you expect to pick it up.

Zip Codes And Main Post Offices

The first three zip code digits, 967, are the same for all of Hawaii (except Honolulu, where it's 968). The last two digits designate the particular post office. The following are the zip codes for the main P.O.s in Hawaii. **Oahu:** Honolulu (downtown, 3600 Aolele St.) 96820, Waikiki 96815; **Kauai:** Lihue 96766; **Maui:** Lahaina 96761, Kihei 96753, Kahului 96732; **Molokai:** Kaunakakai 96748; **Lanai:** 96763; **Hawaii:** Hilo 96720, Kailua-Kona 96740.

NEWSPAPERS

Hawaii's two main English-language dailies are the *Honolulu Star Bulletin,* and the *Honolulu Advertiser.* The *Bulletin* has a circulation of just over 100,000, while the *Advertiser* is just under that figure. The Japanese-English *Hawaii Hochi* has a circulation of 10,000, and the Chinese *United Chinese Press* sells 1,000 copies per day. All are published on Oahu and are available on the other islands.

Weeklies And Magazines

There's a stampede of weeklies in Hawaii; all major islands have at least one and Oahu has at least six. On Kauai look for the *Kauai Times* and the slightly smaller *Garden Island.* The *Maui News,* published in Wailuku, reaches about 16,000 on Maui. The Big Island offers the *Hawaii Tribune Herald* out of Hilo with a circulation of 20,000; *West Hawaii Today,* published in Kailua, reaches 6,000. All of these papers are great for what's happening and for money-saving coupons for restaurants, rentals, and amusements. A few military newspapers are printed on Oahu, along with the *Hawaii Times,* a Japanese-English paper reaching about 10,000 readers.

Over 20 magazines are published in Hawaii, but the ones of most general interest are *Honolulu, Hawaii Business,* and *Waikiki Beach Press* (free).

Tourist Publications And Free Literature

On every island, at airports, hotel lobbies, shopping malls, and main streets are racks filled with free magazines, pamphlets, and brochures. Sometimes the sheer volume is overwhelming, but most have up-to-the-minute information on what's happening and many money-saving coupons. They're also loaded with maps and directions to points of interest. The best, published in a convenient narrow format, are *This Week . . . Oahu, Maui, Kauai, Big Island,* published weekly. *Spotlight,* published weekly for the main islands, is also good, offering information with a strong emphasis on sightseeing. *Guide to . . .* all major islands is in normal magazine format, with good maps. Regional magazines such as *Maui Gold* and *Kona Coast,* are also well worth checking out.

TIDBITS: OFFICIAL AND UNOFFICIAL

Official Hawaii

The state flower is the hibiscus. Over 5,000 species grow in Hawaii. The state tree is the *kukui.* The candlenut was one of the most useful trees of old Hawaii, providing food, medicine, and light. The state bird is the *nene,* a modified goose that came to Hawaii eons ago and adapted to the rugged terrain, becoming a permanent resident and losing its instinct for migration. The humpback whale that visits Hawaii every year was made the official mammal in 1979. Hawaii's nickname is "The Aloha State." The motto, *Ua mau ke ea o ka aina i ka pono* ("The life of the land is perpetuated in righteousness"), came from King Kamehameha III, when in 1843 Hawaii was restored to self-sovereignty after briefly being seized by the British. The anthem, "Hawaii Pono," was written by the "Merry Monarch," King Kalakaua, and put to music by the royal bandmaster, Henri Berger, in 1876. "Hawaii Pono" at one time was the anthem of the Kingdom of Hawaii and later of the Territory before becoming the official state anthem.

Little-Known Facts

The Hawaiian Islands, from Kure Atoll in the north to The Big Island in the south, stretch 1,600 miles. South Point (*Ka Lae*) on the Big Island is the southernmost point of the U.S. The islands are 25 million years old and are entirely created by volcanic activity. Haleakala on Maui is the world's largest inactive volcano, while Hawaii's Mauna Loa is the world's largest active volcano, and Kilauea is *the* most active volcano in the world. Kauai's Mt. Waialeale is the wettest spot on earth, receiving over 600 inches of rain per year. Honolulu's Iolani Palace is the only "Royal Palace" in the United States. Hawaii had the first company (C. Brewer), American school (Lahainaluna), newspaper *(Sandwich Island Gazette)*, bank (First Hawaiian), and church (Pukoo, Molokai) west of the Rocky Mountains.

Tidbits

American captains Shaler and Cleveland brought the first horses aboard the *Lydia Byrd*, and introduced them at Lahaina in 1803. Two were given to Kamehameha the Great, who was not impressed. Tattooing was common in old Hawaii; many people had the date of the death of a loved one tattooed on their body, and gouged their eyes and knocked out their own teeth as signs of mourning. The greatest insult was to inlay a spittoon with the teeth of a defeated enemy. The name of the channel between Maui and Kahoolawe, *Kealaikahiki*, means "the way to Tahiti." Voyagers got their bearings here for the long voyage south. "It will happen when Boki comes back" means something is impossible. Boki was a chief who sailed away in 1829 looking for sandalwood. He never returned. Only 20 of the 500 who sailed with him made it back to Hawaii.

LARGEST CITIES/TOWNS

ISLAND	TOWN/CITY	POP.
Oahu	Honolulu	400,000
	Kailua	36,000
	Kaneohe	35,000
	Pearl City	40,000
	Wahiawa	17,000
	Waipahu	30,000
Maui	Kahului	17,000
	Kihei	11,000
	Lahaina	11,000
Hawaii	Captain Cook	2,500
	Hilo	37,800
	Kailua-Kona	9,000
Kauai	Hanamalu	3,600
	Kapa'a	8,000
	Kekaha	3,300
	Lihue	5,500
Molokai	Kaunakakai	2,300
Lanai	Lanai City	2,400
Niihau		250

DIANA LASICH HARPER

a branch from the ohia lehua *tree*

OAHU

". . . but a diversion, the most common is upon the water . . .
the men lay themselves flat upon an oval piece of plank . . .
they wait the time for the greatest swell that sets on shore,
and altogether push forward with their arms to keep on its top,
it sends them in with a most astonishing velocity . . ."

—James King, c. 1779

BOB RACE

INTRODUCTION

It is the destiny of certain places on earth to be imbued with an inexplicable magnetism, a power that draws people whose visions and desires combine at just the right moment to create a dynamism so strong it becomes history. The result is greatness . . . and Oahu is one of those certain places.

It is difficult to separate Oahu from its vibrant metropolis, Honolulu, whose massive political, economic, and social muscle dominate both the entire state and its home island. But to look at Honolulu *as* Oahu is to look upon only the face of a great sculpture, ignoring the beauty and subtleness of the whole. The words "Honolulu," "Waikiki," and "Pearl Harbor" conjure up visions common to people the world over. Immediately imaginations flush with palm trees swaying, healthy tans, bombs dropping with infamy, and golden moons rising romantically over lovers on white-sand beaches.

Oahu is called the "Gathering Place," and to itself it has indeed gathered the noble memories of old Hawaii, the vibrancy of a bright-eyed fledgling state, and the brawn so necessary for the future. On this amazing piece of land adrift in the great ocean, over 800,000 people live; five times that number visit yearly, and as time passes, Oahu remains strong as one of those certain places."

OVERVIEW

Oahu is partly a tropical garden, bathed by soft showers and sunshine, and swaying with a gentle but firm rhythm. You can experience this feeling all over the island, even in pockets of downtown Honolulu and Waikiki. However, its other side is brash—dominated by the confidence of a major American city perched upon the Pacific Basin whose music is a combination of pounding staccato jackhammer, droning bulldozer, and mechanically screeching crane. The vast majority of first-time and return visitors land at Honolulu International and spend at least a few days on Oahu, usually in Waikiki.

People are amazed by the island's diverse experiences. Besides the obvious (and endless) beach activities, it offers museums, botanical gardens, a fantastic zoo and aquarium,

Waikiki

J.D. BISIGNANI

nightclubs, extravagant shows, free entertainment, cultural classes, theaters, sporting events, a major university, historical sights galore, an exotic cosmopolitan atmosphere, backcountry trekking, and an abundance of camping—all easily accessible via terrific public transportation. Finally, to sweeten the pot, Oahu can be the least expensive of the Hawaiian Islands to visit.

Waikiki

Loosely, this world-famous beach is a hunk of land bordered by the Ala Wai Canal and running eastward to Diamond Head. Early last century these two golden miles were little more than a string of dirty beaches backed by a mosquito-infested swamp. Until 1901, when the Moana Hotel was built, only Hawaii's few remaining *ali'i* and a handful of wealthy *kama'aina* families had homes here. Now, over 125 hotels and condos provide more than 35,000 rooms, and if you placed a $20 bill on the ground, it would barely cover the land it could buy!

This hyperactive area will delight and disgust you, excite and overwhelm you, but never bore you. Waikiki gives you the feeling you've arrived *someplace.* Besides lolling on the beach and walking the gauntlet of restaurants, hotels, malls, and street merchants, you can visit the Waikiki Aquarium or Honolulu Zoo. Then, it's off to ever-present Diamond Head, that monolith of frozen lava so symbolic of Hawaii: it is only a few minutes' drive and a leisurely stroll to its summit. Head eastward around the bulge passing exclusive residential areas and you soon find a string of secluded beaches. Around this tip you pass Koko Head Crater, a trekker's haven; Hanauma Bay, an underwater conservation park renowned for magnificent family-class snorkeling; Sea Life Park, an extravaganza of the deep; and the sleepy village of Waimanalo. Nearby camping at Bellow's Beach makes it hard to believe the city's just 10 miles back.

Downtown Honolulu

Head for downtown and give yourself a full day to catch all the sights. It's as if a huge grappling hook attached to the heart of a Mainland city and hauled it across the sea. But don't get the idea it's not unique, because it is. You'll find a delightful mixture of quaintly historic and future-shock new; exotic and ordinary. The center is Iolani Palace, the only royal palace in America, heralded by the gilded statue of Kamehameha I. Within easy walking radius are the State Capitol and attendant government buildings. Chrome and glass skyscrapers holding the offices of Hawaii's economically mighty shade small stone and wooden structures from the last century: Mission Houses Museum, Kawaiahao Church, and St. Andrew's Cathedral.

Down at the harbor Aloha Tower greets the few passenger ships that still make port; nearby is the floating museum ship, *Falls of Clyde,* a nostalgic reminder of simpler times. Hotel Street takes you to old but not always venerable Chinatown, filled with alleyways housing tiny temples, herbalists, aromatic markets, inexpensive eateries, rough nightspots, dives, and the strong, distinctive flavor of transplanted Asia.

If the hustle and bustle gets to be too much, head for Foster Botanical Gardens. Or hop a special London bus for the serenity of the Bishop Museum and Planetarium, undoubtedly *the* best Polynesian cultural and anthropological museum in the world.

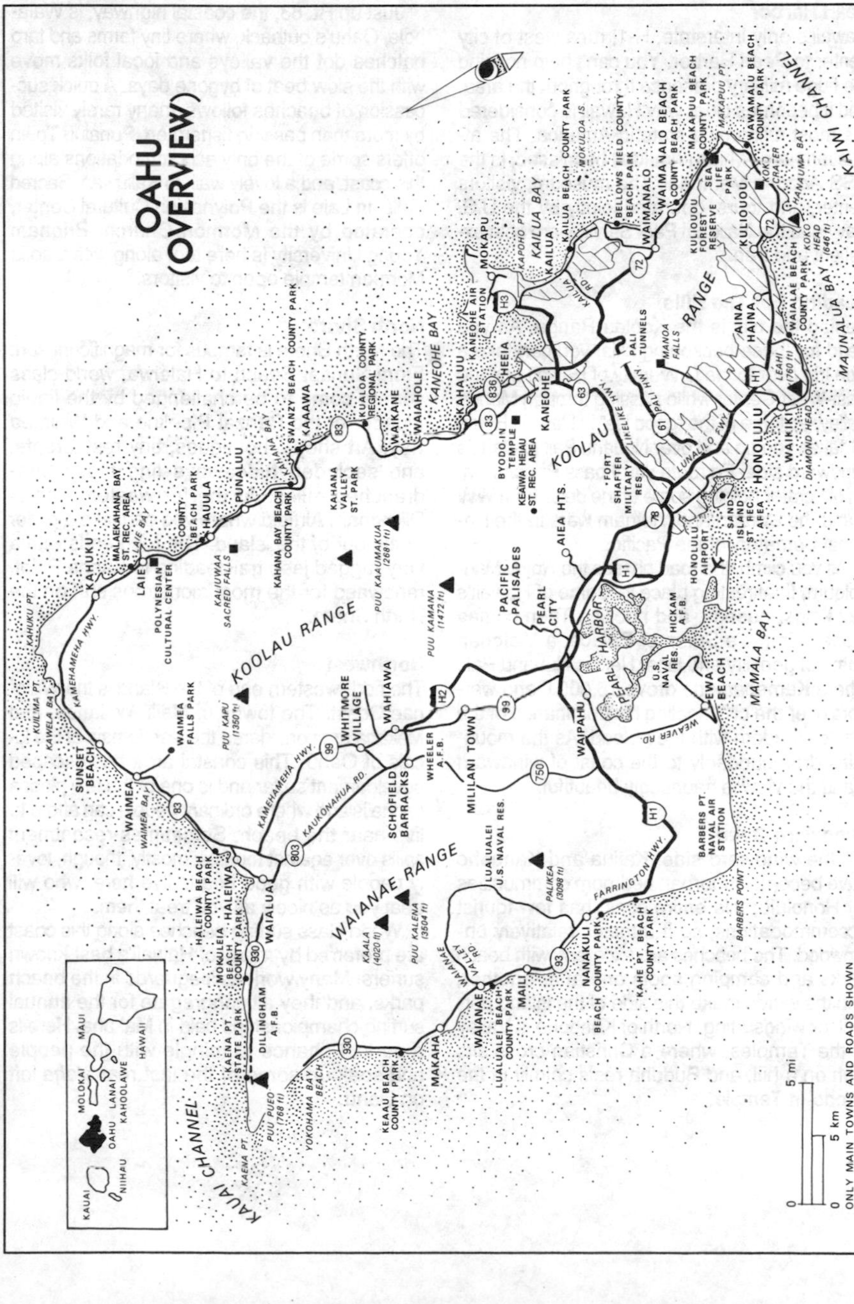

OAHU (OVERVIEW)

KAUAI CHANNEL
KAENA PT.
PUU PUEO (768 ft)
KAENA PT. STATE PARK
DILLINGHAM A.F.B.
MOKULEIA BEACH COUNTY PARK
HALEIWA BEACH COUNTY PARK
HALEIWA
WAIALUA
WAIMEA
WAIMEA BAY
WAIMEA FALLS PARK
SUNSET BEACH
KAWELA BAY
KUILIMA PT.
KAHUKU PT.
KAHUKU
KAMEHAMEHA HWY.
LAIE
LAIE BAY
POLYNESIAN CULTURAL CENTER
MALAEKAHANA BAY ST. REC. AREA
KALIUWAA SACRED FALLS
HAUULA
COUNTY BEACH PARK
PUNALUU
KAHANA BAY BEACH COUNTY PARK
KAHANA VALLEY ST. PARK
KAHANA BAY
SWANZY BEACH COUNTY PARK
KAAAWA
KUALOA COUNTY REGIONAL PARK
WAIKANE
WAIAHOLE
KANEOHE BAY
KAHALUU
HEEIA
KANEOHE AIR STATION
MOKAPU
KAPOHO PT.
KAILUA BAY
MOKULOA IS.
KAILUA
KAILUA BEACH COUNTY PARK
BELLOWS FIELD COUNTY BEACH PARK
WAIMANALO
WAIMANALO BEACH COUNTY BEACH PARK
MAKAPUU BEACH COUNTY PARK
MAKAPUU PT.
SEA LIFE PARK
WAWAMALU BEACH COUNTY PARK
KAIWI CHANNEL
KOKO CRATER
HANAUMA BAY
KOKO HEAD (646 ft)
KULIOUOU
KULIOUOU FOREST RESERVE
WAIALAE BEACH COUNTY PARK
MAUNALUA BAY
AINA HAINA
LEAHI (760 ft)
DIAMOND HEAD
WAIKIKI
HONOLULU
LUNALILO FWY.
MANOA FALLS
PALI TUNNELS
PALI HWY.
LIKELIKE HWY.
KOOLAU RANGE
BYODO-IN TEMPLE
KEAIWA HEIAU ST. REC. AREA
FORT SHAFTER MILITARY RES.
SAND ISLAND ST. REC. AREA
HONOLULU AIRPORT
HICKAM A.F.B.
AIEA HTS.
PACIFIC PALISADES
PEARL CITY
PEARL HARBOR
U.S. NAVAL RES.
MAMALA BAY
EWA BEACH
WEAVER RD.
BARBERS PT. NAVAL AIR STATION
BARBERS POINT
WAIPAHU
MILILANI TOWN
WHEELER A.F.B.
WAHIAWA
WHITMORE VILLAGE
SCHOFIELD BARRACKS
KAUKONAHUA RD.
KAMEHAMEHA HWY.
PUU KAPU (1350 ft)
KOOLAU RANGE
PUU KAUMAKUA (2681 ft)
PUU KAMANA (1472 ft)
WAIANAE RANGE
KAALA (4020 ft)
PUU KALENA (3504 ft)
PALIKEA (3098 ft)
LUALUALEI U.S. NAVAL RES.
FARRINGTON HWY.
KAHE PT. BEACH COUNTY PARK
NANAKULI
BEACH COUNTY PARK
MAILI
LUALUALEI BEACH COUNTY PARK
WAIANAE
WAIANAE VALLEY RD.
MAKAHA
KEAAU BEACH COUNTY PARK
YOKOHAMA BAY BEACH
KAUAI
NIIHAU
OAHU
MOLOKAI
LANAI
MAUI
KAHOOLAWE
HAWAII
0 5 mi
0 5 km
ONLY MAIN TOWNS AND ROADS SHOWN

Pearl Harbor

Hawaii's only interstate, H-1, runs west of city center to Pearl Harbor. You can't help noticing the huge military presence throughout the area, and it becomes clear why Hawaii is considered the most militarized state in America. The attraction here, which shouldn't be missed, is the USS *Arizona* Memorial. The museum, visitors center, and tours, operated jointly by the U.S. Navy and the National Park Service, are both excellent and free.

Heading For The Hills

Behind the city is the Koolau Range. As you head for these beckoning hills, you can take a side trip over to the University of Hawaii and the East-West Center while passing through Manoa Valley, epitome of the "good life" in Hawaii. Route 61 takes you up and over Nuuanu Pali to Oahu's windward side. En route you'll pass Punchbowl, an old crater holding some of the dead from WW II and the Korean and Vietnam wars in the National Cemetery of the Pacific.

As you climb, the road passes the Royal Mausoleum, final resting place for some of Hawaii's last kings, queens, and nobility. Then comes Queen Emma's Summer Palace, a Victorian home of gentility and lace. Next is Nuuanu Pali, where Kamehameha drove 16,000 Oahu warriors over the cliff, sealing his dominance of the island kingdom with their blood. As the mountains drop suddenly to the coast of windward Oahu the view is hauntingly beautiful.

Windward Oahu

On the windward side, Kailua and Kaneohe have become suburban bedroom communities for Honolulu; this entire coast has few tourist accommodations, so it remains relatively uncrowded. The beaches are excellent, with beach parks and camping spots one after another, and the winds make this side of the island perfect for windsurfing. North of Kaneohe is Valley of the Temples, where a Christian cross sits high on a hill, and Buddha rests calmly in the Byodo-In Temple.

Just up Rt. 83, the coastal highway, is Waiahole, Oahu's outback, where tiny farms and taro patches dot the valleys and local folks move with the slow beat of bygone days. A quick succession of beaches follows, many rarely visited by more than passing fishermen. Punaluu Town offers some of the only accommodations along this coast, and a lovely walk to Kaliuwaa, Sacred Falls. In Laie is the Polynesian Cultural Center, operated by the Mormon Church. Brigham Young University is here too, along with a solid Mormon temple open to visitors.

North Shore

The North Shore is famous for magnificent surf. From Sunset Beach to Haleiwa, world-class surfers come to be challenged by the liquid thunder of the Banzai Pipeline and Waimea Bay. Art shops, boutiques, tiny restaurants, and secluded hideaways line these sun-drenched miles. At the far western end is Dillingham Airfield where you can take a glider or air tour of the island. The road ends with a very rugged jeep trail leading to Kaena Point, renowned for the most monstrous surf on the North Shore.

Northwest

The northwestern end of the island is the Waianae Coast. The towns of Maili, Waianae, and Makaha are considered the last domain of the locals of Oahu. This coastal area has escaped development so far and is one of the few places on the island where ordinary people can afford to live near the beach. Sometimes resentment spills over against tourists; mostly, though, lovely people with good hearts live here, who will treat you as nicely as you treat them.

World-class surfing beaches along this coast are preferred by many of Hawaii's best-known surfers. Many work as lifeguards in the beach parks, and they all congregate for the annual surfing championships held in Makaha. Here is a perfect chance to mingle with the people and soak up some of the last real *aloha* left on Oahu.

THE LAND

When Papa, the Hawaiian earth mother, returned from vacationing in Tahiti, she was less than pleased. She had learned through a gossiping messenger that her husband, Wakea, had been playing around. Not simply philandering, he'd been foolish enough to impregnate Hina, a lovely young goddess who bore him island children. Papa, scorned and furious, showed Wakea two could play the same game by taking a handsome young lover, Lua. Their brief interlude yielded the man-child Oahu, sixth of the great island children. Geologically, Oahu is the second oldest main island after Kauai. It emerged from beneath the waves as hissing lava a few million years after Kauai and cooled a little quicker than Papa's temper to form Hawaii's third largest island.

Land Facts

Oahu has a total land area of 608 square miles, and measured from its farthest points is 44 miles long by 30 miles wide. The 112-mile coastline holds the two largest harbors in the state, **Honolulu** and **Pearl.** The **Koolau Mountains** run north-south for almost the entire length of the island, dramatically creating windward and leeward Oahu. The **Waianae Range** is smaller, confined to the northwestern section of the island. It too runs north-south, dividing the **Waianae Coast** from the massive **Leilehua Plateau** of the interior. **Mount Ka'ala,** at 4,020 feet, in the northern portion of the Koolaus, is Oahu's highest peak. The huge Leilehua Plateau is still covered in pineapple and sugarcane and lies between the two mountain ranges running all the way from Waialua on the north shore to Ewa, just west of Pearl Harbor. At its widest point, around Schofield Barracks, it's more than six miles across.

Oahu's most impressive natural features were formed after the heavy volcanic activity ceased and erosion began to sculpt the island. The most obvious is the wall-like cliffs of the **Pali.** Mountain heads were eroded by winds from the east, valleys cut by streams from the west. Perfect examples of these eroded valleys are **Nuuanu** and **Kalihi.** Other impressive examples are **Diamond Head, Koko Head,** and **Punchbowl,** three "tuff-cone" volcanoes created after the heavy volcanic activity of early Oahu. A tuff cone is volcanic ash cemented together to form solid rock. Diamond Head is the most dramatic, formed after a minor eruption about 100,000 years ago and rising 760 feet from its base.

Oahu has the state's longest stream, **Kaukonahua,** which begins atop Puu Kaaumakua at 2,681 feet in the central Koolaus and runs westward for over 30 miles through the Leilehua Plateau. En route, it passes the **Wahiawa Reservoir** which, at 302 acres, forms the second largest body of fresh water in Hawaii. Oahu's tallest waterfalls are 80-foot **Kaliuwaa** (Sacred Falls) just west of Punaluu; and **Waihee Falls** in famous Waimea Park on the North Shore, which have a sheer drop of over 40 feet. Oahu's main water concern is usage that outstrips supply. Major municipal water shortages are expected by the year 2000 unless conservation measures and new technology are employed.

OAHU AVERAGE TEMPERATURE AND RAINFALL

TOWN		JAN.	MARCH	MAY	JUNE	SEPT.	NOV.
Honolulu	high	80	82	84	85	82	81
	low	60	62	68	70	71	68
	rain	4	2	0	0	0	4
Kaneohe	high	80	80	80	82	82	80
	low	67	62	68	70	70	68
	rain	5	5	2	0	2	5
Waialua	high	79	79	81	82	82	80
	low	60	60	61	63	62	61
	rain	2	1	0	0	1	3

Note: rainfall in inches; temperature in °F

Rivers And Lakes
Oahu has no navigable rivers, but there are hundreds of streams. The two largest are Kaukonahua Stream, which runs through central Oahu, and Waikele Stream, which drains the area around Schofield Barracks. A few reservoirs dot the island, like Wahiawa Reservoir and Nuuanu Pali Reservoir, both excellent freshwater fishing spots, but there are no natural bodies of water on Oahu. Hikers should be aware that countless streams and rivulets can quickly turn from trickles to torrents, causing flash floods in valleys that were the height of hospitality only minutes before.

FLORA AND FAUNA

You would think with Oahu's dense human population, little room would be left for animals. In fact, they are environmentally stressed, but they do survive. The interior mountain slopes are home to **wild pigs,** and a small population of **feral goats** survives in the Waianae Range. Migrating **whales** pass by, especially along the leeward coast where they can be observed from lookouts ranging from Waikiki to Koko Head. Half a dozen introduced game birds are found around the island, but Oahu's real animal wealth is its indigenous birdlife.

BIRDS

The shores around Oahu, including those off Koko Head and Sand Island, but especially on the tiny islets of Moku Manu and Manana on the windward side, are home to thriving colonies of marine birds. On these diminutive islands it's quite easy to spot a number of birds from the **tern** family, including the white, gray, and sooty tern. All have a distinctive screeching voice and an approximate wingspan of 30 inches. Part of their problem is they have little fear of humans. Along with the terns are **shearwaters.** These birds have a normal wingspan of about 36 inches, and make a series of moans and wails, oftentimes while in flight. For some reason they're drawn to the bright lights of the city, where they fall prey to house cats and automobiles. Sometimes Moku Manu even attracts the enormous **Laysan albatross** with its seven-foot wingspan. **Tropic birds** with lovely, streamerlike tails, are quite often seen along the windward coast.

To catch a glimpse of exotic birds on Oahu you don't have to head for the sea or the hills. The city streets and beach parks are constantly aflutter with wings. Black **mynah birds** with their sassy yellow eyes are common mimics around town. **Sparrows,** introduced to Hawaii through Oahu in the 1870s, are everywhere, and **munia,** first introduced as cage birds from Southeast Asia, have escaped and are generally found anywhere around the island. Another escaped cage bird from Asia is the **bulbul,** a natural clown that perches on any likely city roost and draws attention to itself with loud calls and generally ridiculous behavior.

If you're lucky, you can also catch a glimpse of the ***pueo*** (Hawaiian owl) in the mountainous areas of Waianae and the Koolaus. Also, along trails and deep in the forest from Tantalus to the Waianae Range you can sometimes see elusive native birds like the ***elepaio, amakihi,*** and fiery red ***'i'iwi.***

Oahu also is home to a number of game birds found mostly in the dry upland forests. These include two varieties of **dove,** the **Japanese quail,** both the **green** and **ring-necked pheasant,** and **Erkel's francolin.** Hunting of these birds occurs year-round and information can be had by contacting the Oahu branch of the Division of Forestry and Wildlife.

Note: Also see The Northwestern Islands chapter for more information on wildlife, including the Hawaiian monk seal, green sea turtle, and various marine birds.

National Wildlife Refuges And Others

Two areas at opposite ends of the island have been set aside as national wildlife refuges (NWR): **James Campbell NWR,** above the town of Kahuku on the extreme northern tip; and **Pearl Harbor NWR,** at the harbor entrance. Both were established in the mid-'70s and managed by the U.S. Fish and Wildlife Service. They serve mainly as wetland habitats for the endangered Hawaiian gallinule *(alae'ula),* stilt *(aeo),* and coot *(alae ke'oke'o).* Clinging to existence, these birds should have a future as long as their nesting grounds remain undisturbed. These refuges also attract a wide variety of other birds, mostly introduced species such as **cattle egrets, herons,** a few species of **doves, munia, cardinals,** and **common finch.**

Much of the area within the refuges is natural marshland, but ponds, complete with water-regulating pumps and dikes, have been built. The general public is not admitted to these areas without permission from the refuge managers. For more information, and to arrange a visit, contact Refuge Manager, Hawaiian and Pacific Islands NWR, U.S. Fish and Wildlife Service, Federal Bldg., Room 5302, Box 50167, Honolulu, HI 96850.

The Nature Conservancy of Hawaii maintains two nature preserves. **Honouliuli,** located on the southeast slope of the Waianae Mountains above Makakilo, is home to more than 45 native plants found nowhere else on earth; guided hikes are offered monthly. Ihi'ihilauakea, in a shallow crater on the dry southeast coastline above Hanauma Bay, has a totally unique vernal pool and a very rare fern, *Marsilea villosa.* Because of the nature of this extremely fragile ecosystem, visitation is limited.

Note

Oahu, a huge tropical garden, has been long planted with every type of flower, tree, fern, and fruit found in the islands. For a description of these and of Hawaii's indigenous flora, please see "Flora and Fauna" in the General Introduction.

BOB RACE

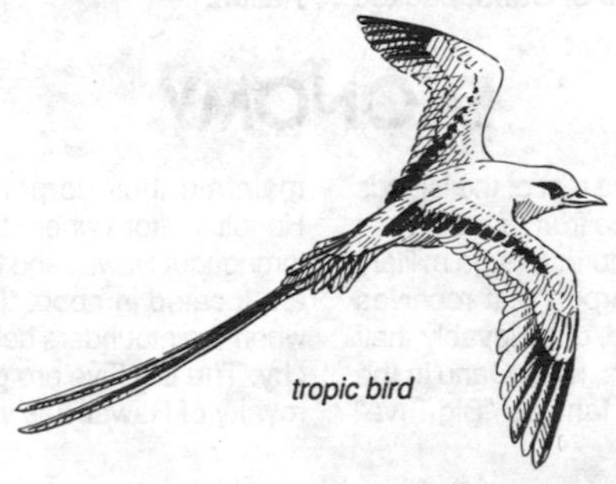

tropic bird

GOVERNMENT

Oahu has been the center of government for about 150 years, since King Kamehameha III permanently established the royal court here in the 1840s. In 1873-74, King David Kalakaua built Iolani Palace as the central showpiece of the island kingdom. Liliuokalani, the last Hawaiian monarch, lived after her dethronement in the nearby residence, Washington Place. While Hawaii was a territory, and for a few years after it became a state, the palace was used as the capitol building, the governor residing in Washington Place. Modern Oahu, besides being the center of state government, governs itself as the **City and County of Honolulu.** The county covers the entire island of Oahu as well as the far-flung Northwestern Islands, except for Midway, which is under federal jurisdiction.

State Representation

Oahu has four times as many people as the other islands combined. Nowhere is this more evident than in the representation of Oahu in the state House and Senate. Oahu claims 19 of the 25 state senators, and 39.7 of the 51 state representatives. (The 0.7 state representative belongs to the district of the north Waianae area of Oahu; the north shore of Kauai chips in with the 0.3 remaining.) These lopsided figures make it obvious Oahu has plenty of clout, especially Honolulu urban districts, which elect more than 50% of Oahu's representatives.

Frequent political battles ensue, since what's good for the city and county of Honolulu isn't always good for the rest of the state. More often than not, the political moguls of Oahu, backed by huge business interests, prevail. The Oahu state senators are overwhelmingly Democratic, except for three Republicans, all from the Honolulu urban districts. State representation is similar: only nine are Republicans, all from urban Honolulu or the suburban communities around Kailua.

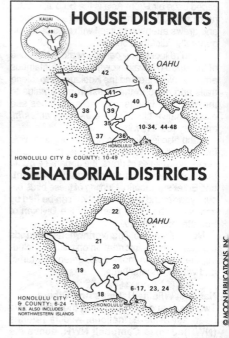

ECONOMY

Economically, Oahu dwarfs the rest of the islands combined. It generates income from government spending, tourism, and agriculture. A huge military presence, an international airport that receives the lion's share of visitors, and, unbelievably, half of the state's best arable lands, keep Oahu in the economic catbird seat. The famous "Big Five" maintain their corporate offices in downtown Honolulu, from where they oversee vast holdings throughout Hawaii and the Mainland. The holdings are located in about the same spots they were when their founders helped overthrow the monarchy. The Big Five are going strong, while the old royalty of Hawaii has vanished.

TOURISM

The flow of visitors to Oahu has remained unabated ever since tourism outstripped sugar and pineapples in the early 1960s, becoming Hawaii's top moneymaker. Of the nearly five million people who visit the state yearly, two-thirds stay on Oahu; almost all the rest, en route to the Neighbor Islands, at least pass through. Hotels directly employ over 15,000 workers, half the state's total, not including the shop assistants, waiters and waitresses, taxi drivers, and everyone else who helps ensure carefree vacations for tourists. Of Hawaii's 60,000 hotel rooms, Oahu claims 34,000. The visitor industry generates over $2 billion of yearly revenue, and this is only the amount that can be directly related to the hotel and restaurant trades. With the flow of visitors seemingly endless, Oahu has a bright economic future.

THE MILITARY

Hawaii is the most militarized state in the U.S., and Oahu is the most militarized island in the state. The U.S. military has been in Hawaii since 1887, when Pearl Harbor was given to the Navy as part of the "Sugar Reciprocity Treaty." The sugar planters were given duty-free treatment for their sugar, while the U.S. Navy was allowed exclusive use of one of the best harbors in the Pacific. In 1894, when the monarchy was being overthrown by the sugar planters, the USS *Boston* sent a contingency of Marines ashore to "keep order," which really amounted to a show of force backing the revolution. The Spanish-American War saw U.S. troops billeted at Camp McKinley at the foot of Diamond Head, Schofield Barracks opened to receive the 5th Cavalry in 1909, and Pearl Harbor's attack, igniting WW II.

About 60,000 military personnel are stationed on Oahu, with a slightly higher number of dependents. The Navy and Marines combined have the most personnel with about 36,000, followed by the Army's 17,000, the Air Force's 6,000, and the Coast Guard's 1,000. Besides this, 20,000 civilian support personnel account for 65% of all federal jobs in Hawaii. The combined services are one of the largest landholders, with over 242,000 acres, accounting for six percent of Hawaiian land. The two major holdings are the 100,000-acre Pohahuloa Training Area on Hawaii and 100,000 acres on Oahu, which is a full 26% of the island. The Army controls 71% of the military lands, followed by the Navy at 25%, and the remainder goes to the Air Force and a few small installations to the Coast Guard. Much of this land, used for maneuvers, is off-limits to the public. Besides Pearl Harbor, so obviously dominated by battleship gray, the largest military lands are around Schofield Barracks and the Kahuku-Kawailoa Training Area.

AGRICULTURE

You'd think that with all the people living on Oahu, coupled with the constant land development, there'd be hardly any room left for things to grow. But that's not the case. The land is productive, though definitely stressed. It is startling to realize that in downtown Honolulu and Waikiki, so many trees have been removed to build parking lots the asphalt becomes overheated from the lack of shade, raising temperatures once moderated by trade winds.

Changing times and attitudes led to a "poi famine" that hit Oahu in 1967 because very few people were interested in the hard work of farming this staple. However, with half the state's best arable land, Oahu manages to produce a considerable amount of sugarcane, pineapples, and the many products of diversified agriculture. Sugar lands account for 33,000 acres, most owned by the James Campbell Estate, located around Ewa, north and west of Pearl Harbor, with some acreage around Waimea and Waialua on the North Shore. Pineapples cover 11,500 acres, with the biggest holdings on the Leilehua Plateau belonging to Dole, a subsidiary of Castle and Cooke. In the hills, entrepreneurs raise *pakalolo,* which has become the state's most productive cash crop. Oahu is also a huge agricultural consumer, demanding more than four times as much vegetables, fruits, meats, and poultry to feed its citizens and visitors than the remainder of the state combined.

THE PEOPLE

For most visitors, regardless of where they've come from, Oahu (especially Honolulu) will be the first place they've ever encountered such an integrated multiracial society. Various countries may be cosmopolitan, but nowhere will you meet so many individuals from such a diversity of ethnic groups, and mixes of these groups. You could be driven to your hotel by a Chinese-Portuguese cab driver, checked in by a Japanese-Hawaiian clerk, served lunch by a Korean waiter, and serenaded by a Hawaiian-Italian-German musician, while an Irish-English-Filipino-French chambermaid tidies your room. This racial symphony is evident throughout Hawaii, but it's more apparent on Oahu, where the large population creates more opportunity for a racial hodgepodge. The warm feeling you get almost immediately upon arrival is that everyone belongs.

Population Figures

Oahu's 800,000 or so residents account for 80% of the state's population. All these people are on an island comprising only 10% of the state's land total. Sections of Waikiki can have a combined population of permanent residents and visitors as high as 90,000 per square mile, making cities like Tokyo, Hong Kong, and New York seem quite roomy by comparison. The good news is that Oahu *expects* all these people and knows how to accommodate them comfortably.

About 400,000 people live in greater Honolulu, generally considered the built-up area from Ewa to Koko Head. The next most populous urban centers after Honolulu are the Kailua-Kaneohe area with about 80,000 residents, followed by Pearl City and Waipahu with a combined total of about 43,000. With all of these people, and such a finite land resource, real estate on the island is sky-high. A typical one-family home sells for $180,000, while a condo averages about $110,000. And for plenty of prime real estate,

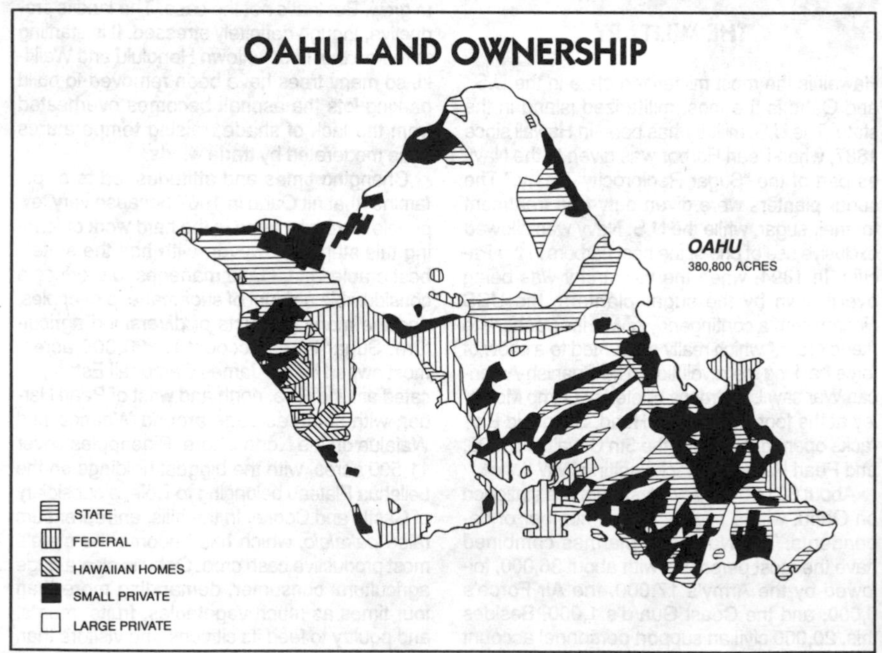

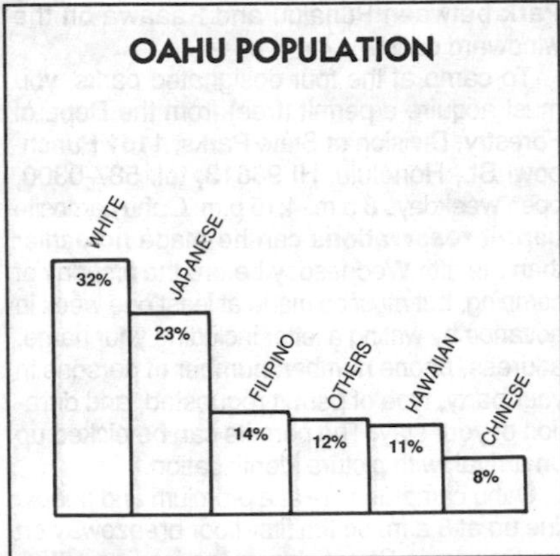

these figures would barely cover the down payment!

So where is everybody? Of the major ethnic groups, you'll find the Hawaiians clustered around Waianae and on the windward coast near Waiahole; the whites tend to be in Wahiawa, around Koko Head, in Waikiki, and in Kailua-Kaneohe; those of Japanese ancestry prefer the valleys heading toward the Pali, including Kalihi, Nuuanu, and Tantalus; Filipinos live just east of the airport, in downtown Honolulu, around Barbers Point, and in Wahiawa; the Chinese are in Chinatown and around the Diamond Head area. As for other ethnic groups, the highest concentration of blacks is in the Army towns around Schofield Barracks; Samoans live along with the Hawaiians in Waianae and the windward coastal towns, though the heaviest concentration is in downtown Honolulu not far from Aloha Tower; Koreans and Vietnamese are scattered here and there, but mostly in Honolulu.

CAMPING AND HIKING

Few people equate visiting Oahu with camping. The two seem mutually exclusive, especially when you focus on the mystique of Waikiki, and the dominance of a major city like Honolulu. But among state, county, and private campgrounds, and even a military reserve or two, you have about 20 spots to choose from all over the island. Camping on Oahu, however, is a little different from the more amenable camping on the Neighbor Islands.

Although legal to camp, and done by both visitors and residents, Oahu's camping problems are widely divergent, with social and financial implications. When the politically powerful tourist industry thinks of visitors, it imagines people sitting by a hotel pool, drinking mai tais, and dutifully spending money. Campers just won't cooperate in parting with their quota of dollars, so there's not much impetus to cater to their wants and needs. Moreover, Honolulu is an international city attracting both the best and worst kinds of people. The tourist industry, supported by the civil authorities, has a mortal dread of low-lifers, loafers, and bums who might ensconce themselves on Oahu's beaches. So on Oahu they keep a close eye on the campgrounds, enforcing the rules, controlling the situation. The campgrounds are patrolled, adding a measure of strictness to a measure of security. Rules can't be bent and nothing is allowed to slide, whereas they normally might on the Neighbor Islands.

An odd inherent social situation adds to the problem. Not too long ago, the local people either lived on the beach or used it extensively, oftentimes for their livelihood. Many, especially fishermen and their families, would set up semipermanent camps for a good part of the year. You can see vestiges of this practice at some of the more remote and ethnically claimed campgrounds. As Oahu, much more than the Neighbor Islands, felt the pressures of growing tourism, beachfront property became astronomically expensive. Local people had to relinquish what they thought of as their beaches. The state and county, in an effort to keep some beaches public and therefore undeveloped, created **beach parks.** This ensured all could use the beaches forever, but it also meant their access would be governed and regulated.

Local people, like visitors, must follow the rules and apply for camping permits limited by the number of days you can spend in any one spot. Out went the semipermanent camp and with it, for the local people, the idea of *our* beach. Now, you have the same right to camp in a spot that may have been used, or even owned, in past generations, by the family of locals next to you. They feel dispossessed, infringed upon, and bitter. And you, especially if you have white skin, can be the focus of this bitterness. This situation, although psychologically understandable, can be a monumental drag. Of course, not all island people have this attitude, and chances are very good nothing negative will happen. But you must be aware of underlying motivations so that you can read the vibes of the people around your camp spot.

If these "problems" haven't made you want to pull up your tent stakes and head into a more congenial sunset, you can have a great and inexpensive time camping on Oahu. All of this is just the social climate you *may* have to face, but most likely, nothing unpleasant will happen, and you'll come home tanned, relaxed, and singing the praises of the great outdoors on Hawaii's capital island.

STATE PARKS

Oahu boasts 23 state parks and recreation areas. The majority offer beaches for day-use, walks, picnicking, toilets, showers, and pavilions. A few of these, including some very important *heiau,* along with **Washington Place,** the state capitol, **Iolani Palace, the Royal Mausolem,** and **Diamond Head** are designated as state monuments.

Oahu state parks close their gates and parking lots at night. Those *not* offering camping are open 7 a.m.-8 p.m., May 1 to September 30, closing during the remainder of the year at 6:30 p.m.

Camping At State Parks

Four state parks currently offer tent camping: **Sand Island State Recreation Area,** just a few minutes from downtown Honolulu; **Keaiwa Heiau State Recreation Area,** in the interior on the heights above Aiea; **Malaekahana Bay State Recreation Area,** a mile north of Laie on the windward coast; and **Kahana Valley State Park** between Punaluu and Kaaawa on the windward coast.

To camp at the four designated parks, you must acquire a permit (free) from the Dept. of Forestry, Division of State Parks, 1151 Punchbowl St., Honolulu, HI 96813, tel. 587-0300, open weekdays 8 a.m.-4:15 p.m. Oahu campsite **permit reservations** can be made no earlier than the fifth Wednesday before the first day of camping, but *must* be made at least one week in advance by writing a letter including your name, address, phone number, number of persons in your party, type of permit requested, and duration of your stay. The permits can be picked up on arrival, with picture identification.

Oahu campsites are at a premium and people line up at 8 a.m. on the first-floor breezeway on the Beretania Street side of the issuing office, just outside the double glass doors, where you are given a number on a first-come, first-served basis (usually no hassle except on three-day holiday weekends). After this, go to the third-floor office.

Note: Camping is allowed *only* from 8 a.m. Friday to 8 a.m. Wednesday (closed all day Wednesday and Thursday to camping, other activities okay). The shutdown is supposedly for regrowth. Camping is allowed for only five consecutive days in any one month, and don't forget a parking permit for your vehicle, which must remain within the locked park gates at night.

COUNTY PARKS

The City and County of Honolulu has opened 13 (changes periodically) of its 65 beach parks around the island to tent camping, and most allow trailers and RVs. Unfortunately, these are the very parks at which you're more likely to encounter hassles. A free permit is required, and camping is allowed for one week from Friday at 8 a.m. until the following Wednesday at 8 a.m., at which time your campsite must be vacated (no camping Wednesday and Thursday evenings). These campsites are also at a premium, but you can write for reservations and pick up your permits on arrival with picture identification. For information and reservations write or visit City and County of Honolulu, Depart-

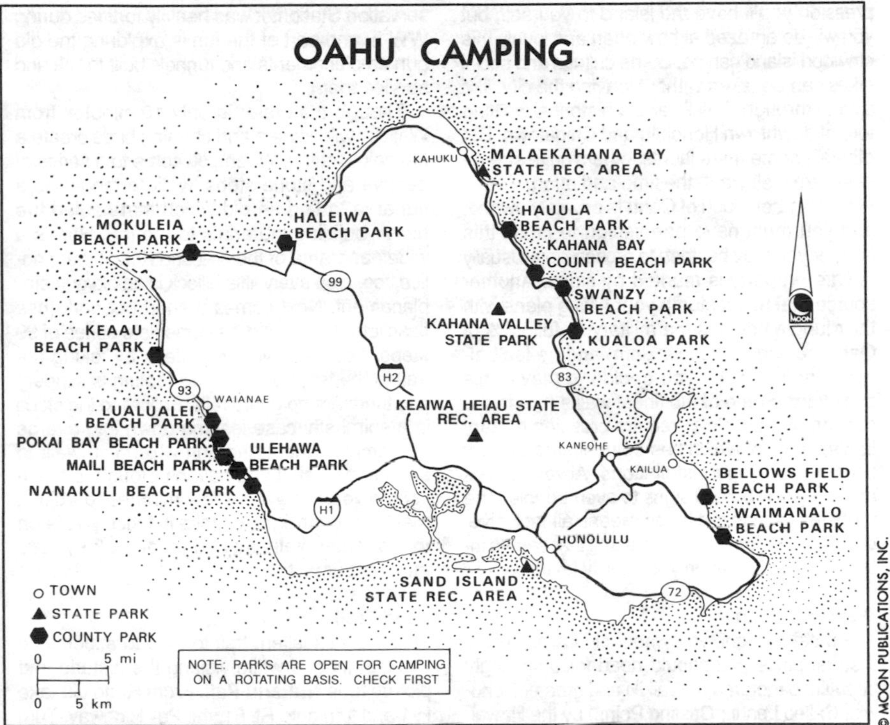

ment of Parks and Recreation, 650 S. King St., Honolulu, HI 96813, tel. 523-4525. Permits are also available from the satellite city halls around the island.

Note: All of the beach parks are closed during designated months (they differ from park to park) throughout the year. This is supposedly for cleaning, but really it's to reduce the possibility of squatters moving in. If you're reserving far in advance, make sure the park will be open when you arrive! Don't count on the Parks and Recreation department to inform you.

Private Campground

A private campground at **Malaekahana Beach** is located virtually next door to Malaekahana Bay State Recreation Area just north of Laie. Contact Network Enterprises, 56-335 Kam Hwy., Laie, tel. 293-1736, Monday, Wednesday, Friday 10 a.m.-6 p.m., other days 3-5 p.m. only.

Camping Gear And Rentals

If you've come without camping gear and wish to rent or purchase some, try: **The Bike Shop,** 1149 S. King St., tel. 531-7071, renting tents at $30 for a weekend, $60 for the week, and backpacks at $20 for the weekend, $40 for the week.; or **Omar the Tentman,** 1336 Dillingham Blvd., tel. 836-8785, who rents a one-size-only tent that sleeps six to eight people (no backpacking tents) at $52 for the weekend, $59 for a week, and backpacks at $17 weekend, $22 week.

HIKING

The best way to leave the crowds of tourists behind and become intimate with the beauty of Oahu is to hike it. Although the Neighbor Islands receive fewer visitors, a higher percentage of people hike them than Oahu. Don't get the impression you'll have the island to yourself, but you will be amazed at how open and lovely this crowded island can be. Some cultural and social hikes can be taken without leaving the city, like a stroll through Waikiki and a historical walking tour of downtown Honolulu and Chinatown. But others—some mere jaunts, others quite strenuous—are well worth the time and effort.

Remember much of Oahu is privately owned, and you must have permission to cross this land, or you may be open to prosecution. Usually private property is marked by signs. Another source that might stomp your hiking plans with their jungle boots is the military. A full 25% of Oahu belongs to Uncle Sam, and he isn't always thrilled when you decide to play in his back yard. Some of the finest walks (like to the summit of Mt. Ka'ala) require crossing military lands, much of which has been altered by very unfriendly looking installations. Always check and obey any posted signs to avert trouble. The following listings are by no means all-inclusive, but should help you choose a trail that seems interesting and is within your ability level.

Diamond Head

The most recognized symbol of Hawaii, this is the first place you should head for a strikingly beautiful panorama of Waikiki and greater Honolulu. Called Leahi ("Casting Point") by the Hawaiians, it was named Diamond Head after a group of wild-eyed English sailors espied what they thought to be diamonds glistening in the rocks. Hawaii had fulfilled so many other dreams, why not a mountain of diamonds? Unfortunately, the glimmer was caused by calcite crystals. No fortune was made, but the name stuck.

To get here, follow Kalakaua Avenue south from Waikiki until it leads onto Diamond Head Road; a sign points you to Diamond Head Crater. Pass through a tunnel and into the heavily militarized section in the crater's center; the trail starts here. Although the hike is moderate, you should bring along water, flashlight (a must), and binoculars if you have them. Run by the Division of State Parks, the park is open daily 6 a.m.-6 p.m. A sign at the beginning describes the rigors you'll encounter, and informs you the trail is seven-tenths of a mile long and was built to the 760-foot summit of Leahi Point in 1908 to serve as a U.S. Coast Artillery Observation Station. It was heavily fortified during WW II, and part of the fun is exploring the old gun emplacements and tunnels built to link and service them.

Though the crater is only 10 minutes from Waikiki, wildflowers and chirping birds create a peaceful setting. When you come to a series of cement and stone steps, walk to the left to a flat area to find an old winch that hauled the heavy building materials to the top. Here's a wide panorama of the sea and Koko Head; notice, too, atop every little hillock is an old gun emplacement. Next comes a short but dark (use flashlight) tunnel and an immediate series of 99 steps. You can avoid the steps by taking the trail to the left, but the trail's footing is slippery and there are no guard rails. Following the steps is a spiral staircase leading down into a large gun emplacement, through which you walk to another tunnel. If you haven't brought a flashlight, give your eyes a few minutes to adjust; there's enough light to make it. Once you're on top, another stairway and ladder take you to the very summit.

Judd Trail

This is an excellent trail to take to experience Oahu's "jungle" while visiting the historic and picturesque **Nuuanu Pali.** From Honolulu take H-1 and turn onto Rt. 61, the Pali Highway. Turn right onto the Old Pali Hwy., then right again onto Nuuanu Pali Drive. Follow it for just under a mile to Reservoir No. 2 spillway. The trail begins on the ocean side of the spillway and leads through fragrant eucalyptus and a dense stand of picture-perfect Norfolk pines. It continues through the forest reserve and makes a loop back to the starting point. En route you pass **Jackass Ginger Pool.** In the immediate area are "mud slides," where you can take a ride on a makeshift toboggan of *pili* grass or ti leaves, or on a piece of plastic if you've brought one. This activity is rough on your clothes, and even rougher on your body. The wet conditions after a rain are perfect. Afterward, a dip in Jackass Pool cleans away mud and refreshes at the same time. Continue down the trail to observe wild ginger, guava, and *kukui,* but don't take any side trails, which can get confusing. If you get lost, head back to the stream and follow it until it intersects the main trail.

Tantalus And Makiki Valley Trails

Great sightseeing and hiking can be combined when you climb the road atop Tantalus. A range of trails in this area offers magnificent views. A few roads lead up Tantalus, but a good one heads past Punchbowl along Puowaina Drive; just keep going until it turns into Tantalus Drive. The road switchbacks past some incredible homes and views until it reaches the 2,013-foot summit, where it changes its name to Round Top Drive, then heads down the other side.

The best place to start a hike is at the top of Tantalus at the **Manoa Cliff Trailhead,** where a number of intersecting trails promise you a selection of adventures. Once you're on Round Top Drive, pass a brick wall with the name Kalaiopua Road imbedded in the stonework, and continue until you pass Forest Ridge Way, right after which is a large turnout on both sides of the road near telephone pole no. 56. To the right is the beginning of half-mile-long **Moleka Trail,** which offers some excellent views and an opportunity to experience the trails in this area without an all-day commitment. The trails are excellently maintained by the Division of Forestry and Wildlife. Your greatest hazard here is mud, but in a moment you're in a lovely stand of bamboo, and in 10 minutes the foliage parts onto a lovely panorama of Makiki Valley, with Honolulu in the background. These views are captivating, but remember to have "small eyes"—check out the varied-colored mosses and fungi, and don't forget the flowers and fruit growing around you.

A branch trail to the left leads to Round Top Drive, and if you continue the trail splits into three: to the right is the **Makiki Valley Trail** that cuts across the valley starting at a Boy Scout camp on Round Top Drive and ending atop Tantalus; **Ualakaa Trail** branches to the left and goes for another half mile, connecting the Makiki Valley Trail with Puu Ualakaa State Park; straight ahead is the **Makiki Branch A Trail,** which descends for a half mile, ending at the Division of Forestry Baseyard at the bottom of the valley.

On the mountainside of the Manoa Cliffs Trailhead is the **Connector Trail.** This pragmatic-sounding trail does indeed connect the lower trails with **Manoa Cliffs Trail,** skirting around the backside of Tantalus and intersecting the **Puu Ohia Trail,** which leads to the highest point on Tantalus and the expected magnificent view.

Maunawili Demonstration Trail

This is one of Oahu's the most easily accessible and newest trails. Soon after passing the Pali Lookout, clearly marked along the Pali Highway, you will go through a tunnel. Almost immediately, a sign points to a scenic overlook. Pull off into the parking area and walk back up the highway for about 100 yards, where you'll see a break in the guardrail and a sign for *"Na'ala Hele,"* the Hawaiian Trail and Access System. The beauty of this trail is that it is reasonably flat with little elevation gain or loss as it winds its way along the windward side of the Koolau Range. The whine of traffic along the Pali Hwy. abates almost immediately and you are suddenly in a brilliant highland tropical forest. You can continue to the end (about three hours one-way) for a full day's hike, or find a secluded spot after a mile or so for a picnic. The views are spectacular and there are vantage points from where you can see the coast all the way from Rabbit Island to Chinaman's Hat. Remember, however, that as with all Hawaiian trails, recent rainfalls make for treacherous footing.

Hauula Loop Trails

Built by the Workers Civilian Conservation Corps (WCCC) during the Depression, these manicured trails run up and down two ridges and deep into an interior valley, gaining and loosing height as they switchback through the extraordinary jungle canopy. The **Gulch and Papali trails,** branches of the Hauula Loop Trail, start from the same place. The Hauula Trail is wide with good footing. There're a few stream crossings, but it's not muddy even after a heavy rain, which can shut down the Sacred Falls Trail just a few miles north. The hard-packed trail, covered with a soft carpet of ironwood needles, offers magnificent coastal views once you reach the heights, or you can look inland into verdant gulches and gulleys (valleys).

You'll be passing through miniature ecosystems very reminiscent of the fern forests on the Big Island, but on a much smaller scale. The area flora is made up of ironwoods, passion fruit, thimbleberries, ohia, wild orchids, and fiddlehead ferns. To get here, head for Hauula on coastal Rt. 83 (Kam Hwy.), and just past the 7-Eleven Store, between mile markers 21-22, look inland for Hauula Homestead Road. Follow it a short distance until you see the well-marked sign leading to the trails.

Sacred Falls

On coastal Rt. 83, between Hauula and Punaluu (mile markers 22 and 23), an HVB Warrior points you to Sacred Falls. Note you *cannot* drive to the falls. An old commercial venture put out this misinformation, which persists to this day. The walk is a hardy stroll, so you'll need jogging shoes, not thongs. The area becomes a narrow canyon, and the sun sets early; don't start out past 3 p.m., especially if you want a dip in the stream. The trail was roughed up by Hurricane Iwa, and a sign along it says "Danger. Do not go past this point." Not necessarily true; the walking is a little more difficult, but safe.

The area's Hawaiian name was Kaliuwaa ("Canoe Leak") and although the original name isn't as romantic as the anglicized version, the entire area was indeed considered sacred. En route, you pass into a very narrow valley where the gods might show disfavor by dropping rocks onto your head. Notice many stones wrapped in ti leaves. This is an appeasement to the gods, so they're not tempted to brain you. Go ahead, wrap a rock. You can hear the falls dropping to the valley floor. Above you the walls are 1,600 feet high, but the falls drop only 90 feet or so. The pool below is ample for a swim, but the water is chilly and often murky. A number of beautiful picnic spots are on the large flat rocks.

North Oahu Treks

Some of the hiking in and around northwest Oahu is quite difficult. However, you should take a hike out to **Kaena Point.** You have two choices: you can park your car at the end of the road past Dillingham Airfield on the north coast and hike in; or you can park your car at the end of the road past Makua on the Waianae coast and hike in. Both routes are about the same distance, and both are hardy but not difficult. The attraction of Kaena Point is huge surf, sometimes 30 feet high. The trail is only two miles, from each end, and few people come here except local fishermen.

Peacock Flat is a good family-style trail that offers primitive camping. Follow Rt. 930 toward Dillingham Airfield and just before getting there turn left onto a dirt road leading toward the Kawaihapi Reservoir. If you want to camp, you need permits from the Division of Forestry and a waiver from the Mokuleia Ranch, tel. 637-4241, which you can get at their office, located at the end of a dirt road just before the one leading to Kawaihapi Reservoir. They also provide instructions and a key for the two locked gates before the trailhead, if you decide to go in from that end. Heading through the Mokuleia Forest Reserve, you can camp anywhere along the trail, or at an established but primitive campground in Peacock Flat. This area is heavily used by hunters, mostly after wild pig.

Dupont Trail takes you to the summit of Mt. Ka'ala, highest point and by far the most difficult hike on the island. The last mile is downright dangerous, and has you hanging on cliff edges, with the bottom 2,000 feet below. This is not for the average hiker. Follow Rt. 930 to Waialua, make a left at Waialua High School onto a cane road, and follow it to the second gate, about 1.5 miles. Park here. You need a hiking permit from the Division of Forestry and a waiver from the Waialua Sugar Company, tel. 637-3521. Atop Ka'ala, although the views are magnificent, you'll also find a mushroom field of FAA satellite stations.

INFORMATION AND EQUIPMENT

Hiking Groups And Information

The following organizations can provide information on wildlife, conservation, and organized hiking trips. The **Department of Land and Natural Resources,** Division of Forestry and Wildlife, 1151 Punchbowl St., Room 325, Honolulu, HI 96813, tel. 548-2861, is helpful in providing trail maps, accessibility information, hunting and fishing regulations, and general forest rules. Their "Recreation Map" (for each island) is excellent and free. **Hawaiian Trail and Mountain Club,** Box 2238, Honolulu, HI 96804, meets behind Iolani Palace Saturday at 10 a.m., and Sunday at 8 a.m. Their hikes are announced in the *Honolulu Star Bulletin*'s "Pulse of Paradise" column. **Hawaii Audubon Society** can be reached at Box 22832, Honolulu, HI 96822.

Sierra Club, 1212 University Ave., Honolulu, HI 96826, tel. 538-6616, can provide you with a packet describing Hawaii's trails, charted by island, along with their physical characteristics and information on obtaining maps and permits. The packet costs $3, postage paid.

SPORTS AND RECREATION

If it can be ridden, sailed, glided, flown, bounced, smashed with a racquet, struck with a club, bat, or foot, or hooked with the right bait, you can find it on Oahu. And lots of it! The pursuit of fun is serious business here, and you can find anything, sportswise, you ever dreamed of doing. The island offers tennis and golf, along with plenty of horseback riding, hiking, hunting, and freshwater fishing. Spectator sports like baseball, basketball, polo, and especially football are popular. Whatever your desire or physical abilities may be, there'll be some activity to strike your fancy.

GOLF

With over 30 private, public, and military golf courses scattered around such a relatively small island, it's a wonder it doesn't rain golf balls. At present 15 links are open to the public, ranging from modest nine-holers to world-class courses whose tournaments attract the biggest names in golf today. Prices range from $25-140 or more. An added attraction of playing Oahu's courses is you get to walk around on some of the most spectacular and manicured pieces of real estate on the island. Some afford sweeping views of the coast, like the **Ko Olina Golf Club,** while others, like the **Pali Golf Course,** have a lovely mountain backdrop, or, like Waikiki's **Ala Wai Golf Course,** are set virtually in the center of the downtown action.

The **Hawaiian Open Invitational Golf Tournament** held in late January or February at the Waialae Country Club brings the world's best golfers. Prize money is close to $1 million, and all three major TV networks cover the event. This is usually the only opportunity the average person gets to set foot on this course.

Military personnel, or those with military privileges, are welcome to golf at a number of courses operated by all four branches of the service. Call the respective bases for information.

TENNIS

Grease up the old elbow, because Oahu boasts over 168 county-maintained tennis courts. Get a complete list of them by writing a letter of inquiry and enclosing a S.A.S.E. to the Department of Parks and Recreation, Tennis Division, 3908 Paki Ave., Honolulu, HI 96815, tel. 923-7927. Also, plenty of hotel and private courts are open to the public for a fee, though a few hotels limit play to guests only. The following chart is a partial listing of what's available.

FISHING

Deep-Sea Fishing

Oahu's offshore waters are alive with game fish. Among these underwater fighters are marlin, *ahi, ono,* mahimahi, and an occasional deep-water snapper. The deep-sea boats generally troll the Penguin Banks and the generally calm waters along the Waianae Coast, from Barbers Point to Kaena Point. Approximate rates are: private full day $400-600, half day $250-350; shared full day $125, half day $85. Full days are eight hours, half days four, with three-quarter days and overnighters available too. Rates depend on the size of the boat, and most anglers opt to share the boat and split costs with others in the party.

The vast majority of Oahu's fleet moors in **Kewalo Basin,** in Honolulu Harbor along Ala Moana Boulevard next to Fisherman's Wharf. The boat harbor is a sight in itself, and if you're contemplating a fishing trip, it's best to head down there the day before and yarn with the captains and returning fishermen. This way you can get a feel for the charter that suits you best.

Charter organizations include **Island Charters,** tel. 536-1555; and **Ocean Fishing Adventures,** tel. 487-9060. Many private boats operating out of Kewalo Basin include: *Alii Kai,* tel. 521-

GOLF COURSES OF OAHU

COURSE	PAR	YARDS	WEEKDAY FEES
Ala Wai Golf Course 404 Kapahulu Ave. Honolulu, HI 96851 tel. 296-4653	70	6,065	$20
Bay View Golf Center 45-285 Kaneohe Bay Dr. Kaneohe, HI 96744 tel. 247-0451	54	2,231	$20
Hawaii Country Club Kunia Rd. Kunia, HI 96759 tel. 621-5654	71	5,664	$55/60
Hawaii Kai Championship Golf Course 8902 Kalanianaole Hwy. Honolulu, HI 96825 tel. 395-2358	72	6,350	$75
Hawaii Kai Executive Golf Course 8902 Kalanianaole Hwy. Honolulu, HI 96825 tel. 395-2358	55	2,433	$25
Hawaii Prince Golf Club 91-100 4th Weaver Rd. Ewa Beach, HI 96706 tel. 944-4567	72	3,076	$50/135
Honolulu Country Club 1690 Ala Puunalu St. Honolulu, HI 96818 tel. 833-4541	73	6,808	$75
Kahuku Golf Course * x P.O. Box 143 Kahuku, HI 96731 tel. 293-5842	35	2,699	$18
Ko Olina Golf Club 92-1220 Alii Nui Dr. Ewa Beach, HI 96707 tel. 676-5300	72	6,867	$135
Links at Kuilima 57-091 Kamehameha Hwy. Kahuku, HI 96731 tel. 293-8574	72	6,795	$115/125
Makaha Valley Country Club 84-627 Makaha Valley Rd. Waianae, HI 96792 tel. 695-7111	71	6,369	$70

GOLF COURSES OF OAHU

COURSE	PAR	YARDS	WEEKDAY FEES
Mid Pacific Country Club 266 Kaelepulu Dr. Kailua, HI 96734 tel. 261-9765	72	6,812	$130
Mililani Golf Club 95-176 Kualelani Ave. Mililani, HI 96789 tel. 623-2254	72	6,815	$75/80
Moanalua Golf Club * 1250 Ala Aolani St. Honolulu, HI 96819 tel. 839-2411	36	2,972	$25
Oahu Country Club 150 Country Club Rd. Honolulu, HI 96817 tel. 595-3256	71	6,000	$110
Olomana Golf Links 41-1801 Kalanianaole Hwy. Waimanalo, HI 96795 tel. 259-7926	72	6,081	$65
Pali Golf Course 45-050 Kamehameha Hwy. Kaneohe, HI 96744 tel. 261-9784	72	6,493	$25
Pearl Country Club 98-535 Kanonohi St. Aiea, HI 96701 tel. 487-3802	71	6,924	$70/75
Sheraton Makaha Resort and Country Club P.O. Box 896, Makaha Valley Rd. Waianae, HI 96792 tel. 695-9544	72	7,091	$135
Ted Makalena Golf Course 93059 Waipio Point Access Rd. Waipahu, HI 96796 tel. 296-7888	71	5,976	$25
Waialae Country Club x √ 4997 Kahala Ave. Honolulu, HI 96816 tel. 734-2151	72	6,529	$65

Note: *= 9-hole course x = no club rentals √ = guests only

TENNIS COURTS OF OAHU

COUNTY COURTS

Under the jurisdiction of the Department of Parks and Recreation, 3908 Paki Ave., Honolulu, HI 96815; tel. 923-7927. Courts listed are in Waikiki and main towns only. There are approximately 30 additional courts around the island.

LOCATION	NAME OF COURT	NO. OF COURTS	LIGHTED
Aiea	Aiea Recreation Center	2	Yes
Ewa	Ewa Beach Community Park	4	Yes
Kahala	Kahala Recreation Center	2	No
Kailua	Kailua Recreation Center	8	Yes
Kaimuki	Kaimuki Recreation Center	2	Yes
Kalakaua	Kalakaua Recreation Center	4	Yes
Kaneohe	Kaneohe District Park	6	No
Keehi	Keehi Lagoon Courts	12	No
Koko Head	Koko Head District Park	6	Yes
Maunawili	Maunawili Park	2	Yes
Pearl City	Pearl City Recreation Center	2	Yes
Sunset Beach	Sunset Beach Neighborhood Park	2	Yes
Wahiawa	Wahiawa Recreation Center	4	Yes
Waialua	Waialua Recreation Center	4	Yes
Waianae	Waianae District Park	8	Yes
Waikiki	Ala Moana Park	10	Yes
Waikiki	Diamond Head Tennis Center	7	No
Waikiki	Kapiolani Tennis Courts	4	Yes
Waimanalo	Waimanalo District Park	4	No
Waipahu	Waipahu Recreation Center	4	Yes

HOTEL AND PRIVATE COURTS OPEN TO THE PUBLIC

LOCATION	NAME OF COURT	NO. OF COURTS	LIGHTED
Honolulu	Hawaiian Regent Hotel (fee)	1	No
Honolulu	Ilikai Hotel, The Westin (fee)	7	Yes
Honolulu	King Street Courts (fee)	4	Yes
Honolulu	Waikiki Malia Hotel (fee for nonguests)	1	No
Kailua	Windward Tennis Club (fee)	5	Yes
Waianae	Makaha Resort (fee)	4	Yes

3969; *Fish Hawk,* tel. 531-8338; *Sea Verse,* tel. 521-8829; **E.L.O. Sport Fishing,** tel. 947-5208.

A few boats operate out of **Pokai Bay,** in Waianae on the northern leeward coast, and there's even a few berthed in Haleiwa on the North Shore.

The state maintains two public freshwater fishing areas on Oahu. The **Wahiawa Public Fishing Area** is 300 acres of fishable waters in and around the town of Wahiawa. It's basically an irrigation reservoir used to hold water for cane fields. Species regularly caught here are large and smallmouth bass, sunfish, channel catfish, *tucunare,* oscar, carp, snakehead, and Chinese catfish. The other area is the **Nuuanu Reservoir no. 4,** a 25-acre restricted watershed above Honolulu in the Koolau Mountains. It's open for fishing only three times per year in

May, August, and November. Fish caught here are tilapia and Chinese catfish.

WATER SPORTS

Oahu has particularly generous underwater vistas open to anyone donning a mask and fins. Snorkel and dive sites in a range of difficulty levels are accessible from the island. Some sites can be perfect for families and first-time snorkelers; some are accessible only to the experienced diver. All over the island are dive shops where you can rent or buy all equipment, and where dive boats and instruction can be arranged. Particular spots are listed under "Beaches and Parks" in the travel chapters, but some well-known favorites are Hanauma Bay, Black Point off Diamond Head, the waters around Rabbit Island, Shark's Cove on the North Shore, Wanalua Bay between Koko Head and Diamond Head (good for green sea turtles), Magic Island near Ala Moana Beach Park, and sunken ships and planes just off the Waianae coast.

Scuba

Scuba divers will have to show "C Cards" in order to rent gear, fill tanks, or go on charter dives. Plenty of outstanding scuba instructors will give you lessons toward certification, and they're reasonable because of the stiff competition. Prices vary, but you can take a three- to five-day semiprivate certification course, including equipment, for about $375 (instruction book, dive tables, logbook extra charge). Divers unaccustomed to Hawaiian waters should not dive alone regardless of their experience. Most opt for dive tours to special dive grounds guaranteed to please. These vary also, but an *accompanied* single-tank dive where no boat is involved goes for about $65. For a single-tank boat dive, expect to spend $65-85. Special charter dives, night dives, and photography dives are available. Most companies pick you up at your hotel, take you to the site, and return you home. Basic equipment rental costs $25-35 for the day, and most times you'll only need the top of a wetsuit.

Snorkeling

Scuba diving requires expensive special equipment, skills, and athletic ability. Snorkeling is much simpler and enjoyable to anyone who can swim. In about 15 minutes you can be taught the fundamentals—you really don't need formal instruction. Other snorkelers or dive shop attendants can tell you enough to get you started. You can go for much greater distances and spend longer in the water than if you were swimming; you can breathe without lifting your head, you get great propulsion from the fins, and you hardly ever need to use your arms. Experienced snorkelers make an art of this sport and you too can see and do amazing things with a mask, snorkel, and flippers. Don't, however, get a false sense of invincibility and exceed your limitations.

You can buy or rent equipment in the dive shops listed below and in department stores. Sometimes condos and hotels offer free snorkeling equipment for their guests, but if you have to rent it, don't do it at a hotel or condo; go to a dive shop where it's much cheaper (see the following section). Expect to spend about $7 a day for mask, fins, and snorkel. Many boats will take you out snorkeling or diving. Prices range from $40 (half day, four hours) to $70 (full day, eight hours); check "Sightseeing Tours" under "Getting Around" later in this chapter for many of the boats that do it all, from deep-sea fishing to moonlight cruises. A hotel's "activities center" can arrange these excursions for no extra charge. Do yourself a favor and wash sand off rented equipment. Most shops irritatingly penalize you $1 if you don't. All want a deposit, usually $30, which they put on a credit card slip and tear up when you return. Underwater camera rentals are now normal at most shops, and go for around $10-12 including film (24 shots), but not developing. Happy diving!

Dive Shops And Rentals

Dive shops with good reputations include the following. **Waikiki Diving,** at 1734 Kalakaua, and at 420 Nahua, tel. 955-5151, closed Sunday, does PADI certification. No snorkeling tours, but they rent snorkeling equipment at $6 for 24 hours. Dive certification courses cost $370. Open-water dive for beginners from shore is $50 one dive, $75 two dives. Also try **Steve's Diving Adventures,** 1860 Ala Moana Blvd., tel. 947-8900; **South Sea Aquatics,** 1050 Ala Moana Blvd; tel. 538-3854; **Hawaiian Divers,** 2344 Kam Hwy., tel. 845-6644; and **American**

Dive Oahu, 3648 Waialae Ave., tel. 732-2877, a full-service dive shop offering certification, shore and boat dives, and snorkeling adventures. **Snorkel Bob's,** tel. 735-7944, at the corner of Kapahulu and Date avenues, has very inexpensive deals on snorkeling equipment (rent the "better equipment," still a deal). Prices start at only $15 per week for full snorkel gear which you can take to Maui, Kauai, and Big Island locations and return there ($3 extra). Snorkel Bob's also has underwater cameras, and boogie boards for reasonable prices.

Surf and Sea, tel. 637-9887, is a complete dive shop on the North Shore in Haleiwa. **Aaron's Dive Shop,** at 602 Kailua Rd., Kailua, tel. 262-2333, open Mon.-Fri 8 a.m.-8 p.m., Saturday till 6 p.m., Sunday till 5 p.m., is a full-service dive shop. A snorkel outfit costs $7 for 24 hours. Their four-day scuba certification course costs $350, PADI. An introductory dive from a boat costs about $75; off the beach costs $75 but you get two dives.

Leeward Dive Center, 87-066 Farrington Hwy., Maili, tel. 696-3414, (800) 255-1574, offers PADI courses for $325. Introductory dives are $75, boat dives $75 for two tanks, night dives $75.They also offer snorkeling with lessons and equipment for $36. The Leeward Dive Center's specially equipped dive boat *Kahanuolo* departs daily from Waianae Boat Harbor at 8:30 a.m. and returns around noon. They'll pick you up and return you to any Waikiki hotel. The above prices include all equipment and lunch aboard the boat.

Aloha Dive Shop, at Koko Marina (on the way to Haunama Bay), tel. 395-5922, does it all, from snorkeling to boat dives. Excellent rates. **Adventure Dive Hawaii,** tel. 235-4217 or 226-9814, owned and operated by Mark and Midori Imhoof, features introductory shore dives at Hanauma Bay for $50, along with private PADI certification courses for $350. They limit their number of divers to six so the impact on the bay is kept to a minimum while the divers get optimum attention.

Snuba Tours Of Oahu

No, that's not a typo. **Snuba,** at 2233 Kalakaua Ave., B-205A, Suite 1271, Honolulu, HI 96815, tel. 396-6163 or 922-7762, offers a hybrid sport that is half snorkeling and half scuba diving. You have a regulator, weight belt, mask, and flippers, and you're tethered to scuba tanks floating 20 feet above you on a sea-sled. The unofficial motto of Snuba is "secure but free." The idea is many people become anxious diving under the waves encumbered by tanks and all the scuba apparatus. Snuba frees you. You would think being tethered to the sled would slow you down, but actually you're sleeker and can make better time than a normal scuba diver. The sled is made from industrial-strength polyethylene and is 2.5 feet wide by 7.5 feet long, consisting of a view window and a belly for the scuba tank. If you get tired, just surface and use the sled as a raft. Snuba was invented by Mike Stafford of Placerville, California, as an aid to disabled people who wished to scuba. He got the idea from modern gold miners in the Mother Lode area who set a scuba tank on the side of the riverbank and run an air line down to the water to look for gold nuggets wedged under boulders. The first raft came off the assembly line in 1988.

Mick Riegel, the owner and operator of Snuba of Oahu, is one of the first to open a commercial venture in this newest of underwater sports. Mick and his staff conduct various tours throughout the day including Snuba at Waikiki, daily 8:30 a.m.-3:30 p.m. on the half hour. Cost is $45. The Snuba Half-Day Adventure at $95 includes lunch.

Surfing

A local Waikiki beachboy by the name of Duke Kahanamoku won a treasure box full of gold medals for swimming at the Olympic Games of 1912, and thereafter became a celebrity who toured the Mainland and introduced surfing to the modern world. Duke is the father of modern surfing, and Waikiki is its birthplace. All the Hawaiian Islands have incredibly good surfing conditions, but Oahu has the best. Conditions here are perfect for both rank beginners and the most acclaimed surfers in the world. Waikiki's surf is predictable, and just right to start on, while the **Banzai Pipeline** and **Waimea Bay** on the North Shore have some of the most formidable surfing conditions on earth. **Makaha Beach** in Waianae is perhaps the best all-around surfing beach, frequented by the living legends of this most graceful sport. If there is such a thing as "the perfect wave," Oahu's waters are a good place to look for it.

Summertime brings rather flat action around the island, but the winter months are a totally different story, with monster waves on the North Shore, and heavy surf, at times even in the relative calm of Waikiki. *Never* surf without asking about local conditions, and remember that "a fool and his surfboard, and maybe his life, are soon parted." See "Festivals, Holidays, and Events" in the Out and About chapter for local and international surfing competitions on Oahu.

Surfing Lessons

A number of enterprises in Waikiki offer beach services. Often these concessions are affiliated with hotels, and almost all hotel activities desks can arrange surfing lessons for you. An instructor and board go for about $25 per hour. A board alone is half the price, but as in skiing, a few good lessons to start you off are well worth the time and money. Some reputable surfing lessons along Waikiki are provided by: Outrigger Hotel, 2335 Kalakaua Ave. tel. 923-0711; Hilton Hawaiian Village, 2005 Kalia Rd., tel. 949-4321; Halekulani Hotel, 2199 Kalia Rd., tel. 923-2311; Big Al Surfing School, 2210 Kalia Rd., tel. 923-4375. Also check near the huge rack of surfboards along Kalakaua Ave., just near Kuhio Beach at the Waikiki Beach Center, where you'll find a number of beachboy enterprises at competitive rates. Good ones are Waikiki Beach Services, tel. 924-4941; and Beach Boys Inc., tel. 923-0711. In Haleiwa on the North Shore, try Surf and Sea, tel. 637-9887.

SAILBOARDING AND BOOGIE BOARDING

The fastest-growing water sport, both in Hawaii and around the world, is sailboarding. Many people call this relatively new sport "windsurfing," after the name of one of the most famous manufacturers of sailboards. Kailua Bay has perfect conditions for this sport, and you can go there any day to see sailboarders skimming the waves with their multihued sails displayed like proud peacocks.

Sailboarding Lessons And Rentals

Far and away the most famous sailboarding beach on Oahu is Kailua Beach Park on the windward coast. Daily, a flotilla of sailboarders glides over its smooth waters, propelled by the always blowing breezes. Along the shore and in town a number of enterprises build, rent, and sell sailboards. There is also sailboarding along the North Shore. Commercial ventures are allowed to operate along Kailua Beach only on weekdays and weekend mornings, but weekend afternoons and holidays are *kapu!* Here are some of the best.

Kailua Sailboard Company, 130 Kailua Rd., tel. 262-2555, open daily 8:30 a.m.-5 p.m., is a full-service sailboard store. Rentals are $30 full day (24 hours), $25 half day, longer term available. Beginners' group lessons are $39 for a three-hour session. During the week they have equipment right at the beach so you don't need a car to transport it. Weekends they provide a push cart or a roof rack at no additional charge. They also rent boogie boards for $7.50 per day, and two-person kayaks for $37.

Naish Hawaii, 155 A Hamakua Dr., tel. 262-6068, open daily 9 a.m.-5 p.m., are very famous makers of custom boards, production boards, sails, hardware, accessories, and repairs. They also have T-shirts, bathing suits, beach accessories, hats, and slippers primarily for men, but plenty of their fashions would be attractive on women as well. Naish is the largest and oldest sailboarding company in Hawaii. The famous Naish Windsurfing School, located at Kailua Beach, gives a half-day lesson which includes 90 minutes of personal instruction for $55 including all equipment; $75 for two people.

On the North Shore in Haleiwa, try **Surf and Sea,** tel. 637-9887.

Boogie Boards

If surfing or sailboarding are a bit too much for you, try a boogie board—a foam board about three feet long that you lie on from the waist up. You can get tremendous rides on boogie boards with the help of flippers for maneuverability. You can learn to ride in minutes and it's much faster, easier, and more thrilling than bodysurfing. Boogie boards are for sale all over the island and are relatively cheap. You can rent one from a dive or surf shop for a couple bucks, or buy your own for $35-70. The most highly acclaimed boogie-boarding beach on Oahu is Sandy Beach. It also has the dubious distinction of being the

Kailua Beach, the sailboarding capital of Oahu

most dangerous beach in Hawaii, with more drownings, broken backs, and broken necks than anywhere in the state. Waikiki is tame and excellent for boogie boarding, while Waimanalo Beach, on the southeast side, is more for the intermediate boogie-boarder.

OTHER WATER SPORTS

The **Windward Boats and Froome Boating Company,** tel. 261-2961, at 789 Kailua Rd., on the corner of Kailua Rd. and the Pali Hwy. just as you're entering town, rents Hobie Cats, powerboats, kayaks, and wave skis. Rates are: kayaks and wave skis, half day $25, full day $30, 24 hours $35; Hobies rent from $60 half day to $350 for the week for a 14-footer; a 16-footer is $80 half day, $400 week. Hobie Cat lessons are available.

If you like water-skiing, **Suyderhoud's Water Ski Center,** tel. 395-3773, at the Koko Marina Shopping Center, can provide equipment, rentals, and lessons. The rate is $49 for two people, skis included, for a half-hour session.

Go Bananas Hawaii, 730 Kapapulu, tel. 737-9514, and at 98-406 Kam Hwy., Pearl City, tel. 484-0606, are into kayaks, wave skis, and water toys. You can go for a guided kayak day-tour (appointment only); kayaks rent for $25 per day, plus $20 per hour for the guide, with reduced prices for longer periods. The store also sells aqua socks for walking on the reef, books, soaps, sunglasses, and T-shirts.

Note: Also see "Sailboarding Lessons and Rentals" above, since many of those companies also rent other water equipment.

Hang Gliding, Parasailing, And Jet Skis

For a once-in-a-lifetime treat try **Aloha Parasail,** tel. 521-2446. Strapped into a harness complete with lifejacket, you're towed aloft to glide effortlessly over the water. Aloha Parasail has free hotel pickup. Others are: **Big Sky Parasail,** at the Koko Marina Shopping Center, tel. 395-2760; and **Hawaii Kai Parasail,** at the Hawaii Kai Shopping Center, tel. 396-9224.

Sport Aviation of Hawaii, tel. 235-6307, sells hang gliders, but doesn't offer lessons. They will, however, give you a lot of tips on where to fly.

Waikiki Beach Services, tel. 924-4941, rents Jet Skis along Waikiki. Their rates are $45 for one hour, or $70 for two people on one ski for one hour. They also have parasailing; "early bird special" at 9 a.m. costs $36. Thereafter, it's $45.

OTHER SPORTS

Horseback Riding

A different and delightful way to see Oahu is from the back of a horse. Here are a few outfits operating trail rides on different parts of the island. **Kualoa Ranch,** tel. 237-8515, by reservation only, in Kualoa on north windward Oahu, offers picnic rides into Ka'a'awa Valley. Hotel pick-up is available. **Turtle Bay Hilton,** tel. 293-8811, on the North Shore welcomes nonguests. Beach rides are offered daily except Monday, with sunset rides on the weekends. **Sheraton Makaha Resort,** tel. 695-9511, offers escorted trail rides through Makaha Valley on leeward Oahu, daily except Monday. Hotel pick-up is available.

Spectator Sports

Oahu is home to a number of major sporting events throughout the year. Many are "invitationals" attracting the cream of the crop from both collegiate and professional levels. Here are the major sports events on the island.

Football is big in Hawaii. The University of Hawaii's Rainbows play during the normal collegiate season at Aloha Stadium near Pearl Harbor. In early January, the **Hula Bowl** brings together two all-star teams from the nation's collegiate ranks. You can hear the pads crack in February, when the NFL sends its best players to the **Pro Bowl.**

Basketball is also big on Oahu. The University of Hawaii's Rainbow Warriors play at the **Neal S. Blaisdell Center,** in Honolulu at 777 Ward Street. Mid-April sees some of the nation's best collegiate hoopballers make up four teams to compete in the **Aloha Basketball Classic.**

You can watch the Islanders of the Pacific Coast League play **baseball** during the regular season at Aloha Stadium. Baseball goes back well over 100 years in Hawaii, and the Islanders receive extraordinary fan support.

Water-sport festivals include surfing events, usually from November through February. The best known are: the **Hawaiian Pro Surfing Championships;** the **Duke Kahanamoku Classic; Buffalo's Big Board Classic;** and the **Haleiwa Sea Spree,** featuring many ancient Hawaiian sports. You can watch some of the Pacific's most magnificent yachts sail into the **Ala Wai Yacht Harbor** in mid-July, completing their run from Los Angeles in the annual **Trans Pacific Yacht Race.**

SHOPPING

You can't come to Oahu and *not* shop. Even if the idea doesn't thrill you, the lure of endless shops offering every imaginable kind of merchandise will sooner or later tempt even the "big-waste-of-time" mumbler through their doors. So why fight it? And if you're the other type, who feels as though a day without shopping is like being marooned on a deserted island, have no fear of rescue, because everywhere on the horizon is "a sale, a sale!"

You can use "much much more" as either an aspersion or a tribute when describing Oahu, and nowhere does this qualifier fit better than when describing its shopping. Over a dozen major and minor shopping centers and malls are in Honolulu and Waikiki alone. Population centers around the island, including those in the interior, the South Shore, windward shore, and North Shore, all have shopping centers in varying degrees—at the very least, a parking lot rimmed with a half-dozen shops can provide immediate necessities. On the Neighbor Islands, a major shopping mall is usually found only in the island's main city, with mom 'n' pop stores and small superettes taking up the slack.

The tourist trade fosters the sale of art and artifacts, jewelry and fashions; numerous boutiques selling these are strung around the island like shells in a necklace. Food costs, in supermarkets, tend to be reasonable because Oahu is the main distribution center, and with all the competition, prices in general seem to be lower than on the other islands. If your trip to Hawaii includes a stop on Oahu, do most of your shopping here, because of the cut-rate prices and much greater availability of goods. When most Hawaiians go on a shopping spree, they head for Oahu. Don't underestimate a simple trip to the grocery store. Often, but not always, you can find uniquely Hawaiian gifts like Kona coffee, macadamia nut liqueur, coconut syrup, and an assortment of juices much cheaper than those in gift shops.

Note: The following are general listings; refer to "Shopping" in the travel chapters for listings of specific shops, stores, and markets.

carver at International Market Place, Waikiki

J.D. BISIGNANI

Honolulu Shopping Centers

Since it serves as the main terminal for TheBus, you could make a strong case that **Ala Moana** Shopping Center is the heart of shopping on Oahu. At one time billed as the largest shopping center in the country, it settles today for being the largest in the state, with hundreds of stores covering 50 acres. It's on Ala Moana Blvd., across from the Ala Moana Beach Park. **The Ward Warehouse** is a few blocks west of Ala Moana Center, at 1050 Ala Moana Boulevard. **Ward Center** on Ala Moana Blvd. across from Ward Warehouse is a relatively new shopping center that's gaining a reputation for some exclusive shops.

Waikiki Shopping

Shopping in Waikiki is as easy as falling off a surfboard. Along two or three blocks of Kuhio and Kalakaua avenues are no less than seven shopping centers. If that's not enough, there are hundreds of independent shops, plus plenty of street vendors. Main shopping centers include **Royal Hawaiian Shopping Center, Waikiki Shopping Plaza,** and **International Market Place,** an open-air shopping bazaar across from the Moana Hotel at 2330 Kalakaua Ave., open daily from 9 a.m. until the vendors get tired at night. **Hyatt Regency Shopping Center** is located on the first three floors of the Hyatt Regency Hotel, at 2424 Kalakaua Ave., tel. 922-5522. **King's Village** is at 131 Kaiulani Ave.; **Waikiki Trade Center** is on the corner of Seaside and Kuhio avenues; and **Rainbow Bazaar** is a unique mall located at the Hilton Hawaiian Hotel, at 2005 Kalia Road.

Around The Island

As you head east from Waikiki on Rt. 72, the first shopping opportunity is **Niu Valley Shopping Center** on your left, about four miles before Hanauma Bay. **Times Supermarket** is known for good prices. Also on the left is **Koko Marina Shopping Center,** just before Hanauma Bay, with a Liberty House, a few art galleries, and **Foodland Supermarket. Kailua** and **Kaneohe** bedroom communities have shopping malls. **Kahaluu Sportswear,** along the Kahekili Hwy., about five minutes north of Byodo-In Temple, is a garment factory outlet store with decent prices and the ugliest collection of mannequins in the Pacific. Numerous shops are found along the North Shore from Haleiwa to Waimea, including surf centers, art galleries, boutiques, and plenty of fast-food places and restaurants. **Pearlridge Shopping Center** in Pearl City at the corner of the Kamehameha Hwy. and Waimano Home Rd. is a full shopping complex with over 150 stores. **Waianae Mall** at 86-120 Farrington Hwy. serves the Waianae coast with a supermarket, drugstore, fast foods, and sporting goods.

Sundries

ABC has over a dozen mini-marts in and around Waikiki. Their prices are generally high, but they do have some good bargains on suntan lotions, sunglasses, and beach mats. The cheapest place to buy **film** is at **Sears, Woolworth,** and **Longs Drugs.** All have good selections, cheap prices, and stores all over the island. **Francis Camera Shop** in the Ala Moana Center, tel. 946-2879, is extremely well stocked with accessories. For a large selection of military surplus and camping goods try the **Big 88** at 330 Sand Island Access Rd., tel. 845-1688.

If gadgetry fascinates you, head for **Shirokiya Department Store** at the Ala Moana and Pearlridge centers and in Waikiki. Besides everything else, they have a wonderful selection of all the jimjicks and doohickeys that Nippon has to offer. The atmosphere is somewhat like that of a trade fair. Those who can't imagine a tour with anything on their feet but Birkenstock can have their tootsies accommodated, but they won't be entirely happy. If you get a sole blowout, **Birkenstock Footprints** at Ala Moana Center, tel. 531-6014, will resole your footwear for $14, but they want a full week to do it. For one-day service, they'll refer you to a shoemaker, **Joe Pacific** at the Ala Moana Center, tel. 946-2998, but he wants a toe-twisting $25 for the service!

Bookstores

Oahu has plenty of excellent bookstores. In Honolulu, try the **Honolulu Book Shops,** with three locations at the Ala Moana Center, tel. 941-2274; in downtown Honolulu at 1001 Bishop St., tel. 537-6224; and at the Pearlridge Center, tel. 487-1548. **Waldenbooks** is at the Pearlridge Center, tel. 488-9488; Kahala Mall, tel. 737-9550; and Waikiki Shopping Plaza, tel. 922-4154. For a fine selection of Hawaiiana try the **Bishop Museum and Planetarium Bookshop,** at the Bishop Museum, 1525 Bernice St., tel. 847-3511; or the **Mission Houses Museum** in downtown Honolulu at 553 S. King St., tel. 531-0481.

Three women, Rachel McMahan, Janice Beam, and Kathryn Decker, have shopped their fingers to the bone for you and have written a small but definitive book entitled *The Shopping Bag.* It lists and describes shops all over Oahu carrying everything from art supplies to toys and sporting goods.

Arts And Crafts

The following are a few of Oahu's many art shops and boutiques, just to get you started. An excellent place to find original arts and crafts at reasonable prices is along **The Fence** surrounding the Honolulu Zoo fronting Kapiolani Park. Island artists come here every weekend 10 a.m.-4 p.m. to display and sell their artwork. The **Honolulu Academy of Arts** at 900 S. Beretania, open Tues.-Sat. 10 a.m.-4:30 p.m., Sunday 1-5 p.m., is not only great to visit, but has a fine gift shop that specializes in Asian art.

The same high-quality and authentic handicrafts are available in both the **Hawaiian Mission Houses Museum** and **Bishop Museum** gift shops (see "Bookstores" above). For Asian art try **Gallery Mikado** and **Garakuta-Do,** both in Waikiki's Eaton Square Complex. Haleiwa's **Ka'ala Art,** tel. 637-7533, is a great one-stop shop for fine arts, pop art, and handicrafts, all by aspiring island artists. The **Punaluu Gallery,** tel. 237-8325, is the oldest gallery on the windward coast. It's been there over 30 years and is now operated by candle maker extraordinaire Scott Bechtol.

Flea Markets And Swap Meets

Amidst the junk, these are the cheapest places to find treasures. Two operate successfully on Oahu and have a regular following. **Aloha Flea Market,** tel. 486-1529, or weekdays tel. 732-9611, is at Aloha Stadium every Wednesday, Saturday, and Sunday and most holidays 6.a.m.-3 p.m. It's the biggest flea market on Oahu, selling everything from bric-a-brac to real heirlooms and treasures.

Kam Swap Meet, tel. 483-5933, Kam Drive-In Theater, 98-850 Moanalua Rd., Pearl City, is open Wednesday, Thursday, Saturday, and Sunday mornings. Regular stall holders to housewives cleaning out the garage offer great fun and bargains.

Food Shopping

Around the island plenty of mom 'n' pop grocery stores provide fertile ground for cultural exchange, but they're expensive. Oahu's large supermarkets include **Times, Safeway, Foodland,** and **Star Market.** Preference is highly individual, but Times has a good reputation for fresh vegetables and good prices. Japanese **Holiday Mart** has stores around the island. They've got some bargains in their general merchandise departments, but because they try to be everything, their food section suffers, especially the fruits and vegetables.

A **Floating Farmers' Market** appears at different times and places around Honolulu. For example, on Wednesday mornings, 9:45-10:45 a.m., it's behind the fire station just north of the Honolulu Zoo in the tennis court (they change locations periodically). The vendors are mostly Filipino, who drive up in small battered trucks and sell wonderful fresh vegetables from their home plots at very reasonable prices. Big shots who bring in fruits and vegies from California and the like have been trying to weed these little guys out. The Honolulu Department of Parks regulates the time and place for the market, and you can get information at 527-6060.

Chinatown offers the **People's Open Market** at the Cultural Plaza, located at the corner of Mauna Kea and Beretania streets. Besides produce, you'll find fresh fish, meats, and poultry. **Oahu Fish Market** is in the heart of Chinatown along King Street. The shops are run-down but clean, selling everything from octopus to *kimchi.*

Health Food Stores

Brown rice and tofu eaters can keep that special sparkle in their eyes with no problem on Oahu—there are some excellent health food stores. Most have a snack bar where you can get a delicious and nutritious meal for bargain prices. **Down to Earth,** 2525 S. King St., tel. 947-7678, is an old standby where you can't go wrong; great stuff at great prices. **Kokua Co-op Natural Foods And Grocery Store,** at the corner of S. Beretania and Isenberg, tel. 941-1921, is open to the public Mon.-Sat. 9 a.m-8 p.m., Sunday 10 a.m.-7 p.m. It's a full-service store with organic and fresh produce, cheese, milk, juices, bulk foods, and breads. **Celestial Natural Foods,** at the Haleiwa Shopping Plaza on the North Shore, tel. 637-6729, is also top-notch. **Vim and Vigor** is at the Ala Moana Center, tel. 955-3600.

BY ALPHONSE PELLION, C. 1819, HAWAII STATE ARCHIVES

ACCOMMODATIONS

The innkeepers of Oahu would be personally embarrassed if you couldn't find adequate lodging on the island. So long as Oahu has to suffer the "slings and arrows" of development gone wild, at least you can find all kinds, qualities, and prices of places in which to spend your vacation. Of the nearly 60,000 rooms available in Hawaii, 35,000 are on Oahu—30,000 of them in Waikiki alone! Some accommodations are living landmarks, historical mementos of the days when only millionaires came by ship to Oahu, dallying as if it were their own private hideaway. When the jumbo jets began arriving in the early '60s, Oahu, especially Waikiki, began to build frantically. The result was hotel skyscrapers that grew faster than bamboo in a rainforest. These monoliths, which offered the "average family" a place to stay, marked a tremendous change in social status of visitors to Oahu. The runaway building continued unabated for two decades, until the city politicians, supported by the hotel keepers themselves, cried "Enough!" and the activity finally slowed down.

Now a great deal of money is put into refurbishing and remodeling what has already been built. Visitors can find breathtakingly beautiful hotels that are the best in the land next door to more humble inns that can satisfy most anyone's taste and pocketbook. On Oahu, you may not get your own private beach with swaying palms and hula performers, but it's easy and affordable to visit one of the world's most exotic and premier vacation resorts. The following is an overview of the accommodations available on Oahu.

Note: For details and listings of specific accommodations, refer to the "Accommodations" sections in specific travel chapters, and to the Hotel Index in the back of the book.

What, Where, And How Much

At almost any time of year, bargains, plenty of them, include fly/drive/stay deals, or any combination thereof, designed to attract visitors while keeping prices down. You don't even have to look hard to find roundtrip airfare, room, and rental car for a week from the West Coast, all for under $500 based on double occupancy. Oahu's rooms are found in all sorts of hotels, condos, and private homes. Some venerable old inns along **Waikiki Beach** were the jewels of the city when only a few palms obscured the views of Diamond Head. However, most of Waikiki's hotels are now relatively new high-rises. In Waikiki's five-star hotels, prices for deluxe accommodations, with all the trimmings, run about $200 per night. But a huge inventory of rooms go for half that amount and less. If you don't mind being one block from the beach, you can easily find nice hotels for $50-60. You can even find these prices in hotels on the beach, though most tend to be a bit older and heavily booked by tour agencies. You, too, can get a room in these, but expect the staffs to be perfunctorily friendly, and the hotels to be a bit worn around the edges. Waikiki's side streets also hold many apartment-hotels that are, in effect, condos. In these you get the benefit of a full kitchen for under $75. Stays of a week or more bring further discounts.

Central Honolulu has few acceptable places to stay except for some no-frills hotels in and around Chinatown. Bad sections of Hotel Street have dives frequented by winos and prostitutes, not worth the hassle for the few dollars saved. Some upscale hotels around Ala Moana put you near the beach, but away from the heavy activity of Waikiki. For those just passing through, a few overnight-style hotels are near the airport.

The remainder of the island, outside Waikiki, was mostly ignored as far as resort development was concerned. In the interior towns, and along the south and most of the windward coasts, you'll be hard pressed to find a room because there simply aren't any. Even today, only a handful of hotels are found on the leeward coast, mostly around **Makaha,** with the exception of the new and luxurious Ihilani Resort and Spa. The area has experienced some recent development with a few condos and full resorts going up, but it remains mostly undeveloped. **Windward Oahu** does have a few established resorts at Turtle Bay and Punaluu, but most of the lodging there is in beachhouse rentals, and tiny, basic inns.

To round things off, there is a network of bed and breakfasts, YM/WCAs, youth hostels, elderhostels, and summer sessions complete with room and board at the University of Hawaii (see "Accommodations" in the Honolulu chapter for details). Oahu's state and county campgrounds offer plenty of spots to pitch a tent.

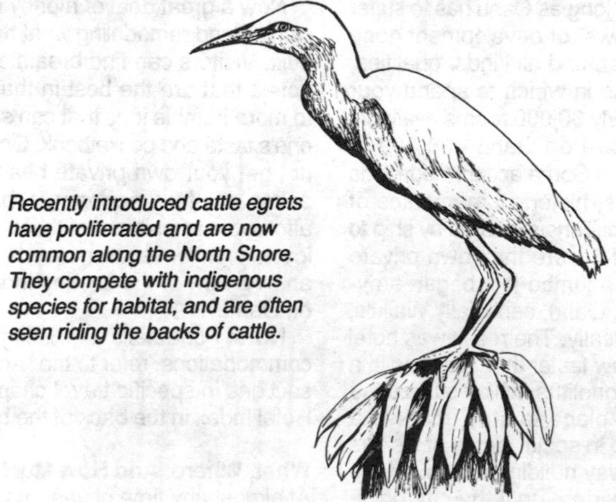

Recently introduced cattle egrets have proliferated and are now common along the North Shore. They compete with indigenous species for habitat, and are often seen riding the backs of cattle.

GETTING THERE

The old adage of "all roads leading to Rome" applies almost perfectly to Oahu, though instead of being cobblestones, they're sea lanes and air routes. Except for a handful of passenger ships still docking at Honolulu Harbor, and some limited nonstop flights to Maui and the Big Island, all other passengers to and from Hawaii are routed through **Honolulu International Airport.** These flights include direct flights to the Neighbor Islands, which means stopping over at Honolulu International and continuing on the same plane, or more likely changing to an interisland carrier whose fare is included in the original price of the flight.

HONOLULU INTERNATIONAL AIRPORT

The state's only international airport is one of the busiest in the country, with hundreds of flights to and from cities around the world arriving and departing daily. In a routine year, over 15 million passengers utilize this facility. The two terminals (directions given as you face the main entranceway) are: the main terminal, accommodating international and Mainland flights, with a small wing at the far left end of the ground floor for a few commuter airlines; and the interisland terminal in a separate building at the far right end of the main terminal.

The ground floor of the **main terminal** is mostly for arriving passengers, and contains the baggage claim area, lockers and long-term storage, car rental agencies, and international and domestic arrival doors (which are kept separate). The second floor is for departing passengers, with most activity centered here, including ticket counters, shops, lounges, baggage handlers, and the entrance to most of the gates. From both levels you can board taxis and TheBus to downtown Honolulu and Waikiki.

The **interisland terminal** services flights aboard Hawaii's own interisland carriers. It has its own snack bars, car rental booths, transportation to and from the city, lounges, information windows, and restrooms.

The stroll between the two terminals is a leisurely five minutes, which is fine if you don't have much baggage; if you do, there are plenty of shuttles every few minutes . . . supposedly! (See "Airport Transportation" below.)

Services, Information, Tips

The main **information booth** is located on the ground level just near the central escalators. Besides general information, they have good maps of the airport, Oahu, Honolulu, and Waikiki. Also, inquiry booths lined up along the ground level and at the interisland terminal are friendly and helpful, but not always stocked with as many maps as the main information booth.

The **lost and found** is located on the ground level of the main terminal, and also at the interisland terminal. The **post office** is across the street from the main entranceway toward the interisland terminal.

Lockers are located on both levels of the main terminal and at the interisland terminal, with a **baggage storage room** only on the ground floor of the main terminal. Locker rental is for a 24-hour period, with a refundable key deposit. You can rent lockers for a month or longer, but you must prepay and leave a deposit. The baggage storage accepts no personal checks, no prepayments, and no pets or perishables. You *must* have your claim ticket to retrieve your belongings. The service is well-run, efficient, and unfriendly.

Money can be a hassle at the airport, especially getting change, which is a downright rip-off, and very bad public relations for visitors. Unfortunately, no one will give you change, putting you at the mercy of $1-bill-change machines located throughout the airport. These machines happily dispense 85 cents for every $1 you put in, so if you want to make a phone call or the like, you're out of luck. The snack bars will only change money for you with a purchase. For a state that prides itself on the *aloha* spirit and depends on good relations with its visitors, this is a ridiculously poor way of greeting people or of giving them a last impression before they return home. The **foreign currency exchange**

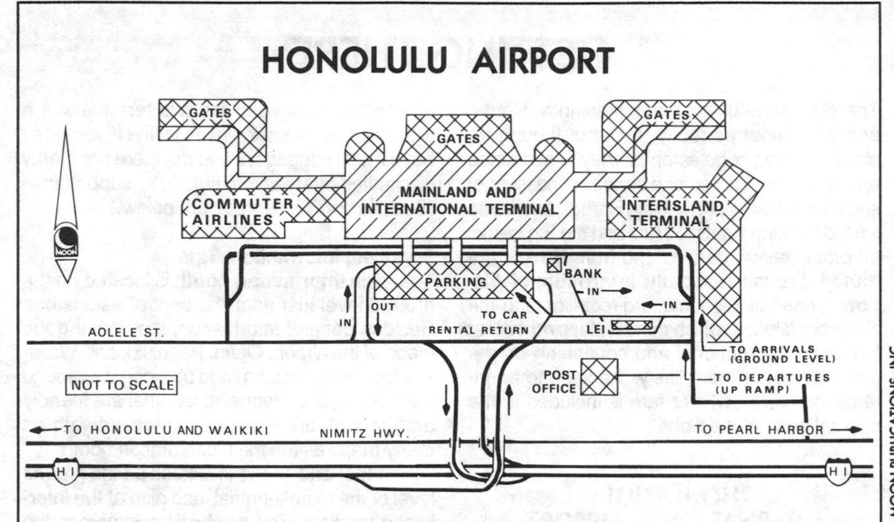

is on the second floor of the main terminal along the concourse behind the United Airlines ticket window. Here, and at a few smaller exchanges on the ground floor, the charge is one percent per transaction on foreign currency, and the same on traveler's checks no matter where they're from, with a minimum charge of $1.50.

To refresh and relax, you might visit the **Airport Mini-Hotel,** tel. 836-3044, on the second level of the terminal's central area. You can have a shower for $8.18, which includes soap, towel, shampoo, deodorant, and hair dryers; an eight-hour sleep in a private little room and a shower for $32.20; or a two-hour nap after 9 a.m. for $19.08. Also try **The Shower Tree,** 3085 N. Nimitz Hwy., tel. 833-1411, only five minutes from the airport with transportation available and luggage storage. Prices are the same as the Airport Mini-Hotel. If these seem a bit pricey, use the airport's public bathrooms for a quick wash, then choose any one of three small gardens near the central concourse to take a little nap. If you're there for just a short snooze, airport security won't bother you.

Airport Transportation

The **Wiki Wiki Shuttle** is a free bus that takes you between the international terminal and the interisland terminal. Staffed by courteous drivers, it is efficient, most of the time. When it's not, a nickname could be the "Tricky Tricky Shuttle." Transfer time between the two terminals is only about 10 minutes, which does not include baggage transfer. If you'll be going on to a Neighbor Island, make sure the carrier you are using has an inter-line agreement with the Hawaiian domestic carrier. If not, you must fetch your own bags, place them on the shuttle, and bring them with you to the interisland terminal. Also, if a flight is delayed, it is up to the carrier to notify the Wiki Wiki Shuttle so adjustments can be made and they wait for you. If your carrier does not contact them, the shuttle bus will follow the normal schedule and may not arrive in time to get you to the interisland terminal. Usually, this is a routine procedure with few problems, but if your connecting schedule is tight, and especially if your carrier has no inter-line agreement (the airline or your travel agent can tell you), be aware of this and leave extra time.

Car rental agencies are lined up at booths on the ground floors of both terminals. Many courtesy phones for car rental agencies not based at the airport are located in and around the baggage claim area; call for free vans to pick you up and take you to their nearby facility. This procedure saves the hassle of maneuvering through heavy airport traffic—you usually wait at the traffic island in the middle of the road just outside the baggage claim area. Make sure to specify the number of the area where you'll wait.

If you're driving to the airport to pick up or drop off someone, you should know about **parking.** If you want to park on the second level of the parking garage for departures, you must either take the elevator up to the fourth floor or down to ground level, and from there cross the pedestrian bridge. There's no way to get across on levels two and three.

Public transportation to downtown Honolulu, especially Waikiki, is abundant. Moreover, some hotels have courtesy phones near the baggage claim area; if you're staying there, they'll send a van to fetch you. Current charges for taxis, vans, TheBus, and limos are posted just outside the baggage claim area, so you don't have to worry about being overcharged.

Taxis to Waikiki cost about $20-25, not counting bags. **Taxi Corporation** tel. 944-8294, charges $18 per car load with no baggage charge. Splitting the fare with other willing passengers can save money. **Grayline** runs a small bus or van to Waikiki for about $5 with no baggage charge. Also, a number of vans and motorcoaches leave from the central traffic island in the roadway just outside the baggage claim. They charge $5, but a wait of up to 45 minutes for one is not out of the ordinary. Moreover, they drop passengers at hotels all over Waikiki, so if yours is not one of the first stops, it could be an hour or so after reaching Waikiki before you're finally deposited at your hotel.

Airport Motor Coach, tel. 839-0911, open daily 6:30 a.m.-10 p.m., hotel pick-up, charges $4 per person from Waikiki to the airport, and $5 per person from the airport to Waikiki.

You can take **TheBus** (no. 8 and no. 20) to Waikiki via the Ala Moana Terminal, from which you can get buses all over the island. If you're heading north pick up buses 20, 51, or 52 just outside the airport. TheBus costs only 85 cents (exact change), but you are allowed only one carry-on bag small enough to hold on your lap. Drivers are sticklers on this point.

GETTING AROUND

Touring Oahu is especially easy, since almost every normal (and not so normal) mode of conveyance is readily available. You can rent anything from a moped to a pedicab, and the competition is very stiff, which helps keep prices down. A few differences separate Oahu from the other islands. To begin with, Oahu has a model public transportation system called TheBus—not only efficient, but very inexpensive. Also, Oahu is the only island that has a true expressway system, though along with it came rush hour and traffic jams. A large part of Oahu's business is processing people, even if it's only to send them on to another island. The agencies operating these businesses on the island are masters at moving people down the road. With the huge volume of tourists who visit every year, it's amazing how smoothly it works. The following is a cross section of what's available and should help you decide how to get around. Have fun!

CAR RENTALS

Every reputable nation-, state-, and island-wide car rental agency is here, along with some car rental hucksters that'll hook you and land you like mahimahi if you're not careful. Most of the latter are located along the main tourist drags of Waikiki. The rule of thumb is, if their deal sounds too good to be true, it is. The competition is so fierce among the reputable agencies, however, that their deals are all equally good. Always check with your travel agency for big savings on fly/drive or stay/drive packages. Make sure your car comes with a flat daily rate and unlimited mileage. If you're lured into renting a "bargain" car, don't be whacked with a mileage charge. Extra benefits from many firms include a free *Drive Guide* that has good maps and lists the island's main attractions; oftentimes you receive a booklet of coupons that entitle you to free or reduced prices on services, admissions, dining, and entertainment. Eight full pages of car rental agencies grace the Honolulu *Yellow Pages,* from firms that rent Mercedes convertibles down to low-budget operations with a few dented and dated Datsuns. Don't get the impression that all the backyard firms are rip-offs. You can get some great deals, but you have to choose wisely and be willing to settle for a less-than-prestigious car.

Reserving a car on Oahu is doubly important because of the huge turnover that can occur at any time. Be aware of **drop-off charges;** for example, if you rent in Waikiki and leave the car at the airport, you'll be charged. It's convenient to rent a car at the airport. But it's also convenient to take an inexpensive shuttle to and from Waikiki (see below) and rent there. Many firms have offices in Waikiki, and you can even rent a car from your hotel desk and have it delivered to you. This saves you the hassle of dealing with traffic and unfamiliar roads during arrival and departure, and avoids drop-off fees—but you don't always get the cheapest rates.

National Agencies

The following national companies have locations in Waikiki. The local phone numbers given are for their main locations at Honolulu International Airport. Call for more details.

One of the best national firms, with an excellent reputation for service and prices, is **Dollar Rent A Car,** tel. 944-1544, (800) 367-7006, or (800) 342-7398 in Hawaii. Their deals and service can't be beat.

Others include: **National Car Rental,** tel. 831-3800, (800) 227-7368; **Hertz,** tel. 831-3500, (800) 654-3131; **Avis,** tel. 834-5536, (800) 331-1212, (800) 831-8000 in Hawaii; **Budget,** tel. 922-3600, (800) 527-0700; **Alamo,** tel. 845-7511, (800) 327-9633; and **Sears,** accepting Sears credit cards, tel. 599-2205, (800) 451-3600.

Local Agencies

These firms offer bargain rates and older cars. Many of them rent without requiring a major credit card, but require a stiff deposit. Sometimes they even rent to those under 21, but you'll have to show reservations at a major hotel. You usually make out all right at: **Aloha Funway Rentals,** airport tel. 831-2277, Waikiki tel. 942-9696, includes exotics, jeeps, and mopeds; **Island,** tel. 839-2222 airport, 946-6666 Waikiki; **Sunshine,** tel. 836-0319 airport, 924-2866 Waikiki; and **VIP** (Very Inexpensive Prices), tel. 946-1671.

Fantasy And Vanity Rentals

The most distinctive and fun-filled cars on Oahu are the hot rods available from Waikiki's **Cruisin' Classics,** 2080 Kalakaua Ave., tel. 951-8331. They have a fleet of completely restored American and European classic cars. Owner Don Pierce operates the company and has done the majority of the work himself on the 1928 Model-A Fords. He has completely reinforced each frame and incorporated a Mustang front suspension, engine, transmission, and rear end. They've all been updated with automatic transmissions and power steering (easy to drive). All are equipped with AM/FM cassette players and *oouugah* horns. Pick a roadster that'll seat four with the rumble seat, or a four-door convertible touring car, which seats five. Recent additions to the fleet are a 1959 pink Cadillac convertible, a 1960 Corvette, and a 1973 Corvette Stingray convertible. Prices start at $89 and can go up to $250 for a stretch limo. The company offers a collision damage waiver for an additional $14.95, or you can accept full responsibility. Insurance for these particular cars is not automatically covered by your credit card company, as it often is with normal rental cars. If your hotel is in the Waikiki area they'll fetch you in their stretch limo, and when you return their car, they'll take you back to your hotel.

Ferrari Rentals, also in Waikiki at 2080 Kalakaua Ave., tel. 942-8725, rents a magnificent Lamborghini Diablo for the equally magnificent price of $1100 per day, while their Ferrari Mondail is $400 per day, and a 1990 Jaguar XJSV-12 convertible goes for a pittance of $250 per day.

Four-Wheel Drives

If you're into 4WDs try **United Car Rental,** tel. 922-4605; or **Aloha Funway Rentals,** tel. 834-1016.

BICYCLES, MOTORCYCLES, AND MOPEDS

Pedaling bicycles around Oahu can be both fascinating and frustrating. The roads are well paved, but the shoulders are often torn up. Traffic in and around Honolulu is horrifying, and the only way to avoid it is by leaving very early in the morning. TheBus has no facilities for transporting your bike out of town, so an early departure is your only alternative. Once you leave the city, traffic, especially on the secondary interior roads, isn't too bad. Unfortunately, all of the coastal roads are heavily trafficked. Instead of a delicate road bike, you're better off renting a **cruiser** or **mountain bike,** which allow for the sometimes poor road conditions and open up the possibilities of off-road biking. Even experienced mountain bikers should be careful on Oahu trails, which are often extremely muddy and rutted. Pedaling around Waikiki, although congested, is usually safe, and a fun way of seeing the sights. Always lock your bike, and take your bike bag.

For info on biking on Oahu, contact **Hawaii Bicycling League,** Box 4403, Honolulu, HI 96813. This nonprofit corporation sponsors rides all over Oahu almost every weekend. Nonmembers are always welcome. The rides are multiple-level ability and are listed in the Hawaii Bicycling League's monthly newsletter, *Spoke-n-Words.* If you're into cycling and want a unique look at Oahu, don't miss these rides.

For bicycle rentals try: good old **Aloha Funway Rentals,** 2025 Kalakaua Ave., tel. 946-2766; and **The Bike Way,** 250 Ward Way, tel. 538-7433. For sales and repairs try: **The Bike Shop,** featuring Fuji, Mongoose, and Schwinn, at 1149 S. King St., tel. 531-7071; **McCully Bicycle,** featuring Specialized, Miyata, and Takara, 2124 S. King, tel. 955-6329; and **The Bike Way,** featuring Bianchi and Univega.

Motorcycles And Mopeds

These two-wheelers are available from: **Aloha Funway Rentals,** tel. 942-9696; **Two Wheel Ventures,** tel. 943-0223; **Discount Moped Rentals,** tel. 941-3623; **Island Scooters,** tel. 946-0013.

PUBLIC TRANSPORTATION

TheBus

If Dorothy and her mates had TheBus to get them down the Yellow Brick Road, she might have chosen to stay in Oz and forget about Kansas. TheBus, TheBus, ThewonderfulBus is the always-coming, slow-moving, go-everywhere friend of the budget traveler. Operated by Mass Transit Lines (MTL) Inc., it could serve as a model of efficiency and economy in any city of the world. What makes it more amazing is it all came together by chance, beginning as an emergency service in 1971. These brown, yellow, and orange coaches go up and down both the windward and leeward coasts, and through the interior, while passing through all of the major and most of the minor towns in between—most often stopping near the best sights.

The **direction** in which TheBus travels is posted on the vehicle after the number and the name of the town. The directions are designated as EB (eastbound toward Diamond Head) and WB (westbound toward the airport). The **fare** is only 85 cents adult, 25 cents student under age 19 or over six, while kids under five who can sit on a parent's lap aren't charged at all. The fare must be paid in exact change upon entering. Even putting a $1 bill into the box and not expecting change is unacceptable. Adult **monthly bus passes,** good at any time and on all routes, are $20, but be aware they are good only from the first to the 31st of every month. If you buy a pass in mid-month, or even later, it is still $20. **Senior Citizens Bus Passes** are $15 and good for four years, or $6 for a discount fare ID also good for four years. Seniors must furnish proof of age, and will be given the pass within a few minutes of having an ID photo taken. Passes are available at **TheBus Pass Office,** open Mon.-Fri. 7:30 a.m.-3:30 p.m., 811 Middle St., tel. 848-4500. The Rt. 1 Kalihi bus stops within a few feet of TheBus Pass Office.

Transfers are free and are issued upon request when entering TheBus, but you can use them only for ongoing travel in the same direction, and on a different line (numbered bus). They are also timed, dated, and good for approximately two hours. For example, you can take no. 8 from Waikiki to the Ala Moana Terminal, get off and do some fast shopping, then use your transfer on no. 20 to continue on to Pearl Harbor.

Get full **route and schedule information** by calling TheBus at tel. 848-5555, or by visiting the information booth at the Ala Moana Terminal, where you can pick up fliers and maps. An excellent, inexpensive little guide is *Hawaii Bus and Travel Guide* by Milly Singletary, available in most bookstores.

Following are popular destinations and their bus numbers, all originating from the Ala Moana Terminal: **Airport,** numbers. 19, 20; ***Arizona* Memorial, Pearl Harbor,** numbers. 20, 50, 51, 52 Wahiawa, (not no. 52 Kaneohe); **Bishop Museum,** no. 2 School; **Chinatown,** numbers. 1, 2, 3, 4, 6, 8, 9, 11, 12, 50, 52 Wahiawa; **Fisherman's Wharf,** no. 8 Airport, no. 20, no. 52 Kaneohe; Hanauma Bay, numbers 1, 57, beach bus (no. 22) weekends; **Honolulu (downtown),** numbers 1, 2, 3, 4, 9, 11, 12; **Pali Lookout,** not serviced; **Polynesian Cultural Center,** both no. 52s, then a shuttle; **Queen Emma Palace,** no. 4; **Sea Life Park,** no. 57; **Waikiki Beach,** numbers. 2, 4, 8, 14, 20.

Circling the island is a terrific way to see the sights and meet people along the way. The circle route takes about four hours if you stay on, but you can use the transfer system to give yourself a reasonable tour of the sights that strike your fancy. The **circle-island** bus is no. 52, but remember that there are two no. 52s, going in different directions. The buses are labeled: **no. 52 Wahiawa Kaneohe,** going inland to Wahiawa, north to Haleiwa, along the North Shore, down the windward coast to Kaneohe, and back over the Pali to Honolulu; **no. 52 Kaneohe Wahiawa,** follows the same route but in the opposite direction. If you'll be taking this bus to Pearl Harbor, be absolutely sure to take no. 52 Wahiawa Kaneohe, because if you took the other, you'd have to circle the entire island before arriving at Pearl!

Other Transportation

A special "beach bus" (no. 22) operates year round and runs from Waikiki to Waimanalo Beach, stopping at Hanauma Bay and Sandy Beach. It has racks for surfboards and leaves every hour (11 a.m.-4 p.m.) from the corner of Monsarrat and Kalakaua avenues. The **Waikiki Trolley,** tel. 526-0112, an open-air bus, will take you on a tour of Waikiki and Honolulu for $15 (all-day pass, so you can board, exit and reboard whenever you like).

Taxis

The law says taxis are not allowed to cruise around looking for fares, so you can't hail them.

But they do and you can, and most policemen have more important things to do than monitor cabs. Best is to summon one from your hotel or a restaurant. All are radio-dispatched, and they're usually there in a flash. The fares, posted on the taxi doors, are set by law and are fair, but still expensive for the budget traveler. The rates do change, but expect to pay about $2.50 for the flag fall, and 50 cents for each additional one-sixth mile. The airport-to-Waikiki is about $25. You pay extra for bags.

Of the many taxi companies, some with good reputations are: **SIDA,** a cooperative of owner-drivers, tel. 836-0011; **Aloha State Taxi,** tel. 847-3566; **Charley's,** tel. 531-1331; City Taxi, tel. 524-2121; and **TheCab,** tel. 533-4999. If you need something special like a Rolls-Royce limo, try **Cloud 9 Limousines,** tel. 524-7999. The **handicapped** can call **Handicabs,** tel. 524-3866.

Hitchhiking

On Oahu, hitchhiking is legal, and you use the tried-and-true style of facing traffic and waving your thumb—but you can only hitchhike from bus stops. Not many people hitchhike and the pickings are reasonably easy, but TheBus is only 85 cents for anywhere you want to go and the paltry sum you save by hitchhiking is lost in "seeing time."

SIGHTSEEING TOURS

Guided land tours are much more of a luxury than a necessity on Oahu. Because of the excellent bus system and relatively cheap rental cars, you spend a lot of money for a narration and to be spared the hassle of driving. If you've come in a group and don't intend to rent a car, a guided land tour may be worth it. Sea cruises and air tours are equally luxurious, but provide glimpses of this beautiful island you'd normally miss. The following partial list of tour companies should get you started.

Note: For all activities, including water sports, horseback riding, parasailing, golf, tennis, etc., please refer to "Sports and Recreation" later in this chapter.

Land Tours

If you're going to take a land tour, you must have the right attitude, or it'll be a disaster. Your tour leader, usually driving the van or bus, is instructor, comedian, and cheerleader, with enough "corn" in his or her jokes to impress an Iowa hog. On the tour, you're expected to become part of one big happy family, and most importantly, to be a good sport. Most guides are quite knowledgeable about Oahu and its history, and they honestly try to do a good job. But they've done it a million times before, and their performance can be as stale as week-old bread. The larger the tour vehicle and the shorter the miles covered, the worse it is likely to be. If you still want a tour, take a full-day jaunt in a small van: you get to know the other people and the guide, who'll tend to give you a more in-depth presentation. Tips are cheerfully accepted. Also, be aware some tours get kickbacks from stores and restaurants they take you to, where you don't always get the best bargains. Most companies offer free hotel pickup and delivery. Lunch or dinner is not included unless specified, but if the tour includes a major tourist spot like Waimea Falls Park or the Polynesian Cultural Center, admission is usually included.

About eight different tours offered by most companies are variations on the same theme; since the prices are regulated, the cost is fairly uniform. The more popular are the **circle island tour,** including stops at Diamond Head, Hanauma Bay, the windward and north shores, Waimea Falls, and perhaps the Mormon Temple and Dole Pineapple Plantation, for about $50, half-price for children. A **night tour** to the Polynesian Cultural Center, including admission and dinner show, costs $50. **Picnic tours,** and tours to **Byodo-In Temple,** go for around $40. Tours to **Punchbowl** and the ***Arizona*** **Memorial** are about $25.

Some reputable companies include: **Akamai Tours,** tel. 971-3131; **Polynesian Adventure Tours,** tel. 922-0888; **Robert's Hawaii Tours,** tel. 523-5187; **Trans Hawaiian Tours,** tel. 735-6467; **E. Noa Tours,** 599-2561; **Dole Pineapple Cannery Tour,** tel. 523-3653; and **Paradise Action Tours,** 307 Lewers St., tel. 926-9193. Companies can arrange everything from Pearl Harbor cruises to dinner shows. They can also arrange condo/hotel reservations, car rental, and interisland tours at competitive prices.

Special Tours

The following are special tours you should seriously consider. **Walking Tour of Chinatown,** tel. 533-3181, by the Chinese Chamber of Commerce, leaves every Tuesday at 9:30 a.m. from in front of their offices at 42 N. King Street. You get a narrated, three-hour tour of Chinatown for about $3, and an optional Chinese lunch for around $4. **Walking Tour of Honolulu, the 1800s,** tel. 531-0481, is a two-hour tour led by a very knowledgeable volunteer from the Mission Houses Museum, who is probably a member of the Cousin's Society and a descendant of one of the original Congregationalist missionaries to Hawaii. You're led on a wonderfully anecdotal walk through the historical buildings of central Honolulu for only $4 for the tour alone, and $7 if you combine it with a museum tour, every Wednesday and Thursday at 9:30 a.m., beginning from The Mission Houses Museum.

Honolulu Time Walks, 2634 S. King St. #3, Honolulu, HI 96826, tel. 943-0731, offer fascinating interpretive walking tours focusing on the city's colorful past. The tours, ranging in price $2-$40 and sometimes including dinner, are thematic and change regularly. Expect topics like "The Revolution of 1893," "The Lighter Side of Old Honolulu," "Scandalous Days of Old Honolulu," and the very popular "Ghosts of Honolulu." Master storyteller Glen Grant, in costume, hosts many of the tours. Extremely authentic and painstakingly researched, these tours are immensely educational and entertaining. You can't find better. Reserve!

The Hawaii Nature Center, 2131 Makiki Heights Dr., Honolulu, HI, tel. 955-0100, is a nonprofit organization dedicated to environmental education through a hands-on approach. Primarily geared toward school-age children, but welcoming the young at heart, the Hawaii Nature Center offers weekend community programs that allow families and the public to share the wealth of Hawaii's magnificent natural environment through interpretive hikes, earth care projects, and nature crafts. This is a wonderful opportunity for visitors to explore Hawaii through direct interaction with the environment.

Oahu By Air

When you soar above Oahu, you realize just how beautiful this island is, and considering that the better part of a million people live in this relatively small space, it's amazing how much undeveloped land still exists in the interior and along the coast. The following are air tours worth considering. All are licensed and regulated for safety. Remember, though, small, one- or two-plane operations come and go as quickly as cloudbursts; if business is bad, the propellers stop spinning.

Novel air tours are offered from Dillingham Airfield in northwest Oahu, a few miles down the Farrington Hwy. from Waialua. You can soar silently above the coast with **Glider Rides,** tel. 677-3404, an outfit offering one- or two-passenger piloted rides infinitely more exciting than the company's name. A plane tows you aloft and you circle within a five-mile radius with a view that can encompass 80 miles on a clear day. The rides are available daily, first-come, first-served, 10 a.m.-5 p.m. Cost is around $50 single, $70 double, and flights, depending upon air currents, last about 20 minutes.

Islands in the Sky is a one-day flying extravaganza offered by the most reputable island-based airline, **Hawaiian Air,** tel. 537-5100. It goes from Honolulu to Kona on the Big Island, on to Maui, and then back to Oahu for about $290.

Panorama Air Tours, tel. 836-2122 or (800) 367-2671, has tailor-made tours of Oahu and an all-encompassing "flightsee Hawaii tour" similar to Hawaiian Air's for about the same price. They fly smaller two-engined aircraft, and include the Big Island, Maui, and Kauai with a ground stop on each.

Helicopter companies rev up their choppers to flightsee you around the island, starting at $50 for a short trip over Waikiki. Prices rise from there as you head for the North Shore. Chopper companies include: **Hawaii Pacific Helicopters,** tel. 836-1561; **Kenai Air Hawaii,** tel. 836-2071, one of the oldest and most reputable companies in the islands; **Papillon Helicopters,** tel. 836-1566, another very well-known and respected company; and **Royal Helicopters,** tel. 941-4683.

Sails And Dinner Cruises

If you're taking a tour at all, your best bet is a sail or dinner cruise. They're touristy, but a lot of

J.D. BISIGNANI

dinner sail, Waikiki

fun, and actually a good value. Many times money-saving coupons for them are found in the free tourist magazines, and plenty of street buskers in Waikiki give special deals. The latter are mostly on the up and up, but make sure you know exactly what you're getting. Most of these cruises depart from the Kewalo Basin Marina near Fisherman's Wharf at 5:30 p.m., and cruise Waikiki toward Diamond Head before returning about two hours later. On board are a buffet, open bar, live entertainment, and dancing. Costs vary but expect to spend about $50-60 per person. Cruises around Pearl Harbor and the ***Arizona* Memorial** cost about $15 and operate out of Kewalo Basin.

Some of the better dinner sails and cruises follow. **Jada Yacht Charters,** tel. 955-0722, sails sister ships *Jada I* and *Jada II,* usually in tandem. Double-masted and with classic lines, they are the sharpest boats off Waikiki. Jada Charters takes you on a real sail, not a booze cruise where you stuff yourself on fried-to-death teriyaki chicken. They disembark from Ke'ehi Harbor, and will send a van to shuttle you from Waikiki.

Aikane Catamarans, tel. 522-1533, is an established company with a number of boats sporting thatched roofs and Polynesian revues. They offer sunset and morning cruises.

Windjammer Cruises, tel. 922-1200, sails out of Kewalo Basin on a sunset booze cruise.

Ali Kai Catamaran, tel. 522-1533, sails from Pier 5 every evening and presents a Polynesian dinner show complete with cocktails and dancing.

Royal Hawaiian Cruises, tel. 573-7001, sails from Pier 6 or Kewalo Basin on a nightly dinner cruise. They also offer Pearl Harbor cruises, and whalewatching in season.

For something different the **International Society for Krishna Consciousness** offers free rides on its *Jaludata,* along with free love feasts on Sunday at 4:30 p.m. For information, *Hare Krishna, hare rama,* call 595-3947.

If you think Oahu is beautiful topside, just wait until you see it below the waves. **Atlantis Submarines,** tel. 973-9800, (800) 548-6262, costs $80 adults, $39 children 12 and under. Pick-up is daily every hour on the hour 7 a.m.-5 p.m. from the Hilton Hawaiian Village, where you board the Hilton Rainbow Catamaran that ferries you to the waiting sub. Once aboard, you're given a few instructions and then it's "run silent, run deep, run excited" for about one hour. The sub is amazingly comfortable. Seats are arranged so everyone gets a prime view through the large windows, and the air is amazingly fresh. In early 1994 a brand-new, futuristic sub was launched measuring 96 feet and able to carry 64 passengers. Outfitted with videocams, it allows passengers to view the undersea world in every direction while listening to explainations of the varied sea life through a multi-language audio system. A thrill of a lifetime.

High-tech hits the high seas on the ***Navatek I,*** tel. 848-6360, a unique, bi-hulled ship that guarantees the "most stable ride in the islands" from Pier 6. You have a choice of an early morning Pearl Harbor cruise, midday luncheon cruise, or ultimate dinner cruise featuring gourmet food and some of the island's best entertainers.

Captain Bob's Picnic Sail, tel. 926-5077 or (800) 262-8798 tours Kaneohe Bay daily and features lunch and all you can drink on its three- to four-hour sail for $65 adults, $45 children. You can work off lunch snorkeling or playing volleyball on the beach. The food is passable, but the setting offshore with the *pali* in the background is world class.

Luau

The **Royal Hawaiian Luau** on the Ocean Lawn of the Royal Hawaiian Hotel, every Monday 6-9 p.m., tel. 923-7311, *is* the classic Hawaiian feast, complete with authentic foods and entertainment, and richly spiced with *aloha*. Authenticity is added by lawn seating on traditional *lau hala* mats (table seating also available) while the sun sets on Waikiki Beach and the stars dance over Diamond Head. Entertainment is an hour-long Polynesian extravaganza featuring Tahitian and traditional hula, a Samoan fire dance, bold rhythmic drumming, and singing by Sam Bernard. The buffet is a lavish feast of *kalua* pig, salmon, mahimahi, steak, and sides of poi and *haupia,* and a sinful but scrumptious table of desserts like coconut cake, *lilikoi* chiffon pie, banana bread, and guava chiffon pie. You are presented with a fresh flower lei and welcomed at the open bar for mai tais and other tropical drinks. The cost is $49.50 adults, $39.50 children under 12.

Chuck Machado's is open every Tuesday, Friday, and Sunday at 7 p.m., tel. 836-0249, at the Waikiki Outrigger Hotel. It's a great show you can enjoy just by strolling on the nearby beach.

Germaine's Luau, often claimed by local people to be *the* best, is held at Ewa Beach, tel. 946-3111.

Paradise Cove Luau boasts a private beach with a shuttle bus departing Waikiki at 4 p.m. and returning by 10 p.m., tel. 945-3571. The **Great Hawaiian Luau** is held at Makapuu Point, tel. 926-8843.

Hawaiian women bleached their hair with a concoction made from burnt coral and an extract of ti. It was also common for both men and women to be elaborately tattooed, oftentimes using their skin to record the date of death of a loved one. Both practices were first reported by Otto Von Kotzebue in 1816.

INFORMATION AND SERVICES

Emergency

Police, fire, and ambulance can be summoned from anywhere on Oahu by calling **911.** Reach the **Coast Guard** for search and rescue at tel. 536-4336 and the **Life Guard Service** at tel. 922-3888.

Health Care

Full-service hospitals include: **Queen's Hospital,** 1301 Punchbowl St., Honolulu, tel. 538-9011; **Kaiser Foundation,** 1697 Ala Moana Blvd., Honolulu, tel. 949-5811.

Medical services and clinics include: **Doctors On Call,** tel. 971-6000 (for Japanese speaking doctors tel. 923-9966), for emergencies and "house calls" to your hotel, 24 hours a day; **Medi-Mart,** Waikiki, Royal Hawaiian Shopping Center, Bldg. A, Room 401, tel. 922-2335, open 9 a.m.-6 p.m.; **Waikiki Health Center,** 277 Ohua Ave., tel. 922-4787, for low-cost care including pregnancy and confidential VD testing, open Mon.-Thurs. 9 a.m-8 p.m., Friday until 4:30 p.m., Saturday until 2 p.m. You can get a free **blood pressure** check at the fire station in Waikiki, corner of Paki and Kapahulu streets, daily 9 a.m.-5 p.m.

For dental referrals call the **Dentist Information Bureau** at 536-2135; a 24-hour service.

Pharmacies around the island include: **Outrigger Pharmacy,** in Waikiki Outrigger Hotel, 2335 Kalakaua Ave., tel. 923-2529; the full-service **Kuhio Pharmacy,** at the corner of Kuhio and Nahua, tel. 923-4466; **Longs Drugs,** in Honolulu at the Ala Moana Shopping Center, tel. 941-4433, and at the Kaneohe Shopping Center, tel. 235-4511; **Pay 'n Save** at 86-120 Farrington Hwy., Waianae, tel. 696-6387.

For **alternative health care** try one of the following. **Acupuncture Clinic,** Waikiki Medical Bldg., 305 Royal Hawaiian Ave., Room 208, tel. 923-6939, open Mon.-Fri. 9 a.m.-4 p.m. Herbalists and acupuncturists are located in Chinatown (see "Shopping" under "Chinatown" in the Honolulu chapter). **Honolulu School of Massage,** 1750 Kalakaua Ave., tel. 942-8552, is open 10 a.m.-6 p.m., with some later hours. **Ed Hoopai** is an excellent masseur whose motto is "You're in good hands." Contact him at 250 Lewers St., second floor of the Outrigger Village Hotel, the suite above the pool, tel. 926-9045. He deals basically in headaches, neck and shoulders, and lower backs. **Chiropractic Referral Service,** 700 Bishop St., tel. 521-5784, offers free information and referral to qualified chiropractors. **Chiropractic Dial-a-Tape** has taped messages for what ails, tel. 737-1111. On the leeward side is **Dr. Tom Smith,** 1222 Oneawa St., Kailua, tel. 261-4511, limited hours.

Visitor Information

The **Hawaii Visitors Bureau** Administrative Office is at the Waikiki Business Plaza, 2270 Kalakaua Ave., Suite 801, Honolulu, HI 96815, tel. 923-1811.

The **Japanese Chamber of Commerce** has special information on things Japanese, tel. 949-5531; the **Chinese Chamber of Commerce** offers information and tours on Chinatown, tel. 533-3181. **State Foundation on Culture and Arts,** 335 Merchant St., Room 202, tel. 548-4657, dispenses information on what's happening culturally on Oahu. For general information, or if you're trying to solve a hassle, try the **Office of Information and Complaints,** tel. 520-4005 or 523-4381. Write to any HVB office and request a copy of ***Hawaii On A Budget,*** a tabloid-style brochure listing some of Hawaii's least expensive accommodations and attractions.

Reading Material

Besides a number of special-interest Chinese, Japanese, Korean, Filipino, and military newspapers, two major dailies are published on Oahu. The *Honolulu Advertiser,* tel. 525-8000, is the morning paper, and the *Honolulu Star Bulletin,* tel. 525-8000, is the evening paper. They combine to make a Sunday paper. A money-saving paper is the *Pennysaver,* tel. 521-9886, featuring classified ads on just about anything. Call for distribution points.

Don't miss out on the **free tourist literature** available at all major hotels, shopping malls, the airport, and stands along Waikiki's streets. They contain up-to-the-minute information on what's happening, and a treasure trove of coupons for various attractions and services either free or at reduced prices. Always featured are events, shopping tips, dining and entertainment, and sightseeing. The main ones are *This Week Oahu,* the best and most complete; and *Spotlight Hawaii,* with good sections on dining and sightseeing. Two free tabloids, *Waikiki Beach Press* and *Island News,* offer entertainment calendars and feature stories of general interest to visitors. *Oahu Drive Guide,* handed out by all the major car rental agencies, has some excellent tips and orientation maps. It's especially useful to get you started from the airport.

Note: For **bookstores,** see "Shopping" or "Practicalities" in the travel chapters.

Post Offices And Libraries

Many small post offices are found in various towns around the island. The main post office in downtown Honolulu is at 3600 Aolele St., tel. 422-0770; in Waikiki at 330 Saratoga Rd., tel. 941-1062; in Kailua at 335 Hahani, tel. 262-7205; in Waianae at 86-015 Farrington Hwy., tel. 696-4032; in Haleiwa at 66-437 Kam Hwy., tel. 637-5755; in Wahiawa at 115 Lehua, tel. 621-8496.

Oahu's libraries include: Hawaii State Library, in Honolulu at 478 S. King St., tel. 548-4775; Kailua Library, 239 Kuulei Rd., tel. 261-4611; Library for the Blind and Physically Handicapped, 402 Kapahulu Ave., tel. 732-7767; Waikiki branch next door, at 400 Kapahulu, tel. 732-2777.

Weather And Surf Conditions

For a weather report call 836-0234; for surfing conditions, call 836-1952; for Hawaiian waters report, call 836-3921.

Helpful Numbers

The area code for all numbers on Oahu is 808. ***Arizona* Memorial,** tel. 922-1626; **babysitting services,** tel. 923-8337, in Waikiki tel. 922-5575; **Bishop Museum,** tel. 922-1626; **Council of Churches,** tel. 521-2666; **Department of Agriculture,** plants, produce, regulations, etc., tel. 836-1415; **directory assistance,** tel. 411; **Honolulu Harbor,** daily ship arrival recording, tel. 537-9260; **Honolulu International Airport,** tel. 836-1411/6431; **time of day,** tel. 983-3211; **whale watch,** tel. 922-1626.

BOB RACE

HONOLULU

Honolulu is *the* most exotic city in America. It's not any one attribute that makes this so; it's a combination of things. Honolulu's like an ancient Hawaiian goddess who can change her form at will. At one moment you see a black-eyed beauty, swaying provocatively to a deep and basic rhythm, and in the next a high-tech scion of the computer age sitting straight-backed behind a polished desk. The city is the terminus of "manifest destiny," the end of America's relentless westward drive after no more horizons were left. Other Mainland cities are undoubtedly more historic, more cultural, and perhaps, to some, more beautiful than Honolulu, but none come close to having all of these features in the same overwhelming combination. The city's face, though blemished by high-rises and pocked by heavy industry, is eternally lovely. The Koolau Mountains form the background tapestry from which the city emerges; the surf gently foams along Waikiki; the sun hisses fire-red as it drops into the sea; and Diamond Head beckons with a promise of tropical romance.

In the center of the city, skyscrapers rise as silent, unshakable witnesses to Honolulu's economic strength. In glass and steel offices, businesspeople wearing conservative three-piece uniforms are clones of any found on Wall Street. Below, a fantasia of people live and work. In nooks and crannies is an amazing array of arts, shops, and cuisines. In a flash of festival the streets become China, Japan, Portugal, New England, old Hawaii, or the Philippines.

New England churches, royal palaces, bandstands, tall-masted ships, and coronation platforms illustrate Honolulu's history. And what a history! You can visit places where in a twinkle of time past, red-plumed warriors were driven to their deaths over an impossibly steep *pali,* or where the skies were alive with screaming Zeros strafing and bombing the only American city threatened by a foreign power since the War of 1812. In hallowed grounds throughout the city lie the bodies of fallen warriors. Some are entombed in a mangled steel sepulchre below the waves, others from three wars rest in a natural bowl of bereavement and silence. And a nearby royal mausoleum holds the remains of those who were "old Hawaii."

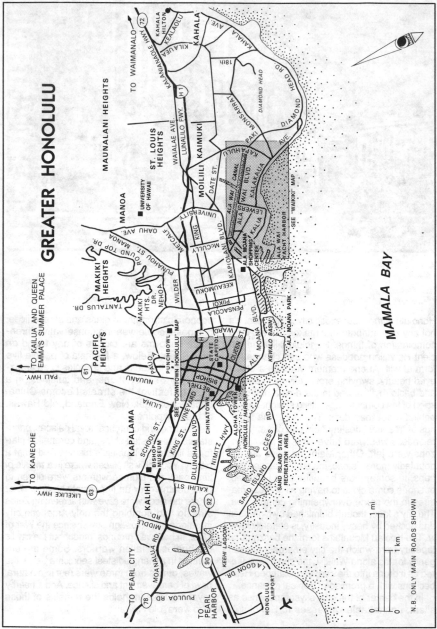

GREATER HONOLULU

N.B. ONLY MAIN ROADS SHOWN

Honolulu is the pumping heart of Hawaii. The state government and university are here. So are botanical parks, a fine aquarium and zoo, a floating maritime museum, and the world's foremost museum on Polynesia. Art flourishes like flowers, as do professional and amateur entertainment, extravaganzas, and local and world-class sporting events. But the city isn't all good clean fun. The seedier side includes "girlie" shows, raucous GI bars, street drugs, and street people. But somehow this blending and collision of East and West, this hodgepodge of emotionally charged history, this American city superimposed on a unique Pacific setting, works well as Honolulu, the "Sheltered Harbor" of people and their dreams.

SIGHTS

The best way to see Honolulu is to start from the middle and fan out on foot to visit the inner city. You can *do* downtown in one day, but the sights of greater Honolulu require a few days to see them all. It's a matter of opinion where the center of downtown Honolulu actually is, but the King Kamehameha statue in front of Aliiolani Hale is about as central as you can get, and a perfect landmark from which to start. If you're staying in Waikiki, leave your rental car in the hotel garage and take TheBus (no. 2) for downtown sightseeing.

Note: For terrific **Living History Walking Tours** see "Sightseeing Tours—Special Tours" under "Getting Around" in the Oahu Introduction.

Parking And Transportation, Downtown Honolulu

If you can't bear to leave your car behind, head for Aloha Tower. When you get to where you can see the Aloha Tower off the S. Nimitz Hwy., look for a sign pointing you left to "Piers 4 and 11, Aloha Tower." Enter to find plenty of parking. The traffic is not as congested here and the large lot is open 24 hours, at $1.00 per hour, with a four-hour maximum on the meter. Bring change, as none is available. You might have to come back and feed the meter again if you want to go as far as Chinatown, but four hours will be plenty of time for the local attractions that are well within walking distance.

For various sights outside the downtown area, your rental car is fine. Some shuttles running out to the *Arizona* Memorial are more expensive than TheBus (85 cents), but so convenient they're worth the extra few coins. The **Waikiki Trolley,** tel. 526-0112, conducts tours throughout the downtown area. For $15 adults, $7.50 children, you can ride it all day long. It looks like a trolley but it's a bus that's been ingeniously converted.

DOWNTOWN HONOLULU

The **Statue of King Kamehameha** is at the junction of King and Mililani streets. Running off at an angle is **Merchant Street,** the oldest thoroughfare in Honolulu, and you might say "the beginning of the road to modernity." The statue is more a symbol of Kamehameha's strength as a ruler and unifier of the Hawaiian Islands than a replica of the man himself. Of the few drawings of Kamehameha that have been preserved, none is necessarily a good likeness. Kamehameha was a magnificent leader and statesman, but by all accounts not very good-looking. This statue is one of three. The original, lost at sea near the Falkland Islands en route from Paris where it was bronzed, was later recovered, but not before insurance money was used to cast this second one. The original is in the town of Kapaau, in the Kohala District of the Big Island, not far from where Kamehameha was born, but although they supposedly came from the same mold, they seem quite different. The third stands in Washington, D.C., dedicated when Hawaii became a state. The Honolulu statue was dedicated in 1883, as part of King David Kalakaua's coronation ceremony. Its black and gold colors are striking, but it is most magnificent on June 11, King Kamehameha Day, when 18-foot lei are draped around the neck and outstretched arms.

Behind Kamehameha stands **Aliiolani Hale,** now the State Judiciary Building. This handsome structure, designed by an Australian architect and begun in 1872, was originally com-

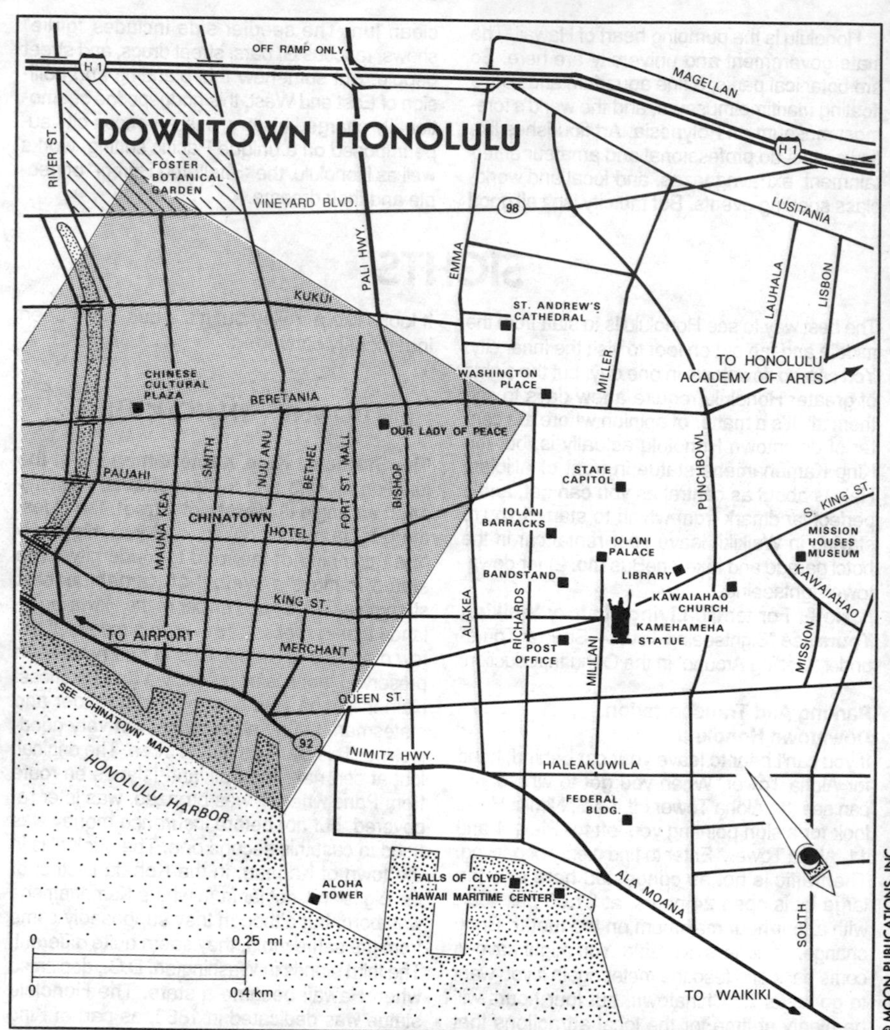

missioned by Kamehameha V as a palace, but was redesigned as a general court building. It looks much more grand than Iolani Palace across the way. Kamehameha V died before it was finished, and it was officially dedicated by King Kalakaua in 1874. Less than 20 years later, on January 17, 1893, at this "hall of justice," the first proclamation by the Members of the Committee of Safety was read, stating that the sovereign nation of Hawaii was no more, and that the islands would be ruled by a provisional government.

Iolani Palace

As you enter the parklike palace grounds, notice the emblem of Hawaii in the center of the large

J.D. BISIGNANI

Iolani Palace, the only royal residence in the United States

iron gates. They're often draped with simple lei of fragrant *maile.* The quiet grounds are a favorite strolling and relaxing place for many government workers, especially in the shade of a huge banyan, purportedly planted by Kalakaua's wife, Kapiolani. The building, with its glass and ironwork imported from San Francisco, and its Corinthian columns, is the only royal palace in America. Iolani ("Royal Hawk") Palace, begun in 1879 under orders of King Kalakaua, was completed in December 1882 at a cost of $350,000. It was the first electrified building in Honolulu, and had a direct phone line to the Royal Boat House.

Non-Hawaiian island residents of the day thought it a frivolous waste of money, but here poignant scenes and profound changes rocked the Hawaiian Islands. After nine years as king, Kalakaua built a **Coronation Stand** that temporarily sat in front of the palace (now off to the left). In a belated ceremony, Kalakaua raised a crown to his head and placed one on his queen, Kapiolani. During the ceremony, 8,000 Hawaiians cheered, while Honolulu's foreign, tax-paying businesspeople boycotted. On August 12, 1898, after only two Hawaiian monarchs, Kalakaua and Liliuokalani (his sister), had resided in the palace, the American flag was raised up the flagpole following a successful coup that marked the U.S.'s official recognition of Hawaii as a territory. During this ceremony, loyal Hawaiian subjects wept bitter tears, while the businesspeople of Honolulu cheered wildly.

Kalakaua, later in his rule, was forced to sign a new constitution that greatly reduced his power to little more than figurehead status. He traveled to San Francisco in 1891, where he died. His body was returned to Honolulu and lay in state in the palace. His sister, Liliuokalani, succeeded him; she attempted to change this constitution and gain the old power of Hawaii's sovereigns, but the businessmen revolted and the monarchy fell. Iolani Palace then became the main executive building for the provisional government, with the House of Representatives meeting in the throne room and the Senate in the dining room. It served in this capacity until 1968.

Iolani Palace is open to one-hour **guided tours only,** Wed.-Sat. 9 a.m.-2:15 p.m.; $5 adults, $2 children, with no children under five admitted. They're popular so make reservations at least a day in advance, and parking is limited, allowed only at certain metered spaces. Tickets are sold at a window at the Barracks, open Tues.-Sat. 8:30 a.m.-2:15 p.m. The Palace shop is open Tues.-Sat. 8:30 a.m.-3:30 p.m. For information and reservations call 522-0832.

Palace Grounds

Kalakaua, known as the "Merry Monarch," was credited with saving the hula. He also hired Henri Berger, first Royal Hawaiian Bandmaster, and together they wrote "Hawaii Pono," the state anthem. Many concerts were given from the Coronation Stand, which became known as the **Royal Bandstand.** Behind it is **Iolani Barracks** (Hale Koa), built in 1870 to house the Royal Household Guards. When the monarchy of Hawaii fell to provisional government forces in 1893, only *one* of these soldiers was wounded in a pathetic show of strength. The barracks were moved to the present site from nearby land on which the State Capitol was erected.

To the right behind the palace are the **State Archives.** This modern building, dating from 1953, holds records, documents, and vintage photos. A treasure trove to scholars and those tracing their genealogy, it is worth a visit by the general public to view the old photos on display. Free, open Mon.-Fri. 7:45 a.m.-4:30 p.m. Next door is the **Hawaii State Library,** housing the main branch of this statewide system. As in all Hawaii state libraries, you are entitled to a card on your first visit, and are then eligible to take out books. The central courtyard is a favorite lunch spot for many of the government workers. Some of the original money to build the library was put up by Andrew Carnegie. For information call 548-4775.

Government Buildings

Liliuokalani was deposed and placed under house arrest in the palace for nine months. Later, after much intrigue that included a visit to Washington, D.C., to plead her case and an aborted counterrevolution, she sadly accepted her fate and moved to nearby **Washington Place.** This solid-looking structure fronts Beretania Street and was originally the home of sea captain John Dominis. It was inherited by his son John Owen Dominis, who married a lovely young Hawaiian aristocrat, Lydia Kapaakea, who became Queen Liliuokalani. She lived in her husband's home, proud but powerless, until her death in 1917. Washington Place is now the official residence of the governor of Hawaii.

To the left of Washington Place is **St. Andrew's Cathedral,** built in 1867 as an Anglican church. Many of its stones and ornaments were shipped from England. Hawaii's monarchs worshipped here, and the church is still very much in use. To the right is the **War Memorial.** Erected in 1974, it replaced an older memorial to the people who perished in WW II. A courtyard and benches are provided for quiet meditation.

Across Beretania is the magnificent **Hawaii State Capitol,** built in 1969 for $25 million. The building itself is a metaphor for Hawaii: the pillars surrounding it are palms, the reflecting pool is the sea, and the cone-shaped rooms of the Legislature represent the volcanoes of Hawaii. It's lined with rich koa wood from the Big Island, and is further graced with woven hangings and murals, with two gigantic, four-ton replicas of the State Seal hanging at both entrances. The inner courtyard has a 600,000-tile mosaic, *Aquarius,* rendered by island artist Tadashi Sato, and to one side is a poignant sculpture of *Father Damien of the Lepers.* The State Legislature is in session January to March, and opens with dancing, music, and festivities at 10 a.m. on the third Wednesday in January, public invited. Peek inside, then take the elevator to the fifth floor for outstanding views of the city.

MISSION HOUSES MUSEUM

The days when tall ships with tattered sails crewed by rough seamen bore God-fearing missionary families dedicated to Christianizing the savage islands are alive in the halls and buildings of The Mission Houses Museum, 553 S. King St., Honolulu, HI 96813, tel. 531-0481. Across from Kawaiahao Church (oldest in Honolulu), the complex includes two main houses, a printing house annex, a library, and a fine, inexpensive gift shop, and is operated by the **Hawaiian Mission Children's Society** (or Cousins' Society), whose members serve as guides and hosts. Many are direct descendants, or spouses of descendants, of the Congregationalist missionaries who built these structures. Tours are conducted Tues.-Sat. 9 a.m.-4 p.m., Sunday 12-4 p.m., closed Monday. Guided tours of the Frame House, oldest wooden structure in Hawaii are held 9:30 a.m.-3 p.m.; $3.50 admission (see "Special Programs" below).

Construction

If you think that precut modular housing is a new concept, think again. The first structure you enter is the **Frame House,** the oldest wooden structure in Hawaii. Precut in Boston, it came along with the first missionary packet in 1819. Since the interior frame was left behind and didn't arrive until Christmas Day, 1820, the missionary families lived in thatched huts until it was erected. Finally the Chamberlain family occupied it in 1821. Many missionary families used it over the years, with as many as four households occupying this small structure at the same time. This is where the Christianizing of Hawaii truly began.

left to right: Frame House, Printing House, and Chamberlain House

The missionaries, being New Englanders, first dug a cellar. The Hawaiians were very suspicious of the strange hole, convinced that the missionaries planned to store guns and arms in this "fort." Though assured to the contrary, King Liholiho, anxious to save face and prove his omnipotence, had a cellar dug near his home twice as deep and large. This satisfied everyone.

Notice the different styles, sizes, and colors of bricks used in the structures. Most of the ships of the day carried bricks as ballast. After unloading cargo, the captains either donated or sold the bricks to the missionaries, who incorporated them into the structures. A common local material was coral stone: pulverized coral was burned with lime to make a rudimentary cement, which was then used to bind cut-coral blocks. The pit used for this purpose is still discernible on the grounds.

Kitchen

The natives were intrigued with the missionaries, whom they called "long necks" because of their high collars. The missionaries, on the other hand, were a little more wary of their "charges." The low fence around the complex was symbolic as well as utilitarian. The missionaries were obsessed with keeping their children away from Hawaiian children, who at first ran around naked and played many games with overt sexual overtones. Almost every evening a small cadre of Hawaiians would assemble to peer into the kitchen to watch the women cook, which they found exceedingly strange because their *kapu* said that *men* did the cooking. In the kitchen, actually an attached cookhouse, the woodburning stove kept breaking down. More often than not, the women used the fireplace with its built-in oven. About once a week, they fired up the oven to make traditional New England staples like bread, pies, cakes, and puddings. The missionaries were dependent on the Hawaiians to bring them fresh water. Notice a large porous stone through which they would filter the water to remove dirt, mud, and sometimes brackishness.

The Hawaiians were even more amazed when the entire family sat down to dinner, a tremendous deviation from their beliefs that separated men and women when eating. When the missionaries assembled to dine or meet at the "long table," the Hawaiians silently stood at the open door to watch the evening soap opera. The unnerved missionaries eventually closed the door and cut two windows into the wall, which they could leave open but draped. The long table later took on further significance. The one you see is a replica. When different missionaries left the islands, they, like people today, wanted a souvenir. For some odd reason, they elected to saw a bit off the long table. As years went by, the table got shorter and shorter until it was useless.

Residents

The house was actually a duplex. Although many families lived in it, two of the best known were the Binghams and the Judds. Much of the furniture here was theirs. Judd, a member of the third missionary company, assumed the duties of physician to all the missionaries and islanders. He often prescribed alcohol of different sorts to the missionary families for a wide variety of ailments; many records remain of these prescriptions, but not one record of complaints from his patients. The Binghams and Judds got along very well, and entertained each other and visitors, most often in the Judds' parlor because they were a little better off. The women would often congregate here to do their sewing, which was in great demand, especially by members of the royal household. Until the missionary women taught island girls to sew, providing clothing for Hawaii's royalty was a tiresome and time-consuming obligation.

The missionaries were self-sufficient, and had the boundless energy of youth, as their average age was only 25. The husbands often built furniture for their families. Reverend Bingham, a good craftsman, was pressed by Queen Kaahumanu to build her a rocking chair after she became enamored of one made for Mrs. Bingham. The queen weighed almost 400 pounds, so building her a suitable chair was no slim feat! Still, the queen could only use it in her later years when she'd lost a considerable amount of weight. After she died, the Binghams asked that it be returned, and it sits in their section of the house. Compare Bingham's chair to another in the Judds' bedroom, jury-rigged by a young missionary husband from a captain's chair. An understatement, found later in his diary, confirmed that he was not a carpenter.

When you enter the Judds' bedroom, note how small it is, and consider that two adults and five children slept here. As soon as the children were old enough, they were sent back to the Mainland for schooling, no doubt to relieve some of the congestion. Also notice that the windows were fixed, in the New England style, and imagine how close it must have been in these rooms. The Binghams' bedroom is also small and not as well furnished. Bingham's shaving kit remains and is inscribed "The Sandwich Isles." In the bedroom of Mary Ward, a missionary woman who never married, the roof was raised to accommodate her canopy bed.

Another famous family who lived in the complex was the Cookes. When the missionary board withdrew its support, the Cookes' petition to buy the duplex was granted. Shortly thereafter, Mr. Cooke, who had been a teacher, formed a partnership with one Mr. Castle, and from that time forward Castle and Cooke grew to become one of Hawaii's oldest and most powerful corporations. The largest building in the compound is the **Chamberlain House.** This barnlike structure was completed in 1831 and used as a warehouse and living quarters for Levi Chamberlain's family. Goods were stored in most of the structure, while the family occupied three modest rooms.

Printing House

The missionaries decided almost immediately that the best way to convert the natives was to speak to them in their own language, and to create a written Hawaiian language which they would teach in school. To this end, they created the **Hawaiian alphabet,** consisting of 12 letters, including the five vowels and seven consonants. In addition, to disseminate the doctrines of Christianity, they needed books, and therefore a printing press. On the grounds still stands the Printing House, built in 1841 but first used as annex bedrooms by the Hall family. The original printing house, built in 1823, no longer exists. In the Printing House is a replica of the Ramage press brought from New England, first operated by Elijah Lewis. He returned to the Mainland when he was 24 and soon died of tuberculosis, but not before he had earned the distinction of being the first printer west of the Rockies. Here were printed biblical tracts, textbooks, or anything that the king or passing captains were willing to pay to have printed. Although it took eight hours of hard work to set up one page to be printed, it is estimated that in the 20 years the press operated under the missionaries, over seven million pages were produced.

Gift Shop

While on the grounds make sure to visit the bookstore and gift shop. It's small but has an excellent collection of Hawaiiana, and some very inexpensive but quality items, such as tapa bookmarks for only 25 cents, and an outstanding collection of Niihau shellwork, considered the finest in Hawaii. The shelves hold tasteful items like woodcarvings, bread boards, hats, weavings, chimes, flags of old Hawaii, and stuffed pillows with classic Hawaiian quilt motifs. Also a good collection of Hawaiian dolls, for kids and adults. Between the bookstore and the research library are restrooms.

Special Programs

Along with other programs, the museum hosts Hawaii's only **living history program,** with actors who dress in fashions of the period and assume the roles of missionaries in 1830s Honolulu. Feel free to interact and ask questions, but remember that they stay in character, so the answers may surprise you. The living history program is usually offered on the last Saturday of the month, 10 a.m.-3 p.m., adult admission $3.50. Other special programs include the "Candlelight Tour of Honolulu, 1831," and tea with the 19th-century Rev. Hiram and Mrs. Sybil Bingham in their parlor; phone 924-1911 for details. Also, consider a "Walking Tour of Honolulu," offered by the museum, that guides you through downtown Honolulu for two hours, hitting all the historic sights with extremely knowledgeable narration by one of the museum's guides (see "Sightseeing Tours—Special Tours" under "Getting Around" in the Oahu Introduction).

KAWAIAHAO CHURCH

This church, so instrumental in Hawaii's history, is the most enduring symbol of the original missionary work in the islands. A sign welcomes you and bestows the blessing, "Grace and peace to you from God our Father." The church was constructed from 1836 until 1842 according to plans drawn up by Hiram Bingham, its minister. Before this, at least four grass shacks of increasing size stood here. One was destroyed by a sailor who was reprimanded by Reverend Bingham for attending services while drunk; the old sea dog returned the next day and burned the church to the ground. Kawaiahao ("Water of Hao") Church is constructed from over 14,000 coral blocks quarried from offshore reefs. In 1843, following Restoration Day, when the British returned the Hawaiian Islands to sovereignty after a brief period of imperialism by a renegade captain, King Kamehameha III uttered here in a thanksgiving ceremony the profound words destined to become Hawaii's motto, *"Ua mau ke ea o ka aina i ka pono"* ("The life of the land is preserved in righteousness").

Other noteworthy ceremonies held at the church were the marriage of King Liholiho and his wife Queen Emma, who bore the last child born to a Hawaiian monarch. Unfortunately, little Prince Albert died at the age of four. On June 19, 1856, Lunalilo, the first king elected to the throne, took his oath of office in the church. A bachelor who died childless, he always felt scorned by living members of the Kamehameha clan, and refused to be buried with them at the Royal Mausoleum in Nuuanu Valley; he is buried in a tomb in the church's cemetery. Buried along with him is his father, Charles Kanaina, and nearby lies the grave of his mother, Miriam Kekauluohi. In the graveyard lies Henri Berger, and many members of the Parker, Green, Brown, and Cooke families, early missionaries to the islands. Liliuokalani's body lay in state in the church before it was taken to the Royal Mausoleum. A jubilation service was held in the church when Hawaii became a state in 1959. Kawaiahao holds beautiful Christmas services with a strong Polynesian and Hawaiian flavor. Hidden away in a corner of the grounds is an unobtrusive adobe building, remains of a schoolhouse built in 1835 to educate Hawaiian children.

HAWAII MARITIME CENTER

The development of this center is a wonderful concept whose time has finally come. It's amazing that a state and former nation, whose discovery and very birth are so intimately tied to the exploration, navigation, and exploitation of the sea, has never had a center dedicated exclusively to these profoundly important aspects of its heritage. Now the Hawaii Maritime Center, at Pier 7, Honolulu Harbor, Honolulu, HI 96813, tel. 523-6151, is exactly that . . . and it needs your support as a visitor. The center, along with its museum in the **Kalakaua Boathouse,** consists of three attractions: Aloha Tower, the beacon of hospitality welcoming people to Hawaii for six decades (not technically part of the center); the classic, and last remaining, fully rigged, four-masted *Falls of Clyde* floating museum; and the reproduction of a Hawaiian sailing canoe, *The Hokule'a,* which recently sailed back in time using ancient navigational methods to retrace the steps of Hawaii's Polynesian explorers. Take bus no. 8 or 20 from Waikiki and you're deposited right in front. Admission is $7 for all attractions. Open daily 9 a.m.-5 p.m.

The Kalakaua Boathouse

The main building of the center is the two-storied Kalakaua Boathouse. Behind it is Coasters, an American standard restaurant (see "Inexpensive" under "Food" later in this chapter), and an area called Kalakaua Park, a garden and observation area perfect for lunch. Eighty-one steps lead to the "crow's nest," and "widow's walk," with great views of the harbor and city.

Upon entering you find a glass case filled with trophies and memorabilia from the days of King Kalakaua. His words have a sadly prophetic ring. "Remember who you are. Be gracious, but never forget from whence you came for this is where your heart is. This is the cradle of your life." Notice the phones installed throughout the capital in 1887, a few years before California had electricity. Kalakaua had previously installed telephones between his boathouse and the palace in 1878, just two years after Bell's invention. The bottom floor of the center recalls ancient fishing methods, and the traditional division of land and sea resources among the people.

Another fascinating display traces the development of surfing through the ages, from original boards, more like seagoing canoes at 18 feet long, until the modern debut of the fiberglass board. You can spot a vintage album of *Surfin' Safari* by The Beach Boys. Here, too, is a land-surfing sled used for games during the Makahiki Festival. It measures six inches wide and 10-14 feet long. Trails to accommodate it were up to a mile long. Built on steep hills, they were paved in stone, layered with earth, and topped with slippery grass. Once they were launched, there was no stopping until the bottom. Yippee!

One corner of the museum is dedicated to tattooing, Polynesian and Western. It shows traditional tattoos worn by both men and women, and then how the Western style be-

HAWAII STATE ARCHIVES

King David Kalakaua

came more popular, as Hawaii was a main berth for sailors, who sported these living souvenirs from around the world. **Mail buoys** sound uninteresting, but these tidbits of old Hawaiiana, alive today, are fascinating objects fashioned from gaily painted metal cans. Passing ships, mainly from Peru and Equador, still radio Honolulu Harbor that they are dropping one. Whoever hears the message fetches the mail buoy. Inside are little gifts for the finder, who sends the enclosed mail on its way.

The second floor is dedicated to the discovery of Hawaii by both Polynesians and Westerners. Through ledgers, histories, and artifacts, it traces original discovery, Western discovery, the death of Captain Cook, and the role of the sea otter pelt and sandalwood, which brought the first whalers and traders. The whaling section drips with blood and human drama. Look at the old harpoons and vintage film footage. Yes, film footage, and photos. A remarkable display is of scrimshaw from the whaling days. Sailors would be at sea for five to seven years, and would have untold hours to create beauty in what were dismal conditions. Suspended from the ceiling are replicas of double-hulled sailing canoes, and one of only two fully restored skeletons of the humpback whale (this one is in diving position). One corner is a replica of H. Hatfield and Co., a whaling supply store of the era. The rear of the second floor shows steamships that cruised between Hawaii, Japan, and the East Coast; offers a nature exhibit of weather, marinelife, and volcanoes; and has an auditorium with a video on the ***Hokule'a*** (see below).

Aloha Tower

When this endearing and enduring tourist cliche was built in 1926 for $160,000, the 184-foot, 10-story tower was the tallest structure on Oahu. As such, this landmark, with clocks embedded in all four walls, and emblazoned with the greeting and farewell *Aloha,* became the symbol of Hawaii. Before the days of air transport, ocean liners would pull up to the pier to allow passengers to disembark. On these "Steamer Days," festive well-wishers from throughout the city would gather to greet and lei the arriving passengers. Even the Royal Hawaiian Band would turn out to welcome the guests ashore.

When you take the escalator up from the parking area, notice the huge U.S. Customs rooms that at one time processed droves of passengers. Today, the crowds are gone and the tower is quiet. Only a few harbormasters on the top floor oversee the comings and goings of cargo ships. When you enter the tower a sign claims that you can only get to the observation area on the top floor by elevator. You can walk up to the ninth floor if you want, but to get to the very top does necessitate taking the elevator, which has the dubious distinction of being one of the first elevators in Hawaii. Once atop the tower, you get the most remarkable view of the harbor and the city. A high-rise planned for just next door will surely ruin the view, but many people with good sense, and luckily with some clout, are fighting this project. A remarkable feature of the vista is the reflections of the city and the harbor in many of the steel and reflective glass high-rises. It's as if a huge mural were painted on them. The tower is open free of charge, daily 8 a.m.-9 p.m., though currently it is temporarily closed due to extensive construction immediately surrounding the building. Check!

Falls Of Clyde

This is the last fully rigged, four-masted ship afloat on any of the world's oceans and has recently been designated a National Historic Landmark. The ship was saved from being scrapped in 1963 by a Seattle bank that was attempting to recoup money on a bad debt. The people of Hawaii learned of its fate and spontaneously raised money to have the ship towed to Honolulu Harbor. The *Falls of Clyde* had always been a worker, never a pleasure craft. It served the Matson Navigation Company as a cargo and passenger liner from 1898 until 1920. Built in Glasgow, Scotland, in 1878, it was converted in 1906 to a sail-driven tanker; a motor aboard was used mainly to move the rigging around. After 1920, the ship was dismantled and towed to Alaska, and became little more than a floating oil depot for fishing boats. Since 1968, the *Falls of Clyde* has been a floating museum, sailing the imaginations of children and grown-ups to times past, and in this capacity has perhaps performed its greatest duty.

Hokule'a

The newest and perhaps most dynamic feature of the center is the *Hokule'a.* This authentic re-creation of a traditional double-hulled sailing canoe captured the attention of the world when in 1976 it made a 6,000-mile roundtrip voyage to Tahiti. Piloted by Mau Piailug, a Caroline Islander, it was guided only by ancient navigational techniques on its successful voyage. This attempt to relive ancient voyages as closely as possible included eating traditional provisions only—poi, coconuts, dried fish, and bananas. Toward the end of the voyage some canned food had to be broken out!

Modern materials such as plywood and fiberglass were used, but by consulting many petroglyphs and old drawings of original craft, the design and lines were kept as authentic as possible. The sails, made from a heavy cotton, were the distinctive crab-claw type. In trial runs to work out the kinks and choose the crew, the canoe almost sank in the treacherous channel between Oahu and Kauai and had to be towed in by the Coast Guard. But the *Hokule'a* performed admirably during the actual voyage. The experiment was a resounding technical success, but it was marred by bad feelings between members of the crew who argued and drew racial boundary lines. Both Hawaiian and white crew members found it impossible to work as a team on the first voyage, thereby mocking the canoe's name, "Star of Gladness." The tension was compounded by the close quarters of more than a dozen men living on an open deck only nine feet wide by 40 feet long. The remarkable navigator Piailug refused to return to Hawaii with the craft and instead sailed back to his native island. Since then, the *Hokule'a* has made five more voyages, logging over 50,000 miles, with many racially mixed crews who have gotten along admirably.

The *Hokule'a,* sponsored by the Polynesian Voyaging Society, makes Pier 7 its home berth when not at sea. This double-hulled canoe, a replica of the ones that Captain Cook found so remarkable, will fascinate you too.

PALI HIGHWAY

Cutting across Oahu from Honolulu to Kailua on the windward coast is Rt. 61, better known as the Pali Highway. Before getting to the famous Nuuanu Pali Lookout at the very crest of the Koolau Mountains, you can spend a full and enjoyable day sightseeing. Stop en route at Punchbowl's National Cemetery, and follow it with an optional side trip to the summit of Tantalus for a breathtaking view of the city (see "Hiking" under "Camping and Hiking" in the Oahu Introduction). You can also visit the **Royal Mausoleum** in the vicinity. Take the H-1 Freeway to Vineyard Boulevard (exit 22), cross the Pali Hwy. to Nuuanu Avenue and follow it to the mausoleum. In a minute or two, if you continue up Nuuanu Avenue, it intersects the Pali Hwy., but you'll have passed the Punchbowl turnoff (see below). This small chapel, built in 1865 by Kamehameha IV, holds the bodies of most of the royal family who died after 1825. Their bodies were originally interred elsewhere but were later moved here. The mausoleum at one time held 18 royal bodies but became overcrowded, so they were moved again to little crypts scattered around the grounds. Few tourists visit this serene place open weekdays 8 a.m-4 p.m., tel. 536-7602.

About two miles past the Punchbowl turnoff, heading up the Pali Hwy. (exit 21-B off H-1), an HVB Warrior points you to the **Walker Home** across from Nuuanu Congregational Church. It's famous for its gardens, and at one time visitors were welcome to come and tour them for a fee. It's hard to tell if this is still happening. The gates are open and no signs tell you to keep out, but an unsmiling housekeeper backed by a steely-eyed German shepherd makes you want to wave from your car and keep rolling. Next come Queen Emma's Summer Palace (see below), the Dai Jingu Temple, a Baptist college, and a Catholic church. It almost seems as though these sects were vying to get farther up the hill to be just a little closer to heaven.

A sign, past Queen Emma's Palace, points you off to **Nuuanu Pali Drive.** Take it! This few-minutes' jog off the Pali Hwy. (which it rejoins) takes you through some wonderful scenery. Make sure to bear right as soon as you pull off and not up the Old Pali Hwy., which has no outlet. Immediately the road is canopied with trees, and in less than a half mile there's a bubbling little waterfall and a pool. The homes in here are grand, and the entire area has a parklike effect. One of the nicest little roads that you can take while looking around, this side trip wastes no time at all.

Queen Emma's Summer Palace

This summer home is more the simple hideaway of a well-to-do family than a grand palace. The 3,000-square-foot interior has only two bedrooms and no facilities for guests. The first person to put a house on the property was John George Lewis. He purchased the land for $800 from a previous owner by the name of Henry Pierce, and then resold it to John Young II. The exterior has a strong New England flavor, and indeed the house was prefabricated in Boston. The simple square home, surrounded by a lanai, was built from 1843 to 1847 by John Young II, Queen Emma's uncle. When he died, she inherited the property and spent many relaxing days here, away from the heat of Honolulu, with her husband King Kamehameha IV. Emma used the home little after 1872, and following her death in 1885 it fell into disrepair.

Rescued from demolition by the Daughters of Hawaii in 1913, it was refurbished and has operated as a museum since 1915. The palace, at 2913 Pali Hwy., tel. 595-3167, is open daily 9 a.m.-4 p.m., admission $6, children under 12 50 cents. Although it's just off the Pali Hwy., the one and only sign comes up quickly, and many visitors pass it by. If you pass the entranceway to the Oahu Country Club just across the road, you've gone too far.

As you enter the palace, notice the tall *kahili,* symbols of noble rank in the entranceway, along with *lau hala* mats on the floor, which at one time were an unsurpassed specialty of Hawaii. Today they must be imported from Fiji or Samoa. The walls are hung with paintings of many of Hawaii's kings and queens, and in every room are distinctive Hawaiian artifacts, such as magnificent feather capes, fans, and tapa hangings.

The furnishings have a very strong British influence. The Hawaiian nobility of the time were enamored with the British. King Kamehameha IV traveled to England when he was 15 years old; he met Queen Victoria, and the two become good friends. Emma and Kamehameha IV had the last child born to a Hawaiian king and queen on May 20, 1858. Named Prince Albert after Queen Victoria's consort, he was much loved but died when he was only four years old, on August 27, 1862. His father followed him to the grave in little more than a year. The king's brother, Lot Kamehameha, a bachelor, took the throne but died very shortly thereafter, marking the end of the Kamehameha line; after that, Hawaii elected its kings. Prince Albert's canoe-shaped cradle is here, made in Germany by Wilhelm Fisher from four kinds of Hawaiian wood. His tiny shirts, pants, and boots are still laid out, and there's a lock of his hair, and one from Queen Emma. In every room are royal memorabilia. The royal bedroom displays a queen-size bed covered with an exquisite pink and purple tapa bedspread. There's vintage Victorian furniture, and even a piano built in London by Collard and Collard. A royal cabinet made in Berlin holds porcelains, plates, and cups. After Queen Emma died, it stood in Charles R. Bishop's drawing room but was later returned. The grounds are beautifully manicured, and the house is surrounded by shrubbery and trees, many of which date from when the royal couple lived here. Restrooms are around back.

Walk around back past the basketball court and keep to the right. Soon you'll see a modest little white building. Look for a rather thick and distinctive rope hanging across the entranceway. This is the Shinto temple **Dai Jingu.** It's not nearly as spectacular as the giant trees in this area, but it is authentic and worth a quick look.

The Daughters of Hawaii have added a gift shop around back, which is open the same hours as the palace. It's small but packed with excellent items like greeting cards, lei, travel guidebooks, beverage trays (reproductions of the early Matson Line menus), little Hawaiian quilt pillows, needlepoint, wraparounds from Tahiti, T-shirts with Queen Emma's Summer Palace logos, and Niihau shellwork, the finest in Hawaii.

Nuuanu Pali Lookout

This is one of those extra-benefit places where you get a magnificent view without any effort at all. Merely drive up the Pali Hwy. to the well-marked turnout and park. Rip-offs happen, so take all valuables. Before you, if the weather is accommodating, an unimpeded view of windward Oahu lies at your feet. Nuuanu Pali ("Cool Heights") lives up to its name; the winds here are chilly and extremely strong, and funnel right through the lookout. You definitely need a jacket or windbreaker. On a particularly windy day just after a good rainfall, various waterfalls tumbling off the *pali* will actually be blown uphill! A number of roads, punched over and through the *pali* over the years, are engineering marvels. The famous "carriage road" built in 1898 by John Wilson, a Honolulu boy, for only $37,500, using 200 laborers and plenty of dynamite, was truly amazing. Droves of people come here, many in huge buses, and they all go to the railing to have a peek. Even so, by walking down the old road built in 1932 that goes off to the right, you actually get private and better views. You'll find the tallest point in the area, a huge, needlelike rock. The wind is quieter here.

Nuuanu Pali figures prominently in Hawaii's legends. It's said, not without academic skepticism, that Kamehameha the Great pursued the last remaining defenders of Oahu to these cliffs in one of the final battles fought to consolidate his power over all of the islands in 1795. If you use your imagination, you can easily feel the utter despair and courage of these vanquished warriors as they were driven ever closer to the edge. Mercy was not shown nor expected. Some jumped to their deaths rather than surrender, while others fought until they were pushed over. The estimated number of casualties varies considerably, from a few hundred to a few thousand, while some believe that the battle never happened at all. Compounding the controversy are stories of the warriors' families, who searched the cliffs below for years, and supposedly found bones of their kinsmen, which they buried. The Pali Lookout is romantic at night, with the lights of Kailua and Kaneohe in the distance, but the best nighttime view is from Tantalus Drive, where all of Honolulu lies at your feet.

PUNCHBOWL, NATIONAL CEMETERY OF THE PACIFIC

One sure sign that you have entered a place of honor is the hushed and quiet nature everyone adopts without having to be told. This is the way it is the moment you enter this shrine. The Hawaiian name, Puowaina ("Hill of Sacrifice"), couldn't have been more prophetic. Punchbowl is the almost perfectly round crater of an extinct volcano that holds the bodies of nearly 25,000 men and women who fell fighting for the United States, from the Spanish-American War to Vietnam. At one time, Punchbowl was a bastion of heavy cannon and artillery trained on Honolulu Harbor to defend it from hostile naval forces. In 1943 Hawaii bequeathed it to the federal government as a memorial; it was dedicated in 1949, when the remains of an unknown serviceman killed during the attack on Pearl Harbor were the first interred.

As you enter the main gate, a flagpole with the Stars and Stripes unfurled is framed by a long, sweeping lawn. A roadway lined with monkeypod trees adds three-dimensional depth to the impressionistic scene, as it leads to the steps of an altarlike marble monument in the distance. The eye has a continuous sweep of the field, as there are no elevated tombstones, just simple marble slabs lying flat on the ground. The field is dotted with trees, including eight banyans, a special tree and symbolic number for the many Buddhists buried here. Brightening the scene are plumeria and rainbow shower trees, often planted in Hawaiian graveyards because they produce flowers year-round as perennial offerings from the living to the dead when they can't personally attend the grave. All are equal here: the famous, like Ernie Pyle, the stalwart who earned the Congressional Medal of Honor; and the unknown who died alone and unheralded on muddy battlefields in godforsaken jungles. To the right just after you enter is the office, open Mon.-Fri. 9 a.m.-5 p.m., with brochures and restrooms. Tour buses, taxis, and limousines are lined up here. Don't leave valuables in your car.

To get to Punchbowl take the H-1 Freeway to Rt. 61, the Pali Hwy., and exit at 21B. Immediately get to the right, where a sign points you to Punchbowl. You'll make some fancy zigzags through a residential area, but it's well marked and you'll come to Puowaina Street, which leads you to the main gate. Make sure to notice landmarks going in, because as odd as it sounds, no signs lead you back out and it's easy to get lost.

The Monument

Like a pilgrim, you climb the steps to the monument, where on both sides marble slabs seem to whisper the names of the 20,000-plus servicepeople, all MIAs whose bodies were never found but whose spirits are honored here. The first slabs on the right are for the victims of Vietnam, those on the left are from WW II, and you can see that time is already weathering the marble. They are honored together, as they fought and died—men, boys, lieutenants, captains, private soldiers, infantrymen, sailors—from everywhere in America. "In proud memory . . . this memorial has been erected by the United States of America."

At the monument itself, built in 1966, is a chapel and in the middle is a statue of a woman: a woman of peace, a heroic woman of liberty. Around her on the walls are etched maps and battles of the Pacific War whose names still evoke passion: Pearl Harbor, Wake, Coral Sea, Midway, Iwo Jima, the Gilbert Islands, Okinawa. Many of the visitors are Japanese. Many of Hawaii's war dead are also Japanese. Four decades ago we battled each other with hatred and malice. Today, on bright afternoons we come together with saddened hearts to pay reverence to the dead.

UNIVERSITY OF HAWAII

You don't have to be a student to head for the University of Hawaii, Manoa Campus. For one, it houses the **East-West Center,** which was incorporated in 1975 and officially separated from the university; here nations from Asia and the Pacific present fascinating displays of their homelands. Also, Manoa Valley itself is one of the loveliest residential areas on Oahu (see below). To get to the main campus follow the H-1 Freeway to exit 24B (University Avenue). Don't make the mistake of exiting at the University's Makai Campus. Follow University Avenue to the second red light, Dole Avenue, and make a right onto campus. Stop immediately at one of the parking lots and get a parking map! Parking restrictions are strictly enforced, and this map not only helps you get around, it saves you from fines or having your car towed away. Parking is 50 cents an hour, even for visitors, so think about taking TheBus, which services this area quite well.

Student Center

Make this your first stop. As you mount the steps, notice the idealized mural of old Hawaii: smiling faces of natives all doing interesting things. Inside is the **Information Center,** which dispenses info not only about the campus, but also about what's happening socially and culturally around town. They even have lists of cheap restaurants, discos, and student hangouts. Next door are typewriters available to nonstudents at $2 per day. The food in the cafeteria is institutional but cheap and has a Hawaiian twist. The best place to eat is **Manoa Gardens** in the Hemingway Center, where you can get a tasty stir-fry or good vegetarian dishes for $3.50 and up.

The **University Bookstore** is excellent, open Mon.-Fri. 8:15 a.m.-4:15 p.m., Saturday 8:15-11:45 a.m. The bookstore is worth coming to for its excellent range of specialty items, like language tapes, and its extensive assortment of travel guidebooks. The free **University Art Gallery** on the third floor is worth a look. The exhibits change regularly. Next to the gallery is a lounge filled with overstuffed chairs and big pillows, where you can kick back and even take a quick snooze. This is not a very social campus. By 4:30 or 5 p.m. the place is shut up and no one is around. Don't expect students gathered in a common reading room, or the activity of social and cultural events. When school lets out at the end of the day, people go home.

East-West Center

Follow Dole Avenue to East-West Road and make a left. Free tours, Wednesdays only at 1:30 p.m., originate from Imin Center-Jefferson Hall opposite Kennedy Theater. For more info contact the Friends of the East-West Center, 1777 East-West Rd., Honolulu, HI 96848, tel. 944-7691. The center's 21 acres were dedicated in 1960 by the U.S. Congress to promote better relations between the countries of Asia and the Pacific with the United States. Many nations, as well as private companies and individuals, fund this institution of cooperative study and research. John Burns Hall's main lobby dispenses information on what's happening, along with self-guiding maps. Imin Center-Jefferson Hall, fronted by Chinese lions, has a serene and relaxing Japanese garden behind it, complete with a rivulet and a teahouse named Jakuan, "Cottage of Tranquility." The murals inside are excellent, and the hall also contains a large reading room with relaxing couches.

The impressive Thai Pavilion was a gift from the king of Thailand, where it was built and sent to Hawaii to be reconstructed. This 23-ton, solid teak *sala* is a common sight in Thailand. The Center for Korean Studies (not part of the East-West Center) is also outstanding. A joint venture of Korean and Hawaiian architects, its inspiration was the classic lines of Kyongbok Palace in Seoul. Most of the buildings are adorned with fine artworks: tapa hangings, murals, calligraphy, paintings, and sculpture. The entire center is tranquil, and along with the John F. Kennedy Theater of Performing Arts just across the road, is indeed fulfilling its dedication to sharing and learning, culture and art.

MANOA VALLEY

Manoa Valley, a tropical palette of green ablaze with daubs of iridescent color, has a unique designation most aptly described as "urban rainforest." Although this is not technically true, the valley's more than 100 inches of rainfall per year makes it exceptionally verdant even by Hawaiian standards. However, it wasn't always so. In the late 1800s, the overpopulated valley was almost denuded of trees, only to be reforested by Dr. Lyon, the founder of Lyon Arboretum, who planted trees gathered from around the world. A literal backwater, the runoff from Manoa would flood relatively dry Waikiki until the Ala Wai Canal was built in the 1920s as a catchment for its torrential flash floods. Only a short drive from arid Waikiki, Manoa was the first place in Hawaii where coffee was grown and where pineapple was cultivated. The great Queen Kaahumanu, who died here in 1832, favored the cool hills of the valley as a vacation spot in which to escape the summer heat. Manoa, favored by royalty ever since, has maintained itself as one of the most fashionable residential areas in Hawaii, even boasting its own country club at the turn of the century—memorialized by the "Manoa Cup" held yearly at the Oahu Country Club. In 1893, just before annexation, a bewildered and beaten group of royalists came to Manoa to hide out. They were subsequently captured by a contingency of pursuing U.S. Marines and imprisoned in an area called "The Pen," located on the grounds of the now-defunct Paradise Park.

Taking Manoa Road past the University of Hawaii (see above), you pass **Punahou School,** one of the oldest and most prestigious high schools in Hawaii. Built in 1841 from lava rock, it was attended by the children of the missionary families of wealthy San Franciscans who got the best possible education west of the Rockies.

Manoa Road eventually crosses Oahu Avenue. Follow it to **Waioli Tea Room,** 3016 Oahu Ave., owned and operated by the Salvation Army, a small park with a snack bar that features fresh-baked pastries and serves lunch daily. Also featured here is the **Little Grass Shack** supposedly lived in by Robert Louis Stevenson when he was a resident of Waikiki. Visit the chapel with its distinctive stained-glass windows. Waioli Tea Room is open daily except Monday, 8 a.m.-3:30 p.m., luncheon served 11 a.m.-2 p.m. Reservations, tel. 988-2131.

Paradise Park, 3737 Manoa Rd. (at the very end), closed in late 1993, is 13 acres of lush tropical plants founded by James Wong about 25 years ago. Magnificent blooms compete with the wild plumage of 50 species of exotic birds. However, the Treetop (literally) Restaurant, located here and offering very good food and superlative views, is still operating.

BISHOP MUSEUM (STATE MUSEUM OF NATURAL AND CULTURAL HISTORY)

This group of stalwart stone buildings holds the greatest collection of historical relics and scholarly works on Hawaii and the Pacific in the world. It refers to itself as a "museum to instruct and delight"; in one afternoon walking through its halls you can educate yourself about Hawaii's history and people and enrich your trip to the islands tenfold.

The founding of the Bernice Pauahi Bishop Museum was directly connected to the last three royal women of the Kamehameha dynasty. Princess Bernice married Charles Reed Bishop, a New Englander who became a citizen of the then-independent monarchy in the 1840s. The princess was a wealthy woman in her own right, with lands and an extensive collection of "things Hawaiian." Her cousin, Princess Ruta Keeikolani, died in 1883 and bequeathed Princess Bernice all of her lands and Hawaiian artifacts. Together, this meant that Princess Bernice owned about 12% of Hawaii! Princess Bernice died less than two years later, and left her land holdings to the **Bernice Pauahi Bishop Estate,** which founded and supported the Kamehameha Schools, dedicated to the education of Hawaiian children. (Though this organization is often confused with the Bishop Museum, they are separate. The school shared the same grounds with the museum, but none of the funds from this organization were, or are, used for the museum.) Bernice left her personal property, including its priceless Hawaiian artifacts, to her husband, Charles. Then, when Queen Emma, her other cousin, died the following year, she too desired Charles Bishop to combine her Hawaiian artifacts with the already formidable collection and establish a Hawaiian museum.

True to the wishes of these women, Bishop began construction of the museum's main build-

Princess Bernice

ing on December 18, 1889, and within a few years the museum was opened. In 1894, after 50 years in Hawaii, Bishop moved to San Francisco, where he died in 1915. He is still regarded as one of Hawaii's most generous philanthropists. In 1961, a science wing and planetarium were added, and two dormitory buildings once occupied by the Kamehameha School for Boys are still used.

Getting There

To get there, take exit 20A off the H-1 Freeway, which puts you on Rt. 63, the Likelike Highway. Immediately get into the far right lane. In only a few hundred yards, turn onto Bernice Street, where you'll find the entrance. Or, exit H-1 onto Houghtailing Street, Rt. 61, exit 20B. Keep your eyes peeled for a clearly marked but small sign directing you to the museum. TheBus no. 2 (School-Middle Street) runs from Waikiki to Kapalama Street, from which you walk two blocks.

Admission And Information

The museum is located at 1525 Bernice St., Honolulu, HI 96817, tel. 847-3511, and is open seven days a week 9 a.m.-5 p.m. Admission is $7.95 adults, $6.95 ages 6-17, ages five and younger free, but some exhibits and the planetarium are closed to children under six. It's sometimes best to visit on weekends because many weekdays bring teachers and young students who have more enthusiasm for running around than checking out the exhibits. Food, beverages, smoking, and flash photography are all strictly prohibited in the museum. The natural light in the museum is dim, so if you're into photography you'll need super-fast film (400 ASA performs only marginally). Before leaving the grounds make sure to visit **Hawaiian Halau,** where a hula is performed Mon.-Fri. at 1 p.m. Throughout the week, the hall offers demonstrations in various Hawaiian crafts like lei-making, featherwork, and quilting. The **planetarium** opens up its skies daily at 11 a.m. and 2 p.m.

Special nighttime shows and family discount days are offered; call 847-3511 for details. The snack shop has reasonable prices, and **Shop Pacifica,** the museum bookstore and boutique, has a fine selection of materials on Hawaii and the Pacific, and some authentic and inexpensive souvenirs. The **museum cafe** has a limited menu of dishes like Hawaiian fruit salad for $3.50; hamburger for $2.85; teriyaki burger for $2.65; and snacks like chili dogs, muffins, chips, and drinks.

Exhibits

It's easy to become overwhelmed by the museum, so just take it slowly. The number of exhibits is staggering: over 100,000 artifacts; almost 20 million (!) specimens of insects, shells, fish, birds, and mammals; an extensive research library; a photograph collection; and a fine series of maps. The main gallery is highlighted by the rich tones of koa, the showpiece being a magnificent staircase. Get a map at the front desk that lists the halls and their themes, and suggests a route to follow. The following is a small potpourri of the highlights you'll discover.

To the right of the main entranceway is a fascinating exhibit of the old Hawaiian gods. Most are labeled "wooden image" and date from the early 19th century. Among them are: Kamehameha's war-god, Ku; the tallest Hawaiian sculpture ever found, from Kauai; an image of a god from a temple of human sacrifice; and lesser gods, personal *aumakua* that controlled the lives of Hawaiians from birth until death. You wouldn't want to meet any of them in a dark alley! Outside, in what's called the **Hawaiian Courtyard,** are implements used by the Hawaiians in everyday life, as well as a collection of plants that are all identified. The first floor of the main hall is perhaps the most interesting because it deals with old Hawaii. Here are magnificent examples of *kahili,* feathered capes, plumed helmets . . . all the insignia and regalia of the *ali'i.* A commoner sits in a grass shack, a replica of what Captain Cook might have seen.

Don't look up! Over your head is a 55-foot sperm whale hanging from the ceiling. It weighed over 44,000 pounds alive. You'll learn about the ukulele, and how vaudevillians spread its music around the world. Bare-breasted, hula-skirted damsels from the 1870s peer provocatively from old photos. Tourists bought these photos even then, although the grass skirts they're wearing were never a part of old Hawaii but were brought by Gilbert Islanders. See authentic hula instruments like a "lover's whistle," a flute played through the nose; and a musical bow, the only stringed pre-European Hawaiian instrument.

Don't miss the koa wood collection. This accomplished artform produced medicine bowls, handsome calabashes, simple bowls for household use, and others reputed to be the earthly home of the wind goddess, which had to be refitted for display in Christianized Iolani Palace. A model *heiau* tells of the old religion, and the many strange *kapu* that governed every aspect of life. Clubs used to bash in the brains of *kapu*-breakers are next to benevolent little stone gods, the size and shape of footballs, that protected humble fishermen from the sea. As you ascend to the upper floors, the time periods approach the present. The missionaries, whalers, merchants, laborers, and Westernized monarchs have arrived. Yankee whalers from New Bedford, New London, Nantucket, and Sag Harbor appear determined and grim-faced as they scour the seas, harpoons at the ready. Great blubber pots, harpoons, and figureheads are preserved from this perilous and unglamorous life. Bibles, thrones—the regalia of power and of the new god are all here.

ART MUSEUMS AND GALLERIES

Honolulu Academy Of Arts

Enjoy the magnificent grounds of this perfectly designed building, a combination of East and West with a Hawaiian roof and thick white stucco walls reminiscent of the American Southwest, created by architect Bertrum Goodhugh and benefactor Mrs. Charles Montague expressly as a museum. The museum, at 900 S. Beretania St. (TheBus no. 2) opposite Thomas Square, tel. 532-8700, is open Tues.-Sat. 10 a.m.-4:30 p.m., Sunday 1-5 p.m., closed Monday, suggested donation $4, free the first Wednesday of the month. Guided tours are conducted Tues.-Sat. at 11 a.m., Sunday at 1 p.m. The academy houses a brilliant collection of classic and modern art, strongly emphasizing Asian artwork.

James Michener's outstanding collection of Japanese *ukiyo-e* is here. The story goes that an unfriendly New York cop hassled him on his way to donate it to a New York City museum, while a Honolulu officer was the epitome of *aloha* when Michener was passing through, so he decided that his collection should reside here. This collection is currently displayed about six months per year, but a decision has been made to display it year-round. Magnificent Korean ceramics, Chinese furniture, and Japanese prints, along with Western masterworks from the Greeks to Picasso, make the academy one of the most well-rounded art museums in America. Some collections are permanent while others change, so the museum remains dynamic no matter how many times you visit.

Enter through the foyer and pass into the courtyard that gets you away from the hustle and bustle of downtown—great for a respite from noise. Pass through double French doors to the galleries with thick white walls that create a perfect atmosphere for displaying fine works of art. Discover delights like Paul Gauguin's *Two Nudes on a Tahitian Beach,* James Whistler's *Arrangement in Black No. 5,* John Singer Sargent's *Portrait of Mrs. Thomas Lincoln Hansen, Jr.* An entire wing is dedicated to religious art, while another holds furniture from medieval Europe. The courtyards are resplendent with statuary from the 6th century A.D. and a standing figure from Egypt, circa 2500 B.C. The Hawaiian climate is perfect for preserving artwork.

Stop at the **Academy Shop,** specializing in art books, museum repros, Hawaii out-of-prints, jewelry, notebooks, and postcards, open Tues.-Sat. 10 a.m.-4:30 p.m., Sunday 1-5 p.m., tel.

532-8704. The **Garden Cafe,** open Tues.-Sat. 11:30 a.m.-1 p.m., Thursday supper at 6:15 p.m., is in a garden under a canopy. They have a light but terrific menu, and besides, a trip to the academy demands a luncheon in the cafe. For menu and details see "Inexpensive Dining Around Town" under "Food" later in this chapter.

The Contemporary Museum

Under the direction of Merrill Rueppel, at 2411 Makiki Heights Dr., tel. 526-1322, the museum welcomes you with two copper-green gates that are sculptures themselves. This open and elegant structure, the former Spaulding House, has yielded six galleries, a shop, and an excellent gourmet restaurant, the Contemporary Cafe. Acquired through the generosity of the *Honolulu Advertiser*'s stockholders, the building was donated to the museum as a permanent home in 1988. Surrounding it are three magnificent acres sculpted into Asian gardens perfect for strolling and gazing at the sprawl of Honolulu far below. The focus is on exhibitions, not collections, although works by David Hockney are on permanent display. Always-changing exhibits reflect different themes in contemporary art. Open Tues.-Sat. 10 a.m.-4 p.m., Sunday noon-4 p.m., closed Monday, admission $4.

Tennent Art Foundation

At 201-203 Prospect St., on the *ewa* (west of Pearl Harbor) slope of Punchbowl, the foundation is open Tues.-Sat. 10 a.m.-noon, and Sunday 2-4 p.m., tel. 531-1987. Free. The library walls hold the paintings of Madge Tennent, one of Hawaii's foremost artists, as well as many other contemporary works. It's beautiful, quiet, and worth a visit.

GARDENS AND GUIDED TOURS

Foster Botanical Garden

Many of these 15 acres of exotic trees have been growing for over 100 years in this manicured garden, at one time the private estate of Dr. Hillebrand, physician to the royal court. He brought many of the seedlings from Asia. Two dozen trees enjoy lifetime protection by the state. Located at 180 N. Vineyard Blvd., tel. 522-7065, open daily 9 a.m.-4 p.m., $1, self-guiding brochures. Guided tours Monday, Tuesday, and Wednesday at 1:30 p.m. Many nature hikes on Oahu and the Neighbor Islands are sponsored by the gardens.

Moanalua Gardens

The private gardens of the Damon Estate, at 1352 Pineapple Pl., tel. 839-5334, were given to the original owner by Princess Bernice Bishop in 1884. Just off the Moanalua Freeway, and open to the public, these gardens are not heavily touristed, a welcome respite from the hustle and bustle of the city. Some magnificent old trees include a Buddha tree from Ceylon and a monkeypod called "the most beautifully shaped tree" in the world by *Ripley's Believe It or Not.* The Moanalua Foundation also sponsors walks deep into Moanalua Valley for viewing the foliage of "natural Hawaii." The free guided walks begin at 9 a.m. usually on weekends; make arrangements by calling 839-5334.

Dole Cannery Square

Look for the giant pineapple rising 200 feet into the air. A landmark of Honolulu, it was built in Chicago and erected here in 1928. It is still used as a reservoir and holds 100,000 gallons of water piped throughout the Dole Cannery, whose outer buildings were transformed in 1988 to a mini-mall that complements the ongoing Dole Cannery Tour. Located at 650 Iwilei Rd., tel. 548-4837; 45-minute tours are conducted daily 9 a.m.-5 p.m., with the last departing at 3 p.m. Admission $5, children under 12 free. Free parking is provided if you take your car, but try the **Pineapple Transit,** tel. 523-DOLE, a van that runs 8:30 a.m.-3:30 p.m., stopping at many Waikiki hotels, 50 cents one-way. Upon entering the atrium area, look high on the walls to see reproductions of Dole Pineapple can labels. They're pop art, and convey a feeling of simpler times past. Here also is the **Food Court,** providing snacks, salads, sandwiches, and soups for quick lunches.

The tour itself begins with a stereophonic slide show that details the development of pineapple as an industry in Hawaii. Plenty of memorabilia and vintage photos help create a sense of the past. You're then conducted right into the factory where workers are busy packing the fruit, and where you learn the process of how it makes it to the kitchen table. Observe the newest generation of the marvelous Ginaca machine, first built in 1913 by Henry Ginaca, a draftsman hired by James Dole to modernize the industry. This whirring wonder can peel, core, cut, slice, and dice 100 fruits per minute. Within 20 minutes of reaching the machine, the canned fruit's ready for the grocer's shelf. After the tour, you're taken to a tasting room where you're offered complimentary . . . guess what?

On the second floor you'll find a cluster of shops laid out as traditional storefronts and featuring items made in Hawaii. Stop at the **Dole Logo Shop** for a T-shirt with a replica of a vintage pineapple-can label, along with hats, gift items, and glassware bearing the Dole logo. The **Island Moo Moo Works,** popular with local people, has racks of affordable muumuu and alohawear. The **Jungle Jerky Shop** has jerky of all sorts and sells life-size stuffed animals, as well as cotton cloth flowers. New shops like **Mamo Howell** and **Island Princess** add elegance with their fashions, or you can take care of your sweet tooth at **Sharyn's Hawaiian Island Cookies.** One of the nicest shops is the **Village Beach Shop.** They're a complete resortwear store with plenty of muumuu, sandals, and even boogie boards to choose from. They have a fine selection of T-shirts with gold designs by Ericka Paeis, a very creative and distinctive designer in the crowded field of Hawaiian T-shirts.

HONOLULU BEACHES AND PARKS

The beaches and parks listed here are found in and around Honolulu's city limits. World-famous Waikiki has its own section in this book (see "Waikiki Beaches and Parks" under "Sights" in the Waikiki chapter). The good thing about having Waikiki so close is that it lures most bathers away from other city beaches, which makes them less congested. The following list contains most of Honolulu's beaches, ending at Fort DeRussy Beach Park, just a few hundred yards from where the string of Waikiki's beaches begin. Also see "Aiea, Pearl City, and Vicinity" in the Central Oahu chapter.

Sand Island State Recreation Area

As you enter this 140-acre park by way of Sand Island Access Road, clearly marked off the Nimitz Hwy., you pass through some ugly real estate—scrap yards, petrochemical tanks, and other such beauties. Don't get discouraged, keep going! Once you cross the metal bridge, a favorite fishing spot for local people, and then pass the entrance to the U.S. Coast Guard base, you enter the actual park, 14 acres landscaped with picnic and playground facilities. Follow the road into the park; you pass two observation towers built in the middle of a grassy field, from where you can get an impressive view of Honolulu, with Diamond Head making a remarkable counterpoint. The park is excellently maintained, with pavilions, cold-water showers, walkways, and restrooms, all for day use only; the park closes at 6:30 p.m. However, the camping area is usually empty (state permit required). The sites are out in the open, but a few trees provide shade.

Unfortunately, you're under one of the main glide paths for Honolulu International Airport. Many local people come to fish, and the surfing is good, but the beaches for snorkeling and swimming are fair at best. Some of the beach area is horrible, piled with broken stone, rubble, and pieces of coral. However, if you follow the road past the tower and park in the next lot, you can turn right and follow the shore up to a sandy beach. The currents and wave action aren't dangerous, but remember that this part of the harbor receives more than its share of pollutants. For delicious and inexpensive plate lunches, make sure to stop at Penny's next door to Dirty Dan's Topless Go-Go Bar on your way down the access road.

La Mariana Yacht Sailing Club

This small marina at 50 Sand Island Access Rd. is a love song in the middle of an industrialized area. The marina is Annette La Mariana Nahinua's labor of love that has remained true since 1955. You can read her fantastic story on the menu of the marina's **Hideaway Restaurant,** which is the only real restaurant on Sand Island. In 1955 this area was forgotten, forsaken, and unkempt. Ms. Nahinua, against the forces of nature, and the even more unpredictable and devastating forces of bureaucracy, took this land and turned it into a yacht harbor. Her main tools were indefatigable determination, God listening to her prayers, and a shovel and rake. It's one of the last enclaves of old Hawaii, a place to come for dinner or a drink, or just to look at the boats. The nighttime bartender, Mr. Lee, is friendly but stoic after decades of seeing and hearing it all. Annette, the founder, is now a little gray-haired woman, a motherly type in Birkenstocks, who lives right here above the Hideaway. In the daytime she wanders around spreading her magic while talking to old salts or new arrivals.

The marina is adjacent to an open waterway, which means that you don't have to pay for anchorage. It comes under the old "rights of sailors" to find a free port in which to berth. This unique setup has created an atmosphere in which a subculture of people have built subsistence shacks on the little islands that dot the bay. Some also live on old scows, shipshape yachts, or very imaginative homemade crafts, afloat and semi-afloat on this tranquil bay. Many are disillusioned and disenfranchised Vietnam vets who have become misanthropes. You'll see the Stars and Stripes flying from their island hooches. Others are yachties who disdain being landlubbers, while still others are poor souls who have fallen through the social net. La Mariana is a unique statement of personal freedom in a city where unique statements are generally not tolerated.

Kakaako (Point Panic) Beach Park
This small facility was carved out of a piece of land donated by the University of Hawaii's Biomedical Research Center. Next to Kewalo Basin Harbor, follow Ahuii Street, off Ala Moana Boulevard. You'll come to some landscaped grounds with a cold-water shower and a path leading to the bathing area. Kewalo Basin, developed in the '20s to hold Honolulu's tuna fleet, is home to many charter boats. If you're lucky, you may even spot a manta ray, which are known to frequent these waters. This area is poor for swimming, known for sharks, but great for bodysurfing. Unfortunately, novices will quickly find out why it's called Point Panic. A long seawall with a sharp drop-off runs the entire length of the area. The wave action is perfect for riding, but waves wash against the wall. Beginners stay out! The best reason to come here is for the magnificent and unobstructed view of the Waikiki skyline and Diamond Head.

Ala Moana Park
Ala Moana ("Path to the Sea") Beach County Park is by far Honolulu's best. Most visitors congregate just around the bend at Waikiki, but residents head for Ala Moana, the place to soak up local color. During the week, this beautifully curving white-sand beach has plenty of elbow room. Weekends bring families who come for every water sport Oahu offers. The swimming is great, with manageable wave action, plenty of lifeguards, and even good snorkeling along the reef. Board riders have their favorite spots, and bodysurfing is excellent. The huge area has a number of restrooms, food concessions, tennis courts, softball fields, a bowling green, and parking for 500 cars. Many Oahu outrigger canoe clubs practice in this area, especially in the evening; it's great to come and watch them glide along. A huge banyan grove provides shade and strolling if you don't fancy the beach, or you can bring a kite to fly aloft with the trade winds. Ala Moana Park stretches along Ala Moana Blvd., between the Ala Wai and Kewalo Basin boat harbors. It's across from the Ala Moana Shopping Center, so you can rush right over if your credit cards start melting in the sun.

Aina Moana ("Land from the Sea") **State Recreation Area** used to be called Magic Island because it was reclaimed land. It is the point of land stretching out from the eastern edge of Ala Moana, and although it has a different name, appears to be part of Ala Moana. All the beach activities are great here, too.

Kahanamoku Beach
This stretch of sand in front of the Hilton Hawaiian Village is named after Hawaii's most famous waterman, Duke Kahanamoku. The manmade beach and lagoon were completed in 1956. A system of pumps pushes water into the lagoon to keep it fresh. The swimming is great, and plenty of concessions offer surfboards, beach equipment, and catamaran cruises.

Fort DeRussy Beach
This is the last beach before you reach the Waikiki beaches proper. You pass through the right-of-way of Fort DeRussy military area, where you'll

find restrooms, picnic facilities, volleyball courts, and food and beverage concessions. Lifeguard service is provided by military personnel—no duty is too rough for our fighting men and women! A controversy has raged for years between the military and developers who covet this valuable piece of land. The government has owned it since the turn of the century, and has developed what once was wasteland into the last stretch of noncement, nonhigh-rise piece of real estate left along Waikiki. Since the public has access to the beach, and since Congress voted a few years back that the lands cannot be sold, it'll remain under the jurisdiction of the military.

If you are fascinated by the military and its history, visit **Battery Randolph** at Fort DeRussy, at the corner of Kalia and Saratoga roads. Plenty of displays and historical artifacts, free guided tour, open Tues.-Sun. 10 a.m.-4:30 p.m., tel. 543-2687. (For complete descriptions see "Sights" under "Free Sights and Curiosities" in the Waikiki chapter.)

ACCOMMODATIONS

The vast majority of Oahu's hotels are strung along the boulevards of Waikiki. Most are neatly clustered, bound by the Ala Wai Canal, and run eastward to Diamond Head. These hotels will be discussed in the Waikiki section. The remainder of greater Honolulu has few hotels, but those that do exist are some of Oahu's cheapest. Most are clean, no-frills establishments, with a few others at the airport, or just off the beaten track.

Oahu's YM/WCAs And YH

Oahu has a number of YMCAs and YWCAs from which to choose, and the only official youth hostel in the state. They vary as far as private room and bath are concerned, facilities offered, and prices. Expect to pay about $30 s with a shared bath, and about $32.50 d with a private bath.

The **YMCA Central Branch** (men only) at 401 Atkinson Dr., Honolulu, HI 96814, tel. 941-3344, is the most centrally located and closest to Waikiki. You can call ahead, but there are no reservations, no curfew, no visitors after 10 p.m.; it has an outside pool, singles, doubles, and private baths. This Y is located just across from the eastern end of Ala Moana Park, only a 10-minute walk to Waikiki.

YMCA Nuuanu (men only), 1441 Pali Hwy., Honolulu, HI 96813, tel. 536-3556, near the intersection of S. Vineyard Blvd., is a few minutes' walk from downtown Honolulu. You'll find a modern, sterile facility with a pool, shared and single rooms, and private or communal showers; reservations accepted.

Armed Services YMCA, open to military personnel and civilians, both men and women, at 250 S. Hotel St., Honolulu, tel. 524-5600. Doesn't accept reservations, but it has a pool, single and double rooms, plenty of sporting facilities, and child care.

YMCA Atherton Branch, 1810 University Ave., Honolulu, tel. 946-0253, is near the University of Hawaii; students are given preferential treatment. Dormitory style, no recreational facilities. Cheapest in town, but there's a three-night minimum and a one-time membership fee.

YWCA Fernhurst, 1566 Wilder Ave., Honolulu, HI 96822, tel. 941-2231, is just off Manoa Road, across from the historical Punahou School. Singles and doubles with shared bath, women only. Weekly rates. Breakfast and dinner are included (except Sunday) for low prices. Doors close at 11 p.m., but the night guard will admit later arrivals. Reservations are limited depending on availability; deposit required. Women can stay for up to one year, and the many women from around the world add an international atmosphere.

The only official American Youth Hostel in Hawaii (more listed under Waikiki) is the **Honolulu International Youth Hostel,** 2323 A Seaview Ave., Honolulu, HI 96822, tel. 946-0591, located near the University of Hawaii. This YH is always busy, but will take reservations. AYH members with identity cards are given priority, but nonmembers are accepted on a space-available, day-by-day basis. For information and reservations write to the manager, and include an S.A.S.E. For information and membership cards write American Youth Hostels, 1332 I St. NW, Suite 895, Washington, D.C. 20005.

Elderhostel, 100 Bolyston St., Suite 200, Boston, MA 02116, offers noncredit courses at

Hawaii Loa College, Oahu. For people 60 years and older. Fees begin at $175 and include course, room, and board.

University Of Hawaii

Two six-week summer sessions beginning late May and in early July are offered at the University of Hawaii at Manoa, Oahu to bona fide students of accredited universities. Reasonable rates are available in residence halls (mandatory meals) and in apartments on campus; special courses emphasize Polynesian and Asian culture and languages, including those of China and Japan. Unbeatably priced tours and outings to points throughout the islands for students and the general public can be arranged at the Summer Session Activities Office. For information, catalog, and enrollment, write Summer Session Office, University of Hawaii, 2500 Dole St., Krauss Hall 101, Honolulu, HI 96822, tel. 944-1014 or 949-0771.

Moderate/Expensive Hotels

The **Kobayashi Hotel** at 250 N. Beretania St., Honolulu, HI 96817, tel. 536-2377, is in Chinatown, and it's an old standby as an inexpensive but clean hotel. It's away from all the Waikiki action, and the spartan, linoleumed rooms rent for under $37. Plenty of travelers pass through here, and the hotel's restaurant serves authentic Japanese food at moderate prices.

The **Nakamura Hotel** is a little bit more "uptown" in both price and location. It's at 1140 S. King St., Honolulu, HI 96814, tel. 537-1951. The rooms are well appointed and carpeted, and have large bathrooms. Some a/c rooms face busy King Street; the *mauka*-side rooms are quieter, with plenty of breezes to keep you cool. You can often find a room at this meticulously clean hotel when others are booked up, only because it's out of the mainstream.

The **Pagoda Hotel,** 1525 Rycroft St., Honolulu, HI 96814, tel. 941-6611 or (800) 367-6060, behind Ala Moana Park between Kapiolani Blvd. and S. King Street. Because this hotel is away from the action, you get very good value for your money. Rooms with kitchenettes start at about $55, with two-bedroom suites at around $90. All rooms have TV, a/c, and parking, and there's a swimming pool as well as access to the well-known Pagoda Restaurant.

Another in the same category is the **Hawaii Dynasty Hotel,** at 1830 Ala Moana Blvd., tel. 955-1111. Rooms here are clean, decent, away from the action, and reasonably priced.

The **Ala Moana Americana,** 410 Atkinson Dr., Honolulu, HI 96814, tel. 955-4811 or (800) 228-3278, is another hotel off the Waikiki strip. It's located just behind Ala Moana Park between Ala Moana and Kapiolani boulevards, with a walking ramp connecting it directly with the Ala Moana Shopping Center. Rooms start at $90 and go up to around $250 for a two-bedroom suite (six people). There's a/c, TV, swimming pools, an all-night coffee shop, and the Summit Supper Club on the top of this 36-story hotel.

Manoa Valley Inn

The Manoa Valley Inn, at 2001 Vancouver Dr., Honolulu, HI 96822, tel. 947-6019 or (800) 634-5115, offers a magnificent opportunity to lodge in turn-of-the-century elegance. Formerly the John Guild Inn, this bed and breakfast was completely restored in 1982 and is listed on the National Register of Historic Places. Innkeeper Lisa Hookan-Holly offers a double bed with a shared bath, including continental breakfast, at a very reasonable $95, or a private suite for $120-175.

The exemplary continental breakfasts are prepared on the premises. In the morning, the aroma of fresh-brewed coffee wafts up the stairs. The breakfast selections are bran muffins, croissants, little sticky buns, fresh seasonal fruit, and hand-squeezed juices. The daily and Sunday newspapers are available. Pick one and sink into the billowy cushions of a wicker chair on the lava-rock-colonnaded back porch. Both inside and out, you'll find coffee tables surrounded by overstuffed chairs and, nearby, decanters of port and sherry and dishes filled with chocolates. Every evening, wine and gourmet cheese, along with crackers and fresh fruits, are presented. All are complimentary for guests.

The original structure was a very modest, two-story, boxlike home. It was situated on seven acres, but the demand for land by growing Honolulu has whittled it down to the present half acre or so. The grounds are well kept but small, so don't expect sweeping grand lawns. The original owner was Milton Moore, an Iowa lumberman. He sold it to John Guild in 1919, a secretary to Alexander and Baldwin, who basically created

Manoa Valley Inn

J.D. BISIGNANI

the structure that you see today. The home went through several owners and even did a stint as a fraternity house. It ended up as low-priced apartment units until it was rescued and refurbished by Rick Ralston, the owner of Crazy Shirts and one of Hawaii's successful self-made men, a patron of arts and antiques. He outfitted the house from his warehouse of antiques with furnishings not original to the house, but true to the period. The original structure was built in 1915. In 1919 the third floor was added, along with the back porch. A cottage with a white-on-white theme is available, and offers seclusion and privacy away from the main house.

FOOD

The restaurants mentioned below are outside the Waikiki area, although many are close, even within walking distance. Others are located near Ala Moana, Chinatown, downtown, and the less touristed areas of greater Honolulu. Some are first-class restaurants; others, among the best, are roadside stands where you can get a satisfying plate lunch. The restaurants are listed according to price range and location, with differing cuisines included in each range. Besides the sun and surf, it's the amazing array of food found on Oahu that makes the island extraordinary.

SHOPPING CENTER DINING

Ala Moana Shopping Center

The following are located at the Ala Moana Shopping Center along Ala Moana Boulevard, which has recently undergone a full face-lift. Most are located in the **Makai Food Court,** a huge central area where you can inexpensively dine on dishes from San Francisco to Tokyo. Counter-style restaurants serve island favorites, reflecting the multi-ethnic culinary traditions from around the Pacific. You take your dish to a nearby communal dining area, which is great for people-watching. The **China House** is open daily for lunch and dinner, tel. 949-6622. This enormous dining hall offers the usual selection of Chinese dishes, but is famous for its dim sum (served 11 a.m.-2 p.m.); you choose bite-sized morsels from carts.

La Cocina, open daily for lunch and dinner, tel. 949-9233, serves Mexican food for under $5 with complimentary chips and salsa. It offers dining facilities and takeout service. Less spicy offerings suit American tastes.

Michel's Baguette, first floor ocean side, is open weekdays 7 a.m.-9 p.m., Saturday till 5:30 p.m., Sunday 8 a.m.-5 p.m., tel. 946-6888. They specialize in French bread, pastries, and croissants baked on the premises. Their good selection of tasty soups, salads, and sandwiches is a change from the ordinary burger.

Patti's Chinese Kitchen, first floor facing the sea, tel. 946-5002, has all the ambience you'd expect from a cafeteria-style Chinese fast-food joint, plus lines about a block long. But don't let either discourage you. The lines move incredibly quickly, and you won't get gourmet food, but it's tasty, plentiful, and cheap. The Princess Special is steamed rice, fried rice or noodles, chow mein, plus two entrees like sweet-and-sour pork or a chicken dish—for around $3. The Queen Special is the same, but add another entree—under $4. You can even have four entrees, which fills two large paper plates. The princesses who eat this much food aren't tiny-waisted damsels waiting for a prince to rescue them—they can flatten anyone who hassles them.

Ward Warehouse

This shopping center, located at 1050 Ala Moana Blvd., has a range of restaurants, from practical to semi-chic, all reasonably priced. **Beni Kai** is a beautifully appointed Japanese restaurant with a rock garden at the entranceway that continues inside. It's bright and airy, neo-Japanese traditional. Prices are reasonable, with set-menu dishes like *unagi kabayaki* for $12.95, or miso-fried fish at $9.25. They have a wide selection of *donburi,* yakitori, and tempura for around $6. Open Mon.-Sat. 11 a.m.-2 p.m. for lunch, and for dinner from 5 p.m.

Nearby is the opposite side of the coin. A small lunch stand sells saimin and yakitori for under $4. Mostly you stand and eat, but there are a few tables in the common mall area. Also, for fast food you'll find **Cookie Kitchen** and **The Old Spaghetti Factory.** The latter serves a wide variety of pasta not quite like Mama makes, but passable, and at a reasonable price.

For those into health foods **Aloha Health Food,** primarily a vitamin and mineral store, has some prepared food and drinks in a cooler. Right across from it is **Coffee Works,** specializing in gourmet coffee and tea. They have a bakery; sandwiches are under $5, croissants $1.50. So take your vitamins on one side and get jazzed on the other. The **Farmers' Market** is not in the Ward Warehouse but just across the street, at 1020 Auahi, where you can pick up fresh produce and flowers.

Orson's Restaurant is a seafood house on the second floor. It's quite elegant considering the location, with a prize-winning sunset view of the small boat harbor at Kewalo Basin across the way. The inside, too, is richly appointed in wood and glass. Prices are $12-15 for fresh catch of the day complemented by an extensive wine list.

The **Chowder House** on the ground floor has fresh-grilled *ahi* ($8.25), snow crab salad ($5.95), Manhattan clam chowder ($2.25), clams and oysters on the half shell ($6), bay shrimp cocktail ($2.95), deep-fried shrimp ($5.85), and daily specials ($5-8).

Ward Center

This upscale shopping center is directly across the street from Ala Moana Park and next door to the Ward Warehouse. The following are some of its restaurants and eateries, where you can enjoy not only class, but quality as well.

R. Fields Wine Co. is not really a restaurant, but a purveyor of exquisite food, fine wines, crackers, cookies, cheeses, imported pastas, and caviar. Most of the wines are top-shelf Californian like Kiestler, Dominus, Opus I, Sutter Home (a fluke, left over from their catering business), and Robert Mondavi, with a nice vertical of their reserve wines going back to 1968. Older French wines, as well as German wines, are also available, and while you're there peruse the humidor for a fine cigar.

Chocoholics would rather visit the **Honolulu Chocolate Company** than go to heaven. Mousse truffles, Grand Marnier truffles, chocolate eggs with pistachio or English walnut—all will send you into eye-rolling rapture. If you enter, forget any resolve about watching your weight. You're a goner!

For a quick lunch try **Mocha Java** or **Crepe Fever.** Both are yuppie, upscale, counter-service-type places with a few tables. Both have a selection of sandwiches with an emphasis on vegetarian. Crepe Fever has stuffed croissants and whole-grain sandwiches. If you want a designer lunch, it's the place to go. For a double-fisted American sandwich with all the trimmings try **Big Ed's.** This deli serves no-nonsense corned beef ($5.35), ham ($4.50), tuna salad ($4.25), or polish sausage. Takeout as well as sit-down service, with a good seating area away from the bustle at the south end of the shopping center.

Al Fresco's on the corner in the Ward Center is an upscale semi-deli and restaurant whose tables spill out into a little courtyard. Stay simple with a small pizza ($8.95) or Caesar salad ($6.95), or move on to smoked chicken with mustard-herb-butter pasta ($13.95), pesto with smoked salmon ($13.95), or boneless chicken breast ($14.95). Specials are available every day, like grilled eggplant for $8.95 or blackened *onaga* for $19.95. This Mediterranean-style cafe is gourmet; while perhaps not designed for an elegant evening, it will give you gourmet food at reasonable prices.

The premier, or at least best-known, restaurant in the complex is **Keo's Thai Restaurant,** known for its mouthwatering Thai dishes and for its beautiful decor. The menu is extensive, with plenty of dishes for nonmeat-eaters. Prices can be quite reasonable for Thai noodles, chicken, shrimp, or vegetarian ($6.95-8.95); house salad ($4.95); green papaya salad ($4.95); spring rolls (four for $4.95); and tofu, shrimp, or chicken satay (under $9). Try the delicious soups like spicy lemongrass or Thai ginger for $3.75 per serving. Entrees like the Evil Jungle Prince have spicy reputations, or tame your tongue down with Asian watercress stir-fried with garlic, yellow bean sauce, and beef, shrimp, or vegies ($6.95-8.95). Keo's has another location, and operates the Mekong I and II, simpler and less expensive restaurants. Keo's is known for its beautiful flower displays of torch ginger, orchids, or plumeria on every table, and you may eat inside or outside.

The **Yum Yum Tree** is an affordable American standard restaurant that features pies and cakes from its bakery, along with home-style fresh pasta. They have an extensive dining area, quite cheerful with dark wood floors, ferns, hanging greenery, and an open-beam ceiling. Breakfast is served 7 a.m.-noon, lunch 11 a.m.-5 p.m., dinner 5 p.m.-midnight, cocktails 7 a.m.-closing.

Compadres Mexican Restaurant, tel. 523-1307, open daily 11 a.m.-10:30 p.m., and until midnight on weekends, although part of a small chain with restaurants in Maui, San Francisco, Sacramento, and Palo Alto, offers made-to-order, health-conscious Mexican cuisine voted as the "Best on Oahu" by the small but discerning local Mexican population. The open-beamed dining room overlooking Ala Moana Park is a mixture of "South Seas" and "south of the border" with plenty of ferns and foliage, round-topped wooden tables, and bent-backed chairs upholstered in primary reds and greens; Mexican masks, bronze parrots and ceramic macaws hang from the walls and ceilings. The huge menu, featuring handmade tortillas of white flour, whole wheat, blue corn, or yellow corn, along with homemade chips and salsa, uses no lard in any of the dishes except in *carnitas,* which are pork anyway. The most unique offerings are the **Quesadillas Internacionales,** priced at $6.95-8.95; flavors vary and can be Greek, filled with feta cheese and lamb; Baja with shrimp, spinach, and Monterey Jack cheese; Texan with chicken or steak and fiery sauce; or German with sausage, Monterey Jack cheese, honey mustard, and "Oh Chihuahua" sauerkraut. Besides quesadillas, there are standard burritos and tacos, and plenty of vegetarian selections like the Santa Fe Tamale or Compadres Tostada filled with beans, avocado, fresh salsa, and chopped olives. No dish is over $9. The bar complements the meal with a full selection of domestic and imported beer, 10 different kinds of tequila, margaritas by the glass or pitcher, and exotic island drinks for under $5. Compadres is an excellent choice for a budget gourmet meal in a hospitable atmosphere where the prices are right and the service excellent. There's even live music offered now and again. You can't go wrong!

Don't let the name **Andrew's Restaurant,** tel. 523-8677, fool you. It's actually an excellent continental restaurant on the second floor that makes its own pasta. Starters include *calamari fritto* ($6.25), wilted spinach salad ($3.50), and minestrone soup ($3); entrees are cannelloni ($13.95), frog legs ($16.75), a variety of veal dishes for under $20, and complete dinners with all the trimmings for $17-25.

Ryan's Grill, open Mon.-Sat. 11:15 a.m.-1:45 a.m., Sunday 5 p.m.-1:45 a.m., is an ultramodern yet comfortable establishment appointed with black leather chairs, chrome railings, marble-topped tables, and a hardwood floor, which are dominated by a huge bar and open kitchen. The menu offers standards along with nouveau cuisine and includes French onion soup ($6.59), sesame chicken salad ($8.50), and linguine with fresh basil and pine nuts ($7.95). Sandwiches are everything from hot Dungeness crab to a grilled chicken club, all under $8. More substantial meals from the grill include Korean chicken ($7.95) or fresh blue marlin. The bar prepares all of the usual exotic drinks and has plenty of draught beer selections from which to choose. Most menu items along with plenty of munchies and *pu pu* are served until 1 a.m., so Ryan's Grill makes a perfect late-night stop.

The Monterey Bay Canners Seafood Restaurant, open for lunch Mon.-Sat. 11 a.m.-4 p.m., for dinner Sun.-Thurs. 4 p.m.-11 p.m., Fri.-Sat. till midnight, Sunday for brunch 10 a.m.-4 p.m., is a small California chain with a reputation for decent seafood at reasonable prices. Lunch from the sandwich board can be bay shrimp, bacon, and avocado ($7.25), a Kona burger ($6.25), or teriyaki chicken ($7.95). "Early bird specials," served daily 4-6 p.m., are priced at $9.95, and include baked mahimahi, blackened salmon, and shrimp or chicken curry. All come with soup or salad. For dinner, entrees might be deep-fried shrimp for $15.95, or the very substantial grilled Seafest Special laden with lobster, crab legs, and shrimp for $18.95 (with chowder and salad add $2; children's menu available). The restaurant has live entertainment nightly 9 p.m.-1:30 a.m., usually provided by a local band like Fresh Catch that plays everything from Hawaiian favorites to contemporary music; happy hour, Wed.-Fri. 4:30-7:30 p.m., also brings live entertainment.

Restaurant Row

This new-age complex at 500 Ala Moana Blvd. (across from the Federal Building) points the way to "people-friendly" development in Honolulu's future. It houses shops and businesses, but mostly restaurants grouped around a central courtyard and strolling area. Some restaurants are elegant and excellent, while others are passable and plain. But the setting is congenial, and you can pick your food style as easily as you'd pick offerings at a buffet. Start at the central fountain area with its multicolored, modernistic, Lego-inspired tower. Every Saturday at 8 p.m. jazz is offered here overlooking the waterfront.

The **Sunset Grill,** tel. 521-4409, is on the corner. With wraparound windows, a long and open bar, and comfortable maple chairs, it lives up to its name. This is the place to come for a quiet evening drink in the downtown area. The food is prepared in full view on a *kiawe*-fired grill, wood-roasting oven, and Italian rotisserie. Choices include a variety of pasta, gourmet salads, calamari, fresh fish, oysters, chicken, veal, and lamb. Lunch is a wide variety of plump and juicy sandwiches of turkey, sausage, beef, fish, or chicken. The chefs at the Sunset aren't afraid to blend East with West in a wide variety of creations. Open daily 11 a.m.-2 a.m., weekends from 9 a.m., with a late-night menu available on weekends.

The Rose City Diner, open Mon.-Thurs. 11 a.m.-11 p.m., Fri.-Sat., 11 a.m.-midnight, Sunday 11 a.m.-11 p.m., will take you back to a more innocent time in America when bobby-soxers sat on the hoods of their boyfriends' Chevys and listened to Buddy Holly on the AM radio. Fabian, Dion, Annette, or Ricky would feel right at home ordering burgers and BLTs from this classic menu, except the food would be better than ever. The waitresses wear pink uniforms with white aprons and jaunty hats. The booths, like a cool Elvis outfit, are pink and black. The walls are covered with pictures of five decades of actors and musicians: Satohmo, Jimmy Stewart, Ronald Reagan, Bogart, Elvis, Marlon, Sophia, Rock, Marilyn, Jayne, Hitchcock, Lucy, Desi, Fred, and Ethel—they're all here. Booths have table-top jukeboxes. Try a slider burger with grilled onions, or a mini-burger served in a basket on top of French fries. Wash it all down with a root beer float, cherry Coke, or a frothy malt.

Fast-food pawns will be happy to hear that **Burger King** is here too. **R. Fields Wine Co.,** for a do-it-yourself meal, offers gourmet wines, crackers, cheeses, escargot, caviar, and pâté. **Cheers** is a small bar open 11 a.m.-2 a.m. Stuck in the corner, it tries to live up to its TV namesake by welcoming the local execs and secretaries in for an after-work drink and chat. It's comfortable, friendly, sports oriented, and smoky.

In the middle of the complex is **The Row,** an outdoor bar with finger food. The **Honolulu Chocolate Co.** is next. Like a smug little devil, it tempts you with chocolate truffles, mocha clusters, and fancy nut rolls. So sin! You're on vacation. The **Paradise Bakery Cafe** is a simple counter restaurant with pie, coffee, and donuts.

Trattoria Manzo, tel. 522-1711, owned by Tony Manzo, offers very special Italian dishes from the Abruzzi, a coastal and mountainous region along the Adriatic known for its hearty cooking. Choose an antipasto from Italian cold cuts to clams in red wine sauce for $7 and under. Assorted soups and salads range from $3 to $6 for *insalata calamari.* Select your favorite pasta, and then cover it with one of 201 delectable sauces, most under $10. Chicken, veal, and steak are grilled, simmered in wine sauce, or made parmigiana style; or choose a traditional lasagna, gnocchi, or good old pizza. The interior is sharp with neon strips, and black marble tables and chairs.

A few others in the Row include **CJ's Seafood,** open for lunch Mon.-Sat. 10:30 a.m.-2:30 p.m., dinner 5-10 p.m., with lunch specials for $5.25, and karaoke Thurs.-Sat. 10 p.m.-1:30 a.m.; and **Cafe Athena,** an indoor-outdoor restaurant with happy hour Mon.-Fri., when domestic beer and wine are $1.50.

INEXPENSIVE DINING AROUND TOWN

The following restaurants are located in and around the greater Honolulu area.

The University of Hawaii, Manoa Campus, hosts a number of restaurants, ranging from an inexpensive cafeteria to international cuisine at the East-West Center. Inexpensive to moderate restaurants include: **Manoa Gardens,** salad and snacks; **Campus Center Dining Room,** for full meals; and the **International Garden,** at Jefferson Hall in the East-West Center. For a great little lunch in a quiet setting in this area see the Waioli Tea Room described in "Manoa Valley" under "Sights" earlier in this chapter.

At the Hawaii Maritime Center you'll find **Coasters Restaurant** tucked away in the rear overlooking Honolulu Harbor. It serves American standards with a full complement from the sandwich board. Not great food, but the setting is great, away from the bustle of Honolulu. More interesting and definitely more local is **Pier Eight Restaurant** sandwiched under the huge elevated pier area just nearby the Maritime Center. Basic Chinese fast food to go, open daily 10 a.m.-5 p.m.

King's Bakery and Coffee Shop is a favorite of local people, at 1936 S. King St. and Pumehana, tel. 941-5211 (one of three locations). They're open 24 hours, and get very busy around 6 p.m. when they allow only groups of two or more to sit in the few booths; the rest eat at the counter. The menu is American/Hawaiian/Asian. Full meals are around $5. Not great, but good and wholesome. The bakery has seven-grain or whole wheat bread, but mostly sells white fluffy stuff with tons of powdered sugar. However, they do offer Tofutti, a soft, ice-creamlike dessert made from healthful tofu. Their other locations are at the Kaimuki Shopping Center and Eaton Square. Across the street from King's Bakery are two inexpensive eateries, **McCully Chop Suey** and **Yoshi's Sushi Yakiniku Restaurant.**

Down to Earth Natural Foods, open Mon.-Sat. 10 a.m.-8:30 p.m., Sunday 10 a.m.-6 p.m., at 2525 S. King St., tel. 947-7678, is a kind of "museum of health food stores" serving filling, nutritious health food dishes for very reasonable prices. Sandwiches, like a whopping avocado, tofu, and cheese, are under $5. Daily full-meal specials, like vegie stroganoff, eggplant parmigiana, and lasagna are around $4, including salad. Plenty of items on the menu will fill you up for under $3. Healthwise, you can't go wrong! Just up the street at 2471 S. King, across from the Star Garden Market, is the tiny **Saimin Bowl Restaurant.** Their name says it all, and you can have a huge, steaming bowl of soup for a few dollars.

Kokua Co-op Natural Foods And Grocery Store, at the corner of S. Beretania and Isenberg, tel. 941-1921, is open to the public Mon.-Sat. 9 a.m-8 p.m., Sunday 10 a.m.-7 p.m. It's a full-service store with organic and fresh produce, cheese, milk, juices, bulk foods, and breads.

Sekiya's Restaurant and Deli at 2746 Kaimuki Ave., tel. 732-1656, looks like a set from a 1940s tough-guy movie. The food is well prepared and the strictly local clientele will be amazed that you even know about the place.

Hale Vietnam, 1140 12th Ave. in Kaimuki, tel. 735-7581, is building an excellent reputation for authentic and savory dishes at very moderate prices. It gets the highest praise from local people, who choose it again and again for an inexpensive evening of delicious dining.

For a quick *bento* or sushi to go, try **Matsuri Sushi,** tel. 949-1111, at the corner of Kapiolani Blvd. and McCully. This quick-stop is a perfect place to pick up lunch on your way out of the Waikiki area.

Suehiro's at 1824 S. King, open daily for lunch and dinner, with takeout service, tel. 949-4584, gets the nod from local Japanese people. The menu here is authentic, the decor strictly Americana, and the food well prepared and moderately priced.

People's Cafe, 1300 Pali Hwy., is open Mon.-Sat. 10 a.m.-7:30 p.m., tel. 536-5789. Two going on three generations of the same Japanese family have been serving the full range of excellent and inexpensive Hawaiian food at this down-home restaurant. It's not fancy, but the food is good and the surroundings clean.

Coco's Coffee House at the corner of Kalakaua Ave. and Kapiolani Blvd. is an American standard that's open all night. It's like a million others in the U.S. where you can order a hot roast beef sandwich for a few bucks, or just sip a coffee into the wee hours, staying out of the weather.

Another of the same type is the **Hungry Lion,** tel. 536-0148, at 1613 Nuuanu Avenue. Open 24 hours, it serves everything from Asian food to steaks. Many local people come here after a night out. Nothing special, but decent wholesome food on Formica tables.

M's Coffee Tavern is a favorite with downtown office workers for great lunches, excellent coffee, and cocktails, at 124 Queen St., tel. 531-5739.

Walli Wok, tel. 943-1WOK, is a Chinese restaurant that delivers, but you must spend a minimum of $8. They'll deliver anywhere in the downtown and Waikiki area, and are perfect for condo dinners or late-night snacks. The food is passable, and the servings are ample.

Two inexpensive yet authentic restaurants sit next door to each other at 1679 Kapiolani Blvd.; the **Kintoki Japanese Restaurant,** tel. 949-8835, and the **Sukyung Korean Restaurant.** This semi-seedy area has plenty of "girlie bars," but the food is good and authentic, with most items priced below $5.

Penny's Plate Lunches, on the Sand Island Access Rd. next to Dirty Dan's Topless Go-Go Joint, is one of the least expensive and most authentic Hawaiian plate-lunch stands you can find. The most expensive lunch is *lau lau,* pork and butterfish wrapped in a ti leaf, at around $3.50. You can also try baseball-sized *manapua* for around 60 cents. Penny's is out of the way, but definitely worth a stop.

You can't get much cheaper than free, and that's what the **International Society for Krishna Consciousness** asks every Sunday at 5:30 p.m. for its vegetarian smorgasbord. Their two-acre compound is just off the Pali Hwy. at 51 Coelho Way, tel. 595-4913. Of course there're a few chants for dessert. *Hare Krishna!*

Downtown Honolulu

In central Honolulu, mostly along Bishop Street's financial district, you'll find excellent and inexpensive restaurants that cater to the district's lunch crowd. One of the best is the **Croissanterie,** tel. 533-3443, at 222 Merchant St., open Mon.-Fri. 6 a.m.-9 p.m., Saturday to 4 p.m., closed Sunday. They serve up gourmet coffee and baskets of croissants stuffed with everything from tuna to strawberries and cream. Also offered are salads, soups, Japanese food, and a pasta table with lasagna and linguine with salad and garlic bread for under $5. The vintage building, which recently housed a bookstore, has brick walls, hardwood floors, and straight-backed cane chairs, all part of the decor in this sidewalk-style European cafe.

Another good place is **Al's Cafe** in the 1100 block of Bishop, open Mon.-Fri. 6 a.m.-4 p.m., Saturday 7 a.m.-1 p.m. Daily lunch specials like tuna or ham-and-cheese sandwiches and a medium soft drink or coffee go for $3. Fast food in the area is **Jack in the Box, Taco Bell,** and **Pizza Hut** across the street from Woolworth's on Hotel Street. Heading down Hotel Street toward Chinatown, you'll pass **Kathy's Kitchen,** at Bethel and Pauahi, where for around $4 you can get a plate lunch.

Art And The Sandwich

In Honolulu there are a few opportunities to feed your mind and soul while satiating your appetite.

The **Garden Cafe,** tel. 531-8865, at the Honolulu Academy of Arts, 900 S. Beretania, is a classy place for lunch, Tues.-Sat. 11:30 a.m.-1 p.m., supper Thursday at 6:15 p.m., set up in a garden of this excellent museum under a canopy. The cafe serves soups like iced pumpkin soup with parsley, salads such as crunchy pea or orange, and sandwiches of ham with pepper jelly. Desserts run $1.50, full luncheon at $7.50. The food is delicious, but be aware that the portions are not for the hungry, being designed primarily for patrons of the arts who seem to be wealthy, waistline-watching matrons from the fashionable sections of Honolulu.

Don't let the Porsches, Mercedeses, and BMWs parked vanity plate to vanity plate in the parking lot discourage you from enjoying the **Contemporary Cafe,** tel. 523-3362 (reservations recommended), at the Contemporary Museum, 2411 Makiki Heights Drive. The small but superb menu is as inspired as the art in the museum, and the prices are astonishingly inexpensive. Dine inside or out, or perch on the porch. Appetizers are pâté, mussels, escargot, or smoked salmon for under $10. Salads are home-smoked mahimahi-and-lingonberry salad, Malaysian shrimp salad, Greek salad, or chicken salad for under $11. A fine selection of sandwiches includes smoked breast of turkey or *ahi* Caesar for under $10. Desserts from cheesecake to pecan pie are available, and beverages include homemade lemonade and cappuccino. For a wonderful cultural outing combined with a memorable lunch, come to the Contemporary Cafe. It's just so . . . contemporary!

Fast Foods And Treats

Fast-food fanciers and fanatics have nothing to fear on Oahu. There are enough quick-stop eateries to feed an army, mainly because there is an Army, plus a Navy and a Marine Corps of young men and women on the island, not to mention the army of tourists. If you're after pizza, burgers, shakes, or fries, choose from 36 **McDonald's,** 13 or so **Jack in the Box,** 24 **Pizza Hut,** 10 or so **Zippy's,** six **Wendy's,** a few **Farrell's,** and a few good old **Dairy Queen** restaurants.

For **shave ice** try the **Waiola Store,** open Mon.-Sat. 7 a.m.-9 p.m., Sunday 8 a.m.-7:30 p.m., on the corner of Paani and Waiola. You can get it in Waikiki, but for the real stuff in all its syrupy glory come here.

MODERATE DINING AROUND TOWN

The following listings are for restaurants where two can dine for around $35. This does not include drinks.

The Hideaway Restaurant, at La Mariana Yacht Sailing Club, 50 Sand Island Access Rd., is the only real restaurant on Sand Island. Henry, for many years a ship's cook, can cook everything well—maybe not great, but well. If a Chinese person came here and wanted chop suey Henry could do it. If a guy wanted steak and potatoes, you got it. Pasta? Here it is. The Hideaway is an out-of-the-way place, local, and real Hawaiiana. This is where all the yachties come. The Hideaway serves appetizers like escargot ($6.75), chicken wings ($5.25), and sautéed button mushrooms ($5.25). From the broiler, rib-eye steak is $11.50. The most expensive broiled item is an eight-ounce filet mignon ($14.95). From the sea, try deep-fried scallops ($10.50), shrimp scampi served over linguine ($10.95), or fresh *ahi* fillet or steak ($10.95). That's the cheapest fresh *ahi* around.

Henry is also known for his onion rings. They're not on the menu; you have to know about them. Now you know. The Sunday brunch is excellent, but basic—eggs, potatoes, a slab of ham, rice, and toast for $3.50. Hard to beat. Inside hang Japanese glass floats that at night are diffused with different colors, providing mood lighting for the cozy black booths and wooden tables with high-backed wicker chairs.

Shiruhachi, at 1901 Kapiolani Blvd., tel. 947-4680, is a completely authentic Japanese sushi bar operated by Hiroshi Suzuki. As a matter of fact, until recently 90% of the clientele was Japanese, either visiting businesspeople or locals in the know, and the menu was in Japanese. However, everyone is more than welcome. With a beer, you get free *otsumami* (nibbles), with a wide selection of sushi and other finger foods like yakitori at about $2 for two skewers. A separate section of the restaurant turns into a cocktail lounge, somewhat like an *akachochin,* a neighborhood Japanese bar where people go to relax. There's taped music and a dance floor. If you're into authentic Japanese, this is a great one.

Auntie Pasto's, at 1099 S. Beretania and the corner of Pensacola, tel. 523-8855, is open daily for lunch and dinner until late at night. The vibe is upbeat pizza parlor, where you can even bring your own wine. Most of the Italian menu is around $6; the specialty is a fish stew loaded with morsels for about $12. Their large salad with garlic bread is cheap, and enough for two. No reservations necessary, quiet, comfortable.

TGI Fridays is a raucous singles' bar known for delectable morsels such as stuffed potatoes and quiches. It's across the street from the Blaisdell Center at 950 Ward Ave., open daily 11 a.m.-2 p.m., tel. 523-5841. Plenty of swingers and college students keep the joint jumpin'.

Wo Fat's, at 115 N. Hotel St., tel. 533-6393, has had a little experience satisfying customers—the oldest eatery in Chinatown, it's been at the same location for over 80 years, and open for business for 100! Besides serving delicious food from a menu with hundreds of Cantonese dishes, it's in a monumentally ornate building. You're entertained just checking out the decor of lanterns, dragons, gilt work, and screens. Most dishes are reasonably priced and start at around $5. This restaurant is highly respected by the people of Chinatown and is part of the Chinatown tour offered by the chamber of commerce.

EXPENSIVE DINING AROUND TOWN

Sometimes only the best will do, and Honolulu can match any city for its fine restaurants. For more fine dining see Waikiki chapter.

Won Kee Seafood Restaurant, 100 N. Beretania, is a splurge joint where you get delicious seafood. Free parking on Maunakea Street. This is the place for Honolulu's in-the-know crowd. Tasteful and elegant surroundings.

The Chart House, at 1765 Ala Moana Blvd. near Ala Wai Yacht Harbor, is open daily 4 p.m. (Sunday 5 p.m.) till 2 a.m., tel. 941-6660. They offer a happy hour until 7 p.m., *pu pu* until midnight, and nightly entertainment. Shellfish specialties start at $15, with chicken and beef dishes a few dollars cheaper.

India House, 2632 S. King St., is open daily for lunch and dinner, tel. 955-7552. Extraordinary Indian dishes prepared by chef Ram Arora include a wide selection of curries, vegetarian dishes, special *nan* bread, kabobs, and fish *tikka.* Specialty desserts of homemade ice cream and toppings.

Windows of Hawaii sits atop the Ala Moana Building at 1441 Kapiolana Blvd., serving American and continental. Great views from this revolving restaurant. Lunch (sandwiches) can be had for under $8, and complete dinners from $15. Extremely popular for its sunset view. For reservations, phone 941-9138. Champagne brunch is served Saturday and Sunday 10 a.m.-2 p.m.

Keo's Thai Restaurant, 625 Kapahulu, open nightly 5:30-11 p.m., tel. 737-8240, has become an institution. It serves great Thai food at expensive prices. They pride themselves on the freshest ingredients, spices tuned up or down to suit the customer, and Keo's recipes taught to each chef personally. There's always a line, with a few benches in the parking lot for waiting customers, but no reservations are taken. The eight-page menu offers most of Thailand's delectables, and vegetarians are also catered to. You can save money and still have the same quality food at **Mekong II,** 1726 S. King, tel. 941-6184, lunch and dinner. Owned by Keo's, it's not as fancy.

Nuuanu Onsen, 87 Laimi Rd. (right off the Pali Hwy., just before Queen Emma's Summer Palace), tel. 538-9184, is one of Honolulu's best-kept secrets. This authentic Japanese teahouse serves a gourmet fixed menu. You leave your cares along with your shoes at the entrance and are escorted by a kimono-clad waitress to your lacquered table, where you sit on tatami mats and enjoy the serenity of the garden framed by shoji screens. The hostess, like a geisha, plays teahouse games if you like. Here, you enjoy the experience as much as the meal.

ENTERTAINMENT

Dancing, Disco, And Lounge Acts

Anna Bannana's, at 2440 S. Beretania, tel. 946-5190, is the "top banana" for letting your hair down and boogying the night away. It's out by the university just across from Star Market. This dance joint has a laid-back atmosphere, reasonable beer prices, a small cover which goes to the band, no dress code, and a friendly student crowd. Dancing is upstairs, light dining downstairs, and there's a backyard in which to cool off between sets. Great place, great fun!

The **Club Jubilee,** at 1007 Dillingham Blvd., tel. 845-1568, sways with Hawaiian music every night but Monday. Listen to hula tunes on the quickly fading tradition of slack key guitar. People from the audience, when moved by the music, will take to the dance floor or the stage for impromptu performances. What they lack in polish they make up for in sincerity. Everybody's welcome. Beer around $3, with plenty of *pu pu,* like watercress with mayonnaise and soy sauce, along with regular island munchies.

University of Hawaii students trumpet the mating call at **Moose McGillycuddy's,** at 1035 University Ave., tel. 944-5525, especially every Thursday, which is "Ladies' Night." Standard but good food priced for the student pocketbook, and plenty of dancing.

Studebaker's, at Restaurant Row, 500 Ala Moana, tel. 526-9888, is a neon-lit, chrome deco bar with two red Studebakers in the window. By day it's a restaurant, but in the evening it's a disco and bar. From 4 to 7 p.m. enjoy its best deal, a one-drink minimum and inexpensive buffet, which can easily be a light dinner. The bartenders and cocktail waitresses climb on stage every hour and jitterbug for the audience, demonstrating classic "American Bandstand" routines and steps. One wall of glass bricks diffuses the light, and from the outside makes the dancers look as if they're in a fishbowl. *Uptown* dress code, male and female peacocks welcome.

Rumours, in the Ala Moana American Hotel, 410 Atkinson St., tel. 955-4811, is an established disco that cranks up around 9 p.m. and features the newest in dance and rock videos. Also, the restaurant atop the building, Windows of Hawaii, supplements your dinner with an evening lounge act.

Tony Roma's, 98-150 Kaonohi St. in the Westridge Mall, Aiea, tel. 487-9911, offers a lounge act Sun.-Fri., and daily happy hour 4:30-8:30 p.m. with a special *pu pu* menu.

TGI Fridays, 950 Ward Ave., tel. 523-5841, is a lively nightspot. Good food, large portions, reasonable prices, and music.

Pecos River Cafe, at 99-016 Kamehameha Hwy., tel. 487-7980, has country music by local country bands.

Note: Also see "Entertainment" in the Waikiki chapter.

Freebies

At **Centerstage,** Ala Moana Center, various shows are presented—mostly music (rock, gospel, jazz, Hawaiian) and hula. Performances usually start at noon. The **Young People's Hula Show,** every Sunday at 9:30 a.m., is fast becoming an institution. Here, hula is being kept alive, with many first-time performers interpreting the ancient movements they study in their *halau.*

The **Royal Hawaiian Band,** founded over 100 years ago, performs Friday at noon on the Iolani Palace Bandstand.

Hilo Hatties, 700 Nimitz Hwy., the largest manufacturer of alohawear in the state, conducts free tours of the factory, complete with complimentary shuttle ride from your hotel. Up to 80,000 garments are on display in the showroom. It's hard to resist spending: prices and craftsmanship are good, and designs are the most contemporary. Open daily 8:30 a.m.-5 p.m., tel. 537-2926.

The giant pineapple water tower off Iwilei Road guides you to the **Dole Pineapple Factory,** which has been completely refurbished into a mini-mall called the Dole Cannery Square, with distinctive Hawaiian shops and a cafeteria. Here, millions of Hawaii's fruit are canned, juiced, and sliced for shipment around the world. Free samples are available. The factory is least busy during the winter months, but something fascinating is always going on. In the summertime, at the height of the harvest, this factory can process over three million cans of fruit per day. No reservations needed for small groups. Contact the Dole Company at 650 Iwilei Rd., tel. 523-3653, open 9 a.m.-3 p.m.

Girlie Bars And Strip Joints
You'll have no excuse if your maiden Aunt Matilda or local chapter of Fed Up Feminists Inc. ever catches you going into one of these joints, sonny boy! There's not even a hint of redeeming social value here, and the only reason they're listed is to let you know where *not to go.* Many of these "lounges," as they're called, are strung along the 1600 and 1700 blocks of Kapiolani Boulevard, and in the little alleys running off it. Mostly, tough-looking Asian men own or operate them, and they open and shut quicker than a streetwalker's heart. Inside are two types of women: the dancers and the "lap sitters," and there's definitely a pecking order in these henhouses. (For a full description, see "Prostitution" under "Health and Safety" in the Out and About chapter.) Most patrons are local men or GI types, with a smattering of tourists. Personal safety is usually not a problem, but a fool and his money are soon parted in these bars.

Here are some places *without* the bad reputations that frequently go along with this type of clip joint. **Misty II Lounge,** operated by a Vietnamese man, has been here for over five years, an eternity in this business; he immediately fires any woman with bad vibes. This club is at 1661 Kapiolani Blvd., tel. 944-1745. Just behind it in the little alleyway are the **Orchid, Musume,** and **Winners Club**—all about the same. Two clubs considered to be good by their patrons are **Butterfly Lounge,** 903 Keeaumoku, tel. 947-3012; and **Stop Lite Lounge,** 1718 Kapiolani, tel. 941-5838.

Chinatown's **Hotel Street** (see "Chinatown Nights" under "Chinatown" later in this chapter) has hookers, both male and female, walking the heels off their shoes. They cruise during the day, but the area really comes alive at night. Mostly, these people are down-and-outers who can't make it against the stiff competition along the main areas of Waikiki. The clientele is usually servicepeople and hard-core locals. A few clubs in this area offer strippers. Always be prepared for fights and bad vibes in any of these joints. A few that tourists have entered and survived include the **Zig Zag, My Way,** and **Hubba Hubba Club.**

SHOPPING

If you don't watch the time, you'll spend half your vacation moving from one fascinating store to the next. Luckily, in greater Honolulu the majority of shopping is clustered in malls, with specialty shops scattered around the city, especially in the nooks and crannies of Chinatown. For a general overview of what the island has for sale, along with listings for bookstores, flea markets, food shopping, sundries, and art shops, see "Shopping" in the Oahu Introduction.

Ala Moana Shopping Center
This is the largest shopping center in the state, and if you want to get all of your souvenir hunting and special shopping done in one shot, this is the place. It's on Ala Moana Blvd. just across from the Ala Moana Beach Park, open weekdays 9:30 a.m.-9 p.m., Saturday 9:30 a.m.-5:30 p.m., Sunday 10 a.m.-5 p.m., tel. 946-2811. Recently, the Ala Moana Shopping Center has taken off its comfortable Hawaiian shirt and shorts and donned designer fashions by Christian Dior and Charles Jourdan. Local people are irritated, and they have a point, to a point. The center has plenty of down-home shopping left, but it now caters as much to the penthouse as it does to the one-room efficiency. It used to be where the *people* shopped, but now sections are aimed at the affluent tourist, especially the affluent Japanese tourists who flaunt designer labels like politicians flaunt pretty secretaries. If anything, the shopping has gotten better, but you'll have to look around a bit more for bargains.

Plenty of competition keeps prices down, with more than enough of an array to suit any taste and budget. There are about 100 stores, including all of Hawaii's major department stores like **Sears, JCPenney,** and **Liberty House.** Utilitarian shops like shoe makers, eateries, banks, and boutiques feature everything from flowers to swim fins. It's also a great place to see a cross-section of Hawaiian society. Another pleasantry is a free hula show every Sunday at 9:30 a.m. on the **Centerstage** (see "Freebies" under "Entertainment" above). The **Hawaii Visitors Bureau** maintains an information kiosk just near Centerstage. The following is a sampling of what you'll find.

The restaurants in the **Makai Food Court** are exceptional, if not for taste, at least for price, and are unbelievable for the variety of cuisines represented. In a huge open area you'll find dishes from Bangkok to Acapulco, from Tokyo to San Francisco. Most of these restaurants have only counters for ordering, with tables in a common dining area. Great for people-watching, too.

A good one-stop store with plenty of souvenir-quality items at affordable prices is good old **Woolworth.** They have all the same sundries the Mainland stores do, but plenty of Hawaiian and Asian baubles fill the shelves, too. The film prices are some of the best.

House of Music sells records and tapes. This is a good store to shop for those island sounds that'll immediately conjure up images of Hawaii whenever they're played. It's on the ground floor, tel. 949-1051.

The Honolulu Book Shop, tel. 941-2274, has the largest selection of books in the state, especially their Hawaiiana section. Books make inexpensive, easy-to-transport, and long-lasting mementos of your trip to Hawaii. It's on ground level near Centerstage.

Francis Camera Shop, tel. 946-2879, is a well-stocked camera store with a fine selection of merchandise sure to please the most avid camera buff. If you need something out of the ordinary for your camera bag, this is a good place to come. The staff is friendly and will spend time giving you advice. However, the best place to buy film is at **Sears** (no credit cards). **Woolworth** and **Longs Drugs** also have good prices, but for cheap and fast developing try **Fromex Photo,** tel. 955-4797, street level, ocean side.

The Crackseed Center, tel. 949-7200, offers the best array of the crackseed (spiced nuts, seeds, and fruits) that have been treats for island children for years. There're also dried and spiced scallops at $68 per pound and cuttlefish at $2.50 per pound—such a deal! Prices are inflated here, but their selection can't be beat, and you can educate yourself about these same products in smaller stores around the island. Crackseed is not to everyone's liking, but it does make a unique souvenir. Spirulina hunters can get their organic fix at **Vim and Vigor,** featuring vitamins, supplements, and minerals.

Shirokiya is a Japanese-owned department store between JCPenney and Liberty House on the mountain side of the complex. They have a fascinating assortment of gadgetry, knickknacks, handy items, and nifty stuff for which Nippon is so famous. It's fun just to look around, and the prices are reasonable. Japanese products are also available at **Iida's,** a local store dating back to the turn of the century, featuring garden ornaments and flower-arrangement sets, tel. 946-0888.

Specialty shops in the center include: **The Ritz Department Store,** with high fashions for men and women; **Hawaiian Island Creations, Products of Hawaii,** and **Irene's,** all selling a wide assortment of island-made goods and souvenirs, from cheap to exquisite; **India Imports,** featuring eelskin products and many unique items from the subcontinent; **Tahiti Imports,** with bikinis, muumuu, and a wide selection of handicrafts from throughout Polynesia; **Jeans Warehouse** for you aloha buckaroos; and **San Francisco Rag Co.** for nice rags sewn together well.

Ward Warehouse

Located just a few blocks west of Ala Moana Center, at 1050 Ala Moana Blvd., open weekdays 10 a.m.-9 p.m., Saturday 10 a.m.-5 p.m., Sunday 11 a.m.-4 p.m., tel. 531-6411, this modern, two-story complex lives up to its name as a warehouse, with a motif from bygone days when stout wooden beams were used instead of steel. The wide array of shops here includes a number of inexpensive restaurants (see "Food"), but the emphasis is on arts and crafts, with no less than 10 shops specializing in this field.

Give the tots their first lesson in impulse buying at **Hello Kiddie's,** a toy store, or at **Junior Co.,** or show them how a pro does it by wandering into **Be Be Sports** or **Blue Ginger** for men's and women's fashionable alohawear.

Kids of all ages will love **Neon Leon,** where you can buy masks, flying bats, puppets, a lot of neon, fake buns (yes, those kind!), and a pineapple head if you've left yours at home.

Waldenbooks, tel. 533-2711, open daily 10 a.m.-9 p.m., Sunday to 6 p.m., has a tremendous selection of printed material. In this first-rate bookstore, you'll find the latest novels, a good section on Hawaiiana, and even travel guidebooks.

Repent past gluttonies at **Aloha Health Food,** primarily a vitamin and mineral store. Or dress your feet at **Thongs and Things,** with everything from spiked golfing thongs to Teva sandals, the best all-around footwear for the island. Upstairs is **Birkenstock Footprints,** with their wonderfully comfortable ugly ducklings. More shops are: **Island Sun Spots** featuring bikinis and sundresses; **Traditions,** a great junk shop; **Cotton Cargo** for comfortable and tasteful dresses; and **JR's Music Shop** for standard and contemporary music with plenty of tunes by local Hawaiian musicians.

Perhaps the premier shop in the Warehouse is **Nohea Gallery** (*nohea* means beautiful or handsome in Hawaiian), tel. 599-7927, owned and operated by Gail and Lorie Baron, who personally choose for display works by over 500 local artists and craftspeople. Some of the finest works are created by over 100 island woodworkers who make everything from rocking chairs and rolltop desks to traditional canoe paddles, using rich grained woods like koa, mango, and rosewood. One of the most acclaimed woodworkers on display is **Kelly Dunn** who, from his shop in Hawi on the Big Island, turns out bowls from Norfolk island pine that are so thin you can actually see through them. Other artists displaying their talents include: **Kurt McVay,** who creates masterpieces in glass primarily in cobalt blues and emerald greens highlighted with daubs of oranges and yellows; **Diana Lehr,** who uses oils and pastels to capture the dramatic skyscapes and colors of Hawaii's sunsets and sunrises; **Fabienne Blanc,** who works in ultravibrant watercolors creating surrealistic close-up images of plants and foliage; **Russell Lowrey,** Fabienne's husband, who uses watercolors and pastels to create soft, feminine images of the islands; a very talented local couple, under the name of **Ulana O Kukui,** who make beautiful jewelry such as rings of gold and silver that they fashion like traditional *lau hala* weaving along with fused and blown glass, and woven baskets of all natural materials; and **Rick Mills,** a University of Hawaii professor, another glass artist who favors cobalt blue. Distinctive and affordable treasures include backgammon games, jewelry boxes, bowls, all kinds of jewelry, prints, and distinctive postcards. Nohea Gallery is where you can see the heart of Hawaii through the eyes of its artists. Have a look!

Ward Center

Across the street from the Ward Warehouse, this relatively new shopping center is gaining a reputation for some exclusive shops. The Ward Center, open weekdays 10 a.m.-9 p.m., Saturday 10 a.m.-5 p.m., Sunday 11 a.m.-4 p.m., tel. 531-6411, is appointed in light wood and accentuated by brick floors that give the feeling of an intimate inside mall, although much is outside.

The Colonnade is a cluster of shops inside the Ward Center. It includes **Regency Shoes, Lady Judith,** a fine apparel shop, and **Willowdale Galleries,** twinkling with elegant antiques, crystal place settings, chandeliers, and candelabra for those closet Liberace wannabes. It's like looking into a giant china closet filled with the best place settings and crystal.

Art A La Carte is a 12-member co-op featuring the works of well-known island artists, including Bunky Bakutis, Gail Bakutis, Connie Hustace, Mary Sylva, and Jackie Tanaguchi. Hanging on the walls are landscapes, seascapes, and a variety of portraits done in oils, paper, and watercolors, while glass cases hold the distinctive pit-fired ceramics of Bunky Bakutis.

Ladies will find exotic to erotic garments at **The Blush Collection,** while gentlemen can find that just-right gift at **Gems of the Pacific,** which mainly deals in coral and black onyx jewelry. **Villa Roma** is a women's high-fashion boutique, while **Size Me Petite** is for the smaller women and young girls, and **Allure** offers designer bikinis and bathing suits.

For a distinctive shop, check out **Hawaiian Heritage,** which brims with lustrous koa furniture—rocking chairs, four-poster beds, planter tables, and dining-room tables and chairs, all beautifully executed.

Vibrating from a remote corner of the mall, where mystics feel more at home, is **Sedona,** tel. 531-8010, a metaphysical new-age store. Their shelves and cases are stocked with aromatherapy and massage oils, natural crystals, agates, books, jewelry, and consciousness-lifting tapes. Recharge your spiritual batteries with a personal psychic reading by practitioners in a private upstairs area.

Downtown Shopping

If you're touring the historical sights of downtown Honolulu, take a short stroll over to the corner of Bishop and King streets, as good a place as any to call the center of the financial district. The names atop the buildings, both vintage and new, trace "big business" in Hawaii. There's good food to be enjoyed in the restaurants in this area (see "Food") along with some shops stuck away in the corners of the big buildings. See also "Shopping" under "Chinatown" in this chapter. An enjoyable time can be had at **Dole Cannery Square,** with shopping in its new minimall. **Longs Drugs,** tel. 534-4551, is at 1088 Bishop, and almost next door is **Woolworth,** tel. 524-8980, for sundries and necessities.

The full-service **Honolulu Bookshop** is on the corner of Bishop and Hotel, tel. 534-6224. The selections are excellent. **Nautilus of the Pacific** is at 1141 Bishop, specializing in estate jewelry and Hawaiian heirlooms, with plenty of sculptures and ceramics from Japan and China. **Hawaiian Islands Stamp and Coin,** tel. 531-6251, at 1111 Bishop St., street level in the International Savings Building, displays rare coins, stamps, and paper money of Hawaii, the U.S., and the world. **Discount Store,** at 65 S. Hotel St., sells TVs, VCRs, radios, and electronic gear. **Amar's Sporting Goods,** tel. 536-0404, at the corner of Bethel and Pauahi, is one of the bigger sporting goods stores on Oahu. The **Lion Coffee Co.,** at 894 Queen St., tel. 521-3479, offers a great tour of their roasting facilities and will mail out a colorful newsletter on request. For classic Hawaiian shirts head for **Bailey's Antique and Thrift Shop,** 758 Kapahulu, tel. 734-7628, where you will find thousands of vintage "collectible garments" on display. The best are made from rayon that was manufactured before 1950. Prices can range $100-2000.

Bargains And Discounts

For discounts and bargains, try the following. **Crazy Shirts Factory Outlet,** at 99-969 Iwaena St., Aiea, tel. 487-9919, sells seconds and discontinued styles, with a minimum savings of 50%. **Swimsuit Warehouse,** 870 Kapahulu Ave., Honolulu, tel. 735-0040, has women's swimsuits under $20, plus shorts and tops. **The Muumuu Factory,** 1526 Makaloa St., offers great sales—get there early and bring your helmet and shoulder pads to fight off the crowds. The **Hawaii Fashion Factory** at 1031 Auahi St., second floor, is just between the Ward Center and the Ward Warehouse. Fashions at factory prices; the public is welcome to visit the showrooms. **Goodwill Thrift Shop,** at 83 N. King, tel. 521-3105, displays the same bargains as on the Mainland, but with a wide assortment of alohawear. **Nearly New Thrift Shop,** 1144 Koko Head Ave., tel. 732-3272, has consignment sales of quality merchandise. **Symphony Thrift Shop,** 1923 Pensacola, tel. 524-7157, is a consignment shop for used clothing in excellent condition, usually name brands. **The Discount Store,** 188 S. Hotel St., tel. 537-4469, boasts excellent prices on tape recorders, tapes, batteries, and electrical equipment. **Paradise Found Factory Outlet,** at 1108 Fort Street Mall, tel. 533-3658, is known for quality shirts that sell for under $20. Tom Selleck, star of "Magnum P.I.," often wore shirts from Paradise Found.

Miscellaneous

Everyone, sooner or later, needs a good hardware store. You can't beat the selection at **Kilgo's,** 180 Sand Island Rd., tel. 845-3266. They have it all.

For camera and photo supplies **Central Camera** is a fine store in the downtown area where the salespeople are very helpful. It's across from Hawaiian Telephone at 1164 Bishop St., tel. 536-6692. Open Mon.-Fri. 8:30 a.m.-4 p.m., Saturday 8:30-11 a.m. (Also see "Ala Moana Shopping Center" above.) For sporting goods try: **Big 88,** 330 Sand Island Rd., tel. 845-1688, many military items; **Amar Sporting Goods,** 1139 Bethel St., tel. 536-0404, sporting goods, sportswear, and a full range of accessories and equipment.

BOB RACE

CHINATOWN

Chinatown has seen ups and downs in the last 130 years, ever since Chinese laborers were lured from Guangdong Province to work as contract laborers on the pineapple and sugar plantations. They didn't need a fortune cookie to tell them that there was no future in plantation work, so within a decade of their arrival they had established themselves as merchants, mostly in small retail businesses and restaurants. Chinatown is roughly a triangle of downtown Honolulu bordered by Nuuanu Avenue on the southeast, N. Beretania Street on the northeast, and S. King Street to form the hypotenuse. Twice this area has been flattened by fire, once in 1886 and again in 1900. The 1900 fire was deliberately set to burn out rats that had brought bubonic plague to the city. The fire got out of control and burned down virtually the whole district. Some contended that the fire was allowed to engulf the district in order to decimate the growing economic strength of the Chinese. Chinatown reached its heyday in the 1930s when it thrived with tourists coming and going from the main port at the foot of Nuuanu Avenue.

Today, Chinatown is a mixed bag of upbeat modernization and run-down sleazy storefronts. Although it is still strongly Chinese, there are Japanese, Laotians, Vietnamese, and even an Irish pub, O'Toole's, on Nuuanu Avenue. This is Asia come to life: meat markets with hanging ducks, and Chinese, Korean, Japanese, and Vietnamese food with their strange aromatic spices all within a few blocks. The entire district takes only 10 minutes to walk and is a world apart from "tourist" Oahu. Crates, live chickens, incredible shops, down-and-outers, tattoo parlors, and temples can be found in this quarter. When Hotel Street meets River Street, with the harbor in the background, it all abruptly ends. This is a different Honolulu, a Pacific port, crusty and exciting.

AROUND CHINATOWN

Look for the pagoda roof of **Wo Fat's** on the corner of Hotel and Maunakea streets. This is the oldest chop suey house in Honolulu, started in 1886 by Mr. Wo Fat, a baker. It's a good landmark for starting your tour. If you want to clear your head from the hustle and bustle, visit the nearby **Kuan Yin Temple,** where Buddha is always praised with sweet-smelling incense. For peace and quiet, or to check out old-timers playing checkers or dominoes, cross the river and enter **Aala Triangle Park.**

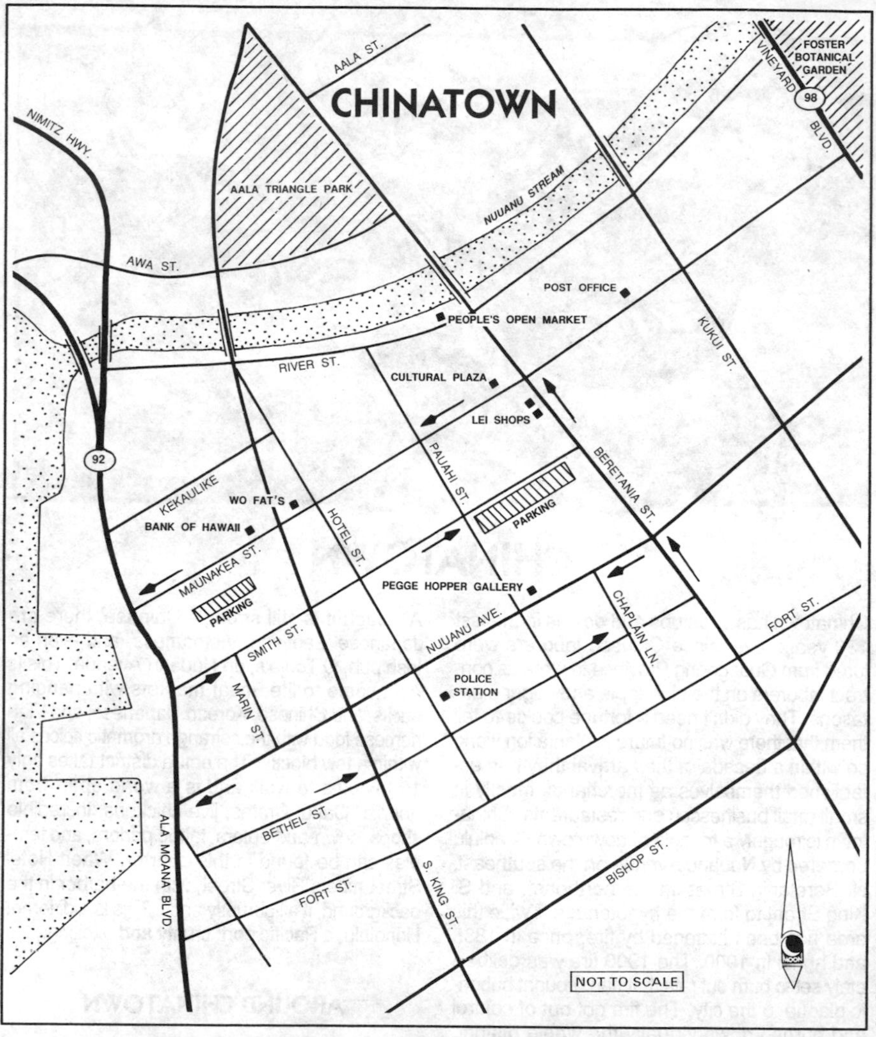

Treat yourself by walking a few minutes to **Foster Botanical Garden** at 180 N. Vineyard for a glimpse of rare and exotic flora from around the world. (See "Galleries and Guided Tours" under "Sights" earlier in this chapter.) While walking River Street, bordering Nuuanu Stream, behind the Cultural Plaza, notice what most people think is a temple but is really **Izumo Taisha Jinja,** a Japanese Shinto shrine. All the accoutrements of a shrine are here—roof, bell, prayer box. This one houses a male deity; you can tell by the cross on its top. There's a ferroconcrete example of a *torii* gate.

Lum Sai Ho Tong, across the street from the Shinto shrine, is a basic Chinese Buddhist temple, very small. Below it is Edwin's Upholstery Shop, part of the temple.

You can easily do Chinatown on your own, but for another view and some extremely knowledgeable guides try the **Chinese Chamber of Commerce** tour, tel. 533-3181, which has been operating as a community service for almost 30 years. They'll guide you around Chinatown for only $4, with an optional $5 lunch at Wo Fat's. Or try the **Hawaiian Heritage Center Tour** from 1026 Nuuanu Ave., tel. 521-2749, every Monday, Wednesday, and Friday at 9:30 a.m., for $4, and a lunch at Wo Fat's for $5. An excellent source of general information is the **Hawaii Chinese History Center,** 111 N. King St., Honolulu, HI 96817.

SHOPPING

For shopping head to the **Cultural Plaza,** on the corner of Maunakea and Beretania streets, but note that it has been struggling lately and shops come and go with regularity. It's more fun to look at than to shop. You'll find **Vin Ching Jade Center, Dragongate Bookstore, Excellent Jewelry Factory,** and **Peninsula Jewelry.** The Cultural Plaza **Moongate Stage** is the centerpiece. Here they perform Chinese dances and plays, and herald the Chinese New Year. If there is a presentation (free), attend.

Nearby at River and S. Beretania you'll find the **People's Open Market,** a cooperative of open-air stalls selling just about everything that Chinatown has to offer at competitive prices, including fresh produce from local gardens. It's held Monday 10 a.m.-11:15 a.m. Follow your nose to the pungent odors of fresh fish at **Oahu Fish Market** on King Street, where ocean delectables can be had for reasonable prices.

Pauahi Nuuanu Gallery, open weekdays 10:30-4, Saturday 9-1, at the corner of Pauahi Street and Nuuanu Avenue, is owned and operated by Lorna Dunn. It's small, but so are diamonds, and inside it's loaded with Hawaiian arts and crafts. The most impressive are the wooden bowls—light as feathers and thin as glass, made by Michael Ilipuakea Dunn, Lorna's son. Besides bowls there are little wooden jewelry boxes by Michael. Mythical carvings by Richard Morgan Howell depict Hawaiian legends in wood and stone. Bruce Clark and Rick Mills, an instructor at the University of Hawaii, are featured glasswork artists. The painters represented are Laka Morton, a Kauai artist; Jianjie Jie; and Douglas Tolantino, a Filipino-Hawaiian; with heavy oils by Ellen Joseph Gilmore. Expensive prices, but quality work.

Waterfall Galleries, owned by award-winning photographer William Waterfall, is at 1160A Nuuanu Ave., tel. 521-6863. William runs the gallery, takes the photos, and collects the artwork. The photography is original. Plenty of the artwork comes from Asia, especially Balinese carvings and celadon pottery from Thailand, which is done in woodburning kilns and signed by the potter. William, while doing travel assignments, buys the artwork and schlepps them back. His gallery is full of sculptures, bas-reliefs, and masks from previous trips. You don't know what you'll get when you come in here, but you can count on it being tasteful and original.

Pegge Hopper Gallery is next door to Waterfall Galleries. Ms. Hopper is one of the three most famous working artists in all of Hawaii. Her original works grace the walls of the most elegant hotels and homes in the islands. If you would like to purchase one of her bold and amazing serigraphs, this shop has the best and widest selection.

Cindy's Flower Shop is just next to Wo Fat's, and they have fresh lei at cheap prices. Located right where S. Beretania turns into N. Beretania, at Smith Street across from the Honolulu Towers, is a garland of flower shops like Lita's Lei and Mauna Kea Lei, famous for good products and prices. Also, at the corner of Pauahi and Maunakea look for **Aloha Lei and Flowers,** tel. 599-7725, who are locally famous for their lei, which they can ship to the Mainland.

The **Wingon Co.,** at 131 Hotel, has porcelain ware, but the feature is the big crocks of crackseed. If you want it the way it *was* made, this is it.

On the corner of Maunakea and Hotel you'll find **New World Fashions,** men's and women's wear, quality, value, and low prices.

Chinese Acupuncturists And Herbalists

Ted J. Kaptchuk, O.M.D., in his excellent book *The Web That Has No Weaver,* says, "Actually,

Chinese medicine is a coherent and independent system of thought that has been developed over two millenia." Chinese practitioners, unlike their Western counterparts, look at the entire individual, not just the acute symptom, and try to pinpoint what they refer to as "internal disharmony." Their diagnosis might be "dampness in the liver" or "fire in the kidney," for which they may prescribe a combination of acupuncture, herbs, dietary supplements, or exercise. The practitioners listed below are all licensed to practice Chinese medicine. A visit, during which they will check your overall appearance and a number of "pulses," costs about $5. The herbs they prescribe, usually dispensed from a wall of drawers labeled with Chinese characters, will probably cost under $10 depending upon the malady.

Yuan Chai Tong Ltd. Oriental Herbs and **Dr. W.S. Lam,** licensed acupuncturist, occupy a storefront on the corner of River and N. King.

Nearby on Maunakea is **Fook Sau Tong's,** another Chinese herb specialist. Look in the window to see coiled snake skin, a few dried-out snakes, some flat-looking lizards, and who-knows-what. If you need the bounce put back in your step, maybe some tonics or a few needles in the ear are just what the doctor will order.

Kam Sang Chun, 1121 Nuuanu Ave., open daily 9 a.m.-noon and again 2-5:30 p.m., Sunday 9 a.m.-noon, is another long-established acupuncturist and herbalist.

Down Smith St. is **Kam Mau Co.,** whose shelves are stacked with every conceivable (and inconceivable) Asian food. This is a great place to sample authentic crackseed. If your tummy revolts or if you need a quick tonic, head next door to **Lai An Tong's** herb shop, where some mashed antelope antler or powdered monkey brain will set you straight again.

CHINATOWN NIGHTS

Chinatown is relatively safe, especially during the daytime, but at night, particularly along infamous Hotel Street, you have to be careful. When the sun sinks, the neon glows and the area fires up. Transvestites and hookers slide down the street, shaking their wares and letting you know that they're open for business. Purchasing might leave you with a few souvenirs that you'd never care to *share* with the folks back home.

Not many tourists come this way. But walking down Hotel Street is really an adventure in and of itself. If you stay on the main drag, right down the middle, you'll be okay.

There are a lot of nondescript places like **China Bar** that open to the street like a wound oozing the odor of stale beer and urine. At Hotel Street and Nuuanu Avenue you'll find the Honolulu Police Department downtown substation.

The **Hubba Hubba Club,** with its live nude shows, no cover, and not too inflated drink prices, is the best of Hotel Street. This is not a place for candy-asses, wimps, or missionaries. Simply put, there are naked women in here doing exotic and bizarre acts. The Hubba Hubba is basically a clip joint on the up and up. Inside are flashing lights, a runway, and $3 beers, with only mild pressure as you sit and watch the act.

As you walk down Hotel Street toward the river it gets sleazier. The **Zig Zag Club** is basically a gin joint. Interspersed is an assortment of peep shows, followed by the **Swing Club,** with disco dancing 10:30 a.m.-2:30 a.m., and then **Two Jacks Bar** (bar and cabaret). **Elsie's Bar,** at 145 N. Hotel St., open 6 a.m.-2 a.m., looks meaner than a tattooed snake, but it's a safe place. So if you want to have a night of fun and relaxation come in here. They offer Hawaiian music by the Puamana Serenaders along with fairly decent Hawaiian food. A few doors down are steps leading upstairs to the **Original Bath Palace.** The *original* place where drunken fools were taken to the cleaners.

FOOD

You can eat delicious ethnic food throughout Chinatown. If not Honolulu's best, the entire district, food-wise, is definitely Honolulu's cheapest. On almost every corner you've got places like **Mini Garden Noodle and Rice Shop** and **Cafe Paradise** for breakfast, lunch, and dinner. They're basic and cheap eateries whose ambience is a mixture of Formica-topped tables and linoleum floors. In almost all, the food is authentic and mostly Asian. You can easily get meals here for $3-5. Some eateries appear greasier than the Alaska Pipeline, so you'll have to feel them out. The local people eat in them regularly, and most are clean enough.

An example is **Neon's Filipino Restaurant** on S. Hotel near the Hubba Hubba Club. The sign says, "Come in and have a halo halo, consists of many delicious fruits and flavor of canned juices. And by the way order a piece of custard." They serve Filipino dishes like *mongo ampalaya,* shrimp *pinakabet,* and *pancit* Canton for around $5.

Right at the corner of N. Hotel and Maunakea, you'll see **Wo Fat's Chinese Chop Suey,** tel. 533-6393, the oldest chop suey house in Hawaii, where you're guaranteed an authentic meal at reasonable prices. A visit to Chinatown is incomplete without lunch at Wo Fat's, or at least a tour of this extremely ornate restaurant. The three floors are covered with paintings of dragons, birds, flowers and a variety of land- and seascapes. Murals, carvings, and hanging lanterns create the mood of "rococo Chinese." The menu is like a small phone book, with literally hundreds of choices of fish, fowl, beef, and vegetarian dishes. It's hard to spend more than $10 per person, with many dishes considerably less.

Rosarina Pizza, New York Style, at N. Pauahi and Maunakea streets, tel. 533-6634, offers an alternative to Asian cuisine. They will sell you a slice of pizza for only $1.40, or a whole pie ranging from a small cheese for $8 to a large combo at $15.25. You can also order a 12-inch sublike pastrami and provolone for $4.75, or an a la carte dinner like spaghetti with meat sauce or sausage, cannelloni, or manicotti, all for under $7.

Doong Kong Lau offers Hakka cuisine and sizzlers. It's on the river side of the Cultural Plaza, open Monday 9 a.m.-9:30 p.m., Tues.-Sun. 8 a.m.-9:30 p.m., tel. 531-8833. Inside it's utilitarian, with leatherette seats and Formica tables. You come here for the food. Savories include stir-fried squid with broccoli for $5.95, stir-fried scallops with garlic sauce for $7.95, stir-fried oysters with black beans for $6.95, sizzle plates like seafood combo at $7.95, and shark fin with shredded chicken, $16.50. The menu reads, "The chief recommends deep fried shrimp with toast." Who's to argue with the chief! **Wan Kee Seafood Restaurant** is another restaurant in the Cultural Plaza. Locals swear by it, especially the lunch specials for $4.95.

The **Royal Kitchen,** tel. 524-4461, in the Cultural Plaza, is very popular with local families and businesspeople. They're especially known for their takeout baked *manapua,* soft dough with pork and spices; and for their Chinese sausage, *lupcheung.* Open very early in the morning.

One place that you shouldn't miss is **Shung Chong Yuein,** a Chinese cake shop at 1027 Maunakea. Look in to see yellow sugar cakes, black sugar cakes, shredded coconut with eggs, salted mincemeat, Chinese ham with egg, lotus seeds, and steamed buns.

Chinatown Joe's, at the corner of Hotel St. and Nuuanu Ave., tel. 534-3677, is a classic tavern complete with dart board and mugs of draft beer. Laid-back, local, and friendly, it's a good place to stop in for a breather, or to have a classic tuna, ham-and-Swiss, or pastrami sandwich.

Chinatown's Vietnamese Restaurants

A recent phenomenon is a number of excellent Vietnamese restaurants that have sprung up like bamboo sprouts along Chinatown's streets. The majority are meticulously clean, and the moderately priced food is "family-pride-gourmet." The decor ranges from oilcloth on tables topped by bouquets of plastic flowers and lazy Susans filled with exotic spices and condiments, to down-to-earth chic with mood lighting, candles, and even linen place settings. As a group, these restaurants represent the best culinary deals on Oahu today. Many selections, like the grilled seasoned meatballs or marinated pork (under $8), come with noodles, fresh lettuce, mint, cucumber, bean sprouts, and ground peanut sauce that you wrap in layers of rice paper to make your own version of what can best be described as an Asian taco. Simply moisten a few sheets of the rice paper in the bowl of water provided and wrap away. Great fun, and they'll show you how. There are plenty of savory vegetarian menu choices as well.

Maxime's Vietnamese Restaurant, 1134 Maunakea St., tel. 545-4188, open Tues.-Fri. 9 a.m.-9 p.m., Sat.-Sun. until 10 p.m., Monday 5 p.m., is as authentic as its name is contrived. To get an idea, ask to use the bathroom. You'll pass through the cramped but meticulously clean kitchen filled with boiling pots that are tended by about three generations of the family. In the dining room, it's Formica tables and red Naugahyde chairs, but the people couldn't be more friendly. Try Maxime's special noodles with pork, shrimp, crab, bean sprouts, lettuce, and pork soup on the side for only $6.50, or an order of shrimp rolls—light aromatic rolls with shrimp, pork, garden vegetables, and rice noodles rolled up in rice paper and served with sauce for $4, or only $1.50 as an appetizer. The selections of *pho* soup, which can be beef or chicken *(pho ga)* come with rice noodles, onions, Chinese parsley, basil, bean sprouts, and wine. You can have the meat either in the soup or on the side, for only $4.50 ($5 for the jumbo size). Beverages are lemonade, iced coffee with condensed milk, jasmine tea, fresh coconut juice, sweet and sour lemon juice, and soybean milk. Top off your meal with desserts like caramel custard or sweet beans with coconut milk for under $2.

Royal Vietnam Restaurant, 1127 Maunakea St., tel. 524-1486, across from Maxime's, open daily 9 a.m.-10 p.m., is just as friendly, makes an attempt at decor, and is slightly higher priced. Specialties include barbecued quail with butter ($9.95) and braised prawns and black pepper gravy ($9.95). The hot-and-sour soups ("poolenty" for two) are wonderful. Try the Royal Seafood combination at $10.95, or catfish or shrimp hot-and-sour soup at $9.95. Less expensive, but great selections, are *bun,* shredded pork and vermicelli with cucumbers, bean sprouts, mint, shredded lettuce, and roasted peanuts for $6.50; or spicy chicken and lemongrass for $6.95. Top off your meal with *che,* a sweet pudding for $1.95.

A Little Bit of Saigon, 1160 Maunakea, tel. 528-3663, open daily 10 a.m.-10 p.m., is the fanciest of the lot, although it is still quite basic. Specialties are "roll ups" that include savory beef, pork, or chicken, served with lettuce, fresh herbs, vegetables, sweet and sour fish sauce, and peanut or pineapple and anchovy sauce, along with thin rice paper that you use to roll-your-own for $5.95-8.95. Good yet inexpensive selections are stir-fried vegetables that you can have either by themselves or with fresh fish, prawns, chicken, beef, tofu, or scallops, all for under $7.95. Those with hearty appetites should try the seven-course dinner for two at $29.95 that gives a good sample of the menu. Finish with agar served with tapioca and coconut milk for $1.75.

Pho May Vietnamese Restaurant, at 1029 Maunakea St., tel. 533-3522, open daily 9 a.m.-9 p.m., is a fine family-operated restaurant. Though it's "ambience free," the food more than makes up for this. Nothing is over $8. Specialties include Vietnamese soups of steak, well-done brisket and flank, tendon, and tripe ($5.95); French bread and juicy beef cube ($5.95); and hot-and-sour soup for two bucks. With the soup they give you a stalk of fresh basil you break up yourself, a spice that resembles cilantro, and sprouts that you add to the soup. Try shrimp and pork salad, crabmeat fried wonton, or spicy chicken curry. For under $10 you'll waddle away totally satiated.

To Chau Vietnamese Restaurant, at 1007 River, tel. 533-4549, and **Ha Bien,** next door to "Tattoo Parlor," serve basic Vietnamese fare for under $7 for most dishes. They're around the corner from the action of Hotel Street, and are family-oriented. Ha Bien is open strange hours, Monday 8 a.m.-4 p.m., Tues.-Sun. until 6 p.m.

Another Vietnamese restaurant is **My Canh,** tel. 599-1866, at 164 N. King St., open Mon.-Sat. 9 a.m.-5 p.m., Sunday 9-3. Their menu reads, "You can select one specialty of the heart warming combination of the followings: rare steak well cooked, brisket and tendon, regular is $4.75, special is $5. BBQ meat spring for roll rice vermicelli is $5.25."

There's a really decent-looking Vietnamese restaurant called **Sau Duong** at 58 N. Hotel, tel. 538-7658, with home-cooked dishes like sour soup with fish ($8), lemongrass-spiced pork chop ($5.50), and house specialties like finely sliced papaya salad with shrimp and pork ($3.75). Open for breakfast, lunch, and dinner.

"It is the meeting place of East and West. The very new rubs shoulders with the immeasurably old. And if you have not found the romance you expected you have come upon something singularly intriguing."

—W. Somerset Maugham

GORDY OHLIGER

WAIKIKI

Waikiki ("Spouting Water") is like a fresh young starlet from the sticks who went to Hollywood to make it big, and did, though maybe too fast for her own good. Everyone always knew that she had a double-dip of talent and heart, but the fast lane has its heartaches, and she's been banged around a little by life. Even though her figure's fuller, her makeup's a little askew, and her high heels are worn down, she has plenty of chutzpah left, and when the curtain parts and the lights come up, she'll play her heart out for her audience.

Waikiki is a classic study of contradictions. Above all, it is an example of basic American entrepreneurialism taken to the nth degree. Along the main strip, high-powered businesspeople cut multimillion-dollar deals, but on the sidewalks it's a carnival midway with hucksters, handbillers, and street people selling everything decent and indecent under the tropical sun. To get a true feeling for Waikiki, you must put this amazing strip of land into perspective. The area covers only seven-tenths of a square mile, which at a good pace, you can walk in 15 minutes. On any given day, about 110,000 people crowd its beaches and boulevards, making it one of the most densely populated areas on earth. Sixty thousand of these people are tourists; 30,000 are workers who commute from various towns of Oahu and cater to the tourists, and the remaining 20,000 actually call Waikiki home. The turnover is about 80,000 new tourists per week, and the pace never slackens. To the head shakers, these facts condemn Waikiki as a mega-growth area gone wild. To others, these same figures make Waikiki an energized, fun-filled place to be, where "if you don't have a good time, it's your own fault."

For the naive or the out-of-touch looking for "grass-shack paradise," the closest they'll come to it in Waikiki is painted on a souvenir ashtray. Those drawn to a smorgasbord of activities, who are adept at choosing the best and ignoring the rest, can't go wrong. People and the action are as constant in Waikiki as the ever-rolling surf.

History

The written record of this swampy area began in the late 1790s. White people, along with their historians, cartographers, artists, and gunpowder, were already an undeniable presence in the islands. Kalanikupule, ranking chief of Oahu, hijacked the *Jackall*, a small ship commanded by Captain Brown, with which he intended to spearhead an attack against Kamehameha I. The chief held the *Jackall* for a while, but the sailors regained control just off Diamond Head and sent the Hawaiians swimming for land. The ship then hastened to Kamehameha to report the treachery and returned with his armada of double-hulled canoes, which beached along Waikiki. The great king defeated Kalanikupule at the famous battle of Nuuanu Pali and secured control of the island. Thereafter Waikiki, pinpointed by Diamond Head, became a well-known landmark.

Waikiki's interior was low-lying swampland, long known to be good for fishponds, taro, rice, and bananas, but hardly for living. The beach, however, was always blessed with sunshine and perfect waves, especially for surfing, a sport heartily loved by the Hawaiians. The royalty of Hawaii, following Kamehameha, made Honolulu their capital and kept beachhouses at Waikiki. They invited many visiting luminaries to visit them at their private beach. All were impressed. In the 1880s, King Kalakaua was famous for his beachhouse hospitality. One of his favorite guests was Robert Louis Stevenson, who spent many months here writing one of his novels. By the turn of the 20th century Waikiki had become a highly exclusive vacation spot.

In 1901 the Moana Hotel was built, but immediately a protest was heard because it interfered with the view of Diamond Head. In 1906, Lucius Pinkham, then director of Hawaii's Board of Health, called the mosquito-infested area "dangerous and unsanitary," and proposed to drain the swamp with a canal so that "the whole place can be transformed into a place of unique beauty." By the early 1920s, the Ala Wai Canal was built, its dredgings were used to reclaim land, and Waikiki was demarcated. By the end of the 1920s, the Royal Hawaiian Hotel, built on the site previously occupied by the royal beachhouse, was receiving very wealthy guests who arrived by ocean liner, loaded down with steamer trunks. They ensconced themselves at Waikiki, often staying for the duration of the season.

For about 40 years, Waikiki remained the enchanted domain of Hollywood stars, dignitaries, and millionaires. But for the brief and extraordinary days of WW II, which saw Waikiki barricaded and barbwired, GIs—regular guys from the Mainland—were given a taste of this "reserved paradise" while on R and R. They brought home tantalizing tales of wonderful Waikiki, whetting the appetite of middle America.

Beginning just before statehood and continuing through the '60s to the mid-'70s, hotels and condos popped up like fertilized weeds, and tourism exploded with the advent of the jumbo jet. Discounted package tours began to haul in droves of economy-class tourists. Businesses catering to the tastes of penny-pinchers and first-timers elbowed their way into every nook and cranny. For the first time Waikiki began to be described as tacky and vulgar. For the old-timers, Waikiki was in decline. The upscale and repeat visitors started to snub Waikiki, heading for hidden resorts on the Neighbor Islands. But Waikiki had spirit and soul, and never gave in. In the last few years, its declining hotels started a campaign to regain their illustrious images. Millions upon millions of dollars have been poured into renovations and remodeling. Luxury hotels renting exclusive and expensive rooms have reappeared and are doing a booming business.

Waikiki Today

The Neighbor Islands are pulling more and more tourists away, and depending on your point of view, this is either a boon or a bust for Waikiki. Direct flights to Maui and the Big Island allow more tourists than ever to bypass Oahu, but still a whopping 80% of the people visiting the islands spend at least one night in a Waikiki hotel, which offer the lowest room rates in Hawaii. The sublime and the gaudy are neighbors in Waikiki. Exclusive shops are often flanked by buskers selling plastic hula dolls. Burgers and beer mingle their pedestrian odors with those of Parisian cuisine. Though Waikiki in many ways is unique, it can also come off as "Anytown, U.S.A." But most importantly it somehow works, and works well. You may not find Waikiki a paradise, but you will find it a willing "dancing partner," and if you pay the fiddler, she'll keep the beat.

Non-Americans, especially Japanese, still flock to Hawaii for dream vacations, mostly staying at Waikiki hotels, 25% of which are owned by

Japanese firms. Mainlanders and locals alike are disgruntled when they see the extent to which Waikiki has become a Japanese town. It's one of the only cities in America where you can have trouble ordering a meal or making a purchase if you don't speak Japanese! The visiting Japanese have been soundly warned by the tour operators before they arrive to never talk to strangers, especially someone on the street. Unfortunately for them, this means a vacation in which they never really leave Japan. They're herded into Japanese-owned shops and restaurants where prices are grossly inflated, and from which the tour operators get kickbacks. Local shopkeepers, not on the list, are aggravated. They say that the once-timid Japanese visitor will now show irritation if the shopkeeper doesn't speak Japanese, and will indignantly head for the door if no one can deal with them in their native tongue. Also, these visitors have been taught to bargain with American shopkeepers, who they are told inflate prices. This makes for some rugged interaction when the price is already fair, but the Japanese visitor won't believe it. Although a survey was done that says the Japanese tourist spends an average of $500 per day, as opposed to a Mainlander who spends $100 per day, the Japanese really don't spread their money around as much as you would think. The money spent in Japanese shops primarily goes back to Japan. It's an incestuous system that operates in Waikiki.

SIGHTS

To see Waikiki's attractions, you have to do little more than perch on a bench or loll on a beach towel. Its boulevards and beaches are world-class for people-watching. Some of its strollers and sunbathers are *visions,* while others are real *sights.* And if you keep your ears open, it's not hard to hear every American accent and a dozen foreign languages. Some actual sights are intermingled with the hotels, boutiques, bars, and restaurants. Sometimes, too, these very buildings are the sights. Unbelievably, you can even find plenty of quiet spots—in the gardens of Kapiolani Park, and at churches, temples, tearooms, and ancient Hawaiian special places sitting unnoticed amidst the grandiose structures of the 20th century. Also, both the Honolulu Zoo and Waikiki Aquarium are well worth a visit.

Getting Around

By far and away the best way to get around Waikiki is on foot. For one, it's easily walked from one end to the other in less than 20 minutes, and walking will save you hassling with parking and traffic jams. Also, TheBus and taxis are abundant, and along with rental cars, have been covered in the Out and About chapter under "Getting Around." Those who have opted for a rental car should note that many of the agencies operate Waikiki terminals, which for some can be more convenient than dropping your car at the airport on the day of departure. Check to see if it suits you. The following information is specific to Waikiki, and offers some limited alternatives.

In mid-1987, **pedicabs,** for all intents and purposes, were outlawed in Waikiki. There used to be 150-160 pedicabs that offered short taxi rides. They took people shopping, sightseeing, and between hotels, but basically they were a joy ride. Mainstream businesspeople considered them a nuisance, and there were rumors that some drivers dealt drugs, so they were finally outlawed. Now only 10-12 legal pedicabs operate in and around Waikiki. They're not allowed to go along Kalakaua Avenue, pick-up or drop-off at hotels, or use any of the main drags. They stay on the backstreets or in the park, where they are constantly watched by the police. Charges are a hefty $3 per minute. The main customers are Japanese tourists who marvel at being pedaled around town by a muscular *gaijin* in a rickshaw-type conveyance no longer seen in their homeland.

The **Waikiki Trolley,** tel. 526-0112, offers tours throughout Waikiki and downtown Honolulu. A day pass costs $15 adults, $7.50 children, and you can get on and off as much as you like. The trolley is really an open-air bus, but it's well done and plenty of fun.

Waikiki does an excellent job of conveying traffic, both auto and pedestrian, along Kalakaua Avenue, the main drag fronting Waikiki. They've

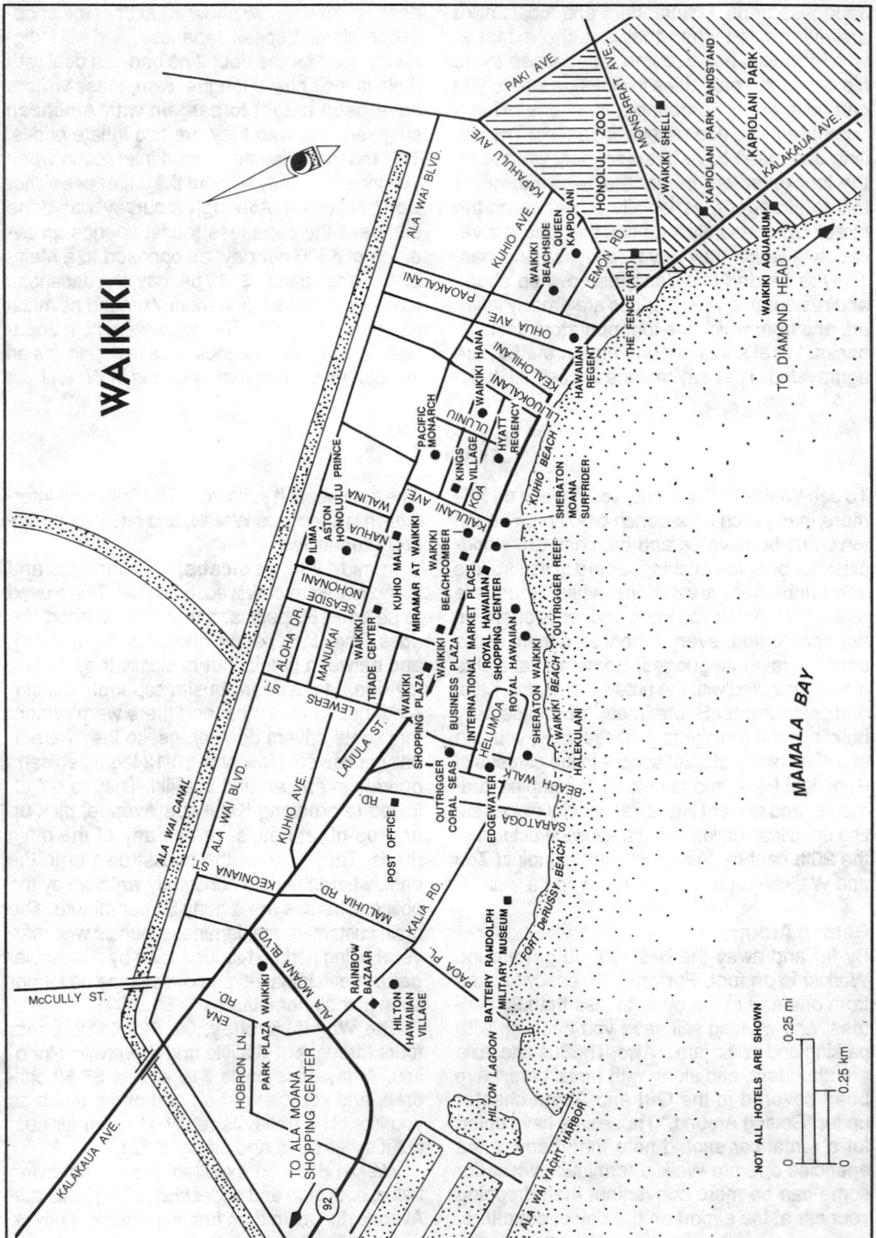

WAIKIKI

MAMALA BAY
TO DIAMOND HEAD
KAPIOLANI PARK
KALAKAUA AVE.
WAIKIKI AQUARIUM
KAPIOLANI PARK BANDSTAND
WAIKIKI SHELL
MONSARRAT AVE.
PAKI AVE.
HONOLULU ZOO
THE FENCE (ART)
LEMON RD.
KAPAHULU AVE.
QUEEN KAPIOLANI
WAIKIKI BEACHSIDE
KUHIO AVE.
OHUA AVE.
HAWAIIAN REGENT
PAOAKALANI
KEALOHILANI
LILIUOKALANI
WAIKIKI HANA
ULUNIU
HYATT REGENCY
PACIFIC MONARCH
KINGS VILLAGE
KOA
KUHIO BEACH
SHERATON MOANA SURFRIDER
KAIULANI AVE.
WALINA
ASTON HONOLULU PRINCE
NAHUA
ILIMA
KUHIO MALL
WAIKIKI BEACHCOMBER
MIRAMAR AT WAIKIKI
NOHONANI
SEASIDE
OUTRIGGER REEF
ROYAL HAWAIIAN SHOPPING CENTER
INTERNATIONAL MARKET PLACE
WAIKIKI BUSINESS PLAZA
WAIKIKI TRADE CENTER
ALOHA DR.
MANUKAI
WAIKIKI SHOPPING PLAZA
LEWERS ST.
ROYAL HAWAIIAN
SHERATON WAIKIKI
WAIKIKI BEACH
HALEKULANI
HELUMOA
OUTRIGGER CORAL SEAS
EDGEWATER
BEACH WALK
SARATOGA RD.
LAUULA ST.
POST OFFICE
KUHIO AVE.
ALA WAI BLVD.
ALA WAI CANAL
KEONIANA ST.
KALIA RD.
MALUHIA RD.
FORT DeRUSSY BEACH
BATTERY RANDOLPH MILITARY MUSEUM
PAOA PL.
RAINBOW BAZAAR
HILTON HAWAIIAN VILLAGE
HILTON LAGOON
ALA WAI YACHT HARBOR
ALA MOANA BLVD.
PARK PLAZA WAIKIKI
ENA RD.
McCULLY ST.
HOBRON LN.
TO ALA MOANA SHOPPING CENTER
92
KALAKAUA AVE.
NOT ALL HOTELS ARE SHOWN
0 0.25 mi
0 0.25 km

installed very clear yet unattractive combinations of stoplights and street names. These are metal L-shaped beams, painted a dull brown, that straddle the roadways, clearly pinpointing your location. Unfortunately, they match the area about as well as work boots match a hula dancer. To give the feeling of an outdoor strolling mall, sidewalks along Kalakaua have been widened and surfaced with red brick.

The **Kapiolani Park Kiosk** is on the corner of Kapahulu and Kalakaua avenues. The kiosk uses vintage photos to give a concise history of Kapiolani Park. An overview map shows all the features of the park. Information is available here concerning events at the Aquarium, Zoo, Waikiki Shell, Kodak Hula Show, Art Mart—island artists selling their creations along the Zoo fence (see "The Fence" under "Shopping" later in this chapter), and Kapiolani Park Bandstand, where you're treated to free concerts by top-name bands and orchestras (see "Free or Small Fee Entertainment" under "Entertainment" later in this chapter).

Public parking in Waikiki can be a hassle, although there are plenty of parking garages. A good place to park not far from the beach is the strip running parallel to Kapiolani Park at one end and along Saratoga Street at the other. There are plenty of two-hour parking meters available, especially if you arrive before 9 a.m. Also, inexpensive (for Waikiki) parking is available at the ramp adjacent to the Waikiki 3 Theaters along Seaside Road, but only after 5:30 p.m.

Note: For terrific "Living History Walking Tours" see "Sightseeing Tours" under "Getting Around" in the Oahu Introduction.

DIAMOND HEAD

If you're not sandwiched in a manmade canyon of skyscrapers, you can look eastward from anywhere in Waikiki and see Diamond Head. Diamond Head *says* Waikiki. Western sailors have used it as a landmark since the earliest days of contact, and the Hawaiians undoubtedly before that. Ships' artists etched and sketched its motif long before the names of the newfound lands of Hawaii, Waikiki, and Oahu were standardized and appeared on charts as Owyhee, Whytete, and Woohoo. The Hawaiian name was Leahi ("Brow of the Ahi"); legend says it was named by Hi'iaka, Madame Pele's younger sister, because she saw a resemblance in its silhouette to the yellowfin tuna. The name "Diamond Head" comes from a band of sailors who found calcite crystals on its slopes and thought they'd discovered diamonds. Kamehameha I immediately made the mountain *kapu* until his adviser John Young informed him that what the seamen had found, later known as "Pele's tears," were, except as souvenirs, worthless. Diamond Head was considered a power spot by the Hawaiians. Previously, Kamehameha had worshipped at a *heiau* located on the western slopes, offering human sacrifice to his bloodthirsty wargod, Ku.

Geologically, the 760-foot monolith is about 350,000 years old, formed in one enormous explosion when seawater came into contact with lava bubbling out of a fissure. No new volcanic activity has been suspected in the last 200,000 years. The huge rock is now Hawaii's state monument and a national natural landmark. Its crater serves as a Hawaii National Guard depot; various hiking trails to the summit bypass installations left over from WW II (see "Camping and Hiking" in the Oahu Introduction). Getting there takes only 15 minutes from Waikiki, either by TheBus no. 57 or by car along Diamond Head Road. The southeast (*makai*) face has some of the most exclusive and expensive real estate in the islands. The Kahala Hilton Hotel here is regarded by many to be one of the premier hotels in the world, and nearby is the super-snobbish Waialae Country Club. Many private estates—homes of multimillionaires, Hollywood stars, and high-powered multinational executives—cling to the cliffside, fronting ribbons of beach open to the public by narrow rights-of-way that oftentimes are hemmed in by the walls of the estates.

KAPIOLANI PARK

In the shadow of Diamond Head is Kapiolani Park, a quiet 140-acre oasis of greenery, just a coconut's roll away from the gray cement and flashing lights of Waikiki. It has proved to be one of the best gifts ever received by the people of Honolulu, ever since King Kalakaua donated this section of crown lands to them in 1877, requesting that it be named after his wife, Queen Kapiolani. In times past, it was the site of horse and car races, polo matches, and Hawaii's unique *pa'u* riders, fashionable ladies in long flowing skirts riding horses decked out with lei. The park was even the site of Camp McKinley, the U.S. Army headquarters in the islands from 1898 to 1907.

It remains a wonderful place for people to relax and exercise away from the hustle of Waikiki. The park is a mecca for jogging and aerobics, with many groups and classes meeting here throughout the day. It also serves as the starting point for the yearly **Honolulu Marathon,** one of the most prestigious races in the world. The beach part of the park, called Sans Souci, is very popular with local people and those wishing to escape the crowds, just a few beach-blanket lengths away.

Its **Waikiki Shell,** an open-air amphitheater, hosts many visiting musical groups, especially during Aloha Week. The Honolulu Symphony is a regular here, providing free concerts, especially on summer evenings. Nearby, the **Kapiolani Park Bandstand** hosts the Royal Hawaiian Band on Sunday afternoons. Also, under the shade of the trees toward Waikiki Beach, plenty of street entertainers, including clowns, acrobats, and jugglers, congregate daily to work out their routines to the beat of conga drums and other improvised music supplied by wandering musicians. Families and large groups come here to picnic, barbecue, and play softball. The park grounds are also home to the free **Kodak Hula Show** (see "Dinner Shows and Polynesian Extravaganzas" under "Entertainment" later in this chapter), Elks Club, prestigious Outrigger Canoe Club founded at the turn of the century, Waikiki Aquarium, and 45-acre Honolulu Zoo.

Just in front of the zoo, by the big banyan, are hundreds and hundreds of pigeons, the "white phantoms of Waikiki." In the morning they are especially beautiful darting through the sunshine like white spirits. Go to the Stop N Go or the ABC Store at the corner of Kapahulu and Kapiolani and buy birdseed. Take a few handfuls and stand among the pigeons. They will perch on your arms, shoulders, and head and peck away. If you're not wearing toe-covering shoes be advised that if you drop seed between your toes, you'll get an instant pedicure by the hungry birds. This is great fun and free!

WAIKIKI AQUARIUM

The first Waikiki Aquarium was built in 1904, its entranceway framed by a *torii* gate. Rebuilt and restocked in 1954, it has just undergone another face-lift with a new entranceway, "touch tanks," and an opening directly to the sea. The aquarium, located at 2777 Kalakaua Ave. (TheBus no. 2), tel. 923-9741, is open daily 9 a.m.-5 p.m., admission $6 adults, $4 seniors, $2.50 youths 13-17, and free to children under 12. A self-guiding book describing the marinelife is available for $5, and an audio tour ("magic wand" device) in English and Japanese is 50 cents.

Although over 300 species of Hawaiian and South Pacific fish, flora, and mammals live in its sparkling waters, the aquarium is much more than just a big fish tank. The floor plan contains four galleries of differing themes, and a seal tank. The **South Seas Marine Life** exhibit shows fish found in waters from Polynesia to Australia. The tanks hold sharks, turtles, eels, rays, clams, a seahorse, and colorful coral displays. Another exhibit, **Micronesia Reef Builders,** is perhaps the most amazing of all. It contains live coral that seem more like extraterrestrial flowers than specimens from our own seas. Some are long strands of spaghetti with bulbous ends like lima beans, others are mutated roses, or tortured camellias, all moving, floating, and waving their iridescent purples, golds, and greens in a watery bouquet.

Watch the antics of the monk seals, shameless hams, from the side of their newly renovated 85,000 gallon tank, which now has a "variegated coastline" of natural nooks and crannies patterned after sections of Oahu's Pupukea and Kahe Point. Hawaiian monk seals are one of only two species of tropical seals on earth. Endangered, only about 1,500 individuals survive, and the "performances" are more of a detailed description of the seals' day-to-day life in their dwindling environment. The three seals inhabiting the tank are all males, since placing a breeding couple in it would almost certainly result in the birth of a pup. Marine biologists anguished over the decision. It was felt that seals raised in captivity and then released back into the natural environment might introduce a devastating disease to the native population. This was considered too great a risk.

The aquarium contains a bookshop with a tremendous assortment of titles on the flora and fauna of Hawaii. Restrooms are behind the bookshop area as you face the main gate. The University of Hawaii offers seminars and field trips through the aquarium, everything from guided reef walks to mini-courses in marine biology; information is available at the aquarium.

The Waikiki Aquarium is a very special opportunity for fun and education that will be enjoyed by the entire family. Don't miss it!

Just near the aquarium is the **Waikiki Natatorium,** a saltwater swimming pool built in 1927 as a WW I memorial, which was allowed to decay over the years until it was closed in 1980. Plans are constantly afoot in the House of Representatives calling for a restoration, which may actually start soon.

HONOLULU ZOO

The trumpeting of elephants and chatter of monkeys emanates from the jungle across the street at the Honolulu Zoo, 151 Kapahulu Ave., tel. 923-7723, open daily 8:30 a.m.-4:30 p.m., with special shows in the summer at 6 p.m., admission $3, yearly pass $5. As you walk along or ride the tram, you find the expected animals from around the world: monkeys, giraffes, lions, big cats, a hippo, even a grizzly bear. The Honolulu Zoo has the *only* reptiles in Hawaii—three snakes in the Reptile House. Many islanders love this exhibit, because snakes in Hawaii are so exotic! But the zoo is much more than a collection of animals. It is an up-close escapade through the jungles of Hawaii, where plants, trees, flowers, and vines are named and described. Moreover, the zoo houses Hawaii's indigenous birdlife, which is fast disappearing from the wild: Hawaiian gallinules, coots, hawks, owls, and *nene,* the state bird, which is doing well in captivity, with breeding pairs being sent to other zoos around the world. The zoo is also famous for its Manchurian cranes, extremely rare birds from Japan, and for successfully mating the Galapagos turtle. A **petting zoo** of barnyard animals is great for kids. A concession stand serves typical junk food and soft drinks.

FREE SIGHTS AND CURIOSITIES

On the beach near the Surfrider Hotel are the ***kahuna* stones,** a lasting remnant of old Hawaii. The Hawaiians believed these stones were imbued with mana by four hermaphroditic priests from Tahiti: Kinohimahu, Kahaloamahu, Kapunimahu, and Kapaemahu (*mahu* in Hawaiian signifies homosexuality). They came to visit this Polynesian outpost in ancient times and left these stones for the people, who have held them in reverence for over 600 years. About 40 years ago, a group of local historians went looking for the stones but couldn't find them. Around that time, there was a bowling alley along the beach, and when it was finally torn down, it was discovered that the stones had been incorporated into the foundation. Today, the vast majority of visitors and islanders alike no longer revere the stones, often using them as a handy spot to scrape sand off their feet. *Kupuna* versed in the old ways say that the mana, once put in and strengthened by reverence, is now dissipating.

The **Urusenke Teahouse** is an authentic teahouse donated to Hawaii by the Urusenke Foundation of Kyoto. It is located at 245 Saratoga Rd., which lies along the Waikiki side of Fort DeRussy. Every Wednesday and Friday 10 a.m.-noon, tea master Yoshibuma Ogawa performs the ancient and aesthetic art of *chanoyu* (tea ceremony). The public is invited (free) to partake of the frothy *matcha,* a grass-green tea made from the delicate tips of 400-year-old bushes. To find delight and sanctuary in this centuries-old ritual among the clatter and noise of Waikiki offers a tiny glimpse into the often puzzling duality of the Japanese soul.

As you walk along Kalakaua Avenue, directly across from Waikiki Beach proper is **St. Augustine Catholic Church.** This modernistic building squashed between high-rises is worth a quick look. The interior, serene with the diffused light of stained glass, looks like a series of A-frames.

Believe it or not, you should pass through the McDonald's at the Royal Hawaiian Shopping Center to see a permanent collection of

Hawaiian art on display. Among the exhibits are carvings, paintings, macrame, and featherwork. Many of the works are by Rocky Kaiouliokahihikoloehu Jensen, a famous island artist.

Even if you're not a guest at the following hotels, you should at least drop by their lobbies for a quick look. Dramatically different, they serve almost as a visual record of Waikiki's changing history. The **Moana Hotel,** the oldest, dating from 1901, is a permanent reminder of simpler times when its illustrious clientele would dance the night away at an open-air nightclub suspended over the sea. The Moana houses the Banyan Court, named for the enormous banyan tree just outside. From here, "Hawaii Calls" beamed Hawaiian music to the Mainland by shortwave for 40 years beginning in 1935. In its heyday, the show was carried by over 700 stations. The hotel's architecture is a classic example of the now quaint "colonial style."

Across the street are the giant, modernistic, twin towers of the **Hyatt Regency.** The lobby, like those in most Hyatts, is wonderful, with a huge waterfall and a jungle of plants, all stepped down the series of floors, making an effect like the "Hanging Gardens of Babylon." The **Pacific Beach Hotel,** at 2490 Kalakaua Ave., is a first-rate hotel and a great place to stay in its own right. But if you don't, definitely visit the lobby, where the Oceanarium Restaurant has an immense three-floor-high aquarium holding 280,000 gallons of seawater. The old mafia dons used to send their rivals to "sleep with the fishes"; here, you have an opportunity to dine with the fishes. Usually you go snorkeling to watch the fish eat, but in this particular instance the fish watch you eat.

The **Royal Hawaiian Hotel,** built in 1927 on the site of the old royal beach house, once had fresh pineapple juice running in its fountains. Now surrounded by towering hotels, it's like a guppy in a sea of whales. However, it does stand out with its Spanish-Moorish style, painted in distinctive pink. In the old days, only celebrities and luminaries came to stay—who else could afford $3 per day? Although it's younger than the Moana, many consider it the grande dame of Hawaiian hotels. The entranceway is elegantly old-fashioned, with rounded archways, overstuffed couches, and lowboys. You pass through the lobby on a shocking cerise and green rug. All the rooms are appointed in the trademark pink, with matching towels, sheets, and pillowcases. When you visit the Royal Hawaiian, the most elegant lobby is not where you check in. Rather, turn right from there and follow the long hallway toward the sea. This becomes an open breezeway, with arches and columns in grand style. You'll come to a small circular area in the hotel. Here is its heart, with Diamond Head framed in the distance.

Battery Randolph Military Museum

The museum at Battery Randolph, guarded by the hulks of tanks, is one long corridor where you feel the strength of the super-thick reinforced walls of this once-active gun emplacement. It's located at Fort DeRussy, on the corner of Kalia and Saratoga roads, and offers a free guided tour. Open Tues.-Sun. 10 a.m.-4:30 p.m., tel. 543-2687. The U.S. Battery Randolph once housed two 14-inch coast artillery rifles meant to defend Honolulu and Pearl harbors. The architecture is typical of the Taft Period forts constructed between 1907 and 1920. The battery is listed in the National Register of Historic Places. As you enter there is a shop dedicated to "things military," from flight jackets to wall posters. Walk the halls to learn the military history of Hawaii traced as far back as Kamehameha I. Here are rifles, swords, and vintage photos of Camp McKinley, a turn-of-the-century military station in the shadow of Diamond Head.

A side room holds models of artillery used to defend Waikiki from times when Battery Randolph was an active installation. One room demonstrates "disappearing guns." The gun would raise up and fire and then disappear. The recoil of the gun would lock it back in position, and after it was reloaded a 50-ton counterweight would pop it up ready to fire. The explosive sound would rattle the entire neighborhood so they were seldom test-fired.

Exhibits show the fledgling days of Army aviation in Hawaii when on July 13, 1913, 14 officers began a military flying school. There are beautiful models of military equipment, especially one of an old truck unit. Then comes the ominous exhibit of "Rising Japan" with its headlong thrust into WW II. Hawaii, grossly overconfident, felt immune to attack because of the strong military presence. Photos from the '30s and '40s depict

J.D. BISIGNANI

Waikiki

the carefree lifestyles of visiting celebrities like Babe Ruth and Shirley Temple, which ended abruptly on December 7, 1941, in the bombing of Pearl Harbor.

An entire room dedicated to the Pearl Harbor attack is filled with models of Japanese planes, aircraft carriers, and real helmets and goggles worn by the Zero pilots. Most interesting are the slice-of-life photos of Hawaii mobilized for war: defense workers, sailors, soldiers, entertainers, and street scenes. Pamphlets from the time read, "Know Your Enemies," and there's a macabre photo of people gathered at a stadium to see a demonstration of the devasting effect of flamethrowers that would be employed upon the Japanese enemy. Bob Hope is here entertaining the troops, while a 442nd Regimental Battle Flag bears testament to the most decorated unit in American history, comprised mostly of *nisei* Japanese from Hawaii. Then come photos and exhibits from the soul-wrenching conflicts in Korea and Vietnam. Finally a room, like a whispering tomb, tells of the heroics of Hawaiian soldiers who have been awarded the Congressional Medal of Honor, almost all posthumously.

Make sure to go outside to the upper-level exhibit where you'll see one of the old guns still pointing out to sea, which seems incongruous with sunbathers just below on the quiet and beautiful stretch of beach. On the upper deck are depth charges, torpedoes, and shells, along with a multimedia slide show. Your eyes will take a few minutes to refocus to the glorious sunshine of Waikiki after the cold gloom of the bunker. Perhaps our hearts and souls could refocus as well.

WAIKIKI BEACHES AND PARKS

In the six miles of shoreline from Gray's Beach fronting the Halekulani Hotel in central Waikiki to Wailupe Beach Park in Maunalua Bay just east of the Kahala Hilton, there are at least 17 choice spots for enjoying surf activities. Most of the central Waikiki beaches are so close to each other you can hardly tell where one ends and another begins. All of these are generally gentle, but as you head east the beaches get farther apart and have their own personalities. Sometimes they're rough customers. As always, never take *moana* for granted, especially during periods of high surf. To get information on the presence of lifeguards, call Honolulu Water Safety, tel. 922-3888; handicapped people can get information on specialized beach facilities and parks by calling 586-8121. Now that you've finally arrived at a Waikiki beach, the one thing left to do is kick back and R-E-L-A-X.

Waikiki Beach stretches for two miles, broken into separate areas. A multitude of concession stands offer everything from shave ice to canoe rides. It's not news that this beach is crowded. Sometimes when you look at the rows of glistening bodies, it appears that if one person wants to tan his other side, everybody else has to roll over with him. Anyone looking for seclusion here is just being silly. Take heart—a big part of the fun is the other people.

Umbrella stands set up along Waikiki Beach fronting Kalakaua rent boogie boards, surfboards, paddle boats, and snorkel gear. They're convenient, but their prices are much higher ($5 for two hours) than those at many shops offering the same equipment (see "Sports and Recreation" in the Oahu Introduction). The guys by the big banyan tree are slightly cheaper than those set up by the breakwater just before Kapiolani Park. However, all offer decent prices for surfing lessons ($15 per hour including board and lesson, standing guaranteed), and a $5 ride on an outrigger canoe, which gets you three waves and about 20 minutes of fun. Bargaining is acceptable.

Gray's Beach

This westernmost section's name comes from Gray's-by-the-Sea, a small inn once located here. The narrow white-sand beach lies in front of the Halekulani Hotel, which replaced Gray's. Take Lewers Street off Kalakaua Avenue and park along Kalia Road; a right-of-way is between the Reef and Halekulani hotels. The sea is generally mild here and the swimming is always good, with shallow waters and a sandy bottom. Offshore is a good break called **No. 3's,** a favorite with surfers.

Next door is **Royal Moana Beach,** lying between Waikiki's oldest manmade landmarks, the Moana and Royal Hawaiian hotels. Access is unlimited off Kalakaua Avenue. The inshore waters here are gentle and the bottom is sandy and generally free from coral. Offshore are three popular surfing areas, **Popular's, Queen's,** and **Canoes.** Many novices have learned to surf here because of the predictability of the waves, but with so many rookies in the water, and beach activities going on all around, you have to remain alert for runaway boards and speeding canoes.

Waikiki Beach Center And Prince Kuhio Beach Center

When people say "Waikiki Beach," this is the section to which they're referring. Both beaches lie along Kalakaua Avenue, fronted by a long sand-retaining wall called Slippery Wall that creates a semi-enclosed saltwater pool. Here, you'll find surfing, canoeing, snorkeling, and safe year-round swimming along the gently sloping, sandy-bottomed shoreline. There are comfort stations, concession stands, and lifeguards. Be careful of the rough coral bottom at the Diamond Head end of Kuhio Beach. Covered with a coating of slick seaweed, Slippery Wall definitely lives up to its name. Though local youngsters play on the wall, the footing is poor and many knees have been scraped and heads cracked after spills from this ill-advised play. The surf on the seaward side of the wall churns up the bottom and creates deep holes that come up unexpectedly, along with an occasional rip current.

Kapiolani Beach Park

This is the only park along Waikiki with facilities for barbecueing and picnicking. Although it's only a short stroll down the beach from Waikiki, it gets much less use. This is where local families and those in the know come to get away from the crowds. In the park and along the beach are restrooms, volleyball courts, picnic tables, lifeguard towers, a bath house, and a concession stand. Activities include surfing, fishing, snorkeling, and year-round safe swimming. Just be careful of the rocky bottom that pops up unexpectedly here and there. Kapiolani Park incorporates **Sans Souci Beach** at the eastern end. This beach, in front of the Colony Surf and Kamaaina hotels, has unlimited access. Changing facilities are found at the deteriorating Honolulu Natatorium, a saltwater pool built in the '20s. Many families with small children come to Sans Souci because it is so gentle.

The **Natatorium** is in a sad state. Battles rage on whether it should be refurbished or torn down. Unless something has been done by the time you arrive, it's better to avoid its murky waters. Be careful of the rocky areas and dangerous dropoffs along the channel, especially in front of the Natatorium. **Kapiolani Park Center** is the beach closest to Waikiki. The swimming is good here, with the best part at the Waikiki end. The beach is at its widest, and the bottom is gently sloping sand. The area called **The Wall** has been designated a special bodysurfing area. Supposedly, board riders are restricted from this area, but if the surf is good they're guaranteed to break the rules. Experts can handle it, but novices, especially those with runaway boards, are a hazard.

Around Diamond Head

Kaluahole Beach is located at the Waikiki side of Diamond Head. The water conditions are safe year-round, but the beach is small and lies along a seawall. Once a large beach, it was paved over for building purposes. It has one public right-of-way, poorly marked and sandwiched between private homes. It's almost at the end at 3837 Kalakaua Avenue. The surfing in this area is generally good, and the breaks are known as "Tongg's," named after a local family that lived along this shore.

Diamond Head Beach Park is an unlimited-access area along Beach Road (marked). It covers almost two acres of undeveloped shoreline. Unfortunately, the beach is very narrow and surrounded by unfriendly rock and coral. The waters, however, are quite protected and generally safe, except in periods of high surf. This area is good for fishing and finding quiet moments.

Kuilei Cliffs Beach Park lies below Diamond Head Road, with access available from three lookout areas along the road. You must walk down the cliff trails to the beaches below. Here are plenty of secluded pockets of sand for sunbathing, but poor swimming. The surf is generally rough, and the area is always frequented by surfers. Offshore is hazardous with submerged rocks, but this makes it excellent for diving and snorkeling—for experts only! Currents can be fierce, and you can be dashed against the rocks. Whales can sometimes be spotted passing this point, and to add to the mystique, the area is considered a breeding ground for sharks. Most visitors just peer down at the surfers from Diamond Head Road, or choose a spot of beach for peace and quiet.

Farther east is **Kaalawai Beach.** The swimming is good here and generally safe because of a protective reef. Many locals come to this area to fish, and it is good for bodysurfing and snorkeling. The waters outside the reef are excellent for surfing, and produce some of the biggest waves on this side of the island. Access is by public right-of-way, marked off Kulumanu Place; or by a small side road running off Kahala Avenue; or by walking along the shoreline from Kuilei Beach.

Kahala Beach, lying along Kahala Avenue, can be reached by a number of marked rights-of-way located between the high fences of estates in the area. The swimming is not particularly good, but there are plenty of pockets of sand and protected areas where you can swim and snorkel. Local people come to fish, and the surfing is good beyond the reef. The Kahala Hilton is located along this beach at the eastern end. The public can use "their" beach by walking from Kahala Beach. The swimming here is always safe and good because the hotel has dredged the area to make it deeper. Concession stands and lifeguards are provided by the hotel.

Wailupe Beach Park lies on the Waikiki side of Wailupe Peninsula in Maunalua Bay, and is the last beach covered by this chapter. This beach park, clearly marked off the Kalaniana'ole Highway, provides restrooms and picnic facilities. The swimming is safe, but the bottom can have either oozy mud or sharp coral in spots. Be careful of the boat channel surrounding the area because the deep dropoff is very abrupt.

ACCOMMODATIONS

Waikiki is loaded with places to stay: 170 properties holding 30,000 rooms jammed into one square mile. And they come in all categories of hotels and condos, from deluxe to dingy. Your problem won't be finding a place to stay, but choosing from the enormous selection. During peak season (Christmas to Easter and again in summer) you'd better have reservations, or you could easily be left out in the *warm.* The good news is that, room for room, Waikiki is the cheapest place to stay in the state. Hotels along the beach tend to be slightly more expensive than their counterparts on a side street or back lane. The beachfront hotels have the surf at the doorstep, but those a block away have a little more peace and quiet. The following listings are not exhaustive. They couldn't be! They describe just the best in each categoriy, which you can use as a barometer.

INEXPENSIVE

Youth Hostels

Hale Aloha Youth Hostel is located in Waikiki at 2417 Prince Edward St., Honolulu, HI 96815, tel. 926-8313. Walk down Kalakaua until you see the Hyatt Regency. Two streets directly behind it is Prince Edward. Directions are also available at the Airport Information Counter. A dorm-room bunk is $12. Couples only can rent a studio for $25, which has to be reserved at least two weeks in advance with first night's deposit. No credit cards. The business office is open 8-10 a.m. and 5-9 p.m. The hostel closes at 11 p.m. and all must leave daily 10 a.m.-5 p.m. The maximum three-day stay, especially during peak seasons, can sometimes be extended at the discretion of the house parent. Requests must be made before 7:30 p.m. the previous day. Baggage may be left for the day for $1. Key deposits will not be returned if keys are not returned by 10 a.m. Visitors are not allowed at any time; nor are alcohol or smoking. Chores are required. Lockers are available.

Inter Club Hostel Waikiki, at 2413 Kuhio Ave., Honolulu, HI 96815, tel. 924-2636, has kitchen and laundry facilities and a relaxed island-style lounge. You must be an international traveler or an American with an onward-going ticket to bunk here. Rooms are dorm style (five beds in each), $15 per night plus $10 returnable "care deposit"; $45 double rooms, $10 key deposit. They accept reservations.

Hawaiian Seaside Hostel, 419 Seaside and Kuhio, Honolulu, HI 96815, tel. 924-3306, is a private hostel for international travelers, who must show a passport and an onward-going ticket. United States citizens are welcomed if they are travelers bound for a foreign destination (onward-going ticket necessary). Rates are $9.75 for the first night, plus a $5.25 deposit refundable upon checkout. After the first night, the rates go up to $13 per night. Accommodations are in nine mixed dorms, each with five bunks. Each dorm has a complete kitchen and a bathroom, and other helpful amenities include free safe-deposit boxes, free long-term storage, laundry facilities, a lounge with a wide-screen TV, and free videos. The hostel, located on a cul-de-sac, is quiet for being so close to the action, and there is a lanai where you can socialize. Most of the international travelers here are Australians, British, Germans, and Swedes.

When the YHs are full try the **Waikiki Prince** just next door to Hale Aloha YH, at 2431 Prince Edward St., tel. 922-1544. Listed as a hotel, it is perhaps the cheapest in Waikiki at about $25-35 per night during low season.

The **Waikiki Hostel** for now, but their name changes regularly, at 1946 Ala Moana Blvd. no. 212, Honolulu, HI 96815, tel. 949-3382, offers dormitory rooms at $10 the first two nights, $14 thereafter, $90 weekly. All dorm rooms have a/c, cable TV, a fridge, and a bath. The hostel provides laundry facilities and limited cooking facilities along with free tea and coffee, boogie boards, and masks. They'll also shuttle you to and from the airport (free) if their van is running.

Honolulu's YM/WCAs and official American Youth Hostel are near, but not technically in, Waikiki. Find a complete list under "Accommodations" in the Honolulu chapter.

Inexpensive Hotels And Condos

The **Waikiki Hana Hotel** at 2424 Koa Ave., Honolulu HI 96815, tel. 926-8841 or (800) 367-5004, sits behind the massive Hyatt Regency on a quiet side street. The hotel has just 73 rooms, so you won't get lost in the shuffle, and the friendly staff go out of their way to make you feel welcome. The Waikiki Hana is surrounded by high-rise hotels, so there's no view, but the peace and quiet just one block from the heavy action more than make up for it. Rooms start at a very reasonable $80 and go to $115 for a superior with kitchenette. All rooms have telephones, a/c, color TV, and in-room safes, and are gaily appointed with bright bedspreads and drapes. The **Super Chef Restaurant,** on the ground floor of the hotel, is one of the best in Waikiki for atmosphere, food, and very reasonable prices. On-site parking is another good feature in crowded Waikiki. For a quiet, decent, but basic hotel in the heart of Waikiki, the Waikiki Hana can't be beat.

The **Waikiki Beachside Apartment Hotel,** at 2556 Lemon Rd., Honolulu, HI 96815, tel. 923-9566, is owned and operated by Mr. and Mrs. Wong, who keep a close eye on who they admit, as they run a very "decent" clean hotel. They rent weekly and monthly, charging $285-1000, off-season cheaper. Per diem rooms are sometimes available, but you have to speak to Mrs. Wong first. Furnished units have full kitchens and baths with twin beds and a convertible sofa, and accommodate up to three people at no extra charge. There are laundry facilities, but no maid service is available. Reservations are reluctantly accepted (they like to see you first), and parking is extra. Mrs. Wong says that they are going to renovate the hotel because it has become run-down. There are no firm plans for completion, but when and if they are carried out, the rates will go up. Be advised!

The **Outrigger Coral Seas Hotel,** at 250 Lewers St., Honolulu, HI 96815, tel. 923-3881 or (800) 367-5170, is an old standby for budget travelers. This is the epitome of the economy tourist hotel and houses **Perry's Smorgy.** It's one of the Outrigger Hotels, and seems to get all the hand-me-downs from the others in the chain. There's a restaurant, cocktail lounge, TV, pool, and parking. Rates are an economical $65-75, extra person $15, and just a few dollars more for a kitchenette. Not to everyone's taste, but with plenty of action, and the beach is only a few steps away.

The **Edgewater Hotel,** at 2168 Kalia Rd., Honolulu, HI 96815, tel. 922-6424, is another budget standby in the palpitating heart of Waikiki. Rates begin at a reasonable $45 s, to $110 for a suite; $15 extra person. Facilities include a swimming pool, a good Italian restaurant, parking, TV, and maid service. Kitchenettes cost slightly extra.

The **Royal Grove Hotel,** at 151 Uluniu Ave., Honolulu, HI 96815, tel. 923-7691, run by the Fong family, gives you a lot for your money. You can't miss its "paint-sale pink" exterior, but inside it's much more tasteful. The older and cheaper wing is about $40 per room, the newer upgraded wing with a/c is around $45-75. Most units are studios or one-bedroom apartments with full facilities. A tiny pool in the central courtyard offers some peace and quiet away from the street. The Royal Grove passes the basic tests of friendliness and cleanliness. It's used but not abused. During low season they offer reduced weekly and monthly rates.

Hale Pua Nui, at 228 Beachwalk, Honolulu, HI 96815, tel. 923-9693 or 921-4398, offers very reasonable accommodations a few minutes' walk from Waikiki Beach. A studio apartment with a kitchenette is only $40 off-season, and $55 during peak season, additional person $5. Hale Pua Nui, clean and adequate, is a touch above spartan, with ceiling fans but no a/c, cable TV, phone, and fully equipped kitchen. Unfortunately, the "House of the Big Flower" is a bit wilted. The hotel is geared to repeat clientele, mostly from Canada, who book a year in advance, and not really open to new clientele, especially those who just drop in. If you want a room, call well in advance, and they will send you a form with the house rules (plenty). Remember, too, that there is no elevator, so you must carry your bags to the upper floors.

A two-minute walk puts you on Waikiki Beach when you stay at the **Waikiki Malihini Hotel,** 217 Saratoga Rd., Honolulu, HI 96815, tel. 923-9644 or 923-3095, which bills itself as a "small, plain hotel with no extra frills. Just a place to stay in an excellent location." And that's just what it is. In a semi-quiet area just across from Fort DeRussy, the hotel's 30 units have kitchenettes, daily maid service, fans (no a/c in most units), rental TV, and convenient but not complimentary parking next door. The management, not unfriendly but not overly congenial either, "strongly requests" that you contact them and fill out a card that will inform them of your dates-of-stay, number-in-party, etc., *before* they will make reservations. A well-laid lava-rock wall in front provides privacy for a small picnic area complete with tables and charcoal grills. Rates are studios $45-48, lanai studios $50-55, and one-bedroom apartments $65-75 (some have a/c). There's a three-day minimum stay during peak season, and payment is by *cash only*.

MODERATE HOTELS AND CONDOS

The **Queen Kapiolani Hotel** is at 150 Kapahulu Ave., Honolulu, HI 96815, tel. 922-1941 or (800) 367-5004. With its off-the-strip location and magnificent views of Diamond Head, this is perhaps the best, and definitely the quietest, hotel for the money in Waikiki. You're only seconds from the beach, and the hotel provides a spacious lobby, parking, a restaurant, TV, a/c, shops, and a swimming pool. Rates range $110 standard to $120 for a superior; a few rooms have kitchenettes. The main lobby has been rejuvenated with a $2-million face-lift. The stately marble columns have been redone, new wallpaper has been applied, and the shopping area has been upgraded. The overall effect is open and airy, with the living mural of Diamond Head in the background. Select rooms have been made first-class with new carpeting, draperies, furnishing, and amenities. Most boast a spectacular view of Diamond Head. An excellent choice for the money; for reservations write directly to Hawaiian Pacific Resorts, 1150 S. King St., Honolulu, HI 96814, tel. 531-5235. Also featured, in the Peacock Dining Room, is one of the best buffets in Waikiki (see "Moderate" under "Food" later in this chapter).

You can't beat the value at the **Pacific Monarch Hotel/Condo** located directly behind the Hyatt Regency at 142 Uluniu Ave., Honolulu, HI 96815, tel. 923-9805 or (800) 777-1700. It offers some great features for a moderately priced hotel. Fully furnished studios begin at $95, one-bedroom apartments at $130, all a/c, with on-site parking; standard rooms are available, too. The rooms are bright and cheery with full baths, living/dining areas, and cable TV. End units of each floor are larger, so request one for a large or shared party. The swimming pool, with a relaxing jacuzzi, perches high over Waikiki on the 34th floor of the hotel, offering one of the best cityscapes in Honolulu. The lobby is sufficient but small. It's accented with a lava fountain and two giant brass doors. A security key allows guests through the main door to the elevators. Save money and have a great family experience by setting up temporary housekeeping at the Pacific Monarch.

The **Outrigger Hotels** chain has 23 locations in and around Waikiki offering thousands of rooms. Many of the hotels are on quiet side streets, others are on the main drags, while still more perch on Waikiki Beach. Although most are not luxurious, they do offer good accommodations and all have pools, restaurants, a/c, TV, and parking. Rates vary slightly from hotel to hotel: some have kitchen facilities and cost $75 d to $300 for a suite, $10-15 extra person. Special discounts of 20% are offered to travelers over 50 years old. For information contact Outrigger Hotels Central Reservations, 3443 S. Galena Dr., Denver, CO 80231, tel. (800) 462-6262. Three of their best hotels in Waikiki are the **Outrigger Reef, Outrigger Waikiki** (both on the beach), and **Outrigger Prince Kuhio.**

You can capitalize on the off-beach location of the **Aston Honolulu Prince,** at 415 Nahua St., Honolulu, HI 96815, tel. 922-1616 or (800) 922-7866, where you'll find a hotel/condo offering remarkably good value for your money. The hotel/condo, under the auspices of general manager Charles St. Sure, invites you into its fully furnished one- and two-bedroom suites. All offer a/c, color cable TV, fully equipped kitchens, and daily maid service. Prices begin at $80 for a standard room, $125 one bedroom, and $145 two bedroom, with substantial discounts during low season. The apartments are oversized, with a huge sitting area that includes a sofa bed for extra guests. The Honolulu Prince is not fancy, but it is clean, decent, and family-oriented. A fine choice for a memorable vacation at affordable prices.

The **Breakers Hotel,** 250 Beach Walk, Honolulu, HI 96815, tel. 923-3181 or (800) 426-0494, is a very friendly family-style hotel, where if you're a repeat visitor, the staff remembers your name. Only minutes from the beach, this little gem of a hotel somehow keeps the hustle and bustle far away. Every room has a kitchenette and overlooks the shaded courtyard of coconut and banana trees. The rates for studios are $88-95 s, $91-97 d, additional person $8. The garden suites, which are equipped for up to four people, are $120-146. All units have a full kitchenette, a/c, color TV, room safe, and limited parking. There is also a swimming pool, and the Hotel Cafe Terrace where you can have a snack or light meal.

The **Waikikian Hotel,** 1811 Ala Moana Blvd., Honolulu, HI 96815, tel. 949-5331 or (800) 367-5124, is at the north end of Waikiki near the Ala Moana Boat Harbor and is surrounded by ultramodern high-rise hotels. This character-laden hotel is only two stories, and is an enclave of peace amidst hustle and bustle. There is a feeling of days gone by as you move down the charming walkway through painstakingly cared-for grounds. Ferns, palms, and flowers line the walk, and at night it is accentuated with lighted torches. If you know what to expect you'll be happy with this hotel; not luxury, but a double dip of character. The grounds front the very safe beach of the Hilton Hawaiian Village Lagoon; from there it's a short walk to the waves of Waikiki. Prices are reasonable, beginning at $77, with family suites for $140.

Sometimes you just hit it lucky, and find yourself in a situation where you get more for your money than you expected, and delightfully so. The **Waikiki Beachcomber Hotel,** 2300 Kalakaua Ave., Honolulu, HI 96815, tel. 922-4646, (800) 622-4646 Mainland, or (800) 338-6233 Canada, is definitely one of those *sometimes* things. The Beachcomber, living up to its name, is just a minute from the beach, and the professional and amiable staff knows exactly what you want and how to deliver it. Each guest room, outfitted in rattan furniture and painted in soothing tropical tones, features a private lanai, a/c, TV, phone, and convenient refrigerator. On the property is a pool, the Beachcomber Restaurant (long famous for its live KCCN Aloha Friday Luncheon Buffet), boutique shops, and a lounge for evening relaxation. The rates for guest rooms range from $120 to $280 for a suite, $15 for an additional person, children under 17 free in their parents' room. A fantastic special at only $99 puts you in a city-view room with a rental car included or a breakfast buffet for two. If you want to stay within a budget while having a quality experience, the Beachcomber is a sure bet.

The **Ilima Hotel,** 445 Nohonai St., Honolulu, HI 96815, tel. 923-1877 or (800) 367-5172, is two streets back from the Ala Wai Canal and overlooks the Ala Wai Golf Course. This condo-style hotel is a few blocks from the beach—quiet atmosphere and budget rates. They have just completed a $1.5-million renovation, featuring waveless waterbeds in their deluxe suites. Studio units begin at a reasonable $86, $10 extra person, one bedroom $109, two bedroom $176. All units have full kitchens, a/c, and TV, along with a pool, parking, and maid service. Good value.

Miramar at Waikiki, 2345 Kuhio Ave., Honolulu, HI 96815, tel. 922-2077 or (800) 367-2303, is in the heart of Waikiki. The hotel, refurbished and renamed in the last few years, offers generous-size rooms, with lanai, a pool, a restaurant, a/c, TV, and parking. Rates range $90-105, $20 extra person.

All you have to do is literally roll out of bed, walk out your door, and pick a spot on Waikiki Beach when you stay at the **Aston Waikiki Shores Condominium,** at 2161 Kalia Rd., Honolulu, HI 96815, tel. 926-4733 or (800) 367-2353. Individually owned, each unit differs in decor, but most are tasteful with island-style furnishings, and all are immense. Typical is a one-bedroom laid out with a sitting area, living room, dining area, two baths with dressing rooms, and kitchen complete with microwave, dishwasher, coffeemaker, and garbage disposal. To make your stay more pleasant, there's daily maid service, private lanai, cable TV, in-room washers and dryers, beach towels, and limited parking. Children stay free with their parents. Rates, especially for what you get, are very reasonable; they start at $150 for a studio with deluxe ocean view, and go up to $385 for a two-bedroom deluxe oceanfront unit (10% off-season discount, ask).

A reasonably priced accommodation is the **Coconut Plaza Hotel,** at 450 Lewers St., tel. 923-8828 or (800) 882-9696. Rate for a double during peak season is about $100. Off-season is cheaper, with a special day rate of $50 for bona fide business travelers. A complimentary continental breakfast is offered daily in the lobby. All rooms are fully air-conditioned, and there is a hotel pool.

Twinkling lights descending the residential valleys of the Koolaus with Diamond Head framed in perfect symmetry are an integral part of the natural room decor of the **Aston Waikiki Sunset Hotel,** 229 Paoakalani St., Honolulu, HI 96815, tel. 922-0511, (800) 922-7866 Mainland, or (800) 321-2558 Hawaii, one of Waikiki's newest suite-hotels. Charmingly refurbished from head to toe in 1991, the Waikiki Sunset, although *feeling* like a condominium, offers all the comfort and conveniences of a hotel, including 24-hour front desk service, daily maid service, and amenities like a swimming pool, sauna, tennis court, travel desk, mini-mart, and restaurant. The entrance, cooled by Casablanca fans whirring over marble floors, sets the mood for this charming hotel tucked away only one block from the Waikiki strip. Suites range from comfortable studios at $119, to deluxe two-bedroom units for $315 (penthouse available). Each features a full kitchen outfitted with a large refrigerator, coffeemaker, electric stove and oven, disposal, and complete utensils for in-room cooking and dining. Each also features a private lanai and entertainment center with remote-control color TV, and a tiled bath with a Japanese-style *ofuro,* a soaking tub perfect for the start of a cozy evening. The larger suites have a sitting room, modern and chic with rattan furniture; a bar/breakfast nook; and separate master bedroom. The **Manbow Inn,** on the sixth floor, open 7:30 a.m.-9 p.m., serves breakfast, lunch, and dinner at reasonable prices. The mini-mart, open 7 a.m.-11 p.m., provides everything from suntan lotion to takeout pizza. Here, too, you can rent sporting equipment like snorkel sets and boogie boards, with a 10% discount offered to hotel guests.

Varying shades of Italian travertine marble covered with pink floral carpets, filigreed mirrors, tables of black lacquer bearing Chinese porcelains, and ornate Louis XV chests under cut crystal chandeliers are the signature touches of the chinoiserie decor (combination of Chinese and European) at the **Aston Waikiki Beachside Hotel,** 2452 Kalakaua Avenue, Honolulu, HI 96815, tel. 931-2100, (800) 922-7866 Mainland, (800) 445-6633 Canada, or (800) 321-2558 Hawaii. A Chinese lord and his concubine sit under an umbrella in a hand-painted silk portrait, while two bronze lions guard the marble staircase leading to a formal parlor on the second floor. Here, white silk couches with puffy pillows, a magnificent Chinese folding screen depicting courtly life, and an 18th-century Chinese secretary in red and black lacquer especially made for the "British market" are the decor. Outside, a tiny courtyard serenaded by a bubbling Italian fountain is set with wooden tables protected by canvas umbrellas. Mornings are perfect here with complimentary coffee and croissants. In the 12 floors above, only 77 luxurious rooms await, ranging in price from $160 for a superior to $290 for a VIP oceanfront (ask for discounted specials). Small, but space-consciously designed, the rooms are vibrant with melba peach carpet and wallpaper counterpointed with black. Amenities include air-conditioning or functional windows to catch the Waikiki breeze, an entertainment center with remote-control color TV and VCR, a mini-fridge stocked with a selection of complimentary soft drinks, and a voice mail message system. Your stay is made even more relaxing with twice-daily maid service and turndown service with a special treat left on your pillow, a free morning newspaper, and concierge service for all activities and travel plans. Tastefully decorated, the rooms are appointed with Chinese vases, folding screens painted with birds and flowers, jewelry boxes, and goosedown pillows imported from London. The bathrooms are done in Italian marble and feature glass shower stalls (no baths), floor-to-ceiling mirrors, pedestal sinks with black fixtures from Germany, his-and-her *yukata* (robes), a makeup mirror, a hair dryer, and bath products including shampoo, moisturizer, and French-milled soaps. Ocean-view rooms have their own lanai, but be aware that some inside rooms are windowless.

A tunnel of white thumbergia tumbling from a welcoming arbor leads to the entrance of the **Aston Waikiki Beach Tower Hotel,** 2470 Kalakaua Ave., Honolulu, HI 96815, tel. 926-6400, (800) 922-7866 Mainland, or (800) 321-2558 Hawaii, one of Waikiki's newest mini-luxury suite hotels. A lustrous patina shines from brown-on-tan marble floors, while glass-topped tables of black and gold lacquer hold magnificent displays of exotic blooms, and fancy French mirrors and cut glass chandeliers brighten the small but intimate reception area. Enter your suite through a vestibule of brown marble and glass onto a white carpet leading to a combination dining/living room. This common area, accented with contemporary paintings and highlighted by koa trim, offers a full wet bar, drum and glass tables, high-backed chairs, a pastel rainbow couch, and an entertainment center with remote-control TV. The ultramodern kitchen is complete with a standard-sized refrigerator with ice maker, a rice cooker, a blender, a coffeemaker, a microwave, a four-burner stove and oven, a dishwasher, a double sink, and koa cabinets. The master bedroom has its own entertainment center and private lanai overlooking Waikiki. The bathroom has a double sink, commode, and shower, and a huge walk-in closet holding a complimentary safe, steam iron and board, and washer and dryer. Rates range from $305 for a one-bedroom superior to $475 for a two-bedroom deluxe, with the two-bedroom penthouse at $575, and the two-bedroom Presidential at $800. Special amenities include twice-daily maid service, turndown service, concierge desk, valet parking, paddle tennis court, swimming pool, spa and sauna, and also meeting rooms and a family plan.

Upon arrival, step onto a path of white tile leading through a tiny but robust garden to a translucent dome sheltering the outdoor reception area of the **Aston Waikiki Joy Hotel,** a lotus flower that blooms in the heart of Waikiki, at 320 Lewers St., Honolulu, HI 96815, tel. 923-2300, (800) 922-7866 Mainland, or (800) 321-2558 Hawaii. Blocks of glass; veined marbles in pinks, whites, and grays; and polished chrome make up its petals. Marble steps rise to a veranda, where every morning a complimentary continental breakfast is served accompanied by the soft background chant of a tiny fountain. The hotel, with only 94 rooms, is divided into two towers, the Hibiscus and the Gardenia (housing only suites). It's intimate enough to make everyone feel like an honored guest. Typical rooms in the Hibiscus Tower, $99-125, are amazingly spacious. You enter through a vestibule to find an ultramodern room of slate blue and pastel pink contrasted with a tan Berber carpet. Two accommodating wicker chairs wait to hug you with their overstuffed pillow arms. At the foot of each bed is an ottoman, great for perching on while dressing, and a dresser built in as part of the wall. Each hotel room features a refrigerator and writing desk, which has a believable rendition of Miss Muffet's tuffet as its chair. A king-size bed with a slanted headboard perfectly designed for propping up pillows is the "nerve center" of the room. Here, within easy reach, are a dimmer switch for all lighting, a temperature control, and a phone featuring a personalized voice message system. In front of the bed is an entertainment center with remote-control color TV and a stereo system with tape deck. The bathroom, done in pastel barber stripes, is a sanctuary of relaxation where you can slide every evening into a large and bubbling jacuzzi tub. Each suite in the Gardenia Tower, $120-220, features a bedroom and sitting area complete with couch, and a large private lanai. Suite kitchens have a standard-size refrigerator, two-burner stove, double sink, microwave, toaster, and coffeemaker. Here too, the bathrooms feature the wonderful jacuzzi tub. The Waikiki Joy is also very special because of its 15-room karaoke studio, the largest and most modern in Waikiki (reservations recommended). The karaoke studio features a lounge at the entrance, open weekdays 5 p.m.-2 a.m., weekends until 4 a.m., where you can order exotic drinks, standard cocktails, assorted iced teas, and island-inspired *pu pu* from tofu to breaded calamari sticks. The hotel restaurant is **Cappucino's,** (see "Food") a European-style bistro featuring live entertainment on the weekends. The Waikiki Joy, aptly named, is the epitome of the adage that "wonderful things come in small packages," but in this case, the wonderful thing *is* the package.

DELUXE

Hilton Hawaiian Village

This glorious first-rate hotel, an oasis of tranquility, sits in its own quiet corner of Waikiki. The Hilton, at 2005 Kalia Rd., Honolulu, HI 96815, tel. 949-4321 or (800) 445-8667, is at the far western end of Waikiki, just below Fort

DeRussy. Enter along 200 yards of the private hotel driveway, passing the Village, a small mall with exclusive shopping and dining. Facing you are the Hilton's "towers"—the Tapa, the Diamond Head, the Rainbow, and the prestigious Alii. Rainbow Tower, so called because of the huge multistoried rainbow on the entire side of this building, is, according to the *Guinness Book of World Records,* the tallest ceramic-tile mosaic in the world. All the rooms are deluxe with magnificent views. Amenities include color TV, a/c, self-service bar, refrigerator, 24-hour room service, voice mail, and a safe for personal belongings. Children will also be delighted with the **Rainbow Express,** a year-round program that entertains and educates with everything from hula lessons to a trip to the Honolulu Zoo ($10 half day, $20 full lunch included).

The Alii Tower pampers you even more with a private pool with nightly gourmet *pu pu,* turndown service, fresh flowers, fruit baskets, concierge service, a fitness center, a sauna, and bath accessories. Rates are $195-350 throughout the Village, and $240-375 in the Alii Tower.

The towers form a semicircle fronting the beach, not a private beach because none can be private, but about as private a public beach as you can get. Few come here unless they're staying at the Hilton. It's dotted with palms—tall royal palms for elegance, shorter palms for shade. The property has three pools. The main pool, surrounded by luxuriant tropical growth, is the largest in Waikiki. The lagoon area creates the music of water in bubbling rivulets, tiny waterfalls, and reflecting pools. Ginger, banana trees, palms, ferns, torches, and rock gardens decorate the grounds. The concierge can arrange a guided tour of the grounds (free) by a groundskeeper, who will explain the habitat, life cycle, and characteristics of each plant.

The *action* of Waikiki is out there, of course, just down the driveway, but you don't feel it unless you want to. Relax and enjoy the sunset and background music at any one of 10 lounges like the **Shell Bar,** or in the main foyer where a small, casual bar swings to the tunes of a piano stylist. Exotic and gourmet dining from throughout the Pacific Rim is available at the Village's 10 restaurants, especially the hotel's signature **Bali by the Sea** and **Golden Dragon** restaurants (see "Food").

J.D. BISIGNANI

Hilton Hawaiian Village

As you pull into the driveway you'll see a geodesic dome, like a giant stereo speaker, where headliner John Hirokawa stars in the **Magic of Polynesia,** a magic show and Polynesian extravaganza performed twice nightly. Also, Charo, a superb flamenco guitarist and comedienne, along with her fabulous international "koochie koochie" show, performs in the Tropic Showroom nightly Tues.-Sat. (see "Entertainment" later in this chapter for both). The hotel has everything to keep its "villagers" contented and happy. As a complete destination resort where you can play, relax, shop, dine, dance, and retreat, the Hilton Hawaiian Village knows what it's about.

Halekulani Hotel

The Halekulani Hotel, in mid-Waikiki at 2199 Kalia Rd., Honolulu, HI 96815, tel. 923-2311 or (800) 367-2343, was an experiment of impeccable taste that paid off. A few years ago the hotel was completely rebuilt and refurnished in the belief that Waikiki could still attract the luxury-class visitor, and that belief has proven accurate. Since opening, the hotel has gained international recognition, and has been named a member of the prestigious Leading Hotels of the World, and Preferred Hotels and Resorts Worldwide. The soothing serenade of the Halekulani begins from the moment you enter the porte cochere, where an impressive floral display of protea, anthuriums, orchids, and ferns arranged in the *sogetsu* style of *ikebana* by Kanemoto-san welcomes you. The property was first developed in 1907 by Robert Lewers as a residential grouping of bungalows, none of which survive. However, still preserved is the **Main Building,** dating from the 1930s when the hotel became a fashionable resort owned by Juliet and Clifford Kimball. The Main Building, a plantation-style mansion, houses the hotel's award-winning **La Mer Restaurant; Orchids Dining Room,** serving breakfast, lunch, and dinner; **Lewer's Lounge** for an intimate cocktail and nightly entertainment; and the very genteel **Living Room,** where you can enjoy afternoon tea and watercress sandwiches (see "Classy Dining" under "Food," or "Entertainment").

Notice the Main Building's distinctive "Dickey Roof," patterned after a Polynesian longhouse, perfectly sloped to catch island breezes and repel sudden rain squalls. Wander the grounds to be pleasantly surprised by the full 50% given to open space accented with trimmed lawn, reflecting pools, and bubbling fountains. The **Orchid Pool,** with its signature mosaic orchid, is always inviting and within earshot of the foaming surf. Close by is **House Without a Key,** an indoor/outdoor buffet restaurant also serving light snacks and perhaps the best locale in all of Waikiki for a sunset cocktail. Upon arrival, you are escorted directly to the privacy of your own guest room, where you register. Awaiting you is fine china bearing fresh fruit and complimentary "Bakeshop" chocolates. Each evening, with turndown service, a dainty orchid and delicate shell are left upon your pillow, along with a once-per-week recipe card from one of the fine hotel restaurants. The guestroom itself, entered via a solid teak door and an antechamber, is done in seven shades of white. The floors are covered in rich Berber carpet while the king-size bed is dressed with a distinctive Hawaiian quilt. For ultimate relaxation and added convenience, all of the rooms feature a writing desk, small couch, reclining chair, and marble-topped accessory tables softly lit by Asian-style lamps. A remote-control entertainment center, a mini-fridge, three telephones, an in-room safe, and a collection of wooden and satin covered hangers complete the amenities. Sliding louvered doors lead to a tiled lanai, private and perfect for in-room dining. The bathroom, with floor-to-ceiling tile, features a deep soaking tub, a shower stall, two sinks, a separate commode, and a hair dryer. The louvered and glass doors can be opened so that you have a view from your tub directly past the lanai to Diamond Head in the distance. Prices are $245-425 guest room, $580-3500 suite, and $45 extra person. Additional amenities include a swimming pool, beach service, daily newspapers, free local telephone calls, and a full-service fitness center where you can sign up to go on a fun run with world-class marathon runner Max Telford. The Halekulani awaits you with its version of classic island charm. You won't be disappointed.

Sheraton Moana Surfrider

The Moana, at 2365 Kalakaua Ave., Honolulu, HI 96815, tel. 922-3111 or (800) 325-3535, is the oldest and most venerable hotel in Waikiki. Now operated by Sheraton Hotels, it has recently completed a $50-million upgrade, which has restored the class and beauty for which the Moana has long been famous. More than just recapturing turn-of-the century grandeur, the Moana has surpassed itself by integrating all of the modern conveniences. The original Italian Renaissance style is the main architectural theme, but like a fine opera, it joins a variety of architectural themes that blend into a soul-satisfying finale. The restoration has connected the three main buildings, the Moana, Ocean Lanai, and Surfrider, to form an elegant complex of luxury accommodations, gourmet dining, and distinctive shopping. The renovated Moana, filled with memories of times past, is magical. It's as if you stood spellbound before the portrait of a beautiful princess of long ago, when suddenly her radiant granddaughter, an exact image, dazzling in jewels and grace, walked into the room.

You arrive under the grand columns of a porte cochere, where you are greeted by doormen in

Sheraton Moana Surfrider Hotel

J.D. BISIGNANI

crisp white uniforms and hostesses bearing lei and chilled pineapple juice. The lobby is a series of genteel parlor arrangements conducive to very civilized relaxation. Art, urns, chandeliers, sofas, koa tables, flowers, vases, and pedestaled glass-topped tables wait in attendance. An elevator takes you to the second floor, where a room filled with 80 years of memorabilia whispers names and dates of the Moana's grand past. After a glass of fresh chilled pineapple juice, you are escorted to check-in.

Upstairs, the rooms are simple elegance. Queen-size beds in the Banyan Wing, rattan chairs, and fat fluffy pillows and bedspreads extend their waiting arms. All rooms have a/c, and the Banyan Wing features a remote-control master keyboard for TV, lights, and music. But this is the Moana! Sachet-scented closets hold *yukata* (robes), terry-cloth slippers, and satin hangers. Bathrooms are tile and marble appointed with huge towels and stocked with fine soaps, shampoos, creams, makeup mirrors, and a bathroom scale, which you can hide under the bed.

The first hotel built in Waikiki, the Moana sits right on the beach with one of the best views of Diamond Head along the strip. A swimming pool with sundeck is staffed with attentive personnel, and the activities center can book you on a host of activities, including a classic outrigger canoe ride or a sunset sail on a catamaran. Three restaurants, a grand ballroom, a snack bar, and two lounges take care of all your dining needs. Rooms in the Moana Wing overlook Banyan Court, scene of nightly entertainment that can be chamber music provided by a pianist or harpist. Open the windows, allowing the breezes to billow the curtains while the waves of Waikiki join with the music below in a heavenly serenade. Rooms are $195-315, with suites priced $260-340; $25 each additional person. The Sheraton Moana Surfrider is a superb hotel offering exemplary old-fashioned service.

Royal Hawaiian Hotel

The Royal Hawaiian, second oldest hotel built along Waikiki, at 2255 Kalakaua Ave., Honolulu, HI 96815, tel. 923-7311 or (800) 325-3535, provides an ongoing contemporary experience in turn-of-the-century charm. The Royal Hawaiian has also recently completed a $25-million restoration, which has recaptured the grand elegance of days past. Doors first opened in 1927, at a cost of $4 million, an unprecedented amount of money in those days for a hotel. The Depression brought a crushing reduction to Hawaiian tourism, sending the yearly total of visitors down from a whopping 22,000 to under 10,000 (today more visitors arrive in one day), and the Royal became a financial loss. During WW II, with Waikiki barbwired, the Royal was leased to the Navy as an R and R hotel for sailors from the Pacific Fleet. After the war, the hotel reverted to Matson Lines, the original owner, and reopened in 1947 after a $2-million renovation.

Sheraton Hotels purchased the Royal in 1959, built the Royal Tower Wing in 1969, sold the hotel in 1975, but continued to remain as operating managers.

Original double doors featured one solid door backed by a louvered door so you could catch the ocean breezes and still have privacy. Today, the hotel is fully air-conditioned, so the old doors have been removed and new solid rosewood doors carved in the Philippines have replaced them. Rooms might have four-poster beds, canopies, twins, or kings, depending upon your preference. All rooms have remote-control TV, refrigerators, electronic safes, and computer hookups on telephones for lap-top computers. Furniture is French provincial, with bathrooms fully tiled. Completely renovated rooms in the original section have kept the famous pink motif, but are slightly more pastel. Each has a marble tile bathroom, a brass butler, louvered drawers, and a huge bed. The tall ceilings are even more elegant, with molded plaster cornices. Guests are treated to banana bread on arrival, a daily newspaper, and turndown service with a complimentary late-night sweet treat. Preferential tee-off times at the Makaha Resort are also offered. Each floor of the original Royal has a pool elevator, so guests in beachwear don't clash with the early evening black-tie set. A Hospitality Suite is provided for early morning check-ins or late checkouts and offers complimentary shower facilities, maid service six times during the day, coffeemaking facilities, and a sitting and lounging area.

Some of the prestige suites are truly luxurious and feature huge balconies with tiled floors, where a party of 25 could easily be entertained. Each tastefully carpeted bedrooms boasts a quilt-covered bed heaped with a half-dozen pillows. The huge bathrooms overlook the beach and have a small, built-in jacuzzi. In the massive Governor's Suite is a formal dining room, two huge bedrooms, and two magnificent sitting areas—one a formal parlor, the other an "informal" rec-room. The Royal Towers, an addition dating from 1969, are preferred by many guests because every room has an ocean view. From the balcony of most, you look down onto the swimming pool, the beach, palm trees, and Diamond Head in the distance. A basic guest room is $235-425, with suites ranging from $350 to over $1600.

If you stay at the Royal Hawaiian, you can dine and sign at the Moana Surfrider, Sheraton Waikiki, or Princess Kaiulani, all operated by Sheraton Hotels. One of the best features of the Royal, open to guest and nonguest, is the remarkable luau every Monday night (see "Hawaiian Foods" under "Food and Drink" in the Out and About chapter), and the extraordinary food and entertainment provided Tues.-Sat. by the Brothers Cazimero in the hotel's famous and elegant Monarch Dining Room (see "Entertainment" later in this chapter). The Royal Hawaiian, a Waikiki classic, is worth a visit even if you don't stay there. (See "Sights" earlier in this chapter.)

Hawaiian Regent Hotel

The Hawaiian Regent, at 2552 Kalakaua Ave., Honolulu, HI 96815, tel. 922-6611 or (800) 367-5370, has a long history of treating guests like royalty. The hotel now stands on what was the original site of Queen Liliuokalani's summer cottage. The Regent was the first major Hawaiian project of master designer Chris Hemmeter, famed for his magnificent Westin Kauai and Hyatt Regency Waikoloa hotels. The grand tradition of the hotel is reflected in the open sweeping style that marks a Hemmeter project. After almost two decades, the Regent appears extremely modern because its design was so visionary when it was built. With almost 1,400 units, the hotel ranks as the third-largest hotel in Hawaii after the Hilton Hawaiian Village and the Sheraton Waikiki. Rates are from $135 for a standard room to $695 for a deluxe suite. Children are especially taken care of with the "Keiki K.A.I. Club," a summer program; and honeymooners can choose a junior suite with special amenities for a reduced price. All rooms are oversized and include cable TV, a/c, nightly turndown service, and in-room safes. You can step across the street to mingle with the fun-seekers on Waikiki Beach, or relax at one of the hotel's two pools. A championship Laykold tennis court is open from sunrise to sunset, with lessons and rackets available. The hotel offers a variety of exclusive shops in an off-lobby mall area, including Shirokiya and Sandcastles for alohawear and evening wear. An on-site beauty shop and Japanese acupressure/massage service can revitalize you after a hard day of fun in the sun. The Regent is renowned for its fine dining, entertainment, and late-night disco. The **Lobby Bar** is a perfect spot at which to perch while relaxing to Hawaiian music. The **Cafe Regent,** an open-air restaurant just off the main lobby, is open for breakfast, buffet, and lunch selections 6 a.m.-2:30 p.m. The **Tiffany Restaurant,** dinner only, has casual dining in an elegant atmosphere, with a stained-glass ceiling and shuttered windows (see "Food"). The **Ocean Terrace,** designed for kicking back and watching life go by, is a poolside bar serving sandwiches and hamburgers at very good prices. The premier restaurant of the hotel, and one of Waikiki's consistently best, is award-winning **The Secret,** previously known as the Third Floor (see "Food"), where you not only dine in Polynesian splendor, but are treated to a magnificent selection of wines collected by Richard Dean, one of only two sommeliers in all of Hawaii.

Enjoy a daily international buffet or spectacular Sunday brunch at **The Summery,** or a traditional Japanese meal at the **Regent Marushin.** You won't be told to hush while you dance or relax to the sounds of live music in **The Library.** And, if you have "dancing feet" take them to **The Point After,** one of Waikiki's swingingest high-tech discos, which will rock you until the wee hours. If you're after peace and quiet, head for the **Garden Courtyard,** a multipurpose area in the center of the hotel. Sit among flowers and full-grown coconut and bamboo trees. Every Monday, Wednesday, and Friday, 10 a.m.-noon, learn lei-making, hula, or Hawaiian checkers from *kupuna* who come just to share their *aloha.* The Hawaiian Regent is a first-class hotel that really knows how to make you feel like a visiting monarch. Rule with joy!

Park Plaza Waikiki

While the valets park your car, climb the marble staircase or take the chrome and glass-etched escalator one floor to the reception area where Jun Keneko's mural, *The Hawaii Wall,* fashioned from colorful tiles, black-and-white painted stripes, and precisely placed painted dots, will mirror your excitement at being in Hawaii. The Park Plaza Waikiki, 1956 Ala Moana Blvd., Honolulu, HI 96815, tel. 941-7275, (800) 367-6070, or (800) 437-7275, one of Waikiki's newest hotels, has only been open since 1992. The main lobby, mostly in tile, is bright and colorful with

J.D. BISIGNANI

Royal Hawaiian Hotel

strong straight lines. Listen for the tinkling notes of a player piano that will lead you to the **Heliconia Bar,** where comfortable leather stools equipped with arm- and backrests are perfect for an afternoon's lounging. Along the bar's walls are original Picasso porcelains: magnificent, provocative, and stunningly simple. Among the works are practical serving plates named *Three Sardines* and a water pitcher shaped like a human face. On the second floor is a reading room with papers from around the world, a pool where room service will deliver snacks and sandwiches, and a complete fitness room where you can exercise or schedule a massage after winding down in the sauna. An entire wing called **The Gallery** is designated an official extension of the Contemporary Museum, and displays the best by Hawaiian artists, with exhibits changing every eight weeks.

The hotel has 313 rooms, including 45 suites that all feature air-conditioning, private lanai, twice-daily maid service, in-room refreshment centers (which include wet bars and complimentary coffee service), in-room safe, hair dryers, bathrobes, daily newspaper, three telephones, voice mail, and remote-control TV and VCR. The Park Plaza also welcomes business travelers with its executive business center, which provides mail service, cellular phones, fax service, and computer hook-ups. There is a splendid meeting facility and a concierge service that will take care of anything from renting snorkel gear to getting you a helicopter ride. Rates are: $120 standard, city or ocean view; $140 superior, city view; $160 deluxe. The Plaza suites are $200-240, with luxury suites going for $400-500; and the grand luxury Royal Amethyst Suite goes for $2000; additional person $25. Corporate rates are available, and children 18 years of age and under stay free when sharing. Rollaway beds and cribs are also complimentary.

In a standard to deluxe room, you enter the wall-to-wall carpeted guest room through a vestibule of textured wallpaper and white-on-tan marble to find a king-size bed with upholstered headboard flanked by two pine end tables, and an armoire that functions as the entertainment center. The small and efficient bathroom features a tub or choice of standard shower or hand-held shower, a pedestal sink, and a fine collection of toiletries. Hotel suites on the top floor, featuring butler service, are named after gemstones. A typical suite, huge by any standard, has a magnificent master bedroom where you can't help feeling like an honored guest in a king-size bed with recessed headboard specially designed to accommodate pillows so that the entire bed becomes a grand chaise lounge from which you can enjoy the view or the private entertainment center. The living area is a combination of dining room complete with oak table, and parlor with beautifully upholstered chairs, a writing desk, a sectional sofa that doubles as a lounge, another entertainment center, and a full wet bar. The bathroom contains a wonderful jacuzzi tub. The Park Plaza, because of its "off the strip" location, is one of the most reasonably priced luxury-class hotels in Waikiki.

Hawaii Prince Hotel

The dynamic seascape of tall-masted ships anchored in the Ala Wai Yacht Harbor is reflected in the shimmering, pink-tinted glass towers of the Hawaii Prince Hotel, at 100 Holomoana St., Honolulu, HI 96815, tel. 956-1111 or (800) 321-6248, the city's newest luxury hotel. Opposite the harbor, and through the main reception area, ultramodern with burnished chrome and lustrous marble, are framed in a sweep of curved glass the busy streets of the city. The twin towers, Diamond Head and Ala Moana, are scaled by a glass elevator affording wide-angled vistas of the Honolulu skyline. Decorated in green and tan with light pine paneling, each room features an ocean view, a marble-topped desk with full mirror, a/c, functional windows, and a full entertainment center with remote-control color TV and VCR. Each room also has its own refrigerator, walk-in closet with complimentary safe and terry-cloth robes, and a king-size bed with fluffy down pillows. The marble bathrooms have separate shower stalls, tubs, and commodes with a full set of toiletries, lighted makeup mirrors, and hair dryers. Rates are from $200 for an Oceanfront Marina room to $330 for an Oceanfront Top room (floors 30-33), while suites range $450-2500, $35 extra person. Special business rates are offered (ask when booking). The Prince Three-Night Special at $550 double occupancy comes with a daily full American breakfast for two, airport limousine transfer, and unlimited golf package. Great deal! Ride the elevator to the fifth floor, where you will find a keyhole-shaped pool and canvas shade umbrellas overlooking the harbor below. Other amenities include three excellent restaurants—the Takanawa, Prince Court, and Hakone (see "Food")—a small but adequate fitness room, turndown service, valet parking, and a Waikiki/Ala Moana Shuttle. The Hawaii Prince boasts its own golf course, the **Hawaii Prince Golf Club,** the only one of its kind belonging to a Waikiki hotel. Located at Ewa Beach, 35 minutes away by complimentary shuttle, the Arnold Palmer-designed 27-hole championship course (see the "Golf Courses of Oahu" chart in the Oahu Introduction) includes a fully equipped golf shop, practice range, putting greens, chipping greens, locker and shower facilities, clubhouse dining, and tennis courts (special golf packages available). The Hawaii Prince, located at the "gateway to Waikiki," is away from the action of the frenetic Waikiki strip, but close enough to make it easily accessible.

Kahala Hilton

Cast-up treasures of sand-tumbled glass is the theme captured in the distinctive, multihued chandeliers that hang from the 30-foot vaulted ceilings of the grand hallway, the entrance to the Kahala Hilton. Long considered a standard-setter for Hawaiian deluxe hotels, the Kahala Hilton, 5000 Kahala Ave., Honolulu, HI 96816, tel. 734-2211 or (800) 367-2525, is not technically in Waikiki, but in Kahala, an exclusive residential area just east of Diamond Head. The hotel, built 30 years ago, is proud that most of its key employees have been here from the first days and that they have formed lasting friendships with guests who happily return year after year. Surrounded by the exclusive Waialae Country Club (not even hotel guests are welcome unless they are members), the hotel gives a true sense of peace and seclusion and rightly boasts a "Neighbor Island Experience" only minutes from bustling Waikiki. A grand staircase fashioned from lava rock wears a living lei of green ferns and purple orchids, as it descends to the **The Maile Lounge,** a formal restaurant, and the last of its kind that still offers dinner dancing. The menu features appetizers like fresh sashimi, Russian caviar, tender breast of duck, and seared fresh foie gras. Soups can be lobster bisque or gazpacho followed by a Maile salad or Caesar salad. Sumptuous entrees are Maine lobster, swordfish, fresh catch prepared various ways, and specialties like roast duckling, chicken Wellington, and roast rack of lamb Provençale. The hotel's informal **Plumeria Cafe** is famous for its impossible-to-resist pastries, while the seaside **Hala Terrace,** open for breakfast, lunch, and dinner, hosts the legendary **Danny Kaleikini Show** (see "Entertainment"). A beach shack offers all kinds of poolside snacks and boasts the best hamburgers on Oahu.

The hotel, fronting sheltered Maunalua Bay, features a perfect crescent beach, swimming pool, and beach cabana. All water-sports gear is available, including kayaks, paddleboats, and scuba gear (free lesson daily). Behind, a waterfall cascading from a free-form stone wall forms a rivulet that leads to a dolphin lagoon (feeding daily at 11 a.m., 2 p.m., and 4 p.m.) and a series of saltwater ponds teeming with reef fish.

Average rooms are extra-large and feature tropic-perfect parquet floors, done in light pastels in a nouveau-European style. All feature either an ocean view or sweeping mountain view that overlooks the manicured golf courses. The marble-tiled bathrooms are also extra-large and await you with *yukata* robes. Each bathroom features a "lady's side" with a *rightfully* larger dressing area, makeup mirror, hair dryer, personal sink, and soaking tub, while the "man's side" holds a mini-fridge and shower stall. Rates are $180-495 d, $495-1800 for a suite. The Kahala Hilton isn't for everyone, but there's no doubt that you get all that you pay for. Recently, because of a lease snafu, the hotel was put up for sale. With the new owners will come extensive renovations that will preserve the spirit and taste so well earned by the classic hotel, but that at the same time will make it glamorous once again.

FOOD

The streets of Waikiki are an international banquet, with over a dozen cuisines spreading their tables for your enjoyment. Because of the culinary competition, you can choose restaurants in the same way that you peruse a smorgasbord, for both quantity and quality. Within a few hundred yards are all-you-can-gorge buffets, luau, dinner shows, fast foods, ice cream, and jacket-and-tie restaurants. The free tourist literature runs coupons, and placards advertise specials for breakfast, lunch, and dinner. Bars and lounges often give free *pu pu* and finger foods that can easily make a light supper. As with everything in Waikiki, its restaurants are a close-quartered combination of the best and the worst, but with a little effort it's easy to find great food, great atmosphere, and mouthwatering satisfaction.

Note: At many of the moderately priced restaurants listed below and at all of the expensive restaurants *reservations are highly recommended.* It's much easier to make a two-minute phone call than it is to have your evening spoiled, so please call ahead. Also, many of the restaurants along the congested Waikiki strip provide valet parking (usually at no charge), or will offer validated parking at a nearby lot. So check when you call to reserve. Attire at most Hawaiian restaurants is casual, but at the better restaurants it is dressy casual, which means closed-toe shoes, trousers, and a collared shirt for men, and a simple but stylish dress for women. At some of the very best restaurants you won't feel out of place with a jacket, but ties are not usually worn. For a list of **luau** in greater Honolulu, including Waikiki, see "Luau" under "Hawaiian Foods" in the "Food and Drink" section of the Out and About chapter.

INEXPENSIVE

Eggs And Things, at 1911 Kalakaua Ave., just where it meets McCully, tel. 949-0820, is a late-night institution open from 11 p.m. until 2 p.m. the following afternoon. A number of discos are just around the corner, so the clientele in the wee hours is a mix of revelers, hotel workers, boat captains, and even a hooker or two. The decor is wooden floors and Formica tables, but the waitresses are top-notch and friendly. The food is absolutely excellent and it's hard to spend over $10. "Daily" specials are offered 1-2 a.m., while the morning special 5-8 a.m. gets you three pancakes and two fresh eggs cooked as you like them for just a few dollars. Waffles and pancakes are scrumptious with fresh fruit or homemade coconut syrup. Besides the eggs and omelettes, the most popular item is the fresh fish usually caught by the owner himself, Mr. Jerry Fukunaga, who goes out almost every day on his own boat. It's prepared Cajun-style, or sautéed in garlic and butter, with two fresh eggs and a choice of pancakes, rice, or home-fried potatoes. Prices vary according to market price. Casual attire is acceptable, and BYO wine or beer is okay.

Around the corner is **The Dynasty Restaurant,** tel. 947-3771, at 1778 Ala Moana Blvd., in Discovery Bay across from the Ilikai Hotel. They have an enormous menu of Chinese cuisines that is acceptable but not memorable. They are friendly and courteous, and open daily 10 a.m.-6 a.m. For a very late-night repast after "doing the town," their food definitely hits the spot.

Almost across the street and tucked into a nook close to the Hilton Hawaiian Village is the **Saigon Cafe,** at 1831 Ala Moana Blvd., tel. 955-4009, open daily 6:30 a.m.-10 p.m. The Saigon Cafe is a friendly, meticulously clean, unpretentious, family-run affair that definitely offers "budget gourmet" food. Order tureens of soup for two, spiced with lemongrass and hot garlic sauce, and floating with dollops of seafood, chicken, beef, tofu, or pork, for under $7. Roll your own spring rolls, which come with slices of meat, fresh vegetables, mint, dipping sauces, and transparently thin rice paper that you dip in water to soften before rolling away. Noodle dishes are large and hearty, while breakfast brings an assortment of eggs, pancakes, and waffles. It's hard to spend more than $10 on a meal that is not only delicious, but fresh, made to order, and healthy as well. Great choice.

Da Smokehouse, 470 Ena Rd., tel. 946-0233, open daily 11:30 a.m.-midnight, is one of those places where the food is excellent, but you wouldn't want to eat there. Why? Because it is primarily a takeout restaurant with only a few booths stuck in the back where *da* smoke and *da* grease from *da* wood-fired smoker is *da* decor. Actually, owner Shirley Jones has recently moved *da* wood-fired smoker out back and added a few new tables. *Da* decor is now compromised. Next will come color-coordinated tableware. God forbid! Your choices are smoked beef, pork, chicken, or ham served picnic style, with two choices of sides including homemade potato salad, baked beans, rice, or coleslaw. Price ranges are chicken, smoked ham, or smoked beef brisket sandwiches for $6; one-quarter barbecue chicken for $5.05; grilled ham, pork spareribs, or beef back ribs for $10.45; or a side of pork for $24. The combo plate of all of the above, which can easily feed four, is only $20. No liquor, so BYO. Free delivery makes Da Smokehouse a perfect alternative to inflated room-service prices at surrounding hotels, or for a home-cooked dinner in your condo. You'll love it.

Ena Restaurant, 432 Ena Rd., tel. 951-0818, open daily 10 a.m.-11:30 p.m., is a small Chinese restaurant with little atmosphere, but with good food at good prices. Appetizers and soups include crispy won ton $2.95, chicken salad $5.95, and scallop soup $2.95. Lunch specials like lemon chicken or beef with vegetables are $4.75; while entrees like mixed seafood and vegetables, fillet of fish in hot red sauce, roast duck, twice-cooked Sichuen-style pork, or Hunan-style tofu are $5.95-8.95. The Ena Restaurant, away from the hustle and bustle, is a good choice for a basic meal with no frills.

Ruffage Natural Foods, at 2442 Kuhio, tel. 922-2042, is one of the very few natural food restaurants in Waikiki. They serve regular as well as nonfish sushi, a wide assortment of tofu sandwiches, natural salads, tofu burgers, fresh island fruits, and smoothies. Everything is homemade, and they try to avoid, as much as possible, processed foods. Just about everything on the menu is less than $5. It's a hole-in-the-wall that's easy to miss. A few tables outside under a portico is the ambience.

Ezogiku is a chain of Japanese restaurants. Open till the wee hours, these no-atmosphere restaurants serve inexpensive hearty bowls of Sapporo *ramen* (renowned as the best), curry rice, and *gyoza.* They have multiple locations in and around Waikiki at 2083 Kuhio Ave., 2420 Koa Ave., 2546 Lemon Rd., and 2141 Kalakaua Avenue. Ezogiku is a no-frills kind of place. Small, smoky, counter seating, and totally authentic. They're so authentic that on their dishes they spell *ramen* as *larmen.* You not only eat inexpensively, but you get a very authentic example of what it's like to eat in Japan . . . cheaply. Eat heartily for around $6.

The Jolly Roger is an American standard restaurant with a Hawaiian flair. If you're after good old-fashioned tuna salad sandwiches, hot roast beef, a tostada even, or just plain soup and salad, this would be your best bet in Waikiki. The Jolly Roger has two locations, at 2244 Kalakaua (always too crowded so the service suffers), and 150 Kaiulani, where it's slightly quieter. Actually the Kaiulani restaurant borders on tasteful, with a dark green decor accented with bronze, pleasant booth seating, and a profusion of ferns and hanging plants. Both are open 6:30 a.m.-1 a.m. Breakfasts are waffles, pancakes, omelettes, and meats, but try their orange bread as standard or French toast. A lunch special is hamburger steak for $4.95. Dinners are well under $10. Happy hour is 6 a.m.-6 p.m., when exotics are poured for $1.75, draft beer $1.50; free *pu pu* from 4-6 p.m. Nightly entertainment in the bar section, especially The Blue Kangaroo at the Kalakaua Ave. Jolly Roger (see "Entertainment" below).

Man Lee's Chinese Restaurant, 124 Kapahulu, tel. 922-6005, is a basic Chinese restaurant that offers daily lunch and dinner specials. The atmosphere is quiet since it's around the corner from most of the action, and the food is acceptable but not great. A belly-filler only.

Wong and Wong, at 1023 Maunakea, tel. 521-4492, is a simple and basic Chinese restaurant where you can have a good and filling meal at a reasonable price. Many people who live and work in and around Waikiki choose to go here for Chinese food.

Perry's Smorgy, at 2380 Kuhio Ave., tel. 926-9872, and at the Coral Seas Hotel, 250 Lewers St., tel. 923-3881, is the epitome of the budget traveler's "line 'em up, fill 'em up, and head 'em out" kind of restaurant. There is no question that you'll waddle away stuffed, but forget about any kind of memorable dining experience. When you arrive, don't be put off by the long lines. They move! First, you run a gauntlet of salads, breads, and potatoes, in the hopes that you'll fill your plate. Try to restrain yourself. Next comes the meat, fish, and chicken. The guys serving up the roast beef are masters of a whole lot of movement and very little action. The carving knife whips around in the air, but does very little damage to the joint of beef. A paper-thin slice is finally cut off and put on your plate with aplomb. The carver then looks at you as if you were Oliver Twist asking for more. Added pressure comes from the long line of tourists behind, who act as if they have just escaped from a Nazi labor camp. The breakfast buffet is actually very good, with all the standard eggs, meats, juices, and rolls, and the food in general, considering the price, is more than acceptable. You can't complain.

Pizzeria Uno, at 2256 Kuhio (and Seaside), tel. 926-0646, is part of a small chain that allows each of its locations to be individual, although the deep-dish "Chicago-style" pizza remains the same. Open daily 11 a.m.-midnight, live entertainment Wed.-Sat., express lunch Mon.-Fri. 11 a.m.-3 p.m., with specials including soup or salad. Appetizers like pizza skins, pizza-flavored potato wedges with onions and zesty cheese for $4.75, and individual-size pizzas for $5.95 keep prices down. Large pizzas like Spinoccoli are flavored with spinach, fresh broccoli, a blend of cheeses, and a little garlic for $10.95. Also, burgers and sandwiches, with names like The Big Frankie, not a teenie-weenie, mark Pizzeria Uno as a casual, fun-filled restaurant. Happy hour, 11 a.m.-6 p.m., is good value with draft beer at 95 cents and all tropical drinks at $1.95. Breakfast is a "sunrise special," two golden-brown pancakes, two strips of bacon, and an egg for $1.99, 6 a.m.-noon. Modern and upbeat with black-and-white decor, this place is on the beaten track, but worth a stop.

The **Waikiki Seafood and Pasta Co.** is at the Outrigger Surf Hotel, 2280 Kuhio Avenue. Dinners are good but not memorable, and range from inexpensive to reasonable. Fresh pasta includes golden-herb pasta for $5.95 and pasta of the day for $6.95. Other dishes are calamari marinara ($9.95), veal picatta ($12.95), and calamari steak Italiana ($10.95). Specials like vegie lasagna are $6.95; the most expensive is veal parmigiana at $14. Good value, and acceptable food. A change from deep-fried mahimahi.

Peking Garden, 307 Royal Hawaiian Ave., tel. 922-3401, is a hole-in-the-wall eatery just behind the Waikiki Medical Center heading *mauka*. They serve Chinese-American food basically in the form of filling plate lunches for around $3.50. A good choice is the Peking fried chicken.

Shorebird Beach Broiler, open for breakfast, lunch, and dinner (from 5 p.m.), is on the beach behind the Outrigger Reef Hotel at 2169 Kalia Rd., tel. 922-2887, giving this budget restaurant the best gourmet location in all of Waikiki. Here you'll find a limited but adequate menu of cook-your-own selections for under $15 (discount tickets save you more). Walk through the lobby to the beach for a remarkable sunset while dining. Included is a good, fresh salad bar of vegetables and fruits. Beverages are included, the setting is wonderful, and the value excellent, but you do pay extra for bread. Karaoke is offered nightly for all those Don Ho "wannabes."

Ferdinand's, in the Coral Reef Hotel, 2299 Kuhio Ave., tel. 923-5581, is a no-nonsense place running specials and discount tickets. Basically it's an American standard restaurant with a Hawaiian flavor. An attempt is made at entertainment, a Don Ho clone singing in the background. The food is decent but not fabulous; with discounts two can eat for around $15. Besides inexpensive food, they have inexpensive drinks at happy hour, beers $1 or $1.25. They also have free *pu pu* 4-6 p.m. The breakfast special is two pancakes or toast and jelly with bacon or sausage, and an egg any style for $2.99.

The **Holiday Inn,** at 2570 Kalakaua Ave., has very reasonable basic American food in the street-level dining room. Breakfast specials for $1.99 bring you pancakes, eggs, and bacon. Dinner features specials for $10 and under, like roast beef for $8.95.

Hamburger Mary's, at 2109 Kuhio, tel. 922-6722, has two claims to fame. It serves home-style food at reasonable prices and has long been famous as a gay and lesbian hangout. The decor, given the open structure of the building facing Kuhio, is actually quite nice. The front is a terrace with a brick floor, round tables, and wrought-iron chairs. The *inside* area has a little grass shack motif, with curios hanging from the ceiling—old glass bottles, chandeliers, a flying angel, even an old surfboard. The back room holds a pool table and a dance floor. Rock and roll is always happening. Breakfast is served all day long. At lunch they feature salads such as a fresh garden salad for $5.25, or a "stuff your own" (your choice of papaya, avocado, or tomato stuffed with chicken, tuna, cream cheese, or cheddar cheese) for $7.25. Big, hearty Hamburger Mary sandwiches are the Mary burger ($4.25), avocado burger ($6.25), and meatless sandwiches like avocado or cheddar cheese (under $6). Soups and sides are plentiful, but try a bowl of homemade beef chili for $3.50. A great people-watching spot with good food at moderate prices.

Waikiki Wailana Restaurant, 2211 Kuhio Ave., in the Outrigger Waikiki Malia Hotel, tel. 923-7621, open 24 hours, offers daily dinner specials for around $7.95. Included is a crisp salad bar and a huge, well-baked potato. The beverages are not included, but for the price, the food is a good value.

The Islander Coffee House, on Lewers St., tel. 923-3233, in the Reef Towers Hotel, open daily 6 a.m.-midnight, has inexpensive breakfasts of two pancakes, eggs, and bacon for $2.69. They also offer steak and eggs Benedict for $4.29, chef's salad for $6, hamburgers for under $5, and inexpensive specials every day. No dining experience whatsoever, but down-home prices in the heart of Waikiki.

The **Mongolian Barbecue,** at the Kuhio Mall, 2301 Kuhio Ave., tel. 923-2445, open daily 11 a.m.-10 p.m., would make Genghis Khan smile. He could feed his army for peanuts. There is no decor, but this is a very good and inexpensive place to eat. For $13.95 you get the Full Mongolian, for which you make a selection of beef, chicken, pork, lamb, vegies, sauces, and spices from chilled serving trays. Then you watch them cook your order in the fire pit. Included are rice and a famous, homemade sesame bun. If you've got the room, you can go back for a second round. Children under 12 get the same treatment for $8.95. If it sounds like too much, try the Quick Mongolian for $6.95, which is the same but the items are selected for you by the servers, with no seconds. The Mini-Mongolian for $5.95 is your choice of beef, lamb, chicken, or pork with vegies, served with rice or homemade bun. Limited fish selections are available as well. Good and "budget gourmet."

The **Beach Street Cafe,** in the Outrigger Reef Hotel, 2169 Kalia Rd., open daily 7 a.m.-9 p.m., is literally on the beach. Breakfast, 7-11 a.m., starts at $2.99 for a scrambled-egg platter, and just $1.95 for cereal and yogurt. Other munchies like burgers and plate lunches are under $4. Cafeteria-style, the cafe has no decor except for a huge open window that frames the living sculpture of Waikiki.

Kapahulu Avenue

Once Kapahulu Avenue crosses Ala Wai Boulevard, it passes excellent inexpensive to moderately priced restaurants, strung one after the other. Kapahulu was the area in which the displaced Chinese community resettled after the great Chinatown fire at the turn of the century. Kapahulu basically means "poor soil," and unlike most areas of Hawaii could barely support vegetables and plants. Undaunted, the Chinese brought in soil with wagons and wheelbarrows, turning the area productive and verdant.

The first is **Rainbow Drive-In,** at the corner of Kanaaina Avenue. It's strictly local, with a kids' hangout feel, but the plate lunches are hearty and well done for under $4. **K C Drive-In,** just up the road a few blocks at 1029 Kapahulu, specializes in waffle dogs and shakes, and even has carhops. Both are excellent places to pick up plate lunches on your way out of Waikiki heading for the H-1 Freeway.

The first sit-down restaurant on the strip is **Irifune Japanese Restaurant,** at 563 Kapahulu, tel. 737-1141, open daily for lunch 11:30 a.m.-1 p.m. and for dinner 5-9:30 p.m., directly across from **Zippy's,** a fast-food joint. Irifune serves authentic, well-prepared Japanese standards in its small dining room. Most meals begin at $6, with a nightly special for around $8. You're also given a card that is punched every time you eat there; after 20 meals, you get one free. Irifune is a great deal for Japanese food, and is much cheaper and easily as good as most other Japanese restaurants on the Waikiki strip. A winner.

The next restaurant in line is **Ono Hawaiian Foods,** 726 Kapahulu Ave., tel. 737-2275, open Mon.-Sat. 10:30 a.m.-7:30 p.m., an institution in down-home Hawaiian cooking. This is the kind of place a taxi driver takes you to when you ask for "the real thing." It's clean and basic, with photos of local performers—all satisfied customers—decorating the wall. If you want to try *lomi lomi* salmon, poi, or *kalua* pig, this is *da kine place, brah!* Prices are cheap. And, if you have a sweet tooth, try **Leonard's Bakery,** 933 Kapahulu Ave., which specializes in *malasadas* and *pao dolce.*

The **Rama Thai Restaurant,** on the corner of Kapahulu and Winam Street, across from New World Chinese Restaurant, open daily for dinner 5-10 p.m., tel. 735-2789, is *uptown* with track lighting and linen tablecloths, but the prices and food are still *downtown* Bangkok. A wonderful choice is *satay* beef appetizer for $6.95; or try chicken and ginger soup in a coconut-milk spicy broth for $6.95. Red Thai curried beef, chicken, or scallops is $6.95. Almost half of the menu is vegetarian. All items are a la carte, so it's not that cheap; a complete meal costs around $15. The fish-ball soup is out of this world, with plenty for two. The tofu in coconut milk is also a great choice.

To round out the multicultural cuisines of Kapahulu Avenue, try **Jo-Ni's Restaurant and Bakery,** at 1017 Kapahulu, tel. 735-8575, serving traditional Filipino dishes as well as many American and Hawaiian standards.

Fast Foods And Snacks

There are enough Formica-tabled, orange-colored, golden-arched, belly-up-to-the-window places selling perfected, injected, and inspected ground cow, chicken, and fish to feed an army . . . and a navy, and marine corps too. Those needing a pre-fab meal can choose from the royal **Burger King** and **Dairy Queen, Jack in the Box, McDonald's, Pizza Hut, Wendy's,** and **Zippy's Drive-In.** Fast food addicts easily find your pushers throughout Waikiki!

Farrell's Restaurant, at the International Market Place and the Royal Hawaiian Center, serves ice cream and a good selection of sandwiches and soups for decent prices. Along Kalakaua Avenue are **Baskin-Robbins** and **Häagen Dazs.** For cheap Italian try the **Noodle Shop** in the Waikiki Sand Villa Hotel, tel. 922-4744.

Minute Chef, across from the Sheraton Moana Surfrider Hotel, on Kalakaua Ave., has hamburgers for 99 cents, cheeseburgers for $1.19, sandwiches for $2.50, and roast beef for about $3.99. A change of pace from the styrofoam box-type fast foods. Not bad, for cheap fast food.

Zorro's, at 2310 Kuhio Ave., tel. 926-5555, is your basic pizza parlor that includes a limited menu of pasta, sandwiches, and salad. The standard 16-inch pizza ranges $10.99-19.89 depending upon toppings. Pastas are all under $6, and sandwiches under $5. Open 10 a.m.-4 a.m. with free delivery.

You can't miss the pink, white, and magenta of **J.R.'s Fast Food Plate Lunch Restaurant,** at the corner of Lewers and Helumoa, where $6 or less will get you a hefty plate of rice, macaroni salad, and a slice of teriyaki beef, roast pork, or mahimahi. The food is fair, the portions hefty, and with a touch of local color the place is far superior to the nondescript national fast-food chains in the area. Upstairs is a dining veranda where you can perch above the endless crowd.

The **Patisserie,** at 2330 Kuhio, tel. 922-9752, offers fresh French pastries, coffee, and sandwiches. They're not bad for this neck of the woods. Fairly decent food at acceptable prices. Good for early mornings if you want just a light breakfast. The **Patisserie** adjacent to the Edgewater Hotel, at 2168 Beach Walk, open 6:30 a.m.-9 p.m., offers sundaes, ice cream, fresh baked pastries, and hefty deli sandwiches like the Black Forest Ham for $4.50; or try lasagna for $3.50. A breakfast special, served 6:30-9 a.m., includes scrambled eggs, toast, and your choice of ham, bacon or Portuguese sausage for only $2.25. If the Waikiki sun is, God forbid, shaded by clouds, you can prepare yourself for its return by focusing on the blazing yellow walls of this sandwich shop. Two more Patisseries can be found around town, one at 33 S. King St., the other in the Amfac Building in downtown Honolulu.

Fatty's Chinese Fast Food, 2345 Kuhio, tel. 922-9600, is very inexpensive. For about $3.50 you get a giant plate of Chinese fast food. A belly-filler only, but not bad.

MODERATE

Roberto and Laura Magni, a couple from Milano, one day discussed moving to Hawaii. With Italian spontaneity and gusto, they looked at each other and simultaneously said, "Perche no!" **Caffelatte,** at 339 Saratoga Rd. (across from the P.O.), tel. 924-1414, open daily 5:30 p.m.-1 a.m., on the second floor of a clapboard "New England-Hawaiian style" house encircled by a veranda, is the result of their impetuousness. The cosmopolitan interior, simple and basic, is white on green, its wrought-iron tables set with starched white linens. Hardwood floors, framed paintings both traditional and modern, a horseshoe bar, and subdued globed lighting complete the casual but stylish effect. The Mediterranean-inspired service is slow, but very friendly, and very professional. Each waitperson is intimately familiar with the menu, and will be happy to recommend and describe each dish. The menu features homemade pasta ranging in price $11.50-20, with offerings like Spaghetti Paradiso with tomato sauce, or *daglia talle,* a flat thin pasta with Italian sausage for $12.50. Traditional favorites are sure to please: lasagna Leonardo da Vinci for $15, various polenta smothered in everything from a simple calamari to *brosola,* a rolled and herb-stuffed steak; gnocchi for $14.50; and ricotta and spinach ravioli for $17. Top off dinner with Italian desserts like peaches and strawberries in wine, or oranges and bananas in Russian vodka. The bar serves Italian wine by the bottle or glass, along with bubbling spumante and various champagnes. Italy in Hawaii? . . . *Perche no?*

The **Super Chef Restaurant,** tel. 926-7199, at the Waikiki Hana Hotel, 2424 Koa Ave., is a sleeper. It is definitely one of *the* best moderately inexpensive restaurants in Waikiki, where you can get an *almost* gourmet meal for a terrific price. It's location in a small hotel on a side street keeps the crowds away, so the quality of the food and service never suffers. The restaurant decor is not spectacular, but it is classy with small linen-covered tables and drum-seat chairs in a open and cheery room. The staff is very friendly, and the chefs prepare each meal individually behind a tile counter. Breakfast, served 6:30-10:30 a.m., features buttermilk pancakes, bacon and ham, or Portuguese sausage with a large juice for just $2.25; or choose a *wiki wiki* breakfast of pastry, juice, and Kona coffee for only $1.75. No lunch menu, but dinner is served 5-10 p.m. One special is a complete dinner of steak with two lobster tails for only $11.95, or rack of lamb for $8.95. The portions are moderate but definitely not minuscule, and on top of it the cooking is just a half step below excellent. Definitely worth a try.

The **Waikiki Broiler,** in the Edgewater Hotel, 2168 Kalia Rd., open daily 6 a.m.-9 p.m., displays multiple personalities depending on where you choose to sit. All are pleasant. Dine alfresco at the Patio Bar and start your day with a "breakfast special" of pancakes, two strips of bacon, and one egg for $2.49. In the afternoon, the Patio Bar, accented with brass rail, comfortable stools, and tables shaded by umbrellas, becomes more of a bistro/beer garden where you can enjoy hand-mixed exotic drinks while listening to a guitarist daily 4-6 p.m. The main dining room, brightened with paintings of flowers and birds, and light fixtures that look like melted ice-cream cones, is as homey as a kindly old *tutu's* kitchen. Here, for lunch, you can order teriyaki chicken breast with rice or fries for $3.49, and for dinner a complete teriyaki steak dinner for two for only $15.95. Evening specials like freshly caught *ahi,* mahimahi, or marlin are a reasonable $13.25. The main lounge area, comfortable with tall wooden stools surrounding drum-topped tables, serves handmade mai tais daily 6-9 p.m., for $1.75. Evenings the inside bar rocks with a live band 9 p.m.-1:30 a.m., with karaoke on Sunday and Monday. The Waikiki Broiler is a terrific, moderately priced restaurant, where the food, if not quite outstanding, is definitely worth the price.

The **Peacock Dining Room,** at the Queen Kapiolani Hotel, 150 Kapahulu, tel. 922-1941, open 5:30-9 p.m., offers one of the most outstanding buffets in Waikiki for both price and quality. Different nights feature different cuisines. All are special but the Japanese buffet on Wednesday and Thursday and the seafood buffet on Friday are extraordinary. Buffet prices range $12.95-15.95. The room itself is tasteful with white tablecloths and full service. Every time you return to the buffet, leave your empty plate on your table and it will be taken away for you. Help yourself to an amazing array of entrees that are expertly prepared. The salad bar is extremely varied, and the desserts will make you wish you saved room. Excellent value.

Tiffany's Steakhouse, at the Hawaiian Regent, 2552 Kalakaua, tel. 922-6611, dinner 6-9:30 p.m., is a casual restaurant featuring thick juicy steaks, a varied and ample salad bar, and a good selection of fresh seafood. Evenings are magical because of a stained-glass ceiling illuminated by backlighting. The furnishings are European contemporary that counterpoint louvered windows all around. Tables are set with pink tablecloths and heavy crystalware; subdued lighting and ceiling fans add comfort and romance to your meal. The menu begins with escargot ($6.95), soups and chowder (under $4), and a seafood bar for $6.95. The house specialties are generous portions of prime rib ($19.95), filet mignon ($21), short rib ($18.50), tempura ($18.50), and seafood Newburg ($17.95). A la carte salad bar is $7.95. Tiffany's is that special blend of elegant and casual where you can dine in style and still be presented with a moderate check.

Carlos Castaneda wouldn't even notice the two psychedelic green cactuses if he walked into **Pepper's,** at 150 Kaiulani Ave., tel. 926-4374, open daily for lunch 11:30 a.m.-4 p.m., dinner 4 p.m.-1:30 a.m. The interior is Yuppie-Mex, with a wraparound rectangular bar with a fat wooden rail, and low ceilings done of Mexican-style stucco. The specialties of the house are prepared in a wood-fired oven for that hearty outdoor flavor in the heart of "Rancho Waikiki." Light meals are chicken taco salad ($9.95), the Pepper club ($6.95), and tuna melt ($5.95), with a good selection of salads. But you can get these anywhere, so go "south of the border" for burrito madness ($8.50), the complete *flautas* dinner ($9.95), or selections from the lava-rock grill like marinated chicken breast ($12.95) or baby-back ribs (full slab, $15.95). You can also pick Mexican favorites like tacos, enchiladas, and fajitas, all served with rice, beans, and Mexican salad. Nothing on the Mexican side is more than $12.95, with most around $9. Eat, *hombre!*

Eating at **Caffe Guccinni,** at 2139 Kuhio Ave., tel. 922-5287, open daily 4-10:30 p.m., is like following a Venetian gondolier to his favorite restaurant. It's not fancy but the food is good and plentiful, and the pasta is made fresh daily. The staff is usually a cook and a waiter who seats you at one of a dozen tables, most outdoors. The place is easy to miss because it's stuck back off the street, which means a nice, quiet area. For a light meal choose garlic bread ($2.50) and Caesar salad ($6.98), or for a full meal try one of the house specialties (with soup or salad), like eggplant parmigiana, pasta contesto, spaghetti and meatballs, or manicotti, all under $11. The cappuccino and espresso are freshly brewed and extraordinarily good. For dessert have *cannoli,* a flaky pastry stuffed with ricotta and smothered with slivers of almond and chocolate—excellent.

Hernando's Hideaway, at 2139 Kuhio, tel. 922-7758, open daily 10:30 a.m.-2 a.m., sits well off the street and is a very casual Mexican restaurant where the emphasis is on plenty of good food and a good time. Most tables are outside under an awning, and every day a special drink is featured, with $2 margaritas during happy hour. Some of the best offerings are the chicken enchilada dinner for $6.75, and an overstuffed calzone for $5.75. Every night, 6-7 p.m. is "power hour," when all well drinks are $1, followed by "pizza hour" 7-8 p.m., when pizza is only $1 per slice. All this activity attracts a younger crowd of both resort workers and vacationers. You can eat until you're as stuffed as a burrito for under $10.

The **New Orleans Bistro,** at 2139 Kuhio, tel. 926-4444, open 5 p.m.-midnight, along with its zesty Cajun and creole dining, offers jazz nightly. The chef, from New Orleans, has put together a small but superb sampler menu of the finest in Cajun cooking. The prices are a touch expensive, but if you're bored with the average offerings of mahimahi and teri chicken, you'll be glad that you found the Bistro. They've done the most with this limited location. The tables, covered in pink tablecloths, are arranged for an intimate and romantic feeling, and somehow the hustle and bustle of Kuhio has been minimized. Appetizers begin at $4.95 and sharpen your palate with deep-fried calamari, oysters Bienville, or Gulf Coast oysters baked on the half shell and topped with New Orleans classic cream sauce laced with shrimp for $10.95. Salads are basically $5 and include beefsteak tomato (Maui Feast) and house salad of hearts of palm ($4.95). Entrees are mesquite-grilled lemon herb chicken ($12.95), Louisiana fresh fried catfish ($14.95), blackened fish du jour (seasonal price), or smoked *kalua* shrimp and angel hair pasta ($15.95). If amphibians and reptiles pique your fancy, try frog legs and alligator tenderloins barbecued, blackened, or deep-fried with cocktail sauce, served with Cajun rice and vegies for $19.95. A good choice for a different dining experience.

Bobby McGee's Conglomeration, at the Colony East Hotel, 2885 Kalakaua, tel. 922-1282, is open Mon.-Thurs. 5:30-10 p.m., Friday, Saturday, and Sunday 5-11 p.m. This is a rip-roaring fun-filled place for the entire family. One of those rare combinations that caters to all ages and all pocketbooks, and foodwise it won't let you down. The waiters and waitresses are in costume, so you might be served your meal by Batman or Annie Oakley. The interior has numerous rooms, so you can sit close to the disco dance floor in case you have the overwhelming urge to twist off a few calories, or you can sit in a quiet room well away from the music. Create your own combos by mixing and matching selections like fried clam strips, top sirloin, deviled crab, and island chicken. Pick any two for $14.95, any three for $16.95, each additional $3.95. Also, traditional dishes are top sirloin for $13.75, mahimahi macadamia for $8.95, or lasagna for $8.25. Children's menu offers selections for under $5. You can also choose from an assortment of sandwiches for $5. All entrees come with the salad bar, which is set up in an old bathtub. If you can't make up your mind where to dine, Bobby McGee's is a sure bet.

Pieces of Eight is in the Coral Seas Hotel, tel. 923-6646, open daily 5-11 p.m., happy hour 4-6 p.m., piano bar nightly. This steak and seafood house has managed to create a comfortable and relaxed atmosphere where they serve up excellent steaks and very good fish dishes at moderate prices. The decor is dark wood and burnished brass in a romantically lit main room. A piano stylist tinkles in the background. It's the kind of restaurant that will match itself to your mood. Come for that special night out or just a casual evening meal. "Early birders" who arrive 5-7 p.m. can pick selections like garlic chicken or fish 'n' chips with salad bar for $6.95. Entrees are 10-ounce top sirloin ($13.95), ground beef sirloin ($8.95), filet mignon ($15.95), and mahimahi amandine ($11.95). All dinners include choice of potato, rice, or bread; salad bar is $3.50 extra. A great choice for good food and a pleasant setting at affordable prices. The **Cellar Bar,** open from noon to the wee hours, serves exotic drinks and light meals like a simple pizza, hamburger, or fish bake combination. If you are out on the town, it is a good place where you can munch while enjoying a video game or a game of pool.

The House of Hong, 260 Lewers St., tel. 923-0202, open daily 11 a.m.-10:30 p.m., Sunday from 4 p.m., is a standard, no-surprises Chinese restaurant with a flair. The decor borders on tasteful, with inlaid wall murals, painted ceilings of China scenes, and some tables outfitted in starched white tablecloths. The Cantonese lunch special is offered weekdays 11 a.m.-3 p.m. for $5.95. "Early bird specials" are served 4-6 p.m.—combinations like egg flower soup, chicken chow mein, sweet and sour pork, crispy wonton, fried rice, fortune cookie, and Chinese tea for $9.95. Not great, but no complaints either.

The **Oceanarium** at the Pacific Beach Hotel, 2490 Kalakaua Ave., tel. 922-1233, offers a full breakfast, lunch, and dinner menu. For lunch, try the tropical fruit plate at $7.50, or an entree such as Cajun five-spice chicken for $7.50. Dinner appetizers like Cajun calamari begin at $4.95, while entrees like New York peppercorn steak are $19.95, and specials like live Maine lobster are $21.95. Also featured are fresh island catches at market prices. The Oceanarium is done in elegant muted colors that make you feel as if you were under water. See "Free Sights and Curiosities" under "Sights" earlier in this chapter for a description of the massive 280,000-gallon aquarium that is the decor.

Trattoria, in the Edgewater Hotel, 2168 Kalia Rd., tel. 923-8415, serves savory dishes from northern Italy. Particularly good are the veal plates with an appropriate bottle of Italian wine. The interior is upscale: bentwood chairs and white linen tablecloths set with crystal. Antipasto selections include escargot ($8.25) and spinach salad ($7.75). Combine these with pasta dishes like spaghetti puttanesca, a savory dish of fillet of anchovy and melted butter cooked in a hot sauce with tomatoes and black olives

($10.75). Complete dinners, ranging in price $17.95-24.95, include choice of minestrone soup or dinner salad, and lasagna, eggplant or tortellini. Trattoria is a good choice for a pleasant atmosphere and better-than-average cooking at a moderate price.

Benihana of Tokyo, at the Hilton Rainbow Bazaar, 2005 Kalia Rd., open daily for lunch 11:30 a.m.-2 p.m., and for dinner 5:30-10:30 p.m., tel. 955-5955, is a medium-priced Japanese restaurant for those who are jittery about the food and prices. Meals are designed to fit *gaijin* taste, and cooks flash their knives and spatulas at your table—as much a floor show as a dining experience. Good, basic Japanese food, *teppan*-style.

Rascals on Kuhio, at the Kuhio Mall, 2301 Kuhio Ave., tel. 922-5566, is open for dinner only, and doubles as a nightclub with late-night suppers served until 3 a.m. and dancing until 4 a.m. Varied menu of seafood, featuring Cajun-style shrimp soup.

Mandarin Palace, at the Miramar Hotel, 2345 Kuhio Ave., tel. 926-1110, is open for lunch and dinner. Highly rated for its Asian cuisine in a full-blown Chinese atmosphere.

The **Seafood Emporium,** Royal Hawaiian Shopping Center, 2201 Kalakaua Ave., tel. 922-5477, is moderately priced for seafood, with one of the island's largest selections of domestic and imported fish. A good choice for a reasonable lunch or dinner.

The Great Wok of China, Royal Hawaiian Shopping Center, 2201 Kalakaua Ave., tel. 922-5373, has decent food. It's fun to eat here as chefs prepare food at your table in, you guessed it, woks. A good assortment of meat, seafood, and vegetable dishes, guaranteed not to be the steam-table variety.

If local people want a buffet they head for **Kengo's Buffet,** 1529 Kapiolani Blvd, tel. 941-2241, which is a sure sign that you get value for your money. Friday evenings are extremely popular, with a special seafood buffet for $14.95. If you're heading for Kengo's, go at lunchtime because you get the exact same buffet for $7.50. Every day is slightly different, but you can count on a huge assortment of food that is sure to please.

White and pink canvas umbrellas shade the outdoor tables of the **Cafe Princess Garden,** just next to its sister restaurant the **Cafe Princess** (indoor restaurant with full table service), both set in a carved garden grotto surrounded by the Royal Hawaiian and Sheraton hotels. Here, in the heart of Waikiki, but buffered from the crowds, you can enjoy a reasonably priced breakfast special of two scrambled eggs, link sausage, and a croissant for $3.50; or lunch specials, served 11:30 a.m.-5 p.m., like soup and a sandwich for $6.50 or a plate lunch for $5.75. Dinner specials served 5-10 p.m. in the Princess Garden include steak and lobster for $18.95, while those opting for the inside Cafe Princess can choose jumbo prawns or charbroiled steak for $16.95, or roast prime rib for $11.95. The outdoor Cafe Princess Garden is an excellent people-watching perch from which to enjoy happy hour drinks, 11:30 a.m.-6 p.m., and 10 p.m. until closing, when mai tais are $2.25, pitchers of Bud are $5.50, and frothy chi-chis are only $3.

CASUAL GOURMET

The following restaurants are unique in that they serve inspired gourmet food in lovely settings for very reasonable prices. Technically not in Waikiki, but located almost next door to each other in Hawaii Kai about 20 minutes away, both are definitely worth the trip.

OnJin Kim creates with food in the same way that a great maestro conducts a symphony orchestra . . . each instrument, distinctive in its own voice, is embraced into the whole. This executive chef draws upon innate talents honed to perfection at the world's finest culinary schools, and then, like a true virtuoso, adds her own intangible ingredients of imagination and heart. The result is the finest dishes of contemporary French, Italian, and Japanese cuisine offered side by side in a glorious melody of flavor and presentation. OnJin is a "nouveau purist," respecting each culinary style, with the blending of taste left to the menu selection. Her creations are offered at the **Hanatei Bistro,** 6650 Kalanianaole Hwy., Honolulu, HI 96825, tel. 396-0777, located in the Hawaii Kai Executive Plaza II, open for dinner daily 5:30-10 p.m. Sunday is extra special, with brunch served 10 a.m.-1:30 p.m.—a fantastic display including sushi bar, snow crab and shrimp cocktails, made-to-order omelettes of all descriptions, carved slabs of prime rib done to perfection, and a "thank the lord it's Sunday and my sins are forgiven" dessert table, all for only $19.95. The dining room, with floor-to-ceiling windows, is very simple with a minimal amount of decoration on a Japanese-inspired theme. The lattice-covered ceiling, hung with tasteful chandelier and huge origami crane, is curved like the roof of a Buddhist temple. The curved roof picks up again over an elevated section reminiscent of a classic tea pavilion. Black and red lacquered partitions separate the two areas while the soothing waters of two miniature ponds purl in the background.

Appetizers are everything from charred *ahi* at $8.50 to curried-chicken spring rolls at $5.95. The sashimi menu features individual classic offerings like *hamachi* at $5; or special orders for two like Nihon Sensu, three sashimi selections presented on a Japanese fan at $12; or the superb Nihonbashi, five sashimi selections presented on a miniature Japanese cedar bridge at $24. Pasta, half orders as appetizers or full orders as entrees, include capellini with black sturgeon and red salmon caviar at $9/$18, and prawn ravioli also at $9/$18. Soups, all $5, range from a seafood *suimono*—a blend of French and Japanese traditions with seafood, mushrooms, tofu, and green onions—to a hearty four-onion soup with glazed croutons.

The entrees, reflecting OnJin's philosophy of "neo-purist" cuisine, include filet mignon in a merlot sauce; tempura-battered seafood and vegetables with dipping sauces; veal scallopini in a savory Madeira sauce; *opakapaka,* luscious Hawaiian pink snapper in a delicate Chinese sesame chile sauce; and *sanshuno sakana,* butterfish in miso, salmon in a salt crust, and teriyaki *unagi* (eel). The most expensive entree is $22, with most priced under $20. The specialty of the house is Bouillabaisse de Chef OnJin, a medley of seafood simmered in saffron, lemongrass, and plum tomatoes at $26. Regional specials are offered with the changing of the seasons. Satiate your taste buds with a scrumptious dessert like creme brulee, spiced apple puff, or tiramisu cheesecake, or throw all caution to the wind and indulge in the very wicked chocolate macadamia nut torte. At Hanatei, the service is impeccable, and a complete wine list complements all dishes. This is adventurous gourmet dining at its best.

The word "genius" is oftentimes overused and misapplied, causing it to lose its oomph, but when it comes to creativity with food, Roy Yamaguchi is a genius, par excellence! **Roy's Restaurant,** 6600 Kalanianaole Hwy. and Keahole Dr., tel. 396-7697, in Hawaii Kai Corporate Plaza, open Sun.-Thurs. 5:30-9:30 p.m., until 10:30 p.m. Fri.-Sat., presents Euro-Asian cuisine (Pacific Rim) at its very best. The young master chef, through experimentation and an unfailing sense of taste, has blended the diverse and distinctive flavors of French, Italian, Chinese, Japanese, Thai, and Hawaiian cuisine into a heady array of culinary delights that destroy the adage that "east is east and west is west." The twain have definitely met, and with resounding success. Roy's dining room is "elegant casual" much like the food, featuring an open kitchen, and although pleasant enough with a superb view, it is not designed for a lengthy romantic evening. Roy's dining philosophy seems to be the serving of truly superb dishes posthaste with the focus on the "food as the dining experience," not the surroundings. The presentation of every dish, under the direction of executive chef Gordon Hopkins, who has been with Roy's since its inception, is flawless, and as pleasing to the eye as it is titillating to the palate. The mastery is in "the blend," which can take you to heights of satiation rarely experienced before.

Start with the wild mushrooms with polenta and macadamia nut oil, or potstickers with lobster miso sauce, or even an individual *imu*-oven pizza smothered with grilled chicken, feta cheese, olives, and pesto, all for under $8. Salads feature island-grown greens and vegetables and include such wonderful concoctions as crispy calamari with lemongrass and vinaigrette at $6.95, and Chinese chicken with candied pecans and soy ginger dressing at $6.95. Entrees are wonders like grilled loin of lamb with rosemary, crabmeat, and risotto sauce at $17.95, or a nightly special such as lemongrass-encrusted mahimahi with crispy duck cakes in *lilikoi* mustard sauce for $22.95. Desserts by pastry chef Rick Chang are also superb, and include individually prepared (order at beginning of dinner) fresh fruit cobbler in sauce anglaise, or a richer than rich chocolate soufflé. Although Roy's has only been open since 1988, it is *the* trendsetter in new and inspired cuisine, receiving the praise and adulation of other fine chefs throughout the islands who try to mimic and match Roy's flair and style.

CLASSY DINING

Halekulani Hotel Dining
Softly the soprano sea sings, while the baritone breeze whispers in melodious melancholy, as you float ephemerally above the waves at **La Mer,** the signature dinner restaurant at the Halekulani Hotel. Splendid in its appointment, the walls, filigreed panels of teak covered in Chinese silk screen, are predominantly browns and whites, the traditional colors of Hawaiian tapa. The ceiling, too, is a work of art, with carved panels trimmed in bronze. Seating is in high-backed upholstered chairs with armrests, and every table is illuminated either by flickering candles or recessed ceiling lamps that seem to drip the soft gold light of the melting sun upon the table. The hotel's executive chef and chef de cuisine of La Mer, George Mavrothalassitis (Chef Mavro), was gifted at birth with all the ingredients of a great chef . . . a passionate Greek heart inherited from his father, an artistic soul from his Austrian mother, and a Frenchman's devoted love affair with food. Using only the finest and best ingredients, Chef Mavro creates culinary masterpieces of Hawaiian regional cuisine that are impeccably presented by a highly professional wait staff. Each dish, prepared by La Mer's 12 cooks at their own stations, must pass final inspection by the chef, and if they are found to be at all flawed or simply unartistic, they never reach the dining room. The menu is magnificent and begins with zucchini torte of sautéed Kahuku prawns at $19, or *kiawe*-wood smoked Norwegian salmon with shallot and chive sauce at $17. Next comes *onaga* baked in thyme and rosemary rock salt crust with a fresh herb sauce at $38, sautéed fish coated with cumin and rosemary in a light curry at $26, or filet mignon with oysters in a pinot noir and chervil sauce at $34. All are wonderful; the best, however, are three selections of full course table d'hôte priced $65-95. Courses are sumptuous and can be poached *papio* with scallop mousse served with lobster sauce, or poached *onaga* with wilted greens and three-caviar sauce. All come with a marvelous selection of fine French cheeses served with walnut bread and a wonderful dessert. Desserts prepared by pastry chef Franz Schier include chilled white nougat with candied fruit and guava coulis, and a warm brownie with cognac sabayon, at $12. La Mer sets the standard of haute Hawaiian regional cuisine, and if you were to choose one restaurant for a night of culinary bliss, this is a perfect choice.

The House Without a Key, open for breakfast buffet 7-10 a.m., lunch 11 a.m.-5 p.m., and dinner 5-9 p.m., is a casual outdoor-indoor restaurant in a magnificent oceanside setting. Named after the first novel written about Charlie Chan, Honolulu's famous fictional detective, the restaurant offers unsurpassed views in every direction, and is perhaps the best spot on the island to enjoy a sunset cocktail. Although casual, the seating is very comfortable with padded chairs at simple wood-trimmed tables. The breakfast buffet, including fresh omelettes, is $18.50. The lunch menu offers main course salads like oriental chicken salad and grilled beef fajita salad; or pasta dishes like seafood penne or spaghetti bolognese, all for under $15. Sandwiches range from a classic triple-decker club sandwich at $12, to grilled mahimahi on nori bread for $15, while entrees are New York steak at $21 or grilled salmon at $19. Dinner starts with cocktail *pu pu,* including chilled jumbo shrimp at $13.50 or scallops wrapped in bacon for $10.50, with sandwiches, salads, and entrees about the same as those on the lunch menu. Desserts, designed to soothe your palate as the setting sun soothes your soul, include chocolate macadamia-nut creme pie, Toblerone chocolate mousse, and *lilikoi* cheesecake all priced at $6. Entertainment, nightly 5-8 p.m., performed by **The Islanders** or by the **Hiram Olsen Trio,** is great for dancing under the stars. Remember, the door is never locked at House Without a Key.

White, purple, and yellow orchids tumble from trellises, cascade from clay planters, and always grace your table at **Orchids Dining Room,** also at the Halekulani. Open daily 7:30-11 a.m. for breakfast, 11:30 a.m.-2 p.m. for lunch, and 6-10 p.m. for dinner, this is another seaside, indoor-outdoor restaurant. Specializing in contemporary American cuisine, Orchids is also famous for its fabulous Sunday brunch at $29.50 adults, $18.50 children. Executive chef Shawn Smith makes freshness a priority, buying ingredients as locally as possible . . . vegetables, beef, prawns, and especially fish. Beautifully appointed with teak wood and Hawaiian eucalyptus flooring, the setting is casual-elegant with white starched linen tablecloths, captain-style chairs with blue and white pillows, and of course heavy silver and crystal. Arranged on a bi-level central dining area that spreads out to a covered veranda, all tables enjoy a panoramic view of the sea with Diamond Head in the distance. Start the day with a continental breakfast including fresh fruit juice, pastry basket, and beverage at $12.50; or an American breakfast with all of the above plus eggs and a breakfast meat at $16.50; or try a Japanese breakfast of grilled fish, steamed rice, pickles, miso soup, seaweed, and green tea at $19.50. There's also a frittata for $13, whole wheat pancakes with macadamia nuts and coconut syrup at $9, or a basket of pastries and coffee for $6.75. The daily brunch is served 8:30-10 a.m., at $20.75. Start your engine with a mimosa, Bloody Mary, screwdriver, or tropical fruit, along with eggs Benedict, frittata, smoked salmon and cream cheese, and various pastries. Lunch begins with an assortment of delicious appetizers like seared *ahi* with mustard shoyu for $15, or a simple salad of mixed greens with various dressings for $6. Soups, all priced at $5, include Portuguese bean and chilled tropical fruit soup. Special dishes are an assortment of pasta under $15, lamb curry or Thai chicken for around $18, and broiled Hawaiian fish with herbs at $18. A full course table d'hôte is $25, and all desserts are $6.50. Dinner entrees are luscious seafood platters of charbroiled *a'u* with Kula tomato and herbed pasta at $27, pepper-crusted *opakapaka* at $29.50, or rack of lamb Provençale at $33. A taster's menu at $54 is a full five-course meal including a symphony of desserts.

Hilton Hawaiian Village Dining

The Hilton Hawaiian Village, at 2005 Kalia Rd., is one of the finest destination resorts in Hawaii. Its two signature restaurants, both *Travel Holiday* award winners, complement the resort perfectly. **Bali by the Sea,** tel. 941-2254, open daily for dinner 6-10 p.m., may sound like Indonesian cuisine, but it's more continental than anything else. The setting couldn't be more brilliant. Sit by the open windows so that the sea breezes fan you as you overlook the gorgeous Hilton beach with Diamond Head off to your left. The room is outfitted in a blue paisley carpet, high-backed, armrest-type chairs, white tablecloths, and classical place settings with silver service. Upon ordering, you are presented with a complimentary platter of hors d'oeuvres. Choose appetizers like gratin of oysters with julienne of duck, or fettuccine with wild mushrooms, prosciutto, and sun-dried tomatoes. Soups are bisque of shrimp and lobster or a classic French onion. Entrees are a magnificent selection of fish from Hawaiian waters baked, sautéed, or broiled and then covered in a variety of sauces from fresh basil to mint and tomato vinaigrette. Meat entrees are breast of chicken and lobster, or medallions of venison simmered in pears, cranberry, and *poivrade* sauce. The meal ends with a fine presentation of desserts, or a complimentary "steaming chocolate Diamond Head." Bali by the Sea is a superb choice for an elegant evening of fine dining.

The **Golden Dragon,** tel. 946-5336, open nightly for dinner 6-10 p.m., would tempt any knight-errant to drop his sword and pick up chopsticks. This too is a fine restaurant where the walls are decorated with portraits of emperors, and the plates carry the Golden Dragon motif. The interior color scheme is a striking vermilion and black, with the chairs and tables shining with a lacquerware patina. The floor is dark koa. Outside, the terrace has pagoda-style canopies under which you may dine. Obviously the Golden Dragon isn't your average chop suey house, but the menu has all of the standard Chinese fare from lemon chicken to . . . well, chop suey, but it doesn't end there. The food is expertly prepared, and two fine choices are the exotic Imperial Beggar's Chicken (for two), which takes 24 hours' notice to prepare, and Chef Dai's Selection (for two), which includes lobster in black bean sauce, shrimp, almond duck, beef in rice wine, duck fried rice, and a special dessert all for only $40. For a first-class restaurant with impeccable food and service, the Golden Dragon offers prices that are very, very reasonable.

Around Waikiki

One of the most laudable achievements in the restaurant business is to create an excellent reputation and then to keep it. **Nick's Fishmarket** at the Waikiki Gateway Hotel, 2070 Kalakaua, tel. 955-6333, open nightly for dinner 6-11:30 p.m., has done just that . . . and keeps doing it. Many gourmets consider Nick's *the* best dining in Waikiki, and it's great fun to find out if they know what they're talking about. Owner Randy Schoch pays personal attention to every detail at Nick's, while executive chef Mariano Lalica creates the culinary magic. Lalica placed first in the "Seafood Olympics" recently held in Hawaii, and is a marvel at preparing fresh fish, which he accents with Thai peanut sauce and balsamic vinegar, rock shrimp sauce with stone ground mustard and macadamia nuts, or roasted garlic and sun-dried tomato vinaigrette. Adventurous and highly skilled, Chef Lalica, like the master of an old sailing ship, will take you to culinary ports of call rarely, if ever, visited. Highly professional waiters, knowledgeable about every dish, are friendly and efficient, and always at hand to suggest just the right wine from the extensive list to perfectly complement your choice of dish.

Start with fresh-baked clams casino ($9.95), smoked salmon ($10.50), or, if you're in the mood, how about beluga caviar (don't ask). For soup order the Fish Market Chowder, while the Caesar salad prepared at your table has long won honors as the best available west of California. Although Nick's is primarily renowned for its fish, don't overlook the veal, steaks, and chicken with sides of pasta. An excellent choice is one of Nick's complete dinners featuring entree, soup or salad, vegetables, and hot drink. Other great choices are veal picatta, succulent rack of lamb with a Hawaiian mango chutney, and perfectly prepared abalone imported from the cold waters of the California coast. The sinless along with those expecting salvation "tomorrow" will enjoy the dessert menu, which features Nick's vanbanna pie, a tempting concoction of banana mousse and almond vanilla ice cream dripping with caramel sauce; New York-inspired cheesecake; or a lighter tropical sorbet. A "Cafe Menu" has recently been added from which you can order until the wee hours while listening to live entertainment in the lounge area. Lobster fried rice, crispy calamari, pasta à la Hawaii, or plump tacos can all be enjoyed and are very reasonably priced under $10. Dancing to live music is featured nightly along with special events such as wine tasting evenings scheduled throughout the year. The bar prepares a host of exotic island drinks along with a fine cup of cappuccino, and is known for its extensive microbrewery beer selections. If you have only one evening in Waikiki and you want to make it memorable, you'd have a hard time doing better than Nick's Fishmarket.

Sergio's, at the Ilima Hotel, 445 Nohonani, open daily for dinner 5:30-11:30 p.m., tel. 926-3388, is one of the finest Italian restaurants in Honolulu. The interior is romantic, subtle, and simple, with a combination of booths and tables. Sergio blends and matches foods from all regions of Italy: hearty peasant soups, fresh salads, antipasti garnished with aromatic cheeses and spicy prepared meats, pasta dishes, entrees, and desserts. The more than a dozen choices of pasta come with sauces of savory meat, delicate vegetables, or seafood. Entrees of chicken, beef, and fresh fish make your taste buds rise and shout, "Bravo! Sergio! Bravo!"

Michel's, at the Colony Surf Hotel, 2895 Kalakaua Ave., tel. 923-6552, open daily 7 a.m.-10 p.m., is literally on the beach, so your appetite is piqued not only by sumptuous morsels, but by magnificent views of the Waikiki skyline boldly facing the Pacific. The interior is "neo-French elegant," with the dining rooms appointed in soft pastels, velour chairs with armrests, white tablecloths, crystal chandeliers, heavy silver service, and tasteful paintings. The serpentine bar is of polished koa. Michel's Sunday brunch is legendary. Choose an entree, and the remainder of the brunch comes with it. Suggestions are baked avocado with crab meat for $26, or the renowned eggs Benedict for $22. You get a choice of broiled fresh grapefruit with sherry, sliced oranges and melon, fresh Hawaiian pineapple slices, or Puna papaya with limes, along with a sparkling champagne cocktail, baskets of banana or blueberry muffins, and Kona coffee. Daily breakfasts are a wild mushroom omelette ($8.50), breakfast steak and eggs

($14.50), Belgian waffles ($9.50), and buttermilk pancakes ($7.50). Lunch can be appetizers like baked oysters Michel ($10), or Michel's Reuben sandwich ($10). Fruits of the sea include steamed king crab leg for $27, and from the grill come spring lamb chops ($17). Dinner is *magnifique* with fresh Maine lobster on ice ($27), delicate baby coho salmon garnished with shrimp served in its own sauce ($37), or tournedos Rossini, a center cut of tenderloin with goose liver and truffles. The dining experience at Michel's is completely satisfying with outstanding food and service in an outstanding setting.

The Secret is the signature restaurant at the Hawaiian Regent, 2552 Kalakaua, tel. 922-6611, open nightly 6-9:30 p.m. As you enter, you pass an arrangement of cornucopias, some holding fresh fruits and fish, others brimming over with gourds, Indian corn, bread turtles, and alligators. A wheelbarrow is loaded with nuts. The decor in the main room is high-back, peacock, wicker chairs, bamboo wraps you in a booth-like atmosphere. The room is open-beam construction overlooking Waikiki Beach. In the center is a koi pond with gas torches lit for that extra touch. Hanging from the ceiling are banners that give you the feeling of being at a medieval feast, Polynesian style. Strolling minstrels, The Anacans, play a seemingly infinite melody of moody contemporary tunes, while a harpist gives an impression of heavenly strains on Monday evenings. Waiters are extremely professional, providing insightful tips to the menu they have memorized. The Secret is renowned for its fine wines, with over 340 selections expertly managed by Richard Dean, one of only two master sommeliers in all of Hawaii. Within the restaurant is a wine room that can hold a private party of 12, who may choose from a special menu. As you peruse the menu you are presented with a plate of freshly baked Indian *nan* bread. Select the hors d'oeuvres bar, which has smoked salmon, caviar, and duck pâté, enough for a meal for a reasonable $14. Specialties are a Casserole des Fruits de Mer (lobster, scallops, shrimp, and *opakapaka* in fennel sauce), and medallions of venison, both priced around $35. The Secret has a long and well-deserved reputation as one of the finest eating establishments in Waikiki. A romantic dinner here will long be remembered.

Matteo's, in the Marine Surf Hotel, 364 Seaside, tel. 922-5551, open 6 p.m.-2 a.m., is a wonderfully romantic Italian restaurant that sets the mood even outside by welcoming you with a red canopy and brass rail that leads to a carved door of koa and crystal. The interior is dark and stylish, with high-backed booths, white tablecloths, and marble-top tables. On each is a rose, Matteo's signature. Dinners begin with hot antipasti priced $7-14, such as stuffed mushrooms a la Matteo or seafood combo, or cold antipasto for two. Light fare of *ensalada e zuppa* (salad and soup), hearts of romaine lettuce, or clam soup matched with garlic bread or pizza bread make an inexpensive but tasty meal. Entree suggestions are chicken *rollatini,* veal *rollatini* (rolled veal stuffed with bell peppers, mushrooms, onions, spinach, and mozzarella), or *bragiola* (rolled beef with mozzarella cheese, garlic, and fresh basil, baked with marinara sauce), all under $20. Complete dinners come with Matteo's special salad, pasta, vegetables, and coffee or tea, and include mahimahi Veronica (sautéed fish in lemon sauce and seedless grapes) or veal parmigiana, priced under $28. Pastas are very reasonable and besides the usual linguine dishes include gnocchi and manicotti a la Matteo. An extensive wine list complements the food. If you are out for a special evening of fine dining and romance, Matteo's will set the mood, and the rest is up to you.

The **Surf Room** is in the Royal Hawaiian Hotel, 2259 Kalakaua Ave., tel. 923-7311. The menu is solid but uninspired. However, the setting couldn't be lovelier, and the buffet is staggeringly huge.

Hy's Steak House, 2440 Kuhio Ave., tel. 922-5555, is one of those rare restaurants that is not only absolutely beautiful, but serves great food as well. Decorated like a Victorian sitting room, it offers things other than steaks and chops, but these are the specialties and worth the stiff-upper-lip price.

Restaurant Suntory, Royal Hawaiian Shopping Center, tel. 922-5511, is a very handsome restaurant with different rooms specializing in particular styles like *shabu shabu, teppanyaki,* and sushi. The prices used to be worse, but they're still expensive. However, the food preparation and presentation are excellent, and the staff is very attentive.

Furusato Sushi, right next to the Hyatt Regency at 2424 Kalakaua Ave., tel. 922-4991, and **Furusato Tokyo Steak,** downstairs, are both expensive but top-notch Japanese restaurants. The food and service are authentic, but they are geared toward the Japanese tourist who expects, and almost demands, to pay high prices. In the steakhouse, expect steak since very little else is on the menu. Upstairs is sushi. Free valet parking is great for this congested part of Waikiki.

The **Hawaii Prince Hotel,** 100 Holomoana St., tel. 956-1111, features three distinctive restaurants. **Takanawa,** with posts of *sugi* pine, floor-to-ceiling windows, and a koi pond in the center of a Japanese garden, is the hotel's sushi bar. **The Prince Court,** the main dining room, offers breakfast, lunch, and dinner. Breakfast, served 5:30-11 a.m., starts with juices and fruits ($4-7), seasonal berries and cream ($6), continental breakfast ($10.50), and a buffet breakfast ($15). Lunches start with appetizers like grilled fresh mozzarella ($6.50), barbecued Pacific oysters and fried onions ($9.50), and Cobb salad with Dungeness crab ($9.50). Sandwiches like sliced avocado, tomato, sprouts, and cucumber in pocket bread start at $6.50, while pasta selections are $9-13.50. Dinner offers entrees like the fresh fish of the day, cooked five possible ways including baked in a cornbread crust or sautéed with angel hair pasta for a reasonable $17.50; or try a mixed grill of local slipper lobster, Kahuku shrimp, and sea scallops for $24. **Hakone,** the hotel's fine Japanese restaurant, is appointed with shoji screens and wooden tables with high-backed chairs in front of a glass wall that frames the still life of the Ala Wai Yacht Harbor. Dishes are typical, with set menus *(teishoku)* of chicken teriyaki ($23), *katsura* steak ($29.50), and the Kaiseki Hakone, a full seven-course meal for $60.

ENTERTAINMENT

Waikiki swings, beats, bumps, grinds, sways, laughs, and gets down. If Waikiki has to bear being called a carnival town, it might as well strut its stuff. Dancing (disco and ballroom), happy hours, cocktail shows, cruises, lounge acts, Polynesian extravaganzas, and the street scene provide an endless choice of entertainment. Small-name Hawaiian trios, soloists, pianists, and sultry singers featured in innumerable bars and restaurants woo you in and keep you coming back. Big-name island entertainers and visiting international stars play the big rooms. Free entertainment includes hula shows, ukulele music, street musicians, jugglers, and artists. For a good time, nowhere in Hawaii matches Waikiki. Also see "Entertainment" in the Honolulu chapter for other listings in and around greater Honolulu.

Bars, Happy Hours, And Lounge Acts

Brother Noland is a local talent who appears here and there around town. He's the cutting edge for ethnic Hawaiian groups playing hot reggae, originals, and plenty of Stevie Wonder, solo or with a group; he shouldn't be missed.

Steve and Theresa are excellent Hawaiian musicians. Their sound is a melodious mixture of traditional and contemporary. Accomplished musicians with beautiful voices, they often appear at various venues around town.

In the Park Shore Hotel, 2586 Kalakaua Ave., **The Bar** is a quiet, relaxing place to have a drink. Sometimes, a guest pianist plays.

The **Irish Rose Saloon,** at 227 Lewers, presents live entertainment nightly with dancing till 4 a.m., and features sporting events on their big-screen TV. Happy hour is 3-8 p.m. It's right across the street from the Outrigger Coral Seas Hotel, just at the entrance to the Al Harrington Show.

A great little bar, the **Brass Rail** serves up cold draft beer and deli sandwiches. They're into sports and especially Monday Night Football, which usually begins in Hawaii at 7:30 p.m. Located on the ground floor of the Outrigger Waikiki Hotel, at 2335 Kalakaua.

The **Rose and Crown Pub** in King's Village has a pianist playing sing-along favorites in what is a very close rendition of an English-style pub. They have daily specials; for example, on Saturday if you wear your Rose and Crown hat you have happy hour prices all night long. So drink hearty, and hold on to your hat! The crowd is intent on swilling beer and partying. Noisy, raucous, and fun.

Key Largo is a *bar,* and bars are not so easy to find in Waikiki. Stuck away at 142 Uluniu St., it attracts a mostly local crowd, especially Wed.-Sat. when they feature live rock 'n' roll bands. Key Largo doesn't have the vibe of a rough joint, but it is the sort of place where a fool and his teeth can easily be parted.

Jolly Roger Restaurant, at 2244 Kalakaua and 150 Kaiulani (see "Food") presents a changing mixture of live music nightly in their lounge, open until 2 a.m. A good spot for listening to music and enjoying conversation around the bar. The **Crow's Nest,** above the Jolly Roger restaurant at 2244 Kalakaua, features local and visiting entertainers. If **Blue Kangaroo,** a hilarious comedy act, is playing, don't miss them. The entertainers, Mike Drager and Jay Cook, have been singing and playing their guitars and various other stringed instruments together for over 25 years. They first played at the Crow's Nest in 1972, and in their own words "can't believe the sumbitch lasted this long." Their ribald songs are extremely egalitarian . . . they insult all races, creeds, and sexes equally. As the night gets later their humor gets raunchier. Be forewarned, and have a ball.

The Grapevine, corner of Prince Edward and Uluniu streets, presents low-key live music. Artists change, but expect a guitarist playing soulful Hawaiian music.

In the International Market Place, the **Cock's Roost Steak House** offers free entertainment, with no minimum or cover.

The Brothers Cazimero have an excellent and well-deserved reputation as one of Hawaii's finest duos, singing a lovely blend of Hawaiian and contemporary music. You can usually catch them at the Royal Hawaiian Hotel's Monarch Room. Dinner and cocktail shows are Tues.-Sat. at 7 p.m. Alohawear is fine, tel. 923-7311.

Baron's Studio, Waikiki Plaza Hotel, tel. 946-0277, is home to jazz vocalist Azure McCall. Open nightly, quiet drinks, fine background tunes.

The **Polynesian Pub,** 2490 Kalakaua, tel. 923-3683, offers happy hour nightly and contemporary Hawaiian music. Right-priced drinks, no cover.

The Garden Bar, Hilton Hawaiian Village, tel. 949-4321, features John Norris and the New Orleans Jazz Band Sunday 2-6 p.m. Also, at the hotel's Paradise Lounge, **Olomana,** a contemporary Hawaiian trio, performs weekend evenings 8 p.m.-midnight, no cover.

The five-star Halekulani Hotel offers superb nightly entertainment. There is no lovelier location for a sunset cocktail than **House Without a Key,** where The Islanders or The Hiram Olsen Trio perform contemporary tunes nightly 5-8:30 p.m. Gracing the stage are two former Miss Hawaii's, Kanoe Miller and Debbie Nakanelua, who perform their inspired hula on alternate evenings. Sunday brunch at the hotel's **Orchids Dining Room** is made even more genteel with the musical strains of harpist Susanne Hussong, accompanied by flutist Susan Gillespie, who perform the hit songs of Broadway musicals. Nightly 9 p.m.-12:30 a.m, from the wood-paneled **Lewers Lounge** flows the liquid sweetness of jazz vocalist Loretta Ables, accompanied by Jim Howard on keyboard and Bruce Hamada on bass. On Sunday and Monday, Billy Kurch, a pianist/vocalist, takes over and performs contemporary tunes.

Flashback, two shows nightly except Sunday, at the Waikiki Terrace Hotel, re-creates the legends of the '50s. Elvis lives!

The Honolulu Comedy Club, nightly except Monday, at the Ilikai Hotel, tel. 922-5998, presents most of Hawaii's and many of the Mainland's hottest comedians.

Discos, Dancing, And Nightclubs

Ballroom dancers will enjoy **Tea Dancing at the Royal** in the Monarch Room of the Royal Hawaiian Hotel, featuring the 14-piece Del Courtney Orchestra, Monday 5:30-8:30 p.m. The **Maile Lounge** at the Kahala Hilton, tel. 734-2211, offers live music for ballroom dancing nightly.

Nick's Fishmarket at the Gateway Hotel, 2070 Kalakaua (see "Food" above), swings with contemporary dance music until 1:30 a.m. A mixed crowd, but mostly a mature crowd who have stayed on to dance after one of the magnificent meals Nick's is known for. Music is provided by No Excuse, headliners who make Nick's their home when not on tour.

The **Paradise Lounge** in the Rainbow Tower of the Hilton Hawaiian Village is a jazz nightclub, perfect for a night of relaxing entertainment. They have a pianist nightly and a polished wooden dance floor. Weekends bring a variety of

J. D. BISIGNANI

the distinctive wall mural at The Wave

jazz ensembles for your listening and dancing pleasure. Perfect for a romantic evening.

The Wave is a rock 'n' roll and new wave hotspot with live music nightly, 1877 Kalakaua Ave., tel. 941-0424. It has become an institution of late-night fun and dancing. The crowd is mixed, and you can choose to dance, perch upstairs in the balcony behind glass to check out the dancers below, or have a few drinks and some conversation. The Wave is a sure bet for a night of fun.

Pink Cadillac, at 478 Ena, is just around the corner from the Wave. Open till 2 a.m., its large dance floors rock with merrymakers ages 18 and up. It's a happening place for younger rockers. Alcohol is served, but if you are under 21 you'll be braceleted, which means you can't drink. The cover charge is $10 for ages 18-21, $5 over 21.

The following are disco nightclubs in and around Waikiki. Most have videos, a theme, and a dress code of alohawear and shoes (no sandals). They start hopping around 9 p.m., with the energy cutoff around 4 a.m.

The **Jazz Cellar,** 205 Lewers St., tel. 923-9952, features mostly live rock 'n' roll and some jazz. The place jumps till 4 a.m. and has plenty of special nights like "Thirsty Tuesdays" and "Ladies' Night." Put on your dancin' shoes and casual attire.

Lewers Street Annex, at 270 Lewers, is a basic disco dance spot featuring Top 40 tunes. The clientele is mostly young visitors and some local workers who stop in for a late-night drink. A special feature is their "12 o'clock high," basically happy hour prices noon-midnight. Standard drinks are $1.50, domestic beers $1.50, margaritas and mai tais $1.50. Good for casual drinking, dancing, and meeting people.

The Infinity, at the Sheraton Waikiki, presents golden oldies and contemporary live music nightly from 8 p.m. Good dance floor.

The **Blue Water Cafe,** 2350 Kuhio Ave., once the home of live music, now has disco and videos. It's distinguished by its copper and brass appointment, including full copper doors to the restrooms, and pillars covered in copper.

The **3-D Ballroom,** 2260 Kuhio, is a crummy little joint two floors up with super-loud music for teeny-boppers and punkers.

The Point After, 2552 Kalakaua Ave., tel. 922-6611, is a local favorite with a dress code. Fatso sofas can be found in this football-theme nightspot.

Red Lion Dance Palace, 240 Lewers St., tel. 922-1027, offers high-tech video, disco, and a pool bar. Beachwear is OK. Open 2 p.m.-4 a.m.

Masquerade and **Phaze,** next door to each other at the corner of McCully St. and Kalakaua Ave., feature heavy sound systems and wild light shows. Cutting-edge videos, great dance floors, and wild tunes till 4 a.m.

Cilly's, 1909 Ala Wai Blvd., tel. 942-2942; **Annabelle's** at the Westin Ilikai, 1777 Ala

Moana Blvd., tel. 949-3811; and **Steel Wings,** also at the Westin Ilikai, are well-known discos where you can't help having a good time. All have reputations as swinging nightspots.

Exotic live dancers, like exotic live plants, need a unique atmosphere in which to bloom. Both seem to crave light, one sunlight, the other a spotlight. Most of the flashy fleshy nightspots of Waikiki used to be a few blocks away along Kapiolani Boulevard (see "Prostitution" under "Health and Safety" in the Out and About chapter), but they have been moving ever closer to the heart of Waikiki. Now they are strung along Kuhio Avenue, where they're easily recognizable by their garish neon lights advertising their wares. The Kuhio Avenue exotic dance spots are supposedly a step up in class from their Kapiolani Boulevard counterparts, but when their dancers strip to the buff, the difference is hardly noticeable . . . or very noticeable, depending upon point of view. The names of the strip joints really don't matter, just look for the Exotic Dancers signs. Usually a $10 cover and $5 for a drink.

Dinner Shows And Polynesian Extravaganzas

The **Don Ho Show,** an institution that played at the Hilton Hawaiian Village for years, is no longer. Mr. Ho has moved to the Waikiki Beachcomber at 2300 Kalakaua Ave., tel. 922-4646, where he plays two shows nightly, Thurs.-Sunday. The 7 p.m. dinner show costs $46, and the 9 p.m. cocktail show is $28. Either show is recommended. Gone are the glitz and glamour, leaving just Ho and his organ performing much the same way he did at Duke Kahanamoku's Club in the 1960s. Don Ho is still a great performer, and "the godfather of modern Hawaiian music."

Professional funster **Frank De Lima** hosts "Tropical Madness" in the Polynesian Palace nightly except Monday, at 9 p.m. De Lima, supported by a cast of loonies, is guaranteed to tickle your funny bone, "island style."

The Kahala Hilton, tel. 734-2211, presents **An Evening With Danny Kaleikini.** This extraordinary island entertainer has been captivating audiences here for almost 30 years. His show has class; it doesn't draw the large, budget-oriented crowds. Two shows nightly except Sunday, dinner show at 7 p.m., cocktail show at 9 p.m.

The Hilton Dome at the Hilton Hawaiian Village fills with magical vibrations when headliner **John Hirokawa** suddenly appears out of nowhere. The **Magic of Polynesia** is a journey into a realm of enchantment and beauty the entire family can enjoy. Sleight of hand, disappearing maidens, swaying hula dancers, fantastic costumes, and audience participation are all part of the magical extravaganza. Two shows nightly: dinner seating at 6:30 p.m., adults $45, children $31; cocktail show at 9 p.m., adults $25, children $17.

Society of Seven, a well-established local ensemble, appears nightly except Sunday at the Outrigger Main Showroom.

If you missed them the first time, here's your chance to see the world's greatest entertainers when unbelievably realistic impersonators perform **Legends in Concert,** a Las Vegas-style spectacular presented nightly at the Aloha Showroom of the Royal Hawaiian Shopping Center.

The Ainahau Showroom at the Sheraton Princess Kaiulani Hotel presents the **Sheraton Spectacular Polynesian Revue,** nightly for dinner and cocktail shows at 5:30 and 8 p.m.

Free Or Small Fee Entertainment

Check the newspapers and free tourist literature of times to the following events.

The **Royal Hawaiian Band** plays free concerts on Sunday afternoons at the bandstand in Kapiolani Park, oftentimes with singers and hula dancers. Also in the park, free concerts are periodically given by a variety of local and visiting musicians at the Waikiki Shell.

The **Kodak Hula Show** (small admission) is very popular. The show is held on Tuesday, Thursday, and Friday at 10 a.m. in Kapiolani Park, but people start lining up at 8 a.m.; be there by 9 if you want a seat. You sit on bleachers with 3,000 people, while Hawaiian *tutu* bedecked in muumuu, lei, and smiles play ukuleles and sing for the ti-leaf-skirted dancers. You can buy film and even rent a camera, as befits the show's sponsor, the Eastman Kodak Company—snap away with abandon. The performance dates back to 1937, and some of the original dancers, now in their eighties, still participate. At the finale, the dancers line up on stage with red-lettered placards that spell out H-A-W-A-I-I, so you can take your own photo of the most famous Hawaiian postcard. Then the audience is invited down for a free hula lesson. People who are too hip hate the show, *kama'aina* shy away from it, but if you're a good sport, you'll walk away like everyone else with a big smile on your face.

A potpourri of contemporary entertainment is also found in Kapiolani Park on weekends. Just across from the zoo, musicians, jugglers, clowns, unicyclists, and acrobats put on a free, impromptu circus. Some of the best are B.J. Patches, Twinkles, and Jingles from a local troupe called Clown Alley.

The **Ukulele Tree Hawaiian Music Show** is held in the Outrigger East Hotel Saturday, Sunday, and Monday 5-7 p.m., free, where local musicians and sometimes well-known guests come to play. For information call 922-5353.

The **Royal Hawaiian Shopping Center** provides free entertainment throughout the week: quilting, *lau hala* weaving, pineapple cutting, and hula lessons every Friday at 10 a.m. with Auntie Maiki Aiu Lake.

Molehu I Waikiki, a nightly torch-lighting ceremony complete with authentic hula performed by various *halau,* is offered to the public free of charge at Kuhio Beach Park. For information contact 923-1094.

Na Mea Hula, under the direction of *kumu hula* Karla Akiona, takes place every Friday 5:30-7 p.m., at the Sheraton Waikiki Hotel, tel. 922-4422. Preceding the hula, the presentation includes lei-making, conch-shell blowing, a *kahiko* procession, and a torch-lighting ceremony.

Aunty Bella's Leis, 2200 Kalakaua Ave., gives free lei-making classes Monday, Wednesday, and Friday at 10:30 a.m. The flowers are free and you keep the lei that you string.

At the Shore Bird Restaurant, 2160 Kalia, a **female bikini beauty** contest is held on Sunday at 4 p.m. You can win $400 for first prize, $150 second prize, $50 third. All finalists receive dinner for two at the Shore Bird Beach Broiler and much more.

Sometimes, "free" tickets to some of Waikiki's most popular Polynesian extravaganzas are handed out by condo time-share outfits stationed in booths along the main drags. For attending their sales presentations, usually 90 minutes, you can get tickets, but they might be the toughest freebies you've ever earned. The presentation is a pressure cooker in which hardened sales pros try every imaginable technique to get you to sign . . . "right now, because this is the only time that this deal can be offered." If you're really interested in time-sharing, the deals aren't too bad, but if you're there only for the tickets, what a waste of time!

SHOPPING

The biggest problem concerning shopping in Waikiki is to keep yourself from burning out over the endless array of shops and boutiques. Everywhere you look someone has something for sale, and with the preponderance of street stalls lining the boulevards, much of the merchandise comes out to greet you. The same rule applies to shopping that applies to everything in Waikiki—class next door to junk. Those traveling to the Neighbor Islands should seriously consider a shopping spree in Waikiki, which has the largest selection and most competitive prices in the islands. A great feature about shopping in Waikiki is that most shops are only a minute or two from the beach. This enables your sale-hound companion to hunt while you relax, or vice versa. There's no telling how much money your partner can save you: "Ingrate! This bathing suit could have cost $50, but I got it for $25. See, you saved $25 while you were lying here like a beached whale." Everyone concerned should easily be mollified. Charge!

The Fence

The best place to find an authentic island-made souvenir at a reasonable price is **The Fence,** located along the fence of the Honolulu Zoo fronting Kapiolani Park. The new official name is **Artists of Oahu/Sunday Exhibit.** Some of the island's best artists congregate here to display and sell their works on Wednesday and on weekends, 10 a.m.-4 p.m. Individual artists are only allowed to display one day a week. The Fence was the good idea of Honolulu's current mayor, Frank Fasi, who decided that Oahu's rich resource of artists shouldn't go untapped. There are plenty of excellent artists whose works are sure to catch your fancy.

artist John Costello with his work at The Fence

Gifts And Souvenirs

If you would really like to return from the islands with a unique gift try **Hawaiian Pillows and Kits,** tel. 734-5032. The pillowcases are excellent renditions of the distinctive style developed in Hawaii after quilting was introduced by the missionaries of last century. Rose Tam-Hoy, the owner, shows her handiwork at the Sheraton Moana's Banyan Courtyard on Friday and at various other hotels throughout the week. Rose is a wealth of knowledge on Hawaiian quilting, and is happy to offer demonstrations and lessons.

Another islander demonstrating and selling Polynesian crafts is Faitu Powell of **Powell's Souvenirs,** tel. 926-6797. Faitu also sets up a small display at the Moana on Friday, and across the way at the Princess Kaiulani on Saturday. She specializes in handmade hula skirts, lei, headbands, *haku,* and a variety of handicrafts. All of her souvenirs are authentic.

Fine Japanese art can be seen and purchased at two outstanding shops in Waikiki's Eaton Square, **Gallery Mikado** and **Garakuta-Do.**

ABC Stores scattered throughout Waikiki were founded by a local man, Sid Kosasa, who learned the retail business from his father. This "everything store" sells groceries, sundries, and souvenirs. Prices are good, especially on specials like lotions and beach mats. Very convenient.

On Kalakaua between Kealohilani and Ohua avenues above the ABC Store is **Lowest Factory Prices.** They've got very good prices on all-cotton shirts and muumuu, a rarity. Every price tag offers 10% off.

Those who just can't return home without a deep Hawaiian tan can be helped by visiting **Waikiki Aloe.** They specialize in skin-care products, lotions, and tanning supplies. You'll find them in the Royal Hawaiian Shopping Center and the Kuhio Mall.

The **Waikiki Business Plaza,** 2270 Kalakaua Ave., houses a number of jewelry stores. In one stop you can get a pretty good idea of prices and availability. Look for jewelry boxes laden with jade, gold, turquoise, pearls, coral, and *puka* shells; and eel, snake, and leather goods.

Military Shop of Hawaii has an entire wall dedicated to military patches, along with clothes, memorabilia, and collectibles. At 1921 Kalakaua Ave., tel. 942-3414.

Those with good taste but a limited budget should check out **Hawaiian Wear Unlimited,** liquidators of alohawear from most of Hawaii's big manufacturers. It's located at the Royal Hawaiian Shopping Center, open daily 9 a.m.-10 p.m. Also, **Robin Claire** "resale boutique" sells used designer clothing at 1901 Kapiolani Blvd., tel. 941-8666.

Kite Fantasy, 2863 Kalakaua Ave., tel. 922-KITE, is sure to have an aerial toy to tickle your fancy. Kapiolani Park across the road is one of the best spots around to fly a kite, and they give free kite-flying lessons regardless of whether you purchase a kite or not; daily display at 11 a.m. and 2 p.m. Next door to the old Natatorium and the New Otani Hotel, the store's multicolored kites float in the breeze. Inside Kite Fantasy is the "finest collection of kites, windsocks, and toys" in Hawaii. The phenomenal winds in Hawaii that generate good waves and good windsurfing conditions also generate excellent kite-flying conditions. Hardly a day goes by that there isn't wind enough to get a kite up. And, because the winds are so gusty and changeable, it makes for some fantastic kite-flying acrobatics. Nearby in the park is what they call the Kite Tree, where kite flyers congregate in the evening. So if you're interested, go fly a kite!

Waikiki Fashion Center, 2310 Kuhio, next door to Zorro's, sells alohawear like plenty of other stores, but the prices are pretty good, and they even feature an ad for $5 off with a purchase of $20 or more.

For a full range of **photo supplies** at bargain prices try: **Woolworth,** 2224 Kalakaua Ave.; **Fox Photo** in the International Market Place and the Waikikian and Reef Towers hotels; and **Photo Stores** here and there along Kalakaua, Kuhio, Kalia, and Lewers streets. **Island Camera and Gift Shop,** on Kalakaua across from the Moana Hotel, is a small but full-service camera store. Handbillers often give money-saving coupons for a variety of photo stores.

Duty-free goods are always of interest to international visitors. You can find a duty free store on Royal Hawaiian Ave., just behind Woolworth. Also, if you want to see a swarm of Japanese jostling for position in a tiny little store trying to feed a buying frenzy, that's the spot.

Waikiki Shopping Centers

The largest credit card oasis is the **Royal Hawaiian Shopping Center.** This massive complex is three stories of nonstop shopping, running for three blocks in front of the Sheraton and Royal Hawaiian hotels. It's open daily 9 a.m.-10 p.m., till 9 p.m. on Sunday, tel. 922-0588. This complex provides an excellent mixture of small intimate shops and larger department stores. There's a **post office** on the second-floor "B" building. The second and third floors of this shopping center are pretty quiet. It's off the street so not as many tourists find their way here. It's a good place to do some comparative browsing before making your purchases.

Where the Royal Hawaiian Shopping Plaza ends the **Waikiki Shopping Plaza** begins, but on the other side of the street. Here, you'll find multilevel shopping. The mall's centerpiece is a five-story waterfall, an impressive sculpture of water and plexiglass. Another feature of this mall is Waikiki Calls, a free hula show. The plaza is open daily 9 a.m.-11 p.m., tel. 923-1191.

The **International Market Place** is an open-air shopping bazaar that feels like Asia. Its natural canopy is a huge banyan, and the entire complex is across from the Moana Hotel at 2330 Kalakaua Ave., open daily from 9 a.m. until the vendors get tired at night, tel. 923-9871. Among some fine merchandise and a treasure or two is great junk. If you're after souvenirs like bamboo products, shellwork, hats, mats, lotions, alohawear, and carvings, you can't do better than the International Market Place. The worst thing is that everything starts to look the same; the best is that the vendors will bargain. Make offers and try hard to work your way through the gauntlet of shops without getting scalped. Check out the Elvis Store and Museum, which must be seen to be believed.

Directly behind the marketplace is the **Kuhio Mall,** at 2301 Kuhio Avenue. Basically the same theme with open-air shops: gifts, fashions, food, and handmade artifacts. Enjoy the free Polynesian Show nightly at 7 and 8 p.m. This is a little older, funkier mall, one grade up from the International Market Place and Duke's Alley. If you want a place to discover "treaure junk" this mall is better than the International Market Place because it's more low-key. There aren't nearly as many customers here and the salespeople are not as pushy.

For those who can't waste an opportunity to shop, pass through **Duke's Alley,** a shortcut between Kuhio and Kalakaua avenues. Here you'll find a row of stalls selling basically the same merchandise found in the International Market Place.

The **Hyatt Regency Shopping Center,** also called the **Atrium Shops,** is located on the first three floors of the Hyatt Regency Hotel, 2424 Kalakaua Ave., tel. 922-5522, open daily 9 a.m.-11 p.m. The 70 or so shops are mighty classy: if you're after exclusive fashions or a quality memento, this is the place. There's a continental-style sidewalk cafe, backed by a cascading indoor waterfall. Free entertainment and fashion shows are often put on by the various shops.

Smaller Malls

King's Village, at 131 Kaiulani Ave., just next to the Hyatt Regency, takes its theme from last century. Boardwalks pass 19th-century look-alike shops, complete with a changing-of-the-guard ceremony nightly at 6:15 p.m. This attractive complex offers free entertainment and attracts some of the best local street artists, who usually set up their stands at night. The **Waikiki Trade Center** on the corner of Seaside and Kuhio avenues has some of Waikiki's most elegant shops, featuring sophisticated fashions, exquisite artwork, and fine dining. The **Rainbow Bazaar** is a unique mall located at the Hilton Hawaiian Village, 2005 Kalia Road. Fun just to walk around, its shops feature three main themes: Imperial Japan, Hong Kong Alley, and South Pacific Court.

The Waikiki Bazaar is on Kalakaua across from a brand-new building called A.N.A. Kalakaua Center, a beautiful, multihued building in pastels reminiscent of newer constructions seen in Japan. The Bazaar is bizarre. Upstairs, and in little booths, is an orgy of porno shops. A person who couldn't read Japanese *katakana* wouldn't know that they said "porno." The Bazaar is expressly for the use of Japanese tourists.

Street Artists And Vendors

You don't have to try to find something to buy in Waikiki—in fact, if you're not careful, the merchandise will come after you! This takes place in the form of street vendors, who have been gaining a lot of attention lately. Some view them as a colorful addition to the beach scene, others as a nuisance. These carnival-type salespeople set up their mobile booths mainly along Kalakaua Avenue, with some on Kuhio Avenue and the side streets in between. In dealing with them you can have a positive experience if you remember two things: they have some pretty nifty junk, and you get what you pay for.

Also, street artists set up their palettes along busy thoroughfares, and especially at the entrances to small shopping malls. Most draw caricatures of patrons in a few minutes for a few dollars—fun souvenirs.

Right here under the Waikiki banyan is a gentleman named Coco who makes coconut-frond hats, basically a dying art. Just near the canoe rides, you'll see his hats and baskets. Depending on the hat, you can get one for $15 or so. The baskets, good for holding fruit, incidentals, or whatever, are a real souvenir of Hawaii. With Coco making them right before your very eyes, you can't get more authentic than that. Coco says you can still learn how to weave in the Hawaiian tradition. His dad, Uncle Harry Kuikai, weaves at the Royal Hawaiian Shopping Center every Tuesday and Thursday 9:30-11:30 a.m. He'll teach you the basics of weaving and you can make your own souvenir (free). For longer-term tourists, there's an eight-week weaving class sponsored by the Kamehameha Schools. Call the high school and inquire as to time and fees.

As you walk around Waikiki you'll see plenty of street-side booths offering unbelievable prices like "Rent a car for $5, a jeep for $15, Pearl Harbor Cruise $5, Don Ho Show $20." Why so cheap? The offers are made by an advertising firm that signs you up to listen to a 90-minute spiel on a time-share condo. What happens during and after the 90-minute hard pitch is up to you, but you do get the payoff at the end.

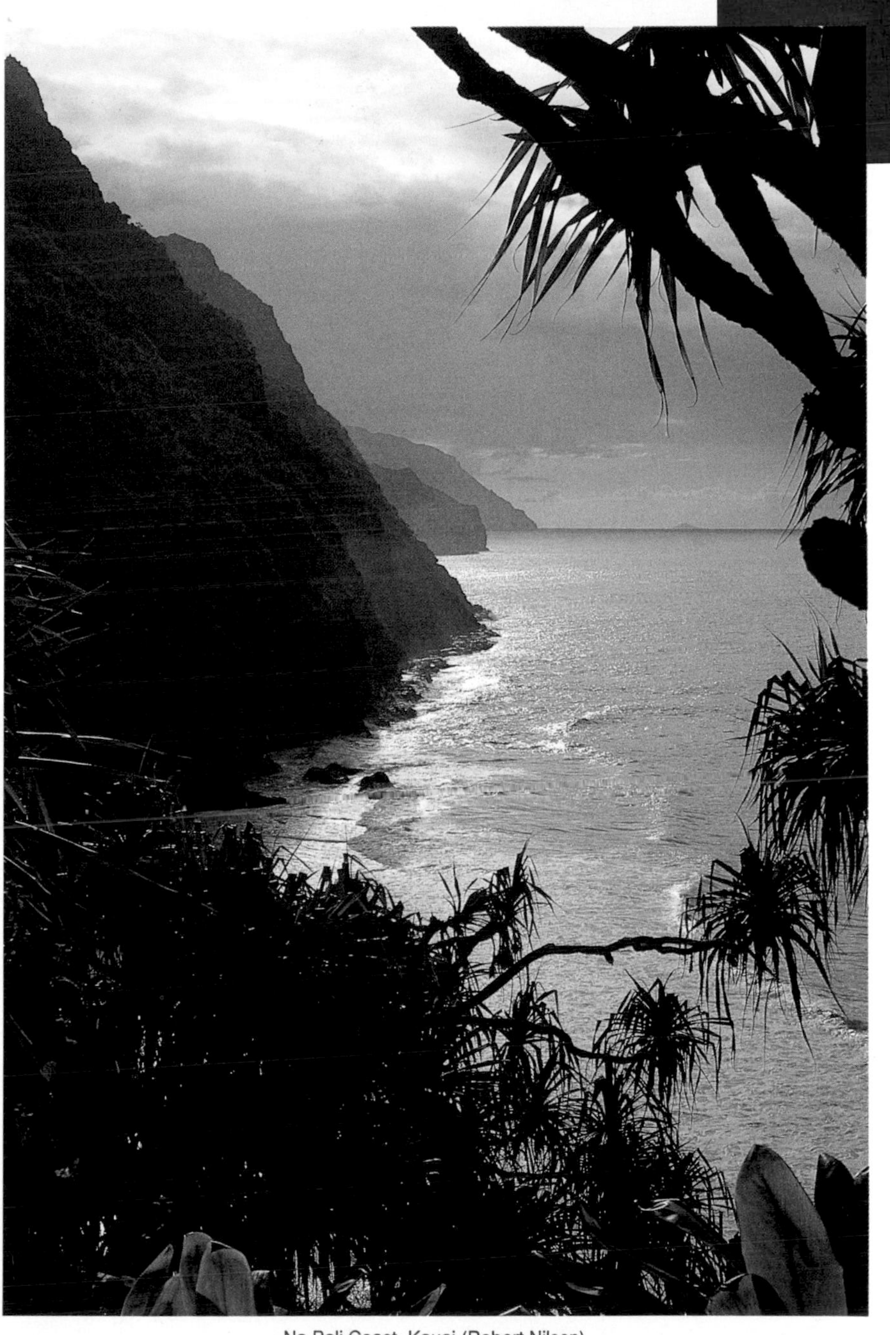

Na Pali Coast, Kauai (Robert Nilsen)

1

2

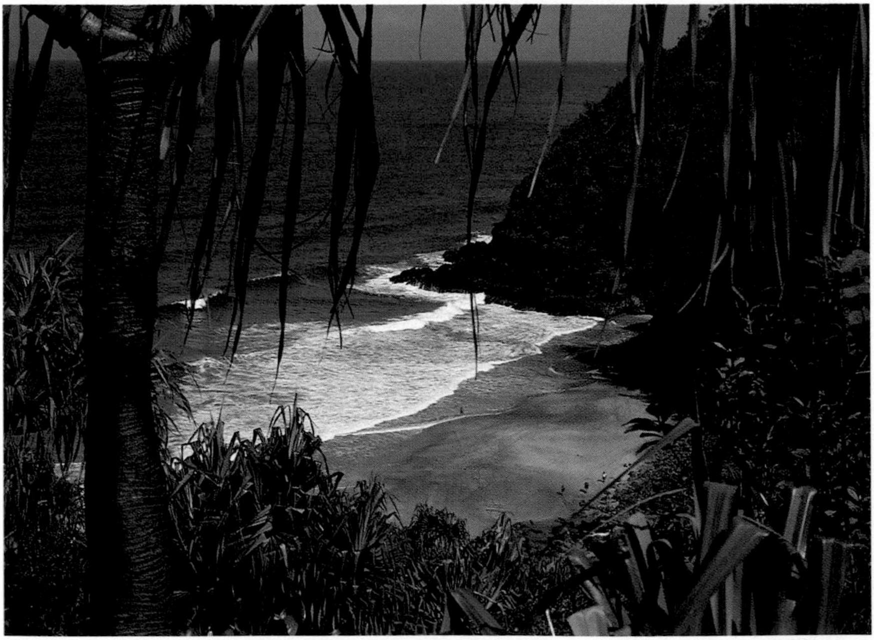

1. Waipio Valley, Hawaii (J.D. Bisignani); 2. Hanakapi'ai Beach, Kauai (Robert Nilsen)

BOB RACE

CENTRAL OAHU

For most uninformed visitors, central Oahu is a colorful blur as they speed past in their rental cars en route to the North Shore. Slow down, there are things to see! For some island residents, the suburban towns of Aiea, Pearl City, Mililani, and Wahiawa are home. Both routes heading north from Honolulu meet in **Wahiawa,** the island's most central town. The roads cross just near the entrance to **Schofield Barracks,** a warm-up target for Japanese Zeros as they flew on their devastating bombing run over Pearl Harbor.

Wahiawa was of extreme cultural and spiritual importance to the early Hawaiians. In town are **healing stones,** whose mystic vibrations were said to cure the maladies of sufferers. In a field not far from town are the **Kukaniloko,** the sacred birthing stones, where the ruling *ali'i* labored to give birth to the future nobles of the islands. While in town you can familiarize yourself with Oahu's flora by visiting the **Wahiawa Botanical Garden,** or take a quick look at a serene Japanese temple.

As you gain the heights of the **Leilehua Plateau,** sandwiched between the Waianae and Koolau ranges, a wide expanse of green is planted in cane and pineapple. Just like on supermarket shelves, Del Monte's **Pineapple Variety Garden** competes with Dole's **Pineapple Pavilion,** a minute up the road. As a traveler's way station, central Oahu blends services, amenities, and just enough historical sites to warrant stretching your legs, but not enough to bog you down for the day.

WAHIAWA AND VICINITY

Wahiawa is like a military jeep: basic, ugly, but indispensable. This is a soldiers' town, with servicepeople from Schofield Barracks or nearby Wheeler AFB shuffling along the streets. Most are young, short-haired, short-tempered, and dressed in fatigues. Everywhere you look are cheap bars, burger joints, run-down discos perfumed with sweat and spilled beer, and used-furniture stores. Route 99 turns into Rt. 80 which goes through Wahiawa, crossing California Avenue, the main drag, then rejoins Rt. 99 near the Del Monte Pineapple Variety Garden. Wahiawa has seemingly little to recommend it, and maybe because of its ugliness, when you do find beauty it shines even brighter.

SIGHTS

Wahiawa Botanical Garden

In the midst of town is an oasis of beauty, 27 acres of developed woodlands featuring exotic trees, ferns, and flowers gathered from around the world. Located at 1396 California Ave., they're open daily except Christmas and New Year's 9 a.m.-4 p.m.; admission is free. The parking lot is marked by an HVB Warrior; walk through the main entranceway and take a pamphlet from the box for a self-guiding tour. When it rains, the cement walkways are treacherously slippery, especially if you're wearing thongs. The nicer paths have been left natural, but they can be muddy. Inside the grounds are trees from the Philippines, Australia, and Africa, and a magnificent multihued Mindanao gum from New Guinea. Your senses will be bombarded with the fragrance of camphor trees from China and Japan, and the rich aroma of cinnamon. Everywhere are natural bouquets of flowering trees, entangled by vines and highlighted by rich green ferns. Most specimens have been growing for a minimum of 40 years, so they're well established.

The Healing Stones

Belief in the healing powers of these stones has been attracting visitors since ancient times. When traveling down Oahi Street (Rt. 80) take a left on California Avenue, and follow it to Kaalalo Place. To glimpse the religion of Hawaii in microcosm, in a few blocks you pass the Riusenji Soto Buddhist Mission, followed by the healing stones, next door to Olive United Methodist Church. If you've never experienced a Buddhist temple, make sure to visit the grounds of **Riusenji Soto Mission.** Usually no one is around, and even if the front doors are locked you can peer in at an extremely ornate altar graced by Buddha, highlighted in black lacquer and gold. On the grounds look for a stone *jizo,* patron of travelers and children. In Japan he often wears a red woven hat and bib, but here he has on a straw hat and muumuu.

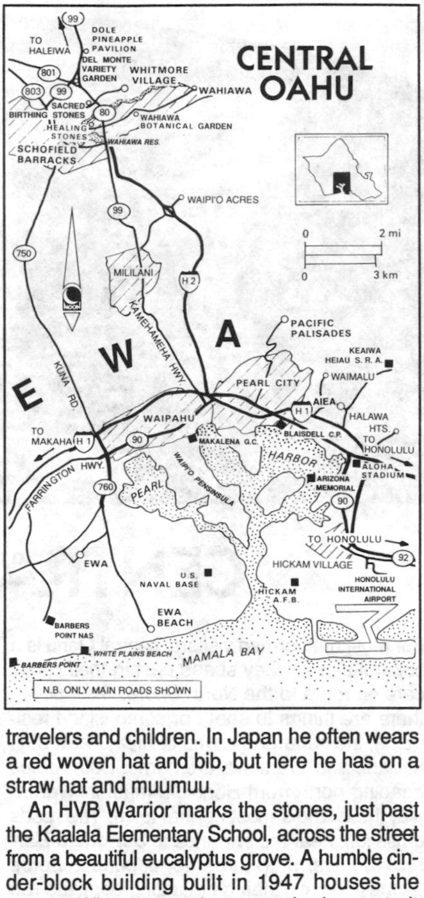

An HVB Warrior marks the stones, just past the Kaalala Elementary School, across the street from a beautiful eucalyptus grove. A humble cinder-block building built in 1947 houses the stones. When you swing open the iron gate it strikes a deep mournful note, as if it were an instrument designed to announce your presence and departure. Inside the building, three stones sit atop rudimentary pedestals. Little scratches mark the stones, and an offertory box is filled with items like oranges, bread, a gin bottle, coins, and candy kisses. A few votive candles flicker before a statue of the Blessed Virgin.

Kukaniloko, The Sacred Birthing Stones

Follow Rt. 80 through town for about a mile. At the corner of Whitmore Avenue is a red light: right takes you to Whitmore Village and left puts you on a dirt track that leads to another eucalyptus grove marking the birthing stones. About 40 large boulders sit in the middle of a field with a mountain backdrop. One stone looks like the next, but on closer inspection you see that each has a personality. The royal wives would come here, assisted by both men and women of the ruling *ali'i,* to give birth to their exalted offspring. The baby's umbilical cord, a sacred talisman, would be hidden in the cracks and crevices of the stones. Near the largest palm tree is a special stone that appears to be fluted all the way around, with a dip in the middle. It, along with other stones nearby, seem perfectly fitted to accept the torso of a woman in a reclining position. Notice that small fires have been lit in the hollows of these stones and that they are discolored with soot and ashes.

Schofield Barracks

Stay on Rt. 99, skirt Wahiawa to the west, and go past the entrance to Schofield Barracks. Schofield Barracks dates from the turn of the century, named after Gen. John Schofield, an early proponent of the strategic importance of Pearl Harbor. A sign tells you that it is still the "Home of the Infantry, Tropic Lightning." If you enter here through the McComb Gate, you can visit the **Tropic Lightning Museum** with memorabilia going back to the War of 1812. There are planes from WW II, Chinese rifles from Korea, and deadly *pungi* traps from Vietnam.

The museum has lost many of its exhibits in recent years. They've been taken to the Army Museum in Waikiki. But the base is still interesting to visit and remains one of the prettiest military installations in the world. With permission, you can proceed to the Kolekole Pass, from where you get a sweeping view of inland and coastal Oahu. While heading north on 99 as you pass Schofield Barracks, notice a few rundown shops about 50 yards past the entrance. Stop here and look behind the shops at a wonderful still life created by the Wahiawa Reservoir (good fishing; see "Freshwater Fishing" under "Sports and Recreation" in the Out and About chapter).

Pineapples

A few minutes past the entrance to Schofield Barracks, Rt. 803 bears left to Waialua, while Rt. 99 goes straight ahead and begins passing rows of pineapple. At the intersection of Rt. 80 is the **Del Monte Pineapple Variety Garden.** You're free to wander about and read the descriptions of the history of pineapple production in Hawaii, and of the genetic progress of the fruit made famous by the islands. This exhibit is much more educational and honest than the **Dole Pineapple Pavilion** just up the road, the one with all the tour buses lined up outside. You too can enter and pay $1.50 for a sad little paper plate half filled with pineapple chunks. Or how about 60 cents for a glass of canned pineapple juice from a dispenser that you'd find in any fast-food store? Unless the pineapple harvest has been abundant, you can't even buy a fresh fruit, and when you can, they're no cheaper or fresher than those in any grocery store. The Dole Pineapple Pavilion is firmly entrenched along the tourist route, but as a positive public relations scheme it is a blunder.

PRACTICALITIES

Food And Shopping

Dot's Restaurant, off California Ave. at 130 Mango St., tel. 622-4115, is a homey restaurant specializing in American-Japanese food that gives a good square meal for your money. The interior is a mixture of Hawaiian/Asian in dark brown tones. Lunch specials include butterfish, teriyaki chicken, pork, or beef plates for around $4.50. Miso soup is $2, and simple Japanese dishes go for about $3.50. The most expensive item on the menu is steak and lobster for $15. Dot's is nothing to write home about, but you definitely won't go hungry.

If you're into fast food, no problem. The streets are lined with places like **Jack in the Box** elbowing **McDonald's,** that's trying to outflash the old **Burger King.**

Wahiawa stores cater to residents, not tourists. This means that the prices are right, and if you need supplies or necessities, this would be a good place to stock up. On the corner of California Avenue and Oahi Street is a **Cornet Store,** an old-fashioned five and dime, where you can buy anything from suntan lotion to a crock pot. The **Big Way Supermarket** is at the corner of California and Kilani avenues.

AIEA, PEARL CITY, AND VICINITY

The twin cities of Aiea and Pearl City, except for the USS *Arizona* Memorial and perhaps a football game at Aloha Stadium, have little to attract the average tourist. Mainly they are residential areas for greater Honolulu, and for the large numbers of military families throughout this area.

PEARL HARBOR: USS *ARIZONA* MEMORIAL

Even as you approach the pier from which you board a launch to take you to the USS *Arizona*, you know that you're at a shrine. Very few spots in America carry such undeniable emotion so easily passed from one generation to another: here, Valley Forge, Gettysburg, not many more. On that beautiful, cloudless morning of December 7, 1941, at one minute before 8 o'clock, the United States not only entered the war, but lost its innocence forever.

The first battle of WW II for the U.S. actually took place about 90 minutes before Pearl Harbor's bombing, when the USS *Ward* sank an unidentified submarine sliding into Honolulu. In Pearl Harbor, dredged about 40 years earlier to allow superships to enter, the heavyweight champions of America's Pacific Fleet were lined up flanking the near side of Ford's Island. The naive deployment of this "Battleship Row" prompted a Japanese admiral to remark that never, even in times of maximum world peace, could he dream that the military might of a nation would have its unprotected chin stuck so far out, just begging for a right cross to the jaw. When it came, it was a roundhouse right, whistling through the air, and what a doozy.

Well before the smoke could clear and the last explosion stopped rumbling through the mountains, 3,581 Americans were dead or wounded, six mighty ships had sunk into the ooze of Pearl, 12 others stumbled around battered and punch-drunk, and 347 warplanes were useless heaps of scrap. The Japanese fighters had hardly broken a sweat, and when their fleet, located 200 miles north of Oahu, steamed away, the "east wind" had indeed "rained." But it was only the first squall of the American hurricane that would follow.

Getting There

There are a few options on how to visit Pearl Harbor and the USS *Arizona* Memorial. If you're driving, the entrance is along Rt. 99, the Kamehameha Hwy., about a mile south of Aloha Stadium; well-marked signs direct you to the parking area. If you're on H-1 west, take exit 15A, and follow the signs. You can also take TheBus, no. 50, 51, or 52 from Ala Moana Center, or no. 20 Airport from Waikiki, and be dropped off within a minute's walk of the entrance. Depending upon stops and traffic, this can take well over an hour.

***Arizona* Memorial Shuttle Bus,** tel. 839-0911, a private operation from Waikiki, takes about 20 minutes and will pick you up at most Waikiki hotels. They charge $2 one-way; reservations are necessary. Returning, no reservations are necessary; just buy a ticket from the woman selling them under the green umbrella in the parking lot.

The ***Arizona* Memorial Visitor Center** is a joint venture of the U.S. Park Service and the Navy, and is free. The Park Service runs the theater and museum, and the Navy operates the shuttle boats that take you out to the memorial shrine. The complex is open daily 7:30 a.m.-5 p.m., with daily programs 8 a.m.-3 p.m. (closed Thanksgiving, Christmas, New Year's Day), when you can visit the museum and the theater, and take the shuttle boats out to the memorial. If the weather is stormy, or waves rough, they won't sail. For recorded information call 422-0561 or 422-2771. As many as 3,000 people visit per day, and your best time to avoid delays is before 9:30 a.m.

Also, a number of boats operate out of Kewalo Basin doing **Pearl Harbor Cruises.** Charging about $15 for an extensive tour of Pearl Harbor, they are not allowed to drop passengers off at the memorial itself.

Bookstore And Theater

As you enter, you're handed a numbered ticket. Until it's called, you can visit the bookstore/gift

NATIONAL ARCHIVES

The Japanese attack on Pearl Harbor set off a chain of events that would make the U.S. the domineering power of the Pacific.

shop and museum, or if the wait is long, the USS *Bowfin* moored within walking distance (see following). The bookstore specializes in volumes on WW II and Hawaiiana. The museum is primarily a pictorial history, with a strong emphasis on the involvement of Hawaii's Japanese citizens during the war. There are instructions of behavior to "all persons of Japanese ancestry," from when bigotry and fear prevailed early in the war, as well as documentation of the 442nd Battalion, made up of Japanese soldiers, and their heroic exploits in Europe, especially their rescue of Texas's "lost battalion." Preserved newspapers of the day proclaim the "Day of Infamy" in bold headlines.

When your number is called you proceed to the comfortable theater, where a 20-minute film includes actual footage of the attack. The film is historically factual, devoid of an overabundance of flag waving and mom's apple pie. After the film you board the launch: no bare feet, no bikinis or bathing suits, but shorts and shirts are fine. Twenty years ago visitors wore suits and dresses as if going to church.

The Memorial

The launch, a large, mostly open-air vessel handled and piloted with professional deftness, usually by women Naval personnel, heads for the 184-foot-long alabaster memorial straddling the ship that still lies on the bottom. Some view the memorial as a tombstone; others see it as a symbolic ship, bent by struggle in the middle, but raised at the ends pointing to glory. The USS *Arizona* became the focus of the memorial because her casualties were so severe. When she exploded, the blast was so violent that it lifted entire ships moored nearby clear out of the water. Less than nine minutes later, with infernos raging and huge hunks of steel whizzing through the air, the *Arizona* was gone. Her crew went with her; nearly 1,100 men were sucked down to the bottom, and only 289 managed to struggle to the surface. To the left and right are a series of black and white moorings bearing the names of the ships tied to them on the day of the attack.

The deck of the memorial can hold about 200 people; a small museum holds the ship's bell, and a chapel-like area displays a marble tablet with the names of the dead. Into a hole in the center of the memorial, flowers and wreaths are dropped on special occasions. Part of the superstructure of the ship still rises above the waves, but it is slowly being corroded away by wind and seawater. The flag, waving overhead, is attached to a pole anchored to the deck of the sunken ship. Sometimes, on weekends, survivors from the attack are aboard to give first-hand descriptions of what happened that day. Many visitors are Japanese nationals, who often stop and offer their apologies to these Pearl Harbor survivors, distinguished by special military-style hats. The Navy ordered that any survivor wishing to be buried with his crew members had that right. In 1982 a diver took a stainless-steel container of the ashes of one of the survivors to be laid to rest with his buddies.

Nearby Attractions

The **USS *Bowfin,*** a WW II submarine moored within walking distance of the *Arizona* Memorial Center, has been turned into a self-guiding museum, open 9:30 a.m.-4:30 p.m., admission $6 adults, $1 children ages 6-12. In the little compound leading to the sub is a snack bar with some tables, a few artillery pieces, and a torpedo or two. As you enter, you're handed a telephonelike receiver; a recorded transmitted message explains about different areas on the sub. The deck is made from teakwood, and the deck guns could go fore or aft depending on the skipper's preference. You'll also notice two anchors; one, under a fresh coat of paint, was salvaged from the pink sub used in the film *Operation Petticoat.*

As you descend, you feel as if you are integrated with a machine, a part of its gears and workings. In these cramped quarters of brass and stainless steel lived 90-100 men, all volunteers. Fresh water was in short supply, and the only man allowed to shower was the cook. Officers were given a dipper of water to shave with, but all the other men grew beards. With absolutely no place to be alone, the men slept on tiny stacked shelves, and only the officers could control their light switches. The only man to have a minuscule private room was the captain.

Topside, twin 16-cylinder diesels created unbelievable noise and heat. A vent in the passageway to the engine room sucked air with such strength that if you passed under it, you'd be flattened to your knees. When the sub ran on batteries under water, the quiet became maddening. The main bunk room, not much bigger than an average bedroom, slept 36 men. Another 30 or so ran the ship, while another 30 lounged. There was no night and day, just shifts. Coffee was constantly available, as well as fresh fruit, and the best mess in all the services. Subs of the day had the best radar and electronics available. Aboard were 24 high-powered torpedoes, and ammo for the topside gun. Submariners, chosen for their intelligence and psychological ability to take it, knew that a hit from the enemy meant certain death. The USS *Bowfin* is fascinating and definitely worth a visit.

The Navy holds an **open house** on one of its ships berthed at Pearl Harbor on the first Saturday of each month. For information call 474-8139. You must enter through the main Nimitz Gate, and then follow the signs to the ship, which is usually at the Bravo or Mike piers. On your way to the docking area you stop at the Family Services area where you can pick up snacks or ice cream at a Baskin-Robbins concession. The sailors conducting the tour are polite and knowledgeable, and the tour is free. You can always spot the officers—the guys with the white shoes. Take TheBus to the Nimitz Gate, or if you've visited the *Arizona* Memorial, a convenient shuttle connects it with the gate for only 50 cents.

The **Pacific Submarine Museum** is also reached through the Nimitz Gate. It's free but you need a pass from the gate. It's open Wed.-Sun. 9:30 a.m.-5 p.m., tel. 471-0632.

BEACHES AND SIGHTS

As you travel up Aiea Heights Road, an exit off H-1, you get a world-class view of Pearl Harbor below. It's not glorious because it is industrialized, but you do ride through suburban sprawl Hawaiian style until you come to the end of the road at **Keaiwa Heiau State Recreation Area.** In the cool heights above Aiea, these ancient grounds have a soothing effect the minute you enter. Overnight tent camping is allowed here, in exceptionally large sites (permit needed, see "Camping and Hiking" in the Oahu Introduction); for the few other visitors, the gates open at 7 a.m. and close at 6:30 p.m. As you enter the well-maintained park (a caretaker lives on the premises), tall pines to the left give a feeling of alpine coolness. Below, Pearl Harbor lies open, like the shell of a great oyster.

Keaiwa Heiau was a healing temple, surrounded by gardens of medicinal herbs tended by Hawaii's excellent healers, the *kahuna lapa'au.* The garden's, roots, twigs, leaves, and barks were ground into potions and mixed liberally with prayers and love. These potions were amazingly successful in healing Hawaiians before white people brought their diseases. As you walk onto the stone floor of the *heiau,* the air is somehow warmer and the winds seem quieter. Toward the floor's center are numerous offerings, simple stones wrapped in ti leaves. Some are old, while others are quite fresh. Follow the park road to the **Aiea Loop Trail,** which heads back 4.5 miles roundtrip onto one of the ridges descending from the Koolaus. Pass through a forest of tall eucalyptus trees, viewing canyons to the left and right. Notice, too, the softness of the "spongy bark" trees growing where the path begins. Allow three hours for the loop.

Blaisdell County Park's waters, which can be considered part of Pearl Harbor, are too polluted for swimming. It's sad to think that at the turn of the century they were clear and clean enough to support oysters. Pearl Harbor took its name from Waimomi, "Water of Pearls," which were indeed harvested from the oysters and a certain species of clam growing here. Today, sewage and countless oil spills have done their devastation. Recently, oysters from the Mainland's East Coast have been introduced, and are being harvested from the mudflats. Supposedly, they're fit to eat. Facilities include a pay phone, tables, and restrooms. Access is off Rt. 99 just past Aloha Stadium and before you enter Pearl City.

Keehi Lagoon Beach Park is also polluted, but some people do swim here. The park is at the northern tip of Keehi Lagoon, at 465 Lagoon Dr., just past the **Pacific War Memorial** on Rt. 92 (the Nimitz Highway). Here are restrooms, picnic facilities, and a pay phone. Local people use the area for pole fishing and crabbing.

The **Hawaii Plantation Village,** 94-695 Waipahu St., Waipahu, HI 96797, tel. 677-0110, offers a stroll down memory lane into a once working plantation village. The small group of homes is a testament to the hard work performed by Hawaii's plantation communities. Reservations are recommended, and admission is by donation.

PRACTICALITIES

Accommodations

Except for long-term stays, accommodations are virtually nonexistent in this area. Luckily a few **bed and breakfast** homes provide alternatives (see "Bed and Breakfast" under "Accommodations" in the Out and About chapter). One of the most interesting is the home of Corry and Helga Trummel, who reside in Pacific Palisades above Pearl City. What started out as a tract house has become a living museum. Helga has been collecting and inheriting art since she was a little girl in prewar Germany. Every nook and cranny has a curio from Europe, Asia, or Hawaii, and Helga loves to share her artwork and the fascinating stories of her youth. The first floor is completely dedicated to the guests. There's a music room, a library with a fine collection of books on WW II and the western U.S., two bedrooms, and a separate cottage in the back. Out back too are a small pool, dry sauna, and observation platform high on the hill. Inside, as you mount the steps to the second floor you're greeted by a wooden statue of a woman with a bowl on her head, original oil paintings, and a grandfather clock, all from the last century. Enter the breakfast nook and suddenly you're in a German hunting lodge. The green and white table and benches painted with flowers are over 100 years old. Gaze around at a stuffed bear, an antique sitar, a mountain goat, stag, stuffed ducks, a collection of beer steins, a white moose head, pronghorn, and a bar. All in what was once a tract house kitchen! The main house is furnished like a very rich German chocolate cake; maybe not to everyone's taste, but definitely filling.

The **Pepper Tree Apartment Hotel,** at 98-150 Lipoha Pl., Aiea, HI 96701, tel. 488-1993, offers furnished studios and apartments, all with complete kitchens and baths, TV, and phones. A laundromat and swimming pool are also available. Many military personnel use this facility as temporary housing.

Shopping, Dining, And Services

The main shopping center in Aiea is the **Pearlridge Shopping Center,** tel. 488-0981, open Mon.-Sat. 10 a.m.-9 p.m., Sun. to 5 p.m., with prices geared toward island residents, not tourists, so you have a good chance of coming away with a bargain. Some of the larger stores include Liberty House, JCPenney, Sears, Star Market, Longs Drugs, Waldenbooks, and Woolworth. There are also 16 theaters, two food courts with over 30 restaurants, plus 150 smaller boutiques and specialty shops. The entire complex is air-conditioned and serviced by an in-house monorail for your shopping convenience.

Buzz's Steak House, 98-751 Kuahao Pl. (at the corner of Moana Loa and Kaahumanu), tel. 487-6465, sometimes open for lunch, nightly for dinner, is futuristic, like something a kid would build with an erector set. It'd be perfect if it were down by the sea, where you could see something, but from where it's located you can peer at Pearl Harbor in the distance or have a world-class view of the freeway. The steakhouse is owned and operated by an old island family whose business grew into a small chain of restaurants from their original location in Kailua. This is one of the remaining three. Buzz's is an institution where islanders go when they want a sure-fire good meal. There's a salad bar and you prepare your own charbroiled steaks and fish. The prices are reasonable.

The **Waimalu Shopping Plaza,** located along Kaahumanu St. between the Kamehameha Hwy. (Rt. 99) and the H-1 Freeway, has a small cluster of shops and restaurants. There's a **Times Supermarket,** open 24-hours with its pharmacy and deli, and the **Good Health Store,** open 9 a.m.-7 p.m., Sat. 11 a.m.-6 p.m., selling food supplements and minerals. In the same complex is **Stuart Anderson's Cattle Co.,** tel. 487-0054, open daily for lunch and dinner. The lounge is open until 2 a.m. weekends, serving huge steaks and all the trimmings.

Across the road is the **Elephant and Castle Restaurant,** at 98-1247 Kaahumanu, tel. 487-5591, open daily for lunch and dinner, breakfast only on weekends. This restaurant has done an excellent job of creating an English-style pub atmosphere. The interior is cool and rich with red velvet, heavy chairs, tapestries, open beams, with a pool table and dart boards in the pub area. Nightly, it's one of the best places in the area for a beer and a chat. The food is good too. For example, try English fish 'n' chips ($4.95), a burger platter ($5), hot sandwiches ($5), or soup and sandwich ($4.75). Specials on weekends are English prime rib dinner, (queen-sized $10.95, king-sized $14.95), New York steak ($14.95), and seafood scampi ($10.95). Enjoy merry old England Hawaiian style.

The **Pearl City Tavern,** at 905 Kamehameha Hwy. (corner of Waimano Home Dr.), tel. 455-1045, is the best restaurant in the Pearl City/Aiea area. The cuisine is a combination of seafood, steaks, and mainstream Japanese. They're famous for their "monkey bar," which houses rhesus monkeys behind the bar in a glass cage. After a couple of stiff belts some customers think they're looking into a mirror. There's a fish tank bubbling away and a separate tank for live Maine lobsters, a specialty of the house. Choose a table or romantic booth in the huge dining room appointed with Japanese scrolls, a huge lantern, and shoji screens. For lunch try escargot ($5.50), seafood *pu pu* ($2.15), chef salad ($8), shrimp Louie ($7.50), or a bowl of Boston clam chowder for only $1.50. Dinner is delicious with a choice of chicken oriental salad ($6), prime rib ($15.75), fillet of mahimahi ($15), or seafood Newburg ($15.75). Or choose three different entrees for $25 from: soft-shell crab, shrimp and scallops, king crab legs, and roast prime rib. Dinners include won-ton soup or salad, potatoes, and French bread and butter. Complete Japanese dinners at $17.25 per person consist of miso soup and trimmings, rice and tea, and a choice of any three of the following entrees: broiled fish, sashimi, beef teriyaki, butterfish *misoyaki,* or chicken teriyaki. If you're in the Pearl Ridge/Aiea area and want a special night out, this is the place.

DIANA LASICH HARPER

triton shell

BOB RACE

SOUTHEAST OAHU

KOKO HEAD TO WAIMANALO

It's amazing how quickly you can leave the frenzy of Waikiki behind. Once you round the bend past Diamond Head and continue traveling east toward Koko Head, the pace slackens measurably . . . almost by the yard. A minute ago you were in traffic, now you're cruising. It's not that this area is undeveloped; other parts of the island are much more laid-back, but none are so close to the action of the city. In the 12 miles you travel from Honolulu to Waimanalo, you pass the natural phenomenon of Koko Crater, a reliable blowhole, the most aquatically active underwater park in the islands, and a string of beaches, each with a different personality.

Humans have made their presence felt here, too. The area has some of the most exclusive homes on the island, as well as Hawaii Kai, a less exclusive project developed by the visionary businessman Henry Kaiser, who 20 years ago created this harbinger of things to come. There's Sea Life Park, offering a day's outing of fun for the family, plus shopping centers, the mostly Hawaiian town of Waimanalo, and Bellows Air Force Base, unused by the military and now one of the finest camping beaches on the island. Other than campsites, few accommodations are found out here, and few restaurants. This lack of development preserves the area as scenic and recreational, prized attributes that should be taken advantage of before this sunny sandbox gets paved over.

SIGHTS, BEACHES, AND PARKS

The drive out this way accounts for half of the 360 degrees of what is called **The Circle Route.** Start by heading over the Pali Hwy. down to Kailua, hitting the sights on the way, or come this way first along Diamond Head Road to Rt. 72 as you make the loop back to the city. The only consideration is what part of the day you'd rather stop at the southeast beaches for a dip. For the most part, the beaches of this area *are* the

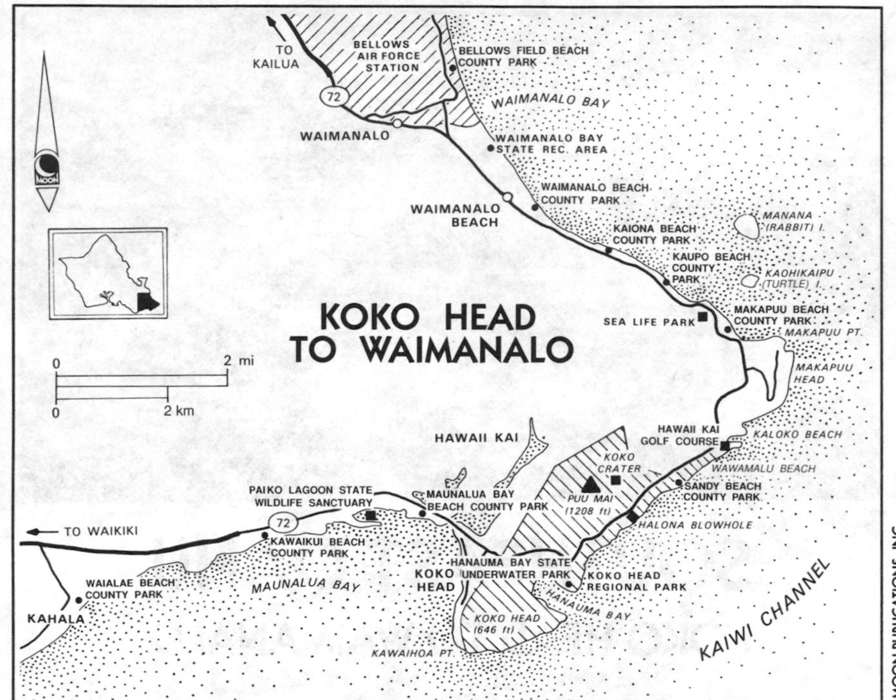

sights, so both are combined in this one section. The road abounds with scenic points and overlooks. This is the part of Oahu that's absolutely beautiful in its undevelopment. It's hard to find a road on any of the Hawaiian islands that's going to be more scenic than this. At first the countryside is dry because this is the leeward side. But as you approach Waimanalo it gets much more tropical. The road is a serpentine ribbon with one coastal vista after another, a great choice for a joy ride just to soak in the sights. The following listings assume that you follow Rt. 72 from Waikiki to Waimanalo. For beaches between Waikiki and the following, please see "Waikiki Beaches and Parks" under "Sights" in the Waikiki chapter.

Maunalua Bay

Maunalua ("Two Mountain") Bay is a four-mile stretch of sun and surf between Diamond Head and Koko Head, with a beach park about every half mile. The first is **Waialae Beach County Park** in Kahala. Go straight ahead on Kahala Avenue for one minute instead of going left on Rt. 72 to join H-1 on to Hanauma Bay. This section is the Beverly Hills of Honolulu, as many celebrities like Tom Selleck and Carol Burnett have homes here. The least expensive home in this section easily pushes the $1 million asking price. Waialae is a popular windsurfing spot, crowded on weekends. It's a small beach park with basic amenities in a beautiful location where Makapuu Head wraps around and gives the impression that there are two islands off in the distance, but it's just the way Oahu bends at this point.

Next comes **Kawaikui Beach County Park.** No lifeguard, but the conditions are safe year-round, and the bottom is shallow, muddy, and overgrown with seaweed. In times past, islanders came to the confluence of a nearby spring to harvest special *limu* that grow only where fresh water meets the ocean. You'll find unlimited access, parking stalls, picnic facilities, and restrooms. Few people use the park, and it's ideal for sunning, but for frolicking in the water, give it a miss.

In quick succession come **Niu and Paiko beaches,** lying along residential areas. Although there is public access, few people take advantage of them because their coral and mud bottoms are less than ideal for swimming. Some residents have built a pier at Niu Beach past the mudflats, but it's restricted to their private use. Paiko Lagoon is a state wildlife sanctuary; binoculars will help you sight a variety of coastal birds.

The residential area in the hills behind **Maunalua Bay Beach County Park** is Hawaii Kai, built by Henry Kaiser, the aluminum magnate. The controversial development was often denigrated as "suburban blight." Many felt it was the beginning of Oahu's ruination. The park fronts Kuapa Pond, at one time a huge fishpond, later dredged by Kaiser, who used the dredged material to build the park, which he donated to the city in 1960. Now, most of the land has been reclaimed except for Koko Marina, whose boat launch constitutes the primary attraction of the park. You'll find a large sandy parking area where **Paradise Jet Skis** (look for a tent) rents self-powered skis, pricey at $40 per hour, tel. 235-1612.

Except for the boat launch (the only one on this side of the island), the area is of little recreational use because of the mud or coral bottom. However, swimming is possible and safe, but be careful of the sudden drops created by the dredged boat channels. Two undeveloped parks are located at the end of Poipu Drive, **Koke'e and Koko Kai parks.** The currents and beach conditions make both unsuitable for swimming, but they're popular with surfers. Few others come here, but the views of the bay are lovely with glimpses of Molokai floating on the horizon to the south.

Hanauma Bay State Underwater Park

One of the premier beach parks in Hawaii is located in the sea-eroded crater of an extinct volcano just below Koko Head. People flock here to snorkel, scuba, picnic, and swim. During the day, the parking lot at the top of the hill overlooking the crescent bay below looks like a used car lot, jammed with Japanese imports, vans, and tour buses. A shuttle bus (75 cents) runs up and down the hill, and you can rent snorkeling equipment at the concession stand for $10 per day, but quantities are limited. If you want to avoid the crowds, come in the early morning or after 4 p.m., when the sun dips behind the crater and most tourists leave on cue. There's still plenty of daylight, so plan your trip accordingly.

The reef protects the bay and sends a maze of coral fingers right up to the shoreline. A large sandy break in the reef, **Keyhole,** is a choice spot for entering the water and for swimming. The entire bay is alive with tropical fish. Many have become so accustomed to snorkelers that they've lost their fear entirely, and willingly accept food from your fingers—some so rudely you had better be careful of getting your fingers nibbled. The county provides lifeguards, restrooms, showers, picnic facilities, a pavilion, and a food concession.

Before you enter the water, do yourself a favor and read the large bulletin board near the pavilion that describes conditions. It divides the bay into three areas ranging from beginner to expert, and warns of sections to avoid. Be especially careful of **Witches Brew,** a turbulent area on the right at the mouth of the bay that can wash you into the **Molokai Express,** a notoriously dangerous rip current. Follow a path along the left-hand seacliff to **Toilet Bowl,** a natural pool that rises and falls with the tides. If the conditions are right, you can sit in it to float up and down in a phenomenon very similar to a flushing toilet.

Environmental Alert: Because severe overuse was threatening the fragile ecosystem of the bay, tour companies are now banned from dropping people in the park expressly for snorkeling. Tour buses can now only stop at the top of the hill for a 15-minute overview, and then must leave. People wishing to explore the bay may come by rental car, moped, bicycle, or city bus, which has a stop within the park. However, if you drive, once the parking lot is filled, it is closed! And, the park is closed to visitors on Wednesday mornings until noon for sorely needed maintenance. Also, please do not feed the fish anything but approved fish food. Peas and bread are only appetizing to large-mouthed fish and severely cut down on the variety of fish that would normally live within the reef. Most importantly, the very reef is being destroyed by people walking upon it. Please do everything you can to avoid this. A few tour companies have continued bringing people into the park and have found ways to violate the *spirit,* if not the *letter,* of the restrictions. Please do not patronize them. With care, Hanauma Bay will remain beautiful for future generations.

Koko Head Hike

For a sweeping view, hike to the summit of **Koko Head,** not to be confused with Koko Crater, another good hike but farther east on Rt. 72 (see following). To start your trek, look for a paved road closed off to vehicles by a white metal fence, on the right before the road to the parking lot. A 15-minute hike takes you to the 646-foot summit of Koko ("Blood") Head. This was the last place where young, wandering Madame Pele attempted to dig herself a fiery nest on Oahu; as usual, she was flooded out by her jealous sister. From the summit you get an unobstructed view of Molokai 20 miles across the Kaiwi Channel, the bowl of Hanauma Bay at your feet, and a sweeping panorama of Diamond Head and the Koolau Mountains. Below are two small extinct craters, Nono'ula and Ihi'ihilauakea.

Koko Crater

Koko Crater's Hawaiian name is Kohelepelepe ("Fringed Vagina"). Legend says that Pele's sister, Kapo, had a magical "flying vagina" that could fly and that she could send anywhere. Kamapua'a, the pig-god, was intent on raping Pele when Kapo came to her aid. She dispatched her vagina to entice Kamapua'a, and he followed it to Koko Head, where the vagina made the crater and then flew away. Kamapua'a was unsuccessful when taking a flying leap at this elusive vagina.

You can either hike or drive to the crater. To begin the hike, look for the road to the "Hawaii Job Corp Training Center" just across from Hanauma Bay. Follow the road down past a rifle range and park at the job training building. Behind it is an overgrown tramway track. The remaining ties provide a rough but adequate stairway to the top. At the 1,208-foot summit is an abandoned powerhouse and tramway station. The wood is rotted and the floors are weak! The crater itself lies 1,000 feet below. An easier but less exciting route is to follow Rt. 72 for two miles to Wawamalu Beach near the Hawaii Kai Golf Course, and then take a left on Kealahou Street. Nearby is a walking path that leads into the crater. On the floor of Koko Crater is a botanical garden that, due to the unique conditions, specializes in succulents.

Halona Cove

As you round a bend on Rt. 72 you come to the natural lookout of Halona Cove, which means "The Peering Place," an excellent vantage point from which to see whales in season. Just before Halona, a sign will point you to the **Honolulu Japanese Casting Club,** with a stone wall and a monument. The monument at one time was of O Jisan, the Japanese god of protection, destroyed by overzealous patriots during WW II. The current monument was erected after the war, and O Jisan was carved into it. Below is a secluded little beach that's perfect for sunbathing. The only way to it is to scramble down the cliff. Swim only on calm days, or the waves can pull you out to sea and then suck you into the chamber of the famous **Halona Blowhole** just around the bend. There's a turnout at the blowhole for parking. The blowhole is a lava tube at the perfect height for the waves to be driven into it. The water is compressed, and the pressure sends a spume into the air. Be extremely cautious around the blowhole. Those unfortunate enough to fall in face almost certain death.

Sandy Beach County Park

Sandy Beach is one of the best bodysurfing beaches on Oahu, and the most rugged of them all. More necks and backs are broken on this beach than on all the other Oahu beaches combined. But because of the east-breaking waves, and bottom, the swells are absolutely perfect for bodysurfing. The lifeguards use a flag system to inform you about conditions. The **red flag** means "stay out." When checking out Sandy Beach, don't be fooled by bodysurfers who make it appear easy. These are experts, intimately familiar with the area, and even they are injured at times. Local people refer to the beach as "Scene Beach" because this is where young people come to strut their stuff. This is where the boys are because this is where the

J.D. BISIGNANI

The lifeguards do a great job at Sandy Beach.

girls are. There are restrooms, a large parking area, and two lifeguard towers. Rip-offs have happened, so don't leave valuables in your car. *Kaukau* wagons park in the area, selling a variety of refreshments.

As the road skirts the coastline, it passes a string of beaches that look inviting but are extremely dangerous because there is no protecting reef. The best known is **Wawamalu,** where people come to sunbathe only. Across the road is **Hawaii Kai Golf Course,** tel. 395-2358. You have a choice of two courses: the Championship, offering a full round of golf with beautiful views, challenging holes, and excellent greens; or the Executive, a shorter par-three course for those with limited time. This is an excellent public course, but the greens fee is high.

Makapuu Beach County Park

This beach park is below Makapuu ("Bulging Eye") Point, a projection of land marking Oahu's easternmost point, and a favorite launch pad for hang gliding. Makapuu is *the* most famous bodysurfing beach in the entire state, but it can be extremely rugged; more people are rescued here than at any other beach on Oahu (except Sandy Beach). In winter the conditions are hazardous, with much of the beach eroded away, leaving exposed rocks. With no interfering reef, the surf can reach 12 feet—perfect for bodysurfing, if you're an expert. Board riding is prohibited. In summer, the sandy beach reappears, and the wave action is much gentler, allowing recreational swimming. There are restrooms, lifeguard towers with a flag warning system, and picnic facilities.

Offshore is **Manana ("Rabbit") Island.** Curiously, it does resemble a rabbit, but it's so named because rabbits actually live on it. They were released here in the 1880s by a local rancher who wanted to raise them but who was aware that if they ever got loose on Oahu they could ruin much of the crop lands. During the impotent counterrevolution of 1894, designed to reinstate the Hawaiian monarchy, Manana Island was a cache for arms and ammunition buried on its windward side. Nearby is tiny Kaohikaipu ("Turtle") Island, which, along with Manana, is a seabird sanctuary.

Sea Life Park Hawaii

Overlooking Makapuu Point and nestled below the lush Koolau Mountains is Sea Life Park Hawaii, a cluster of tanks holding an amazing display of marine animals that live freely in the ocean just a few hundred yards away. Admission for adults is $19.95, juniors $8.95, and children $3.95. Open daily 9:30 a.m.-5 p.m., Friday until 10 p.m., tel. 259-7933 or (800) 767-8046. A free shuttle bus runs from major Waikiki hotels (call for details), or take TheBus no. 57 from Ala Moana Center, or no. 58, which comes straight up Kuhio Avenue. The park hosts a variety of shows by trained seals, whales, and dolphins, along with the informative Ocean Science Theater. The park's most impressive feature is the **Hawaiian Reef Tank,** a massive 300,000-gallon fishbowl where guests come face to face with over 2,000 specimens of the island's rich marinelife as they descend three fathoms down an exterior ramp. At **Whaler's Cove,** tall tales and legends of old Hawaii are retold while the park's dolphins cavort using offshore Rabbit Island as a backdrop.

Outside the entrance turnstile is a shopping complex and the new **Sea Lion Cafe.** Here too is the **Pacific Whaling Museum,** free admission, housing one of the largest collections of whaling artifacts and memorabilia in the Pacific. The Whaler's Cove has a replica of a whaling ship called the *Essex Nantucket.* Sea lion food is available, and there are public feedings daily at 11:30 a.m., 1:30 p.m., and 3:30 p.m., also 5 p.m. on Friday. Sea Life Park Hawaii is a great learning and entertaining experience for the entire family, or for anyone interested in exploring Hawaii's fascinating marinelife.

Kaupo Beach County Park

This is the first park that you come to along the southeast coast that is safe for swimming. It is between Sea Life Park and Waimanalo. The park is undeveloped and has no lifeguards, so you are advised to exercise caution. The shore is lined with a protective reef or rocks, and the swimming is best beyond the reef. Close to shore, the jutting rocks discourage most swimmers. Surfers frequent Kaupo, especially beginners, lured by the ideal yet gentle waves.

Kaiona Beach County Park

Just before you enter the ethnically Hawaiian town of Waimanalo, you pass Kaiona Beach County Park, which you can spot because of the semipermanent tents pitched here. Local people are very fond of the area, and use it extensively. Look inland to view some remarkable cliffs and mountains that tumble to the sea. The area was at one time called Pahonu, "Turtle Fence," because a local chief who loved turtle meat erected a large enclosure in the sea into which any turtle that was caught by local fishermen had to be deposited. Parts of the pond fence can still be seen. Facilities include restrooms, showers, and a picnic area. Swimming is safe year-round, and tent and trailer camping are allowed with a county permit.

Waimanalo

This small rural town was at one time the center of a thriving sugar plantation owned by the *hapa* Hawaiian nobleman, John Cummins, who was responsible for introducing rabbits to Manana Island. It has fallen on hard times ever since the plantation closed in the late 1940s, and now produces much of Honolulu's bananas, papayas, and anthuriums from small plots and farms. The town sits in the center of Waimanalo Bay, which is the longest (3.5 miles) stretch of sand beach on Oahu. To many people, especially those from Oahu, it is also the best. Few but adequate travelers' services are in town (see "Services" below).

The **Olomana Golf Links,** tel. 259-7926, is a 6,000-yard, relatively easy, par-72 course, inexpensive and close to town. It's also a good place to go for breakfast. You think you're in Waimanalo when you pass a 7-Eleven Store and McDonald's in a built-up area, but this isn't it. Keep going about a mile or two, and you'll come to the older section of town which is Waimanalo proper.

Waimanalo Beach County Park, as you enter town by the 7-Eleven and McDonald's, provides camping with a county permit. The beach is well protected and the swimming is safe year-round. Snorkeling is good, and there are picnic tables, restrooms, and recreational facilities, including a ball park and basketball courts. This park is right in town, and not secluded from the road. Although the facilities are good, the setting could be better.

Just outside of town is **Waimanalo Bay State Recreation Area,** which remains largely undeveloped, and is much better situated. The access road is hard to spot, but just after McDonald's look for a tall wire fence with the poorly marked entrance in the center. It is good for picnicking and swimming, which can sometimes be rough. The area, surrounded by a dense ironwood grove, is called "Sherwood Forest," due to many rip-offs by thieves who fancy themselves as Robin Hood, plundering the rich and keeping the loot for themselves. Guess who the rich guys are? Fortunately, this problem of breaking into cars is diminishing, but take necessary precautions. This is the best beach on this section of the island.

Bellows Field Beach County Park, a onetime active Air Force base, is now one of Oahu's finest beach parks, and there's camping, too. As you enter a sign warns that "This military installation is open to the public only on the following days: weekends—noon Friday to 6 a.m. Monday; federal and state holidays—6 a.m. to 6 a.m. the following day. Camping is authorized in this park by permit from the City and County of Honolulu, Parks and Recreation Board, only." They mean it! The water is safe for swimming year-round, but lifeguards are on duty only during the above-stated hours. Bodysurfing and board surfing are also excellent in the park, but snorkeling is mediocre. Surfboards are not allowed in the area between the two lifeguard towers. After entering the main gates, follow the road for about two miles to the beach area. You'll find picnic tables, restrooms, and cold-water showers. The combination of shade trees and adjacent beach makes a perfect camping area. The park is marked by two freshwater streams, Waimanalo and Puha, at either end.

SERVICES

Except for the excellent camping, you're limited when it comes to accommodations in this area. **Hawaiian Family Inns,** a small cooperative of private homes in and around Hawaii Kai, provides European-style bed and breakfast. Each home differs slightly, but most have a private entrance, bath, yard and beach privileges, and some kitchen facilities. Daily rates are a reasonable $35, less during the off-season, with weekly and monthly discounts available. The three homes involved can be reached by calling 395-3710, 395-4130, or 395-8153.

The first place to pick up supplies as you head east on Rt. 72 is at the **Times Supermarket** in the **Niu Valley Shopping Center,** located about halfway between Diamond Head and Koko Head. In the shopping center is **The Swiss Inn,** tel. 377-5447, an authentic Swiss restaurant where the owner/chef pours love and attention into every dish. The food is superb, well prepared, and reasonably priced for the quality. After your meal, have dessert at **Dave's Ice Cream,** also in the center.

Note: For Hawaii Kai's two outstanding gourmet restaurants, **Roy's** and **Hanatei,** see "Casual Gourmet" under "Food" in the Waikiki chapter.

Koko Marina Shopping Center

Located along the highway in Hawaii Kai, this center is the largest and most accessible shopping center that you'll find on the way to Hanauma Bay. For photo supplies and sundries, try **Thrifty Drugs, Ben Franklin, Clic Photo,** and **Surfside Camera.** There are two banks, a **Waldenbooks,** and a satellite city hall for camping permits (tel. 395-4481). **Foodland** provides most supplies for picnics and camping, and you can dine at **Chuck's Steak House, McDonald's, Magoo's Pizza, Baskin-Robbins Ice Cream, Sizzler, Kentucky Fried Chicken,** and **Kozo Sushi.**

The **Aloha Dive Shop** at the Koko Marina is a full-service dive shop. You can rent or buy snorkeling and scuba gear. So, if you haven't picked up rentals from Waikiki and you're heading out to Hanauma Bay, come here. They have plenty of different dives. They start at $52 for beginners, $62 for certified divers, and $295 for certification courses (three days), featuring all-boat diving at Maunalua Bay, Koko Head, and Diamond Head.

The Japanese own the Koko Marina Center. In the center are thrill-ride (Jet Skis, parasails, etc.) booking agencies that will take tourists, but are more for the Japanese who come here by the busload and immediately head out on one of the rides. They've already booked from Japan, so it's all set up and off they go.

Upstairs, on the water side of Koko Marina, is **American Sports Ltd.,** tel. 395-5319. They offer Jet Skiing and snorkeling, and can book you into parasailing and scuba diving as well. Their special deal is Jet Skiing, snorkeling, plus lunch for $49. Lunch is a sandwich and French fries, or, *bento* if you prefer.

Waimanalo And Vicinity Practicalities

For a tasty and inexpensive lunch try any of a number of *kaukau* wagons around Sandy Beach.

As you enter Waimanalo, look on the right for a sandwich-board sign painted with a bright red chili pepper that marks the **Bueno Nalo Cafe** at 41865 Kalanianaole Hwy. (next door to Bobby's Market), tel. 259-7186, open daily 11:30 a.m.-9 p.m., which offers a very tasty and inexpensive selection of Mexican food a la Hawaiiana. Hearty *menudo* soup covered in melted cheese is only $3.95 while a la carte tacos, tostadas, tamales, and burritos range $2.25-3.50, and combination dinners are priced at $8.95-9.95. The service is friendly, the atmosphere relaxed, and the food much better than average.

A short "mile" past Bueno Nalo is **Mel's Market,** where you can pick up almost all camping supplies. Waimanalo town is growing up. As you enter you'll find a **7-Eleven** and **McDonald's.** The **Waimanalo BBQ,** just near the 7-Eleven and the P.O., open daily 10 a.m.-5 p.m., is an open-air "cafe" that prepares huge plate lunches including *kalua* pig, shrimp, pork adobo, and grilled mahimahi for only $4. They also have a mixed plate of three items for $5, and shave ice for dessert. The food is delicious, the atmosphere as local as you can get, and the service friendly. It's a great stop to pick up a picnic lunch. The restrooms, unfortunately, leave a little to be desired.

Keep going along Kalanianaole Hwy. for a mile or so to find **Waimanalo Shopping Center** in the middle of town. Here are **Jack in the Box, Subway Sandwiches, Dave's Ice Cream,** two gas stations, and a bank. You can do all your business, pick up lunch and supplies, and head on down the road or go to the beach. In the shopping center are also a **visitor information booth, Woolworth,** and **Waimanalo Market.**

Frankie's Drive-In, at the bottom of the hill a minute or so past Jack in the Box, is a local favorite plate lunch drive-in, where you can fill up on teriyaki beef or chicken, fried mahimahi, or hamburger steak along with two big scoops of rice and a whack of mac-salad for under $5. Frankie's is great for takeout that can be enjoyed at one of the nearby beaches. Their specialty is a *lilikoi* milkshake, a true island delight.

Pine Grove Village is an open-air bazaar where local people come to sell handmade products and produce. The majority of items are authentic and priced well below similar products found in Honolulu. Participants and times vary, but a group is usually selling daily until 6 p.m. Some excellent buys include local fruits and vegetables, lei, shellwork, hand-dipped candles, bikinis, jewelry, and leather goods. Price haggling is the norm; when the seller stops smiling, that's about the right price.

The **Olomana Golf Course,** at 41-1801 Kalanianaole Hwy., Waimanalo, is a good place to go for breakfast. The menu is uninspired American-standard with an island twist, but the view is very good and the prices reasonable.

the hibiscus, Hawaii's state flower

BRIAN BARDWELL

WINDWARD OAHU

Oahu's windward coast never has to turn a shoulder into a harsh and biting wind. The trades do blow, mightily at times, but are always tropical warm, perfumed with flowers, balmy and bright. Honolulu is just 12 miles over the hump of the *pali,* but a world apart. When *kama'aina* families talk of going to "the cottage in the country," they're most likely referring to the windward coast. In the southern parts, the suburban towns of **Kailua** and **Kaneohe** are modern in every way, with the lion's share of the services on this side. Kailua has Oahu's best windsurfing beach and a nearby *heiau,* preserved and unvisited, while Kaneohe sits in a huge bay dotted with islands and reef. The coastal **Kamehameha Highway** (Rt. 83) turns inland to the base of the *pali,* passing the **Valley of the Temples,** resplendent with universal houses of worship. At **Kahaluu** starts a string of beaches running north, offering the full range of Oahu's coastal outdoor experience. You can meander up side roads into the mountains near the Hawaiian villages of **Waiahole** and **Waikane,** where the normal way of life is ramshackle cottages on small subsistence farms.

The coast bulges at **Ka'a'awa,** where the **Crouching Lion,** a natural stone formation, seems ready to pounce on the ever-present tour buses that disturb its repose. North is **Punaluu,** famous for **Pat's,** the only resort in the immediate area, and for **Sacred Falls State Park,** a short hike to a peak at Oahu's beautiful and natural heart (if it isn't muddy). Suddenly, you're in manicured **Laie** where Hawaii's Mormon community has built a university, a temple perfect in its symmetry, and the **Polynesian Cultural Center,** a sanitized replica of life in the South Seas, Disney style. The northern tip at **Kahuku,** site of one of Oahu's oldest sugar mills, is where the **North Shore** begins. Kahuku Point houses two refuges, one for wildlife, and the other for Oahu's only nudist camp, both protecting endangered species from humanity's prying eyes.

It makes little difference in which direction you travel the windward coast, but the following will be listed from south to north from Kailua to Kahuku. The slight advantage in traveling this direction is that your car is in the right-hand lane, which is better for coastal views. But, as odd as it may seem, this dynamic stretch totally changes its vistas depending upon the direction that you travel. You can come one way and then retrace your route convinced you've never seen it before. The road is clearly marked with mile markers. The numbers on the mile markers decrease as you head north from Kaneohe on Rt. 83, the Kamehameha Highway. Also see "Camping and Hiking" in the Oahu Introduction for trails in the area.

Beaches And Parks

Over a dozen beaches line the 24 miles of the windward coast from Kailua to Kahuku. The majority offer a wide range of water sports and camping. A few offshore islands, refuges for Hawaiian waterbirds, can be visited and explored. You can walk to these islands during low tide, and even camp there. See "Camping and Hiking" in the Oahu Introduction for other state and county parks not along the coast.

KAILUA AND VICINITY

The easiest way into Kailua ("Two Seas") is over the Koolaus on Rt. 61, the Pali Highway. As soon as you pass through a long tunnel just after the Nuuanu Pali Lookout (see "Sights" in the Honolulu chapter) and your eyes adjust to the shocking brilliance of sunshine, look to your right to see Mt. Olomana. Its 1,643-foot peak is believed to be the volcanic origin of Oahu, the first land to emerge from the seas. Below lies Kailua and the Kawainui swamp, perhaps the oldest inhabited area on this side of the island. Kamehameha I, after conquering Oahu in 1795, gave all this land to the chiefs who fought for him. The area became a favorite of the ruling *ali'i* until the fall of the monarchy at the turn of this century. The Kawainui Canal drains the marsh and runs through Kailua. A good vantage point from which to observe it is along Kalaheo Ave., the main road running along the coast in Kailua. Kailua has approximately 45,000 people, technically making it the state's largest windward city. It's developed with shopping centers, a hospital, and the *best* windsurfing beach in the state (see below). For a full description of windsurfing activities at Kailua Beach please refer to "Sports and Recreation" in the Oahu Introduction. Four golf courses surround the town, and a satellite city hall dispenses **camping permits.**

SIGHTS

A good tour loop is to continue straight on Rt. 61 until it comes to the coast. Turn right onto Kalaheo Road, which takes you along the coast to Kailua Beach County Park. In the waters offshore will be a spectacle of windsurfers, with their sails puffed out like the proud chests of multicolored birds. To the left of the beach is **Mokapu** ("Sacred Area") **Peninsula,** home of the Kaneohe Marine Corps Air Station. Notice that the rock that separates the peninsula creates a large natural archway navigable by sizable boats. Most of the little islands in the bay are bird sanctuaries. The farthest, **Moku Manu,** is home to terns and man-o'-wars, birds famous for leading fishermen to schools of fish. Up on the coastal bluffs is a gray house with a flat roof, the residence of a local woman called the "Birdlady of Kailua." The woman has a reputation for taking care of any sick or injured birds that people bring to her. Her entire home is carved from rock, including the chairs and table. Every once in a while tours of the house are offered for a few dollars. They're irregular, so check the local papers, and you may be lucky enough to be there at just the right time.

A'alapapa Drive traverses the heights from the beach and takes you through an area of beautiful homes until you come to **Lanikai Beach.** At one time trees came down to the shoreline, but it has steadily eroded away. The Navy attempted to start a retaining reef by dumping bargeloads of white bath tile just offshore. Their efforts were not successful, but many homes in town now have sparkling-new, white-tiled bathrooms. As A'alapapa Drive loops back to town, its name changes to Mokulua; a turnout here affords an expansive panorama of the bay below. By daytime it's enjoyable, but in the evening local kids come here to hang out and drink beer.

Ulupo Heiau

Ulupo is dedicated to the Ulu line of *ali'i,* who were responsible for setting up *heiau* involving

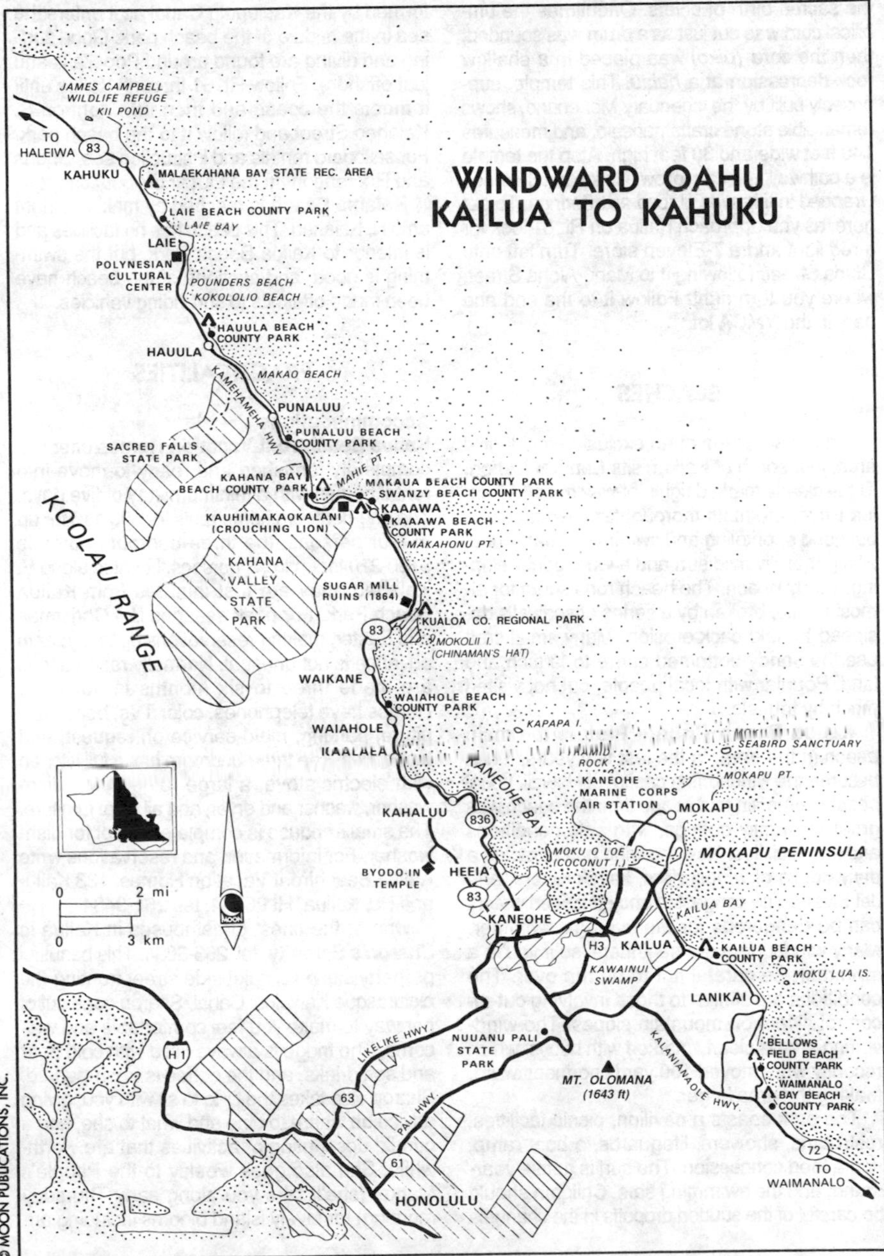
WINDWARD OAHU
KAILUA TO KAHUKU
JAMES CAMPBELL
WILDLIFE REFUGE
KII POND
TO
HALEIWA
83
KAHUKU
MALAEKAHANA BAY STATE REC. AREA
LAIE BEACH COUNTY PARK
LAIE BAY
LAIE
POLYNESIAN
CULTURAL
CENTER
POUNDERS BEACH
KOKOLOLIO BEACH
HAUULA BEACH
COUNTY PARK
HAUULA
MAKAO BEACH
KAMEHAMEHA HWY
PUNALUU
PUNALUU BEACH
COUNTY PARK
SACRED FALLS
STATE PARK
MAHIE PT
KAHANA BAY
BEACH COUNTY PARK
MAKAUA BEACH COUNTY PARK
SWANZY BEACH COUNTY PARK
KAUHIIMAKAOKALANI
(CROUCHING LION)
KAAAWA
KAAAWA BEACH
COUNTY PARK
MAKAHONU PT.
KOOLAU RANGE
KAHANA
VALLEY
STATE
PARK
SUGAR MILL
RUINS (1864)
KUALOA CO. REGIONAL PARK
MOKOLII I.
(CHINAMAN'S HAT)
WAIKANE
WAIAHOLE BEACH
COUNTY PARK
WAIAHOLE
KAPAPA I.
SEABIRD SANCTUARY
ROCK
MOKAPU PT.
KANEOHE BAY
KANEOHE
MARINE CORPS
AIR STATION
KAHALUU
836
MOKAPU
MOKU O LOE
(COCONUT I.)
MOKAPU PENINSULA
BYODO-IN
TEMPLE
HEEIA
83
KANEOHE
KAILUA BAY
0 2 mi
0 3 km
MOON
H3
KAILUA
KAILUA BEACH
COUNTY PARK
KAWAINUI
SWAMP
MOKU LUA IS.
LANIKAI
LIKELIKE HWY.
NUUANU PALI
STATE
PARK
KALANIANAOLE HWY
H1
BELLOWS
FIELD BEACH
COUNTY PARK
MT. OLOMANA
(1643 ft)
WAIMANALO
BAY BEACH
COUNTY PARK
63
PALI HWY
72
61
TO
WAIMANALO
HONOLULU
© MOON PUBLICATIONS, INC.

the sacred birth of chiefs. Oftentimes the umbilical cord was cut just as a drum was sounded, then the cord *(piko)* was placed in a shallow rock depression at a *heiau*. This temple, supposedly built by the legendary Menehune, shows remarkable stone craftsmanship, and measures 140 feet wide and 30 feet high. Atop the temple is a pathway you can follow. Notice small stones wrapped in ti leaves placed as offerings. To get here, as you approach Kailua on Rt. 61 look for a red light and a 7-Eleven store. Turn left onto Uluoa Street, following it to Manu Aloha Street, where you turn right. Follow it to the end and park in the YMCA lot.

BEACHES

Along the shoreline of an exclusive residential area, just south of Kailua, sits **Lanikai Beach.** Three clearly marked rights-of-way run off Mokulua Drive, the main thoroughfare. No facilities, but good snorkeling and swimming year-round, with generally mild surf and a long, gently sloping, sandy beach. The beach runs south for almost a mile, broken by a series of seawalls designed to hold back erosion. Many small craft use the sandy-bottomed shore to launch and land. Popular with local people, but not visited much by tourists.

Kailua Beach County Park is the main beach in the area. In the last few years, it has become the windsurfing capital of Hawaii. Local people complain that at one time the beach was great for family outings, with safe conditions and fine facilities. Now the wind has attracted a daily flotilla of windsurfers, kayak racers, and Jet Skiers. The congested and contested waters can be dangerous for the average swimmer. Many windsurfers are beginners, so if you're a swimmer, be careful not to be run over. The conditions are similar to those involving out-of-control skiers on mountain slopes. The windsurfing area is clearly marked with buoys, which recently were moved 100 yards northeastward, making the area larger.

The park boasts a pavilion, picnic facilities, restrooms, showers, lifeguards, a boat ramp, and a food concession. The surf is gentle year-round, and the swimming safe. Children should be careful of the sudden dropoffs in the channels formed by the Kaelepulu Canal as it enters the sea in the middle of the beach park. Good surfing and diving are found around Popoi'a Island just offshore. Follow Rt. 61 through Kailua until it meets the coast, and then turn right on S. Kalaheo Street and follow it to the beach park. For sailboard rentals and instruction see "Sports and Recreation" in the Out and About chapter.

Kalama Beach is reached by making a right onto N. Kalaheo. This beach has no facilities and is inferior to Kailua Beach Park, but the swimming is good, and sections of the beach have been made off-limits to surf-riding vehicles.

PRACTICALITIES

Accommodations

Kailua Beachfront Vacation Homes offer two completely furnished and ready-to-move-into rental homes with a minimum stay of five days. The one-bedroom home rents for $95-110 for up to four persons, the three-bedroom home is $190-220 for up to six persons. Located along S. Kalaheo, they are just minutes from Kailua Beach Park. For peak seasons like Christmas and Easter, making reservations up to a year in advance is not unusual. Normally reservations are made three to six months in advance. Homes have telephones, color TVs, beach furniture, parking, maid service on request, and barbecues. The three-bedroom has a full kitchen with electric stove, a large refrigerator, dishwasher, washer and dryer, and all lanai furniture. The smaller house is complete except for dishwasher. For information and reservations write Kailua Beachfront Vacation Homes, 133 Kailuana Pl., Kailua, HI 96734, tel. 261-3484.

One of the finest guesthouses in Kailua is **Sharon's Serenity,** tel. 263-3634. This beautiful property sits on a quiet side street fronting the picturesque Kawainui Canal. Sharon goes out of her way to make you feel comfortable and welcome. The fridge is always filled with cold beer and soft drinks, and the coffee is fresh-perked. Sharon also takes the time to sit with you, giving advice on where to dine and what to see, and a candid description of activities that are worthwhile. She also goes weekly to the People's Market (she'll take you along early Thursday morning) for lovely island blooms including anthuriums, ginger, and heliconia, which she arranges and places throughout the home to add touches of beauty. The meticulously clean, beautifully appointed home features guest rooms with color TV, Mexican tile throughout, spacious family room, swimming pool, lanai, and beautiful views of the *pali* and the bay. The main guest room has its own attached private bath done in tile and oak cabinetry. In here, the bed is queen-size, and next to it is a comfortable leather recliner with green-shaded reading lamp close at hand. Another bedroom could easily accommodate a family, with a large double bed and a twin bed set up like a daybed. It features in-room sliding doors for privacy and its own bath just across the hall. Rates are $45-50 s, $60-65 d. A self-contained but very tiny and inexpensive "Lemon Room" (named for its color, not because you'll be squeezed) is available on request. The price includes a continental or bacon-and-egg breakfast (bacon and eggs available every day but Thursday), which Sharon will have waiting in the morning. Sharon's Serenity is an excellent choice for the windward coast, and perfect for getting away from it all.

Pacific Hawaii Bed and Breakfast lists private homes in and around Kailua. Rates and homes differ dramatically, but all are guaranteed to be comfortable and accommodating. For details see "Bed and Breakfast" under "Accommodations" in the Out and About chapter.

Food

The **Kailua Shopping Center,** 540 Kailua Rd., has one of the very best restaurants for value in Kailua, **Barbecue East,** tel. 262-8457, open Mon.-Sat. 11 a.m.-9 p.m., Sunday 1-9 p.m., last Sunday of the month 5-9 p.m. The prices are terrific, the service friendly, and the food delicious in this Formica and linoleum decor restaurant. It demonstrates the international potpourri Hawaii is famous for, because with every plate you get Korean *kimchi,* Japanese miso soup, Hawaiian fish, American macaroni salad, and a bit of coleslaw. If that's not all the peoples of Hawaii accounted for, then what is? Specials include butterfish, scallops *jun,* or *ahi jun* or teriyaki for $6.95. The sashimi special is *ahi* sashimi with fried scallops, fried oysters, *kalbi* beef, barbecued chicken, and sides for $10.75. You can even have a sashimi mixed plate of barbecued chicken and beef, sashimi, and the works for only $7.45. Korean specials are *kalbi* beef, *pulgogi,* or chicken *mando* and all the trimmings for $8.95. They also serve beer and wine. The best choice for the money in Kailua, but no decor whatsoever.

If you want to save even more, at the other end of the shopping plaza is **Okazu-ya,** just a takeout lunch window, Japanese and Korean style. In the same small complex is **Chef's Grill Sandwich and Plate Lunch,** and a **Baskin-Robbins** for your sweet tooth.

Hekili Street: Kailua's Restaurant Row

The 100 block of Hekili Street could be Kailua's version of Honolulu's Restaurant Row. Along this street is the **No Name Bar,** tel. 261-8725, just across from the bowling alley. The No Name Bar is for beer-drinking types who want a good meal as well. They have Sunday morning football at 7:30 a.m., and serious Monday night football at 6:30 p.m. Open Mon.-Fri. 3 p.m.-2 a.m., Saturday 11 a.m.-2 a.m., Sunday 3 p.m.-midnight, happy hour 4-7 p.m., with live entertainment nightly. Choices include salads like Cobb salad for $6.50, or No-name salad of ham, turkey, Swiss, provolone, eggs, and cukes for $6.95. Mixed plates can be empanadas—fresh-baked pastry filled with chick peas, olives, cheddar, and spicy Mexican sauce ($6.95)—or sausage bread ($5.95 small, $7.50 large). Chili is $3.95, and sandwiches are under $7.

The **Princess Chop Suey** is your basic chop suey joint two doors down from the No Name. It's open Mon.-Sat. 10:30 a.m.-9 p.m., Sunday noon-9 p.m., tel. 839-0575. Expect Naugahyde booths and Formica tables. Everything is under $7.95.

Next door is **Sisco's Cantina,** tel. 262-7337, featuring complete Mexican cuisine, open Sun.-Thurs. 11 a.m.-10 p.m., Friday and Saturday 11 a.m.-11 p.m. Tostadas, tacos, burritos, enchiladas, and chiles rellenos are all under $10. More expensive dishes are shrimp Veracruz ($14), fajitas ($16.25, for two $20.95). All come with Mexican corn, sautéed Tex-Mex mushrooms, and salad. Inside, the south-of-the-border atmosphere is created with hanging piñatas, stucco walls, and blue-tile tables. A minute down the street is **Detroit Italian Deli,** featuring subs and ice cream.

Onesto's Ristorante Italiano, at 117 Hekili St., tel. 261-8688, is open daily except Monday; lunch is 11 a.m.-2 p.m., dinner is 5:30 p.m.-9:30 p.m., Fri.-Sat. until 10 p.m. Onesto's has brought a touch of "la dolce vita" Italian-style to Kailua. The lunch menu starts with appetizers like antipasto for two at $3.80, sautéed mushrooms for $3.80, and Caesar salad for two or more at $3.80 per person. Pasta dishes, a staple of Onesto's, are linguine with chicken, anchovy linguine with mushrooms, or linguine arrabiata with tomato sauce and sautéed bacon, all priced under $8. Seafood offerings are calamari marinara for $6.80, or the fresh catch (usually *ono*), which is prepared scampi style with picante or garlic sauce for under $10. Poultry entrees are chicken Marsala ($7.50) and chicken Sorrentino with eggplant, mozzarella cheese, mushrooms, butter, and Marsala wine ($8.50). Dinner entrees are *"un poco molto expensivo"* than lunch. Good choices are Sicilian chicken with roasted potatoes and onions served with linguine ($10.80), or shrimp linguine ($11.80). Seafoods like calamari marinara or shrimp saltimbocca with eggplant, mozzarella cheese, prosciutto, mushrooms, butter, and white wine are $11.80. Pasta dishes, in small (about $2 less) and regular-size servings, are linguine with meat sauce, rigatoni with ricotta, and fettuccine Alfredo, all for under $10. There's even a small deli area selling bread and pasta by the pound. Desserts include amaretto or cappuccino gelato, and New York-style cheesecake, for about $3, but opt for the *torta delicato Italiano,* also $3. Onesto's, although not quite haute cuisine, offers a pleasant setting and very decent food, especially for the money.

Around Town

Let the pungent aroma of garlic frying in olive oil lead you to **Assaggio's Ristorante Italiano,** 354 Uluniu St., tel. 261-2772, open Mon.-Fri. for lunch, 11:30 a.m.-2:30 p.m., dinner nightly 5-10 p.m. You are welcomed into a bright and open room done in striking black, red, teal, and magenta. A wall running down the center of the restaurant separates the bar from the dining room, where tables covered in white linen and black upholstered chairs line the long window area. The typical Italian menu, served with crusty Italian bread, begins with antipasti priced $5.90-9.90, fresh clam scampi at $6.90, and the light and classic prosciutto and melon at $6.90. Soups are pasta fagioli (macaroni and beans, the favorite of Italian *contadina*), minestrone, tortellini *imbrodo* (tortellini with ricotta in broth), or vichysoisse served as a cup or bowl, for $1.90 or $2.90. Pasta ranging in price $8-12 includes linguine, fettuccine, and ziti. Servings come in two sizes, small (about $2 less) and regular, covered with your choice of marinara, clam, carbonara, or pesto sauce. Entrees are chicken cacciatore or chicken *rolatini* (stuffed with ricotta cheese), both at $12.90; baked ziti with eggplant and mozzarella for $9.90; or lasagna for $11.90. Meat dishes are New York steaks, pork chops, or *osso bucco* (veal shanks with onions), all for around $14.90. From the sea comes fresh fish sautéed in garlic oil for $15.90; scallops and shrimp in wine, garlic butter, and snow peas for $17.90; or calamari alla parmigiana at $12.90. Desserts are homemade cheesecake, cannelloni, spumoni, and chocolate mousse, all around $4. The full bar serves imported and domestic beers, liquors, coffees, espressos, and plenty of wine varietals.

El Charro Avitia, 14 Oneawa St., tel. 263-3943, open daily for lunch and dinner, is a better than average Mexican restaurant. Simple yet tasteful, the south-of-the-border inspired decor is achieved with adobelike arches, wooden tables, Mexican ceramics placed here and there, and plenty of cacti and hanging plants. The menu features combination dinners of burritos, chile verde, enchiladas, or tacos, all priced under $10. The specialty of the house is the fresh fish Veracruzana, as good as you'll find anywhere, *carne asada,* or *camarones al mojo de ajo* (jumbo shrimp sautéed in butter, garlic, and white wine), all for under $14, and all served with rice, black beans, fresh vegetables, and a fresh fruit garnish. Less expensive dishes at around $9 are chimichangas, burritos, taco salad, and Mexican pizza, which is two deep-fried tortillas topped with cheddar cheese, jack cheese, beans, tomatoes, olives, and lettuce. *Huevos Mexicana, rancheros,* and *revueltos,* served throughout the day, are $7.50. The bar mixes a mean margarita, which come in normal sizes up to a fiesta 40-ounce that will definitely have you yelling *¡Olé!* El Charro Avitia is definitely worth the money.

Just up Oneawa St., across from the **Taco Bell,** is **Ching Lee Chop Suey,** a down-home, inexpensive Chinese restaurant where you can have a complete meal for under $5.

You'll first notice **Someplace Else,** at the corner of Aulike and Kuulei Rd., tel. 262-8833, because of the huge multicolored umbrellas in the outside patio area. This is Kailua's upscale yuppie restaurant. It's open 11 a.m.-2 a.m., food service till 10 p.m., no breakfast except Sunday brunch from 9 a.m. It's a jungle in here with hanging plants, ferns, and flowers in every nook and cranny. Lunch brings a broiled *ono* sandwich ($7.25), chicken almond salad ($6.25), or crab-stuffed tomato ($8.95). The extensive menu continues with omelettes; appetizers like escargot ($6.95) and stuffed mushrooms ($6.95); and soups like clam chowder, French onion, gazpacho, and soup of the day for under $5. South-of-the-border selections are burritos, chimichangas, and the like for around $8. The broiler fires up with top New York steak ($16.95), barbecued ribs ($13.95), and chicken Marsala ($12). If you are looking for a place to "do lunch," or an evening of civilized conversation, don't go anywhere until you've tried Someplace Else.

Buzz's Original Steakhouse, at 413 Kawailoa Rd., tel. 261-4661, is really *the* original steakhouse of this small island chain owned by the Schneider family. Buzz's is just across the road from Kailua Beach Park, situated along the canal. This restaurant is an institution with local families. It's the kind of place that "if you can't think of where to go, you head for Buzz's." The food is always good, if not extraordinary. They have top sirloin ($14.95), pork chops ($13.95), chicken teriyaki ($11.75), fresh fish (usually about $18), and mahimahi ($12.95). Salad bar is included with all entrees; separately it costs $7.95. Everything is charbroiled.

Saeng's Thai Cuisine, at 315 Hahani, tel. 263-9727, open Sat.-Sun. 5-9:30 p.m., Mon.-Fri. 11 a.m.-2:30 p.m. and again 5-9:30 p.m., offers spicy Thai food with an emphasis on vegetarian meals. Appetizers and starters are Thai crisp noodles ($5.25), sautéed shrimp ($9.95), green papaya salad ($5.25), *yum koong* (shrimp salad, $7.95), and chicken coconut soup ($6.95). Specialties include spicy stuffed calamari ($9.95), Thai red curry ($7.95), and a la carte beef, pork, and chicken dishes, all under $8. Vegetarians can pick from mixed vegies with yellow bean paste ($5.95), mixed vegies with oyster sauce ($5.95), or zucchini tofu ($5.95). Saeng Thai is a good change of pace at a decent price.

Orson's Bourbon House, along the main drag at 5 Hoolai St., tel. 262-2306, is just behind the Burger King on a little side street. This Cajun-style restaurant prepares blackened *ahi* as a medium-rare fish (wonderful as an appetizer, but can do as an entree for $9), fried calamari ($7.95), and *mufaletas* (a sub sandwich New Orleans style). Special of the day could be fresh silver salmon sautéed for $12.50. The decor emphasizes fine dining with white starched tablecloths and fresh flower bouquets, while the bar area is rich with koa wood trim. Nightly entertainment is lively with everything from Hawaiian to jazz.

Captain Bob's Picnic Sail, tel. 926-5077 or (800) 262-8798, tours Kaneohe Bay daily and features lunch and all-you-can-drink on its three- to four-hour sail, $65 adults, $45 children. You can work off lunch snorkeling or playing volleyball on the beach. The food is passable, but the setting offshore with the *pali* in the background is world class. Captain Bob also has a good reputation for community spirit, often taking local children's groups out on his boats. For people desiring to see the waters along the windward coast while spending a pleasant afternoon, this is a best bet.

Uluniu Street: Inexpensive Dining

Uluniu Street has inexpensive places to eat, one after the other. After making a left from Kuulei Road (Rt. 61) onto Oneawa, a main thoroughfare, turn right onto Uluniu just at the large Kailua Furniture. First is an authentic hole-in-the-wall Japanese restaurant, **Kailua Okazuya.** They specialize in *donburi,* a bowl of rice smothered with various savories. Try their *oyako donburi,* chicken and egg with vegetables over rice for under $4. They serve plate lunches and a sushi special that can't be beat, which includes fresh fish, shrimp, abalone, and octopus for only $5. Next door is **Insam Korean Restaurant,** with more of the same Korean style; and up the street is the **New Chinese Garden,** a basic Chinese restaurant with decent prices. None of these restaurants are remarkable, but will fill you up with good enough food for a very reasonable price.

Shopping And Services

The two towns of Kailua and Kaneohe have the lion's share of shopping on the windward coast. You can pick up basics in the small towns as you head up the coast, but for any unique or hard-to-find items, Kailua/Kaneohe is your only bet. The area offers a few shopping centers. The **Windward Mall,** at 46-056 Kamehameha Hwy., Kaneohe, tel. 235-1143, open weekdays 9:30 a.m.-9 p.m., Saturday to 5:30 p.m., Sunday 10 a.m.-5 p.m., is the premier, full-service mall on the windward coast. Besides department stores like Liberty House and Sears, there are shops selling everything from shoes to health foods.

The **Kaneohe Bay Mall** across from the Windward Mall is a little more down-home, and features a Longs Drugs, especially good for photo supplies. The **Aikahi Park Shopping Center** along Kaneohe Bay Dr., at the corner of Mokapu Blvd., is a limited shopping center whose main shops are a Safeway and a Sizzler Restaurant. The **Kailua Shopping Center,** at 540 Kailua Rd., also has limited shopping that includes a **Times Supermarket,** open till 10 p.m.; and a well-stocked **Honolulu Bookshop,** tel. 261-1996, open Mon.-Fri. 9:30-9, Saturday 9:30-5:30, Sunday till 5 p.m., for a full range of reading material. There's also a **Cornet Store** along Kailua Ave. for sundries, lotions, and notions, and a **Longs Drugs.**

Thursday mornings bring a **farmers' market** into town for only one hour, 8:50-9:50 a.m. Those in the know arrive early to get a number at their favorite stalls, which can sell out within minutes of opening. Great for fresh flowers and fruits.

You might pick up an heirloom at **Heritage Antiques,** at the corner of Kailua Rd. and Amakua St., tel. 261-8700, open daily 10-5:30, which is overflowing with Asian, Hawaiian, and Americana antiques. Here too are **jewelers** H.W. Roberts and J.K. Phillips, who also specialize as gemologists. **Hunter Antiques,** across the street from Heritage Antiques, specializes in Depression-era glass.

You'll find just about anything at **Holiday Mart** on Hahani Rd., or picnic supplies at the landmark **Kalapawai Store,** at the corner of Kailua and Kalaheo roads, which marks the best entrance to Kailua's windsurfing beaches.

Campers can reach the **satellite city hall** for information and permits by calling 261-8575. A **post office** is at the corner of Kailua and Hahani, just across from the Hawaiian National Bank. Medical aid is available from **Castle Medical Center,** tel. 261-0841. **Family and Urgent Medical Care** is at 660 Kailua Rd., tel. 263-4433.

KANEOHE AND VICINITY

The bedroom community of Kaneohe ("Kane's Bamboo") lies along Kaneohe Bay, protected by a huge barrier reef. Within the town is **Hoomaluhia Regional Park,** so large that guided hikes are offered on a daily basis. Offshore is Moku o' Loe, commonly called **Coconut Island.** It became famous as the opening shot in the TV show "Gilligan's Island," although the series itself was shot in California. In ancient times, it was *kapu* and during WW II served as an R and R camp for B-29 crews. Many of the crews felt the island had bad vibes, and reported having streaks of bad luck. In recent times, Frank Fasi, Honolulu's current mayor, suggested that Hawaii's gate-crashing guests, Ferdinand and Imelda Marcos, should lease Coconut Island. It never happened.

SIGHTS

In the northern section of town is **Heeia Pier,** launching area for the *Coral Queen,* tel. 247-0375, a glass-bottomed boat that sails throughout the bay. It is a popular attraction, so make reservations. Fortunately, in recent years, the once crystal-clear bay, which was becoming murky with silt because of development, is clearing again due to conservation efforts.

A sandbar building up in the center of Kaneohe Bay makes a perfect anchorage for yachts and powerboats. These boat people drop anchor, jump off, and wade to the bar through waist-deep, clear waters. It has become an unofficial playground where you can

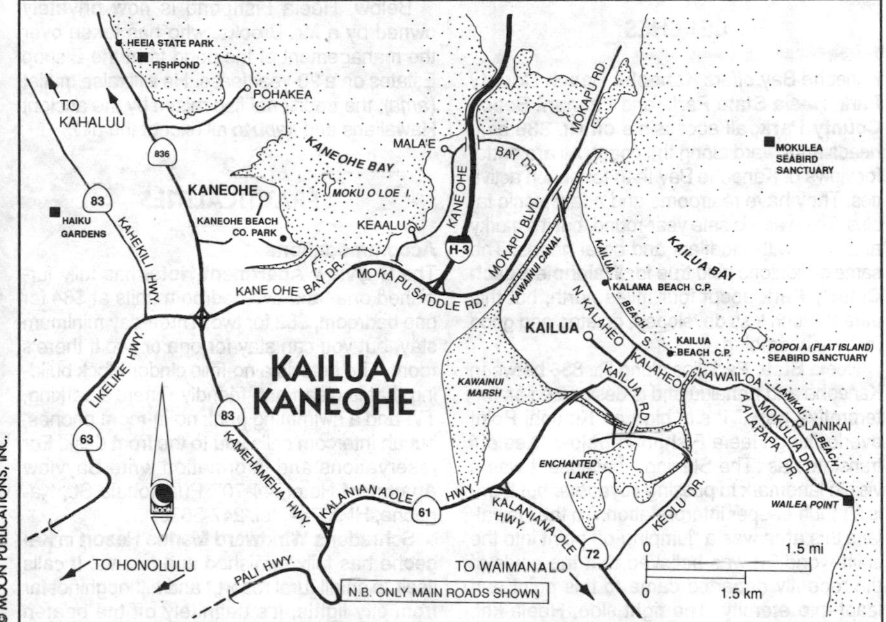

fling a Frisbee, drink beer, fly a kite, or just float around. Part of the sandbar rises above the water and some barbecue chefs even bring their hibachis and have a bite to eat. Surrounding you is Kaneohe Bay with Chinaman's Hat floating off to your right, and a perfect view of the *pali* straight ahead. The epitome of la dolce vita, Hawaiian style.

Senator Fong's Plantation, at 47-285 Pulama Rd., Kaneohe, HI 96744 (near Kahaluu), tel. 239-6775, is open daily 9 a.m.-4 p.m., with guided tram tours running 10:30 a.m.-3 p.m., admission $8.50 adults, $5 children. Hawaii's newest attraction is a labor of love created by Senator Hiram Fong, who served as the state senator from 1959 to 1976. Upon retirement he returned to his home, and ever since has been beautifying the gardens he started over 40 years ago. The result is 725 acres of natural beauty. When you first arrive, you'll see a large open-air pavilion housing a snack window serving sandwiches, plate lunches, and saimin. Also inside the pavilion is a small but well-appointed souvenir shop where you can get everything from aloha shirts to postcards. Notice a table set with baskets of flowers where you can make your own keepsake lei for $5.

For a fun-filled day on Kaneohe Bay, far from the crowds of Waikiki, try **North Bay Boat Club's** "A Day on the Bay," located on the grounds of Schrader's Windward Marine Resort, 47-039 Lihikai Dr., Kaneohe, tel. 239-5711, ext. 112. "Your day" includes hotel pick-up, barbecue lunch, open bar, windsurfing, kayaking, snorkeling, and sailing. Scuba introductory dives and Jet Ski rides are also available at extra cost from **Wave Riders of Kaneohe,** tel. 239-5711, who offer a self-propelled tour around the bay on Jet Skis for $40 per hour, or $60 for two people for an hour.

All Hawaii Cruises, tel. 926-5077, features a snorkel/sail with Captain Bob, who has an excellent reputation with local people. Your adventure includes hotel pick-up, barbecue lunch, open bar, a four-hour sail, glass-bottom viewing, and reef walking. This is an excellent opportunity to view the awesome beauty of the windward coast.

BEACHES

Kaneohe Bay offers **Kaneohe Beach County Park, Heeia State Park,** and **Laenani Beach County Park,** all accessible off Rt. 836 as it heads northward along the coast. All are better for views of Kaneohe Bay than for beach activities. They have restrooms and a few picnic tables. The water is safe year-round, but it's murky and lined with mudflats and coral heads. The same conditions hold true for **Waiahole Beach County Park** about four miles north, but this area is much less developed, quieter, and good for beachcombing.

Heeia State Park lies along Rt. 836 between Kaneohe and Kahaluu and is designated an "interpretive park." It sits high on Kealohi Point overlooking Heeia Fishpond below. Kealohi translates as "The Shining," because it was a visible landmark to passing voyagers, but there is a much deeper interpretation. To the Hawaiians this area was a "jumping-off point into the spirit world." It was believed that the souls of the recently departed came to this point and leapt into eternity. The right side, Heeia-kei, was the side of light, while the left side, Heeia-uli, was the domain of darkness. The wise *kahuna* taught that you could actually see the face of God in the brilliant sun as it rises over the point.

On the grounds are a main hall, pavilion, restrooms, and various short walks around the entire area with magnificient views of Kaneohe Bay. The park contains numerous indigenous plants and mature trees, the perfect laboratory for the educational goals set by The Friends of Heeia State Park. As an interpretive park, it offers programs for the community and visitors alike. Bernadette Lono, the Director of Hawaiian Studies, gives personal tours of the area. Her family has been part of this *ahupua'a* (ancient land division) for countless generations. Bernadette first acquaints you with the area by asking you to sit Hawaiian style on the grass. The earth or *aina* is fundamental to the Hawaiian belief system, and you should start connected to it. She goes on to explain the symbiotic relationship between inland farmers whose fields stretched to Eolaka, the top of the *pali,* and the fishermen who plied the waters of Mokapu on the other side of the peninsula.

Below, Heeia Fishpond is now privately owned by a Mr. Brooks, who has taken over the management of the pond from the Bishop Estates on a 20-year lease. He will raise mullet (*ama*), the traditional fish raised by the ancient Hawaiians and *kapu* to all except the *ali'i.*

PRACTICALITIES

Accommodations

The **Bayview Apartment Hotel** has fully furnished one- and two-bedroom units at $64 for one bedroom, $82 for two. Three-day minimum stay, but you can stay for one or two if there's room. The hotel is a no-frills cinder-block building that is clean and friendly. There's parking, TV, and a swimming pool; no in-room phones, but an intercom calls you to the front desk. For reservations and information write Bayview Apartment Hotel, 44-707 Puamohala St., Kaneohe, HI 96744, tel. 247-3635.

Schrader's Windward Marine Resort in Kaneohe has fully furnished apartments. It calls itself "a small rural resort," and although not far from city lights, it's definitely off the beaten track—literally on the edge of Kaneohe Bay, so close that it boasts fishing from the lanai of some apartments. Follow Rt. 836 from Kahaluu for a few minutes until you spot the Pineapple Hut (a tourist trap) and St. John's by the Sea Church. Turn here down Lihikai Drive to the resort.

There are 53 units here, but they differ greatly as they sprawl along the bay. The gray building, a housing-project clone along the road front, is part of the place, and oddly enough has some of the most expensive units at $85-100 per night. All units have living rooms, color TV, phones, daily maid service, refrigerators, and a/c, but only 19 have stoves and these rent for $65-200 per night. The least expensive unit with a full kitchen is $65. The rooms are spotless but old. Because of the age of the building, it's as if you've gone back 30 years to old Hawaii. The resort houses a fair number of TLM people (Temporary Lodging for Military). This is the only place for them to stay on the island.

The best deal for the money is a one-bedroom away from the road and facing the bay. If you call and specify any unit with a lanai, you're going to get at least a partial view of the bay. The resort also offers motorboats, kayaks, sailboards, and small sailboats through its sister organization, North Bay Boat Club. Get a break at Wave Runners of Kaneohe (Jet Skis) and Twilight Cruise, a narrated cruise of the bay every Tuesday evening on a pontoon boat. Discounts are offered on long stays.

For information write Schrader's Windward Marine Resort, 47-039 Lihikai Dr., Kaneohe, HI 96744, tel. 239-5711; (800) 367-8047, ext. 239; (800) 423-8733, ext. 239, Canada.

Dining And Nightlife

Fortunately, or unfortunately, Kaneohe is a bit of a wasteland as far as tourist services, nightlife, and eating out are concerned. Most people who live here head for the action in Honolulu. There are a few limited choices. **Fuji's Delicatessen,** at 45-270 Wm. Henry Rd., tel. 235-3690, is a local favorite known for its down-home Japanese, Korean, and Hawaiian cooking served family style on long communal tables.

If you're looking for a real cultural experience, head for **Bob's Saimin,** at 46-132-A Kahuhipa St., tel. 247-7878, especially late in the evening where you can get hearty bowls of soup and a selection of barbecued meats for inexpensive prices. The best deal in town is at **Kim Chee One,** at 46-010 Kamehameha Hwy., tel. 235-5560, which has a few sister restaurants scattered around Oahu. The setting is plain, but you'll have trouble finishing the excellent Korean mixed-barbecue plate for $6.95, easily enough for two.

KAHEKILI HIGHWAY

Where Rt. 83 intersects the Likelike Hwy. on the southern outskirts of Kaneohe, it branches north and changes its name from the Kamehameha Hwy. to the Kahekili Hwy. until it hits the coast at Kahaluu. This four-mile traverse passes two exceptionally beautiful valleys: Haiku Valley and the Valley of the Temples. Neither should be missed.

SIGHTS

Haiku Gardens

Haiku ("Abrupt Break") Gardens is a lovely section of a commercial area that includes a restaurant (see below) and some quiet condominiums. After you pass a community college, Haiku Road is past two red lights. Turn left here and proceed for about a half mile until you see the entrance. The gardens date from the mid-1800s, when Hawaiian *ali'i* deeded 16 acres to an English engineer named Baskerville. He developed the area, creating a series of spring-fed lily ponds, building a number of estate homes, and planting flowers, fruits, and ornamental trees. Later a restaurant was built, now owned by the Ing family, and the grounds became famous for their beauty, often used for outdoor weddings and special gatherings.

You're welcome to walk through the gardens. Proceed from the restaurant down a grassy area to a pond, where perhaps you'll attract an impromptu entourage of ducks, chickens, and guinea fowl that squawk along looking for handouts. Amidst the lush foliage is a grass shack used for weddings. A path leads around a larger pond whose benches and small pavilions are perfect for contemplation. The path passes beneath a huge banyan, while a nearby bamboo grove serenades you with sonorous music if the wind is blowing.

Valley Of The Temples

The concept of this universal-faith cemetery is as beautiful as the sculpted *pali* that serves as its backdrop. A rainy day makes it better. The *pali* explodes with rainbowed waterfalls, and the greens turn a richer emerald, sparkling with dewdrops. Don't miss the Valley of the Temples Memorial Park, 47-200 Kahekili Hwy., tel. 239-8811. Admission is $2 per person or *kama'aina* rates of $5 per carload, but you have to prove you're from Hawaii. High on a hill sits a Christian chapel, an A-frame topped by a cross. The views can be lovely from up here, but unfortunately the large windows of the chapel perfectly frame some nondescript tract housing and a Pay 'n Save supermarket below. Great planning!

The crown jewel of the valley is **Byodo-In Temple** ("Temple of Equality"), a superbly appointed replica of the 900-year-old Byodo-In of Uji, Japan (depicted on the 10-yen coin). This temple dates from June 7, 1968, 100 years to the day when Japanese immigrants first arrived in Hawaii. It was erected through the combined efforts of an American engineering firm headed by Ronald Kawahara in accordance with a plan designed by Kiichi Sano, a famed Kyoto landscape artist. A three-ton brass bell, which you're invited to strike after making an offering, creates the right vibrations for meditation, and symbolically spreads the word of Amidha Buddha. Remove your shoes before entering the temple. The walls hold distinctive emblems of different Buddhist sects. Upstairs wings are roped off, with no entry permitted.

Stand on the gravel path outside the main temple, which is fronted by a grating with a circle cut in the middle. Through the circle you can see the perfectly framed contemplative visage of Buddha. Cross a half-moon bridge to the left of the temple and follow the path to a small gazebo. Here a rock, perfectly and artistically placed, separates a stream in two, sending the water to the left and right. The pagoda at the top of the path is called the Meditation House. Go to this superbly manicured area to get a sweeping view of the grounds. In front of the Meditation House is a curious tree; pick up one of the fallen leaves, and feel the natural velvet on the backside.

The grounds are alive with sparrows and peacocks, and from time to time you'll hear a curious-sounding "yip, yip, yip" and clapping hands. Follow it to discover Mr. Henry Oda, who will be surrounded by birds taking crumbs from his fingers, and by a boiling cauldron of koi in the waters below with mouths agape demanding to be fed. He has taken over for the recently retired Mr. Hisayoshi Hirada, the original "Birdman of Byodo-In." Mr. Hirada translates his first name into "long live a good man," and he, well into his 80s, is living proof. Mr. Hirada began training the birds and carp of Byodo-In after his *first* retirement. He would come daily to feed the fish, clapping his hands while he did so. Soon the Pavlovian response took over. Simultaneously, a small and courageous bird, which Hirada-san calls Charlie, began taking crumbs from his fingers.

Mr. Oda does a great job of showing visitors around, but old-timers say that there is no one like Mr. Hirada, and if he happens to be there while you're visiting, you have been blessed by the great Buddha of Byodo-In. A small gift shop selling souvenirs, cards, and some refreshments is to the right of the temple. If you wish to photograph the complex, it's best to come before noon, when the sun is at your back as you frame the red and white temple against the deep green of the *pali*.

Kahaluu

This town is at the convergence of the Kahekili Hwy. and the Kamehameha Hwy. (Rt. 83) heading north. Also, Rt. 836, an extension of the Kamehameha Hwy., hugs the coastline heading down to Kailua/Kaneohe. It offers some of the most spectacular views of a decidedly spectacular coast, with very few tourists venturing down this side road. Kahaluu town is a gas station and a little tourist trap selling junk just in case you didn't get enough in Waikiki. The Hygienic Store sells liquor, groceries, soda, and ice, all you'll need for an afternoon lunch. The Waihee Stream, meandering from the *pali*, empties into the bay and deposits fresh water into the ancient **Kahaluu Fish Pond.** So picture-perfect is the tropical setting that it has provided scenery for TV and Hollywood productions such as "Jake and the Fat Man," *Parent Trap II,* and the famous airport and village scene in *The Karate Kid II.* All of the movie sets have been torn down, but you can still see the fishpond by taking a short walk just behind the bank in town.

WAIAHOLE AND VICINITY

If you want to fall in love with rural, old-time Oahu, go to the northern reaches of Kaneohe Bay around Waiahole and Waikane, a Hawaiian grassroots area that has so far eluded development. Alongside the road are many more fruit stands than in other parts of Oahu. For a glimpse of the area look for the Waiahole Elementary School, and turn left up Waiahole Valley Road. The road twists its way into the valley, becoming narrower until it turns into a dirt track. Left and right in homey, ramshackle houses lives down-home Hawaii, complete with taro patches in the back yards. Another road of the same type is about a one-half mile up Rt. 83 just before you enter Waikane. If you're staying in Waikiki, compare this area with Kuhio Avenue only 45 minutes away.

Route 83 passes a string of beaches, most with camping. Offshore from Kualoa County Park is Mokolii ("Small Reptile") Island, commonly called **Chinaman's Hat** (between mile markers 30 and 31) due to its obvious resemblance to an Asian chapeau. If the tides are right, you can walk out to it (sneakers advised because of the coral), where you and a few nesting birds have it to yourself. Kualoa Park has undergone extensive renovations. There is an expansive parking area, plenty of picnic tables, and a huge grassy area fronting the beach. The road passes through what was once sugarcane country. Most of the businesses failed last century, but you will see the ruins of the Judd Sugar Works a mile or so before Ka'a'awa. The dilapidated mill stands although it was closed more than a century ago. Entering is not advised!

Kualoa County Regional Park

With the *pali* in the background, Chinaman's Hat island offshore, and a glistening white strand shaded by swaying palms, Kualoa is one of the finest beach parks on windward Oahu. It was also one of the most sacred areas on Oahu; the *ali'i* brought their children here to be reared and educated, and the area is designated in the National Register of Historic Places. It has a full range of facilities and services, including lifeguards, restrooms, and picnic tables. The park is open daily 7 a.m.-7 p.m., with overnight camping allowed with a county permit (mandatory). The swimming is safe year-round along a shoreline dotted with pockets of sand and coral. The snorkeling and fishing are good, but the real treat is walking the 500 yards to Chinaman's Hat at low tide. You need appropriate footgear (old sneakers are fine) because of the sharp coral heads. The island is one of the few around offshore Oahu that is not an official bird sanctuary, although many shorebirds do use the island and should not be molested.

Because of its exposure to winds, Kualoa is sometimes chilly. Although the park is popular, it is not well marked. It lies along Rt. 83, and if you're heading north, look for a red sign to the Kualoa Ranch. Just past it is an HVB Warrior pointing to the park and Chinaman's Hat. As you head south the entrance is just past the HVB Warrior pointing to the Kualoa Sugar Mill ruins.

PRACTICALITIES

Food And Shopping

The **Haiku Gardens Restaurant,** true to its name, sits surrounded by a fragrant garden in a lovely, secluded valley (see "Kahekili Highway" above). After massive renovations, the restaurant has reopened as a **Chart House,** a small chain with an excellent reputation for good food at reasonable prices.

The **Hygienic Store** along Rt. 83 just past the Valley of the Temples sells groceries and supplies. It's flanked by stalls selling fruits and shellwork at competitive prices.

Kahaluu Sportswear, at 47-102-A1 Wailehua Rd., along the Kahekili Hwy. about five minutes past Byodo-In Temple, open daily until 10 p.m., is a garment factory outlet store that sells inexpensive alohawear. Some is made from unbearable and unwearable polyester, but a great deal are made from cotton or rayon. Prices are about 10-20% cheaper than what you'll find in the malls, or city area, though the mannequins, mostly armless and legless, are a sad lot.

Follow the Kahekili Hwy. to Rt. 83 past Waiahole and Waikane, where you'll find some of the best roadside fruit stands on Oahu. One is located just near the Waiahole Elementary School (mile marker 34.5), and another just a few minutes north along Rt. 83 has cold drinking coconuts. Do yourself a favor and have one. Sip the juice and when it's gone, eat the custardlike contents. A real island treat, nutritious and delicious.

KA'A'AWA TOWN AND VICINITY

SIGHTS

When you first zip along the highway through town you get the impression that there isn't much, but there's more than you think. The town stretches back toward the *pali* for a couple of streets. On the ocean side is **Ka'a'awa Beach County Park,** a primarily local hangout. Across the road is the post office, and the **Ka'a'awa Country Kitchen,** which serves breakfast and plate lunches, where you can easily eat for $5. They have a few tables, but the best bet is to get your plate lunch and take it across the street to the beach park. Next door is a **7-Eleven** with gas and incidentals. Behind the post office is **Pyramid Rock,** obviously named because of its shape.

Oahu's *pali* is unsurpassed anywhere in the islands, and it's particularly beautiful here. Take a walk around. Stroll the dirt roads through the residential areas and keep your eyes peeled for a small white cross on the *pali* just near Pyramid Rock. It marks the spot where a serviceman was killed during the Pearl Harbor invasion. His spirit is still honored by the perpetually maintained bright white cross. While walking you'll be treated to Ka'a'awa's natural choir—wild roosters crowing any time they feel like it, and the din of cheeky parrots high in the trees. A pair of parrots escaped from a nearby home about 10 years ago, and their progeny continue to relish life in the balmy tropics.

As you come around the bend of Mahie Point, staring down at you is a very popular stone formation, the **Crouching Lion.** Undoubtedly a tour bus or two will be sitting in the lot of the Crouching Lion Inn. As with all anatomical rock formations, it helps to have an imagination. Anyway, the inn is much more interesting than the lion; it was built by George Larsen in 1928 from rough-hewn lumber from the Pacific Northwest. The huge stones were excavated from the site itself. The inn went public in 1951 and has been serving tourists ever since (for menu and prices see "Practicalities" below).

Ka'a'awa And Kahana Bay Beaches

Three beach parks in as many miles lie between Ka'a'awa Point and Kahana Bay. The first as you head north is **Ka'a'awa Beach County Park,** a popular camping beach (county permits) with restrooms, lifeguards, and picnic facilities. An offshore reef running the entire length of the park makes swimming safe year-round. There's a dangerous rip at the south end of the park at the break in the reef.

Swanzy Beach County Park, two minutes north, also allows camping with a county permit. The sand-and-rubble beach lies below a long retaining wall, often underwater during high tide. The swimming is safe year-round, but is not favorable because of the poor quality of the beach. Swanzy is one of the best squidding and snorkeling beaches on the windward coast. A break in the offshore reef creates a dangerous rip, which should be avoided.

Kahana Bay Beach County Park is a full-service park with lifeguards, picnic facilities, restrooms, the area's only boat launch, and camping (county permit). Swimming is good year-round, although the waters can be cloudy at times. A gentle shorebreak makes the area ideal for bodysurfing and beginner board riders. This entire beach area is traditionally excellent for *akule* fishing, with large schools visiting the offshore waters at certain times of year. It once supported a large Hawaiian fishing village; remnants of fishponds can still be seen. On the mountainside is **Kahana Valley State Park** amidst a mixture ironwoods and coconut trees. It has restrooms, fresh water, and picnic tables. Few visit here, and it's perfectly situated for a quiet picnic.

Huilua Fishpond lies between Ka'a'awa and Punaluu, not far from the Paniola Cafe (about mile marker 25.8). Look to the mountainside for Trout Farm Road, and immediately to your right, on the ocean side, is the fishpond. You'll spot a small bridge and a great launching area for a canoe, kayak, or flotation device. Once in the area, go left by foot under the traffic bridge. Follow Kahana Stream as it gets narrower and narrower (but passable) as it heads inland. You

J.D. BISIGNANI

near Ka'a'awa

can use the overhanging ferns to pull yourself along. The water is deep so be aware. If you go to the right, you'll reach the bay. It's fairly safe until you come to open ocean. TheBus stop is directly across from the launching area so you can get off here, enjoy the sights, and then continue on.

PRACTICALITIES

Crouching Lion Inn

There was a time when *everyone* passing through Ka'a'awa stopped at the Crouching Lion Inn. Built in 1926, it was the only place *to* stop for many, many years. The inn has seen its ups and downs, and now, fortunately, it is under new management and on the upswing again. The inn, along Rt. 83 in Ka'a'awa, tel. 237-8511, open daily for lunch 11 a.m.-3:30 p.m., and for dinner 5-9 p.m., is beautiful enough to stop at just to have a look, but if you want a reasonably quiet meal, avoid lunchtime and come in the evening when the tour buses have long since departed. Sitting high on a verdant green hill, the inn has an architectural style that's a mixture of Southwestern and Hawaiian-country. Inside it is cozy with a few fireplaces as well as open-beamed ceilings, while the view from the veranda is especially grand. Lunch can be a simple order of Portuguese bean soup that comes with a delicious flavored bun at only $3.75 per bowl, or appetizers like royal shrimp cocktail, sashimi, honey garlic shrimp, or oysters on the half shell ($6.25-8.95). Salad entrees are a Crunchy Lion Louie with your choice of shrimp or snow crab at $8.95, or a papaya stuffed with tuna salad for $7.25. Regular entrees are chopped steak, chicken macadamia, or *kalua* pork plate all priced under $10. Sandwiches like a grilled Reuben are under $8, while various burgers cost $6.50-8. Dinner entrees, with fresh-baked rolls, soup or salad, vegetables, and choice of rice, potatoes, or garlic pasta, include pepper steak, teriyaki steak, filet mignon, or prime rib for $18.50-22.95. Chicken macadamia, broiled chicken, and *kalua* pork go for $14.95, while seafood selections and vegetarian-pleasing stir-fry tempura complete the menu. The inn's famous mile-high coconut pie, macadamia nut cream pie, or double-crusted banana pie for under $4, are absolutely delicious. To complement your menu selection a full bar serves cocktails, beer, wine, and liquors.

On the premises is the **Livingstone Galleries,** open daily 11 a.m.-7 p.m., tel. 237-7165, which display original prints, sculptures, and edition prints of both internationally acclaimed and local island artists. The artists displayed include: **Jiang, He Neng,** and **Hede Guang,** all of the Yunnan School of Art that emerged in China after long years of repression under the Mao regime. Using various media including pastels, watercolors, and chalk, the Yunnan artists have created works reminiscent of stained-glass windows that seemingly pre-existed inside their souls waiting for the light to illuminate their beauty. Other artists include father and son Edgardo and Walfrido Garcia. Dad, Edgardo, lives on the North Shore and does sunsets, waves, and wind-tortured palm trees, while Walfrido specializes in fantastic seascapes that often include Pele, the goddess of fire. Also on display are the works of **Tony Bennett,** the famous crooner, which burst with intense emotion; the fantastic underwater-earth-cosmic paintings of **John Pitre** or **Dana Queen,** his wife and colleague; the foggy coasts and misty *pali* captured by **Somner;** bronze sculptures by University of Hawaii economics professor **Bruce Stanford;** and the terminally cute children rendered by **Mary Koski.** Also represented are **Beverly Fettig,** an Oahu artist long renowned for her land and seascapes; and **Dawson,** who sculpts faces and masks in a neoclassic Greek style.

PUNALUU AND HAUULA

PUNALUU

When islanders say Punaluu ("Coral Diving") they usually combine it into the phrase "Pat's at Punaluu" because of the famous resort that's been delighting local people and visitors for years (at mile marker 23.2). It's a favorite place to come for a drive in the "country." Punaluu is a long and narrow ribbon of land between the sea and the *pali.* Its built-up area is about a mile or so long, but only a hundred yards wide. It has gas, supplies, camping, and some of the cheapest accommodations anywhere on Oahu, along with the **Punaluu Art Gallery,** operated by Scott Bechtol, famous candle artist (for both see "Practicalities" following). On the northern outskirts of town, a sign points to **Sacred Falls,** an excellent hike, weather permitting (see "Camping and Hiking" in the Oahu Introduction).

A few hundred yards south of Pat's is **St. Joachim Church.** There's nothing outstanding about this one-room church meekly sitting on a plot of ground overlooking the sea. But it's a real home-grown place where the people of this district come to worship. Just look and you might understand the simple and basic lifestyle that persists in this area.

HAUULA

This speck of a town is just past Punaluu between mile markers 21 and 22. The old town center is two soda machines, two gas pumps, and two limited supply stores, **Masa's** and **Ching Jong Leong's.** Another store, **Segame's,** sells cold beer and liquor. At the estuary of a stream is **Aukai Beach County Park,** a flat little beach right in the middle of town. A **7-Eleven** and a little church up on the hill with the *pali* as a backdrop add the seemingly mandatory finishing touches. Just near the bus stop on the south end, look for a local man who is usually there selling lei. The flowers and vines are fresh-picked from the immediate area, and the prices and authenticity are hard to beat.

Outdoor enthusiasts will love the little-used **Hauula Loop Trails.** These ridge trails head up the valleys gaining height along the way. They offer just about everything that you can expect from a Hawaiian trail: the mountains, the valleys, and vistas of the sea. Built by the Civilian Conservation Corps during the Depression, the trails are wide, and the footing is great even in rainy periods which can shut down the nearby **Sacred Falls Trail.** (See "Camping and Hiking" in the Oahu Introduction.)

BEACHES

Right along the highway is **Punaluu Beach County Park.** Punaluu provides shopping, and the beach park has restrooms, cooking facilities, camping by permit (recently closed, so check), but no lifeguards. The swimming is safe year-round inside the protected reef. Local fishermen, usually older Filipino men who are surf-casting, use this area frequently. They're friend-

2

1. Captain Dave Ventura and friend; **2.** aloha, *paniolo* style;
3. motorcycle madonna (all photos by J.D. Bisignani)

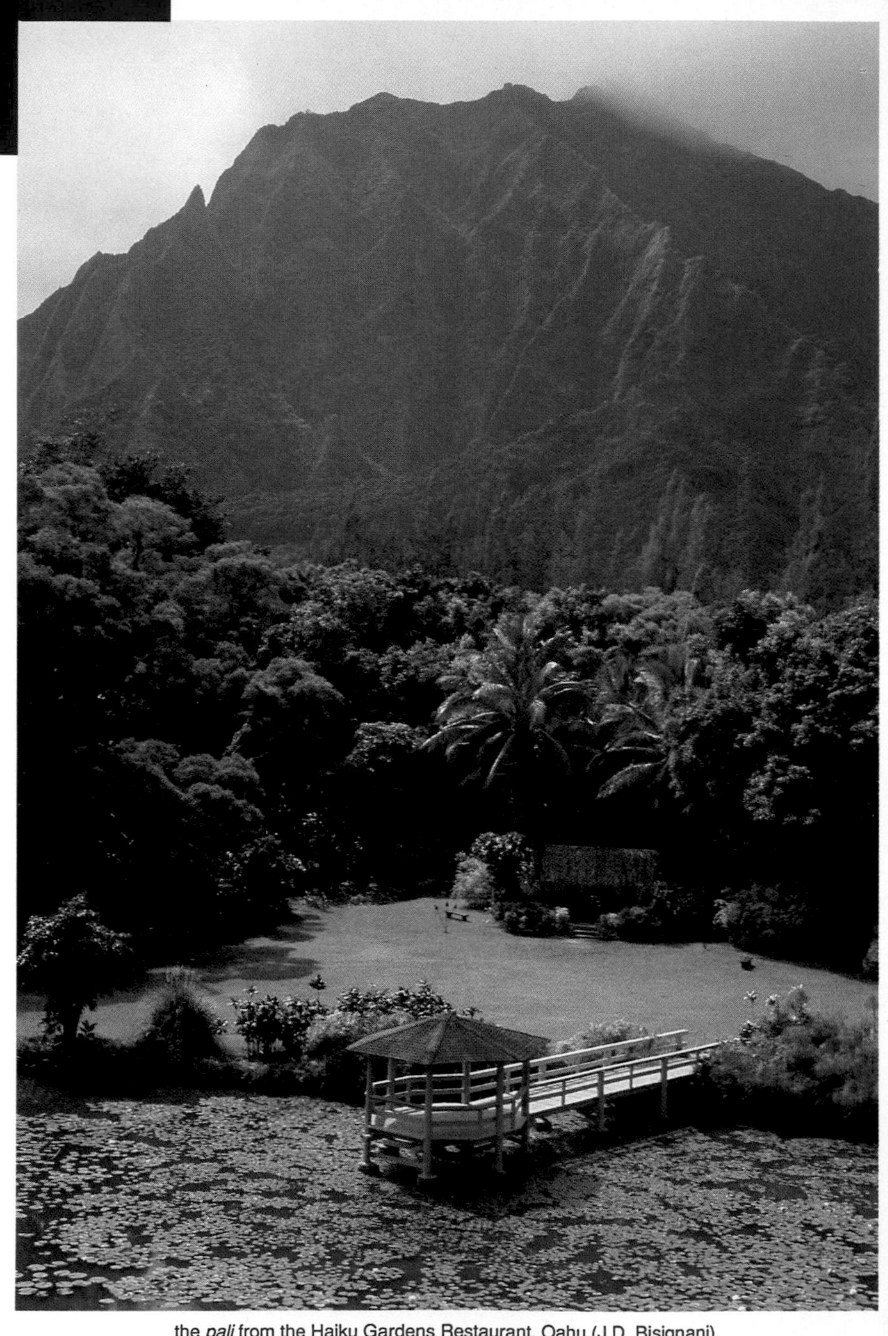

the *pali* from the Haiku Gardens Restaurant, Oahu (J.D. Bisignani)

ly and a great source of information for anyone trying to land a fish or two. They know the best baits and spots to dunk a line.

Hauula Beach County Park is an improved beach park with lifeguards, picnic facilities, restrooms, pavilion, volleyball court, and camping (permit). Safe swimming year-round inside the coral reef, with good snorkeling; surfing is usually best in the winter months. Rip currents are present at both ends of the beach at breaks in the reef, and deep holes in the floor of a brackish pond are formed where Maakua Stream enters the sea. Across the road are the ruins of the historic **Lanakila Church** (1853), partially dismantled at the turn of the century to build a smaller church near Punaluu.

PRACTICALITIES

Accommodations

Pat's at Punaluu Condominium, at mile marker 23.2, P.O. Box 359, Hauula, HI 96717, tel. 293-8111 or (800) 845-8799, is definitely in the budget category, so don't expect deluxe accommodations. The "used but not too abused" units are clean, and you will get what you pay for. Rates on a sliding scale depend upon the length of your stay: $68-76 for a guest room; $72-80 for a large deluxe; $76-84 one bedroom; $120-140 three bedroom. Pat's has a great beach, parking, TV, a restaurant, a swimming pool, and weekly maid service. They offer a "room 'n' wheels" package, and discounts on long stays. Pat's is off the beaten track, so definitely call ahead to check room availability. Turning up and expecting a room is a foolish gamble. This is a condo, not a hotel, so one-night stays are not the norm, and few services are provided. Next to the restaurant is a small convenience store that may or may not look open. But inside (separate business) is a small desk, open 8:30 a.m.-1 p.m., where you register. Another rental office on the property is open until 9 p.m., but check-in after that costs extra since someone has to stay around to let you in.

The **Countryside Cabins** are a wonderful, inexpensive, and definitely funky place to stay. They're owned and operated by Margaret Naai, still sparkling at 92 years old. The entrance is hard to spot, but it's located *mauka* about 5-10 minutes past Pat's at Punaluu. Look for the small white sign that says "Cabins." Completely furnished studios are $25 daily, $175 weekly, $475 monthly. Unfurnished rooms are $20 nightly, $140 weekly, $300 monthly. Margaret will reserve a room for you if you send a $10 deposit. She's a peach, but she's getting on in years, so it would be best to send a S.A.S.E. with your deposit and not count on her to remember. For information and reservations, write Countryside Cabins, 53-224 Kamehameha Hwy., Hauula HI 96717, tel. 237-8169.

Food And Shopping

The **Punaluu Art Gallery,** in Punaluu around mile marker 24, tel. 237-8325, open daily 10:30 a.m.-6:30 p.m., formerly owned by Dorothy Zoler, is the oldest art gallery on windward Oahu. The new owner, candle artist Scott Bechtol, remains dedicated to showcasing the works of the finest artists on the North Shore. Scott is well known for his wonderful sculpted candles, all made from the finest beeswax. Some are lanterns shaped like a huge pita bread with the top third cut off. Each lantern is sculpted with a scene that glows when the candle is lit. Others are huge tikis, dolphins, or flowers, all inspired by the islands; there's even a 10-foot whale. Some of the larger candles are $70, and the man-size tiki is about $800, but smaller candles are only $5, and Scott's unique "crying tiki" sells for only $20. Scott creates all of this beautiful glowing art with just one precision carving tool . . . a Buck knife. Another artist shown is Bill Cupit, who creates "bananascapes." Bill removes the outer bark from the banana tree, which he then tears and cuts to make a scene of boats or mountains. The result is a three-dimensional piece. Bill's wife is an artist who specializes in seascapes made with seaweed, while Christine Diana uses fossilized wood to render "Tiny Treasures," miniature paintings of Hawaiian scenes. Also take a look at Janet Holiday's silk screen prints, Peter Hayward's oil paintings, and the dramatic tropical beauty of the North Shore captured by longtime resident Edgardo Garcia. The Punaluu Art Gallery is a jewel case of manmade beauty surrounded by natural beauty. They harmonize perfectly.

The **Sacred Falls Bazaar,** seaside on the north end of Punaluu, open daily 9:30 a.m.-6:30 p.m., sells an assortment of neat touristy junk including aloha shirts, shell lei, tie-dyed T-shirts, and fresh island fruit. A minute farther north is the **Jhing Leong Store,** painted shocking pink, where you can pick up a smattering of supplies.

In Hauula look for the **Hauula Kai Center,** a small shopping center with a **post office** and a **Pay 'n Save** for everything from film to swim fins, and the **Village Food Mart,** open weekdays 9-9, Sunday 9-5 for all food needs. Also, look for **Lotus Inn Chop Suey,** tel. 293-5412, where you'll get a tasty and filling meal daily 10 a.m.-9 p.m. for under $6. A full menu of Cantonese-style food includes ginger chicken, shrimp, and beef. Happy hour runs 3-7 p.m., when well drinks cost $1.25 and are accompanied by free *pu pu.* The shopping center also features the **Bethlehem Baking Company,** open daily 6:30 a.m.-6 p.m., with an assortment of yummies including sweet homemade breads of pineapple and coconut.

Also in Hauula is the **Rainbow Shopping Plaza,** an unabashed tourist trap, classic in its obvious tastelessness. Here you'll find beads and baubles, the **Rainbow Barbecue** for something to eat, and the **Rainbow Lounge** where you can have a drink.

LAIE TO KAHUKU

LAIE

The "Saints" came marching into Laie ("Leaf of the Ie Vine") and set about making a perfect Mormon village in paradise. What's more, they succeeded. The town itself is squeaky clean, with well-kept homes and manicured lawns that hint of suburban Midwest America. Dedicated to education, the Mormons built a branch of **Brigham Young University** (BYU) that attracts students from all over Polynesia, many of whom work in the nearby Polynesian Cultural Center. The students vow to live a clean life, free of drugs and alcohol, and not to grow beards. In the foyer of the main entrance look for a huge mural depicting Laie's flag-raising ceremony in 1921, which symbolically established the colony. The road leading to and from the university campus is mazelike but easily negotiable.

The first view of the **Mormon Temple,** built in 1919, is very impressive. Square, with simple architectural lines, this house of worship sits pure white against the *pali,* and is further dramatized by a reflecting pool and fountains spewing fine mists. This tranquil, shrinelike church is open daily 9 a.m.-9 p.m., when a slide show telling the history of the Laie colony is presented, along with a guided tour of the grounds. "Smoking is prohibited, and shirts (no halter tops) must be worn to enter." The temple attracts more visitors than any other Mormon site outside of the main temple in Salt Lake City.

Polynesian Cultural Center

The real showcase is the Polynesian Cultural Center. PCC, as it's called by islanders, began as an experiment in 1963. Smart businesspeople said it would never thrive way out in Laie, and tourists didn't come to Hawaii for *culture* anyway. The PCC now rates as one of Oahu's top tourist attractions, luring about one million visitors annually. Miracles do happen. PCC is a nonprofit organization, with proceeds going to the Laie BYU and to the center's maintenance.

Covering 42 acres, the primary attractions are seven model villages that include examples from Hawaii, Samoa, the Marquesas, Fiji, New Zealand, Tonga, and Tahiti. Guides lead you through the villages either on a walking tour, or by canoe over artesian-fed waterways. A shuttle tram runs outside the center and will take you on a guided tour to the BYU campus, the temple, and a the community (which would be okay except for the missionary hard sell). The villages are primarily staffed with people from the representative island homelands. Remember that most are Mormons, whose dogma colors the attitudes and selected presentations of the staffers. Still, all are genuinely interested in dispensing cultural knowledge about their traditional island ways and beliefs, and almost all are characters who engage in lighthearted bantering with their

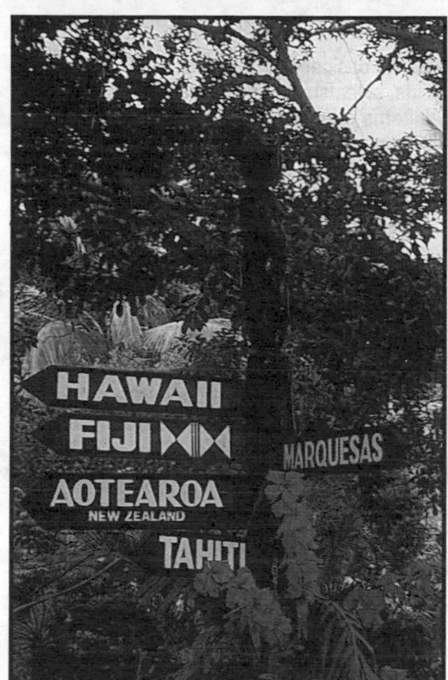

J.D. BISIGNANI

Polynesian Cultural Center

willing audience. The undeniable family spirit and pride at PCC make you feel welcome, while providing a clean and wholesome experience, with plenty of attention to detail.

The show begins with the **Fiafia Festival,** a lei greeting that orients you to the center. Next comes **Music Polynesia,** a historical evolution of island music presented by singers, musicians, and dancers. A brass band plays from 5:30 p.m., touring the different villages, and the **Pageant of Canoes** sails at 2 and 3 p.m. The largest extravaganza occurs during an evening dinner show called **This is Polynesia.** Beginning at 7:30 p.m., the center's amphitheater hosts about 3,000 spectators for this show of music, dance, and historical drama. The costumes and lighting are dramatic and inspired; it's hard to believe that the performers are not professionals. Soon to open is an **Imax,** a wrap-around movie screen that attempts to give you a real sense of what it's like to take a canoe around the shores of Fiji, or to tramp the mountains of New Zealand.

Food is available from a number of snack bars, or you can dine at the **Gateway,** which serves you a buffet dinner as part of a package including the Polynesian extravaganza. A luau or a Mission Buffet are offered now and again, usually at 5:30 p.m., so there's plenty of time to eat and then catch the show if you desire.

PCC is open daily except Sunday 12:30 p.m.-9 p.m. General admission to the center is $25 adults, $12.50 children, under five free. A variety of packages are available, including an all-day pass with dinner buffet and evening show for around $50, children $25. For more information contact PCC at 293-3333 or (800) 367-7060. TheBus no. 52 from Ala Moana gets to the center in about two hours. Most island hotels can arrange a package tour to PCC.

PRACTICALITIES

Accommodations

The **Laniloa Lodge Hotel,** 55-109 Laniloa St., Laie, HI 96762, tel. 293-9282 or (800) 526-4562, is just outside the Polynesian Cultural Center, and has been recently given a face-lift. Rooms are $70-85 standard, $90-105 deluxe, $100-130 two-bedroom deluxe, $10 additional person. They also offer a special rate if you purchase two all-day tickets to the Polynesian Cultural Center. All rooms have a/c and TV, and there's parking, a pool, and a restaurant that closes early on Sunday, but McDonald's is next door.

Kekeala Hale is a condominium rental fronting Kekeala Beach, at 55-113 Kamehameha Hwy., Laie, HI 96762, tel. 293-9700. They call themselves "private Polynesia at its best," and being as secluded as they are, they have a point. Cottages are over a thousand square feet with a full kitchen and bath, with one king and four twin beds in each unit. The property features a tennis court. Rates for cottages that sleep 6-12 (using foam pads) are $240 daily, $600 for a weekend, $1440 weekly. Rates for a cottage sleeping four to six are $120 daily, $720 weekly. All require a three-day minimum.

Lora Dunn's House is at 55-161 Kamehameha Hwy., Laie, HI 96762, tel. 293-1000 (between mile markers 19 and 20, ocean side). Lora admits people on a first-come, first-served basis, but will happily take phone reservations for which she requires a deposit. Chances of turning up and finding a vacancy are poor, so at least call from the airport to check availability. A separate studio for two people is $175, while the downstairs self-contained unit of her home, which is larger and can accommodate four people, runs about $350 per week. Good value in a quiet, if not spectacular, setting.

Note: Also see "Beaches" following, some of which have camping facilities.

Food And Shopping

When you enter Laie you will be greeted by the Stars and Stripes flying over the entrance of the Polynesian Cultural Center. Next door is a whopper of a **McDonald's,** and in keeping with the spirit of Polynesian culture, it looks like a Polynesian longhouse. Just next door is the **Laniloa Lodge,** tel. 293-5888, whose restaurant features breakfast specials for under $4, and complete dinners with soup, salad, vegies, and Kona coffee for only $10.95. They're open every day for breakfast until 8 p.m., except Sunday when the restaurant closes at 2 p.m. The food is wholesome but ordinary.

On the ocean side of the road is **Masa's Market,** which couldn't be more local with counters stocked with everything from lotus root to lamb. At the north end of Laie, you'll pass **TT Surf Shop,** about the only shop in this neck of the woods offering snorkeling equipment, surfboards, and boogie boards. A few minutes south is the **Hauula Kai Shopping Center** (see "Food and Shopping" under "Practicalities" in the "Punaluu and Hauula" section earlier in this chapter), which provides a small variety of dining spots and shopping.

Between Kahuku and Laie is a new **Laie Shopping Center,** where you'll find a large and modern **Foodland** along with a **Bank of America** and a small convenience store, **Lindy's Food.** The most interesting shop is the **Hawaiian-Polynesian Cultural Supply,** tel. 293-1560, open weekdays 9:30 a.m.-5 p.m., Saturday half day, a rare and unique hula supply store. They feature fine Polynesian crafts used in the hula like *ipu* (gourd drums), hula skirts, headdresses, beads, and shell lei. There are other accoutrements and art items like koa bowls, carved turtles, and mother-of-pearl necklaces. All items are handmade in Tahiti, Samoa, Tonga, and Hawaii, basically from throughout Polynesia. T-shirts, sweatshirts, and suntan oil are also sold. All items offered are authentic, and the storekeepers are friendly and informative regarding the hula. A great store in which to browse and to pick up a unique and *real* souvenir. Also see "Practicalities" under "Kahuku" following.

BEACHES

At the southern end of Laie is **Pounder's Beach,** so named by students of BYU because of the pounding surf. The park area is privately owned, open to the public, with few facilities (a few portable outhouses and picnic tables). This beach experiences heavy surf and dangerous conditions in the winter months, but its excellent shoreline break is perfect for bodysurfing. The remains of an old pier at which interisland steamers once stopped is still in evidence.

Laie Beach County Park is an unimproved beach park with no facilities, but a one-mile stretch of beach. The shoreline waters are safe for swimming inside the reef, but wintertime produces heavy and potentially dangerous surf. Good snorkeling, fishing, and throw-netting by local fishermen; get there by following the stream from the bridge near the Laie Shopping Center.

Camping Beaches

Kakela Beach was a privately owned facility where camping was allowed. Now under the Department of State Parks, it is being renovated and may open again for camping. (See "Camping and Hiking" in the Oahu Introduction for information.)

Malaekahana Bay State Recreation Area is the premier camping beach along the north section of the windward coast. Separated from the highway by a large stand of shade trees, it offers showers, restrooms, picnic facilities, and camping (state permit). Offshore is Moku'auia, better known as **Goat Island.**

The island is only a stone's throw from shore. Reef walkers or tennis shoes are advised. You can reach this seabird sanctuary by wading across the reef during low tide. You'll find a beautiful crescent of white-sand beach and absolute peace and quiet. The swimming inside the reef is good, and it's amazing how little used this area is for such a beautiful spot. Be aware that there are two entrances to the park. The north entrance, closest to Kahuku, puts you in the day-use area of the park, where there are restrooms and showers. Farther offshore, about 200-300 yards, is a small island. *You cannot wade to this island. It is too far, and the currents are strong.* The entrance to the camping section is south a minute or two (around mile marker 17) and is marked by a steel gate painted brown and a sign welcoming you to Malaekahana Bay State Recreation Area. You must be aware that the gates open at 7 a.m. and close at 6:45 p.m.

KAHUKU

This village, and it is a village, is where the *workers* of the North Shore live. Kahuku is "fo' real," and a lingering slice of what *was* not so long ago. Do yourself a favor, and turn off the highway for a two-minute tour of the dirt roads lined by proudly maintained homes that somehow exude the feeling of Asia.

Practicalities

You can pick up supplies at the **Kahuku Superette** clearly marked along Rt. 83, or better yet look for a little white ***kaukau* wagon** that sits across the roadway from the school. It sells great food brought from Honolulu's Chinatown fresh every day. Unfortunately, the wagon is here only during school hours, when you can pick up a tasty and inexpensive lunch.

Keep a sharp eye out for a truck and a sign featuring fresh shrimp for $6.95 just along the road. Follow it to **Ahi's Kahuku Restaurant,** operated by Roland Ahi and son, open daily 10 a.m.-9 p.m. The shrimp couldn't be fresher, as it comes from Pacific Sea Farms, an aquaculture farm just a few minutes away. The longest that these plump babies have been out of the water is 48 hours, so you are definitely getting *the* best. In this no-frills but super-friendly restaurant, you can have your shrimp cooked to order—deep-fried, sautéed, tempura, a cocktail, or as scampi. You get about eight shrimp, depending on the size. The shrimp is the pièce de résistance, but they have basic sandwiches like tuna and hamburger, both under $4, and entrees like spaghetti with meat sauce for $5.95, and steak and mahimahi combo for $10.95. Complete meals come with green salad, fresh vegetables, rice, and tea. They also serve beer and wine, and on Friday nights, Charlie Kualoha, a wonderfully talented local musician, performs everything from country to contemporary Hawaiian. Ahi's serves all of its great food with authentic *aloha.* Stop in! You'll be glad you did.

On the north end of town is the **Mill Shopping Center,** which is really the town's old sugar mill that has been recycled. The interior is dominated by huge gears and machinery, power panels, and crushers that are the backdrop for a string of shops, a restaurant, and the Kahuku Theater. The 10-foot gears and conveyor belts, painted bright colors, seem like a display of modern art. Outside is a **Circle K** food store and gas station, **Lee's Gifts and Jewelry, Island Snow** for shave ice, **Tropical Memories Jeweler,** and a post office.

Chucho's Mexican Restaurant and **J-Gem's Plate Lunches** defy the adage that "two things can't occupy the same space at the same time." These "window service" restaurants, tel. 293-2110, open daily except Sunday 7 a.m.-8 p.m., are separate establishments serving very different menus but operating out of the same window. They're located under the veranda behind the gas station at the Mill Shopping Center. J-Gem's offers breakfast selections like Portuguese sausage, eggs, and rice ($2.99), or a stack of pancakes ($1.99). The most expensive plate lunch is a teri beef combo ($4.99), or choose a fishburger ($2.25) or *lumpia,* an island favorite by way of the Philippines ($3.99). Chucho's offers tacos, tostadas, burritos, quesadillas, and taquitos all for under $2.95, and dinner combinations with rice and beans ($3.65-4.95). Both get the "thumbs up" from local people, who say their food is great.

About one mile northwest of Kahuku heading toward Haleiwa, you'll pass the **Royal Hawaiian Prawn and Shrimp Farm.** Notice a patchwork quilt of ponds shored up with mud, very similar to rice paddies, where the succulent crustaceans are raised. The general public is invited to stop by and purchase the little beauties.

Just past the farm is the **Tanaka Plantation Store,** at 56-901 Kamehameha Hwy., Kahuku, a refurbished turn-of-the-century company store that now houses a clutch of boutiques and shops. Make sure to visit **Paul Wroblewski's Antiques and Collectibles,** open daily 10 a.m.-5:30 p.m., "unless they are closed." Blown to Oahu's North Shore from Kauai by Hurricane Iniki, Paul has reopened his shop and once again jammed it with Hawaiian artifacts, old bottles, costume jewelry, license plates, fishing floats, netsuke, scrimshaw, a collection of Marilyn Monroe memorabilia, and a full line of antique jewelry. Paul's an amiable fellow, and is open to any reasonable offer.

Next door is **Fairly Galleries,** featuring posters, prints, and a bit of jewelry. **Coconuts** is open daily 9 a.m.-6 p.m., tel. 293-7865, with bathing suits, T-shirts, straw hats, alohawear, towels, silver jewelry, and postcards. They also have a snack counter featuring sandwiches and espresso.

Perhaps the most interesting shop in the complex is the **Amazonian Forest Store,** open daily 11 a.m.-6 p.m., owned and operated by Brazilian world travelers Cesar Olivera and Katia Ferz. They specialize in authentic artifacts gathered from the Amazon and other rainforest regions around the world, including Hawaii and Indonesia. Some of the most amazing artifacts are headdresses and paintings by Brazil's Xindu Indians, along with basketry, parasols, coconut purses, string and cotton hammocks, and semiprecious gemstones gathered from throughout South America. If these aren't enough to make you bug-eyed perhaps a Brazilian string bikini will.

Geographical Note

The following chapter, "The North Shore," begins at the west end in Waialua/Haleiwa and works eastward toward Kahuku. That's because most people visiting the North Shore proceed in this direction, while those heading for windward Oahu start in Kailua/Kaneohe and proceed up the coast. So, the end of this chapter connects geographically with the end of "The North Shore" chapter. Don't let it throw you.

seal

BOB RACE

THE NORTH SHORE

This shallow bowl of coastline stretches from Kaena Point in the west to Turtle Bay in the east. **Mount Ka'ala,** verdant backdrop to the area, rises 4,020 feet from the Waianae Range, the highest peak on Oahu. The entire stretch is a day-tripper's paradise with plenty of sights to keep you entertained. But the North Shore is synonymous with one word: surfing. Thunderous winter waves, often measuring 25 feet (from the rear!) rumble along the North Shore's world-famous surfing beaches lined up one after the other—**Waimea Bay, Ehukai, Sunset, Banzai Pipeline.** They attract highly accomplished athletes who come to compete in prestigious international surfing competitions. In summertime *moana,* the sea, loses its ferocity and becomes gentle and safe for anyone.

Haleiwa, at the junction of the Farrington Hwy. (Rt. 930) heading west along the coast and the Kamehameha Hwy. (Rt. 83) heading east, is fast becoming the central town along the North Shore. The main street is lined with restaurants, boutiques, art galleries, small shopping malls, and sports equipment stores. **Waialua,** just west, is a sugar town with a few quiet condos for relaxation. Farther west is **Dillingham A.F.B.** (inactive), where you can arrange to fly above it all in a small plane or soar silently in a glider. The road ends for vehicles not far from here, and then your feet have to take you to Kaena Point, where *the* largest waves pound the coast. Heading east, you'll pass a famous *heiau* where human flesh mollified the gods. Then come the great surfing beaches and their incredible waves. Here and there are tidepools rich with discovery, a monument to a real local hero, and **Waimea Falls Park,** the premier tourist attraction of the North Shore.

BEACHES AND SIGHTS

The main attractions of the North Shore are its beaches. Interspersed among them are a few sights definitely worth your time and effort. The listings below run from west to east. The most-traveled route to the North Shore is from Honolulu along the H-2 Freeway, and then directly

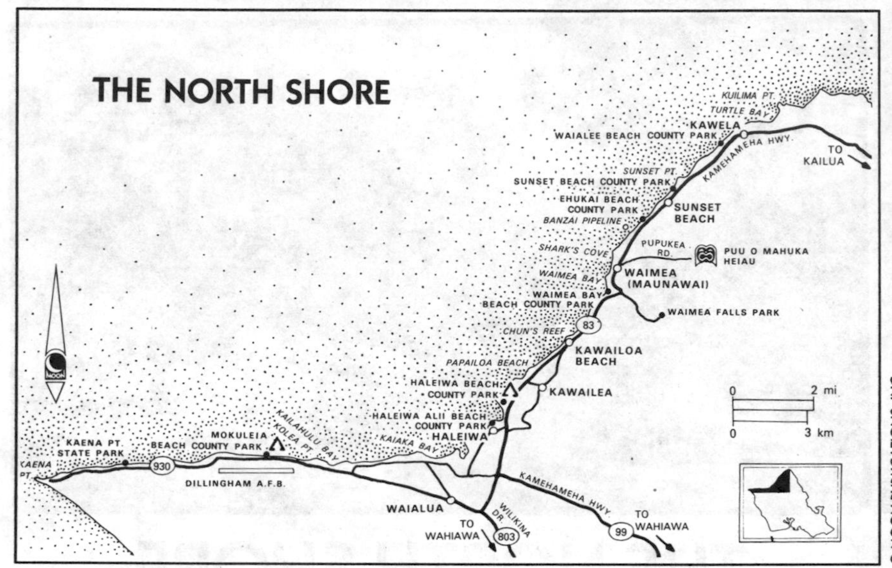

to the coast along Rt. 99 or Rt. 803. At Weed Circle or Thompson Corner, where these routes reach the coast, turn left along the Farrington Hwy., following it to road's end just before Kaena Point, or turn right along the Kamehameha Hwy. (Rt. 83), which heads around the coast all the way to Kailua.

Be aware that *all* North Shore beaches experience very heavy surf conditions with dangerous currents from October through April. The waters, at this time of year, are not for the average swimmer. Please heed all warnings. In summertime, leap in!

ALONG THE FARRINGTON HIGHWAY, RT. 930

Waialua

The first town is Waialua ("Two Waters"). Take Waialua Beach Road just off the Weed Traffic Circle coming north on Rt. 99, or follow the signs off the Farrington Highway. At the turn of the century, Waialua, lying at the terminus of a sugar-train railway, was a fashionable beach community complete with hotels and vacation homes. Today, it's hardly ever visited, and it's not uncommon to see as many horses tied up along the main street as it is to see parked cars in this real one-horse town. Sundays can also attract a rumble of bikers who kick up the dust on their two-wheeled steeds.

The sugar mill, an outrageously ugly mechanical monster, is still operating and is central to the town. Quiet Waialua, with its main street divided by trees running down the middle, *is* rural Oahu. There's a general store for supplies, a post office, and snacks at the **Sugar Bar,** a restaurant in the old Bank of Hawaii building. If you're returning to Haleiwa take Haleiwa Road, a back way through residential areas. Look for Paalaa Road on the right and take it past a small Buddhist temple that holds an *o bon* festival honoring the dead, traditionally observed in July.

Mokuleia Beach County Park And Dillingham Airfield

Mokuleia is the main public access park along the highway. It provides picnic facilities, restrooms, lifeguards, a playground area, and camping (county permit). In summertime, swimming is possible along a few sandy stretches protected by a broken offshore reef. Mokuleia Army

Beach, across from the airfield, is a wider strand of sand. It's very private, and the only noise interrupting your afternoon slumber might be planes taking off from the airfield. A minute farther toward Kaena is an unofficial area with a wide sand beach. During the week you can expect no more than half dozen people on this 300-yard beach. Remember that this is the North Shore and the water can be treacherous. Careful! Five minutes past the airfield, the road ends. This is a good place to check out giant waves.

Across the road is **Dillingham Airfield,** small but modern, with restrooms near the hangars and a new parking area. A public phone is available in hangar G-1. Most days, especially weekends, a few local people sell refreshments from their cars or trucks. The main reason for stopping is to take a small plane or glider ride. **Glider Rides,** tel. 677-3404, takes you on a 20- to 30-minute flight for $40 single, $60 double. The owner is Bill Star, who has been flying from here since 1970. They fly seven days a week starting at about 10 a.m. on a first-come, first-served basis. They suggest you bring a camera and arrive before 5 p.m. to get the best winds. There's always a pilot with you to make sure that your glider ride is a *return* trip. Another glider operation is **Mile High Glider Rides.** They fly for 30 minutes and offer a sit-up-front-and-try-the-controls-type ride complete with acrobatics and instruction. They fly out of hangar no. 10, and charge about $80 per ride. **Surf Air Tours,** tel. 637-7003, flies Cessna 172s or 206s for a half-hour along the North Shore for $30 per person, or a longer "circle-island tour" for $50 per person. It's worthwhile, but the glider ride is exceptional.

In quick succession west after Dillingham Airfield come undeveloped **Kealia Beach,** safe during calm periods, and **Mokuleia Army Beach,** improved and open to the public. Local people have erected semipermanent tents in this area and guard it as if it were their own. **Camp Harold Erdman** is next, one of the best-known camps on Oahu. This YMCA facility is named after a famous Hawaiian polo player killed in the '30s. The facility is used as a summer camp for children, throughout the year for special functions, and as a general retreat area by various organizations. Access is limited to official use.

Kaena Point

Kaena Point lies about 2.5 miles west down the dirt track after the pavement gives out. Count on three hours for a return hike and remember to bring water. The point can also be reached from road's end above Mahuka on the Waianae (leeward) side of the island. Kaena has *the* largest waves in Hawaii on any given day. In wintertime, these giants can reach above 40 feet, and their power, even when viewed safely from high ground, is truly amazing. Surfers have actually plotted ways of riding these waves, which include being dropped by helicopter with scuba tanks. Reportedly, one surfer named Ace Cool has already done it. For the rest of us mortals . . . "who wants to have that much fun anyway?" Kaena Point is the site of numerous *heiau.* Due to its exposed position, it, like similar sites around the islands, was a jumping-off point for the "souls of the dead." The spirits were believed to wander here after death, and once all worldly commitments were fulfilled, they made their "leap" from earth to heaven. Hopefully, the daredevil surfers will not revive this tradition.

HALEIWA AND VICINITY

Haleiwa ("Home of the Frigate Birds") has become the premier town of the region, mainly because it straddles the main road and has the majority of shopping, dining, and services along the North Shore. **Haleiwa Ali'i Beach County Park** is on the western shores of Waialua Bay, which fronts the town. This beach park is improved with restrooms, lifeguard tower, and a small boat launch. Lifeguards staff the tower throughout the summer, on weekends in winter. The shoreline is rocks and coral with pockets of sand, and although portions can be good for swimming, the park is primarily noted for surfing, in a break simply called "Haleiwa."

When you come into Haleiwa, just past Pizza Hut and McDonald's, notice on the right-hand side of the road a sign that says "Weinberg Village." Look and you will see one-room, decent, modern . . . shacks. The idea was good—"to create low rent homes for the poor and homeless" with funds bequeathed for this purpose by Mr. Weinberg, a social-minded philanthropist. However, each of the tiny units costs $40,000 to build, and the people residing here have to pay $300 per month rent. Moreover, they are supposed to be torn down in five years.

Head eastward and cross the **Anahulu River Bridge.** Park for a moment and walk back over the bridge. Look upstream to see homes with tropical character perched on the bank with a bevy of boats tied below. The scene is reminiscent of times gone by.

A much better park is **Haleiwa Beach County Park,** clearly marked off the highway on the eastern side of Waialua Bay. Here you'll find pavilions, picnic facilities, lifeguards, restrooms, showers, food concessions, and camping (county permit). The area is good for fishing, surfing, and most importantly, for swimming year-round. It's about the only safe place for the average person to swim along the entire North Shore during winter.

Kawailoa Beach is the name given to the general area stretching all the way from Haleiwa Beach County Park to Waimea Bay. A string of beaches, **Papailoa, Laniakea,** and **Chun's Reef,** is just off the road. Cars park where the access is good. None of these beaches is suitable for the recreational swimmer. All are surfing beaches, with the most popular being Chun's Reef.

WAIMEA BAY AND VICINITY

The two-lane highway along the North Shore is pounded by traffic; be especially careful around Waimea Bay. The highway sweeps around till you see the steeple of **St. Peter and Paul Mission** with the bay below. The steeple is actually the remains of an old rock-crushing plant on the site. **Waimea Bay Beach County Park** has the largest rideable waves in the world. This is the heart of surfers' paradise. The park is improved with a lifeguard tower, restrooms, and a picnic area.

During a big winter swell, the bay is lined with spectators watching the surfers ride the monumental waves. In summertime, the bay is calm as a lake. People inexperienced with the sea should not even walk along the shorebreak in winter. Unexpected waves come up farther than expected, and a murderous rip lurks only a few feet from shore. The area is rife with tales of heroic rescue attempts, many ending in fatalities. A plaque commemorates Eddie Aikau, a local lifeguard credited with making thousands of rescues. In 1978, the *Hokule'a,* the Polynesian Sailing Society's double-hulled canoe, capsized in rough seas about 20 miles offshore. Eddie was aboard and launched his surfboard to swim for help. He never made it, but his selfless courage lives on.

Waimea Falls Park

Look for the well-marked entrance to Waimea Falls Park, mountain side from the bay, and then drive for quite a way into the lush valley before coming to the actual park entrance. Along with the Bishop Museum, the park is the most culturally significant travel destination on Oahu. Although open to the public and more than happy to welcome visitors, Waimea Falls Park has not lost sight of its ancient *aloha* soul, which it honors while providing a wonderful day of excitement and education. Primarily a botanical garden, with a fascinating display of flowers and plants all labeled for your edification, the Waimea Arboretum collects, grows and preserves extremely rare specimens of Hawaii's endangered flora. If you choose not to walk, an open-air tour bus will take you through, narrating all the way. A thrilling event is the professional diving from the 55-foot rock walls into the pool below Waimea Falls, along with the feeding of peacocks, geese, guinea fowl, and jungle fowl scheduled throughout the day. Culturally enlightening are displays of ancient hula *(kahiko)* performed by very accomplished dancers, a display of Hawaiian games, carving demonstrations, and walks along forest paths that end at fascinating historical sites. On the property is Hale O Lono, one of the island's largest and most ancient *heiau* dedicated to the god Lono. Admission is $19.95 adults, $8.95 juniors, and $3.95 children, open daily 10 a.m.-5:30 p.m., tel. 638-8511. The **Proud Peacock** (see "Food" under "Practicalities" later in this chapter) serves dinner until 9 p.m. Monthly (check the free tourist literature), on the Friday night closest to the full moon, beginning at 8:30 p.m., the park offers a free, guided moon-viewing tour.

Pupukea Beach County Park

A perfect place to experience marinelife is the large tidepool next to Pupukea Beach Park, the first one north of Waimea Bay, across the street

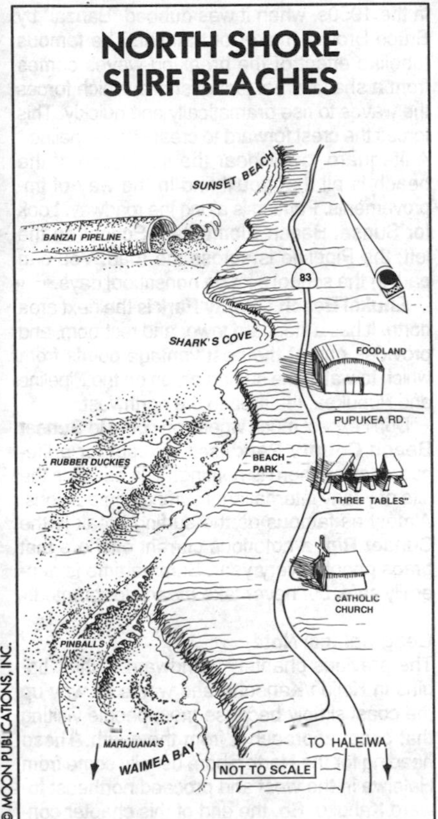

from the Shell gas station. A long retaining wall out to sea forms a large and protected pool at low tide. Wear footgear and check out the pools with a mask. Don't be surprised to find large sea bass. A sign warns against spearing fish, but the local people do it all the time. Be careful not to step on sea urchins, and stay away from the pool during rough winter swells, when it can be treacherous. The beach park has restrooms, picnic facilities, and fair swimming in sandy pockets between coral and rock, but only in summertime. County camping with a permit used to be allowed at this beach park, and may be available again.

The middle section of the park is called **Shark's Cove,** though no more sharks are here than anywhere else. The area is terrific for snorkeling and scuba in season. Look to the mountains to see **The Mansion** (see following), and next to it the white sculpture of the **World Unity Monument.** If you had to pick a spot from which to view the North Shore sunset, Pupukea Beach Park is hard to beat.

Farther down the road, as you pass mile marker 9 you can't help noticing a mammoth redwood log that has been carved into a giant statue representing an ancient Hawaiian. Peter Wolfe, the sculptor, has done a symbolic sculpture for every state in the union, this being his 50th. This statue is extremely controversial. Some feel that it looks much more like a Native American than a Hawaiian, and that the log used should have been a native koa instead of an imported redwood from the Pacific Northwest. Others say that its *intention* was to honor the living and the ancient Hawaiians, and that is what's important. Just off to the left a small shop sells plants, towels, and shellwork from the Philippines.

Puu O Mahuka Heiau

Do yourself a favor and drive up the mountain road leading to the *heiau* even if you don't want to visit it. The vast and sweeping views of the coast below are incredible. About one mile past Waimea Bay the highway approaches a Foodland on the right. Turn here up Pupukea Road and follow the signs. There is a warning at the beginning of the access road, but the road is well maintained and many people ignore the sign.

Puu O Mahuka Heiau is large, covering perhaps five acres. Designated a state historical site, it has a floorplan of huge steps, with one area leading to another just below. The *heiau* was the site of human sacrifice. People still come here to pray, as is evidenced by many stones wrapped in ti leaves placed on small stone piles lying about the grounds. In the upper section is a raised mound surrounded by stone in what appears to be a central altar area. The *heiau's* stonework shows a high degree of craftsmanship throughout, but especially in the pathways. The lower section of the *heiau* appears to be much older, and is not as well maintained.

Drive past the access road leading to the *heiau* and in a minute or so make a left onto

Alapio Road. This takes you through an expensive residential area called **Sunset Hills** and past a home locally called **The Mansion**—look for the English-style boxwood hedge surrounding it. The home was purported to be Elvis Presley's island hideaway. Almost next door are the grounds of the **Nichiren Buddhist Temple,** resplendent with manicured lawns and gardens. This area is a tremendous vantage point from which to view Fourth of July fireworks lighting up Waimea Bay far below.

THE GREAT SURFING BEACHES

Sunset Beach runs for two miles, the longest white-sand beach on Oahu. Winter surf erodes the beach, with coral and lava fingers exposed at the shoreline, but in summertime you can expect an uninterrupted beach usually 200-300 feet wide. The entire stretch is technically Sunset Beach, but each world-famous surfing spot warrants its own name though they're not clearly marked and are tough to find . . . exactly. Mainly, look for cars with surfboard racks parked along the road. The beaches are not well maintained either. They're often trashed, and the restrooms, even at Waimea Bay, are atrocious. The reason is politics and money. Efforts all go into Waikiki, where the tourists are. Who cares about a bunch of crazy surfers on the North Shore? They're just a free curiosity for the tourists' enjoyment.

The **Banzai Pipeline** is probably the best-known surfing beach in the world. Its notoriety dates from *Surf Safari,* an early surfer film made in the 1950s, when it was dubbed "Banzai" by Bruce Brown, maker of the film. The famous tubelike effect of the breaking waves comes from a shallow reef just offshore, which forces the waves to rise dramatically and quickly. This forces the crest forward to create "the Pipeline." A lifeguard tower near the south end of the beach is all that you'll find in the way of improvements. Parking is along the roadway. Look for Sunset Beach Elementary School on the left; the Pipeline is across the road. You can park in the school's lot on nonschool days.

Ehukai Beach County Park is the next area north. It has a lifeguard tower and restroom, and provides one of the best vantage points from which to watch the surfing action on the Pipeline and Pupukea, the area to the northwest.

Don't expect much when you come to **Sunset Beach County Park** itself. Except for a lifeguard tower, there is nothing. This beach is the site of yearly international surfing competitions. Almost as famous as the surfing break is the **Sunset Rip,** a notorious current offshore that grabs people every year. Summertime is generally safe, but never take *moana* for granted.

Geographical Note

The previous chapter, "Windward Oahu," begins in Kailua/Kaneohe and works its way up the coast simply because most people visiting that coast approach it from the south. Those heading for the North Shore usually come from Haleiwa in the west and proceed northeast toward Kahuku. So, the end of this chapter connects geographically with the end of the "Windward Oahu" Chapter. Don't let it throw you.

PRACTICALITIES

ACCOMMODATIONS

Places to stay are quite limited along the North Shore. The best deals are beach homes or rooms rented directly from the owners, but this is a hit-and-miss proposition, with no agency handling the details. You have to check the local papers. The homes vary greatly in amenities. Some are palaces, others basic rooms or shacks perfect for surfers or those who consider lodging secondary. Check the bulletin boards outside the Surf and Sea dive shop in Haleiwa, and the Foodland supermarket along the highway north of Waimea Bay.

Deluxe

The **Turtle Bay Hilton Golf and Tennis Resort** is a first-class resort on Turtle Bay, the northern extremity of the North Shore, P.O. Box 187, 57-091 Kamehameha Hwy., Kahuku, HI 96731, tel. 293-8811 or (800) HILTONS. Once a

J.D. BISIGNANI

Turtle Bay

Hyatt hotel, it was built as a self-contained destination resort and is surrounded by sea and surf on Kuilima Point, which offers protected swimming year-round. The entrance road to the hotel is lined by blooming hibiscus that outline a formal manicured lawn. In 1993, *Golf Magazine* rated the 27-hole, Arnold Palmer-inspired Links at Kuilima one of the "top 10 best new courses in the U.S.," while *Tennis Magazine* rated the hotel's tennis facilities among the top 50 tennis resorts in the entire world. The resort also offers a pool, full water activities including windsurfing and scuba lessons, horseback riding, shopping, and the fanciest dining on the North Shore (see "Food" following). Since the hotel is an oasis unto itself, you should *always* call ahead to book any of these activities, even as a guest staying at the hotel, to avoid disappointment. There's very little shopping in this area, so if you're after film, or basic picnic supplies, stop at the hotel's mini-mall. The resort's newest feature is a seaside **wedding chapel,** splendid with open-beamed ceiling, stained glass, and eight-foot beveled windows that can be thrown open to allow the ocean breezes to waft through. All guest rooms have ocean views, but not all are oceanfront. Oceanfront is slightly more expensive, but is worth the price, especially from December to April when humpback whales cavort in the waters off the point. Each room is furnished with full bath, a mini-fridge, a dressing room, a large vanity, ample closets, a/c, and remote-control cable TV. Junior suites come complete with a library, a large bathroom and changing room, two couches, a sitting area, a queen-size bed, and a large enclosed lanai. The Hilton has upgraded and refurbished with new carpets, drapes, bedspreads, and hibiscus-patterned wallpaper. Rates are: ocean view $170; ocean lanai $190; oceanfront $210; cabanas $320; and suites $390-$1350; $25 extra person. The Hilton family plan allows children free when they stay in a room with their parents. The Hilton is a first-class destination resort, but because of its fabulous yet out-of-the-mainstream location, you get much more than what you pay for. The Turtle Bay Hilton is an excellent choice for a vacation with the feel of being on a Neighbor Island.

Ke Iki Hale is a small condo complex operated by Alice Tracy, 59-579 Ke Iki Rd., Waimea, HI 96712, tel. 638-8229. Pass the Foodland supermarket heading north from Waimea, and look for a school sign. Turn left to the beach to find the condo. The property has 200 feet of private beach with a sandy bottom that goes out about 300 feet (half that in winter). The condo is quiet with a home-away-from-home atmosphere. Rates are: one-bedroom beachfront, $125 per day, $770 per week, $2400 per month; two-bedroom beachfront, $150 per day, $975 per week, $2500 per month. Units on the grounds with no beachfront are about 25% less.

Surfer Rentals

The North Shore of Oahu has long been famous for its world-class surfing. The area attracts enthusiasts from around the world who are much more concerned with the daily surfing report than they are with deluxe accommodations. The Kamehameha Hwy. is dotted with surfer rentals from Haleiwa to Turtle Bay. Just outside their doors are the famous surfing breaks of Marijuana's, Rubber Duckies, and Pinballs, all famous and known to world-class surfers. Some of these accommodations are terrific, while others are barely livable. Here's a sample of what's offered.

Backpacker's Vacation Inn and Hostel, 59-788 Kamehameha Hwy., Haleiwa, HI 96712, tel. 638-7838 (courtesy phone at airport, no charge), specializes in budget accommodations for surfers, backpackers, and families. Owned and operated by the Foo Family, the main building in this small cluster of buildings is at mile marker 6, the fourth driveway past the church tower coming from Waimea Bay. There are a number of facilities and room styles which could put you on the beach or mountainside, depending on availability and your preference. Basic rates are $14-16 for a bunk in the hostel-style rooms, which includes cooking and laundry facilities, and TV in the communal room. Each room has four bunks, microwaves, a shower, and a bath. The feeling is definitely not deluxe, but it is adequate. A complex on the beach, $70 daily, $420 weekly, sleeps four, has a complete kitchen, two double beds, a roll-out couch, a ceiling fan, and a world-class view of the beach from your lanai. The back house, on the mountainside, is farther away from traffic and is among the trees. It's on stilts and has an open ceiling and rustic common area. Rates are $40 for the main rooms (two people), $25 for a private loft (it gets hot up there), or $14 for a shared bunk. The Vacation Inn asks only this: use common sense, and clean up after yourself. They provide free boogie boards and snorkeling gear. Airport transportation (directly opposite the baggage claim) is free *to* the inn and $5 for the return trip. Everyone's friendly and laid-back. Book ahead. A good choice.

The **Plantation Village** at 59754 Kamehameha Hwy., tel. 638-7838, operated by Backpacker's (see above) lies across from Three Tables Beach by Shark's Cove, between mile markers 6 and 7. It's on TheBus line and only a five-minute walk from a Foodland store for supplies. The Plantation Village, once a real Filipino working village, has cottages by the sea, secure behind a locked gate, and furnished with cable, stereo, linens, a full kitchen, dishes, washers and dryers, ice machines, and cleaning service. Many of the fruit trees on the grounds provide the guests with complimentary bananas, papayas, breadfruit, or whatever is ripe. The price is $16 for a shared room and bath with two or three others. Ask for Unit 2, which is the same price, but a tiny private room. The small (300 square feet) private cottages, once the homes of real plantation workers, sleep two and are $40 per night, or $245 per week. A $100 per night deluxe cottage sleeps four, and you get a large front lanai, two couches, wicker furniture in a sitting room, cable TV, a/c, fan, full bath with vanity, and kitchen fully furnished with microwave, stove, and fridge. The Backpacker's van (see above) also services the Plantation Village. During surfing season the place is booked out. Reserve one month in advance, full deposit during high season (Dec.-Feb.), half deposit other months. No refund policy in high season.

FOOD

Inexpensive

McDonald's golden arches rise above Haleiwa as you enter town. Historic Haleiwa Theater was torn down so that the world could have another Egg McMuffin. Here too is a **7-Eleven** convenience store. Almost next door is **Pizza Hut.** Besides pizza, their salad bar isn't bad.

Between the two, but a culinary world apart, **Celestial Natural Foods,** tel. 637-6729, open weekdays 9 a.m.-6:30 p.m., Sunday 10-6, sells natural and health foods, and serves vegetarian meals at the snack bar. Smoothies are $2.50; most sandwiches and a variety of salads are under $3.50. The food is healthful and nutritious, but portions are definitely not for the hungry.

Cafe Haleiwa, a hole-in-the-wall eatery on your left just as you enter town, serves one of the best breakfasts on Oahu. Their "dawn patrol" 6-7 a.m. includes eggs and whole-wheat pancakes for $2.50. Specials of the house are whole-wheat banana pancakes, French toast, spinach and mushroom quiche, and steaming-hot Kona coffee. One of the partners, Jim Sears, is called "the wizard of eggs" and has built up a local following. The cafe attracts many surfers, so it's a great place to find out about conditions.

If you're tired or just need a pick-me-up, head for the North Shore Marketplace (after McDonald's, mountain side), where you'll find the **Coffee Gallery,** open daily 6 a.m.-9 p.m., tel. 637-

5571, which has the largest selection of fresh roasted gourmet coffees in Hawaii, including Kona coffees and international selections of organically grown coffee from Sumatra, Indonesia, Guatemala, and South America. You can enjoy a steaming cup from their full-service espresso bar along with fresh carrot juice, and vegan pastry made without dairy products or eggs. Other more bliss-inducing pastries are blackberry apple crumble pie, super chocolatey brownies, fresh fruit bars, and various cookies and muffins. Every day there is a homemade soup and fresh salad. A fine selection of deli sandwiches priced around $5 range from a vegetarian garden burger on a whole wheat bun with lettuce and tomatoes, Maui onion, guacamole, and a side of tortilla chips, to a turkey sandwich, or pita bread filled with eggplant, pesto, and vegies. Sit outside in the shaded and screened dining area and watch the "characters" of the North Shore come and go.

The **China Inn** serves a variety of inexpensive dishes like sweet and sour pork ($3.50), sweet and sour fish ($3.25), and hamburgers. Take your food out to the shade of the lanai. A minute past it is the **Haleiwa Chinese Restaurant,** tel. 637-3533, open daily 10 a.m.-9 p.m. The interior is basic but the food is very good. Their steamed sea bass and *kung pao* chicken are both excellent. A gigantic bowl of tofu soup is $4, while most main courses are under $6. One of the best inexpensive eateries on the North Shore.

You can tell by the tour buses parked outside that **Matsumoto's** is a very famous store on the North Shore. What are all those people after? Shave ice. This is one of the best places on Oahu to try this island treat. Not only do the tourists come here, but local families often take a "Sunday drive" just to get Matsumoto's shave ice. Try the Hawaiian Delight, a mound of ice smothered with banana, pineapple, and mango syrup.

The **Country Drive-In** is across from Haleiwa Shopping Center. They have plate lunches (20 varieties), smoothies, and country breakfasts like corned-beef hash and fried eggs with breakfast meat for $2.25. Quick and good.

The tiny town of Waialua (see "Along The Farrington Highway, Rt. 930" under "Beaches and Sights" earlier in this chapter) is home to **The Sugar Bar,** located in the old Bank of Hawaii Building. Their international cuisine features everything from American hot dogs to German bratwurst. *Magnifique!*

East from town, across from Shark's Cove, is **Shark's Shack,** a *usually* open lunch wagon that'll fix you a sandwich or rent you snorkeling gear. Next door is **Pupukea Shave Ice** for an island treat. Farther toward Sunset Beach (around mile marker 9) look for **Diamico's Pizza,** open for breakfast, lunch, and dinner (slow but friendly service), and the Sunset Beach store, home of Ted's Bakery.

Moderate/Expensive

Steamer's in the Haleiwa Shopping Plaza, tel. 637-5071, is a clean and modern restaurant serving seafood, beef, and chicken. There's plenty of brass, paneled walls, and low lighting. Lunches are especially good with a wide choice of omelettes from $5, including one made from crab, shrimp, and mushrooms; all come with blueberry or French muffins. Whet your appetite with sushi or steamed clams, or have a full fish dinner starting at $10. Dining daily 11 a.m.-11 p.m., bar until 2 a.m.

Rosie's Cantina, also in the plaza, open Sun.-Thurs. 7 a.m.-10 p.m, Fri.-Sat. 7 a.m.-11 p.m., prepares hearty Mexican dishes for a good price. The inside is "yuppie Mex" with brass rails, painted overhead steam pipes, and elevated booths. Expect to pay $4 for enchiladas and burritos, while meat dishes are $8-9. Order the enchilada stuffed with crab for $9, add a salad, and two could easily make this a lunch. **Pizza Bob's** across the way has an excellent local reputation, and its little pub serves up delicious pizza, salad, lasagna, and sandwiches.

The **Proud Peacock,** Waimea Falls Park, tel. 638-8531, is open daily for lunch and dinner. It's fun to dine here even if you don't enter the park. From the dining room, you can look into some of the nicest gardens while feeding crumbs to the peacocks. The beautiful mahogany bar was made in Scotland almost 200 years ago. You can have a light soup and salad, but their seafood *pu pu* platter is hard to beat. Roast pork and roast beef are well-prepared favorites here. A Moonlight Buffet 5-9 p.m. is served to adults for $9.95, children 12 and under $5.95, on two full-moon nights a month. Included are prime rib, chicken, mahimahi, and Hawaiian-style pork. Guided tours begin at 8:30 p.m. sharp.

Jameson's by the Sea, 62-540 Kamehameha Hwy., tel. 637-4336, is open daily for lunch, dinner, and cocktails. Located at the north end of Haleiwa overlooking the sea, its outdoor deck is perfect for a romantic sunset dinner. Inside, the romantic mood continues with track lighting, shoji screens, cane chairs with stuffed pillows, shaded candles, and tables resplendent with fine linen. Appetizers include a salmon plate ($8.95), stuffed mushrooms with escargot ($6.50), and fresh oysters ($8.95). Chowder and salad are under $7. Try the Yokohama soup, as well as salad with homemade dressing. Main dishes like mahimahi, stuffed shrimp, shrimp curry with mango chutney, and sesame chicken range $16-25. For dessert have the lemon macadamia nut chiffon pie for $3.50. The bar is quiet at night and serves a variety of imported beers; try South Pacific, imported from New Guinea. The dining room closes at 10 p.m. and the bar an hour later. Reservations are highly recommended; request a window seat for the sunset.

The **Chart House,** at 66-011 Kamehameha Hwy., Haleiwa, tel. 638-8005, open daily for dinner 5-10 p.m., for lunch Thurs.-Sun. 11 a.m.-3 p.m., is part of a small chain known for good food, located in a green cinder-block building on the left before you cross the Anahulu River bridge. Although purely utilitarian on the outside, the inside is modern and tasteful with plenty of tilework, track lighting, bent-wood chairs, and ceiling fans. Most appetizers, ranging from artichokes to chowder, are under $5, while the salad bar (included with an entree) is $11.95 a la carte. Steaks, the specialty of the house, are priced $17.95-22.95, while chicken breast teriyaki is a reasonable $15.95, and seafood from salmon to shrimp Santa Fe is all under $22. Specials are offered daily, and there's a "wine of the month" chosen to enhance your meal. For dessert try the mud pie or the key lime pie. Although the Chart House is not quite gourmet, the food is good and wholesome, with the price right for what you get.

Classy Dining

If you're looking for gourmet dining in an incredibly beautiful setting, head for the Turtle Bay Hilton Golf and Tennis Resort (see "Accommodations" above). The **Cove Restaurant,** open 6-9:30 p.m. (reservations advised), is the signature restaurant at the resort and welcomes you for an evening of fine dining. Slowly stroll a wooden walkway leading past tiny waterfalls and a profusion of plants to the main room that overlooks the manicured grounds and pool. Start with lobster bisque in a puff pastry shell or a variety of fresh island salads for $6. Move on to filet mignon, veal chops, fresh tiger prawns, or lobster that you choose fresh from the tank. The fresh catch, always an excellent choice, is a very reasonable $19.95. If you really want to treat yourself, order the North Shore potpourri, a silver bowl mounded with ice that cradles *opihi,* shrimp, sashimi, oysters, and fresh fish that come with savory dipping sauces from a basic shoyu and hot mustard to a papaya salsa. Enjoy dessert while gazing through floor-to-ceiling windows that frame the living mosaic of Turtle Bay turned brilliant by a legendary North Shore sunset.

The **Seatide Room** is synonymous with Sunday brunch. It enjoys a wonderful reputation, and if friends or family come visiting, islanders take them here to impress them. Brunch is buffet style 9 a.m.-2 p.m. and features mounds of fresh fruits and pastries, fresh-squeezed fruit juices, imported cheeses, eggs Florentine and Benedict, fresh fish, seafood, sashimi, shrimp, crab claws, and flowing champagne. Reservations not taken, $25 adults. Expect a wait, which goes easily as you enjoy the magnificent scenery.

The **Palm Terrace** is the most "ordinary" of the hotel's restaurants, but ordinary par excellence. Open 6:30 a.m.-10 p.m., the restaurant serves hearty American favorites from all 50 states, supplemented by dishes from around the world. You can dine on smoked Pacific fish, saimin with crispy bread, curried chicken papaya, or a seafood tostada. You will enjoy lunch sandwiches like Portuguese sausage on rye or a clubhouse special. There are hamburgers, of course—the basic burger, right down to a North Shore burger with grilled onions and peppers. For dessert order a cinnamon tulip: macadamia nut ice cream, split bananas, chocolate, and Kahuku watermelon all in a cinnamon tostada pastry shell. The views overlooking Turtle Bay combined with excellent value for the money make the Palm Terrace the best *ordinary* restaurant on the North Shore.

A wonderful culinary addition to the hotel is the **Asahi,** open Thurs.-Mon. 5:30-9:30 p.m., a Japanese restaurant with a full-service sushi bar. Dine on delectables made right before your eyes by master sushi chefs from Japan. The more timid can choose a Japanese standard like teriyaki chicken, or the Asahi combination dinner of beef teriyaki and lobster tail. Complete meals are served with salad, rice, and miso soup.

The **Bay View Lounge** is a casual restaurant/nightclub offering a deli-luncheon buffet. It's open 11:30 a.m.-1 a.m. and serves complimentary *pu pu* around sunset, which is a perfect time to drop in. On weekends the Bay View Lounge is the hot-spot disco, ID required after 9 p.m.; dress code is collared shirts and closed-toe shoes.

SHOPPING AND SERVICES

Art Galleries And Shops

As you enter Haleiwa, across from McDonald's, you'll see **Ka'ala Art,** open 9 a.m.-6 p.m. daily, tel. 637-7065. It's a perfect place to stop, with some of the best shopping on the North Shore. The brothers Costello, John and Jim, who own and operate the shop, are knowledgeable, longtime residents of the North Shore who don't mind dispensing directions and information. The premier items are John's original artwork, wonderful paintings that are impressionistic and magical, with many of these unique designs silk-screened onto 100% cotton T-shirts or made into inspiring posters. John has also turned his hand to carvings of dolphins and other Hawaiian themes. Also featured are fine carvings from Tonga, Tahiti, and Bali that John has handselected on his travels, along with excellent examples of local Hawaiian woodcarvings. Small but wonderful items are tapa cloth made by Sella, a Tongan woman who lives nearby, batiks from Thailand, and jewelry made locally and in Asia. The Costello brothers travel to buy, and they have a keen eye for what's happening and distinctive. Brother Kevin offers a fine selection of imported clothing from Thailand, which is available through the gallery by appointment. A rainbow has spilled in a corner of the shop, where 100% cotton pareau ($18-35) from Hawaii, Tahiti, and Indonesia vibrate in living color. More "art-clothing" includes a rack of beach cover-ups designed by John, and tie-dyed and silk-screened using ecological nontoxic colors. There's also a fine postcard selection just to remind the folks back home that you are in Hawaii.

Iwa Gallery, open daily except Tuesday 10:30 a.m.-6:30 p.m., is across the street from the Protestant church, founded in 1892, and next door to Aoki's Shave Ice. This co-op shows the efforts of local artists who have been juried in order to place their artwork on consignment. Featured are the fine candle sculptures of **Scott Bechtol** (see "Punaluu and Hauula" in the Windward Oahu chapter). Other artists displayed at the gallery include: Angela Kanas, a watercolor artist who does fanciful renditions of Hawaiian gods, goddesses, and traditional folk; Janet Stewart, who depicts island themes like Madame Pele lying with the blood of her hot lava flowing from her body, or a *keiki* hula dancer with a look of concentration on her face, or a kindly *tutu* in a red muumuu; Bill Cupit, who uses the bark of banana trees to create entire island scenes like ships departing a sheltered harbor; Peter Hayward, well into his eighties, who works in oils to create translucent waves crashing on lonely shores. Serigraphs and cards by Janet Holaday often depict of flowers in bold primary colors; Peggy Pai, born and raised in China, creates silk batik with ephemeral, beautiful, cloudy landscapes; James Rack uses his palette and brush to catch scenes of idyllic Hawaii; and Norman Kelly catches children at play or surfers on towering waves in his fluid watercolors.

Wyland Gallery, across the street from the Haleiwa Shopping Center, is open daily 9 a.m.-6 p.m., tel. 637-7498. Wyland is a famous environmental artist known for his huge whale and marinelife murals, in addition to watercolors and fine oil paintings. The gallery is large, spacious, and well lit. Everything has a Hawaiian or sea theme, and there's even a huge fish tank filled with tropical fish. Delight at the magnificent bronze sculptures by Dale Evers, depicting whales and manta rays in sublime frozen movement. You'll see modern sepia-tone photos by Kim Taylor Reese, watercolors of Hawaiian maidens by Janet Stewart, lithographs by Roy Tabora of palm trees and cliffs with Michelangelo skies, bronze dolphins by Christopher Bell, wood sculptures by Kerry Sweet, Margaret Keene's lithographs of children with big eyes, and Sue

Phillipson's oils of island flowers. You can walk away with a limited-edition lithograph by Wyland with original watercolor mark framed in koa for $940. If the original artwork is too expensive, choose from posters, mini-prints, and postcards. Wyland's gold jewelry sculpture is also beautiful, distinctive, and affordable.

North Shore Marketplace

The North Shore Marketplace, along the Kamehameha Hwy. between McDonald's and the Haleiwa Shopping Center, is a small complex with some inexpensive and unique shops. The most interesting shop is **Jungle Gem's,** tel. 637-6609, open 10 a.m.-6 p.m., with a metaphysical assortment of crystals, crystal balls, African trading beads, and gems. The shop specializes in locally made jewelry reasonably priced and of excellent quality. The owners, Brent Landberg and Kimberley Moore, are knowledgeable gemologists and fine jewelers who do much of the work on display. Next door, the **Island Wear Factory Outlet** has inexpensive alohawear.

Another good shop is **More or Less Beach Wear,** tel. 638-6859, open daily 9 a.m.-6 p.m., where they make custom bathing suits and sell hand-painted T-shirts by local artists. The owner and chief designer, Lucinda Vaughen, will personally fit and design just the right suit for you.

Birds of Aloha, open daily except Monday 10:30 a.m.-5:30 p.m., tel. 638-5214, specializes in hand-fed baby parrots, macaws, cockatoos, and African grays. These living rainbows of color cost $1500-5000, and can be brought back to the Mainland without being quarantined. Rossi Baker, the owner, hatched the birds herself and is happy to talk about them. She'll allow you to hold the birds and take pictures.

Northshore Books, tel. 637-3202, open 10 a.m.-6:30 p.m., is a general-purpose bookstore with racks of used books emphasizing Hawaiiana, metaphysics, new age, and children's literature. The bookstore also has selections of posters, note cards, and bookmarks.

Along The Kamehameha Highway

As you move down the Kamehameha Hwy. from west to east you'll pass the **Haleiwa Flower Shop** on the left selling lei and fresh-cut flowers. Next comes **Oogenesis Boutique,** with original fashions for women. Almost next door is **Haleiwa Acupuncture Clinic,** tel. 637-4449, with Richard Himmelmann, in cooperation with **Healing Touching Massage** by Brenda McKinnon, and chiropractic care by Dr. Edward Bowles, who will make house calls.

On the right is **A Guy Selling Shells.** He specializes in hanging baskets made from bubble and cowrie shells. Prices range $5-50, with most shells coming from the Philippines.

The **Consignment Shop,** behind the Country Kitchen, sells well-chosen junk, previously owned women's apparel and accessories, artwork, clothing, and towels.

Haleiwa Shopping Center

This shopping center provides all the necessities in one-stop shopping: boutiques, pharmacy, photo store, and general food and merchandise. It's in the center of Haleiwa, tel. 622-5179. Some shops are: **Rix** with jewelry, women's fashions, and alohawear; **Exotic Gourmet Ice Cream Palace; Et Cetera's,** a tiny but jam-packed souvenir store with woodcarvings, teas, alohawear, and shells; **Space And Lace,** selling hats, slippers, shoes, towels, and sunglasses; **Liquor Galley,** open daily 9 a.m.-midnight, a full-service liquor store; and **Haleiwa Family Health Center** a walk-in clinic, tel. 524-2527, open daily 8 a.m.-5 p.m., closed Sunday.

Food Shopping

For food and picnic supplies try the **Haleiwa IGA,** tel. 637-5004, in the Haleiwa Shopping Center, or **Foodland,** along the highway north of Waimea Bay, tel. 638-8081.

Services

The best sources of general **information** for the North Shore are the bulletin boards outside Surf and Sea dive shop in Haleiwa, and outside the Foodland supermarket along the highway north of Waimea Bay.

As you enter Haleiwa from the west, you'll pass a **Shell** gas station and a full-service **post office.**

Sporting Goods And Rentals

The following shops are all located along the Kamehameha Hwy., the main drag through Haleiwa, heading from west to east.

Across the road from the Shell gas station just as you enter the west end of town is **Excell Wet Suits and Water Sports,** a full-service surf shop that rents snorkeling gear. On the right is **Kayak Oahu,** tel. 637-6565, that rents kayaks and will provide tips on where to go.

Raging Isle Sports, in the North Shore Marketplace, tel. 637-7707, open daily 10 a.m.-6 p.m., is primarily a surf shop and manufacturer of Barnfield's Raging Isle Boards, but they rent and sell bikes, and you can pick up items from a pair of shorts to a tennis racket. The bikes are an assortment of beach cruisers and mountain bikes that rent $10-20 daily and $55-115 weekly. The shop also services and repairs bikes.

Race Hawaii, 66-249 Kamehameha Hwy., tel. 637-SURF, open daily 9 a.m.-6 p.m., 8 a.m.-7 p.m. during high season, is a famous surfboard design shop owned by Scott Bucknall, who has patented the x-fin skeg design. The shop rents boards during the surf season and sells bathing suits, biking pants, and T-shirts bearing its logo.

Hawaii Surf and Sail, 66-214 Kamehameha Hwy., open 8:30 a.m.-7:30 p.m., tel. 637-5373, has surfboards (rental $10 per day), sailboards, and accessories.

For a full range of surfing, snorkeling, and diving equipment try **Surf and Sea** near the Union 76 gas station in Haleiwa. It's got boogie boards, masks and fins, tanks, weights, surfboards, and sailboards. The store can even arange flights from Dillingham Airfield.

Fantasy Cycles, 66-134 Kamehameha Hwy., tel. 637-3221, open 10 a.m.-7 p.m., Sunday 10 a.m.-3 p.m., is owned by Bob Frattin. He rents bikes for $15 per day or $63 per week. Bob will start off entry-level riders with a map and riding pointers and will also take riders on trail tours that include lunch. You must be experienced, and the ride is not for the beginner or couch potato.

unique figurine of Neckar Island

BOB RACE

THE LEEWARD COAST

The Waianae ("Mullet Waters") coast, the leeward face of Oahu, is separated physically from the rest of the island by the Waianae Range. Spiritually, culturally, and economically, the separation is even more profound. This area is Oahu's last stand for ethnic Hawaiians, and for that phenomenal cultural blending of people called *locals.* The idea of "us against them" permeates the consciousness of the area. Guidebooks, government pamphlets, and word of mouth warn tourists against going to Waianae because "the natives are restless." If you follow this poor advice, you not only miss the last of undeveloped coastal Oahu, but the absolute pleasure of meeting people who will treat you with genuine *aloha.* Along the coast are magnificent beaches long known for their surf, new condos and developments nestled in secure valleys, and prime golfing. Inland, roads will take you to the roof of Oahu. Waianae is the home of small farms, run-down shacks, and families who hold luau on festive occasions, where the food and entertainment are the real article. Anyone lucky enough to be invited into this quickly disappearing world will be blessed with one of the last remaining authentic cultural experiences in Hawaii.

Warnings about hassles shouldn't be minimized because they do happen, but every aggressor needs a victim. The biggest problem is thievery, of the sneak-thief variety. You're marked as a tourist because of your new rental car. If you leave valuables in it, or lying unattended on the beach, they have a good chance of disappearing. But who does silly things like this *anywhere* in the U.S.? You won't be accosted or held up at gunpoint, but if you bother a bunch of local guys drinking beer, you're asking for trouble. Moreover, the toughness of Waianae is self-perpetuating, and frankly the locals *like* the hard reputation. A few years back a feature writer reported that when he visited Waianae some toughs threw rocks at him. No one had ever reported this before, but after a big stink was made about it, more and more people had rocks thrown at them when they visited here. In recent years *pakalolo* has had a tremendous effect on the area. Local guys began growing and smoking it. This brought some money back into the depressed region, and it changed the outlook of some of the residents. They felt a camaraderie with other counterculture people, many of whom happened to be *haole.* They could relax and not feel so threatened by the elusiveness of the materialistic path. Many became more content with their laid-back lifestyle and genuinely less interested in the materialistic trip all the way around.

In truth, *we* shouldn't be warned about *them,* but vice versa. The people of Waianae are the ones being infringed upon, and it is they who, in the final analysis, will be hassled, ripped off, and ultimately dispossessed. Recent articles by Oahu's Development Conference strongly state that future development will center on the island's northwestern shore . . . the Waianae coast. A few rocks are poor weapons against developmental progress, which is defined by the big boys with the big dreams and the big bucks to back them up.

BEACHES AND SIGHTS

The Waianae coast is very accessible. One road brings you here. Simply follow the H-1 Freeway from Honolulu until it joins the Farrington Hwy. (Rt. 93). It runs north, opening up the entire coast. A handful of side roads leads into the interior, and that's about it. A strange recommendation, but sensible on this heavily trafficked road, is to drive north to the end of the line and then stop at the scenic sights on your way back south. This puts you on the ocean side of the highway where you won't have to worry about cutting across two lanes of traffic, which can be a steady stream that's tough to navigate. TheBus no. 51 runs the entire Waianae coast and stops at all of the following beaches.

Note: Many of the beach parks along this coast offer **camping,** but their status periodically changes to **no camping** without notice. Many campers are local people in semipermanent structures; the reason that the status changes quickly is to prevent these people from squatting. Also, remember that this is the leeward coast, which gets plenty of sunshine. Many of the beach parks do not have shade trees, so be prepared. June is the prettiest month because the flowers are in bloom, but it's one of the worst times for sunburn. The entire coast is great for snorkeling, with plenty of reef fish. However, keep your eyes on the swells, and always stay out of rough seas, when waves can batter you against the rocks. The parks listed below run from south to north.

HEADING NORTH

Barbers Point Beach County Park

The first beach is Barbers Point Beach County Park, at the end of Kalaeloa Boulevard. Turn down it where H-1 and the Farrington Hwy. join. The point was named after Capt. Henry Barber, who was shipwrecked here in 1795. Few people, even island residents, visit this beach park. It's in an industrial area and the shoreline is rocky. One pocket of white-sand beach is open to the public, though it fronts a private residence. The swimming is safe only in summer, and you'll find picnic facilities, restrooms, and camping (county permit).

Kahe Point And Hawaiian Electric Beach County Parks

Kahe Point and Hawaiian Electric beach county parks are just where the Farrington Hwy. curves north along the coast. They're the first two *real* Waianae beaches, and they're symbolic. You come around the bend to be treated to an absolutely pristine view of the coast with the rolling sea, a white-sand beach, a cove, and the most hideous power plant you've ever seen. Kahe Point Beach County Park offers restrooms, a pavilion, and picnic facilities. The beach is poor except for a section just east of the improved park. Swimming is dangerous except on calm summer days. The Hawaiian Electric Beach Park, across from the power plant, is known as "Tracks" to island surfers because of the railroad tracks that run along the shore here. Facilities include picnic tables, a pavilion, restrooms, showers, and parking along the highway. The white-sand beach is wide, and the swimming generally safe. The mild waves are perfect for learning how to surf. If you keep your eyes trained out to sea, the area is beautiful. Don't look inland!

Nanakuli Beach County Park

Nanakuli Beach County Park is on the southern outskirts of Nanakuli ("Pretend to be Deaf") town, which is the first real town of the Waianae coast. If you get to the red light you've gone a little too far. The beach park is community-oriented, with recreational buildings, basketball courts, a baseball diamond, and kiddies' play area. Camping has been permitted with a county permit. Lifeguards work on a daily basis, and the swimming is generally safe except during periods of high winter surf. The northern end of the beach, called Kalanianaole, is generally calmer than the southern end. They're divided by a housing project, but connected by a walkway. The southern section is fronted by a cliff with a small cove below. During periods of calm surf, the waters are crystal clear and perfect for snorkeling.

Ulehawa Beach County Park

Ulehawa Beach County Park, just north of Nanakuli, offers restrooms, picnic facilities, lifeguards, and sometimes camping. The best swimming is in a sandy pocket near the lifeguard tower. Surf conditions make for good bodysurfing. Most of the park, along a rocky cliff, is undeveloped. Here you'll find unlimited fishing spots. A shallow lagoon is generally safe for swimming year-round. As always, it's best to check with the local people on the beach.

Maili Beach County Park

Maili Beach County Park is at the southern end of Maili ("Many Small Stones") town. It lies between two streams coming down from the mountains. Amenities include restrooms, picnic facilities, a lifeguard tower, and camping . . . sometimes! The best swimming is in front of the lifeguard tower. The beach is broken into three parts by a housing development. In wintertime the beach disappears, but it returns wide and sandy for the summer. Most of the park is undeveloped. In town are a **7-Eleven** and gas stations. As you drive through town notice a giant outcropping, Maili Point, which meets the sea like a giant fist. It has the same dominant presence as Diamond Head. When you go through town you'll see what's been happening around here since development has come to Waianae. Pull off at Maili Beach County Park, and to your right are the modest homes of local people. Look up the coast to where the mountains come down to the sea. Out on that headland you can see a giant resort and on the bending back-

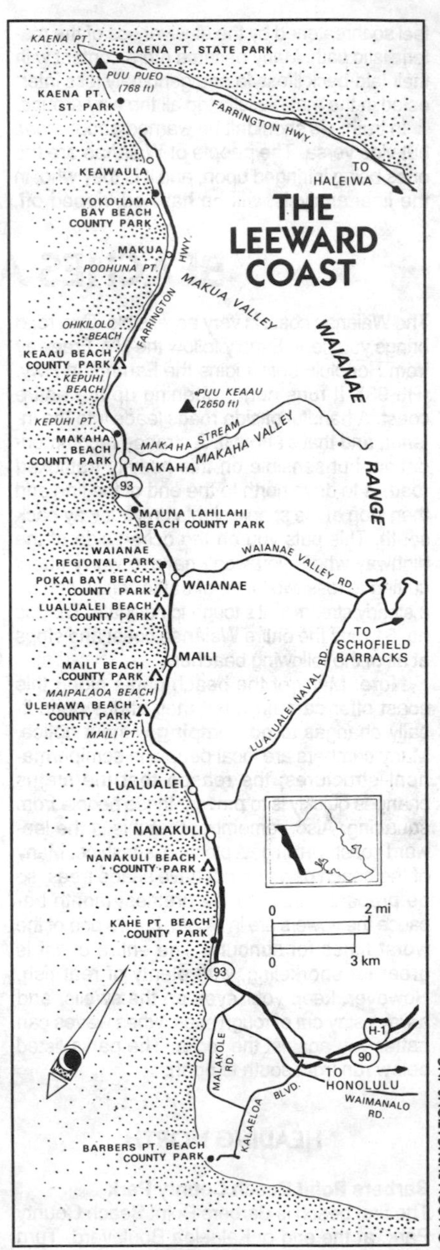

bone leading up to it modest homes of the local people. The beach is at least 300 yards long, and family-oriented. Plenty of coral pockets offer good snorkeling. Don't just jump in. Ask the locals or swing by the lifeguard tower to make sure that it's safe.

Lualualei Beach County Park
Lualualei Beach County Park has restrooms, camping sometimes, and picnic facilities. The entire park is largely undeveloped and lies along low cliffs and raised coral reef. Swimming is almost impossible. It's primarily good for fishing and looking.

Pokai Bay Beach County Park
Pokai Bay Beach County Park is one of the nicest along the Waianae coast, located just south of Waianae town. It provides restrooms, camping sometimes, lifeguards, and a boat ramp, which brings plenty of small craft into the area. Don't be surprised to see a replica of a double-hulled canoe, often used for publicity purposes. It last appeared in a beer commercial. The park is clean, well maintained, reasonably secure, and family-oriented. There's surfing, snorkeling, and safe swimming year-round. If you're heading for one beach along Waianae, this is a top choice.

To get a look at a small working harbor or to hire a fishing boat, visit **Waianae Boat Harbor** as you head north from town. Huge installed stones form an impressive manmade harbor for everything from luxury yachts to aluminum fishing boats. To head inland take **Waianae Valley Road.** You quickly gain the heights of the Waianae Range, and eventually come to a sentry box with a soldier inside. From here Kolekole Road is closed to the public, but if you stop and identify yourself, you'll be given permission to go to **Kolekole Pass.** The awesome view is well worth the trip.

Makaha Beach County Park
Makaha Beach County Park is famous for surfing, and as you approach, you can't help spotting a dominant headland called **Lahi Lahi,** which was a one-time island. Called "Black Rock" by the local fishermen, and used as a landmark, it still marks Makaha. Surfing competitions have been held here since the Makaha International Surfing Competition began in 1952. In recent years, a local lifeguard named Richard "Buffalo" Keaulana, known to all who've come here, has begun the Annual Buffalo Big Board Riding Championship. Paul Strauch, Jr., inventor of the "hang five," comes to Makaha whenever he has a chance, along with Buffalo's sons and other pro surfers, many of whom live in the area. The swimming can be dangerous during high surf, but excellent on calm days. Winter brings some of the biggest surf in Hawaii. Always pay heed to the warnings of the lifeguards.

Although Makaha can translate as "water breaking out to sea" because of the area's propensity of damming runoff waters from the mountains behind the beach until enough pressure forces it to "break out," there is another meaning for Makaha that doesn't help its image. The second translation, meaning "Fierce," aptly describes a gang of bandits who long ago lived in the surrounding hills and terrorized the region. They would wait for small bands of people walking the road, then swoop down and relieve them of their earthly goods. If you follow Makaha Valley Road inland, you pass condos and high-rises clinging to the arid walls of this leeward valley. Surrounded by an artificial oasis of green, this developed resort area provides golfing and all the amenities of a destination resort. Stop in at the Sheraton Makaha to ask permission to visit the **Kaneaki Helau,** a 17th-century temple restored by the resort under the direction of the Bishop Museum. This temple was dedicated to Lono, the benevolent god of harvest and fertility. The grass and thatched huts used as prayer and meditation chambers, along with a spirit tower, have all been replicated.

Once past Makaha, the road gets rugged, with plenty of private places to pull off. This crab claw of land, which ends at Kaena Point, forms a bay. The seascape demands attention, but look into the interior. The mountains seem naturally terraced as they form dry, deep valleys. All are micro-habitats, each different from the other. On top of one notice a gigantic golf ball, really a radar tracking station, that lets you know you're coming to the end of the passable road.

Keaau Beach County Park
Keaau Beach County Park has restrooms, picnic facilities, and camping (county permit). The

improved part of the park has a sandy beach, but most of the park is fronted by coral and lava and is frequented by fishermen and campers. The unimproved section is not good for swimming, but it does attract a few surfers, and is good for snorkeling and scuba but only during calm periods. The improved section is a flat grassy area with picnic tables, shade trees, and pavilions.

Yokohama Bay

Yokohama Bay is the end of the line. The pavement ends here, and if you're headed for Kaena Point (see "Beaches and Sights" in the North Shore chapter) you'll have to walk. Yokohama Bay is a long stretch of sandy beach that is mostly unimproved. A lava-rock bathhouse is on the right, just after the entrance. The area was named for the multitude of Japanese fishermen who came to this lonely site to fish. It's still great for fishing. The swimming can be hazardous because of the strong wave action and rough bottom, but the snorkeling is superb. Mostly the area is used by surfers and local people, including youngsters who dive off the large lava rocks. This is inadvisable for people unfamiliar with the area. Yokohama is a great place to come if you're after a secluded beach. Weekdays, you'll have it to yourself, with a slightly greater number of people on the weekends. Definitely bring cold drinks, and remember that there are no shade trees, so a hat or beach umbrella is a necessity. Many camp here unofficially.

Notice a rugged beach area, marked by dumped household appliances, just south of Yokohama Bay. Notice broken-down vans and makeshift tents of ripped tarps put up by local people who have staked out this area and who live here semipermanently. If you're looking for trouble, you've found the right spot.

Kaneana Cave is a few minutes south on your left as you head back down the coast. You probably didn't notice it on your way north because of the peculiar land formation that conceals the mouth in that direction. Unfortunately, people have come here with spray cans and trashed the cave. If you can overlook that, it's a phenomenon—a big one. You can spot it by looking for three cement blocks, like road dividers, right in front of the entrance. It's at the foot of a 200-foot outcropping of stone. When you see local people defacing the natural beauty like this, it's hard to believe that the Hawaiians had such a spirit bond with the *aina*.

J.D. BISIGNANI

buffalo at Makaha Beach County Park

PRACTICALITIES

ACCOMMODATIONS

Except for camping, there are no inexpensive places to stay along the Waianae coast. Some local people let rooms for a good rate, but there is no way to find this out in advance. Your best bet is to check out the **bulletin board** at the Food Giant Supermarket in Waianae. Accommodations range from moderate to expensive, with Makaha Valley being the most developed resort area of Oahu outside of Waikiki. Except for the Sheraton Makaha Resort, all lodgings are condos and require a minimum stay of seven days.

The **Maili Cove** rents one-bedroom apartments for $350-450 per week. They have a swimming pool, parking, and TV; a few hotel units are available. Located at 87-561 Farrington Hwy., Waianae, HI 96792, tel. 696-4447.

The **Makaha Beach Cabanas** are in Makaha along the beach just past the high school. All units have a lanai overlooking the water. They're not fancy, but are spotlessly clean and serviceable. All units are fully furnished with complete kitchens; from $350 per week. Contact the Makaha Beach Cabanas, 84-965 Farrington Hwy., tel. 696-7227.

The **Makaha Shores** are privately owned units that overlook a beautiful white-sand beach and provide great viewing of the surfers challenging the waves below. All units are fully furnished with weekly rates of $290 studio, $400 one-bedroom, and $500 two-bedroom. Contact the condo at 84-265 Farrington Hwy., Makaha, HI 96792, tel. 696-7121.

The least expensive accommodations are at the **Makaha Surfside.** The beach is rocky near the condo, but it makes up for this with two pools and a sauna. All units are individually owned and fully furnished. Weekly rates begin at $290 studio to $400-475 for a one-bedroom. Daily rates range $30-60. For information write Makaha Surfside, 85-175 Farrington Hwy., Makaha, HI 96792, tel. 696-2105.

Makaha Valley Towers rise dramatically from Makaha Valley, but they don't fit in. They're a testament to either human achievement or ignorance, depending on your point of view. In keeping with the idea of security, you drive up to a gate staffed by two guards. You're stopped, asked your business, and sent unsmilingly on your way. The condo provides fully furnished units, a/c, TV, and pool. Weekly rates are $365 studio, $400-500 one-bedroom. If you're staying in this ill-fitting high-rise, at least try to get a top floor where you can take advantage of the remarkable view. For rates and information: Makaha Valley Towers, 84-740 Kili Dr., Makaha, HI 96792, tel. 695-9055.

The **Sheraton Makaha Resort** is famous for its hideaway golf course, among the top five on Oahu. The Sheraton has done an exemplary job with the units, some of the nicest on the island. This is a true destination resort with a complete list of activities, including horseback riding, tennis, two swimming pools, and a full complement of hotel-sponsored beach and water activities (although the ocean is a few miles away). Rooms begin at $110; a suite costs $340. For information and reservations, write Sheraton Makaha Resort, P.O. Box 896, Waianae, HI 96792, tel. 695-9511 or (800) 325-3535.

The courtiers anxiously waited for the grand night when the torches would be lighted and the drums beaten to announce the lovely princess as she was presented to the assembled *ali'i.* Those closest to the young beauty were confident that their years of training had refined the grace and nobility that matched her dignified heritage. She had proven to be an enthusiastic and willing student, endearing herself to all because of her gaiety, sweetness, and loving heart. But to assume her rightful place with the most powerful in the land, she would have to gain the self-assurance that comes only with the wisdom of experience. It is much the same with the **Ihilani Resort and Spa,** at 92-1001 Olani St., Kapolei, HI 96707, tel. 679-0079, (800) 626-4446, Oahu's newest luxury resort that officially opened its doors in December 1993. The hotel, an alabaster specter floating amidst the 640 emerald green acres of the Ko Olina Resort, rises above a white-sand beach 25 minutes southwest of the airport (simply follow the H-1

J.D. BISIGNANI

typical camping at the leeward coast

expressway to the clearly marked Ko Olina exit). You approach the resort by way of a cobblestone drive that winds up to a porte cochere, where valets and lei-bearing hostesses greet you. The open breezeway leads to a towering glass-domed atrium brightened by cascading trellised flowers, and ringed by living green ferns. Below, rivulets trickle through a series of freeform ponds, some like glass-reflecting sculptures, others alive and tinkling a natural refrain. The guest rooms, huge at almost 700 square feet, are pleasantly appointed in pastels and white. All feature a/c, ceiling fans, louvered doors, remote-control entertainment centers, in-room safes, minibars, and luxurious cushioned teak furniture including a dining table and lounge on your private lanai. A futuristic feature is a bedside master-control telephone system from where you can regulate the room's lighting, a/c, and voice mail service at the touch of a finger. Bathrooms, an intricate play of marble and tile, feature double sinks, hair dryers, a basket of fine toiletries, separate commode and shower stalls, and deep over-sized tubs. Evening brings turndown service when little gifts of mineral bath gels or soothing facial compresses are left on your pillow, compliments of the spa. Other amenities are 24-hour room service, concierge service, tennis courts, and a beauty salon.

The green velvet of the **Ko Olina Championship Golf Course,** designed by Ted Robinson, and already named as one of the finest courses in America by the prestigious *Golf Digest,* fronts the hotel. Open since 1990, the course is fully matured and has already hosted a number of prestigious tournaments.

Dining at the Ihilani is in the masterful and infinitely creative hands of executive chef Katsuo Sugiura (Chef Suki), who has created dishes he describes as "Tropical Pacific." This fantastic blending of East and West relies heavily on locally grown herbs, vegetables, meats, and most importantly, island seafood. It is a blissful marriage of Mediterranean, Asian, and Hawaiian cuisines that can easily be influenced by Scandinavian, Caribbean and Southwestern ingredients. Chef Suki is an artist who constantly experiments and creates new presentations on a daily basis. Using smoking techniques he has perfected over the years, Suki not only creates distinctive individual dishes, he creates them especially for each guest, sealing the recipe and repeating it when you return, if you so desire. The Ihilani's signature restaurant is the dinner-only **Azul,** complemented by a magnificent wine cellar, with breakfast, lunch, and dinner served at the open-air **Naupaka Terrace.** Health-conscious cuisine is offered at the **Spa Cafe,** on the fourth level of the Ihilani Spa; traditional Japanese fare is prepared at the **Kyuan Restaurant.** Golfers or those into a more casual setting will enjoy clubhouse dining at the Ko Olina Golf Course's **Niblick Restaurant.**

Located in a separate facility just a short walk across from the main entrance is the **Ihilani Spa,** a magnificently soothing, revitalizing, and uniquely Hawaiian spa experience. Under the direction of Lisa Dobloug, the facility is centered around Thalasso water therapy, a computer-controlled water-jet massage utilizing fresh seawater and seaweed. After being immersed in this state-of-the-art tub, you move on to the Vichy Shower, Grand Jet, or Needle Pavilion, where 12 shower heads poke stimulating sprays into every nook and cranny. Next, the superbly trained staff offers therapeutic massage including Swedish, *lomi lomi,* and shiatsu. You can also opt for a manicure, pedicure, or skin-rejuvenating facial. To keep trim and supple, head for the fitness facility on the third level, where you will find a lap pool, jacuzzi, aerobics room, and strengthening equipment. With time and maturity, the Ihilani Resort and Spa, tucked away from the madding crowd, gives every indication of becoming one of Oahu's premier destinations.

FOOD

For anyone with an urge to eat a two-scoop plate lunch, no problem. Little drive-in lunch counters are found in almost every Waianae town. Each serves hearty island food such as teriyaki chicken, pork, or mahimahi for under $5. A good one is the **Makaha Drive-In.** Another popular spot is **Red Baron Pizza** in the Waianae Mall, tel. 696-2396.

You also see plenty of fruit sellers parked along the road. Their produce couldn't be fresher, and stopping provides you not only with the perfect complement to a picnic lunch but with a good chance to meet some local people.

For your shopping and dining needs in Nanakuli, try the **Pacific Shopping Mall,** where you'll find **Sac and Save Supermarket,** the largest in the area. In the complex is **Nanakuli Chop Suey Restaurant,** open 10 a.m.-8:30 p.m., tel. 668-8006, serving standard Chinese fare at local down-home prices (chicken dishes under $5, beef or pork to $4.75). Just behind McDonald's is the **Eden BBQ Lounge,** with sit-down and takeout Korean food at moderate prices, tel. 668-2722, open daily 10-9.

The **Waianae Mall** is a complete shopping facility. Don't worry about bringing supplies or food if you're on a day excursion. You'll find all that you need at the mall, which includes Cathay Deli, Red Baron Pizza, Subway Sandwiches, Woolworth, Big-Way Supermarket, and Pay 'n Save Drugs. Have no fear if you're addicted to fast foods. Some major franchises have decided that your trip to leeward Oahu wouldn't be complete without something processed in a styrofoam box. **Burger King** is in the mall, and in town **McDonald's** golden arches rise alongside the highway just across from **Taco Bell.** If you're looking for ethnic flavor try the **Tamura Supermarket,** which stocks plenty of ingredients used in ethnic foods. You'll spot a number of gas stations in the middle of town, along with a **Domino's Pizza, Circle K,** and **7-Eleven** convenience store.

Makaha has **Makaha Drive-In,** a plate lunch stand, **Woolworth,** and a shopping basket of neighborhood markets.

Salvatore's, 87-064 Farrington Hwy., tel. 696-6121, open daily 8 a.m.-10 p.m., is located about halfway between Waianae and Maili, and is the hot spot in these parts serving the best food for the money in Makaha. Weekend entertainment sometimes features a live band. Located on the second floor, it's a pretty good perch from which to view the coast. Painted sea-blue and cloud-white, the open beamed interior has a nautical theme with ship's ladders, glass lanterns, and heavy cargo nets placed here and there. Half of Salvatore's is a full bar, and the other a dining area. The breakfast menu offers French toast at $2.95, all-you-can-eat hotcakes for $5.95, eggs Benedict for $6.95, and a variety of omelettes priced $4.95-5.95. The lunch buffet, offered daily except Sunday 11 a.m.-3 p.m., gives you a choice of fresh fruits, salads, vegetables, chili, rice, soup, pasta of the day, and chicken and fish prepared various ways. The regular lunch menu includes burgers from $4.95; French-dip, barbecue, teriyaki, and turkey club sandwiches at $5.95, and a salad bar for $5.95. The dinner menu features gourmet pasta priced $6.95-13.95, grilled garlic chicken or ground sirloin for $9, fish and chips for $7.95, and combination dinners like barbecued teriyaki beef, ribs, and chicken basket at $13.95. From the bar order domestic or imported beer, cocktails of every description, or one of the house wines.

The **Sheraton Makaha** has a number of restaurants ranging from sandwich bars to elegant dining. The **Kaala Room** features an impressive menu of fresh fish, steaks, and continental cuisine. Get a table with a long sweeping view of the valley, wonderful at sunset. Open daily for dinner, tel. 695-9511. The hotel's **Pikake Cafe** serves breakfast, lunch, and dinner with an assortment of sandwiches and international dishes.

The **Food Giant** grocery store in Waianae has a good selection of Asian and Hawaiian food. To find out what's happening along the Waianae coast, check out the bulletin board in front.

Note: For other restaurant choices see the Ihilani Resort and Spa under "Accommodations" above.

Arts And Crafts

The **Waianae Hawaiian Cultural and Art Center** offers workshops in lei-making, *lau hala* weaving, hula, and the Hawaiian language. They welcome people to either observe or participate in their programs. For times and schedules contact the **State Foundation of Culture and Arts,** tel. 586-0300.

Sports And Recreation

The **Leeward Dive Center,** tel. 696-3414 or (800) 255-1574, is a full-service dive shop offering rentals, scuba and snorkel excursions and certification courses. See "Water Sports" under "Sports and Recreation" in the Oahu Introduction.

monk seal

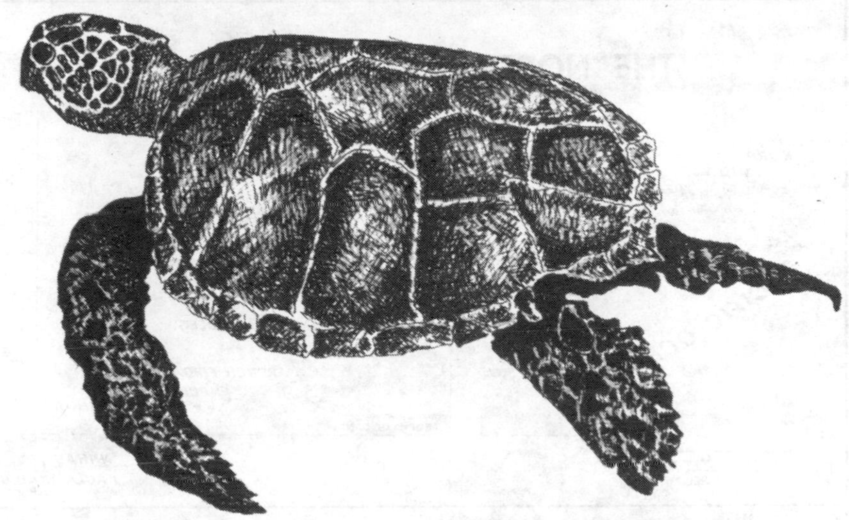

THE NORTHWESTERN ISLANDS

Like tiny gems of a broken necklace, the Northwestern Hawaiian Islands spill across the vast Pacific. Popularly called the **Leewards,** most were discovered last century, oftentimes by hapless ships that ground to a sickening halt on their treacherous, half-submerged reefs. The ship captains left their names: Lisianski, Kure, French Frigate Shoals, Hermes, and Pearl. Even today, craft equipped with the most modern navigational devices must be wary in these waters. They remain among the loneliest outposts on the face of the earth.

Land And Climate

The Leewards are the oldest islands of the Hawaiian chain, believed to have emerged from the sea at least six million years ago; some experts say 25 million years! Slowly they floated northward past the suboceanic hot spot as the other islands were built. Measured from **Nihoa Island,** about 100 miles off the northern tip of Kauai, they stretch for just under 1,100 miles to **Kure Atoll,** last of the **Midway Islands.** There are 13 islets, shoals, and half-submerged reefs in the chain. Most have been eroded flat by the sea and wind, but a few tough volcanic cores endure. Together they make up a landmass of approximately 3,400 acres, the largest being the Midways at 1,280 acres, and the smallest the **Gardner Pinnacles** at just over 2.5 acres. The climate is similar to that of the main islands with a slightly larger variance. Temperatures sometimes dip as low as 50 degrees and climb as high as 90 degrees.

Administration And History

Politically, the Leewards are administered by the City and County of Honolulu, except for the Midway Islands, which are under federal jurisdiction. None are permanently inhabited, except for some lonely military and wildlife field stations on Midway, Kure, and the French Frigate Shoals. All are part of the **Hawaiian Islands National Wildlife Refuge,** established at the turn of the century by Theodore Roosevelt. In pre-contact times, some of the islands supported a Tahitian culture markedly different from the one that emerged on the main Hawai-

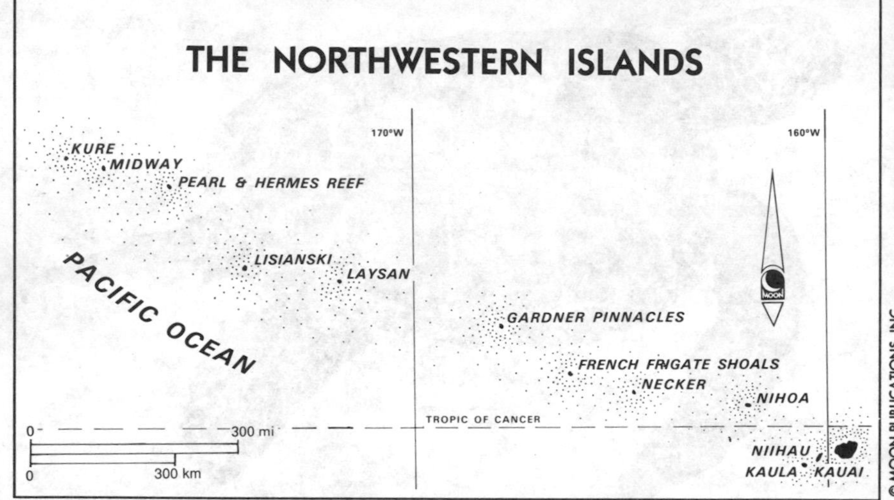

ian islands. Necker Island, for example, was the only island in the entire Hawaiian archipelago on which the inhabitants carved stone figures with a complete head and torso. On many of the others, remains of *heiau* and agricultural terracing attribute to their colonization by precontact Hawaiians. Over the years, natives as well as Westerners have exploited the islands for feathers, fertilizer, seals, and fish.

The islands are closely monitored by the U.S. Fish and Wildlife Agency. Permission to land on them is granted only under special circumstances. Studies are underway to determine if the waters around the islands can support commercial fishing, while leaving a plentiful supply of food for the unique wildlife of these lonely islands.

Wildlife

Millions of seabirds of various species have found permanent sanctuary on the Leewards, using them as giant floating nests and rookeries. Today the populations are stable and growing, but it hasn't always been so. On Laysan, at the turn of the century, egg hunters came to gather countless albatross eggs, selling the albumen to companies making photographic paper. They brought their families along, and their children's pets, which included rabbits. The rabbits escaped and multiplied wildly. In no time they invaded the territories of the **Laysan honeycreeper, rail,** and **millerbird,** rendering them extinct. Laysan has recovered and is refuge to over six million birds, including the rare and indigenous **Laysan teal** and **finch.**

An amazing bird using the rookeries is the **frigate bird.** During mating rituals, the male can inflate its chest like a giant, red, heart-shaped balloon. Also known as **man-o'-war birds,** they oftentimes pirate the catches of other birds, devour chicks, and even cannibalize their own offspring.

Some of the most prolific birds of the Leewards are terns, both the delicate all-white **fairy tern** and its darker relative the **sooty tern.** Other distinctive species include a variety of boobies, and the **Laysan albatross,** which has a wingspan of 10-12 feet, the world's largest.

Besides birds, the islands are home to the **Hawaiian monk seal,** one of only two species of indigenous Hawaiian mammals. These beautiful and sleek animals were hunted to near extinction for their skins. Humans encroached on their territory more and more, but now they are protected as an endangered species. About 1,000 individuals still cling to existence on various islands.

The **green turtle** is another species that has found a haven here. They were hunted to near extinction for their meat and leather, and of the few colonies around the world, the largest in the U.S. is on the French Frigate Shoals.

MAUI

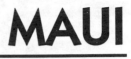

KAHOOLAWE, LANAI, AND MOLOKAI

"How shall we account for this nation spreading itself so far over this vast ocean? We find them from New Zealand to the south, to these islands to the north and from Easter Island to the Hebrides; . . . how much farther is not known . . ."

—Captain James Cook

BOB RACE

INTRODUCTION

The Kumulipo, the ancient genealogical chant of the Hawaiians, sings of the demigod Maui, a half-human mythological sorcerer known and revered throughout Polynesia. Maui was a prankster on a grand scale who used guile and humor to create some of the most amazing feats of derring-do ever recorded. A Polynesian combination of Paul Bunyan and Hercules, Maui had adventures known as "strifes." He served humankind by fishing up the islands of Hawaii from the ocean floor, securing fire from a tricky mud hen, lifting the sky so humans could walk upright, and slowing down the sun god by lassoing his genitals with a braided rope of his sister's pubic hair. Maui accomplished this last feat on the summit of the great mountain Haleakala ("House of the Sun"), thus securing more time in the day to fish and to dry tapa. Maui met his just but untimely end between the legs of the great goddess, Hina. This final prank, in which he attempted to crawl into the sleeping goddess's vagina, left his feet and legs dangling out, causing uproarious laughter among his comrades, a band of warrior birds. The noise awakened Hina, who saw no humor in the situation. She unceremoniously squeezed Maui to death. The island of Maui is the only island in Hawaii and throughout Polynesia named after a god. With such a legacy the island couldn't help but become known as *"Maui no ka oi"* ("Maui is the best").

AN OVERVIEW

In a land of superlatives, it's quite a claim to call your island *the* best, but Maui has a lot to back it up. Maui has more miles of swimmable beach than any of the other islands. Haleakala, the massive mountain that *is* East Maui, is the largest dormant volcano in the world, and its hardened lava rising over 30,000 feet from the sea floor makes it one of the heaviest concentrated masses on the face of the earth. There are legitimate claims that Maui grows the best onions and potatoes, but the boast of the best *pakalolo* may only be a pipe dream, since all the islands have great soil, good weather, and many enterprising gardeners.

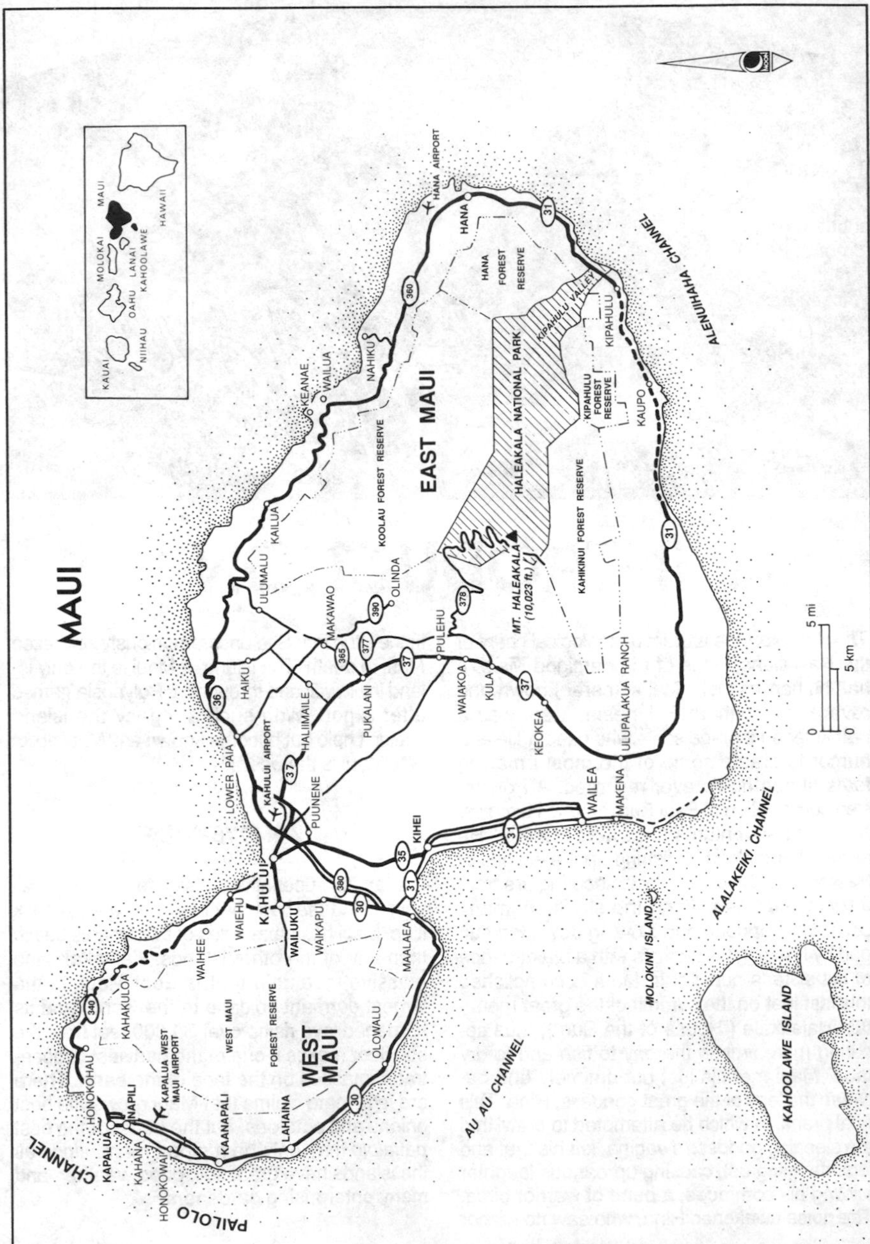

MAUI

KAUAI
NIIHAU
OAHU
MOLOKAI
LANAI
KAHOOLAWE
MAUI
HAWAII

PAILOLO CHANNEL
KAPALUA
KAHANA
HONOKOWAI
NAPILI
HONOKOHAU
KAPALUA WEST MAUI AIRPORT
KAANAPALI
LAHAINA
340
KAHAKULOA
WEST MAUI
WEST MAUI FOREST RESERVE
OLOWALU
30
WAIHEE
WAIEHU
KAHULUI
WAILUKU
WAIKAPU
MAALAEA
380
30
31
35
AU AU CHANNEL
KIHEI
31
WAILEA
MAKENA
MOLOKINI ISLAND
ALALAKEIKI CHANNEL
KAHOOLAWE ISLAND
LOWER PAIA
KAHULUI AIRPORT
37
PUUNENE
HALIIMAILE
36
HAIKU
PUKALANI
365
377
MAKAWAO
390
OLINDA
ULUMALU
KAILUA
37
PULEHU
WAIAKOA
KULA
37
KEOKEA
ULUPALAKUA RANCH
378
MT. HALEAKALA (10,023 ft.)
KOOLAU FOREST RESERVE
EAST MAUI
KEANAE
WAILUA
NAHIKU
360
HALEAKALA NATIONAL PARK
KAHIKINUI FOREST RESERVE
31
KIPAHULU FOREST RESERVE
KAUPO
KIPAHULU
KIPAHULU VALLEY
HANA FOREST RESERVE
HANA
HANA AIRPORT
31
ALENUIHAHA CHANNEL
0 5 mi
0 5 km

Maui's Body

If you look at the silhouette of Maui on a map, it looks like the head and torso of the mythical demigod bent at the waist and contemplating the uninhabited island of Kahoolawe. The head is West Maui, and its profile is that of a wizened old man whose wrinkled brow and cheeks are the West Maui Mountains. The highest peak here is **Puu Kukui,** at 5,778 feet, located just about where the ear would be. If you go to the top of the head you'll be at Kapalua, a resort community recently carved from pineapple fields. Fleming Beach begins a string of beaches that continues down over the face, stopping at the neck, and picking up again on the chest, which is Southeast Maui. Kaanapali is located at the forehead; its massive beach continues almost uninterrupted for four miles, an area that in comparison would take in all of Waikiki, from Diamond Head to Ala Moana. Sugarcane fields fringe the mountain side of the road, while condos are strung along the shore. The resorts here are cheek to jowl, but the best are tastefully done with uninterrupted panoramic views and easy and plentiful access to the beach.

Lahaina is located at the Hindu "third eye." This town is where it's "happening" on Maui, with concentrations of craftspeople, artists, museums, historical sites, restaurants, and nightspots. Used in times past by royal Hawaiian *ali'i* and then by Yankee whalers, Lahaina has always been somewhat of a playground, and the good-times mystique still lingers. At the tip of the nose is Olowalu, where a lunatic Yankee trader, Simon Metcalfe, decided to slaughter hundreds of curious Hawaiians paddling toward his ship just to show them he was boss. From Olowalu you can see four islands: Molokai, Lanai, Kahoolawe, and a faint hint of Hawaii far to the south. The back of Maui's head is an adventurer's paradise, complete with a tourist-discouraging rugged road posted with overexaggerated "Proceed No Farther" signs. Back here are tremendous coastal views, bird sanctuaries, *heiau,* and Kahakuloa, a tiny fishing village reported to be a favorite stomping ground of the great Maui himself.

The Isthmus

A low, flat isthmus planted primarily in sugarcane is the neck that connects the head of West Maui to the torso of East Maui, which is Haleakala. The Adam's apple is the little port of Maalaea, which has a good assortment of pleasure and fishing boats, and provides an up-close look at a working port not nearly as frenetic as Lahaina. The nape of the neck is made up of the twin cities of Wailuku, the county seat, and Kahului, where visitors arrive at Maui's airport. These towns are where the "people" live. Some say the isthmus, dramatically separating east and west, is the reason Maui is called "The Valley Isle." Head into Iao Valley from Wailuku, where the West Maui Mountains have been worn into incredible peaked monolithic spires. This stunning valley area played a key role in Kamehameha's unification of the Hawaiian Islands, and geologically seems to be a more fitting reason for Maui's nickname.

East Maui/Haleakala

Once you cross the isthmus you're on the immensity of Haleakala, the one mountain that makes up the entire bulging, muscled torso of the island. A continent in microcosm, it encompasses alpine terrain, baking desert, moonscape, blazing green jungle, pastureland, and lava-encrusted wasteland. The temperature, determined by altitude, ranges from subfreezing to subtropical. If you head east along the spine, you'll find world-class sailboarding beaches, artists' villages, last-picture-show towns, and a few remaining family farms planted in taro. Route 360, the only coastal road, rocks and rolls you over more than 600 documented curves and shows you more waterfalls and pristine pools than you can count. After crossing more than 50 bridges, you come to Hana. Here, the "dream" Hawaii that people seek still lives. Farther along is Kipahulu, and Oheo Gulch's fantastic pools and waterfalls. Close by is where Charles Lindbergh is buried, and many celebrities have chosen the surrounding hillsides for their special retreats.

On Haleakala's broad chest are macho cowboy towns complete with Wild West rodeos, a contrast to the gentle atmosphere but riotous colors of carnation and protea farms. Polipoli State Park is here, a thick forest canopy with more varieties of imported trees than anywhere else in Oceania. A weird cosmic joke places Kihei just about where the armpit would be. Kihei is a mega-growth condo area ridiculed as an example of what developers shouldn't be allowed to do. Oddly enough, Wailea, just down the road, exemplifies a reasonable and aesthetic planned community and is highly touted as a "model" development area. Just at the belly button, close to the kundalini, is Makena, long renowned as Maui's "alternative free beach," but rapidly losing its status.

Finally, when you make the pilgrimage to the summit of Haleakala, it'll be as if you've left the planet. It's another world: beautiful, mystical, raw, inspired, and freezing cold. When you're alone on the crater rim with the world below garlanded by the brilliance of sunrise or sunset, you'll know that you have come at last to great Maui's heart.

THE LAND

After the Big Island of Hawaii, Maui is the second largest and second youngest of the main Hawaiian Islands. The land was formed from two volcanoes: the **West Maui Mountains** and **Haleakala.** The West Maui Mountains are geologically much older than Haleakala, but the two were joined by subsequent lava flows that formed a connecting low, flat isthmus. **Puu Kukui**, at 5,778 feet, is the tallest peak of the West Maui Mountains. It's the lord of a mountain domain whose old weathered face has been scarred by a series of deep crags, verdant valleys, and inhospitable gorges. Rising over 30,000 feet from the ocean floor, Haleakala is by comparison an adolescent with smooth, rounded features looming 10,023 feet above sea level, with a landmass four times larger than West Maui's. The two parts of Maui combine to form 728.8 square miles of land with 120 linear miles of coastline. At its widest, Maui is 25 miles from north to south, and 40 miles east to west. The coastline has the largest number of swimmable beaches in Hawaii, and the interior is a miniature continent with almost every conceivable geological feature evident.

CLIMATE

Maui's weather is similar to that of the rest of the Hawaiian Islands, though some aficionados claim that it gets the most sunshine of all. The weather on Maui depends more on where you are than on what season it is. The average yearly daytime temperature hovers around 80° F and is moderated by the trade winds. Nights are just a few degrees cooler. Since Haleakala is a main feature on Maui, you should remember that altitude drastically affects the weather. Expect an average drop of three degrees for every

MAUI AVERAGE TEMPERATURE AND RAINFALL

TOWN		JAN.	MARCH	MAY	JUNE	SEPT.	NOV.
Lahaina	high	80	81	82	83	84	82
	low	62	63	68	68	70	65
	rain	3	1	0	0	0	1
Hana	high	79	79	80	80	81	80
	low	60	60	62	63	65	61
	rain	9	7	2	3	5	7
Kahului	high	80	80	84	86	87	83
	low	64	64	67	69	70	68
	rain	4	3	1	0	0	2

Note: rainfall in inches; temperature in °F

1,000 feet of elevation. The lowest temperature ever recorded in Hawaii was atop Haleakala in 1961, when the mercury dropped well below freezing to a low, low 11°.

Precipitation

Rain on Maui is as much a factor as it is elsewhere in Hawaii. On any day, somewhere on Maui it's raining, while other areas experience drought. A dramatic example of this phenomenon is a comparison of Lahaina with Mt. Puu Kukui, both on West Maui and separated by only seven miles. Lahaina, which translates as "Merciless Sun," is hot and arid, and gets only 17 inches of rainfall annually, while Puu Kukui can receive close to 500 inches (40 *feet!*) of precipitation. This rivals Mt. Waialeale on Kauai as the wettest spot on earth. The windward (wet) side of Maui, outlined by the Hana Road, is the perfect natural hothouse. Here, valleys sweetened with blossoms house idyllic waterfalls and pools that visitors treasure when they happen upon them. On the leeward (dry) side are Maui's best beaches: Kapalua, Kaanapali, Kihei, Wailea, and Makena. They all sit in Haleakala's rain shadow. If it happens to be raining at one beach, just move a few miles down the road to the next. Anyway, the rains are mostly gentle, and the brooding sky, especially at sundown, is even more spectacular than an unclouded one.

FLORA AND FAUNA

Maui's indigenous and endemic plants, trees, and flowers are both fascinating and beautiful. Unfortunately, they, like everything else that was native, are quickly disappearing. The majority of flora found interesting by visitors was either introduced by the original Polynesians or by later white settlers. Maui is blessed with state parks, gardens, undisturbed rainforests, private reserves, and commercial nurseries; combined they offer brilliant and dazzling colors to the landscape.

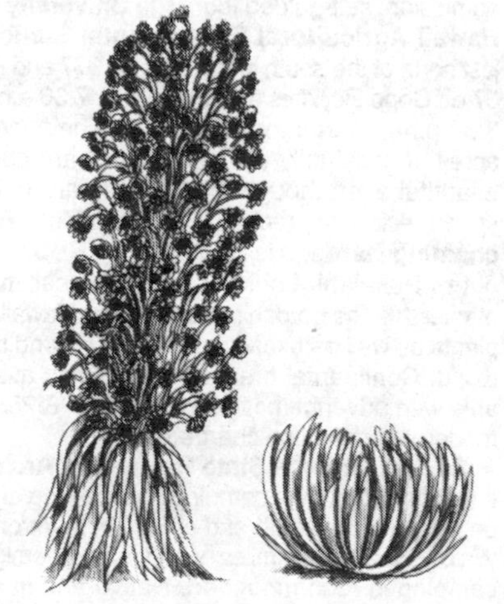
silversword

Silversword

Maui's official flower is a tiny pink rose called a *lokelani.* The island's unofficial symbol, however, is the silversword. The Hawaiian name for silversword is *ahinahina,* which translates as "gray gray," and the English name derives from a silverfish, whose color the plant is said to resemble. The silversword belongs to a remarkable plant family that claims 28 members, with five in the specific silversword species. It's kin to the common sunflower, and botanists say the entire family evolved from a single ancestral species. Hypothetically, the members of the silversword family can interbreed and produce remarkable hybrids. Some plants are shrubs, while others are climbing vines, and some even become trees. They grow anywhere from desert to steamy jungles. On Maui, the silversword is only found on Haleakala, above the 6,000-foot level, and is especially prolific in the crater. Each plant lives 5-20 years and ends its life by sprouting a gorgeous stalk of hundreds of purplish-red flowers. It then withers from a majestic six-foot plant to a flat gray skeleton. An endangered species, silverswords are totally protected. They protect themselves, too, from radiation and lack of moisture by growing fuzzy hairs all over their swordlike stalks. You can see them along the Haleakala Park Road at **Kalahaku Overlook,** or by hiking along **Silversword Loop** on the floor of the crater.

Protea

These exotic flowers are from Australia and South Africa. Because they come in almost limitless shapes, sizes, and colors, they captivate everyone who sees them. They are primitive and almost otherworldly in appearance, and exude a life force more like that of an animal than a flower. The slopes of leeward Haleakala between 2,000 and 4,000 feet are heaven to protea—the growing conditions could not be more perfect. Here are found the hardiest, highest-quality protea in the world. The days are warm, the nights are cool, and the well-drained volcanic soil has the exact combination of minerals on which protea thrive. Haleakala's crater even helps by creating a natural air flow that produces cloud cover, filters the sun, and protects the flowers. Protea make excellent gifts that can be shipped anywhere. As fresh-cut flowers they are gorgeous, but they have the extra benefit of drying superbly. Just hang them in a dark, dry, well-ventilated area and they do the rest. You can see protea, along with other botanical specialties, at the following: **Kula Botanical Garden,** Rt. 377 (Kekaulike Ave.) just a mile from where Rt. 377 joins Rt. 37 at the south end; **Cloud's Rest Protea Farm,** on Upper Kimo Drive one mile off Haleakala Hwy. (Rt. 377); **The Protea Gift Shoppe,** next to Kula Lodge on Haleakala Hwy.; **Protea Gardens of Maui,** on Hapapa Road off Rt. 377 not far from Kula Lodge; and **Sunrise Protea Farm,** on Haleakala Hwy. above the turnoff from Rt. 377.

Carnations

If protea aren't enough to dazzle you, how about fields of carnations? Most Mainlanders think of carnations stuck in a groom's lapel, or perhaps have seen a table dedicated to them in a hothouse, but not fields full of carnations! The Kula area grows nonchalant rows of carnations like cabbages. They fill the air with their unmistakable perfume, and they are without doubt a joy to behold. You can see family and commercial plots throughout the upper Kula area.

Prickly Pear Cactus

Interspersed in countless fields and pastures on the windward slope of Haleakala, adding that final nuance to cattle country, are clusters of prickly pear cactus. The Hawaiians call them *panini,* which translates as "very unfriendly," undoubtedly because of the sharp spines covering the flat, thick leaves. These cactus are typical of those found in Mexico and the southwestern United States. They were introduced to Hawaii before 1810 and established themselves, coincidently, in conjunction with the cattle brought at that time. It's assumed that Don Marin, a Spanish adviser to Kamehameha I, was responsible for bringing the cactus. Perhaps the early *paniolo* felt lonely without them. The *panini* can grow to heights of 15 feet and is now considered a pest, but nonetheless looks as if it belongs. The cactus has beautiful yellow and orange flowers that develop into small pear-shaped fruits—quite delicious. Hikers who decide to pick them should be careful of small yellowish bristles that can burrow under the skin and become very irritating.

Botanical Gardens, Parks, And State Forests

Those interested in the flora of Maui will find a visit to any of the following both educational and entertaining. In the Kula area visit: **Kula Botanical Gardens,** clearly marked along Rt. 377 (Kekaulike Ave.) just a mile from where Rt. 377 joins Rt. 37 at the south end, tel. 878-1715. The five acres of plants and trees include koa in their natural settings. Open daily 7 a.m.-4 p.m., admission, self-guided tour. The **University of Hawaii Agricultural Experimental Station,** just north of the south junction of Rt. 377 and Rt. 37 off Copp Road, is open Mon.-Fri. 7:30 a.m.-3:30 p.m., closed for lunch, free. The twenty acres of constantly changing plants are quite beautiful even though the grounds are uninspired, scientific, rectangular plots. **Maui Enchanting Gardens** is located along Rt. 37 just out of Pukalani. Look for the sign near mile marker 10. The garden features native Hawaiian plants as well as exotic plants from around the world. Continental breakfast and lunch available with advance notice by calling 878-2531; moderate admission charged.

Polipoli Springs State Recreation Area is the finest Upcountry camping and trekking area on Maui. At the south end of Rt. 377, turn onto Waipoli Road for 10 miles of bad road. Overnight camping is recommended. Native and introduced birds, and magnificent stands of redwoods, conifers, ash, cypress, sugi, cedar, and various pines may be found here. The park is known for delicious Methley plums that ripen in early June. For more info contact the Division of State Parks in Wailuku, tel. 243-5354.

Hosmer Grove, within Haleakala National Park, is an experimental forest project from the last century. Here are fine examples of introduced trees like cedar, pine, juniper, and sugi originally planted in hopes of finding a commercial, economically marketable wood for Hawaii. A short trail now winds through the no-longer-orderly stands of trees.

Keanae Arboretum, about 15 miles west of Hana on the Hana Road (Rt. 360), is always open, no fee. Native, introduced, and exotic plants, including Hawaiian food plants, grow in a natural setting with walkways, identifying markers, tropical trees, and mosquitoes. Educational and a must.

Kahanu Gardens, a branch of the Pacific Tropical Botanical Gardens, is located on the rugged lava coast east of Hana at the site of Piilanihale Heiau. Open Tues.-Sat. 10 a.m.-2 p.m. for self-guided tours. You'll find stands of breadfruit and coconut trees, a pandanus grove, and numerous other tropical plants from throughout the world. Located 1.5 miles down the rough and graveled Ulaine Road; admission is $5. Call 284-8912 for more information.

Maui Zoo and Botanical Garden in Wailuku is easily accessible. You can get a basic introduction to flora at this tiny zoo, which is good for tots and mildly interesting. In Central Maui try **Kepaniwai Park,** on Rt. 32 leading to Iao Needle. The park provides a tropical setting for formalized gardens from different nations. Open daily, no fee.

Finally, for excellent information concerning Maui's environment and its impact upon native species, contact **The Nature Conservancy,** P.O. Box 1716, Makawao, HI 96768, tel. 572-7849. The Conservancy is especially active in preserving a section of rainforest at Waikamoi Ridge on the road to Hana, where you can take a self-guided nature walk.

KAREN McKINLEY

Hawaiian stilt

Maui's Endangered Birds

Maui's native birds are disappearing. The island is the last home of the **crested honeycreeper** *(akohe'kohe),* which lives only on the windward slope of Haleakala from 4,500 to 6,500 feet. It once lived on Molokai, but no longer. It's rather a large bird, averaging over seven inches long, and predominantly black. Its throat and breast are tipped with gray feathers, and it has bright orange on its neck and underbelly. A distinctive fluff of feathers forms a crown believed to gather pollen from the ohia flowers that are the bird's primary food, helping propagate the ohia. The **parrotbill** is another endangered bird, found only on the slopes of Haleakala above 5,000 feet. It has an olive-green back and a yellow body. Its most distinctive feature is its parrotlike bill, which it uses to crack open branches and pry out larvae.

Two waterbirds found on Maui are the **Hawaiian stilt** *(ae'o)* and the **Hawaiian coot** *(alae ke'oke'o).* The stilt is about 16 inches tall and lives at Kanaha and Kealia ponds. Primarily black with a white belly, it has pink, sticklike legs. The adults will pretend to be hurt, putting on an excellent "broken wing" routine in order to lure predators away from their nests. The Hawaiian coot is a web-footed waterbird that resembles a duck. It's found on all the main islands but mostly on Maui and Kauai. Primarily a dull gray, it has a white bill and tail feathers. It builds a large floating nest and vigorously defends its young.

The **dark-rumped petrel** is slightly different than others in its family that are primarily marine birds. This petrel is found around the visitors center at Haleakala Crater about one hour after dusk May through October. The ***amakihi*** and the ***'i'iwi*** are endemic birds that aren't endangered at the moment. The *amakihi* is one of the most common native birds. It's yellowish-green and frequents the high branches of ohia, koa, and sandalwood looking for insects, nectar, or fruit. It's less specialized than most other Hawaiian birds, the main reason for its continued existence. The *'i'iwi* is a bright red bird with a salmon-colored hooked bill. It's found only on Maui, Hawaii, and Kauai in forests above 2,000 feet. It, too, feeds on a variety of insects and flowers. The *'i'iwi* is known for its harsh voice that sounds like a squeaking hinge, but is also capable of a melodious song.

The ***poouli*** is a dark brown, five-inch bird with a black mask and dark brown feet. Its tail is short, and it sports a conical bill. It was saved from extinction through the efforts of the Sierra Club and Audubon Society, who successfully added it to the Federal List of Endangered Species. The bird has one remaining stronghold deep in the forests of Maui.

Other indigenous birds found on Maui are the **wedge-tailed shearwater, white-tailed tropic bird, black noddy, American plover,** and a large variety of escaped exotic birds.

THE HUMPBACKS OF MAUI

Humpbacks are named for the way they expose their dorsal fin when they dive, which gives them a humped appearance. Having a dorsal fin puts them into the **roqual** family. There are about 7,000-8,000 humpback whales alive today, down from an estimated 100,000 at the turn of the century. They are divided into three separate global populations: North Atlantic, North Pacific, and South Pacific groups. About 600 North Pacific humpbacks migrate from coastal Alaska beginning in November. Migration peaks in February, when humpbacks congregate mostly in the waters off Maui, with a few heading for the waters off Kona on Hawaii. Within the last few years, all of the waters surrounding Maui County (including the Lahaina Roads but not the water around Kahoolawe) have been designated the **Hawaiian Islands Humpback Whale National Marine Sanctuary,** hoped to be a perpetual safe haven for whales.

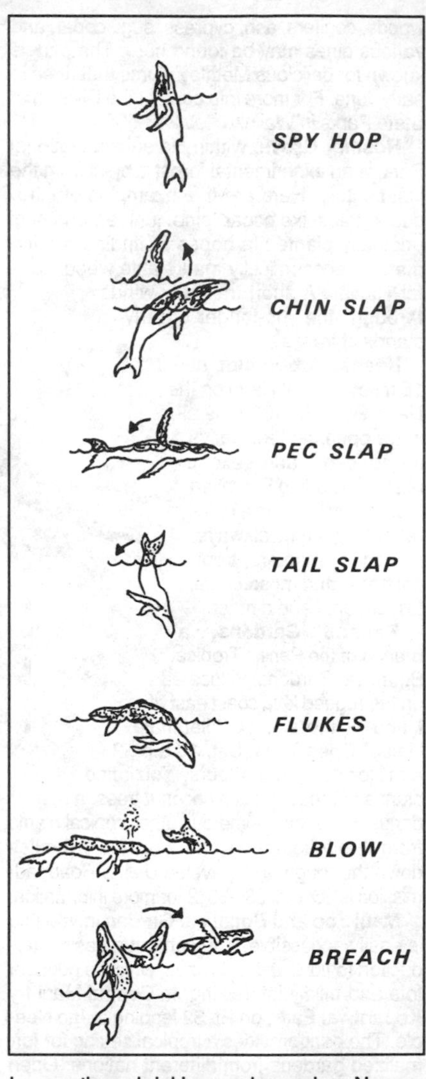

The Humpback's Song

Unlike other whales, humpbacks have the special ability to sing. They create their melodies by grunting, shrieking, and moaning. No one knows exactly what the songs represent, but it's clear they're a form of communication. The singers appear to be "escort males" that tag along with, and seem to guard, a mother and her calf. Amazingly, all the whales know and sing the same song, and the song changes from year to year. The notes are so forceful they can be heard above and below the water for miles. Some of the deep bass notes can even carry underwater for 100 miles.

Good recordings of the humpbacks' songs can be heard aboard the *Carthaginian II,* a restored 19th-century square-rigged ship just to the right of the loading dock in Lahaina Harbor. It serves as a floating museum dedicated to whales and whaling. As you descend into the ship's hold and bright sunlight fades to cool shadow, you become a visitor to the watery world of the humpback whale. The mysterious songs of the humpback provide the background music and set the mood. Sit on comfortable captain's chairs and watch the excellent audiovisual display. The photos of whales are by Flip Nicklin, courtesy of the National Geographic Society. The *Carthaginian II* is a project of the Lahaina Restoration Foundation, P.O. Box 338, Lahaina, HI 96761, tel. 661-3262. The foundation is a nonprofit organization dedicated to educational and historical restoration in Lahaina; open 9:30 a.m.-4:30 p.m., $3 adults, $2 seniors, free to children accompanied by an adult.

Whalewatching

If you're in Hawaii from late November to early May, you have an excellent chance of spotting a humpback. You can often see a whale from a vantage point on land, but this is nowhere near as thrilling as seeing one up close from a boat. Either way, binoculars are a must. Telephoto and zoom lenses are also useful, and you might even get a nifty photo into the bargain. But don't waste your film unless you have a fairly high-powered zoom: fixed-lens cameras give pictures with a lot of ocean and a tiny black speck. If you're lucky enough to see a whale breach (jump clear of the water), keep watching—it will often repeat this a number of times. If a whale dives and lifts its fluke high in the air, expect it to be down for at least 15 minutes and not come up in the same spot. Other times a whale will dive shallowly, then bob up and down quite often. From shore you're likely to see whales anywhere along Maui's south coast. If you're staying at one of the hotels or condos along Kaanapali or Kihei and have an ocean view, you can spot them from your lanai or window. A good vantage spot is Papawai Point along Rt. 30 and up the road heading west just before the tunnel. Maalaea Bay is another favorite nursing ground for female whales and their calves; here you can also see a small working harbor up close. Another excellent viewpoint is Makena Beach, on the spit of land separating Little and Big beaches. If you time your arrival near sunset, even if you don't see a whale you'll enjoy a mind-boggling light show.

Note: For whalewatching cruises see "Ocean Tours" under "Getting Around" in this chapter.

HISTORY

The Kumulipo sings that Maui was the second island child of Wakea and Papa. Before the coming of white people and their written record, it's clear the island was a powerful kingdom. Wars raged throughout the land and kings ruled not only Maui, but the neighboring islands of Lanai and Kahoolawe. By the 16th century, a royal road called the *Alaloa* encircled the island and signified unity. Today, on West Maui, the road is entirely obliterated; only a few portions remain on East Maui. When white people began to arrive in the late 1700s, Maui became their focal point. Missionaries, whalers, and the new Hawaiian kings of the Kamehameha line all made Lahaina their seat of power. For about 50 years, until the mid-19th century, Maui blossomed. Missionaries built the first permanent stone structures in the islands. An exemplary New England-style school at Lahainaluna attracted students even from California cities. Here, too, a famous printing press brought not only revenue but refinement, through the written word. The sugar industry began in secluded Hana and fortunes were made; a new social order under the Plantation System began. But by the turn of this century, the glory years were over. The whaling industry faded away and Oahu took over as the central power spot. Maui slipped into obscurity. It was revived in the 1960s when tourists rediscovered what others had known: Maui is a beauty among beauties.

Maui's Great Kings

Internal turmoil raged in Hawaii just before Captain Cook's arrival in 1778. Shortly after contact, the great Kamehameha would rise and consolidate all the islands under one rule, but in the 1770s a king named Kahekili ruled Maui. (Some contend Kahekili was Kamehameha's father.) The Hana District, however, was ruled by Kalaniopuu of Hawaii. He was the same king who caused the turmoil on the day Captain Cook was killed at Kealakekua.

In 1776, Kalaniopuu invaded Maui, but his forces were annihilated by Kahekili's warriors at Sand Hill near Wailuku, which means Bloody Waters. On November 26, 1778 Captain Cook spotted Maui, but bypassed it because he could find no suitable anchorage. It wasn't until May 28, 1786 that a French expedition led by Commander La Perouse came ashore near Lahaina after finding safe anchorage at what became known as La Perouse Bay. Maui soon became a regular port of call. In 1790 Kamehameha finally defeated Kahekili's forces at Iao Needle and brought Maui under his domain. The great warrior Kahekili was absent from the battle, during which Kamehameha used a cannon from the *Fair American,* a small ship seized a few years before. Davis and Young, two marooned seamen, provided the technical advice for these horrible but effective new weapons.

Maui's Rise

The beginning of the 19th century brought amazing changes to Hawaii, many of which came through Maui—especially the port of Lahaina. In 1793, Captain Vancouver visited Lahaina and confirmed LaPérouse's report that it was a fine anchorage. In 1802 Kamehameha stopped with his enormous Pelelu fleet of war canoes on his way to conquer Oahu. He lingered for over a year collecting taxes and building his Brick Palace at Lahaina. The bricks were poorly made, but marked the first Western-style structure in the islands. He also built a fabulous straw house for his daughter Princess Nahienaena that was so well constructed it was later used as the residence of the U.S. Consul. In 1819 the first whaler, *The Bellina,* stopped at Lahaina and marked Hawaii's ascendancy as the capital of the whaling industry, a position that lasted until the majority of the whaling fleet was lost in the Arctic in 1871. During Lahaina's heyday, over 500 ships visited the port in one year. Also in 1819, the year of his death, Kamehameha built an observation tower in Lahaina so he could watch for returning ships, many of which held his precious cargo. In that prophetic year the French reappeared, with a warship this time, and the drama began. The great Western powers of the period maneuvered to upstage each other in the quest for dominance of this Pacific jewel.

The Missionaries

In 1823 the first Christian mission was built in Lahaina under the pastorage of Reverend Richards, and the conversion of Hawaii began in earnest. In that year Queen Keopuolani, the first great convert to Christianity, died. She was buried in Lahaina not according to the ancient customs accorded an *ali'i,* but as a reborn child of Christ.

The Reverend Richards and Queen Kaahumanu worked together to produce Hawaii's first Civil Code based on the Ten Commandments. The whalers fought the interference of the missionaries to the point where attempts were made on Reverend Richards's life, including a naval bombardment of his home. Over the next decade, the missionaries, ever hard at work, became reconciled with the sailors, who donated funds to build a Seaman's Chapel. This house of worship was located just next to The Baldwin Home, an early, permanent, New England-style house, which still stands on Front Street. The house originally belonged to the Spaulding family, but the Baldwins were such an influence that it was known by their name. Lahainaluna High School, situated in the cool of the mountains just north of Lahaina, became the paramount institution of secondary learning west of the Rocky Mountains. The newly wealthy of Hawaii and California sent their progeny here to be educated along with the nobility of the Kingdom of Hawaii.

Maui Fades

If the following 30 years of Maui's historical and sociological development were put on a graph, it would show a sharp rise followed by a crash. By mid-century, Maui boasted the *first* Constitution, Catholic Mass, Temperance Union, Royal Palace, and steamship service. A census was taken and a prison built to house reveling seamen. Kamehameha III moved the capital to Honolulu and the 1850s brought a smallpox epidemic, the destruction of Wainee Church by a "ghost wind," and the death of David Malo, a classic historian of pre-contact Hawaii. By the late 1860s, the whaling industry was dead, but sugar would rise to take its place. The first successful sugar plantation was started by George Wilfong in 1849 along the Hana coast, and the first great sugar mill was started by James Campbell in 1861. The 1870s saw the planting of Lahaina's famous Banyan Tree by Sheriff W.O. Smith, and the first telephone and telegraph cable linking Paia with Haiku.

The 20th Century

When the Pioneer Hotel was built in 1901, Lahaina was still important. Claus Spreckels, King Sugar himself, had large holdings on Maui and along with his own sugar town, Spreckelsville, built the Haiku Ditch in 1878. This 30-mile ditch brought 50 million gallons of water a day from Haiku to Puunene so the "green gold" could flourish. The entrepreneur was able to buy the land for his sugar plantation cheaply. The highly superstitious Hawaiians of the time didn't value this particular plot of land, believing that the souls of those who had not made the leap to heaven were condemned to wander the wasteland. To them it was obviously cursed, supporting only grasses and scrub bushes, and they felt that they were getting the bargain, off-loading it onto the unsuspecting *haole.* Moreover, Spreckels was a gambler. In a series of late-night poker games with Kamehameha III he was able to win the water rights to a dozen or so streams in the area, thereby creating the possibility for his Haiku Ditch. Sugar and Maui became one.

Then, because of sugar, Lahaina lost its dominance and Paia became *the* town on Maui during the 1930s, where it housing plantation workers in camps according to nationality. Maui slid more and more into obscurity. A few luminaries brought passing fame: Tandy MacKenzie, for example, born in Hana in 1892, was a gifted operatic star whose career lasted until 1954. In the 1960s, Maui, as well as all of Hawaii, became accesssible to the average tourist. It was previously discovered by men like Sam Pryor, retired vice-president of Pan Am who made his home in Hana and invited Charles Lindbergh to visit, then to live and finally die in this idyllic spot. In the mid-'60s, the Lahaina Restoration Foundation was begun. It dedicated itself to the preservation of Old Lahaina and other historical sites on the island. It now attempts to preserve the flavor of what once was while looking to future growth. Today, Maui is once again in ascendancy, the second most visited island in Hawaii after Oahu.

GOVERNMENT

The boundaries of Maui County are a bit oddball, but historically oddball. Maui County encompasses Maui Island, as well as Lanai, Molokai, and the uninhabited island of Kahoolawe. The apparent geographical oddity consists of an arc on East Maui, from Makawao past Hana and along the south coast almost to Kihei, which is a "shared" political area, aligned with the Kohala District of the Big Island since Poly-

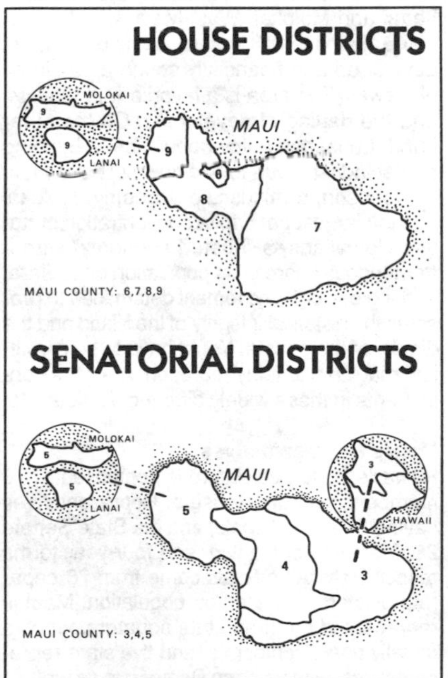

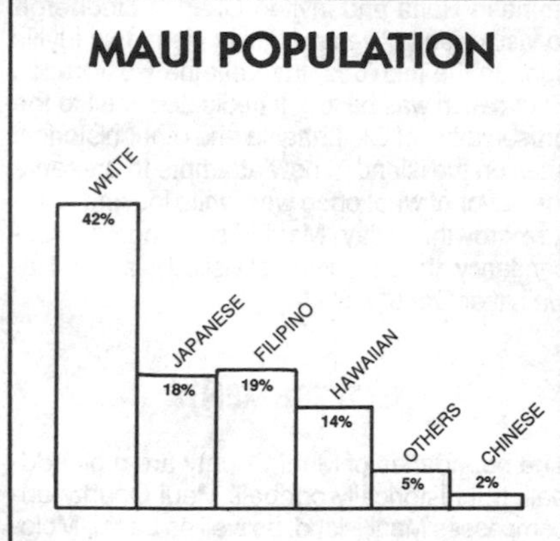

nesian times. These two districts were joined with each other, so it's just a traditional carryover. The real strangeness occurs in Maui's 5th Senatorial District and its counterpart, the 9th Representative District. These two political areas include West Maui and the islands of Lanai and Molokai. West Maui, with Kaanapali, Lahaina, and Kapalua, is one of the most developed and financially sound areas in all of Hawaii. The area is a favorite with tourists, and the darling of developers. On the other hand, Lanai has a tiny population, a budding tourist industry due to two new hotels, and, in comparison, a minuscule economy. Molokai has the largest per capita concentration of native Hawaiians, a "busted economy" with a tremendous share of its population on welfare, and a grassroots movement determined to preserve the historical integrity of the island and the dignity of the people. You'd have to be a political magician to fairly represent all of the constituents in these widely differing districts.

Maui's Representatives

Hawaii's State Legislature is comprised of 76 members, with the House of Representatives having 51 elected seats, and the State Senate 25. Members serve two- and four-year terms respectively. All officials come from 76 separate electorates based on population. Maui is represented by three state senators, who've usually been Democrats, and five state representatives, who've been Democrats as well.

ECONOMY

Maui's economy is a mirror image of the state's economy: it's based on tourism, agriculture, and government expenditures. The primary growth is in **tourism,** with Maui the second most frequently chosen Hawaiian destination after Oahu. Over 17,000 rooms are available on Maui in all categories, and they're filled 70% of the time. On average, Maui attracts about one million tourists per year, and on any given day there are about 16,000 visitors enjoying the island. The majority of the rooms are in Kihei-Wailea, but with the building trades still booming, the Kaanapali area is catching up fast.

Agriculturally, Maui generates revenue through cattle, sugar, pineapples, and flowers, along with a substantial subculture economy in *pakalolo.* **Cattle grazing** occurs on the western and southern slopes of Haleakala, where 20,000 acres are owned by the Ulupalakua Ranch, and over 32,000 acres by the Haleakala Ranch. The upper slopes of Haleakala around Kula are a gardener's dream. Delicious onions, potatoes, and all sorts of garden vegetables are grown, but are secondary to large plots of gorgeous flowers, mainly carnations and the amazing protea.

Sugar, actually in the grass family, is still very important to Maui's economy, but without federal subsidies it wouldn't be a viable cash crop. The largest acreage is in the central isthmus area, virtually all of which is owned by Alexander and Baldwin Inc. Large sugarcane tracts along Kaanapali and the west coast that are owned by Amfac and Maui Land and Pineapple. Those lodging in Kaanapali will become vividly aware of the cane fields when they're burned off just prior to harvesting. Making these unsightly burnings even worse is the fact that the plastic pipe used in the drip irrigation of the fields is left in place. Not cost-efficient to recover, it is burned along with the cane, adding its noxious fumes to the air.

Pineapples grow in central east Maui between Paia and Makawao, where Alexander and Baldwin own most of the land. Another area is the far west coast north of Napili where Maui Land and Pineapple controls most of the holdings. Renegade entrepreneurs grow patch-

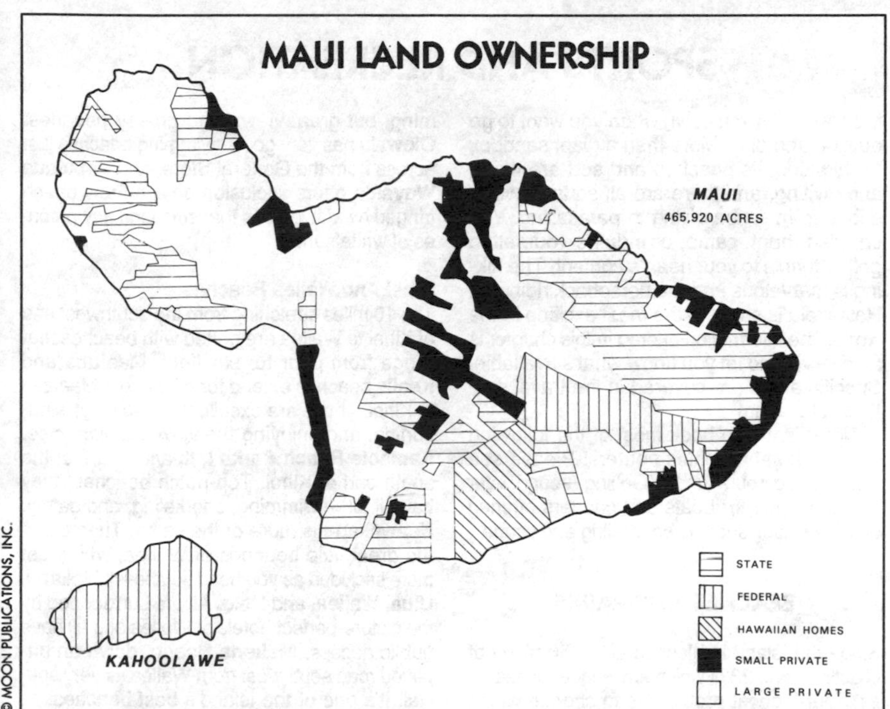

es of *pakalolo* wherever they can find a spot that has the right vibes and is away from the prying eyes of the authorities. Deep in the West Maui Mountains and along the Hana coast are favorite areas.

Government expenditures in Maui County are just over $40 million per year. The small military presence on Maui amounts to a tiny Army installation near Kahului and the Navy's ownership of the target island of Kahoolawe. With tourists finding Maui more and more desirable every year, and with agriculture firmly entrenched, Maui's economic future is bright.

Tourism-Related Problems

Two prime examples of the best and the worst development can be found on Maui's south shore at Kihei and Wailea, less than five miles apart. In the late '60s Kihei experienced a development-inspired "feeding frenzy" that made the real sharks offshore seem about as dangerous as Winnie the Pooh. Condos were slapped up as fast as cement can dry, their architecture reminiscent of a stack of shoeboxes. A coastline renowned for its beauty was overburdened, and the view was wiped out in the process. Anyone who had the bucks built, and now parts of Kihei look like a high-rise, low-income, federally funded housing project. You can bet that those who made a killing doing the building don't live here.

Conversely, just down the road is Wailea, a model of what development could (and should) be. The architecture is tasteful, low-rise, unobtrusive, and designed with people and the preservation of the scenery in mind . . . mostly. It's obviously more exclusive, but access points to the beaches are open to everyone, and the view is still there for all to enjoy. Wailea points the way for the development of the future.

SPORTS AND RECREATION

Maui won't let you down when you want to go outside and play. More than a giant sandbox for big kids, its beaches and surf are warm and inviting, and there are all sorts of water sports from scuba diving to parasailing. You can fish, hunt, camp, or indulge yourself in golf or tennis to your heart's content. The hiking is marvelous and the horseback riding on Haleakala is some of the most exciting in the world. The information offered in this chapter is an overview to let you know what's available. Specific areas are covered in the travel sections. Have fun!

Note: You can book most of the following through hotel activities centers. Please see "Sightseeing Tours" under "Getting Around" later in this chapter for boats and charters offering other activities such as snorkeling and scuba.

BEACHES AND PARKS

Since the island is blessed with 150 miles of coastline, over 32 of which are wonderful beaches, your biggest problem is to choose which one you'll grace with your presence. The following should help you—but before you romp, pick up and read the brochure *Maui Beach Safety Tips* by the American Red Cross.

Southwest Maui Beaches

The most plentiful and best beaches for swimming and sunbathing are on the south coast of West Maui, strung along 18 glorious miles from Kapalua to Olowalu. For an all-purpose beach you can't beat **Kapalua Beach** (Fleming Beach) on Maui's western tip. It has everything: safe surf (except in winter), great swimming, snorkeling, and bodysurfing in a first-class, family-oriented area. Then come the Kaanapali beaches along Rt. 30, bordered by the hotels and condos. All are open to the public, and "rights of way" pass just along hotel grounds. **Black Rock** at the Sheraton is the best for snorkeling. West of Lahaina is **Lahaina Beach,** convenient but not private; southeast of town, **Launiupoko Wayside** and **Puamana Beach** have only fair swimming, but great views and grassy beaches. **Olowalu** has very good swimming beaches just across from the General Store, and **Papalaua Wayside** offers seclusion on a narrow beach fringed by *kiawe* trees that surround tiny patches of white sand.

Kihei And Wailea Beaches

The 10 miles stretching from the southwest end of Kihei to Wailea are dotted with beaches that range from poor to excellent. **Maalaea** and **Kealia** beaches extend for miles from Maalaea to Kihei. These are excellent for walking, windsurfing, and enjoying the view, but little else. **Kamaole Beach Parks I, II,** and **III** are at the south end of Kihei. Top-notch beaches, they have it all—swimming, snorkeling, and safety. **Keawakapu** is more of the same. Then come the great little beaches of Wailea, which get more secluded as you head southeast: **Mokapu, Ulua, Wailea,** and **Polo.** All are surrounded by the picture-perfect hotels of Wailea and all have public access. **Makena Beach,** down an unpaved road southwest from Wailea, is very special. It's one of the island's best beaches. At one time, alternative people made Makena a haven and it still attracts free-spirited souls. There's nude bathing here in secluded coves, unofficial camping, and freedom. It gets the highest compliment when locals, and those staying at hotels and condos around Maui, come here to enjoy themselves.

Wailuku And Kahului

Poor ugly ducklings! These are shallow, unattractive beaches in both towns where no one spends any time. However, **Kanaha Beach** between Kahului and the airport isn't bad at all. **Baldwin Beach Park** has a reputation for hostile locals protecting their turf, but the beach is good and you won't be hassled if you "live and let live." **Hookipa Beach** just east of Paia isn't good for the average swimmer but is the "sailboarding capital" of Hawaii, and you should visit here just to see the exciting, colorful spectacle of people skipping over the ocean with bright sails.

Hana Beaches
Everything about Hana is heavenly, including its beaches. There's **Red Sand Beach,** almost too pretty to be real. **Waianapanapa** is surrounded by the state park and good for swimming and snorkeling, even providing a legendary cave whose waters turn blood red. **Hana Bay** is well protected and safe for swimming. Farther along at **Oheo Stream** (Seven Sacred Pools) you'll find the paradise you've been searching for—gorgeous freshwater pools at the base of wispy waterfalls, fronted by a tremendous sea of pounding surf only a few yards away.

Freshwater Swimming
The best places for freshwater swimming are in various stream pools on the road to Hana. One of the very best is **Twin Falls,** up a short trail from Hoolawa Bridge. **Helio's Grave** is another good swimming spot between Hana and Oheo Stream, which are excellent themselves, especially the upper pools. Also, you can take a refreshing dip at Iao Valley Stream when you visit Iao Needle, or at Waihee Stream in the next valley north.

SNORKELING AND SCUBA

Maui is as beautiful beneath the waves as it is above. There is world-class snorkeling and diving at many coral reefs and beds surrounding the island. You'll find the best, coincidentally, just where the best beaches are: mainly from Kihei to Makena, up around Napili Bay and especially from Olowalu to Lahaina. Backside Maui is great (but mostly for experts), and for a total thrill, try diving Molokini, the submerged volcano, peeking above the waves and designated a Marine Life Conservation District.

Great Underwater Spots
These are some of the best on Maui, but there are plenty more (see "Sights" in individual chapters). Use the same caution when scuba diving or snorkeling as when swimming. Be mindful of currents. It's generally safer to enter the water in the center of a bay than at the sides, where rips are more likely to occur. The following sites are suitable for beginners to intermediates. On Maui's western tip try **Honolua Bay,** a Marine Life Conservation District; nearby **Mokuleia Bay,** known as "Slaughterhouse," is gentle. Napili Bay usually has good and safe conditions. In Kaanapali you'll enjoy **Black Rock** at the Sheraton Hotel. At **Olowalu,** the ocean is very gentle with plenty to see. Also try **Kamaole Parks II** and **III** in Kihei, and **Ulua, Polo,** and **Wailea** beaches in Wailea. On the windward side, **Baldwin Beach Park** in Paia and **Waianapanapa State Park** near Hana are both generally good. Under no circumstances should you miss taking a boat out to Molokini. It's worth every penny!

For **scuba divers,** there are underwater caves at **Nahuna** ("Five Graves") **Point** between Wailea and Makena, great diving at Molokini, magnificent caves out at the **Lanai Cathedrals,** and a sunken Navy sub (the USS *Bluegill*) to explore. Advanced divers *only* can attempt the backside of West Maui, the Seven Sacred Pools, and beyond Pu'uiki Island in Hana Bay.

Equipment
Sometimes condos and hotels offer snorkeling equipment free to their guests, but if you have to rent it, don't do so from a hotel or condo; go to a dive shop where rentals are much cheaper. Expect to spend $5-7 per day for mask, fins, and snorkel. One of the best snorkel deals is through **Snorkel Bob's,** tel. 879-7449 Kihei, 661-4421 Lahaina, or 669-9603 Napili. Old Snorkel Bob will dispense info and full snorkel gear for only $15 weekly, which you can return on a Neighbor Island, if you'll be heading that way before the week is up. **A & B Rentals and Sportswear,** in Honokowai in Da Rose Mall at 3481 Lower Honoapiilani Hwy., tel. 669-0027, open daily 9 a.m.-5 p.m., rents snorkel gear for $2.50 per day, and $10 per week.

Scuba divers can rent gear for about $40 from most shops. All the shops listed below rent snorkel gear as well. In Lahaina rent from: **Lahaina Divers,** tel. 667-7496, at 710 Front St., one of the best all-around shops/schools on Maui; **Dive Maui,** Lahaina Market Place, tel. 667-2080; **Hawaiian Reef Divers,** 156 Lahainaluna Rd., tel. 667-7647, snorkel sets for $2 per day, good instruction, and a reasonably priced snorkel/sail to Molokini/Lanai; **Captain Nemo's Emporium,** 150 Dickenson, tel. 661-

5555 or (800) 367-8088 Mainland; **Fun Rentals of Maui,** 193 Lahainaluna Rd., tel. 661-3053, snorkel sets $2.50 for 24 hours or $12 per week, rentals of miscellaneous items like binoculars and baby strollers for parents who wish to stay fit.

In Kihei all-around dive shops are **Maui Dive Shop,** Azeka Pl., tel. 879-3388 (other locations see "Snorkel and Scuba Excursions" following); **Dive and Sea Center,** 1975 S. Kihei Rd., tel. 874-1952; and **Molokini Divers,** 1993 S. Kihei Rd., tel. 879-0055. You might also consider renting an underwater camera. Expect to spend $15-20, including film.

Note: See "Shopping" in individual travel chapters for rental equipment in that area.

Scuba Certification

A number of Maui companies take you from your first dive to PADI, NAUI, or NASDS certification. Prices range from $50 for a quickie refresher dive up to around $350 for a four- to five-day certification course. Courses or arrangements can be made with any of the dive shops listed above or with **Ocean Activities Center,** tel. 879-4485; **Beach Activities of Maui,** tel. 661-5500; **Destination Pacific,** tel. 874-0305; or **Aquatic Charters,** tel. 879-0976.

Snorkel And Scuba Excursions

Many boats will take you out snorkeling or diving. Prices range from $30 (half day, four hours) to $60 (full day, eight hours) for a snorkeling adventure, and $50-80 for scuba diving. Check "Ocean Tours" under "Getting Around" later in this chapter for many of the boats that do it all, from deep-sea fishing to moonlight cruises. Hotel activities centers can arrange these excursions for no extra charge; check "Sightseeing Tours" under "Getting Around" in this chapter for names and numbers.

Mike Severns, tel. 879-6596, is one of the most experienced and respected divers on Maui. As a marine scientist/explorer, he is extremely knowledgeable about Maui above and below the waves. Mike has his own boat and accepts both beginning and advanced divers. Diving with Mike is an extraordinary educational experience.

The Dive and Sea Center, 1975 S. Kihei Rd., tel. 874-1952, open daily 7 a.m.-5 p.m., and until noon on Sunday, is a full-service dive shop offering scuba dives, four-day certification classes for $250, air refills, and equipment rentals (scuba gear $19.95 per day, snorkel gear $5 per day). Dive/snorkel trips to Molokini Crater (snorkelers $49, one tank beginner dive $80) are on a six-passenger Mako boat so that you are given individual attention and full value for your money.

The **Maui Dive Shop,** at Azeka II Shopping Center along S. Kihei Road, tel. 879-3388 (call for other locations and phone numbers), is a full-service water sports store that also operates snorkel ($49) and scuba dives ($85 two tanks) to Molokini Crater and the south shore, departing daily at 7 a.m. and 10 a.m., aboard either the *India Express* or the *Kanapihi.*

For a magnificent day of sailing, exploring, and snorkeling, you can't beat **Trilogy Excursions,** tel. 661-4743, whose sleek catamarans leave Lahaina Harbor for a day trip to Lanai.

Captain Nemo's Emporium, tel. (800) 367-8088 Mainland or 661-5555 in Hawaii, located at 150 Dickenson Street, is owned and operated by an excellent diver, Lynn Palmer. She is actively concientious about understanding and preserving the ecology of Hawaii. Nemo's offers certification classes, three-day open water $169; beach dives $59; and night dives $59. This full-service scuba/snorkel store's daily rental rates (weekly discounts) are: $25 scuba; $2.50 snorkel; $4 boogie boards. Captain Nemo's is an excellent booking agency for everything from helicopters to scuba trips (their specialty), with a complete repair facility and air fill station for those already certified.

Hawaiian Reef Divers, at 156 Lahainaluna Rd., tel. 667-7647, offer a snorkel trip to Lanai or Molokini Crater (alternating days) for $49, or a scuba dive (one tank $55, two tanks $75, introductory dive $69) including a continental breakfast, picnic lunch, free snorkel map, and all the equipment. For departures to Molokini, check-in is at 6:30 a.m., with a return about 1 p.m.; to Lanai, check-in is at 7:30 a.m., with a return about 2 p.m. Four-day scuba certification courses run about $249-299.

Lahaina Divers, at 710 Front St., Lahaina, tel. 667-7496, offer a scuba ($75 one tank) or snorkeling ($45) experience to Lanai that includes all gear and a light lunch. They also offer a scuba certification course and night dive.

J.D. BISIGNANI

Hobie Cats at Kealia Beach

With a name like **Chuck Thorne,** what else can you expect but a world-class athlete of some kind? Well, Chuck is a diver who lives on Maui. He's written *The Divers' Guide to Maui,* the definitive book on all the best dive/snorkel spots on the island. Chuck's is a one-man operation, so unfortunately he must limit his leadership and instruction to advanced divers only. People have been known to cancel flights home to dive with Chuck, and he receives the highest accolades from other water people. Some feel that Chuck is Maui's "Rambo" diver. He's a no-nonsense kind of guy who's out to show you some great spots, but never forgets about safety first. He'll arrive in a pickup truck, oftentimes with ladders on the roof. These might come in handy later when he drives you to a remote area and you've got to climb down the cliff to get to the dive spot. No pencil-necked wimps! You can buy his book at many outlets or write: Maui Dive Guide, P.O. Box 1461, Kahului, HI 96732.

For a pure snorkeling adventure besides those offered by the dive shops and tour boats above, try **Snorkel Maui,** tel. 572-8437, with Ann Fielding, the naturalist author of *Hawaiian Reefs and Tide Pools.* Her newest book, *Underwater Guide To Maui,* details many of the invertebrates and reef fish you will encounter on one of her fantastic dives. Ms. Fielding will instruct you in snorkeling and in the natural history and biology of what you'll be seeing below the waves. She tailors the dive to fit the participants, and does scuba as well. A basic snorkel dive, about two hours, costs $40.

Snuba

No, that's not a typo. Snuba is half snorkeling and half scuba diving. You have a regulator, weight belt, mask, and flippers, and you're tethered to scuba tanks that float 20 feet above you on a sea-sled. The idea is many people become anxious diving under the waves encumbered by tanks and scuba apparatus. Snuba frees you. You would think being tethered to the sled would slow you down, but actually you're sleeker and can make better time than a normal scuba diver. If you would like to start diving, this is a wonderful and easy way to begin. Try **The Four Winds,** tel. 879-8188, a snorkel-dive boat that goes to Molokini Crater and is the only outfit offering Snuba on Maui at this time.

MORE WATER SPORTS

Bodysurfing

All you need are the right waves, conditions, and ocean bottom to have a ball bodysurfing. Always check conditions first, as bodysurfing has led to very serious neck and back injuries for the ill-prepared. The following are decent areas: Ulua, Wailea, Polo, or Makena beaches; the north end of Kamaole Beach Park I in Kihei; Napili Bay; and Baldwin Park.

Surfing And Boogie Boarding

For good surfing beaches try: Lower Paia Park, Napili Bay, Baldwin Park, Maalaea, and Hookipa. The **Maui Surfing School** offers lessons at the beach just southeast of Lahaina Harbor. Call 877-8811 and ask for Andrea Thomas. Specializing in "beginners and cowards," they guarantee results after one lesson. **Kaanapali**

Windsurfing in Kaanapali, tel. 667-1964, also offers lessons.

Fun Rentals of Maui, at 193 Lahainaluna Rd., Lahaina, tel. 661-3053, open daily 8:30 a.m.-5 p.m., Sunday until 3 p.m., rents **skim boards** at $12 per day and **surfboards** at $20 per day, with weekly discounts available.

Hawaiian Reef Divers, at 156 Lahainaluna Rd., tel. 667-7647, rents boogie boards at $3 per day.

Snorkel Bob's, at 161 Lahainaluna Rd., tel. 661-4421, rents boogie boards at $13 per day or $26 per week, and their advice, whether you need it or not, is always plentiful and free.

A & B Rentals and Sportswear, in Honokowai's Da Rose Mall at 3481 Lower Honoapiilani Hwy., tel. 669-0027, open daily 9 a.m.-5 p.m., rents boogie boards, surfboards, and fishing poles per day or week for reasonable rates.

Sailing/Boating

The most popular day sails are from Maui to Molokai or Lanai (fully discussed in "Ocean Tours" under "Getting Around" later in this chapter). Your basic half-day snorkel-and-swim sail will be $50. For serious sailors, some top-notch boats in Lahaina and Maalaea harbors are open for lengthy charters. Try: **Alihilani Yacht Charters,** tel. 871-1156; **Scotch Mist Sailing Charters,** tel. 661-0368; **SeaEscape U-Drive Boat Rental,** tel. 879-3721; **Island Sports Rental,** tel. 667-0449; or **Lavengro,** tel. 879-8188, at Maalaea Harbor.

For more **kayaking** and **rafting** alternatives, see "Ocean Tours" in "Getting Around" later in this chapter.

Windsurfing

This is one of the world's newest sports, and unlike in surfing, which tends to be male-dominated, women who windsurf are highly visible. Hookipa Beach, just east of Paia, is the "windsurfing capital of the world," and the **O'Neill International Championship** is held here every year in March and April. Kanaha Beach Park, in nearby Kahului, has perfect, gentle winds and waves for learning the sport, and Kealia Beach in Kihei is the choice of many. Summer is best for windsurfing because of the wind characteristics. Mornings, when winds are lighter, are good for the novice. As winds pick up in the afternoon the more advanced board riders hit the water. Any sailboard shop will point you in the right direction for location and gear according to your skill level.

To rent boards and to take instructions, try: **Sailboards Maui,** 430 Alamaha, Suite 103, Kahului, tel. 871-7954; and **Kaanapali Windsurfing School,** tel. 667-1964. Also check the **Maui Windsurfing Company,** tel. 877-4816 or (800) 872-0999. They have rentals from $45 per day to $495 for three weeks, and lessons for about $60. Remember—start with a big board and a small sail! Take lessons to save time and energy.

THRILL CRAFT

A recent controversy has focused on what has been called "thrill craft." Usually this term refers to Jet Skis, water-skiing boats, speedboats, parasailing, and even sailboards. The feeling among conservationists is that these craft disturb humans, and during whale season disturb the whales who come to nest in the rather small Lahaina Roads. This is definitely a case of "one person's pleasure is another person's poison." On March 31, 1991 a law was passed that bans these types of craft from operating in west and south Maui waters during whale season, December 15 through May 15.

Parasailing

If you've ever wanted to soar like an eagle, here's your chance—no prior experience necessary. Basically, a parasail is a parachute tethered to a speedboat. And away we go! **Lahaina Parasail,** tel. 661-4887, located in downtown Lahaina on the south end of the breakwater, is a family-run business that was the first of its kind on Maui. These folks know what they're doing and have taken tens of thousands of people aloft on their thrill-of-a-lifetime ride. The most dangerous part, according to the crew, is getting in and out of the shuttle boat that takes you to the floating platform about 1,000 yards offshore from where you take off. Awaiting you is a powerboat with special harness attached to a parachute. You're put in a life vest, and strapped to the harness that forms a cradle upon which you sit while aloft. Make sure, once you're up, to pull the cradle as far under your thighs as you can. It's much more comfortable. Don't be afraid to loosen your steel grip on the guide ropes, because they're not what holds you anyway. In the air, you are as free as a bird and the unique view is phenomenal. You don't have time to fret about going up. The boat revs and you're airborne almost immediately. Once you're up, you feel very secure. The technology is simple, straightforward, and safe. Relax and have a ball. Cost is $48 for this 8- to 10-minute joy ride.

Other companies include **West Maui Parasail,** tel. 661-4060; **UFO Parasail,** tel. 661-7UFO; and **Para-Sail Hawaii,** tel. 661-5322.

Jet Skiing

To try this exciting sport, contact: **Kaanapali Jet Ski** at Whaler's Village, tel. 667-7851; or **Jammin Jet Skis** in Kihei, tel. 879-6662, with rates $30-60, seasonal prices for the use of Kawasakis or Yamaha Wave Runners.

Water-Skiing

Kaanapali Water Skiing, tel. 661-3324, can

TENNIS COURTS OF MAUI

COUNTY COURTS

Under jurisdiction of the Department of Parks & Recreation, 200 High St., Wailuku, Maui, tel. 244-7750; there are three additional locations around the island. Courts listed are in or near visitor areas.

NAME	LOCATION	NO. OF COURTS	LIGHTED
Hana	Hana Ball Park	2	Yes
Kahului	Kahului Community Center	2	Yes
Kihei	Kalami Park	4	Yes
Kihei	Seaside of Maui Sunset Condo	4	Yes
Lahaina	Lahaina Civic Center	8	Yes
Lahaina	Malu-ulu-olele Park	4	Yes
Makawao	Eddie Tam Memorial Center	2	Yes
Pukalani	Pukalani Community Center	2	Yes
Wailuku	Maui Community College tel. 244-9181 courts available after school hours	4	No
Wailuku	Wailuku Community Center	7	Yes
Wailuku	Wailuku War Memorial	4	Yes

HOTEL AND PRIVATE COURTS OPEN TO THE PUBLIC (fees vary)

NAME	LOCATION	NO. OF COURTS	LIGHTED
Kaanapali	Maui Marriott Resort	5	No
Kaanapali	Hyatt Regency	5	Yes
Kaanapali	Royal Lahaina Resort	11	six are
Kaanapali	Sheraton Maui Hotel	3	Yes
Kaanapali	Whaler	4	No
Kapalua	Tennis Club	10	four are
Kapalua	Tennis Garden	10	four are
Kihei	Luana Kai	6	No
Kihei	Maui Schooner Resort	4	No
Kihei	Maui Sunset	2	No
Makena	Makena Tennis Club	6	No
Napili Bay	Napili Kai Beach Club	2	No
Wailea	Wailea Tennis Club	14	three are

GOLF COURSES OF MAUI

COURSE	HOLES	PAR	YARDS	RATES	CART
Kapalua Golf Club*					
Kapalua, HI 96791; tel. 669-8044					
Bay Course	18	72	6,151	$110	Incl.
Village Course	18	71	6,601	$110	Incl.
Plantation Course	18	73	6547	$110	Incl.
Makena Golf Course*	18	72	6,823	$110	Incl.
Kihei, HI 96753; tel. 879-3344	36	72	6,876	$110	
Maui Country Club					
Paia, HI 96779; tel. 877-0616 (Monday only for visitors)					
Front Course	9	37	3,148	$50	Incl.
Back Course	9	37	3,247	$50	Incl.
Pukalani Country Club	18	72	6,494	$62	$11
Pukalani, HI 96788; tel. 572-1314					
Royal Kaanapali*					
Kaanapali, HI 96761; tel. 661-3691					
North Course	18	71	6,136	$110	Incl.
South Course	18	71	6,067	$110	Incl.
Sandalwood Country Club	18	72	6,000	$65	Incl.
Wailuku, HI 96793; tel. 242-4653,					
Silversword Golf Course*	18	71	6,400	$65	Incl.
Kihei, HI 96753; tel. 874-0777					
Waiehu Municipal Golf Course	18	72	6,330	$25	$12.50
Waiehu, HI 96793; tel. 243-7300					
Waikapa Valley Country Club	18	72	6,200	$85	Incl.
tel. 244-7888					
Wailea Golf Club					
Wailea, HI 96753; tel. 879-2966					
Blue Course	18	72	6,152	$125	Incl.
Orange Course	18	72	6,304	$125	Incl.

* Weekday and special twilight rates in effect. Call for details.

arrange an outing with lessons. Another place to try is **Lahaina Water Ski,** tel. 661-5988, offering professional instructors and a wide range of equipment.

HORSEBACK RIDING

Those who love sightseeing from the back of a horse are in for a big treat on Maui. Stables dot the island, so you have a choice of terrain for your trail ride: breathtaking Haleakala Crater, or the backwoods ride at the Seven Sacred Pools. Unfortunately, none of this comes cheap. A bale of alfalfa, which goes for under $5 on the Mainland, fetches $18-22 on Maui. If you plan to do some serious riding, it's advisable to bring jeans (jogging-suit bottoms will do) and a pair of boots, or at least jogging shoes.

The Rainbow Ranch

The Rainbow Ranch is operated by Kimo Harlacher and his top hands. Beginners ride daily at 9 a.m. for $30 on gentle horses; experienced riders can take sunset, mountain, pineapple field, or extended trips for $45-65. The West

Maui Adventure, $55 for two hours, runs through the foothills of the mountains. Picnic rides (bring your own) for $50 depart at 10 a.m. and return at 1 p.m. No dress code, but long pants and closed-toe shoes required. Rainbow Ranch, P.O. Box 10066, Lahaina, HI 96761, tel. 669-4991, is located at mile marker 29 along Rt. 30 toward Kapalua.

Makena Stables

Makena Stables, tel. 879-0244, is located just past Polo Beach in Wailea on Old Makena Road; owners Helaine and Pat Borge will take you on a two-and-a-half-hour ride through low-elevation rangeland and lava flows, and along the mountain trails of Ulupalakua Ranch.

Haleakala And Environs

A few Upcountry companies offer trail rides through the crater or over the mountain. Wear *warm* clothes. Here are some of the best. **Charley's Trailride and Pack Trips** takes you on day-trips or overnight camping trips atop Haleakala, arranging for cabins and supplying all meals. The company is run by Charles Aki, c/o Kaupo Store, Hana, HI 96713, tel. 248-8209. Rates on rides for more than two people (rates for only two people are higher) are: $150 per person per night, which includes food and cabin fees or camping equipment if a campsite is used; $125 per night without food included. Early reservations are required, along with a $75 deposit well in advance. A hat, warm clothing, rain ponchos, and boots are recommended for all rides. Meet at Charley's residence in Kaupo for a 9 a.m. departure.

Pony Express Tours offers Maui's only trail rides into Haleakala Crater; full day $123, partial day $98, lunch provided. One- and two-hour rides ($25 and $45 respectively) are also offered across private ranch land high on the slope of this volcanic mountain. Contact Pony Express Tours, P.O. Box 535, Kula, HI 96790, tel. 667-2200.

Thompson Ranch Riding Stables, a family-operated stable that will even mount up children under 10, guides you over the slopes of Haleakala on one of Maui's oldest cattle ranches. Contact Thompson Stables, Thompson Rd., Kula, HI 96790, tel. 878-1910.

Adventures On Horseback offers waterfall rides along the north coast over lands of a private estate; the maximum is six riders. For reservations and information, call 242-7445, or write P.O. Box 1771, Makawao, Maui, HI 96768.

Hotel Hana-Maui Stables

The hotel guests are given priority for use of the horses, but you can call ahead to arrange a trail ride on this truly magnificent end of the island. For information call 248-7238.

TENNIS AND GOLF

Maui specializes in these two sports. The high-class resort areas of Kaanapali and Wailea are built around golf courses, and tennis courts are available all over the island. See the accompanying charts for more information.

CAMPING AND HIKING

A major aspect of the "Maui experience" is found in the simple beauty of nature and the outdoors. Some visitors come to Maui to luxuriate at resorts and dine in fine restaurants, but everyone heads for the sand and surf, and most are captivated by the lush mountainous interior. What better way to savor this natural beauty than by hiking slowly through it or pitching a tent in the middle of it? Maui offers a full range of hiking and camping, and what's more, most of it is easily accessible and free. Camping facilities are located near many choice beaches and amid the most scenic areas of the island. They range in amenities from full-housekeeping cabins to primitive "hike-in" sites. Some restrictions to hiking apply because much of the land is privately owned, so you may require advance permission to hike. But plenty of public access trails along the coast and deep into the interior would fill the itineraries of even the most intrepid trekkers. If you enjoy the great outdoors on the Mainland, you'll be thrilled by these "mini-continents," where in

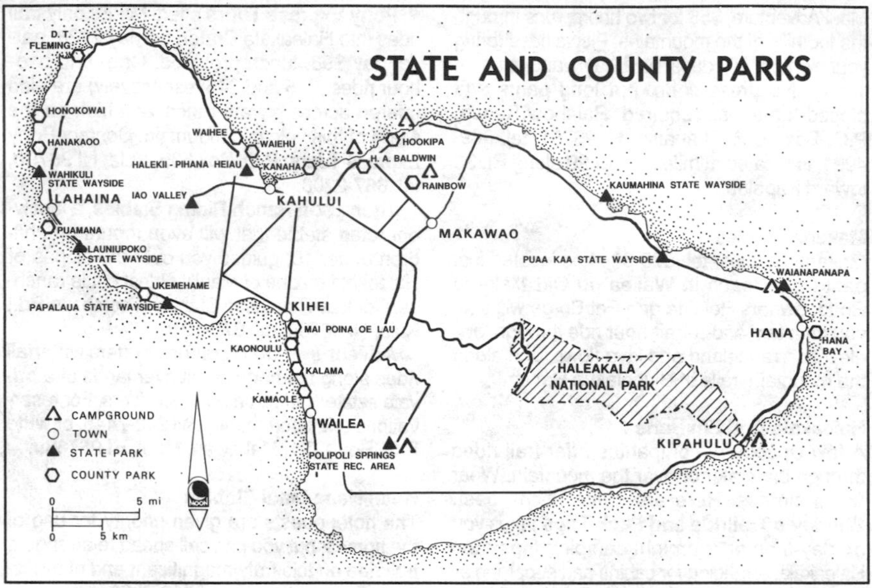

STATE AND COUNTY PARKS

one day you can go from the frosty summits of alpine wonderlands down into baking cactus-covered deserts and emerge through jungle foliage onto a sun-soaked subtropical shore.

Note: Descriptions of individual state parks, county beach parks, and Haleakala National Park, along with directions on how to get there, are given under "Sights" in the respective travel chapters.

HALEAKALA NATIONAL PARK

Camping at Haleakala National Park is free, but there is an automobile entrance fee of $4, with a senior-citizen discount. Permits are not needed to camp at Hosmer Grove, just a short drive from park headquarters, or at Kipahulu Campground along the coastal road 10 miles south of Hana. Camping is on a first-come, first-served basis, and there's an official three-day stay limit, but it's a loose count, especially at Kipahulu, which is almost always empty. The case is much different at the campsites located inside Haleakala Crater proper. On the floor of the crater are two primitive tenting campsites, one at Paliku on the east side and the other at Holua on the north rim. For these you'll need a wilderness permit from park headquarters. Because of ecological considerations, only 25 campers per night can stay at each site, and a three-night, four-day per month maximum stay is strictly enforced, with tenting allowed at any one site for only two consecutive nights. However, because of the strenuous hike involved, campsites are open most of the time. You must be totally self-sufficient, and equipped for cold-weather camping, to be comfortable at these two sites.

Also, Paliku, Holua, and another site at Kapalaoa on the south rim offer cabins. Fully self-contained with stoves, water, and nearby pit toilets, they can handle a maximum of 12 campers each. Cots are provided, but you must have your own warm bedding. The same maximum-stay limits apply as in the campgrounds. Stays at these cabins are at a premium—they're popular with visitors and residents alike. They're geared toward the group, with rates at $19 s, $23 d, $9 extra person (limit 12). To have a chance at getting a cabin you must make reservations, so write well in advance for complete information to: Haleakala National Park, P.O. Box 369, Makawao, HI 96768, or call 572-9306. For general information write: National Park Service, 300 Ala Moana Blvd., Honolulu, HI 96850, or call 546-7584.

STATE PARKS

There are nine state parks on Maui, managed by the Department of Land and Natural Resources through their Division of State Parks. These facilities include everything from historical sites to wildland parks accessible only by trail. Some are only for looking at, some are restricted to day use, and two of them have overnight camping. Polipoli and Waianapanapa offer free tenting, and self-contained cabins are available on a sliding fee; reservations highly necessary. Permits are required at each, and RVs technically are not allowed.

Park Rules

Tent-camping permits are free and good for a maximum stay of five nights at any one park. A permit to the same person for the same park is again available only after 30 days have elapsed. Campgrounds are open every day. You can arrive after 2 p.m. and you should check out by 11 a.m. The minimum age for park permits is 18, and anyone under that age must be accompanied by an adult. Alcoholic beverages are prohibited, as is nude sunbathing. Plants and wildlife are protected, but reasonable amounts of fruits and seeds may be gathered for personal consumption. Fires are allowed on cookstoves or in designated pits only. Dogs and other pets must be under control at all times and are not permitted to run around unleashed. Hunting and freshwater fishing are allowed in season only with a license; ocean fishing is permitted unless prohibited by posting. Permits are required for certain trails, so check at the state parks office.

Cabins And Shelters

Housekeeping cabins are available as indicated on the accompanying chart. As with camping, permits are required, with the same five-day maximum stay. Reservations are absolutely necessary, especially at Waianapanapa, and a 50% deposit at time of confirmation is required. There's a three-day cancellation requirement for refunds, and payment is to be made in cash, money order, certified check, or personal check, the latter only if it's received 30 days before arrival so that cashing procedures are possible. The balance is due on date of arrival. Cabins are on a sliding scale of $10 s, $14 d, and about $5 for each person thereafter. They are completely furnished down to the utensils, with heaters for cold weather and private baths.

Permit-Issuing Office

Permits can be reserved up to one year in advance, but you must confirm at least seven days prior to arrival by writing a timely letter including your name, address, phone number, number of persons in your party, type of permit requested, and duration of your stay. They can be picked up on arrival with proof of identification. Office hours are Mon.-Fri. 8 a.m.-4:15 p.m. Usually, tent-camping permits are no problem to secure on the day you arrive, but reserving one ensures you a space and alleviates anxiety. The permits are available from the Maui (Molokai also) Division of State Parks, 54 S. High St., Wailuku, HI 96793, tel. 243-5354; or write P.O. Box 1049 Wailuku, HI 96793.

COUNTY PARKS

There are 16 county parks scattered primarily along Maui's coastline, and because of their locations, they're generally referred to as **beach parks.** Most are day-use parks only, where visitors fish, swim, snorkel, surf, picnic, and sunbathe, but two have overnight camping. The rules governing use of these county parks are just about the same as those for state parks. The main difference is that besides requiring a use permit, county beach parks charge a fee for overnight use. Again, the differences between individual parks are too numerous to mention, but the majority have a central pavilion for cooking, restrooms, cold-water showers, and individual firepits and picnic tables. Electricity is usually available only at the central pavilion. RVs are allowed to park in appropriate spaces. One safety point to consider is that beach parks are open to the general public and most are used with regularity. This means that quite a few people pass through, which increases your chances of encountering a hassle or running into a rip-off.

STATE PARKS OF MAUI

PARK NAME	RESTROOMS	OVERLOOKS	PICNIC TABLES	OUTDOOR STOVES	DRINKING WATER	SWIMMING	SHELTERS	TENT CAMPING	CABINS	SHOWERS
Halekii-Pihana Heiau State Historical Monument		•								
Iao Valley State Park	•	•			•		•			
Kaumahina State Wayside	•	•	•	•	•					
Keanae-Wailua Lookout		•								
Launiupoko State Wayside	•		•	•	•	•				•
Papalaua State Wayside						•				
Polipoli Springs State Recreation Area	•		•	•	•			•	•	
Wahikuli State Wayside	•		•	•	•	•	•			•
Waianapanapa State Park	•	•	•	•	•	•	•	•	•	•

COUNTY PARKS OF MAUI

PARK NAME	RESTROOMS	OVERLOOKS	PICNIC TABLES	OUTDOOR STOVES	DRINKING WATER	SWIMMING	SHELTERS	TENT CAMPING	CABINS	SHOWERS
D.T. Fleming	•		•		•	•				•
H. A. Baldwin	•		•	•	•	•	•	•		•
Hana Bay	•		•	•	•	•	•			•
Hanakaoo						•				
Honokowai	•		•		•					•
Hookipa	•	•	•	•	•		•			•
Kalama	•		•	•	•	•	•			•
Kamaole	•					•				
Kanaha	•		•	•	•	•	•			•
Kaonoulu	•		•	•	•	•				
Mai Poina Oe Iau	•		•	•	•	•	•			•
Rainbow	•		•	•	•	•	•			
Puamana					•					
Ukumehame					•					
Waiehu										
Waihee	•		•	•	•					

Fees And Permits

The fees are quite reasonable at $3 per night per person, 50 cents for children, with no more than three consecutive nights at any park. To get a permit and pay your fees for use of a county beach park, either write in advance or visit the following issuing office (Mon.-Fri. 9 a.m.-5 p.m.): Deparment of Parks and Recreation, Recreation Division, 1580 Kaahumanu Ave. (in the War Memorial Gym), Wailuku, HI 96793, tel. 243-7389.

HIKING

The hiking on Maui is excellent; most times you have the trails to yourself, and hikes can range widely from a family saunter to a strenuous trek. Most trails are on public lands. Some cross private property, not a problem on well-established routes, but for others you'll need special permission.

Haleakala Hikes

The most spectacular hikes on Maui are through Haleakala Crater's 30 miles of trail. **Halemauu Trail** is 10 miles long, beginning three miles up the mountain from park headquarters. It quickly winds down a switchback descending 1,400 feet to the crater floor. It passes Holua Cabin and goes six more miles to Paliku Cabin, offering expansive views of Koolau Gap along the way. A spur leads to Sliding Sands Trail and a short walk to the visitors center. Halemauu Trail also passes Silversword Loop and the Bottomless Pit, two attractions in the crater. **Sliding Sands Trail** might be considered the main trail, beginning from the visitors center at the summit and leading 10 miles over the crater floor to Paliku Cabin. It passes Kapalaoa Cabin en route and offers the best walk through the crater, with up-close views of cinder cones, lava flows, and unique vegetation. **Kaupo Trail** begins at Paliku Cabin and descends rapidly through the Kaupo Gap, depositing you in the semi-ghost town of Kaupo. Below 4,000 feet the lava is rough and the vegetation thick. You pass through the private lands of the Kaupo Ranch along well-marked trails. Without a pick-up arranged at the end, this is a tough one because the hitching is scanty.

West Maui Trails

The most frequented trails on West Maui are at Iao Needle. From the parking area you can follow the **Tableland Trail** for two miles, which gives you beautiful panoramas of Iao Valley as you steadily climb to the tableland above, or you can descend to the valley floor and follow Iao Stream to a series of small but secluded swimming holes. **Waihee Ridge Trail** is a three-mile trek leading up the windward slopes of the West Maui Mountains. Follow Rt. 34 around the backside to Maluhia Road and turn up it to the Boy Scout camp. From here the trail rises swiftly to 2,560 feet. The views of Waihee Gorge are spectacular. The **Waihee Trail** runs into this narrow valley. North of the town of Waihee turn left at the Oki Place road sign. Proceed as far as you are able to drive, park your car, and walk up along the flume. This level track takes you over two suspension footbridges, through a bamboo forest, and under huge banyan trees until you reach the head dam. By crossing the river here, you can follow a smaller trail farther up the valley. **Kahakuloa Valley Trail** begins from this tiny forgotten fishing village on Maui's backside along Rt. 34. Start from the schoolhouse, passing burial caves and old terraced agricultural sites. Fruit trees line the way to trails ending two miles above the town.

Kula And Upcountry Trails

Most of these trails form a network through and around Polipoli Springs State Recreation Area. **Redwood Trail,** 1.7 miles, passes through a magnificent stand of redwoods, past the ranger station and down to an old Civilian Conservation Corps camp where there's a rough old shelter. **Tie Trail,** a half mile, joins Redwood Trail with **Plum Trail,** so named because of its numerous plum trees, which bear during the summer. **Skyline Trail,** 6.5 miles, starts atop Haleakala at 9,750 feet, passing through the southwest rift and eventually joining the **Haleakala Ridge Trail,** 1.6 miles, at the 6,500-foot level; it then descends through a series of switchbacks. You can join the Plum Trail or continue to the shelter at the end. Both the Skyline and Ridge trails offer superb vistas of Maui.

Others throughout the area include: **Polipoli,** 0.6 miles, passing through the famous forests of the area; **Boundary Trail,** four miles, leading from the Kula Forest Reserve to the ranger's cabin, passing numerous gulches still supporting native trees and shrubs; **Waiohuli Trail,** descending the mountain to join Boundary Trail and overlooking Keokea and Kihei with a shelter at the end; and **Waiakoa Trail,** seven miles, beginning at the Kula Forest Reserve Access Road. It ascends Haleakala to the 7,800-foot level and then descends through a series of switchbacks, covering rugged territory and passing a natural cave shelter. It eventually meets up with the three-mile **Waiakoa Loop Trail.** All of these trails offer intimate forest views of native and introduced trees, and breathtaking views of the Maui coastline far below.

Coastal Trails

Along Maui's southernmost tip the **King's Highway Coastal Trail,** 5.5 miles, leads from La Perouse Bay through the rugged and desolate lava flow of 1790, the time of Maui's last volcanic eruption. Kihei Road leading to the trail gets extremely rugged past La Perouse and should not be attempted by car, but is easy on foot. It leads over smooth stepping stones that were at one time trudged by royal tax collectors. The trail heads inland and passes many ancient Hawaiian stone walls and stone foundation sites. Spur trails lead down to the sea, including an overview of Cape Hanamanioa and its Coast Guard lighthouse. The trail eventually ends at private land. **Hana Waianapanapa Coastal Trail,** three miles, is at the opposite side of East Maui. You start from Waianapanapa State Park or from a gravel road near Hana Bay and again you follow the flat, laid stones of the King's Highway. The trail is well maintained but fairly rugged due to lava and cinders. You pass natural arches, a string of *heiau,* blowholes, and caves. The vegetation is lush, and long fingers of black lava stretch out into cobalt-blue waters.

Hiking Tour

This special Maui tour is an extraordinary one-man show. **Hike Maui,** P.O. Box 330969, Kahului, HI 96733 (tel. 879-5270), as its name implies, offers walking tours to Maui's best scenic areas accompanied by Ken Schmitt, a professional nature guide. Ken has dedicated years to hiking Maui and has accumulated an unbelievable amount of knowledge about this awesome island. He's proficient in Maui archaeology, botany, geology, anthropology, zoology, history, oceanography, and ancient Hawaiian cosmology. Moreover, he is a man of dynamic and gracious spirit who has tuned in to the soul of Maui. He hikes every day and is superbly fit, and though he will tailor his hikes for anyone, good physical conditioning is essential. Ken's hikes are actually workshops in Maui's natural history. As you walk along, Ken imparts his knowledge but never intrudes on the beauty of the site itself.

The hikes require a minimum of two people and a maximum of six. Ken offers gourmet breakfasts, lunches, and snacks with an emphasis on natural health foods. All special equipment, including snorkel gear and camping gear, is provided. The hikes take in sights from Hana to West Maui to the summit of Haleakala, and range from the moderate to the hardy ability level. Half-day hikes last about five hours and all-day hikes go for at least 12 hours. The rates vary from $75 (about half that for children) to $110. By special arrangement, overnighters can be arranged with prices quoted upon request. A day with Ken Schmitt is a classic outdoor experience. Don't miss it.

SHOPPING

This chapter provides information about shopping on Maui for general merchandise, books, arts, crafts, and specialty items. Specific shops are listed in the "Shopping" section of each travel chapter. The following overview of what's available and where should get your pockets twitching and credit cards smoldering. Happy bargain hunting!

SHOPPING CENTERS

Those who enjoy one-stop shopping will be happy with the choices in Maui's various malls. You'll find familiar department stores as well as small shops featuring island-made goods. The following are Maui's main shopping malls. For food markets and health food stores see "Food" later in this chapter.

Kahului/Wailuku

Along Kaahumanu Avenue, you'll find **Kaahumanu Shopping Center,** tel. 877-3369, the largest on the island. Here's everything from **Sears** and **Liberty House** to **Sew Special,** a tiny store featuring island fabrics. The mall is full-service with apparel stores, shoe stores, computer centers, art shops, music stores, a gourmet coffee shop, and **Waldenbooks.** You can eat at numerous restaurants, buy ice-cream cones, or enjoy a movie at **Holiday Theaters.**

Down the road is **Maui Mall,** tel. 877-5523, featuring photo centers, **Longs Drugs** for everything from aspirin to film, **Woolworth, JCPenney, Waldenbooks,** sports and swimwear shops, and numerous restaurants and food outlets. Sandwiched between these two modern facilities is **Kahului Shopping Center,** tel. 877-5527. It's definitely down-home with old-timers sitting around outside. The shops here aren't fancy, but they are authentic and you can make some offbeat purchases by strolling through.

Across the street from Maui Mall is the **Old Kahului Store,** a refurbished mini-mall with apparel shops, restaurant, deli, surf shop, video store, and other specialty shops.

Lahaina And Vicinity

You can't beat Lahaina's Front Street for the best, worst, most artistic, and tackiest shopping on Maui. This is where the tourists are, so this is where the shops are . . . shoulder to shoulder. The list is endless, but you'll find art studios, galleries, kites, T-shirts galore, scrimshaw, jewelry, silks, boutiques, leathers, souvenir junk, eelskins, and even a permanent tattoo memory of Maui. No wimps allowed! Front Street has the best special-interest shopping on Maui (see "Shopping" under "Lahaina" in the West Maui chapter).

The following are the local malls. **The Wharf Shopping Center** on Front Street, tel. 661-8748, has a multitude of eating establishments, as well as stores and boutiques in its multilevel shopping facility. When you need a break, get a coffee and browse the fine selections at The Whaler's Book Shoppe—great selections and a top-notch snack bar. **Lahaina Market Place,** tel. 667-2636, tucked away on Front Street, features established shops along with open-air stalls. **Lahaina Square Shopping Center,** tel. 242-4400, **Lahaina Shopping Center,** and **Lahaina Business Center,** all between Rt. 30 and Front Street, have various shops, and are probably the most *local* of the Lahaina malls. The **505 Front Street Mall,** tel. 667-2514, at the south end of Front Street, offers distinctive and quiet shopping away from the frenetic activity.

The Lahaina Cannery Shopping Mall, tel. 661-5304, is a newly opened center on Lahaina's west end, featuring restaurants, boutiques, specialty shops, fast food, and plenty of bargains. It's the largest mall on West Maui and has some of the best shopping under one roof on the island. The newest center, and potentially the largest, is the **Lahaina Center,** located along Front Street at Papalaua Street. While the center is not yet full, its stores include Hilo Hatties, Lahaina Licks, and a Hard Rock Cafe.

Kaanapali And Vicinity

Whaler's Village, tel. 661-4567, is a Kaanapali mall set right on the ocean, which features a decent self-guided museum. It has various eateries, bottle shops, boutiques, galleries, a **Liberty House,** and a **Waldenbooks.** It's a great place at which to stroll, shop, and learn a few things about Maui's past. The **Sheraton, Marriott, Westin Maui, Hyatt Regency,** and **Royal Lahaina** hotels all have shopping arcades. You'll need a suitcase stuffed with money to buy anything there, but it's a blast just walking around the grounds and checking out the big-ticket items.

Up the road from Kaanapali is the **Kahana Gateway Shopping Center,** just outside the village of Honokowai. Here you'll find one of Maui's finest restaurants, a hardware store, a number of apparel shops, and a sporting goods store. Farther along in Kapalua is the recently opened **Napili Plaza** with restaurants, shops, and travel services.

Kihei And Wailea

Azeka Place, tel. 874-8400, is along Kihei Road. Here there's food shopping, a **Liberty House,** a dive shop, and an activities center, among many other specialty shops. Strung along Kihei Road, one after another, are **Kukui Center, Kihei Town Center, Dolphin Shopping Plaza, Kamaole Beach Center, ABC Shopping Center, Kamaole Shopping Center,** and **Rainbow Mall,** where restaurants, food outlets, boutiques, and gift shops can be found. Kihei's newest malls include **Azeka Place II, Longs Shopping Center, The Kukui Center,** and the **Kihei Gateway Plaza.** The exclusive **Wailea Shopping Village,** tel. 879-4474, has an assortment of both chic and affordable boutiques near the Inter-Continental, Stouffer's, Four Seasons, and Grand Wailea Resort and Spa hotels, all of which have shopping arcades of their own.

SPECIALTY SHOPS, ART, AND NEAT THINGS

Some truly nifty and distinctive stores are wedged in among Maui's run-of-the-mill shopping centers; however, for real treasures you'll find the solitary little shop the best. Lahaina's Front Street has the greatest concentration of top-notch boutiques; others are dotted here and there around the island. The following is a sampling of the best; many more are listed in the individual chapters.

Tattered sails on a rotted mast, tattooed sea-dogs in wide-striped jerseys, grim-faced Yankee captains squinting at the horizon, exotic (probably extinct) birds on the wing, flowers and weather-bent trees, and the beautiful, open faces of Polynesians staring out from ancient days are faithfully preserved at **Lahaina Printsellers Ltd.,** one of the most unusual purveyors of art on Maui. Their six shops, like mini-museums, are hung with original engravings, drawings, maps, charts, and naturalist sketches ranging in age from 150 to 400 years. Each, marked with an authenticity label, can come from anywhere in the world, but the Hawaiiana collection is amazing in its depth. Many works feature a nautical theme, reminiscent of the daring explorers who opened the Pacific. The Lahaina Printsellers have been collecting for over 15 years, and are the largest collectors of material relating to Captain Cook in the entire Pacific Basin. Prices range from $25 for the smallest antique print, up to $150,000 for a rare museum-quality work. The Lahaina Printsellers keep Maui's art alive by representing modern artists as well. Their production end is located at the historic Hale Aloha, an old-time meeting house, at 636 Luakini St., Lahaina, tel. 661-5120, (800) 669-7843, free brochure upon request. Three of the shops are in malls—one at the Whaler's Village in Kaanapali, tel. 667-7617, another at the Wailea Shopping Village, tel. 879-1567, and the third at Lahaina Cannery Mall, tel. 667-7843—with the fourth shop located at the Grand Hyatt Wailea, tel. 874-9310. The Cannery Mall Shop features a tri-weekly demonstration of *intaglio,* engraving and printing, by renowned artist Steve Strickland. This fascinating free demonstration is now being offered Monday, Wednesday, and Friday at 2 p.m., but times may vary so call to confirm.

For a unique memento of Maui, have your photo taken along Front Street near Pioneer Square. Here, you'll become the human perch for macaws and cockatoos. The birds are very tame, natural hams, and are the only thing on Maui guaranteed to be more colorful than your Hawaiian shirt. For $15-20 you can have your picture taken and your photos delivered the next day. You also might run across "Bud the Birdman." Strolling the streets of Lahaina, with birds perched on his shoulders or hanging from his fingers, he will take photos of you with his birds and deliver the pictures the next day.

Paia is quickly becoming the unofficial art center of Maui, as well as the windsurfing capital of Hawaii. Lahaina has slicker galleries, but you come much closer to the source in Paia. The **Maui Crafts Guild** is an exemplary crafts shop that displays the best in local island art. All artists must be selected by active members before their works can be displayed. All materials used must be natural, with an emphasis on those found only in Hawaii. Located nearby is **Hana Hou Gallery,** hung with distinctive island works, and **Deybra's,** featuring the whimsical art of Deybra. A few miles past Paia, you turn up an old road to the **Old Pauwela Cannery,** where artists like Piero Resta have honeycombed studios into this massive old building.

Upcountry's Makawao is a wonderful and crazy combination of old-time *paniolo,* matured hippies who now worry about their kids using drugs, and sushi-munching yuppies. This hodgepodge makes for a town with tack shops, hardware stores, exclusive boutiques, art shops, gourmet coffee shops, and nondairy guaranteed-to-be-good-for-you ice-cream stores. All are strung along two Dodge City-like streets.

Near Kahului Airport visit the **Pink and Black Coral Factory.** Local craftspeople make distinctive coral jewelry from the amazing corals found under Maui's seas. Each year some divers lose their lives while harvesting these fantastic corals. **Maui Swap Meet** at Maui County Fairgrounds in Kahului, off Puunene Avenue (Hwy. 35), is open every Saturday 8 a.m.-1 p.m.; admission 50 cents. Great junk!

Wailuku is Maui's attic turned out on the street. About five odd little shops on Market Street display every kind of knickknack, curio, art treasure, white elephant, grotesque and sublime piece of furniture, jewelry, stuffed toy, game, or oddity that ever floated, sailed, flew, or washed up on Maui's beaches.

ACCOMMODATIONS

With over 17,000 rooms available, and more being built every day, Maui is second only to Oahu in the number of visitors it can accommodate. There's a tremendous concentration of condos on Maui (approximately 10,000 units predominately in the Kihei area), plenty of hotels (the majority in Kaanapali), and a growing number of bed and breakfasts. Camping is limited to a handful of parks, but what it lacks in number it easily makes up for in quality.

Your Choices

Over 80 hotels and condos have sprouted on West Maui, from Kapalua to Lahaina. The most expensive are in **Kaanapali** and include the Hyatt Regency, Marriott, Westin Maui, and Sheraton, strung along some of Maui's best beaches. The older condos just west in Honokowai are cheaper, with a mixture of expensive and moderate as you head toward Kapalua. **Lahaina** itself offers only a handful of places to stay: condos at both ends of town, the famous nonluxury Pioneer Inn, and four hotels. Most people find the pace a little too hectic; you couldn't get more in the middle of *it* if you tried. **Maalaea Bay,** between Lahaina and Kihei, has 11 quiet condos. Prices are reasonable, the beaches are fair, and you're within striking distance of the action in either direction.

Kihei is "condo row," with well over 50 of them along the six miles of Kihei Avenue, plus a few hotels. This is where you'll find top-notch beaches and the best deals on Maui. **Wailea** just up the road is expensive, but the hotels here are world-class and the secluded beaches are gorgeous. **Kahului** often takes the rap for being an unattractive place to stay on Maui. It isn't all that bad. You're within striking distance of Maui's best sights, and the airport is minutes away for people staying only a short time. Prices are cheaper and Kanaha Beach is a sleeper, with great sand, surf, and few visitors. **Hana** is an experience in itself. You can camp, rent a cabin, or stay at an exclusive hotel; always reserve in advance. Consider arranging your stay on Maui so that you can spend your last few nights in Hana. Then you can really soak up this wonderful area without worrying about rushing back along the Hana Highway.

Tips

Like all of Hawaii, Maui has an **off-season** that runs from after Easter to just before Christmas; the fall months are particularly beautiful. During this period you can save 25% or more on accommodations. If you'll be staying for over a week, get a condo with cooking facilities or a room with at least a refrigerator; you can save a bundle on food costs. You'll pay more for an ocean view, but along Maui's entire south shore from Kapalua to Wailea, you'll have a cheaper and cooler room if you're mountainside, away from the sun.

Hotel/Condo Booking And Reservations

The following is a partial list of booking agents handling a number of properties on Maui. **Aston Hotels and Resorts,** 2250 Kuhio Ave., Honolulu, HI 96815, tel. 931-1400, (800) 922-7866 Mainland, (800) 445-6633 Canada, (800) 321-2558 Hawaii, offers plenty of condos from Kaanapali to Kihei. Some are Aston's while others are managed by this professional organization. **Maui Condominium and Home Realty,** 2511 S. Kihei Rd., P.O. Box 1840 Kihei, HI 96753, tel. 879-5445, (800) 822-4409 Mainland and Canada, has over 300 listings in all price categories with most in the Kihei area. **AA Oceanfront Condo Rentals,** 2439 S. Kihei Rd., Kihei, HI 96753, tel. 879-7288, (800) 488-6004, has over three dozen units from Kihei to Makena priced $65-150. **Condominium Rentals Hawaii,** 362 Huku Lii Pl., Kihei, HI 96753, tel. 879-2778, (800) 367-5242, offers five properties in and around Kihei at $60-210.

Note: Also see "Bed and Breakfast" under "Accommodations" in the General Introduction.

FOOD

FOOD MARKETS AND SUPERMARKETS

If you're shopping for general food supplies and are not interested in gourmet, specialty, or organic items, you'll save money by shopping at the big-name supermarkets located in Lahaina, Kahului, and Kihei, often in malls. Smaller towns have general stores, which are adequate but a bit more expensive. You can also find convenience items at commissaries in many condos and hotels, but these should be used only for snack foods or when absolutely necessary, because the prices are too high.

Kahului

The greatest number of supermarkets is found in Kahului. They're all conveniently located along Rt. 32 (Kaahumanu Avenue) in or adjacent to the three malls, one right after the other. **Foodland,** open seven days 8:30 a.m.-10 p.m., is in the **Kaahumanu Shopping Center.** Just down the road in the **Kahului Shopping Center** is the ethnic **Ah Fooks** (open daily 8 a.m.-7 p.m., closes early Saturday and Sunday), specializing in Japanese, Chinese, and Hawaiian foods. Farther along in the **Maui Mall** is **Star Market,** open Mon-Sat. 8:30 a.m.-9 p.m., and until 7 p.m. Sunday. Just behind the Maui Mall on E. Kamehameha Avenue is a **Safeway.** Wailuku doesn't have shopping malls, but if you're taking an excursion around the top of West Maui, make a "last chance" stop at **T.K. Supermarket** at the end of N. Market Street in the Happy Valley area. They're open 7 days, but close early on Sunday afternoons. **Ooka Supermarket,** just off Main Street, is the biggest and most well-stocked in town. Its hours are Mon.-Wed. and Saturday 7:30 a.m.-8 p.m., Thursday and Friday until 9 p.m., and Sunday until 6 p.m.

Kihei

In Kihei you've got a choice of three markets, all strung along S. Kihei Road, the main drag. **Foodland** in the Kihei Town Center, and **Star Market** just down the road, offer standard shopping. The most interesting is **Azeka's Market** in Azeka Plaza. This market is an institution, and is very famous for its specially prepared (uncooked) ribs, perfect for a barbecue. In Wailea you'll find **Wailea Pantry** in the Wailea Shopping Village, open seven days a week, 8 a.m.-7 p.m., but it's an exclusive area and the prices will make you sob.

Lahaina And Vicinity

In Lahaina you can shop at **Foodland** in Lahaina Square off Rt. 30. More interesting is **Nagasako's** in the Lahaina Shopping Center off Front Street. They've got all you need, plus a huge selection of Chinese and Japanese items. Nagasako's is open daily 7 a.m.-9 p.m., and Sunday until 7 p.m. If you're staying at a condo and doing your own cooking, the largest and generally least expensive supermarket on West Maui is the **Safeway,** open daily, 24 hours, in The Cannery Shopping Mall. West of Lahaina in Honokowai, you'll find the **Food Pantry.** Although there are a few sundry stores in various hotels in Kaanapali, this is the only real place to shop. It's open daily 8 a.m.-9 p.m. In Napili, pick up supplies at **Napili Village Store,** a bit expensive, but well-stocked and convenient. In Olowalu, south of Lahaina, you can pick up limited items at the **Olowalu General Store.**

Hana

In Hana is the **Hana Store,** which carries all the necessities and even has a selection of health foods and imported beers. Open daily 7:30 a.m.-6:30 p.m.

Around And About

Other stores where you might pick up supplies include the following. **Komoda's** in Makawao is famous throughout Hawaii for their cream buns, which are sold out by 8 a.m. At **Pukalani Superette** in Pukalani, open seven days a week, you can pick up supplies and food to go, including sushi. In Paia try **Nagata's** or **Paia General Store** on the main drag.

HEALTH FOOD

Those into organic foods, fresh vegetables, natural vitamins, and takeout snack bars have it made on Maui. Try the following: in Wailuku, **Down to Earth** is an excellent health food store complete with vitamins, bulk foods, and a snack bar. This Krishna-oriented market, on the corner of Central and Vineyard, is open Mon.-Fri. 8 a.m.-6 p.m., to 5 p.m. Saturday, and to 4 p.m. Sunday. Formerly Lahaina Natural Foods, **Westside Natural Food** is now relocated on Dickenson Street. Open daily, they're a full-service health food store, featuring baked goods and Herbalife vitamins. **Paradise Fruit Company** on S. Kihei Road is terrific. It's not strictly a health food store, but it does have plenty of wholesome items. Their food bar is among the best, and you can't go wrong. In Paia is **Mana Natural Foods,** open daily 8 a.m.-8 p.m., and possibly the best health food store on Maui. You can pick up whatever you need for your trip to Hana. **Maui Natural Foods,** tel. 877-3018, in the Maui Mall in Kahului, is open daily. It has a fair selection of fresh foods and refrigerated deli items, and a huge selection of vitamins, minerals, herbs, and supplements.

Fresh Fish And Fruit

What's Hawaii without its fruits, both from the sea and from the vine? For fresh fish try the **Maalaea Fish Market and Cafe** at Maalaea Harbor. They get their fish right from the boats, but they do have a retail counter and a limited menu. In Wailuku, both **Nagasako Fishery** on Lower Main and **Wakamatsu Fish Market** on Market Street have a great selection of fresh fish daily. In Kihei, **Azeka's Market** is the place to go; however, some enterprising fishermen set up roadside stands along S. Kihei just west of Azeka's whenever they have a good day. Look for their coolers propping up a sign.

For the best and freshest fruits, vegies, cheese, and breads search out **The Farmers' Market.** Gardeners from Kula bring their fresh vegetables to roadside stands on Monday and Thursday 7:30 a.m.-1:30 p.m. in Honokowai along the Lower Honoapiilani Hwy.; also every Tuesday and Saturday, 1:30 p.m until the vendors decide to call it a day, in the parking lot of Suda's Store along the *mauka* side at 61 S. Kihei Road. Be early for the best selections. Family fruit stands are tucked along the road to Hana. Many times no one is in attendance and the very reasonably priced fruit is paid for on the honor system.

Take Home Maui, at 121 Dickenson St., Lahaina, mail order tel. (800) 545-MAUI, is a food store and delicatessen that specializes in packaging "agriculturally inspected" Maui produce such as pineapples, papayas, Maui onions, protea, potato chips, macadamia nut products, and Kona coffee, which they will deliver to you at the airport.

RESTAURANTS

If you love to eat, you'll love Maui. Besides great fish, there's fresh beef from Maui's ranches and fresh vegetables from Kula. The cuisines offered are as cosmopolitan as the people: Polynesian, Hawaiian, Italian, French, Mexican, Filipino, and Asian. The following are just hors d'oeuvres. Check the "Food" sections of the travel chapters for full descriptions.

Classy Dining

Five-star restaurants on Maui include: the **Prince Court** at the Maui Prince Hotel, Makena; **Raffles** at Stouffer's Wailea Resort; **The Grand Dining Room** at the Grand Wailea Resort; **Seasons** at The Four Seasons, Wailea; **Kea Lani, The Restaurant** at the Kea Lani, Wailea; **Plantation Veranda** at the Kapalua Bay Hotel; and **The Grill** at the Ritz-Carlton Kapalua. You won't be able to afford these every day, but for that one-time blowout, take your choice.

Fill 'Er Up

For more moderate fare, try these no-atmosphere restaurants that'll fill you up with good food for "at home" prices: **Ma Chan's** in Kahului; **Kitada's** in Makawao for the best bowl of saimin on the island; and both restaurants at the **Silversword** and **Makena golf courses.** For great sandwiches try the snack bars at all of the island's health food stores, especially **Paradise Fruit Co.** in Kihei, and **Picnics** in Paia. The best inexpensive dining is in Kahului/Wailuku.

Can't Go Wrong

There is great Mexican food (some vegetarian, no lard) at **Polli's Restaurant** in Makawao. **Longhi's** in Lahaina is well established as a gourmet cosmopolitan/Italian restaurant. Also do yourself a flavor and dine in Lahaina at **Avalon,** or **Gerard's**—both out of this world, with **David Paul's** adding to the gourmet delight. **Mama's Fish House** in Paia receives the highest compliment of being a favorite with the locals, and **The Grill and Bar** at the Kapalua Golf Course is extraordinarily good and always consistent. **The Moana Terrace** at the Kaanapali Marriot has an outstanding breakfast and dinner buffet. **Erik's Seafood Grotto** in Kahana is good value, and **Leilani's** is an up-and-comer in the Whaler's Village. The Sunday brunches at **Raffles** at Stouffer's in Wailea and at the **Maui Prince** hotel in Makena are legendary. Two new restaurants building a steady reputation for superb food are the **Haliimaile General Store** in Haliimaile, and **Roy's** in Honokowai.

LUAU

The luau is an island institution. For a fixed price of about $40, you get to gorge yourself on a tremendous variety of island foods, and have a night of entertainment as well. Eat light on your luau day so you'll have room for the many delights offered. A few of the many luau choices are listed below.

Old Lahaina Luau, on the beach near the 505 Front Street Mall, tel. 667-1998, has an excellent reputation because it is as close to authentic as you can get. Seating is Mon.-Sat. 5:30-8:30 p.m., but reserve at least three to six days in advance to avoid disappointment, especially during peak season. The luau, featuring a "local's favorite," all-you-can-eat buffet and all-you-can-drink bar, costs $55 adults, half price childen 3-12. The traditional hula dancers use ti-leaf skirts, and the music is *fo' real.* The Old Lahaina Luau is one of the oldest and best luau on the island.

Stouffer's Wailea Beach Resort, tel. 879-4900, recounts tales of old Hawaii with its very authentic and professional hula show and luau every Thursday at 6 p.m. Host Rod Guerrero spins yarns and tales of Maui's past, and then bursts into song with his intriguing falsetto voice. Dramatically, a fire dancer appears, and the show moves on into the evening as you dine on a wonderful assortment of foods expertly prepared by Stouffer's chefs. Price includes open bar at $48 adults, $24 children 12 and under. Reservations are required.

The Aloha Luau, tel. 661-3500, every night 5-8 p.m. at the Sheraton Maui, is a fun time of feasting and entertainment on one of the most beautiful sunset beaches on Maui. Price, including full buffet, bar, and entertainment, is $42; children under 12 pay $19.

The **Royal Lahaina Resort,** tel. 661-3611, has been offering a nightly luau and entertainment for years in their Luau Gardens. The show is still spectacular and the food offered is authentic and good. Prices are $49 adults, $24 children; reservations suggested.

Others include **Wailea's Finest Luau,** tel. 879-1922, Tuesday, Thursday, and Friday from 5:30 p.m., $48 adults, $24 children 6-10, at the Maui Inter-Continental Wailea; Hyatt Regency Maui's **Drums of the Pacific,** tel. 661-1234, every evening but Sunday and Thursday at 5:30 p.m., $44 adults, $36 for children 6-12; and **Aloha Friday Luau,** tel. 661-0011, 5:30 p.m. at Kaanapali Beach Hotel, $37.50 adults, $18.75 children 5-12.

For something a little different try the **Hawaiian Country Revue** at Maui Tropical Plantation, tel. 242-8605, in Waikapu near Wailuku. Here you get a *yippee yai yo kai yeah* good time complete with hula and square dancing. The grill is fired up and sizzles with savory steaks, and there's a big pot of chili and all the fixin's. The price is $48, and the fun happens every Monday, Wednesday, and Friday from 5:30 p.m. Host is Uncle Buddy Fo, who lassoes everyone into the good time with his singing, dancing, and drumming.

New on the scene is the Pioneer Inn's **Whaling Party,** tel. 661-3636. This show will take you back to the days of historic Lahaina town, where you will be entertained by cancan dancers on stage, sailors in the crowd, and bar girls from the balcony. And of course the missionaries are there as well to try to keep you from being led astray. The evening is rounded out by a buffet dinner and open bar. Every Sunday and Monday at 6 p.m., $45 adults, $22.95 children ages 6-12.

GETTING THERE

Maui, the Hawaiian destination second only to Oahu, attracts over a million visitors per year. A limited number of direct flights from the Mainland is offered, but most airlines servicing Hawaii, both domestic and foreign, land at Honolulu International Airport and then carry on to Maui or offer connecting flights on "interisland carriers." In most cases the connecting flights are part of the original ticket price with no extra charge. Different airlines have "interline" agreements with different Hawaiian carriers so check with your travel agent. All major and most smaller interisland carriers service Maui from throughout Hawaii with over 100 flights per day in and out of Kahului Airport and several dozen a day to Kapalua-West Maui airport.

Maui's Airports

There are three commercial airports on Maui, but the vast majority of travelers will be concerned with **Kahului Airport,** which accommodates 95% of the flights in and out of Maui. Kahului Airport is only minutes from Kahului city center, on the north-central coast of Maui. A full-service facility with most amenities, it has car rental agencies, information booths, and limited public and private transportation. This airport is currently undergoing a major expansion—opposed by many island residents—that will allow it to land the biggest commercial planes and handle a great increase in traffic, including direct international flights. The first phase was completed in 1990 and work will continue for the next several years, causing only minor inconvenience to travelers. Major roads lead from Kahului Airport to all primary destinations on Maui.

Hawaiian Airlines opened **Kapalua-West Maui Airport** in early 1987. This brand-new facility is conveniently located between Kaanapali and the Kapalua resort areas, on the *mauka* side of the Honoapiilani Hwy. at Mahinahina just a few minutes from the major Kaanapali hotels. If possible, this is definitely the airport you want to use if you are staying anywhere on West Maui. Though Hawaiian Air no longer connects flights to West Maui, seven other commuter airlines have contracted to use the facility, but for now only Aloha Island Air and Panorama Air Tours have a booth. The facility opens West Maui to its first-ever service to all the Hawaiian Islands, the South Pacific, and the Mainland's West Coast. The new airport is very user-friendly with a snack bar, sundries, and car rental agencies or courtesy phones for car rental pick-up. A free trolley bus connects you with major Kaanapali hotels.

The third airstrip is **Hana Airport,** an isolated runway with a tiny terminal on the northeast coast just west of Hana. It has no amenities and transportation is available only to the Hotel Hana Maui via the hotel shuttle. People flying into Hana Airport generally plan to vacation in Hana for an extended period and have made prior arrangements for being picked up. The only rental cars available in Hana can be arranged by calling 248-8391—call before you come.

Nonstop Flights

Until recently, **United Airlines** was the only carrier that offered nonstop flights from the Mainland to Maui. United, tel. (800) 241-6522, flies one daily nonstop to Maui from both San Francisco and Los Angeles. Denver, Portland, and Seattle passengers fly via San Francisco or Los Angeles. Now, **Delta Airlines,** tel. (800) 221-1212, flies once daily direct from Los Angeles, with other flights originating in Los Angeles and San Francisco going through Honolulu at no extra charge. **Hawaiian Air,** tel. (800) 367-5320, offers daily flights via San Francisco and Los Angeles through Honolulu.

Interisland Carriers

Hawaiian Air, tel. (800) 367-5320 Mainland, (800) 882-8811 Hawaii, 244-9111 on Maui, offers more flights to Maui than any other interisland carrier. The majority of flights are to and from Honolulu (average flight time 30 minutes), with over 30 per day in each direction. Hawaiian Air flights to Kahului, Maui, from Honolulu begin at 5:30 a.m., with flights thereafter about every 30 minutes until 8 p.m. Flights from Kahului to Honolulu begin at 6:30 a.m. and go all day until 9 p.m. There are two flights to/from Hilo daily,

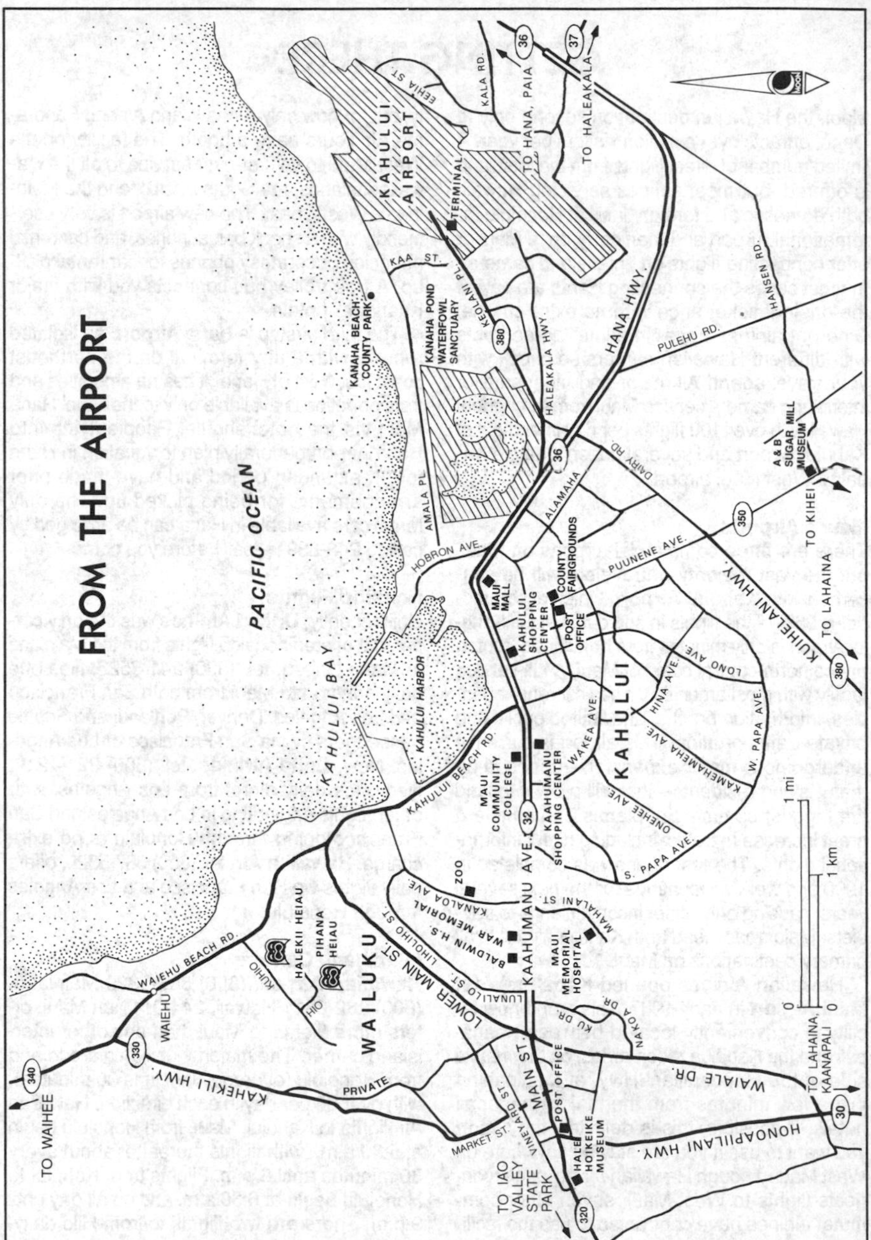

FROM THE AIRPORT

PACIFIC OCEAN
KAHULUI BAY
KAHULUI AIRPORT
TERMINAL
KAHULUI HARBOR
KANAHA BEACH COUNTY PARK
KANAHA POND WATERFOWL SANCTUARY
KAHULUI
WAILUKU
WAIEHU
TO WAIHEE
TO HANA, PAIA
TO HALEAKALA
TO KIHEI
TO LAHAINA
TO LAHAINA, KAANAPALI
TO IAO VALLEY STATE PARK
EEHIA ST.
KALA RD.
KAA ST.
KEOLANI PL.
HALEAKALA HWY.
HANA HWY
PULEHU RD.
HANSEN RD.
AMALA PL.
ALAMAHA
DAIRY RD.
A & B SUGAR MILL MUSEUM
HOBRON AVE.
PUUNENE AVE.
KUIHELANI HWY.
MAUI MALL
KAHULUI SHOPPING CENTER
POST OFFICE
COUNTY FAIRGROUNDS
LONO AVE.
HINA AVE.
WAKEA AVE.
KAMEHAMEHA AVE.
W. PAPA AVE.
ONEHEE AVE.
S. PAPA AVE.
KAHULUI BEACH RD.
MAUI COMMUNITY COLLEGE
KAAHUMANU SHOPPING CENTER
KAAHUMANU AVE.
KANALOA AVE.
ZOO
WAR MEMORIAL
BALDWIN H.S.
MAHALANI ST.
MAUI MEMORIAL HOSPITAL
LIHOLIHO ST.
LUNALILO ST.
LOWER MAIN ST.
MAIN ST.
KU DR.
NAKOA DR.
WAIALE DR.
HONOAPIILANI HWY.
VINEYARD ST.
MARKET ST.
POST OFFICE
HALE HOIKEIKE MUSEUM
PRIVATE
KAHEKILI HWY.
WAIEHU BEACH RD.
HALEKII HEIAU
PIHANA HEIAU
KUHIO
HIO
340
330
320
30
32
36
37
350
380
0 1 mi
0 1 km
MOON

one in the morning and one in mid-afternoon. Kona, on the Big Island, is serviced with three daily flights from Kahului (two in the morning and one in the late afternoon), and three from Kona to Kahului on about the same time schedule. There is one direct flight between Maui and Molokai, leaving Maui at 10:20 a.m. and Molokai at 12:30 p.m. on Dash 7 prop planes. Molokai and Lanai are connected by twice-weekly flights, both going through Honolulu.

Aloha Airlines, tel. 244-9071, (800) 367-5250, with its all-jet fleet of 737s, flies from Honolulu to Maui over 30 times per day beginning at 5:35 a.m. with the last flight at 8 p.m.; to Honolulu at 6:35 a.m., last flight at 9 p.m. Multiple flights throughout the day from Kauai depart 6:35 a.m. until 7 p.m.; to Kauai at 6:35 a.m. and throughout the day until 6:50 p.m. From Hilo there are two flights, the first at mid-morning and the second at 5:30 p.m.; to Hilo there are three flights from 8:30 a.m. until 4:30 p.m.; from Kona six flights leave from 9:25 a.m. until 6:55 p.m.; to Kona five flights leave from 7:15 a.m. until 6:20 p.m.

Commuter Airlines

Aloha Island Air, tel. (800) 323-3345 Mainland, (800) 652-6541 Hawaii, 877-5755 Kahului, offers daily flights connecting Maui with all the major islands. Along with two of the state's main airports (Honolulu and Kahului), they service the smaller and sometimes more convenient airports of Kapalua and Hana on Maui, Princeville on Kauai, and Kalaupapa on Molokai. Over a dozen flights a day connect Honolulu to Kahului (most via Molokai, Lanai, or Kapalua-West Maui) beginning at 7:30 a.m. (6:10 from Honolulu) and run until 6:20 p.m., with one late-night flight at 11:59 p.m. to Kahului, and 1 a.m. from Kahului to Honolulu. Five daily flights run from Molokai to Kahului (6:30 a.m. to 5 p.m.), with two from Lanai (6:45 a.m. and 2:05 p.m.); from Maui you can catch a connecting flight to either of these islands. There are daily flights to/from Kahului and Hana, and to Princeville via Molokai. Direct flights to/from Honolulu from West Maui Airport run from 7:50 a.m. to 4:55 p.m. There are regular flights to Kalaupapa on Molokai from Kahului, Molokai, and Honolulu, but only with a reservation on one of the organized tours (see "The Kalaupapa Experience—Getting There" under "Middle Molokai and Kalaupapa" in the Molokai chapter).

Air Molokai, tel. 521-0090 on Oahu, 877-0026 Maui, 567-6881 Molokai, has flights connecting Oahu, Molokai, Maui, and Lanai upon request only. There are four flights throughout the day between Oahu and Molokai; two daily flights connect Molokai and Kahului, Maui.

Charter Airlines

If you've got the bucks or just need to go when there's no regularly scheduled flight, try either **Paragon Air,** tel. 244-3356, or **Trans Air,** tel. 833-5557, (800) 634-2094 Hawaii, for islandwide service.

GETTING AROUND

If it's your intention to *see* Maui when you visit, and not just lie on the beach in front of your hotel, the only efficient way is to rent a car. Limited public transportation, a few free shuttles, taxis, and the good old thumb are available, but all these are flawed in one way or another. Other unique and fun-filled ways to tour the island include renting a bike or moped, or hopping on a helicopter, but these conveyances are highly specialized and are more in the realm of sports than touring.

RENTAL CARS

Maui has about 40 car rental agencies that can put you behind the wheel of anything from a Mercedes convertible to a used station wagon with chipped paint and torn upholstery. There are national companies, interisland firms, good local companies, and a few fly-by-nights that'll rent you a clunker. Eleven companies are clustered in little booths at the Kahului Airport, a few at Kapalua-West Maui Airport, and none at Hana Airport, but the Hana Hotel can arrange a car for you or you can do it yourself by calling Purdee's at 248-8391. The rest are scattered around the island, with a heavy concentration on Dairy Road in Kahului, at the Kaanapali Transportation Center, and along S. Kihei Road. Those without an airport booth either have a courtesy phone or a number to call; they'll pick you up and shuttle you to their lots. Stiff competition tends to keep the prices more or less reasonable. Good deals are offered off-season, with price wars flaring at any time and making for real savings. Even with all these companies, it's best to book ahead. You might not save money, but you can save youself headaches.

National Companies

The following are major firms that have booths at Kahului Airport. **Dollar,** tel. 877-2731, 667-2651 Kahului, (800) 342-7398 Hawaii, (800) 800-4000 worldwide, has an excellent reputation and very competitive prices. Dollar rents all kinds of cars as well as jeeps and convertibles. Great weekly rates, and all major credit cards are accepted. **Alamo** has good weekly rates, tel. (800) 327-9633, 871-6235 Kahului, 661-7181 Kaanapali. **National Car Rental,** tel. 871-8851 or (800) 227-7368 Mainland, has cars, vans, jeeps, and station wagons. **Avis,** tel. 871-7575, 661-4588 Kaanapali, or (800) 831-8000 Mainland, features late-model GM cars as well as most imports and convertibles. **Budget,** tel. 871-8811 Kahului, 661-8721 Kaanapali, or (800) 527-0700 Mainland, offers competitive rates on a variety of late-model cars. **Hertz,** tel. 661-3195, (800) 654-3131 Mainland, perhaps the best known company, offers a wide variety of vehicles with some special weekly rates. Hertz has locations at Kaanapali and Wailea.

Local Companies

The following companies are based in Hawaii and either have booths at the airport or pick-up services through courtesy phones. **Word of Mouth Rent a Used Car,** at 150 Hana Hwy., tel. 877-2436 or (800) 533-5929, pick-up van provided, offers some fantastic deals on their used, but not abused, cars. All cars, standard shift or automatic, can go for as little as $90 per week (good price for windsurfers) with a three-day minimum, or $15.95 per day, but expect to spend $119 per week for a nice four-door, a/c, late-model car. The office is open 8 a.m.-5 p.m., but they will leave a car at the airport at earlier or later hours with prior arrangement. Others include: **Andres,** tel. 877-5378; **Kihei Rent A Car,** tel. 879-7257; and **Atlas,** tel. 871-2860.

Four-Wheel Drive

Though 4WDs much more expensive than cars, some people might feel safer in them for completely circling Maui. Also unlike cars, rented 4WDs are given no restrictions on driving past the Seven Sacred Pools or around the head of West Maui (roads subject to closure, check). Obtain 4WDs from **Maui Rent A Jeep,** tel. 877-6626; **Hertz,** tel. 877-5167; **Atlas,** tel. 871-2860; and a few others. Rates vary from company to company; most are $60-70 per day, depending on availability and length of rental.

Mopeds

For running around town or to the beach, mopeds are great. Expect to pay $5-10 per hour, $35-50 per day, or up to $125 per week. Contact **Go Go Bikes** at the Kaanapali Transportation Center, tel. 661-3063 or 669-6669; **A & B Rentals and Sportswear,** in Honokowai in Da Rose Mall, tel. 669-0027, renting mopeds for $10 for two hours, $25 per day, and $125 per week; **Fun Rentals of Maui,** at 193 Lahainaluna Rd., Lahaina, tel. 661-3053, renting scooters at $8 per hour, and $50 per day; and **Rainbow Rent A Car,** also in Lahaina, tel. 661-8734.

PUBLIC TRANSPORTATION

The **Akina** Bus Service, tel. 879-2828, handles airport runs to/from Kihei and throughout East Maui. They leave every hour on the half hour *from* Kahului airport, 7:30 a.m.-7:30 p.m., and from various stops throughout Makena, Wailea, and Kihei *to* the airport, 8 a.m.-8 p.m., every hour on the hour. One-way fares are $12; children under seven accompanied by an adult travel free. Reservations are a must. Use the free direct-line courtesy phone at Kahului Airport or visit their booth in the rental car building.

Trans Hawaiian, tel. 877-7308, operates a similar service to/from Lahaina, Kaanapali, and various points throughout West Maui. They operate *to* Kahului Airport, 8 a.m.-7 p.m., and *from* Kahului Airport, 8:50 a.m.-7:50 p.m. A courtesy phone and ticket booth are available at Kahului Airport across from baggage carousel no. 2. Fares are $13.50 one-way.

The free **Kaanapali Trolley** runs along the Kaanapali strip about every half hour throughout the day, stopping at all major resorts, golf courses, Whaler's Village shopping center, and the Sugar Cane Train station. Look for the green jitneys. Service starts at 7 a.m. and runs until 11 p.m. About a dozen of these buses run to Kapalua-West Maui airport 8:25 a.m.-4:05 p.m., while those from the airport run 8:15 a.m.-5:15 p.m. Pick up free printed tourist literature or ask at any hotel desk for the schedule.

Also free is the **Lahaina Express** shuttle, which runs 9:10 a.m.-9:45 p.m. connecting various stops in Lahaina to Kaanapali. The major pick-up point in Lahaina is at the rear of the Wharf Cinema Center along Front Street.

Transportation to the new Lahaina Cannery Mall is provided by the free **Lahaina Cannery Shuttle** from major hotels and the Whaler's Village shopping center in Kaanapali, and from Honokowai.

For those riding the Sugar Cane Train, free transportation aboard the **Sugar Cane Trolley** is available from Front Street and the Lahaina Harbor to the Lahaina Station.

For those in the Wailea area the **Wailea Resorts Shuttle** is free and stops at all Wailea Beach hotels and condos, the Wailea Shopping Village, the golf course, and tennis courts, throughout the day. A new free shuttle also operates between Wailuku and Kahului (see "Services" under "Kahului" in the Central Maui chapter).

Taxis

About 18 taxi companies on Maui more or less operate in a fixed area. Most, besides providing normal taxi service, also run tours all over the island. Taxis are expensive and metered by the distance traveled. For example, a ride from Kahului Airport to Kaanapali is $45 and to Wailea about $30. Try: **Yellow Cab of Maui,** tel. 877-7000; **Kahului Taxi Service,** tel. 877-5681; **Alii Cabs** in Lahaina at 661-3688; **Kaanapali Taxi,** tel. 661-5258; **Wailea Taxi,** tel. 874-5000; **Kihei Taxi,** tel. 879-3000.

ALTERNATIVE TRANSPORTATION

Hitchhiking

The old tried-and-true method of hitchhiking—with thumb out, facing traffic, a smile on your interesting face—is "out" on Maui! It's illegal, and if a policeman sees you, you'll be hassled, if not outright arrested. You've got to play the game. Simply stand on the side of the road facing traffic with a smile on your interesting face, but put away the old thumb. In other words, you can't actively solicit a ride. People know what you're doing; just stand there. You can get around quite well this way, if you're not on a schedule. The success rate of getting a ride to the number of cars that go by isn't great, but you will get picked up. Locals and the average tourist with family will generally pass you by. Recent residents and single tourists will most often pick you up, and 90% of the time these will be white males. Hitching short hops along the resort beaches is easy. People can tell by the way you're dressed that you're not going far and will give you a lift. Catching longer rides to Hana or up to Haleakala can be done, but it'll be tougher because the driver will know that you'll be with him or her for the duration of the ride. Under no circumstances should women hitch alone.

Bicycles

Bicycle enthusiasts should be thrilled with Maui, but the few flaws might flatten your spirits as well as your tires. The countryside is great, the weather is perfect, but the roads are heavily trafficked and the most interesting ones are narrow and have bad shoulders. Pedaling to Hana will give you an up-close personal experience, but for bicycle safety this road is one of the worst. Haleakala is stupendous, but with a rise of more than 10,000 feet in less than 40 miles it is considered one of the most grueling rides in the world. A paved bike path running from Lahaina to Kaanapali is tame enough for everyone and you can even arrange a bicycle tour of Lahaina. In short, cycling on Maui as your primary means of transportation is not for the neophyte; because of safety considerations and the tough rides, only experienced riders should consider it.

Getting your bike to Maui from one of the Neighbor Islands is no problem. All of the interisland and commuter carriers will let you take it with you on your same flight for $20-25—just check it in as baggage. If you plan ahead, you can send your bike the previous day by air freight. Aloha Airlines has an excellent system promising 24-hour delivery. You don't have to box or disassemble your bike, but you must sign a damage waiver. This is usually okay because the awkwardness of a bike almost ensures that it will be placed on the top of the baggage out of harm's way. The freight terminal at Kahului is just a few minutes' walk from the passenger terminal and opens at 7 a.m. You can also take your bike free on the interisland ferry, the *Maui Princess* (see "By Interisland Ferry" below).

Getting your bike to Hawaii from the Mainland will depend upon which airline you take. Some will accept bicycles as baggage traveling with you (approximate additional charge of $30) if the bikes are properly broken down and boxed in a bicycle box, while others will only take them as air freight, in which case the rates are exorbitant. Check with the airlines well before you plan to go, or explore the possibility of shipping your bike by sea through a freight company.

Bicycle Rentals

Some bicycle rental shops will tell you the Park Service does not allow you to take your bike up to Haleakala National Park—horse pucky! You *cannot* ride the bike on the hiking paths, but going up the road (40 miles uphill) is okay if you have the steam. You are given this misinformation because the bike rental shops don't want the wear and tear on their bikes, but for the prices they charge, they shouldn't squawk.

Fun Rentals, at 193 Lahainaluna Rd., Lahaina, tel. 661-3053, open daily 8:30 a.m.-5 p.m., Sunday until 3 p.m., is a semi-benign bike service and rental shop. Semi-benign because their prices are high, but they could be higher, and because they have the best selection around. This full-service bike shop sells and rents everything from clunkers for around town to world-class Tomasso racing bikes. Rates are: cruisers, $5 per hour for one to four hours, and $45 per week; 21-speed Cannondale mountain bikes, $10 per hour for one to four hours, and $65 per week; road-racing bikes, $25 per day, and $85 per week (more rates available).

South Maui Bicycles, 1913 S. Kihei Rd., tel. 874-0068, open daily 9 a.m.-5 p.m., and Sunday 10 a.m.-2 p.m., is a rental and bike repair shop that boasts the largest fleet on Maui from which to choose. Rates are: one-speed city bikes $10 per day, $50 per week; beach cruisers $15 per day, $68 per week. Also available are mountain bikes and touring bikes at competitive rates. Frank Hackett, the shop owner, will take time to give you tips including routes and the best times to travel.

Maui Mountain Bike Adventures, at 3600 L. Honoapiilani Hwy., 5-A Rent a Space, Honokowai, tel. 669-1169, open weekdays 8 a.m.-6 p.m., weekends 10 a.m.-3 p.m., rents bicycles and operates tours on West Maui and Hana, and will custom-tailor any tour to meet your needs, including free pickup and delivery. Rental rates are $19 per day, $15 per day for three days or more, $79 weekly; rate includes lock, helmet, and free water bottle.

For other bike rentals, try **Go Go Bikes Hawaii** in Kaanapali, tel. 661-3063. **A & B Rentals and Sportswear,** in Honokowai at 3481 Lower Honoapiilani Hwy., tel. 669-0027, open daily 9 a.m.-5 p.m., rents basic street bicycles at $10 for 24 hours, $50 per week.

Cruiser Bob's, tel. 579-8444, rents Schwinn mountain bikes for $20 per day and $100 per week.

BY INTERISLAND FERRY

Molokai-Maui Interisland Ferry

From time to time, ferry companies have operated in Hawaii, but very stiff competition generated by the airline industry and the notoriously rough waters of the Hawaiian channels have combined to scuttle their opportunity for success. However, a new company has opened, making daily runs between Molokai (Kaunakakai) and Maui (Lahaina) aboard their 118-foot vessel, the ***Maui Princess.*** Fares are $50 roundtrip, half price for children, $25 one-way. Bicyclists will be especially happy because no extra fee is charged to transport your wheels. The *Maui Princess* makes the one and one-half-hour roundtrip once a day, departing Lahaina Harbor at 7 a.m. and arriving at Molokai's Kaunakakai Pier at 8:45 a.m. It departs Molokai at 3:55 p.m. and arrives at Lahaina Harbor at 5:45 p.m. For information and reservations call (800) 833-5800, 553-5736 Molokai, 661-8397 Maui. The boat, a converted oil-platform personnel carrier from Louisiana, has been retrofit for Hawaii and includes a sun deck and hydraulic stabilizers, which take some of the roll out of the rocky crossing. In effect, it's still a work boat, carrying workers from Molokai to Lahaina, along with some light cargo. As beautiful as the Hawaiian Islands are from the air, this is a wonderful opportunity to experience them from sea level. The cabin is comfortable and air-conditioned, and the crew, all local people, play guitar and ukulele, and sing old island tunes. The majority of the passengers are islanders, so if you're looking for a colorful and cultural experience, this is one of the best opportunities. The snack bar serves soft drinks and snacks for under $2, but no alcohol.

Lanai-Maui Interisland Ferry

A passenger ferry, *Expeditions,* now plies the ocean between Lahaina and Manele Bay on Lanai. This shuttle service is not luxury travel but offers a speedy, efficient, and convenient transportation alternative to the Pineapple Island. You are allowed to take luggage free of charge, but there's an extra $10 fee for a bicycle. The one-hour crossing leaves Lahaina's public launch pier daily at 6:45 a.m., 9:15 a.m., 3:15 p.m., and 5:45 p.m.; departures from Manele Bay are at 8 a.m., 10:30 a.m., 4:30 p.m., and 6:45 p.m. Adults pay $25 one-way, and children under 11 pay $20. This shuttle takes 64 passengers, but it is best to reserve your place. For information and reservations contact Expeditions, tel. (800) 695-2624, 661-3756; or write P.O. Box 1763, Lahaina, HI 96767.

SIGHTSEEING TOURS

Tours are offered that will literally let you cover Maui from head to foot; you can walk it, drive it, sail around it, fly over it, or see it from below the water. Almost every major hotel has a tour desk from which you can book.

Booking Agencies

The biggest, **Ocean Activities Center,** happens to be the best agency for booking any and all kinds of activities on Maui. For many of the fun events like snorkeling, scuba diving, whalewatching, sunset cruises, and deep sea fishing, the center has its own facilities and equipment, which means they not only provide you with an excellent outing, but offer very competitive prices. Ocean Activities can also book you on helicopters, parasails, and land tours, and rent and sell boogie boards, snorkel equipment, sailboards, and surfboards. They have sun and surf store/booking agencies in the Kihei/Wailea area at: the Maui Inter-Continental Resort, tel. 879-7466; the Maui Prince Hotel, tel. 879-7218; Stouffer's Wailea Beach Resort, tel. 879-0181; Mana Kai Hotel, tel. 879-6704; Maui Hill Hotel, tel. 879-0180; Azeka Place, tel. 879-0083; the Lahaina Cannery Mall, tel. 661-5309; the Maui Marriott in Kaanapali, tel. 661-3631; and the Embassy Suites in Honokowai, tel. 667-7116. Ocean Activities also runs a boat from the beach at the Maui Prince Hotel to the underwater fantasy of Molokini Crater. Prices on all of their activities are very reasonable, and the service is excellent. If you had to choose one agency for all your fun needs, this would be your best bet.

For personalized attention by very knowledgeable Maui residents, check out **Donya and Tracy** at the Maui Hill Condominium, tel. 879-0180. They've got the inside scoop on many of the activities, and can book you on the best and save you money at the same time.

One of the easiest ways to book an activity and sightsee at the same time is to walk along the Lahaina Wharf—an information booth here is operated by many of the companies who rent slips at the harbor. Check it out first, and then plan to be here when the tour boats return. Asking the passengers, right on the spot, if they've had a good time is about the best you can do. You can also check out the boats and do some comparative pricing of your own.

In Lahaina along Front Street try any of the **Fantasy Island Activities and Tours** kiosks, or call 661-5315. Also try the **Visitor Info & Ticket Center** in the Wharf Shopping Center, tel. 661-5151, or **Tom Barefoot's Cashback Tours,** tel. 661-8889. You will find a horde of other activities desks up and down Front Street; you almost don't have to search for them—they'll find you, especially to make an exhausting, high-pressured pitch for time-shares! An organization with a solid reputation is the **Activities Information Center,** tel. 667-7777, at 888 Wainee St. in the Lahaina Business Center.

For boats and a full range of activities out of quiet Maalaea Harbor, contact Jerome at **Maalaea Activities,** tel. 242-6982. They do it all, from helicopters to horseback. They specialize in the boats berthed at Maalaea.

Captain Nemo's Emporium, tel. 661-5555, (800) 367-8088 Mainland, located at 150 Dickenson Street, is an excellent booking agency for everything from helicopters to their specialty, scuba trips.

To get information about these tours and other activities, and general information on Maui, a convenient telephone service has been set up to assist you. Call **Teleguide Information Service** at 877-4266 and punch in a four-digit code for the specific activity, or wait for an operator. For a list of the codes, pick up a brochure at any information stand around the island.

Land Tours

It's easy to book tours to Maui's famous areas such as Lahaina, Hana, Kula, Iao Valley, and Haleakala. Normally they're run on either half- or full-day schedules (Hana is always a full day) and range $20-80 with hotel pick-up included. Big bus tours are run by **Grayline,** tel. 877-5507, and **Roberts,** tel. 871-6226. These tours are quite antiseptic—you sit behind tinted glass in an air-conditioned bus. Smaller companies like **No Ka Oi Tours,** tel. 871-9008, hit all the high spots and offer competitive prices. **Ekahi Tours,** tel. 572-9775, specializes in all-day, catered trips to Hana for $60. **Polynesian Adventure Tours,** tel. 877-4242, offers tours to Hana for $65, or a Haleakala, Central Maui, and Iao Valley tour for $42.

Temptation Tours, RR 1, P.O. Box 454, Kula, Maui 96790, tel. 878-2911, operates the ultimate in luxury van tours for the discriminating traveler. Their deluxe vans, more like limousines, seat each of the eight passengers in a comfortable captain's chair for the trip to Hana. Once in Hana, you will be provided either with a gourmet lunch at the famous Hotel Hana Maui ($139), where you get the run of the menu, or with an upscale picnic at a secluded black-sand beach ($110) complete with linens and crystal. Vegetarians and special dietary needs will be accommodated. Temptation Tours also offers an optional **helicopter tour** either down to or back from Hana, with the van making the connections. Priced at $225, the tour provides lunch and a personalized video of your experience.

For those who desire a go-at-your-own pace alternative to van tours, yet want the convenience of an escort, **Best of Maui Cassette Tours** may be for you. Your choice of quality tapes to the Hana Highway or the road to Haleakala comes with a cassette player; a small guidebook of sights, history, and legends; bird and flower handbooks; a route map; and a free T-shirt. Rental is $25, and you can pick up cassettes 6:30 a.m.-12:30 p.m.; reservations are appreciated. Call Best of Maui at 871-1555 or stop by their office at 333 Dairy Rd., Kahului, HI 96732.

For a truly wonderful hiking tour with Maui's foremost naturalist, Ken Schmitt, see "Hiking—

Hiking Tour" under "Camping and Hiking" earlier in this chapter.

Bicycle Tours

An adventure on Maui that's become famous is a 40-mile ride on a specially equipped bike from the summit of Mt. Haleakala to Paia at the bottom. A pioneer in this field is **Maui Downhill**, 199 Dairy Rd., Kahului, tel. 871-2155, (800) 535-BIKE. Included in the $106 bike ride are: two meals (continental breakfast, brunch or a gourmet picnic lunch), windbreakers, gloves, and helmets. To drench yourself in the beauty of a Haleakala sunrise, you have to pay your dues. You arrive at the base yard in Kahului at about 3:30 a.m. after being picked up at your condo by the courtesy van. Here, you'll muster with other bleary-eyed but hopeful adventurers and munch donuts and coffee, which at this time of the morning is more like a transfusion. Up the mountain, in the van, through the chilly night air takes about one and one-half hours, with singing and storytelling along the way. Once atop, find your spot for the *best* natural light show in the world: the sun goes wild with colors as it paints the sky and drips into Haleakala Crater (see "Haleakala National Park" under "Camping and Hiking" earlier in this chapter). This is your first reward. Next comes your environmental bicycle cruise down the mountain, with vistas and thrills every inch of the way. For the not-so-early risers, a 6:30-a.m. mountain descent for $79 is also available.

Cruiser Bob's, at 99 Hana Hwy., Box B, Paia, HI 96779, tel. 579-8444 or (800) 654-7717, offers a variation on the same theme. You get a similar experience for about the same amount of money ($105), and their breakfast is an all-you-can-eat buffet at the Kula Lodge. A picnic ride lasting 7 a.m.-3 p.m. is also available. Cruiser Bob's limits their groups to 13 people. **Maui Mountain Cruiser** of Makawao, tel. 572-0195, offers basically the same services. **Chris's Bike Adventures,** tel. 871-BIKE, offers a variation on the theme, taking you on a mountain-bike adventure down Haleakala including a tour of the Tedeschi Winery, and a walk along the lava fields around La Perouse Bay, all for $89. Or you can take an afternoon ride for $61, winding up at the winery where you can soothe your beaten bottom with a glass of *vino.* Chris also offers a "boat and bike" experience for $150 that includes a boat trip to Lanai and a bike trip on Molokai with continental breakfast and lunch included.

Maui Mountain Bike Adventures, at 3600 L. Honoapiilani Hwy., 5-A Rent a Space, Honokowai, tel. 669-1169, open weekdays 8 a.m.-6 p.m., weekends 10 a.m.-3 p.m., operates tours on West Maui and Hana, and will custom-tailor any tour to meet your needs, with free pick-up and delivery. For downhilling you have to be a fair rider; those under 16 require parental release. All riders must be at least five feet tall; pregnant women are not allowed; and proper clothing, shoes, and glasses must be worn. The rides are popular, so reserve well in advance. This outfit offers tamer tours of Lahaina and the beach resorts, including admissions into historical sites and museums. There's no gripe with the Haleakala experience; it's guaranteed thrills, and since they have you for eight hours including two meals and pick-up service, the price isn't too hard to take.

For those who like to strike out on their own, two routes are recommended. One takes you for a 50-mile loop from Wailuku (or Lahaina) up the Kaanapali coast and around the head of Maui back to Wailuku. The road starts out in good condition, but the traffic will be heavy until you pass Kapalua. Here the road begins to wind along the north coast. The road surface eventually turns to gravel, so a mountain bike with wide tires is a necessity. Traffic around the north end is almost nonexistent, and the road will be yours—but there is no place to get service, either. Go prepared.

The second route is from Kahului up to Kula or Pukalani via Pulehu Road and back down the mountainside via Paia, Haiku, or Ulumalu, taking you through irrigated cane fields, the cool Upcountry region, the lush, sculpted north slope of Haleakala, and along the back of Maui.

Air Tours

Maui is a spectacular sight from the air. A few small charter airlines, a handful of helicopter companies, and one sailplane outfit swoop you around the island. These joy rides are literally the highlight of many people's experiences on Maui, but they are expensive. The excursions vary, but expect to spend at least $100 for a basic half-hour tour. The most spectacular ones take you over Haleakala Crater, or perhaps to the remote West Maui Mountains, where inaccessible gorges lie at your feet. Other tours are civilized; expect a champagne brunch after you visit Hana. Still others take you to nearby Lanai or Molokai to view some of the world's most spectacular seacliffs and remote beaches. Know, however, that many hikers and trekkers have a beef with the air tours: after they've spent hours, or maybe days, hiking into remote valleys in search of peace and quiet, out of the sky comes the mechanical whir of a chopper to spoil the solitude.

For a slightly different thrill, experience a Maui joy ride out of Kahului Airport with **Paragon Airlines**, tel. 244-3356. **Scenic Air Tours,** tel. 871-2555 or (800) 352-3722, has five all-day tours leaving daily from the Kahului Airport commuter terminal. All tours are narrated and conducted in 10-seat Beachcraft planes so everyone has good viewing. **Biplane Barnstormers,** tel. 878-2860, offers open-cockpit biplane rides for as little as $59. This is an opportunity to fly in a new edition of a classic plane, a great contrast to the super jet that brought you to Hawaii.

Helicopters

Kenai Helicopter, tel. 871-6463, (800) 622-3144, is one of the better and more experienced companies. All their rides are smoothly professional. **Papillon Helicopters,** tel. 669-4884, (800) 562-5641 Maui, (800) 367-7095 Mainland, is also one of the larger and more experienced firms. Flights cost from $95 for a 30-minute West Maui excursion to $245 for one and one-half-hour flights to Hana or Molokai. Recently Papillon introduced a discount "Hawaii Flightsee" rate as low as $49. The price was in response to the "Kauai Reborn Campaign" that offered discount fares on that island after the devastation caused by Hurricane Iniki.

Among the local Maui companies: **Hawaii Helicopter,** tel. 877-3900, (800) 346-2403, has plush interiors for your comfort, but they squeeze four people in the back, so the two middle ones don't always get a good view. **Sunshine Helicopter,** tel. 871-0722, (800) 544-2520, is another local, family-run outfit. The seating is two-by-two, and owner and chief pilot Ross Scott goes out of his way to give you a great ride over Maui, which he knows intimately after thousands of hours in the air. Sunshine sometimes offers a 20-minute "special" for only $49. Others are: **Blue Hawaiian Helicopters,** tel. 871-8844, (800) 247-5444, featuring wide-body A-Stars; and **Alex Air,** tel. 871-0792.

Tours by all companies are narrated over specially designed earphones; some companies offer a video of your helicopter tour of Maui as a souvenir at the end of the flight. On certain flights the craft will touch down for a short interlude, and on some flights a complimentary lunch will be served (see the preceding description of Temptation Tours under "Land Tours"). Most companies will make special arrangements to drop off and pick up campers in remote areas, or will design a package especially for you. Chopper companies are competitively priced, with tours of West or East Maui at around $100, with a trip to Hana about $120. Circle-island tours are approximately $175. The best tour would be one including a trip to Molokai at approximately $200, in order to experience the world's tallest seacliffs along the isolated windward coast. All flights leave from the heliport at the back side of Kahului Airport.

OCEAN TOURS

You haven't really seen Maui unless you've seen it from the sea. Tour boats operating out of Maui's Lahaina and Maalaea harbors take you fishing, sailing, whalewatching, dining, diving, and snorkeling. You can find boats that offer all of these or just sail you around for pure pleasure—Maui presents one of the premier sailing venues in the Pacific. Many take day-trips to Lanai or to Molokai, with a visit to Kalaupapa included. Others visit Molokini, a submerged volcano with half its crater rim above water. It has been designated a Marine Life Conservation District. The vast majority of Maui's pleasure boats are berthed in Lahaina Harbor and most have a booth right there on the wharf where you can sign up. Other boats come out of Maalaea, and a few companies are based in Kihei. The following are limited to sailing/dining/touring activities, with snorkeling often part of the experience. If you're interested in other ocean activities such as scuba and fishing, see "Sports And Recreation" earlier in this chapter.

That section includes activities such as waterskiing or Jet Skiing, parasailing, sailboarding, and surfing.

Excursions/Dinner Sails
Sunset cruises are very romantic, and very popular. They last for about two hours and cost $35-45 for the basic cruise; but for a dinner sail expect to spend $50-80. Remember, too, that the larger established companies are usually on Maui to stay, but that smaller companies come and go with the tide. The following are general tour boats that offer a variety of cruises.

Trilogy Excursions, tel. 661-4743, (800) 874-2666, founded and operated by the Coon family, is a success in every way; their Lanai Cruise is the best on Maui. Although the handpicked crews have made the journey countless times, they never forget it's your first time. They run trimarans and catamarans, including the 54-foot *Trilogy II,* which carries up to 50 passengers to Lanai. Once aboard, you're served a mug of steaming Kona coffee, fresh juice, and Mama Coon's famous cinnamon rolls. After the boat anchors in Manele Bay, a tour van picks you up and you're driven to Lanai City. Along the way, the driver, a Lanai resident, tells stories, history, and anecdotes about the Pineapple Island. After the tour, you return to frolic at Hulopoe Bay, which is great for swimming and renowned as an excellent snorkeling area. All gear is provided. While you play, the crew is busy at work preparing a delicious barbecue at the picnic facilities at Manele Harbor. You couldn't have a more memorable or enjoyable experience than sailing with Trilogy. But don't spoil your day; be sure to bring along (and use!) a wide-brim hat, sunglasses, sunscreen, a long-sleeve shirt, and a towel. For this full-day experience, adults pay $139, children half price. Trilogy Excursions also runs a popular half-day trip to Molokini Crater, sailing daily from Maalaea Harbor (see "Kihei" in the East Maui chapter) at 6:30 a.m., adults $75, children half price, which includes breakfast, lunch, and all snorkeling gear (scuba available at additional cost).

If you've had enough of Front Street Lahaina, **Club Lanai,** tel. 871-1144, (800) 531-5262, is a Maui-based company that runs day excursions to its developed facilities on the east side of Lanai (whalewatches and dinner cruises, too). Besides Trilogy Excursions, Club Lanai is the only company with permission to land on Lanai. You board one of two catamarans at Lahaina Harbor, leaving at 7:30 a.m. and returning around 3:30 p.m. after a full day. En route you're served a breakfast of assorted donuts, coffee cake, juices, and coffee. The boats cruise to Club Lanai's private beach just near old Halepaloa Landing, between the deserted villages of Keomuku and Naha, on Lanai's very secluded eastern shore. Awaiting you is an oasis of green landscaped beach. Palm trees provide shade over manmade lagoons, and hammocks wait for true relaxation. The club provides you with snorkel gear, wave skis, kayaks with instruction, bicycles for exploring the area, horseshoes, volleyball, and even a guided historic wagon tour. Scuba diving can also be arranged at an extra charge. On the grounds are a gift shop and a Hawaiian village where you can learn handicrafts from local or visiting artists. The bar serves exotic drinks and is open all day. Lunch is a buffet featuring barbecued beef, chicken, mahimahi, juices, fresh fruit, and salads. The entire day including sail, meals, and use of facilities is reasonably priced at $79; children 4-12 pay $29, and ages 13-20 pay $59. Family oriented with plenty of activities for children of all ages, Club Lanai lets you set your own pace . . . do it all, or do nothing at all.

Scotch Mist, tel. 661-0386, has one racing yacht, *The Scotch Mist II.* They are the oldest sailing charters on Maui (since 1970) and claim to be the fastest sailboats in the harbor: boasting the lightest boat, the biggest sail, and the best crew. You can cruise/snorkel West Maui for $45 per person (four hours from 12:30 p.m.), sail and snorkel Lanai for a half day for $55 per person (four hours from 8 a.m.), or be one of 25 passengers on a sunset sail complete with champagne for $35 per person. When the time is right, a moonlight starlight sail and a whalewatching sail are offered, for $35 each.

The ***Navatek II,*** a snow-white manta ray, has risen from Maui's waters. This state-of-the-art marvel, built on Oahu and engineered expressly for use in Hawaii, is actually a SWATH vessel (Small Water Plane Twin Hull) of revolutionary design that features two submerged hulls—remote-controlled submarines, connected by two half-moon arching struts that support the above-water superstructure. The design means the $5-million, 82-foot-long, 36-foot-wide cruise ship handles the waves with amazing dexterity, since no part of the above-water decks come into actual contact with the waves. The result is the island's most steady, nimble, and comfortable craft. Once welcomed aboard by the courteous and highly professional crew, you make your way to the upper deck where the captain stands watch in a glass-enclosed pilothouse. At the touch of his finger, ballast tanks in the submersibles can be either flooded or blown to balance the craft, while a joystick raises or lowers the bow, and a polished aluminum ship's wheel the size of a hockey puck steers the agile SWATH. Fronting the pilothouse is stepped amphitheater seating, perfectly designed for spotting whales, observing the undulating coastline, or quietly watching the golden sun dipping into the azure sea. Behind is a tanning deck comfortable with lounge chairs, restrooms, and even hot showers—very welcome after a swim or snorkeling adventure. The glass-enclosed lower deck converts to a floating restaurant, with stage, dance floor, full table settings, kitchen, and complete bar.

The Navatek II offers the **Lanai Voyage of Discovery,** $120 adults, $60 children ages 5-12, leaving daily except Sunday from Lahaina Harbor at 7 a.m. and returning at 1 p.m. The cruise offers a delicious breakfast buffet, barbecue lunch, snorkeling, and entertainment while circumnavigating the lightly visited island of Lanai. The **Sunset Odyssey Dinner Cruise,** adults $78, children ages 5-12 $39, departs Maalaea Harbor nightly at 5:30 p.m. and returns at 7:30 p.m. It features *pu pu,* cocktail hour, and a three-course dinner and dessert served at your individual table by a professional wait staff. For details contact Navatek II, a division of Royal Hawaiian Cruises, tel. 848-6360 or (800) 852-4183.

One of the least expensive cruises is a cocktail sail aboard the 44-foot catamaran ***Frogman,*** tel. 667-7622. It departs from Maalaea Harbor and serves *pu pu,* mai tais, and beer on its trade wind sail. Also departing Maalaea Harbor is the champagne sunset dinner sail offered by Ocean Activities Center, tel. 879-4485, aboard their 65-foot catamaran ***Wailea Kai.*** They sail Monday, Wednesday, Friday, and Saturday. Also out of Maalaea Harbor is the ***Mahana Maia,*** tel. 871-8636, a 58-foot cat that'll carry 50 passengers out to Molokini.

The ***Prince Kuhio,*** tel. (800) 468-1287, 242-8777 on Maui, offers a different kind of trip altogether. Comfort, luxury, and stability come with this 92-foot ship. Departing from Maalaea Harbor Tues.-Thurs. and Sat.-Sun., the *Prince* does a four-hour snorkel cruise to Molokini ($80 adults, $42 children under 12) that includes a continental breakfast, buffet lunch, open bar, and champagne on the return voyage. On Monday, Wednesday, and Friday 7:15 a.m.-3 p.m. the *Prince* sails a Molokini-Club Lanai Adventure including continental breakfast, snorkeling on Molokini, and the full bar and buffet of Club Lanai for $135 adults, $90 children under 12.

Perhaps the quickest way to Molokini, which means more time in the water, is aboard the catamaran ***Kai Kanani,*** tel. 879-7218, or call Ocean Activities at 879-4485. It departs from Makena Beach in front of the Maui Prince Hotel. Equipment and food are provided.

From Kaanapali the ***Sea Sails*** makes an evening dinner sail from its anchorage at the Sheraton Beach; contact **Sea Sport Activities Center,** tel. 667-2759. Others with good reputations that you might try are: ***Prodive,*** tel. 875-4004, berthed at Maalaea, offering dives and snorkeling to Molokini; ***Extended Horizons,*** tel. 667-0611, berthed at Lahaina's Mala Wharf with snorkel/dive sails to Lanai; the ***Maui E-Ticket,*** tel. 669-8000, a high-tech, glass-bottomed viewing vessel; ***The Manutea,*** tel. 879-4485, a 50-foot catamaran offering a deluxe dinner sail for $59; ***Zip-Purr,*** tel. 667-2299, one of Maui's newest catamarans, offering a morning snorkel sail, sunset sail, and whalewatch in season with an Earthtrust scientist aboard for interpretation (some money goes to Earthtrust)—this family-operated, 41-foot catamaran was built in Hawaii expressly for Hawaiian waters; ***First Class,*** tel. 667-7733, a 65-foot yacht custom-built for Maui waters, offering everything from a $25 whalewatch to a $55 sunset sail complete with mai tais and champagne; the ***Lavengro,*** tel. 879-8188, a 60-foot "Roaring 20s" pleasure craft that even saw coastal duty during WW II and that now offers you a lovely sail on a tall, two-masted ship; and the ***Lahaina Princess,*** tel. 661-8397, a sleek motor yacht offering $65 dinner cruises that include open bar, dinner, entertainment, and dancing.

Some of the above companies offer a variety of cocktail sails and whalewatches for much cheaper prices, but many tend to pack people in so tightly they're known derisively as "cattle boats." Don't expect the personal attention you'd receive on smaller boats, and always check number of passengers when booking. However, all the boats going to Molokai or Lanai will take passengers for a one-way trip. You won't participate in the snorkeling or the food, but the prices (negotiable) are considerably cheaper. This extra service is offered only if there's room. Talk to the individual captains.

Unique Ocean Tours

For a totally different experience, try a rafting trip with: **Blue Water Rafting,** tel. 879-7238, P.O. Box 10172, Lahaina, HI 96761, departing from the Kihei Boat Ramp and primarily offering snorkel trips to Molokini (whalewatching in season); and **Ocean Riders,** tel. 661-3586, departing from Mala Wharf in Lahaina for trips to Lanai and Molokini. Their vessels are highly maneuverable, totally seaworthy, high-tech motorized rafts whose main features are their speed and ability to get intimate with the sea as their supple form bends with the undulations of the water.

Located in the Rainbow Mall at 2439 S. Kihei Rd., **South Pacific Kayaks,** tel. 875-4848, (800) 776-2326, open daily 8 a.m.-5 p.m., offers a half-day introductory trip for $55, or an advanced explorer trip along the remote coastline of East Maui for $79. Both tours include lunch along with plenty of snorkeling opportunities as you glide in and out tiny bays fashioned from jutting lava-rock fingers. South Pacific Kayaks offers per-day rentals of single kayaks at $20 and double kayaks at $40.

SeaEscape U-Drive Boat Rental, 1979 S. Kihei Rd., tel. 879-3721, offers seagoing motorized rafts that you can pilot yourself to all the snorkel, dive, and picturesque spots of the Lahaina Roads. Rates begin at $80 per hour (two-hour minimum, additional hours $35) for a 16-foot Zodiac with a 25 hp motor; larger boats are available.

Whalewatching

Anyone on Maui from November to April gets the added treat of watching humpback whales as they frolic just off Lahaina, one of the world's major wintering areas for the humpback. Almost every boat in the harbor runs a special whalewatch during this time of year.

Whales Alive Maui, tel. 242-7075, is a fantastic organization of dedicated scientists who have made a career of studying the magnificent humpback whale and who operate whalewatches every day in season. Stan Butler, the director of Whales Alive Maui, like most of the involved scientists, began his love affair with the sea as an 11-year-old surfer who realized that he was the "visitor" in the ocean home of enormous, powerful, yet wonderfully gentle whales and dolphins. Stan began his formal whale work in 1988 with Earthtrust, when he was appointed the manager of Save the Whales International. Now, through his direction, Whales Alive Maui operates two-hour whalewatches for a reasonable $25 through the **Ocean Activities Center,** tel 879-4485. Part of the proceeds is donated to this fine organization. Whales Alive Maui leaves daily at noon and again at 3 p.m. from Maalaea Harbor on the *Makakai,* at 1:30 p.m. from Maalaea Harbor on the *Wailea Kai,* and at 2 p.m. from Lahaina Harbor on the *Manueta.* On each of these stable and seaworthy catamarans is a fully trained Whales Alive Maui naturalist who offers a very educational and entertaining interpretive narration. When one of the wonderful whales shows itself by breaching, spouting, or slapping a pectoral fin, the on-board scientist will make every effort to inform you of what's going on, especially how it relates to the social pattern of whale life. There is no better way to have a truly Hawaiian experience of sea, surf, and natural beauty than a whalewatch sail with Whales Alive Maui.

Another highly educational whalewatch is sponsored by the **Pacific Whale Foundation,** located at Kealia Beach Plaza, Suite 25, 101 N. Kihei Rd., Kihei, HI 96753, tel. 879-8811, open daily 8 a.m.-5 p.m. A nonprofit organization founded in 1980, it is dedicated to research, education, and conservation, and is one of the only research organizations able to survive by generating its own funds through membership, donations, and excellent whalewatch cruises.

They have one of the best whalewatches on the island aboard their own two ships, the *Whale I* and *II*, berthed for your convenience at Maalaea and Lahaina harbors. The scientists and researchers who make up the crew rotate shifts and come out on the whalewatch when they're not out in the Lahaina Roads getting up close to identify, and make scientific observations of, the whales. Most of the information dispensed to tourists by other whalewatchers is generated by the Pacific Whale Foundation. Departures from Maalaea and Lahaina harbors are four times daily 7 a.m.-4:30 p.m.; adults $27.50 whalewatch only, and $44.25 for a whalewatch and snorkel excursion. The foundation also offers an "Adopt-a-whale Program" and various reef and snorkel cruises that run throughout the year.

Since Lahaina Harbor is an attraction in itself, take a stroll along it to handpick your own boat. Many times the whalewatch is combined with a snorkel and picnic sail, so prices vary accordingly.

Note: For further information on **whales,** see "Whales" under "Flora and Fauna" in the General Introduction. To make reservations for a whalewatch see **"Booking Agencies"** under "Sightseeing Tours" above. For more boats offering whalewatches see **"Ocean Tours"** above and **"Snorkeling and Scuba"** under "Sports and Recreation" earlier in the chapter. Many of these boats offer whalewatches in season.

OTHER TOURS ON LAND

The Sugar Cane Train

The old steam engine puffs along from Lahaina to Kaanapali pulling old-style passenger cars through cane fields and the Kaanapali golf course. The six miles of narrow-gauge track are covered in 25 minutes (each way) for a cost of $6 one-way and $9 roundtrip adults; $3 one-way and $4.50 roundtrip children 3-12. A free double-decker bus shuttles between Lahaina Station and the waterfront to accommodate the most popular tour on Maui. The train runs throughout the day 8:55 a.m.-4:40 p.m. It's very popular so book in advance. All rides are narrated and there may even be a singing conductor. It's not only great fun for children, everybody has a good time. All kinds of combination tours are offered as well: some feature lunch, a tour of Lahaina with admission into the Baldwin House and the *Carthaginian II,* or even a cruise on a glass-bottomed boat. They're tame, touristy, and fun. The price is right. Call the Lahaina Kaanapali and Pacific Railroad at 661-0089.

Private Tour Guides

These are individualized tours arranged with your needs and desires in mind. You provide the rental car, they drive and provide the knowledge and expertise about the island. Try **Personal Maui** for a half-day ($60), full-day ($110), or two-day Hana overnight ($200) trip; add $10 for each additional passenger. For one or two people the prices are a bit steep, but for three or more, fares become competitive with those of other tour companies. Contact Dan Kuehn, P.O. Box 1834, Makawao, HI 96768, tel. (800) 326-5336, or 572-1589 in Hawaii. Another reputable company offering similar services is **Guides of Maui.** Call (800) 228-6284 or 877-4042 in Hawaii; or write 333 Dairy Rd., Suite 104-B, Kahului, HI 96732.

INFORMATION AND SERVICES

EMERGENCY AND MEDICAL CARE

To summon the police, the fire department, or an ambulance to any part of Maui, dial **911.** This help number is available throughout the island. **Helpline,** the island's crisis center, is 244-7407. **Maui Memorial Hospital** is located at Mahalani St., Wailuku, tel. 244-9056; **Kihei-Wailea Medical Center,** 41 E. Lipoa St., Kihei, tel. 874-8100 (near Star Market) offers a number of physicians in varying specialties. **Pharmacies** include: Kahului, tel. 877-0041; Kihei, tel. 879-8499; Lahaina, tel. 661-3119; Pukalani, tel. 572-8244.

SERVICES FOR THE DISABLED

Beaches

On December 30, 1993 a measure was passed to make four Maui beaches wheelchair accessible: Kihei's Kamaole Beaches I, II, and III (see "Kihei" in the East Maui chapter), and Kahului's Kanaha Beach Park (see "Sights" under "Kalului" in the Central Maui chapter). Construction, mandated to be finished within a year, will include large, clearly marked parking spaces, and an elevated boardwalk leading to the beach. Contact Maui's Department of Parks and Recreation, tel. 243-7626, for up-to-the-minute details.

Maui Services

Upon your arrival at Kahului Airport, you'll find parking spaces directly in front of the main terminal. The restaurant here has steps; however, food will be brought to you in the cocktail lounge. There are no special emergency medical services, but visitor information is available at 877-6431. There is no centralized medical service, but Maui Memorial Hospital in Wailuku will refer, tel. 244-9056. Getting around can be tough because there is virtually no public transportaion on Maui, and no tours or companies to accommodate non-ambulatory persons. However, both Hertz and Avis rent cars with hand controls. Health care is provided by **Maui Center for Independent Living,** tel. 242-4966. Medical equipment is available at Hawaiian Rentals, tel. 877-7684, and at Maui Rents, tel. 877-5827. Special recreation activities referrals are made by Easter Seal Society, tel. 877-4443, or by the Commission on Persons with Disabilities, tel. 243-5441.

Over The Rainbow, 186 Mehani Circle, Kihei, HI 96753, tel. 879-5521, is a private company, owned and operated by Dave McKown, who has traveled the world with his brother, a paraplegic. Dave knows first hand the obstacles faced by disabled people. Over The Rainbow provides: a full-service travel agency, with bookings into hotels, condos, and private homes set up for the handicapped; an activities desk featuring everything from water sports to helicopter rides; u-drive cars and vans with hand controls and wheelchair lifts; airport arrangements; and scenic tours.

INFORMATION SOURCES, ETC.

The **Maui Visitors Bureau** is at 250 Alamaha St., Suite N-16, Kahului, HI 96732, tel. 244-3530.

The state operates two **visitors' kiosks** at Kahului Airport. Open daily 6 a.m.-9 p.m., they have plenty of practical brochures. **Teleguide,** tel. 877-3324, is a 24-hour telephone activities information service. Use a touch-tone phone to enter a four-digit code for the particular tourist information desired. Brochures listing codes can be picked up at any tourist literature stand. **On Call,** tel. 244-8934, offers free service also via touch-tone codes (see the front of any telephone book) to access community services, entertainment, shopping, news, sports, and cultural information. The **Maui Chamber of Commerce** is located at 26 Puunene Ave., Kahului, tel. 871-7711. For **consumer complaints,** call 243-5387. For **time,** call 242-0212. The **area code** for all Maui telephone numbers is 808.

Before you leave for the islands, information can be accessed from the ***Official Recreation Guide*** through travel agents who have a Sabre hookup. Information can be garnered on transportation, travel activities, and cultural events, and reservations can be made.

Reading Material

For bookstores try **Waldenbooks:** at Maui Mall, Kahului, tel. 877-0181; at Kaahumanu Shopping Center, tel. 871-6112; at Lahaina Cannery Shopping Center, tel. 667-6172; at Whaler's Village, tel. 661-8638; and at the Kukui Mall, tel. 874-3688. There's also **The Whaler's Book Shoppe** at The Wharf Shopping Center, Front Street, Lahaina, tel. 667-9544.

Libraries: the main branch is at 251 High St., Wailuku, tel. 243-5945; other branches may be found in Kahului, Lahaina, Makawao, Kihei, and Hana. Open a hodgepodge of hours throughout the week, they are usually closed Friday or Saturday.

Free tourist literature is well done and loaded with tips, discounts, maps, happenings, etc. Find it in hotels and restaurants and at street stands. They include: ***This Week Maui,*** every Friday; ***Guide to Maui*** on Thursday; ***Maui Beach Press,*** newspaper format and in-depth articles, every Friday; ***Maui Gold,*** one for each season; ***Drive Guide,*** excellent maps and tips, given out free by all car rental agencies, bimonthly; ***TV Maui,*** a weekly television and entertainment guide with feature articles and local events; and ***A Taste of Maui,*** all about food.

Newspapers include the following. ***Maui News,*** a local newspaper for 25 cents, contains good "Datebook" listings of local events. It's published Mon.-Fri., tel. 244-3981. ***The Gold Coast News*** has local-interest stories; ***Lahaina News*** is a community paper of news, feature stories, and entertainment listings; ***Island Living*** specializes in dining and entertainment; the ***Island Calendar of Events*** is an alternative "event and networking newsletter"; ***ECO Report*** is an environmental paper with local and global focus; and to keep abreast of what's happening on the local scene read the ***Kama'aina News.***

Parks And Recreation

Contact State Parks in Wailuku at 243-5354; County Parks in Wailuku at 243-7389; Haleakala National Park Headquarters at 527-7749.

Weather And Whales

For all Maui weather, tel. 877-5111; for recreational areas, tel. 877-5054; for Haleakala, tel. 571-5054; for marine weather, tel. 877-3477; for whale sighting and reports in season, tel. 661-8527. Or try **On Call,** a free 24-hour telephone service offering all of the above.

Storage

As there are no storage facilities at the Kahului Airport, private storage companies must be used. Try **Store and Lock** in Kahului, tel. 871-4240, for various-sized lockers—daily, weekly, or monthly rates. Others can be found through the phone book. Guests of the Northshore Inn in Wailuku can use the on-site storage rooms for everything from backpacks to surfboards to bicycles.

Post Offices

In Wailuku, tel. 244-4815; in Kahului, tel. 871-4710; in Kihei, tel. 879-2403; in Lahaina, tel. 667-6611. Other branch offices are scattered around the island.

Legal Help

For advice on legal problems while on Maui, contact **Legal Aid Society,** tel. 244-3731.

Maui Facts

Maui is the second youngest and second largest Hawaiian island after Hawaii. Its nickname is the Valley Island. Its color is pink and its flower is the *lokelani,* a small rose.

BOB RACE

CENTRAL MAUI: THE ISTHMUS

KAHULUI

It is generally believed that Kahului means "The Winning," but perhaps it should be "The Survivor." Kahului suffered attack by Kamehameha I in the 1790s, when he landed his war canoes here in preparation for battle at Iao Valley. In 1900 the settlement was purposely burned to thwart the plague, then rebuilt. Combined with Wailuku, the county seat just down the road, this area is now home to 22,000 Mauians, over one-third of the island population. Here's where the people live. It's a practical, homey town, the only deep-water port from which Maui's sugar and pineapples are shipped. Although Kahului was an established sugar town by 1880, it's really only grown up in the last 20 years. In the 1960s, Hawaiian Commercial and Sugar Co. began building low-cost housing for its workers, which became a model development for the whole of the U.S. Most people land at the airport, blast through for Lahaina or Kihei, and never give Kahului a second look. It's in no way a resort community, but it has the best general-purpose shopping on the island, a few noteworthy sites, and a convenient location to the airport.

SIGHTS

Kanaha Pond Waterfowl Sanctuary

This one-time royal fishpond is 1.5 miles southwest of the airport at the junctions of Routes 36 and 37. It's on the migratory route of various ducks and Canada geese, but most importantly it is home to the endangered Hawaiian stilt *(ae'o)* and the Hawaiian coot *(alae ke'oke'o)*. The stilt is a slender, 16-inch bird with a black back, white belly, and sticklike pink legs. The coot is a gray-black, ducklike bird, which builds large floating nests. An observation shelter is main-

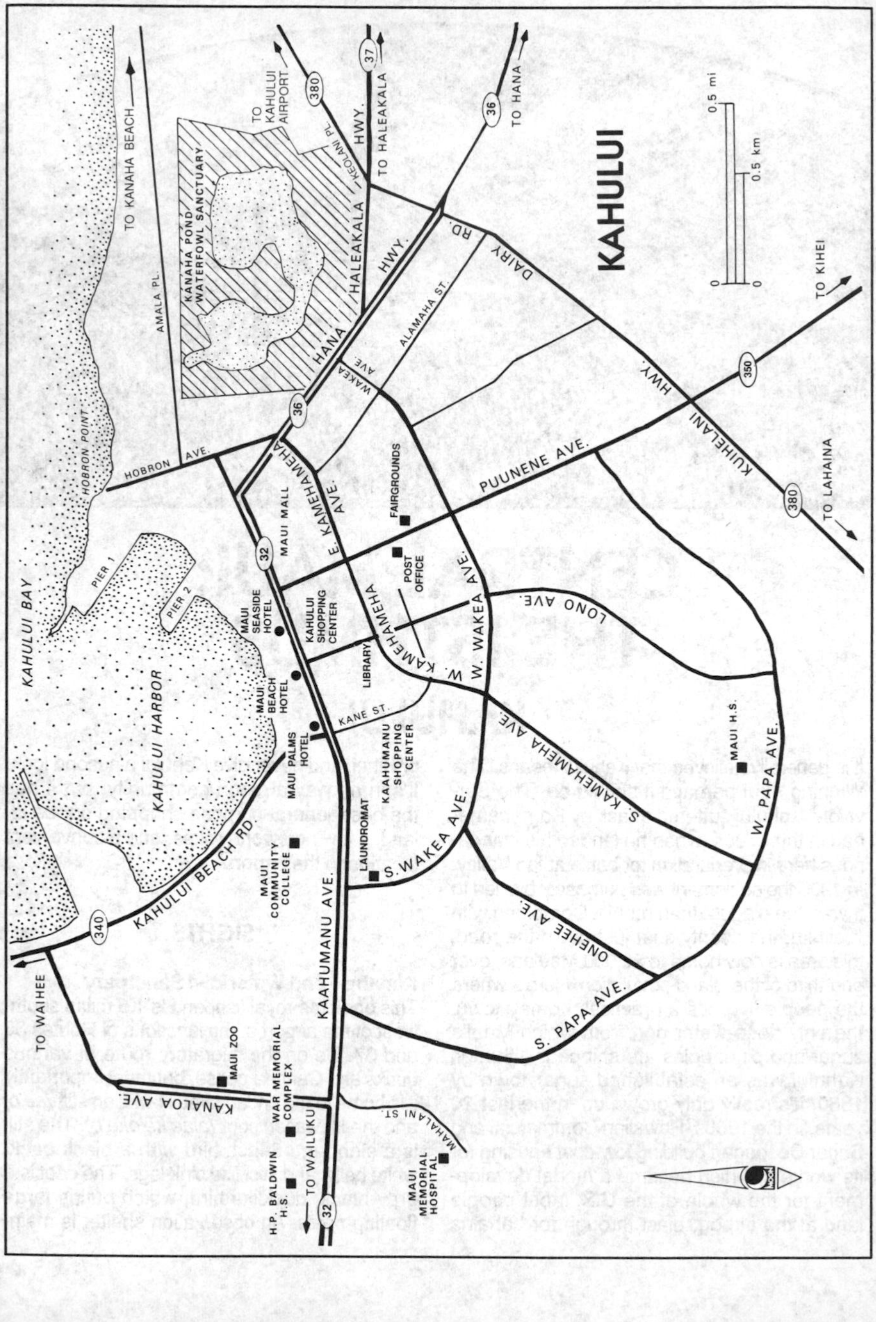

KAHULUI

0 0.5 mi
0 0.5 km

KAHULUI BAY
KAHULUI HARBOR
HOBRON POINT
PIER 1
PIER 2
TO KANAHA BEACH
AMALA PL.
HOBRON AVE.
KANAHA POND WATERFOWL SANCTUARY
TO KAHULUI AIRPORT
KEOLANI PL.
HANA HWY.
HALEAKALA HWY.
TO HALEAKALA
TO HANA
DAIRY RD.
ALAMAHA ST.
WAKEA AVE.
E. KAMEHAMEHA AVE.
MAUI MALL
FAIRGROUNDS
POST OFFICE
PUUNENE AVE.
KUIHELANI HWY.
TO KIHEI
TO LAHAINA
LONO AVE.
W. WAKEA AVE.
W. KAMEHAMEHA
LIBRARY
KAHULUI SHOPPING CENTER
MAUI SEASIDE HOTEL
MAUI BEACH HOTEL
MAUI PALMS HOTEL
KANE ST.
KAAHUMANU SHOPPING CENTER
LAUNDROMAT
MAUI COMMUNITY COLLEGE
S. KAMEHAMEHA AVE.
S. WAKEA AVE.
MAUI H.S.
W. PAPA AVE.
ONEHEE AVE.
S. PAPA AVE.
KAHULUI BEACH RD.
KAAHUMANU AVE.
TO WAIHEE
KANALOA AVE.
MAUI ZOO
WAR MEMORIAL COMPLEX
H.P. BALDWIN H.S.
TO WAILUKU
MAHALANI ST.
MAUI MEMORIAL HOSPITAL
32
36
37
340
350
380

tained along Rt. 37. Kanaha Pond is always open and free of charge. Bring binoculars.

Maui Community College

Just across the street from the Kaahumanu Shopping Center on Rt. 32, the college is a good place to check out the many bulletin boards for various activities, items for sale, and cheaper long-term housing. The **Student Center** is conspicuous as you drive in, and is a good place to get most information. The library is adequate.

Maui Zoo And Botanical Gardens

These grounds are more aptly described as a children's park. Plenty of young families enjoy themselves in this fenced-in area. The zoo houses various colorful birds such as cockatoos, peacocks, and macaws, as well as monkeys, baboons, and a giant tortoise that looks like a slow-moving boulder. The chickens, ducks, and swans are run-of-the-mill, but the ostriches, over seven feet tall, are excellent specimens. With pygmy goats and plenty of sheep, the atmosphere is like a kiddies' petting zoo. It's open daily 9 a.m.-4 p.m., free. Turn at the red light onto Kanaloa Avenue off Rt. 32 about midway between Kahului and Wailuku.

Also at this turn is **Wailuku War Memorial Park and Center.** Here you'll find a stadium, gymnasium, swimming pool, and free hot showers. To the left, at the entrance to the gym, you can pick up county camping permits (see "County Parks" under "Camping and Hiking" in the Maui Introduction).

Alexander And Baldwin Sugar Mill Museum

The museum is located at the intersection of Puunene Ave. (Rt. 350) and Hanson Rd., about a half mile from Dairy Rd. (Rt. 380), tel. 871-8058, open Mon.-Sat. 9:30 a.m.-4:30 p.m., admission $3 adults, $1.50 children, free for children ages five. (Avoid the area around 3 p.m., when the still-working mill changes shifts.) This small but highly informative museum could easily be your first stop after arriving at Kahului Airport only 15 minutes away, especially if you're heading to Kihei. Once you get off the plane, you'll realize that you're in the midst of sugarcane fields. If you want to know the history of this crop and the people who worked and developed it, visit the museum. The vintage building was the home of the sugar mill supervisor, who literally lived surrounded by his work. Inside is a small but well-stocked bookstore and gift shop featuring Hawaiiana and handmade clothing and artifacts, with goodies like passion fruit syrup and raw sugar. Among the unique items for sale are *waraji,* Japanese sandals fashioned from bulrushes by a 92-year-old *sensei,* Kinichi Tasaka, from Kauai. He has recently suffered a stroke but not before he passed on the tradition to his daughter. These sandals are traditional in Japan, often used by pilgrims to the 88 Sacred Temples of Shikoku, and for making the climb up Mt. Fuji. The handicraft is dying even in Japan, so take the opportunity to see and to buy these distinctive gifts from days gone by.

As you begin your tour, notice in the corner the ancient refrigerator still used by the staff. In the first room, you are given a brief description of the natural history of Maui, along with a rendition of the legends of the demigod Maui. Display cases explain Maui's rainfall and use of irrigation for a productive sugarcane yield. You'll see an old-fashioned copper rain gauge along with pragmatic artifacts from the building of the Haiku Ditch. A collection of vintage photos features the Baldwin and Alexander families, while a historical plaque recalls when workers lived in ethnic camps, each with its own euphemistic name (Chinese at Ah Fong, Japanese at Nashiwa, Portuguese at Cod Fish). This setup was designed to discourage competition (or cooperation) between the ethnic groups during labor disputes, and to ease the transition to the new land. These people are represented by everything from stuffed fighting cocks to baseball mitts from the '30s. The museum is in the shadow of the mill, and you can hear the wheels turning and the mill grinding. It's not an antiseptic remembrance, but a vital one in which the history continues.

Kanaha Beach County Park

This is the only beach worth visiting in the area. Good for a swim and a picnic. Follow Rt. 380 toward the airport and turn left on Kaa Street. Alternately, from Kaahumanu Avenue, turn left onto Hobron Avenue, and then immediately right onto Amala Street, and follow the signs to the park. It's also *the* best place to begin learning sailboarding. The wind is steady but not too strong, and the wave action is gentle.

ACCOMMODATIONS

Kahului features motel/hotels because most people are short-term visitors, heading to or from the airport. These accommodations are bunched together across from the Kahului Shopping Center on the harbor side of Kaahumanu Avenue (Rt. 32). The best are the **Maui Beach Hotel,** tel. 877-0051; and just across a parking lot, its sister hotel, **The Maui Palms Hotel,** tel. 877-0071. The Maui Beach has a pool on the second floor, and its daily buffet is a good value. The central courtyard, tastefully landscaped, is off the main foyer, which has a Polynesian flavor. The Red Dragon Room provides the only disco (Friday and Saturday nights) on this part of the island. Rates for the Maui Beach are $79-138; for the Maui Palms $50-74 ($10 less in the off-season). For reservations, call (800) 367-5004, (800) 272-5275 interisland. The one other hotel, 100 yards to the east, is the **Maui Seaside Hotel** (now combined with the Maui Hukilau), tel. 877-3311, part of the Sand and Seaside Hotels, an island-owned chain. Rates are $55-79, $71-95 with rental car. For reservations, call (800) 367-7000.

FOOD

The Kahului area has some elegant dining spots as well as an assortment of inexpensive yet good eating establishments. Many are found in the shopping malls. Here are some of the best.

Inexpensive

Ma Chan's, tel. 877-7818, is a cement-floored, no-atmosphere restaurant across from the fire station at 199 Dairy Rd., located in the fading pink-on-green Maui Plantation Shops. Open daily for breakfast and lunch until 6 p.m., Ma Chan's has a variety of inexpensive sandwiches, burgers, and plate lunches, all with an island twist. The restaurant is a little worse for wear, but the staff is very friendly, and the food is very good.

Maui Bagel and Bakery, nearby at 201 Dairy Rd., tel. 871-4825, open daily except Sunday 6:30 a.m.-5:30 p.m., makes fresh (preservative-, fat-, and cholesterol-free) rye, blueberry, whole wheat, garlic, poppy seed, sesame, and onion bagels. Choose a buttered bagel for $1, or one smothered in a layer of cream cheese for $1.50, and have it wrapped to go, or eat it at one of the tables. Tasty deli sandwiches, served on bagels, French bread, or rye, include turkey breast, chicken salad, and even curry for under $6. The bakery also makes mouthwatering cinnamon and walnut coffee cake, fudge brownies, strudel, and loaves of French, rye, and whole wheat bread. Specialties are egg sesame bread, challah, garlic Parmesan bread, and sourdough. A deli case holds a variety of drinks and flavored cream cheeses.

Follow your nose in the Kaahumanu Shopping Center to **The Coffee Store,** tel. 871-6860, open daily 7 a.m.-6 p.m., till 9 p.m. on Thursday and Friday, and Sunday 9 a.m.-3 p.m. Light lunches include savories like a hot croissant for $1.95 or a spinach roll pastry puff for $3.95. Coffee by the cup is under $2.25, refills 35 cents. The coffees, roasted on the premises, are from 40 gourmet varieties handpicked in Africa, South America, and Indonesia, and include exotic beans like Jamaican Blue Mountain. Gifts and giftwear, too.

The **Maui Mall**, off Puunene Ave., has a terrific selection of inexpensive eateries. **Matsu Restaurant,** tel. 877-0822, is a fast-food Japanese restaurant with an assortment of daily specials for under $4; or try a steaming bowl of one of various types of saimin for $3.80. Very authentic, like a *soba-ya* in Japan. Japanese standards include *katsu donburi,* tempura, or curry rice, all for under $5. Adjacent is **Siu's Chinese Kitchen,** where most of their typical Chinese dishes are under $4. **Sir Wilfred's,** tel. 877-3711, is another gourmet coffee shop that offers a commodious setting for sipping fresh-brewed coffee and eating gourmet sandwiches, like their hot pastrami for under $5. It's good place for an inexpensive lunch with some atmosphere. **Luigi's Pizza Factory** serves up decent pizza. **SW Barbecue** is a terrific indoor/outdoor fast-food restaurant with Korean favorites, plate lunches under $5, and a delicious grilled chicken sandwich for only $2.25.

Try the **Original Maui Sweet Baked Ham Deli,** open weekdays 8 a.m.-5 p.m., Saturday 9 a.m.-4 p.m., Sunday 10 a.m.-3 p.m., across from the Maui Mall in the Old Kahului Store, for any of their filling sandwiches, deli salads, soups, or lunch baskets (great for the trip to Hana). Their gift shop has "hog" motif items in keeping with their motto: "Maui No Ka Oink."

At counter-seating in the back of **Toda Drugs,** in the Kahului Shopping Center, open daily 8:30 a.m.-4 p.m., tel. 877-4550, locals enjoy daily specials of Hawaiian and other ethnic foods. Better than you'd think! Daily special under $5.

Next door you'll find **Ichiban,** another authentic and inexpensive Japanese restaurant, tel. 871-6977, open daily except Sunday 8 a.m.-2 p.m., dinner 5-9 p.m., featuring full and continental breakfasts, along with Japanese, American, and local specialties. The lunch menu includes teriyaki chicken or shrimp tempura for $5.95; chicken cutlet for $4.95; pork, chicken, shrimp, or beef *donburi* under $5; and a variety of *udon*, $2.95 for basic noodles or $4.95 for *udon nabeyaki* with shrimp tempura, boiled egg, and fish cake. Sandwiches are everything from a BLT to baked ham for under $5. Dinner features combination plates, with your choice of any two items like shrimp and vegetable tempura, sashimi, or teriyaki chicken for $9.95, along with special combinations like steak and lobster at $18.95, the most expensive item on the menu. The interior is basic American with a pinch of Japanese.

Others worth trying include **Shirley's** and **Dairy Queen,** near each other on Lono Avenue. Both serve good and inexpensive plate lunches and sandwiches, and Shirley's is open early mornings.

Finally, for those who need their weekly fix of something fried and wrapped in styrofoam, Kahului's main streets are dotted with McDonald's (Puunene Ave.), Pizza Hut (Kamehameha Ave.), Burger King (Kaahumanu Ave.), and Kentucky Fried Chicken (Wakea Ave.); there are more at Maui Mall and Kaahumanu Shopping Center.

Moderate

The Maui Beach Hotel's **Rainbow Dining Room** serves food in the second-floor dining room. You can fill up here at their lunch buffet 11 a.m.-2 p.m. for $6.50 ($5.50 salad bar only), or come for dinner 6-9 p.m. (except Monday) to the **Red Dragon Restaurant** for their "Cantonese Buffet Dinner," offered for a very reasonable $9.95 ($5.25 children under 11). Prime rib and seafood dinners are also served. Breakfast (from 7 a.m.) features fresh-baked goods from $5.75. For reservations, call 877-0051.

Maui Palms Hotel's **East-West Dining Room,** tel. 877-0071, offers an "Imperial Teppanyaki Japanese Buffet," every day 5:30-8:30 p.m. for $15. The food, although plentiful, is prepared for the undiscerning conventioneer, and is either fried to death or is a generic mish-mash of Japanese cuisine. All-you-can-eat salad bar daily for lunch, 11 a.m.-1 p.m., costs $6.

Across from the Maui Mall, **Aurelio's,** tel. 871-7656, presents a selection of Italian dishes, plate lunches, and daily specials ($5 off most entrees). The restaurant is not fancy, but the local staff is very friendly, and the atmosphere is that of a neighborhood tavern where all are welcome. Open for lunch and dinner for chef's or tuna salad for under $7; sandwiches ranging from French dip to a tuna, jack, and avocado for under $6; and juicy burgers smothered in mushrooms, bacon, cheddar cheese, and avocado for $5.50. Plate lunches priced $5.95-6.95 are teriyaki steak, roast pork, and oyster chicken. Specials include prime rib with mushrooms and gravy for $12.95, shrimp fettuccine for $12.95, or boneless chicken breast with cream paragon for $11.95. Aurelio's also features daily entertainment (see "Entertainment" following).

At **Ming Yuen,** tel. 871-7787, for under $9 you can dine on Cantonese or Sichuan specialties like braised oysters with ginger and scallions. The hot-and-sour soup ($5.25) is almost a meal in itself. Inexpensive lunch 11 a.m.-5 p.m. except Sunday, dinner nightly 5-9 p.m. Located behind the Maui Mall at 162 Alamaha St., off E. Kamehameha Avenue. Reservations are suggested; takeout is available.

Across the street from Ming Yuen is **Lopaka's Bar and Grill,** tel. 871-1135. Open for lunch and dinner Mon.-Sat. 11 a.m. to closing; there is entertainment nightly—no cover. Lunches are mostly burgers, salads, plate lunches, sandwiches for less than $7.75. Full dinners of steak, seafood, or chicken cost up to $10.95.

Vi's Restaurant, tel. 877-3311, is at the Maui Seaside Hotel. Breakfast, served 7-9:30 a.m., includes omelettes, hotcakes, and other island favorites. Dinner is served 6-8 p.m; Vi's offers over 20 of them for under $10.

Expensive

The Chart House, on Kahului Bay at 500 N. Puunene Ave. (also in Lahaina), tel. 877-2476, is a steak and seafood house that's not really expensive. This is a favorite with businesspeople and travelers in transit to or from the airport. The quality is good and the atmosphere is soothing. Open for dinner nightly 5:30-10 p.m.

Wolfgang's Bistro, in the Kahului Building at 33 Lono Ave., tel. 871-7555, open for lunch Mon.-Fri. with slightly cheaper prices, and dinner Tues.-Sat., is the only semi-elegant restaurant in Kahului. They specialize in island fish, prepared seven different ways. Expect to spend $17 and up per person for dinner.

Liquor

Maui Wine and Liquor at 333 Dairy Rd. (out near the airport), tel. 871-7006, is an excellent liquor store. They have an enormous wine selection, over 80 different types of imported beer, and even delivery service. For a quick stop at a basic bottle shop try **Party Pantry** on Dairy Rd., **Ah Fooks Supermarket,** or **Star Market.**

ENTERTAINMENT

The **Red Dragon Disco** at the Maui Beach Hotel is the only disco and dance spot on this side of the island. It's open Friday and Saturday 10 p.m.-2 a.m. With a reasonable dress code and cover charge, it's a favorite with local people under 25.

The **Maui Palms Hotel** hosts the "Sakuras" every Friday and Saturday (no cover). They specialize in "oldies," and their large repertoire includes Top 40, country, and even Hawaiian and Japanese ballads. Good for listening and dancing! A favorite with local people, whose children might be partying at the Red Dragon. On Tuesday, Wednesday, and Thursday, 8 p.m.-midnight, stop in for karaoke night.

Aurelio's, tel. 871-7656, across from the Maui Mall, is a friendly local tavern serving island and Italian cuisine and featuring daily entertainment. Happy hour, Wed.-Fri. 3-7 p.m., brings Kenny Roberts, a talented local musician who performs contemporary music. Other groups, including Kona Winds, After Hours, Local Fashion, and Youth, play Wed.-Sat. respectively, 9 p.m.-12:30 a.m., when the restaurant becomes a swinging nightspot.

Holiday Theater, tel. 877-6622, is at the Kaahumanu Shopping Center, and **The Maui Theater,** tel. 877-3560, is at the Kahului Shopping Center. In addition, legitimate theater is offered by the **Maui Community Theater,** tel. 242-6969, at 68 N. Market St., Wailuku. Major productions occur four times a year.

SHOPPING

Because of the three malls right in a row along Kaahumanu Avenue, Kahului has the best all-around shopping on the island. Here you can find absolutely everything you might need (see "Shopping" in the Introduction). Don't miss the **Maui Swap Meet,** tel. 877-3100, at the fairgrounds on Puunene Avenue every Saturday. You can also shop almost the minute you arrive or just before you leave at two touristy but good shops along Airport Road. At the **Little Airport Shopping Center** a half mile from the airport are the **T-shirt Factory,** with original Maui designs and custom T-shirts $7-19 (displayed on the walls); and **Hawaiian Ali'i Coral Factory,** for pink and black coral and jewelry set with semiprecious stones. When Airport Road turns into Dairy Road you'll find **Airport Flower and Fruits,** which can provide you with produce that's pre-inspected and admissible to the Mainland. They also have a large selection of lei, which can be packed to go.

The **Kaahumanu Shopping Center**, along Kaahumanu Avenue, is the largest and has the widest selection of stores. You'll find **Liberty House, Sears, Ben Franklin,** apparel stores, shoe stores, computer centers, art shops, music stores, and a dozen inexpensive eateries. **Waldenbooks** is also here, tel. 871-6112, open Mon.-Sat. 9 a.m. to mall closing at 5:30 p.m., Thursday and Friday to 9 p.m., and Sunday to 3 p.m., for the best selection of books on Maui. A great store for a relaxing cup of coffee or light lunch is **The Coffee Store.**

At the **Maui Mall** just up the road is **Longs Drugs** for everything from aspirin to film, **Woolworth,** and another **Waldenbooks,** tel. 877-0181, open Mon.-Thurs. 9 a.m.-6 p.m., Friday 9 a.m.-9 p.m., Saturday 9 a.m.-5:30 p.m., Sunday 10 a.m.-4 p.m. **Affordable Fashions** has a full selection of action and resortwear. A **Postal Center,** open Mon.-Fri. 9 a.m.-5 p.m., offers full mailing services.

At the **Kahului Shopping Center,** 47 Kaahumanu Ave., you will find **Ah Fooks Supermarket,** specializing in Asian foods; **Noda Market,** a local market with more of the same; **Peggy and Johnny's,** selling Levi's to formal attire; the **Island Biker,** a full-service bicycle shop; **Burger King; Toda Drugs** and its locally famous lunch counter; and the inexpensive but authentic **Ichiban Restaurant.**

The Old Kahului Shopping Center, at 55 Kaahumanu Ave., across from the Maui Mall, is just that, an old building from 1916 that held a bank and a series of shops that has been modernized and brought back to life. It is now one of the best groupings of boutiques on Maui, each store distinctive and well presented. **Lightning Bolt,** tel. 877-3484, specializes in surfboards and surf attire by Billabong, and in modern fashions by Patagonia and Quicksilver. They also feature women's apparel, dancewear, swimwear, and aloha shirts, along with a good selection of hats, sunglasses, and waterproof wristwatches. Other shops include women's apparel stores **Tiger Lily** and **Jazzed**; **Tropica,** another surf store; a futon and furniture shop; a video store; **Seahorses,** a toy emporium with kites, dolls, stuffed whales, and baskets of magnificent protea blooms that sell for as little as 50 cents; and **Tester's Shoe Repair,** tel. 877-7140, open daily 9 a.m.-6 p.m., Saturday 10 a.m.-3 p.m., specializing in Birkenstocks repair starting at $21.50.

SERVICES

Free Shuttle Bus

The County of Maui offers a free shuttle connecting Wailuku and Kahului, *for now* operating weekdays only 8 a.m.-4 p.m., tel. 877-7651 for current information. The stops are too numerous to mention, but they definitely include all of the shopping centers and main roads.

Miscellaneous

There is a **Bank of Hawaii,** tel. 871-8250, on Puunene Avenue. **City Bank,** tel. 871-7761, is at the Kaahumanu Shopping Center. And find **First Hawaiian Bank,** tel. 877-2311, at 20 W. Kaahumanu Avenue.

The Kahului **post office** is on Puunene Ave. (Rt. 350) just across the street from the fairgrounds, tel. 871-4710.

The **library,** at 90 School St., tel. 877-5048, has irregular hours.

If you're looking for a laundromat, **W & F Washerette** features video games to while away the time, 125 S. Wakea, tel. 877-0353.

The **East West Clinic,** at 444 Hana Hwy., Suite 111, Kahului, tel. 871-4722, has licensed practitioners who offer acupuncture, massage therapy, naturopath health care, dietary counseling, weight-loss programs, and treatments for smokers who wish to kick the habit.

WAILUKU

Often, historical towns maintain a certain aura long after their time of importance has passed. Wailuku is one of these. Today Maui's county seat, Wailuku earned its name, "Bloody Waters," from a ferocious battle fought by Kamehameha I against Maui warriors just up the road in Iao Valley. The slaughter was so intense that over four miles of the local stream literally ran red with blood. Last century the missionaries settled in Wailuku, and their architectural influences, such as a white-steepled church and the courthouse at the top of the main street, give an impression of a New England town.

Wailuku is a pretty town, especially its backstreets. Its location on the rolling foothills of the West Maui Mountains adds character—unlike the often-flat layout of many other Hawaiian towns. You can "do" Wailuku in only an hour, though most people don't even give it this much time. They pass through on their way to Iao Needle, where everyone goes, or to Happy Valley and on to Kahakuloa, around the backside, where the car companies hope that no one goes. You *can* see Wailuku's sights from the window of your car, but don't short-change yourself this way. Definitely visit the Bailey House, now called **Hale Hoikeike,** and while you're out, walk the grounds of **Kaahumanu Church.** Market Street, just off Main, has a clutch of intriguing shops you can peek into while you're at it. With new restaurants, art galleries, a community theater, and a cultural center, Wailuku is taking on the trappings of a cultural center.

SIGHTS

Kaahumanu Church

It's fitting that Maui's oldest existing stone church is named after the resolute but loving Queen Kaahumanu. This rock-willed woman is the "Saint Peter" of Hawaii, upon whom Christianity in the islands was built. She was *the* most important early convert, often attending services in Kahului's humble grass-hut chapel. In 1832 an adobe church was built on the same spot and named in her honor. Washed away by rain and time it was replaced by the island's first stone structure in 1837. In 1876 the church was reduced to about half its original size, and what remained is the white and green structure we know today. Oddly enough, the steeple was repaired in 1984 by Skyline Engineers, who hail from Massachusetts, the same place from which the missionaries came 150 years earlier. You can see the church sitting here on High Street (Rt. 30), but it's usually closed during the week. Sunday services are at 9 a.m., when the Hawaiian congregation sings the Lord's praise in their native language. An excellent cultural and religious event to attend.

Hale Hoikeike

This is the old **Bailey House,** built from 1833 to 1850, with various rooms added throughout the years. In the 1840s it housed the "Wailuku Female Seminary," of which Edward Bailey was principal until it closed in 1849. Bailey then went on to manage the Wailuku Sugar Company. More important for posterity, he became a prolific landscape painter of various areas around the island. Most of his paintings record the period from 1866 through 1896 and are now displayed in the "annex," known as the Bailey Gallery. This one-time seminary dining room was his actual studio. In July 1957 the old missionary homestead formally became the Maui Historical Society Museum, at which time it acquired its new name of Hale Hoikeike, "House of Display." It closed in 1973, then was refurbished and reopened in July 1975.

You'll be amazed at the two-foot-thick walls the missionaries taught the Hawaiians to build, using goat hair as the binding agent. Years of whitewashing make them resemble new-fallen snow. The rooms inside are given over to various themes. **The Hawaiian Room** houses excellent examples of the often practical artifacts of pre-contact Hawaii; especially notice the fine displays of tapa cloth and calabashes. Hawaiian tapa, now a lost art, was considered Polynesia's finest and most advanced. Upstairs is the bedroom. It's quite large and dom-

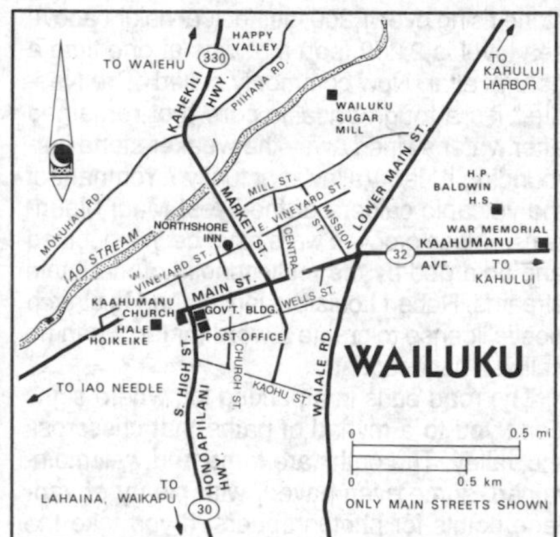

inated by a canopied bed. There's a dresser with a jewelry box and fine lace gloves. Peek behind the wooden gate in the rear of the bedroom to see swords, dolls, walking canes, toys, and muskets—now only a jumble, one day they'll be a display. Upstairs at the front of the house is the old office. Here you'll find roll-top desks, ledgers, and excellent examples of old-time wicker furniture, prototypes of examples you still see today. Downstairs you'll discover the sitting room and kitchen, heart of the house: the "feelings" are strongest here. There are excellent examples of Hawaiian adzes, old silverware, and plenty of photos. The lintel over the doorway is as stout as the spirits of the people who once lived here. The stonework on the floor is well laid and the fireplace is totally homey.

Go outside! The lanai runs across the entire front and down the side. Around back is the canoe shed, housing accurate replicas of Hawaiian-sewn sennit outrigger canoes, as well as Duke Kahanamoku's redwood surfboard. On the grounds you'll also see exhibits of sugarcane, sugar pots, *konane* boards, and various Hawaiian artifacts. Hale Hoikeike is open daily 10 a.m.-4:30 p.m., on Main Street (Rt. 320) on your left, just as you begin heading for Iao Valley. Admission is well worth $2 (children 50 cents). Tours are usually self-guided, but guides are available free if arrangements are made in advance. The bookstore/gift shop has a terrific selection of souvenirs and Hawaiiana at better-than-average prices. The office of the Maui Historical Society is in the basement.

Kepaniwai Park

As you head up Rt. 320 to Iao Valley, you're in for a real treat. Two miles after leaving Wailuku, you come across Kepaniwai Park and Heritage Gardens. Here the architect, Richard C. Tongg, envisioned and created a park dedicated to all of Hawaii's people. See the Portuguese villa and garden complete with an outdoor oven, a thatch-roofed Hawaiian grass shack, a New England "salt box," a Chinese pagoda, a Japanese teahouse with authentic garden, and a bamboo house; any of these could be the little "sugar shack" that songs and dreams are made of. Admission is free and there are pavilions with picnic tables. This now-tranquil spot is where the Maui warriors fell to the invincible Kamehameha and his merciless patron war god, Ku. *Kepaniwai* means "Damming of the Waters"—literally with corpses. Kepaniwai is now a monument to higher human nature: harmony and beauty.

John F. Kennedy Profile

Up the road toward Iao Valley you come to a scenic area long known as Pali Ele'ele, or Black Gorge. This stream-eroded amphitheater canyon has attracted attention for centuries. Amazingly, after President Kennedy was assassinated, people noticed his likeness portrayed here by a series of large boulders; mention of a profile had never been noted or recorded here before. A pipe stuck in the ground serves as a rudimentary telescope. Squint through it and there he is, with eyes closed in deep repose. The likeness is uncanny, and easily seen, unlike those in most of these formations, for which you have to stretch your imagination to the breaking point.

Maui Tropical Plantation

This new attraction is somewhat out of the ordinary. The Maui Tropical Plantation presents a model of a working plantation that you can tour by small tram. Most interesting is an up-close look at Maui's agricultural abundance. Displays of products are situated around the taro patches at the plantation village. An $8 ($3 for children), 45-minute tram ride (optional) takes you through fields of cane, banana, mango, papaya, pineapple, and macadamia nuts; flowers here and there add exotic color. The plantation, with a restaurant, gift shop, and tropical flower nursery, is in Waikapu, a small village along Rt. 30 between Wailuku and Lahaina. It's open daily 9 a.m.-5 p.m., tel. 244-7643. As an added attraction, have your photo taken with a brightly feathered parakeet or cockatiel and transformed into a picture postcard (overnight service) by **Birds of Paradise.** Buddy Fo's **Hawaiian Country Show** is put on here Monday, Wednesday, and Friday evenings, 5-9 p.m.

Tropical Gardens Of Maui

This private garden of tropical flowers and fruits is located on the way to Iao Valley, tel. 244-3085, open 9 a.m.-5 p.m., admission $4. The gift shop has a good display of flowers, certified for mailing to the Mainland; also a deli counter for sandwiches, burgers, ice cream, and beverages.

IAO VALLEY STATE PARK

This valley has been a sacred spot and a place of pilgrimage since ancient times. Before Westerners arrived, the people of Maui, who came here to pay homage to the "Eternal Creator," named this valley *Iao,* "Supreme Light." In the center of the velvety green valley is a pillar of stone rising over 1,200 feet (actual height above sea level is 2,250 feet) that was at one time a natural altar. Now commonly called "The Needle," it's a tough basaltic core that remained after water swirled away the weaker stone surrounding it. Iao Valley is actually a remnant of the volcanic caldera of the West Maui Mountains, whose grooved walls have been smoothed and enlarged by the restlessness of mountain streams. Robert Louis Stevenson had to stretch poetic license to create a word for Iao when he called it "viridescent."

The road ends in a parking lot, where signs point you to a myriad of paths that crisscross the valley. The paths are tame and well maintained, some even paved, with plenty of vantage points for photographers. If you take the lower path to the river below, you'll find a good-sized, popular swimming hole; but remember, these are the West Maui Mountains, and it can rain at any time! You can escape the crowds even in this heavily touristed area by following the path toward The Needle until you come to the pavilion at the top. As you head back, take the paved path that bears to the right. It soon becomes dirt, skirting the river, and the tourists magically disappear. Here are a number of pint-sized pools where you can take a refreshing dip.

Iao is for day-use only. On your way back to Wailuku you might take a five-minute side excursion up to Wailuku Heights. Look for the

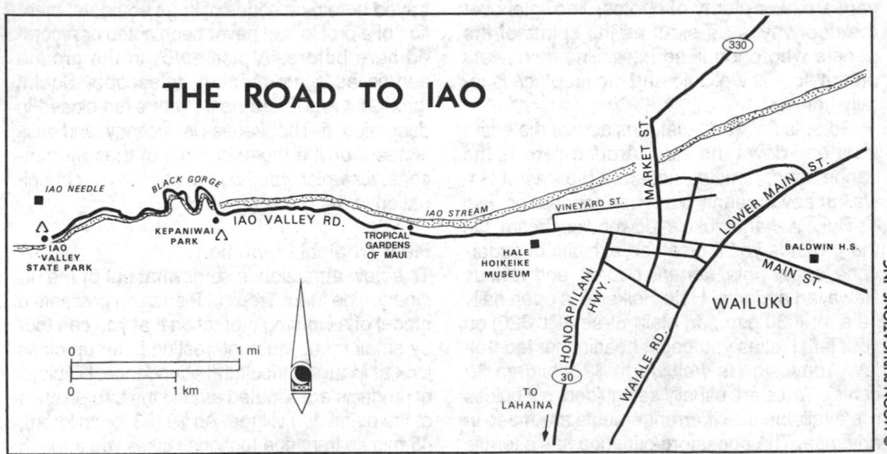

road on your right. There's little here besides a housing development, but the view of the bay below is tops.

PRACTICALITIES

Accommodations

Visitors to Wailuku mostly stay elsewhere on Maui because there really isn't any place to lodge in town except for a few very specialized and very humble hotels. The newest and most pleasant is the **Northshore Inn,** tel. 242-8999, at 2080 Vineyard St., easily spotted with its row of international flags fluttering from the second-floor balcony. After several months of cleaning and painting (it was previously the fleabag, drug-infested Wailuku Grand Hotel), this clean, light, and comfortable inn caters mostly to young independent travelers and surfers. Skylights brighten the upstairs; potted plants add color to the beige walls; and the homey sitting room offers a place for the international guests to talk, listen to music, or watch television. The balcony is a fine place to catch the evening air. A bulletin board is filled with helpful information about Maui and the other islands. Bunk rooms go for $15 a bed, single rooms $39, and double rooms $43, all sharing four spotless bathrooms. Not only is this an easygoing, well-cared-for place, the owners (who live on the premises) are environmentally conscious—they recycle and use low-wattage light bulbs, solar-heated water, and low-flow shower heads. There are laundry facilities; storage facilities for sailboards, backpacks, and large items; a full communal kitchen; free morning coffee; and a small garden in the back with an 80-year-old banyan tree and tropical fruit trees. The Northshore Inn also has a shuttle van with pick-up and delivery service to the airport. Time permitting, they offer island-wide tours, including trips to Haleakala, Hana, and various beaches, at very affordable prices. Ask about their deal with Word of Mouth Rental Cars for low daily rates. The owners have won the respect of the community for transforming this inn into a viable business and dealing equitably with the locals.

The **Banana Bungalow Two** is at 310 N. Market St., Wailuku, HI 96793, in Happy Valley, tel. 244-5090 or (800) 846-7835, office hours 7 a.m.-11 p.m. Rates are $34.90 s, $42.50 d, or $16.40 for bunk rooms sleeping three to four persons; weekly and monthly rates available. Until very recently, this was a flophouse for locals who were down on their luck. Now it's a clean and spartan hotel, with a fresh coat of paint and new bathrooms up and down. Typically, you're liable to hear languages from a dozen countries, and if you're into sailboarding or after a cross-cultural experience, this is the spot. The Banana offers basic accommodations; if you care more about wind and surf conditions than about what your bedroom looks like, it's the place for you. If you leave a message, they *will* return your call anywhere in the world. Make sure to give international area codes. Extra services include: bicycle rentals at $5 per day; boogie boards and two-person sea kayaks at $10 per day; a free and convenient airport/beach shuttle; adventure tours such as crater hikes or kayaking trips; and inexpensive meals at an outdoor cafe.

The **Vineyard Inn,** above the Maui Boy Restaurant, at 2102 Vineyard St., tel. 244-7243, is owned and operated by Bob Kato, the owner of the Maui Boy. The rooms are small, basic, clean, and very inexpensive at only $20 per night, $38 double. There's an area out back to store your surfboard, clean communal bathrooms with plenty of hot water, a public phone, private entrance, and private parking. Check in at the Maui Boy, or at the small hotel office if open.

Molina's Bar and Rooms, at 197 Market St., offers utilitarian rooms at $350 per month, $25 per night, $125 per week, with private bath and room service. Bogart playing a character with a five-day-old beard and a hangover would be comfortable waking up at this basic, clean, and friendly fleabag.

Food

The establishments listed below are all in the bargain or reasonable range. The decor in most is basic and homey, with the emphasis placed on the food. Wailuku has the best and the most inexpensive restaurants on Maui.

Sam Sato's is at 318 N. Market St., open Mon.-Sat. (closed Thursday) 8 a.m.-4 p.m. (Happy Valley). Sato's is famous for *manju,* a pufflike pastry from Japan filled with sweets, meats, or *adzuki* beans. Local residents *must* bring Sato's *manju* on visits to friends or relatives off-island. Lunch is served only until 2 p.m. A specialized place, but worth the effort.

Maui Boy Restaurant, tel. 244-7243, open daily 7:30 a.m.-9 p.m., at 2102 Vineyard St., owned and operated by Bob Kato, the friendly greeter, is a down-home place with excellent local food for under $7. Sandwiches, miso, Portuguese bean soup, and Maui omelettes are all delicious and reasonably priced. Dishes like teri beef and *katsu don* are under $6, but the real specialties are Hawaiian foods like *kalua* pork or *lau lau* under $9.

Across the street is the new **Canto's Creative Cuisine,** tel. 242-9758. Open 8 a.m.-8 p.m., except Sunday, this restaurant specializes in sandwiches, pastries, fresh-baked bread, and pies; there are several lunch and dinner specials daily.

The **Maui Bake Shop and Deli,** owned and operated by Jose and Claire Krall, at 2092 Vineyard St., tel. 242-0064, open weekdays 6 a.m.-6:30 p.m., Saturday 7 a.m.-5 p.m., Sunday 7 a.m.-1 p.m., has a full selection of home-baked goods and sandwiches at very reasonable prices. Sandwich selections include turkey-ham, roast beef, pastrami, or vegie for $3.25, with soup du jour, $5.25. Daily specials can be pizza, quiche, filled croissants, or lox and bagels for under $5. Tantalizing baked goods include apple fritters, coconut macaroons, apricot twists, and fruit tarts; or choose from a menagerie of butter and cream pigs, rabbits, and frogs. Enjoy your selection with an espresso, cappuccino, or hot tea.

Siam Thai is a small restaurant painted black and white at 123 N. Market, tel. 244-3817, open weekdays 11 a.m.-2:30 p.m. and 5-9:30 p.m., Saturday and Sunday 5-9:30 p.m. only. They serve excellent Thai food with an emphasis on vegetarian cuisine, at very reasonable prices.

Saeng's, at 2119 Vineyard (Lahaina location too—see "Food" under "Lahaina" in the West Maui chapter), open weekdays for lunch and dinner, weekends for dinner only, tel. 244-1567, serves excellent Thai food at great prices. Dishes include appetizers like Thai crisp noodles for $4.95, green papaya salad for $5.50, and shrimp salad at $6.95. The savory soups, enough for two, include spicy fish or shrimp soup for $7.50, and *poh teak,* a zesty seafood combination soup for $8.95. Thai specialties such as shrimp asparagus, cashew chicken, and seafood garlic shrimp are all under $9, while vegetarian selections like mixed vegetable curry, and watercress with tofu, are under $7. The best seating, although the interior is quite tasteful with linen tablecloths and paisley booths, is outside in a garden area where a small waterfall gurgles pleasantly. Saeng's and its friendly competitor Siam Thai are the two best, reasonably priced restaurants in town.

Just up the street is the **Vineyard Tavern,** tel. 242-9938, with dynamite burgers.

Hamburger Mary's, at the corner of N. Main and E. Market streets, tel. 244-7776, open daily 7 a.m.-2 a.m., is a very friendly bar and restaurant, where people of all sexual lifestyles are welcome, and where you can have a quiet beer or boogie the night away to rock music. The interior, like the inside of a big kid's toy box, is brightened with Humpty Dumpty falling off his wall, the man in the moon hanging from the ceiling, a manikin riding a horse, a winged mermaid floating in celestial bliss, Japanese fans, surfboards, a small mirrored dance floor, and cherubic angels and fairies perched here and there about the room. Start your day with a breakfast of Portuguese sausage and eggs for $5, create-your-own omelettes for $5, or Mary's short stack for $3.50. The lunch menu has *pu pu* like homefried melt for $3; Mary's macho nachos with black olives, jalapeños, and cheddar cheese for $3.50; and an assortment of fresh salads and homemade soups for under $5. Large two-fisted sandwiches and burgers include avocado burger for $5.25, meatless patty burger for $5.95, and the bird of paradise sandwich with cheddar cheese, sliced bacon, turkey, and avocado for $7.95. You can also enjoy a gigantic char-broiled steak with salad for $10.25, or Mary's mahimahi or a breast of chicken for $9.25. Happy hour, daily 3-9 p.m., features $1.75 well drinks and domestic beers, while Saturday and Sunday specials are a choice of Bloody Mary's, screwdrivers, or greyhounds for $2. Dee-jay music and dancing are offered Thurs.-Sat. 9 p.m.-closing, when Mary's comes alive and everybody rocks.

The **Maui Grill Restaurant,** tel. 244-7776, on the corner of Main and Market streets, has American and Mexican food at prices under $7.

Down To Earth, at 1910 Vineyard, tel. 242-6821, open Mon.-Sat. until 6:30 p.m., sells natural and health foods and has an excellent snack bar—basically a little window around back with a few tables. Really filling!

Both **Wakamatsu** on Market Street and **Nagasako Fish Market** on Lower Main offer a wide variety of fresh fish.

Food Off The Main Drag

If you get off the main highway and take Mill Street and Lower Main, the beachside roads connecting Kahului and Wailuku, you'll be rewarded with some of the *most* local and *least* expensive restaurants on West Maui. They are totally unpretentious, and serve hefty portions of tasty, homemade local foods. If your aim is to *eat,* search out one of these. **Tasty Crust Restaurant,** at 1770 Mill St., tel. 244-0845, is open daily 5:30 a.m.-1:30 p.m., and again 5-10 p.m., closed Monday night. If you have to carbo-load for a full day of sailing, snorkeling, or windsurfing, order their famous giant homemade hotcakes for only 80 cents.

Or try **Nazo's Restaurant,** at 1063 Lower Main St., second floor of the Puuone Plaza, an older yellowish two-story building, tel. 244-0529. Park underneath and walk upstairs. Daily specials cost under $6, but they're renowned for their oxtail soup, $5.50, a clear-consommé broth in which peanuts and water chestnuts float—a delicious combination of East and West.

Tokyo Tei, in the same complex, tel. 242-9630, open daily 11 a.m.-1:30 p.m. for lunch and 5-8:30 p.m. for dinner, open Sunday for dinner only, is another institution around for decades; they serve Japanese dishes to a devoted clientele. Eating here is as predictable as eating at grandma's kitchen, with traditional Japanese dishes like tempura, *donburi,* and seafood platters. If you want to sample real Japanese food at affordable prices, come here!

LOUISE FOOTE

Hale Lava is a little cafe/lodge serving Japanese and American food. For under $7, you can get a full meal. Located at 740 Lower Main, tel. 244-0871, it's open 5:30 a.m.-1:30 p.m., closed Monday.

A favorite with locals, **Archie's Place** serves full meals for $6, specializing in Japanese. Located at 1440 Lower Main, tel. 244-9401, it's open daily 10:30 a.m.-2 p.m., 5-8 p.m., closed Sunday.

And, for a different taste treat, try the *mochi* made fresh daily at Wailuku's **Shishido Manju Shop,** 758 Lower Main Street. Nearby on Lower Main are **Maui Coffee Roasters**—stop in for a variety of the world's best beans roasted on the spot—and **Tropical Chocolate.**

Shopping

Most shopping in this area is done in Kahului at the three big malls. But for an interesting diversion try one of these stores on or around Main or Market Street. **T-Shirt Factory Outlet** can save you money on T-shirts that you'll see all over the island. For better clothes and accessories visit **Tropical Emporium. St. Anthony's Thrift Shop** on lower Main is open Wednesday and Friday 8 a.m.-1 p.m.; you'll find used articles from irons to aloha shirts. **Maui Wholesale Gold** sells gold, jewelry, and eelskin items; **Treasure Imports** sells the same type of articles, as does **Take's. Miracles Unlimited,** on Central Street, has what you need in the way of crystals, metaphysical books, and jewelry. **New Maui Fishing Supply** has all you need to land the big ones.

Wailuku's attic closets are overflowing. Several discovery

shops in a row hang like prom-night tuxedos, limp with old memories. Each has its own style. Look for these shops on the elevated portion of the 100 block of N. Market as you head toward Happy Valley. Here you'll find **Ali'i Antiques,** tel. 244-8012, open daily 9 a.m.-5 p.m., offering Depression glass, dolls, china, photos, chandeliers, 200-year-old kimonos, ranks of toy soldiers, African trading beads, and netsuke miniatures. **Traders of the Lost Art** specializes in carvings from the Pacific, especially from New Guinea. Here as well are **Memory Lane,** for curios and collectibles, and **Wailuku Gallery** just a few doors away. In the same row, look for **Helen's Treasures Antiques and Collectibles,** tel. 242-6977, open Mon.-Sat. 9:30 a.m.-5 p.m. (though if the sun's shining Helen is often gone), specializing in antique jewelry, glassware, pottery, and vintage clothing. Helen shares space with **Makani Ltd.** that handles only Hawaiiana, from aloha shirts to hula dolls. Also along antique row search out **Bird of Paradise,** tel. 242-7699, open Mon.-Sat. 9:30 a.m.-5:30 p.m., where owner Joe Myhand sells Blue Willow china, vintage bottles, Depression and carnival glass, license plates from around the world, and a smattering of antique furniture.

Free Shuttle Bus

The County of Maui offers a free shuttle connecting Wailuku and Kahului, *for now* operating weekdays only 8 a.m.-4 p.m., tel. 877-7651 for current information. The stops are too numerous to mention, but they definitely include all of the shopping centers and main roads.

Services

There's a **Bank of Hawaii** at 2105 Main, tel. 871-8200; and a **First Interstate** at 2005 Main, tel. 244-3951. The **post office** is on High St., next to the state government building, and the **library** is at 251 High St., tel. 244-3945.

For conventional health care, go to **Maui Memorial Hospital,** off Rt. 32, tel. 244-9056; or to **Kaiser Permanente's Wailuku Clinic** near the hospital.

Camping permits for county parks are available at the War Memorial Gym, Room 102, Rt. 32, tel. 244-9018. They cost $3 adults, 50 cents children, per person per night. State park permits can be obtained from the State Building, 54 S. High St., tel. 243-5354 (see "State Parks" under "Camping and Hiking" in the Maui Introduction).

KAHAKULOA—WEST MAUI'S BACKSIDE

To get around to the backside of West Maui you can head northeast from Kaanapali, but the majority of those few who defy the car companies and brave the bad road strike out northwest from Wailuku.

Note: Rt. 340 is rugged and a sign warns that it is closed to all but local residents. Although the ordinance is not enforced, be extremely cautious on this road, especially during or just after bad weather.

Before you start this rugged 18-mile stretch, make sure you have adequate gas, water, and food. It'll take you a full three hours to go from Wailuku to Kapalua. Start heading north on Market Street, toward the area of Wailuku called **Happy Valley** (good restaurants—see "Food" above). At the end of Market Street (Rt. 330) you'll find **T.K. Supermarket,** your best place to buy supplies (open seven days). At mile marker 2, Rt. 330 turns into Rt. 340, which you'll follow toward Kahakuloa Bay and all the way around. In a few minutes, just when you come to the bridge over Iao Stream, will be Kuhio Place on your right. Turn here to **Halekii and Pihana Heiau.** Although uninspiring, this area is historical and totally unvisited.

Back on Rt. 340 you come shortly to **Waihee** ("Slippery Water"). There's a little store here, but even if it's open it's probably understocked. On the right, a sign points you to **Waiehu Golf Course,** tel. 243-7400. Mostly local people golf here; fees are $25 for nonresidents, $12.50 club rental. The fairways, strung along the sea, are beautiful to play. **Par Five Restaurant** is an adequate little eatery at the golf course. Also here are two county beach parks: **Waiehu** and **Waihee.** They're secluded and frequented mostly by local people. Some come here to spear fish inside the reef. Although for day-use only, they'd probably be okay for an unofficial overnight stay. For Waihee, turn at the Kiwanis Park (softball on Saturday) and go left just before the golf course parking lot along the fence; for Waiehu take Lower Waiehu Road, off Rt. 340, at the north end of Wailuku—follow the "shoreline access" signs.

At mile marker 11 the pavement begins to deteriorate. The road hugs the coastline and gains elevation quickly; the undisturbed valleys are resplendent. At mile marker 11, just past the Boy Scout camp, you'll see a metal gate and two enormous carved tikis. No explanation, just sitting there. You next enter the fishing village of **Kahakuloa** ("Tall Hill") with its dozen weatherworn houses and tiny white church. Here the road is at its absolute roughest and narrowest! The valley is very steep-sided and beautiful. Supposedly, great Maui himself loved this area. Two miles past Kahakuloa, you come to **Pohaku Kani,** the bell stone. It's about six feet tall and the same in diameter, but graffiti spoils it. Here the seascapes are tremendous. The surf pounds along the coast below and sends spumes skyward, roaring through a natural blowhole. The road once again becomes wide and well paved and you're soon at **Fleming Beach County Park.** Civilization comes again too quickly.

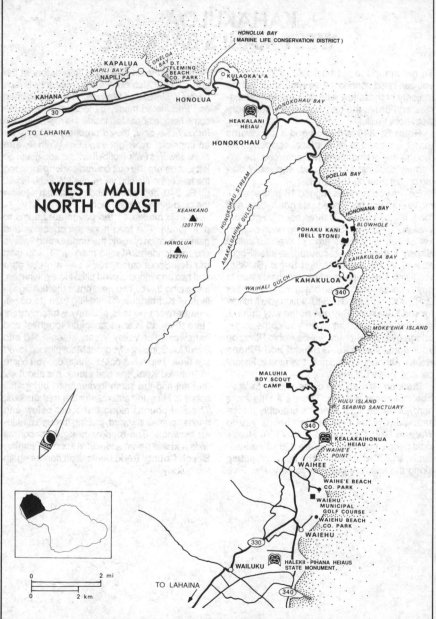

WEST MAUI NORTH COAST

HONOLUA BAY
(MARINE LIFE CONSERVATION DISTRICT)
KAPALUA
NAPILI BAY
NAPILI
ONELOA BAY
D.T. FLEMING BEACH CO. PARK
KULAOKA'E'A
KAHANA
HONOLUA
30
TO LAHAINA
HEAKALANI HEIAU
HONOKOHAU BAY
HONOKOHAU
POELUA BAY
HONOKOHAU STREAM
ANAKALUAHINE GULCH
KEAHKANO (2017ft)
HANOLUA (2627ft)
HONONANA BAY
BLOWHOLE
POHAKU KANI (BELL STONE)
KAHAKULOA BAY
WAIHALI GULCH
KAHAKULOA
340
MOKE'EHIA ISLAND
MALUHIA BOY SCOUT CAMP
HULU ISLAND SEABIRD SANCTUARY
340
KEALAKAIHONUA HEIAU
WAIHE'E POINT
WAIHEE
WAIHE'E BEACH CO. PARK
WAIEHU MUNICIPAL GOLF COURSE
WAIEHU BEACH CO. PARK
WAIEHU
330
WAILUKU
HALEKII - PIHANA HEIAUS STATE MONUMENT.
0 2 mi
0 2 km
TO LAHAINA
340
MOON

1. waterfall at Hawaii Tropical Botanical Gardens, Hawaii (J.D. Bisignani);
2. Waimea Canyon, Kauai (J.D. Bisignani); **3.** Hanalei Valley, Kauai (Robert Nilsen)

1

2

3

1. the Pololu Valley, Hawaii; **2.** Hana Road waterfalls, Maui;
3. Road to MacKenzie State Recreation Area, Hawaii (all photos by J.D. Bisignani)

BOB RACE

WEST MAUI

LAHAINA

Lahaina ("Merciless Sun") is and always has been the premier town on Maui. It's the most energized town on the island as well, and you can feel it from the first moment you walk down Front Street. Maui's famed warrior-king Kahekili lived here and ruled until Kamehameha, with the help of newfound cannon power, subdued Kahekili's son in Iao Valley at the turn of the 19th century. When Kamehameha I consolidated the island kingdom, he chose Lahaina as his seat of power. It served as such until Kamehameha III moved to Honolulu in the 1840s. Lahaina is where the modern world of the West and the old world of Hawaii collided, for better or worse. The *ali'i* of Hawaii loved to be entertained here; the **royal surf spot,** mentioned numerous times as an area of revelry in old missionary diaries, is just south of the Small Boat Harbor. Kamehameha I built in Lahaina the islands' first Western structure in 1801, known as the **Brick Palace;** a small ruin still remains. Queens Keopuolani and Kaahumanu, the two most powerful wives of the great Kamehameha's harem of over 20, were local Maui women who remained after their husband's death and helped to usher in the new order.

The whalers came preying for "sperms and humpbacks" in 1819 and set old Lahaina Town a-reelin'. Island girls, naked and willing, swam out to meet the ships, trading their favors for baubles from the modern world. Grog shops flourished, and drunken sailors with their brown-skinned doxies owned the debauched town. The missionaries, invited by Queen Keopuolani, came praying for souls in 1823. Led by the Reverends Stuart and Richards, they tried to harpoon moral chaos. In short order, there was a curfew, a *kapu* placed on the ships by wise but ineffectual old Governor Hoapili, and a jail and a fort to discourage the strong-arm tactics of unruly captains. The pagan Hawaiians transformed like willing children to the new order, but the Christian sailors damned the meddling missionaries. They even whistled a few cannonballs into the Lahaina homestead of Reverend Richards, hoping to send him speedily to his eternal reward. Time, a new breed of sailor, and the slow death of the whaling industry eased the tension.

Meanwhile, the missionaries built the first school and printing press west of the Rockies at **Lahainaluna,** in the mountains just above the town, along with downtown's **Wainee Church,** the first stone church on the island. Lahaina's glory days slipped by and it became a sleepy "sugar town" dominated by the Pioneer Sugar Mill that has operated since the 1860s. In 1901, the **Pioneer Inn** was built to accommodate interisland ferry passengers, but no one *came* to Lahaina. In the 1960s, Amfac Inc. had a brilliant idea. They turned Kaanapali, a magnificent stretch of beach just west, into one of the most beautifully planned and executed resorts in the world. The Pioneer Sugar Mill had long used the area as a refuse heap, but now the ugly duckling became a swan, and Lahaina flushed with new life. With superb farsightedness, the **Lahaina Restoration Foundation** was begun in those years and almost the entire town was made a national historical landmark. Lahaina, subdued but never tamed, throbs with its special energy once again.

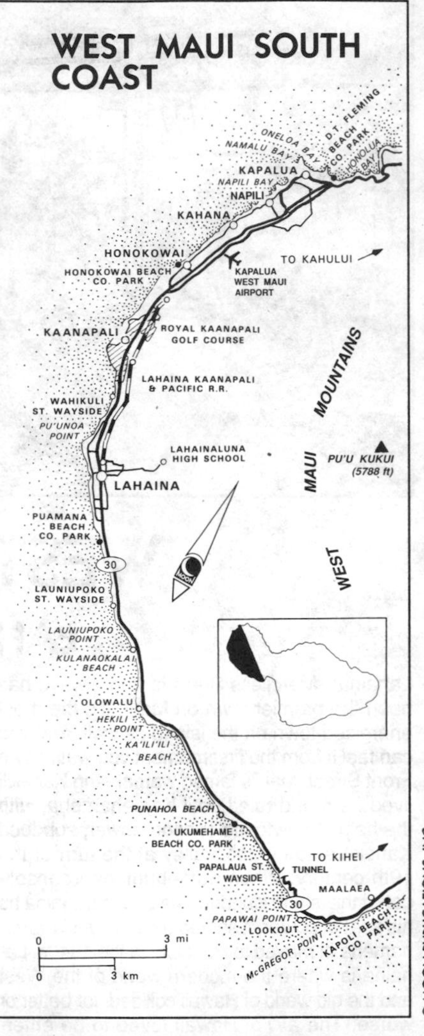

SIGHTS

In short, strolling around Lahaina offers the best of both worlds. It's busy, but it's bite-sized. It's engrossing enough, but you can "see" it in half a day. Most of the main attractions are downtown within a few blocks of each other. Lahaina technically stretches, long and narrow, along the coast for about four miles, but you'll only be interested in the central core, a mere mile or so. All along Front Street, the main drag, and the side streets running off it are innumerable shops, restaurants, and hideaways where you can browse, recoup your energy, or just wistfully watch the sun set. Go slowly and savor, and you'll feel the dynamism of Lahaina past and present all around you. Enjoy!

Parking

Traffic congestion is a problem that needs to be addressed. Be parked and settled 4:30-5:30 p.m., when traffic is heaviest. While there still are no traffic lights on Front Street, a spree of construction in the last several years has increased the number of lights on the highway from two to over half a dozen. The other thing to know to make your visit carefree is where to stash your car. The parking lot on the corner of Wainee and Dickenson streets is centrally located and charges a reasonable daily rate. There's another large lot on Prison Street, just up from

Front (free three-hour limit), two smallish lots along Luakini Street, and small lots behind the Baldwin Home, the Lahaina Hotel, and Burger King on Front Street. The Lahaina Shopping Center has three-hour parking. Most of the meters in town are a mere one hour, and the most efficient people on Maui are the "meter patrol!" ($15-20 per parking ticket). Your car will wind up in the pound if you're not careful! The best place to find a spot is down at the end of Front Street past the Kamehameha III School and along Shaw. You'll have to walk a few minutes, but it's worth it. For those staying in Kaanapali, leave your car at your hotel and take the Lahaina Express for the day. (See "Public Transportation" under "Getting Around" in the Maui Introduction for details.)

The Banyan Tree

The best place to start your tour of Lahaina is at this magnificent tree at the corner of Hotel and Front. You can't miss it as it spreads its shading boughs over almost an entire acre. Sit on the benches and reconnoiter while the sun, for which Lahaina is infamous, is kept at bay. Children love the banyan, which seems to bring out the Tarzan in everyone. Old-timers sit here chatting, and you might be lucky enough to hear Ben Victorino, a tour guide who comes here frequently, entertain people with his ukulele and endless repertoire of Hawaiian tunes. The tree was planted in April 1873 by Sheriff Bill Smith in commemoration of the Congregationalist Missions' golden anniversary. One hundred years later, a ceremony was held here and over 500 people were accommodated under this natural canopy. Just left of the banyan, down the lane toward the harbor, was a canal and the Government Market. All kinds of commodities, manufactured and human, were sold here during the whaling days, and it was given the apt name of "Rotten Row."

The Courthouse

Behind the banyan on Wharf Street is the Courthouse. Built in the 1850s from coral blocks recycled from Kamehameha III's ill-fated palace, Hale Piula ("House of Iron"), it also served as the police station, complete with a jail in the basement. Today, the jail is home to the **Lahaina Art Society,** where paintings and artifacts are kept behind bars, waiting for patrons to liberate them. Adjacent is **The Fort,** built in the 1830s to show the sailors they couldn't run amok in Lahaina. It was more for show than for force, though. When it was torn down, the blocks were hauled over to Prison Street to build the real jail, **Hale Pa'ahao.** A corner battlement of the fort was restored, but that's it, because restoring the entire structure means mutilating the banyan.

Small Boat Harbor

Walking along the harbor stimulates the imagination and the senses. The boats waiting at anchor sway in confused syncopation. Hawser ropes groan and there's a feeling of anticipation and adventure in the air. Here you can board for all kinds of seagoing excursions. In the days of whaling there was no harbor; the boats tied up one to the other in the "roads," at times forming an impromptu floating bridge. The whalers came ashore in their chase boats; with the winds always up, departure could be made at a moment's notice. The activity here is still dominated by the sea.

The *Carthaginian II*

The masts and square rigging of this replica of the enterprising freighters that braved the Pacific tower over Lahaina Harbor. You'll be drawn to it . . . go! It's the only truly square-rigged ship left afloat on the seas. It replaced the *Carthaginian I* when that ship went aground in 1972 while being hauled to Honolulu for repairs. The Lahaina Restoration Foundation found this steel-hulled ship in Denmark; built in Germany in 1920 as a two-masted schooner, it tramped around the Baltic under converted diesel power. The foundation had it sailed 12,000 miles to Lahaina, where it underwent extensive conversion until it became the beautiful replica that you see today. The sails have yet to be made due to lack of funds.

The *Carthaginian II* is a floating museum dedicated to whaling and to whales, open daily 9:30 a.m.-4:30 p.m., but arrive no later than 3:45 to see all the exhibits and videos. Admission is $3 adults, $2 seniors, and free to children accompanied by an adult. Richard Widmark, the actor, narrates a superb film documenting the life of humpbacks. Belowdecks is the museum containing artifacts and implements from the whal-

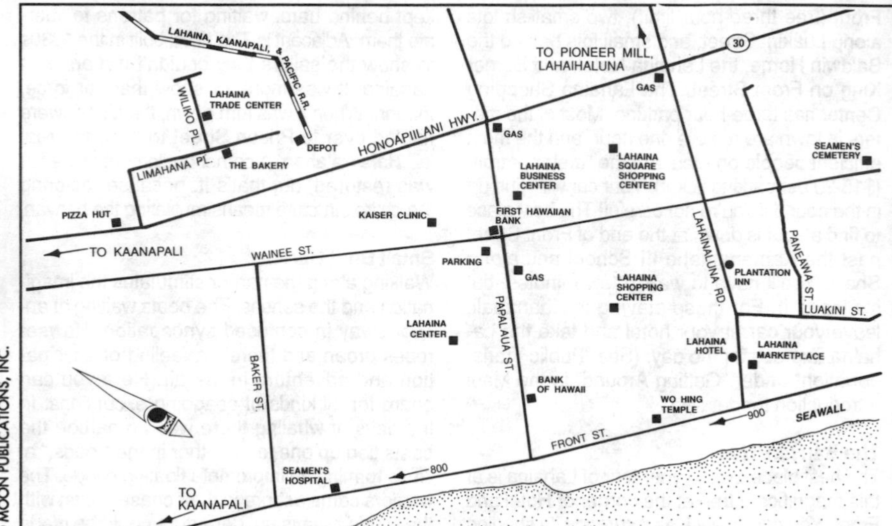

ing days. There's even a whaling boat found intact in Alaska in the 1970s. The light below decks is subdued, and while you sit in the little "captain's chairs" the humpbacks chant their peaceful hymns in the background. Flip Nicklin's sensitive photos adorn the bulkheads.

Pioneer Inn

This vintage inn, situated at the corner of Hotel and Wharf streets, is exactly where it belongs. Stand on its veranda with the honky-tonk piano playing in the open bar behind you and gaze at the *Carthaginian II.* Presto . . . it's magic time! You'll see. It was a favorite spot for actors like Errol Flynn and later Spencer Tracy, when he was in Lahaina filming *Devil at Four O'clock.* The green and white inn was built in 1901 to accommodate interisland ferry passengers, but its style seems much older. If ironwork had been used on the veranda, you'd think you were in New Orleans. A new wing was built behind it in 1965 and the two form a courtyard. Make sure to read the hilarious rules governing behavior posted in the main lobby. The inn is still functional. The rooms in the old wing are colorfully seedy—spotlessly clean, but with character and atmosphere. The off-level wooden stairway, painted red, leads upstairs to an uneven hallway lined with a threadbare carpet. The interior smells like the sea. There's no luxury here, but you might consider one night just for the experience. (See "Accommodations" following for details.) Downstairs the **Harpooner's Lanai Terrace** serves dinner, and you can't find a better place to watch life go by with a beautiful sunset backdrop than the **Old Whaler's Saloon.**

The Brick Palace

This rude structure was commissioned by Kamehameha I in 1801 and slapped together by two forgotten Australian ex-convicts. It was the first Western structure in Hawaii, but unfortunately the substandard materials have for the most part disintegrated. Kamehameha never lived in it, but it was occupied and used as a storehouse until the 1850s. Just to the right of the Brick Palace, as you face the harbor, is **Hauola Stone,** marked by an HVB Warrior. Formed like a chair, it was believed by the Hawaiians to have curative powers if you sat on it and let the ocean bathe you. Best view is at low tide.

Baldwin Home

One of the best attractions in Lahaina is the Baldwin Home, on the corner of Front and Dickenson. It was occupied by Doctor/Reverend

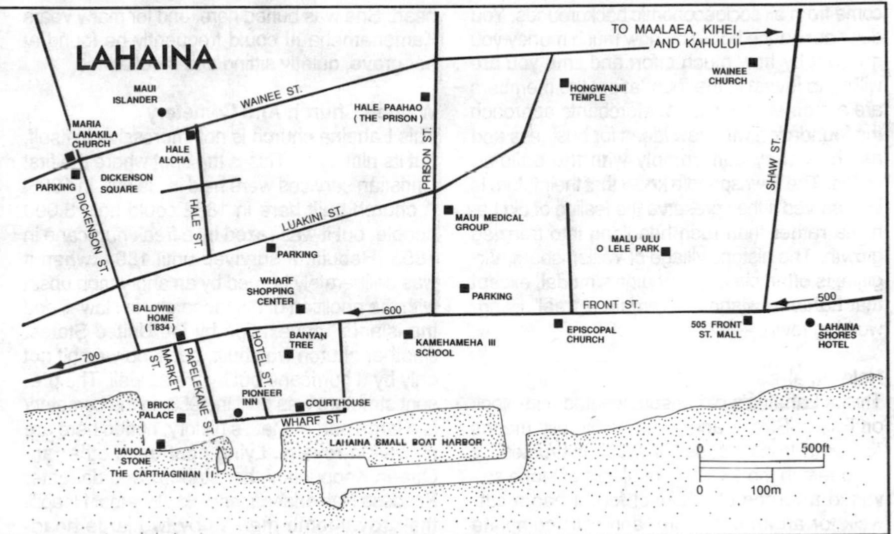

Dwight Baldwin, his wife Charlotte, and their eight children. He was a trained teacher, as well as the first doctor/dentist in Hawaii. The building served from the 1830s to 1868 as a dispensary, meeting room, and boarding home for anyone in need. The two-foot-thick walls are made of cut lava, and the mortar made of crushed coral over which plaster was applied. As you enter, notice how low the doorway is, and that the doors inside are "Christian doors"—with a cross forming the upper panels and an open Bible at the bottom. The Steinway piano that dominates the entrance was built in 1859. In the bedroom to the right, along with all of the period furniture, is a wooden commode. Also notice the lack of closets; all items were kept in chests. Upstairs was a large dormitory where guests slept.

The doctor's fees are posted and are hilarious. Payment was by "size" of sickness: very big $50, diagnosis $3, refusal to pay $10. The Reverend Baldwin was 41 when he arrived in Hawaii from New England and his wife was 25. She was supposedly sickly (eight children!) and he had heart trouble, so they moved to Honolulu in 1868 to receive better health care. The home became a community center, housing the library and meeting rooms. Today, the Baldwin Home is a showcase museum of the Lahaina Restoration Society. It's open daily 9:30 a.m.-5 p.m., admission $2, kids free accompanied by a parent.

Master's Reading Room

Originally a missionaries' storeroom, the Master's Reading Room was converted to an officers' club in 1834. This venerable building and the Baldwin Home next door constitute the oldest Western structures on Maui. Fittingly, this uniquely constructed coral stone building is home to the Lahaina Restoration Foundation. The building is not really open to the public, but you can visit to pick up maps, brochures, and information about Lahaina.

The **Lahaina Restoration Foundation,** begun in 1962, is headed by Jim Luckey, a historian in his own right who knows a great deal about Lahaina and the whaling era. The main purpose of the foundation is to preserve the flavor and authenticity of Lahaina without stifling progress—especially tourism. The foundation is privately funded and has managed to purchase many of the important historical sites in Lahaina. They own two of the buildings mentioned, the restored Wo Hing Temple, and the land under the U.S. Seamen's Hospital, and they'll own the plantation house next door in 18 years. The 42 people on the board of directors come from all socioeconomic backgrounds. You don't get on the board by how much money you give but by how much effort and time you are willing to invest in the foundation; the members are extremely dedicated. Merchants approach the foundation with new ideas for business and ask how they can comply with the building codes. The townspeople know that their future is best served if they preserve the feeling of old Lahaina rather than rush headlong into frenzied growth. The historic village of Williamsburg, Virginia, is often cited as Lahaina's model, except that Lahaina wishes to remain a "real" living, working town.

Hale Pa'ahao

This is Lahaina's old prison, located mid-block on Prison Street, and its name literally means "Stuck-in-Irons House." It was constructed by prisoners in the 1850s from blocks of stone salvaged from the old defunct fort. It had a catwalk for an armed guard, and cells complete with shackles for hardened criminals, but most were drunks who'd yahooed around town on the Sabbath, wildly spurring their horses. The cells were rebuilt in 1959, the gatehouse in 1988, and the structure is maintained by the Lahaina Restoration Foundation. The cells, curiously, are made of wood, which shows that the inmates weren't that interested in busting out. It's open daily, admission free.

Malu'ulu O Lele Park

This nondescript area at the corner of Shaw and Front was at one time the most important spot in Lahaina. Here was a small pond with a diminutive island in the center. The pond, Mokuhinia, was home to a *moo,* a lizard spirit. The tiny island, Mokuula, was the home of the Maui chiefs, and the Kamehamehas, when they were in residence. It became a royal mausoleum, but later all the remains were taken away and the pond was filled and the ground leveled. King Kamehameha III and his sister Princess Nahienaena were raised together in Lahaina. They fell in love, but the new ways caused turmoil and tragedy. Instead of marrying and producing royal children, a favored practice only 20 years earlier, they were wrenched apart by the new religion. He, for a time, numbed himself with alcohol, while she died woefully from a broken heart. She was buried here, and for many years Kamehameha III could frequently be found at her grave, quietly sitting and meditating.

Wainee Church And Cemetery

This Lahaina church is not impressive in itself, but its history is. This is the spot where the first Christian services were held in Hawaii, in 1823. A church built here in 1832 could hold 3,000 people, but it was razed by a freak hurricane in 1858. Rebuilt, it survived until 1894, when it was deliberately burned by an angry mob upset with the abolition of the monarchy in Hawaii and the islands' annexation by the United States. Another church was built, but it too was hit not only by a hurricane but by fire as well. The present structure was built in 1953. In the cemetery is a large part of Maui's history: buried here are Hawaiian royalty. Lying near each other are Queen Keopuolani, her star-crossed daughter Princess Nahienaena, and old Governor Hoapili, their royal tomb marked by two large headstones surrounded by a wrought-iron fence. Other graves hold missionaries such as William Richards and many infants and children.

Churches And Temples

You may wish to stop for a moment at Lahaina's churches and temples dotted around town. They are reminders of the mixture of faiths and peoples that populated this village and added their cultural styles. **The Episcopal Cemetery** on Wainee Street shows the English influence in the islands. Many of the royal family, including King Kalakaua, became Anglicans. This cemetery holds the remains of many early Maui families, and of Walter Murray Gibson, the notorious settler, politician, and firebrand of the 1880s. Just behind is **Hale Aloha,** "House of Love," a small structure built by Maui residents in thanksgiving for being saved from a terrible smallpox epidemic that ravaged Oahu but bypassed Maui in 1858. The structure was restored in 1974. Also on Wainee is **Maria Lanakila Church,** the site of the first Roman Catholic Mass in Lahaina, celebrated in 1841. The present structure dates from 1928. Next to the church's cemetery is the **Seamen's Cemetery** where many infirm from the ships that came to Lahaina were buried. Most stones have been obliterated by time and only a few remain. Herman Melville came here to pay his last respects to a cousin buried in this yard. **Hongwanjii Temple** is also on Wainee, between Prison and Shaw. It's a Buddhist temple with the largest congregation in Lahaina and dates from 1910, though the present structure was raised in 1927.

The **Wo Hing Temple** on Front Street is the Lahaina Restoration Foundation's newest reconstruction. It was opened to the public in 1984 and shows the Chinese influence in Lahaina. Downstairs are displays, upstairs is the altar. In the cookhouse next door, you can see film clips of Hawaii taken by the Edison Company in 1899 and 1906. It's open daily 9 a.m.-4 p.m., from 10 a.m. Sunday, admission $1. **Holy Innocents Episcopal Church,** built in 1927, is also on Front Street, near Kamehameha III School. Known for its "Hawaiian Madonna," its altar is resplendent with fruits, plants, and birds of the islands.

The **Lahaina Jodo Mission** is at the opposite end of Front Street, near Mala Wharf on Ala Moana Street. When heading west, you'll leave the main section of town and keep going until you see a sign over a building that reads "Jesus is Coming Soon." Turn left toward the beach and you'll immediately spot the three-storied pagoda. Here the giant bronze Buddha sits exposed to the elements. The largest outside of Asia, it was dedicated in 1968 in commemoration of the centennial of the arrival of Japanese workers in Hawaii. The grounds are impeccable and serenely quiet. You may stroll around, but the buildings are closed to the public. If you climb the steps to peek into the temple, kindly remove your shoes. A striking cemetery is across the street along the beach; the tombstones set in sand seem incongruous. The entire area is quiet and a perfect spot for lunch or solitary meditation if you've had enough of frenetic Lahaina.

U.S. Seamen's Hospital

This notorious hospital was reconstructed by the Lahaina Restoration Foundation in 1982. Here is where sick seamen were cared for under the auspices of the U.S. State Department. Allegations during the late 1850s claimed that the care here extended past the grave! Unscrupulous medicos supposedly charged the U.S. government for care of seamen who had long since died. The hospital is located at Baker and the end of Front Street, heading toward Kaanapali, near the Jodo Mission. The hospital now houses a TV production company, and in the front yard is a 10,000-pound, swivel-end Porter anchor, found off Black Rock in Kaanapali.

Lahainaluna

Head up the mountain behind Lahaina on Lahainaluna Road for approximately two miles. On your left you'll pass the **Pioneer Sugar Mill,** in operation since 1860. Once at Lahainaluna ("Above Lahaina") you'll find the oldest school west of the Rockies, opened by the Congregationalist missionaries in 1831. Children from all over the islands, and many from California, came here if their parents could afford to send them to boarding school. Today, the school is West Maui's public high school, but many children still come here to board. The first students were given not only a top-notch academic education, but a practical one as well. They built the school buildings, and many were apprentices in the famous **Hale Pa'i** ("Printing House") that turned out Hawaii's first newspaper and made Lahaina famous as a printing center.

One look at Hale Pa'i and you think of New England. It's a white stucco building with blue trim and a wood-shake roof. It was restored in 1982 and is open by appointment only (contact the Lahaina Restoration Foundation or the Baldwin Home). If you visit the campus when school is in session, you may go to Hale Pa'i, but if you want to walk around the school grounds, please sign in at the vice-principal's office. Lahainaluna High School is dedicated to the preservation of Hawaiian culture. Every year, in April, they celebrate the anniversary of the death of one of their most famous students, David Malo. Considered Hawaii's first scholar, he authored the definitive *Hawaiian Antiquities.* His final wish was to be buried "high above the tide of foreign invasion" and his grave is close to the giant "L" atop Mt. Ball, behind Lahainaluna. On the way back down to Lahaina, you get a wide, impressive panorama of the port and the sea.

Heading East

Five miles east of Lahaina along the coastal road (Rt. 30) is the little village of **Olowalu.** Today, little more than the Olowalu General Store and Chez Paul French restaurant are here. This was the site of the Olowalu Massacre perpetrated by Captain Metcalf, whose far-reaching results greatly influenced Hawaiian history (see "History" in the General Introduction for details). Two American seamen, Young and Davis, were connected with this incident, and with their help Kamehameha I subdued all of Hawaii. Behind the general store a half-mile dirt track leads to **petroglyphs;** make sure you pass a water tower within the first few hundred yards because there are three similar roads here. You'll come to the remains of a wooden stairway going up a hill. There once was an HVB Warrior here, but it might be gone. Claw your way up the hill to the petroglyphs, which are believed to be 300 years old.

If you continue east on Rt. 30, you'll pass **Papawai** and **McGregor Point,** both noted for their vistas and as excellent locations to spot migrating whales in season. The road sign merely indicates a scenic lookout.

BEACHES

The best beaches around Lahaina are west of town in Kaanapali, or east toward Olowalu. A couple of adequate places to spread your towel are right in Lahaina, but they're not quite on a par with the beaches just a few miles away.

Malu'ulu O Lele Park

"The Breadfruit Shelter of Lele" is in town and basically parallels Front Street. It's crowded at times and there's plenty of "wash up" on this beach. It's cleaner and quieter at the east end down by Lahaina Shores Hotel, a one-time favorite with the *ali'i.* There are restrooms, the swimming is fair, and the snorkeling is acceptable past the reef. **Lahaina Beach** is at the west end of town near Mala Wharf. Follow Front to Puunoa Place and turn down to the beach. This is a good place for families with tots because the water is clear, safe, and shallow.

Puamana Beach County Park

About two miles before you enter Lahaina from the east along Rt. 30, you'll see signs for this beach park, a narrow strip between the road and the sea. The swimming and snorkeling are only fair. The setting, however, is quite nice with picnic tables shaded by ironwood trees. The views are terrific and this is a great spot to eat your plate lunch only minutes from town. **Launiupoko State Wayside**, a mile farther east, has restrooms and showers, but no beach. This is more of a pit stop than anything else, although many come to sunbathe on the grass below the coconut trees.

Wahikuli State Wayside

Along Rt. 30 between Lahaina and Kaanapali, the park is a favorite with local people and excellent for a picnic and swim. Restrooms and tennis courts are across the street. The park is very clean and well maintained. Just up the highway, as if connected to this wayside park, is **Hanakaoo Beach County Park.** This beach runs north past some of the most exclusive hotels on the island. Often the local canoe club will put their canoes in the water here and at certain times of the year paddling events will be held at this beach.

ACCOMMODATIONS

Lodging in Lahaina is limited, surprisingly inexpensive, and an experience . . . of sorts. Most visitors head for Kaanapali, because Lahaina tends to be hot and hot to trot, especially at night. But you can find good bargains here, and if you want to be in the thick of the "action," you're in the right spot.

Pioneer Inn

This is the oldest hotel on Maui still accommodating guests, located at 658 Wharf St., Lahaina, HI 96761, tel. 661-3636 or (800) 457-5457. Absolutely no luxury whatsoever, but a double scoop of atmosphere: the place to come if you want to save money and be the star of your own movie with the Pioneer Inn as the stage set. Enter the tiny lobby full of memorabilia, and follow the creaking stairway up to a wooden hallway painted green on green. This is the old wing. Clean but basic rooms open out onto the building-long lanai overlooking the harbor; all rooms have ceiling fans. Rates are about $35 with shared bath, private bath (showers) are a few dollars extra; music and the sounds of life from the bar below late in the evening at no extra charge. The "new wing," basic modern, circa 1966, is attached. Starting at $70, its rooms are no bargain. Each room offers a private lanai, bath, and a/c, and overlooks the central courtyard. The old section is fun; the new section is only adequate.

The Plantation Inn

If Agatha Christie were seeking inspiration for *the* perfect setting for one of her mysteries, this is where she would come. The neo-Victorian building is appointed with posted verandas, hardwood floors, and natural wood trim around windows and doors, counterpointed by floral wall coverings and bedspreads. Rays of sunlight stray through stained-glass windows and wide double doors. Each room is comfortable, with overstuffed couches, four-poster beds, and private tiled baths with bold brass fixtures. The complete illusion is turn-of-the-century, but the modern amenities of a/c, remote-control TV and VCR, a hidden fridge, daily maid service, and a soothing spa and pool are included. A new addition in the back brings the total room count to 17. Most of the 10 new units have lanais overlooking the garden, pool, spa, and guest pavilion. Prices are a reasonable $99-125 deluxe, $145 superior, $175 suite (some with kitchenette and jacuzzi), and all include a breakfast buffet at Gerard's, the fine French restaurant on the first floor. The Plantation Inn also has money-saving options for dinner at Gerard's, rental car, and package deals. For full information contact the inn at 174 Lahainaluna Rd., Lahaina, HI 96761, tel. 667-9225 or (800) 433-6815 Mainland; they will accept collect calls from Canada. Set on a side street away from the bustle, it's simply one of the best accommodations Lahaina has to offer.

Lahaina Hotel

Is nothing sacred? Will Birkenstocks be on *every* foot, quiche on *every* table, and a sensible Volvo in *every* driveway? The old, down-at-the-heels, traveler's classic, Lahainaluna Hotel, at 127 Lahainaluna Rd., Lahaina, HI 96761, tel. 661-0577 or (800) 669-3444, has been completely renovated and remodeled. This one-time dowdy orphan, now renamed, has emerged a lovely lady. Gone from this cockroach paradise are the weather-beaten linoleum floors, bare-bulbed musty rooms, and rusted dripping faucets. In their place are antique-stuffed, neo-Victorian, tastefully appointed rooms that transport you back to the late 1800s. Period pieces include everything from wardrobes to nightstands, rugs, ceramic bowls, mirrors, pictures, lamps, and books. The only deferences to modernity are the bathrooms with their new but old-style fixtures, the air-conditioning, telephone, and safes—no TV. You can still peer from the balcony of this vintage hotel—each room has a lanai with two hardwood rocking shairs and a table—or observe the masses below from behind heavy drapes and lace curtains. The 13 units include three spacious suites. Rates are $89-129 for the parlor suites, and include a complimentary continental breakfast, served every morning from about 7:30 a.m. at the sideboard at the end of the hall. The Lahaina Hotel's only drawback is the complete lack of parking facilities. You must either park in a lot (one to the rear charges $8 overnight, $3 to hotel guest) or find a place on the street. Overnight parking in downtown Lahaina is officially prohibited, but the fine is less than the cost of most parking lots.

Maui Islander

Located a few blocks away from the hubbub, at 660 Wainee St., Lahaina, HI 96761, tel. 667-9766 or (800) 367-5226, the Maui Islander is a very adequate hotel offering rooms with kitchenettes, studios, and suites of up to three bedrooms for seven guests or more. All with a/c and TV, plus pool and tennis courts. Homey atmosphere with daily planned activities. Basic hotel rooms start at $85, studios $98, one bedroom $110; two- and three-bedroom suites are also available.

Lahaina Shores

This six-story condo was built before the Lahaina building code limited the height of new structures. Located at the east end of town, at 475 Front St., Lahaina, HI 96761, tel. 661-4835 or (800) 628-6699, the condo has become a landmark for incoming craft. The Shores offers a swimming pool and spa and is located on the only beach in town. From a distance, the Southern-mansion facade is striking; up close, though, it becomes painted cement blocks and false colonnades. The rooms, however, are good value for the money. The basic room contains a full bathroom, powder room, large color TV, and equipped kitchen. They're all light and airy, and the backside views of the harbor or frontside of the mountains are the best in town. Studios begin at $105, one-bedroom suites range $147-172, penthouse ranges $192-227, additional guests $8; rates reduced about 20% for the low season.

Lahaina Roads
This condo/apartment is at the far west end of town at 1403 Front St., Lahaina, HI 96761, tel. 661-3166, (800) 624-8203. All units have fully equipped kitchens, TV, and maid service on request. One-bedroom units (for two) run $85 ($105 high season), two-bedroom units (for four) $105-150 ($125-200 high season); $10 for each additional guest. There is a three-night minimum stay. Two nights' deposit is required for reservations. Select credit cards are honored except for the weekly or longer-stay discounts. There is no beach as the building sits right along the seawall, but there is a pool, and you couldn't have a better view; all units are ocean-view deluxe at a standard price.

Puamana
A private community of condos, located one mile southeast of town on the ocean, Puamana is a quiet hideaway away from the hustle and bustle of town. One-bedroom units (fully equipped) begin at $105 in the low season, for up to four people; $140 garden, $170 ocean, Two-bedroom units range $155-210, and three-bedroom townhouses cost $260. Rates are higher mid-December to mid-April. Discounts for long stays. Puamana features an oceanside swimming pool, tennis, badminton, volleyball courts, and a sauna. Write P.O. Box 515, Lahaina, HI 96767, tel. 667-2551, (800) 367-5630 Mainland, (800) 423-8733, ext. 255 in Canada. Check in at the clubhouse, the local sugar plantation's former manager's house.

B&Bs And Cottages
Aloha Tony's, 13 Kauaula Rd., Lahaina, HI 96761, tel. 661-8040 or (800) 57-ALOHA, off Front Street, is a neat, cozy, and clean guesthouse, a minute from downtown Lahaina. Tony Mamo, the owner and operator, rents rooms $40-60.

The **Guesthouse B&B,** 1620 Ainakea Rd., Lahaina, HI 96761, tel. 661-8085, (800) 621-8942, is a well-appointed B&B where the host will provide free snorkel gear, and scuba lessons for a fee. Rates are $65-105.

John and Sherry Barbier's **Old Lahaina House,** P.O. Box 10355, Lahaina, HI 96761, tel. 667-4663, (800) 847-0761, just two blocks from Old Lahaina Towne, has four rooms (two with private bath). All rooms include a/c, telephone, TV, and access to the swimming pool; $50-95 per night, breakfast included.

The **Garden Gate B&B,** 67 Kaniau Rd., Lahaina, HI 96761, tel. 661-8800, owned and operated by Ron and Welmoet Glover, offers quiet accommodations just north of Lahaina toward Kaanapali. Choose a private garden studio with its own lanai that can accommodate up to five people for $75-95, or the Molokai Room with its own private bath at $50 for two. Breakfast is eggs, fresh-baked pastry, cereal, fruit, juices, and coffee.

FOOD

Lahaina's menu of restaurants is gigantic. All palates and pocketbooks can easily be satisfied: there's fast food, sandwiches, sushi, happy hours, and elegant cosmopolitan restaurants. Because Lahaina is a dynamic tourist spot, restaurants and eateries come and go with regularity. The following is not an exhaustive list of Lahaina's food spots—it couldn't be. But there is plenty listed here to feed everyone at breakfast, lunch, and dinner. *Bon appétit!*

Inexpensive
Seaside Inn, 1307 Front St., tel. 661-7195, serves local plate lunches and Japanese *bento* during the day for about $5; steam-table dishes include teriyaki chicken, beefsteak tomatoes, and chicken curry. The evening menu offers American and Asian selections like rib-eye steak for $7.50, tempura, *tonkatsu,* or various tofu dishes for under $5; for a complete dinner add $2 and receive miso soup, salad, and *tsukemono.* This is where local people and those in the know come for a very good but no-frills meal. If eating hearty without caring about the ambience (actually the sunset view couldn't be better)

is your aim, come here. An added attraction is the karaoke sing-along on Friday and Saturday from 8 p.m.

The **Thai Chef,** tel. 667-2814, will please any Thai food lover who wants a savory meal at a good price. Search for this restaurant stuck in a corner at the Lahaina Shopping Center, open Mon.-Sat. 11:30 a.m.-2 p.m. for lunch, nightly 5-10 p.m. for dinner. As in most Thai restaurants, vegetarians are well taken care of with plenty of spicy tofu and vegetable dishes. The extensive menu offers everything from scrumptious Thai soups with ginger and coconut for $7.25 (enough for two) to curries and seafood. Most entrees are under $8, with a good selection under $6. It's not fancy, but food-wise you won't be disappointed.

Zushi's is a hole-in-the-wall, very reasonably priced Japanese restaurant selling sushi and various other Japanese dishes at the Lahaina Business Center, across the street from McDonald's. It's stuck away in the corner, so look for it around the back. They serve lunch (takeout too) 11 a.m.-2 p.m., and dinner 5-9 p.m. The food is authentic, with most items under $5. Also in the plaza next to the Activities Information Center is a small takeout window with the imaginative name **Local Food,** which sells local food in the form of plate lunches. Basic, cheap, filling, and good.

Snug Harbor and the South Seas Patio, at the historic Pioneer Inn along Front St., serves breakfast 7-11:30 a.m., offering hotcakes for $4.50, and eggs with bacon or sausage for $5.25. Lunch is a hot roast beef sandwich for $5.75, Southern deep-fried chicken for $6.75, or chili dogs, turkey sandwiches, ham and cheese, and mini-pizzas, all for under $4. They also have ice cream and shave ice. Since the Pioneer Inn is the oldest hotel in town, and a true landmark with a great lanai from which you can view the harbor, the experience is really the history and the atmosphere and not the food, although it is passable.

Sunrise Cafe, open 5:30 a.m.-10 p.m. at 693 Front St., tel. 661-8558, is the kind of place locals keep secret. It's a tiny little restaurant where you can have excellent coffee, a sandwich, or more substantial gourmet food, at down-home prices. The food, provided by the excellent Village Cafe in Kapalua, includes breakfast specials like strudels and croissants for under $3, and lunch salads from Caesar to fresh island fruit priced under $6. Heartier appetites can choose daily specials like vegie lasagna with French bread for under $6, or from various sub sandwiches that come with pasta salad, macaroni salad, or Maui-style chips, all for under $5.50. A deli case holds scrumptious pastries that can be complemented by a fine selection of freshly brewed coffees and herbal teas. The cafe is owned and operated by Kathleen and Larry Leonard, who operate Lappert's Ice Cream just up the street, where you can choose a yummy dessert.

The open-air **Cheeseburger in Paradise** at 811 Front St., tel. 661-4855, open 11 a.m.-11 p.m., live music nightly (see "Entertainment" following), is a joint down by the sea overlooking the harbor out back. Served are burgers for $6.50, tofu burgers for $6.95, the famous spinach and nut burger for $6.95, the *haole* hot dog covered with cheese and grilled onions for $5.95, or the Maui classic BLT for $5.95. Other selections include the aloha fish and seasoned fries at $7.95, a huge Upcountry salad for $6.95, and a bowl of chili for only $3.50. Cheeseburger also has a full bar that sells a range of both imported and domestic beer, along with tropical concoctions. If you were going to pick one spot to have a beer, soak in the sights, and capture the flavor of old Lahaina, "the Burg" has all the trimmings.

The tiny **Sushiya Deli** is a local plate lunch, *bento,* and saimin place on Prison Street just after you turn toward the mountains off Front Street. Look for it across the street from the public parking lot. Open weekdays 6 a.m.-4 p.m., they make their own sushi but are usually sold out by early afternoon. You can also choose from a full selection of plate lunches like beef teriyaki for $4.75, or a hamburger plate for only $3.50. This is a very local restaurant with unbeatable prices.

Your sweet tooth will begin to sing the moment you walk into **The Bakery** at 911 Limahana, near the Sugar Cane Train Depot off Honoapiilani Hwy. (Rt. 30) as you head toward Kaanapali. You can't beat their stuffed croissants for under $2, or their sandwiches for under $4. Coffee is a mere 40 cents and their pastries, breads, and pasta are gooood! Open daily 7 a.m.-5 p.m., until noon on Sunday, tel. 667-9062.

Lahaina Coolers in the Dickenson Square serves breakfast, lunch, and dinner. Lunch specials daily, and the bar has happy hour 4-6 p.m. and 10-midnight "eight days a week." The most expensive item on the menu is about $10. Bright and breezy; tables are also set out in the courtyard.

Wiki Wiki Pizza across from the Cannery Mall, at 1285 Front St., tel. 661-5686, has a takeout window featuring an eight-inch lunch pizza for only $3.95, 12-inch $8.95, 16-inch $11.95, toppings extra, and sandwiches from $5.99. A deck-patio on the premises gives you a quiet nook to eat in as you overlook Mala Wharf and the Lahaina Roads. If you're in a nearby condo, they'll deliver free.

The Wharf Shopping Center at 658 Front St. includes the inexpensive **Blue Lagoon Saloon** on the ground floor, open daily 9 a.m.-10 p.m. The offerings are steam-table counter style, but the surroundings in the courtyard are pleasant. Most everything on the menu is under $8.50. A few entrees like mahimahi at $11.95, fish and chips for $10.25, and New York steak for $13.95 round out the menu. The Blue Lagoon offers daily specials like a clam basket for about $7.95, and soup and sandwich for under $7. **Orange Julius** dispenses its famous drinks, along with hot dogs and sandwiches for a quick, cheap meal. **Taco Jo's** is a passable Mexican restaurant stuck away in the corner where you can get a full meal for around $7.95. Taco Jo's has happy hour 3-6 p.m. and again 9-11 p.m., when you can have a draft beer for $1.25 and a margarita for $1.99. Jo's live music from 9 p.m. until midnight features various island artists. To the rear on the opposite side is **Song's Oriental Kitchen.** This unpretentious restaurant is of the precooked steam-table variety, but you can stuff yourself on meals like beef stew for $3.95 or barbecued chicken for $3.85, all with two-scoop rice and macaroni salad. **Chun's Chinese Barbecue** on the second level offers plate lunches, *bento,* a full selection of Chinese food, and some Korean favorites.

Moondoggies, at 666 Front St., tel. 661-3966, open daily 7:30-11 a.m. for breakfast, and 11 a.m.-10 p.m. for lunch and dinner, sits high above the action, and along with reasonably priced food, offers daily entertainment and a bird's-eye-view of the human tide ebbing and flowing below. The menu offers fresh fruit pancakes at $6.95, meatball sandwiches for $6.95, a turkey club at $6.95, pasta dishes like marinara for $8.95 or shrimp Alfredo for $15.95, and various pizzas ranging in price $7.95-14.95. Moondoggies is an excellent choice for a cool beer, followed by a light meal, and makes a perfect escape from Lahaina's frenetic action.

The Hard Rock Cafe, at the Lahaina Shopping Center on the corner of Front and Papalaua streets, tel. 667-7400, open daily from 11 a.m., is a large, breezy, screened restaurant keeping the rock 'n' roll faith. Over the bar is a '59 Cadillac convertible, and on the walls are electric guitars including a Gibson autographed by The Grateful Dead. The floors have a shiny patina, and the raised stools and round-topped tables give you a view of the street and the sea beyond. Menu prices are moderate, with Maui onion rings at $3.95, guacamole and salsa for $5.50, Caesar salad for $6.50, barbecued chicken for $10.95, and natural vegie burger for $6.50. The bar serves house wine, champagne, domestic and imported beer, mixed drinks, soft drinks, and coffee.

Chili's Bar and Grill, also at the Lahaina Shopping Center, open Sun.-Thurs. 11:30 a.m.-10 p.m., Fri.-Sat. to 11 p.m., serves up savory Southwestern and Mexican food. The interior, predominantly gray-on-green, is cooled by ceiling fans, while the tile floor, grooved ceilings, tile-topped tables, and a touch of brickwork complete the illusion of a border-town cantina. The *carta* offers munchies like buffalo wings for $4.95, chicken quesadillas for $6.45, or grilled Caribbean chicken for $7.95. From the grill you can order Monterey chicken for $9.95, burgers for under $6.95, and a variety of tacos for under $7. Full bar.

Aside from the full range of produce, vitamins, and health foods, the **Westside Natural Food and Deli** on Dickenson has some reasonably priced and healthy prepared foods and fruit drinks.

Fast Food And Snacks

Fanatics can get their fix at: **Burger King,** on Front Sreet near the banyan tree; **Pizza Hut** at 127 Hinau St.; or the The Lahaina Shopping Center, which has **Jack in the Box, McDon-**

ald's, Kentucky Fried Chicken, and **Denny's** across the street.

Lappert's Ice Cream, at the Pioneer Inn Mall, not only has ice cream, shave ice, and cookies, but also serves fat- and sugar-free ice cream, about the only thing on Maui that is fat-free!

A good one for a quick snack is **Mr. Sub,** tel. 667-5683, at 129 Lahainaluna Road. They feature double-fisted sandwiches and packed picnic lunches.

Take Home Maui at 121 Dickenson St., mail order tel. (800) 545-MAUI, is a food store and delicatessen that specializes in packaging agriculturally inspected Maui produce such as pineapples, papayas, Maui onions, protea, potato chips, macadamia nut products, and even Kona coffee, which they will deliver to you at the airport before your departing flight. For an on-the-spot treat they prepare deli sandwiches like roast beef or ham for under $5.50, a variety of quiches, and sides of macaroni and potato salad. Take Home Maui is famous for its fresh-fruit smoothies, homemade soups, and picnic lunches. Choose a shaded spot on their veranda and enjoy your lunch while taking a break from the jostle of Front Street.

The **Harbor Front Restaurant** on the second floor at The Wharf Shopping Center on Front Street, tel. 667-8212, has a logo that reads "Established a long time ago." Lunch up to $10, sandwiches $6.50, dinners $19. A display case at the entrance holds the fresh catch-of-the-day. The interior is surprisingly well done with many hanging plants in distinctive planters, high-backed wicker chairs, and white tables with bright orange table settings.

Harpooner's Lanai is in the Pioneer Inn, tel. 661-3636. Daily breakfast from 7 a.m., lunch from 11:30 a.m. Basic but good foods including pancakes and Portuguese bean soup. Most dishes and sandwiches are under $8.

Kimo's, 845 Front St., tel. 661-4811, is friendly and has great harbor and sunset views on the lower level. If you're in Lahaina around 6 p.m. and need a break, head here to relax with some "Kimo therapy." Popular, but no reservations taken. They offer seafood from $12, with most entrees $15-25, and are known for their catch-of-the-day, usually the best offering on the menu; limited menu for children. The downstairs bar has top-notch well drinks featuring brand-name liquors.

Moose McGillycuddy's, 844 Front St., tel. 667-7758, is almost an institution. A wild and zany place, it has music nightly (live on Friday and Saturday), daily specials, "early bird specials" (both breakfast and dinner), and a happy hour 4-8 p.m. Their large portions are filling, and the menu reads like a book.

Moderate

You won't be a pawn when you walk onto the black-and-white checkered floor at **Longhi's,** 888 Front St., tel. 667-2288, open daily 7:30 a.m.-10 p.m. Longhi owns the joint and he's a character. He feels that his place has "healing vibes" and that the basic food of humans is air. Prices at Longhi's may seem high but the portions are enormous and can easily fill two. Better yet, order a half-order for half-price. With all meals and salads comes a wonderful basket of jalapeño and pizza breads. Sometimes people complain about the service. It *is* different! No written menu, so when you sit down, you might feel ignored, especially when they're busy. Don't! The waiter or waitress will come around and explain the menu to you. Mornings you can order *frittatas,* like spinach, ham, and bacon, $7.50, easily enough for two. A good lunch choice is pasta Siciliana with calamari, spicy with marinara sauce; for dinner, the prawns amaretto and shrimp Longhi are good. Save room for the fabulous desserts. It's hard not to have a fine meal here. There's always a line, reservations accepted, no dress code, and complimentary valet parking. There's also entertainment in the upstairs bar, with live dance music Friday and Saturday from 10:30 p.m.

Kobe Japanese Steak House is at 136 Dickenson at the corner of Luakini, tel. 667-5555, open daily for dinner from 5:30 p.m. Service is *teppan yaki*-style, which means that the chef comes to you. His sharp blade flashes through the air and thumps the table, keeping the culinary beat as it slices, dices, and minces faster than any Veg-o-matic you've ever seen. The delectables of marinated meat, chicken, and vegetables are then expertly flash-fried at your own grill, oftentimes with aplomb in a ball of sake-induced flame. The experience is fun, the food very good, and the interior authentic Japanese. *Teppan* meals come complete with soup, tea, and dessert. Expect to spend at least $15 for an entree, $10 for an appetizer; or have sake or beer while munching at the sushi bar.

Saeng's Thai Cuisine, one of the best restaurants in Wailuku, has opened a sister restaurant in Lahaina at 1312 Front St., tel. 667-0822, open for lunch Mon.-Fri. 11 a.m.-2:30 p.m., dinner nightly 5-10 p.m. The large menu includes savory appetizers and salads like sautéed tofu, Thai crisp noodles, green papaya salad, and *yum-muer*—sliced beef, lemongrass, kafir, lime leaves, and onions served on fresh lettuce—all priced $5-9. Exotically spiced Thai soups, plenty for two, are priced under $7.50. For an entree try Thai garlic or ginger beef or pork, shrimp asparagus, cashew chicken delight, or the evil prince shrimp and fish, all for under $12.95. Vegetarians can choose from an assortment of dishes including eggplant tofu or eggplant curry. Money-saving daily specials, especially at lunch, are tempting; try the chili chicken for $9.50, kung pao shrimp for $11.95, or kung pao chicken for $9.95. Saeng's Thai Cuisine is a "budget gourmet" restaurant where the service is very friendly and the location is away from the madding crowd.

Benihana of Tokyo, at the Wharf Shopping Center, 658 Front St., tel. 667-2244, open daily 11:30 a.m.-2 p.m. for lunch, and 5-10 p.m. for dinner, has been a pioneer in introducing Japanese cuisine to the West. Chefs from Japan prepare dishes like seafood *bento* for $13.75, or the special Benihana *bento* for $16.75. Traditional Japanese foods include hibachi-cooked chicken, steak, or scallops ranging in price $14.50-19.25. Lighter appetites will enjoy *yaki soba* (fried *soba* noodles) for $6.50, or chicken cutlets at $6.75.

The Old Lahaina Cafe, located at the 505 Front Street Mall, is famous for offering one of the best luau on Maui (see "Food and Drink" in the Out and About chapter). The post-and-beam cafe, tel. 661-3303, open daily 7:30 a.m.-10 p.m., happy hour noon-6 p.m., is blue-on-blue with shutters that open to the sea breezes. Breakfast entrees are served 7:30-11:30 a.m., with Sunday brunch 8 a.m.-3 p.m., and include the *paniolo* breakfast of two eggs, Portuguese sausage, pineapple sausage, bacon, or papaya wedge, along with rice or homefried potatoes, for $5.95. You can build your own omelette from $4.95, or forget about your arteries and order a loco moco, two fried eggs over hamburger steak with gravy on a bed of rice for $5.95. Lunch, served noon-3:30 p.m., offers very reasonable selections like soup du jour for $3.25, sandwiches $5.95-8.95, and plate lunches for under $7.95. Dinner entrees, served 5:30-10 p.m., include fresh island fish broiled over *kiawe* or sautéed in a papaya and ginger sauce, or the luau dinner (without the entertainment) that includes *kalbi* ribs, chicken long rice, *lomi lomi* salmon, sweet potatoes, rice, and *kalua* pork for $16.95. Broiled lobster tail and a selection of beef and chicken entrees are priced $11.95-21.95. The Old Lahaina Cafe has very good food at reasonable prices in a congenial atmosphere and is worth the money.

The Lahaina Fish Company at 831 Front St., tel. 661-3472, open daily noon-5 p.m. for happy hour and 5-11 p.m. for dinner, operates its own fishing boat so that the fish is guaranteed fresh. Belly up to the Hammerhead Bar, fashioned from glass and brass, or choose a table that looks directly out onto Lahaina Harbor. Notice the vintage Coca Cola vending machine, and a display of knots tied by the old salts who visited Lahaina. Happy hour brings domestic beer, house wine, and well drinks for $2, while imports and exotic drinks are only $2.50. The evening menu starts with dinner salads at only $1.95, a smoked fish platter at $9.95, or a bowl of fresh fish chowder for $3. Entrees can be mahimahi fish and chips at $7.95; fisherman's pasta with fish and vegetables sautéed in garlic, white wine, lemon butter, and herbs for $14.95; or the Lahaina fish fry, a combination of shrimp, oysters, calamari, and clams for $5.95. Meat and poultry dishes include honey-fried chicken for $8.95, teriyaki beef kabob for $11.95, or blackened rib-eye steak for $14.95. The fresh fish, depending on what's caught that day, is grilled, oven broiled, or blackened Cajun style and offered at market price. Every day brings a chef's special that ranges $16.95-21.95.

The Lahaina Broiler, at 889 Front St., tel. 661-3111, is a family affordable restaurant with indoor/outdoor seating. The menu offers Maui onion salad or seafood salad for $9.95, deep-fried calamari or fresh steamed clams for $8.95, and steaming bowls of their highly touted

French onion soup for $3.75. The Lahaina burger, a mahimahi burger, or a soup-and-sandwich combo are very affordable. Dinner specialties are seafood fettuccine for $19.95 or cioppino for $23.50; also served are inexpensive items like Hawaiian fish and fries for $11.95. The Lahaina Broiler offers a "mai tai sunset dinner" 5-9 p.m. that includes sautéed mahimahi and teriyaki chicken, salad bar, and a mai tai all for $12.95. You can also enjoy nightly entertainment 8 p.m.-1:30 a.m., anything from karaoke to rhythm and blues.

Hecock's at the 505 Front Street Mall, tel. 661-8801, open daily 7 a.m.-10 p.m. for food service, bar open until 2 a.m., is owned and operated by Tom and Nancy, a husband-and-wife team who bring you good food at reasonable prices. Hecock's breakfast could be ranch eggs with a sirloin steak for $6.95, or a three-egg scampi omelette for $9.95, along with the classics like French toast or buttermilk pancakes with the trimmings for under $8. The lunch menu offers a chef salad for $6.95, assorted burgers and sandwiches priced $6.95-7.50, and pasta dishes like cheese tortellini or fettuccine Alfredo for under $8.95. The dinner bill of fare includes sausage and rigatoni for $15.95, New York steak at $17.95, and *huli huli* chicken for 15.95. A children's menu, happy hour with complimentary *pu pu,* daily specials, and an "early bird special" offered 5-6:30 p.m. for $9.95, help keep prices down.

J.J.'s Beach Grill, at the 505 Front Street Mall, tel. 667-4341, open daily 11 a.m.-3 p.m. for lunch, 5:30-10 p.m. for dinner, is one of the newest additions to the Lahaina food scene. Away from the central action, it's a great bet for always finding a table. The sunset view and classic interior of Italian marble floors and triton shell chandeliers add that special touch for a great evening. J.J.'s lunch menu offers starters like steamed clams at $9.95, salad of tomato and mozzarella for $5.95, and chicken Caesar salad for $8.95. You can also choose from a variety of sandwiches ranging $6.95-9.95 that include a *kiawe* chicken sandwich. Try a New York steak with sautéed mushrooms, or one of the pasta dishes priced around $9.95. Dinner starts with soft-shelled crab or seared sashimi for $9.95, French onion soup or clam chowder at $4, or a Greek salad for $7.95. Entrees like chicken picatta at $14.95 or New York steak at $18.95 come with tossed Caesar salad, baked potato, pasta, or French fries.

Tree House Restaurant in the Maui Marketplace off Front Street serves dinner 5-9 p.m. In keeping with their name, there is a second floor surrounded by trees where you can perch and eat. Most entrees are only $12.95, with appetizers around $7. Lunch at $5.95-7.95 and afternoon *pu pu* are also served. An open-air restaurant away from the action and where you can always get a good seat, the Tree House has a full bar. Expect a reasonable meal, but not gourmet.

The Chart House at the far west end of Lahaina at 1450 Front St., tel. 661-0937, serves dinner nightly 5-9:30 p.m. No reservations, and a wait is common. They have another, less crowded restaurant in Kahului; both offer a good selection of seafood and beef. It's reasonably priced with a decent salad bar, and though the food is usually very good, it can slip to mediocre, depending upon the daily chef. There's no way of telling, so you just have to take a chance.

Gourmet Dining

When you feel like putting a major dent in your budget and satisfying your desire for gourmet food, you should be pleased with one of the following.

Whoever said "East Is East and West is West" would have whistled a different tune if only they'd had the pleasure of dining at the **Avalon,** 844 Front St. just below Moose McGillycuddy's, tel. 667-5559, open daily for lunch, dinner, and late snacks. Owner/chef Mark Ellman, assisted by his sister, Gerry, have put together a uniquely blended menu they've dubbed "Pacific Basin cuisine." Here are dishes from Sausalito to Saigon, and from Mexico City to Tokyo, with a bit of Nebraska and Hong Kong thrown in for good measure. Moreover, they've spiced, herbed, and garnished their delectables by mixing and matching the finest and most refined tastes from all the geographical areas, creating a culinary extravaganza. If you're tired of the same old appetizers, try Maui onion rings with tamarind-chipotle catsup, or don't resist the combination platter with a selection of the best appetizers for $16.95 (enough for two). Move on to mixed greens and crispy noodles in a tempting ginger sesame dressing, or *gado-gado* on a bed of brown rice turned sumptuous by a Balinese peanut sauce. Drift the Pacific through their grill selections like whole *opakapaka* in Thai sauce, or savor the flavors of succulent Asian prawns either with shiitake mushrooms or in a sun-dried tomato and basil cream sauce. If you need more convincing, try the house specialty of whole Dungeness crab and clams in a garlic and black bean sauce ($50 for two), or the mouthwatering Asian pasta like mama-*san* wished she could make. If only people could get along together as well as this food! The full lunch menu and late nights are special, too, with snacks at the bar. Choose indoor seating where you dine in air-conditioned comfort, or dine alfresco in the court-yard. The Avalon boasts a fine wine list along with champagne by the glass, served with crushed raspberries. The restaurant's single dessert, caramel Miranda, is made fresh daily and sure to please.

Gerard's elegant restaurant is in the **Plantation Inn,** at 174 Lahainaluna Rd., tel. 661-8939, open nightly for dinner 6-10 p.m., validated free parking nearby. Fronting the building is a small dining garden; the interior is rich with hardwood floors and oak bar. The epitome of neo-Victorian charm, the room is comfortable with puff-pillowed wicker chairs and fine crystal table settings atop starched linen. Chef Gerard Reversade, trained in the finest French culinary tradition since age 14, creates masterpieces. He feels that eating is *the* experience of life, around which everything else that is enjoyable revolves. He is aided by his friend Pierre, the hospitable wine steward, who intimately understands the magical blend of wine and food, bringing out the best in both. Gerard insists that the restaurant's waiters and waitresses share his philosophy, so along with the excellent food comes excellent service. The menu changes, but it's always gourmet. Some superb choices are the island greens with raspberry vinaigrette dressing, and crusty French bread. Appetizers feature mouthwatering choices like shiitake and wild mushrooms in puff pastry. Full entrees like herbed rack of lamb, or savory veal in a light tomato sauce with a side of spinach- and cheese-filled ravioli, titillate the palate. Confit of duck with potato *galette* served with mixed greens in a walnut-oil dressing is one of their superb signature dishes. Even if you possess great self-control, you have less than an even chance of restraining yourself from a luscious dessert like raspberry and chocolate *vacherin* with passion fruit *coulis,* chocolate mousse with shambot liqueur, or fresh berries with home-made sherbets.

David Paul's Lahaina Grill, at 127 Lahainaluna Rd., tel. 667-5117, open Mon.-Fri. 11 a.m.-2:30 p.m. for lunch, dinner nightly 6-11 p.m., complimentary cheese and specially priced wines by the glass, is Lahaina's newest gourmet restaurant. Owner David Paul, famous for his sauces, presents "artwork on a plate." The dining room is quite lovely, with coved and molded ceilings from which hang punchbowl chandeliers illuminating the starched white and green table settings. Unfortunately, the chairs are more cafe style, not meant for a long evening of salubrious relaxation. The waiters and waitresses, professional, friendly, and well-dressed in black pants and Paris-by-way-of-Texas formal tops, definitely give you attentive service, but their body language combined with a speedy presentation of the bill lets you know that they are waiting to seat the next lucky patrons . . . immediately! The menu is wonderful. Start with rich black bean soup, roasted pepper and sweet corn chowder, or Mediterranean cioppino, ranging in price $6-8.95. A lovely appetizer is the fried Dungeness crabmeat served over pasta ladled with a sesame sauce and avocado relish for $9.95, or *griglia mista,* local vegetables grilled over *kiawe* coals and brushed with olive oil and *croustad* for $7.95. Entrees include David Paul's signature dish, the "seafood painted desert," a savory creation of grilled seafood served on a bed of chardonnay and Gorgonzola sauce, and three pepper-flavored butters that David uses to paint cacti and a red setting sun. Other wonderfully prepared dishes are tequila shrimp and firecracker rice, another signature entree, made from tiger prawns marinated in chili oil, lemon juice, cilantro, cumin, and brown sugar in a blend of vanilla bean and chili rice for $21.95; or Kona coffee roasted lamb for $24.95. The very wicked dessert tray, with everything priced at $5, combined with a cup of rich roasted coffee, ends a wonderful meal.

Alex's Hole-in-the-Wall, down an alleyway at 834 Front St., tel. 661-3197, will put a small hole in your wallet and a big smile on your face. The food is Italian, with delights like veal parmigiana for $23, and chicken Marsala for $16. The pasta is locally made and fresh. Open for dinner daily except Sunday, 6-10 p.m. Lunch, offers Mon.-Fri. 11 a.m.-2:30 p.m., consists of less expensive salads, sandwiches, and pasta.

Chez Paul, five miles east of Lahaina in Olowalu, tel. 661-3843, seatings daily at 6:30 and 8:30 p.m., reservations only, credit cards accepted, is secluded, romantic, very popular, and French—what else? Local folks into elegant dining give it two thumbs up. The wine list is tops, the desserts fantastic, and the food *magnifique!* Start with luscious hors d'oeuvres like warm Maine lobster salad with a brandy cocktail sauce, homemade country pâté, a more simple bay shrimp salad, or a bowl of soup du jour, all priced $5-12. Entrees are delightful: fresh island fish poached in champagne, scampi smothered with fresh mushrooms, lobster in a sorrel sauce, veal in a Madeira wine sauce, or a medley of island vegetables, all priced $21-31. Chez Paul is definitely worth the trip from Lahaina; a short stroll along the beach is recommended as a perfect *aperitif.*

ENTERTAINMENT

Lahaina is one of those places where the real entertainment is the town itself. The best thing to do here is stroll along Front Street and people-watch. As you walk along, the street feels like a block party with the action going on all around you—as it does on Halloween. Some people duck into one of the many establishments along the south side of Front Street for a breather or a drink, or just to watch the sunset. It's all free, enjoyable, and safe.

Art Night

Friday night is Art Night in Lahaina. In keeping with its status as the cultural center of Maui, Lahaina opens the doors of its galleries, throws out the welcome mat, sets out food and drink, provides entertainment, and usually hosts a well-known artist or two for this weekly party. It's a fine social get-together where the emphasis is gathering people together to appreciate the arts and not necessarily on making sales. Take your time and stroll Front Street from one gallery to the next. Stop and chat with shopkeepers, munch the goodies, sip the wine, look at the pieces on display, corner the featured artist for comment on his/her work, soak in the music of the strolling musicians, and strike up a conversation with the person next to you who is eyeing that same piece of art with the same respect and admiration. It's a party. People dress up, but don't be afraid to come casually. Take your time and immerse yourself in the immense variety and high quality of art on display in Lahaina.

Halloween

This is one of the big nonofficial events of the year. It seems that everyone dresses in costume, strolls Front Street, parties around town, and gets into the spirit of the evening. It is a party in the street with lots of people, dance, music, color, and activities. In fact, it's becoming so popular with some that they fly in from Honolulu just for the night.

Nightspots/Discos

All of Lahaina's evening entertainment is in restaurants and lounges (see corresponding restaurants in "Food" for details). The following should provide you with a few laughs.

Free Hawaiian music and dance are featured at the **Wharf Shopping Center** courtyard as announced in the free tourist literature, and jam sessions and popular combos at the **Whale's Tale.** At **Taco Jo's,** island musicians treat you to their Maui sounds nightly 9 p.m.-midnight.

You, too, can be a disco king or queen on **Longhi's** black-and-white chessboard dance floor every weekend. Longhi's has live music on Friday and Saturday nights featuring island groups like The Ripe Tomatoes, or island songster Joe Cano. **Moose McGillycuddy's** (just listen for the loud music on Front Street) is still a happening place with nightly music though it's becoming more of a cruise joint for post-adolescents. Those who have been around Lahaina for a while usually give it a miss, but if you want to feast your eyes on prime American two-legged beef on the hoof, this place is for you.

The new experience in town is **Studio 505,** upstairs at the 505 Front Street Mall, open nightly 9 p.m.-2 a.m., cover $5, where you can dance to live music five nights per week, and disco on the other two.

The open-air **Cheeseburger in Paradise** at 811 Front St., tel. 661-4855, open 11 a.m.-11 p.m., rocks with live music nightly. There's no cover charge, and you can sit upstairs or down listing to the tunes.

The Lahaina Broiler, at 889 Front St., tel. 661-3111, swings with nightly entertainment that can be karaoke, rhythm and blues, country and western, or contemporary Hawaiian.

Cinema

Lahaina Cinemas, the only multiplex theater on West Maui, is located on the third floor of the Wharf Shopping Center. First-run features start at about noon and run throughout the day. Adults $5, kids 12-16 $3.50, seniors and children $2.50; all seats $2.50 until 5 p.m.

Hawaii Experience Omni Theater at 824 Front St. has continuous showings on the hour 10 a.m.-10 p.m. (45-minute duration), adults $5.95, children 12 and under $3.95. The idea is to give you a total sensory experience by means of the giant, specially designed concave screen that surrounds you. You will tour the islands as if you were sitting in a helicopter or diving below the waves. And you'll be amazed at how well the illusion works. You'll soar over Kauai's Waimea Canyon, dip low to frolic with humpbacks, and rise with the sun over Haleakala. If you can't afford the real thing, this is about as close as you can get. The lobby of the theater doubles as a gift shop where you can pick up souvenirs like carved whales and T-shirts, and a variety of inexpensive mementos, including Maui chips.

Hookers

Lahaina had more than its share last century, and thankfully they haven't had a great resurgence, as in Waikiki. In the words of one longtime resident, "There's no prostitution in Lahaina. People come as couples. For single people, there's so much free stuff around that the pros would go hungry." Skin merchants in Honolulu, operating under the thin guise of escort services or masseuses, will fly their practitioners to Maui, but anyone going to this length would be better off at home on their knees praying for any kind of a clue to life!

SHOPPING

Everybody loves to do the "Lahaina Stroll." It's easy. Just act cool and nonchalant, and give it your best strut as you walk the gauntlet of Front Street's exclusive shops and exotic boutiques. The fun is just in being here. If you begin in the evening, go to the east end of town and park down by Prison Street; it's much easier to find a spot and you walk westward, catching the sunset.

The Lahaina Stroll

On Prison Street, check out **Dan's Green House,** open daily 9 a.m.-5 p.m., specializing in *fukubonsai,* miniature plants originated by David Fukumoto. They're mailable (except to Australia and Japan), and when you get them home, plop them in water and presto . . . a great little plant, $14-98. Dan's also specializes in exotic birds like African gray parrots, macaws from Australia, common cockatoos, and various cheeky parrots. Dan's is a great place to browse, especially for families.

As you head west on Front, **Pearls of Tahiti,** open Mon.-Fri. 10 a.m.-8 p.m., and every other Saturday until 6 p.m., tel. 661-8833, will make you swoon with its assortment of fine jewelry and beads. It's the only store on Maui featuring Tahitian black pearls and 18-karat gold jewelry. Owned and managed by Mark Bennett, a longtime island resident who is more than willing to chat if time permits, Pearls of Tahiti has its own in-house designer who will create a one-of-a-kind piece, destined to become a family heirloom. Visit the "pin and ink" artist upstairs at **Skin Deep Tattooing,** at 626 Front St., tel. 661-8531, open daily 9 a.m.-10 p.m., until 5 p.m. Sunday, where you can get a permanent memento of your trip to Maui. They feature "new age primal, tribal tattoos," Japanese-style intricate beauties; female artists are available for shy female clientele. The walls are hung with sample photos and Harley-Davidson T-shirts that say Maui or Hawaii. A sobriety test is necessary to get tattooed. No wimps allowed! **Cammellia** is a treasure chest laden with gifts and jewelry made from gold, silver, and ivory. **Pricilla's Maui** sells T-shirts, towels, beach blankets, sunglasses, and other assorted items.

Moving Down The Line

The following shops are all located along Front Street. **Luana's** features contemporary resortwear, hand-painted accessories, and jewelry. **Seabreeze Ltd.** is a souvenir store with fake lei and generic muumuu that are no better or worse than others you'll find along Front Street, but their prices are good, especially for film. **The South Seas Trading Post** is just across from the Wo Hing Temple, at 851 Front St., tel. 661-3168, open daily 8:30 a.m.-10 p.m., and is the second oldest shop in modern Lahaina, dating back to 1871. They indeed have artifacts from the South Pacific, like tapa cloth from Tonga, but also colorful rugs from India, primitive carvings from Papua New Guinea, and Burmese *kalaga* wall hangings with their beautiful and intricate stitching. Prices range $30-300. You can pick up a one-of-a-kind bead necklace for only a few dollars, or a real treasure that would adorn any home, for a decent price. Both antiques and reproductions are sold; the bona fide antiques have authenticating dates on the back or bottom sides. **Maui Clothing Co.** has racks of hand-screened men's, women's, and kids' apparel; nice stuff. **Crazy Shirts** has a great assortment of T-shirts and other clothes. Also in this store at 865 Front Street is the tiny but intriguing **Lahaina Whaling Museum** (free) that displays antiques, nautical instruments, scrimshaw, harpoons, and other whaling artifacts. Open Mon.-Sat. 9 a.m.-10 p.m., Sunday until 9 p.m.

Just between the Pioneer Inn and the seawall, walk onto the sandy floor of the Polynesian-style **Gecko Store** where all the items including shorts, T-shirts, bathing suits, and sweatshirts bear the bug-eyed, sucker-footed logo of Hawaii's famous clicking geckos. Nearby is the **Lahaina Hat Co.,** where you can find the perfect chapeau to shield your head from the "merciless" Lahaina sun; and **Maui Mercantile,** which offers a great selection of really neat junk.

Noah himself would have been impressed with the **Endangered Species Store,** open daily 9 a.m.-10:30 p.m., tel. 661-0208, where a life-sized mountain gorilla, coiled python, flitting butterflies, and fluttering birds bid you welcome to this lovely jam-packed menagerie. The shelves hold world globes, maps, cuddly panda bears, posters of trumpeting elephants, sculptures of soaring eagles, parlor games, postcards, and memento flora- and fauna-inspired T-shirts of 100% cotton designed by local artists. A percentage of the profits from every purchase is set aside to advance environmental issues of all kinds. Moreover, the store deals with vendors who also contribute to the well-being of endangered species and the environment.

Christopher James, along Front Street, just next to the seawall, is a premier luggage boutique specializing in Dooney and Bourke leather handbags and luggage, and in distinctive silkscreened cotton canvas bags made by the Italian firm Prima Classe. With prices ranging from $140 for a tiny clutch bag to $750 for a medium-sized suitcase, the store caters to the well-heeled traveler.

Tropical Blues, next door to the Royal Art Gallery, presents the T-shirt art of Mark and Irene Ciaburri, who create all the designs for their cotton shirts. A display case holds the shimmering rhinestones and twinkling gold of costume jewelry.

The **Whaler's Locker,** at 780 Front St., open 9 a.m.-10 p.m., is a sea chest filled with hand-engraved scrimshaw on fossilized walrus and mammoth ivory. Lahaina, historically a premier whaling port, has long been known for this sailor's art etched on everything from pocket knives to whale tooth pendants. Display cases also hold gold and amber jewelry, Niihau shellwork, Japanese netsuke, and coral necklaces. If you are looking for a distinctive folk-art gift that truly says Maui, the Whaler's Locker is an excellent store from which to make your choice.

Lahaina Scrimshaw, 845 Front St. (across from Wo Hing Temple), tel. 661-8820, (800) 642-7021, open daily 9 a.m.-10 p.m., boasts their own master scrimshander, John Lee, who works in the window every day about 7:30 a.m.-noon, and who is friendly and willing to answer questions about this seaman's art. Most of the scrimshaw is done on antique whale's teeth from the whaling era or on fossilized walrus and mastodon tusks. The scrimshaw offered is authentic, and made by about 40 artists, most of whom are from Hawaii.

The "sexually incorrect" will love **David's of Hawaii,** at 815 Front St., where you can find all kinds of lewd postcards, T-shirts, and souvenirs. If T-shirts bearing sexually implicit puns offend you, keep strolling—it's nasty in there.

The Wharf Shopping Center

The Wharf Shopping Center at 658 Front St. offers three floors of eateries (see "Food" above) and shops. Browse **Lahaina Shirt Gallery** for fine aloha shirts, or **Crazy Shirts** with their excellent selection of quality T-shirts. Next door is **Gigi's Leather Boutique** for everything from jackets to purses. **Casablanca's** offers women's tropical sportswear; nearby is **Island Swimwear** with bathing suits for men and women, and **The Coral Tree** with a mixture of junk and fine jewelry. **The Whaler's Book Shoppe** on the third floor is well stocked with books, everything from Hawaiiana to bestsellers. Relax and read in the coffee bar. The **Mad Hatter** has an unbelievable variety of straw (and a few cloth) hats. If you can't find something here to fit your head, your style, and your pocketbook, you won't find it anywhere. **Island Coins and Stamps** on the second floor is a shop as frayed as an old photo album. They specialize in philatelic supplies. For postal needs and gifts, stop by the **Lahaina Mail Depot** on the lower level at the rear. Across the walk is a free exhibit about the lighthouses of Hawaii, a project of the Lahaina Restoration Foundation. The Fresnel lens on display was once in the lighthouse at Kalaupapa on Molokai. Next door to this display is **Island Sandals,** a small shop run in the honest old-style way that produces fully adjustable tie sandals, styled from the days of Solomon. As the gregarious sandalmaker says, he creates the right sandal for $85 and gives you the left as a gift. Stop in and have him trace your feet for an order (or mail in tracings). As he works, he'll readily talk about political, social, or local island issues.

505 Front Street Mall

The 505 Front Street Mall, with most shops open daily 9 a.m.-9 p.m., offers a barrelful of shops, stores, a disco, and restaurants at the south end of Front Street, away from the heavier foot traffic. The mall is like a New England village, and the shopping is good and unhurried with free underground parking for customers. Some shops include **The Bikini Corner** for swimwear, and **Sea Level Trading Co.** for affordable hand-painted cotton clothing $7.50-60, with a design emphasis on Hawaiian flowers and marinelife.

Lee Sands Eelskins is filled with accessories, clothing, handbags, briefcases, purses, and belts made from reptile and other unique animal skins. If "you are what you wear," set your own standards by adorning yourself in something made from pig, cobra, shark, stingray, peacock, or even chicken skin.

Emanuelle is a women's apparel shop that features high fashion in basic black. **KPOA FM Music Shop** offers the latest in cassettes and CDs, with an emphasis on local Hawaiian sounds. **Bisous** is a distinctive shop with a kissing-lips logo that offers men's and women's clothing from France. Silk shirts average $80, while print dresses made from antique rayon are priced around $110.

The Lahaina Shopping Center

The Lahaina Shopping Center, just behind Longhi's, has a few inexpensive shops, a drugstore, and **Nagasako's Market**, known for its good selection of local and Asian food. Across the street are the **Lahaina Square Shopping Center,** with a **Foodland,** and the **Lahaina Business Center** with many more shops. Across Papalaua Street is the new **Lahaina Center** with **Hilo Hatties, Hard Rock Cafe,** and other shops yet to be determined.

Golden Reef is at 695 Front St., tel. 667-6633, open daily 10 a.m.-10 p.m. Inside is all manner of jewelry, from heirloom quality to costume baubles, made from black, gold, red, and pink coral, malachite, lapis, and mother of pearl. All designs are created on the premises. Everyone will be happy shopping here because prices range from $1 to $1000 and more. Golden Reef is also very happy to create one-of-a-kind work for you and you alone.

In the **Old Poi Factory** at 819 Front St., **Pacific Visions** sells hand-painted local garments done at Haiku, and art-deco items from Los Angeles, San Francisco, and New York. Pick up a plumeria lei out front at **Nito's Handicrafts,** where Tongan islander Mrs. Nito, usually sitting in a lawn chair, will make you one on the spot for only $5. She also makes hula skirts from raffia and *hau* tree fronds, while the tikis, carved from *milo,* are made by her husband Rafael. Here, the **Laura Rose Gallery** sells "art to wear" hand-painted by Laura Peterson, the proprietress. One of the oldest shops at the Poi

Factory is **Valley Isle Promotions,** opened in 1974, which specializes in children's and women's clothing, along with 14-karat gold jewelry designed in Indonesia by Jeanette, the store's owner. **Fox Photo** one-hour lab is on Front Street just across the street.

Off The Main Drag

Just off Front Street and Lahainaluna Rd. is **The Lahaina Market Place,** a collection of semi-open-air stalls, open daily 9 a.m.-9 p.m. Some vendors have roll-up stands and sell trinkets and baubles. It's junk, but it's neat junk. An interesting shop is **Donna's Designs** for tie-dyed T-shirts and sweatshirts in wild colors. For only $15 they make distinctive beachwear that will dazzle the eyes. **Crystal Creations** has fine examples of Austrian crystal and pewterwear, and **Annie's Candle Shop** deals in hand-dipped candles.

Nagamine Camera at 139 Lahainaluna Rd., tel. 667-6255, open daily 8:30 a.m.-8:30 p.m., is a full-service, one-hour-developing camera store. They're the best on West Maui for any specialized photo needs. Prices on film, however, could be better.

To save some money, try **991 Limahana Place** just near the Sugar Cane Train Depot off Hwy. 30. Here you'll find **Posters Maui,** which features a wide selection of the same posters that you'll spot on Front Street, but at a more reasonable price; **J.R.'s Music Shop** has a great selection of music, from "Beyond the Reef" to new age, but the prices aren't much cheaper than elsewhere.

The **Salvation Army Thrift Shop** on Shaw Street just up from Front Street has the usual collection of inexpensive used goods but occasionally some great buys on older aloha shirts. Open Mon.-Sat., regular business hours.

Take Home Maui, at 121 Dickenson St., mail order tel. (800) 545-MAUI, is a food store and delicatessen that specializes in packaging agriculturally inspected Maui produce.

The Lahaina Center

Lahaina's newest shopping center, at the corner of Front and Papalaua streets on the northwest end of town, had the finishing touches put on it in early 1993, and still awaits full occupancy by its merchants. The signature establishment of the center is the **Hard Rock Cafe,** filled with memorabilia of rock 'n' roll greats, and serving American standards and cold beer. Counterpointing the Hard Rock cafe is **Chili's Bar and Grill,** (see "Food" above) in neo-classic style, serving everything from quesadillas to mushroom burgers. Also in the center you will find **Local Motion Hawaii,** a hip clothing store selling tank tops, swimwear, and locally designed T-shirts that can be stenciled on the premises. **Bebe Sports** welcomes you with a "full dress" Harley Davidson, giant size, is a designer clothing store filled with jeans, leather jackets, and ladies' evening wear. They boast that if you saw "it" in L.A., you can buy it here on Maui. **Tropix** bills itself as "Lahaina's Nightclub" and offers dancing nightly. A Maui-style sign reads Dress With Style, No Beachwear.

Lahaina Cannery Shopping Center

As practical looking as its name on the outside, the center's bright and well-appointed interior features some of the best and most convenient shopping on West Maui, open daily 9:30 a.m.-9:30 p.m. It is located at 1221 Honoapiilani Highway. If you'll be staying at a condo and doing your own cooking, the largest and generally least expensive supermarket on West Maui is the Cannery's **Safeway,** open daily 24 hours. To book any activities, from a whalewatch to a dinner cruise, you'll find the **Ocean Activities Center** offers the most activities on Maui for the right price. Quickies can be picked up at the **ABC Sundry Store,** and you can beat the sun's glare by stopping into **Shades of Hawaii.** Chocoholics will be happy to discover the **Rocky Mountain Chocolate Factory,** where they even have sugarless chocolates for diabetics. **Dolphin Galleries** is an art shop specializing in whales and other mammals of the sea. Food is available at **Burger King, Marie Callendar's,** and **Padres Mexican Grill.** Although the mall is new, don't let that fool you because some of Lahaina's oldest and best shops, like **Lahaina Printsellers** and **Gem Creations,** are here. **Waldenbooks** has one of its excellent, well-stocked stores in the mall, open daily 9:30 a.m.-9:30 p.m., tel. 667-6172. One of the most unusual shops is **The Kite Fantasy,** featuring kites, windsocks, and toys for kids of all ages. You can buy kites like a six-foot flexifoil for $105 or a simple triangular plastic kite for only $2.50.

Cloth kites made from nylon with nice designs are a reasonable $15.95.

If you're into designer coffees, come to **Sir Wilfred's.** They also feature lunches like roast beef on a baguette for $4.25 and quiche for $2.50. Their great selection of roasted coffees makes terrific gifts. **Longs Drugs** is one of the cheapest places to buy and develop film. You can also find a selection of everything from aspirin to boogie boards.

Arts, Crafts, And Photos

Make sure to visit the **Lahaina Art Society** in the basement of the old jail in the courthouse. The artists here are up and coming, and the prices for sometimes remarkable works are reasonable. The **Waterfront Gallery and Gifts,** located at the Pioneer Inn Shopping Mall, will tickle big kids with their fine ships, models, and imported sheepskins.

The Village Galleries, with two locations at 120 Dickenson St., tel. 661-4402, (800) 346-0585, open daily 9 a.m.-9 p.m., and The Lahaina Cannery Mall, tel. 661-3208, open daily 9:30 a.m.-9 p.m., were founded by Lynn Shue in 1970, and are among the oldest continuous galleries featuring original works of Maui artists. Enter to find a small showcase brimming with everything from painted eggs to glass bead necklaces. The central area is given to sculptures of whales and mermaids done in both wood and metal. Some of the accomplished artists on display are: George Allan, who works in oils; Joyce Clark, another oil painter noted for her seascapes; Betty Hay-Freeland, a landscape artist; Fred Kenknight, who uses watercolors to depict island scenes; Lowell Mapes, who uses oils to render familiar landmarks like the Pioneer Inn. The galleries also have inexpensive items like postcards, posters, and limited-edition prints—perfect mementos.

Lahaina Printsellers at the Lahaina Cannery Mall, open daily 9:30 a.m.-9 p.m., tel. 667-7843, (800) 669-7843, has walls festooned with beautiful prints of old Hawaii, including endangered birds and historical figures that featured prominently in Hawaii's past. The Printsellers specialize in antique maps, especially those depicting the Pacific Basin, and Captain Cook memorabilia. Original antique prints and maps, many from the beginning of last century, start at only $25, and can go all the way up to $100,000. Lahaina Printsellers also offer hand-rubbed koa frames, and will be happy to send you a brochure if you would like to choose your artwork at home.

The Wyland Gallery, at 711 Front St., tel. 667-2285, open daily 9 a.m.-10 p.m., showcases the works of Wyland, renowned worldwide for his "whaling wall" murals of cavorting whales. Wyland's visionary oil and watercolor paintings of marvelous aquatic scenes adorn the walls, while his compassionate bronze renderings of whales and dolphins sing their soul songs from white pedestals. Signed limited-edition prints range $165-1000, original works $2500-250,000. Also displayed are the organic sculptures of Dale Joseph Evers, a pioneer in functional furnishings, who has turned bronze and acrylic into dolphin-shaped tables. Outside is a quiet lanai overlooking the harbor, where more aquatic-inspired glass sculptures counterpoint the living sea. Just down the street, **The Wyland Gallery Annex,** at 697 Front St., tel. 661-7097, open daily 9 a.m.-10 p.m., vibrates with fantastic colors and images created by Hawaii's premier artists. The gallery holds the dramatic, thundering seascapes of Roy Gonzales Tabora, a third-generation Filipino regarded as the best seascape artist in Hawaii; the liquidly poetic "sea-to-air" sculptures of Douglas Wylie; and the conjured magic of James Coleman, a renowned animator at Walt Disney Studios. Prices start from $400 for a numbered lithograph to $45,000 for published originals.

The **Lassen Gallery,** along Front Street, tel. 661-1101, open daily 10 a.m.-11 p.m., showcases original and limited-edition prints by Christian Lassen, who boldly applies striking colors to bring to life his two-worlds perspective of sea and earth. Typical of his dynamic vision is a displayed painting entitled *Majestic Encounters,* which depicts a pond alive with whales and dolphins who are being observed by a fierce-eyed tiger, who in turn is espied by the fixed and ageless glare of a stony-eyed sphinx. Originals are priced $10,000-200,000 and limited-edition prints $400-5000. Complementing the exaggerated hues of Lassen's works is the subtle patina of Richard Steirs's cast-iron sculptures of supple whales and dolphins. Mr. Steirs, an Upcountry resident, is among the most admired sculptors on Maui; his limited-edition castings sell for $150-250, and originals from $1,700 to as high as $13,000.

The Lahaina Galleries, 728 Front St., open daily 9 a.m.-10 p.m., tel. 667-2152 (branch galleries at Whaler's Village and at the Kapalua Shops), one of the oldest galleries on the island, showcases the lyrical paintings of **Robert Lynn Nelson,** who presents wide-angle views of the earth and water. The gallery, with a central room and two in the rear, is hung with the works of Frederick Hart and Dario Campanile, two widely acclaimed painters.

The Royal Art Gallery, at 752 Front St., open daily 9 a.m.-10:30 p.m., is alive with the works of Dennis Williams, who depicts impressionistic whales and dolphins in polished bronze; Jerry Joslyn, who is in love with mermaids; Linda Andelain, who paints the flowers of Hawaii; Caroline Young, a Westerner raised in Hong Kong, who depicts mythical priestesses and goddesses on silk; Anthony Casay, a world-class marine artist; and Michael Ward, whose futuristic world is filled with whales, spaceships, and elephants.

The Metropolitan Art Gallery, at 802 Front St., tel. 661-5033, open daily 10 a.m.-10 p.m., presents a mixture of local and internationally famous artists. They include: John Petri, a fantasy-surrealist who portrays everything from maidens communing with dolphins to whales cavorting in cosmic space; Annenberg, a marine artist who paints scenes of Neptune's paradise; Dick Kearney, a pioneer in marine art; John Stobart, who captures dramatic bygone harbor scenes; and Gil Bruvel, a Frenchman who paints "fantasy women" emerging from a feathered pen, or sporting wings in outer space. Prices in the gallery range from $300 for a limited-edition print to $100,000 and more for an original.

Food/Liquor Stores

The following markets/supermarkets are in and around Lahaina. The larger ones stock beer, wine, and liquor.

Safeway, at the Lahaina Cannery Shopping Center, open 24 hours, tel. 667-4392, is a large supermarket complete with deli, fish market, floral shop, and bakery.

Foodland, tel. 661-0975, at the Lahaina Square Shopping Center, is also a well-stocked supermarket.

Nagasako Supermarket, at the Lahaina Shopping Center, tel. 661-0575, open daily 7 a.m.-9 p.m., Sunday until 7 p.m., is a local supermarket with plenty of ethnic Hawaiian, Japanese, Chinese, and Korean foods, along with liquor selections. The market is also known for its fresh fish and produce.

The Olowalu General Store, tel. 661-3774, located five miles east of Lahaina along Rt. 30, open daily 5:30 a.m.-6 p.m., is fairly well stocked and the only place to pick up supplies in this area. Their light snacks like sandwiches and hot dogs make them a perfect stop if you are snorkeling or swimming on the nearby beaches.

Sports, Excursions, And Equipment

The **Maui Dive Shop,** at 624 Lahaina Ave., tel. 661-5388, open daily 8 a.m.-9 p.m., is a full-service dive shop offering tours, and snorkel and scuba rentals (see "Sports and Recreation" in the Maui Introduction).

Fun Rentals of Maui, at 193 Lahainaluna Rd., tel. 661-3053, open daily 8:30 a.m.-5 p.m., Sunday until 3 p.m., rents everything from snorkels to kayaks. Snorkel sets rent for $2.50 for 24 hours or $12 per week; skim boards $12 per day; surfboards $20 per day with weekly discounts available; kayaks $40 per day. They also rent miscellaneous items like binoculars, and baby joggers for parents who wish to stay fit.

Hawaiian Reef Divers, at 156 Lahainaluna Rd., tel. 667-7647, is a full-service dive shop that can arrange a two-hour, scientist-narrated whalewatch or a half-day snorkel/scuba excursion, rent snorkel/scuba gear, and provide scuba certification courses.

Snorkel Bob's, at 161 Lahainaluna Rd., tel. 661-4421, rents snorkel gear for $15 per week, which you can take to a neighboring island and return there. Boogie boards are available at $13 per day or $26 per week, and Snorkel Bob's advice, whether you need it or not, is plentiful and free.

SERVICES AND INFORMATION

Emergency

For fire, police, or ambulance, dial *911* throughout the Lahaina area.

Banks
In Lahaina during normal banking hours try **Bank of Hawaii** in the Lahaina Shopping Center, tel. 661-8781; **First Interstate** at 135 Papalaua St., tel. 667-9714; or **First Hawaiian,** 215 Papalaua St., tel. 661-3655.

Post Office
The post office is on the west edge of town toward Kaanapali, well marked, tel. 667-6611. **Lahaina Mail Depot** is a post office contract station located at the Wharf Shopping Center, 658 Front St., tel. 667-2000. They're open 10 a.m.-5 p.m. (Saturday until 1 p.m.) and along with the usual stamps, etc., they specialize in sending packages home. They've got mailing boxes, tape, and packaging materials. They also sell souvenir packs of coffee, nuts, candies, and teas, which might serve as last-minute purchases, but are expensive. In the Lahaina Shopping Center you'll find the **Mail Room** for shipping and packaging services. Hours are Mon.-Fri. 9:30 a.m.-6 p.m., Saturday until 3:30 p.m.; closed for lunch.

Medical Treatment
A concentration of all types of specialists is found at **Lahaina Medical Group,** located at Lahaina Square, tel. 667-2534. Look also at the **Maui Medical Group,** tel. 661-0051, on Prison Street, open Mon.-Fri. 8 a.m.-5 p.m. and Saturday 8 a.m.-noon; call for emergency hours. Professional medical care can also be found at the **Kaiser Permanente Clinic** on Wainee Street, tel. 661-0081. Alternatively, the **Lahaina Health Center,** 180 Dickenson St. at Dickenson Square, Suite 205, tel. 667-6268, offers acupuncture, chiropractic, therapeutic massage, and podiatry. Most practitioners charge approximately $30 for their services. In Suite 218 of the Dickenson Square are **Doctors On Call,** tel. 667-7676. They see patients in the office or will make house or hotel calls daily 7 a.m.-11 p.m. Pharmacies in Lahaina include: **Lahaina Pharmacy** at the Lahaina Shopping Center, tel. 661-3119, and **Valley Isle** at 130 Prison St., tel. 661-4747.

Next door to Lahaina Health Center is **Lahaina Nautilus Center,** tel. 667-6100, with exercise machines, free weights, and massage by appointment. The center's hours are Mon.-Fri. 6:30 a.m.-10 p.m., Saturday 8 a.m.-8 p.m., and Sunday 9 a.m.-2 p.m. Daily, weekly, and monthly (from $50 for one month to $499 for one year) rates are available. One-hour massages run $32 members and $47 nonmembers.

Services
For **laundromats** try **Fabritek Cleaners,** Lahaina Shopping Center, tel. 661-5660. For self-service try **Cabanilla Kwik'n Kleen,** also at the Lahaina Shopping Center, or the 24-hour **First Hawaiian Laundry** on Limahula Street, behind Pizza Hut, tel. 661-3061.

For Shear, tel. 667-2866, is a very local, semi-open-air **hair salon** for men, women, and children. Men's haircuts are about $15 and women's start at $20.

Information
The following groups and organizations should prove helpful. **Lahaina Restoration Foundation,** P.O. Box 338, Lahaina, HI 96761, tel. 661-3262, can also be found in the "Master's Reading Room" along Front Street. They are a storehouse of information about historical Maui; make sure to pick up their brochure, *Lahaina, A Walking Tour of Historic and Cultural Sites.* **The library** is at 680 Wharf St., tel. 661-0566, open Monday through Thursday. Stop in at **Whaler's Book Shoppe** in the upper level of the Wharf Shopping Center along Front Street. They have an excellent book selection as well as a gourmet coffee and sandwich shop if you get tired of browsing. See also "Information and Services" under the Maui Introduction for general information sources.

KAANAPALI AND VICINITY

Five lush valleys, nourished by streams from the West Maui Mountains, stretch luxuriously for 10 miles from Kaanapali north to Kapalua. All along the connecting **Honoapiilani Highway** (Rt. 30), the dazzle and glimmer of beaches is offset by black volcanic rock. Two sensitively planned and beautifully executed resorts are at each end of this drive. Kaanapali Resort is 500 acres of fun and relaxation at the southwest end. It houses six luxury hotels, six beautifully appointed condos, a shopping mall and museum, 36 holes of world-class golf, tennis courts galore, and epicurean dining in a chef salad of cuisines. Two of the hotels, the **Hyatt Regency** and **Westin Maui,** are inspired architectural showcases that blend harmoniously with Maui's most beautiful seashore surroundings. At the northeast end is another gem, the **Kapalua Resort,** 750 of Maui's most beautifully sculpted acres with its own showcase, the **Kapalua Bay Hotel.** Here, too, are prime golf and **Fleming Beach,** plus exclusive shopping, horseback riding, and tennis aplenty.

Kaanapali, with its four miles of glorious beach, is Maui's westernmost point. In general, it begins where Lahaina ends, and continues north along Route 30 until a mile or so before the village of Honokowai. Adjacent to each other at the north end are the villages of Honokowai and Kahana, which service the condos tucked away here and there along the coast and mountainsides. Both are practical stops where you can buy food, gas, and all necessary supplies to keep your vacation rolling. The accommodations are not as grand, but the beaches and vistas are. Along this entire southwestern shore, Maui flashes its most captivating pearly white smile. The sights all along this coast are either natural or manmade, but not historical. This is where you come to gaze from mountain to sea and bathe yourself in natural beauty. Then, after a day of surf and sunshine, you repair to one of the gorgeous hotels or restaurants for a drink, a meal, or just to promenade around the grounds.

History

Southwestern Maui was a mixture of scrub and precious *lo'i,* land, reserved for taro, the highest life-sustaining plant given by the gods. The farms stretched to Kapalua, skirting the numerous bays all along the way. The area was important enough for a "royal highway" to be built by

Chief Piilani, and it still bears his name. Westerners used the lands surrounding Kaanapali to grow sugarcane, and **The Lahaina, Kaanapali, and Pacific Railroad,** known today as the "Sugar Cane Train," chugged to Kaanapali Beach to unburden itself onto barges that carried the cane to waiting ships. Kaanapali, until the 1960s, was a blemished beauty where the Pioneer Sugar Mill dumped its rubbish. Then Amfac, one of the "Big Five," decided to put the land to better use. In creating Hawaii's first planned resort, they outdid themselves. Robert Trent Jones was hired to mold the golf course along this spectacular coast, while the Hyatt Regency and its grounds became an architectural marvel. The Sheraton-Maui was built atop, and integrated with, Puu Kekaa, "Black Rock." This area is a wave-eroded cinder cone, and the Sheraton architects used its seacliffs as part of the resort's walls. Here, on a deep underwater shelf, daring divers descend to harvest Maui's famous black coral trees. The Hawaiians believed that Puu Kekaa was a very holy place where the spirits of the dead left this earth and migrated into the spirit world. Kahekili, Maui's most famous 18th-century chief, often came here to leap into the sea below. This old-time daredevil was fond of the heart-stopping activity, and made famous "Kahekili's Leap," an even more treacherous seacliff on nearby Lanai. Today, the Sheraton puts on a sunset show during which this "leap" is reenacted.

Unfortunately, developers picked up on Amfac's great idea and built condos up the road starting in Honokowai. Interested in profit, not beauty, they earned that area the dubious title of "condo ghetto." Fortunately, the Maui Land and Pineapple Co. owned the land surrounding the idyllic Kapalua Bay. Colin Cameron, one of the heirs to this holding, had visions of developing 750 acres of the plantation's 20,000 into the extraordinary **Kapalua Bay Resort.** He teamed up with Rockresort Management, headed by Laurence Rockefeller, and the complex opened in 1979.

Transportation

Kaanapali is serviced by the **Kaanapali Trolley** and by the **Lahaina Cannery Shuttle** as far as that center. The Sugar Cane Train offers a day of fun for the entire family. The Kapalua-West Maui Airport is the most convenient for air travel to this end of the island. For details see "Maui's Airports" under "Getting There" and "Public Transportation" under "Getting Around" in the Maui Introduction.

Kaanapali Extras

Two situations in and around Kaanapali mar its outstanding beauty—you might refer to them as "Kaanapali Perfumes." There are still plenty of sugarcane fields in the area, and when they're being burned off, the smoke is heavy in the air; the soot falls at this time are called "black snow" by locals. Also, the sewage treatment plant is inadequate, and even the constantly blowing trade winds are insufficient to push the stench out to sea.

BEACHES

The four-mile stretch of pristine sand at Kaanapali is what people come to experience in Maui, and they are never disappointed.

Hanakoo Beach

This uninterrupted stretch of sand runs from the Hyatt Regency to the Sheraton. Although these are some of the most exclusive hotels on the island, public access to the beach is guaranteed in the state's constitution. There are "rights of way," but parking your car is definitely a hassle. A good idea is to park at **Wahikuli State Wayside** and walk westward along the beach. You can park (10 cars) in the Hyatt's lower lot and enter along a right of way. There's access between the Hyatt and the Marriott (pay parking ramp) and between the Marriott and the Kaanapali Alii, which also has limited parking. There is also some parking near the Sheraton and at the Whaler's Village Mall parking ramp, but you must pass through the gauntlet of shops.

Black Rock

One of the most easily accessible and visually engaging snorkeling spots on Maui is located at the Sheraton's Black Rock. Follow the main road past the Sheraton until it climbs the hill around back. Walk up the hill and through the hotel grounds until you come to a white metal fence. Follow the fence down toward the sea.

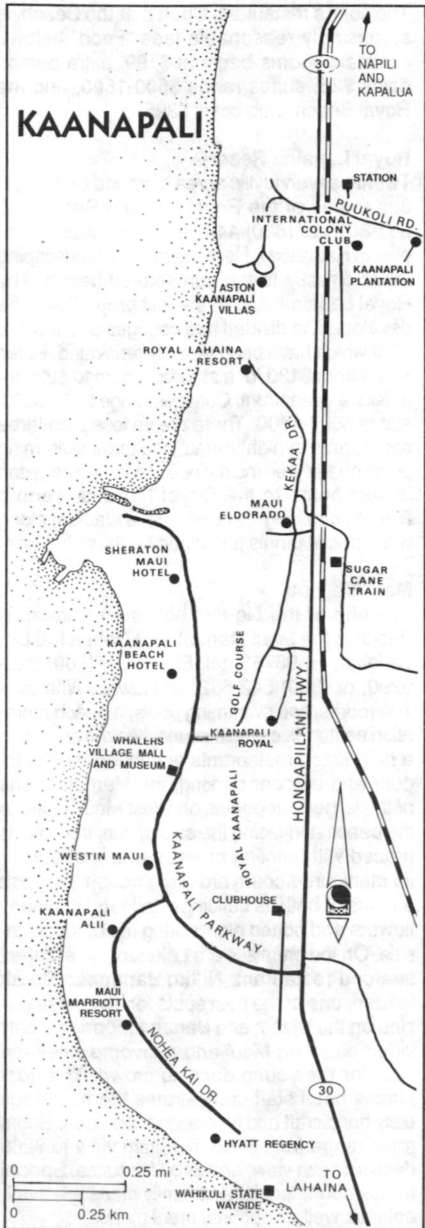

You'll come to a spur of rock jutting out, and that's it. The entire area is like an underwater marine park. Enter at the beach area and snorkel west around the rock, staying close to the cinder cone. There are schools of reef fish, rays, and even a lonely turtle. If you want to play it safe, park at the small parking lot at the far west end of Kaanapali near the Aston Kaanapali Villas. It's only a 10-minute walk away.

Sports

For a full listing of the sporting facilities and possibilities in the Kaanapali area, contact the information center in the Whaler's Village Mall or any of the activities desks at the hotels on the strip. **Golf** at the Royal Kaanapali North/South costs $90, par 72, tel. 661-3691. For **tennis,** the most famous is the Royal Lahaina Tennis Ranch with 11 courts, tennis clinics, and tournaments. The Hyatt and Marriott have five courts each, The Whaler has three courts, and the Kaanapali Royal has one. For **water sports,** catamarans are available twice a day from Kaanapali Beach. Contact any major hotel activities desk in the resort area, or **Maui Beach Center** at the Whaler's Village, tel. 667-4355.

ACCOMMODATIONS

The Kaanapali Resort offers accommodations ranging from "moderate deluxe" to "luxury." There are no budget accommodations here, but just northwest toward Honokowai are plenty of reasonably priced condos. As usual, they're more of a bargain the longer you stay, especially if you can share costs with a few people by renting a larger unit. And as always, you'll save money on food costs. The following should give you an idea of what's available.

Hyatt Regency Maui

The moment you enter the main lobby of this luxury hotel the magic begins. A multi-tiered architectural extravaganza opens to the sky, birds fly freely, and magnificent potted plants and full-sized palm trees create the atmosphere of a modern Polynesian palace located at Kaanapali's southern extremity, at 200 Nohea Kai Dr., Lahaina, HI 96761, tel. 661-1234 or (800) 233-1234. Nooks and crannies abound where you can lounge in kingly wicker thrones. Peacocks strut their regal stuff amid impeccable Japanese gardens, and ducks and swans are floating alabaster on landscaped ponds. The swimming pools, inspired by the islands, have built-in grottoes, caves, and waterfalls, and a huge slide. A swinging wooden bridge connects the sections, and you can have an island drink at a sunken poolside bar. There are two five-star *Travel Holiday* award-winning restaurants, one doubling as a disco for human peacocking. The "Elephant Walk" is a covey of specialty shops and boutiques. Rates are: $230-240 for terrace rooms, $345-360 for deluxe ocean-view rooms. Rates are higher for the special Regency floor. If you visit, valet parking is in front of the hotel, complimentary if you validate your ticket by dining at Spats or the Palm Court, or spend $25 in one of the shops. Or you can self-park around back.

Sheraton-Maui Hotel

The 505 rooms of the Sheraton Maui, 2605 Kaanapali Pkwy., Lahaina, HI 96761, tel. 661-0031 or (800) 325-3535, are built around Kaanapali's most conspicuous natural phenomenon, Puu Kekaa, "Black Rock." Room rates are $129 in the Molokai wing, $170 standard, $300 oceanfront, $25 extra person. The snorkeling around Black Rock is the best in the area. There are two pools, and the view from the upper-level **Sundowner Bar** is worth the price of a drink. A catamaran is available to guests. You can rent snorkeling equipment at a poolside kiosk, but the prices are triple what you pay at a dive shop.

The Westin Maui

The newest in luxury hotels to spring up along Kaanapali, at 2365 Kaanapali Pkwy., Lahaina, HI 96761, tel. 667-2525 or (800) 228-3000, is actually a phoenix, risen from the old Maui Surf Hotel. True to the second life of that mythical bird, it is a beauty. The Westin is known for its fabulous entranceways, lobbies, and quiet nooks. A series of strolling paths takes you through resplendent manicured grounds that surround an extensive pool area. Waterfalls, water slides, and natural rock formations blend to create civilized paradise. To the left of the main lobby is a collection of exclusive boutiques. The hotel's restaurant, **Cook's at the Beach,** is surprisingly reasonable (see "Food" below). Standard rooms begin at $199, extra person costs $25, suites range $500-1600, and the Royal Beach Club costs $395.

Royal Lahaina Resort

Twenty-seven idyllic acres surround 542 luxurious rooms of the Royal Lahaina Resort, tel. 661-3611 or (800) 447-6925, the largest complex in Kaanapali. Here the tropical landscaping leads directly to the sun-soaked beach. The Royal Lahaina, one of the first properties to be developed, is divided into cottages and towers, all of which have been recently renovated. Rates range from $130 for a standard room to $235 for a deluxe oceanfront. Cottages range $225-$290, suites $600-1500. There are no less than three restaurants, a nightly luau, and three swimming pools on the well-maintained grounds. The resort is also home to the **Royal Lahaina Tennis Ranch,** boasting 11 courts and a stadium along with special tennis packages for those inclined.

Maui Marriott

The fifth of the big five hotels on Kaanapali Beach is the Maui Marriott, 100 Nohea Kai Dr., Lahaina, HI 96761, tel. 667-1200, (800) 228-9290, or (800) 542-6821 in Hawaii. With over 700 rooms, two swimming pools, a beach recreation center, five tennis courts, two dozen shops, a half dozen restaurants and lounges, and indoor and outdoor parking, the Marriott is one of the largest properties on West Maui. Open to the beach and facing the setting sun, the hotel is graced with cooling breezes that waft across its manicured courtyard and through the open atriums of both its buildings. Indoors, the many flowers and potted plants bring the outdoors inside. On the premises are **Lokelani,** an excellent seafood restaurant; **Nikko Japanese Steak House,** one of the best spots for Japanese cuisine on the island; and **Banana Moon,** the only video disco on Maui and a favorite weekend spot for the young dancing crowd. The hospitable hotel staff orchestrates the numerous daily handicraft and recreational activities. Room rates range from $185 mountain view to $260 deluxe ocean view, and $400 for suites. Special honeymoon, tennis, and family plans are available, as well as optional meal plans.

Kaanapali Beach Hotel
Not as luxurious as its famous neighbors, but an excellent hotel nonetheless, at 2525 Kaanapali Pkwy., tel. 661-0011 or (800) 657-7700. For Kaanapali, this hotel is a bargain. Standard rooms range $135-175 for an ocean view; suites are priced at $525. A distinctive whale-shaped pool and tennis privileges at the Royal Lahaina are some of the amenities. This is perhaps the most "Hawaiian" of the hotels in Kaanapali.

Condos
Generally less expensive than the hotels, condos begin at around $100 per night and offer full kitchens, some maid service, swimming pools, and often convenience stores and laundry facilities. Off-season rates and discounts for longer stays are usually offered. Combinations of the above are too numerous to mention, so it's best to ask all pertinent questions when booking. Not all condos accept credit cards, and a deposit is the norm when making reservations. The following should give you an idea of what to expect.

The Aston Kaanapali Shores: The green tranquility of this created oasis fronting Kaanapali Beach at 3445 Lower Honoapiilani Hwy., tel. 667-2211 or (800) 922-7866, offers an unsurpassed view of sun-baked Lanai and Molokai just across the channel. You enter a spacious and airy open lobby, framing a living sculpture of palms and ferns. Water melts over a huge copper painting-sculpture of the moon. The grounds are a trimmed garden in large proportions dappled with sunlight and flowers. Soak away your cares in two whirlpools, one tucked away in a quiet corner of the central garden area for midnight romance, the other near the pool. Shop at **Beachside Casuals,** a special children's boutique of handpicked toys, clothing, and games (big people's clothes, too). You can enroll the little ones in **Camp Kaanapali,** a program for children ages 3-8, operated Mon.-Fri. 8 a.m.-2 p.m., $10 per child, plus $6 if lunch is included. Parents can indulge themselves at the **beauty salon,** or work off those rich meals at the **fitness center,** equipped with Nautilus weights, a Stairmaster, and a Lifecycle. Enjoy a romantic dinner at **The Beach Club,** a beautifully appointed restaurant serving delectables ranging from *pasta primavera* to the fresh catch-of-the-day. All units have been recently refurbished with new drapes, carpets, and furniture, and include gourmet kitchens, sweeping lanais, TV, and a/c. Prices range from $129 for an affordable studio to $280 for a two-bedroom oceanfront suite; or you can choose a simple hotel room at $109 that has a mini-kitchen equipped with small fridge, microwave, coffeemaker, and dishware for two. The Aston Kaanapali Shores offers great value for the money.

The Mahana at Kaanapali: The second that you walk into these reasonably priced condos and look through a large floor-to-ceiling window framing a swimming pool and the wide blue sea, your cares immediately begin to slip away. The condo sits on a point of beach at 110 Kaanapali Shore Pl., Lahaina, HI 96761, tel. 931-1400 or (800) 922-7866, which allows all apartments to have an ocean view at no extra cost. Rates range $105-160 for studios to $240 for huge two-bedrooms (up to six people). Enjoy a complete kitchen plus pool, sauna, tennis, maid service, and a money-saving family plan.

Aston Kaanapali Villas: Enjoy the surroundings of 11 sculpted acres at this affordable condo at 2805 Honoapiilani Hwy., Lahaina, HI 96761, tel. 667-7791 or (800) 922-7866. The extensive grounds of cool swaying palms harbor three pools, a jacuzzi, and tennis courts. Rates run $149 for a hotel room, $164-179 for studio suites, and $215 for a one-bedroom with a/c, cable TV, small refrigerator, and coffee pot, plus maid service. This property, located at the far north end of the Kaanapali development, has the added bonus of peace and quiet along with the best of the Kaanapali beaches, although you remain just minutes from the action. You're also a few minutes' walk from Black Rock, a superb snorkeling area. The units are very large with spacious bedrooms; even a one-bedroom is capable of handling four people.

Across the street from the villas is the **Lahaina Health Club,** tel. 667-6684, a private club open to walk-in guests. There is a room full of exercise machines, free weights, bicycle machines, and floor mats; aerobic classes are also given. Rates range from a $10 one-day fee to a $300 one-year membership.

Other accommodations in Kaanapali include **International Colony Club** on the *mauka* side of Rt. 30, tel. 661-4070 or (800) 526-6284 during weekday business hours. It offers individual cottages: one bedroom at $95, two bedrooms at $110, and three bedrooms at $130, extra person $10, four-day minimum. **Maui Eldorado,** tel. 661-0021 or (800) 367-2967, is surrounded by the golf course, rates $124-214. **Kaanapali Plantation,** tel. 661-4446, offers accommodations from $85 with a $10 discount for 14 days or longer, plus maid service and most amenities. **Kaanapali Royal,** a golfer's dream right on the course, tel. 661-7133 or (800) 367-5637, has rooms from $160 with substantial low-season and long-term discounts. Next to the Whaler's Village Mall is **The Whaler,** tel. 661-4861 or (800) 367-7052 Mainland. Rates range $160-525 for studio, one-, and two-bedroom units. **Kaanapali Alii,** tel. 667-1400 or (800) 642-6284, has one- and two-bedroom suites ranging $205-550.

FOOD

Every hotel in Kaanapali has at least one restaurant, and numerous others are scattered throughout the area. Some of the most expensive and exquisite restaurants on Maui are found in these hotels, but surprisingly, at others you can dine very reasonably, even cheaply.

The Beach Club

Whether you're a guest or not, a quiet and lovely restaurant in which to dine is **The Beach Club** at the Aston Kaanapali Shores. One of Kaanapali's best-kept secrets, the restaurant is centered in the condo's garden area and opens directly onto the sea. Request a table on the terrace overlooking the pool for an especially romantic setting. The interior is classy, with comfortable chairs and tables topped with crisp starched linens. The restaurant changes throughout the day, from a casual cafe in the morning to a more formal candlelit room in the evening, but the service is always friendly. Breakfast, served 7-11:30 a.m., with "early bird specials" until 9 a.m., can be *paniolo* French toast, scrambled eggs and bacon, or lox and bagels for $5.95, a variety of gourmet omelettes for $5.50, or a simple stack of pancakes and coffee for $4.95. Lunch, served 11:30 a.m.-3 p.m., offers roast beef, turkey, or tuna sandwiches with trimmings for $5.95; breast of chicken for $6.95; mahimahi burger for $8.95; or seafood melt on an English muffin, topped with jack cheese and served with fries for $6.95. The evening dinner menu, served 5:30-9:30 p.m., whets your appetite with sautéed mushrooms for $5.95, or Cajun *ahi* served with *wasabi* and shoyu for $9.95. The soup of the day is a reasonable $2.95 and the Caesar salad for two is only $4.95; combined, they make an inexpensive and light meal. "Sunset specials" are a limited menu of mahimahi, sautéed or broiled with lemon and garlic butter; grilled breast of chicken; or barbecued baby back ribs, all priced under $10.95. Main entrees are chicken Marsala at $13.95, grilled scallops at $16.95, or clams pesto with linguine for $15.95. A children's menu is offered.

Nanatomi's

This Japanese restaurant is located upstairs in the clubhouse at the Royal Kaanapali Golf Course, tel. 667-7902. Every night a sushi chef from Japan entertains with his dexterous hands at the 15-seat sushi bar, followed by a karaoke sing-along until 1 a.m. Open for breakfast, lunch, and dinner. An "early bird" breakfast special is featured 7-8:30 a.m. for $1.99, eggs Benedict for $5.75, and homemade buttermilk pancakes for $2.75. Lunch is 11 a.m.-3 p.m.—a wide selection of sandwiches and burgers under $6, Korean ribs for $5.75, or a chef salad for $5.75. The dinner menu offers a wide variety of *donburi,* meaning everything from fish to pork served in a bowl of rice. A holdover from when Nanatomi's was a Mexican restaurant is their happy hour, featuring stiff margaritas. You can come here to drink Mexican style, lounge Hawaiian style, and eat Japanese style.

Luigi's

This is one of three locations for Luigi's, formerly Apple Annie's, located just off Honoapiilani Hwy. at the entrance to Kaanapali Resort. Pizza prices range from $7.99 for a regular cheese-only item to $29.99 for a large super-combination pizza smothered with toppings; or you can nibble a salad for only $2.99. Pasta ranges from $8.99 for marinara sauce to $12.99 for bolognese. Full-course meals include scallops Luigi for $16.99, and steak Luigi for $17.99. This is a family-oriented restaurant. Don't expect food like mama used to make, but it's not bad for adopted Italians. For information and reservations call 661-3160.

Of special interest to those vacationing in condos who want to eat in but don't want to cook is **Chicken Express,** downstairs from Luigi's, tel. 661-4500. They offer a takeout service for pizza, barbecued ribs, chicken, and sub sandwiches. Dinners are as little as $5.49 for three pieces of chicken, biscuits, potatoes, slaw, and salad. You can eat there or have them deliver—free from Kapalua to Puamana.

Cook's At The Beach
You'll be surprised to find how reasonable this open-air restaurant at the deluxe Westin Maui can be, especially their evening barbecue buffet. The regular menu includes various seafood platters for under $17, and a selection of wok-prepared items for under $12.50. The all-you-can-eat prime rib buffet is the best deal at $19.75. The salad bar is all you can eat, and live music soothes you as the sun dips into the sea. The restaurant opens at 6:30 a.m. with a breakfast buffet for $13.75, lunch from 10:30 a.m., and dinner 5-9 p.m. For information call 667-2525. Free valet parking.

Royal Lahaina Resort
You have no less than three establishments from which to choose, plus a luau. Follow your nose nightly to the Luau Gardens, adults $48.96, children (under 12) $24.48, reservations required, tel. 661-3611, where the biggest problem after the Polynesian revue is standing up after eating mountains of traditional food. **Moby Dick's** is a seafood restaurant open for dinner only, tel. 661-3611. Entrees are priced at $16-27, or you can opt for an all-you-can-eat ticket for $18.95. **Royal Ocean Terrace,** tel. 661-3611, is open daily for breakfast, lunch, and dinner, offering a breakfast buffet and better-than-average salad bar. Sunday brunch 9 a.m.-2 p.m. is a winner. **Chopsticks** is a "dinner-hour only" restaurant that serves a variety of Asian dishes similar to Chinese dim sum.

Swan Court
Save this one for a very special evening. You don't come here to eat, you come here to dine, peasant! Anyone who has been enraptured by those old movies where couples regally glide down a central staircase to make their grand entrance will have his or her fantasies come true. Although it's expensive, you get your money's worth because of the attention to detail; prosciutto is served with papaya, ginger butter with the fresh catch-of-the-day, and pineapple chutney with the oysters. The wine list is a connoisseur's delight. The Swan Court offers a sumptuous breakfast/brunch buffet daily from 6:30 a.m., $13.95 per person, and worth the price for the view alone. Located in the Hyatt Regency, daily breakfast and dinner, tel. 661-1234.

Spats II is also at the Hyatt, tel. 661-1234, dinner only. They specialize in Italian food, with the average entree around $18. At night the place becomes a disco, and fancy duds are in order. **Lahaina Provision Co.** could only survive with a name like that because it's at the Hyatt. Regular broiled fare, but you get a complimentary bowl of ice cream and are free to go hog-wild with chocolate toppings at their famous chocoholic bar. Guaranteed to make you repent your sins!

Discovery Room
Located at the Sheraton, tel. 661-0031, open daily for breakfast and dinner. Entrees include island fish $26-31, chicken Kaanapali $27, and noisettes of lamb $29.95. Entertainment is offered at dinner. The **Aloha Luau** uncovers its *imu* daily at 5:30 p.m. beachside at the Sheraton, adults $36, children $19. The luau features Chief Faa, a fire/knife dancer, rum punch, Hawaiian arts and games, and a Polynesian revue. For reservations call 667-9564.

Lokelani
At the Maui Marriott, tel. 667-1200, Lokelani is open for dinner only, from 6 p.m. Full seafood dinners such as sautéed catch-of-the-day are served with trimmings from $21. Also at the Marriott, **Nikko Japanese Steak House,** tel. 667-1200, dinner from 6 p.m. No cheap imports here; prices are high, but the Japanese chef works right at your table slicing meats and vegetables quicker than you can say "samurai." An expensive but fun meal.

Kaanapali Beach Hotel Restaurants
The hotel might be fancy but the restaurants are down-to-earth. Try the **Tiki Terrace** restau-

rant for meat, poultry, and seafood; or the **Koffee Shop** for their great-priced breakfast, lunch, and dinner buffets. Call 661-0011.

Whaler's Village Mall

This shopping mall has a half dozen or so dining establishments. You can find everything from pizza and frozen yogurt to lobster tails. Prices range from bargain to moderate.

An up-and-comer is **Leilani's,** tel. 661-4495, where the downstairs Beachside Grill is open 11:30 a.m.-11 p.m., and the upstairs fine-dining section is open for dinner 5-10:30 p.m. A daily dinner special is featured 5-6:30 p.m. The Beachside Grill offers plate lunches of Azeka's famous barbecued ribs, *paniolo* steak, or teriyaki chicken all priced at $9.95, along with appetizers like sashimi at a daily quote, and creamy seafood chowder for $2.95. Their burgers range $5.95-7.95. Dinner from the broiler can be fresh fish of the day, Cajun style, filet mignon for $19.95, or pastas for $15.95; or the less expensive spinach, mushroom, and cheese raviolis for $9.95. A children's menu helps keep prices down, and cocktails are served until 1 a.m.

El Crab Catcher, tel. 661-4423, is open daily 8:30-10:30 a.m. for breakfast, 11:30 a.m.-3 p.m. for lunch, 5:30-10 p.m. for dinner; happy hour is twice daily 3-5 p.m. and again at 10 p.m. This well-established restaurant features seafood and a variety of crab dishes, steaks, and chops. It has a sunken bar, music nightly, and a swimming pool only a stride or two away from the beach. Entrees at El Crab Catcher range from approximately $19.95 for the fresh fish of the day to $28.95 for New York steak and lobster, with a filet mignon and king crab going for $29.95. Many of their dishes are served in wicker baskets, especially at the *pu pu* poolside bar, which begins serving dinner from 3 p.m.

The **Rusty Harpoon,** previously a "do-it-yourself" broiler, has remodeled and changed its image. It offers a completely new menu and pleasing atmosphere. Its bar, which claims to serve the best daiquiris on Maui, also offers two happy hours: 2-6 p.m. and again from 10:30 p.m. until closing. Breakfast, served 8-10:45 a.m., gets you started for the day with a three-egg-build-your-own omelette for $7.50; a home-style breakfast with potatoes, eggs, and sausage links for $6.95; a continental breakfast at $7.50; and a Belgian waffle bar with your choice of various fruit toppings and garnishes for $7.50. Lunch, served from 11:30 a.m.-3 p.m., has an extensive menu that begins with appetizers like a starter salad for $3.75, bucket of clams for $9.25, and shrimp cocktail for $8.95. Sandwiches and burgers are priced $7.50-9, or choose a seafood salad with cheddar on a croissant for $8.75. Dinner, 5-10 p.m., offers entrees priced $15.95-21.95 that include seafood sautéed in Madeira, chicken Marsala, and stir-fried beef. To save you money The Rusty Harpoon offers an "early bird special" 5-6 p.m., when most dishes are priced at $10.95.

Chico's Cantina, tel. 667-2777, where you will be greeted by an old "Woody" station wagon at the door, has a special happy hour 3-7 p.m., when deluxe nachos, usually $5.95, are half price; all other menu items are $1 off; and draft beer is only $1, mixed drinks only $2. "Cinco de Chico's" is a special offered the fifth of every month, when you get happy hour prices all day long. Chico's offers a pleasant atmosphere in a cool stucco setting with plenty of cooling breezes to counterbalance the fiery-hot dishes. Chico's is popular with the young crowd, who tend to gather late at night (taco bar goes until 11 p.m.). Stop in for reasonably priced, south-of-the-border food.

The **Beach Barbecue** is a fast-food restaurant offering hot dogs, hamburgers, and salads, with everything under $5.95.

Yami Yogurt, tel. 661-8843, sells wholesome, well-made sandwiches for $3 and under. Salads, too, and yogurt, of course. Seating outside.

ENTERTAINMENT

If you're out for a night of fun and frivolity, Kaanapali will keep you hopping. The dinner shows accompanying the luau at the Hyatt Regency feature pure Island entertainment. "Drums of the Pacific" is the kind of musical extravaganza you would expect from the Hyatt. It features torch-lit processions and excitingly choreographed production numbers, with all the hula-skirted *wahines* and *malo*-clad *kanes* you could imagine. Flames add drama to the setting, and the grand finale is a fire dance. At both shows you're dined and entertained by mid-evening.

2

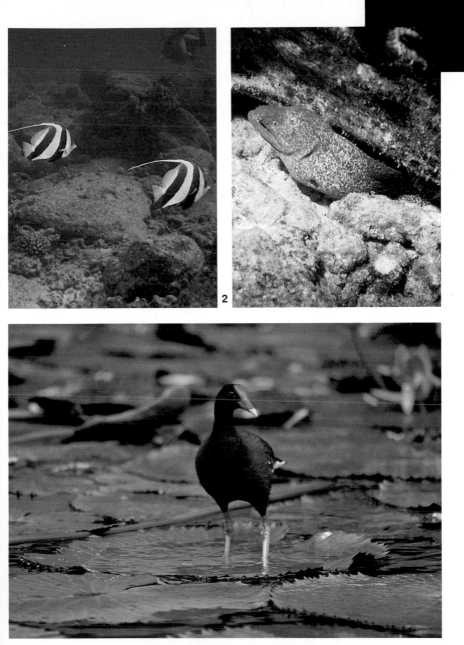

1. banner butterfly fish (Dr. Greg Leo); **2.** moray eel (Dr. Greg Leo);
3. Hawaiian gallinule (R.J. Shallenberger)

1

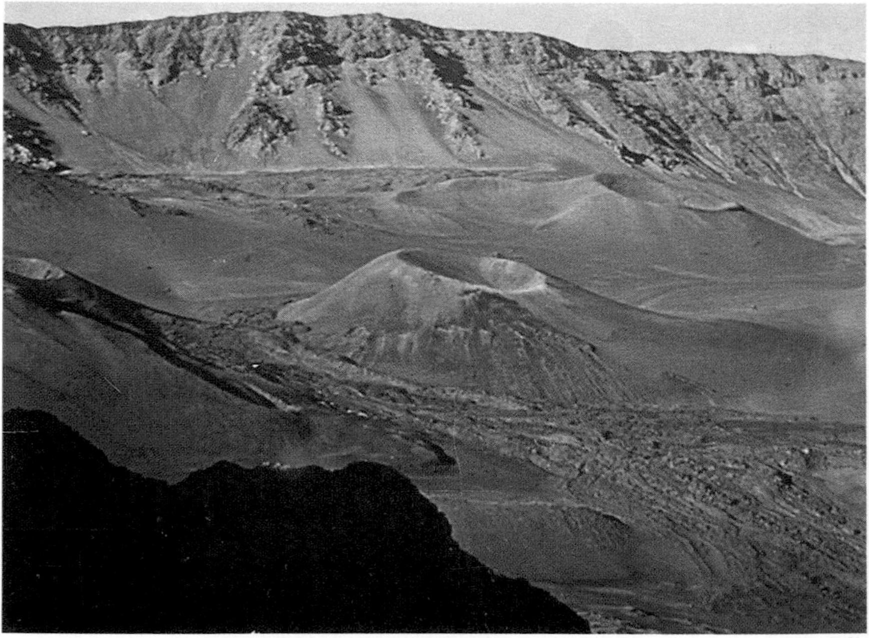

2

1. Kalalau Valley, Kauai (D. Stanley); **2.** Haleakala National Park, Maui (Dr. Janos Balogh)

Those with dancing feet can boogie the night away at the Hyatt's **Spats II.** There is a dress code and plenty of room for those "big dippers" on this very large dance floor. Practice your waltzes for the outdoor **Pavilion Courtyard** at the Hyatt.

El Crab Catcher at Whaler's Village Mall offers nightly entertainment, mostly soft island tunes to accompany your dinner.

SHOPPING

Kaanapali provides a varied shopping scene: the **Whaler's Village Mall,** which is affordable; the **Maui Marriott** for distinctive purchases; and the **Hyatt Regency** and **Westin Maui,** where most people get financial jitters window-shopping.

Whaler's Village Mall And Museum

This whaling museum has a few outside displays but most items are in the enclosed section on the top floor of the mall (free). The compact display area is full of whaling history, photographs, drawings, artifacts from whaling ships, a reconstructed section of a ship, and many informative descriptions of and stories about the whaling industry, whaling life, and the whalers themselves. Also, every Saturday 9-11:30 a.m. there is a sand sculpture demonstration at the mall.

You can easily find anything you need at this mall. Some of the shops are: **Wyland Galleries** (see "Shopping" under "Lahaina" in this chapter for details), for fantastic above-below the waves sculpture and painting; **Whaler's Fine Wine and Spirits,** a full-service bottle shop; **Kula Bay,** for upscale tropical clothing; the **Maui Clothing Company** for more of the same; **Outta the Blue,** a very wild art and design shop with distinctive dresses, handbags, and T-shirts; **Canoe Clothing Co.** for a selection of fine men's clothing specially designed for the tropics; the **Village Slipper and Sandal Shop** offering everything from flip-flops to dancing shoes; the exclusive **Louis Vuitton Shop** for designer luggage; **Dolphin Gallery,** with beautiful creations in glass, sculptures, paintings, and jewelry; **Lahaina Scrimshaw Factory,** tel. 661-4034, for fine scrimshaw pieces and other art objects ranging from affordable to expensive; **Blue Ginger Designs,** for women's and children's resortwear and alohawear; **Lahaina Galleries,** featuring paintings and sculptures of animals; **Endangered Species Store,** where you are greeted by a stuffed python and proceeds help endangered species; **Jessica's Gems,** featuring the work of designer David Welty, along with coral jewelry and black Tahitian pearl rings; **Paradise Clothing,** for inexpensive alohawear and beachwear.

Selections are wide and varied at **Waldenbooks** on the lower level of the mall, tel. 661-8638, open daily 9:30 a.m.-9:30 p.m. The bookstore has it all, from light mysteries for beach reading to travel books to guide you happily around the island. **The Eyecatcher** will take care of your eyes with shades from $150 Revos to $5 cheapies. There are many other shops tucked away here and there. They come and go with regularity.

A fascinating new shop is **Lahaina Printsellers and Engravings** (see "Shopping" under "Lahaina" in this chapter), tel. 667-7617, open daily 8:30 a.m.-10:30 p.m. The shop features original engravings, drawings, maps, charts, and naturalist sketches ranging in age from 150 to 400 years, each with an authenticity label. The collection comes from all over the world, but the Hawaiiana collection is amazing in its depth, with many works featuring a nautical theme reminiscent of the amazing explorers who opened the Pacific. The Lahaina Printsellers, although new as a store, have been collecting for over 15 years, and are the largest purveyor of material relating to Captain Cook in the entire Pacific Basin. Prices range from $25 for the smallest antique print up to $150,000 for rare museum-quality work.

Note: The Whaler's Village Mall also has plenty of fast-food shops and restaurants. Please see "Food" above for details.

The Hyatt Regency Mall

Off the main lobby and surrounding the gardens is a number of exclusive shops. They're high-priced, but their offerings are first class. Call 667-7421 and ask for the store of your choice. **Elephant Walk** specializes in primitive art such as tribal African masks and carved wooden statues. **Sandal Tree** has footwear for men and women with the emphasis on sandals.

Mark Christopher is a chain store selling jewelry, glassware, fabrics, and beachwear.

Maui Marriott Mall

The main store here is **Liberty House,** tel. 667-6142, with the emphasis on clothing. The **Maui Sun and Surf,** tel. 667-9302, is a well-stocked dive and swimwear store where you'll find everything from visors to top-notch snorkeling equipment. **Friendship Store**'s art objects, clothing, silks, and goods are from the Republic of China. The mall also has more clothing stores and jewelry shops.

Westin Maui Mall

Stroll the series of exclusive boutiques just left of the main lobby. Fine women's apparel is available at **Collections,** or you can purchase a superb diamond at **Edward Thomas Jewels.**

Beachside Casuals

You'll find a specialized boutique geared toward children at the Aston Kaanapali Shores. It's small, but jammed like a 12-year-old's closet. They feature handpicked fashions, resortwear, toys, swimsuits, books, mementos, and even snorkel gear. Big people can choose from a few racks, rent a video, or have those special photos developed in 24 hours. Open daily 9 a.m.-9 p.m.

SERVICES AND INFORMATION

Banks

There are no banks in Kaanapali; the closest are in Lahaina. Most larger hotels can help with some banking needs, especially with the purchasing or cashing of traveler's checks.

Medical

Dr. Ben Azman maintains an office at the Whaler's Village Mall, tel. 667-9721, or after hours tel. 244-3728.

Camera Needs

Shops are: **Fox Photo** in the Whaler's Village Mall, or **Island Camera and Gift** at the Sheraton and Royal Lahaina hotels.

Laundromat

The Washerette Clinic is located in the Sheraton.

Information

For complete information on all aspects of the Kaanapali area, contact Kaanapali Beach Operators Association, P.O. Box 616, Kaanapali, HI 96761, tel. 661-3271.

HONOKOWAI AND KAHANA

You head for Honokowai and Kahana if you want to enjoy Maui's west coast and not spend a bundle of money. They're not quite as pretty as Kaanapali or Kapalua, but proportionate to the money you'll save, you come out ahead. To get there, travel along the Honoapiilani Hwy., take Lower Honoapiilani Hwy. through Honokowai, and continue on it to Kahana.

Beaches

Honokowai Beach County Park is right in Honokowai just across from the Food Pantry. Here you have a large lawn with palm trees and picnic tables, but a small beach. The water is shallow and tame—good for tots. The swimming is not as nice as at Kaanapali, but take a dip after shopping. Snorkeling is fair, and you can get through a break in the reef at the west end. **Kahana Beach** is near the Kahana Beach Resort; park across the street. Nothing spectacular, but the protected small beach is good for tots. There's a great view of Molokai and the beach is never crowded.

ACCOMMODATIONS

At last count there were well over three dozen condos and apartment complexes in the three miles encompassing Honokowai and Kahana. There are plenty of private homes out here as well, which gives you a good cross-section of Hawaiian society. A multimillion-dollar spread may occupy a beach, while out in the bay is a

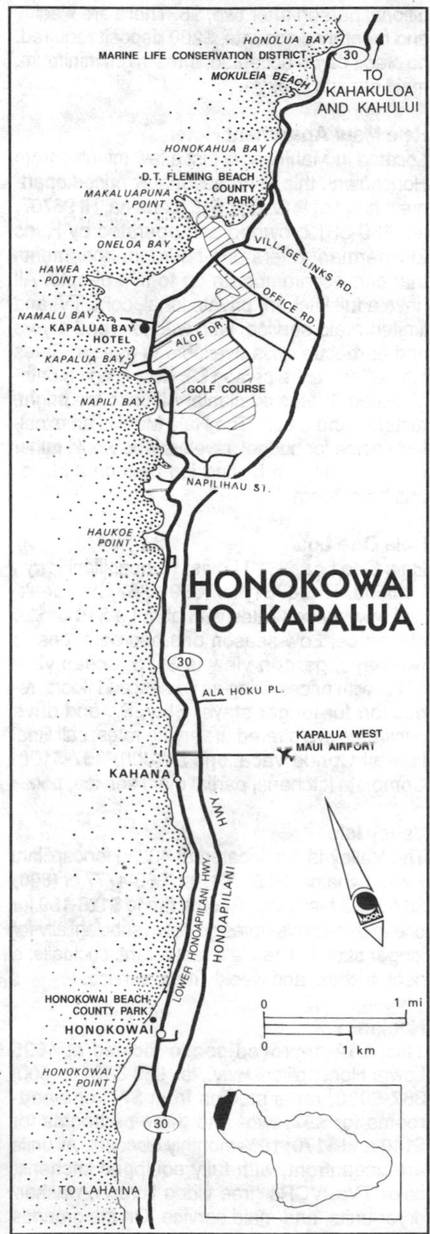

local fisherman with his beat-up old boat trying to make a few bucks for the day. Many of the condos built out here were controversial. Locals refused to work on some because they were on holy ground, and a few actually experienced bad luck jinxes as they were being built. The smarter owners called in *kahuna* to bless the ground and the disturbances ceased.

Paki Maui Resort

Situated between Kaanapali and Kapalua at 3615 Lower Honoapiilani Hwy., Lahaina, HI 96761, tel. 669-8235, (800) 535-0085 Mainland, (800) 219-9700 Hawaii, this excellent-value condo presents airy and bright rooms with sweeping panoramas of the Lahaina Roads. Well-appointed studios begin at $109, a two-bedroom apartment for up to six people costs $160, additional guests $10. Amenities include maid service, a/c, cable TV, complete kitchens, pool with spa, and coin laundry facilities. Every unit has a private lanai overlooking a gem of a courtyard or the ocean. You can save money by getting a garden-view studio without sacrificing that delightful feeling that you are in the tropics. Although the Paki Maui is in town, it feels secluded the moment you walk onto this property, which forms a little oasis of tranquility. There is no sand beach fronting the condo, but the snorkeling along the reef is excellent.

Sands Of Kahana

Your pleasure begins when you spot the distinctive blue tile roofs of this gracious complex, which forms a central courtyard area at 4299 Honoapiilani Hwy., Lahaina, HI 96761, tel. 669-0400, (800) 367-6046 Mainland, (800) 663-1118 Canada. The condo boasts a tennis and pro shop and the poolside **Kahana Terrace Restaurant and Lounge.** The sandy-bottomed beach fronting the property is very safe and perfect for swimming and sunbathing. The Sands of Kahana gives you extraordinarily large units for the money, and to sweeten the pot, they're beautiful and well appointed, mostly in earth tones and colors of the islands. One-bedroom units from $189, two-bedroom units from $245, and three-bedroom units from $310 are massive with two lanais, two baths with a tub built for two, walk-in closets, and great ocean views. Each unit offers a gourmet kitchen, cable TV (free HBO), daily maid service, and washer/dryer units. The property, with pool, three tennis courts, putting green, and spa, exudes a sense of peace and quiet, and although there are plenty of guests, you never feel crowded. This is where you come when you want to get away from it all, but still be within reach of the *action.*

Kahana Villa

Across the street from the Sands of Kahana, at 4242 Lower Honoapiilani Hwy., tel. 669-5613 or (800) 535-0085, this modern, five-story condo steps up the hillside and looks out over the channel to Lanai and Molokai. Pleasantly and casually attractive with contemporary designs and Hawaiian artwork, each of the large units features a complete kitchen, color TV and video equipment, washer/dryer, and daily maid service. On the property are a pool, jacuzzi, barbecue grills, tennis and volleyball courts, an activities desk, and a sundries store. A complimentary continental breakfast of juice, coffee, and homemade pastries is served daily 8-9 a.m. at the front desk. An added special feature is highly acclaimed Erik's Seafood Grotto, privately operated but located on the property. High-season rates start at $125 for a one-bedroom garden-view unit to $205 for a deluxe ocean-view two-bedroom unit.

Honokowai Palms

At 3666 Lower Honoapiilani Hwy., Lahaina, HI 96761, tel. 669-6130 or (800) 669-6284, this condo is an old standby for budget travelers. A basic two-story cinder-block affair, it was originally used as housing for workers constructing the Sheraton down the road. The manager's office is near the pool. Amenities include Ping-Pong, barbecue grills, book exchange, and color TVs. The Palms is older, but not run-down, no tinsel and glitter, but neat and clean. A coin laundry is on the premises. Each unit is fully furnished with kitchen, full bath, and queen-size hide-a-bed, and has been recently upgraded with new carpets, drapes, bedspreads, and ceiling fans. Forget about the ocean-view rooms. They don't have a great view anyway. Save money by taking the standard rooms. You can get a one-bedroom ocean-view unit with lanai for $65 or without ocean view for $60, or a two-bedroom with lanai but no view for $65, each additional person after two, $6. There are weekly and monthly discounts, $200 deposit required, no credit cards accepted, three-night minimum; maid service is extra.

Hale Maui Apartment Hotel

Located in Mahinahina just a few minutes from Honokowai, this very reasonably priced apartment hotel at P.O. Box 516, Lahaina, HI 96767, tel. 669-6312, owned and operated by Hans Zimmerman, offers one-bedroom apartments that can accommodate up to five people. All have a full kitchen, private lanai, color TV, and limited maid service, with washers and dryers and barbecue grills available to guests. Rates are $65-85, extra person $8, weekly and monthly discount rates available. All units are bright, tasteful, and clean. The Hale Maui is an excellent choice for budget travelers who would rather spend money on having fun than on a luxurious hotel room.

Hale Ono Loa

Hale Ono Loa, 3823 Lower Honoapiilani Hwy., Lahaina, HI 96761, tel. 669-6362, has peak- and low-season rates with about a $10 or $20 difference. Low-season one-bedroom, one to two days, garden view is $115, ocean view $125, with prices rising as you ascend floors, reduction for longer stays. Stay, fly, and drive packages are offered at varying rates; call Real Hawaii Condo vacations at (800) 367-5108. Complete kitchens, partial maid service, pool.

Valley Isle

The Valley Isle is located at 4327 Honoapiilani Hwy., Lahaina, HI 96761, tel. 669-4777 or (800) 367-6092 Mainland. Rooms range $128-189 for one to three days (rates go down substantially for longer stays). There's a restaurant, cocktails, a pool, a shop, and weekly maid service.

Noelani

This AAA-approved condo located at 4095 Lower Honoapiilani Hwy., tel. 669-8374 or (800) 367-6030, rents studios from $77, one-bedrooms for $97, two- and three-bedrooms for $140 and $170; 10% monthly discount. All units are oceanfront, with fully equipped kitchens, color TVs, VCRs (free video library), washer/dryer units, and maid service. On the grounds are two pools and a barbecue area. You're welcomed on the first morning with a complimentary continental breakfast served poolside, where you are given an island orientation by the concierge.

Kahana Sunset

Finely sculpted gardens and trellised lanai set off these attractive and privately owned condo units sitting along on a small protected bay. All units have full kitchens, color televisions, and daily maid service. There is a three-night minimum. Rates for two people are $135 for a one-bedroom unit, and $165-215 for a two-bedroom. A 10% monthly discount is given; no credit cards are accepted. Write P.O. Box 10219, Lahaina, HI 96761, or call 669-8011 or (800) 367-8047.

Kahana Falls Condo Hotel

You'll know immediately that the Kahana Falls, the area's most recent arrival, should have worn sunblock when you see the "sunburn pink" exterior of this upscale condo located at 4260 Lower Honoapiilani Hwy., Lahaina, HI 96761, tel. 669-1050 or (800) 635-MAUI. Otherwise resplendently appointed, the Kahana Falls has a central courtyard with cascading falls, tropical landscaping, swimming pool, kiddie pool, koi pond, sand-bottomed whirlpool spa, and fitness center. Rates are one bedroom $160, up to four persons; two bedrooms, two baths $200 up to six people (complimentary manager's mai tai party). Units have remote-control color TV; full kitchens complete with microwaves, dishwasher, and self-cleaning range; a/c and ceiling fans; service bar; spacious double sink bathrooms with whirlpool tubs; and washers and dryers. The white-on-pink rooms are beautifully accented with marble-topped counters and tables, high-backed chairs, and twill wool carpets. A private lanai overlooks the grounds. The master bedroom has its own TV, wet bar, and microwave. The Kahana Falls offers excellent value for the money.

FOOD AND ENTERTAINMENT

Roy's Kahana Bar And Grill

Finally McDonald's has a culinary purpose—to landmark Roy's Kahana Bar and Grill, located at the new Kahana Gateway Shopping Center, 4405 Honoapiilani Hwy., Kahana, tel. 669-6999, open daily for dinner 5:30-9:30 p.m. Roy Yamaguchi, the restaurant's founder and inspirational chef, and David Abella, the executive chef, work kitchen magic preparing the best in Pacific Rim cuisine. Roy has a penchant for locating his restaurants in pragmatic shopping malls; the original Roy's in Honolulu, established in 1988, is in a corporate plaza as well. At Roy's Kahana, the surroundings are strictly casual, like a very upscale cafeteria. The enormous room, reverberating with the clatter of plates and the low hum of dinner conversations, has 40-foot vaulted ceilings, a huge copper-clad preparation area, heavy koa tables and booths, track lighting, and windows all around. Roy's philosophy is to serve truly superb dishes posthaste, but impeccably, focusing on the *food* as the dining experience, not the surroundings. Start your culinary extravaganza with dim sum and appetizers like potstickers in a lobster Thai peanut sauce for $5.75; wood roasted Sichuan baby back pork ribs for $6.95; lobster bisque with crunchy croutons for $6.50; or treat yourself to *penne* pasta with grilled shrimp or pesto and tomato sauce for $8.95. There's also individual *imu* pizzas, and fresh basil pizzas for only $5.95, or Roy's Thai-style chicken pizza for $6.95. Salads include garden fresh greens with vinaigrette for only $4.25, grilled eggplant with Big Island goat cheese for $6.25, or the savory fresh mahimahi with cilantro vinaigrette for $7.95. Move on to entrees like hibachi-style chicken at $12.95, bistro-style filet mignon for $17.95, *imu*-roasted pork with island-style ginger and applesauce for $17.50, or seared Tex-Mex grilled marlin with smoked scallops and risotto for $21.95. Desserts by pastry chef Casey A. Logsdon feature the chocolate macadamia tart for $5.50 or a fluffy dark chocolate soufflé at $5.95 (allow 20 minutes to prepare). The full bar serves beer, mixed drinks, and personally selected wine by the bottle or glass. Roy's "elegant cafeteria" is no place to linger over a romantic cocktail. The experience is more like sipping the world's finest champagne from a beer mug. But the best by any other name is still the best.

Nicolina

Nicole Yamaguchi has a restaurant named in her honor, just next door to her dad's place at the Kahana Gateway, open daily from 5:30 p.m., tel. 669-5000. Under the skilled hand of executive chef Jacqueline Lau, imported from Roy's original resaurant on Oahu, the restaurant features Euro-Asian cuisine heavily spiced with California and Southwestern dishes. For example, try one of Jackie's gourmet pizza-like flatbreads covered in red onions, tomatoes, and pesto; or Cajun shrimp and handmade sausage for under $6. Appetizers can be pan-fried calamari with anchovy mayonnaise, or seared goat cheese and eggplant with cilantro pesto and red pepper vinaigrette for under $6. Entrees are delicious and fascinating offerings like smoked and peppered duck with ginger sweet potatoes at $11.95, or Yankee pot roast with mashed potatoes and garlic spinach for only $11.95. If dad's place is filled up, you'll love Nicolina, a "Sichuan-spiced taco chip off the old block."

China Boat

This seafood restaurant at 4474 Lower Honoapiilani Hwy. in Kahana, tel. 669-5089, is open daily for lunch 11:30 a.m.-2 p.m., dinner 5-10 p.m., karaoke Friday and Saturday 10 p.m.-1:30 a.m. Since its opening, the China Boat has been gaining respect from locals and visitors alike. It's tastefully decorated, almost elegant with its highly polished, black lacquer furniture, white linens, and island-inspired prints. Reasonably priced with lunch specials at $5.95 and "early bird specials" at $8.95, the large *MSG-free* menu offers chicken and garlic sauce for $10.95, beef with broccoli for $9.50, and shrimp with lobster sauce at $12.95. Hearty appetites will appreciate the China Boat special: sautéed lobster meat, chicken white meat, and scallops with kung pao sauce for $21.95. The typically large Chinese menu offering seafood, beef, chicken, vegetables, pork, and noodles can satisfy all at a reasonable price.

Dollie's

Located at 4310 Honoapiilani Hwy. in the Kahana Manor Shops, tel. 669-0266, open daily 10 a.m.-midnight, happy hour 4-6 p.m., Sunday brunch 8 a.m.-1 p.m., Dollie's features wide-screen TVs for sporting events, cappuccino, delivery service in the immediate area, and weekend entertainment. The good food and fair prices on Dollie's menu feature 20 sandwiches from which to choose, all priced around $6.50; plates of lasagna or chicken marinara for $6.95; pizza by the tray or slice; and plenty of finger foods. The sandwiches and other entrees are good, but the pizza is the best. The bar has a wide selection of domestic and imported beer, wines, and a daily exotic drink special. Dollie's, one of the few eateries in the area, is usually a laid-back pub/pizzeria but can get hopping on the weekend and is perhaps the most happening place for late-night get-togethers in Kahana.

Erik's Seafood Grotto

At 4242 Lower Honoapiilani Hwy., second floor of Kahana Villa, tel. 669-4806, Erik's is open daily for dinner 5-10 p.m. An "early bird special" is offered 5-6 p.m. for $11.95; menu changes daily. Dinners include chowder, bread basket, and potato or rice. Most dinners run $16-19 with a good selection of appetizers. Erik's is known to have *the* best selection of fresh fish on Maui. This is a quality restaurant with fair prices.

Kahana Keyes

Located at the Valley Isle Resort, tel. 669-8071, the Kahana Keyes is open for dinner only, with music 7:30 p.m.-12:30 a.m. seven nights a week. "Early bird specials" 5-7 p.m. include whole lobster and prime rib, $13.95; steak and crab, $11.95; prime rib, $9.95; or mahimahi $9.95. They're well known for their salad bar and fresh fish. This restaurant is the only show in town around here, and luckily it ain't bad! Local bands perform all types of music from rock to Hawaiian, and the intimate dance floor is hardly ever crowded.

Lin's Kitchenette

Small, simple, clean, and adequate, Lin's is located at Da Rose mall, 3481 Lower Honoapiilani Hwy., tel. 669-5725, open daily until 4 p.m. They offer takeout or delivery service along with a few red picnic tables out front where you can eat. They prepare plate lunches and simple Chinese food. Prices are $4.95 two items and $6.95 four items that can be pork, chicken, or fish plus steamed or fried rice or noodles. They also have containers of beef, pork, or chicken for takeout, $5.95.

Pizza Hut
Located at 5-A Rent a Space at 3600 Lower Honoapiilani Hwy., tel. 669-6996, open Sun.-Thurs. 11 a.m.-11 p.m., weekends until midnight, this standard pizzeria offers carry-out and delivery pizza.

SHOPPING AND SERVICES

Honokowai Food Pantry
The only real place west of Lahaina to shop for groceries and sundries is the Food Pantry located at 3636 Lower Honoapiilani Hwy., tel. 669-6208, open daily 6:30 a.m.-11 p.m. The prices are just about right at this supermarket. Condo convenience stores in the area are good in a pinch but charge way too much. Stock up here; it's worth the drive.

The **Honokowai P.O.** is at the Honokowai Food Pantry. Never busy, this full-service post office accepts packages.

Convenience Stores
The Valley Isle Resort has the **Kahana Pantry,** a mini-mart and grocery store selling everything from beer to sunglasses. **The Villa** has almost the same items plus fresh fruits and vegetables. The **ABC Store,** in Honokowai, hours 6:30 a.m.-11 p.m., tel. 669-0271, is a mini-market selling everything from resortwear to wine.

5-A Rent A Space Mall
A new mall has opened in Honokowai called 5-A Rent a Space, at 3600 Lower Honoapiilani Highway. Here you'll find **Posters Maui**, open daily 9 a.m.-8 p.m., tel. 669-5404, where you can get a vibrant visual memento of Maui, framed and ready for your wall back home. Well-known island artists represented here include Robert Lynn Nelson, Anthony Casay, Pegge Hopper, Diana Hanson Young, Guy Buffet, and photographer Robert Talbot. An upcoming new artist featured by Posters Maui is Richard Fields, who creates poster-paintings in the realistic-fantastic mode, like *Haleakala Sunrise.* Posters Maui claims the highest quality posters and lowest prices on the island with prices ranging $5-50. They do custom framing, along with packaging and shipping.

If you're staying at one of the condos in the area, **Kelly's Video,** tel. 669-6004, can provide the evening's entertainment. Also in the small mall is **Rio de Janeiro Beauty Shop,** tel. 669-0274, a full-service beauty salon where the entire family is welcome (walk-ins okay).

Maui Mountain Bike Adventures, tel. 669-1169, open weekdays 8 a.m.-6 p.m., weekends 10 a.m.-3 p.m., rents bicycles and operates tours of West Maui and Hana, and will custom-tailor any tour to meet your needs, including free pick-up and delivery. Rental rates are $19 per day, $15 per day three days or more, $79 weekly; lock, helmet, and water bottle are included.

Kahana Manor Shops
Aside from **Dollie's** (see above), there is the **Two Doors Down** convenience store for food items, wine, spirits, and sundries; a **Videoland;** a one-hour photo shop; and **5th Ave. Mile,** a women's clothing store that also rents snorkel gear and boogie boards.

Da Rose Mall
Look for this tiny mall located at the south end of town at 3481 Lower Honoapiilani Hwy., where you'll find **A & B Rentals and Sportswear,** tel. 669-0027, open daily 9 a.m.-5 p.m., specializing in mopeds, bicycles, snorkel gear, boogie boards, and surfboards. Prices are: mopeds $10 for two hours or $125 per week; bicycles $10 for 24 hours, $50 per week; snorkeling gear, $2.50 per day and $10 per week. Boogie boards, surfboards, and even fishing poles are rented by the day or week. The sportswear includes Lycra mini-dresses, tie-dyed dresses, T-shirts, and men's printed shirts. In front is **Lin's Kitchenette** (see "Food" above); **One Hour Wiki Wiki Photo,** whose name says it all; the **Honokowai Nut Shop,** selling gifts and souvenirs; and **The Ebb Tide Gallery,** with distinctive hand-painted T-shirts.

Next door is **Leola's Family Funwear,** where you'll find inexpensive beach towels, cover-ups, and T-shirts. In the same building is the **Lahaina Gift and Shell Shop,** loaded with hanging shell baskets, coconut bird feeders, backscratchers, and nifty tourist junk.

Kahana Gateway Shopping Center
At this newest shopping addition to the Kahana area, easily spotted along Rt. 30 by **McDonald's** golden arches, you'll find a **Shell gas sta-**

tion, a convenience **grocery store,** a **laundromat,** and a **beauty shop.** However, the premier stops are **Roy's Restaurant** (see "Food" above), one of the finest gourmet restaurants on Maui; and **Nicolina's** next door, a more moderate restaurant operated by Roy's. Also at the center is the **Maui Dive Shop,** tel. 669-3800, a full-service water activities store where you can rent snorkel equipment, scuba gear, and beach accessories. More shops include **Posters Unlimited,** a **Bank of Hawaii,** and **Polynesian's Children's Shop.** Next door are the **Maui Ski Company,** offering fine beachwear, sunglasses, sweatshirts, and alohawear; and **O'Rourke's Tourist Trap,** for a 99-cent beach mat, artificial lei, or postcards. If you just can't live without a toggle bolt or tile grout, there's the **Kahana Do-it-yourself Hardware Center.** Out front giving McDonald's some competition is **Bob's Big Boy.**

KAPALUA AND NAPILI—THE WEST END

Kapalua sits like a crown atop Maui's head. One of the newest areas on Maui to be developed, it's been nicely done. Out here is the **Kapalua Bay Resort,** golf, horseback riding, and terrific beaches.

BEACHES AND SPORTS

Some of the very best beaches Maui has to offer are clustered in this area. The following listing proceeds from south to north.

Napili Bay
There are rights of way to this perfect, but condo-lined, beach. Look for beach access signs along Napili Place near the Napili Shores and Napili Surf Beach Resort, and on Hui Drive near the Napili Sunset and Napili Bay condos. They're difficult to spot, but once you're on the beach you'll find better-than-average swimming, snorkeling, and a good place for beginning surfers.

Kapalua Beach
Along Lower Honoapiilani Hwy. look for access just past the Napili Kai Beach Club. Park in the public lot and follow the path through the tunnel to the beach, another beautiful crescent that's popular, though usually not overcrowded. The well-formed reef has plenty of fish for snorkeling. Also here are restrooms, showers, and beach concessions.

D.T. Fleming Beach County Park
One of Maui's best, clearly marked just past mile-marker 31 on Lower Honoapiilani Highway. Here you'll find parking, showers, barbecue grills, and excellent swimming except in winter, when there's a pounding surf. Fair snorkeling and good surfing.

Oneloa Beach
Located a short mile before Fleming's, Oneloa is a small sandy beach down a steep path. Those who brave it can camp without a hassle from the officials.

Mokuleia Beach
Also known as "Slaughterhouse." You can spot it because the R.V. Deli, a lunch wagon, is usually parked here, about 200-300 yards after mile marker 32. This beach has great bodysurfing, but terribly dangerous currents in the winter when the surf is rough. Be careful. Follow the trail to the left for the beach. The path straight ahead takes you to a rocky lava flow. This entire area, plus all of adjacent Honolua Bay, is a Marine Life Conservation District and the underwater life is fabulous.

Honolua Bay
Just past Mokuleia Bay heading north, look for a dirt road, then park. Some can try the road, but it's very rugged. The bay is good for swimming, snorkeling, and especially surfing. Many people stay the night without much problem.

Sports
The following are offered in the Kapalua area: **Kapalua Golf Club,** Bay Course, par 72; Village Course, par 71; and Plantation Course, par 73. Greens fee for all courses is $110, golf cart included. **Tennis** is found at the Napili Kai Beach Club, $9 guests; also the Kapalua Bay

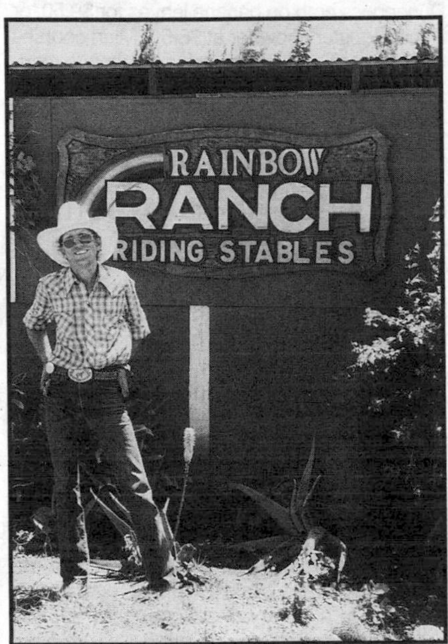

J.D. BISIGNANI

Hotel **Tennis Garden,** free to guests, $4 others, dress code, tel. 669-5677. There's **horseback riding** at the Rainbow Ranch; see "Sports and Recreation" in the Maui Introduction for details.

ACCOMMODATIONS

Napili, just south of Kapalua Bay, sports a string of condos and a hotel or two. Almost all front the beach, which is hardly ever crowded in this still largely underdeveloped area of Maui.

Napili Point Condominium

Napili Point is one of the most beautifully situated complexes on Maui. The low-rise complex sits on its own promontory of black lava separating Kahana and Napili, located at 5295 Honoapiilani Hwy., Napili, HI 96761, tel. 669-9222 or (800) 922-7866. The reef fronting the condo is home to a colorful display of fish and coral, providing some of the best snorkeling on the west end. Though the complex is not graced with a sand beach (100 yards north along a path), nature was generous in another way. Each room commands an unimpeded panorama with a breathtaking sunset view of Lanai and Molokai. You get a deluxe room for a standard price. Because of the unique setting, little development has occurred in the area, and the condo is very secluded though convenient to shops and stores. The two-story buildings offer fully furnished one- and two-bedroom units from a very affordable $159 to $215, with full kitchens, washers and dryers, walk-in closets, and large dressing and bath areas. Up to four people can be accommodated, rollaway $10, and this includes maid service, two pools, and a family plan. Two-bedroom units on the second floor include a loft with its own sitting area. Floor-to-ceiling windows frame the living still life of sea and surf so you can enjoy the view from every part of the apartment.

Ritz-Carlton Kapalua

The green sweep of tended lawns fading into the distant, foaming azure sea heralds your entrance into an enchanted realm as you wind your way down the serpentine roadway leading to the Ritz-Carlton Kapalua, One Ritz-Carlton Dr., Kapalua, HI 96761, tel. 669-6200 or (800) 241-3333. At the porte cochere a waiting bellhop will park your car. Enter the main hall and relax in the formal parlor of overstuffed chairs, marble-topped tables, and enormous flower arrangements. Evenings in the hall bring mellow entertainment softly illuminated by emerald green chandeliers. Register, then peer through a huge set of double doors that look straight out into the central courtyard. Walk ahead to the terrace built from Chinese slate, and look into the floral heart of the hotel grounds. Below are seashell-shaped swimming pools and fluttering palms. The roof line of the great hotel, borrowed from Asia, covers the two wings that descend the hill toward the sea, creating an enormous central area between. Stroll the halls hung with fine works by prominent island artists like George Allan, Betty Hay Freeland, Joyce Clark, and Fred Kenknight. Sit in a tiny alcove and let the music of sea and wind lull you into deep relaxation and contemplation.

On the beach, a sweeping crescent of white sand is embraced by two sinewy arms of jet-black lava. It becomes immediately obvious why the diminutive promontory was called Kapalua, "Arms Embracing the Sea," by the ancient Hawaiians who lived here. Notice on the rise above the sea a rounded shoulder of banked earth separated from the main hotel grounds by a low hedge: the spirits of the ancient *ali'i* linger here in this ancient burial ground. The original construction plans were altered and the hotel was moved away from the area in an attempt to protect it. A *kahuna* was asked to perform the ancient *mele* to appease the spirits, and to reconsecrate the land, passing the *kahu* (caretaking) of it to the Ritz. Although the small parcel was deeded to the state, the hotel management and staff alike take their responsibility very seriously.

The hotel's **Village Tennis Center,** combined with the Kapalua Tennis Garden a few minutes away, represents the largest private tennis facility in the state. The Village Tennis Center has 10 courts, five lighted for evening play, and a full-service pro shop. At the Kapalua Golf Club, a few minutes away by shuttle, are three championship **golf courses:** the Plantation Course, the Village Course, and the Bay Course. Both golf and tennis packages are available. The hotel also has a fitness center complete with Stairmasters, massage therapists, beauty salon, sauna, and steam rooms.

Dining at the Ritz-Carlton is a wonderful gastronomic experience. There are three main restaurants from which to choose, plus a lobby and sunset lounge, and a beachside cafe, all under the skillful management of executive chef Patrick Callarec. **The Terrace Restaurant,** open daily for breakfast 6:30-11:30 a.m. (buffet to 10:30) and for dinner 5-10:30 p.m., informal and relaxed, overlooks the central courtyard with the dramatic sea vista beyond. Tastefully appointed in green and burgundy, the restaurant features Pacific Rim and Asian food, with an emphasis on Japanese cuisine. Although there is an extensive a la carte breakfast menu, the house specialty is a breakfast buffet for $16.50 or a lighter selection for $12. Apple blintzes, eggs royal and Benedict, Molokai French toast, plump sausages, grilled potatoes, and sizzling strips of bacon are surrounded by fruits, fresh juices, and jams. For dinner, Chef Pierre Albaladejo starts you with tiger prawns and sweet potato cake for $10.50, Dungeness crab on banana leaves for $9.50, or Pacific lobster chowder at $6.50. Main courses include horseradish-basted tenderloin in rosemary essence for $24; chow mein noodles with clams, shrimp, and scallops in a ginger sauce for $18.50; or simple grilled *ahi* with vegetables and papaya mango relish for $12. Wednesday brings an Italian night buffet for $19.50; on Friday it's seafood, with a la carte selections or a buffet for $24.

The Grill, serving dinner nightly except Sunday 6-9:30 p.m., and Sunday champagne brunch 10:30 a.m.-2:30 p.m., $29 including champagne, is the hotel's most elegant restaurant. Formal yet intimate, the Grill offers Hawaiian regional cuisine prepared by master chef Roy Basilio. Appetizers, salads, and soups fit for the *ali'i* are lehua honey seared squab for $14.50; steamed vegetable tofu *lau lau* with garlic black bean sauce for $10.50; smoked duck and green papaya soup for $6.50, and *ahi* pastrami salad with arugula, watercress, and goma-seed dressing for $9.60. The finest entrees include fresh island fish grilled, poached, or sautéed, in a variety of sauces, from $25. Or try the wonderful sesame-seed rack of lamb with poha berries and pineapple chutney for $30. Desserts are caramel macadamia nut torte, warm hazelnut cake, or a fluffy soufflé of the day prepared just for you.

The Banyan Tree, an informal poolside restaurant open for lunch and appetizers 11:30 a.m.-5 p.m., is a good stop on your way to or from the beach. Fashioned like a Mediterranean court with stone floor and copper-and-green tiled bar, the restaurant offers seating in high-backed chairs at teakwood tables, with mood lighting reminiscent of old oil lamps. Dine alfresco on the redwood deck and watch cavorting whales just offshore. Selections start with beefsteak tomatoes and grilled eggplant with Maui onions and buffalo mozzarella for $6.75; Pacific seafood gazpacho for $5.25; or *penne* pasta smothered in a sauce of roma tomatoes, basil, fried capers, Romano cheese, and garlic for $9.75. Families will enjoy a selection of gourmet pizzas, from calzone with Hawaiian pineapple and ham for $9.50 to smoked shrimp, anchovies, and eggplant for $14. Down by the beach, on a patio surrounded by a manicured coconut grove, is the **Beachhouse,** serving tropical libations, healthy fruit smoothies, burgers, and sandwiches for $12.

Located in two wings off the main reception hall, the luxury rooms, each with their own private lanai and sensational view, are a mixture of kings, doubles, and suites. Done in muted neutral tones, the rooms feature handcrafted quilts, twice-daily room attendance, turndown service complete with complimentary orchid and Ghirardelli chocolates, remote-control color TV, 24-hour room service, fully stocked honor bar, and in-room safe. Wardrobes, hung with plush terrycloth robes and plump satin hangers, feature automatic lights, steam irons, and small ironing boards. The spacious bathrooms, regal with calcatta fabricatta Italien marble, offer wide, deep tubs, separate commodes, and shower stalls, along with dressing and vanity mirrors, double sinks, hair dryers, and name-brand grooming products. Rates begin at $285 for a garden view to $455 for a deluxe oceanfront room (off-season rates available). The Ritz-Carlton Club, an exclusive floor with its own concierge, and featuring continental breakfast, light lunch, cocktails, cordials, and a full spread of evening hors d'oeuvres, is $495. Suites from an executive one-bedroom to the magnificent Ritz-Carlton Suite run $625-2800.

Kapalua Bay Hotel And Villas

This, like other grand hotels, is more than a place to stay; it's an experience. The main lobby is partially open and accented with an enormous skylight. Plants trail from the ceiling. Below are a tropical terrace and restaurant; all colors are soothing and subdued. Although relaxing, this hotel is the kind of a place where you feel underdressed if you don't wear an evening gown to go to the bathroom. In January 1988 renovations were completed to the tune of $20,000 per room, which added ultra-luxury details like silk wallpaper in the already beautiful suites. The least expensive room in the hotel itself is one with a garden view at $185. The villas with a mountain view are $275 and climb rapidly to the $375-475 range. You can choose the American plan, consisting of breakfast and dinner, for an extra $40. You must make a three-nights' deposit, refundable only with 14 days' notice. There are five restaurants in the complex, magnificent golf at the Kapalua Village Course, tennis at the Tennis Club, a multitude of daily activities, and a small arcade with plenty of shops. Contact the hotel at One Bay Drive, Kapalua, HI 96761, tel. 669-5656 or (800) 367-8000.

Napili Kai Beach Club

Located at 5900 Honoapiilani Hwy., Lahaina, HI 96761, tel. 669-6271 or (800) 367-5030, the Napili Kai Beach Club, the dream-come-true of now deceased Jack Millar, was built before regulations forced properties back from the beach. The setting couldn't be more idyllic, with the beach a crescent moon with gentle wave action. The bay itself is a swim-only area with no pleasure craft allowed. Jack Millar's ashes are buried near the restaurant under a flagpole bearing the U.S. and Canadian flags. It's expensive at $195 per studio to $295 for a beachfront luxury suite, but you do have a kitchenette, complimentary snorkel gear, putting green, jacuzzi, croquet, daily tea party, and all the amenities of home. Special packages are available. There are four pools, putting greens, tennis courts, and the Kapalua Golf Course just a nine-iron away. All rooms have Japanese touches complete with shoji screens. There's dancing and entertainment at their famous Sea House Restaurant.

Napili Shores

Overlooking Napili Bay from the lava-rock shoreline is Napili Shores condominium, 5315 Honoapiilani Hwy., tel. 669-8061 or (800) 367-6046 for reservations. All units surround a tropical garden, fishpond, manicured lawn, and swimming pool. Although not large, each unit is comfortable and contains a full kitchen, color TV, large lanai, and some of the best views on the island. Rates run $130-170, with an additional $15 for extra persons. The **Orient Express Thai Restaurant** is one of two restaurants on the premises. **Kalena's Groceries and Gifts** offers food items, gifts, and sundries.

Napili Bay

There's no minimum stay at 33 Hui Drive, Lahaina, HI 96761, tel. 669-6044. For this neck of the woods, the place is reasonably priced from $85 (four people) for a studio off the ocean. All have queen-size beds, lanai, full kitchens, and maid service; laundromat available.

Napili Surf Beach Resort
Located at 50 Napili Pl., Lahaina, HI 96761, tel. 669-8002 or (800) 541-0638, these full condo units operate as a hotel at the south end of Napili Beach. Studios from $84, discount is 12% for 28 days or longer, 15% for 45 days. Preferred views and one-bedroom units from $128, $300 deposit. Minimum stay is four nights. The grounds are not luxurious but are nicely manicured, with plenty of pride put into the property. Very clean rooms with full kitchens have their own lanai and open onto the central grounds area with the sea in the background. Two pools, fantastic beach, maid service, and laundry. Their adjacent Puamala building with its studio apartments is somewhat cheaper.

FOOD

The Grill And Bar
Don't underestimate this excellent restaurant (lunch and dinner), tel. 669-5653, at the Kapalua Golf Club, which is not nearly as utilitarian as its name suggests. What's more, local people consider it one of the most consistently good and affordable restaurants in the area. The soothing main room is richly appointed with koa wood, and large windows frame a sweeping view of the super-green fairways of the golf course. The lunch menu offers a side of pasta for $8.95, or a large salad for only $3.50. Dinner entrees are tempting, with fettuccine pescatore from $16.95, to filet mignon and lobster for $24.95, and plenty of selections for around $20.95. To relax and soak up the scenery you can order dessert like amaretto creme caramel at $2.95, or sip wine selected from an extensive list. The best restaurant for the money in the area.

Kapalua Bay Resort Restaurants
There's a complete menu of restaurants, so you can choose anything from sandwich shops to elegant dining. **Market Cafe**, found in the "shops" area, tel. 669-4888, has foods from around the world, including wines, meats, cheeses, and pastries. All kinds of gourmet items, and delicious but expensive sandwiches, cost from $7. **Bay Club,** tel. 669-8008, offers lunch daily 11:30 a.m.-2 p.m., dinner 5:30-9:30 p.m., on a promontory overlooking the beach and Molokai in the distance. The pool is right here. Dress code; expect to spend $25 for a superbly prepared entree.

The Plantation House
Above Kapalua on the road leading to the Plantation Golf Course Club House, you'll find the lovely Plantation House Restaurant, open daily 8-11 a.m. for breakfast, 11 a.m.-3 p.m. for lunch, and 5-9 p.m. for dinner, tel. 669-6299. Inside, the split-level floor, gabled roof, natural wood, and carpeted and marbled floor add elegance, but the real beauty is the natural still life that pours through the floor-to-ceiling French doors. Napili and Kapalua lie at your feet, Molokai floats upon the still blue sea, and the West Maui Mountains rise behind in a paisley of emerald green, indigo, and cloud-dappled grays. For breakfast, the extensive menu offers light fare like home-baked muffins for $2.95, whole grain muesli for $2.50, or a hearty rancher's breakfast of three eggs, toast, two scoops of rice, breakfast potatoes, and grilled ham, bacon, or Portuguese sausage all for $6.45; fresh catch and eggs costs $9.95. For lunch, start with pan-fried crab cakes served with green peppercorns, lime, and mayonnaise for $7.95; a "home-on-the-range" chicken salad for $6.75; or blackened chicken Caesar for $6.95. Personal pizzas are available for under $9; a half-pound double-fisted Plantation House burger for $5.95; a vegetarian sandwich for $6.25; or a grilled chicken breast sandwich for $7.50. The dinner menu tempts your palate with shrimp *anu anu,* chilled and served with homemade cocktail sauce for $7.95; hot and spicy seared sashimi at a daily quote; and warm goat cheese on a bed of fresh, mixed local greens, raw onion, and tomatoes for $6.95. The chef prepares *pasta al giorno* for $15.95, or tops it with scallops or shrimp for $18.95. Try the fresh catch, charbroiled, brushed with citrus, and served with mango chutney. The Fishermen's *hui hui,* a mix of shrimp, scallops, mussels, or clams, and fresh fish sautéed with garlic and basil in a cream sauce, costs $20.95. The Plantation House mixed grill of broiled lamb chop, blackened fresh fish, and curried chicken sausage costs $21.95. To complement your dinner, the mostly Californian wine list also offers a smattering of French and Italian wines, and the full bar can prepare any drink you may desire.

Napili Plaza Restaurants
The following restaurants are all located at Napili Plaza, easily spotted just off the highway. **Koho's Bar and Grill,** an American standard comfortably appointed with booths and tables, ceiling fans, and wide-screen TVs, also has a full-service bar. The menu offers a fried clam basket for $5.75, soups and dinner salads for $2.45, and a taco salad for $5.85. A sandwich board offers everything from BLTs to a club sandwich, all for under $6, while full-dress burgers are priced around $5. Plate lunches, all under $6, include teriyaki beef or chicken, and mahimahi. More substantial entrees are fettuccine Alfredo, $7.95, shrimp fettuccine, $8.95, and steak and shrimp $12.95. Daily specials, like a 16-ounce T-bone steak, are only $12.95.

Pizza Fresh Cafe, open weekdays 11:30 a.m.-9 p.m., Saturday from 3 p.m., local deliveries only 4-9 p.m., is owned and operated by the husband-and-wife team of Craig and Elizabeth. Besides the obvious pizza ranging in price from a basic small at $7.75 to an extra large with "the works" for $23.95, the small cafe offers espresso and fine baked goods. You can't beat a salad for two plus an oven-roasted turkey breast sandwich for $6.25, or an original Caesar salad for $5.95. Pasta lovers will delight in the fresh lasagna from $5, and the spinach linguine at $9.95. Pizza Fresh is an excellent choice for tasty homemade food at great prices, and is also perfect for a picnic takeout lunch enjoyed on a nearby beach.

Subway Submarine, open daily 7 a.m.-10 p.m., Friday and Saturday to midnight, serves double-fisted fatso sandwiches.

Napili Shores Resort
Two restaurants are located at this resort, 5315 Honoapiilani Hwy., about one mile before Kapalua town. The **Orient Express,** tel. 669-8077, is open for dinner nightly 5:30-10 p.m. The restaurant serves Thai and Chinese food with a flair for spices; duck salad and stuffed chicken wings are specialties. The "early bird special," served before 7 p.m., is a five-course dinner for $11.95. An extensive menu of finely spiced foods includes their well-known curry dishes; takeout available.

The **Gazebo,** tel. 669-5621, open 7:30 a.m.-2 p.m., one of the best-kept secrets in the area, is a little brown gazebo with louvered windows next to the resort pool. Locals in the know come here for a breakfast of the Gazebo's famous banana, pineapple, and especially macadamia nut pancakes for $4.95. There are also eggs and omelettes of all sorts under $6.95. The lunch menu features a range of sandwiches $3.95-6.95, along with burgers under $5.75. You can enjoy a world-class view sitting outside the Gazebo for down-home prices.

The Sea House
The Restaurant of the Maui Moon, perhaps the nicest restaurant name on the island, has changed to the Sea House, at the Napili Kai Beach Club, 5900 Honoapiilani Hwy., tel. 669-6271, open daily for breakfast 8-11 a.m., lunch 12-3 p.m., and dinner 5:30-9 p.m., reservations suggested. At Sunday's breakfast lunch you can order eggs Benedict or fresh banana-macadamia pancakes. If you want to soak up the rays and gorgeous view of Napili Bay, you can wear your swimwear and have a cool drink or light fare on the **Sea Breeze Terrace.** This newly opened addition was a stroke of luck after the federal government redid an old flood project ditch and allowed the hotel to build on the newly reclaimed land.

Inside the semi-open-air restaurant, appetizers range from sliced Maui onions and tomatoes for $3.95 to a bucket of littleneck clams for $11.95. Soups and salads start at a reasonable $1.95 and go up to $13.95 for cold seafood salad with shrimp and scallops stuffed in a papaya. Dinner choices are fresh catch (priced daily); beef teriyaki, $14.95; filet and lobster; and special "lite" fare. Every night also brings specials that range from baked mahimahi on Monday to seafood Newburg on Wednesday, all for around $12.95, but the best is the lobster tail on Thursday. A full wine list includes selections from California and France. There is Hawaiian music nightly and a wonderful Friday night Napili Kai Foundation show (seating at 6 p.m. $25 adults, $20 children) put on by local children who have studied their heritage under the guidance of the foundation.

Honolua Store
Just on the right before the Ritz-Carlton, this small general store (see "Shopping" below)

also serves reasonably priced light meals and sandwiches. The breakfast menu, served 7-10 a.m. offers "The Hobo": eggs, sausage, and rice for $3.50; or you can have two pancakes for $2.75. The dairy case holds a variety of lunch meats, or you can order a prepared sandwich of ham, corned beef, turkey, or pastrami for $4.45. Specials like baked potatoes with broccoli and cheese are only $2.95, and plump hot dogs go for a buck. Sit at a table on the front porch and overlook the exclusive planned community of Kapalua.

Others

Another restaurant to try is **Pineapple Hill,** tel. 669-6129, surrounded by—what else—pineapple fields and overlooking the Kapalua Golf Course. It has an extensive list of seafood and meat selections. A bit on the pricy side but it has a good reputation. The **Village Cafe** at the clubhouse serves light meals, better than you would expect from a small snack shop with outdoor seating. They are especially famous for their hot dog, a steamed Vienna all-beef quarter pounder with all the trimmings on a French roll, supposedly the best on the island.

Note: Please see "Accommodations" above for more fine dining at Kapalua's great hotels.

SHOPPING

The Napili Plaza

Napili's newest shopping center offers **Pizza Fresh Cafe** for espresso and pizza; **First Hawaiian Bank,** a full service bank; **Napili Supermarket** open daily 6:30 a.m.-11 p.m., featuring fresh fish; **Mail Services Plus,** open daily 9 a.m.-6 p.m., Saturday until 1 p.m., closed Sunday, for all your postal needs; **Subway Submarine** for two-fisted sandwiches; and **Koho Grill and Bar,** an American-standard restaurant.

Kapalua Resort And Shops

A cluster of exclusive shops service the resort, including **McInerny** with fine women's apparel; **Kapalua Kids** for the younger set; and **Kapalua Logo Shop** if you want to show off that you've at least been to the Kapalua Resort, since all items of clothing sport the butterfly logo. **Mandalay Imports** has a potpourri of silks and cottons from the East, especially Thailand. Visit **La Perle** for pearls, diamonds, and other jewels. **Distant Drums** sports an amazing collection of offbeat artifacts from Asia, and **Lahaina Galleries** has a wonderful collection of island artists on display.

Whaler's General Store

Located at the Napili Village Shopping Center, tel. 669-6773, this well-stocked little store and landmark is good for last-minute items, with fairly good prices for where it is. You can pick up picnic items and sandwiches. Next door is **Snorkel Bob's,** tel. 669-9603, where you can rent snorkel equipment (prescription masks available) and boogie boards for only $15 per week—one of the best prices on Maui (also in Kihei). **Kalena's Groceries and Gifts** at Napili Shores is mainly a convenience store for last-minute items.

Honolua Store

This well-stocked, reasonably priced store just on the right before the Ritz-Carlton Kapalua, open daily 6:30 a.m.-8 p.m., is a rare find in this expensive neck of the woods. The shelves hold beer, wine, and liquors; basic food items from bananas to sweets; and a smattering of sunglasses, shorts, hats, and aloha shirts. They are also by far the cheapest place in the area to eat.

KEITH PERKINS

EAST MAUI

KIHEI

Kihei ("Shoulder Cloak") takes it on the chin whenever anti-development groups need an example at which to wag their fingers. For the last two decades, construction along both sides of Kihei Road, which runs the length of town, has continued unabated. Since there was no central planning for the development, mostly high-rise condos and a few hotels were built wherever they could be squeezed in: some are lovely, some are crass. There's hardly a spot left where you can get an unobstructed view of the beach as you drive along. That's the "slam" in a nutshell. The good news is that Kihei has so much to recommend it that if you refrain from fixating on this one regrettable feature, you'll thoroughly enjoy yourself, and save money, too.

The developers went "hyper" here because it's perfect as a tourist area. The weather can be counted on to be the best on all of Maui. Haleakala, looming just behind the town, catches rain clouds before they drench Kihei. Days of blue skies and sunshine are taken for granted. On the other side of the condos and hotels are gorgeous beaches, every one open to the public. Once you're on the beach side, the condos don't matter anymore. The views out to sea are unobstructed vistas of Lanai, Kahoolawe, Molokini, and West Maui, which gives the illusion of being a separate island. The buildings are even a buffer to the traffic noise! Many islanders make Kihei their home, so there is a feeling of real community here. It's quieter than Lahaina, with fewer restaurants and not as much action; but for sun and surf activities, this place has it all.

Sights

The six-mile stretch bordered by beach and mountain that makes up Kihei has always been an important landing spot on Maui. Hawaiian war canoes moored here many times during countless skirmishes over the years; later, Western navigators such as Capt. George Vancouver found this stretch of beach a congenial anchor-

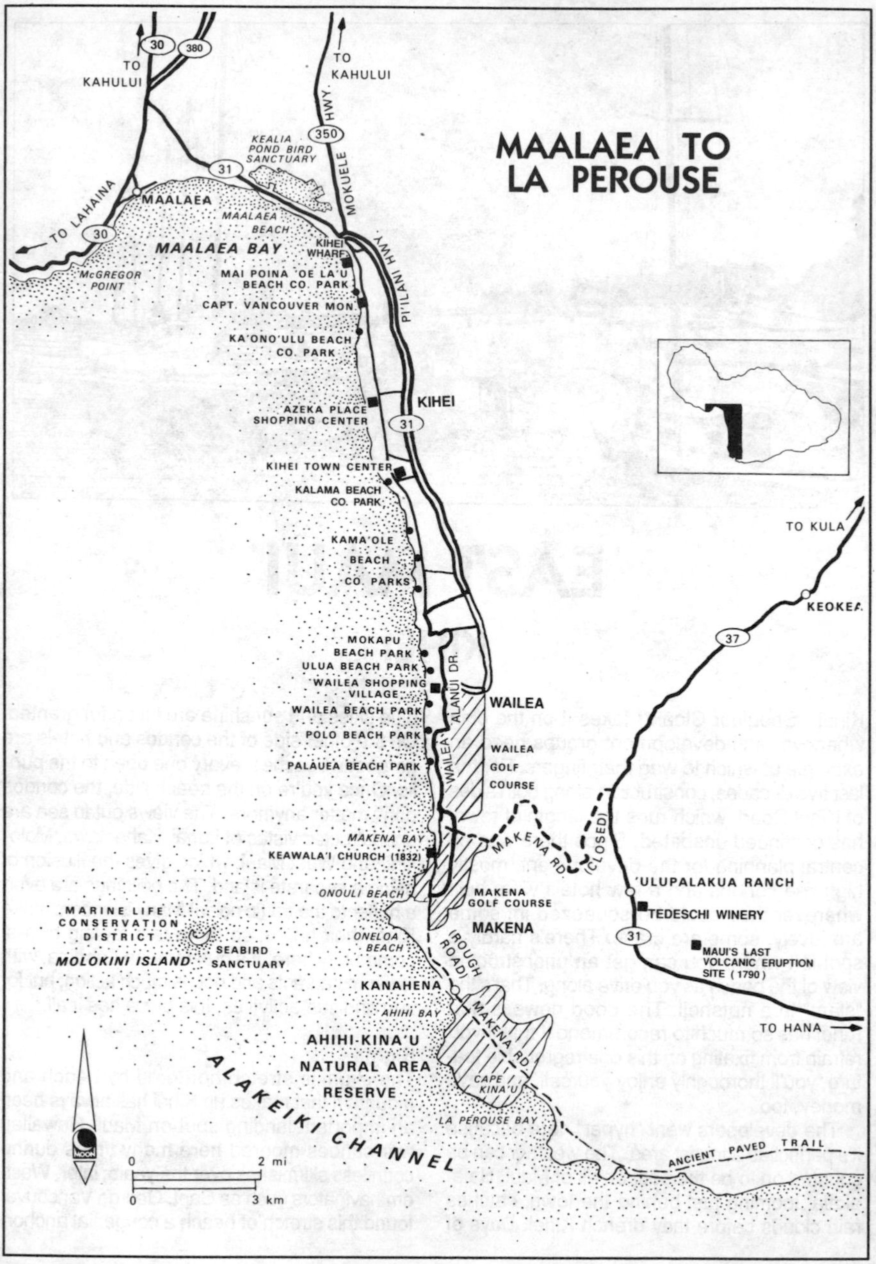

MAALAEA TO LA PEROUSE

30
380
TO KAHULUI
TO KAHULUI
MOKUELE HWY.
350
KEALIA POND BIRD SANCTUARY
31
TO LAHAINA
30
MAALAEA
MAALAEA BEACH
MAALAEA BAY
McGREGOR POINT
KIHEI WHARF
PI'ILANI HWY
MAI POINA 'OE LA'U BEACH CO. PARK
CAPT. VANCOUVER MON.
KA'ONO'ULU BEACH CO. PARK
KIHEI
AZEKA PLACE SHOPPING CENTER
31
KIHEI TOWN CENTER
KALAMA BEACH CO. PARK
KAMA'OLE BEACH CO. PARKS
TO KULA
KEOKEA
37
MOKAPU BEACH PARK
ULUA BEACH PARK
WAILEA SHOPPING VILLAGE
WAILEA ALANUI DR.
WAILEA
WAILEA BEACH PARK
POLO BEACH PARK
PALAUEA BEACH PARK
WAILEA GOLF COURSE
MAKENA BAY
KEAWALA'I CHURCH (1832)
MAKENA RD (CLOSED)
'ULUPALAKUA RANCH
ONOULI BEACH
MAKENA GOLF COURSE
TEDESCHI WINERY
MARINE LIFE CONSERVATION DISTRICT
MAKENA
31
ONELOA BEACH
(ROUGH ROAD)
MAUI'S LAST VOLCANIC ERUPTION SITE (1790)
MOLOKINI ISLAND
SEABIRD SANCTUARY
KANAHENA
AHIHI BAY
MAKENA RD
TO HANA
AHIHI-KINA'U NATURAL AREA RESERVE
CAPE KINA'U
ALAKEIKI CHANNEL
LA PEROUSE BAY
ANCIENT PAVED TRAIL
MOON
0 2 mi
0 3 km

age. A totem pole across from the **Maui Lu Resort** marks the spot where Vancouver landed. During WW II, when a Japanese invasion was feared, Kihei was considered a likely spot for an amphibious attack. Overgrown pillboxes and rusting tank traps are still found along the beaches. Many look like cement porcupines with iron quills. Kihei is a natural site with mountain and ocean vistas. It's also great for beachcombing down toward Maalaea, but try to get there by morning because the afternoon wind is notorious for creating minor sandstorms.

BEACHES

Maalaea Beach And Harbor

Consisting of three miles of windswept sand partially backed by Kealia Pond and a bird sanctuary, Maalaea Beach has many points of access between Maalaea and Kihei along Rt. 31. The strong winds make the beach undesirable for sunning and bathing, but it's a windsurfer's dream. The hard-packed sand is a natural track for joggers, profuse in the morning and afternoon. The beachcombing and strolling are quiet and productive. If you're up by 6 a.m. you can see the Kihei canoe club practice here; they put their canoes in the water near the Kihei wharf just across the road from Suda's Store.

Maalaea Harbor is a bite-sized working harbor sprinkled with a half-dozen homes and businesses that make up Maalaea Village. With the coming and going of all types of craft, the harbor is colorful, picturesque, and always busy. Upon entering from Kihei, you are greeted by a small U.S. Coast Guard installation at one end, or by Buzz's at the Wharf (see "Food" below), a well-known restaurant, at the other. Nearby you will find restrooms.

Mai Poina Oe Lau Beach County Park

On Kihei's western fringe, fronting Maui Lu Resort, this beach has limited paved parking; otherwise park along the road. Showers, tables, and restrooms front the long and narrow white-sand beach, which has good safe swimming but is still plagued by strong winds by early afternoon. A sailboarder's delight, here you can see upwards of 100 sporting enthusiasts out trying the wind when conditions are optimal.

Kaonoulu Beach County Park

You'll find parking, picnic tables, showers, and barbecues here, also very safe swimming and lesser winds. A small beach but not overcrowded.

Kalama Beach County Park

The park, located in the middle of town, is more suited to family outings and enjoying the vista than it is for beach activities. Kalama has a large lawn ending in a breakwater, a small beach in summer, and none in winter. However, there are 36 acres of pavilions; tables; barbecue pits; volleyball, basketball, and tennis courts; a baseball diamond; a soccer field; and plenty of expanse to throw a Frisbee. With its great views of Molokai and Haleakala, it is considered the best family park in the area.

Kamaole I, II, And III

These beach county parks are at the south end of town near Kihei Town Center. All three have beautiful white sand, picnic tables, lifeguards, and all the amenities. Shopping and dining are nearby. The swimming and bodysurfing are good. Kamaole III has a kiddie playground. Snorkeling is good for beginners on the reef between II and III, where much coral and many colorful reef fish abound.

ACCOMMODATIONS

The emphasis in Kihei is on condos. With keen competition among them, you can save money while having a homey vacation. Close to 100 condos, plus a smattering of vacation apartments, cottages, and even a few hotel resorts, are strung along Kihei Road. As always, you pay more for ocean views. Don't shy away from accommodations on the *mauka* side of Kihei Road. You have total access to the beach and some superior views of Haleakala, and you usually pay less money.

Hotels

The Kihei area offers two hotels that are reasonably priced and well appointed. **Maui Lu Resort,** 575 S. Kihei Rd., Kihei, HI 96753, tel. 879-5881, (800) 922-7866 Mainland, (800) 321-2558 in Hawaii, attempts to preserve the feeling of old Hawaii with its Aloha Department and its emphasis on *ohana*. Activities here include a first-class prime-rib buffet in the evening, tennis, a Maui-shaped pool, and tiny private beaches strung along its 28 acres. Rooms, located mostly in the new wing that is mountainside and quieter, are priced $89-140, $10 extra person, and include refrigerators and hot pot. This full-service hotel pampers you in the old Hawaiian style.

The Wailea Ocean Front Hotel is at 2980 S. Kihei Rd., Kihei, HI 96753, tel. 879-7744 or (800) 367-5004. This is a very affordable and well-maintained hotel recently given a complete makeover including buildings, furnishings, and grounds. The hotel fronts a long sandy beach, located just before you get to Wailea at the south end of town. Rates (with a rental car) are $77 standard (up to three persons), $85 superior (up to three persons), and $96 deluxe (two people); $15 extra person, off-season $10 lower, free morning coffee and donuts. The hotel amenities include a/c, room refrigerators, and a jacuzzi. You can't go wrong at this terrific little hotel.

The Maui Coast Hotel, 2259 S. Kihei Rd., Kihei, HI 96753, tel. 874-6284, (800) 426-0670 Mainland, (800) 371-2402 in Hawaii, is Kihei's newest hotel, completed in 1993. The rooms and suites are bright and cheerful, blending Southwestern pastels and Hawaiian-style furniture. Adding to your comfort are standard amenities like remote-control color TV, a/c and ceiling fans, complimentary in-wall safes, refrigerator, slippers to pad around in, full bathrooms that include a jacuzzi bathtub and a "who asked for one" bathroom scale. A microwave and wet bar are in all the larger suites. Guests are treated to morning coffee, and washers and dryers on every other floor. The hotel offers two spas with whirlpools, swimming pool, lighted tennis court, fitness center, restaurant, cocktail lounge, sundries shop, and free parking. Rates are $99-109 for a standard room, $139-149 for a suite, $10 additional person, with discounted off-season and weekly rates. The Maui Coast Hotel, set back from busy Kihei Road, offers a small oasis of peace and tranquility with excellent rates for the standard of rooms and amenities offered.

Condos, Cottages, And B&Bs

At **Kamaole Sands,** 2695 S. Kihei Rd., Kihei, HI 96753, tel. 879-0666, reservations tel. (800) 922-7866, all apartments come completely fur-

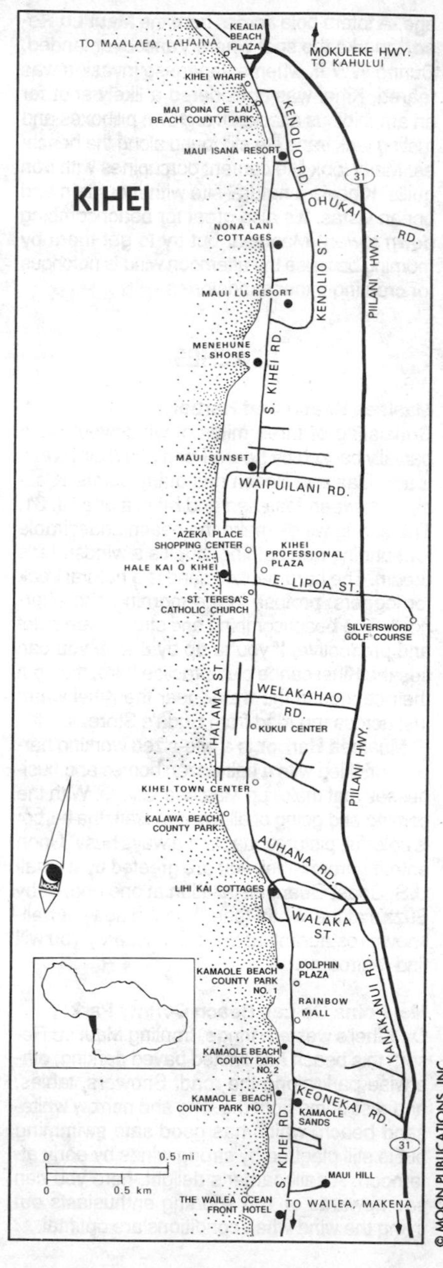

nished with a full bath and kitchen, roomy living area, and lanai. Prices are: $110-125 one bedroom, $145-185 two bedrooms, $205-215 three bedrooms; 15% discount off-season, and rental car package available. The Kamaole Sands is a full-service, family-oriented condo geared toward making the entire family comfortable. One-bedroom units offer 900 square feet, and two-bedroom units are 1,300 square feet. **Great Fettucini, Etc.,** situated poolside, serves inexpensive breakfasts, lunches, and dinners featuring fresh island fish and pasta—most dinners from $9.95. A marine biologist visits on Wednesday and presents a slide show of the flora and fauna of Maui, and Hawaiian women come on Thursday to sell their locally made crafts. One of the main features of the Kamaole Sands is its wonderful tennis courts, free to guests, with a tennis instructor to help you work on the fine points of your game. The Kamaole Sands is bright and cheerful, and gives you a lot for your money.

Maui Hill is located at 2881 S. Kihei Rd., Kihei, HI 96753, tel. 879-6321, (800) 922-7866 Mainland, (800) 342-1551 Hawaii. If you want to rise above it all in Kihei, come to this upbeat condo with a Spanish motif. The hotel sits high on a hill and commands a sweeping view of the entire area. The one-, two-, or three-bedroom suites are spacious, bright, and airy; all have ceiling fans and a/c, cable TV, daily maid service, and gourmet kitchens. A concierge service helps with your every need and arranges all sun and surf activities. The grounds are secluded and beautifully maintained, and offer a pool, tennis courts, and spa. The Maui Hill sits between Kihei and Wailea, so you get a deluxe area at reasonable prices. Rates are: one bedroom from $125 (up to four people), two bedrooms from $145 (up to six people), three bedrooms from $165 (up to seven people); $30 higher during peak season. A weekly complimentary mai tai party complete with games, singing, and door prizes is held for guests, along with a continental breakfast at 8 a.m. that offers an orientation to island activities. Guests can also enjoy a weekly afternoon lei-making class, and a poolside scuba orientation at 10 a.m. four days per week.

Ann and Bob Babson's Vacation Rentals, 3371 Keha Dr., Kihei, HI 96753, tel. 874-1166 or (800) 824-6409, offers B&B rooms, a separate studio apartment, and a private cottage in the quiet residential area of Maui Meadows perched on the hillside between Kihei and Wailea. From this vantage point, you can watch the sun set over the Lahaina Roads with Kahoolawe, Molikini, Lanai, and even Molokai floating on the horizon. All rentals include cable TV, telephone, and laundry facilities. Ann and Bob are happy to recommend their favorite scenic spots, activities, and restaurants, and will provide you with towels and a cooler for a day at the beach. Rates in the main home's B&B rooms are $60-70 and include an all-you-can-eat breakfast. The Hibiscus Hideaway, a first-floor studio priced at $70, has its own bath, kitchen, separate bedroom, and garden. A two-bedroom cottage that can sleep six comfortably, offers a sweeping ocean view, cathedral ceilings, two private baths, and full kitchen, rents for $95. Ann and Bob go out of their way to make your stay enjoyable, having mastered the art of allowing you to enjoy it yourself.

Lihi Kai Cottages are located at 2121 Ili'ili Rd., Kihei, HI 96753, tel. 879-2335 or (800) 544-4524. These nine cottages are such a bargain they're often booked by returning guests, particularly during winter months. They're not plush and there's no pool, but they're homey and clean, with little touches like banana trees growing on the property. Rates are $59 s or d daily for three to five nights, $54 s or d for six or more nights, monthly rates available on request, off-season cheaper, deposit required (no credit cards). For reservations, write well in advance c/o Manager, at the above address.

Nona Lani Cottages, 455 S. Kihei Rd., Kihei, HI 96753, tel. 879-2497 or (800) 733-2688, are owned and operated by Dave and Nona Kong. The clean and neat units on the *mauka* side of Kihei Road have full kitchens and baths, queen beds, and daybeds. Laundry facilities, public phones, and barbecues are on the premises. Rates are $75 during peak season, seven-night minimum. There is a four-night minimum in the slow season, but call to find out if anything's available on a shorter basis or for their off-season weekly rates. Additional person is $7.

Sunseeker Resort is at 551 S. Kihei Rd., tel. 879-1261, write P.O. Box 276, Kihei, HI 96753. Rates are: studio with kitchenette $39, one bedroom $49, two bedrooms $60, additional person $7. Special rates for off-season and long-term stays. Deposit required. Not bad at all.

Nani Kai Hale is at 73 N. Kihei Rd., Kihei, HI 96753, tel. 879-9120 or (800) 367-6032. Very affordable at $42.50 for a room and bath only; $73.50 for studio with kitchenette; or $125 for two bedrooms and two baths. Substantial savings during off-season, seven-day minimum high-season, monthly rates, children under five free. There's a good beach plus sheltered parking, pool, laundry facilities, private lanai, and barbecues on premises. Good views.

Menehune Shores, 760 S. Kihei Rd., mailing address P.O. Box 1327, Kihei, HI 96753, tel. 879-5445 or (800) 822-4409, is a huge, family-oriented and moderately priced condo on the beach overlooking an ancient fishpond. The building is highlighted by replicas of Hawaiian petroglyphs, and on the first floor is **Akina's Restaurant.** All units have an ocean view and rates are $95 one bedroom, $120 two bedrooms, $140 three bedrooms, five-day minimum. No credit cards are accepted, but monthly discounts and off-season rates are offered. Full kitchens with dishwasher, washer and dryer, and disposals are in all units, which are individually owned, so furnishings vary. The majority of units are well appointed, and the condo gives a lot for the money.

Maui Sunset, 1032 S. Kihei Rd., Kihei, HI 96753, tel. (800) 843-5880, is two large buildings containing over 200 units; some are on a timeshare basis and usually have nicer furnishings. High- and low-season rates for the one-, two- and three-bedroom units run $85-200. Full kitchens. Pitch-and-putt golf green, pool, jacuzzi, sauna, rec room, beachfront, and quality tennis courts are on the premises.

One of the newest resorts in Kihei is the **Maui Isana Resort,** 515 N. Kihei Rd., Kihei, HI 96753, tel. 879-7800 or (800) 633-3833. These fully equipped condos are located near the popular windsurfing beach Mai Poina Oe Lau. One-, two-, and three-bedroom units have full kitchens and dining areas, cable TV, and maid service. Room rates run $110-160 per day; weekly rates available. A pool, jacuzzi, and Japanese restaurant are also on the premises.

Hale Kai O Kihei, 1310 Uluniu Rd., Kihei, HI 96753, tel. 879-2757, has reasonable weekly rates based on double occupancy ranging $345-525 (high season) for one bedroom, $495-695 (high season) for two bedrooms with up to four people, $8.50 additional person. Long-stay rates available. No children under six. Pool, shuffleboard, parking, coin-laundry, and maid service on request. The apartment-like cinder-block affair is simple and utilitarian, but clean, well kept, and cute for what it is.

Kauhale Makai is at 930 S. Kihei Rd., contact Maui Condo and Home Realty, P.O. Box 1840, Kihei, HI 96753, tel. 879-5445, (800) 822-4409 Mainland, (800) 648-3301 Canada. Rates from $60 studio, $70 one bedroom, $85 two bedrooms, $7.50 additional person, five-night minimum. Swimming pool, kiddie pool, barbecues, putting green, and sauna are available.

FOOD

Inexpensive

Azeka's Snacks, Azeka Place, S. Kihei Rd., is open daily except Sunday, 9:30 a.m.-4 p.m. Basically takeout, featuring $1 hamburgers and a variety of plate lunches for $4.50. Azeka's is popular with locals and terrific for picnics. A good bargain is the salad bar for only $4.95 (salad bar usually closes by 8 p.m.). Go inside to their bake shop and try a mini-pie for $2.39.

International House of Pancakes is toward the rear of Azeka Place. Open daily 6 a.m.-midnight, Friday and Saturday until 2 a.m. Same American standards as on the Mainland with most sandwiches and plate lunches under $7, dinners under $10, and breakfasts anytime around $5. Not exotic, but basic and filling with a good reputation in the area for inexpensive but passable fresh fish and daily specials.

Let the rich aroma of 40 different types of roasting coffee lure you to **The Coffee Store** at Azeka Place II, 1279 S. Kihei Rd., tel 875-4244, open Sun.-Thurs. 7 a.m.-9 p.m., Friday and Saturday until 10 p.m. A recent popular vote distinguished the shop as having the best cup of cappuccino on the island. Breakfast fare, served all day, features quiche for $3.75 or a breakfast quesadilla for $4. Lunch selections, always served with crusty homemade bread, include a Caesar salad at $3.75—or $5.95 for the large size that can easily feed two—and sandwiches like tuna, turkey, or ham for $5.50. Pizza, on a six-inch Boboli crust, range $6.50-10. Daily homemade soup for $3.50 including bread and coffee, and stuffed quesadillas of all sorts for $4-6, complete the menu. Enjoy coffee drinks that range in price $1-2.50, along with hot and iced herbal teas, hot chocolate, and Italian cream sodas. A deli case filled with luscious desserts is sure to satisfy any sweet tooth. You can purchase bulk coffee, espresso machines, distinctive aprons, kitchen gadgets, and T-shirts as well. Dine inside, or sit outside, especially in the evening to hob-nob with local residents who come here to chat and enjoy a rich cup of coffee and snack.

Tie-dyed "Dead-heads" or heat-flushed tourists hoping to chill out should head for **Stella Blue's Cafe and Deli,** located at Longs Shopping Center, 1215 S. Kihei Rd., tel. 874-3779, open daily 8 a.m.-8 p.m., Sunday 8 a.m.-5 p.m. Inside, the full coffee bar serves up the standards from a cup of house blend to a mocha, along with fresh hot bagels for $2.50, a tuna salad plate for $7.25, or a tossed green salad for $2.25. Sandwiches, everything from roast beef to vegie, average about $6. From the grill you can have a tuna melt, vegie burger, or pastrami melt for under $7.50. Breakfast, served 8-11 a.m., features a continental breakfast for $4.85 and homestyle waffles for $6.25. Also, Stella pours frothy mugs of ice-cold beer, perfect to help cool you down before returning to the beach. A few racks hold a small selection of *pareau* and alohawear, as well as psychedelic T-shirts, tie-dyed fashions, and stickers.

Kalbi House, in a corner of Longs Shopping Center, open daily except Sunday 9 a.m.-9 p.m., offers Korean standards like barbecued short ribs, fried squid, chicken teriyaki, noodles, and small-intestine soup for under $7 (dinner about $1 more). The restaurant, appointed with bright Formica and linoleum, is basic but clean.

And then there's **Subs of Paradise,** also in Longs Shopping Center, where you can get an overstuffed six- or 12-inch submarine sandwich of all descriptions ranging in price $3.79-5.99.

For a gourmet Italian deli try **Bello Cibo** at the Kukui Center, tel. 875-0669, open Mon.-Thurs. 8 a.m.-11 p.m., Fri.-Sat. 11 a.m.-9 p.m., and Sunday 12-8 p.m., where the pudgy ravioli filled with spinach, ricotta, shrimp, and mushrooms, along with the spicy sausage, are imported from New Jersey. The deli case is filled with mouthwatering items like artichoke hearts, pasta salad, prosciutto, oven-roasted turkey, pastrami, and Italian roast pork; sandwiches on crusty homemade Italian bread cost $7. Bello Cibo also offers daily specials like lasagna, crisp Caesar salads, and fresh-baked goods. The shop has a few tables for dining, and the service is very friendly. You can't go wrong, *paisano!*

Paradise Fruit Co., at the Rainbow Mall, 2439 S. Kihei Rd., tel. 879-1723, open daily 6 a.m.- 9 p.m., serves health-conscious food. Daily house specials like lasagna are under $7.50, while the snack bar offers hearty sandwiches for under $5.50, along with a selection of crisp salads. Try the pita melt for $4.25, and a smoothie, purported to be the best on the island. Take your food out, or dine alfresco at a few tables out front.

Wiki Wiki Pizza, at the Kamaole Beach Center, 2411 S. Kihei Rd., tel. 874-9454, open 11 a.m.-10 p.m., offers table service or free pizza and deli delivery with a $10 purchase. The restaurant, using only the freshest ingredients, offers a range of pizzas, from a small cheese for $8.95 to a large vegetarian delight for $18.95. The menu also includes salads, most for under $4.50, along with lasagna, spaghetti, and calzone for under $7.

Sports Page Bar and Grill, also at the Kamaole Beach Center, tel. 879-0602, open 11 a.m.-midnight for cocktails and 11:30 a.m.-10 p.m. for food service, scores big with a full bar and a large-screen TV. Order a mug of beer and a light snack like oyster shooters for $1 or teriyaki chicken breast strips for $5.95. The burger and sandwich menu goes all the way with a San Francisco '49er burger topped with bacon and cheese, a Chicago Cubs hot dog, or a Boston Celtics turkey sandwich, all for under $7. Families and even the athletically challenged will be comfortable here and more than welcome.

If you've been having too much fun and need a reviving cup of espresso, stop in at the **Kihei Caffe,** 1945 S. Kihei Rd., tel. 878-2230, open daily 5 a.m.-3 p.m., and enjoy your coffee along with an excellent assortment of sandwiches and baked goods. This full coffee bar serves up coffee drinks costing $1-2.75. Order a complete breakfast of eggs, bacon, home fries, and biscuits with gravy for $3.75, or a giant raisin muffin for $1.50. Sandwiches, all under $6.50, are served on homemade herb bread. Lighter fare includes couscous salad for $4.50, or honey cashew chicken salad for $5.95. The cafe provides a few tables and stools inside, and more outside where you can watch the action on Kihei Road.

Alexander's Fish and Fowl, at 1913 S. Kihei Rd., tel. 874-0788, open 11 a.m.-9 p.m., is definitely a cut above most fast-food restaurants. The limited menu offers fresh fish sandwiches like mahimahi for $4.95, or chicken, beef, or fish barbecue for $5.95, all served with coleslaw, French fries, or rice. There's not much decor or atmosphere, but the food is delicious and makes a perfect takeout meal that can be enjoyed at the beach.

At the north end of Kihei as you approach from Kahului or Lahaina, look for **Surfer Joe's Bar and Grill,** at 61 S. Kihei Rd., tel. 879-8855, open daily for food 11 a.m.-10 p.m., bar until 2 a.m., happy hour 11 a.m.-7 p.m. This is a friendly and unpretentious local bar where you can have yourself a cold draft beer. The menu offers a totally awesome tostada for $5.50, a Joe's "da kine" burger for $5, a hang-ten tempura fish for $6.50, a garden salad for $4.50, or groomed shrooms for $4. Joe's is not fancy, and if you want to meet "the people" this is the place to come. Next door is **Suda's Snack Shop** where you can order a combination pizza, a steaming bowl of saimin, or a deluxe burger for very reasonable prices.

Maalaea Fish Market and Cafe, tel. 244-9633, at Maalaea Harbor, open Mon.-Sat. 10 a.m.-5 p.m., is a rare find. The menu offers shrimp cocktail for $3.95, fish and shrimp combo for $8.95, and tuna salad with tomatoes for only $4, all prepared with fresh fish straight off the boat. Eat out on the lattice-covered veranda and avoid the fishy odor inside. If you are lodging in a condo and have kitchen facilities, the fish market is an excellent place to purchase fresh ingredients for dinner.

Moderate

Margarita's Beach Cantina, at 101 N. Kihei Rd., tel. 879-5275, open daily 11:30 a.m.-midnight, has a well-deserved reputation for good food at fair prices. Formerly vegetarian, they now serve a variety of meat and chicken dishes but still use the finest ingredients, cold-pressed oils, and no lard or bacon in their bean dishes. The decor is classical Mexican with white stucco walls and tiled floors. There's an outdoor deck affording a great sunset view. The *carta* offers taco salads for $7.95, combination plates for $8.95-12.95, and money-saving daily lunch specials like *carnitas burrito* for under $7. Well drinks are $3, imported beers $3.50; during happy hour 2:30-5:30 p.m., margaritas are only 96 cents or $3 by the pitcher.

La Bajia is a friendly and reasonably priced Mexican restaurant at Kai Nani Village Plaza, 2511 S. Kihei Rd., tel. 875-1007, across from Kamaole Park II. Most dishes are under $10 and are made with locally grown ingredients when possible. All soups are homemade. Happy hour 2-6 p.m. features traditional margaritas for $1.50. Pleasant waitresses, good service, well-prepared large portions, and a terrific sunset view make La Bajia a good choice.

Tucked behind La Bajia in the Kai Nani Village Plaza is the **Greek Bistro,** tel. 879-9330, a wonderful addition to the restaurant scene, where the flavors and textures of the Mediterranean dishes served by the Arabatzi family will excite your palate. Lunch and dinner are served 12:30 p.m.-9:30 p.m. and include two kinds of gyros, spanakopita, moussaka, and lamb kabob, all ranging $9.95-16.95. If you're in doubt as to what would be tasty, try the Greek Gods Platter, a sampling of each homemade entree on the menu. Salads and island dishes are also served for the less adventurous.

Chuck's Steak House at the Kihei Town Center, tel. 879-4488, open daily for lunch 11:30 a.m.-2:30 p.m., dinner nightly from 5:30 p.m., fresh fish and steaks available from 11 a.m., closed Sunday, is a family restaurant featuring American standards with an island twist. With a gray-on-gray interior, the restaurant provides a pleasant atmosphere, and although they do not take reservations, they will tell you how busy they are if you call ahead. The lunch menu is affordable, with selections like a Reuben sandwich for $5.95, tavern ham and roast beef sandwiches for $6.95, and plate lunches for under $6. The "early bird special," priced at a reasonable $9.95, is normally fresh fish or barbecued chicken, and includes the salad bar, homemade bread, and a choice of white rice or French fries.

The dinner menu includes steaks and ribs for $19.95, *kalbi* ribs for $14.95, and a petite top sirloin priced at $10.95. Chuck's seafood selections include fresh fish for $15.95, lobster tail for $24.95, and chicken, prime rib, and lobster tail for $36.95.

The **Island Fish House,** at 1945 S. Kihei Rd., tel. 879-7771, has a very good reputation and offers money-saving "early bird specials." Entrees include seafood salad, shrimp Polynesian, and a variety of beef and chicken dinners priced $15-21. The house specialty is the fresh catch that is prepared seven different ways. *Pu pu* range from escargot to a sample platter for two for $15.95, with most priced $3.50-7. For a complete sampling, try the "king's platter for two," featuring two types of fresh fish, sautéed lobster, deep-fried shrimp and scallops, New York steak, and scampi, all for $64.95. Sharing the same building is **Ferrari's,** tel. 879-1535, open daily for dinner from 5:30 p.m., an Italian restaurant featuring homemade pasta, fresh fish, fine wines, and desserts. Their kitchen offers fried calamari for $6.95, seared *ahi* priced daily, eggplant Parmesan for $14.95, and steak Italiano priced at $23.95. Lighter appetites will enjoy a medley of salads ranging $5-7, along with a pizza. Top off your dinner with one of the rich desserts and a cup of espresso.

Chum's at the Rainbow Mall, 2439 S. Kihei Rd., tel. 874-9000, open daily 6:30 a.m.-11 p.m., breakfast until 11 a.m., specializes in local and island-style food at moderate prices. Breakfast specials are Chum's fried rice with two eggs for $5.10 or stuffed French toast for $3.40. American breakfasts like eggs with sausage or ham go for $3.99. Lunch and dinner items are a mixture of standard and local favorites like steaming bowls of Portuguese bean soup, seafood chowder, and burgers and sandwiches $4.75-5.25. Combination plate luncheons like pork *katsu* or teriyaki beef cost under $6. If you are interested in sampling some *local* cuisine, order *lau lau,* seasoned pork and butterfish wrapped in ti leaf; or *kalua* pork. Both come with macaroni salad, Hawaiian chile pepper water, onions with Hawaiian salt, and *lomi lomi* salmon, and both cost under $7. Chum's also has nightly entertainment, with the bar open until 2 a.m., so this is a regular stop for many of the hotel and lounge workers in the area (see "Entertainment" below). Chum's is not fancy, but the service is friendly and the food ample, very well prepared for the price.

Try **Luigi's Pasta and Pizzeria** at Azeka Place Shopping Center, tel. 879-4446, for live entertainment, pasta, seafood, and pizza plus "early bird specials" 4-6 p.m.; moderately priced but mediocre food. Music nightly with a live band Wed.-Sat. evenings, $3 cover.

At the **Kamaole Shopping Center,** the larger mall next door to the Rainbow Mall, you'll find three reasonably priced restaurants. **Denny's** serves food just like on the Mainland but with a few more island specialties. A portion of Denny's called **The Cactus and Rose Cantina** features Mexican food from enchiladas to *chile verde,* all for under $10, and a full-service bar. **Erik's Seafood Broiler,** tel. 879-8400, has a very good reputation for fresh fish (the biggest selection on Maui) and fair prices. "Early bird specials" 5-6:30 p.m. run $12.95. The **Canton Chef**, open for lunch 11 a.m.-2 p.m., and dinner 5-9:30 p.m., tel. 879-1988, is a moderately priced restaurant with the usual Chinese selections and specialties like Sichuan scallops with hot garlic sauce for $8.50; *kung pao* scallops, $8.50; noodles and rice dishes from $5.25; and chicken dishes $6-9. Seafood is slightly more expensive, with selections such as fresh fish with black bean sauce for $8.50.

Silversword Golf Course Restaurant, tel. 879-0515, open daily for lunch 11 a.m-3:30 p.m., is located at Maui's newest golf course, 1345 Piilani Hwy., above and parallel to Kihei Road. From the porticolike dining room, you get an extraordinary view, not only of the sweeping fairways, but of Kihei's coast below and the Neighbor Islands in the distance. The food is very good, and the prices are unbeatable. You can order a hefty sandwich like pastrami or lox and bagels for under $6, or a variety of salads from $4. But the best deals are the lunch entrees, like shrimp silversword, beef stroganoff, or hamburger steak for under $7.50.

Expensive

The **Waterfront Restaurant** at the Milowai Condo in Maalaea Harbor, tel. 244-9028, is the most elegant and most gourmet restaurant in the Kihei area. It's owned and operated by the Smith brothers, Gary and Rick, out front greeting and seating, and brother Ron, creating sumptuous dishes in the kitchen. Choose a horseshoe-shaped booth tucked around the room's perimeter, and order a bottle of wine from their extensive international list. For starters, consider the Caesar salad for $5.50, Pacific oysters on the half shell at $8.50, or exotic Indonesian escargot for $6.50. Definitely order the Maine lobster chowder, a famous specialty, for $4.25. Entrees like chicken picatta or scampi cost $22.95, while savory Colorado rack of lamb in a lemon pepper, garlic, and olive oil base is priced at $26.95. However, the best choice is the fresh island fish, priced daily, which is prepared in a variety of ways: Sicilian, Cajun, and Hawaiian, or *a là manoir* in a white wine sauce with lemon. Save room for one of the prize-winning desserts—white-chocolate and cream cheese cake, upside-down apple pie, chocolate mousse, or tropical strudel. The Waterfront provides an excellent dining experience, from the fine service to the wonderful food, and is well worth the price.

Buzz's at the Wharf at Maalaea Harbor, tel. 244-5426, open daily 11 a.m.-11 p.m., specializes in seafood. The waterfront atmosphere and second-story views are unbeatable. *Pu pu* selections include steamed clams for $12.95, escargot on the shell for $7.95, Buzz's salmon for $6.95, and fresh Pacific oysters on the half shell for $11.95. The lunch menu offers a tossed salad with shrimp for $11.95, an assortment of burgers and fries for under $10, and a Cajun open-faced chicken sandwich for $9.95. For dinner, try prawns Tahitian at $19.95, the Captain's Seafood Platter for $16.95, or a mouthwatering cut of prime rib au jus for $20.95 (lady's cut, $18.95). Enjoy a liter of house wine for $10.50 or cocktail for $5. End your meal with dessert followed by a stroll around the moonlit harbor.

Overlooking a rocky beach is the appropriately named **Ocean Terrace,** located at the Mana-Kai Condo, 2960 S. Kihei Rd., tel. 879-2607, open daily for breakfast 7-11 a.m., lunch 11:30 a.m.-2 p.m., dinner 5 p.m. till closing, bar 10 a.m.-10 p.m., Sunday brunch 10:30 a.m.-1:30 p.m. This is perhaps the most gloriously situated restaurant in Kihei. From the elevated terrace, swaying palms perfectly frame Kahoolawe and Molokini Crater just offshore, while the West Maui Mountains appear to float in the distance, giving the illusion of a separate island. Breakfast eggs are fixed to order and accompanied with sausage, bacon, or ham for $6.75; New York steak or fresh fish and eggs cost about $10.95. Choose the lighter continental breakfast for $5.75, or dive into a stack of old-fashioned buttermilk pancakes for $4.95, or the scrumptious banana-macadamia pancakes for $6.50. Lunch and dinner menus start with seafood trout chowder for $3.95, or choose a *pu pu* platter for two for at $13.95 that is heaped with steamed artichokes, sautéed mushrooms, zucchini strips, scallops, shrimp, and more. Always wonderful is the fresh Hawaiian fish sautéed in lemon butter and garlic, or charbroiled or poached, daily quote. Try the Kona lime shrimp, sweet and tangy for $19.95, or prawns Tahitian at $19.95. Less-expensive chicken dishes with an Asian flavor are all under $16. Hearty appetites will be satisfied with the New York steak and teriyaki chicken combination for $17.95, or the King's Platter for two—fresh fish, lobster, New York steak, scampi, deep-fried shrimp, and scallops for $64.95. Relax and savor the dramatic sun-splashed panorama along with your dessert at the Ocean Terrace.

Upstairs from La Bajia Restaurant at the Kai Nani Village Plaza at 2511 S. Kihei Rd. is **Kihei Prime Rib House,** open from 5 p.m., tel. 879-1954, offering most entrees for $18-30, including a well-stocked salad bar (by itself, $9.95). Sashimi, lobster, and stuffed mushroom appetizers are under $10, and the "early bird specials," 5-6 p.m. are $11.95, salad bar included. One of the best choices is rack of lamb for $21.95. An island ambience is created with carvings by Bruce Turnbull and paintings by Sigrid, both well-known local artists.

Located at the Menehune Shores Condo overlooking the beach, **Akina's** at 760 S. Kihei Rd., tel. 874-5787, is open nightly for dinner from 4 p.m., and offers a money-saving "early bird special." Start your meal with *pu pu* like artichoke hearts, chicken yakitori, or seared *ahi* for $5-10. Seafood pasta costs $21.95, while beef dishes like New York strip loin or steak and shrimp scampi are priced around $20. Less expensive dishes are chicken teriyaki or lemon chicken for under $14.95, or the salad bar for $10.95. Akina's seafood is charbroiled with garlic, sautéed in lemon butter, blackened, or prepared island-style with papaya and Bermuda onions, and is priced daily. A children's menu, with everything priced under $5, also helps keep prices down.

The **Maui Lu Resort** at 575 S. Kihei Rd., tel. 879-5881, offers a prime rib buffet and Polynesian revue in the hotel's longhouse nightly for $29.95. A full breakfast and dinner menu is available, as well as an "early bird" dinner special for $9.95. The hotel still offers its famous Aloha Mele Luncheon, but only on the third Thursday of the month.

Isana Shogun, located at the Maui Isana Resort, 515 N. Kihei Rd., tel. 874-5034, open nightly 5-10 p.m., is one of the best Japanese restaurants in the area. You can either sit at the sushi bar or have dinner cooked at your table in the *teppan* style. Upstairs is the Mermaid Bar, which has a karaoke sing-along after 10 p.m. *Teppan yaki* dinners featuring, shrimp, chicken, or beef along with green salad, miso soup, *teppan* vegetables, and rice range $15.95-25.95. There's a lower-priced children's menu, and a full selection of beer and sake.

ENTERTAINMENT

Kihei isn't exactly a hot spot when it comes to evening entertainment. A **Polynesian revue** is offered nightly along with their prime rib buffet at the Maui Lu Resort. You can dance at **Margarita's Beach Cantina** now and again, and at **Luigi's** nightly, with karaoke as part of the entertainment. **Chum's** offers karaoke Sun.-Thurs., with the local **Hawaiian Diamonds** swinging with contemporary dance music on the weekends. The **Isana Shogun Restaurant** provides karaoke nightly from 10 p.m., where you can become the star performer (heaven help us all!). Many of the restaurants offer entertainment on a hit-and-miss basis, usually one artist with a guitar, a small dinner combo, or some Hawaiian music. These are usually listed in the free tourist brochures.

SHOPPING AND PRACTICALITIES

While driving the length of Kihei, you will find shopping centers, both large and small, strung along the entire coastal area like shells on a dime store lei. At many you can buy food, clothing, sporting goods, camping and picnic supplies, sundries, photo equipment, cosmetics, resortwear, ice cream, pizza, dinner, and liquor. You can also book activities, order a custom bikini, or relax with an ice cold beer while your partner satisfies his or her shopping addiction. In Kihei, you have more than ample opportunity to spend your hard-earned vacation money that would be a sin to take back home. $Aloha$!

Note: Most of the restaurants listed below are described under "Food," above.

Azeka Place I

At the **Azeka Place Shopping Center,** along S. Kihei Rd. in the center of town, you'll find **Azeka's Market,** well stocked and featuring famous Azeka ribs for barbecues. There's also a great community bulletin board listing apartments, yard sales, and odds and ends. Most shops are open daily 9 a.m.-9 p.m. with shorter Sunday hours, including **Ben Franklin** for everything from reading glasses to thumbtacks, and a small **Liberty House** for island fashions. **Rainbow Connection,** tel. 879-5188, features personalized and Polynesian gifts. **Lelani's** has towels, beachwear, hats, and postcards; next door is **O'Rourke's Tourist Trap,** where the junk ain't bad, and neither are the prices. **Maui Water Wear** features alohawear, dresses, shirts, and a good selection of bathing suits. **Island Memories** is stocked with carved koa boxes, shells, earrings, woven basketry, a good selection of pottery, and hula instruments, all made in Hawaii. **Leather of the Sea** sells eelskin handbags, shoulder bags, belts, and briefcases. **Wings on the Wind** will send your spirits soaring with fantastic kites of all kinds, shapes, and colors. **Tropical Tantrum** specializes in hand-painted clothing by local artists, mostly for women but with a few selections for men as well.

Also here are **American Savings Bank,** tel. 879-1977, the Kihei **post office** at 1254 S. Kihei Rd.; and a gas station. **Kihei Acupuncture Clinic,** tel. 874-0544, is run by Dr. Nancy Macauley, who specializes in gentle needling techniques and offers a full selection of Chinese herbs. **Fox Photo One-Hour Lab** does quick developing and is a good place to buy film. **Ocean Activities Center,** tel. 875-4544, has a desk from which you can book all types of activities.

Azeka Place II
Located across the street from the original Azeka's, this new shopping center features the **Maui Dive Shop,** tel. 879-3388, a full service dive shop (see "Snorkeling and Scuba" under "Sports and Recreation" in the Maui Introduction); **The Coffee Store,** a great place for a cup of coffee (40 kinds), a light lunch, or a late-night snack; **In's Eel Skins** for bags, belts, and accoutrements made from eel; **Rapre,** whose shelves hold distinctive shells and gifts of Maui; **Liberty House,** a department store with tasteful island fashions; **Kihei Ace Hardware** in case you need a toggle bolt; **Bank of Hawaii,** a full-service bank; **Roland's Shoes** for everything from slippers to hiking boots; **Elephant Walk** for gifts and boutique items; and **Tradewinds Treasures** for distinctive souvenirs.

Longs Shopping Center
Located at 1215 S. Kihei Rd. near Azeka Plaza, this shopping center is dominated by a huge **Longs Drugs** stocked with electronics, photo equipment, sundries, cosmetics, stationery, and sporting goods. At the center you will find the **T-Shirt Factory** featuring all kinds of discounted T-shirts; **A-1 Photo** for quick one-hour photos; **Kalbi Korean Barbecue** featuring inexpensive Korean food; and next door **Affordable Fashions,** a discount clothing store selling everything from alohawear to bathing suits. For a quick lunch try **Subs of Paradise,** where you can satisfy any appetite with a foot-long sub sandwich, or **Stella Blue's,** an outdoor/indoor coffee house and deli. Boys and girls will find tasteful island fashions at the **The Children's Shop,** and you can do everything from faxing to packing and shipping at **Mail Boxes Etc.**

Kihei Town Center
This small shopping center just south of Azeka Place offers a 24-hour **Foodland,** a bank, an art gallery, a **Maui Dive Shop,** and a few clothing and gift stores.

International Market Place
Look for this bargain-filled, semi-open-air mall at 1945 S. Kihei Rd. that offers everything from tourist trinkets to fine art. Among its shops you will find **Serendipity,** open 10 a.m.-7 p.m., a small, well-appointed boutique that displays imported items mainly from Malaysia and Brazil. Nearby is **Made In Hawaii,** tel. 874-3760, open daily 9 a.m.-5 p.m., a store that specializes in a variety of locally made items. One of the best indoor/outdoor shops is **Bunga Maui,** open daily 9 a.m.-6 p.m., that specializes in women's fashions from Bali, personally designed by shop owner Rene. Recently she has introduced a line of men's aloha shirts, with more men's fashions planned for the future. Both the price and quality of the merchandise are very good.

Kamaole Shopping Center
This new mall at the east end of town features **Denny's, Erik's Seafood, Canton Chef, Cinnamon Roll Fare,** and various clothing, souvenir, and sundries stores. From its two floors of shops you can buy baubles, beads, and some nicer pieces at **Jewels and Gifts of Paradise;** a tangle of novelty items and sundries at **O'Rourke's Tourist Trap;** and groceries, liquor, and souvenirs at **Whaler's General Store. Lappert's Ice Cream** sells island-made delights and fat-free yogurt. Also in the center is **Maui Dive Shop,** a complete diving and water-sports store offering rentals, swimwear, snorkels, cruises, and windsurfing lessons.

Dolphin Shopping Plaza
This small, two-story plaza along S. Kihei Road includes **Miki's** for swimwear and alohawear, and **Pro Photo and Gifts,** featuring 40-minute processing. You can take care of your sweet tooth by visiting the **Kihei Bakery,** open daily 6 a.m.-9 p.m., tel. 879-8666, where they make fresh bread, blueberry donuts, and bagels. Here, too, the **New York Deli** is a clone of any found in the Big Apple. If you have a craving for pizza, try **Pizza Hut.**

Rainbow Mall
Yet another mall just up the road at 2439 S. Kihei Rd. features **Tropical Trappings,** a clothing store with resortwear; **South Pacific Kayaks;** and **Auntie Snorkel,** a booth out front that rents snorkel gear and boogie boards for very reasonable prices (see "Dive Shops and Marine Rentals" following). Other shops in the mall are the **T-shirt Factory; L.A. Rage,** selling women's apparel; **The Bridge,** a men's apparel store; **Topaz,** a fine jewelry store; and **Maui**

Custom Beach Wear, where you can buy off the rack or have a bikini made especially for you (tops and bottoms sold separately). **Kihei Discount Liquor** and the **Paradise Fruit Company,** offering health-conscious fare, are also located in the mall.

Kamaole Beach Center
This small group of shops between Dolphin Plaza and Rainbow Mall includes the **Sports Page Grill and Bar, Wiki Wiki Pizza, E-Z Discount Store, TCBY Yogurt Shop,** and **Hobie Sports Store.**

Kukui Center
At the new **Kukui Center** along S. Kihei Road are **Waldenbooks, Valley Isle Produce,** a cash-and-carry store, **Kihei Kukui Laundromat, J.R.'s Music Store,** several apparel stores, **Kihei Art Gallery, Wings On The Wind Kites** for all sorts of flying objects, **Whaler's General Store** for sundries, and **Maui Dive Shop.**

Kihei Gateway Plaza
Kihei's newest shopping mall has opened along the Piilani Hwy. (Rt. 31), the main thoroughfare above Kihei that parallels Kihei Road. The entrance to the plaza is marked by **Gas Express.** Continue on the service road past the gas station, and turn at the second right onto another service road that leads into the **Kihei Commercial Center.** Here you'll find **Kihei Wine and Spirits,** the best bottle shop in Kihei; and the **Pikake Bakery,** the best gourmet bakery in the Kihei area.

Swap Meet And Farmers' Market
If you're looking for a bargain on clothes, gifts, crafts, or odds and ends, try the **Kihei swap meet** every Saturday 7 a.m.-4 p.m. across the road from Kalama Beach Park.

A **farmers' market** is held in the parking lot near Suda's Store at 61 S. Kihei Rd., every Tuesday and Saturday from 1:30 p.m. until the vendors decide to call it a day. Besides fresh produce, stalls sell shells, T-shirts, and knickknacks.

North End Shopping
At the very north end of Kihei as you approach from Kahului or Lahaina is the **Sugar Beach General Store,** tel. 879-6224, with a small clutch of shops selling resortwear, snacks, gifts, and jewelry. Nearby at **Kealia Beach Plaza** is the **Kealia General Store** and the **Pacific Whale Foundation** office. **Suda's Kihei Store** is a basic little market with limited food items, but with cold beer, and sits along the *mauka* side at 61 S. Kihei Road. A few minutes down the road from Suda's heading for Kihei, look for the **Nona Lani Cottages** where you can pick up a fresh flower lei for a reasonable price.

At Maalaea Harbor look for the **Maalaea General Store,** open daily except Monday 8 a.m.-5 p.m., where you have a much better chance of buying fishing tackle than you do a loaf of bread. They do have a very limited selection of groceries, sundries, and gasoline.

Food/Liquor Stores
Azeka's Market at Azeka Place is famous for its delicious marinated ribs, sought after by local barbecue artists, along with selections of exotic Asian foods and spices, as well as shelves stocked with national brands and an assortment of general merchandise. **Foodland** at Kihei Town Center (open 24 hours) and **Star Market** at 1310 S. Kihei Rd. are full-service supermarkets with complete liquor, wine, and beer sections. **Kihei Discount Liquor** at the Rainbow Mall along S. Kihei Road has a good selection of liquor, imported beers, and wine.

Kihei Wine and Spirits, located at the Kihei Commercial Center, the second right behind Gas Express above Kihei on the Piilani Hwy., tel. 879-0555, open daily 10 a.m.-7 p.m., Saturday until 5 p.m., has a fantastic selection of wine and beer and a great little gourmet food section. Along with your liquor, pick up some imported pasta, sun-dried zucchini or tomatoes, olives, and fancy cheese. Even the most discriminating yuppie will find all they need for a first-class picnic at Kihei Wine and Spirits.

The **Pikake Bakery,** open daily 8 a.m.-6 p.m. except Sunday, tel. 879-7295, next door to Kihei Wine and Spirits, is owned and operated by Peter and Tina Teimorabadi, who bake the best breads and pastries in Kihei. Choose a bread flavored with red onions and olives or red potatoes and rosemary, or the *pane* fraciliano made with semolina flour. Order a cup of cappuccino and choose a cinnamon roll with macadamia nuts; a walnut muffin; cheese, custard, or chocolate bear claw; or an apple muffin. All breads and pastries are made fresh with the finest ingredients.

DIVE SHOPS AND MARINE RENTALS

The **Maui Dive Shop,** at its Kihei locations (Azeka Place II, tel. 879-3388; Kamaole Shopping Center, tel. 879-1533; Kihei Town Center, tel. 879-1919) and at the Wailea Shopping Village, tel. 879-3166, offers a full range of equipment, lessons, and rentals.

The Dive and Sea Center, 1975 S. Kihei Rd., tel. 874-1952, open daily 7 a.m.-5 p.m., and until noon on Sunday, is a full-service dive shop offering scuba dives, four-day certification classes for $250, air refills, equipment rentals (scuba gear $19.95 per day, snorkel gear $5 per day), and dive/snorkel trips to Molokini Crater (snorkelers pay $49, a one-tank beginner dive costs $80) on a six-passenger Mako boat so that you are given individual attention and full value for your money.

Snorkel Bob's, tel. 879-8225, is easy to spot at 1913 S. Kihei Road. The weekly prices can't be beat at $15 for snorkel gear or boogie boards (day rentals available too). You also get snorkel tips, a fish ID card, and the semi-soggy underwater humor of Snorkel Bob.

Auntie Snorkel and Aloha Destinations, tel. 879-6263, located in a booth in front of the Rainbow Mall along S. Kihei Road, and operated by Melissa and Mike McCoy, rents snorkel gear at $3.95 per day or $11.95 per week, along with boogie boards, beach chairs, and ice chests. Theirs are among the lowest prices in the area.

Located at the Rainbow Mall along S. Kihei Road, **South Pacific Kayaks,** tel. 875-4848 or (800) 776-2326, open daily 8 a.m.-5 p.m., offers a half-day introductory trip for $55, or an advanced explorer trip along the remote coastline of East Maui for $79. Both tours include lunch along with plenty of snorkeling opportunities as you glide in and out tiny bays fashioned from jutting lava rock fingers. South Pacific Kayaks offer rentals of single kayaks at $20 per day, and double kayaks at $40 per day.

SeaEscape U-Drive Boat Rental, at 1979 S. Kihei Rd., tel. 879-3721, offers seagoing motorized rafts that you can pilot yourself to all the snorkel, dive, and picturesque spots of the Lahaina Roads. Rates begin at $80 per hour (two-hour minimum, additional hours $35) for a 16-foot Zodiac with a 25 hp motor. Larger boats are available.

Ocean Activities Center, tel. 879-4485, is at the Kamaole Shopping Center (look for the Denny's sign along S. Kihei); you can book every fun activity on Maui and purchase anything you'll need for sun and surf at this excellent one-stop store.

SERVICES

For a full-service bookstore browse at **Waldenbooks** at the Kukui Center, open daily 9 a.m.-9 p.m., Sunday 10 a.m.-5:30 p.m., tel. 874-3688. You will find shelves stocked with all kinds of books and titles from fiction to travel guidebooks. Also at the Kukui Center is a **Kukui Laundromat,** tel. 879-7211, open weekdays 10 a.m.-5 p.m., Saturday 10 a.m.-2 p.m., featuring self- or full-service.

Mail Boxes Etc. at Longs Shopping Center, 1215 S. Kihei Rd., open weekdays 8 a.m.-6 p.m., Saturday 9 a.m.-5 p.m., Sunday 10 a.m.-3 p.m., offers fax services, copies, notary, and packing and shipping.

The main **U.S. post office** in Kihei is located near Azeka Place at 1254 S. Kihei Rd., tel. 879-2403.

For medical emergencies try: **Kihei Physicians,** tel. 879-7781, at 1325 S. Kihei Rd., Suite 103, open 8 a.m-8 p.m. (till 5 p.m. Saturday, 1 p.m. Sunday); **Kihei-Wailea Medical Center,** tel. 874-8100, at 41 E. Lipoa St., with physicians, a pharmacy, physical therapy, and a clinical laboratory (same hours as Kihei Physicians); or **Kihei Clinic and Wailea Medical Service,** tel. 879-7447, at 1993 S. Kihei Rd., open 24 hours a day. Chiropractic services are available at the **Chiropractic Clinic of Kihei,** tel. 879-7246, at 1819 S. Kihei Rd., which specializes in nonforce techniques.

KEITH PERKINS

WAILEA AND BEYOND

Wailea ("Waters of Lea" or "Joyful Waters") isn't for the hoi polloi. It's a deluxe resort area custom-tailored to fit the egos of the upper class like a pair of silk pajamas. This section of southeastern Maui was barren and bleak until Alexander and Baldwin Inc. decided to landscape it into an emerald 1,450-acre oasis of world-class golf courses and destination resorts. Every street light, palm tree, and potted plant is a deliberate accessory to the decor so that the overall feeling is soothing, pleasant, and in good taste. To dispel any notions of snootiness, the five sparkling beaches that front the resorts were left open to the public and improved with better access, parking areas, showers, and picnic tables—a gracious gesture even if state law does require open access! You'll know when you leave Kihei and enter Wailea. The green, quiet, and wide tree-lined avenues give the impression of an upper-class residential area. Wailea is where you come when quality is the most important aspect of your vacation. The brilliant five-star resorts are first-rate architecturally, and the grounds are exquisite botanical jewel boxes.

Onward And Backward

If you turn your back to the sea and look toward Haleakala, you'll see its cool, green forests and peak wreathed in mysterious clouds. You'll want to run right over, but you can't get there from here! Outrageous as it may sound, you have to double back 18 miles to Kahului and then head down Rt. 37 for another 20 miles to get to the spot on Rt. 37 you can so easily see. On the map a neat little road called **Makena Road** connects the Wailea/Makena area with Upcountry in a mere two-mile stretch, but it's closed. An ongoing fight over who's responsible for its maintenance keeps it that way. Once this appalling situation is rectified, you'll be able to travel easily to the **Tedeschi Winery** and continue on the "wrong way" to Hana, or go left to Kula and Upcountry. For now, however, happy motoring!

BEACHES

If you're not fortunate enough to be staying in Wailea, the best reason for coming here is its beaches. These little beauties are crescent moons of white sand that usually end in lava outcroppings on both ends. This makes for sheltered swimmable waters and good snorkeling and scuba. Many of the hotel guests in Wailea seem to hang around the hotel pools, maybe peacocking or just trying to get their money's worth, so the beaches are surprisingly uncrowded. The following beaches are listed from north to south, toward Makena.

Keawakapu
The first Wailea beach, almost a buffer between Kihei and Wailea, is just past the Mana Kai Resort. Turn left onto Kamala Place, or proceed straight on S. Kihei Road until it dead-ends. Plenty of parking at both accesses, but no amenities. Keawakapu is a lovely white-sand beach with a sandy bottom. Good swimming and fair snorkeling. There's also a beginner's dive spot offshore where an underwater junkyard of a few hundred cars forms an artificial reef.

Mokapu And Ulua
These two beaches are shoulder to shoulder, separated only by a rock outcropping. Turn right off Wailea Alanui Drive at the first turn past the Inter-Continental Resort. The beach is clearly marked, and there's a parking area, showers, and restrooms. Being resort beaches, they're both particularly well kept. Beautiful white sand and protected waters are perfect for swimming. There's good snorkeling at the outcropping separating the beaches, or swim out to the first reef just in front of the rocks for excellent snorkeling.

Wailea Beach
Travel a half mile past the Wailea town center and turn right onto a clearly marked access road; at the beach there's good parking, also showers and toilets. A short but wide beach of pure white sand, Wailea offers good swimming and bodysurfing, but the snorkeling is only fair.

Polo Beach
Follow Wailea Alanui Drive toward Makena. Turn right at the clearly marked sign near Polo Beach condo. Here also are paved parking, showers, and toilets. Polo Beach is good for swimming and sunbathing, with few tourists. There's excellent snorkeling in front of the rocks separating Polo from Wailea Beach—tremendous amounts of fish, and one of the easiest spots to get to.

ACCOMMODATIONS

Stouffer's Wailea Beach Resort
Always a beauty, Stouffer's, at 3550 Wailea Alanui Dr., Wailea, HI 96753, tel. 879-4900 or (800) 992-4532, is like a rich red cabernet that

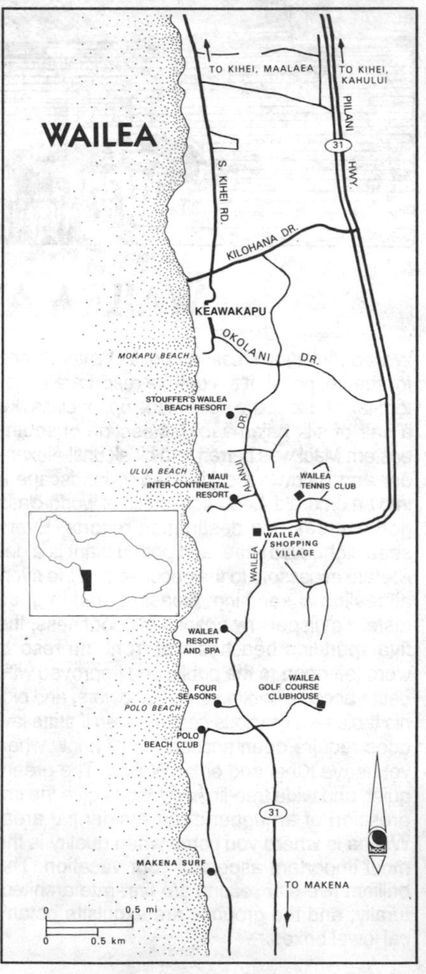

has aged superbly. Now under the direction of general manager Greg Nelson, the hotel has been given a magnificent $45-million face-lift, which included every guest room ($63,000 per room), public area, and nook and cranny. Stouffer's is a superbly appointed resort with attention given to the minutest detail of comfort and luxury. When you enter the main lobby, you're actually on the fifth floor; the ones below terrace down the mountainside to the white-sand beach. The lobby has huge oak and brass doors, original artwork on the walls, and a sweeping marble staircase leading down to the Palm Court Restaurant. The pool area has also been renovated. A bubbling spa fashioned from lava rock is surrounded by vines and flowering trees; another spa contains three little pools and a gurgling fountain, so that while the therapeutic water sooths your muscles, the music of the fountain soothes your nerves. The hotel boasts the best beach in the area, long known as an excellent vantage point from which to view humpback whales in season. The impeccable grounds have grown into an actual botanical garden, with all plants identified. And everywhere there is water, cascading over tiny waterfalls, tumbling in brooks, and reflecting the amazing green canopy in tranquil lagoons.

The white-on-tan rooms are appointed with koa and rattan furniture. Beds are brightened with quilted pillows and each room is accented with standing lamps, paintings of Hawaiian flora, an entertainment center with VCR and remote-control TV, a wall safe, a glass-topped writing desk, a fully stocked wet bar, double closets with padded hangers, even matching *yukata* for an evening of lounging. Sliding doors lead to a lanai where you can relax or enjoy a quiet in-room meal. The luxurious bathrooms have double marble-topped sinks, queen-size tub, pulsing shower head, vanity mirror, hair dryer, and quality lotions, soaps, and creams.

The hotel features the very private **Mokapu Beach Club,** a detached low-rise wing complete with its own pool and daily continental breakfast, where the hotel's impeccable service reaches higher levels with limousine and valet service and 24-hour concierges. Room rates are $215 for a standard to $390 for an ocean view; $400 for the Mokapu Beach Club; $585 for a one-bedroom suite; $25 additional person. Varying rates include a family plan, in which children under 18 stay free in their parents' room, and also golf and tennis packages.

Stouffer's Wailea Beach Resort has been acclaimed as a "Five-Diamond Resort" by the AAA motor club for 10 consecutive years, while **Raffles Restaurant** has won not only official culinary awards but the praise of local residents, particularly for its magnificent Sunday brunch. You will also enjoy the **Palm Court,** another restaurant; the poolside **Maui Onion;** a cocktail lounge; and a luau held twice weekly. Stouffer's offers valet parking, 24-hour room service, a fitness center, a free daily newspaper, and an **Ocean Activities Center** to book you into every kind of outdoor Maui activity. The most amazing feature of the resort is its peace and tranquility.

Maui Inter-Continental Resort

The Maui Inter-Continental Resort, at 3700 Wailea Alanui Dr., Wailea, HI 96753, tel. 879-1922 or (800) 367-2960, is a class act. Even the Wrong Way signs politely state, "*Please,* Do Not Enter." The main lobby, supported by gigantic wooden beams, is inviting with overstuffed chairs in a formal setting, while a wall of glass frames a wide panorama of the sea and Lanai floating on the horizon. Walk out onto a stone-tiled portico and below, in a central courtyard ringed by palms, is a series of quiet koi ponds highlighted with red torch ginger. Stroll the 22 meticulously landscaped acres, and dip into either of the two pools: one for relaxing, the other a lap pool designed to give the illusion that you are swimming out to sea.

At least 70% of the rooms have ocean views, which in most cases are actually oceanfront. Rooms are coordinated with light pastel tones of green-on-tan and beige, and are appointed with marble-topped writing desks and incidental tables. Each has a large entertainment center with remote-control TV, a fully stocked minibar, a coffeemaker, and a double closet with full-length mirror. Marble bathrooms are lavish with full bath and shower, double sinks, and separate dressing area. Doors open to a terra-cotta floored lanai, flushed with sunshine and sea breezes, from where you have a private view of the Lahaina Roads. More amenities include 24-hour room service, self-service laundry, valet parking, beauty salon, and fitness center. Rates

Stouffer's Wailea Beach Resort sets the standard of excellence in Wailea.

run $159 for a standard to $279 for a deluxe; suites are available from $750, $30 per extra person. Special family, room and car, honeymoon, and golf packages are available.

Four Seasons Resort Wailea
The Four Seasons Resort Wailea, 3900 Wailea Alanui, Wailea, HI 96753, tel. 874-8000 or (800) 334-6284, situated at the south end of Wailea Beach, is oriented to the setting sun and opens itself up to the sweet sea breezes. Casually elegant, the open-air lobby is full of cushy chairs and couches, fountains, flowers, fans, and a grand staircase that glides down to the huge pool at beach level. The pool and the colonnade of lobby pillars above it hint at a Romanesque architectural influence, yet the ambience and colors of the hotel say island natural. Original artwork and reproductions hang throughout the lobby and hallways, while huge fossilized sea anemones are displayed on lobby tables, and birds and plants bring the outdoors inside. Countless little details make this resort pleasant and special.

The Four Seasons is a study of cream-on-cream, and this color scheme runs throughout the resort, offset by coral, almond, muted greens, and other pastels. Each large unit has a bedroom and sitting area, a bath with separate shower and deep tub, a well-stocked wet bar, TV and complimentary video, a room safe, and a private lanai; 85% of the rooms have an ocean view and all have twice-daily room service. While air-conditioning is standard, rooms also have sliding screen doors or louvered French doors and overhead fans. Double rooms and suites are even more spacious, with the addition of a second bathroom and/or a dining area. Rates run $325-500 for a partial-to-full ocean view, $75 extra person, and $650-2200 for a suite. Rates on the Club Floor, which includes on-floor check-in, complimentary continental breakfast, afternoon tea, sunset cocktails and hors d'oeuvres, and a personal concierge, run an additonal $100 a day for two people, $80 extra person. The club lounge on this floor provides books, newspapers, magazines, and board games. Golf, family, room and car, and other special packages are available.

Other amenities include a lounge, a games bar with a fine collection of surfing memorabilia, meeting rooms for conventions, complimentary valet parking, 24-hour room service, and an early arrival-late departure lounge where you can relax and enjoy the hotel services, store a small bag, or shower off the grit of travel. On-site are two tennis courts; lawn croquet; an expanded health club with exercise machines and a steam room; and organized beach activities. Five shops are also here, among them **Viewpoint** for alohawear; **Hildgund Jewelers;** and **Lamonts,** a gift and sundries shop. A hotel-supervised, full-day (9 a.m.-5 p.m.) children's activities program is available for youngsters 5-12 years old.

The Four Seasons' three **restaurants** are the Seasons, Pacific Grill, and poolside Cabana Cafe. With its table linen, crystal, classical music, and a jacket requirement for men, **Seasons** is elegant but not stuffy—the decor is weathered bamboo, the windows are open to let in sea breezes and moonlight, and the island cuisine is offered in a "homelike" presentation. Dinner is 6-10 p.m. nightly, and reservations are recommended. Open all day, the **Pacific Grill** is more casual, with alohawear and activewear the norm. Breakfast offers a choice of buffets. The lunch menu includes sandwiches, salads, and pasta. Dinner entrees are from Asia and the Pacific, some cooked in view of the guests at the "oriental exhibition kitchen." For a quick bite, try a burger, *pu pu,* or a tropical drink at the **Cabana Cafe** 11 a.m.-7 p.m.

Kea Lani Hotel

While Aladdin napped and dreamed of high adventure, his genie was at work building a pleasure dome more splendid than the great Khan's Xanadu. The Kea Lani Hotel, 4100 Wailea Alanui, Wailea, HI 96753, tel. 875-4100 or (800) 659-4100, is an alabaster fantasy bazaar where turrets and cupolas cover vaulted and coved ceilings suspended above towering pillars. Enter the central lobby, an open-air court with a bubbling fountain, completely sculpted and gilded; sultan's slippers would be appropriate here to pad around on the mosaic floors. A staircase leads to a tranquil pool area fronting a wide sweep of grass and perpetual blue sea. On the second level is a parlor, formal but comfortable, with giant shoji-like mirrors and sculpted harps and lyres embedded in the walls.

Lodging at the Kea Lani is in one-bedroom luxury suites priced $235-385, or in opulent two- and three-bedroom villas priced $695-995 that include a car and private pool. Enter a suite, very roomy at just under 900 square feet, to see the rich embossed weave of a Berber carpet contrasting with white-on-white walls. Double doors open to the master bedroom with its own entertainment center, minibar, large dresser/vanity, and brass valet. The parlor, formal but comfy, is appointed with puff-pillowed chairs, a queen-size sleeper sofa, an entertainment center, marble-topped tables, and a full bar with microwave and coffeemaker. All rooms are air-conditioned, but there are also ceiling fans. The bathroom, marble from floor to ceiling, features an oversized tub, two pedestal sinks, a huge stall shower, Neutrogena bath products, a full-length mirror, a hair dryer, and a vanity mirror. Cotton *yukata* are yours for a day of lounging. A steam iron and board are available for last-minute touch ups.

The villas are magnificent. Outside each is a private courtyard complete with table, cotton-clad chaise lounges, and a plunge pool, slightly heated and perfect for two. Inside, the bi-level villa includes a completely tiled living room furnished with an oriental rug, glass-topped tables, couches and chairs, and a complete entertainment center. The kitchen includes a fridge, stove, microwave, trash compactor, dishwasher, and laundry room. Two downstairs bedrooms, each with full baths, pamper you with queen-size beds. Upstairs, an alcove leads to the master bedroom self-contained with entertainment center; minibar; two pedestal sinks; a deep, almost two-person tub; and a huge shower area. The walk-in closet, as large as many hotel rooms, features a wall safe.

The hotel's pool area is grand, just right for frolicking or for savoring an afternoon siesta. A free-form upper pool, boasting a swim-to bar, and serviced by the **Polo Beach Grill,** is connected to the lower pool by a 140-foot water slide. The lower area is family oriented with a football-shaped children's pool, but escape is at hand at the casbah pool, inlaid with multihued tiles forming an entwined moon and sun; adults can shelter in Camelot-like tents providing shade and privacy.

Other amenities include a video library, a complimentary fitness center, a clutch of swank boutiques, a jewelry store, and a hair salon. The children have their own **Keiki Kealani,** "Children's Heaven," open daily 9 a.m.-3 p.m., where for $15 children ages 5-12 are fed lunch and entertained with a mixture of fun and educational activities.

For casual dining visit **Cafe Ciao,** rich with the smell of espresso, where the shelves hold homemade jellies, jams, chutney, peppercorn ketchup, and Italian olives. Choose fresh-baked bread, pastries, a spicy focaccia, pesto salad, even ready-to microwave Italian rigatoni and chicken Parmesan.

Towering glass and wooden doors open into **Kealani, the Restaurant,** where you're guaranteed an elegant dining experience in this sanctuary hung with huge chandeliers and capped with a molded ceiling. Ocean breezes flow freely through louvered windows into the white-on-gray great hall furnished with marble-topped tables. For a romantic evening, choose a table in a more intimate area, where a lowered ceiling, and a massive sideboard filled with wine and set with pottery, create a warmer, candlelit atmosphere. At the entrance to the restaurant is a lounge area with a hand-rubbed wooden bar that offers evening entertainment, usually a jazz or Hawaiian ensemble.

Grand Wailea Resort And Spa

A sublime interplay of cascading water, light diffused and brilliant, and the music of natural sound, has been entwined with fine art, sculpted landscaping, and brilliant architecture to create the intangible quality of grandeur so apparent at the astounding Grand Wailea Resort and Spa, 3850 Wailea Alanui Dr., Wailea, HI 96753, tel. 875-1234. On arrival the spume of a thunderous waterfall, misting a heroic sculpture of the warrior king, Kamehameha, is the tangible spirit of the grand hotel. Inside the towering reception atrium, alive with the essences of over 10,000 plants, flowers, and ferns, the interplay of water and sculpture continues. Hula dancers both male and female, some with arms outstretched to the sun, others in repose or in a stance of power, sing silent *mele* of ancient times. A mermaid, bronzed, bare-breasted, offers a triton shell of sweet water, and behind, sleek canoes float on a pond of blue. Alcoves and arches frame dramatic scenes in every direction. Ahead the glimmering sea, foaming surf, and wind-tossed palms dance to their immortal tunes. Left and right, Fernando Botero's sculpted women—enormous, buxom, and pleasant—lie in alluring repose. Bellhops, in starched white livery, lead you to your room over marble floors embossed with mosaic tiles and laid with rich carpets.

Rooms, the least expensive of which has an ocean view, feature private lanai that look out over the water and flower gardens below, while inside they are sanctuaries of pure luxury. Each is appointed in soothing earth tones with comfortable puff-pillowed chairs, complete entertainment center with remote-control color TV, VCR, mini-fridge and bar, in-room safes, multiple phones, twice-daily maid service, and turndown service. Rates are $350-425 standard room, $500 Regency Club, and $700-8000 luxury suite.

If Nero had had the health and relaxation resources found at the hotel's **Spa Grande,** his fiddle playing would have vastly improved and Rome would never have burned. You enter the facility and the magic begins as soon as you shed your clothing and don a fluffy terrycloth robe. Walk the marble floors and choose a loofah scrub or dip first into a Japanese *o furo* that unjangles nerves and soothes muscles. From there, take a cold dip to revitalize your body and then go into the **Terme Circuit,** a series of baths, each more intriguing than the last. Choose from a Jell-O green papaya bath, a dark green *limu* bath, a mud bath, or the crystal waters of an aroma bath. Special to the facility are the Hawaiian rejuvenating bath, made from Hawaiian alaea salt and a number of spices, and the tropical enzyme bath, especially good for the skin. From there a cascading waterfall massages you with watery fingers, or a jet bath sends 50 penetrating streams of water in varying temperatures that let you know you are indeed alive. Awaiting you are private massage rooms where you can choose from seven different types of massage and five different types of facials. Each room opens to the sea, whose eternal rhythm helps create complete relaxation.

The pool area surrounds a "volcano" and fronts Wailea Beach. Here, a formal fountain, surrounded by royal palms, is reflected in a rectangular pool inlaid with white and gold tile forming a giant hibiscus. A canyon riverpool, complete with gentle current, glides you through a series of pools, and past small grottoes where you can stop to enjoy a jacuzzi, swing like Tom Sawyer on a suspended rope, swim up to a bar for your favorite drink, or just slip along until you are deposited in the main pool. Waiting is the world's only water elevator that lifts you to the top again and again.

The resort's eclectic mix of restaurants—all landscaped around the central theme of water, art, and flowers—offers cuisines catering to all tastes and appetites. **The Grand Dining Room**

Maui is French with an Asian twist. Start with wonderful appetizers like lobster noodle soufflé at $12.50, Maui onion broth with Gruyère for $6, or Mandarin chicken salad for $11. Entrees beginning at $27 range from grilled *ahi* Nicoise, to Hoisin encrusted lamb loin. A fun and informal restaurant more reasonably priced is **Bistro Molokini,** Italiano with antipasti for under $9; pasta smothered in everything from shrimp to pancetta for under $19; pizza with fresh tomato, cheeses, and Italian meats for under $16; and main dishes like picatta milanese (veal dipped in Parmesan and served with risotto) for $27. **Humuhumu** is a thatched-roof Polynesian restaurant afloat on its own lagoon complete with 2,000 varieties of tropical fish. The specialties prepared at Humuhumu come from throughout the Pacific. *Pu pu* like fried coconut shrimp for $12, or a dim sum basket for $9.50, are great to nibble on while enjoying a special exotic drink like a Humu Heaven. Entrees are delightful offerings like wok-seared scallops SIchuan for $27, or an enormous porterhouse steak for $30.

The **Cafe Kula** specializes in "spa cuisine," dishes especially prepared with dynamic health in mind. Here the freshest fruits, organic vegetables, and whole grains provide the foundation for most dishes. For breakfast enjoy fresh carrot juice $4.50, housemade granola at $7, or apple-stuffed crepes with fresh brandied currants for $8. Appetizers are spicy black bean chili for $6, or summer oranges with raspberries and papaya for $6. Healthful entree choices are Basmati rice torte for $11.50, or grilled salmon at $13. Perhaps the most elegant restaurant is **Kincha,** serving superb Japanese cuisine. Enter over stepping stones past a replica of a golden tea kettle used by Toyotomi Hideyoshi, revered as both a great warrior and a master of the *chanoyu,* tea ceremony. Follow the stones past stone lanterns that light your way over a hump-backed bridge, a symbol of life, that crosses a tiny stream brimming with orange and white koi. Inside a raised tatami area awaits you with sushi chefs ready to perform their magic. Private rooms, comfortable with *zabuton* backrests, are perfect for a very refined full meal. For a treat order the sashimi *moriawase,* a sampler of the best sashimi for $40; or start with a hot appetizer like *kani shumai,* deep-fried croquette of crab for $10. Soups and salads are *wafu* salad, greens in a Japanese dressing for $7; *miso wan,* a traditional soup for $3; or *cha soba,* tea flavored buckwheat noodles for $10. Entrees are Japanese favorites like *hamachi* teriyaki, broiled yellowtail tuna at $30, or tempura, regular or deluxe $35-$55.

To make a family visit perfect, there is **Camp Wallea,** $35 per day, for children ages 3-15. The day camp, run by professionals, features movies, a preschool playroom, arts and crafts, a computer learning center, a video-game room, and a kids' restaurant with their own dance floor and soda fountain. **Rock Wailea** is a nightclub for teenagers, with dance floor, light show, and nonalcoholic bar. The nondenominational **chapel** is a miniature cathedral with floor to ceiling stained-glass windows by renowned Indonesian artist Yvonne Cheng. Finally, there's a number of exclusive shops and boutiques for your shopping pleasure.

Destination Resorts

This complex is located at 3750 Wailea Alanui, Wailea, HI 96753, tel. (800) 367-5246 Mainland; (800) 423-8773, ext. 510, Canada; and 879-1595 collect in Hawaii. It is made up of four separate villages: **Ekolu,** $135-160, near the golf course; **Ekahi,** the least expensive, from $130 near the tennis courts; **Elua,** the most expensive, from $265 near the sea; and **Grand Champions,** from $175 on the golf links. Rates are lower during the off-season, and special golf and car packages are available. There is a three-night minimum stay, $20 fee for extra person, and daily housekeeping service. All units are plush and fully furnished, with swimming pools and tennis courts on the premises. The beach, two golf courses, and additional tennis courts are nearby.

FOOD

Raffles Restaurant

Glide regally down the marble and burnished brass central staircase from the main lobby of Stouffer's Wailea Beach Resort to Raffles Restaurant, tel. 879-4900, reservations a must, dinner 6:30-10:30 p.m. nightly except Monday, dress semi-formal. Pass through enormous double doors into a formal room with boldly upholstered high-backed chairs, wrought-iron tables, a full-service marble bar, a grand piano, and an intimate hardwood dance floor. Inspired by the famed Raffles of Singapore, this restaurant lives up to the founders' tradition. Sashimi, lobster, and crab cocktails tantalize your taste buds, preparing them for the entrees. Salads galore, including mushroom, spinach, and Manoa lettuce—all in savory dressings—complement lobster bisque or Maui onion soup. Roast rack of lamb, *onaga* with baby spinach and caviar, or veal grenadine in whiskey cream are just some of the delights prepared by the chefs. Wines are from the best vineyards around the world, and magnificent desserts make you pray for just a little more room.

Raffles Sunday Brunch, 9 a.m.-2 p.m., is legendary. For $29 you choose from a selection of the best island fruits and vegetables, and a table laden with rich and creamy desserts. Omelettes made to order are stuffed with seafood, crunchy vegetables, or plump Portuguese sausages. The entree table groans with chops, steaks, fresh fish, caviar, prosciutto, crab, lobster, eggs Benedict, and more. Steaming pots of coffee are brought to every table while waiters continually change used table settings. Be smart and sample slowly; this is gourmet food that demands a gourmet attitude.

The **Palm Court** is Stouffer's main dining room. Walk though the lobby and look over the rail to the partially open-air restaurant below, open for breakfast 6-11 a.m. and for dinner nightly from 6 p.m. The menu offers a different buffet every night, featuring cuisines ranging from Italian to Southwestern. The Palm Court is a first-rate restaurant with very reasonable prices, the best in its category in Wailea.

Stouffer's **Sunset Terrace** is a delightful perch on which to have a drink and survey the grounds and beach below. Every evening brings a dramatic torch-lighting ceremony. The drums reverberate and the liquid melancholy of the conch trumpet sends a call for meditation at day's end. Drinks include the full complement of island specialties, and you can order wonderful gourmet-quality *pu pu.*

The **Maui Onion** is a convenient snack-type restaurant at poolside. Burgers, sandwiches, salads, smoothies, and Maui onion rings, their specialty, are on the limited menu. Prices are reasonable, especially if you don't want to budge from your lounge chair. On Wednesday and Friday evenings 5:30-8:30 p.m., relax here and dine under the stars on a limited choice of entrees.

Hula Moon

The Maui Inter-Continental's Hula Moon, open daily for lunch and dinner, is a casual indoor/outdoor restaurant draped with awnings for shade and privacy. The name Hula Moon derives from the writings of Don Blanding, Hawaii's poet laureate, who arrived by steamship in 1924, dead broke, and remained for over 40 years, all the while singing the island's praises. At the restaurant's entrance are opened drawers from Don Blanding's desk filled with memories—Lucky Strike cigarettes, round sunglasses, a box camera, matchboxes, and playing cards—all whispering of the time when Hawaii was a distant land where only the rich and famous came to escape. Choose a table or horseshoe booth and for lunch dine on everything from a juicy foot-long hot dog for $6.95 to an *ahi caballero*—fresh grilled tuna strips with spices, pepper, onions, and tomatoes served with warm flour tortillas for $10.50. The poolside menu, basically appetizers, offers Chinese spring rolls for $4.50, or an assortment of sandwiches like a tuna pocket for $9. For dinner, the menu begins with coconut-fried shrimp and spicy marmalade for $8.50, or chicken sautéed with peanut sauce for $6.50. A famous specialty is Oh Joy's steamed seafood basket—scallops, lobster, fish, prawns, Chinese dim sum, and Alaskan crab legs brushed with herb butter, all served with a trio of dipping sauces for $38. Enjoy a mixed seafood grill for $28.95, a whole Maine lobster at market price, or grilled shrimp and scallops for $18.95. Hula Moon has an extensive wine list, with selections from France to Australia, and a full bar serving exotic drinks.

A special **Sunday Champagne Brunch** is offered in the Makani Room 9 a.m.-1 p.m. for $28. Let the piano accompaniment soothe your soul as you satiate your body with made-to-order omelettes; fresh fruits and pastries; or mouthwatering entrees of fish, poultry, and meat. Another hotel restaurant is the **Lanai Terrace,** an all-day restaurant where you can have a great meal at an affordable price.

The **Inu Inu Lounge** is a full-service bar where you can dance to live music Tues.-Sat. 9 p.m.-closing. Completely open and protected by floor-to-ceiling glass, the lounge offers a romantic view of the beach and ocean in the background. Enjoy **Maui's Merriest Luau** every Tuesday, Thursday, and Friday from 5:30 p.m. (see "Luau" under "Hawaiian Foods" in the "Food and Drink" section of the Out and About chapter).

Seasons

Located in the Four Seasons Resort, this elegant restaurant is an experience in fine dining. Luxuriate in the teal and bamboo surroundings, or sit on the terrace and look out over the ocean at the sunset. Emphasis is on island seafood such as pan-fried pink snapper with braised fennel and apple raisin curry sauce, sashimi, gazpacho, and prawns for $25-39. Open 6-10 p.m., tel. 874-8000, reservations recommended and proper dress required.

The all-day and casual **Pacific Grill** restaurant combines a large selection of foods from East and West; the breakfast buffet is a long-established special. For sandwiches and tropical drinks anytime until sundown, try the **Cabana Cafe** at poolside. At dusk, catch the Hawaiian music and hula dancers at the cafe or stroll up to **Lobby Lounge** to catch the multi-hued sunset curtain descending upon this beautiful tropical setting.

Sandcastle Restaurant

Located at Wailea Shopping Village, tel. 879-0606, this moderate restaurant is far enough out of the way that you can count on getting a table, but reservations are recommended anyway. The restaurant, overlooking a small courtyard, has wraparound glass and mirrors, vaulted ceilings, and latticework partitions allowing for some privacy. Lunch, served daily 11 a.m.-3 p.m., offers a full range of sandwiches at $5.95-10.95. Lighter appetites will enjoy a full salad selection at $6.95-8.95, which you can combine with a pizza for a full yet inexpensive meal. "Early bird specials," offered 5-6 p.m., are complete dinners for $9.95-14.95. Otherwise the dinner menu offers entrees like roasted rack of lamb for $19.95, filet mignon for $18.95, fresh catch at the daily quote, and prime rib of beef au jus for $16.95. The Sandcastle has a full bar and an excellent wine list.

Golf Ball Soup

The following restaurants are located at the golf links in the area. **The Chart House,** on the 15th fairway of Wailea Blue Course across from the Wailea Shopping Village, 100 Wailea Ike Dr., tel. 879-2875, open nightly for dinner from 5:30 p.m., is part of a small chain that deserves its reputation for consistently well-prepared and reasonably priced food. The menu has starters like artichoke salad for $5.25, shrimp cocktail for $8.95, or Caesar salad for $8.95. Entrees include New York pepper steak for $24.95, prime rib for $21.95, grilled chicken breast for $16.50, and shrimp Santa Fe at $19.95. There's a children's menu with most dinners priced under $6.95. Also on the premises is the **Sunset Lounge,** an open-air bar open 5 p.m.-closing, where you can enjoy an evening cocktail.

The Maui Lobster Cove Restaurant, tel. 879-7677, across from The Chart House, open nightly 5:30-10 p.m., is a seafood restaurant that also makes sushi. Delicious appetizers include warm lobster salad in a ginger cocktail sauce for $10.95, or fresh lobster cakes for $10.95. Entrees include Maine and Pacific lobster, and Dungeness crab, all at market price, as well as fresh fish served poached, sautéed, or broiled. Lobster Cove specialties are grilled *ahi* for $20.95, sautéed prawns over pasta for $18.95, and sushi and sashimi from **Harry's Sushi and Pupu Bar,** which you can order as appetizers or as a Japanese meal.

Fairway Restaurant, at the Wailea Golf Course clubhouse, tel. 879-4060, is across the street from the entrance to Polo Beach. Open from 7:30 a.m. for breakfast, which is everything from eggs Benedict for $5.95 to a simple omelette for $4.75 to buttermilk pancakes, all you can eat, for $3.50. Lunch offers burgers and sandwiches at $5-7. Dinner selections, $15-20, include filet mignon, New York pepper steak, veal parmigiana, or salad bar for $11.95. Although the dining room isn't ultra fancy, there's a terrace, and the ambience is peaceful and unhurried. A good place to eat in an area not known for budget restaurants.

At the Wailea Tennis Club is the **Set Point Cafe,** tel. 879-3244. Stop here for breakfast or light lunch after a game.

ENTERTAINMENT, SHOPPING, AND SERVICES

Entertainment

If you haven't had enough fun on the Wailea beaches during the day, you can show off your best dance steps at the Inter-Continental's **Inu Inu Room** that swings with live music and disco dancing nightly, or you can dance the night away at Four Seasons' **Sunset Bar.**

Golf And Tennis

Two of the main attractions in Wailea are the fantastic golf and tennis opportunities. **Wailea Golf Club,** tel 879-2966, has two magnificent golf courses laid out on Haleakala's lower slopes, both open to the public. Tennis is great at the **Wailea Tennis Club,** tel. 879-1958, and many of the hotels and condos have their own championship courts. Please see the Tennis and Golf charts in the Maui Introduction for rates and specifics.

Wailea Shopping Village

The only shopping in this area is at Wailea Shopping Village, open daily 9 a.m.-7 p.m., Sunday 10 a.m.-6 p.m., just east past the Inter-Continental Hotel off Wailea Alanui Drive. It has the usual collection of boutiques and shops. **Superwhale** offers alohawear for children. **Kiwina's** sells fine jewelry, while **Miki's** has racks of alohawear at very competitive prices. More exclusive shops are: **Sea and Shells** with a range of gifts from the iṣlands; **Isle Style,** a fine-arts gallery with works by local artists; the **Elephant Walk,** a shopping gallery of fine crafts; **Alexia's** for natural fiber fashions; **For Your Eyes Only,** which sells sunglasses for every eye and lifestyle. Money needs are handled by the **First Hawaiian Bank; Island Camera** offers accessories and processing; **Whaler's General Store** sells food and liquor; and **Ed and Don's** sells fast food, sandwiches, ice cream, beverages, and gift-food items. The **Maui Dive Shop** is a full-service dive shop with snorkel and scuba rentals, sales, and diving excursions.

The major hotels have an arcade of shops for quick and easy purchases. One of note is the **Coast Gallery, Maui** at the Inter-Continental, which displays a wide range of mostly island art, including some unique wood and pottery pieces not usually on display at art galleries.

Transportation

The **Wailea Shuttle** is a complimentary jitney that stops at all major hotels and condos, the Wailea Shopping Village, and golf and tennis courts in Wailea about every 20 minutes. It operates 6:30 a.m.-10:30 p.m. With a little walking, this is a great way to hop from one beach to the next.

MAKENA TO LA PEROUSE

Just a skip south down the road is Makena Beach, but it's a world away from Wailea. This was a hippie enclave during the '60s and early '70s, and the freewheeling spirit of the times is still partially evident in the area even though Makena is becoming more refined, sophisticated, and available to visitors. For one thing, "Little Makena" is a famous clothes-optional (unofficial) beach, but so what? You can skinny-dip in Connecticut. What's really important is that Makena is *the last* pristine coastal stretch in this part of Maui that hasn't succumbed to undue development . . . yet. As you head down the road you'll notice Hawaii's unofficial bird, the building crane, arching its mechanical neck and lifting girders into place. The Japanese firm of Seibu Hawaii has built the Maui Prince Hotel, and more luxury accommodations are on the rise. Wailea Point, a promontory of land between Wailea and Makena, is the site of one, and others will be across the road near the golf courses.

Aside from the sundries shop at the Maui Prince Hotel, there's nothing in the way of amenities past Wailea, so make sure to stock up on supplies. The police come in and sweep the area now and again, but mostly it's mellow. They do arrest the nudists on Little Makena to make the point that Makena "ain't free no more"

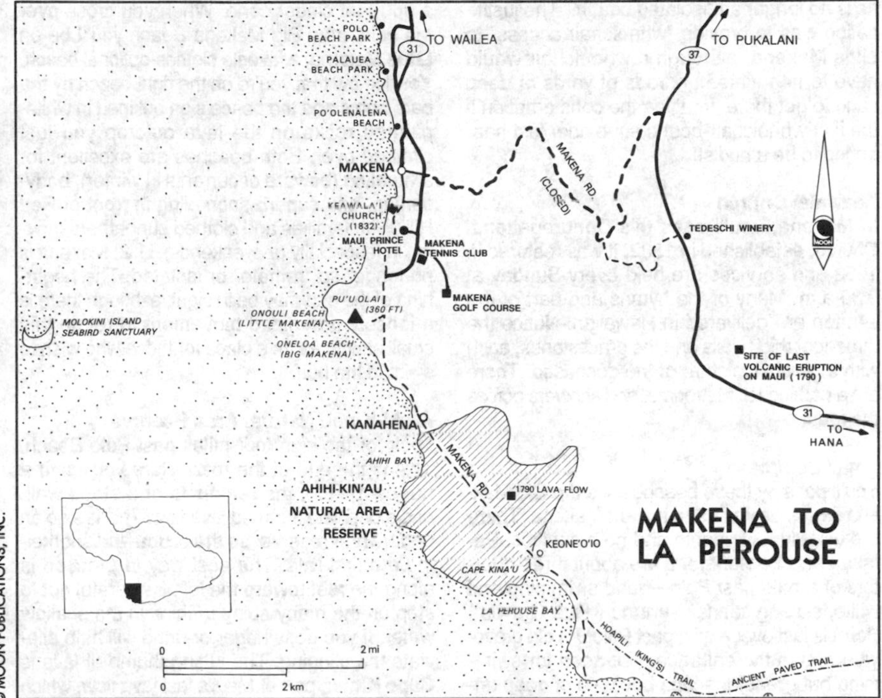

(see "The Naked Truth" below). Rip-offs can be a problem, so lock your car, hide your camera, and don't leave anything of value. Be careful of the *kiawe* thorns when you park; they'll puncture a tire like a nail.

Makena is magnificent for bodysurfing and swimming. Whales frequent the area and come quite close to shore during the season. Turtles waddled on to Makena to lay their eggs in the warm sand until early in this century, but too many people gathered the eggs and the turtles scrambled away forever. The sunsets from **Red Hill** (Puu Olai), the cinder cone separating Big Makena from Little Makena, are among the best on Maui; you can watch the sun sink down between Lanai, Kahoolawe, and West Maui. The silhouettes of pastel and gleaming colors are awe-inspiring. Oranges, russets, and every shade of purple reflect off the clouds caught here. Makena attracts all kinds: gawkers, burn-outs, adventurers, tourists, free spirits, and a lot of locals. It won't last long, so go and have a look now!

The Naked Truth

Some years ago in an extremely controversial episode, the Maui police came down hard on the nudists. They arrested nine top-free women from various parts of the U.S. and from foreign countries. The police acted in defiance of a recent Hawaii Supreme Court ruling that a woman's breasts when uncovered in appropriate circumstances (i.e., isolated beaches) do not violate the state's "open lewdness" statute. The women, defended by attorney Anthony Ranken, sought compensation for malicious prosecution. Some point directly at former Mayor Hannibal Tavares for running a personal crusade against the au naturel sun-worshippers. To show the extent of the conflict, one hare-brained scheme actually proposed was to pave a walkway to Puu Olai ("Red Hill") so that Little Makena is no longer an "isolated beach." The justification was to provide "wheelchair access" to Little Makena, although a wheelchair would have to negotiate hundreds of yards of deep sand to get there. Imagine the consternation if the first wheelchair-bound sunbather just happened to be a nudist!

Keawalai Church

In Makena, you'll pass this Congregational Church, established in 1832. It was restored in 1952 and services are held every Sunday at 9:30 a.m. Many of the hymns and part of the sermon are delivered in Hawaiian. Notice the three-foot thick walls and the gravestones, each with a ceramic picture of the deceased. There are a parking lot, restrooms, and showers across the road.

Small Beaches

You'll pass by these beaches, via the Old Makena Road, as you head toward Makena. There are usually few people and no amenities. **Palauea** and **Poolenalena** are about three-quarters of a mile past Polo—good swimming and white, sloping sands. **Nahuna** ("Five Graves") **Point** is just over a mile past Polo. An old graveyard marks the entrance. Not good for swimming but great for scuba because of deep underwater caves. Snorkelers can enjoy this area, too. A short distance farther on is the **Makena Boat Landing** (water, restrooms, showers), a launch site for boaters and scuba divers. **Papipi** is along the road 1.5 miles past Polo, but its small sand beach is too close to the road. **Onouli** ("Black Sand Beach") on the north side of Red Hill actually has a salt-and-pepper beach. Turn down a rutted dirt road for a third of a mile. Not good for swimming, but good diving, unofficial camping, and shore fishing. No amenities.

Makena Beach

A few minutes past the Maui Prince Hotel, look for a *kaukau* wagon on the left where you might pick up a snack before turning right along an access road. Negotiate the excessive speed bumps for a few hundred yards to the parking lot and a few portable toilets; a second beach access is a few hundred yards farther on. This is **Oneloa Beach,** generally called **Makena Big Beach.** Right leads you to **Puu Olai** ("Red Hill"), a 360-foot cinder cone. When you cross over the point from Big Makena Beach you'll be on **Little Makena,** a favorite clothes-optional beach. You'll know that you're on the right beach by the bare bums and the peace sign outlined in white-painted rocks on the lava outcrop you just climbed over. Both beaches are excellent for swimming (beware of currents in winter), bodysurfing, and superb snorkeling in front of Red Hill. With families and clothed sunbathers moving in (especially on weekends), Little Makena is no longer so "remote" or isolated. The beginning of the end may be in sight, although there is a loosely organized movement to retain this small sanctuary as a place for those who wish to swim in the buff.

Ahihi-Kinau Natural Area Reserve

Look for the sign four miles past Polo Beach. This is the end of the road. Here you'll find a narrow beach, the remnants of a stone wall, and a desolate, tortured lava flow. This is also an underwater reserve, so the scuba and snorkeling are first-rate. The best way to proceed is along the reef toward the left. Be careful not to step on the many spiny urchins in the shallow water. If you do, vinegar or urine will help alleviate the stinging. The jutting thumb of lava is **Cape Kinau,** part of Maui's last lava flow, which occurred in 1790.

La Perouse Bay

Just shy of six miles from Polo Beach, the bay is named after the French navigator Jean-François La Pérouse, first Westerner to land on Maui in May 1786. The bay is good for snorkelers and divers, but beware of the urchins on entry. If you walk left you'll come across a string of pocket-sized beaches. The currents can be tricky along here. Past the bay are remains of the **Hoapili** ("King's") **Trail,** still hikable along some of its distance.

PRACTICALITIES

A gleaming white hexagonal building, understated and almost stark on the outside, the **Maui Prince Hotel,** 5400 Makena Alanui Rd., Kihei, HI 96753, tel. 874-1111 or (800) 321-6284, is a fabulous destination resort that opens into an enormous central courtyard, one of the most beautiful in Hawaii. Japanese in its architecture and its sense of beauty, the courtyard is a protected haven of cascading waters, black lava rock, stone lanterns, breeze-tossed palms, and raked Zen-like gardens. Lean over the hardwood rails of the balconies on each floor and soak in the visual pleasure of the landscape below, where from these balconies cascade flowers and ferns in sympathetic mimicry of Maui's waterfalls. Every evening the water is turned off in the central courtyard, and the natural melody is replaced by the duo **Prince Classics,** who perform soothing music for all to enjoy; on Tuesday and Friday evenings an authentic hula show is featured.

All rooms have an alcove door so that you can open your front door to allow the breeze to pass through yet still have privacy. Ocean-view and oceanfront rooms ranging $220-350 are beautifully accentuated in earth tones and light pastels. Each bathroom has a separate commode and a separate shower and tub. Each one-bedroom suite, priced $400-800, features a giant living room, three lanais, a large-screen TV and VCR, and *yukata* robes for lounging. The master bedroom has its own TV, listening center, and king-size bed. A nonsmoking wing is also available, along with honeymoon packages, tennis and golf packages, and a complimentary children's program. The Prince also offers the very reasonable Prince Special that includes an ocean-view room, mid-size rental car, and buffet breakfast for two priced only $189 per night per couple (call for information).

The Maui Prince faces fantastic, secluded Maluaka Beach, almost a small bay, with two points of lava marking it as a safe spot for swimming and snorkeling. Seven sea turtles live on the south point and come up on the beach to nest and lay their eggs. To the left you can see Puu Olai, a red cinder cone that marks Makena. **Ocean Activities Center** arrives each morning with its beach launch and will take you snorkeling to Molokini or arrange other activities throughout the island. The pool area is made up of two circular pools—one for adults, the other a wading pool for kids—and a poolside snack bar. There's volleyball, a children's program (free), croquet, six plexi-pave tennis courts with a pro on the staff, and the 36 holes of the Makena Golf Course, designed by Robert Trent Jones Jr., the main attraction of the Maui Prince. The **concierge desk** offers a variety of complimentary activities including a snorkel and scuba introduction. Sign up here for **Makena Adventures,** an interpretive tour through the entire Makena area via a hotel mini-van.

The Prince has three restaurants, at which head chef Roger Dikon is building an island-wide reputation for exquisite dining. The fanciest restaurant is the **Prince Court,** featuring fine dining for dinner only, except for their truly exceptional Sunday brunch. The evening fare is Hawaiian regional cuisine and then some. Start with appetizers like orange-cured smoked salmon with warm Maui onions for $11.50, or soups and salads that include Hawaiian-style conch chowder with Portuguese sausages and warm Molokini bread for $6. Thai-style hot and sour seafood stew with Manila clams, rock shrimp, scallops, and papaya costs $9.50. From the grill, entrees include Hawaiian slipper lobster curry with coconut milk, Thai yellow curry and ginger chips for $32, or a Napoleon of the fresh catch-of-the-day nestled in collard greens and shiitake mushrooms. Sautéed pink snapper with avocado, artichoke, and lime costs $26. The room's subdued elegance is highlighted with snow-white tablecloths and sparkling crystal. The view is serene facing the courtyard, or dramatic looking out to sea.

When chefs from the best restaurants on Maui want to impress visiting friends with a **brunch,** they come to the Maui Prince on Sunday. For only $24 ($15 for children) you can surpass most of your dining fantasies. You start with a table laden with exotic fruits and fresh-squeezed juices. Nearby are plump and steaming rolls, croissants, and pastries rich in chocolates and creams. Then comes an omelette gauntlet, where you pick and choose your ingredients and an attendant chef creates it before your eyes. Hot entrees for the gastronomically timid are offered, from roast beef to fresh fish. But the real delights are the cornucopia of smoked seafood and shellfish. To the left pâté, to the right sushi, and sashimi straight ahead, or choose cracked crab to nibble while you decide. Fat yellow rounds of imported cheeses squat on huge tables. Waiters and waitresses attend you with fresh plates, champagne by the glass, and pots of coffee. You couldn't possibly eat like this every day, but *sacrifice* yourself at least once while on Maui.

Hakone is a Japanese restaurant and sushi bar with chefs from Japan. They serve complete dinners like sukiyaki or tempura for under $29, and they also serve sushi and sashimi. Traditional seven- to nine-course *kaiseki* dinners run $42-50 per person. In keeping with the tradition of Japan, the room is subdued and simple, with white shoji screens counterpointed by dark open beams. The floor is black slate atop packed sand, a style from old Japan.

The main dining room is **Cafe Kiowai,** open for breakfast, lunch, and dinner, located on the ground level, opening to the courtyard and fishponds. Lunch choices are almost endless, beginning with appetizers like a trio of mini-croissant sandwiches with crab and shrimp, prime rib, and sliced turkey with tomato for $8, or Maui onion soup with jack cheese in a bread bowl for $5. Main courses are seafood curry with mango chutney, coconut flakes, and macadamia nuts at $16, or picatta of veal for $18. Desserts are sinfully rich and delicious. For now, food and accommodations in Makena mean the Maui Prince. The only exception is the **Makena Golf Course Restaurant,** which serves soups, salads, sandwiches, and grilled items for lunch for under $10.

Recreation

As the Maui Prince Hotel is a destination resort, on-site recreation possibilities include the beach, the swimming pool, and a catamaran ride to Molokini with Ocean Activities, which leaves directly from the beach in front of the hotel. Golf at Makena Golf Course and tennis at Makena Tennis Club are just across the road and offer world-class courts and links. See the Golf and Tennis charts in the Maui Introduction for specifics.

Services

Except for phones at the Maui Prince, Makena Golf Course and Tennis Club, the boutique and sundries shops at the hotel, and the showers and restrooms at Keawalai Church, you won't find any amenities.

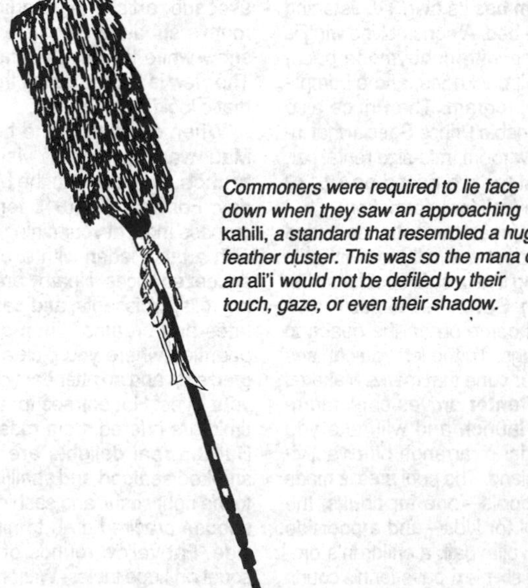

Commoners were required to lie face down when they saw an approaching kahili, *a standard that resembled a huge feather duster. This was so the mana of an* ali'i *would not be defiled by their touch, gaze, or even their shadow.*

UPCOUNTRY

Upcountry is much more than a geographical area to the people who live here: it's a way of life, a frame of mind. You can see Upcountry from anywhere on Maui by lifting your gaze to the slopes of Haleakala. There are no actual boundaries, but this area is usually considered as running from Makawao in the north all the way around to Kahikinui Ranch in the south, and from below the cloud cover up to about the 3,000-foot level. It encircles Haleakala like a large green floral bib patterned by pasturelands and festooned with wild and cultivated flowers. In this rich soil and cool-to-moderate temperatures, cattle ranching and truck farming thrive. Up here, *paniolo* ride herd on the range of the enormous 20,000-acre **Haleakala Ranch,** spread mostly around Makawao, and the even larger 30,000 acres of the **Ulupalakua Ranch**, which *is* the hills above Wailea. **Pukalani,** the largest town, is a way station for gas and supplies. **Makawao** is a real cowboy town with saddleries, rodeos, and hitching posts. It's also sophisticated, with some exclusive shops and fine dining.

Kula is Maui's flower basket. This area is one enormous garden producing brilliant blooms and hearty vegetables. **Polipoli State Recreation Area** is a forgotten wonderland of tall forests, a homoğenized stand of trees from around the world. **Tedeschi Winery** in the south adds a classy touch to Upcountry; you can taste wine in a historic jailhouse. There are plenty of commercial greenhouses and flower farms to visit all over Upcountry, but the best activity is a free Sunday drive along the mountain roads and farm lanes, just soaking in the scenery. The purple mists of mountain jacaranda and the heady fragrance of eucalyptus encircling a mountain pasture manicured by herds of cattle portray the soul of Upcountry.

MAKAWAO

Makawao is proud of itself; it's not *like* a cowboy town, it *is* a cowboy town. Depending on the translation you consult, it means "Eye of the Dawn" or "Forest Beginning." Both are appropriate. Surrounding lowland fields of cane and pineapples give way to upland pastures rimmed with tall forests, as Haleakala's morning sun shoots lasers of light through the town. Makawao was settled late last century by Portuguese immigrants who started raising cattle on the upland slopes. It loped along as a *paniolo* town until WW II, when it received an infusion of life from a nearby military base in Kokomo. After the war it settled back down and became a sleepy village again, where as many horses were tethered on the main street as cars were parked. The majority of its false-front, one-story buildings are a half-century old, but their prototype is strictly "Dodge City, 1850." During the 1950s and '60s, Makawao started to decline into a bunch of worn-out old buildings. It earned a reputation for drinking, fighting, and cavorting cowboys, and for a period was derisively called "Macho-wao."

In the 1970s it began to revive. It had plenty to be proud of and a good history to fall back on. Makawao is *the* last real *paniolo* town on Maui and, with Kamuela on the Big Island, is one of the last two in the entire state. At the Oskie Rice Arena, it hosts the largest and most successful rodeo in Hawaii. Its Fourth of July parade is a marvel of homespun humor, *aloha,* and an old-fashioned good time. Many people ride their horses to town, leaving them to graze in a public corral. They do business at stores operated by the same families for 50 years. Though much of the dry goods are country-oriented, a new breed of merchant has come to town. You can buy a sack of feed, a rifle, designer jeans, and an imported silk blouse all on one street. At its eateries you can have lobster, vegetarian or Mexican food, or a steaming bowl of saimin, reputed to be the best on Maui.

Everyone, old-timers and newcomers alike, agrees that Makawao must be preserved, and they work together. They know that tourism is a financial lifeline, but shudder at the thought of Makawao becoming an Upcountry Lahaina. It shouldn't. It's far enough off the track to keep the average tourist away, but easy enough to reach and definitely interesting enough to make the side trip absolutely worthwhile.

Getting There

The main artery to Makawao is through Paia as you travel Rt. 36 (Hana Hwy.). In Paia turn right onto Baldwin Avenue at the corner marked by the gaily painted "Ice Creams and Dreams" shop. From here it's about six miles to Makawao. You can also branch off Rt. 37 (Haleakala Hwy.) in Pukalani, onto Rt. 365 (some maps show it as Rt. 400) that'll lead you to the town.

SIGHTS

En route on Baldwin Avenue, you pass the **sugar mill,** a real-life Carl Sandburg poem. It's a green monster trimmed in bare lightbulbs at night, groaning with sounds of turning gears, cranes, and linkbelts, all surrounded by packed, rutted, oil-stained soil. Farther along Baldwin Avenue sits **Holy Rosary Church** and its sculpture of Father Damien. The rendering of Damien is idealized, but the leper, who resembles a Calcutta beggar, has a face that conveys helplessness while at the same time faith and hope. It's worth a few minutes' stop. Coming up next is **Makawao Union Church,** and it's a beauty. Like a Tudor mansion made completely of stone with lovely stained-glass windows, it has an entrance framed by two tall and stately royal palms. Farther up is **Rainbow State Park,** one of the few noncoastal parks on Maui and one of two set up for tent camping (see "Camping and Hiking" in the Maui Introduction).

The back way reaches Makawao by branching off Rt. 36 through Ulumalu and Kokomo. Just where Rt. 36 turns into Rt. 360, there's a road to the right. This is Kaupakulua Road, or Rt. 365. Take it through backcountry Maui, where horses graze around neat little houses. Haleakala looms on the horizon; guavas, mangos, and bananas grow wild. At the first Y-intersec-

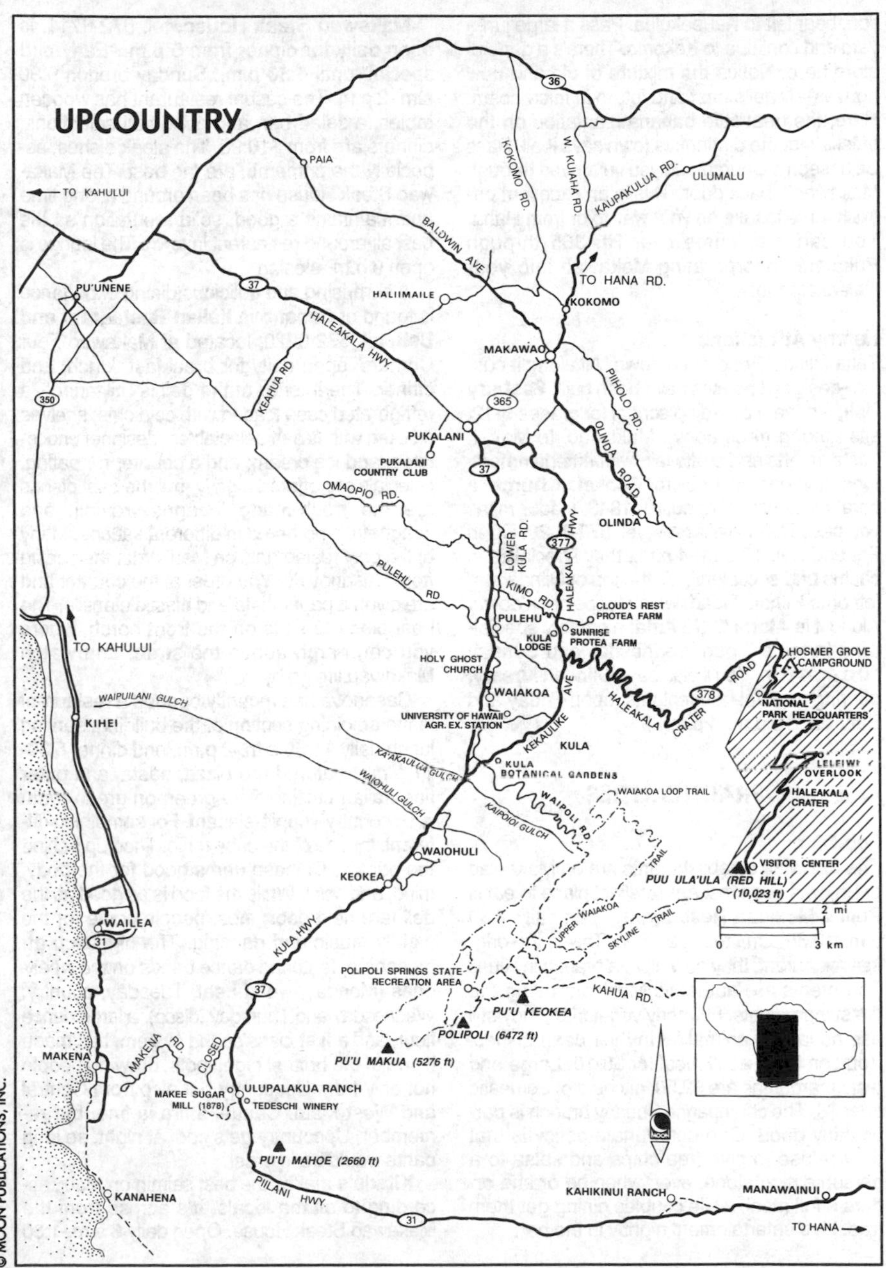
UPCOUNTRY
TO KAHULUI
PAIA
36
KOKOMO RD.
W. KUIAHA RD.
KAUPAKULUA RD.
ULUMALU
BALDWIN AVE
TO HANA RD.
PU'UNENE
37
HALIIMAILE
KOKOMO
HALEAKALA HWY
MAKAWAO
KEAHUA RD
PIIHOLO RD.
350
365
OLINDA ROAD
PUKALANI
PUKALANI COUNTRY CLUB
37
OMAOPIO RD.
OLINDA
LOWER KULA RD.
377
HALEAKALA HWY
PULEHU RD
KIMO RD.
PULEHU
CLOUD'S REST PROTEA FARM
SUNRISE PROTEA FARM
KULA LODGE
TO KAHULUI
HOLY GHOST CHURCH
HOSMER GROVE CAMPGROUND
CRATER ROAD
378
NATIONAL PARK HEADQUARTERS
WAIPUILANI GULCH
WAIAKOA
KIHEI
UNIVERSITY OF HAWAII AGR. EX. STATION
KEKAULIKE AVE
HALEAKALA CRATER
KULA
LELEIWI OVERLOOK
KA'AKAULUA GULCH
WAIOHULI GULCH
KULA BOTANICAL GARDENS
HALEAKALA CRATER
WAIAKOA LOOP TRAIL
WAIPOLI RD.
KAIPOIOI GULCH
WAIOHULI
TRAIL
VISITOR CENTER
KEOKEA
PUU ULA'ULA (RED HILL) (10,023 ft)
WAILEA
UPPER WAIAKOA
SKYLINE TRAIL
0
2 mi
0
3 km
31
KULA HWY
37
POLIPOLI SPRINGS STATE RECREATION AREA
KAHUA RD.
PU'U KEOKEA
POLIPOLI (6472 ft)
PU'U MAKUA (5276 ft)
MAKENA
MAKENA RD.
CLOSED
ULUPALAKUA RANCH
MAKEE SUGAR MILL (1878)
TEDESCHI WINERY
MOON
PU'U MAHOE (2660 ft)
PIILANI HWY
KANAHENA
KAHIKINUI RANCH
MANAWAINUI
31
TO HANA

tion, bear left to Kaupakulua. Pass a large junkyard and continue to Kokomo. There's a general store here. Notice the mixture of old and new houses—Maui's past and future in microcosm. Here, the neat little banana plantation on the outskirts of the diminutive town says it all. Pass St. Joseph's Church and you've arrived through Makawao's back door. This is an excellent off-track route to take on your way to or from Hana. You can also come over Rt. 365 through Pukalani, incorporating Makawao into your Haleakala trip.

Nearby Attractions

Take Olinda Road out of town. All along it custom-designed houses have been built. **Seabury Hall,** a private boarding school for grades 6-12, sits among trees above Makawao. In May, it hosts an arts and crafts fair, with entertainment, food, and games. Look for **Pookela Church,** a coral-block structure built in 1843. In four miles you pass **Rainbow Acres,** tel. 572-8020. Open Fri. and Sat. 10 a.m.-4 p.m., they specialize in cactus and succulents. At the top of Olinda turn left onto Piiholo Road, which loops back down. Along it is **Aloha O Ka Aina,** a nursery specializing in ferns, open Wednesday and Sunday 10 a.m.-4 p.m. You'll also pass **Olinda Nursery,** offering general houseplants, open Friday and Saturday 10 a.m.-4 p.m.

PRACTICALITIES

Food

The following establishments are on Makawao or Baldwin avenues. An excellent place to eat is **Polli's Mexican Restaurant,** open daily 7:30 a.m.-10:30 p.m., tel. 572-7808. This is the original restaurant; they now have a branch in Kihei. The meals are authentic Mexican, using the finest ingredients. Formerly vegetarian, they still use no lard or animal fat in their bean dishes. You can have a full meal for $8-10. Large and tasty margaritas are $2.50, pitchers of domestic beer $6. The champagne Sunday brunch is particularly good. One unfortunate policy is that they refuse to give free chips and salsa to a person dining alone, even when he or she orders a full meal, while couples dining get them free. Live entertainment nightly in the bar.

Makawao Steak House, tel. 572-8711, is open daily for dinner from 5 p.m. "Early bird special" until 6:30 p.m., Sunday brunch 9:30 a.m.-2 p.m. The casual restaurant has wooden tables, a salad bar, and good fish selections; dinners are from $10.95. The steak dishes, especially the prime rib, are the best. The Makawao Steak House has been around a long time and maintains a good, solid reputation as the best all-around restaurant in town. The lounge is open 9 p.m.-closing.

A surprising and delicious dining experience is found at **Casanova Italian Restaurant and Deli,** tel. 572-0220, located at Makawao Four Corners, open daily for breakfast, lunch, and dinner. The interior of the deli is utilitarian—a refrigerated case loaded with cold cuts; shelves stocked with Italian delectables, designer chocolates, and ice cream; and a counter for eating. Specials are offered nightly, but the best dishes are the fresh-made lasagna, ravioli, and spaghetti, smothered in different sauces. Many of the best restaurants on Maui order their pasta from Casanova's. You order at the counter and are given a paper plate and plastic utensils. The best place to sit is on the front porch, where you can perch above the street and watch Makawao life go by.

Casanova has recently opened a restaurant in the adjoining section of the building, serving lunch daily 11:30 a.m.-2 p.m., and dinner 5:30-11 p.m. Featured are pizza, pasta, and other fine Italian cuisine. The green-on-green room is Upcountry-yuppie-elegant. For something different, try one of the Jade tonics lined up behind the bar . . . Chinese herbs good for the body, mind, and spirit. While the food is as good as the deli fare next door, most people come for the nightly music and dancing. The nightclub atmosphere, featuring dance bands on the weekends (Monday, world beat; Tuesday, country; Wednesday and Thursday, disco), a large dance floor, and a first-class sound system, has made it one of the hottest nightspots, drawing people not only from Upcountry but also from Central and West Maui. Casual attire is fine, but remember, Upcountry gets cool at night, so long pants would be in order.

Kitada's makes the best saimin on Maui, according to all the locals. It's across from the Makawao Steak House. Open daily 6 a.m.-1:30

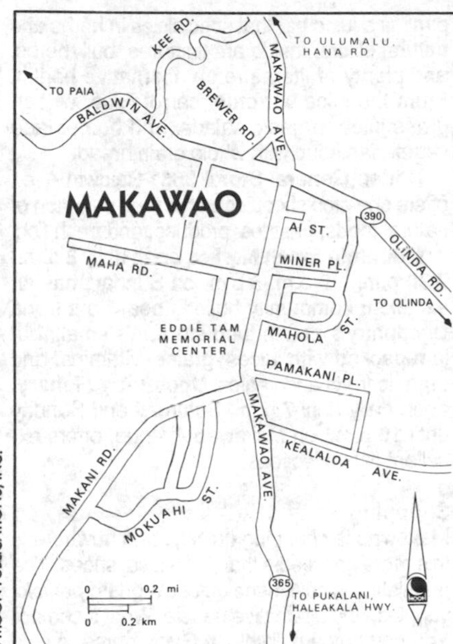

p.m., tel. 572-7241. The 77-year-old owner, Takeshi Kitada, does all the prep work himself. Walk in, pour yourself a glass of water, and take a hardboard-topped table. The saimin is delicious and only $2. There are plate lunches, too. On the walls are paintings of Upcountry by local artists; most show more heart than talent. Bus your own table while Kitada-*san* calculates your bill on an abacus. His birthday, May 26, has become a town event.

Komoda's is a corner general store that has been in business for over 50 years. They sell everything, but their bakery is renowned far and wide. They open at 6:30 a.m., when people are already lined up outside to buy their cream buns and homemade cookies—all gone by 9 a.m.

The **Cross Roads Cafe,** at the corner of Makawao and Baldwin avenues, tel. 572-1101, open daily 8-10:30 a.m. breakfast, 11 a.m.-4 p.m. lunch, 6-8:30 p.m. dinner except Sunday, and 11 a.m.-3 p.m. Sunday brunch, is owned and operated by Neal and Jean Kunin, who have turned their corner into a budget-gourmet restaurant. Sit at the wooden-and-ceramic counter and order a cappuccino, caffe latte, or espresso, accompanied by a fresh-baked pastry, Belgian waffle, bagel, or breakfast burrito. For lunch choose a small Caesar salad at $2.95, a bowl of curried turkey for $3.95, or a vegie burger for $4.95 (with a side of salad $5.95). Dinner, priced $8.95-14.95, brings vegetarian dishes from a cuisine that changes every night and might be Italian, French, Caribbean, Middle Eastern, or Greek.

One of the newest establishments in Makawao is **Circle of the Sun Cafe and Convergence Center.** Open from 7 a.m. for breakfast and lunch, it serves all vegetarian food items. Taking a holistic approach, the center supports programs that are health-conscious, peace oriented, environmentally sound, and financially unexploiting. In esssence, its focus is a campaign for the earth and the uplifting of humanity. A bulletin board here alerts you to similar happenings throughout the island.

The **Courtyard Deli** at the Courtyard of Makawao, 3620 Baldwin Ave., tel. 572-3456, open daily 7:30 a.m.-6 p.m., Sunday brunch 8:30 a.m.-3 p.m., is a gourmet deli and espresso bar. Owner Cynthia Burke and her staff prepare homemade soups, desserts made with honey, and an array of fresh salads every day. Enjoy a pastry and cappuccino, or a luscious sandwich of fresh-roasted turkey breast and a salad for under $8. If you want a break from sightseeing in Makawao, come to the Courtyard Deli, especially for Sunday brunch.

The **Haliimaile General Store Restaurant,** open daily except Monday 11 a.m.-3 p.m., and again 6-10 p.m., with a Sunday brunch 10 a.m.-2:30 p.m., tel. 572-2666, serves elegant gourmet food to anyone lucky enough to find this Upcountry roadhouse. Located in Haliimaile village along Haliimaile Rd. between Baldwin Ave., which leads from Paia to Makawao (mile marker 5), and Rt. 37, also called the Haleakala Hwy., the restaurant is housed in what was this pineapple town's general store. Climb the steps to a wide veranda and enter to find the vintage utilitarian interior transformed into an airy room of white-on-pink with tropical fish hung from the ceiling, primitive ceramics and sculptures placed here and there, and paintings of brilliant tulips. Choose a drum-topped glass table in the casual front room; perch on a bent-back stool at the classic wooden bar; or choose a table in the back room, more formal with dark wood paneling, ceiling fans, track lighting, and floral displays. Master chef Beverly Gannon presents magnificent "Hawaiian regional cuisine with an American and international twist," while her Irish husband, master schmoozer Joe Gannon, presents an equally magnificent Blarney Stone atmosphere. The lunch menu starts with soup of the day for $3.50, or the mini-bun sandwich and soup for $7. Salads are the famous house salad for $4, a Caesar salad at $7, and a Niçoise salad, which is the catch of the day grilled and served with new potatoes, olives, tomatoes, artichoke hearts, and cucumbers, for $10. There's a good selection of vegetarian specialties like *caprese*—fresh mozzarella, tomatoes, grilled eggplant, fresh basil—and vegetable torte for $9, or Brie and grape quesadilla for $7. Sandwiches, priced under $9, are special and include the grilled catch-of-the-day, the Haliimaile BOLT (bacon, lettuce, tomato, and Maui onion), or a complete selection of foccacia topped with everything from artichoke hearts to seasoned prawns. Dinner at Haliimaile opens with appetizers like the sashimi sampler for $12, or Peking duck salad for $9. Entrees include pasta primavera for $13, *paniolo* ribs for $16, coconut seafood curry for $20, or range-fed, yearling rib-eye steak for $23. The restaurant is also part boutique and art gallery, the walls hung with original works, and the old grocery shelves filled with distinctive gift items like porcelain plates, dishes, and teapots. The Haliimaile General Store has been reborn, and its spirit lives on in this great restaurant.

Food Markets And Liquor

Down to Earth Natural Foods, 1161 Makawao Ave., tel. 572-1488, open daily 8 a.m.-8 p.m., is a first-rate health food store that originated in Wailuku and recently opened a branch here in Makawao. Inside you'll find shelves packed with minerals, vitamins, herbs, spices, and mostly organic fruits and vegetables. Bins hold bulk grains, pastas, honey, and nut butters, while a deli case holds sandwiches and drinks. Down to Earth has a philosophy by which it operates: "To promote the living of a healthy lifestyle by eating a natural vegetarian diet; respect for all forms of life; and concern for the environment."

Nature's Nectar, 3647 Baldwin Ave., tel. 572-9122, open daily except Sunday 9 a.m.-6 p.m., is a juice bar that specializes in herbs and natural elixirs. Inside are tinctures, bulk herbs, and plenty of literature on alternative health. From the juice bar order carrot juice, wheatgrass juice, organic salads, and homemade vegetarian soup with whole grain bread.

Rodeo General Store, 3661 Baldwin Ave., offers one-stop shopping with a wide selection of natural foods, pastries, produce, and fresh fish.

Mountain Fresh Market, open daily 8 a.m.-7:30 p.m., 10 a.m.-6 p.m. on Sunday, has an excellent community bulletin board out front. Upcountry's health food store, it's small, but jam-packed with juices, grains, vitamins, and organic fruits and vegies. **Upcountry Fishery,** open daily until 7 p.m., Saturday and Sunday until 10 p.m., on Makawao Avenue, offers excellent fish selections.

Shopping

Makawao is changing quickly, and nowhere is this more noticeable than in its local shops. The population is now made up of old-guard *paniolo,* yuppies, and alternative people. What a combo! You can buy a bullwhip, a Gucci purse, a cold Bud, or sushi all within 100 feet of each other. Some unique and fascinating shops here can provide you with distinctive purchases.

When Mimi Merrill opened **Miracles Bookery Too,** at 3682 Baldwin Ave., tel. 572-2317, hours Mon.-Sat. 9:30 a.m.-9 p.m., Sunday 9:30 a.m.-5 p.m., she put her heart, soul, and all of her resources into the place, running out of funds before she could finish the floor. Her friends, building off the "miracles do happen" theme of the store, got together and painted it. Every evening for a week they came, and with regular house paint created a mosaic of stones, bricks, and flowers, fashioning what the local people call "the stained-glass floor." Miracles Bookery Too specializes in new age spiritualism, astrology, tarot, children's classics, Hawaiiana, general novels and poetry, "pre-loved" books, and even travel guide books! A different astrologer, palmist, or tarot reader is "in residence" every day, and on the third Saturday of every month there's an open house with free readings all day long. Miracles also has unique gift items: angels and more angels, petroglyph reproductions, Native American jewelry, bumper stickers with an attitude, T-shirts with a message, posters, and music of all kinds from spiritual to rock.

The Courtyard of Makawao is a consortium of shops at 3620 Baldwin Ave. where you can dine, buy fine art, or watch as a glassblowing family pursues alchemical art. Here, **Maui Hands,** tel. 572-5194, open daily except Sunday 10 a.m.-6 p.m., specializes in Maui-made art and crafts like semiprecious stone necklaces, sterling and gold jewelry, prints, bamboo work, raku pottery, primitive basketry, and even T-shirts. **Viewpoints Gallery,** tel. 572-5979, open daily 10 a.m.-6 p.m., is an artists' cooperative specializing in locally created paintings, sculptures, handcrafts, and jewelry. On display are: Cathy Riley's tapestries of handspun and hand-dyed yarn; handmade paper almost like paintings by Pam Peterson; oil paintings by Kathleen MacDonald; impressionistic oils by George Allen; and the mixed-media art of Joelle Chiche-bortiche. Most of the artists live in the area, and with enough notice will come to meet you if time permits. The shop is perfectly suited as a gallery with track lighting and movable partitions, so even the room itself is quite artistic with a feeling of brightness. It is a perfect place to spend an afternoon perusing the contemporary art scene so vibrant in Upcountry, Maui. Outside is a pleasant courtyard where you will find Bill and Sally Worcester making magic at **Hot Island Glass,** open daily 10 a.m.-5 p.m., tel. 572-4527. These very talented glassblowers, assisted by their son Michael, turn molten glass into everything from simple paperweights to gorgeous vases. Just line up at their window and watch the artists work. Between mother, father, and son they have won almost every meaningful art award on Maui and in their former Oregon home. This includes the *Art Maui Award,* which they have brought home every year since 1985.

Moondance Fine Collectibles, tel. 572-5172, open daily 11 a.m.-6 p.m., Sunday until 4 p.m., is an overstuffed closet of collectible clothing from all over the world, owned and operated by Margarite, master seamstress. Hanging in the closet are dresses, aloha shirts, kimonos, and leather articles and men's silk shirts done on the premises. Shelves also hold barrettes, bracelets, hats, handbags, African belts, baskets from Lumbach, and silk carpets from China. Margarite says, "If we don't have it, we'll make it."

Upcountry Legends, open daily 10 a.m.-6 p.m., Sunday 11 a.m.-5 p.m., sells hand-painted tuxedo shirts, batik and silk shirts, sterling silver jewelry, raku pottery by Rick Cosci, stained-glass kaleidoscopes for big kids, and children's clothing.

Collections Boutique, tel. 572-0781, open daily till 9 p.m., imports items from throughout Asia: batik from Bali, clothes from India, jewelry and handicrafts from various countries. The store is operated by Pam Winans.

Silversword Stoves, tel. 572-4569, formerly Outdoor Sports, has the largest line of wood-burning stoves in Hawaii. That's right, stoves! Nights in the high country can get chilly, and on top of Haleakala downright cold. Also here is a good selection of cutlery, and a few leftovers from when this was a great hardware and tack store. The owner, Gary Moore, is a relative newcomer who helped restore the integrity of Makawao and became a town historian in his own right.

For fine art, check out **David Warren's Studio,** tel. 572-1864, along Baldwin Avenue. David is one of the featured artists at the prestigious Maui Crafts Guild in Paia, but chose Upcountry for his studio.

Other shops along Baldwin Avenue include **Children's Paradise,** a children's boutique with new and used clothing. **Gecko Trading Co.,** tel. 572-0249, open daily 10 a.m.-5:30 p.m., Sunday 11 a.m.-4 p.m., bright with fashions for men, women, and children, also sells sterling silver and amber jewelry, handbags, teddy bears, and imported clothing from Thailand and Guatemala. Close by is **Country Flowers,** tel. 572-1154, for lei or arranged flowers. Listen for tinkling wind chimes to locate **Goodies,** tel. 572-0288, open daily 9:30 a.m.-5:30 p.m., Sunday 10 a.m.-5 p.m., a boutique that looks like a spilled treasure chest. Crystals, silk and cotton casual and elegant clothing, dolls, children's wear, stuffed animals, locally crafted trays, and magic wands fill this shop.

Down a narrow alley a few steps from the intersection of Baldwin and Makawao avenues is **The Dragon's Den,** tel. 572-2731, a shop stuffed full of Chinese herbs and medicines, minerals, crystals, teas, gifts, and books on Eastern healing arts. Also in the alley are **Graceland Rejuvenation Center,** tel. 572-6091, for therapeutic massage and colonic therapy; and **Grace Clinic,** tel. 572-6091, which specializes in traditional Asian medicine—new features on the ever-changing face of this Upcountry community.

Hui Noeau ("Club of Skills") Visual Arts Center, at 2841 Baldwin Ave., tel. 572-6560, open daily except Monday 10 a.m.-4 p.m., is a local organization that features traditional and modern arts housed at Kaluanui, a mansion built in 1917 by the Baldwin family on their nine-acre estate just down the road from Makawao on the way to Paia. Their member artisans and craftspeople produce everything from ceramics to *lau hala* weaving. Throughout the year classes, lectures, and exhibits are offered, along with an annual Christmas Fair featuring their creations. One of the best features of visiting Hui Noeau is the resplendent mansion itself. Built in a neo-Spanish motif with red-tiled roof and light-pink stucco exterior, Kaluanui sits among the manicured grounds that feature a reflection pond just in front of the portico.

Events

Makawao has a tremendous rodeo season every year. Most meets are sponsored by the Maui Roping Club. They start in the spring and culminate in a massive rodeo on July 4, with over $22,000 in prize money. These events attract the best cowboys from around the state. The organization of the event is headed by longtime resident Brendan Balthazar, who welcomes everyone to participate with only one rule, "Have fun, but maintain safety."

KULA

Kula could easily provide all of the ingredients for a full-course meal fit for a king. Its bounty is staggering: vegetables to make a splendid chef salad, beef for the entree, flowers to brighten the spirits, and wine to set the mood. Up here, soil, sun, and moisture create a garden symphony. Sweet Maui onions, cabbages, potatoes, grapes, apples, pineapples, lettuce, and artichokes grow with abandon. Herefords and black Anguses graze in knee-deep fields of sweet green grass. Flowers are everywhere: beds of proteas, camellias, carnations, roses, hydrangeas, and blooming peach and tangerine trees dot the countryside like daubs from van Gogh's brush. As you gain the heights along Kula's lanes, you look back on West Maui and a perfect view of the isthmus. You'll also enjoy wide-open spaces and rolling green hills fringed with trees like a lion's mane. Above, the sky changes from brooding gray to blazing blue, then back again. Kula is a different Maui—quiet and serene.

Getting There

The fastest way is the same route to Haleakala Crater. Take Rt. 37 through Pukalani, turn onto Rt. 377, and when you see Kimo Road on your left and right, you're in Kula country. If you have the time, take the following scenic route. Back in Kahului start on Rt. 36 (Hana Hwy.), but as soon as you cross Dairy Road look for a sign on your left pointing to Pulehu-Omaopio Road. Take it! You'll wade through acres of sugarcane, and in six miles these two roads will split. You can take either, but Omaopio to the left is better because, at the top, it deposits you in the middle of things to see. Once the roads fork, you'll pass some excellent examples of flower and truck farms. You'll also go by the cooperative **Vacuum Cooling Plant** where many farmers store their produce. Then Omaopio Road comes again to Rt. 37 (Kula Hwy.). Don't take it yet. Cross and continue until Omaopio dead ends, in a few hundred yards. Turn right onto Lower Kula Road and watch for Kimo (Lower) Drive on your left, and take it straight uphill. This brings you through some absolutely beautiful countryside and in a few miles crosses Rt. 377, where a right will take you to Haleakala Crater Road.

PUKALANI

This way-station town, at the intersection of routes 37 and 365, is a good place to get gas and supplies for a walking or driving trek through Kula. There's a shopping mall and several mini-malls where you can pick up just about anything. **Bullock's** restaurant, just past the T-intersection with Makawao Ave., serves a wide assortment of good-value sandwiches. The Moonburger is a tradition, but a full breakfast here for under $6 will give you all the energy you'll need for the day ahead. They also have plate lunches and some tropical fruit-flavored shakes.

Also at this intersection is the **Pukalani Superette,** a well-stocked grocery store, especially for this neck of the woods, and next door is a tiny **post office** that can take care of basic mailing needs. Here, too, you'll find a **gas station** and the famous golden arches heralding a **McDonald's.**

The **Upcountry Cafe,** just past McDonald's in the pink and gray building, tel. 572-2395, open daily except Tuesday 6:30 a.m.-3 p.m., Sunday until noon, has brought upscale yet unpretentious dining to Upcountry. Inside, wooden tables, bent-back chairs, a tiled counter, and a black-on-white Holstein motif set the ambience in this American-island standard restaurant. Their breakfast menu has a cholesterol bomb for $5.95, a Belgian waffle for $4.50, "Supermoo" eggs with bacon or Portuguese sausage and wheat toast for $4.75, or a vegetarian fritatta for $4.75. Lunch brings a traditional Reuben for $4.95, or a Crab Supreme on Boboli bread for $7.50. You can also order entrees like sautéed mahimahi for $5.95, or vegetarian lasagna for $6.25. The Upcountry Cafe is a perfect breakfast or lunch stop while touring Kula.

In the Pukalani Terrace Center are **Hua Restaurant** for a wide variety of Chinese foods, a

Subway sandwich shop, and **Y's Okazu-Ya and Crack Seed Shop.**

One of the best restaurants in the area is the **Pukalani Terrace,** open daily 10 a.m.-9 p.m, tel. 572-1325, at the Pukalani Country Club. They have a salad bar and sandwiches, but specialize in local Hawaiian foods such as *kalua* pig and *lau lau* at reasonable prices. Most patrons are local people, so you know they're doing something right. The only Upcountry golf course on Maui, **Pukalani Country Club,** offers 18 holes of inexpensive golf. In the bargain come spectacular views over the isthmus and up toward Haleakala. See "Tennis and Golf" under "Sports and Recreation" in the Maui Introduction for specifics.

SIGHTS, GARDENS, AND PROTEA FARMS

The Protea Gift Shoppe

An extension of the Hawaii Protea Corporation, the shop is next door to the Kula Lodge and open Mon.-Fri. 9 a.m.-4:30 p.m., tel. 878-6464 or (800) 367-8047, ext. 215. Don't miss seeing these amazing flowers. (For a full description see "Flora and Fauna" in the Maui Introduction.) Here you can purchase a wide range of protea that can be shipped back home. Live or dried, these flowers are fantastic. Gift boxes starting at $30 are well worth the price. The salespeople are friendly and informative, and it's educational just to visit.

Upper Kimo Road

If you want to be intoxicated by some of the finest examples of Upcountry flower and vegetable farms, come up here. First, head back north along Rt. 377 past the Kula Lodge and turn on Upper Kimo Road on your right. One mile up, at the very end, is **Cloud's Rest Protea Farm,** open daily 8 a.m.-4:30 p.m., Rt. 1, Box 485F, Upper Kimo Dr., Kula, HI 96790, tel. 878-2544; for phone orders call (800) 332-8233. They have over 50 varieties of protea and other flowers. You can walk the grounds or visit the gift shop, where they offer gift packs and mail orders. Although harvests are year-round since something is always blooming, the ultimate time for viewing and sending protea as gifts is Sept.-January.

Sunrise Protea Farm

This farm and gift shop is less than a half mile up Haleakala Highway. The shop sells gift items, local Maui produce, homemade sweets, and fruit juices. In the flower shop you'll find fresh and dried flowers and arrangements that can be sent anywhere in the country. An easy stop on the way back from Haleakala Crater. Open weekdays 8 a.m-4 p.m., weekends 7 a.m-5 p.m., tel. 878-2119 or (800) 222-2797 for phone orders.

Kula Botanical Gardens

Follow Rt. 377 south (it turns into Kekaulike Ave.) and look for the gardens on your left just before the road meets again with Rt. 37. The gardens are open daily 7 a.m.-4 p.m; be sure to start by 3 p.m. to give yourself enough time for a thorough walk-around. Admission is $3, children under 12, 50 cents, tel. 878-1715. Here are five acres of identified plants (mostly trees and flowering bushes—few flowers) on a self-guided tour. There are streams and ponds on the property, and plants include native koa and *kukui,* as well as many introduced species. The gardens are educational and will give names to many flowers and plants you've observed around the island. They make for a relaxing afternoon, with picnic tables provided.

Polipoli State Recreation Area

If you want quietude and mountain walks, come here, because few others do. Just past the botanical gardens look for the park sign on your left leading up Waipoli Road. This 10-mile stretch is only partially paved, and the second half can be very rutted and muddy. As always, it's worth it. Polipoli is an established forest of imported trees from around the world: eucalyptus, redwoods, cypress, and *sugi* pines. You can hike the **Redwood Trail** to a shelter at the end. Camping permits are required and are available from the Division of State Parks, P.O. Box 1049, Wailuku, HI 96793, tel. 244-4354. The cabin here is a spacious three-bedroom affair with bunks for up to 10 people. It starts at $10 single and goes up about $5 per person. It's rustic, but all camping and cooking essentials are provided, including a wood-burning stove. If you want to get away from it all, this is your spot.

Others

The University of Hawaii maintains an agriculture experimental station of 20 acres of flowers that change with the seasons. It's located off Copp Road above Rt. 37, open Mon.-Fri. 7:30 a.m.-3:30 p.m. A self-guided tour map is available at the office, which is closed during the lunch hour. **Holy Ghost Church** on Lower Kula Road, in Waiakoa, is an octagonal building raised in 1897 by the many Portuguese who worked the farms and ranches of Upcountry. There's a gas station here, as well as **Morihara Store, Kula Country Store and Deli,** and the **Hawaii Institute of Astronomy.**

Keokea

Continue south on Rt. 37 through the town of Keokea, where you'll find gas, two general stores, and an excellent park for a picnic. At the far end of the village are two new establishments. **Keokea Gallery** displays works by Maui artists, and next door is **Grandma's Maui Coffee.** Grandma's is open every day 7:30 a.m.-5 p.m. You can enjoy fresh pastries for breakfast, and sandwiches, saimin, and pies for lunch. The real treat, however, is the coffee, grown on the slope below and roasted in an old-fashioned coffee machine in the shop. Stop in for a sip or buy a package to go.

Tedeschi Winery

Past Keokea you'll know you're in ranch country. The road narrows and herds of cattle graze in pastures that look like manicured gardens highlighting *panini* (prickly pear) cactus. You'll pass Ulupalakua Ranch and then come to the Tedeschi Winery tasting room on the left. Open for tasting daily 9 a.m.-5 p.m., tel. 878-6058, they sell bottles of all their wines and cushioned boxes for transporting it back to the Mainland. Fifteen-minute tours of the winery are offered as well, but there is no set schedule and tours are started whenever enough people ask for one. Here, Emil Tedeschi and his partner Pardee Erdman, who also owns the 30,000-acre Ulupalakua Ranch, offer samples of their wines. This is the only winery in all of Hawaii. When Erdman moved here in 1963 from California and noticed climatic similarities to the Napa Valley, he knew that this country could grow decent wine grapes. Tedeschi comes from California, where his family has a small winery near Calistoga. The partners have worked on making their dream of Maui wine a reality since 1973.

It takes time and patience to grow grapes and turn out a vintage wine. While they waited for their carnelian grapes (a cabernet hybrid) to mature and be made into a sparkling wine, they fermented pineapple juice, which they call Maui Blanc. If you're expecting this to be a sickeningly sweet syrup, forget it. Maui Blanc is surprisingly dry and palatable. In 1984 the first scheduled release of the winery's carnelian champagne, Maui Brut, celebrated the patience and craftsmanship of the vintners. Maui Blush, a zinfandel-like light dinner wine, and the most recent, Maui Nouveau, a young red wine, round out the line as the two still wines. You can taste the wines at the 100-year-old tasting room, which is a plaster and coral building. It served as the jailhouse of the old Rose Ranch owned by James Makee, a Maui pioneer sugarcane planter. Look for the 22-acre vineyard one mile before the tasting room on the ocean side of the highway. Tedeschi wines are available in restaurants and stores around the island.

Across the street are remains of the old **Makee Sugar Mill.** Down the road across from the Ulupalakua Ranch office, sitting on the front porch of a woodworking shop, are four carved and painted lifelike figues. A cowboy, sea captain, farmhand, and Filipino with his fighting cock represent the varied people who contributed to Maui's history.

ACCOMMODATIONS

Kula Lodge

The Kula Lodge, RR 1, Box 475, Kula, HI 96790, tel. 878-1535 or (800) 233-1535, is on Rt. 377 past Kimo Road and before Haleakala Crater Road. Lodging here is in five $100-150 chalets. Two have fireplaces with wood provided, four have lofts for extra guests, and all have lanai and excellent views of lower Maui. The lobby and dining areas are impressively rustic. The walls are covered with high-quality photos of Maui: windsurfers, silverswords, sunsets, cowboys, and horses. The main dining room has a giant bay window with a superlative view. Breakfast is served daily from 6:30 a.m., lunch 11:30 a.m.-5 p.m., dinner 5:30-9 p.m. Entertainment in the evenings. Perhaps the only drawback is the clamor created 6:30-7:30 a.m. when riders on the Haleakala downhill bike trips arrive in a large group for breakfast. Be up early so as not to be disturbed.

In the basement of the lodge is the **Curtis Wilson Cost Art Gallery.** One of Maui's premier artists, Cost captures scenes reflecting the essence of Upcountry Maui; handles color, light, and shadow to perfection; and portrays the true pastoral nature of the area. Stop in and browse daily 8:30 a.m.-4:30 p.m.

Ahinahina Farm B&B, 210 Ahinahina Pl., Kula, HI 96790, tel. 878-6096 or (800) 241-6284, owned and operated by Annette and Mike Endres, offers country accommodations on this working lime and orchid farm. Available are a studio apartment at $75 for multiple-night stays, $10 extra person, complete with private entrance, queen-size bed, efficiency kitchen, full bath and reading area; and a two-bedroom cottage, at $90 for multiple night stays, $15 extra person, with its own private drive, living room, full kitchen and bath, TV, and VCR. Both accommodations are of natural wood in an open-beam style with great views from large covered decks.

Kula View B&B, P.O. Box 322, 140 Holopuni Rd., tel. 878-6736, hosted by Susan Kauai, offers a room on the upper level of the home with private entrance, private lanai, and sweeping views of Upcountry. Because the place is surrounded by two lush acres, peace is assured in your bright and cheery room appointed with queen-size bed, wicker furniture, breakfast nook, and private shower. Rate is $75, including breakfast, with weekly discounts available.

BOB RACE

HALEAKALA

Haleakala ("House of the Sun") is spellbinding. As with seeing Niagara Falls or the Grand Canyon for the first time, it makes no difference how many people have come before you; the experience is undiminished, powerful, and personal. The mountain is a power spot, a natural conductor of cosmic energy. *Kahuna* brought their novitiates here to perform final rites of initiation. During their heyday, intense power struggles took place atop the mountain between the *kahuna lapa'au,* the healing practitioners, and their rivals the *kahuna ana'ana,* the "black magic" sorcerers of old Hawaii. **Kawilinau,** the "Bottomless Pit," a natural feature on the crater floor, was the site of an ancient battle between Pele and one of her siblings, and thus held tremendous significance for both schools of *kahuna.* Average Hawaiians did not live on Haleakala, but came now and again to quarry tool-stones. Only *kahuna* and their apprentices lived here for any length of time, as a sort of spiritual preparation and testing ground. Today, students of higher consciousness from around the world are attracted to this natural cosmic empire because of the rarefied energy. They claim it accelerates personal growth, and compare it to remote mountain and desert areas in the Holy Lands. Even the U.S. Air Force has a facility here, and their research indicates Haleakala is *the* strongest natural power point in America. Not only is there an energy configuration coming from the earth itself, but there is also a high focus of radiation coming from outside the atmosphere. No one is guaranteed a spiritual experience on Haleakala, but if you're at all sensitive, this is fertile ground.

Natural Features

Haleakala is the world's largest dormant volcano, composed of amazingly dense volcanic rock, almost like poured cement. Counting the 20,000 feet or so of it lying under the sea makes it one of the tallest mountains on earth. Perhaps this mass accounts for the strange power of Haleakala as it sits like a mighty magnetic pyramid in the center of the North Pacific. The park's boundaries encompass 27,468 variable acres, which stretch from Hosmer Grove to Kipahulu and include dry forests, rainforests, desert, and subtropical beaches.

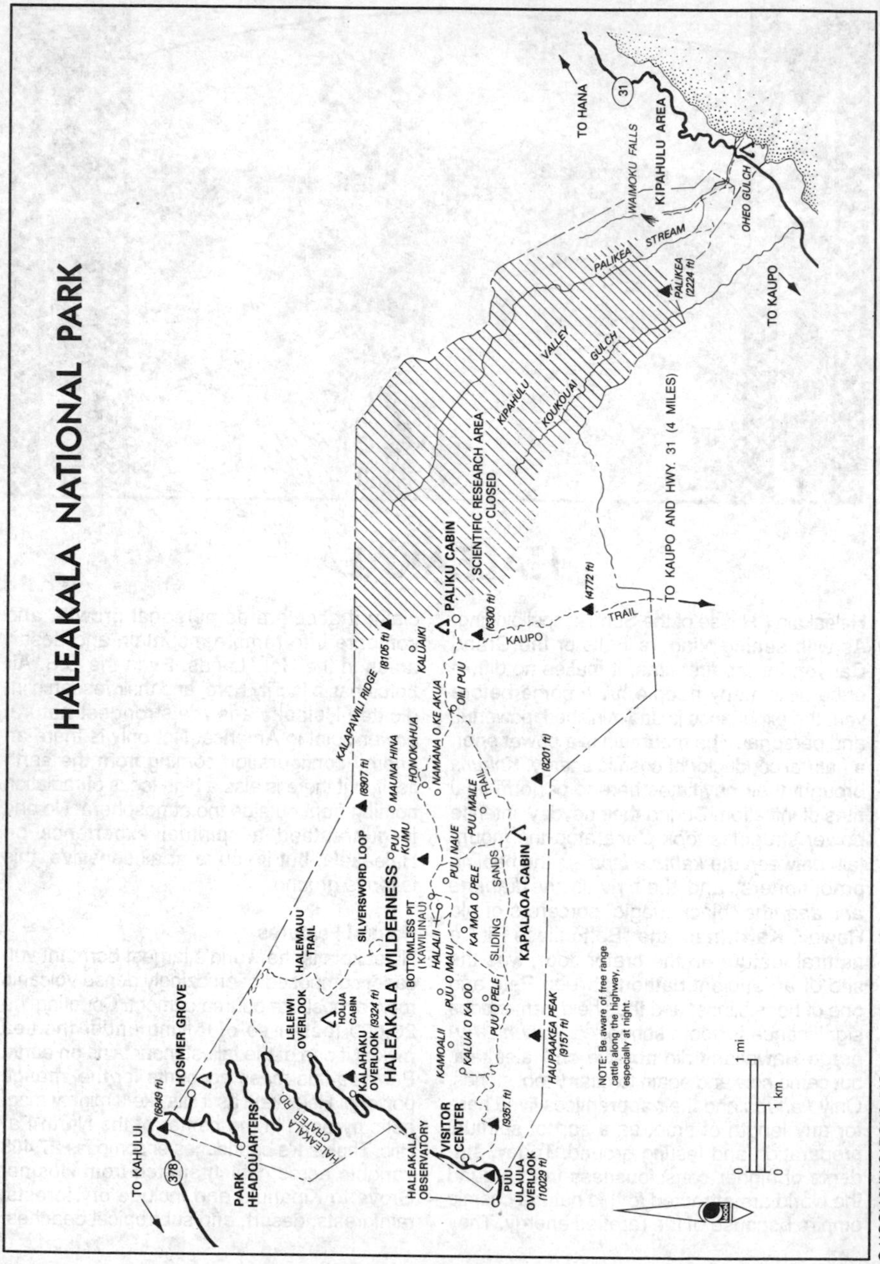

HALEAKALA NATIONAL PARK

TO KAHULUI
378
(6849 ft)
HOSMER GROVE
PARK HEADQUARTERS
HALEAKALA CRATER RD.
LELEIWI OVERLOOK
HALEMAUU TRAIL
HOLUA CABIN
KALAHAKU OVERLOOK (9324 ft)
SILVERSWORD LOOP
(8907 ft)
KALAPAWILI RIDGE
(8105 ft)
HALEAKALA WILDERNESS
PUU KUMU
MAUNA HINA
HONOKAHUA
KALUAIKI
HALEAKALA OBSERVATORY
BOTTOMLESS PIT (KAWILINAU)
HALALII
VISITOR CENTER
KAMOALII
PUU O MAUI
PUU NAUE
NAMANA O KE AKUA
OILI PUU
PALIKU CABIN
KALUA O KA OO
KA MOA O PELE
PUU MAILE
TRAIL
SCIENTIFIC RESEARCH AREA CLOSED
PUU O PELE
SLIDING SANDS
(6300 ft)
(9357 ft)
PUU ULAULA OVERLOOK (10029 ft)
KAPALAOA CABIN
KAUPO TRAIL
HAUPAAKEA PEAK (9157 ft)
(8201 ft)
KIPAHULU VALLEY
KOUKOUAI GULCH
(4772 ft)
PALIKEA STREAM
TO HANA
WAIMOKU FALLS
31
KIPAHULU AREA
TO KAUPO AND HWY. 31 (4 MILES)
PALIKEA (2224 ft)
OHEO GULCH
TO KAUPO

NOTE: Be aware of free range cattle along the highway, especially at night.

0 — 1 mi
0 — 1 km

The most impressive feature is the crater itself. It's 3,000 feet deep, 7.5 miles long, and 2.5 miles wide, accounting for 19 square miles, with a circumference of 21 miles. A mini-mountain range of nine cinder cones marches across the crater floor. They look deceptively tiny from the observation area, but the smallest is 600 feet, and the tallest, Puu O Maui, is 1,000 feet high. Haleakala was designated as a national park in 1961. Before that it was part of the Big Island's Volcanoes National Park. The entire park is a nature preserve dedicated to Hawaii's quickly vanishing indigenous plants and animals and is recognized as an International Biosphere Reserve by the United Nations. Only Volcanoes and Haleakala are home to the ***nene,*** the Hawaiian wild goose, and the **silversword,** a fantastically adapted plant. (For full descriptions, see "Flora and Fauna" in the Maui Introduction.)

The Experience

If you're after *the* experience, you must see the sunrise or sunset. Both are magnificent, but both perform their stupendous light show with astonishing speed. Also, the weather must be cooperative. Misty, damp clouds can surround the crater, blocking out the sun, or pour into the basin, obscuring even it from view. The *Maui News* prints the hours of sunrise and sunset (on a daily basis) as they vary with the season, so make sure to check. The National Weather Service provides a daily weather recording at 871-5054. For more specific information, you can call the ranger station at 572-7749 for a recorded message, or call 572-9306 for a ranger. Plan on taking a minimum of one and one-half hours to arrive from Kahului, and to be safe, arrive at least 30 minutes before dawn or dusk, because even one minute is critical. The sun, as it rises or sets, infuses the clouds with streaks, puffs, and bursts of dazzling pastels, at the same time backlighting and edging the crater in glorious golds and reds. Prepare for an emotional crescendo that will brim your eyes with tears at the majesty of it all. Engulfed by this magnificence, no one can remain unmoved.

Note: If you want to avoid downhill bikers and tourists, you can also get a great view from the Kalahaku Overlook.

Crater Facts

Haleakala was formed primarily from *pahoehoe* lava. This lava is the hottest natural substance on earth, and flows like swift fiery rivers. Because of its high viscosity, it forms classic shield volcanoes. Plenty of *'a'a* is also found in the mountain's composition. This rock comes out partially solidified and filled with gases, then breaks apart and forms clinkers. You'll be hiking over both, but be especially careful on *'a'a,* because its jagged edges will cut you as quickly as coral. The crater is primarily formed from erosion, not from caving in on itself. Erosion in Hawaii is quite accelerated due to carbonic acid build-up, a by-product of the quick decomposition of abundant plantlife. The rocks break down into smaller particles of soil which are then washed off the mountain by rain, or blown off by wind. Natural drainage patterns form, and canyons begin to develop and slowly eat their way to the center. The two largest are **Keanae Valley** in the north and **Kaupo Gap** in the south. These canyons, over time, moved their heads past each other to the center of the mountain, where they took several thousand feet off the summit and formed a huge, amphitheaterlike crater.

Some stones you encounter while hiking will be very light in weight. They once held water and gases that evaporated. If you knock two together, they'll sound like crystal. Also, be observant for **Maui diamonds.** They are garnet stones, a type of pyroxene or crystal. The cinder cones in the crater are fascinating. They're volcanic vents with a high iron content and may form electromagnetic lines from the earth's center. Climbing them is not recommended, since it violates park rules made to protect endangered plants and the threatened insects that pollinate them. On top, the craters are like funnels, transmitters and receivers of energy, natural pyramids. Notice the color of the compacted earth on the trails. It's obvious why you should remain on them. All the plants (silverswords, too) are shallow-rooted and live by condensing moisture on their leaves. Don't walk too close to them because you'll compact the earth around them and damage the roots. The ecosystem on Haleakala is very delicate, so please keep this in mind to better preserve its beauty for future generations.

SIGHTS

You'll start enjoying Haleakala long before you reach the top. Don't make the mistake of simply bolting up the mountain without taking time to enjoy what you're passing. Route 37 from Kahului takes you through Pukalani, the last place to buy supplies. Here it branches to clearly marked Rt. 377; in six miles it becomes the zigzag of Rt. 378 or **Haleakala Crater Road.** Along the way are forests of indigenous and introduced trees, including eucalyptus, beautifully flowering jacaranda, and cactus. The vistas change rapidly from one vantage point to the next. Sometimes it's the green rolling hills of Ireland, and then it's the tall, yellow grass of the plains. This is also cattle country, so don't be surprised to see all breeds, from Holsteins to Brahmans.

Headquarters

The first stopping point in the park is **Hosmer Grove Campground** (see "Camping" under "Practicalities" below) a short way down a secondary park road on your left. Proceed past here a few minutes and you'll arrive at **park headquarters,** open 7:30 a.m.-4 p.m. Campers can get their permits here, and others will be happy to stop for brochures and information, for water, or to use the toilet. There are some silverswords outside, and a few *nene* can occasionally be seen wandering the area. After you pass the park headquarters, there's trail parking on your left (see "Hikes" below). Following are two overlooks, **Leleiwi** and **Kalahaku.** Both offer tremendous views and different perspectives on the crater. They shouldn't be missed—especially Kalahaku, where there are silverswords and the remains of a travelers' lodge from the days when an expedition to Haleakala took two days.

Visitors Center

At road's end is the visitors center, approximately 10 miles up the mountain from headquarters. It's open sunrise-3 p.m. and contains a clear and concise display featuring the geology of Haleakala. Maps and books are available, and the ranger talks, given every hour on the hour, are particularly informative, delving into geology and the legends surrounding the great mountain. Various ranger-led hikes are also given, including the hike down Sliding Sands Trail, a daily interpretive talk at the summit, and the Hosmer Grove forest walk. Check with the park headquarters or the visitors center for times and days of programs.

Walks

One of the outside paths leads to **Pakaoao** ("White Hill"). An easy quarter-mile hike will take you to the summit, and along the way you'll pass stone shelters and sleeping platforms from the days when Hawaiians came here to quarry the special tool-stone. It's a type of whitish slate that easily flakes but is so hard that when you strike two pieces together it rings almost like iron. Next comes **Puu Ulaula Overlook** ("Red Hill"), the highest point on Maui, at 10,029 feet. Atop is a glass-encased observation area (open 24 hours). This is where many people come to view the sunrise and sunset. From here, if the day is crystal clear, you can see all of the main Hawaiian Islands except Kauai. Behind you on the slope below is **Haleakala Observatory,** a research facility staffed by the University of Hawaii and the Department of Defense. It is not open to the public.

Hikes

There are three trails in Haleakala Wilderness Area: Halemauu, Sliding Sands, and Kaupo. **Halemauu Trail** starts at the 8,000-foot level along the road about four miles past the park headquarters. It descends quickly to the 6,600-foot level on the crater floor. En route you'll pass Holua Cabin, Silversword Loop, the Bottomless Pit (a mere 65 feet deep), and a portion of Sliding Sands Trail, which takes you back to the visitors center. You shouldn't have any trouble hitching to your car from here.

Sliding Sands begins at the summit of Haleakala near the visitors center. This is the main crater trail and gives you the best overall hike. It joins the Kaupo Trail at Paliku Cabin; alternatively, at Kapaloa Cabin you can turn left to the Bottomless Pit and exit via Halemauu Trail. This last choice is one of the best, but you'll have to hitch back to your car at the visitors center, which shouldn't be left for the dwindling late-evening traffic going up the mountain.

The **Kaupo Trail** is long and tough. It follows the Kaupo Gap to the park boundary at 3,800 feet. It then crosses private land, which is no problem, and after a steep and rocky downhill grade deposits you in the semi-ghost town of Kaupo. This is the rugged part of the Hana loop that is forbidden by the car rental companies. You'll have to hitch west just to get to the scant traffic of Rt. 31, or head nine miles east to Kipahulu and its campground, and from there back along the Hana Road.

For those inclined, crater walks are conducted by the rangers during the summer months. These vary in length and difficulty, so check at the ranger station. There are also horseback tours of the crater (see "Sports and Recreation" in the Maui Introduction). Hikers should consider a day with the professional guide, Ken Schmitt, of **Hike Maui.** His in-depth knowledge and commentary will make your trip not only more fulfilling, but enjoyably informative as well. (See "Getting Around" in the Maui Introduction.)

PRACTICALITIES

Making Do

If you've come to Hawaii for sun and surf and you aren't prepared for alpine temperatures, you can still enjoy Haleakala. For a day-trip, wear your jogging suit or a sweater, if you've brought one. Make sure to wear socks, and bring an extra pair to use as makeshift mittens. Use your dry beach towel inside your sweater as extra insulation, and consider taking your hotel blanket to wrap around you. Make rain gear from a large plastic garbage bag with holes cut for head and arms; this is also a good windbreaker. Take your beach hat, too. Don't worry about looking ridiculous in this get-up—you will! But you'll also keep warm. Remember that for every thousand feet you climb, the temperature drops three degrees Fahrenheit, so the summit is about 32° cooler than at sea level. As the sun reaches its zenith, if there are no rain clouds, the crater floor will go from about 50 to 80 degrees. It can flip-flop from blazing hot to dismal and rainy a number of times in the same day. The nights will drop below freezing, with the coldest recorded temperature a bone-chilling 14°. Dawn and dusk are notorious for being bitter. Because of the altitude, be aware that the oxygen level will drop, and those with any impairing conditions should take precautions. The sun is ultra-strong atop the mountain and even those with deep tans are subject to burning. Noses are particularly susceptible.

Trekkers

Serious hikers or campers must have sturdy shoes, good warm clothes, rain gear, canteens, down bags, and a serviceable tent. Hats and sunglasses are needed. Compasses are useless because of the high magnetism in the rock, but binoculars are particularly rewarding. No cookfires are allowed in the crater, so you'll need a stove. Don't burn any dead wood—the soil needs all the decomposing nutrients it can get. Drinking water is available at all of the cabins within the crater but the supply is limited so bring what you will need. This environment is particularly delicate. Stay on the established trails so that you don't cause undue erosion. Leave rocks and especially plants alone. Don't walk too close to silverswords or any other plants because you'll compact the soil. Leave your pets at home; ground-nesting birds here are easily disturbed. If nature "calls," dig a very shallow hole, off the trail, and pack out your used toilet paper since the very dry conditions are not conducive to it biodegrading.

Camping

Admission to the park is $4, good for seven days (discounted passes for U.S. senior citizens), but camping is free with a necessary camping permit from park headquarters. The Hosmer Grove campground is at the 6,800-foot level, just before park headquarters; the free camping here is limited to 25 people, but there's generally room for all to use the sites, water, pit toilets, grills, and a pavilion. The grove was named after Ralph Hosmer, who tried to save the watershed by planting fast-growing foreign trees like cedars, pines, and junipers. He succeeded, but this destroyed any chance of the native Hawaiian trees making a comeback. While here, take a stroll along the half-mile forest loop that threads its way through the grove of trees that Hosmer planted.

Kipahulu Campground is a primitive camping area over near Oheo Stream. It's part of the park, but unless you're an intrepid hiker and descend all the way down the Kaupo Trail, you'll come to it via Hana (see "Beyond Hana" later in this chapter).

There are campsites in the crater at **Holua, Paliku,** and **Kapalaoa.** All three offer cabins, and tent camping is allowed at the first two. Camping at any of these is extremely popular, and reservations for the cabins must be made months in advance by mail using a special cabin reservation request form. A lottery of the applicants chosen for sites keeps it fair for all. Environmental impact studies limit the number of campers to 25 per area per day. Camping is limited to a total of three days, with no more than two days at each spot. Rates for cabin use are $19 s, $23 d, plus $9 extra person to a maximum of 12 people. For complete details and reservation form write: Haleakala National Park, P.O. Box 369, Makawao, HI 96768, tel. 572-9306.

The Hawaiians were the finest adze makers in Polynesia. One of the best quarries was atop Haleakala.

LOUISE FOOTE

BCB RACE

NORTHEAST MAUI

THE HANA ROAD

On the long and winding road to Hana's door, most people's daydreams of "paradise" come true. A trip to Maui without a visit to Hana is like ordering a sundae without a cherry on top. The 50 miles that it takes to get there from Kahului are some of the most remarkable in the world. The Hana Hwy. (Rt. 36) starts out innocently enough, passing **Paia.** The inspiration for Paia's gaily painted storefronts looks like it came from a jar of jelly beans. Next come some north-shore surfing beaches where windsurfers fly, doing amazing aquabatics. Soon there is a string of "rooster towns," so named because that's about all that seems to be stirring. Then Rt. 36 becomes Rt. 360 and at mile marker 3 the *real* Hana Road begins.

The semi-official count tallies over 600 rollicking turns and more than 50 one-lane bridges, inducing everyone to slow down and soak up the sights of this glorious road. It's like passing through a tunnel cut from trees. The ocean winks azure blue through sudden openings on your left. To the right, streams, waterfalls, and pools sit wreathed with jungle and wildflowers. Coconuts, guavas, mangos, and bananas grow everywhere on the mountainside. Fruit stands pop up regularly as you creep along. Next comes **Keanae** with its arboretum and taro farms indicating that many ethnic Hawaiians still live along the road. There are places to camp, picnic, and swim, both in the ocean and in freshwater streams.

Then you reach **Hana** itself, a remarkable town. The great Queen Kaahumanu was born here, and many celebrities live in the surrounding hills seeking peace and solitude. Past Hana, the road becomes even more rugged and besieged by jungle. It opens up again around **Oheo Stream** (or Seven Pools). Here waterfalls cascade over stupendous cataracts, forming a series of pools until they reach the sea. Beyond is a rental car's no-man's land, where the passable road toughens and Haleakala shows its barren volcanic face scarred by lava flows.

LOWER PAIA

Paia ("Noisy") was a bustling sugar town that took a nap. When it awoke, it had a set of whiskers and its vitality had flown away. At the turn of the century, many groups of ethnic field workers lived here, segregated in housing clusters called "camps" that stretched up Baldwin Avenue. Paia was the main gateway for sugar on East Maui, and even a railroad functioned here until 20 years ago. During the 1930s, its population, at over 10,000, was the largest on the island. Then fortunes shifted toward Kahului, and Paia lost its dynamism, until recently. Paia was resuscitated in the 1970s by an influx of paradise-seeking hippies, and then in the '80s came another shot in the arm from windsurfers. These two groups have metamorphosed into townsfolk and have pumped new life into its old muscles. The practical shops catering to the pragmatic needs of a "plantation town" were replaced. The storefronts were painted and spruced up. A new breed of merchants with their eye on passing tourists has taken over. Now Paia (Lower) focuses on boutiques, crafts, artwork, and food. Since you've got to pass through on your way to Hana, it serves as a great place not only to top off your gas tank, but also to stop for a bite and a browse. The prices are good for just about everything, and it boasts one of the island's best fish restaurants and art shops. Paia, under its heavy makeup, is still a vintage example of what it always was—a homey, serviceable, working town.

Sights

A mile or so before you enter Paia on the left is **Rinzai Buddhist Temple** located on Alawai Road—reached by going through H.P. Baldwin Park. The grounds are pleasant and worth a look. **Mantokuji Buddhist Temple** on the eastern outskirts of Paia heralds the sun's rising and setting by ringing its huge gong 18 times at dawn and dusk.

H.P. Baldwin Beach County Park is on your left about seven miles past Kahului on Rt. 36, just past Maui Country Club; this spacious park is good for swimming, shell-collecting, and decent winter surfing. There are tent and trailer camping (county permit required) and full amenities. Unfortunately, Baldwin has a bad reputation. It's one of those places locals have staked out with the attitude of "us against them." Hassles and robberies have been known to occur. Be nice, calm, and respectful. For the timid, to be on the safe side, be gone.

Hookipa Beach County Park is about 10 minutes past Paia. There's a high grassy sand dune along the road and the park is down below, where you'll enjoy full amenities—unofficial camping is done. Swimming is advisable only on calm days, as there are wicked currents. Primarily a surfing beach now regarded as one of the best sailboarding areas in Hawaii, this is home to the **O'Neill International Windsurfing Championship,** held yearly during early spring. The world's best sailboarders come here, trying to win the $10,000 prize. The colorful spectacle is often televised. Bring binoculars.

Accommodations

About the only place to lodge in Paia is at the **Nalu Kai Lodge,** located just behind Corner Wines and Liquors at the corner of Baldwin Avenue and the Hana Hwy., tel. 579-8009; ask for Myrna. This plain and simple two-story cement building offers clean, quiet, adequate rooms with refrigerators but no stoves. Rates vary—Myrna bargains—but expect to spend about $30 for one night, or $20 for multiple nights.

Food

Picnic's, along Baldwin Ave., tel. 579-8021, is open daily 7:30 a.m.-7 p.m. Breakfast and lunch offer everything from roast beef to vegetarian sandwiches like a scrumptious spinach nut burger or tofu burger, all under $5. The best news are boxed picnic lunches that add a special touch if you're heading to Hana (few restaurants there). They start from the basic "Countryside," which includes sandwiches and sides at $7.95 per person, to the "Executive" with sandwiches, *kiawe*-broiled chicken, sides, nut bread, condiments, cheeses, and even a tablecloth all in a styrofoam ice chest for $42.50. (Supposedly feeds two, but with extra buns it will feed four.) Picnic's is one of the best stops along the Hana Road even for a quick espresso, cappuccino, or frozen yogurt. Or treat yourself to the fresh-baked pastries like macadamia nut sticky buns

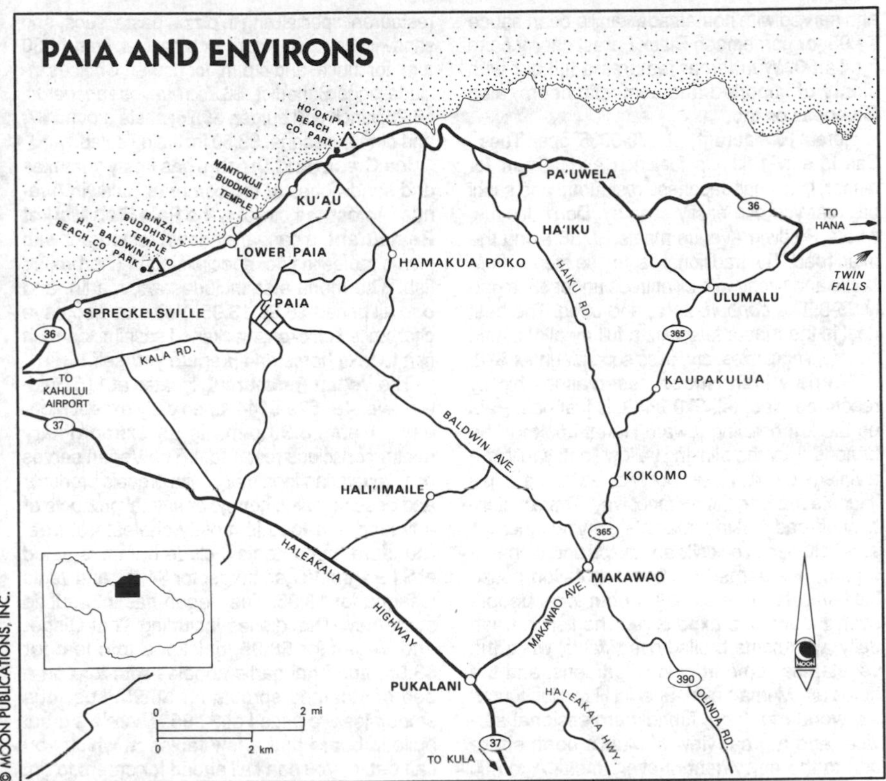

or apple and papaya turnovers: worth the guilt! Also, ask for the *free* Hana Road map.

Another place for boxed picnic lunches is **Peach's and Crumble Cafe and Bakery,** at 2 Baldwin Ave., tel. 579-8612, open 6:30 a.m.-6 p.m., Thursday and Friday to 7:30 p.m., where you can enjoy a scone, the famous peach crumble, and a cup of cappuccino. For a boxed lunch try the Hana Bay box at $6.95, or the continental for $6.85. Peach's also serves sandwiches, smoothies, great spinach lasagna, and fresh pastries of all sorts.

Wunderbar, in downtown Paia, tel. 579-8808, open daily 7:30 a.m.-2 a.m., takes care of you from morning till night in their very agreeable dining room dominated by a grand piano, or alfresco in the beer garden. The breakfast menu offers rolled crepes for $3; *menemen,* Turkish scrambled eggs fried in a spicy mixture of onions, bell pepper, and tomatoes for $4; or yogurt with fresh fruit, $4.50. There's also Kona coffee, espresso, cappuccino, fruit juice, Portuguese sausage, steamed rice, and plenty of omelettes. Lunch can be an Alpine plate of cured meats and imported cheeses served with authentic Bavarian bread for $10, an assortment of pasta dishes priced from $6.50, or seafood stewed in plum tomatoes for $10. There are also burgers with all the trimmings, and great sandwiches made with German luncheon meats. Evening entrees include picatta milanaisse, breast of turkey lightly coated in a fluffy egg batter, Hungarian goulash, and smoked pork cutlets and sauerkraut, all priced $13.95-18.95. German-style desserts are "wunderbar": baked apple slices turned in cinnamon sugar and served with homemade vanilla bean sauce $4.95, or homemade Black Forest cherry cake for $4.50. Wunderbar features a full bar with plenty of imported and domestic beers, also Guinness on tap.

Kihata Restaurant, tel. 579-9035, open Tues.-Sat. 11 a.m.-1:30 p.m. for lunch, and 5-9 p.m. for dinner, is a small Japanese restaurant and sushi bar that you can easily pass by. Don't! It's just where Baldwin Avenue meets Rt. 36 along the main road. The traditional Japanese menu offers *bento* and sushi, with all entrees under $8, mostly $5-6, like *donburi, soba,* and *udon*. The best deal is the Kihata *teishoku,* a full meal of steak, shrimp, vegetables, and miso soup for under $12.

Mama's Fish House, reservations highly recommended, tel. 579-8488, is just past Paia on the left heading toward Hana. Look for the turnoffs near the blinking yellow light; you'll see a vintage car with a sign for Mama's and a ship's flagpole marking the entranceway. There's plenty of offroad parking. Mama's, serving lunch 11 a.m-2:30 p.m., cocktails and *pu pu* until dinner at 5 p.m., has earned the best reputation possible—it gets the thumbs-up from local people even though it is expensive. The fish is fresh daily, with some broiled over *kiawe,* while the vegetables come from local gardens, and the herbs are Mama's own. Special Hawaiian touches, wonderful food, friendly professional service, and a great view of Maui's north shore add to the enjoyment of every meal. A terrific idea is to make reservations here for the evening's return trip from Hana.

Cafe Paradiso, tel. 597-8819, an indoor/outdoor cafe with a courtyard area surrounded by palm trees, open Tues.-Sat. 6-10 p.m., features Mediterranean dining for a reasonable price. Antipasti are combination seafood, meat, cheese, and marinated vegetables for $13.95, or homemade bread topped with prosciutto and mozzarella cheese for $6.95. Soup du jour is $4.50, spinach salad $7.95, and a locally grown salad with mozzarella cheese, roasted peppers, and sun-dried tomatoes is $9.95. Fresh pasta topped with pesto, smoked salmon in a cream sauce, or cannelloni stuffed with crab, scallops, shrimp, and catch-of-the-day, are sure to please. *Bon appetito!*

For a quick bite you have **Charlie P. Woofers,** tel. 579-9453, a saloon with pool tables and a restaurant specializing in pizza, pasta, subs, and sandwiches, open 7 a.m. for breakfast, from 11:30 a.m. for lunch, and 4 p.m. for dinner. Choices include eggs Benedict, $6.75; *huevos rancheros,* $6.25; lunch chili burger, $5.75; pasta around $7; and dinner lasagna, $8.50 including salad.

Ice Cream and Dreams has frosty yummies and sandwiches at the corner of Baldwin Avenue. Across the street is the **Paia Fish Market Restaurant,** a casual sit-down restaurant with picnic tables inside, specializing in charbroiled fish. The menu also includes *ahi,* marlin, and *ono* all priced $8.95-13.95. You can also have charbroiled chicken, blackened sashimi, or fresh fish to take home and prepare yourself.

The **Vegan Restaurant,** located at 115 Baldwin Ave., tel. 579-9144, open daily except Monday 11 a.m.-8:30 p.m., is an extraordinary health-conscious restaurant. The Vegan serves only vegetarian food made with organic products and uses no dairy, honey, or animal products of any kind; the food is mostly cholesterol free. Standard menu items include hummus salad at $4.95, the Vegan burger for $4.75, and vegie lasagna for $8.95. The Vegan has introduced some new Thai dishes including Thai Ginger and Vegas for $8.95, chickpea tofu loaf for $8.95, and Thai garlic noodles with tofu on a bed of steamed sprouts for $8.95. Luscious smoothies are priced at $2.95. There's a great bulletin board and a few tables at which you can eat, or you can call ahead for orders to go.

Mana Natural Foods, at 49 Baldwin Ave., tel. 579-8078, open daily 8 a.m.-8 p.m., is a well-stocked health-food store, maybe the best on Maui. Inside the old building you'll find local organic produce, and vitamins, grains, juices, bulk foods, and more. Outside, check out the great community bulletin board for what's selling and happening around Paia.

For boxed and canned goods and picnic items try either of the old-time shops, **Nagata Store** or **Horiuchi.**

The **Wine Corner,** appropriately located at the corner of Baldwin Avenue and the Hana Hwy., is a well-stocked bottle shop with wines, liquor, and ice-cold beer.

Shopping

Maui Crafts Guild is on the left just before entering Paia, at 43 Hana Hwy., P.O. Box 609,

Paia, HI 96779, tel. 579-9697. Open daily 9 a.m.-6 p.m., the Crafts Guild is one of the best art outlets in Hawaii. It's owned and operated by the artists themselves, all of whom must pass a thorough jurying by present members. All artists must be islanders, and they must use natural materials found in Hawaii to create their work except for some specialized clay, fabrics, and printmaking paper. Items are tastefully displayed and you'll find a wide variety of artwork and crafts including pottery, furniture, beadwork, woodcarving, bamboowork, stained glass, batik, and jewelry. Different artists staff the shop on different days, but business cards and phone numbers are available if you want to see more of something you like. Prices are reasonable and this is an excellent place to make that one "big" purchase.

In downtown Paia (two blocks along the highway) is **Tropical Emporium** with resortwear; and the **Paia Trading Co.,** a discovery shop open Mon.-Fri. 9 a.m.-5 p.m., with collectibles like old glass, telephones, aloha shirts, lanterns, jewelry, license plates, oil lamps, and a smattering of pottery and antique furniture. Next door is the **Boutique Two,** open daily 10 a.m.-6 p.m., Sunday to 4 p.m., filled with women's fancy apparel and alohawear. **Jaggers,** open daily 9 a.m.-5 p.m., features alohawear, fancy dresses, and replicas of vintage aloha shirts for men.

Hana Hou Gallery Fine Arts and Jewelry, owned and operated by Peter Medwick, tel. 579-8185, open daily 9 a.m.-6 p.m., specializes in Hawaiiana. Most artists displayed are from Maui, with the rest from the Neighbor Islands. The gallery displays the works of Loren Adams, who does surrealistic, bright oils capturing the brilliance of Maui sunshine; and Eddie Flotte, who captures the nobility inherent in the "everyday" people of Maui in his sensitive yet realistic paintings. Hana Hou also showcases exquisite wood bowls, serving trays, and boxes along with basketry, jewelry, and some porcelains. Great inexpensive souvenir items, priced $9-50, are painted fish by Manali made into everything from dangly earrings to mobiles.

Just You and Me Kid is an apparel store for *keiki* and their moms, where they can even find matching alohawear. **Picture This, Art and Framing Boutique,** open daily 9 a.m.-6 p.m., does custom framing and features the works of local artists. Some artists represented are: Tracy Dudley, who works in oils, acrylics and watercolors, capturing the flora and fauna of Hawaii; Jos, who does the whimsical, cartoonish works; and Avi Kiriaty, an Israeli who has perfected the technique of linoleum block prints that capture the spirit of Hawaii and the South Seas. **Deybra's** features the art of Deybra, where you are greeted by a life-sized black-and-white papier mâché cow. Deybra works in mixed media of acrylic, pastel, and inks, creating primitive, bright colorful artworks, many of which are three-dimensional sculptures, that celebrate the joy of island life.

The **Tee Shirt Factory** sells T-shirts that are more expensive elsewhere. **Paia Gifts and Gallery,** tel. 579-8185, open daily 8 a.m.-7 p.m., displays art by local artists.

For the sailboarder, look for boards and gear at **Hi-Tech Sailboards, Paia Sail Company, Sailboards Maui, North Swell Maui,** or **Paia Sports Inc.**

Walk along Baldwin Avenue for a half-block and you'll find a drawerful of boutiques and fashion shops. **Nuage Bleu,** a boutique open daily 10 a.m.-5 p.m., features distinctive fashions and gift items, mostly for women. **Studio 27,** 27 Baldwin Ave., tel. 557-9984, open daily 8:30 a.m.-7 p.m., is an apparel store filled with resortwear, jewelry, aloha shirts, and shorts, all made in Indonesia exclusively for Studio 27. **Ice Cubes,** open daily 9 a.m.-6 p.m., painted blue and splashed with tropical fish, sells sunglasses, sandals, hats, bikinis (a specialty), and T-shirts—all in the brightest, newest fashions. Next door is **Maui Gecko,** shining with "cheapy" jewelry, trinkets, T-shirts, and basic alohawear. **Yoki's Boutique,** tel. 579-9249, open daily 10 a.m.-5 p.m., has jewelry, gifts, and designer apparel by Betsey Johnson. The walls also hold lace and beaded lingerie from Europe and Asia that's hotter than the tropical sun. If you've forgotten your fish-net nylons at home, you can pick up a pair at Yoki's. Next door is **Northshore Silks,** open daily 11 a.m.-6 p.m, sometimes closed on Sunday, tel. 579-9478, a Victorian-style women's store filled with satin and lace, angels, cherubs, scented pillows, perfume oils, custom-scented lotions, lithographs, and semiprecious stone jewelry. **Maui Girl** has antique aloha shirts; sexy, custom-made bikinis; and men's surf fashions made by Billabong, Gotcha, and O'Neill. The

Creative Culture Boutique, on the right going up Baldwin Avenue, sells decorated shirts, shorts, colorful backpacks, and pouches.

Also along Baldwin Avenue are the **Bank of Hawaii,** the **post office,** a *washerette,* and **Paia 30-minute Photo,** open Mon.-Sat. 8 a.m.-6 p.m. with shorter hours on Sunday.

Unocal 76 is the last place to fill your tank before reaching Hana. Next door is **Paia General Store** for supplies and sundries, with a takeout snack window called the **Paia Drive Inn.** Across the street is the **Paia Mercantile Shopping Complex,** a collection of shops ranging from a surfing-equipment store to **Clementine's** for women's clothing to **Tropical Blossoms** wholesale outlet for gift items.

Heading down the road to Hana you'll see the **Maui Community Center** on your left. Soon, just past mile marker 12, look for W. Kuiaha Road and make a right toward the old **Pauwela Cannery,** which is less than five minutes up the road. This huge tin can of a building has been divided into a honeycomb of studios and workshops housing fine artists, woodworkers, cabinetmakers, potters, and sailboard makers. All welcome guests to browse and buy. In the rear is Resta Studio, the workshop of Piero Resta. Along with his son Luigi, he graciously welcomes visitors (call first, tel. 575-2203) and with Italian hospitality makes you feel at home with a cup of cappuccino. To qualify as a real Italian gentleman you must have imagination! Without it you're like pasta with no sauce, or pesto with no basil. You must possess, and be willing to share, opinions on life, politics, religion, and philosophy, and moreover you must be a lover . . . of art, women, music, and food, preferably all in the same evening! Piero Resta is an Italian gentleman. His studio with loft (necessary to be a real artist) is a vision of dynamism. His works are bold, colorful, neo-Renaissance personal statements of semi-abstract reality. Broad-hipped women with classical Greek faces pose or stride nonchalantly across a surrealistic collage of vibrant Maui colors. Carved wooden pillars wait to adorn a modern portico, while a mythical yellow tiger on a bold red background opens its mouth in anticipation of eating its own tail. The studio and the artwork surround you like a colorful wave. Soul-surf with Piero. You'll be glad you did!

Paia has two gas stations: **Unocal,** which has made-to-order sandwiches; and **Chevron,** open 24 hours.

THE ROAD BEGINS

The road to Hana holds many spectacles and surprises, but one of the best is the road itself . . . it's a marvel! The road was hacked out from the coastline in 1927, every inch by hand using pick and shovel. An ancient Hawaiian trail followed the same route for part of the way, but mostly people moved up and down this coastline by boat. What makes the scenery so special is that the road snakes along Maui's windward side. There's abundant vegetation and countless streams flowing from Haleakala, carving gorgeous valleys. There are a few scattered villages with a house or two that you hardly notice, and the beaches, although few, are empty. Mostly, however, it's the "feeling" that you get along this road. Nature is close and accessible, and it's so incredibly "South Sea island" that it almost seems artificial. But it isn't.

Hana Road Tips

You've got 30 miles of turns ahead when Rt. 36 (mile marker 22) becomes Rt. 360 (mile marker 0) and the fun begins. The Hana Road has the reputation of being a "bad road," but this isn't true. It's narrow, with plenty of hairpin turns, but it's well banked and has clearly marked bridges, and there's always maintenance going on (which can slow you up). Years back, it was a harrowing experience. When mud slides blocked the road, drivers were known to swap their cars with those on the opposite side and carry on to where they were going. The road's reputation sets people up to expect an ordeal, so they make it one, and unfortunately, drive accordingly. Sometimes it seems as though tourists demand the road to be rugged, so that they can tell the folks back home that they, too, "survived the road to Hana." This popular slogan appears on T-shirts, copyrighted and sold by Hasegawa's famous (though recently burned down and reopened) store in Hana, and perpetuates this belief. You'll have no problem, and you'll see much more if you just take it easy.

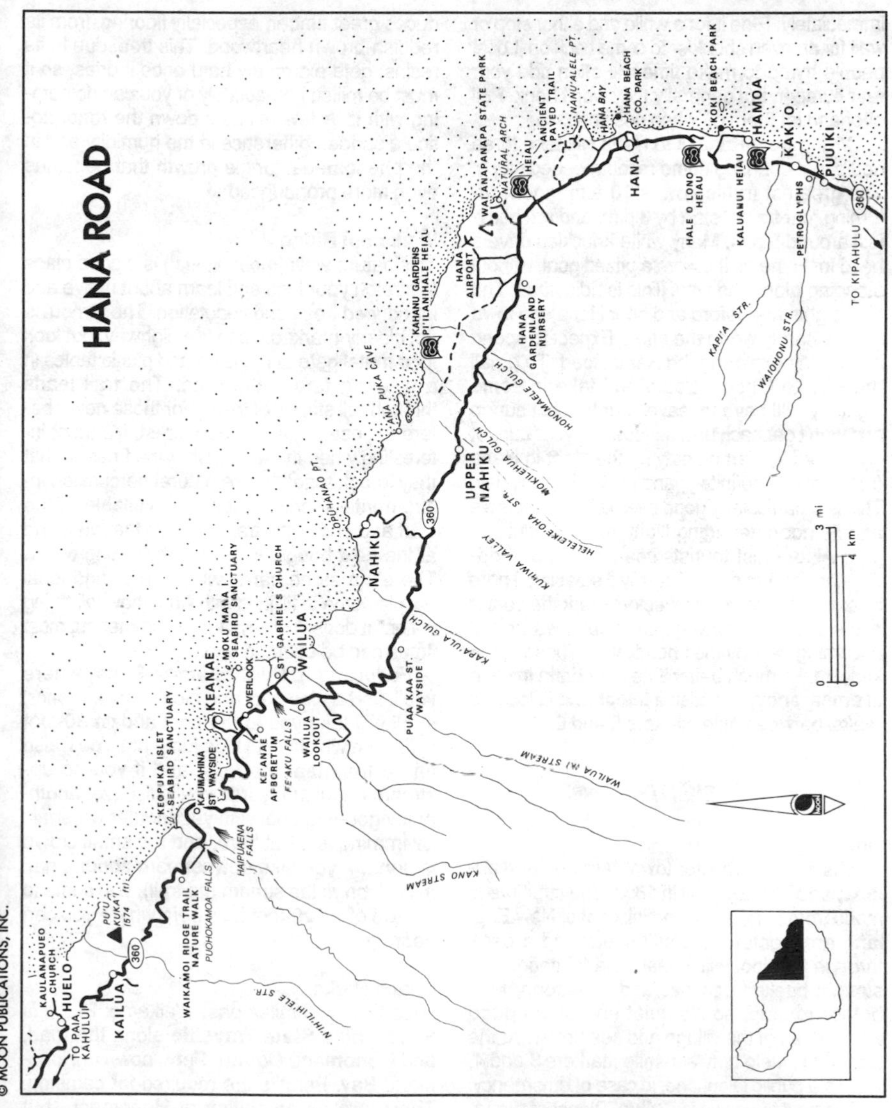

Your speed will often drop below 10 miles per hour and will rarely exceed 25. Standard-shift cars are better for the turns. Cloudbursts occur at any time so be ready for slick roads. A heavy fall of fruit from roadside mango trees can also coat the road with slippery slime. Look as far up the road as possible and don't allow yourself to be mesmerized by the 10 feet in front of your hood. If your tire dips off a rough shoulder, don't risk losing control by jerking the wheels back on immediately. Ride it for a while and either stop or wait for an even shoulder to come back on. Local people trying to make time will often ride your rear bumper, but generally they won't honk. Pull over and let them by when possible.

Driving from Kahului to Hana will take three hours, not counting some recommended stops. The greatest traffic flow is 10 a.m.-noon; returning "car trains" start by 3 p.m. and are heaviest around 5 p.m. Many white-knuckled drivers head for Hana as if it were a prized goal, without stopping along the way. This is ridiculous. The best sights are before and after Hana; the town itself is hardly worth the effort. Expect to spend a long day exploring the Hana Road. To go all the way to Oheo Stream and take in some sights, you'll have to leave your hotel at sunup and won't get back until sundown. If your budget can afford it, plan on staying the night in Hana (reservations definitely) and return the next day. This is a particularly good alternative if you have an afternoon departing flight from Kahului Airport. Also, most tourists seem terrified of driving the road at night. Actually it's easier. There is far less traffic, road reflectors mark the center and sides like a runway, and you're warned of oncoming cars by their headlights. Those in the know make much better time after dark! In case of **emergency,** a roadside **telephone** is located *makai* between mile markers 5 and 6.

SIGHTS

Huelo

This is a quiet "rooster town" famous for **Kaulanapueo Church** built in 1853. The structure is made from coral and is reminiscent of New England architecture. It's still used, and a peek through the door will reveal a stark interior with straight-backed benches and a platform. Few bother to stop, so it's quiet and offers good panoramas of the village and sea below. At the turnoff to Huelo between mile markers 3 and 4, there's a public telephone, in case of emergency.

The next tiny town is **Kailua.** Plenty of mountain apple trees flourish along this stretch. The multicolored trees are rainbow eucalyptus, introduced late last century from Australia and some of the most beautiful trees in Hawaii. Close by is a cousin, *Eucalyptus robusta,* which produces great timber, especially flooring, from its reddish-brown heartwood. This tree, due to its resins, gets extremely hard once it dries, so it must be milled immediately or you can do nothing with it. A few minutes down the road, notice a sudden difference in the humidity and in the phenomenal jungle growth that becomes even more pronounced.

Waikamoi Ridge

This nature walk (mosquitoes!) is a good place to stretch your legs and learn about native and introduced trees and vegetation. The turnout is not clearly marked along the highway, but look for a metal gate at roadside and picnic tables in a clearing above the road. The trail leads through tall stands of trees. For those never before exposed to a bamboo forest, it's most interesting when the wind rustles the trees so that they knock together like natural percussion instruments. Picnic tables are available at the start and end of the trail. Back on the road, and at the next bridge, is excellent drinking water. There's a stone barrel with a pipe, and local people come to fill jugs with what they call "living water." It doesn't always run in summer but most times can be counted upon.

Following is **Puohokamoa Falls,** where you'll find a nice pool and picnic table. A short stroll will take you to the pool and its 30-foot cliff, from which local kids jump off. You'll also find a trail near the falls, and if you go upstream about 100 yards you'll discover another invigorating pool with yet another waterfall. Swimming is great here, and the small crowd is gone. If you hike downstream about a half mile *through* the stream (no trail), you come to the top of a 200-foot falls from where you can peer over the edge.

Beach Parks

Less than two miles past Waikamoi Ridge is **Kaumahina State Wayside** along the road, and **Honomanu County Park,** down at Honomanu Bay. Permits are required for camping. There are no amenities at Honomanu, but Kaumahina has them all. Camping here is in a rainforest with splendid views out to sea overlooking the rugged coastline and the black-sand beach of Honomanu Bay. Puohokamoa Falls are just a short walk away. Honomanu is not good for swimming because of strong currents, but is good for surfing.

Keanae

Honomanu Valley, just before the Kaenae Arboretum, is the largest valley on the north side of Haleakala. Most of the big valleys that once existed, especially on East Maui, were filled in by lava flows, greatly reducing their original size. But Honomanu goes back about five miles toward the center of the mountain, and has 3,000-foot cliffs and 1,000-foot waterfalls. Unfortunately, the trails are quite difficult to find and to negotiate.

Clearly marked on the right will be **Keanae Arboretum.** A hike through this facility will exemplify Hawaiian plantlife in microcosm. There are two sections, one of tropical plants (identified) and the other of Hawaiian domestic plants. Toward the upper end of the arboretum are taro fields, and the hillsides above are covered with the natural rainforest vegetation. You can picnic and swim along Piinaau Stream. Hardier hikers can continue for another mile through the rainforest; at the end of the trail are a pool and waterfall. As there is a gate across the entrance (located at a sharp curve in the road), pull well off the road to park your car and walk in.

Camp Keanae YMCA is just before the arboretum. It looks exactly as its name implies, set in a gorgeous natural pasture. There are various bunkhouses for men and women. Arrival time is between 4 and 6 p.m., cost is $8. For more information call the camp at 248-8355. All accommodations are by reservation only. For reservations contact the Kahului YMCA office at 244-3253.

Keanae Peninsula is a thumblike appendage of land formed by a lava flow that came down the hollowed-out valley from Haleakala Crater. A fantastic lookout is here—look for a telephone pole with a tsunami loudspeaker atop, and pull off here. Below you'll see neat little farms, mostly raising taro. Shortly before this lookout, a public road heads down into the peninsula to a turnaround. Most people living here are native Hawaiians. They still make poi the old-fashioned way: listen for the distinctive thud of poi-pounding in the background. Though *kapu* signs abound, the majority of people are friendly. If you visit, be aware that this is one of the last patches of ground owned by Hawaiians and tended in the old way. Be respectful, please. Notice the lava-rock missionary church. Neat and clean, it has straight-backed, hardwood pews and a pleasant altar inside. The cemetery to the side is groomed with tropical flowers while the grounds are rimmed by coconut trees. Next comes the lonely **Wailua Peninsula.** It, too, is covered in taro and is a picturesque spot. Only 3,000 people live along the entire north coast of East Maui leading to and including Hana.

Fruit Stands

Do yourself a favor and look for **Uncle Harry's Fruit Stand,** clearly marked on the left past the Keanae Peninsula just beyond the Keanae school. Unfortunately, this *kahuna* who knew a great deal of the natural pharmacology of old Hawaii, and was a living encyclopedia on herbs and their healing properties, has passed away, but his spirit lives on. Past Keanae between mile markers 17 and 18 is another roadside stand where you can buy hot dogs, shave ice, and fruit. Notice the picture-perfect, idyllic watercress farm on your left. Past mile marker 18 on the right is a fruit stand operated by a fellow named Joseph. He not only has coconuts, pineapples, and papayas, but little-tasted exotic fruits like mountain apples, star fruit, strawberry guavas, and Tahitian lemons. An authentic fruit stand worth a stop. Another one, operated by a Hawaiian woman, is only 50 yards on the left. If you have a hankering for fruit, this is the spot.

Wailua

At mile marker 18, you come to Wailua. Turn left here on Wailua Road, following signs for **Coral Miracle Church.** Here, too, you'll find the **Miracle of Fatima Shrine,** so named because a freak storm in the 1860s washed up enough coral onto Wailua Beach that the church could be constructed by the Hawaiian congregation. Here also are St. Gabriel's Church and St. Augustine's Shrine. There is a lovely and relatively easy-access waterfall nearby. Pass the church, turn right, and park by the large field. Look for a worn path (may be private, but no signs or hassle) that leads down to the falls.

Puaa Kaa State Wayside

This lovely spot is about 14 miles before Hana. There's no camping, but there are picnic tables,

54 BRIDGES OF HANA, MAUI, HAWAII

No.	Bridge	Meaning	No.	Bridge	Meaning
1	O'o-pu-ola	life maturing	28	Pu-a-pa-pe	baptismal
2	Ma-ka-na-le	bright vision	29	Ka-ha-wai-ha-pa-pa	extensive valley
3	Ka-ai-ea	breathtaking view	30	Ke-a-a-iki	burning star (sirius)
4	Wai-a-ka-mo'i	waters of the king	31	Wai-oni (Akahi)	first ruffled waters
5	Pu-oho-ka-moa	sudden awakening	32	Wai-oni (Elua)	second ruffled waters
6	Hai-pue-na	glowing hearts	33	Lani-ke-le	heavenly mist
7	Ko-le'a	windborne joy	34	He-lele-i-ke-oha	extending greetings
8	Hono-manu	bird valley	35	Ula-i-no	intense sorrow
9	Nu'a-'ai-lua	large abundance	36	Moku-lehua	solemn feast
10	Pi-na-ao	kind hearted	37	'O-i-lo-wai	first sprouting
11	Pa-lauhulu	leaf sheltered	38	Hono-ma-'e-le	land of deep love
12	Wai-o-ka-milo	whirling waters	39	Ka-wai-pa-pa	the forbidden waters
13	Wai-kani	sounding waters	40	Ko-holo-po	night traveling
14	Wai-lua-nui	increasing waters	41	Ka-ha-wai-'oka-pi-a	frugal valley
15	Wai-lua-iki	diminishing waters	42	Wai-o-honu	water of the turtle
16	Ko-pi-li-ula	sacred ceremony	43	Papa'a-hawa-hawa	strenghold
17	Pu'a-aka-a	open laughter	44	Ala-ala-'ula	reawakening
18	Wai-o-hu-e	deceptive waters	45	Wa-i-ka-ko'i	time of demand
19	Wai-o-hu-e-'lua	second deceptive water	45	Pa-'ihi	place of majesty
20	Pa-akea	spacious enclosure	47	Wai-lua	water spirits
21	Ka-pa-'ula	to hold sacred	48	Wa-'i-lua	scattered spirits
22	Hana-wi (Akahi)	first whistling wind	49	Pu'u-ha-o-a	burning hill
23	Hana-wi (Elua)	second whistling wind	50	Pae-hala	pandanus clusters
24	Ma-ka-pi-pi	desire for blessings	51	Maha-lawa	place of rest
25	Ku-hiwa	precious love	52	Hana-lawe	proud deduction
26	Ku-pu-koi	claiming tribute	53	Pua-a-lu-'u	prayer blossoms
27	Ka-ha-la-o-wa-ka	lightning flash	54	O'he'o	enduring pride

Inez MacPhee Ashdown's translations of the Hana Road bridges; layout by artist Sam Eason, a longtime Hana resident

grills, and restrooms. Nearby are Kopiliula and Waikani falls. A stream provides some smaller falls and pools suitable for swimming.

Nahiku

The village, named after the Hawaiian version of the Pleiades, is reached by a steep and bumpy three-mile road and has the dubious distinction of being one of the wettest spots along the coast. The well-preserved and tiny village church was constructed in 1867. The turnaround at ocean-side is where many locals come to shore-fish. Every evening during the summer months, beginning around 3 p.m., an extended family pod of dolphins enters Nahiku Bay to put on an impromptu performance of water acrobatics just for the joy of it. There's a picnic bench to sit on, and after the white bridge, a rope swing dangles above a refreshing freshwater pond. At one time Nahiku was a thriving Hawaiian village with thousands of inhabitants. Today it's home to only about 70 people, the best-known being former Beatle George Harrison. A few inhabitants are Hawaiian families, but mostly the people are wealthy Mainlanders seeking isolation. After a few large and attractive homes went up, the real estate agents changed the description from "desolate" to "secluded." What's the difference? About $500,000 per house! At the turn of the century it was the site of the Nahiku Rubber Co., the only commercial rubber plantation in the United States. Many rubber trees still line the road, although the venture collapsed in 1912 because the rubber was poor due to the overabundance of rainfall. Some people have augmented their incomes by growing *pakalolo* in the rainforest of this area. However, the alternative people who first came here and have settled in have discovered that there is just as much money to be made raising ornamental tropical flowers ($5000-10,000 per acre), and have become real "flower children." Many have roadside stands (you'll find others along the Hana Hwy.) where payment for the flowers displayed is on the honor system. Leave what is requested—prices will be marked.

Hana Gardenland Nursery

Continue on the Hana Hwy. to Hana Gardenland Nursery, open daily 9 a.m.-5 p.m., where you're free to browse and picnic. They sell fresh-cut flowers, and the prices are some of the best on Maui. On the premises is the **Hana Gardenland Cafe,** a "semi-gourmet window restaurant" (see "Food and Shopping" below). This certified nursery, which can ship plants or cut flowers to the Mainland, sits on more than five acres, over which you can take a $5 self-guided tour complete with map, and acquaint yourself with the spectacular plantlife that you will encounter throughout the Hana area. Inside the main building is a **fine arts and gift gallery** featuring local artists (others also). Included are: magnificent photos by Brad Lewis; inspired paintings by Bradford Binning; bronze sculptures by Marielis Faue; Bruce Turnbull's evocative wood sculptures; porcelains by Karen Jennings; freeform paper creations by Nicole Dean; imaginative basketry by Arlene Taus; and masterful oils and watercolors by Dick Lewis. The shelves hold perfume, a smattering of books on Hawaii, postcards, handmade jewelry, and koa wood boxes. Hana Gardenland is a perfect rest and fun stop for the entire family.

Kahanu Gardens

Past Gardenland and leading left is Ulaino Road. Here, the pavement soon gives way to a rough track and leads to Kahanu Gardens, tel. 248-8912, located past a shallow stream. Recently closed, but rumored to reopen, the gardens may be visited Tues.-Sat. 10 a.m.-2 p.m. for self-guided tours, admission $5. The gardens may be closed at any time if, because of heavy rains, the stream (no bridge) is too high or moving too swiftly to cross. This 120-acre tropical garden runs down to the tortured lava coastline. Part of the Pacific Tropical Botanical Garden, the Kahanu Gardens contain a huge variety of domestic and imported tropical plants, including a native pandanus forest and large and varied collections of breadfruit and coconut trees. Also within the gardens is **Piilanihale Heiau,** Hawaii's largest, with massive walls that rise over 50 feet.

Past Kahanu Gardens, Ulaina Road continues to roughen and ends at a parking area. Walking along the coast from there you will arrive at **Venus Pool,** a clothing-optional swimming spot where a waterfall drops fresh water into an oceanside pool.

Hana Airport

Less than a mile past Ulaino Road, on Alalele Road, a sign points left to Hana Airport, where **Aloha Island Air,** tel. (800) 323-3345, or 248-8328 in Hana, operates five daily flights to Kahului. All flights to Hana go through Kahului, from where you can get connecting flights to other Hawaiian cities and the Mainland. Hotel Hana Maui operates a shuttle between the airport and the hotel for its guests. There is no public transportation in Hana, and only Dollar Rent A Car, tel. 248-8237, can arrange wheels for you—make reservations before arriving in Hana.

Even though you're in a remote section of the island, adventure can still be found in Hana. Both Hawaii Helicopters and Soar Maui operate out of the Hana Airport. **Hawaii Helicopters,** tel. 877-3900, has various flight packages over the eastern half of the island, and **Soar Maui,** tel. 248-7433, a sailplane company, can thrill you with an engine-less glide along the mountainside. Its four offerings vary from a 20-minute Introductory Scenic Flight for $75 ($90 for two people) to a 75-minute Haleakala Crater Flight, $225-250. For the steel-stomach enthusiast, adventure comes by way of the Acrobatic Flight ($175), during which you can have your thrills with loops, spins, and gravity-defying stunts. Instruction and rentals available.

Waianapanapa State Park

Only three miles outside Hana, this state park offers not only tent camping but cabins sleeping up to six on a sliding scale, $10 single up to $30 for six. The cabins offer hot water, full kitchens, electricity, and bedding. A deposit is required. They're very popular so book far in advance by writing Division of State Parks (see "Camping and Hiking" in the Maui Introduction). Even for those not camping, Waianapanapa is a "must stop." Pass the office to get to the beach park and its black-sand beach. The swimming is dangerous during heavy surf because the bottom drops off quickly, but on calm days it's mellow. The snorkeling is excellent. Offshore is a clearly visible natural stone bridge. Contact P.O. Box 1049, Wailuku, HI 96753, tel. 244-4354.

A short, well-marked trail leads to **Waianapanapa Caves.** The tunnel-like trail passes through a thicket of vines and *hao,* a bush used by the Hawaiians to mark an area as *kapu.* The two small caves are like huge smooth tubs formed from lava. The water trapped inside is crystal clear. These caves mark the site of a Hawaiian legend, in which a lovely princess named Popoalaea fled from her cruel husband Kakae. He found her hiding here and killed her. During certain times of the year millions of tiny red shrimp invade the caves, turning the waters red, which the Hawaiians say is a reminder of the poor slain princess. Along the coastline here are remnants of the ancient Hawaiian **paved trail** that you can follow for a short distance.

Helani Gardens

Your last stop before Hana town, clearly marked on the right, these gardens are a labor of love begun 30 years ago by Howard Cooper, founder and longtime Hana resident. The gardens were recently sold to commercial flower growers, and it is not decided if they will be reopened to the public; if so, definitely go. The lower gardens are five formally manicured acres, but the 65 acres of upper garden are much more wild and open to anyone wishing to stroll around. The lower gardens have flowering trees and shrubs, vines, fruit trees, flowers, and potted plants everywhere. People see many of these plants in nurseries around the country, and may even have grown some varieties at home, but these specimens are huge. There are baobab trees, ginger plants, carp ponds, even papyrus. The fruit trees alone could supply a supermarket. The upper gardens are actually a nursery where plants from around the world are raised. Some of the most popular are heliconia and ginger, and orchids galore. In Mr. Cooper's own words, "Helani Garden is where heaven touches the earth." Be one of the saved!

At the entrance of Helani Gardens sits longtime Hana resident **John the Basketmaker,** who is here every day unless he's gone fishing . . . life Hana-style. John adeptly fashions palm-frond baskets, receiving the highest acclaim of local people who come to him when they need a basket. John has plenty of *aloha* and will "talk story" and demonstrate his craft if time permits, which is usually the case.

HANA

Hana is about as pretty a town as you'll find anywhere in Hawaii, but if you're expecting anything stupendous you'll be sadly disappointed. For most it will be a quick stopover at a store or beach en route to Oheo Stream: the townsfolk refer to these people as "rent-a-car tourists." The lucky who stay in Hana, or those not worried about time, will find plenty to explore throughout the area. The town is built on rolling hills that descend to Hana Bay; much of the surrounding lands are given over to pasture, while trim cottages wearing flower corsages line the town's little lanes. Before the arrival of white people, Hana was a stronghold that was conquered and reconquered by the kings of Maui and those of the north coast of the Big Island. The most strategic and historically laden spot is Kauiki Hill, the remnant of a cinder cone that dominates Hana Bay. This area is steeped in Hawaiian legend, and old stories relate that it was the demigod Maui's favorite spot. It's said that he transformed his daughter's lover into Kauiki Hill and turned her into the gentle rains that bathe it to this day.

Changing History

Hana was already a plantation town in the mid-1800s when a hard-boiled sea captain named George Wilfong started producing sugar on his 60 acres here. Over the years the laborers came from the standard mixture of Hawaiian, Japanese, Chinese, Portuguese, Filipino, and even Puerto Rican stock. The *luna* were Scottish, German, or American. All have combined to become the people of Hana. Sugar production faded out by the 1940s and Hana began to die, its population dipping below 500. Just then, San Francisco industrialist Paul Fagan purchased 14,000 acres of what was to become the **Hana Ranch.** Realizing that sugar was *pau,* he replanted his lands in *pangola* range grass and imported Hereford cattle from another holding on Molokai. Their white faces staring back at you as you drive past are now a standard part of Hana's scenery.

Fagan loved Hana and felt an obligation to and affection for its people. He also decided to retire here, and with enough money to materialze just about anything, he decided that Hana could best survive through limited tourism. He

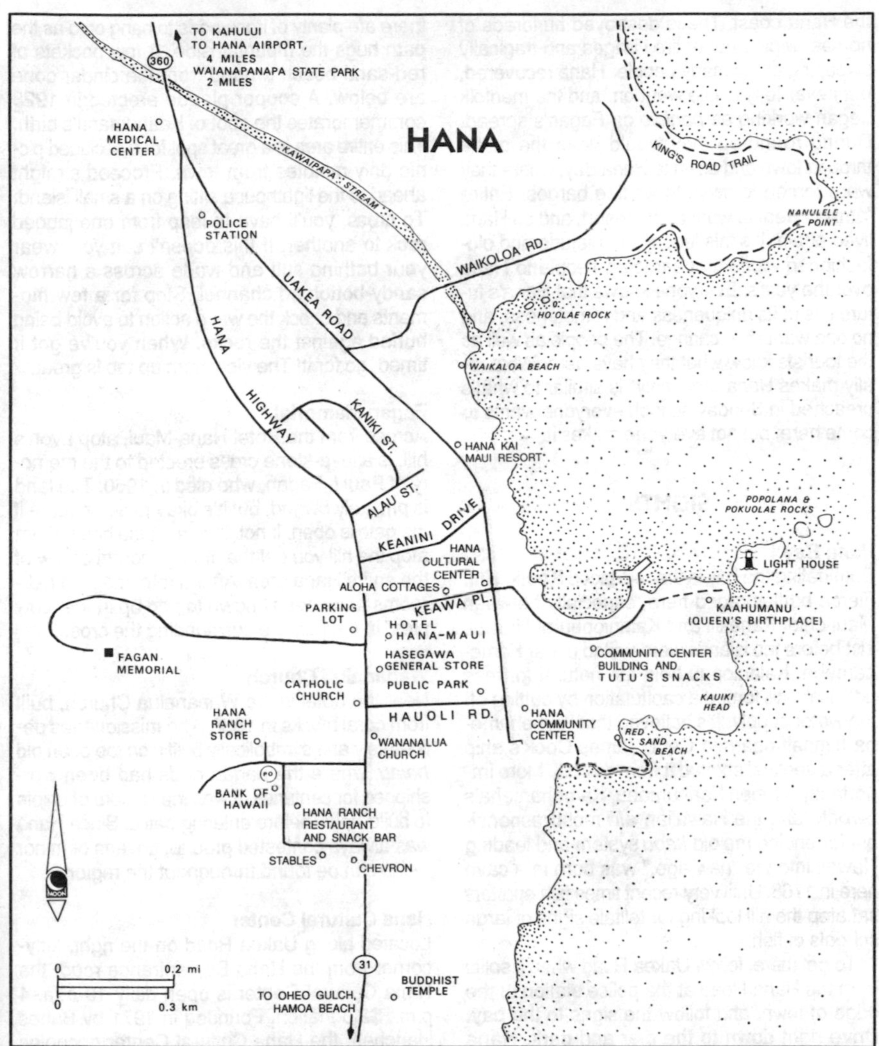

built the **Hotel Hana-Maui,** which catered to millionaires, mostly his friends, and began operation in 1946. Fagan owned a baseball team, the San Francisco Seals, and brought them to Hana in 1946 for spring training. This was a brilliant publicity move because sportswriters came along; becoming enchanted with Hana, they gave it a great deal of copy and were probably the first to publicize the phrase "Heavenly Hana." It wasn't long before tourists began arriving.

Unfortunately, the greatest heartbreak in modern Hana history occurred at just about the same time, on April 1, 1946. An earthquake in Alaska's Aleutian Islands sent huge tidal waves that raked the Hana coast. These destroyed hundreds of homes, wiping out entire villages and tragically sweeping away many people. Hana recovered, but never forgot. Life went on, and the menfolk began working as *paniolo* on Fagan's spread. During round-up they would drive the cattle through town and down to Hana Bay, where they were forced to swim to waiting barges. Entire families went to work at the resort, and so Hana lived again. It's this legacy of quietude and old-fashioned *aloha* that attracted people to Hana over the years. Everyone knows that Hana's future lies in its uniqueness and remoteness, and no one wants it to change. The people as well as the tourists know what they have here. What really makes Hana "heavenly" is similar to what's preached in Sunday school: everyone wants to come here, but not everyone makes it.

SIGHTS

Hana Bay

Dominating the bay is the red-faced **Kauiki Hill.** Fierce battles raged here, especially between Maui chief Kahekili and Kalaniopuu of Hawaii, just before the islands were united under Kamehameha. Kalaniopuu held the natural fortress until Kahekili forced a capitulation by cutting off the water supply. It's believed that Kamehameha himself boarded Capt. James Cook's ship after a sentinel spotted it from this hill. More importantly, Queen Kaahumanu, Kamehameha's favorite and the Hawaiian *ali'i* most responsible for ending the old *kapu* system and leading Hawaii into the "new age," was born in a cave here in 1768. Until very recent times fish-spotters sat atop the hill looking for telltale signs of large schools of fish.

To get there, follow Uakea Road when it splits from the Hana Road at the police station at the edge of town, and follow the signs to the bay. Drive right down to the pier and park. Hana Beach has full amenities and the swimming is good. It's been a surfing spot for centuries, although the best breakers occur in the middle of the bay. To explore Kauiki look for a pathway on your right and follow it. Hana disappears immediately; few tourists come out this way. Walk for a few minutes until the lighthouse comes clearly into view. The footing is slightly difficult but there are plenty of ironwoods to hang onto as the path hugs the mountainside. A few pockets of red-sand beach eroded from the cinder cone are below. A copper plaque erected in 1928 commemorates the spot of Kaahumanu's birth. This entire area is a great spot for a secluded picnic only minutes from town. Proceed straight ahead to the lighthouse sitting on a small island. To cross, you'll have to leap from one jagged rock to another. If this doesn't suit you, wear your bathing suit and wade across a narrow sandy-bottomed channel. Stop for a few moments and check the wave action to avoid being hurled against the rocks. When you've got it timed, go for it! The view from up top is great.

Fagan Memorial

Across from the Hotel Hana-Maui, atop Lyon's hill, is a lava-stone cross erected to the memory of Paul I. Fagan, who died in 1960. The land is privately owned, but it's okay to go up there if the gate is open. If not, inquire at the hotel. From atop the hill you get the most panoramic view of the entire Hana area. After a rain, magic mushrooms have been known to pop up in the "cow pies" in the pasture surrounding the cross.

Wananalua Church

Near the hotel is the Wananalua Church, built from coral blocks in 1838. The missionaries deliberately and symbolically built it on top of an old *heiau,* where the pagan gods had been worshipped for centuries. It was the custom of chiefs to build *heiau* before entering battle. Since Hana was always contested ground, dozens of minor *heiau* can be found throughout the region.

Hana Cultural Center

Located along Uakea Road on the right, kitty-corner from the Hana Bay entrance road, the Hana Cultural Center is open daily 10 a.m.-4 p.m., $2 donation. Founded in 1971 by Babes Hanchett, the Hana Cultural Center occupies an unpretentious building (notice the beautifully carved doors, however) on the grounds of the old courthouse and jail. The center houses fine examples of quiltwork: one, entitled "Aloha Kuuhae," was done by Rosaline Kelinoi, a Hana resident and the first woman voted into the State Legislature. There are pre-contact stone implements, tapa cloth, and an extensive shell collection. Your $2 entitles you to visit the courthouse and jail. Simple but functional, with bench and witness stand, it makes "Andy of Mayberry" look big-time. The jail was used from 1871 to 1978, and the townsfolk knew whenever it held an inmate because he became the groundskeeper and the grass would suddenly be mowed.

BEACHES

Red Sand Beach

This is a fascinating and secluded beach area, but unfortunately the walk down is treacherous. The path, after a while, skirts the side of a cliff, and the footing is tough because of unstable and crumbly cinders. Grave accidents have occurred, and even locals won't make the trip. Follow Uakea Road past the turnoff to Hana Bay. Proceed ahead until you pass the public tennis courts on your right and Hana School on your left. The road dead-ends a short way later. Look left for the worn path and follow it around the Hana Ranch property fence. Ahead is a Japanese cemetery with its distinctive headstones. Below are pockets of red sand amidst fingers of black lava washed by sky-blue water. There are many tidepools here. Keep walking around Kauiki Head until you are obviously in the hollowed-out amphitheater of the red cinder cone. Pat the walls to feel how crumbly they are—the red "sand" is eroded cinder. The water in the cove is fantastically blue against the redness.

Across the mouth of the bay are little pillars of stone, like castle parapets from a fairy kingdom, that keep the water safe for swimming. This is a favorite fishing spot for local people and the snorkeling is good, too. The beach is best in the morning before 11 a.m.; afterwards it can get hot if there's no wind and rough if the wind is from the north. The coarse red sand massages your feet, and there's a natural jacuzzi area in foamy pools of water along the shore.

Koki Beach Park

The beach park is a mile or so out of town heading toward the Seven Pools. Look for the first road to your left with a sign directing you to Hamoa Village/Beach. Koki is only a few hundred yards on the left. The riptides are fierce in here so don't swim unless it's absolutely calm. The winds can whip along here, too, even though at Hamoa Beach, less than a mile away, it can be dead calm. Koki is excellent for beachcombing and for a one-night's unofficial bivouac.

A very special person named Smitty lived in a cave on the north side of the beach. Hike left to the end of the beach and you'll find a rope ladder leading up to his platform. A distinguished older man, he "dropped out" a few years back and came here to live a simple monk's existence. He kept the beach clean and saved a number of people from the riptide. He was a long-distance runner who would tack up a "thought for the day" on Hana's public bulletin board. People loved him and he loved them in return. In 1984 the roof of his cave collapsed and he was killed. When his body was recovered, he was in a kneeling position. At his funeral, all felt a loss, but there was no sadness because all were sure that Smitty had gone home.

Hamoa Beach

Follow Hamoa Road a few minutes past Koki Beach until you see the sign for Hamoa. Between Hamoa and Koki are the remains of an extensive Hawaiian fishpond, part of which is still discernible. This entire area is an eroding cinder cone known as **Kaiwi O Pele** ("The Bones of Pele"). This is the spot where the swinish pig-god, Kamapua'a, ravished the goddess. Pele also fought a bitter battle with her sister here, who dashed Pele on the rocks, giving them their anatomical name. Out to sea is the diminutive Alau Island, a remnant left by Maui after he finished up the Hawaiian Islands. You can tell that Hamoa is no ordinary beach the minute you start walking down the paved, torch-lined walkway. This is the semiprivate beach of the Hotel Hana-Maui. But don't be intimidated, because no one can own the beach in Hawaii. Hamoa is terrific for swimming and bodysurfing. The hotel guests are shuttled here by buses throughout the day that depart the hotel on the hour, so if you want this lovely beach to yourself arrive before mid-morning and stay after late afternoon. There is a pavilion that the hotel uses for its Friday night luau, as well as restrooms and showers.

Waioka Pool

Also called Venus Pool, a myth-legend says it was once used exclusively by Hawaiian royalty.

At the bridge near the Hana Ohana Plantation Houses office, cross over the fence and hike (public access trail) through the fields above the river to its mouth. Here you'll find a spring-fed, freshwater pool scoured out of the solid rock walls of this water course. This is a refreshing, usually solitary, place for a swim or to sunbathe on the smooth rocks. Be safe and stay out of the ocean—the surf, which is just over the narrow sandbar, is strong. At certain times of the year you may see giant turtles just off the rocks a short way farther down the coast. They are best seen from the road a quarter mile past the river at a sharp turn in the highway. In the fields above Waioka Pool are the remains of an old sugar mill, and part of the King's Hwy., a paved pathway that once ran along the coast.

ACCOMMODATIONS

Hotel Hana-Maui

The Hotel Hana Maui, Hana, HI 96713, tel. 248-8211 or (800) 325-3535, is the legacy of Paul Fagan, who built it in the late '40s. It operates as close to a family-run hotel as you can get. Most personnel have been here from the beginning, or their jobs have passed to their family members. Guests love it that way, proven by an astonishing 80% in repeat visitors, most of whom feel like they're staying with old friends. The hotel has had only five managers in the last 45 years. The present manager, Fred Orr, came on board in 1990 when the management of the hotel was taken over by ITT Sheraton Hotels. In 1989 the hotel was sold to Keola Hana Maui, Inc. (a group of local Hawaiian, Japanese, and English investors), which has had the good sense to leave well enough alone. What has changed has been for the better. All rooms have been extensively renovated and the hotel can now proudly take its place among the truly luxury hotels of Hawaii. Rooms, each with their own lanai, surround the beautifully appointed grounds, where flowers add a splash of color to the green-on-green blanket of ferns and gently sloping lawn. Inside, the colors are subdued shades of white and tan. Morning light, with the sun filtering through the louvered windows, is especially tranquil. Each suite has a wet bar and large comfortable lounge area with rattan furniture covered in billowy white pillows. A glass-topped table is resplendent with a floral display, and a tray of fresh fruit greets you. A refrigerator is stocked with a full choice of drinks, and there's even fresh Kona coffee that you grind and brew yourself. The floors are a deep rich natural wood counterpointed by a light reed mat in the central area. The queen-size bed is covered with a handmade Hawaiian quilt, while Casablanca fans provide all the cooling necessary. The guest-cottage rooms have large free-standing pine closets; all rooms have two walk-ins. The bathrooms, as large as most sitting rooms, are tiled with earth-tone ceramic. You climb a step to immerse yourself in the huge tub, then open eye-level windows that frame a private mini-garden like an expressionist's still life.

The hotel staff adds an intangible quality of friendliness and *aloha* that sets the hotel apart from others. Housekeepers visit twice a day, leaving beige terry-cloth robes, and plumeria or orchids on every pillow. There is a library for use by guests, and a few shops for clothes, necessities, and gifts. Other facilities and activities include a wellness center, two heated swimming pools, tennis courts, superb horseback riding, a three-hole practice golf course, free bicycle use by guests, hikes to archaeological sites, and a famous luau held every Tuesday 6 p.m., at the hotel's facilities on Hamoa Beach. Activities are easily arranged by visiting the activities desk; it can be counted on to keep family and children happy with Hawaiian language lessons, lei-making, or swaying hula lessons.

Meals become a long-remembered sumptuous event. Follow the hostesses to your table in the new dining room. Here, breakfasts are all manner of fresh exotic fruits and juices; hot pastries; banana macadamia-nut waffles; and eggs poached or herbed into omelettes accompanied with petite steaks, fresh fish, or Hana Ranch sausages. Lunches, which upon request are prepared as very civilized picnics in wicker baskets, include chilled seafood chowder, oriental sesame chicken salad, smoked turkey and bacon sandwich, *kiawe*-grilled chicken breast, and a potpourri of vegetables. Special dinner menus are prepared daily, but you can begin with a sashimi plate or sautéed chicken with peanut sauce, and move on to an assortment of grilled and roasted fowl, seafood, wild boar, or locally grown beef and lamb, all basted in a variety of gourmet sauces. Vietnamese whole fish for two is especially tantalizing. Desserts are too tempting to resist, and if you can somehow save the room try lime or macadamia-nut pie, banana cream cake, coconut mousse, or a rainbow of rich and creamy ice creams and sherbets.

Rates start at $305 for a garden-view room and progress up to $795 for the sea ranch cottage suites. An option, for an additional $95, includes three meals under the full American plan. Otherwise you can pay as you eat. The entire scene isn't stiff or fancy, but a memorable first-class experience.

Heavenly Hana Inn

The second most famous Hana hotel, the Heavenly Hana, resembles a Japanese *ryokan* (inn). Walk through the formal garden and remove your shoes on entering the open-beamed main dining hall. Though now undergoing renovations, the inn is still open for business. The four suites seem like little apartments broken up into sections by shoji screens. Rates are $65-100 for up to four guests. The inn is homey and delightful. Two other rental units, a one-bedroom cottage and a family cottage, are also available in town. Write P.O. Box 146, Hana, HI 96713, tel. 248-8442.

Joe's Place

Across the road from the Heavenly Hana Inn is Joe's Place, tel. 248-7033, a very modest but clean self-serve guesthouse. A Maui-style sign reads, "If our office is closed, check key rack at left, and you may use a room and either pay in the morning or lock payment and key to the room before leaving, two persons to a room." Rooms cost $45, cash or traveler's checks only. Checkout is 10 a.m. and check-in is 2 p.m. "or as soon as room is available." Reservations are held until 4 p.m. There's kitchen access, a communal TV room, and maid service on request at an extra charge.

Hana Ohana Plantation Houses

Hana Ohana Plantation Houses offer a unique service enabling you to rent a private house on the lush, tropical Hana coast. You have 14 or so homes to choose from, ranging from the Plantation House—a deluxe cedar one-bedroom, sleeping four and complete with lanai, full kitchen, barbecue, and your own private koi pond and mini-garden, all in a coconut grove for $140—to the Lanai Makaalae Studio, a Japanese-style studio for two at $80. Several other newly remodeled homes are available in town and near Hamoa Beach, like the two-story Hale Kipa plantation house ($100-140) that has full amenities as well as an outdoor jacuzzi; and a four-bedroom, three-bath house that can easily accommodate up to 10 people for $300 per night. Contact Hana Ohana Plantation Houses at P.O. Box 489, Hana, HI 96713, tel. 248-7868, or (800) 258-4262 for reservations. Check-in is at Hana Gardenland, open daily 8:30 a.m.-5 p.m., just past mile marker 30, *mauka* side before entering Hana. Late check-ins call the listed number for directions.

Aloha Cottages

These are owned and operated by Zenzo and Fusae Nakamura and are the best bargain in town. The cottages are meticulously clean, well built, and well appointed. For $55-88 d, $10 per additional guest, you get two bedrooms, a full kitchen, living room, deck, and outdoor grills. Mrs. Nakamura is very friendly and provides daily maid service. The fruit trees on the property provide free fruit to guests. Contact them at P.O. Box 205, Hana, HI 96713, tel. 248-8420.

Hana Kai Maui Resort

These resort apartments, P.O. Box 38, Hana, HI 96713, tel. 248-8426 or (800) 346-2772, directly overlooking Hana Bay, are well maintained and offer a lot for the money. Rates are: studios from $103, deluxe one-bedrooms $125-158. All have private lanai with exemplary views of the bay, maid service, laundry facilities, and barbecues. The views couldn't be more spectacular as the grounds, laid out in a lovely garden highlighting the interplay of black lava rock and multihued blooms, step down the mountainside to the bay.

Hana Bay Vacation Rentals

Stan and Paula Collins offer nine private cottages, cabins, two-bedroom houses, and duplexes in and around Hana for rent by the day, week, or month. Discounts of 10% are given on stays of seven days or longer. Rates start at $65 and go up to $170. Their rentals include everything from a rustic cabin to a half-million-dollar, three-bedroom, beachfront home with banana and breadfruit trees and fishpond in the front yard. This small company has an excellent reputation for quality and service. Write P.O. Box 318, Hana, HI 96713; or call 248-7727 or (800) 959-7727.

Hana Kai Holidays
A second agency in Hana renting everything from a seaside cottage to large plantation homes scattered throughout the Hana area. Hana Kai Holidays has rates ranging $65-225 per night. Write P.O. Box 536, Hana, HI 96713; or call 248-7742 or (800) 548-0478.

Hana Hou Hale
Brand new, this plantation-style guesthouse, tel. 248-8913 or 248-7067, offers a wraparound deck, large shuttered windows, hot tub, vaulted ceilings, and knotty pine floors. The units, two one-bedrooms at $85, and one two-bedroom at $145, have mini-kitchens complete with fridge, microwave, toaster oven, and electric coffee pot, along with color TV, VCR, and ceiling fans. The entire front of the building is nothing but window offering a panoramic view of the distant bay.

FOOD AND SHOPPING

As far as dining out goes, there's little to choose from in Hana. The **Hotel Hana-Maui** main dining room offers breakfast, lunch, and dinner buffets. Prices vary according to your choice, but expect to spend $10 for breakfast, $15 for lunch, and $40 for dinner. Reservations recommended. The hotel also has a self-serve coffee shop.

Note: Except for Thursday through Saturday evenings at the Hana Ranch Restaurant, there is no place besides the Hotel Hana-Maui to get an evening meal. Dinner at the hotel is from 6 p.m., and if you are going to be in Hana, be sure to make reservations. Hotel guests have first preference, but the hotel will try their hardest to seat. Also, aside from the nightly Hawaiian music at the hotel bar, the only evening **entertainment** in Hana is at the Hana Ranch Restaurant, offered about once a month when a local band performs dance music. Or you may find the frequent evening baseball games at the ballpark an alternative.

The **Hana Ranch Restaurant** serves very tasty family-style meals, but they can be stampeded by ravenous tourists heading up or down the Hana Road. Breakfast, daily 6:30-10 a.m., is served from an adjoining service window only, but a shaded area with picnic tables is provided. Lunch, also served from the service window, daily 11 a.m.-4 p.m., is sandwiches, saimin, or plate lunches. An inside **lunch buffet,** served daily 11 a.m.-3 p.m., adults $12.95, children $6.50, salad only $7.95, includes barbecued beef ribs, teriyaki chicken, baked beans, assorted vegetables, and baked potato. A **dinner buffet** similar to lunch is served Friday and Saturday evenings 5-9 p.m., and a pizza and salad bar is served on Thursday evenings. Besides the Hotel Hana-Maui, this is the only place to have an evening meal in Hana.

Tu Tu's Snack Shop, open daily for breakfast and lunch, is at the community center building at Hana Bay; window service with tables available. Salads $2-3, saimin $2.60, plate lunches about $4, hamburgers, sandwiches, drinks, and ice cream. This building was donated by Mrs. Fagan, the wife of Paul Fagan, the original owner of the Hotel Hana-Maui, to the community.

Sit surrounded by the blooms and ferns of the Hana Gardenland Nursery and enjoy the delicious food prepared by the **Hana Gardenland Cafe,** a bamboo- and rattan-fronted "window restaurant" open daily 9 a.m.-5 p.m. Start your day with the sunrise continental breakfast of Maui bagels served hot with cream cheese and guava jelly for $1.75, or steamed eggs and salsa served with whole wheat toast for $4.75. Lunch and snack time brings guacamole, made fresh with hand-picked Gardenland avocado and served with taro chips for $4.95, along with gourmet sides like pesto pasta for only $2.50, or soup for $3.25. Sandwiches are smoked turkey with cheddar cheese topped by Tony's homemade cranberry relish with a side of baby greens for $6.75, or a fresh *ahi* tuna salad sandwich for $6.75. Refreshing beverages include espresso, cappuccino, fresh-squeezed orange or carrot juice, fruit smoothies, and tropical fruit iced tea for only $1.50. The cafe will be happy to prepare your food to go.

Hasegawa's General Store
In the ranks of general stores, Hasegawa's, formerly south of town on the Hana Road, would be

commander-in-chief. This institution, run by Harry Hasegawa, had been in the family for 75 years before it burned to the ground in the fall of 1990. While your gas tank was being filled, you could buy anything from a cane knife to a computer disk. There were rows of food items, dry goods, and a hardware and parts store out back. Cold beer, film, blue jeans, and picnic supplies—somehow it was all crammed in there. Everybody went to Hasegawa's, and it was a treat just to browse and people-watch.

The store, now temporarily housed in the old movie theater in downtown Hana, open daily 8 a.m.-5:30 p.m., Sunday 9 a.m.-3:30 p.m., tel. 248-8231, plans to rebuild, but until then it still serves the community and visitors that for so long sustained it.

Hana Ranch Store

From the Hana Road, make the first right past St. Mary's Catholic Church and go up to the top of the hill to find the Hana Ranch Store, open daily 7 a.m.-6:30 p.m., tel. 248-8261, a general store with an emphasis on foodstuffs. They carry a supply of imported beers, a wide selection of food items, film, videos, and some gifts. The bulletin board here gives you a good idea of what's currently happening in town.

Hana Treasures

In the small complex across from the Hana Ranch Restaurant, look for Hana Treasures, open Mon.-Fri. 10 a.m.-4 p.m., Saturday 10:30 a.m.-2:30 p.m., closed Sunday, operated by Cheryl, a Hana resident who is friendly and willing to offer local information. The small shop features airbrushed T-shirts by Hana artists, an assortment of Hawaiian gifts (particularly those made in the Hana area), and two display cases of silver necklaces, bracelets, and rings.

SERVICES, INFORMATION, GETTING AROUND

Hana Hou Charters

Also known as Hana from the Sea, tel. 877-7369, this charter is operated by husband-and-wife team Captain Mark and Nani. They will take you on their glass-bottomed 38-foot *Pacific Safari* along one of Hawaii's most spectacular coastlines. Departure is from Hana Pier Mon.-Fri. at 9 a.m.; reservations are highly recommended 24 hours in advance. Hana Hou offers a 90-minute sightseeing and photo cruise complete with snacks and beverage for only $29.95; or a three and one-half-hour snorkel cruise for $59.95 complete with catered lunch. The boat leaves Hana Bay, passing the famous spot of Queen Kaahumanu's birth, and then rounds Kauiki Head for the trip south along the coast where waterfalls tumble from the emerald green *pali*. A great view is ensured since the boat holds only 28 passengers, nine of whom can perch on the top deck to look for the telltale spouts of humpback whales who shelter along this coast from November through March (see "Whales" under "Flora And Fauna" in the General Introduction). After snorkeling, the boat continues south, passing Wailua Waterfall, the tallest on Maui, a silver thread shimmering from the scalloped shoreline of stone and jungle. Captain Mark and Nani, who often perform community service work like taking the local school children out for excursions, are members of Earthtrust, and a percentage of their profits goes directly back to that organization.

Hana Medical Center

Along the Hana Road, clearly marked on the right just as you enter town, tel. 248-8294, the center is open Mon.-Fri. 8 a.m.-noon and again 2-5 p.m., Saturday 8 a.m.-noon only, closed Sunday. For emergencies, use the phone at the hospital entrance.

Police Station

The station is at the Y-intersection between Hana and Uakea roads, just as you enter town. For emergencies call 911.

Services

The Bank of Hawaii, tel. 248-8015, is open Mon.-Thurs. 8:30 a.m.-4:30 p.m., Friday 3-6 p.m.; the **post office** is open weekdays 8 a.m.-4:30 p.m. Both are next door to the Hana Ranch Restaurant. The **library** is at Hana School, open Mon.-Fri. 8 a.m.-5 p.m., tel. 248-7714.

Gas

The only gas available in town is at the Chevron station, next to the horse stables and below the Hana Ranch Restaurant.

Rental Cars
Dollar Rent A Car, tel. 248-8237, is the only show in town. It's best to call in advance to ensure a reservation. Cars may be available on short notice during low season, but don't count on it.

Hauoli Lio Stable
The stable is open through the day for horseback-riding adventures on the Hana Ranch. Rides include one-hour trips ($27.50 per person) through the macadamia nut plantation or tropical rainforest, and near the beach. Book through the activities desk at the Hotel Hana-Maui.

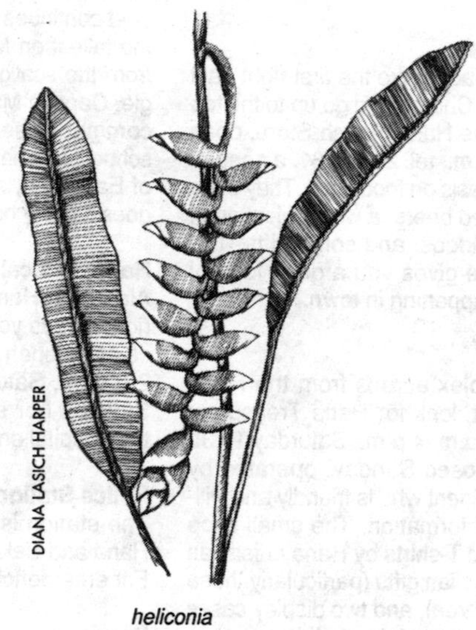

heliconia

BEYOND HANA

Now you're getting into adventure. The first sign is that the road gets steadily worse after Hana. It begins to narrow, then the twists and turns begin again, and it's potholed. Signs warn "Caution: Pig Crossing." There are no phones and no gas; a fruit stand or two and one store can be counted on only to be closed. The faint-hearted should turn back, but those with gumption are in for a treat. There are roadside waterfalls, cascading streams filling a series of pools, a hero's grave, and some forgotten towns. If you persevere all the way, you pop out at the Tedeschi Winery, where you can reward yourself with a glass of bubbly before returning to civilization.

Wailua Falls

About seven miles out of Hana, Wailua and Kanahualui falls tumble over steep lava *pali,* filling the air with a watery mist and filling their pools below. They're just outside your car door, and a minute's effort will take you to the mossy grotto at the base. There's room to park. If not for Oheo up ahead, this would be a great picnic spot, but wait! Sometimes roadside artists park here. In a few minutes you pass a little shrine cut into the mountain. This is the **Virgin by the Roadside.** It's usually draped with a fresh lei.

KIPAHULU: THE COASTAL BOUNDARY OF HALEAKALA NATIONAL PARK

This is where the enormous **Kipahulu Valley** meets the sea. Palikea Stream starts way up on Haleakala and steps its way through the valley, leaving footprints of waterfalls and pools until it spends itself in the sea. The area was named the Seven Sacred Pools by a publicity person in the late '40s. The area should have been held sacred, but it wasn't. You can feel the tremendous power of nature: bubbling waters, Haleakala red and regal in the background, and the sea pounding away. Hawaiians lived here but the *heiau* that you would surely expect are missing. Besides that, there aren't seven pools; there are more like 24! The name "Seven Sacred Pools" is falling into disfavor because it is inaccurate, with local people and the National Park Service preferring the proper name Kipahulu, or Oheo Gulch, instead.

Getting There

Head 10 miles out of Hana on Rt. 31. You'll come to a large cement arched bridge (excellent view) and then a parking area to your left with a ranger's station, restrooms, and public telephone. A short way beyond, a dirt trail turns off the highway to the left and leads down to the large grassy camping area.

Warnings And Tips

Before doing any exploring, try to talk to the rangers, Eddie Pu and Perry Bednorse, generally found around the parking area. They know a tremendous amount of natural history concerning the area and can inform you about the few dangers in the area, such as the flash flooding that occurs in the pools. Ranger Pu has received a Presidential Citation for risking his life on five occasions to pluck drowning people from the quickly rising streams. For those intending to hike or camp, bring your own water. Don't be put off by the parking area, which looks like a used-car lot for Japanese imports; 99% are gone by sundown. The vast majority of the people go to the easily accessible lower pools, but a stiff hike up the mountain takes you to the upper pools, a bamboo forest, and a fantastic waterfall.

The Lower Pools

Head along the clearly marked path from the parking area to the flat, grass-covered peninsula. The winds are heavy here as they enter the mouth of the valley from the sea. A series of pools to choose from are off to your left. It's delightful to lie in the last one and look out to the sea crunching the shore just a few yards away. Move upstream for the best swimming in the largest of the lower pools. Be careful, because you'll have to do some fairly difficult rock-climbing. The best route is along the right-hand side as you face up the valley. Once you're satiated, head back up to the road along the path on the left-hand side. This will take you up to the bridge that you crossed when arriving, one of the best vantage points from which to look up and down this amazing valley.

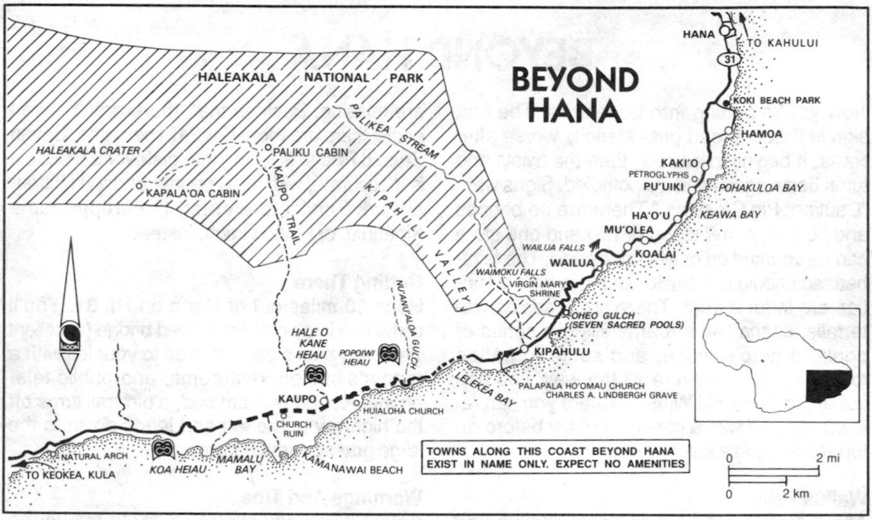

The Upper Pools

Very few people head for the upper pools. However, those who do will be delighted. The trail is called **Waimoku Falls Trail,** and begins at the ranger station. The falls at Makahiku are a half mile uphill and Waimoku Falls is two miles distant. The toughest part is at the beginning as you huff-puff your way straight uphill. The trail leads to a fenced overlook from where you can see clearly the lacelike falls at Makahiku as they plummet 181 feet to the rugged valley floor below. Behind you a few paces and to the left will be a waterworn, trenchlike path. Follow it to the lip of the falls and a gorgeous little pool. You can swim safely to the very edge of the falls. The current is gentle here, and if you stay to the right you can peer over the edge and remain safe behind encircling boulders. Be extremely conscious of the water rising, and get out immediately if it does!

After refreshing yourself, continue on the path through a grassy area. Here you'll cross the creek where there's a wading pool, and then zigzag up the opposite bank. After passing some enormous mango trees, you start going through a high jungle area. Suddenly you're in an extremely dense bamboo forest. The trail is well cut as you pass through the green darkness of this stand. If the wind is blowing, the bamboo will sing a mournful song for you. Emerge into more mangos and thimbleberries and there's the creek again. Turn left and follow the creek, without crossing yet, and the trail will become distinct once more. There's a wooden walkway, and then, eureka! . . . Waimoku Falls. It cascades over the *pali* and is so high that you have to strain your neck back as far as it will go. It's more than a waterfall; it's silver filigree. You can stand in the shallow pool below surrounded by a sheer rock amphitheater. The sunlight dances in this area and tiny rainbows appear and disappear. There is periodically a ranger-led hike to the falls (check bulletin board for schedule).

Camping

Kipahulu is part of Haleakala National Park, and camping is free for a three-day limit (no one counts too closely) and no permit is necessary. The campgrounds are primitive and mostly empty, except on holiday weekends when they can be packed. From the parking lot follow the camping sign and continue straight ahead on the dirt track. Bear right to a large grassy area overlooking the sea, where signs warn you not to disturb an archaeological area. Notice how spongy the grass is here. You'll see a very strange palm tree that bends and twists from the ground like a serpent. Move to the trees just behind it to escape the wind. Here are clean outhouses and barbecue grills, but no potable water, so make sure to bring your own.

BEYOND OHEO GULCH

Route 31 beyond Oheo is genuinely rugged and makes the car companies cry. It can be done, and even the tourist vans make it part of their regular route. Be aware, however, that rough weather can bring landslides, and that the road can be closed by a locked gate with access available only for official business and local residents. Check! In 1.5 miles you come to **Palapala Hoomau Church** (St. Paul's) and its tiny cemetery where Charles Lindbergh is buried. People, especially those who are old enough to remember the "Lone Eagle's" historic flight, are drawn here like pilgrims. The public is not really encouraged to visit, but the human tide cannot be stopped. If you go, please follow all of the directions posted. Up ahead is Samuel F. Pryor's Kipahulu Ranch. Mr. Pryor was a vice-president of Pan Am and a close chum of Lindbergh's. It was he who encouraged Lindbergh to spend his last years in Hana. Sam Pryor raises gibbons and lives quietly with his wife. Past Sam Pryor's place is B.B. Smith's fruit stand (which isn't always open), and another follows shortly. Here the road really begins to get rugged.

Kipahulu Ranch has seen other amazing men. Last century a Japanese samurai named Sentaro Ishii lived here. He was enormous, especially for a Japanese of that day, over six feet tall. He came in search of work, and at the age of 61 married Kehele, a local woman. He lived in Kipahulu until he died at the age of 102.

Kaupo Store

The vistas open up at the beginning of the Kaupo Gap just when you pass **Huialoha Church,** built in 1859. The village of Kaupo and the Kaupo Store follow Huialoha Church. A sign reads "This store is usually open Mon.-Fri., around 7:30 to 4:30. Don't be surprised if it's not open yet. It soon will be unless otherwise posted. Closed Saturday and Sunday and when necessary." Check out the bulletin board; it's full of business cards from all over the world. Only a few families live in Kaupo, old ones and new ones trying to live independently. Kaupo is the last of a chain of stores that stretched all the way from Keanae and were owned by the Soon Family. Nick Soon was kind of a modern-day wizard. He lived in Kaupo, and among his exploits he assembled a car and truck brought piecemeal on a barge, built the first electric generator in the area, and even made a model airplane from scratch that flew. He was the son of an indentured Chinese laborer.

Auntie Jean's

Wonders never cease! Just across from the Kaupo Store is a recently opened *kaukau* wagon, owned and operated by Auntie Jean Aki, who (along with her husband Charles) owns and operates a Kaupo cattle ranch. Their organic beef is made into the large juicy burgers offered on the limited menu. Definitely stop by if only just to "talk story" with Auntie Jean, a lifelong Hawaii resident, who came to the Kaupo area 30 years ago. Open from "about 11 a.m. to about when the sun goes down, everyday except Wednesday or Thursday, probably," Auntie Jean offers big juicy regular burgers, or teriyaki burgers for $3, along with ice cream and soda. Also along with her husband, Jean owns and operates **Charley's Trail Rides,** offering guided day-trips and overnighters from Kaupo to Haleakala Crater. Auntie Jean has "plenty *aloha*" that is as nourishing to the soul as her burgers are to the belly. Fill up!

Once you get to the Kaupo Gap, the tropical vegetation suddenly stops and the landscape is barren and dry. Here Haleakala's rain shadow creates an environment of yellow grassland dotted with volcanic rock. Everywhere are *ahu,* usually three stacked stones, that people have left as personal prayers and wishes to the gods.

Just after Kaupo, the dirt road becomes a beat-up, hard surface that wheels along the sheer cliff face with the ocean far below. Around mile markers 29 and 30, notice an ancient lava flow that spilled into the sea and created a huge arch. Also, be aware that free-range cattle can be in the middle of the road around any turn. Enjoy the road, because in a few minutes the pavement will improve and you'll be back in the civilized world.

Found above 3,000 feet, the small, gray Hawaiian thrush, the oma'o, is a probable descendant of a Townsend's solitaire.

KAHOOLAWE

OVERVIEW

The island of Kahoolawe is clearly visible from many points along Maui's south shore, especially when it was lit up like a firecracker during heavy bombardment by the U.S. Navy. Until recently Kahoolawe was a target island, uninhabited except for a band of wild goats that refuse to be killed off. Kahoolawe was a sacred island born to Wakea and Papa, the two great mythical progenitors of Hawaii. The birth went badly and almost killed Papa, and it hasn't been any easier for her ill-omened child ever since. Kahoolawe became synonymous with Kanaloa, the man-god. Kanaloa was especially revered by the *kahuna ana'ana,* the "black sorcerers" of old Hawaii. Kanaloa, much like Lucifer, was driven from heaven by Kane, the god of light. Kanaloa held dominion over all poisonous things and ruled in the land of the dead from his power spot here on Kahoolawe. There are scores of archaeological sites and remains of *heiau* all over the bomb-cratered face of Kahoolawe. A long, bitter feud has raged between the U.S. Navy, which wanted to keep the island as a bombing range, and Protect Kahoolawe Ohana, a Hawaiian native-rights organization that wants the sacred island returned to the people. In a recent turn of events, the Navy has agreed to stop bombing and return the island to the state of Hawaii, bringing the Ohana one step closer to its goal.

The Land

Kahoolawe is 11 miles long and six miles wide, with 29 miles of coastline. The tallest hill is **Lua Makika** in the northeast section at 1,477 feet. There are no natural lakes or ponds on the island, but it does get some rain and a stream runs through Ahupu Gulch.

MODERN HISTORY

It's perfectly clear that small families of Hawaiians lived on Kahoolawe for countless generations and that religious rites were carried out by many visiting *kahuna* over the centuries, but mostly Kahoolawe was left alone. In 1917 Angus

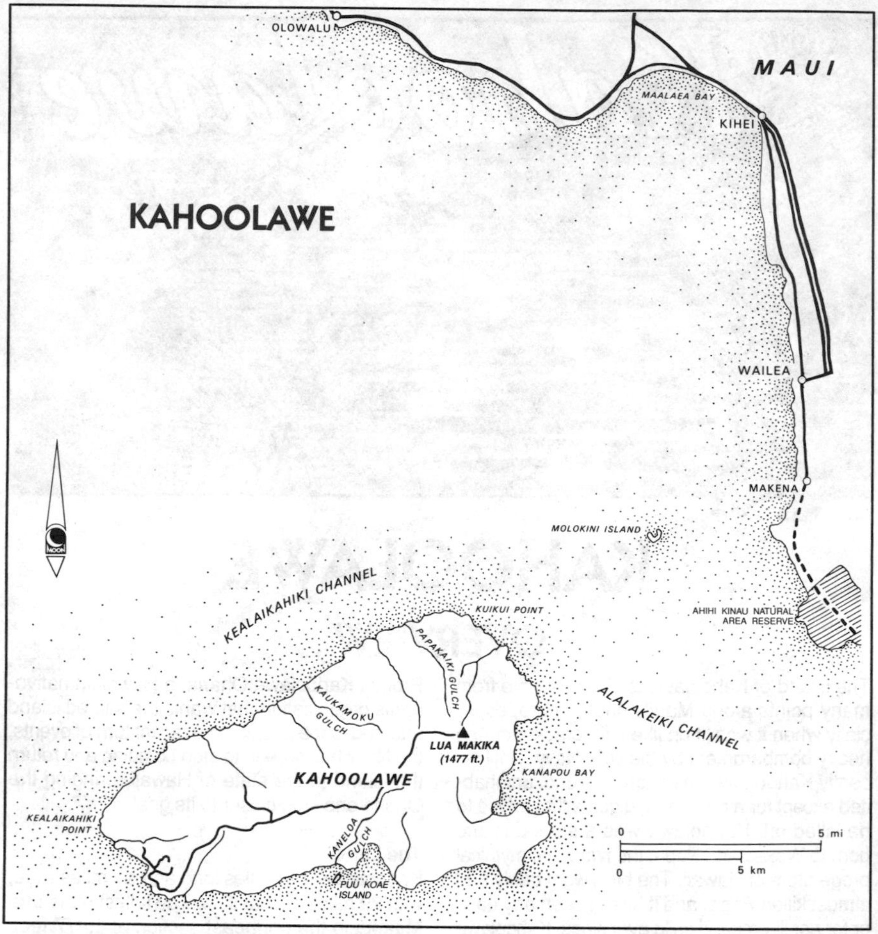

MacPhee, a cattleman, leased Kahoolawe from the territorial government for $200 per year. The lease would run until 1954 with a renewal option, if by 1921 MacPhee could show reasonable progress in taming the island. Harry Baldwin bought into the **Kahoolawe Ranch** in 1922, and with his money and MacPhee's know-how, Kahoolawe turned a neat profit. The island then supported indigenous vegetation such as ohia, mountain apples, and even Hawaiian cotton and tobacco. MacPhee planted eucalyptus and range grass from Australia, which caught on well and stopped much of the erosion. Gardens were planted around the homestead and the soil proved to be clean and fertile. Within a few years Kahoolawe Ranch cattle were being shipped regularly to markets on Maui.

The Navy Arrives

In 1939, with the threat of war on the horizon, MacPhee and Baldwin, stimulated by patriotism, offered a small tip of Kahoolawe's southern shore to the U.S. Army as an artillery range. One day after the attack on Pearl Harbor, the

J.D. BISIGNANI

The Protect Kahoolawe Ohana resolutely builds a longhouse, pitting traditional Hawaiian beliefs aganst naval artillery.

U.S. Navy seized all of Kahoolawe to further the "war effort" and evicted MacPhee, immediately disenfranchising the Kahoolawe Ranch. Kahoolawe has since become the most bombarded piece of real estate on the face of the earth. During WW II the Navy praised Kahoolawe as being *the* most important factor in winning the Pacific War, and it held Kahoolawe until the fall of 1990.

The Book On Kahoolawe

Inez MacPhee Ashdown lived on the island with her father and was a driving force in establishing the homestead. She has written a book, *Recollections of Kahoolawe,* available from Topgallant Publishing Co., Honolulu. This book chronicles the events from 1917 until the military takeover and is rife with myths, legends, and historical facts about Kahoolawe. Mrs. Ashdown is in her late eighties, going blind and in failing health, but her mind remains brilliant. She resides on Maui.

The Protect Kahoolawe Ohana: A.K.A. PKO

The Protect Kahoolawe Ohana is an extended group, favoring traditional values based on *aloha aina* (love of the land), which is the primary binding force for all Hawaiians. They would like the island to return to Hawaiian Lands inventory and the *kahu* (stewardship) to the hands of native Hawaiians. The point driven home by the Ohana is that the military has totally ignored and belittled native Hawaiian values, which are now beginning to be asserted. They maintain that Kahoolawe is not a barren wasteland, but a vibrant part of their history and religion. Indeed, Kahoolawe was placed on the National Register of Historic Sites.

The Ohana currently has legal access to the island for 10 days per month, for 10 months of the year. They have built a *halau* (longhouse) and use the time on Kahoolawe to dedicate themselves to religious, cultural, and social pursuits. The Ohana look to Kahoolawe as their *pu'uhonua* (refuge), where they gain strength and knowledge from each other and the *aina.* Hopefully Kahoolawe's future as a sacred island is now secure.

Recent Developments

In 1990, then-president George Bush issued an order to immediately halt the bombing of Kahoolawe, and at the same time established a congressional commission to create the terms and conditions for returning the island to the state. At that time, Ka Lahui Hawaii, the Native Nation of Hawaii, founded in Hilo in 1987, demanded that the island, as "totally ceded lands," be given to them as part of their sovereign nation. The Protect Kahoolawe Ohana, in a more moderate stance, suggested "land banking" the island under the control of the state or federal government until the United States recognizes the sovereignty of the Ka Lahui Hawaii. In the meantime, the PKO continues to lobby for exclusive rights to the stewardship of Kahoolawe. Finally, as of May 7, 1994, Kahoolawe was returned to the state of Hawaii. It is tough to conjecture what the final result will be, though it seems to be moving in the direction of native Hawaiian management.

BOB RACE

LANAI

INTRODUCTION

Lanai, in the long dark past of Hawaiian legend-history, was a sad and desolate place inhabited by man-eating spirits and fiendish blood-curdling ghouls. It was redeemed by spoiled but tough Prince Kaululaau, exiled here by his kingly father, Kakaalaneo of Maui. Kaululaau proved not only brave, but wily too; he cleared Lanai of its spirits through trickery and opened the way for human habitation. Lanai was for many generations a burial ground for the *ali'i* and therefore filled with sacred mana and *kapu* to commoners. Later, reports of its inhospitable shores filled the logs of old sailing vessels. In foul weather, captains navigated desperately to avoid its infamously treacherous waters, whose melancholy whitecaps still outline Shipwreck Beach and give credence to its name.

The vast majority of people visiting the Hawaiian Islands view Lanai from Lahaina on West Maui but never actually set foot upon this lovely quiet island. For two centuries, first hunters and then lovers of the humpback whale have come to peer across the waters of the Auau Channel, better known as the "Lahaina Roads," in search of these magnificent giants. Lanai in Hawaiian means "Hump," and it's as if nature built its own island-shrine to the whale in the exact spot where they are most plentiful. Lanai is a victim of its own reputation. Its nickname is the "Pineapple Island"; most visitors are informed by even longtime residents that Lanai is a dull place covered in one large pineapple plantation. It's true that Lanai has the largest pineapple plantation in the world, 12,000 cultivated acres, which accounts for about 90% of U.S. production. But the island has 74,000 acres that remain untouched and perfect for exceptional outdoor experiences. Besides, the pineapple fields are themselves interesting: endless rows of the porcupine plants, sliced and organized by a labyrinth of roads, contoured and planted by improbable-looking machines, and tended by mostly Filipino workers in wide-brimmed hats and goggles.

Around And About

The people of Lanai live in one of the most fortuitously chosen spots for a working village in the world: Lanai City. All but about two dozen of the island's 2,600 permanent residents make their homes here. (See "Changing Lanai" under "History" below.) Nestled near the ridge of mountains in the northeast corner of the Palawai Basin, Lanai City (1,600 feet) is sheltered, cooled, and characterized by a mature and extensive grove of Norfolk pines planted in the early 1900s by the practical New Zealand naturalist, George Munro. This evergreen canopy creates a parklike atmosphere about town while reaching tall green fingers to the clouds. A mountainous spine tickles drizzle from the water-bloated bellies of passing clouds for the thirsty, red, sunburned plains of Lanai below. The trees, like the bristled hair of an annoyed cat, line the **Munro Trail** as it climbs Lanaihale, the highest spot on the island (3,370 feet). The Munro Trail's magnificent panoramas encompass sweeping views of no fewer than five of the eight major islands as it snakes along the mountain ridge, narrowing at times to less than 30 yards across. Here are limitless paths for trekking and four-wheel driving.

Maunalei Gulch, a vast precipitous valley visible from "The Trail," was the site of a last-ditch effort by Lanai warriors to repel an invasion by the warrior king of the Big Island at the turn of the 18th century. Now its craggy arms provide refuge to mouflon sheep as they execute death-defying leaps from one rocky ripple to the next. On the valley floors roam axis deer, and on the northwest grasslands is the remainder of an experimental herd of pronghorn antelope brought from Montana in 1959. After saturating yourself with the glories of Lanai from the heights, descend and follow a well-paved road from Lanai City to the southern tip of the island. Here, **Manele** and **Hulopoe** bays sit side by side. Manele is a favorite spot of small sailing craft that have braved the channel from Lahaina. Hulopoe Bay, just next door, is as salubrious a spot as you can hope to find. It offers camping and all that's expected of a warm, sandy, palm-lined beach. With its virtually untouched underwater marine park, Hulopoe is regarded as one of the premier snorkeling spots in the entire island chain.

Adventure

You can take a hike or 4WD to Kaunolu Bay, one of the best-preserved ancient Hawaiian village sites. Kamehameha the Great came to this ruggedly masculine shore to fish and frolic his summers away with his favorite cronies. Here, a retainer named Kahekili leaped from a seacliff to the ice-blue waters below, and challenged all other warriors to prove their loyalty to Kamehameha by following his example and hurtling themselves off what today is known as **Kahekili's Leap.**

You can quickly span a century by heading for the southeast corner of Lanai and its three abandoned villages of **Lopa, Naha,** and **Keomuku.** Here legends abound. *Kahuna* curses still guard a grove of coconut trees, which are purported to refuse to let you down if you climb for their nuts without offering the proper prayers. Here also are the remnants of a sugar train believed to have caused its cane enterprise to fail because the rocks of a nearby *heiau* were disturbed and used in its track bed. An enchanting abandoned Hawaiian church in Keomuku insists on being photographed.

You can head north along the east shore to **Shipwreck Beach,** where the rusting hulk of a Liberty ship, along with timbers and planks from the great wooden square-riggers of days gone by, lie along the beach, attesting to the authenticity of its name. Shipwreck Beach is a shore stroller's paradise, a real beachcomber's boutique. Also along here are some thought-provoking petroglyphs. Other petroglyphs are found on a hillside overlooking the "pine" fields of the Palawai Basin.

If you hunger for a totally private beach, head north for the Polihua Trail. En route, you'll pass through a fantastic area of ancient cataclysm aptly called **The Garden of The Gods.** This raw, baked area of monolithic rocks and tortured earth turns incredible shades of purple, red, magenta, and yellow as the sun plays upon it from different angles. You have a junction of trails here. You can bear left to lonely **Kaena Point,** where you'll find Lanai's largest *heiau,* a brooding setting full of weird power vibrations. If you're hot and dusty and aching for a dip, continue due north to trail's end where the desolation of the garden suddenly gives way to the gleaming brightness of virtually unvisited **Polihua Beach.**

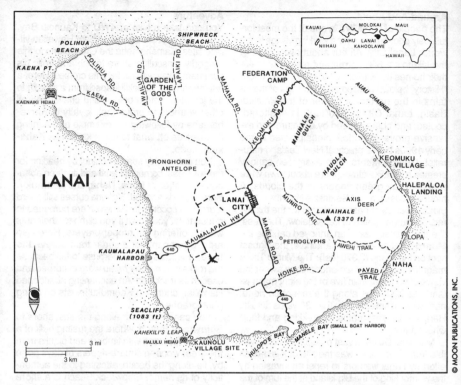

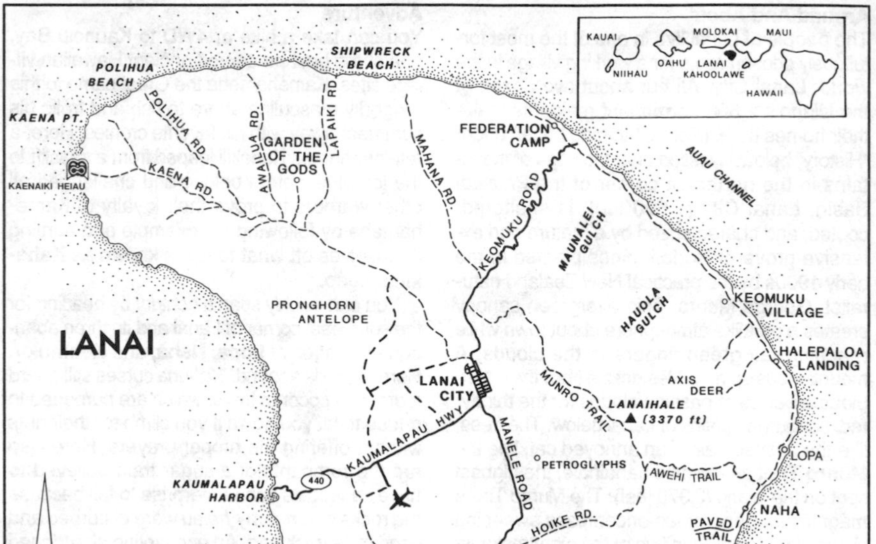

After these daily excursions, return to the green serenity of Lanai City. Even if you're only spending a few days, you'll be made to feel like you're staying with old friends. You won't have to worry about bringing your dancing shoes, but if you've had enough hustle and bustle and yearn to stroll in quietude, sit by a crackling fire, and look up at a crystal-clear sky, head for Lanai. Your jangled nerves and ruffled spirit will be glad you did.

THE LAND

The sunburned face of Lanai seems parched but relaxed as it rises in a gentle, steady arc from sea level. When viewed from the air it looks like an irregularly shaped kidney bean. The sixth largest of the eight main islands, Lanai is roughly 140 square miles, measuring 18 miles north to south and 13 miles east to west at its longest points. A classic single-shield volcano, at one time Lanai was probably connected to Maui and Molokai as a single huge island. Marine fossils found at the 1,000-foot mark and even higher in the mountains indicate its slow rise from the sea. Its rounded features appear more benign than the violent creases of its closest island neighbors; this characteristic earned it the unflattering Hawaiian name of "Hump." More lyrical scholars, however, have refuted this translation and claim the real meaning has been lost to the ages, but Lanai does look like a hump when viewed from a distance at sea.

Its topography is simple. A ridge of rugged mountains runs north to south along the eastern half of the island, and their entire length is traversed by the Munro Trail. The highest peak is

LANAI CITY AVERAGE TEMPERATURE AND RAINFALL

	JAN.	MARCH	MAY	JUNE	SEPT.	NOV.
high	70	71	75	80	80	72
low	60	60	62	65	65	62
rain	3	3	2	0	2	4

Note: rainfall in inches; temperature in °F

Lanaihale (3,370 feet). This area is creased by precipitous gulches: the two deepest are Maunalei and Hauola at more than 2,000 feet. The topography tapers off steadily as it reaches the sea to the east. A variety of beaches stretch from the white sands of Polihua in the north, and along the salt-and-pepper sands of Naha on the east, ending with the beautiful rainbow arches of Manele and Hulopoe in the south. Palawai, Lanai's central basin, is completely cultivated in manicured, whorled fields of pineapple. Early this century, Palawai was covered in cactus. The west coast has phenomenal seacliffs accessible only by boat. Some of the most majestic are the **Kaholo Pali,** which run south from Kaumalapau Harbor, reaching their most amazing ruggedness at Kaunolu Bay. At many spots along this area the sea lies more than 1,500 feet below. Starting at Lanai City in the center, a half-hour of driving in any direction presents a choice of this varied and fascinating geography.

Climate

The daily temperatures are quite balmy, especially at sea level, but it can get blisteringly hot in the basins and on the leeward side, so be sure to carry plenty of water when hiking or four-wheel driving. Lanai City gets refreshingly cool in the evenings and early mornings, but a light jacket or sweater is adequate, although thin-blooded residents bundle up.

Water

Lying in the rain shadow of the West Maui Mountains, even Lanai's windward side receives only 40 inches of rainfall a year. The central basins and leeward shores taper off to a scant 12 inches, not bad for pineapples and sun worshippers. Lanai has always been short of water. Its scruffy vegetation and red-baked earth are responsible for its inhospitable reputation. There are no real rivers; the few year-round streams are found only in the gulches of the windward mountains. Most ventures at colonizing Lanai, both in ancient and modern times, were kept to a minimum because of this water shortage. The famous Norfolk pines of Lanai City, along with other introduced greenery, greatly helped the barrenness of the landscape and provided a watershed. But the rust-red earth remains unchanged, and if you get it onto your clothes, it'll remain there as a permanent souvenir.

FLORA AND FAUNA

Most of Lanai's flora and fauna have been introduced. In fact, introduction of the Norfolk pine and the regal mouflon sheep was a deliberate attempt by humans to improve the natural, often barren habitat. These species have adapted so well they now symbolize Lanai, along with, of course, the ubiquitous pineapple. Besides the mouflon, Lanai boasts pronghorns, axis deer, and a few feral goats. A wide variety of introduced game birds include the Rio Grande turkey, ring-necked pheasant, and an assortment of quail, francolins, and doves. Like the other Hawaiian Islands, Lanai, unfortunately, is home to native birds headed for extinction. Along the Munro Trail and on the windward coast you pass through forests of Norfolk and Cook Island pines, tall eucalyptus stands, shaggy ironwoods, native koa, and silver oaks. Everywhere, dazzling colors and fragrances are provided by Lanai's flowers.

Flowers

Although Lanai's official flower is the *kaunaoa,* it's not really a flower, but an airplant that grows wild. It's easily found along the beach at Keomuku. It grows in conjunction with *pohuehue,* a pinkish-red, perennial seashore morning glory. Native to Hawaii, the *pohuehue* grows in large numbers along Lanai's seashore. It's easy to spot, and when you see a yellow-orange vinelike airplant growing with it, you've found Lanai's *kaunaoa,* which is traditionally fashioned into lei. The medicinal *ilima,* used to help asthma sufferers, is found in large numbers in Lanai's open fields. Its flat, open yellow flower is about one inch in diameter and grows on a waist-high shrub. Two other flowers considered pests by some are the purple *koali* morning glory and the miniature red and yellow flowering lantana, known for its unpleasant odor. Both are abundant on the trail to the Garden of the Gods.

Norfolk Pines

These pines were discovered by Captain Cook and named after Norfolk Island in the South Pacific, on which they were found. Imported in great numbers by George Munro, they adapted well to Lanai and helped considerably to attract moisture and provide a firm watershed. Exquisitely ornamental, they can also be grown in containers. Their perfect cone shape makes them a natural Christmas tree, used as such in Hawaii; some are even shipped to the Mainland for this purpose.

Endemic Birds

The list of native birds found on Lanai gets smaller every year, and those still on the list are rarely seen. The *amakahi* is about five inches long with yellowish-green plumage. The males deliver a high-sounding tweet and a trilling call. Vegetarians, these birds live mostly on grasses and lichen, building their nests in the uppermost branches of tall trees. Some people believe that the *amakahi* is already extinct on Lanai. The *'ua'u* or Hawaiian petrel is a large bird with a 36-inch wingspan. Its head and back are shades of black, its underbelly white. This "fisherbird" lives on squid and crustaceans that it regurgitates to its chicks. Unfortunately, the Hawaiian petrel nests on the ground, sometimes laying its eggs under rocks or in burrows, which makes it easy prey for predators. Its call is reported to sound like a small yapping dog. The *apapane* is abundant on the other main islands, but dwindling rapidly on Lanai. It's a chubby red-bodied bird about five inches long with a black bill, legs, wingtips, and tail feathers. It's quick and flitty, and has a wide variety of calls and songs from beautiful warbles to mechanical buzzes. Its feathers were sought by Hawaiians for distinctive ornate featherwork.

Axis Deer

This shy and beautiful creature came to Lanai via Molokai, where the first specimens arrived in 1868 as a gift from the Hawaiian consul in Hong Kong. Its native home is the parkland forests of India and Sri Lanka. The coats of most axis deer are golden tan with rows of round lifetime spots, along with a black stripe down the back and a white belly. They stand three to four feet at the shoulder, with bucks weighing an average of 160 pounds and does about 110. The bucks have an exquisite set of symmetrical antlers that always form a perfect three points. The antlers can stand 30 inches high and more than 20 inches across, making them coveted trophies. Does are antlerless and give birth to one fawn, usually from November to February, but Hawaii's congenial weather makes for good fawn survival any time of year. Axis deer on Lanai can be spotted anywhere from the lowland *kiawe* forests to the higher rainforests along the Munro Trail. Careful and proper hunting management should keep the population stable for many generations. The meat from axis deer is reported to have a unique flavor, different from Mainland venison—one of the finest tasting of all wild game.

Mouflon Sheep

Another name for these wild mountain sheep is Mediterranean or European bighorn. One of only six species of wild sheep in the world, mouflon are native to the islands of Sardinia and Corsica, whose climates are quite similar to Hawaii's. They have been introduced throughout Europe, Africa, and North America. Although genetically similar to domestic sheep, they are much more shy, lack a woolly coat, and only infrequently give birth to twins. Both rams and ewes are a similar tannish brown, with a snow-

BOB RACE

pronghorn

white rump, which is all that most people get to see of these always-alert creatures as they quickly and expertly head for cover. Rams weigh about 125 pounds (ewes a bit less) and produce a spectacular set of recurved horns. They need little water to survive, going for long periods only on the moisture in green plants. On Lanai they are found along the northwest coast in the grasslands and in the dry *kiawe* forests.

Pronghorns

Not a true antelope, this animal is a native to the Western states of North America. Both males and females produce short black antlers that curve inward at the tip. Males average 125 pounds, females about 90. Pronghorns are a reddish tan with two distinct white bands across the neck and a black patch under the ear. They can also flare the hair on their rumps to produce a white flag when alarmed. In 1959, 38 pronghorn were brought to Lanai in an attempt to introduce another big game animal. Lanai's upper grasslands seemed perfectly suited to the pronghorn, closely resembling the animal's natural habitat in Montana, and hopes ran high for survival. At first the herd increased, but then the numbers began to slowly and irreversibly dwindle. Experts felt that the animals were confused by the nearby salt water and those that drank it quickly died. Also, the new grasses of Lanai caused digestion problems. Poaching added even more problems to the troubled pronghorns. It's tough to spot the few that remain, but with good field glasses and perseverance you might catch some browsing on *haole koa* in the north-central grasslands of Lanai. The fact that even a few pronghorn remain decades after introduction gives some hope that these noble animals can still beat the odds of extinction and make a permanent home for themselves in Hawaii.

HISTORY

Kakaalaneo peered across the mist-shrouded channel between West Maui and Lanai and couldn't believe his eyes. Night after night, the campfire of his son Kaululaau burned, sending its faint but miraculous signal. Could it be that the boy was still alive? Kaululaau had been given every advantage of his noble birth, but still the prince had proved to be unmanageable. King Kakaalaneo had even ordered all children born on the same day as his son to be sent to Lahaina, where they would grow up as his son's friends and playmates. Spoiled rotten, young Kaululaau had terrorized Lahaina with his pranks and one day went too far: he destroyed a new planting of breadfruit. Even the chief's son could not trample the social order and endanger the livelihood of the people. So finally the old *kahuna* had to step in. Justice was hard and swift: Kaululaau must be banished to the terrible island of Lanai, where the man-eating spirits dwelled. There he would meet his fate, and no one expected him to live. But weeks had passed and Kalulaau's nightly fires still burned. Could it be some ghoulish trick? Kakaalaneo sent a canoe of men to investigate. They returned with incredible news. The boy was fine! All the spirits were banished! Kaululaau had cleansed the island of its evil fiends and opened it up for the people to come and settle.

Oral History

In fact, it's recorded in the Hawaiian oral genealogical tradition that a young Kaululaau did open Lanai to significant numbers of inhabitants in approximately A.D. 1400. Lanai passed through the next few hundred years as a satellite of Maui, accepting the larger island's social, religious, and political dictates. During this period, Lanai supported about 3,000 people, who grew taro and fished. Most inhabited the eastern shore facing Maui, but old home sites show that the population became established well enough to homestead the entire island. Lanai was caught up in the Hawaiian wars that raged in the last two decades of the 1700s, and was ravaged and pillaged in 1778 by the warriors of Kalaniopuu, aging king of the Big Island. These hard times marked a decline in Lanai's population; accounts by Western sea captains who passed even a few years later noted that the island looked desolate, with no large villages evident. Lanai began to recover and saw a small boost in population when Kamehameha the Great established his summer residence at Kaunolu on the southern shore. This kept Lanai vibrant for a few years at the beginning of the 19th century, but it began to fade soon thereafter. The decline continued until only a handful of Hawaiians remained by the 20th century. The old order ended completely when one of the last traditional *kanaka,* a man named Ohua, hid the traditional fish-god, Hunihi, and died shortly thereafter in his grass hut in the year 1900.

Early Foreign Influences

No one knows his name, but all historians agree that a Chinese man tried his luck at raising sugarcane on Lanai in 1802. He brought boiling pots and rollers to Naha on the east coast, but after a few years of hard luck gave up and moved on. About 100 years later a large commercial sugar enterprise was attempted in the same area. This time the sugar company even built a narrow-gauge railroad to carry the cane. A story goes that after the venture disrupted a local *heiau* to make ballast for the rail line, the water in the area, never in great abundance to begin with, went brackish. Again sugar was foiled.

In 1854 a small band of Mormon elders tried to colonize Lanai by starting a "City of Joseph" at Palawai Basin. This began the career of one of Hawaii's strangest, most unfathomable, yet most charismatic early leaders. Walter Murray Gibson came to Palawai to start an idyllic settlement for the Latter-day Saints. He energetically set to work improving the land with funds from Utah and hard work of the other Mormon settlers. The only fly in Gibson's grand ointment occurred when the Mormon Church discovered that the acres of Palawai were not registered to the church at all but to Walter Murray Gibson! He was excommunicated, and the bilked settlers relocated. Gibson went on to have one of the strangest political careers in Hawaiian history, including championing native rights and enjoying unbelievable influence at the royal Hawaiian court. His land at Palawai passed on to his daughter, who became possessed by the one evil spirit Kaululaau failed to eradicate: she tried to raise sugarcane, but was fated, like the rest, to fail.

A few other attempts proved uneconomical, and Lanai languished. The last big attempt at cattle raising produced The Ranch, part of whose lands make up the Cavendish Golf Course in Lanai City. This enterprise did have one bright note. A New Zealander named George Munro was hired as the manager. He imported all manner of seeds and cuttings in his attempt to foliate the island and create a watershed. The Ranch failed, but Munro's legacy of Norfolk pines stands as a proud testament to this amateur horticulturalist.

The Coming Of Pineapples

The purchase of Lanai in 1922 was one of the niftiest real estate deals in modern history. James D. Dole, the most enterprising of the pineapple pioneers, bought the island—lock, stock, and barrel—from the Baldwins, an old missionary family, for $1.1 million. That comes to only $12 per acre, though many of those acres were fairly scruffy, not to mention Lanai's bad economical track record. Dole had come from Boston at the turn of the century to figure out how to can pineapple profitably. Dole did such a remarkable job of marketing the "golden fruit" on the Mainland that in a few short years, Midwestern Americans who'd never even heard of pineapples before were buying cans of it regularly from the shelves of country grocery stores. In 1922, Jim Dole needed more land for his expanding pineapple fields, and the arid basin of Palawai seemed perfect.

Lanai Plantation was an oligarchy during the early years, with the plantation manager as king.

One of the most famous of these characters was H. Broomfield Brown, who ran Lanai Plantation in the '30s. He kept watch over the fields from his house through a telescope. If anyone loafed, he'd ride out into the fields to confront the offender. Mr. Brown personally "eyeballed" every new visitor to Lanai: prostitutes, gamblers, and deadbeats were turned back at the pier. An antilitter fanatic, he'd reprimand anyone who trashed the streets of Lanai City. During the labor strikes of the 1960s, workers' grievances were voiced and Lanai began to function as a more fair enterprise. With pineapple well established on the world market, Lanai finally had a firm economic base. From a few thousand fruits in the early days, the flow today can reach a million fruits per day during the height of the season. They're shipped from the manmade port at Kaumalapau, which was specially built to accommodate Lanai's "pines."

Crushed Pineapples

Lanai's 12,000 acres of pineapples made up the largest single pineapple plantation in the world. Virtually the entire island was operated by The Dole Co., whose name had become synonymous with pineapples. In one way or another, everyone on Lanai owed their livelihood to pineapples, from the worker who twisted his ankle in a pine field to the technician at the community hospital who X-rayed it. Now, all has changed and only a few plots remain, mostly for use by the hotels.

Foreign production, especially in the Philippines, has greatly increased, and the Lanai pineapple industry has virtually folded. As Dole has taken acreage out of pineapple production, and as the population of the island and number of visitors have increased, the company has experimented with raising various organic vegetables, grains, and cattle to diversify the island's economy. This seems to be a pet project of David Murdoch, and the hope is to make the economy of Lanai more locally sustainable and less dependent on imports from the other islands and the Mainland.

Changing Lanai

Most are amazed that George Munro's pines still shelter a tight-knit community that has remained untouched for so long. But all that's changing, and changing quickly. Two new hideaway luxury hotels have risen, and they're beauties. Both are Rock Resorts. **The Lodge at Koele,** with 102 rooms, is just a five-minute walk from downtown Lanai City. An upland hotel befitting this area of trees and cool summers, it's like a grand country home of the landed gentry, in neo-Victorian style. Amenities include lawn bowling, an orchid house for pure visual pleasure, a swimming pool, tennis courts, golf course, stables and horseback riding, and hunting. The other hotel, **Manele Bay,** houses 250 villas and suites. The architecture is a blend, both classical and island-inspired, a *kama'aina* Mediterranean masonry style with tiled roofs. Outdoor features include the unobstructed natural beauty of Hulopoe Bay (all rooms have a view), tennis courts, swimming pools, snorkeling, and fishing.

The coming of these resorts has brought the most profound changes to Lanai since James Dole arrived at the turn of the century. Castle and Cooke, practically speaking, owns the island (98%). David Murdoch is the CEO of Castle and Cooke, and the hotels are his babies. He developed them through a newly formed company called Lanai Resort Partners. The hotels employ a staff of 600 or so, more than all the workers needed to tend the pineapple fields, which was just over 500 people. The hotels have brought an alternative job market, new life to the downtown area, and a housing spurt. One fact was undeniable concerning Lanai: if you wanted to make a living you either had to work the pineapple fields, or leave. Now that has changed. To stop the disenfranchisement of the local people, which was generally the case with rapid development, Castle and Cooke has built several new housing projects, that have come with a promise. Local people, according to seniority with the company and length of residence on Lanai, have first choice. One group of houses is multiple-family, geared to the entry-level buyer. The second is single-family homes, and the third is for middle-management types. The future also calls for million-dollar homes that will line the fairways of the new golf courses, for people like David Murdoch and his associates. This isn't all *heart* on the part of Castle and Cooke. They want to ensure that the hotels will have a steady and contented workforce to keep them running without a hitch.

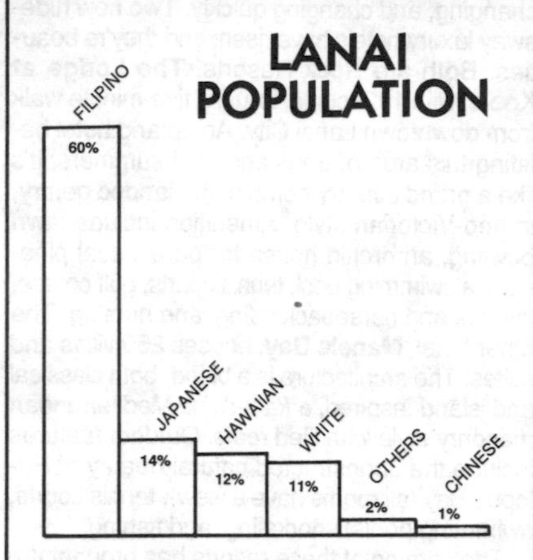

Downtown Lanai is inadequate. It couldn't possibly handle the hotel guests and all the new workers and their families who have moved to the island. Old buildings have been refurbished, some torn down and replaced, with more upscale businesses taking their place. The tired little shops in town are on Castle and Cooke property, most with month-to-month leases. Castle and Cooke again promises to be fair, but like the rest of Lanai, they'll have a choice: progress or perish. Most islanders are optimistic, keeping an open mind and adopting a "wait and see" attitude concerning the inevitable changes and the promises that have been made for a better life.

THE PEOPLE

Lanai is characterized by the incredible mix of racial strains so common in Hawaii—Filipino, Japanese, Hawaiian, Chinese, and Caucasian. It is unique, however, in that 50-60% of its people are Filipino. The Filipinos, many recent immigrants, were solicited by Castle and Cooke to work as laborers on the pineapple plantation. Mostly 18- to 25-year-old men, the majority speak Ilocano and many have come to join relatives already on Lanai. Most arrive on their own; they learn English and from Lanai they spread out. As workers they're perfect: industrious and quiet. At night you wonder where they all are. Due to the tremendous shortage of eligible women, most workers stay home or fish or have a beer in the backyard with buddies. And on Sunday, there is the illegal (officially nonexistent) cockfight. For high living, everyone heads for Maui or Oahu.

The next largest racial groups are Japanese (18%) and whites (11%). The Japanese started as the field workers before the Filipinos, but now, along with the whites, are Lanai's professionals and middle management. The races coexist, but there are still unseen social strata. There's even a small Chinese population (one percent) who continue their traditional role as shopkeepers. A good nine percent of Lanaians are Hawaiians. Finally, almost 10% fall into the "mixed" category, with many of these Filipino-Hawaiian.

Community

Lanai has a strong sense of community and uniqueness that keeps the people close. For example, during a bitter three-month strike in 1964, the entire community rallied and all suffered equally: laborers, shopkeepers, and management. All who remember say that it brought out the best in the island tradition of *aloha*. If you really want to meet Lanaians, just sit in the park in the center of Lanai City for an hour or two. You'll notice a lot of old-timers, who seem very healthy. You could easily strike up a conversation with some of them.

Other Faces

It should strike you that most of the people you see around Lanai are men. That in itself is a social comment about Lanai. Where are the women? They're in the traditional roles at home, nurturing and trying to add the pleasantries of life. Some are field workers too. You might notice that there are no famous crafts of Lanai and no artists working commercially. This is not to say there is no art on Lanai, but the visitor rarely sees it. One reason that Lanai produces so little commercial art is that it's a workers' island with virtually no unemployment, so everyone is busy making a living. Old-timers are known to make superb fishing poles, nets, and even their own horseshoes. The island women are excellent seamstresses and with the rising interest in hula, make lovely lei from the beautiful *kaunaoa*,

Lanai's flower. If you turn your attention to the young people of Lanai, you'll see the statewide problem of babies having babies. Teenage pregnancy is rampant, and teenage parents are common. Young guys customize their 4WDs although there's no place to go. If as a young person you wish to remain on Lanai, then in almost every case your future will be tied to Dole. If you have other aspirations, it's "goodbai to Lanai." These islanders are some of the most easygoing and relaxed people you'll encounter in Hawaii, but with the electronic age extending its long arms of communication, even here they're not nearly as "backwater" as you might think.

GETTING THERE

By Air

Hawaiian Air, tel. (800) 367-5320 Mainland and Canada, (800) 882-8811 or 565-6977 on Lanai, flies Dash-7 turbo-prop planes to Lanai. They currently have flights only from Honolulu that run Friday and Saturday every other week, and one on Monday on the alternate week.

Daily flights are available to and from Lanai by **Aloha Island Air,** tel. 833-3219 Oahu, (800) 652-6541 Neighbor Islands, (800) 323-3345 Mainland. They fly to and from Honolulu 10 times daily, with extra flights on Monday and Friday. There is also one early-morning flight daily from Molokai, two from Kapalua West Maui Airport, and five from Kahului. Flights originating in Princeville go via Honolulu and those from Hana and Kamuela go through Kahului.

Lanai Airport is a practical little strip out in the pineapple fields about four miles southwest of Lanai City. The one-room terminal offers *no* shops, car rental booths, lockers, public transportation, or even access to a toilet, unless there's a scheduled flight. A bulletin board near the waiting-room door has all the practical information and phone numbers you'll need to get to Lanai City, and a courtesy phone outside connects you with Lanai City Service/Dollar Rent A Car for those who have not arranged a car before arriving.

By Boat

Expeditions, a new passenger ferry, now plies between Lahaina and Manele Bay. No luxury transportation, this shuttle offers speedy and convenient alternative transportation to the island. The crossing takes one hour and the ferry leaves Manele Bay at 8 a.m., 10:30 a.m., and 4:30 p.m. From Lahaina's public loading pier, ferries leave at 6:45 a.m., 9:15 a.m., and 3:45 p.m. There are late departures from both ends on Thursday, Friday, and Sunday evenings. The adult fare is $25 one-way while children under 11 pay $20; luggage goes free, except for a $10 charge for bicycles. As this shuttle takes only 24 passengers, it's best to reserve a place. For information and reservations call 661-3756, or write P.O. Box 1763, Lahaina, HI 96767.

One other possibility for getting to Lanai is going by pleasure boat from Maui. Many Lanai and Maui residents travel by this route and receive special *kama'aina* rates. These are basically tour boats specializing in snorkeling, dinner cruising, whalewatching, and the like, but they're willing to drop you off and pick you up at a later date. It's an enjoyable and actually inexpensive way of going. You'll have to make your own arrangements with the boat captains, most berthed at Lahaina Harbor. This alternative is particularly attractive to campers, as the boats anchor on Lanai at Manele Bay, just a five-minute walk from the campsites at Hulopoe. There are no fixed rates for this service, but *kama'aina* pay about $20. Expect to pay more but use this as a point of reference. One company to try is Trilogy, tel. 661-4743. Another outfit is Club Lanai, tel. 871-1144, but they anchor at their own private beach on very remote East Lanai, with no way of getting anywhere except by a long and dusty hike. Remember that, in effect, you're going standby with these companies, but there is generally room for one more.

GETTING AROUND

Public Transportation

No public bus transportation operates on Lanai, but **Lanai City Service,** tel. 565-7227, or 565-7065 after-hours, operates an airport limousine service if you're renting a car/jeep from them. Otherwise their service to/from the airport to anywhere in Lanai City is $5, and to Manele Bay, $10. They also run throughout the day from Lanai City to Manele Bay for $10, and from the bay to the Manele Bay Hotel for $2.50. You can call them anytime for service anywhere on Lanai.

Car And 4WD Rental

For a car, or better yet, a jeep, try **Lanai City Service, Dollar Rent A Car,** Lanai City, HI 96763, tel. 565-7227 or (800) 800-4000. You'll be outfitted with wheels and given information about road conditions and where to go. Pay heed! Make sure to tell them your plans, especially if you're heading for a remote area. That way, if you have problems and don't return, they'll know where to send the rescue party! Lanai City Service is a subsidiary of Trilogy Excursions and has a franchise with Dollar Rent A Car. It rents compacts for $50 per day, and 4WDs (mostly jeeps) for $100 per day (insurance compulsory), eight-passenger mini-vans for $109, and 15-passenger maxi-vans for $139 per day.

Using A 4WD Rental

With only 30 miles of paved road on Lanai and rental cars firmly restricted to these, there is no real reason to rent one. The *real* adventure spots of Lanai require a 4WD vehicle, which on Lanai is actually useful and not just a yuppie showpiece, since mind-boggling spots on Lanai are reachable only on foot or by 4WD. Unfortunately, even the inveterate hiker will have a tough time because the best trailheads are quite a distance from town, and you'll spend as much time getting to them as hiking the actual trails.

Many people who have little or no experience driving 4WDs are under the slap-happy belief that they are unstoppable. Oh, that it were true! They do indeed get stuck, and it's usually miserable getting them unstuck. The rental agencies will give you up-to-the-minute info on the road conditions, and a fairly accurate map for navigation. They tend to be a bit conservative on where they advise you to take "their" vehicles, but they also live on the island and are accustomed to driving offroad, which balances out their conservative estimates. Also, remember road conditions change rapidly: a hard rain on the Munro Trail can change it from a flower-lined path to a nasty quagmire, or wind might lay a tree across a beach road. Keep your eye on the weather and if in doubt, don't push your luck. If you get stuck, you'll not only ruin your outing and have to hike back to town, but you'll also be charged for a service call, which can be astronomical, especially if it's deemed to be due to your negligence. Most of your offroad driving will be in *compound* 4WD, first gear, low range.

Sightseeing Tours

Lanai City Service offers a number of personalized escorted tours to various spots on the island. Since they are subject to change, it's best to call in advance to get the rates and times. One of the best is the **Historic Guided Tour** (two to three hours, refreshment included, $30) given Tuesday, Thursday, and Saturday, departing at 2 p.m. from the Manele Bay Hotel. On this tour you visit the pineapple fields, Koele Lodge, and Keomuku Lookout. From there you take a short tour of Lanai City and its historic "Alcatraz of Lanai," the formidable jailhouse that's about as big as a closet, and about as difficult to escape from. You then head for the pineapple wharf at Kaumalapau Harbor, and finally for the petroglyph sites.

Hitchhiking

Hitching is technically illegal on Lanai, but the islanders are friendly and quite good about giving you a lift. Lanai, however, is a workers' island and the traffic is really skimpy during the day. You can only reasonably expect to get a ride from Lanai City to the airport or to Manele Bay, since both are on paved roads frequented by normal island traffic. There is only a very slim chance of picking up a ride out through the pine fields toward the Garden of the Gods or Kaunolu, for example, so definitely don't count on it.

Around Town

Lanai City streets running east-west are numerical starting with 3rd Street and running to 13th Street; the streets running north-south have alphabetical first letters and include Frazier, Gay, Houston, Ilima, Jacaranda, Koele, and Lanai avenues, with a few more beyond in a residential area. If you manage to get lost in Lanai City you should seriously consider never leaving home.

ACCOMMODATIONS

The Manele Bay Hotel
Glass doors, curved in a traditional Roman arch, sympathize with the surging Pacific as you enter the seaside Manele Bay Hotel, P.O. Box 774, Lanai City, HI 96763, tel. 565-3800 or (800) 321-4666, Lanai's newest luxury resort fashioned in a fusion of Mediterranean, Asian, and Hawaiian architecture. The open reception area, all marble and glass, holds two massive murals of Lanai and the wide Pacific dotted with islands. Heroic paintings depict pioneering Polynesians in a double-hulled canoe sighting the Hawaiian Islands, and the rascal Prince Kaululaau, redeemer of Lanai, standing triumphantly on a windswept beach after banishing the vexing specters of Lanai. Underfoot, a fern and pineapple motif is woven into the rich carpet, and overhead chandeliers hang from coved and molded ceilings. Throughout the hotel are sitting areas and niches where you will find velvet-covered chairs and marble-topped or lacquer tables. Mythical dragons fashioned from mirrors and gold filigree, lamps of Chinese flute players, carved elephant tusks, and billowy curtains add a touch of style. For an elegant evening, order a drink and have it in the hotel **library,** a salubrious room filled with leather-bound tomes, globes, and models of sailing ships. Overhead, the recessed wooden ceiling has been painted with emblems of Hawaii; the floor is an intricate paisley of tasseled Persian carpets. Sit in a high-backed chair near the library's balcony and enjoy the view of Hulopo'e Court below.

From the main reception area, descend a grand staircase and pass a formidable lava rock wall draped with the purples and pinks of living bougainvillea. Here is the grand cloverleaf pool encircled by a marble apron where you can relax upon white chaise lounges softened with billowy pillows and shaded by white canvas umbrellas. Near the pool is the hotel spa and fitness center, complete with steam rooms, saunas, fitness machines, free weights, and professional staff. The formal gardens, two on the east and three on the west, are tranquil oases where rivulets drop into koi ponds surrounded by patches of broad-leafed taro and swaying stands of bamboo.

The hotel rooms and suites are mainly in two wings, east and west. East rooms bear marine names derived from the sea; the west rooms are named after flowers. These oversized guest rooms ranging in price $295-475, designed with Mediterranean and Asian themes, offer wool carpets, four-poster mahogany beds covered with thick quilts, double-wide louvered closets, wicker lounge chairs, wet bars, and user-friendly entertainment centers. The tiled bathrooms, a study in relaxation with thick white carpets on marble floors, feature extra-deep soaking tubs, double sinks and vanity, separate commodes, glass-enclosed shower stalls big enough for two, name-brand bath products, hair dryers, and slippers and robes for lounging. Each room has its own private lanai that either overlooks one of the gorgeous gardens, or offers an ocean panorama. The hotel also offers 12 suites that range in price $599-2000. A typical mid-range suite offers a formal parlor and separate master bedroom with a dressing room attached. Butlers will pack and unpack clothing, make dinner reservations, and act as your personal liaison at the hotel. They will draw hot baths, pour cold champagne, and tuck you and your teddy bear in for the night.

Executive Chef Philippe Padovani, renowned for his magnificent fare created at the exclusive La Mer Restaurant at Waikiki's Halekulani and at the Ritz-Carlton Mauna Lani, has been lured by the quiet charms of Lanai's Manele Bay Hotel. Learning his trade from some of the finest French chefs, Philippe combines skilled preparation and superb ingredients so that he can "push every dish to its peak point and make it come out fabulous." The master chef, aided by a handpicked staff at the hotel's formal **Ihilani Dining Room** (jackets requested but not required) offers two fixed menus nightly, along with a complete menu of a la carte suggestions. Begin with ravioli of Hawaiian goat cheese in a sauce of parsley and sun-dried tomatoes for $20, or Maine lobster with Hayden mango and arugula salad for $19. Your second course can be a delicately roasted squab breast in a marmalade of onions and a Molokai sweet potato puree for $34. Entrees are roasted Chinese duck with Hawaiian seasoning, oriental rice, and pickled ginger plum sauce for $25, or an array of curries from Thai shrimp red curry to

Hotel Lanai

J.D. BISIGNANI

pan-fried *onaga* in a North Indian style for under $28. Grill selections include catch-of-the-day for $28, or Colorado lamb chops with polenta topped by a roasted garlic sauce for $29.

The less formal but still extremely elegant **Hulopo'e Court** offers breakfast, lunch, and dinner of contemporary Hawaiian regional cuisine. Begin the day with a continental breakfast of assorted pastries, sliced fruits, a selection of cereals, chilled juices, and rich Kona coffee for $12, or choose all manner of traditional favorites from the breakfast buffet for $18 (a la carte selections available as well). Lunch and dinner begin with appetizers like Chinese spring rolls for $9.50, seared *ahi* in a spicy crust for $14, or a fresh dim sum basket for $12. Soups and salads include Maui onion soup for $6.50, Caesar salad with croutons for $9, or Lanai field greens in a *lilikoi* vinaigrette for $7. Entrees are fresh pasta for $19, Chinese noodles with duck covered in a chili oyster sauce for $17, or *penne* pasta primavera for $20 (about $5 less as appetizers). You can also have a gourmet pizza of Tandoori chicken or Peking duck for around $15. An excellent selection of domestic and imported beer and wine completes the meal.

The least formal dining setting is poolside at **The Pool Grill,** an alfresco restaurant serving appetizers like chicken quesadilla or cocktail of Pacific shrimp. Lighter appetites will enjoy main course salads including marinated grilled vegetables, Cobb salad, or seafood salad priced $13-15. The sandwich board features a good old-fashioned club, a grilled beef burger, or a hot dog. Special offerings are Hawaiian favorites like grilled fresh catch for $17, or a steaming bowl of savory saimin for $12.

The hotel also offers valet parking, a Lanai City shuttle, tennis courts, a children's program, and a cocktail lounge. At the Manele Bay Hotel Gift Shop you can get a windbreaker, polo shirt, sweatshirt, children's alohawear, stuffed animals, incidental bags, jewelry, or light reading material. Saturdays and Sundays are special with *keiki* hula dancers who come to perform their special magic in the Hulopo'e Court. Complimentary afternoon tea is served here daily as well. Another treat is to walk a few minutes to the hotel's **Lanai Conference Center,** where the antechamber holds museum-quality artifacts. In glass cases, you will find stone implements ranging from *ulu maika* (Hawaiian bowling stones similar to Italian boccie) to *poho kukui* (*kukui* nut oil lamps). Most of these implements, including a petroglyph stone, have been gathered from Lanai. There is also a very impressive replica of a Hawaiian double-hulled canoe.

The Lodge At Koele

A stately row of Norfolk pines bids you welcome as they line the red brick driveway leading to this grand manor house perched in genteel quietude above the town. The Lodge at Koele ("Koele" is variously interpreted as black sugarcane, the banging together of hula sticks, or the summoning of a commoner to do tithe work for an *ali'i*), P.O. Box 774, Lanai City, HI, 96763, tel. 565-3800 or (800) 321-4666, with its encircling veranda and sweep of broad lawn, exudes gracious relaxation. You enter the Great Hall, where the entire roof is a translucent skylight through which the sun casts diffused beams onto the formal Victorian parlors below. Encircled by a rich koa balcony, the great room holds two immense fireplaces, the largest in Hawaii. Parlor settings of green velvet chairs, lace doilies, pink couches, wicker lounges, credenzas covered in flowers and ferns, and lustrous end tables are perfect for a lazy afternoon of perusing the newspapers and magazines of the world.

At each corner of the Great Hall is a hexagonal room of beveled windows: one for dining; one for music; one a library; and the last a game room with backgammon, chess, and dominoes. Out front is a bowling green, to the side croquet, and out back through glass French doors are a swimming pool and jacuzzi, Japanese strolling garden, orchid house, and executive putting green. The green being a professionally designed "miniature" but real golf course. Here with putter, a glass of chilled champagne, and chocolate-dipped strawberries, you can test your skill against tiny sand traps, puddle-sized water traps, and challenging Chihuahua-inspired dog legs left and right.

Walk along the covered veranda past a row of rocking chairs to the two wings off the Great Hall, where you will find the guest rooms that range in price from $295 for a garden view to $975 for the best suite, $30 extra person. Once inside, you can take the brass-doored elevator—but climb instead the sweeping wooden staircases bearing carved pineapples, the symbol of hospitality, and walk the hardwood hall hung with the works of island artists (ask concierge for hotel art list). Rooms are furnished in a combination of wicker and heavy knotty pine, with a four-poster bed covered by a downy quilt; billowy printed curtains flutter across a window seat. Along with this turn-of-the-century charm comes a full entertainment center with remote-control color TV, video viewer, in-room safe, and wet bar. Each room has its own lanai with tile floor and wooden furniture. The bathroom, perhaps blue- or black-on-white marble, features a pedestal sink and deep soaking tub with old-fashioned brass knobs, a full assortment of name-brand bath care products, huge towels, and separate commode. Each room also has multiple phones, ceiling fans, even walking sticks for an afternoon foray into the surrounding hills.

In harmony with the rest of the hotel, the dining rooms are impeccably furnished. **The Terrace,** set off the Great Hall and the more casual of the two restaurants, looks out over the exotic gardens, while the separate **Formal Dining Room** lends itself to evening attire. Breakfast selections include continental breakfast, $7.50; eggs Benedict, $8.50; and sweet rice waffles with *lilikoi*-coconut chutney, $7.50. At midday satisfy your hunger with jumbo shrimp with papaya relish for $8.50, pan-fried Kona crab cakes with a spicy remoulade for $8.25, grilled pastrami of striped marlin on a tomato fennel salad for $8, spinach pasta with grilled scallops for $14.50, or smoked salmon and herbed goat cheese on a salad of field greens and vegetables with cilantro dressing for $15. Simple tastes might also enjoy barbecued pork sandwich on a sesame bun with cabbage slaw for $9.50; or ask for a picnic basket for two and find a shady tree where you can enjoy an alfresco lunch. Dinner, like the other daily fare, is made from the freshest island ingredients. Choose standards like rack of lamb, prime rib, a superbly prepared catch-of-the-day, or, for a special treat, the Lanai mixed pheasant, quail, and axis deer sausage with pinot noir sauce.

You can find sundries at the hotel shop, open 8 a.m.-9 p.m. All hotel and island activities, including croquet, tennis, golf, hunting, horseback riding, jeep tours, and beach and boating activities, can be arranged by the concierge. There is free shuttle service to meet all arriving and departing planes, to and from Lanai City, and to Manele and Hulopoe bays.

Hotel Lanai

It being the only hotel on the island until 1990, you'd think the lack of competition would have made Hotel Lanai, P.O. Box A-119, Lanai City, HI 96763, tel. 565-7211 or (800) 624-8849, arrogant, indifferent, and expensive. On the contrary: it is delightful. The hotel has gone through a few cosmetic changes since it was built in 1923 as a guest lodge primarily for visiting executives of Dole Pineapple Co., which still owns it. Its architecture is simple Hawaiiana, and its setting among the tall Norfolk pines fronted by a large lawn is refreshingly rustic. With a corrugated iron roof, board and batten walls inside and out, and two wings connected by a long enclosed veranda, it looks like the main building at a Boy Scout camp. But don't be fooled. The 10 remodeled rooms may not be plush, but they are cozy as can be. All have been painted lively colors and are immaculate with private baths, but no phones or TVs. All have comfortable beds, pine dressers, and ceiling fans. A newly renovated cottage behind the main building, at one time the manager's house, has its own private yard and bath. Room rates are $95-120.

The hotel has the only in-town bar on its enclosed veranda, where guests and at times a few islanders have a quiet beer and twilight chat. The main dining room (see "Restaurants" below) is large, and lined with hunting trophies. So if you're lured by the quiet simplicity of Lanai and wish to avail yourself of one of the last family-style inns of Hawaii, stay at the lovely little Hotel Lanai.

Bed And Breakfast

For a more homey stay on the Pineapple Island, try one of the few bed-and-breakfast inns on Lanai. Contact: Phyllis Cole, tel. 565-6223, who rents rooms with shared bath; Josephine Endira, tel. 565-6593, who rents rooms; Dreams Come True, tel. 565-6961, a true B&B; and Lucille Graham, tel. 565-6378, a delightful B&B. Also, for information and reservations contact any of the bed and breakfast associations listed in the Out and About chapter (see "Accommodations").

Okamoto Realty

Lanai's first house rental agency recently opened for business. All houses are completely furnished including linens, kitchen utensils, washer/dryer, and TV, and are rented by the day, week, or month. Write Kay Okamoto Realty, Lanai City, HI 96763, tel. 565-7519.

Camping

The only official camping permitted to nonresidents is located at Hulopoe Bay, administered by the Lanai Land Company. Reservations for one of the six official campsites here are a must, although unbelievably there's usually a good chance of getting a space. Lanai Land Co. officials state that they try to accommodate any "overflow" unreserved visitors, but don't count on it. Since Lanai is by and large privately owned by Castle and Cooke Inc., the parent company of Koele, you really have no recourse but to play by their rules. It seems they want to hold visitors to a minimum and keep strict tabs on the ones who do arrive.

Nonetheless, the campsites at Hulopoe Bay are great. Lining the idyllic beach, they're far enough apart to afford some privacy. The showers are designed so that the pipes, just below the surface, are solar heated. This means a good hot shower during daylight and early evening. Campsite use is limited to seven nights. The fee includes a one-time $5 group registration and is $5 per person per night. For reservations write to the Lanai Land Co., Box L, Lanai City, HI 96763, tel. 565-7400. Permits, if not mailed in advance, are picked up at the Koele office. If you're visiting on the spur of the moment from a neighboring island, it's advisable to call ahead.

Note: While you're hiking or four-wheel driving the back roads of Lanai, especially along Naha, Shipwreck, and Polihua beaches, a multitude of picture-perfect camping spots will present themselves, but they can be used only by Lanai residents, although there's little supervision. A one-night bivouac would probably go undetected. No other island allows unofficial camping and unless it can be statistically shown that potential visitors are being turned away, it seems unlikely that the Koele Co. will change its policies. If you're one of the unlucky ones who have been turned down, write your letter of protest to parent company Castle and Cooke, 965 N. Nimitz Hwy., Honolulu, HI 96817, tel. 548-6611.

RESTAURANTS

Aside from the new hotels, Lanai City is the only place on the island where you can dine, shop, and take care of business. The food situation on Lanai can be discouraging. Most everything has to be brought in by barge. There's very little fresh produce and hardly any fresh fish, and even chicken is at a premium. People surely eat differently at home, but in the two tiny restaurants open to the traveler, the fare is restricted to the "two-scoop rice and teri beef" variety, with fried noodles and Spam as the *pièce de résistance.* Salad to most islanders means a potato-macaroni combination sure to stick to your ribs and anything else on the way. Vegetables are usually a tablespoon of grated cabbage and soy sauce. But, "the times they are a changin'."

By far the best restaurant in town is at the **Hotel Lanai,** tel. 565-7211. The meals that come out of this kitchen are wholesome home cooking, done under the supervision of the chefs at the Lodge at Koele. The hotel bakes pies and provides fresh fish and vegetables whenever possible. Budgeters can order a large stuffed potato, salad, soup of the day, and drink for under $8. Restaurant hours are breakfast 7-9 a.m., lunch 11:30 a.m.-1:30 p.m., dinner 6:30-8:30 p.m. The best dish is the fresh fish when available, and all go for under $15 except for a steak dinner.

The banging screen doors announce your presence as you enter the plantation-era wainscoted **Blue Ginger Cafe,** tel. 565-6363, open Mon.-Fri. 7 a.m.-2 p.m., and again in the afternoon 5-9:30 p.m., weekends 7 a.m.-9 p.m. The place could actually be called chic for Lanai. Baked goods in a case let you know that not long ago it was **Dahang's Bakery,** a Lanai institution whose motto, "Mo betta grind ova hea," has also survived. The restaurant offers a full breakfast menu with choices like two eggs with sausage for $4.50, along with plenty of side orders, and fresh pastries. Plate lunches are $5 or so, while a bowl of saimin goes for $2.85, and mahimahi on a bun for $5.95. For a taste treat, choose a local item like fried *akule* for $5.95, or *chow fun* with "toss" salad for $4.95. Dinner specials, served with rice or French fries and "toss" salad or macaroni salad, are fresh *aku* for $8.95, or stir-fried shrimp for $8.50. Eat inside or on the veranda, where you can see everything there is to see in Lanai City.

An authentic workers' restaurant and sundries store, **S.T. Property,** open daily except Wednesday for breakfast 6:30-10:30 a.m., lunch until 1 p.m., is one of those places you must visit at least for morning coffee. It's totally down-home and a pure cultural experience. Arrive before 7 a.m. when many of the old pineapple workers come to "talk story." Just one look around at the crinkled faces will reveal the tough but sweet spirit of Lanai.

Note: For superb gourmet food you must visit the restaurants at the Lodge at Koele, or at the Manele Bay Hotel (see "Accommodations" above). Also, the **Club House** at the **Experience at Koele** golf course has recently opened and sells excellent soups, sandwiches, and salads at very reasonable prices. Everyone is welcome, and the standing room only lets you know that the food is very good.

SHOPPING

The two grocery stores in town are fairly well stocked with basics, but anyone into health foods or vegetarianism should carry supplies and use the markets for staples only. The markets are almost next door to each other: **Pine Isle Market,** run by Kerry Honda, and **Richards Shopping Center,** both open Mon.-Sat. 8 a.m.-5:30 p.m. They supply all your basic camping, fishing, and general merchandise needs, including clothing and medicines.

Also in town are **Akamai Trading Company,** which sells furniture and gifts; **International Food and Clothing Center,** where you can pick up not only things to eat and wear, but also hardware and hunting supplies; and **Lanai Family Store** for video tape rentals.

Island Collections, housed in a vintage plantation-era building in downtown Lanai, open daily 9 a.m. until approximately 7 p.m., is bright with the paintings, sculptures, and handicrafts of its contributing artists, all island and mostly Lanai residents. The artwork displayed is constantly changing, but some of the regulars include: Nancy Poes and Margaret Leach, whose watercolors capture the simple spirit of Lanai life; Steve Lance, a longtime resident who moved away but whose surrealistic paintings are filled with the vibrant colors of the islands (Steve is also a very talented wood sculptor and some of his pieces are displayed as well); Sandy Phillips, who creates primitive basketry and paintbrushes from Lanai bamboo and axis deer hair; Sherry Menze, current Lanai harbormaster and former fisherwoman and boat captain, who has captured her love of the sea in the Japanese technique of *gyotaku,* or fish printing; and Ruth

GOLF COURSES OF LANAI

COURSE	PAR	YARDS	FEES	CART
Cavendish Golf Course* Koele Company, P.O. Box L, Lanai City, HI 96763; tel. 565-9993	36	3071	free	
Experience At Koele	72	5,425-7,014	$140 nonguest* $95 guest	
Challenge At Manele tel. 565-3500	72	4,890-7,088	$140*	

*clubs, shoes, lessons available

Puchek, who arrived on Lanai in 1972 and has captured the mysterious moods of the islands in her paintings (she also sells postcards of her original works). Also exhibited are the works of Rony Doty, a watercolorist who paints the flowers and fauna of Lanai.

The **Lanai Art Program,** tel. 565-7503, open weekdays 9 a.m.-4 p.m. (closed for lunch), and a few irregular hours on the weekend, has taken the spirit of the Zimbabwe saying "If you can walk, you can dance," and changed it into "If you've got life, you've got art." This co-op of local Lanai citizens, banded together under the direction of Aprylisa Snyder, is a nonprofit organization dedicated to developing the artistic talents of its members. Classes, chaired by guest artists, are periodically offered in photography, woodworking, Japanese doll-making, fabric-making, drama, and pen and ink drawing. The showroom offers purchases like hand-dyed silk scarves, stenciled T-shirts, naturally dyed incidental bags, notecards, lovely *pareau* for women, and homemade jams and jellies. The work is always changing, but you are sure to find a distinctive island memento that couldn't be more genuine. All are welcomed, resident or not, so you can drop in on a workshop, pay for your supplies, and create your own art.

OUTDOOR SPORTS

No question that Lanai's forte is its natural unspoiled setting and great outdoors. Traffic jams, neon lights, blaring discos, shopping boutiques, and all that jazz just don't exist here. The action is swimming, hiking, snorkeling, fishing, horseback riding, and some hunting. Tennis and golf round out the activities. Lanai is a place to revitalize your spirits—you want to get up with the birds, greet the sun, stretch, and soak up the good life.

Snorkeling, Scuba, And Swimming

Lanai, especially around Manele/Hulopoe Bay, has some of the best snorkeling and scuba in Hawaii. If you don't have your own equipment, and you're not a guest at one of the hotels, your only choice is to buy it from Pine Isle or Richards markets, but their prices are quite high. If you're the adventurous sort, you can dive for spiny lobsters off Shipwreck or Polihua, but make absolutely sure to check the surf conditions as it can be super-treacherous. It would be best to go with a local person.

Trilogy Excursions operates the brand-new *Trilogy III* from Manele Boat Harbor for a combination snorkel ($75) and scuba adventure ($95 certified divers, $115 introductory). Departure is daily at 8:45 a.m.; book through the concierge desk at the Manele Bay Hotel or at the Lodge at Koele. Lunch, prepared by the Manele Bay Hotel, is gourmet with an excellent assortment of luncheon meats, cheeses, sushi, and fresh-baked cookies. Trilogy, in the business for years, has worked out all the kinks, and their boat, crew, and services are truly state-of-the-art. No matter how many times they make the trip, they never seem to forget that it's a new and exciting adventure for you, and they go out of their way to be helpful, upbeat, and caring without being intrusive. *Trilogy III*'s aft is set up for

TENNIS COURTS OF LANAI

LOCATION	NAME OF COURT	NO. OF COURTS	LIGHTED	COMMENTS
The Lodge At Koele		3	yes	guests complimentary, nonguests $9 per day
Lanai School	Lanai City	2	yes	open to the public; call for availability

easy entry and exit, with steps going down to the water level. Just make like a seal and slither in and out. If the winds are up, Captain Pat and his crew will be happy to set sail as they head toward Kahekili's Leap and other famous Lanai landmarks. The experience is not just underwater, but also in the magnificent views of this pristine island that hasn't changed since the days of the Polynesian explorers. You return in the early afternoon with plenty of time left for more sightseeing or relaxing.

Spinning Dolphin Charters, owned and operated by Capt. Jeff Menze, a longtime Lanai resident, P.O. Box 491, Lanai City, HI 96763, tel. 565-6613, will take you fishing (children welcome), snorkeling, and whalewatching in season. Captain Jeff is a commercial fisherman and master diver who knows all of the best spots in Lanai's waters. Rates are: full-day adventures, 8 a.m-3 p.m., $110; half day, 8 a.m.-noon Tuesday, Thursday, and Saturday, and at 12:30-4:30 p.m. Sunday, Wednesday, and Friday, $70. The special children's adventure, 2:30-4:30 p.m., is $25 per child, and $40 for moms and dads if they come along. Special off-the-beaten-path-dives and private boat charters are also available.

Lanai City has a brand-new swimming pool. Located in town near the high school, it's open to the public daily during summer, and on a limited schedule during other seasons.

Tennis And Golf

You can play tennis at three (two lighted) courts at the Lanai School. They have rubberized surfaces called Royal Duck and are fairly well maintained—definitely okay for a fun game. The Lodge at Koele and the Manele Bay Hotel have new Plexipave courts that are free to hotel guests, and $9 per day to Lanai residents, but not open to nonresident nonguests. Equipment rental (rackets and ball machines) and court times are arranged by the concierge. Private lessons and clinics are available.

Golfers will be delighted to follow their balls around Cavendish Golf Course on the outskirts of Lanai City. This nine-hole, 3,071-yard, par-36 course is set among Norfolk pines. It's free to all, but unless you're familiar with the course, the first tee is hard to find.

The **Experience at Koele,** a Greg Norman designed course, ws designated Best New Golf Course of 1991 in *Fortune Magazine*. This magnificent course, set in the mountains above the Lodge, not only offers challenging links, but a fantastic series of views of Molokai and Maui on a shimmering canvas of sea. With four sets of tees ranging from forward to tournament, the course yardage varies accordingly from 5,425 yards to 7,014 yards. The course also boasts the only bent grass greens in the state. Two of the finest holes are the no. 8, 444-yard par-four, which cascades from mountaintop to glen below, and the short but maximum water-challenged no. 9, 180-yard par-three.

The Challenge at Manele, designed by the legendary Jack Nicklaus, officially opened on Christmas Day 1993. Employing the five-tee concept, the par-72 course ranges in length from 4,890 to 7,088 yards. Three of the main holes, including the signature no. 16 par-three hole, demand a tee shot over the greatest water hazard in the world, the wide Pacific.

Horseback Riding

The **Stables at Koele,** open daily except Monday, a few minutes from the Lodge at Koele (contact concierge at the hotel) offers a variety of mounted excursions. The beginners' Plantation Trail Ride lasts one hour and costs $25, while the Paniolo Lunch Ride lasts three hours, includes lunch, and costs $50. Other rides are available, including a children's pony ride. Lanai enjoys a ranching heritage that goes back to the 1870s. Many of the trails that you'll follow date from those early days. Riders must be in good health, weigh less than 225 pounds, and wear long pants and shoes. Safety helmets will be provided.

Hunting

The first cliché you hear about Lanai is that it's one big pineapple plantation. The second is that it's a hunter's paradise. Both have some truth. The big game action is provided by mouflon sheep and axis deer. Also spotted are the protected yet failing population of pronghorns which, thankfully, can only be shot with a camera. Various days are open for the hunting of game birds, which include ring-necked and green pheasant; Gambel, Japanese, and California quail; wild turkey; and a variety of doves, francolins, and partridges. Hunting of mouflon sheep and axis deer is open to the public only in the northwest area of the island, which is leased to the state of Hawaii by the Koele Company. Brochures detailing all necessary information can be obtained free of charge by writing to Department of Land and Natural Resources, 1151 Punchbowl St., Honolulu, HI 96813. The Lanai regional office is at 338 8th St., Lanai City, HI 96763. Licenses are required ($10 resident, $20 nonresident) and can be purchased by mail from the Department of Land and Natural Resources or picked up in person at their office on Lanai.

Public archery hunting of mouflon sheep is restricted to the first and second Sundays of August and rifle season occurs on the third and fourth Sundays, but hunters are restricted by public drawing. Axis deer regular season (rifle, shotgun, and bows) opens on the nine consecutive Sundays up to and including the last Sunday in April; it's also restricted by public drawing. Archery season for axis deer is the two Sundays preceding the regular season. Bag limits are one mouflon ram and one deer.

Axis deer are hunted year-round on the private game reserves of the Koele Co., although the best trophy season is May through November. The rates are $200 per day for a regular hunting permit, $50 for an archery hunting permit. Guide service is not officially mandatory, but you must prove that you have hunted Lanai before and are intimately knowledgeable about its terrain, hunting areas, and procedures. If not, you must acquire the services of either Kazu Ohara or Gary Onuma, two excellent rangers on Lanai. Guide service is $750 a day. This service includes all necessities, except lodging and meals, from airport pick-up to shipping the trophy. For full details write to Chief Ranger, Koele Co., Box L, Lanai City, HI 96763, tel. 565-6661.

Fishing

Only one charter fishing boat operates out of Lanai (see the description of Spinning Dolphin Charters preceding), but that's not to say there are no fish. On the contrary, one of the island's greatest pastimes is this relaxing sport. Any day in Lanai City Park, you'll find plenty of old-timers you can ask where the fish are biting. If you have the right approach and use the right smile, they just might tell you. Generally, the best fishing and easiest access on the island is at Shipwreck Beach running north toward Polihua. Near the lighthouse ruins is good for *papio* and *ulua,* the latter running to 50 pounds. Many of the local fishermen use throw nets to catch the smaller fish such as *manini,* preferred especially by Lanai's elders. Throw-netting takes skill usually learned from childhood, but don't be afraid to try even if you throw what the locals call a "banana" or one that looks like Maui (a little head and a big body). They might snicker, but if you laugh too, you'll make a friend.

Mostly you'll fish with rod and reel using frozen squid or crab, available at Lanai's general stores. Bring a net bag or suitable container. Shipwreck Beach offers is the best beachcombing on the island and it's also excellent diving for spiny lobster. There is good shore fishing (especially for *awa*) and easy accessibility at Kaumalaupu Harbor, from where the pineapples are shipped. It's best to go after 5 p.m. when wharf activity has slowed down. There is also superb offshore fishing at Kaunolu, Kamehameha's favorite angling spot on the south shore. You can catch *aku* and *kawakawa,* but to be really successful you'll need a boat. Finally, Manele Hulopoe Marine Life Conservation Park has limited fishing, but as the name implies, it's a conservation district so be sure to follow the rules prominently posted at Manele Bay.

PRACTICALITIES

Information

Maps, brochures, and pamphlets on all aspects of staying on Lanai are available free from **Destination Lanai,** P.O. Box 700, Lanai City, HI 96763, tel. 565-7600.

Money

Try full-service **First Hawaiian Bank** in Lanai City for your banking needs. **First Federal Savings** has also established a branch here. All major businesses accept traveler's checks. Banks are open Mon.-Thurs. 8:30 a.m.-3 p.m. (First Federal to 4 p.m.), and until 6 p.m. on Friday.

Post Office

The Lanai P.O., tel. 565-6517, is across the street from the Koele offices on Lanai Avenue. Open daily 8 a.m.-4:30 p.m., it's full service but does not sell boxes or padded mailers to send home beachcombing treasures. You can get these at the two stores in town.

Laundromat

The laundromat, located next to Island Collections, is open every day from "morning until nighttime."

Useful Phone Numbers

Lanai City Service and Dollar Rent A Car, tel. 565-7227; Hotel Lanai, tel. 565-7211; Lanai Land Co. (for camping and hiking info), tel. 565-7400; Department of Land and Natural Resources, tel. 565-6688; Lanai Airport, tel. 565-6757; Lanai Community Library, tel. 565-6996; police, tel. 565-6525; Lanai Community Hospital, tel. 565-6411; Lanai Family Clinic, tel. 565-6423; Dr. Nick's Family Dentistry, tel. 565-7801, for emergency tel. 565-6527; Lanai City Travel, tel. 565-7635. The area code for all Lanai numbers is 808.

Norfolk pine

DIANA LASICH HARPER

EXPLORING LANAI

LANAI CITY

Lanai City (pop. 2,600) would be more aptly described and sound more appealing if it were called Lanai Village. A utilitarian town, it was built in the 1920s by Dole Pineapple Company. The architecture, field-worker plain, has definitely gained "character" in the last 60 years. It's an excellent spot for a town, sitting at 1,600 feet in the shadow of Lanaihale, the island's tallest mountain. George Munro's Norfolk pines have matured and now give the entire town a green, shaded, parklike atmosphere. It's cool and breezy—a great place from which to launch in the morning and a welcome spot to return to at night. Most visitors head out of town to the more spectacular sights and never explore the backstreets.

Houses

As you'd expect, most houses are square boxes with corrugated roofs, but each has its own personality. Painted every color of the rainbow, they'd be garish any other place, but here they break the monotony and seem to work. The people of Lanai make their living from the land and can work wonders with it. Around many homes are colorful flower beds, green gardens bursting with vegetables, fruit trees, and flowering shrubs. When you look down the half-dirt, broken-pavement roads at a line of these houses, you can't help feeling that a certain nobility exists here. The houses are mud-spattered where the rain splashes red earth against them, but inside you know they're sparkling clean. Even some modern suburban homes sprawl on the south end of town. Most of these belong to Lanai's miniature middle class and would fit unnoticed in any up-and-coming neighborhood on the Mainland.

Downtown

If you sit on the steps of Hotel Lanai and peer across its huge front yard, you can scrutinize the heart of downtown Lanai City. Off to your right are the offices of the Dole and Koele companies sitting squat and solid. In front of them, forming a type of town square, is Dole Park, where old-timers come to sit and young mothers bring their kids for fresh air. No one in Lanai City rushes to do anything. Look around and you'll discover a real fountain of youth: many octogenarians with a spring in their step. Years of hard work without being hyper or anxious is why they say they're still around. The park is surrounded by commercial Lanai. There's nowhere to *go* except over to the schoolyard to play tennis or to Cavendish Golf Course for a round of nine holes. Lanai City had a movie theater, but it screened its last picture show a while back. You can plop yourself at the Blue Ginger Cafe or S.T. Property for coffee, or stay in the park if you're in the mood to strike up a conversation—it won't take long.

Meander down Lanai Avenue past a complex of agricultural buildings and shops. Heavy equipment leaks grease in their rutted dirt lots, where Lanai shows its raw plantation muscle. Just down the street is a complex of log buildings with shake-shingled roofs. These rustic barracks are for the summer help that come to pick the pineapples—often Mormon kids from Utah out to make some money and see a bit of the world. They're known to be clean-living and quiet, and it's ironic that Lanai was once a failed Mormon colony. Do yourself a favor—get out of your rental car and walk around town for at least 30 minutes. You'll experience one of the most unique villages in America.

MUNRO TRAIL

The highlight of visiting Lanai is climbing the Munro Trail to its highest point, Lanaihale (3,370 feet), locally called **The Hale.** As soon as you set foot on Lanai the silhouette of this razorback ridge with its bristling coat of Norfolk pines demands your attention. Set off for The Hale and you're soon engulfed in its cool stands of pines, eucalyptus, and ironwoods, colored with ferns and wildflowers. George Munro, a New Zealander hired as the manager of the Lanai Ranch a short time before Jim Dole's arrival, is responsible. With a pouchful of seeds and clippings from his native New Zealand, he trudged all over Lanai planting, in an attempt to foliate the island and create a permanent watershed. Driven by that primordial human desire to see things grow, he climbed The Hale time and again to nurture his leafy progeny. Now, all benefit from his labors.

Getting There

There are two basic ways to go to The Hale: by foot or by 4WD. Some local people go on horseback. Head out of town on Rt. 440 toward Shipwreck Beach. Make sure to start before 8 a.m.; cloud cover is common by early afternoon. After less than two miles, still on the Lanai City side of the mountains, take the first major gravel road to the right, heading for the new upcountry golf course. In about a quarter mile the road comes to a Y-intersection—go left. You immediately start climbing and pass through a forested area past a series of gulches. Continue and the road forks; again bear left. Always stay on the more obviously traveled road. The side roads look muddy and overgrown and it's obvious which is the main one. Robert Frost would be disappointed.

The Trail

As you climb, you pass a profusion of gulches, great red wounds cut into Lanai's windward side. First comes deep and brooding **Maunalei** ("Mountain Lei") **Gulch,** from where Lanai draws its water through a series of tunnels bored through the mountains. It's flanked by **Kuolanai Trail,** a rugged and dangerous footpath leading all the way to the coast. Next is **Hookio Gulch,** a battleground where Lanai's warriors were vanquished in 1778 by Kalaniopuu and his ferocious fighters from the Big Island. All that remains are a few room-sized notches cut into the walls where the warriors slept and piled stones to be hurled at the invaders. After Hookio Gulch, a trail bears left, bringing you to the gaping mouth of **Hauola Gulch,** over 2,000 feet deep. Keep your eyes peeled for axis deer, which seem to defy gravity and manage to cling to and forage along the most unlikely and precipitous cliffs. Be very careful of your footing—even skilled Lanai hunters have fallen to their deaths in this area.

The jeep trail narrows on the ridge to little more than 100 feet across. On one side are the

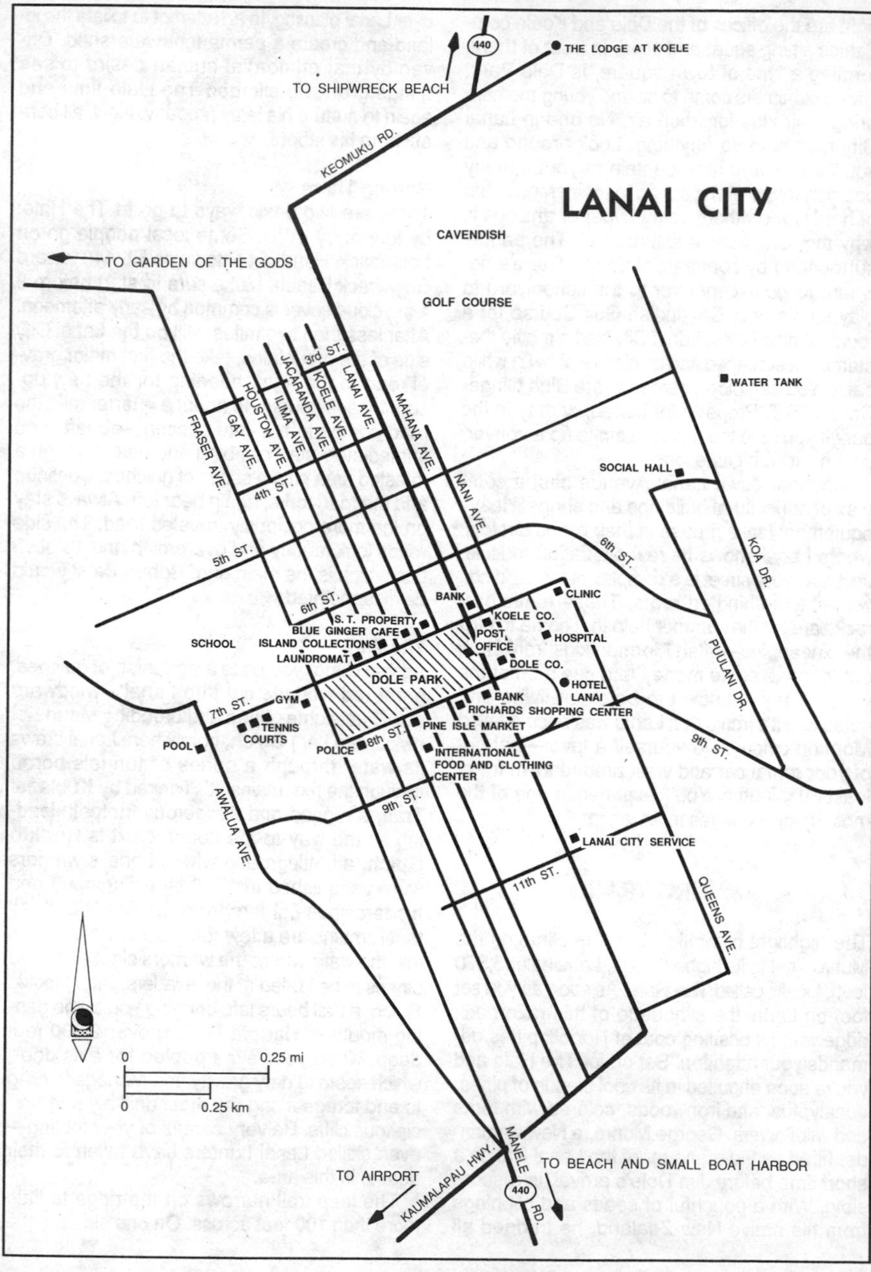

LANAI CITY

THE LODGE AT KOELE
440
TO SHIPWRECK BEACH
KEOMUKU RD.
CAVENDISH
TO GARDEN OF THE GODS
GOLF COURSE
WATER TANK
3rd ST.
LANAI AVE.
KOELE AVE.
JACARANDA AVE.
ILIMA AVE.
HOUSTON AVE.
GAY AVE.
FRASER AVE.
MAHANA AVE.
4th ST.
5th ST.
NANI AVE.
SOCIAL HALL
6th ST.
KOA DR.
6th ST.
BANK
CLINIC
S. T. PROPERTY
BLUE GINGER CAFE
KOELE CO.
POST OFFICE
HOSPITAL
SCHOOL
ISLAND COLLECTIONS
LAUNDROMAT
PUULANI DR.
DOLE CO.
DOLE PARK
HOTEL LANAI
BANK
7th ST.
GYM
RICHARDS SHOPPING CENTER
TENNIS COURTS
PINE ISLE MARKET
9th ST.
POOL
POLICE
8th ST.
INTERNATIONAL FOOD AND CLOTHING CENTER
9th ST.
AWALUA AVE.
LANAI CITY SERVICE
11th ST.
QUEENS AVE.
0 0.25 mi
0 0.25 km
MOON
TO BEACH AND SMALL BOAT HARBOR
TO AIRPORT
KAUMALAPAU HWY.
MANELE RD.
440

wild gulches, on the other the bucolic green, whorling fingerprints of the pineapple fields. Along the trail you can munch strawberries, common guavas, and as many thimbleberries as you can handle. At the crest of The Hale, let your eyes pan the horizon to see the main islands of Hawaii (except Kauai). Rising from the height-caused mirage of a still sea is the hazy specter of Oahu to the north, with Molokai and Maui clearly visible just 10 miles distant. Haleakala, Maui's magical mountain, has a dominant presence viewed from The Hale. Sweep your gaze right to see Kahoolawe, bleak and barren, its body shattered by the bombs of the U.S. Navy, a victim of their controversial war games. Eighty miles south of Kahoolawe is the Big Island, its mammoth peaks, Mauna Loa and Mauna Kea, floating like ethereal islands in the clouds.

Just past the final lookout is a sign for **Awehi Trail,** which leads left to Naha on the beach. It's extremely rough and you'll definitely need a 4WD in compound-low to get down. Most people continue straight ahead and join up with Hoike Road that flattens out and takes you through the pineapple fields until it joins with Rt. 440 just south of Lanai City. If you have time for only one outing on Lanai or funds budgeted for only one day of 4WD rental, make sure to treat yourself to the unforgettable Munro Trail.

HEADING SOUTH

Joseph Kaliihananui was the last of the free Hawaiian farmers to work the land of Lanai. His great-grandson, Lloyd Cockett, still lives in Lanai City. Joseph made his home in the arid but fertile Palawai Basin that was later bought by Jim Dole and turned into the heart of the pineapple plantation. Just south of Lanai City on Rt. 440 (Manele Road), the Palawai Basin is the crater of the extinct single volcano of which Lanai is formed. Joseph farmed sweet potatoes, which he traded for fish. He gathered his water in barrels from the dew that formed on his roof and from a trickling spring. His lands supported a few cattle among its now-extinct heavy stands of cactus. Here, too, Walter Murray Gibson attempted to begin a Mormon colony, which he later aborted, supposedly because of his outrage over the idea of polygamy. Nothing noteworthy remains of this colony, but high on a hillside overlooking Palawai are the Luahiwa Petroglyphs, considered some of the best-preserved rock hieroglyphics in Hawaii.

Luahiwa Petroglyphs

The route through the maze of pineapple roads that leads to the petroglyphs is tough to follow, but the best recipe for success is being pointed in the right direction and adding a large dollop of perseverance. Heading south on Manele Road, look to your left for the back side of a triangular yield sign at Hoike Road, the main pineapple road. Hoike Road was once paved but has now disintegrated into gravel. After turning left onto Hoike, head straight toward a large water tank on the hill. You pass two round-bottomed irrigation ditches, easily spotted as they're always green with grass due to the water they carry. At the second ditch turn left and follow the road, keeping the ditch on your right. Proceed until you come to a silver water pipe about 12 inches in diameter. Follow this pipe as it runs along a hedgerow until you reach the third power pole. At the No Trespassing sign, bear left.

Follow this overgrown trail up the hill to the boulders on which appear the petroglyphs. The boulders are brownish-black and covered in lichen. Their natural arrangement resembles an oversized Japanese rock garden. Dotted on the hillside are sisal plants that look like bouquets of giant green swords. As you climb to the rocks be very careful of your footing—the ground is crumbly and the vegetation slippery. The boulders cover a three-acre area; most of the petroglyphs are found on the south faces of the rocks. Some are hieroglyphics of symbolic circles, others are picture stories complete with canoes gliding under unfurled sails. Dogs snarl with their jaws agape, while enigmatic triangular stick figures try to tell their stories from the past. Equestrians gallop, showing that these stone picture-books were done even after the coming of white people. The Luahiwa Petroglyphs are a very special spot where the ancient Hawaiians still sing their tales across the gulf of time.

Hulopoe And Manele Bays

Proceed south on Rt. 440 to Lanai's most salubrious spots, the twin bays of Manele and Hulopoe. At the crest of the hill, just past the milepost, you can look down on the white, inviting sands of Hulopoe to the right, and the rockier small boat harbor of Manele on the left. The island straight ahead is Kahoolawe, and on very clear days you might be able to glimpse the peaks of Hawaii's Mauna Loa and Mauna Kea. Manele Bay is a picture-perfect anchorage where a dozen or so small boats and yachts are tied up on any given day. Tour boats from Maui also tie up here, but according to local sailors the tourists don't seem to come on the weekends. Manele and Hulopoe are a Marine Life Conservation District with the rules for fishing and diving prominently displayed on a large bulletin board at the entrance to Manele. Because of this, the area is superb for snorkeling.

Hulopoe Bay offers very gentle waves and soothing, crystal-clear water. The beach is a beautiful expanse of white sand fringed by palms with a mingling of large boulders that really set it off. This is Lanai's official camping area, and six sites are available. All are well spaced, each with a picnic table and firepit. A series of shower stalls made of brown plywood provides solar-heated water and just enough privacy, allowing your head and legs to protrude. After refreshing yourself you can fish from the rock promontories on both sides of the bay. It's difficult to find a more wholesome and gentle spot anywhere in Hawaii.

Kaumalapau Harbor

A side trip to Kaumalapau Harbor is worth it. This manmade facility, which ships more than a million pineapples a day during peak harvest, is the only one of its kind in the world. Besides, you've probably already rented a vehicle and you might as well cover these few paved miles from Lanai City on Rt. 440 just to have a quick look. En route you pass Lanai's odoriferous garbage dump, which is a real eyesore. Hold your nose and try not to notice. The harbor facility itself is no-nonsense commercial, but the coastline is reasonably spectacular, with a glimpse of the island's dramatic seacliffs. Also, this area has super-easy access to some decent fishing, right off the pier area. An added bonus for making the trek to this lonely area is that it is one of the best places on Lanai from which to view the sunset, and you usually have it all to yourself.

KAUNOLU: KAMEHAMEHA'S GETAWAY

At the southwestern tip of Lanai is Kaunolu Bay. At one time, this vibrant fishing village surrounded Halulu Heiau, a sacred refuge where the downtrodden were protected by the temple priests who could intercede with the benevolent gods. Kamehameha the Great would escape Lahaina's blistering summers and come to these very fertile fishing waters with his loyal warriors. Some proved their valor to their great chief by diving from Kahekili's Leap, a manmade opening in the rocks 60 feet above the sea. The remains of over 80 house sites and a smattering of petroglyphs dot the area. The last inhabitant was Ohua, elder brother of Joseph Kaliihananui, who lived in a grass hut just east of Kaunolu in Mamaki Bay. Ohua was entrusted by Kamehameha V to hide the *heiau* fish-god, Kuniki; old accounts by the area's natives say that he died because he mishandled this stone god. The natural power still emanating from Kaunolu is obvious, and you can't help feeling the energy that drew the Hawaiians to this sacred spot.

Getting There

Proceed south on Manele Road from Lanai City through Palawai Basin until it makes a hard bend to the left. Here, a sign points you to Manele Bay. Do not go left to Manele, but proceed straight and stay on the once-paved pineapple road. At a dip by a huge silver water pipe, go straight through the pineapple fields until another obvious dip at two orange pipes (like fire hydrants) on the left and right. Turn left here onto a rather small road—pineapples on your left and tall grass along the irrigation ditch on your right. Follow the road left to a weather-worn sign that actually says "Kaunolu Road." This dirt track starts off innocently enough as it begins its plunge toward the sea. Only two miles long, it is considered by locals to be the roughest road on the island. It *is* a bone-cruncher, but if you take it super-slow, you should have no real problem. Plot your progress against the lighthouse on the coast. This area is excellent for spotting axis deer. The deer are nourished by *haole koa,* a green bush with a brown seedpod that you see growing along the road. This natural feed also supports cattle, but is not good for horses, causing the hair on their tails to fall out.

Kaunolu

The village site lies at the end of a long dry gulch that terminates at a rocky beach, suitable in times past as a canoe anchorage. This entire area is a mecca for archaeologists and anthropologists. The most famous was the eminent Dr. Kenneth Emory of the Bishop Museum; he filed an extensive research report on the area. At its terminus, the road splits left and right. Go right to reach a large *kiawe* tree with a rudimentary picnic table under it. Just in front of you is a large pile of nondescript rocks purported to be the ruined foundation of Kamehameha's house. Unbelievably, this sacred area has been trashed out by disrespectful and ignorant picnickers. Hurricane Iwa also had a hand in changing the face of Kaunolu, as its tremendous force hit this area head on and even drove large boulders from the sea onto the land. As you look around, the ones that have a whitish appearance were washed up on the shore by the fury of Iwa.

The villagers of Kaunolu lived mostly on the east bank and had to keep an ever-watchful eye on nature because the bone-dry gulch could suddenly be engulfed by flash floods. In the center of the gulch, about 100 yards inland, was **Paao,** the area's freshwater well. Paao was *kapu* to menstruating women, and it was believed that if the *kapu* was broken, the well would dry up. It served the village for centuries. It's totally obliterated now; in 1895 a Mr. Hayselden tried to erect a windmill over it, destroying the native caulking and causing the well to turn brackish—an example of Lanai's precious water being tampered with by outsiders, causing disastrous results.

The Sites

Climb down the east bank and cross the rocky beach. The first well-laid wall close to the beach on the west bank is the remains of a canoe shed. Proceed inland and climb the rocky bank to the remains of Halulu Heiau. Just below in the undergrowth is where the well was located. The *heiau* site has a commanding view of the area, best described in the words of Dr. Emory himself: "The point on which it is located is surrounded on three sides by cliffs and on the north rises the magnificent cliff of Palikaholo, terminating in Kahilikalani crag, a thousand feet above the sea. The ocean swell entering Kolokolo Cave causes a rumbling like thunder, as if under the *heiau*. From every point in the village the *heiau* dominates the landscape." As you climb the west bank, notice that the mortarless walls are laid up for over 30 feet. If you have a keen eye you'll notice a perfectly square firepit right in the center of the *heiau*.

This area still has treasures that have never been cataloged. For example, you might chance upon a Hawaiian lamp, as big and perfectly round as a basketball, with an orange-sized hole in the middle where *kukui* nut oil was burned. Old records indicate that Kuniki, the temple idol itself, is still lying here face down no more than a few hundred yards away. If you happen to discover an artifact, do not remove it under any circumstance. Follow the advice of the late Lloyd Cockett, a *kupuna* of Lanai, who said, "I wouldn't take the rock because we Hawaiians don't steal from the land. Special rocks you don't touch."

Kahekili's Leap

Once you've explored the *heiau*, you'll be drawn toward the seacliff. **Kaneapua Rock,** a giant towerlike chunk, sits perhaps 100 feet offshore. Below in the tidepool are basinlike depressions in the rock-salt evaporation pools, the bottoms still showing white residue. Follow the cliff face along the natural wall obstructing your view to the south. You'll see a break in the wall about 15 feet wide with a very flat rock platform. From here, **Shark Island,** which closely resembles a shark's fin, is perfectly framed. This opening is Kahekili's Leap, named after a Lanai chief, not the famous chief of Maui. Here, Kamehameha's warriors proved their courage by executing death-defying leaps into only 12 feet of water, and clearing a 15-foot protruding rock shelf. Scholars also believe that Kamehameha punished his warriors for petty offenses by sentencing them to make the jump. Kahekili's Leap is a perfect background for a photo. Below, the sea surges in unreal aquamarine colors. Off to the right is Kolokolo Cave, above which is another, even more daring, leap at 90 feet. Evidence suggests that Kolokolo is linked to Kaunolu Gulch by a lava tube that has been sealed and lost. On the beach below Kahekili's

Leap the vacationing chiefs played *konane,* and many stone boards can still be found from this game of Hawaiian checkers.

Petroglyphs
To find them, walk directly inland from Kaneapua Rock, using it as your point of reference. On a large pile of rocks are stick figures, most with a bird-head motif. Some heads even look like a mason's hammer. This entire area has a masculine feeling to it. There aren't the usual swaying palms and gentle sandy beaches. With the stones and rugged seacliffs, you get the feeling that a warrior king would enjoy this spot. Throughout the area is *pili* grass, used by the Hawaiians to thatch their homes. Children would pick one blade and hold it in their fingers while reciting, *"E pili e, e pili e, au hea kuu hale."* The *pili* grass would then spin around in their fingers and point in the direction of home. Pick some *pili* and try it yourself before leaving this wondrous, powerful area.

THE EAST COAST: KEOMUKU AND NAHA

Until the turn of this century, most of Lanai's inhabitants lived in the villages of the now-deserted east coast. Before the coming of Westerners, 2,000 or so Hawaiians lived along these shores, fishing and raising taro. It was as if they wanted to keep Maui in sight so that they didn't feel so isolated. Numerous *heiau* from this period still mark the ancient sites. The first white people also tried to make a go of Lanai along this stretch. The Maunalei Sugar Co. tried to raise sugarcane on the flat plains of Naha but failed and pulled up stakes in 1901—the last time this entire coastline was populated to any extent. Today, the ancient *heiau* and a decaying church in Keomuku are the last vestiges of habitation, holding out against the ever-encroaching jungle. You can follow a jeep trail along this coast and get a fleeting glimpse of times past.

Getting There
Approach Keomuku and Naha from one of two directions. The most straightforward is from north to south. Follow Rt. 440 (Keomuku Road) from Lanai City until it turns to dirt and branches right (south) at the coast. This road meanders for about 15 miles all the way to Naha. Though the road is partial gravel and packed sand and not that rugged, you definitely need a 4WD. It's paralleled by a much smoother road that runs along the beach, but it can only be used at low tide. Many small roads connect the two, so you can hop back and forth between them every 200-300 yards. Consider two tips: first, if you take the beach road, you can make good time and have a smooth ride, but could sail past most of the sights since you won't know when to hop back on the inland road; second, be careful of the *kiawe* trees—the tough, inch-thick thorns can puncture tires as easily as nails. The other alternative is to take Awehi Trail, a rugged jeep track, about halfway between Lopa and Naha. This trail leads up the mountain to the Munro Trail, but because of its ruggedness it's best to take it down from The Hale instead of up. A good long day of rattling in a jeep would take you along the Munro Trail, down Awehi Trail, then north along the coast back to Rt. 440. If you came south along the coast from Rt. 440, it would be better to retrace your steps instead of heading up Awehi. When you think you've suffered enough and have been bounced into submission by your jeep, remember that many of these trails were carved out by Juan Torqueza. He trailblazed alone on his bulldozer, unsupervised, and without benefit of survey. Now well into his 70s, he can be found in Dole Park in Lanai City, except when he's out here fishing.

A new island venture based on Maui, called **Club Lanai,** tel. 871-1144, has recently opened the remote east coast of Lanai to visitors. Basically they transport tourists from Maui aboard their boats to their private facility for a day of fun, games, and feasting. For full information see "Ocean Tours" under "Getting Around" in the Maui Introduction.

Keomuku Village
There isn't much to see in Keomuku ("Stretch of White") Village other than an abandoned Hawaiian church. Though this was the site of the Maunalei Sugar Co., almost all the decaying buildings were razed in the early 1970s. A few hundred yards north and south of the town site are examples of original fishponds. They're tough to see (overgrown with mangrove), but a

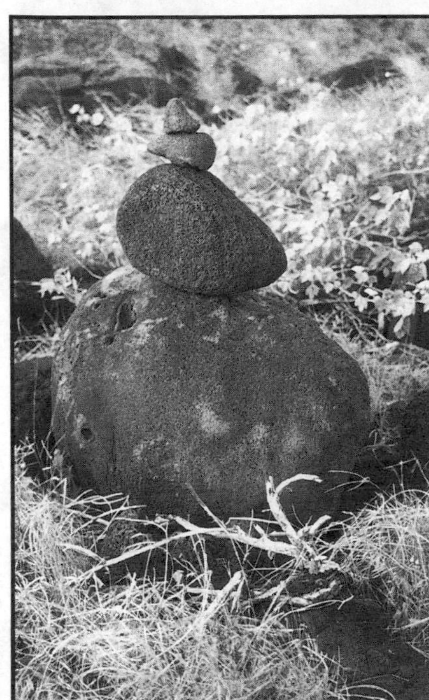
J.D. BISIGNANI

ahu, *a traveler's wish for happy trails*

close observation gives you an idea of how extensive they once were. The **Hawaiian church,** now being refurbished, is definitely worth a stop —it almost pleads to be photographed. From outside, you can see how frail it is, so if you go in, tread lightly—both walls of the church are caving in and the floor is humped in the middle. The altar area, a podium with a little bench, remains. A banner on the fading blue-green walls reads *"Ualanaano Jehova Kalanakila Malamalama,* October 4, 1903." Only the soft wind sounds where once strong voices sang vibrant hymns of praise.

A few hundred yards south of the church is a walking trail. Follow it inland to **Kahea Heiau** and a smattering of petroglyphs. This is the *heiau* disturbed by the sugarcane train; its desecration was believed to have caused the sweet water of Keomuku to turn brackish. The people of Keomuku learned to survive on the brackish water and kept a special jug of fresh water for visitors.

Heading South

Farther south a Japanese cemetery and monument were erected for the deceased workers who built **Halepaloa Landing,** from where the cane was shipped. Today, only rotting timbers and stonework remain, but the pier offers an excellent vantage point for viewing Maui, and it's a good spot to fish. The next landmark is a semi-used getaway called "Whale's Tale." A boat sits in the front yard. This is a great place to find a coconut and have a free roadside refreshment. Also, a very fruitful *kamani* nut tree sits right at the entrance. The nut looks like an oversized bean. Place your knife in the center and drive it down. The *kamani,* which tastes like a roasted almond, is 99% husk and one percent nut.

The road continues past **Lopa,** ending at **Naha.** You pass a few coconut groves on the way. Legend says that one of these was cursed by a *kahuna*—if you climb a tree to get a coconut you will not be able to come down. Luckily, most tourists have already been cursed by "midriff bulge" and can't climb the tree in the first place. When you get to Naha check out the remnants of the paved Hawaiian walking trail before slowly heading back from this decaying historical area.

SHIPWRECK BEACH

Heading over the mountains from Lanai City to Shipwreck Beach offers you a rewarding scenario: an intriguing destination point with fantastic scenery and splendid panoramas on the way. Head north from Lanai City on Rt. 440 (Keomuku Road). In less that 10 minutes you crest the mountains, and if you're lucky the sky will be clear and you'll be able to see the phenomenon that guided ancient navigators to land: the halo of dark brooding clouds over Maui and Molokai, a sure sign of landfall. Shorten your gaze and look at the terrain in the immediate vicinity. Here are the famous precipitous gulches of Lanai. The wounded earth bleeds red while offering patches of swaying grass and wildflowers. It looks as if the canyons of Arizona have been dragged to the rim of the sea. As you wiggle your way down Keomuku Road, look left to see the rusting hull of a WW II Liberty Ship sitting on the shallow reef almost completely out of the water. For most, this derelict is the destination point on Shipwreck Beach.

The Beach

As you continue down the road, little piles of stones, usually three, sit atop a boulder. Although most are from modern times, these are called *ahu,* a traditional Hawaiian offering to ensure good fortune while traveling. If you have the right feeling in your heart and you're moved to erect your own *ahu* it's okay, but under no circumstances disturb the ones already there. Farther down, the lush grasses of the mountain slope disappear, and the scrub bush takes over. The pavement ends and the dirt road forks left (north) to Shipwreck Beach, or straight ahead (south) toward the abandoned town of Naha. If you turn left you'll be on an adequate sandy road, flanked on both sides by thorny, tire-puncturing *kiawe* trees. In less than a mile is a large open area to your right. If you're into unofficial camping, this isn't a bad spot for a one-night bivouac—the trees here provide privacy and an excellent windbreak against the constant strong ocean breezes. About two miles down the road is Federation Camp, actually a tiny village of unpretentious beach shacks built by Lanai's workers as "getaways" and fishing cabins. Charming in their humbleness and simplicity, they're made mostly from recycled timbers and boards that have washed ashore. Some have been worked on quite diligently and skillfully and are actual little homes, but somehow the rougher ones are more attractive. You can drive past the cabins for a few hundred yards, but to be on the safe side, park just past them and begin your walk.

Petroglyphs

At the very end of the road is a cabin that a local comedian has named the "Lanai Hilton." Just off to your left *(mauka)* are the ruins of a lighthouse. Look for a cement slab where two graffiti artists of bygone days carved their names: "John Kupau and Kam Chee, Nov. 28, 1929." Behind the lighthouse ruins an arrow points you to "The Bird Man of Lanai Petroglyphs." Of all the petroglyphs on Lanai these are the easiest to find; trail-marking rocks have been painted white by Lanai's Boy Scouts. Follow them to a large rock bearing the admonition "Do Not Deface." Climb down the path with a keen eye—the rock carvings are small, most only about 10 inches tall. Little childlike stick figures, they have intriguing bird heads whose symbolic meaning has been lost.

Hiking Trail

The trail along the beach goes for eight long hot miles to Polihua Beach. That trip leads through the Garden of the Gods and should be done separately, but at least walk as far as the Liberty Ship, about a mile from the cabins. The area has some of the best beachcombing in Hawaii; no telling what you might find. The most sought-after treasures are glass floats that have bobbed for thousands of miles across the Pacific, strays from Japanese fishnets. You might even see a modern ship washed onto the reef, like the Canadian yacht that went aground in the spring of 1984. Navigational equipment has improved, but Shipwreck Beach can *still* be a nightmare to any captain caught in its turbulent whitecaps and long ragged coral fingers. This area is particularly good for lobsters and shore fishing. And you can swim in shallow sandy-bottom pools to refresh yourself as you hike.

Try to time your return car trip over the mountain for sundown. The tortuous terrain, stark in black and white shadows, is awe-inspiring. The larger rocks are giant sentinels: it's easy to feel the power and attraction they held for the ancient Hawaiians. As you climb the road on the windward side with its barren and beaten terrain, the mystique attributed to spiritual Lanai is obvious. You come over the top and suddenly see the valley—manicured, rolling, soft, and verdant with pineapples, the few lights of Lanai City beckoning.

THE GARDEN OF THE GODS AND POLIHUA

The most ruggedly beautiful, barren, and inhospitable section of Lanai is out at the north end. After passing through a confusing maze of pineapple fields, you come to the appropriately named Garden of the Gods. Waiting is a fantasia of otherworldly landscapes—barren red earth, convulsed ancient lava flows, tortured pinnacles of stone, and psychedelic striations of vibrating colors, especially moving at sunrise and sunset. Little-traveled trails lead to Kaena Point, a wasteland dominated by seacliffs where adulterous Hawaiian wives were sent into exile for a short time in 1837. Close by is Lanai's largest *heiau,* dubbed Kaenaiki, so isolated and forgotten that its real name and function were lost even to Hawaiian natives by the middle of the 19th century. After a blistering, sun-baked, 4WD drubbing, you emerge at the coast on Polihau, a totally secluded, pure-white beach where sea turtles once came to bury their eggs in the natural incubator of its soft warm sands.

Getting There

Lanai doesn't hand over its treasures easily, but they're worth pursuing. To get to the Garden of the Gods you have to tangle with the maze of pineapple roads. Head for the Lodge at Koele, and turn right onto the road that runs next to the tennis courts. After about one minute, the road will turn right. Follow it, keeping the prominent ridge on your right. Proceed until you come to a tunnel of spindly pine trees and a fenced area. In about 10 minutes, you'll come to a sign pointing to Kaena Point. Proceed until you cross a cattle guard. In a minute or so, a sign points to Kuamo'o. Don't follow it! Go straight ahead and shortly, a marker points you off to the right onto Lapaiki Road. This is a bit out of the way, but if you follow it you'll get a good view of the garden, and eventually wind up at Shipwreck Beach. It's better, however, to proceed straight ahead to another marker pointing you down Awailua Trail to the right and Polihua straight ahead. Follow Polihua Trail, and soon you begin to see large boulders sitting atop packed red earth, the signal that you're entering the Garden of the Gods. Finally comes another marker for Kaena Road, which leads to magnificent seacliffs and Kaenaiki Heiau.

Note: These roads are very confusing, and oftentimes the signs, due to heavy weather and vandalism, are missing. Check at Lanai City Service for up-to-the-minute road conditions and instructions. Definitely do not attempt the lower reaches of this road without 4WD.

Hiking

Anyone wishing to hike this area should drive to the end of the pineapple fields. It's at least half the distance and the scenery is quite ordinary. Make sure to bring plenty of water and a windbreaker because the heavy winds blow almost continuously. Sturdy shoes and a sun hat are also needed. There is no official camping at Polihua Beach, but again, anyone doing so overnight probably wouldn't meet with any hassles. Those with super-keen eyes might even pick out one of the scarce pronghorn that live in the fringe of surrounding grasslands.

The Garden Of The Gods

Here, a shocking assault on your senses, is the bleak, red, burnt earth, devoid of vegetation, heralding the beginning of the garden. The flowers here are made of rock, the shrubs are the twisted crusts of lava, and trees are baked minarets of stone, all subtle shades of orange, purple, and sulfurous yellow. The jeep trail has been sucked down by erosion and the garden surrounds you. Stop many times to climb a likely outcropping and get a sweeping view. The wind rakes these badlands and the silence penetrates to your soul. Although eons have passed, you can feel the cataclysmic violence that created this haunting beauty.

Polihua Beach

Abruptly the road becomes smooth and flat. Straight ahead, like a mirage too bright for your eyes, an arch is cut into the green jungle, framing white sand and moving blue ocean. As you face the beach, to the right it's flat and expansive and the sands are white, but the winds are heavy; if you hike eight miles, you'll reach Shipwreck Beach. More interesting is the view to the left, which has a series of lonely little coves. The sand is brown and coarse and large black lava boulders are marbled with purplish-gray rock embedded in long, faulted seams. Polihua is not just a destination point where you come for a quick look. Coming and going here requires so much effort that you should plan on having a picnic and a relaxing afternoon before heading back through the Garden of the Gods and its perfectly scheduled sunset light show.

MOLOKAI

INTRODUCTION

Molokai is a sanctuary, a human time capsule where the pendulum swings inexorably forward, but more slowly than in the rest of Hawaii. It has always been so. In ancient times, Molokai was known as *Pule-oo,* "Powerful Prayer." The small, underpopulated refuge was protected by its supreme chiefs not through legions of warriors but through the chants of their *kahuna.* This powerful, ancient mysticism, handed down directly from the goddess Pahulu, was known and respected throughout the archipelago. Its mana was the oldest and strongest in Hawaii, and its practitioners were venerated by nobility and commoners alike—they had the ability to "pray you to death." The entire island was a haven, a refuge for the vanquished and *kapu*-breakers of all the islands. It's still so today, beckoning to determined escapees from the rat race!

The blazing lights of super-modern Honolulu can easily be seen from western Molokai, while Molokai as viewed from Oahu is fleeting and ephemeral, appearing and disappearing on the horizon. The island is home to the largest number of Hawaiians. In effect it is a tribal homeland: over 2,500 of the island's 6,000 inhabitants have more than 50% Hawaiian blood and, except for Niihau, it's the only island where they are the majority. The 1920s Hawaiian Homes Act allowed *kuleana* of 40 acres to anyone with more than 50% Hawaiian ancestry. *Kuleana* owners form the grassroots organizations that fight for Hawaiian rights and battle the colossal forces of rabid developers who have threatened Molokai for decades.

AN OVERVIEW

Kaunakakai And West

Kaunakakai, the island's main town, is like a Hollywood sound stage where Jesse James or Wyatt Earp would feel right at home. The town is flat, treeless, and three blocks long. Ala Malama, its main shopping street, is lined with false-front stores; pickup trucks are parked in front where horses and buggies ought to be. To the west are the prairielike plains of Molokai. The northern section of the island contains **Palaau State Park,** where a campsite is always easily found, and **Phallic Rock,** a natural shrine where island women came to pray for fertility. Most of the west end is owned by the mammoth 70,000-acre **Molokai Ranch.** Part of its lands supports 6,000 head of cattle, **Wildlife Safari Park,** and herds of axis deer imported from India in 1867.

The 40-acre *kuleana* are here, as well as abandoned Dole and Del Monte pineapple fields. The once-thriving pineapple company towns of **Maunaloa** and **Kualapuu** are now semi-ghost towns since the pineapple companies pulled up stakes in the last few years. Maunaloa is trying to hold on as an embryonic artists' colony, and the Kualapuu area attracts its scattered Filipino workers mostly on weekends, when they come to unofficially test their best cocks in the pit.

On the western shore is the Kaluakoi Resort and a handful of condos perched above the island's best beaches. Here, 7,000 acres sold by the Molokai Ranch to the Louisiana Land and Exploration Company are slated for development. This area, rich with the finest archaeological sites on the island, is a hotbed of contention between developers and preservationists. The Kaluakoi, however, is often pointed to as a well-planned development, a kind of model compromise between the factions. Its first-rate architecture, in low Polynesian style, blends well with the surroundings and is not a high-rise blight on the horizon.

The East Coastal Road

Highway 450 is a magnificent coastal road running east from Kaunakakai to Halawa Valley. A slow drive along this writhing country thoroughfare rewards you with easily accessible beach parks, glimpses of fishponds, *heiau,* wildlife sanctuaries, and small one-room churches strung along the road like rosary beads. Almost every mile has a historical site, like the **Smith and Bronte Landing Site** where two pioneers of transpacific flight ignominiously alighted in a mangrove swamp, and **Paikalani Taro Patch,** the only one from which Kamehameha V would eat poi.

On Molokai's eastern tip is **Halawa Valley,** a real gem accessible by car. This pristine gorge has a just-right walk to a series of invigorating waterfalls and their pools, and a beach park where the valley meets the sea. The majority of the population of Halawa moved out in 1946 when a 30-foot tsunami washed their homes away and mangled their taro fields, leaving a thick salty residue. Today a handful of mostly alternative lifestylers lives in the valley among the overgrown stone walls that once marked the boundaries of manicured and prosperous family gardens. Just south on the grounds of Puu O Hoku Ranch is **Kalanikaula,** the sacred *kukui* grove of Lanikaula, Molokai's most powerful *kahuna* of the classic period. This grove was planted at his death and became the most sacred spot on Molokai. Today the trees are dying.

The Windward Coast

Kalaupapa leper colony, a lonely peninsula completely separated from the world by a hostile pounding surf and a precipitous 1,500-foot *pali,* is a modern story of human dignity. Kalaupapa was a howling charnel house where the unfortunate victims of leprosy were banished to die. Here humanity reached its lowest ebb of hopelessness, violence, and depravity, until one tiny flicker of light arrived in 1873—Joseph de Veuster, a Belgian priest known throughout Hawaii as Father Damien. In the greatest example of pure *aloha* yet established on Hawaii, he became his brothers' keeper. Tours of Kalaupapa operated by well-informed former patients are enlightening and educational.

East of Kalaupapa along the windward (northeast) coast is a series of amazingly steep and isolated valleys. The inhabitants moved out at the beginning of this century except for one pioneering family that returned a few years ago to carve out a home. Well beyond the farthest reaches of the last road, this emerald green primeval world awaits. The *pali* here mark the tallest seacliffs in the world, and diving headfirst is **Kahiwa** ("Sacred One") **Falls,** the highest in Hawaii at 1,750 feet. You get here by helicopter excursion, by boat in the calmer summer months, or by foot over dangerous and unkempt mountain trails.

For now, Molokai remains a sanctuary, reminiscent of the Hawaii of simpler times. Around it the storm of modernity rages, but the "Friendly Island" awaits those willing to venture off the beaten track.

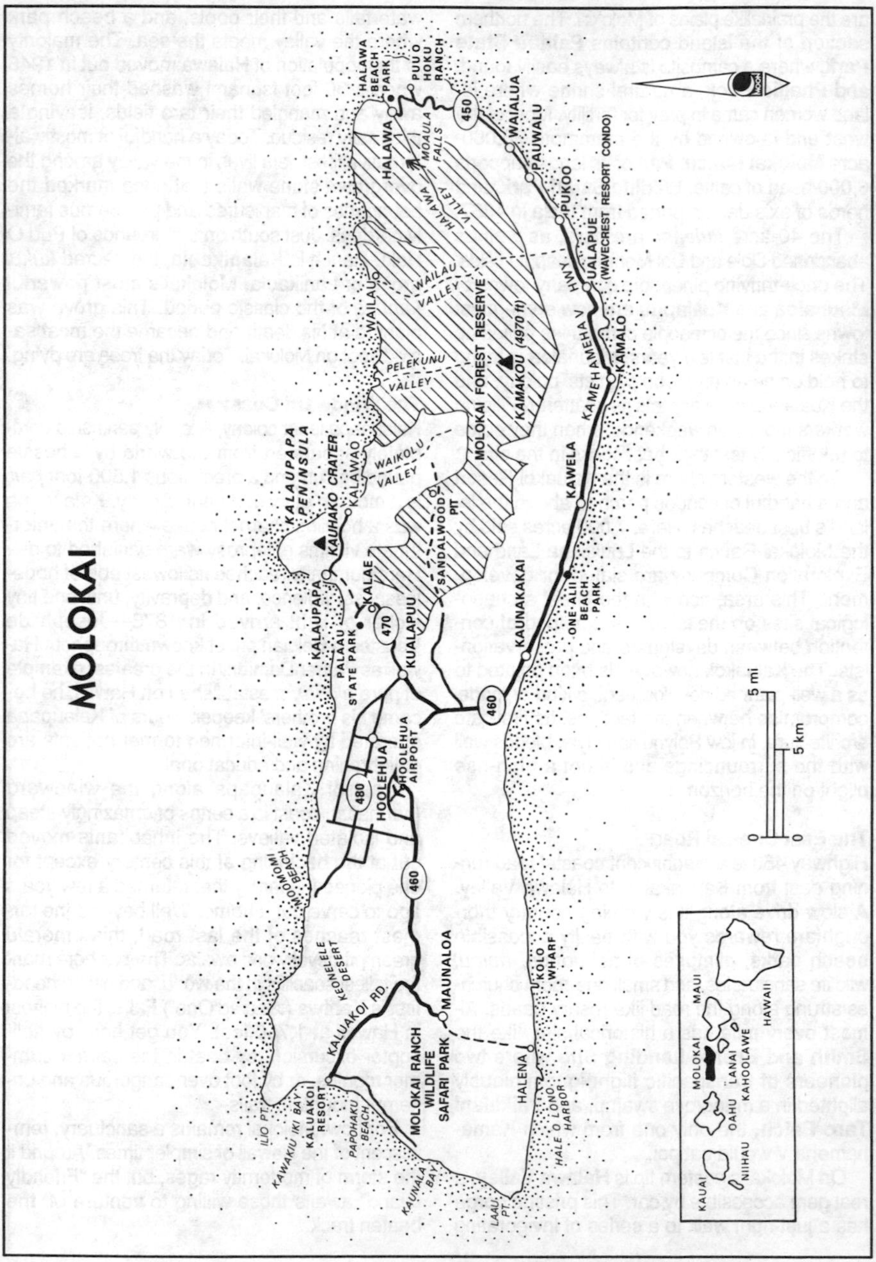

MOLOKAI

KALAUPAPA PENINSULA
KALAUPAPA
KAUHAKO CRATER
KALAWAO
KALAE
PALAAU STATE PARK
KUALAPUU
470
WAIKOLU VALLEY
SANDALWOOD PIT
PELEKUNU VALLEY
WAILAU VALLEY
WAILAU
HALAWA VALLEY
HALAWA
MOAULA FALLS
HALAWA BEACH PARK
PUU O HOKU RANCH
450
WAIALUA
PAUWAU
PUKOO
UALAPUE (WAVECREST RESORT CONDO)
KAMALO
KAMEHAMEHA V HWY.
MOLOKAI FOREST RESERVE
KAMAKOU (4970 ft)
KAWELA
ONE ALII BEACH PARK
KAUNAKAKAI
460
HOOLEHUA
HOOLEHUA AIRPORT
480
MOOMOMI BEACH
KEONELELE DESERT
MAUNALOA
KALUAKOI RD.
MOLOKAI RANCH WILDLIFE SAFARI PARK
KALUAKOI RESORT
PAPOHAKU BEACH
KAWAKIU IKI BAY
ILIO PT.
KAUNALA BAY
HALENA
KOLO WHARF
HALE O LONO HARBOR
LAAU PT.
5 mi
5 km
KAUAI
NIIHAU
OAHU
MOLOKAI
LANAI
MAUI
KAHOOLAWE
HAWAII

THE LAND

Molokai is the fifth largest Hawaiian island. Its western tip, at Ilio Point, is a mere 22 miles from Oahu's eastern tip, Makapuu Point. Resembling a jogging shoe, Molokai is about 38 miles from heel to toe and 10 miles from laces to sole, totaling 165,760 acres, with just over 88 miles of coastline. Most of the arable land on the island is owned by the 70,000-acre Molokai Ranch, primarily on the western end, and the 14,000-acre Puu O Hoku Ranch on the eastern end. Molokai was formed by three distinct shield volcanos. Two linked together to form Molokai proper, and a later eruption formed the flat Kalaupapa Peninsula.

Physical Features

Although Molokai is rather small, it has a great deal of geographical diversity. Western Molokai is dry with rolling hills, natural pastures, and a maximum elevation of only 1,381 feet. The eastern sector of the island has heavy rainfall, the tallest seacliffs in the world, and craggy narrow valleys perpetually covered in a velvet cloak of green mosses. Viewed from the sea it looks like a 2,000-foot vertical wall from surf to clouds, with tortuously deep chasms along the coastline. Mount Kamakou is the highest peak on Molokai, at 4,970 feet. The south-central area is relatively swampy, while the west and especially northwest coasts around Moomomi have rolling sand dunes. Papohaku Beach, just below the Kaluakoi Resort on western Molokai, is one of the most massive white-sand beaches in Hawaii. A controversy was raised when it was discovered that huge amounts of sand were dredged from this area and hauled to Oahu; the Molokai Ranch was pressured and the dredgings ceased. The newly formed and very political Office of Hawaiian Affairs (OHA) became involved, and a court case on behalf of native Hawaiian rights is pending. A hefty section of land in the north-central area is a state forest where new species of trees are planted on an experimental basis. The 240-acre Palaau State Park is in this cool upland forested area.

Manmade Marvels

Two manmade features on Molokai are engineering marvels. One is the series of ancient fishponds strung along the south shore like pearls on a string—best seen from the air as you approach the island by plane. Dozens still exist, but the most amazing is the enormous **Keawanui Pond,** covering 54 acres and surrounded by a three-foot tall, 2,000-foot long wall. The other is the modern **Kualapuu Reservoir** completed in 1969. The world's largest rubber-lined reservoir, it can hold 1.4 billion gallons of water. Part of its engineering dramatics is the Molokai Tunnel, which feeds the reservoir with water from the eastern valleys. The tunnel is eight feet tall, eight feet wide, and almost 27,000 feet (five miles) long.

Climate

The average island temperature is 75-85° F (24° C). The yearly average rainfall is 30 inches; the east receives a much greater percentage than the west.

FLORA AND FAUNA

The land animals on Molokai were brought by humans. The island is unique in that it offers **Molokai Ranch Wildlife Safari Park** on the grounds of Molokai Ranch in the western sector, with more than 400 animals mostly imported from the savannahs of Africa (see "Molokai's West End" later in this chapter). And who knows? Perhaps in a few thousand years after some specimens have escaped there might be such a thing as a "Molokai giraffe" that will look like any other giraffe except that its markings resemble flowers.

Birdlife

A few of Hawaii's endemic birds can be spotted by a determined observer at various locales around Molokai. They include: the **Hawaiian petrel** *('ua'u);* **Hawaiian coot** *(alae ke'oke'o),* prominent in Hawaiian mythology; **Hawaiian stilt** *(ae'o),* a wading bird with ridiculous stick legs that protects its young by feigning wing injury and luring predators away from the nest; and the Hawaiian owl *(pueo),* a bird that helps in its own demise by being easily approached. Molokai has a substantial number of introduced game birds that attracts hunters throughout the year (see "Game Animals" under "Hunting" below).

KAUNAKAKAI, MOLOKAI AVERAGE TEMPERATURE AND RAINFALL

	JAN.	MARCH	MAY	JUNE	SEPT.	NOV.
high	79	79	81	82	82	80
low	61	63	68	70	68	63
rain	4	3	0	0	0	2

Note: rainfall in inches; temperature in ˚F

Flora

The *kukui* or candlenut tree is common to all the Hawaiian Islands; not only is it the official state tree, its tiny white blossom is Molokai's flower. The *kukui,* introduced centuries ago by the early Polynesians, grows on lower mountain slopes and can easily be distinguished by its pale green leaves.

Conservation Controversy

It has long been established and regretted that introduced animals and plants have destroyed Hawaii's delicate natural balance, leading to the extinction of many of its rare native species. A number of well-meaning groups and organizations are doing their best to preserve Hawaii's habitat, but they don't always agree on the methods employed. Feral pigs, indiscriminate in their relentless hunt for food, are ecological nightmares that virtually bulldoze the rainforest floor into fetid pools and gouged earth where mosquitoes and other introduced species thrive while driving out the natives. Molokai's magnificent Kamakou Preserve, Upper Pelekunu, and Central Molokai Ridges are the last remaining pockets of natural habitat on the island. The Kamakou Preserve, 2,774 pristine acres, is covered, like the others, in ohia forest, prime habitat for the almost-extinct *oloma'o* (Molokai thrush), *kakawahie* (creeper), and hearty but beleaguered *apapane* and *amakihi.* No one disagrees that the wild boar must be managed to protect these areas, but they do not agree on *how* they should be managed. The Nature Conservancy, in their dedication to preserving the rainforest, backed a policy to snare the wild boar, maintaining that this was the best possible way of eliminating these pests while placing the forest under the least amount of stress. In opposition to the practice of snaring is Pono, a local organization of native Molokai hunters that maintains snaring pigs is inhumane, causing the animals to starve to death or to die slowly from strangulation. *Pono* also abhors the wasting of the meat, and the indiscriminate killing of sows, the future of pigs on Molokai.

Another grassroots group, *Na Ala Hele,* with branches on all islands, is dedicated to opening the ancient and extensive Hawaiian trail and access system. As part of their lobbying to open these trails, many of which now cross private property, they are trying to free landowners from any liability while the trails are used. So far progress has been very slow.

HISTORY

The oral chant *"Molokai nui a Hina . . ."* ("Great Molokai, child of Hina") refers to Molokai as the island-child of the goddess Hina and the god Wakea, male progenitor of all the islands; Papa, Wakea's first wife, left him in anger as a result of this unfaithfulness. Hina's cave, just east of Kaluaaha on the southeast coast, can still be visited and has been revered as a sacred spot for countless centuries. Another ancient spot, Halawa Valley, on the eastern tip of Molokai, is considered one of the oldest settlements in Hawaii. As research continues, settlement dates are pushed further back, but for now scholars agree that early wayfarers from the Marquesas Islands settled Halawa in the mid-seventh century.

Molokai, from earliest times, was revered and feared as a center for mysticism and sorcery. **Ili'ili'opae Heiau** was renowned for its powerful priests whose incantations were mingled with the screams of human sacrifice. Commoners avoided Ili'ili'opae, and even powerful *kahuna* could not escape its terrible power. One, Kamalo, lost his sons as sacrifices at the *heiau* for their desecration of the temple drum. Kamalo sought revenge by invoking the help of his personal god, the terrible shark deity, Kauhuhu. After the proper prayers and offerings, Kauhuhu sent a flash flood to wipe out Mapulehu Valley where Ili'ili'opae was located. All perished except for Kamalo and his family, who were protected by a sacred fence around their home.

This tradition of mysticism reached its apex with the famous Lanikaula, "Prophet of Molokai." During the 16th century, Lanikaula lived near Halawa Valley and practiced his arts, handed down by the goddess Pahulu, who even predated Pele. Pahulu was the goddess responsible for the "old ocean highway," which passed between Molokai and Lanai and led to Kahiki, lost homeland of all the islanders. Lanikaula practiced his sorcery in the utmost secrecy and even buried his excrement on an offshore island so that a rival *kahuna* could not find and burn it, which would surely cause his death. Hawaiian oral history does not say why Kawelo, a sorcerer from Lanai and a friend of Lanikaula, came to spy on Lanikaula and observed him hiding his excrement. Kawelo burned it in the sacred fires, and Lanikaula knew that his end was near. Lanikaula ordered his sons to bury him in a hidden grave so that his enemies could not find his bones and use their mana to control his spirit. To further hide his remains, he had a *kukui* grove planted over his body. **Kalanikaula** ("Sacred Grove of Lanikaula") is still visible today, though most of the trees appear to be dying.

Western Contacts

Captain James Cook first spotted Molokai on November 26, 1778, but because it looked bleak and uninhabited he decided to bypass it. It wasn't until eight years later that Capt. George Dixon sighted the island and decided to land. Very little was recorded in his ship's log about this first encounter, and Molokai slipped from the attention of the Western world until Protestant missionaries arrived at Kaluaaha in 1832 and recorded the native population as approximately 6,000.

In 1790 Kamehameha the Great came from the Big Island as a suitor seeking the hand of Keopuolani, a chieftess of Molokai. Within five years he returned again, but this time there was no merrymaking: he came as a conquering emperor on his thrust westward to Oahu. His war canoes landed at Pakuhiwa Battleground, a bay just a few miles east of Kaunakakai; it's said that warriors lined the shores for more than four miles. The grossly outnumbered warriors of Molokai fought desperately, but even the incantations of their *kahuna* were no match for Kamehameha and his warriors. Inflamed with recent victory and infused with the power of their horrible war god Ku ("of the Maggot-dripping Mouth"), they slaughtered the Molokai warriors and threw their broken bodies into a sea so filled with sharks that their feeding frenzy made the waters appear to boil. Thus subdued, Molokai slipped into obscurity once again as its people turned to quiet lives of farming and fishing.

Molokai Ranch

Molokai remained almost unchanged until the 1850s. The Great Mahele of 1848 provided for private ownership of land, and giant tracts were formed into the Molokai Ranch. About 1850, German immigrant Rudolph Meyer came to Molokai and married a high chieftess named Dorcas Kalama Waha. Together they had 11 children, with whose aid he turned the vast lands of the Molokai Ranch into productive pastureland. A man of indomitable spirit, Meyer held public office on Molokai and became the island's unofficial patriarch. He managed Molokai Ranch for the original owner, Kamehameha V, and remained manager until his death in 1898, by which time the ranch was owned by the Bishop Estate. In 1875, Charles Bishop had bought half of the 70,000 acres of Molokai Ranch; his wife Bernice, a Kamehameha descendant, inherited the remainder. In 1898, the Molokai Ranch was sold to businessmen in Honolulu for $251,000. This consortium formed the American Sugar Co., but after a few plantings the available water on Molokai turned brackish and once again Molokai Ranch was sold. Charles Cooke bought controlling interest from the other businessmen in 1908, and Molokai Ranch remains in the Cooke family to this day.

Changing Times

Very little happened for a decade after Charles Cooke bought the Molokai Ranch from his partners. Molokai did become famous for its honey production, supplying a huge amount to the world up until WW I. During the 1920s, political and economic forces greatly changed Molokai. In 1921, Congress passed the **Hawaiian Homes Act,** which set aside 43,000 acres on the island for people who had at least 50% Hawaiian blood. By this time, however, all agriculturally productive land in Hawaii had already been claimed. The land given to the Hawaiians was very poor and lacked adequate water. Many Hawaiians had long since left the land, and were raised in towns and cities. Now out of touch with the simple life of the taro patch, they found it very difficult to readjust. To prevent the Hawaiians from selling their claims and losing the land forever, the Hawaiian Homes Act provided that the land be leased to them for 99 years. Making a go of these 40-acre parcels *(kuleana)* was so difficult that successful homesteaders were called "Molokai Miracles."

In 1923 Libby Corporation leased land from Molokai Ranch at Kaluakoi and went into pineapple production; Del Monte followed suit in 1927 at Kualapuu. Both built company towns and imported Japanese and Filipino field laborers, swelling Molokai's population and stabilizing the economy. Many of the native Hawaiians subleased their tracts to the pineapple growers, and the Hawaiian Homes Act seemed to backfire. Instead of the homesteaders working their own farms, they were given monthly checks and lured into a life of complacency. Those who grew little more than family plots became, in effect, permanent tenants on their own property. Much more importantly, they lost the psychological advantage of controlling their own future and regaining their pride as envisioned in the Hawaiian Homes Act.

Modern Times

For the next 50 years life was quiet. The pineapples grew, providing security. Another large ranch, **Puu O Hoku** ("Hill of Stars") was formed on the eastern tip of the island. It was originally owned by Paul Fagan, the amazing San Francisco entrepreneur who also developed Hana on Maui. In 1955, Fagan sold Puu O Hoku to George Murphy, a Canadian industrialist, for a meager $300,000, about five percent of its present worth. The ranch, under Murphy, became famous for beautiful white Charolais cattle, a breed originating in France.

In the late 1960s "things" started quietly happening on Molokai. The Molokai Ranch sold about 7,000 acres to the Kaluakoi Corp., which they controlled along with the Louisiana Land and Exploration Company. In 1969 the long-awaited Molokai reservoir was completed at Kualapuu; finally west Molokai had plenty of water. Shortly after Molokai's water problem appeared to be finally under control, Dole Corp. bought out Libby in 1972, lost millions in the next few years, and shut down its pineapple production at Maunaloa in 1975. By 1977 the 7,000 acres sold to the Kaluakoi Corp. was developed, and the Molokai Sheraton (now the Kaluakoi Resort) opened along with low-rise condominiums and home sites selling for a minimum of $150,000. Lo and behold, sleepy old Molokai with the tiny Hawaiian Homes farms was now prime real estate and worth a fortune.

To complicate the picture even further, Del Monte shut down its operations in 1982, throwing more people out of work. In 1986 they did resume planting 250-acre tracts, but now all the pineapple is gone. Recently, a Brazilian company has been experimenting with and exploring the possibilities of marketing new varieties of coffee, and a New Zealand interest in the Molokai Company has brought sheep and cattle to Molokai. These new avenues of diversification are still in their infant stages but might possibly lead to greater economic stength and stability. Today Molokai is in a period of flux in other ways. There is great tension between developers, who are viewed as "carpetbaggers" interested only in a fast buck, and those who consider themselves the last survivors of a lost race holding on desperately to what little they have left.

ECONOMY

If it weren't for a pitifully bad economy, Molokai would have no economy at all. At one time the workers on the pineapple plantations had good steady incomes and the high hopes of the working class. Now with all the jobs gone, Molokai

J.D. BISIGNANI

Small private enterprises like gathering coconuts help bolster Molokai's flagging economy.

has been transformed from an island with virtually no unemployment to a hard-luck community where a whopping 80-90% of the people are on welfare. Inexplicably, Molokai also has the highest utility rates in Hawaii. Some say this is due to the fact that the utility company built a modern biomass plant, and didn't have enough biomass to keep it operating—the people were stuck with the fuel tab. The present situation is even more ludicrous when you consider that politically Molokai is part of Maui County. It is lumped together with Kaanapali on Maui's southern coast, one of Hawaii's most posh and wealthy areas, where the vast majority of people are recent arrivals from the Mainland. This amounts to almost no political-economic voice for grassroots Molokai.

Agriculture

The word now bandied about is "diversified" agriculture. What this means is not pinning all hope on one crop like the ill-fated pineapple, but planting a potpourri of crops. Attempts at diversification are evident as you travel around Molokai. Fields of corn, wheat, fruits, and nuts are just west of Kaunakakai; many small farmers are trying truck farming by raising a variety of garden vegetables they hope to sell to the massive hotel food industry in Honolulu. The problem is not in production, but transportation. Molokai raises excellent crops, but little established transport exists for the perishable vegetables. A barge service, running on a loose twice-weekly schedule, is their only link to the market. No storage facilities on Molokai makes it tough to compete in the hotel food business, which requires the freshest produce. Unfortunately, vegetables don't wait well for late barges.

Development

A debate rages between those in favor of tourist development, which they say will save Molokai, and grassroots organizations championed by OHA (Office of Hawaiian Affairs), which insist unchecked tourism development will despoil Molokai and give no real benefit to the people. A main character in the debate is the Kaluakoi Corp., which wants to build condos and sell lots for $500,000 each. They claim that this, coupled with a few more resorts, will bring in jobs. The people know that they will be relegated to service jobs (maids and waiters), while all the management jobs go to outsiders. Most islanders feel that only rich people from the Mainland can afford million-dollar condos, and that eventually they will become disenfranchised on their own island. Claims are that outsiders have no feeling for the *aina* (land), and will destroy important cultural sites whenever growth dictates.

A few years back the Kaluakoi Corp. hired an "independent" research team to investigate Kawakiu Iki Bay, known to be an ancient adze quarry. After weeks of study, this Maui-based research team reported that Kawakiu was of "minor importance." Hawaii's academic sector went wild. The Society of Hawaiian Archaeology dispatched its own team under Dr. Patrick Kirch, who stated that Kawakiu was one of the richest archaeological areas in Hawaii. In one day they discoverd six sites missed by the "independent" research team, and stated that a rank amateur could find artifacts by merely scraping away some of the surface. Reasonable voices call for moderation. Both sides agree Molokai must grow, but the growth must be controlled, and the people of Molokai must be represented and included as beneficiaries.

THE PEOPLE

Molokai is obviously experiencing a class struggle. The social problems hinge on the economy—the collapse of pineapple cultivation and the move toward tourism. The average income on Molokai is quite low and the people are not consumer-oriented. Tourism, especially "getaway condos," brings in the affluent. This creates friction; the "have-nots" don't know their situation until the "haves" come in and remind them. Today, most people hunt a little, fish, and have small gardens. Some are small-time *pakalolo* growers who get over the hard spots by making a few dollars from backyard plants. There is no organized crime on Molokai. The worst you might run into is a group of local kids drinking on a weekend in one of their favorite spots. It's a territorial thing. If you come into their vicinity they might feel their turf is being invaded, and you could be in for some hassles. All this could add up to a bitter situation except that the true nature of most of the people is to be helpful and friendly. Be sensitive to smiles and frowns, and give people their space.

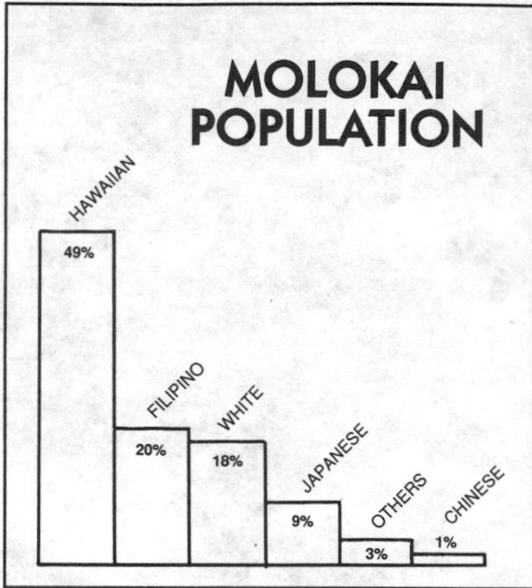

Ho'opono'opono is a fascinating family problem-solving technique still very much employed on Molokai. The process is like "peeling the onion," wherein a mediator, usually a respected *kupuna,* tries to get to the heart of a problem. Similar to group therapy, it's a closed family ordeal, never open to outsiders, and lasts until all emotions are out in the open and all concerned feel "clean."

Ethnic Identity

An underground link exists between Molokai and other Hawaiian communities such as Waianae on Oahu. Molokai is unusual in that it is still Hawaiian in population and influence, with continuing culturally based outlooks that remain unacceptable to Western views. Ethnic Hawaiians are again proud of their culture and heritage, as well as politically aware and sophisticated, and have now entered the political arena.

Social problems on Molokai relate directly to teenage boredom and hostility in the schools, fueled by a heavy drinking scene. A disproportionate rate of teen pregnancy is a direct byproduct. Teachers unofficially admit that they prefer a student who has smoked *pakalolo* to one who's been drinking. It mellows them out. The traditional educational approach is failing.

GETTING THERE

Hawaiian Air, tel. (800) 882-8811, or 567-6510 on Molokai, has regularly scheduled flights throughout the day arriving from all the major islands. Depending on the flight, the planes are either DC-9s or four-engine turbo-prop Dashes. There are 10 daily 30-minute flights from Honolulu starting at 6:40 a.m. and going until 5:30 p.m. Six of those flights originate in Kauai. The one morning flight from Kahului originates in Hilo on the Big Island.

Aloha Island Air, tel. 833-3219 Oahu, (800) 652-6541 Neighbor Islands, (800) 323-3345 Mainland, offers flights connecting Molokai with Oahu, Kauai, Maui, Lanai, and the Big Island. There are a dozen daily flights from Honolulu 6:05 a.m.-5:45 p.m. with five of these originating in Princeville, Kauai. The five daily flights from Hana and Kamuela go through Kahului, from where there are an additional three daily flights. There are also two direct flights from Kapalua West Maui to Molokai, and two daily from Lanai with an extra on Monday morning and Friday evening.

Air Molokai, tel. 553-3636 on Molokai, 877-0026 on Maui, and 556-7217 on Lanai, offers flights connecting Molokai, Kahului, Lanai, and Honolulu. There are twice-daily flights between Molokai and Kahului, and four throughout the day between Molokai and Honolulu. For either trip the fare is $83 roundtrip for adults and $53.25 for children. Because the connection to Lanai has been opened recently, the frequency of flights between Molokai and the Pineapple Island is still being settled. Rates are $78 roundtrip for adults and $54.60 for children.

Molokai Airport

At the Hoolehua Airport you'll find a lounge and lunch counter with not too bad prices, but avoid the hamburgers, which are made from mystery meat. Pick up a loaf of excellent Molokai bread, the best souvenir available, or a lei from the small stand. Tropical, Avis, Dollar, and Budget have rental cars here. If you rent a car make sure to top off in Kaunakakai before returning it. The price is much higher at the car companies' pumps. There is also a state tourist information booth at the terminal where you can pick up brochures, maps, and helpful hints about what to see and do.

By Sea

The only scheduled ferry service to Molokai connects the island to Maui. The ***Maui Princess*** sails daily from Kaunakakai Wharf at 5:45 a.m. and 3:45 p.m. Roundtrip fares are $42 for adults and $21 for children.

GETTING AROUND

Public Transportation

No public bus transportation services Molokai. The following are taxi and limousine services that also provide limited tours: **Kukui Tours and Limousines,** tel. 553-5133, a 24-hour taxi service, reservations 8 a.m.-5 p.m.; **Molokai Limousine Taxi,** tel. 553-3979, offering 24-hour taxi service and stretch limousines at hourly rates; **Molokai Off-road Tours and Taxi,** tel. 553-3369, offering narrated tours by van or 4WD, open Mon.-Sat., reservations required.

Rental Cars

Molokai offers a limited choice of car rental agencies—make reservations to avoid being disappointed. You should arrive before 6 p.m., when most companies close. Special arrangements can be made to pick up your car at a later time. All rental car companies on Molokai dislike their cars being used on dirt roads (there are plenty), and strongly warn against it. No jeeps are available on Molokai at this time, but it's always in the air that one of the car companies will make them available in the future. All companies are located at the airport.

Dollar Rent A Car, tel. 567-6156, provides professional and friendly service, also offering some of the best rates on the island; **Budget,** tel. 567-6877, is the only other option.

Hitchhiking

The old thumb gives fair to good results on Molokai. Most islanders say they prefer to pick up hitchers who are making an effort by walking along, instead of lounging by the side of the road. It shows that you don't have a car, but do have some pride. Getting a ride to or from Kaunakakai and the airport is usually easy.

GUIDED TOURS

Only a few limited tours are offered on Molokai. Mostly, it's you and your rental car. **Friendly Isle Tours,** tel. 553-9046, or 553-1233 (no charge to calling party), the only booking agency on Molokai, runs a Grand Isle Tour for $40 (others available) that will take you from the Kaluakoi Resort to Maunaloa, stop at a macadamia nut farm, and then go on to the Kalaupapa Lookout, Halawa Valley, a string of fishponds, and finally Kaunakakai.

One of the most fun-filled cultural experiences you can have is an afternoon on the **Molokai Wagon Ride,** tel. 558-8380 or 567-6773. Rates are $30 for the ride, or $37 with lunch at the Hotel Molokai. The experience starts and ends from a hidden beach just past mile marker 15 on the east end of the island along Rt. 450. As you drive, look to the right for a sign to Mapulehu

Mango Grove; you'll follow the road to a small white house and a picnic area prepared on the beach. The wonderful aspect of this venture is that it is a totally local operation devoid of glitz, glamour, and hype. It's run by three local guys: Junior Rawlins the wagonmaster, Kalele Logan, and Larry Helm, master of ceremonies, musician, and all-around merrymaker.

After loading, the wagon leaves the beach and rolls through the **Mapulehu Mango Grove,** one of the largest in the world, with over 2,000 trees. Planted by the Hawaiian Sugar Co. in the 1930s in an attempt to diversify, trees came from all over the world, including Brazil, India, and Formosa. Unfortunately, most of the U.S. was not educated about eating exotic fruits, so the mangos rotted on the tree unpicked, and the grove became overgrown. The ride proceeds down a tree-shrouded lane with Larry Helm playing guitar, singing, and telling anecdotes along the way. In about 20 minutes you arrive at **Ili'ili'opae Heiau,** among the largest Hawaiian places of worship in the islands. Again Larry takes over, telling you the history of the *heiau,* pointing out exotic fruits and plants in the area, and leading you atop the *heiau* for a photo session. You then return to the beach for a demonstration of coconut husking, throw-netting—one of the oldest and most fascinating ways of catching fish—and maybe even a hula lesson. You can also count on the Hawaiian tradition of hospitality. These guys know how to treat you well, but remember that this is a *real* experience, so don't expect anything fancy or pretentious.

For tours to **Kalaupapa** see "Middle Molokai and Kalaupapa" later in this chapter.

Helicopter And Airplane Flights

An amazing way to see Molokai is by helicopter. This method is admittedly expensive, but dollar for dollar it is *the* most exciting way of touring and can get you places no other means can. A handful of companies operate mostly from Maui and include overflights of Molokai. One of the best is **Papillon Helicopters** on Maui, tel. 669-4884. Their 60-minute "West Maui/Molokai" flight costs $185, and the 75-minute "Molokai Odyssey," which includes a stop on Kalaupapa, costs $270. Though they'll put a big hole in your budget, most agree they are among the most memorable experiences of a trip.

Air Molokai, tel. 553-3638, the island's own airline, is intimately familiar with Molokai and offers scenic air tours including trips down to Kalaupapa, $40 roundtrip; similar service is offered by **Aloha Island Air,** tel (800) 652-6541.

Scenic Air Tours, tel. 836-0044, has various flights from Maui and Oahu that fly by Molokai, most in combination with other islands and one that takes you to Kalaupapa. These day-long flights are in the $110 range.

SHOPPING

Coming to Molokai in order to shop is like going to Waikiki to find a grass shack on a deserted beach. Molokai has only a handful of shops where you can buy locally produced crafts and Hawaiiana. Far and away, most of Molokai's shopping is centered along Ala Malama Street in downtown Kaunakakai. All three blocks of it! Here you'll find the island's only health food store, three very good food markets, a drugstore that sells just about everything, and a clutch of souvenir shops. Away from Kaunakakai the pickin's get mighty slim. Heading west you'll find the **Kualapuu** General Store off Rt. 470 on the way to Kalaupapa, and a sundries store along with a **Liberty House** at the Kaluakoi Resort on the far west end. The Maunaloa Road (Rt. 460) basically ends in Maunaloa town. Go there! The best and most interesting shop, **The Big Wind Kite Factory,** is in town and is worth a visit in its own right. Also in Maunaloa you'll find a market and a small homey restaurant. East from Kaunakakai is another shoppers' wasteland with a few, almost dry, oases. The **Hotel Molokai** has one souvenir shop, then comes a convenience store at the **Wavecrest Condominium.** The **Mapulehu Glass House,** near mile marker 15, offers gift boxes of Molokai's flowers and a free guided tour.

BEACHES, OUTDOORS, AND SPORTS

Since Molokai is a great place to get away from it all, you would expect an outdoor extravaganza. In fact, Molokai is a "good news, bad news" island when it comes to sports, especially in the water. Molokai has few excellent beaches with the two best, Halawa and Papohaku, on opposite ends of the island; **Papohaku Beach** on the west end is treacherous during the winter months. Surfers, windsurfers, and Hobie Cat enthusiasts will be disappointed with Molokai except at a few locales at the right time of year, while bathers, sun worshippers, and families will love the small secluded beaches with gentle waves located around the island.

Molokai has a small population and plenty of undeveloped "outback" land. This *should* add up to great trekking and camping, but most of the land is privately owned and the tough trails are poorly maintained. However, permission is usually granted to trek across private land, and those bold enough to venture into the outback will virtually have it to themselves. Day-hiking trails and lightly used camping areas with good facilities are no problem. Molokai has tame, family-oriented beach parks along its southern shores, superb hunting and fishing, two excellent golf courses, and fine tennis courts. Couple this with clean air, no industrial pollution, no city noise, and a deliciously casual atmosphere, and you wind up with the epitome of relaxation.

Eastern Beaches

The beaches of Molokai have their own temperament, ranging from moody and rebellious to sweet and docile. Heading east from Kaunakakai along Rt. 450 takes you past a string of beaches that varies from poor to excellent. Much of this underbelly of Molokai is fringed by a protective coral reef that keeps the water flat, shallow, and at some spots murky. This area was ideal for fishponds but leaves a lot to be desired as far as beaches are concerned. The farther east you go, the better the beaches become. The first one you come to is at **One Ali'i Park,** about four miles east of Kaunakakai. Here you'll find a picnic area, campsites, good fishing, and family-class swimming where the kids can frolic with no danger from the sea. Next you pass **Kakahaia Beach Park** and **Kumimi Beach,** one of a series of lovely sandy crescents where the swimming is fine. Just before you reach Pukoo, a small dirt road on your right goes to a hidden beach perfect for a secluded swim.

Halawa Bay, on Molokai's far east end, is the best all-around beach on the island. It's swimmable year-round, but be extra careful during the winter months. The bay protects the beach for a good distance; beyond its reach the breakers are excellent for surfing. The snorkeling and fishing are good to very good.

West End Beaches

The people of Molokai favor the beaches on the northwest section of the island. **Moomomi Beach** is one of the best and features good swimming, fair surfing, and pleasurable snorkeling along its sandy, rocky bottom. You have to drive over a very rutted dirt road to get here. Although car rental agencies are against it, you can make it, but only in dry weather. From Moomomi you can walk west along the beach and find your own secluded spot.

Very few visitors go south from Maunaloa town, but it is possible and rewarding for those seeking a totally secluded area. As you enter Maunaloa town a dirt track goes off to your right. Follow it through the Molokai Ranch gate (make sure to close it behind you). Follow the rugged but passable track down to the coast, the ghost town of Halena, and **Hale O Lono Harbor,** start of the Aloha Week Outrigger Canoe Race. A tough jeep track also proceeds east to collapsing **Kolo Wharf** and very secluded areas. The swimming is only fair because of murky water but the fantasy-feeling of a deserted island is pervasive.

Papohaku and **Kepuhi** beaches below the Kaluakoi Resort are excellent, renowned for their vast expanses of sand. Unfortunately, they're treacherous in the winter with giant swells and heavy rips, which make them a favorite for surfers. Anyone not accustomed to strong sea conditions should limit themselves to sunning and wading only to the ankles. During the rest of the year this area is great for swimming, becoming like a lake in the summer months. North of Kepuhi Bay is an ideal beach named **Kawakiu.** Although it's less than a mile up the coast, it's more than 15 miles away by road. You have to branch off Rt. 460 and follow the seven-mile dirt track north well before it forks toward the Kaluakoi. This area is well established as an archaeological site, and access to the beach was a hard-fought controversy between the people of Molokai and the Molokai Ranch. Good swimming, depending upon tide conditions, and free camping on weekends.

GOLF COURSES OF MOLOKAI

COURSE	PAR	YARDS	FEES	CART
Ironwood Hills Golf *	34	6148	$12 (9 hole)	$8
Course Del Monte,			$15 (18 hole)	$11
Molokai, HI 96757				
tel. 567-6000				
club rental $6				
2-people special $40 incl. cart				
Twilight special $18 for 2 people incl. cart, after 7 p.m.				
Kaluakoi Golf Course	72	6618	$55 guest	cart incl.
P.O. Box 26, Maunaloa, HI 96770			$75 nonguest	cart incl.
tel. 552-2739				

*9-hole course

Snorkeling And Scuba

Some charter fishing boats arrange scuba and snorkeling excursions, but scuba and snorkeling on Molokai is just offshore and you don't need a boat to get to it. Beginners will feel safe at **One Ali'i Park,** where the sea conditions are mild, though the snorkeling is mediocre. The best underwater area is the string of beaches heading east past mile marker 18 on Rt. 450, and especially at mile marker 20. You'll wind up at Halawa Bay, which is tops. Moomomi Beach on the northwest shore is very good, and Kawakiu Beach out on the west end is good around the rocks, but stay away during winter.

Molokai Fish and Dive in Kaunakakai, tel. 553-5926, is a full-service snorkel shop. They have very good rental rates, can give you directions to the best spots, and arrange excursions.

Bill Kapuni's Snorkel and Dive, tel. 553-9867, is an excellent way to enjoy Molokai's underwater spectacle with Bill Kapuni, a native Hawaiian, who is intimately familiar with both the marinelife that you will encounter and the Hawaiian myths and legends of his heritage. Bill's trips, 7:30 a.m., 10:30 a.m., and 1 p.m., including complimentary snacks, are $45 for snorkeling, and $85 for a one-tank dive. Bill offers professional PADI instruction, and has a compressor to fill tanks for certified divers. If you are contemplating a tour with Bill, make arrangements through Fantasy Island Activities, tel. 661-4919.

Ma'a Hawaii, Molokai Action Adventures

Walter Naki knows Molokai—its mountains, seas, shores, trails, flowers, trees, and birds. His one-man company, **Ma'a Hawaii,** P.O. Box 1269, Kaunakakai, HI 96748, tel. 558-8184, loosely translates as "used to, accustomed to, familiar with Hawaii." As a native Hawaiian raised on the island and versed in its myths and mysteries, his spirit is strengthened and revitalized by the *aina* to which he is so closely attached. Walter has won the Hawaiian decathlon five times—a ten-event competition that includes sprinting, spear throwing, heaving a 28-pound stone, and swimming. He has also proven one of Hawaii's most renowned athletes in statewide spearfishing and free diving contests, training himself to stay underwater for over two minutes while descending to depths of 85 feet. Walter's modest but lovingly tended home, which he shares with his two children, is lined with his trophies. Outside, a pet deer, Pua ("Flower"), that he has raised since she was a tiny fawn, comes when he calls, loves sweets, and follows his truck like a puppy whenever he leaves. If it has to do with the outdoors Walter does it. Hunting for axis deer, wild boar, or goats costs $150 per day for bow hunters, and $250 per day for rifle hunts (10 hunters per day only). Hiking and "camera safaris" over many of the same hunting trails cost $50 for a half day (up to six people only), while snorkeling, skin diving, spearfishing, and reef fishing are $50 per half day; kayak trips are available on request. Walter is extremely ecologically minded, employing practical knowledge that he has learned from years of living *with* the land and sea. The wild game that he hunts is used for food, and by taking pig, goats, and deer, he helps manage the forest, balancing the destruction caused by these introduced animals so that native species can survive.

Walter is a great guide, but he is definitely "fo' real," absolutely genuine with no glitz or glamour. He transports his gear, much of which is homemade and which he pulls from a shed in his backyard, in a used but not abused old truck, and he takes you to sea in a very seaworthy but basic Boston Whaler. Walter will do everything that he can to make your day safe and enjoyable, even stopping at his friend's taro patch to give you a glimpse of preserved island life. Remember, however, that it is up to you to be completely honest about your physical abilities, especially underwater, because with Walter's great skills and enthusiasm, it is easy for him to push you to your limit while he is just taking a stroll in the park. If you seek a unique experience in which you can touch the spirit of Molokai, travel for a day with Walter Naki. It will make all the difference.

Surfing

The best surfing is out on the east end past mile marker 20. Pohakuloa Point has excellent breaks, which continue eastward to Halawa Bay. Moomomi Beach has decent breaks; Kawakiu's huge waves are suitable only for experts during the winter months.

Horseback Riding

The Molokai Ranch, tel. 552-2767, offers a variety of horseback rides over their ranch lands.

GOLF AND TENNIS

Molokai's two golf courses are as different as custom-made and rental clubs. The **Kaluakoi Golf Course,** tel. 552-2739, is a picture-perfect beauty that would challenge any top pro. Laid out by master links designer Ted Robinson, it's located out at the Kaluakoi Resort. The 6,618-yard, par-72 course winds through an absolutely beautiful setting including five holes strung right along the beach. There's a complete pro shop, driving range, and practice greens. Golf lessons by the hour are also available. Greens fees for 18 holes are $30 for resort guests and $50 for nonguests. The PGA head pro is Marty Keiter, the director Ben Neeley.

Molokai's other golf course is the homey **Ironwood Hills Golf Club,** tel. 567-6000. This rarely used but well-maintained mountain course is nine holes, par-34, and 6,148 yards long. Pay the affordable greens fee, $12 for nine holes and $15 if you want to loop the course twice, to a groundskeeper who will come around as you play (two-people special and twilight special offered). The course is located up in the hills in Kalae, just before the Meyer Sugar Mill—look for the sign. The Ironwood Hills Golf Course is turning from a frog to a prince. Recent work has concentrated on improving the grounds. Even today there is no building, pro shop, or snack shop—these will come in time.

Tennis

The best courts are at the **Kaluakoi Resort:** four lighted Lakloyd courts, free for resort guests and $3 per hour for nonguests. They offer a free tennis clinic Friday at 4 p.m.; call 552-2555, ext. 548, to reserve. Two courts are available at

TENNIS COURTS OF MOLOKAI

These tennis courts are open to the public; call ahead to check availability.

LOCATION	NAME OF COURT	NO. OF COURTS	LIGHTED
Kepuhi Beach	Kaluakoi Resort	4	Yes
Kaunakakai	Community Center	2	Yes
Molokai High	Hoolehua	2	Yes
Star Route	Wavecrest	2	No

the **Ke Nani Kai Condos,** near the Kaluakoi, which are free to guests. Two courts at the **Wavecrest Condo** east of Kaunakakai on Rt. 450 are also free to guests. Public courts are available at Molokai High School and at the Community Center in Kaunakakai, but you may have to reserve a spot with the office in the Mitchell Pauole Center next door.

FISHING

The Penguin Banks of Molokai are some of the most fertile waters in Hawaii. Private boats as well as the commercial fishing fleets out of Oahu come here to try their luck. Trolling produces excellent game fish such as marlin; mahimahi; *ahi,* a favorite with sashimi lovers; and *ono,* reputedly the best-tasting fish in Hawaii. Bottom fishing, usually with live bait, yields *onaga* and *uku,* a gray snapper favored by local people. Molokai's shoreline, especially along the south and west, offers great bait-casting for *ulua* and *ama ama. Ulua* is an excellent eating fish, and with a variance in weight from 15 to 110 pounds, can be a real whopper to catch from shore. Squidding, *limu* gathering, and torch-fishing are all quite popular and productive along the south shore, especially around the old fishpond sites. These remnants of Hawaii's one-time vibrant aquaculture still produce the *ali'i's* favorite mullet, an occasional Samoan crab, the less desirable introduced tilapia, and the better-left-alone barracuda.

Fishing Boats

The ***Shon-a-lei,*** Shon-a-lei Sports and Marine, P.O. Box 1018, Kaunakakai, HI 96748, tel. 553-5242 or (800) 998-3474, is operated by Steve Schonley, who's so very well-acquainted with the local waters that he states, "If the fish are biting, I'll find them." Steve operates an air-conditioned, 35-foot Bertrum twin-diesel, which he uses to fish for tuna, marlin, mahimahi, or *ono,* or even for bottom fishing. All tackle is provided for half-day, full-day, or overnight fishing trips. Whalewatches, custom charters, and diving and snorkeling can be arranged as well. You can't go wrong fishing with Steve, and if you're after a trophy fish, this is your best bet.

The ***Alyce C.,*** tel. 558-8377, is a 31-foot, fully equipped diesel-powered fishing boat, owned and operated by Capt. Joe Reich. He can take you for full- or half-day charters, and offers whalewatching tours in season.

The **Molokai Fish and Dive Co.,** tel. 553-5926, also arranges deep-sea charters as well as excursions and shoreline sailing.

Sailing

Molokai is nearly devoid of charter sailboats. However, for those who like to feel the salty sea breeze in their hair, hear the snap of a full-furled sail, or enjoy the sunset from the deck of a sailing ship, try an excursion with **Molokai Charters,** tel. 553-5852, on their 42-foot sloop. A two-hour sunset sail is $30, a half-day of sailing is $40, and a full-day trip to Lanai runs $75. Four-person minimum.

HUNTING

The best hunting on Molokai is on the private lands of the 44,000-acre **Molokai Ranch,** tel. 552-2767, open to hunting year-round. However, the enormous fees charged by the ranch have effectively stopped hunting on their lands for all but the very determined or very wealthy. A permit to hunt game animals, including black buck and aoudad, a type of antelope, costs $450 per day for a guided hunt with an additional fee of $200 per person (up to three). Limited black buck hunting in the ranch's Trophy Park is also permitted, but it's restricted to certain times and locations. Fees are the same, except that the trophy fee here is $1,500! Bird hunting is also offered Nov.-Jan., weekends only, at $50 per day.

Public hunting lands on Molokai are open to anyone with a valid state hunting license (see "Hunting" under "Sports and Recreation" in the Out and About chapter). Wild goats and pigs can be hunted in various hunting units year-round on weekends and state holidays. Bag limits are two animals per day (moratorium in effect on hunting axis deer). Hunting game birds (ring-necked pheasants, various quails, wild turkeys, partridges, and francolins) is open on public lands from the first Saturday in November to the third Sunday in January. A special dove season opens in January. For full information, license, and fees (as well as State Park and Forest Service camping permits), contact the Division of Forestry and Wildlife, Puu Kapeelua Ave. near the intersection of Farrington Rd. (Rt. 480), Hoolehua, HI 96729, tel. 567-5019.

Also see "Ma'a Hawaii, Molokai Action Adventures" above.

Game Animals

The earliest arrival still extant in the wild is the *pua'a* (pig). Molokai's pigs live in the upper wetland forests of the northeast, but they can actually thrive anywhere. Hunters say the meat from pigs that have lived in the lower dry forest is superior to meat from pigs that acquire the muddy taste of ferns from the wetter upland areas. Pigs on Molokai are hunted mostly with the use of dogs, who pin them by the ears and snout while the hunter approaches on foot and skewers them with a long knife.

A pair of **goats** left by Captain Cook on the island of Niihau spread to all the islands, and were very well adapted to life on Molokai. Originally from the arid Mediterranean, goats could live well without any surface water, a condition quite prevalent over most of Molokai. They're found primarily in the mountainous area of the northeast.

The last free-roaming arrivals to Molokai were **axis deer** (hunting moratorium). Molokai's deer came from the upper reaches of the Ganges River, sent to Kamehameha V by Dr. William Hillebrand while on a botanical trip to India in 1867. Kamehameha V sent some of the first specimens to Molokai, where they prospered. Today they are found mostly on western Molokai, though some travel the south coast to the east.

Note: Also see "Flora and Fauna" earlier in this chapter.

CAMPING AND HIKING

The best camping on Molokai is at **Pala'au State Park** at the end of Rt. 470, in the cool mountains overlooking Kalaupapa Peninsula. It's also the site of Molokai's famous Phallic Rock. Here you'll find pavilions, grills, picnic tables, and fresh water. What you won't find are crowds; in fact, most likely you'll have the entire area to yourself. The camping here is free, but you need a permit, good for seven days, from the Department of Land and Natural Resources in Hoolehua, tel. 567-6618. Camping is permitted free of charge at **Waikolu Lookout** in the Molokai Forest Reserve, but you'll have to follow a tough dirt road (Main Forest Road) for 10 miles to get to it. A free permit must be obtained from the Division of Forestry in Hoolehua, tel. 553-5019.

Seaside camping is allowed at **One Ali'i Park** just east of Kaunakakai, and at **Papohaku Beach Park** west of Kaunakakai. These parks have full facilities but due to their beach location and easy access just off the highway they are often crowded, noisy, and bustling. Also, you are a target here for any rip-off artists. A county permit ($3 per day) is required and available from County Parks and Recreation in Kaunakakai, tel. 553-3204.

The Hawaiian Homelands Department in Hoolehua, tel. 567-6104, offers camping at **Kioea Park,** one mile west of Kaunakakai. The permit to this historical coconut grove is $5 per day. One of the most amazing royal coconut groves in Hawaii, it's a treat to visit, but camping here, though quiet, can be hazardous. Make sure to pitch your tent away from any coconut-laden trees if possible, and vacate if the winds come up.

Private camping on the **Molokai Ranch,** tel. 552-2767, is allowed at Halena, Moomomi Beach, Hale O Lono, and Puulakima. Rates are: $5 key charge, $10 per day camping fee, $30 per day for use of the pavilion at Halena, plus a refundable $50 deposit. Contact the Molokai Ranch office.

You can also camp free at **Moomomi Beach** on the island's northwest shore on a grassy plot where the pavilion used to be. You can't officially camp at Halawa Bay Beach Park, but if you continue along the north side of the bay you'll come to a well-used but unofficial campground fringed by ironwoods and recognizable by old firepits. This area does attract down-and-outers so don't leave your gear unattended.

Trekking

Molokai should be a hiker's paradise and there are exciting, well-maintained, easily accessible trails, but others cross private land, skirt guarded *pakalolo* patches, are poorly maintained, and are tough to follow. This section provides a general overview of the trekking possibilities available on Molokai. Full info is given in the respective "Sights" sections.

One of the most exciting hassle-free trails descends the *pali* to the **Kalaupapa Peninsula.** You follow the well-maintained mule trail down, and except for some "road apples" left by the mules, it's a totally enjoyable experience suitable for an in-shape family. You *must* have a reservation with the guide company to tour the former leper colony (see "Getting There" under "The Kalaupapa Experience" in the "Middle Molokai and Kalaupapa" section).

Another excellent trail, at Halawa Valley, follows **Halawa Stream** to cascading Moaula Falls, where you can take a refreshing dip if the famous *mo'o,* a mythical lizard said to live in the pool, is in the right mood. This trail is strenuous enough to be worthwhile and thrilling enough to be memorable.

Molokai Forest Reserve, which you can reach by driving about 10 miles over the rugged Main Forest Road (passable by 4WD only in the dry season), has fine hiking. At road's end you'll find the Sandalwood Measuring Pit. The hale and hearty who push on will find themselves overlooking Waikolu and Pelekunu, two fabulous and enchanted valleys of the north coast.

The most formidable trail on Molokai is the one that completely crosses the island from south to north and leads into **Wailau Valley.** It starts innocently enough at Ili'ili'opae Heiau about 15 miles east of Kaunakakai, but as you gain elevation it gets increasingly tougher to follow. After you've trekked all day, the trail comes to an abrupt halt over Wailau. From here you have to pick your way down an unmarked, slippery, and treacherous 3,000-foot *pali.* Don't attempt this trail alone. It's best to go with the Sierra Club, which organizes a yearly hike, or with a local person who knows the terrain. Wailau Valley is one of the last untouched valleys of bygone days. Here are bananas, papayas, and guavas left over from the last major inhabitants who left early in this century. The local people who summer here, and the one family who lives here year-round, are generous and friendly, but also very aware and rightfully protective of the last of old Hawaii in which they live. If you hike into Wailau Valley remember that in effect you are a guest. Be courteous and respectful and you'll come away with a unique and meaningful island experience.

MOLOKAI: INFORMATION PLEASE

Destination Molokai, tel. 553-3876 or (800) 800-6367, is an excellent organization that can help with every aspect of your trip to Molokai. Barbara Schonely and her friendly staff dispense up-to-the-minute information on hotels, car rentals, activities, and services. Destination Molokai should be your first contact if you are contemplating a visit to Molokai.

Telephone numbers for service agencies you might find useful: emergency, 911; ambulance, 553-5911; police, 553-5355; hospital, 553-5331; County Parks and Recreation, 553-5141; Department of Land and Natural Resources, 567-6618; Division of Forestry, 553-5019; Fire Department, 553-5401; Hawaiian Homelands, 567-6104; library, 553-5483; Office of Hawaiian Affairs (OHA), 553-3611; pharmacy, 553-5790; post office, 553-5845. The area code for all Molokai phone numbers is 808.

KAUNAKAKAI

No matter where you're headed on the island you have to pass through Kaunakakai ("Beach Landing"), the tiny port town that is Molokai's hub. An hour spent walking the three blocks of Ala Malama Street, the main drag, gives you a good feeling for what's happening. As you walk along you might hear a mechanical whir and bump in the background—Molokai's generating plant almost in the middle of town. If you need to do any banking, mailing, or shopping for staples, Kaunakakai's the place. Hikers, campers, and even day-trippers should get all they need here since shops, both east and west, are few and far between, and understocked. Evenings are quiet with no bars or nightspots in town.

SIGHTS

Head toward the lagoon and you'll see Kaunakakai's wharf stretching out into the shallow harbor for over a half mile. Townsfolk like to drive their cars onto it, but it's much better to walk out. The fishing from the wharf isn't great but it's handy and you never can tell. If you decide to stroll out here, look for the remains of Lot Kamehameha's summer house near the canoe shed on the shore.

Kapuaiwa Coconut Grove

A three-minute drive or a 10-minute walk west brings you to this royal coconut grove planted in the 1860s for Kamehameha V (Lot Kamehameha), or Kapuaiwa to his friends. Kapuaiwa Coconut Grove was originally built because there were seven pools here in which the *ali'i* would bathe, and the grove was planted to provide shade and seclusion. The grove also symbolically provided the king with food for the duration of his life. The grove has diminished from the 1,000 trees originally planted, but more than enough remain to give a sense of grandeur to the spot. Royal coconut palms are some of the tallest of the species, and besides providing nuts, they served as natural beacons pinpointing the spot inhabited by royalty. Now the grove has a parklike atmosphere and mostly you'll have it to yourself. Pay heed to the signs warning of falling coconuts. An aerial bombardment of hefty five pounders will rudely customize the hood of your rental car. Definitely do not walk around under the palms if the wind is up. Just next to the grove is **Kiowea Park,** where camping is permitted for $5 per day through the Hawaiian Homelands Department (see "Camping and Hiking" in the Molokai Introduction).

Church Row

Sin has no chance against this formidable defensive line of churches standing altar-to-altar along the road across from Kapuaiwa Coconut Grove. A grant from Hawaiian Homelands provides that a church can be built on this stretch of land for any congregation that includes a minimum number of Hawaiian-blooded parishioners. The churches are basically one-room affairs that wait quietly until Sunday morning when worshippers come from all over the island. Let there be no doubt: old Satan would find no customers around here, as all spiritual loopholes are covered by one denomination or another. Visitors are always welcome, so come join in. Be wary of this stretch of road—all services seem to let out at the same time on Sunday morning, causing a minuscule traffic jam.

Classic Fishponds

Molokai is known for its fishponds, which were a unique and highly advanced form of aquaculture prevalent from at least the early 13th century. Molokai, because of an abundance of shallow, flat waters along its southeastern shore, was able to support a network of these ponds numbering over five dozen during their heyday. Built and tended by the commoners for the royal *ali'i,* they provided succulent fish that could easily be rounded up at any time for a meal or impromptu feast. The ponds were formed in a likely spot by erecting a wall of stone or coral. It was necessary to choose an area that had just the right tides to keep the water circulating, but not so strong as to destroy the encircling walls. Openings were left in the wall for this purpose. **Kalokoeli Pond** is about two miles east of Kau-

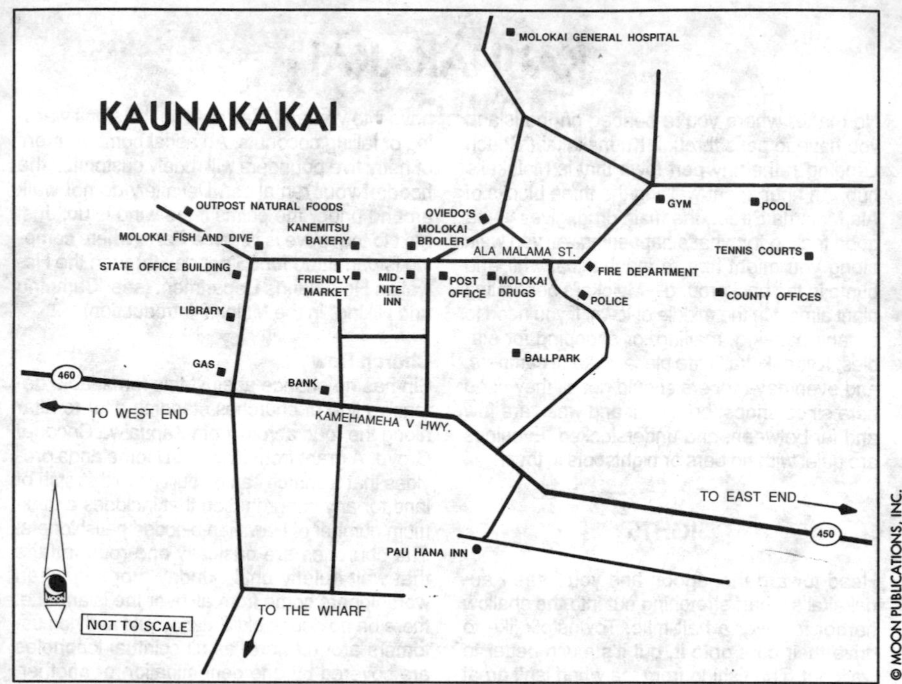

nakakai along Rt. 450. Easily seen from the road, it's an excellent example of the classic fishpond. You can proceed a few more minutes east until you come to a large coconut grove a half mile before One Ali'i Beach Park. Stop here for a sweeping view of **Ali'i Fishpond,** another fine example.

ACCOMMODATIONS

Besides campsites, Kaunakakai has three places to stay. The only other places to lodge outside of town are way out on the west end at the exclusive Kaluakoi Resort or the three condos that surround it, and at the Wavecrest Condo east of Kaunakakai along the south coast. Head for Kaunakakai and its limited but adequate accommodations if you want to save money. The choices are all along the *makai* side of Rt. 450 as you head east from town.

Pau Hana Inn

For years the Pau Hana ("Work's Done") Inn had the reputation of being *the* budget place to stay on Molokai. Now all that's left is the reputation, although it's still not too expensive. The new owners are Molokai Beach, Ltd., affiliated with Aston Hotels and Resorts, and many changes have been made; rooms are refurbished and the whole place is spiffed up. Special touches still remain, though, like the open windows of the dining room through which birds can fly to peck crumbs off the floor. A fireplace is lit in the morning to take the chill off; hanging over it is a noble stag with wide, perfect antlers and tearful eyes. Outside, in the courtyard bar, a magnificent Bengalese banyan provides the perfect setting to sit back and relax. The waitresses are friendly and go out of their way to make you feel welcome and comfortable. The Pau Hana Bar is a favorite with local people. Friday and Saturday nights feature live music and dancing under the banyan tree. Rates are: Long House, a clean barracks-type building with newly carpeted floors $45; studio with kitchenette $90; poolside unit $75; oceanfront unit $90; suite $125; extra person $10; no minimum stay. For reservations contact Pau Hana Inn, P.O. Box 546, Kaunakakai, HI 96748, tel. 553-5342 or (800) 423-6656.

Molokai Shores

This is a relatively new condo a few minutes east of the Pau Hana with full kitchens, large living rooms, and separate bedrooms. The white walls contrasting with the dark-brown floors are hung with tasteful prints. Plenty of lounge furniture is provided along with a table for outside dining and barbecues. The upper floor of the three-story building offers an open-beam ceiling including a full loft. Some units have an extra bedroom built into the loft. The grounds are very well kept, quiet, and restful. The swimming pool fronts the gentle but unswimmable beach, and nearby is a classic fishpond. The only drawback is the architecture: it's pragmatic and neat, but not beautiful. Rates are $95 one-bedroom deluxe; $125 two-bedroom deluxe, two baths; $10 for each additional person. For information contact Hawaiian Islands Resorts, P.O. Box 212, Honolulu, HI 96810, tel. 531-7595 or (800) 367-7042; or contact Molokai Shores, P.O. Box 1037, Kaunakakai, HI 96748, tel. 553-5945 or (800) 367-7042.

Hotel Molokai

The hotel was built in 1966 by an architect (Mr. Roberts) enamored with the South Seas, who wanted to give his hotel a Polynesian village atmosphere. He succeeded. The buildings are two-story, semi-A-frames with swaybacked roofs covered with split wood shingles. Outside staircases lead to the large, airy studios that feature lanai with swings. No cooking facilities, but a refrigerator in every room is handy. Although the Hotel Molokai is a semi-condo, there are hotel amenities like full maid service, a friendly staff, a well-appointed gift shop, a swimming pool, and a poolside bar. The rates vary from $55 standard, $69 garden, $85 deluxe upper lanai, $115 deluxe family unit (sleeps up to six), and $99 oceanfront; add $10 for each additional person. Currently, registration takes place at the Pau Hana Inn. Like the Pau Hana Inn, Motel Molokai is under the new ownership of Molokai Beach, Ltd. For information contact Hotel Molokai, P.O. Box 546, Kaunakakai, HI 96748, tel. 553-5347 or (800) 423-6656.

Also see **Wavecrest Resort Condominium** (under "East to Halawa Valley" later in this chapter) for the only other accommodation on this end of the island.

FOOD AND ENTERTAINMENT

As with the hotels, Molokai has only a handful of places to eat, but among these are veritable institutions that if missed make your trip to Molokai incomplete. The following are located on Kaunakakai's main street, or just a minute away. Ask anyone where they are.

Around Town

The 50-year-old **Mid-Nite Inn,** tel. 553-5302, in "downtown" Kaunakakai, was started as a saimin stand by Mrs. Kikukawa, the present owner's mother. People would come here to slurp noodles while waiting for the midnight interisland steamer to take them to Honolulu. The steamers are gone but the restaurant remains, sort of. The Mid-Nite Inn burned down but is scheduled to reopen on the same spot if all plans go smoothly. The Mid-Nite was well known for its large, tasty, island-inspired meals, and very friendly service. When it reopens, you can count on those to remain the same.

Gone, too, is the venerable **Hop Inn,** another Kaunakakai institution. Located across from the Mid-Nite Inn, the site is going to house the brand-new **Molokai Broiler.** This restaurant will feature do-it-yourself steaks, chops, chicken, and fresh fish.

The **Kanemitsu Bakery** has been in business for almost 70 years, and is still run by the same family. The bakery is renowned for its Molokai breads, boasting cheese and onion among the best of its 19 varieties. Small interisland airlines even hold up their planes to get their shipment from the bakery. Mrs. Kanemitsu's cookies are scrumptious, and anyone contemplating a picnic or a day-hike should load up. The bakery is open 5:30 a.m.-8 p.m., closed Tuesday. There's a lunch counter in the back where you can get eggs, pancakes, and omelettes for breakfast, and local Hawaiian foods for lunch and dinner, open daily except Tuesday 5:30 a.m.-2 p.m., and again 5-8 p.m.

Oviedo's Filipino Restaurant is the last building on the left along Ala Malama, as you head east. Every item on the menu is about $5. Choose from ethnic selections like pork *adobo,* chicken papaya, tripe stew, sweet and sour ribs, pig's feet, mongo beans, and a good selection of ice cream for dessert. Oviedo's is small, rundown, but clean. The decor is worn linoleum floors and Formica tables, and the cooling is provided by breezes that readily pass through large cracks in the walls.

Don't let the name **Molokai Pizza Cafe** fool you! Although this bright and cheery restaurant makes designer pizza, the emphasis is on *cafe.* Co-owned by George and Pamela Goll and Julie and Shawn Connolly, the cafe is operated by the partners. It's located in Kaunakakai wharfside of the junction of routes 450 and 460, and open daily 11 a.m.-10 p.m., depending upon business. Molokai's answer to upscale dining, the cafe serves fast food with a flair. Pizzas come in three sizes and range in price from a Molokai small for $7.80 for up to a giant Big Island with everything including green peppers, onions, sausage, beef, and bacon for $21.95. Sandwiches can be an Italian sub laden with turkey, ham, and roast beef for $6.75, or a plump fresh-baked pocket sandwich for $5.95. Hearty appetites will enjoy meals made by Chef Regan De George, like pasta in marinara sauce for $5.25, barbecued spareribs at $10.49 (great!), or the fresh catch, usually under $11. Order it! Caught in these waters, the fish comes in the back door, is filleted, cooked, and served to you as fresh as it can be. For dessert, you can be repentant and go for a low-fat frozen yogurt, be brazen and order the strawberry shortcake, or let the devil take the hindmost and order the chocolate suicide. The Molokai Pizza Cafe delivers, perfect for anyone staying in a condo.

The **Molokai Drive-In,** open daily 6 a.m.-10 p.m., is about one minute out of town along the Kamehameha V Highway in a bluish-gray, flat-roofed building. You order from the window, and then take your meal to eat under an awning, or go inside to find a few tables. Breakfast offers omelettes, eggs, Spam, bacon, or ham along with sides of rice, hash browns, or toast for under $3.50. Lunch is chili dogs, nachos, subs, fish, shrimp, and chicken burgers, with a special featured every day. The drive-in is actually tasteful, bright, and clean. It's a local place with decent food and very affordable prices. It would make a great stop for a picnic lunch to go, especially if you're heading to Halawa and points east.

Note: Also see the description of **Outpost Natural Foods** following.

Hotel Restaurant/Entertainment

The **Pau Hana Inn** offers a full menu with most dinners under $15. Start with breakfast for under $5.25, or carbo-load on French toast with meat for $4.75, made from famous Molokai bread dipped in a banana egg batter, coffee and tea included. Lunches are $5-6, with offerings like chef salad, mahimahi, and French dip (sounds contagious!). Full dinners under $15 include chicken or shrimp tempura. The Pau Hana Bar has a daily happy hour with *pu pu* 4-6 p.m., when beer is only $1.75, and well drinks $2.25. Here you can relax under the famous banyan tree for an early evening cocktail. Friday and Saturday evenings bring live music and dancing, but there is an annoying cover charge, even for hotel guests who only want a quiet drink.

Shopping

Molokai Fish and Dive in downtown Kaunakakai, tel. 553-5926, sounds very practical, and it is, but along with its fishing equipment it has a good selection of souvenirs, T-shirts and fashions, books, and jewelry, and a good assortment of film. They can give you detailed information about fishing and water sports on Molokai, and they rent some water gear like snorkel sets for $7 and boogie boards for $6.

Molokai Island Creations, open daily 9:30 a.m.-4:30 p.m., adjacent to Molokai Fish and Dive, features authentic Molokai designs on women's blouses, tank tops and men's T-shirts. They also have original Molokai glasswear, china, and porcelain, along with Hawaiian cards and notebooks. Fashions also include *pareau,* children's alohawear, shorts, hats, aloha shirts, muumuu, swimwear, a good selection of jewelry, and a rack of cosmetics and perfumes in island scents.

Imamura's, open daily except Sunday 8:45 a.m.-5:45 p.m., is a very friendly down-home shop that sells everything from flip-flops to fishnets. They specialize in lei-making needles, and have a great selection of inexpensive luggage. The shelves hold beach mats and hats, T-shirts, pots and pans, and kitchen utensils. The sales staff, friendly and slow-paced, will tell you where to go for cheaper items. When you return, they'll smile a welcome.

Lourdes Shoes Clothing and Jewelry is a basic local shop offering a smattering of alohawear, handbags, jogging shoes, baby clothes, towels, and women's clothing. **Molokai Sight and Sound,** tel. 553-3600, open daily 9 a.m.-8:30 p.m., is a video store also stocked with records and tapes, film, and T-shirts. Two exotic birds squawk in the corner as you peruse. The selection of *Jahawaiian* and modern Hawaiian sounds is excellent. There is no theater on Molokai, so if you want to see a movie, only the VCR in your condo will serve. The store rents camcorders and even sells a smattering of snorkel gear.

Molokai Surf, open daily except Sunday 9 a.m.-6 p.m., has bathing suits, sandals, T-shirts, shorts, and alohawear. Nearby, **Togs and Things,** open daily 9 a.m.-8 p.m., and Sunday 10 a.m.-5 p.m., is a T-shirt shop with a good collection of Hawaiiana books, jewelry, alohawear, dresses, and handbags. **Dudoit Imports,** just up the street, features wicker baskets, rattan furniture, and handcrafted items made on Molokai.

The **Molokai Hotel Gift Shop** has a good selection of resortwear, sundries, and gift items.

Grocery Stores

For those into wholesome health food, **Outpost Natural Foods** is at 70 Makaena Place near Kalama's Gas Station. It's the only store of its kind on Molokai, and it's excellent. They're open Sun.-Thurs. 9 a.m.-6 p.m., Friday 9 a.m.-3 p.m., closed Saturday, tel. 553-3377. The fruits and vegetables are locally and organically grown as much as possible. Along with the usual assortment of health foods you'll find bulk grains, granola, nuts, and dried fruits. The jam-packed shelves also hold rennetless cheese, fresh yogurt, nondairy ice cream, vitamins, minerals, supplements, and a good selection of herbs, oils, and spices. If you can't find what you need, ask Dennis, the general manager. Their Oasis Juice Bar, open Sun.-Fri. 10 a.m.-3 p.m., has huge tofu, avocado, chicken, and cheese sandwiches for up to $3.95; burritos $2.50; salad $4.95; tempeh burger $4.95; daily lunch specials for $5; and fresh juice and smoothies. Shaded picnic tables are provided out back.

For general shopping along Ala Malama Street, the **Friendly Market,** open Mon.-Fri. 8:30 a.m.-8:30 p.m., Saturday 8:30 a.m.-to 6:30 p.m., is by far the best-stocked grocery store on Molokai.

Just down the street, **Takes Variety Store** and **Misaki's Groceries and Dry Goods** sell just about everything in food and general merchandise you'll require. Across from the Mid-Nite Inn is the mini-mart **C. Paascua Store** for snack items and drinks.

The **Kaunakakai Market,** along the main drag, open 7 a.m.-10:30 p.m., is fairly well-stocked, with a selection of canned goods and fresh veggies.

For that special evening, try **Molokai Wines and Spirits,** open Sun.-Thurs. 9 a.m.-10 p.m. and until 10:30 p.m. Friday and Saturday, which has a small but good selection of vintage wines as well as beer, and gourmet treats.

Molokai Drugstore, tel. 553-5790, is open daily 8:45 a.m.-5:45 p.m., closed Sunday. Don't let the name fool you because they sell much more than potions and drugs. You can buy anything from sunglasses to film, watches, toys, baby food, small appliances, and garden supplies. They have the best selection of film on Molokai, with a very good selection of books, especially on Hawaiiana. Film processing, including slides, takes 48 hours.

For **fresh fish** check out the Chevron gas station at the light at the crossroads in Kaunakakai. Local fishermen bring their catch here, where it's sold from ice chests. You'll have to take pot luck on there being any catch that day.

Services And Information

The following phone numbers may be of use in Kaunakakai: Police Department, 553-5355; Bank of Hawaii, tel. 553-3273; Fire Department, tel. 553-5401; Maui Community College, tel. 553-3605; Molokai Family Health Center, tel.

553-5353; Molokai Drugstore, tel. 553-5790; Molokai General Hospital, tel. 553-5331. The Friendly Market has a community bulletin board outside. It might list cars for sale, Hawaiian genealogies, or fund-raising sushi sales. Have a look! There is a laundromat behind the Outpost Natural Food Store.

EAST TO HALAWA VALLEY

The east end of Molokai, from Kaunakakai to Halawa Valley, was at one time the most densely populated area of the island. At almost every milepost is a historical site or point of interest, many dating from pre-contact times. A string of tiny churches attests to the coming of the missionaries in the mid-1800s, and a crash-landing site was an inauspicious harbinger of the deluge of Mainlanders bound for Hawaii in this century. This entire stretch of Rt. 450 is almost entirely undeveloped, and the classical sites such as *heiau,* listening stones, and old battlegrounds are difficult to find, although just a stone's throw from the road. The local people like it this way, as most would rather see the south shore of Molokai remain unchanged. A determined traveler might locate the sites, but unless you have local help, it will mean hours tramping around in marshes or on hillsides with no guarantee of satisfaction. Some sites such as **Ili'ili'opae Heiau** are on private land and require permission to visit. It's as if the spirits of the ancient *kahuna* protect this area.

SIGHTS

It's a toss-up whether the best part about heading out to the east end is the road itself or the reward of Halawa Valley at the end. Only 30 miles long, it takes 90 minutes to drive. The road slips and slides around corners, bends around huge boulders, and dips down here and there into coves and inlets. The cliff face and protruding stones have been painted white so that you can avoid an accident, especially at night. Sometimes the ocean and road are so close that spray splatters your windshield. Suddenly you'll round a bend to see an idyllic house surrounded by palm trees with a gaily painted boat gently rocking in a protected miniature cove. Behind is a valley of verdant hills with colors so vibrant they shimmer. You negotiate a hairpin curve and there's Lanai and Maui, black on the horizon, contrasted against the waves as they come crashing in foamy white and blue. Down the road chugs a pickup truck full of local people. They wave you a "hang loose" as their sincere smiles light up your already glorious day. Out in one of the innumerable bays are snorkelers, while beyond the reef, surfers glide in exhilarating solitude.

The local people think of the road as "their road." Why not? They use it as a sidewalk, playground, and extension of their backyards. Dogs snooze on it, while the rumps of grazing stock are only inches away from your fender. The speed limit is 35, but go slower and enjoy it more. The mile markers stop at mile 17, then four miles farther you come to the best part. Here, the well-tended two-lane highway with the yellow stripe plays out. The road gets old and bumpy, but the scenery gets much more spectacular. It's about nine miles from where the bumpy part begins until you reach the overlook at Halawa Valley. Come with a full tank of gas, plenty of drinking water, a picnic lunch, and your sense of wonder.

One Ali'i Beach Park

Five minutes past the Hotel Molokai brings you to a stand of perhaps 80 coconut palms. Here is a little-used, unnamed beach park with an excellent view of one of the string of fishponds that are famous in this area. One Ali'i Beach Park, only a few minutes farther along, is open for camping. It's too close to the road, not well shaded, and a bit too overused to be comfortable. The swimming here is only fair for those who like a challenging surf, but excellent for families with little children who want calm waters. Clean restrooms and showers are available and the grounds are generally in good shape. Those not camping here would find it pleasant enough

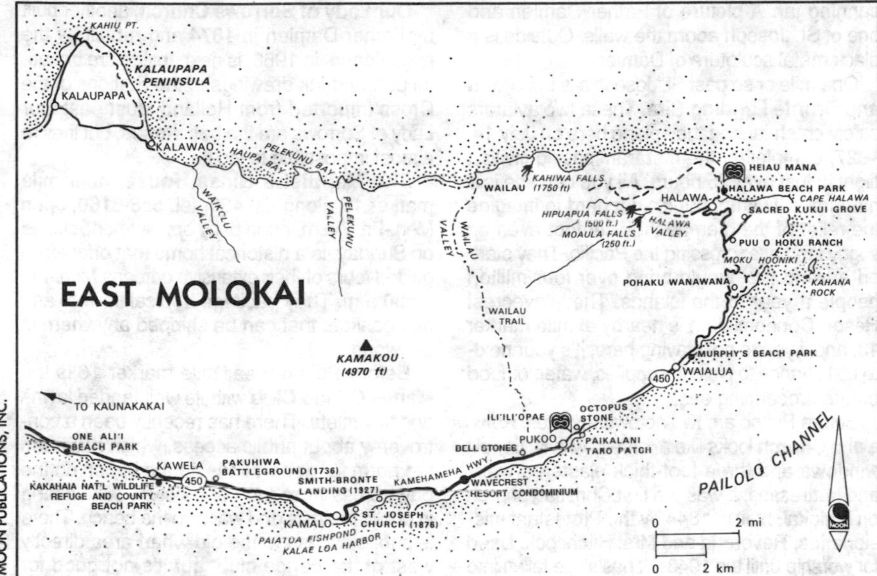

for a day excursion, but it's nothing compared with what's farther east along the road.

About two minutes past One Ali'i, Makanui Road leads up the hillside on the *mauka* side of the road. A two-minute ride up this road exposes the beginnings of a condo development. As you gain height (on one of the only roads that allows you to do so) you'll have an excellent view of the coastline with a panorama of the fishponds below and Lanai and Maui out to sea. Beyond this road is another just like it, leading into a future subdivision with much the same overview.

Kawela

The Kawela area was a scene of tragedy and triumph in Molokai's history. Here was Pakuhiwa, the battleground where Kamehameha I totally vanquished the warriors of Molokai on his way to conquering Oahu. In nearby Kawela Gulch was Pu'u Kaua, the fortress that Kamehameha overran. The fortress oddly doubled as a *pu'uhonua,* a temple of refuge, where the defeated could find sanctuary. Once the battle had been joined, and the outcome inevitable, the vanquished could find peace and solace in the very area they had so recently defended.

Today the area offers refuge as **Kakahai'a County Beach Park and National Wildlife Refuge.** The beach park is not used heavily: it, too, is close to the road. The fishpond here is still used though, and it's not uncommon to see people in it gathering *limu.* This is also an excellent area for coconut trees, with many nuts lying on the ground for the taking. At the wildlife refuge, birdwatchers can still be captivated by the sight of rare endemic birds.

Kamalo To Pukoo

This six-mile stretch is loaded with historical sites. Kamalo is one of Molokai's natural harbors and was used for centuries before most of the island commerce moved to Kaunakakai. **Kamalo Wharf** (turn right down the dirt road at mile marker 10) still occasionally gets large sailboats from throughout the islands. It's a great place to meet local fishermen and inquire about crewing on island-cruising boats. A daily boat for Maui may give you a lift for $20.

Saint Joseph Church, next in line, was built in 1876 by Father Damien. It's small, no more than 16 by 30 feet, and very basic. Inside is a small wooden altar adorned with flowers in a canning jar. A picture of Father Damien and one of St. Joseph adorn the walls. Outside is a black metal sculpture of Damien.

One mile or so past St. Joseph's is the **Smith and Bronte Landing Site.** These two aviators safely crash-landed their plane here on July 14, 1927, completing the first transpacific civilian flight in just over 25 hours. All you can see is a mangrove swamp, but it's not hard to imagine the relief of the men as they set foot even on soggy land after crossing the Pacific. They started a trend that would bring over four million people a year to the islands. The Wavecrest Resort Condominium is nearby at mile marker 13, and if you're not staying here, it's your next-to-last chance to pick up supplies, water, or food before proceeding east.

Before Pukoo are two noteworthy sites. **Kalua'aha Church** looks like a fortress with its tiny slit windows and three-foot-thick plastered walls and buttresses. It was the first Christian church on Molokai, built in 1844 by the Protestant missionaries, Reverend and Mrs. Hitchcock. Used for worship until the 1940s, it has since fallen into disuse. The roof is caving in, but the parishioners have repair plans.

Then comes **Ili'ili'opae Heiau,** one of Hawaii's most famous human-sacrifice temples, and a university of sorcery, as it were, where *kahuna* from other islands were tutored. (For a unique tour of this area, along with nearby Mapulehu Mango Grove, see the description of the **Molokai Wagon Ride,** under "Guided Tours" in the Molokai Introduction.) The wooden structures on the 267-foot stone platform have long since disappeared. Legend holds that all of the stone was carried across the island from Wailau Valley and perfectly fitted in one night of amazing work. Legend also holds that the sorcerers of Ili'ili'opae once sacrificed nine sons of a local *kahuna*. Outraged, he appealed to a powerful shark god for justice. The god sent a flash flood to wipe out the evil sorcerers, washing them into the sea where the shark god waited to devour them. The trailhead for Wailau Valley begins at Ili'ili'opae, but since the temple is now on private land it is necessary to receive permission to visit it. The easiest way to go about this is to stop at the activities desk of any of the island hotels or condos. They have the right telephone numbers and procedures.

Our Lady of Sorrows Church, another built by Father Damien in 1874 and rebuilt by the parishioners in 1966, is next. Inside are beautiful pen-and-ink drawings of the Stations of the Cross imported from Holland. Just past Our Lady of Sorrows are the **bell stones,** but they're almost impossible to locate.

The Mapulehu Glass House, near mile marker 15 along Rt. 450, tel. 558-8160, open Mon.-Fri. 7 a.m.-noon or by appointment, closed on Sunday, is a historical home that offers free guided tours of their extensive gardens Mon.-Fri. 10:30 a.m. They package tropical flowers and fruit baskets that can be shipped anywhere in the world.

Before Pukoo, near mile marker 16 is the **Manee Canoe Club** with its well-tended lawns and tiny inlets. There has recently been a controversy about public access, which has been the norm for generations, to the beach on the bay across from the canoe club, culminating in public protests and walks to the beach. There is public access to the old wharf area directly west of the canoe club, but it's not good for swimming.

Just past Pukoo is the **octopus stone,** a large stone painted white next to the road. It is believed that this is the remainder of a cave inhabited by a mythical octopus, and that the stone still has magical powers.

More East End Beaches

Waialua Beach, almost at mile marker 19, is one of the best beaches on the island for swimming, snorkeling, and beginner surfing. A freshwater stream entering the ocean is very convenient for rinsing off.

Two minutes past mile marker 19 is a sand and coral beach where you can walk knee-deep out to the reef. At high tide, the water is chest high.

Mile Marker 20 Beach, with its huge strand of white sand and protected lagoon, is the main beach on the east end. Pull off at a handy spot and enjoy the great snorkeling, and only mediocre swimming. It's very safe and perfect for a family outing.

Note: All of these beaches have sharp coral. Wear a pair of reef walkers or good old sneakers. You do not want to go out there barefoot!

J.D. BISIGNANI

picturesque coconut grove and fishpond typical of east Molokai

On To Halawa Valley

Past Pukoo, the road gets spectacular. Many blow-your-horn turns pop up as you wind around the cliff face following the natural roll of the coastline. Coming in rapid succession are incredibly beautiful bays and tiny one-blanket beaches, where solitude and sunbathing are perfect. Be careful of surf conditions! Some of the fruitful valleys behind them are still cultivated in taro, and traditional community life beckons young people from throughout the islands to come and learn the old ways. Offshore is the crescent of **Moku Ho'oniki Island,** and Kanaha Rock in front. The road swerves inland, climbing the hills to the 14,000 acres of **Puu O Hoku** ("Hill of Stars") **Ranch.** People often mistake one of the ranch buildings along the road for a store. It's a print shop, but the people inside can direct you to an overlook where you can see the famous and sacred *kukui* grove where Lanikaula, one of the most powerful sorcerers of Molokai, is buried. The distinctive-looking cattle grazing these hilly pastures are French Charolais, imported by Puu O Hoku Ranch and now flourishing on these choice pasturelands. The road comes to a hairpin turn where it feels like you'll be airborne. Before you is the magnificent chasm of Halawa Valley with its famous waterfalls sparkling against the green of the valley's jungle walls. Hundreds of feet below, frothy aquamarine breakers roll into the bay.

Halawa Valley And Bay

This choice valley, rich in soil and watered by Halawa Stream, is believed to be the first permanent settlement on Molokai, dating from the early 7th century. Your first glimpse is from the road's overlook, where you get a spectacular panorama across the half-mile valley to Lamaloa Head forming its north wall, and eastward, deep into its four-mile cleft, where lies Moaula Falls. Many people are so overwhelmed when they gaze from the overlook into Halawa that they don't look around. Turn to your right and walk only 15 yards directly away from Halawa. This view gives a totally different perspective of a deep-V valley and the pounding surf of its rugged beach—so different from the gently arching haven of Halawa Bay. For centuries, Halawa's farmers carved geometric terraces for taro fields until a tidal wave of gigantic proportions inundated the valley in 1946, and left a plant-killing deposit of salt. Most people pulled out and left their homes and gardens to be reclaimed by the jungle.

Follow the paved road into the valley until you see a house that was obviously a church at one time. Cross Halawa Stream and follow the road as far as you can. Here you have a choice of bathing in the cool freshwater stream or in the surf of the protected bay. Don't go out past the mouth of the bay because the currents can be treacherous. This area is great for snorkeling and fishing, one of the only good surfing beaches on Molokai.

Halawa Bay is a beach park, but it's not well maintained. There are toilet facilities and a few dilapidated picnic tables, but no official overnight camping, and the water is not potable. You can bivouac for a night on Puu O Hoku Ranch land at the far north end of Halawa Bay under a canopy of ironwood trees, but be aware that this area attracts rip-offs and it's not safe to leave your gear unattended. Living just near the mouth of the bay is an island fisherman named Glenn and his wife Cathy. Glenn is an expert seaman and knowledgeable about the waters on this side of Molokai. He is willing to take people to Wailau Valley for $30 one-way. The only problem is he has no phone, so you'll have to catch him at home or leave a note saying where he can contact you. Things are less efficient at Halawa Bay, and that's the beauty of it.

Parking

If you're going to Moaula Falls, when you come to the end of the road you'll see a parking lot where a gentleman named Dupre Dudoit sells sodas, chips, etc. He'll promise to watch your car and will give you a map of the walk up the valley for only $5! You can park free, just as long as it's not in his lot. If you have no valuables to lose, forget it. For the $5, this stalwart watchman is just as likely to take a nap or go swimming or fishing as he is to actually watch your car. Most times, he's not here anyway, so park farther along the road in an established public parking lot.

Moaula Falls

One of *the* best walks on Molokai, mosquitoes notwithstanding, is to the famous 250-foot Moaula ("Red Chicken") Falls. Depending on recent rainfall, the trail can be very difficult and poorly maintained. Valley residents claim that a full 50% of the people headed for Moaula never get there. They start out wrong! After parking at the turnout at the bottom of the road, follow the dirt road past the little church and the group of houses for about 10 minutes (a half mile) until it turns into a footpath. Pass a few houses and head toward Halawa Stream, keeping the stone wall on your left. This is where most people go wrong. *Sometimes* yellow arrows point you to the falls, but they come and go with the heavy rains or at the whim of vandals. A foolproof method is to follow a white PVC waterpipe that leads along the left bank of the stream to the falls.

Halawa Stream can be a trickle or torrent, depending upon recent rains. If the stream's roaring, Moaula will be spectacular. The trail continues under a thick canopy of giant mango trees. The luscious fruits are ripe from early spring to early fall. The trail goes up a rise until it forks at another trail paralleling the stream. Take the left fork and follow the trail on this side of the stream. This entire area harbors the remains of countless taro patches and home sites. Groves of *kamani* trees mark the sites where *ali'i* were buried; their tall trunks at one time were used by Hawaiian fishermen and later by sailors as a landmark. Start listening for the falls and let your ears guide you.

Legend recalls that a female lizard, a *mo'o,* lives in the gorgeous pool at the bottom of the falls. Sometimes she craves a body and will drag a swimmer down to her watery lair. The only way to determine her mood is to place a ti leaf (abundant in the area) in the pool. If it floats you're safe, but if it sinks the lady lizard wants company—permanently! Minor gods who live in the rocks above Moaula Falls pool want to get into the act too. They'll drop tiny rocks on your head unless you make an offering (a penny under a ti leaf will do).

Before crossing a side stream, a branch trail leads to the right up the cliff where it divides again in about 150 yards. If you take the left fork you come to another pool at the bottom of **Upper Moaula Falls,** but you have to scale the almost-vertical cliff face aided only by a wire cable attached to the rock wall. The right fork leads you into heavy brush, but if you persevere for 500 yards or so you come to the cascading brilliance of 500-foot **Hipuapua Falls** and its smaller but totally refreshing swimming hole.

Accommodations

Depending on your point of view the **Wavecrest Resort Condominium** is either a secluded hideaway, or stuck out in the sticks away from all the action. It's east of Kaunakakai on Rt. 450 at mile marker 13. You'll find *no* hustle, bustle, anxiety, nightlife, restaurants, or shopping except for a tiny general store that sells the basics for not too much of a mark-up. The Wavecrest sits on five well-tended acres fronting a lovely-to-look-at lagoon that isn't good for swimming. Enjoy a putting green, shuffleboard court, swimming pool, and two lighted tennis courts free to guests. Even if you feel that you're too far from town, remember nothing is going on there anyway. Another attraction is that local fishermen put in next to the Wavecrest and sell their fish for unbeatable prices. Guests can barbecue on gas grills provided. Rates: one-bedroom ocean-view $75, car-condo $95, oceanfront $85, car-condo $105, up to two people; two-bedroom ocean-view $95, with car $125; two-bedroom oceanfront $115, with car $135, up to four people; $5 extra person; three-night minimum. Attractive monthly and low-season discounts. For information write Wavecrest Resort, Star Route, Kaunakakai, HI 96748, tel. 558-8101 or (800) 367-2980.

The **Wavecrest Condo Store** is at the entrance of the Wavecrest. They have a small selection of staples and a good selection of beer and wine. More importantly, local fishermen put in at the Wavecrest beach—it's your best chance to get fresh fish at a very reasonable price.

Kamalo Plantation, H.C. 01, Box 300, Kaunakakai, HI 96748, tel. 558-8236, is a five-acre working lime orchard, where Glenn and Akiko Foster welcome guests. About 11 miles east of Kaunakakai, and across from Father Damien's St. Joseph Church, Kamalo Plantation is surrounded by fully matured manicured grounds and even has a *heiau* on the property. The Fosters can accommodate you in a fully contained private cottage for $75, or as a B&B guest in two private rooms in the main house for $55-65. A breakfast and a tour of the grounds are part of the price.

mourning gecko, a natural flycatcher

DIANA LASICH HARPER

MIDDLE MOLOKAI AND KALAUPAPA

As you head west from Kaunakakai on Rt. 460 toward Hoolehua Airport, you pass fields planted in various crops. These are Molokai's attempt at diversified agriculture since the demise of pineapple a few years ago. Iowalike corn fields make it obvious that the experiment is working well and has a chance, if the large corporations and the state government get behind it. The cultivated fields give way to hundreds of acres filled with skeletons of dead trees. It's as if some eerie specter stalked the land and devoured their spirits. Farther along and just before a bridge, the **Main Forest Road** intersects, posted for 4WD vehicles but navigable in a standard car during dry weather. This track leads to the Sandalwood Measuring Pit, a depression in the ground that is a permanent reminder of the furious and foolhardy trading of last century. Here too along little-used trails are spectacular views of the lost valleys of Molokai's inaccessible northeast shore.

West on Rt. 460 another branch road, Rt. 470, heads due north through Kualapuu, Del Monte's diminished pineapple town, to road's end at Palaau State Park, Molokai's best camping area and home to the famous Phallic Rock. Near the state park entrance is the lookout for Kalaupapa Peninsula and the beginning of the mule trail, which switchbacks down over 1,600 feet to the humbling and uplifting experience of Kalaupapa.

KUALAPUU

Kualapuu was a vibrant town when pineapples were king and Del Monte was headquartered here, but the vibrancy has flown away. Now, there is Brazilian money and expertise in town trying to grow and market a domestic coffee that would fall somewhere between the aromatic Kona and cheaper South American varieties. Still, it is the only town where you can find basic services on the way to Kalaupapa.

Turn left off Rt. 470 onto Rt. 480 (Farrington Ave.) and in a minute you'll come to the **Kuala-**

puu Market, open daily 8:30 a.m.-6 p.m. except Sunday. Here you'll find a limited selection of foodstuffs, fresh produce and beef, and general merchandise as well as the only gas pump in the area. The post office is located to the rear.

Across the street is the **Kualapuu Cookhouse,** tel. 567-6185, open daily except Sunday 7 a.m.-8 p.m., Saturday until 4 p.m., serving country-cooked local foods like saimin and teriyaki beef or chicken. The Kualapuu Cookhouse, headquarters of "The Slow Food Chain," is very friendly, meticulously clean, reasonably priced, and, well . . . slow! The Friday evening special is pizza, which you can enjoy to live entertainment.

Notice also the world's largest rubber-lined reservoir across the highway from town. Holding 1.4 billion gallons, it gets its water via a five-mile long, eight-foot round tunnel from the water-filled valleys to the east.

Meyer Sugar Mill Museum

Along Rt. 470, two miles past Kualapuu in the village of Kalae, you'll discover the old R.W. Meyer Sugar Mill (see "History" in the Molokai Introduction), tel. 567-6436. Open daily 10 a.m.-noon, it charges an entrance fee of $2.50 adults, $1 students. Built in 1878, this restored mill, in functioning order, shows the stages of creating sugar from cane. A museum and cultural center will be added within the next few years. They will focus on preserving Hawaiian handicrafts like quilting, *lau hala* weaving, and woodcarving, and on demonstrating arts like lei-making and hula. The idea is to share and revive the arts of Hawaii, especially those of Molokai, in this interpretive center.

A minute or two past the sugar mill is a surrealistic scene amidst the bucolic highland fields of knee-deep grass. Keep your eyes peeled for a tall cyclone fence topped with nasty-looking barbed wire. Inside are row after row of tiny green A-frames, like the pup tents of a brigade of G.I.'s on bivouac. Restrained by leashes just long enough to prevent mortal combat, are hundreds of plumed, crowing roosters. Molokai's Filipino population has long been known for cockfighting, an illegal activity, but no law prevents the raising of the fighting birds. These glorious cocks, displaying their feathers while clawing the earth, challenge each other with quite a show of devil-may-care bravado. The spectacle is easily seen from the road.

Palaau State Park

A few minutes past Kualapuu are the temporarily closed stables for Molokai Mule Rides, which take you down to Kalaupapa. Even if you're not planning a mule ride, make sure to stop and check out the beauty of the countryside surrounding the mule stables. Follow the road until it ends at the parking lot for Palaau State Park.

In the lot, two signs direct you to the Phallic Rock and to the Kalaupapa Overlook (which is not the beginning of the trail down to the peninsula). Palaau State Park offers the best camping on Molokai although it's quite a distance from the beach (see "Camping and Hiking" in the Molokai Introduction). Follow the signs from the parking lot for about 200 yards to **Phallic Rock** ("Kauleomamahoa"). Nanahoa, the male fertility god inhabiting the anatomical rock, has been performing like a champ and hasn't had a "headache" in centuries! Legend says that Nanahoa lived nearby and one day sat to admire a beautiful young girl who was looking at her reflection in a pool. Kawahuna, Nanahoa's wife, became so jealous when she saw her husband leering that she attacked the young girl by yanking on her hair. Nanahoa became outraged in turn and struck his wife, who rolled over a nearby cliff and turned to stone. Nanahoa also turned to stone in the shape of an erect penis and there he sits pointing skyward to this day. Barren women have come here to spend the night and pray for fertility. At the base of the rock is a tiny pool the size of a small bowl that collects rainwater. The women would sit here hoping to absorb the child-giving mana of the rock. You can still see offerings and of course graffiti. One says "Zap"—parents thankful for twins maybe.

Return to the parking lot and follow the signs to **Kalaupapa** ("Flat Leaf") **Overlook.** Jutting 1,600 feet below, almost like an afterthought, is the peninsula of Kalaupapa, which was the home of the lost lepers of Hawaii, picked for its remoteness and inaccessibility. The almost-vertical *pali* served as a natural barrier to the outside world. If you look to your right you'll see the mule trail winding down the cliff. Look to the southeast sector of the peninsula to see the almost perfectly round **Kauhako Crater,** the remnant of the separate volcano that formed Kalaupapa.

THE KALAUPAPA EXPERIENCE

No one knew how the dreaded disease came to the Hawaiian Islands, but they did know that if you were contaminated by it your life would be misery. Leprosy has caused fear in the hearts of people since biblical times, and last century King Kamehameha V and his advisors were no exception. All they knew was that lepers had to be isolated. Kalawao Cove, on the southeast shore of Kalaupapa Peninsula, was regarded as the most isolated spot in the entire kingdom. So it was to Kalawao that the lepers of Hawaii were sent to die. Through crude diagnostic testing, anyone who had a suspicious skin discoloration, ulcer, or even bad sunburn was rounded up and sent to Kalawao. The islanders soon learned that once sent, there was no return. So the afflicted hid. Bounty hunters roamed the countryside. Babies, toddlers, teenagers, wives, grandfathers—none were immune to the bounty hunters. They hounded, captured, and sometimes killed anyone who had any sort of skin ailment. The captives were ripped from their villages and loaded on a ship. No one would come near the suspected lepers on board and they sat open to the elements in a cage. They were allowed only one small tin box of possessions. As the ship anchored in the always choppy bay at Kalawao, the cage was opened and the victims were tossed overboard. Their contaminated cage was followed by a few sealed barrels of food and clothing that had been collected by merciful Christians. Those too weak or sick or young drowned; the unlucky made it to shore. The crew waited nervously with loaded muskets in case any of the howling, walking nightmares on shore attempted in their delirium to board the ship.

Hell On Earth

Waiting for the newcomers were the forsaken. Abandoned by king, country, family, friends, and apparently the Lord himself, they became animals—beasts of prey. Young girls with hardly a blemish were raped by reeking deformed

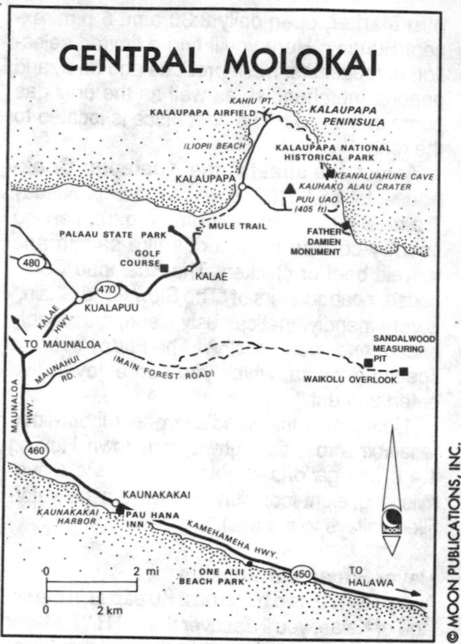

men in rags. Old men were bludgeoned, their tin boxes ripped from their hands. Children and babies cried and begged for food, turning instinctively to the demented women who had lost all motherly feelings. Finally too weak even to whimper, they died of starvation. Those victims who could made rude dwellings of sticks and stones, while others lived in caves or on the beach open to the elements. Finally, the conscience of the kingdom was stirred in 1866: the old dumping ground of Kalawao was abandoned and the lepers were exiled to the more hospitable Kalaupapa Peninsula, just a few hundred yards to the west.

The Move To Kalaupapa

The people of the sleepy village of Kalaupapa couldn't believe their eyes when they saw the ravaged ones. But the lepers now sent to Kalaupapa were treated more mercifully. Missionary groups and *kokua* ("helpers") provided food and rudimentary clothing. An end was put to the lawlessness and depravity. Still, the lepers were kept separate. For the most part they lived outdoors or in very rude huts. They never could come in direct contact with the *kokua.* If they met a healthy person walking along a path, they had to grovel at the side. Most fell to the ground, hiding their faces and attempting to crawl like beaten dogs under a bush. Many *kokua,* horrified by Kalaupapa, left on the next available boat. With no medical attention, death was still the only release from Kalaupapa.

Father Damien just weeks before his death from Hansen's disease

Light In Hell

It was by accident or miracle that **Joseph de Veuster, Father Damien,** a Catholic priest, came from Belgium to Hawaii. His brother, also a priest, was supposed to come but he became ill and Father Damien came in his place. Damien spent a few years in Hawaii, building churches and learning the language and ways of the people, before he came to Kalaupapa in 1873. What he saw touched his heart. He was different from the rest, having come with a sense of mission to help the lepers and bring them hope and dignity. The other missionaries saw Kalaupapa not as a place to live, but to die. Damien saw the lepers as children of God, who had the right to live and be comforted. When they hid under a bush at his approach, he picked them up and stood them on their feet. He carried water all day long to the sick and dying. He bathed their wounds and built them shelters with his own two hands. When clothes or food or materials ran short, he walked topside and begged for more. Other church groups were against him and the government gave him little aid, but he persevered. Damien scraped together some lumber and fashioned a flume pipe to carry water to his people, who were still dying mainly from pneumonia and tuberculosis brought on by neglect. Damien worked long days alone, until he dropped exhausted at night.

Father Damien modified **St. Philomena Church,** a structure originally built in Honolulu by Brother Bertrant in 1872, and shipped to Molokai in segments. Father Damien invited his flock inside, but those grossly afflicted could not control their mouths, so spittle would drip to the floor. They were ashamed to soil the church, so Damien cut squares in the floor through which they could spit onto the ground. Slowly a light began to shine in the hearts of the lepers and the authorities began to take notice. Conditions began to improve, but there were those who resented Damien. Robert Louis Stevenson visited the settlement, and after meeting Damien wrote an open letter that ended ". . . he is my father." Damien contracted leprosy, but by the time he died in 1889 at age 49, he knew his people would be cared for. In 1936, Damien's native Belgium asked that his remains be returned. He was exhumed and his remains sent home, but a memorial stands where he was interred at Kalaupapa.

The Light Grows Brighter

Mother Mary Ann Cope, a Franciscan nun from Syracuse, New York, arrived in 1888 to carry on Damien's work. In addition, many missionary groups sent volunteers to help at the colony. Thereafter the people of Kalaupapa were treated with dignity and given a sense of hope. In 1873, the same year that Damien arrived at Kalaupapa, Norwegian physician Gerhard Hansen isolated the bacteria that causes leprosy, and shortly thereafter the official name of the malady became Hansen's disease. By the turn of this century, adequate medical care and good living conditions were provided to the patients at Kalaupapa. Still, many died, mostly from complications such as TB or pneumonia. Families could not visit members confined to Kalaupapa unless they were near death, and any children born to the patients—who were now starting to marry—were whisked away at birth and adopted, or given to family members on the outside. Even until the 1940s people were still sent to Kalaupapa because of skin ailments that were never really diagnosed as leprosy. Many of these indeed did show signs of the disease, but there is always the haunting thought that they may have contracted it after arrival at the colony. Jimmy, one of the guides for Damien Tours, was one of these. He had some white spots as a child that his Hawaiian grandmother would treat with herbs. As soon as she stopped applying the herbs, the spots would return. A public health nurse at school saw the spots, and Jimmy was sent to Kalaupapa. At the time he was given only 10 years to live.

In the mid-1940s sulfa drugs were found to arrest most cases of Hansen's disease, and the prognosis for a normal life improved. By the 1960s further breakthroughs made Hansen's disease noncontagious, and the patients at Kalaupapa were free to leave and return to their homes. No new patients were admitted, but most, already living in the only home they'd ever known, opted to stay. The community of resident patients is less than 100 today, and the average age is about 60. Kalaupapa will be turned into a national park soon, but the residents are ensured a lifetime occupancy.

Getting There

It shouldn't be a matter of *if* you go to Kalaupapa, but *how* you go. You have choices. You can fly, walk, or walk and fly (or maybe ride in on a mule, see below). No matter how you go, you *cannot* walk around Kalaupapa unescorted. You *must* take an official tour, and children under 16 are not allowed. If you're going by air (or mule), arrangements are made for you by the companies, but if you're walking you have to call ahead to **Damien Tours,** tel. 567-6171, the only tour company now operating, and they will give you an exact place and time to meet once down on the peninsula. Damien Tours charge $22 for a fascinating, four-hour tour conducted by one of the residents. Definitely worth the money; the insight you get from the resident tour guide is priceless and unique. No food or beverages, except water, are available to visitors, so make sure to bring your own.

"I'd rather be riding a mule on Molokai" was until very recently an eye-catching bumper sticker sported by those lucky enough to have made the descent to Kalaupapa aboard sure-footed mules. Unfortunately, the **Molokai Mule Rides** ceased operations after many years due to an insurance snafu. Rumor has it that the Molokai Mule Rides will resume soon. For up-to-the-minute information, contact **Destination Molokai,** tel. 553-3876, (800) 800-6367. The well-trained mules will transport you down the 1,600-foot *pali,* expertly negotiating 26 hairpin switchbacks on the trail to the bottom.

If you're walking to Kalaupapa, follow the mule trail, cut by Manuel Farinha in 1886. Go about 200 yards past the stables and look for a road to the right. Follow this track down past pastureland to the trailhead, where there is a small metal building with an odd sign that reads "Advance Technology Center Hawaii USA" just near an an overgrown observation point for the peninsula. The three-mile, 90-minute trail going down the steep north face of the *pali* is well maintained and only mildly strenuous. It will be rutted and muddy in spots so wear hiking boots if possible.

You can fly in and out, or out only, which is a good alternative and relatively cheap. Both **Air Molokai** and **Aloha Island Air** offer roundtrip flights for $40, one-way for $20. Flights are limited so call for schedules. When you fly in you must still arrange for the ground tour through Damien Tours before you will be sold a ticket. Occasionally, **Scenic Air Tours** runs a trip to Kalaupapa in combination with a Maui fly-by for $119. **Papillon Helicopters,** tel. 669-4884, flies over Kalaupapa from Maui but doesn't land; they charge $185 per person. If you decide to fly, notice the breakers at the end of the runway sending spray 90 feet into the air. The pilots time their take-off to miss the spray!

MAIN FOREST ROAD

Head west on Rt. 460 from Kaunakakai, and just before mile marker 4, turn right over a bridge (just past the Seventh-day Adventist Church). After a few hundred yards is a red dirt road called Main Forest or Maunahui Road that heads into the mountains. Your car rental agency will tell you that this road is impassable except in a 4WD, and they're right—if it's raining! But, even if it isn't, this road is rough. Follow the rutted road up into the hills and you'll soon be in a deep forest of ohia, pine, eucalyptus, and giant ferns thriving since their planting early this century. The cool, pleasant air mixes with rich, earthy smells of the forest. In just under six miles is a main intersection where you turn right. Proceed a few hundred yards and look for a sign pointing out a Boy Scout/Nature Conservancy Camp. Ignore many small roads branching off.

After 10 miles, look for the road sign, "Kamiloloa"; park 100 yards past in a turnout and walk five minutes to the **Sandalwood Measuring Pit** *(Lua Na Moku Iliahi).* It's not very spectacular, and this is a long way to go to see a shallow hole in the ground, but the Sandalwood Pit is a permanent reminder of the days of mindless exploitation in Hawaii when money and possessions were more important than the land or the people. Hawaiian chiefs had the pit dug to measure the amount of sandalwood necessary to fill the hold of a ship. They traded the aromatic wood to Yankee captains for baubles, whiskey, guns, manufactured goods, and tools. The traders carried the wood to China where they made huge profits. The trading was so lucrative that the men of entire villages were forced into the hills to collect it, even to the point where the taro fields were neglected and famine gnawed at the door. It only took a few years to denude the mountains of their copious stands of sandalwood, even more incredible when you consider that all the work was done by hand and all the wood was carried to the waiting ships on the coast using the *maka'ainana* as beasts of burden.

Travel past the Sandalwood Pit (beware of the mud) for about one mile and you'll come to **Waikolu** ("Three Waters") **Overlook.** From here you can peer down into this pristine valley 3,700 feet below. If rains have been recent, hundreds of waterfalls spread their lace as they fall to the green jungle. The water seeps into the ground, which soaks it up like a huge sponge. A water tunnel, bored into the valley, collects the water and conducts it for more than five miles until it reaches the 1.4-billion-gallon Kualapuu Reservoir. Only drive to this area on a clear day, because the rain will get you stuck in mud and obscure your view with heavy cloud cover.

Hiking trails through this area are poorly marked, poorly maintained, and strenuous—great qualifications for those who crave solitude and adventure. Up-to-the-minute information and maps are available from the Department of Land and Natural Resources in Hoolehua, tel. 567-6618. **Hanalilolilo Trail** begins not far from Waikolu Lookout and winds through high mountain forests of ohia until it comes to a breathtaking view of **Pelekunu** ("Foul Smelling, No Sunshine") **Valley.** Don't let the name fool you. Hawaiians lived happily and well in this remote, north shore valley for centuries. Time, aided by wind and rain, has turned the 4,000-foot seacliffs of Pelekunu into the tallest in the world. Today, Pelekunu is more remote and isolated than ever. It has no permanent residents although islanders come sporadically to camp in the summer, when the waters are calm enough to land.

The Hanalilolilo Trail is in the 2,774-acre **Kamakou Preserve,** established by the Nature Conservancy of Hawaii in 1982. It seeks to preserve this unique forest area, home to five species of endangered Hawaiian birds, two of which are endemic only to Molokai. There are 250 species of Hawaiian plants and ferns, 219 of which grow nowhere else in the world. Even a few clusters of sandalwoods tenaciously try to make a comeback. The land was donated by the Molokai Ranch, but they kept control of the water rights. Two officials of the ranch are on the conservancy board, which causes some people to look suspiciously at their motives. The Kamakou Preserve manager is Ed Misaki. Most trails have been mapped and hunting is encouraged throughout most of the area. If interested in obtaining a map, ask the preserve manager.

MOLOKAI'S WEST END

Long before contact with the Europeans, the west end of Molokai was famous throughout the Hawaiian Islands. The culture centered on Maunaloa, the ancient volcanic mountain that formed the land. On its slopes the goddess Laka learned the hula from her sister and spread its joyous undulations to all the other islands. Not far from the birthplace of the hula is Kaluakoi, one of the two most important adze quarries in old Hawaii. Without these stone tools, no canoes, bowls, or everyday items could have been fashioned. Voyagers came from every major island to trade for this perfect stone of Kaluakoi. With all this coming and going, the always-small population of Molokai needed godly protection. Not far away at Kalaipahoa, the "poison wood" sorcery gods of Molokai lived in a grove that supposedly sprouted to maturity in one night. With talismans made from this magical grove, Molokai kept invading warriors at bay for centuries.

Most of the island's arable land is out here. The thrust west began with the founding of the Molokai Ranch, whose 70,000 acres make up 50% of the good farmland on the island. The ranch was owned last century by Kamehameha V, and after his death was sold to private interests who began the successful raising of Santa Gertrudis cattle imported from the famous Texas King Ranch. The ranch employs *paniolo,* with the life of riding the range and rodeo still strong.

THE NORTHWEST

The northwest section of Molokai, centered at **Hoolehua,** is where the Hawaiian Homes parcels are located. The entire area has a feeling of heartland America, and if you ignore the coastline in the background you could easily imagine yourself in the rolling hills of Missouri. Don't expect a town at Hoolehua. All that's there are a little post office and a government office.

The real destination is **Moomomi** ("Jeweled Reptile") **Beach.** Follow Rt. 460 until it branches north at Rt. 480 a mile east of the airport. Follow Rt. 480 until it turns left onto Farrington Avenue in Hoolehua, and continue for about four miles until it turns into a red dirt road. This road can be extremely rutted, even tipping your car at a very precarious angle. Be advised! Continue for about 10 minutes, bearing right at the main intersection until you come to an area where a foundation remains of a burned bathhouse. Below you is Moomomi. This area is a favorite with local people who come here to swim, fish, and surf. The swells are good only in winter, but the beach becomes rocky at that time of year. The tides bring the sand in by April and the swimming until November is good.

Moomomi Beach goes back in Hawaiian legend. Besides the mythical lizards that inhabited this area, a great shark god was born here. His mother was a woman who became impregnated by the gods. Her husband was angry that her child would be from the spirit world, so he directed her to come and sit on a large rock down by the beach. She went into labor and began to cry. A tear, holding a tiny fish, rolled down her cheek and fell into the sea to become the powerful shark god. The rock upon which his mother sat is the large black one just to the right of the beach.

If you feel adventurous you can head west along the beach. Every 10 minutes or so you come to a tiny beach that you have entirely to yourself. Because the area is so isolated, be extremely careful of surf conditions. About two miles west of Moomomi is **Keonelele,** a miniature desert of sand dunes. The wind whips through this region and carries the sand to the southwest shore. Geologists haunt this area trying to piece together Molokai's geological history. The Hawaiians used Keonelele as a burial site, and strange footprints found in the soft sandstone supposedly foretold the coming of white people. Today, Keonelele is totally deserted; although small, it gives the impression of a vast wasteland. Camping (no permit necessary) is allowed on the grassy area overlooking Moomomi Beach, but since a fire claimed the bathhouse, there are no showers or toilets. Water is available from a tap near the old foundation. You should be personally safe camping here, but if you leave gear unattended it could walk off.

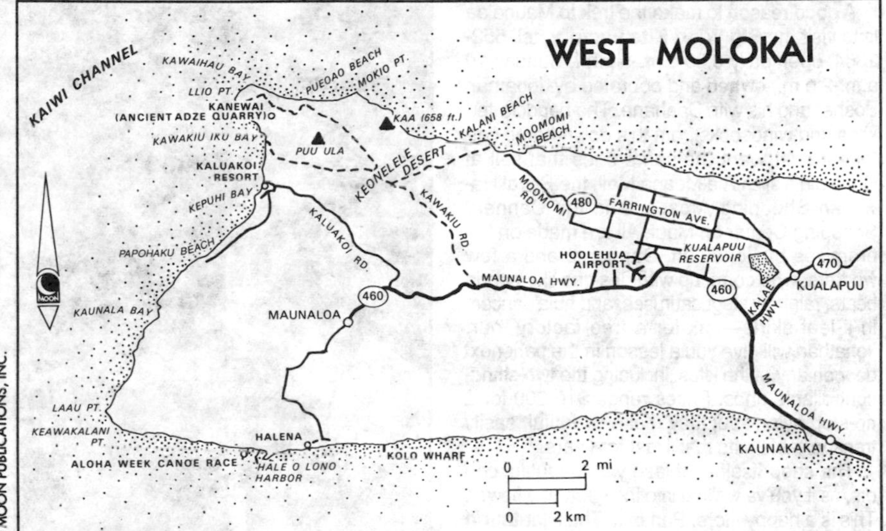

Kawakiu Beach

This secluded and pristine beach in the far northwestern corner of Molokai was an item of controversy between the developers of the Kaluakoi Corp. and the grassroots activists of Molokai. For years access to the beach was restricted, and the Kaluakoi Corp. planned to develop the area. It was known that the area was very important during pre-contact times, and rich in unexplored archaeological sites. The Kaluakoi Corp. hired a supposed team of "experts" that studied the site for months, and finally claimed the area had no significant archaeological importance. Their findings were hooted at by local people and by scholars from various institutions who knew better. This controversy resulted in Kawakiu Beach being opened to the public with plans of turning it into a beach park; the archaeological sites will be preserved.

The swimming at Kawakiu is excellent with the sandy bottom tapering off slowly. To get here go to the Paniolo Hale Condo at Kaluakoi Resort (see following) and park at the end of the dirt road that heads toward the sea, past the last paved parking lot of the condo. Walk across the golf course fairway of the 10th or 11th hole to the beach. Follow it north for three-quarters of a mile, dodging the tide until you come to Kawakiu. You can also drive here by following the dirt road past the condos until it branches inland. It eventually swings back and takes you to Kawakiu. The road is rough, and the hike mildly strenuous, but Kawakiu is definitely worth it.

MAUNALOA

Most people heading east-west between Kaunakakai and the Kaluakoi Resort never make it into Maunaloa town. That's because Rt. 460 splits just east of Maunaloa, and Kaluakoi Road heads north toward the Kaluakoi Resort and away from the town. With the pineapple gone and few visitors coming, the town is barely hanging on. Maunaloa is a wonderful example of a plantation town. As you pull in, there's a little patch of humble but well-kept workers' houses carved into a field. In front you're likely to see a tethered horse, a boat, or glass fishing floats hanging from the lanai. Overhead you may see a kite flying—that's your beacon that you've arrived in Maunaloa. The townsfolk are friendly and if you're looking for conversation or a taste of Hawaiian history, the old-timers hanging around the shaded lean-to near the post office are just the ticket.

A good reason to make the trek to Maunaloa is to visit the **Big Wind Kite Factory,** tel. 552-2364, open daily 8:30 a.m.-5 p.m., Sunday 10 a.m.-2 p.m., owned and operated by Jonathan Sosher and his wife Daphane. The handcrafted kites and windsocks from this down-home cottage industry are the same ones that sell at Honolulu's slick Ala Moana Mall, the Royal Hawaiian Shopping Arcade, and the Cannery Shopping Center on Maui. All are made on the premises by Jonathan, Daphane, and a few workers, who come up with designs like panda bears, rainbow stegosauruses, and hula dancers in ti-leaf skirts—ask for a free factory tour. Jonathan will give you a lesson in the park next door on any of the kites, including the two-string-controllable ones. Prices range $10-200 for a rip-stop nylon kite; they make beautiful, easily transportable gifts that'll last for years.

The shop itself is ablaze with beautiful colors, as if you've walked into the heart of a flower. This is a happy store. Part of it, **The Plantation Gallery,** sells a variety of crafts by local artists—Hawaiian quilt pillowcases, Pacific isle shell jewelry, scrimshaw (on deerhorn), black coral necklaces, earrings, bracelets, boxes, and other wood objects. Island cypress, Japanese *sugi* from a local tree, and *milo* have been carved by a local artist named Robin. **Bali Hale,** part of the boutique, has batiks, Balinese masks, woodcarvings, and sarongs; especially nice are carved mirror frames of storks, birds, and flowers. And if you just can't live without a blowgun from Irian Jaya, this is the place. After you've run through a million tourist shops and are sick of the shell lei, come here to find something truly unique. The Big Wind Kite Factory is *the* most interesting shop on Molokai. Before you leave, ask Jonathan to take you out back so you can try your hand at the rubber band "shooting gallery."

Just up the road from the kite factory is **Dolly Hale** (House of Dolls). This one-room house sitting on the right, usually open 9 a.m.-5 p.m., is where Laurie Cavenaugh fashions coconut fiber dolls ranging in price $7.95-20. If Dolly Hale is closed, you can purchase one of Laurie's creations at the Big Wind Kite Factory.

One minute up the hill from the kite factory is **Under the Banyan Tree,** tel. 552-0012, open daily except Sunday 9 a.m.-5 p.m., a boutique in a refurbished plantation house that specializes in gifts, books, jewelry, fine arts, and natural health and beauty aids. Chris Johnson, artist-in-residence, handmakes his jewelry from semiprecious stones including turquoise, moonstone, malachite, and onyx. The store has quite a collection of new-age books with plenty of titles on metaphysics and self-help. The wainscotted walls are hung with the works of local artists, including the fantastic world of mythical princesses rendered by White Eagle, and the bold seascapes, portraits, and mountainscapes of Evie Dayman. Under the Banyan Tree is also a frame shop and has a small rack of distinctive women's clothing as well.

J.D. BISIGNANI

Jonathan displays a handcrafted kite.

Maunaloa General Store, tel. 552-2868, open daily 9 a.m.-7 p.m., Sunday 10 a.m.-7 p.m., has been taken over by Hansa and Girish Patel from India via Connecticut. It's a well-stocked store where you can pick up anything you'll need if you'll be staying in one of the condos at Kaunakakai. You can buy liquor, wine, beer, canned goods, meats, and vegetables.

The same family has also purchased **Jo Jo's,** tel. 552-2803, the only restaurant in town—have a look at the restaurant menu posted in the general store.

THE SOUTHWEST COAST

If wanderlust draws you to the secluded beaches around **Halena** on the south shore, make sure to ask one of the local old-timers hanging around Maunaloa about road conditions (which change with every storm). Before you enter town proper, a dirt road is to the right. Follow it for just under three miles to the sometimes-unlocked gate of the Molokai Ranch (this gate is heavily padlocked at times, and the only way of knowing is by calling the Molokai Ranch office located in Maunaloa, tel. 552-2767). Proceed, closing the gate behind you, and bounce and rattle down the road for just under two miles. At the fork, go right and then almost immediately left. Follow the road to the end and then walk a few hundred yards to Halena. You'll have the entire area and shoreline to yourself. Ask at the ranch office if you want to camp here. Obviously you must bring all the food and water you'll require.

If you go west from Halena, you'll come to **Hale O Lono** in about one mile, the launch point for the annual outrigger canoe race to Oahu. There's an old harbor area from which sand from Papohaku Beach was shipped to Oahu for building purposes. If you go east back at the fork to Halena, you'll come to the dilapidated **Kolo Wharf** (two miles), from which Molokai once shipped its pineapples. The road is even more remote and rougher, so getting stuck by vehicle will mean a long hike out and an astronomical towing charge. It's best to walk from Halena along the coast.

Accommodations

Much of the west end of Molokai is the Kaluakoi Resort, owned by the Louisiana Land and Exploration Company. The complex includes the Kaluakoi Resort, Ke Nai Kai Condominiums, world-famous Kaluakoi Golf Course, private home sites, and Papohaku, Hawaii's largest white-sand beach.

The **Kaluakoi Resort and Golf Course,** P.O. Box 1977, Maunaloa, HI 96770, tel. 552-2555 or (800) 777-1700, is the destination point for most of the people coming to Molokai. The low-rise buildings, made primarily of wood, blend with the surrounding countryside. The well-kept grounds, covered in manicured trees and shrubbery, provide a miniature botanical tour. All rooms have color TVs, VCRs, and refrigerators, and those on the second floor have open-beam construction. Most rooms sit along the fairways of the golf course and have at least a partial ocean view. Because of the constant cool breezes, no air-conditioning is necessary, but there are ceiling fans.

The rooms, newly refurbished, are done in light pastels and earth colors, all very harmonious and pleasing to the senses. Dynamic color is provided by the large windows that open onto the fairways and the sea beyond. The least expensive room is $100; rates go up to $240 for a one-bedroom ocean cottage. The best deal at the Kaluakoi is the **Colony Club** that includes rooms, partial American plan, greens fees, and all activities.

Consult the lobby bulletin board for happenings at the resort, and the activities desk for what's doing around the island. Make sure to avail yourself of the in-house activities. You can have a ball playing volleyball, swimming at the beach or in the freshwater pool, taking nature walks, riding very good bicycles, or taking lei-making and hula lessons. Every Saturday there's a Hawaiian handicrafts and art presentation in the courtyard, with demonstrations on quilting, weaving, woodwork, pottery, and coconut fiber art. In the evenings there are free top-rated movies, while the bar offers daily specials, usually exotic drinks at great prices.

Four lighted tennis courts are free to guests, open 7 a.m.-10 p.m. Also on the property you'll find a small Liberty House, along with a sundries store selling snacks, magazines, and liquor, and a jewelry shop. Past the 10th hole, which is basically the far north end of the property, you overlook a very private beach. No rules or prying eyes here, so if you would like to swim au naturel, this is the place.

Some of the units at the resort complex, collectively called the **Kaluakoi Villas,** are managed by the Castle Group. Each studio and cottage has been tastefully decorated and includes a color television, lanai, and refrigerator; guests can use the resort's restaurants and all its recreational facilities. Rates range from $85 for a studio to $185 for a suite. Call (800) 525-1470, or write Kaluakoi Villas, P.O. Box 200, Maunaloa, HI 96770.

Ke Nani Kai Condos are *mauka* of the road leading to the Kaluakoi Resort, and they charge $105-130 for one of their fully furnished one-bedroom apartments; two bedrooms rent at $135-155. The complex is relatively new, and all apartments are in excellent condition. Contact Ke Nani Kai, P.O. Box 126, Maunaloa, HI 96770, tel. 552-2761 or (800) 888-2791.

Paniolo Hale is another condo complex nearby. Studios start at $95, one bedroom $115, two bedrooms $145. Two-bedroom units have a hot tub and enclosed lanai. Guests of the Paniolo Hale can use the Kaluakoi Resort's tennis courts for a small fee. Contact Paniolo Hale, P.O. Box 146, Maunaloa, HI 96770, tel. 552-2731 or (800) 367-2984.

Food

The Kaluakoi Resort's **Ohia Lounge** is now an uninspired, pre-prepared, steam-table, buffet restaurant serving breakfast at $10.95, and dinner at $21.95, with a special prime rib buffet at $23 on Friday evenings. The gardenside **snack bar,** open daily 11 a.m.-5 p.m. and 6-8 p.m. on Friday and Saturday, sells sandwiches, burgers, and plate lunches, with most everything under $4.50.

Jo Jo's, tel. 552-2803, in Maunaloa, owned and operated by Hansa and Girish Patel, is open for lunch 12-2 p.m., and for dinner 5-7 p.m., every day except Wednesday and Sunday, but these hours may change with the season and influx of tourists so be sure to call ahead to inquire about the current days and hours of business. Most lunch items go for less than $8 with plenty of plate lunches around $6, while dinner includes shrimp curry $7.99, Korean ribs $14.99, or the fresh catch for $12.99. Desserts like apple pie and cheesecake, along with a good selection of beer and wines, are also part of the menu. The cafe, a one-time bar, is in an old board-and-batten plantation building kept neat and clean as a pin. Check out the architecture while getting a feeling for a simpler Hawaii.

Note: Except for Jo Jo's, the Ohia Room, and the snack window at the Kaluakoi, there are no other options for dining on the west end. Wednesday and Sunday when Jo Jo's is closed is a particular problem. Be prepared!

Excursions And Attractions

The **Molokai Ranch Wildlife Safari Park** is a one-square-mile preserve on the ranch lands, open to the public, which houses over 800 grazing animals from Africa and India. Among the exotic occupants are giraffes, kudu, ibex, antelopes, and ostriches that have lost their fear of humans and can be seen at very close quarters. Bring your camera! The environment and grazing of west Molokai are almost identical to those of the animals' home in East Africa; because of this and the exemplary care afforded by the caretaker, Pilipo Solotario, the wildlife park has one of the best reputations in the world. Weather permitting, tours depart from the Kaluakoi Resort four times daily 8 a.m.-3 p.m. The tour costs $25 for adults and $10 for children under 12. Reservations are required 24 hours in advance; minimum of four persons, maximum of eight. For information call 552-2555 or 552-2767.

Papohaku Beach, the best attraction in the area, doesn't have a price tag. Papohaku Beach is the giant expanse of white sand running south from the Kaluakoi Resort. The sands here are so expansive they were dredged and taken to Oahu in the 1950s. During the winter months a great deal of sand is stripped away and large lava boulders and outcroppings are exposed. Every spring and summer the tides carry the sand back and deposit it on the enormous beach. Camping is permitted at the **Papohaku Beach County Park.** Pick up your permit at the Mitchell Pauole Center in Kaunakakai, tel. 553-3221, before you come all the way out here. You'll find a large grassy play area, toilets, showers, picnic tables, grills for cooking, and a virtually empty beach. A sign on the road past the park tells you to watch out for wild turkeys! The road runs through a future home development area, with several beach access roads and parking areas that lead to other spots along the huge expanse of beach.

BIG ISLAND

"In what other land save this one is the commonest form of greeting not 'Good Day,' . . . but 'Love?' . . . Aloha . . . It is the positive affirmation of one's own heart giving."

—Jack London, 1916

BOB RACE

INTRODUCTION

The island of Hawaii is grand in so many ways. Its two nicknames, "The Orchid Island" and "The Volcano Island," are both excellent choices: the island produces more of the delicate blooms than anywhere else on earth; and Pele, the fire goddess who makes her mythological home here, regularly sends rivers of lava from the world's largest and most active volcanoes. However, to the people who live here, Hawaii has only one real nickname, "The Big Island." Big isn't necessarily better, but when you combine it with beautiful, uncrowded, traditional, and inexpensive, it's hard to beat.

The Big Island was the first to be inhabited by the Polynesian settlers, yet it's geologically the youngest of the Hawaiian Islands at barely a million years old. Like all the islands in the Hawaiian chain, it's a mini-continent whose geographical demarcations are much more apparent because of its size. There are parched deserts, steaming fissures, jet-black sand beaches, raw semi-cooled lava flows, snow-covered mountains, entire forests encased in hardened stone, and lush valleys where countless waterfalls break through the rock faces of 1,000-foot-tall chasms. There are small working villages time has passed by, the state's most tropical city, and an arid coast stretching over 90 miles where the sun is guaranteed to shine. You'll find some of the islands' least expensive accommodations as well as some of the world's most exclusive resorts.

Historically, the Big Island is loaded with religious upheavals, the births and deaths of great people, vintage missionary homes and churches, reconstructed *heiau,* and even a royal palace. Here is the country's largest privately owned ranch, where cowboy life is the norm; America's only coffee plantations; and enclaves of the counterculture, where people with alternative lifestyles are still trying to keep the faith of the '60s.

Sportspeople love it here, too. The Big Island is a mecca for triathletes and offers snow skiing in season, plenty of camping and hiking, and the best marlin waters in all the oceans of the world.

There are direct flights to the Big Island, where the fascination of perhaps not "old" Hawaii, but definitely "simple" Hawaii, still lingers.

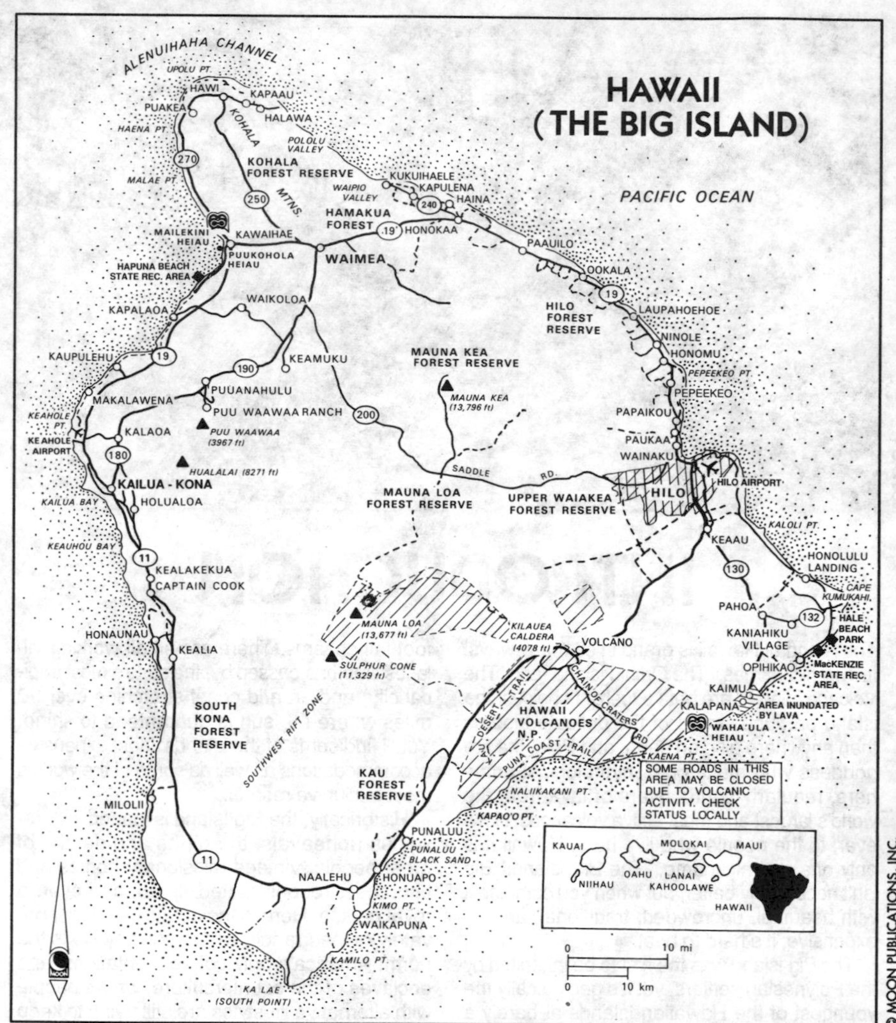

OVERVIEW

Hilo on the east coast and Kailua-Kona on the west are the two ports of entry to the Big Island. At opposite ends of the island as well as of the cultural spectrum, the two have a friendly rivalry. It doesn't matter at which one you arrive, because a trip to the Big Island without visiting both is unthinkable. Better yet, split your stay and use each as a base while you tour. The Big Island is the only Hawaiian island big enough that you can't drive around it comfortably in one day, nor should you try. Each of the six districts is interesting enough to spend at least one day exploring.

Hilo And Vicinity

Hilo is the oldest port of entry, the most tropical town in Hawaii, and the only major city built on the island's windward coast. The city is one tremendous greenhouse where exotic flowers and tropical plants are a normal part of the landscape, and entire blocks canopied by adjoining banyans are taken for granted. The town, which hosts the yearly Merrie Monarch Festival, boasts an early morning fish market, Japanese gardens, the Lyman House Museum, and a profusion of natural phenomena, including Rainbow Falls and Boiling Pots. Plenty of rooms in Hilo are generally easily available, and its variety of restaurants will titillate anyone's taste buds. Both go easy on the pocketbook while maintaining high standards.

Saddle Road begins just outside of Hilo. It slices directly across the island through a most astonishing high valley or "saddle" separating the mountains of Mauna Loa and Mauna Kea. Passable, but the bane of car rental companies, it heads 13,796 feet up to the top of Mauna Kea, where a series of astronomical observatories peer into the heavens through the clearest air on earth.

Northeast

Hamakua refers to the entire northeast coast, where streams, wind, and pounding surf have chiseled the lava into towering cliffs and precipitous valleys known locally by the unromantic name of "gulches." All the flatlands here are awash in a green sea of sugarcane. A spur road from the forgotten town of Honomu leads to Akaka Falls State Park, whose waters tumble over a 442-foot cliff—the highest sheer drop of water in Hawaii. North along the coastal road is Honokaa, a one-street town of stores, restaurants, and crafts shops. The main road bears left here to the cowboy town of Waimea, but a smaller road inches farther north. It dead-ends at the top of Waipio Valley, cradled by cliffs on three sides with its mouth wide open to the sea. The valley is reachable only by foot, 4WD vehicle, or horseback. On its verdant floor a handful of families live simply by raising taro, a few head of cattle, and horses. Waipio was a burial ground of Hawaiian *ali'i,* where *kahuna* traditionally came to commune with spirits. The enchantment of this "power spot" remains.

Southeast

Puna is the area which lies south of Hilo and makes up the majority of the southeast coast. Here are the greatest lava fields that have spewed from Kilauea, the heart of Volcanoes National Park. An ancient flow embraced a forest in its fiery grasp, entombing trees that stand like sentinels today in Lava Tree State Monument. Cape Kumukahi, a pointed lava flow that reached the ocean in 1868, is officially the easternmost point in Hawaii. Just below it is a string of beaches featuring ebony-black sand. Past the small village of Kalapana, the road skirts the coast before it dead-ends where it has been covered over by lava. Chain of Craters Road is now passable only *from* Hawaii Volcanoes National Park. Wahaula Visitor Center has been torched by lava, but the Wahaula Heiau, where human sacrifice was introduced to the islands, survived and can be reached on foot if conditions permit. Chain of Craters Road spills off the mountain through a forbidding, yet vibrant, wasteland of old lava flows until it comes to the sea, where this living volcano fumes and throbs. Atop the volcano, miles of hiking trails crisscross the park and lead to the very summit of Mauna Loa. You can view the natural phenomena of steaming fissures, boiling mud, Devastation Trail, and Thurston Lava Tube, large enough to accommodate a subway train. Here, too, you can lodge or dine at Volcano House, a venerable inn carved into the rim of the crater.

Kau, the southern tip of the island, is primarily a desert. On well-marked trails leading from the main road you'll discover ancient petroglyphs and an eerie set of footprints left by an ill-fated band of warriors who were smothered under the moist ash of a volcanic eruption and whose demise marked the ascendancy of Kamehameha the Great. Here are some lovely beaches and state parks you'll have virtually to yourself. A tiny road leads to Ka Lae ("South Point"), the most southerly piece of ground in the United States.

Kona

Kona, the west coast, is in every way the opposite of Hilo. It's dry, sunny, and brilliant, with large expanses of old barren lava flows. When watered, the rich soil blossoms, as in South Kona, renowned for its diminutive coffee plantations. The town of Captain Cook, named after the intrepid Pacific explorer, lies just above the very beach where he was slain because of a terrible miscommunication two centuries ago. Ironically, nearby is the restored Pu'uhonua o Honaunau Heiau, where mercy and forgiveness were rendered to any *kapu*-breaker or vanquished warrior who made it into the confines of this safe refuge.

Kailua-Kona is the center of Kona. The airport is just north and here is a concentration of condos and hotels. The town itself boasts an array of art and designer shops; world-class triathletes come here to train, and charter boats depart in search of marlin. Within Kailua is Mokuaikaua Church, a legacy of the very first packet of missionaries to arrive in the islands; and Hulihee Palace, vacation home of the Kamehameha line of kings.

Northward, the Kona District offers a string of beaches. Just outside Kailua is a clothing-optional beach, one of very few in Hawaii, and farther up the coast in South Kohala is Hapuna Beach, best on the island. In 1965, Laurence Rockefeller opened the Mauna Kea Resort here. For the last three decades, this resort, along with its sculptured, coast-hugging golf course, has been considered one of the finest in the world. Just south is the Kona Village Resort, whose guests can arrive at a private airstrip to spend the night in a "simple" grass shack on the beach. Its serenity is broken only by the soothing music of the surf and by the not-so-melodious singing of "Kona nightingales," a pampered herd of wild donkeys that frequents this area. The Hilton Waikoloa Village is here, billed as the most fabulous resort on earth, and just down the road is the Mauna Lani, another first-rate hotel.

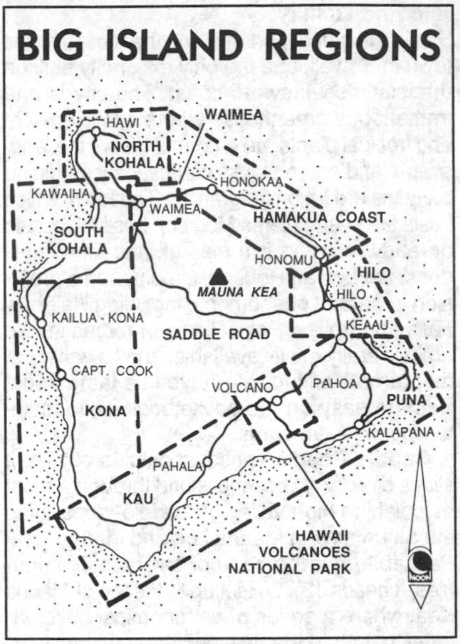

North

North Kohala is primarily the peninsular thumb on the northern extremity of the island, although the area does dip south along the coast and eastward into rolling hills. At its base is Waimea (Kamuela), center of the enormous Parker Ranch. Here in the cool mountains, cattle graze in chest-high grass and *paniolo,* astride their sturdy mounts, ride herd in time-honored tradition. Hunters range the slopes of Mauna Kea in search of wild goats and boars, and the Fourth of July is boisterously acknowledged by the wild whoops of cowboys at the world-class Parker Ranch Rodeo. Along the coast are beach parks, empty except for an occasional local family picnic. A series of *heiau* dot the coast, and on the northernmost tip a broad plain overlooking a sweeping panorama marks the birthplace of Kamehameha the Great. The main town up here is Hawi, holding on after the sugar companies pulled out a few years ago. Down the road is Kapaau, where Kamehameha's statue resides in fulfillment of a *kahuna* prophecy. Along this little-traveled road, a handful of artists offer their crafts in small shops. At road's end is the overlook of Pololu Valley, where a steep descent takes you to secluded beaches and camping in an area once frequented by some of the most powerful sorcerers in the land.

BIG ISLAND REGIONS

THE LAND

Science and the oral history of *The Kumulipo* differ sharply on the age of the Big Island. Scientists say Hawaii is the youngest of the islands, being a little over one million years old; the chanters claim it was the first "island-child" of Wakea and Papa. It is, irrefutably, closest to the "hot spot" on the Pacific floor, evidenced by Kilauea's frequent erruptions and by **Loihi Seamount,** located 30 miles off the southeast coast, which is even now steadily growing about 3,000 feet below the waves. The geology, geography, and location of the Hawaiian Islands, and their ongoing drifting and building in the middle of the Pacific, make them among the most unique pieces of land on earth, and the Big Island is the *most* unique of them all.

Size

The Big Island dwarfs all the others in the Hawaiian chain at 4,038 square miles and growing. It accounts for about 63% of the state's total land mass; the other islands could fit within it two times over. With 266 miles of coastline, the island stretches about 95 miles from north to south and 80 miles from east to west. Cape Kumukahi is the easternmost point in the state, and Ka Lae ("South Point") is the southernmost point in the country.

The Mountains

The tremendous volcanic peak of **Mauna Kea** ("White Mountain"), located in north-central Hawaii, has been extinct for over 4,000 years. Its seasonal snowcap earns Mauna Kea its name and reputation as a good skiing area in winter. Over 18,000 feet of mountain below the surface rises straight up from the ocean floor—making Mauna Kea actually 31,796 feet tall, a substantial 2,768 feet taller than Mt. Everest; some consider it the tallest mountain in the world. At 13,796 feet above sea level, it is without doubt the tallest peak in the Pacific. Near its top, at 13,020 feet, is **Lake Waiau,** the highest lake in the state and third highest in the country. Mauna Kea was obviously a sacred mountain to the Hawaiians, and its white dome was a welcome beacon to seafarers. On its slope is the largest adze quarry in Polynesia, from which high-quality basalt was taken to be fashioned into prized tools. The atmosphere atop the mid-Pacific mountain, far from pollutants, is the most rarefied and cleanest on earth. The clarity makes Mauna Kea a natural for astronomical observatories. The complex of telescopes on its summit is internationally staffed and provides data to scientists around the world.

The **Kohala Mountains** to the northwest are the oldest. This section looks more like the other Hawaiian Islands, with deep gorges and valleys along the coast and a forested interior. As you head east toward Waimea from Kawaihae on Rt. 19, for every mile you travel you pick up about 10 inches of rainfall per year. This becomes obvious as you begin to pass little streams and rivulets running from the mountains.

Mount Hualalai at 8,271 feet is the backdrop to Kailua-Kona. It's home to many of the Big Island's endangered birds and supports many of the region's newest housing developments. Just a few years ago, Mt. Hualalai was thought to be extinct, since the last time it erupted was in 1801. Recently, volcanologists using infrared technology have discovered the mountain to be red-hot again. The U.S. Geological Survey has listed this sleeper as the fourth most dangerous volcano in the U.S., because when it does erupt, it's expected to produce a tremendous amount of lava that will pour rapidly down its steep sides. The scientists, whose opinion is seconded by local Hawaiians, say that the mountain will blow within the next 10 years. The housing developers don't say anything.

Even though **Mauna Loa** ("Long Mountain") measures a respectable 13,677 feet, its height isn't its claim to fame. This active volcano, 60 miles long by 30 wide, is comprised of 10,000 cubic miles of iron-hard lava, making it the densest and most massive mountain on earth. In 1950, a tremendous lava flow belched from Mauna Loa's summit, reaching an astonishing rate of 6,750,000 cubic yards per hour. Seven lava rivers flowed for 23 days, emitting over 600 million cubic yards of lava covering 35 square

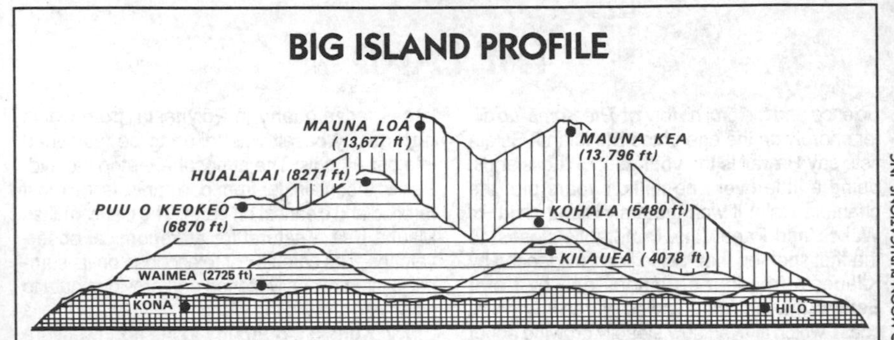

miles. There were no injuries, but the villages of Kaapuna and Honokua were partially destroyed along with the Magoo Ranch.

Kilauea, whose pragmatic name means "The Spewing," is the world's most active volcano. In the last hundred years, it has erupted an average of once every 11 months. The Hawaiians believed that the goddess Pele inhabited every volcano in the Hawaiian chain, and that her home is now Halemaumau Crater in Kilauea Caldera. Kilauea is the most scientifically watched volcano in the world, with a permanent observatory built right into the crater rim. When it erupts, the flows are so predictable observers run toward the mountain, not away from it. The flows, however, can burst from fissures far from the center of the crater in areas that don't seem "active." This occurs mainly in the Puna District. In 1959, Kilauea Iki Crater came to life after 91 years, and although the flow wasn't as massive as others, it did send blazing fountains of lava 1,900 feet into the air. Kilauea has been very active within the last few years, with eruptions occurring at least once a month and expected to continue. Most activity has been from a yet unnamed vent below Pu'uo. You might be lucky enough to see this phenomenon while visiting.

Beaches, Ponds, And The Coast

The Big Island takes the rap for having poor beaches—this isn't true. They are certainly few and far between, but they are spectacular. Hawaii is big and young, so distances are greater than on other islands, and the wave action hasn't had enough time to grind the new lava into sand. The Kona and Kohala coast beaches, along with a few nooks and crannies around Hilo, are gorgeous. Puna's beaches are incredible black sand, and the southern part of the island has a string of hidden beaches enjoyed only by those intrepid enough to get to them. Full listings are found in the various travel chapters under "Beaches."

Makalawena, just north of Keahole Airport on a rough coastal trail, has a beautiful white-sand beach. Inland is its associated wetland pond, probably the most important one on the Big Island. This fragile and archaeologically important area is managed by the Bishop Estate, tel. 322-6088. Currently entry is not allowed, except with a U.S. Fish and Wildlife Service official or a state biologist. However, the Sierra Club and Audubon Society are permitted to enter, and you can arrange to accompany them on a field trip. If you wish to visit this beautiful area, consider contacting these organizations long before your trip to the Big Island. The second most important body of water is near Honokohau Beach.

Tsunami

Hilo has been struck with the two worst tidal waves in modern history. A giant wave smashed the islands on April 1, 1946, and swept away 159 people and over 1,300 homes; Hilo sustained most of these losses. Again, on May 23, 1960, Hilo took the brunt of a wave that rumbled through the business district killing 61 people. There is an elaborate warning system throughout the island; emergency procedures and Inundation Maps can be found in the front of the telephone directory.

ENVIRONMENTAL ISSUES

Currently controversy is raging over an attempt to place anchoring pins in the hard lava rock just off the Kailua-Kona Coast. Boats could latch onto them, and by doing so would not drag their anchors across the fragile coral reef, as is now the case. The Dive Council in Kona isn't known for agreement on many issues because they represent so many different factions, but they agreed unanimously the pins should be put in place. The process is environmentally sound, and the pins have been used successfully all over the world. In fact, the technology specifically needed for drilling in lava rock was developed at the University of Hawaii. After three years elapsed, during which the Department of Land and Natural Resources debated whether it was their responsibility or that of the Hawaii Department of Transportation to implement the program, the Dive Council went ahead and put in the pins, without the moorings. Upstaged, the Department of Land and Natural Resources was furious. At meetings they tried to find a scapegoat at which they could throw their bureaucratic book, though their energy would have been better spent protecting the reef.

In a separate issue, the Department of Land and Natural Resources is attempting to trade 450 acres of state land surrounding Kua Bay (just north of the airport in Kona). This magnificent area has a secluded beach that is very popular with local people, and is well documented as having significant archaeological sites. In return, from international land developers, the state will receive 340 acres of rocky coastal land that isn't nearly as beautiful, and coincidentally would be difficult to develop as a resort.

Geothermal Controversy

Pele's blood-red lava is cool compared to the uncompromising debate now sizzling between native rights groups allied with environmentalists, and geothermal advocates who view the Big Island's molten core as an infinite source of power. Governor John D. Waihee, with strong support from the state's legislators, has sanctioned the construction of a geothermal well within the 27,000 acres that make up the **Wao Kele O Puna Rainforest**—the *only* tropical lowland rainforest in the United States. Another 20 power plants will bore into the east rift of Kilauea Volcano, and all will require huge steam collection systems, power plants, power lines, and towers that will march across the island's most expansive and pristine panoramas. Adding to the magnitude of this engineering feat (the largest developmental plan of any type ever attempted in Hawaii) will be a deep ocean cable stretching from the Big Island to Maui, and on to Oahu. Traversing an unstable ocean canyon over 6,500 feet deep, the cable, with an estimated cost of $3 billion, will lie at more than seven times the depth of any cable laid thus far anywhere in the world. The major developers, Hawaii's Campbell Estates, and True Geothermal of Casper, Wyoming, envision generating about 500 megawatts of electricity, close to four times the amount needed by the Big Island at the present rate of consumption. The power will be used to further develop Kona on the Big Island; the substantial excess will be exported to Oahu and Maui. Residents of Puna, where the development will occur, can see no benefit in despoiling their homes and environment in order to fuel the ravenous demands generated by tourism on the islands.

One of the constituents of the anti-geothermal coalition, the **Pele Defense Fund,** views the development as a desecration of the land not sanctioned by traditional religion; they believe that each well is a puncture wound in Pele's side. To these local people, many of whom are native Hawaiians who trace their lineage directly to Pele, and who feel protected by her, the drilling amounts to no less than sacrilege. Having recently lost a local court battle in which they claimed the area has religious significance, they plan to carry the fight all the way to the Supreme Court. The Pele Defense Fund points out the wells are being drilled over extremely unstable land that is susceptible to a rampaging lava flow at any time. A destroyed well could pump incalculable volumes of hydrogen sulfide gas into the atmosphere. They also contend most of the jobs at the sites are low-paying maintenance jobs that will hardly benefit the local economy, and the higher-paying managerial positions will be given to new arrivals brought in from the Mainland.

BIG ISLAND AVERAGE MAXIMUM/MINIMUM TEMPERATURE AND RAINFALL

TOWN		JAN.	MARCH	MAY	JUNE	SEPT.	NOV.
Hilo	high	79	79	80	82	82	80
	low	62	62	61	70	70	65
	rain	11	15	7	10	10	15
Kona	high	80	81	81	82	82	81
	low	62	64	65	68	68	63
	rain	4	3	2	0	2	1

Note: rainfall in inches; temperature in °F

To environmentally aware botanists and entomologists, the despoiling of any of the precious and dwindling rainforest is a nightmare. Even one footprint in a 2,000-year-old bog-floored rainforest can take months and even years to disappear. Native species of plants could be made extinct through the introduction of foreign species inadvertently carried by workers and machinery, while the ruts left by construction could become stagnant pools breeding mosquito larvae that affect native birds. The destruction caused by heavy trucks, earth-moving machinery, site deforestation, and the constant maintenance of the site, in these fragile environs is incalculable. The Sierra Club Legal Defense Fund has been attempting to force the Environmental Protection Agency, Army Corps of Engineers, U.S. Geological Survey, Department of Energy, and National Park Service—the federal agencies involved in the project—to prepare an environmental impact statement ,which, unbelievably, has not been done to date. The Sierra Club seeks a moratorium placed on construction until a study is done. All scientists agree that once a rainforest is destroyed, or disturbed, it is virtually gone forever.

Proponents of the geothermal power plants point to the fact that Hawaii is *the* most oil-dependent state in America. They say that the building of the pollution-free plants will save millions of barrels of oil over the years, reduce air pollutants, and help reduce the threat to Hawaii's coastline due to oil spills. Ormat Energy Systems of Sparks, Nevada, who purchased Puna Geothermal Venture, the previous plant operator, claims its geothermal technology provides for a "closed system" that will pump any residual geothermal brine and steam back into the earth, while absolutely eliminating any foul smell of hydrogen sulfide gas. Opponents say that the vast majority of Hawaii's imported petroleum is used for automobiles and aircraft, and the development of alternative sources of power like solar and wind energy, along with increased conservation, could easily make up for the purported savings.

The real issue in the development of geothermal electrical power generation on the Big Island is the priorities of modern American society: power and profits now for large developers and corporations, or the preservation of the earth's wild places for future generations. Neither seems able to wait.

CLIMATE

The average temperature around the island varies between 72 and 78° F. Summers raise the temperature to the mid-80s and winters cool off to the low 70s. Both Kona and Hilo seem to maintain a year-round average of about 80 degrees. As usual, it's cooler in the higher elevations, and Waimea (Kamuela) sees most days in the mid-60s to low 70s, while Volcanoes maintains a steady 60°. Atop Mauna Kea, the temperature rarely climbs above 50° F or dips below 30, while the summit of Mauna Loa is about 10° warmer.

Rainfall

Weatherwise the Big Island's climate varies not so much in temperature, but precipitation. Hawaii has some of the wettest and driest coastal (tourist) areas in the islands. The line separating wet from dry can be dramatic. Waimea, for example, has an actual dry and wet side of town, as if a boundary line split the town in two. Houses on the dry side are at a premium. Kona and Hilo are opposites. The Kona Coast is almost guaranteed to be sunny and bright, receiving as little as 15 inches of rainfall per year. Both Kona and the Kau Desert to the south are in the rain shadow of Mauna Loa, and most rain clouds coming from east to west are pierced by its summit before they ever reach Kona. Hilo is wet, with predictable afternoon and evening showers—they make the entire town blossom. Though this reputation keeps many tourists away, the rain's predictability makes it easy to avoid a drenching while exploring the town. Hilo does get as much as 150 inches of rainfall per year, with a record of 153.93 inches set in 1971. It also holds the dubious honor of being the town with the most rainfall recorded by the National Weather Service in a 24-hour period—a drenching 22.3 inches in February 1979.

FLORA AND FAUNA

The indigenous plants and birds of the Big Island have suffered the same fate as those of the other Hawaiian Islands: they're among the most endangered species on earth and disappearing at an alarming rate. There are some sanctuaries on the Big Island where native species still live, but they must be vigorously protected. Do your bit to save them; enjoy but do not disturb.

COMMON FLORA

The Hawaiians called the **prickly pear cactus** *panini,* which translates as "very unfriendly," undoubtedly because of the sharp spines covering the flat, thick leaves. The cactus is typical of those found in Mexico and the southwestern United States. It was introduced to Hawaii before 1810 and established itself coincidentally with the cattle brought in at the time; *panini* is very common in North Kohala, especially on the Parker Ranch lands. It is assumed that Don Marin, a Spanish advisor to Kamehameha I, was responsible for importing the plant. Perhaps the early *paniolo* (cowboy) felt lonely without it. The *panini* can grow to heights of 15 feet and is now considered a pest, but nonetheless looks as if it belongs. The cactus blooms in beautiful yellow and orange flowers measuring three inches across. It develops small, delicious, pear-shaped fruits. Hikers who decide to pick the fruit should be careful of small, yellowish bristles that can burrow under the skin and irritate. An attempt is being made to control the cactus in *paniolo* country. *El cosano rojo,* the red worm found in the bottom of Mexican tequila, has been introduced to destroy the plant. It burrows into the cactus and eats the hardwood center, causing the plant to wither and die.

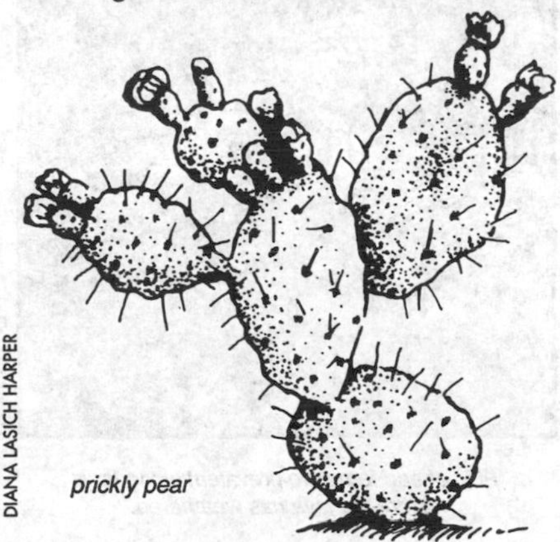

DIANA LASICH HARPER

prickly pear

More species of **lobelia** grow in Hawaii than anywhere else in the world. A common garden flower elsewhere, in Hawaii it grows to tree height. You'll see some unique species covered with hair or with spikes. The lobelia flower is tiny and resembles a miniature orchid with curved and pointed ends, like the beak of the native *'i'iwi.* This bird feeds on the flower's nectar; it's obvious that both evolved in Hawaii together and exhibit the strange phenomenon of nature mimicking nature.

The Big Island has more species of **gesneriad,** the African violet family, than anywhere else on earth. Many don't have the showy flowers that you normally associate with African violets, but have evolved into strange species with huge, fuzzy leaves.

The ***puahanui,*** meaning "many flowers," is Hawaii's native hydrangea; it is common in the upland forests of the Big Island.

Ferns

If you travel to Volcanoes National Park you will find yourself deep in an amazing, high-altitude tropical rainforest. This unique forest exists because of the 120 inches of annual rainfall, which turn the raw lava into a lush forest. Besides stands of ohia and koa, you'll be treated to a primordial display of ferns. All new fronds on ferns are called "fiddleheads" because of the way they unfurl and resemble the scrolls of violin heads. Fiddleheads were eaten by Hawaiians during times of famine. The most common ferns are *hapu'u,* a rather large tree fern, and *amauamau,* a smaller type with a more simple frond. A soft, furry growth around the base of the stalks is called *pulu.* At one time *pulu* was collected for stuffing mattresses, and a factory was located atop Volcanoes. But *pulu* breaks down and forms a very fine dust after a few years, so it never really became generally accepted for mattresses.

At high altitudes, young ferns and other plants will often produce new growth that turns bright red as protection against the sun's ultraviolet rays. You'll see it on new foliage before it hardens. Hawaiians called this new growth *liko.* Today, people still make lei from *liko* because it has so many subtle and beautiful colors. Ohia *liko* is a favorite for lei because it is so striking.

BIRDS

You'll spot birds all over the Big Island, from the coastal areas to the high mountain slopes. Some are found on other islands as well, but the ones listed below are found only or mainly on the Big Island. Every bird listed is either threatened or endangered.

Hawaii's Own

The ***nene,*** or Hawaiian goose, deserves special mention because it is Hawaii's state bird and is making a comeback from the edge of extinction. The *nene* is found only on the slopes of Mauna Loa, Hualalai, and Mauna Kea on the Big Island, and in Haleakala Crater on Maui. By the 1940s, fewer than 50 birds lived in the wild. Now approximately 125 birds live on Haleakala and 500 on the Big Island. Although the birds can be raised successfully in captivity, their life in the wild is still in question.

The *nene* is believed to be a descendant of the Canada goose, which it resembles. Geese are migratory birds that form strong kinship ties, mating for life. The *nene* is smaller than its Canadian cousin, has lost a great deal of webbing in its feet, and is perfectly at home away from water, foraging and nesting on rugged and bleak lava flows.

Good places to view *nene* are in Volcanoes National Park at Kipuka Nene Campground,

J.D. BISIGNANI

Fiddlehead ferns are prevalent along trails where the lava has weathered.

BOB RACE

The nene, *the state bird, lives only on the slopes of Mauna Loa and Mauna Kea on the Big Island and in the crater of Haleakala, Maui.*

Summit Caldera, Devastation Trail, and at Volcanoes Golf Course, at dawn and dusk. They gather at the golf course because they love to feed on grasses. The places to view them on the Kona side are at Puulani, a housing development north of Kailua-Kona; or at Kaloka Mauka, another housing development on the slopes of Mt. Hualalai. At the top of the road up Mt. Hualalai is a trail, a good place to see the *nene*. Unfortunately, as the housing developments proliferate and the residents invariably acquire dogs and cats, the *nene* will disappear. The *nene* is a perfect symbol of Hawaii: let it be, and it will live.

The **Hawaiian crow,** or *alala,* is reduced to less than 12 birds living on the slopes of Hualalai and Mauna Loa above the 3,000-foot level. It looks like the common raven but has a more melodious voice and sometimes dull brown feathers. The *alala* breeds in early spring, and the greenish-blue, black-flecked eggs hatch from April to June. It is extremely nervous while nesting and any disturbance will cause it to abandon its young.

The **Hawaiian hawk** *('io)* primarily lives on the slopes of Mauna Loa and Mauna Kea below 9,000 feet. It travels from there to other parts of the island and can often be seen kiting in the skies over Hawaii Volcanoes National Park, upland from Kailua-Kona, and in remote spots like Waimanu Valley. This noble bird, the royalty of the skies, symbolized the *ali'i.* The *'io* population was once dwindling, and many scientists feared that the bird was headed for extinction. The hawk exists only on the Big Island for reasons that are not entirely clear. The good news is that the *'io* is making a dramatic comeback, also for reasons that are still unclear. Speculation has it that it may be gaining resistance to some diseases, including malaria, or that it may have learned how to prey on the introduced rats, or even that it may be adapting to life in macadamia nut groves and other alternate habitats.

The ***akiapola'au*** is a five-inch yellow bird hardly bigger than its name. It lives mainly on the eastern slopes in ohia and koa forests above 3,500 feet. It has a long, curved upper beak for probing and a smaller lower beak it uses woodpecker-fashion. The *akiapola'au* opens its mouth wide, strikes the tree bark with its lower beak, and then uses the upper beak to scrape out any larvae or insects. Listen for the distinctive rapping sound to spot this melodious singer. The *akiapola'au* can be seen at the Hakalau Fish and Wildlife Preserve; south of Powerline Road off the Saddle Road; and along the Pu'u O'o Volcano Trail from Volcanoes National Park.

Marine Birds

Two coastal birds that breed on the high slopes of Hawaii's volcanoes and feed on the coast are the **Hawaiian petrel *('ua'u)*** and the **Newell shearwater *('a'o).*** The *'ua'u* lives on the barren high slopes and craters, where it nests in burrows or under stones. Breeding season lasts from mid-March to mid-October. Only one chick is born and nurtured on regurgitated squid and fish. The *'ua'u* suffers heavily from predation. The *'a'o* prefers the forested slopes of the interior. It breeds April-Nov., and spends its days at sea and nights inland. Feral cats and dogs reduce its numbers considerably.

Forest Birds

The following birds are found in the upland forests of the Big Island. The ***elepaio*** is found on other islands but is also spotted in Volcanoes National Park. This long-tailed (often held upright), five-inch brown bird (appearance can vary considerably) can be coaxed to come within touching distance of the observer. Sometimes it will sit on lower branches above your head and scold you. This bird was the special *aumakua* (personal spirit) of canoe builders in ancient lore. Fairly common in the rainforest, it is basically a flycatcher.

The ***amakihi*** and ***'i'iwi*** are endemic birds not endangered at the moment. The *amakihi* is one of the most common native birds; yellowish green, it frequents the high branches of the ohia, koa, and sandalwood looking for insects, nectar, or fruit. It is less specialized than most other Hawaiian birds, the main reason for its continued existence. The *'i'iwi* is a bright red bird with a salmon-colored, hooked bill. It's found on Hawaii in the forests above 2,000 feet. It too feeds on a variety of insects and flowers. The *'i'iwi* is known for a harsh voice that sounds like a squeaking hinge, but it's also capable of a melodious song. The *'i'iwi* can be spotted at the top of Kaloka Mauka (a housing development north of Kailua-Kona), at Powerline Road, which goes south off the Saddle Road, and at Puu O'o Trail in Volcanoes National Park.

'io

BOB RACE

The ***apapane*** is abundant on Hawaii, especially atop Volcanoes, and being the most common native bird, is the easiest to see. It's a chubby, red-bodied bird about five inches long with a black bill, legs, wingtips, and tail feathers. It's quick and flitty and has a wide variety of calls and songs, from beautiful warbles to mechanical buzzes. Its feathers were sought by Hawaiians to produce distinctive capes and helmets for the *ali'i.*

The **Hawaiian thrush *('oma'o)*** is a fairly common bird found above 3,000 feet in the windward forests of Hawaii. This eight-inch gray bird is a good singer, often seen perching with distinctive drooping wings and a shivering body. The *'oma'o* is probably descended from Townsend's solitaire. The best place to look for it is at the Thurston Lava Tube, where you can see it doing its baby-bird shivering-and-shaking act. A great mimic, it can sound like a cat or even like an old-fashioned radio with stations changing as you turn the dial. Another good place to see the *'oma'o* is along Powerline Road, off the Saddle Road.

The ***akepa*** is a four- to five-inch bird. The male is a brilliant orange to red, the female a drab green and yellow. It is found mainly on Hualalai and in windward forests.

The six-inch, bright yellow ***palila*** is found only on Hawaii in the forests of Mauna Kea above 6,000 feet. It depends exclusively upon *mamane* trees for survival, eating its pods, buds, and flowers. *Mamane* seedlings are destroyed by feral sheep. The Department of Land and Natural Resources for some inexplicable reason attempted to introduce sheep on the land that is the main refuge for the *palila,* which greatly endangered the bird's survival. The Sierra Club and Audubon Society immediately sued to prevent this environmental fiasco and were successful in winning their case in the local courts. The Department of Land and Natural Resources insisted on fighting the decision all the way to the Supreme Court. They lost and reluctantly got rid of the sheep. But instead of letting a bad decision fade away, they compounded their folly by introducing a different type of sheep. They were sued again, lost again, and again fought it all the way to the Supreme Court, wasting taxpayers' money every laborious inch of the way. As goes the *mamane,* so goes the *palila.* As goes the *palila,* so goes humanity's attempt to live in harmony with nature.

The ***po'ouli*** is a dark-brown, five-inch bird with a black mask and dark-brown feet. Its tail is short, and it sports a conical bill. It was saved from extinction through efforts of the Sierra Club and Audubon Society, who successfully had it added to the Federal List of Endangered Species. The bird has one remaining stronghold deep in the forests of Maui, although it has been purportedly spotted from time to time on Puu Ula Ula, a peak just off the Saddle Road that rises to 7,421 feet.

MAMMALS AND OTHERS

Hawaii had only two indigenous mammals: the monk seal, found throughout the islands (see

The Northwestern Islands chapter), and the hoary bat, found mainly on the Big Island. The remainder of the Big Island's mammals are transplants. But like anything else, including people, that has been in the islands long enough, they have taken on characteristics that make them "local."

The following animals are found primarily on the Big Island. The **Hawaiian hoary bat *('ope'ape'a)*** is a cousin of the Mainland bat, a strong flier that made it to Hawaii eons ago and developed its own species. Its tail has a whitish coloration, hence its name. Small populations of the bat are found on Maui and Kauai, but the greatest numbers of them are on the Big Island, where they have been spotted even on the upper slopes of Mauna Loa and Mauna Kea. The hoary bat has a 13-inch wingspan. Unlike other bats, it is a solitary creature, roosting in trees. It gives birth to twins in early summer and can often be spotted over Hilo and Kealakekua bays just around sundown.

Introduced Animals

The **feral dog *(ilio)*** is found on all the islands but especially on the slopes of Mauna Kea, where packs chase feral sheep. Poisoned and shot by local ranchers, it is diminishing in number. Black dogs, thought to be more tender, are still eaten in some Hawaiian and Filipino communities.

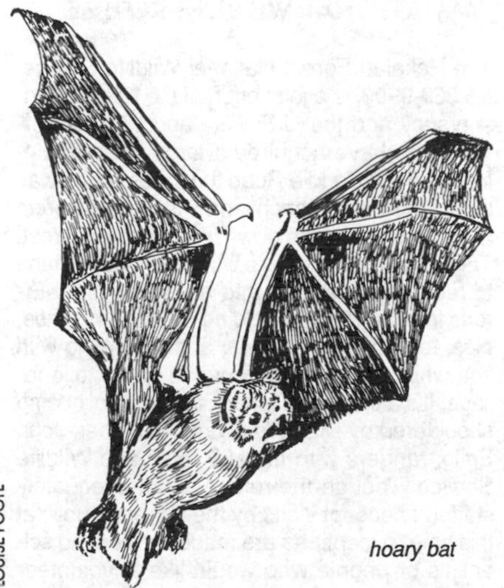

hoary bat

LOUISE FOOTE

The **feral sheep** is an escaped descendant of animals brought to the islands by Captain Vancouver in the 1790s, and of merinos brought to the island later and raised for their exceptional woolly fleece. It exists only on the Big Island, on the upper slopes of Mauna Loa, Mauna Kea, and Hualalai; by the 1930s, its numbers topped 40,000 head. The fleece is a buff brown, and its two-foot-wide curved horns are often sought as hunting trophies. Feral sheep are responsible for the overgrazing of young *mamane* trees, necessary to the endangered bird, *palila.* In 1979, a law was passed to exterminate or remove the sheep from Mauna Kea so that the native *palila* could survive.

The **mouflon sheep** was introduced to Lanai and Hawaii to cut down on overgrazing and serve as a trophy animal. This Mediterranean sheep can interbreed with feral sheep to produce a hybrid. It lives on the upper slopes of Mauna Loa and Mauna Kea. Unfortunately, its introduction has not been a success. No evidence concludes that the smaller family groups of mouflon cause less damage than the herding feral sheep, and hunters reportedly don't like the meat as much as feral mutton.

The **feral donkey,** better known as the "Kona nightingale," came to Hawaii as a beast of burden. Domesticated donkeys are found on all islands, but a few wild herds still roam the Big Island along the Kona Coast, especially near the exclusive Kona Village Resort at Kaupulehu.

Feral cattle were introduced by Captain Vancouver, who gave a few domesticated head to Kamehameha; immediately a *kapu* (taboo) against killing them went into effect for 10 years. The lush grasses of Hawaii were perfect and the cattle flourished; by the early 1800s they were out of control and were hunted and exterminated. Finally, Mexican cowboys were brought to Hawaii to teach the locals how to be range hands. From this legacy sprang the Hawaiian *paniolo.*

MARINELIFE

Humpback whales migrate to Hawaiian waters yearly, arriving in late December and departing by mid-March. The best places to view them are along the South Kona Coast, especially at Kealakekua Bay and Ka Lae ("South Point"), with many sightings off the Puna coast around Isaac Hale Beach Park, and in North Kohala just in front of Mookini Luakini Heiau.

Hawksbill Turtle

Hawaii Volcanoes National Park stretches from the top of Mauna Kea all the way down to the sea. It is here, around Apua Point, that three of the last-known nesting sites of the very endangered hawksbill turtle are found. This creature has been ravished in the Pacific, where it is ruthlessly hunted for its shell which is made into women's jewelry, especially combs. It is illegal to bring items made from turtle shell into the U.S., but the hunt goes on.

Billfish

Although these magnificent game fish occur in various South Sea and Hawaiian waters, catching them is easiest in the clear, calm waters off the Kona Coast. The billfish—swordfish, sailfish, marlin, and *a'u*—share two distinctive common features: a long, spearlike or swordlike snout, and a prominent dorsal fin. The three main species of billfish caught are the blue, striped, and black marlin. Of these three, the **blue marlin** is the leading game fish in Kona waters. The blue has tipped the scales at well over 1,000 pounds, but the average fish weighs in at 300-400 pounds. When alive, this fish is a striking cobalt blue, but death brings a color change to slate blue. It feeds on skipjack tuna; throughout the summer, fishing boats look for schools of tuna as a tip-off to blues in the area. The **black marlin** is the largest and most coveted catch for blue-water anglers. This solitary fish is infrequently found off the banks of Kona. Granddaddies can weigh 1,800 pounds, but the average is a mere 200. The **striped marlin** is the most common commercial billfish, a highly prized food served in finer restaurants and often sliced into sashimi. Its coloration is a remarkable royal blue. Its spectacular leaps when caught gives it a great reputation as a fighter. The striped marlin is smaller than the other marlins, so a 100-pounder is a very good catch. For more information see "Sports and Recreation" later in this chapter.

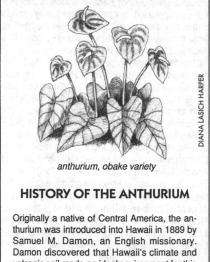

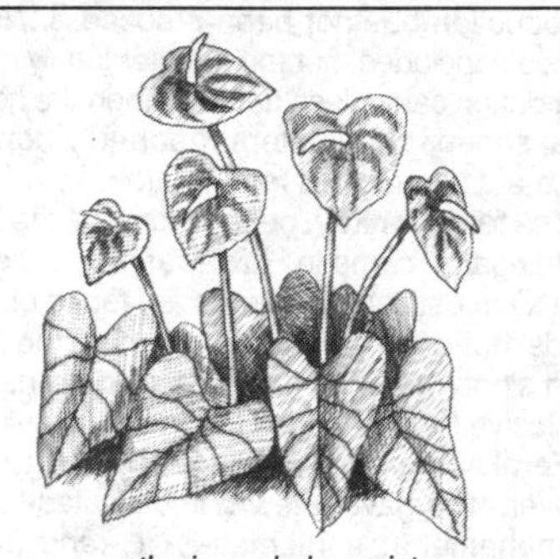

anthurium, obake variety

HISTORY OF THE ANTHURIUM

Originally a native of Central America, the anthurium was introduced into Hawaii in 1889 by Samuel M. Damon, an English missionary. Damon discovered that Hawaii's climate and volcanic soil made an ideal environment for this exotic flower. Over the years since then, anthurium production has turned into a million-dollar export industry with all the major growers located on the Big Island.

THE HAKALAU FOREST NATIONAL WILDLIFE REFUGE

The Hakalau Forest National Wildlife Refuge, tel. 969-9909, is a joint effort of the Nature Conservancy and the U.S. Fish and Wildlife Service, who have acquired a large tract of rainforest off the Saddle Road that goes all the way up to the Parker Ranch lands. It's upland forest and scrub that drifts down into solid rainforest. These two agencies are working hand-in-hand to reconvert the area into natural habitat. Efforts include fencing; ridding the area of cattle, pigs, feral dogs, and cats; and replanting with koa while removing introduced and exotic foliage. It's a tremendous task that's mainly being shouldered by Dick Watts and his helper, John Emig, rangers with the U.S. Fish and Wildlife Service. Though the refuge is not adequately staffed to accept visits by the general public at this time, exceptions are made for working scientists or people who would like to volunteer for an ongoing project. If you *truly* have a dedication to help and aren't afraid to get your hands dirty, contact Dick for a rewarding experience. The logistics of setting up your visit require you be willing to work for at least an entire day in physically demanding conditions. The refuge is very beautiful, a diamond in the rough, which encompasses an incredible rainforest unlike any on the Big Island.

HISTORY

The Big Island plays a significant role in Hawaii's history. A long list of "firsts" have occurred here. Historians generally believe (backed up by oral tradition) the Big Island was the first to be settled by the Polynesians. The dates now used are from A.D. 600 to 700. Hawaii is geographically the closest island to Polynesia; Mauna Loa and especially Mauna Kea, with its white summit, present easily spotted landmarks. Psychologically, the Polynesian wayfarers would have been very attracted to Hawaii as a lost homeland. Compared to Tahiti and most other South Sea Islands (except for Fiji), it's huge. It *looked* like the "promised land." Some may wonder why the Polynesians chose to live atop an obviously active volcano, and not bypass it for a more congenial island. The volcanism of the Big Island is comparatively gentle, and the lava flows follow predictable routes and rarely turn killer. The animistic Hawaiians would have been drawn to live where the godly forces of nature were so apparent. The mana would be exceptionally strong, and therefore the *ali'i* would be great. Tahitians eclipsed this power and introduced human sacrifice to Hawaii at Wahaula Heiau in the Puna District in the 13th century, and from there *luakini* (human sacrifice temples) spread throughout the islands.

The Great One

The greatest native son of Hawaii, Kamehameha, was born under mysterious circumstances in the Kohala District, probably in 1753. Kamehameha became a renowned warrior and a loyal retainer to his uncle, Kalaniopuu, the *moi* (ruler) of Hawaii. Before Kalaniopuu died, he made Kamehameha the keeper of the feathered family war god, Kukailimoku, or Ku the Land Snatcher, while Kamehameha's cousins Kiwalao and his half-brother Keoua engaged in a civil war over land rights. Kamehameha, aided by disgruntled chiefs from Kona, waged war on both, and at Mokuohai, Kiwalao was killed. Kamehameha went on to fight on Maui. By this time he had acquired a small ship, the *Fair American,* and using cannon manned by two white sailors, Isaac Davis and John Young, he defeated the Maui warriors at Iao Valley. If he could defeat Keoua at home, he would be king of all Hawaii.

The Gods Speak

A great oracle from Kauai announced war would end on Hawaii only after a great *heiau* was built at Puukohola, dedicated by the corpse of a great chief. Kamehameha instantly set about building this *heiau,* and through cunning, wisdom, and true belief placed the conquest of Hawaii in the hands of the gods. Meanwhile, a fleet of war canoes belonging to Kahekili of Maui attacked Kamehameha's forces at Waimanu, near Waipio. Aided again by the *Fair American* and Davis and Young, Kamehameha won a decisive battle and subdued Kahekili once and for all. Keoua seized this opportunity to ravage Kamehameha's lands all the way from Waipio to Hilo. He sent his armies south through Kau, but when the middle legions were passing the foot of Kilauea, it erupted and suffocated them with poisonous gas and a heavy deposit of ash. Footprints, encased in the cementlike ash, still mark their last steps.

Kamehameha and Keoua both took this as a direct sign from the gods. Kamehameha returned to Puukohala and finished the *heiau.* Upon completion he summoned Keoua, who came by canoe with a small band of warriors resplendent in feather helmet and cape. He knew the fate that awaited him, and when he stepped ashore he was slaughtered by Keeaumoku. Keoua's body was laid on the altar, and at that moment the islands of Hawaii were united under one supreme ruler, Kamehameha, The Lonely One. He ruled until his death in 1819, and his passing marked the beginning of the end for old Hawaii.

Great Changes

The great navigator and explorer, Captain Cook, was killed at Kealakekua Bay on February 14, 1779. Kalaniopuu was still alive at the time and Kamehameha was only a minor chief, although Cook had previously written about him in the ship's log when he came aboard off Maui. During Kamehameha's reign ships from the United States, England, and various European countries came to trade. Americans monopolized the lucrative sandalwood business with China, and New England whalers discovered the rich whaling waters. The Englishman, Captain Vancouver, became a trusted advisor of Kamehameha and told him about the white people's form of worship, while introducing plants and animals such as oranges, grapes, cows, goats, and sheep. He even interceded for Kamehameha with his headstrong queen, Kaahumanu, coaxing her out from her hiding place under a rock at Pu'uhonua o Honauanau, where she had sought refuge from Kamehameha's wrath.

When Kamehameha died in 1819, Hawaii was ripe for change. His two great queens, Kaahumanu and Keopuolani, realized the old ways were coming to an end. They encouraged Liholiho (Kamehameha II) to end the *kapu* system. Men and women were forbidden to eat together, and those who violated this principal *kapu* were immediately killed to placate the gods before they retaliated with grave destruction. Keopuolani defied this belief when she sat down with Kauikeaouli, the seven-year-old brother of Liholiho. The gods remained quiet. Encouraged, Liholiho called for a great *luau* at Kailua, and openly sat down to eat with his chiefs and chieftesses. Symbolically, the impotent gods were toppled with every bite, and *heiau* and idols were razed throughout the land.

Into this spiritual vortex sailed the brig ***Thaddeus*** on April 4, 1820. They had set sail from Boston on October 23, 1819, lured to the Big Island by Henry Opukahaia, a local boy born at Napoopoo in 1792. Coming ashore at Kailua, the first missionary packet convinced Liholiho to give them a one-year trial period. Hawaii changed forever in those brief months. By 1824 the new faith had such a foothold that Chieftess Keopuolani climbed to the firepit atop Kilauea and defied Pele. This was even more striking than the previous breaking of the food *kapu* because the strength of Pele could actually be seen. Keopuolani ate forbidden *ohelo* berries and cried out, "Jehovah is my God." Over the next decades the governing of Hawaii slipped away from the Big Island and moved to the new port cities of Lahaina, and later, Honolulu. In 1847, the Parker Ranch began with a two-acre grant given to John Parker. He coupled this with 360 acres given to his *ali'i* wife Kipikane by the land division known as the Great *Mahele.*

GOVERNMENT

The county of Hawaii is almost entirely Democratic with a token Republican state senator or representative here and there. Of the 25 State Senatorial Districts, Hawaii County is represented by three. The 1st District is the whole southern part of the island, from Puna to Kailua; its representative is one of the few Republicans holding office on the island. The 2nd District is mainly Hilo. The 3rd District takes in the whole northern section and is a shared district with East Maui. The combination of these two areas has been traditional, even from old Hawaiian times.

Of 51 seats in the State House of Representatives, Hawaii County has six. The 6th District is again shared with East Maui and takes in most of South Kohala. At this time, all representatives are Democrats, except for a Republican representing Kailua-Kona, 5th District.

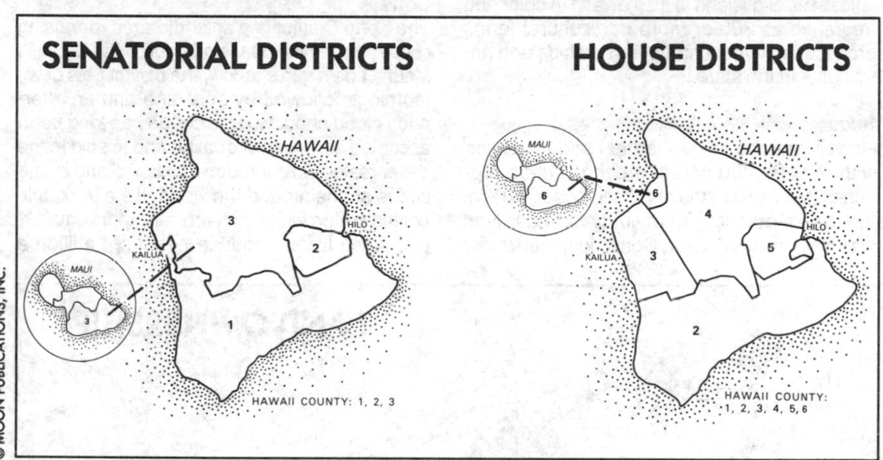

ECONOMY

The Big Island's economy is the most agriculturally based in the state. Over 6,000 farmhands, horticultural workers, and *paniolo* work the land, producing over half of the state's vegetables and melons, and over 75% of the fruit, leading all other islands, especially in papayas. The Big Island produces 33 million pounds of macadamia nuts, all the state's production, except for a small farm here and there on the other islands. The Big Island is also awash in color and fragrance as 300 or more horticultural farms produce the largest number of orchids and anthuriums in the state.

Sugar

Hawaii was the state's largest sugar grower, with over 90,000 acres in cane. These produced four million tons of refined sugar, 40% of the state's output. The majority of sugar land was along the Hamakua Coast, long known for its abundant water supply. At one time, the cane was even transported to the mills by water flumes. Another large pocket of cane fields is found on the southern part of the island, mostly in Puna. Recently, the Hamakua Sugar Company laid off most of its personnel and the future of the Big Island's sugar production is in a state of great flux.

Coffee

The Kona District is a splendid area for raising coffee; it gives the beans a beautiful tan. Lying in Mauna Loa's rain shadow, the district gets dewy mornings followed by sunshine and an afternoon cloud shadow. This coffee has long been accepted as gourmet quality, and is sold in the better restaurants throughout Hawaii and in fine coffee shops around the world. It's a dark, full-bodied coffee with a rich aroma. Approximately 650 small farms produce nearly $4 million a

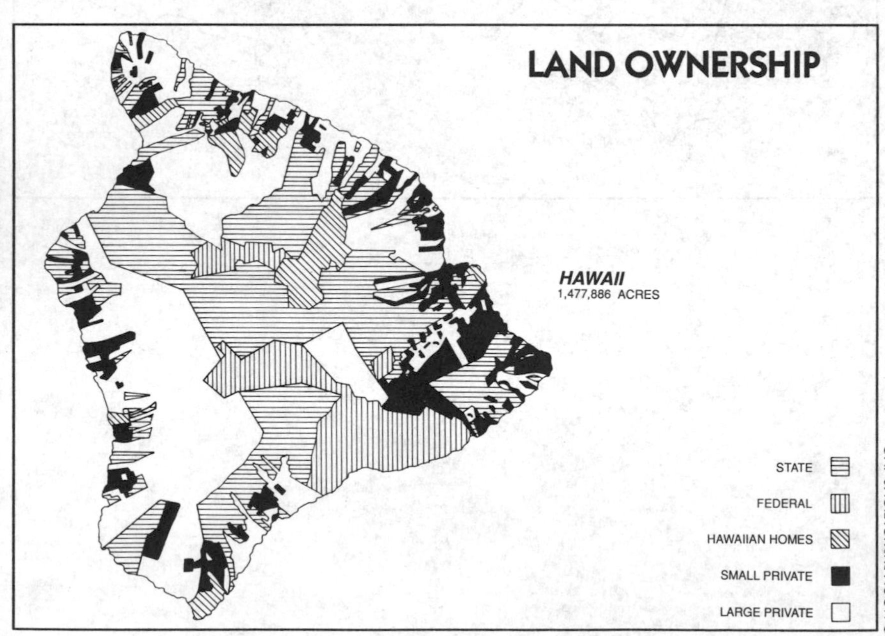

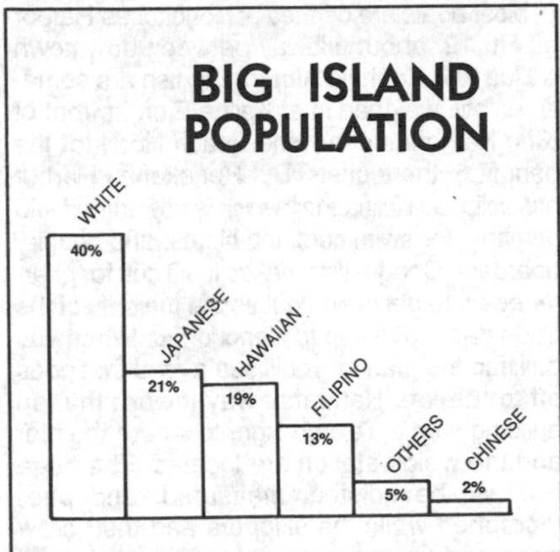

year in coffee revenue. Few, however, make it a full-time business.

Cattle

Hawaii's cattle ranches produce over 18 million pounds of beef per year, 65% of the state's total. More than 360 independent ranches are located on the island, but they are dwarfed both in size and production by the massive Parker Ranch, which alone is three-quarters the size of Oahu.

The Military

There are just under 200 Army personnel on the island, with about the same number of dependents. Most of these people are attached to the enormous Pohakuloa Military Reserve in the center of the island. There are also a few minor installations around Hilo and at Kilauea.

Tourism

Over 4,000 island residents are directly employed by the hotel industry, and many more indirectly serve the tourists. There are slightly more than 7,500 hotel rooms, with the greatest concentration in Kona and South Kohala. They have the lowest occupancy rate in the state, which rarely rises above 60%. Of the major islands, Hawaii receives the fewest tourists annually, only about 7,500 on any given day.

PEOPLE

With 120,000 people or so, the Big Island has the second-largest island population in Hawaii, just under 10% of the state's total. However, it has the smallest population density of the main islands, with barely 25 people per square mile. Hilo has the largest population with 38,000 residents, followed by Kailua-Kona with under 10,000, and Captain Cook with 2,500 or so. The ethnic breakdown of the 120,000 people is as follows: 40% Caucasian, 21% Japanese, 19% Hawaiian, 13% Filipino, 2% Chinese, 5% other.

SPORTS AND RECREATION

You'll have no problem having fun on the Big Island. Everybody goes outside to play. You can drive golf balls over lagoons, smack tennis balls at over 50 private and public courts, ski, snorkel, windsurf, gallop a horse, bag a wild turkey, or latch on to a marlin that'll tail-walk across a windowpane sea. Choose your sport and have a ball.

DEEP-SEA AND FRESHWATER FISHING

Hawaii has some of the most exciting and productive blue waters in all the world. You'll find a sportfishing fleet made up of skippers and crews who are experienced professional anglers. You can also fish from jetties, piers, rocks, or shore. If rod and reel don't strike your fancy, try the old-fashioned throw net, or take along a spear when you go snorkeling or scuba diving. There's nighttime torch fishing that requires special skills and equipment, and freshwater fishing in public areas. Streams and irrigation ditches yield introduced trout, bass, and catfish. While you're at it, you might want to try crabbing for Kona and Samoan crabs, or working low-tide areas after sundown hunting octopus, a tantalizing island delicacy.

Fishing Boats And Charters

The fishing around the Big Island's Kona Coast ranges from excellent to outstanding! It's legendary for marlin fishing (see "Deep Sea Fishing" under "Sports and Recreation" in the Out and About chapter for a complete description of these marvelous fish), but there are other fish in the sea. The vast majority of charter boats are berthed at Honokohau Small Boat Harbor just north of Kailua-Kona (see "Honokohau Marina" under "Sights" under "Kailua-Kona and Vicinity" in the Kona chapter). The best times of year for marlin are July-September and January-March (when the generally larger females arrive). August is the optimum month. Rough seas can keep boats in for a few days during December and early January, but by February all are generally out.

You can hire a boat for a private or share charter, staying out for a full day or half day. Boat size varies, but four anglers per mid-size boat is about average. Approximate rates are: private, full day $400-600, half day $250-350; share, full day $125, half day $85. Full days are eight hours, half days four, with three-quarter days and overnighters available too. No licenses are required and all gear is provided. Bring your own lunch, beverages, and camera. Some of the best boats with top-notch reputations include *Summer Rain, Notorious,* and *Kona Rainbow.*

To charter a boat contact the individual captains directly, check at your hotel activities desk, or book through one of the following agencies. **Kona Marlin Center** at Honokohau Harbor, tel. 329-7529 or (800) 648-7529, is owned by Jim Dahlberg, who was born and raised on the Big Island. This is the main booking facility in the area. If you're after a company that's knowledgeable about getting you onto a boat that will bring you to waters where you'll have the opportunity to catch one of the twirling and gigantic "big blues," this is the place to call. Other general booking agencies include: **Kona Activities Center** in Kailua-Kona, tel. 329-3171; **Kona Coast Activities** at Honokohau Harbor, tel. 329-2971; **Kona Charter Skippers Assoc.,** Box 806, Kailua-Kona, HI 96740, tel. 329-3600; **Mauna Kea Beach Hotel,** Travel Desk, Box 218, Kamuela, HI 96743, tel. 882-7222; and **Jack's Kona Charters,** tel. 325-7558 or (800) 545-5662, who can put you on any number of boats.

Most boats are berthed at Honokohau Harbor off Rt. 19, about midway between downtown Kailua and Keahole Airport. Big fish are sometimes still weighed in at Kailua Pier, in front of King Kamehameha Kona Beach Hotel for the benefit of the tourists. But Honokohau Harbor has eclipsed Kailua Pier, which is now tamed and primarily for swimmers, triathletes, and boogie-boarders. Congestion makes it difficult for charter boats to get in and out so the majority of the trade has moved up to Honokohau. When you pull into the marina, you'll see a road that goes off to the left. Head that way toward the tan building with a Texaco sign, to where the pier and the weigh-station are located. The huge fish will be hoisted, measured, and photographed while the skippers and their crew clean and prepare the boat for the next day's outing. If you're into deep-sea fishing, this is your chance to pick a likely boat and to get acquainted with the crew.

An excellent publication listing boats and general deep-sea fishing information is ***Fins and Fairways, Hawaii,*** Box P, Kailua-Kona, HI 96745, tel. 325-6171, published by Capt. Tom Armstrong. This tabloid, available free at newsstands and in hotel/condo lobbies, is filled with descriptions of boats, phone numbers, captains' names, maps, and photos of recent catches. Write for subscription rates.

Deep-Sea Fishing

Most game-fishing boats work the waters on the calmer Kona side of the island. Some skippers, carrying anglers who are accustomed to the sea, will also work the much rougher windward coasts and island channels where the fish bite just as well. Trolling is the preferred method of deep-sea fishing; this is done usually in waters of 1,000-2,000 fathoms (a fathom is six feet). The skipper will either "area fish," which means running in a crisscross pattern over a known productive area, or "ledge fish," which involves trolling over submerged ledges where the game fish are known to feed. The most advanced marine technology, available on many boats, sends sonar bleeps searching for fish. On deck, the crew and anglers scan the horizon in the age-old Hawaiian tradition—searching for clusters of seabirds feeding on baitfish pursued to the surface by the huge and aggressive game fish.

"Still fishing," or "bottom fishing" with hand-lines, yields some tremendous fish.

Coastal And Freshwater Fishing

You don't have to hire a boat to catch fish! The coastline is productive too. *Ulua* are caught all along the coast south of Hilo, and at South Point and Kealakekua Point. *Papio* and *halalu* are caught in bays around the island, while *manini* and *'ama'ama* hit from Kawaihae to Puako. Hilo Bay is easily accessible to anyone, and the fishing is very exciting, especially at the mouth of the Wailuku River.

Licensed fishing is limited to the **Waiakea Public Fishing Area,** a state-operated facility in downtown Hilo. This 26-acre pond offers a variety of saltwater and brackish-water species. A license is required. You can pick one up at sporting goods stores or at the Division of Conservation and Resources Enforcement Office, 75 Aupuni St., Hilo, HI 96720, tel. 961-7291.

SNORKELING, SCUBA, AND OTHER WATER SPORTS

Scuba

Those in the know consider the deep diving along the steep drop-offs of Hawaii's geologically young coastline some of the best in the state. The ocean surrounding the Big Island has not had a chance to turn the relatively new lava to sand, which makes the visibility absolutely perfect, even to depths of 150 feet or more. There's also 60-70 miles of coral belt around the Big Island, which adds up to a magnificent diving experience. Only advanced divers should attempt deep-water dives, but beginners and snorkelers will have many visual thrills inside the protected bays and coves. (See "Beaches" in the travel sections.)

Snorkel/Scuba Companies And Equipment Rentals

Snorkel and scuba rental gear as well as escorted dives and lessons are available from the following.

One of the best outfits to dive with on the Big Island is **Dive Makai** in Kona, tel. 329-2025, operated by Tom Shockley and Lisa Choquette. These very experienced divers have run this service for years and have many dedicated customers. Both Tom and Lisa are conservationists who help preserve the fragile reef. They've worked very hard with the Diver's Council to protect dive sites from fish collectors and to protect the reef from destruction by anchors. Their motto, "We care," is not a trite saying, as they continue to preserve the reef for you and your children.

Another excellent diving outfit is **Jack's Diving Locker,** tel. 329-7585 or (800) 345-4807, in the Kona Inn Shopping Village—a responsible outfit that does a good job of watching out for their customers and taking care of the reef. They run diving and snorkeling excursions along the Kona Coast from Kealakekua Bay to Keahole Point, which takes in over 50 dive sites (most of which have permanent moorings to protect the reef from damage by anchoring). Jack's also specializes in snorkel sales and rentals ($7.50 for 24 hours), scuba rentals, certification classes, and dive classes. You can do a five-hour snorkel/sail on the *Blue Dolphin* departing at 8:30 a.m., or on their larger *Na Pali Kai II* (ask for rates).

King Kamehameha Divers in the King Kamehameha Kona Beach Hotel, Kailua-Kona, tel. 329-5662, offers a daily boat charter that gives you a two-tank certified dive with your own gear for $65, $75 with their gear. An introductory dive is $95, and snorkeling is $35. This includes continental breakfast, lunch, and soft drinks. Rental rates for snorkeling gear run $7.50 for 24 hours, boogie boards $15.

Big Island Divers, tel. 329-6068, in the Honokohau Small Boat Harbor, offers a scuba certification course for only $59.95 that's given on four consecutive Saturdays or Wednesdays, so you must intend to stay on the Big Island for that length of time. The normal four-day course costs $450. They also rent complete snorkel gear for only $6 for 24 hours.

Kohala Divers, located along Rt. 270 in Kawaihae, open daily 8 a.m.-5 p.m., tel. 882-7774, offers scuba certification for $300, snorkel rentals for $10 (24 hours), and scuba rentals for $22. They lead two-tank dives for $75, and will take snorkelers along if they have room on the boat ($15). It's a bit far to go from Kailua-Kona but it's a big savings, and they're the only dive company along the Kohala coast.

Snorkel Bob's, tel. 329-0770, in the parking lot next to the Kona Hilton right in front of Huggo's Restaurant, offers snorkel gear for $15

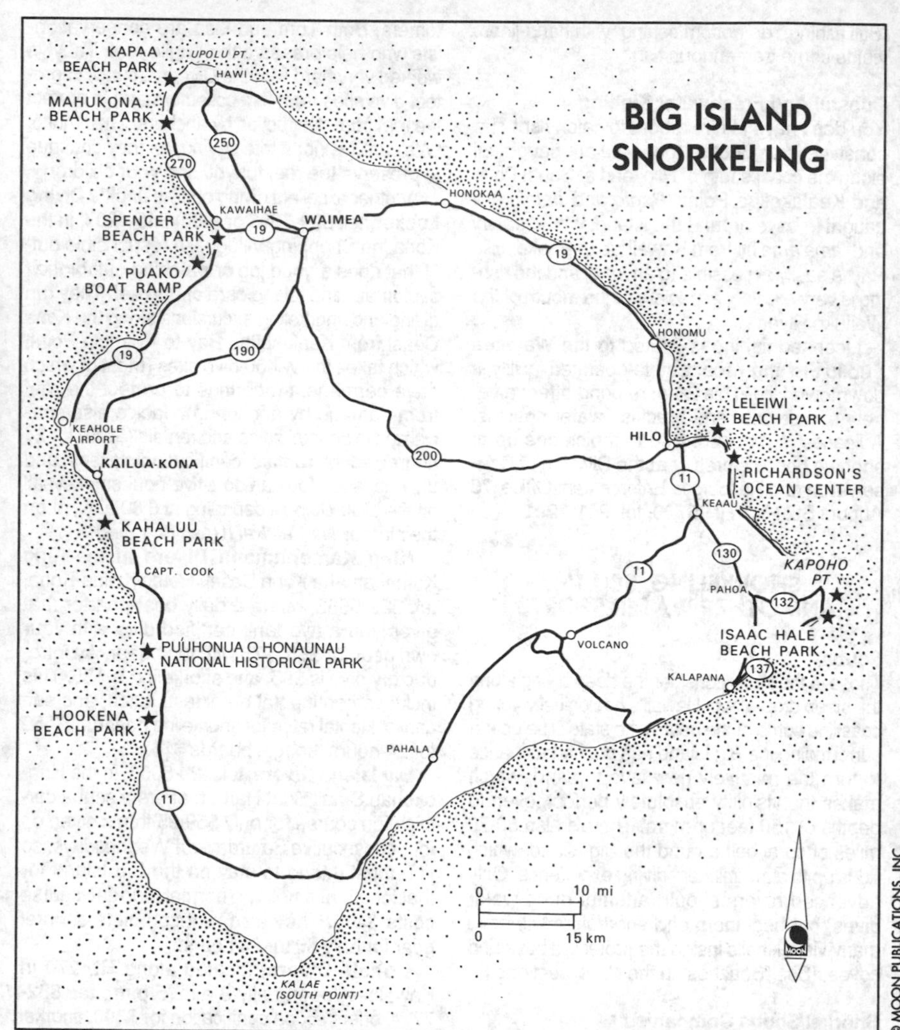

per week for basic equipment. Upgrading to a comfortable surgical silicone mask with Italian fins is $27. Boogie boards are $9-15 per day, $22-35 per week depending on quality.

The **Nautilus Dive Center,** 382 Kamehameha Ave., Hilo, tel. 935-6939, is one of the only dive companies on the Hilo side, and offers a free informative dive map.

Snuba, tel. 326-7446, offers a new underwater concept that is perfect for an introductory underwater adventure. Tethered to a flotation raft bearing a scuba tank, you are unencumbered by the normal scuba equipment and your descent is limited to under 20 feet. For those who feel timid about scuba diving or who just want a new, fun-filled adventure, Snuba might be

TENNIS COURTS OF THE BIG ISLAND

PUBLIC COURTS

Under jursidiction of the Department of Parks and Recreation, 25 Aupuni St., Hilo, HI 96720, tel. 961-8311.

LOCATION	NAME OF COURT	NO. OF COURTS	LIGHTED
Hilo	Ainaole Park	1	No
Hilo	Hakalau Park	2	No
Hilo	Hilo High School	1	No
Hilo	Hoolulu Park	8	Yes
Hilo	Lincoln Park	4	Yes
Hilo	Mohouli Park	2	No
Hilo	University of Hawaii-Hilo College	2	No
Honokaa	Honokaa Park	2	Yes
Kapaau	Kamehameha Park	2	Yes
Kau	Kau High School	2	Yes
Keaau	Keaau Park	2	No
Kona	Greenwell Park	1	Yes
Kona	Kailua Park (Old Kona Airport)	4	Yes
Kona	Kailua Playground	1	Yes
Kona	Keauhou Park	1	No
Waimea	Waimea Park	2	Yes
Waimea	Hawaii Prep Academy	4	Yes

HOTEL AND PRIVATE COURTS OPEN TO THE PUBLIC

LOCATION	NAME OF COURT	NO. OF COURTS	LIGHTED
Kailua-Kona	King Kamehameha Kona Beach Hotel (fee)	2	Yes
Kailua-Kona	Kona Hilton Beach and Tennis Resort (fee)	4	Yes
Kamuela	Waimea Park	2	Yes
Keauhou-Kona	Keauhou Beach Hotel (fee)	6	Yes
Keauhou-Kona	Kona Surf Hotel Racket Club (fee)	7	Yes
Kona	Country Club Villas	2	No
Pahala	Seamountain Tennis Center (fee)	4	No
Waikoloa	Waikoloa village (fee)	2	Yes

the answer. Prices are $49 for a beach dive, $40 for a boat dive.

Larger hotels often have snorkel equipment for guests, but if it isn't free, it always costs more than if you rented it from a dive shop. Scuba and snorkel cruises are booked through the various activities centers mentioned in "Sightseeing Tours" under "Getting Around" later in this chapter, and at your hotel travel desk.

An alternative to boat dives is shore diving. *Shore Diving in Kona* is a great book listing sites, equipment, regulations, and suggestions for successful and safe dives. If your budget is limited and you're an experienced shore diver, it's a way to have a great outing at a reasonable price.

Snorkel/Scuba Dive Boats

Snorkeling, scuba, and some snuba excursions are provided by the following: The **Fair Wind,** tel. 322-2788, leaving daily from magnificent Keauhou Bay (snuba too); **The Body Glove,** tel. 326-7122 (snuba too); **Capt. Cook VI,** tel. 329-6411;

GOLF COURSES OF THE BIG ISLAND

LOCATION	COURSE	PAR	YARDS	FEES	CART
South Kohala	Hapuna Golf Course, One Mauna Kea Beach Dr., Kohala Coast, HI 96743, tel. 882-1035	72	6069	$90	incl.
South Kohala	Mauna Kea Beach Hotel Golf Course, Box 218, Kamuela, HI 96743, tel. 882-7222	72	6365	$130	incl.
South Kohala	Mauna Lani Resort, Frances H. I'i Brown Golf Courses, Box 4959, Kawaihae, HI 96743, tel. 885-6655	North 72	6361	$150	incl.
		South 72	6370	$150	incl.
South Kohala	Waikoloa Beach Golf Courses, Box 5100, Waikoloa, HI 96743, tel. 883-6060	Beach 70	5958	$95	incl.
		King's 72	6010	$95	incl.
South Kohala	Waikoloa Village Golf Course, Box 3068, Waikoloa, HI 96743, tel. 883-9621	72	6142	$75	incl.
Waimea	Waimea Country Club, Box 2155, Kamuela, HI 96743, tel. 885-8053	72	6661	$50	incl.
Kailua-Kona	Kona Country Club, 78-7000 Ali'i Dr., Kailua-Kona, HI 96740, tel. 322-2595	Mountain 72	5828	$100	incl.
		Ocean 72	6165	$100	incl.

Kamanu Charters, tel. 329-2021; **Sea Quest,** tel. 329-7238; and **Captain Beans',** tel. 329-2955. Also see "Sightseeing Tours" under "Getting Around" later in this chapter.

Surfing And Sailboarding

The surfing off the Big Island is rather uninspiring compared to that off the other islands. The reefs are treacherous and the surf is lazy. Some surfers bob around off the north section of Hilo Bay, and sometimes in Kealakekua and Wailua bays on the Kona side. Puna also attracts a few off Isaac Hale and Kaimu beaches, and up north off Waipio Valley Beach. However, the winds are great for sailboarding.

Jet Skiing, Parasailing, And Water-Skiing

For those interested in thrill rides, **Kona Water Sports,** tel. 329-1593, rents Jet Skis and conducts water-skiing and parasailing excursions.

SKIING

Bored with sun and surf? Strap the "boards" to your feet and hit the slopes of Mauna Kea. There are no lifts so you'll need a 4WD to get to the top, and someone willing to pick you up again at the bottom. You can rent 4WDs from the car rental agencies already mentioned, but if that seems like too much hassle, contact **Ski Guides**

GOLF COURSES OF THE BIG ISLAND

LOCATION	COURSE	PAR	YARDS	FEES	CART
Kailua-Kona	Makalei Hawaii Country Club, 72-3890 Hawaii Belt Rd., Kailua-Kona, HI 96740, tel. 325-6625	72	6101	$77	incl.
Kau	Discovery Harbor, Kau District, HI 96772, tel. 929-7353	72	6640 (closed Tues.)	$20	incl.
Kau	Seamountain Golf Course, Box 85, Pahala, HI 96777, tel. 928-6222	72	6106	$36	$14
Kau	Volcano Golf and Country Club, Box 46, Volcanoes National Park, HI 96718, tel. 967-7331	72	5936	$52	incl.
Hilo	Hilo Municipal Golf Course, 340 Haihai St., Hilo, HI 96720, tel. 959-7711	71	6320	$6 (weekdays) $8 (weekends and holidays)	$14.50
Hilo	Naniloa Country Club, 120 Banyan Dr., Hilo, HI 96720, tel. 935-3000	36	2875	$35 (9 holes)	$14 (for 18)
Hamakua Coast	Hamakua Country Club, Box 344, Honokaa, HI 96727, tel. 775-7244	33	2520 (9 holes) (no club rental)	$10	(no carts)

Hawaii, Box 2020, Kamuela, HI 96743, tel. 885-4188 or 889-6747. Here you can rent skis and they'll provide the "lifts" to the top. You can expect snow Dec.-May, but you can't always count on it.

GOLF

The Big Island has some of the most beautiful golf links in Hawaii. Robert Trent Jones Sr. and Jr. have both built exceptional courses here. Dad built the Mauna Kea Beach Hotel course, while the kid built his at the Waikoloa Beach Resort. Both links are in South Kohala, as is another spectacular course at the nearby Mauna Lani. If these are too rich for your blood, you can hit nine holes in Hilo for about $10. How about golfing at Volcano Golf Course, where if you miss a short putt, you can blame it on an earthquake?

TENNIS

Many tennis courts dot the Big Island, and plenty of them are free. County courts are under the control of the Department of Parks and Recreation, which maintains a combination of lighted and unlit courts in Hilo, Kona, and Waimea. Some private and hotel courts are open to the public for a fee, while others restrict play to guests only.

HUNTING

Huge unpopulated expanses of grassland, forest, and scrubby mountainside are very good for hunting. The Big Island's game includes feral pig, sheep, and goats, plus a variety of pheasant, quail, dove, and wild turkey. Mauna Kea Beach Hotel guests can hunt on the Parker Ranch, while the **McCandless Ranch** near Captain Cook supplies guides for its 30,000 acres. For information contact Steve Arrington, Box 63 G, Captain Cook, HI 96704, tel. 328-2349/2389. Public game lands are located throughout the island; a license is required to take birds and game. For full information, write Division of Forestry and Wildlife, 1643 Kilauea Ave., Box 4849, Hilo, HI 96720, tel. 961-7221.

HORSEBACK RIDING

Waipio Naalapa Trail Rides, operated by Sherri Hannum, tel. 775-0419, offers the most unique rides on Hawaii. Sherri and her family have lived in Waipio Valley for 20 years and know its history, geology, and legends intimately. She offers pick-up service from Kukuihaele for the half-day rides ($65). Sherri treats guests like family. If you have time, don't miss this wonderful adventure! Another great activity is a mule-drawn tour of the magnificent Waipio Valley with **Waipio Valley Wagon Tour,** tel. 775-9518, owned and operated by Peter Tolin. The two-hour tours leave four times daily at 9 a.m., 10:30 a.m., 12:30 p.m., and 2 or 4 p.m. The cost is $35, children under 12 half price, children two and under free. For full information on both the above rides, see "Activities" under "Waipio Valley" in the Hamakua Coast chapter.

H.R.T. Waipio Tour Desk, tel. 775-7291, located in the Hawaiian Holiday Macadamia Nut Factory in Honokaa, offers van and horseback riding through fabulous Waipio Valley (see "Honokaa to Kukuihaele" in the Hamakua Coast chapter). Daily van tours at 9:30 a.m. and 1 p.m. (pick-up service from your hotel costs extra) usually last 90 minutes, including a short shuttle to Waipio, and cost $26 per person. The horseback rides start at the same times but last two and a half hours and cost $65, including transportation from Honokaa to Waipio. Make reservations 24 hours in advance.

Enjoyable rides are also offered by the **Mauna Kea Beach Hotel** (to nonguests also), tel. 882-7222. They have an arrangement with the Parker Ranch, which will supply a *paniolo* to guide you over the quarter-million acres of open range on the slopes of Mauna Kea. The stables are at Parker Ranch headquarters in Waimea.

King's Trail Rides, tel. 323-2388, has offices along Rt. 11 high above the Kona Coast on the outskirts of Kealakekua. Prices are $50 for a one-and-one-half-hour trail ride, $60 for two hours, and $79 for a five-hour adventure, half of which is on horseback (lunch included). After being driven to the 4,200-foot level, you mount up to ride the Kealakekua Ranch lands, a 20,000-acre working spread. This is the "real McCoy."

CAMPING AND HIKING

The Big Island has the best camping in the state, with more facilities and less competition for campsites than on the other islands. Over three dozen parks fringe the coastline and sit deep in the interior; almost half offer camping. The others boast a combination of rugged hikes, easy strolls, self-guided nature walks, swimming, historical sites, and natural phenomena. The ones with campgrounds are state-, county-, and nationally operated, ranging from remote walk-in sites to housekeeping cabins. All, except the national park, require inexpensive camping permits, and although there is usually no problem obtaining sites, always write for reservations well in advance, allowing a minimum of one month for letters to go back and forth.

General Information

Most campgrounds have pavilions, fireplaces, toilets (sometimes pit), and running water, but usually no individual electrical hookups. Pavilions often have electric lights, but sometimes campers appropriate the bulbs, so it's wise to carry your own. Drinking water is available, but at times brackish water is used for flushing toilets and for showers, so read all signs regarding water. Backcountry shelters have catchment water, but never hike without an adequate supply of your own. Cooking fires are allowed in established firepits, but no wood is provided. Charcoal is a good idea. When camping in the mountains, be prepared for cold and rainy weather. Women, especially, should never hike or camp alone, and everyone should exercise precaution against theft, though it's not as prevalent as on the other islands.

County Parks

The county-maintained parks are open to the public for day-use, and permits are only required for camping (tents or RVs). For information write: Department of Parks and Recreation, County of Hawaii, 25 Aupuni St., Hilo, HI 96720, tel. 961-8311. You can pick up your permits here, but only during business hours Mon.-Friday. If you'll be arriving after hours or on a weekend, have the permits mailed to you. Branch offices are located at Hale Halawai in Kailua-Kona, tel. 323-3046; at Captain Cook, tel. 323-3046; and at Waimea, tel. 885-5454. Fees are $1 per adult per day; children ages 13-17, 50 cents; youngsters free. Pavilions for exclusive use are $5 per day with kitchen, $2 without.

State Parks And Cabins

Day-use of state parks is free, with no permit required, but you will need one for tent camping and for cabins. If you want a cabin, at least one week's notice is required regardless of availability. You can pick up your permit if you arrive during normal business hours, but again it saves time if you do it all by mail. Write: Department of Land and Natural Resources, Division of State Parks, Box 936 (75 Aupuni St.), Hilo, HI 96720, tel. 961-7200.

Cabins or A-frames are offered at Mauna Kea State Recreation Area's Pohakuloa Camp, tel. 935-7237; Hapuna Beach State Recreation Area, tel. 882-7995; Kalopa State Recreation Area, tel. 775-7114; and Niaulani Cabin at Kilauea State Recreation Area. Fees and regulations vary slightly so when writing for permits specify exactly which facility you require, for how long, and for how many people. For example, A-frames are a flat $7 per night, while cabins start at $10 s, up to $30 for a party of six.

Hawaii Volcanoes National Park

Both day-use and overnight camping at Hawaii Volcanoes National Park are free and no permits are required. The drive-in campgrounds throughout the park can be reserved, but usually operate on a first-come, first-served basis. Your stay is limited to seven days per campground per year. A-frame cabins are provided at Namakani Paio Campground, and arrangements are made through Volcano House, Hawaii Volcanoes National Park, HI 96718, tel. 967-7321. There are free walk-in trail cabins and shelters throughout the park; you can't reserve them and you should expect to share them with other hikers. Coleman stoves and lanterns are sometimes provided (check), but you provide the fuel. Basic bedding and cooking utensils are also there for your convenience. Shelters, in the park along the coast, are three-sided, open affairs that offer only a partial covering against the elements. For information on camping and hiking in the park, write Hawaii Volcanoes National Park, Information Services, Volcano, HI 96718.

Hiking The Big Island

Hiking on the Big Island is stupendous. There's something for everyone, from civilized walks to the breathtaking Akaka Falls to huff-puff treks to the summit of Mauna Loa. The largest number of trails, and the most outstanding according to many, is laced across Volcanoes National Park. After all, this is the world's most active volcano. You can hike across the crater floor, spurred on by the knowledge that it can shake to life at any moment. Or dip down off the mountain and amble the lonely trails in the Kau Desert or remains of the King's Coastal Trail in Puna.

The most important thing to do, before heading out in Volcanoes, is to stop at park headquarters and inquire about trail conditions. Make absolutely sure to register, giving the rangers your hiking itinerary. In the event of an eruption, they will be able to locate you and send a helicopter if necessary. Follow this advice; your life may depend upon it. Without any danger whatsoever, everyone can enjoy vistas on Devastation Trail, at Sulfur Bank, or at the Thurston Lava Tube. In the north you'll find Waipio, Waimanu, and Pololu valleys. All offer secluded hiking and camping where you can play Robinson Crusoe on your own beach and gather a variety of island fruits from once-cultivated trees gone wild.

Precautions
Always tell a ranger or official of your hiking intentions. Supply an itinerary and your expected route, then stick to it. Be aware of current lava flows, and heed all posted advice. If lost, walk on ridges and avoid the gulches, which have more obstacles and make it harder for rescuers to spot you. Be careful of elevation sickness, es-

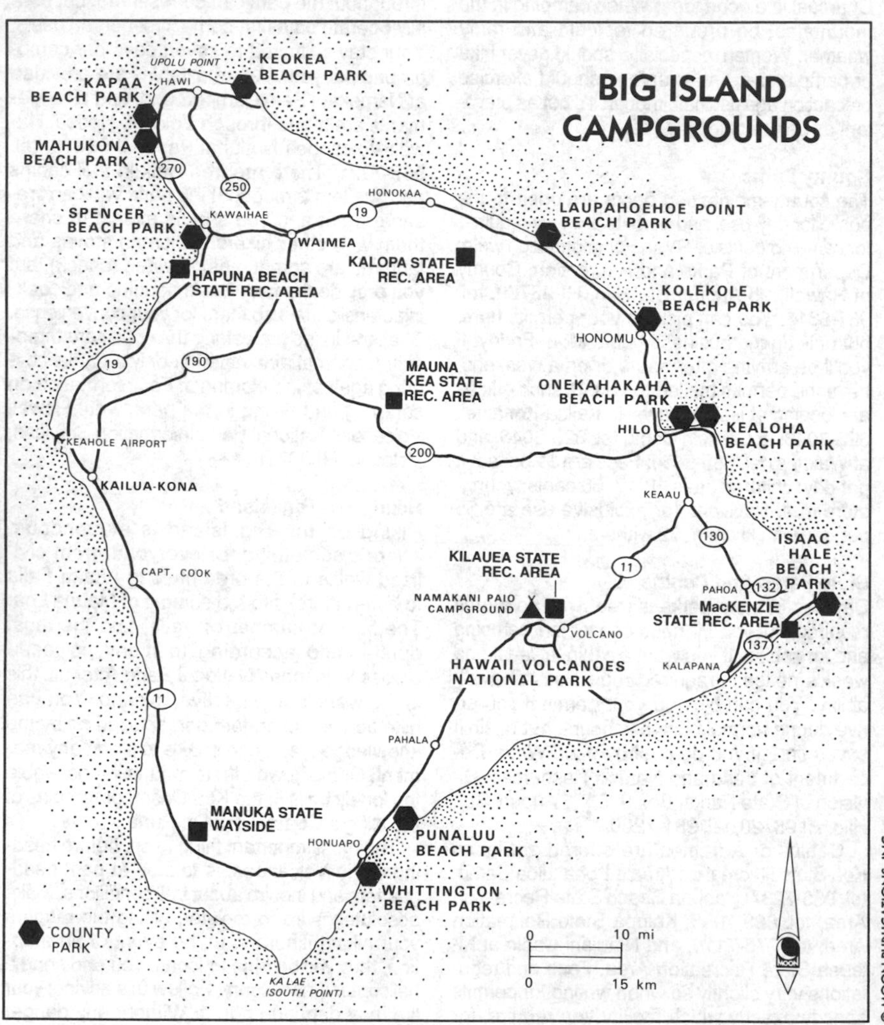

pecially on Mauna Loa and Mauna Kea. The best cure is to descend as soon as possible.

Heat can cause you to lose water and salt. If you become woozy or weak, rest, take salt, and drink water as you need it. Remember, it takes much more water to restore a dehydrated person than to keep hydrated; take small, frequent sips.

Be mindful of flash floods. Small creeks can turn into raging torrents with upland rains. Never camp in a dry creekbed. Fog is only encountered at elevations of 1,500-5,000 feet, but be careful of disorientation. Generally, stay within your limits, be careful, and above all else, enjoy yourself.

Camping Equipment

Camping equipment is available for rent from **Pacific United Rent All,** 1080 Kilauea Ave., Hilo, tel. 935-2974. It can also be purchased at **Gaspro,** tel. 935-3341 Hilo or 329-7393 Kona; **J&J Sporting,** tel. 329-2610 Kona; and **The Surplus Store,** tel. 935-6398 Hilo, 329-1240 Kona.

Hilo's **Basically Books,** downtown at 46 Waianuenue St., tel. 961-0144, has an unbeatable selection of maps. You can get anywhere you want to go with their nautical charts, road maps, and topographical maps, which include sectionals for serious hikers and trekkers. Their collection covers most of the Pacific.

SHOPPING

The following is an overview of the main shopping areas and their locations around the island. Almost every town has at least a gas station and market, and they will be listed in the travel chapters under "Shopping." Look there for directions to and descriptions of specific malls, art shops, and boutiques in the area. Supermarkets, health food stores, and local markets are listed in the individual travel chapters, generally in the "Food" sections.

SHOPPING CENTERS

General shopping centers are found in Hilo, Kailua-Kona, Waimea, and Captain Cook. Like most shopping malls, these have a variety of stores whose offerings may include apparel, dry goods, sporting goods, food, photography supplies, or outdoor rentals.

Hilo Malls

The main shopping center in Hilo is the **Prince Kuhio Plaza** at 111 E. Puainako. This shoppers' paradise is Hilo's newest and the island's largest shopping mall. An older but still full-service shopping center is **Kaiko'o Mall** at 777 Kilauea Avenue. The **Hilo Shopping Center** is about a half mile south on Kilauea Ave. at the corner of Kekuanoa Street. This smaller mall has a handful of local shops. **Puainako Town Center** is located at 2100 Kanoelehua Avenue. **Waiakea Shopping Plaza,** at 100 Kanoelehua Ave., has a small clutch of stores.

Kona Malls

Two commodities you're guaranteed in Kailua-Kona are plenty of sunshine and plenty of shopping. **Kona Inn Shopping Village** is located in central Kailua at 75-5744 Ali'i Dr. and has more than 40 shops selling everything from fabrics to fruits. **World Square** is smaller and just across the road. **Kona Banyan Court,** also in central Kailua, has a dozen shops with a medley of goods and services. **Kailua Bay Inn Shopping Plaza** is along Ali'i Drive, **Akona Kai Mall** is across from Kailua Pier, while the **Kona Coast Shopping Center** and the **North Kona Shopping Plaza** are both along Palani Road. **Lanihau Center,** at 75-5595 Palani Rd., tel. 329-9333, is one of Kailua-Kona's newest shopping additions. **King Kamehameha Kona Beach Hotel Mall** is an exclusive shopping haven on the first floor of the hotel, while **Rawson Plaza,** at 74-5563 Kaiwi St., is in the industrial area and offers bargains. **Waterfront Row** is a new shopping and food complex at the south end of downtown Kailua-Kona that's done in period architecture with rough-cut lumber.

Keauhou Shopping Village is conveniently located at the corner of Ali'i Dr. and Kamehameha III Rd. at the far southern end of Kailua-Kona. Here you'll find everything from a post office to a supermarket. Continuing south on Rt. 11, you'll spot **Kainaliu Village Mall** along the main drag.

Kealakekua Ranch Center, in Captain Cook, is a two-story mall with fashions and general supplies.

Waimea (Kamuela) Malls

After the diversity of shopping malls in Kailua and Hilo, it's like a breath of fresh air to have only one choice. In Waimea try the **Parker Ranch Shopping Center,** which has over 30 shops, including a pharmacy, grocery, and general merchandise. A small herd of shops in this center also features ranch and Western-wear with a Hawaiian twist. **Parker Square Shopping Mall,** along Rt. 19, has a collection of fine boutiques and shops. **Waimea Center,** also along Rt. 19, is one of Waimea's newest shopping malls.

BOOKSTORES

Two aspects of a quality vacation are knowing what you're doing and thoroughly relaxing while doing it. Nothing helps you do this better than a good book. The following stores offer full selections.

Hilo has excellent bookstores. **Basically Books,** downtown at 46 Waianuenue St., tel. 961-0144, has a good selection of Hawaiiana and out-of-print books, and an unbeatable selection of maps. You can get anywhere you want to go with their nautical charts, road maps, and topographical maps, which include sectionals for serious hikers and trekkers. Their collection covers most of the Pacific. They also feature a very good selection of travel books, and flags from countries throughout the world. The **Book Gallery,** tel. 959-7744, at Prince Kuhio Plaza, is a full-selection bookstore featuring Hawaiiana, hardcovers, and paperbacks. **Waldenbooks,** also at Prince Kuhio Plaza, tel. 959-6468, open daily 9 a.m.-9 p.m., is the largest and best-stocked bookstore in the Hilo area. **Bookfinders of Hawaii,** at 150 Haili St., tel. 961-5055, specializes in hard-to-find and out-of-print books. If you want it, they'll get it.

Kailua-Kona bookstores include **Waldenbooks** in Lanihau Center on Palani Rd., tel. 329-0015; **Middle Earth Bookshop** at 75-5719 Ali'i Dr., in the Kona Plaza Shopping Arcade, tel. 329-2123; **Keauhou Village Bookshop** at Keauhou Shopping Village, tel. 322-8111, open Mon.-Fri. 9 a.m.-9 p.m., Saturday 9 a.m.-6 p.m., Sunday 9 a.m.-5 p.m.

Waimea offers books at the **Waimea General Store,** located at the Parker Square Shopping Mall, tel. 885-4479, open Mon.-Sat. 9 a.m.-5 p.m., Sunday 10 a.m.-4 p.m.

SPECIALTY SHOPS, ART, AND NEAT THINGS

You can stroll in and out of flower shops, T-shirt factories, and a panoply of boutiques offering ceramics, paintings, carvings, and all manner of island handicrafts. Art and crafts shops are always a part of the Big Island's shopping malls, and in even the smallest village you can count on at least one local artist displaying his or her creations. The following list of artists and shops is by no means exhaustive, but for the most part, they are in out-of-the-way places and worth a visit. Art shops and boutiques in specific areas will be covered in the travel sections under "Shopping."

In Hilo, **Hawaiian Handcrafts** at 760 Kilauea Ave., tel. 935-5587, specializes in woodcarvings. **Halemanu Crafts** is a shop at 195 Kinole St. where senior citizens from the Hilo area display their fine *lau hala* weavings. **Sugawara Lauhala and Gift Shop** at 59 Kalakaua St. is a virtually unknown Hilo institution making genuine *lau hala* weavings. The **Crystal Grotto** at 290 Kamehameha Ave., tel. 935-2284, is a metaphysical bookstore filled with crystals, jewelry, videotapes, tarot cards, incense, and oils, and a full line of magnificently crafted beadwork. **Old Town Printer and Stationers** at 201 Kinoole St., open weekdays 8 a.m-5 p.m., has been in business for 35 years selling stationery, office supplies, postcards, notecards, and a terrific selection of calendars. **Sig Zane Design** at 122 Kamehameha Ave., tel. 935-7077, is one of the most unique and distinctive shops on the island. Here, owner and designer Sig Zane creates distinctive island wearables in 100% cotton.

While heading up the Hamakua Coast, make sure to visit **The Hawaiian Artifacts Shop** along the main drag in downtown Honokaa. **Waipio Valley Artworks** in Kukuihaele, tel. 775-0958, showcases exclusive artwork of distinguished island artists.

If you are after an exquisite piece of art, a unique memento, or an inexpensive but distinctive souvenir, make sure to visit the **Volcano Art Center** in Hawaii Volcanoes National Park.

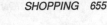

J.D. BISIGNANI

ipu, *a drum used to accompany hula*

In Kona's World Square shopping center, visit the **Showcase Gallery** for its offerings of glasswork, beadwork, featherwork, enamelling, and shell lei from the islands, with emphasis on the Big Island. Across the way, the **Coral Isle Art Shop** presents modern versions of traditional Hawaiian carvings. **Collectors Fine Art** in the Kona Inn Shopping Village is a perfect labyrinth of rooms and hallways showcasing fine art from around the world. Here too, **Crystal Visions** has incense, perfume, metaphysical books, and the channeling of personal and cosmic vibrations through its large selection of crystals, crystal balls, and pyramids. **Kona Inn Jewelry,** for world treasures, is one of the oldest and best-known shops for a square deal in Kona. **Alapaki's,** at Keauhou Shopping Village, sells traditional island arts and crafts. **The Glass Blower,** across from the seawall along Likana Ln., is a very interesting shop where you can watch the artist actually blowing the glass.

The mountain village of Holualoa has become an artists' haven. As you enter the village you'll spot **Kimura's Lauhala Shop,** which has been selling and producing its famous *lau hala* hats ever since local weavers began bartering their creations for groceries in 1915. In town you'll find a converted coffee mill, gaily painted and decorated, that's the home of the **Kona Art Center,** a community art-cooperative run by Robert and Carol Rogers since 1965. The premier shop in town, **Studio 7,** is owned and operated by Hiroki Morinoue, who studied at the Kona Art Gallery as a young man. The shop showcases Hiroki's work along with that of about 35 Big Island artists, including famous *raku* potter Chiu Leong. A separate shop in the same building is **Goldsmithing by Sam Rosen,** featuring unusual, one-of-a-kind works mostly in gold, silver, and precious stones.

In the nearby village of Kainalu look for **The Blue Ginger Gallery,** tel. 322-3898, displaying the art of owners Jill and David Bever, as well as artists' works from all over the island. **Elizabeth Harris and Co.** in Kealakekua, tel. 323-2447, displays shirts, T-shirts, and dresses made by 13 local seamstresses and artists. The **Kahanahou Hawaiian Foundation,** tel. 322-3901, is along the road in Kealakekua. They deal in ancient Hawaiian handicrafts, including masks, hula drums, and hula accoutrements.

The Little Grass Shack is an institution in Kealakekua. It looks like a tourist trap, but don't let that stop you from going in and finding some authentic souvenirs, most of which come from the surrounding area. **Tropical Temptations in Kealakekua,** tel. 326-2007, turns the best available grade of local fruits, nuts, and coffee beans into delicious candies. **Country Store Antiques** is next door to the Manago Hotel, just as you're entering Captain Cook. Owned and operated by E.L. Mahre, it's filled to the brim with kerosene lamps, dolls, glassware, old bottles, and Hawaiian antique jewelry.

Along the north shore in Kapaau across from the Kamehameha statue is **Ackerman Gallery I and II,** where you'll find the work of artist Gary Ackerman along with displays of local pottery, carvings, and one-of-a-kind jewelry. **Hana Koa** is a woodworking shop owned by artist Don Wilkinson. Don, a friendly storehouse of information, lives along Rt. 250 heading into Hawi from Waimea. Another local artist is **David Gomes,** a guitar and ukulele maker who works in koa. His small shop is located about a half mile on the Kapaau side of the junction of routes 270 and 250.

In the *paniolo* town of Waimea you can pick up down-home cowboy items or sophisticated artwork at the following shops. At the **Parker Ranch Shopping Center,** the **Paddock Shop** sells boots, cowboy hats, shirts, skirts, and buckles and bows. **Nikko Natural Fabrics,** in the Kamuela Country Plaza, will dress you in cottons, woolens, and silks, and adorn your walls with batiks and fine fiber arts, tel. 885-7661. In the **Parker Square Shopping Mall** along Rt. 19, the **Gallery of Great Things,** tel. 885-7706, really is loaded with great things—everything from a carousel horse to koa hair sticks. Here too, **Gifts in Mind** has novelty items, and a very good selection of aloha shirts and dresses; **Mango Ranch** sells duds for cowpokes, including bow ties, fancy shirts, and cowboy hats. Across the road **Kamaaina Woods** sells locally created wood handicrafts.

ACCOMMODATIONS

Finding suitable accommodations on Hawaii is never a problem. At only 65%, the 7,000-plus rooms available have the lowest annual occupancy rate of any in the islands. Except for during the height of the high seasons and during the Merrie Monarch Festival in Hilo, you can count on finding a room at a bargain. Many places offer kitchenettes and long-term discounts as a matter of course. The highest concentration of rooms is strung along Ali'i Drive in Kailua-Kona—over 4,500 in condos, apartment hotels, and standard hotels. Hilo has almost 2,000 rooms; many of its hotels have "gone condo," and you can get some great deals. The rest are scattered around the island in small villages from Naalehu in the south to Hawi in the north, where you can almost count on being the only off-island guest. You can comfortably stay in the cowboy town of Waimea, or perch above Kilauea Crater at one of the oldest hotel sites in the islands. Also on the island are bed and breakfasts, and the camping is superb, with a campsite almost guaranteed at any time.

The Range

The Big Island has a tremendous range of accommodations. A concentration of the world's greatest luxury resorts are within minutes of each other on the Kohala coast: The Mauna Kea Beach Hotel, Mauna Lani Bay Hotel, Ritz-Carlton Mauna Lani, and Kona Village Resort. The Mauna Kea, built by Laurence Rockefeller, has everything the name implies. The others are just as superb, with hideaway "grass shacks," exquisite art collections as an integral part of the grounds, world-ranked golf courses, and perfect crescent beaches.

Kona has fine hotels like the King Kamehameha Kona Beach Hotel and Kona Hilton in downtown Kailua. Just south toward Keahou is a string of reasonably priced yet luxurious hotels. Interspersed among the big hotels are little places with homey atmospheres and great rates. Hilo offers the best accommodations bargains. Luxury hotels such as the Hilo Hawaiian and Naniloa Surf are priced like mid-range hotels on the other islands. There are also semi-fleabags in town that pass the basic cleanliness test and go for as little as $20 per day, along with gems like the Dolphin Bay Hotel that gives you so much for your money it's embarrassing. And for a real treat, head to Hawaii Volcanoes National Park and stay at one of the bed and breakfasts tucked away there, or at Volcano House where raw nature has thrilled kings, queens, and luminaries like humorist Mark Twain for over a century.

If you want to get away from everybody else, it's no problem, and you don't have to be rich to do it. Pass-through towns like Captain Cook and Waimea have accommodations at very reasonable prices. You can try a self-growth retreat in the Puna District at Kalani Honua Culture Center or at the Wood Valley Buddhist Temple above Pahala. Want ultimate seclusion? Head down to Tom Araki's Hotel or the Treehouse in Waipio Valley, or spend the night at a defunct, century-old girls' boarding school in Kapaau.

KONA HILTON BEACH AND TENNIS RESORT

Kona Hilton Beach and Tennis Resort

Hotel/Condo Booking And Reservations

The following is a partial list of booking agents handling a number of properties on the Big Island. They include but are not limited to: **Kona Vacation Resorts,** tel. (800) 367-5168; **Hawaiian Holiday Rentals & Management,** tel. (800) 462-6630; **Hawaii Resort Management,** tel. (800) 553-5053; and **Keahou Property Management,** tel. (800) 745-5662. The Big Island is blessed with a profusion of **B&B homes** in unique and dramatic settings. You will find these pleasant lodgings in Volcano Village; at South Point; in Hawaii'c picturocquo townc; and overlooking Waipio Valley. For specific homes please see the following Big Island travel chapters, and for B&B booking agencies please see "Bed and Breakfast" in the "Accommodations" section of the General Introduction.

Residence Information

If you have been considering moving to the Big Island, or would just like to explore the possibility, contact **The Big Island by Mail,** Box 333, Kailua-Kona, HI 96745, tel. 329-7688. Owner Barbara Uechi will mail you an order blank listing an assortment of books, magazines, and newspapers especially chosen to guide the homeowner or businessperson looking to relocate to Hawaii. She can also offer information on moving and storage, education, building codes, and the economy.

Hostels

The Big Island has two very reasonably priced hostels operating at this time. **Arnott's Lodge,** 98 Apapano Rd., Hilo, HI 06720, tol. 060-7007 or (800) 368-8752 Mainland, or (800) 953-7773 Hawaii, offers a dormitory bunk for $15, and semiprivate rooms with a shared bath, kitchen and living room for $26 s, $36 d. Arnott's also offers inexpensive hiking and snorkeling excursions.

Patey's Place, 75-5731 Ala Hou St., Kailua-Kona, HI 96740, tel. 326-7018 or (800) 972-7408 (recently moved from 75-195 Ala Onaona St.), will set you up in a bunk for $15, a private room for $35, or a room with bath and kitchen for $45.

FOOD

Groceries and supplies can be purchased in almost every town on the island. Many of the markets in the smaller towns also sell a limited supply of sundries and dry goods. The general rule is: the smaller the market, the higher the prices. The largest and least expensive stores with the biggest selections are found in Hilo and Kailua-Kona. The following is a sampling of what you'll find. More extensive listings are found under "Shopping" in the individual district chapters.

Supermarkets in Hilo include **Food Fair,** 194 Kilauea Ave.; **Safeway,** 333 Kilauea Ave.; **Foodland** at Puainako Town Center; **Mall Foods** in Kaiko'o Mall; **Pick and Pay,** Hilo Shopping Center. In Kona, **K. Tanaguchi Market** at Kona Coast Shopping Center and **Food for Less** in Lanihau Center, are two of the main supermarkets. **KTA Supermarket** is at the Keauhou Village Mall, at the extreme south end of Ali'i Drive.

Around The Island

These smaller markets should meet your needs as you travel around the Big Island. Along the eastern Hamakua Coast you'll find **Ishigo's General Store** in Honomu Village en route to Akaka Falls. Further north along Rt. 24 in Honokaa are **T. Kaneshiro Store** and **K.K. Market.** In Kukuihaele, the last village before Waipio Valley, look for the **Last Chance Market.**

In Waimea, **Sure Save Supermarket** is at the Parker Ranch Shopping Center. Meat lovers can't go wrong at the **Kamuela Meat Market,** also at the center, selling Parker Ranch beef at home-town prices. On the Kohala peninsula look for **Kohala Market** in Kawaihae, **M. Nakahara** for general supplies and liquor in Hawi, and Kapaau's **Union Market** for a good assortment of grains, nuts, fruit, and locally made pastries and breads.

In Hilo, shop **Da Store,** which offers groceries and sundries, open 24 hours, at 776 Kilauea Avenue. South of Hilo you'll find in Pahoa Town **Pahoa Cash and Carry.** Along the Puna coast is the **Kalapana General Store.** In Volcano Village try **Kilauea Store** along Rt. 11 just before entering Hawaii Volcanoes National Park.

South of Kailua-Kona town center is **Casa De Emdeko Liquor and Deli. Kamigaki Store** and **Sure Save** are in Kealakekua. **Shimizu Market** is south on Rt. 11 in Honaunau. Farther south between mile markers 77 and 78 you'll find the very well-stocked **Ocean View General Store.** In the Kau District look for **Wong Yuen Market** in Waiohinu, and **Pick and Pay** in Naalehu, which bills itself the southernmost market in the United States.

Health Food, Fruit Stores, And Farmers' Markets

Abundant Life Natural Foods is in downtown Hilo at 90 Kamehameha Hwy., at the corner of Waianuinui Street. On Saturday morning, check out the **farmers' market** along Kamehameha Ave. fronting the bay, in the center of the downtown area. For a real treat visit the early morning (over by 8 a.m.) **Suisan Fish Auction** at 85 Lihiwai St. in Hilo.

Kona keeps you healthy with **Kona Healthways** in the Kona Coast Shopping Center. In Honokaa try the **Homestead Market and Cafe** for herbs, bulk foods, dairy products, and vitamins. In Kainaliu look for the well-stocked **Ohana O Ka Aina Food Co-op.** In Naalehu the **Naalehu Fruit Stand** is a favorite with local people for its fresh fruit, grains, minerals, vitamins, and health foods. While heading south from Hilo to Volcanoes, stop along Rt. 11 at **Keaau Natural Foods;** or in Pahoa at **Pahoa Natural Groceries,** which specializes in organic fruits and juices and is one of the finest health food stores on the Big Island.

A **farmers' market** held in Waimea every Saturday 7:30 a.m.-noon is where local farmers come to sell their produce, much of which is organic. Look for a dozen or so stalls in the parking lot of the Hawaiian Homelands Building located along Rt. 19, about two miles east of town center heading toward Honokaa.

Luau

The following is a listing of the luau available on the Big Island at the present time. For full descriptions including prices, menus, and times, see the listings in the appropriate district chapters. The luau include: **The Kona Hilton Resort,** tel. 329-3111; **The Royal Waikoloan,** tel. 885-6789; **King Kamehameha Kona Beach Hotel,** tel. 329-2911; **Kona Village Resort,** tel. 325-5555; **Mauna Kea Beach Resort,** tel. 822-7222.

GETTING THERE

Almost all travelers to the Big Island arrive by air. A few lucky ones come by private yacht, and in season the cruise ship SS *Constitution* docks in Hilo on Sunday mornings, then sails around the island to Kailua. For the rest, the island's two major airports are at Hilo and Kailua-Kona, with a few secondary strips here and there. Almost every flight to the Big Island has a stopover, mostly in Honolulu, but these are efficient and at no extra cost. The following should help you plan your arrival.

Note: Handicapped travelers, please see "Health and Safety" in the General Introduction.

The Airports

The largest and only international airport on the Big Island is **Hilo International Airport,** tel. 935-0809, which services Hilo and the eastern half of the island. It's a modern facility with full amenities and its runways can handle all jumbo jets. The two-story terminal has an information center, a restaurant, a number of vendors (including lei shops), and lockers. Most major car rental agencies have booths outside the terminal; a taxi for the three-mile ride to town costs about $6.50. The airport features 20 acres of landscaped flowers and an assortment of fountains and waterfalls supplied by rainwater collected on the terminal's roof.

Keahole Airport, tel. 329-2484, is nine miles north of Kailua-Kona and handles the air traffic for Kona. The terminal is a series of open-sided, Polynesian-style buildings. Here too are lockers, food, visitor information, various vendors, and most car rental agencies. The Gray Line limousine can take you to Kailua for under $10, while a private cab to your hotel is $15 or more.

Waimea-Kohala Airport, tel. 885-4520, is just outside Waimea (Kamuela). There are few amenities and no public transportation to town. **Upolu Airport,** tel. 889-9958, is a lonely strip on the extreme northern tip of the island, with no facilities whatsoever. Both are serviced only on request by small charter airlines.

Nonstop Flights

United Airlines operates the only nonstop flight to the Big Island from the Mainland. The San Francisco flight departs daily at 8:50 a.m. and arrives at Keahole Airport on the Kona Coast at 11:16 a.m. In the past during peak season, United has run a flight to Hilo International Airport, but it's an on-and-off affair depending on the number of travelers. It's also interesting to note that the Hilo Airport is an international one, and most island flights landed there in the past. Now, with the Kona Coast gaining popularity, many domestic flights have shifted to that side of the island.

Stopover Flights

All major carriers have arrangements for getting you to the Big Island. American carriers such as Hawaiian Air, Delta, Continental, and American, along with foreign carriers like Canadian Pacific, Qantas, and Japan Airlines, land at Honolulu. There they have an inter-line agreement with island carriers, including Hawaiian Air and Aloha Airlines, which then take you to the Big Island. This sometimes involves a plane change, but your baggage can be booked straight through. Hawaiian Air has expanded to Mainland flights from San Francisco and Los Angeles, with connecting flights in Honolulu to Kona. They offer the convenience of dealing with just one airline.

Interisland Carriers

Getting to and from the Big Island via the other islands is easy and convenient.

Hawaiian Air, tel. (800) 367-5320 Mainland or (800) 882-8811 Hawaii, offers the most flights. From Honolulu to Kona, 17 flights (about 40 minutes) are spread throughout the day running approximately 5:40 a.m.-7:05 p.m. The same scheduling applies to Hilo, except there are slightly fewer flights, the last departing Honolulu at 7:15 p.m. Hawaiian Air also offers daily flights from Kauai, Molokai,

Lanai, and Maui to both Hilo and Kona. Most are aboard DC-9 jet aircraft, with some on the four-prop Dash Transits. About the same number of flights from Hilo and Kona *to* Honolulu and the above destinations are spread throughout the day.

Aloha Airlines, tel. 935-5771 or (800) 367-5250, services the Big Island with flights from the neighboring islands. Their 24 daily Honolulu-Kona runs start at 5:40 a.m., with the last at 7 p.m.; 16 Honolulu-to-Hilo flights depart throughout the day, 5:35 a.m.-6:35 p.m. Aloha flies from Kauai to Hilo and Kona with a dozen or so flights to each approximately 6:30 a.m.-6:30 p.m. Maui flights to Hilo and Kona are much fewer, with usually only four flights per day, two in the morning and two in the afternoon.

Aloha Island Air, tel. (800) 323-3345 Mainland or (800) 652-6541 Hawaii, offers scheduled flights to and from Honolulu, Princeville on Kauai, Molokai, and Lanai; and from Kahului, Kapalua, and Hana airports on Maui. There are three flights from Honolulu, with the first at 6:10 a.m. and the last at 5 p.m. Flights to and from the other destinations are scheduled at one or two per day and often involve a stopover.

Big Island Air, tel. 329-4868 or (800) 367-8047, ext. 207, operates out of Kailua-Kona and has a regularly scheduled flight between Kona and Hilo on the Big Island only. The roundtrip flight leaves and returns daily between 11 a.m. and noon. Check for specifics. Big Island Air also features jet charter service, and flightsee tours around the Big Island.

GETTING AROUND

The first thing to remember when traveling on the Big Island is that it *is* big, over four times larger than Rhode Island. A complete range of vehicles is available for getting around, everything from helicopters to mopeds. Hawaii, like Oahu, has good public transportation. Choose the conveyance that fits your style, and you should have no trouble touring the Big Island.

CAR RENTALS

Car Rental Tips

The best way to tour the island is in a rented car, but keep these tips in mind. Most car companies charge you a fee if you rent the car in Hilo and drop it off in Kona, and vice versa. The agencies are prejudiced against the Saddle Road and the spur road leading to South Point, both of which offer some of *the* most spectacular scenery on the island. Their prejudice is unfounded because both roads are paved, generally well maintained, and no problem if you take your time. They'll claim the insurance will not cover you if you have a mishap on these roads. A good automobile policy at home will cover you in a rental car, but definitely check this before you take off. It's even possible, but not recommended, to drive to the top of Mauna Kea if there is no snow. Plenty of signs to the summit say "4WD only"; heed them, not so much for going up, but for needed braking power coming down (see Saddle Road chapter). Don't even hint of these intentions to the car rental agencies, or they won't rent you a car.

No way whatsoever should you attempt to drive down to Waipio Valley in a car! The grade is unbelievably steep, and only a 4WD compound first gear can make it. Put simply, you have a good chance of being killed if you try it in a car.

Gas stations are farther apart than on the other islands, and sometimes they close very early. As a rule, fill up whenever the gauge reads half full.

Both General Lyman Field (Hilo Airport) and Keahole Airport (Kona) have a gauntlet of car rental booths and courtesy phones outside the terminals.

National Companies

The following are national firms represented at both airports. Kona numbers begin with "329," Hilo with "961" or "935." One of the best national firms with an excellent reputation for service and prices is **Dollar Rent A Car,** tel. 329-2744, 961-2101, (800) 367-7006 Mainland, (800) 342-7398 in Hawaii. Others include: **National Car Rental,** tel. 329-1674, 935-0891, (800) 227-7368; **Hertz,** tel. 329-3566, 935-2896, or (800) 654-3131; **Avis,** tel. 329-1745, 935-1290, (800) 331-1212 Mainland, (800) 831-8000 in Hawaii;

Budget, tel. 329-8511, 935-9678, or (800) 527-0700; and **Alamo,** tel. 329-8896, 961-3343, or (800) 327-9633.

Local Companies

The following companies have booths or courtesy phones at the airport(s) (telephone prefixes 326 and 329 are for Kona; 935, 961, and 969 are for Hilo). Sometimes, if business is slow, they'll give you a deal on their prices. Firms include: **Sunshine Rent A Car,** tel. 329-2926, 935-1108, or (800) 522-8440; **VIP Car Rental,** tel. 326-9466, 329-7328; **Harper,** 969-1478; **World Rent A Car,** tel. 329-1006; and **Ciao Exoticar,** tel. 326-2426. Remember that local companies come and go with regularity, so call first to make sure that they are still in business. Harper and Ciao Exoticar carry 4WD rigs, excellent and necessary for a drive up to the summit of Mauna Kea.

PUBLIC TRANSPORTATION

The county of Hawaii maintains the Mass Transportation System (MTS), known throughout the island as the **Hele-On Bus.** For information, schedules, and fares contact the MTS at 25 Aupuni St., Hilo 96720, tel. 961-6722 or 935-8241. The main bus terminal is in downtown Hilo at Mooheau Park, at the corner of Kamehameha Avenue and Mamo Street. Recently, it's been completely rebuilt and modernized. Like bus terminals everywhere, it has a local franchise of derelicts and down-and-outers, but they leave you alone. What the Hele-On Bus lacks in class, it more than makes up for in *color* and affordability. The Hele-On operates Mon.-Sat. approximately 6 a.m.-6 p.m., depending on the run. It goes just about everywhere on the island—sooner or later—but recently many of the routes have been curtailed. If you're in a hurry definitely forget about taking it, but if you want to meet the people of Hawaii, there's no better way. The base fare is 50 cents, which increases whenever you go into another zone. You can also be charged an extra $1 for a large backpack or suitcase. Don't worry about that—the Hele-On is one of the best bargains in the country. The routes are far too numerous to mention, but one goes from Kealia, south of Captain Cook, through Kailua, and all the way to Hilo on the east coast via Waimea, Honokaa, and Honomu. This journey covers 110 miles in just over four hours and costs about $8, the most expensive fare in the system. You can take the southern route through Kau, passing through Naalehu and Volcano, and continuing on to Hilo. This trip takes just over two hours and costs $6.

J.D. BISIGNANI

Waipio Valley Shuttle

The county also maintains the **Banyan Shuttle** in Hilo. This bus does five runs Mon.-Fri. 9 a.m.-2:55 p.m. The Shuttle costs 50 cents but you can buy a $2 pass for one-day's unlimited use. The Shuttle runs from the Hukilau Hotel at the end of Banyan Dr. to the Mooheau Bus Terminal in downtown Hilo. En route it stops at the better hotels, Puainako Town Center, Hilo and Kaiko'o malls, Lyman Museum, and Rainbow Falls, where you're allowed 10 minutes for a look.

Kailua-Kona also has the **Ali'i Shuttle** that cruises flower-lined Ali'i Drive. This red, white, and blue bus runs every 45 minutes, 7:45 a.m.-10 p.m.

Taxis

General Lyman Field in Hilo and Keahole Airport north of Kailua always have taxis waiting for fares. From Hilo's airport to downtown costs about $12, and from Keahole to most hotels along Ali'i Drive in Kailua is $22. Obviously, a taxi is no way to get around if you're trying to save money. Most taxi companies, both in Kona and Hilo, run sightseeing services for fixed prices. In **Kona** try: Kona Airport Taxi, tel. 329-7779; Paradise Taxi, tel. 329-1234; Marina Taxi, tel. 329-2481. In **Hilo** try: Hilo Harry's, tel. 935-7091; A-1 Bob's Taxi, tel. 959-4800; ABC Taxi, tel. 935-0755; or Hawaii Taxi, tel. 959-6359.

Note: Inquire at the County Transit Authority, tel. 935-8241, about money-saving coupons for "shared-ride taxi service." They allow door-to-door taxi service within nine miles of the urbanized areas of Hilo, Waimea, and Kona. Service hours and other restrictions apply.

ALTERNATIVE TRAVEL

Hitchhiking

The old thumb works on the Big Island about as well as anywhere else. Some people hitchhike rather than take the Hele-On Bus not so much to save money as to save time. It's a good idea to check the bus schedule (and routes), and set out about 30 minutes before the scheduled departure. If you don't have good luck, just wait for the bus to come along and hail it down. It'll stop.

Bicycles

Pedaling around the Big Island can be both fascinating and frustrating. The roads are well paved, but the shoulders are often torn up. With all the triathletes coming to Hawaii, and all the fabulous, little-trafficked roads, you'd think the island would be great for biking. It is, but you are better off bringing your own bike than renting. If you do rent, instead of a delicate road bike, you're better off getting a **cruiser** or **mountain bike** that can handle the sometimes poor road conditions as well as open up the possibilities of offroad biking. Even experienced mountain bikers should be careful on trails, which are often extremely muddy and rutted.

For rentals, try the following. **Hawaiian Pedals Unlimited,** tel. 329-2294, in the Kona Inn Shopping Plaza, rents mountain bikes at $10.50 per day for four to seven days, $12 per day for two to three days, $15 for 24 hours; tandems cost $25 per day. They also offer tours. **Island Cycle Rentals** is at Jack's Diving Locker at the Kona Inn Plaza, tel. 329-7585. **Dave's Bike and Triathlon Shop,** 75-5626 Kuakini Hwy., Kailua-Kona, tel. 329-4522, rents road bikes at $15 first day, $12 second day, $10 third day, or $60 per week; they also rent mountain bikes. **Pacific United Rental** at 1080 Kilauea Ave., Hilo, tel. 935-2974, has rentals limited to the Hilo area at $8 per day for single-speed bikes.

Teo's Safaris in Keaau, just south of Hilo, tel. 982-5221, rents bicycles and leads mountain tours. Rentals for 21-speed mountain bikes are $10 per day, $15 for 24 hours, $20 two days, or $50 for the week. Teo leads a rainforest ride which includes bike and helmet for $20 (call 24 hours in advance). Teo also has panniers, bike racks, and camping equipment available for people renting his bikes (rates subject to length of rental).

For information on biking in Hawaii, contact **Hawaii Bicycling League,** Box 4403, Honolulu, HI 96813. This nonprofit corporation publishes a monthly newsletter, *Spoke-n-Words,* filled with tips and suggested rides.

SIGHTSEEING TOURS

Tours are offered that will literally let you cover the Big Island from top to bottom. You can drive it, fly it, dive below it, or sail around it.

Note: For snorkel/scuba, deep-sea fishing, and horseback-riding tours, see the "Sports and Recreation" section earlier in this chaper.

Van And Bus Tours

Narrated and fairly tame island tours are operated by **Grayline,** tel. 329-9337 or 935-2835; **Robert's Tours,** tel. 935-2858; **Jack's Tours,** tel. 961-6666; and **Polynesian Tours,** tel. 329-8008. All cost about $50, and all offer a "circle island tour" that takes in Kilauea Caldera.

Four-wheel-drive tours include: **Waipio Valley Shuttle,** tel. 775-7121, offering a two-hour tour down to Waipio Valley ($25) and a Mauna Kea summit tour ($75); and **H.R.T. Waipio Tour Desk,** 775-7291, offering van and horseback riding tours through the Waipio Valley.

Paradise Safaris, tel. 322-2366, Box A-D, Kailua-Kona, HI 96745, owned and operated by Pat Wright, has been taking visitors on high-adventure trips around the Big Island for the last seven years. Pat, originally from New Mexico, is a professional guide who's plied his trade from the Rockies to New Zealand, and has taken people on trips ranging from mountaineering to white-water rafting. Your comfort and safety, as you roam the Big Island, are ensured as you ride in sturdy GMC High Sierra vans with 4WD and a/c. The premier trip offered by Paradise Safaris is an eight-hour journey to the top of Mauna Kea. Pat not only fills your trip with stories, anecdotes, and fascinating facts during the ride, he tops off the safari by setting up an eight-inch telescope so you can get a personal view of the heavens through the rarified atmosphere atop the great mountain. Pat will pick you up at your hotel in Kailua-Kona at about 4 p.m. If you're staying on the Hilo side, he will meet you at a predetermined spot along the Saddle Road. The price is $105-110, with hot savory drinks and good warm parkas included. Paradise Safaris will also tailor special trips for your interests in photography, hiking, astronomy, or shore fishing.

Tour Tapes

For a unique concept, rent Tour Tapes, narrated by Russ Apple, Ph.D., a retired national-park ranger and 1987 winner of the *Historic Hawaii Foundation Award.* Russ dispenses his knowledge about the Big Island as you drive along prescribed routes, mostly in and around Hawaii Volcanoes National Park. Tapes and decks are available in Hilo from the Hilo Hawaiian Hotel, Aston Hawaii Naniloa Resort, and Lyman House Museum. They are also available at the Volcano Art Center.

Helicopter And Air Tours

Air tours are a great way to see the Big Island, but they are expensive, especially when the volcano is putting on a mighty display. Expect to spend a minimum of $135-275 for a front-row seat to watch the amazing light show from the air. An eruption at Kilauea is like winning the lottery for these small companies, and many will charge whatever the market will bear.

Tip: to get the best view of the volcanic activity, schedule your flight for the morning, and no later than 2 p.m. Any later, clouds and fog may set in, obstructing your view.

Volcano Helitours, tel. 967-7578, owned and operated by David Okita, is intimately familiar with the volcano area. Their heliport sits atop Kilauea and is located just off a fairway of the Volcano Golf and Country Club. Rates are extremely competitive, and because your flight originates atop the volcano, you waste no air time going to or from the eruption sites. The helicopter is a four-passenger (all seats have windows) Hughes 500D.

Helicopter flights from Hilo International Airport are very competively priced, with savings over the companies operating out of Kailua-Kona. Two good companies include **Hilo Bay Air,** tel. 969-1545, and **Io Aviation,** tel. 935-3031. Also try **Kainoa Aviation** from Hilo tel. 961-5591, or **Mauna Kea Helicopters,** tel. 885-6400, which flies from the small Kamuela Airport in Waimea.

At mile marker 75 along Rt. 19 heading north from Kailua-Kona is the turnoff to Waikaloa Village. Just here is a heliport that services the helicopter companies on the Kona side. One of the major island firms, **Papillon Helicopters,** tel. 329-0551 or (800) 367-7095, not only flies from here, but maintains its office here. Prices range from $153 for a 45- to 50-minute flight along the Kohala Coast, to $295 for a Pele Spectacular that flies you over the volcano, dips low over Waipio Valley, and then runs along the Kohala Coast. All seats cost the same price, but the premier seats are up front with the pilot.

Kenai Helicopters, in a small booth next door to Papillon, tel. 329-7424 or (800) 622-3144, is in direct, but friendly, competition with Papillon. Their prices are about the same, but they do have the advantage of being one of the oldest and most knowledgeable helicopter companies on the Big Island. They offer the "Fire and Rain Tour," which includes a rainforest and Puna Coast flyover for $145, and the "Creation of Pele," which takes you over the active volcano zone, past Hilo, up the Hamakua Coast, and back to Waikoloa for $297. A ride with Kenai is a once-in-a-lifetime thrill.

For fixed-wing air tours try one of the following: **Big Island Air** offers small-plane flights from Keahole Airport, two-person minimum, tel. 329-4868. They fly a two-hour circle-island tour in an eight-passenger Cessna 402. This tour passes over the volcanic activity. **Hawaii Airventures,** tel. 329-0014, offers sightseeing and photographic tours from Keahole Airport, as does **Classic Aviation,** tel. 329-8687 or (800) 695-8100, who can take you on a number of flying adventures in their open-cockpit biplane. **Hawaii Pacific Aviation,** tel. 961-5591, or **Island Hoppers,** tel. 969-2000, will take you topside from Hilo International Airport.

Ocean Tours

Captain Zodiac, tel. 329-3199, Box 5612, Kailua-Kona, HI 96745, will take you on a fantastic ocean odyssey beginning at Honokohau Small Boat Harbor just north of Kailua-Kona, from where you'll skirt the coast south all the way to Kealakekua Bay. A Zodiac is a very tough, motorized rubber raft. It looks like a big, horseshoe-shaped inner-tube that bends itself and undulates with the waves like a floating waterbed. These seaworthy craft, powered by twin Mercury 280s, have five separate air chambers for unsinkable safety. They'll take you for a thrilling ride down the Kona Coast, pausing along the way to whisk you into sea caves, grottoes, and caverns. The Kona Coast is also marked with ancient ruins and the remains of villages, which the captains point out, and about which they relate historical anecdotes as you pass by. You stop at Kealakekua Bay, where you can swim and snorkel in this underwater conservation park. Roundtrips departing at 8 a.m., and again at 1 p.m., take about five hours and cost $62 adults, $52 children under 11. Captain Zodiac provides a light tropical lunch of fresh exotic fruit, taro chips, fruit juice, iced tea, and sodas. All you need are a bathing suit, sun hat, towel, lotion, camera, and sense of adventure.

Atlantis Submarine, tel. 329-6626, allows everyone to live out the fantasy of Captain Nemo on a silent cruise under the waves off Kailua-Kona. After checking in at their office in the King Kamehameha Kona Beach Hotel Mall, you board a launch at Kailua Pier that takes you on a 10-minute cruise to the waiting submarine tethered offshore. You're given all of your safety tips on the way there. As you descend, notice that everything white, including teeth, turns pink, because the ultraviolet rays are filtered out. The only colors you can see clearly beneath the waves are blues and greens, because water is 800 times denser than air and filters out the reds and oranges. Everyone has an excellent seat with a viewing port; there's not a bad seat in the submarine, so you don't have to rush to get on. Don't worry about being claustrophobic either—the sub is amazingly airy and bright, with white space-age plastic on the inside walls, and aircraft-quality air blowers over your seat.

The Atlantis Sub is getting some competition from the **Nautilus II,** tel. 326-2003, a semi-submersible very similar to the famous "ironsides" first used in the Civil War. This high-tech model offers a narrated one-hour tour in its spacious, air-conditioned lower deck. Departures are daily from Kailua Pier.

The ***Maile,*** berthed at Kawaihae Harbor, Box 44335, Kamuela, HI 96743, tel. (800) 726-SAIL, is a 50-foot Gulfstar sloop available for luxury sailing charters and shorter-term whalewatching, snorkeling, and fishing expeditions. Skippered by Ralph Blancato, a U.S. Coast Guard-certified Master, the sloop offers competitive prices on half- or full-day charters, sunset sails, and long-term rental.

For more conventional sailing and boating adventures, try one of the following. **Captain Beans',** tel. 329-2955, is a Kona institution that will take you aboard its glass-bottomed boat. Departures leave daily at 5:15 p.m. from Kailua Pier, $45 per adult. During the very tame cruise you'll spot fish, listen to island music, and enjoy a sunset dinner. ***Captain Cook VII,*** tel. 329-6411, is also a glass-bottomed boat. Its tour includes snorkeling and lunch for $25 per adult.

Whalewatch Cruises

In season (Nov.-April), these fascinating adventures are provided by **Royal Hawaiian Cruises,** tel. 329-6411. Cruises usually last about three hours and cost $35 per adult. Accompanied by naturalists from the University of Hawaii, the educational cruise advertises that you will "see a whale, or get a coupon for another whale watch free." For a day of snorkeling, sailing and whalewatching in season, contact **Kamanu Charters,** tel. 329-2021. From Waikoloa, try **Ocean Sports,** tel. 885-5555; they offer snorkeling and whalewatching cruises with five departures per day.

Camping/Hiking Tours

Hawaiian Island Kamping Excursions, Box 726, Pahoa, HI 96778, tel. 965-7293 or (800) 726-4453, offers adventure hiking tours ranging from a 12-day deluxe tour covering the Big Island and Kauai, to a five-day Waimanu Valley escape to this pristine area along the Big Island's north coast. The tours are designed to include a great deal of personal attention, with a maximum of 16 people per group allowed. Tour leaders, intimately versed in the flora, fauna, geology, history, and ancient cosmology of the islands, share their knowledge as you trek along. All interisland flights, accommodations (ranging from tents to condos), and meals are provided. A deposit is required to confirm a place on a tour and to receive a packet containing information necesary to make your tour enjoyable.

An organization offering camping and hiking trips to the Big Island is **Wilderness Hawaii,** Box 61692, Honolulu, HI 96839, tel. (808) 737-4697. Led by Sheena Sandler, Wilderness Hawaii offers courses that range from a 4- to a 12-day sojourn where the experiential journey takes place as much within yourself as on the hiking trail.

Note: For more about ecotourism in Hawaii see "Getting There" in the General Introduction.

Bicycling Tours

For those interested in bicycle touring, contact one of the following for their specialized bike trips. The owners and tour leaders of **Island Bicycle Adventures,** 569 Kapahulu Ave., Honolulu, HI 96815, tel. 734-0700 or (800) 233-2226, are intimately familiar with bicycle touring and are members of the Hawaii Bicycling League. They offer tours to Maui, the Big Island, and Kauai. **Backroads,** 1516 5th St., Suite PR, Berkeley, CA 94710, tel. (510) 527-1555 or (800) 462-2848, also goes easy on the environment with their bicycle and hiking trips to the Big Island. **Teo's Safaris** in Keaau, just south of Hilo, tel. 982-5221, rents bicycles and leads a rainforest ride. The $20 fee includes bike and helmet. Call 24 hours in advance.

INFORMATION AND SERVICES

EMERGENCY AND MEDICAL CARE

For police, fire and ambulance, dial **911** from anywhere on the island.

Hospitals: Hilo Hospital, tel. 969-4111; Kona Hospital, tel. 322-9311; Honokaa Hospital, tel. 775-7211; Kohala Hospital, tel. 889-6211; Kau Hospital, tel. 928-8331.

Drugstores: Longs Drugs, Hilo, tel. 935-3357, or Kona, tel. 329-1380; Kona Coast Drugs, Kailua, tel. 329-8886; Village Pharmacy, Waimea, tel. 885-4418.

Hawaii Services For The Disabled

At Hilo Airport there are no facilities for deplaning nonambulatory people from propeller planes, only from jets and on the jetways. Interisland flights should be arranged only on jets. Ramps and a special elevator provide access in the bilevel terminal. Parking is convenient in designated areas. At Kona Airport, boarding and deplaning is possible for the handicapped. Ramps make the terminal accessible. To get around, **Handi-Vans** are available in Hilo, tel. 961-6722. **Kamealoha Unlimited** has specially equipped vans, tel. 966-7244. **Parking permits** are available from the Department of Finance, tel. 961-8231. Medical help, nurses, and companions can be arranged through **Big Island Center for Independent Living,** tel. 935-3777. Doctors are referred by **Hilo Hospital,** tel. 961-4211, and **Kona Hospital,** tel. 322-9311. Medical equipment is available from **Kamealoha Unlimited,** tel. 966-7244; **Medi-Home,** tel. 969-1123; **Pacific Rentall,** tel. 935-2974.

ALTERNATIVE HEALTH CARE

The Big Island is blessed with some of the finest natural healers and practitioners in the state. For a holistic healing experience of body, mind, and soul, the following are highly recommended.

At the **School of Hawaiian Lomi Lomi,** Box 221, Captain Cook, HI 96704, tel. 323-2416 or 328-2472, Margaret Machado, assisted by her husband Daniel, provides the finest *lomi lomi* and traditional Hawaiian herbal cures in the islands. Both are renowned *kupuna* who dispense a heavy dose of love and concern with every remedy prescribed.

Acupuncture and Herbs is the domain of Angela Longo. This remarkable woman is not only a superbly trained, licensed practitioner of traditional Chinese medicine and acupuncture, but she covers all bases by holding a Ph.D. in biochemistry from U.C. Berkeley. For a totally holistic health experience, contact Angela at her Waimea/Kamuela office, tel. 885-7886.

Angela's top student, **Karen MacIsaac,** has opened a Chinese herb and acupuncture clinic by appointment only, tel. 329-4393, at 75-5995 Kuakini Hwy., Suite 126, Kailua-Kona, HI 96740.

The **Hawaiian Islands School of Body Therapy,** tel. 322-0048, owned and operated by Peter Wind and Lynn Filkins-Wind, offers state-certified massage courses and mini-courses for the beginning or experienced therapist. A full range of massage, anatomy, and physiology are part of the coursework preparing the student for a Hawaii State License. Programs include a basic massage program taking 150 hours, an advanced massage program of 450 hours, and a third-level course designed for the professional that takes a minimum of one year's intensive study to complete. Under Peter and Lynn's tutelage you'll learn *lomi lomi,* reflexology, hydrotherapy, aromatherapy, trigger point therapy, and treatment therapy. Lynn specializes in treatment therapy, which she teaches by the European, hands-on approach, while Peter is a hydrotherapist and colonics therapist. They are assisted by Gigi Goochey, the anatomy and physiology instructor. Lynn and Peter are dedicated professionals who have clued in, body and soul, to the art of healing.

Brain Gym Hawaii, tel. 889-5937, Box 1421, Kapaau, HI, is owned and operated by

Jan Ellison, whose motto is, "Movement is the door to learning." A practitioner of educational kinesthesiology, Jan offers classes in how movement relates to performance, and how the practice of "Edu-K" helps you realize your full potential. The practice integrates the body, mind, and spirit, aligning them to put you in control of your entire self. Costs for therapy sessions are on a sliding scale, and Jan will arrange to meet you at the time and place of your convenience.

To revitalize those aching muscles and put a spring in your step, visit massage practitioners with magic in their hands: **Kiauhou Massage and Spa** at the Kiauhou Beach Hotel, tel. 322-3441, Room 227, is open Tuesday, Thursday, and Saturday 10 a.m.-5 p.m., and Monday, Wednesday, and Friday 5-8 p.m.

To get that just-right chiropractic adjustment, try **Rodgers Chiropractic Arts** with Howard Rodgers, D.C., in the WOW Building, Kailua, tel. 329-2271; or try **Kohala Chiropractic** with Dr. Bob Abdy, Kamuela, tel. 885-6847. Also in Waimea is **Kohala Coast Massage,** tel. 885-5442, and the **Chiropractic Clinic** of Dr. Kenneth C. Williams, tel. 885-7719, emergency tel. 885-6812.

A wonderful healing center is **Halemana** in Pahoa, tel. 965-7783, where they'll soothe you with acupuncture and massage. For full details, see "Route 130 and the Southeast Coast" in the Puna chapter.

Academy of Therapeutic Massage, c/o Nancy Kahalewai P.M.T., 197 Kinoole St., Hilo, HI 96720, tel. 935-1405, focuses on prelicensing programs with an emphasis on sports massage, injury prevention and care, and inner changes of body psychology. Semesters include a summer intensive and regular winter and fall classes. Nancy, a longtime member of the Hawaii Board of Massage Advisory Committee, has been practicing her healing arts in the islands for about 15 years. She not only has the "golden touch" but is a terrific resource for all types of alternative medicines available on the Big Island. All massages, given by students, are completely supervised. This is a great opportunity to receive a quality massage at a reasonable price while visiting Hilo.

HVB AND OTHER INFORMATION

Big Island HVB Offices

The best information is dispensed by the **Hawaii Visitors Bureau,** 250 Keawe St., Hilo, HI 96720, tel. 961-5797; HVB Kona Branch, 75-5719 W. Ali'i Dr., Kailua-Kona, HI 96740, tel. 329-7787.

The **State Visitor Information** centers at the airports, tel. 935-1018 (Hilo) or 329-3423 (Kona), are good sources of information available on arrival.

The **Chamber of Commerce** can be consulted in Hilo, 180 Kinoole St., Hilo, HI 96720, tel. 935-7178; or in Kailua-Kona, 75-5737 Kuakini Hwy., Suite 207, Kailua-Kona, HI 96740, tel. 329-1758.

For all kinds of up-to-the-minute information, including sports (both local and national), weather, surf report, and news, call 935-1666 and then enter a four-number code as instructed (free 24 hours a day). Receive 24-hour recorded information regarding volcanic activity by calling 967-7977.

The area code for all telephone numbers on the Big Island is 808.

Reading Material

Make sure to pick up copies of the following free literature. Besides maps and general information, they often include money-saving coupons. Available at most hotels/condos and at all tourist areas, the weekly publications include: *Guide to Hawaii, Big Island Beach Press,* and *This Week Big Island.* Island newspapers include: *Hawaii-Tribune Herald,* a Hilo publication; and *West Hawaii Today,* published in Kona.

Libraries are located in towns and schools all over the island. The main branch is at 300 Waianuenue Ave., Hilo, tel. 935-5407. They provide information regarding all branch libraries. In Kailua-Kona, the library is at 75-140 Hualalai Rd., tel. 329-2196. For bookstores, please refer to "Shopping" earlier in this chapter.

Post Office

Branch post offices are found in most major towns. Window service is offered Mon.-Fri. 8:30

a.m.-4 p.m.; some offices are open Saturday 10 a.m.-noon. The following are the main offices: Hilo, tel. 935-2821; Kailua, tel. 329-1927; Captain Cook, tel. 323-3663; Waimea/Kamuela, tel. 885-4026; Volcano, tel. 967-7611; Hawi, tel. 889-5301.

Island Facts
Hawaii has three nicknames: the Big Island, the Volcano Island, and the Orchid Island. It's the youngest, most southerly, and largest (4,038 square miles) island in the Hawaiian chain. Its color is red, and the island lei is fashioned from the *ohia-lehua* blossom.

BOB RACE

HILO

Hilo is a blind date. Everyone tells you what a beautiful personality she has, but . . . But? . . . it rains: 133 inches a year. Mostly the rains come in winter and are limited to predictable afternoon showers, but they do scare some tourists away, keeping Hilo reasonably priced and low key. In spite of, and because of, the rain, Hilo is gorgeous. It's one of the oldest permanently settled towns in Hawaii and the largest on the windward coast of the island. Hilo's weather makes it a natural greenhouse. Twenty acres of exotic orchids and flowers line the runways at the airport. Botanical gardens and flower farms surround Hilo like a giant lei, and shoulder-to-shoulder banyans canopy entire city blocks. To counterpoint this tropical explosion, Mauna Kea's winter snows backdrop the town. The crescent of Hilo Bay blazes gold at sunrise, while a sculpted lagoon, Asian pagodas, rock gardens, and even a tiny island connected by footbridge line its shores. Downtown's waterfront has the perfect false-front buildings that always need a paint job. They lean on each other like "old salts" that've had one too many. Don't make the mistake of underestimating Hilo, or of counting it out because of its rainy reputation. For most, the blind date with this exotic beauty turns into a fun-filled love affair.

SIGHTS AND BEACHES

SIGHTS

Hilo is a unique town in a unique state in America. You can walk down streets with names like Puueo and Keawe, and they could be streets in Anywhere, U.S.A., with neatly painted houses surrounded by white picket fences. Families live here. There are roots, and traditions, but the town is changing. Fishermen still come for the nightly ritual of soul-fishing and story-swapping from the bridge spanning the Wailuku River, while just down the street newly arrived chefs prepare Cajun blackened fish at a yuppie restaurant as midnight philosophers sip gourmet coffee and munch sweets next door. Hilo is a classic

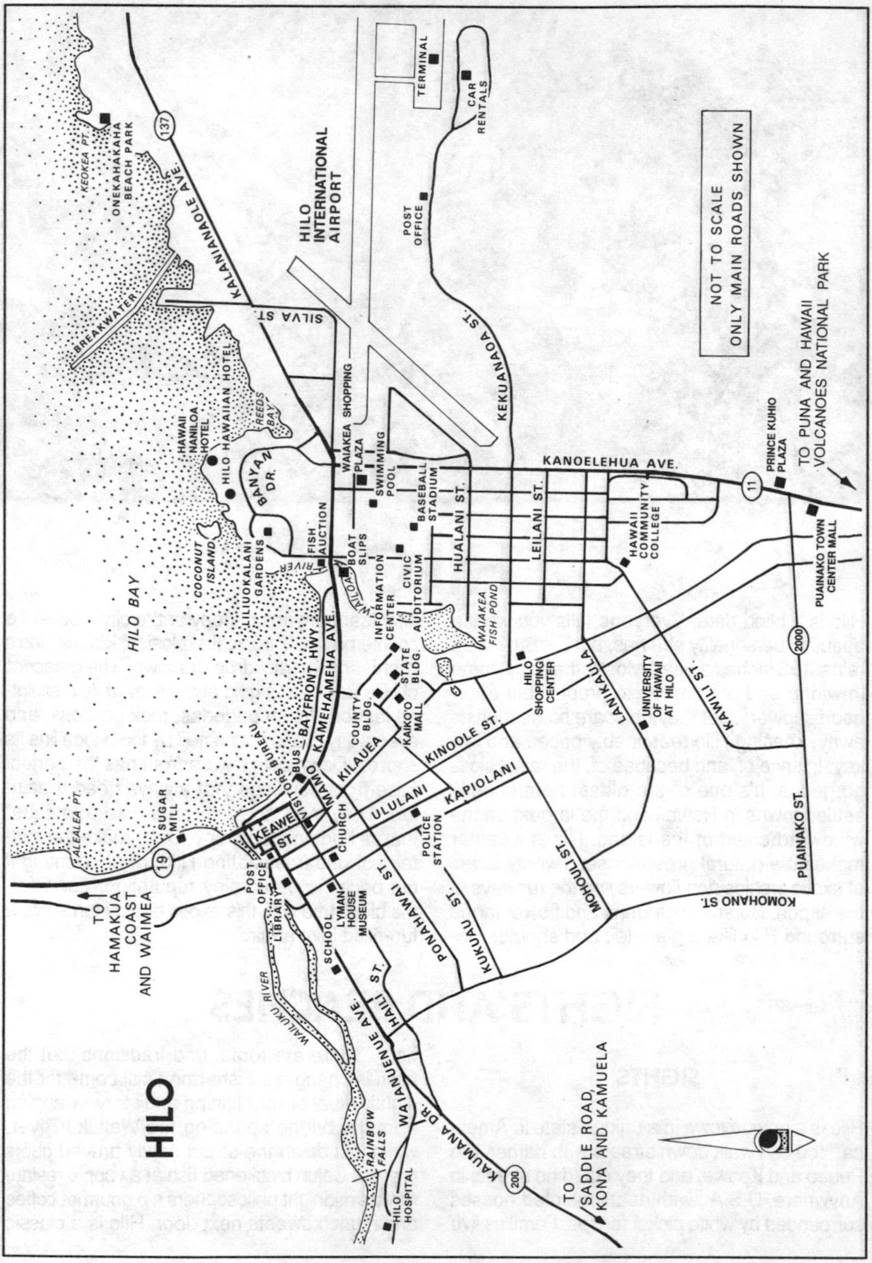

HILO
HILO BAY
TO HAMAKUA COAST AND WAIMEA
ALEALEA PT.
SUGAR MILL
19
KEAWE ST.
POST OFFICE
LIBRARY
SCHOOL
LYMAN HOUSE MUSEUM
CHURCH
VISITORS BUREAU
BUS
MAMO
KAMEHAMEHA AVE.
BAYFRONT HWY.
KILAUEA
COUNTY BLDG.
KAIKO'O MALL
STATE BLDG.
INFORMATION CENTER
CIVIC AUDITORIUM
BOAT SLIPS
WAILOA
RIVER
FISH AUCTION
LILIUOKALANI GARDENS
COCONUT ISLAND
BANYAN DR.
HILO HAWAIIAN HOTEL
HAWAII NANILOA HOTEL
REEDS BAY
BREAKWATER
ONEKAHAKAHA BEACH PARK
KEOKEA PT.
137
KALANIANAOLE AVE.
SILVA ST.
HILO INTERNATIONAL AIRPORT
TERMINAL
CAR RENTALS
POST OFFICE
WAIAKEA SHOPPING PLAZA
SWIMMING POOL
BASEBALL STADIUM
KEKUANAOA ST.
KANOELEHUA AVE.
HUALANI ST.
LEILANI ST.
WAIAKEA FISH POND
HILO SHOPPING CENTER
KINOOLE ST.
ULULANI
KAPIOLANI
POLICE STATION
PONAHAWAI ST.
KUKUAU ST.
MOHOULI ST.
LANIKAULA
UNIVERSITY OF HAWAII AT HILO
HAWAII COMMUNITY COLLEGE
KAWILI ST.
2000
PUAINAKO ST.
KOMOHANA ST.
PUAINAKO TOWN CENTER MALL
11
PRINCE KUHIO PLAZA
TO PUNA AND HAWAII VOLCANOES NATIONAL PARK
NOT TO SCALE
ONLY MAIN ROADS SHOWN
WAILUKU RIVER
RAINBOW FALLS
HILO HOSPITAL
WAIANUENUE AVE.
HAILI ST.
KAUMANA DR.
200
TO SADDLE ROAD, KONA AND KAMUELA
MOON

tropical town. Some preserved buildings, proud again after new face-lifts, are a few stories tall and date from the turn of the century when Hilo was a major port of entry to Hawaii. Sidewalks in older sections are covered with awnings because of the rains and add a turn-of-the-century gentility. Because Hilo is a town, most Americans can relate to it: it's big enough to have one-way streets and malls, but not so big that it's a metropolis like Honolulu, or so small that it's a village like Hana. You can walk the central area comfortably in an afternoon, but the town does sprawl, and it's *happening.* Teenagers in "boom box" cars cruise the main strip which is lined with fine restaurants, high-tech discos, and mom-and-pop shops. There's even a down-and-out section where guys hunker down in alleyways, smoking cigarettes and peering into the night. But in the still night, there's the deep-throated sound of a ship's foghorn, a specter of times past when Hilo was a vibrant port. Hilo is the opposite of Kailua-Kona both spiritually and physically. There, everything runs super-fast; it's a clone of Honolulu. In Hilo the old beat, the old music, that feeling of a tropical place where rhythms are slow and sensual, still exist. Hilo nights are alive with sounds of the tropics and the heady smell of fruits and flowering trees wafting on the breeze. Hilo remains what it always was—a town, a place where people live.

Hilo is the eastern hub of the island. Choose a direction, and an hour's driving puts you in a time-lost valley deep in *paniolo* country, or on the blackness of a recent lava flow, or above the steaming fumaroles of Hawaii Volcanoes National Park. In and around town are museums, riverbank fishing, cultural centers, plenty of gardens, waterfalls, a potholed riverbed, and lava caves. Hilo's beaches are small, rocky, and hard to find—perfect for keeping crowds away. Hilo is bite-sized, but you'll need a rental car or the Banyan Shuttle to visit most of the sights around town.

The main thoroughfares through town are Kilauea Street, which merges into Keawe Street and runs one-way toward the Wailuku River; and Kinoole Street, which runs one-way away from the river. Basically they feed into each other and make a big loop through the downtown area. Kamehameha Avenue fronts the town area and runs along the bay.

Lyman Mission House And Museum

The preserved New England-style homestead of David and Sarah Lyman, Congregationalist missionaries who built it in 1839, is the oldest frame building still standing on the Big Island. Lyman House, at 276 Haili St., Hilo, HI 96720, tel. 835-5021, open Mon.-Sat. 9 a.m.-5 a.m., Sunday 1-4 p.m., admission $4.50 adults, $2.50 children 6-18, opened as a museum in 1932! In 1856, a second story was added, which provided more room and a perfect view of the harbor. In 1926, Haili Street was extended past the home, and at that time the Wilcox and Lyman families had the house turned parallel to the street so that it would front the entrance.

The furniture is authentic "Sandwich Isles" circa 1850, the best pieces fashioned from koa. Much of it has come from other missionary homes, although many pieces belonged to the original occupants.

The floors, mantels, and doors are deep, luxurious koa. The main door is a "Christian door," built by the Hilo Boys Boarding School. The top panels form a cross and the bottom depicts an open Bible. Many of the artifacts on the deep windowsills are tacked down because of earthquakes. One room was used as a schoolroom/dayroom where Mrs. Lyman taught arithmetic, map-making, and proper manners. The dining room holds an original family table that was set with the "Blue Willow" china seen in a nearby hutch. Some of the most interesting exhibits are of small personal items like a music box that still plays, and a collection of New England autumn leaves that Mrs. Lyman had sent over to show her children what that season was like. Upstairs are bedrooms that were occupied by the parents and the eight children (six were boys). Their portraits hang in a row. Mrs. Lyman kept a diary and faithfully recorded eruptions, earthquakes, and tsunamis. Scientists still refer to it for some of the earliest recorded data on these natural disturbances. The master bedroom has a large bed with pineapples carved into the bedposts, crafted by a ship's carpenter who lived with the family for about eight months. The bedroom mirror is an original, in which many Hawaiians received their first surprised look at themselves. A nursery holds a cradle used by all eight children. It's obvious that the Lymans did not live luxuriously, but they were comfortable in their new island home.

Next door to the Lyman House, in a modern two-story building, is the museum. The first floor is designated the **Island Heritage Gallery.** The entry is a replica of a Hawaiian grass house, complete with thatched roof and floor mats. Nearby are Hawaiian tools: hammers of clinkstone, chisels of basalt, and state-of-the-art "stone age" polishing stones with varying textures used to rub bowls and canoes to a smooth finish. Hawaiian fiberwork, the best in Polynesia, is the next display. As well as coconut and pandanus, the Hawaiians used the pliable air root of the *'ie'ie.* The material, dyed brown or black, was woven into intricate designs. You'll also see fishhooks, stone lamps, mortars and pestles, *lomi lomi* sticks, and a display on *kahuna,* with a fine text on the *kapu* system. Pre-contact displays give way to kimonos from Japan, a Chinese herbal medicine display, and a nook dedicated to Filipino heritage. Saying good-bye is a bust of Mark Twain, carved into a piece of the very monkeypod tree that he planted in Waiohinu in 1866.

Upstairs is the **Earth Heritage Gallery.** The mineral and rock collection here is rated one of the top 10 in the entire country, and by far the best in Polynesia. Marvel at thunder eggs, agates, jaspers, India blue mezolite, aquamarine lazurite from Afghanistan, and hunks of weirdly shaped lava. These displays are the lifelong collection of the great-grandson of the original Reverend Lyman. Anything coming from the earth can be exhibited here: shells named and categorized from around the world, petrified wood, glass paperweights, crystals, and Chinese artifacts. Other exhibits explain the geology and volcanology of Kilauea and Mauna Kea, and an entire section is dedicated to the vanishing flora and fauna of Hawaii. The museum is an educational delight.

Natural Sites And Walking Tour

Start your tour of Hilo by picking up a pamphlet/map entitled *Discover Downtown Hilo, A Walking Tour of Historic Sites,* free at most restaurants, hotels, and shops. This self-guiding pamphlet takes you down the main streets and back lanes where you discover the unique architecture of Hilo's glory days. The majority of the vintage buildings have been restored and the architecture varies from the continental style of the Hawaiian Telephone Building to the Zen Buddhist Taishoji Shoto Mission.

A remarkable building is the old police station just across from Kalakaua Park. Behind it, in a classic plantation building, is the home of the **East Hawaii Culture Center,** a nonprofit organization which supports local arts and hosts festivals, performances, and workshops throughout the year (see "Entertainment" under "Practicalities" later in this chapter).

After you leave the Lyman Museum, it's a short walk over to Hilo's library, 300 Waianuenue Avenue. Sitting at the entrance are two large stones. The larger is called the **Naha Stone,** known for its ability to detect any offspring of the ruling Naha clan. The test was simple: a baby was placed on the stone, and if the infant remained silent, he or she was Naha; if the baby cried, he or she wasn't. It is believed that this 7,000-pound monolith was brought from Kauai by canoe and placed near Pinao Temple in the immediate vicinity of what is now Wailuku Drive and Keawe Street. Kamehameha the Great supposedly fulfilled a prophecy of "moving a mountain" by budging this stone. The smaller stone is thought to be an entrance pillar of the Pinao Temple. Just behind the library is the Wailuku River. Pick any of its bridges for a panoramic view down to the sea. Often, local fishermen try their luck from the Wailuku's grassy banks. The massive boulder sitting in the river's mouth is known as Maui's Canoe.

A few miles out of town, as you head west on Waianuenue Avenue, are two natural spectacles definitely worth a look. Just past Hilo High School a sign directs you to Wailuku River State Park. Here is **Rainbow Falls,** a most spectacular yet easily visited natural wonder. You'll look down on a circular pool in the river below that's almost 100 feet in diameter; cascading into it is a lovely waterfall. The falls deserve their name because as they hit the water below, their mists throw flocks of rainbows into the air. Underneath the falls is a huge cavern. Most people are content to look from the vantage point near the parking lot, but if you walk to the left a stone stairway leads to a private viewing area directly over the falls. Here the river, strewn with volcanic boulders, pours over the edge. Follow the path for a minute or so along the bank to a gigantic banyan tree and a different vantage point.

Follow Waianuenue Avenue for two more miles past Hilo Hospital to the heights above town. A sign to turn right onto Pee Pee Falls Street points to the **Boiling Pots.** Usually no one is here. At the parking lot are an emergency phone and toilets. Follow the path past No Swimming signs to an overlook. Indented into the riverbed below is a series of irregularly shaped holes that look as though a peg-legged giant left his peg prints in the hot lava. Seven or eight resemble naturally bubbling jacuzzis. Turn your head upriver to see Pee Pee Falls, a gorgeous, five-spouted waterfall. You'll have this area to yourself, and it's great for a quiet picnic lunch.

Around Banyan Drive

If your Hilo hotel isn't situated along Banyan Drive, go there. This bucolic road skirts the edge of the Waiakea Peninsula that sticks out into Hilo Bay. Lining the drive is an almost uninterrupted series of banyans forming a giant hedgerow, while the fairways and greens of the Banyan Golf Course take up the center of the tiny peninsula. Park your car at one end and take a 15-minute stroll through this parklike atmosphere; the banyans have been named for well-known American luminaries. Boutiques and a variety of restaurants sit in the coolness under the trees.

Liliuokalani Gardens are formal Japanese-style gardens located along the west end of Banyan Drive. Meditatively quiet, they offer a beautiful view of the bay. **Coconut Island** just offshore is connected by a footbridge leading from the gardens. Along the footpaths are pagodas designed for relaxing, *torii* gates, stone lanterns, and half-moon bridges spanning a series of ponds and streams. Few people visit. If it weren't for the striking fingers of black lava and coconut trees, you could easily be in Japan.

Suisan Fish Market is at the corner of Banyan Drive and Lihiwai Street, which crosses Kamehameha Avenue. This fish auction draws island fishermen of every nationality. The auctioneer's staccato is pure pidgin. Restaurateurs, housewives, and a smattering of tourists gather by 7:30 a.m. to eyeball the catch of the day. Boats tie up and fishermen talk quietly about the prices. Next door, a small snack shop sells sandwiches and piping-hot coffee. Grab a cup and walk over to the gardens through a nearby entrance—you'll have them to yourself.

Cross Lihiwai Street heading south. **Waiakea Pond,** a brackish lagoon where people often fish, is on your right. To the left are **Hoolulu County Park, Civic Center Auditorium,** and a city nursery brimming with orchids. The **Culture Center Nihon** is here too, at 123 Lihiwai St.; it displays artwork and cultural exhibits from Japan. The center is also a restaurant and sushi bar, with a special room set aside for the "tea ceremony." (For more details see "Food" in the "Practicalities" section below.)

On the opposite side of Waiakea Fish Pond (drive down Kamehameha Avenue and make a left onto Pauahi Street since no bridges cross), you'll find **Wailoa Information Center** dispensing all manner of brochures and pamphlets on Hilo and Big Island activities. The walls of this 10-sided building are used to display works of local artists and cultural/historic exhibits, changed on a monthly basis. Across the parking lot in a grassy area is the Tsunami Memorial, dedicated to those who lost their lives in the devastating tidal waves that raked the island. Volcanic stone, inlaid with blue and green tile, has been laid to form a circular wall that undulates and peaks like a wave. It's worth a look.

Hilo's Gardens

Hilo's greatest asset is its flowers. Its biggest cash crops are orchids and anthuriums. Flowers grow everywhere, but to see them in a more formalized way, visit one of the following nurseries in and around town. Most have excellent prices for floral arrangements sent to the Mainland. They'll do a Hawaiian bouquet with heliconia, anthuriums, and orchids for around $25 including shipping. The flowers arrive neatly packaged but unassembled, with a picture of the arrangement so that you can put them together yourself. These hearty cut flowers will look fresh and vibrant for as long as two weeks, so a few days in the mail won't hurt them. (Also see the description of Hawaii Tropical Botanical Gardens under "Scenic Drive" below.)

Hilo Tropical Gardens and Gallery (formerly Kong's Floraleigh), 1477 Kalanianaole Ave., Hilo, HI 96720, tel. 935-4957, is open daily 9 a.m.-5 p.m. The admission price of $3 (children under 12 free) includes a cup of Kona coffee. Here you can go on a self-guided tour through the gardens; all plants have been labeled. Everything's here: plumeria, lipstick trees, anthuriums, orchids, birds of paradise, even pineapples, coconuts, and papayas. You can purchase all manner of dried and fresh-cut flowers, seeds, packaged plants, seedlings, and corsages. The Gallery Gift Shop features art and local crafts of the Big Island, including prints, books, wood items, and pottery. The "no-pressure" salespeople are courteous and friendly. Shipping purchases is no problem.

Along Kilauea Avenue, between Lanikaula and Kawili streets, the Department of Natural Resources, Division of Forestry maintains the **Hilo Arboretum,** open Mon.-Fri. 7:45 a.m.-4:30 p.m., closed Saturday, Sunday, and holidays; free. This tree nursery contains most of the trees present in Hawaii, including indigenous and imported specimens. The office will provide you with a mimeographed sheet entitled "Hilo Nursery Arboretum." It's basically a self-guided tour, but the clerks will warn you that it's not very good. It attempts to name the trees by matching them with points on the map as you pass by, instead of referring to signs on each specimen. However, the trees are magnificent and you will have this quiet area virtually to yourself. The site was originally an animal quarantine station operated by the Territory of Hawaii; the 19.4 acres of the arboretum were established in 1920 by Brother Mathias Newell. Brother Newell was a nurseryman employed by the Catholic boys' school in Hilo. At that time the Division of Forestry was already actively introducing plant species from all over the world. For the 40 years from 1921-61 the department was engaged in the development and maintenance of arboretums consisting primarily of plant species from Australia and Africa. Arboretum sites ranged from sea level to Mauna Kea. Plant materials were exchanged and thousands of breadfruit cuttings were exported. Over 1,000 different tree species and 500 different fruit trees were field tested. Here at the Hilo Arboretum over 1,000 trees were planted. A few trees such as the paper bark and some pines are more than 50 years old. Presently a small number of timber species is grown for reforestation purposes. Essentially the Hilo site is utilized for the propagation of rare and endangered plant species, for research, and for experimental pursuits.

Nani Mau Gardens are some of the largest in and around Hilo, and touring these spectacular displays is well worth an afternoon. Located at 421 Makalika St. (off Rt. 11), Hilo, HI 96720, tel. 959-3541, the gardens are open daily 8:30 a.m.-5 p.m. Admission is $5, golf cart for touring $6. The gardens consist of 20 sculpted acres; 33 more are being developed. More than a botanical garden, Nani Mau is a "floral theme park" designed as a tourist attraction. Walks throughout the garden are very tame but very beautiful; umbrellas are provided during rainy weather, which adds its own dripping, crystalline charm to the experience. Plants are labeled in English, Latin, and Japanese. The gardens are a huge but ordered display of flowers, flowering trees, and shrubbery. The wildly colored plumage of tropical birds here and there competes with the colors of the exotic blooms. The gardens are broken off into separate areas: fruit orchards, heliconia garden, ginger garden, anthurium garden, orchid garden, orchid pavilion, gardenia garden, and bromeliad garden. The new 33 acres include an annual garden, white-sand beach, small volcano, picture garden for photos, and orchids and more orchids. It also features floral sculptures, a small reflective pond, and an assortment of flowers and shrubs laid out in geometric patterns, hearts, mountains, and even "aloha" and "Hilo Hawaii" spelled out in blooms. The tourist shop and snack area is exactly like a Japanese *omiyagi* (souvenir) shop. No wonder, since it's owned by Japanese, and the tour buses coming here are filled with Japanese. If you enjoy a clean, outdoor experience surrounded by magnificent flowers, this is the place.

Tanaka's is an excellent nursery from which to buy and to send flowers. They call themselves Jewel Box Orchids and also The Orchidarium, Hawaii Inc., at 524 Manono St., Hilo, HI. It's off the main track. Follow Rt. 11 toward Volcano, make a right on Kekuanaoa Street, and go down four blocks to Manono. Make a right and they're a few hundred yards down on the left. For beautiful orchids at unbeatable prices, search them out.

While in the neighborhood, visit **Paradise Plants** at 575 Hinano St., tel. 935-4043, a complete garden center specializing in indoor-outdoor plants and tropical fruit trees. They send orchids and other live flowers to the Mainland. Also featured is a large gift area with gifts from around the world. While browsing, check out their free orchid garden, which ranks as Hilo's oldest.

Kualoa Farms is at the corner of Mamaki (off Rt. 11) and Kealakai streets, tel. 959-4565, open daily 8 a.m.-4 p.m. A guided tour takes you over some of the 62 acres planted in anthuriums, ti plants, torch ginger, and macadamia and papaya orchards.

Mauna Loa Macadamia Nut Factory is located along Mauna Loa Road, eight miles out of Hilo on Rt. 11 toward Volcanoes National Park. Head down the drive until you come to the visitors center. Inside will be a free video explaining the development and processing of macadamia nuts in Hawaii. Take a self-guided tour through the orchards, where all trees and plants are identified. Then return to the snack shop for mac-nut goodies like ice cream and cookies. The gift shop has a wide assortment of mac-nut items at considerably lower prices than anywhere else on the island.

Panaewa Rainforest Zoo

Not many travelers can visit a zoo in such a unique setting where the animals virtually live in paradise. The road to the zoo is a trip in itself, getting you back into the country. Follow Rt. 11 toward Volcanoes National Park for a few miles until you see the sign pointing down Mamaki Street to the zoo. On a typical weekday, you'll have the place to yourself. The zoo, operated by the Department of Parks and Recreation, is open Mon.-Fri. 9 a.m.-4 p.m., Saturday 11 a.m.-2 p.m., gates locked at 4:15 p.m., closed Christmas and New Year's Day. Admission is free.

Here you have the feeling that the animals are not "fenced in" so much as you are "fenced out." The collection includes ordinary and exotic animals from around the world. You'll see a giant anteater from Costa Rica, pygmy hippos from Africa, and a wide assortment of birds like pheasants and peacocks. The zoo is also a botanical garden with many of the trees, shrubs, and ferns labeled. The zoo hosts many endangered animals indigenous to Hawaii like the Laysan duck, Hawaiian coot, *pueo,* Hawaiian gallinule, and even a feral pig in his own stone mini-condo. There are some great iguanas and mongooses, lemurs, and an aviary section with exotic birds like yellow-fronted parrots and blue and gold macaws. The central area is a tigers' playground; a tall fence marks this rather large area where tigers still rule their domain. It's got its own pond and tall grasses that make the tigers feel at home, but also make them hard to spot.

A touching place is the **Astronaut Grove,** in memory of the astronauts who were killed in the regrettable explosion of the space shuttle *Challenger.* All are remembered, especially Ellison Onizuka, a native son of the Big Island. The zoo makes a perfect side trip for families or for anyone wishing to get off the beaten track.

Scenic Drive

Route 19 heading north from Hilo toward Honokaa is a must, with magnificent inland and coastal views one after another. (See the Hamakua Coast chapter for full coverage of the northern section leading to Waipio.) Only five minutes from Hilo, you'll come to Papaikou town. Look for a small convenience store on the right. Just here is a road posted as a scenic drive which dips down toward the coast. Take it! Almost immediately a sign says Narrow Winding Road, 20 MPH, letting you know what kind of area you're coming into. Start down this lane past some very modest homes, and into the jungle that covers the road like a living green tunnel. Prepare for tiny bridges crossing tiny valleys. Stop, and you can almost hear the jungle growing. For those who have heard of the road to Hana, Maui, the Scenic Drive is a mini-version of what it has to offer.

In a few minutes you'll come to **Hawaii Tropical Botanical Gardens,** tel. 964-5233, open daily 8:30 a.m.-5:30 p.m., with the last shuttle van departing for the garden from the registration area at 4:30 p.m. Admission is $12, children under 16 free. Remember that the $12 entrance fee not only allows you to walk through the best-tamed tropical rainforest on the Big Island, but helps preserve the area in perpetuity. The gardens were established in 1978 when Dan and Pauline Lutkenhouse purchased the property in order to educate the public to the beauty of tropical plants in their natural setting. The gardens have been open for viewing since 1984. Mr. Lutkenhouse, a retired San Francisco businessman, purchased the 25-acre valley and

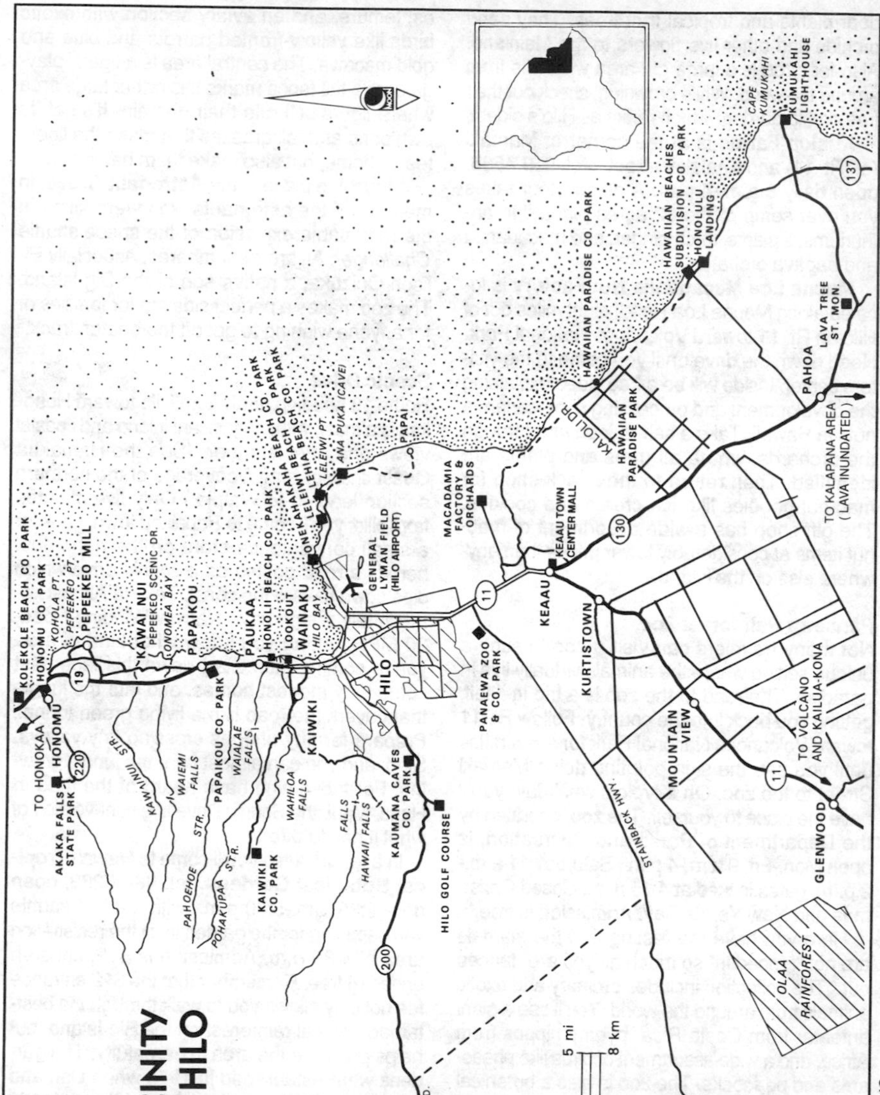

VICINITY OF HILO

TO HONOKAA
AKAKA FALLS STATE PARK
HONOMU
KOLEKOLE BEACH CO. PARK
HONOMU CO. PARK
KOHOLA PT.
PEPEEKEO PT.
PEPEEKEO MILL
KAWAI NUI
PEPEEKEO SCENIC DR.
ONOMEA BAY
PAPAIKOU
PAUKAA
HONOLII BEACH CO. PARK
LOOKOUT
WAINAKU
HILO BAY
ONEKAHAKAHA BEACH CO. PARK
LELEIWI BEACH CO. PARK
LEHIA BEACH CO. PARK
LELEIWI PT.
ANA PUKA (CAVE)
PAPAI
GENERAL LYMAN FIELD (HILO AIRPORT)
HILO
KAIWIKI
KAWAINUI STR.
WAIEMI FALLS
PAHOEHOE STR.
PAPAIKOU CO. PARK
WAIALAE FALLS
POHAKUPAA STR.
KAIWIKI CO. PARK
WAHILOA FALLS
FALLS
HAWAII FALLS
KAUMANA CAVES CO. PARK
HILO GOLF COURSE
SADDLE RD.
TO WAIMEA AND KAILUA-KONA
PANAEWA ZOO & CO. PARK
MACADAMIA FACTORY & ORCHARDS
KEAAU
KEAAU TOWN CENTER MALL
KURTISTOWN
MOUNTAIN VIEW
STAINBACK HWY.
KULANI HONOR CAMP
OLAA RAINFOREST
TO VOLCANO AND KAILUA-KONA
GLENWOOD
KALOLI DR.
HAWAIIAN PARADISE PARK
HAWAIIAN PARADISE CO. PARK
HAWAIIAN BEACHES SUBDIVISION CO. PARK
HONOLULU LANDING
TO KALAPANA AREA (LAVA INUNDATED)
PAHOA
LAVA TREE ST. MON.
KUMUKAHI LIGHTHOUSE
CAPE KUMUKAHI
19
11
130
137
200
220
0 5 mi
0 8 km

personally performed the work that transformed it into one of the most exotic spots in all of Hawaii. The locality was amazingly beautiful but inaccessible because it was so rugged. Through a personal investment of nearly $1 million and six painstaking years of toil aided only by two helpers, he hand-cleared the land, built trails and bridges, developed an irrigation system, acquired more than 2,000 different species of trees and plants, and established one mile of scenic trails and a large water-lily lake stocked with koi and tropical fish. A shuttle van takes you on a five-minute ride down to Onomea Bay where the gardens are located. Onomea was a favorite spot with the Hawaiians, who came to fish and camp for the night. The valley was a fishing village called Kahlili in the early 1800s. Later on it became a rough-water seaport used for shipping sugarcane and other tropical products. Recently, a remake of *Lord of the Flies* was filmed here, and it's easy to see why the area made the perfect movie set.

The van drops you off at a staging area in the garden where you'll find self-guiding maps, drinking water, restrooms, umbrellas for your convenience, and jungle perfume—better known as mosquito repellent! Plants from the four corners of the globe, including Iran, Central China, Japan, tropical Africa, India, Borneo, Brazil, East Indies, South Pacific Islands, tropical America, and the Philippines, are named with a full botanical description. Native plants from Hawaii are included. Listen for the songs of birds: the white-tailed tropic bird, black-crowned heron, Pacific golden plover, Hawaiian hawk, Japanese white eye, common mynah, and northern cardinal. Choose one of the aptly named trails like Ocean Trail or Waterfall Trail and lose yourself in the beauty of the surroundings. You are in the middle of a tamed jungle, walking along manicured paths. Stroll the Ocean Trail down to the sea, where the rugged coastline is dramatically pummeled by frothy waves. You can hear the waves entering submerged lava caves, where they blow in and out like a giant bellows. Away from the sea you'll encounter screened gazebos filled with exotic birds like cockatoos from Indonesia and blue-fronted Amazon parrots. Walk the inland trails past waterfalls, streams, a bamboo grove, and innumerable flowers. For at least a brief time you get to feel the power and beauty of a living Garden of Eden.

Hawaiian Artifacts, just a minute down Scenic Drive past the gardens, is a shop owned and operated by Paul Gephart, tel. 964-1729, open Mon.-Sat. 9 a.m.-5 p.m. Paul creates wood sculptures mainly from koa and ohia that he turns into whales, dolphins, birds, and poi bowls. Here's also a small but tasteful collection of jewelry and seashells, all at very decent prices.

Continue for another two to three miles, and you'll come to a wooden bridge with a white railing overlooking a cascading mountain stream with a big swimming hole. Great for a freshwater dip, but always be careful: these streams can be torrential during a heavy rain. The side road rejoins Rt. 19 at Pepeekeo, a workers' village where you can get gas or supplies. (For points north see the Hamakua Coast chapter.)

BEACHES

If you define a beach as a long expanse of white sand covered by a thousand sunbathers and their beach umbrellas, then Hilo doesn't have any. If a beach, to you, can be a smaller, more intimate affair where a good but not gigantic number of tourists and families can spend the day on pockets of sand between fingers of black lava, then Hilo has plenty. Hilo's best beaches all lie to the east of the city along Kalanianaole Avenue, which runs six miles from downtown Hilo to its dead end at Leleiwi Point. Not all beaches are clearly marked, but they are easily spotted by cars parked along the road or in makeshift parking lots.

Hilo Bayfront Park is a thousand yards of black sand that narrows considerably as it runs west from the Wailoa River toward downtown. At one time it went all the way to the Wailuku River and was renowned throughout the islands for its beauty, but commercialism of the harbor has ruined it. By the 1960s, so much sewage and industrial waste had been pumped into the bay that it was considered a public menace, and then the great tsunami came. Reclamation projects created the Wailoa River State Recreation Area at the east end, and shorefront land became a buffer zone against future inundation. Few swimmers come to the beach because the water is cloudy and chilly, but the sharks don't seem to mind! The bay is terrific for fishing and picnicking, and the sails of small craft and windsurfers can always be seen. It's a perfect spot for canoe races, and many local teams come here to train. Notice the judging towers and canoe sheds. Toward the west end, near the mouth of the Wailuku River, surfers catch long rides during the winter months, entertaining spectators.

Coconut Island Park is reached by footbridge from a spit of land just outside Liliuokalani Gardens. It was at one time a *pu'uhonua* ("place of refuge") opposite a human sacrificial *heiau* on the peninsula side. Coconut Island has restrooms, a pavilion, and picnic tables shaded by tall coconut trees and ironwoods. A favorite picnic spot for decades, it has a diving tower and a sheltered natural pool area for children. The only decent place to swim in Hilo Bay, it also offers the best panorama of the city, bay, and Mauna Kea beyond.

Reeds Bay Beach Park is on the east side of the Waiakea Peninsula at the end of Banyan Drive. It too is technically part of Hilo Bay, and offers good swimming, though the water is notoriously cold because of a constantly flowing freshwater spring. Most people just picnic here, and fishermen frequent the area.

Keaukaha Beach, located on Puhi Bay, is the first in a series of beaches as you head east on Kalanianaole Avenue. Look for Baker Avenue and pull off to the left into a parking area near an old pavilion. This is a favorite spot with local people, who swim at "Cold Water Pond," a spring-fed inlet at the head of the bay. A sewage treatment plant fronts the western side of Puhi Bay. Much nicer areas await you just up Kalanianaole Avenue.

Onekahakaha Beach County Park has it all: safe swimming, white-sand beach, lifeguards, all amenities, and camping. Turn left onto Machida Lane and park in the lot of Hilo's favorite "family" beach, although very recently a number of local homeless people have been living in this area. Swim in the large, sandy-bottomed pool protected by the breakwater. Outside the breakwater the currents can be fierce and drownings have been recorded. Walk east along the shore to find an undeveloped area of the park with many small tidal pools. Beware of sea urchins.

James Kealoha Park is next; people swim, snorkel, and fish, and during winter months it's a favorite surfing spot. A large grassy area is shaded by trees and a picnic pavilion. Just offshore is an island known as Scout Island because local Boy Scouts often camp here. This entire area was known for its fishponds, and inland, just across Kalanianaole Avenue, is Loko'aka Pond, a commercial operation providing the best mullet on the island.

Leleiwi Beach County Park lies along a lovely residential area carved into the rugged coastline. Part of the park is dedicated to the Richardson Ocean Center, and the entire area is locally called **Richardson's Beach.** Look for Uwau Street, just past the Mauna Loa Shores Condo, and park along the road here. Look for a fancy house surrounded by tall coconut trees and follow the pathway through the grove. Use a shower that's coming out of the retaining wall surrounding the house. Keep walking until you come to a seawall. A tiny cove with a black-sand beach is the first in a series. This is a terrific area for snorkeling, with plenty of marinelife. Walk east to a natural lava breakwater. Behind it are pools filled and flushed by the surging tide. The water breaks over the top of the lava and rushes into the pools, making natural jacuzzis. This is one of the most picturesque swimming areas on the island. At Leleiwi Beach Park proper (three pavilions), the shore is open to the ocean and there are strong currents; it's best to head directly to Richardson's.

Lehia Park is the end of the road. When the pavement stops, follow the dirt track until you come to a large, grassy field shaded by a variety of trees. This unofficial camping area has no amenities whatsoever. A series of pools like those at Richardson's are small, sandy-bottomed, and safe. Outside of the natural lava breakwater, currents are treacherous. Winter often sends tides surging inland here, making Lehia unusable. This area is about as far away as you can get and still be within a few minutes of downtown Hilo.

PRACTICALITIES

ACCOMMODATIONS

Accommodations in Hilo are hardly ever booked out, and they're reasonably priced. Sounds great, but many hotels have "gone condo" to survive while others have simply shut their doors, so there aren't as many as there once were. During the Merrie Monarch Festival (late April), the entire town is booked solid. The best hotels are clustered along Banyan Drive, with a few gems tucked away on the city streets.

Banyan Drive Hotels

The following hotels lie along Banyan Drive. They range from moderate to deluxe; all are serviced by the Banyan Shuttle (see "Public Transportation" under "Getting Around" earlier in this chapter).

Prices at the classy **Hilo Hawaiian Hotel,** 71 Banyan Dr., Hilo, HI 96720, tel. 935-9361 or (800) 272-5275, start at $99-122; all rooms have a/c, phone, and TV, plus there's a pool. The Hilo Hawaiian occupies the most beautiful grounds of any hotel in Hilo. From the vantage of the hotel's colonnaded veranda, you overlook formal gardens, Coconut Island, and Hilo Bay. Designed as a huge arc, the hotel's architecture blends well with its surroundings and expresses the theme set by Hilo Bay, that of a long, sweeping crescent. The hotel buffet, especially the Friday and Saturday seafood version, is absolutely out of this world (see the description of Queen's Court under "Food" below). As a deluxe hotel, the Hilo Hawaiian is the best that Hilo has to offer.

Hawaii Naniloa Hotel, 93 Banyan Dr., Hilo, HI 96720, tel. 969-3333 or (800) 442-5845, is a massive, 386-room hotel offering deluxe accommodations. Rates start at $96 standard, $119 superior, $144 deluxe with private balcony. Private suites are available from $189. A third person costs $15 additional; children under 17 sharing with parents are free. They offer a/c, TV, hotel parking, a restaurant, and a pool setting—just above the lava—that is the nicest in Hilo. The original hotel dates back over 60 years and has built up a fine reputation for value and service. The Hawaii Naniloa has recently undergone extensive renovations and is now as beautiful as ever.

Uncle Billy's Hilo Bay Hotel is sandwiched between much larger hotels at 87 Banyan Dr., Hilo, HI 96720, tel. 961-5818 or (800) 367-5102. Rooms here begin at $59 d (including breakfast for two), $69 for a kitchenette, and $74 for a room-and-car package. The Hilo Bay's blue metal roof and orange louvered shutters make it look a bit like "Howard Johnson's Meets Polynesia." The lobby's rattan furniture and thatched longhouse theme are pure '50s-kitsch Hawaii. There are parking and a pool, all rooms are clean and air-conditioned, and each one has a TV and phone. The hotel offers excellent value for the money. Uncle Billy's Polynesian Marketplace, where you can buy everything from beer to sundries, is part of the complex.

You can't miss the orange-and-black **Hilo Seaside Hotel,** 126 Banyan Dr., tel. 935-0821 or (800) 367-7000. This is the budget hotel on Banyan Drive. It's island-owned by the Kimi family, and like the others in this small chain, it's clean and well kept and has Polynesian-inspired decor. Room prices are $49 standard, $59 superior, $66 deluxe, and $76 kitchenette. Add approximately $20 for a room/car package. Ask about off-season rates, and they will sometimes offer a better rate depending on the amount of business at the time. The grounds are laid around a central courtyard and the pool is secluded away from the street. At this family-style hotel with a motel atmosphere, the friendly staff goes out of its way to make you feel welcome.

The **Country Club Condo Hotel,** 121 Banyan Dr., tel. 935-7171, is a basic hotel/condo with very reasonable rates. Standard rooms are $39, deluxe ocean $59, one-bedroom suites $80. Weekly and monthly rates are available. Since this is a condo hotel, the rooms vary from unit to unit, but most have either double beds or a queen-size bed.

Downtown Hotels

The following hotels are found along Hilo's downtown streets. Some are in quiet residential areas,

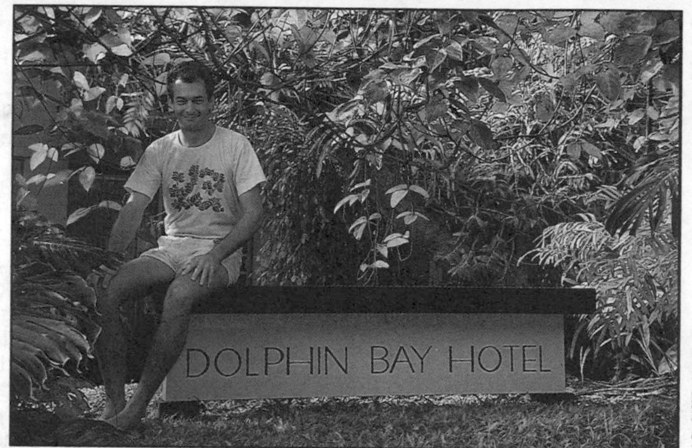

John Alexander of the Dolphin Bay Hotel

J.D. BISIGNANI

while others are along busy thoroughfares. They are moderately to inexpensively priced.

Dolphin Bay Hotel is a sparkling little gem—simply the best hotel bargain in Hilo, one of those places where you get more than you pay for. It sits on a side street in the Puueo section of town at the north end of Hilo Bay: 333 Iliahi St., Hilo, HI 96720, tel. 935-1466. John Alexander, the owner/manager, is at the front desk every day. He's a font of information about the Big Island and will happily dispense advice on how to make your day-trips fulfilling. The hotel was built by his father, who spent years in Japan, and you'll be happy to discover this influence when you sink deep into the *ofuro*-type tubs in every room. All 18 units have full modern kitchens. Rates are single studio apartment $39 s, $49 d; superior $49 s, $59 d; one bedroom $69 d; two-bedroom, fully furnished unit $79 d, $10 additional guest. Deluxe units upstairs have open-beam ceilings and lanai, and with three spacious rooms feel like apartments. No swimming pool or a/c, but there are color TVs and fans with excellent cross-ventilation. The grounds and housekeeping are immaculate. Hotel guests can partake of free bananas, papayas, and other exotic fruits found in hanging baskets in the lobby, as well as free coffee. Weekly rates range from $315 for a studio to $525 for a two-bedroom deluxe. Make reservations, because everyone who has found the Dolphin Bay comes back again and again.

The Wild Ginger Inn, at 100 Puueo St., Hilo, HI 96720, tel. 935-5556 or (800) 882-1887, is a refurbished plantation-style hotel, painted shocking pink and green, that bills itself as a bed-and-breakfast inn. An open-air lobby leads to an encircling veranda overlooking the central courtyard area, with a view of the bay in the distance. Each of the wainscoted rooms, very basic but very clean, has a refrigerator, private shower-bath, cross ventilation, and one double and one twin bed. A double hammock and vintage chairs in the lobby area are for your relaxation. Rates are standard room $39 d, deluxe rooms with cable TV $49-59, special weekly and monthly rates, and extra person $10. The homestyle Hawaiian buffet is terrific: guava-passion fruit juice, milk, local coffee with macadamia nuts, granola, yogurt, muffins, hard-boiled eggs, island fruits in season, turkey-ham, cheese, and toast. The inn is completely nonsmoking with a special area provided for smokers in the garden. The Wild Ginger Inn, with a friendly staff and good service, is an excellent choice for budget accommodations, and gives more than full value for the money.

The **Hilo Hotel** is downtown at 142 Kinoole St., Hilo, HI 96720, tel. 961-3733. This vintage hotel originally opened in 1888 and was managed by Uncle George Lycurgus, who was more famous as manager of Volcano House. The present buildings date from 1955, and although additions have been made over the years, a sense of nostalgia lingers. Basic rooms in the old wing, each with phone and fridge, are $39-45; deluxe new-wing suites, quieter and with a/c, are $85-115. A big front porch is great for relaxing, and complimentary coffee is served at the pool every morning. The Hilo Hotel is also home to the Fuji Restaurant (see "Food" below). This is a classic hotel where you get full value for your money, and where the staff takes pride in doing things the right way.

The **Iolani Hotel,** 193 Kinoole St., Hilo, HI 96720, and the **Kamaaina Hotel** at 110 Haili St., are your basic fleabag dives. You can get a room at either for about $30 per night or $135 per week if you can find someone to check you in. For information contact Mrs. Beatie at The Surplus Store, 284 Keawe St., tel. 935-6398, only after noon. She doesn't seem overly anxious to rent these rooms, so you'll have to persevere.

Arnott's Lodge, 98 Apapane Rd., Hilo, HI 96720, tel. 969-7097, (800) 368-8752 Mainland, (800) 953-7773 Hawaii, is a very reasonably priced hostel offering a dormitory bunk for $15, and semiprivate rooms with shared bath, kitchen, and living room for $26 s, $36 d. Arnott's also offers inexpensive hiking and snorkel excursions.

If a hotel is not your style, and if you would appreciate something a little more . . . well, homey, try **Holmes' Sweet Home B&B,** at 107 Koula St., Hilo, HI 96720, tel. 961-9089, the residence of John and Charlotte Holmes. Located on a quiet cul-de-sac with a view of Hilo Bay, the home provides two rooms priced $60-70 (no credit cards) that each feature private entrance, bath, guest refrigerator, and microwave. A continental breakfast is included.

FOOD

Inexpensive Dining

Named after the famous all-Japanese fighting battalion that even predated the famous "442," the **Cafe 100,** at 969 Kilauea Ave., open Mon.-Thurs. 6:45 a.m.-8:30 p.m., Fri.-Sat. until 9:30 p.m., is a Hilo institution. The Miyashiro family has been serving food at their indoor-outdoor restaurant here since the late '50s. Although the loco moco, a cholesterol atom bomb containing a hamburger and egg atop rice smothered in gravy, was invented at Hilo's Lincoln Grill, the Cafe 100, serving it since 1961, has actually patented this belly-buster and turned it into an art form. There are the regular loco moco, the teriyaki loco, the sukiyaki loco, the hot dog loco, the *oyako* loco, and for the health-conscious, the mahi loco. With a few exceptions, they cost $2 or less. So, if your waistline, the surgeon general, and your arteries permit, this is *the* place to have one. Breakfast choices include everything from bacon and eggs to coffee and donuts, while lunches feature beef stew $3.75, mixed plate $3.95, fried chicken $3.25, and an assortment of sandwiches from teri beef to a good old BLT for $2 or so. Make your selection and sit at one of the picnic tables under the veranda to watch the people of Hilo go by.

All trips to Hilo must include a brief stop at **Low's International Food,** long occupying the corner of Kilauea and Ponahawai streets, tel. 969-6652, open daily except Wednesday, 9 a.m.-8 p.m., where *everyone* comes for the unique bread. Some of the more fanciful loaves are made from taro, breadfruit, guava, mango, passion fruit, coconut, banana, pumpkin, and cinnamon. The so-you-want-to-taste-it-all rainbow bread is a combination of taro, guava, and sweet bread. Loaves cost $4.25-5.25, and arrangements can be made to ship them home by Federal Express. Lunches, most under $5, range from their famous pot-roast pork tail with black bean sauce to turkey plate to lamb curry stew. Choose a table under the pavilion and enjoy your picnic in downtown Hilo.

Jasper's Espresso Cafe at 110 Kalakaua, tel. 969-6686, is open daily for lunch and dinner 11 a.m.-7:45 p.m., Friday and Saturday until 9:45 p.m., and for Sunday brunch 9 a.m.-2 p.m. It is not only a politically correct, community-oriented restaurant housed in a vintage bakery building from the 1920s, but it also has the most ceiling fans per square foot in Hilo, and the town's most elegant toilet (worth a visit regardless of whether nature is calling!). Jasper, the owner, serves "food with an attitude," and tries to keep it organic, island-fresh, mostly vegetarian, and wholesome. Racks hold environmental and peace-oriented magazines that you can browse while sipping espresso and listening to quiet acoustic guitar most evenings, or poetry on Fridays. The menu offers garden salad of mixed greens $3.50 (with soup $6.50), Caesar salad $6.50 (with soup $9.50), garden burger $5.50, or a good old crunchy peanut butter sandwich $2 (half orders available). The best deal, however, is an order of pinto beans and brown rice ($3.75) made more savory with toppings of salsa, sour cream, cheese, onions, and jalapeños (add 50 cents). Desserts are scrumptious: homemade Hilo ice cream, chocolate-caramel-macadamia nut cake $3.50, and brownies made with cream cheese, mac nuts, chocolate, and peanut butter $1.50. Jasper's is a terrific spot to relax and catch up on world events at the same time. Prices are unbeatable, and the service is friendly.

Mun Cheong Lau is a cheap Chinese joint in downtown Hilo at 172 Kilauea Ave., tel. 935-3040 (takeout too), open daily 11 a.m.-11 p.m., closed Tuesday. If you want to eat with "the people," this is the spot. Soups on the front of the menu are $3.50; those on the back are $2.50, and are about the same except they don't contain noodles. The servings are generous. Entrees like crispy chicken in oyster sauce for under $5 are delicious at any price. Seafoods include abalone with vegies for $3.40, abalone with black mushrooms $4.50, and shrimp with corn $3.75. A variety of pork or beef dishes are all priced under $3.50, while pineapple spareribs are $2.70 and boneless chicken with mushrooms is $3.75. These are full plates served with steamed rice, 60 cents extra if you want fried rice. For under $4 you can fill up in this place. It's clean, service is friendly, and the dining experience, while certainly not fancy, is definitely authentic.

Owned and operated by Dotty and Rey Frasco, **Dotty's Coffee Shop and Restaurant,** tel. 959-6477, at the Puainako Town Center, is open for breakfast daily 7-11 a.m., for lunch Mon.-Sat. 10:30 a.m.-2 p.m., and for dinner Mon.-Thurs. 5-8 p.m., Friday 5-9 p.m. Dotty's is an institution where local people come for the large and hearty portions. Breakfast is known for the corned beef hash and eggs and for French toast made with thick slices of sweet bread from Punaluu covered with real maple or coconut syrup at $3.75. Lunch favorites are grilled chicken supreme with mushrooms and Swiss cheese $4.65, or Dotty's ultimate steak sandwich with slices of sirloin, sautéed mushrooms, onions, and Swiss cheese on a grilled potato roll $5.65. Those in the know come from around the island to dine on Dotty's famous oven-roasted turkey, fresh catch-of-the-day, barbecued pork ribs with their own smoke-flavored sauce, and an amazing combination plate for $9.85 that gives you a choice of two: top sirloin, teriyaki steak, ribs, scampi, sautéed shrimp, or catch-of-the-day. Fresh vegetables, real mashed potatoes, and homemade soups (great chowder on Friday) come with all full meals. The decor is "American standard" with a Formica counter and leatherette booths. Check out the black-and-white photos hanging on the walls.

Ting Hao Mandarin Kitchen is a family affair run by Alice Chang and her sister, also in the Puainako Town Center, tel. 959-6288, open weekdays 11 a.m.-8:30 p.m., weekends 5-8:30 p.m. Seek them out for a mouthwatering, home-cooked meal. The two most expensive items on the menu are Seafood Treasure for $6, and half a tea-smoked duck for $7; all others are under $5. Service is slow due to individual-order cooking, and those in the know pick up a hand-out menu and call to place their orders 30 minutes before arriving. Also at Puainako Town Center is **Five Spice** with an assortment of *bento* for under $4 and quick snacks like chili and rice $1.90, chili dogs $1.95.

Bear's Coffee Shop, at 106 Keawe, tel. 935-0708, just down the street from Roussel's, is an upscale coffee shop renowned for its breakfast, served daily 7-11:30 a.m. It features Belgian waffles (made from malted flour) and an assortment of egg dishes for $2.95. Lunch is hearty sandwiches of turkey, pastrami, chicken fillet, tuna, or ham for under $5, along with a small but zesty selection of Mexican food as well as salads. Beverages include Italian sodas, homemade lemonade, and a large selection of coffee, cappuccino, and caffe latte from their full espresso bar. All perfect with desserts like carrot cake, Bear's brownies, cheesecake, and pies. A great place to relax, read the morning paper, and watch Hilo life go by.

Kay's Family Restaurant, at 684 Kilauea Ave., tel. 969-1776, open Tues.-Sun. 5 a.m.-2 p.m. and 5-9 p.m., can't be beat for a good square meal of Asian, Hawaiian, or American standards. Sandwich favorites like hamburgers, fish burgers, grilled cheese, and tuna are all under $3. Large bowls of saimin and wonton soups are under $4. Their grilled plates, like Korean barbecued beef or *kalbi* (short ribs), are cooked over an open wood fire and are delicious. Combo plates of their grilled offerings are $5.95 for one choice, $6.95 for two choices, and $7.95 for three choices, and include rice, miso soup, four kinds of *kimchi,* and vegetables. Kay's isn't much to look at, with leatherette booths and Formica tables, but it's a winner.

The **Ichiban Deli,** at 415 Kilauea Ave., across from the Hilo Hongwanji Temple, open Tues.-Sat. 7 a.m.-2 p.m. and 5-8:30 p.m., takeout available, is a basic Japanese-Hawaiian-American restaurant with breakfast like eggs with bacon or link sausage or corned beef hash $3.35, and lunches like fried chicken or spareribs, each at $4.25. The Japanese meals are standards like *bento* or tempura for under $5. No decor at all, but the prices are very reasonable.

Satsuki's, along the 200 block of Keawe St., receives the highest recommendation because when local people want a good meal at an inexpensive price they head here. Open for lunch 10 a.m-2 p.m., dinner 4:30-9 p.m., closed Tuesday. Specialties are oxtail soup, the lunch special for $4.25, and the Okinawa *soba* plate lunch for only $3.95. Dinner specials are beef teriyaki for $5.70, *tonkatsu* $5.65, and fish teriyaki $7.50. Plenty of traditional favorites like *donburi* and *nabemono.* All meals come with miso soup, Japanese pickles and condiments, rice, and tea. No decor, but spotlessly clean and friendly. Excellent food at excellent value.

Sachi's Gourmet, only a few seconds away at 250 Keawe St., open Monday 8 a.m.-2 p.m. only, Tues.-Sat. 8 a.m.-2 p.m. and dinner 5-9 p.m., Sunday dinner only 5-9 p.m., is the same type of restaurant as Satsuki's, with its own loyal local clientele. The food is excellent here, too, and the prices are unbeatable. You'll walk away stuffed on traditional Japanese food for about $8 for a full meal.

Dick's Coffee House in the Hilo Shopping Center, tel. 935-2769, is American standard with a Hawaiian twist. Open daily 7 a.m.-7 p.m., Sunday 7-10:30 a.m., this place could be Smalltown, U.S.A., where the walls are covered with pennants, except that the waitresses wear outrageously colorful, Hawaiian-style uniforms. Excellent prices for decent food—full meals with soup, salad, dessert, and coffee go for $4.50.

Hukilau Restaurant at the Hilo Seaside Hotel (see above), 126 Banyan Dr., is open daily 7 a.m.-1 p.m. and 4-9 p.m. For breakfast you can have steak and eggs $6.95, fish and eggs $2.95, two eggs and toast $1.85, ham omelette $2.75, or a full choice of hotcakes and waffles at reasonable prices. The lunch menu offers a choice of Reuben sandwich, steak and rice, baked chicken, or hamburger deluxe; each choice comes with a buffet salad bar for a fixed price of $5.25. The dinner menu is reasonable with T-bone steak $10.95, steak and lobster $14.95, oven roast prime rib $9.95, or the Captain's Platter (fried fish, shrimp, scallops, and oysters) for $9.95. All dinners come with soup of the day and salad bar. The decor is orange Naugahyde booths and brown Formica tables. Some of the vegetables come out of a can, and the deep-fried offerings have enough grease to clog the Alaska pipeline, but the view of Hilo Bay is exceptional and helps with digestion.

The **New China Restaurant,** at 510 Kilauea Ave., tel. 961-5677, open daily 10 a.m.-10 p.m., serves basic Chinese combo plates of chicken, duck, pork, beef, and seafood. The most expensive seafood on the menu is $7 for abalone and Chinese mushrooms. Special plates include steamed chicken with ginger, onion sauce, and steamed rice for $3.80; beef broccoli and crispy chicken for $2.80. Not much class—almost like a McDonald's of Chinese food—but it's bright, shiny, and sparkly.

When a Hilo resident wants a plate lunch, and that's saying something, they go to **Hilo Lunch Shop,** at the corner of Kalanikoa and Piilani, open daily except Sunday 6:15 a.m.-1:30 p.m. At this very basic restaurant, you pick and choose each separately priced item for your plate: tempura 90 cents; mahimahi 50 cents; vegetables 45 cents; for about $3 your plate will be huge. A minute away is **Snappy's Korean Barbecue,** a fairly new restaurant where dishes are priced well under $5.

Down Piilani, just at the Kentucky Fried Chicken, make a right onto Hinano Street and in a minute you'll see **Don's Grill,** tel. 935-9099, open daily except Monday 10:30 a.m.-9 p.m., and to 10 p.m. on Friday. This American/Hawaiian restaurant is known for good food at reasonable prices. Inside find wood-trimmed blue Formica tables in a very modern yet functionally tasteful setting. Breakfast starts with two eggs and toast $2.50, omelettes $4.95, and on weekends only, sweet bread French toast $2.75. Lunch can be taco salad $4.95, Philadelphia cheese steak $5.95, club sandwich $4.50, or your own burger creation starting at $4.25. Entrees are barbecued ribs, pork chops, or fillet of fish, all priced under $6. There's homemade pie, cheesecake, and pudding to top off your meal. Don's is a basic American standard restaurant where you can get a good square meal for a good price.

Stratton's at 121 Banyan Dr., tel. 961-6815, is a sports bar/restaurant where many of the local people go for a few laughs and a few beers. The breakfast menu, offered daily 6:30-11 a.m., includes two large eggs and choice of sausage, ham, Portuguese sausage, or Spam along with toast, rice, or hash browns $4.25; mahimahi and eggs $4.50; breakfast special $2.95; and a full pancake breakfast for only $3.95. Lunch, served daily 11 a.m.-3 p.m., includes specials like teriyaki beef $5.65, and the Captain's Platter (a combination of shrimp, oysters, and mahimahi) $7.95; or sandwiches like roast beef with sautéed onions $5.65 and a good old BLT $4.95. (Also see "Entertainment" below).

Fast Foods And Snacks

Okay! For those who must, **McDonald's** is at 88 Kanoelehua Ave. and 177 Ululani St., and **Pizza Hut,** which actually has a decent salad bar, is at 326 Kilauea Avenue. Fast-food junkies will be totally happy at the **Puainako Town Center,** where glass and Formica cubes hold endless boxes of munchies from **McDonald's, Pizza Hut, Subway Sandwiches, and Taco Bell.**

On Banyan Drive just outside of the Hilo Hawaiian Hotel, get delicious scoops of ice cream in island flavors like macadamia nut at the **Ice Cream Factory.** Nearby is the **Banyan Snack Shop,** which dispenses whopping plate lunches like the loco moco—two scoops of rice and a hamburger covered in fried egg and gravy—for only $2.75. The breakfast specials here are very cheap too.

The Chocolate Bar, next door to Bear's Coffee Shop (see above) at 98 Keawe St., will tempt you with fine candies and ice cream. Everything's homemade, from Gummi Bears to rolled chocolates. **Hilo Seeds and Snacks** next to Lehua's Restaurant at 15 Waianuenue Ave. sells sandwiches and authentic crackseed. The **Kilauea Preserve Center,** at the corner of Kilauea and Ponahawai streets, also sells authentic crackseed.

Lanky's Pastries and Deli, Hilo Shopping Center, tel. 935-6381, open 6:30 a.m.-9 p.m., deli side from 6 a.m., is a perfect place to head if you have a sweet tooth that *must* be satisfied. The deli/bakery is especially known for its "long johns,"—long, thin sugar donuts filled with custard—but they also have all kinds of baked goods from bread to apple turnovers. Their deli case holds sandwiches priced under $3, along with an assortment of *bento,* perfect for a picnic lunch.

Cathy's Lunch Shop, at 270 Kamehameha Ave., is a tiny little place with two tables, where only a few dollars will get you breakfast, a plate lunch, a hamburger, or even a taco.

Moderately Priced

Restaurant Miwa, at Hilo Shopping Center, 1261 Kilauea Ave., tel. 961-4454, is open daily 10 a.m.-9 p.m., sometimes until 10 p.m. for meals, and until 2 a.m. at the bar. Very beautifully appointed, Miwa is a surprise, especially since it's stuck back in the corner of the shopping center. Enter to find traditional shoji screens and wooden tables adorned with fine linens, along with a classic sushi bar. The waitresses wear kimonos, though most are local women, and not necessarily Japanese. The menu is excellent, with appetizers like sake-flavored steamed clams for $4.95 and crab *sunomono* (seaweed, cucumber slices, and crab meat) for $4.25. A specialty is *nabemono,* a hearty and zesty soup/stew, prepared at your table, with a two-order minimum. Traditional favorites popular with Westerners include beef sukiyaki and *shabu shabu* (each $14. Combination dinners give you a wider sampling of the menu at good value. Restaurant Miwa is an excellent choice for a gourmet meal at a reasonable price in a congenial setting.

Soontaree Gervais, a native Thai who wears a chef's hat about as big as she is, is the owner of **Soontaree's,** also at the Hilo Shopping Center, tel. 934-SIAM, open for lunch Tues.-Fri. 11 a.m.-2 p.m., dinner Tues.-Sun. 5:30-9 p.m. Here, you can have an excellent Thai meal for a very reasonable price. Although there is no view at all,

Soontaree's is nicely furnished with pink and blue tablecloths and full place settings. Like many Thai restaurants, they take care of the vegetarian. Meatless items on the menu are identified by a carrot icon next to them. Appetizers could be curry puff $2.95, chicken satay $6.95, grilled eggplant salad $4.95, or grilled Thai shrimp salad $8.95. Luscious Thai soups range from Thai *Tomyam* (mixed seasonal vegetables) for $5.95 to *Tom Kar Gar* (a hearty soup of coconut broth, chicken, and lemongrass) for $6.95. Entrees are exciting; choices include Thai barbecued chicken $7.95, an assortment of yellow or red curry $5.95-8.95, and *me grob* (crispy noodles with bay shrimp) $7.95. Desserts include traditional *haupia* (coconut custard Hawaiian style) and sticky rice pudding with coconut milk, both $1.95. Soontaree's offers exotic gourmet food at very reasonable prices in a setting that may not be elegant, but is definitely acceptable for a special meal.

Modern and chic with a checkerboard floor, gray-on-black tables and chairs, ceiling fans, and the calming effect of ferns and flowers, **Cafe Pesto,** at 308 Kamehameha Ave., tel. 969-6640, is open Sun.-Thurs. 11 a.m.-9 p.m., Fri.-Sat. 11 a.m.-10 p.m. One of Hilo's newest restaurants, it offers affordable gourmet food in an unpretentious and comfortable setting. The one-size pizza from their wood-fired oven can be anything from *quattro formaggio* (four cheeses) $5.95 to chicken bianco with wild mushrooms, sun-dried tomatoes and basil cream sauce $9.95. Combined with dinner salads of "wild greens" at $3.50, the pizza or a calzone makes a great meal for two. Delectable yet inexpensive items are foccacia with rosemary and Gorgonzola for $3.50, *crostini* (fresh bread with a creamy, fresh herb garlic butter) for $2.95, and soup of the day for only $3.25. Heartier appetites will be satisfied with bouillabaisse, rich with morsels of lobster, shrimp, fresh fish, clams, garlic, tomatoes, and sweet fennel, served with crusty bread for $12.95; or with chicken Lallo Rosa, a breast of chicken, greens, Maui onions, cherry tomatoes, and coriander dressing for $7.95. Pasta lovers will be happy with ceviche pasta salad $7.95; smoked salmon with fettuccine $12.95; and the *delizioso* lobster with *penne,* a delightful mix of noodles, spinach, roasted red peppers, cream sauce, and lobster $14.95. Cafe Pesto also has a brass-railed espresso bar where you can order caffe latte or iced cappuccino to top off your meal.

Fiasco's, a good restaurant and nightspot, is at the Waiakea Shopping Plaza, 200 Kanoelehua Ave., tel. 935-7666, open Sun.-Thurs. 11 a.m.-10 p.m., weekends to 11 p.m., with dancing 9 p.m. until closing on weekends (see "Entertainment" below). Featuring a country inn flavor, Fiasco's has a cobblestoned entrance that leads you to the cozy, post-and-beam dining room appointed with stout wooden tables and captain's chairs, with semi-private booths lining the walls. The mahogany bar, a classic with polished lion's-head brass rails, offers comfortable stools and black leather booths. The menu begins with appetizers like fried mozzarella $4.25, escargot $5.95, or a big plate of onion rings at $2.75. Lighter appetites might enjoy the salad bar buffet $6.50, or a taco salad with beef or chicken $6.25 (with refried beans $5.25). Sandwiches range from the croissant club $6.75 to French dip $5.95 to a classic burger $5.25. Entrees include Mexican fare like tacos $6.25 and American standards like rib-eye steak or prime rib $14.95. Families can save money with a special children's menu.

Uncle Billy's at the Hilo Bay Hotel along Banyan Drive, tel. 935-0861, is open for breakfast (featuring a $1.99 "aloha special") 6:30-9 a.m., dinner 5-8:30 p.m. Enjoy the free nightly hula show 6:30-7:30 p.m. The interior is neo-Polynesian with a Model T Ford as part of the decor. It's basically a fish and steak restaurant serving up shrimp scampi for $9.95, steaks for $11, and catch-of-the-day from $7.75—a good, fun place to dine.

Ken's Pancake House is one of a chain but you can have a good meal for a good price (cocktails too). Open 24 hours, it's conveniently located on the way to the airport at 1730 Kamehameha Ave., tel. 935-8711.

Nihon Culture Center, 123 Lihiwai St., tel. 969-1133 (reservations required), presents authentic Japanese meals, an excellent sushi bar, and combination dinners along with cultural and artistic displays. Open daily for breakfast, lunch, and dinner until 9 p.m., sushi bar until 10 p.m.

Reuben's Mexican Restaurant will enliven your palate with its zesty dishes. The food is well prepared and the atmosphere is homey.

Beer, wine, and margaritas are available. Open daily 10 a.m.-11 p.m., Sunday 4-9 p.m., 336 Kamehameha Ave., tel. 961-2552. ¡Olé!

Expensive Restaurants

Queen's Court Restaurant at the Hilo Hawaiian Hotel on Banyan Drive, tel. 935-9361, offers a nightly buffet that is *the* best in Hilo. Connoisseurs usually don't consider buffets to be gourmet quality, but the Queen's Court proves them wrong. Each night has a different food theme but the Friday- and Saturday-evening seafood buffet would give the finest restaurants anywhere a run for their money. The dining room is grand, with large archways and windows overlooking Hilo Bay. A massive table is laden with fresh island vegetables and 15 different salads. On seafood night, you choose from oysters, shrimp, crab, sushi, and sashimi. Then the chefs take over. Resplendent in white uniforms and chef's hats, they stand ready to sauté or broil your choice of fish from selections that always include swordfish or *ono*. Beverages include white, rosé, and rich red wines, plus fresh-squeezed guava and orange juice. The dessert table entices you with fresh fruits and imported cheeses, and dares you to save room for cream pies, fresh-baked cookies, and éclairs. The price is an unbelievable $20.95. Sunday champagne brunch is more of the same quality at $16.95. Make reservations, especially on seafood night, because the Hilo Hawaiian attracts many Hilo residents who love great food.

Roussel's, at 60 Keawe St., tel. 935-5111, open for lunch Mon.-Fri., dinner Mon.-Sat., with service all day in the lounge 11:30 a.m.-10 p.m., closed Sundays, is one of the newest additions to Hilo's upscale dining. The building housing the restaurant—the Bishop Trust Building—dates from the 1920s, and the restaurant is in a section that was formerly a bank. Roussel's is owned by Herbert Roussel, who joined with a Louisiana friend, Spencer Oliver, to create the restaurant. They changed the facade of the building to evoke a New Orleans French Quarter style, but preserved the original hardwood floor and hand-molded plaster walls and ceilings. Also, the vault has been converted to a private dining room, brightened by black-and-white checkered floors, mirrors, track lighting, and drumhead tables and chairs. Roussel's specializes in spicy Cajun food. The shrimp and oyster gumbo are outstanding, as is the blackened fish, crisp on the outside and succulent on the inside. Whet your appetite with escargots and garlic and tomato $6.75, blackened sashimi at market price, or crab and shrimp cocktail $7.50. Delightful salads are greens *beaucoup* (a mixture of romaine and butter leaf lettuce with crumbled blue cheese) $3.75, tempting avocado vinaigrette salad with homemade shallot-vinaigrette dressing $3.25, or Creole Caesar $3.95. Move on to the Cajun entrees of chicken Pontalba (sautéed boneless chicken breast with béarnaise sauce) $14.95, duck in orange sauce $18.75, or prime rib, seasoned and flash-cooked $19.75. Seafood entrees delight with meunière amandine (boneless fillet sautéed with sliced almonds and brown butter sauce) $13.85; fresh local catch blackened, broiled, or sautéed with white wine; and a Louisiana favorite, shrimp Creole $16.25. The menu also includes vegetarian dishes like pasta in garden vegetables sauté and linguine with vegetables, each $13.45. Choose from an assortment of cakes, pies and mousses, baked daily; complement the meal with a choice wine; and end with a wonderful cognac or armagnac. Roussel's is the place to see and be seen. It's upscale Cajun cooking, down on the bayou here in Hilo.

Sicilian fishermen would feel right at home at **Pescatore Ristorante,** 235 Keawe St., tel. 969-9090, open daily for lunch 11 a.m.-2 p.m., dinner 5:30-9 p.m. and until 10 p.m. Friday and Saturday. The building housing Pescatore is part of the *Main Street U.S.A. Project* evident in downtown Hilo. The building has had multiple uses over the years, and as part of its colorful past, served as a house of ill repute. Completely redone, it has been transformed into a bright, cheery room with high-backed, red velvet armchairs and formally set tables with green linen tablecloths. Italian-style chandeliers, lace curtains, exposed beams, and koa trim add to the elegance. You can also request a "Portofino Room," a separate area for romance and privacy. Lunch fare begins with antipasto of marinated fish with olive oil, garlic, and vinegar, or of fresh clams, when available. *Primo piatti* can be *pollo Marsala* $8.95, or *scalopini Marsala* (tender veal sautéed with mushrooms and onion in a wine sauce) $13.95. If your taste turns to pasta, go for the primavera with fresh vegetables in tomato sauce for a very reasonable $7.95. Or try the *putanesca,* a famous dish cooked by the Italian ladies of the evening for their clientele; it's made from garlic, anchovies, sun-dried tomatoes, black olives, capers, and olive oil and costs $7.95. For dinner, start with their special minestrone $3.50, or the *ensalata* of sliced tomatoes, mozzarella, and spinach with Italian vinaigrette dressing $4.95. For a dinner antipasto try the hearts of artichokes sautéed with fresh basil, garlic, and tomatoes, and sprinkled with Parmesan cheese $5.95. Dinner entrees bring *cioppino clasico alla pescatore,* swimming with morsels of lobster, mussels, clams, shrimp, fish, and scallops served with garlic bread $24.95; *gamberetti Alfredo* (large shrimp sautéed in butter, garlic, fresh basil, and Parmesan cheese in a white-wine sauce); or *vongole* (steamed clams and choice of red or white clam sauce) $17.95. Pescatore's offers elegant, gourmet dining for reasonable prices.

Lehua's Bar and Restaurant, at 11 Waianuenue Ave., tel. 935-8055, open for lunch 11 a.m.-4 p.m., dinner 5-9:30 p.m., is another upscale restaurant in a restored building. The mood is set with track lighting, Casablanca fans, and an excellent sound system. The decor is gray-on-gray with cane chairs and art deco silverware; the walls hold works of local artists. Owners Mark and Larry, transplanted from Oahu where they spent years in the nightclub business, have joined with Chef Corey Giannalone to create a restaurant inspired by island-style cuisine. Lunch offerings feature Lehua's homemade soup for $2.95 per bowl, Caesar salad for $4.25, and shrimp Lehua for $7.75. Also charbroiled burgers $6.95, club sandwiches $6.95, charbroiled chicken $6.50, and barbecued ribs $7.95. Evenings, dine on appetizers like jumbo prawns $5.25; shrimp Lehua salad $7.25; catch of the day $14.50; and mixed grill of prawns, chicken, and teriyaki steak $16.95. Specialties are angel-hair pasta with fresh tomato, basil, and garlic at $7.25; and pork spareribs at $9.25. The dinner menu also includes cioppino $15.95, sautéed medley of stir-fried vegetables over white or brown rice with teriyaki or oyster sauce $7.95, boneless marinated chicken $9.95, and a whopping 16-ounce porterhouse steak $18.95. Friday and Saturday nights bring live entertainment, mostly jazz and Hawaiian music. Lehua's is upbeat with delicious food, and fun thrown in for free.

Sandalwood Room is the main restaurant of the Hawaii Naniloa Hotel on Banyan Drive, tel. 935-0831. Here, in an elegant room overlooking the bay and lined with aromatic sandalwood, you can feast on dishes from around the world. Zesty curries, rich French sauces, chops done in wine, and Polynesian-inspired dishes are offered on this full and expensive menu.

Fuji Restaurant, as its name implies, is a Japanese restaurant at the Hilo Hotel, 142 Kinoole St., tel. 961-3733. Specialties are *teppan yaki* (beef cut thinly and cooked right at your table), tempura, and various *teishoku* (full meals) at $12-24. From the menu choose barbecued chicken $7.25, *zarusoba* (a traditional Japanese dish of cold buckwheat noodles served with seaweed and a cold dip) $4.25, *ten donburi* (rice topped with shrimp, fish, and vegetable tempura) $7.75, and teriyaki *teishoku* (a full meal) $9.75. Seafood entrees are *ahi teishoku* for $7.75, or a *soba* seafood *bento* (a combination box lunch with egg roll, shrimp tempura, grilled fish, cold buckwheat noodles, and potato salad) for $10.75. There's even a "ladies' menu" with shrimp tempura, chicken cutlet, potato salad, and egg rolls at $9.25, and combination meals like *soba* and seafood *bento* at $13.25. All the chefs are from Japan, and the food is authentic.

KK Tei Restaurant, 1550 Kamehameha Ave., tel. 961-3791, is a favored restaurant of many local people. The centerpiece is a bonsai garden complete with pagodas and arched moon bridges. Cook your own beef, chicken, or fish at your tableside hibachi and dip it into an array of savory sauces—or the chefs will prepare your selection from their full menu of Japanese dishes. Entrees cost about $10 in this unique Asian setting. Those in the know accord this restaurant gourmet status.

Harrington's, at 135 Kalanianaole Ave., tel. 961-4966, is open nightly for dinner 5:30-10 p.m., Sunday 5:30-9 p.m., lounge open 5:30-closing. The setting couldn't be more brilliant, as the restaurant overlooks the bay. A sunset cocktail or dinner is even more romantic with the melodic strains of live jazz, contemporary, or

Hawaiian music playing softly in the background. The continental cuisine features appetizers like shrimp cocktail $7.50, seafood chowder $3.50, mushroom tempura $5.25, escargot in casserole $7.50, and a variety of salads. Special vegetarian dishes like eggplant parmigiana are $12.50, while seafood selections of prawns scampi are $19.95, scallops chardonnay $18.25, and calamari meunière $15.25. Meat and fowl dishes are tempting: Slavic steak $15.50, prime rib au jus $18.95, and chicken Marsala $15.25.

Chapman's, tel. 935-7552, at the corner of Laukapu and Piilani streets, is open for lunch Mon.-Fri. 11:30 a.m.-2 p.m., dinner nightly 5:30-10 p.m., Sunday brunch 10:30 a.m.-2 p.m., piano bar Thursday 6-10 p.m., and live lounge music on weekend evenings. Chapman's lunch menu features tortellini chicken salad with spinach, macadamia nuts, cherry tomatoes, fresh mushrooms, strips of chicken breast and Caesar dressing $7.95; Alaskan snow crab salad $9.95; roast beef sandwich $5.95; chicken pesto salad $6.95; Korean ribs $8.95; and various burgers from $5.95. For dinner start with calamari oriental (crispy fried calamari topped with black bean sauce) $5.95, sashimi at market price, or tempura *soba* salad (tender crisp shrimp tempura served atop buckwheat noodles and garnished with daikon, carrots, and cucumbers) $11.95. Entrees are chicken Victoria (sautéed chicken breast topped with chunks of lobster and fresh whole mushrooms) $15.95, Chapman's crab cakes cooked to a light golden crispness and complemented by a Louie basil cream sauce served with saffron rice $13.95, or Asian-style rack of lamb $18.95. On a side street, away from downtown Hilo, Chapman's is a good place to dine with the local people at an upscale but casual restaurant.

ENTERTAINMENT

Hilo doesn't have a lot of nightlife, but it's not a morgue either. You can dance, disco, or listen to quiet piano music at a few lounges and hotels around town. **Note:** Since most of these entertainment spots are also restaurants, their addresses and phone numbers can be found above in "Food."

In a classic plantation building behind the old police station, on Kalakaua between Keawe and Kinoole streets, is the **East Hawaii Culture Center,** a nonprofit organization that supports local art by showcasing the works of different artists monthly on a revolving basis in the large entrance hall of the old police station. They also host **Shakespeare in the Park,** a local repertory of performers who stage, direct, design, and enact Shakespearean plays under the large banyan in Kalakaua Park during the month of July. If you're in Hilo at this time, it shouldn't be missed. The Big Island Arts Guild and the Dance Council also meet here. The bulletin board is always filled with announcements of happenings in the local art scene.

Lehua's Bar and Restaurant, 11 Wainuenue Ave., offers a mixed bag of jazz, Hawaiian, or contemporary music on weekends. Occasionally there is a comedy night. Upbeat vibes with good food as well.

Stratton's at 121 Banyan Dr., tel. 961-6815, becomes a sports bar daily 3-9 p.m. You can enjoy everything from boxing to football on their big-screen TV. After 9 p.m. until closing Sun.-Thurs., Stratton's features local singers performing their best *karaoke* tunes, and on Friday and Saturday you can dance your heart out at Stratton's disco.

Hilo has its own little sleaze bar, **The Green Onion,** at 885 Kilauea Ave., where exotic dancers can *sometimes* be coaxed on stage if the clientele takes up a collection and offers them a minimum amount of money. Sound good to you? Things *can't* be that bad!

Chapman's, tel. 935-7552, at the corner of Laukapu and Piilani streets, offers a piano bar Thursday 6-10 p.m., and live lounge music on weekend evenings.

Fiasco's at the Waiakea Shopping Plaza, 200 Kanoelehua Ave., tel. 935-7666, swings with a full venue of live music, disco, or comedy on most weekends. Doors open at 9 p.m., with a $2 cover and relaxed dress code.

If you're looking for a night out, you can't beat the **Wai'oli Lounge** at the Hilo Hawaiian Hotel, where live music every night ranges from contemporary Hawaiian to rock. **Uncle Billy's** at the Hilo Bay Hotel has two dinner hula shows nightly at 6:30 and 7:30 p.m. **Harrington's,** one of Hilo's most romantic nightspots, offers live jazz, contemporary, or Hawaiian music nightly. Perfect for dinner or just for relaxing.

Others

To catch a flick try the **Waiakea Theaters** I, II, and III at Waiakea Shopping Plaza on Kanoelehua Avenue, tel. 935-9747; and the **Prince Kuhio Theaters I & II** at the Prince Kuhio Plaza. You'll enjoy great listening on **KIPA Rainbow Radio** (AM 620). This station plays an excellent selection of contemporary music with few commercial interruptions. It sounds the way FM used to. K-BIG FM 98 is worth listening to, and KAOI FM 95 from Maui puts out some really good tunes.

SHOPPING

Shopping Malls

Hilo has the best general-purpose shopping on the island. Stock up on film and food before you do any touring or camping. **Prince Kuhio Plaza,** at 111 E. Puainako, open weekdays 9:30 a.m.-9 p.m., Saturday to 5:30 p.m., Sunday 10 a.m.-5 p.m., is Hilo's newest and the island's largest shopping mall. Restaurants, jewelry shops, shoe stores, supermarkets, and large department stores like Sears and Liberty House make it a one-stop shopper's paradise. Here too you'll find Longs Drugs for film, and Waldenbooks for an extensive selection of reading material. An older but still full-service shopping center is **Kaiko'o Mall** at 777 Kilauea Ave., which includes a JCPenney, Ben Franklin, Mall Foods, The Book Gallery, and Longs Drugs. **Hilo Shopping Center** is about a half mile south on Kilauea Avenue at the corner of Kekuanaoa Street. This smaller mall has only a handful of local shops, but it does have some excellent inexpensive restaurants and a fine pastry shop. **Puainako Town Center** is located at 2100 Kanoelehua Ave. (Rt. 11 south toward Volcanoes), with lots of shops, Sack 'n' Save Market, and plenty of fast foods. **Waiakea Shopping Plaza,** handy to the airport at 100 Kanoelehua Ave., has a small clutch of stores that include Mail With Us, with full fax and mailing services; Koreana restaurant and lounge; and Fiasco's, a local restaurant known for its nightly entertainment (see above).

For Hilo's real treasures see "Hilo's Gardens" under "Sights and Beaches," above, where you'll find listings for the wonderful commercial flower gardens that surround the city. They are experts at preparing and shipping vibrant and colorful floral arrangements. Prices are reasonable and no other gift says Hawaii like a magnificent bouquet of exotic flowers.

Food Markets

For groceries and supplies try: **Food Fair,** 194 Kilauea Ave.; **Safeway,** 333 Kilauea Ave.; **Sack 'n' Save** at Puainako Town Center; or **Mall Foods** in Kaiko'o Mall. For a real treat visit the early morning (over by 8 a.m.) **Suisan Fish Auction** at 85 Lihiwai Street. A retail fresh-fish market is next door. Also see "Fast Foods and Snacks" under "Food," above.

Health Food And Fruit Stores

Abundant Life Natural Foods, owned and operated by Leslie Miki since 1977, is in downtown Hilo at 292 Kamehameha Ave., open daily 8:30 a.m.-6 p.m., Saturday until 5 p.m., and Sunday 10 a.m.-2 p.m., tel. 935-7411. The store's kitchen puts out daily specials of soup, salads, sandwiches, and *bento,* all for well under $5, while the shelves are stocked with an excellent selection of fresh fruits and vegies, bulk foods, cosmetics, vitamins, and herbs. The bookshelves cosmically vibrate with a selection of tomes on metaphysics and new-age literature.

On Wednesday and Saturday morning, check out the **farmers' market** along Kamehameha Avenue fronting the bay in the center of the downtown area. Great for bargains and local color.

Bookstores

Hilo has excellent bookstores (also see "Shopping Malls" above). **Basically Books,** downtown at 46 Waianuenue St., tel. 961-0144, has a good selection of Hawaiiana, out-of-print books, and an unbeatable selection of maps. You can get anywhere you want to go with their nautical charts, road maps, and topographical maps. The selection includes sectionals for serious hikers and trekkers. Their collection covers most of the Pacific. They also feature a very good selection of travel books, and flags from countries throughout the world.

one of Hilo's many vintage buildings

J.D. BISIGNANI

The **Book Gallery** at Prince Kuhio Plaza, tel. 959-7744, is a full-selection bookstore featuring Hawaiiana, hardcovers, and paperbacks. **Waldenbooks,** also at Prince Kuhio Plaza, tel. 959-6468, open daily 9 a.m.-9 p.m., is the largest and best-stocked bookstore in the Hilo area.

Bookfinders of Hawaii at 150 Haili St., tel. 961-5055, specializes in hard-to-find and out-of-print books. If you want it, they'll get it.

Gifts And Crafts

If you're looking for that special island memento or souvenirs to bring home to family and friends, Uncle Billy covers all the bases and along with everything else offers the **Polynesian Marketplace,** adjacent to the Hilo Bay Hotel. Open daily 8 a.m.-8 p.m., the marketplace sells a lot of good junk, liquor, and resortwear. **Hilo Hatties** at Prince Kuhio Plaza has all you need in island clothing, tourist style. **Hawaiian Handcrafts** at 760 Kilauea Ave., tel. 935-5587, specializes in woodcarvings. Here, Dan DeLuz uses exotic woods to turn out bowls, boxes, and vases, and sells shells from around the Pacific.

Sugawara Lauhala and Gift Shop at 59 Kalakaua St. is a virtually unknown Hilo institution operated by the Sugawara sisters, who have been in business for most of their 70-plus years. They make genuine *lau hala* weavings right on the premises of their character-laden shop. Their best hats sell for $75 up, and they also have baskets from $15. If you are after the genuine article made to last a lifetime, you'll find it here.

The **Crystal Grotto,** at 290 Kamehameha Ave., tel. 935-2284, open weekdays 10 a.m.-5:30 p.m., Saturday until 3:30 p.m., is a metaphysical bookstore filled with crystals, jewelry, videotapes, tarot cards, incense, and oils, and a full line of magnificently crafted beadwork. Different psychic readers are available throughout the week; they specialize in everything from astrology to tarot, with prices around $15 for an introductory reading. Just walking into the shop with its attuned vibes might do anything from balancing your aura to causing a past life regression. You never know, unless, of course, you're a psychic reader.

Old Town Printer and Stationers, at 201 Kinoole St., open weekdays 8 a.m-5 p.m., has been in business for 35 years selling stationery, office supplies, postcards, notecards, and a terrific selection of calendars.

Sig Zane Design, at 122 Kamehameha Ave., tel. 935-7077, open Mon.-Sat. 9:30 a.m.-5 p.m., is one of the most unique and distinctive shops on the island. Here, owner and designer Sig Zane creates distinctive island wearables in 100% cotton. All designs are not only Hawaiian/tropical, but also chronicle useful and medicinal Hawaiian plants, ancient implements, and hula instruments. Zig's wife, Nalani, who helps in the shop, is a *kumu hula* who learned the intricate dance steps from her mother, Edith Kana-

1

2

3

1. lantana; **2.** plumeria; **3.** anthurium (all photos by J.D. Bisignani)

1

2

1. Byodo-In Temple, Oahu (J.D. Bisignani); **2.** Rural church (Bob Cowan)

kaole, a legendary dancer who has been memorialized with a local tennis stadium that bears her name. You can get shirts for $49, dresses around $75, and *pareau* for $24, as well as affordable house slippers, sweatshirts, T-shirts, *hapi* coats, and even futon covers. The shelves also hold *lau hala* hats, hand-bound koa notebooks, and basketry made from natural fibers. Outfit yourself from head to toe at Sig's shop and be totally in style and comfort.

Dragon Mama, a lovely boutique at 266 Kamehameha Ave., features natural-fiber futons, fine bedding, wool, cotton fabrics, custom covers, meditation pillows, and Japanese rice paper.

Maile's Hawaii, at 216 Kamehameha Ave., open weekdays 9 a.m.-5 p.m., Saturday until 4 p.m., is a hula supply store where the shelves hold *ipu,* flutes, drums, and rattles, along with crafts items and an extensive collection of books on Hawaiiana.

Caravan Town at 194 Kamehameha Ave. is open daily except Sunday 8 a.m.-4:30 p.m., Friday until 5:30 p.m., and Saturday until 4 p.m. It is one of the most interesting junk stores in Hilo. The shelves hold an internationally eclectic mix of merchandise that includes pendulum clocks, plaster Greek goddesses, luggage, and paper lanterns. Also, the shop specializes in over-the-counter Chinese herbs and medicines purportedly effective for everything from constipation to impotence.

The 100 block of Keawe Street, between Shipman and Kalakaua streets, is Hilo's **yuppie row.** Designer-shoulder-to-designer-shoulder are the **Chocolate Bar,** with fine handmade temptations; **The Futon Connection,** with baskets, futons, and futon furniture; the **Picture Frame Shop and Cunningham Gallery** for fine arts; and **The Most Irresistible Shop in Hilo,** with Ciao backpacks and bags. Here too is **The Fire Place Store,** featuring coffee pots, Mexican piñatas, children's toys, greeting cards, *pareu,* T-shirts, and a good selection of cosmetics.

The other side of yuppie row is down-home Hilo. Some downtown shops along Keawe Street are **Kodani's Florist** for fresh-cut flowers and lei; and **Hawaii Sales and Surplus,** featuring raincoats, hats, military supplies, knives, backpacks, rubber rafts, and plenty of old and new military uniforms.

Big Island Estate Jewelry and Pawn Shop, at 164 Kilauea St., open Sun.-Thurs. 10 a.m.-3 p.m., is a must-stop. Inside are the expected cameras and guitars, but you'll also find Japanese miniature dolls, glassware, and hula supplies. **Northern Lights Antiques,** diagonally across on Ponahawai Street, is another treasure chest overflowing with antiques, curios, lamps, beads, and Asian heirlooms.

The **Modern Camera Center,** at 165 Kiawe St., tel. 935-3279/3150, is one of the few full-service camera shops in Hilo.

SERVICES AND INFORMATION

Emergencies

When in need call: **police** 935-3311; **fire-ambulance** tel. 961-6022; **Hilo Hospital** at 1190 Waianuenue St., tel. 961-4211. Keiko Gido has an office at 140 Kinoole St., where she practices the ancient healing arts of acupuncture and shiatsu and various therapeutic massages.

Information

The following will be helpful: **Hawaii Visitors Bureau,** at the corner of Keawe and Haili streets, tel. 961-5797, open Mon.-Fri. 8 a.m.-noon and 1-4:30 p.m.; and the **Chamber of Commerce,** 180 Kinoole St., tel. 935-7178. Both are good sources of maps and helpful brochures. Also try the **Hilo Public Library,** 300 Waianuenue Ave., tel. 935-5407; or the **University of Hawaii** in Hilo at 1400 Kapiolani St., tel. 961-9311.

Banks And Post Office

For your money needs try the following: **City Bank** at Kaiko'o Mall, tel. 935-6844; **Central Pacific,** 525 Kilauea Ave., tel. 935-5251; or **First Hawaiian,** 1205 Kilauea Ave., tel. 969-2211.

The central **post office,** open weekdays 9 a.m.-4:30 p.m., Saturday 9 a.m.-12:30 p.m., is an efficiently run, modern post office, clearly marked on the access road to the airport. It is extremely convenient for mailings prior to departure.

BOB RACE

THE SADDLE ROAD

Slicing west across the Hilo District with a northward list is Rt. 200, the Saddle Road. Everyone with a sense of adventure loves this bold cut across the Big Island along a high valley separating the two great mountains, Mauna Loa and Mauna Kea. Along it you pass explorable caves, a *nene* sanctuary, camping areas, and a spur road leading to the very top of Mauna Kea. Besides, it's a great adventure for anyone traveling between Hilo and Kona. Keep your eyes peeled for convoys of tanks and armored personnel carriers as they sometimes sally forth from Pohakuloa Military Camp.

Getting There

The car rental companies cringe when you mention the Saddle Road. Some even intimidate you by saying their insurance won't cover you on this road. They're terrified you'll rattle their cars to death. For the most part these fears are groundless. For a few miles the Saddle Road is corrugated because of heavy use by the military but, by and large, it's a good road, no worse than many others around the island. However, it *is* isolated, and there are no facilities along the way. If you bypass it, you'll miss some of the best scenery on the Big Island. From Hilo, follow Waianuenue Avenue west past Rainbow Falls. Saddle Road (Rt. 200) splits left within a mile or two and is clearly marked. If you follow it across the island, you'll intersect Rt. 190 on which you can turn north to Waimea or south to Kona. For information on professional guide service to the top of Mauna Kea, see "Sightseeing Tours" under "Getting Around" in the Big Island Introduction. For skiing expeditions contact Ski Guides Hawaii, Box 2020, Kamuela, Hi 96743, tel. 885-4188 or 889-6747.

KAUMANA CAVES

In 1881 Mauna Loa's tremendous eruption created a huge flow of lava. The lava became rivers that crusted over, forming a tube through which molten lava continued to flow. Once the eruption ceased, the lava inside siphoned out, leaving the tube now called Kaumana Caves. The caves are only five miles out of Hilo along Rt. 200, clearly marked next to the road. Oddly enough, they are posted as a fallout shelter. Follow a staircase down into a gray hole draped with green ferns and brightened by wildflowers. You can walk about 50 yards into the cave before you'll need a flashlight. It's a thrill to turn around and look at the entrance, where blazing sunlight shoots through the ferns and wildflowers. The floor of the cave is cemented over for easy walking. Another cave visible across the way is undeveloped and more rugged to explore.

Two miles past Kaumana Caves is **Hilo Municipal Golf Course,** a 5,991-yard, par-72 course where you can golf for under $10.

MAUNA KEA

The lava along both sides of the road is old as you approach Mauna Kea ("White Mountain"). The lowlands are covered with grass, ferns, small trees, and mossy rocks. Twenty-seven miles out of Hilo, a clearly marked road to your right leads to the summit of 13,796-foot Mauna Kea. A sign warns you that this road is rough, unpaved, and narrow, with no water, food, fuel, restrooms, or shelters. Moreover, you can expect winds, rain, fog, hail, snow, and altitude sickness. Intrigued? Proceed: it's not as bad as it sounds. A 4WD vehicle is highly advised, and if there's snow the road is impossible without one. A normal rental car isn't powerful enough, mainly because you're gaining more than 8,000 feet of elevation in 15 miles, which plays havoc with carburetors. But the real problem is coming down. For a small car with not very good gearing you're going to be riding your brakes for 15 miles. If they fail, you'll stand a very good chance of becoming a resident spirit of the mountain!

Four miles up you pass **Hale Pohaku** ("House of Stone"), which looks like a ski resort; many of the scientists from the observatory atop the mountain live here. A sign says that you need a permit from the Department of Land and Natural Resources (in Hilo) and a 4WD vehicle to proceed. Actually, the road is graded, banked, and well maintained, with the upper four miles paved so that dust is kept to a minimum to protect the sensitive "eyes" of the telescopes. As you climb, you pass through the clouds to a barren world devoid of vegetation. The earth is a red, rolling series of volcanic cones. You get an incredible vista of Mauna Loa peeking through the clouds and what seems like the entire island lying at your feet. In the distance the lights of Maui flicker. **Lake Waiau,** which unbelievably translates as "Swim Water," is almost at the top at 13,020 feet, making it the third-highest lake in the U.S. If the vistas aren't enough, bring a kite along and watch it soar in the winds of the earth's upper atmosphere. Off to your right is Puu Kahinahina, a small hill whose name means "hill of the silversword." It's one of the only places on the Big Island where you'll see this very rare plant. The mountaintop was at one time federal land, and funds were made available to eradicate feral goats, one of the worst destroyers of the silversword and many other native Hawaiian plants.

Mauna Kea is the only spot in the tropical Pacific that was glaciated. The entire summit of the mountain was covered in 500 feet of ice. Toward the summit, you may notice piles of rock which are the terminal moraine of these ancient glaciers. The snows atop Mauna Kea are unpredictable. Some years it is merely a dusting, while in other years, as in 1982, there was enough snow to ski from late November to late July. The ski run comes all the way down from the summit, giving you about a four-mile trail.

Here and there around the summit are small caves, remnants of ancient quarries where Hawaiians came to dig a special kind of fired rock that is the hardest in all Hawaii. They hauled roughed-out tools down to the lowlands, where they refined them into excellent implements that became coveted trade items.

A natural phenomenon is the strange thermal properties manifested by the cinder cones that dot the top of the mountain. Only 10 feet or so under their surface is permafrost which dates back 10,000 years to the Pleistocene Epoch. If you drill into the cones for only 10-20 feet and put a pipe in, during daylight hours air will be sucked into the pipe. At night, warm air comes out of the pipe with sufficient force to keep a hat levitating.

Evening brings an incredibly clean and cool breeze that flows down the mountain. The

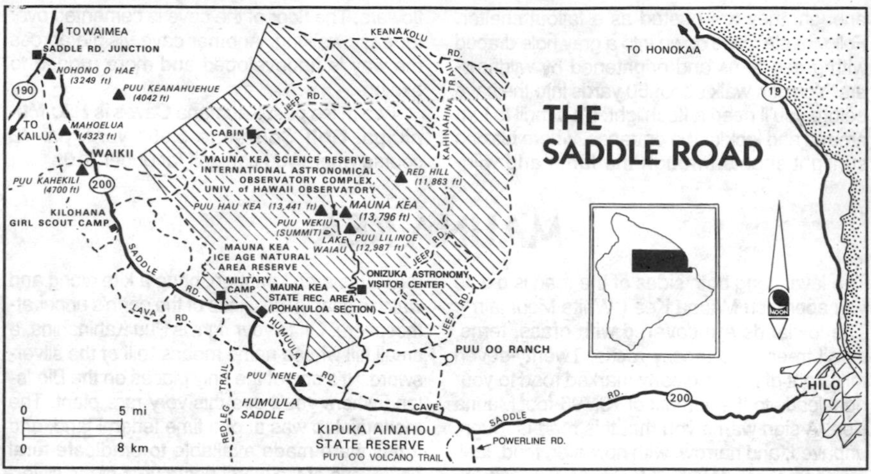

Hawaiians called it the Keihau Wind, whose source, according to ancient legend, is the burning heart of the mountain. To the Hawaiians, this inspiring heavenly summit was the home of Poliahu, The Goddess of Snow and Ice, who vied with the fiery Pele across the way on Mauna Loa for the love of a man. He could throw himself into the never-ending embrace of a mythical ice queen, or of a red-hot mama. Tough choice, poor fellow!

Mauna Kea Observatory Complex

Atop the mountain is a mushroom grove of astronomical observatories, as incongruously striking as a futuristic earth colony on a remote planet of a distant galaxy. The crystal-clear air and lack of dust and light pollution make the Mauna Kea Observatory site *the* best in the world. At close to 14,000 feet, it is above 40% of the earth's atmosphere. Although temperatures generally hover around freezing, there's only 9-11 inches of precipitation annually, mostly in the form of snow. The astronomers have come to expect an average of 325 crystal-clear nights per year, perfect for observation. The state of Hawaii leases the tops of the cinder cones, upon which institutions from all over the world construct telescopes. These institutions in turn give the University of Hawaii up to 15% of their viewing time. The university sells the excess viewing time for $5,000-10,000 a night, which supports the entire astronomy program and makes a little money on the side. Those who work up here must come down every four days because the thin air seems to make them forgetful and susceptible to making minor calculation errors.

Scientists from around the world book months in advance for a squint through one of these phenomenal telescopes. Teams from Great Britain, The Netherlands, Canada, France, and Japan as well as from the U.S. maintain permanent outposts here. The first telescope that you see on your left is the U.K.'s **James Clark Maxwell Telescope,** a radio telescope with a primary reflecting surface over 15 meters in diameter. It was dedicated by Britain's Prince Philip, who rode all the way to the summit in a Rolls Royce. The **Canada-France-Hawaii Telescope,** built in 1977 for $33 million, was the first to spot Halley's comet in 1983, and still can see it.

The newest eye to the heavens atop Mauna Kea is the **W.M. Keck Observatory,** completed in March 1993 at a cost of $94 million. The Keck Foundation, a philanthropic organization from Los Angeles, funded the telescope, one of the world's most high tech, powerful, and expensive. Operated by the California Association for Research in Astronomy (CARA), a joint project of the University of California and Cal Tech, the telescope has an aperture of 400 inches and employs entirely new and unique types of technology. The primary reflector is fashioned from a mosaic of 36 hectagonal mirrors, each only three inches thick and six feet in diameter. These "small" mirrors have been very carefully joined together to form one incredibly huge, actively controlled light reflector surface. Each of the mirror segments is separately positionable to an accuracy of a millionth of an inch, and is computer-controlled to bring the heavenly objects into perfect focus. This titanic eyeball has already spotted both the most distant known galaxy and the most distant known object in the universe, 12 and 13 billion light years from earth, respectively. The light received from these objects today was emitted not long after the "Big Bang" creating the universe theoretically occurred. In a very real sense, these scientists are looking back toward the beginning of time!

The Keck Observatory includes a public gallery, closed until mid-1996 due to construction of Keck II, Son of Cyclops. When it is completed and linked with the original Keck telescope, scientists will have an immensely more powerful tool for their earthbound exploration of the heavens.

The entire mountaintop complex is managed by the University of Hawaii. Visitors are welcome to tour the complex and to have a look through the telescopes on special weekends May-September. Reservations are a must; arrangements can be made by calling the **Mauna Kea Support Services** in Hilo at tel. 935-3371. The **Onizuka Astronomy Center** at the 9,000-foot level, named in honor of space shuttle *Challenger* astronaut Ellison Onizuka, is a must-stop for stargazers. It allows visitors a chance to acclimatize to the thin, high-mountain air, another must—a stay of one hour here is recommended before heading up to the 13,796-foot summit. (Because of the high altitude and the remoteness of the mountaintop from emergency medical facilities, children under age 16 are prohibited from venturing to the summit. Those with cardiopulmonary or respiratory problems are also discouraged from attempting the trip.) The visitors center provides the last public restrooms before the summit and is a good place to stock up on water, also unavailable higher up. The visitors center also conducts free stargazing tours. Call 961-2180 for more information.

DIANA LASICH HARPER

the red-bodied apapane

If you plan on continuing up to the summit, you must provide your own transportation. Observatory personnel suggest calling **Harper Car and Truck Rentals** in Hilo, tel. 969-1478, or **Ciao Rentals** in Kailua-Kona, tel. 326-2426, both of which offer 4WD rentals. Take extra layers of warm clothing—it can snow up there any month of the year—and your camera. Photographers, using fast film, get some of the most dazzling shots *after* sunset. During the gloaming, the light show begins. Look down upon the clouds to see them filled with fire. This heavenly light is reflected off the mountain to the clouds and then back up like a celestial mirror in which you get a fleeting glimpse of the soul of the universe.

MAUNA KEA STATE RECREATION AREA

This area, known as Pohakuloa ("Long Stone"), is five miles west of the Mauna Kea Observatory Road (33 miles from Hilo). The altitude is 6,500 feet and the land begins to change into the rolling grasslands for which this *paniolo* country is famous. Here you'll find a cluster of seven cabins that can be rented (arrange in advance) from the Department of Land and Natural Resources, Division of State Parks, 75 Aupuni St., Hilo, HI 96720, tel. 961-7200. The cabins are completely furnished with cooking facilities and hot showers. You'll need warm clothing, but the days and nights are unusually clear and dry with very little rain. The park is within the Pohakuloa Game Management Area, so expect hunting and shooting in season. A few minutes west is the Pohakuloa Military Camp, whose manuevers can sometimes disturb the peace in this high mountain area. Follow the Saddle Road about 20 miles west to intersect Rt. 190 on which you can turn right (north) to Waimea—seven miles—or left (south) to Kailua—33 miles.

Birdwatchers or nature enthusiasts should turn into Koa Kipuka, a bite-sized hill just near mile marker 28. (A *kipuka* is a very special area, usually a hill or gully, in the middle of a lava flow that was never inundated by lava and therefore provides an old, original, and established ecosystem.) Look for Powerline Road and Puu O'o Volcano Trail. Follow either for a chance to see the very rare *akiapola'au* or *apapane,* and even wild turkeys. For descriptions of these birds, see "Birds" under "Flora and Fauna" in the Big Island Introduction.

HAMAKUA COAST

Inland the Hamakua Coast is awash in a rolling green sea of sugarcane, while along the shore, cobalt waves foam into razor-sharp valleys where cold mountain streams meet the sea at lonely pebbled beaches. Along a 50-mile stretch of the Belt Road (Rt. 19) from Hilo to Waipio, the Big Island has grown its cane for 100 years or more. Water is needed for sugar, a ton to produce a pound, and this coast has plenty. Huge flumes once carried the cut cane to the mills. Last century so many Scots worked the plantations hereabouts that Hamakua was called the "Scotch Coast." Now most residents are a mixture of Scottish, Japanese, Filipino, and Portuguese ancestry. Side roads dip off Rt. 19 into one-family valleys where modest, weatherbeaten homes of plantation workers sit surrounded by garden plots on tiny, hand-hewn terraces. These valleys, as they march up the coast, are unromantically referred to as "gulches." From the Belt Road's many bridges, you can trace silvery-ribboned streams that mark the valley floors as they open to the sea. Each is jungle-lush with wildflowers and fruit trees transforming the steep sides to emerald green velvet.

Note: For more on the southern section of the Hamakua Coast, please see "Scenic Drive" under "Sights and Beaches" in the Hilo chapter.

HONOMU TO LAUPAHOEHOE

The ride alone, as you head north on the Belt Road, is gorgeous enough to be considered a sight. But there's more! You can pull off the road into sleepy one-horse towns where dogs are safe snoozing in the middle of the road. You can visit a plantation store in Honomu on your way to Akaka Falls, or take a cautious dip at one of the seaside beach parks. If you want solitude, you can go inland to a forest reserve and miles of trails. The largest town on the coast is Honokaa, with supplies, handmade mementos, and a macadamia nut factory. You can veer west to Waimea from Honokaa, but don't. Take the spur road, Rt. 240, to Waipio Valley, known as the "Valley of Kings," one of the most beautiful in all of Hawaii.

HONOMU AND VICINITY

During its heyday, Honomu ("Silent Bay") was a bustling center of the sugar industry boasting saloons, a hotel/bordello, and a church or two for repentance. Now Honomu is only a stop as you head somewhere else. It's 10 miles north of Hilo and a mile or so inland on Rt. 220, which leads to Akaka Falls. As you enter Honomu you'll see a string of false-front buildings doing a good but unofficial rendition of a living history museum. It's as if the entire town has taken a nap and is about to wake up at any moment. At the south end of town, just at the turn to Akaka Falls, notice the **Odaishasan,** a beautifully preserved Buddhist temple. Honomu is definitely worth a stop. It takes only five minutes to walk the main street, but those five minutes can give you a glimpse of history that will take you back 100 years.

Practicalities

Before entering town proper you'll spot **Jan's,** a convenience store selling cold beer and groceries. As you enter town look for **The Plate Lunch,** offering sushi, shave ice, sub sandwiches, and frozen bananas, about as down-home as you can get. In town at **Akaka Falls Flea Market,** the merchandise changes so you never know what to expect, but they claim "all new quality merchandise at reduced prices." And, in case you're suddenly struck by an irresistible urge for a permanent memento of Honomu, there's the **Akaka Falls Tattoo Club** in town.

As you walk the main street of Honomu, make sure to stop into **Ishigo's General Store,** tel. 963-6128, open Mon.-Fri. 7 a.m.-6 p.m., Saturday and Sunday 7 a.m.-5 p.m., to see a real plantation store still in operation. Owned and operated by Hideo Ishigo, the original store began in 1910 when his forebears, Inokichi Ishigo and his wife Maki, emigrated from Fukuoka, Japan to begin a new life in Hawaii. They began with a bakery, employing recipes they learned from all the ethnic groups in Hawaii. They passed their knowledge down to their children, who still use the same recipes in the bakery section of the store. The general store section has food, ice cream, sandwiches, and pizza, but the real treats are in the bakery. Here in a

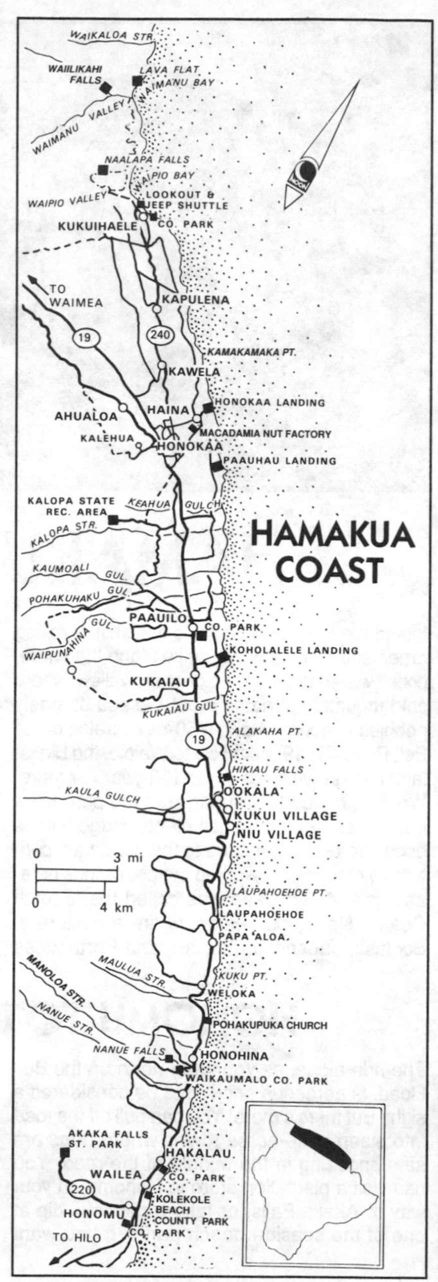

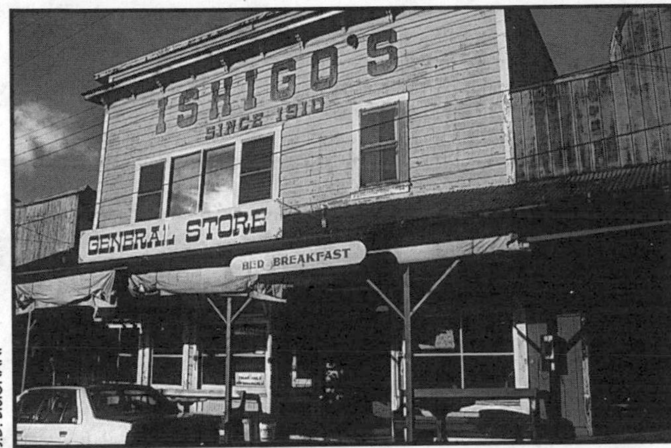

J.D. BISIGNANI

Ishigo's General Store

self-serve case are familiar munchies like blueberry, pineapple, and coconut turnovers along with taro bread. But according to Mr. Ishigo, the old-timers around here go right for the cream buns and the *anpan* with *adzuki* beans. So if you want to get some *real* local flavor, pick one of these and sit out front sipping a cup of Kona coffee. Mr. Ishigo is very friendly and will "talk story" about Honomu, and may even invite you to a relative's orchid farm in the nearby area. If he's around, it's an added treat, but you can give yourself a small history course of Honomu by checking out the antiques, mementos, and vintage photos that have been placed around the store. Most photos are of Japanese couples who immigrated to the area. Check out the bottles of *okolehau,* local moonshine, that could easily fuel the space shuttle, and an old HVB roadside warrior made of wood.

Next door to Ishigo's, **Akaka Falls Gallery,** tel. 963-6700, is owned and operated by Deborah Jenks, who specializes in island art. Since most of the pieces are on consignment, the gallery display will constantly change, but the philosophy of art based on island themes and created by island artists will remain constant. Part of the gallery is the **Bamboo Cafe,** where you can munch an assortment of sweets and bakery items while enjoying a cup of coffee or espresso from beans prepared by the Big Island's own **Badass Coffee Company** (see "Shopping" under "Central and South Kona" in the Kona chapter).

Akaka Falls

Follow Rt. 220 from Honomu past dense sugarcane fields for 3.5 miles to the parking lot of Akaka Falls. From here, walk counterclockwise along a paved "circle route" that takes you through everybody's idea of a pristine Hawaiian valley. For 40 minutes you're surrounded by heliconia, gingers, orchids, ferns, and bamboo groves as you cross bubbling streams on wooden footbridges. Many varieties of plants that would be in window pots anywhere else are treelike giants here. An overlook views Kahuna Falls as it spills into a lush green valley below. The trail becomes an enchanted tunnel through hanging orchids and bougainvillea. In a few moments you arrive at Akaka Falls. The mountain cooperates with the perfect setting, forming a semicircle from which the falls tumble 420 feet in one sheer drop. After heavy rains expect a mad torrent of power; during dry periods marvel at liquid-silver threads forming mist and rainbows. The area, maintained by the Division of State Parks, is one of the most easily accessible forays into Hawaii's beautiful interior.

Kolekole Beach County Park

Look for the first tall bridge (100 feet high) a few minutes past Honomu, where a sign points to a small road that snakes its way down the valley to the beach park below. Amenities include showers, restrooms, grills, electricity, picnic tables, and a camping area (county permit).

Kolekole is very popular with local people, who use its five pavilions for all manner of special occasions, usually on weekends. A black-sand beach fronts an extremely treacherous ocean. The entire valley was inundated with over 30 feet of water during the great 1946 tsunami. The stream running through Kolekole comes from Akaka Falls, four miles inland. It forms a pool complete with waterfall that is safe for swimming but quite cold.

LAUPAHOEHOE

This wave-lashed peninsula is a finger of smooth *pahoehoe* lava that juts into the bay. Located about halfway between Honomu and Honokaa, the valley at one time supported farmers and fishermen who specialized in catching turtles. Laupahoehoe was the best boat landing along the coast, and for years canoes and, later, schooners would stop here. A plaque commemorates the tragic loss of 20 schoolchildren and their teacher who were taken by the great tsunami of 1946. Afterwards, the village was moved to the high ground overlooking the point. Laupahoehoe Beach County Park now occupies the low peninsula; it has picnic tables, showers, electricity, and a county camping area. The sea is too rough to swim but many fishermen come here, along with some daring surfers. Laupahoehoe makes a beautiful rest stop along the Belt Road.

Ten miles inland from Laupahoehoe Point along a very rugged jeep trail is **David Douglas Historical Monument.** This marks the spot where the naturalist after whom the Douglas fir is named lost his life under mysterious circumstances. Douglas, on a fact-gathering expedition on the rugged slopes of Mauna Kea, never returned. His body was found at the bottom of a deep pit that was used at the time to catch feral cattle. Douglas had spent the previous night at a cabin occupied by an Australian who had been a convict. Many suspected that the Australian had murdered Douglas in a robbery attempt and thrown his body into the pit to hide the deed. No hard evidence of murder could be found, and the death was officially termed accidental.

Practicalities

Luckily for all of us traveling the Hamakua Coast, French Canadian Charles Peladeau and his fiancée Judy had a dream. They dreamed of swaying palms, days of bright, sun-splashed beaches, and a vintage 1940s-style diner in which they could prepare food the old-fashioned way. *Voilà!* **The Local Cafe,** tel. 962-6669, open weekdays 7:30 a.m.-7:30 p.m., Saturday 10 a.m.-7:30 p.m., Sunday 10 a.m.-5 p.m., is located in a brightly painted vintage building *in* Laupahoehoe Village between mile markers 24 and 25. Inside, the decor, thanks to Judy, is "modern-classic-chic" appointed with black floor, white wainscotted walls, and turquoise stools, countertop, and ceiling. Musty encyclopedias, dog-eared books, framed photos, and a collection of bottles turned translucent with age whisper the faded memories of days gone by. Overhead, lively paintings of "stoned" parrots and stuffed cloth fish, whales, and sharks dangle from the ceiling, shouting "Today!" The breakfast menu brings "Charlie's eggs to go," a muffin mounded with egg, ham, and cheese $2.25; a three-egg cheese omelette $4.50; and plenty of sweets, treats, and side orders. Living up to its name, the Local Cafe just has to offer a full range of plate lunches like meatball platters, chicken delight, and teriyaki chicken, all for around $5. Burgers and sandwiches include everything from a half-pound beef burger for the very hungry at $4.50, to an assortment of jumbo sandwiches like ham and cheese or turkey with all the trimmings for under $4. Charlie, like a true Frenchman—sort of—claims unabashed bragging rights to the islands' best pizza, served daily from 10:30 a.m. and ranging in price from a small plain pie for $7.95 to Frankie's Delight covered with the works and large enough to feed five for $20.95. Although all of Charlie's food is wholesome and delicious, his pièces de résistance are homemade, deep-dish, fruit and berry pies, topped with homemade ice cream from Hilo (oftentimes gone by early afternoon). Drop in at the Local Cafe and share Charlie's and Judy's dream. You'll be glad you did.

HONOKAA TO KUKUIHAELE

HONOKAA AND VICINITY

With a population of nearly 2,000, Honokaa ("Crumbling Bay") is the major town on the Hamakua Coast. Here you can continue on Rt. 19 to Waimea, or take Rt. 240 through Honokaa and north to Waipio, which you should not miss. First, however, stroll the main street of Honokaa, where a number of shops specialize in locally produced handicrafts. This is also the best place to stock up on supplies or gasoline. The surrounding area is the center of the macadamia nut industry. If you are proceeding north along Rt. 240, the coastal route heading to Waipio Valley, just past mile marker 6 on the left, keep an eye peeled for a lava-tube cave right along the roadway. This is just a tease of the amazing natural sights that follow. (See "Waipio Valley" later in this chapter.)

Kalopa State Recreation Area

This spacious natural area is 12 miles north of Laupahoehoe (two miles south of Honokaa), and two miles inland on a well-marked secondary road. Little used by tourists, it's a great place to get away from it all. Hiking is terrific throughout the park on a series of nature trails where much of the flora has been identified. All trails are well marked and vary widely in difficulty. The park provides an excellent opportunity to explore some of the lush gulches of the Hamakua Coast, as well as tent camping (state permit) and furnished cabins that can house up to eight people (see "State Parks and Cabins" under "Camping and Hiking" in the Big Island Introduction).

Hawaiian Holiday Macadamia Nut Factory

This factory, open 9 a.m.-6 p.m., is on a side road that leads from the middle of town down a steep hill toward the sea. A self-guided tour explains how John MacAdams discovered the delicious qualities of these nuts and how they were named after him. The macadamia nut industry was started in Honokaa when W.H. Purvis, a British agriculturalist who had been working in Australia, brought the first trees to Honokaa in 1881, one of which is still bearing! In 1924, W. Pierre Naquin, then manager of the Honokaa Sugar Co., started the first commercial nut farm in the area. You can buy a large variety of macadamia items, from butters to candies. A delicious and nutritious munchy is a five-ounce, vacuum-packed can of nuts that make a great souvenir or add a special touch to a picnic lunch. The Nut Factory also has a small deli selection and ice cream. Inside the same facility is the **H.R.T. Waipio Tour Desk,** tel. 775-7291, where you can arrange a van or horseback tour through fabulous Waipio (see "Waipio Valley" later in this chapter).

Practicalities

Centrally located along Rt. 240 is the **Hotel Honokaa Club.** Contact Marilyn Otake, Manager, Box 185, Honokaa, HI 96727, tel. 775-0678. What it lacks in elegance it makes up for in cleanliness and friendliness. The hotel, mostly used by local people, is old and appears rundown. Upstairs rooms (view and TV) are $42 s, $44 d. The more spartan but very clean downstairs rooms go for $32 s, $35 d, and have their own baths. The hotel dining room serves the best meals in town. Breakfasts are served weekends only 6:30-11 a.m., lunch Mon.-Fri. 11 a.m.-2 p.m., and dinner nightly 5:30-8 p.m. The cooking is home-style with a different dinner special nightly, such as a seafood platter for $8.75, or lobster and steak for $20.95. Specials come with rice, potatoes, salad, and coffee. The hotel lounge serves a full range of cocktails and beer daily during lunch and dinner, and depending on business will stay open to 2 a.m.

Local people thought that Jolene was such a good cook, they recently talked her into opening **Jolene's Kau Kau Corner** in downtown Honokaa, tel. 775-9598, open daily except Sunday 10 a.m.- 8 p.m. Most tried-and-true recipes were handed down by her extended family, who also lend a hand in running the restaurant. They currently serve only lunch and dinner, with breakfast a possibility in the near future. The restaurant, located in a vintage storefront, is trim and neat, and the menu includes a variety of plate lunches like beef tips teriyaki $4.95, shrimp plate $5.50, and a steaming bowl of beef stew $4.85. Saimin in two sizes is $1.95 and $3.50, while most burgers and fries are under $4.50. The dinner menu brings broiled mahimahi $7.75, shrimp tempura $8.25, shrimp and chicken baskets around $5, and the enormous captain's plate of Alaska snow crab leg, shrimp, and New York steak $15.95. Jolene's is as down-home and local as you can get, and what she lacks in atmosphere, she more than makes up for in friendly service, hearty dishes, and reasonable prices. One of the best places to eat along the northern Hamakua Coast.

Dragon Chop Suey, tel. 775-0553, is open daily except Monday 11 a.m.-8 p.m. Along with standard Chinese dishes, it features vegetarian foods like vegetable soup $3.75, vegetarian saimin $3.75, and egg foo young $3.95. Basic Chinese dishes are ginger chicken, pork broccoli chow mein, and pot stickers, all $5-6. Dim sum plate lunches give you a choice of four items for $4.75.

Herb's Place, in downtown Honokaa, is open for breakfast, lunch, and dinner Mon.-Fri. from 5:30 a.m., Saturday from 8:30 a.m., closed Sunday. You get basic meals and cocktails in this little roadside joint.

C.C. Jon's is a plate-lunch, local fast-food stand, just as you enter town. Most of their dishes are under $4.50.

You can pick up supplies and even a few health food items at **T. Kaneshiro Store** and **K.K. Market,** two well-stocked markets in town.

If you are at all interested in the history of Hawaii, make sure to stop by the **The Hawaiian Artifacts Shop** along the main drag in downtown Honokaa. Look for a carved mermaid and a strobe light blinking you into the shop. This amazing curio and art shop is owned and operated by James and Lokikamakahiki "Loki" Rice. The Rices, both elderly and in failing health, keep no set hours, opening when they feel like it. They're usually here for a few hours in the afternoon, but never before 2 p.m. At first glance the shop may look unauthentic, but once you're inside, that impression quickly melts away. Loki, a full-blooded Hawaiian, was born and raised in Waipio Valley, and James has traveled the Pacific for years. Between the two, the stories from the old days are almost endless. Notice a tiki that serves as a main beam, and two giant shields against the back wall. They belonged to Loki's father, a giant of a man just under seven feet tall and over 450 pounds who had to have a special coffin made when he was buried on the island of Niihau. Local people bring in their carvings and handicrafts to sell, many of which are hula implements and instruments like drums and rattles. Some of the bric-a-brac is from the Philippines or other South Sea islands, but Jim will identify them for you. Mingled in with what seems to be junk are some real artifacts like poi pounders, adzes, and really good drums. Many have come from Loki's family, while others have been collected by the Rices over the years. But the real treasures inside the shop are Jim and Loki, who will share their *aloha* as long as time permits. Jim is also a **clockmaker** who not only makes clocks, but repairs them as well.

Kamaaina Woodworks, in Honokaa halfway down the hill leading to Hawaiian Holiday Macadamia Nut Factory, tel. 775-7722, is usually open daily except Sunday 9 a.m.-5 p.m., but this depends on the weather, their inclination, and how the spirits are moving on any particular day. The shop is owned and operated by Bill Keb and Roy Mau, talented woodworkers who specialize in fabulous bowls turned from native woods like koa, milo, extremely rare *kou,* and a few introduced woods like mango and Norfolk Island pine. All of the wooden artpieces, priced at $20-1000, are one-of-a-kind, and are designed to be utilitarian. Less expensive items are koa or milo bracelets $10-20, letter openers $5, and rice paddles $4. When you first enter the shop, don't be surprised if it looks like someone's home with a TV on in the sitting room and glass cases filled with Hawaiian flora and fauna.

On the right, just near the Hotel Honokaa Club, is the **Honokaa Trading Co.,** selling new and used goods, antiques, and collectibles. On the south end of town as you enter, **Seconds To Go,** open daily except Sunday 9:30 a.m.-5 p.m., is owned and operated by Elaine Carlsmith, and is a collectibles and antique shop specializing in Hawaiian artifacts. The shop brims over with articles like classic Hawaiian ties and shirts from the '50s, dancing hula-doll lamps, antique hardware and building materials, clawfoot bathtubs, old books, Japanese bowls, a good collection of plates and saucers, and a ukelele. Elaine also has used fishing gear in case you want to try your luck.

In town, **S. Hasigara** has a few racks of local fashions, and a few bolts of traditional Japanese cloth. Look for the very ethnic **Filipino Store** along the main drag to soak up a cultural experience and to find an array of exotic spices and food ingredients. You can do most of your banking needs at **Bank of Hawaii,** also located in the downtown area. Gas can be purchased at either a **Union 76** or a **Chevron,** both well marked along the main drag.

KUKUIHAELE

For all of you looking for the "light at the end of the tunnel," Kukuihaele ("Traveling Light") is it. On the main road, the **Last Chance** grocery and gas station, open daily 9 a.m.-6 p.m., stocks basic supplies plus a small assortment of handicrafts and gift items. The Last Chance has an excellent selection of domestic and imported beers, along with light snacks for a picnic lunch. The store attendants are friendly and don't mind answering a few questions about the Waipio area if they are not too busy.

Waipio Valley Artworks, tel. 775-0958, open daily 9 a.m.-5 p.m., is an excellent shop in which to pick up an art object. There are plenty of offerings in wood that include carvings and bowls, but the shop also showcases various Hawaii-based artists working in different media. Definitely check out inspired prints by Sue Sweardlow, who has tuned in to the soul of Hawaii, and paintings by Carli Oliver and Kim Starr. You'll also find tikis, earrings, basketry made from natural fibers, and ceramics by Robert Joiner and Ann Rathbun. The shop features a snack window serving ice cream, sandwiches, and soft drinks. Out back, a small boutique offers designer T-shirts, alohawear, a smattering of souvenir items, and a fairly extensive collection of books mostly on Hawaiiana. Waipio Valley Artworks is also the meeting place for **Waipio Valley Shuttle,** tel. 775-7121, which will take you down to Waipio Valley (see below).

Accommodations

Waipio Wayside, Box 840, Honokaa, HI 96727, tel. 775-0275, the vintage home of the one-time plantation manager, is now owned and operated by Jackie Horne as a congenial B&B. Look for a white picket fence and two driveways exactly two miles toward Waipio from the Honokaa post office. You enter through double French doors, onto a rich wooden floor shining with a well-waxed patina. The walls are hand-laid vertical paneling, the prototype that modern paneling tries to emulate. The home contains five double bedrooms ranging in price $50-80 s, $65-85 d for multiple-night stays; $5 extra for single-night stays; $15 extra person. One large master bedroom is in its own little space out back, but attached to the house. The room, rich with knotty pine, is spacious and airy with plenty of windows. Every bedroom has beautiful curtains that are hand-painted originals by Jackie's friend, Laura Lewis, a local island artist. The back deck, where you will find hammocks in which to rock away your cares, overlooks manicured grounds that gently descend, affording a panoramic view of the coast. Jackie, whose meticulous and tastefully appointed home is straight from the pages of *Ladies' Home Journal,* is also a gourmet cook. Breakfast is sometimes waffles with strawberries and whipped cream, sometimes omelettes and biscuits, with fresh fruit from the property. Beverages are pure Kona coffee, juices, and an assortment of 24 gourmet teas from around the world. A stay at Waipio Wayside is guaranteed to be civilized, relaxing, and affordable.

Hale Kukui, tel. 775-7130 or (800) 444-7130, Box 5044, Kukuihaele, HI 96727, owned and operated by William and Sarah McCowatt, is a secluded B&B on four acres perched high on the *pali* from which you get a sweeping view of Waipio Valley and the wide Pacific. Follow the main road *through* Kukuihaele and look for a sign pointing you down a private drive that leads about 200 yards to the comfortable cottage. Inside, the units are tasteful with vaulted ceilings, black ceiling fan, white wicker furniture, and woven wool carpets. The bedroom is large, and the complete kitchen features a two-burner range, refrigerator, sink and preparation area, microwave, table and chairs, and utensils. The private lanai has a barbecue grill, and a TV can be provided on request. The grounds have been improved with a trail that leads down to a semi-private stream where you'll find a small but refreshing freshwater pool. The units include a self-contained studio and a two-bedroom unit which can be combined into a three-bedroom unit for large families or a group of friends. Rates based on double occupancy are studio (440 square feet, sleeps 2-4) $75; two-bedroom unit (660 square feet, sleeps 4-6) $95; three-bedroom unit (both combined) $150; additional person $10. A five percent discount is offered to members of Greenpeace, the Sierra Club, or any other recognized national environmental organization.

Enjoy the privacy of **Hamakua Hideaway,** Box 5104, Kukuihaele, HI 96727, tel. 775-7425. This B&B is only a 15-minute walk from Waipio Overlook. The entire home, s/d, is $60 daily, with reduced weekly and monthly rates available.

WAIPIO VALLEY

Waipio is the way the Lord would have liked to fashion the Garden of Eden, if he hadn't been on such a tight schedule. You can read about this incredible valley, but you really can't believe it until you see it for yourself. Route 240 ends a minute outside of Kukuihaele at an overlook, and 1,000 feet below is Waipio ("Arching Water"). The valley is a mile across where it fronts the sea at a series of high sand dunes. It's vibrantly green, always watered by Waipio Stream and lesser streams that spout as waterfalls from the *pali* at the rear of the valley. The green is offset by a wide band of black-sand beach. The far side of the valley ends abruptly at a steep *pali* that is higher than the one on which you're standing. A six-mile trail leads over it to Waimanu Valley, smaller, more remote, and more luxuriant.

Travelers have long extolled the amazing abundance of Waipio. From the overlook you can make out the overgrown outlines of garden terraces, taro patches, and fishponds in what was Hawaii's largest cultivated valley. Every foodstuff known to the Hawaiians once flourished here; even Waipio pigs were said to be bigger than pigs anywhere else. In times of famine, the produce from Waipio could sustain the populace of the entire island (estimated at 100,000 people). On the valley floor and alongside the streams you'll still find avocados, bananas, coconuts, passion fruit, mountain apples, guavas, breadfruit, tapioca, lemons, limes, coffee, grapefruit, and pumpkins. The old fishponds and streams are alive with prawns, wild pigs roam the interior, and there are abundant fish in the sea.

But the lovingly tended order, most homes, and the lifestyle were washed away in the tsunami of 1946. Now Waipio is unkempt, a wild jungle of mutated abundance. The valley is a neglected maiden with a dirty face and disheveled, windblown hair. Only love and nurturing can refresh her lingering beauty.

Getting There

The road leading down to Waipio is outrageously steep and narrow. If you attempt it in a regular car, it'll eat you up and spit out your bones. Over 20 fatalities have occurred since people started driving it, and it has only been paved since the early 1970s. You'll definitely need 4WD, low range, to make it; downhill vehicles yield to those coming up. There is very little traffic on the road except when surfing conditions are good. Sometimes Waipio Beach has the first good waves of the season and this brings out the surfers en masse. **Waipio Valley Shuttle,** tel. 775-7121, has their office at Waipio Valley Artworks in Kukuihaele. They still have a few super-tough and adventurous open Land Rovers for their 90-minute descent and tour, but mostly you'll ride in air-conditioned comfort in 4WD vans. The tour costs $25.80. Buy your ticket at the Artworks, and then proceed to the Waipio Overlook from where the vans leave every hour on the hour. This is the tamest, but safest, way to enjoy the valley. If you decide to hike down or stay overnight, you can make arrangements for the van to pick you up or drop you off for an added cost. The same company also offers a trip to the top of Mauna Kea.

If you have the energy, the hike down the paved section of the road is just over one mile, but it's a tough mile coming back up! Expect to take three to four hours down and back, adding more time to swim or look around. (For details, see "Camping in Waipio" below.)

ACTIVITIES

For a fun-filled experience guaranteed to please, try horseback riding with **Waipio Naalapa Trail Rides,** tel. 775-0419. Sherri Hannum, a young mother of three who moved to Waipio from Missouri almost 25 years ago, and her husband Mark, own and operate the trail rides. Both are enamored with the valley, and as fate would have it, have become the old-timers of Waipio. They gladly accept the charge of keeping the ancient accounts and oral traditions alive. The adventure begins when Mark picks you up at 9:30 a.m. at Waipio Valley Artworks (see "Kukuihaele" above). You begin a 40-minute 4WD ride down to the ranch, which gives you an excellent tour of the valley in and of itself, since their spread is even deeper into the valley than the end of the line for the commercial valley tour! En route you cross three or four streams, as Mark tells you some of the history and lore of Waipio. When you arrive, Sherri has the horses ready to go. Sherri knows the trails of Waipio intimately. She puts you in the saddle of a surefooted Waipio pony and spends all day telling you legends and stories while leading you to waterfalls, swimming holes, gravesites, and finally a *heiau.* The lineage of the horses of Waipio dates from the late 1700s. They were gifts to the *ali'i* from Capt. George Vancouver. Waipio was especially chosen for the horses because they were easy to corral here and could not escape. Today, over 150 semiwild progeny of the original stock roam the valley floor. Technically, you should bring your own lunch for the ride, since you can't always count on the fruits of Waipio to be happening. But if they are, Sherri will point them out and you can munch to your heart's delight. Tours lasting two and one-half hours cost $65 and start at 9:30 a.m. and 1 p.m. Full-day tours can be arranged, but a minimum of two and a maximum of four riders is required. Sorry, no children under 12 or riders weighing more than 230 pounds. Go prepared with long pants, shoes, and swimsuit. A ride with Sherri isn't just an adventure; it's an experience with memories that will last a lifetime.

Waipio Valley Wagon Tour, Box 1340, Honokaa, HI 96727, tel. 775-9518, owned and operated by Peter Tolin, is the newest and one of the most fun-filled ways of exploring Waipio. This surrey-type wagon, which can hold about a dozen people, is drawn by two Tennessee mules. The fascinating two-hour tours depart four times per day at 9 a.m., 10:30 a.m., 12:30 p.m., and either 2 or 4 p.m. Cost is $35, children under 12 half price, children two and under free. To participate, make reservations 24 hours in advance. Then check in 30 minutes before departure at the Waipio Overlook, where a 4WD vehicle will come to fetch you. The overlook also has a pay phone from which you can call the Wagon Tour to see if there is last-minute room for you, but a space is definitely not guaranteed. Lunch is not included, but if you bring your own, you can walk down to the beach and have a great picnic. The original wagon was built by Peter himself from parts that he ordered from the Mainland. Unfortunately, every part that he ordered broke down over a nine-month trial period. Peter had all new parts made at a local machine shop, only three times thicker than the originals! Now that the wagon has been *Waipionized,* the problems have ceased. The only high-tech aspect of the wagon ride is a set of small loudspeakers through which Peter narrates the history, biology, and myths of Waipio as you roll along.

Note:
In the summer of 1992, the Bishop Museum requested an environmental impact survey for Waipio Valley because the frequency of visitors to the valley had increased tremendously. Old-time residents were complaining not only about the overuse of the valley, but about the loss of their quiet and secluded lifestyle. Sherri Hannum of Waipio Naalapa Trail Rides and Peter Tolin of Waipio Valley Wagon Tour cooperated fully and did their best to help in the preservation and reasonable use of one of Hawaii's grandest valleys. They have complied with the regulations imposed by the Bishop Museum even when it meant a significant financial loss to themselves. Because of the impact study, the commercial tours are not allowed to go to the beach area, which is now open to foot traffic only, and the valley is **closed on Sunday** to commercial tours. Other tour operators, resentful of the Bishop Museum, were not as cooperative as Sherri and Peter, and apparently have put personal gain above the preservation of Waipio.

HISTORY

Legend And Oral History

Waipio is a mystical place. Inhabited for over 1,000 years, it figures prominently in old Hawaiian lore. In the primordial past, Wakea, progenitor of all the islands, favored the valley, and oral tradition holds that the great gods Kane and Kanaloa dallied in Waipio intoxicating themselves on *awa.* One oral chant relates that the demigod Maui, that wild prankster, met his untimely end here by trying to steal baked bananas from these two drunken heavyweights. Lono, god of the Makahiki, came to Waipio in search of a bride. He found Kaikilani, a beautiful maiden who lived in a breadfruit tree near **Hiilawe Waterfall,** which tumbles 1,300 feet to the valley below and is Hawaii's highest single falls.

Nenewe, a shark-man, lived near a pool at the bottom of another waterfall on the west side of Waipio recently fenced in so access is no longer available. The pool was connected to the sea by an underwater tunnel. All went well for Nenewe until his grandfather disobeyed a warning never to feed his grandson meat. Once Nenewe tasted meat, he began eating Waipio residents after first warning them about sharks as they passed his sea-connected pool on their way to fish. His constant warnings roused suspicions. Finally, a cape he always wore was ripped from his shoulders, and there on his back was a shark's mouth! He dove into his pool and left Waipio to hunt the waters of the other islands.

Pupualenalena, a *kupua* (nature spirit), takes the form of a yellow dog who can change his size from tiny to huge. He was sent by the chiefs of Waipio to steal a conch shell that mischievous water sprites were constantly blowing, just to irritate the people. The shell was inherited by Kamehameha and is now in the Bishop Museum. Another dog-spirit lives in a rock embedded in the hillside halfway down the road to Waipio. In times of danger, he comes out of his rock to stand in the middle of the road as a warning that bad things are about to happen.

Finally, a secret section of Waipio Beach is called **Lua o milu,** the legendary doorway to the land of the dead. At certain times, it is believed, ghosts of great *ali'i* come back to earth as "Marchers of the Night," and their strong chants and torch-lit processions fill the darkness in Waipio. Many great kings were buried in Waipio, and it's felt that because of their mana, no harm will come to the people who live here. Oddly enough, the horrible tsunami of 1946 and a raging flood in 1979 filled the valley with wild torrents of water. In both cases, the devastation to homes and the land was tremendous, but not one life was lost. Everyone who still lives in Waipio will tell you that somehow, they feel protected.

The remains of **Paka'alana Heiau** are in a grove of trees on the right-hand side of the beach as you face the sea. It dates from the 12th century and was a "temple of refuge" where *kapu* breakers, vanquished warriors, and the weak and infirm could find sanctuary. The other restored and more famous temple of this type is Pu'uhonua O Honaunau in Kona (see "Central and South Kona" in the Kona chapter). Paka'alana was a huge *heiau* with tremendous walls that were mostly intact until the tsunami of 1946. The tidal wave sounded like an explosion when the waters hit the walls of Paka'alana, according to first-hand accounts. The rocks were scattered, and all was turned to ruins. Nearby, **Hanua'aloa** is another *heiau* in ruins. Archaeologists know even less about this *heiau,* but all agree that both were healing temples of body and spirit, and the local people feel that their positive mana is part of the protection in Waipio.

Recorded History

Great chiefs have dwelt in Waipio. King Umialiloa planted taro just like a commoner, and fished with his own hands. He went on to unite the island into one kingdom in the 15th century. Waipio was the traditional land of Kamehameha the Great, and in many ways was the basis of his earthly and spiritual power. He came here to rest after heavy battles, and offshore was the scene of the first modern naval battle in Hawaii. Here, Kamehameha's war canoes faced those of his nemesis, Keoua. Both had recently acquired cannons bartered from passing sea captains. Kamehameha's artillery was supervised by two white sailors, Davis and Young, who became trusted advisors. Kamehameha's forces won the engagement in what became known as the "Battle of the Red-Mouthed Gun."

When Captain Cook came to Hawaii, 4,000 natives lived in Waipio; a century later only 600 remained. At the turn of this century many Chinese and Japanese moved to Waipio and began raising rice and taro. People moved in and out of the valley by horse and mule and there were schools and a strong community spirit. Waipio was painstakingly tended. The undergrowth was kept trimmed and you could see clearly from the back of the valley all the way to the sea. WW II arrived and many people were lured away from the remoteness of the valley by a changing lifestyle and a desire for modernity. The tidal wave in 1946 swept away most of the homes, and the majority of the people pulled up stakes and moved away. For 25 years the valley lay virtually abandoned. The Peace Corps considered it a perfect place to build a compound in which to train volunteers headed for Southeast Asia. This too was abandoned. Then in the late '60s and early '70s a few "back to nature" hippies started trickling in. Most only played "Tarzan and Jane" and moved on, especially after Waipio served them a "reality sandwich" in the form of the flood of 1979.

Waipio is still very unpredictable. In a three-week period from late March to early April of 1989, 47 inches of rain drenched the valley. Roads were turned to quagmires, houses washed away, and more people left. Part of the problem is the imported trees in Waipio. Until the 1940s, the valley was a manicured garden, but now it's very heavily forested. All of the trees that you will see are new; the oldest are mangroves and coconuts. The trees are both a boon and a blight. They give shade and fruit, but when there are floods, they fall into the river, creating log jams that increase the flooding dramatically. Waipio takes care of itself best when humans do not interfere. Now the taro farmers are having problems because the irrigation system for their crops was washed away in the last flood. But, with hope and a prayer to Waipio's spirits, they'll rebuild, knowing full well that there will be a next time. And so it goes.

Waipio Now

Waipio is at a crossroads. Many of the old people are dying off, or moving topside (above the valley) with relatives. Those who live here learn to accept life in Waipio and genuinely come to love the valley, while others come only to exploit its beauty. Fortunately, the latter underestimate the raw power of Waipio. Developers have eyed the area for years as a magnificent spot in which to build a luxury resort. But even they are wise enough to realize that it is nature that rules Waipio. For now the valley is secure. A few gutsy families with a real commitment have stayed on and continue to revitalize Waipio. The valley now supports perhaps 50 residents. A handful of elderly Filipino bachelors who worked for the sugar plantation continue to live here. About 50 more people live topside, but come down to Waipio to tend their gardens. On entering the valley, you'll see a lotus-flower pond, and if you're lucky enough to be here in December, it will be in bloom. It's tended by an 80-year-old Chinese gentleman, Mr. Nelson Chun, who wades into the chest-deep water to harvest the sausage-linked lotus roots by clipping them with his toes! Margaret Loo comes to harvest wild ferns served at the exclusive banquets at the Mauna Kea Beach Resort. Seiko Kaneshiro is perhaps the most famous taro farmer because of his poi factory that produces "Ono Ono Waipio Brand Taro." Another old-timer is Charlie Kawashima, who still grows taro the old-fashioned way, as an art passed from father to son. He harvests the taro with an *o'o* (digging stick) and after it's harvested cuts off the corm and sticks the *huli* (stalk) back into the ground, where it begins to sprout again in a week or so.

Harrison Kanakoa, recently deceased, mostly lived topside because of failing health in his later years. He was born in a house built in 1881 near Kauiki Heiau, one of the biggest and most powerful *heiau* in the valley. Harrison loved to "talk story," relating tales of when his family was the keeper of the *heiau.* When he was a small boy his grandfather took him to the *heiau,* where he rolled away an entrance stone to reveal a small tunnel that went deep inside. He followed his grandfather in a ways, but his child's courage failed, and he turned away and ran out. He said his grandfather yelled after him something in Hawaiian like, "You coward," and refused to show him that place again. In 1952, C.H. Brewer, a very powerful sugarcane company in this area, bulldozed the *heiau* and planted macadamia trees on top. The trees still bear nuts, but the *heiau* was obliterated.

Camping In Waipio

For camping in Waipio Valley you must get a permit from the Hamakua Sugar Co., tel. 776-1511. The office is located about 15 minutes from the overlook in Paauilo and you must pick up the permit in person. Camping is allowed in designated areas only on the east side of Waipio Stream. Many hikers and campers have stayed in Waipio overnight without a permit and have had no problem. Remember, however, that most of the land, except for the beach, *is* privately owned.

Waipio Beach, stretching over a mile, is the longest black-sand beach on the island. The surf here can be very dangerous and there are many riptides. During the summer the sands drift to the western side of the valley; in winter they drift back east. If there is strong wave action, swimming is not advised. It is, however, a good place for surfing and fishing.

The **Waipio Valley Aqueduct Trail,** which follows the clearly marked water system of the recently defunct Hamakua Sugar Plantation, has just opened up to the public. Not overly vigorous, the rather flat trail (except for one spot that requires scrambling down a ladder) skirts the rear of the valley where the natural flora is still thriving. In some places, the sugar company followed an irrigation system laid by native Hawaiians over 1,000 years ago that watered ancient terraces growing wetland taro.

Accommodations

Waipio has a hotel! Owned and operated by Tom Araki, it was built by his dad to serve as a residence for teachers who came to teach at the local school, and was later used for officers of a nearby, now defunct Peace Corps training camp. You'll find eight basic but clean rooms. Light is provided by kerosene lamp, and you must bring your own food to prepare in a communal kitchen. Tom, at 84, is a treasure house of information about Waipio, and a "character" who's more interested in tending his taro patch, telling stories, and drinking wine than he is in running a hotel. His philosophy, which has enabled him to get along with everyone from millionaires to hippies, is a simple "live and let live." The Waipio Hotel has become known and it's even fashionable to stay here. For reservations, write Tom Araki, 25 Malama Pl., Hilo, HI 96720, or call Tom down in Waipio Valley at tel. 775-0368. Expect to pay about $15 per person.

Ever fantasized about running off to a tropical island and living a life of "high" adventure? *The* most secluded accommodation in all of Hawaii is **The Treehouse,** owned and operated by Linda Beech and her partner, Mark Singleton, a technological tinkerer *extraordinaire* who keeps most of the alternative water, phone, and electrical systems up and running. The Treehouse is located deep in Waipio Valley on three acres of land completely surrounded by holdings of the Bishop Museum. Linda or Mark will fetch you from topside in a sturdy 4WD and ferry you across at least five rivers until you come to their idyllic settlement at the foot of Papala Waterfall. Tumbling 1,800 feet over the towering *pali,* the falls provide the water for a hydroelectric power plant (solar backup) that runs everything from stereos to ceiling fans. Linda purchased the land about 25 years ago after returning to Hawaii, the place of her birth. She has had a most interesting life, traveling throughout Asia. In Japan she was a famous personality starring in a very popular and long-running TV sitcom entitled *"Uchi no okasan, tonari no mama-san"* (The lady of the house and the mama-san next door).

The Treehouse was built in 1972 by master boatbuilders Eric Johnson and Steven Oldfather, who chose a 65-foot monkeypod tree as its perch. Secured by an ingenious "three pin anchoring system," the Treehouse sways like a moored boat, allowing the tree to grow without causing structural damage. It has survived 120 mph winds and has proven to be a most "seaworthy" treehouse. Eric Johnson came back about four years ago to reroof the structure and found it still square and level. Both men have given up professional boatbuilding and have become very famous on the Big Island as custom home builders.

The Treehouse is fascinating, but basic. As you climb the steps, the first landing holds a flushing toilet. Inside, the Treehouse is plain wood and screened windows, not much more. It's very comfortable with island-style furnishings, and provides a full kitchen and all utensils, but it is not luxurious. The luxury is provided by Waipio itself, which floods the interior with golden light and the perfume of tropical flowers wafting on the breeze. All around, the melodious songs of indigenous birds, the ever-present wind, and cascading waters serenade you day and night. If you don't wish to perch high in a tree, Linda also offers **The Hale,** an earthbound but commodious structure where the walls of glass and screen open to the magnificent still-life surrounding you. All guests are invited to use a traditional Japanese *ofuro,* a hot tub, brought back by Linda from her travels in the East. Remember, however, that The Treehouse is a vacation rental, not a B&B, and that you will be required to bring all of your own food and to do your own light housekeeping.

Because The Treehouse, tel. 775-7160 (same as Waipio Valley Wagon Tours), Box 5086, Honokaa, HI 96727, is so remote, it is necessary to make reservations well in advance. Rates at The Treehouse, which can handle two "very friendly" couples, are $200 per couple first day, $150 per day thereafter, and $25 per additional person over 12 years old. Rates for The Hale, which can sleep up to six, are $75 double occupancy, $25 per additional person. A 50% deposit is requested with the reservation, and a two-week cancellation notice prior to arrival is necessary for a refund. Nature still rules Waipio, and about 10 days per year the streams are flooded and it is impossible to get either in or out. If you can't get in, a prompt refund will be made, and if you're lucky enough to be marooned, complimentary lodging and food will be cordially provided for the duration of your stay.

WAIMANU VALLEY, CAMPING AND HIKING

The hike down to Waipio and over the *pali* to Waimanu Valley 12 miles away is one of the top three treks in Hawaii. You must be fully prepared for camping and in excellent condition to attempt this hike. Also, water from the streams and falls is not always good for drinking due to irrigation and cattle grazing topside; bring purification tablets or boil or filter it to be safe. To get to Waimanu Valley, a switchback trail leads over the *pali* about 100 yards inland from Waipio Beach. The beginning of the switchback trail has a post with a painting that reads "Warning Menehune." Waimanu was bought by the State of Hawaii about 12 years ago, and they are responsible for trail maintenance. The trail ahead is rough, as you go up and down about 14 gulches before reaching Waimanu. At the ninth gulch is a trail shelter. Finally, below is Waimau Valley, half the size of Waipio but more verdant, and even wilder because it has been uninhabited for a longer time. Cross Waimanu Stream in the shallows where it meets the sea. For drinking water (remember to treat it), walk along the west side of the *pali* until you find a likely waterfall. To stay overnight in Waimanu Valley you must have a (free) camping permit available through the Division of Forestry and Wildlife, Box 4849, Hilo, HI 96721, tel. 933-4221, open Tues.-Fri. 8 a.m.-4 p.m., Monday 10 a.m.-4 p.m. Your length of stay is limited to seven days and six nights. Each of the nine designated campsites has a fireplace and a composting outhouse. Carry out what you carry in!

Early this century, because of economic necessity brought on by the valley's remoteness, Waimanu was known for its *okolehau* (moonshine). Solomon, one of the elders of the community at the time, decided that Waimanu had to diversify for the good of its people. He decided to raise domesticated pigs introduced by the Chinese, who roasted them with spices in rock ovens as a great delicacy. Solomon began to raise and sell the pigs commercially, but when he died, out of respect, no one wanted to handle his pigs, so they let them run loose. They began to interbreed with feral pigs, and after a while there were so many pigs in Waimanu that they ate all the taro, bananas, and breadfruit. The porkers' voracious appetites caused a famine which forced the last remaining families of Waimanu to leave in the late 1940s. Most of the trails that you will encounter are made by wild-pig hunters who still regularly go after Solomon's legacy.

According to oral tradition the first *kahuna lapa'au* (healing doctor) of Hawaii was from Waimanu Valley. His disciples crossed and recrossed Waipio Valley, greatly influencing the development of the area. Some of the *heiau* in Waipio are specifically dedicated to the healing of the human torso; their origins are traced to the healing *kahuna* of Waimanu.

LOUISE FOOTE

PUNA

The Puna District was formed from rivers of lava spilling from Mauna Loa and Kilauea again and again over the last million years or so. The molten rivers stopped only when they hit the sea, where they fizzled and cooled, forming a chunk of semi-raw land that bulges into the Pacific—marking the state's easternmost point at **Cape Kumukahi.** These titanic lava flows have left phenomenal reminders of their power. **Lava Tree State Monument** is a former rainforest whose giant trees were covered with lava, like hot dogs dipped in batter. The encased wood burned, leaving hollow stone skeletons. You can stroll through this lichen-green rock forest before you head farther east into the brilliant sunshine of the coast. Little-traveled side roads take you past a multitude of orchid, anthurium, and papaya farms, oases of color in a desert of solid black lava. A lighthouse sits atop Cape Kumukahi, and to the north an ancient paved trail passes beaches where no one ever goes.

Southward is a string of popular beaches—some white, some black. You can camp, swim, surf, or just play in the water to your heart's delight. Villages have gas and food, and all along the coast you can visit natural areas where the sea tortured the hot lava into caves, tubes, arches, and even a natural bathtub whose waters are flushed and replenished by the sea. There are historical sites where petroglyphs tell vague stories from the past, and where generations of families placed the umbilical cords of their newborn into manmade holes in the rock. On Puna's south coast are remains of ancient villages, including Kamoamoa where you can camp. The park **visitors center,** which used to stand before the beginning of Chain of Craters Road, burned down in the summer of 1989 when lava surged across the road, severing this eastern gateway to Volcanoes National Park. (The road is still closed, with no opening scheduled for the near future. See "Chain of Craters Road" in the chapter on Hawaii Volcanoes National Park.) The

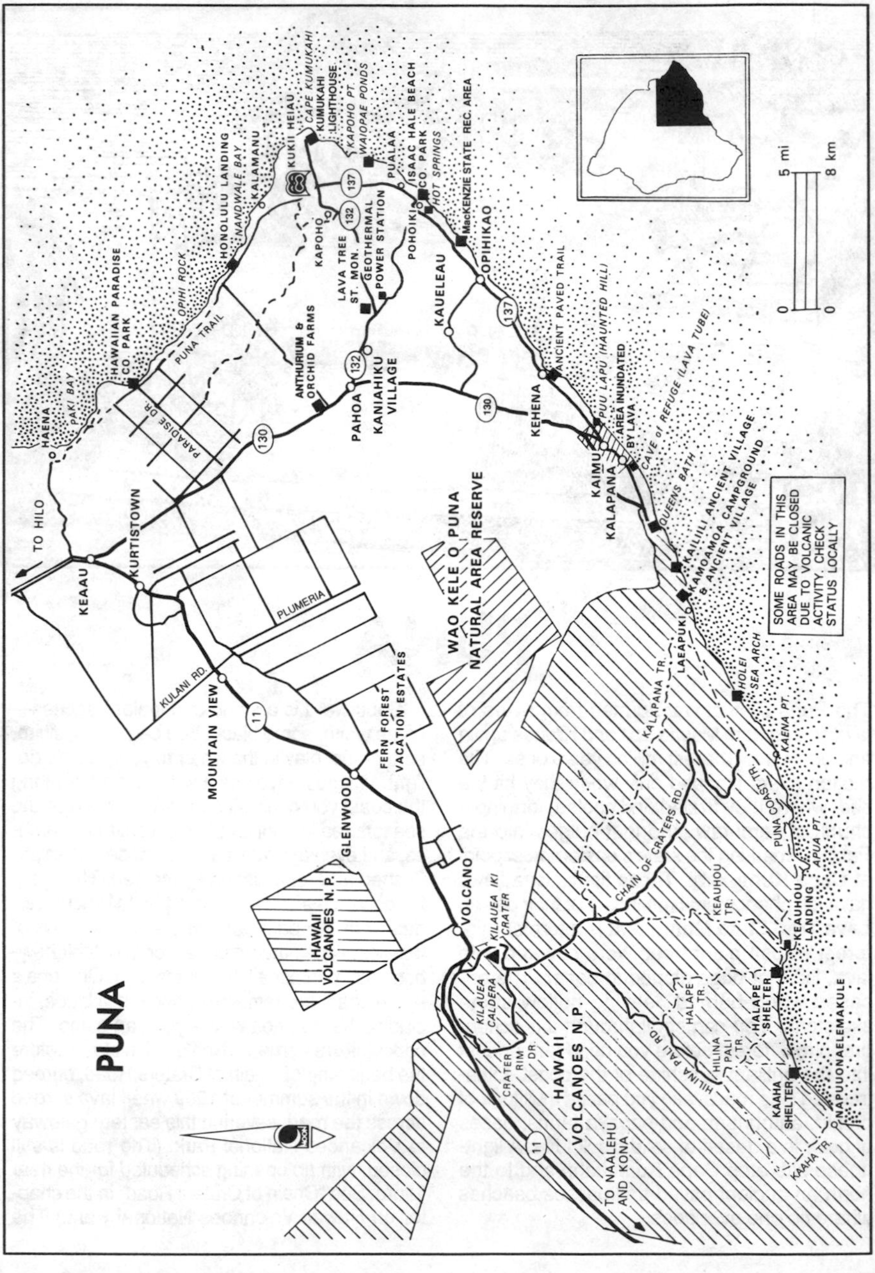

PUNA
TO HILO
KEAAU
KURTISTOWN
HAENA
PAKI BAY
HAWAIIAN PARADISE CO. PARK
PARADISE DR.
PUNA TRAIL
OPIHI ROCK
HONOLULU LANDING
NANAWALE BAY
KALAMANU
KUKII HEIAU
CAPE KUMUKAHI
KUMUKAHI LIGHTHOUSE
KAPOHO PT.
WAIOPAE PONDS
KAPOHO
LAVA TREE ST. MON.
GEOTHERMAL POWER STATION
PUALAA
ISAAC HALE BEACH CO. PARK
POHOIKI
HOT SPRINGS
MacKENZIE STATE REC. AREA
OPIHIKAO
KAUELEAU
ANTHURIUM & ORCHID FARMS
PAHOA
KANIAHIKU VILLAGE
KEHENA
ANCIENT PAVED TRAIL
PUU LAPU (HAUNTED HILL)
AREA INUNDATED BY LAVA
KAIMU
KALAPANA
CAVE of REFUGE (LAVA TUBE)
QUEENS BATH
KAILIILI ANCIENT VILLAGE
KAMOAMOA CAMPGROUND & ANCIENT VILLAGE
LAEAPUKI
HOLEI SEA ARCH
SOME ROADS IN THIS AREA MAY BE CLOSED DUE TO VOLCANIC ACTIVITY. CHECK STATUS LOCALLY
WAO KELE O PUNA NATURAL AREA RESERVE
PLUMERIA
KULANI RD.
MOUNTAIN VIEW
FERN FOREST VACATION ESTATES
GLENWOOD
VOLCANO
HAWAII VOLCANOES N.P.
KILAUEA IKI CRATER
KILAUEA CALDERA
CRATER RIM DR.
CHAIN OF CRATERS RD.
KALAPANA TR.
KEAUHOU TR.
HALAPE TR.
HILINA PALI RD.
HILINA PALI TR.
PUNA COAST TR.
KAENA PT.
APUA PT.
KEAUHOU LANDING
HALAPE SHELTER
KAAHA SHELTER
KAAHA TR.
NAPUUONAELEMAKULE
TO NAALEHU AND KONA
11
130
132
137
0
5 mi
8 km

Hawaii Belt Road (Rt. 11) is a corridor cutting through the center of Puna. It goes through the highlands to Volcanoes National Park, passing well-established villages and scattered housing developments as new as the lava on which they precariously sit. Back in these hills, new-wave gardeners grow "Puna Butter" *pakalolo,* as wild and raunchy as its name. On the border of Puna and the Kau District to the south is **Hawaii Volcanoes National Park.** Here the goddess Pele resides at Kilauea Caldera, center of one of the world's most active volcanoes.

HAWAII BELT ROAD— HILO TO VOLCANOES

Route 11 (Hawaii Belt Road) splits in Keaau and passes through the high mountain villages of Mountain View, Glenwood, and Volcano, then enters Hawaii Volcanoes National Park. It takes a full day and then some to see and appreciate Volcanoes, so if "making time" is your main consideration, this is the way to go. The Belt Road, although only two lanes, is straight, well surfaced, and scrupulously maintained. However, if you want much more exciting scenery and a host of natural and historic sites, head south on Rt. 130 toward Pahoa and the east coast. Route 130 shouldn't be traveled at night, however. In short, if time is on your side, take one day to visit Volcanoes, using the Belt Road for convenience, and another to "Sunday drive" Rt. 130 along the coast.

KEAAU

Keaau is the first town south of Hilo (10 miles) on Rt. 11, and although pleasant enough, it's little more than a Y in the road. At the junction of Rt. 11 and Rt. 130 is **Keaau Town Center,** a small shopping mall with a handful of variety stores, a laundromat, a post office, restaurants, and a sizable **Ben Franklin.** Here, the **Sure Save Supermarket** has not only groceries but plenty of sundries and a decent camera department, along with a public fax service.

Food

The local **Dairy Queen,** in the Keaau Town Center, not only makes malts and sundaes but serves breakfast, lunch, and dinner. Plate specials, burgers, and sandwiches like a Reuben with French fries go for $4.95. Next door to the Sure Save Supermarket, the **New Seoul Barbecue,** open daily except Sunday 9 a.m.-9:30 p.m., is an inexpensive, shocking-yellow Formica-and-linoleum Korean restaurant offering tasty meals like barbecued beef, chicken, rice, macaroni salad, pickle, and squash jam all for $4.95; or combination plates of steak, chicken, shrimp, sashimi, rice, and macaroni salad for $8.50. Next door is a tiny hole-in-the-wall eatery, **Lunch at Miu's,** that sells an assortment of *manapua* and spring rolls for under $1, steaming bowls of saimin, and plate lunches. For those who want to try an island treat like crackseed or shave ice, visit the center's **Kaeo Krack Seed,** open daily except Sunday 9 a.m.-5 p.m.

Across the street, and a few hundred yards down Rt. 130, is **Keaau Natural Foods** with a large stock of organic food items, herbs, and grains but no juice or snack bar. However, premade sandwiches like tempeh burgers with all the trimmings are $5, and fresh-baked goods are always available.

Tonya's Cafe is a tiny place next door to Keaau Natural Foods; hours are Mon.-Fri. 11 a.m.-7 p.m., closed Saturday and Sunday. Tonya, tiny herself but of big spirit, has surfer specials, sandwiches, and side orders like nachos and tostadas, but the main cuisine is "international vegetarian" featuring an eclectic selection of recipes—anything from Thai to Jamaican. Tonya's is a mix of funky and yuppie in a moderate but tasteful decor where you can read the latest metaphysical tome while eating a frozen yogurt. Her hours can be irregular, but when she's there she serves up some of the best vegetarian food (organic when possible) on this side of the island.

Catty-corner to the shopping mall, just near the red light, look for **Lorenzo's Badass Coffee Bar and Cafe,** open from about 8 a.m. to 10:30

p.m., where you can have an "individually made" cup of coffee or espresso from beans roasted by the Big Island's own Badass Coffee Company (see "Shopping" under "Central and South Kona" in the Kona chapter). You can also munch on an assortment of bagels and cream cheese $1.50, tuna melt or fish sandwiches $2.95, pizza by the slice, and salads—or forget the waistline and go for ice cream and pie. The corner location makes Lorenzo's perfect for people-watching.

A few hundred yards down Rt. 130 heading toward Pahoa, you'll see **Verna's Drive-In,** and behind it is a small mall with a **Wiki Wiki Mini-Mart.**

MOUNTAIN VILLAGES

South along Rt. 11, at approximately 10-mile intervals, are Mountain View, Glenwood, and Volcano. **Mountain View** is a village of nurseries specializing in anthuriums. Many of them sport signs inviting you to a free tour. Along Rt. 11 is a mini-mart and **Verna's Too Snack Shop** serving plate lunches, burgers, and shakes. As you pass through, take a minute to explore the short side-road into the village itself. Every house has a garden of ferns, flowers, and native trees. In the village is **Mt. View Bakery,** home of the famous stone cookies; and the **Mt. View Village Store,** which is fairly well supplied.

Look for a vintage plantation house painted blue between mile markers 12 and 13. This is **Tinny Fisher's Antique Shop,** owned and operated by Charles and Dorothy Wittig. What started as "yard sale treasures" about 10 years ago has turned into a unique curio, antique, and collectibles shop. Open daily except Monday, noon-6 p.m., the shop has all kinds of antiques and collectibles from Asia and Hawaii, including glass balls, Asian furniture, jewelry, and glassware galore. Tinny's also features a good Hawaiiana collection, with artifacts from the ancient days like *kukui* nut lamps, poi pounders, and stone knives.

Glenwood, between mile markers 19 and 20, offers a gas station and **Hirano's General Store** for basic provisions. A few minutes down the road you pass **Akatsuka Tropical Orchids and Flower Gardens,** open daily 8:30 a.m.-5 p.m. If tour buses don't overflow the parking lot, stop in for a look at how orchids are grown or to use the clean restrooms. They offer a complimentary orchid to all visitors. Just before you enter Volcanoes National Park, a sign points to the right down a short side road to **Volcano village** (see "Small Detours" under "Kilauea Caldera," and "Accommodations, Food, and Shopping" under "Practicalities," all in the Hawaii Volcanoes National Park chapter).

ROUTE 130 AND THE SOUTHEAST COAST

The most enjoyable area in the Puna District is the southeast coast, with its beaches and points of natural and historical interest. If you take Rt. 130 south from Keaau, in about 12 miles you pass **Pahoa.** As in Keaau, Pahoa is primarily a crossroad. You can continue due south on Rt. 130 to the seaside villages of **Kaimu** and **Kalapana,** where Rt. 130 joins coastal Rt. 137, feeding into Chain of Craters Road which has been buried by recent lava flows and is impassable. (For more information see "Chain of Craters Road" in the Hawaii Volcanoes National Park chapter.) Along Rt. 130, about halfway between Pahoa and Kaimu, look for a small, unobtrusive sign that reads "Scenic Overlook." Pull off and walk toward the sea until you find four hot steam vents. Many local people use them as natural saunas.

You might go directly east from Pahoa along Rt. 132. This lovely, tree-lined country road takes you past **Lava Tree State Monument,** which shouldn't be missed, and then branches northeast, intersecting Rt. 137 and terminating at **Cape Kumukahi.** If this seems *too* far out of the way, head down **Pohoiki Road,** just past Lava Tree. You bypass a controversial geothermal power station, then reach the coast at **Isaac Hale Beach County Park.** From here, Rt. 137 heads southwest down the coast to Kalapana, passing the best Puna beaches en route. Fortunately for you, this area of Puna is one of those places where no matter which way you decide to go, you really can't go wrong.

PAHOA AND VICINITY

You can breeze through this "one-street" town, but you won't regret stopping if even for a few minutes. A raised wooden sidewalk passing false-front shops is fun to walk along to get a feeling of the last century. Most of the shops lining it are family-run fruit and vegetable stands supplied by local gardeners. Selections depend upon whether the old pickup truck started and made it to town that day. At one time Pahoa boasted *the* largest sawmill in America. Its buzz saw ripped ohia railway ties for the Santa Fe and other railroads. It was into one of these ties that the *golden spike* uniting the East and West coasts of the Mainland was driven. Many local people earned their livelihood from ohia charcoal they made and sold all over the island until it was made obsolete by the widespread use of kerosene and gas introduced in the early 1950s. Pahoa's commercial heart went up in flames in 1955. Along the main street was a tofu factory that had a wood-fired furnace. The old fellow who owned the factory banked his fires as usual before he went home for the night. Somehow, they got out of control and burned all the way down to the main alley dividing the commercial district. The only reason the fire didn't jump the alley was because a papaya farmer happened to be around and had a load of water on the back of his truck, which he used to douse the buildings and save the town.

Pahoa is attempting to become part of the *Main Street U.S.A. Project* which will protect and revitalize its commercial center and bring new life to vintage buildings like the Akebono Theater, where classic movies will be shown. Pahoa has one of the highest concentrations of old buildings still standing in Hawaii that are easily accessible. Although it has been bypassed by a new road, make sure to enter the town and stroll along the tiny back roads. The town is attempting to become the anthurium capital of the world, and they have a good start on it. In virtually every garden, surrounded by distinctive lava-rock walls, you'll see black shade mesh under which are magnificent specimens of the normal red flowers, plenty of white ones, a few green, and even black anthuriums.

Lava Tree State Monument

In 1790, slick, fast-flowing *pahoehoe* lava surged through this ohia forest, covering the tree trunks from the ground to about a 12-foot level. The moisture inside the trees cooled the lava, forming a hardened shell. At the same time, tremors and huge fissures cracked the earth in the area.

When the eruption ended, the still-hot lava drained away through the fissures, leaving the encased tree trunks standing like sentinels. The floor of the forest is so smooth in some areas that the lava seems like asphalt. Each lava tree has its own personality; some resemble totem poles, and it doesn't take much imagination to see old, craggy faces staring back at you. The most spectacular part of the park is near the entrance. Immense trees loom over cavernous cracks *(puka)* in the earth and send their roots, like stilled waterfalls, tumbling down into them. To get to Lava Tree, take Rt. 132 east from Pahoa for three miles and look for the well-marked entrance on the left. Brochures are available as you enter.

Cape Kumukahi

It's fitting that Kumukahi means "First Beginning" since it is the easternmost point of Hawaii and was recognized as such by the original Polynesian settlers. Follow Rt. 132 past Lava Tree for about 10 miles until it hits the coast, where a lighthouse sits like an exclamation point. Along the way, get an instant course in volcanology: you can easily chart the destructive and regenerative forces at work on Hawaii. At mile marker 5 an HVB Warrior points out the lava flow of 1955. Tiny plants give the lava a greenish cast, and shrubs are already eating into it, turning it to soil. Papaya orchards grow in the raw lava of an extensive flat basin. The contrast between the black, lifeless earth and the vibrant green trees is startling. In the center of the flatland rises a cinder cone, a caldera of a much older mini-volcano unscathed by the modern flows; it is gorgeous with lush vegetation. An HVB Warrior points out the lava flow of 1960, and you can see at a glance how different it was from the flow of five years earlier. When Rt. 132 intersects Rt. 137, go straight ahead east down a paved road for two miles to the Cape Kumukahi Lighthouse. People in these parts swear that on the fateful night in 1960 when the nearby village of Kapoho was consumed by the lava flow, an old woman (a favorite guise of Madame Pele) came to town begging for food and was turned away by everyone. She next went to the lighthouse asking for help, and was cordially treated by the lighthouse keeper. When the flow was at its strongest, it came within yards of the lighthouse and then miraculously split, completely encircling the structure but leaving it unharmed as it continued out to sea for a considerable distance.

Practicalities

When you pull into Pahoa you are greeted by the **Pahoa Village Center,** a small shopping center where you'll find a **laundromat** and a video store. Almost adjacent is **The Rib House,** basically counter service offering baby-back ribs, chicken, and burgers at reasonable prices. Here too is **Dairy Queen,** open daily 7 a.m.-8:30 p.m. for breakfast, lunch, and dinner. They serve everything from banana splits to chicken, pizza, and plate lunches. A minute down the road is **Pahoa Cash and Carry** grocery store, **7-Eleven,** and the **Pahoa Casherette,** which are enough for any supplies or incidentals you may need. Close by is **Pahoa Chop Suey,** a down-home restaurant where you can eat cheaply; and down the street is **Luquin's Place,** open daily 11 a.m.-9 p.m., tel. 965-9990, a reasonably priced Mexican restaurant that offers enchiladas, burritos, tacos, and combination platters for $5-7.

Pahoa Natural Groceries, tel. 965-8322, open weekdays 9 a.m.-9 p.m., Sunday 9 a.m.-6 p.m., specializing in organic fruits and juices, is one of the finest health food stores on the Big Island. They have an excellent selection of fresh vegies, organic grains, herbs and minerals, and deli items, and a very good bakery selection (see The Bamboo House in the following "Accommodations" section). Adjacent is **The Emporium,** open daily 10 a.m.-6 p.m., with a small but excellent selection of jewelry, Guatemalan clothing, gifts, magazines, and cards. The Emporium also displays artwork, some by local artists, and a colorful selection of rugs. Their shirts and dresses, all 100% cotton, cost $25-50.

Halemana, tel. 965-7783, open Mon.-Fri. 9 a.m.-5 p.m. or by appointment, adjacent to the health food store, is an acupuncture and massage clinic. The acupuncturists are Françoise Hesselink, Jocelyn Mayeux, and Rhonda Ashby. Relax as you lie on the table and breezes blow through the vintage rooms. Let one of these fine practitioners energize and revitalize your spirit and put spring back into your aching muscles.

The **Puna Sands Restaurant,** a block away, makes luscious banana, papaya, or passion fruit smoothies for $2. Sandwiches, all under $5, include roast beef with peppers sautéed in olive oil on a French roll, barbecued ham with homemade sauce, and Italian sausage and peppers with spaghetti sauce. There's also a breakfast special for $1.95. The Pahoa **Coffee Shop** along the main drag specializes in breakfast, but is open for lunch and dinner too. Next door is the **Pahoa Lounge** that rocks with live music every Friday and Saturday night.

Along the elevated boardwalk, you'll spot shops like **Ernie's Produce;** a laundromat; and **T-shirt Boutique,** tel. 965-9776, open daily except Sunday 10 a.m.-4 p.m, where Alva sells tees of all description, from tie-dyed to originals by local artists. Or bring home a permanent souvenir from **Through the Looking Glass, Skin Illusions,** where one hour and $125 will get you an "entry level" tattoo at this fully licensed parlor (only pre-sterilized, single-service utensils and tools are used). Before you decide on a tattoo, maybe you should drop in next door at **Pacific Mystics,** a new-age shop, and consult the tarot while browsing among books, crystals, surfboards, and a cosmic smattering of clothes and sunglasses. Up the walk is **Threads,** open daily except Sunday, 10 a.m.-4:30 p.m., where seamstress Mariko Jones will tailor shirts, blouses, and pants to your specifications. She also sells new and used alohawear.

It's a toss-up whether the name **Kukui Hale,** "The Nut House," more aptly describes the characters running this offbeat art shop or the pieces they create, open 10 a.m.-5 p.m. sort of, daily sort of, depending upon their mood. Hanging around the shop are "coconotes" (painted coconuts that can be sent through the mail) for $20 and coconut fiber (sennet) baskets at $20-60. From the ceilings, $12 "angels of the rainforest" (coconuts made into cherubs) smile down upon you. Judith Pearl, one of the owners, also paints mythical renderings of Pele, or whales floating in a pink and azure sky. Next door, look for **Simply Natural,** open daily except Sunday 10:30 a.m.-7:30 p.m., serving sandwiches, shave ice, homemade Hilo ice cream, high-protein shakes, and daily specials like chili and sandwiches. Simply Natural also has a smattering of silver jewelry, penny candy, and antiques. Adjacent is **Naung Mai Thai Food,** open daily for lunch and dinner, tel. 965-8186, where you can dine on Thai spring rolls $4.95; red, green, or yellow curried shrimp, chicken, or beef $8.95; or a hearty bowl of Thai chicken-coconut soup $6.95. A full vegetarian selection, including tofu and eggplant curry $5.95, and rice and noodles $7.95, completes the menu.

One of the best places to eat in Pahoa is **Paradise West Coffee Shop,** tel. 965-9733, open daily 7 a.m.-2 p.m., breakfast until noon, owned and operated by Dave and Carrie Marry. Dave has a remarkable knowledge of Pahoa's history that he is willing to share if time permits. Breakfast is served with hash browns, rice, and buttermilk biscuits, and includes eggs with bacon $4.95, two eggs with fresh catch priced daily, and their very famous hollandaise sauce that tops eggs Benedict. One of the best deals is *huevos rancheros* with tortillas, beans, and salsa for $3.95. The lunch menu is basic cheeseburgers, tempeh burgers, and turkey sandwiches, all priced under $5.50. The menu changes daily, but you can count on fresh fish, tender steaks, and pasta for $5.95 that can be covered with sun-dried tomatoes, olive oil, Parmesan, and fresh basil. They also take care of the vegetarians with tofu scramble and a daily vegie special (see Marry Whale's Hotel in the following "Accommodations" section).

Wetlands Saloon, tel. 964-7488, on Pahoa's main street, features live music every weekend that can include local groups like To the Max or Pat Pauline playing everything from rock to blues. Next door is **Koho Okazuya,** open from 7 a.m., a window restaurant serving continental breakfast $2.60, and a variety of lunches like pineapple chicken, beef stew, and hamburger patties. A minute further down the elevated sidewalk is **Da Store** with groceries, a deli case, beer, and liquor.

Let your mind and stomach be soothed with cosmic vibrations and libations at **Huna Ohana,** open daily except Sunday for breakfast 8-11 a.m., lunch 11 a.m.-5:30 p.m., tel. 965-9661. The metaphysical bookstore (open until 6 p.m.) and cafe is owned and operated by Dawn Hurwitz. Vegetarian breakfast dishes include egg soufflé or tofu scramble served with cottage potatoes and multigrain toast at $3.95; bagels and cream cheese $1.75; and an assortment of croissants and special muffins such as purple sweet potato, chocolate zucchini, blueberry, and poppy seed with raspberry filling. Lunch brings pita pizza $3.95, vegie sandwiches $3.50, filling garden burgers (a blend of mushrooms, onions, rolled oats, lowfat mozzarella, brown rice, cottage cheese, eggs, cheddar, bulgur wheat, walnuts and spices) $4.75, or Jamaican patties (a curry pastry turnover with mixed vegie or spinach-and-squash filling) $2. To get those cosmic vibes kicked into high gear, order a cup of espresso, mocha latte, or cappuccino, choose a likely tome from the bookstore section, and kick back on an overstuffed couch or outside in the garden area.

A pipe dream that came true is **The Hawaiian Hemp Company,** open weekdays 10 a.m.-9 p.m., Sunday noon-6 p.m., tel. 965-8600. The shop is filled from floor to ceiling with hemp, one of the oldest and most useful plants known to humanity. The organic, all-hemp products include fanny packs, "Pakaloha" shirts, hip sun hats, shoulder bags, vests, twine, paper, and even hemp oil—nutritionally valuable, with a high concentration of essential fatty acids important to the immune system and in helping to fight cholesterol. Some fashions come from Macao and contain a blend of cotton, while others are made and designed in Hawaii from cloth woven in China. A mini-museum features hemp and its many uses around the world in music, art, medicine, and religious rites, and as a mind-altering drug. For excellent products and a mind-opening education, make sure to stop in at the Hawaiian Hemp Company.

Yo Pizza, tel. 965-7033, open daily except Monday 11 a.m.-10 p.m., uses homemade sauces and dough to make small, medium, and large traditional pizzas costing $4.90-14.90. They also have Italian Caesar salads $4.50, garden salad $2.75, garlic bread $1.50, and hot, rich cappuccino and espresso, perfect with slices of homemade pie. Lunch can be sub sandwiches $4.50, or you can dine on dinner specials like lasagna or spaghetti and meatballs for $6.50. The decor is "basic pizza parlor" sautéed in olive oil and garlic.

Accommodations

Out behind the Paradise West Coffee Shop (see above) is the **Marry Whales Hotel,** a one-time house of ill repute. Japanese entertainment troupes used to lodge here while performing at one of three major theaters in town. The hotel has 14 rooms, a quiet courtyard filled with flowers and cacti, and a Japanese *ofuro* which is now an outside bath painted by a local artist to look like the inside of an aquarium. The classically designed redwood structure is in remarkably good shape. Monthly rates only are $250-300 including utilities. Shared bathrooms are clean and newly painted but basic. No reservations are accepted because of the limited number of rooms, but always check with Dave at the coffee shop because he knows of other people in the area willing to rent rooms.

Pahoa Natural Groceries (see above) rents **The Bamboo House,** $45 d first night, $35 three nights or more, with rates for four people, just a minute's walk from the store. Small, basic, and clean, it features a bedroom with a queen-size bed, fold-out couch, private bath, and cable color TV. Write the Bamboo House, Box 1429, Pahoa, HI 96778; or phone the health food store at 965-8322. A 25% deposit is required.

Whittaker's B&B, Box 1324, Pahoa, HI 96778, tel. 965-7015, offers two bedrooms with private baths in a new home located in the Puna rainforest. Each room, large enough for a small family, rents for $50 d, children under 12 free.

KAIMU AND KALAPANA

Note

Kaimu and Kalapana have been annihilated by the advancing lava flow. For a full description of **Chain Of Craters Road** see the section by that name in the chapter on Hawaii Volcanoes National Park. Parts of the road are still open, but only *from* Volcanoes National Park.

Sights

Star of the Sea Catholic Church is a small but famous structure better known as **The Painted Church.** An effort to save the historic church from the lava was mounted, and it has been moved. It now sits along the road waiting for a permanent home. A brief history of the area asserts that the now-inundated Kalapana was a spiritual magnet for Roman Catholic priests. Old Spanish documents support evidence that a

Spanish priest, crossing the Pacific from Mexico, actually landed very near here in 1555. Father Damien, famous priest of the Molokai Leper Colony, established a grass church about two miles north and conducted a school when he first arrived in the islands in 1864. The present church dates from 1928, when Father Everest Gielen began its construction. Like an inspired but much less talented Michelangelo, this priest painted the ceiling of the church, working mostly at night by oil lamp. Father Everest was transferred to Lanai in 1941, and the work wasn't completed until 1964, when Mr. George Heidler, an artist from Atlanta, Georgia, came to Kalapana and decided to paint the unfinished lower panels in the altar section. The artwork can only be described as gaudy but sincere. The colors are wild blues, purples, and oranges. The ceiling is adorned with symbols, portraits of Christ, the angel Gabriel, and scenes from the Nativity. Behind the altar, a painted perspective gives the impression that you're looking down a long hallway at an altar that hangs suspended in air. The church is definitely worth a few minutes at least.

End Of The Road

Just near the lava-inundated village of Kalapana, routes 130 and 137 come to an abrupt halt where Madame Pele has repaved the road with lava. At the end of the line you come to a barricaded area. A bulletin board informs you about the current volcanic activity that has continued virtually unabated since January 1983, when lava fountains soared 1,500 feet into the sky and produced a cone over 800 feet tall. The initial lava flow was localized at Puu O'o vent, but after dozens of eruptive episodes it shifted to Kupaianaha, which has continuously produced about half a million cubic yards of lava per day. The lava flows eight miles to the sea, mostly through lava tubes. It has inundated almost 20,000 acres, caused $25 million worth of property damage, and added more than 100 acres of new land to the Puna Coast. (For more information see "Eruptions" in the "Introduction" of the Hawaii Volcanoes National Park chapter.)

A sign strongly warns you against walking out onto the lava. Some hazards that you may encounter are brushfires, smoke, ash, and extremely explosive methane gas. You can also fall through the thin-crusted lava into a tube which will immediately reduce you to a burnt offering to Pele, and unceremoniously deposit your ashes into the sea! New lava can cut like broken glass, and molten lava can be flung through the air by steam explosions, especially near the coastline. Seacliffs collapse frequently, and huge boulders can be tossed several hundred feet into the air. The steam clouds contain minerals that can cause burning eyes, throat and skin irritations, and difficulty breathing.

If you are still intrigued, realize that you are on the most unstable piece of land on the face of the earth. For those maniacs, fools, adventurers, and thrill-seekers who just can't stay away, the walk to the sea takes about 25 minutes. Give yourself up for dead, and proceed. Follow the old roadbed, up and down, over the lava. When you can no longer discern the road, look off to your left and you'll see a large steam cloud rising. Pick your way to it, but don't get too close. Observers say that every day, huge chunks fall off into the sea in this area. As you look back at the mountain you can see heat waves rising from the land upon which you are standing. A camera with a zoom lens or a pair of binoculars accentuates this phenomenon. The whole mountain wavers in front of you. As you walk closer to the sea, the lava cools and you can see every type there is: rope lava, lava toes, lava fingers. The tortured flow, that crinkles as you walk over it, has created many imaginative shapes: gargoyles, medieval faces, dolphins, and mythical creatures. At the coast, the lava pours into the sea, creating a white spume of steam lifting 200-300 feet into the air. No other place in the world gives you the opportunity to be the first person to tread upon the earth's newest land.

Practicalities

Keoki's Mart, inland from the former Kaimu black-sand beach, still stands but has been surrounded by lava. As of this writing, it is closed.

Kalani Honua, Box 4500, Kalapana, HI 96778, tel. 965-7828, is an international conference and retreat center, a haven where people come when they truly want to get away from it all. The entrance is located a few miles north of Kalapana on Rt. 137 between mile markers

17 and 18. Look for a large pink Visitors Welcome sign and proceed until you see the office area and a gift and sundries shop. Depending upon the yearly schedule, they offer a variety of activities that include holistic massage, meditation, yoga, and lei-making. Contact them to find out what's happening when you'll be on the Big Island. The grounds have a commune-type atmosphere, with a rain-fed swimming pool, hot tub, jacuzzi, assembly studios, classrooms, and cedar lodges with kitchen facilities. It's the only place along the Puna Coast that offers lodging and vegetarian fare. Rates are $28 s for a dorm room with shared bath, $52 s and $62 d for a private room with shared bath, $65 s and $75 d for a private room with private bath, guest cottage $85. A conch shell calls you to breakfast at 8 a.m. and to dinner at 6 p.m. (nonguests welcome). The meals cost $6 and $10 respectively, with a meal ticket prepurchased at the office. Lights go out at 10:30 p.m., but candles are provided for night owls. Kalani Honua is not for everyone, but if you are looking for unpretentious peace and quiet, there's no better place on the island.

Hale Kipa O Kiana, tel. 965-8661, a modern guesthouse owned and operated by Diana Allegra, is located along Rt. 137 very close to the now lava-inundated Harry K. Brown Beach Park. Diana is a wonderful cook and loves to do breakfast, which is $5 extra per person and consists of home-baked bread, fresh locally grown fruit, homemade jams, and coffee. The knotty pine guest room, suitable for one or two people, is of open-beam design, is fully carpeted, and has tasteful artwork on the walls. This room features louvered wooden doors, extra-large closet, desk, private sink, and private bath. Rates are $30 s, $35 d, $10 additional person, and $200 weekly. Accommodations include use of the massage room complete with dance barre, wall mirror, and a smattering of free weights. The house is styled in a beautiful neo-Hawaiian classical design, and the upstairs, where Diana resides, has a huge porch which extends over the downstairs area, so you have your own lanai with wrought-iron furniture and a chaise lounge. The home overlooks a dramatic landscape of sea and lava, and is only a short walk from two newly formed black-sand beaches.

BEACHES, PARKS, AND CAMPGROUNDS

All of Puna's beaches, parks, and campgrounds lie along coastal Rt. 137 stretching for 20 miles from Pohoiki to Kamoamoa (recently wiped out by lava flow, see "Chain of Craters Road" in the Hawaii Volcanoes National Park chapter). Surfers, families, transients, and nude-sunbathing "buffs" have their favorite beaches along this southeast coast. For the most part, swimming is possible, but be cautious during high tide. There are plenty of sun, snorkeling sites, and good fishing, and the campgrounds are almost always available.

Isaac Hale Beach County Park

You can't miss this beach park located on Pohoiki Bay, at the junction of Rt. 137 and Pohoiki Road. Just look for a jumble of boats and trailers parked under the palms. At one time Pohoiki Bay served the Hawaiians as a canoe landing, then later became the site of a commercial wharf for the Puna Sugar Company. It remains the only boat launching area for the entire Puna Coast, used by pleasure boaters and commercial fishermen. Due to this dual role, it's often very crowded. Full amenities include pavilions, restrooms, and showers (county permit). Experienced surfers dodge the rip-current in the center of the bay, and swimming is generally good when the sea is calm. Pohoiki Bay is also one of the best scuba sites on the island. Within walking distance of the salt-and-pepper beach are hot springs that bubble into lava sinks surrounded by lush vegetation. They're popular with tourists and residents, and provide a unique and relaxing way to wash away sand and salt. To find them, face away from the sea and turn left, then look for a small but well-worn path that leads through the jungle. The pools are warm, small, and tranquil. Harmless, tiny brine shrimp nibble at your toes while you soak.

MacKenzie State Recreation Area

This popular state park was named for forest ranger A.J. MacKenzie, highly regarded throughout the Puna District and killed in the area in 1938. The park's 13 acres sit among a cool grove of ironwoods originally planted by MacKenzie. A

the Puna coast

portion of the old King's Highway, scratched out by prisoners last century as a form of community service, bisects the area. Many people who first arrive on the Big Island hang out at MacKenzie until they can get their start. Consequently, the park receives its share of hard-core types, which has earned it a reputation for rip-offs. Mostly it's safe, but if you're camping, take precautions with your valuables. The entire coastline along MacKenzie is bordered by rugged black-lava seacliffs. Swimming is dangerous, but the fishing is excellent. Be extremely careful when beach-walking, especially out on the fingers of lava; over the years, people have been swept away by freak waves. MacKenzie Park is located along Rt. 137, two miles south of Isaac Hale. Full amenities and state permits for overnight camping are available.

Puala'a Beach Park

Quietly opened by the County of Hawaii on July 4, 1993, this lovely, 1.3-acre beach park (short on parking) was an ancient fishing village on the boundary of the *ahupua'a* of Leapao'o and Puala'a. Located along the *red road* between Kapoho and Opihikao, the park features a brackish pond warmed by underground volcanic activity. The swimming is safe except for periods of very high surf, and the park is perfect for families with young children.

Kehena

Kehena is actually two pockets of black-sand beach below a low seacliff. Entrance to the beach is marked only by a scenic pulloff on Rt. 137, about five miles south of MacKenzie; usually a half-dozen cars are parked here. At one time Kehena was very popular, and a stone staircase led down to the beach. In 1975 a strong earthquake jolted the area, breaking up the stairway and lowering the beach by three feet. Now access is via a well-worn path, but make sure to wear sneakers because the lava is rough. The ocean here is dangerous, and often pebbles and rocks whisked along by the surf can injure legs. Once down on the beach, head north for the smaller patch of sand, because the larger patch is open to the sea and can often be awash in waves. The black sand is hot, but a row of coconut palms provides shade. The inaccessibility of Kehena makes it a favorite "no-hassle" nude beach with many "full" sunbathers congregating here.

Note: Unfortunately, recent lava flows have completely covered the very popular **Kaimu Beach Park,** also known as Black Sand Beach, and **Harry K. Brown Beach Park.** Now, raw and rugged lava meets the sea to be slowly turned into beach parks for future generations.

BOB RACE

HAWAII VOLCANOES NATIONAL PARK

INTRODUCTION

Hawaii Volcanoes National Park (HVNP) is an unparalleled experience in geological grandeur. The western end of the park is the summit of stupendous **Mauna Loa,** the most massive mountain on earth. The park's heart is **Kilauea Caldera,** encircled by 11 miles of **Crater Rim Drive.** At the park visitors center you can give yourself a crash course in geology while picking up park maps and information. Nearby is **Volcano House,** Hawaii's oldest hotel, which has hosted a steady stream of adventurers, luminaries, royalty, and heads of state ever since it opened its doors in the 1860s. Amidst the natural wonders is a golf course—for those who want to boast they've done it all after hitting a sand wedge from a volcanic fissure. Just down the road is one of Hawaii's last remaining indigenous forests, providing the perfect setting for a bird sanctuary. Mauna Loa Road branches off Crater Rim Drive and ends at a foot trail for the hale and hearty who trek to the 13,677-foot summit.

The rim drive continues past steam vents, sulphur springs, and tortured faultlines that always seem on the verge of gaping wide and swallowing. You can peer into the maw of **Halemaumau Crater,** home of the fire goddess, Pele, and you'll pass **Hawaii Volcano Observatory** (not open to public), which has been monitoring geologic activity since the turn of the century. Nearby is the **Thomas A. Jaggar Museum,** an excellent facility where you can educate yourself on the past and present volcanology of the park. A fantastic walk is **Devastation Trail,** a paved path across a desolate black lava field where gray, lifeless trunks of a suffocated forest lean like old gravestones. Within minutes is **Thurston Lava Tube,** a magnificent

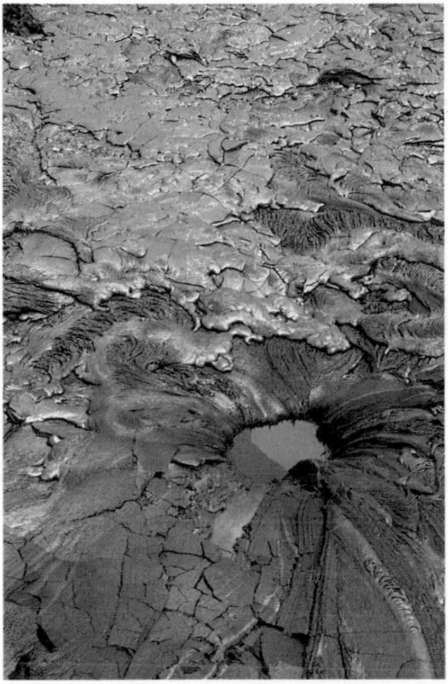

2

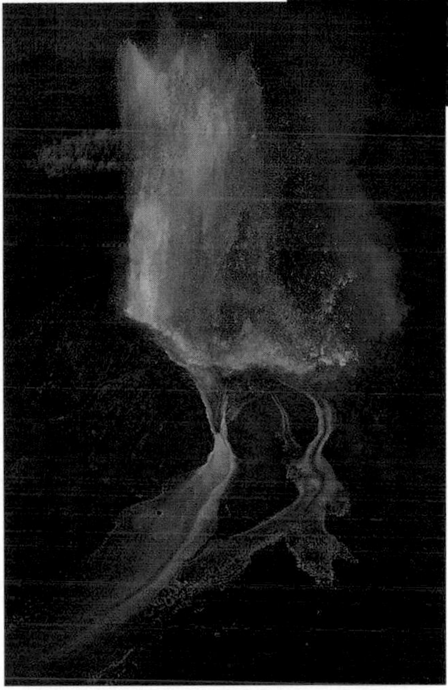

1. lava pool, Hawaii (J.D. Bisignani);
2. and **3.** awesome volcanic power, 1989 eruption, Hawaii (U.S. Geological Survey, J.D. Griggs)

1

2

3

1. Waikiki skyline, Honolulu, Oahu (J.D. Bisignani); **2.** Pololu Valley meets the sea, Hawaii (J.D. Bisignani); **3.** Wailua Falls, Kauai (Robert Nilsen)

natural tunnel "leid" by amazingly vibrant fern grottoes at the entrance and exit.

The indomitable power of Volcanoes National Park is apparent to all who come here. Mark Twain, enchanted by his sojourn in Volcanoes in the 1860s, quipped, "The smell of sulphur is strong, but not unpleasant to a sinner." Amen brother! Wherever you stop to gaze, realize that you are standing on a thin skin of cooled lava in an unstable earthquake zone atop one of the world's most active volcanoes.

Note: For a description of the villages along Rt. 11 heading to Volcanoes, please see "Mountain Villages" under "Hawaii Belt Road—Hilo to Volcanoes" in the Puna chapter.

Geologic History: Science Versus Madame Pele

The goddess Pele is an irascible old dame. Perhaps it's because she had such a bad childhood. All she wanted was a home of her own where she could house her family and entertain her lover, a handsome chief from Kauai. But her sea goddess sister, Namakaokaha'i, flooded her out wherever she went after Pele seduced her husband, and the pig god, Kamapu'a, ravished Pele for good measure. So Pele finally built her love nest at Halemaumau Crater at the south end of Kilauea Caldera. Being a goddess isn't as heavenly as one would think, and whenever the pressures of life get too much for Pele, she blows her stack. These tempestuous outbursts made Pele one of the most revered gods in the Hawaiian pantheon because her presence and might were so easily felt.

For a thousand years Pele was appeased by offerings of pigs, dogs, sacred *ohelo* berries (her favorite), and now and again an outcast man or two (never women) who would hopefully turn her energy from destruction to more comfortable pursuits. Also, if Pele was your family's personal goddess, your remains were sometimes allowed to be thrown into the firepit as a sign of great respect. In the early 1820s, the chieftess Keopuolani, an ardent convert to Christianity, officially challenged Pele in an attempt to topple her like the other gods of old. Keopuolani climbed down into Pele's crater and ate the sacred *ohelo* berries, flagrantly violating the ageless *kapu*. She then took large stones and defiantly hurled them into the firepit below while bellowing, "Jehovah is my God. It is He, not Pele, that kindled these flames."

Yet today, most residents, regardless of background, have an inexplicable reverence for Pele. The goddess has modernized her tastes, switching from *ohelo* to juniper berries that she prefers in liquid form as bottles of gin! The Volcano Post Office receives an average of three packages a week containing lava rocks taken by tourists as souvenirs (sometimes 30 per day). Some hold that Pele looks upon these rocks as her children and taking them from her is kidnapping. The accompanying letters implore the officials to return the rocks because ever since the offender brought them home, luck has been bad. The officials take the requests very seriously, returning the rocks with the customary peace offering: a bottle of gin. Many follow-up "thank you" letters have been written to express relief that the bad luck has been lifted. There is no reference in Hawaiian folklore to this phenomenon, although Hawaiians did hold certain rocks sacred. Park rangers will tell you that the idea of "the bad-luck rocks" was initiated a few decades back by a tour bus driver who became sick and tired of tourists getting his bus dirty by piling aboard their souvenirs. *Voilà*—another ancient Hawaiian myth! Know, however, that the rocks in Hawaii Volcanoes National Park are protected by federal law, much meaner and more vindictive than Pele ever imagined being.

Pele is believed to take human form. She customarily appears before an eruption as a ravishing beauty or a withered old hag, often accompanied by a little white dog. She expects to be treated cordially, and it's said that she will stand by the roadside at night hitching a ride. After a brief encounter, she departs and seems to mysteriously evaporate into the ether. Kindness on your part is the key; if you come across a strange woman at night, treat her well—it might not help, but it definitely won't hurt.

Eruptions

The first white man atop Kilauea was Rev. William Ellis, who scaled it in 1823. Until the 1920s, the floor of the caldera was exactly what people thought a volcano would be: a burning lake of fire. Then the forces of nature changed, and the fiery lava subsided and hardened over. Today, Kilauea is called the only

VOLCANOES NATIONAL PARK
TO LOOKOUT AND MAUNA LOA TR.
PU'U O'O VOLCANO TR. (PRIV.)
TO HILO
11
HAWAIIAN TROPICAL ORCHIDS
KIPUKA KULALIO
MAUNA LOA RD.
BIRD PARK PICNIC AREA
TREE MOLDS
VOLCANO C.C. GOLF COURSE
KILAUEA MILITARY CAMP
PARK HEADQUARTERS, VISITOR CENTER, ART CENTER AND MUSEUM
VOLCANO
POWERLINE RD.
NAMAKANI PAIO CAMPGROUND
STEAMING BLUFF
VOLCANO HOUSE
KILAUEA STATE REC. AREA
OVERLOOK
KILAUEA CALDERA
VOLCANO OBSERVATORY
THOMAS A. JAGGAR MUSEUM
KILAUEA IKI OVERLOOK
THURSTON LAVA TUBE
HALEMAUMAU TR.
WALDRON LEDGE
HAWAII BELT ROAD
HALEMAUMAU (3412 ft)
LOOKOUT 9
DEVASTATION TR.
TREE FERN & OHIA FOREST
CRATER RIM DR.
KEAMOKU LAVA FLOW
KAU DESERT TR.
CRATER RIM TR.
LUA MANU CRATER
PUHIMAU CRATER
CONE PEAK (3652 ft)
KOKOOLAU CRATER
SOUTHWEST RIFT ZONE
DEVILS THROAT
TO NAALEHU AND KONA
HIIAKA CRATER
1974 LAVA FLOW
KAU DESERT
NAPAU CRATER TR.
MAUNA ULU (3480 ft)
ALOI CRATER (SITE)
HILINA PALI RD.
KALANAOKUAIKI PALI
EAST RIFT ZONE
FOOTPRINTS IN ASH
CONE CRATER
PIT CRATERS
PUU KOAE (3250 ft)
KALAPANA TR.
MAUNA IKI (3032 ft)
MAUNA IKI TR.
PALI LEIE O KALI HIPOA
CHAIN OF CRATERS RD.
AINAHOU RANCH
0
2 mi
0
3 km
KIPUKA PAPALINAMOKU PALI
KEAUHOU TR.
MAU LOA O MAUNA ULU
MOON
TO HILINA PALI LOOKOUT
KIPUKA NENE CAMPGROUND
TO COAST
MULIWAI A PELE

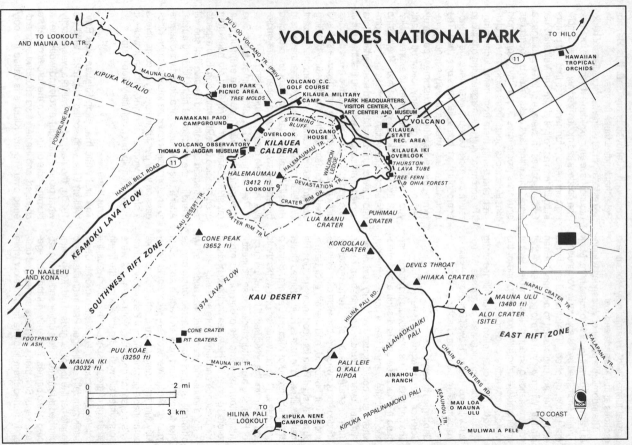

"drive-in" volcano in the world, and in recent years has been one of the most active, erupting almost continuously since 1983. When it begins gushing, the result is not a nightmare scene of people scrambling away for their lives, but just the opposite; people flock *to* the volcano. Most thrill-seekers are in much greater danger of being run over by a tour bus hustling to see the fireworks than of being entombed in lava. The volcanic action, while soul-shakingly powerful, is predictable and almost totally safe. The Hawaiian Volcano Observatory has been keeping watch since 1912, making Kilauea one of the best-understood volcanoes in the world. The vast volcanic field is creased by rift zones, or natural pressure valves. When the underground magma builds up, instead of *kaboom!* as in Mt. St. Helens, it bubbles to the surface like a spring and gushes out as a river of lava. Naturally, anyone or anything in its path is burned to a cinder, but scientists routinely walk within a few feet of the still-flowing lava to take readings. In much the way canaries detect mine gas, longtime lava observers pay attention to their ears. When the skin on top begins to blister, they know they are too close. The lava establishes a course that it follows much like an impromptu mountain stream caused by heavy rains.

This does not mean that the lava flows are entirely benign, or that anyone should visit the area during an eruption without prior approval by the Park Service. When anything is happening, the local radio stations give up-to-the-minute news, and the Park Service provides a recorded message at tel. 967-7977. In 1790 a puff of noxious gases was emitted from Kilauea and descended on the Kau Desert, asphyxiating a rival army of Kamehameha's that just happened to be in the area. Eighty people died in their tracks. In 1881 a flow of lava spilled toward undeveloped Hilo and engulfed an area within today's city limits. In 1942, a heavy flow came within 12 miles of the city. Still, this was child's play in comparison with the unbelievable flow of 1950. Luckily, this went down the western rift zone where only scattered homes were in its path. It took no lives as it disgorged well over 600 million cubic yards of magma that covered 35 square miles! The flow continued for 23 days and produced seven huge torrents of lava that sliced across the Belt Road in three different areas. At its height, the lava front traveled six miles per hour and put out enough material to pave an eight-lane freeway twice around the world. In 1960, a flow swallowed the town of Kapoho on the east coast. In 1975, Hawaii's strongest earthquake since 1868 caused a tsunami to hit the southeast coast, killing two campers and sinking almost the entire Puna Coast by three feet.

The most recent, and very dramatic, series of eruptions that spectacularly began on January 3, 1983, have continued virtually unabated ever since. Magma bubbled to the surface about two miles away from Puu O'o. The gigantic fissure fountained lava and formed Puu O'o Cinder Cone that is now 830 feet high and almost 1,000 feet across. Over a three-and-a-half-year period, there were 47 eruptions from this vent. On July 20, 1986 a new fissure, comprised of approximately two miles of fountaining lava, broke upon the surface at Kupaianaha and has since formed a lava lake about one acre in size and 180 feet deep. At the end of April 1987 all activity suddenly stopped and the lava drained from the lake and tube system, allowing scientists to accurately gauge the depth. About a week later, it all started up again when lava poured back into the lake, went through the tube system, and flowed back down to the ocean. The output is estimated at 650,000 cubic yards per day, which is equal to 55,000 truckloads of cement, enough to cover a football field 38 miles high.

From that point, the flow turned destructive and started taking homes. It moved to the coast in tubes, wiping out Kapaahu, parts of Kalapana, and most of the Royal Gardens Subdivision, with over 70 homes incinerated. In May 1989 it moved into the national park proper, and on June 22, it swallowed the park visitors center at Waha'ula. So far, it has spared Waha'ula Heiau (see "Chain of Craters Road" later in this chapter). The destruction has caused over $25 million worth of damage. Many of the homesteaders in the worst areas of the flow were rugged individualists and back-to-nature alternative types who lived in homes that generally had no electricity, running water, or telephones. The homes were wiped out. Some disreputable insurance companies with legitimate policy holders tried to wiggle out of paying premiums for lost homes, although the policies specifically stipulated loss by lava flow. The insurance companies whined that the 2,000° lava never really touched some of the homes, and therefore, they were exonerated from paying the coverage. Their claims were resoundingly repudiated in the courts, and people were paid for their losses. One gentleman, however, has been forced to continue living in the middle of the lava flow. He's been there from the beginning because his insurance company will not pay if he leaves, claiming that the house was abandoned and therefore not covered. He sits in the middle of the lava plain with the flows all around him. For the last seven years, he's ridden a bicycle out from his house to the road. From there he goes to work and goes about his business, then goes back in on his bicycle. Sometimes in the middle of the night, or while he's gone, a lava flow occurs and he has to wait a couple of days for it to crust over before he can get in and out. Makes you want to rush right out and pay your premium to your caring friends in the insurance business. A prayer to Pele would easily be more effective. There is only one way to treat the power of Hawaii's magnificent volcanoes: not with fear, but with the utmost respect.

Mauna Loa

At 13,677 feet, this magnificent mountain is a mere 117 feet shorter than its neighbor Mauna Kea, which is the tallest peak in the Pacific, and by some accounts, tallest in the world. Measured from its base, 18,000 feet beneath the sea, it would top even Mt. Everest. Mauna Loa is the most massive mountain on earth, containing 10,000 cubic miles of solid, iron-hard lava. This titan weighs more than California's entire Sierra Nevada range! In fact, Mauna Loa ("Long Mountain"), at 60 miles long and 30 wide, occupies the entire southern half of the Big Island, with Volcanoes National Park merely a section of its great expanse.

Note

Everything in the park—flora and fauna, rocks, buildings, trails—is protected by federal law. Be respectful! The ***nene,*** Hawaii's state bird, is endangered. By feeding these birds, visitors have taught them to stand in parking lots and by the roadside. What appears to be a humane and harmless practice actually helps kill these rare birds. Automobiles running them over has become the leading cause of death of adult birds in the park. Please look, but do not try to approach, feed, or harass the *nene* in any way.

KILAUEA CALDERA

The sights of Hawaii Volcanoes National Park are arranged one after another along **Crater Rim Drive.** Off the beaten track but worth a look are **Mauna Loa Road** (which takes you to places of special interest such as **Tree Molds** and **Bird Park**—10-minute detours) and **Kau Desert Trail,** about eight miles south of the visitors center on the Hawaii Belt Road, Hwy. 11. Most of the sights are the "drive-up" variety, but plenty of major and minor trails lead off here and there.

Admission to the park is $5 per vehicle (good for multiple entry over a seven-day period), $15 for an annual permit, $3 for bicycle traffic, and free to those 62 and over with a *golden age permit.*

Tips

Expect to spend a long full day atop Kilauea to take in all the sights, and never forget that you're on a rumbling volcano where a misstep or loss of concentration at the wrong moment can lead to severe injury, or even loss of life. Try to arrive by 9 a.m. with a picnic lunch to save time and hassles. Kilauea Caldera, at 4,000 feet, is about 10° cooler than the coast. It's often overcast and there can be showers. Wear your walking shoes and bring a sweater and/ or windbreaker. Binoculars, sunglasses, and a hat will also come in handy.

Warning! Small children, pregnant women, and people with respiratory ailments should note that the fumes from the volcano can cause problems. Stay away from sulphur vents and don't overdo it, and you should be fine.

A very dramatic way to experience the awesome power of the volcano is to take a **helicopter tour.** The choppers are perfectly suited for the up-close maneuverability necessary to get an intimate bird's-eye view. The pilots will fly you over the areas offering the most activity, often dipping low over lava pools, skimming still-glowing flows, and circling the towering steam clouds rising from where lava meets the sea. When activity is really happening, tours are jammed, and prices, like lava fountains, go sky-high. Remember, however, that there is growing resentment by hikers or anyone else trying to have a quiet experience, and that new regulations might limit flights over the lava area. Also, choppers do go down, and it is the park rangers and their rescue units who must go to their aid. (For full details see "Sightseeing Tours under "Getting Around" in the Big Island Introduction.)

VISITORS CENTER AREA

The best place to start is at the visitors center/park headquarters. The turnoff is clearly marked off Belt Road (Hwy. 11). By midmorning it's jammed, so try to be an early bird. The center is well run by the National Park Service. They offer a free lecture and film about geology and volcanism, with tremendous highlights of past eruptions, and with plenty of detail on Hawaiian culture and natural history. It runs every hour on the hour starting at 9 a.m. Also, a self-guided natural history museum gives more information about the geology of the area, with plenty of exhibits of the flora and fauna. You will greatly enrich your visit if you take a half-hour tour of the museum. Actually, the visitors center has been eclipsed by the state-of-the-art information available at the **Thomas A. Jaggar Museum** a few minutes up the road (see a description under "Crater Rim Drive" below).

For safety's sake, anyone trekking to the backcountry *must* register with the rangers at the visitors center, especially during times of eruption. Do not be foolhardy! There is no charge for camping (see "Camping and Hiking" under "Practicalities" later in this chapter), and the rangers can give you up-to-the-minute information on trails, backcountry shelters, and cabins. Trails routinely close due to lava flows, tremors, and rock slides. The rangers cannot help you if they don't know where you are. Many day trails leading into the caldera from the rim road are easy walks that need no special preparation. The backcountry trails can be very challenging, and detailed maps (highly recommended) are sold at the center along with special-interest geology and natural history publications prepared by the Hawaii Natural History Association. The visitors center is open daily 9 a.m.-5 p.m.; call 967-7311 for trail and camping information, or 967-7977 for a recorded message concerning the latest news on volcanic activity.

Volcano House

Have you ever dreamed of sleeping with a goddess? Well, you can cuddle up with Pele by staying at Volcano House (for details see "Accommodations, Food, and Shopping" under "Practicalities" later in this chapter). If your plans don't include an overnight stop, go in for a look. Sometimes this is impossible, because not only do tour buses from the Big Island disgorge here, but tour groups are flown in from Honolulu as well. A stop at the bar provides refreshments and a tremendous view of the crater. Volcano House still has the feel of a country inn, although in reality it's a Sheraton Inn. This particular building dates from the 1940s, but the site has remained the same since a grass hut was perched on the rim of the crater by a sugar planter in 1846. He charged $1 a night. A steady stream of notable visitors has come ever since: almost all of Hawaii's kings and queens dating from the middle of last century, as well as royalty from Europe. Mark Twain was a guest, followed by Franklin Roosevelt. Most recently, a contingent of astronauts lodged here and used the crater floor to prepare for walking on the moon. In 1866 a large grass hut replaced the first, and in 1877 a wooden Victorian-style hotel was built. It is now the Volcano Art Center, and has been moved across the road. Volcano House was owned and operated longest by Mr. George Lycurgus, who took over management of the hotel in the 1890s. His son, Nick, followed him and managed the hotel until the 1960s.

Volcano Art Center

Art and history buffs should walk across the street to the Volcano Art Center, tel. 967-7511, which is the original 1877 Volcano House, Hawaii's oldest hotel. You not only get to see some fine arts and crafts, you can take a self-guided tour of this mini-museum, open daily 9 a.m.-5 p.m. A new show featuring one of the many superlative island artists on display is presented monthly. Some prominent artists represented are John Wisnosky, who teaches at the University of Hawaii; Chiu Leong, who has a studio nearby where he turns out inspired *raku* pottery; Rick Mills, the best young glass artist in the state; Dietrich Varez, who makes affordable and distinctive woodblock prints; Garron Alexander, who does *raku* marinelife; Wilford Yamazawa, another amazing glassworker; Marin Burger, a young artist who lives in Volcano, known as one of the best naturalist painters around; Kathy Long, creator of insightful pencil drawings of local people; Pam Barton, who does whimsical fiber arts; woodworker Jack Straka, famous for his rich turned bowls; and Boone Morrison, the center's founder, a photographer and architect who apprenticed under Ansel Adams. There is also a profusion of less expensive but distinctive items like posters, cards, and earthy basketry made from natural fibers collected locally. One of the functions of the art center is to provide interpretation for the national park. All of the 250-plus artists who exhibit here do works that in some way relate to Hawaii's environment. Volcano Art Center is one of the finest art shops in the entire state, boasting works from the best the islands have to offer.

J.D. BISIGNANI

friendly and knowledgeable salesperson at the Volcano Art Center

CRATER RIM DRIVE

There are so many intriguing nooks and crannies to stop at along Crater Rim Drive that you'll have to force yourself to be picky if you intend to cover the park in one day. Crater Rim Drive is a circular route; it matters little which way you proceed. Take your choice, but the following sights are listed counterclockwise beginning from Kilauea Visitors Center. Your biggest problem will be timing your arrival at the "drive-in" sights to avoid the steady stream of tour buses.

Sulphur Banks

You can easily walk to Sulphur Banks from Volcano Art Center along a 10-minute trail. If you're driving, signs along Rim Drive direct you, and your nose will tell you when you're close. As you approach these fumaroles, the earth surrounding them turns a deep reddish-brown, covered over in yellowish-green sulphur. The rising steam is caused by surface water leaking into the cracks where it becomes heated and rises as vapor. Kilauea releases hundreds of tons of sulphur gases every day, with Sulphur Banks being an example. This gaseous activity stunts the growth of vegetation. And when atmospheric conditions create a low ceiling, the gases sometimes cause the eyes and nose to water. The area is best avoided by those with heart and lung conditions.

Steam Vents

Next you'll come to steam vents which are also fumaroles, but without sulphur. The entire field behind the partitioned area steams. The feeling is like being in a sauna. There are no strong fumes to contend with here, just the tour buses. **Kilauea Military Camp** beyond the vent is not open to the public. The camp serves as an R and R facility for military personnel.

Hawaii Volcano Observatory

This observatory has been keeping tabs on the volcanic activity in the area since the turn of the century. The actual observatory is filled with delicate seismic equipment and is closed to the public, but a lookout nearby gives you a dentist's view into the mouth of Halemaumau Crater ("House of Ferns"), Pele's home. Steam rises and you can feel the power, but until 1924 the view was even more phenomenally spectacular: a lake of molten lava. The lava has since sunk below the surface, which is now crusted over. Scientists do not predict a recurrence in the near future, but no one knows Pele's mind. This is a major stop for the tour buses, but a two-minute saunter along the hiking trail gives you the view to yourself. Information plaques in the immediate area tell of the history and volcanology of the park. One points out a spot from which to observe the perfect shield volcano form of Mauna Loa—most times too cloudy to see. Another reminds you that you're in the middle of the Pacific, an incredible detail you tend to forget when atop these mountains. Here too is Uwekahuna ("Wailing Priest") Bluff, where the *kahuna* made offerings of appeasement to Pele. A Hawaiian prayer commemorates their religious rites.

Thomas A. Jaggar Museum

This newest addition to the national park is located next door to the Hawaii Volcano Observatory, and offers a fantastic multimedia display of the amazing geology and volcanology of the area. The state-of-the-art museum, complete with a mini-series of spectacular photos on movable walls, topographical maps, inspired paintings, and TV videos, is open daily 8:30 a.m.-5 p.m., admission free. The expert staff constantly upgrades the displays to keep the public informed on the newest eruptions. The 30-45 minutes it takes to explore the teaching museum will enhance your understanding of the volcanic area immeasurably. Do yourself a favor and visit this museum before setting out on any explorations.

Moon Walks

A string of interesting stops follows the observatory. One points out the **Kau Desert,** an inhospitable site of red-earth plains studded with a few scraggly plants (see "Small Detours" below). Next comes the **Southwest Rift,** a series of cracks running from Kilauea's summit to the sea. You can observe at a glance that you are standing directly over a major earthquake fault. Dated lava flows follow in rapid succession until you arrive at **Halemaumau Trail.** The well-maintained trail is only a quarter mile long and gives an up-close view of the crater. The area is rife with fumaroles and should be avoided by those with respiratory problems. At the end you're treated to a full explanation of Halemaumau. Farther along the road, a roped-off area was once an observation point that caved in. You won't take the ground under your feet for granted! Close by is **Keanakakoi,** a prehistoric quarry from which superior stone was gathered to make tools. It was destroyed by a flow in 1877. If that seems in the remote past, realize that you are now on a section of road that was naturally paved over with lava from a "quickie" eruption in 1982!

Most visitors hike along **Devastation Trail,** which could aptly be renamed "Regeneration Trail." The half mile it covers is fascinating, one of the most-photographed areas in the park. It leads across a field devastated by a tremendous eruption from **Kilauea Iki** ("Little Kilauea") in 1959, when fountains of lava shot 1,900 feet into the air. The area was once an ohia forest that was denuded of limbs and leaves, then choked by black pumice and ash. The vegetation has regenerated since then, and the recuperative power of the flora is part of an ongoing study. Blackberries, not indigenous to Hawaii, are slowly taking over. The good news is that you'll be able to pick and eat blackberries as you hike along the paved trail, but note that the rangers are waging a mighty war against them. Notice that many of the trees have sprouted aerial roots trailing down from the branches: this is total adaptation to the situation, as these roots don't normally appear. As you move farther along the trail, tufts of grass and bushes peek out of the pumice. Then the surroundings become totally barren and look like the nightmare of a nuclear holocaust.

Thurston Lava Tube

If the Devastation Trail produced a sense of melancholy, the Thurston Lava Tube makes you feel like Alice walking through the looking glass. Inside is a fairy kingdom. As you approach, the expected billboard gives you the lowdown on the geology and flora and fauna of the area. Take the five minutes to educate yourself. The paved trail starts as a steep incline which quickly enters a fern forest. All about you are fern trees, vibrantly green, with native birds flitting here and there. As you approach the lava tube, it seems almost manmade, like a perfectly formed tunnel leading into a mine. Ferns and moss hang from the entrance, and if you stand just inside the entrance looking out, it's as if the very air is tinged with green. If there were such things as elves and gnomes, they would surely live here. The walk through takes about 10 minutes, and the tube rolls and undulates through narrow passages and into large "rooms." At the other end, the fantasy world of ferns and moss reappears.

SMALL DETOURS

Volcano Village

You shouldn't miss taking a ride through the village of Volcano, a beautiful settlement with truly charming houses and cottages outlined in ferns. Tiny gravel roads lace the development, which sits virtually atop one of the world's undeniable "power spots." The area is so green and so vibrant that it appears surrealistic. With flowers, ferns, and trees everywhere, it is hard to imagine a more picturesque village in all of America.

Volcano Golf And Country Club

What's most amazing about this course is where it is. Imagine! You're teeing off atop an active volcano surrounded by one of the last pristine forests in the state. At the right time of year, the surrounding ohia turn scarlet when they are in bloom. The fairways are carved from lava, while in the distance Mauna Loa looms. A poor shot, and you can watch your ball disappear down a steam vent. The course began about 70 years ago when a group of local golfers hand-cleared three "greens," placing stakes that served as holes. Later this was improved to sand greens with tin cans for holes, and after an eruption in 1924 blanketed the area with volcanic ash that served as excellent fertilizer, the grass grew and the course became a lush green. After WW II the course was extended to 18 holes, and a clubhouse was added. Finally, Jack Snyder, a well-known course architect, redesigned the course to its present par-72, 6,119-yard layout. Rate is $30 with shared cart. To beat the heavy lunch crowd at Volcano House, try the restaurant at the course, tel. 967-7331 (see "Other Food and Shopping" below). The course is located just north of the Belt Road, about two miles west of the park entrance. Phone 967-7550 for more information.

Mauna Loa Road

About 2.5 miles west of the park entrance on the Belt Road, Mauna Loa Road turns off to the north. This road will lead you to the Tree Molds and a bird sanctuary, as well as to the trailhead for the Mauna Loa summit trail. As an added incentive, a minute down this road leaves 90% of the tourists behind.

Tree Molds is an ordinary name for an extraordinary place. Turn off Mauna Loa Road soon after leaving the Belt Road and follow the signs for five minutes to a cul-de-sac. At the entrance, a billboard tries hard to dramatically explain what occurred here. In a moment, you realize that you're standing atop a lava flow, and that the scattered potholes are entombed tree trunks, most likely the remains of a once-giant koa forest. Unlike at Lava Tree State Monument, where the magma encased the trees and flowed away, the opposite happened here. The lava stayed put while the tree trunks burned away, leaving 15- to 18-foot-deep holes.

Kipuka Puaulu is a sanctuary for birds and nature lovers who want to leave the crowds behind, just under two miles from Rt. 11 down Mauna Loa Road. The sanctuary is an island atop an island. A *kipuka* is a piece of land surrounded by lava but not inundated by it, leaving the original vegetation and land contour intact. A few hundred yards away, small scrub vegetation struggles, but in the sanctuary the trees form a towering canopy a hundred feet tall. The first sign for Bird Park takes you to an ideal picnic area; the second, 100 yards beyond, takes you to Kipuka Puaulu Loop Trail. As you enter the trail, a bulletin board describes the birds and plants, some of the last remaining indigenous fauna and flora in Hawaii. Please follow all rules.

The trail is self guided, and pamphlets describing the stations along the way are dispensed from a box 50 feet down the path. The loop is only one mile long, but to really assimilate the area, especially if you plan to do any birdwatching, expect to spend an hour minimum. It doesn't take long to realize that you are privileged to see some of the world's rarest plants, such as a small, nondescript bush called *aalii.* In the branches of the towering ohia trees you might see an *elepaio* or an *apapane,* two birds native to Hawaii. Common finches and Japanese white eyes are imported birds that are here to stay. There's a fine example of a lava tube and an explanation of how ash from eruptions provided soil and nutrients for the forest. Blue morning glories have taken over entire hillsides. Once considered a pest and aggressively eradicated, they have recently been given a reprieve and are now considered good ground cover—perhaps even indigenous. When you do come across a native Hawaiian plant, it seems somehow older, almost prehistoric. If a pre-contact Hawaiian could come back today, he or she would recognize only a few plants and trees even here in this preserve. More than four times as many plants and animals have become extinct in Hawaii in the last 200 years as on the entire North American continent. As you leave, listen for the melodies coming from the treetops, and hope the day never comes when no birds sing.

Mauna Loa Road continues westward and gains elevation for approximately 10 miles. At the end of the pavement, at 6,662 feet, you find a parking area and lookout. A trail leads from here to the summit of Mauna Loa. (See following "Camping and Hiking" section.) It takes three to four days to hike. Under no circumstances should it be attempted by novice hikers or those unprepared for cold alpine conditions.

Olaa Track

Off Rt. 11 close to Volcano Village, turn onto Wright Road (or County Road 148) heading toward Mauna Loa (on a clear morning you can see Mauna Kea). Continue for approximately three miles until you see a barbed-wire fence. The fence is distinctive because along it you'll see a profusion of *hapu'u* ferns which are in sharp contrast to the adjacent property. Here is an *ola'a* rainforest, part of the national park and open to the public, although park scientists like to keep it quiet. Be aware that the area is laced with lava tubes. Most are small ankle twisters, but others can open up under you like a glacial crevasse. Here is a true example of a quickly disappearing native forest. What's beautiful about an endemic forest is that virtually all species coexist wonderfully. The ground cover is a rich mulch of decomposing ferns and leaves, fragrant and amazingly soft. This walk is for the intrepid hiker or naturalist who is fascinated by Hawaii's unique foliage.

Remember, trails in this section of the park are poorly marked and quite confusing. You can get lost, and if no one knows you're in here, it could be life threatening. Also, be aware that you may be trampling native species, and could be inadvertently introducing alien species. The Park Service is trying to bring the area back to its native Hawaiian rainforest condition through eradication of alien plants and elimination of feral pigs.

Kau Desert Trail

Kau Desert Trail starts about eight miles south of the visitors center along Rt. 11, between mile markers 37 and 38. It's a short hike from the trailhead to the **Kau Desert Footprints.** People going to or from Kailua-Kona can see them en route, but those staying in Hilo should take the time to visit the footprints. The trek across the small section of desert is fascinating, and the history of the footprints makes the experience more evocative. The trail is only 1.6 miles roundtrip and can be hustled along in less than 30 minutes, but allow at least an hour, mostly for observation. The predominant foliage is a red bottlebrush that contrasts with the bleak surroundings—the feeling throughout the area is one of foreboding. You pass a wasteland of *'a'a* and *pahoehoe* lava flows to arrive at the footprints. A metal fence in a sturdy pavilion surrounds the prints, which look as though they're cast in cement. Actually they're formed from pisolites: particles of ash stuck together with moisture, which formed mud that hardened like plaster.

In 1790 Kamehameha was waging war with Keoua over control of the Big Island. One of Keoua's warrior parties of approximately 80 people attempted to cross the desert while Kilauea was erupting. Toxic gases descended upon them and the warriors and their families were enveloped and suffocated. They literally died in their tracks, but the preserved footprints, although romanticism would wish otherwise, were probably made by a party of people who came well after the eruption. This unfortunate occurrence was regarded by the Hawaiians as a direct message from the gods proclaiming their support for Kamehameha. Keoua, who could not deny the sacred signs, felt abandoned and shortly thereafter became a human sacrifice at Puukohola Heiau, built by Kamehameha to honor his war god, Kukailimoku.

CHAIN OF CRATERS ROAD

The Chain of Craters Road that once linked Volcanoes National Park with Kalapana village on the east coast has been severed by an enormous lava flow and can only be driven from Volcanoes down to where the flow crosses the road near the now-inundated and inaccessible Kamoamoa Campground. Remember that the volcanic activity in this area is unpredictable, and that the road can be closed at a moment's notice. Flying volcanic ash, mixed with the frequent drizzle, can be as slippery as ice. As you head down the road, every bend—and they are countless—offers a panoramic vista. There are dozens of pulloffs, many of which are named, like Naulu ("Sea Orchards"); plaques provide geological information about past eruptions and lava flows. The grandeur, power, and immensity of the forces that have been creating the earth from the beginning of time are right before your eyes. The lower part of the road is spectacular. Here, blacker-than-black seacliffs, covered by a thin layer of green, abruptly stop at the sea. The surf rolls in, sending up spumes of seawater. In the distance, steam billows into the air where the lava flows into the sea. At road's end you will find a barricade staffed by park rangers. Heed their warnings. The drive from atop the volcano to the barricade takes about 30 minutes. If you are going in the evening, when the spectacle is more apparent, bring a flashlight. A ranger will escort you onto the flow, giving an interpretive talk as you walk along. To experience the lava flow from the Kalapana side, see "Kaimu and Kalapana" under "Route 130 and the Southeast Coast" in the Puna chapter.

When the road almost reaches the coast, look for a roadside marker that indicates the **Kau Puna Trail.** Just across the road is the **Puu Loa Petroglyph Field.** The Kau Puna Trail leads you along the coast, where you can find shelters at Keauhou and Halape. Rain catchment tanks provide drinking water. All campers must register at the Kilauea Visitors Center. In 1975 an earthquake rocked the area, generating a tidal wave that killed two campers; more than 30 others had to be helicoptered to safety. Only registering will alert authorities to your whereabouts in case of a disaster. A number of trails cross this area and you can take them back up to Chain of Craters Road or continue on a real expedition through the Kau Desert. The Kau Puna Trail requires full trekking and camping gear.

Puu Loa Petroglyphs

The walk out to Puu Loa Petroglyphs is delightful and highly educational, and only takes one hour. The trail, although it traverses solid lava, is discernible. The tread of feet over the centuries has discolored the rock. As you walk along, note the *ahu,* traditional trail markers that are piles of stone shaped like little Christmas trees. Most of the lava field leading to the petroglyphs is undulating *pahoehoe* and looks like a frozen sea. You can climb bumps of lava, 8-10 feet high, to scout the immediate territory. Mountainside, the *pali* is quite visible and you can pick out the most recent lava flows—the blackest and least vegetated. As you approach the site, the lava changes dramatically and looks like long strands of braided rope.

The petroglyphs are in an area about the size of a soccer field. A wooden walkway encircles them and ensures their protection. A common motif of the petroglyphs is a circle with a hole in the middle, like a donut; you'll also see designs of men with triangular-shaped heads. Some rocks are entirely covered with designs while others bear only a symbolic scratch or two. If you stand on the walkway and trek off at the two o'clock position, you'll see a small hill. Go over and down it, and you will discover even better petroglyphs that include a sailing canoe about two feet high. At the back end of the walkway, a sign proclaims that Puu Loa meant "Long Hill," which the Hawaiians turned into the euphemism "Long Life." For countless generations, fathers would come here to place pieces of their infants' umbilical cords into small holes as offerings to the gods to grant long lives to their children. Concentric circles surrounded the holes that held the umbilical cords. The entire area, an obvious power spot, screams in utter silence, and the still-strong mana is easily felt.

Waha'ula Heiau

Waha'ula Heiau, "Temple of the Red Mouth," radically changed the rituals and practices of the relatively benign Hawaiian religion by introducing the idea of human sacrifice. The 13th century marked the end of the frequent comings and goings between Hawaii and the "Lands to the South" (Tahiti), and began the isolation which would last 500 years until Captain Cook arrived. Unfortunately, this last influx of Polynesians brought a rash of conquering warriors carrying ferocious gods who lusted for human blood before they would be appeased. Paao, a powerful Tahitian priest, supervised the building of Waha'ula. He brought in a new chief, Pili, to strengthen the mana of the Hawaiian chiefs, which was diminished by their practice of intermarriage with commoners. Waha'ula became the foremost *luakini* (human sacrifice) temple in the island kingdom and held this position until the demise of the old ways in 1819. The *heiau* is not at all grandiose, merely an elevated rock platform smoothed over with pebbles.

Note: This entire area is now completely inundated by recent lava flows, and for all intents and purposes, is unreachable. The *heiau* itself is now a small island in a sea of black lava that has so far miraculously escaped destruction. Only Pele's benevolence will continue to save it.

PRACTICALITIES

CAMPING AND HIKING

Campgrounds And Cabins

The main campground in Volcanoes, **Namakani Paio,** clearly marked off Rt. 11, is situated in a stately eucalyptus grove. There is no charge for tent camping and no reservations are required. A cooking pavilion has fireplaces, but no wood or drinking water are provided. **Cabins** are available through Volcano House (see "Accommodations, Food, and Shopping" below). Each accommodates four people and costs $32 s/d, $6 additional person. A $10 refundable key deposit gives you access to the shower and toilet; and a $5 refundable deposit gets you linens, soap, towels, and a blanket (extra sleeping bag recommended). Each cabin contains one double bed and two single bunk beds and an electric light, but no electrical outlets. Outside are a picnic table and barbecue grill but you must provide your own charcoal and cooking utensils. Check in at Volcano House at 3 p.m. and check out by noon.

Kipuka Nene is another campground, approximately 10 miles south of park headquarters down Hilina Pali Road. Many fewer people camp here and it too is free, with no permit required, but be aware that the campground is subject to closure during the *nene* nesting period, which runs from fall to early winter. You'll find a cooking pavilion and fireplaces, but no firewood or drinking water.

Niaulani Cabin is operated by the Division of State Parks. The cabin is outside the park along Old Volcano Road, about a half mile south of the Village General Store in Volcano village. The cabin is completely furnished with full kitchen and bathroom facilities. It accommodates up to six people, and the rates are on a sliding scale determined by number of people and length of stay: one person for one day is $10, two people $14, and six people $30. Reservations and a deposit are required. For full details write Department of Land and Natural Resources, Divison of State Parks, Box 936, Hilo, HI 96720, tel. 961-7200. Pick up the key at the Divison of State Parks office at 75 Aupuni St., Hilo, 7:45 a.m.-4:30 p.m. Holidays and weekends the key is left at the Hilo Airport information booth.

Hiking
The slopes of Mauna Loa and Volcanoes National Park are a trekker's paradise. You'll find trails that last for days or for an hour or two. Many have shelters, and those trails that require overnight stays provide cabins. Because of the possibility of an eruption or earthquake, it is *imperative* to check in at park headquarters, where you can also pick up current trail info and maps (see "Visitors Center Area" in the Introduction of this chapter).

The hike to the summit of **Mauna Loa** (13,677 feet) is the most grueling. The trailhead is at the lookout at the end of the pavement of Mauna Loa Road. Hikers in excellent condition can make the summit (roundtrip) in three days, but four would be more comfortable. There is a considerable elevation gain so expect freezing weather even in summer, and snow in winter. Altitude sickness can also be a problem. En route you pass through *nene* country, with a good chance to spot these lava-adapted geese. Fences keep out feral goats, so remember to close gates after you. The first cabin is at Red Hill (10,092 feet) and the second is at the summit. Water is from roof catchment and should be boiled. The summit treats you to a sweeping panorama that includes Haleakala. Mauna Loa's Mokuaweoweo Caldera is over three miles long and has vertical walls towering 600 feet. From November to May, if there is snow, steam rises from the caldera. The trail cabin is on the rim.

The **Crater Rim Loop Trail** begins at park headquarters and follows Crater Rim Drive, crossing back and forth a number of times. Hiking the entire 11 miles takes a full day, but you can take it in sections as time and energy permit. It's a well-marked and maintained trail; all you need are warm clothing, water, and determination. For your efforts, you'll get an up-close view of all of the sights outlined along Crater Rim Drive.

Kilauea Iki Trail begins at the Thurston Lava Tube, or at park headquarters via the Waldron Ledge Trail. This five-mile trail generally takes three to four hours as it passes through the center of Kilauea Iki Caldera. It's easy to link up with the Byron Ledge Trail or with the Halemaumau Trail. You can return north to park headquarters or continue on either of these two trails to the Halemaumau parking area directly south of park headquarters.

Halemaumau Trail provides the best scenery for the effort. It begins at park headquarters and descends into Kilauea Caldera, covering six miles (five hours). If possible, arrange to be picked up at the Halemaumau parking area due south of park headquarters.

ACCOMMODATIONS, FOOD, AND SHOPPING

If you intend to spend the night atop Kilauea, your choices of accommodations are few and simple. Volcano House provides the only hotel, but cabins are available at the campgrounds, there are plenty of tenting sites, and there is a wonderful assortment of bed and breakfasts.

Kilauea Lodge
This superb addition to the Volcano area, tel. 967-7366, Box 116, Volcano Village, HI 96785, owned and operated by Lorna Larsen-Jeyte and Albert Jeyte, is the premier restaurant and lodge atop Volcano, as well as one of the very best on the island. The solid stone and timber structure was built in 1938 as a YMCA camp and functioned as such until 1962, when it became a "mom and pop operation," often failing and changing ownership. It faded into the ferns until Lorna and Albert revitalized it in 1987, opening in 1988. The lodge is a classic, with a vaulted, open-beamed ceiling. A warm and cozy "international fireplace" dating from the days of the YMCA camp is embedded with stones and plaques from all over the world, along with coins from countries such as Malaysia, Japan, Singapore, Australia, New Zealand, Finland, Germany, and Italy, to name a few.

The **Kilauea Lodge Restaurant,** open for dinner nightly 5:30-9 p.m., reservations a must, is an extraordinary restaurant serving gourmet continental cuisine at reasonable prices. Choose a seat below the neo-Victorian windows or at a table from which you can view the vibrant green ferns and manicured trees of the grounds. A very friendly and professional staff serves the excellent food prepared by Albert, and starts you off with a fresh "loafette" studded like their fireplace, but with sunflowers and sesame seeds. Appetizers such as mushroom caps stuffed with crab and cheese will titillate your palate. Entrees, ranging $13-26, include soup, salad, and vegetables. Vegetarians will be delighted with Eggplant Supreme, a stew of Mediterranean vegetables served atop fettuccine at $13.50, while shrimp tempura at $18.50 adds an Asian touch. Dinner features Seafood Mauna Kea (succulent pieces of seafood served atop a bed of fettuccine), and paupiettes of beef (prime rib slices rolled around herbs and mushrooms in a special sauce), both for under $20. Always a great choice, the catch-of-the-day is baked, broiled, or sautéed with a savory sauce. Desserts are wonderful, and you can top off the meal with a cup of Irish or Italian coffee.

Kilauea Lodge is also an exquisite inn with an assortment of rooms ranging $85-110, including a complete breakfast. The architect, Virginia McDonald, a Volcano resident, worked magic in transforming the brooding rooms of the original section into bright, comfortable, and romantic suites. Each bathroom, with vaulted 18-foot ceilings, has a skylight. The sink and grooming area is one piece of Corianne with a light built into it, so that the entire sink area glows. The rooms, all differently appointed, range in decor from Hawaiian-European to Asian with a motif of Japanese fans. Each has a working fireplace, queen-size bed, and swivel rocking chair. A separate one-bedroom cottage features a wood-burning stove (central heat too), a queen-size bed, private bath, and small living room with queen-size pull-out sofa. In 1991, Kilauea Lodge opened seven new units centered around a commodious common room where you can read and snooze by a crackling fire. All rooms in the new section are tastefully furnished with wicker furniture, white curtains, vaulted ceilings, oak trim, Japanese and Hawaiian art prints, and fluffy quilts to keep off the evening chill. The Kilauea Lodge provides one of the most *civilized* atmospheres in Hawaii in one of its most powerful natural areas. The combination is hard to beat.

Bonnie Goodell's Guest House

This very friendly hideaway, tel. 967-7775, Box 6, Volcano, HI 96785, is on the back roads of Volcano Village. The fully furnished house is designed as a self-sufficient unit where the guests are guaranteed peace and quiet on a lovely six-acre homesite. Bonnie grew up in Hawaii and was for many years the education director for the Honolulu Botanic Gardens. She *knows* her plants and is willing to chat with her guests. The place is particularly good for families. Children have plenty of room to play, while parents can roam the orchards on the property. The two-story guest home is bright and airy. Enter into a combo living room, kitchen, and dining area with a large bathroom off to the right. Upstairs is a sleeping area with two twin beds and a queen-size fold-out bed; downstairs is another fold-out bed. Futons can sleep even more. Another cottage, smaller but more luxurious (wheelchair-accessible) is nearing completion. Plans call for a fireplace, and the romantic mood is designed for honeymoon couples who want to be alone. The rate is $50 d, $5 for each additional person, $40 off-season, minimum stay two nights. Sometimes Bonnie will allow an emergency one-night stay if the house is not booked, but she charges $10 extra because the entire house has to be cleaned.

Volcano B&B

This gingerbread house, Hawaiian style, tel. 967-7779, Box 22, Volcano, HI 96785, is owned and operated by Jim and Sandy Pedersen. The home is in the old Volcano Village and was originally built in 1912 as a vacation getaway for a local Hawaiian family. Additions and improvements followed over the years until it was purchased by the Pedersens, who have transformed it into a serene mountain bungalow. All windows are original, and along with the vaulted ceilings give the common rooms an open and airy feel. One of the finest features is a lovely sun porch, bedecked in white with blue-trimmed wicker furniture. Morning on the porch is especially beautiful—greet the sunshine and view a garden of ferns, flowers, and trees. Filling the house at breakfasttime is the homey smell of baking muffins, which you will enjoy with a large bowl of fresh fruit, yogurt-fruit sauce, fluffy golden pancakes that are becoming famous, and 100% pure organic Kona coffee. The B&B has three very comfortable guest rooms. They're small, but rich with the feeling of absolute hominess and relaxation expressed in varying decor. All are immaculate. Rates are $50 s, $55 d, and $65 d with two beds. The second and third floors of the house are dedicated to the guests, with the exception of the kitchen. The Pedersens live below. The common area and sun porch are separated from the living room by two sets of French doors. The living room, equipped with TV and VCR, also serves as a reading room and piano room. The hosts help with small items like coolers, water bottles, and flashlights with which to view the volcano after dark.

Hale Ohia Cottages

Follow a private mountain lane for a few minutes into an enchanted clearing where the artwork of a meticulous Japanese garden surrounds a New England gabled-and-turreted home and its attendant cottages of red-on-brown rough-cut shingles. Once the hideaway of the Dillinghams, an old and influential *kama'aina* family, Hale Ohia, Box 758, Volcano Village, HI 96785, tel. 967-7986 or (800) 455-3803, is now owned and operated by Michael D. Tuttle, who recently purchased the property after falling hopelessly in love at first sight. The main house holds the Dillingham Suite ($85), with its own sitting room, bath, fireplace, and glass-covered lanai. Simple and clean, with hardwood floors and wainscotted walls, the home is the epitome of country elegance, Hawaiian style.

Hale Ohia, once the gardener's cottage, has two stories, with the bottom floor occupied by the Iiwi ($60) and Camellia ($65) suites, which are wheelchair-accessible and can be combined for larger groups ($85). Stained-glass windows with a calla lily-and-poppy motif add a special touch, while the low ceilings are reminiscent of the captain's quarters on a sailing ship. The first floor has a full kitchen and a covered lanai complete with barbecue grill that makes it perfect for evening relaxation. Narrow stairs lead to a full bath located on the first landing, from where you get a sweeping view of the grounds while performing your morning meditation. Upstairs opens into a bright and airy parlor and adjacent bedrooms that can sleep five comfortably.

Hale Lehua, once a private study, is secluded down its own lava footpath. Enter to find a wall of windows framing the green-on-green grounds. The interior is cozy with its own fireplace, bamboo and wicker furniture, self-contained bathroom, covered lanai, and partial kitchen with microwave, toaster, and refrigerator. Another "Hale" still unnamed and under construction will feature an outdoor shower, skylight, fireplace, and leaded glass windows through which the surrounding fern forest will emit its emerald radiance.

To make your stay even more delightful, room rates include an "extended" continental breakfast, and guests are welcome to immerse themselves in the bubbling jacuzzi that awaits you under a canopy of Japanese cedars and glimmering stars.

Chalet Kilauea

Peeking from the *hapu'u* fern forest in a manicured glen is **Chalet Kilauea,** tel. 967-7786 or (800) 937-7786, Box 998, Volcano Village, HI 96785, where you will be cordially accommodated by owners Lisha and Brian Crawford. Enter the second level of the main house to find a guest living room where you can wile away the hours playing chess, listening to a large collection of CDs, or gazing from the wraparound windows at a treetop view of the surrounding forest, ferns, and impeccable grounds. Just out the door, a make-over of a one-time Japanese *ofuro* resulted in a gurgling fountain, inside of which a miniature volcano blazes and smokes. (Downstairs are a hot tub and outdoor lounge area, and a black-and-white checkerboard dining room where wrought-iron tables sit before a huge picture window.) Breakfasts (changeable daily), friendly and relaxed but with formal table settings, are remarkable: lox and bagels, fresh Volcano onions and tomatoes, macadamia nut or banana pancakes with strawberry topping, fresh papaya and squeezed juices, and Brian's own house blend Kona coffee with a hint of cinnamon.

The main house holds three unique theme rooms (European, African, Asian) that rent for $75 d. The Oriental Jade Room is richly appointed with Chinese folding screens, samurai murals, an oriental carpet, and jade-green bedspread. Plush terry-cloth robes are available for all guests, and a large shared bath of rich blue tile is on the ground level. Connected by a deck to the main house is the Treehouse Suite ($95 d), a two-story unit, with a bath and sitting room downstairs, and a large bedroom on the upper floor. Also on the property are the Ohia Holiday Cottage ($75) and the Hoku Hawaiian House ($100). However, the prize is the very special Hapuu Forest Cabin ($145), nestled at the end of its own driveway and footpath about 50 yards from the main house. The cabin, with a covered porch all around, is post-and-beam with plenty of knotty pine. A 20-foot-high vaulted ceiling, wood-burning stove on a lava-rock base, and Persian carpet help set the cabin's mood. Wherever it is possible to have glass, there is glass! The bathroom has an enormous tub perfect for a couple who wants to sip champagne in pure luxury while throwing open the windows to the night air and the soothing whispers of rustling ferns. A narrow staircase leads to a loft where four skylights allow moonbeams to illuminate the comfy, queen-size bed. There's a full kitchen (breakfast at the main house included) where you can fix your own meals and snacks, and even a TV if you are so inclined. Lisha and Brian also own and operate **Volcano Reservations,** a B&B reservation service with guest homes available statewide.

Hale Kilauea

Green pines and native ohia shade Hale Kilauea, tel. 967-7591, Box 28, Volcano, HI 96785, owned and operated by Maurice Thomas. In the main lodge, a central common room is very comfortable with reading materials, fireplace, parlor games, and TV. The spacious and airy rooms in the main lodge, $65-85 d, $15 extra person, all with private baths, are comfortable but not luxurious. Upstairs rooms are more deluxe with plush carpeting, knotty pine trim, refrigerator, small divan, and private lanai. Ask for a room in the rear so that you can overlook the quiet green forest instead of the parking area. Two rooms across from the main building are warm and cozy, although quite small. They are private, and the least expensive is $55. The best deal, however, is a refurbished plantation cottage that sits across the road. The rate is $85 d, with special weekly and monthly rates. The wainscotted cottage provides a small but serviceable kitchen, separate bedroom, and living room that can sleep a few more. Don't expect luxury, but a night in the cottage is a window into Hawaii's past of humble workers in humble homes. With all the rooms, including the cottage, a hearty breakfast of hot and cold cereals, various breads, cheeses, plump sausages, and occasionally quiche, waffles, or pancakes is provided.

Lokahi Lodge

Built in 1992 specifically as a B&B by Patrick Dixon and Danny DiCastro, Lokahi Lodge, tel. 985-8647 (on Oahu, Maui, and Kauai tel. 922-6597 or 800-457-6924), Box 7, Volcano, HI 96785, offers quiet country comfort. A rocking-chair veranda, perfect for keeping off sun and showers, completely surrounds the spacious ranch house. Enter into a common sitting room of 16-foot vaulted ceilings where you can relax on overstuffed couches and chairs while warming yourself in front of a red enameled free-standing stove. An old-fashioned, crank-handled telephone hangs on the wall, and an ensemble of organ, piano, and harp awaits anyone inclined to make their own music. A continental breakfast of homemade banana bread, fresh papaya and pineapple, fruit juices, jams, jellies, coffee, and tea assortment is offered at a huge banquet table surrounded by high-backed chairs. The stardust-speckled hallway is lined with vintage lei collected by owner Danny DiCastro, a famous hula dancer. Rooms, $65 d, $15 extra person, are triple-insulated for guaranteed quiet, are fully carpeted, offer large closets, and have differing decor—for example, billowy paisley curtains and bedspreads with matching wallpaper. Comfortable furniture for private relaxation, tasteful oil prints, and bathrooms with tub, shower, and pedestal sink complete the rooms. For the most privacy request the "yellow or blue rooms" at the far end of the hallway. Each room has a private entrance leading onto the veranda, so that you may come and go without disturbing anyone. Lokahi Lodge definitely lives up to its name, which translates as "peace and harmony."

Carson's Volcano Cottages

Deep in the fern forest, Carson's Volcano Cottages, tel. 967-7683 or (800) 845-LAVA, Box 503, Volcano, HI 96785, owned and operated by Tom and Brenda Carson, offers four B&B rooms, one in its own studio cottage, and the others in a three-room cottage. The accommodations all have private baths, entrances, and decks, and there's a hot tub for use by guests on the deck of the main house. Two of the rooms have kitchens. The one-acre property is naturally landscaped with ohia and ferns, while moss-covered sculptures of Balinese gods peeking through the foliage escort you through the grounds. The studio cottage, $75 d, a miniature plantation house with corrugated roof, has a kitchen and a bath with skylight. Appointed with fluffy pillows and downy quilts, this would be a perfect rendezvous for a "Victorian lady" and her paramour. The three-room cottage, $70 d per room, has vaulted ceilings, beds with wooden headboards, wicker furniture, and vintage photos on the walls. In one room, the snow-white bedspreads are helped by electric blankets, while a free-standing credenza from the '30s adds a touch of charm. Leaded glass windows open to a private porch. Another room, all in pink, also with its own vaulted ceiling and free-standing wardrobe, is appointed with vintage kitsch bric-a-brac like hula dancer glasses and lamps. A retired "lady of the evening" could easily relive her memories in this room. Finally, the Oriental Room, striking in black and white, features Balinese masks and a Japanese doll mural. Located at the side of the cottage, this room has a more private entrance and a tiny kitchenette. Tom and Brenda provide a continental breakfast that might include banana bread, French toast, passion fruit juice, bagels and lox, strawberry crepes, or mai tais made with lemon juice. The Carsons also rent out two other homes in the Volcano Village area. One is a vintage two-bedroom home at $85, the other is a one-bedroom cedar home, recently built, that features a living room, full kitchen, bath, and white-pane windows. Another two-bedroom home, in Kapoho, one lot back from the sea, rents for $85.

Volcano House

If you decide to lodge at Volcano House, tel. 967-7321 or (800) 325-3535, Box 53, Hawaii Volcanoes National Park, HI 96718, don't be frightened away by the daytime crowds. They disappear with the sun. Then Volcano House metamorphoses into what it has always been: a quiet country inn. The 37 rooms are comfy but old-fashioned. Who needs a pool or TV when you can look out your window into a volcano caldera? Unfortunately, the management of this venerable hotel has been in a state of flux lately, and there have been reports of indifferent service. Be advised! Room rates are: main building with crater view $131, noncrater view $105, Ohia Wing noncrater view $79, $10 additional person. No charge for children under 12 occupying the same room as their parents. Also see Namakani Paio Cabins under "Camping and Hiking" above.

Volcano House Restaurant offers a breakfast buffet, $7.50 per person daily 7-10:30 a.m., with hot and cold cereals, assorted juices, pancakes topped with ohia berries and macadamia nuts, sweet bread French toast, scrambled eggs, bacon, chili links, and Portuguese sausage. A lighter continental breakfast is $4.50. The lunch buffet ($11 adults, $6.75 children, served daily 11 a.m.-1:30 p.m.), often terribly crowded because of the tour buses, offers salads, fresh fruits, sautéed mahimahi, teriyaki beef, honey-dipped chicken, soft drinks, coffee, and tea. Dinner nightly, 5:30-9 p.m., starts with appetizers like sautéed shrimp $6.50 and special salad of the night $6.50. It moves on to entrees like seafood linguine $18.50, filet mignon $19.95, and Volcano House scampi $17.50. Hearty appetites will enjoy the prime rib of beef and shrimp combination at $23. The quality is fair and the prices reasonable; however, the lunchtime buffet is overwhelmingly crowded and should be avoided if possible.

Other Lodging

A B&B with an excellent reputation is **My Island,** tel. 967-7216, Box 100, Volcano, HI 96785. Rates range from a very reasonable $30 s with shared bath to $60 for a double with private bath, and there's even a private studio.

Victoria Rose, a one-room B&B, tel. 967-8026, owned and operated by Louisa and Pat Edie, is a fancy jewelry box done in maroon, pink, and lace, lots of lace. A four-poster "pineapple" bed and a private bath ensure privacy and comfort. Pat is an accomplished astrologer who, on request, will fill your evenings with the stars.

Bonnie Goodell (see above) recommends a similar cottage owned by her friend Beverly Jackson, tel. 967-7986. The setup is just about the same as Bonnie's, except that Beverly's cottage is closer to the road, which makes it more convenient, but a bit less secluded.

Other Food And Shopping

If you are after an exquisite piece of art, a unique memento, or an inexpensive but distinctive souvenir, be sure to visit the **Volcano Art Center** (see "Visitors Center Area" under "Kilauea Caldera" earlier in this chapter).

You can get away from the crowds and have a satisfying meal at **Volcano Country Club Restaurant** at Volcano Golf Course. The cuisine is quite good. Complete breakfast is served daily 7-10 a.m., a full lunch menu daily 11 a.m.-3 p.m., and light snacks and *pu'pu* until 5 p.m. Selections include hearty sandwiches for $6 and under; burgers with trimmings; luncheon New York steak smothered in onions for $7; and a seafood plate with shrimp, fish, and onion rings for $7.75. There is also a good selection of local favorites like loco moco and chili with rice for under $6. The bar is well stocked, serving name-brand liquor, exotic drinks, and beer and wine. Next to the Kilauea Lodge, this is the best place for lunch in the area.

A **farmers' market** opens on the first and third Sunday of the month and sells local produce, baked goods, and used books. It's located at the Community Center at the corner of Wright Road (the north entrance to the village) and Rt. 11, between mile markers 26 and 27.

Volcano Store, tel. 967-7210, open daily 6 a.m.-7 p.m., is in the middle of Volcano Village and sells gasoline, film, and a good selection of basic foods. In front are a few **telephone booths,** and next door is a full-service **post office.**

On the porch of Volcano Store is a **window service restaurant,** open Mon.-Thurs. 8 a.m.-4:30 p.m., Fri.-Sat. until 5 p.m., Sunday until 4 p.m., with seating available. Breakfasts are everything from coffee and a sweet roll to meat and eggs for $3.95, or a special of steak or fish and eggs for $4.99. Lunches are burgers and fries for around $3, and an assortment of plate lunches for under $5.

Behind Volcano Store, **Woodcarver's Corner,** open Wed.-Sun. 10 a.m.-5 p.m., tel. 985-8518, is run by a husband-and-wife team who sell bowls, trays, bracelets, and even totem poles. Prices are good, and the items are a mixture of semi-art and authentic junk.

Just down the road, **Kilauea General Store,** open 6 a.m.-7:30 p.m., Sunday 6:30 a.m.-6:30 p.m., also sells gas, and although it is not as well stocked as a grocery, it does have a deli case, a good stock of beer and liquor, and an excellent community bulletin board.

tree fern

KONA

Kona is long and lean, and takes its suntanned body for granted. This district *is* the west coast of the Big Island and lies in the rain shadows of both Mauna Loa and Mauna Kea. You can come here expecting brilliant sunny days and glorious sunsets, and you won't be disappointed; this reliable sunshine has earned Kona the nickname "The Gold Coast." Offshore, the fishing grounds are legendary, especially for marlin that lure game-fishing enthusiasts from around the world. There are actually two Konas, north and south, and both enjoy an upland interior of forests, ranches, and homesteads while most of the coastline is low, broad, and flat. If you've been fantasizing about swaying palms and tropical jungles dripping with wild orchids, you might be in for "Kona shock," especially if you fly directly into Keahole Airport. Around the airport the land is raw black lava that can appear as forbidding as the tailings from an old mining operation. Don't despair. Just north is one of the premier resorts in Hawaii, with a gorgeous white-sand beach lined with dancing coconut palms, and throughout Kona the lava has been transformed into beautiful gardens with just a little love and care.

Kailua-Kona is the heart of North Kona, by far the most developed area in the district. Its **Ali'i Drive** is lined with shops, hotels, and condos, but for the most part the shoreline vista remains intact because most of the buildings are low-rise. To show just how fertile lava can be when tended, miles of multihued bougainvillea and poinsettias line Ali'i Drive like a lei that leads to the flowerpot of the **Kona Gardens.** East of town is **Mt. Hualalai** (8,271 feet), where local people still earn a living growing vegetables and taro on small truck farms high in the mountain coolness.

South Kona begins in the town of **Captain Cook.** Southward is a region of diminutive coffee plantations, the only ones in the U.S. The bushes grow to the shoulder of the road and the air is heady with the rich aroma of roasting coffee. Farther south, rough but passable roads branch from the main highway and tumble toward hidden beaches and tiny fishing villages where time slips away. From north to south, Kona is awash in brilliant sunshine, and the rumble of surf and the plaintive cry of seabirds create the music of peace.

KAILUA-KONA AND VICINITY

SIGHTS

The entire Kona District is both old and historic. This was the land of Lono, god of fertility and patron of the Makahiki Festival. It was also the spot where the first missionary packet landed and changed Hawaii forever, and it's been a resort since the 19th century. In and around **Kailua** are restored *heiau,* a landmark lava church, and a royal palace where the monarchs of Hawaii came to relax. The coastline is rife with historical sites: lesser *heiau,* petroglyph fields, and curious amusement rides dating from the days of the Makahiki. Below the town of Captain Cook is **Kealakekua Bay,** the first and main *haole* anchorage in the islands until the development of Honolulu Harbor. This bay's historical significance is overwhelming, alternately being a place of life, death, and hope from where the spirit of Hawaii was changed for all time. Here on the southern coast is a Hawaiian "temple of refuge," restored and made into a National Historical Park. The majority of Kona's sights are strung along Rt. 11. Except for Kailua-Kona, where a walking tour is perfect, you need a rental car to visit the sights; the Big Island's Hele-On Bus is too infrequent to be feasible. The sights listed below are arranged from Kailua heading south.

Ali'i Shuttle

If you want to concentrate on the scenery and not on driving, take the Ali'i Shuttle. Painted red, white, and blue, the bus runs daily every 45 minutes along Ali'i Drive 7:45 a.m.-10 p.m., and charges $1 each direction. The terminal points are Lanihau Shopping Center on the north end and Kona Surf Resort on the south end, with pick-ups at major hotels along the way. You can hail the bus and it will stop if possible.

Mokuaikaua Church

Kailua is one of those towns that would love to contemplate its own navel if it could only find it. It doesn't really have a center, but if you had to pick one, it would be the 112-foot steeple of Mokuaikaua ("The trees are felled, now let us eat") Church. This highest structure in town has been a landmark for travelers and seafarers ever since the church was completed in January 1838. The church claims to be the oldest house of Christian worship in Hawaii. The site was given by King Liholiho to the first Congregationalist missionaries who arrived on the brig *Thaddeus* in 1820. The actual construction was undertaken in 1836 by the Hawaiian congregation under the direction of Rev. Asa Thurston. Much thought was given to the orientation of the structure, designed so the prevailing winds blow through the entire length of the church to keep it cool and comfortable. The walls of the church are fashioned from massive, rough-hewn lava stone, mortared with plaster made from crushed and burned coral that was bound with *kukui* nut oil. The huge cornerstones are believed to have been salvaged from a *heiau* built in the 15th century by King Umi. The masonry is crude but effective—still sound after 150 years.

Inside, the church is extremely soothing, expressing a feeling of strength and simplicity. The resolute beams are native ohia, pegged together and closely resembling the fine beamwork used in barns throughout 19th-century New England. The pews, railings, pulpit, and trim are all fashioned from koa, a rich brown, lustrous wood that begs to be stroked. Although the church is still used as a house of worship, it also has the air of a museum, housing paintings of historical personages instrumental in Hawaii's Christian past. The crowning touch is an excellent model of the brig *Thaddeus,* painstakingly built by the men of the Pacific Fleet Command and presented to the church in 1934. The church is open daily from sunrise to sunset, and volunteer hostesses answer your questions 10 a.m.-noon and 1-3:30 p.m. Mokuaikaua Church is a few hundred yards south of Kailua Pier on the *mauka* side of Ali'i Drive.

Hulihee Palace

Go from the spiritual to the temporal by walking across the street from Mokuaikaua Church and entering Hulihee ("Flight") Palace. This two-story Victorian structure commissioned by

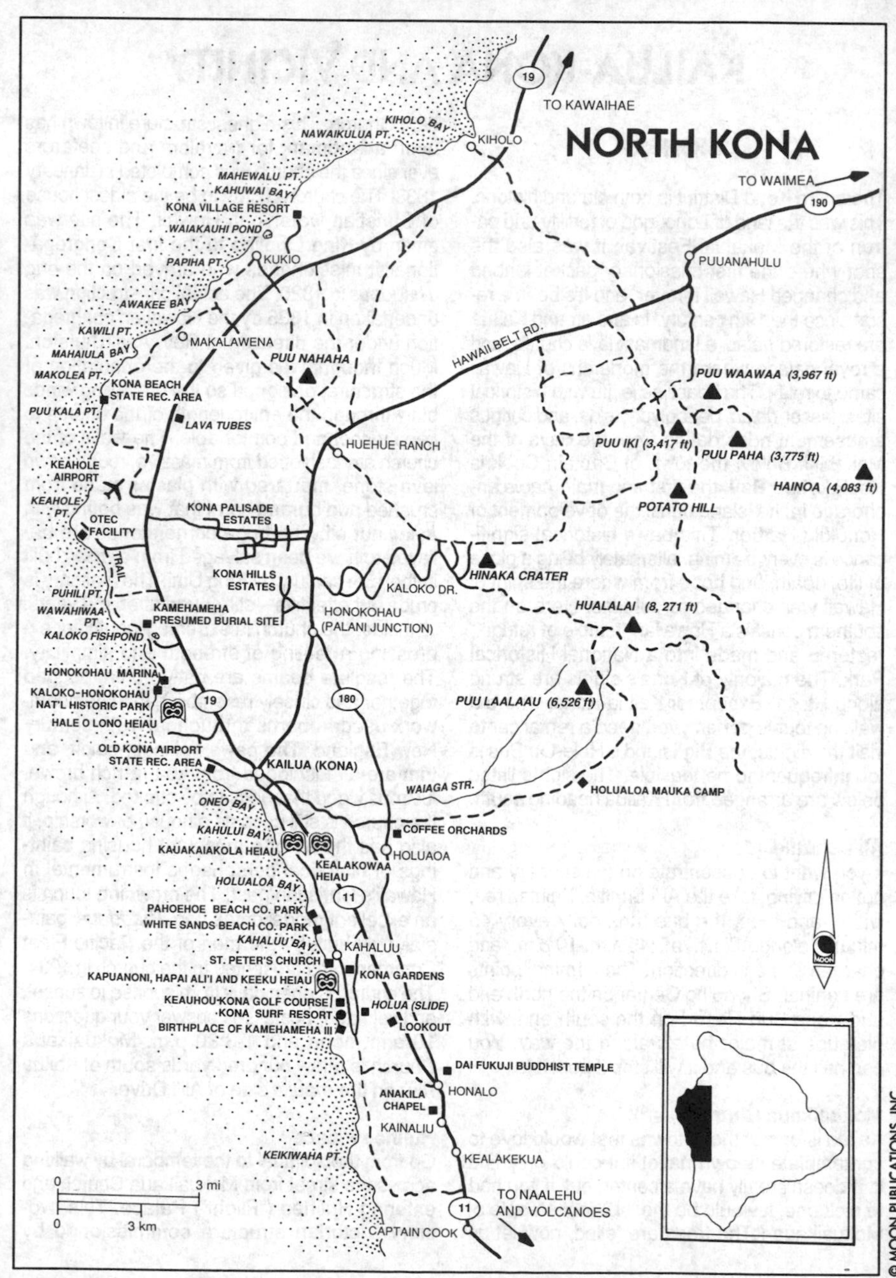
NORTH KONA
19
TO KAWAIHAE
KIHOLO BAY
NAWAIKULUA PT.
KIHOLO
TO WAIMEA
190
MAHEWALU PT.
KAHUWAI BAY
KONA VILLAGE RESORT
WAIAKAUHI POND
PAPIHA PT.
KUKIO
PUUANAHULU
AWAKEE BAY
KAWILI PT.
MAKALAWENA
MAHAIULA BAY
HAWAII BELT RD.
PUU NAHAHA
MAKOLEA PT.
KONA BEACH STATE REC. AREA
PUU WAAWAA (3,967 ft)
PUU KALA PT.
LAVA TUBES
PUU IKI (3,417 ft)
PUU PAHA (3,775 ft)
HUEHUE RANCH
KEAHOLE AIRPORT
HAINOA (4,083 ft)
KEAHOLE PT.
POTATO HILL
KONA PALISADE ESTATES
OTEC FACILITY
TRAIL
HINAKA CRATER
KONA HILLS ESTATES
PUHILI PT.
KALOKO DR.
WAWAHIWAA PT.
HONOKOHAU (PALANI JUNCTION)
KAMEHAMEHA PRESUMED BURIAL SITE
HUALALAI (8, 271 ft)
KALOKO FISHPOND
HONOKOHAU MARINA
KALOKO-HONOKOHAU NAT'L HISTORIC PARK
HALE O LONO HEIAU
19
180
PUU LAALAAU (6,526 ft)
OLD KONA AIRPORT STATE REC. AREA
KAILUA (KONA)
WAIAGA STR.
HOLUALOA MAUKA CAMP
ONEO BAY
KAHULUI BAY
COFFEE ORCHARDS
KAUAKAIAKOLA HEIAU
HOLUAOA
KEALAKOWAA HEIAU
HOLUALOA BAY
11
PAHOEHOE BEACH CO. PARK
WHITE SANDS BEACH CO. PARK
KAHALUU BAY
KAHALUU
ST. PETER'S CHURCH
KAPUANONI, HAPAI ALI'I AND KEEKU HEIAU
KONA GARDENS
KEAUHOU-KONA GOLF COURSE
HOLUA (SLIDE)
KONA SURF RESORT
BIRTHPLACE OF KAMEHAMEHA III
LOOKOUT
MOON
DAI FUKUJI BUDDHIST TEMPLE
HONALO
ANAKILA CHAPEL
KAINALIU
KEIKIWAHA PT.
KEALAKEKUA
0
3 mi
0
3 km
11
TO NAALEHU AND VOLCANOES
CAPTAIN COOK

J.D. BISIGNANI

Ahuena Heiau

Hawaii's first governor, John Kuakini, also dates from 1838. A favorite summer getaway for all the Hawaiian monarchs who followed, especially King Kalakaua, it was used as such until 1916. At first glance, the outside is unimpressive, but the more you look the more you realize how simple and grand it is. The architectural lines are those of an English country manor, and indeed Great Britain was held in high esteem by the Hawaiian royalty. Inside, the palace is bright and airy. Most of the massive carved furniture is made from koa. The most magnificent pieces include a huge formal dining table, 70 inches in diameter, fashioned from one solid koa log. Upstairs is a tremendous four-poster bed that belonged to Queen Kapiolani, and two magnificent cabinets built by a Chinese convict who was serving a life sentence for smuggling opium. King Kalakaua heard of his talents and commissioned him to build the cabinets. They proved to be so wonderfully crafted that after they were completed the king pardoned the craftsman.

Prince Kuhio, who inherited the palace from his uncle, King Kalakaua, was the first Hawaiian delegate to Congress. He decided to auction off all the furniture and artifacts to raise money, supposedly for the benefit of the Hawaiian people. Providentially, the night before the auction each piece was painstakingly numbered by the royal women of the palace, and the name of the person bidding for the piece was dutifully recorded. In the years that followed, the **Daughters of Hawaii,** who now operate the palace as a museum, tracked down the owners and convinced many to return the items for display. Most of the pieces are privately owned, and because each is unique, the owners wish no duplicates to be made. It is for this reason, coupled with the fact that flashbulbs can fade the wood, that a strict *no photography* policy is enforced.

Delicate and priceless heirlooms on display include a tiger-claw necklace belonging to Kapiolani. You'll also see a portrait gallery of Hawaiian monarchs. Personal and mundane items are on exhibit as well—there's an old report card showing a 68 in philosophy for King Kalakaua—and lining the stairs is a collection of spears reputedly belonging to the great Kamehameha himself.

Hulihee Palace, tel. 329-1877, is on the *makai* side of Ali'i Drive, open daily except Sunday 9 a.m.-4 p.m., last tour at 3:30, admission $4. A hostess knowledgeable in Hawaiiana is usually on duty to answer most questions.

The **Palace Gift Shop,** small but with quality items, is on the grounds next door to the palace. It offers a fine selection of koa sculptures of fish, sharks, and even a turtle, along with Hawaiiana books and postcards. Just outside is a saltwater pond with tropical fish.

Ahuena Heiau

Directly behind the King Kamehameha Kona Beach Hotel, at the north end of "downtown"

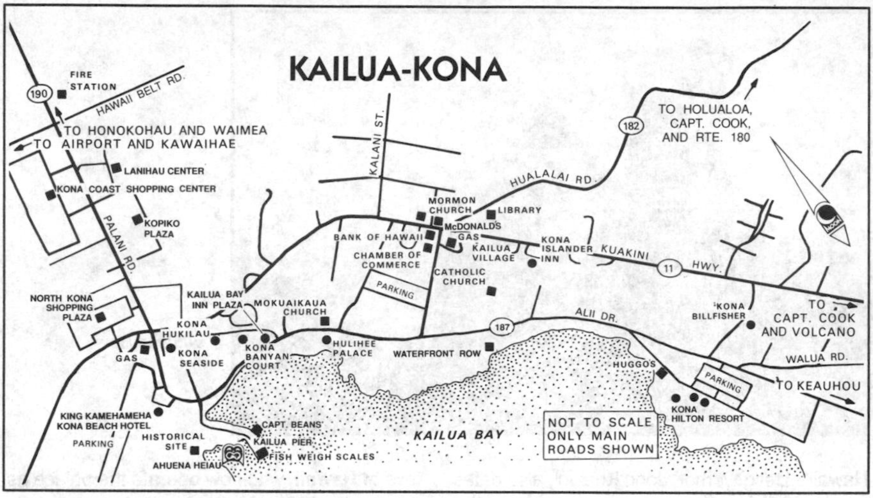

KAILUA-KONA

Kailua, is the restored Ahuena Heiau. Built around Kamakahonu ("Eye of the Turtle") Beach, it's in a very important historical area. Kamehameha I, the great conqueror, came here to spend the last years of his life, settling down to a peaceful existence after many years of war and strife. The king, like all Hawaiians, reaffirmed his love of the *aina* and tended his own royal taro patch on the slopes of Mt. Hualalai. After he died, his bones were prepared according to ancient ritual on a stone platform within the temple, then taken to a secret burial place just north of town which is believed to be somewhere near Wawahiwaa Point. It was Kamehameha who initiated the first rebuilding of Ahuena Heiau, a temple of peace and prosperity dedicated to Lono, god of fertility. The rituals held here were a far cry from the bloody human sacrifices dedicated to the god of war, Kukailimoku, held at Puukohola Heiau, which Kamehameha had built a few leagues north and a few decades earlier. At Ahuena, Kamehameha gathered the sage *kahuna* of the land to discourse in the Hale Mana (main prayer house) on topics concerning wise government and statesmanship. It was here that Liholiho, Kamehameha's son and heir, was educated, and it was here that as a grown man he sat down with the great queens, Keopuolani and Kaahumanu, and broke the ancient *kapu* of eating with women, thereby destroying the old order.

The tallest structure on the temple grounds is the *anuu* (oracle tower), where the chief priest, in deep trance, received messages from the gods. Throughout the grounds are superbly carved *kia akua* (temple images) in the distinctive Kona style, considered some of the finest of all Polynesian art forms. The spiritual focus of the *heiau* was humanity's higher nature, and the tallest figure, crowned with an image of the golden plover, was that of Koleamoku, a god of healing. Another interesting structure is a small thatched hut of sugarcane leaves, Hale Nana Mahina, which means "house from which to watch the farmland." Kamehameha would come here to meditate while a guard kept watch from a nearby shelter. The commanding view from the doorway affords a sweeping panorama from the sea to the king's plantations on the slopes of Mt. Hualalai. Though the temple grounds, reconstructed under the auspices of the Bishop Museum, are impressive, they are only one-third their original size. The *heiau* is open daily 9 a.m.-4 p.m., and admission is free. You can wander around following a self-guided tour, or take the free tour offered by the King Kamehameha Kona Beach Hotel, tel. 329-2911, which includes a tour of their own hotel grounds as well. The hotel portion of the tour includes a walk through the lobby, where various artifacts are displayed, and features an extremely informative botanical tour that highlights the medicinal herbs of old Hawaii. The hotel tours begin at 10 a.m. and 1:30 p.m. Don't miss this excellent educational opportunity, well worth the time and effort!

While in the area, make sure to visit the **Kailua Pier,** across the street from the *heiau.* Fishing boats are in and out all day, with most charters returning around 5 p.m. You'll have a chance to see some of the marlin for which Kona is noted, but if you have a sympathetic heart or weak stomach it might not be for you. This area is frantic with energy during the various "billfish tournaments" (see "Festivals, Holidays, and Events" in the General Introduction) held throughout the year.

Honokohau Marina

Honokohau Harbor, three miles north of Kailua-Kona, is a new boat harbor and deep-sea fishing facility that has eclipsed the old Kailua Pier. The harbor area is full of fishing-oriented shops, and is also home to **Captain Zodiac Cruises** (see "Sightseeing Tours" under "Getting Around" in the Big Island Introduction) and **Harbor House** (see "Food" below), formerly Atilla's Bar and Grill, where you can have a yarn with Kona's old salts. Primarily, this is where you come to see huge marlin caught that day and to talk to the skippers of the deep-sea fishing boats that go after them. (For a description of deep-sea fishing see "Sports and Recreation" in the Big Island Introduction.) Be at the harbor at 4 p.m. when all the boats come in every day like clockwork. When you pull into the marina, you'll see a road that goes off to the left. Head that way toward the tan building with a Texaco sign, to where the pier and the weigh-station are located. The huge fish will be hoisted, measured, and photographed while the skippers and their crew clean and prepare the boat for the next day's outing. If you're into deep-sea fishing, this is your chance to pick a likely boat and to get acquainted with the crew.

OTEC Natural Energy Labs

These amazing Ocean Technology facilities are located just south of the airport between mile markers 95 and 94, where you'll find a turnoff heading toward the sea. Incredible things are being done here. For example, cold water from several thousand feet below the surface of the ocean is placed in a turbine with warm surface water, a process that generates electricity and also provides desalinated water. In addition, the cold water is used for raising very un-Hawaiian things such as giant strawberries, lobsters, prawns, abalone, and kelp. Tours are offered Thursdays at 2 p.m. Make sure you call ahead, tel. 329-7341, to ensure a place on a tour.

Along Ali'i Drive

Ali'i Drive heads south from Kailua, passing the majority of Kona's resorts. On the mountain side of the road, a continuous flow of flowers drapes the shoulder like a femme fatale's seductive boa, while seaside the coastline slips along, rugged and bright, making Ali'i Drive a soothing sight.

At your first stop, near White Sands Beach, look for the historic **Ohana Congregational Church** built in 1855 by Rev. John D. Paris. Services are still held every Sunday at 8 a.m. The base of the church is mostly original lava rock topped with a new roof. The cemetery area is peaceful and quiet and offers a perfect meditative perch from which to scan the coast below. Back on the road, look for signs to Kahaluu Beach Park; pull in and park here. On the rocky northern shore of this bay is **St. Peter's Catholic Church.** Its diminutive size, capped by a blue tin roof that winks at you from amidst the lava like a bright morning glory in an ebony vase, has earned it the nickname **Little Blue Church.** Built in 1889 on the site of an old, partially reclaimed *heiau,* the church is a favorite spot for snapshots. Inside, the epitome of simplicity reigns with bare wood walls and a simple crucifix. The only splash of color is a bouquet of fresh flowers on the altar. To the right of the church as you face it are the remains of **Kuemanu Heiau,** and within a 10-minute walk heading south from the church along the coast are strung the remains of **Kapuanoni, Hapai Ali'i, and Keeku *heiau.*** All are unrestored historical sites that still show signs of being used, and all offer fantastic vantage points from which to view the coast.

Do yourself a favor and visit the grounds of the **Kona Surf Resort,** which have graciously been opened to the public. You're free to stroll around on your own, and nonguests can take a tour on Wednesday and Friday at 9 a.m. Here are 14 acres of ponds and gardens glorious with the perfumes and blooms of over 30,000 plants, flowers, fruits, and shrubs gathered from throughout Polynesia. Complementing the natural setting of the grounds is a profusion of Asian and Hawaiian artwork. Inside, the main hallways of the hotel's four wings are resplendent with over a million dollars' worth of wall hangings and tapestries. For a special treat, visit in the evening, when the hotel shines spotlights on the water and attracts a flock of manta rays.

A short stroll or a minute's drive south brings you to **Keauhou Bay.** Here you'll find a cluster of historical sites and the pier for the Fair Winds Snorkel Dive and Charter. Look for a monument marking the birthplace of Kamehameha III in 1814. Local people come to fish from the pier around 5 p.m. for *halalu,* a tough little fish to catch. Ask at the Keauhou Bay Hotel for a free area map. Along the shoreline is a number of partially developed *heiau* sites. You'll also find a *holua,* grass-covered rocks slicked with water to form a slide. Hawaiians rode it on wooden sleds, especially during the Makahiki Festival. A small home stuck on a point of land on the edge of the bay is where John Wayne married his wife Pilar in 1954 and marks the site of the first modern house built on the bay.

BEACHES AND PARKS

If Kona is short on anything, it is beaches. The ones it has are adequate and quite striking in their own way, but they tend to be small, few, and far between. Most people expecting a huge expanse of white sands will be disappointed. These beaches do exist on the Big Island's west coast, but they are north of Kailua-Kona in the Kohala District. Kona does, however, have beaches alive with marinelife, providing excellent and safe snorkeling and top-notch tidepooling.

Note: The following are the main beaches in Kailua-Kona and North Kona. For descriptions of South Kona beaches like Milolii, Hookena, and Keei, see "Honalo to Captain Cook and Vicinity" under "Central and South Kona" later in this chapter.

Kamakahonu Beach

You couldn't be more centrally located than at "Eye of the Turtle" Beach. Find it in downtown Kailua-Kona near Kailua Pier and the King Kamehameha Kona Beach Hotel. Local people refer to it as "Kids' Beach" because it is so gentle and perfect for a refreshing dip. Big kids come here to play too, when every year world-class athletes churn the gentle waters into a fury at the start of the Ironman Triathlon. Rent snorkel gear, kayaks, and Hobie Cats for reasonable prices from the **Beach Shack,** located on the beach itself. Restrooms are on the pier.

Old Kona Airport State Recreation Area

In 1970 the old Kona Airport closed and the state of Hawaii turned it into a beach park. To get there, simply walk along the shoreline for a few hundred yards north of the King Kamehameha Kona Beach Hotel. If driving, follow Ali'i Drive to the junction just before the North Kona Shopping Plaza and turn left on the Kuakini Highway Extension. Facilities include showers, restrooms, and picnic area. Parking is unlimited along the old runway. The white-sand beach is sandwiched between water's edge and the runway. You can enter the water at some shallow inlets, but the bottom is often rocky and the waters can be treacherous during high surf. The safest spot is a little sandy cove at the southern end of the beach. Snorkeling is good at the northern end of the beach, and offshore a break makes Old Airport popular with Kona surfers. There is no official camping at the park, but people often do camp at the north end. A heated controversy erupted when a developer purchased the land adjacent to the north end of the park, then closed it to camping. Local fishermen had camped here for years. Protesting in 1981, they raised a tent village named Kukai-limoku, which disbanded when the leaders were arrested for trespassing. It's also disputed whether the developer has claimed eight acres that actually belong to the state. The controversy goes on.

Honokohau Beach

All types of people come to Honokohau Beach, including fishermen, surfers, and snorkelers, but it's primarily known as a **clothes optional beach.** This status has been drastically changing ever since the area officially became part of **Kaloko-Honokohau National Historical Park.** Follow Rt. 19 north from Kailua-Kona for three miles and turn left on the marked road leading to the Honokohau Small Boat Harbor.

Stay to the right and park almost at the end of the access road near the "boat graveyard" in a dirt parking lot. Don't walk straight ahead onto land being claimed by the Pai 'ohana, a local Hawaiian family trying to establish a homestead within the "sovereign jurisdiction of the Kingdom of Hawaii." Instead clamber over the berm, follow the well-worn path into the vegetation, and keep walking for a few minutes to the beach.

This area, more toward Kaloko, was heavily populated during old Hawaiian days, and plenty of archaeological sites—mostly fishponds, ruins of houses, and a few petroglyphs—are found along the shoreline. Most of these sites are closed to protect them for posterity; if you come to an archaeological area, obey all posted signs and approach with great care and respect. Remember, it is imperative that you do not touch, disturb, or remove any historical artifacts. The beach offers safe swimming in somewhat shallow water, and except for a composting toilet, has no facilities.

The status of nudity along the beach is changing, and as part of the General Management Plan, the "proposed action" is to make nudity illegal. Camping and open fires, now illegal, are citable offenses under federal regulations. Walk to the north end of the beach, where a trail leads inland through thick vegetation. Follow it to the "Queen's Bath" (officially called the "Anchialine Bath" by the Park Service), a brackish pond surrounded by rock cairns. Because it is under consideration as a historical site, swimming in the pond is not recommended. There's sometimes a ranger back in here, and although the park is officially open, visitation is neither encouraged nor discouraged. On the way out, pause at the active small-boat harbor. Although shark warning signs are posted, snorkelers frequent the bay.

Kaloko Beach, about a 10-minute hike north of Queen's Bath, has great snorkeling in only 10-20 feet of water. Here, you can explore a series of sea arches. The entire area is a favorite with green sea turtles, who make their presence known mainly in the evenings.

North Kona Beaches

The first beach you come to heading north from Kailua-Kona is the famous **Pine Trees** surfing beach, located near the OTEC facility (see above) just south of the airport between mile markers 95 and 94. Look for a well-worn dirt road leading to the left away from OTEC, and follow it to Pine Trees. Although famous with surfers and the site of many competitions, Pine Trees (none of which is in evidence) is not a good swimming beach. There are a few one-towel coves along the rocky shoreline where you can gain access to the water, but mostly it's a place from which to observe the action. You can also follow the road toward the OTEC facility until you find a large, sandy, public beach, fronted by rock and coral. Here are a few volleyball nets, a restroom, and some picnic tables.

Recently opened and well marked, **Kona Beach State Recreation Area** is about two miles north of the airport between mile markers 91 and 90. Follow the rugged but passable dirt road for about 1.5 miles to one of the closest beaches to Kailua-Kona. The semi-improved area has a lavatory and dilapidated picnic tables built around palm trees. The land rises before getting to the beach, and to the left are the remains of a concession stand. The swimming here is safe in season, but always be careful.

Before you get to the official parking area for Kona State Beach Park, notice a walking path off to the right. It is a five-minute walk to **Mahaiula Bay.** En route, you'll pass a portable toilet (clean), and about 200 yards farther along is magnificent Mahaiula Beach. This crescent of white sand stretches for about 200 yards, with shade trees coming down almost to the water's edge. Completely unimproved and secluded, it's a great beach to "get away from it all" for the day.

Two miles further north, between mile markers 89 and 88, look for a cinder cone whose vegetation has been given a crew cut by the trade winds. Turn here on a very rugged, 4WD-only dirt road that takes you down to **Makalawena Beach.** En route to this totally secluded area, you'll pass over rough lava and coral and eventually come to a gate, where you park. Proceed on foot, and you'll have your choice of three wonderful beaches, ranging in size from 30 to 100 yards long—all frequented by green sea turtles. Walk to the left past the biggest beach, and look for a path behind it that leads to a brackish but mostly freshwater pond where you can rinse off. Don't be alarmed by the harmless brine shrimp that nibble at your toes. They're much too small to do any real damage. If you do not have 4WD, you can still enjoy this area, but it means a hike of about 30 minutes. Be sure to bring water, especially if you intend to spend the day. From Mahaiula Beach (see above), walk north along a path and in about five minutes you'll come to the remains of an abandoned estate that once belonged to the Magoon Family, longtime island residents and major stockholders in Hawaiian Airlines. The state has purchased this land—which was at one time being eyed by a Japanese firm that wished to build a luxury resort—and it is now, thankfully, in the public domain. After enjoying your short coastal hike, you will come to Makalawena, where you will be totally secluded. Remember not to take any chances during high surf, since there is no safety supervision whatsoever.

A few minutes farther north, just past the cinder cone, you'll find another road that starts off paved but almost immediately turns to lava and coral. If you have 4WD you can go to the end of the road, and then walk to the beach, but you can also walk for about 15 minutes from the turnout near the highway. The well-worn path leads you to **Kua Bay,** a famous swimming and boogie-boarding beach. Finally, just before you get to the luxury resorts of South Kohala, you'll find **Kiholo Bay** and **Luahinewai Pond,** considered yet another Queen's Bath. Look for a stand of royal palms marking the spot, and follow the rough but passable road down to the beach, where you will find a large round wooden house that once belonged to Loretta Lynn. Close by, a path leads over the lava to a tiny cove made more dramatic by a black-sand beach.

Ali'i Drive Beaches

The following beaches are strung one after the other along Kailua-Kona's Ali'i Drive. The first is **Pahoehoe Beach County Park,** about three miles south of town center. It's not much of a swimming beach, with only one small pocket of white sand next to a low seawall, but it's a handy spot to pull off for a view of the coastline or for a picnic.

White Sands Beach County Park (a.k.a **Magic Sands** or **Disappearing Sands**) is an excellent spot for a dip—if the sand is there. Every year, usually in March and April, the sands are stripped away by heavy seas and currents, exposing rough coral and making the area rugged for the average swimmer. People still come during those months because it's a good vantage point for observing migrating humpback whales. The sands always come back and when they do, the beach is terrific for all kinds of water sports, including bodysurfing and snorkeling. The annual **Magic Sands Bodysurfing Contest** is held during the winter months. The best board surfing is just north of the beach in a break the locals call "Banyans." White Sands' amenities include picnic pavilions, showers, and restrooms, making the beach a favorite spot with local people and tourists.

Kahaluu Beach Park on Kahaluu Bay has always been a productive fishing area. Even today, fishermen come to "throw net." You'll occasionally see large family parties surrounding their favorite fish with a huge *hukilau* net, then sharing their bounty among all participants. Because of this age-old tradition, the area has not been designated a Marine Life Conservation District. Kahaluu became a beach park in 1966. This ensured that the people of Kona would always have access to this favorite spot, which quickly became surrounded by commercial development. Amenities include picnic tables, showers, restrooms, and a basketball court. The swimming is very good, but the real attraction is snorkeling. The waters are very gentle and Kahaluu is a perfect place for families or beginning snorkelers. However, stay *within* the bay because a powerful and dangerous rip current lurks outside, and more rescues are made on this beach than on any other in Kona. The shoreline waters are alive with tropical fish: angelfish, parrotfish, the works. Bring bread or cheese with you, and in a minute you'll be surrounded by a live rainbow of colors. Some fish are even bold enough to nip your fingers. It's very curious that when these semi-tame fish spot a swimmer with a spear gun, they'll completely avoid him. They know the difference! Unfortunately, Kahaluu is often crowded, but it is still worth a visit.

ACCOMMODATIONS

Almost all of Kona's accommodations lie along the six miles of Ali'i Drive from Kailua-Kona to Keauhou. Most hotels/condos fall in the moderate to expensive range, including one super-luxury hotel just north of Kailua-Kona. A few inexpensive hotels are scattered here and there along Ali'i Drive, and back up in the hills are a "sleeper" or two that are cheap but decent. The following list should provide you with a good cross section.

Camping Note

It's sad but true: except for the limited beach park in the village of Milolii, 25 miles south of Kailua-Kona, there is *no* official camping in all of the Kona District. Campers wishing to enjoy the Kona Coast must go north to the Kohala District to find a campground, or south to Kau. Some unofficial camping does exist in Kona (see "Beaches and Parks" above), but as always, this generates certain insecurities. Bivouacking for a night or two in any of the unofficial camp spots should be hassle free. Good luck!

Inexpensive

For a reasonable and homey hotel, try the **Kona Tiki,** 75-5968 Ali'i Dr., Box 1567, Kailua-Kona, HI 96745, tel. 329-1425, featuring refrigerators in all rooms (some kitchen units) and complimentary continental breakfast daily. Island fruits and a few old fishing poles are also furnished for the guests. The hotel is close to the road so it's a bit noisy in the day but quiets down at night. Rooms are clean, with ceiling fans, and have been recently refurnished with new curtains and bedspreads of pastel blue. All units face the ocean so everyone gets a view. There's a lovely lanai, a pool, and a trim little garden of raked sand. Prices are $50 s/d, kitchenette unit $55, extra person $6, three-day minimum. Rooms have a/c, but no phones or TVs.

The **Kona Bay Hotel,** at 75-5739 Ali'i Dr., Kailua-Kona, HI 96740, tel. 329-1393 or (800) 367-5102, is a locally owned downtown hotel run by Uncle Billy and his Kona family. Its best feature is the friendly and warm staff. The hotel is a remaining wing of the old Kona Inn, the rest of which was torn down to accommodate the shopping center across the road. The Kona Bay is built around a central courtyard and garden containing the Banana Cafe, pool, and bar. As at Uncle Billy's Hilo Bay Hotel, the motif is "cellophane Polynesian," highlighted by some artificial palms. The rooms are a combination of basic and superior with a/c, TV, green carpeting, one wall papered and the other bare cinder block. Each room has a mini-fridge, and some can be outfitted with kitchenettes. Rates begin at $59 s, $74 d, add $10 for a kitchenette; car rental package available.

Kona White Sands apartment hotel is a two-story building just across from the famous White (Disappearing) Sands Beach, but all units now appear rented to long-term residents. All units are fully furnished, with electric kitchens, lanai, and cross ventilation; prices run $60/80 s/d, $6 extra person, three-day minimum. For information write Kona White Sands Apartments, Box 594, Kailua-Kona, HI 96745, tel. 329-3210 or (800) 553-5035.

Kona Magic Sands condominium is next door to Jameson's Restaurant at 77-6452 Ali'i Dr., Kailua-Kona, HI 96740, tel. 326-5622. Bookings are made through Kona Vacation Resorts at 77-6435 Kuakini Hwy., Kailua-Kona, HI 96740, tel. (800) 367-5168 Mainland, (800) 800-KONA Canada, and 329-6488 locally. Prices start at $65 and $85 nightly for a studio and one-bedroom with substantial savings on weekly and especially monthly rates. You can also call the resident manager at this time, Don Buchnowski, tel. 326-5622, for up-to-the-minute rates and availability. There is a three-night minimum stay and an off-season deal of seven nights for the price of six. The Kona Magic Sands is a landlord-green cinder-block building that is modest, clean, and well maintained. The units are homey and basic with the usual amenities, including TV, parking, cocktail lounge, pool, and maid service on request.

Kona Hukilau Hotel is another downtown hotel at 75-5646 Palani Rd., Kailua-Kona, HI 96740, tel. 367-7000 or (800) 367-7000. It's part of the island-owned Sands, Seaside, and Hukilau chain. Its sister hotel, the **Kona Seaside,** is just up the road; they share pools and other facilities. Most rooms have a/c, cross ventilation, and lanai, but no TV. There's a sun deck and central area with enclosed courtyard and lobby. Prices range from $55 standard to $76 deluxe, double occupancy. A car package adds $10 daily.

Patey's Place, 75-5731 Ala Hou St., Kailua-Kona, HI 96740, tel. 326-7018 or (800) 972-7408 (recently moved from 75-195 Ala Onaona St.) is a reasonably priced hostel that will set you up in a bunk for $15 or give you a private room for $35, with bath and kitchen $45.

Moderate

Aston Kona by the Sea, 75-6106 Ali'i Dr., Kailua-Kona, HI 96740, tel. 327-2300 or (800) 922-7866, is a rather new and beautifully situated condominium with extraordinary coastal views. Like many of Kona's properties, it has no beach, but there is a freshwater pool on the premises, and a saltwater pool run by the state only a minute away. From the balcony of your suite overlooking a central courtyard, you can watch the aqua-blue surf crash onto the black lava rocks below. Each spacious one- or two-bedroom unit has two bathrooms, tiled lanai, modern kitchen complete with dishwasher and garbage disposal, living room with fold-out couch, dining room, color cable TV, and central air. Furniture differs slightly from unit to unit but is always tasteful and often includes rattan with plush cushions, and mauve and earth-toned rugs and walls. Prices are a very reasonable $155-180 for one bedroom, $200-215 for two. Aston Kona by the Sea, like most of the Aston properties, offers excellent value for a peaceful Kona vacation.

Kanaloa at Kona, 78-261 Manukai St., Kailua-Kona, HI 96740, tel. 322-2272 or (800) 657-7872, is situated in an upscale residential area at the southern end of Kailua-Kona and is one of those special places where you feel you get more than you pay for. The one- to three-bedroom units are enormous. Big isn't always better, but in this case it is. Each unit comes equipped with a complete and modern kitchen, two baths, a lanai with comfortable outdoor furniture, and a wet bar for entertaining. Rates for the tastefully furnished units range from $125 for one bedroom to $205 for three bedrooms; the rooms can accommodate four and six people respectively at no extra charge. A security officer is on duty, and on the grounds you'll find three pools, lighted tennis courts, jacuzzis, gas barbecues, an activities desk with free morning coffee, and a restaurant and cocktail lounge overlooking the black-sand beach. The complex itself is made up of low-rise units around a central courtyard. If you would like to escape the hustle and bustle but stay near the action, the Kanaloa at Kona is the place.

The **Keauhou Beach Hotel,** 78-6740 Ali'i Dr., Kailua-Kona, HI 96740, tel. 322-3441 or (800) 446-8990, is built on a historic site that includes the remains of a *heiau* and a reconstruction of King Kamehameha III's summer cottage. The hotel is famous for its bougainvillea that plummets over the seven-story face of the hotel. Kahaluu Beach Park is adjacent, and the entire area is known for fantastic tidepools. This famous Kona hotel has been undergoing extensive renovation over the past few years, but is open to guests. Rates range from $95 standard up to $400 for a three-bedroom suite. Each has a/c, TV, phone, private lanai, and small refrigerator. The hotel offers free shuttle service to local shopping, golfing, and dining.

Casa De Emdeko is a condominium that receives the best possible praise: people who have lodged here once always return. It's a quiet, low-rise condo surrounding a central courtyard with freshwater and saltwater pools, maid service every three days, and a sauna. All units have a/c, full kitchen, and lanai. Prices start at $75 d, $10 extra person, for a garden-view apartment, with every seventh night free. Contact Casa De Emdeko at 75-6082 Ali'i Dr., Kailua-Kona, HI 96740, tel. 329-2160 (resident manager); or the booking agent of Kona Vacation Resort, tel. 329-6488 or (800) 367-5168. Office hours are weekdays only 8 a.m.-5 p.m.; check-in is at 1 p.m., checkout at 11 a.m. The office is closed on weekends and holidays but special arrangements can be made to accommodate you, and a buzzer at the front desk summons the resident manager.

Kona Islander Inn condominium apartments are well appointed for a reasonable price. Conveniently located within walking distance of downtown Kailua-Kona, they're next door to the Spindrifter Restaurant. The style is "turn-of-the-century plantation" shaded by tall palms. All 100 units have phone, offroad parking, a/c, and TV. For information write Kona Islander Inn, 75-5776 Kuakini Hwy., Kailua-Kona, HI 96740, tel. 329-3181; or Aston Resorts, tel. (800) 367-5124 Mainland, (800) 342-1551 in Hawaii.

Kailua Plantation House, at 75-5948 Ali'i Dr., Kailua-Kona, HI 96740, tel. 329-3727, is a *designed* bed-and-breakfast neo-Victorian home with an island twist. Each different-theme room, prices ranging $120-175, has color cable TV, refrigerator, full bath stocked with Paul Mitchell products, private lanai, a/c and ceiling fans, and soundproofing—there are no common walls, ensuring peace and quiet. The first-floor premier suite, done in shades of pastel blue and white, has its own jacuzzi, skylights for enjoying the brilliant Kona stars, and a location close enough to the beach that the lapping waves sing you to sleep with a soothing lullaby. Up the central staircase is the rose-colored Victorian Room, dominated by a four-poster bed. Turn-of-the-century furniture includes kerosene-lamp replicas that have been electrified. Another room features a double shower with windows for peering out to sea. The wild Africa Room has a zebra-striped bedspread and black-on-white motif. Rose Singarella, the hostess, takes special care in preparing a healthy breakfast that varies daily. Generous servings always include fresh island fruit and juices, and homemade muffins and cereals. Entrees can be quiches of all sorts, pancakes, or basmati rice.

High above Kailua-Kona on the road to Holualoa perches **Hale Maluhia B&B,** 76-770 Hualalai Rd., tel. 329-1123 or (800) 559-6627, a hideaway lovingly tended by hosts Ken and Ann Smith. Built and furnished in a mixture of rustic Hawaiian with a Victorian twist, the B&B offers accommodations in the main house and two separate cottages. The interiors feature open-beam ceilings, plenty of natural wood trim, koa cabinets, full kitchens, and private baths. There's even a functional office with a computer, laser printer, and fax machine for those forced to mix business with pleasure. On the property are an outdoor spa, massage table, and two lanai from which to soak in the views; all are wheelchair friendly. Rates begin at $45 for a single bed and shared bath in the main house to $235 for the entire two-bedroom, three-bath house. The Banyan Cottage is $110, and The Gatehouse $135.

A few reasonably priced and attractive condominium apartments include the following. **Kona Mansion,** a quarter mile from downtown, offers one-bedroom suites for up to four persons $55-60. There's a swimming pool, parking, TV, and maid service on request, with a minimum stay of five nights. Contact Hawaiian Apartment Leasing, 1240 Cliff Dr., Laguna Beach, CA 92651, tel. (714) 497-4253 or (800) 854-8843, or in California tel. (800) 472-8449. **Ali'i Villas,** oceanside just a half mile from Kailua-Kona, offers full kitchens, lanais, TVs, parking, a pool, and barbecues. Rates vary from one-bedroom units at $45 daily, $252 weekly (two to three guests), to two bedrooms (all units waterfront) from $60 daily, $380 weekly (up to four guests). Additional guests cost extra. There is a 20% monthly discount, and every seventh night is free. For bookings, contact Norma C. Edens, Kona Sun Coast Properties, tel. (800) 326-4751. **Kona Billfisher,** tel. (808) 329-9277, near downtown, offers full kitchens, pool, barbecues, limited maid service, and gazebo. One-bedroom units rent from $40 daily for up to four persons, two-bedrooms from $60 for up to six guests. Weekly and monthly rates and discounts. **Kona Plaza,** tel. 329-1132, downtown, has a swimming pool and sun decks and is wheelchair accessible. Daily rates are $40 d, $50 up to four. Weekly, monthly, and off-season rates available.

Expensive

The **Aston Royal Sea Cliff Resort,** winner of an American Automobile Association Three Diamond Award, offers classy condo apartments. The white alabaster building features rooms fronting a central courtyard where you'll find the pool and spa. The unobstructed views of the coast from most rooms are glorious, with sunsets enjoyed on your private lanai a perfect day-ending activity. Full amenities are offered, such as free tennis, daily maid service, two swimming pools, cable color TV, activities desk, jet spa and sauna, and sundries shop. Rates start with a studio at $140, and move to a one-bedroom $160-180, two-bedroom $180-200, and oceanfront villa $400; special 15% rate reduction during the off-season, and a "family plan." Contact Royal Sea Cliff Resort, 75-6040 Ali'i Dr., Kailua-Kona, HI 96740, tel. 329-8021, (800) 922-7866 Mainland, (800) 445-6633 Canada, (800) 342-1551 Neighbor Islands.

The **Kona Hilton Resort,** tel. 329-3111 or (800) 452-4411 in Hawaii, (800) 445-8667 Mainland, Box 1179, Kailua-Kona, HI 96745, has figuratively and literally become a Kona landmark. The rooms are spacious and each includes a lanai (so protected from public view that it easily serves as an outdoor room). The tennis facilities are superb, and an ocean-fed pool is sheltered from the force of the waves by huge black lava boulders. Rates run from $130 for a standard room to $200 for a deluxe. The hotel, built like rising steps with the floor below larger than the one above, commands a magnificent view from its perch atop a beautiful promontory of black lava. On the property, you can dine in the Lanai Restaurant, the main dining room open for dinner only, or have breakfast and lunch in the Lanai Coffee Shop, which has a beautiful veranda with a magnificent view of the surrounding coastline (for details see "Food" below). At both you'll be treated to the wonderful creations of executive chef Hiroshi Omori. The hotel also boasts a mini-shopping mall with a sundries store. The Windjammer, an open-air bar with nightly entertainment, features jazz and contemporary music throughout the week (see "Entertainment and Activities" below). The hotel pool, completely refurbished, has an upper kiddie pool and a lower retiled main pool adjacent to the rolling surf. Between the main building and the beach tower is the coconut grove. The *imu* is fired up every Monday, Wednesday, and Friday, and the luau comes complete with island entertainment that fills the grounds with music and laughter. The tennis courts, attended by hotel pro Adrian Canencia, are lighted for nighttime play and are open to the public. Costs are a reasonable $6 per hour per court, or $7 for all day; nonguests pay $7 and $9 respectively. Other full-service amenities include laundry, free parking, beauty salon, babysitters, and no charge for children, regardless of age, if they share a room with their parents. The Kona Hilton keeps alive the tradition of quality service at a quality hotel.

King Kamehameha Kona Beach Hotel is located in downtown Kailua-Kona at 75-5660 Palani Rd., Kailua-Kona, HI 96740, tel. 329-2911 or (800) 367-6060, on a spot favored by Hawaiian royalty; Kamehameha the Great spent the last days of his life here. It's one of the only Kona hotels that has its own beach, adjacent to the restored Ahuena Heiau. The walls of the lobby are lined with artifacts of ancient battles, and a hotel staff member gives historical and botanical tours of the grounds. Rooms (each with a/c, TV, refrigerator, safe, and phone), are appointed in shades of blue with rattan furniture, and each features a lanai with a sweeping panorama of the bay and Mt. Hualalai. Prices range from $105 for a standard room up to $500 for a three-bedroom suite, additional person $20, and children under 18 free when sharing their parents' room. The hotel features restaurants, a famous luau (see "Food" below), cocktail lounges, tennis courts, shops, and a pool.

The **Kona Surf Resort,** 78-128 Ehukai St., Kailua-Kona, HI 96740, tel. 322-3411 or (800) 367-8011, is located at Keauhou Bay, six miles south of Kailua-Kona. The building, comprised of four wings and lined with over $1 million worth of art, is architecturally superb. The impeccable hotel grounds are a magnificent match for the building and are open to the public (see "Sights" above). The hotel features the S.S. *James Makee* restaurant and nightly entertainment in their Puka and Poi Pounder rooms. All 535 rooms have a/c, phones, and TVs. Prices begin at $99 and go to $365 for a suite. There are two swimming pools, lighted tennis courts, and the Keauhou-Kona Golf Course next door, with special rates and starting times for hotel guests.

FOOD

Inexpensive

"So, budget traveler," you've been asking yourself, "which is the best restaurant in town, with the most food at the lowest prices, with that down-home atmosphere?" **The Ocean View Inn,** tel. 329-9998, is it! The gigantic menu of Chinese, American, Japanese, and Hawaiian food is like a mini-directory. Lunch and dinner range $6-12, and a huge breakfast goes for about $3.50. The most expensive dinner is T-bone steak at $12.95. They're open daily except Monday, 6:30 a.m.-2:45 p.m. and 5:30-9 p.m., with the bar open daily 6:30 a.m.-9 p.m. Located across from the seawall near the King Kamehameha Kona Beach Hotel, they're always crowded with local people, a sure sign that the food is good.

Stan's Restaurant, tel. 329-1655, is an open-air establishment one notch up in both price and atmosphere from the Ocean View Inn next door. Here you have a cocktail lounge and a stab at atmosphere with some cozy lighting and rattan furniture. Breakfast is pleasing, with an assortment of island-inspired hotcakes and a spe-

J.D. BISIGNANI

Many of Kailua-Kona's restaurants are found in shopping plazas like the "Waterfront Row."

cial for $3.95; no lunch is served. Dinner specials, starting at 5 p.m., are hibachi chicken or fillet of mahimahi $7.85, fresh island fish $9.95, and the captain's seafood dinner $11.50. All include salad, rice or whipped potatoes, fresh fruit, and dinner bread. However, the best items are their many Hawaiian foods like *kalua* pig and *lala poi* for under $5. The food is good, but not great, and you generally get a square meal for a very reasonable price.

The **Royal Jade Garden,** tel. 326-7288, open daily 10:30 a.m.-10:30 p.m., in the Lanihau Center, is a Chinese restaurant where you can get an amazing amount of well-prepared food for a moderate price. They have the normal run-of-the-mill chow meins for $5.50-7.50, noodle soups around $5, and meat dishes of chicken, duck, pork, or beef for $5.95-7.50. More expensive items include lobster with black bean sauce for $18.95, and a variety of fresh fish and seafoods for $8 and up. But they have an unbeatable special every night: you choose three entrees plus fried rice or fried noodles for only $5.50 (fewer choices less expensive). The food is pre-prepared and placed on a steam table, but it's not cooked to death. You wind up with so much food that the most difficult part is keeping it on your plate. In the Royal Jade there's no decor, but if you are hungry and on a tight budget, this is one of the best values in town.

Yuni's Special Korean Barbecue, tel. 329-3167, also at the Lanihau Center, open daily 9 a.m.-9 p.m., is a basic steam-table-type Korean restaurant where you can enjoy a variety of combo-plates from $4.75. Your choices include *kalbi* beef, barbecued short ribs, and Korean chicken. No decor, but the prices are right, and the dishes make a perfect picnic or lunch.

Kona's **old industrial area,** although it doesn't sound inviting, is a great place to find inexpensive food, along with stores where the *people* shop. To get to the industrial area, head for the airport, and about one minute north of the junction of Rt. 19 (the airport road) and Palani Road, make a left on Kaiwi Street. Or follow Kuakini Road, a major intersection off Palani Road just a minute from the seawall, to Kaiwi Street. The triangle formed by Kaiwi and Kuakini is primarily the old industrial area. The **French Bakery,** Kaahumanu Plaza, 74-5467 Kaiwi St., tel. 326-2688, open weekdays 5:30 a.m.-4 p.m., Saturday 5:30 a.m.-3 p.m., is a budget gourmet deli/restaurant where the food is great and the prices are low. Not only does it have the full range of pastries you would expect, it has wonderful sandwiches like pizza roll with cheese for only $1.25 and with ham or bacon for $1.50. All of the sandwiches are under $4, and the European-style coffee is full-bodied and rich.

Su's Thai Kitchen, in the industrial area (see above) at 74-5588A Pawai Pl. (just off Kaiwi St.), tel. 326-7808, open for lunch weekdays 11 a.m.-2:30 p.m. and for dinner nightly 5-9 p.m., is a semi-open-air restaurant with a distinctive touch of southeast Asia. You can sit inside, but choose a spot on the veranda, where there is absolutely no view but where the breezes blow and bamboo curtains are dropped for a feeling of privacy. The extensive menu offers a *pu pu* platter (a combination of all the appetizers including spring roll, shrimp, and chicken sauté served with homemade plum sauce and peanut sauce) for $10.95. Other choices are lightly breaded and pan-fried shrimp combined with fresh mint, lime juice, garlic, and kafir for $8.95; savory Thai soups mostly with a coconut base, with morsels of fish, scallops, or pork $6.95-9.95; salads $4.95-9.95; and a full selection of curries $7.95-9.95. Vegetarians will be happy with vegetable curry, vegetable stir-fry, or sweet-and-sour vegetables. The daily lunch special for $5.95 might be a mini *pu pu* platter; green curry with chicken and eggplant accompanied by a bowl of white rice; or yellow curry with chicken, potatoes, carrots, and onions with a bowl of white rice. The service is friendly, the portions large for the money. Su's is a favorite with local people—the highest recommendation.

A friendly gorilla greets you at the **Pot Belli Deli** (in the industrial area, see above) at 74-5543 Kaiwi St., tel. 329-9454, open weekdays 6 a.m.-4 p.m. The refrigerated deli case holds chicken, ham, or tuna salad sandwiches for $2.65; jumbos of all at $3.95; spinach pie $4.25; and bagels with cream cheese. The shelves hold all the condiments and extras you would need for a terrific picnic lunch. You can get your order to go, or eat at one of the few booths inside.

Tom Bombadill's menu takes its inspiration from Tolkien's Middle Earth, but its location is a lot noisier, perched over Ali'i Drive and overlooking the Hilton's tennis courts. They talk about the ocean view, but your neck will have to stretch like the mozzarella on their pizza to see it. The bar pours domestic beers at $2.50, imports at $3.50, and pitchers for $8.50. The menu includes all sorts of hamburgers for under $6; soups $3; and a variety of chicken, fish, and shrimp platters from $6.50. All of these meals are good, but the real specialty is pizza, from $9 up depending upon size and toppings. Open daily 11 a.m.-10 p.m., tel. 329-1292.

Harbor House, formerly Attilla's Bar and Grill, at the Honokohau Small Boat Harbor, tel. 326-4166, open daily 10:30 a.m.-8:30 p.m., features Kona's longest bar. Harbor House is more or less an open-air pavilion, but it is actually quite picturesque as it overlooks the harbor. If you are interested in a charter fishing boat, this is the best place to come to spin a yarn with the local skippers who congregate here nightly at about 4:30 p.m. Over the bar hangs a gigantic 1,556-pound marlin, almost as big as the Budweiser sign. Strategically placed TVs make it a good sports bar, and the jukebox has a great selection of oldies and contemporary tunes. A variety of draft beers from Steinlager to Coors Light come in 16-ounce chilled schooners for only $2.50, Heineken and Carlsburg $2.75. Sunday and Monday, the frothy schooners are only $2, with the same price daily during happy hour 3-6 p.m. The bill of fare offers grilled bacon cheeseburgers with fries for $6.50, shrimp and chips $6.75, crab-salad sandwich $5, clam chowder $3.25, and chili and rice $4.25. Try their delicious macadamia nut pie for $2.50. Harbor House is one of the truly *colorful* places in Kailua-Kona, and one of the best places to relax and have a hassle-free brew.

Giuseppe's, tel. 329-7888, in the Kailua Bay Inn Shopping Plaza at 75-5699F Ali'i Dr. across from the Kona seawall, open daily except Sunday for lunch 11:30 a.m.-3 p.m. and for dinner 5-9 p.m., serves dishes of savory pasta in a tiny but tasteful restaurant where you can dine in or take out. Lunch specials served until 4 p.m. range from spaghetti marinara for $4.95 to fettuccine with artichoke hearts for $6.25. Dinner is *delisioso* with choices like chicken Marsala $11.75 and scampi Mediterranean $14.25, which includes pasta, dinner salad, and a choice of cheese bread. The minestrone soup served all day for $3.25 per bowl is excellent. The menu is rounded out with a small selection of sandwiches and various dishes from the children's menu for only $3.95. Bring your own beer or wine. During the triathlon, Giuseppe's offers all the pasta you can eat for $10.

Ali'i Sunset Plaza, 75-5799 Ali'i Dr. across from the seawall at the south end of town, has a cluster of inexpensive to moderately priced restaurants that more or less cover the major international cuisines. **King Yee Lau,** tel. 329-7100, open Mon.-Sat. 11 a.m.-9 p.m., Sunday 4-9 p.m., offers an all-you-can-eat lunch buffet, and the usual Chinese dishes like pressed crisp duck, beef with ginger sauce, and shrimp with seasoned vegetables, all priced under $7.95. Vegetarians can dine on tofu with oyster sauce or a variety of chow mein for under $6.50. **Thai Rin,** tel. 329-2929, open weekdays for lunch 11 a.m.-2:30 p.m., dinner 5-9:30 p.m., weekends dinner only 5-9:30 p.m., fills the air in the small plaza with the aromas of its savory Thai spices. The menu offers spring rolls $4.95; fried noodles Chinese-style $6.95; vegetarian dishes like Thai fried rice $7.95; stir-fried chicken, beef, or pork $7.95; and Thai garlic shrimp or squid $8.95. Thai Rin features a variety of lunch specials for about $5.95. And for a fast snack and a smattering of Hawaiian fare, stop in at **Huli Huli Chicken,** where $5 will get you a plate lunch featuring island barbecued chicken.

Fast Foods And Snacks

At the Kona Inn Shopping Village, try one of the following. **Mrs. Barry's Cookies** are homemade yummies that include macadamia nut, chocolate chip, and peanut butter, gift boxed to send home. Follow your nose to the **Coffee Cantata** and drink a cup in the little courtyard. **Kona Kai Farms Coffee House** features a sampler cup of Kona coffee. **Be Happy Cafe** has plate lunches like beef stew, chicken garlic, teriyaki beef/shrimp combo, and chicken and fries for $5-6.

Around town, the **Bartender's Ocean Breeze** serves up 12-ounce mugs of ice-cold beer for $1 and grill-your-own burgers for $2.75. Other snacks are available on Ali'i Drive, near the Kona Hilton tennis courts, tel. 329-7622. **McGurk's** is a fill-er-up joint next door to Marty's Steak and Seafood in the Kailua Bay Inn Shopping Plaza in downtown Kailua-Kona. They serve an evening special like the Wednesday fish buffet for $6.95 that includes mac-nut coleslaw and French fries. Basically a takeout place with a limited sit-down menu, McGurk's isn't special, but the food is worth the money.

In the Kona Marketplace, **Chili by Max,** open Mon.-Sat. 10 a.m.-8 p.m., Sunday 11 a.m.-8 p.m., is famous for its award-winning oven-baked chili, made with beef or turkey. Also on the bill of fare are kosher hot dogs, chili dogs, chili nachos, baked potatoes, and ice cream.

Across Sarona Road from Kona Marketplace and down toward Kuakini Hwy. there's **Subway Sandwiches,** a chain selling double-fisted sandwiches to go. On Kuakini Hwy. next to **McDonald's** golden arches is a **7-Eleven,** open 24 hours, and along Palani Road is **Taco Bell,** next door to **Pizza Hut,** which is across the road from **Burger King.**

In the **Lanihau Center** along Palani Road, you can snack at **Gifu Bento,** a sidewalk cafe where you'll find a Japanese-style plate lunch for under $5. **Buns In The Sun,** open Tues.-Sat. 5 a.m.-5 p.m., Sunday 6 a.m.-5 p.m., Monday to 4 p.m., is a bakery-deli serving everything from croissants to apple turnovers. Also enjoy sandwiches priced $3.75-6.50 while sitting at a few wrought-iron tables under their outdoor canopy. The center also houses **Kentucky Fried Chicken** and **Penguin's Frozen Yogurt** (where you can order a smoothie).

Rocky's Pizza, tel. 322-3223, open daily 11 a.m.-9 p.m. at the Keauhou Shopping Village, offers whole pizzas for $9.95-14.95 or slices for $1.75 each. Rocky's also features delicious sub sandwiches like hot pastrami on crusty bread; they are favorites with the locals who like good food at a good price.

In the **Kopiko Plaza,** along Palani Road and just down from the Lanihau Center, you'll find **Cynthia's Hawaiian Kitchen** for inexpensive local foods; **Kaminari's,** a cafeteria-style Japanese restaurant with affordable prices; **Domino's Pizza,** for eat in, takeout, or delivery; **Mask,** a bar and grill so new it hasn't developed a personality yet; and **Kona Mix Plate** for inexpensive plate lunches.

The **Kona Coast Shopping Center,** also along Palani Road, has a number of small local and ethnic restaurants where you can get inexpensive but savory meals. **Kim's Place,** open weekdays 10 a.m.-8 p.m., Saturday 10 a.m.-4 p.m., closed Sunday, tel. 329-4677, features takeout and catering, and has a few tables with umbrellas; enjoy Korean items like *kalbi, pulgogi,* Korean chicken, and even tempura. Prices for most items are under $5. For the health-conscious, **Kona Health Ways,** open Mon.-Fri. 9 a.m.-7 p.m., Saturday 9 a.m.-6 p.m., Sunday 9:30 a.m.-5 p.m., is a full-service health food store that makes ready-to-eat sandwiches, salads, and soups geared toward the vegetarian. **Mother India,** also in the mall, serves chicken curry $4.95, lamb curry $5.95, chicken biriani $5.95, and mixed vegetables $4.95. The best place to eat, however, is **Bianelli's,** an Italian pizzeria and more (see under "Moderate" below).

The Kona Square Shopping Center is home to the very inexpensive **Stumble Inn.** They have breakfast specials for $1.99, and a lunch special. Unfortunately, there is little that's special about their food, but they are open at 5:30 a.m. for those going fishing who need a very early breakfast.

On your way to Pu'uhonua O Honaunau (see "Honalo to Captain Cook and Vicinity" under "Central and South Kona" later in this chapter) you might consider stopping at **Barry's Nut Farm** along Rt. 160. They'll give you a free tour of the gardens and nursery, or you can browse for pottery or buy sandwiches and drinks. Open daily 9 a.m.-5 p.m., tel. 328-9930.

Moderate

Cafe Sibu, in the Kona Banyan Court, open daily 11:30 a.m.-9 p.m., tel. 329-1112, is an Indonesian restaurant serving savory marinated meats and vegetables spiced with zesty sauces and flame grilled. The restaurant, across from the seawall under the big banyan tree, has only a few outside tables, and makes a light attempt at decor with a few antique Indonesian masks and *wayang* (Indonesian puppet theater) puppets hanging on the walls. They do, however, win the prize for the most ventilated restaurant in all of Hawaii, with nine ceiling fans whirring in a 10- by 10-foot room! To make the menu even more varied, the Italian owner offers a daily pasta dish, using recipes over 100 years old that have been handed down by her grandmother. *Delizioso!* If you're hungry, go for the *gado gado* for $9.50, an Indonesian salad layered with spices and peanut sauce that can be dinner for one or a salad entree for two or three. Stir-fried vegetables with chicken or tofu are $9.95; chicken and vegetable curries are $10.50 and $8 respectively; and Balinese chicken marinated in tarragon, garlic, and spices is $10.95. The combination plates are the best deals: you get a stir-fry, chicken curry, and choice of sauté for $11.95. Lunch prices on all of the above are about $2 cheaper. Cafe Sibu serves *the* best and *the* most interesting moderately priced food in Kailua-Kona.

The **Kona Ranch House** is a delightful restaurant with something for everyone. It has two rooms: the family-oriented Paniolo Room, where hearty appetites are filled family style; and the elegant Plantation Lanai, where both palate and sense of beauty are satiated. This restaurant, highlighted by copper drainpipes, brass ceiling fans, wicker furniture, and latticework, all against a natural wood-and-brick background, epitomizes plantation dining. The Kona Ranch House is a classy establishment where you get more than what you pay for. Prices range from reasonable to expensive, and the menus in the two separate rooms reflect this. Open daily 6:30 a.m.-10 p.m., and Sunday for brunch. Reservations are needed for the Plantation Lanai. The restaurant is located two minutes from downtown at the corner of Kuakini Hwy. and Palani Road, tel. 329-7061.

The **Jolly Roger,** walking distance from downtown at 75-5776 Ali'i Dr., tel. 329-1344 (formerly the Spindrifter), is another Kona restaurant with a remarkable seaside setting. The gently rolling surf lapping at the shore is like free dessert. Full breakfasts are served 6:30 a.m.-noon and start at $4, with waffles and pancakes cheaper. Lunch is served 11 a.m.-4 p.m., dinner 5:30-10 p.m. Sandwiches start at $3; assorted salads are $5; full salad bar is $5.95; and entrees of fresh fish, seafood, and beef are from $10. Happy hour daily, 11 a.m.-6 p.m., features an assortment of *pu pu.* A daily special of steak and eggs Benedict, available 6:30 a.m.-noon, costs $4.75. The decor is bent bamboo with puffy cushions, and the tile-floored veranda has marble-topped tables and white wrought-iron chairs.

Banana Bay Buffet, tel. 329-1393, is located in the courtyard of Uncle Billy's downtown Kona Bay Hotel. Following in the semi-plastic Polynesian tradition of Uncle Billy, they serve a fair to passable buffet for $8.95. A stuffed marlin, seemingly too huge and colorful to be real, gazes down at everyone from the wall. Sometimes free hula shows are part of the bargain. Open daily at 6:30 a.m. (breakfast specials $4.95), this restaurant could be an "old reliable" with a touch more care in the food preparation.

Reuben's Mexican Cafe, open daily 11 a.m.-11 p.m., Sunday 3-11 p.m., tel. 329-7031, is tucked away in the downtown Kona Plaza and serves up hefty portions of south-of-the-border fare at good prices. There's a full menu, from *chiles rellenos* to *huevos rancheros,* all $5-7. The only "slam" against Reuben's is that the dishes are a bit too tame. Reuben's does have the best prices on imported beers—offering Dos Equis, Corona, and Heineken for only $2.

Marty's Steak and Seafood House, open daily for lunch 11 a.m.-3 p.m., dinner 5-10 p.m., tel. 329-1571, was a former Buzz's Steak House. They serve hefty orders of chops, steaks, fresh fish, and Korean-style barbecued ribs for under $15. Fresh, hot bread and the salad bar are filling and priced reasonably. A nightly buffet special of barbecued beef-back ribs is $12.95, while crab is $21.95. Sunday nights bring a special of prime rib for $10.95, or a larger cut at $13.95. Marty's has reliable quality and is located upstairs in the Kailua Bay Inn Shopping Plaza. The atmosphere in this open and airy perch overlooking the bay is congenial.

Don Drysdale's Club 53, open daily 10 a.m.-2 a.m., tel. 329-6651, is owned by the famous Dodger pitcher, and in the good sense of the word can best be described as a saloon. The amiable bar and grill serves reasonably priced beer, drinks, and sandwiches until 1 a.m. Sports fans away from home can always catch their favorite events on the bar's TV. Fare includes soup and salads from $2.50, a wide variety of *pu pu* from $4, sandwiches $3-5, plus the special peanut-butter cream pie at $2.35. Drysdale's is one of the most relaxing and casual bars in town, overlooking the bay at the Kona Inn Shopping Village.

Cafe Calypso, tel. 349-5550, along Ali'i Drive just near the pier, is open 11 a.m.-4 p.m. for lunch, and 4-9 p.m. for dinner. The koa-covered menu offers a full range of appetizers from $5.95, with one of the most outstanding being escargots with special garlic herb butter topped with melted cheese. For light but inexpensive meals, choose the homemade soup and dinner salad for $5.50, or roasted garlic chicken atop tossed Caesar salad for $7.50. The Calypso's grill cooks a special Calypso burger, a monster made from a half pound of fresh ground beef, grilled onions, and melted jack cheese, served with the works and fries for $6.95. The Calypso Natural is made from fresh avocado, tomato, cucumber, carrots, red onion, lettuce, sprouts, and French bread, and is served with French fries or salad greens for $5.95. Among the best entrees are grilled chicken linguine with tomato, mushrooms, garlic, fresh basil, and virgin olive oil; and boneless breast of chicken fixed with papaya wedges and bay shrimp swimming in a special curry sauce. Each is $9.95. The Calypso, with its soothing, semi-open-air dining room, is a well-established Kona favorite and well worth the money.

Quinn's is Kona's socially eclectic bar and grill where everyone from local bikers to pink-roasted tourists are welcomed. It's also a roost for nighthawks who come here to munch and have a beer when everything else in town is closed. Quinn's, across from the King Kamehameha Kona Beach Hotel, is open daily for lunch 11 a.m.-5:30 p.m. and dinner 5:30 p.m.-1 a.m. (Sunday until 10 p.m.), tel. 329-3822. The local in-crowd comes to the patio for sandwiches, vegetarian specialties, and seafood. The inside bar is cozy, friendly, and sports oriented. For lunch, a gigantic mound of shrimp and crab salad for $8.95 is wonderful. The fresh catch-of-the-day sandwiches with salad for $7.75 are a deal, but they're not always available. Reasonably priced specialties include tenderloin tips sautéed in brandy with onions for $8.95, shrimp and chips for $8.95, and fish and chips for $6.95. Dinner entrees are savory: sautéed scallops $15.95, chicken stir-fry $12.95, and fresh catch sautéed or baked for $18.50 up. All include soup or dinner salad, vegetable, rice, and Quinn's homefried potatoes.

When you enter the Kaloko Industrial Park, just past mile marker 97 heading north from Kailua-Kona, the setting makes you think you're after plumbing supplies. What you'll find is terrific food prepared by one of Hawaii's greatest chefs, at **Sam Choy's Restaurant,** tel. 326-1545, open weekdays 5 a.m.-2 p.m., Saturday 6:30 a.m.-2 p.m., and Wed.-Sat. 5-9 p.m. for dinner, reservations suggested. To get there, make a right along the main road as soon as you enter the industrial park, and pass a gas station (a good place to fuel if you're returning your rental car to the airport). About 50 yards past the gas station, make a left and look for Sam's in a nondescript gray building halfway up the hill on the right. The atmosphere is pleasant enough, but those in the know who have dined on Sam's sumptuous creations, either here or at the Hilton (where he used to be executive chef), come for the food! Breakfasts like the ultimate stew omelette (a three-egg omelette filled with Sam's beef stew) $6, steak and eggs $7.95, or the local favorite of fried rice and egg for $3.50 will keep you going most of the day. The regular menu also includes fresh island fish prepared *poke* style and then flash-fried for $5.95; Kaloko steak marinated in teriyaki sauce with grilled onions $7.95; and Kaloko noodle mania (chow mein noodles cooked with fresh vegetable and meat and served in a crispy wonton ball) for $6. Or try one of the specials, such as fresh *ahi* sauté $6.75. Local people also come here for the lunch favorites like deep-fried breaded shrimp for $6, or homemade beef stew for $5.50. For a gourmet dinner, choose oriental lamb chops with shiitake mushrooms $14.95, vegetable pasta $16.95, macadamia nut chicken breast grilled with papaya and pineapple compote $12.95, or stuffed shrimp Christopher and broiled fillet of beef at $17.95, all with soup and salad. Sam prepares wonderful food, and being a dad himself, he doesn't forget the kids—they have their own menu.

Calling **Bianelli's** "just a pizza shop" is like calling a Ferrari "just a car." Although they make pizza, and it is superb, they also have a full deli counter and plenty of delicious lunch and dinner entrees, all of which they deliver. Bianelli's has two locations, at the Kona Coast Shopping Center along Palani Road, tel. 329-1484, and at the Pine Plaza at 75-240 Nani-Kailua between Hualalai Road and the Kona Belt Road, tel. 326-4800. Specialty sandwiches like a Philly steak are scrumptious, and meals like manicotti, a variety of spaghetti dishes, and lasagna are all well under $10. Bianelli's makes their own pizza dough, and they offer pizza pies ranging from $7.95 for a hand-tossed, New York-style mini-pizza to an exotic pie smothered in garlic and herb sauce, layered with Parmesan and buffalo-milk-mozzarella cheeses, and topped with whole peeled tomatoes and fresh herbs for around $15.95. Vegetarian pizza topped with artichoke hearts, eggplant, sun-dried tomatoes, and Maui onions costs about $14. The wine cellar is outstanding, with over 64 different selections ranging from California merlot to French pinot noir; prices range from about $14 to over $200 per bottle. Bianelli's also has a tremendous selection of domestic and imported beers. Open daily for lunch and dinner at the Palani Road location, and 4-10 p.m. at Pine Plaza, both restaurants are small but are tastefully decorated in Italian-American style with the mandatory red-checkered tablecloths. The food and service at both are excellent. *Delizioso!*

Kona Amigos, tel. 326-2840, across the seawall in downtown Kailua-Kona at 75-5669 Ali'i Dr., is open daily 11 a.m.-midnight. This bar and restaurant features Mexican cuisine, with special dishes like crab enchiladas for $13.50, or enchilada rancheros for $10.50. Less expensive but savory items include a fiesta tostada $8.75, *chiles rellenos* $10.50, and the Miss Manaloa (roasted pork rolled in a flour tortilla) $10.50. The Southwestern Caesar salad for $8.95 comes with either grilled chicken breast or grilled fresh fish. Sit on the veranda to people-watch or to survey the entire harbor area. In season, the Kona Triathlon starts and finishes in front of this restaurant.

Kaminari's, open Mon.-Sat. 5:30-9 p.m., tel. 326-7799, is an authentic and moderately priced Japanese restaurant located in the Kopiko Plaza along Palani Road just near the Lanihau Center. The decor is functional cafeteria style, and the menu includes *tempura tonkatsu donburi* (deep-fried shrimp, vegetables, and pork cutlet atop rice) $7; an assortment of *teishoku,* including soup, salad, pickles, and rice for $11.80; sashimi priced daily; Japanese-style steak $13.80; and yakitori (grilled chicken) $5.50.

Expensive

The **Lanai Restaurant** at the Kona Hilton Resort, tel. 329-3111, offers premier dining 5-9:30 p.m. in a magnificent setting. Executive chef Hiroshi Omori and his assistant chefs start you off with sashimi for $8.95, or jumbo shrimp cocktail for $7.95. Soups are Kona's best seafood chowder at $4.95, or old-fashioned Portuguese soup for $4.25, which you can combine with the gourmet salad bar for an excellent yet moderately priced meal. Seafood, from sautéed mahimahi Eurasian style (tender white fillets of seasoned fish sautéed in shiitake mushroom shoyu butter sauce) to sizzling lobster tail, comes with rice pilaf and fresh vegetables. Entrees include prime rib $19.95 and pineapple smoked pork loin $12.95. The phenomenally hungry can order the Ali'i Platter (not on the menu, daily quote), which comes laden with sashimi, shrimp, crab claws, sirloin steak, chicken macadamia, *kalua* pig, chicken *sate,* sliced lobster, and a personal beach boy or two to help lift you from your chair. Choose a table in the richly appointed dining room, or perch on the veranda for an outdoor setting. A remodeling done in 1985 lifted the floor 12 inches so that everyone is ensured a spectacular view through the wraparound windows. The Hilton's Sunday champagne brunch is considered the best in Kailua-Kona by local people (see "Expensive" under "Accommodations" above). Seatings are 9 a.m.-12:30 p.m., with reservations strongly recommended. The Kona Hilton's Lanai Restaurant offers truly fine dining in an elegant hotel. If you're into something simpler in a casual setting, try the hotel's **Lanai Coffee Shop,** open daily for breakfast, lunch, and dinner. The breakfast menu ranges from steak and eggs for $9.85 to Belgian waffles smothered in nuts, berries, and fresh fruits for $7.25. Lunch could be an assortment of burgers and sandwiches priced under $8, or a crisp chef salad laden with ham, roast beef, and turkey for $7.75.

Oui oui monsieur, but of course we have zee restaurant *Français.* It is **La Bourgogne,** tel. 329-6711, open Mon.-Sat. 5:30-10 p.m., located in Kuakini Plaza South, five minutes from downtown Kailua-Kona along Rt. 11. Guy Chatelard, the original owner of La Bourgogne, has recently sold the restaurant to master chef Ron Gallagher and his manager wife Colleen Moore. Guy stayed on for a transition period, sharing his recipes and food philosophy with Ron and Colleen, who are dedicated to keeping up the fine service and cuisine. For those who just can't live without escargots, shrimp Provençal, or pheasant, you've been saved. How much? Plenty, *mon petit!* Cold and hot appetizers include *pâté du chef* for $6, jumbo shrimp cocktail for $10.50, and mussels baked in garlic butter for $6. Soups of the day are scrumptious: French onion at $4.50, and homemade lobster soup when available at $5.75. For salads, order greens with Roquefort dressing at $3, or Caesar salad for two at $8. Titillating seafood and poultry entrees feature fresh catch-of-the-day $18.50; jumbo shrimp in butter, parsley, and garlic sauce $21; and sliced breast of roast duck with lemon-orange sauce $15. Meat courses are delectable roast saddle of lamb with creamy mustard sauce $26, or veal in creamy white wine and mushroom sauce $25. Top off your gourmet meal with fresh, made-in-house desserts. This restaurant, small and slightly out of the way, is definitely worth a visit for those who enjoy exceptional food.

Jameson's-by-the Sea (formerly Dorian's), tel. 329-3195, open weekdays for lunch 11 a.m.-2:30 p.m. and dinner every night 5:30-10 p.m., is located at 77-6452 Ali'i Dr. next to Kona Magic Sands Condo. Jameson's makes a good attempt at elegance with high-backed wicker chairs, crystal everywhere, white linen table settings, and a back-lit fish tank in the entry. The sea foams white and crashes on the shore just outside the restaurant's open windows. The quality of the food is very good, but just shy of gourmet. The bar serves domestic beer for $2.75, imported beer $3.50, well drinks $3, and exotics $5, which you can take to the veranda with some *pu pu* to enjoy the sunset. The lunch menu lists appetizers like sashimi, salmon pâté, fried calamari, and shrimp cocktail, all from $7.95. Jameson's Yokohama soup, which is a hearty fish soup with fresh spinach and cream at $4, could complement a dinner salad for around $3.75 to make a light meal. Lunch sandwiches are hearty fish of the day, grilled ham and cheese, or teriyaki steak for around $8. A number of seafood Louie salads made with crab, shrimp, or other seafood cost around $10. The dinner menu offers the same appetizers but adds a seafood platter with sashimi, shrimp, and fresh oysters for $9.50. The dinner entrees range from fresh catches like *opakapaka, ono,* and mahimahi at market price, to fried shrimp and scallops with oyster sauce and Chinese pea pods for $16.95. Other full meals include filet mignon with béarnaise sauce for $21.95, veal picatta $21.95, and sesame chicken $15.95. There's also shrimp curry with mango chutney for $16.95. For dessert save room for their assortment of homemade chiffon pies from $4.50.

At **Huggo's Restaurant,** tel. 329-1493, on Ali'i Drive next door to the Kona Hilton, it's difficult to concentrate on the food because the setting is so spectacular. If you were any closer to the sea, you'd be in it, and of course the sunset is great. Because it is built on a pier, you can actually feel the floor rock. When you are having dinner, ask the waitperson for some bread between courses so that you can feed the fish. Huggo's is open Mon.-Fri. 11:30 a.m.-2:30 p.m. for lunch and 5:30-10 p.m. for dinner, with entertainment most nights (see "Entertainment and Activities" below). Waiters and waitresses are outfitted in alohawear, and the heavy wooden tables are inlaid with maps of the Pacific. Huggo's executive chef, John Halligan, and the head chef, Peter Bartsch from Switzerland, have created a combination of continental, Hawaiian, and Pacific Rim cuisine that is extraordinarily good, and affordable. Lunch is reasonable, with tasties like Huggo's club; or a spicy, hot Italian sandwich prepared with pepperoni and aged Italian salami, Greek olives, and tomatoes for under $9. Huggo's burgers are around $8 and include the classic Huggo (with onions and mushrooms and your choice of Swiss or American cheese), the garden burger (a nonmeat patty with all the trimmings), the fresh-catch burger (priced daily), and the teriyaki chicken burger. Lunch salads include the Kona Caesar for $7.25 and the Chinese chicken salad for $7.50. Meat-lovers must try Huggo's "almost world famous" barbecued ribs with beans for $7.95—more on your plate than you can eat—served only on Tuesday and Thursday. The dinner menu is superb and starts with fresh sashimi (which can be seared on request) about $9; escargot $8.95; and seafood chowder made from clams and fresh fish and seasoned with sherry, cream sauce, and butter, a reasonable $3.50 per cup or $5.25 per bowl. The best entrees come from the sea just outside the door and are priced daily at around $22. A fantastic selection is the stuffed fish, delicious with an exotic blend of tender bay shrimp and Dijonaise sauce. The Korean shrimp at $19.95, or the oriental surprise sautéed in a spicy sauce, are also excellent. Huggo's has been in business for over 25 years, and is consistently outstanding. Enjoy free *pu pu* Mon.-Fri. 4-6 p.m. while sipping a cocktail as the red Kona sun dips into the azure sea.

S.S. *James Makee*, tel. 322-3411, is a fancy continental restaurant at the Kona Surf Resort. The nautical decor is commemorative of the restaurant's namesake, an old island steamer. The limited menu includes shrimp Kamehameha, teriyaki steak, various veals, and filet mignon. Fresh fish of the day is always well prepared and a good choice. A major part of the minimum $20 per person dining experience is the atmosphere. Open daily for dinner at 6 p.m. by reservation only—of course, matey!

The Kona Inn Restaurant at the Kona Inn Shopping Village, tel. 329-4455, open daily for lunch and dinner, is a lovely but lonely carryover from the venerable old Kona Inn. Part of the deal for tearing down the Kona Inn and putting up the Kona Inn Shopping Village was giving the restaurant a prime location. On entering, notice the marlin over the doorway and a huge piece of hung glass through which the sunset sometimes forms prismatic rainbows. The bar and dining area are richly appointed in native koa and made more elegant with a mixture of turn-of-the-century wooden chairs, high-backed peacock thrones, polished hardwood floors, and sturdy open-beam ceilings. If you want to enjoy the view, try a cocktail and some of the *pu pu* served all day, or try one of the light choices like guacamole and chips $5.95, pasta and chicken salad $7.95, shrimp salad $8.95, or a six-pack of oyster shooters $6.95. Lunch is reasonable: steak sandwich $10.95, or Hawaiian chicken sandwich on whole-wheat bun with pineapple and cheese $6.95. The dinner menu starts with Boston or Manhattan chowder $2.95, and mixed green salad of crisp romaine tossed with Caesar dressing and topped with bay shrimp for a very reasonable $3.95. The specialties are local fish like *ono, ahi, opakapaka,* or mahimahi for around $20; and seafood pasta topped with shrimp, scallops and mussels for $18.95. Less expensive selections include stir-fried chicken for $13.95, and chicken chardonnay (chicken lightly sautéed with chardonnay, simmered in a Dijon cream sauce, and served over fettuccine with leeks and mushrooms) for $15.95. The Kona Inn Restaurant epitomizes Kona beachside dining and the view is simply superb.

Adjacent is **Fisherman's Landing,** tel. 326-2555, open daily for lunch 11:30 a.m.-5 p.m. in the Captain's Deck section, and dinner 5-10 p.m. in the main dining section. You walk down a cobblestone pathway to a group of five Hawaiian dining huts separated by koi ponds and wooden bridges. A bronze cannon sits in a reflecting pool, while a gigantic blue marlin is a still-life billboard promising fresh seafood within. The decor is tasteful: glass fishing floats, bronze lanterns, and bamboo tables and chairs. Entrees at Fisherman's Landing (dinner only) feature fresh catch-of-the-day to $22.95, lobster tail $24.95, scampi Alfredo $17.95, top sirloin $14.95, New York steak $17.95, and shrimp tempura $19.95. Lunch specials served under large shade umbrellas in the open-air Captain's Deck are cold peel-and-eat shrimp $7.95, skipper's chicken salad and soup $6.95, teriyaki beef skewers $6.95, and pasta with calamari $7.95. There are also plenty of Asian selections. Oyster shooters at $1.95 are great when washed down with mugs of beer. Create your own entertainment every Wednesday 9 p.m.-midnight with *karaoke,* or dance to the live music of Sugar Sugar, Sun.-Thurs. 7:30-11:30 p.m. Fisherman's Landing is a perfect Kona restaurant for a relaxing and romantic evening.

Philip Paolo's, tel. 329-4436, in Waterfront Row at 75-5770 Ali'i Dr., is run by Tim O'Higgin—a true Italian if there ever was one. It is open for lunch daily 11 a.m.-2 p.m., and for dinner at 5:30 p.m. Savory selections include antipasto for two at $11.95, minestrone soup for $3.95, and specialty salads that could make a meal, like scallops, crab, and shrimp marinated in olive oil, garlic, and fresh herbs for $10.95. For lunch, try garlic cheese bread for $2.95, tropical salad $6.95, angel-hair Caesar salad $6.95, hot sandwiches like grilled chicken $7.95, or pasta dishes like linguine with clam sauce $5.95. Dinners are served with pasta sautéed in garlic, olive oil, and fresh herbs. The menu suggests dinner specials for $9.95 that include pasta primavera or angel-hair pasta, served with mushrooms and Maui onions sautéed in spinach-and-cream sauce. Other suggestions are fresh island chicken breast with lemon butter sauce for $12.95, or all-you-can-eat spaghetti with zesty marinara sauce sautéed with fresh tomatoes, onions, olive oil, basil, garlic, and Parmesan cheese for $12.95. More expensive dishes are soft-shell crab for $24.95, veal parmigiana $21.95, chicken parmigiana $15.95, or the house specialties like fettuccine Giuseppe (meat sautéed in creamy garlic butter and onions) $18.95. The extensive wine list offers varietals from Italy, France, Australia, and California. The large room is appointed with open-beam ceilings joined by distinctive copper couplings, and Casablanca fans.

Also in Waterfront Row, the **Chart House,** tel. 329-2451, open daily for dinner 5-10 p.m., is part of a small chain of restaurants that have built a good reputation for service, value, and well-prepared food. Primarily, they are a steak and seafood house with most meals costing $16-25. The location is very pleasant, away from the street noise and with a good view of the sea.

Kanazawa-tei, tel. 326-1881, open for dinner daily except Sunday, 6-9:30 p.m. (call to confirm lunch openings), is at 75-5845 Ali'i Dr. across from the Kona Hilton. The Japanese restaurant and sushi bar boasts chefs brought over from Japan. Specialties include sukiyaki, teriyaki, and tempura. The dinner menu lists appetizers like *age* tofu $3.95, small tempura $7.45, and butterfish *misoyaki* $9.95. Evening *bento* are extensive; the *Kanazawa-tei bento* includes tempura, sashimi, *yakimoto, nimono,* rice, miso soup and *tsukemono* for $25.50. Other *bento* are Japanese-style steak for $22.95, *sushi moriwase* (assorted sushi) $25.50, and teriyaki chicken $12.25. Kanazawa-tei is an authentic and gourmet Japanese restaurant.

The Continent meets Asia on a Pacific island by way of the magnificent creations of master chef Daniel Thiebaut at the **Palm Cafe,** Coconut Grove Marketplace, 75-5819 Ali'i Dr., tel. 329-7765, open daily 5:30-10 p.m., reservations suggested. Perched above Ali'i Drive, with the sea in the distance, the restaurant has an elegant interior comfortably done in a soothing green-on-green motif with high-backed chairs, linen tablecloths, large louvered windows, and subdued lighting. Start with seared *ahi* served on a bed of crisp leeks and jicama stir-fry $7.50, or Chinese ravioli stuffed with ground pork, shiitake mushrooms, balsamic vinegar, and ginger butter sauce. Salads range from Big Island field greens with Portuguese sweet bread and croutons for $5.50 to the Palm Cafe Caesar for a very reasonable $4.50. Vegetarians will be pleased with vegetable and tofu tempura $16.50, or timbale of vegetables with a Hawaiian chili curry sauce and brown rice $15. The fresh fish dishes are the best, whether prepared with lemon and cilantro butter; Kona style, with ginger, green onions, shoyu, and hot peanut oil;

or with an elegant vinaigrette of Kau orange and *benishoga*. The fish itself is grilled or steamed; daily quote about $22. Another specialty is baked *ono* with almond sesame crust, papaya, and Kona tomato relish, made piquant with ginger lime sauce. The wine selection is superb and can be counted on to complement the meal perfectly. To top off your meal, choose one of the devilish pastry selections, and end with the Earl Gray Tea liqueur.

The **Kona Beach Restaurant,** tel. 329-2911, at the King Kamehameha Kona Beach Hotel, is open daily for breakfast, lunch, and dinner and is especially known for its Sunday brunch served 9 a.m.-1 p.m. Appetizers include crab cakes for $6.95 and sashimi medley $7.95, while entrees range from *kiawe*-smoked prime rib of beef at $17.95 to barbecued baby-back ribs for $13.95. More moderately priced pastas are made scrumptious with Cajun prawns or sautéed with herbs and spices. Fresh catch or broiled salmon combined with prime rib is $19.95. Hearty luncheon sandwiches are reasonably priced—served with French fries for under $8. The restaurant itself is tasteful, but the best feature is an unobstructed view of the hotel's beach, especially fine at sunset.

Luaus, Buffets, Etc.

The **Keauhou Beach Hotel Buffet,** tel. 322-3441, at the hotel's Ocean Terrace, is legendary. People in the know flock here especially for the *Seafood Prime Rib Buffet* for $19.95, children $9.95, served Fri.-Sun. 5-9 p.m. Fill your plate again and again with Alaskan snow crab legs, prime rib (excellent), seafood Newburg, sautéed mahimahi, fresh teriyaki marlin, deep-fried oysters, New England clam chowder, sashimi, *poki,* and boiled shrimp. They also have a great dessert bar with Boston cream pies, strawberry shortcake, rich double-chocolate carrot cake, and banana cream pie. A Chinese buffet is offered Mon.-Thurs. for $12.95, children $8.95, and features roast duck, dim sum, Mandarin salad, and a medley of Cantonese and Sichuan selections. The restaurant has a beautiful view of the coast, and dinner is rounded off with live nightly entertainment.

The **Kona Hilton Luau,** tel. 329-3111, held every Monday, Wednesday, and Friday at the hotel's Coconut Grove, offers an authentic evening of entertainment and feasting, Hawaiian style. The *imu* ceremony begins at 6 p.m. and is followed by an open bar, lavish buffet, and thrilling entertainment for three fun-filled hours. Many supposedly authentic luaus play-act with the *imu*-baked pig, but here it is carved and served to the guests. Prices are $36 adults, $20 children under 12, with reservations strongly recommended.

A sumptuous feast is held at the **Kona Village Resort,** just north of Kailua-Kona (see "Practicalities" in the South Kohala chapter). It's worth attending this luau just to visit and be pampered at this private hotel beach. Adults pay around $40, children under 12 half-price. Held every Friday, by reservation only, tel. 325-5555. The *imu* ceremony is at 6 p.m., followed by no-host cocktails; the luau and Hawaiian entertainment begin at 8 p.m. Also, limited reservations are accepted during the week for lunch, dinner, and special dinners and buffets.

The **King Kamehameha Kona Beach Hotel,** tel. 329-2911, sways with Hawaiian chants during its famous luau held every Sunday, Tuesday, Wednesday, and Thursday. The pig is placed into the *imu* every morning at 10:15 a.m. and the festivities begin in the evening with a lei greeting at 5:30 p.m. and a torch-lighting *imu* pageant at 6:15 p.m. Cocktails flow 6-8 p.m.; the luau dinner is served 6:30-9 p.m. Prices are $45 adults, $15 children 6-12. Reservations are required. **Kona Beach Restaurant,** tel. 329-2911, also at the King Kamehameha Kona Beach Hotel (see above) features a breakfast buffet at $7.95, Mon.-Sat. 6:30-10:30 a.m., Sunday to 9:30 a.m. As good as the breakfast buffet may be, the restaurant is very famous for its **King's Brunch,** served Sunday 10 a.m-1 p.m., $19.95 adults, $9.95 children 6-12. The long tables are laden with fruit, vegetables, pasta salad, peel-and-eat shrimp, omelettes, waffles, hot entrees from fresh catch to sashimi, and desserts so sinful you'll be glad that someone's on their knees praying at Sunday services. Every night of the week brings a different theme buffet for around $15.95 where you can always count on tempura, shrimp, and prime rib as part of the offerings. Weekends are special because of the scrumptious seafood buffet.

Captain Beans' Dinner Cruise departs Kailua Pier daily at 5 p.m. and returns at 8 p.m.

You are entertained while the bar dispenses liberal drinks and the deck groans with all-you-can-eat food. And you get a terrific panorama of the Kona Coast from the sea. You can't help having a good time on this cruise, and if the boat sinks with all that food and booze in your belly, you're a goner—but what a way to go! Minimum age is 21 years, $30 includes tax and tip. Reservations suggested; call 329-2955.

ENTERTAINMENT AND ACTIVITIES

Kona nights come alive mainly in the restaurants and dining rooms of the big hotels. The most memorable experience for most is free: watching the sunset from Kailua Pier, and taking a leisurely stroll along Ali'i Drive. All of the luaus previously mentioned have "Polynesian revues" of one sort or another, which are generally good, clean, sexy fun, but of course these shows are limited only to the luau guests. For those who have "dancin' feet" or wish to spend the evening listening to live music, there's a small but varied selection from which to choose. **Note:** The hotels and restaurants listed below have been previously mentioned in either the "Accommodations" or "Food" sections, so please refer there for addresses and directions.

Around Town

Huggo's Restaurant, with its romantic waterfront setting along Ali'i Drive features music 8:30 p.m.-12:30 a.m. The entertainment changes nightly; *karaoke* on Tuesday features Juni Maderas. Excellent local bands like Mango, Nightlife, and Kona Blend offer smooth Jahwaiian and other mellow contemporary sounds with a touch of rock now and again.

The **Keauhou Beach Hotel** soothes you with easy listening, Hawaiian style, nightly at their famous buffet. Weekends bring live bands like Holua, and Nightlife who will rock you with everything from original tunes to classic Hawaiian numbers. Also, Uncle George Naope, a renowned *kumu hula,* delights audiences with members of his local dance troupe on the Kuakini Terrace, Friday 11 a.m.-1:30 p.m. and again 5:30-9:30 p.m., Saturday 5:30-9 p.m., Sunday 10 a.m.-1 p.m. (usually!).

At the **Kona Surf Resort** a quiet piano tinkles in the S.S. *James Makee* Restaurant 6-11 p.m., or you can glide around the dance floor in the Puka Bar to live music 9 p.m.-closing. More yet! The Poi Pounder Nightclub beats out "top 40" dancin' tunes Tues.-Sat. 9 p.m. until the wee hours.

At the **Kona Hilton** piano bar you can enjoy happy hour 4:30-6 p.m. with free *pu pu* while listening to the mellow piano, which begins at 4:30 p.m. and goes until closing. Windjammer Lounge, an open-air bar, features jazz on Sunday, the contemporary sounds of the Silk and Steel band Mon.-Wed., and The Fortunes, a blues and rock 'n' roll band Thurs.-Saturday. Music nightly 8:30 p.m.-closing.

In downtown Kailua-Kona you can pick your fun at the **King Kamehameha Kona Beach Hotel.** Here, the Billfish Bar has live entertainment nightly 6-10:30 p.m., featuring mellow Hawaiian music by Hapalaka. The bar is open 10:30 a.m.-10:30 p.m. with happy hour 5-7 p.m.

Around town, the **Eclipse Restaurant** has dance music 10 p.m.-1:30 a.m. every night. **Jolly Roger Restaurant** offers a variety of live music throughout the week beginning at 8:30 p.m. At the **Keauhou-Kona Golf Course Restaurant** you can enjoy live contemporary Hawaiian music performed by local artists every evening from 7 p.m. For a quiet beer, sports talk, or just hanging out with the local people try **Quinn's, Drysdale's, Ocean View Inn,** or **Sam's Hideaway,** all in downtown Kailua-Kona.

At **Fisherman's Landing Restaurant,** *karaoke* is presented every Wednesday 9 p.m.-midnight. They also have live music and dancing nightly to the tunes of Sugar Sugar, a local dance band; Fri.-Sat. 6-9 p.m. a solo musician plays a mixed bag of country, classic rock 'n' roll, and Hawaiian music.

The Tech, one of Kailua-Kona's newest discos and hangouts, is open nightly on the premises of the Poo Ping Restaurant II. The restaurant is located at Kamehameha Square, a small shopping mall a few minutes from town along Kuakini Hwy. leading to the airport. It draws a younger, local crowd, but is friendly and what's happening now.

For movies try the **World Square Theater** in the Kona Marketplace or the **Hualalai Theater** in Kailua-Kona.

The **Aloha Theater** in Kainaliu (see "Accommodations and Food" under "Central and South Kona" later in this chapter) has a semi-professional local repertory company, the Aloha Community Theater. It puts on plays about six times per year that run for about three weeks each. Showtime in the completely refurbished and well-appointed theater is usually 8 p.m., and admission is a very reasonable $8 (senior discount). Check the local newspaper or the HVB office, or look for posters here and there around town.

SHOPPING

Shopping Note

Below is an overview of Kona-area malls, including a general idea of what they contain. For specific shops see the sub-categories following, i.e., "Markets, Health Food Stores, Bookstores, Specialty Shops."

Kailua-Kona Malls

The Kailua-Kona area has an abundance of two commodities near and dear to a tourist's heart: sunshine and shopping malls.

One of the largest malls in Kailua is the **Kona Inn Shopping Village** at 75-5744 Ali'i Drive. This shopping village boasts more than 40 shops selling fabrics, fashions, art, fruits, gems and jewelry, photo and music needs, food, and even exotic skins.

The **Kona Marketplace** in central Kailua-Kona offers a variety of shops selling everything from burgers to bathing suits. The **Kona Banyan Court,** also in central Kailua-Kona, has a dozen shops with a medley of goods and services. Distinctive shops include: **Kona Fine Woods** for souvenir-quality woodcarvings; **Unison,** a surfing shop with T-shirts, sandals, hats, and boogie boards; and**South Sea Silver Company,** whose name says it all. The most impressive shop in the complex is **Big Island Jewelers,** tel. 329-8571, open Mon.-Sat. 9 a.m.-9 p.m., Sunday 10 a.m.-6 p.m., owned and operated by brothers Flynn and Gale Carpenter, master goldsmiths. The shop motto, "Have your jewelry made by a Carpenter," applies to custom-made jewelry fashioned to their or your personal design. **Big Island Jewelers,** in business for over 10 years, does repairs and also carries a full line of pearls and loose stones that they will mount into any setting you wish. You'll also find **Kailua Bay Inn Shopping Plaza** along Ali'i Drive and **Akona Kai Mall** across from Kailua Pier.

The **King Kamehameha Kona Beach Hotel Mall,** fully air-conditioned, features a cluster of specialty shops and a Liberty House. One excellent shop is **Kona Kapa,** which features beautiful hand-stitched Hawaiian quilts and less expensive items like throw pillows. Open Mon.-Sat. 9 a.m.-6 p.m., Sunday 9 a.m.-5 p.m., tel. 326-7119, the shop also sells koa wood items from carvings to jewelry boxes. One distinctive item is a koa wood whale that folds out to form a serving bowl. Also in the mall are **Gifts For All Seasons** (jewelry), **Jafar** (high fashion), and **Tots and Teens** (clothes for children).

The **Lanihau Center,** tel. 329-9333, at 75-5595 Palani Rd., is one of Kailua-Kona's newest shopping meccas. It offers **Longs Drugs** for sundries and photo supplies; an assortment of restaurants (see "Food"); apparel and shoe stores including **Feet First; Waldenbooks,** an excellent all-purpose bookstore; **Radio Shack** for electronic gizmos of all sorts; and **Zac's Photo,** a very friendly and professional photo store (see "Photo Needs" below).

Kopiko Plaza, along Palani Road just down from the Lanihau Center, is a small mall containing **J.R.'s Music Shop,** where you can purchase records, tapes, and CDs of your favorite artists; **Scott's Knife Center** for a fine piece of cutlery from a carving knife to a Swiss Army knife; **Wall Art and Frame;** a video store; and **Action Sports** for the largest selection of sporting equipment in town. The mall also has a smattering of inexpensive restaurants, both for takeout and eat-in (see "Fast Foods and Snacks" above).

Waterfront Row is a relatively new shopping and food complex at the south end of downtown Kailua-Kona. Built of rough-cut lumber, it's done in period architecture reminiscent of an outdoor promenade in a Boston shipyard at the turn of the century. **Pacific Vibrations,** a surf shop, sells everything from postcards to hats, backpacks, and aloha shirts. **Pleasant Hawaiian Holidays** maintains a booth here from where you can book a wide range of activities. **Crazy**

Kona's best treats are available from roadside stands.

Shirts sells unique island creations, and **Kona Jack's** offers distinctive unisex apparel featuring its logo. Restaurants include the **Chart House** for steaks and seafood, **Philip Paolo's** for Italian cuisine, and **Jolly Roger** for American and Hawaiian cuisine (see "Food" above).

Rawson Plaza, at 74-5563 Kaiwi St., is just past the King Kamehameha Kona Beach Hotel in the industrial area. This practical, no-frills area abounds in "no-name" shops selling everything you'll find in town but at substantial savings.

Kona Coast Shopping Center along Palani Road features **Pay 'n Save** for sundries and everything from scuba gear to styrofoam coolers; **KTA Market** (see below); the **Undercover Shop,** with fine lingerie; **Hallmark Cards;** and a smattering of clothing, accessory, and shoe stores.

South Of Kailua Malls

If, god forbid, you haven't found what you need in Kailua, or if you suddenly need a "shopping fix," even more malls are south on Rt. 11. **Keauhou Shopping Village** is at the corner of Ali'i Drive and Kamehameha III Road. Look for flags waving in the breeze high on the hill marking the entrance. This mall houses apparel shops, restaurants, a post office, and photo-processing booths. You can find all your food and prescription needs at **KTA Supermarket,** the largest in the area. **Keauhou Village Bookshop** is a full-service bookstore. **Kona-kai Cafe,** an espresso and coffee shop open daily 8:30 a.m.-6 p.m., will take care of your sweet tooth and drooping energy; you can also buy a pound or two of fresh Kona coffee there. **Drysdale's** is an indoor/outdoor bar and grill where you can relax over a cold beer or choose from their extensive sandwich menu. Other shops include: the **Showcase Gallery,** for glassware, paintings, ceramics, and local crafts; and **Alapaki's,** for island goods from black coral jewelry to colorful muumuu.

Continuing south on Rt. 11, you'll spot the **Kainaliu Village Mall** along the main drag.

Food Markets, Etc.

KTA Market is generally the cheapest market in town and is located at the Kona Coast Shopping Center along Palani Road. They're well stocked with sundries; an excellent selection of Asian foods, fresh vegies, fish, and fruit; and a smattering of health food that's mixed in with the usual food items. Sugar Pops and *kimchi,* anyone? **KTA Supermarket,** open Mon.-Sat. 8 a.m.-10 p.m., Sunday 8 a.m.-9 p.m., is at the Keauhou Village Mall, at the extreme south end of Ali'i Drive at its junction with Kamehameha III Road. You can save time and traffic hassles by shopping here. The market also offers a full-service pharmacy.

Across the road, **Sack 'n' Save,** in the Lanihau Center, open 24 hours, is one of the main supermarkets in town.

Kona Wine Market, in the small Kamehameha Square Shopping Center, 75-5626 Kuakini Hwy., tel. 329-9400, open daily 10 a.m.-8 p.m., Sunday noon-4 p.m., is the best wine shop on the Kona coast. They feature an impressive international selection of wine and varietals from California, Italy, Spain, France, Chile, and Australia. Prices range from $4.95 for a table wine to $200 for a bottle of select boutique wine. A large cooler holds a fine selection of beer, both domestic and imported, and the store shelves hold wonderful gourmet munchies like Indian chutney, Sicilian olives, mustards, dressings, marinades, smoked salmon, hearty cheeses, and pasta imported from Italy.

Casa De Emdeko Liquor and Deli is south of town center at 75-6082 Ali'i Drive. It's well stocked with liquor and groceries, but at convenience-store prices. Other markets include **King Kamehameha Pantry,** tel. 329-9191, selling liquors, groceries, and sundries; and **Keauhou Pantry,** tel. 322-3066, in Keauhou along Ali'i Drive, selling more of the same.

Health Food Stores

Kona keeps you healthy with **Kona Healthways** in the Kona Coast Shopping Center, tel. 329-2296, open Mon.-Fri. 9 a.m.-7 p.m., Saturday 9 a.m.-6 p.m., Sunday 9:30 a.m.-5 p.m. Besides a good assortment of health foods, they have cosmetics, books, and dietary supplements. Vegetarians will like their ready-to-eat sandwiches, salads, and soups. Shelves are lined with teas and organic vitamins. They also have a cooler with organic juices, cheeses, and soy milk. A refrigerator holds organic produce, while bins are filled with bulk grains.

Bookstores

Waldenbooks, in the Lanihau Center on Palani Road, tel. 329-0015, open Mon.-Thurs. 9:30 a.m.-6 p.m., Friday 9:30 a.m.-9 p.m., Sunday 10 a.m.-5 p.m., not only has the well-stocked and far-ranging selection this national chain has become famous for, but features an in-depth Hawaiiana collection and some Hawaiian music tapes.

In Kailua-Kona be sure to venture into **Middle Earth Bookshop** at 75-5719 Ali'i Dr., in the Kona Plaza Shopping Arcade, tel. 329-2123, open Mon.-Sat. 9 a.m.-9 p.m., Sunday to 6 p.m. This jam-packed bookstore has shelves laden with fiction, nonfiction, paperbacks, hardbacks, travel books, maps, and Hawaiiana. A great place to browse.

Keauhou Village Bookshop at Keauhou Shopping Village, tel. 322-8111, open Mon.-Sat. 9 a.m.-6 p.m., Sunday 9 a.m.-5 p.m., is a full-service bookstore with plenty of Hawaiiana selections, general reading material, a children's section, and a good travel guide section.

Photo Needs

Zac's Photo, in the Lanihau Center, tel. 329-0006, open daily 7 a.m.-9 p.m., develops prints in one hour and slides in two days. Zac, a native of Belgium, will even make minor camera repairs free of charge. Prices are very competitive and you can save more by clipping two-for-one and 20% discount coupons from the free tourist brochure, *This Week, Big Island.* **Longs Drugs,** in the same mall, also has excellent prices on film and camera supplies.

Ali'i Photo Hut, in the parking lot in front of Huggo's Restaurant along Ali'i Drive, open daily 7:30 a.m.-5:30 p.m., develops prints and rents underwater cameras. Rental rate is $17.95 for camera plus a roll of 36 exposures. A 20% discount on developing is offered with rental.

The **Kona Photo Center** in the North Kona Shopping Plaza, at the corner of Palani Road and Kuakini Hwy., tel. 329-3676, is open Mon.-Sat. 8 a.m.-6 p.m. It is a *real* photography store where you can get lenses, cameras, filters, telescopes, and binoculars. Their processing is competitive, and they offer custom developing.

Art And Specialty Shops

In the King Kamehameha Kona Beach Hotel, the **Kona Kapa** sells carvings, jewelry, and magnificent quilts (see "Expensive" under "Accommodations" above), while **The Shellery** lives up to its name with baubles, bangles, and beads made from shells, along with a selection of fine jewelry and pearls.

Island Togs, tel. 329-2144, is across from the Kona Beach Restaurant at the King Kamehameha Kona Beach Hotel. This long-established shop hidden from the main tourist gauntlet is known by the locals as one of the best places to purchase women's bathing suits and bikinis. They also feature very reasonable prices on resortwear, shorts, and an assortment of tops.

In the World Square Shopping Center visit **Coral Isle Art Shop** for modern versions of traditional Hawaiian carvings. You'll find everything from tikis to scrimshaw, with exceptionally good carvings of sharks and whales for a pricey $75 or so.

Enjoy the beauty of Hawaii with flowers from **Editha's Lei Stand,** located in front of Huggo's Restaurant (see above), open daily 10:30 a.m.-6 p.m. Editha creates lovely lei that run from $3.75 for a basic strand to $20 for a magnificent triple-stand. Editha also does fresh-cut flower arrangements, and she can arrange for shipment to the Mainland. Also in the parking lot in front of Huggo's Restaurant, along Ali'i Drive, look for a little truck business called **Nikki's** that sells Kona coffee at $8.49 per pound and macadamia nuts at $6.95 per pound, both decent prices.

At the **Kona Inn Shopping Village** you can buy custom jewelry at **Jim Bill's Gemfire.** Featured at the **T-shirt Company,** a.k.a. **Island Salsa,** are designer tee's that are some of the best in Kona. Prices are normally around $18, but they run specials all the time. You can pick up one-of-a-kind creations by Roberta, the owner/artist, for around $10. **Collectors Fine Art** is a perfect labyrinth of rooms and hallways showcasing the acclaimed works of international artists. Not a shop at which to buy trinkets; prices range $300-250,000 for some of the finer paintings and sculptures by internationally acclaimed artists. **Hula Heaven,** open daily 9 a.m.-9 p.m., is situated in a stone tower dating from 1927 and specializes in vintage Hawaiian shirts and modern reproductions. Prices range from $50 for the "look alikes" to $1000 for the rarest of the classics. Because many of the items on display date from the '40s and '50s, the shop is like a trip back in time. Another distinctive shop is **Crystal Visions** for incense, perfume, metaphysical books, and a large selection of crystals, crystal balls, and pyramids. A sign proclaims, "Shoplifting is bad karma," and a shop assistant claims that the owner looked at her *aura,* not her resume, when she was hired. Crystal Visions also stocks essential oils and small, handmade beaded bags for carrying your precious items. A unique item of interest to travelers might be the azurite spheres for expansion of consciousness and astral travel—in case you have lost your airline tickets or your flight has been delayed. If you're feeling low, and your cosmic vibrations need a boost, come in to Crystal Visions.

At **Kona Inn Flower and Lei** you can pick up flowers to add that perfect touch to a romantic evening. Nearby **Chrestel's Collectibles** has stuffed toys, stuffed pillows, and some clothing. **Kona Inn Jewelry,** for worldwide treasures, is one of the oldest and best-known shops for a square deal in Kona. Owned and operated by Joe Goldscharek and his family, they take time to help you choose just the right gift. Inside you'll find stained-glass hangings, jewelry, fine gemstones, and a collection of hand-painted fish. The family tries to pick unique items from around the world that can be found in no other Kona shop. Be aware that the shop is protected by Mama Cat, a sleeping ball of fur honored with her own postcard, who if you're not careful will purr you to death.

Other shops in the center include: **Flamingo's** for contemporary island clothing and evening wear mainly for women; **Big Island Hat Co.** for headgear ranging from pith helmets to sombreros; **The Treasury,** specializing in jewelry, T-shirts, beachwear, hats, sunglasses, backpacks, shoulder bags, and postcards; **Tahiti Fabrics,** offering bolts of cloth and a nice collection of Hawaiian shirts; **Alley Gecko's,** showcasing colorful gifts from around the world; and the **Old Hawaiian Gold Co.,** which can bedeck you in gold chains or pearl and coral jewelry.

At the **Kona Marketplace** in the downtown area, look for **Kona Jewelery,** specializing in fine jewelry and ceramics. Good for trinkets is **Kona Bazaar Affordables.** Or pick up a pair of eelskin cowboy boots at **Lee San's Eelskin.** The jam-packed **Aloha From Kona** specializes in baubles, bangles, postcards, handbags, and purses. In contrast is **Ali'i Nexus,** for fine jewelry, one of the nicest and most low-key shops in town. The **Kona Flea Market** stuck to the rear of the mall sells inexpensive travel bags, shells, beach mats, suntan lotion, and all the junk you could want. **Island Salsa** features original silk-screened T-shirts, alohawear for the entire family, women's evening wear, swimwear, and dinner clothes. **Goodies of Hawaii** sounds like a candy store but they actually sell beach towels, T-shirts, wind chimes, wooden postcards, distinctive beach bags, and a good selection of candles and ceramics.

Kona Gold, tel. 327-9373, in the Kailua Bay Inn Shopping Plaza, open daily except Sunday 9 a.m.-9 p.m., has excellent prices on custom-made jewelry by Harold Booton, the goldsmith and proprietor. Harold also imports jewelry from around the world, especially silver, and if it's not on sale, bargaining is definitely okay. The store stocks coral jewelry, a smattering of T-shirts, and lifelike wooden sculptures of whales and marine animals, many of which come from Indonesia. Kona Gold is a perfect shop in which to purchase a lifelong memento at a very reasonable price.

Alapaki's, at Keauhou Shopping Village (see "South of Kailua Malls" above), sells distinctive island arts and crafts. Inside you'll find pink, gold, and black coral jewelry; lei of shells and seeds; and *tutu* dolls bedecked in colorful muumuus. Distinctive items include koa bowls, each signed by the artist; and a replica of a Hawaiian double-hulled canoe made of coconut and cloth with traditional crab-claw sails. Original paintings by R.K. McGuire feature Hawaiian animals; basketry, fans, and jewelry made from ironwood needles are by local artist Barb Walls. Some of the finest artworks displayed are feather lei by Eloise Deshea and woodcarvings by Thomas Baboza.

For practical purchases at wholesale prices check out **Kona Jeans** for shirts, tops, footwear, and jeans, at 74-5576 Kaiwi Street. **Liberty House Penthouse** at Keauhou Shopping Village will appeal to bargain hunters. This outlet store sells items cleared and reduced from the famous Liberty House stores. You can save on everything from alohawear to formal dresses.

Kailua Candy Company, in the industrial section (see "Inexpensive" under "Food" above) on the corner of Kuakini and Kiawi, tel. 329-2522 or (800) 622-2462, is open weekdays 8 a.m.-6 p.m., weekends 10 a.m.-6 p.m. It was recognized as one of the "top 10 chocolate shops in the United States" in the February 1993 issue of *Bon Appetit* magazine. All the chocolates are made of the finest ingredients available, and all would try the willpower of Gandhi, but the specialty is the macadamia nut *honu,* Hawaiian for turtle. The best sampler is the one-pound Kailua Candy Company Assortment, hand-packed with a quarter pound each of *honu,* the award-winning Kona coffee swirl, dark macadamia nut clusters, and white coconut Mauna Kea snowballs. It costs $17.10, or $21 shipped anywhere on the Mainland. Shipping is available at the cost of postage plus $1 handling fee; shipments are guaranteed to be in perfect condition or they will be replaced free.

Two shops along Ali'i Drive, diagonally across from Hulihee Palace, are **Noa Noa,** featuring hand-painted, one-of-a-kind original clothing, mostly from Indonesia; and **Hawaiian Wear Unlimited,** where you can pick up alohawear for a very reasonable price. Just up the road, **The Glass Blower,** across from the seawall along Likana Lane, is a very interesting shop where you can watch the artist blow the glass. This shop is the perfect place to purchase a distinctive treasure. Next door is **Ululani Fresh Cut Flowers,** a reasonably priced lei stand. **Goodies** just up the alley has gift boxes of jams and jellies, Maui onion mustard, macadamia nuts, an assortment of coffees, and various perfumes and scents.

Real treasure hunters will love the **Kona Gardens Flea Market** held every Wednesday and Saturday 8 a.m-2 p.m. at the road fronting the Kona Botanical Gardens along Ali'i Drive. Unfortunately, this formerly huge flea market is now only a shadow of its former self and is always tottering on the brink of closure. The latest rumor has it moving to the old airport, so check.

SERVICES AND INFORMATION

Emergencies

For **ambulance and fire** assistance call 961-6022; for **police** in Kona communities call 323-2645; the **Kona Hospital** is in Kealakekua, tel. 322-9311. The most convenient **pharmacies** are Kona Coast Drugs in Kailua, tel. 329-8886; and Pay 'n Save Drugs, tel. 329-3577. For **alternative health care services and massage,** both well established in Kailua-Kona, see "Alternative Health Care" under "Information and Services" in the Big Island Introduction.

Information And Services

An **information gazebo** is open daily 7 a.m.-9 p.m. along the boardwalk in the Kona Inn Shopping Village. They can handle your questions about everything from dining to diving. The **Hawaii Visitors Bureau** maintains an office in the Kona Plaza, at 75-5719 Ali'i Dr., tel. 329-7787. The staff is friendly, helpful, and extremely knowledgeable about touring the Big Island. The **library** is at 75-140 Hualalai Rd., tel. 329-2196. The Hele Mai **laundromat** is at the North Kona Shopping Center, at the corner of Kuakini Hwy. and Palani Road, tel. 329-3494.

An excellent **tourist map** highlighting restaurants, accommodations, and businesses is available free at the HVB office and at many shops in Kona and throughout the Big Island. The map is published by the Island Map Company, 159 Kiawe St., Suite 1, Hilo, HI 96720, tel. 934-9007.

Banks, Post Office, Etc.

First Interstate Bank, tel. 329-4481, is at 75-5722 Kuakini Hwy.; **First Hawaiian Bank,** in the Lanihau Center on Palani Road, can be reached at tel. 329-2461; **Bank of Hawaii** maintains two area offices, one in Kailua at tel. 329-7033, the other in Kealakekua at tel. 322-9377. The main **post office** is on Palani Road, tel. 329-1927, just past the Lanihau Center. There is also mail service at the **General Store,** a market along Ali'i Drive in central Kailua-Kona. **Mail Boxes U.S.A.,** at the Lanihau Center, Palani Road, open weekdays 8:30 a.m.-6:30 p.m., Saturday to 3 p.m., provides Western Union, a notary public, typing service, money orders, gift wrapping, and the boxing and shipping of parcels.

BOB RACE

CENTRAL AND SOUTH KONA

Kailua-Kona's Ali'i Drive eventually turns up the mountainside and joins Rt. 11, which in its central section is called the **Kuakini Highway.** This road, heading south, quickly passes the towns of **Honalo, Kainaliu** ("Bail the Bilge"), **Kealakekua,** and **Captain Cook.** You'll have ample opportunity to stop along the way for gas, picnic supplies, or browsing. These towns have some terrific restaurants, specialty shops, and boutiques.

At Captain Cook, you can dip down to the coast and visit a working coffee mill, or continue south to **Pu'uhonua O Honaunau,** a reconstructed temple of refuge, the best in the state. Farther south still, little-traveled side roads take you to the sleepy seaside villages of **Hookena** and **Milolii,** where traditional lifestyles are still the norm.

Or for an alternative, instead of heading directly south out of Kailua-Kona on Rt. 11, take Hualalai Road (Rt. 182) to Rt. 180, a high mountain road that parallels Rt. 11 and takes you to the artist community of **Holualoa** from where you get an expansive view of the coastline below.

HOLUALOA

Holualoa ("The Sledding Course") is an undisturbed mountain community perched high above the Kailua-Kona Coast. Get there by taking the spur Rt. 182 off Rt. 11 from Kailua-Kona, or by taking Rt. 180 from Honalo in the south or from Honokohau in the north. Climbing Rt. 182 affords glorious views of the coast below. Notice the immediate contrast of the lush foliage here with the vegetation of the lowland area. On the mountainside, bathed in tropical mists, are tall forest trees interspersed with banana, papaya, and mango trees. Flowering trees pulsating in the green canopy explode in vibrant reds, yellows, oranges, and purples. If you want to get away from the Kona heat and dryness, head up to the well-watered coolness of Holualoa.

Practicalities

After you wind your way up Rt. 182 through this verdant jungle area, you suddenly enter the village and are greeted by **Kimura's Lauhala Shop,** open daily 9 a.m.-5 p.m., closed Sunday.

The shop, still tended by Mrs. Kimura and her daughters, Alfreida and Ella, has been in existence since 1915. In the beginning, Kimura's was a general store, but they always sold *lau hala* and became famous for their hats, which local people would make and barter to Kimura's for groceries. Only *Kona-side* hats have a distinctive pull-string that makes the hat larger or smaller. All *lau hala* weavings are done on the premises, while some of the other gift items are brought in. Choose from authentic baskets, floor mats, handbags, slippers, and of course an assortment of the classic sun hats that start at $35.

After Kimura's follow the road for a minute or so to enter the actual village, where the **post office** and a cross atop a white steeple welcome you to town. The tiny village, complete with its own elementary school, is well kept, with an obvious double helping of pride put into this artists' community by its citizens. Numerous art shops line the main street. Look for the **Holualoa Gallery,** open Tues.-Sat. 10 a.m.-5 p.m., a pottery studio where Matt and Mary Levine produce excellent *raku.* The shop also features paintings, prints, and wearable art. **Paul's Place,** a well-stocked country store, is open weekdays 7 a.m.-8 p.m., weekends 8 a.m.-8 p.m.

Along the main road is a converted coffee mill, gaily painted and decorated, and currently the home of the **Kona Art Center,** open Tues.-Sat. 10 a.m.-4 p.m., run by Robert and Carol Rogers. Uncle Bob and Aunt Carol, as they are affectionately known to many, have extensive backgrounds in art teaching. They moved from San Francisco to Holualoa in 1965 and began offering community workshop classes. Carol says, "I love Kona because we share, care, and love with our people here." Across the road is a restored building, a one-time country church rescued from the ravages of weather and termites, that now proudly displays the works of the center's members. In here you will find everything from hobby crafts to serious renderings that might include paintings, basketry, sculptures, and tie-dyed shirts. The center is very friendly and welcomes guests with a cup of Kona coffee. The building is rickety and old, but it's obviously filled with good vibrations and love. However, time moves on and things change. The building has been recently sold, and the new owners—who tried to cooperate with the center by keeping it housed here—were advised by a number of outside architects that the building is beyond saving and must be torn down. The idea is to replace it with a new center that will house a restaurant and various shops, and provide space for the art center in the rear. This is all in the planning stage.

Across the road from the Kona Art Center is **Vahlia's Flower Shop,** tel. 324-1421, open daily except Sunday 9:30 a.m.-4:30 p.m., specializing in tropical flower arrangements, mums, and fresh *maile* lei. The prices are excellent and they offer shipping to the Mainland and Canada.

Opposite the Holualoa Library is the **Country Frame Shop,** open Mon.-Fri. 9:30 a.m.-4:30 p.m., Saturday 9:30 a.m.-1:30 p.m. It specializes in framing, but also has prints by famous local artists. The owner, Chuck Hart, accepts credit cards and will ship anywhere. Check out the distinctive koa wood frames that add a special island touch to any artwork—especially that of **Kim Starr,** a famous island artist who recently moved to the Mainland but whose works still grace the walls here. The frame shop also showcases the splendid furniture of wood artist Ty Lake, who learned the rudiments of his trade by apprenticing to his dad, a master carpenter. Ty's high-backed chairs, tulip-legged tables, and stout sideboards in rich, hand-rubbed mountain koa sell for $700-5000. The Country Frame Shop is well worth a visit, if only to browse.

The premier shop in town, **Studio 7,** open Tues.-Sat. 10 a.m.-4 p.m., is owned and operated by Hiroki Morinoue, who studied at the Kona Art Center as a young man. The shop showcases Hiroki's work along with that of about 35 Big Island artists. Hiroki works in many media, but primarily does large watercolors or woodblock prints. Setsuko, Hiroki's wife, is a ceramicist and displays her work with about six other potters, including the famous Chiu Leong. Check out the "neoclassical" silkscreen by contemporary Japanese artist Hideo Takeda, one of seven contemporary Japanese printmakers represented in the shop. Affordable items include free-form bowls, signed by the artist, and wooden bracelets. To the rear of the shop is a wooden walkway over gray lava gravel that looks out

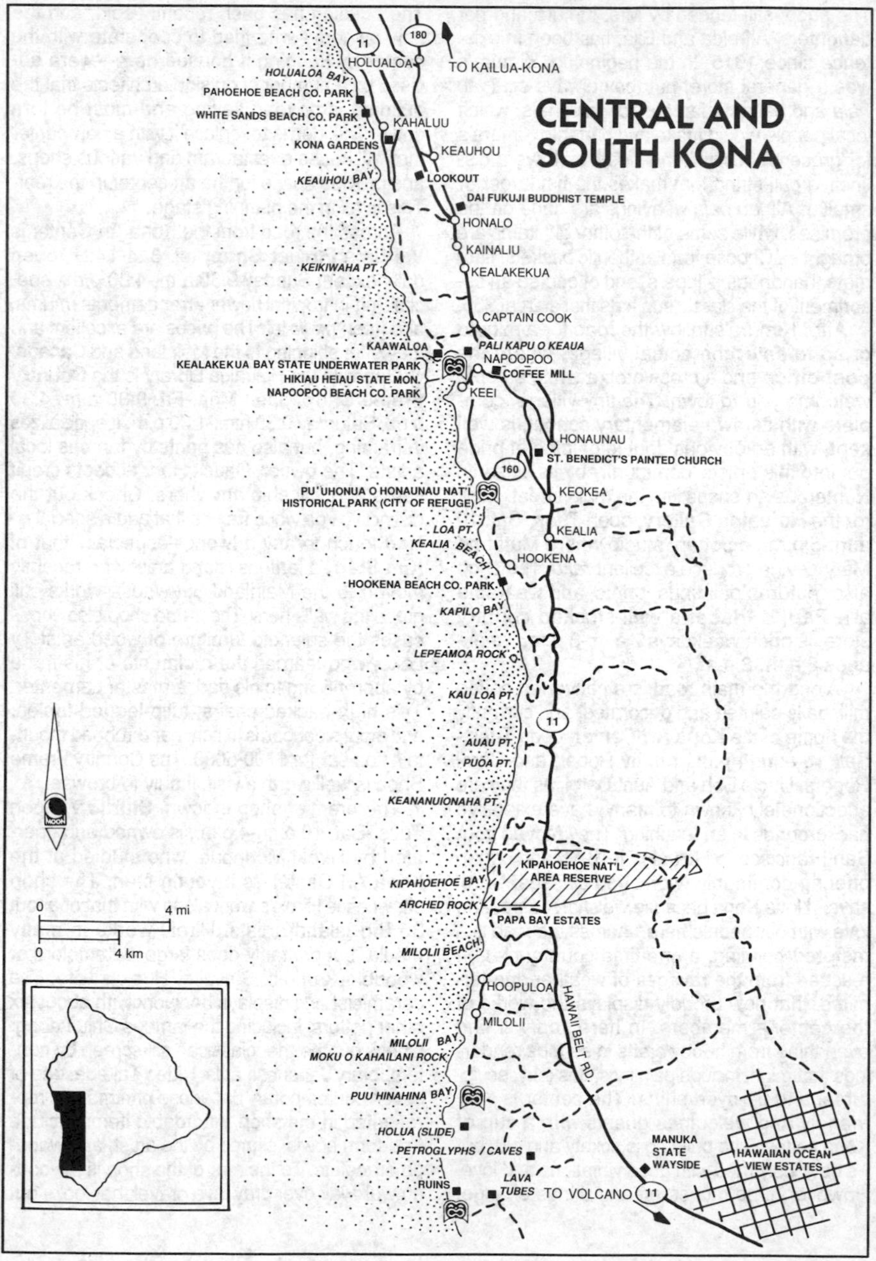

CENTRAL AND SOUTH KONA

11
180
HOLUALOA
TO KAILUA-KONA
HOLUALOA BAY
PAHOEHOE BEACH CO. PARK
WHITE SANDS BEACH CO. PARK
KAHALUU
KONA GARDENS
KEAUHOU
KEAUHOU BAY
LOOKOUT
DAI FUKUJI BUDDHIST TEMPLE
HONALO
KAINALIU
KEALAKEKUA
KEIKIWAHA PT.
CAPTAIN COOK
PALI KAPU O KEAUA
KAAWALOA
NAPOOPOO
KEALAKEKUA BAY STATE UNDERWATER PARK
COFFEE MILL
HIKIAU HEIAU STATE MON.
NAPOOPOO BEACH CO. PARK
KEEI
HONAUNAU
ST. BENEDICT'S PAINTED CHURCH
160
PU'UHONUA O HONAUNAU NAT'L HISTORICAL PARK (CITY OF REFUGE)
KEOKEA
LOA PT.
KEALIA
KEALIA BEACH
HOOKENA
HOOKENA BEACH CO. PARK
KAPILO BAY
LEPEAMOA ROCK
KAU LOA PT.
11
AUAU PT.
PUOA PT.
KEANANUIONAHA PT.
MOON
KIPAHOEHOE NAT'L AREA RESERVE
KIPAHOEHOE BAY
ARCHED ROCK
0
4 mi
0
4 km
PAPA BAY ESTATES
MILOLII BEACH
HOOPULOA
HAWAII BELT RD.
MILOLII
MILOLII BAY
MOKU O KAHAILANI ROCK
PUU HINAHINA BAY
HOLUA (SLIDE)
PETROGLYPHS / CAVES
MANUKA STATE WAYSIDE
HAWAIIAN OCEAN VIEW ESTATES
LAVA TUBES
RUINS
TO VOLCANO
11

onto a Japanese-style garden. It's worth the trip to Holualoa just to visit Studio 7.

A separate shop in the same building is **Goldsmithing by Sam Rosen.** Sam works mostly in gold, silver, and precious stones, but will work in coral if it's unusual. He can also supply the stones from his collection, which includes amazing specimens like malachite and polyhedroid, a quartz from Brazil. All works have a distinctive island theme.

The **Kona Hotel,** along Holualoa's main street, tel. 324-1155, primarily rents its 11 units to local people who spend the work-week in Kailua-Kona's seaside resorts and then go home on weekends. They are more than happy, however, to rent to any visitor passing through and are a particular favorite with Europeans. The Inaba family opened the hotel in 1926, and it is still owned and operated by Goro Inaba and his wife Yayoko, who will greet you at the front desk upon arrival. A clean room with bare wooden floors, a bed and dresser, and a shared bath down the hall goes for $18-28. Call ahead for reservations. No meals are served, but Mrs. Inaba will make coffee in the morning if you wish. The hotel is simple, clean, and safe.

The enticing aroma of rich coffee has been wafting on the breeze in this mountain community ever since the **Holuakoa Cafe,** owned and operated by Meggi Worbach, opened its doors in mid-1992. Just up the hill from the Kona Hotel, the cafe, open Mon.-Sat. 6:30 a.m.-5 p.m., Thursday 7-10 p.m. (hours vary) for live music, tel. 322-2233, serves wonderful sticky buns, bagels, muffins, and coffee and espresso from mocha frappés to double cappuccinos. Other offerings include smoothies, juices, and herbal teas. The cafe also serves as a revolving art gallery for local artists who may include Bob Smith, known for carving koa canoe paddles in the ancient tradition; and Pamela Coulton-Thomas, creator of distinctive postcards and a famous poster entitled *Shadow Dance.* The cafe displays a few boutique and souvenir items, including jewelry from Indonesia, perfume, massage oils, and a smattering of wooden art pieces. You can sit inside at a table, perch at the counter, or enjoy your coffee and pastry alfresco on the veranda, from where the two-block metropolis of Holualoa sprawls at your feet.

HONALO TO CAPTAIN COOK AND VICINITY

The following mountainside communities lie along a five-mile strip of Rt. 11, and if it weren't for the road signs, it would be difficult for the itinerant traveler to know where one village ends and the next begins. However, if you are after budget accommodations, unique boutique shopping, inexpensive island cuisine, and some off-the-beaten-track sightseeing, you won't be disappointed.

When leaving Holualoa, and if heading for Captain Cook and points south, stay on Rt. 180, the Mamalahoa Hwy., a gorgeous road that gives great views from the heights.

Note: The following are the sights that you will encounter along routes 180 and 11. For accommodations and food, and shopping in the villages along this route, see those sections following this one.

Fuku Bonsai Center

About three miles south of Holualoa on Rt. 180, you come to the Fuku Bonsai Gardens, open daily 8 a.m.-5 p.m., tel. 322-9222, offering a self-guided tour, $5 per person. A series of nine gardens over an improved path covers a 3.5-acre area and depicts the evolution of different types of bonsai, which traces its *roots* to ancient China. All plants are labeled. A souvenir shop allows you to purchase a living memento that can be shipped home. You can also follow the path to a ceramics studio, where artist-in-residence Jon Pacini creates earthy *raku.*

Near the Fuku Bonsai Center is a cutoff to Rt. 11, the main highway, but if you continue straight, you'll come to Keauhou and an understocked general store that for some inexplicable reason has a large inventory of bicycle parts. Open most days 9:30 a.m.-5 p.m., it's a good place to get a cold drink, and that's about it.

Honalo

This dot on the map is at the junction of routes 11 and 180. Not much changes here, and the town is primarily known for **Dai Fukuji Buddhist Temple** along the road. It's open daily 9 a.m.-4:30 p.m., free. Inside are two ornate altars; feel free to take photos but please remember to remove your shoes. There's a **Circle K** for sundries, food, and gasoline; and **Teshima's Inn and Restaurant,** an old standby for budget travelers (see "Accommodations and Food" below).

Royal Kona Coffee Mill And Museum

In the town of Captain Cook, **Napoopoo Road** branches off Rt. 11 and begins a roller-coaster ride down to the sea, where it ends at Kealakekua Bay. En route it passes the well-marked Royal Kona Coffee Mill. Along the way you can't help noticing the trim coffee bushes planted along the hillside. Many counterculture types have taken up residence in semi-abandoned "coffee shacks" throughout this hard-pressed economic area, but the cheap, idyllic, and convenience-free life isn't as easy to arrange as it once was. The area is being "rediscovered" and getting more popular. For those just visiting, the tantalizing smell of roasting coffee and the lure of a "free cup" are more than enough stimulus to make you stop. Mark Twain did! The museum is small, of the nontouchable variety with most exhibits behind glass. Mostly they're old black-and-white prints of the way Kona coffee country used to be. Some heavy machinery is displayed out on the back porch. The most interesting is a homemade husker built from an old automobile. While walking around be careful not to step on a couple of lazy old cats so lethargic they might as well be stuffed. Perhaps a cup of the local "java" in their milk bowl would put a spring in their feline step! Inside, more or less integrated into the museum, is a small gift shop. You can pick up the usual souvenirs, but the real treats are gourmet honeys, jellies, jams, candies, and of course coffee. Buy a pound of Royal Kona Blend for about $6, or 100% Royal Kona for around $10. Actually, it's cheaper at other retail outlets and supermarkets around the island, but you can't beat the freshness of getting it right from the source. Refill, anyone? The museum is open daily 8 a.m.-4:30 p.m., tel. 328-2511. Mailing address: Mauna Kea Coffee Co., Box 829, Captain Cook, HI 96704.

Kealakekua Bay

Continue down Napoopoo Road through the once-thriving fishing village of Napoopoo ("Holes"), now just a circle on the map with a few houses fronted by neat gardens. At road's end, you arrive at Kealakekua ("Road of the God") Bay. Relax a minute and tune in all your sensors because you're in for a treat. The bay is not only a **Marine Life Conservation District** with a fine beach and top-notch snorkeling (see "Napoopoo Beach County Park" below), but it drips with history. *Mauka,* at the parking lot, is the well-preserved **Hikiau Heiau,** dedicated to the god Lono, who had long been prophesied to return from the heavens to this very bay to usher in a "new order." Perhaps the soothsaying *kahuna* were a bit vague on the points of the new order, but it is undeniable that at this spot of initial contact between Europeans and Hawaiians, great changes occurred that radically altered the course of Hawaiian history.

The *heiau* is carved into the steep *pali* that form a well-engineered wall. From these heights the temple priests had a panoramic view of the ocean to mark the approach of Lono's "floating island," heralded by tall white tapa banners. The *heiau* platform was meticulously backfilled with smooth, small stones; a series of stone footings, once the bases of grass and thatch houses used in the religious rites, is still very much intact. The *pali* above the bay is pocked with numerous burial caves that still hold the bones of the ancients.

Captain James Cook, leading his ships *Resolution* and *Discovery* under billowing white sails, entered the bay on the morning of January 17, 1778, during the height of the Makahiki Festival, and the awestruck natives were sure that Lono had returned. Immediately, traditional ways were challenged. An old crew member, William Watman, had just died, and Cook went ashore to perform a Christian burial atop the *heiau.* This was, of course, the first Christian ceremony in the islands, and a plaque at the *heiau* entrance commemorates the event. On February 4, 1778, a few weeks after open-armed welcome, the goodwill camaraderie that had developed between the English voyagers and their island hosts turned sour, due to terrible cultural misunderstandings. The sad result was the death of Captain Cook. During a final conflict, this magnificent man, who had resolutely sailed and explored the greatest sea on earth, stood helplessly in knee-deep water, unable to swim to rescue-boats sent from his waiting ships. Hawaiians, provoked to a furious frenzy because of an unintentioned insult, beat, stabbed, and clubbed the great captain and four of his marines to death. (For a full accounting of these events, see "The World Discovers Hawaii" under "History" in the General Introduction.) A 27-foot obelisk of white marble erected to Cook's memory in 1874 "by some of his fellow countrymen" is at the far northern end of the bay. Another plaque is dedicated to Henry Opukahaia, a young native boy taken to New England, where he was educated and converted to Christianity. Through impassioned speeches begging for salvation for his pagan countrymen, he convinced the first Congregationalist missionaries to come to the islands in 1820.

The land around the monument is actually under British rule, somewhat like the grounds of a foreign consulate. Once a year, an Australian ship comes to tend it, and sometimes local people are hired to clear the weeds. The monument fence is fashioned from old cannons topped with cannon balls. Here too is a bronze plaque often awash by the waves that marks the exact spot where Cook fell. You can see the marble obelisk from the *heiau,* but actually getting to it is tough. Expert snorkelers have braved the mile swim to the point, but be advised it's through open ocean, and Kealakekua Bay is known for sharks that come in during the evening to feed. A rugged jeep/foot trail leads down the *pali* to the monument, but it's poorly marked and starts way back near the town of Captain Cook, almost immediately after Napoopoo Road branches off from Rt. 11. If you opt for this route, you'll have to backtrack to visit the coffee museum and the *heiau* side of the bay.

Kona Historical Society Museum

The main building of the Kona Historical Society Museum was originally a general store built in the mid-1800s by local landowner and businessman H.L. Greenwell using native stone and lime mortar made from burnt coral. Now on both the Hawaiian and national registers of historic places, the building served many uses, including the warehousing and packaging of sweet oranges raised by Greenwell, purported to be the largest, sweetest, and juiciest in the world. The Kona Museum, Box 398, Captain Cook, HI 96704, tel. 323-3222, is open weekdays 9 a.m.-3 p.m. and every second Saturday 10 a.m.-2 p.m.; admission is by donation. To get there, as you approach Kealakekua along Rt. 11, look on the right for a sign that reads "Kona Meat Company Market." Pull onto this road and follow it around to the back of the meat market, where you will find the parking lot for the museum.

The main artifact is the building itself, but inside, you will find a few antiques like a surrey and glassware, and the usual photographic exhibit with themes like coffee-growing—part of the legacy of Kona. The basement of the building houses archives filled with birth and death records of local people, photographs both personal and official, home movies, books, and maps, most of which were donated by the families of Kona. The archives are open to the public by appointment only. According to the director, Jill Olsen, the main purpose of the Historical Society is the preservation of Kona's history and the dissemination of historical information. Sometimes the society sponsors lectures and films (nominal charge), which are listed in the local newspapers. They also offer 4WD tours of the Kona area ($55) three times per year, usually in March, July, and November, and a historical boat tour in late January ($20) that takes you from Kailua-Kona south along the coast. There is no fixed schedule, but if you are in the area during those times of year, it would be well worth the trouble to contact the museum to find out if these excellent tours are being offered.

Napoopoo Beach County Park

Kealakekua Bay has been known as a safe anchorage since long before the arrival of Captain Cook and still draws boats of all descriptions. The area, designated a **Marine Life Conservation District,** lives up to its title by being an excellent scuba and snorkeling site. Organized tours from Kailua-Kona often flood the area with boats and divers, but the ocean expanse is vast and you can generally find your own secluded spot to enjoy the underwater show. If you've just come for a quick dip or to enjoy the sunset, look for beautiful, yellow-tailed tropic birds that frequent the bay. Napoopoo Beach County Park has full amenities, including showers, picnic tables, and restrooms.

Heading For Pu'uhonua O Honaunau

This historical park, the main attraction in the area, shouldn't be missed. Though it was once known as City of Refuge Park, the official name is coming into more use in keeping with the emergence of Hawaiian heritage. The best way to get here is to bounce along the four miles of coastal road from Kealakekua Bay. En route, you pass a smaller, more rugged road to **Keei;** this side trip ends at a black-sand canoe launch area and a cozy white-sand beach good for swimming. A channel to an underwater grotto has been sliced through the coral. On the shore are the remains of Kamaiko Heiau, where humans were once sacrificed.

The other, more direct way to Pu'uhonua O Honaunau is Rt. 160 at Keokea, where it branches off Rt. 11 at mile marker 104. Whether you are going or coming this way, make sure to take a five-minute side trip off Rt. 160 to **St. Benedict's Painted Church.** This small house of worship is fronted by latticework and with its gothic-style belfry looks like a little castle. Inside, a Belgian priest, John Berchman Velghe, took house paint and, with a fair measure of talent and religious fervor, painted biblical scenes on the walls. His masterpiece is a painted illusion behind the altar that gives you the impression of being in the famous Spanish cathedral in Burgos. Father John was pastor here from 1899 until 1904, during which time he did these paintings, similar to others he did in small churches throughout Polynesia. Before leaving, visit the cemetery to see its petroglyphs and homemade pipe crosses.

Pu'uhonua O Honaunau National Historical Park

The setting of Pu'uhonua O Honaunau couldn't be more idyllic. It's a picture-perfect cove with many paths leading out onto the sea-washed lava flow. The tall royal palms surrounding this compound shimmer like neon against the black lava so prevalent in this part of Kona. Planted for this purpose, these beacons promised safety and salvation to the vanquished, weak, and war-tossed, as well as to the *kapu*-breakers of old Hawaii. If you made it to this "temple of refuge," scurrying frantically ahead of avenging warriors or leaping into the sea to swim the last desperate miles, the attendant *kahuna,* under pain of their own death, had to offer you sanctuary. *Kapu*-breakers were particularly pursued because their misdeeds could anger the always moody gods, who might send a lava flow or tidal wave to punish all. Only the *kahuna* could perform the rituals that would bathe you in the sacred mana, and thus absolve you from all wrongdoing. This *pu'uhonua* ("temple of refuge") was the largest in all Hawaii, and be it fact or fancy, you can feel its power to this day.

The temple complex sits on a 20-acre finger of lava bordered by the sea on all sides. A massive, 1,000-foot-long mortarless wall, measuring 10 feet high and 17 feet thick, borders the site on the landward side and marks it as a temple of refuge. Archaeological evidence dates use of the temple from the mid-16th century, and some scholars argue that it was a well-known sacred spot as much as 200 years earlier. Actually, three separate *heiau* are within the enclosure. In the mid-16th century, Keawe, a great chief of Kona and the great-grandfather of Kamehameha, ruled here. After his death, he was entombed in *Hale O Keawe Heiau* at the end of the great wall, and his mana reinfused the temple with cleansing powers. For 250 years the *ali'i* of Kona continued to be buried here, making the spot more and more powerful. Even the great Queen Kaahumanu came here seeking sanctuary. As a 17-year-old bride, she refused to submit to the will of her husband, Kamehameha, and defied him openly, often wantonly giving herself to lesser chiefs. To escape Kamehameha's rampage, she made for the temple. Kaahumanu chose a large rock to hide under, and she couldn't be found until her pet dog barked and gave her away. Kaahumanu was coaxed out only after a lengthy intercession by Capt. George Vancouver, who had become a friend of the king. The last royal personage buried here was a son of Kamehameha who died in 1818. Soon afterwards, the "old religion" of Hawaii died and the temple grounds were abandoned but not entirely destroyed. The foundations of this largest city of refuge in the Hawaiian Islands were left intact.

In 1961, the National Park Service opened Pu'uhonua O Honaunau after a complete and faithful restoration was carried out. Careful consultation of old records and vintage sketches from early ships' artists gave the restoration a true sense of authenticity. Local artists used traditional tools and techniques to carve giant ohia logs into faithful renditions of the temple gods. They now stand again, protecting the *heiau* from evil. One of the most curious is a god-figure, with his maleness erect, glaring out to sea as if looking for some voluptuous mermaid. All the buildings are painstakingly lashed together in the Hawaiian fashion, but with nylon rope instead of traditional cordage, which would have added the perfect touch. Entrance to the park is $1, children under 16 free. Stop at the visitors center to pick up a map and brochure for a self-guided tour. Exhibits line a wall, complete with murals done in heroic style. Push a button and the recorded messages give you a brief history of Hawaiian beliefs and the system governing daily life. Educate yourself; the visitors center, tel. 328-2326, is open daily 7:30 a.m.-5:30 p.m. Rangers give tours 10 a.m.-3:30 p.m. The beach park section (see below) is open 6 a.m.-midnight. Follow the refuge wall toward the northwest to a large, flat rock perfect for lying back and watching the sun set.

Hookena

If you want to see how the people of Kona still live, visit Hookena. A mile or two south of the Pu'uhonua O Honaunau turnoff, or 20 miles south of Kailua-Kona, take a well-marked spur road *makai* off Rt. 11 and follow it to the sea. The village is in a state of disrepair, but a number of homey cottages and some semi-permanent tents are used mostly on weekends by local fishermen. Hookena also boasts a beach park with showers and picnic tables but no potable water or camping. For drinking water, a tap is attached to the telephone pole near the beginning of your descent down the spur road. The black-sand (actually gray) beach is broad, long, and probably *the* best in South Kona for both swimming and bodysurfing. If the sun gets too hot, plenty of palms lining the beach provide not only shade but a picture-perfect setting. Until the road connecting Kona to Hilo was finally finished in the 1930s, Hookena shipped the produce of the surrounding area from its bustling wharf. At one time, Hookena was the main port In South Kona and even hosted Robert Louis Stevenson when he passed through the islands in 1889. Part of the wharf remains, and nearby a fleet of outrigger fishing canoes is pulled up on shore. The surrounding cliffs are honeycombed with burial caves. If you walk a half mile north, you'll find the crumbled walls and steeple of Maria Lanakila Church, leveled in an earthquake in 1950. The church was another "painted church," done by Father John Velghe in the same style as St. Benedict's.

Milolii

This active fishing village is approximately 15 miles south of Pu'uhonua O Honaunau. Again, look for signs to a spur road off Rt. 11 heading *makai.* The road, leading through bleak lava flows, is extremely narrow but worth the detour. Milolii ("Fine Twist") earned its name from times past when it was famous for producing *'aha,* a sennit made from coconut-husk fibers; and *olona,* a twine made from the *olona* plant and best for fishnets. This is one of the last villages in Hawaii where traditional fishing is the major source of income and where old-timers are heard speaking Hawaiian. Fishermen still use small outrigger canoes, now powered by *outboards, to catch *opelu,* a type of mackerel that schools in these waters. The method of catching the *opelu* has remained unchanged for centuries. Boats gather and drop packets of chum made primarily from poi, sweet potatoes, or rice. No meat is used so sharks won't be attracted. In the village, a small, understocked store is operated by Willie Kaupiko, though the whole family pitches in. Milolii has a **beach park** that is a favorite with local people on the weekends. Technically, it's a county park (permit), but no one checks. Tents are pitched in and around the parking lot, just under the ironwoods at road's end. Notice that a number of them appear to be semi-permanent. There are flushing toilets, a basketball court, and a brackish pond in which to rinse off, but no drinking water, so bring some. Swimming is safe inside the reef and the tidepooling in the area is some of the best on the south coast. A 15-minute trail leads south to Honomalino Bay where a white-sand beach is secluded and great for swimming. But always check with the local people first about conditions!

ACCOMMODATIONS AND FOOD

Accommodations

So you came to Kona for the sun, surf, and scenery and couldn't care less about your room so long as it's clean and the people running the hotel are friendly? Well, you can't go wrong with any of the following out-of-the-mainstream hotels. They're all basic, but not fleabags. At all of these inexpensive hotels, it is very important to get your rooms first thing in the morning if you don't have reservations. They are very, very, tough to get into. People know about them, so the rooms are at a premium.

Manago Hotel in Captain Cook has been in the Manago family for 75 years, and anyone who puts his name on a place and keeps it there that long is doing something right. The old section of the hotel along the road is clean but a little worse for wearre and doesn't impress much because it looks like a storefront. Walk in to find a bridgeway into a garden area that's open, bright, and secluded away from the road. The rates with common bath are $22 s, $25 d, $28 t. First-floor rooms with private bath and lanai run $35 s, $38 d, $41 t. For $50-53, extra person $3, you're accommodated in the new wing, where you have a lanai and private bath and can train your eyes to catch the brilliance of the Kona sunset by practicing on the orange floor and pink furniture. Psychedelic! The views of the Kona Coast from the hotel grounds are terrific. You can dine in a restaurant in the old section, open for breakfast 7-9 a.m., lunch 11 a.m.-2 p.m., dinner 5-7:30 p.m., closed Monday, where people come from all over the island for the legendary pork chop dinners. For information, write to: Herald Manago, c/o Manago Hotel, Box 145, Captain Cook, Kona, HI 96704, tel. 323-2642.

Teshima's Inn, tel. 322-9140, is a small, clean, family-run hotel in the mountain village of Honalo at the junction of routes 180 and 11. Operated by Mr. and Mrs. Harry Teshima and family, it's somewhat like a Japanese *minshuku* with all rooms fronting a Japanese garden. To be sure of getting a room, call three days to a week in advance, and to reserve you must send at least one night's deposit. If you just turn up, you have a slim chance of getting one of the 11 rooms, five of which are generally rented long term. Check-in is at the restaurant section, which is closed 2-5 p.m., so time your arrival accordingly. The rooms, at $20 s, $30 d, $250-300 monthly, are spartan but very clean.

Howard and Marge Abert's B&B in Kealakekua, tel. 322-2405, is a friendly place where the home's ground floor is given over to the guests. Both former Peace Corps volunteers, the Aberts are now retired and have taken up tropical gardening, as well as opening their home to travelers.

The Dragonfly Ranch, Box 675, Honaunau, HI 96762, tel. 328-9570 or (800) 487-2159, owned and operated by David and Barbara Link, offers "tropical fantasy lodging" at a country estate. Rooms are remarkable and range from the "Hale in the Trees" to the "Honeymoon Suite" featuring an outdoor water bed. All rooms include a wet bar and refrigerator, private outdoor shower, cable TV, stereo, and small Hawaiiana library. Rates run $70 for a suite in the main house, $120 for the Redwood Cottage and Writer's Studio, and $160 for the Honeymoon Suite (substantial discounts for longer stays).

Food

All of the restaurants in this section happen to fall in the inexpensive range. None merits a special trip, but all are worth a stop if you're hungry when you go by. Some are great, especially for breakfast and brunch. For markets and health food stores, see "Shopping," below.

Teshima's Restaurant, tel. 322-9140, open daily 6:30 a.m.-1:45 p.m. and 5-9:30 p.m., at the junction of routes 11 and 180 in the mountain village of Honalo, is just like the small, clean, and homey Teshima's Inn that adjoins it. Here, in unpretentious surroundings, you can enjoy a full American, Hawaiian, or Japanese lunch for about $6.50, a filling daily special for $7, and dinner at $7.50-11. Another specialty is a *bento,* a box lunch for $5 that includes riceballs, luncheon meat, fried fish, teriyaki beef, *kamaboku* (fish cake), and Japanese roll. If you're interested in a good square meal, you can't go wrong.

Aloha Theater Cafe, open daily 8 a.m.-8 p.m., tel. 322-3383, is part of the lobby of the Aloha Theater in Kainaliu. The enormous breakfasts ($4-8) feature locally grown eggs, homemade muffins, and potatoes. Lunchtime sandwiches, $5-8.50, are super-stuffed with varied morsels from tofu and avocado to vegetarian tempeh burgers. There's also a variety of soups and salads and Mexican dishes like a quesadilla *especial* for $7.50. Full dinners like fresh *ahi* and *ono* are $13.95, filet mignon goes for $15.95, and pasta and shells are $12.95. For a snack choose from an assortment of homemade baked goods that you'll enjoy with an espresso or cappuccino. Order at the counter first (table service for dinner), and then sit on the lanai that overlooks a bucolic scene of cows at a watering trough, with the coast below. This is an excellent place to have breakfast or to pick up a picnic lunch on your way south. Also, check out the bulletin board for local happenings, sales, services, and the like.

The **Korner Pocket Bar and Grill,** tel. 322-2994, serving lunch and dinner weekdays 11 a.m.-10 p.m., until midnight Friday and Saturday, is a family-oriented/friendly biker bar where you can get excellent food at very reasonable prices. To get here, turn left off Rt. 11 in Kealakekua onto Halekii St. between the 76 gas station and McDonald's, and look for the Korner Pocket in the small shopping center on the left. Start with *pu pu* like twice-baked potato for $1.50, calamari strips $4.25, chicken hot wings $4.95, and chilled shrimp cocktail $5.95. Grill selections are a poolroom burger $4.95, mahimahi sandwich $5.50, or scrumptious bistro burger of grilled beef on crusty sourdough topped with fresh mushrooms sautéed in wine garlic sauce $6.50. Dinners are tempting: garlic scampi $12.95; chicken *aiko* accented with zesty Japanese sauce of lemon, apple, laurel, and spices; and prime rib eight ball, their encore entree at $10.95. The complete bar is well stocked with wines and spirits, or you can wash down your sandwich with an assortment of draft beers. The Korner Pocket looks as ordinary as a Ford station wagon, both inside and out, but the food is surprisingly good, and the owners, Paul and Judy, are very friendly.

Just beyond **McDonald's** golden arches as you enter Kealakekua, look for the **Canaan Deli,** a luncheonette with an Italian flair. The owners, Gigi and Guy Gambone, hail from Philadelphia, and bring the "back East" deli tradition of a lot of food for a little money along with them. You can't go wrong with a Philly cheese-steak sub for $5.50, or a 12-inch lunch pizza for only $6. All sauces, breads, and the pizza dough are homemade.

There are very few places in Captain Cook where you can get a meal. On the right as you enter town is a takeout restaurant with barbecued ribs, chicken, hot biscuits, coleslaw, and salad. You can also try **Hong Kong Chop Suey** in the Ranch Center, which is as basic as can be with most items at $5, including sides. Also, try the legendary pork chop dinner served at the **Manago Hotel** restaurant in downtown Captain Cook (see "Accommodations" above).

SHOPPING

Kainaliu

Badass Coffee Company, tel. 322-9196, open daily 7:30 a.m.-6 p.m., is a coffee and espresso bar where they roast their own beans on the premises in a *Royal No. 4 Roaster* manufactured in 1910, probably the last operational roaster of its type left in the state. Pure Kona coffee of the best grade sells for $9.95 per pound. After watching the roasting, take your cup of coffee and a homemade pastry to the rear of the shop, where you'll find an indoor stone grotto area away from the noise of the street.

Crystal Star Gallery specializes in cosmic vibrations and how to get in tune with them. You can feel the vibes as soon as you walk into this lavender-and-purple shop stocked with alluring crystals for channeling and massage, plus crystal balls and two racks filled with new-age books.

The Blue Ginger Gallery, tel. 322-3898, open Mon.-Sat. 9 a.m.-5 p.m., showcases the art of owners Jill and David Bever, as well as artists' works from all over the island. David creates art pieces in stained glass, fused glass, and wood. The small but well-appointed shop brims over with paintings, ceramics, sculptures, woodworking, and jewelry. A rack holds one-of-a-kind clothing items like sarongs and aloha shirts. Jill paints on silk, creating fantasy works in strong primary colors. The Blue Ginger Gallery is a perfect place to find a memorable souvenir of Hawaii.

Formerly at the south end of town in the C.H. Aina Shopping Center, the **Ohana O Ka Aina Food Co-op** is now located in a little shopping strip called Mango Court in Kainaliu on the *makai* side. The co-op is open weekdays 8 a.m.-7 p.m., Saturday 9 a.m.-6 p.m., and Sunday 9 a.m.-4 p.m. This full-range health food store serves freshly made soup and sandwiches from their deli. You can buy fresh orange and ginger lemonade made on the premises. The co-op, the last of its kind in Hawaii, has a large supply of herbs, plenty of vitamins and minerals,

the Blue Ginger Gallery in Captain Cook

J.D. BISIGNANI

a smattering of fresh produce, and an excellent assortment of bulk grains.

Oshima's General Store is well stocked with cameras and film, drugs, fishing supplies, magazines, and some wines and spirits. Also in town are a **Ben Franklin, Ace Hardware,** and **Kimura's Market,** a general grocery store with some sundries.

Kealakekua

Elizabeth Harris and Co., tel. 323-2447, is open Mon.-Fri. 9 a.m.-5 p.m., and displays shirts, T-shirts, and dresses made by 13 local seamstresses and artists who come in to showcase their works. You'll be greeted by the manager, Mary Harper, who'll be sitting behind a Singer sewing machine or hand-painting shirts. Take a look at the ceramics and glasswork as well. A great stop for truly distinctive clothing.

Right next door to the Kona Central Union Church is **Changing Hands,** a resale shop owned by Norma Hand that specializes in vintage clothing, glassware, and mostly Hawaiian antiques and bric-a-brac. It's open weekdays 10:30 a.m.-4:30 p.m., occasionally Saturday. You can pick up a treasure ranging in cost from a dollar or two to a few hundred.

The **Kahanahou Hawaiian Foundation,** tel. 322-3901, deals in ancient Hawaiian handicrafts, including masks, hula drums, and hula accoutrements. This nonprofit organization serves as an apprenticeship school for native Hawaiians who are trying to revitalize traditional arts. Unfortunately, no one seems to be in attendance in the shop, and you are instructed to ring the buzzer. A sign says, "If you're just here to browse and to kill time don't kill ours; we can't afford the luxury." That sets the tone of your greeting when someone finally appears to scowl at you. Obviously the foundation is not into preserving *aloha.*

The Grass Shack, a.k.a. Little Grass Shack, open Mon.-Sat. 9 a.m.-5 p.m., sometimes Sunday noon-5 p.m., tel. 323-2877, is an institution in Kealakekua. It looks like a tourist trap, but don't let that stop you from going in and finding some authentic souvenirs, most of which come from the area, the workshop next door, or rehabilitation centers around the island. The items *not* from Hawaii are clearly marked with a big orange sign that says Sorry These Items Were Not Made In Hawaii. But the price is right. There are plenty of trinkets and souvenir items, as well as a fine assortment of artistic pieces, especially wooden bowls, hula items, and Hawaiian masks. A shop specialty is items made from curly koa. Each piece is signed with the craftsperson's name and the type of wood used. One of the artisans displayed here is master woodworker Jack Straka. Items are also made from Norfolk pine and milo. A showcase holds jewelry and tapa cloth imported from Fiji. The shop is famous for its distinctive *lau hala* hats, the best hat for the tropics.

Tropical Temptations, tel. 326-2007, open Mon.-Sat. 10 a.m.-5 p.m., is housed in a gaily painted yellow and green building. Climb the steps to the porch, where you'll find a service buzzer that will summon owner and chief tempter Lance Dassance, who will smile a welcome into his candy kitchen. Remember, however, that most of the business is wholesale and not really set up for drop-in visitors. Lance turns the best available grade of local fruits, nuts, and coffee beans into delicious candies. The fresh-fruit process uses no preservatives, additives, waxes, or extenders, and no sugars except in the chocolate, which is the best grade possible. A slow-drying process is used, so as few nutrients as possible are lost. A shop specialty is candy made from rare white pineapple, which grows for only eight weeks per year. Lance, if not too busy, will be happy to take you on a tour of the facility. He takes a personal pride in making the best candy possible and stresses that he uses only fruit ripened in the last 24 hours. Tropical Temptations, the healthiest candy store in Hawaii, has an outlet booth in Kailua-Kona at the Kona Inn Shopping Village.

Konakai Coffee Farms has a tasting room and restaurant at the south end of Kealakekua. They produce and serve cups of Kona coffee plain, or as espresso, cappuccino, and caffe latte. Check the racks of fresh-roasted pure Kona coffee at about $12 per pound.

The **Kamigaki Store** is also in Kealakekua, and **Sure Save** is in Kealakekua Shopping Center.

Captain Cook

Next door to the Manago Hotel, just as you're entering town, is **Country Store Antiques.** Owned and operated by E.L. Mahre, open Mon.-Fri. 9 a.m.-3 p.m., it's filled to the brim from back to front. Inside you'll find kerosene lamps, dolls, glassware, old bottles, and Hawaiian antique jewelry. The shop is more like a museum than an antique store. There are plenty of purse- and suitcase-sized items that will travel well and make lasting mementos of your trip. On the other side of the Manago Hotel is the **Manaloa Gallery and Thrift Store,** another bric-a-brac shop filled with art objects and curiosities.

The **Kealakekua Ranch Center,** in Captain Cook, is a two-story mall with fashions, food, and general supplies. Here you'll find a True Value hardware store, Ben Franklin, and Sure Save Supermarket.

Other Shopping

A row of international flags waving along the roadside might lure you into **Kona Plantation Coffee,** an upscale tourist trap. They offer free coffee 8 a.m.-6 p.m., and the prices on the souvenir-quality items are cheaper than in Kailua-Kona. Peer from the elevated platforms to the coast below before entering. Inside you'll find Kona coffee, T-shirts, carved coconuts, towels, beads, and paper lei. Ask them for directions to the lava tube that you are allowed to tour free of charge. Exotic caged birds are also part of the experience.

Bong Brothers, about a mile past the Kona Country Fair, is an authentic fruit store. Check it out for the atmosphere and the fresh local fruit. The **Shimizu Market** is south on Rt. 11 in Honaunau. Farther south between mile markers 77 and 78 you'll find the very well-stocked **Ocean View General Store,** tel. 929-9966, which sells groceries, snacks, and gas. It's the last place to stock up before Naalehu, at the southern tip of the island.

KAU

The Kau District is as simple and straightforward as the broad, open face of a country gentleman. It's not boring, and it does hold pleasant surprises for those willing to look. Formed entirely from the massive slopes of Mauna Loa, the district presents some of the most ecologically diverse land in the islands. The bulk of it stretches 50 miles from north to south and almost 40 miles from east to west, tumbling from the snowcapped mountain through the cool green canopy of highland forests. At lower elevations it becomes pastureland of belly-deep grass ending in blistering-hot black sands along the coast encircled by a necklace of foamy white sea. At the bottom of Kau is **Ka Lae** ("South Point"), the southernmost tip of Hawaii and the southernmost point in the U.S. It lies at a latitude 500 miles farther south than Miami and twice that below Los Angeles. Ka Lae was probably the first landfall made by the Polynesian explorers on the islands. A variety of archaeological remains supports this belief.

Most people dash through Kau on the Hawaii Belt Road, heading to or from Volcanoes National Park. Its main towns, **Naalehu** and **Pahala,** are little more than pit stops. The Belt Road follows the old Mamalahoa Trail where, for centuries, nothing moved faster than a contented man's stroll. Kau's beauties, mostly tucked away down secondary roads, are hardly given a look by most unknowing visitors. If you take the time and get off the beaten track, you'll discover black- and green-sand beaches, the world's largest macadamia nut farm, Wild West rodeos, and an electricity farm sprouting windmill generators. The upper slopes and broad pasturelands are the domain of hunters, hikers, and *paniolo,* who still ride the range on sure-footed horses. In Kau are sleepy plantation towns that don't even know how quaint they are, and beach parks where you can count on finding a secluded spot to pitch a tent. Time in Kau moves slowly, and *aloha* still forms the basis of day-to-day life.

SIGHTS AND BEACHES

The following sights are listed from west to east along Rt. 11, with detours down secondary roads indicated whenever necessary. The majority of Kau's pleasures are accessible by standard rental car, but many secluded coastal spots can be reached only by 4WD. For example, **Kailiki,** just west of Ka Lae, was an important fishing village in times past. A few archaeological remains are found here, and the beach has a green cast due to the lava's high olivine content. Few tourists ever visit; only hardy fishermen come here to angle the coastal waters. Spots of this type abound, especially in Kau's remote sections. But civilization has found Kau as well: when you pass mile marker 63, look down to the coast and notice a stand of royal palms and a large brackish pond. This is Luahinivai Beach, one of the finest on the island, where country and western star Loretta Lynn has built a fabulous home. Those willing to abandon their cars and to hike the sparsely populated coast or interior of Kau are rewarded with areas unchanged and untouched for generations.

Manuka State Wayside

If hoofing it or four-wheel-driving isn't your pleasure, consider a stop at Manuka State Wayside, 12 miles before you get to South Point Road and just inside the Kau District. This civilized scene has restrooms, pavilions, and trails through manicured gardens surrounded by an arboretum. Shelter camping (no tents) is allowed on the grounds. All plants are identified. This is an excellent rest or picnic stop. The forested slopes above Manuka provide ample habitat for introduced, and now totally successful, colonies of wild pigs, pheasants, and turkeys. Some popular hiking areas are covered in the chapter on Volcanoes National Park. Be advised that the entire district is subject to volcanic activity and, except where indicated, has no water, food, shelter, or amenities.

South Point

The Hawaiians simply called this Ka Lae, "The Point." Some scholars believe Polynesian sailors made landfall here as early as A.D. 150, and that their amazing exploits became navigating legend long before colonization began. A paved, narrow, but passable road branches off Rt. 11 approximately six miles west of Naalehu, and drops directly south for 12 miles to land's end. Luckily the shoulders are firm, so you can pull over to let another car go by. The car rental agencies warn against using this road, but their fears are unfounded. You proceed through a flat, treeless area trimmed by free-ranging herds of cattle and horses: more road obstacles to be aware of. Suddenly, incongruously, huge mechanical windmills appear, beating their arms against the sky. This is the **Kamoa Wind Farm.** Notice that this futuristic experiment at America's most southern point uses windmills made in Japan by Mitsubishi! The trees here are bent over by the prevailing wind, demonstrating the obviously excellent wind-power potential of the area. Farther along, a road sign informs you that the surrounding countryside is controlled by the **Hawaiian Homeland Agency,** and that you are forbidden to enter. That means you are not welcome on the land, but you do have right-of-way on the road.

Here the road splits left and right. Go right until road's end, where you'll find a parking area usually filled with the pickup trucks of local fishermen. Walk to the cliff and notice attached ladders that plummet straight down to where the fishing boats are anchored. Local skippers moor their boats here and bring supplies and their catch up and down the ladders. Proceed south along the coast for only five minutes and you'll see a tall white structure with a big square sign on it turned sideways like a diamond. It marks the true *South Point,* the southernmost tip of the United States. Proceed to the sea and notice the tidepools, a warning that the swells can come high onto the rocks, and that you can be swept away if you turn your back on *moana.* Usually, a few people are line fishing for crevalle or pompano. The rocks are covered with Hawaiian dental floss—monofilament fishing line that has been snapped. Survey the mighty Pacific and realize that the closest continental landfall is Antarctica, 7,500 miles to the south.

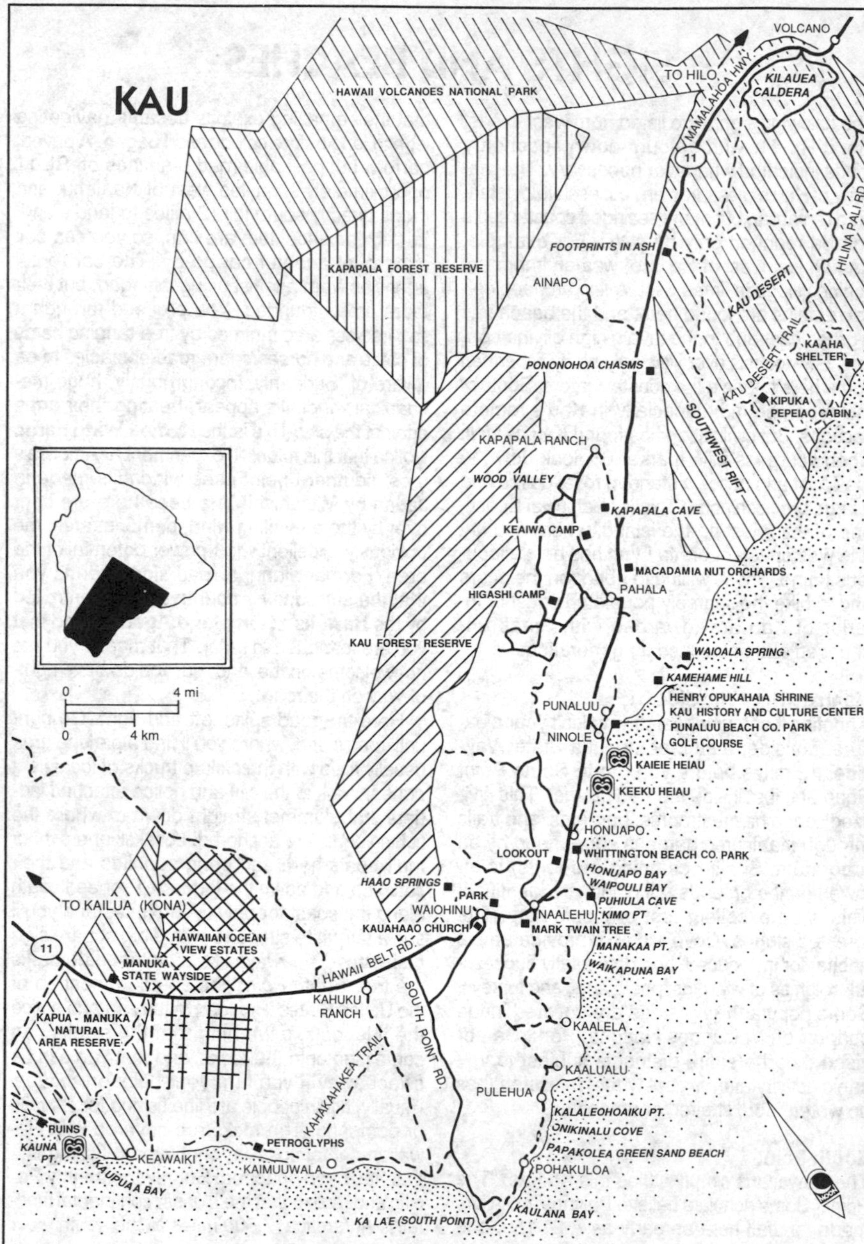

KAU

HAWAII VOLCANOES NATIONAL PARK
VOLCANO
TO HILO
MAMALAHOA HWY.
11
KILAUEA CALDERA
HILINA PALI RD.
FOOTPRINTS IN ASH
KAU DESERT
KAPAPALA FOREST RESERVE
AINAPO
KAAHA SHELTER
PONONOHOA CHASMS
KAU DESERT TRAIL
SOUTHWEST RIFT
KIPUKA PEPEIAO CABIN
KAPAPALA RANCH
WOOD VALLEY
KAPAPALA CAVE
KEAIWA CAMP
MACADAMIA NUT ORCHARDS
PAHALA
HIGASHI CAMP
KAU FOREST RESERVE
WAIOALA SPRING
KAMEHAME HILL
0 4 mi
0 4 km
PUNALUU
HENRY OPUKAHAIA SHRINE
KAU HISTORY AND CULTURE CENTER
PUNALUU BEACH CO. PARK
GOLF COURSE
NINOLE
KAIEIE HEIAU
KEEKU HEIAU
HONUAPO
LOOKOUT
WHITTINGTON BEACH CO. PARK
HONUAPO BAY
WAIPOULI BAY
HAAO SPRINGS
PARK
PUHIULA CAVE
KIMO PT
TO KAILUA (KONA)
WAIOHINU
NAALEHU
KAUAHAAO CHURCH
MARK TWAIN TREE
HAWAIIAN OCEAN VIEW ESTATES
MANAKAA PT.
11
WAIKAPUNA BAY
HAWAII BELT RD.
MANUKA STATE WAYSIDE
KAHUKU RANCH
SOUTH POINT RD.
KAPUA - MANUKA NATURAL AREA RESERVE
KAALELA
KAHAKAHAKEA TRAIL
KAALUALU
PULEHUA
KALALEOHOAIKU PT.
ONIKINALU COVE
RUINS
PETROGLYPHS
PAPAKOLEA GREEN SAND BEACH
KAUNA PT.
KEAWAIKI
KAIMUUWALA
POHAKULOA
KAUPUAA BAY
KA LAE (SOUTH POINT)
KAULANA BAY

Back at the Hawaiian Homes sign, follow the road left and pass a series of WW II barracks being reclaimed by nature. This road, too, leads to a parking area and a boat ramp where a few seaworthy craft are bobbing away at their moorings. Walk toward the the navigational marker and you may notice small holes drilled into the stone. These were used by Hawaiian fishermen to secure their canoes to shore by long ropes while the current carried them a short way offshore. In this manner, they could fish without being swept away. Today fishermen still use these holes, but instead of canoes they use floats or tiny boats to carry only their lines out to sea. The *ulua,* tuna, and *ahi* fishing are renowned throughout this area. The fishing grounds here have always been extremely fertile, and thousands of shell and bone fishhooks have been found throughout the area. Scuba divers say the rocks off South Point are covered with broken fishing line that the currents have woven into wild macrame.

When the *kona* winds blow out of the South Pacific, South Point takes it on the chin. The weather should always be a consideration when you visit. In times past, any canoe caught in the wicked currents was considered lost. Even today, only experienced boaters brave South Point, and only during fine weather.

There are no official camping or facilities of any kind at South Point, but plenty of boat owners bivouac for a night to get an early start in the morning. The lava flow in this area is quite old and grass-covered, and the constant winds act like a natural lawn mower.

Green Sand Beach

From the boat ramp, a footpath leads east toward Kaulana Bay. All along here are remnants of pre-contact habitation, including the remains of a *heiau* foundation. If you walk for three miles, you'll come to Papakolea, better known as Green Sand Beach. The lava in this area contains olivine, a green semiprecious stone that weathered into sandlike particles distributed along the beach. The road heading down to Green Sand Beach is incredible. It begins as a very rugged jeep trail and disintegrates from there. Do not attempt this walk unless you have closed-toe shoes. Thongs will not make it. You're walking into the wind going down, but it's not a rough go—there's no elevation gain to speak of. The lava in the area is *'a'a,* weathered and overlaid by a rather thick ground cover. Follow the road, and after 10 minutes, the lava ends and rich, green pastureland begins. An ancient eruption deposited 15-18 feet of ash right here, and the grasses grew.

Continue for approximately 35 minutes, until you see what is obviously an eroded cinder cone at the edge of the sea. (About 15 minutes back, you'll have noticed an area where many 4WDs have pulled off at an overlook. That isn't it!) Peer over the edge to see the beach with its definite green tinge. This is the only *beach* along the way, so it's hard to mistake. Getting down to it is absolutely treacherous. You'll be scrambling over tough lava rock, and you'll have to make drops of four to five feet in certain spots. The best approach is to go over the edge as soon as you come to the cinder cone area; don't walk around to what would be the south point of the caldera where the sand is. Once you get over the lip of heavy-duty rock, the trail down is not so bad. When you begin your descent, notice overhangs, almost like caves, where rocks have been piled up to extend them. These rocked-in areas make great shelters, and you can see remnants of recent campfires in spots perfect for a night's bivouac.

Green Sand Beach definitely lives up to its name, but don't expect emerald green. It's more like an army green, a dullish khaki green. Down at the beach, be very aware of the wave action. Watch for at least 15 minutes to be sure breakers are not inundating the entire beach. Then you can walk across it, but stay close to the lava rock wall. The currents can be wicked here and you should only enter the water on very calm days. No one is around to save you, and you don't want to wind up as flotsam in Antarctica.

Waiohinu

Back on the highway, as you head east toward Naalehu, you pass through the tiny town of Waiohinu. A tall church steeple welcomes you to town just after you wiggle your way down a long hill to the coast. There's nothing remarkable about this village, except that as you pass through you'll be seeing an example of the real Hawaiian lifestyle as it exists today. Just past the well-marked Shirakawa Motel (see "Practicalities," below) on the *mauka* side of the road is the **Mark Twain Monkeypod Tree.** Unfortunately, Waiohinu's only claim to fame except for its undisturbed peace and quiet blew down in a heavy windstorm in 1957. Part of the original trunk, carved into a bust of Twain, is on display at the Lyman House Museum in Hilo. Now, a few shoots have begun sprouting from the original trunk and in years to come the Monkeypod Tree will be an attraction again.

Naalehu

Next you come to sizable Naalehu, the largest town in the area and the most southern town in the U.S. Naalehu is lush. Check out the overhanging monkeypod trees. They form a magnificent living tunnel as you go down Rt. 11 through the center of town. Between Naalehu and Punaluu, the coastal area is majestic. You've left the mountains behind and stretching out into the aqua-blue sea is a tableland of black lava with waves crashing against it, a surrealistic seascape that seems to go on forever.

Whittington Beach County Park

Three miles north of Naalehu, just past mile marker 61, is a county park with full amenities and camping. This park is tough to spot from the road because it's not clearly marked. As you're coming down a steep hill from Naalehu you'll see a bridge at the bottom. Turn right and you're there. The park is a bit run down, but never crowded. If you follow the dirt roads to its undeveloped sections you encounter many old ruins from the turn of the century when Honuapo Bay was an important sugar port.

Ninole And Punaluu

Whittington Beach Park is followed by Ninole, where you'll find Punaluu Beach County Park (mile marker 56), famous for its black-sand beach (see below). Punaluu was an important port during the sugar boom of the 1880s and even had a railroad. Notice the tall coconut palms in the vicinity, unusual for Kau. Punaluu means "Diving Spring," so-named because freshwater springs can be found on the floor of the bay. Native divers once paddled out to sea, then dove with calabashes that they filled with fresh water from the underwater springs. This was the main source of drinking water for the region.

Ninole is also home to the **Seamountain Resort and Golf Course,** built in the early 1970s by a branch of C. Brewer and Company. The string of flat-topped hills in the background is the remains of volcanoes that became dormant about 100,000 years ago. In sharp contrast with them is **Loihi Seamount,** 20 miles offshore and about 3,000 feet below the surface of the sea. This very active submarine volcano is steadily building and should reach the surface in the next thousand years or so. Near Ninole is **Hokuloa Church,** which houses a memorial to Henry Opukahaia, the Hawaiian most responsible for encouraging the first missionaries to come to Hawaii to save his people from damnation.

Punaluu Beach County Park

Between Pahala and Naalehu is Punaluu Beach Park, a county park (permit) with full amenities. Here you'll find a pavilion, bathrooms, telephone, and open camping area. During the day there are plenty of tourists around, but at night the beach park empties, and you virtually have it to yourself. Punaluu boasts some of the only safe swimming on the south coast, but that doesn't mean it can't have its treacherous moments. Head for the northeast section of the beach near the boat ramp. Stay close to shore because a prevailing rip current lurks just outside the bay. Just near the beach is **Joe and Pauline's Curio Shop.** If you have time, stop in; these people have a reputation for being more interested in offering *aloha* than in selling you a trinket. **Ninole Cove Park,** part of the Seamountain Resort, is within walking distance and open to the public. For day-use, you might consider parking near the pro shop. As you walk to the beach from here you pass a freshwater pond, quite cold but good for swimming.

Pahala

Eight miles east of Ninole and 22 miles from Volcanoes is Pahala, clearly marked off Rt. 11. The Hawaii Belt Road flashes past this town, but if you drive into it, heading for the tall stack of the Kau Sugar Co., you'll find one of the best-preserved examples of a classic sugar town in the islands. It was once gospel that sugar would be "king" in these parts forever, but the huge stone stack of the sugar mill puffs erratically, while in the background the whir of a modern macadamia nut-processing plant breaks the stillness. Another half hour or so of driving from Pahala puts you in Hawaii Volcanoes National Park (for Kau desert footprints, see "Small Detours" under "Kilauea Caldera" in the Hawaii Volcanoes National Park chapter).

Wood Valley Temple

Also known as Nechung Drayang Ling, "Island of Melodious Sound," the Wood Valley Temple, Box 250, Pahala, HI 96777, tel. 928-8539, is true to its name. This Tibetan Buddhist temple sits like a sparkling jewel surrounded by the emerald green velvet of its manicured grounds. To get here, enter Pahala Village, proceed to the stop sign in the village center, and turn right onto Pikake Street. The road will open up into a very wide cane road where you should be aware that monstrous cane trucks can lumber down it at any moment. Proceed for five miles until you come to a Y, where you go left. Follow this small road for a few hundred yards through an aromatic stand of majestic eucalyptus trees and look for two tall prayer poles on the right. Pull into the parking lot and you'll see the temple, gaily painted red, yellow, orange, and green, glistening on top of the hill. Here Marya and Miguel, the caretakers and administrators, will greet you if they are not off on one of their frequent trips to Asia.

Buddha gave the world essentially 84,000 different teachings to pacify, purify, and develop the mind. In Tibetan Buddhism there are four major lineages, and this temple, founded by Tibetan master Nechung Rinpoche, is a classic synthesis of all four. Monks and scholars from different schools of Buddhism are periodically invited to come and lecture as resident teachers. The Dalai Lama came in 1980 to dedicate the temple, and many lama have come since then. Two affiliate temples are located in Dharamsala, India, and in Lhasa, Tibet. Programs vary, but people genuinely interested in Buddhism come here for meditation and soul-searching as well as for peace, quiet, relaxation, and direction. Morning and evening services at 7 a.m. and 7 p.m. are led by Debala, the Tibetan monk in residence. Formal classes depend upon which invited teacher is in residence (write ahead for a schedule of programs).

The retreat facility is called the Tara Temple and at one time housed a Japanese Shingon Temple in Pahala. When the Shingon sect moved to a new facility in Kona, this building was abandoned and given to Wood Valley Temple. A local contractor moved it to its present location, cranked it up one story, and built the dormitories underneath. The grounds, hallowed and consecrated for decades, already held a Nichiren temple, the main temple here today, that was dismantled in 1919 and rebuilt on its present site to protect it from lowland flooding. Rates at the retreat facility are private room $25 s, $150 s weekly, $35 d, $210 d weekly. A bunk in the dorm is $15 with use of a large communal kitchen and shared bath. Definitely call or write to make reservations, since you could be disappointed if you just turn up.

The majority of the flowering and fruit trees on the premises are imports. Plenty of parishioners are into agriculture, and there is a strong movement by the temple members to slowly replant the grounds with native vegetation they collect from various sites in and around Pahala. The grounds, like a botanical garden, vibrate with life and energy. Buddhism strives for its followers to become wise and compassionate people. The focus of the temple is to bring together all meditation and church groups in the community. Plenty of local Christian and Buddhist groups use the nonsectarian facilities. Any group that is spiritually, socially, and community oriented and that has a positive outlook is welcome. Wood Valley Temple can't promise *nirvana,* but they can point you to the path.

PRACTICALITIES

One thing you won't be hassled with in the Kau District is deciding on where to eat or spend the night. The list is short and sweet.

ACCOMMODATIONS

The **Shirakawa Motel,** tel. 929-7462, Box 467, Naalehu, HI 96772, is a small, clean, comfortable hotel where your peace and quiet are guaranteed. Open since 1928, it is run by a Japanese family as quiet and unobtrusive as *ninja*. Prices are a reasonable $27 s, $36 s with kitchen, $40 d with kitchen, with a 10% discount for a one-week stay, 15% for longer. You'll be greeted by two dogs—Rex, a Doberman pinscher, and Kai, a golden Lab—both of whom have given up aggression and opted for the "hang loose, no worries" island lifestyle.

Seamountain Resort at Punaluu, tel. 928-8301 or (800) 367-8047, Box 340, Pahala, HI 96777, is a condominium/hotel complex. Prices range from $67 for a studio to $114 for a two-bedroom apartment (two-day minimum stay). Because of its rural location, Seamountain can offer deluxe accommodations for moderate prices. Your condo unit will be a low-rise, Polynesian-inspired bungalow with a shake roof. Outside your door are the resort's fairways and greens, backdropped by the spectacular coast. If you're after peace and quiet, Seamountain is hard to beat. Besides golf, amenities include a nearby restaurant, tennis courts, pool, and weekly maid service.

Becky's Bed & Breakfast, tel. 929-9690 or (800) 235-1233, Box 673, Naalehu, HI 96772, about 100 yards past the theater on the left, is owned and operated by Becky and Chuck McLinn. Available in this modest but cheery 60-year-old home is a spacious room with a queen bed and private bath for $50 s, $60 d; a room with two double beds and private bath at $55 s, $65 d; and a room with queen bed and shared bath $45 s, $55 d, additional person $10. There is no official policy, but if you'll be staying four nights or longer, a discount can be arranged. To help you relax, the B&B features a backyard deck with a barbecue grill, inviting hammock, and hot tub to unjangle nerves. Becky serves a full breakfast of juice, fruit, and either Hawaiian French toast or hotcakes with bacon or sausage.

South Point Bed & Breakfast, tel. 929-7466, HC1 92-1408 Donala Dr., Captain Cook, HI 96704, is owned and operated by Bruce and Robin Hall. They offer rooms at $55 d, with a discount for longer stays.

For unique and distinctive accommodations see **Wood Valley Temple** above.

FOOD AND SHOPPING

The Kau Drive-in Restaurant is open for breakfast, lunch, and dinner. You pass it on the left between mile markers 78 and 77, near a Texaco gas station. The food is simple but good, and makes a perfect lunch.

A mile further south is **South Point Bar and Restaurant,** tel. 929-9343, which has been changing owners regularly but is making a valiant effort to stay open. The restaurant is open for dinner Wed.-Fri. 5-8 p.m., and for breakfast Sat.-Sun. 8 a.m.-1 p.m. Wednesday is Mexican night. On the other evenings you can expect barbecued boneless chicken $9.95, steak dinner $15.95, and an assortment of burgers and sandwiches. The bar is open weekdays noon-8 p.m., and weekends 8 a.m.-8 p.m. The South Point Bar and Restaurant is the only place to stop for food until you get to Naalehu.

Kau Ice and Fishing Center in Waiohinu offers fresh local fish that would make a perfect self-prepared meal for anyone heading back to a condo in Kailua-Kona. Down the road, you can pick up supplies at **Wong Yuen General Store and Gas Station,** open Mon.-Sat. 8:30 a.m.-5 p.m., Sunday to 3 p.m., tel. 929-7223.

Naalehu Shopping Center is along the road at the west end of town. In the small complex you'll find Food Mart, Ed's Laundromat, and **Greensan's Shop,** where you can pick up sandwiches and plate lunches.

As you are entering the west side of town, a large, easily spotted sign on the left marks the

Punaluu Bake Shop and Visitor's Center, open daily 9 a.m.-5 p.m. The bake shop, with all kinds of tempting pastries, is especially known for its *pao dolce,* sweet bread. Park and follow a cement pathway to the retail shop for baked goods, coffee, and a smattering of souvenirs.

In **Naalehu** you can gas yourself or your car at the **Luzon Liquor Store,** open Mon.-Sat. 7 a.m.-7:30 p.m., Sunday till 6 p.m., closed Tuesday, tel. 929-7103. For a quick sandwich or full meal try the **Naalehu Coffee Shop,** open daily, tel. 929-7238. Many of the local people call this restaurant Roy's, after the owner's first name. The menu is typical island cuisine with a Japanese flavor; the best item is the fresh fish from local waters. The restaurant is basic and clean, with most meals on the menu around $7. They also have a wide assortment of souvenirs and tourist junk, and a large koi pond outside. Look for the big yellow building just near the shopping center as you enter town.

Naalehu Fruit Stand, tel. 929-9009, open Mon.-Thurs. 9 a.m.-6:30 p.m., Friday and Saturday till 7 p.m., Sunday till 5 p.m., is a favorite with local people, always a tip-off that the food is great. Along with fresh fruit, they sell submarines, hot dogs, pizza, salads, sodas, teas, coffee, and a good selection of grains, minerals, vitamins, and health foods. The owners, John and Dorene Santangelo, are very friendly and willing to give advice about touring the Kau area. This is the best place on the south coast for a light meal or picnic lunch.

Across the road from the Naalehu Fruit Stand, notice the baseball park. Here **Lilly's Plate Lunch** serves hearty sandwiches and island favorites ready to go.

In **Pahala Village** (see "Pahala" under "Sights and Beaches" above) you'll find the basics like a gas station, small shopping center, post office, Bank of Hawaii, Mizumo's Superette, and take-out plate lunch restaurant.

SPORTS AND ACTIVITIES

The only organized sporting facility in Kau is at the Seamountain Resort. Here you'll find four unlit tennis courts and a 6,106-yard, 18-hole, par-72 course. Greens fees are $30, cart $16, and clubs $10.

The **Southern Star Theater** is a large building on the left as soon as you drive into Naalehu. It's a classic old-time theater usually open on weekends, adults $3.25, children $1.75.

The best **sailboarding** in the area is at Kaulana Bay. Head down South Point Road, and about a half mile before you get to the windmills is a passable dirt road to the left. You can only see about a half mile down it when you first start out, but keep going. Pass through cattle gates and make absolutely sure to close them behind you. When you get to the bay, go to the left-hand side for the best entry. Remember that down here, no help is available, and you are totally on your own!

Kau Windsurfing in Naalehu, next to the Naalehu Fruit Stand, rents and sells sailboards, fins, snorkels, and masks.

BOB RACE

SOUTH KOHALA

The Kohala District is the peninsular thumb in the northwestern portion of the Big Island. At its tip is **Upolu Point,** only 40 miles from Maui across the **Alenuihaha Channel.** Kohala was the first section of the Big Island to rise from beneath the sea. The long-extinct volcanoes of the Kohala Mountains running down its spine have been reduced by time and the elements from lofty, ragged peaks to rounded domes of 5,000 feet or so. Kohala is divided into North and South Kohala. South Kohala boasts *the* most beautiful swimming beaches on the Big Island, along with good camping and world-class hotels. Inland is **Waimea** (Kamuela), the *paniolo* town and center of the massive Parker Ranch. Founded last century by John Parker, its 200,000 acres on the western slopes of Mauna Kea now make it the largest privately owned ranch in America.

Getting There From Hilo

If you're approaching Kohala from Hilo or the east side of the island, you can take two routes. **The Saddle Road** (Rt. 200) comes directly west from Hilo and bypasses Mauna Kea and the Observatory Road. This very scenic road has the alluring distinction of being the least favorite route of the car rental agencies. The Saddle Road intersects Rt. 190, where you can turn north for six miles to Waimea, or south for 32 miles to Kailua-Kona (see the chapter on The Saddle Road). **Route 19,** the main artery connecting Hilo with the west coast, changes its "locally known" name quite often, but it's always posted as Rt. 19. Directly north from Hilo as it hugs the Hamakua Coast it's called the "Hawaii Belt Road." When it turns west in Honokaa, heading for Waimea, it's called the "Mamalahoa Highway." From Waimea directly west to Waikui on the coast Rt. 19 becomes "Kawaihae Road," and when it turns due south along the coast heading for Kailua-Kona its moniker changes again to "Queen Kaahumanu Highway." The routes heading to Kohala from Kailua-Kona are discussed in the following sections. Many are "sights" in and of themselves, with lovely panoramas and leisurely back-lane rides.

THE COAST

The shoreline of South Kohala, from Anaehoomalu Bay north to Kawaihae Bay, is rich in perhaps the finest super-deluxe resorts in the state. This coast's fabulous beaches are known not only for swimming and surf, but for tidepooling and awe-inspiring sunsets as well. Also, the two main beaches offer camping and rental cabins. There are little-disturbed and rarely visited archaeological sites, expressive petroglyph fields well off the beaten track, the educational **Puukohola Heiau,** and even a rodeo. No "towns" lie along the coast, in the sense of a laid-out community with a main street and attendant businesses and services. The closest facsimile is Kawaihae, with a small cluster of restaurants, shops, and gas station. Waikoloa Village also provides some services, with exclusive boutique shopping in the resorts.

Route 19, Queen Kaahumanu Highway

As you begin heading north from Kailua-Kona on coastal Rt. 19 (Queen Kaahumanu Hwy.), you leave civilization behind. There won't be a house or any structures at all, and you'll understand why they call this the "Big Island." Perhaps to soften the shock of what's ahead, magnificent bushes loaded with pink and purple flowers line the roadway for a while. Notice too that friends and lovers have gathered and placed white coral rocks on the black lava, forming pleasant graffiti messages such as "Aloha Mary" and "Love Kevin."

Suddenly you're in the midst of enormous flows of old *'a'a* and *pahoehoe* as you pass through a huge and desolate lava desert. At first it appears ugly and uninviting, but the subtle beauty begins to grow. On clear days you can see Maui floating on the horizon, and *mauka* looms the formidable presence of Mauna Kea streaked by sunlight filtering through its crown of clouds. Along the roadside, wisps of grass have broken through the lava. Their color, a shade of pinkish gold, is quite extraordinary and made more striking juxtaposed against the inky-black lava. Caught by your headlights at night, or especially in the magical light of dusk, the grass wisps come alive, giving the illusion of wild-haired gnomes rising from the earth. In actuality, it's fountain grass imported from Africa.

Around mile marker 70, the land softens and changes. The lava is older, carpeted in rich green grass appearing as rolling hills of pastureland. No cows are in evidence, but be aware of "Kona nightingales," wild jackasses that roam throughout this area and can be road hazards. Also, these long, flat stretches of road can give you "lead foot." Be careful! The police patrol this strip heavily, using unmarked cars (high-performance Trans Ams and the like are favorites) and looking for unsuspecting tourists who have been "road hypnotized." From Kailua-Kona to the Royal Waikoloan Hotel at Anaehoomalu is about 30 miles, with another 10 miles to the Mauna Kea Beach Hotel near Kawaihae. If you're day-tripping to the beaches, expect to spend an hour each way.

SIGHTS AND NEARBY COMMUNITIES

The following sights, beaches, and accommodations are listed from south to north. Since most of the accommodations of South Kohala are themselves sights, and lie on the best beaches, make sure to cross-reference the following sections. All, except for Waikoloa Village, lie along coastal Rt. 19, which is posted with mile markers, so finding the spots where you want to stop is easy.

Waikoloa Road

If you're interested in visiting Waimea (Kamuela) as well as seeing the South Kohala coast, you might consider turning right off Rt. 19 between mile markers 74 and 75 onto Waikoloa Road. This is a great deal of territory to cover in one day! This route cuts inland for 13 miles, connecting coastal Rt. 19 with inland Rt. 190, which leads to Waimea. About halfway, you pass the planned and quickly growing community of **Waikoloa Village** (about six miles inland from Waikoloa Resorts) that is unfortunately heralded

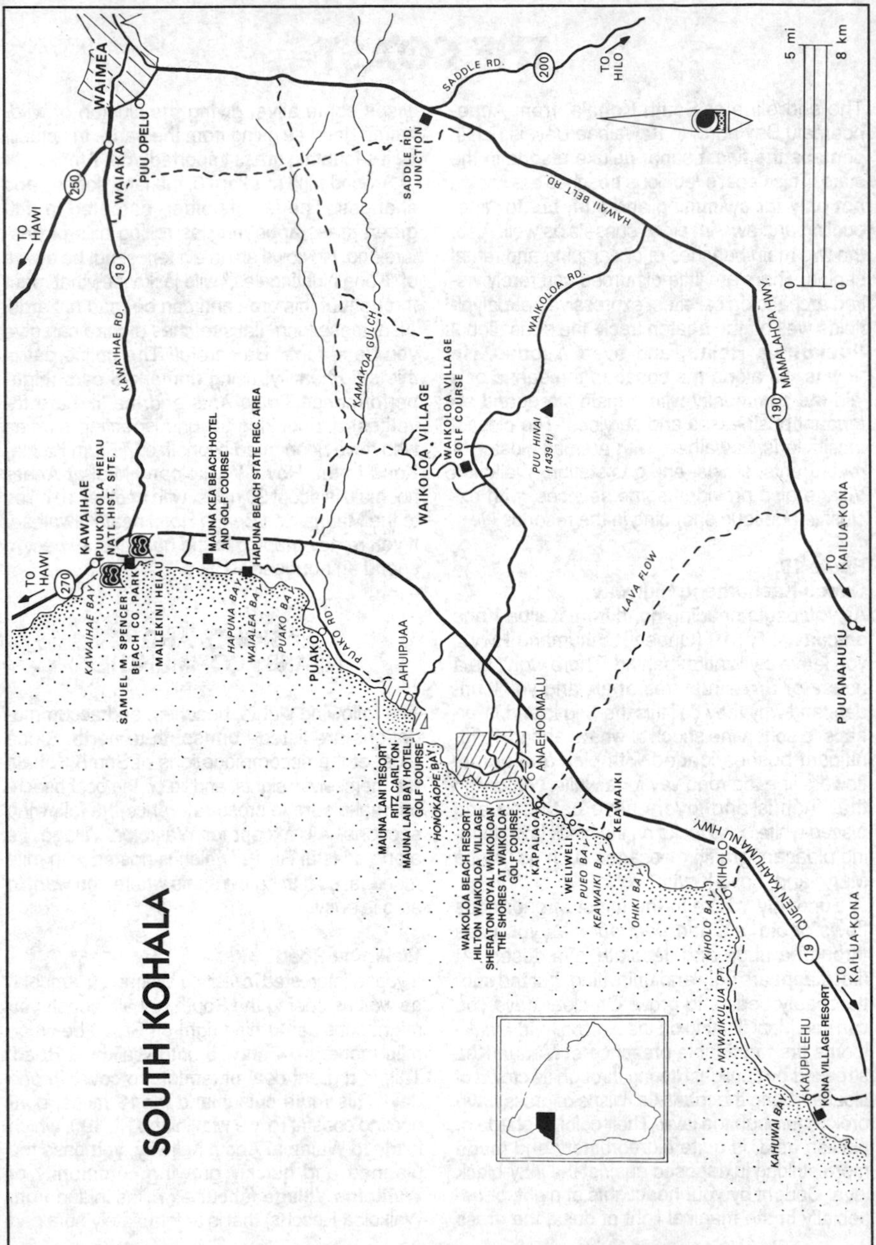

SOUTH KOHALA
TO HAWI
270
KAWAIHAE
KAWAIHAE BAY
PUUKOHOLA HEIAU NATL. HIST. SITE.
SAMUEL M. SPENCER BEACH CO. PARK
MAILEKINI HEIAU
MAUNA KEA BEACH HOTEL AND GOLF COURSE
HAPUNA BAY
WAIALEA BAY
HAPUNA BEACH STATE REC. AREA
PUAKO BAY
PUAKO
PUAKO RD.
MAUNA LANI RESORT
RITZ CARLTON
MAUNA LANI BAY HOTEL
GOLF COURSE
LAHUIPUAA
HONOKAOPE BAY
WAIKOLOA BEACH RESORT
HILTON WAIKOLOA VILLAGE
SHERATON ROYAL WAIKOLOAN
THE SHORES AT WAIKOLOA
GOLF COURSE
KAPALAOA
ANAEHOOMALU
WELIWELI
PUEO BAY
KEAWAIKI BAY
KEAWAIKI
OHIKI BAY
LAVA FLOW
KIHOLO BAY
NAWAIKULUA PT.
KIHOLO
QUEEN KAAHUMANU HWY.
KAHUWAI BAY
KAUPULEHU
KONA VILLAGE RESORT
19
TO KAILUA-KONA
PUUANAHULU
TO KAILUA-KONA
190
MAMALAHOA HWY.
TO HAWI
250
WAIMEA
WAIAKA
19
KAWAIHAE RD.
PUU OPELU
KAMAKOA GULCH
WAIKOLOA VILLAGE
WAIKOLOA VILLAGE GOLF COURSE
PUU HINAI (1439 ft)
WAIKOLOA RD.
HAWAII BELT RD.
SADDLE RD. JUNCTION
SADDLE RD.
200
TO HILO
MOON
0
5 mi
0
8 km

by a condo complex of stark gray in neo-Alcatraz design which would aptly be called "Prisoners of Paradise" but is misnamed "The Greens." Try to overlook them, and head for the village itself, which is low-rise and quite tasteful.

The village is serviced by the **Waikoloa Highlands Center,** a small but adequate shopping mall with a gas station, full-service supermarket, Bank of Hawaii, Straw Hat Pizza, postal service store, small medical center, and a few restaurants and shops. This is also the home of **Waikoloa Stables,** tel. 883-9335, which hosts a number of rodeos and Wild West shows. They offer saddle horses and a variety of trail rides for the visitor. Here too is the **Waikoloa Village Golf Course,** tel. 883-9621, a private course open to the public. You can chase that little white ball for par 72 over 6,316 yards for about $40 including cart.

In the village you'll find **Waikoloa Villas,** Box 3066, Waikoloa Village Station, Kamuela, HI 96743, tel. (800) 367-7042 or 883-9588 on the Big Island. Rates are one bedroom $65-80 d, two bedrooms $85-95 d, three bedrooms (loft) $105-115 d, $8 extra person, two-night minimum stay. Amenities include swimming pool, nearby golf, and weekly maid service. All units are fully furnished with complete kitchens. The condo offers a money-saving condo/car package.

Puako

This alluring area is located *makai* on a side road off Rt. 19 about four miles south of Kawaihae. Hawaiians lived here in times past, but a modern community has been building along the three miles of Puako Bay since the 1950s. A thin ribbon of white sand runs the length of the beach that provides fair swimming, good fishing and snorkeling, and terrific tidepooling. Sunsets here are magnificent and you'll usually have a large stretch of beach to yourself, but remember your flashlight for the walk back because there's no lighting. Near-shore scuba diving is excellent, with huge caverns and caves to explore, and a colorful concentration of coral and marinelife.

Along Puako Road is **Hokuloa Church,** built by Rev. Lorenzo Lyons in 1859. This musically talented reverend mastered the Hawaiian language and composed lovely ballads such as "Hawaii Aloha," which has become the unofficial anthem of the islands. Follow the road through the village to where it ends at a green gate; this is the beginning of the extensive field of **Puako Petroglyphs.** The entrance is marked by an HVB Warrior; the path leading to the rock carvings takes about 20 minutes each way. Access is also available by way of a well-marked self-guiding trail starting from the Mauna Lani Resort area. Any of the large hotels here offer brochures and information concerning the petroglyph field. The markings are considered some of the finest and oldest in Hawaii, but carvings of horses and cattle signify ongoing art that happened long after Westerners appeared. Circles outlined by a series of small holes belonged to families who placed the umbilical cords of their infants into these indentations to tie them to the *aina* and give them strength for a long and good life. State archaeologists and anthropologists have reported a deterioration of the site due to vandalism, so please look but don't deface, and stay on established paths.

Puukohola Heiau

Don't miss this completely restored Hawaiian temple, a National Historical Site located one mile south of Kawaihae where coastal Rt. 19 turns into Rt. 270 heading into North Kohala. This site, covering 77 acres, includes **Mailekini Heiau** and the nearby **John Young House** site. Administered by the National Park Service, it is open daily 7:30 a.m.-4 p.m.; admission is free. As you enter, pick up a map highlighting the main points of interest. It's worthwhile checking out the visitors center, where Ranger Benjamin Saldua and others provide excellent information. Puukohola ("Whale Hill") received its name either because the hill itself resembles a whale, or because migrating whales pass very close offshore every year. It was fated to become a hill of destiny.

Kamehameha I built this *heiau* in 1790 on the advice of Kapoukahi, a prophet from Kauai who said that Kamehameha would unify all the islands only after he built a temple to his war god Kukailimoku. Kamehameha complied, building this last of the great Hawaiian *heiau* from mortarless stone that when finished measured 100 by 224 feet. The dedication ceremony of the *heiau* is fascinating history. Kamehameha's last rival was his cousin, Keoua Kuahuula. This warlike chief, through prophecy and advice from his own *kahuna,* realized that it was Kamehameha who would rise to be sovereign of all the islands. Kamehameha invited him to the dedication ceremony, but en route Keoua, in preparation for the inevitable outcome, performed a death purification ceremony by circumcising his own penis. When his canoes came into view, they were met by a hail of spears and musket balls. Keoua's body was carried to Kukailimoku's altar. Kamehameha became the unopposed sovereign of the Big Island and, within a few years, of all of Hawaii.

Near the *heiau* is the house site of John Young, an English seaman who became a close adviser to Kamehameha, who dubbed him Olohana, "All Hands." Young taught the Hawaiians how to use cannons and muskets and fought alongside Kamehameha in many battles. He turned Mailekini Heiau into a fort, and over a century later it was used during WW II by the U.S. Army as an observation area. Young became a respected Hawaiian chief and grandfather of Queen Emma. He's one of only two white men buried at the Royal Mausoleum in Nuuanu Valley on Oahu.

Kawaihae Town

The port marks the northern end of the South Kohala coast. Here Rt. 19 turns eastward toward Waimea, or turns into Rt. 270 heading up the coast into North Kohala. Kawaihae town is basically utilitarian, with wharfs and fuel tanks. A service cluster has a shop or two and the Harbor Hut, a reasonably priced restaurant in the vicinity.

BEACHES, PARKS, AND CAMPGROUNDS

Anaehoomalu Bay

After almost 30 miles of the transfixing monochrome blackness of Kohala's lava flows, a green standout of palm trees beckons in the distance. Between mile markers 76 and 77, on the Waikoloa Resorts road, another well-marked access road heads *makai* to the Royal Waikoloan Hotel and historic **Anaehoomalu Bay.** The bay area, with its freshwater springs, coconut trees, blue lagoon, and white-sand beach, is a picture-perfect seaside oasis. Between the large coconut grove and the beach are two well-preserved fishponds where mullet was raised *only* for consumption by the royalty who lived nearby or were happening by in seagoing canoes. Throughout the area along well-marked trails are **petroglyphs,** a segment of the cobblestoned **King's Highway,** and numerous archaeological sites including house sites and some hard-to-find burial caves. The white-sand beach is open to the public, with access, parking, and beautiful lava-stone showers/bathhouses. Although the sand is a bit grainy, the swimming, snorkeling, scuba, and windsurfing are fine. A walk north along the bay brings you to an area of excellent tidepools and waters heavily populated by marinelife. The next beach north is at Puako Bay (see "Puako" under "Sights and Nearby Communities" above).

Holoholokai Beach Park

Located near the Ritz-Carlton Mauna Lani Hotel on a well-marked access road, the picturesque beach park, open to the public daily 6:30 a.m.-7 p.m., is improved with a bathhouse, running water, picnic tables, and resort-quality landscaping. Unfortunately, the beach itself is mostly coral boulders with only tiny pockets offering very limited water access. However, the park is used very little and is perfect for relaxing under a palm tree or for a leisurely stroll to explore the many tidepools.

Hapuna Beach State Recreation Area

Approximately 12 miles north of Anaehoomalu is the *second*-best, but most accessible, white-sand beach on the island. (The best, Kauna'oa, is listed next.) **Camping** is available in six A-frame screened shelters that rent for approximately $7 per night per person and accommodate up to four. Provided are sleeping platforms (no bedding), electric outlets, cold-water showers, and toilets in separate comfort stations, plus a shared range and refrigerator in a central pavilion. Check in at 2 p.m., check out at 10 a.m. The A-frames are very popular, so reservations and deposit are required. You can receive full information by contacting the Division of State Parks, Box 936 (75 Aupuni St.), Hilo, HI 96720, tel. 933-4200. However, reservations are made by contacting the concessionaire, Hawaii Untouched Parks & Recreation Inc., Box

390962, Kailua-Kona, HI 96739, tel. 882-1095. There is unofficial camping south along **Waialea Bay** that you can get to by walking or taking the turnoff at mile marker 69.

Hapuna Beach is wide and spacious, almost 700 yards long by 70 wide in summer, with a reduction by heavy surf in winter. A lava finger divides the beach into almost equal halves. During good weather the swimming is excellent, but a controversy rages because there is no lifeguard here. During heavy weather, usually in winter, the rips are fierce, and Hapuna has claimed more lives than any other beach park on all of Hawaii! At the north end is a small cove almost forming a pool that is always safe, a favorite with families and children. Many classes in beginning scuba and snorkeling are held in this area, and shore fishing is good throughout. At the south end, good breaks make for tremendous bodysurfing (no boards allowed), and those familiar with the area make spectacular leaps from the seacliffs.

Kauna'oa Beach

Better known as **Mauna Kea Beach** because of the nearby luxury hotel of the same name, Kauna'oa is less than a mile north of Hapuna Beach and is considered the best beach on the Big Island. In times past, it was a nesting and mating ground for green sea turtles, and although these activities no longer occur because of human pressure on the habitat, turtles still visit the south end of the beach. Mauna Kea Beach is long and wide, and the sandy bottom makes for excellent swimming. It is more sheltered than Hapuna, but can still be dangerous. Hotel beach boys, always in attendance, are unofficial lifeguards who have saved many unsuspecting tourists. During high surf, the shoreline is a favorite with surfers. All beaches in Hawaii are public, but *access* to this beach was won only by a lawsuit against the Mauna Kea Beach Hotel in 1973. The ruling forced the hotel to open the beach to the public, which they did in the form of 10 parking spaces, a right of way, public shower, and toilet facilities. To keep the number of nonguests down, only 10 parking passes are handed out each day on a first-come, first-served basis. Pick them up at the guardhouse as you enter the hotel grounds. These entitle you to spend the day on the beach, but on weekends they're gone by 9:30 a.m. You can wait for someone to leave and then get the pass, but that's unreliable. The hotel also issues a pass for a one-hour visit to the hotel grounds (overstaying results in a $10 fine). You can use this pass to drop off family, friends, beach paraphernalia, and picnic supplies, then park at Hapuna and return via an easy mile-long **nature trail** connecting Hapuna and Mauna Kea beaches, the route used by the majority of people unable to get a pass. Also, the hotel issues a "food and drink" pass that entitles you to stay as long as you wish, if you get it validated at one of the restaurants or snack bars. So as long as you're in there, you might as well use the beach for the price of a soft drink. In time the hotel will catch on, so test the waters before winding up with a fine.

Spencer Beach County Park

Look for the entrance a minute or two past Puukohola Heiau on Rt. 19 just before entering Kawaihae. Trails lead from the beach park up to the *heiau*, so you can combine a day at the beach with a cultural education. The park is named after Samuel Mahuka Spencer, a longtime island resident who was born in Waimea, served as county mayor for 20 years, and died in 1960 at Honokaa. The park provides pavilions, restrooms, cold-water showers, electricity, picnic facilities, and even tennis courts. Day use is free, but tent and trailer **camping** is by county permit only, at $1 per day (see "County Parks" under "Camping and Hiking" in the Big Island Introduction). Spencer Beach is protected from wind and heavy wave action by an offshore reef and by breakwaters built around Kawaihae Bay. These make it the safest and best swimming beach along South Kohala's shore and a favorite with local families with small children. The wide, shallow reef is home to a wide spectrum of marinelife, making the snorkeling easy and excellent. The shoreline fishing is also excellent.

PRACTICALITIES

RESORTS AND ACCOMMODATIONS

Except for a few community-oriented restaurants in Waikoloa Village, and a few reasonably priced roadside restaurants in Kawaihae, all of the food in South Kohala is served in the elegant but expensive restaurants of the luxury hotels. These hotels also provide the **entertainment** along the coast, mostly in the form of quiet musical combos and dinner shows. The **shopping,** too, is in the exclusive boutiques found in the hotel lobbies and mini-malls. The following hotels lie along coastal Rt. 19 and are listed from south to north. For more "Practicalities" listings please see "Sights and Nearby Communities" above.

Kona Village Resort

So you want to go "native," and you're dreaming of a "little grass shack" along a secluded beach? No problem! The Kona Village Resort is a once-in-a-lifetime dream experience. Located on Kahuwai Bay, a picture-perfect cove of white sand dotted with coconut palms, the village lies seven miles north of the airport, surrounded by 12,000 open acres promising seclusion. The accommodations, called "beachcomber hales," are individual renditions of thatch-roofed huts found throughout Polynesia. They are simple but luxurious, and in keeping with the idea of getting away from it all have no TVs, radios, or telephones. All, however, do have ceiling fans and louvered windows to let the tropical breezes blow through. Beds are covered with distinctive quilts and pillows. Each hut features a wet bar, fridge, coffeemaker, and extra-large bathroom. Your Do Not Disturb sign is a coconut that you place upon your private lanai, and messages are hand-delivered and placed in a basket, also on the lanai. At one time you had to fly into the hotel's private airstrip, but today you can arrive by car. You enter by an access road that leads through the tortured black lava fields of South Kohala. Don't despair! Down by the sea you can see the shimmering green palm trees as they beckon you to the resort. Kona Village gives you your money's worth, with tennis, Ping-Pong, lei greetings, water sports, and a variety of cocktail parties and luaus. Guided tours are also offered to the many historic sites in the area. Rates start at $295 s, $370 d, full American plan (three meals). There is a strict reservations and refund policy, so check. For information, contact Kona Village Resort, Box 1299, Kailua-Kona, HI 96740, tel. 325-5555 or (800) 367-5290.

Meals are served in the Hale Moana, the main dining room; and at the Halemoana Terrace, where a luncheon buffet is served daily 12:30-2 p.m. (reservations recommended for dinner). At Hale Ookipa, "House of Hospitality," a luau is held on Friday night, and a steak-fry happens every Wednesday. The restaurants are open to nonhotel guests; a buffet lunch costs $24 per person.

A public tour offered weekdays from 11 a.m. includes a 15-acre petroglyph field on the property that you can inspect if you make prior arrangements. You will be instructed to meet a tour guide at the main gate at about 10:50 a.m. The hotel manager is Fred Dewar, who's been at the facility since 1966, along with most of his highly professional and seasoned personnel. They take pride in the hotel and do everything they can to help you have a rewarding, enjoyable, and relaxing stay at this premier resort. The Kona Village is a Hawaiian classic that deserves its well-earned reputation for excellence.

Royal Waikoloan Hotel

The Sheraton chain wanted to enter the luxury hotel market with a splash, so in 1981 they opened the $70-million, 545-room Sheraton Royal Waikoloan Hotel. They found the perfect spot at Anaehoomalu Bay (between mile markers 77 and 78), and produced a class act. The hotel lobby is a spacious open-air affair, beautifully appointed in koa and objets d'art. All rooms are tastefully decorated and provide a/c, color TV, king-size beds, and private lanai. Rates range $100-155 s/d for a standard, $250 for a cabana, and $550 for a suite; $20 additional person. For reservations, write: Royal Waiko-

J.D. BISIGNANI

hale at Kona Village Resort

loan, HCO2 Box 5300, Waikoloa, HI 96743, tel. 885-6789, (800) 462-6262 Mainland. On the superbly kept grounds are six tennis courts, numerous ponds, and a swimming pool. Special features include a small shopping arcade with a dozen or so choice shops, horseback riding, and free shuttle service throughout Waikoloa. The focal points, however, are two marvelous golf courses designed by Robert Trent Jones Jr. He learned his trade from his dad, whose masterpiece is just up the road at the Mauna Kea Resort.

You have a choice of dining facilities. The **Garden Cafe** features American cuisine, open daily for breakfast, lunch, and dinner. The atmosphere is relaxed and the prices are affordable for such a hotel. **The Tiare** offers elegant dining in elegant surroundings for elegant prices. The continental cuisine includes shrimp nouvelle, rack of lamb, lobster, and roast duckling served to the melodious notes of an accomplished harpist. Open Wed.-Sun. 6:30-10 p.m., tel. 885-6789, reservations recommended. The **Royal Terrace** opens its doors to the sea for breakfast and provides island entertainment with dinner nightly 6:30-10:30 p.m. Featured are nightly theme buffets which can be anything from seafood to Chinese. Expensive.

The Shores At Waikoloa

The Shores at Waikoloa are secluded luxury condominiums nestled away in the planned community of Waikoloa at HCO2, Box 5460, Waikoloa, HI 96743, tel. 885-5001; for reservations phone Aston Hotel and Resorts, tel. (800) 922-7866 Mainland, (800) 445-6633 Canada, (800) 321-2558 Hawaii. To get there, turn off Rt. 19 into well-marked Waikoloa at mile marker 76, and proceed straight ahead past the King's Shops, a small shopping area. Keep going for a few minutes and you will come to a sign that says "Condominiums," and another marker that points you to "The Shores at Waikoloa." Enter through a security gate to see the peaceful and beautifully manicured grounds of the low-rise condominium. A few minutes away are the best beaches on Hawaii and all of the activities offered by the large luxury hotels, if you wish to participate. The condominium offers an activities desk where you can arrange a snorkeling or sailing excursion or hire a babysitter. A swimming pool and jacuzzi are open until 10 p.m., and two complimentary tennis courts (and a few rackets too) are available. The condos are decorated by the individual owners so each room is unique, but there are guidelines and standards so that every unit is tastefully and comfortably decorated, mostly in an island motif. All units are extremely spacious, with many boasting marble and terra-cotta floors; huge bathrooms with double tubs, showers, and sinks; full modern kitchens; and light and airy sitting rooms complete with state-of-the-art entertainment centers. Rates range $165 for a one-bedroom to $295 for a two-bedroom golf villa. Low season brings a 25% reduction, and The Shores offers an unbeatable low-season "golf package" of $145 per night and one round of free golf (usually $95) at either of Waikoloa's two superb courses: the Beach Course, designed by Robert Trent Jones Jr. and the King's Course, designed by Tom Wieskopf and Jay Morrish. If you are after a luxury vacation within a vacation where you can get away from it all after you've gotten away from it all, The Shores at Waikoloa is a superb choice.

The Ritz-Carlton, Mauna Lani

In a tortured field of coal-black lava made more dramatic by free-form pockets of jade-green lawn rises the ivory-white Ritz-Carlton Mauna Lani, at One N. Kaniku Dr., Kohala Coast, HI 96743, tel. 885-2000 or (800) 845-9905. A rolling drive lined with *haku lei* of flowering shrubs entwined with stately palms leads to the open-air porte cochere. Enter to find koa and marble reflecting the diffused and soothing light of the interior. Straight ahead, off the thrust-proscenium Sunset Terrace, a living blue-on-blue still-life of sea and sky is perfectly framed. Nature, powerful yet soothing, surrounds the hotel. Stroll the grounds where gentle breezes always blow, and where the ever-present surf is the back beat of a melody created by trickling rivulets and falling waters as they meander past a magnificent pool and trimmed tropical gardens of ferns and flowers.

The hallways and lobbies, opening from the central area like the delicate ribs of a geisha's fan, are delightfully elegant with comfortable parlor settings of wonderful soft couches attended by stout tables and portly credenzas. Overhead hang magnificent cut-crystal chandeliers of differing designs. The floors, fringed by marble and covered with luxurious Persian carpets, lead past museum-quality displays of porcelains, sculptures, antiques of all descriptions, and the fine needlework of Hawaiian quilts. On the walls hang 18th- and 19th-century oil paintings—many of tall-masted ships that sail the imagination into Hawaii's proud seafaring past—and in the main hallway just past the concierge desk is a model, executed in the most minute detail, of a three-masted ship under full sail. Koa-paneled elevators have their own chandeliers and Persian rugs, and every set of stairs has a velvety smooth koa banister carved with the pineapple motif, the Hawaiian symbol of hospitality.

Located in two, six-story wings off the main reception hall, the 541 hotel rooms, each with its own private lanai and sensational view, are a mixture of kings, doubles, and suites. Done in neutral tones, the stylish and refined rooms feature handcrafted quilts, twice-daily room attendance, turndown service complete with a complimentary orchid and Ghirardelli chocolates, remote-control color TV, 24-hour room service, fully stocked honor bar, and in-room safe. Wardrobes, hung with plush terry-cloth robes and plump satin hangers, feature automatic lights, along with steam irons and small ironing boards. The spacious marble bathrooms, with wide, deep tubs, separate commodes, and shower stalls, are appointed with dressing and vanity mirrors, double sinks, hair dryers, and name-brand grooming products. Rates range $285 for a garden view to $455 for a deluxe oceanfront room (low-season rates available). The Ritz Carlton Club, an exclusive floor with its own concierge, offers extra amenities—$495 will get you a room as well as continental breakfast, light lunch, cocktails, cordials, and a full spread of evening hors d'oeuvres. Suites range from an executive one-bedroom to the magnificent Ritz-Carlton Suite and cost $625-2800.

The hotel offers first-rate guest services, amenities, and activities that include a small shopping mall with everything from sundries to designer boutiques, complimentary shuttle to and from Waikoloa's famous championship golf courses, bag storage, 11 tennis courts (with seven lit for evening play), complimentary use of fitness center and snorkel equipment, an enormous swimming pool and sun deck, bicycles for short tours, safe-deposit boxes, on-property car rental, a comfortable amphitheater showing first-run movies, and babysitting. **Ritz Kids** is a special instructional day-camp program for children ages 4-12. Reasonably priced and offered half or full days, Ritz Kids includes lunch and matinee movies, and lets kids engage in a variety of fascinating activities such as making shell jewelry, stringing lei, exploring petroglyphs, painting, and playing Hawaiian games and water sports.

Dining at the Ritz can be everything from poolside casual (burgers and fries) to haute cuisine (fine delectables from around the world.) The executive chef, Amy Ferguson-Ota, a native Texan, and her talented staff create sumptuous dishes, combining island ingredients like guava, passion fruit, thimbleberries, and papaya with wild boar, fresh *ahi,* and free-range chicken. The result is a unique cuisine *"mai ka aina a me ke kai,"* "from land and sea." **The Dining Room,** where you will be comfortable in tasteful resortwear, is open Tues.-Sat. 6:30-9:30 p.m., with mellow Hawaiian music from 7 p.m. It is Chef Ferguson-Ota's signature restaurant. The cosmopolitan room, with coved ceiling, gorgeous chandelier, and massive floral centerpiece, is relaxed and comfortable. Tables covered with snow-white linen bear the familiar Ritz cobalt-blue-trimmed plates and crystal. Appetizers range from chicken consommé with angel-hair pasta and enoki mushrooms $12 to Maine lobster in an herbed vinaigrette $22. Entrees from $34 include sautéed Black Angus beef in a three-peppercorn sauce, and roasted squab breast.

At **The Grill,** open for dinner 6:30-9:30 p.m., cocktails and dancing until closing, the dishes are beef and seafood Hawaiian style. Whet your palate with fresh Pacific oysters, sashimi, or carpaccio $12-16, and move on to breadfruit vichyssoise or island seafood chowder for about $7. Salads range from a traditional Caesar to Maui onions and Waimea tomatoes for about $7. Entrees include a wonderful selection of fresh island fish grilled, roasted, or poached in banana curry, saffron herb sauce, or black bean and Kau lime butter. Beef dishes include tenderloin, veal medallions, or Kahua prime rib for under $35. Specialties are rack of lamb; Hawaiian Fisherman's stew (wonderful!); and lobster, scallops, and prawns in a Riesling herb sauce. Fresh pasta topped with grilled shrimp, or linguine with smoked chicken, go for around $22.

The Cafe is open daily for breakfast and dinner. Sunday brunch, 10 a.m.-2 p.m., costs $24.50 adults, $12.50 children ages 5-12. The Cafe is a casual restaurant featuring Pacific Rim and American standard fare, and including both a children's and a you-can-run-but-you-can't-hide fitness menu. Prices for standard complete breakfasts are $14-20; the fitness breakfast $11; and a Japanese breakfast of grilled fish, miso soup, steamed rice, and pickles $18. Meal selections include pasta, California-style pizza, lamb chops, and Thai green chicken curry with eggplant. Those annoyingly-thin-why-don't-you-stay-home-anyway fitness fanatics can graze on spicy peppered shrimp salad, followed by chilled carrot soup. The Cafe features Hawaiian music nightly, and hula nightly except Sunday.

The poolside **Ocean Bar and Grill,** open daily for lunch, is the hotel's most casual restaurant, where you dine alfresco in a garden setting. Offerings range from healthful salads to jumbo hot dogs with fries. House specialties are Kahua beef chili and rice, and charbroiled chicken breast. The Ocean Bar and Grill also serves fresh pasta, scrumptious desserts, and pizzas with eclectic toppings like Peking duck, smoked chicken, and Puna goat cheese. And at your feet a perfect crescent of white-sand beach opens to the great Pacific.

Mauna Lani Bay Hotel

As soon as you turn off Rt. 19, the entrance road, trimmed in purple bougainvillea, sets the mood for this $70-million, 350-room hotel that opened in 1983. The per-unit cost of $200,000 was the most ever spent in Hawaii up to that time, and it shows in the oversized rooms emphasizing relaxation and luxury, the majority with an ocean view. The hotel has a tennis garden with 10 courts, a lovely beach and lagoon area, a health spa, exclusive shops, and swimming pools. Enter through a great portico, whose blue tile floor, a mimic of the ever-present sea and sky, immediately creates a sense of sedate but beautiful grandeur. Below is a central courtyard, where full-sized palms sway amidst a lava-rock water garden; cascading sheets of clear water splash through a series of koi ponds, making naturally soothing music. A short stroll leads you through a virtual botanical garden to a white-sand beach perfect for island relaxation.

Surrounding the hotel is the marvelous **Francis I'i Brown Golf Course,** whose artistically laid-out fairways, greens, and sand traps make it a modern landscape sculpture. The course is carved from lava, with striking ocean views in every direction. It's not a tough course, though it measures 6,813 yards, par 72. Greens fees are expensive, with preferred starting times given to hotel guests. (Call the Pro Shop at 882-7255 for more information.)

The Mauna Lani's rooms range $275 garden view to $425 oceanfront, with suites from $725 and royal bungalows for $2500-3000 (includes a personal chef, valet, live-in maid, and swimming pool). The hotel also offers ocean villas starting at $350 for one bedroom to $550 for three bedrooms, weekly and monthly rates available and three-night minimum required. For full information, contact: Mauna Lani Bay Hotel, One Mauna Lani Dr., Kohala Coast, HI 96743, tel. 885-6622, (800) 367-2323 Mainland, (800) 992-7987 in Hawaii.

Le Soleil, the hotel's award-winning signature restaurant, offers imaginative Mediterranean cuisine, dinner only, 6:30-9:30 p.m. (jackets for men required). Starters can be *ahi* carpaccio or a half lobster roasted with enoki and shiitake mushrooms. Entrees starting at $30 are superb and can be anything from steamed *opakapaka* in a fennel saffron broth to grilled lamb chops in a zesty anchovy garlic puree. But the finest culinary delight is the ever-changing "Chef's Tasting Menu," a five-course extravaganza for $65 that offers delectables like Thai spiced clam soup, grilled scallops on a bed of greens flavored with a sweet-and-sour ginger vinaigrette, fillet of beef with a crab-and-wild-mushroom polenta cake, and a specially prepared dessert.

The **Bay Terrace,** open daily for breakfast, lunch, and dinner, offers the most casual but still superb dining. Daily offerings include everything from full-course breakfasts to dinner entrees like rack of lamb. Weekend nights feature a fabulous seafood buffet that shouldn't be missed, and the Sunday brunch served 11:30 a.m.-2 p.m. is legendary.

The **Canoe House,** open daily for dinner, delights with Pacific Rim cuisine. Not as formal as Le Soleil, this oceanfront restaurant features special *pu pu* like roast Chinese duck with avocado salsa, nori-wrapped tempura *ahi* with soy-mustard sauce and tomato-ginger relish, and a variety of soups and salads like corn chowder made with red Thai curry and coconut milk, and a house salad of organically grown greens. Main dishes tantalize: baked Hawaiian swordfish in a Thai-curry crab crust on a crispy potato pillow with fennel chive vinaigrette, Bangkok-grilled half-chicken on a Korean-style salad, and pan-roasted lamb chop with macadamia nut coconut-honey crust and star anise sauce.

The **Ocean Grill,** where you'll be comfortable in bathing suit and cover-up, serves lunches and cocktails. **Knickers,** located at the golf clubhouse and known for its sunsets, open daily 6:30 a.m.-9:30 p.m., is a full-service restaurant serving everything from ham-and-eggs to pasta with shrimp and capers. **The Gallery,** on the grounds at the Racquet Club, is an award-winning dinner restaurant and probably the least expensive fine-dining restaurant at the resort. Here, you can dine on medallions of pork tenderloin or wild-mushroom tortellini for under $20.

Hilton Waikoloa Village

At the Hilton Waikoloa Village (formerly Hyatt Regency Waikoloa), 69-425 Waikoloa Beach Dr., Kamuela, HI 96743, tel. 885-1234 or (800) 445-8667, the idea was to create a reality so beautiful and naturally harmonious that anyone who came here, sinner and saint alike, would be guaranteed a glimpse of paradise.

The architecture, "fantasy grand," is subdued and understated, not gaudy. The three main towers, each enclosing a miniature fern-filled botanical garden, are spread over the grounds almost a mile apart and are linked by pink flagstone walkways, canals navigated by hotel launches, and a quiet, space-age tram. Everywhere sculptures, art treasures, and brilliant flowers soothe the eyes. Songs of rare tropical birds and the wind whispering through a bamboo forest surround you with a natural melody. You can swim in a private lagoon accompanied by dolphins, dine in magnificent restaurants, explore surrounding ranchlands, or just let your cares slip away as you lounge in perfect tranquility.

From Keahole (Kona) Airport, travel north on Rt. 19 for about 15 minutes. Look for mile marker 76, and turn beachside toward Waikoloa. Follow the roadway through the lava fields until you arrive at the hotel. Valets will park your car.

Inside, attention to the smallest detail is immediately apparent. Elevators are done in rich woods and burnished brass. An alcove may hold a dozen superbly hand-carved puppets from Indonesia. Halls are bedecked with chandeliers, marble-topped tables, and immense floral displays. Even cigarette receptacles are artworks: large Asian pots or ceramic dolphins with mouths agape, filled with black sand.

A museum promenade displays a Hawaiiana collection of carved koa bowls and feather lei, along with carvings from Thailand, paintings from Japan, and porcelains from China. Fantastic pots, taller than a person, are topped with handles of gold elephant faces and tusks. Look through archways at perfectly framed grottoes harboring koi ponds and waterfalls. Sit on royal thrones and benches next to intricately carved credenzas and tables and simply delight at the beauty.

The hotel's restaurants are culinary extravaganzas, and every taste is provided for. **Donatoni's** features classic Italian; **Palm Terrace** is a Polynesian buffet; **Imari** serves traditional Japanese fare; **Kamuela Provision Co.** specializes in steak and seafood; and the hotel's bars, lounges, and casual poolside dining options are surprisingly moderately priced.

The beach fronting the property offers excellent snorkeling, while three gigantic pools and a series of lagoons are perfect for water activities and sunbathing.

Take the amazing "Behind the House" tour of the facility (free). You are led below ground, deep into the heart of the hotel, where you get to see how everything works. An underground service roadway, complete with stop signs and traffic cops, runs for over a mile and is traveled by employees on bicycles and motorized utility carts. As you pass offices with signs that read *Wildlife Director, Curator of Art, Astronomer,* you come to realize how distinctive an undertaking the hotel is. Next come the florist shop, the butcher, the baker, the laundry (with more output than any other laundry in the state of Hawaii—22 pounds of linen go in each room) and wardrobe, responsible for outfitting the hotel's 1,300 employees. You're given staggering figures: 750,000 gallons of fresh water is needed for the pools; over 18 million gallons of seawater is pumped through the canals daily; each motor launch costs $300,000; the 41 chandeliers weigh over 24 tons; the hotel's 300 computers are linked by over 28 miles of cable. On and on, the statistics match the magnificence of what you see.

With all this splendor, still, the most talked-about activity at the hotel is **Dolphin Quest.** A specially constructed saltwater pond, 65 times larger than federal regulations require, is home to Atlantic bottlenose dolphins from Florida's Gulf Coast where they're found in bays and lagoons living most of their lives in water 16-20 feet deep. Here, their pond is 22 feet deep in the center, 350 feet long, and contains 2.5 million gallons of naturally filtered seawater.

Daily, on a lottery basis, guests are chosen to "interact with the dolphins." Dolphin Quest is trying to steer the program away from the concept of "swimming with dolphins," and more toward an educational experience. The program was founded by two highly respected marine veterinarians, Drs. Jay Sweeney and Rae Stone, both prominent in their field for their efforts to protect and preserve marine mammal populations. It was their idea to bring a new experience to the public in which the interaction was from the dolphin's point of view. Instead of a typical stadium-type setting where the dolphins are performers and the people are spectators, they created something more natural so the dolphins would enjoy the experience as much as the people.

Here you don't ride the dolphins and they don't do tricks for you. In the half-hour session, typically 10 minutes are spent in the free pool, where people wade in chest-deep water with the dolphins gliding by. If the dolphins want to be petted they stop, if not they move past like a torpedo. The rest of the time you spend on the dock, where you are given information concerning not only dolphins, but all marinelife and human interdependence with it. The experience is voluntary on the dolphins' part—*they* choose to swim with *you* as a guest in their domain.

Much of the proceeds from the program goes toward marine research. Using funds raised by Dolphin Quest, a team from the University of California at Santa Cruz was recently housed, funded, and provided with boats to investigate a way to save the more than 100,000 spinner dolphins caught in tuna nets every year.

This futuristic and fantastic hotel complex, a relative newcomer to the scene, has set a new standard against which all future resorts will be measured. Of course, as you would expect, all this luxury comes at a price; rates are $200-295 standard, $250-325 deluxe ocean view, $525-3500 suites. Experience and time will surely mature the Hilton Waikoloa Village into one of the finest resorts on earth.

The Mauna Kea Beach Hotel
This hotel has set the standard of excellence along Kohala's coast ever since former Hawaii Governor William Quinn interested Laurence Rockefeller in the lucrative possibilities of building a luxury hideaway for the rich and famous. Beautiful coastal land was leased from the Parker Ranch, and the resort opened in 1965. The Mauna Kea was the only one of its kind for a few years until the other luxury hotels were built along this coast. It's getting a bit older, and getting stiff competition from newer nearby luxury resorts, but class is always class and the Mauna Kea receives very high accolades as a fine resort.

The hotel's classic, trendsetting **golf course** designed by the master, Robert Trent Jones, has been voted among America's 100 greatest courses and Hawaii's finest. Also, *Tennis Magazine* includes the hotel among the "50 greatest U.S. tennis resorts." The hotel itself is an eight-story terraced complex of simple, clean-cut design. The grounds and lobbies showcase over 1,000 museum-quality art pieces from throughout the Pacific, and over a half-million plants add greenery and beauty to the surroundings. The landings and lobbies, open and large enough to hold full-grown palm trees, also display beautiful tapestries, bird cages with their singing captives, and huge copper pots on polished brick floors. The Mauna Kea offers a modified American plan (breakfast and dinner), the best beach on the island, and its own dive boat for seagoing adventure. Million-dollar condos grace the grounds. Guests tend to come back year after year. The beautifully appointed rooms, starting at $260 d (European plan, no meals), $25 extra person, are free of TVs, but feature an extra-large lanai and specially made wicker furniture. For full information contact the Mauna Kea Beach Hotel, One Mauna Kea Beach Dr., Kohala Coast, HI 96743, tel. 882-7222 or (800) 882-6060.

Sumptuous dining is presented by Chef Jean-Marc Heim in the **Batik Room,** dinner nightly 7-10 p.m., where the Sri Lankan-inspired decor adds a touch of Eastern mystery and romance. Intricate batik tapestries, brass liner plates, and regal *houdah* (elephant thrones) set the mood for the exotic menu. Begin your feast with Italian-inspired ravioli stuffed with abalone and wild mushrooms $13.25, or with island *ahi* tartar cake $12.50. Soups ranging from a light beef consommé with truffles to lobster bisque Armagnac cost $4.50-6.75. Entrees, magnificent creations from around the world starting at $26, include roasted duck in a papaya and coriander sauce; a variety of island fish grilled, steamed, or sautéed; and zesty Thai curries made from beef, lamb, chicken, or shrimp. A titillating dessert is chocolate soufflé topped with macadamia nuts, champagne sauce, Grand Marnier, or fresh blueberries.

The Garden, another of the hotel's fine dining restaurants, open nightly for dinner 6:30-9 p.m., and now under the skillful hand of Chef Bruce MacVicar, set the standards in the mid-1980s when it was one of the first restaurants to offer Hawaiian regional cuisine. The Garden starts you with appetizers like Trio of Island Sashimi and Poke with lime rice cake for $12.75, or the famous "Firecracker," deep-fried salmon wrapped in nori and garnished with a hot-and-sour chili dip at $8.25. Soups and salads are rock lobster with wonton $6.25, Waimanu chowder made with smoked chicken and sweet Maui onions $5.50, Kamuela spinach with papaya seed dressing $6.50, and hearts of Waimea butter lettuce in a papaya, avocado, and *lilikoi* dressing $5.50. Entrees range from red prawns in coconut curry $32, to sugarcane- and *kiawe*-grilled free-range veal to coffee-smoked rack of lamb. Also in keeping with the Hawaiian regional theme are grilled rare *ahi* steaks and breast of range chicken with Waipio taro pancakes. Desserts like the banana chocolate mousse Napoleon would have soothed even the most belligerent at Waterloo.

The Terrace, informal and alfresco, serves breakfast, lunch, and dinner. Breakfast is either a la carte—from a simple continental breakfast to a traditional American with eggs, potatoes, juice, and bacon—or a lavish buffet offering fresh fruits, cereals, French toast, Belgian waffles, the finest and most delectable breakfast meats, steaming pots of Kona coffee, pineapple crepes, and even *huevos rancheros.* Lunch can similarly be a la carte—*paniolo* steak sandwiches or Cobb salad, for example—or a magnificent buffet of chilled seafood, sashimi, salmon, steaks, chops, lox, a cornucopia of island fruits and vegetables, and a dessert bar.

Dinner offers starters like *fritto misto,* shrimp cocktail, or Mediterranean Caesar salad, all from $7. Sweet onion soup or brown bean soup with orzo are sure to please. Entrees are a variety of pasta dishes or grilled lamb chops, medallions of fresh *ono,* veal T-bone, or jumbo prawns for under $30.

For light fare and quick snacks try the hotel's beachside **Hau Tree Cafe,** serving lunch and cocktails 11:30 a.m.-3:30 p.m.; or **The 19th Hole,** adjoining the pro shop, where you can snack on everything from burgers to sushi daily 11 a.m.-4:30 p.m. The Mauna Kea is also famous for its Saturday-evening **clambake** at the Hau Tree Cafe, where you can feast on Maine lobster, garlic shrimp, and sumptuous steamed clams while the sun sets to the melodious strains of musician extraordinaire George Kahumoku and Friends. Tuesday is extra special, featuring the Mauna Kea's world-famous **Old Hawaiian Aha'aina Luau.** As the sun sends blazing shafts of red and gold over the Luau Gardens at North Pointe, you dine on island favorites like *lau lau, huli huli* pork, Korean short ribs, island-grown steaks, and snow crab claws. The evening entertainment includes a torch lighting ceremony, traditional hula presented by *kumu hula* Nani Lim Yap, and the dramatic Samoan fire dance.

Puako Beach Apartments

Puako Village has the only reasonably priced accommodations in this diamond-studded neck of the woods. The 38 modern units go for $50-$120 (four bedrooms), $5 extra person. All units have a kitchen, laundry facilities, lanai, and twice-weekly maid service. You'll find ample parking, TV, and a swimming pool. Write Puako Beach Apartments, 3 Puako Beach Dr., Kamuela, HI 96743, tel. 882-7711.

FOOD, SHOPPING, AND ENTERTAINMENT

The following is a list of the very limited food, shopping, and entertainment in South Kohala, independent of that offered at the luxury resorts, hotels, and condominiums. Please refer to "Resorts and Accommodations" above for coverage of these topics at the hotels.

King's Shops

The planned resort community of Waikoloa has its own small but adequate shopping center, The King's Shops, tel. 885-8811, open daily 9:30 a.m.-9:30 p.m., that features over 40 different shops and restaurants, along with entertainment (see below), special events, and a **tourist information center.** A number of the shops feature Hawaiian artifacts, with museum-quality exhibits here and there, and even some petroglyphs that offer a link to the mythology of ancient Hawaii. The shops include: **Benetton's** and **Crazy Shirts** for distinctive tops, shirts, and tees; **Zac's** for your photo needs; **Ocean Splash** for everything from masks and snorkels to boogie boards; **Tutu Nene** for women's fine clothing and art objects; **Liberty House** for department-store merchandise; **Whaler's General Store** for light groceries and sundries; **Waikoloa Hat Company** for lids of all descriptions, but especially those made from natural fibers. **Noa Noa** has an excellent selection of imported fashions from throughout Southeast Asia, especially Indonesia. Fabrics range from rayon to silk; the batik prints were individually designed. Excellent prices. **Endangered Species** welcomes you with a python overhead. Most items, from T-shirts to sculptures, have an animal or floral motif. A portion of the proceeds from all sales goes to the World Wildlife Foundation. **Tiki Trading Post** is a terrific shop featuring mainly island-stylish men's clothing. Inside are jogging shorts, T-shirts, sweatshirts, aloha shirts, and some shoes. Their motto, "Dress like you live here," says it all.

Restaurants at the King's Shops include: **Hama Yu Japanese Restaurant,** open daily 11:30 a.m.-2 p.m. and 5:30-9 p.m. Choose appetizers ($4.50-7) like soft-shell crab, yakitori, and a variety of sashimi and sushi. Dinners include tempura $24, Japanese steak $26, and *tonkatsu* $19. For a smaller and more moderately priced meal try **Hawaiian Chili by Max,** a window restaurant where you can have a variety of chili and hot dogs, all well prepared and health-conscious.

Kawaihae Center

The Kawaihae Shopping Center can take care of your rudimentary shopping needs. It sits at the Y-junction of routes 19 and 270 and is situated so that the upper floors face Rt. 19 and the lower floors are along Rt. 270. There's a **7-Eleven** convenience store, **Kohala Kollections** for artwork and antiques, the **Cactus Tree** for alohawear, and **Tropical Dreams** for homemade ice creams and sorbets. Restaurants are on both levels (see below). Across the road are a **76 gas station** and **Laau's Fish Market** (open Mon.-Sat. 6 a.m.-6 p.m.).

Kohala Divers

Located along Rt. 270 in Kawaihae, open daily 8 a.m.-5 p.m., tel. 882-7774, Kohala Divers offers scuba certification for $300, snorkel rentals for $10 (24 hours), and scuba rentals for $22. They lead two-tank dives for $75 and will take snorkelers along if they have room on the boat ($15). It's a bit far to go from Kailua-Kona, but they offer big savings, and they're the only dive company along the Kohala coast.

Blue Dolphin

In Kawaihae Village along Rt. 270 is a takeout-window restaurant, the Blue Dolphin, run by a husband-and-wife team, tel. 882-7771, open weekdays 10 a.m.-3 p.m. Their limited menu features lemonade made from organically grown island lemons, and plate lunches like teriyaki beef $4.95, sautéed mahimahi $5.50, and a mixed plate for $4.95. If you're heading north and want to picnic along the way, the Blue Dolphin will fill the bill.

Cafe Pesto

Who'd expect a yuppie upscale restaurant in the sleepy village of Kawaihae? Cafe Pesto, tel. 882-1071, open Sun.-Thurs. 11 a.m.-9 p.m., Fri.-Sat. 11 a.m.-10 p.m., has a chic interior design with black-and-white checkerboard flooring and black-and-white tables. The bold gourmet menu tantalizes you with starters like *crostini* (French bread with a fresh, creamy herb garlic butter) $2.95 and freshly made soups from $3.25. Daily specials might be scallop-and-Brie bisque $6.95, wild green salad $3.50, blue Caesar salad $3.95, or Greek pasta salad $6.95. Pasta dishes are scrumptious: smoked-salmon pasta with spinach, capers, sun-dried tomatoes, and fettuccine in saffron cream sauce $12.95; or chipotle shrimp and hot Calibrese sausage, red onions, and sweet peppers over cilantro-tossed linguine $13.95. Lunch, served 11 a.m.-4 p.m., brings an assortment of hot sandwiches that includes everything from smoked ham to a chicken pita for under $8. Cafe Pesto also serves gourmet pizza with crust and sauces made fresh daily. Among their best pizzas are shiitake mushrooms and artichokes with rosemary and Gorgonzola sauce, seafood pesto pizza, and pizza luau, all ranging in price from $5.95 for a small to $16.95 for a large (also served by the slice for $2). Cafe Pesto is *the* perfect place to stop for a civilized lunch as you explore the Kohala coast.

Tres Hombres Beach Grill

Pancho Villa in aloha shirt and sombrero and riding a surfboard (!) would be instantly at home in Tres Hombres, tel. 882-1031, located in the Kawaihae Center, open 11:30 a.m.-midnight, dinners to 9 p.m. on weekdays, and to 10 p.m. weekends. Besides being a south-of-the-border restaurant, run by Popeye, an old-time waterman from Southern California, Tres Hombres is an unofficial surfing museum filled with a fine collection of surfboards and surfing memorabilia donated by such legendary greats as Dewey Weber, Greg Knoll, and Jack Wise. Some of the tables are fashioned from surfboards made of balsa wood with mahogany striping, others from green-and-white Mexican tiles. Bar stools are of provincial Mexican design topped with leather. The bamboo-appointed interior has a relaxed tropical effect. The extensive menu, presented on a miniature surfboard, offers savories like nachos $7.95, quesadillas $6.95, and a selection of rolled tacos $6.95. Salads include Caesar for $5.95 and chicken taco (easily a full meal) for $10.95. For combination dinners you have your choice of Mexican favorites like enchiladas, *chiles rellenos,* tostadas, and burritos, for $9.95. Full-dinner entrees can be roasted chicken $11.95; steak, shrimp, or chicken fajitas $14.95; or simple but delicious fish tacos $11.95. The full bar serves not only all the island favorites, but adds special concoctions like K-38s, Swamis, and Popeye's grog, with *pu pu* served daily 3-6 p.m. Relax with an ice-cold margarita on the lanai of this tastefully casual restaurant, and experience an excellent change of pace from the luxury hotels just down the road.

Golf Cart Vendor
You can actually buy a well-made sandwich, a hot dog with all the trimmings, soft drinks, and beer from the strategically placed and gaily canopied Golf Cart Vendor at the Mauna Lani Resort Golf Course. Follow Kaniku Drive toward the Ritz-Carlton Hotel and look for the access road pointing to Holoholokai Beach Park. Follow it, and in about 100 yards just where the golf cart track crosses the road, look to the right for the cart. This makes a perfect stop if you're heading to the Puako Petroglyphs or to the beach park. The sandwiches, fairly hearty, are under $4, the hot dogs $2.50, and the beer, soda, and snacks are priced amazingly right for this exclusive neck of the woods.

Entertainment
Free entertainment is offered at the **King's Shops** at Waikoloa every Thursday 6-8 p.m., when local musicians come to perform contemporary Hawaiian music. The Royal Waikoloan Hotel offers *pu pu* and refreshments at the event for a nominal charge. The evening is popular with both tourists and local people and is an excellent chance to have fun Hawaiian style.

The prepared fronds of the screw pine, or lau hala, *are used in traditional weaving of hats, mats, and trays.*

WAIMEA (KAMUELA)

Waimea is in the South Kohala District. But because of its inland topography of high mountain pasture, mostly covering Mauna Kea's western slopes, Waimea could be considered a district in its own right. It also has a unique culture inspired by the range-riding *paniolo* of the expansive **Parker Ranch.** This spread, founded early last century by John Palmer Parker, dominates the heart and soul of the region. Waimea revolves around ranch life and livestock. A herd of rodeos and "Wild West shows" is scheduled throughout the year. But a visit here isn't one-dimensional. In town are home accommodations and inspired country dining. For fun and relaxation there's a visitor and ranch center; Puuopelu, the Parker mansion and art collection; a wonderful museum operated by John Parker's great-great granddaughter and her husband; a litany of historic shrines and churches; and an abundance of fresh-air and wide-open spaces, the latter not so easily found in the islands.

The town is split almost directly down the center—the east side is the wet side, and the west is the dry side. Houses on the east side are easy to find and reasonable to rent; houses on the dry side are expensive and usually unavailable. You can literally walk from verdant green fields and tall trees to dry desert in a matter of minutes. This imaginary line also demarcates the local social order: upper-class ranch managers (dry), and working-class *paniolo* (wet). However, the air of Waimea, refreshed and cooled by fine mists *(kipuupuu),* combines with only 20 inches of rainfall a year into the best mountain weather in Hawaii. Waimea is equally known as Kamuela, the Hawaiianized version of Samuel, after one of John Parker's grandsons. Kamuela is used as the post office address, so as not to confuse Waimea with a town of the same name on the island of Kauai. The village is experiencing a growth spurt. In 1980 it had no traffic lights and was home to about 2,000 people. Now the population has grown fivefold and there are traffic jams. Waimea is modernizing, and its cowboy backwoods character is rapidly changing.

Getting There

The main artery connecting Waimea and Kailua-Kona is Rt. 190, also known as the Hawaii Belt Road. This stretch is locally called the Mamalahoa Highway. From Kailua-Kona, head out on Palani Road until it turns into Rt. 190. As you gain elevation heading into the interior, look left to see the broad and flat coastal lava flows. Seven miles before reaching Waimea, Saddle Road (Rt. 200) intersects the road from the right, and now the highlands, with grazing cattle amidst fields of cactus, look much more like Marlboro Country than the land of *aloha*. The Saddle Road and Rt. 19, connecting Waimea with Hilo and points east, have been fully described in the chapters on The Saddle Road and South Kohala. The **Waimea-Kohala Airport,** tel. 885-4520, is along Rt. 190 just a mile or so before you enter town. Facilities amount to a basic restroom and waiting area with a few car rental windows. Unless a flight is scheduled, even these are closed. For a description of Rt. 250 leading to Kapaau and Hawi on the coast, see "Getting There" in the North Kohala chapter.

SIGHTS

HISTORIC HOMES AND ART COLLECTION AT PUUOPELU

Richard Smart, heir to the fantastic Parker Ranch, opened Puuopelu, a century-old family mansion, to the public just a few years before he passed away on November 12, 1992. Inside this living museum, the works of over 100 prominent artists, including Degas and Renoir, are displayed. On the grounds, original and reconstructed Parker Ranch homes are also open to visitors. Puuopelu is located along Rt. 190 a few minutes south of town and is open daily 10 a.m.-5 p.m., admission $7.50 adults, $3.75 children.

A formal drive lined with stately eucalyptus leads to the mansion. Begin your tour in an elegant sitting room illuminated by a crystal chandelier. The home was begun in 1852 by John Palmer Parker II. In 1910 Richard Smart's grandmother, Aunt Tootsie, added the living room, kitchen, and fireplace. In 1969 Richard Smart, who inherited the ranch lands and home from Aunt Tootsie, gutted the home and raised the ceiling to 19 feet to accommodate his art collection. He added elegant French doors and skylights. Part of the kitchen was converted into a dining room, the Gold Room was created, and the koa doorways were raised to match. Richard Smart became a well-known actor. He studied at the Pasadena Playhouse in the late '20s, and appeared on Broadway with famous names such as Carol Channing and Nannette Fabray. Mr. Smart performed in plays all over the U.S., and recordings of him singing songs in Italian, French, and Spanish provide the background music as you tour the art collection. You've heard of actors becoming ranchers; well, he was a rancher who became an actor. The tour is self guided with all art pieces named. Besides works of famous artists, there are magnificent pieces like a tall wooden cabinet with carved yellow Chinese Peiping glass from the 19th century, silver tea sets, decanters for pouring wine at elegant functions, large cut-crystal punch bowls, and magnificent chandeliers hung from the skylights overhead. Make sure to see the little side bedroom, called the Venetian Room, aptly decorated with paintings of gondolas and appointed with treasures from Venice. Lighting the room are two chandeliers, one pink and the other turquoise. Here, the filigreed art-deco mirrors are fabulous. The feeling is of genteel elegance, but notice that the walls are rather rough board and battten covered with beautiful artwork. You get a feeling of class, but it's obvious that you are on a ranch. In the emerald green kingdom that is the Parker Ranch, Puuopelu is the crowning jewel.

Just outside Puuopelu is the reconstructed **Mana Home** (included in admission), the original Parker Ranch homestead. A knowledgeable tour guide, Judy Apo, leads you through and provides historical anecdotes about the Parker family. The home was built in 1847 by family patriarch John Palmer Parker from the durable native koa found at high elevations on the ranch lands. The exterior of the original home, covered by a heavy slate roof, was too brittle to move from its original site 12 miles away, but the interior was removed, numbered, and put back together again like a giant jigsaw

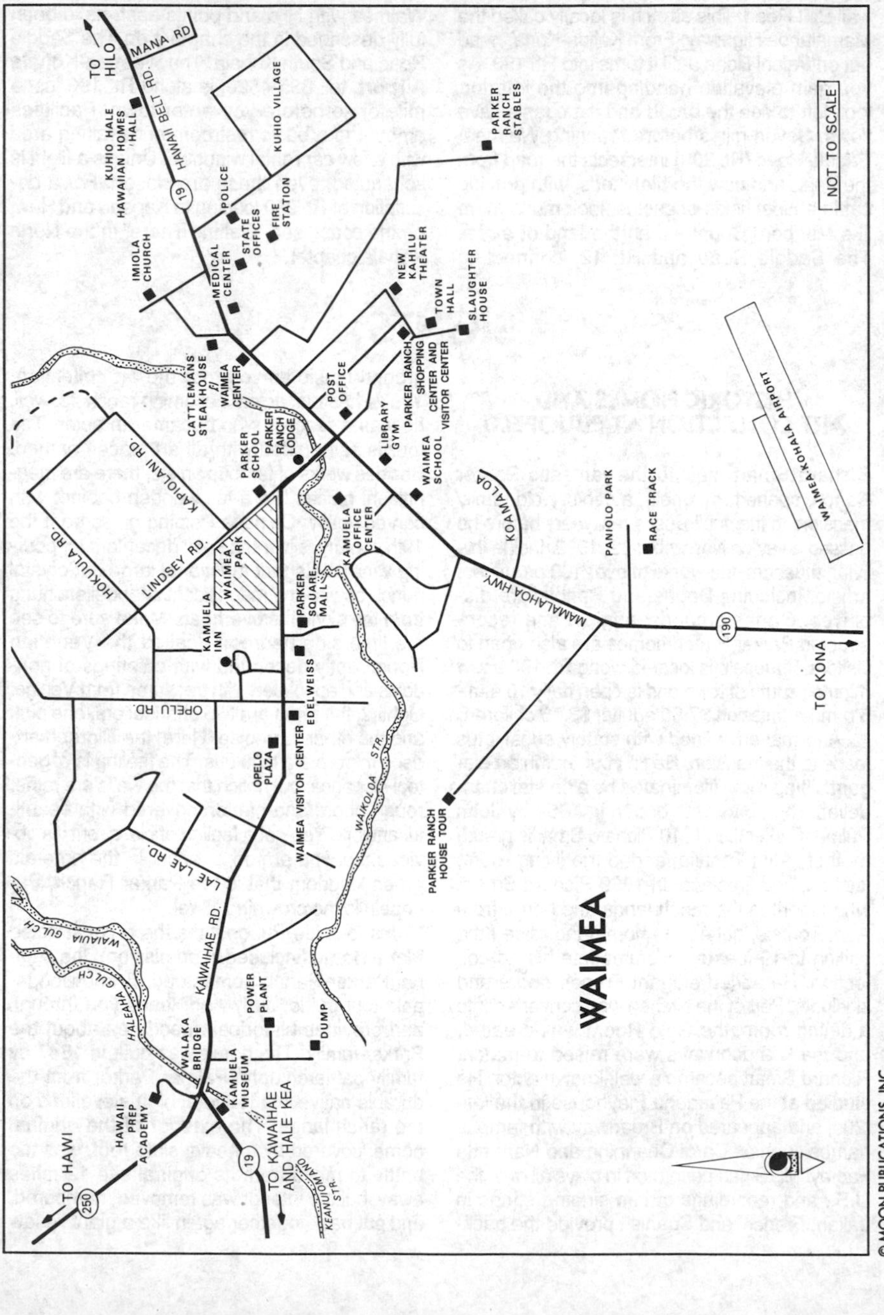

WAIMEA
NOT TO SCALE
TO HILO
MANA RD
KUHIO VILLAGE
19
HAWAII BELT RD.
KUHIO HALE HAWAIIAN HOMES HALL
PARKER RANCH STABLES
POLICE
FIRE STATION
STATE OFFICES
IMIOLA CHURCH
MEDICAL CENTER
NEW KAHILU THEATER
TOWN HALL
SLAUGHTER HOUSE
CATTLEMANS STEAKHOUSE
WAIMEA CENTER
POST OFFICE
PARKER RANCH SHOPPING CENTER AND VISITOR CENTER
LIBRARY GYM
WAIMEA SCHOOL
PARKER SCHOOL
PARKER RANCH LODGE
KAPIOLANI RD.
HOKUULA RD.
LINDSEY RD.
WAIMEA PARK
KAMUELA OFFICE CENTER
KOANI LOA
PANIOLO PARK
RACE TRACK
WAIMEA-KOHALA AIRPORT
MAMALAHOA HWY.
190
TO KONA
PARKER SQUARE MALL
KAMUELA INN
EDELWEISS
OPELU RD.
WAIMEA VISITOR CENTER
OPELO PLAZA
WAIKOLOA STR.
PARKER RANCH HOUSE TOUR
LAE LAE RD.
KAWAIHAE RD.
POWER PLANT
DUMP
WAIAKA GULCH
HALEAHA GULCH
WALAKA BRIDGE
KAMUELA MUSEUM
HAWAII PREP ACADEMY
TO HAWI
250
19
TO KAWAIHAE AND HALE KEA
KEANUIOMANO STR.

puzzle in the reconstructed home. A model in the living room shows you what the original site looked like back in the 1800s. To preserve the rich wood interior of the home, all that's required is to wipe it down once a year with lemon oil. A collection of fine calabashes handed down over the generations is on display. At first the structure seems like a small cabin, just what you'd expect from the 1850s, but in actuality it's a two-story home with one bedroom downstairs and three upstairs.

The Parker dynasty (see "Parker Ranch Visitor Center," following, for more information) began when John Palmer Parker jumped ship and married Rachel Kipikane, the granddaughter of Kamehameha. They bought two acres of land for $10, and Parker with his two sons built the Mana Home. In later years Kipikane, being the granddaughter of the king, received 640 acres. The two sons, John Palmer Parker II and Ebenezer, who were by then married, built two homes on it, and as children came, added more rooms in the sprawling New England tradition. They also built one large community kitchen, at which the entire family cooked and dined. A replica shows how the home grew over the years, and it is a good indicator of how the Parker fortunes grew along with it. As the children's children got older, they needed a schoolhouse, so they built one at the corner of the original site. It still stands and is maintained by a *paniolo* and his family, who live there. Unfortunately, many members of the Parker family died young. The first-born, John Palmer Parker II, married Hanai. His brother, Ebenezer, married Kilea, a woman from Maui, who bore him four children. One of their boys was Samuel Parker, known in Hawaiian as Kamuela, the co-name of Waimea. Samuel married Napela, and together they had nine children. Samuel's father Ebenezer died at age 26 after swallowing the bone of a flubber (a little bird the size of a pigeon) that punctured his intestine. Kilea could never get over his death and visited his grave daily. Finally, she decided that she wanted to return to her family on Maui. She was advised by the people of the island not to go because of rough seas. Kilea did not heed the advice, and along with her entourage was lost at sea. Meanwhile, John Palmer Parker II and Hanai gave birth to only one boy who died within 12 months. Childless, they adopted one of their nephew Samuel's nine children as a *hanai* child in a practice that continues to this day. He was the fifth child, John, who became John Palmer Parker III and who later married Elizabeth Dowsick, known as Aunt Tootsie. They had one girl, Thelma Parker, before John III died of pneumonia at age 19. Aunt Tootsie raised Thelma as a single parent and somehow managed to purchase Samuel Parker's and his eight children's half of the ranch. Thelma Parker married Gillian Smart. They had one boy, Mr. Richard Smart, before his mother Thelma died at age 20 of tuberculosis. Aunt Tootsie literally took the bull by the horns to keep the ranch going, and when she passed away in 1943 she left everything to her grandson Richard. The ranch prospered under his ownership and spread to its present 225,000 acres with 50,000 head of cattle that supply fully one-third of the beef in the Hawaiian Islands.

SIGHTS IN TOWN

Hale Kea

On 11 emerald green rolling acres, typical of *paniolo* country, sits Hale Kea ("White House"), tel. 885-6094, the restored residence of the top hand on the Parker Ranch. Located on Kawaihae Road before you enter Waimea from Kohala, Hale Kea is open daily at 10 a.m. Admission is free, and a shuttle van from the Kohala coast is available by reservation. On the premises are boutique shops, art galleries, and **Hartwell's Restaurant** (see "Food" and "Shopping" following). Built in 1897 for the Parker Ranch's first manager, A.W. Carter, the residence served the Carter family for a total of 60 years in this capacity; 35 years for A.W., and then another 25 years for his son, Hartwell Carter, who took over as manager.

You enter through a large, breeze-catching veranda, which leads into a formal parlor and sitting room. Here velveteen chairs, wicker furniture from 1899, and a baby grand piano bring genteel civility to the heart of a hard-working ranch. The veranda, sprinkled with dining tables and chairs, and most of the rooms in the main house, serve as dining rooms for the restaurant. Feel free to wander around and look at the displays. One of the larger rooms is a formal private dining room with a striking blue carpet and a huge table that could comfortably seat more than a dozen diners. An intimate room called the "Library" was built by Laurence Rockefeller in 1969, and is appointed in rich koa and lined with a collection of rare tomes and sporting arms. Another informal room is the *"Paniolo,"* with heavy, well-worn tables and chairs where you can almost smell the coffee brewing and bacon sizzling as the cowboys prepared to meet the day. Every room holds usable antiques, furniture, fixtures, and artifacts still very serviceable and in use.

Leave the main house and amble around out back, where modest outbuildings that once served as bunkhouses, stables, and storage sheds now house unique shops selling original artwork, designer clothing, and "souvenirs Hawaii." The grounds are made more lovely with rose, flower, and vegetable gardens, and with a gazebo perfect for a soothing contemplation of this striking upcountry land.

Parker Ranch Visitor Center And Museum

This is the first place to stop while in town. The visitors center, at the Parker Ranch Shopping Center, is open daily 9 a.m.-4 p.m., tel. 885-7655, adults $5, children $3.75 (joint admission to Puuopelu available). After spending an hour at the center's two museums and taking in the slide presentation, you'll have a good overview of the history of the Parker Ranch and, by extension, Waimea. Exhibits at the **John Palmer Parker Museum** depict the history and genealogy of the six generations of Parkers who have owned the ranch. At the entrance is a photo of the founder, John Parker, a seaman who left Newton, Massachusetts, on a trading vessel in 1809 and landed in Kealakekua, becoming a fast friend of Kamehameha the Great. Parker, then only 19, continued his voyages, returning in 1814 and marrying Kipikane, a chieftess and granddaughter of Kamehameha. In the interim, domesticated cattle, a present from Captain Vancouver to Kamehameha, had gone wild due to neglect and were becoming a dangerous nuisance all over the Big Island. Parker was hired to round up the best of them and to exterminate the rest. While doing so, he chose the finest head for his own herd. In 1847 King Kamehameha III divided the land by what was known as the Great *Mahele,* and John Parker was granted Royal Deed No. 7, for a two-acre parcel on the northeast slopes of Mauna Kea. His wife, being royal born, was entitled to 640 acres, and with these lands and tough determination, the mighty 225,000-acre Parker Ranch began. It remains the largest privately owned ranch in the U.S., and on its fertile pastures over 50,000 cattle and 1,000 horses are raised.

In the museum, old family photos include one of Rev. Elias Bond, who presided over the Christian marriage of Parker and his Hawaiian wife in 1820. Preserved also are old Bibles, clothing from the era, and an entire koa hut once occupied by woodcutters and range riders. There are fine examples of quilting, stuffed animals, an arsenal of old weapons, and a vintage printing press. A separate room is dedicated to **Duke Kahanamoku,** the great Hawaiian Olympian and "Father of Modern Surfing." Inside are paddles he used; his bed and dresser; legions of the medals, cups, and trophies he won; and Duke's walking sticks. The 15-minute video in the comfortable **Thelma Parker Theater** begins whenever enough people have assembled after going through the museum. The video presents a thorough and professional rendition of the Parker Ranch history, along with sensitive glimpses of ranch life of the still very active *paniolo.*

Imiola Church

Head east on Rt. 19 to "church row," a cluster of New England-style structures on the left, a few minutes past the Parker Ranch Shopping Center. Most famous among them is Imiola ("Seeking Life") Church. It was built in 1857 by the Rev. Lorenzo Lyons, who mastered the Hawaiian language and translated some of the great old Christian hymns into Hawaiian, as well as melodic Hawaiian chants into English. The current minister is a friendly and urbane man, Rev. Bill Hawk, a new arrival who is assisted by his wife Sandra. The yellow clapboard church with white trim would be at home along any New England village green. When you enter, you'll notice an oddity: the pulpit is at the near side and you walk around it to face the rear of the church. The walls and ceilings are of rich brown koa, but the pews, supposedly of the same lustrous wood, have been painted pink! The hymnals contain many of the songs translated by Father Lyons. Outside is a simple monument to Reverend Lyons, along with a number of his children's gravesites. A tour of the church is free and definitely worth the time.

Kamuela Museum

The Kamuela Museum, largest privately owned museum in Hawaii, is a fantastic labor of love. For the octogenarian owners, founders, and curators, Albert and Harriet Solomon, it's a vocation that began in 1968 and fulfilled a prophecy of Albert's grandmother, who was pure Hawaiian and a renowned *kahuna* from Pololu Valley. When Albert was only eight years old, his grandmother foretold that he would build "a great longhouse near three mountains and that he would become famous, visited by people from all over the world." This prediction struck him so much that he wrote it down and kept it throughout his life. When grown, he married Harriet, the great-great granddaughter of John Palmer Parker, and the two lived in Honolulu for most of their adult lives, where Albert was a policeman. For 50 years the Solomons collected, collected, and collected! Harriet, being a Parker, was given heirlooms by family members which are also on exhibit. The museum is west of town center on Rt. 19—50 yards after the junction with Rt. 250 heading toward Hawi. The museum is open every day of the year 8 a.m.-5 p.m., tel. 885-4724, $5 adults, $2 children under 12.

As you enter, the screen door bangs like a shot to signal Albert and Harriet that another visitor has arrived. Although the tour is self guided, Mrs. Solomon directs you through the museum, almost like a stern "schoolmarm" who knows what's best for you, but actually she's a sweetheart who has plenty of time for her guests and is willing to "talk story." Inside it's easy to become overwhelmed as you're confronted with everything from sombreros to a stuffed albatross, moose head, and South American lizard. An extensive weapons collection includes Khyber rifles, Japanese machine guns, swords, and knives. If you enjoy Hawaiiana, there's *kahili, konane* boards, poi pounders, stone sinkers and hooks, wooden surfboards, and a very unique "canoe buster." The museum has a few extremely rare stone idols and a good collection of furniture from the Hawaiian nobility, including Prince Kuhio's council table. Antiques of every description include Japanese and Hawaiian feathered fans, carved Chinese furniture, a brass diving helmet, some of the first Hawaiian Bibles, and even buffalo robes used by the pioneers. Everywhere are old photos commemorating the lives of the Parkers down through the years. Before you leave, go into the front room, where the view through a huge picture window perfectly frames a pond and three round-topped mountains in *paniolo* country.

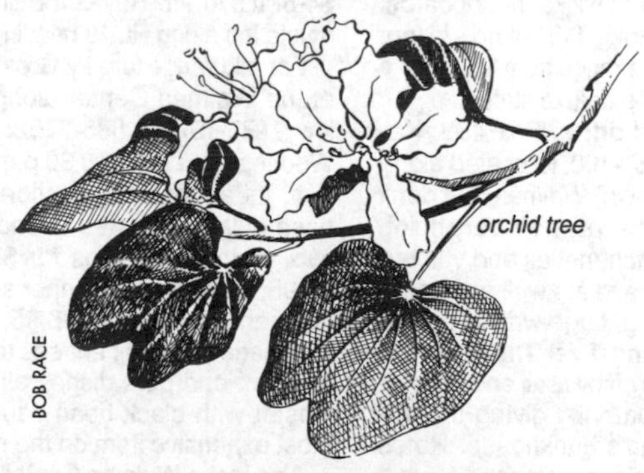

orchid tree

PRACTICALITIES

ACCOMMODATIONS

As far as staying in Waimea is concerned, you won't be plagued with indecision. Of the two hotels in town, both are basic and clean, one inexpensive and the other upscale.

The **Kamuela Inn,** Box 1994, Kamuela, HI 96743, tel. 885-4243, a one-time basic cinder-block motel with 19 units, has been transformed into a bright and airy 31-unit boutique hotel. It is located down a small cul-de-sac off Rt. 19 just before Opelu Road. Office hours are 7:15 a.m.-8 p.m., but a key and instructions will be left for late arrivals. The new owner, Carolyn Cascavilla, takes personal pride in the hotel and offers each guest a complimentary continental breakfast. The small but pleasant grounds are appointed with flowers and manicured trees and you'll find a swing to lull you into relaxation. A new wing features the deluxe "Executive Suite" and a "Penthouse" where Governor John Waihee, among other dignitaries, has found peace and quiet. The new wing is comfortable and tasteful with hardwood floors, queen-size beds, a full kitchen, and a small anteroom that opens onto a private lanai, perfect for a quiet morning breakfast. The Penthouse is upstairs, and breaks into two joinable units that can accommodate up to six guests. The basic motel rooms are small, neat, and tidy with twin beds with wicker headboards, private bathrooms, and color TV, but no a/c (not needed) or phones. Prices range from $54 s for a basic room to $165 for the deluxe suites.

The Parker Ranch Lodge, Box 458, Kamuela, HI 96743, tel. 885-4100, is located along Lindsey Road in "downtown" Waimea, but don't let "downtown" fool you because it's very quiet. The rooms, most with kitchenettes and vaulted ceilings, have full baths, and are well appointed with rich brown carpeting, large writing desks, easy chairs, phones, and TVs. The barn-red board-and-batten inn sits off by itself and lives up to being in *paniolo* country by giving the impression of a gentleman's bunkhouse. Rates are $74 standard, $85.15 for a kitchenette unit, $10 additional person.

FOOD

Inexpensive/Moderate

One of the cheapest places in Waimea to get good standard American/Hawaiian food is the **Kamuela Drive-In Deli.** This no-nonsense eatery, frequented by local people, is next door to the Parker Ranch Shopping Center. They get the folks in these parts started at 5 a.m. with a hearty breakfast for under $5. Plate lunches of teriyaki beef and the like sell for $5-6. If you're into food and not atmosphere, this is the place.

Auntie Alice's, tel. 885-6880, open daily 6 a.m.-6 p.m., is a small restaurant/bakery in the Parker Ranch Shopping Center serving home-made pies and breakfast for under $5, with hefty sandwiches around $6.

Su's Thai Kitchen, tel. 885-8688, offers indoor seating in a great restaurant owned and operated by the same folks who run the Su's Thai Kitchen in Kona (see the "Inexpensive" section under "Food" under "Kailua-Kona and Vicinity" in the Kona chapter). This new location has the same menu as the original place but also features American breakfast and American, Chinese, and Japanese lunch specials.

Massayo's is another basic eatery open daily 5 a.m.-3 p.m., where you can get hearty breakfasts and plate lunches with an Asian twist for $4-5. It's in the Hayashi Building near the Kamuela Inn along Rt. 19 heading west out of town.

For mid-range fare try **Great Wall Chop Suey** at the Waimea Center along the Mamalahoa Hwy. (Rt. 19), tel. 885-7252, open daily except Wednesday 11 a.m.-8:30 p.m., lunch 11 a.m.-3 p.m. Its appealing selection of standard Chinese dishes includes a lunch special of one, two, or three choices for $3.95, $4.95, and $5.95, respectively. Dinner specials are an all-you-can-eat buffet at $6.95, and fresh *manapua* made daily. For entrees try a variety of beef, chicken, and pork dishes all around $5.50, or lobster with black bean sauce at $12.50, the most expensive item on the menu.

Also in the Waimea Center is **Young's Kalbi,** a Korean restaurant open daily except Monday,

10:30 a.m.-9 p.m., that serves dishes like *kalbi* chicken, shrimp tempura, oyster-sauce chicken, and spicy pork, all priced under $6.

Cattleman's Steakhouse, tel. 885-4077, next door to the Waimea Center along Rt. 19 heading east, is a terrific place to soak up the local scene and to enjoy basic but hearty food. At this recently renovated restaurant, the menu is steak and more steak, all from the Parker Ranch. Tuesday-Sat. 3-5:30 p.m. they have the *Pau Hana* Relaxer (happy hour). Also *karaoke* Tuesday and Wednesday, Hawaiian music Thursday by Smitty and Charlie, and everything from country to rock 'n' roll by groups like Ecstasy on the weekends. The bill of fare starts with scampi or sautéed mushrooms for $6.95, and moves on to peppercorn steak, steak Diane, steak and scampi, or New York steak for $17.95. Other entrees include Hawaiian chop steak $15.95, chicken oriental $15.95, seafood pasta $17.95, and baked manicotti $15.95. A limited children's menu helps keep prices down, with everything under $10. The soup-and-salad buffet is just $9.95. Cattleman's Steakhouse is not a *great* restaurant, but the service is friendly, and the scene couldn't be more authentic.

Paniolo Country Inn, tel. 885-4377, in town center, open daily for breakfast 7-11 a.m., lunch 11 a.m.-5 p.m., dinner 5-8:45 p.m., specializes in full breakfasts, flame-broiled steaks, burgers, and plate lunches. Breakfast selections include omelettes with one item $3.75, and the *wikiwiki* breakfast of English muffin, banana bread or wheat toast, coffee, and small fruit juice $3.25. Lunches can be the Rodeo Special (a bun heaped with pepperoni, salami, bell peppers, mushrooms, and onions and smothered with pizza sauce and melted cheese) $5.95, or the *Paniolo Country* (a sandwich made with layers of spiced ham, turkey breast, bacon, tomato, onion, melted cheese, mayonnaise, and sprouts) $6.50. Hamburgers range from $5.75 for a regular burger to $6.95 for the deluxe with the works. Soups and salads are $4.25, the *paniolo* taco salad $6.25, and the tostada grande salad $6.95. Plate lunches are standards like teriyaki short ribs $7.25, while a dinner plate could be top sirloin $12.50. The Paniolo Country Inn even has pizza, and a children's menu to keep prices down. The food is wholesome, the atmosphere American standard, and the service prompt and friendly.

Don's Pake Kitchen, about two miles east of town on Rt. 19, open daily 10 a.m.-9 p.m., has a good reputation for food at reasonable prices even though most of their selections are of the steam-table variety. Chef's specials are ginger beef, oyster chicken, and shrimp-sauce pork all priced under $6. Steamed rice sold by the pint is $1.20. Don's also specializes in large pans of food that can feed entire families. Next door is **The Vegetable Stop,** open Monday, Wednesday, and Saturday 9 a.m.-5 p.m. Most of the best vegies and fruits, homegrown but not necessarily organic, are gone by noon.

Fine Dining

One of the best benefits of Waimea's coming of age is the number of excellent restaurants that have recently opened. The competition among gourmet-food establishments is stiff, so each one tries to find its culinary niche.

The Edelweiss on Rt. 19 across from the Kamuela Inn is Waimea's established gourmet restaurant, where chef Hans-Peter Hager, formerly of the super-exclusive Mauna Kea Beach Hotel, serves gourmet food in rustic but elegant surroundings. The Edelweiss is open Tues.-Sat. for lunch 11:30 a.m.-1:30 p.m. and for dinner 5-9:30 p.m., tel. 885-6800. Inside, heavy posts and beams exude that "country feeling," but fine crystal and pure white tablecloths let you know you're in for some superb dining. The wine cellar is quite extensive, with selections of domestic, French, Italian, and German wines. Affordable lunches include offerings like soup, turkey sandwiches, and chicken salad in papaya for under $8.50. Dinner starts with melon with prosciutto at $4.95, escargot for $5.75, onion soup at $4.25, and Caesar salad for $4.25. Some Edelweiss specialties are sautéed veal, lamb, beef, and bacon with pfefferling for $19.50; roast duck braised with a light orange sauce at $17.50; half spring chicken diablo at $15.50; and of course German favorites like Wiener schnitzel at $16.50, and roast pork and sauerkraut for $15.50. The cooking is rich and delicious; the proof a loyal clientele who return again and again.

Gentlemen ranchers and their ladies love **The Parker Ranch Broiler,** open daily for lunch 11 a.m.-2 p.m. in the dining room and 2-3 p.m. in the bar (limited menu), dinner 5-10 p.m., in the Parker Ranch Shopping Center, tel. 885-7366.

Put on your best duds and sashay into the cushy green-velvet saloon, or into the tasteful koa-paneled main dining area. Local lunchtime favorites include Hawaiian chopped steak $7.95, teriyaki beef plate $8.75, and Hawaiian beef stew $8.95. For lighter fare try the Caesar salad, Parker Ranch chef salad, or fiesta taco salad, each for $7.95. Soups are reasonable at $3.75 per bowl—there is always Portuguese bean soup and a soup du jour. Start dinner with appetizers like escargots $7.95, sautéed mushrooms $5.75, and Chinese chicken salad $8.95. Fulfilling the name of Parker Ranch Broiler, the chef chooses the best cuts of Parker Ranch beef to create a variety of savory meat dishes such as top sirloin $14.95, or a 12-ounce New York cut $19.95. Other entrees include Pulehu chicken $14.95, shrimp scampi and seafood linguine, and even the fresh fish of the day at market price. Even if you don't dine here, it's worth a trip to the bar just for the atmosphere and to immerse yourself in one of the traditions of "*Paniolo* Country."

Merriman's, tel. 885-6822, open for Sunday brunch 10:30 a.m.-1:30 p.m., lunch weekdays 11:30 a.m.-1:30 p.m., dinner 5:30-9 p.m., in the Opelo Plaza along Rt. 19, has been receiving a great deal of praise from travelers and residents alike for its excellent food. The restaurant, resembling a small house from the outside, is stylish with pink and gray tablecloths, multicolored Fiestaware settings, and black- or pink-cushioned chairs of bent bamboo. Chef Peter Merriman creates classical European and American haute cuisine from local ingredients like Kohala lamb, Parker Ranch beef, Waimea lettuce, Puna goat cheese, and vine-ripened tomatoes. The menu changes every few months, but perennial appetizer favorites are corn and Kahuku shrimp fritters $6.75, vine-ripened Lokelani tomatoes with Maui onions $4.50, and spinach salad with balsamic vinaigrette dressing $4.50. Lunch fare is coconut grilled chicken with peanut dipping sauce and rice $5.75; grilled eggplant with Puna goat cheese, basil, and hot sauce $5.75; and grilled papaya salad with shrimp and peanuts for $8.50. Entrees are superb: Oahu chicken ginger-grilled with Indonesian peanut sauce $14.50; seafood sausage, chicken, fish, and shellfish in a saffron sauce at $21.50; and Thai-style shrimp curry for $21.50. Vegetarians can graze on linguine with tomato capers and snow peas $13.50, or on stir-fried vegetables with spicy curry for $12.50. Some of the most delicious offerings, however, are the fresh catch at market price, prepared in various gourmet styles including wrapped in nori and sautéed with *wasabi,* or herb-marinated and grilled with mango-lime sauce, with banana, mango, and coconut relish. Merriman's is destined to become a Big Island classic. Enjoy!

Dine in turn-of-the-century elegance at **Hartwell's Restaurant,** located at **Hale Kea,** the one-time country estate of the Parker Ranch's manager (for complete details see "Hale Kea" under "Sights in Town" above). The restaurant, tel. 885-6094, is open daily for lunch 11 a.m.-3:30 p.m., dinner 5-9:30 p.m., Sunday brunch 10 a.m.-3 p.m. A free shuttle bus is available by reservation from the Kohala Coast resorts. Choose your dining-room style, which can range from "down-home country" to "landed gentry," from any of the converted rooms of the New England-style rambling home. The lunch menu offers the chef's kettle, an edible bread bowl filled with a hearty stew or tangy chili for $6.95, oriental salad made from grilled marinated chicken breast tossed with fried wonton $9.95, or the restaurant's famous baby-back ribs basted in barbecue sauce and served with cornbread and coleslaw. Sunday brunch is a full choice from the breakfast menu for $11.95-14.95. Light suppers are presented 5-6:30 p.m. with entrees like herbed breast of chicken for $14.95 and veal scallopini $17.95. Full dinners start with appetizers like Chesapeake Bay crab cakes $6.95, grilled shrimp $7.95, and a variety of soups and salads from $4.95. For an entree choose Alaska king crab, New York sirloin, or island fresh lamb raised in Kau, all $20-25.

SHOPPING

Shops And Boutiques

Waimea's accelerated growth can be measured by the shopping centers springing up around town. One new center, still under construction across from the Parker Ranch Shopping Center, has some people concerned, as it will surround the Spencer House, a classical home from the ranch period. People were not thrilled when this area was denuded of its stately trees to accommodate the shopping center.

There is shopping in and around town, but the greatest concentration of shops is at the **Parker Ranch Shopping Center,** with over 30 specialty stores selling shoes, apparel, sporting goods, toys, and food. The **Parker Ranch Store** sells boots, cowboy hats, shirts, skirts, and buckles and bows. Many handcrafted items are made on the premises. Open daily, tel. 885-4977. **Setay,** a unique fine-jewelry shop, sells china, crystal, silver, and gold, tel. 885-4127. **Panda Imports,** tel. 885-8558, offers colorful handwoven cotton imports from Guatemala—everything from baby clothes to hammocks. Here too you'll find **Ben Franklin,** for sundries; **Keep In Touch,** with books and stationery; and **Honolulu Sporting Goods.**

The **Waimea Center,** most stores open weekdays 9 a.m.-5 p.m. and Saturday 10 a.m.-5 p.m., well marked along the Mamalahoa Hwy. near McDonald's, is the town's newest shopping mall. Among its shops you will find a **KTA Superstore** with everything from groceries to pharmaceuticals; **Zac's Photo** for developing and all photo needs; **Kona Fashion Club** for women's apparel; the **Men's Shop,** whose name says it all; **Kamuela Kids** for children's clothing; **Postmart** for all mailing and packaging needs including fax service; **Rhythm and Reading** with tapes, CDs, records, videos, and gifts; **Capricorn Book Store** for a fine selection of reading materials ranging from magazines to best-sellers; and the **Competitive Edge Triathalon Center,** an excellent sporting goods store featuring bicycles, swimming gear, and Rollerblades. The Waimea Center also has some fast-food eateries like **TCBY Yogurt** and **Subway Sandwiches** for a fast sandwich. Two inexpensive restaurants are **Great Wall Chop Suey** and **Young's Kalbi,** a Korean restaurant (see "Food" above for a description).

Make sure to tour **Hale Kea,** the converted but preserved country estate of the Parker Ranch's manager (for complete details see "Hale Kea" under "Sights in Town" above). The "White House," tel. 885-6094, and its distinctive boutique shops are open daily from 10 a.m. Admission is free, and complimentary shuttle from the Kohala Coast resorts is available by reservation. In the rambling home, appointed with period furniture and *paniolo* memorabilia, and in the attendant outbuildings, you will find: **Grande Gems and Galleries** offering fine jewelry and original artwork; **Noa Noa,** a shop with a reputation for designer clothes from Southeast Asia made of materials from rayon to silk at excellent prices; **Tutu Nene** for women's fashions; and the **Island Heritage Collection** for distinctive gifts by island artisans.

Around town try: **Waimea Design Center** along Rt. 19, tel. 885-6171, offering Asian handicrafts and Hawaiian koa bowls and furniture; or **The Warehouse,** a small shopping complex whose specialty shops sell books, coffees, spices, flowers, and alohawear, tel. 885-7905.

The **Rosetta Stone,** on Rt. 19, about two miles out of town toward Hilo, tel. 885-7211, open Tues.-Sat. 10 a.m.-6 p.m., Sunday and Monday noon-6 p.m., owned and operated by Suzanne Collins, vibrates with new-age books on metaphysics. Shelves are stocked with minerals, jewelry, incense, music, and sacred artifacts from around the world. Shoppers will find elegant hairpieces, fantastic boas, baskets filled with stones from around the world, tarot cards, the *I-ching,* smudging sticks, and a few tie-dye dresses. Just walking in can help balance your aura, while the fair prices will help balance your budget.

Parker Square Shopping Mall, along Rt. 19 heading west from town center, has a collection of fine boutiques and shops. Here, the **Gallery of Great Things,** tel. 885-7706, open Mon.-Sat. 9 a.m.-5 p.m., really is loaded with great things. Inside you'll find novelty items like a carousel horse, silk dresses—pricey at $200—straw hats, koa paddles for $700, a Persian *kris* for $425, vintage kimonos, an antique water jar from the Chiang Mai area of northern Thailand for $925, Japanese woodblock prints, enormous bronze fish that once fit the entranceway of a palatial estate, and less expensive items like shell earrings for $8 and koa hair sticks for $4. The Gallery of Great Things, with its museum-quality items, is definitely worth a browse. Also in the mall, **Waimea Body Works** features swimsuits and outdoor gear for the active traveler. **Gifts in Mind** has novelty items and a very good selection of aloha shirts and dresses. **Mango Ranch** sells duds for cowpokes, including bow ties, fancy shirts, and cowboy hats. **Bentley's** specializes in ceramics and tableware. **Noa Noa** imports its fashions from Indonesia, offering beautiful batik creations mostly for women, but there are some items for men. Don't let the name **Waimea General Store** fool you. It mostly sells sundries with plenty of stationery, children's games, stuffed toys, and books on Hawaiiana.

Opelo Plaza, along Rt. 19 heading west from town center, is one of Waimea's newest shopping malls. It features **Gallery of the Pacific** as well as **The Bread Depot** and **Merriman's,** two of Waimea's best restaurants in their categories (see "Food" above).

Food Markets And Sundries

For **food shopping** at the Parker Ranch Shopping Center there's **Sure Save Supermarket; Kamuela Meat Market,** featuring fine cuts of Parker Ranch beef; and **Big Island Natural Foods,** selling snacks, sundries, lotions, potions, notions, and coffee.

The **Circle K** convenience store, with food items and gasoline, is located along Rt. 19 heading west out of town.

A **farmers' market** is held in Waimea every Saturday 7:30 a.m.-noon, when local farmers come to sell their produce, much of which is organic. Look for a dozen or so stalls in the parking lot of the Hawaiian Homelands Building located along Rt. 19 about two miles east of town center heading toward Honokaa. In one of the first stalls is Marie McDonald, a Hawaiian woman (don't let the name fool you) who is an expert at fashioning *haku lei,* a beautiful and intricate form of lei-making with multiple strands of intertwined flowers and ferns. Ms. McDonald and her daughter, who often helps at the stand, will take time to "talk story" and to inform you about medicinal herbs and some of the unique produce found at the market.

SERVICES AND INFORMATION

Entertainment

There ain't much happening around the old town entertainment-wise, but **free hula lessons** are given at the Parker Ranch Visitor Center on Monday afternoons. Enjoy live music and dancing nightly at **Cattleman's Steakhouse** (see "Food" above).

Emergency/Health

Police can be be reached at 885-7334, **ambulance and fire** at 961-6022.

Physicians are available at Lucy Henriques Medical Center, tel. 885-7921.

Chiropractic care is available from Dr. Bob Abdy at **Kohala Chiropractic,** tel. 885-6847, open Monday, Wednesday, and Friday 9 a.m.-noon and 2-5 p.m.; Tuesday and Thursday 9 a.m.-1 p.m. Dr. Abdy's office is in a small shopping center across from the Edelweiss restaurant, west of town on Rt. 19. He has an excellent reputation. In the Ironwood Center, east of town on Rt. 19 (across from the Circle K) is **Hamakua Kohala Coast Massage,** tel. 885-5442, and the **chiropractic clinic** of Dr. Kenneth C. Williams, tel. 885-7719.

Angela Longo, Ph.D., tel. 885-7886, located in the Kamuela Office Center, is a practitioner of **acupuncture** and a Chinese herbalist. Angela, who graduated from U.C. Berkeley with a Ph.D. in biochemistry, combines principles from both East and West into a holistic approach to health and well-being. Besides attending to her demanding practice, Angela is a devoted single parent and a classical Indian dancer who performs at special functions around the island. She is one of the most amazing health practitioners in the entire state.

Dr. Richard Leibman is a **naturopathic physician,** in town at 885-4611.

Information/Services

The **post office** is located in the Parker Ranch Shopping Center. Mailing address for Waimea is Kamuela, so as not to confuse it with the Waimeas on Oahu and Kauai.

The **Waimea visitors center** is west of town along Rt. 19, almost directly across from the Opelo Plaza. They hand out free maps and brochures of the area and provide public restrooms.

The **Chock Inn Launderette** is west on Rt. 19, tel. 885-4655.

BOB RACE

NORTH KOHALA

Jungle trees with crocheted shawls of hanging vines stand in shadowed silence as tiny stores and humble homes abandoned by time melt slowly back into the muted North Kohala earth. This secluded region changes very little, and very slowly. It also has an eastward list toward the wetter side of the island, so if you're suffering from "Kona shock" and want to see flowers, palms, banana trees, and Hawaiian jungle, head for the north coast. Here the island of Hawaii lives up to its reputation of being not only big, but bold and beautiful as well.

North Kohala was the home of Kamehameha the Great. From this fiefdom he launched his conquest of all the islands. The shores and lands of North Kohala are rife with historical significance, and with beach parks where no one but a few local people ever go. Here cattle were introduced to the islands in the 1790s by Captain Vancouver, an early explorer and friend of Kamehameha. Among North Kohala's cultural treasures are **Lapakahi State Historical Park,** a must-stop offering "touchable" exhibits that allow you to become actively involved in Hawaii's traditional past; and **Puukohola Heiau,** one of the last great traditional temples built in Hawaii. Northward is **Kamehameha's birthplace**—the very spot. And within walking distance is **Mookini Heiau,** one of the oldest in Hawaii and still actively ministered by the current generation of a long line of *kahuna.*

Hawi is a sugar town whose economy recently turned sour when the sugar company drastically cut back its local operations. Hawi is making a comeback, along with this entire northern shore, which has seen an influx of small, boutiquelike businesses and art shops. In **Kapaau,** a statue of Kamehameha I peering over the chief's ancestral dominions fulfills an old *kahuna* prophecy. On a nearby side road stands historic **Kalahikiola Church,** established in 1855 by Rev. Elias Bond. On the same side road is the old **Bond Homestead,** the most authentic yet virtually unvisited missionary home in all of Hawaii. Financially strapped, but lovingly tended by the remaining members of the Bond family, it's on the National Historical Record, and even rents *the* cheapest rooms on all of the Big Island. The main coastal road ends at **Pololu Valley Lookout,** where you can overlook one of the premier taro-growing

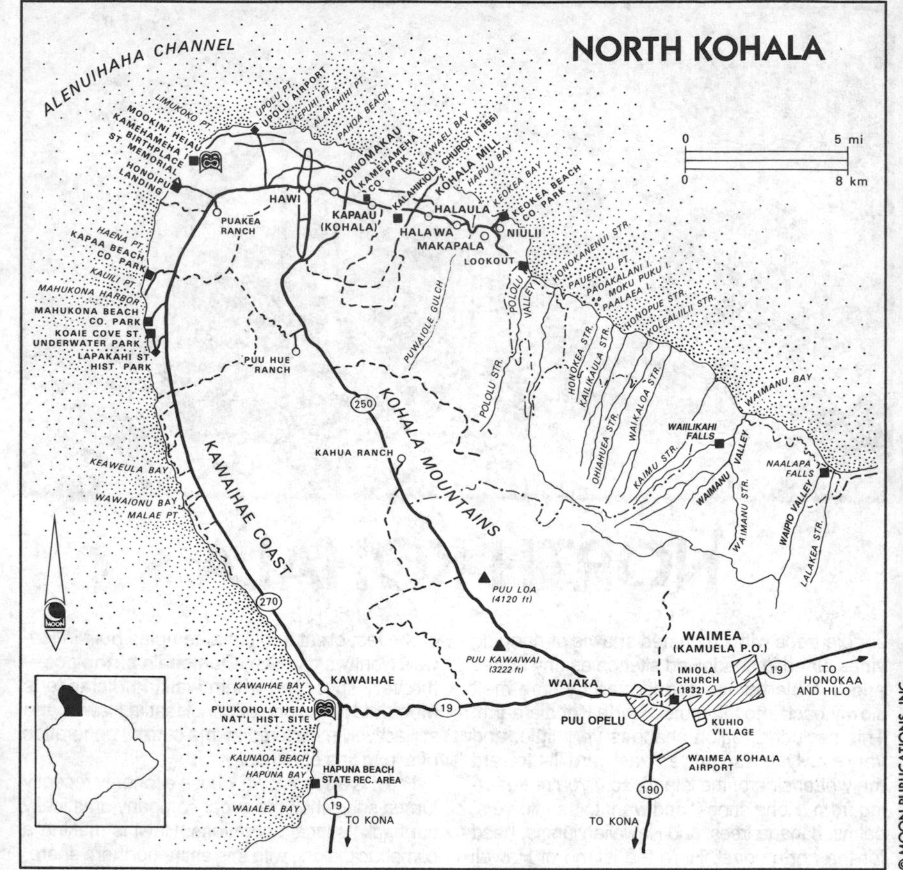

valleys of old Hawaii. A walk down the steep *pali* into this valley is a walk into timelessness, where civilization disappears like an ebbing tide.

Getting There

In Kawaihae, at the base of the North Kohala peninsula, Rt. 19 turns east and coastal Rt. 270, known as the Akoni Pule Hwy., heads north along the coast. It passes through both of North Kohala's two major towns, Hawi and Kapaau, and ends at the *pali* overlooking Pololu Valley. All the historical sites, beach parks, and towns in the following sections are along this route, listed from south to north.

Route 250, the back road to Hawi, is a delightful country lane that winds through gloriously green grazing lands for almost 20 miles along the leeward side of the Kohala Mountains. It begins in the western outskirts of Waimea and ends in Hawi on the far north coast. One of the most picturesque roads on the island, it's dotted with mood-setting cactus and small "line shacks." Suddenly vistas open to your left, and far below are expansive panoramas of rolling hills tumbling to the sea. At mile marker 8 is **Von Holt Memorial Park,** a scenic overlook perfect for a high mountain picnic. Around mile marker 19, keep your eyes peeled for a herd of llamas on the left. At the coast, Rt. 250 splits. Right takes you to Kapaau, and left to Hawi. If you're coming along the coastal Rt. 270 from Kapaau toward Hawi, look for K. Naito's store, and make a left there to go back over Rt. 250 to Waimea; you don't have to go all the way to Hawi to catch Rt. 250.

Upolu Airport, tel. 889-9958, is a lonely strip at Upolu Point, the closest spot to Maui. A sign points the way at mile marker 20 along coastal Rt. 270. Here, you'll find only a bench and a public telephone. The strip is serviced only on request by the small propeller planes of charter and commuter airlines.

SIGHTS, BEACHES, AND TOWNS

KAWAIHAE COAST

Lapakahi State Historical Park

This 600-year-old reconstructed Hawaiian fishing village, combined with adjacent **Koai'e Cove Marine Life Conservation District,** is a standout hunk of coastline 12 miles north of Kawaihae. Gates are open daily 8 a.m.-4 p.m., when park guides are in attendance. Sometimes, especially on weekends, they take the day off; it's okay to park outside the gate and take the self-guided tour, although the guides' knowlegeable anecdotes make the tour much more educational.

The small grass shack near some *lau hala* trees at the entrance stocks annotated brochures and yellow water jugs. As you walk counterclockwise around the numbered stations, you pass canoe sheds and a fish shrine dedicated to Ku'ula, to whom the fishermen always dedicated a portion of their catch. A salt-making area demonstrates how the Hawaiians evaporated seawater by moving it into progressively smaller "pans" carved in the rock. There are numerous homesites along the wood-chip trail. Particularly interesting to children are exhibits of games like *konane* (Hawaiian checkers) and *ulimika* (a form of bowling using stones) that the children are encouraged to try. Throughout the area, all trees, flowers, and shrubs are identified, and as an extra treat, migrating whales come close to shore Dec.-April. Don't leave without finding a shady spot and taking the time to look out to sea. For information write Lapakahi State Park, Box 100, Kapaau, HI 96755, tel. 889-5566.

Mahukona And Kapaa Beach Parks

Mahukona Beach County Park is a few minutes north of Lapakahi down a well-marked side road. As you approach, notice a number of abandoned buildings and warehouses; Mahukona was once an important port from which the Kohala Sugar Co. shipped its goods. Still, there is a pier with a hoist used by local fishermen to launch their boats. The harbor is filled with industrial debris which makes for some good underwater exploring, and snorkeling the offshore reef rewards you with an abundance of sealife. Swimming off the pier is also good, but all water activities are dangerous during winter months and high surf. Picnic facilities include a large pavilion and tables; a large green tank holds drinking water. There are also cold-water showers and restrooms, and electricity is available in the pavilion. Although numerous signs close to the pavilion say No Camping, both tent and trailer camping are allowed with a county permit near the parking lot.

Kapaa Beach County Park is five minutes farther north. Turn *makai* onto a side road and cross a cattle grate as you head toward the sea. This park is even less visited than Mahukona. The rocky beach makes water entry difficult. It's primarily for day-use and fishing, but there are showers, a restroom, and a pavilion. Camping is allowed with a county permit. Neither of these two beaches is spectacular, but they are secluded and accessible. If you're interested in a very quiet spot at which to contemplate a lovely panorama of Maui in the distance, this is it.

Mookini Heiau And Kamehameha's Birthplace

At mile marker 20 turn down a one-lane road to Upolu Airport. Follow it until it reaches the dead end at the runway. Turn left here on a *very* rough dirt road to Mookini Heiau. This entire area is one of the most rugged and isolated on the Big Island, with wide, windswept fields; steep seacliffs; and pounding surf. Pull off at any likely spot along the road and keep your eyes peeled for signs of cavorting humpback whales that frequent this coast yearly Nov.-May. After bumping down the road for about two miles look for a tall transmission tower pointing its bony metal finger skyward that marks the road to the *heiau.* Sometimes the road is closed with a locked gate and you'll have to walk five minutes uphill to gain access, but if the gate is open, you can drive in.

Only *ali'i* came to the *heiau* to purify themselves and worship, sometimes offering human sacrifices. In 1963, Mookini Heiau was the first Hawaiian site to be listed in the National Historical Sites Registry. Legend says that the very first temple at Mookini was built as early as A.D. 480. This incredible date implies that Mookini must have been built immediately upon the arrival of the first Polynesian explorers, who many scholars maintain arrived in large numbers a full two centuries later. More believable oral history relates that the still-standing foundation of the temple was built by the Tahitian high priest Paao, who came with conquering warriors from the south in the 12th century, bringing the powerful mana of the fierce war god Kukailimoku. The oral tale relates that the stones for the temple were fitted in a single night, passed hand to hand by a human chain of 18,000 warriors for a distance of 14 miles from Pololu Valley. They created an irregular rectangle measuring 125 by 250 feet, with 30-foot-high and 15-foot-thick walls all around.

When you visit the *heiau,* pick up a brochure from a box at the entrance (often empty); if none is available, a signboard nearby gives general information. Notice that the leeward stones are covered in lichens, giving them a greenish cast and testifying to the age of the *heiau.* Notice a huge, flat stone near another embedded in the ground with the menacing atmosphere of a sacrificial altar. Nearby is a clone of the famous "Phallic Rock" on Molokai. Please be respectful as you walk around, as this temple is still in use, and stay on the designated paths cordoned off by woven rope. To the rear is an altar area where recent offerings are often seen; the floor of the temple is carpeted with well-placed stones and tiny green plants that give a natural mosaic effect. For at least eight and perhaps 15 centuries, members of the Mookini family have been the priests and priestesses of the temple. Today, the inherited title of *kahuna nui* rests with Leimomi Mookini Lum, a nearby resident. The entire *heiau* is surrounded by a wavelike hump, perhaps the remnant of an earlier structure, that resembles a castle moat. Be sure to visit the nearby "little grass shack," one of the best examples of this traditional Hawaiian architecture in the islands. Check how sturdy the walls are and what excellent protection is provided by the grass-shingled roof. Also, be aware of the integration of its stone platform and how perfectly suited the shack is to provide comfort against the elements in Hawaii. Look through the door at a timeless panorama of the sea and surf.

J.D. BISIGNANI

original Kamehameha statue

A minute from the *heiau* along the dirt road, an HVB Warrior points to Kamehameha's birthplace, **Kamehameha Akahi Aina Hanau.** The entrance to the area is at the back side, away from the sea. Inside the low stone wall, which always seems to radiate heat, are some large boulders believed to be the actual "birthing stones" where the high chieftess Kekuiapoiwa, wife of the warrior *ali'i* Keoua, gave birth to Kamehameha sometime around 1752. This male child, born as his father prepared a battle fleet to invade Maui, would grow to be the greatest of the Hawaiian chiefs—a brave, powerful, but lonely man, like the flat plateau upon which he drew his first breath. The temple's ritual drums and haunting chants dedicated to Ku were the infant's first lullabies. He would grow to accept Ku as his god, and together they would subjugate all of Hawaii. In this expansive North Kohala area, Kamehameha was confronted with unencumbered vistas and sweeping views of neighboring islands, unlike most Hawaiians, whose outlooks were held in check by the narrow, confining, but secure walls of steep-sided valleys. Only this man with this background could rise to become "The Lonely One," high chief of a unified kingdom.

HAWI, KAPAAU, AND VICINITY

Hawi

As you come into Hawi along Rt. 270, you'll see a line of false-front buildings leaning shoulder-to-shoulder like patient old men knowing that something *will* happen. One of the buildings is an ancient movie theater that still shows films. Introducing you to the town are Sacred Heart Church and Hawi Jodo Buddhist Mission, two lovely temples of worship and symbols of Hawaii's diversified spirituality. In the middle of town, Rt. 250, crossing the Kohala Mountains from Waimea, intersects the main road.

Hawi was once a bustling sugar town that boasted four movie theaters in its heyday. In the early 1970s, the Kohala Sugar Co. pulled up stakes, leaving the one-industry town high and dry. Still standing is the monumental stack of the sugarworks, a dormant reminder of what once was. The people of Hawi have always had grit, and instead of moving away they're hanging in and doing a good job of revitalizing their town. Spirit, elbow grease, and paint are their chief allies. Toughing it out is a handful of local shops selling food and household goods, an information center, a hotel (the only functional one in North Kohala), a restaurant or two, a pizza parlor, and some remarkable crafts shops and boutiques (see below).

Kapaau

Kapaau is a sleepy community, the last town for any amenities on Rt. 270 before you reach the end of the line at Pololu Overlook. There's a gas station, grocery store, library, bank, and police station. Most young people have moved away seeking economic opportunity, but the old folks remain, and macadamia nuts are bringing some vitality back into the area. Here too, but on a smaller scale than in Hawi, local artists and some new folks are starting shops and businesses catering to tourists. The main attraction in town is **Kamehameha's Statue,** in front of the Kapaau Courthouse. The statue was commissioned by King Kalakaua in 1878, at which time an old *kahuna* said that the statue would feel at home only in the lands of Kamehameha's birth. Thomas Gould, an American sculptor living in Italy, was hired to do the statue, and he used John Baker, a part Hawaiian and close friend of Kalakaua, as the model. Gould was paid $10,000 to produce the remarkable and heroic sculpture, which was sent to Paris to be bronzed. It was freighted to Hawaii, but the ship carrying the original statue sank just off Port Stanley in the Falkland Islands, and the nine-ton statue was thought lost forever. With the insurance money, Gould was recommissioned and he produced another statue that arrived in Honolulu in 1883, where it still stands in front of the Judiciary Building. Within a few weeks, however, a British ship arrived in Honolulu, carrying the original statue that had somehow been salvaged and unceremoniously dumped in a Port Stanley junkyard. The English captain bought it there and sold it to King Kalakaua for $850. There was only one place where the statue could be sent: to the then-thriving town of Kapaau in the heart of Kamehameha's ancestral homelands. Every year, on the night before Kamehameha Day, the statue is freshly painted with a new coat of house paint; the bronze underneath remains as strong as the great king's will.

Kamehameha County Park, down a marked side road, has a full recreation area, including an Olympic pool open to the public, basketball courts, and weight rooms in the main building along with outside tennis courts with night lighting and a driving range. There is a kiddie area, restrooms, and picnic tables, all free.

Kalahikiola Church

A few minutes east of town an HVB Warrior points to a county lane leading to Kalahikiola Congregational Church. The road is delightfully lined with palm trees, pines, and macadamias like the formal driveway that it once was. Pass the weathering buildings of the **Bond Estate** and follow the road to the church on the hill. This church was built by Rev. Elias Bond and his wife Ellen, who arrived at Kohala in 1841 and dedicated the church in 1855. Reverend Bond and his parishioners were determined to overcome many formidable obstacles in building Kalahikiola ("Life from the Sun") Church, so that they could "sit in a dry and decent house in Jehovah's presence." They hauled timber for miles, quarried and carried stone from distant gulches, raised lime from the sea floor, and brought sand by the jarful all the way from Kawaihae to mix their mortar. After two years of backbreaking work and $8,000, the church finally stood in God's praise, 85 feet long by 45 feet wide. The attached bell tower, oddly out of place, looks like a shoe box standing on end topped by four mean-looking spikes. Note that the doors don't swing, but slide—some visitors leave because they think it's locked. Inside, the church is dark and cool, and inexplicably the same type of spikes as on the bell tower flank both sides of the altar. There is also a remarkable koa table. Pamphlets (25 cents) describe the history of the church.

The Bond Estate

The *most* remarkable and undisturbed missionary estate still extant in Hawaii is the old Bond Homestead and its attendant buildings, including the now defunct but renovated Kohala Girls School. The estate is kept up by 10 surviving cousins of the Bond family, who have recently formed the nonprofit Iole Mission Homestead Foundation. Chaired by Mrs. Noreen Alexander of Honolulu, the Foundation is dedicated to preserving the home and opening it and the surrounding grounds to public tours in the very near future. It's already on the National Historical Register. However, age and the loss of that caring touch of a family actually living in the home have taken their toll. The Foundation is refurbishing the home and strengthening the basic structure so that this venerable old house can take the extra stress created by the traffic of future visitors. Until the renovations are completed, the Bond Estate is closed to the public; please remember this. Mr. Walter Fruitiger, a North Kohala resident and board member of the Foundation, has graciously dedicated his time to answering questions concerning the future visitation of the Bond Estate. If you have any questions or interest in future developments, please contact Mr. Fruitiger at 889-5267. Note, however, that you can rent a room in the refurbished Kohala Girls school for the cheapest rates in Hawaii (see "Practicalities" below).

When you enter the grounds, the clock turns back 100 years. The first buildings were completed in 1841 by Rev. Isaac Bliss, who preceded Elias and Ellen Bond. The main buildings, connected in New England farm fashion, have steep-pitched roofs designed to keep off the "back East" snows. They worked equally well here to keep rainwater out, as the roofs were originally thatched. The original furniture and family possessions are placed as if the residents are out for the afternoon, although the family has not lived in the house since 1925, when it was occupied by Dr. Benjamin Bond. In the majority of missionary homes and museums in Hawaii, suitable period furniture had to be purchased or replicas made to fill the house, but here it is all original. The homey dining and writing room is dominated by a large table that can take six leaves because the Bonds never knew how many there would be for dinner—four, or 60 who might have landed by schooner in the middle of the afternoon. A full set of dishes waits undisturbed in the sideboard. A cozy little parlor has comfortable wicker rocking chairs and a settee under a photo of Elias Bond himself. The reverend built the settee and most of the furniture in the house. His furniture from New England arrived on a ship after he did, but because it was Sabbath, the reverend refused to have it unloaded. Unfortunately, the ship caught fire and all the Bonds' personal possessions were lost. In the kitchen area a refrigerator dating from the '20s looks like a bank vault. It ran on electricity from a generator on the homestead that was frequently used by local plantation owners to recharge their batteries. Off in a side room, an old wooden bathtub is as sound as it was the day it was built. In Reverend Bond's bedroom is a crocheted "primer" dated 1817, made by his sister Eliza who died before he came to Hawaii; he brought it as a memento and it still hangs on the wall. Upstairs are two large rooms in disrepair, which contain a treasure trove of antiques. Notice too, the sturdy, barn-style architecture of pegs and beams.

The small wing attached to the main house, called "The Cottage," was built when Dr. Benjamin Bond was first married. The family ate together in the main house, using the cottage as a Victorian bedroom and sitting room that now abounds with photos and antiques. The attached bathroom was once a summerhouse that was dragged to the present location by a steam tractor, then plumbed. As you look around, you'll feel that everything is here except for the people.

Keokea Beach County Park

Two miles past Kapaau toward Pololu you pass a small fruit stand and an access road heading *makai* to secluded Keokea Beach County Park. The park, on the side of the hill going down to the sea, is very picturesque and luxuriant. It is a favorite spot of North Kohala residents, especially on weekends, but receives little use during the week. The rocky shoreline faces the open ocean, so swimming is not advised except during summer calm. There are a pavilion, restrooms, showers, and picnic tables. A county permit is required for tent and trailer camping.

POLOLU VALLEY AND BEYOND

Finally you come to Pololu Valley Overlook. Off to the right is a small home belonging to Bill Sproat, a man of mixed Hawaiian ancestry and a longtime resident of Pololu. Bill, whose vim and vigor belie his 81 years, was a mule skinner throughout the area for 50 years. He is a treasure house of knowledge and homespun wisdom, and speaks fluent Hawaiian. His mother was a Hawaiian who became a schoolteacher down in Pololu, and his dad was an adventurer who came to Hawaii in the 1890s. Bill's grandmother was a *kahuna* who lived in the valley and never converted to Christianity. Most of the folks feared her dark powers, but not Bill who, although a strong Christian, learned much about Hawaii and its ways from his grandmother. If Bill is in his yard, perhaps tending a mule, make sure to stop and talk with him.

It's about 12 miles from Pololu to Waipio Valley, with five U-shaped valleys in between, including Honokea and Waimanu, two of the largest. From the lookout it takes about 15 minutes to walk down to the floor of Pololu. The trail is well maintained as you pass through a heavy growth of *lau hala,* but it can be slippery when wet. At the bottom is a gate that keeps grazing animals in; make sure to close it after you! **Kohala Ditch,** a monument to labor-intensive engineering, is to the rear of these valleys. It carried precious water to the sugar plantations. Pololu and the other valleys were once inhabited and were among the richest wet taro plantations of old Hawaii. Today, abandoned and neglected, they have been taken over by introduced vegetation. The black-sand beach fronting Pololu is lined with sand dunes, with a small sandbar offshore. The rip current here can be very dangerous, so enter the water only in summer months. The rip fortunately weakens not too far from shore; if you're caught, go with it and ride the waves back in. Many people hike into Pololu for seclusion and back-to-nature camping. Make sure to boil the stream water before drinking. Plenty of wild fruits can augment your food supply, and the shoreline fishing is excellent. The trails leading eastward to the other valleys are in disrepair and should not be attempted unless you are *totally* prepared, and better yet, accompanied by someone who knows the terrain.

PRACTICALITIES

ACCOMMODATIONS

You won't spend a lot of time wondering where you'll be staying in North Kohala. If you don't intend to camp, you can count your lodging options on one hand, without even using your thumb.

The Kohala Lodge in Hawi, Box 521, Kapaau, HI 96755, tel. 889-5433, was long known as Luke's Hotel. The hotel has always catered to local working people or island families visiting the area. It is basic, adequate, and used. Located in central Hawi, it has a quiet little courtyard, restaurant, swimming pool, and TV. Rooms are a reasonable $37 per night, $125 per week, $450 per month, $6 additional person; discounts on long stays and for sharing a bathroom.

Hawaiian Plantation House (Aha Hui Hale), Box 10, Hawi, HI 96719, tel. 889-5523, was once a plantation manager's house. The white clapboard structure sits on four lush acres, letting its two-bedroom suites for $65 d, $10 extra person, communal kitchen.

The manager of the Iole Development Corp., tel. 889-5217 or 889-6989, rents modest rooms in the old **Kohala Girls School** section of the Bond Estate (see above). These buildings are very old, but the conveniences and amenities have been upgraded. Basically, you'll have to take care of yourself as no housekeeping services are provided. The manager *prefers* renting these rooms to school and civic organizations, but he will rent to travelers if they are the right sort, which translates as clean, quiet, and respectful! Rates are $275 per month, with shared bath and kitchen. Daily rates available upon request.

Wo On Gallery and Guest House, tel. 889-5002, owned and operated by Leslie Patten, Box 1065, Kapaau, HI 96755, is a rustic lodging in Halawa. Leslie has opened a gallery dedicated to local artists in the historic Wo On ("Harmony and Peace") General Store that served the Chinese community during plantation days. To the rear of the gallery is an attached, fully furnished, one-room apartment, complete with kitchen. The unit, which can sleep four, rents for $50 daily, $250 weekly, and $800 monthly. Breakfast is rarely provided due to Leslie's hectic schedule, which includes minding twin daughters, but a steaming pot of Gevalia coffee is always offered. Next door is lovely and historically significant Tong Wo Cemetery and Temple, well worth a visit.

RESTAURANTS

You can get a good, inexpensive meal at **Honey's Country Kitchen,** tel. 889-0294, in the "food wing" of the Kohala Hotel in downtown Hawi, open Mon.-Sat., breakfast 7-11 a.m., lunch 11 a.m.-2 p.m., dinner 5-8 p.m., cocktail lounge 8 p.m.-midnight, closed Sunday. Omelettes with the works are under $5, cheeseburgers and most sandwiches under $3.50, and a range of plate lunches around $5.95. More substantial meals are hamburger steak $8.95, mahimahi $12.95, and New York steak $13.95. Honey's is a basic restaurant with good food, reasonable prices, and friendly service.

Ohana Pizza & Beer Garden, tel. 889-5888, also in downtown Hawi, features very good pizza for $5.50-10.75 depending upon size and toppings. This clean, friendly restaurant also offers hefty sandwiches for $2.95, and pasta dinners (like homemade lasagna) served with dinner salad and homemade garlic bread for $6. Salads are $1.50, and homemade garlic bread $1. You can order wine or a chilled domestic beer for $1.75, or an import for $2.50. The staff of local people is friendly and hospitable. A great place to pick up a picnic lunch.

Mits Drive-In, tel. 889-6474, is a small, inexpensive roadside restaurant in Kapaau where you can pick up a fast hamburger, hot dog, soft drink, or snack.

Don's Family Deli, tel. 889-5822, open daily for breakfast and lunch until 6 p.m., across the street from the Kamehameha Statue in Kapaau, is a taste of New York in North Kohala. How can a visit to tropical paradise be complete without bagels and lox, lasagna, or a thick slice of quiche? Don's features Dreyer's ice cream, coffee and cappuccino, and homemade biscotti filled with nuts and that zesty anisette flavor. Don Rich, a longtime Kohala resident, will also fix you up with a tofu or mahimahi burger, and offers a wide selection of meats and breads if you prefer to make your own picnic lunch.

Tropical Dreams Gourmet Shop, in bustling downtown Kapaau, open daily 10 a.m.-5 p.m., Sunday 1-5 p.m., serves freshly made ice cream (macadamia nut is great), and fresh fruit sorbet in season.

SHOPPING

For food shopping try: **Union Market,** tel. 889-6450, along Rt. 270 coming into Kapaau, which sells not only general merchandise and meats, but also a hefty assortment of grains, nuts, fruits, and locally made pastries and breads. **H. Naito** is a general grocery, dry goods, and fishing supplies store in Kapaau, tel. 889-6851. Also in Kapaau, **Kohala Spirits,** open Mon.-Sat. 10 a.m.-10 p.m., stocks a fairly wide range of liquor, beer, and wine. **K. Takata** is a well-stocked grocery store in Hawi, tel. 889-5261. **Kohala Health Food,** in downtown Hawi, tel. 889-0277, Is open daily except Sunday 10:30 a.m.-6:30 p.m.; its shelves are filled with herbs, vitamins, minerals, and local organic produce when available.

For a special treat try **Tropical Dreams,** a locally owned company in Kohala that handmakes gourmet macadamia nut butters. Some of their mouthwatering butters are flavored with Kona coffee, chocolate, or lehua honey. Contact Tropical Dreams for their full brochure at Box 557, Kapaau, HI 96755, tel. 889-5386 or (800) 548-8050. Gift package assortments a specialty.

In Kapaau, across from the Kamehameha statue, is **Ackerman Gallery,** open daily 9 a.m.-5:30 p.m., tel. 889-5971, owned and operated by artist Gary Ackerman. Besides showcasing his own sensitive, island-inspired paintings, he displays local pottery, carvings, and one-of-a-kind jewelry. He also carries a smattering of artwork from throughout the Pacific. The artwork selections are tasteful, but expensive. You can also choose a reasonably priced gift item, especially from the handmade jewelry section. Make sure to check out the beautiful hand-blown glass display by a local artist named Yamazawa. The distinctive, iridescent glaze is achieved by using volcanic cinders—you can bring home a true island memento that includes a bit of Madame Pele herself. Almost next door is **Kohala Sporting,** with a selection of boogie boards, T-shirts, and hunting licenses.

Gary has expanded and has opened another **Ackerman Gallery** also in Kapaau across from Tropical Dreams. This lovely gallery, housed in a turn-of-the-century building, showcases the fine art of local island artists like Greg Pontius, Kelly Dunn (magnificent bowls), and Gary Ackerman (inspired painting).

Hana Koa is a woodworking shop owned by artist Don Wilkinson, who learned the trade of making fine antique furniture replicas from his father. His excellent work, primarily in koa, focuses on the early-20th-century period. Don, a friendly storehouse of information, lives along Rt. 250 heading in from Waimea, tel. 889-6444.

Hale Wood, tel. 889-5075, in Hawi across from the launderette, open mostly by appointment, is owned and operated by husband-and-wife team Buck and Juli, woodworker and finisher, respectively. They work mostly in koa, fashioning hope chests, coat racks, and glass-tiled tables. A small gift shop offers some reasonably priced items like curly koa chopsticks for $5. Some of their pricier items bear tags for their "Friend to a Tree" program, that promises a purchase and planting of a koa tree in your name.

Another local artist is **David Gomes,** tel. 889-5100, a guitar and ukulele maker. He works in koa and other woods and does inlay in shell, abalone, and wood. His beautiful instruments take four to six months to complete. His small shop is located about a half mile on the Kapaau side of the junction of routes 270 and 250. Next door is a hobby and crafts store.

In Hawi, **Dawn's,** tel. 889-5112, open daily except Sunday 9 a.m.-5 p.m., sells sports clothes, T-shirts, and alohawear. The **Heritage Tree** is a specialty hula supply store in Kapaau across from the Kamehameha statue. If you're looking for a small variety of traditional arts and crafts, this shop is worth a stop.

SERVICES AND INFORMATION

The **Kohala Visitor Center** dispenses maps, information, and *aloha.* It's open daily and located just near the junction of routes 270 and 250 in Hawi. Next door is the local **laundromat,** a semi-open-air affair that can be used just about all the time. **Police** can be reached at 889-6225, emergency **fire** and **ambulance** at 961-6022.

The area **post office** is a new and large facility on Rt. 270 between Hawi and Kapaau just near the H. Naito Store.

The full-service **Kamehameha Pharmacy** is along Rt. 270 in downtown Kapaau.

BOB RACE

axis deer

KAUAI

"O, how my spirit languishes

to step ashore in the Sanguishes . . ."

—Robert Louis Stevenson,
c. 1888

INTRODUCTION

Kauai is the oldest of the main Hawaiian Islands, and nature has had ample time to work, sculpting Kauai into a beauty among beauties. Flowers and fruits burst from its fertile soil, but the "Garden Island" is much more than greenery and flora, it's the poetry of land itself. Its mountains have become rounded and smooth, and its streams tumbling to the sea have cut deep and wide, giving Kauai the only navigable river in Hawaii. The interior is a dramatic series of mountains, valleys, and primordial swamp. The great gouge of Waimea Canyon, called the "Grand Canyon of the Pacific," is an enchanting layer of pastels where uncountable rainbows form prismatic necklaces from which waterfalls hang like silvery pendants. The northwest is the seacliffs of Na Pali, mightiest in all of Oceania, looming 4,000 feet above the pounding surf.

After only 27 minutes (100 miles) by air from Honolulu, you land just about the time you're finishing your in-flight cocktail. Everything seems quieter here, rural but upbeat, with the main town being just that, a town. The pursuit of carefree relaxation is unavoidable at five-star hotels, where you're treated like a visiting *ali'i,* or at campsites deep in interior valleys or along secluded beaches where reality *is* the fantasy of paradise.

Kauai is where Hollywood comes when the script calls for "paradise." The island has a dozen major films to its credit, everything from idyllic scenes in *South Pacific* to the lurking horror of Asian villages in *Uncommon Valor. King Kong* tore up this countryside in search of love, and Tattoo spotted "de plane, boss" in "Fantasy Island." In *Blue Hawaii,* Elvis's hips mimicked the swaying palms in a famous island grove, while torrid love scenes from *The Thorn Birds* were steamier than the jungle in the background. Perhaps the greatest compliment to Kauai is that other islanders come here to look at the scenery.

AN OVERVIEW

Kauai is the most regularly shaped of all the major islands, more or less round, like a partially deflated beach ball. The puckered skin around the coast forms bays, beaches, and inlets, while the center is a no man's land of mountains,

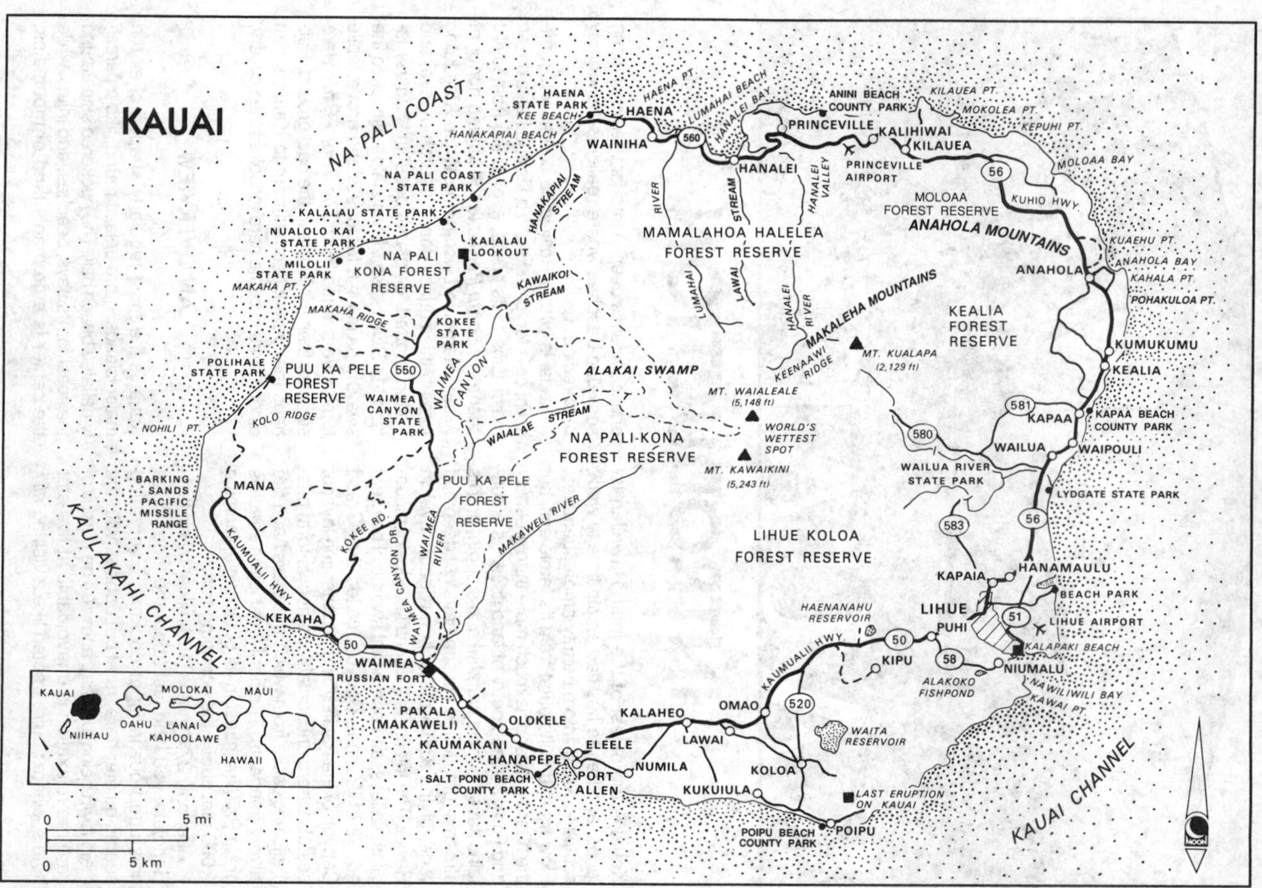

KAUAI
NA PALI COAST
HAENA STATE PARK
KEE BEACH
HAENA PT.
HAENA
LUMAHAI BEACH
HANALEI BAY
ANINI BEACH COUNTY PARK
KILAUEA PT.
MOKOLEA PT.
KEPUHI PT.
HANAKAPIAI BEACH
WAINIHA
560
PRINCEVILLE
KALIHIWAI
KILAUEA
HANALEI
PRINCEVILLE AIRPORT
56
MOLOAA BAY
KUHIO HWY.
NA PALI COAST STATE PARK
KALALAU STATE PARK
NUALOLO KAI STATE PARK
MILOLII STATE PARK
MAKAHA PT.
KALALAU LOOKOUT
NA PALI KONA FOREST RESERVE
HANAKAPIAI STREAM
RIVER
STREAM
HANALEI VALLEY
MOLOAA FOREST RESERVE
ANAHOLA MOUNTAINS
MAMALAHOA HALELEA FOREST RESERVE
KUAEHU PT.
ANAHOLA
ANAHOLA BAY
KAHALA PT.
POHAKULOA PT.
KAWAIKOI STREAM
MAKAHA RIDGE
KOKEE STATE PARK
LUMAHAI
LAWAI
HANALEI RIVER
MAKALEHA MOUNTAINS
KEALIA FOREST RESERVE
KEENAAWI RIDGE
MT. KUALAPA (2,129 ft)
KUMUKUMU
KEALIA
POLIHALE STATE PARK
PUU KA PELE FOREST RESERVE
550
WAIMEA CANYON
ALAKAI SWAMP
MT. WAIALEALE (5,148 ft)
WAIMEA CANYON STATE PARK
581
KAPAA
KAPAA BEACH COUNTY PARK
KOLO RIDGE
NOHILI PT.
WAIALAE STREAM
WORLD'S WETTEST SPOT
580
NA PALI-KONA FOREST RESERVE
MT. KAWAIKINI (5,243 ft)
WAILUA
WAIPOULI
WAILUA RIVER STATE PARK
BARKING SANDS PACIFIC MISSILE RANGE
MANA
PUU KA PELE FOREST RESERVE
LYDGATE STATE PARK
KOKEE RD.
MAKAWELI RIVER
583
56
KAULAKAHI CHANNEL
KAUMUALII HWY.
WAIMEA CANYON DR.
WAIMEA RIVER
LIHUE KOLOA FOREST RESERVE
KAPAIA
HANAMAULU
BEACH PARK
HAENANAHU RESERVOIR
LIHUE
51
LIHUE AIRPORT
KEKAHA
50
PUHI
KAUMUALII HWY.
50
KALAPAKI BEACH
WAIMEA
RUSSIAN FORT
KIPU
58
NIUMALU
ALAKOKO FISHPOND
NAWILIWILI BAY
KAWAI PT.
KAUAI
MOLOKAI
MAUI
NIIHAU
OAHU
LANAI
KAHOOLAWE
HAWAII
PAKALA (MAKAWELI)
OLOKELE
KALAHEO
OMAO
520
KAUMAKANI
ELEELE
LAWAI
WAITA RESERVOIR
HANAPEPE
NUMILA
KOLOA
SALT POND BEACH COUNTY PARK
PORT ALLEN
KUKUIULA
LAST ERUPTION ON KAUAI
KAUAI CHANNEL
0 5 mi
0 5 km
POIPU BEACH COUNTY PARK
POIPU
MOON
© MOON PUBLICATIONS, INC.

canyon, and swamp. Almost everyone arrives at the major airport in Lihue, although another small strip in Princeville has limited service by commuter aircraft. Lihue is the county seat and major town with government agencies, full amenities, and a wide array of restaurants and shopping. Lihue also boasts some of the least expensive accommodations on the island, in small family-operated hotels; however, most visitors head north for Wailua/Kapa'a or Princeville, or west to the fabulous Poipu Beach area. Lihue's Kauai Museum is a must stop, where you'll learn the geological and social history of the island, immensely enriching your visit.

On the outskirts of town is the oldest Lutheran church in the islands, and the remarkably preserved Grove Farm Homestead, a classic Hawaiian plantation so intact all that seems to be missing is the workers. At Nawiliwili Bay you can see firsthand the Menehunes' handiwork at the Menehune (Alakoko) Fish Pond, still in use. Just north are the two suburbs of Kapaia and Hanamaulu. Here too you'll find shops and restaurants and the junction of Rt. 583 leading inland through miles of sugarcane fields and terminating at a breathtaking panorama of Wailua Falls.

East Coast

Heading northeast from Lihue along Rt. 56 takes you to Wailua and Kapa'a. En route, you pass Wailua Municipal Golf Course, beautiful, cheap, and open to the public. Wailua town is built along the Wailua River, the only navigable stream in Hawaii. At the mouth of the river are two enchanting beach parks and a temple of refuge, while upstream are more *heiau,* petroglyphs, royal birth stones, the heavily touristed yet beautiful Fern Grotto, and the Kamokila Hawaiian folk village, all within the Wailua River State Park. Here too are remarkable views of the river below and the cascading Opaekaa Waterfalls. Heavily damaged by Hurricane Iniki, but making a comeback, Wailua's The Coco Palms Resort was an island institution set in the heart of the most outstanding coconut grove on Kauai. Its evening torch-lighting ceremony was the best authentic fake-Hawaii on the island.

Along Rt. 56 toward Kapa'a you pass the Coconut Plantation Market Place, an extensive mall that'll satisfy your every shopping need and then some. In the vicinity, a clutch of first-rate yet affordable hotels and condos line the beach. Kapa'a is a workers' town with more down-home shopping, and good, inexpensive restaurants. Heading north toward Hanalei, you pass Pohakuloa Point, an excellent surfers' beach; Anahola Beach Park, where the water and camping are fine; and Moloa'a Bay, a secluded beach you often will have to yourself.

North Coast

Before entering Kilauea, the first town in the Hanalei District, unmarked side roads lead to secret beaches and unofficial camp spots. A small coastal road leads you to Kilauea Lighthouse, a beacon of safety for passing ships and for a remarkable array of birds that come to this wildfowl sanctuary. Princeville is next, the largest planned resort in Hawaii, featuring its own airstrip. Here an entire modern village is built around superb golf courses and an exclusive deluxe resort.

Down the narrowing lane and over a single-lane steel-strut bridge is Hanalei. Inland is a terraced valley planted in taro just like in the old days. Oceanside is Hanalei Bay, a safe anchorage and haven to seagoing yachts that have made it a port of call ever since Westerners began coming to Hawaii. On the outskirts is Waioli Mission House, a preserved home and museum dating from 1837. Then comes a string of beaches, uncrowded and safe for swimming and snorkeling. You pass through the tiny village of Wainiha, and then Haena, with the island's "last resort." In quick succession come Haena Beach County Park, the wet and dry caves, and the end of the road at Ke'e Beach in Haena State Park. Here are beach houses for those who want to get away from it all, *Kaulu Paoa Heiau* dedicated to hula, and the location where the beach scenes from *The Thorn Birds* were filmed. From here only your feet and love of adventure take you down the Kalalau Trail to back-to-nature camping. You pass along a narrow foot trail down the Na Pali Coast, skirting emerald valleys cut off from the world by impassable 4,000-foot seacliffs, mightiest in the Pacific. All along here are *heiau,* ancient village sites, caves, lava tubes, and the romantic yet true Valley of the Lost Tribe just beyond trail's end.

South Coast

From Lihue west is a different story. Route 50 takes you past the Kukui Grove Shopping Center and then through Puhi, home of Kauai Community College. As the coastal Hoary Head Mountains slip past your window, Queen Victoria's Profile squints down at you. Maluhia Road, famous for its tunnel-like line of eucalyptus, branches off toward Koloa, a sugar town now rejuvenated with shops, boutiques, and restaurants. Continuing to the coast is Poipu Beach, the best on Kauai with its bevy of beautiful hotels and resorts.

Westward is a string of sugar towns. First is Kalaheo, where an island philanthropist, Walter McBride, gave the munificent land gift that has become Kukui O Lono Park. Here you'll find a picture-perfect Japanese garden surrounded by an excellent yet little-played golf course. West on Rt. 50 is Hanapepe, a good supply stop and famous for its art shops and inexpensive restaurants. The road skirts the shore, passing Olokele, a perfect caricature of a sugar town with its neatly trimmed cottages, and Pakala, an excellent surfing beach. Quickly comes Waimea, where Captain Cook first came ashore, and on the outskirts is the Russian Fort, dating from 1817, when all the world powers were present in Hawaii, jockeying to influence this Pacific gem.

In Waimea and farther westward in Kekaha, the road branches inland, leading along the rim of Waimea Canyon. This is what everyone comes to see, and none are disappointed. The wonderfully winding road serves up lookout after lookout and trail after trail. You end up at Koke'e State Park and the Kalalau Valley Lookout, where you're king of the mountain, and 4,000 feet below is your vast domain of Na Pali. Past Kekaha is a flat stretch of desert vast enough that the military has installed Barking Sands Missile Range. The pavement ends and a good tourist-intimidating "cane road" takes over, leading you to the seclusion of Polihale State Park, where you can swim, camp, and luxuriate in privacy. If Madame Pele had had her choice, she never would have moved.

THE LAND

Kauai, 100 miles northwest of Oahu, is the northernmost of the six major islands and fourth largest. It is approximately 33 miles long and 25 miles wide at its farthest points, with an area of 554 square miles and 90 miles of coastline. The island was built by one huge volcano that became extinct about six million years ago. Mount Waialeale in central Kauai is its eastern rim, and speculation holds that Niihau, 20 miles off the west coast, was at one time connected. The volcanic "hot spot" under Kauai was sealed by the weight of the island; as Kauai drifted northward the hot spot burst through again and again, building the string of islands from Oahu to Hawaii.

A simplified but chronologically accurate account of Kauai's emergence is found in a version of the Pele myth retold in *The Kumulipo.* It depicts the fire-goddess as a young, beautiful woman who visits Kauai during a hula festival and becomes enraptured with Lohiau, a handsome and mighty chief. She wants him as a husband and determines to dig a firepit home where they can reside in contented bliss. Unfortunately, her unrelenting and unforgiving sea-goddess sister pursues her, forcing Pele to abandon Kauai and Lohiau. Thus, she wandered and sparked volcanic eruptions on Oahu, Maui, and finally atop Kilauea Crater on Hawaii, where she now resides.

Phenomenal Features Of Kauai

Located almost smack-dab in the middle of the island are **Mount Kawaikini** (5,243 feet) and adjacent **Mount Waialeale** (5,148 feet), highest points on Kauai. Mount Waialeale is an unsurpassed "rain magnet," drawing an estimated 480 inches (40 feet) of precipitation per year, and earning itself the dubious distinction of being "the wettest spot on earth." Don't be intimidated—this rain is amazingly localized, with only 20 inches per year falling just 20 miles away. Visitors can now enter this mist-shrouded world aboard helicopters which fly through countless rainbows and hover above a thousand waterfalls.

Draining Waialeale is **Alakai Swamp,** a dripping sponge of earth covering about 30 square miles of trackless bog (construction of an elevated boardwalk is underway). This patch of

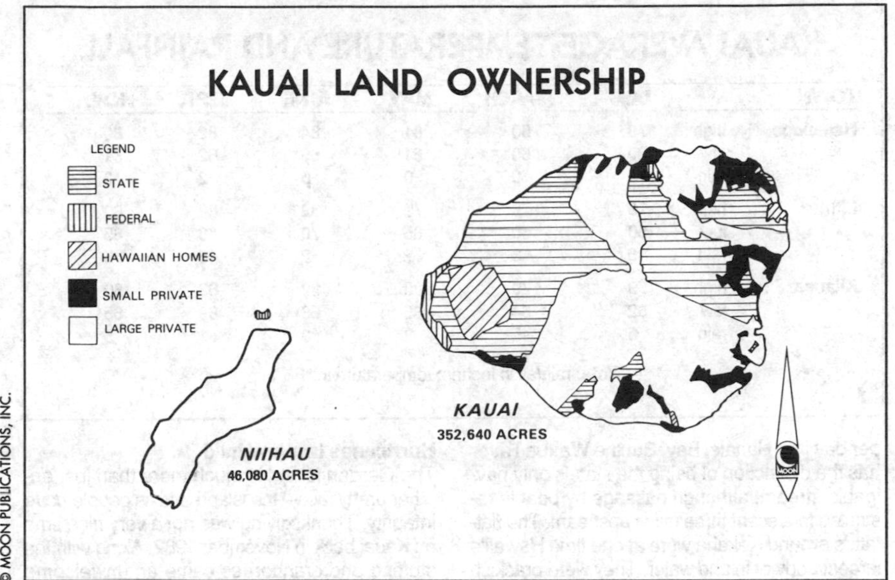

mire contains flora and fauna found nowhere else on earth. For example, ohia trees, mighty giants of upland forests, grow here as natural bonsai that could pass as potted plants.

Boardering the Alakai Swamp on the west is **Waimea Canyon,** where eons of whipping winds, pelting rain, and the incessant grinding of streams and rivulets have chiseled the red bedrock to depths of 3,600 feet and expanses 10 miles wide. On the western slopes of Waimea Canyon is the **Na Pali Coast,** a scalloped, undulating vastness of valleys and *pali* forming a bulwark 4,000 feet high.

Other mountains and outcroppings around the island have formed curious natural formations. The **Hoary Head Mountains,** a diminutive range barely 2,000 feet tall south of Lihue, form a profile of Queen Victoria. A ridge just behind Wailua gives the impression of a man in repose and has been dubbed The Sleeping Giant. Another small range in the northeast, the **Anahola Mountains,** had until recently an odd series of boulders that formed "Hole in the Mountain," mythologically created when a giant hurled his spear through sheer rock. Erosion has collapsed the formation, but the tale lives on.

Land Ownership

Of Kauai's total usable land area of 398,720 acres, 62% is privately owned. Of this, almost 90% is controlled by only half a dozen or so large landholders, mainly Gay and Robinson, Amfac, Alexander and Baldwin, C. Brewer and Co., and Grove Farm. The remaining 38%, which includes a section of Hawaiian Homes lands, is primarily owned by the state, and a small portion is owned by the county of Kauai and the federal government. As everywhere in Hawaii, no one owns the beaches and public access to them is guaranteed.

Channels, Lakes, And Rivers

Kauai is separated from Oahu by the **Kauai Channel.** Reaching an incredible depth of 10,900 feet and a width of 72 miles, it is by far the state's deepest and widest channel. Inland, manmade **Waita Reservoir** north of Koloa is the largest body of fresh water in Hawaii, covering 424 acres with a three-mile shoreline. The **Waimea River,** running through the floor of the canyon, is the island's longest at just under 20 miles, while the **Hanalei River** moves the greatest amount of water, emptying 150 million gallons

KAUAI AVERAGE TEMPERATURE AND RAINFALL

TOWN		JAN.	MARCH	MAY	JUNE	SEPT.	NOV.
Hanapepe	high	79	80	81	84	82	80
	low	60	60	61	65	62	61
	rain	5	2	0	0	2	3
Lihue	high	79	79	79	82	82	80
	low	60	60	65	70	68	65
	rain	5	3	2	2	5	5
Kilauea	high	79	79	80	82	82	80
	low	62	64	66	68	69	65
	rain	5	5	3	3	1	5

Note: rainfall in inches; temperature in °F .

per day into Hanalei Bay. But the **Wailua River** has the distinction of being the state's only navigable stream, although passage by boat is restricted to a scant three miles upstream. The flatlands around Kekaha were at one time Hawaii's largest body of inland water. They were brackish and drained last century when the Waimea Ditch was built to irrigate the cane fields.

CLIMATE

Kauai's climate will make you happy. Along the coastline the average temperature is 80° F in spring and summer, and about 75 during the remainder of the year. The warmest areas are along the south coast from Lihue westward, where the mercury can hit the 90s in midsummer. To escape the heat any time of year, head for Koke'e atop Waimea Canyon, where the weather is always moderate.

Precipitation

Although Mt. Waialeale is "the wettest spot on earth," in the areas most interesting to visitors, rain is not a problem. The driest section of Kauai is the southwestern desert, from Polihale to Poipu Beach (five inches per year) up to a mere 20 inches around the resorts. Lihue receives about 30 inches. As you head northeast toward Hanalei, rainfall becomes more frequent but is still a tolerable 45 inches per year. Cloudbursts in winter are frequent but short-lived.

Hurricanes Iwa And Iniki

The Garden Island is much more than just another pretty face—the island and its people have integrity. Thanksgiving was not a very nice time on Kauai back in November 1982. Along with the stuffing and cranberries came an unwelcome guest who showed no *aloha,* **Hurricane Iwa.** What made this rude 80-mile-per-hour partycrasher so unforgettable was it was only the fourth such storm to come ashore on Hawaii since records have been kept and the first since the late 1950s. All told, Iwa caused $200 million dollars' worth of damage. A few beaches were washed away, perhaps forever, and great destruction was suffered by beach homes and resorts, especially around Poipu. Thankfully, no lives were lost. The people of Kauai rolled up their sleeves and set about rebuilding. In short order, the island recovered, and most residents thought "that was that."

Unfortunately on Friday, September 11, 1992, **Hurricane Iniki,** with unimaginable ferocity, ripped ashore with top wind speeds of 175 mph, and slapped Kauai around like the moll in a Bogart movie. Iniki (whose two meanings in Hawaiian are "piercing winds" or "pangs of love," both devastatingly painful in their own way) virtually flattened or tore to shreds everything in its path. No one was immune from the savage typhoon. Renowned director, Steven Spielberg and his cast, including Laura Dern, Jeff Goldblum, Richard Attenborough, and Sam Neill, were on the island filming scenes for the blockbuster

Jurassic Park. They along with other guests, bellhops, maids, groundskeepers, and cooks, rode out the storm huddled in the ballroom of the Westin Kauai Lagoons, which has still not recovered. Afterward, Mayor JoAnn Yukimura and her staff worked day and night from her now roofless office in Lihue. Hanalei taro farmers opened their humble doors to homeless neighbors and strangers alike, while a general manager of a luxury resort on the eve of his wedding pleaded with invited guests to give donations to various charitable organizations in lieu of gifts. Hardly a structure on the entire island wasn't damaged in one way or another. Proud yachts were thrown like toy boats into a jangled heap; cars were buried whole in the red earth; a full third of Kauai's 20,000 homes were broken into splinters; and 4,200 hotel rooms were a tangled heap of steel and jagged glass. By the grace of god, and because of a very competent warning system, only two lives were regrettably lost, and less than 100 people had to be admitted to the hospital due to injury. Psychologically, however, many people who lost everything were scared, though special counseling services were set up to offer techniques to deal with the stress and sense of loss. Insurance companies were stressed to the breaking point, with some very slow to pay. Locals checked their policies and prayed desperately that they wouldn't be "HIG-positive"; Hawaii Insurance Group, a popular island-based insurance company, literally went broke trying to pay all of the claims brought against it.

Estimates are still coming in, but *Business Trends,* a financial report published by the Bank of Hawaii, related that the state suffered $1.6 billion worth of damage, and that Kauai accounted for $1.58 billion of this total, a full eight times the amount of damage caused by Hurricane Iwa. Undaunted and with pride and will that far surpassed the fury of the storm, Kauai's people immediately set about rebuilding homes, while nature took care of the rest. Some philosophical souls hold *Kauai* wasn't hurt at all, and only a bunch of manmade buildings were destroyed. They contend in its millions of years of existence, Kauai has been through many storms, and Hurricane Iniki was merely a "$1.5 billion pruning . . . for free." Though trees were twisted from the ground and bushes were flattened, Kauai is strong and fertile and the damage was temporary. Now, Iniki is mostly a memory and Kauai has emerged a touch more self-assured and as beautiful as ever.

FLORA AND FAUNA

Kauai exceeds its reputation as the Garden Island. It has had a much longer time for soil building and rooting of a wide variety of plantlife, so it's lusher than the other islands. Lying on a main bird migratory route, lands such as the **Hanalei National Wildlife Sanctuary** have long since been set aside for their benefit. Impenetrable inland regions surrounding Mt. Waialeale and dominated by the Alakai Swamp have provided a natural sanctuary for Kauai's own bird- and plantlife. Because of this, Kauai is home to the largest number of indigenous birds extant in Hawaii, though even here they are tragically endangered. As on the other Hawaiian Islands, a large number of birds, plants, and mammals has been introduced in the past 200 years. Most have either aggressively competed for, or simply destroyed, the habitat of indigenous species. As the newcomers gain dominance, Kauai's own flora and fauna slide inevitably toward oblivion.

Indigenous Forest Birds

Kauai's upland forests are still home to many Hawaiian birds; they're dwindling but holding on. You may be lucky enough to spot some of the following. The **Hawaiian owl *(pueo)***, one of the friendliest *aumakua* (ancestral spirit) in ancient Hawaii, hunts by both day and night. It was an especially benign and helpful guardian. Old Hawaiian stories abound in which a *pueo* comes to the aid of a warrior in distress or a defeated army. Under a tree in which a *pueo* perches, they are safe from their pursuers and are under the protection of "the wings of an owl." The many introduced barn owls in Hawaii are easily distinguished from a *pueo* by their heart-shaped faces. The *pueo* is about 15 inches tall with a mixture of brown and white feathers. The eyes are large, round, and yellow, and the legs are heavily feathered, unlike those of a barn owl. *Pueo* chicks are a distinct yellow.

The ***elepaio*** is an indigenous bird found around Koke'e and so named because its song sounds like its name. A small brown bird with white rump feathers, it's very friendly and can even be prompted to come to an observer offering food.

Found above 2,000 feet, feeding on a variety of insects and flowers, is the ***'i'iwi,*** a bright red bird with a salmon-colored hooked bill. While most often sounding like a squeaking hinge, it can also produce a melodious song.

Anianiau is a four-inch yellow-green bird found around Koke'e. Its demise is due to a lack of fear of humans. The ***nukupu'u,*** extinct on the other islands except for a few on Maui, is found in Kauai's upper forests and on the borders of the Alakai Swamp. It's a five-inch bird with a drab green back and a bright yellow chest.

the friendly elepaio

LOUISE FOOTE

Birds Of The Alakai Swamp

The following scarce birds are some of the last indigenous Hawaiian birds, saved only by the inhospitability of the Alakai Swamp. All are endangered species and under no circumstances should they be disturbed. The last survivors include: the ***o'u,*** a chubby seven-inch bird with a green body, yellow head, and lovely whistle ranging half an octave; the relatively common **Hawaiian creeper,** a hand-sized bird with a light green back and white belly, which travels in pairs and searches bark for insects; the **puaiohi,** a dark brown, white-bellied seven-inch bird so rare its nesting habits are unknown.

O'o'a'a', although its name may resemble the sounds you make getting into a steaming hot tub, is an eight-inch black bird which played a special role in Hawaiian history. Its blazing yellow leg feathers were used to fashion the spectacular capes and helmets of the *ali'i.* Even before white people came, this bird was ruthlessly pursued by specially trained hunters who captured it and plucked its feathers. Finally there is the ***akialoa,*** a seven-inch greenish-yellow bird with a long, slender, curved bill.

Marine And Water Birds

Among the millions of birds that visit Kauai yearly, some of the most outstanding are its marine and water birds. Many beautiful individuals are seen at **Kilauea Point,** where they often nest in the trees on the cliff or on **Moku'ae'ae Islet.** The **Laysan albatross** ***(moli)*** is a far-ranging Pacific flier whose 11-foot wingspan carries it in effortless flight. This bird has little fear of man, and while on the ground is easily approachable. It also nests along Barking Sands. The **wedge-tailed shearwater** ***(ua'u kani)*** is known as the "moaning bird" because of its doleful sounds. These birds have no fear of predators and often fall prey to feral dogs and cats. Also seen making spectacular dives for squid off Kilauea Point is the **red-footed booby,** a fluffy white bird with a blue bill and a three-foot wingspan. Kiting from the same cliffs is the **white-tailed tropic bird,** snow-white elegance with a three-foot wingspan and a long, wispy, kitelike tail. One of the most amazing is the **great frigate bird,** an awesome specimen with an eight-foot wingspan. Predominantly black, the male has a red throat pouch it inflates like a balloon. These giants, the kings of the rookery, often steal food from lesser birds. They nest off Kilauea Point and are also seen along Kalalau Trail, and even at Poipu Beach.

Many of Kauai's waterbirds are most easily found in the marshes and ponds of **Hanalei National Wildlife Refuge,** though they have also been spotted at some of the island's reservoirs, especially at **Menehune Fish Pond** in the **Huleia National Wildlife Refuge** and its vicinity. The **Hawaiian stilt** ***(ae'o)*** is a one-and-a-half-foot-tall wading bird with pink stick-like legs. The **Hawaiian coot** ***(alae ke'oke'o)*** is a gray-black, ducklike bird with a white belly and face. The

Hawaiian gallinule ***(alae ula)***, an endemic Hawaiian bird often found in Hanalei's taro patches, has a ducklike body with a red face tipped in yellow. It uses its huge, chickenlike feet to hop across floating vegetation. The **Hawaiian duck** ***(koloa maoli)*** looks like a mallard, and because of interbreeding with common ducks, is becoming rarer as a distinctive species.

Introduced Common Birds

Kauai is rich in all manner of birds, from migratory marine birds to upland forest dwellers. Many live in areas you can visit; others you can see by taking a short stroll and remaining observant. Some, of course, are rare and very difficult to spot. Some of the most easily spotted island birds frequent almost all areas from the Kekaha Salt Ponds to Kalalau and the upland regions of Koke'e, including the blazing red **northern cardinal;** the comedic, brash **common mynah;** the operatic **western meadowlark,** introduced in 1930 and found in Hawaii only on Kauai; the ubiquitous **Japanese white eye;** sudden fluttering flocks of **house finches;** that Arctic traveler the **golden plover,** found along mudflats everywhere; the **cattle egret,** a white, 20-inch-tall heron found anywhere from the backs of cattle to the lids of garbage cans (introduced from Florida in 1960 to control cattle pests, they have so proliferated they are now considered a pest by some).

Introduced Fauna And Game Animals

One terribly destructive predator of native ground-nesting birds is the **mongoose.** Introduced to Hawaii last century as a cure for a rat infestation, the mongoose has only recently made it to Kauai, where a vigorous monitoring and extermination process is underway. Game mammals found in Kauai's forests include feral goats and pigs, although they too have caused destruction by uprooting seedlings and by overgrazing shrubs and grasses. Game fowl that have successfully acclimatized include francolins, ring-necked pheasants, and an assortment of quail and dove. All are hunted only at certain times of year. Bag limits and hunting seasons vary so check with the Division of Forestry and Wildlife for details.

One game animal found in Hawaii only on Kauai is the **black-tailed deer.** Kauai's thriving herd of 700 started as a few orphaned fawns from Oregon in 1961. These handsome animals, a species of western mule deer, are at home on the hilly slopes west of Waimea Canyon. Although there is little noticeable change in seasons in Hawaii, bucks and does continue to operate on genetically transmitted biological time clocks. The males shed their antlers during late winter months and the females give birth in spring. Hunting of black-tails is allowed only by public lottery in October.

Botanical Gardens

For those interested in the flora of Kauai, beyond what can be seen out of the car window, a visit to the following will be both educational and inspiring. **Koke'e Natural History Museum,** just past the Koke'e State Park Headquarters, has exhibits explaining the geology, plants, and animals of the park and the surrounding upper mountain and swamp regions of the island, tel. 335-9975. Free; open daily 10 a.m.-4 p.m.

Pacific Tropical Botanical Gardens in Lawai is the only research facility for tropical plants in the country and the premier botanical garden on Kauai (see "Lawai" under "West to Hanapepe" in the Southwest Kauai chapter). Lasting about two and a half hours, tours are given twice daily during the week and once a day on weekends. The visitor center/museum/gift shop is open daily 7:30 a.m.-4 p.m. for walk-in visitors. Here you can take a short self-guided tour (map provided) of the plants around

BOB RACE

the mongoose, an experiment gone bad

this building, but to go into the gardens you need reservations in advance. Call 332-7361 for information.

Nearby in Kalaheo is the **Olu Pua Gardens.** Formerly the manager's estate of the Kauai Pineapple Plantation, these gardens are open to the public for a limited time daily at 9:30 a.m., 11:30 a.m., and 1:30 p.m. The 12.5-acre site includes *kaukau,* hibiscus, palm, and jungle gardens, as well as a front lawn of flowering shade trees. Reservations may be made by calling 332-8182 (see "Kalaheo" under "West to Hanapepe" in the Southwest Kauai chapter).

The **Kiahuna Plantation Gardens** are located at the Kiahuna Plantation Resort in Poipu. Over a 27-year period during the mid-1900s, five acres of this former plantation site were cultivated with about 2,500 plants from Africa, the Americas, the Pacific, and India, and include cactus and aloe sections. Open daily during daylight hours; free guided tours of the property are given weekdays at 10 a.m. Call 742-6411 for more information (see "Poipu" in the Poipu and Koloa chapter).

Smith's Tropical Paradise, a finely manicured and well-kept botanical and cultural garden with a bountiful, beautiful collection of ordinary and exotic plants (many labeled), is on 30 riverfront acres adjacent to the Wailua marina. Have a look here before heading upcountry. Open until 4:30 p.m. (see "Sights" in the Wailua chapter). For information call 822-4654.

HISTORY

Kauai is the *first* of the Hawaiian islands in many ways. Besides being the oldest main island geologically, it's believed Kauai was the first island to be populated by Polynesian explorers. Theoretically, this colony was well established as early as A.D. 200, which predates the populating of the other islands by almost 500 years. Even Madame Pele chose Kauai as her first home and was content here until her sister drove her away. Her fires went out when she moved on, but she, like all visitors, never forgot Kauai.

Written History

The written history of Hawaii began when Capt. James Cook sailed into Waimea Bay on Kauai's south shore on the afternoon of September 20, 1778, and opened Hawaii to the rest of the world. In the years just preceding Cook's discovery, Hawaii was undergoing a unique change. Kamehameha the Great, a chief of the Big Island, was in the process of conquering the islands and uniting them under his rule. King Kaumualii of Kauai was able to remain independent from Kamehameha's rule by his use of diplomacy, guile, and the large distances separating his island from the others. Finally, after all the other islands had been subjugated, Kaumualii joined Kamehameha through negotiations, not warfare; he retained control of Kauai by being made governor of the island by Kamehameha. After Kamehameha died, his successor, Kamehameha II, forced Kaumualii to go to Oahu, where arrangements were made for him to marry the great queen Kaahumanu, the favorite wife of Kamehameha, and the greatest surviving *ali'i* of the land. Kaumualii never returned to his native island.

Hawaii was in a great state of flux at the beginning of the 1800s. The missionaries were coming, along with adventurers and schemers from throughout Europe. One of the latter was George Scheffer, a Prussian in the service of Czar Nicholas of Russia. He convinced Kaumualii to build a Russian fort in Waimea in 1817, which Kaumualii saw as a means of discouraging other Europeans from overrunning his lands. A loose alliance was made between Kaumualii and Scheffer. The adventurer eventually lost the czar's support, and Kaumualii ran him off the island, but the remains of **Fort Elizabeth** still stand. Around the same time, George Kaumualii, the king's son who had been sent to Boston to be educated, was accompanying the first missionary packet to the islands. He came with Rev. Sam Whitney, whom Kaumualii invited to stay, and who planted the first sugar on the island and taught the natives to dig wells. **Waioli Mission House,** just north of Hanalei, dates from 1836 and is still standing as a museum. Nearby, Hanalei Bay was a commercial harbor for trading and whaling. From here, produce such as oranges was shipped from Na

Pali farms to California. In Koloa, on the opposite end of the island, a stack from the Koloa Sugar plantation, started in 1835, marks the site of the first successful sugar-refining operation in the islands.

Another successful enterprise was **Lihue Plantation.** Founded by a German firm in 1850, it prospered until WW I, when anti-German sentiment forced the owners to sell out. In Lihue Town, you can still see the Haleko Shops, a cluster of four two-story buildings that show a strong German influence. If you go into the **Lihue Lutheran Church** you can view an ornate altar very similar to ones found in old German churches.

During the 1870s and '80s, leprosy raged throughout the kingdom and strong measures were taken. Those believed to be afflicted were wrenched from their families and sent to the hideous colony of Kalaupapa on Molokai. One famous Kauaian leper, Koolau, born in 1862 in Kekaha, refused to be brought in and took his family to live in the mountain fortress of Na Pali. He fought the authorities for years and killed all those sent to take him in. He was made popular by Jack London in his short story, "Koolau, the Leper."

When WW II came to Hawaii, Nawiliwili Harbor was shelled on December 31, 1941, but there was little damage. The island remained much the same, quiet and rural until the late 1960s when development began in earnest. The first resort destination on the island was the Coco Palms Hotel in Wailua, followed by development in Poipu, and more in Princeville. Meanwhile, Hollywood had discovered Kauai and featured its haunting beauty as a "silent star" in dozens of major films. Today, development goes on, but the island remains quiet, serene, and beautiful.

GOVERNMENT, ECONOMY, AND PEOPLE

GOVERNMENT

Kauai County

Kauai County is comprised of the inhabited islands of Kauai and Niihau, and the uninhabited islands of Kaula and Lehua. Lihue is the county seat. It's represented by two state senators elected from the 24th District, a split district including north Kauai and the Waianae coast of Oahu, and the 25th District, which includes all of southern Kauai and Niihau. Kauai has three state representatives from the 49th District, which is again a split district with north Kauai and the Waianae coast, the 50th District around Lihue, and the 51st District, which includes all of southwestern Kauai and Niihau.

ECONOMY

The economy of Kauai, like that of the entire state, is based on agriculture, the military, and tourism, the fastest-growing sector.

Tourism

Kauai, in a tight race with the Big Island, is the third-most-visited island after Oahu and Maui. Regaining momentum after Hurricane Iniki, it is once again attracting about one million visitors annually, accounting for 17% of the state's total. When completely recovered, approximately 7,200 hotel and condo units will be available, averaging a 70% occupancy rate. At one time, Kauai was the most difficult island on which to build a resort because of a strong grassroots antidevelopment faction. This trend has been changing due to the recession that hit everyone after Hurricane Iwa, and then Iniki scared off many tourists. Island residents realized how much their livelihood was tied to tourism, and a recent ad campaign depicting tourists as visitors (rather than unwelcome invaders) has helped their acceptance. The resorts being built on Kauai are first rate, and the developers are savvy enough to create "destination areas" instead of more high-rise boxes of rooms. Also, Kauai's "quality of room" compared to price is the state's best.

Agriculture

Agriculture still accounts for a hefty portion of Kauai's income, although **sugar,** once the backbone of the agricultural economy, has taken a downward trend because of stiff foreign competition. Kauai produces about six percent of the state's diversified agricultural crop, with a strong yield in **papayas.** In 1982, California banned the importation of Kauai's papayas because they were sprayed with EDB, a fumigant used to control fruit flies. The chemical is no longer used, and the papaya market has rebounded. Hanalei Valley and many other smaller areas produce five million pounds of taro that is quickly turned into poi, and the county produces two million pounds of guavas, as well as pineapples, beef, and pork for its own use. A growing aquaculture industry produces prawns. In the mid-1980s, large acreage near Kalaheo was put into coffee, tea, and macadamia nut production. Since then, it has turned into a thriving industry.

Military

The military influence on Kauai is small but vital. NASA's major tracking facilities in Koke'e Park were turned over to the Navy and Air Force. At **Barking Sands,** the Navy operates BARSTUR, an underwater tactical range for training in antisubmarine warfare. Also along Barking Sands (a fitting name!) is the **Pacific Missile Range,** operated by the Navy but available to the Air Force, Department of Defense, NASA, and the Department of Energy. Civilian visitors to these facilities are few and far between, and as welcome as door-to-door encyclopedia salespeople.

PEOPLE

Kauai County's 50,947 people account for only four percent of the state's total population, making it the least populous county. Also, 325 military personnel and their dependents live on the island. The largest town is Kapa'a with 8,149 people, followed by Lihue with 5,536. Ethnically, there is no clear majority on Kauai. The people of Kauai include: 35% Caucasians, 25% Filipinos, 20% Japanese, 15% Hawaiians including those of mixed blood, and 1.5% Chinese. The remaining 3.5% is Koreans, Samoans, and a smattering of African-Americans and Native Americans.

Mu And Menehune

Hawaiian legends give accounts of dwarflike aborigines on Kauai called the Mu and the Menehune. These two hirsute tribes of pixielike creatures were said to have lived on the island before and after the arrival of the Polynesians. The Mu were fond of jokes and games, while the Menehune were dedicated workers, stonemasons par excellence, who could build monu-

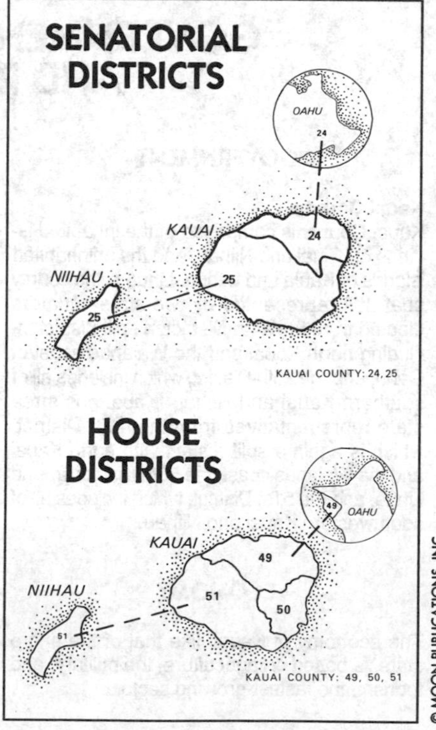

© MOON PUBLICATIONS, INC.

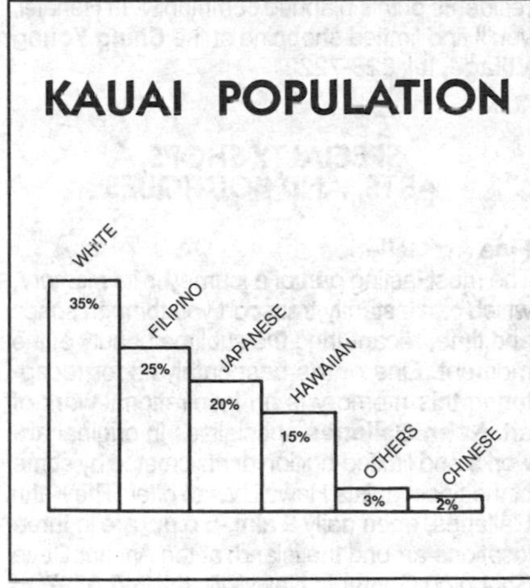

mental structures in just one night. Many stoneworks that can still be seen around the island are attributed to these hardworking nocturnal people, and a wonderfully educational exhibit concerning these pre-contact leprechauns is presented at the Kauai Museum.

Anthropological theory supports the logends that say some non-Polynesian peoples actually did exist on Kauai. According to oral history, their chief felt there was too much interplay and intermarriage with the Polynesians. He wished his race to remain pure so he ordered them to leave on a "triple-decker floating island," and they haven't been seen since, though if you ask a Kauaian if he or she believes in the Menehune, the answer is likely to be, "Of course not! But they're there, anyway." Speculation holds they may have been an entirely different race of people, or perhaps the remaining tribes of the first Polynesians. It's possible they were cut off from the original culture for so long they developed their own separate culture, and the food supply was so diminished their very stature was reduced in comparison to other Polynesians.

SHOPPING

Kauai has plenty of shops of all varieties: food stores in every town, boutiques, and specialty stores here and there. There are health food stores and farmers' markets, two extensive shopping malls, and a flea market.

Note

The following is an overview; specific stores, with their hours and descriptions, are covered in the appropriate travel sections.

SHOPPING CENTERS

Shopping Centers In And Around Lihue

The **Kukui Grove Center,** tel. 245-7784, is one of the two largest malls on Kauai. It's a few minutes west of Lihue along the Kaumualii Hwy. (Rt. 50). Clustered around an open courtyard, its more than 50 shops have everything from food to fashions, sports gear to artwork. Across Rt. 58 and toward the city from this complex is a cluster of offices and shops that includes fast-food restaurants, banks, the Kauai Athletic Club, Kauai Medical Group offices, Island Helicopter office, and Kukui Grove Cinema.

Lihue has four small shopping centers off Rice Street. **Lihue Shopping Center,** tel. 245-3731, is a small clutch of shops, a restaurant or two, a bank, a supermarket, and a discount store. The **Rice Shopping Center,** tel. 245-2033, features variety stores, a natural food and nutrition center, and Rob's Pub, a goodtime karaoke bar. Down the road, on the opposite side, is **Pay 'n Save** with a row of shops, including Cameralab and Daylight Donuts. In Nawiliwili is the **Pacific Ocean Plaza,** with clothing stores, several restaurants, and **Legends,** Lihue's hot nightspot.

Shopping Centers In And Around Kapa'a

The Coconut Market Place, tel. 822-3641, an extensive shopping mall, is along the Kuhio Hwy. (Rt. 56) in Waipouli between Wailua and Kapa'a. The Market Place is even larger than Kukui Grove and offers over 70 shops in a very attractive open-air setting. Aside from the clothing and gift shops, there are a bookstore, a cinema, a good activity and information center, and over a dozen eateries. In its courtyard are a huge banyan tree, a lookout tower, and colorful sculptures made of pipes, fittings, and machinery from old sugar mills.

The **Kauai Village,** built on the theme of an 18th-century "Main Street" and boasting its own museum, is modern, large and diverse. One of Kauai's newest shopping centers, it is located at 4-831 Kuhio Hwy. between Wailua and Kapa'a and offers a **Safeway Supermarket,** open 24 hours; **Pay 'n Save,** a complete variety store with photo equipment, and a **pharmacy;** an **ABC Store** for everything from suntan lotion to beach mats; a well-stocked **Waldenbooks; Blockbuster Video,** for home/condo entertainment; a cluster of fast-food restaurants, and small inexpensive eateries; **Papaya's Market Cafe,** the island's best natural health food store; and the **Pacific Cafe,** a fantastic restaurant featuring Pacific Island cuisine prepared by master chef Jean-Marie Josselin (see "Food" under "Kapa'a and Vicinity").

Along the Kuhio Hwy., in Wailua, Waipouli, and Kaapa, are five smaller shopping centers. Starting from the Rt. 580 turnoff, they are the **Kinipopo Shopping Village** just across from Sizzler; and, in rapid succession, **Waipouli Town Center, Waipouli Plaza,** and **Waipouli Complex** on the *mauka* side of the highway. Finally, just before you enter the main part of Kapa'a, you'll see **Kapa'a Shopping Center,** tel. 245-2033, the largest of these complexes with the greatest variety of stores.

Shopping Centers In And Around Poipu

Across the road from the Kiahuna Plantation Condominiums in Poipu is the **Poipu Shopping Center,** tel. 851-1200, an attractive cluster of shops and restaurants geared toward the tourist. The proletarian **Ele'ele Shopping Center,** tel. 245-2033, at the Rt. 541 turnoff to the Port Allen harbor, is the only one farther to the west along the south shore.

Shopping Centers Along The North Shore

The north coast has but two shopping centers. **Princeville Center,** tel. 826-3320, the newest and largest, provides the main shopping for the residents of this planned community. In Hanalei, you'll find limited shopping at the **Ching Young Village,** tel. 826-7222.

SPECIALTY SHOPS, ARTS, AND BOUTIQUES

Fine Art Galleries

The most lasting part of a journey is its memory, which can instantly transport you through space and time, recapturing the sublime beauty of the moment. One of the best catalysts for recapturing this memory is an inspirational work of art. **Kahn Galleries** specializes in original artworks and limited-edition prints created by some of the finest artists Hawaii has to offer. The Kahn Galleries, open daily 9 a.m.-5 p.m., are in three locations around the island: at the Anchor Cove Shopping Center in Nawiliwili, tel. 245-5397; at Kapa'a's Coconut Plantation Market Place, tel. 822-4277; and at the Kilohana Plantation, just west of Lihue, tel. 246-4454. Some of the master artists shown by Kahn Galleries include: Tabora, who specializes in dramatic seascapes of wind-whipped palm trees and crashing surf illuminated by glorious sunsets; George Sumner, who does surrealistic yet super-real renderings of dolphins hovering in the stratosphere, or two magnificent gulls winging their way past a mythical Hawaiian waterfall along a silhouetted *pali;* Randy Puckett, who expresses himself in finely detailed sculptures; and David Lee (impressionistic paintings) and Jan Parker, both masters of vibrant island color.

If the price of original artwork puts too much strain on your budget, then **Island Images,** offering fine art prints and posters, might have just what you need at an affordable price. Island Images, open daily 9 a.m.-5 p.m., has three stores around the island: in Koloa next to Lappert's Ice Cream, tel. 742-7447; at Kapa'a's Coconut Plantation Market Place, tel. 822-3636; and in Hanalei, tel. 826-6677. Posters average $30, with framing and shipping available.

Old Hanapepe Town has a string of fine art shops and studios along the main drag. The first is the **James Hoyle Gallery,** housed in a two-story building just as you enter town, tel. 335-3582, open daily 9 a.m.-6 p.m. and by appointment. James Hoyle has been able to capture the spirit of Hawaii through color and movement. His medium is oil, pastel, and polymer that he applies on canvas in a distinctive style of macro-pointillism. Each daub, like a molted jelly bean, is a fantastic shade of deep purple, orange, magenta, yellow, or green. The result is a blazing sunset swirling with color, backlighting a tortured lava mountain that broods over a tiny pool of water speckled with green taro. Another painting may depict palm trees laid low by the wind while storm clouds whistle overhead, while below in humble elegance is the bare wood home of a Filipino plantation family clinging to life in a lovely tropical setting. The sense permeating Hoyle's work is that in Hawaii humankind can not conquer nature, but must learn to live in harmony with the *aina,* which is very much alive. These fine works range in price $800-40,000.

A minute down the road is the **Lele Aka Studio and Gallery,** wild with fantastic demons rising from the sea and goddesses with silvery moonbeams emanating from their foreheads. In stark contrast are painted portraits of the lovely bright faces of Kauai's children.

Another minute's stroll brings you to **Kauai Fine Arts,** 3848 Hanapepe Rd., Hanapepe, P.O. Box 1079, Lawai, HI, tel. 335-3778, open Mon.-Fri. 10 a.m.-5 p.m., Saturday and Sunday by appointment only. Inside, floor-to-ceiling hardwoods and pine give the impression you are inside a handcrafted jewelry box. Owned and operated by Caribbean islander Mona Nicolaus, Kauai Fine Arts specializes in original engravings, original antique prints mainly of the Pacific Islands, antique maps, and vintage natural science photos from as far afield as Australia and Egypt. The shelves also hold a collection of antique bottles.

A co-op of four goldsmiths displays its craftsmanship at **The Goldsmith's Gallery,** tel. 822-4653, in the Kinipopo Shopping Village, Waipouli.

Nearly three dozen first-rate Island artists display their artwork at the **Artisans' Guild of Kauai,** tel. 826-6441, in Hanalei.

Specialty Shops And Boutiques

You can't go wrong in the following shops. The **Kauai Museum Shop** on Rice Street in Lihue, tel. 245-6931, has perhaps the island's best selection of Kauaian arts and crafts at reasonable prices, as well as books on Hawaii. **Kapaia Stitchery,** tel. 245-2281, has beautiful handmade quilts, embroideries, and 100% cotton alohawear. Many shops can be found at **Kilohana,** tel. 245-5608, west of Lihue on the way to Puhi. Most rooms in this 1930 plantation estate of Gaylord Wilcox have been turned into boutiques featuring gifts, artwork, clothing, jewelry, antiques, and plants. **Remember Kauai,** 4-734 Kuhio Hwy. between Wailua and Kapa'a, tel. 822-0161, sells a wide selection of coral and shell necklaces, featuring famous Niihau shellwork, bracelets, earrings, buckles, and chains.

Artisans International, tel. 828-1918, a new shop in Kilauea, stocks only handmade gifts and household items. The old standby here is **Kong Lung Store,** which prides itself on being an "exotic gift emporium" and offers such things as jewelry, Niihau shells, upscale gift items including gourmet food and drinks, children's clothes, and books.

Flea Markets, Etc.

Excellent bargains are found at **Spouting Horn Flea Market** near Poipu Beach, where buskers set up stalls selling cut-rate merchandise.

At the **Roxy Swap Meet,** held in central Kapa'a every Saturday, tel. 822-7027, tables are set up under numerous tents. People from all over come to barter and sell everything and anything. See also "Farmers' Markets and Fresh Fish" under "Food Stores" below.

Bookstores

The most extensive bookstores on Kauai are the **Waldenbooks** shops, at the Kukui Grove Shopping Center in Lihue, tel. 245-7162; at the Coconut Plantation Market Place in Waipouli, tel. 822-9362; and at The Kauai Village between Wailua and Kapa'a, tel. 822-7749. All are generally open (some variance) Mon.-Sat. 9 a.m.-8 p.m., Sunday 9 a.m.-5 p.m., and feature racks of books on everything from Hawaiiana to travel, along with maps, postcards, stationery and souvenirs.

Perhaps the place with the widest selection of Hawaiiana, Kauaiana, and guidebooks is the **Kauai Museum Shop.** Other stores to check for these books are the **Koke'e Natural History Museum** in Koke'e State Park, the **Hawaiian Art Museum and Bookstore** and **Kong Lung Store** in Kilauea, and **Happy Talk** and **Hanalei**

Camping and Backpacking in Hanalei. Books on metaphysics, spirituality, and self-help, along with books on health, cooking, and natural foods, can be found at **Papaya's Natural Foods** in Kapa'a, and at **Hanalei Health and Natural Foods** in Hanalei.

FOOD STORES

Supermarkets

Groceries and picnic supplies can be purchased in almost every town on the island. Many of the markets in the smaller towns also sell a limited selection of dry goods and gifts. The general rule is: the smaller the store, the higher the price. The largest and cheapest stores with the biggest selections are in Lihue and Kapa'a. **Big Save Value Centers** sell groceries, produce, and liquors in Eleele, Hanalei, Kapa'a, Koloa, Lihue, and Waimea. Most stores are open weekdays 8:30 a.m.-9 p.m., weekends until 6 p.m.

Foodland supermarkets, open 24 hours, operate large stores at the Waipouli Town Center and at the Princeville Center. The Princeville store is the largest and best-stocked market on the north shore.

Star Market is a well-stocked store in the Kukui Grove Shopping Center, while the smaller but well-stocked **Menehune Food Marts** are found in Kekaha, Kalaheo, and Kilauea.

Safeway, open 24 hours, in the Kauai Village Shopping Center along the Kuhio Hwy. and in Waipouli between Wailua and Kapa'a, is a large, well-stocked supermarket.

Smaller individual markets around the island include **Kojima's** and **Pono Market** in Kapa'a, where you can stock up not only on food items and dry goods, but on local color as well. Heading north from Kapa'a are **Whalers General Store** in Anahola, **The Farmers Market** in Kilauea, and the "last chance" limited-selection **Wainiha Store** in Wainiha.

Note: The following stores in and around the Poipu area are making a comeback since Hurricane Iniki. Some are up and running, while others are still under repair. Along the south coast look for **Sueoka Store** in Koloa, **Kukuiula Store** at the turnoff to Spouting Horn, **Whalers General Store** in the Kiahuna Shopping Village, **Matsuura Store** in Lawai, **Mariko's Mini Mart** in Hanapepe, and **Ishihara Market** in Waimea.

Health Food Stores

Papaya's, a natural food cafe and market at the Kauai Village Shopping Center, 4-831 Kuhio Hwy., open daily except Sunday 10 a.m.-8 p.m., tel. 823-0190, is not only the largest, but the best natural food store on Kauai. Coolers and shelves are stocked with organic fruits and vegetables, whole grain breads, organic teas and flavored coffees, grains, dried beans, spices, homeopathic medicines, cruelty-free cosmetics, vitamins, minerals, and an assortment of biodegradable cleaning products. The cafe section has a display case filled with cheesecakes and other goodies, salads and entrees by the pound, and freshly made sandwiches, packed and ready to go. If you are into healthy organic food, there is no place better than Papaya's.

If not the best, at least the most down-to-earth health food store on Kauai is **Ambrose's Kapuna Natural Foods,** tel. 822-7112, along the Kuhio Hwy. across from the Foodland Supermarket in Kapa'a. Ambrose is a character worth visiting just for the fun of it. His store is well stocked with juices, nuts, grains, island fruits, vitamins and minerals, and plenty of bananas. Ambrose has one of the largest collections of big boards and old surfboards on the island (new ones too). If he's not in the store just give a holler around the back. He's there!

General Nutrition Center, tel. 245-6657, in the Kukui Grove Shopping Center, is a full-service health food store.

Hale O' Health, tel. 245-9053, in the Rice Shopping Center in Lihue, open Mon.-Fri., 8 a.m.-5 p.m., Sat.-Sun. until 3 p.m., specializes in vitamins and minerals. The shelves are stocked with everything from whole wheat flour to spices, organic pastas, oils, and a good selection of teas. The back deli case holds a small selection of fresh organic vegetables and prepared deli sandwiches.

On the north shore try **Hanalei Health and Natural Foods** in the Ching Young Village. Although cramped, this little store has a good vibe and a reasonable selection of bulk foods, fresh produce, hand-squeezed juices, vitamins, and books. It is open daily 8:30 a.m.-8:30 p.m.

Farmers' Markets And Fresh Fish

The farmers' markets on Kauai must have at least 20 vendors each. The **Sunshine Farmers' Market,** featuring surplus backyard produce, is held six days a week: Monday at the baseball field in Koloa at noon; Tuesday at 3 p.m. in Hanalei at Waipa, on the west side of Hanalei Bay; Wednesday at the beach park in Kapa'a at 3 p.m.; Thursday on the lawn of the First United Church of Christ in Hanapepe 4 p.m.-6 p.m.; Friday at 3 p.m. in Lihue at Vidinha Stadium; and two on Saturday, both at noon, one at the Waldorf School in Kilauea and the other in Kekaha. Local gardeners bring their produce to town; a large selection of island produce is had at very good prices. The stories and local color are even more delicious than the fruit. Contact the County Information and Complaint Office, tel. 245-3213, for exact times and places.

Every Tuesday 3-5 p.m., pick up farm-fresh fruit and vegetables from the **Hawaiian Farmers of Hanalei** farmers' market located a half mile west of Hanalei, in Waipa, on the road to Haena. Look for the sign along the road on the left.

An excellent fish store is the **Pono Fish Market** in Kapa'a, open Mon.-Sat. 9 a.m.-8:30 p.m. and Sunday until 6 p.m. They have fresh fish daily and often offer specials.

G's Fishco, 4361 Rice St., Lihue, tel. 246-4440, open weekdays 10 a.m.-8 p.m., Saturday until 7 p.m., and Sunday until 5 p.m., offers cold cases filled with whole fish, *pokei,* sashimi, and assorted seafood.

Ara's Sakamaya, open Mon.-Sat. 9 a.m.-7 p.m., Sunday 9 a.m.-5 p.m., tel. 245-1707, in the Hanamaulu Plaza in Hanamaulu, clearly marked along Rt. 56, is a takeout deli-restaurant that offers plate lunches, Japanese *bento,* boxed lunches, and **fresh fish** daily.

Other stores include **The Fish Express** at 3343 Kuhio Hwy. in Lihue, and at **Nishimura's Market** in Hanapepe.

ACCOMMODATIONS

Kauai is very lucky when it comes to places to stay, a combination of happenstance and planning. Kauai was not a major Hawaiian destination until the early '70s. By that time, all concerned had wised up to the fact that what you *didn't do* was build endless miles of high-rise hotels and condos that blotted out the sun and ruined the view of the coast. Besides that, a very strong grassroots movement here insisted on tastefully done low-rise structures that blend into and complement the surrounding natural setting. This concept mandates "destination resorts," the kind of hotels and condos that lure visitors because of their superb architecture, artistic appointments, and luxurious grounds. There is room for growth on Kauai, but the message is clear: Kauai is the most beautiful island of them all and the preservation of this delicate beauty benefits everyone. The good luck doesn't stop there. Kauai leads the other islands in offering the best quality rooms for the price.

Hotel/Condo Choices

Kauai has approximately 75 properties with a total of 7,200 available rooms, of which 35% are condominium units. Almost all the available rooms on Kauai are split between four major destinations: Poipu Beach, Lihue, Wailua/Kapa'a, and Princeville/Hanalei. Except for Koke'e Lodge overlooking Waimea Canyon and Waimea Plantation Cottages in Waimea, little is available west of Poipu. Specialized and inexpensive accommodations are offered inland from Poipu at Kahili Mountain Park, but these very basic cottages are just a step up from what you'd find at a Boy Scout camp. Long stretches along the coast between the major centers have no lodgings whatsoever. The north shore past Hanalei has one resort, a few condos, and some scattered guest homes, but you won't find any large concentration of rooms. Aside from hotel/condo or cottage rooms, rental homes are peppered throughout the island.

Poipu, the best general-purpose beach and most popular destination on Kauai, has three major hotels (two are rebuilding following Hurricane Iniki) and a host of condos. Prices are reasonable to expensive, and most of the condos offer long-term discounts.

For years Lihue had only one luxury hotel, the Kauai Surf, which became the fabulous

Westin Kauai. Heavily hit by Iniki, its fate is still undetermined. In and around Lihue are most of Kauai's inexpensive hotels, guest cottages, and one mandatory "fleabag." Small hotels, and especially the guest cottages, are family run. They're moderately priced, very clean, and more than adequate. However, they are in town and you have to drive to the beach. Just a few minutes away is the Outrigger Beach Hotel and its neighbor, the Aston Kauai Beach Villas, two fine properties that are affordable.

Wailua/Kapa'a on the east coast has good beaches and a concentration of accommodations, mostly hotels. Here you'll find the Kauai Resort, which traditionally has brought most of the big-name entertainment to Kauai. The Coco Palms in Wailua is a classic. Used many times as a Hollywood movie set, it has a very loyal clientele, the sure sign of a quality hotel. Unfortunately, The Coco Palms was heavily hit by Iniki, and it too has not yet recovered. The Coconut Plantation is just east of Coco Palms and has an extensive shopping center, three large hotels, and a concentration of condos. Almost all sit right on the beach and offer superior rooms at a standard price.

Princeville is a planned "destination resort." It boasts a commuter airport, shopping center, 1,000 condo units, and the Sheraton Princeville Hotel, a showcase resort overlooking Hanalei Bay. From here to Haena are few accommodations until you get to the Hanalei Colony Resort, literally "the last resort."

Hotel/Condo Booking And Reservations

Another way to find vacation or long-term rentals is through a rental/real estate agent. This can be handled either on Kauai or through the mail. If handled through the mail, the process may take considerably longer, and you take a chance getting the type of place you want. Throughout the island, everything from simple beach homes to look-alike condominiums and luxurious hideaways are put into the hands of rental agents. They have descriptions of the properties and terms of the rental contracts, and many will furnish photographs. When contacting an agency, be as specific as possible about your needs, length of stay, desired location, and how much you're willing to spend. Write several months in advance. Be aware high-season rentals are at a premium, and if you're slow to inquire the pickings may be slim.

The following is a partial list of booking agents handling a number of properties on Kauai. They include, but are not limited to: **Aston Hotels and Resorts,** 2250 Kuhio Ave., Honolulu, HI 96815, tel. 931-1400, (800) 922-7866 Mainland, (800) 445-6633 Canada, and (800) 321-2558 Hawaii (some are Aston's while others are managed by this professional organization); **Marc Resorts Hawaii,** 2155 Kalakaua Ave., Honolulu, HI 96815, tel. 926-5900, (800) 535-0085; **North Shore Properties and Vacation Rentals,** Princeville Center, Princeville, HI 96714, tel. 826-9622, (800) 488-3336; **Grantham Resorts,** P.O. Box 983, Poipu, HI 96756, tel. 742-1412, (800) 325-5701; **Kauai Vacation Rental and Real Estate,** 4480 Ahukini Rd., Lihue, HI 96766, tel. 245-8841, (800) 367-5025; **R.R. Realty and Rentals,** 2827 Poipu Rd., Koloa, HI 96756, tel. 742-7555, (800) 367-8022; **Aloha Rental Management,** tel. 826-7288, (800) 487-9833; **Kauai Paradise Vacations,** tel. 826-7444, (800) 826-7782.

Note: For Bed and Breakfast rental agencies, see "Bed and Breakfast" under "Accommodations" in the Out and About chapter.

SPORTS AND RECREATION

Kauai is an exciting island for all types of sports enthusiasts, with golf, tennis, hunting, fresh- and saltwater fishing, and all manner of water sports. You can rent horses or relax on a cruise. The following should start the fun rolling.

Note

For renting **Zodiacs, kayaks, or other boats** see "Zodiacs-Kayaks-Cabin Cruisers and Sailing Ships" under "Sightseeing Tours" in "Getting Around" later in this chapter.

SWIMMING AND BEACHES

With so many to choose from, the problem on Kauai is picking which beach to visit. If you venture farther than the immediate area of your hotel, the following sample listing will help you decide where you'd like to romp about. For more details see the specific listings in the appropriate travel chapters.

Lihue Area Beaches

Kalapaki Beach in Lihue is one of the best on the island, and convenient to Kauai's principal town center. This beach's gentle wave action is just right for learning how to bodysurf or ride the boogie board; snorkeling is fair. Two small crescent beaches lie below the lighthouse at the far end of the beach. Water is rougher there, with much exposed rock; snorkeling should be done on calm days only. Also accessible but less frequented is **Hanamaulu Bay,** just up the coast, with a lagoon, picnic spots, and camping with permit at **Ahukini Recreation Pier State Park.**

Kapa'a, Wailua And Vicinity

Like its accommodations, the beaches of Wailua are few but very good. **Lydgate Beach** has two lava pools, and the beaches below Wailua Municipal Golf Course offer seclusion in sheltered coves where there's fine snorkeling. **Waipouli Beach** and **Kapa'a Beach** flank the well-developed town of Kapa'a, while out along a cane road near Pohakuloa is the little-frequented **Donkey Beach,** known for its good surfing and snorkeling. The undertow is quite strong at Donkey Beach so don't venture out too far if you don't swim well (a permit issued by the Lihue Sugar Co. is technically necessary to use the cane road).

Anahola Beach, at the south end of Anahola Bay, has safe swimming in a protected cove, freshwater swimming in the stream that empties into the bay, picnicking, and camping with permit. Snorkel a short distance up the shore where the reef comes in close—an area where locals come for shore fishing. Still farther north is **Moloa'a Beach,** a little-visited half-moon swath of sand.

North Kauai Beaches

Just south of Kilauea is **Secret Beach,** with all that its name implies. At the end of a tiny dirt road, the start of which eludes many people, is a huge stretch of white sand. You're sure to find it nearly empty. Camping is good, and no one is around to bother you. North of town is **Kalihiwai Beach,** great for swimming and bodysurfing during the right conditions. People camp in the ironwood trees that line the beach. There is a park at **Anini Beach,** a great place to snorkel as it has the longest exposed reef in Kauai, and a wonderful place to learn windsurfing because of the shallow water inside the reef.

Hanalei Bay is a prime spot on the north coast. Swim at the mouth of the Hanalei River (but watch out for boats) or on the far side of the bay. Experienced surfers ride the waves below the Sheraton; snorkeling is good closer to the cliffs. West of Hanalei is **Lumahai Beach,** a beautiful curve of white sand backed by cliffs and thick jungle that was the silent star of the movie *South Pacific.* The inviting water here has a fierce riptide, so enter only when the water is calm. **Haena Beach** and nearby **Tunnels** are terrific swimming and snorkeling spots.

At the end of the road is **Ke'e Beach,** a popular place with some amenities—good swimming in summer with adequate snorkeling. Many secluded beaches at the foot of the Na Pali cliffs dot the coast to the west along the Kalalau Trail.

Hanakapi'ai Beach is reached after one hour on the trail and is fine for sunbathing; the water, especially in winter, can be torturous so stay out. **Kalalau Beach** is a full day's hike down this spectacular coast, while the others can only be reached by boat.

South Kauai Beaches

The **Poipu Beach** area is the most developed on the island. Accommodating, tame, and relaxing, it lets you swim, snorkel, and bodysurf to your heart's content.

Down the coast are **Salt Pond Beach,** one of the island's best and good for swimming and windsurfing, and **Pakala Beach,** popular with surfers but also good for swimming and snorkeling. The golden strand of **Kekaha Beach** runs for miles with excellent swimming, snorkeling, and surfing, and stretches into Barking Sands Military Base, where you can go, with permission, for good views of Niihau when no military exercises are in progress.

Polihale Beach is the end of the road. Swimming is not the best as the surf is high and the undertow strong, but walk along the shore for a view of the south end of the great Na Pali cliffs.

SCUBA AND SNORKELING

The best beaches for snorkeling and scuba are along the northeast coast from Anahola to Ke'e. The reefs off Poipu, roughed up by Hurricane Iwa and Iniki, are making a remarkable comeback. Those interested can buy or rent equipment in dive shops and department stores. Sometimes condos and hotels offer snorkeling equipment free to their guests, but if you have to rent it, don't do it from a hotel or condo; go to a dive shop where it's much cheaper. Scuba divers can rent gear for $50-60 from most shops. To get just what you need at the right price, be sure to call ahead and ask for particulars about what each company offers.

Scuba/Snorkel Rentals

The following full service shops rent/sell snorkel/scuba equipment, and most offer scuba certification courses.

Kauai Water Ski and Surf, tel. 822-3574, open daily 9 a.m.-7 p.m., in the Kinipopo Shopping Village, 4-356 Kuhio Hwy., Wailua, HI, 96746 is a complete water sports shop offering snorkel gear by the day or week.

Aquatic Adventures, at 4-1380 Kuhio Hwy., Kapa'a, HI 96746, tel. 822-1434, open Mon.-Fri. 7:30 a.m.-7 p.m.; Sat.-Sun. 7:30 a.m.-5 p.m., owned and operated by Janet Moore, is a full service dive shop offering rentals, excursions, and certification courses. Janet also sells a full complement of underwater gear.

Also in Kapa'a **Bubbles Below,** tel. 822-3483, runs the most unusual dives (and perhaps the most expensive), as they go to Lehua Island off Niihau—but dives there, where the water is clear to depths of over a hundred feet, is tops. **Sea Fun,** another Kapa'a shop, tel. 822-0211, has everything from snorkel to certification courses, underwater photography, and video.

The second concentration of dive shops is in Koloa. **Fathom Five Divers,** tel. 742-6991, also a well-respected professional group, offers diving charters with their own boat and certification courses at competitive prices.

Kauai Sea Sports, located at the Poipu Plaza, 2827 Poipu Road, tel. 742-9303, is a snorkel/dive shop and a sports boutique where you can rent masks, fins, and snorkels. They also offer surfing, snorkel, and scuba lessons.

The **Captain's Cargo Company,** tel. 338-0333, 9984 Kaumualii Hwy. (Rt. 50), Waimea, and the office of **Liko Kauai Cruises,** is operated by Debra Hookano, wife of Captain Liko. Rental rates are $2 per hour, or $5 per day for mask, fins, and snorkel.

Good old **Snorkel Bob,** at 4480 Ahukini Rd., Lihue, tel. 245-9433, offers some of the best deals for snorkel rental in Hawaii. Basic gear is $15 per week (day rental available) with better gear also available. If you're island hopping, Snorkel Bob allows you to drop off the gear at a Snorkel Bob location on another island.

Others are: **Sea Sports Divers,** tel. 742-7288; **Ocean Odyssey,** tel. 245-8661; **South Shore Activities,** tel. 742-6873, in Poipu; **Pedal and Paddle,** tel. 826-9069, and the **Hanalei Surf Co.,** tel. 826-9000, in Hanalei; **Ray's Rentals and Activities,** 1345 Kuhio Hwy., downtown Kapa'a, tel. 822-5700.

For additional information about scuba diving and diving clubs in Hawaii, contact **Hawaii**

Council of Dive Clubs, P.O. Box 298, Honolulu, HI 96809.

SURFING, SAILBOARDING, AND BOOGIE BOARDING

Surfing has long been the premier water sport in Hawaii. Locals, and now "surfies" from all over the world, know where the best waves are and when they come. While Anahola Beach was a traditional surfing spot for Hawaiians of yesterday, the north shore has the beaches of choice today. The east side of Hanalei Bay provides a good roll in winter for experts, as does Tunnels. Quarry Beach, near Kilauea, and Donkey Beach, north of Kapa'a, are used mostly by locals. On the south coast, the surfers' favorite is the area in front of the Waiohai Resort, or west of there near Pakala. Listen to local advice as to where and when to ride and why. The sea is unforgiving, and particularly unpredictable in winter.

Surfing lessons are available. Contact: **Mike Smith International Surfing School,** tel. 245-3882; world champion **Margo Oberg,** who runs a school on Poipu Beach, tel. 822-5113; or Nancy Palmer of **Garden Island Windsurfing,** tel. 826-9005, who offers surfing lessons at the Lawai Beach Resort.

Kauai Water Ski and Surf, tel. 822-3574, open daily 9 a.m.-7 p.m., in the Kinipopo Shopping Village, 4-356 Kuhio Hwy., Wailua, HI 96746, is a complete water sports shop that offers surfboard and boogie board rentals by the day or week. They also offer water-skiing, complete with boat, driver, equipment, and instruction if necessary. Kayaks are available.

Kauai Sea Sports, located at the Poipu Plaza, 2827 Poipu Road, tel. 742-9303, is a full service snorkel/scuba/surf shop.

Hanalei Surf Co., tel. 826-900, just a few minutes from a great beginners' surfing area at Hanalei, offers sailboarding, and surfing lessons and board rentals without lessons (boogie boards too). Hanalei Bay goes completely flat in summer, so call ahead for surfing conditions.

The **Captain's Cargo Company,** tel. 338-0333, 9984 Kaumualii Hwy. (Rt. 50) and office of **Liko Kauai Cruises** (see "Cabin Cruisers and Sailing Ships" under "Sightseeing Tours" in the Kauai Introduction) rents and sells surfboards and boogie boards. Rental rates are boogie boards $5 per hour or $15 per day; surfboards $5 per hour, or $20 per day.

Sailboarding

Sailboarding has become very popular on Kauai in the last few years. The best spots for beginners are at Anini Beach on the north coast, and Poipu Beach on the south. For the advanced only, Haena Beach on the north coast is preferred.

For windsurfing rental gear and other beach rentals and sales, contact **Hanalei Sailboards,** tel. 826-9733; they're the best in the business. Also contact **Pedal And Paddle,** tel. 826-9069, and **Sand People,** tel. 826-6981, in Hanalei; **Kalapaki Beach Center,** tel. 245-5595, in Nawiliwili; **South Shore Activities,** tel. 742-6873, in Poipu; **Ray's Rentals and Activities,** 1345 Kuhio Hwy., downtown Kapa'a, tel. 822-5700; or any of the sports shops on the island.

WATER-SKIING

When you think of recreation on Kauai, water-skiing might not necessarily come to mind. **Kauai Water Ski and Surf Co.** tel. 822-3574, open daily 9 a.m.-7 p.m., in the Kinipopo Shopping Village, 4-356 Kuhio Hwy., Wailua, HI 96746, has established itself as the main water-skiing company. Skimming placid Wailua River, freshwater skiers pass tour boats going to and from the Fern Grotto. Water-skiing fees include boat, driver, gas, skis, and other equipment; instruction at all levels can be arranged. They also sell beach clothes and water sports equipment. Rentals include kayaks, surfboards, boogie boards, and snorkel equipment. Inquire here about the Terheggen International Ski Club.

FISHING

Deep-Sea Fishing Charters

There are excellent fishing grounds off Kauai, especially around Niihau, and a few charter boats for hire. Most are berthed at Nawiliwili Harbor, with some on the north coast. Rates vary, as do the length of outings (usually four, six, or eight hours) and number of passengers allowed on the boats, so call for information be-

GOLF COURSES OF KAUAI

COURSE	PAR	YARDS	FEES
Kauai Lagoons Golf Club	72	6,942 (Lagoons)	$145
Lagoons and Kiele Courses P.O. Box 3330 Kalapaki Beach, Lihue, HI 96766 tel. 241-6000 or (800) 634-6400	72	7,070 (Kiele)	$100
Kiahuna Golf Course Route 1, Box 73 Koloa, HI 96756 tel. 742-9595	70	6,353	$45
Kukui O Lono Golf Course P.O. Box 987 Lihue, HI 96766 tel. 335-9940	36	2,981	$5
Princeville Makai Golf Courses P.O. Box 3040 Princeville, HI 96722 tel. 826-3580	36 36 36	3,157 (Ocean) 3,149 (Woods) 3,445 (Lake)	$110 $110 $110
Princeville Prince Course P.O. Box 3040 Princeville, HI 96722 tel. 826-3580	72	7,309	$140
Poipu Bay Resort Golf Course 2250 Ainako St. Koloa, HI 96756 tel. 742-8711 or (800) 858-6300	72	6,959	$95
Wailua Municipal Golf Course P.O. Box 1017 Kapa'a, HI 96746 tel. 241-6666	72	6,981	$18 ($20 weekends)

fore planning a trip. Some private yachts offer charters, but these come and go with the tides. Fishing excursions run in the vicinity of $75 half day to $125 full day shared, and $350 half day to $500 full day exclusive.

Charter boats with good reputations are: ***Lucky Lady,*** tel. 822-7590, runs a 33-foot twin-diesel craft off Niihau for the big ones, for whalewatching in season, or bottom fishing "Hawaiian style; ***Alana Lynn Too,*** tel. 245-7446; ***Gent-Lee,*** tel. 245-7504; **Coastal Charters,** tel. 246-1551.

Sea Breeze IV, tel. 828-1285, with skipper Bob Kutowski, specializes in bottom fishing. He and **Robert McReynolds,** tel. 828-1379, leave from Anini Beach. McReynolds uses medium tackle and fishes the area off Kilauea Lighthouse. A trip with him is perhaps the best introduction to sportfishing in Kauai.

Freshwater Fishing

Kauai has trout and bass. Rainbow trout were introduced in 1920 and thrive in 13 miles of fishable streams, ditches, and reservoirs in the Koke'e Public Fishing Area. Large and small bass and the basslike tucunare are also popular game fish on Kauai. Introduced in 1908, they're hooked in reservoirs and in the Wailua River and its feeder streams.

TENNIS COURTS OF KAUAI

COUNTY COURTS

Under jurisdiction of the Department of Parks and Recreation, P.O. Box 111, Lihue, HI 96766, tel. 245-4751. Courts listed are in Lihue and near the Wailua and Poipu areas. There are also additional locations around the island.

LOCATION	NAME OF COURT/LOCATION	NO. OF COURTS	LIGHTED
Hanapepe	next to stadium	2	Yes
Kekaha	next to park	2	Yes
Kalahea	Kalawai Park	2	Yes
Kapa'a	New Park	2	Yes
Koloa	next to fire station	2	Yes
Lihue	next to convention hall	2	Yes
Wailua	Wailua Park	4	Yes
Waimea	next to high school	4	Yes

HOTEL AND PRIVATE COURTS OPEN TO THE PUBLIC

LOCATION	NAME OF COURT/LOCATION	NO. OF COURTS	LIGHTED
Hanalei	Hanalei Bay Resort	8	Yes
Kapa'a	Holiday Inn Kauai Beach	3	No
Poipu	Poipu Kai Resort (fee for nonguests)	9	No
Poipu Beach	Kiahuna Beach and Tennis Resort	10	Yes
Princeville	Princeville Resort and Complex	6	No

Note: a fee may be required

Fishing Licenses And Regulations

No license is needed for recreational saltwater fishing. A freshwater game fishing license is needed for certain freshwater fish during their seasons (inexpensive temporary visitor's licenses available). Licenses and a digest of fishing laws and rules are available from the State Division of Conservation and Resources Enforcement or from most sporting goods stores. For free booklets and information, write Division of Aquatic Resources, 1151 Punchbowl St., Honolulu, HI 96813. On Kauai, write to Division of Aquatic Resources, Department of Land and Natural Resources, P.O. Box 1671, Lihue, HI 96744, or stop by Room 306 of the state office building in Lihue, tel. 241-3400.

Nearly all game fish may be taken year-round, except trout. Trout, only in the Koke'e Public Fishing Area on Kauai, may be taken for 16 days commencing on the first Saturday of August. Thereafter, for the remainder of August and September, trout can be taken only on Saturday, Sunday, and state holidays.

Note

Whalewatching cruises run from January through April. Many of the above charter companies, plus some of the companies listed under "Sightseeing Tours," run special whalewatching tours.

HUNTING

All game animals on Kauai have been introduced. Some are adapting admirably and becoming well entrenched, while the existence of others is still precarious. Feral pigs are escaped domestic pigs and are found on all islands except Lanai. The stock is a mixture of original Polynesian pigs and all that came later. Because the pigs are hunted with dogs and usually killed with a spear or long knife, pig hunting is not recommended for the timid or tenderhearted. These beasts' four-inch tusks and fighting spirit make them tough and dangerous. Feral goats come in a variety of colors. Found on all islands except Lanai, they have been known to cause erosion and are considered pests in some areas. They are openly hunted on all islands; their meat when cooked properly is considered delicious. Black-tailed deer come from Oregon. Forty were released on Kauai in 1961; the herd is now stabilized at around 700 and they're hunted in October by public lottery. Because they thrive on island fruits, their meat is sweeter and less gamey than that of Mainland deer.

Game Birds

A number of game birds are found on Kauai. Bag limits and hunting seasons vary, so check with the Division of Forestry and Wildlife for details. Ring-necked pheasants are one of the best game birds. Francolins—gray, black, and Erkel's—from India and the Sudan are similar to partridges. They are hunted with dogs and are great roasted. There are also chukar from Tibet, found on rugged mountain slopes; a number of quail, including the Japanese and California varieties; and spotted and zebra doves.

HORSEBACK RIDING

There are two stables on Kauai. You can hire mounts from **CJM Country Stables,** tel. 742-6096, just past the Hyatt in Poipu. CJM offers three rides: a one-hour beach ride for $25; a two-hour ride through woods and sugarcane fields and down along the beach for $50; and a three-hour beach breakfast ride for $75, where your meal is prepared by your "galloping gourmet guide."

Pooku Stables, tel. 826-6777, along Rt. 56 near Princeville, also has three rides. One is an hour-long valley ride across ranch land in Hanalei Valley. Another is a two-hour shoreline ride near Anini Beach. The most adventurous is a three-hour waterfall picnic ride where you can rest halfway, swim in a waterfall pool, and munch trail snacks before your return.

GOLF

Kauai offers varied and exciting golfing around the island. Kukui O Lono Golf Course, a mountaintop course in Kalaheo, is never crowded and is worth visiting just to see the gardens. Wailua Golf Course is a public course with a reasonable greens fee, considered excellent by visitors and residents. Princeville boasts 46 magnificent holes sculpted around Hanalei Bay. Kauai Lagoons Golf Club has been a favorite for years; recently added Kiele Course was designed by Jack Nicklaus. Kiahuna Golf Course and the new Poipu Bay Resort Golf Course designed by Robert Trent Jones Jr. are fabulous courses in Poipu.

TENNIS

The preceeding chart lists private and public tennis courts. Many hotel tennis courts are open to nonguests, usually for a fee. The Mirage Princeville Tennis Club has a few clay courts for those who prefer that surface.

FITNESS CENTERS

If you are interested in staying fit or getting fit while vacationing, Kauai has the facilities.

Large and well equipped, the **Kauai Athletic Club,** tel. 245-5381, is across from the Kukui Grove Shopping Center outside Lihue. Its sister club is **Hanalei Athletic Club,** tel. 826-7333, in the Princeville Golf Course clubhouse. Affordable and with convenient hours, both offer aerobic classes, free weights, Nautilus machines, swimming pool, jacuzzi, steam room, sauna, and massage by appointment. Nutrition programs can be set up with the staff, who also have information about running courses.

The **Anara Spa and Fitness Center,** at the Hyatt in Poipu, tel. 742-1234, offers total immersion into health and fitness along with therapeutic massage, water treatments, herbal wraps, and general pampering of aching muscles, overworked egos, and jangled nerves.

CAMPING AND HIKING

Kauai is very hospitable to campers and hikers. More than a dozen state and county parks offer camping, and a network of trails leads into the interior. There are different types of camping to suit everyone: you can drive right up to your spot at a convenient beach park, or hike for a day through incredible country to build your campfire in total seclusion. A profusion of "secret beaches" have unofficial camping, and the State Division of Forestry maintains free campsites along its many trails. Koke'e State Park provides affordable self-contained cabins. RV camping is permitted only at Koke'e and Polihale state parks, and at Haena, Hanamaulu, and Niumalu county parks.

Hikers can take the Kalalau Trail, perhaps the premier hiking experience in Hawaii, or go topside to Koke'e and follow numerous paths to breathtaking views over the bared-teeth cliffs of Na Pali. Hunting trails follow many of the streams into the interior; or, if you don't mind mud and rain, you can pluck your way across the Alakai Swamp (boardwalk under construction). Wherever you go, enjoy but don't destroy, and leave the land as beautiful as you find it.

CAMPING

General Information

All the campgrounds, except for the state parks along Na Pali, provide grills, pavilions (some with electricity), picnic tables, cold-water showers, and drinking water. No one can camp "under the stars" at official campgrounds; all must have a tent. Campsites are unattended,

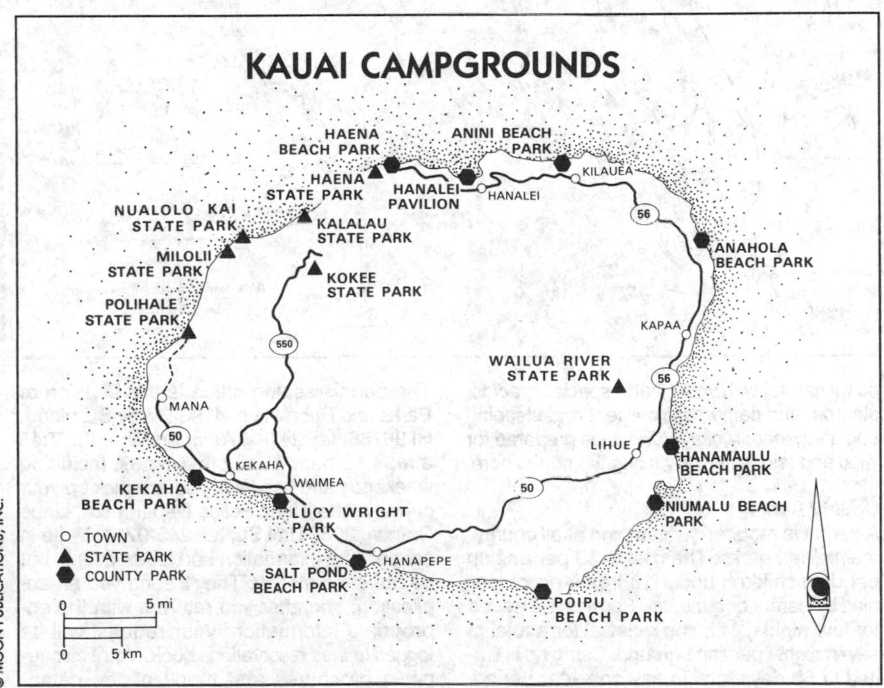

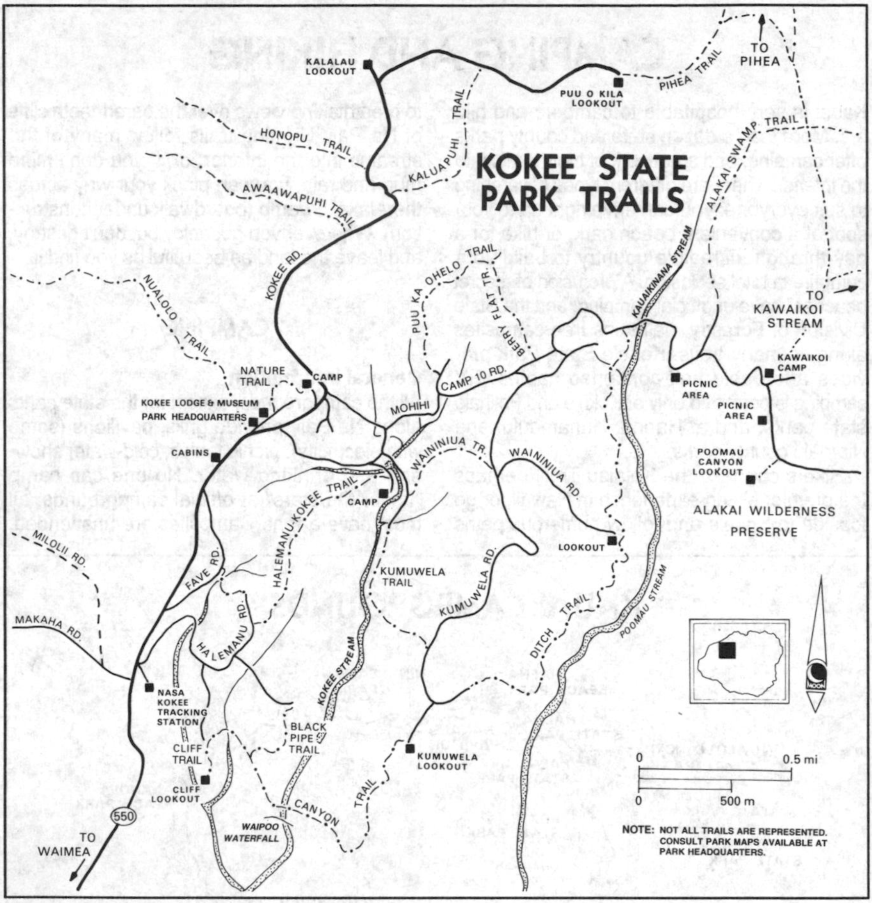

KOKEE STATE PARK TRAILS

NOTE: NOT ALL TRAILS ARE REPRESENTED. CONSULT PARK MAPS AVAILABLE AT PARK HEADQUARTERS.

so be careful with your gear, especially radios, stereos, and cameras. Your tent and sleeping bag are generally okay. Always be prepared for wind and rain, especially along the north shore.

County Parks

A permit is required for camping at all county-maintained parks. The cost is $3 per person per day, children under 18 free if accompanied by parent or guardian. Permits are issued for four nights, with one renewal for a total of seven nights per campground. Camping is limited to 60 days total in any one-year period. The permit-issuing office is the Division of Parks and Recreation, 4193 Hardy St., Lihue, HI 96766, tel. 241-6670, open Mon.-Fri. 7:45 a.m.-4:15 p.m. At all other times, including weekends and holidays, you can pick up your permit at the Kauai Police Department, Lihue Branch, 3060 Umi St., tel. 245-9711. Write in advance for information and reservations, but do not send money. They'll send you an application, and after you return it with the appropriate information, your request will be logged in their reservations book. You'll also receive brochures and maps of the campgrounds. You must pick up and pay for your permit when you arrive at the Parks and Recreation office, or at the police station.

State Parks

A camping permit is required at all state parks. Permits are free, and camping is restricted to five nights within a 30-day period per campground, with a two- and three-night maximum at some of the stopovers along the Kalalau Trail. You can pick up the permits at the Department of Land and Natural Resources, Division of State Parks, 3060 Eiwa St., Room 306, Lihue, HI 96766, tel. 241-3444. Permits can be picked up Mon.-Fri. 8 a.m.-4 p.m. only. *No* permits will be issued without proper identification. You can write well in advance for permits which will be mailed to you, but you must include photocopies of identification for each camper over 18. Children under 18 will not be issued a permit, and they must be accompanied by an adult. Allow at least one month for the entire process, and no reservations are guaranteed without at least a seven-day notice. Include name, dates, number of campers including photocopy ID, and tents.

Camping is allowed at Koke'e State Park. **Koke'e Lodge** also provides self-contained housekeeping cabins. They are furnished with stoves, refrigerators, hot showers, cooking and eating utensils, bedding, and linen; wood is available for the fireplaces. The cabins vary from one large room that accommodates three, to two-bedroom units that sleep seven. The cabins are tough to get on holidays, during trout fishing season (August and September), and during the wild plum harvest in June and July. For reservations write Koke'e Lodge, Box 819, Waimea, Kauai, HI 96796, tel. 335-6061. Please include a S.A.S.E., number of people, and dates requested. One night's deposit is required for confirmation of reservation. Write well in advance. Check-in is from 2 p.m. (call if you will arrive after 5 p.m.), checkout is before noon. The lodge is open Mon.-Thurs. 8:30 a.m.-5:30 p.m., and until 10 p.m. Friday and Saturday. Breakfast and lunch are served daily, while dinner is available Friday and Saturday 6-9 p.m. The lodge has a bar and small shop selling sundries and snacks. The nearest town, Kekaha, is 15 miles down the mountain, on the coast.

Rental Equipment And Sales

A full range of backpacking and camping equipment is rented and sold by **Hanalei Camping and Backpacking,** Ching Young Village, Box 1245, Hanalei, HI 96714, tel. 826-6664. They rent everything from rain gear to tents and sleeping bags daily, overnight, or weekly. They also provide backpack storage and hiking information, and sell books and maps. Unfortunately, they were financially hurt by Hurricane Iniki, and although holding on for the time being, were considering closing. Check!

Other camping supply sales outlets are: **Dan's Sports Shop,** in the Kukui Grove Shopping Center, tel. 246-0151; and **Jungle Bob's** in Hanalei, tel. 826-6664. Also try the very local **Mandala Store,** at 3122 Kuhio Hwy. in Lihue, which carries mosquito nets and hammocks.

HIKING

Over 90% of Kauai is inaccessible by road, making it a backpackers' paradise. Treks range from overnighters requiring superb fitness and preparedness to 10-minute nature loops just outside your car door. Most trails are well marked and maintained, and all reward you with a swimming hole, waterfall, panoramic overlook, or botanical or historical information.

Through its various divisions, the Department of Land and Natural Resources, 3060 Eiwa St., Lihue, Kauai, HI 96766, provides free detailed maps and descriptions of most trails. For state park trails (Kalalau and Koke'e), direct letters to the Department's Division of State Parks; for forest reserve trails, Division of Forestry; for hunting trails, write to the Division of Fish and Game.

Tips And Warnings

Many trails are used by hunters after wild boar, deer, or game birds. Oftentimes these forest reserve trails, maintained by the State Division of Forestry, have a check-in station at the trailhead. Trekkers and hunters must sign a logbook, especially if they intend to use the camping areas along the trails. The comments by previous hikers are worth reading for up-to-the-minute information on trail conditions. Many roads leading to the trailheads are marked for

4WD vehicles only. Heed the warning, especially during rainy weather, when roads are very slick and swollen streams can swallow your rental car. Also remember that going in may be fine, but a sudden storm can leave you stranded.

Maps of the trails are usually only available in Lihue from the various agencies, not at trailheads. Water found along the trails is unsafe to drink unless treated, so carry your own or drink only from catchment barrels. Expect wind and rain at any time along the coast or in the interior. Make sure to check in at stations and leave your itinerary. A few minutes of filling in forms could save your life.

Koke'e State Park Trails

Maps of Koke'e's trails are available at the ranger's booth at park headquarters. The Koke'e Natural History Museum has additional maps and information. Never attempt to climb up or down the park's *pali* (cliffs). You *cannot* go from Koke'e down to the valleys of Na Pali. Every now and again someone attempts it and is killed. The *pali* are impossibly steep and brittle, and your handholds and footholds will break from under you. Don't be foolish.

If you're going into the Alakai Swamp, remember all the birds and flora you encounter are unique, most of them fighting extinction. Also, your clothes will become permanently stained with swamp mud, a wonderful memento of your trip. Before attempting any of the trails, please sign in at park headquarters.

A number of trails start along Koke'e Drive or the dirt roads that lead off from it; most are marked and well maintained. The first you encounter heading up from the coast is **Cliff Trail,** only a few hundred yards long and leading to a spectacular overview of the canyon. Look for feral goats on the canyon ledges. **Canyon Trail** continues off Cliff Trail for one and a half miles. It's a strenuous trail that dips down to Waipoo Waterfall before climbling out of the canyon to Kumuwela Lookout. **Halemanu-Koke'e Trail** begins off a secondary road, from the old ranger station just before the military installation. It travels just over a mile and is a self-guiding nature trail. With plenty of native plants and trees, it's a favorite area for indigenous birds.

One of the best trails off Koke'e Road is the **Kukui Trail.** The well-marked trailhead is between mile markers 8 and 9. The trail starts with the **Iliau Nature Loop,** an easy, 10-minute, self-guided trail that's great for sunset lovers. Notice the pygmy palms among the many varieties of plants and flowers. The sign-in hut for the Kukui Trail is at the end of the Nature Loop. Read some of the comments before heading down. The trail descends 2,000 feet through a series of switchbacks in two and a half miles. It ends on the floor of the canyon at Wiliwili Campsite. From here the hale and hardy can head up the Waimea River for a half mile to the beginning of the **Koaie Canyon Trail.** This three-mile trail takes you along the south side of Koaie Canyon, along which are plenty of pools and campsites. This trail *should not* be attempted during rainy weather because of flash flooding. You can also branch south from the Kukui Trail and link up with the **Waimea Canyon Trail,** which takes you eight miles to the town of Waimea. Because it crosses private land, you must have a special permit available at the trailhead. There is no camping south of Waialeale Stream.

At pole no. 320 near park headquarters, you find the beginning of **Mohihi Camp 10 Road.** This road is recommended for 4WDs, but can be crossed with a regular car *only* in dry weather. It leads to a number of trails, some heading into valleys, others out along ridges, and still others into the Alakai Swamp. **Berry Flat,** a one-mile trail, and **Puu Ka Ohelo,** under a half mile, are easy loops that give you an up-close look at a vibrant upland forest. Under the green canopy are specimens such as sugi pine, California redwoods, eucalyptus from Australia, and native koa. Locals come here in June to harvest the methley plums, for which the area is famous. Off the Camp Road is the entrance to the Forest Reserve at **Sugi Grove,** where camping is limited to three days. **Kawaikoi Stream Trail** begins three-quarters of a mile past Sugi Grove. This three-and-a-half-mile trail is moderately strenuous and known for its scenic beauty. It follows the south side of the stream (trout), crosses over, and loops back on the north side. Avoid it if the stream is high.

The **Alakai Swamp Trail** is otherworldly, crossing one of the most unusual pieces of real estate in the world. It begins off Camp Road at a parking area a quarter mile north of the Na Pali Forest Reserve entrance sign. The trails de-

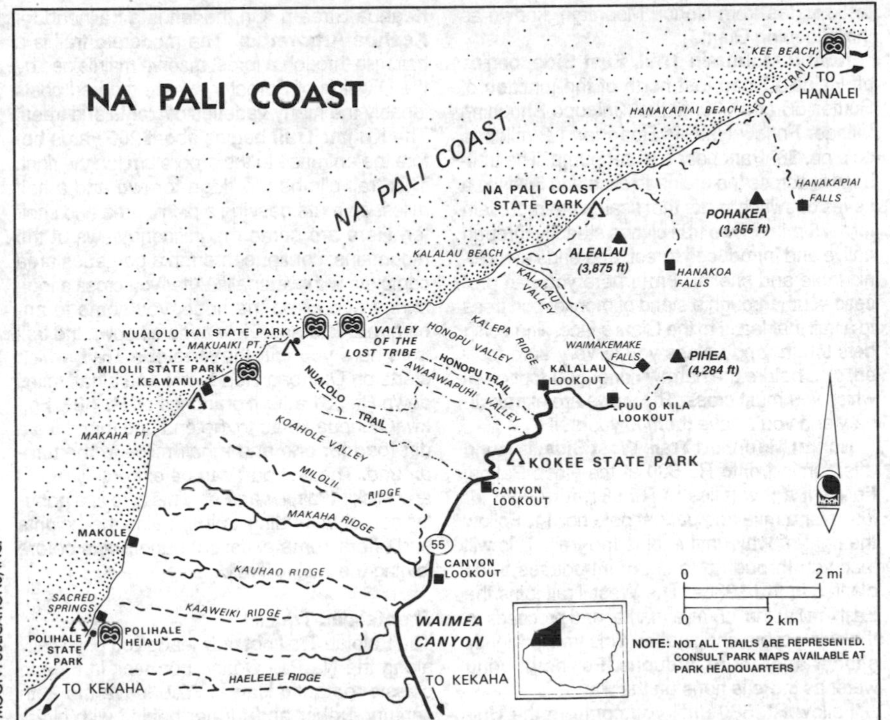

scends into the swamp for three and a half miles and is very strenuous. Because you cross a number of bogs, be prepared to get wet and muddy. Good hiking shoes that won't be sucked off your feet are a must! The trail follows abandoned telephone poles from WW II, and then a series of brown and white (keep an eye out) trail markers. Along the way, if you smell anise, that's the *mokihana* berry, fashioned with *maile* for wedding lei. The trail ends at Kilohana, where there's an expansive vista of Wainiha and Hanalei Valley.

One of the most rewarding trails for the time and effort is **Awaawapuhi Trail.** The trailhead is after park headquarters, just past pole no. 152 at the crest of the hill. It's three miles long and takes you out onto a thin finger of *pali,* with the sea and an emerald valley 2,500 feet below. The sun dapples the upland forest that still bears the scars of Hurricane Iwa. Everywhere flowers and fiddlehead ferns delight the eyes, while wild thimbleberries and passion fruit delight the taste buds. The trail is well marked and slightly strenuous. At the three-mile marker the **Nualolo Trail,** which starts near park headquarters, connects with Awaawapuhi. It's the easiest trail to the *pali* with an overview of Nualolo Valley.

Pihea Trail begins at the end of the paved road near the Puu O Kila Overlook. It's a good general-interest trail because it gives you a great view of Kalalau Valley, then descends into the Alakai Swamp where it connects with the Alakai Swamp Trail. It also connects with the Kawaikoi Stream Trail, and from each you can return via Camp 10 Road for an amazing loop of the area.

East Kauai Trails

All these trails are in the mountains behind Wailua. Most start off Rt. 580, which parallels the Wailua River. Here are an arboretum and fantastic vistas from Nonou Mountain, known as the "Sleeping Giant."

Nonou Mountain Trail, East Side, begins off Haleilio Road just north of the junction of Routes 56 and 580, at the Kinipopo Shopping Village. Follow Haleilio Road for 1.2 miles to pole no. 38. Park near a water pump. The trailhead is across the drainage ditch and leads to a series of switchbacks that scales the mountain for 1.75 miles. The trail climbs steadily through native and introduced forest, and ends at a picnic table and shelter. From here you can proceed south through a stand of monkeypod trees to a trail that leads to the Giant's face. The going gets tough, and unless you're very sure-footed, stop before the narrow ridge (500-foot drop) which you must cross. The views are extraordinary and you'll have them to yourself.

Nonou Mountain Trail, West Side, is found after turning onto Rt. 580 at the Coco Palms. Follow it a few miles to Rt. 581, turn right for just over a mile and park at pole no. 11. Follow the right of way until it joins the trail. This will lead you through a forest of introduced trees planted in the 1930s. The West Trail joins the East Trail at the 1.5-mile marker and proceeds to the picnic table and shelter. This trail is slightly shorter and not as arduous. For both, bring water as there is none on the way.

Follow Rt. 580 until you come to the University of Hawaii Experimental Station. Keep going until the pavement ends and then follow the dirt road for almost a mile. A developed picnic and freshwater swimming area is at Keahua Stream. On the left is a trailhead for **Keahua Arboretum.** The moderate trail is a half mile through a forest reserve maintained by the Division of Forestry, where marked posts identify the many varieties of plants and trees. The **Kuilau Trail** begins about 200 yards before the entrance to the arboretum, on the right. This trail climbs the ridge for two and a half miles, en route passing a picnic area and shelter. Here are some magnificent views of the mountains; continue through a gorgeous area complete with waterfalls. After you cross a footbridge and climb the ridge, you come to another picnic area. A few minutes down the trail from here you join the **Moalepe Trail,** which starts off Olohena Road, one and a half miles down Rt. 581 after it branches off Rt. 580. Follow Olohena Road to the end and then take a dirt road for one and a half miles to the turnaround. The last part can be extremely rutted and slick in rainy weather. This hike is a popular horseback-riding trail. It gains the heights and offers some excellent panoramas before joining the Kuilau Trail.

The Kalalau Trail

The Kalalau Trail not only leads you physically along the Na Pali Coast, but back in time to classic romantic Hawaii. You leave the 20th century further and further behind with every step and reenter a time and place where you can come face to face with your *nature self.* This hike is *the* premier hike on Kauai and perhaps in the entire state.

GETTING THERE

Kauai's Lihue Airport is connected to all the Hawaiian Islands by direct flight, but no nonstop flights from the Mainland are currently operating. Mainland and international passengers arrive via Honolulu, from which the three major interisland carriers offer numerous daily flights.

Average flying times to Kauai are 35 minutes from Honolulu, one to two hours from the Big Island depending upon stops, and just over one hour from Maui, including the stop in Honolulu. Outgoing and incoming flights are dispersed equally throughout the day.

Kauai's Airports

Lihue Airport, less than two miles from downtown Lihue, receives the vast majority of Kauai's flights. No public transportation to or from the airport is available, so you must rent a car or hire a taxi. The new terminal, long and low, has a restaurant and cocktail lounge, snack shop, flower shop, gift shop, restrooms, and a handful of suitcase-size coin lockers ($1) in the lobby. The gift shop sells pre-inspected island fruit that's boxed and ready to transport; tel. 245-6273. All major car rental agencies and a good number of local firms maintain booths outside the main entranceway; other agencies send vans to the airport to pick up customers. Baggage pick-up is at either end of the building, Aloha and United to the left, and Hawaiian Air to the right, as you enter the terminal from the plane—follow the signs. Check-in counters are along the outside corridor; Hawaiian Air is on the left, and Aloha and United are on the right, as you look at the terminal building. All non-carry-on baggage must go through an agricultural inspection at the terminal entrance; carry-on luggage is run through X-ray machines.

Princeville Airport is basically a strip servicing Princeville. Located along Rt. 56 east of town, it is used only by Aloha Island Air and Papillon Helicopters. The terminal is a cute little building made inconspicuous by the immense beauty surrounding it. Found here are a toilet, telephone, Amelia's Cafe and lounge, and Hertz and Avis car rental offices. Located on the second floor, with windows looking out onto the runway and open to the lobby below, Amelia's serves drinks, sandwiches, hot dogs, nachos, and chili—most for under $7. The rental car booths stay open until the last incoming flight has arrived.

Airline Carriers

Hawaiian Airlines, tel. (800) 367-5320 Mainland, (800) 882-8811 Hawaii, offers the largest number of daily flights. From Honolulu, Oahu, 26 nonstop flights operate 5:45 a.m.-8 p.m.; from Kahului, Maui, 15 flights run 6:55 a.m.-7:10 p.m., two nonstop; from Kona, Hawaii, six flights 6:45 a.m.-3:20 p.m. stop in Maui or Honolulu; from Hilo, Hawaii, eight flights 6:45 a.m.-6:40 p.m. stop in Maui or Honolulu; from Lanai, two afternoon flights run via Honolulu; and from Molokai, two flights operate at 7:05 a.m. and 11 a.m., via Honolulu.

Aloha Airlines, tel. 245-3691, (800) 367-5250 Mainland, has an all-jet fleet of 737s that connects Kauai to Honolulu on Oahu, Maui, and both Kona and Hilo on Hawaii. Aloha's routes to Lihue are: from Honolulu, 16 flights 5:40 a.m.-8 p.m.; from Maui, 16 flights via Honolulu 6:35 a.m.-7 p.m.; from Kona, 11 flights via Honolulu and/or Maui 6:50 a.m.-5:50 p.m.; and from Hilo, 11 flights 6:50 a.m.-6:40 p.m.; from Lanai, two flights at 11:50 a.m. and 4:25 p.m.

Commuter Airlines

Aloha Island Air, tel. (800) 323-3345 Mainland, (800) 652-6541 Hawaii, is a commuter airline operating flights to and from Princeville Airport on Kauai's north shore. Flying comfortable 18-passenger Twin Otter De Havilland aircraft, they connect the resort community of Princeville with airports on all the islands. There are five daily nonstop flights from Honolulu 6:55 a.m.-4:50 p.m.; four flights from Molokai 8:15 a.m.-3:10 p.m., via Honolulu; four flights from Kapalua, West Maui 8 a.m.-2:50 p.m.; three flights from Kahului, Maui 7:35 a.m.-1:50 p.m.; three flights from Lanai 7:05 a.m.-1 p.m.; and one flight from Kamuela (Waimea) at 7:25 a.m., via Honolulu.

Pacific Aviation, tel. 335-5009 or (800) 245-9696, operates a nine-passenger Commander 840, from Burns Field at Port Allen Airport to Honolulu three times per day. They also provide charter flights at your convenience.

Charter Airlines

If you've got the bucks or just need to go when there's no regularly scheduled flight, try either **Paragon Air,** tel. 244-3356, or **Trans Air,** tel. 833-5557, (800) 634-2094 Hawaii, for island-wide service.

GETTING AROUND

The most common way to get around Kauai is by rental car. Plenty of agencies keep prices competitive. As always, reserve during peak season, and take your chances by shopping around to score a good deal in the off-season. Kauai also has limited shuttle bus service, expensive taxis, bicycle, mopeds and scooter rentals, and the good old thumb.

Car Rental Companies

The following are major firms that either maintain a booth or courtesy pick-up vans at Lihue Airport. **Dollar,** tel. 245-3651, (800) 342-7398 Hawaii, (800) 800-4000 worldwide, has an excellent reputation and very competitive prices. Dollar rents all kinds of cars as well as jeeps and convertibles. Great weekly rates, and all major credit cards accepted.

Alamo has good weekly rates, tel. 245-8953 or (800) 327-9633.

National Car Rental, tel. 245-3502, (800) 227-7368 Mainland, features GM and Nissan cars and accepts all major credit cards. They sometimes rent without a credit card if you leave a $100 per day deposit, less if you take full insurance coverage.

Avis, tel. 245-3512, 826-9773 in Princeville, or (800) 831-8000 Mainland, features late-model GM cars as well as most imports and convertibles.

Budget, tel. 245-1901 or (800) 527-0700, offers competitive rates on a variety of late-model cars.

Hertz, tel. 245-3356 or (800) 654-3131, is competitively priced with many fly/ drive deals. They also maintain desks at the Princeville Airport.

A local company with a reliable reputation is **Westside-U-Drive,** tel. 332-8644.

Scooters And Mopeds

These tiny two-wheelers are available from **South Shore Activities,** tel. 742-6873, at Poipu Beach; **Budget** at Kiahuna Plantation in Poipu; and **Pedal and Paddle** in Hanalei, tel. 826-9069.

BUSES AND TAXIS

One of the benefits to come out of the destruction caused by Hurricane Iniki is the establishment of limited public transportation. The **Iniki Express,** free for the time being, is a federally funded shuttle bus that runs the entire length of the island from Princeville to Waimea. Wait at any of the designated bus stops, or just hail them down.

Taxis are metered and charge hefty prices for their services; all have the same rates. Airport taxis have a monopoly on pick-ups at the airport, although others can drop off there. Sample fares are $5.50 from Lihue and $35 from Poipu to the airport, $30 from Lihue to Poipu, $60 from Lihue to Princeville, and $25 from Princeville to Ke'e Beach and the Kalalau trailhead. Reputable companies include: **Akiko's,** tel. 822-3613, in Wailua; **A-1,** tel. 742-1390, in Poipu; **North Shore Taxi,** tel. 826-6189, in Hanalei; **Kauai Cab, tel. 246-9554, in Lihue.**

ALTERNATIVES

Bicycles

Except for the road up to Koke'e State Park, riding a bike around Kauai is fairly easy, thanks to the lack of big hills. Traffic is moderate, especially in the cool of early morning, the best time to make some distance. Roads are generally good, but shoulders aren't wide and are sometimes nonexistent. Peak season brings a dramatic increase in traffic and road congestion. Take care! Perhaps the best riding is by mountain bike on the cane haul roads that head into the interior.

Shipping your own bicycle interisland costs about $20, and from the Mainland another $25 if it goes on a different airline. You must provide your own box and pack the bike yourself.

Outfitters Kauai, an ecology-minded sports shop offering kayaking and mountain biking, is owned and operated by Rick and Julie Havilend. Located in the Poipu Plaza, at 2827-A Poipu Road, P.O. Box 1149, Poipu Beach, HI 96756, tel. 742-9667, they're open Mon.-Sat. 9 a.m.-5 p.m., Sunday by arrangement. Their Poipu "interpretive bike course," self-guided with map and narrative information, also featuring tidepooling and snorkeling, is $26 per person with bike and snorkel gear included. Mountain bike rentals, 9 a.m.-5 p.m., helmet and water bottles included, are $20 (multi-day discounts). Outfitters Kauai offers mountain bike ecotours to Koke'e Thursday 9 a.m.-1:30 p.m., or by special arrangement. The 16-mile relaxed-pace ride with a few vigorous climbs focuses on the natural history of the area and includes cold drinks and snacks at $58 per person. Rick and Julie are excellent athletes who know the mountains and seas of Kauai intimately. Their tours are educational as well as highly adventuresome.

An excellent choice is **Bicycle John's,** a full-service bicycle shop offering sales, repairs, and rentals. It has two convenient locations, including the main store along Rt. 56 as you enter Lihue, tel. 245-7579, and the other in Kapa'a also along Rt. 56 at 4504 Kakue St., tel. 822-3495. The shops are open Mon.-Fri. 9 a.m.-5 p.m., Saturday 10 a.m.-4 p.m. Rental bicycles range from an 18-speed basic cruiser to a custom road bike. Prices range from $25 per day to $65 for four days, with a price break for multi-day rentals.

Bicycle Kauai, at 1379 Kuhio Hwy., Kapa'a, tel. 822-3315, open Mon.-Fri. 9 a.m.-6 p.m., Saturday 9 a.m.-4 p.m., Sunday 10 a.m.-3 p.m., is a complete bicycle shop with sales, repairs, helmets, riding clothes, and rentals. Trek mountain bikes are $20 per day or $100 per week (seven-day week), which includes helmet, lock, and car rack. The staff is friendly and knowledgeable and will offer plenty of advice on bike routes, and on where and when to ride.

Other rental shops include: **Aquatics Kauai,** tel. 822-9213, in Kapa'a; **Shore Activities,** tel. 742-6873, at Poipu Beach; and **Pedal and Paddle,** tel. 826-9069, in Hanalei. Or try **Dan's Sport Shop,** tel. 246-0151, a full-service sporting goods store located at the Kukui Grove Shopping Center.

Hitchhiking

Using your thumb to get around is legal on Kauai, but you must stay off the paved portion of the road. For short hops in and around the towns, like from Koloa to Poipu or from the airport to Lihue, thumbing isn't difficult. But getting out to the Kalalau Trail or to Polihale on the west end when you're toting a backpack and appear to be going a longer distance is tough. As on all the islands, your best chance of being picked up is by a visiting or local *haole.* Sometimes locals in pickup trucks will stop to give you a ride for short distances. Women *should not* hitch alone!

SIGHTSEEING TOURS

Magnificent Kauai is fascinating to explore by land, sea, or air. Looking around on your own is no problem, but some of the most outstanding areas are more expediently seen with a professional guide. Some options are discussed below.

Van And Bus Tours

On Kauai, most tour companies run vans, but some larger companies also use buses. Though cheaper, tours on a full-sized coach are generally less personalized. Wherever a bus can go, so can your rental car, but on a tour you can relax and enjoy the scenery without worrying about driving. Also, the drivers are very experienced with the area and know many stories and legends with which they annotate and enrich your trip. Coach tours vary, but typical trips go to Hanalei and the north coast, or to Waimea Canyon and the south coast sights, or combine one of these tours with the Wailua River. Each agency has its own route and schedule, but all hit the major tourist sites.

Rates sometimes include entrance fees and lunch. Half-day fares run about $35-45, while full-day fares run $55-65; children's fares are about one-quarter less. Fares also vary according to area of pick-up and route. Tours are usually run with a minimum number of people, but it is possible to join another group to fill a van. Often a tour to the Fern Grotto is considered the "highlight" . . . that should say it all! Companies offering these tours include **Trans Hawaiian,** tel. 245-5108; and **Robert's Hawaii,** tel. 245-9558.

One unique tour company is **Kauai Mountain Tours, Inc.** tel. 245-7224 or (800) 222-7756, or write P.O. Box 3069, Lihue, HI 96766. It alone is licensed to operate tours in the Na Pali

Kona Forest Reserve. Knowledgeable guides take you into the back country over dirt roads by 4WD GMC Suburbans, with an informed narrative on the way. They let you see a part of Kauai not reached by anyone who doesn't walk in. Traveling is rough but the sights are unsurpassed; truly, this is one of the few ways in Kauai to get off the beaten path. Their guides, like Anthony, a native Hawaiian, are excellent. Anthony has a tremendous amount of knowledge about the island's flora and fauna, and he has been known to bring in specimens of very rare plants and flowers so that local artists can sketch them for posterity. However, he won't tell where he found them! This seven-hour adventure costs $72 plus tax ($51.90 for children under 11), and includes a picnic lunch prepared by the Green Garden Restaurant. Tours start about 8 a.m. There is free pick-up in the Wailua and Poipu areas, but an extra $15 is charged for pick-up in Princeville. A shorter, four-and-a-half- to five-hour trip is also available, costing $55 plus tax with no lunch, but it is not as highly recommended, since much less time is spent in the actual backcountry.

Helicopter Tours

Flying in a chopper is a thrilling experience, like flying in a light plane . . . with a twist. They take you into those otherwise inaccessible little nooks and crannies. Routes cover the entire island, but the highlights are flying through Waimea Canyon, into the Mt. Waialeale crater, where it almost never stops raining, and over the Alakai Swamp, where you see thousands of waterfalls and even 360-degree rainbows floating in mid-air. Then, to top it off, you fly to the Na Pali Coast, swooping along its ruffled edge and dipping down for an up-close look at its caves and giant seacliffs. Earphones cut the noise of the aircraft and play soul-stirring music as a background to the pilot's narration. The basic one-hour around-the-island flight runs about $130 per person; other flights are 45-75 minutes in length. Some companies let you tailor your own flight, which might include a swim at a remote pool along with a champagne lunch, but these are more costly. Niihau Helicopters also flies periodically to points on Niihau. Its flights are more expensive, but are the only way to see this island up close. Discounts of up to 15% from some of the companies are featured in the ubiquitous free tourist brochures, and are occasionally offered through tourist activity and information centers.

Outdoor purists disparage this mode of transport, saying, "If you can't hike in you shouldn't be there," but that's tunnel vision and not always appropriate. To go deep into the mist-shrouded interior, especially through the Alakai Swamp, the average traveler "can't get there from here" . . . it's just too rugged and dangerous. The only reasonable way to see it is by helicopter, and except for the noise, choppers actually have less of an impact on the ecosystem than hikers. A compromise, limiting numbers and times of flights, seems the best answer.

Everyone has an opinion on which company offers the best ride, the best narration, or the best service. All the helicopter companies on Kauai are safe and reputable, and most fly Bell Jet Ranger equipment or Hughes 550-D models. Some helicopters accommodate only four passengers while others take five; some have two-way microphones so you can ask questions of the pilot. Make sure that everyone has a window seat or at least an unobstructed view out the front bubble window.

Of the nearly two dozen helicopter companies on Kauai, the majority operate from Lihue Airport, a handful from Burns Field in Hanapepe, and one from Princeville Airport. The following have top-notch reputations. **Ohana Helicopter Tours,** 3220 Kuhio Hwy., Suite #A, Lihue, HI 96766, tel. 245-3996 or (800) 222-6989, is an owner-operated company that gives personalized service. Ohana offers complimentary shuttle service (Kapa'a and Poipu areas) to their office, where flight procedures will be explained. They want you to have the time of your life—not hard with this experience. The pilot, Bogart Kealoha, has years of commercial and military experience, and *knows* this island of his birth. From smooth liftoff to gentle landing, you are in good hands.

The granddaddy of them all is **Jack Harter Helicopters,** Box 306, Lihue, HI 96766, tel. 245-3774. Jack, along with his wife Beverly, literally started the helicopter business on Kauai, and has been flying the island for over 20 years. Jack doesn't advertise but he is always booked up. He knows countless stories about Kauai and just about everywhere to go on the island.

J.D. BISIGNANI

tourist boat on the Wailua River cruising to the Fern Grotto

He gives you a full hour and a half in the air, and his logo, "Imitated by all, equalled by none," says it all.

The slickest new company is **Papillon Helicopters,** Box 339, Hanalei, HI 96714, tel. 826-6591 or (800) 367-7095. They fly from their own heliport at Princeville, just past mile marker 26, with some flights leaving from Lihue Airport, and offer the largest variety of tours. Besides taking you around the island, one tour features a drop-off with gourmet picnic lunch at a secluded hideaway. At their facilities in Princeville, you are treated to a pre-flight video orientation, while hostesses offer munchies, juice, and wine.

Other companies with good reputations and competitive prices flying out of Lihue Airport are: **Island Helicopters,** Box 3101, Lihue, HI 96766, tel. 245-8588, owned and piloted by Curt Lofstedt, who also hires Rudy Dela Cruz, a local instructor with the Air National Guard; **South Seas Helicopters,** P.O. Box 1445, Lihue, HI 96766, tel. 245-7781 or (800) 367-2914; **Kenai Helicopters,** tel. 245-8591 or (800) 622-3144, which also operates on the Big Island; **Will Squyre Helicopters,** tel. 245-8881, a one-man operation with personalized service from a man who loves his work; and **Safari Aviation Inc.,** tel. 246-0136 or (800) 326-3356, flying deluxe Astar 350s featuring a/c and a three-camera video recording system.

The following reputable companies fly from Burns Field in Hanapepe. **Inter-Island Helicopters,** P.O. Box 156, Hanapepe, HI 96716, tel. 335-5009 or (800) 245-9696, offers tailor-made group flights and aerial photography options in addition to its tourist flights. Inter-Island Helicopters is also contracted by the state and county to do search-and-rescue work. Their pilots are considered among the most skillful on the island. Also try **Bruce Needham Helicopters,** tel. 335-3115; and **Bali Hai,** tel. 332-7331.

Niihau Helicopters, P.O. Box 370, Makaweli, HI 96769, tel. 335-3500, also flies out of Burns Field. The primary purpose of Niihau Helicopters is to provide medical and emergency treatment for the residents of Niihau. However, to defray costs, occasional, nonscheduled tourist charters are offered on its twin-engine Agusta 109A. Two of their flights last 90 and 110 minutes, each with 30-minute stops on secluded beaches on Niihau; fares are $185 and $235, respectively. Two other options are an overflight of Niihau for $135, and a tour of the Na Pali Coast with a Niihau overflight for $235. While it cannot compete with helicopter companies that regularly fly only over Kauai, its does offer you the only way to see Niihau up close. Let pilot Tom Mishler show you a bit of this Forbidden Island.

Wailua River Cruises

You too can be one of the many cruising up the Wailua River on a large canopied, motorized barge. The Fern Grotto, where the boat docks, is a natural amphitheater festooned with hanging ferns, and one of the most touristed spots in Hawaii. The oldest company is **Smith's Motor Boat Service,** tel. 822-4111, in operation since 1947. The extended Smith family still operates the business and members serve in every capacity. During the 20-minute ride upriver you're entertained with music and recounting of legends, and at the Fern Grotto a small but well-done medley of island songs is performed. Daily cruises depart every half hour from Wailua Marina 9 a.m.-4 p.m. Adults $12, children $6. Evening cruises are arranged for large groups by special request.

Waialeale Boat Tours, tel. 822-4908, is Smith's only competition. Also at the marina, they're a smaller operation with competitive rates.

Zodiacs

The opposite experience of the tame Wailua River trip is an adventurous ride down the Na Pali Coast in a very tough motorized rubber raft that looks like a big, horseshoe-shaped inner-tube and undulates with the waves like a floating waterbed. These seaworthy craft, powered by twin engines, have five separate air chambers for unsinkable safety. They'll take you for a thrilling ride down the Na Pali Coast, pausing along the way to whisk you into caves and caverns. Once at Kalalau Valley, you can swim and snorkel before the return ride; the roundtrip, including the stop, takes about five hours. If you wish, you can stay overnight and be picked up the next day, or hike in or out and ride only one way; this service is $60 one-way, $105 roundtrip. You roll with the wind and sea going down the coast and head into it coming back. The wind generally picks up in the afternoon, so for a more comfortable ride, book the morning cruise.

Other Zodiac trips include a hike to an archaeological site at Nualolo Kai Beach, a whale-watching tour, and a trip to Kipu Kai or up little-visited rivers on the south coast. All are popular so make reservations. Rates vary with the season and particular expedition, but the ultimate once-in-a-lifetime ride is around $105. Shorter trips vary from $60-65. Bring bathing suit, snorkel gear (rental available), lunch, drinks (cooler provided), camera (in a plastic bag for protection), sneakers for exploring, and windbreaker for the return ride. Summer weather permits excursions almost every day, but winter's swells are turbulent and these experienced seamen won't go if it's too rough. Take their word for it! Pregnant women and those with bad backs are not advised to take the ride.

Oldest and best known of the Zodiac companies is **Na Pali Zodiac,** Box 456, Hanalei, HI 96714, tel. 826-9371 or (800) 422-7824, owned and operated by "Captain Zodiac," Clancy Greff, and his wife Pam. They now operate on Maui and Hawaii, too.

Another extremely reputable company is **Hanalei Sea Tours,** P.O. Box 1447 Hanalei, HI 96714, tel. 826-7254 or (800) 733-7997. Their trips include: a Nualolo Day Trip, a five- to six-hour trip down the Na Pali Coast for $100, and a half-day, four-hour trip down the Na Pali Coast for $75, lunch and snorkeling gear included; a mini-tour, two and a half hours, which includes whalewatching in season, for $55, beverages provided; and a Kalalau Valley camper drop-off service May-Sept. for $60 one-way, $130 roundtrip. Hanalei Sea Tours also offers a catamaran adventure (see "Cabin Cruisers and Sailing Ships," following).

Kayaks

Outfitters Kauai, an ecology-minded sports shop offering kayaking, and mountain biking, is owned and operated by Rick and Julie Havilend. Located in the Poipu Plaza, at 2827-A Poipu Road, P.O. Box 1149, Poipu Beach, Kauai, 96756, tel. 742-9667, is open they're open Mon.-Sat. 9 a.m.-5 p.m., Sunday by arrangement. Outfitters Kauai's most thrilling adventure is the "South Shore Sea Kayaking Tour" offered Tuesday or Friday, or by arrangement. Check-in is at 1:15 p.m, return is by 5 p.m. Single- or double-person kayaks are available, and the adventure includes snacks and cold drinks at $48 per person. Also offered is the Na Pali Kayak Adventure or River Kayak Adventure which takes you up Kauai's navigable rivers for $45 for a double kayak or $30 for a single. Rick and Julie are excellent athletes and environmentalists who know the mountains and seas of Kauai intimately. Their tours are educational as well as highly adventuresome, and you couldn't find a better outfit to travel with.

Kayak Kauai, P.O. Box 508, Hanalei, HI 96714, tel. 826-9844, has extensive experience, since its owners are world-class kayak experts and the staff are sensitive people who provide good service while having a good time. Two-person Metzeler inflatable kayaks ($48 or $58) and one- and three-person hard-shell kayaks ($35-75) are available. May-Oct. they lead ocean tours up the Na Pali Coast for $95. They also rent and sell surf-skis, boogie boards, masks, fins, *tabi,* tents, and other beach and camping gear. They will rig your car to carry an inflatable kayak, and will provide drop-off and pick-up service at Ke'e Beach for $7, or at Polihale State Park for $35, when it's safe to be on the ocean. During the summer, guided tours are taken along the Na Pali Coast, and when conditions are too harsh there, trips are run to Kipu Kai along the south coast or up the Huleia Stream in Nawiliwili. All of the above are good family-style fun.

Kauai Water Ski and Surf tel. 822-3574, open daily 9 a.m.-7 p.m., in the Kinipopo Shopping Village, 4-356 Kuhio Hwy., Wailua, HI 96746, is a complete water sports shop that offers kayak rentals (for complete details see "Shopping" in the Wailua chapter).

Ray's Rentals and Activities, 1345 Kuhio Hwy., downtown Kapa'a, tel. 822-5700, rents kayaks at reasonable prices. **Kayak Kauai** (see above) has a rental outlet across the road from Ray's, open daily 9 a.m.-4 p.m., tel. 822-9179.

Cabin Cruisers And Sailing Ships

For those who want adventure but a smooth ride, try a cabin cruiser, Boston whaler, or catamaran. Boston whalers are stable V-hulled ships, the fastest on the coast, and catamarans ride on two widely spaced hulls. Both provide smooth sailing down the coast and get you back in great comfort. Like the Zodiacs (see above), each ventures into the sea caves (sea conditions permitting), stops for you to snorkel, and provides complimentary snacks after your swim. Tours vary, but typically are: half day for about $65; five hours, with a hike to an ancient fishing village site at Nualolo Kai, for $90; whale-watching trips on the north and south coasts for $45-65; and during the summer, sunset tours for $80. When calling be sure to ask about the particulars of each trip and what "extras" each company provides.

Liko Kauai Cruises, P.O. Box 18, Waimea, HI 96796, tel. 338-0333, is a new cruise company owned and operated by native Hawaiian Captain Liko Hookano. Unlike all the other cruises, Liko Kauai takes you down the Na Pali Coast from the *west end* departing from Kikiaola Harbor just two miles from Waimea, offering vistas and sights unseen by any of the other companies. Born and raised on Kauai, Captain Liko worked for 10 years as a supervising lifeguard on the west end, and no one knows these waters better than he. After boarding the 38-foot cabin cruiser and setting sail down the coast, Captain Liko begins telling Hawaiian tales, especially about Niihau, the island of his ancestors. En route you pass Barking Sands Pacific Missile Range, Polihale, secluded Milolii Beach, and little-visited Marconi or Treasure Beach where the snorkeling is superb. The tour offers a lunch of sandwiches, chips, sides, and soft drinks (BYO beer okay). On the way back, since the boat is completely outfitted for fishing charters, some lucky person gets to reel in whatever bites. The boat, built not only for speed but for comfort, has a large comfortable bathroom, and fresh-water showers for rinsing off. The four- to five-hour tour meets at 8:30 a.m., at **Captain's Cargo Company,** 9984 Kaumualii Hwy. (Rt. 50), clearly marked just as you enter Waimea from the east end. Rates are $85 adults, $65 children 4-14, under age 4 free.

Paradise Adventure Cruises, Inc., P.O. Box 1379, Hanalei, HI 96714, tel. 826-9999, owned by Byron Fears, runs the most personalized charter boat trips on the island, taking a maximum of six passengers on his Boston whalers. All his captains know the coast well, and one may even take out his guitar and serenade you while you're scarfing down the provided crackers, cheese, and soft drinks. Byron is the only operator to provide free use of simple underwater cameras—bring ASA 400 film.

The following two companies run catamarans. **Hanalei Sea Tours,** tel. 826-7254, (800) 733-7997, P.O. Box 1447 Hanalei, HI 96714, offers Zodiac (see previously) and catamaran trips along the spectacular Na Pali Coast. This reputable company features comfortable boats with limited passengers, and knowledgeable skippers and friendly crews. Definitely one of the best. Or contact **Na Pali Adventures,** P.O. Box 1017, Hanalei, HI 96714, tel. 826-6804.

Blue Odyssey Kauai, tel. 826-9033, runs a 50-foot cabin cruiser on both the north and south coasts, half-day trips for $65, $70 when combined with a one-way Zodiac ride on the north coast. Their dinner cruise is $49.95. From Port Allen, the **Na Pali Cruise Line** operates the island's finest cruise ship. This 130-foot liner takes you from Port Allen around the west end of the island and up the Na Pali Coast in comfort and elegance for $85, or $110 if you combine it with a Zodiac ride partway along the coast. A sunset dinner cruise is also available—very romantic.

Running under sail is also possible around Kauai. Captain Andy of **Captain Andy's Sailing Adventures,** tel. 822-7833, lets the wind power his 40-foot trimaran along the south coast in winter and the north coast in summer. A real jolly fellow, he will take you for a half day of sailing, snorkeling, and beachcombing for $65, or a two-hour sunset cruise for $35. **Bluewater Sailing Kauai,** tel. 822-0525, runs a 33-foot sloop and a 42-foot ketch-rigged yacht, also on the south coast in winter and the north coast in summer. Half-day rates are $60, all day $100, and a sunset sail is $35. Hourly, daily, or weekly charters can be arranged.

INFORMATION AND SERVICES

Emergency: 911
For the police, fire, and ambulance anywhere on Kauai, dial 911.

To reach the **Coast Guard Search and Rescue on Kauai** call 245-4521, (800) 552-6458.

Civil defense: In case of natural disaster such as hurricanes or tsunamis on Kauai call 245-4001.

Crisis Intervention Helpline, tel. 245-3411; Rape Crisis Hotline, tel. 245-4144; and Kauai Hotline, tel. 822-4114.

Ask-2000, Information and Referral Service, tel. 275-2000.

Aloha Pages, tel. 246-4441, is a free 24-hour "talking telephone" information service on a variety of topics including entertainment, sports, health, weather, and community services. For specific information, dial the above number or check your local Hawaiian phone book for a complete listing of available topics.

The area code for all Kauai telephone numbers is 808.

MEDICAL SERVICES

Hospitals
Wilcox Memorial is at 3420 Kuhio Hwy., Lihue, tel. 245-1100; **Kauai Veterans** is in Waimea, tel. 338-9431; and **Samuel Mahelona Hospital** is in Kapa'a, tel. 822-4961.

Medical Clinics And Physicians
Kauai Medical Group is at 3420 B Kuhio Hwy., tel. 245-1500, after hours call 245-1831. Office hours are "urgent care clinic" Mon.-Sat. 9 a.m.-6 p.m., Sunday 10 a.m.-4 p.m.; "regular clinic," weekdays 8 a.m. to 5 p.m. and weekends 8 a.m. to noon. Offices also at Kapa'a, Koloa, Kukui Grove Shopping Center, Kilauea, and Princeville.

Garden Island Medical Group is in Waimea, tel. 338-1645, after hours call 338-9431. Office hours are weekdays 8 a.m.-5 p.m. and weekends 8 a.m.-noon. They also have offices at Eleele and Koloa. Hawaiian Planned Parenthood can be reached at 245-5678.

Contact **Natural Health and Pain Relief Clinic** at 245-2277.

A fine **pediatrician** with four young children of his own is Dr. Terry Carolan, at 4491 Rice St., Lihue, tel. 245- 8566.

Pharmacies
Southshore Pharmacy in Koloa, tel. 742-7511, gives senior discounts. **Westside Pharmacy** is in Hanapepe, tel. 335-5342; **Shoreview Pharmacy** is in Kapa'a, tel. 822-1447; **Longs Drugs** is in the Kukui Grove Shopping Center, tel. 245-7771; and **Pay 'n Save** is in Lihue, tel. 245-8896. Hospitals and medical groups have their own pharmacies.

Alternative Health Care And Massage
Aunty Daisy, Tongan born, but raised on Fiji, affirms that she is alive today because of the *aloha* hands of her grandmother, Tama Tuiileila. At the age of 10, Aunty Daisy contracted German measles, which left her young body painfully crippled. Although her English-born father took her to the best doctors available, nothing could

be done. For five years her young body degenerated until she was a total invalid in chronic pain. Finally, an interisland steamer brought Grandmother Tama on a long-awaited visit. When she laid eyes for the first time upon her granddaughter, she knew what must be done. With total focus she began her ancient incantations while laying hands upon the child. For two torturous days and nights she continuously massaged, all the while infusing the twisted little body with the *aloha* that flowed through her hands. From that day forward, Daisy began to blossom. Within a few years, the lovely young woman was married with children of her own. For the next 20 years Daisy lived her life as wife and mother in Australia where she had moved with her husband. But, when Grandmother Tama passed away, Aunty Daisy was suddenly filled with the desire to help people through massage and knew innately she was somehow imbued with the *aloha* touch. Aunty Daisy carries Tama in her heart and memory. Wherever she goes, even in her tiny massage studio, Grandmother Tama is there too. You can feel this touch at **Aunty Daisy's Polynesian Massage,** in the small Waipouli Complex at 971 D Kuhio Hwy., tel. 822-0305, open Tuesday and Wednesday 8:30 a.m.-5:30 p.m.; Thursday and Friday 11 a.m.-10 p.m.; Saturday 9:30 a.m.-2:30 p.m. If your heart, spirit, or body aches, give them to "the lady with *aloha* hands."

Kapa'a Health and Massage at the dragon-guarded New Pacific House, 4504 Kukui St. in downtown Kapa'a, open daily except Sunday 7 a.m.-7 p.m., tel. 823-6723, is a therapists' cooperative where practitioners offer all types of massage, acupuncture, stress management, aromatherapy, and chiropractic (out calls available).

VISITOR INFORMATION AND SERVICES

The **Kauai HVB** is at 3016 Umi St., Suite 207, Lihue, HI 96766, tel. 245-3971

Reading Material

The central **library** is at 4344 Hardy St., Lihue, tel. 245-3617. Branch libraries are located in Hanapepe, Kapa'a, Koloa, and Waimea. Check with the main library for times and services.

Free tourist literature, such as ***This Week Kauai, Spotlight Kauai,*** and ***Kauai Beach Press,*** is available at all hotels and most restaurants and shopping centers around the island. They come out every Monday and contain money-saving coupons and up-to-the-minute information on local events. ***Kauai Drive Guide*** is available from the car rental agencies and contains tips, coupons, and good maps. The AAA Hawaii ***Tourbook*** is also very useful.

There are two island newspapers, ***The Garden Island,*** published four times weekly, and the ***Kauai Times,*** appearing once a week. Hawaii's two main English-language dailies are the ***Honolulu Star Bulletin,*** and the ***Honolulu Advertiser.*** The Japanese-English ***Hawaii Hochi*** and the Chinese ***United Chinese Press*** are also available. The last four are published on Oahu but are available on Kauai. Magazines to look for that deal with Kauai are ***The Sandwich Islands Quarterly, The North Shore Quarterly, Kauai,*** and ***Kauai Dining.*** Others of interest that have ads, stories, and information, about all the islands are ***Art to Onions,*** a fine art and leisure magazine, and the inflight magazines of Aloha and Hawaiian airlines.

Weather, Surf, And Time

For a recorded message 24 hours a day, call 246-4441, then for local weather ext. 1520, for surf reports ext. 1521. For marine weather call 245-3564; for **time,** call 245-0212.

Consumer Protection

If you encounter accommodations problems, bad service, or downright rip-offs, try the following, all on Kauai: Chamber of Commerce, tel. 245-7363; Hawaii Hotel Association, tel. 923-0407; Office of Consumer Protection, tel. 241-3365; and the Better Business Bureau of Hawaii of Oahu, tel. 942-2355.

Parks

For information about state parks in Kauai contact the Division of State Parks, State Bldg., 3060 Eiwa St., Box 1671, Lihue, HI 96766, tel. 241-3444; for lodging at Koke'e State Park, write Koke'e Lodge, Box 819, Waimea, HI 96796, tel. 335- 6061. For **county parks** information contact Division of Parks and Recreation, 4193 Hardy St., Lihue, HI 96766, tel. 241-6670; open for permits Mon.-Fri. 7:45 a.m.-4:15 p.m., or when closed, permits are available at the Lihue Police Station, 3060 Umi St., Lihue, HI 96766, tel. 245-6721.

Post Offices

Normal business hours are Mon.-Fri. 8 a.m.-4:30 p.m., Saturday 8 a.m.-noon. The central post office on Kauai is at 4441 Rice St., Lihue, tel. 245-4994. Main branches are located at Kapa'a, tel. 822- 5421, and Waimea, tel. 338-9973, with 13 others scattered throughout the island. Most larger hotels offer limited postal services.

Laundromats

Self-service laundromats are Lihue Washerette in the lower level of the Lihue Shopping Center and Kapa'a Laundry Center in the Kapa'a Shopping Center.

Island Facts

Kauai's nickname is "The Garden Island," and it is the oldest of the main Hawaiian Islands. Its lei is made from the *mokihana,* a small native citrus fruit of purple color.

KEITH PERKINS

LIHUE

The twin stacks of the **Lihue Sugar Company** let you know where you are: in a plantation town on one of the world's most gorgeous islands. Lihue ("Open To Chill") began growing cane in the 1840s, and its fields are still among Hawaii's most productive. The town has correspondingly flourished, and boasts all the modern conveniences, complete with chrome and glass shopping centers, libraries, museums, and a hospital. But the feeling is still that of a sugar town. Lihue, the county seat, has 4,000 residents and two traffic lights. It isn't the geographical center of the island (Mt. Waialeale has that distinction), but it is halfway along the coastal road that encircles the island, making it a perfect jumping-off point for exploring the rest of Kauai. It has the island's largest concentration of restaurants, the most varied shopping, a major resort, and right-priced accommodations. If you're going to find any nightlife at all beyond the lounges at the big resorts, it'll be here—but don't expect much. Good beaches are within a five-minute drive, and you can be out of town and exploring long before your shave ice begins to melt.

KAUAI MUSEUM

If you really want to enrich your Kauai experience, this is the first place to visit. Spending an hour or two here infuses you with a wealth of information regarding Kauai's social and cultural history. The two-building complex is at 4428 Rice St. in downtown Lihue, tel. 245-6931, open Mon.-Fri. 9:30 a.m.-4:30 p.m., Saturday until 1 p.m., admission $3, under 18 free. The main building was dedicated in 1924 to Albert Spencer Wilcox, son of pioneer missionaries at Hanalei. It has a Greco-Roman facade, and was the public library until 1970. Its two floors house the main gallery, dedicated to ethnic heritage and island art exhibits that are changed on a regular basis. The **Museum Shop** sells books, Hawaiiana prints, and a fine selection of detailed U.S. Geological Survey maps of the entire island. Some inexpensive but tasteful purchases include baskets, wooden bowls, and selections of tapa. (The tapa is made in Fiji, but native craftspeople are studying Fijian techniques and hope to re-create this lost art.) The main room

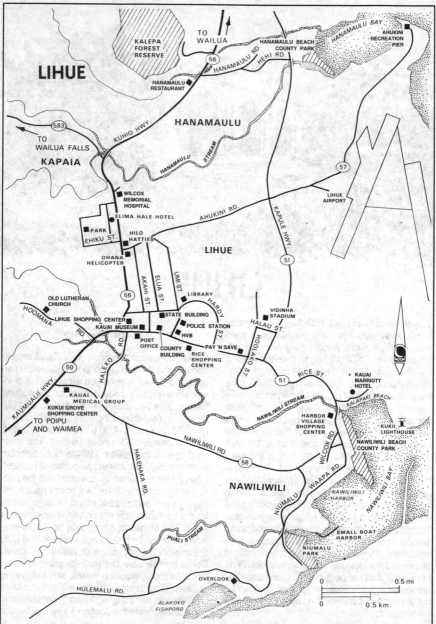

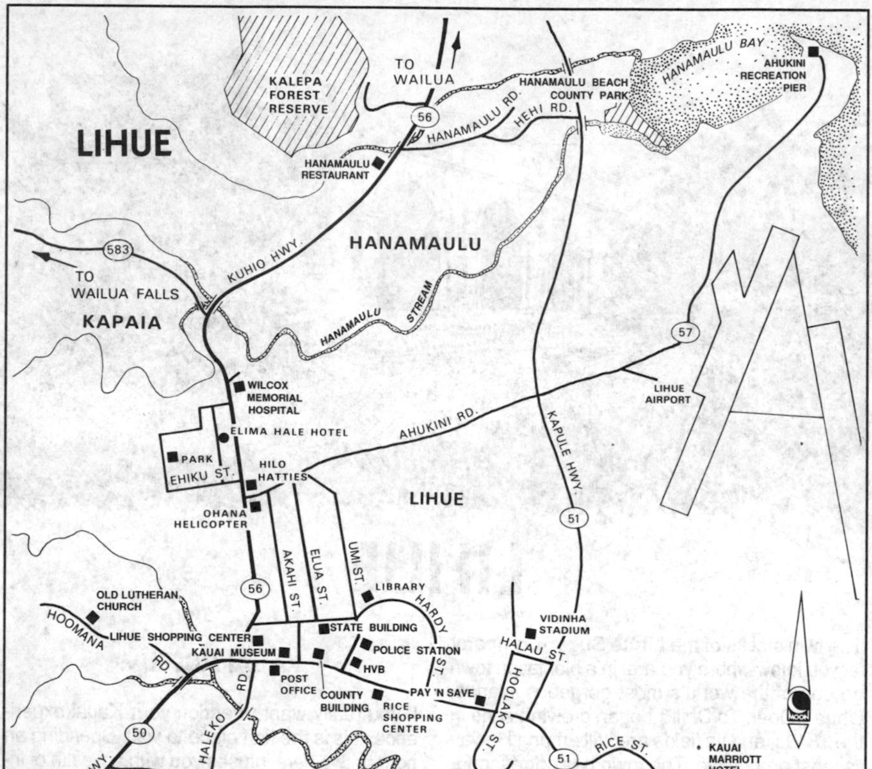

LIHUE

TO WAILUA
KALEPA FOREST RESERVE
56
HANAMAULU BEACH COUNTY PARK
HANAMAULU BAY
AHUKINI RECREATION PIER
HANAMAULU RD.
HEHI RD.
HANAMAULU RESTAURANT
HANAMAULU
583
TO WAILUA FALLS
KUHIO HWY.
KAPAIA
HANAMAULU STREAM
57
LIHUE AIRPORT
WILCOX MEMORIAL HOSPITAL
ELIMA HALE HOTEL
AHUKINI RD.
KAPULE HWY.
PARK
EHIKU ST.
HILO HATTIES
OHANA HELICOPTER
LIHUE
51
AKAHI ST.
ELUA ST.
UMI ST.
56
LIBRARY
HARDY ST.
OLD LUTHERAN CHURCH
HOOMANA RD.
LIHUE SHOPPING CENTER
STATE BUILDING
VIDINHA STADIUM
HALAU ST.
KAUAI MUSEUM
POLICE STATION
HVB
POST OFFICE
COUNTY BUILDING
RICE SHOPPING CENTER
PAY 'N SAVE
HOOLAKO ST.
HALEKO RD.
50
51
RICE ST.
KAUAI MARRIOTT HOTEL
KALAPAKI BEACH
KAUMUALII HWY.
KAUAI MEDICAL GROUP
KUKUI GROVE SHOPPING CENTER
NAWILIWILI STREAM
HARBOR VILLAGE SHOPPING CENTER
KUKII LIGHTHOUSE
TO POIPU AND WAIMEA
NAWILIWILI RD.
WILCOX RD.
NAWILIWILI BEACH COUNTY PARK
58
HALEHAKA RD.
NAWILIWILI
WAAPA RD.
NIUMALU
NAWILIWILI BAY
NAWILIWILI HARBOR
PUALI STREAM
SMALL BOAT HARBOR
NIUMALU PARK
OVERLOOK
HULEMALU RD.
ALAKOKO FISHPOND
0 0.5 mi
0 0.5 km
MOON

contains an extensive and fascinating exhibit of calabashes, koa furniture, quilts, and feather lei. One large calabash belonged to Princess Ruth, who gave it to a local child. Its finish, hand rubbed, still shows a fine luster produced by the original *kukui* nut oil. The rear of the main floor is dedicated to the **Senda Gallery,** with its collection of vintage photos shot by W.J. Senda, a Japanese immigrant from Matsue who arrived in 1906. These black-and-whites are classics, opening a window onto old Kauai.

Kauai's fascinating natural and cultural history begins to unfold when you walk through the courtyard into the second half of the museum, the **William Hyde Rice Building.** Notice the large black iron pot used to cook sugarcane. The exhibits are self-explanatory, chronicling Kauai's development over the centuries. The windows of the Natural History Tunnel show the zones of cultivation on Kauai, along with its beaches and native forests. Farther on is an extensive collection of Kauai shells, old photos, and displays of classic muumuu. The central first-floor area has a model of a Hawaiian village with an extensive collection of weapons, some fine examples of adzes used to hollow canoes, and a model of HMS *Resolution* at anchor off Waimea. An excerpt from the ship's log records Captain Cook's thoughts on the day he discovered Hawaii for the rest of the world.

As you ascend the stairs to the second floor, history continues to unfold. Missionaries stare from old photos, their countenances the epitome of piety and zeal. Just looking at them makes you want to repent! Most old photos record the plantation era. Be sure to see the **Spaulding Shell Collection,** gathered by Colonel Spaulding, an Ohio Civil War veteran who came to Kauai and married the daughter of Capt. James Makee, owner of the Makee Sugar Company. Besides shells from around the world, you'll see magnificent koa furniture, table settings, children's toys, dolls, and photos of Niihau that are about all the outside world ever sees of the "Forbidden Island."

Follow the stairs to the ground floor and notice the resplendent feather capes on the wall. On the main floor, in an alcove by the front door, push the button to begin a 15-minute aerial-view video of Kauai. This pictorial is a treat for the eyes; soothing Hawaiian chanting in the background sets the mood. The final treat, a thorough, well-done exhibit, teaches you about the legendary Menehune and Mu—their kings, work habits, beliefs, and disappearance from Kauai.

GROVE FARM HOMESTEAD

Grove Farm is a plantation started in 1864 by George Wilcox, the son of missionaries who preached at Hanalei. George earned his degree in engineering in Honolulu and returned to Kauai to work for the original owner of the surrounding acreage. The first owner saw no future in the parched land and sold 500 acres to Wilcox for $1000. Through a system of aqueducts, Wilcox brought water down from the mountains and began one of the most profitable sugar plantations in Hawaii. The homestead was a working plantation until the mid-1930s, when George died and operations were moved elsewhere. The remaining family continued to occupy the dwellings and care for the extensive grounds. In 1971, Mabel Wilcox, a niece of the founder, dedicated the family estate to posterity. Well advanced in years but spirited in mind, she created a nonprofit organization to preserve Grove Farm Homestead as a museum. Reap the benefits of her efforts by visiting this self-sufficient farm every Monday, Wednesday, and Thursday. Well-informed guides take you on a two-hour tour of the grounds and various buildings. Admission is $3 adults, $1 children under 12. Tours are by *reservation only!* Call 245-3202 at least 24 hours in advance to make arrangements. Mail reservations are accepted up to three months in advance; write Grove Farm Homestead, P.O. Box 1631, Lihue, HI 96766. The homestead is located off Nawiliwili Road; precise directions are given when you call. Drop-in visitors will be turned away. Group size is limited to give full attention to detail and minimize wear and tear on the buildings. Tours begin at 10 a.m. and 1 p.m. Be prompt please!

Living History

The first thing you notice when entering Grove Farm is the rumble of your tires crossing a narrow-gauge railroad track. The tracks meant sugar, and sugar meant prosperity and change for old

Hawaii. The minute you set foot upon Grove Farm Homestead you can feel this spirit permeating the place. This is no "glass-case" museum. It's a real place with living history, where people experienced the drama of changing Hawaii.

George Wilcox never married. In love once, he was jilted, and that ended that. In 1870 his brother Sam came to live on the homestead. In 1874 Sam married Emma, daughter of missionaries from the Big Island. She had been educated in Dearborn, Michigan, and had recently returned to Hawaii. The couple had six children, three boys and three girls. Two of the boys survived to manhood and managed the farm, but both met later with tragic deaths. Of the girls only Henrietta, the oldest, married. The two other sisters, Miss Elsie and Miss Mabel, were single all their lives. Elsie became very involved in politics, while Mabel went to Johns Hopkins University and earned a degree as a registered nurse. Her parents wouldn't let her leave home until she was 25 years old, when they felt she could cope with the big, bad world. She returned in 1911 and opened a public health office on the grounds.

The Tour

The buildings, furnishings, orchards, and surrounding lands are part of what was the oldest, intact sugar plantation in Hawaii. You meet your guide at the plantation office, which has a safe dating from 1880, when it was customary to pay for everything in cash. On top sits a cannonball that's been there as long as anyone can remember. Perhaps it was placed there by Mr. Pervis, the original bookkeeper. As time went on the safe's combination, which is in letters, not numbers, was lost. Recently a safecracker was hired to open it, and inside was the combination written in a big, bold hand . . . B-A-L-L.

You cross the grounds to a simple dwelling and enter the home of the Moriwakis. Mrs. Moriwaki came to Grove Farm as a "picture bride," though she was born in Hawaii and taken back to Japan as a child. She was the cook at the big house for almost 50 years; after the grounds opened to the public, she returned on tour days to explain her role in running the homestead, until her death in 1986. Her home is meticulously clean and humble, a symbol of Japanese plantation workers' lives on Hawaii. Notice the food safe. There were no ice boxes for most workers in Hawaii; they kept vermin away from the safes by placing sardine cans filled with water or kerosene inside them, into which the pests fell. A small print of Mt. Fuji and a geisha doll in a glass case are simple yet meaningful touches. Together they are the memory of the past along with the hope of the brighter futures plantation workers sought for their children.

As you walk around, notice how lush and fruitful the grounds are, with all sorts of trees and plants. At one time the workers were encouraged to have their own gardens. A highlight is a small latticework building half submerged in the ground. This is the **fernery,** at one time a status symbol of the good life in Hawaii. There was great competition among the ladies of Victorian Hawaii who were proud of their ferns, and you became an instant friend if you presented a new and unique variety while on a social visit. Behind the Wilcox Home is a small schoolhouse built in 1900. It later became Mabel Wilcox's public health office; now a depository for of artifacts and memorabilia, it's called the **Trunk Room.** A photo of Mabel shows her in a Red Cross uniform. By all accounts, Mabel was a serious but not humorless woman. Her dry and subtle wit was given away by her sparkling eyes, obvious in the photo.

Wilcox Home

Shoes are removed before entering this grand mansion. The Wilcoxes were pleasant people given to quiet philanthropy, but their roots as New England missionaries made them frugal. The women always wore homemade cotton dresses, and in the words of a tour guide, "Nothing was ever thrown away by this family." The home is comfortable and smacks of culture, class, and money—in the old-fashioned sense. As you enter, you'll be struck with the feeling of space. The archways were fashioned so they get smaller as you look through the house. This shrinking perspective gives an illusion of great length. The walls and staircase are of rich, brown koa. Much of the furniture was bought secondhand from families returning to the Mainland. This was done not out of a sense of frugality, but simply because it often was the only good furniture available.

The piano here belonged to Emma Wilcox; the profusion of artwork includes many original pieces, often done by visitors to the homestead. One longtime visitor, a sickly girl from the East Coast, did some amazing embroidery. Her finest piece on display took 10 years to complete. Portraits of the family include a good one of George Wilcox. Notice a Japanese chest Miss Mabel won in a drawing while she was in Japan with her sister Elsie and Uncle George in 1907. Notice too the extensive collection of Hawaiiana the family accumulated over the decades. In the separate kitchen wing is a stove that is still functional after 100 years of hard use. A porch, so obviously homey during rainstorms, looks out onto a tea house. Everything in the home is of fine quality and in good taste. It's a dwelling of peace and tranquility.

The Cottage

Finally you arrive at the private home of a private man, George Wilcox himself. It is the picture of simplicity. Only an old bachelor would have chosen these spartan surroundings. Inveterate cigar smokers, he and his brother Sam were forbidden by the ladies to smoke in the main house. Here, George did as he pleased. Maybe the women were right; George died of throat cancer . . . in 1933 at the age of 94!

The first room you enter is his office. George was a small man and a gentleman. Whenever he left the house, he donned a hat. You'll notice a collection of his favorites hanging on pegs in the hallway. One of his few comforts was a redwood tub he'd soak in for hours. This self-made millionaire kept his soap in an old sardine tin, but he did use fine embroidered towels. His bedroom is simple, bright, and airy. The mattress is of extremely comfortable horsehair. Outside his window is a profusion of fruit trees, many of which George planted himself. As the tour ends you get the feeling that these trees are what Grove Farm is all about—a homestead where people lived, and worked, and dreamed.

OTHER SIGHTS

Kilohana Plantation

The manor house at Kilohana Plantation was built in 1935 by the wealthy *kama'aina* planter, Gaylord Wilcox, to please his wife, Ethel. She was enamored with Hollywood and with its glamorous Tudor-type mansions, which were the rage of the day. Sparing no expense, Gaylord spent $200,000 to build an elaborate 16,000-square-foot home estimated to have cost about $3 million by today's standards. A horse and carriage waits (nominal fee) to take visitors on a tour of the 35 lush acres surrounding the home that was the center of a working farm, a feeling that lingers. Inside, **Gaylord's Restaurant** occupies the actual dining room (see "Fine Dining" under "Food" below). Original furniture includes a huge table that seats 22, and a stout sideboard fit for a truly regal manor house. As you pass from room to room, some of which are occupied by fine boutiques, jewelry shops, and art galleries, notice the coved ceiling, lustrous wood molding, and grand staircase. A mirror from the '30s (mirrors in Hawaii have a tough time holding up because of the moisture) hangs just inside the atriumlike tiled main entranceway. Walk straight through a set of double doors onto the flagstone veranda (also occupied by Gaylord's for alfresco dining) to view a living tapestry of mountain and cloud, even more ethereal when mist shrouds magical Mt. Waialeale in the distance. To get there take Rt. 50 (Kaumuali Hwy.) west from Lihue for about two miles toward the tiny village of Puhi, and look mountainside for the clearly marked entrance.

Lihue's Churches

When Rt. 56 becomes Rt. 50 just as you pass the Lihue Sugar Mill, look for the HVB Warrior pointing you to the **Old Lutheran Church.** Just before the bridge, follow Hoomana Road to the right through a well-kept residential area. Built in 1883, it has everything a church should have, including a bell tower and spire, but it's all miniature-sized. The church reflects a strong German influence that dominated Lihue and its plantation until WW I. The turn-of-the-century pastor was Hans Isenberg, brother of the plantation founder and husband to Dora Rice from the old *kama'aina* family. Pastor Rice was responsible for procuring the Lihue Horse Trough, an ornate marble work imported from Italy in 1909, now on display at the Haleko Shops' botanical gardens in downtown Lihue. The outside of the church is basic New England, but inside, the ornate altar is reminiscent of baroque Germany.

Headstones in the yard to the side indicate how old this congregation is.

On a nearby hill is **Lihue Union Church,** once mostly attended by workers and their families. Its cemetery is filled with simple tombstones, and plumeria trees eternally produce blossoms for the departed ones. If you follow the main road past the Lutheran church it dead-ends at an enormous cane field. This sea of green runs to the mountains and lets you know how much sugar still dominates the way of life in Lihue and on Kauai in general.

Around Town

Across the street from Lihue Shopping Center, a stone's throw from the twin stacks of the sugar mill, are four solid-looking buildings known as the **Haleko Shops.** Once the homes of German plantation managers before they gave up their holdings during WW I, they're now occupied by restaurants and shops—part of the shopping center across the road. Around them is a botanical garden. Each plant carries a description of its traditional use and which ethnic group brought it to the island. (Look for the Lihue Horse Trough imported by Pastor Isenberg.)

Follow Umi Street off Rice to Hardy Street. At the corner is the **Kauai Library.** In the entrance is a batik wall hanging by Jerome Wallace, the largest painting of its type in the world.

Follow Rice Street toward Nawiliwili Harbor and it turns into Rt. 51, known as Waapa Road. At its junction with Rt. 58 (known as Nawiliwili Road), take Nawiliwili Road toward the bay to Niumalu Road and turn left, following it to Hulemalu Road. You pass the predominantly Hawaiian settlement of Niumalu. Along Hulemalu Road is a lookout, below which is **Alakoko** ("Rippling Blood") **Pond,** commonly known as Menehune Fishpond. You have a sweeping view of Huleia Stream, the harbor, and the Hoary Head Mountains in the background. The 900-foot mullet-raising fishpond is said to be the handiwork of the Menehune. Legend says they built this pond for a royal prince and princess, and that they made only one demand: that no one watch them in their labor. In one night, the indefatigable Menehune passed the stones needed for the construction from hand to hand in a double line that stretched for 25 miles. But the royal prince and princess could not contain their curiosity, and climbed to a nearby ridge to watch the little people. They were spotted by the Menehune, who stopped building, leaving holes in the wall. They turned the royal pair into the twin pillars of stone still seen on the mountainside overlooking the pond.

Wailua Falls

Heading north, in Kapaia Rt. 583 branches from Rt. 56 and heads into the interior. As the road lifts up and away from the ocean, you realize that the rolling terrain surrounded by lofty mountain peaks is completely given over to sugarcane. To the left and right are small homes with the usual patches of tropical fruit trees. Route 583 ends at mile marker 3. Far below, Wailua Falls tumbles 80 feet over a severe *pali* into a large round pool. It's said that the *ali'i* would come here to dive from the cliff into the pool as a show of physical prowess; commoners were not considered to be infused with enough mana to perform this feat.

Many of the trees here are unwilling trellises for rampant morning glory. Pest or not, its blossoms are still beautiful as it climbs the limbs. A trail down to the falls is particularly tough and steep. If you make it down, you'll have the falls to yourself, but you'll be like a goldfish in a bowl with the tourists, perhaps jealously, peering down at you.

BEACHES AND PARKS

Lihue has very convenient beaches. You can sun yourself within 10 minutes from anywhere in town, with a choice of beaches on either Nawiliwili or Hanamaulu bays. Few tourists head to Hanamaulu Bay, while Nawiliwili Bay is a classic example of "beauty and the beast." There is hardly a more beautiful harbor than Nawiliwili's, with a stream flowing into it and verdant mountains all around. However, it is a working harbor complete with rusting barges, groaning cranes, and petrochemical tanks. Private yachts and catamarans bob at anchor with their bright colors reflecting off dappled waters, and as your eye sweeps the lovely panorama it runs into the dull gray wall of a warehouse where raw sugar is stored before being shipped to the Mainland to be processed. It's one of those places that sep-

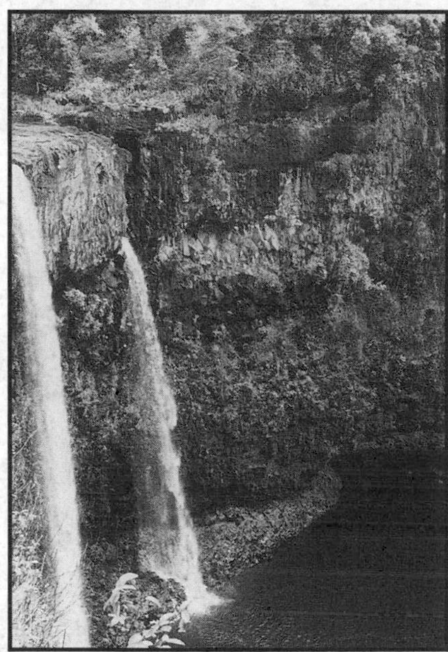
J.D. BISIGNANI

Wailua Falls

arates perspectives: some see the "beauty" while others focus on the "beast."

Kalapaki Beach

This most beautiful beach at Nawiliwili fronts the lavish Mariott Kauai. Follow Rice Street until it becomes Rt. 51, where you'll soon see the bay and the entrance to the hotel on your left. The hotel serves as a giant screen, blocking out most of the industrial area and leaving the lovely views of the bay. Park in the visitors' area at the hotel entrance, or to the rear of the hotel at the north end of Nawiliwili Beach Park, where a footbridge leads across the Nawiliwili Stream to the hotel property and the beach. Access to the beach is open to anyone, but if you want to use the hotel pool and showers, you'll have a lot less hassle if you order a light breakfast or lunch at one of the restaurants. The homemade ice cream at the hotel ice cream shop is delicious!

The wave action at Kalapaki is gentle at most times, with long swells combing the sandy-bottomed beach. Kalapaki is one of the best swimming beaches on the island, fair for snorkeling, and a great place to try bodysurfing or to begin on a board. Two secluded beaches in this area are generally frequented by local people. Head through the hotel grounds following the road to the right past the few private homes that overlook this bay. From here you'll see a lighthouse on Ninini Point. Keep the lighthouse to your left as you walk across the golf course to the bay. Below are two small crescent beaches, both good for swimming and sunbathing. The right one has numerous springs that flow up into the sand. You can also head for **Nawiliwili Beach County Park** by following Rt. 51 downhill past the Mariott Kauai until you come to the water; on the left is the beach park. Here are showers, picnic tables, and a pavilion along with some shady palm trees for a picnic. A seawall has been erected here, so for swimming and sunning it's much better to walk up to your left and spend the day at Kalapaki Beach.

Niumalu Beach County Park

This county-maintained beach park is along the Puali Stream on the west end of Nawiliwili Harbor. Many small fishing and charter boats are berthed nearby and local men use the wharf area to fish and "talk story." There is no swimming and you are surrounded by the industrial area. However, you are very close to Lihue and there are pavilions, showers, toilets, and camping both for tents and RVs (permit required). To get there take Rt. 51 to Nawillwill Harbor. Continue on Waapa Road along the harbor until you arrive at the beach park.

Ahukini Recreation Pier

As the name implies, this state park is simply a pier from which local people fish. And it's some of the best fishing around. Follow Rt. 57 to Lihue Airport. With the airport to your right, keep going until the road ends at a large circular parking lot and fishing pier. The scenery is only fair, so if you're not into fishing give it a miss.

Hanamaulu Beach County Park

This is a wonderful beach, and although it is very accessible and good for swimming, very few tourists come here. There is not only a beach, but to the right is a lagoon area with pools formed by Hanamaulu Stream. Local fam-

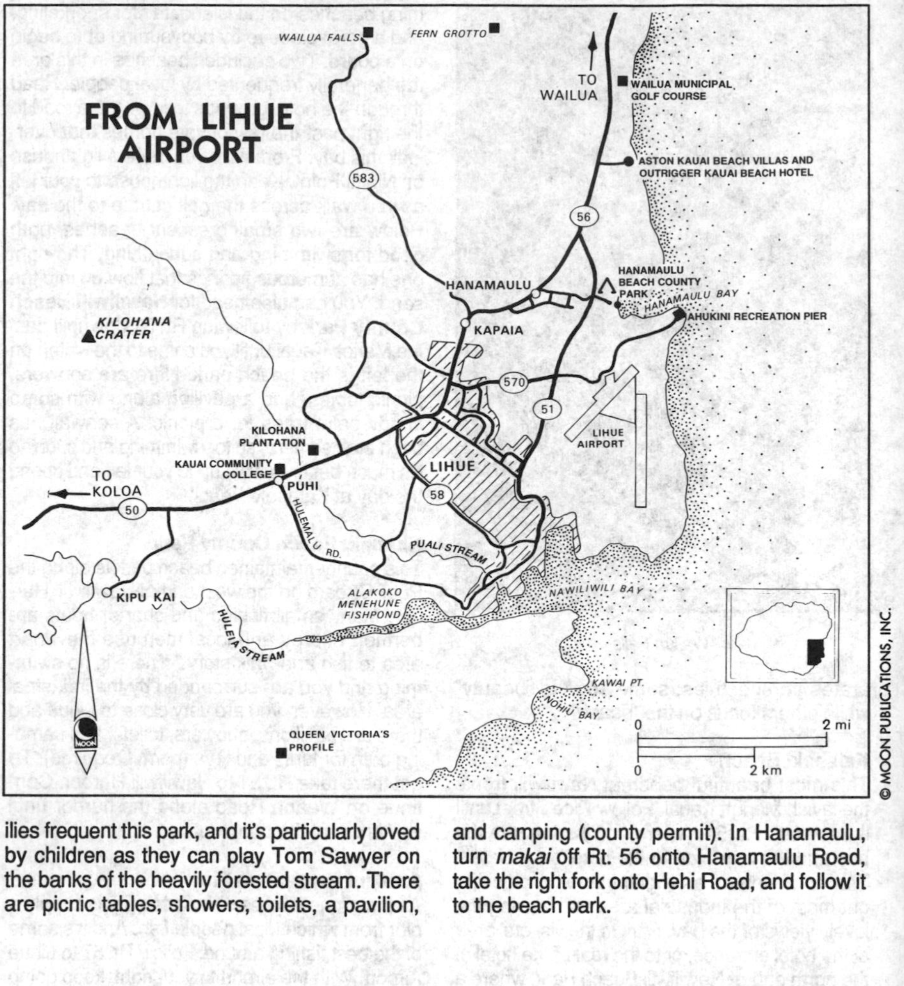

FROM LIHUE AIRPORT

ilies frequent this park, and it's particularly loved by children as they can play Tom Sawyer on the banks of the heavily forested stream. There are picnic tables, showers, toilets, a pavilion, and camping (county permit). In Hanamaulu, turn *makai* off Rt. 56 onto Hanamaulu Road, take the right fork onto Hehi Road, and follow it to the beach park.

ACCOMMODATIONS

If you like simple choices, you'll appreciate Lihue; it has only two fancy resorts. The rest are either family-run hotel/motels or apartment hotels. Prices are also best here because Lihue isn't considered a prime resort town. But it makes an ideal base, because from Lihue you can get *anywhere* on the island in less than an hour. Although it's the county seat, the town is quiet, especially in the evenings, so you won't have to deal with noise or hustle and bustle.

Inexpensive

Motel Lani, owned and operated by Janet Naumu, offers clean, inexpensive rooms at 4240 Rice Street. For reservations write: Motel Lani, Box 1836, Lihue, HI 96766, tel. 245-2965. The lobby is actually an extension of Janet's home, where she and her children often watch TV. There are 10 sunburn-pink units, three of which offer cooking facilities, and although close to the road they're surprisingly quiet. All rooms have a small desk, dresser, bath, fan, refrigerator, and cross ventilation; no TVs. Janet usually doesn't allow children under three years old, especially if they misbehave, but she's reasonable and will make exceptions. A small courtyard with a barbecue is available to guests. Rates for two nights $27-40 double, from $40 triple, additional person $12, slightly more for one night. Rooms with cooking facilities (hard to get) start at $38.

The loved but worse-for-wear Ocean View Motel, built and operated by the irascible but lovable Spike Kanja, is now the new, refurbished, and very attractive **Garden Island Inn,** at 3445 Wilcox Rd., Nawiliwili, HI 96766, tel. 245-7227 or (800) 648-0145. The new owners, Steve and Susan Lange have done a wonderful job of turning the once character-laden but dilapidated hotel into a bright and cheery inn. Head down Rice Street toward Nawiliwili, and at the corner of Wilcox Road, across from Nawiliwili Beach Park and just a stroll from Kalapaki Beach, is the inn. The ground-floor rooms, $55 d, are appointed with textured bamboo-motif wallpaper, and are cooled by louvered windows and ceiling fans. Each room has a color TV, microwave, refrigerator, and coffeemaker. Second-floor rooms, $65 d, are about the same, but each has its own lanai. The best rooms, $75-85, are on the third floor, from where you look down on a fully matured banana grove. "Is this the tropics or what!" More like mini-suites, third-floor units have two full rooms that can comfortably accommodate four people. The front sitting room, doubling as a kitchen, is bright with a wrap-around lanai from where you can watch the goings-on in Nawiliwili Harbor and have an unobstructed view of the cement works! For the money, the Garden Isle Inn is one of the best deals on Kauai.

The **Kauai Inn,** formerly the Hale Niumalu Motel, is off the main drag near the boat harbor in Niumalu. The buildings were at one time overflow accommodations for a big hotel, but are now independently owned. The rooms are large and well kept but plain. The best feature is a screened lanai in the old building with a profusion of hanging plants. No longer the deal it used to be, the inn charges $69-89, weekly rates available. Located across from Niumalu Park at the corner of Niumalu and Hulemalu roads, the Kauai Inn was battered by Iniki but hopes to reopen. For information phone (800) 326-5242 or 245-3316.

Hale Lihue, 2931 Kalena St., Lihue, HI 96766, tel. 245-3151, *was* a quiet, clean, and basic motel owned and operated for many years by a lovely Japanese couple, Mr. and Mrs. Morishige, whose hospitality made it an institution. They retired in 1984 and sold the hotel to a "man from Los Angeles," whose name Mrs. Morishige couldn't remember. She'd been assured that he would keep "everything the same," but Hale Lihue seems a little worse for wear. Rates are $28 s, $30 d, for a basic room with ceiling fan, and $30 s, $44 d, for kitchenettes.

The **Tip Top Motel,** 3173 Akahi St., reservations Box 1231, Lihue, HI 96766, tel. 245-2333, is a combination lounge, restaurant, and bakery popular with local folks. It's a functional, two-story, cinder-block building painted light gray. The lobby/cafe/bakery is open daily except Monday 6:45 a.m.-9 p.m. The rooms are antiseptic in every way, a plus as your feet stay cool on the bare linoleum floor. All are air-conditioned. Just to add that mixed-society touch, instead of a Gideon's Bible in the dresser drawer, you get *The Teachings of Buddha,* placed there by the Sudaka Society of Honolulu. Rates are $50 for four, with a few cheaper rooms available.

If you want to get out of town you can find basic accommodations at the **Elima Hale Hotel,** near the Wilcox Memorial Hospital, on Elima Street between Hanamaulu and Lihue. They offer rooms (some with private baths) with TVs, refrigerators, and use of a kitchen. Rates for this deluxe flophouse are $30 s, $44 d, with monthly and weekly rates. For information write: Elima Hale Hotel, 3360 Elima St., Lihue, HI 96766, tel. 245-9950.

Moderate/Deluxe Accommodations

The **Aston Kauai Beach Villas** at 4330 Kauai Beach Dr., Lihue, HI 96766, tel. 245-7711, (800) 922-7866 Mainland, (800) 445-6633 Canada, (800) 321-2559 Hawaii, are perfectly located midway between the airport and Kapa'a. The fine condominium resort has consistently earned the AAA "Three-diamond Award." The spacious units, a signature of Aston Resorts, differ slightly, but expect a terra-cotta foyer leading to a living room with comfortable bamboo furniture, puff pillows, a fold-out couch, and remote-control color TV with Spectravision. The dining area has a marble-topped table with high-backed chairs adjacent to the full kitchen with refrigerator, dishwasher, garbage disposal, coffeemaker, four-burner electric stove, hood fan, microwave oven, toaster, and all the necessary utensils. A washer-dryer combination is tucked in its own utility closet. Master bedrooms have queen-size beds, private baths, plenty of closet space, and complimentary safes. Ceiling fans, a/c, and phones are part of the amenities. Each unit has a lanai with outdoor tables, chairs, and lounges. Rates are $99 for a studio with kitchen, $140 one bedroom, $195 two bedrooms with garden view, and $255 for a two-bedroom, two-bath suite with ocean view. The Aston Kauai Beach Villas are adjacent to the Outrigger Kauai Beach Hotel (a former Hilton) with which it shares all amenities, including the free-form pool.

The **Outrigger Kauai Beach,** tel. 245-1955 or (800) 733-7777, is one of Kauai's newest hotel/condos. On 25 landscaped acres overlooking Hanamaulu Beach, it offers 350 hotel rooms, all with mini-refrigerators, and 136 villas with full kitchens and laundry facilities. The hotel pool is in three sections connected by tiny waterfalls and cascades. Dining amenities include late-night room service, lobby lounge, pool bar and restaurant, **Gilligan's** for drinks and dancing, and the casual **Jacaranda Terrace,** the hotel's main dining hall. There are four tennis courts, two whirlpools, and water sports equipment. Prior to the nightly luau a torch-lighting ceremony is performed, and a wide range of events is run by the activities desk. Rates are hotel $125-175, one-bedroom villa $140-200, two-bedroom villa (up to four people) $190-250. Special honeymoon, tennis, and golf packages are available.

Oh how the mighty have fallen! Reopened only in 1987 after refurbishing and new construction, the **Westin Kauai** at Kauai Lagoons was the island's fanciest and most modern resort complex. It was heavily damaged by Hurricane Iniki. Marriott International has purchased the property and plans to reopen it in July 1995 as the **Kauai Marriott.** For-up-to-the-minute information phone 245-5050 or (800) 228-9290.

FOOD

Dining in Lihue is a treat. The menu of restaurants in and around town is the most extensive on the island. You can have savory snacks at saimin shops or at bargain-priced eateries frequented by local people. You'll find pizza parlors and fast-food chains. Stepping up in class, there are continental, Italian, and Japanese restaurants, while moderately priced establishments serve up hearty dishes of Mexican, Chinese, and good old American fare. Finally, fancier dining is found in some of the big hotels. The dining in Lihue is good to your palate and to your budget.

Inexpensive In And Around Lihue

If you ask anyone in Lihue where you can chow down for cheap, they'll send you to **Ma's Family Inc.**, an institution owned and operated by matriarch Akiyo Honjo, a third-generation Kauaian, who is assisted at times by her great-grandchildren. To arrive make a right off Rice Street onto Kress Street, and follow it to the corner where you'll find Ma's at 4277 Halenani St., open daily 5 a.m.-1:30 p.m., Saturday, Sunday, and holidays 5 a.m.-10 a.m. (or until customers stop coming), tel. 245-3142. The building is old and a bit run-down, but clean. A few tourists find it, but mostly local working people come here for hearty and filling meals. Lunches are good, but the super deals are breakfast and the Hawaiian food specialties. The coffee, free with breakfast and seved with condensed milk, arrives in a large pot about as soon as your seat hits the chair. The menu is posted above the kitchen. You can start the day with the special with "the works," which includes potatoes or fried noodles with bacon or sausage and toast for $5. From the Hawaiian menu try *kalua* pork with two eggs and rice, poi and *lomi* salmon, or Kauai sausage, all for under $6. For the famished or traveling wrestling team, the menu offers a pound of *kalua* pork. (If this last item is ordered by one guy who appears grumpy before his gallon of morning coffee, don't bother him!) Ma also serves hamburgers from $1.75, and an assortment of sandwiches including teriyaki beef, the most expensive at $2.50.

Hamura Saimin Stand, at 2956 Kress St., tel. 245-3271, open daily 10 a.m.-2 a.m. (depending upon business), is just around the corner from Ma's. People flock to this orange counter-topped restaurant all day long where they perch on short stools to eat giant steaming bowls of saimin. But the real show is around 2 a.m. when all the bars and discos let loose their revelers. There is no decor, just good food, but a sign admonishes, Please Do Not Stick Gum Under Counter. Your first time, try the "saimin special" of noodles, slivers of meat and fish, vegetables, wonton, and eggs, all floating in a golden broth. Other items on the small menu are variations on the same theme, with nothing over $5. On the counter will be hot sauce, mustard, and shoyu, condiments that you mix yourself in the small bowls that accompany your soup. Enjoy not only the saimin, but the truly authentic Kauai experience.

Halo Halo Shave Ice occupies a second counter in the same building—use the side entrance. Here you can get some of the best throat coolers on the island.

Yokozuna's Ramen has taken the place of Judy's Saimin, but has kept on serving good food at cheap prices. This little shop is at 4444 Rice St., tel. 246-1008, on the lower street level of the Lihue Shopping Center.

Garden Isle Kitchen has an odd location—it's in the grease bay of an old gas station that's made from lava rock and has a false grass-shack roof fashioned from cement. Open Mon.-Fri. 8 a.m.-5 p.m. and until 2 p.m. Saturday, they serve Hawaiian and Filipino food, including box lunches, plate lunches, *manapua, lumpia,* and *halohalo,* and run a catering service as well. In the Garden Island Plaza, tel. 246-9021.

Tip Top Restaurant/Bakery, at 3173 Akahi St. between Rice St. and Rt. 57, open daily except Monday 6:45 a.m.-9 p.m., tel. 245-2333, doubles as the downstairs lobby of the Tip Top Motel. At this local favorite with unpretentious but clean surroundings, the food is wholesome but uninspired, just like the service. Breakfast is the best deal for around $5, and the macadamia nut pancakes are delish! Plate lunches are under $6 and dinners under $8. You can choose anything from pork chops to teriyaki chicken, and you get soup, salad, rice, and coffee. The *bento* (box lunches), either American style or Asian, are a good deal. Visit the bakery section and let your eyes tell your stomach what to do. The *malasadas* are fresh daily.

Dani's, 4201 Rice St. toward Nawiliwili near the fire department, open Mon.-Fri. 5 a.m.-1:30 p.m., Saturday 5 a.m.-1 p.m., closed Sunday, tel. 245-4991, is a favorite with local people. It's been around a while and has a good reputation for giving you a hearty meal for a reasonable price. The food is American-Hawaiian-Japanese. Most full meals range $4.50-8 and include selections like *lomi* salmon, tripe stew, teri beef and chicken, and fried fish. Unpretentious, the cafeteria-style decor is Formica-topped tables and linoleum floors. Service is friendly, and the food is good.

Kunja's Korean Restaurant opened recently and is the only place in town serving authentic Korean food, sit down or takeout. Dishes include short ribs, marinated beef strips, mixed rice and vegetables, and various noodle soups, priced $3.25-5.75. Many are made with the Hawaiian palate in mind, but for a real spicy dish try *O-jing-o Po Kum* for $4.50 or *kimchi* soup for $5.50. Clean and tidy, with only eight tables. Open Mon.-Sat. 9:30 a.m.-8 p.m., Kunja's is located at 4252 Rice St., across from N. Yoneji's Store, tel. 245-8792.

Look for an anchor chain marking the two-tone blue **Kalapaki Beach Burgers,** open daily except Sunday 10 a.m.-4 p.m., at the bottom of Rice St., just before Nawiliwili Harbor. This upscale window-restaurant offers limited seating in the upstairs "crow's nest" from where you get a great view of the harbor. Brand new, but with an excellent reputation already, it serves lunches like fish and chips, mahimahi, and charbroiled chicken for under $6. The specialty is large, juicy buffalo burgers with all the fixings. Unpretentious, Kalapaki Beach Burgers is an excellent choice for lunch in the Nawiliwili area.

Savory bowls of saimin and inexpensive *bento,* Japanese boxed lunches, are available from **OK Bento and Saimin,** tel. 245-6554, located at 4100 Rice St., in the small shopping center adjacent to Pay 'n Save, open Mon.-Fri. 8 a.m.-8:30 p.m., Saturday, 8 a.m.-2 p.m., closed Sunday. A basic bowl of saimin is only $2.35, and the "saimin special," a complete meal in a bowl with vegetables, wonton, egg, and pieces of pork floating in golden broth, is only $3.35 (large size available) . Other menu selections include wonton mein for $3.60, OK bento for $4.25, and hamburger steak or teri beef or chicken for under $6. Formica-topped tables and Japanese fans are the decor in this basic, clean, and right-priced restaurant.

Next door is **Tammy's Okazu-ya,** open Mon.-Sat. 7 a.m.-2 p.m., tel. 246-0460, a very local plate lunch restaurant where you choose items from the menu to build your own plate lunch. Typical savories include: fried shrimp 80 cents, fried chicken 85 cents, mahimahi 90 cents, cone sushi $1.50, and pork or chicken long rice 90 cents. A prepared *bento* for $5 containing "two scoop rice," hash, Spam, teriyaki beef, fried chicken, and chow fun is perfect for a picnic lunch at the beach. The food is good, wholesome, and as local as you can get.

Don't let the name **Lihue Bakery and Coffee Shop** fool you into thinking of just the familiar styrofoam cup of coffee and powdered donut. Located in the Rice Shopping Center, open Mon.-Sat. 5:30 a.m.-6 p.m., Sunday 5 a.m.-1 p.m., this storefront restaurant specializes in Filipino foods and pastries. Choose your selection from a steam table laden with ethnic dishes like *pinkabet* and chicken or pork *adobo.* You can have from one to three selections costing $4, $4.50, and $5, and top it off with a Filipino pastry.

The **Kukui Grove Shopping Center** has a number of sit-down and sidewalk restaurants. They include: the **Deli and Bread Connection,** a kitchenware store with a deli counter offering sandwiches for around $3, and an assortment of soups and salads; **Kauai Cinnamons,** a bake shop specializing in cinnamon rolls; **Si Cisco's,** a Mexican restaurant, nicely appointed with a tile floor and a full bar; **Joni Hana,** a walk-up counter with *bento* and plate lunches priced $2-5; and **J.V. Snack Bar,** featuring shave ice and light sandwiches.

One of the mall's best restaurants for Cantonese food at very reasonable prices is **Ho's Garden,** where most dishes are under $7.

Fast Food

Yes, the smell of the Colonel's frying chicken overpowers the flower-scented air, and the Golden Arches glimmer in the bright Kauai sun. **Pizza Hut, Jack in the Box, McDonald's, Kentucky Fried Chicken, Zack's Frozen Yogurt, Domino's, Baskin-Robbins** and **Subway Sub Shop** are all located along Rt. 56 as you enter Lihue. **Burger King** and **Taco Bell** are at the Kukui Grove Shopping Center, and a **Dairy Queen** brazier can be found on Rice Street across from the Rice Shopplng Center.

Moderate In And Around Lihue

The restaurants in and around Lihue charge as little as $5 for an entree, with the average around $10. Most of these restaurants advertise specials and discounts in the free tourist literature.

Restaurant Kiibo serves authentic Japanese meals without a big price tag. Many Japanese around town come here to eat. The low stools at the counter are reminiscent of a Japanese *akachochin* or *sushiya.* The sushi bar is a recent addition. Savory offerings of *udon,* tempura, teriyaki, and a variety of *teishoku* (specials) are accompanied by a picture showing you just what you'll get. The service is quick and friendly; most offerings are under $10. Restaurant Kiibo is *ichiban!* Located just off Rice Street, at 2991 Umi Street. Open for lunch 11 a.m.-1 p.m. (attracts many office workers) and for dinner 5:30-9 p.m., closed Sunday and holidays, tel. 245-2650. Just around the corner is the **Lihue Cafe** for Japanese and Chinese food. Unpretentious setting, basic food. Open Mon.-Sat. 4:30 p.m.-9 p.m. (to 10 pm. on Friday), tel. 245-6471.

The **Barbecue Inn,** 2982 Kress St., tel. 245-2921, has been in business for three decades, and if you want a testimonial, just observe the steady stream of local people, from car mechanics to doctors, heading for this restaurant. Word has it that it's better for lunch than dinner. The atmosphere is "leatherette and Formica," but the service is homey, friendly, and prompt. Japanese and American servings are huge. Over 30 entrees range from a chicken platter to seafood and prime rib. The Friday teriyaki platter is a good choice. The scampi is perhaps the best for the price on the island. Most meals are complete with soup/salad, banana bread, vegetables, beverage, and dessert for around $6 and up. Breakfast goes for a reasonable $2, with lunch at bargain prices. The homemade pies are luscious. Cocktails are available. No credit cards accepted. Open daily 7:30 a.m.-8:45 p.m.

Tokyo Lobby, in Nawiliwili at the Pacific Ocean Plaza, 3501 Rice St., Suite 103, tel. 245-8989, open for lunch Mon.-Sat. 11:30 a.m.-2:30 p.m., dinner nightly 5 p.m.-9:30 p.m., prides itself on the freshness of the food, especially the seafood. Appointed with shoji screens, a pagoda-style roof over the sushi bar, paper fans, and paper lanterns, the Tokyo Lobby creates an authentic Japanese atmosphere. Most meals are presented in a small wooden boat, the signature of the restaurant. For lunch start with combination *nigiri* sushi or sashimi priced $8.50-9.50, various *donburi* (a bowl of rice topped with savory bits of meat, egg, and vegetables) for $6.50-7.95, or *nabeyaki* (assorted seafood with vegetables and noodles in broth) for $8.95. The dinner menu starts with appetizers like chicken teriyaki or deep-fried soft-shell crab for $3.75-8.95. Soups and salads include miso soup for $1.50, or *sunomono,* seafood and cucumber in a light vinegar sauce, for $4.50. Sashimi and sushi platters are served with soup and *tsukemono* (cabbage salad), and range $8.95-18.95 for the deluxe combination. Dinner entrees include calamari steak, curried chicken, and beef teriyaki all priced under $13.95. Combination dinners like sesame chicken with sashimi cost $14.95. The house specialty is the Tokyo Lobby Love Boat, including soup, steamed rice, New York steak, teri chicken, California roll, sashimi, and tempura at $19.95 per person.

Kauai Chop Suey, tel. 245-8790, open daily except Monday for lunch 11 a.m.-2 p.m., and for dinner 4:30-9 p.m., is a reasonably priced Chinese restaurant also located in Nawiliwili's Pacific Ocean Plaza. The restaurant's two dining rooms, separated by a keyhole archway, are alive with plants and brightened by Chinese lanterns hanging from the open-beamed ceiling. The simple but pleasing decor also features tables set with white linen, all dominated by large lazy Susans, perfect for easy sampling of the savory dishes chosen from the menu. Begin with scallop soup or seafood tofu soup, priced under $7. Entrees include sizzling shrimp with lobster sauce for $6.95, boneless chicken with mushrooms for $6.45, beef or pork with tomato for under $7, and abalone with black mushrooms for $8.75. House specials are Kauai Chop Suey for only $5.85, and a variety of noodle dishes, all under $7. Kauai Chop Suey also offers plate lunches and dinners to go, and although relatively new, has a steady local clientele, a sure sign of good food at reasonable prices.

Rob's Goodtime Grill (formerly Kay's) is one of Lihue's only "neighborhood bars" where you can watch sports on a big-screen TV, hobnob with the locals, sing your heart out when the karaoke fires up, and have a reasonable meal. It's located in the Rice Shopping Center, open daily 10 a.m.-2 a.m., with takeout orders available 10 a.m.-midnight, tel. 246-0311. The menu begins with zucchini sticks, shrimp cocktail, chef salad, or Pacific catch salad (seafood, crabmeat, and jumbo shrimp) priced $5-6.75. Sandwiches include pastrami and Swiss for $5.50, vegie for $5.25, and burgers for under $6. Entrees include a mahi platter or stir-fry for $6.75, with a "special" offered daily. The interior is a mixture of booths, table, and bar seating, and the service and atmosphere are friendly. (See "Entertainment" below for karaoke).

Hanamaulu Dining

In Hanamaulu clearly marked along Rt. 56 is the **Hanamaulu Restaurant and Tea House and Sushi Bar,** where they must be doing something right to have lasted in the same location for over 70 years! Open Tues.-Fri. 10 a.m.-1 p.m. for lunch, Tues.-Sun., 4:30-9 p.m. for dinner, tel. 245-2511, the menu, which includes sushi, *yakiniku,* and a variety of other Japanese and Chinese dishes, is priced right. Ho Tai, the pudgy happy Buddha, greets you as you enter the room shining with parquet flooring and partitioned by shoji screens and hanging plants. Next door and part of the same restaurant is **a sushi bar** with *tatami*-floored rooms that overlook a fishpond and a lovely Japanese garden. In the sushi bar section are sliding screens and an elevated *tatami* section made private by sliding screens. The gardens behind and next door to the restaurant are wonderful, and well worth a stroll.

The Planter's also sits along Rt. 56 in Hanamaulu, tel. 245-1606. The menu is long and varied, but the specialty is *kiawe*-broiled prime rib and steak. Most meals run in the $10-14 range. Open windows let in the breeze, but also the traffic noise along the highway. The bar is open 3:30-10:30 p.m., happy hour until 5:30 p.m., and dinner is served daily except Sunday 5-9:30 p.m. In the large green building next door (built 1908) are the post office, a few shops, and the **Big Wheel Donut Shop** for a quick sugar fix.

Hanamaulu Plaza in Hanamaulu is clearly marked along Rt. 56 in a small but practical shopping center featuring a **laundromat** and **Ara's Sakamaya,** open Mon.-Sat. 9 a.m.-7 p.m., Sunday 9 a.m.-5 p.m., tel. 245-1707. It is a takeout deli-restaurant that offers plate lunches, Japanese *bento* boxed lunches, and **fresh fish** daily.

Across the street are a **7-Eleven** and a **Shell gas station.**

Fine Dining

The rear flagstone veranda and original dining room at Kilohana, the restored 1935 plantation estate of Gaylord Wilcox, have been turned into the breezy **Gaylord's at Kilohana,** at 3-2087 Kaumualii Hwy., Lihue, tel. 245-9593, open daily for lunch 11 a.m.-3:30 p.m., Sunday brunch 9:30 a.m.-3 p.m., and dinner from 5 p.m. daily; reservations recommended. Visiting the vintage estate is a must, and if you don't fancy a full meal, go for *pu pu,* served daily 3:30 p.m. until closing. Choose items like fresh shrimp cocktail at $7.95, baked Brie in phyllo $7.95, *lumpia* (an island favorite similar to plump spring rolls, stuffed with chicken and coconut milk) $4.95, or good old-fashioned American onion rings for $4.95. Lunch starts with salads like smoked tuna Caesar, shrimp Louie, or Kilohana fruit platter, all around $9. The sandwich board brings shrimp avocado, turkey, beef and Brie, or hot teriyaki chicken, priced $7.95-9.95, and a grilled cheese or peanut butter sandwich for the children for $3.95. Enjoy a light supper, 5-6:30 p.m., of smoked chicken breast or fresh island fish $15.95-18. The dinner menu begins with appetizers like escargot, blackened prawns, or sashimi priced $4.95-8.95. Dinner entrees include marinated New York steak, veal chops, smoked chicken breast, Alaskan king crab, and Peking duck, and range in price $19.95-22.95. Gaylord's famous baby-back ribs garnished with crisp onion rings are a reasonable $16.95. For dessert choose fabulous Kilohana mud pie, rich cheesecake, or raspberry decadence cake, all guaranteed to please. Finish your meal with a cappuccino or coffee mocha prepared with a century-old espresso machine, resplendent in its battered yet burnished glory. Gaylord's prides itself on having one of the largest wine collections on Kauai, featuring over 200 wines from around the world representing more than two dozen varietals. Sunday brunch, basically a la carte, features the hearty Plantation Breakfast, cheese blintzes, French toast, Gaylord's eggs Benedict, and Gaylord's waffle topped with real maple syrup or the special topping of the day. Breakfast meats served with all types of eggs and omelettes include ham, bacon, Portuguese sausage, and even spring ham. Prices for a complete brunch are $10.95-14.95, and include a fresh baked sweet roll, potatoes, and a dessert from the pastry chef. If you want to move away from the breakfast menu, try the a special Sunday pasta, bagels and lox, teriyaki chicken, or even a hamburger. (For a complete description of the home, see previous "Kilohana Plantation" under "Other Sights" earlier in this chapter).

The heady aroma of sauteéd garlic, mixed with the sweet scents of oregano and rosemary floats from the kitchens of **Cafe Portefino,** to be caught and spread like a tempting balm by the soft breezes over Nawiliwili. This authentic Italian restaurant, owned and operated by Giuseppi Avocadi, is located on the second level of the Pacific Ocean Plaza, tel. 245-2121, and is open for lunch Mon.-Fri. 11 a.m.-2 p.m., nightly for dinner 5-10 p.m. Sliding wooden doors open to the distinctive wooden bar, a bold statement of high chic, topped with pink and black marble and surrounded by marble-topped tables and floral upholstered captain's chairs. The open-beamed wooden ceiling is dotted with fancy fans and track lighting, with a baby spot illuminating a coal-black piano. The main dining room, encased by beveled glass windows, contains formally set gray-on-pink tables counterpointed by a black-and-white tiled floor. Flowers and ferns add island color, and an outdoor veranda is perfect for a romantic evening. The dinner menu begins with antipasto Portefino for $6.75, or steamed clams, calamari friti, or escargot for $7.75. Salads include the house salad for $3.75 or *ensalate de patate,* a warm potato salad with bacon strips for $4.75. Soups of the day like minestrone Portefino are priced at $4.25. Tempting Italian entrees are spaghetti marinara at $12.50, fettuccine Cafe Portefino (noodles sauteéd in tomato, mushroom, garlic, butter, oregano, and cheese sauce) for $13.75, and specialties of the house like scampi with fettuccine for $17.75, or eggplant parmigiana at $13.75. Fresh fish, broiled, baked, or sauteéd, is served with fresh homemade condiments, daily quote, while chicken dishes, from cacciatore to *al forno,* are priced around $12.50. There is a full wine list, and desserts are complemented by a cup of coffee or cappuccino from the full espresso bar. The lunch menu is smaller, both in portion size and price, with most offerings under $10. Cafe Portofino is an excellent choice for an evening of romance and fine dining. *Bon appetito!*

Farmers' Market

If you're making your own meals while visiting Kauai, remember that locally grown fresh fruit and vegetables are available from vendors at the farmers' market every Friday at 3 p.m. at Vidinha Stadium in Lihue.

ENTERTAINMENT

Lihue is not the entertainment capital of the world, but if you have the itch to step out at night, there are a few places where you can scratch it.

Legends, tel. 249-0491, on the second floor of Nawiliwili's Pacific Ocean Plaza swings with dancing and live music Tues.-Sat. 8 p.m.-2 a.m. The spacious interior is chic with pink and black tile, brass rails for those who came to pose, high-backed stools on which to perch, and plenty of ceiling fans to cool you off in case you begin to sizzle uncontrollably. Thursday is special with well drinks and draft beer for $1 until midnight, and Tuesday and Wednesday offer classic rock 'n' roll by *A Triple Threat.* The reasonable dress code prohibits tank tops and thongs. No other rules apply except to have a good time.

The **Outrigger Kauai Beach Hotel** has dancing and entertainment at **Gilligan's.** Weekends are popular here with locals from Lihue and Kapa'a who are looking for a night out on the town. The music seems to get louder as the night wears on, and the dance floor is seldom empty. Open Sun.-Thurs. 8 p.m.-2 a.m., Friday and Saturday 8 p.m.-4 a.m. Dress code.

If you desire slower dancing and quieter music, find your way to the **Lihue Neighborhood Center,** tel. 822-4836, any Friday evening 7:30-9:30 p.m. for down-home square dancing. A $1 donation is asked for at the door. Records provide the music, and a caller helps even the novice become proficient by the end of the evening.

Sometimes the **Kukui Grove Shopping Center** presents free entertainment, usually of a Hawaiian nature. The schedule varies but these shows mainly occur on weekends. Check the free tourist literature to see if anything's going on—they're worth the effort.

Enjoy a night of shared karaoke fun at **Rob's Goodtime Grill** (formerly Kay's Pub), open Mon.-Sat. 10 a.m.-1 a.m. in the Rice Shopping Center. The would-be crooner is given the microphone and sings along with the music, the video and words to which are projected on a screen in the corner. A funky, dark little place with booths and Formica tables, it's become a local hangout. Even if your own mom asked you to stop singing in the shower, join in the fun. Everyone gets applause, and beer and drinks are reasonably priced (see also "Food" above).

If you're lucky, you can "strike out" at the **Lihue Lanes Bowling Alley,** in the Rice Shopping Center, 4303 Rice St., tel. 245-5263, open daily 9 a.m.-11 p.m.

Hap's Hideaway Tavern is a friendly neighborhood bar where you can have a quiet beer. The address is 2975 Ewalu St., tel. 245-3473, and although you'll see the sign on Rice Street, you have to go around back to enter.

Other possibilities for evening entertainment are the nightly luau and torch-lighting ceremony at the Outrigger Kauai Beach Hotel.

THEATER

For 20 years the **Kauai Community Players** has presented the island with virtually its only theatrical performances. Four times a year, November, February, April, and July, this nonprofessional, community theater group puts on well-known and experimental plays, usually in the Lihue Parish Hall across Nawiliwili Road from the Kukui Grove Shopping Center. Curtain time is 8 p.m., and ticket prices are $7 adults, $5 students and senior citizens—a dollar less with advance purchase. For information on what's currently showing call 822-7797.

SHOPPING

Lihue makes you reach for your wallet, with good cause. A stroll through one of its four shopping centers (see "Shopping" in the Kauai Introduction) is guaranteed to send you home with more in your luggage than you came with. Kauai's best selections and bargains are found here. It helps that Lihue is a *resort* town, second to being a *living* town. Kauaians shop in Lihue, and the reasonable prices that local purchasing generates are passed on to you.

Shopping Centers

The **Rice Shopping Center,** at 4303 Rice St., tel 245-2033, has a laundromat, bowling alley, inexpensive eateries, health food store, pet center, and karaoke bar.

The Lihue Shopping Center, in downtown Lihue along Rt. 56, features **Gem,** a large discount store filled with everything from sporting goods to aloha wear, and the **Big Save Supermarket,** open daily 7 a.m.-11 p.m.

The **Kukui Grove Shopping Center,** tel. 245-7784, along Rt. 50 a few minutes west of Lihue, is Kauai's largest shopping mall. The center's main stores include: **Liberty House** for general merchandise and apparel; **Longs Drugs and Woolworth** for sundries, sporting goods, medicines, and photo needs; **Sears Roebuck and JCPenney** major department stores; **Footlocker, Kinney's Shoes, and Thom McAn** where you can dress your tootsies; and **Waldenbooks,** a first-class complete bookstore. Distinctive boutiques and shops at the mall include: **Alexandra Christian,** for racks of ladies' high fashion including cocktail dresses and evening gowns; **Deja Vu,** primarily a children's boutique with all the latest in name-brand clothing; **Runway 7,** a bargain store filled with T-shirts, women's and men's resortwear, sun hats, jewelry, and shorts; **Shades of California** will protect your eyes with a large assortment of sunglasses; and **Zale's and Prestige Jewelers** for fine jewelry. To pick up classic, contemporary or island tunes head for **J.R. Music Shop,** and for anything electrical that beeps or buzzes head for **Radio Shack.** Other shops include: **Pictures Plus** for island prints and custom framing; **Rave,** another store for the younger set with dresses, bikinis, and alohawear; **Kauai Beach Co.,** a great shop for T-shirts and distinctive men's and women's fashions; **Dan's Sports Shop** for golf clubs, tennis rackets, baseball caps, mitts, dartboards, and water gear (see "Bicycles" under "Alternatives" in the "Getting Around" section of the Kauai Introduction); **General Nutrition Center** for the health-conscious; and finally the **Indo Pacific Trading Co.,** the most intriguing store in the mall (see "Arts, Crafts, and Souvenirs" following).

Note: For more details of specific shops in the centers see "Food" or "Entertainment," above, and "Clothing and Specialty Shops," below. Also refer to "Supermarkets" and "Health Food Stores" under "Shopping" in the Kauai Introduction.

Clothing Specialty Shops

Don't pass up **Hilo Hatties,** an alohawear institution, to at least educate yourself on products and prices. Though their designs may not be one of a kind, their clothing is very serviceable and well made. Specials are always offered in the free tourist literature, along with clearance racks at the store itself. They also have a selection of gifts and souvenirs. Among the plenty of incentives to get you in are the free hotel pick-up from Poipu to Kapa'a, a tour of the factory, free refreshments while you look around, and free on-the-spot alterations. Look for them at 3252 Kuhio Hwy., at the intersection of Rt. 57. Open every day 8:30 a.m.-5 p.m., tel. 245-3404.

Kapaia Stitchery is where you can find handmade and distinctive fashions. This shop is along Rt. 56 in Kapaia, a tiny village between Hanamaulu and Lihue. The owner is Julie Yukimura, who, along with her grandmother and a number of very experienced island seamstresses, creates fashions, quilts, and embroideries that are beautiful, painstakingly made, and priced right. You can choose a garment off the rack or have one tailor-made from the Stitchery's wide selection of cotton fabrics. You can't help being pleased with this fine shop!

Clothing at discount prices is found at **Garment Factory to You** in the Lihue Shopping Center. This store is as practical as its name.

Bamboo Lace, in the **Pacific Ocean Plaza** at 3501 Rice St., tel. 245-6007, almost in Nawiliwili, offers dresses, blouses, hats, jewelry, and a smattering of alohawear.

Arts, Crafts, And Souvenirs

Kahn Galleries specializes in original artworks and limited-edition prints created by some of the finest artists Hawaii has to offer. The Kahn Galleries, open daily 9 a.m.-5 p.m., are located in the Anchor Cove Shopping Center, 3416 Rice St., tel. 245-5397, and at the Kilohana Plantation, just west of Lihue, tel. 246-4454. (For details see "Specialty Shops, Arts, and Boutiques" under "Shopping" in the Kauai Introduction).

If you're after a shopping basket filled with trinkets and gimcracks for family and friends back home, go to **Gem** in Lihue, or **Longs Drugs** in the Kukui Grove Shopping Center. Their bargain counters are loaded with terrific junk for a buck or two.

Indo Pacific Trading Co. at the Kukui Grove Center, tel. 246-2177, is a distinctive boutique selling artifacts, incense, local island perfumes, and cotton and rayon clothing mostly from Indonesia and Thailand. Artworks include sculpted ducks, fish, and a beautiful collection of Balinese masks. Richly embroidered Burmese tapestries, baskets, hammocks, and wind chimes imported from Java, Sumatra, and other parts of Oceania hang on the walls. Amazing pieces of furniture including handcarved teak chests, a beveled intricately etched glass mirror, a Balinese temple door, prancing horses, and bentback chairs, are also on display. Part of the shop is an **espresso bar** serving coffees, pastries, and light vegie-oriented lunches.

For better-quality souvenirs, along with custom jewelry, try **Linda's Creations** at 4254 Rice Street. This shop, owned and operated by Joe and Linda Vito, is well stocked with items ranging from silk wallets for $2 to lovely vases for over $100.

Kauai Museum Shop at the Kauai Museum has authentic souvenirs and items Hawaiian at competitive prices.

The Gift Gallery, at the Pacific Ocean Plaza at 3501 Rice St. near Nawiliwili Harbor, open Tues.-Sat. 10 a.m.-9 p.m., is filled with stuffed animals, koa woodwork, tile whales, decorative exotic birds, mugs, wind chimes, serving platters, glasswork, and a good collection of postcards.

Longi's Crackseed Center, in the Rice Shopping Center, open Mon.-Fri. 8:30 a.m.-9 p.m., Saturday 8:30 a.m.-4:30 p.m., Sunday 10 a.m.-4 p.m., is packed with large glass jars filled with crackseed, preserved and spiced fruits, seeds, and nuts.

Photo Needs

For a full-line photo store go to **Don's Camera Center,** 4286 Rice St., tel. 245-6581. Find all you'll need in their wide selection of famous brands, camera repair, and one-day processing. **Longs Drugs, Woolworth,** and **Kauai 1-hour Photo** at the Kukui Grove Shopping Center have inexpensive film and processing. **Cameralab** near McDonald's on the Kuhio Hwy. develops film in one hour, and **Senda Studio** at 4450 Hardy St. is a studio and supply shop.

KEITH PERKINS

WAILUA

Wailua ("Two Waters") is heralded by the swaying fronds of extra tall royal palms, and whenever you see these, like the *kahili* of old, you know you're entering a special place. The Hawaiian *ali'i* knew a choice piece of land when they saw one, and they cultivated this prime area at the mouth of the Wailua River as their own. Through the centuries they built many *heiau* in the area, some where unfortunates were slaughtered to appease the gods, others where the weak and vanquished could find succor and sanctuary. The road leading inland along the Wailua River was called the King's Highway. Commoners were confined to traveling along this road and could approach the royal settlement by invitation only. The most exalted of the island's *ali'i* traced their proud lineage to Puna, a Tahitian priest who, according to the oral tradition, arrived in the earliest migrations and settled here.

Even before the Polynesians came, the area was purportedly settled by the semimythical Mu. This lost tribe may have been early Polynesians who were isolated for such a long time that they developed physical characteristics different from those of their ancestral stock. Or perhaps they were a unique people altogether, whom history never recorded. But like another island group, the Menehune, they were dwarfish creatures who shunned outsiders. Unlike the industrious Menehune, who helped the Polynesians, the Mu were fierce and brutal savages whose misanthropic characters confined them to solitary caves in the deep interior along the Wailua River, where they led unsuspecting victims to their deaths.

Wailua today has a population of over 1,500, but you'd never know it driving past, as most houses are scattered in the hills behind the coast. Though an older resort area, it's not at all overdeveloped. The natural charm is as vibrant as ever. Depending on conditions, the beaches can be excellent, and shops, restaurants, and nightlife are close at hand. With development increasing both to the east and west, perhaps now, as in days of old, the outstanding beauty of Wailua will beckon once again.

SIGHTS

Wailua is primarily famous because of two attractions, one natural, the other manmade. People flock to these, but there also exists, in the hills behind the settlement along the King's Highway deserted *heiau,* sacred birthing stones, old cemeteries, and meditative views of the river below.

Fern Grotto

Nature's attraction is the Wailua River itself, Hawaii's only navigable stream, which meanders inland toward its headwaters atop forbidding Mt. Waialeale. Along this route is the **Fern Grotto,** a tourist institution of glitz, hype, and beauty rolled into one. Two local companies run sightseeing trips to the grotto on large motorized barges. As you head the two miles upriver, the crew tells legends of the area and serenades visitors with Hawaiian songs. You are encouraged to get up and swing along with the hula demonstration. The grotto is a huge rock amphitheater, whose ever-misty walls create the perfect conditions for ferns to grow. And grow they do, wildly and with abandon, filling the cavern with their deep musty smell and penetrating green beauty. Partially denuded of its lush green coat by Hurricane Iniki, the grotto is slowly filling in and becoming the beauty it once was. It's smaller than you might imagine; the resonating acoustics are wonderful from inside the grotto. Musicians break into the Hawaiian Wedding Song in this natural cathedral, where over the years a steady stream of brides and grooms have come to exchange vows. The Fern Grotto trip is an amusement ride, but it's also the only way to get there. It's enjoyable and memorable if you stay in the right frame of mind; otherwise it's easily put down. For tour information see "Sightseeing Tours" under "Getting There" in the Kauai Introduction.

Smith's Tropical Paradise

Set along the Wailua River is this 30-acre botanical and cultural garden. A large entranceway welcomes you, and proclaims it a "tropical paradise." Most plants are labeled; many are ordinary island foliage, others are rare and exotic even for the Garden Island. The entire area is sheltered and well watered, and it's easy to imagine how idyllic life was for the original Hawaiians. The buildings include a luau house and lagoon theater used in the evenings for an international musical show and luau. Peacocks and chickens pecking beneath the trees are natural groundskeepers, preventing insects and weeds from overpowering the gardens. The "villages"—Japanese-, Filipino-, and Polynesian-inspired settlements—are plywood facsimiles. However, the grounds themselves are beautifully kept and very impressive. For those who won't be trekking into the Kauai backcountry, but especially for those who will, this garden provides an excellent opportunity to familiarize yourself with Kauai's plants, flowers, and trees. You are welcome to walk where you will, but signs guide you down a recommended walk. Scheduled mini-trams carry tourists around the grounds for an additional fee. Entrance fees are $5 adults, $2.50 children ages 2-11; the tram tour is an additional $3 for adults, $2 for children. The entrance fee is good 8:30 a.m.-4:30 p.m., after which the gardens are readied for the evening entertainment. The luau/musical show costs $43.75 for adults, $26 children ages 2-11, and $10.50 and $5.25 respectively for the show only. Reservations are necessary for both. Rated the favorite luau show on the island, the spectacle features Hawaiian music, a fiery volcanic eruption, and dances from all over the Pacific. For information call 822-4654, 822-9599, or 822-3467, or pick up tickets at Smith's booth across from the entrance to the Coco Palms on the north side of the rivermouth. To get to the gardens, follow the road past the Wailua Marina on the south side of the river and park in the large lot.

Historical Sites And *Heiau*

The King's Highway (Rt. 580) running inland from Wailua, and Rt. 56, the main drag, have a number of roadside attractions and historical sites dating from the precontact period. Most are just a short stroll away from your car and well worth the easy effort. The mountains behind Wailua form a natural sculpture of a giant in repose, aptly called **The Sleeping Giant.** You have to stretch your imagination a little to see him (his outline is clearer from farther up, toward Kapa'a), and although not entirely a bore, like most giants, he's better left asleep. This giant and his green cover are part of the Nounou Forest Reserve.

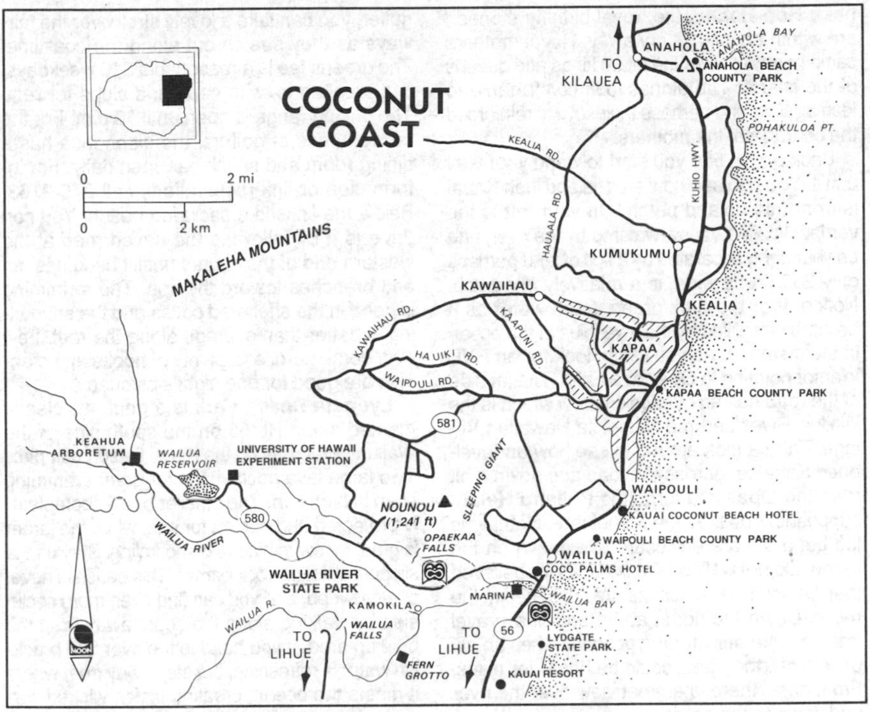

Along Rt. 56 just before the Coco Palms, a tall stand of palms on the east side of the Wailua River is part of Lydgate State Park, and marks **Hauola O' Honaunau,** a temple of refuge that welcomed offending *kapu*-breakers of all social classes. Here miscreants could atone for their transgressions and have their spiritual slates wiped clean by the temple priests, enabling them to return to society without paying with their lives. Both the refuge and **Hikina Heiau** are marked by a low encircling wall. The area is extremely picturesque here, where the Wailua River meets the sea. Perhaps it's knowledge about the temple of refuge that creates the atmosphere, but here, as at all of these merciful temple sites, the atmosphere is calm and uplifting, as if some spiritual residue has permeated the centuries. It's a good spot to relax in the cool of the grove, and picnic tables are available.

As Rt. 580 meanders inland, you pass **Wailua River State Park.** Immediately look for **Poaiahu Arboretum** and its convenient turnout. The arboretum is merely a stand of trees along the roadside. Across the road is **Holo Holo Ku Heiau,** where the unfortunate ones who didn't make it to the temple of refuge were sacrificed to the never-satisfied gods. This temple is one of Kauai's most ancient; the altar is the large slab of rock near the southwest corner. Behind the *heiau,* a silver guard rail leads up the hill to a small, neatly tended Japanese cemetery. The traditional tombstones chronicling the lives and deaths of those buried here turn green with lichens against the pale blue sky. As if to represent the universality of the life-death cycle, **Po-**

haku Hoo Hanau, the "royal birthing stones," are within an infant's cry away. Royal mothers came here to deliver the future kings and queens of the island. The stones look comfortable to lean against and perhaps their solidity reinforced the courage of the mothers.

Back on Rt. 580 you start to wend your way uphill. You can see how eroded and lush Kauai is from this upland perch. On your left is the verdant Wailua Valley, watered by the river, and on your right, separated by a spit of land perhaps only 200 yards wide, is a relatively dry gulch. Notice, too, the dark green, fresh water as it becomes engulfed by the royal blue of the ocean in the distance. As you climb, look for an HVB Warrior pointing to **Opaeka'a Falls.** The far side of the road has an overlook, below which is the Wailua River and the Kamokila Hawaiian Village. Take a look around to see how undeveloped Kauai is. Across the road and down a bit from the Opaeka'a turnoff is **Poliahu Heiau,** supposedly built by the Menehune. Nothing is left but a square enclosure overgrown on the inside. Do not walk on the walls, as it's believed that the spirits of ancestors are contained in the rocks. Down the ridge, at the end of a gravel track, are the **bell stones;** pounded when an *ali'i* gave birth, their peal could be heard for miles. From here, there is a great view over the river and down to the coast.

Beaches, Parks, And Recreation

Wailua has few beaches, but they're excellent. **Wailua Municipal Golf Course** skirts the coast, fronting a secluded beach, and because of its idyllic setting is perhaps the most beautiful public links in Hawaii. Even if you're not an avid golfer, you can take a lovely stroll over the fairways as they stretch out along the coastline. The greens fee is a reasonable $10 weekdays, $11 weekends, with carts and clubs for rent. The driving range is open until 10 p.m. For the convenience of golfers, the clubhouse has a dining room and snack bar open daily. For information or link reservations call 245-2163. Below the links is a secluded beach. You can drive to it by following the paved road at the western end of the course until it becomes dirt and branches toward the sea. The swimming is good in the sheltered coves and the snorkeling is better than average along the reef. Few ever come here, and plenty of nooks and crannies are good for one night's bivouac.

Lydgate Beach Park is a gem. It's clearly marked along Rt. 56 on the south side of the Wailua River, behind the Kauai Resort complex. Two large lava pools make for great swimming even in high surf. The smaller pool is completely protected and perfect for tots, while the larger is great for swimming and snorkeling. Stay off the slippery volcanic rock barrier. This beach is never overcrowded, and you can find even more seclusion by walking along the coast away from the built-up area. If you head to the river, the brackish water is refreshing, but stay away from where it meets the ocean, creating tricky, wicked currents. **Lydgate State Park** also provides sheltered picnic tables under a cool canopy provided by a thick stand of ironwoods, plus grills, restrooms, and showers, but no camping.

The beach across the river fronting the Coco Palms is treacherous and should only be entered on calm days when lifeguards are in attendance.

ACCOMMODATIONS AND FOOD

ACCOMMODATIONS

The hotel scene in Wailua is like the beaches, few but good. Your choices are the famous Coco Palms or the Kauai Resort, with its admirable location fronting Lydgate State Park.

The **Kauai Resort,** at 3-5920 Kuhio Hwy., Kapa'a, HI 96746, reservations Hawaiian Pacific Resorts, tel. 245-3931 or (800) 367-5004, has a lovely setting above Lydgate State Park, with the Hauola Temple of Refuge adjacent to the grounds. Incorporated into the architecture are a series of cascading pools and a koi pond that boils with frenzied color during feeding time. The main lobby is a huge affair with swooping beams in longhouse style. Enjoy a Polynesian revue five nights a week, or a luau. The hotel buffet receives the ultimate compliment of high attendance by local people. The hotel is one of the best places on Kauai for name entertainment—Mainland performers such as Jesse Colin Young, and Hawaii's own, like the Peter Moon Band. Every night except Monday, the lobby lounge features music—often jazz—by local artists; a good place to people-watch and wind down after a hard day. Rooms are well decorated and most have ocean views. Rates are $79 standard, $109 deluxe oceanfront, and $89 for cabanas with kitchenettes, which are separate from the main facility with unobstructed views of the beach.

A unique alternative for lodging is at the **Fern Grotto Inn,** a bed and breakfast surrounded by Wailua River State Park. This plantation home on the Wailua River offers three tastefully furnished bedrooms with private baths, gourmet breakfast especially tailored for the health-conscious traveler, and a private garden, perfect for an evening stroll. Rates range $80-100 per night, or the entire home can be rented for $1250 per week. For information contact the Fern Grotto Inn at 4561 Kuamoo Rd., Wailua, HI 96746, tel. 822-2560, or 521-5521 on Oahu.

The **Coco Palms Resort,** tel. 823-0760 or (800) 338-1338, is a classic Hawaiian hotel, one of the first tourist destinations built on the island, but it took a terrible beating during Hurricane Iniki. Promising to reopen soon, the Polynesian-inspired buildings are interspersed amidst a monumental coconut grove planted by a German immigrant in the early 1800s. His aspiration was to start a copra plantation, and although it failed, his plantings matured into one of the largest stands of coconut trees in the islands. Nightly, the hostelry's famous torch-lighting ceremony takes place under the palm canopy that encircles a royal lagoon, once used to fatten succulent fish for the exclusive use of the *ali'i.* Everyone is welcome to the ceremony, hotel guest or not, and you should definitely go if you're in the area around sundown. The Lagoon Terrace Lounge, with soft evening entertainment, and the Lagoon Dining Room have superb front-row seats. Some may put the performance down as "fake traditional," but it's the *best* fake traditional on the island, both dramatic and fun. It was started by the recently-retired Grace Guslander, the congenial hostess famous for her cocktail parties.

The hotel grounds are inspiring, and often when Hollywood needed "paradise" they came here. Parts of past movie sets still remain. Notice the authentic-looking cement palm trees used to accent the construction of some of the buildings. There's a small zoo, museum, and a chapel built by Columbia Pictures for Rita Hayworth in the movie *Sadie Thompson.* More than 2,000 marriages have been performed in this chapel since, and not all to Zsa Zsa Gabor and Liz Taylor! When Tattoo informs Mr. Rourk about "De plane, boss," in the popular TV series "Fantasy Island," it is into the Coco Palms grove that he drives the jeep. Elvis came here to film *Blue Hawaii,* and segments of *South Pacific* were shot on the grounds. Frank Sinatra found out who the "chairman of the board" really was when one day he was swept out to sea from a nearby beach. "Old Blue Eyes" used his velvet voice to scream for help and was rescued by local men from the fire department using a surfboard. After the rescue, Sinatra discovered that they had no boat; showing the class he's famous for, he bought them a spanking new Chris-Craft.

The hotel bought the beach house known as the "Sinatra House" and rented it out. Sinatra was later upstaged when John Kennedy visited a number of times, and the house was renamed the "President's House." The hotel divested itself of this property recently. As soon as you walk onto the Coco Palms' grounds you feel romantic. You can't help it. No one's immune; the Coco Palms is a peaceful garden. Let it surround you.

FOOD

Part of the pattern, the food scene is akin to Wailua's accommodations and beaches: not a smorgasbord to choose from, but a good range of prices and cuisine.

Inexpensive

Two ethnic restaurants with good food at decent prices are both located behind the Sizzler Steakhouse at 4361 Kuhio Highway. **Mema Thai Cuisine,** tel. 823-0891, open for dinner 5-9:30 p.m., is upscale, even gooey-romantic. Pink tablecloths on glass-topped tables, bent-back black bamboo chairs, and welcoming sculptures of Thai goddesses and a reclining Buddha in a small temple nook set the mood. The menu is classic Thai with most dishes under $10.

Next door is the pick-and-choose, steam-table style **Manila Fastfood Restaurant,** tel. 823-0521, serving breakfast 7 a.m.-9:30 a.m., lunch 10 a.m.-3 p.m., and dinner 4-7 p.m. A mixture of Filipino and American dishes is served for around $5.

Wah Kung Chop Suey is in the Kinipopo Shopping Village just across from the Sizzler Steakhouse, open daily 11 a.m.-8:30 p.m., tel. 822-0560. The clean, no-decor restaurant offers Chinese and local food. Lunch specials from 11 a.m.-2 p.m. can be kung pao chicken with vegetables, rice or noodles, beef broccoli, fried chicken, lemon chicken, or egg foo young, all for around $5. Soups made from scallops, abalone, and pork are $4.50-5.50. Standards like chop suey and chow mein are under $6, while shrimp, scallops, and mahimahi is the most expensive dish for $7.50. Wah Kung has a good reputation with local people, so they must be doing something right.

Moderate

The **Wailua Marina Restaurant,** tel. 822-4311, overlooking the Wailua River, offers inexpensive to moderately priced "local-style" food, and free hotel pick-up in the Wailua area for dinner. If you're going on a Fern Grotto boat trip, consider eating here. Breakfast, 8:30-11 a.m., is under $3; lunches, until 2 p.m., are plates like a small tenderloin, fries, and a tossed green salad for $6.25; dinner, 5-9 p.m., features entrees like Korean barbecued ribs or breaded veal cutlets in mushroom sauce for under $9. It's convenient, and there's never a wait after the last boat upriver.

Perhaps the best moderately priced meals in Wailua are the buffets at the **Pacific Dining Room** in the Kauai Resort. Generally, buffets are ho-hum, but the Saturday night prime rib buffet ($13.25) or the seafood extravaganza every Sunday, Tuesday, and Friday ($18.50) are terrific, with as many local people as hotel guests. The seafood includes the catch-of-the-day, steamed shrimp, crab, clams, oysters, and sushi, plus fried chicken and roast beef along with tables laden with salads and desserts. Dinner is served 6-8:30 p.m. For reservations call 245-3931. The Kauai Resort also features a luau every night except Monday and Friday, beginning with an *imu* ceremony at 6 p.m. Even with plenty of food, lei greeting, and Polynesian show, somehow this luau isn't quite as good as the buffet, especially since it costs almost double at $38. The Kauai Resort provides free shuttle service to most area hotels. Reservations are suggested.

The **Seashell Restaurant,** part of the Coco Palms Resort (scheduled reopening spring 1995), has long been a favorite with visitors and residents. Well-prepared island fish entrees and a salad bar are offered.

A more romantic setting is the open-air **Lagoon Dining Room,** also opening soon, the Coco Palms' main restaurant. The menu is average, the service friendly, and the setting exceptional—overlooking the hotel's lagoon, long famous as the setting for the nightly torch-lighting ceremony.

Some will be happy and others sad to hear that the aroma of fast food wafts on the breezes of Wailua. Just past the venerable Coco Palms is **The Sizzler Steakhouse,** at 4361 Kuhio Hwy., tel. 822-7404, open Fri.-Sat. 6 a.m.-11 p.m., Sun.-Thurs. 6 a.m.-10 p.m., serving breakfast and the familiar steaks, burgers, and salad bar, in this better than average fast-food environment.

Expensive

The Japanese legend of Kintaro, a pint-sized boy born to an old couple from inside a peach pit, is slightly less miraculous than this excellent and authentic Japanese restaurant owned and operated by a Korean gentleman, Don Kim. From the outside **Restaurant Kintaro** is nothing special, but inside it is transformed into the simple and subtle beauty of Japan. The true spirit of Japanese cooking is presented, with the food as pleasing to the eye as to the palate. The sushi bar alone, taking up an entire wall, is worth stopping in for. The dinners are expertly and authentically prepared, equaling those served in fine restaurants in Japan. If you have never sampled Japanese food before, Restaurant Kintaro is the best place to start. Those accustomed to the cuisine can choose from favorites like tempura, sukiyaki, a variety of *soba,* and the old standby, teriyaki. Open nightly for dinner only, 5:30-9:30 p.m., along Rt. 56 just past the Coco Palms. Reservations often necessary; call 822-3341.

SHOPPING

The **Kinipopo Shopping Village,** a diminutive mall, seaside at 4-356 Kuhio Hwy., across from Sizzler Steakhouse, offers most of Wailua's one-stop shopping. Here you can find **The Goldsmith's Gallery,** tel. 822-4653, open Mon.-Sat. 9:30 a.m.-5:30 p.m., Friday until 7 p.m., a store shimmering with brilliant jewelry. Five jewelers make the individual pieces, and for their artistry were awarded the 1992 "Jewel Designers of the Year" title for the State of Hawaii. Diamonds, gold, and Australian opals add brilliance (and a hefty price tag) to the artwork. Much of the jewelry is commissioned, but there is plenty on display to choose from. One of their distinctive lines with an island motif features pieces shaped like flowers, clamshells, sailfish, petroglyphs, birds, and tropical fish, fashioned into bracelets, earrings, brooches, and charms.

Kauai Water Ski and Surf, tel. 822-3574, open daily 9 a.m.-7 p.m., also in the Kinipopo Shopping Village, is a complete water sports shop. Bathing suits, bikinis, sun visors, men's shorts, surfboards, boogie boards, wetsuits, fins, masks, snorkels, underwater watches, and a few backpacks and daypacks line the shelves of this small but jam-packed shop. Rentals include: water-skiing, complete with boat, professional driver, all equipment, and instructions for beginners to advanced for $85 per hour; kayaks, $25 per day single, $50 per day double; snorkel gear, $5 per day, $20 per week; boogie boards, $5 per day, $20 per week; and surfboards, $10 per day, $30 per week.

Bachman's, also in the Kinipopo Shopping Village, handles clothes, shells, and gift items. **A Unique Emporium,** open daily except Monday, 10 a.m.-5 p.m., tel. 823-0455, is a cutesy-pie shop. Dolls, umbrellas, quilts, pillows, some wicker furniture, and a few display cases filled with jewelry make it as sweet as a double-fudge brownie.

Tony's Minit Mart and the **Shell Station Mini-Mart** next door sell sundries, snacks, beer, and packaged foods.

May and Joy of Hawaii, tel. 823-6276, across the street, is a surprisingly neat souvenir stand. Inside you will find cut flowers and lei, and a good selection of touristy "junque" including fine lei fashioned from amethyst and other semiprecious stones.

Almost next door, the **Kinipopo General Store** sells groceries, sundries, and liquors.

D.S. Collections, next to Kintaro's Restaurant, just past the Kinipopo Shopping Village, is a women's fine apparel store, with a smattering of jewelry and some lovely ceramic bowls.

BOB RACE

KAPA'A AND VICINITY

Kapa'a means "fixed" or "crystallized," as in "fixed course." In the old days when the canoes set sail to Oahu, they'd always stop first at Kapa'a to get their bearings, then make a beeline directly across the channel to Oahu. Yachts still do the same today. Kapa'a is a different kind of town, with unusual contrasts. At the south end is **Waipouli** ("Dark Water"), a separate municipality along the main drag, though you'd never know it. Clustered here are newish hotels, condos, a full-service shopping mall, restaurants, nightlife—a "live-in resort" atmosphere. The heart of Kapa'a itself is a workers' settlement, with modest homes, pragmatic shops, down-home eateries, and a funky hotel.

Actually, a few more people live here than in Lihue, and the vibe is a touch more local. There are no sights per se. You spend your time checking out the shops, scanning the color-mottled mountains of the interior, and combing the beaches, especially those to the north, toward Hanalei. Two minutes upcoast you're in wide-open spaces. Cane roads cut from Rt. 56 and rumble along the coast. Small oceanside communities pop up, their residents split between beachhouse vacationers and settled *kama'aina.* What distinguishes Kapa'a is its unpretentiousness. This is "everyday paradise," where the visitor is made to feel welcome and stands in line with everyone else at the supermarket. Generally the weather is cooperative throughout the area, prices on all commodities and services are good, beaches are fair to spectacular, and the pace is unhurried. Kapa'a isn't the choicest vacation spot on the island, but you can have a great time here and save money.

Beaches And Parks

Central Kapa'a's beaches begin at **Waipouli Beach County Park,** fronting the cluster of hotels just north of the Coconut Plantation Market Place, and ending near the royal coconut grove by the Kauai Coconut Beach Hotel. The town interrupts the beach for a while this side of the Waikaea Canal, and then the beach picks up again at **Kapa'a Beach County Park,** running north for almost a mile until it ends near a community swimming pool and the Kapa'a Library. A number of small roads lead from Rt. 56 to the nearby stretch of beach. Kapa'a Beach County Park has just over 15 acres, with a pavilion, picnic tables, showers, toilets, and grills. The beach is pretty to look at, but this section of town is run-down. The feeling here is it *belongs* to the locals, although no undue hassles have been reported.

As soon as you cross the Kapa'a Stream on the north end of town you're in the one-store village of Kealia. Past mile marker 1, look for Ray's Auto Saloon, and turn off onto the cane road. At the junction is **Kealia Beach.** This wide, white strand curves along the coast for a half mile. Not a beach park, so no facilities, but during calm weather the swimming is good, particularly at the north end, and few people come here except local fishermen and surfers.

Continue along the cane road (watch for oncoming trucks) for just over two miles (technically you need a permit issued at the office of the Lihue Sugar Co. in Lihue). As you skirt the coastline, heading for **Pohakuloa Point** and a surfing beach the locals call **Donkey Beach,** the ride is much more picturesque than Rt. 56. Look for a tall stand of ironwoods, a makeshift rutted pulloff, and a wide sandy beach below. A footpath leads down to it. This area is very secluded and good for unofficial camping. Unfortunately, the undertow is severe, especially during rough weather, and only experienced surfers challenge the waves here. You can sunbathe and take dips, but remain in the shallows close to shore. Continue north on the cane road until it intersects Rt. 56 again. Be even more careful of the monolithic cane trucks because a sign here (which everyone ignores) points "One Way" in the *other* direction—and who are you to argue, in a subcompact whose only trace of extreme foolhardiness would be a grease spot in the road?

ACCOMMODATIONS

Inexpensive

Hotel Coral Reef is relatively inexpensive and definitely has character. Toward the north end of Kapa'a between the main road and the beach, this humble hotel has a deluxe view of the bay. Although it closely resembles one, the Coral Reef isn't a fleabag, because it's clean and well tended, and attracts decent clientele. One of the first hotels in the area, this 33-year-old establishment is friendly, homey, and funky, and it has recently been refurbished. The lobby is small, not conducive to relaxing, adorned only by a fish tank and color TV. Rooms in the old wing, with limited views of the ocean, are clean and cheap at $41-46. More modern and brighter, the new wing has an A-plus view of the bay. Large and airy rooms with lanai, sliding glass doors, and refrigerators go for only $67-75. For reservations, write Hotel Coral Reef, 1516 Kuhio Hwy., Kapa'a, HI 96746, or call 822-4481 or (800) 843-4659.

For those visiting the island "who value their personal health, and who seek inner growth and the opening of creative potential," the **Keapana Center,** at 5620 Keapana Rd., Kapa'a, Kauai, HI 96746, tel. 822-9978 or (800) 822-7968, may be the place for you. Gabriela, the owner, is a dance and meditation instructor who has lived on Kauai for over 20 years. An avid hiker and outdoor person, Gabriela is very accommodating in giving tips on hikes and nature trails, and is well-versed on Hawaiian culture, especially the healing arts. In touch with local practitioners, she can make arrangements for instruction or sessions of massage and body work, naturopathic medicine, yoga, tai chi, the twelve-step program, and other healing and wellness programs in this restful but stimulating nonsmoking environment. Guest rooms are very island, very Hawaiian. Floors are covered with sisal matting, and most furniture is bent-back rattan or wicker. Shoji-screen paper lanterns add soft lighting, and beautiful floral displays brighten every room. Beds are covered with batik bedspreads, while Balinese masks, Chinese peasant hats, and hula skirts hang from the walls. The common area, open to the elements, is serene with its own indoor/outdoor garden. The lanai offers sweeping vistas over the lush hillside that descends to the beach only five minutes away. A solar jacuzzi awaits to knead the muscles of intrepid hikers. Rooms with shared/private baths are $35/50 s, $50/65 d, and $300/350 a week. Each morning the continental breakfast includes homemade bread, health-conscious muffins, and unique island fruits like soursop or star fruit that grow on the property and are delightfully unfamiliar to most guests. Bowls of papayas and hands of bananas, all organic and from the property as well, are left in the downstairs area for the guests. There are no actual kitchen facilities, but a refrigerator and microwave are available.

The Royal Drive Cottages, at 147 Royal Dr., Kapa'a, HI 96746, tel. 822-2321, owned and operated by Bob Levine, are nestled in the mountains high above Kapa'a. Very private, the self-contained cottages are complete with kitchenettes, $75 d, with weekly discounts available.

Moderate

Part of the Hawaiian-owned Sand and Seaside Hotels, **Kauai Sands** is a better-than-average budget hotel with a convenient location, spacious grounds, accommodating staff, large relaxing lobby, budget restaurant, two pools, and beach access. Recently renovated, all rooms have two double beds, refrigerator, a/c, ceiling fan, TV, telephone, and lanai. What it lacks in luster it makes up for in price. Daily rates range from $75 for a standard room to $135 for a junior suite. Excellent room and car packages are offered. For reservations, write Sand and Seaside Hotels, 2222 Kalakaua Ave., Suite 714, Honolulu, HI 96815, tel. (800) 367-7000. The hotel is located behind the Coconut Plantation Market Place, at 420 Papaloa Rd., Wailua, HI 96746, tel. 822-4951.

For a better-than-average hotel at moderate prices, you can't go wrong with the **Kauai Beachboy Hotel,** located along the coastline at the Coconut Plantation. Cool and quiet, most rooms surround a central courtyard and pool. All rooms have a shower (no tub), color TV, a small fridge, and a lanai. The decor is pleasant "Hawaiian style"; each unit has a powder room, large closet, and full mirror. The hotel also offers a poolside bar, shuffleboard, volleyball, tennis facilities, and free daily scuba lessons for guests. The hotel's Perry's Smorgy restaurant is an all-you-can-eat place with reasonable prices. Rates for a double are: $78 garden room, $83 superior, and $93 deluxe oceanfront room, $15 each additional person; high-season rates, December 20-March 31, are $10 more. For reservations, contact Kauai Beachboy, 4-484 Kuhio Hwy. #100, Kapa'a, HI 96746, tel. 822-0843 or (800) 367-8047.

Between the Beachboy and Kauai Sands hotels is the **Islander on the Beach Hotel,** a bright white hotel with a front veranda on all levels,

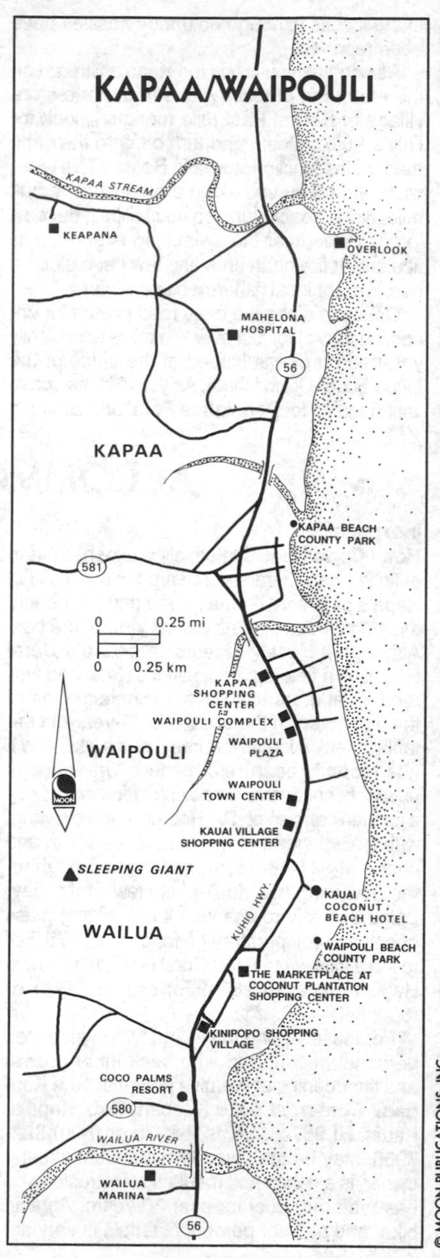

giving it a Southern plantation look. The studio apartments have been changed into hotel rooms each with wet bar, refrigerator, coffeemaker, color TV, and lanai. Set right on the beach, the hotel has a pool, beach activities center, and gift shop. Room rates are $95 for a standard to $185 for an oceanfront suite; add $10 more for high season. Write Islander on the Beach, 484 Kuhio Hwy., Kapa'a, HI 96746, or call 822-7417 or (800) 847-7417.

Kapa'a also has several condos in the moderate price range. The **Kapa'a Shore Condo** is along the main road just north of the Coconut Plantation, at 40-900 Kuhio Hwy., Kapa'a, HI 96746, tel. 822-3055. These one- and two-condo units offer a swimming pool, heated jacuzzi, tennis courts, and maid service on request. All units are bright and cheerful, with a full kitchen and dishwasher. One-bedroom garden-view units accommodate up to four for $110; one-bedroom ocean-view units run $120; and two-bedroom ocean-view units house up to six for $150. For reservations, call Kauai Vacation Rentals, tel. 245-8841 or (800) 367-5025.

Another reasonably priced condominiums in the area is the **Kapa'a Sands,** with pool and maid service. The oldest condo on the island—since 1968—Kapa'a Sands is kept clean and up-to-date. It is situated on old Japanese grounds once the site of a Shinto shrine. The Japanese motif is still reflected in the roofline of the units and the torii design above each door number. Each unit has a full kitchen, ceiling fan in all rooms, and lanai. Two-bedroom units are on two levels, and even the garden units have a limited view of the ocean. Room rates are $75 for garden studios, $85 for oceanfront studios, $99 for two-bedroom garden units, and $109 for two-bedroom oceanfront units. Monthly rates are available; minimum stay is three days, except during winter when it is seven days. For reservations write Kapa'a Sands, 380 Papaloa Rd., Kapa'a, HI 96746, or call 822-4901 or (800) 222-4901.

The **Pono Kai,** at 1250 Kuhio Hwy., Kapa'a, HI 96746, is a step up in class, offering one-bedroom units at $109-135, and two bedrooms at $135-160. All units have a full kitchen, color cable TV, and lanai. For reservations call Kauai Vacation Rentals, tel 245-8841 or (800) 367-5025.

The **Plantation Hale,** at 484 Kuhio Hwy., Kapa'a, HI 96746, tel. 822-4911 or (800) 462-6262, is a condominium that also offers daily rates. It's across the street from Waipouli Beach County Park just beyond the Market Place at Coconut Plantation. Units have only one bedroom; however, each is like a small apartment with full kitchen, bath, dining room, and living area. Rates for up to four people are $105-120.

Expensive

Amidst a huge grove of swaying palms sits the **Kauai Coconut Beach Hotel,** at P.O. Box 830, Coconut Plantation, Kapa'a, HI 96746, tel. 822-3455 or (800) 222-5642. The palm grove once belonged to the family of famous swimmer and actor Buster Crabbe of "Buck Rogers" fame. He and his twin brother, Bud, were born and raised right here, and Buster learned to swim along this very coast. The lobby is alive with trees, flowers, and vines trellised from the balconies. Wicker chairs, stained glass, a huge carpet sculpture, and a 40-foot waterfall add comfort and grandeur. The Voyage Room is an indoor/outdoor restaurant featuring original artwork. Have a drink and listen to nightly entertainment at Cook's Landing, or try the hotel luau, one of the best on the island. (For the hotel's luau and Flying Lobster Restaurant, see "Fine Dining, Luau, and Buffets" under "Food" below.)

Make sure to check out the fine photos hanging along the main hall, and the superb replica of a double-hulled sailing canoe. Also, the charts in the Chart Room that look like those nifty old ragged-edged maps of yore are the real McCoy. The hotel has just undergone a massive sprucing-up. The rooms have new handcarved wooden furniture, textured wallpaper, and remote-control TVs. Each has its own refrigerator, small lanai, and original artwork. Bathrooms and dressing rooms are spacious. The fourth floor offers enormous, high-ceilinged deluxe rooms, and breathtaking views of the coast. Rates are $95 for a standard room to $250 for a VIP suite, which includes a full buffet breakfast.

Colony Resorts manages two deluxe condos in and around the Coconut Plantation. A touch classier than their Plantation Hale is the **Lae Nani,** offering one- and two-bedroom units on the beach. The rich decor varies by unit, but all have a full kitchen, a lanai, ceiling fans, and a bath and a half; most have an ocean view. There are a laundry room, daily maid service, a swimming pool, tennis courts, and barbecue grills on the lawn. A small *heiau* is on the property beachside. One-bedroom units for up to four people are $150-179, and two-bedroom units are $185-205, maximum six persons; rates are $20 cheaper during low season. The condo is at 410 Papaloa Rd., Kapa'a, HI 96746. The **Lanikai** is next door at 390 Papaloa Rd., tel. 822-7456. Here the two-bedroom, two-bath units rent for $200 a day, $20 cheaper during low season. For reservations contact Colony Resorts, 32 Merchant St., Honolulu, HI 96813, tel. 822-4938 or (800) 367-6046.

FOOD

From the Coconut Plantation Market Place to the north edge of Kapa'a, there are dozens of places to eat. The vast majority are either inexpensive diners or mid-priced restaurants, but there is one fine restaurant, several luau and buffets, the ubiquitous fast-food chains, and several bakeries, fruits stands, markets, and grocery stores.

Inexpensive Food In Shopping Malls

Surrounded by hotels and condos is the **Market Place at Coconut Plantation,** the island's larget shopping center. In this huge complex are more than a dozen eateries.

For a quick, cool snack try Lappert's for ice cream, or **Rainbow Frozen Yogurt** for the competition. For quick counter food try **The Fish Hut, Island Chicken,** or **JJ's Dog House.** JJ's has hot dogs for $1.95-2.70, serves beer, and looks onto one of the center's intriguing fountains.

For more substantial food check out: **South of the Border,** a restaurant and cantina, serving steak and Mexican food, that even has live music now and again, especially on weekends; **Pop's Restaurant,** open Mon.-Sat. 5 a.m.-9 p.m., Sunday from 8 a.m, with complete breakfasts for $4.95, *bento* lunches for $4.95, and American standard dinner specials with a Hawaiian twist like roast pork, meatloaf, or chicken in a basket for about $5; **Tradewinds, A South Sea Bar,** open 10 a.m.-2 a.m., serving drinks and food, and offering karaoke nightly; **Taco Dude,** which receives high praise from local people, open for lunch and dinner, serving beef, chicken, or bean tacos for $1.75, tostadas for $2.25, burritos at $3.75-4.75, and taco salad for $4.75. A counter restaurant, they serve fresh food made to order at reasonable prices. Or try the **Banyan Tree Cafe** or **Bella Rosa Pizza.** At **Don's Deli and Picnic Basket** you can get a large sandwich for $2.50-4.50, subs, or a picnic basket for your day on the beach or trip to the north coast. For a cup of fine coffee and baked goods, try the **Cafe Espresso.** For your sweet tooth, step in to see what mouthwatering delicacies the **Rocky Mountain Chocolate Factory** and **Nut Cracker Sweet** shops have to offer.

A short way up the highway, *mauka* from the road, is the **Waipouli Town Center,** marked by **McDonald's** and **Pizza Hut.** Near the yogurt shop is **Waipouli Restaurant,** a cafeteria-style eatery with breakfast specials, Mexican food, seafood, and saimin, open Monday 7 a.m-3 p.m., Tues.-Sun. 7 a.m.-3 p.m. and 5-9 p.m. In the next two little complexes up, the Waipouli Plaza and Waipouli Complex, are four restaurants where you can get good hearty ethnic meals.

The Waipouli Town Center has one of the best moderately priced restaurants on the island, **The King and I,** tel. 822-1642, open daily 4:30-9:30 p.m. This Thai restaurant serves wonderful food that will make your taste buds stand up and be counted. Most dinners are $5-8. Also in the center is the Chinese restaurant **Dragon Inn** that has a well-deserved reputation for filling meals at reasonable prices. The menu is an arm long, and most dinners go for $5-7. Stop in for lunch Tues.-Sat. 11 a.m.-2 p.m. and nightly for dinner 4:30-9:30 p.m.

In the Waipouli Complex is the **Aloha Diner,** tel. 822-3851. Open daily except Sunday 11:30 a.m.-3 p.m. and 5:30-9 p.m., this diner serves Hawaiian food. It offers a la carte selections like *kalua* pig, chicken luau, *lomi* salmon, rice and poi, *haupia,* and *kulolo.* Dinner specials run around $5-6, with full dinners $7.50-9.50. Take-outs are available. There is no atmosphere, the service is slow and friendly, and most people eating here are residents. Next door is the Japanese **Restaurant Shiroma,** which serves Chinese standards as well. The daily lunch and dinner specials include items like shrimp tempura, pork tofu, teriyaki steak, or seafood combo. A money-saving lunch is a huge bowl of *wonton mein* and a side of rice. And you must have a slice of the homemade pineapple or passion fruit chiffon pie for $1. Shiroma's is open Fri.-Sun. 7 a.m.-9 p.m., and Monday, Wednesday, and Thursday 7 a.m.-2 p.m., closed Tuesday.

For inexpensive plate lunches, try the **Barbeque House** in the Kapa'a Shopping Center, open Mon.-Sat. 10:30 a.m.-8 p.m., where most selections are under $5.

Papaya's, a natural food cafe and market at the Kauai Village Shopping Center, 4-831 Kuhio Hwy., open daily except Sunday 10 a.m.-8 p.m., tel. 823-0190, is not only the largest, but best natural food store/cafe on Kauai. From the cafe section (outdoor tables available) come daily specials like vegan baked tofu over brown rice with green salad for $4, a tri-plate with your choice of three salads (one pound) for $6.75, soup du jour $1.95-4.95 depending upon bowl size, and two-fisted sandwiches like vegie with cheese ($4.50), nutty burger ($5.25), or a good old-fashioned tempeh burger for $4.95. Gourmet coffees, herbed teas, and fresh juices are also a specialty. Papaya's is famous for their hot entrees, including stuffed peppers, vegetarian lasagna, chicken enchiladas, spanakopita (a Greek dish with feta cheese and filo dough), and stuffed baked potatoes, all sold by the pound from about $3.50 and up; all can be packed to go. If you are into healthy organic food, there is no place better than Papaya's! (For a complete description of the market section see "Small Food Stores" under "Shopping" in the "Other Practicalities" section below.)

Inexpensive Eateries In And Around Kapa'a

In Kapa'a proper are several more convenient restaurants. **Fast Freddy's Diner** serves no-nonsense food in no-nonsense surroundings, tel. 822-0488. Try their Deuces Wild breakfast special of two eggs, two pancakes, two sausage links, and two strips of bacon for $2.22. Dinner specials are scampi for $9.95 and mahimahi for $5.95. Breakfast is served from 8 a.m., dinner from 5:30 p.m. except Wednesday; closed on Sunday.

A diner with Formica tables and a lunch counter, **T. Higashi Store** caters mostly to local residents, tel. 822-5982. Serving everyday Japanese food, they are open 6 a.m.-8 p.m.

Look for yellow and white umbrellas shading a few picnic tables that mark **Bubba's,** at 1384 Kuhio Hwy., Kapa'a, tel. 823-0069, open Mon.-Sat. 10:30 a.m.-6 p.m., sometimes on Sunday. You can have a Bubba burger for $2.25, or a Big Bubba for $4.40. Other menu items include a "Slopper," an open-faced burger smothered in Bubba's famous Budweiser beer chili for $3.95; a Hubba Bubba, a scoop of rice, hamburger, and grilled hot dog smothered in beer chili with diced onion for $4.95; or a simple order of fish and chips, chicken burger, or corn dog, all for under $4. Sides include french fries, onion rings, and "frings," a combo of both. On entering, you can try your hand at a coin toss, and if you manage to place it in the right slot, you win a soda, lunch, or a T-shirt. Also, check out the community bulletin board to see what's happening and what's for sale in the Kapa'a area. Bubba's is a throwback to the days when the owner was the short-order cook, and all the burgers were hand-made. Rock 'n' roll, grease, and Elvis Lives, man!

Michel's Cafe and Bakery, near Bubba's at 1381 Kuhio Hwy., tel. 823-6008, open Mon.-Sat. 7:30 a.m.-9 p.m., occupies an old bank building, and to keep up with the "catch your eye" local paint jobs, is bright orange. Here too, everything is homemade, but instead of old-fashioned burgers, the offerings are mostly organic and healthful. From the bakery case choose cheese or whole grain bread, cinnamon-raisin rolls, blackberry bran muffins, white chocolate mac-nut almond cookies, or a quivering slab of bread pudding. Enjoy your choice with a rich cup of cappuccino or caffe latte from the full espresso bar. Every day brings a different "special sandwich" like chicken breast, tuna, or hummus and vegies with all the trimmings on homemade bread for under $5.50. You can also enjoy homemade soups like spring garlic and potato, and black bean chili over rice with sour cream, both including bread for $3.75. In the evening, there are two daily entrees like vegetarian lasagna or enchiladas, served with bread and salad for under $10. On Friday and Saturday evenings, in keeping with the coffeehouse tradition, they have live music which could be a harpist, solo guitarist, small Hawaiian combo, or classical jazz. Michel's is unpretentious, homey, healthful, and "culinarily correct," a welcome haven for yuppies and born-again hippies. Peace, brotherhood, Birkenstocks, and Volvos forever!

Hana-Ya Sushi, an authentic sushi bar in downtown Kapa'a, at 1394 Kuhio Hwy., tel. 822-3878, open Mon.-Fri. 11:30 a.m.-2 p.m. for lunch, Mon.-Sat. 5:30-9:30 p.m. for dinner, owned by sushi chef Matomu Hanaya, serves up tasty tidbits and classic Japanese dishes. For lunch try *oyaku donburi* for $5.95, or chicken *katsu* for $5.95, or a 16-piece tray of assorted sushi for $8.55. Dinner prices are about $1 more for the fixed dishes, and $16.55 for a tray of 19 pieces of assorted sushi. Hanaya-*san* has no liquor license but it's okay to bring your own sake or beer.

The **Olympic Cafe,** a fixture in Kapa'a for over half a century, but torn up by Hurricane Iniki, is back in business at 1387 Kuhio Hwy., Kapa'a, tel. 822-5731, open daily except Wednesday, 6 a.m.-11 a.m. for breakfast; 11 a.m.-1:45 p.m. for lunch; 5 p.m.-8:45 p.m. for dinner. This linoleum and Formica restaurant fixes American and Hawaiian standards. Breakfasts of eggs, meats, rice, and potatoes are under $5, and lunches of chopped steak or breaded pork cutlets are under $6. Island favorites like saimin and pork soup are about $4, and the mahi plate is under $5. Beer, wine, and cocktails are served. There's no atmosphere, but the service is friendly and the food plentiful and good.

Sidezout, tel. 822-0082, a neighborhood bar and restaurant in downtown Kapa'a, open daily 11 a.m.-1:30 a.m., offers inexpensive sandwiches, burgers, and light meals along with cold drafts, wine, liquor, and imported beer. Sidezout patrons are a fun-filled potpourri of sunburned tourists, tattooed locals, and multi-earringed men and women of alternative sexual persuasions. The restaurant has a dining deck out back and plans to build a volleyball court.

Moderate

The **Ono Family Restaurant,** downtown Kapa'a at 4-1292 Kuhio Hwy., open daily 7 a.m.-2 p.m., closed Sunday evenings, tel. 822-1710, is cozy and functional, with nice touches like carpeted floors, ceiling fans, and a chandelier. Creative breakfasts include eggs Canterbury (a takeoff on eggs Benedict) with turkey, tomatoes, and hollandaise sauce over poached eggs and an English muffin; pancakes; and a variety of omelettes like a "Local Boy," which combines Portuguese sausage and *kimchi.* Lunch salads run about $4.50, and the "island's best burger" is $5.50. For dinner you can't go wrong with a mushroom melt burger for $6.95, and from the broiler or grill try sirloin steak, barbecued ribs, or teri chicken. For those with a taste for the exotic, you can get a real buffalo burger here, from American bison raised in Hanalei and Kansas. The daily fish special is always terrific, and depending upon the catch goes for about $13.

When you don't want to fool around deciding where to get a good meal, head for the north end of Kapa'a and the local favorite, **Kountry Kitchen,** open daily 6 a.m.-9 p.m. The tables are usually packed with regulars during peak dining hours. Breakfasts are full meals of hefty omelettes for $3-4 to the "Hungryman Special" for over $6. Lunches range $4-6, and full dinners like country ribs, sesame shrimp, and baked ham served with soup, bread, potatoes/rice, and vegies are $7-9. The food is tasty, the service prompt and friendly, and the portions large. The Kountry Kitchen is at 1485 Kuhio Hwy., tel. 822-3511.

Nearby is the **Makai Restaurant,** tel. 822-3955, which serves Hawaiian, Mediterranean, and continental food. Try their fish and chips, gyros, or moussaka; you can get it to go. The open windows let in the breeze and morning sunlight, but as it is close to the road, they also let in the sounds of passing cars.

Norberto's El Cafe is a family-run Mexican restaurant from *sombrero* to *zapatos.* Then what's it doing on a side street on a Pacific island, you ask? Hey, gringo, don't look a gift burro in the face! They serve nutritious, delicious, wholesome food, and they cater to vegetarians, as all dishes are prepared without lard or animal fats. The smell of food wafting out of the front door around dinnertime is its best advertisement. They serve the best Mexican food on the island. Full-course meals of burritos, enchiladas, and tostadas are $9-10, children's plates are $5, while a la carte dishes are $4-5. The best deals are the chef's specials of burrito El Cafe, Mexican salad, and chiles rellenos, all for under $6, or fajitas for $11.95. Other entrees are rellenos Tampico, chimichangas, tacos, and quesadillas. Dinners are served with soup, beans, and rice; chips and salsa are complimentary. There's beer on tap, or if you really want to head south of the border (by way of sliding under the table), try a pitcher of margaritas. If you have room after stuffing yourself like a chimichanga, try a delicious chocolate cream pie or homemade rum cake. The cafe is extremely popular with local folks, so tables fill as soon as they're empty. Look for Norberto's at the intersection of Kukui St. and Rt. 56 in downtown Kapa'a, tel. 822-3362; open nightly 5:30-9:30 p.m.

JJ's Broiler Room, tel. 822-4411, is in the Coconut Plantation Market Place. You won't go wrong here if you're after steak or beef, though chicken and fish are also available. Open daily for dinner and cocktails from 5 p.m., they offer beef kabobs, steak and lobster, and the famous "Slavonic steak" of thinly sliced meat broiled in wine and garlic, all for under $14.95; a salad bar is offered too. Check out their "early bird specials" 5-6 p.m. or late evening specials 9-10 p.m.

At the Coconut Plantation Market Place is **Buzz's Steak and Lobster** restaurant, tel. 922-7491. Lunch is 11 a.m.-3 p.m., *pu pu* and happy hour 3-5 p.m., and dinner 5-10:30 p.m. Word on the street says the salad bar here is the best. Two of the many appetizers are deep-fried artichokes or calamari. Various st;eaks run $10.95-16.95, 12-ounce prime rib $18.95, lobster trap combo $21.95, and other seafood $8.95-18.95. A light dining menu of mahimahi, ginger chicken kabob, and seafood brochette is offered for the more health and nutrition conscious. As an added benefit, you can sit at the bar after dinner and listen to nightly entertainment 9 p.m.-midnight.

The **Jolly Roger Restaurant,** open 6 a.m.-2 a.m., claims to have the longest happy hour on the island—6:30 a.m.-7 p.m. They're not known for exceptional food, but you always get hearty, substantial portions no matter what time of day you come to dine. A breakfast special brings pancakes, eggs, and bacon for $2.99. You can find Jolly Roger behind the Coconut Plantation Market Place near the Islander on the Beach Hotel, tel. 822-3451.

Al and Don's Restaurant in the Kauai Sands Hotel is open daily 7 a.m.-8 p.m., tel. 822-4221. The service and food are good but not memorable. However, the view from the spacious booths overlooking the seacoast is magnificent. Prices for their numerous dinner and breakfast selections are reasonable. Perhaps this is the problem: though you don't get the bum's rush, the place feels like one of those feeding troughs in Waikiki that caters to everyone and pleases no one. However, you can't complain about the large portions; breakfast is $3.85 for all-you-can-eat hotcakes, one egg, grilled ham, and coffee. And you won't be disappointed with their "build-your-own-omelette." Most breakfasts are under $4, and there are plenty of evening specials, with most dinners under $10. Dinner includes soup and salad bar with adequate entrees like *ahi*, swordfish, top sirloin, or chicken exotica. The bar serves good drinks for reasonable prices. When you leave Al and Don's, you won't feel like complaining, but you won't rush back, either.

The **Bull Shed,** known for its prime rib, is also praised for its chicken and seafood ($9.95-18.95). The wine list is better than average and includes Domaine Chandon champagne ($22.95). Insiders go for the extensive salad bar at only $6.95, but be forewarned, the pickings get all jumbled together as the night goes on, and the salad bar peaks out by 7:30. The Bull Shed is open nightly for cocktails and dinner 5:30-10 p.m. at 796 Kuhio Hwy., down the lane across from McDonald's, tel. 822- 3791.

Ginger's Grille, in Kauai Village, tel. 822-5557, offers soups and sandwiches 10 a.m.-10 p.m., dinner 5-10 p.m., cocktails until 11:30 p.m., and live music Thurs.-Sat. 9-11 p.m. The interior is subdued and intimate. The menu offers appetizers like mozzarella sticks or wing-dings for under $6, and salads including Cobb salad, chicken salad, or seafood salad, for under $10. From the sandwich board, you can have a burger ($5.25), mahi fillet sandwich ($6.95), or teriyaki chicken sandwich ($6.95). Dinner brings beef, chicken, or shrimp stir-fry ($11.95), New York steak ($13.95), and scampi ($11.95).

Fine Dining, Luau, And Buffets

Master chef Jean-Marie Josselin knows a good thing when he sees it, and moreover knows how to prepare it exquisitely. With a handful of other colleagues creating their culinary magic in

Hawaii, Chef Josselin is on the cutting edge of an exciting new cuisine called Pacific Rim. Based on the finest traditions of European cooking, Pacific Rim boldly adds the pungent spices and sauces of Asia, the fantastic fresh vegetables and fish of Hawaii, and, at times, the earthy cooking methods of the American Southwest. The result is a cuisine of fantastic tastes, subtle yet robust, and satiating but health-conscious, the perfect marriage of fresh foods prepared in a fresh way. You can enjoy this excellent food at the **Pacific Cafe** at the Kauai Village Shopping Center, 4-831 Kuhio Hwy., tel. 822-0013, open 5:30 p.m.-10 p.m. Although in a shopping center, the Pacific Cafe creates a casually elegant atmosphere appointed with a coved and molded ceiling, ferns and flowers placed here and there, bent-back bamboo chairs, and an open kitchen so that you can watch the food preparation. Start with mouthwatering appetizers like smoked chicken *lumpia* served with curried citrus dip, deep-fried sashimi with *wanna* sauce, or poached scallops ravioli with *tobiko* and lime ginger sauce, all for under $6. Soups and salads, always accompanied by fresh-baked bread and a saucer of herbed olive oil and balsamic vinegar, are delightful with hand-picked organic greens for $4.25. Entrees, served with rice and seasoned vegetables and prepared on a wood-fired grill, include grilled swordfish with shrimp and eggplant cannelloni served with gazpacho sauce ($21.25), grilled *ahi* with eggplant puree ($20.75), angel hair pasta with Chinese pesto and grilled Hawaiian fish skewers ($17.95), or specialties like crusted peanut lemongrass pork loin with yellow curry sauce ($18.75). Special dishes prepared for the vegetarian include organic potato and tofu lasagna with ginger and scallion pesto for $8.50, or grilled Japanese eggplant and mesclun salad with a chile pepper and soy vinaigrette for $9.50. The Pacific Cafe is an excellent restaurant with the perfect mixture of fine food, fine service, and superb presentation; the best that the area has to offer.

The **Voyage Room** at the Kauai Coconut Beach Hotel offers a sumptuous breakfast buffet including vegetarian and health-conscious fare like fresh fruit, yogurt, and cereal along with the traditional breakfast fixings of sausage, home-fried potatoes, eggs, and a good assortment of croissants and pastries. In the evenings, the Voyage Room transforms into **The Flying Lobster.** All meals are served with salad and *pu pu* bar. Try slipper lobster, $20 for two tails; or spiny lobster favored by local people, $27 for two tails. Teriyaki top sirloin, baby-back ribs, garlic shrimp, vegetarian lasagna, and combinations like mahi with lobster are all priced $13.50-22. A weekly special like crispy oriental chicken is $16. Top off your meal with Coconut Beach Hawaiian Sand Pie, a trio of coffee, chocolate, and vanilla ice cream atop a macadamia nut crust; or the Flying Lobster Banana Coupe, spiced banana flambéed in brown sugar, butter, and a blend of fine liqueurs, poured atop rich vanilla ice cream.

The real treat is the hotel luau which everyone agrees is one of the best on the island. It's held every night except Monday in the special luau *halau* (longhouse) under a canopy of stars and palm trees. The luau master is Mr. Lopaka, who starts the *imu* every morning; stop by and watch. He lays the hot stones and banana stalks so well that the underground oven maintains a perfect 400°. In one glance he can gauge the weight and fat content of a succulent porker and decide just how long it should be cooked. The water in the leaves covering the pig steams and roasts it so that the meat falls off a fork. Mr. Lopaka says about his luau, "All that you can't eat in the *imu* are the hot stones." You arrive at 6:30 p.m. to see the torch-lighting ceremony, followed by the *imu* ceremony. Cocktails are ongoing and at 8 p.m. the luau begins at tables laden with pork, chicken, oriental beef, salmon, fish, exotic fruits, salads, coconut cake, and *haupia*. Then at 8:30 you recline and watch authentic Hawaiian hula and entertainment choreographed by Kawaikapookalawai, a.k.a. Frank Hewett. Prices are: $45 adults, $22.94 children under 12, $20 show only. Reservations suggested; tel. 822-3455, ext. 651.

On a day that you can eat a lot, want to try a little bit of everything, and don't want to bust your wallet, stop in at **Buffet,** at the Aston Kauai Beachboy Hotel. Long tables are laden with food, all you care to eat. Breakfast for $3.95 is served 7-10:30 a.m. Some of the selections are sausage and eggs, hotcakes, toast, fruit, and pastries. Lunch at $5.45 runs 11 a.m.-2:30 p.m., and offers such tasty morsels as fried chicken, stews, pasta, and salads. At $7.95, dinner can hardly be beat. The five main entrees are complemented by fruit and a salad bar. While the dining isn't elegant, the surroundings are pleasant, and you certainly get your money's worth.

OTHER PRACTICALITIES

ENTERTAINMENT

The night scene in Kapa'a isn't very extensive, but there is enough to satisfy everyone. In the area you'll usually find at least one good disco, dinner show, easy-listening music, and Polynesian extravaganza.

The **Jolly Roger Restaurant** at the Coconut Plantation Market Place offers karaoke nightly. You can listen, sing, and dance nightly 9 p.m.-1:30 a.m. The atmosphere is casual, the talk friendly. A good watering hole where you can find cool drinks and conversation is the **Tradewind's South Sea Bar** at the Coconut Plantation Market Place. Also in the Market Place, **South of the Border,** a Mexican cantina, sometimes has live music, especially on weekends. Nearby Buzz's has nightly entertainment as well, usually a small band playing contemporary, original, and country and western music. You can sit at the bar and enjoy the casual Polynesian setting.

The Coconut Plantation Market Place hosts a free **Polynesian Hula Show** Thurs.-Sat. at 4 p.m. The young local dancers and musicians put as much effort into their routines as if this were the big time. Be forewarned that local sneak thieves rifle cars in the parking lot, knowing their owners are occupied watching the show. Also at the shopping center are the **Plantation Cinemas 1 and 2** for movie-goers.

The **Kauai Coconut Beach Hotel** offers a little of everything. You can enjoy free *pu pu* and entertainment at Cook's Landing, just off the gardens and pool deck—happy hour 4-6 p.m. Every evening 8-11 p.m. listen to pop, contemporary, and standard hits by local musicians. The dinner show in the Paddle Room presents a full performance of Hawaiian dance and music. And swing, rock, and Hawaiian music, as well as the hula of the Polynesian Show, accompany the luau (see above).

Michel's Espresso Bar, in downtown Kapa'a (see preceeding), in keeping with coffeehouse tradition, offers live music on weekend evenings which could be a harpist, solo guitarist, small Hawaiian combo, or classical jazz.

Ginger's Grille, in Kauai Village, tel., 822-5557, has live music Thurs.-Sat. 9-11 p.m.

SHOPPING

Kapa'a teems with shopping opportunities. Lining Kuhio Hwy. are a major shopping mall, the Coconut Plantation Market Place, and several other smaller shopping plazas. All your needs are met by food stores, health stores, drug stores, a farmers' market, fish vendors, and some extraordinary shops and boutiques tucked away here and there. You can easily find photo supplies, sporting equipment, "treasures," and inexpensive lei to brighten your day. As when dealing with the sun, enjoy yourself, but don't overdo it.

Coconut Plantation Market Place

The name doesn't lie about this cluster of over 70 shops, restaurants, galleries, and movie theaters, all amid coconut trees. Prices are kept down because of the competition of so many shops, and each tries to "specialize," which usually means good choices for whatever strikes your fancy. As you walk around, notice the photo blowups that give you glimpses into old Hawaii. **Ye Old Ship Store** displays the best collection of scrimshaw on Kauai and sea paintings by local artists. Any of the jewelry shops have enough stock on hand to drop even Mr. T to his knees. With so many apparel and footwear shops, the job of finding just the right aloha shirt, muumuu, or sports clothing shouldn't be a problem. **Waldenbooks** has the corner on books and magazines. **Pottery Tree** overflows with everything from junk to fine pieces. Select from stained-glass chandeliers, I Love Hawaii mugs, and cheap yet nice shell mobiles. **High as a Kite** is great for high fliers that will add fun to any beach outing. **Kahn Galleries** (two other locations) features the fine work of Hawaii's artists along with basketry, sculpture, woodcarvings, and superb jewelry for expensive, but once-in-a-lifetime purchases. (For complete details see "Specialty Shops, Arts, and Boutiques" under "Shopping" in the Kauai Introduction.) If the price of original artwork puts too much strain on your budget, then **Island Images,** offering fine art prints and posters, might have what you need at an affordable price. Island Images, open daily 9 a.m.-5 p.m., tel. 822-3636, offers posters for around $30, framing and shipping available.

If your heart desires Hawaiian delicacies like Kona coffee, Maui onion mustard, macadamia nuts, island candy, Kauai Kookies, Kukui jams and jellies, and much more, head for **The Nut Cracker Sweet** shop and see if you can pull yourself away. For the ordinary purchase, head for **Whaler's General Store. Foto Freddie** will develop film, **Hawaiian Air** will confirm a plane reservation, and **Kauai Visitor's Center** can give you information about things to see, places to go, and adventures to explore.

Kauai Village

Built around the theme of an 18th-century "Main Street," the Kauai Village is a very modern, very large, and very diverse shopping center with its own museum. Located at 4-831 Kuhio Hwy., it is one of the newest and best Kauai has to offer. In the village you will find: a convenient **Safeway Supermarket,** open 24 hours; **Pay 'n Save,** a complete variety store with photo equipment and a **pharmacy; an** ABC Store for everything from suntan lotion to beach mats; a well-stocked **Waldenbooks,** with everything from Hawaiiana to travel; **Blockbuster Video,** for home/condo entertainment; and a cluster of fast-food restaurants and small inexpensive eateries. Also located here are **Papaya's Market Cafe,** the island's best natural health food store (for the "Cafe" see "Food" above, and for the "Market" see "Small Food Stores" following, also "Food Stores" under "Shopping" in the Kauai Introduction), and the **Pacific Cafe,** a fantastic restaurant featuring Pacific Rim cuisine prepared by master chef Jean-Marie Josselin (see "Food" above).

Kapa'a Shopping Center

Marked by a **Shell Station,** and **Burger King** at 4-1105 Kuhio Hwy., is the bite-sized and pragmatic Kapa'a Shopping Center. Here, you'll find a **Big Save Market,** a well-stocked food store, **Clic Photo** for inexpensive film and fast developing, **Kapa'a Bakery** filled with goodies, **Kapa'a Laundry** for do-it-yourselfers, **Kapa'a Sports Center** with all kinds of sporting goods, and **Kauai Video.** Also in this shopping center are the Kapa'a clinic of the **Kauai Medical Group,** a full service **U.S. post office,** an inexpensive restaurant or two (see "Food" above), and **Mail Boxes Kauai** for mailboxes, faxes, and mailings of all sorts.

Small Shopping Malls

Across the highway from another Shell station, in the **Waipouli Complex,** is Popo's Cookies. Closed Mon.-Wed., it is open Thurs.-Fri. 8 a.m.-5 p.m., till 3 p.m. on Saturday, and till 2 p.m. on Sunday. Nearby in the **Waipouli Plaza** are several clothing shops and a seashell merchant that sells retail and wholesale. Farther down the road in the **Waipouli Town Center** you'll find **Foodland,** open 24 hours, Fun Factory arcade for games, and JM's jewelry store.

Boutiques And Souvenirs

On the Kuhio Hwy., across from Foodland, is a tiny lei shop, owned and operated by **Liz, the lei lady.** When she has a supply of fresh flowers, she puts out a sign that simply says Lei. If she's open, rush in because they won't last long. She'll make you a lovely lei for around $6, and what she calls "flower jewelry" of necklaces, hair adornments, and brooches for $5. Liz usually opens around 11 a.m. and stays open as late as 7 p.m.

Remember Kauai, 4-734 Kuhio Hwy., tel. 822-0161, past the Kauai Coconut Beach Hotel, specializes in unique Hawaiian jewelry like necklaces made from shells, beads, wood, and gold. The counters shine with belt buckles, pins, and gemstones from around the world. Niihau shellwork is available, and fine specimens run up to $1200. The scrimshaw, worked by Kauai artists on fossilized walrus ivory, adds rich texture to everything from knives to paperweights. Any place like this one with a rainbow painted on its roof is worth a look.

Cathy and Karlos travel to Indonesia where they purchase magnificent fabrics of 100% cotton or rayon that they design into exclusive clothing for their shop **Bokumarue,** at 1388 Kuhio

Hwy., Kapa'a HI 96746. tel. 822-1766, open 10 a.m.-6 p.m. Affordable yet classy, the garments include dresses, shirts, and *pareau,* all of which are either hand stamped or hand painted. Other distinctive items include *ikat* blankets, at $20 a real deal; temple carvings; and gaily painted masks, angels, and winged creatures priced $30-50. There is even some amazing primitive basketry from Borneo. Bokumarue, although not typically Hawaiian, is a real find.

Earth Beads, owned by Kavan and Stacey Crane, a step away from Bokumarue, tel. 822-0766, open daily 10 a.m.-6 p.m., specializes in beads and imported items from India, Africa, and South America. Shimmering in the tiny shop are earrings, belts, incidental bags, and sterling silver jewelry from Thailand. Woven cotton "throws" which would work equally well as rugs, blankets, or wraparounds are $55. A smattering of primitive basketry, Guatemalan woven hats and purses, incense, perfumed oils, and very unusual greeting cards complete the stock of this great little shop.

Old Kapa'a Town Antiques, in downtown Kapa'a, tel. 823-6919, open daily 9 a.m.-6 p.m., rattles a greeting with racks filled with old Hawaiian bottles. On the walls and shelves are tin signs, vintage aloha shirts, radios, model airplanes, toy tractors, jewelry, and old license plates. Next door is **Cajun Shave-Ice,** 31 flavors in all sorts of concoctions. Although shave ice is well known in Hawaii, gourmets will tell you that the best is served in New Orleans . . . but don't tell that to the locals!

Look for **M. Miura Store,** at the north end of Kapa'a, mountain side, open Mon.-Sat. 9 a.m.-5 p.m. Local people shop at this dry goods store for alohawear, T-shirts, caps, men's and women's shorts, and a good selection of bikinis.

Yellow Fish Trading Company, in the dragon-guarded New Pacific House, catercorner to the ABC Store, at 4504 Kukui St., Kapa'a, HI, is a bi-level store owned and operated by Gritt Benton, filled with Hawaiiana, contemporary and antique furniture, and artwork. Some of the most intriguing furniture is made from tiger bamboo—a light, mottled bamboo with ebony-colored ends. As you look around, notice lampshades from Indonesia, basketry in all shapes and sizes, old drapery, gaily painted kitchen chairs, carvings from South America's tropical rain forest, and Hawaiian tapa wall hangings. An exquisite silk kimono hangs on the wall in stark contrast to devil masks from Africa and Borneo, while an 18th-century German trunk and a vintage desk from France complete the mélange. For a memento you can also choose from a smattering of jewelry, a rack of postcards, or contemporary island prints. Open Mon.-Fri. 10 a.m.-6 p.m., Saturday noon-6 p.m., tel. 823-6717.

Old and used books, records, CDs, and comics rise from the dead at **Lazerus Books,** 4-1353 Kuhio Hwy., downtown Kapa'a, tel. 822-4420, open Sun.-Fri. noon-6 p.m., Saturday 10 a.m.-6 p.m.

The **Roxy Swap Meet,** held in central Kapa'a every Saturday, tel. 822-7027, features tables set up under tents. People from all over come to barter and sell everything and anything.

Photo Needs

Across from Remember Kauai on Kuhio Hwy. is **Cameralab,** tel. 822-7338, for all your photofinishing needs. In downtown Kapa'a, **Pono Studio** develops film, carries photographic equipment, and has a studio for portraits. At the Coconut Plantation Market Place, **Foto Freddie** and **Plantation Camera and Gifts** do photo developing.

Small Food Stores

Papaya's, a natural food cafe and market, at the Kauai Village Shopping Center, 4-831 Kuhio Hwy., open daily except Sunday 10 a.m.-8 p.m., tel. 823-0190, is not only the largest but the best natural food store/cafe on Kauai. Coolers and shelves hold items like wild tropical guava juice, organic sprouted hot dog buns, and mainstays like organic fruits and vegetables, yogurt, whole grain bread, and bulk foods. There is also a good selection of organic teas and flavored coffees. Spices, oils, vinegars, organic pre-made salad dressings, homeopathic medicines, cruelty-free cosmetics, vitamins, minerals, and biodegradable cleaning products are well represented. A large display case holds all kinds of goodies like cheesecake, pumpkin and carrot cakes, mango moussecake, and chocolate flan. If you are into healthy organic food, there is no place better than Papaya's! (For a complete description of the cafe section see preceding "Inexpensve Food in Shopping Malls" under "Food.")

There are several other markets and groceries in the Waipouli/Kapa'a area where you can pick up your food needs if you're cooking for yourself. **Ambrose's Kapuna Natural Foods** (in a funky yellow building) across from Foodland in the Waipouli Town Center serves the community's tofu, fruits, and bulk and health food needs. Ambrose and his friends are real storehouses of information about the island; they have the "scoop" on what's happening and where it's at. If you have kids, check next door at the children's shop. (Also see "Food Stores" under "Shopping" in the Kauai Introduction, and "Sports and Recreation" below).

In downtown Kapa'a there's a **farmers' market** every Wednesday at 3 p.m. at the beach park, while the local **Pono Market** is stuffed to the gills. **Kojima's** grocery, for produce, meat, liquor, beer, and picnic supplies, is beyond the Aloha Lumber yard at the north end of town. Currently painted blue, this well-stocked store is on the mountain side of the road.

Sports And Recreation

One of the best bike shops on the island for sales and repair is **Bicycle Kauai,** tel. 822-3315, at 1379 Kuhio Hwy. in Kapa'a. Stop in and talk to the guys; they can give you great advice on where to ride your type of bike. (See "Alternatives" under "Getting Around" in the Kauai Introduction.)

Aquatic Adventures, at 4-1380 Kuhio Hwy., Kapa'a HI 96746, tel. 822-1434, open Mon.-Fri. 7:30 a.m.-7 p.m., Sat.-Sun. 7:30 a.m.-5 p.m., owned and operated by Janet Moore, is a full-service dive shop offering rentals, excursions, and certification courses. PADI courses, lasting three to five days for open water certification, are $395 for the total package; $195 for a refresher course. Beginners can start with an introductory shore dive for $100; a boat dive is $120. Other prices include: two-tank boat dive $70, with equipment $90; one-tank shore dive $60, with equipment $80; and one-tank night dive $70, with equipment, $90. Janet also sells a full complement of underwater gear including knives, wetsuits, masks, fins, spearfishing gear, and carry bags.

There's no problem planning a fun-filled day with the help of **Ray's Rentals and Activities,** 1345 Kuhio Hwy., downtown Kapa'a, tel. 822-5700. Ray's rents boogie boards, snorkel gear, bicycles, surfboards, video cams, powerboats, and kayaks. They also are a booking agency for activities like helicopter rides, scuba diving, snorkeling, and luau. They claim "to beat all prices," so it's worth calling to see what they can do.

Kayak Kauai, across the road from Ray's, open daily 9 a.m.-4 p.m., tel. 822-9179, rents two-person kayaks for $50 per day, and single kayaks for $25 per day. (For a full description see "Kayaks" under "Sightseeing Tours" under "Getting Around" in the Kauai Introduction.)

Ambrose of **Ambrose's Kapuna Natural Foods,** in a funky yellow building across from Foodland in the Waipouli Town Center (see above) is a surfer's advocate, philosopher, and general good guy. He has one of the largest collections of big boards and old surfboards on the island; and some new ones too. If you are a surfer coming on vacation and you let Ambrose know in advance what you want and are qualified to use, he'll have it waiting when you get here. He doesn't rent boards, but he'll buy back the ones he sells at a very equitable rate.

INFORMATION AND SERVICES

Aside from the hotel activities desks, there are four places in Waipouli/Kapa'a where you can get tourist information. Very helpful is the **Kauai Visitor's Center** in the Coconut Plantation Market Place, tel. 245-3882. They have a complete range of free information on all the island's activities, are able to make reservations, and have an eye for the deals. **K.B.T.C.** also has the full range of information and sometimes gets discount deals. Stop at their main booth at the Pono Kai Condo or at their cubbyhole office below Jimmy's Grill in downtown Kapa'a; or call 822-7447.

Information of another sort can be had at **The Rosetta Stone** on the north end of Kapa'a near the Shiatsu International Massage Clinic and the Kapa'a Chiropractic Clinic. The Rosetta Stone is a metaphysical resource center that taps into the spiritual elements on the island. Books, tapes, crystals, flower essences, gem elixirs, and more are sold, a reference library is being started, and a used-book shelf is also beginning. If you're interested in the mystic arts, spiritual and healing workshops, channeling, psychic guidance, homeopathic remedies, and practitioner referrals, stop in at 1536 Kuhio Hwy. or call Susan at 822-2745.

For a rejuvenating and revitalizing massage contact **Aunty Daisy's Polynesian Massage,** in the small Waipouli Complex at 971 D Kuhio Hwy., tel. 822-0305, open Tuesday and Wednesday 8:30 a.m.-5:30 p.m.; Thursday and Friday 11 a.m.-10 p.m.; Saturday 9:30 a.m.-2:30 p.m. She's "the lady with *aloha* hands." (For complete information see "Alternative Health Care" under "Medical Services" under "Information and Services" in the General Introduction.)

KEITH PERKINS

THE NORTH SHORE

The north shore is a soulful song of wonder, a contented chant of dream-reality, where all notes of the Garden Island harmonize gloriously. The refrain is a tinkling melody, rising, falling, and finally reaching a booming crescendo deep in the emerald green of Na Pali. In so many ways this region is a haven: tiny towns and villages that refused to crumble when sugar pulled out; a patchwork quilt of diminutive *kuleana* homesteads of native Hawaiians running deep into luxuriant valleys where ageless stone walls encircle fields of taro; a sanctuary for migrating birds and gritty native species desperately holding on to life; a haven for visitors—the adventuring, vacationing, life-tossed, or work-weary who come to its shores seeking peace of body and soul.

The north shore is only 30 miles long, but oh, what miles! Along its undulating mountains, one-lane roads, and luminescent bays are landlocked caves still umbilically tied to the sea; historical sites, the remnants of peace or domination once so important and now reduced by time; and living "movie sets," some occupied by villas of stars or dignitaries, enough to bore the worst name-dropper. Enduring, too, is the history of old Hawaii in this fabled homeland of the Menehune, overrun by the Polynesians who set up their elaborate kingdoms built on strict social order. The usurpers' *heiau* remain, and from one came the hula, swaying, stirring, and spreading throughout the island kingdoms.

Starting in **Kilauea,** an old plantation town, you can search out the spiritual by visiting two intriguing churches, visit an "everything" general store, or marvel at the coastline from bold promontories pummelled by the sea. Then there are the north shore beaches, fans of white sand, some easily visited as official parks, others hidden, the domains of simplicity and free spirits. **Princeville** follows, a convenient but incongruous planned community, vibrant with its own shopping mall, airport, and flexing condo muscles. Over the rise is **Hanalei,** more poetic than its lovely name, a tiny town, a yachties' anchorage with good food, spirited, slow, a bay of beauty and enchantment. The cameras once rolled at neighboring **Lumahai Beach,** and an entire generation shared the dream of paradise when they saw this spot in *South Pacific.* Next in rapid succession are **Wainiha** and **Haena,** the latter with its few amenities, the road's last available indoor lodging, restaurant, bar, and a little of the world's most relaxed lifestyle. The road ends at **Ke'e Beach,** where adventure begins on the Na Pali Coast Trail. The north shore remains for most visitors the perfect place to seek and maybe actually find peace, solitude, the dream, yourself.

HEADING NORTH: ANAHOLA AND VICINITY

Route 56 north from Kapa'a is a visual treat. Out your window, the coastline glides along in an ever-changing panorama. Development is virtually nonexistent until you get to Kilauea in the Hanalei District. To your left are the **Anahola Mountains,** jagged and intriguing. Until recently, you could crane your neck to see **Hole-in-the-Mountain,** a natural arrangement of boulders that formed a round *puka.* Legend says it was formed by an angry giant who hurled his spear with such force that he made the hole. But time and storms have taken their toll and the hole has collapsed.

Villages, Beaches, And Practicalities

The first village that you come to is **Anahola.** Just before mile marker 14 is the **Whaler's General Store,** open Mon.-Sat. 10 a.m.-6 p.m., selling groceries, souvenirs, vegetables, and liquor. If you'd like to brighten your day or evening with an inexpensive orchid or plumeria lei, call ahead and order one from **Albert Christian** in Anahola at 822-5691.

Next door to the general store is a **post office** and **Duane's Ono Charburger,** open Mon - Sat. 10 a.m.-6 p.m., Sunday from 11 a.m., a clean, friendly roadside stand where you can get burgers or fish 'n' chips. He has an island-wide reputation for good food. Prices are a bit stiff, but the burgers are large, delicious, and heavy with cheese and trimmings. Tables for a quick lunch are provided, but better to hold your appetite and picnic at the nearby beach.

Just a minute up the road, look to your right for Aliomanu (Oil of the Shark) Road and follow it for a few minutes to the mouth of the Anahola River as it spills into the bay. Or take Anahola Road off Rt. 56 just before the Whaler's General Store to a long strand of white sand that forms one of the best beaches on the north shore. The south end of the bay is **Anahola Beach County Park** with a developed picnic area, shower, grills, restrooms, and camping (county permit). Tall ironwoods provide a natural canopy. The swimming is safe in the protected cove near the beach park, as is a refreshing dip in the freshwater river. As you walk north the waves and rips get tougher—Anahola means "Easily Broken." It's not advisable to enter the water, although some experienced board riders do challenge the waves here as the Hawaiians did long ago. The reef comes close to shore at this end, and any sheltered pocket is good for snorkeling. Local anglers love this spot for near-shore fishing. The entire area is popular with local people, and at times begins to look like a tent-city of semipermanent campers and squatters. This is a place to camp for a few days, or just to stop in for a

J.D. BISIGNANI

Anahola Village Church backdropped by the distinctive Anahola Mountains

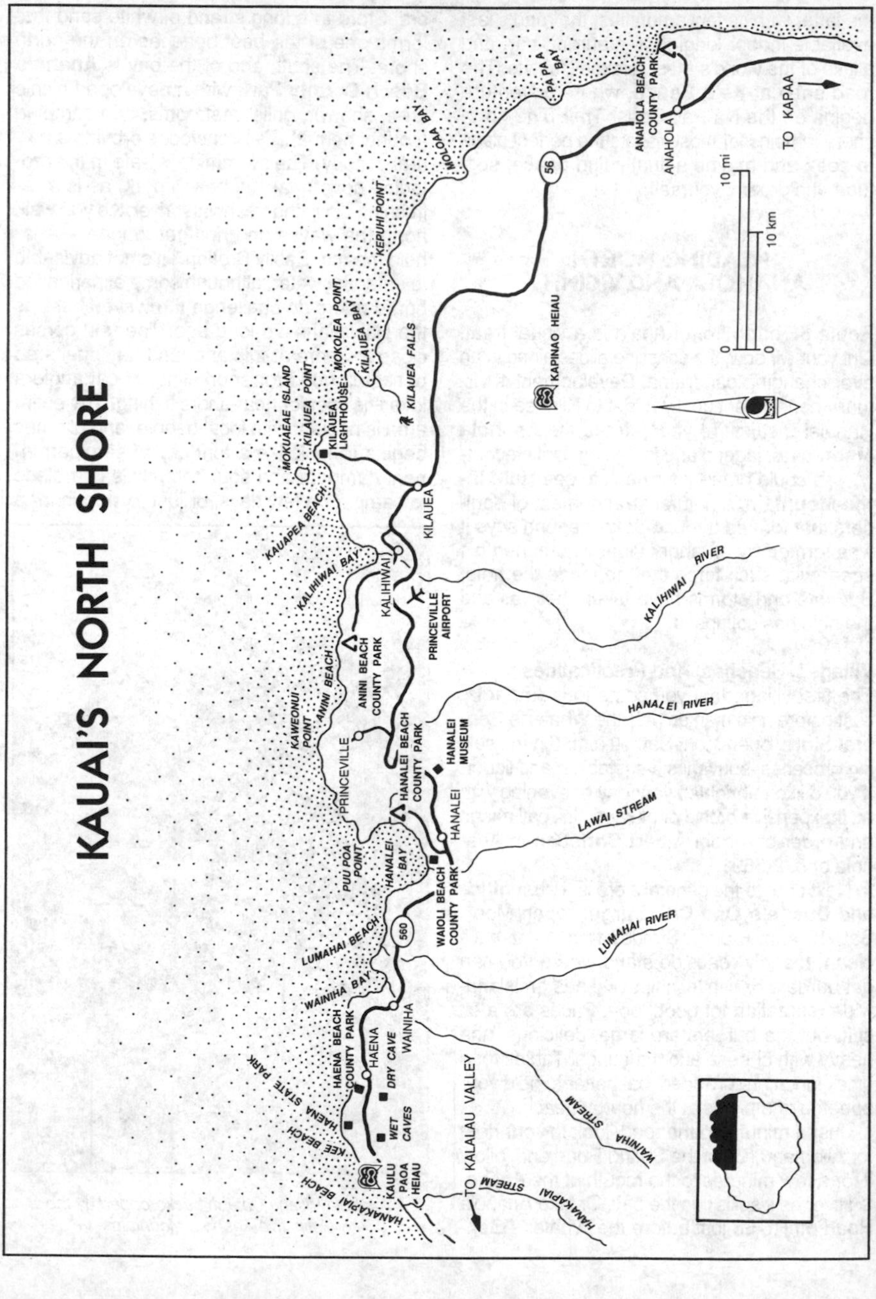

KAUAI'S NORTH SHORE

HANAKAPIAI BEACH
KEE BEACH
HAENA STATE PARK
KAULU PAOA HEIAU
WET CAVES
HAENA BEACH COUNTY PARK
HAENA
DRY CAVE
WAINIHA
WAINIHA BAY
LUMAHAI BEACH
560
PUU POA POINT
HANALEI BAY
WAIOLI BEACH COUNTY PARK
HANALEI
HANALEI BEACH COUNTY PARK
HANALEI MUSEUM
PRINCEVILLE
KAWEONUI POINT
ANINI BEACH
ANINI BEACH COUNTY PARK
PRINCEVILLE AIRPORT
KALIHIWAI
KALIHIWAI BAY
KAUAPEA BEACH
KILAUEA
MOKUAEAE ISLAND
KILAUEA POINT
KILAUEA LIGHTHOUSE
KILAUEA FALLS
MOKOLEA POINT
KILAUEA BAY
KEPUHI POINT
MOLOAA BAY
56
PAPAA BAY
ANAHOLA BEACH COUNTY PARK
ANAHOLA
TO KAPAA
KAPINAO HEIAU
0 10 mi
0 10 km
KALIHIWAI RIVER
HANALEI RIVER
LAWAI STREAM
LUMAHAI RIVER
WAINIHA STREAM
HANAKAPIAI STREAM
TO KALALAU VALLEY

refreshing plunge on the way to or from the north shore.

The turnoff to Moloa'a ("Matted Roots") Bay is announced by the **Moloa'a Sunrise** roadside fruit stand and information center at mile marker 17. The fruit stand, an outlet for a nearby papaya farm, has the best prices and most succulent fruit on the island. Turn down the rough Koolau Road, follow it to Moloa'a Road, and take this narrow but paved road to the end. Look for the brilliant poinsettias blooming in early winter along Koolau Road—they are the island's clue that Christmas and New Year are near. **Moloa'a Bay** is a magnificent but rarely visited beach. The road leading down is a luscious little thoroughfare, cutting over domed hillocks by a series of switchbacks. The jungle canopy is thick and then it opens into a series of glens and pastures. Off to the sides are vacation homes perched on stilts made from telephone poles. A short drive takes you to road's end and a small cluster of dwellings where there is limited space to put your vehicle. Park here and follow the "Right of way to the beach" signs. Here, a stream comes into the bay providing a great place to wash off the ocean water after a dip. The beach is lovely, bright, and wide, forming a crescent moon. To the north the beach ends in a grassy hillock, and south it's confined by a steep *pali*. Swimming at all north shore beaches is advised only during calm weather, and is best at the south end of the beach. Snorkeling is good, but you'll have to swim the channel out to the base of the *pali* which is unadvisable if the waves are rough. Although a few homes are around, Moloa'a is a place of peaceful solitude. Sunsets are lightshows of changing color, and you'll probably be a solitary spectator.

KILAUEA

There's no saying *exactly* where it begins, but Kilauea is generally considered the gateway to the north shore. The village was built on sugar, which melted away almost 20 years ago. Now the town holds on as a way station to some of the most intriguing scenery along this fabulous coast. Notice the bright, cheery, and well-kept homes as you pass through this community. The homeowners, perhaps short on cash, are nonetheless long on pride, and surround their dwellings with lovingly tended flower gardens. The bungalows, pictures of homey contentment, are ablaze with color.

To get into town, look for mile marker 23 and a **Shell gas station** on your right, and **Hale O Health,** a small health food store with some general groceries. This is where you turn onto Kolo Road, following the signs to Kilauea Lighthouse and National Wildlife Refuge. The promontory it occupies, Kilauea Point, is the northernmost tip of the main Hawaiian Islands. A second way into Kilauea Town is to turn off the highway at **Pu'u Lani Fruit Stand** (a farmers' market is held every Saturday at noon in the Waldorf schoolyard next door). Drive one block and turn left. Pass St. Sylvester's Church, and proceed over a bridge past the Kilauea School into town.

Sights

As you head down Kolo Road from the gas station, you pass the post office. Where Kolo intersects Kilauea Road sits **Christ Memorial Episcopal Church** on the right. Hawaii seems to sprout as many churches as bamboo shoots, but this one is special. The shrubbery and flowers immediately catch your eye, their vibrant colors matched by the stained-glass windows imported from England. The present church was built in 1941 from cut lava stone. Inside is a hand-hewn altar, and surrounding the church is a cemetery with old tombstones for long-departed parishioners. Go in, have a look, and perhaps meditate for a moment.

Before turning on Kilauea Road have a look at **St. Sylvester's Catholic Church.** This church is octagonal with an odd roof. Inside are murals painted by Jean Charlot, a famous island artist. The church, built by Friar John Macdonald, was an attempt to reintroduce art as one of the bulwarks of Catholicism.

Head down Kilauea Road past the Kong Lung Store, and keep going until Kilauea Road makes a hard swing to the left. Proceeding straight ahead up Mihi Road brings you to a little Japanese cemetery on your right. This road has been blocked as it's now privately owned and closed to the public, but it leads to Mokolea Point's **Crater Hill,** where 568 feet straight down is the Pacific, virtually unobstructed until it hits Asia. The seacliff is like a giant stack of pancakes, layered and jagged, with the edges eaten by age, and covered with a green syrup of lichen and mosses. The cliff is undercut, and gives you the sensation of floating in midair. There is a profusion of purple and yellow flowers all along the edge. The cliffs are a giant rookery for seabirds, and along with Mokolea Point to the east are now part of the **Kilauea National Wildlife Refuge** that also encompasses Kilauea Point.

For a more civilized experience of the same view with perhaps a touch less drama, head down Kilauea Road to the end and park at **Kilauea Lighthouse,** a designated national historical landmark. This facility, built in 1913, was at one time staffed by the Coast Guard, but is now under the jurisdiction of the Department of the Interior's Fish and Wildlife Service. Boasting the largest "clamshell lens" in the world, it is capable of sending a beacon 90 miles out to sea. The clamshell lens has not been used since the mid-'70s, and a small, high-intensity light now shines as an important reference point for mariners.

The area is alive with permanent and migrating birds. Keep your eyes peeled for the **great frigate bird** kiting on its eight-foot wingspan, or the **red-footed booby,** a white bird with black wingtips darting here and there, and always wearing red dancing shoes. At certain times of the year Hawaiian monk seals and green turtles can be seen along the shore and around Mokuaeae Island just off Kilauea Point. Dolphins and whales are also spotted offshore. Information at the visitors center gives you a fast lesson in birdlife and a pictorial history of the lighthouse—worth reading. A good selection of books on Hawaiian flora, fauna, history, and hiking, as well as maps of the islands, are available. The center lends out binoculars to view the birds, and there are usually informative docents in the yard with monoculars trained on a particular bird or nesting site on the nearby cliffs.

The Kilauea Wildlife Refuge is attempting to relocate albatrosses from the Midway Islands, where they nest on runways. The refuge has successfully relocated more than 40, and you can watch them floundering around on nearby Albatross Hill.

A leisurely walk takes you out onto this amazingly narrow peninsula, where you can learn more about the plant and bird life in the area. Don't keep your eyes only in the air, however. Look for the coastal *naupaka* plants that surround the parking lot and line the walk to the lighthouse. Common along the seashore and able to grow in arid regions, these plants have bunches of bright green, moisture-retaining, leathery leaves; at their centers are white half-flowers the size of fingernails, and small white seeds.

The refuge plans to establish a four-mile walking trail from Kilauea Point around Crater Hill to Mokolea Point, to be used strictly for tours led by refuge personnel. The lighthouse facility is open Mon.-Fri. 10 a.m.-4 p.m., closed weekends and

great frigate bird

LOUISE FOOTE

federal holidays. The entrance fee is $2 adults, children under 16 free; an annual refuge permit is $10. The Golden Eagle Pass, Golden Access Pass, Golden Age Pass, and Federal Duck Stamp are also honored for free entrance.

Beaches

The Kilauea area has some fantastic beaches. One is a beach park with full amenities and camping, one is hidden and rarely visited, while others are for fishing or just looking.

Kauapea Beach, more commonly called **Secret Beach,** lives up to everything its name implies. After passing through Kilauea, look for Banana Joe's tropical fruit stand on the left; past it is Kalihiwai Road. Make a right onto Kalihiwai and then take the very first dirt road on the right. Follow this tiny road for about one mile until it turns right at an iron gate. Continue down the hill to a parking area and a little homemade sign saying "Beach Trail." Follow the signs that point you to the beach—if there are signs it can't be too secret. Even some local residents ruefully admit that the "secret" is out. However, if you venture to this beach, be conscious that there are private homes nearby and that it's a place locals come to enjoy away from the crowds of tourists.

Walk beside the barbed-wire fence and down the slippery slope to the beach. You pass through some excellent jungle area before emerging at Secret Beach in less than 15 minutes. If you expect Secret Beach to be small, you're in for a shock. This white-sand strand is huge. Off to the right you can see Kilauea Lighthouse, dazzling white in the sun. Along the beach is a fine stand of trees providing shade and perfect for pitching a tent. A stream coming into the beach when you come down the hill is okay for washing in, but not for drinking. For drinking water head south along the beach and keep your eyes peeled for a freshwater spring coming out of the mountain. What more can you ask for? The camping is terrific and generally free of hassles.

Kilauea Bay offers great fishing, unofficial camping, and beautiful scenery. Proceed through Kilauea along Kilauea Road past Kong Lung Store. About 100 yards past the Martin Farm produce stand, take the second dirt road to the right (it angles through cane fields). Follow this rutted, gravel road one and a half miles down to what the local people call **Quarry Beach,** also called Kahili Beach. At the end of the road is the now-abandoned Kahili Quarry. Although easy to get to, this wide sandy beach is rarely visited. Characteristic of Kauai, Kilauea Stream runs into the bay. From the parking lot, you must wade across the stream to the beach. The swimming is good in the stream and along the beach, but only during calm periods. Local residents come here to surf or use boogie boards; do this only if you have been on the bay before and are experienced with Hawaiian waters. Plenty of places along the streambank or on the beach are good for picnicking and camping. Many local fishermen come here to catch a transparent fish called *oio* that they use for bait. It's too bony to fry, but they have figured out an ingenious way to get the meat. They cut off the tail and roll a soda pop bottle over it, squeezing the meat out through the cut. They then mix it with water, pepper, and bread crumbs to make delicious fish balls.

Kalihiwai Beach is just past Kilauea off Rt. 56 and down Kalihiwai Road. If you go over the Kalihiwai River you've gone too far, even though another section of the Kalihiwai Road also leads from there down to the coast. This road was once part of the coastal road, but the devastating tsunami of 1946 took out the lower bridge and the road is now divided by the river. As on many such rivers in Kauai, a ferry was used here to ease early transportation difficulties. In less than a half mile down the first Kalihiwai Road you come to an off-the-track, white-sand beach lined by ironwoods. The swimming and bodysurfing are outstanding given the right conditions. The river behind the ironwoods forms a freshwater pool for rinsing off, but there are no amenities whatsoever. People can camp among the ironwoods without a problem. The second Kalihiwai Road leads you to the beach on the west side of the river where some people come to fish.

Go over the bridge and turn right on the second Kalihiwai Road. Follow this to a Y, taking the left fork, Anini Road, ending at the remarkable **Anini Beach County Park.** The reef here is the longest exposed reef off Kauai; consequently the snorkeling is first-rate. It's amazing to snorkel out to the reef in no more than four feet of water and then to peer over the edge into waters that seem bottomless. Windsurfers also love this area, and their bright sails can be seen year-round. Those in the know say this is the *best* spot on Kauai for beginning windsurfers as the winds are generally steady, the bottom shallow, and the beach protected. Several shops in Hanalei give lessons here.

Follow the road to the end where a shallow brackish lagoon and large sandbar make the area good for wading. This beach has full amenities with toilets, picnic tables, grills, and a pavilion. There are private homes at both ends of this beach so be considerate when coming and going.

A polo ground is across the road from the open camping area, and several Sundays per month matches are held 3-5 p.m. Admission is $3 per person or $6 per car, and the exciting match is both fun and stylish. The local horsemen are excellent players who combine with their trusty mounts to perform amazing athletic maneuvers.

Food, Shopping, And Services

An institution in this area is **Kong Lung Store,** which has been serving the needs of the north shore plantation towns for almost a century. But don't expect bulk rice and pipe fittings. Kong Lung prides itself on being an "exotic gift emporium," with shelves of gourmet cheeses, fine wines, and all the accoutrements necessary for a very civilized picnic. Another section is a clothing boutique selling name-brand beach duds, casual clothes, and alohawear. Enter an adjoining room to find an art gallery specializing in carvings, pottery, jewelry, and Niihau shellwork. Notice too the old-fashioned rag carpets woven with modern pastel material. A children's section and shelves of cards and books of Kauaiana and Hawaiiana round out this unique store. Kong Lung is located along Kilauea Lighthouse Road at the intersection of Keneke Street, tel. 828-1822, open daily 9 a.m.-5 p.m.

Windows all around open onto a miniature garden and lanai patio where you can dine alfresco, at **Casa di Amici Ristorante.** Located next door to Kong Lung Store, open for dinner 5:30-9 p.m., tel. 828-1388, it is the best Italian restaurant on the north shore. Chef Randall Yates and his professional staff make you feel right at home in this "house of friends." The classic *ristorante* has green-topped tables trimmed in wood, and comfortable chairs with padded armrests. In the center, a diminutive fountain performs a tinkling melody, while an ensemble of magnificent Hawaiian flowers dances gently with the breeze. Start with antipasti, a plate laden with greens, pepperoncini, olives, eggs, provolone, salami, prosciutto, and anchovies for $7; or try the polenta, a specialty of northern Italy, garnished with fresh tomatoes, basil, and Parmesan, also for $7. For a light meal combine these with homemade *zuppa* like *straciatella,* an egg-drop broth flavored with Parmesan cheese, or a classic minestrone, both priced at $5. Pasta, priced $12-15, comes in all shapes and sizes: linguine, rigatoni, fettuccine, covered with sauces like sun-dried tomato pesto or cilantro macadamia-nut pesto. Main courses are veal scallopini ($22), chicken with Marsala sauce, ($15), fettuccine marino, fresh fish, mussels, prawns, and calamari for $22, or a plate of lasagna for only $12. The *ristorante* also has a full-service bar serving top shelf liquors and imported draft beers, along with a fine wine selection prominently displayed for your perusal. There's espresso or cappuccino to complete your meal, and to add to your dining pleasure, soothing piano music is performed nightly.

Just behind the Casa di Amici is **The Kilauea Bakery and Pau Hana Pizza,** open daily except Sunday, 6:30 a.m.-10 p.m., tel. 828-2020. Using all natural ingredients, Kilauea Bakery supplies some of the best restaurants along the north shore. The extensive list of baked goods is tempting, and occasionally they put out something a bit offbeat like pumpkin coconut muffins. As with the other shops in this little complex, Kilauea Bakery succeeds in offering something special. Their gourmet pizzas are made with organically grown California olive oil and whole milk mozzarella on a whole wheat or sourdough crust. Prices are $6 for a small to $15 for a 16-inch large, $1-2.25 by the slice. Toppings are sauteéd mushrooms, feta cheese, grated Parmesan, homemade pesto, sun-dried tomatoes, or locally grown peppers. Enjoy your treat inside, or sit on the tiny veranda under a shade umbrella. Coffee, made by the cup, is also served.

Directly behind Kong Lung Store is the **Lighthouse Gallery,** tel. 828-1828. Open every day except Sunday, this shop carries paintings, prints, and woodwork by statewide artists. Concentrating on local themes, these items are in the mid-price range, and the object of the gallery is to offer something different from what is seen in the ordinary tourist shops.

Next door to Casa di Amici is the Kilauea neighborhood center and theater, and beyond that are the **Farmers' Market** and a deli/grocery store open 9 a.m.-9 p.m. The deli carries food items and beverages, and makes homemade and filling (but not cheap) soup and sandwiches if you want something substantial but don't want a full sit-down meal. Behind the center is a small community park.

Martin Farm Produce Stand is just beyond town. Open Mon.-Sat. 9 a.m.-5 p.m., it operates on the self-service honor system. Select what you want, add up the cost marked on each item, and drop your payment in the box. Nearby, at the corner of Oka Street, is the Kilauea clinic of the **Kauai Medical Group.**

Across Lighthouse Road from Kong Lung Store is the Kilauea Plantation Center, a low lava-rock building. Recently remodeled, it has several shops, boutiques, and offices, one of which is **Artisan's International,** tel. 828-1918. Open Mon.-Sat. 10:30 a.m.-5:30 p.m., this shop is chock-a-block with quality household items, fine furnishings, gifts, craft items, jewelry, clothes, and collectables—not an inch is left bare. All items are handmade, and this helps create a real "feeling" store, as Jeri, the owner, likes to say.

At the intersection of Kolo and Kilauea roads, across from the Episcopal church, is the **Hawaiian Art Museum.** A project of Aloha International, it seems more like a gift shop with books, tapes, gift items, postcards, and a few arts and crafts for sale.

After visiting all these places, you need a rest. The perfect stop is west of town at **Banana Joe's** fruit stand, *mauka* of the highway, tel. 828-1092. Run by Joe Halasey, his wife, and friends, this little yellow stand offers fresh fruit, smoothies and other drinks, packaged fruit baskets, baked goods with fruit, and other fruit products. They have more kinds of fruit than you've ever heard of—try something new. If you're interested and they have the time, you may be able to visit the farm behind the stand and talk to Banana Joe himself, but you'll have to ask first. Not to be outdone in the "related to a tropical fruit" department, just before Banana Joe's is **Mango Mama's Fruitstand.** What's next? Sister Soursop and Brother Breadfruit?

Accommodations

The **Mahi Ko Inn,** General Delivery, Kilauea, HI 96754, tel. 828-1103 or (800) 458-3444, is a restored plantation home hosted by Cathy and Doug Weber. Rates are $75-135, with a continental breakfast included.

The **Kai Mana,** Box 612, Kilauea, HI, tel. 828-1280, is filled with the healing vibrations of its internationally acclaimed owner, Shakti Gawain, author of *Creative Visualization,* and by the powerful natural forces so evident on Kauai. Here, the emphasis of your vacation is not only on relaxation, but on revitalization. Part of your stay can be private counseling with Shakti when she is in residence, or a session with a massage practitioner or meditation instructor, or a simple nature attunement excursion. Rates are: standard room $75 s, $95 d; deluxe corner room $95 s, $115 d; and self-contained cottage $125 per night, $750 per week. All rooms have private entrances and private baths. Light breakfast food is provided and a kitchenette is open to guests.

PRINCEVILLE

Princeville is 11,000 acres of planned luxury overlooking Hanalei Bay. Last century the surrounding countryside was a huge ranch, Kauai's oldest, established in 1853 by the Scotsman R.C. Wyllie. After an official royal vacation on the ranch by Kamehameha IV and Queen Emma in 1860, the name was changed to Princeville in honor of their son, Prince Albert. The young heir unfortunately died within two years and his heartbroken father soon followed.

Since 1969, Consolidated Gas and Oil of Honolulu has taken these same 11,000 acres and developed them into a prime vacation community dedicated to keeping the humdrum world far away. Previously owned by the Princeville Development Corp., a subsidiary of Quitex Australia, and now owned by the Japanese firm Santuri and the Mitsui Corporation, Princeville provides everything: accommodations, shopping, dining, recreational facilities (especially golf and tennis), a fire and police force, and an airport. First-rate condos are scattered around the property and a new multitiered Sheraton Mirage Hotel perches over the bay. The guests expect to stay put, except for an occasional daytrip. Management and clientele are in league to provide and receive satisfaction. And without even trying, that's just about guaranteed.

Note: Mileage markers on Hwy. 56 going west are renumbered from one (1) at Princeville. It is 10 miles from here to the end of the road at Ke'e Beach.

RECREATION

Golf, Tennis, And Athletic Clubs

Those addicted to striking hard, dimpled white balls or fuzzy soft ones have come to the right spot. In Princeville, golf and tennis are the royal couple. The **Princeville Makai Golf Course** offers 27 holes of magnificent golf designed by Robert Trent Jones, Jr. This course, chosen as one of America's top 100, hosted the 26th annual World Cup in 1978, and is where the LPGA Women's Kemper Open is played. Radiating from the central clubhouse are three nine-hole par-36 courses you can use in any combination. They include the **Woods, Lake,** and **Ocean** courses, the names highlighting their special focus.

Opened in 1987, the 18-hole **Prince** course, tel. 826-3580 for information and reservations, also welcomes the public. It's located off Hwy. 56 just east of the Woods course and has its own clubhouse. For this course, accuracy and control are much more important than power and distance. Many expert golfers judge the Prince extremely difficult, perhaps the most challenging in Hawaii—one par-six hole, one hole with the tee 300 feet above the fairway, and ravines and streams to play over, are among the obstacles. Nine-hole twilight golf on any course is available on weekdays after 3 p.m. for a reduced fee. The clubhouse has an extensive pro shop, a snack shop, and club storage. The driving range is open during daylight hours. Plenty of package deals to the resort include flights, accommodations, rental car, and unlimited golf.

You can charge the net on 22 professional tennis courts, day or night at the **Princeville Tennis Club,** tel. 826-3620. There are two pro shops, lessons of all sorts, racquet rental, ball machines, and even video playback so you can burn yourself up a second time while reviewing your mistakes. Several condos in Princeville, such as The Cliffs and the Hanalei Bay Resort, also have tennis courts, but these are for their guests only.

Note: Also see the Golf and Tennis charts under "Sports and Recreation" in the Kauai Introduction.

On the lower level of the Princeville Clubhouse is the **Hanalei Athletic Club,** open weekdays 7 a.m.-8 p.m., Saturday 8 a.m.-6 p.m., and Sunday 11 a.m.-5 p.m., tel. 826-7333. This is a sister club of the Kauai Athletic Club in Lihue, so you can use both if you are a member. Available are aerobics classes, Nautilus machines, free weights, outdoor pool, jacuzzi, and sauna. It also has designated running courses throughout the Princeville resort area. Daily, weekly, and monthly rates are available with discounts for couples offered. For those with small children, a babysitting service is available by appointment weekdays 8:30-10 a.m. Operating through the health club is **Hanalei Health and Sports Massage.** For an appointment, call 826-1455. Licensed professional staff give *lomi lomi,* shiatsu, Swedish, Esalen, and sports massages.

Other Activities

Two miles east of Princeville is the Princeville Airport. **Papillon Helicopters,** tel. 826-6591, operates its magical mystery tours deep into Kauai's interior from here. Once-in-a-lifetime, unforgettable experiences, the flights range anywhere from the "Discover" at 30 minutes to the "Odyssey," which includes a complete view of the island and a two-hour picnic stop.

If flying isn't your pleasure, how about loping along on horseback? **Pooku Stables,** tel. 826-6777, is located a half mile east of Princeville Center and is open Mon.-Sat. 7:30 a.m.-4 p.m. You can rent a mount here for one of three group rides that take you throughout the area's fascinating countryside. Prices are $30, $50, and $75 for the Hanalei Valley, shoreline, and waterfall picnic rides. Hanalei Stampede, Kauai's largest rodeo, is held at Pooku Stables in early August. Call for details.

ACCOMMODATIONS

The condos and hotel rooms in Princeville all fall into the high-moderate to expensive range. The best deals naturally occur off-season (fall), especially if you plan on staying a week or more. Oddly enough, a project like Princeville should make booking one of its many condos an easy matter, but it's sadly lacking on this point. Lack of a centralized organization that handles reservations causes the confusion. Each condo building can have half a dozen booking agents, all with different phone numbers and widely differing rates. The units are privately owned and the owners simply choose one agency or another. If you're going through a travel agent at home, be aware of these discrepancies and insist on the least expensive rates. Reducing the number of units available is condo conversion to complete time-share programs. Some still offer rental units with their time-share units, so check out the possibilities.

Set high on the bluff overlooking the Pacific Ocean, with one of the nicest views in the area, is **The Cliffs At Princeville,** tel. 826-6219 or (800) 367-7052. Each one-bedroom condo unit has a full-size bath and a small wet bar in the room; a second full bath is off the entryway. At the far end of the L-shaped living and dining room is the fully equipped kitchen; you can prepare everything from a fresh pot of morning coffee to a five-course meal at your leisure and in the comfort of your own living space. Two large lanai, one at each end of the unit, offer both an ocean view and a mountain view. Carpets run throughout the unit, and the furniture is of contemporary style. Fresh flowers, potted plants, Hawaiian prints, and artwork counter the pastel colors and the subdued floral patterns of the bedroom linen. The bedroom has a king-size bed and the cushy living-room couch pulls out to sleep two more. Each unit also has a color TV, video and stereo systems, compact washer and dryer, iron and ironing board, small safe for valuables, and daily maid service. Some units on the third floor have two bedrooms. These are basically the same as the one-bedroom units except that the second bedroom is in a loft and the living-room ceiling slants up to the second floor. One-bedroom units are $75-150; two-bedroom units run $95-200; and three to four bedrooms run $150-450. The property has a pool and tennis courts free to the guests, and a breezy common room off the pool with a large-screen TV, reading material, and a laundry room.

The best deal in Princeville is offered by **Sandpiper Village** condominiums. By chance they stumbled onto a good thing. When they first opened they priced their units low to attract clientele. The response was so good, with so many repeat visitors, that they have decided to keep it that way . . . for the time being. For $55-100, you get a roomy one-bedroom unit (one to two people), for $65-135 a two-bedroom, two-bath unit (one to four people), or for $100-175 a three-bedroom unit. (Minimum stay often required, inquire.) A few unadvertised one-room studios with bath for $45 per night are available on a limited basis, but you must specifically ask about these. All units have garden views. Each has a full kitchen with dishwasher, laundry facilities, color TV, and private lanai. Maid service is available every four days. On the grounds are a pool, a jacuzzi, barbecue grills, and a recreational building, all surrounding well-tended gardens. For reservations and information contact Sandpiper Village at 826-9613, or phone their booking agents, Kauai Paradise Vacations at (800) 826-7782, Oceanfront Realty at (800) 222-5541.

The **Hanalei Bay Resort,** P.O. Box 220, Hanalei, HI 96714, physically at 5380 Honoiki Road, Princeville, tel. 826-6522 or (800) 827-4427, is a combination condo/hotel, with some private units. You enter through a spacious open area paved with flagstone, and face the **Bali Hai Bar,** done in longhouse style with palm-frond roof and magnificent koa long bar matched by a koa canoe. From the bar you have a spectacular panorama of Bali Hai Mountain dappled by the passing clouds, and of Hanalei Bay's sheet of foam-fringed azure. Evening brings live music, with everything from jazz to a local slack-key combo. Stepping down the hillside from the bar is the resort's free-form pool complete with a 15-foot waterfall, surrounded by landscaping inspired by the area's natural beauty. The resort buildings are like two outstretched arms ready to embrace the bay, and all units are guaranteed to have a stupendous view. Amenities include laundry facilities, full kitchens in the condo units, TV, phone, tennis courts, and a/c. Rates are $70 for a hotel room, $250 for a three-bedroom condo.

Other condos in the development are expensive, charging a minimum of $100 per night. They're out to please and don't skimp on the luxuries. For example, the **Ka'eo Kai,** tel. (800) 367-8047, gives you a massive, 2,300-square-foot unit with lanai, custom kitchen, fireplace, stereo, and big-screen TV. Each unit accommodates seven comfortably. The **Pali Ke Kua** condos sit right on the cliffs, and along with the nearby **Pu'u Po'a,** and the **Hale Moi** condominiums are managed by Marc Resorts Hawaii; for reservations call (800) 535-0085. One of the best restaurants on the north coast, the Beamreach, is at the Pali Ke Kua. More luxurious, the Pu'u Po'a is slightly more expensive than the Pali Ke Kua; overlooking the golf course, the Hale Moi is about half the price.

Other good options include the **Alii Kai II** (like the Sandpiper and Hanalei Bay Resort, managed by Hawaiiana Resorts), where all units are $100; and the **Paniolo** and weathered-gray Cape Cod-ish **Sealodge.** Reservations for both can be made by calling Hanalei Aloha Rental Management, Box 1109, Hanalei, HI 96714, tel. 826-9833 or (800) 367-8047

The **Princeville Hotel,** operated by Sheraton Hotels, is a dramatic architectural feat, built in tiers stepping down the point of a rugged peninsula. From its perch, all but 16 of the 250 rooms offer a breathtaking view of Hanalei Bay as it stretches toward Bali Hai Peak down the coast. The others offer a panoramic view of Puu Poa Marsh, a wildlife conservation wetlands area that offers sanctuary to exotic birdlife. The hotel, at one time offering a Hawaiian plantation motif, is now coming back as an elegant European-inspired hotel. The lobby, opened to encompass a sweeping view of Hanalei Bay, is graced with light timbers, marble flooring, and silent waterfalls naturally illuminated by skylights. Over $4 million of art and antiques add to the visual pleasures. A main feature is the Living Room, just off the main lobby, providing a library, a 16th-century restored piano, and a fireplace for an evening of quiet contemplation and relaxation. Each room features a bathroom with double vanity, gold fixtures, and deep tub. Bathroom doors are of liquid crystal that can be controlled to change from opaque for privacy to clear so that you can enjoy the view while you soak away. Rooms also feature minibar, refrigerator, TV, and VCR with free videos. A sweet welcome awaits you on your first day, when a little jar of warm brownies will be placed in your room. In addition, there are three restaurants (see below), two lounges, a swimming pool, gift shops, an art gallery, an activities desk, and a white-sand beach on the bay. Free shuttle service is provided to and from the golf course, tennis courts, shopping center, and Princeville Airport. A standard room ranges $295-410, and suites $450-2300; third-person charge is $35. For information write Princeville Hotel, 5520 Kahaku Rd., Princeville, HI 96722, or call 826-9644, (800) 826-4400, or (800) 325-3535.

FOOD

Princeville's restaurants, many located within the condos, are expensive but good. The **Bali Hai,** open daily, tel. 826-7670, an open-air restaurant in the Hanalei Bay Resort, enjoys an excellent reputation not only for its food, but for its superb atmosphere and prize-winning view of the sunset. The bamboo, batik, and tapestries hung in this bilevel restaurant add an informal elegance. The Bali Hai, under the direction of Chef Geoff Anderson, offers breakfast, lunch, and dinner. Chef Anderson, who grows his own herbs on the premises, insists on fresh local vegetables, meat, and fish for his Pacific Rim cuisine. Breakfast and lunch could be eggs, omelettes, salads, or sandwiches; a substantial dinner menu is offered.

Lanai Restaurant, tel 826-6226, at the Princeville clubhouse, is an open-air restaurant right on the fairways—great sunsets over the course. It receives the most consistent praise of any eatery in Princeville. The Lanai serves continental and American fare, with a touch of Asian. Open at 4 p.m. for cocktails; sunset dinners start at 6 p.m. Light entertainment is provided nightly by local musicians.

The **Princeville Hotel** is home to three restaurants. The **Cafe Hanalei** is open for breakfast, lunch, and dinner and offers indoor or outdoor seating in a casual setting. The contemporary American cuisine specializes in fresh island fish. **La Cascata,** open daily for dinner and Sunday for brunch, offers tremendous views of the island's inland waterfalls. Designed after a famous restaurant in Positano, Italy, the restaurant's decor includes elegant hand-painted terra-cotta floors and murals. The cuisine is southern Italian in this casually elegant *ristorante.* For light meals try the hotel's **Beach Bar and Restaurant,** where you can order snacks and sandwiches in this pavilion-type casual restaurant.

At the Princeville Center you'll find **Chuck's Steak House** and **Cafe Zelo's Deli & Espresso Bar.** Chuck's has a good reputation for meat dishes and a loyal local clientele. Both are open for lunch and dinner, and entrees are $12-18. Zelo's is the place to go for breakfast. Definitely more casual and *simpatico* than the hotel restaurants, this little cafe is open Mon.-Sat. 8 a.m.-6 p.m., until 3 p.m. on Sunday, tel. 826-9700. Breakfasts include omelettes, crepes, and bagels, most under $4.50; lunch is various sandwiches and salads, most under $6. Pastries, desserts, fruit drinks, and coffee are served anytime. Sit inside under the high arched ceiling or out on the patio, and order coffee from the largest selection on the north coast. The decor's subdued grays and whites bring out the brighter colors in the wall hangings of tropical birds, fish, and vegetation. On occasion, you'll be lucky to catch one of the local musicians strumming softly on his guitar in the corner.

Also at the Princeville Center, **Lappert's Ice Cream** will fill a cone for you, **Sweet Temptation Bakery** will tempt you to come in and try a mouthwatering treat, and you can order guess what at the **Pizza Burger.** Don't forget **Amelia's** at the Princeville Airport for sandwiches, snacks, and drinks on your way into or out of town.

ENTERTAINMENT

There is little in the way of evening entertainment in Princeville, so you may have to be creative and make your own. However, the following are worth checking out. The **Lanai Restaurant** hosts live music nightly, ranging from Hawaiian to jazz to contemporary sounds. At the **Bali Hai Restaurant** you can listen to Hawaiian music five nights a week. The **Ukiyo Lounge** at the Sheraton (dress code) is a disco that stays open Sun.-Thurs. until midnight, and until 2 a.m. on Friday and Saturday.

SHOPPING AND SERVICES

Aside from the few shops, the Princeville Hotel, the clubhouse, and the tennis pro shop, the shopping in Princeville is clustered in the Princeville Center complex. A few stores sell souvenirs and gifts, but since Princeville is a self-contained community, most are practical shops: bank, hardware store, sporting goods outlet, real estate offices, Kauai Medical Group clinic, post office, restaurants, and **Foodland** supermarket. The latter is important because it offers the cheapest food prices on the north shore. Before it was built, the local people would drive to Kapa'a to shop; now they come here. The last gas station on the north shore is **Princeville Chevron.** If your gauge is low make sure to tank up if you're driving back down the coast. They're open Mon.-Thurs. 7 a.m.-7 p.m., Friday and Saturday until 8 p.m., and Sunday until 6 p.m.

HANALEI

If Puff the Magic Dragon had resided in the sunshine of Hanalei instead of the mists of Hanalee, Little Jackie Paper would still be hangin' around. You know you're entering a magic land the minute you drop down from the heights and cross the Hanalei River. The narrow, one-lane bridge is like a gateway to the enchanted coast, forcing you to slow down and take stock of where you are. To add to your amazement, as you look "up valley" over a sea of green taro, what else would you expect to find but a herd of buffalo? (They're imported by a local entrepreneur trying to cross-breed them with beef cattle.)

Hanalei ("Lei-making Town") compacts a lot into a little space. You're in and out of the town in two blinks, but you'll find a small shopping center, some terrific restaurants, beach and ocean activities, historical sites, and a cultural and art center. You also get two superlatives for the price of one: the epitome of a north shore laid-back village, and a truly magnificent bay. In fact, if you were forced to choose the most beautiful bay in all of Hawaii, Hanalei (and Lumahai, the silent star of the movie *South Pacific,* just north of town), would definitely be among the finalists.

SIGHTS

The sights around Hanalei are exactly that, beautiful sweeping vistas of **Hanalei Valley** and the sea, especially at sunset. People come just for the light show and are never disappointed. When you proceed past the Princeville turnoff, keep your eyes peeled for the Hanalei Valley scenic overlook. Don't miss it! Drifting into the distance is the pastel living impressionism of Hanalei Valley—most dramatic in late afternoon when soft shadows from deeply slanting sun rays create depth in this quilt of fields. Down the center, the liquid silver Hanalei River flows to the sea where the valley broadens into a wide flat fan. Along its banks vibrate impossible shades of green as the valley extends inland for almost nine miles, cradled in the protective arms of 3,500-foot *pali.* Turned on or off by rains, waterfalls tumble over the *pali* like lace curtains billowing in a gentle wind, or with the blasting power of a fire hose. Local wisdom says that "when you can count 17 waterfalls it's time to get out of Hanalei." The valley has always been one of the most accommodating places in all of Hawaii to live in, and its abundance was ever-blessed by the old gods. Madame Pele even sent a thunderbolt to split a boulder so that the Hawaiians could run an irrigation ditch through its center to their fields.

In the old days, Hanalei produced taro, and deep in the valley the outlines of the ancient fields can still be discerned. Then white settlers raised coffee that failed, sugar that petered out, and cattle that overgrazed the land. During these times Hanalei had to *import* poi from Kalalau. Later, when Chinese plantation laborers moved in, the valley was terraced again, but this time the wet fields were given to rice. This crop proved profitable for many years and was still grown as late as the 1930s. Then, amazingly, the valley began to slowly revert back to taro patches.

In 1972, 917 acres of this valley were designated **Hanalei National Wildlife Refuge.** Native waterbirds such as the Hawaiian coot, stilt, duck, and gallinule reclaimed their ancient nesting grounds. Today, the large, green, heart-shaped leaves of taro carpet the valley, and the abundant crop supplies about half of Hawaii's poi. You can go into Hanalei Valley; however, you're not permitted in the designated wildlife areas except along the river for fishing or hiking. Never disturb nesting birds. Look below to where a one-lane bridge crosses the river. Just there, Ohiki Road branches inland. Drive along it slowly to view the simple and quiet homesteads, old rice mill, nesting birds, wildflowers, and terraced fields of this enchanted land.

Overlooking the bay, on a tall bluff, are the remains of an old Russian fort (1816), from the days when Hawaii was lusted after by many European powers. It's too difficult to find, but knowing it's there adds a little spice. As you enter town look for the Hanalei Trader on your right. Past it on the left is the **Hanalei Museum,** one of Hawaii's funkiest. Often closed, and seemingly an addendum to a small stand selling

J.D. BISIGNANI

Waioli Mission House

plate lunches and saimin, it's great just because it is so unostentatious. Perhaps the most intriguing things in this two-room, rough-wood building are the photographs from the early years of the century. Go around back to the outhouselike shed holding a few rusty, muddy items, like an old sink and a mirror. The experience is cultural, like being invited into someone's backyard.

Down the block, on the right next to Napali Zodiac, an old building (the old Ching Young Store) houses the **Native Hawaiian Trading and Cultural Center.** Don't get *too* excited because this good idea doesn't have its act together yet. Aside from a very small museum (open daily 10 a.m.-5 p.m.), they have some authentic Hawaiian crafts, and some awful touristy junk, too. You can buy handmade jewelry, shells, clothes, and sweets, but some of the really worthwhile items are lovely fresh plumeria lei and flowers. Upstairs is the Artisans Guild of Kauai, a fine co-op where local artists display and sell their arts and crafts.

Waioli Mission House Museum

As you leave town, look to your left to see **Waioli Hui'ia Church.** If you're in Hanalei on Sunday do yourself a favor and go to the 10 a.m. service, where you will be uplifted by a choir of rich voices singing enchanting hymns in Hawaiian. They do justice to the meaning of *Waioli,* which is "Healing or Singing Waters." The **Waioli Mission House** is a must-stop whenever you pass through. You know you're in for a treat as soon as you pull into the parking lot, which is completely surrounded by trees, creeping vines, ferns, and papaya. You walk over steppingstones through a formal garden with the jagged mountains framing a classical American homestead. Most mission homes are New England-style, and this one is too, inside. But outside it's Southern, because the missionary architect was a Kentuckian, Rev. William P. Alexander, who arrived with his wife Mary Ann in 1834 by double-hulled canoe from Waimea. Although a number of missionary families lived in the home the first few years after it was built in 1837, in 1846 Abner and Lucy Wilcox arrived, and the home became synonymous with this family. Indeed, it was owned and occupied by the *kama'aina* Wilcox family until very recently. It was George, the son of Abner and Lucy, who founded Grove Homestead over by Lihue. Miss Mabel Wilcox, his niece who died in 1978, and her sister Miss Elsie, who was the first woman representative of Hawaii in the '30s, set up the nonprofit educational foundation that operates the home.

Your first treat will be meeting Joan, the lovely tour guide. A "fuss pot" in the best sense of the word, she's like a proper old auntie who gives you the "hairy eyeball" if you muss up the doily on the coffee table. Joan knows an unbelievable amount of history and anecdotes, not only about the mission house, but about the entire area and Hawaii in general. The home is great, and she makes it better. The first thing she says, almost apologetically to Mainlanders, is, "Take off your shoes. It's an old Hawaiian custom and feels good to your feet."

You enter the parlor where Lucy Wilcox taught native girls who'd never seen a needle and thread to sew. Within a few years, their nimble fingers were fashioning muumuu to cover their pre-Christian nakedness. In the background an old clock ticks. In 1866 a missionary coming to visit from Boston was given $8 to buy a clock; here it is, keeping time more than 120 years later. The picture on it is of the St. Louis Courthouse. Paintings of the Wilcoxes line the walls. Lucy looks like a happy, sympathetic woman. Abner's books line the shelves. Notice old copies of *Uncle Tom's Cabin* and *God Against Slavery.* Mr. Wilcox, in addition to being a missionary, was a doctor, teacher, public official, and veterinarian. His preserved letters show that he was a very serious man, not given to humor. He and Lucy didn't want to come to Waioli at first, but they learned to love the place. He worried about his sons, and about being poor. He wrote letters to the king urging that Hawaiian be retained as the first language, English as a second. He and Lucy returned to New England for a visit in 1869, where both took sick and died.

During the time this was a mission household, nine children were born in the main bedroom, eight of them boys. Behind it is a nursery, the only room that has had a major change; Lucy and Mabel had a closet built and an indoor bathroom installed here in 1921. Upstairs is a guest bedroom the Wilcoxes dubbed the "room of the traveling prophet," because it was invariably occupied by visiting missionaries. Also used by Abner Wilcox as a study, the room contains the original primers printed on Oahu. The homestead served as a school for selected boys who were trained as teachers.

The house has been added to several times and is surprisingly spacious. It was also a self-sufficient farm where chickens and cattle were raised. In the home are artifacts, dishes, and knickknacks from the last century; notice candle molds, a food locker, a charcoal iron, and the old butter churn. Lucy Wilcox churned butter that she shipped to Honolulu in buckets, which brought in some good money. Most of the furniture is donated period pieces; only a few were actually used by the Wilcoxes. From the upstairs window you can still see the view that has remained unchanged from the last century: Hanalei Bay, beautifully serene and timeless. The Waioli Mission House is open Tuesday, Thursday, and Saturday 9 a.m.-3 p.m., and admission is free. There is a bucket for donations; please be generous.

BEACHES

Since the days of the migrating Polynesians, Hanalei Bay has been known as one of the Pacific's most perfect anchorages. Used as one of Kauai's three main ports until very recently, it's still a favorite port of call for world-class yachts. They start arriving in mid-May, making the most of the easy entrance and sandy bottom, and stay throughout the summer. They leave by October, when even this inviting bay becomes rough, with occasional 30-foot waves. When you drive to the bay, the section under the trees near the river is called **Black Pot.** It received this name from an earlier time when the people of Hanalei would greet the yachties with island *aloha,* which of course included food. A fire was always going with a large black pot hanging over it, to which everyone contributed and then shared the meal. Across the road and upriver a few hundred yards is **Hanalei Canoe Club.** This small local club has produced a number of winning teams in statewide competitions, oftentimes appearing against much larger clubs.

The sweeping crescent bay is gorgeous. The Hanalei River (and three smaller streams) empties into it, and mountains embrace it protectively. A long pier is in the center, and two reefs front the bay, **Queen** to the left and **King** to the right. The bay provides excellent sailing, surfing, and swimming, mostly in the summer. The swimming is good near the river (but watch out for boats and Zodiac rafts launched from here!) and at the west end, but rip currents can appear anywhere, even around the pier area, so be careful. The best surf rolls in at the outside reef below Puu Poa Point on the east side of the bay, but it's definitely recommended only for expert surfers. Beginners can try the middle of the bay during summer when the surf is smaller and gentler. The state maintains three parks on the bay: Black Pot at the Hanalei River mouth, Pine Trees in the middle of the bay, and Waipa on the west side. Black Pot and Pine Trees have picnic areas, restrooms, and showers. Camping is permitted only at Pine Trees. A small *kaukau* wagon sells plate lunches near the river; local fishermen launch their boats in the bay and are often amenable to selling their catch.

Lumahai Beach is a *femme fatale,* lovely to look at but treacherous. This hauntingly beautiful beach, meaning "Twist of Fingers," is what dreams are made of: white sand curving perfectly at the bottom of a dark lava cliff with tropical jungle in the background. The riptides here are fierce even with the reef, and the water should never be entered except in very calm conditions during the summer. Look for a vista point past mile marker 4. Cars invariably park here. It's a sharp curve, so make sure to pull completely off the road or the police may ticket you. An extensive grove of *hala* trees appears just as you set off down a steep and often muddy footpath leading to the east end of the beach. The best and easiest place to park is among the ironwood trees at the west end of the beach near the bridge that crosses the Lumahai River; an emergency phone is across the road from this parking area. From here you can walk to the south end if you want seclusion.

ACCOMMODATIONS

The inexpensive **Mahikoa's Hanalei Bay Inn** is on the west side of town across from the school. It is tucked among flowering bushes and trees; with only six units, it's a quiet, relaxing place. Five units have a living/bedroom area with a queen-size bed or two twins, an efficiency kitchen sufficient to make a light meal, and a full bath; one of the units has an additional separate bedroom. The efficiency studios run $55 ($45 after two days) and the one-bedroom is $65 ($55 after two days). In addition, a bed-and-breakfast room maintained in the innkeeper's cottage goes for $50 plus tax. Maid service is available after four days. For more information call 826-9333 or write to Edmund Gardien, Innkeeper, Mahikoa's Hanalei Bay Inn, P.O. Box 122, Hanalei, HI 96714.

Bed, Breakfast, and Beach, P.O. Box 748, Hanalei, HI 96714, tel. 826-6111 or 826-6038, offers five rooms of various sizes all with private bath and queen-size beds. The rooms are completely furnished with antique oak furniture, and a healthful island breakfast is served on the second-floor lanai from where you can enjoy views of the magnificent countryside. The B&B is walking distance from downtown Hanalei, and offers rooms from a 700-square-foot suite on the third floor, to a first-floor room with its own kitchenette and outdoor shower for $60-80 d.

Private rental homes, generally listed through property and rental agencies, are available in town (and farther along the coast). For information contact **Na Pali Properties, Inc.,** P.O. Box 475, Hanalei, HI 96714, tel. 826-7272; **North Shore Properties, Ltd.,** P.O. Box 607, Hanalei, HI 96714, tel. 826-9622; or **Ironwood Rentals,** Hanalei, HI, tel. 826-7533.

FOOD AND FOOD SHOPPING

Hanalei has a number of eating institutions, ranging from excellent restaurants to *kaukau* wagons. The food is great at any time of day, but those in the know time their arrival to coincide with sunset. They watch the free show and then go for a great meal.

The **Hanalei Gourmet,** in the old schoolhouse at the Hanalei Center, open daily 8 a.m.-10 p.m., tel. 826-2524, is a born-again-hippie, semi-yuppie, one-stop nouveau cuisine deli, gourmet food shop, and good-time bar. To top it off, it's friendly, the food is exceptionally good, the price is right, and there's live entertainment. It is broken into two sections: to the right is the deli with cases filled with lunch meats, cheeses, salads, and smoked fish, while to the left is the bar-dining area. Here, ceiling fans keep you cool, while blackboards, once used to announce hideous homework assignments, now herald the daily specials. Behind the bar, windows through which reprimanded childhood daydreams once flew, open to frame green-silhouetted mountains. Original hardwood floors, white walls bearing local artworks and hanging plants, two big-screen TVs for sports enthusiasts, and a wide veranda with a few tables for dining alfresco complete the restaurant. Breakfast, served from 8 a.m., can be a half-papaya with other fresh fruit for $4.75, bagels, lox, and cream cheese for $6.50, muesli topped with fresh fruit for $4.25, or *huevos Santa Cruz* for $6.25. You can also enjoy a cup of Lappert's coffee and a pastry for around $3. Lunch sandwiches, all around $6, are huge wedges filled with pastrami, smoked ham, and gourmet cheeses. Dinner is served 5:30-9:30 p.m., and features specials like Oregon Bay shrimp served open-face on brown bread with melted cheese and remoulade sauce for $7.50, or smoked Alaskan king salmon on a French baguette for $9.95. A terrific Hawaiian seafood sampler features smoked ahi, mahimahi, and marlin served on Hawaiian sea salt, with soft breadsticks for $9.75. You can also order a picnic lunch to go, side salads, plenty of baked goods, or a fine bottle of wine. The Hanalei Gourmet definitely lives up to its name, and is the perfect spot for a meal or social beer.

You've got to stop at the **Tahiti Nui,** tel. 826-6277, if just to look around and have a cool drink. The original owner, Louise Marston, a real Tahitian although her name doesn't sound like it, was dedicated to creating a friendly, family atmosphere and she succeeded admirably. The restaurant is now run by her daughter and son-in-law, but the tradition carries on. Inside, it's pure Pacific island. The decorations are modern Polynesian longhouse, with blowfish lanterns and stools carved from palm tree trunks. The bar, open noon-2 a.m., is the center of action. Old-timers drop in to "talk story" and someone is always willing to sing and play a Hawaiian tune. The mai tais are fabulous. Sit out on the porch, kick back, and sip away. The lunch and dinner menu is limited and prices run $10-15. It includes fresh fish, beef, and chicken, all prepared with an island twist. You sit at long tables and eat family-style. The Tahiti Nui is famous for its luau-style party, Wednesday and Friday at 6:30 p.m. There's singing, dancing, and good cheer all around, a perfect time to mingle with the local people. The food is real Hawaiian, and the show is no glitzy extravaganza or slick production. This luau is very down to earth, casual, and Kauaian, and everybody has a good time. Adults $30, children $15.

Located next to Tahiti Nui, in the Kauhale Center, the **Hanalei Wake-Up Cafe,** open daily 6 a.m.-noon, tel. 826-5551, owned and operated by Lani, is the perfect breakfast place in Hanalei. Cubbyhole small, it has a few tables out on the veranda. The cheery help, smell of freshly brewed coffee, and good home cookin' should start off your day on the right foot. Try a giant muffin for $2, Over the Falls French toast for $4.75, or Hanalei in the Tube (a quesadilla with scrambled eggs, onions, and bell peppers in a flour tortilla with rice or hash browns) for $6.50. You can also have a vegie tofu saute of fresh vegetables, served with rice or hash browns for $5.75. Baked goods include bagel with cream cheese for $2; or have a nutritious sunrise smoothie, flavored with fresh pineapple, banana, or papaya for $2.75.

Just down the walkway in this group of shops is the **Black Pot Luau Hut** restaurant and bar, tel. 826-9871, serving mostly Hawaiian food. Open on a variable schedule for lunch and dinner, usually 11:30 a.m.-2:30 p.m. and 5:30 p.m.-9 p.m., Black Pot offers saimin $2.55-4.25, teri chicken or beef sticks at $1, hamburgers $2.55-3.40, and a selection of sandwiches like fishmelt, crabmelt, teri beef, or teri chicken for under $5. The Hawaiian/local food choices, served with two-scoop rice and potato or macaroni salad, includes *kalua* pig for $7.95, stir-fry chicken for $6.50, and a teri chicken plate at $4.95. Down-home basic Black Pot is very friendly, very local, and very good.

For a mouthwatering burger with all the trimmings, a plate lunch, or an undisputedly luscious bowl of saimin (the latter only in the evening), try the food stand at the **Hanalei Museum** on your left just as you enter town. Or try **Tropical Taco,** a *kaukau* wagon that dispenses great food at cheap prices. Open about noon, Tropical Taco is usually parked next to the Hanalei Trader as you enter town.

In the Ching Young Village, **Pizza Hanalei,** open daily 11 a.m.-9 p.m., delivery in the Hanalei/Princeville area 5-8:30 p.m., tel. 826-9494, serves the area's only pizza, and it's delicious. Made with thin, white, or whole-wheat crusts, these pizzas run $9-17.95. There is pizza by the slice 11 a.m.-5 p.m. Green and pasta salads, garlic bread, lasagna, and pizzarittos (pizza filling rolled up in a pizza shell like a burrito) are also on the menu. They do cholesterol-free tofu pizza as well, using Tofurella.

Next to Pizza Hanalei is **Hanalei Natural Foods,** open daily 8:30 a.m.-8:30 p.m., tel. 826-6990. Inside are bulk foods, fresh fruits and vegetables, baked breads, freshly squeezed juices, deli foods, and sandwiches, as well as books and vitamins. They also have a good selection of cosmetics, incense, candles, and massage oils. If you're into natural foods and healthful living, stop in, look around, and chat.

If the little hunger monster gets hold of you and a slab of tofu just won't do, walk across the courtyard to **The Village Snack And Bake Shop.** Open daily 6 a.m.-6 p.m., it serves just what its name implies, along with light breakfasts.

In a century-old building across the street from the Ching Young Center and next door to the Old Hanalei School is **Hanalei Wishing Well Shave Ice,** where Diana, the proprietress, will be happy to scoop you up what many claim to be the best shave ice on the island. Colorful long-necked bottles hold flavors like pistachio, raspberry, and coconut. If you are a neophyte shave ice eater, get the rainbow, a tour de force of multiple flavors. Diana also serves light snacks like barbecued teri chicken and beef sticks for $1.50, with rice $2, homemade saimin for $2, and coffee, tea, and hot chocolate.

Every Tuesday 3-5 p.m., pick up farm-fresh fruit and vegetables from the **Hawaiian Farmers of Hanalei** farmers' market located a half mile west of town in Waipa, on the road to Haena. Look for the sign along the road on the left.

An umbrella marks a stand by the old Hanalei School that sells hot dogs and vegie chili, both for around $2.

SHOPPING AND SERVICES

The **Ching Young Village** in the center of town is a small shopping center. Among its shops are **Big Save Supermarket,** a number of variety and gift stores, a few clothing shops, a **Foto Freddie,** a **Bank of Hawaii** office, and the **See Kauai** activity and information booth; the post office is next door (also see "Food and Food Shopping" above, and "Sporting Goods and Services" below).

If you are looking for arts and crafts, you're in luck. Check out the **Artisan's Guild of Kauai,** a co-op of local artists displaying and selling paintings, prints, pottery, cloth, shellwork, metalwork, and items in other media. Friendly, with a good selection. Prices are not out of sight.

The **Hanalei Trader** is the first building as you enter town. Here you'll find **Ola's** handcrafted novelty items, **Sand People** beach clothes and rentals, and **Hanalei Sailboards.** The **Hanalei Liquor Store** is on the right up the road, and across the street, next to the Hanalei Museum, is the **Hanalei Sea Tours** office.

Across the alley from Tahiti Nui in the Kauhale Center is **Happy Talk,** open Mon.-Wed. 1-6 p.m., Thurs.-Sat. 1-7 p.m., and closed Sunday. They offer paperback books, music, Hawaiiana, cameras, film, processing, and video rentals.

Down the lanai is **Aku's Hawaiian Express** one-hour photo-finishing service. Next to Blue Odyssey boat charter company at the west end of town are massage and hair-cutting salons.

Island Images, offering fine art prints and posters, open daily 9 a.m.-5 p.m., is in the Hanalei Center, tel. 826-6677. Posters average $30, with framing and shipping available (see "Specialty Shops, Arts, And Boutiques" under "Shopping" in the Kauai Introduction).

SPORTING GOODS AND SERVICES

Hanalei is alive with outdoor activities. The following is a sample of what's available.

Na Pali Zodiac, tel. 826-9371, does stupendous rides up the Na Pali Coast in a seagoing rubber raft. Hiking drop-off service is also available. Another reputable company is **Hanalei Sea Tours,** tel. 826-7254. (For a complete description see "Zodiacs" under "Sightseeing Tours" in the "Getting Around" section of the Kauai Introduction.)

For boat rides up the coast contact **Na Pali Adventures,** tel. 826-6804; **Hanalei Sea Tours,** tel. 826-7254; and **Luana of Hawaii,** tel. 826-9195.

The company to patronize for a kayaking adventure up the Hanalei River or during summer along the coast is **Kayak Kauai,** tel. 826-9844. A variety of sailing and fishing adventures is available from **Hawaiian Z-boat Co.,** tel. 822-5113; **Robert McReynolds,** tel. 822-5113; and Captain Andy's **Blue Water Sail-**

ing, tel. 822-0525. The sailboats run only during the summer.

The **Hanalei Surf Co.,** in the Hanalei Center, tel. 826-9000, is a water sports shop that rents and sells snorkeling equipment, sailboards, boogie boards, and surfboards. Rental rates are: sailboards $45 for 24 hours, and $60 for an optional three-hour lesson; surfboards $15 per day; boogie boards $7 per day; snorkel equipment $8 per day; money-saving weekly rates available on all rentals. The store is stocked with a good selection of shirts, shorts, thongs, bathing suits, *pareau,* incidental bags, sunglasses, sunblock, and dresses.

An extensive range of backpacking and hiking equipment to rent or buy is available from **Hanalei Camping and Backpacking** in the Ching Young Village, tel. 487-1567. They are *the* camping and hiking information center on the island, and have a great selection of books. Lanterns, tents, hiking boots, canteens, and sleeping pads are all available.

Pedal and Paddle, tel. 826-9069, also in the Ching Young Village, rents and sells snorkel gear, bikes, boats, sailboats, surfboards, and sailboards.

North Shore Taxi, tel. 826-6189, runs not only a pick-up and delivery service, but tours as well. The ordinary fare from Hanalei to Princeville is just a few bucks, to the end of the road at Ke'e Beach $18, and to Lihue Airport $50.

ROAD'S END

Past Hanalei you have six miles of pure magic until the road ends at Ke'e Beach. To thrill you further and make your ride even more enjoyable, you'll find historical sites, natural wonders, a resort, a restaurant, a grocery store, and the *heiau* where the hula was born, overlooking a lovely beach.

Sights, Accommodations, And Services

As you drive along you cross one-lane bridges and pass little beaches and bays, one after another, invariably with small streams flowing into them. Try not to get jaded peering at "just another gorgeous north shore beach."

Over a small white bridge is the village of **Wainiha** ("Angry Water"), with its tiny **Wainiha Store,** open daily 10 a.m.-7 p.m., where you can pick up a few supplies and sundries. They also rent snorkel gear, $6 per day, (Tunnels Beach, just down the road, offers great snorkeling), and offer storage for hikers and bikers going down the Kalalau Trail, $1.50 per day per bag, $2.50 per day per bike. Talk to Janet if you're looking for a place to stay; people from around the area come to the store to post fliers if they have rooms to rent. You can still get a shack on the beach or in among the banana trees!

Attached to the store are **Wainiha Sandwiches** and a T-shirt/gift shop. Sandwiches around $4 include turkey and Swiss, roast beef, ham, or tuna, all with sprouts, tomatoes, mustard, mayonnaise, and vegie salt. It's not hard to find a bunch of local guys hanging around, perhaps listening to reggae music, who could brighten your day by selling you some of the local produce.

Next up, look for signs to the **Hanalei Colony Resort,** literally the "last resort." You can rent very comfortable, spacious, two-bedroom condos here, each with a full kitchen, shower/tub, and lanai. The brown board-and-batten buildings blend into the surroundings. The resort has a jacuzzi and swimming pool, complimentary snorkel gear, barbecue grills, coin-operated washers and dryers, and maid service every fourth day. The beach in front of the resort is great for a stroll at sunset, but is not good for swimming because of the strong currents. Based on single or double occupancy, units rent from $95 for a garden view to $190 for a premium oceanfront. Car rental packages are available if arranged before arriving on Kauai. For information contact Hanalei Colony Resort, Box 206, Hanalei, HI 96714, tel. 826-6235 or (800) 626-3004.

On the premises is **Charo's Restaurant**—yes, *that* Charo! Unfortunately heavily damaged by Hurricane Iniki, it is scheduled to reopen limited operations soon with light lunches, bar service, and a big-screen TV.

Past Hanalei Resort, between mile markers 7 and 8 on the highway, look for the entrance to the **YMCA Camp Naue.** The turnoff is the one by the phone booth. Here, several buildings hold bunks and a separate toilet area and cooking facilities. The camp caters to large groups but is open to single travelers for the staggering sum of $10 per night. Kauai residents pay $9, children half price; a tent and one person cost $8, each additional person in the tent $5. The bunk houses lie under beachside trees and campers stay in the yard. As with most YMCAs, there are many rules to follow. You can get full information from YMCA headquarters in Lihue or by writing YMCA of Kauai, Box 1786, Lihue, HI 96766, tel. 246-9090, 742-1200, or 826-6419 in Haena.

About a half mile past the YMCA, a driveway turns off the highway to **Tunnels Beach** (look for a two-story house with a green roof). It's superb for snorkeling and scuba, with a host of underwater caves off to the left as you face the sea. Both surfing and windsurfing are great, and the swimming is, too, if the sea is calm. Watch out for boats that come inside the reef to anchor. Off to the right and down a bit is a nude beach. Be careful not to sunburn delicate parts!

Haena Beach County Park, just before road's end, is a large, flat, fieldlike area, where you carve out your own camping site. For your convenience the county provides tables, a pavilion, grills, showers, and camping (permit required). The sand on this long crescent beach is rather coarse, and the swimming is good only when the sea is gentle, but in summer a reef offshore is great for snorkeling. Some Zodiac boats are launched a few hundred yards down the beach to the east. The cold stream running through the park is always good for a dip. Kuulei's *kaukau* wagon is usually parked in this lot every day from about 10 a.m.

Across the road is **Maniniholo dry cave.** Notice the gorgeous grotto of trees, and the jungle wild with vines. You walk in and it feels airy and very conducive to living here. Luckily, it hasn't been trashed. Up the road, after you enter **Haena State Park,** an HVB Warrior points the way to the **wet caves.** Right along the road is Waikanaloa, and 150 yards up the side of a hill is Waikapalae. Their wide openings resemble gaping frogs' mouths, and the water is liquid crystal. Amazingly, the dry cave is down by the sea, while Waikapalae, subject to the tides, is inland and uphill. Look around for ti leaves and a few scraggly guavas. Above you, different lavas that have flowed over the eons create a stacked pancake effect. The best time to come is an hour before or after noon, when the sun shoots rays into the water. If azure could bleed, it would be this color.

The road ends at **Ke'e Beach,** a popular spot with restrooms and showers. Here is the beginning of the Kalalau Trail. As always, the swimming is mostly good only in summer. A reef offshore is great for snorkeling. If conditions are right and the tide is out, you can walk left around the point to get a dazzling view of the Na Pali cliffs. Don't attempt this when the sea is rough! This path takes you past some hidden beach homes. One was used as the setting for the famous love rendezvous in *The Thorn Birds.* Past the homes, another path takes you up the hill to the site of the ancient Kaulu Paoa *heiau,* birthplace of the hula. The views from up here are remarkable and worth the climb, especially during winter when the sun drops close to the cliffs, backlighting Lehua Island, and sinks into its molten reflection. After the novitiate had graduated from the hula *heiau,* she had to jump into the sea below and swim around to Ke'e Beach as a sign of her dedication. Tourists aren't required to perform this act.

BOB RACE

POIPU AND KOLOA

Poipu-Koloa is the most well-established and developed tourist area on Kauai, but it's now fielding competition from developments in Kapa'a and Princeville. On the site of what was the island's oldest sugar mill—a stone chimney remains to mark the spot—Koloa has been transformed from a tumbledown sugar town to a thriving tourist community where shops, restaurants, and boutiques line its wooden sidewalks. Nearby is the site of Hawaii's first Catholic mission. On the oceanfront in Poipu, luxury accommodations and fine restaurants front the wide, accommodating beach, the water beckons, and the surf is gentle. Flanking this resort community on the east is Pu'uhi Mount, where the island's last volcanic eruption occurred; to the west, beyond Prince Kuhio's birthplace, is the Spouting Horn, a plume of water that jets up through an opening in the volcanic rock shore with every incoming wave. Whether you're exploring the sights, cultivating a tan on the beach, combing the shops for your gift list, or sampling island treats, Poipu-Koloa will not fail to provide.

KOLOA

Five miles west of Lihue, Maluhia Road (Rt. 520) dips south off Rt. 50 and heads for Koloa. As you head down Maluhia Road, you pass through **Tunnel of Trees,** a stand of rough-bark *Eucalyptus robustus,* sometimes referred to as "swamp mahogany." Brought from Australia, they're now very well established, adding beauty, a heady fragrance, and shade to over a mile of this narrow country lane.

Koloa Town attracts a large number of tourists and packs them into a small area. There are plenty of shops, restaurants, and water sport equipment rentals in town. Nearly all the old shops are remodeled plantation buildings. Dressed in red paint and trimmed with white, they are festooned with strings of lights as if decorated for perpetual Christmas festivity.

The traffic is hectic around 5:30 p.m. and parking is always a problem, but you can easily solve it. Just as you are entering town look to your right to see a weathered stone chimney standing alone in a little field. Park here and simply walk across the street, avoiding the hassles. This unmarked edifice is what's left of the **Koloa Sugar Plantation,** established in 1835, site of the first successful attempt to refine sugar in the islands. Although of major historical significance, the chimney is in a terrible state of disrepair—many broken beer bottles litter the inside. Notice, too, that shrubs are growing off the top and that a nearby banyan has thrown an aerial root engulfing the structure. Unless action is taken soon, this historical site will be lost forever.

On this overgrown corner lot is a circle of over a dozen varieties of sugarcane, each with a short explanation of its characteristics and where it was grown. A plaque and sculpture have recently been added to this site. Reading the plaque will give you an explanation of and appreciation for the sugar industry on Hawaii, the significance of the Koloa Sugar Plantation, and the people who worked the fields. The bronze sculpture portrays individuals of the seven ethnic groups that provided the greatest workforce for the sugar plantations of Hawaii: Hawaiians, Chinese, Japanese, Portuguese, Puerto Ricans, Koreans, and Filipinos. (From the 1830s to the first decade of this century, smaller numbers of English, Scots, Germans, Scandinavians, Poles, Spaniards, American blacks, and Russians also arrived to work. All in all, about 35,000 immigrants came to Hawaii to make the sugar industry the success it has been.) Koloa is the birthplace of the Hawaiian sugar industry, the strongest economic force in the state for over a century. More than anything else, it helped shape the multi-ethnic mixture of Hawaii's population. While the original mill is gone, the fields surrounding Koloa still produce cane for the McBryde Sugar Co., Ltd., which has a mill to the east of town.

The tall steeple on the way to Poipu belongs to **Koloa Church,** locally known as the White Church. Dating from 1837, it was remodeled in 1929. For many years the steeple was an official landmark used in many land surveys. If you turn left from Maluhia onto Koloa Road, right on Weliweli Road, and then follow Hapa Road to its end, you come to **St. Raphael's Catholic Church,** marking the spot that in 1841 the first Roman Catholic mission was permitted in the islands. The stone church itself dates from 1856, when it was built by Friar Robert Walsh. The roof of the church can be seen sticking above the trees from Kiahuna Golf Course in Poipu.

PRACTICALITIES

Most of the accommodations, restaurants, and shopping in the Koloa area are centered around Poipu. Please refer to the following "Poipu" section for these topics also.

Accommodations

Kahili Mountain Park is a gem, *if* you enjoy what it has to offer: it's like a camp for big people, at Box 298, Koloa, HI 96756, tel. 742-9921. To get there follow Rt. 50 west about a half mile past the turnoff to Koloa, and look for the sign pointing mountainside up a cane road. Follow it for about one mile to the entranceway. The surroundings are absolutely beautiful, and the only noises, except for singing birds, are from an occasional helicopter flying into Waimea Canyon and the children attending the school on the premises. The high meadow is surrounded by mountains, with the coast visible and Poipu Beach about 15 minutes away. In the middle of the meadow is a cluster of rocks, a mini-replica of the mountains in the background. A spring-fed pond is chilly for swimming, but great for catching bass that make a tasty dinner. There are three types of accommodations: cabinettes, cabins, and deluxe cabins. Cabinettes are one-room units, usually with a double or twin beds, and full kitchen that rent for $25 d, $6 extra person. A few of the original rustic cabinettes with no running water, bare wood walls, open ceilings, and cement floors remain, but the majority didn't survive Hurricane Iniki. The cabinettes are in a cluster facing a meadow and each is surrounded by flower beds and trees. All dishes and utensils are provided, but you must do your own housekeeping. Bathrooms and showers are in a central building, with separate laundry facilities available. A relaxing Japanese *ofuro*

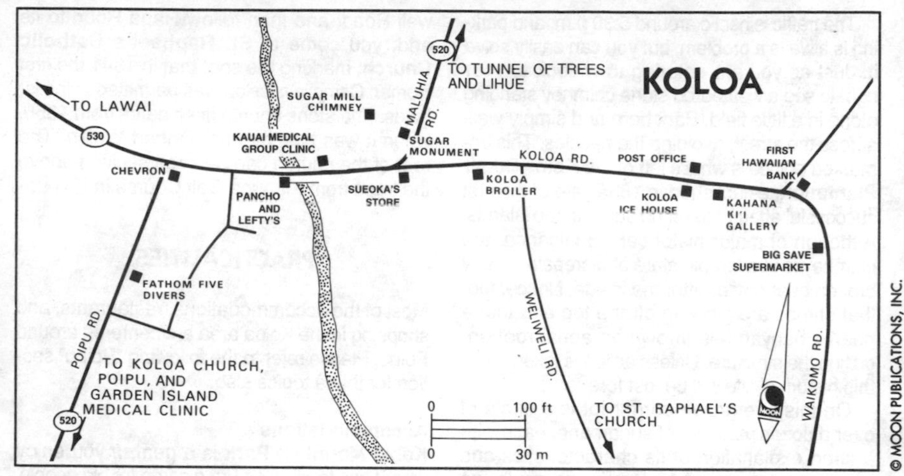

(hot tub) is open to guests. The cabins are raised wooden-floor houses with full kitchen; bedrooms with chairs, tables, and dressers; private toilets; and outdoor showers. They are priced reasonably at $35 d, $6 for an extra person. Deluxe cabins, renting at $50, are about the same, but a bit larger and upgraded with queen-size and two twin beds, an inside shower, and complete kitchen with large refrigerator. The park has been open for about 25 years and has recently been purchased by the Seventh-day Adventist Church, which runs the school while retaining the rental units. The grounds and the facility are beautifully kept by the original caretakers, Ralph and Veronica.

More expensive, yet still tranquil, is **Halemanu Bed And Breakfast Inn.** Perched atop a hill overlooking Waita Reservoir, Halemanu ("House of Birds") Inn offers seclusion in a rustic setting, with nothing here but clean air and sweeping vistas of the ocean, cane fields, and mountains. Wooden buildings from the mid-1880s were moved to this site from other parts of the island and remodeled. There are four bedrooms, a spacious sitting room, and a breezy kitchen. Each tastefully appointed room has simple period-piece furniture and a private bath; decorations are at a minimum. An English breakfast is provided daily. Room rates are $125 and $150. The first night's deposit is required for any reservation. For information and directions contact Valdemar or Karma Knutsen at 742-1288, or write Halemanu, P.O. Box 729, Koloa, HI 96756.

Food

Koloa Ice House, open daily 10:30 a.m.-9 p.m., tel. 742-6063, is on the right along Koloa Road after you make a left into town from Maluhia Road. It seems more like a deli than a restaurant, but you can have sit-down meals. They feature ice cream, shave ice, and mud pies. Tempting treats also include sandwiches, cheeses, fresh juices, fancy pastries, and lox and bagels.

Lappert's Aloha Ice Cream in downtown Koloa dishes up creamy scoops of delicious Hawaii-made ice cream. Connoisseurs of the dripping delight consider it among the best in the world. The ice-cream parlor doubles as an espresso bar, with pastries thrown in for good measure.

Adjacent to Sueoka's Market in downtown Koloa is a **plate-lunch window** that dishes out hearty, wholesome food until early afternoon. It's difficult to spend more than $5 here.

Rosie's Kaukau Wagon, parked at the entrance to Koloa's baseball diamond (near the firehouse) especially on Monday when the **farmers' market** is operating (see "Shopping" below), dishes up traditional island favorites weighty enough to sink a Boston whaler for only $5.

If you want pampering, keep walking past the **Koloa Broiler,** but if you want a good meal at an unbeatable price, drop in. The decor is the weather-beaten, wainscotted building itself, with a few neglected potted ferns here and there because someone probably told them they ought to have some. This cook-it-yourself restaurant is centrally located on Koloa Road, and is open daily for lunch, dinner, and cocktails 11 a.m.-10 p.m., happy hour 3-5 p.m., tel. 742-9122. At the Koloa Broiler *you* are the chef. Order top sirloin, beef kabob, mahimahi, and barbecued chicken for $10.95-11.95, or a beef burger for $6 until 4 p.m., and $7 after. Your uncooked selection is brought to your table, and you take it to a central grill where a large clock and a poster of cooking times tell you how long your self-made dinner will take. The feeling is like being at a potluck barbecue, and you can't help making friends with the other "chefs." There is a simple salad bar with sticky rice and a huge pot of baked beans from which you can help yourself. Waiters bring fresh-baked bread and a pitcher of ice water. Put your selection on the grill, fix and eat a salad, and it's just about time to turn your meat on the barbecue. Just before it's done, toast some bread on the grill. The **Koloa Broiler Bar** attracts a good mixture of tourists and local people with its friendly neighborhood atmosphere. After dinner order a cup of coffee or one of their special drinks like Mighty Mai Tai, Passionate Margarita, Forbidden Fruit, or the famous Konanut Cooler. The bartenders and patrons are friendly, and you couldn't find a better place for a beer while "shootin' the breeze."

Pancho and Lefty's Cantina and Restaurante, in downtown Koloa, tel. 742-7377, open daily for breakfast, lunch, and dinner 8 a.m.-11 p.m., is south-of-the-border cool with ceiling fans, knotty pine paneling, a green-and-white open-beamed ceiling, heavy wooden tables, and captain's chairs with armrests. In the bar area you can't help but notice a neon flying horse, the world's largest sombrero, and an old-fashioned barber's chair stuck in a corner. The breakfast menu offers *huevos rancheros* or scrambled eggs with Mexican sausage for $7.95, Mexican omelettes for $8.95, macadamia nut pancakes for $4.95, and sides like fresh papaya or English muffins for under $2. A good deal is the "early riser special," two eggs any style with hash browns and your choice of toast or biscuits for $4.95. The lunch and dinner menu tantalize with *calientitas,* mild jalapeño peppers stuffed with cheese and deep fried for $6.95; Pancho's nachos for $6.95; or Lefty's nachos, which contain chips, refried beans, spicy beef and cheese, guacamole, and sour cream for $7.95. The chips and salsa, in true Mexican tradition, are made on the premises. Salads include seafood salad for $9.95, taco salad for $7.95, and a small dinner salad for $2.25. Dinners are enchiladas rancheros, tamales, and burritos with rice and beans $8.95-9.95. Their luscious specialty is steak or chicken fajitas at $13.95, or $20.95 for two. Daily specials could be anything from pork chops to chicken-fried steak for $9.95, and on weekends they feature prime rib for $15.95. Pastries include Mexican pie, cheesecake, and cinnamon crisps. Pancho and Lefty's is a superb choice for a moderately priced, family-style restaurant in the Poipu area. A pleasing atmosphere where you can't go wrong.

Follow the raised wooden sidewalk to the **Koloa Cultural Center** where you will find **Taisho Restaurant,** open for dinner only Mon.-Sat. from 5 p.m., where you can enjoy a full Japanese meal or pick and choose tidbits from the sushi bar. Classic entrees include tempura at $12.95, chicken *katsu* for $7.95, and mushroom chicken for $8.95. A specialty is Taisho *bento,* a full meal with tempura, sesame chicken, sashimi, *gyoza,* salad, and rice soup for $13.95. A full menu of *donburi* (a bowl of rice topped with vegetables, egg, tofu, or meat) starts at only $5.50, with the most expensive *donburi* $8.95. This intimate restaurant with only a dozen or so tables is very simple, with a few strokes of Japanese decor like shoji partitions.

Shopping

In Koloa, shops and boutiques are strung along the road like flowers on a lei. You can buy everything from original art to beach towels. Jewelry stores, surf shops, gourmet stores, even a specialty shop for sunglasses are just a few; Old Koloa Town packs a lot of shopping into a small area. It's fun just walking the raised sidewalks of what looks very much like an old Western town.

Koloa Town's shops run along the main street and for a few hundred yards down Poipu Road. **Island Images,** offering fine art prints and posters, is open daily 9 a.m.-5 p.m., next to Lappert's Ice Cream, tel. 742-7447. Posters average $30, with framing and shipping available (see "Specialty Shops, Arts, And Boutiques" under "Shopping" in the Kauai Introduction). **Crazy Shirts** is a Hawaiian firm selling some of the best T-shirts and islandwear available. **Koloa Gold** and **Koloa Jewelry** offer rings, necklaces, and scrimshaw. **Paradise Clothing** has alohawear; **Progressive Expressions** has surfboards, surf gear, and islandwear; and **Kahana Ki'i Art Gallery** offers quality island art.

Kauai One Hour Photo, tel. 742-1719, along Poipu Road in Koloa, offers camera supplies, film, and processing.

The **Blue Orchid,** at the end of the raised wooden sidewalk in the Koloa Cultural Center, open Mon.-Sat. 9:30 a.m.-5:30 p.m., is a women's boutique selling dresses, alohawear, earrings, jewelry, and fresh cut flowers. Arlene, the owner, hand-paints the dresses and T-shirts, all of which are made from cotton, rayon, or silk. Prices start at $30 for the dresses and $12 for the T-shirts.

When you see Weliweli Road at the end of the raised wooden sidewalk, look for a sign pointing to St. Raphael's Church and follow it for a minute to **Chang's Tao Wai,** a discount variety store. Inside is a tangle of touristy junk, and nifty items including beach mats, T-shirts, hats, fishing supplies, and inexpensive cotton aloha shirts.

Stuck in a corner near Chang's is **Nileen's Enterprises,** tel. 742-9727, a nutrition center about as large as your average closet. Open Monday, Wednesday, and Friday 12:30-5 p.m., and Saturday 9:30 a.m.-2:30 p.m., Nileen sells nutritional supplements, vitamins, minerals, homeopathic remedies, and skin care products.

Food Shopping

In Koloa, a **Big Save Supermarket** is on Koloa Road, at its junction with Waikomo Road. **Sueoka's Store** in downtown Koloa is a local grocery and produce market. Both carry virtually everything you'll need for condo cooking.

Pick up fresh fruits and vegetables at the **farmers' market,** every Monday at noon at the baseball field in Koloa (turn near the fire station). Depending on what's happening on the farms, you can get anything from coconuts to fresh cut flowers while enjoying a truly local island experience.

Services

Koloa's **public restrooms** are in the courtyard behind Pancho and Lefty's Mexican restaurant.

The **Koloa Post Office** is along Koloa Road, tel. 742-6565. At the east end of Koloa Road is **First Hawaiian Bank,** the area's only bank.

Note: For outdoor activities in and around Koloa, see "Sports and Recreation" under "Poipu" below.

POIPU

Poipu Road continues south from Koloa for two miles until it reaches the coast. En route it passes a cane road (traffic signal) reaching Hanapepe via Numila, and a bit farther passes Lawai Road, which turns right along the coast and terminates at the Spouting Horn. Poipu Road itself bends left past a string of condos and hotels, into what might be considered the town, except nothing in particular makes it so. Both Hoonani and Hoowili roads lead to different sections of the beach. As you pass the mouth of Waikomo Stream (along Hoonani Road), you're at **Koloa Landing,** once the island's most important port. When whaling was king, dozens of ships anchored here to trade with the natives for provisions. Today nothing remains. Behind Poipu is **Pu'uhi Mount,** believed to be the site of the last eruption on Kauai.

Along Poipu Road look for the driveway into the Kiahuna Plantation Resort on the right across the street from the Poipu Shopping Village. This is the site of the **Kiahuna Plantation Gardens,** formerly known as the Moir Gardens (the central area retains this name). The 35 lovely acres are adorned with over 3,000 varieties of tropical flowers, trees, and plants, and a lovely lagoon. The gardens were heavily battered by Hurricane Iwa and again by Iniki, but the two dozen full-time gardeners have restored them to their former beauty. These grounds, originally part of the old sugar plantation, were a "cactus patch" started by manager Hector Moir and his wife back in 1938. Over the years the gardens grew more and more lavish until they became a standard Poipu sight. The Kiahuna Plantation has greatly expanded the original gardens, opening them to the public during daylight hours, free of charge. Many plants are identified.

The Great Poipu Beaches

Although given a lacing by Hurricane Iniki, **Poipu Beach Park** is on the mend and is Poipu's best developed beach park. Located at the eastern end of Poipu, it provides a pavilion, tables, showers, toilets, playground, and lifeguards. The swimming, snorkeling, and bodysurfing are great. A sheltered pool rimmed by lava boulders is gentle enough for anyone, and beyond it is the more exciting wave action often used by local surfers. Follow the rocks out to Nukamai Point, where there is a number of tidepools. Following the shoreline around to the east, you'll end up at Brennecke's Beach, a good spot at which to boogie board and watch locals shore fish.

At the eastern end of the Hyatt is an access road leading to **Mahaulepu Beach,** now improved with a pavilion containing restrooms and showers. The Hyatt hotel has also developed a nearby walkway affording fantastic seascapes as you amble along it.

Follow Poipu Road past the Hyatt and in a few minutes you will come to **Shipwreck Beach,** a long strand of white sand. One of the only beneficiaries of Hurricanes Iwa and Iniki, the beach was broadened and widened with huge deposits of sand to make it bigger and better than ever. The swimming and snorkeling are good, but as at all secluded beaches, use extra caution. There is no official camping here, but local people sometimes bivouac in the ironwoods at the east end; beyond is a rocky bluff from which you have a fine view of the coastline east of here. The only people who regularly frequent the beach are fishermen, *au naturel* sunbathers, and surfers when the waves are right.

Continue along Poipu Road past the golf course and take a right on the dirt road toward CJM Stables. Park before the hill gets too steep (4WD okay) and walk 10 minutes down to a wonderful beach with breaks in the reef that make it good for swimming. You can also continue on Poipu Road to the very end (don't turn toward stables) and you will be at the far end of **Keoniloa Bay.** Here too is a safe family swimming beach, but again, be careful during heavy wave action.

West End

Turn onto Lawai Road to pass **Kuhio Park,** the birthplace of Prince Kuhio. Loved and respected, Prince Cupid (his nickname) was Hawaii's delegate to Congress from the turn of the century until his death in 1922. He returned to the shores of his birth whenever his duties permitted.

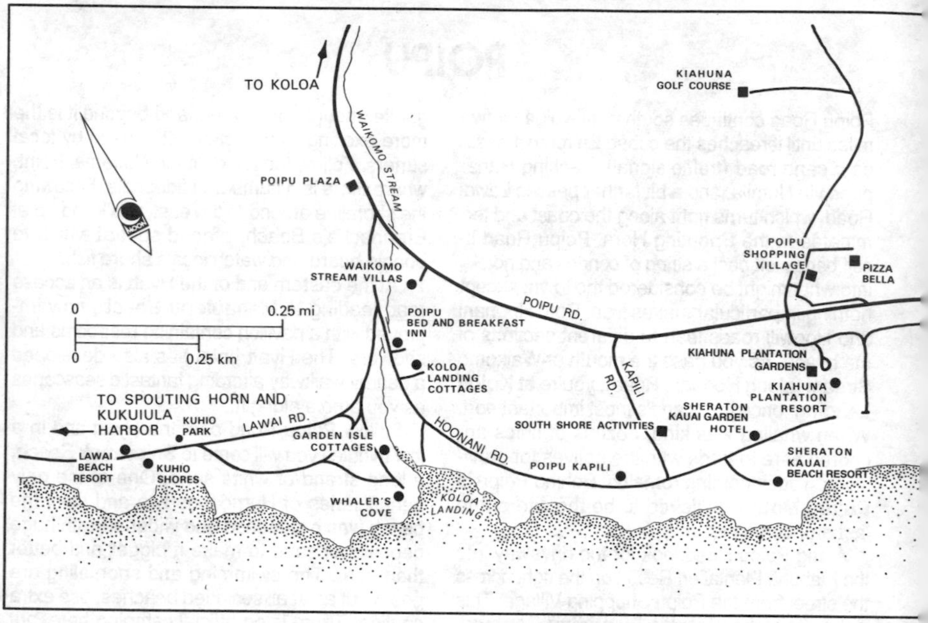

Decked with a statue and monument, lava terrace walls, palm trees, and a pool, this well-manicured acre faces the sea. Farther along is **Kukui'ula Bay.** Before Hurricane Iwa and later Iniki pummelled this shoreline, the bay was an attractive beach park where many small boats anchored. Today you can launch a boat here, but the surrounding area is still recovering. Sailing cruises leave from this harbor in winter, shore fishermen come to try their luck, and scuba divers explore the coral reef offshore, but no swimming is allowed.

In a moment you arrive at the **Spouting Horn.** A large parking area has many slots marked for tour buses. At the **flea market** here you can pick up trinkets and souvenirs. Don't make the mistake of looking just at the Spouting Horn. Have "big eyes" and look around at the full sweep of this remarkable coastline. The Spouting Horn is a lava tube that extends into the sea with its open mouth on the rocky shore. The wave action causes the spouting phenomenon, which can blow spumes quite high, depending on surf conditions. They say it shot higher in the old days, but the salt spray damaged nearby cane fields. Supposedly, the plantation owners had the opening made larger so that the spray wouldn't carry as far. Photographers wishing to catch the Spouting Horn in action have an ally. Just before it shoots, a hole behind the spout makes a large belch, and a second later the spume flies. Be ready to click.

ACCOMMODATIONS

Most of Poipu's available rooms are found in medium- to high-priced condos. However, there are some first-class hotels, a handful of cottages, and bed and breakfasts.

Note: Also see "Accommodations" under "Practicalities" under "Koloa" above.

Cottages, Cabins, And B&Bs

Koloa Landing Cottages at 2749 Hoonani Rd. are modern units in a quiet residential area, and some of Poipu's least expensive accommodations. Two-bedroom, two-bath units for up to five people are available. Each has a full kitchen with dishwasher, and a color television. Rates

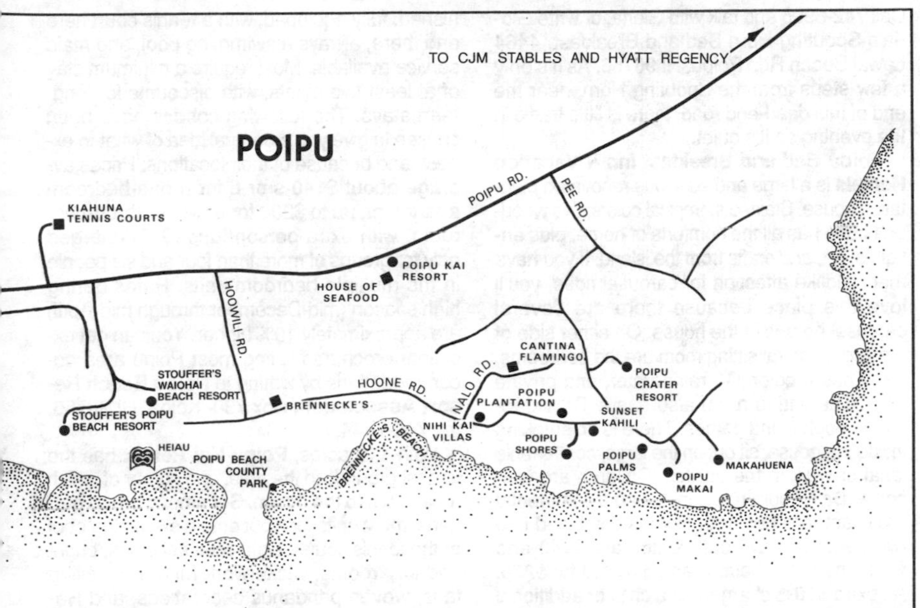

are $65 for one or two persons, $75 for three or four, and $5 for an additional person. Studios, also equipped with a kitchen and color TV, run $45 for one or two people. Laundry facilities are on the premises. Reservations are suggested; four nights' deposit is required, 25% for stays longer than 14 days. Contact Sylvia at 742-1470, Hans at 742-6436, or write to Koloa Landing Cottages, RR 1, Box 70, Koloa, HI 96756.

Garden Isle Cottages are tucked away at the west end along Hoona Road between Poipu Beach and the Spouting Horn. They sit on the beach surrounded by lush foliage, offering privacy. The cottages are operated by artists Robert and Sharon Flynn, whose original works highlight each of the units. All units, from studios to two-bedroom apartments, are self-contained and fully equipped. Prices range $52-75 for a single or double in a studio with bath and lanai but no kitchen (refrigerator, coffee pot, and toaster only), to $130-135 for a two-bedroom, two-bath unit for up to four people; $6 per additional person in any unit. Weekly maid service is provided for the studios. Four nights' deposit is required; 25% if staying over 14 days. Phone 742-6717 daily 9 a.m.-noon, or write Garden Isle Cottages, 2666 Puuholo Rd., Koloa, HI 96756.

You will find no bedroom closer to the gentle surf than at **Gloria's Spouting Horn Bed and Breakfast.** A remodeled plantation worker's house from the 1940s, its white wood walls make it bright and airy, and antique furniture and tasteful decorations make it feel like home. Three units are downstairs, two upstairs; only one doesn't have an ocean view, but it looks out on a koi pond. Overlooking a rocky beach, its stepped front lanai is about 40 feet from the water. Lie on the grass, swing in a hammock, or sit on the side lanai out of the sun; in the sitting room, a TV, a piano, chess, and books on Hawaii are provided for your use. Rooms are not large but they're cozy and comfortable—just right for newlyweds. Each room has a TV, refrigerator, and ceiling fan. Two of the downstairs rooms have a shared bath. No children under 14, no pets, no smoking inside. Room rates, which include a daily continental breakfast, range $50-80 a night; discounts can be arranged for stays of a week or more; add 20% for the Christmas season. Reservations are necessary.

Call 742-6995 and talk with Gloria, or write Gloria's Spouting Horn Bed and Breakfast, 4464 Lawai Beach Rd., Poipu, HI 96756. As it's only a few steps from the Spouting Horn, near the end of this dead-end road, there is little traffic in the evening so it's quiet.

Poipu Bed and Breakfast Inn & Vacation Rentals is a large and spacious renovated plantation house. Stained in tropical colors, this wooden house has all the comforts of home, plus antiques, art, and crafts from the island. If you have that childlike affection for carousel rides, you'll love this place because there are several carousel horses in the house. On either side of the large, central sitting room are the bedrooms. Each has a color TV, refrigerator, and private bath. The sitting room also has a TV, videotapes, books, and games. There is no smoking inside the house; sit out on the large, comfortable lanai or walk in the garden. Children are welcome. Daily room rates, including a continental breakfast, are $65-100. Rooms combined into two-bedroom, two-bath suites are $140 and $155; the entire house can be rented for $250. An extra $10 is charged for a child or additional person; $5 less for single occupancy. For information and reservations call 742-1146 or (800) 552-0095, or write to Poipu Bed and Breakfast Inn, 2720 Hoonani Rd., Koloa, HI 96756.

Pua Hale ("Flower House"), at 2381 Kipuka St., Koloa, HI 96756, tel. 742-1700 or (800) 745-7414, is a lovely, deluxe 750-square-foot house where your privacy and serenity are assured. With a touch of Japan, Pua Hale features shoji screens, cool wooden floors, a relaxing *ofuro* (Japanese bath), custom furniture and decorating, and a complete kitchen and laundry. This self-contained unit, only minutes from Poipu, is surrounded by a privacy fence and a manicured garden, so you make the decision on whether you want to socialize or simply enjoy the glorious quietude. Rates are a reasonable $100 per night, or $650 per week. You can't find better.

Moderate

Although the prices in Poipu can be a bit higher than elsewhere on Kauai, you get a lot for your money. Over a dozen well-appointed modern condos are lined up along the beach and just off it, with thousands of units available. Most are a variation on the same theme: comfortably furnished, fully equipped, with a tennis court here and there, always a swimming pool, and maid service available. Most require a minimum stay of at least two nights, with discounts for long-term stays. The following condos have been chosen to give you a general idea of what to expect, and because of their locations. Prices average about $140 s or d for a one-bedroom apartment, up to $200 for a two- or three-bedroom, with extra-person fees ($10) charged only for groups of more than four and six people in the multiple-bedroom units. Rates during high season (mid-December through mid-April) are approximately 10% higher. You can get excellent brochures listing most Poipu area accommodations by writing to **Poipu Beach Resort Association,** Box 730, Koloa, HI 96756, tel. 742-7444.

With 110 acres, **Poipu Kai Resort** has the largest grounds in the area, one corner of which runs down to the ocean. Set among broad gardens, most units look out onto a swimming pool or the tennis courts. Light color schemes, bright and airy rooms, wickerwork furniture, ceiling fans, woven pandanus decorations, and Hawaiian art prints typify the decor. Most units have a queen-size bed and a walk-in closet with a chest of drawers; bathrooms have a large shower/tub and double sinks. For your convenience, color TV, economy washer and dryer unit, iron and ironing board, and floor safe are in each unit. Daily maid service is provided. Kitchens are fully equipped with electric utilities and sufficient cookware to prepare a full-course meal. Dining rooms adjoin spacious living rooms, which open onto broad lanai. There are one- and two-bedroom units, in 15 different floor plans. Some are Hawaiian in theme, others Spanish with stucco and arched entryways. Modern units show more glass and chrome, while a few may resemble your own Mainland home. A handful of three-bedroom homes is also available in the adjacent housing estate. Room rates (high/low season) are $130-150/$115-135 for one-bedroom units, $175-240/$160-210 for two bedrooms and two baths, and $205/$180 for the homes. Facilities on the grounds include nine tennis courts (free for guests), a pro shop (open 8 a.m.-noon and 2-6 p.m.) with a resident tennis pro, five swimming pools, one outdoor jacuzzi, and numerous barbecue grills. The activity center, open to nonguests as well 8 a.m.-1 p.m. and 2:30-4 p.m., can arrange everything from a towel for the beach to a helicopter tour of the island. Across the walkway from the resort office is the House of Seafood, the area's premier seafood restaurant; open only for dinner. For reservations write to Poipu Kai Resort, RR 1, Koloa, HI 96756, or call 742-6464 or (800) 367-6046.

The **Poipu Shores** condo is at the east end of the beach, surrounded by other small condos. They're slightly less expensive than the rest, allowing up to six people at no extra charge for certain two- and three-bedroom units. Try their one-bedroom units for $110; a standard two-bedroom is $150, a deluxe two-bedroom is $160, and a three-bedroom unit runs $165. Rates are $10-20 cheaper off-season. There is a three-night minimum stay. Maid service is provided free every other day. All units are clean, spacious, and airy, with the area's best beaches a short stroll away. Write Poipu Shores, 1775 Pe'e Rd., Koloa, HI 96756, tel. 742-7700 or (800) 367-8047.

Poipu Kapili is a three-story condo that looks more like a "back East" bungalow. Directly across the road from the beach, all units have ocean views. The pool is located in the center of the property. Also on the premises are free, lighted tennis courts, racquets and balls provided. The bedrooms are huge, with ceiling fans and wicker headboards; kitchens are spacious with full stoves and dishwashers. Each unit has its own private lanai. Rates range from $125-225 for a one-bedroom unit to $185-300 for a two-bedroom unit; monthly and weekly discounts are available. The condo also offers a convenient activities desk which will book you into any activity that strikes your fancy. Write Poipu Kapili, 2221 Kapili Rd., Koloa, HI 96756, tel. 742-6449 or (800) 443-7714.

Other condos also dot this wonderful shore. The smaller condos generally cluster at the east end of the beach. **Makahuena** sits on Makahuena Cliff with the crashing waves below, tel. 742-7555 or (800) 367-8022; **Poipu Crater Resort** snuggles inside a small seaside caldera, tel. (800) 367- 8020. Or contact **Poipu Makai,** tel. (800) 367-5025; **Poipu Palms,** tel. (800) 367-8022; **Sunset Kahili,** tel. (800) 827-6478; **Poipu Plantation,** tel. 742-6757 or (800) 733-1632; or **Nihi Kai Villas,** tel. (800) 367-5025. All run in quick succession across the cliff at the east end of Poipu Beach. On the west end: **Grantham Resorts** and **Waikomo Stream Villas** (also managed by Grantham Resorts) are next door to each other along the stream, tel. (800) 325-5701. On the far side of Koloa Landing is **Whaler's Cove,** tel. (800) 367-7052; and at Lawai Beach are **Lawai Beach Resort,** tel. (800) 777-1700, and **Kuhio Shores,** tel. 742-1319.

Deluxe

A parade of royal palms lines the grand boulevard that ends at the elegant porte cochere. There, towering panes of glass, open to the sea roiling beneath a periwinkle sky, front the **Hyatt Regency Kauai Resort and Spa,** 1571 Poipu Rd., Koloa, HI, 96756, tel. 742-1234 or (800) 233-1234. This magnificent 600-room hotel, deceptive in size, is architecturally designed so that its five floors rise no taller than the surrounding palms. A bellhop pulls the golden frond handles on double doors opening to the main hall, where a floor of green and white marble is covered by an enormous Persian rug bearing a tropical island motif. To the left and right, larger-than-life replicas of poi bowls especially fashioned for the royal *ali'i* mark a formal sitting area illuminated by a magnificent chandelier of cut crystal. Ahead is a central courtyard, tiled to create a sundial effect. As you progress through the heart of the hotel, greenery and flowers, both wild and tamed, are a living lei of floral beauty. Lustrous koa tables bear gigantic anthuriums and torch ginger ablaze with color. Artwork, tapa wall hangings, and bird cages filled with flitting plumage and trilling songs line the hallways, while the interplay of marble floors and rich carpet is counterpointed by weathered bronze. Enter the **Stevenson Library,** one of the Hyatt's bars, to find overstuffed chairs, beveled glass windows, pool and billiard tables, a grand piano, and ornate chess sets waiting for the first move. Outdoors, walking paths scented by tropical blooms lead through acres of fresh and saltwater pools featuring slides, a rivulet flowing through a "gorge," and the watery massaging fingers of cascading waterfalls and bubbling whirlpools.

Heavy mahogany doors open into guest rooms done in soothing pastels with white-on-tan textured wallpaper. Each room features a full entertainment center with remote-control color TV, private lanai with outdoor furniture, minibar, and double closets. Mahogany furniture, overstuffed chairs and footstools, and Chinese-style lamps ensure tasteful relaxation. Each spacious bathroom contains separate commode with its own telephone, double marble-top sinks, hair dryer, large soaking tub, and cotton *yukata* (robe). Rates are from $230 garden view to $345 deluxe oceanfront; Regency Club $410; and suites $425-1800.

Restaurants at the Hyatt range from casual to elegant (see "Food" below for a complete description). **Dondero's,** the hotel's signature restaurant, offers superb Italian food, while the **Tidepool Restaurant,** in South Pacific style, offers fresh fish and seafood. The **Ilima Terrace,** at the bottom of a sweeping staircase, is open for breakfast, lunch, and dinner and presents everything from a Philadelphia cheese steak to a children's menu. The **Seaview Terrace,** with its vaulted ceiling, magnificent chandeliers, and carved marble-topped tables, is perfect for a sunset drink, while **Kuhio's,** with its sunken parquet dance floor, is perfect for an intimate rendezvous.

In its own facility fronted by a courtyard is the distinctive green tile roof of the horseshoe-shaped **Anara Spa.** The treatment rooms offer ancient Hawaiian methods for capturing energy and rejuvenation. You begin with *kapu kai* ("sacred sea"), a steam bath, followed by a body scrub with *'alaea* clay and Hawaiian sea salt. Next you may be immersed in a tub of *limu* (seaweed) and then kneaded by a massage therapist who specializes in *lomi lomi,* the Hawaiian massage favored by the *ali'i.* All therapy rooms are indoor/outdoor, with mini-gardens and the serenade of falling waters to help unjangle nerves. Hibiscus tea and cool water are always available. Once finished, you are conducted into the locker rooms where you can shower and pamper yourself with lotions and potions. The Anara Spa also offers health-conscious cuisine, lap pool, aerobics room, and complete training equipment including Lifecycles, treadmills, and Stairmasters.

Coming Back

The following properties in and around Poipu were extensively damaged by Hurricane Iniki. Although physically battered, their spirits are intact, and all will be reopening as soon as renovations are completed. Call directly, or check with **Kauai Today,** tel. (800) 262-1400. All are excellent choices.

The **Kiahuna Plantation Resort** surrounds the lovely Kiahuna Gardens. Most units feature cross ventilation through louvered windows and have full bathrooms, kitchens, and enormous lanai. You get a lot for your money at the Kiahuna Plantation, with up to five and seven people at no extra charge in the appropriate units. Housekeeping is available, laundry facilities are on the premises, and there is an activities director. Activities include scuba and surfing lessons, golf at the Kiahuna Golf Course, tennis, and swimming at the resort pool. Write Kiahuna Plantation Resort, RR 1, Box 73, Koloa, HI 96756, tel. 742-6411 or (800) 367-7052.

The **Sheraton Kauai Garden Hotel,** tel. 742-2442 or (800) 325-3535, is partially open, with renovations still underway. The **Sheraton Kauai Beach Resort,** tel. 742-1661 or (800) 325-3535, though very heavily damaged, hopes to reopen soon. Located just a minute from Poipu Beach, both are premier luxury resorts.

Stouffer's Waiohai Beach Resort is another first-rate luxury hotel that hopes to open soon; no reopening date is scheduled at this time. **Stouffer's Poipu Beach Resort** is friendly, with a family atmosphere. Construction is underway, with an opening date not set as of yet. For information on the status of either Stouffer's resort, call 742-9511 or (800) 468-3571.

FOOD

Inexpensive

On your right as you approach Poipu from Koloa is a small complex called the Poipu Plaza. Here, at **Taqueria Nortenos,** you can fill up on Mexican fast food for under $4. They make their tacos and burritos a bit differently than do most Mexican food stands: a taco is simply rice and beans in a taco shell. If you want the standard cheese, tomato, and lettuce, you have to ask for it at an extra charge. The flavorful food is homemade but precooked, waiting in heating trays. Vegetarian meals are also served. Order at the walk-up window and take your tray to one of the picnic tables in the next room; they do takeout as well. Filling, good, but not special, the Taqueria Nortenos is open daily except Wednesday, 11 a.m.-11 p.m.

Shipwreck Subs in the Poipu Shopping Village can fix you up with sub sandwiches like tuna delight, cheese combo, or vegetarian, $6 large and $4.50 small.

Brennecke's Snack Bar is located just off Poipu Beach, below Brennecke's restaurant; open 10:30 a.m.-4 p.m. The best deals are takeout hot dogs, burgers, and filling plate lunches.

For a bit more sophistication, try the hotels' poolside grills and cafes for a light lunch.

Moderate

Located on the terrace of the Kiahuna Plantation Resort (once the plantation manager's home), under towering trees and surrounded by lush greenery, the **Plantation Garden Cafe** emanates a strong Hawaiian atmosphere. *Pu pu* run $3.95-6.95 and whet your appetite for the meal to come. For a main course, try Hawaiian chicken, shrimp tempura, or the pasta special, all $12.95. Or sample the seafood or vegetable salads, and sandwiches. After dinner have a mouthwatering dessert or walk across the lobby for a tropical drink in the lounge.

Brennecke's Beach Broiler, an open-air, second-story deck directly across from Poipu Beach County Park, offers a view that can't be beat. Seafood is the dinner specialty but *kiawe*-broiled meat and chicken and pasta are also served. Prices range $9.95-22.50. All entrees are served with soup, salad, pasta primavera (instead of regular old potatoes), and garlic bread. Salads and sandwiches are served for lunch, and *pu pu* until dinner starts. There is a children's menu for both lunch and dinner. Lunch is 11:30 a.m.-3 p.m., happy hour 2-4 p.m., and dinner 5-10:30 p.m.; tel. 742-7588.

Keoki's Paradise, at the Poipu Shopping Village, tel. 742-7534, serves the fresh fish of the day, plus steaks and ribs ($9.95-19.95). Evening specials ($7.95) are served 5:30-6:15 p.m., and the house wine list is better than most. Keoki's has tables inside, and under the stars next to the fishpond; have dinner by torchlight. Their seafood and taco bar (a good place for conversation for single travelers) is open 4:30 p.m.-midnight. Have an island drink before going into dinner, served 5:30-10 p.m.

Venturi's, at the Poipu Shopping Village, open Mon.-Fri. 6 a.m.-9 p.m., weekends 11 a.m.-9 p.m. for lunch and dinner, tel. 742-9168, is an indoor/outdoor restaurant that offers a decent meal and live Hawaiian music nightly except Monday. It is decorated in simple island style with wooden shutters, terra-cotta floor, round-topped drum tables, windows all around, and a few picnic tables under an awning. At night when the shopping center quiets down, magic sets in, and Venturi's suddenly feels like a European bistro. Breakfast, easily under $6, is hearty with omelettes, Portuguese sausage, and loco mocos (an island concoction that's delicious but greasy enough to clog the Alaskan pipeline). Lunch specials range from the basic burger with cheese and fries for $4.25, to a double-fisted vegie sandwich for $5.25. Pasta of the day or a fresh mahimahi sandwich are around $6, while island salads and fresh fruit platters are priced $4.75-5.25. Lighter appetites will enjoy *pu pu* like hot and spicy chicken wings, quesadillas, and fried zucchini for $3.25-4.25. Dinner offers grilled chicken, shrimp Venturi with pasta, vegetable platter, or seafood salad, $8.25-12.50, and yummy fresh-baked pie for dessert. Beer and wine are available.

Pizza Bella, at the Poipu Shopping Village, tel. 742-9571, is a happening place with very good food. The restaurant, open daily for breakfast 6:30 a.m.-10;30 a.m. (basic and around $5), and then11:30 a.m.-10 p.m. for the full menu, also offers takeout (and delivery service in the Poipu-Koloa area). Black-and-white tiled floor, mirrored walls, glass blocks under the counter backlit by pink neon lights, ceiling fans, and lots of potted plants and trees give this eatery a contemporary feel. You can get medium or large combination pizzas $9.95-21.95 on thick whole wheat or white crust, or pizza by the slice until 4:30 p.m. for $2.65. If you want something more unusual try one of the gourmet pizzas: *quattro formaggi* with homemade sauce of olive oil, crushed garlic, and spices, and four kinds of cheese; barbecue chicken with red onion; seafood; Mexican, with meat, beans, cheese, bell pepper, black olives, and jalapeños; or Cajun seafood. Sound great? Hot and cold sandwiches, salads, pasta dishes, beer, and wine are also served. Pizza Bella has earned a good reputation.

If you don't want Mexican pizza but still want south-of-the-border food, try the homey **Cantina Flamingo,** tel. 742-9505, on Nalo Road in among the condos—follow the pink flamingos! Sizzling fajitas are the specialty of the house and a real treat; other items on the menu are enchiladas tasca, flamingo burritos, *taquitos rancheros, flautas* Kauai, appetizers, soups, and salads. Chips and salsa are free. Nothing on the menu is over $9.95. You can't go wrong here. How about deep-fried ice cream for dessert? If not, head to the next room, beyond the wall aquarium, for a cool-down drink at the cantina. There you can choose one of at least nine kinds of fruit margaritas. (Imagine what it's like to peer through the distortion of the aquarium divider after a few of these potent concoctions!) Food is served daily 3:30-9:30 p.m., *pu pu* free 3:30-5:30 p.m.; takeout is available for some menu items. Hanging greenery, pink flamingos, and piñatas lend this eatery its distinctive touch.

You can find other mid-price restaurants at the hotels and clubhouses in Poipu. Try the **Poipu Bay Grill,** in the clubhouse of the Poipu Bay Resort Golf Course. This moderately priced restaurant serving American standards has fantastic views of the surrounding mountains and sea.

Fine Dining

Exquisite dining can be enjoyed at various restaurants that have perfect positions along Poipu's beaches for catching the setting sun. Prices are high, but the surroundings are elegant and the service impeccable.

The House of Seafood has windows framing living still-lifes of palm fronds, flower gardens, and the ocean in the background. It consistently has the largest selection of fresh fish in the area, generally 8-12 varieties, and its ways of preparing fish are very creative—baked in puff pastry, sautéed with macadamia-nut sauce, or steamed in a ginger sauce, to name a few. Ask the waiter for the best choice of the day. Start your meal off with an appetizer, soup, or salad, and finish with a creamy island-fruit dessert or drink. Entrees run $17-35; on a children's menu they're $9-11. Located at Poipu Kai Resort; call 742-5255 for reservations.

The main dining room at the Hyatt, tel. 742-1234, is the **Ilima Terrace,** open daily for breakfast, lunch, and dinner. Descend a formal staircase and step onto a slate floor covered with an emerald green carpet. The tables, bright with floral-patterned tablecloths, have high-backed wicker chairs. Floor-to-ceiling beveled glass doors look out onto the lovely grounds, while lighting is provided by massive chandeliers fashioned like flowers. Start your day with a choice of fresh chilled juices, and move on to hearty servings of eggs or omelettes accompanied by *paniolo* corned beef or chicken hash, priced at $8.50. Other selections are Belgian waffles or buckwheat or buttermilk pancakes for around $7.50, or simple sides like English muffins, hash browns, or steamed rice for around $3. The wonderful Ilima Breakfast Buffet at $14.75 daily, $17 on Sunday, offers specialties like eggs Benedict, stuffed blintzes, freshly made omelettes, fresh fish, and a wide assortment of breakfast meats. The health-conscious can choose from homemade muesli, granola, and an assortment of fresh island fruit. Lunch brings starters like quesadillas, tossed salad, and *ahi* sashimi for $4.25-8. Try the lemon barbecued chicken salad or Niçoise salad with albacore tuna for around $8. Move on to grilled salmon with Bibb lettuce, tomato, and sprouts for $9.25, or you can have a personal pizza topped with mushrooms, pepperoni, and cheese for $12. A daily pasta could be linguine with roasted chicken for $9.75, while sandwiches range from a Philly cheese steak to a Reuben for around $9. Dinner offers fresh Hawaiian fish prepared with *hulakoi* pineapple sauce for $19, grilled chicken for $17, and vegetable and shrimp tempura for $18. Desserts include papaya cheesecake, triple chocolate torte, and coconut cream pie. There is a full-service bar, with wine, beer, and cappuccino, and the children's menu is loaded with goodies like alphabet soup, grilled cheese sandwiches and chips, and hamburgers, all for under $4.

Dondero's, featuring classic Italian cuisine, is the Hyatt's signature restaurant, open for dinner only. To enter, you descend a marble staircase highlighted with green tiles into which have been embedded scallop shells. The continental room is formal with high-backed upholstered armchairs, and tables covered in white linen and set with crystal and silver. Each has a view through floor-to-ceiling windows facing the manicured gardens. Dinner begins with antipasti, or crepes with porcino mushrooms for $7.50, or sautéed shrimp with lemon and spinach pasta for $9.50. Try the open ravioli with seafood, Caesar salad for $4.50, or fresh buffalo mozzarella with tomato and basil for $5. Soups include minestrone or delicate pasta squares in chicken broth for $4. Entrees are pasta primavera for $18, whole wheat pizza topped with feta cheese for only $12, and special dishes like *spaghettini, gnocchi, farfalle, penne* or *risotto del giorno* for under $22. An excellent dish is cioppino, a heady mixture of sautéed scallops, shrimp, lobster, and clams in a tomato broth for $26.

Slightly more casual is the hotel's **Tidepool Restaurant,** a mushroom cluster of thatched "huts" supported by huge beams forming an indoor/outdoor restaurant overlooking the tidepools. They boast the island's freshest fish, broiled, seared, grilled, and steamed with a medley of sauces and toppings to choose from.

ENTERTAINMENT

If, after a sunset dinner and a lovely stroll along the beach, you find yourself with "dancing feet" or a desire to hear the strains of your favorite tunes, Poipu won't let you down. Many restaurants in the area feature piano music or small combos, often with a Hawaiian flair.

Venturi's in the Poipu Shopping Village gently sways with Hawaiian music nightly except Monday 6-9 p.m. Come for dinner or a quiet beer and *pu pu,* and let your cares drift away.

SHOPPING

Shopping in Poipu is varied and reasonably extensive for such a small area. The Poipu Shopping Village has the largest concentration of shops, but don't forget Poipu Plaza, the hotel arcades, and the Spouting Horn flea market.

Food Stores

Poipu has the generally well-stocked **Kukuiula Store** at Poipu Plaza, open Mon.-Fri. 8 a.m.-8:30 p.m., Saturday and Sunday 8 a.m.-6:30 p.m., where you'll find groceries, produce, bakery goods, sundries, and liquor. **Whaler's General Store,** at Poipu Shopping Village, is a well-stocked convenience store with a good selection of wines and liquors, and **Brennecke's Mini Mart,** heavily hurricane damaged but coming back, is across from Poipu Beach County Park.

Note: If you're staying in a Poipu condo, you may save money by making the trip to a larger market in one of the nearby towns if you're buying large amounts of food. See "Food Shopping" under "Practicalities" under "Koloa" above.

Boutiques, Gifts, And Apparel

In Poipu, the **Koloa Gallery** in the Sheraton sells pearls, coral jewelry, and handcrafted tiles by local artists. The **Poipu Shopping Village** offers unique one-stop shopping in a number of shops, including: **The Ship Store Gallery** for all things nautical, including sea-inspired art; **The Black Pearl Collection** for pearls and jewelry; **Traders of Kauai,** featuring distinctive gifts, children's wear, and alohawear; **Tropical Shirts** for original airbrush designs on shirts; and **For Your Eyes Only** for distinctive sunglasses.

Photo Needs

Poipu Fast Photo, tel. 742-7322, in the Poipu Shopping Village sells cameras and film, and does processing.

SPORTS AND RECREATION

The Koloa-Poipu area has many surf and sailing shops that rent sports equipment and diving gear, and sponsor boating excursions. **South Shore Activities,** tel. 742-6873, offers just about all you'll need for sun and surf in Poipu. They feature all activities, from horseback riding to helicopter tours, rent all kinds of ocean equipment and provide lessons, and rent bicycles and mopeds. Call for exact rental rates and stipulations; open 9 a.m.-5 p.m. except Sundays. **Brennecke's Ocean Sports,** tel. 742-6570, specializes in snorkel and scuba lessons, and also rents surfboards, boogie boards, and sailboards. Canoe rides and charter boats are also available.

Fathom Five Divers in Koloa, about 100 yards after you make the left turn onto Poipu Road, tel. 742-6991, open daily 9 a.m.-6 p.m., owned and operated by Karen Long, is a complete diving center offering lessons, certification, and rentals. Two-tank boat dives for certified divers, including gear is $85; if you have your own equipment, $70. Introductory dives and lesson including gear is $120, and a one-tank shore dive is $60. Certification courses take five days and average about $350; tank refills are available. Fathom Five's half-day snorkeling cruises include lessons and gear for $60. Snorkel rental is $5 per day, or $15 per week.

Outfitters Kauai, an environment-concious sports shop offering kayaking and mountain biking, is owned and operated by Rick and Julie Havilend. They are located in the Poipu Plaza at 2827-A Poipu Road, P.O. Box 1149, Poipu Beach, HI, 96756, tel. 742-9667, is open Mon.-Sat. 9 a.m.-5 p.m., Sunday by arrangement. Their Poipu "interpretive bike course," self-guided with map and narrative information and featuring tidepooling and snorkeling, is $26 per person with bike and snorkel gear included. Outfitters Kauai's most thrilling adventure is the "South Shore Sea Kayaking Tour" offered Tuesday or Friday, or by arrangement, check in at 1:15 p.m, return by 5 p.m. Single or double-person kayaks are available, and the adventure includes snacks and cold drinks at $48 per person. Also offered is the Na Pali Kayak Adventure or River Kayak Adventure, which takes you up Kauai's navigable rivers, $45 for a double kayak or $30 for a single. Mountain bike rental, 9 a.m.-5 p.m., helmet and water bottle included, is $20 (multi-day discounts). Outfitters Kauai offer mountain bike ecotours to Koke'e on Thursday, 9 a.m.-1:30 p.m., or by special arrangement. The 16-mile relaxed-pace ride with a few vigorous climbs focuses on the natural history of the area and includes cold drinks and snacks at $58 per person. Outfitters Kauai retails biking and kayaking incidentals in its shop along with Patagonia clothing—shorts, sweatshirts, shirts, and hats. This company is highly recommended.

Kauai Sea Sports, at Poipu Plaza, 2827 Poipu Road, tel. 742-9303, is a full-service snorkel/scuba/surf shop. Rentals include: snorkel masks, fins, and snorkels at $5 per hour, $15 per day (includes complimentary lesson), and $30 for a reef tour; surfboard at $5-10 per hour, $15-20 per day depending on quality, and surfing lessons at $30; two-tank introductory scuba dive $150, one-tank certified dive $60, and three-day certification course $295. Kauai Sea Sports is also a sports boutique with boogie boards, surfboards, underwater equipment, T-shirts, sandals, and unique bags designed like sharks and colorful reef fish. Also try the **Poipu Dive Co.,** tel. 742-7661, for rentals of all kinds.

World surfing champion **Margo Oberg,** tel. 742-9533, will teach you how to mount a board and ride gracefully over the shimmering sea.

Captain Andy's Sailing Adventures runs a catamaran along the lovely, sculpted south coast during winter. Famous are the sunset trips with this jovial seaman; call 822-7833 for information. He also sails the north shore during the summer. **Bass Guides of Kauai,** tel. 822-1405, operates charter tours for two people in 17-foot aluminum boats on the reservoirs near Koloa. All equipment is provided.

If you're into horseback riding try **CJM Country Stables** for any of their three scheduled rides. The one-hour, easy beach ride leaves at 12:30 p.m. and costs $20. Departing at 2:30 p.m., the two-hour $40 ride is more extensive, wandering along the beach, into the ironwood trees and cane fields, and over sand dunes. Leaving at 8:30 a.m., the beach breakfast ride takes you to a secluded beach girdled by high mountains where you relax while breakfast is prepared for you; $55, three hours. CJM is located two miles past Poipu Kai Resort on the dirt road. For information and reservations, call 742-6096 or 245-6666.

Designed by Robert Trent Jones Jr., the **Kiahuna Golf Club** course is the best on the south shore. This 18-hole, par 70 course is up the road from Poipu Shopping Village and is open for play 7 a.m. until sunset; the pro shop hours are 6:30 a.m.-6:30 p.m. Reservations are requested a week in advance if possible. The club restaurant serves breakfast (from 7 a.m.), lunch (until 3:30), and dinner (to 9 p.m. except Monday and Tuesday), and happy hour is 3:30-5 p.m. For information and tee time reservation call 742-9595.

SERVICES AND INFORMATION

Medical, Emergency, And Health

At the Koloa Clinic, the **Kauai Medical Group,** tel. 742-1621, offers medical services Mon.-Fri. 8 a.m.-5 p.m., Saturday 8 a.m.-noon, and after hours by arrangement at tel. 245-6810. This clinic is located by the stream, next to the Koloa Sugar Mill chimney. **Garden Island Medical Group, Inc.,** tel. 742-1677, has an office at 3176 Poipu Rd. in Koloa. Hours are the same as above; for after-hours appointments call 338-9431. The **South Shore Pharmacy,** tel. 742-7511, is next door in the same building; open Mon.-Fri. 9 a.m.-5 p.m., and Saturday 9 a.m.-1 p.m., closed Sunday. It not only has a prescription service, but first-aid supplies, skin care, and health care products. (If they can't help, the Kauai Mortuary is right next door!)

DIANA LASICH HARPER

bird of paradise

SOUTHWEST KAUAI

The sometimes turbulent but forever enduring love affair between non-Polynesian travelers and the Hawaiian Islands began in southwest Kauai, when Captain Cook hove to off Waimea Bay and a longboat full of wide-eyed sailors made the beach. Immediately, journals were filled with glowing descriptions of the loveliness of the newly found island and its people, and the liaison has continued unabated ever since.

The **Kaumualii Highway** (the "Royal Oven" road—Rt. 50) steps west from Lihue, with the **Hoary Head Mountains** adding a dash of beauty to the south and Queen Victoria's Profile winking down from the heights. Soon, **Maluhia** ("Peaceful") **Road** branches to the south through an open lei of fragrant eucalyptus trees lining the route to Koloa and Poipu. Quickly come the towns of **Omao, Lawai,** and **Kalaheo,** way stations on the road west. Hereabouts three separate botanical gardens create a living canvas of color in blooms.

After Kalaheo, the road (Rt. 540) dips south again and passes **Port Allen,** a still-active harbor, followed by Ele'ele, then goes on to **Hanapepe** at the mouth of the Hanapepe River, whose basin has long been known as one of the best taro lands in the islands. Tiny "sugar towns" and hidden beaches follow until you enter **Waimea,** whose east flank was once dominated by a Russian fort, the last vestige of a dream of island dominance gone sour. Captain Cook landed at Waimea in the mid-afternoon of January 20, 1778, and a small monument in the town center commemorates the great event. A secondary road leading north from Waimea and another from Kekaha farther west converge inland, then meander along Waimea Canyon, the Pacific's most superlative gorge. **Kekaha,** with its belching sugar stacks, marks the end of civilization, and the hard road gives out just past the **Barking Sands Missile Range.** A "cane road" carries you to the wide sun-drenched beach of **Polihale** ("Protected Breast"), the end of the line, and the southernmost extremity of the Na Pali Coast.

SIGHTS, VILLAGES, AND BEACHES

The **Koloa District** starts just west of the Hoary Head Mountains and ends on the east bank of the Hanapepe River. It mostly incorporates the ancient *ahupua'a,* a land division shaped like a piece of pie with its pointed end deep in the Alakai Swamp and the broad end along the coast. *Koloa* means "duck," probably chosen because of the preponderance of ponds throughout the district that attract these water-loving fowl. The district's villages are strung along Rt. 50, except for Koloa and Poipu, which lie south of the main road.

The adjoining *ahupua'a* is the **Waimea District,** whose broad end continues from Hanapepe until it terminates about midway up the Na Pali Coast. Waimea means "Red Waters," named after the distinctive color of the Waimea River that bleeds from Mt. Waialeale. It cuts through Waimea Canyon, depositing the rich red soil at its mouth.

Kauai's southwest underbelly has the best beaches on the island. They're not only lovely to look at, but at most the surf is inviting and cooperative, and they lie in the island's sunbelt. At some you can camp, at all you can picnic, and a barefoot stroll is easy to come by just about anywhere along these 30 sun-drenched miles.

Note: Accommodations, Dining, And Other Practicalities

Lodging in the southwest mostly means staying in the Poipu area (see "Accommodations" under "Poipu" above). Otherwise, avail yourself of facilities in the county beach parks (for permits and general information see "Camping and Hiking" in the Kauai Introduction), Classic Cottages, the Koke'e Lodge Cabins, the Waimea Plantation Cottages, and Kahili Mountain Park, which sits at the foot of Mt. Kahili ("Tower of Silence") off Rt. 50. (See listings in the Hotel Index.) Since the following villages are quite small, practicalities, usually given under a separate heading, will be part of the descriptive text.

WEST TO HANAPEPE

PUHI

This village is technically in Lihue District, but since it's the first settlement you pass heading west, it's included here. Two road signs tip you off that you're in Puhi, one for **Kauai Community College** and the other for **Queen Victoria's Profile** scenic overlook turnout. It's beneficial to keep abreast of what's happening at the college by reading the local newspaper and free tourist brochures. Oftentimes, workshops and seminars concerning Hawaiian culture, folk medicine, and crafts are offered, most open to the general public free of charge. Queen Victoria's Profile isn't tremendously remarkable, but a definite resemblance to this double-chinned monarch has been fashioned by nature on the ridge of the Hoary Head Mountains to the south. More importantly, look for the **People's Market** across from the college. Here, you can pick up fruit and vegetables, and they offer excellent prices for freshly strung plumeria lei, an inexpensive way to brighten your day. Next door is the brown-wood **Puhi Store,** a small sundries shop that has the feel of bygone days (built in 1917). Also in Puhi is the Grove Farms Co., Inc., office, **Lappert's Ice Cream, Kauai Sausage, Sea Star** store for windsurfing and ocean gear supplies, and a **Shell station,** with gas slightly cheaper than in Lihue or Koloa.

LAWAI

In times past *ali'i* from throughout the kingdom came to Lawai (along Rt. 50 near the intersection of Rt. 530, which comes up from Koloa) to visit an ancient fishpond in the caldera of an extinct volcano. Legend says this was the first attempt by Madame Pele to dig herself a fiery home. From more recent times, look into the valley below town to see an abandoned pineapple factory. In town next to the **post office,** at

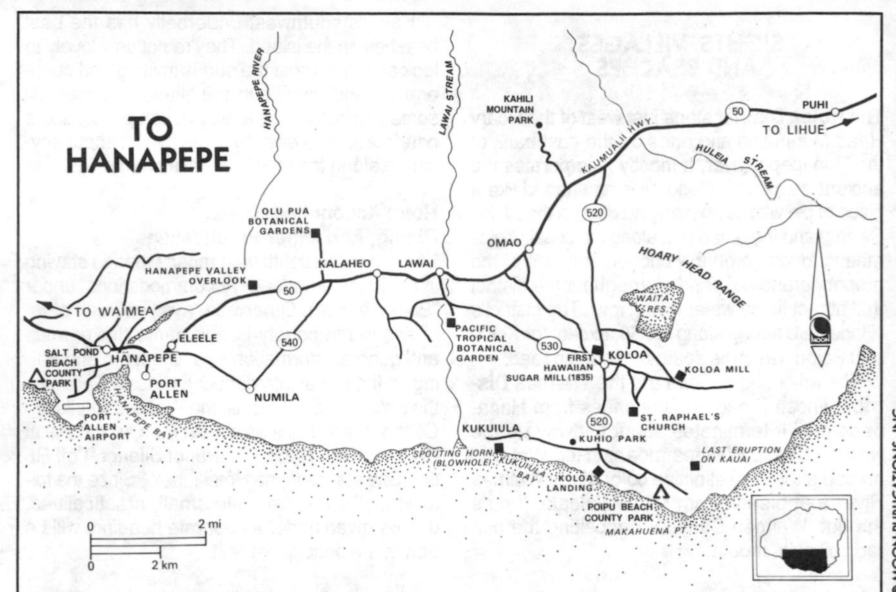

mile marker 10 is **Matsuura's Store,** a reasonably well-stocked way station open Mon.-Sat. 6 a.m.-6:30 p.m., Sunday 6 a.m.-5 p.m. Next door is the **Lawai Restaurant,** open daily 7 a.m.-9 p.m., a very local restaurant that serves American standard and a smattering of Filipino food at very reasonable prices.

At the intersection of Routes 50 and 530 is the **Hawaiian Trader** gift shop and **Mustard's Last Stand** snack shop. Mustard's features over a dozen varieties of hot dogs and sausages, sandwiches, and delicious scoops of island-flavored Lappert's ice cream. Living up to its name, the condiment/mustard table has Dijon, Poupon, horseradish, salsas, and all the trimmings to flavor your dog. Picnic tables in a pleasant grove of coconut, breadfruit, orange African tulip, and purple Hong Kong orchid trees sit next to a miniature golf course ($1 to play as long as you like). Everything at Mustard's is made out of old surfboards. Notice the bottles that have been embedded into the cement floor, and to the rear is a wave fashioned from plaster where you can stand on a surfboard and have your picture taken. Mustard's is excellent for what they offer, and the service is friendly. It is a big hit with the kids and reminds parents of roadside joints of times past.

The **Hawaii Trader,** referred to by locals as "the tourist trap," sells a mind-boggling variety of handcrafted items as well as a large selection of souvenirs, treasures, and tourist junk. Featured are goods made from eelskin and other exotic leathers (chicken feet, python, lizard . . .). Other selections include T-shirts, jewelry, carvings, and an excellent display of shells that should be featured but are stuck away on a back counter. For $10 or so, you can treat a lot of people back home with purchases from here.

The 186 acres of the **Pacific Tropical Botanical Garden**—now part of the National Botanical Gardens—constitute the only tropical plant research facility in the country. Its primary aims are to preserve, propagate, and dispense knowledge about tropical plants. This is becoming increasingly important as large areas of the world's tropical forests are being destroyed. Chartered by Congress in 1964, this nonprofit botanical and horticultural research and educational organization is supported by private contributions.

Currently, the garden's living collection has over 6,000 species of tropical plants, and about

1,000 individual plants are added each year. The staggering variety of tropical plants flourishing here ranges from common bamboo to romantic orchids. The gardens are separated into individual sections that include plants of nutritional value, medicinal value, herbs and spices, and rare and endangered species in need of conservation; other groups include plants of special ethnobotanical interest, plants of unexploited potential, tropical fruits, and ornamentals. This garden also maintains two satellite gardens, one in the wetter Limahuli Valley on the north coast of Kauai (1,000 acres), and another at Hana, Maui (120 acres), which contains Piilanihale Heiau, the largest *heiau* in the islands.

These gardens are so enchanting that many visitors regard them as one of the real treats of their trip. The visitors center (with a small museum and gift shop) is open Mon.-Fri. 7:30 a.m.-4 p.m., and from there you can take a self-guided walking tour of the lawn surrounding the center and its two dozen labeled plants. Organized tours at 9 a.m. and 1 p.m. on weekdays, Saturday at 9 a.m., and Sunday at 1 p.m. (come at least 15 minutes early) take you by van into the gardens proper, and include a two-mile walk. The tour, led by knowledgeable horticultural staff or a Na Lima Kokua ("Helping Hands") volunteer, lasts about two and a half hours and costs $15. The weekday tours include a walk into the Allerton Estate, while the weekend tours include a partial tour of the estate and more time in the gardens. Wear good walking shoes, carry an umbrella if it looks like showers, and bring mosquito repellent! Reservations are needed and should be made four to five days in advance—longer during the Christmas and Thanksgiving seasons. Call the visitors center at 332-7361, or write well in advance to the reservations secretary at Box 340, Lawai, HI 96765. Annual membership, from $35 and up, entitles you to many benefits not glven casual visitors—write to the membership chair at the address above.

Adjoining these gardens is the 100-acre Allerton Garden, started by John Allerton, a member of the Mainland cattle-raising family that founded the First National Bank of Chicago. This garden dates from the 1870s when Queen Emma made the first plantings here at one of her summer vacation homes. John Allerton (grandson of the original owner), assisting and carrying on the work of his father Robert, scoured the islands of the South Pacific to bring back their living treasures. Oftentimes, old *kama'aina* families would send cuttings of their rarest plants to be included in the collection. For 20 years, father and son, helped by a host of gardeners, cleared the jungle and planted. The Lawai River runs through the property, and pools and statuary help set the mood. To reach the gardens, go 2.8 miles north from Koloa (or turn onto Rt. 530 from Rt. 50 if coming from Lihue). Turn into Hailima Road (the third right if coming from Rt. 50) and follow the gravel driveway past the Dead End sign to the visitors center.

Maukalani, 2381 Kipuka St., Koloa, HI 96756, tel. 742-1700 or (800) 745-7414, is a deluxe 650-square-foot cottage in a quiet residential area of Lawai. This one-bedroom unit offers a professionally decorated interior, complete kitchen, full bath, and total privacy. Prices are a very reasonable $55 d, and $450 weekly. Maukalani is a perfect getaway for those who desire peace and quiet.

KALAHEO

The area around Kalaheo is springing up with many new housing subdivisions, and large tracts of coffee, tea, and macadamia nut trees are tinting the hillsides in new shades of green. In town are three gas stations, a liquor store, a post office, a medical clinic, two restaurants, a Menehune Food Mart, and a new office/shopping plaza, all along Rt. 50, making Kalaheo the first sizable town between Lihue and Hanapepe where you can pick up anything you may need before continuing west.

Those in condos or with cooking facilities mlght even stop In at **Medelro's Farm,** just up the hill toward Kukui O Lono Park, for fresh poultry and eggs. If you're interested in a pizza or sandwich, stop in at **Brick Oven Pizza,** open Tues.-Sat. 11 a.m.-10 p.m., Sunday noon-10 p.m., tel. 332-8561 (if you're heading to Waimea or Polihale, call ahead to have a pizza ready for you), located mountain side in a brand-new building as you enter Kalaheo. Pizzas range in price from a 10-inch cheese pizza at $7.35 to a large 15-inch deluxe with all the toppings for $22.85. Brick Oven also prepares vegetarian sandwiches and hot sausage sandwiches for around $5.75, along with pizza bread for $2.35, and a variety of salads $1.70-5.95. Wine, beer, and soft drinks are available. Brick Oven has a well-deserved excellent local reputation for good pizza.

Another option for food is the blue and white **Camp House Grill,** specializing in burgers, Hawaiian-style barbecued chicken, and box lunches, open for breakfast daily except Wednesday 6:30-10:30 a.m., and daily for lunch and dinner 11 a.m.-9 p.m., tel. 332-9755. They're located across from the Menehune Food Mart. Menu items are basic American standard with a Hawaiian twist and include specials like hot-spiced barbecued chicken with *kimchi* on the side for $5.95, and burgers topped with pineapple and cheddar cheese $3.95-5. Camp House is very local, very friendly, and priced right.

Kukui O Lono Park is a personal gift from Walter D. McBryde, the well-known plantation owner who donated the land to the people of Kauai in 1919. Accept it! It's off the beaten track, but definitely worth the trip. Turn left in Kalaheo at the Menehune Food Mart and go up the hill following the road for one mile until you come to (the second) Puu Road (the first Puu Road skirts the hill below the park). A sharp right turn brings you through the large stone and metal-picket gate—gates open 6:30 a.m. and close 6:30 p.m. Inside the park are a golf course and Japanese-style garden. The entrance road leads through a tunnel of eucalyptus trees to a commemorative plaque to McBryde. A flock of green parrots that nest in the tall eucalyptus trees on the grounds can be heard in a symphony of sound in the early evening.

For the gardens and McBryde's memorial, head straight ahead to the parking lot; to get to the clubhouse follow the road to your right for about a half mile. At the clubhouse are a pro shop and snack bar run by a very accommodating man, Mr. Kajitani. He knows a lot about the park and the surrounding area and is willing to chat. A round of golf on the par-72 course is under $10; carts and clubs are rented at a similarly reasonable rate. Lessons are $15 per half-hour and must be arranged with the pro.

From the top of the hill the sweeping views in all directions are striking. Unfortunately, placed in the center of one of the nicest views are a microwave antenna and dish. Set amidst a grove of towering trees, the Japanese garden offers peace and tranquility. A short stone bridge crosses a small pool, around which finely sculpted shrubs and small lanterns have been set; unusually, flowers line the adjoining walks. Many weddings are held here. The whole scene is conducive to Zenlike meditation.

Olu Pua Botanical Gardens are the former formal gardens of the Kauai Pineapple Plantation, now open to the public. West of Kalaheo, just past the turnoff for Rt. 540, a sign on the right indicates the private drive to this 12-acre garden and plantation estate. Olu Pua ("Floral Serenity") typifies the atmosphere of these grounds. There are basically four gardens: the *kaukau* garden filled with fruit trees and other edible and exotic plants, a hibiscus garden, a palm garden that lives up to its name, and a jungle garden thick with tropical exotics like mahogany, vanilla orchids, and heliconia. The broad open lawn, dotted with flowering shade trees, leads up to the handsome plantation house.

Since the property is private, the garden manager wants to control the flow of visitors. The gardens are open daily at limited times for guided tours (around $12), 9:30 a.m., 11:30 a.m., and 1:30 p.m. Reservations are requested, so call ahead; drive-in guests are accommodated *only* if there is room. Soon (the manager says), the gardens will only be open to more expensive organized tour groups as part of a trip to Waimea Canyon or the shopping trips to Old Koloa Town and Kiahuna Shopping Village; call Kauai Island Tours for these arrangements, tel. 245-9382. In regard to the present entrance situation, be sure to check with the Olu Pua Gardens office, P.O. Box 518, Kalaheo, HI 96741, tel. 332-8182, *before* you drive up.

Classic Cottages, owned and operated by Wynnis and Richard Grow, at 2687 Onu Place, P.O. Box 901, Kalaheo, HI 96741, tel. 332-9201, are six homey units where you can expect low daily rates while enjoying excellent access to nearby beaches, golf courses, and tennis courts. Rates are $55 for a garden studio and $60 for an oceanview, breakfast add $5, third person add $10; jacuzzi available.

PORT ALLEN AND VICINITY

As you roll along Rt. 50 from Kalaheo to Port Allen, you're surrounded by sugarcane fields, and the traditional economy of the area is apparent. About halfway an HVB Warrior points to **Hanapepe Valley Overlook,** no farther away than your car door, served up as easily as a fast-food snack at a drive-through window. Definitely worth a stop—for no effort, you get a remarkable panorama of a classic Hawaiian valley, much of it still planted in taro.

In a moment you pass through **Ele'ele** (home of the famous Kauai Kookie Kompany—macadamia shortbread, Kona coffee, guava macadamia and coconut krispies cookies, among others, now available statewide) and **Port Allen,** separate communities on the east bank of the Hanapepe River, with Hanapepe on the west. At mile marker 16, at the junction with Rt. 541 leading to Port Allen, is the **Ele'ele Shopping Center.** Here, along with various eateries, are a post office, **Big Save Supermarket,** laundromat, bank, Chevron station, and **The Garden Isle Medical Group clinic,** tel. 335-3107. The **Port Allen Pub,** open daily from 6:30 a.m., serves sandwiches and light fare. On the road to the Port Allen small boat harbor are the offices of **Na Pali Coast Cruise Line,** tel. 335-5079, for touring, and **Bluewater Sailing,** tel. 335-6440, for charter.

HANAPEPE

Hanapepe ("Crushed Bay"), billing itself "Kauai's Biggest Little Town," is divided into two sections. One lies along Rt. 50. The other is Old Hanapepe, a "must see" along Hanapepe Road, off to the right at the Y-intersection near the Green Garden Restaurant (see "Old Hanapepe" following).

The **Green Garden Restaurant,** an old standby, is marked by the tangle of vegetation that almost makes the building look overgrown, open daily for breakfast, lunch, and dinner 7 a.m.-2 p.m. and 5-9 p.m., closed Tuesday evenings, tel. 335-5422. This family-owned restaurant offers tourist-quality food offered in large portions, with *aloha* service. The new section of the restaurant is set up to hold busloads of tourists who arrive for lunch; go a little earlier or a little later than noon. The old room has a few plants, but the name is really held up by the decor: green walls, chairs, tables, placemats, and bathrooms. If you see anything on the menu you want to mix and match, just ask. Substitutions are cheerfully made. The full meal selections, including beverage, are mostly under $10. The homemade pies are famous, and always delicious.

Immediately past the restaurant look for a tiny white building housing **Susie's Cafe,** tel. 335-3989, an excellent down-home health-conscious restaurant where you can have everything from a smoothie to Susie's beef stew and rice. Breakfast is particularly scrumptious, with farm-fresh eggs, or pancakes made with rice and bananas topped with macadamia nuts. Almost next door is a **Lappert's Ice Cream** stand. Then on your left is another island institution and oddity, the combination **Conrad's** and **Wong's** restaurants, open daily for breakfast, lunch, and dinner, closed after 2 p.m. Monday; tel. 335-5066. Defying the adage "two things can't occupy the same space at the same time," they are different restaurants with different menus in one giant dining room that's reminiscent of a small-town banquet hall that caters to local bowling leagues. Both are very reasonably priced, but they too are a favorite with the tour buses and can be crowded. When you go in to the cafeteria-style dining room, you're handed two separate menus. Feel free to order from each. Conrad's (formerly Mike's—his dad) has standard American fare with a Hawaiian twist. Most sandwiches are under $6, main course dinners under $8. Wong's specialties are Chinese and Japanese dishes, all under $10, with many around $7. The service is friendly, the portions large, but the cooking mediocre, except for the pies. You won't complain, but you won't be impressed either.

If that isn't enough, next door is **Omoide's Deli and Bakery,** and across the street, in a russet-colored building, is **Kauai Kitchens,** a local coffee shop. Both are open early in the morning for breakfast.

Even if you tried, you couldn't miss **Sinaloa Tacqueria,** open daily except Wednesday, lunch 11 a.m.-2 p.m., dinner 5-9 p.m., tel. 335-0006, a huge piñata of a bright turquoise metal building trimmed in yellow and green. The inside is more colorful than a Kauai sunset, with pink, yellow, green, blue, and turquoise chairs, and yellow and blue tiles. Dishes include spicy Mexican fare like burritos, *chile verde, carne asada, pollo poblano,* Mazatlan *chiles rellenos,* eggplant enchiladas, and seafood burritos, all served with extras like chips and salsa, guacamole, and sour cream. For lunch, these dishes cost $7-12, and for dinner about $2 more. The bar serves imported beers like Bohemia, Tecate, and Pacifico, and they also have pitchers of Miller Lite and Bud. The house standard is Cuervo Gold Margaritas for $4, or by the pitcher for $12.50.

In the center of town, along Rt. 50, look for the **Soto Zen Temple Zenshuji** on your left. It's quite large and interesting to people who haven't visited a temple before. Also along the highway in town are the **Westside Pharmacy,** tel. 335-5342; a library; **Bali Hai Helicopter** offices, tel. 335-3166; **Mariko Mini-Mart**; **Inter-Island Helicopters,** tel. 335-5009; and several gas stations.

As you leave town heading west along Rt. 50, a small gift shop called **The Station** sits on the right. A friendly young woman there sells yarn, crochet material, and Hawaiian-style needlepoint designs.

On the western outskirts of town, just past The Station, a sign points *makai* down Rt. 543 to the Kauai Humane Society and Hanapepe Refuse Disposal. Follow the sign to a small Japanese cemetery (there are several others nearby) where an HVB Warrior points to **Salt Pond Beach County Park,** the best beach and windsurfing spot on this end of the island. This beach is at the west end of the Port Allen Airport runway, once the major airport for the island but now servicing only a few helicopters and a glider company. The local people from around Hanapepe enjoy this popular beach park with its pavilions, tables, toilets, showers, and camping (with county permit). The swimming and snorkeling are excellent, and a natural breakwater in front of the lifeguard makes a pool safe for tots. Surfers enjoy the breaks here, and a constant gentle breeze makes the area popular with windsurfers. Along the road to Salt Pond Beach, you pass the actual salt ponds, evaporative basins cut into the red earth that have been used for hundreds of years. The sea salt here is still harvested but isn't considered *pure* enough for commercial use, though the local people know better. They make and harvest the salt in the spring and summer, and because of its so-called impurities that add a special flavor, it is a sought-after commodity and an appreciated gift for family and friends. If you see salt in the basins, it belongs to someone, but there won't be any hassles if you take a *small* pinch. Don't scrape it up with your fingers because the sharp crystals can cut you, and you'll rub salt into your own wounds in the process.

Old Hanapepe

Much more interesting, Old Hanapepe is a time-frozen still life of vintage false-front buildings housing a palette of art studios, local dry goods stores, a tavern, and an excellent restaurant/coffee shop that's a must-stop.

At the eastern approach to town, along Rt. 50 at the Green Garden Restaurant, bear right at the Y-intersection and you'll soon be heading down the main drag. Look up to your right and, if it is early winter, notice an entire hillside of bougainvilleas ablaze with a multicolored patchwork of blossoms. Following this road into the center of the old town, you pass the **James Hoyle Gallery,** the **Lele Aka Studio Gallery,** and **Kauai Fine Arts.** For a complete description see "Specialty Shops, Arts, and Boutiques" under "Shopping" in the Kauai Introduction. Also lining the main drag is the **Sandbox,** a bar about as "local" as you can get; the **Bank of Hawaii;** grocery stores; and for a real treat, **Shimonishi Orchid Nursery.** The nursery has hundreds of varieties of this tropical favorite; this is *the* place on the island to buy and ask about this flower.

Hanapepe Book Store, Tropical Scents, and Espresso Bar, open Wed.-Sun. 8 a.m.-3 p.m., Thursday 8 a.m.-4:30 p.m., breakfast until 11 a.m., lunch until 2 p.m., dinner Thurs.-Sat. 5:30-9:30 p.m. with live music, tel. 335-5011, is a fantastic eclectic restaurant for mind and body operated by Chris and Larry, who are still working out the multiple hyphenation possibilities of their last name. Housed in the town's drugstore, circa 1939, the espresso bar/restaurant section is fashioned from the original soda fountain counter tastefully modernized with a black-and-white checkerboard motif. The food is health-conscious vegetarian with an attempt at organic and locally grown whenever possible, but always fresh and definitely savory and satisfying. Breakfast is terrific with homemade pastries and pies washed down by steaming hot cups of espresso, hot chocolate, cappuccino, caffe latte, and an assortment of herbal teas priced $1.75-2.75. Lunch brings a garden burger made from rolled oats, low-fat mozzarella cheese, cottage cheese, bulgur wheat, walnuts, the kitchen sink, and sautéed mushrooms for $5.95; Chris's Caesar salad for $3.50; or a large bowl of homemade minestrone soup. All are served with fresh bread or a croissant. Dinner is always vegetarian Italian a la Hawaii, and could be baked lasagna al forno, linguine with pesto, or artichokes with cannelloni, all with soup, salad, and bread for $12-16. Dinner music is usually provided by a solo local performer playing everything from slack key to classical flute music. The original wide-board floor and simple shelves in the bookstore/boutique section is reminiscent of an old-time general store. The focus is mostly on Hawaiiana, with Hawaii-made or -related items that include a whale or gecko lightswitch plate, coral jewelry, and genuine Niihau shellwork. For a scent of the islands choose from a bouquet of Hawaiian perfumes, or select a woodcarving or a straw hat. The bookshelves are filled with magazines, postcards, and books on Hawaii. If you crave a snack, quiet cup of coffee, full meal, or good read, you can't beat the Hanapepe Bookstore, Tropical Scents, and Espresso Bar.

A **farmers' market** operates on the lawn of the First United Church of Christ every Thursday 4-6 p.m. Those in the know are on time because the best pickings are gone in the first hour. The late bird gets the wormy apple!

HANAPEPE TO POLIHALE

Sugar Towns:Hanapepe to Waimea

The road hugs the coast after Hanapepe, bypassing a series of still-working "sugar towns" until you arrive in Waimea. **Kaumakani,** a small cluster of homes with a few dirt lanes, has a post office, mini-mart, and the **Niihau Helicopter** office, tel. 335-3500. Put to use mostly for medical emergencies and air-lifting supplies to the island, the helicopter schedules occasional tours to Niihau. This company has the exclusive landing rights on Niihau, and offers the only way to get there without a special invitation.

Olokele is another sugar town. Drive through it to draw your own conclusions about the quality of life. You'll find small homes kept up with obvious pride. The road dips down to the sugar refinery, the focus of the town; the main street is lined with quaint lampposts that recall the last century.

Next is **Pakala,** noted more for its surfing beach than for the town itself. At mile marker 21, cars pulled off the road means "surf's up." Follow the pathway to try the waves yourself, or just to watch the show. Popular with surfers, this beach is not an official park. Walk down past the bridge to a well-worn pathway leading through a field. In a few minutes you'll come to a 500-yard-long horseshoe of white sand. Off to the left is a rocky promontory popular with local fishermen. The swimming is fair, and the reef provides good snorkeling, but the real go is the surf. The beach is nicknamed "Infinity" because the waves last so long. They come rolling in graceful arcs to spill upon the beach, then recede in a regular, hypnotic pattern, causing the next wave to break and roll perfectly. Sunset is a wonderful time to come here for a romantic evening picnic.

WAIMEA

The remains of the Russian fort guard the eastern entrance to Waimea town. Turn left at the sign for Russian **Fort Elizabeth State Park.** The fort, shaped like a six-pointed star, dates from 1817 when a German doctor, George Anton Scheffer, built it in the name of Czar Nicholas of Russia, naming it after the potentate's daughter. Scheffer, a self-styled adventurer and onetime Moscow policeman, saw great potential in the domination of Hawaii, and built other forts in Honolulu and along the Waioli River, which empties into Hanalei Bay on Kauai's north shore. Due to political maneuverings with other European nations, Czar Nicholas never warmed to

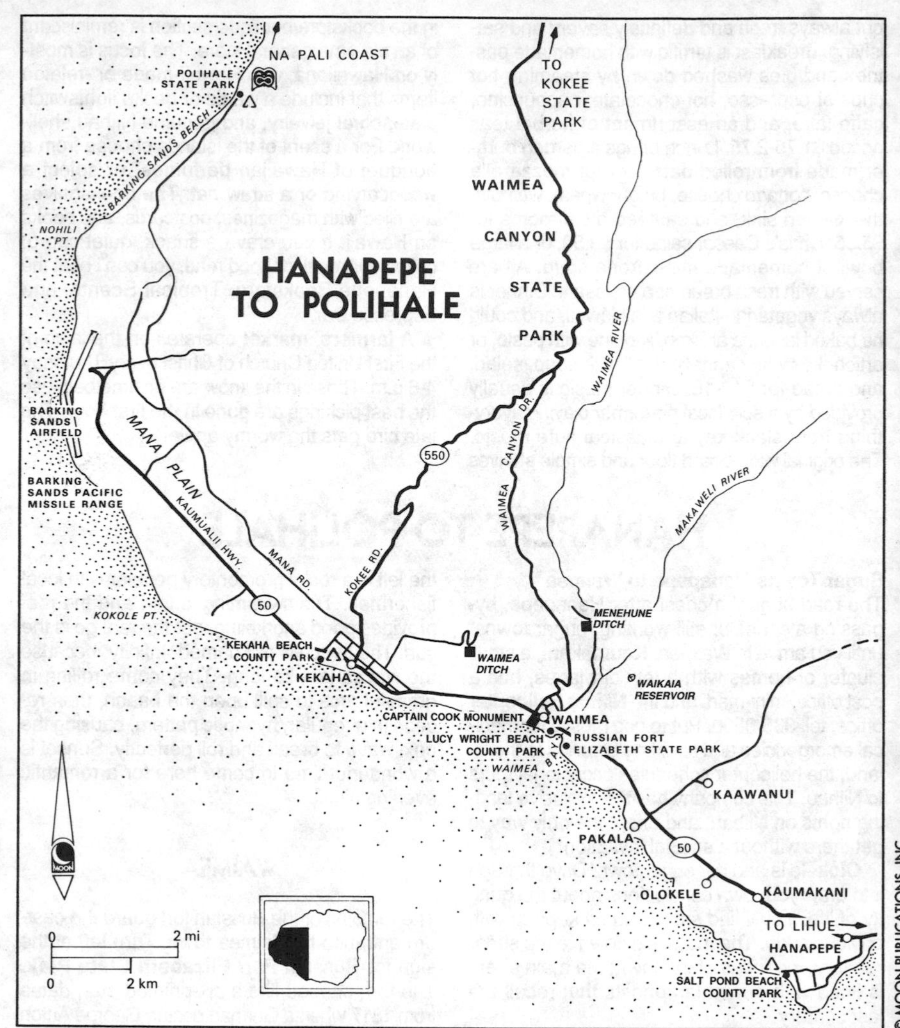

Scheffer's enterprises and withdrew official support. For a time, Kauai's King Kaumuali'i continued to fly the Russian flag, perhaps in a subtle attempt to play one foreign power against another. The fort fell into disrepair and was virtually dismantled in 1864, when 38 guns of various sizes were removed. The stout walls, once 30 feet thick, are now mere rubble, humbled by time-encircling, nondescript underbrush. However, if you climb onto the ramparts you'll still get a commanding view of Waimea Bay.

Just after you cross the Waimea River, signs point to **Lucy Wright Beach County Park,** a five-acre park popular with the local folk. There's a picnic area, restrooms, showers, playground, and tent camping (with county permit). Pick up supplies in Waimea. The park is situated around the mouth of the river, which makes the water a bit murky. The swimming is fair if the water is clear, and the surfing is decent around the river mouth. A few hundred feet to the west of this park is a recreational pier. Good for fishing, it can be reached by walking along the beach or down a back street behind the Waimea Library.

Captain Cook's achievements were surely more deserving than the uninspiring commemorative markers around Waimea indicate. Whether you revere him as a great explorer or denigrate him as an opportunistic despoiler, his achievements in mapping the great Pacific were unparalleled, and changed the course of history. In his memory are **Captain Cook's Landing,** a modest marker near Lucy Wright Beach Park, commemorating his "discovery" of the Sandwich Islands at 3:30 p.m. on September 20, 1778, and **Captain Cook's Monument,** on a little median strip in downtown Waimea. If you're fascinated by Kauai's half-legendary little people, you might want to take a look at the **Menehune Ditch,** a stone wall encasing an aqueduct curiously built in a fashion unused by and apparently unknown to the Polynesian settlers of Hawaii. The oral tradition states that the ditch was built by order of Ola, high chief of Waimea, and that he paid his little workers in *opae,* a tiny shrimp that was their staple. On payday, they supposedly sent up such a great cheer that they were heard on Oahu. Today, the work is greatly reduced, as many of the distinctively hand-hewn boulders have been removed for use in buildings around the island, especially the Protestant church in Waimea. Some steadfastly maintain that the Menehune never existed, but a census taken in the 1820s, at the request of capable King Kaumuali'i, officially listed 65 persons living in Wainiha Valley as Menehune!

Waimea Town is of little interest as far as sights go, but an unescorted walking tour introduces you to the major historical sites in town. Ask at the library (tel. 338-1738) for the free map and description of each site. The walk should take about one and a half hours. Waimea does have some reasonably good restaurants and shopping.

The **Captain's Cargo Company,** tel. 338-0333, 9984 Kaumualii Hwy. (Rt. 50) and office of **Liko Kauai Cruises** (see "Cabin Cruisers and Sailing Ships" under "Sightseeing Tours" under "Getting Around" in the Kauai Introduction) is operated by Debra Hookano, wife of Captain Liko. The small but tasteful boutique, open daily 8 a.m.-5 p.m., offers jewelry, fashionable dresses, shorts, T-shirts, and brocaded vests. The boutique also rents and sells surfboards, boogie boards, and snorkel equipment. Rental prices are boogie boards $5 per hour or $15 per day; surfboards $5 per hour, or $20 per day; and snorkel gear $2 per hour, or $5 per day.

Along the main road, facing Captain Cook's statue, is **Ishihara's Market,** where you'll find all the necessities. Kitty-corner across the intersection is the police station; the street running inland from here goes to the Menehune Ditch. Across the street is a well-stocked **Big Save Supermarket.** Their lunch counter, believe it or not, features terrific local dishes at very reasonable prices. In town are three gas stations, **Da Booze Shop,** laundromat, photography supply shop, bank, discount clothing shop, **Kiyoki's Art Gallery,** and **West Side Sporting Goods. Dairy Queen** is at the west end of town, along with the **Menehune Pharmacy,** and a half mile up Waimea Canyon Road is **Kauai Veterans Memorial Hospital.**

Waimea Plantation Cottages

Aside from a few private rental homes, **Waimea Plantation Cottages** is virtually the only place to stay along the south shore west of Poipu, and what a place it is. Owned and operated by the Kikiaola Land Company, Ltd., this oceanfront property is set in a grove of over 750 coconut palms and a few huge banyan trees at the west end of Waimea. Not giving in to big bucks or modern resort development, worker and supervisor cottages and the manager's house from the former Waimea sugar plantation have been renovated and preserved, and the grounds maintained in an old-style way. Here you are treated to a touch of the past. While some modern amenities such as full kitchens, bathrooms, and color cable TVs have been added for comfort and convenience, an effort has been made to keep each unit as much in its original state as possible (1920-'30s period); period furniture and other furnishings add to the feel of that bygone era. Most buildings have bare wood floors and painted wood walls. Nearly all have ceiling fans and lanai. Weekly housekeeping and linen service are included. Complimentary washers and dryers are available on the premises. A swimming pool in the 1930s style has been constructed on the lawn, along with a court and the Grove Dining Room (see below). In accordance with this philosophy of preservation, the land behind the company office, instead of being developed for profit, houses low- or no-rent cottages for longtime employees of the plantation (no longer a functioning entity).

Presently, there are 48 units, including 11 cottages moved from the Kekaha Plantation. Rates for one-, two-, three-bedroom cottages are $80-180 d; The Director's Cottages are $215 daily, or $1330 weekly; The Manager's House has only a weekly rate at $2275. The average length of stay is over 10 days, with a 35% return rate; make your reservations several months in advance. Low-key and unpretentious, this institution aims to please and offers a chance for seclusion and serenity. What could be better than to relax and read a favorite book on your breezy lanai, watch the sunset through the coconut grove, or take a moonlight stroll along the gently lapping shore? Waimea Plantation Cottages also manages a six-bedroom house and a one-bedroom cottage on the beach in Hanalei. If you are going to the north coast and need a place to stay, check with the office here about these two accommodations. The manager, Mr. Raymond Blouin, or either of the very helpful office workers can provide additional information. Call 338-1625 or (800) 992-4632 Mon.-Fri. 8 a.m.-5 p.m., or write Waimea Plantation Cottages, P.O. Box 367, Waimea, HI 96796.

The Grove Dining Room, open Tues.-Fri. 11:30 a.m.-2 p.m. for lunch, Tues.-Sat. for dinner, and Sunday for brunch ($16.75 adults, $9 children), is adjacent to the new administrative center. The lunch menu starts with appetizers like fresh Kauai sashimi $6.75, fresh fruit plate $8.50, and soup du jour $1.75 a cup. Sandwiches are served with marinated cucumber salad and choice of soup or salad and include everything from thinly sliced seasoned vegetables to charbroiled hamburgers to open-faced shrimp and seafood salad, ranging in price $6.50-8.50. Entree salads include tender fresh *ahi* with sliced vegetables, $10.50, marinated breast of chicken or Caesar $8.75 with half-orders at a reduced price. For dessert there are cheesecake, chocolate mousse, and an assortment of ice creams, in addition to banana bread with vanilla ice cream and fresh pineapple.

WAIMEA CANYON AND KOKE'E STATE PARKS

The "Grand Canyon of the Pacific" is an unforgettable part of your trip, and you shouldn't miss it for any reason. Waimea Canyon Drive (near the Dairy Queen) begins in Waimea, heading inland past sugarcane fields for six miles, where it joins Koke'e Road (Rt. 550) coming up from Kekaha Town. Either route is worthwhile, and you can catch both by going in on one leg and coming out on the other. In about a mile you enter **Waimea Canyon State Park,** a ridgetop park that flanks the road to Koke'e. This serpentine route runs along a good but narrow road into Kauai's cool interior with plenty of fascinating vistas and turnouts along the way. The passenger, going up, gets the better view. Behind you, the coastal towns and their tall refinery stacks fade into the pale blue sea, while the cultivated fields are a study of green on green.

Ever climbing, you feel as though you're entering a mountain fortress. The canyon yawns, devouring clouds washed down by draughts of sunlight. The colors are diffuse, blended strata of gray, royal purple, vibrant red, russet, jet black, and schoolgirl pink. You reach the thrilling spine, obviously different, where the trees on the red bare earth are gnarled and twisted. The road becomes a roller coaster whipping you past raw beauty, immense and powerful. Drink deeply, contemplate, and move on into the clouds at the 2,000-foot level where the trees get larger again. As you climb, every lookout demands a photo. At **Waimea Canyon Lookout** (3,400 feet) you have the most expansive view of the canyon and across to valleys that slice down from the lofty peak. From here it's obvious why this canyon was given its nickname. Watch for soaring birds, mountain goats, and low-flying helicopters.

From **Po'okapele Lookout,** Waipoo Waterfall is seen tumbling forcefully off the hanging valley across the canyon. A small rest area with a few picnic tables lies across the road. **Po'ohinahina Lookout** (3,500 feet) provides the best views

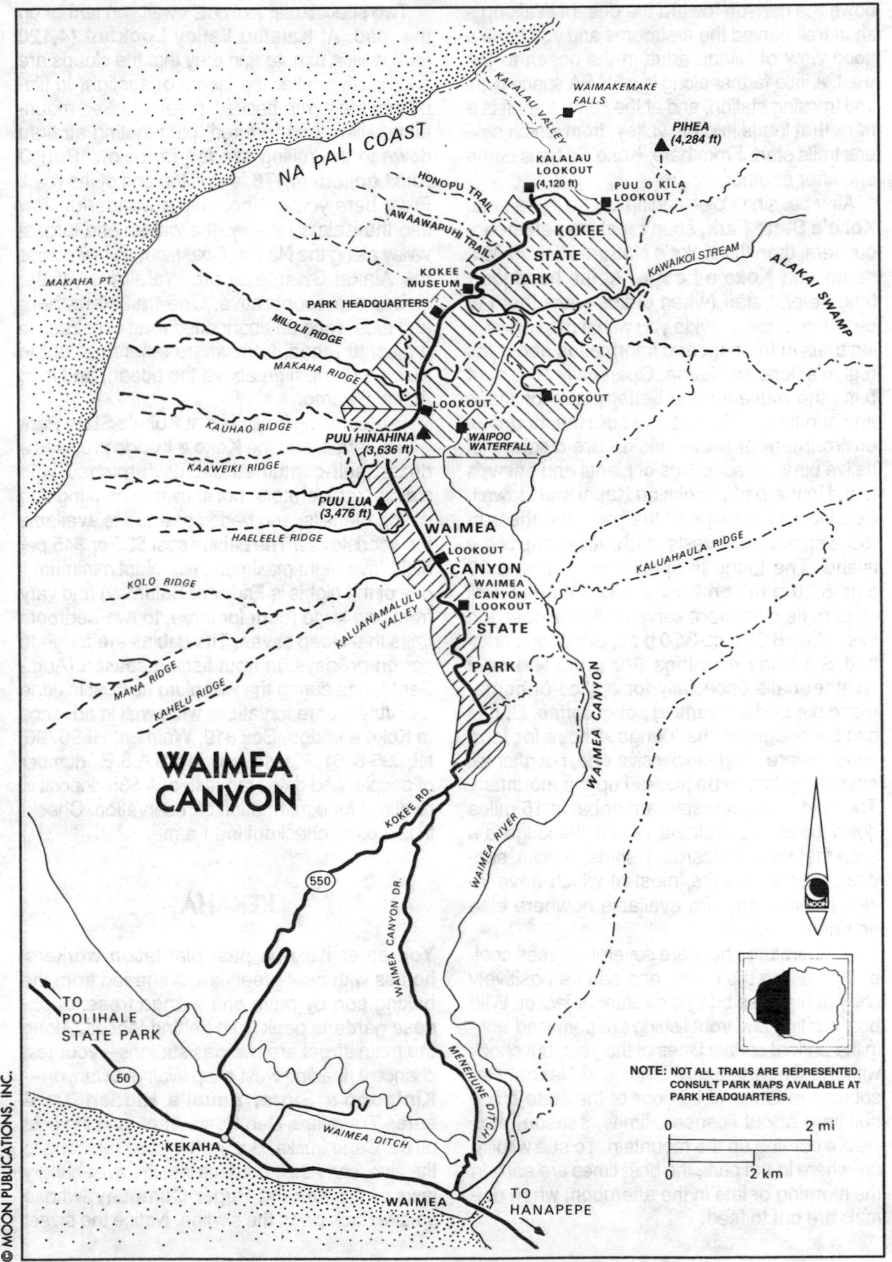

NA PALI COAST
KALALAU VALLEY
WAIMAKEMAKE FALLS
PIHEA (4,284 ft)
KALALAU LOOKOUT (4,120 ft)
PUU O KILA LOOKOUT
HONOPU TRAIL
AWAAWAPUHI TRAIL
KOKEE STATE PARK
KAWAIKOI STREAM
ALAKAI SWAMP
KOKEE MUSEUM
MAKAHA PT.
PARK HEADQUARTERS
MILOLII RIDGE
MAKAHA RIDGE
LOOKOUT
LOOKOUT
KAUHAO RIDGE
PUU HINAHINA (3,636 ft)
WAIPOO WATERFALL
KAAWEIKI RIDGE
PUU LUA (3,476 ft)
WAIMEA CANYON
HAELEELE RIDGE
LOOKOUT
KALUAHAULA RIDGE
KOLO RIDGE
WAIMEA CANYON LOOKOUT
STATE PARK
KALUANAMALULU VALLEY
MANA RIDGE
KAHELU RIDGE
WAIMEA CANYON
WAIMEA CANYON
KOKEE RD.
WAIMEA RIVER
550
WAIMEA CANYON DR.
MOON
TO POLIHALE STATE PARK
50
MENEHUNE DITCH
NOTE: NOT ALL TRAILS ARE REPRESENTED. CONSULT PARK MAPS AVAILABLE AT PARK HEADQUARTERS.
0 2 mi
0 2 km
KEKAHA
WAIMEA DITCH
WAIMEA
TO HANAPEPE

down the canyon toward the ocean. Walk up a short trail behind the restrooms and you have a good view of Niihau adrift in the ocean to the west. A little farther along is a NASA space flight and tracking station, and at the same turnoff is a track that leads into the valley, from which several trails start. From here, Koke'e's trails come one after another.

After passing Po'ohinahina Lookout you enter **Koke'e State Park,** soon reaching park headquarters, then the **Koke'e Natural History Museum** and **Koke'e Lodge.** At the headquarters, helpful staff (when duties allow them to be present) can provide you with a map of walking trails in the park and information about the region's flora and fauna. Open daily 10 a.m.-4 p.m., the museum is a better place for maps and additional information about the mountain environment of Kauai. Inside are displays of native birds, descriptions of plants and animals found in the park, books on Kauai and Hawaii, detailed hiking maps of the park and the surrounding national forests, and a relief map of the island. The lodge is open Sun.-Thurs. 8:30 a.m.-5:30 p.m., on Friday and Saturday until 10 p.m. Its restaurant serves full breakfast and lunch daily 8:30 a.m.-3:30 p.m., dinner on Friday and Saturday evenings 6-9 p.m. The cool weather calls especially for a slice of homemade pie and a steaming pot of coffee. Drinks can be bought at the lounge. Prices for food and drink are on the expensive side, but after all, everything has to be trucked up the mountain. The next nearest restaurant or bar is 15 miles down the road at Kekaha. Also in the lodge is a shop that sells postcards, T-shirts, snacks, sundries, and souvenirs, most of which have island themes and are available nowhere else on Kauai.

Temperatures here are several degrees cooler than along the coast, and can be positively chilly at night, so bring a sweater or jacket. Wild boar hunting and trout fishing are permitted within the park at certain times of the year, but check with the Department of Land and Natural Resources in Lihue (third floor of the state office building) about licenses, limits, season, etc., *before* coming up the mountain. To see wildlife anywhere in the park, the best times are early in the morning or late in the afternoon, when animals are out to feed.

Two spectacular lookouts await you farther up the road. At **Kalalau Valley Lookout** (4,120 feet) walk a minute and pray that the clouds are cooperative, allowing lasers of sunlight to illuminate the hump-backed, green-cloaked mountains, silent and tortured, plummeting straight down to the roiling sea far, far below. **Puu O Kila Lookout** (4,176 feet) is the end of the road. From here you get not only a wonderful view into the Kalalau Valley, the widest and largest valley along the Na Pali Coast, but a view across the Alakai Swamp to Mt. Waialeale—if the clouds are cooperative. One trail starts here and runs along an abandoned road construction project to Pihea, from where others run out to Alealau Point, high above the ocean, and in to Alakai Swamp.

Tent camping is allowed at **Koke'e State Park** with a permit, and the **Koke'e Lodge** provides a dozen self-contained cabins furnished with stoves, refrigerators, hot showers, cooking and eating utensils, and bedding; wood is available for woodstoves. The cabins cost $35 or $45 per night (five-night maximum; two-night minimum if one of the nights is Friday or Saturday) and vary from one large room for three, to two-bedroom units that sleep seven. The cabins are tough to get on holidays, in trout-fishing season (Aug.-Sept.), and during the wild plum harvest in June and July. For reservations write well in advance to Koke'e Lodge, Box 819, Waimea, HI 96796, tel. 335-6061. Please include a S.A.S.E., number of people, and dates requested. A $35 deposit is required for confirmation of reservation. Check-in is 2 p.m., checkout is 11 a.m.

KEKAHA

You enter Kekaha past plantation workers' homes with neat green lawns shaded from the baking sun by palm and mango trees. Japanese gardens peek from behind fences. Along the main street are two gas stations—your last chance if heading west or up Waimea Canyon—**Kinipopo's Store, Kauai's Hidden Treasures, Traveler's Den Restaurant,** and the post office. Cane trucks, like worker bees returning to the hive, carry their burdens into the ever-hungry jaws of the **Kekaha Sugar Company,** whose smokestack owns the skyline. Notice the sweet molasses smell in the air. The turnoff for Rt. 550 leading to Waimea Canyon and to Koke'e 15 miles away branches off in the center of town. At this intersection are a few other shops and **Menehune Food Market,** your last chance for snacks and sundries. Every Saturday at noon there is a farmers' market where you can pick up fresh produce. As the location changes, ask around for the current spot. Kekaha isn't large, so it shouldn't be hard to find.

Route 50 proceeds along the coast. When still in town, you pass **H.P. Faye Park.** Then the golden sands of **Kekaha Beach County Park** stretch for miles, widening as you head west, with pull-offs and shade-tree groves now and again. The sun always shines, and the swimming and surfing are excellent. Pick your spot anywhere along the beach. The area is good for swimming and snorkeling during calm weather, and fair for surfing, although the reef can be quite shallow in spots. In town, across the road from H.P. Faye Park, are Kekaha Beach County Park's pavilion, tables, toilets, and grills. Since there's no tourist development in the area, it's generally quite empty.

The sea sparkles, and the land flattens wide and long, with green cane billowing all around. Dry gulches and red buttes form an impromptu inland wall. In six miles are the gates of **Barking Sands Airfield and Pacific Missile Range.** Here howl the dogs of war, leashed but on guard. You can use the beach and even arrange to camp for a few days if maneuvers are not in progress by calling 335-4111. The area is hot, shadeless, and pounded by unfriendly surf, but affords the best view of **Niihau,** a purple Rorschach blot on the horizon —the closest you're likely to get to the "Forbidden Island." The beach has the largest sand dunes on the island, due to the ocean's shallowness between the two islands. Supposedly, if you slide down the dunes, made from a mixture of sand and ground coral, the friction will cause a sound like a barking dog.

Route 50 curves to the right after you pass the missile range, and an HVB Warrior points left to **Polihale State Park.** The approach is five miles of well-graded dirt cane road. The earth is a definite buff color here, unlike the deep red that predominates throughout the rest of the island. At a stop sign at a crossroads, you're pointed to Polihale ("Home of the Spirits"). You can day-trip to soak up the sights and you'll find pavilions, showers, toilets, and grills. Both RV and tent camping are allowed with a state park permit. The camping area is atop the dune on the left before you get to the pavilions. There are generally no hassles, but the rangers do come around, and you should have a permit because it's a long way back to Lihue to get one.

From the parking area at the chain gate, walk over the dune and down to the beach. The swimming can be dangerous, but the hiking is grand. The powdery white-sand beach stretches for nearly three miles, pushing up against the Na Pali cliffs to the north and meeting the Mana Plain to the east. Literally at the end of the road, this beach takes you away from the crowds but you'll hardly ever be all by yourself. Here the cliffs come down to the sea, brawny and rugged, with the Na Pali Coast beginning around the far bend. Where the cliffs meet the sea is the ruin of **Polihale Heiau.** This is a powerful spot, where the souls of the dead made their leap from land into infinity. The priests of this temple chanted special prayers to speed them on their way, as the waters of life flowed from a sacred spring in the mountainside.

BOB RACE

NIIHAU

THE FORBIDDEN ISLAND

The only thing forbidding about Niihau is its nickname, "The Forbidden Island." Ironically, it's one of the last real havens of peace, tranquility, and tradition left on the face of the earth. This privately owned island, operating as one large cattle and sheep ranch, is staffed by the last remaining pure Hawaiians in the state. To go there, you must have a personal invitation from the owners or one of the residents. Some people find this situation strange, but simply dropping by would be no stranger than walking up to an Iowa farmhouse unannounced and expecting to be invited in to dinner. The islanders are free to come and go as they wish, and are given the security of knowing that the last real Hawaiian place is not going to be engulfed by the modern world. Niihau is a reservation, but a *free-will* reservation, that anyone who has felt the world too much with them could easily admire.

Helicopter Tours

Niihau Helicopters, tel. 335-3500, offers limited tours to the island. For complete details see "Helicopter Tours" under "Sightseeing Tours" under "Getting Around" in the Kauai Introduction.

The Land And Climate

The 17-mile **Kaulakahi Channel** separates Niihau from the western tip of Kauai. The island's maximum dimensions are 18 miles long by six miles wide, with a total area of 73 square miles. The highest point on the island, **Paniau** (1,281 feet), lies on the east-central coast. There are no port facilities on the island, but the occasional boats put in at **Kii** and **Lehua landings,** both on the northern tip. Since Niihau is so low and lies in the rainshadow of Kauai, it receives only 30 inches of precipitation per year, making it rather arid. Oddly enough, low-lying basins, eroded from the single shield volcano that made the island, act like a catchment system. In them are the state's largest naturally occurring lakes, **Halalii** and the slightly larger 182-acre **Halulu.** The two uninhabited islets nearby are **Lehua,** off the northern tip and exceptional for scuba diving, and **Kaula** a few miles off the southern tip; each barely covers one-half square mile, and join Niihau as part of Kauai County.

HISTORY

After the goddess Papa returned from Tahiti and discovered that her husband, Wakea, was playing around, she left him. The great Wakea did some squirming, and after these island-parents reconciled, Papa became pregnant and gave birth to Kauai. According to the creation chants found in *The Kumulipo,* Niihau popped out as the afterbirth, along with Lehua and Kaula, the last of the low reef islands.

Niihau was never a very populous island because of the relatively poor soil, so the islanders had to rely on trade with nearby Kauai for many necessities, including poi. Luckily, the fishing grounds off the island's coastal waters are the richest in the area, and Niihauans could always trade fish. The islanders became famous for Niihau mats, a good trade item, made from *makaloa,* a sedge plant plentiful on the island. Craftspeople also fashioned *ipu pawehe,* a geometrically designed gourd highly prized in the old days. When Captain Cook arrived and wished to provision his ships, he remarked the Niihau natives were much more eager to trade than those on Kauai, and he secured potatoes and yams that seemed to be in abundant supply.

Kamehameha IV Sells

Along with Kauai, Niihau became part of the kingdom under Kamehameha. It passed down to his successors, and in the 1860s Kamehameha IV sold it to the Robinson family for $10,000. This Scottish family, which came to Hawaii via New Zealand, has been the sole proprietor of the island ever since, although they now live on Kauai. They began a sheep and cattle ranch, hiring the island's natives as workers. No one can say exactly why, but it's evident this family felt a great sense of responsibility and purpose. Tradition passed down over the years dictated that islanders could live on Niihau as long as they pleased, but that visitors were not welcome without a personal invitation. With the native Hawaiian population decimated, the Robinsons felt that these proud people should have at least one place to call theirs and theirs alone. To keep the race pure, male visitors to the island were generally asked to leave by sundown.

Niihau Invaded

During WW II, Niihau was the only island of Hawaii to be occupied by the Japanese. A Zero pilot, after hitting Pearl Harbor, developed engine trouble and had to ditch on Niihau. At first the islanders took him prisoner, but he somehow managed to escape and commandeer the machine guns from his plane. He terrorized the island, and the residents headed for the hills. One old woman who refused to leave was a Hawaiian Barbara Fritchie. She told the Japanese prisoner to shoot her if he wished, but to please stop making a nuisance of himself, it wasn't nice! He would have saved himself a lot of trouble if he had only listened. Fed up with hiding, one huge *kanaka,* Benehakaka Kanahele, decided to approach the pilot with *aloha.* He was convinced the intruder would see the error of his ways. This latter-day samurai shot Mr. Kanahele for his trouble. Ben persisted and was shot again. An expression of pain, disgust, and disbelief at the stranger's poor manners spread across Ben's face, but still he tried pleading with the prisoner, who shot him for the third time. Ben had had enough, and grabbed the astonished pilot and flung him headlong against a wall, cracking his skull and killing him instantly. This incident gave rise to two wartime ditties. One went, "Don't shoot a Hawaiian three times or you'll make him mad." The other was a song entitled "You can't conquer Niihau, nohow." Mr. Kanahele lived out his life on Niihau and died in the 1960s.

LIFE TODAY

The only reliable connections that the islanders have with the outside world are a WW II vintage landing craft they use to bring in supplies from Kauai, and a new Agusta helicopter used for medical emergencies, supplies, and aerial tours. Until recently homing pigeons were used to send messages, but they have been replaced by two-way radios. There's no communal electricity on the island, but people do have generators to power refrigerators and TVs. Transistor radios are very popular. Most people get around on horseback or in pickup trucks. The population numbers around 230 people, 95% of whom are Hawaiian and 5% Japanese. There is one elementary school, in which English is used, but most people speak Hawaiian at home. The children go off to Kauai for high school, but after they get a taste of what the world at large has to offer, a surprisingly large number return to Niihau.

After Hurricane Iwa battered the island a few years back, and Hurricane Iniki followed suit in 1992, the state was very eager to offer aid. The people of Niihau thanked them for their concern, but told them not to bother, they would take care of things themselves. Niihau was the only island to reject statehood in the plebiscite of 1959. In November 1988, when a group of environmentally conscious Kauaians took a boat to Niihau to clear beaches of floating sea junk that had washed up on shore, the Niihauans felt that the island was being trespassed upon—they didn't want such help in any case—and a few shots were fired, as if to say, "Back off." Still unsettled, the controversy focuses on the question of who owns the beach—all beaches in Hawaii are open to free access, yet the entire island of Niihau is privately owned.

Today, some people accuse the Robinson family of being greedy barons of a medieval fiefdom, holding the Niihauans as virtual slaves. This idea is utter nonsense. Besides the fact that the islanders have an open door, the Robinsons would make immeasurably more money selling the island off to resort developers than running it as a livestock ranch. As if the spirit of old Hawaii had sent a sign, Niihau's official lei is fashioned from the *pupu,* a rare shell found only on the island's beaches; and island's color is white, the universal symbol of purity.

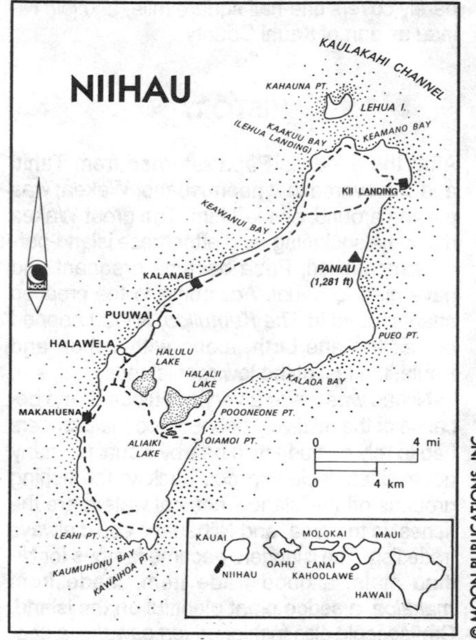

Niihau Shellwork

The finest shellwork made in Hawaii comes from Niihau, in a tradition passed down over the generations. The shells themselves—tiny and very rare *kahelelani* and *kamoa*—are abundant only in the deep waters off the windward coast. Sometimes, the tides and winds are just right and the shells are deposited on Niihau's beaches, but rarely more than three times per year. Islanders then stop everything and head for the shore to painstakingly collect them. The shells are sorted according to size and color, and only the finest are kept: 80% are discarded. The most prized are so tiny that a dozen fit on a thumbnail. Colors are white, yellow, blue, and the very rare gold. The best-quality shells are free from chips or cracks and, after sorting, the shells are drilled. Various pieces of jewelry are fashioned, but the traditional pieces are necklaces and lei. These can be short single-strand chokers, or the lovely *pikake* pattern, a heavy double strand. The *rice* motif is always popular; these are usually multistranded, with the main shells clipped on the ends and colored shells strung in as highlights.

A necklace takes long, painstaking hours, with every shell connected by intricate and minute knots. Usually the women of Niihau do this work. Clasps are made from a type of cowrie shell found only on Niihau. No two necklaces are exactly alike. They sell by the inch, and the pure white and golden ones are very expensive, most handed down as priceless heirlooms. Although Niihau shellwork is available in fine stores all over the state, Kauai, because it's closest, gets the largest selection. If you're after a once-in-a-lifetime purchase, consider Niihau shellwork.

GALLERIES, GARDENS, LIBRARIES, MUSEUMS, AND ZOOS

BIG ISLAND

Bond Mission House, Hawi, HI 96719. Contact Lyman Bond at 889-5108 for an appointment. An original, unrestored, off-the-beaten-track missionary house. See North Kohala sights for more information.

Hawaiian Volcanoes National Park, Thomas A. Jaggar Memorial Museum. Open daily 7:30 a.m.-5 p.m. Natural history exhibits emphasize volcanology, but include ethnology, zoology, and botany. A must-see.

Hulihee Palace, Box 1838, Kailua, HI 96740, tel. 329-1877. Downtown Kailua-Kona; features exhibits of artifacts and furniture of 19th-century Hawaii, particularly items connected with members of the royal family.

Kamuela Museum, Box 507, Kamuela, HI 96743, tel. 885-4724, open daily 8 a.m.-5 p.m. Mr. and Mrs. Solomon, are the owners-curators. Hawaiian artifacts from ancient Hawaii through the monarchy period are displayed, including items from ethnic groups arriving in the 19th century.

Kona Historical Society, Box 398, Captain Cook, HI 96704, tel. 323-3222, features a small collection of materials on the Kona section of the island.

Libraries: Libraries are located in main communities all over Hawaii. The central number in Hilo is 935-5407.

Liliuokalani Gardens Park: See Hilo map for location. Peace and quiet may be found amidst the surroundings of a classical Japanese-style park.

Lyman House Memorial Museum, 276 Haili St., Hilo, HI 96720, tel. 935-5021, by appointment Saturday. The collection has 5,600 publications, 10,000 photos, and 600 newspapers. An inventory is in process on correspondence, diaries, and business records. There are church school records and maps and photos of the island of Hawaii. The collection dates to 1832. It is also one of the best private rock and mineral collections in the world.

Panaewa Zoo and Equestrian Center, 25 Apuni St., Hilo, HI 96720, tel. 961- 8311, has exhibits of animal and plant specimens. It is both an educational and recreational facility.

Pu'uhonua O Honaunau National Historical Park, Box 129, Honaunali, HI 96726, tel. 328-2326, has preserved and interpretive sights associated with the temple of refuge. Excellent, parklike atmosphere. Shouldn't be missed. See South Kona sights for more information.

OAHU

Libraries: Oahu has more than a dozen libraries all over the island. The Central Administration number is 988-2194. Library for the blind and physically handicapped is at 402 Kapahulu Ave., tel. 732-7767.

Aloha Tower and Maritime Museum, at Ala Moana Blvd. and Bishop St., Honolulu, HI 96813, tel. 536-6373 or 548-5713. A landmark that said "Hawaii" to all who arrived by sea before planes took over. Great harbor and city views from top of tower. See also "Hawaii Maritime Center" below.

Army Museum, Fort DeRussy, P.O. Box 8064, Honolulu, HI 96815, tel. 543-2639. Official records, private papers, and photos documenting activities of the U.S. Army in east Asia and the Pacific Islands. Access to holdings is by appointment.

Bishop Museum and Planetarium,1525 Bernice St., Honolulu, HI 96819, tel. 847-3511. Open daily 9 a.m.-5 p.m., $7.95 for adults, $6.95 ages 6-17, five and under free. The best collection in the world on Polynesia in general and Hawaii specifically. A true cultural treat. Should not be missed.

Children's Museum of Natural History, 1201 Ala Moana Blvd., Honolulu HI 96814, Mon.-Fri. 9 a.m.-4 p.m., Saturday 9 a.m.-noon. Natural history and science exhibits.

The Contemporary Museum, under the direction of Merrill Rueppel, at 2411 Makiki Heights Rd., tel. 526-1322, open Tues.-Sat. 10 a.m.-4 p.m., Sunday noon-4 p.m., closed Monday, admission $4. The focus is on exhibitions, not collections, althought works by David Hockney are on permanent display. Changing exhibits reflect different themes in contemporary art.

East-West Center, Burns Hall 4076, 1777 East-West Rd., University of Hawaii, Honolulu, HI 96848, tel. 944-7691. Cultural institute bringing together the peoples, art, history, and ways of East and West.

Episcopal Church in Hawaii, Queen Emma Square, Honolulu, HI 96813, tel. 536-7776. Records and photos of church ministry in Hawaii from 1862.

Foster Botanical Garden, 180 N. Vineyard Blvd. Open daily 9 a.m.-4 p.m., tel 522-7065. Fifteen-acre oasis of exotic trees and rare plants.

Friends of Waipahu Cultural Garden Park, P.O. Box 103, Waipahu, HI 96797, tel. 677-0110. Recreation of plantation village in the style of a living museum.

Hawaiian Historical Society, 560 Kawaiahao St. Honolulu, HI 96813, tel. 537-6271. Open Mon.-Fri. 10 a.m.-4 p.m. Extensive collection of 19th-century materials on Hawaiian Islands, including 3,000 photos, 10,000 books, maps, microfilm. Adjacent to Hawaiian Mission Children's Society. Should be seen together. Should not be missed.

Hawaiian Mission Children's Society, 553 S. King St., Honolulu, HI 96813, tel. 531-0481. Open Tues.-Sat. 9 a.m.-4 p.m., Sunday noon-4 p.m., closed Monday. Admission is $3.50 adults, 75 cents children. Records, personal journals, letters, and photos of early 19th-century Congregational missionaries to the Hawaiian Islands; archive of the Congregational Church in the Pacific. Shouldn't be missed.

Hawaii State Archives, Iolani Palace Grounds, Honolulu, HI 96813, tel. 547-2355. Open Mon.-Fri. 7:45 a.m.-4:30 p.m. Archives of the government of Hawaii. Private papers of Hawaiian royalty and government officials, photos, illustrations, etchings recording Hawaiian history. For anyone seriously interested in Hawaii. Shouldn't be missed.

Hawaii Chinese Historical Center, 111 N. King St. Room 410, Honolulu, HI 96813, tel. 536-9302. Open 12 hours per week. Rare books, oral histories, and photos concerning the history of Chinese in Hawaii.

Hawaii Maritime Center at Pier 7, Honolulu Harbor, HI 96813, tel. 523-6151. Open daily 9 a.m.-5p.m., admission is $7. A museum chronicling the exploration and exploitation of Hawaii by the seafarers who have come to its shores. Visit the famous double-hulled conoe *Hokule'a* and the tall-masted *Falls of Clyde.*

Hawaii Medical Library, Inc., 1221 Punchbowl St., Honolulu, HI 96813, tel. 536-9302. History of medicine in Hawaii.

Hawaii Pacific College Library. For college information call 544-0200.

Honolulu Academy of Arts, 900 S. Beretania St., Honolulu, HI 96814, tel. 532-8700. Object is to collect, preserve, and exhibit works of art (to conduct a public art education program related to the collection). Permanent and special exhibitions. Tours, classes, lectures, and films.

Honolulu Zoo, 151 Kapahulu Ave:, tel. 521-3487. Open daily 9 a.m.-5 p.m. Quiet respite from hustle of Waikiki. Includes a collection of tropical birds as well as pandas, zebras, and gibbon apes. Great for kids of all ages.

Iolani Palace, P.O. Box 2259, Honolulu, HI 96804, tel. 536-3552. Iolani Palace Grounds. Performs all aspects of historic research, restoration, and refurbishing of palace. The only royal palace in the United States. Vintage artwork, antiques.

Kamehameha Schools, Kapalama Heights Rd., Honolulu, HI 96813, tel. 842-8620. Open Mon.-Fri 7:30 a.m.-4 p.m. Traditional school for children of Hawaiian descent. Rare books, periodicals, slides on Hawaiiana.

Libraries: Oahu has more than a dozen libraries all over the island. The Central Administration number is 988-2194. Library for the Blind and Physically Handicapped is at 402 Kapahulu Ave., tel. 732-7767.

Punahou School, 1601 Punahou St., Honolulu, HI 96822, tel. 944-5823. Collection available by special arrangement. Institutional archives of the oldest private school in Hawaii.

Queen Emma's Summer Palace, 2913 Pali Hwy., Honolulu, HI 96817, tel. 595-3167. Restored historic home, built about 1848. Furniture and mementos of Queen Emma and her family. Some items belong to other members of the royal family.

Sea Life Park, Makapuu Point, Waimanalo, HI 96795, tel. 259-7933. Varieties of Pacific marine plant and animal life, including several species of dolphins and whales. Feeding pool, Kaupa Village, turtle lagoon, restaurant, gift shop.

USS *Arizona* Memorial and Pacific Submarine Museum, Arizona Memorial Dr., Pearl Harbor, HI 96818, tel. 422-2771. A free tour of the sleek 184-foot white concrete structure that spans the sunken USS *Arizona*. Free Navy launches take you on the tour of "Battleship Row." Open Tues.-Sun. 8 a.m.-3 p.m. No reservations, first-come, first-served. Launches every 15 minutes. Visitor center offers graphic materials and films reflecting events of the Pearl Harbor attack.

USS *Bowfin*, 11 Arizona Memorial Dr., Pearl Harbor, HI 96818, tel 423-1341. Open daily 9:30-4:30 p.m.Fully restored WWII submarine. Insight into the underwater war. Self-guided tours. Fascinating. Next door to *Arizona* Memorial.

MAUI

Alexander & Baldwin Sugar Museum, 3957 Hansen Rd., Kahului, tel. 871-8058, explains the history of sugar in Hawaii along with how it is grown and harvested. Open Mon-Sat. 9:30 a.m.-4:30 p.m., $3 adults, $1.50 children 6-17.

Baldwin Home, Front St., Lahaina. Open daily 9:30 a.m.-5 p.m., $2, tel. 661-3262. Two-story home of medical missionary Dwight Baldwin.

***Carthaginian II* Floating Museum,** Lahaina Harbor, Lahaina. Open daily 9 a.m.-5 p.m. Replica of a 19th-century brig. Features whaling artifacts and exhibits on the humpback whale.

Hale Hoikeike, 2375-A Main St., Wailuku, tel. 244-3326. Also known as the Bailey House Museum, it is a repository of Hawaiian historical objects, artifacts from Kahoolawe, and the renowned paintings of Edward Bailey.

Hale Pa'i Printshop Museum, P.O. Box 338, Lahaina, tel. 667-7040. Located on the grounds of Lahainaluna school. Operational relics of original printing press, original Lahainaluna press publications, and an exhibit of Lahainaluna school past and present. Open by appointment only—contact the Lahaina Restoration Foundation or the Baldwin Home.

Hana Cultural Center, P.O. Box 27, Hana, tel. 248-8622. Preserves and restores historical sites, artifacts, photos, documents, etc.

Kahanu Gardens, on Ulaina Road in Hana. This 20-acre garden, part of the National Tropical Botanical Garden, contains commercial and decorative varieties of tropical plants, as well as **Piilanihale Heiau,** one of the largest in all of Hawaii. Open Tues.-Sat. 10 a.m.-2 p.m., $5.

Kula Botanical Gardens, Hwy. 377 to Upper Kula Rd., tel. 878-1715. Open daily 7 a.m.-4 p.m. Excellent arrangements of tropical plants and flowers in upcountry Maui.

Lahaina Arts Society, P.O. Box 991, Lahaina, tel. 661-0111, was established to perpetuate and further Hawaiian culture, the arts, and crafts. Sponsors two galleries, an annual scholarship, traveling exhibitions, and helps maintain Lahaina district courthouse.

Libraries: Maui's main library in Wailuku is at tel. 244-3945. Lanai Public Library, tel. 565-6996. Molokai Library, tel. 553-5483.

Lahaina Restoration Foundation, P.O. Box 991, Lahaina, HI 96761, tel. 661-3262. James C. Luckey, director. Open Mon.-Sat. 10 a.m.-4 p.m. Organization dedicated to the preservation of historical Lahaina. Sponsors restorations, archaeological digs, and renovation of cultural and historical sites. Operates Baldwin Home and Brig *Carthaginian II,* among others.

Maui Historical Society, 2375-A Main, Wailuku, tel. 244-3326. Open 25 hours per week. Housed in the Bailey House Museum. Promotes interest in and knowledge of history of Hawaii and Maui County. Free lectures during the year.

Whaler's Village Museum, Whaler's Village Shopping Center, Kaanapali, tel. 661-5992. Whaling artifacts and a 30-foot sperm whale skeleton are set among gift shops. A self-guided learning experience while you shop.

KAUAI

Coco Palms Museum, Coco Palms Resort, P.O. Box 631, Wailua, HI 96766. Seldom visited except by hotel guests, this collection of Hawaiiana, the personal belongings of Mrs. Grace Guslander, the former hotel manager, is open to everyone. Each item tells a tale of the island, its people, and visitors. The Coco Palms, scheduled to re-open in 1995, is a must-see in itself. See "Accommodations" in the Wailua chapter for more information.

Grove Farm Homestead, P.O. Box 1631, Lihue, HI 96766, tel. 245-3202, is open by appointment only. Displayed are the records, business, and personal papers of early sugar planter George N. Wilcox. Plantation owner's house, workers' cottages, outbuildings, and garden. Definitely worth a visit. Personalized tours.

Hanalei Museum, P.O. Box 91, Hanalei, HI 96714, tel. 826-6783. Local history on display. Small collection of native items, but many turn-of-the-century photos. Open 10 a.m.-5 p.m., no admission charge.

Kauai Museum, 4428 Rice, Lihue, HI 96766, tel. 245-6931. Open Mon.-Fri. 9:30 a.m.-4:30 p.m. Two buildings. The story of Kauai told through art and ethnic exhibits. Hawaiiana books, maps, and prints available at museum shop.

Koke'e Natural History Museum, P.O. Box NN, Koke'e State Park, Lihue, HI 96752, tel. 335-9975. Open daily 10-4; free. Exhibits interpreting the geology and unique plants and animals of Kauai's mountain wilderness. Great to visit while at Waimea Canyon.

Libraries: Kauai's central library is at 4344 Hardy St., Lihue, HI 96766, tel. 245-3617. Branch libraries are in Hanapepe, Kapa'a, Koloa, and Waimea.

Waioli Mission House, Waioli Corporation, P.O. Box 1631, Lihue, HI 96766, call 245-3202 for information. Open Tuesday, Thursday, and Saturday 9-3; free.

Note: For Kauai's excellent **Botanical Gardens** see "Botanical Gardens" under "Flora and Fauna" in Kauai's Introduction.

HAWAII NATIONAL WILDLIFE REFUGES

NAME AND ADDRESS; LOCATION; WILDLIFE; HABITAT AND INFORMATION

Pearl Harbor NWR (Oahu), c/o Hawaiian and Pacific Islands NWRs, 300 Ala Moana Blvd., P.O. Box 50167, Honolulu, HI 96850, tel. 541-1201; Located within Pearl Harbor Naval Base; Hawaiian gallinule, Hawaiian coot, Hawaiian stilt, *koloa* (Hawaiian duck), and black-crowned night herons.; 61 acres of manmade wetlands. Contact manager for tours.

James C. Campbell NWR (Oahu), c/o Hawaiian and Pacific Islands NWRs, 300 Ala Moana Blvd., P.O. Box 50167, Honolulu, HI 96850, tel. 541-1201; Near Kahuku on the northeastern shore of the island of Oahu; Hawaiian gallinule, Hawaiian coot, Hawaiian stilt, *koloa* (Hawaiian duck), black-crowned night herons, introduced birds, migratory shorebirds and waterfowl; 142 acres in two units: Punamano Pond is a natural spring-fed marsh. The Kii Unit is manmade ponds once used as sugarcane waste settling basins. Contact manager for tours.

Kilauea Point NWR (Kauai), c/o P.O. Box 87, Kilauea, HI 96754, tel. 541-1201; One mile N of Kilauea on a paved road. Headquarters and parking area on Kilauea Point; red-footed boobies, shearwaters, great frigate birds, brown boobies, red-tailed and white-tailed tropic birds and Laysan albatross, green sea turtles, humpback whales and dolphins; 31 acres of cliffs and headlands with native coastal plants. Open Mon.-Fri., 10 a.m.-4 p.m. Binoculars are available to borrow.

Huleia NWR (Kauai), c/o P.O. Box 87, Kilauea, HI 96754, tel. 541-1201; Viewing is best from the Menehune Fish Pond overlook along Hulemalu Rd. W of Puhi Rd.; *koloa* (Hawaiian duck), Hawaiian coot, Hawaiian gallinule, and Hawaiian stilt; 238 acres of seasonally flooded river bottomland, and wooded slopes of the Huleia River Valley. No general admittance. Contact manager for special permission.

Hanalei NWR (Kauai), c/o P.O. Box 87, Kilauea, HI 96754, tel. 541-1201; one and a half miles E of Hanalei on Hwy. 56. Observe wildlife from Ohiki Rd. which begins at the W end of Hanalei River bridge; *koloa* (Hawaiian duck), Hawaiian coot, Hawaiian gallinule, and Hawaiian stilt; 917 acres of riverbottom land, taro farms, and wooded slopes in the Hanalei River Valley on the N coast of Kauai. By special permit only. Contact manager.

Hakalau Forest NWR (Hawaii), 300 Ala Moana Blvd., P.O. Box 50167, Honolulu, HI 96850, tel. 541-1201; Located between the 3,900 and 7,200 foot elevation on the windward slope of Mauna Kea. Take Saddle Rd. Turn right (N) on Keanakolu Rd., and continue for six miles. Keanakolo Rd. is the refuge's upper boundary; *akiapolaau,* Hawaiian *akepa,* Hawaiian creeper, Hawaiian hawk, *ou,* Hawaiian hoary bat, *amakihi,* Hawaiian thrush, *elepaio, iiwi,* and *apapane;* 11,000 acres of koa-ohia habitat. Instrumental in sustaining the naturally evolving mid-elevation rainforest. Entry is authorized only by special use permit. Contact manager.

Kakahaia NWR (Molokai), c/o Hawaiian and Pacific Islands NWRs, 300 Ala Moana Blvd., P.O. Box 50167, Honolulu, HI 96850, tel. 541-1201; five miles E of Kaunakakai along Hwy. 450; Hawaiian coot and Hawaiian stilt; 40 acres of freshwater pond and marsh with dense thickets of bullrush. Arrange visits with the refuge manager.

Hawaiian Islands NWR, c/o Hawaiian and Pacific Islands NWRs, 300 Ala Moana Blvd., P.O. Box 50167, Honolulu, HI 96850, tel. 541-1201; Far-flung islands and atolls strung 1,000 miles N of main Hawaiian Islands; seabirds, Laysan and black-footed albatrosses, sooty terns, white terns, brown and black noddies, shearwaters, and petrels, red-tailed tropic birds, frigate birds, and boobies; a string of widely separated tiny islands and reefs. 1,000 miles long, reaching almost to Midway Island. Rugged volcanic remnants, sparsely vegetated low sandy islands in the NW. By charter or private boat only. Special permission from managers.

Baker, Howland, Jarvis and Johnston Island NWRs, c/o Hawaiian and Pacific Islands NWRs, 300 Ala Moana Blvd., P.O. Box 50167, Honolulu, HI 96850, tel. 541-1201; Near the equator. Lies about 1,600 miles SW of Honolulu. Jarvis is about 1,300 miles S of Honolulu. Johnston Atoll is located about 825 miles SW of Honolulu; seabird nesting rookeries, sooty terns, gray-backed terns, shearwaters, red-footed boobies, brown boobies, masked boobies, lesser and great frigate birds, red-tailed tropic birds, and brown noddies; 11,000 acres of koa-ohia habitat. The refuge has been instrumental in sustaining the naturally evolving mid-elevation rainforest. Entry to refuge is authorized only by special use permit obtained from the refuge manager.

BOOKLIST

INTRODUCTORY

Aloha, The Magazine of Hawaii and the Pacific. Davick Publications, P.O. Box 49035, Escondido, CA 92046. This excellent bimonthly magazine is much more than slick and glossy photography. Special features focus on sports, the arts, history, flora and fauna, or just pure island adventure. *Aloha* is equally useful as a "dream book" for those who wish they could visit Hawaii, and as a current resource for those actually going. One of the best for an overall view of Hawaii, and well worth the subscription price.

Barrow, Terrence. *Incredible Hawaii.* Rutland, VT: Tuttle, 1974. Illustrated by Ray Lanternman. A pocket-sized compilation of oddities, little-known facts, trivia, and superlatives regarding the Hawaiian Islands. Fun, easy reading, and informative.

Cohen, David, and Rick Smolan. *A Day in the Life of Hawaii.* New York: Workman, 1984. On December 2, 1983, 50 of the world's top photojournalists were invited to Hawaii to photograph a variety of normal-life incidents occurring on that day. The photos are excellently reproduced, and are accompanied by a minimum of text.

Day, A.G., and C. Stroven. *A Hawaiian Reader.* New York: Appleton, Century, Crofts, 1959. A poignant compilation of essays, diary entries, and fictitious writings that takes you from the death of Captain Cook through the "statehood services."

Emphasis International. *On the Hana Coast.* Honolulu: Emphasis International Ltd., 1983. Text by Ron Youngblood. Sketches of the people, land, legends, and history of Maui's northeast coast. Beautifully illustrated with line drawings, vintage photos, and modern color work. Expresses true feeling and insight into people and things Hawaiian by letting them talk for themselves. An excellent book capturing what's different and what's universal about the people of the Hana District.

Friends of the Earth. *Maui, The Last Hawaiian Place.* New York: Friends of the Earth, 1970. A pictorial capturing the spirit of Maui in 61 contemporary color plates along with a handful of historical illustrations. A highly informative as well as beautiful book printed in Italy.

Hawaii Magazine. 1400 Kapiolani Blvd., Suite B, Honolulu, HI 96814. This magazine covers the Hawaiian Islands like a tropical breeze. Feature articles on all aspects of life in the islands, with special departments on travel, happenings, exhibits, and restaurant reviews. Up-to-the-minute information, and a fine read.

Hopkins, Jerry. *The Hula.* Edited by Rebecca Crockett-Hopkins. Hong Kong: APA Productions, 1982. Page after page of this beautifully illustrated book sways with the dynamic vibrancy of ancient Hawaii's surviving artform. Hopkins leads you from legendary dances to those of past and present masters captured in vintage and classic photos. For anyone interested in the history and spirit of Hawaii portrayed in its unique style of expressive motion.

Island Heritage Limited. *The Hawaiians.* Norfolk Island, Australia: Island Heritage Ltd., 1970. Text by Gavan Daws and Ed Sheehan. Primarily a "coffee table" picture book that lets the camera do the talking. Limited yet informative text.

Judd, Gerritt P., comp. *A Hawaiian Anthology.* New York: MacMillan, 1967. A potpourri of observations from literati such as Twain and Stevenson who have visited the islands over the years. Also, excerpts from ordinary people's journals and missionary letters from early times down to a gleeful report of the day that Hawaii became a state.

Krauss, Bob. *Here's Hawaii.* New York: Coward, McCann Inc., 1960. Social commentary in a series of humorous anecdotes excerpted from this newspaperman's column from the late '60s. Dated, but in essence still useful because people and values obviously change very little.

Lueras, Leonard. *Surfing, The Ultimate Pleasure.* New York: Workman Publishing, 1984. An absolutely outstanding pictorial account of Hawaii's own sport—surfing. Vintage and contemporary photos are surrounded by well-researched and written text. Bound to become a classic.

McBride, L.R. *Practical Folk Medicine of Hawaii.* Hilo, HI: Petroglyph Press, 1975. An illustrated guide to Hawaii's medicinal plants as used by the *kahuna lapa'au* (medical healers). Includes a thorough section on ailments, diagnosis, and the proper folk remedy. Illustrated by the author, a renowned botanical researcher and former ranger at Volcanoes National Park.

Michener, James A. *Hawaii.* New York: Random House, 1959. Michener's fictionalized historical novel has done more to inform *and* misinform readers about Hawaii than any other book ever written. A great tale with plenty of local color and information that should be read for pleasure and not considered fact.

Naturist Society Magazine. P.O. Box 132, Oshkosh, WI 54920. This excellent magazine not only *uncovers* bathing-suit-optional beaches throughout the islands, giving tips for naturalists visiting Hawaii, but also reports on local politics, environment, and conservation measures from the health-conscious nudist point of view. A fine publication.

Piercy, LaRue. *Hawaii, This and That.* Hilo, HI: Petroglyph Press, 1981. Illustrated by Scot Ebanez. A 60-page book filled with one-sentence facts and oddities about all manner of things Hawaiian. Informative, amazing, and fun to read.

Rose, Roger G. *Hawaii: The Royal Isles.* Honolulu: Bishop Museum Press, 1980. Photographs by Seth Joel. A pictorial mixture of artifacts and luminaries from Hawaii's past. Includes a mixture of Hawaiian and Western art depicting island ways. Beautifully photographed with highly descriptive accompanying text.

Wilkerson, James A., M.D., ed. *Medicine for Mountaineering.* 3rd ed. Seattle: The Mountaineers, 1985. Don't let the title fool you. Although the book focuses on specific health problems that may be encountered while mountaineering, it is the best first-aid and general health guide available today. Written by doctors for the layperson to use until help arrives, it is jam-packed with easily understandable techniques and procedures. For those intending extended treks, it is a must.

HISTORY/POLITICAL SCIENCE

Albertini, Jim, et al. *The Dark Side of Paradise, Hawaii in a Nuclear War.* Honolulu: cAtholic Action of Hawaii. Well-documented research outlining Hawaii's role and vulnerability in a nuclear world. This book presents the antinuclear and antimilitary side of the political issue in Hawaii.

Apple, Russell A. *Trails: From Steppingstones to Kerbstones.* Honolulu: Bishop Museum Press, 1965. This "Special Publication #53" is a special-interest archaeological survey focusing on Hawaii's trails, roadways, footpaths, and highways throughout the years. Many "royal highways" from pre-contact Hawaii are cited.

Ashdown, Inez MacPhee. *Old Lahaina.* Honolulu: Hawaiian Service Inc., 1976. A small, pamphlet-type book listing most of the historical attractions of Lahaina Town, past and present. Ashdown is a lifelong resident of Hawaii and gathered her information firsthand by listening to and recording stories of ethnic Hawaiians and old *kama'aina* families.

—*Ke Alaloa o Maui.* Wailuku, HI: Kama'aina Historians Inc., 1971. A compilation of the history and legends of sites on the island of Maui. Ashdown was at one time a "lady in waiting" for Queen Liliuokalani and has since been proclaimed Maui's "Historian Emeritus."

Bell, Roger. *Last Among Equals: Hawaiian Statehood and American Politics.* Honolulu: University of Hawaii, 1984. Documents Hawaii's long and rocky road to statehood, tracing political partisanship, racism, and social change.

Cameron, Roderick. *The Golden Haze.* New York: World Publishing, 1964. An account of Capt. James Cook's voyages of discovery throughout the South Seas. Uses original diaries and journals for an "on the spot" reconstruction of this great seafaring adventure.

Daws, Gavan. *Shoal of Time, A History of the Hawaiian Islands.* Honolulu: University of Hawaii Press, 1968. A highly readable history of Hawaii dating from its "discovery" by the Western world down to its acceptance as the 50th state. Good insight into the psychological makeup of the influential characters who formed Hawaii's past.

Department of Geography, University of Hawaii. *Atlas of Hawaii.* 2nd ed. Honolulu: University of Hawaii Press, 1983. Much more than an atlas filled with reference maps, it also contains commentary on the natural environment, culture, and sociology, as well as a gazetteer and statistical tables. Actually a mini-encyclopedia.

Feher, Joseph. *Hawaii: A Pictorial History.* Honolulu: Bishop Museum Press, 1969. Text by Edward Joesting and O.A. Bushnell. An oversized tome laden with annotated historical and contemporary photos, prints, and paintings. Seems like a big "schoolbook," but extremely well done. If you are going to read one survey about Hawaii's historical, social, and cultural past, this is the one.

Fuchs, Lawrence. *Hawaii Pono.* New York: Harcourt, Brace and World, 1961. A detailed, scholarly work presenting an overview of Hawaii's history, based upon psychological and sociological interpretations. Encompasses most socioethnological groups from native Hawaiians to modern entrepreneurs. A must for social historical background.

Handy, E.S., and Elizabeth Handy. *Native Planters in Old Hawaii.* Honolulu: Bishop Museum Press, 1972. A superbly written, easily understandable scholarly work on the intimate relationship of pre-contact Hawaiians and the *aina* (land). Much more than its title implies, this book should be read by anyone seriously interested in Polynesian Hawaii.

The Hawaii Book. Chicago: J.G. Ferguson, 1961. Insightful selections of short stories, essays, and historical and political commentaries by experts specializing in Hawaii. Good choice of photos and illustrations.

Hawaiian Children's Mission Society. *Missionary Album.* Honolulu: Mission Society, 1969. Firsthand accounts of the New England missionaries sent to Hawaii and instrumental in its conversion to Christianity. Down-home stories of daily life's ups and downs.

Heyerdahl, Thor. *American Indians in the Pacific.* London: Allen and Unwin Ltd., 1952. Theoretical and anthropological accounts of the influence on Polynesia of the indigenous peoples along the Pacific coasts of North and South America. Fascinating reading, with unsubstantiated yet intriguing theories.

Ii, John Papa. *Fragments of Hawaiian History.* Honolulu: Bishop Museum, 1959. Hawaii's history under Kamehameha I as told by a Hawaiian who actually experienced it.

Joesting, Edward. *Hawaii: An Uncommon History.* New York: W.W. Norton Co., 1972. A truly uncommon history told in a series of vignettes relating to the lives and personalities of the first white people in Hawaii, Hawaiian nobility, sea captains, writers, and adventurers. Brings history to life. Absolutely excellent!

Lee, William S. *The Islands.* New York: Holt, Rinehart, 1966. A sociohistorical set of stories concerning *malihini* (newcomers) and how they influenced and molded the Hawaii of today.

Liliuokalani. *Hawaii's Story By Hawaii's Queen.* Rutland, VT: Tuttle, 1964. A moving personal account of Hawaii's inevitable move from monarchy to U.S. Territory by its last queen, Liliuokalani. The facts can be found in other histories, but none provides the emotion or point of view as expressed by Hawaii's deposed

monarch. A must-read to get the whole picture.
Nickerson, Roy. *Lahaina, Royal Capital of Hawaii.* Honolulu: Hawaiian Service, 1978. The story of Lahaina from whaling days to present, spiced with ample photographs.

Smith, Richard A., et al., eds. *The Frontier States.* New York: Time-Life Books, 1968. Short and concise comparisons of the two newest states: Hawaii and Alaska. Dated information, but good social commentary and an excellent appendix suggesting tours, museums, and local festivals.

Takaki, Ronald. *Plantation Life and Labor in Hawaii, 1835-1920.* Honolulu: University of Hawaii Press, 1983. A perspective of plantation life in Hawaii from a multiethnic viewpoint. Written by a nationally known island scholar.

MYTHOLOGY AND LEGENDS

Beckwith, Martha. *Hawaiian Mythology.* Honolulu: University of Hawaii Press, 1970. Forty-five years after its original printing, this work remains the definitive text on Hawaiian mythology. Beckwith compiled this book from many sources, giving exhaustive cross-references to genealogies and legends expressed in the oral tradition. If you are going to read one book on Hawaii's folklore, this should be it.

Colum, Padraic. *Legends of Hawaii.* New Haven: Yale University Press, 1937. Selected legends of old Hawaii reinterpreted, but closely based upon the originals.

Elbert, S., comp. *Hawaiian Antiquities and Folklore.* Honolulu: University of Hawaii Press, 1959. Illustrated by Jean Charlot. A selection of the main legends from Abraham Fornander's great work, *An Account of the Polynesian Race.*

Melville, Leinanai. *Children of the Rainbow.* Wheaton, IL: Theosophical Publishing, 1969. A book on higher spiritual consciousness attuned to nature, which was the basic belief of pre-Christian Hawaii. The appendix contains illustrations of mystical symbols used by the *kahuna.* An enlightening book in many ways.

Thrum, Thomas. *Hawaiian Folk Tales.* Chicago: McClurg and Co., 1907. A collection of Hawaiian tales from the oral tradition as told to the author from various sources.

Westervelt, W.D. *Hawaiian Legends of Volcanoes.* Boston: Ellis Press, 1916. A small book concerning the volcanic legends of Hawaii and how they related to the fledgling field of volcanism at the turn of the century. The vintage photos alone are worth a look.

NATURAL SCIENCES

Abbott, Agatin, Gordon MacDonald, and Frank Peterson. *Volcanoes in the Sea.* Honolulu: University of Hawaii Press, 1983. A simplified yet comprehensive text covering the geology and volcanism of the Hawaiian Islands. Focuses upon the forces of nature (wind, rain, and surf) that shape the islands.

Boom, Robert. *Hawaiian Seashells.* Honolulu: Waikiki Aquarium, 1972. Photos by Jerry Kringle. A collection of 137 seashells found in Hawaiian waters, featuring many found nowhere else on earth. Broken into categories with accompanying text including common and scientific names, physical descriptions, and likely habitats. A must for shell collectors.

Brock, Vernon, and W.A. Gosline. *Handbook of Hawaiian Fishes.* Honolulu: University of Hawaii Press, 1960. A detailed guide to most of the fishes occurring in Hawaiian waters.

Carlquist, Sherwin. *Hawaii: A Natural History.* New York: Doubleday, 1970. Definitive account of Hawaii's natural history.

Carpenter, Blyth, and Russell Carpenter. *Fish Watching in Hawaii.* San Mateo, CA: Natural World Press, 1981. A color guide to many of the reef fish found in Hawaii and often spotted by snorkelers. If you're interested in the fish you'll be looking at, this guide will be very helpful.

Fielding, Ann, and Ed Robinson. *An Underwater Guide to Hawaii.* Honolulu: University of Hawaii Press, 1987. If you've ever had a desire to snorkel/scuba the living reef waters of Hawaii and to be familiar with what you're seeing, get this small but fact-packed book. The amazing array of marinelife found througout the archipelago is captured in glossy photos with accompanying informative text. Both the scientific and common names of specimens are given. This book will enrich your underwater experience and serve as an easily understood reference guide for many years.

Hamaishi, Amy, and Doug Wallin. *Flowers of Hawaii.* Honolulu: World Wide Distributors, 1975. Close-up color photos of many of the most common flowers spotted in Hawaii.

Hawaii Audubon Society. *Hawaii's Birds.* Honolulu: Hawaii Audubon Society, 1981. A field guide to Hawaii's birds, listing the endangered indigenous species, migrants, and introduced species that are now quite common. Color photos with text listing distribution, description, voice, and habits. Excellent field guide.

Hosaka, Edward. *Shore Fishing in Hawaii.* Hilo, HI: Petroglyph Press, 1984. Known as the best book on Hawaiian fishing since 1944, this book receives the highest praise because it has bred many Hawaiian fishermen.

Hubbard, Douglass, and Gordon MacDonald. *Volcanoes of the National Parks of Hawaii.* Volcanoes, HI: Hawaii Natural History Association, 1982. The volcanology of Hawaii, documenting the major lava flows and their geological effect on the state.

Island Heritage Limited. *Hawaii's Flowering Trees.* Honolulu: Island Heritage Press. A concise field guide to many of Hawaii's most common flowering trees. All color photos with accompanying descriptive text.

Kay, E. Alison, comp. *A Natural History of the Hawaiian Islands.* Honolulu: University of Hawaii Press, 1972. A selection of concise articles by experts in the fields of volcanism, oceanography, meteorology, and biology. An excellent reference source.

Kuck, Lorraine, and Richard Togg. *Hawaiian Flowers and Flowering Trees.* Rutland, VT: Tuttle, 1960. A classic field guide to tropical and subtropical flora illustrated in watercolor. A "to the point" description of Hawaiian plants and flowers with a brief history of their places of origin and their introduction to Hawaii.

Merlin, Mark D. *Hawaiian Forest Plants, A Hiker's Guide.* Honolulu: Oriental Publishing, 1980. A companion guide for trekkers into Hawaii's interior. Full-color plates identify and describe the most common forest plants encountered.

—*Hawaiian Coastal Plants.* Honolulu: Oriental Publishing, 1980. Color photos and botanical descriptions of many of the plants and flowers found growing along Hawaii's varied shorelines.

Merrill, Elmer. *Plant Life of the Pacific World.* Rutland, VT: Tuttle, 1983. The definitive book for anyone planning a botanical tour to the entire Pacific Basin. Originally published in the 1930s, it remains a tremendous work.

Nickerson, Roy. *Brother Whale, A Pacific Whalewatcher's Log.* San Francisco: Chronicle Books, 1977. Introduces the average person to the life of earth's greatest mammals. Provides historical accounts, photos, and tips on whalewatching. Well written, descriptive, and the best "first-time" book on whales.

Sohmer, S.H., and R. Gustafson. *Plants and Flowers of Hawaii.* Honolulu: University of Hawaii Press, 1987. Sohmer and Gustafson range the vegetation zones of Hawaii, from mountains to coast, introducing you to the wide and varied floral biology of the islands. They give a good introduction to the history and unique evolution of Hawaiian plantlife. Beautiful color plates are accompanied by clear and concise plant descriptions, with the scientific and common Hawaiian names listed.

Stearns, Harold T. *Road Guide to Points of Geological Interest in the Hawaiian Islands.* Palo Alto, CA: Pacific Books, 1966. The title is almost as long as this handy little book that lets you know what forces of nature formed the islands' scenery.

van Riper, Charles, and Sandra van Riper. *A Field Guide to the Mammals of Hawaii.* Honolulu: Oriental Publishing. A guide to the surprising number of mammals introduced into Hawaii. Full-color pages document description, uses, tendencies, and habitat. Small and thin, makes a worthwhile addition to any serious trekker's backpack.

TRAVEL

Morey, Kathy. *Kauai Trails.* Berkeley: Wilderness Press, 1993. Morey's books are specialized, detailed trekker's guides to Hawaii's outdoors. Complete with useful maps, historical references, official procedures, and plants and animals encountered along the way. If you're focused on hiking, these are the best to take along. *Maui Trails, Hawaii Trails,* and *Oahu Trails* are also available.

Riegert, Ray. *Hidden Hawaii.* Berkeley, CA: And/Or Press, 1992. Ray offers a "user friendly" guide to the islands.

Stanley, David. *South Pacific Handbook.* 5th ed. Chico, CA: Moon Publications, 1993. The model upon which all travel guides should be based. Simply the best book in the world for travel throughout the South Pacific.

Sutton, Horace. *Aloha Hawaii.* New York: Doubleday, 1967. A dated but still excellent guide to Hawaii providing sociological, historical, and cultural insight. Horace Sutton's literary style is the best in the travel guide field. Entertaining reading.

Thorne, Chuck. *The Diver's Guide to Maui.* Kahului, HI: Maui Dive Guide, 1984. A no-nonsense snorkeler's and diver's guide to Maui waters. Extensive maps, descriptions, and "straight from the shoulder" advice by one of Maui's best and most experienced divers. A must for all levels of divers and snorkelers.

Thorne, Chuck, and Lou Zitnik. *A Diver's Guide to Hawaii.* Kihei, HI: Hawaii's Diver's Guide, 1984. An expanded diver's and snorkeler's guide to the waters of the six main Hawaiian Islands. Complete list of maps with full descriptions, tips, and ability levels. A must for all levels of snorkelers and divers.

Warner, Evie, and Al Davies. *Bed and Breakfast Goes Hawaiian.* Kapa'a, HI: Island Bed and Breakfast, 1990. A combination bed-and-breakfast directory and guide to sights, activities, events, and restaurants on the six major islands.

COOKING

Alexander, Agnes. *How to Use Hawaiian Fruit.* Hilo, HI: Petroglyph Press, 1984. A full range of recipes using delicious Hawaiian fruits.

Fitzgerald, Donald, et al., eds. *The Pacific House Hawaii Cookbook.* Pacific House, 1968. A full range of Hawaiian cuisine including recipes from traditional Chinese, Japanese, Portuguese, New England, and Filipino dishes.

Gibbons, Euell. *Beachcombers Handbook.* New York: McKay Co., 1967. An autobiographical account of this world-famous naturalist as a young man living "off the land" in Hawaii. Great tips on spotting and gathering naturally occurring foods, survival advice, and recipes. Unfortunately, the lifestyle described is long outdated.

Margah, Irish, and Elvira Monroe. *Hawaii, Cooking with Aloha.* San Carlos, CA: Wide World, 1984. Island recipes including *kalua* pig, *lomi* salmon, and hints on decor.

LANGUAGE

Boom, Robert, and Chris Christensen. *Important Hawaiian Place Names.* Honolulu: Boom Enterprises, 1978. A handy pocket-sized book listing most of the major island place-names and their translations.

Elbert, Samuel. *Spoken Hawaiian.* Honolulu: University of Hawaii Press, 1970. Progressive conversational lessons.

Elbert, Samuel, and Mary Pukui. *Hawaiian Dictionary.* Honolulu: University of Hawaii, 1971. The best dictionary available on the Hawaiian language. The *Pocket Hawaiian Dictionary* is a less expensive, condensed version of this dictionary adequate for most travelers with a general interest in the language.

GLOSSARY

Words marked with an asterisk (*) are used commonly throughout the islands.

'A'a*—rough clinker lava. *A'a* has become the correct geological term to describe this type of lava found anywhere in the world.

ahupua'a—pie-shaped land divisions running from mountain to sea that were governed by *konohiki,* local *ali'i* who owed their allegiance to a reigning chief

aikane—friend; pal; buddy

aina—land; the binding spirit to all Hawaiians. Love of the land is paramount in traditional Hawaiian beliefs.

akamai—smart; clever; wise

akua—a god, or simply "divine." You'll hear people speak of their family or personal *aumakua* (ancestral spirit). Favorites are the shark or the *pueo* (Hawaiian owl).

ali'i*—Hawaiian chief or noble

aloha*—the most common greeting in the islands; can mean both hello or goodbye, welcome or farewell. It can also mean romantic love, affection, or best wishes.

aumakua—personal or family spirit, usually an ancestral spirit

aole—no

auwe—alas; ouch! When a great chief or loved one died, it was a traditional wail of mourning.

ewa—crooked; place-name for west Honolulu, used as a directional term

halakahiki—pineapple

halau—originally a longhouse, now used mostly to describe hula halau, i.e., a hula school

hale*—house or building. Often combined with other words to name a specific place such as Haleakala ("House of the Sun") or Hale Pai ("Printing House").

hana*—work; combined with *pau* means end of work or quitting time

hanai—literally "to feed." Part of the true *aloha spirit.* A *hanai* is a permanent guest, or an adopted family member, usually an elderly person or a child. In this enduring cultural phenomenon in Hawaii, a child from one family (perhaps that of a brother or sister, and quite often one's grandchild) is raised as one's own without formal adoption.

haole*—a word that at one time meant foreigner, but which now means white person or Caucasian. Many etymological definitions have been put forth, but none satisfies everyone. Some feel that it signified a person without a background, because the first white people could not chant their genealogies as Hawaiians commonly could.

hapa*—half, as in a mixed-blooded person being referred to as *hapa haole*

hapai*—pregnant; used by all ethnic groups when a *keiki* is on the way

haupia*—coconut custard dessert often served at luau

heiau*—traditional Hawaiian temple or platform made of skillfully fitted rocks, upon which structures were built and offerings made to the gods

holomuu*—ankle-length dress much more fitted than a muumuu, often worn on formal occasions

hono—bay, as in Honolulu ("Sheltered Bay")

ho'oilo—traditional Hawaiian winter that began in November

hoolaulea—any happy event, but especially a family outing or picnic

hoomalimali*—sweet talk; flattery

huhu*—angry; irritated

hui*—group; meeting; society. Often used to refer to Chinese businesspeople or family members who pool their money to get businesses started.

hukilau—traditional shoreline fish-gathering in which everyone lends a hand to *huki* (pull) the huge net and share the *lau* (food). It is much more like a party than hard work, and if you're lucky you'll be able to take part in one.

hula*—native Hawaiian dance in which the rhythm of the islands is captured by swaying hips and stories told by lyrically moving hands. A *halau* is a group or school of *hula.*

huli huli—barbecue, as in *huli huli* chicken

i'a—fish in general. *I'a maka* is raw fish.

imu*—underground oven filled with hot rocks and used for baking. The main cooking feature at luau, used to steam-bake pork and other succulent dishes. The tending of the *imu* was traditionally for men only.

ipo—sweetheart; lover; girlfriend or boyfriend

kahili—tall pole topped with feathers, resembling a huge feather duster. It was used by an *ali'i* to announce his or her presence.

kahuna*—priest; sorcerer; doctor; skillful person. *Kahuna* had tremendous power in old Hawaii, which they used for both good and evil. The *kahuna ana'ana* was a feared individual because he practiced "black magic" and could pray a person to death, while the *kahuna lapa'au* was a medical practitioner bringing aid and comfort to the people.

kai—the sea. Many businesses and hotels employ *kai* as part of their name.

kalua—roasted underground in an *imu.* A favorite island food is *kalua* pork.

kama'aina*—child of the land; old-timer; long-time island resident of any ethnic background; resident of Hawaii or native son or daughter. Hotels and airlines often offer discounts called "*kama'aina* rates" to anyone who can prove island residency.

kanaka—man or commoner; later used to distinguish a Hawaiian from other races. Tone of voice can make it a derisive expression.

kane*—means man, but actually used to signify a relationship such as husband or boyfriend. Written on a door, it means "Men's Room."

kaola*—any food that has been broiled or barbecued

kapu*—forbidden; taboo; keep out; do not touch

kaukau*—slang word meaning food or chow; grub. Some of the best food in Hawaii comes from the *"kaukau* wagons," trucks that sell plate lunches and other morsels.

kauwa—landless, untouchable caste once confined to living on reservations. Members of this caste were often used as human sacrifices at *heiau.* Calling someone *kauwa* is still considered a grave insult.

kava—a mildly intoxicating traditional drink made from the juice of chewed *awa* root, spat into a bowl, and used in religious ceremonies

keiki*—child or children; used by all ethnic groups. "Have you hugged your *keiki* today?"

kiawe—algaroba tree from South America commonly found in Hawaii along the shore. It grows a nasty long thorn that can easily puncture a tire. Legend has it that the trees were introduced to the islands by a misguided missionary who hoped the thorns would coerce natives into wearing shoes. Actually, they are good for fuel, as fodder for hogs and cattle, and for reforestation, none of which you'll appreciate if you step on one of their thorns or flatten a tire on your rental car!

koa—hard, fine-grained native Hawaiian wood preferred in fashioning furniture and bowls

kokua—help. As in "Your *kokua* is needed to keep Hawaii free from litter."

kona* wind—muggy subtropical wind that blows from the south and hits the leeward side of the islands. It usually brings sticky hot weather and one of the few times when air-conditioning is appreciated.

konane—traditional Hawaiian game, similar to checkers, played with pebbles on a large flat stone used as a board

koolau—windward side of the island

kuhina nui—the highest regent in the days of the monarchy

kukui—candlenut tree, whose pods are polished and then strung together to make beautiful lei. Traditionally, the oil-rich nuts were strung on the rib of a coconut leaf and used as a candle.

kuleana—homesite; the old homestead; small farms. Especially used to describe the small spreads on Hawaiian Homes Lands on Molokai.

Kumulipo*—ancient Hawaiian genealogical chant that records the pantheon of gods, creation, and the beginning of humankind

kupuna—grandparent or old-timer; usually means someone who has gained wisdom. The statewide school system now invites *kupuna* to talk to the children about the old ways and methods.

la—the sun. Often combined with other words to be more descriptive, such as *La*haina ("Merciless Sun") or Haleaka*la* ("House of the Sun").

lanai*—veranda or porch. You'll pay more for a hotel room if it has a lanai with an ocean view.

lani—sky or the heavens

lau hala*—traditional Hawaiian weaving of mats, hats, etc., from the prepared fronds of the pandanus (screw pine)

lei*—traditional garland of flowers or vines. One of Hawaii's most beautiful customs. Given at any auspicious occasion, but especially to a person arriving in or leaving Hawaii.

lele—stone altar at a *heiau*

limu—edible seaweed of various types. Gathered from the shoreline, it makes an excellent salad. It's used to garnish many island dishes and is a favorite at luau.

lomi lomi—traditional Hawaiian massage; also, raw salmon made into a vinegared salad with chopped onion and spices

lua*—the toilet; the head; the bathroom

luakini—human-sacrifice temple. Introduced to Hawaii in the 13th century at Wahaula Heiau on the Big Island.

luau*—Hawaiian feast featuring poi, *imu*-baked pork, and other traditional foods. Good ones provide some of the best gastronomical delights in the world.

luna—foreman or overseer in the plantation fields. They were often mounted on horseback and were renowned either for their fairness or cruelty. They represented the middle class, and served as a buffer between plantation workers and white plantation owners.

mahalo*—thank you. *Mahalo nui* means "big thanks" or "thank you very much."

mahele—division. The "Great Mahele" of 1848 changed Hawaii forever when the traditional common lands were broken up into privately owned plots.

mahimahi*—favorite fish for eating. Often called a dolphin, but a mahimahi is a true fish, not a cetacean.

mahu—homosexual; often used derisively like "fag" or "queer"

maile—fragrant vine used in traditional lei. It looks ordinary but smells delightful.

maka'ainana—commoner; person "belonging" to the *aina* (land), who supported the *ali'i* by fishing and farming and as a warrior

makai*—toward the sea; used by most islanders when giving directions

make—dead; deceased

malihini*—newcomer; tenderfoot; recent arrival

malo—native Hawaiian loincloth. Never worn anymore except at festivals or pageants.

mana*—power from the spirit world; innate energy of all things animate or inanimate; the grace of god. Mana could be passed on from one person to another, or even stolen. Great care was taken to protect the *ali'i* from having their mana defiled. Commoners were required to lie flat on the ground and cover their faces whenever a great *ali'i* approached. *Kahuna* were often employed in the regaining or transference of mana.

manauahi—free; gratis; extra

manini—stingy; tight. A Hawaiianized word taken from the name of Don Francisco *Marin,* who was instrumental in bringing many fruits and plants to Hawaii. He was known for never sharing any of the bounty from his substantial gardens on Vineyard Street in Honolulu.

mauka*—toward the mountains; used by most islanders when giving directions

mauna—mountain. Often combined with other words to be more descriptive, such as Mauna Kea ("White Mountain").

mele—song or chant in the Hawaiian oral tradition that records the history and genealogies of the *ali'i*

Menehune—the legendary "little people" of Hawaii. Like leprechauns, they are said to have shunned humans and possess magical powers. Stone walls said to have been completed in one night are often attributed to them. Some historians argue that they actually existed and were the aboriginals of Hawaii, inhabiting the islands before the coming of the Polynesians.

moa—chicken; fowl

moana*—the ocean; the sea. Many businesses and hotels as well as places have *moana* as part of their name.

moe—sleep

moolelo—ancient tales kept alive by the oral tradition and recited only by day

muumuu*—a "Mother Hubbard," an ankle-length dress with a high neckline introduced by the missionaries to cover the nakedness of the Hawaiians. It has become fashionable attire for almost any occasion in Hawaii.

nani—beautiful

nui—big; great; large; as in *mahalo nui* (thank you very much)

ohana—family; the fundamental social division; extended family. Now used to denote a social organization with grass-roots overtones, as in the "Protect Kahoolawe Ohana."

okolehau—literally "iron bottom"; a traditional booze made from ti root. *Okole* means "rear end" and *hau* means "iron," which was descriptive of the huge blubber pots in which *okolehau* was made. Also, if you drink too much it'll surely knock you on your *okole.*

ono*—delicious; delightful; the best. *Ono ono* means "extra or absolutely delicious."

opihi—a shellfish or limpet that clings to rocks and is gathered as one of the islands' favorite *pu pu.* Custom dictates that you never remove all of the *opihi* from a rock; some are always left to grow for future generations.

opu—belly; stomach

pahoa—dagger, as used by ancient Hawaiians

pahoehoe*—smooth, ropey lava that looks like burnt pancake batter. *Pahoehoe* is now the correct geological term used to describe this type of lava found anywhere in the world.

pakalolo—marijuana; the state's most productive cash crop

pake—Chinese person. Can be derisive, depending on tone in which it is used. It is a bastardization of the Chinese word meaning "uncle."

pali*—cliff; precipice. Hawaii's geology makes them quite common. The most famous are the *pali* of Oahu, where a major battle was fought.

paniolo*—Hawaiian cowboy. Derived from the Spanish *espaniola.* The first cowboys brought to Hawaii during the early 19th century were Mexicans from California.

papale—hat. Except for the feathered helmets of the *ali'i* warriors of old Hawaii, hats were generally not worn. However, once the islanders saw their practical uses and how fashionable they were, they began weaving them from various materials and quickly became experts at manufacture and design.

pau*—finished; done; completed. Often combined into *pau hana,* which means end of work or quitting time.

pa'u—long split skirt often worn by women when horseback riding. Last century, an island treat was *pa'u* riders in their beautiful dresses at Kapiolani Park in Honolulu. The tradition is carried on today at many of Hawaii's rodeos.

pilau—stink; bad smell; stench

pilikia—trouble of any kind, big or small; bad times

poi*—glutinous paste made from the pounded corm of taro which ferments slightly and has a light sour taste. Purplish in color, it's a staple at luau, where it is called "one-, two-, or three-finger" poi, depending upon its thickness.

pono—righteous or excellent

pua—flower

puka*—hole of any size. *Puka* is used by all island residents, whether talking about a pinhole in a rubber boat or a tunnel through a mountain.

punalua—tradition of sharing mates in practice before the missionaries came. Western seamen took advantage of it, and this led to the spreading of contagious diseases and eventually to the ultimate demise of the Hawaiian people.

punee*—bed; narrow couch. Used by all ethnic groups. To recline on a *punee* on a breezy lanai is a true island treat.

pu pu*—appetizer; snack; hors d'oeuvres; can be anything from cheese and crackers to sushi. Oftentimes, bars or nightclubs offer them free.

pupule—crazy; nuts; out of your mind

pu'u—hill, as in Pu'u Ulaula ("Red Hill")

tapa*—traditional paper cloth made from beaten bark. Intricate designs were stamped in using beaters, and natural dyes added color. The tradition was lost for many years but is now making a comeback, and provides some of the most beautiful folk art in the islands.

taro*—staple of old Hawaii. This plant with a distinctive broad leaf that produces a starchy root was brought by the first Polynesians and was grown on magnificently irrigated plantations. According to oral tradition, the life-giving properties of taro hold mystical significance for Hawaiians, since it was created by the gods at about the same time as humans.

ti—broad-leafed plant used for many purposes, from plates to hula skirts (never grass). Especially used to wrap religious offerings presented at the *heiau.*

tutu*—grandmother; granny; older woman. Used by all as a term of respect and endearment.

ukulele*—*uku* means "flea" and *lele* means "jumping," so literally "jumping flea"—the way the Hawaiians perceived the quick finger movements used on the banjolike Portuguese folk instrument called a *cavaquinho.* The ukulele quickly became synonymous with the islands.

wahine*—young woman; female; girl; wife. Used by all ethnic groups. When written on a door, it means "Women's Room."

wai—fresh water; drinking water

wela—hot. *Wela kahao* is a "hot time" or "making whoopee."

wiki*—quickly; fast; in a hurry. Often seen as *wiki wiki* (very fast), as in "Wiki Wiki Messenger Service."

HOTEL INDEX

LANAI

MOLOKAI

BIG ISLAND

KAUAI

RESTAURANT INDEX

MAUI

INDEX

Italicized page numbers indicate information in captions, charts, illustrations, maps, or special topics.

F

G

I

J

K

QR

S

UV

WXYZ

ABOUT THE AUTHOR

Joe Bisignani is a fortunate man because he makes his living doing the two things that he likes best: traveling and writing. Joe has been with Moon Publications since 1979 and is the author of *Japan Handbook, Big Island of Hawaii Handbook, Kauai Handbook, Honolulu-Waikiki Handbook,* and *Maui Handbook.* When not traveling, he makes his home in Northern California.

ABOUT THE COVER ARTIST

Artist Roy Gonzalez Tabora, whose art is featured on all the covers of the Hawaii handbooks series, was born into a family of painters. At the age of 20, already an accomplished realist painter, he continued his education and received his degree in fine arts from the University of Hawaii. He never simply copies from a photograph or relies solely upon his imagination, choosing instead to render an artful blend using his heart and mind to produce what are considered some of the finest and most unforgettable seascapes in the world. He is currently represented by Kahn Galleries, 4569 Kukui St., Kapa'a, HI 96746, tel. (808) 822-5281, fax (808) 822-2756.

THE METRIC SYSTEM

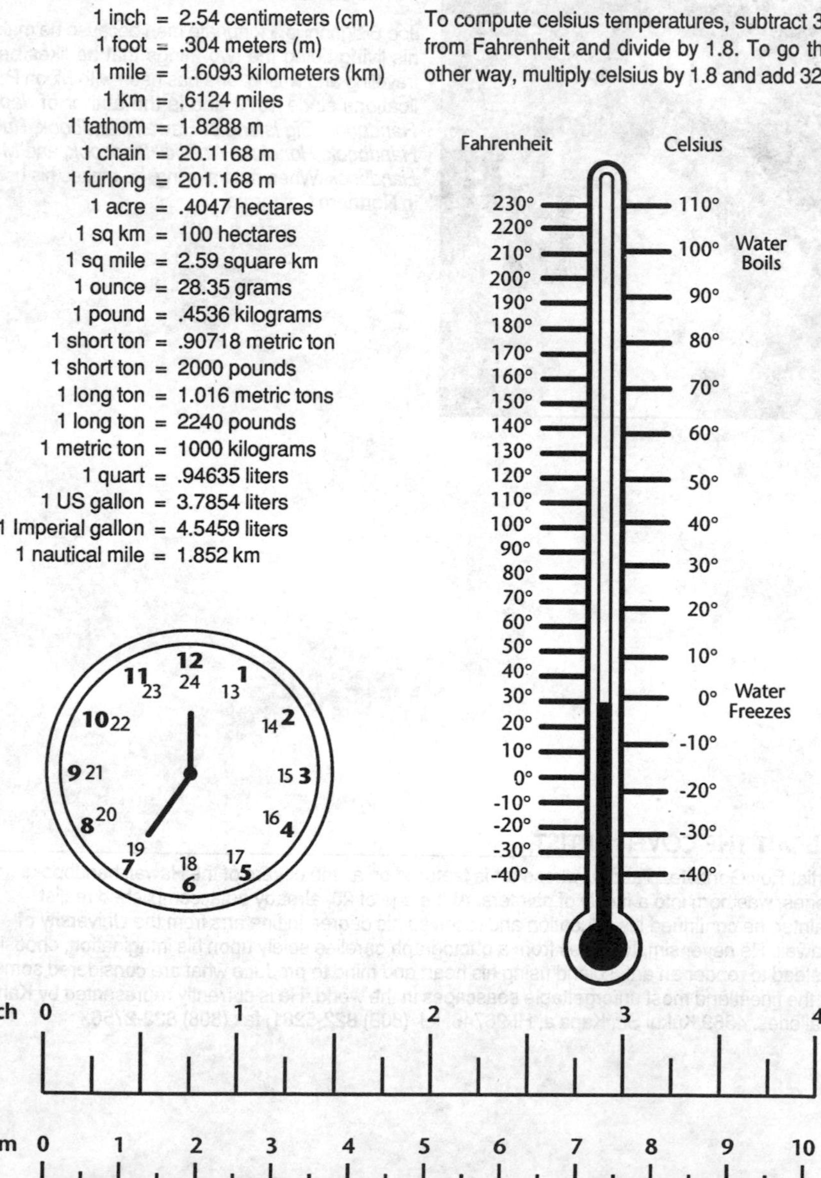

1 inch = 2.54 centimeters (cm)
1 foot = .304 meters (m)
1 mile = 1.6093 kilometers (km)
1 km = .6124 miles
1 fathom = 1.8288 m
1 chain = 20.1168 m
1 furlong = 201.168 m
1 acre = .4047 hectares
1 sq km = 100 hectares
1 sq mile = 2.59 square km
1 ounce = 28.35 grams
1 pound = .4536 kilograms
1 short ton = .90718 metric ton
1 short ton = 2000 pounds
1 long ton = 1.016 metric tons
1 long ton = 2240 pounds
1 metric ton = 1000 kilograms
1 quart = .94635 liters
1 US gallon = 3.7854 liters
1 Imperial gallon = 4.5459 liters
1 nautical mile = 1.852 km

To compute celsius temperatures, subtract 32 from Fahrenheit and divide by 1.8. To go the other way, multiply celsius by 1.8 and add 32.

MOON HANDBOOKS—THE IDEAL TRAVELING COMPANIONS

Moon Handbooks provide travelers with all the background and practical information he or she will need on the road. Every Handbook begins with in-depth essays on the land, the people, their history, arts, politics, and social concerns—an entire bookshelf of introductory information squeezed into a one-volume encyclopedia. The Handbooks provide accurate, up-to-date coverage of all the practicalities: language, currency, transportation, accommodations, food and entertainment, and services, to name a few. Moon Handbooks are ideal traveling companions: informative, entertaining, and highly practical.

To locate the bookstore nearest you that carries Moon Travel Handbooks or to order directly from Moon Publications, call: (800) 345-5473, Monday-Friday, 9 a.m.-5 p.m. PST.

THE PACIFIC/ASIA SERIES

BALI HANDBOOK by Bill Dalton
Detailed travel information on the most famous island in the world. 428 pages. **$12.95**

BANGKOK HANDBOOK by Michael Buckley
Your tour guide through this exotic and dynamic city reveals the affordable and accessible possibilities. Thai phrasebook. 222 pages. **$13.95**

BLUEPRINT FOR PARADISE: How to Live on a Tropic Island by Ross Norgrove
This one-of-a-kind guide has everything you need to know about moving to and living comfortably on a tropical island. 212 pages. **$14.95**

FIJI ISLANDS HANDBOOK by David Stanley
The first and still the best source of information on travel around this 322-island archipelago. Fijian glossary. 198 pages. **$11.95**

INDONESIA HANDBOOK by Bill Dalton
This one-volume encyclopedia explores island by island the many facets of this sprawling, kaleidoscopic island nation. Extensive Indonesian vocabulary. 1,200 pages. **$25.00**

JAPAN HANDBOOK by J.D. Bisignani
In this comprehensive new edition, award-winning travel writer J.D. Bisignani offers to inveterate travelers, newcomers, and businesspeople alike a thoroughgoing presentation of Japan's many facets. 950 pages. **$22.50**

MICRONESIA HANDBOOK: Guide to the Caroline, Gilbert, Mariana, and Marshall Islands by David Stanley
Micronesia Handbook guides you on a real Pacific adventure all your own. 345 pages. **$11.95**

NEW ZEALAND HANDBOOK by Jane King
Introduces you to the people, places, history, and culture of this extraordinary land. 571 pages. **$18.95**

OUTBACK AUSTRALIA HANDBOOK by Marael Johnson
Australia is an endlessly fascinating, vast land, and *Outback Australia Handbook* explores the cities and towns, sheep stations, and wilderness areas of the Northern Territory, Western Australia, and South Australia. Full of travel tips and cultural information for adventuring, relaxing, or just getting away from it all. 355 pages. **$15.95**

PHILIPPINES HANDBOOK by Peter Harper and Evelyn Peplow
Crammed with detailed information, *Philippines Handbook* equips the escapist, hedonist, or business traveler with thorough coverage of the Philippines's colorful history, landscapes, and culture. 600 pages. **$17.95**

SOUTHEAST ASIA HANDBOOK by Carl Parkes
Helps the enlightened traveler discover the real Southeast Asia. 873 pages. **$21.95**

SOUTH KOREA HANDBOOK by Robert Nilsen
Whether you're visiting on business or searching for adventure, *South Korea Handbook* is an invaluable companion. Korean glossary with useful notes on speaking and reading the language. 548 pages. **$14.95**

SOUTH PACIFIC HANDBOOK by David Stanley
The original comprehensive guide to the 16 territories in the South Pacific. 740 pages. **$19.95**

TAHITI-POLYNESIA HANDBOOK by David Stanley
All five French-Polynesian archipelagoes are covered in this comprehensive guide by Oceania's best-known travel writer. 235 pages. **$11.95**

THAILAND HANDBOOK by Carl Parkes
Presents the richest source of information on travel in Thailand. 568 pages. **$16.95**

THE HAWAIIAN SERIES

BIG ISLAND OF HAWAII HANDBOOK by J.D. Bisignani
An entertaining yet informative text packed with insider tips on accommodations, dining, sports and outdoor activities, natural attractions, and must-see sights. 350 pages. **$13.95**

HAWAII HANDBOOK by J.D. Bisignani
Winner of the 1989 Hawaii Visitors Bureau's Best Guide Award and the Grand Award for Excellence in Travel Journalism, this guide takes you beyond the glitz and high-priced hype and leads you to a genuine Hawaiian experience. Covers all 8 Hawaiian Islands. 1,005 pages. **$19.95**

KAUAI HANDBOOK by J.D. Bisignani
Kauai is the island Hawaiians visit to get away from it all. 274 pages. **$13.95**

MAUI HANDBOOK by J.D. Bisignani
"No fool-'round" advice on accommodations, eateries, and recreation, plus a comprehensive introduction to island ways, geography, and history. Hawaiian and pidgin glossaries. 393 pages. **$14.95**

HONOLULU~WAIKIKI HANDBOOK: The Island of Oahu by J.D. Bisignani
A handy guide to Honolulu, renowned surfing beaches, and Oahu's countless other diversions. Hawaiian and pidgin glossaries. 354 pages. **$14.95**

THE AMERICAS SERIES

ALASKA-YUKON HANDBOOK by Deke Castleman and Don Pitcher
Get the inside story, with plenty of well-seasoned advice to help you cover more miles on less money. 460 pages. **$14.95**

ALBERTA AND THE NORTHWEST TERRITORIES HANDBOOK : Including Banff, Jasper, and the Canadian Rockies by Andrew Hempstead and Nadina Purdon
Explore the rich history, rustic towns, and rugged wilderness of the pristine Canadian countryside. 466 pages. **$17.95**

ARIZONA TRAVELER'S HANDBOOK by Bill Weir
This meticulously researched guide contains everything necessary to make Arizona accessible and enjoyable. 445 pages. **$16.95**

ATLANTIC CANADA HANDBOOK: New Brunswick, Nova Scotia, Labrador, Prince Edward Island, and Newfoundland by Mark Morris and Nan Drosdick
Canada's eastern seaboard provinces boast a varied European heritage manifested in local cuisine, crafts, and architecture. 450 pages. **$17.95**

BAJA HANDBOOK: Mexico's Western Peninsula including Cabo San Lucas by Joe Cummings
A comprehensive guide with all the travel information and background on the land, history, and culture of this untamed thousand-mile-long peninsula. 362 pages. **$15.95**

BELIZE HANDBOOK by Chicki Mallan
Complete with detailed maps, practical information, and an overview of the area's flamboyant history, culture, and geographical features, *Belize Handbook* is the only comprehensive guide of its kind to this spectacular region. 263 pages. **$14.95**

BRITISH COLUMBIA HANDBOOK by Jane King
With an emphasis on outdoor adventures, this guide covers mainland British Columbia, Vancouver Island, the Queen Charlotte Islands, and the Canadian Rockies. 381 pages. **$15.95**

CANCUN HANDBOOK by Chicki Mallan
Covers the city's luxury scene as well as more modest attractions, plus many side trips to unspoiled beaches and Mayan ruins. Spanish glossary. 257 pages. **$13.95**

CENTRAL MEXICO HANDBOOK: Mexico City, Guadalajara, and Other Colonial Cities by Chicki Mallan
Retrace the footsteps of Cortés from the coast of Veracruz to the heart of Mexico City to discover archaeological and cultural wonders. 391 pages. **$15.95**

CATALINA ISLAND HANDBOOK: A Guide to California's Channel Islands by Chicki Mallan
A complete guide to these remarkable islands, from the windy solitude of the Channel Islands National Marine Sanctuary to bustling Avalon. 245 pages. **$10.95**

COLORADO HANDBOOK by Stephen Metzger
Essential details to the all-season possibilities in Colorado fill this guide. Practical travel tips combine with recreation—skiing, nightlife, and wilderness exploration—plus entertaining essays. 416 pages. **$17.95**

COSTA RICA HANDBOOK by Christopher P. Baker
Experience the many wonders of the natural world as you explore this remarkable land. Spanish-English glossary. 574 pages. **$17.95**

GEORGIA HANDBOOK by Kap Stann
Discover the Old South of mint juleps and magnolia blossoms, and enjoy Georgia's legendary hospitality. Includes detailed information on the upcoming 1996 Summer Olympic Games. 350 pages. **$16.95**

IDAHO HANDBOOK by Bill Loftus
A year-round guide to everything in this outdoor wonderland, from whitewater adventures to rural hideaways. 282 pages. **$14.95**

JAMAICA HANDBOOK by Karl Luntta
From the sun and surf of Montego Bay and Ocho Rios to the cool slopes of the Blue Mountains, author Karl Luntta offers island-seekers a perceptive, personal view of Jamaica. 230 pages. **$14.95**

MONTANA HANDBOOK by W.C. McRae and Judy Jewell
The wild West is yours with this extensive guide to the Treasure State, complete with travel practicalities, history, and lively essays on Montana life. 427 pages. **$15.95**

NEVADA HANDBOOK by Deke Castleman
Nevada Handbook puts the Silver State into perspective and makes it manageable and affordable. 450 pages. **$16.95**

NEW MEXICO HANDBOOK by Stephen Metzger
A close-up and complete look at every aspect of this wondrous state. 375 pages. **$14.95**

NORTHERN CALIFORNIA HANDBOOK by Kim Weir
An outstanding companion for imaginative travel in the territory north of the Tehachapis. 765 pages. **$19.95**

NORTHERN MEXICO HANDBOOK: The Sea of Cortez to the Gulf of Mexico
by Joe Cummings
Directs travelers from the barrier islands of Sonora to the majestic cloud forests of the Sierra Madre Oriental to traditional villages and hidden waterfalls in San Luis Potosí. 500 pages. **$16.95**

OREGON HANDBOOK by Stuart Warren and Ted Long Ishikawa
Brimming with travel practicalities and insiders' views on Oregon's history, culture, arts, and activities. 461 pages. **$16.95**

PACIFIC MEXICO HANDBOOK by Bruce Whipperman
Explore 2,000 miles of gorgeous beaches, quiet resort towns, and famous archaeological sites along Mexico's Pacific coast. Spanish-English glossary. 428 pages. **$15.95**

TEXAS HANDBOOK by Joe Cummings
Seasoned travel writer Joe Cummings brings an insider's perspective to his home state. 483 pages. **$13.95**

UTAH HANDBOOK by Bill Weir
Weir gives you all the carefully researched facts and background to make your visit a success. 445 pages. **$16.95**

WASHINGTON HANDBOOK by Archie Satterfield and Dianne J. Boulerice Lyons
Covers sights, shopping, services, transportation, and outdoor recreation, with complete listings for restaurants and accommodations. 419 pages. **$15.95**

WYOMING HANDBOOK by Don Pitcher
All you need to know to open the doors to this wide and wild state. 495 pages. **$14.95**

YUCATAN HANDBOOK by Chicki Mallan
All the information you'll need to guide you into every corner of this exotic land. Mayan and Spanish glossaries. 391 pages. **$15.95**

THE INTERNATIONAL SERIES

EGYPT HANDBOOK by Kathy Hansen
An invaluable resource for intelligent travel in Egypt. Arabic glossary. 522 pages. **$18.95**

MOSCOW-ST. PETERSBURG HANDBOOK by Masha Nordbye
Provides the visitor with an extensive introduction to the history, culture, and people of these two great cities, as well as practical information on where to stay, eat, and shop. 260 pages. **$13.95**

NEPAL HANDBOOK by Kerry Moran
Whether you're planning a week in Kathmandu or months out on the trail, *Nepal Handbook* will take you into the heart of this Himalayan jewel. 378 pages. **$12.95**

NEPALI AAMA by Broughton Coburn
A delightful photo-journey into the life of a Gurung tribeswoman of Central Nepal. Having lived with Aama (translated, "mother") for two years, first as an outsider and later as an adopted member of the family, Coburn presents an intimate glimpse into a culture alive with humor, folklore, religion, and ancient rituals. 165 pages. **$13.95**

STAYING HEALTHY IN ASIA, AFRICA, AND LATIN AMERICA
by Dirk G. Schroeder, Sc D, MPH
Don't leave home without it! Besides providing a complete overview of the health problems that exist in these areas, this book will help you determine which immunizations you'll need beforehand, what medications to take with you, and how to recognize and treat infections and diseases. Includes extensively illustrated first-aid information and precautions for heat, cold, and high altitude. 200 pages. **$10.95**

TIBET HANDBOOK: A PILGRIMAGE GUIDE by Victor Chan
This remarkable book is both a comprehensive trekking guide to mountain paths and plateau trails, and a pilgrimage guide that draws on Tibetan literature and religious history. 1104 pages. **$30.00**

IMPORTANT ORDERING INFORMATION

FOR FASTER SERVICE: Call to locate the bookstore nearest you that carries Moon Travel Handbooks or order directly from Moon Publications:

(800) 345-5473 • Monday-Friday • 9 a.m.-5 p.m. PST • fax (916) 345-6751

PRICES: All prices are subject to change. We always ship the most current edition. We will let you know if there is a price increase on the book you ordered.

SHIPPING & HANDLING OPTIONS: 1) Domestic UPS or USPS first class (allow 10 working days for delivery): $3.50 for the first item, 50 cents for each additional item.

Exceptions:

- **Moonbelt** shipping is $1.50 for one, 50 cents for each additional belt.
- Add $2.00 for same-day handling.
- UPS 2nd Day Air or Printed Airmail requires a special quote.
- International Surface Bookrate (8-12 weeks delivery): $3.00 for the first item, $1.00 for each additional item. Note: Moon Publications cannot guarantee international surface bookrate shipping.

FOREIGN ORDERS: All orders that originate outside the U.S.A. must be paid for with either an International Money Order or a check in U.S. currency drawn on a major U.S. bank based in the U.S.A.

TELEPHONE ORDERS: We accept Visa or MasterCard payments. Minimum order is US$15.00. Call in your order: (800) 345-5473, 9 a.m.-5 p.m. Pacific Standard Time.

MOONBELTS

Made of heavy-duty Cordura nylon, the Moonbelt offers maximum protection for your money and important papers. This all-weather pouch slips under your shirt or waistband, rendering it virtually undetectable and inaccessible to pickpockets. One-inch-wide nylon webbing, heavy-duty zipper, one-inch quick-release buckle. Accommodates traveler's checks, passport, cash, photos. Size 5 x 9 inches. Black. **$8.95**

New travel handbooks may be available that are not on this list.
To find out more about current or upcoming titles,
call us toll-free at (800) 345-5473.

ORDER FORM

Be sure to call (800) 345-5473 for current prices and editions or for the name of the bookstore nearest you that carries Moon Travel Handbooks • 9 a.m.–5 p.m. PST

(See important ordering information on preceding page)

Name: ______________________ Date: ______________

Street: ______________________________________

City: ______________________ Daytime Phone: ______________

State or Country: ______________________ Zip Code: ______________

QUANTITY	TITLE	PRICE

Taxable Total ______

Sales Tax (7.25%) for California Residents ______

Shipping & Handling ______

TOTAL ______

Ship: ☐ UPS (no PO Boxes) ☐ 1st class ☐ International surface mail

Ship to: ☐ address above ☐ other ______________________

Make checks payable to: **MOON PUBLICATIONS, INC.** P.O. Box 3040, Chico, CA 95927-3040 U.S.A. We accept Visa and MasterCard. **To Order:** Call in your Visa or MasterCard number, or send a written order with your Visa or MasterCard number and expiration date clearly written.

Card Number: ☐ **Visa** ☐ **MasterCard**

☐☐☐☐ ☐☐☐☐ ☐☐☐☐ ☐☐☐☐

Exact Name on Card: ______________________

expiration date: ______________________

signature ______________________

S/95

WHERE TO BUY THIS BOOK

BOOKSTORES AND LIBRARIES:
Moon Publications Handbooks are sold worldwide. Please contact our sales manager for a list of wholesalers and distributors in your area that stock our travel handbooks.

TRAVELERS:
We would like to have Moon Publications Handbooks available throughout the world. Please ask your bookstore to contact us for ordering information. If your bookstore will not order our guides, please contact us for a free newsletter and catalog.

MOON PUBLICATIONS, INC.
P.O. BOX 3040
CHICO, CA 95927-3040 U.S.A.
TEL: (800) 345-5473
FAX: (916) 345-6751
e-mail: **travel@moon.com**

TRAVEL MATTERS

Travel Matters is Moon Publications' quarterly newsletter. It provides today's traveler with timely, informative travel news and articles.

TRAVEL MATTERS

Ecotourism: Trojan Horse Or Savior Of The Last, Best Place?

You'll find resourceful coverage on:

- **Money**—What does it cost? Is it worth it?
- **Low impact travel**—tread lightly travel tips
- **Special interest travel**—cultural tours, environmental excursions, outdoor recreation, adventure treks, and more
- **Travel styles**—families, seniors, disabled travelers, package and theme tours
- **Consumer reviews**—books, language aids, travel gadgets, products, and services
- **Facts and opinions**—reader's letters and Moon Handbook author news
- **Moon Handbook booklist**—the latest titles and editions, and where and how to purchase them

To receive a free copy of *Travel Matters*, write Moon Publications Inc., P.O. Box 3040, Chico, CA 95927-3040, or call toll-free (800) 345-5473, Monday–Friday, 9 a.m. – 5 p.m. Pacific Standard Time.